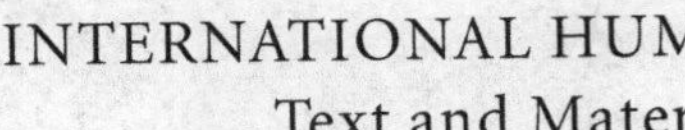

INTERNATIONAL HUM

Text and Mater

The successor to International Human Rights in Context:
Law, Politics and Morals

INTERNATIONAL HUMAN RIGHTS

THE SUCCESSOR TO INTERNATIONAL HUMAN RIGHTS IN CONTEXT: LAW, POLITICS AND MORALS

Text and Materials

PHILIP ALSTON

John Norton Pomeroy Professor of Law at New York University School of Law

RYAN GOODMAN

Anne and Joel Ehrenkranz Professor of Law at New York University School of Law
Professor of Politics and Professor of Sociology at New York University

The authors are co-directors of the
Center for Human Rights and Global Justice at New York University School of Law

OXFORD
UNIVERSITY PRESS

Great Clarendon Street, Oxford, OX2 6DP,
United Kingdom

Oxford University Press is a department of the University of Oxford. It furthers the University's objective of excellence in research, scholarship, and education by publishing worldwide. Oxford is a registered trade mark of Oxford University Press in the UK and in certain other countries

British Library Cataloguing in Publication Data
Data available

ISBN 978–0–19–957872–6

Printed in Great Britain by
Ashford Colour Press Ltd, Gosport, Hampshire

Preface

This course book is a successor to *International Human Rights in Context* (Oxford University Press, 1996, 2000 and 2008). The lead author of all three editions of that volume was Professor Henry Steiner, who founded and directed Harvard Law School's Human Rights Program from 1984 to 2005. Henry was the driving force behind those volumes, and they stand as a tribute to his depth of understanding, his endlessly probing intellect and his vision of how human rights should be taught. Although this book has been prepared without Henry's participation, it retains the essential structure and the basic understanding of the issues that were reflected in the predecessor volume. The current authors take this opportunity to express their gratitude to him for his immense contribution to the past, as well as the new, version of this course book.

Basic purposes

Almost seven decades after the human rights regime emerged out of the disasters of the Second World War, human rights norms and institutions deeply inform the rhetoric, practice and theory of international law and politics, as well as the internal constitutional structures of many states. Although the frailties of human rights as an ideal, an ideology or practice are evident, the concept of human rights has become a part of modern consciousness, a lens through which to see the world, a universal discourse, a potent aspiration. The course book uses the term 'human rights regime' to include post-1945 governmental, intergovernmental and nongovernmental institutions and practices in both national and international contexts in the recognition and protection of human rights.

However striking and disheartening its major failures and inadequacies, the regime has shown staying power and growth, as well as a remarkably broad dissemination of its message. Its claims of permanence carry ever greater credibility. Today's university curriculum dwarfs what was available for study in this field as few as 25 years ago. It evidences the significance of international human rights for fields of study as diverse as law, government, international relations, moral theory, public health, world financial institutions, the environment, economic development, ethnic conflict, religion, education, cultural studies and social anthropology.

Although the human rights regime now forms an indelible part of our legal, political and moral landscape, and indeed perhaps precisely because of that status, recent years have witnessed some of the deepest challenges to the foundations upon which the regime has been built, its aspirations to universality, and its claims of growing success in spreading and realizing its message. In response to these challenges, the book seeks to examine the regime's failures as well as triumphs and dilemmas in seeking to achieve human rights ideals across the world's many histories and cultures.

The book builds on the premise that a basic course in human rights should educate students to see the 'big picture'. Of course it should enable students to master the history, doctrine and institutional structures of the regime. But it should also persuade students to think critically about the subject as a whole. Thus the text and materials describe, analyse, criticize and propose, all from a range of political, cultural, moral and geopolitical perspectives. They do not impose any single dogma, direction or method for thinking about the history or the future of human rights.

These vexing issues are for the student to work out. The book prepares students to work with commitment and critical reflection in a range of roles related to human rights: concerned citizen, advocate, teacher, scholar, activist in a governmental or nongovernmental organization, policy analyst.

Principal features of the book

The conceptual framework for the book consists, in sequence, of the historical development and character of human rights discourse and basic norms; the dilemmas of rights and duties, and of universalism and cultural relativism; the architecture of international institutions as well as their functions, powers and interplay with norms; and the interaction of states with international law and organizations as well as with each other. Certain major themes run through the different parts of the book — for example, changing notions of autonomy and sovereignty, the changing configuration of the public-private divide in human rights ordering, the interplay of duties and rights in the gradual expansion of the human rights regime, the escalating tensions between international human rights and national security, the striking evolution of ideas about the nature and purposes of the regime itself.

Some of our premises about the study of international human rights inform the book as a whole:

1. Human rights are violated within individual states. One might therefore argue that the study of rights should concentrate on different countries — say, human rights *in* Nigeria, Peru, China, the United States, Iran, France. Such a book could offer contextual studies of human rights issues — police brutality, political participation, housing, discrimination, education, freedoms of and from religion, health care and so on — that would draw on different national histories and political cultures. It would have the character and high value of studies in comparative law, history and culture.

This book follows a different path. The distinctive aspect of the human rights regime of the last six decades has been its invention and development on the international level. Hence the stress is on the *international* human rights system, as well as on the vital relationships between that system and states' internal orders. Although many illustrations throughout the book draw on human rights violations within one or another state, most of the materials address international norms, processes and institutions (governmental and nongovernmental), both in their own terms and in terms of their interaction with states.

2. What are the sensible boundaries of a book that has an important focus on 'law'? Clearly, the course book could not achieve its goals if it held to a formal or positivist conception and omitted closely related fields of inquiry. Thus diverse readings from many fields interact with formal legal materials to form a network of interrelated ideas.

This range of readings is readily accessible to university students with academic backgrounds as varied as law, government, political economy, philosophy, education, theology, cultural studies, business or public health. Human rights courses benefit greatly by including students from such varied backgrounds, as well as from diverse countries and cultures. The three editions of this book's predecessor — *International Human Rights in Context* — served as the principal course book in universal human rights courses in several countries, in both graduate schools and colleges that included faculties and departments of law, government and international relations.

3. A book that concentrates on international human rights might presume that students have a rudimentary knowledge of international law. How else can a class discuss matters like treaties and custom, intergovernmental institutions and processes or internalization of treaty or customary norms within a state? In practice, however, a substantial percentage of students taking basic courses on human rights lacks that background knowledge.

How to handle this situation? In its early chapters, the book provides an introduction to basic conceptions, sources, processes and norms of international law. This introduction hardly achieves the depth and sophistication of a course devoted principally to that rich subject. But it suffices to enable students to grapple with the themes of the course book.

4. The study of human rights norms without attention to the international organizations that implement, develop, apply and enforce them would create an air of unreality about the entire enterprise. The architecture, powers, functions and processes of international human rights organizations, intergovernmental and non-governmental, figure importantly in the book. The student is made aware throughout of the pervasive relationships among norms, institutions and processes at the international as well as national levels.

5. No one substantive human rights problem and no one region dominate the book. The text and readings draw on many problems to illustrate their themes: free speech and the right to education; torture and discrimination against ethnic minorities; laws of war and the right to health care. The chapters illustrate those themes by drawing on many parts of the world, developed and developing, internationally powerful and weak states, and the book examines conflicts between regions and cultures in their approaches to and understandings of human rights.

Changes from the predecessor volume

This course book is entirely up to date, at least to the best of our knowledge. Among the more significant changes by comparison with the predecessor volume are two new chapters: one on fact-finding (Chapter 10); and one involving empirical research on the effectiveness of the human rights regime (Chapter 14). We also include new sections, for example, on sexual orientation discrimination (in Chapter 3) and diplomatic assurances for the prevention of torture (in Chapter 5). Finally, the book involves substantial revision of the discussion of prior topics — including women's rights, economic and social rights, the UN human rights machinery, the International Criminal Court, the responsibility to protect, universal jurisdiction and conflicts in culture and traditional practices (e.g., religious symbols; female genital mutilation) — to name but a few.

Practical details on materials

Rather than require students to purchase a separate booklet, we have set forth basic documents like treaties, declarations and constitutions that are necessary companions to the course book's materials in a Documents Supplement on the Online Resource Centre associated with the book: www.oxfordtextbooks.co.uk/orc/alston_goodman/. Most of these documents have been edited to eliminate sections not relevant to the course book's discussions.

We have sharply edited most of the primary and secondary materials in order to make the readings as compact as possible. Omissions (except for footnotes) are indicated by the conventional use of ellipses. Retained footnotes are renumbered within the consecutive footnote numbering of each chapter.

Acknowledgements

The authors wish to express appreciation to Audrey Watne for her superb assistance in the preparation of the volume for publication. Philip Alston also wishes to express his appreciation to Gráinne de Búrca and Mara Bustelo for their invaluable advice, to Sarah Knuckey for extremely helpful comments, to Kate Cornford and Jessye Freeman for excellent research assistance and to Holly Mowforth, Adrienne Lucas and Poonam Singh for their assistance with the permissions process. Ryan Goodman gives his thanks to Naomi Loewith, Brandon Miller and David Zionts for exceptional research assistance and to Derek Jinks for advice on several chapters.

Philip Alston
Ryan Goodman
NYU School of Law, June 2012

Summary of Contents

PART C: RIGHTS, DUTIES AND DILEMMAS OF UNIVERSALISM

PART D: INTERNATIONAL HUMAN RIGHTS ORGANIZATIONS

PART E: STATES AS PROTECTORS AND ENFORCERS OF HUMAN RIGHTS

PART F: CURRENT TOPICS

Contents

Acknowledgements

We gratefully acknowledge the permissions extended by the following publishers and authors to reprint excerpts from the indicated publications:

AMS Press. Excerpts from Jomo Kenyatta, Facing Mount Kenya: The Tribal Life of the Gikuyu (1965).

Acta Juridica. Excerpts from Professor Colonel G.I.A.D. Draper, Humanitarian Law and Human Rights, Acta Juridica 193 (1979).

African Commission on Human and Peoples' Rights. Excerpts from the 17th Annual Activity Report of the African Commission on Human and Peoples' Rights, Annex II (2003–2004).

Agence France Presse. Excerpts from Ines Bel Aiba, Women on the Back Foot in the Arab Spring (5 March 2012).

American Anthropological Association. Excerpts from American Anthropological Association, Statement of Human Rights, 49 American Anthropologist No. 4, 539 (1947); Bettina Shell-Duncan, From Health to Human Rights: Female Genital Cutting and the Politics of Intervention, 110 American Anthropologist 225 (2008).

American Law Institute. Excerpts from Restatement (Third), The Foreign Relations Law of the United States, section 402 (1987).

American Journal of Political Science. Excerpts from Katerina Linos, Diffusion Through Democracy, 55 American Journal of Political Science 678 (2011).

American Political Science Review. Excerpts from R. Grant and R. Keohane, Accountability and Abuses of Power in World Politics, 99 American Political Science Review 29 (2005).

American Society of Comparative Law. Excerpts from Ruth Rubio Marin, A New European Parity-Democracy Sex Equality Model and Why It Won't Fly in the United States, 60 American Journal of Comparative Law 99 (2012)

American Society of International Law. Excerpts from The Attorney-General of the Government of Israel v. Eichmann, 56 American Journal of International Law 805 (1962); Task Force on U.S. Policy Toward the ICC Final Report (2010); James Cavallaro and Stephanie Brewer, Reevaluating Regional Human Rights Litigation in the Twenty-First Century: The Case of the Inter-American Court, 102 American Journal of International Law 678 (2008); Frank Hoffmeister, Case Note: Cyprus v Turkey, 96 American Journal of International Law 445 (2002); Anthea Roberts, Traditional and Modern Approaches to Customary International Law: A Reconciliation, 95 American Journal of International Law 757 (2001)Donna Sullivan, Advancing the Freedom of Religion or Belief Through the UN Declaration on the Elimination of Religious Intolerance and Discrimination, 82 American Journal of International Law 487 (1988); Ryan Goodman, Human Rights Treaties, Invalid Reservations, and State Consent, 96 American Journal of International Law 531 (2002).

Amnesty International. Excerpts from Death Sentences and Executions 2011 (2012); Rwanda: The Troubled Course of Justice (26 April 2000); Rwanda — GACACA: A Question of Justice (17 December 2002).

The Aristotelian Society. Excerpts from James Griffin, The Presidential Address: Discrepancies Between the Best Philosophical Account of Human Rights and the International Law of Human Rights, 101 Proceedings of the Aristotelian Society (2000). Reprinted by courtesy of the Editor of the Aristotelian Society ©2000.

Australian National University, Centre for International and Public Law. Excerpts from Hilary Charlesworth, Swimming to Cambodia: Justice and Ritual in Human Rights After Conflict, 29 Australian Year Book of International Law (2010).

Australian National University, Centre for International and Public Law. Excerpts from Michael Kirby, United Nations Procedures: A Response to Professor Hilary Charlesworth, 29 Australian Year Book of International Law (2010).

Beacon Press. Excerpts from Martha Minow, Between Vengeance And Forgiveness (1998). Copyright ©1998 by Martha Minow, reprinted with permission of Beacon Press, Boston.

Bobbs-Merrill. Excerpts from Louis Sohn & Thomas Buergenthal, International Protection of Human Rights (1973).

Boston Review. Excerpts from Yael Tamir, Hands off Clitoridectomy, 31 Boston Review 21 (Summer 1996).

Brill Academic Publishers. Excerpts from Oscar Schachter, International Law In Theory And Practice (1991); Myron Weiner, Child Labour in Developing Countries: The Indian Case, 2 International Journal of Children's Rights 121 (1994); Philip Alston, The Historical Origins of the Concept of 'General Comments' in Human Rights Law in L. Boisson de Chazournes and V. Gowlland-Debbas (eds.), The International Legal System in Quest of Equity and Universality: Liber Amicorum Georges Abi-Saab (2001); Christine Parker and John Howe, Ruggie's Diplomatic Project and its Missing Regulatory Infrastructure in R. Mares (ed.), The UN Guiding Principles on Business and Human Rights: Foundations and Implementation (2012); Nicolas Valticos, Foreward in B.G. Ramcharan (ed.), International Law and Fact-Finding in the Field of Human Rights (1982); Cole Durham, Perspectives on Religious Liberty: A Comparative Framework, in Johan van der Vyver & John Witte (eds.), Religious Human Rights in Global Perspective (1996); Dinah Shelton & Alexandre Kiss, A Draft Model Law on Freedom of Religion, in Johan van der Vyver & John Witte, Jr. (eds.), Religious Human Rights in Global Perspective (1996); Virginia Leary, International Labour Conventions and National Law (1982).

Brittanica. Excerpts from Burns H. Weston, Human Rights, Britannica, Academic Edition (2012).

Brookings Institutional Press. Excerpts from Ted Piccone, Catalysts for Rights: The Unique Contribution of the U.N.'s Independent Experts on Human Rights, Final Report of the Brookings Research Project on Strengthening U.N. Special Procedures (Oct. 2010).

B'Tselem. Excerpts from Jessica Montell, No Closure in Killing of 21 Gaza Family Members, (8 May 2012).

Business Ethics Quarterly. Excerpts from Peter Muchlinski, Implementing the New UN Corporate Human Rights Framework: Implications for Corporate Law, Governance, and Regulation, 22 Business Ethics Quarterly 145 (2012).

California Western International Law Journal. Excerpts from Jack Donnelly, In Search of the Unicorn: The Jurisprudence and Politics of the Right to Development, 15 Calif. Western Int. L. J. 473 (1985).

Cambridge University Press. Excerpts from Emilie M. Hafner-Burton, Trading Human Rights: How Preferential Trade Agreements Influence Government Repression, 59:3 International Organization (2005); Phil Clark, The Gacaca Courts, Post-Genocide Justice and Reconciliation in Rwanda (2010); Henry Steiner, Individual Claims in a World of Massive Violations: What Role for the Human Rights Committee? in P. Alston and J. Crawford (eds.), The Future of UN Human Rights Treaty Monitoring (2000); Andrew Moravcsik, The Origins of Human Rights Regimes: Democratic Delegation in Postwar Europe, 54 International Organisation 217 (2000); Alec Stone Sweet, A Cosmopolitan Legal Order: Constitutional Pluralism and Rights Adjudication in Europe, 1 Journal of Global Constitutionalism 53 (2012); Louise Arbour, In Our Name and on Our Behalf, 55 International and Comparative Law Quarterly 511 (2006); Sandesh Sivakumaran, Binding Armed Opposition Groups, 55 International and Comparative Law Quarterly 369 (2006); Intergovernmental Panel on Climate Change, Climate Change 2007: Impacts, Adaptation and Vulnerability, Working Group II Contribution to the Intergovernmental Panel on Climate Change, Fourth Assessment Report, Summary for Policymakers, April 2007; Michael P. Van Alstine, The Role of Domestic Courts in Treaty Enforcement in D. Sloss (ed.), Treaty Enforcement: A Comparative Study (2009); Ryan Goodman & Thomas Pegram, National Human Rights Institutions, State Conformity, and Social Change, in R. Goodman & T. Pegram (eds.), Human Rights, State Compliance, and Social Change: Assessing National Human Rights Institutions (2012); Beth A. Simmons, Mobilizing for Human Rights: International Law in Domestic Politics (2009).

Cato Institute. Excerpts from David Kelley, A Life of One's Own: Individual Rights and the Welfare State (1998).

Center for Economic and Social Rights and the Central American Institute for Fiscal Studies. Excerpts from Rights or Privileges? Fiscal Commitment to the Rights to Health, Education and Food in Guatemala (2009).

Center for Strategic and International Studies. Excerpts from Marc Grossman, Remarks on American Foreign Policy and the International Criminal Court (May 6, 2002).

Chicago Journal of International Law. Excerpts from Ellen Lutz and Kathryn Sikkink, The Justice Cascade: The Evolution and Impact of Foreign Human Rights Trials in Latin America, 2 Chicago Journal of International Law 1 (2001).

Columbia University Press. Excerpts from Elvin Hatch, Culture and Morality: The Relativity of Values in Anthropology (1983).

Congressional Research Service, Excerpts from Luisa Blanchfield, The UN Convention on the Elimination of All Forms of Discrimination Against Women (CEDAW): Issues in the US Ratification Debate, Congressional Research Service (28 June 2011).

Council of Europe. Excerpts from Steering Committee for Human Rights (CDDH), Final Report on Measures Requiring Amendment of the European

Convention on Human Rights, Doc. CDDH (2012) R74 Addendum I, (15 February 2012).

DePaul Law Review. Excerpts from Beth Stephens, Individuals Enforcing International Law: The Comparative and Historical Context, 52 DePaul Law Review 433 (2002).

Economic and Political Weekly. Excerpts from Jean Drèze, Democracy and the Right to Food in P. Alston and M. Robinson (eds.), Human Rights and Development: Towards Mutual Reinforcement (2005) (reprinted with permission from Economic and Political Weekly, Vol 39, Issue no. 17, April 24, 2004).

Emory International Law Review. Excerpts from Sandra Coliver, Jennie Green, and Paul Hoffman, Holding Human Rights Violators Accountable by Using International Law in US Courts: Advocacy Efforts and Complementary Strategies, 19 Emory International Law Review 169 (2005).

European Journal of International Law. Excerpts from Darryl Robinson, Serving the Interests of Justice: Amnesties, Truth Commissions and the International Criminal Court, 14 European Journal of International Law 481 (2003); Kenneth Anderson, The Ottawa Convention Banning Landmines, The Role of International Non-Governmental Organizations and the Idea of International Civil Society, 11 European Journal of International Law 92 (2000).

The Federation Press. Excerpts from Michael Kirby, The Role of International Standards in Australian Courts in P. Alston and M. Chiam (eds.), Treaty-Making and Australia: Globalization versus Sovereignty (1995).

Foreign Affairs. Excerpts from Jonathan D. Tepperman, Truth and Consequences, 81 Foreign Affairs (March/April 2002).

Foreign Policy. Excerpts from Helena Cobban, Think Again: International Courts, Foreign Policy (March/April 2006).

Global Policy. Excerpts from Robert Howse & Ruti Teitel, Beyond Compliance: Rethinking Why International Law Really Matters, (2010).

Ryan Goodman & Derek Jinks. Excerpts from Socializing States: Promoting Human Rights Through International Law (forthcoming 2013).

The Guardian. Excerpts from Tamasin Ford, Wronged Women of Liberia Reluctant to Revisit Human Rights Abuses (28 February 2012); Ronald Dworkin, Even Bigots and Holocaust Deniers Must Have Their Say (14 February 2006).

The Hague Academy of International Law. Excerpts from Louis Henkin, International Law: Politics, Values and Functions. General Course on Public International Law, Collected Courses of The Hague Academy of International Law, Vol. 216 (1989).

The Hague Academy of International Law Workshop. Excerpts from Georges Abi-Saab, The Legal Formulation of a Right to Development in Rene-Jean Dupuy (ed.), The Right to Development at the International Level (1980).

Hamline University School of Law. Excerpts from Robert Cover, Obligation: A Jewish Jurisprudence of the Social Order, 5 Journal of Law and Religion 65 (1987).

Hart Publishing. Excerpts from James Cavallaro And Sebastian Albuja, The Lost Agenda: Economic Crimes and Truth Commissions in Latin America and Beyond in Kieran McEvoy and Lorna McGregor (eds.), Transitional Justice from Below:

Grassroots Activism and the Struggle for Change (2008); Sanjay Patel, Founding Legitimate Expectations on Unincorporated Treaties, 15 Judicial Review 74 (2010).

Harvard Civil Rights-Civil Liberties Law Review. Excerpts from Michael A. Rebell, The Right to Comprehensive Educational Opportunity, 47 Harvard Civil Rights-Civil Liberties Law Review 47 (2012).

Harvard Human Rights Journal. Diane F. Orentlicher, Bearing Witness: The Art and Science of Human Rights Fact-Finding, 3 Harvard Human Rights Journal 83 (1990); Abdullahi Ahmed An-Na'im, Human Rights in the Muslim World, 3 Harvard Human Rights Journal 13 (1990).

Harvard Journal of Law and Gender. Excerpts from Tracy Higgins, Anti-Essentialism, Relativism, and Human Rights, 19 Harvard Women's Law Journal 89 (1996).

Harvard Journal of Law and Public Policy. Excerpts from Ganesh Sitaraman, The Use and Abuse of Foreign Law in Constitutional Interpretation, 32 Harvard Journal of Law and Public Policy 653 (2009).

Harvard University Press. David Garland, Peculiar Institution: America's Death Penalty in an Age of Abolition (2010); Amartya Sen, The Idea of Justice (2009); Samuel Moyn, The Last Utopia (2010); Duncan Kennedy, A Critique of Adjudication (1997)

Human Rights Brief. Excerpts from Aryeh Neier, Social and Economic Rights: A Critique, 13/2 Human Rights Brief (2006); Lauren Birchfield and Jessica Corsi, The Right to Life is the Right to Food: People's Union for Civil Liberties v. Union of India and Others 17/3 Human Rights Brief (2010).

ILSA Journal of International and Comparative Law. Excerpts from Nancy Kaymar Stafford, A Model War Crimes Court: Sierra Leone, 10 ILSA Journal of International and Comparative Law 117 (2003).

The Independent. Excerpts from Callum Macrae, Sri Lanka: A Child is Summarily Executed (11 March 2012).

INGO Accountability Charter, International Non-Governmental Organizations' Accountability Charter (2005).

International Center for Transitional Justice. Excerpts from The Special Court for Sierra Leone: The First Eighteen Months (March 2004).

International Commission of Jurists. Excerpts from Nicholas Howen, Business, Human Rights and Accountability, Speech delivered at the International Commission of Jurists' 'Business and Human Rights' Conference, Copenhagen (21 September 2005).

International Committee of the Red Cross. Excerpts from Louise Doswald-Beck and Sylvain Vité, International Humanitarian Law and Human Rights Law, 293 International Review of the Red Cross 94 (1993); Andrew Clapham, Human Rights Obligations of Non-State Actors in Conflict Situations, 863 International Review of the Red Cross 491 (2006).

International Service for Human Rights. GA Third Committee Deletes 'Sexual Orientation' From Resolution on Extrajudicial Execution (22 November 2010).

Intersentia. Excerpts from Olivier de Frouville, Building a Universal System for the Protection of Human Rights: The Way Forward, in M. Cherif Bassiouni & W. Schabas (eds.), New Challenges for the UN Human Rights Machinery: What

Future for the UN Treaty Body System and the Human Rights Council Procedures? (2001); Manfred Nowak, It's Time for a World Court of Human Rights, in M. Cherif Bassiouni & W. Schabas (eds.), New Challenges for the UN Human Rights Machinery: What Future for the UN Treaty Body System and the Human Rights Council Procedures? (2001).

The Johns Hopkins University Press. Excerpts from Kenneth Roth, Defending Economic, Social and Cultural Rights: Practical Issues Faced by an International Human Rights Organization, Human Rights Quarterly 26:1 (2004) ©2004 by The Johns Hopkins University Press; Stanley Cohen, Government Responses to Human Rights Reports: Claims, Denials, and Counterclaims, Human Rights Quarterly 18:3 (1996) ©1996 by The Johns Hopkins University Press. Reprinted with permission of The Johns Hopkins University Press.

Journal of Human Rights Practice. Excerpts from Eitan Felner, Closing the 'Escape Hatch': A Toolkit to Monitor the Progressive Realization of Economic, Social, and Cultural Rights, 1 (2009).

Kluwer Law International. Excerpts from Martti Koskenniemi, Between Impunity and Show Trials, in J.A. Frowein and R. Wolfrum (eds.) Max Planck Yearbook of United Nations Law, vol. 6 (2002); Christof Heyns & Frans Viljoen, The Impact of the United Nations Human Rights Treaties on the Domestic Level (2002).

Law Quarterly Review. Excerpts from Philip Sales and Joanne Clement, International Law in Domestic Courts: The Developing Framework, 124 Law Quarterly Review 338 (2008).

Lessons Learnt and Reconciliation Commission, Report of the Commission of Inquiry on Lessons Learnt and Reconciliation.

Lynne Rienner Publishers. Excerpts from Dinah PoKempner, Valuing the Goldstone Report, 16 Global Governance 144 (2010).

Michigan Law Review. Excerpts from Martti Koskenniemi, The Pull of the Mainstream, 88 Michigan Law Review 1946 (1990).

ProQuest, UMI Dissertation Publishing. Excerpts from Patricia B. Minikon, Truth Commissions in Africa: Learning Over a Decade (2 September 2011).

MIT Press. Excerpts from Jack Snyder and Leslie Vinjamuri, Trials and Errors: Principle and Pragmatism in Strategies of International Justice, 28 International Security 5 (2003/04).

The New Republic. Excerpts from Amartya Sen, Freedoms and Needs, The New Republic (January 10 and 17, 1994).

New York Review of Books. Excerpts from Kenneth Roth, The Court the U.S. Doesn't Want (19 Nov. 1998); Amartya Sen, More Than 100 Million Women are Missing (20 Dec. 1990); Women and Islam: A Debate with Human Rights Watch (22 March 2012).

New York Times. Excerpts from Keith Bradsher, China Moves to Stop Transplants of Organs after Executions (23 March 2012); Barbara Crossette, Inquiry Says UN Inertia in '94 Worsened Genocide in Rwanda (17 Dec. 1999); Edmund Andrews, German Churches, Ever Giving, Ask to Receive (6 Jan. 1998); Alessandra Stanley, Pope Tells India His Church Has Right to Evangelize (8 Nov. 1999); Barbara Crossette, Testing the Limits of Tolerance as Cultures Mix (6 March 1999).

New York University School of Law. José Alvarez, Opening Remarks, How Best to Assure the Independence of the ICC Prosecutor (11 November 2011).

New York University Law Review. Excerpts from Jed Rubenfeld, Unilateralism and Constitutionalism, 79 New York University Law Review 1971 (2004); David S. Law and Mila Versteeg, The Declining Influence of the United States Constitution, 87 New York University Law Review 3 (2012).

New York University Journal of International Law & Policy. Excerpts from Eric Posner, Some Skeptical Comments on Beth Simmons's Mobilizing for Human Rights, 44 NYU Journal of International Law & Policy 819 (2012); Edward T. Swaine, Ersatz Treaties, 44 NYU Journal of International Law & Policy 833 (2012); Beth A. Simmons, Reflections on Mobilizing for Human Rights, 44 NYU Journal of International Law & Policy 729 (2012).

Northern Ireland Legal Quarterly. Excerpts from W.L. Twining and P.E. Twining, Bentham on Torture, 24 Northern Ireland Legal Quarterly 305 (1973).

Notre Dame Law Review. Excerpts from Cass R. Sunstein, Rights and Their Critics, 70 Notre Dame Law Review 727 (1995).

Organization of American States Inter-American Commission on Human Rights. Excerpts from Detainees in Guatanamo Bay, Cuba Request for Precautionary Measures; Response of the United States to Request for Precautionary Measures, Detainees in Guantanamo Bay, Cuba; Detainees in Guantanamo Bay, Cuba, Reiteration and Further Amplification of Precautionary Measures; Resolution No. 2/06 on Guantanamo Bay, Precautionary Measures; Resolution No. 2/11 Regarding the Situation of the Detainees at Guantanamo; Press Release, 10 Years After Detentions in Guantanamo Began, the IACHR Repeats its Call to Close the Detention Center; Report on Terrorism and Human Rights.

Overseas Development Institute. Excerpts from Claire Melamed, After 2015: Contexts, Politics and Processes for a Post-2015 Global Agreement on Development, Overseas Development Institute, Research Reports and Studies (4 January 2012).

Oxford University Press. Excerpts from Antonio Cassese, A Plea for a Global Community Grounded in the Core of Human Rights, in Realizing Utopia: The Future of International Law (2012); P. Craig and G. de Búrca, EU Law: Text, Cases, and Materials (5th edn. 2011); Dominic McGoldrick, Human Rights Committee: Its Role in the Development of the ICCPR (1991); Sandra Fredman, Human Rights Transformed: Positive Rights and Positive Duties (2008); Sanford Levinson, Contemplating Torture: An Introduction, in Sanford Levinson (ed.), Torture: A Collection (2004); Amartya Sen, Development as Freedom (1999); Eugene Kamenka, Human Rights, Peoples' Rights, in James Crawford (ed.), The Rights of Peoples (1988); Ann Janette Rosga & Margaret L. Satterthwaite, Measuring Human Rights: U.N. Indicators in Critical Perspective, in K. Davis, A. Fisher, B. Kingsbury & S. Merry (eds.), Governance by Indicators: Global Power through Quantification and Rankings (2012;)Dinah Shelton, Introduction: Law, Non-Law and the Problem of 'Soft Law' in Dinah Shelton (ed.), Commitment and Compliance: The Role of Non-Binding Norms in the International Legal System (2000); Henry Steiner, Some Characteristics of the Liberal Political Tradition, in H. Steiner & P. Alston, International Human Rights in Context (1996); J.H.H. Weiler,

Editorial, State and Nation; Church, Mosque and Synagogue – The Trailer, 8 International Journal of Constitutional Law 157 (2010). By permission of Oxford University Press.

PLAN. Excerpts from Tradition and Rights: Female Genital Cutting in West Africa (2006).

The Philosophical Quarterly. Excerpts from James W. Nickel, Poverty and Rights, 55 The Philosophical Quarterly 385 (2005).

Pretoria University Law Press. Excerpts from Lucy A. Williams, The Role of Courts in the Quantitative-Implementation of Social and Economic Rights: A Comparative Study, 3 Constitutional Court Review 2010 [South Africa] (2011).

Princeton University Press. Excerpts from David Scheffer, All the Missing Souls: A Personal History of the War Crimes Tribunals (2012); David Kennedy, The Dark Side of Virtue (2004); Frederick Schauer, The Exceptional First Amendment, in Michael Ignatieff, American Exceptionalism and Human Rights (2005).

Random House. Excerpts from Mary Ann Glendon, A World Made New (2001).

Republic of Rwanda. Reply to Amnesty International's Report 'Rwanda: The Troubled Course of Justice' (May 2000).

Thomas Risse & Kathryn Sikkink. Excerpts from Conclusion, in T. Risse, S. Ropp & K. Sikkink (eds.), From Commitment to Compliance: The Persistent Power of Human Rights (forthcoming 2013).

Routledge. Excerpts from Peter Malanczuk, Akehurst's Modern Introduction to International Law, 7th rev. edn. (1997); Priscilla B. Hayner, Unspeakable Truths: Confronting State Terror and Atrocity, 2d edn. (2011).

Sally Engle Merry. Excerpts from The Problem of Human Rights Indicators (unpublished manuscript, 2012).

Shoe String Press. Excerpts from H. Lauterpacht, International Law And Human Rights (1950).

Singapore Academy of Law. Excerpts from Konakuppakatil Gopinathan Balakrishnan, Growth of Public Interest Litigation in India, 21 Singapore Academy of Law Journal 1 (2009), ©2009 author and Singapore Academy of Law. Reproduced with permission.

South African Government. Excerpts from Report of Truth and Reconciliation Commission of South Africa (2003).

South African Journal on Human Rights. Excerpts from Sandra Fredman, Engendering Socio-Economic Rights, 25 South African Journal on Human Rights 410 (2009).

Stanford University Press. Excerpts from Lars Waldorf, Like Jews Waiting For Jesus: Posthumous Justice in Post-Conflict Rwanda, in Rosalind Shaw and Lars Waldorf (eds.), Localizing Transitional Justice (2010).

Truth and Reconciliation Commission of Sierra Leone. Excerpts from the Final Report of the Truth and Reconciliation Commission of Sierra Leone: Witness To Truth (2004).

United Nations Development Program. Excerpts from Yash Ghai and Jill Cottrell, The Millennium Declaration, Rights and Constitutions (2011).

Universidad de Deusto. Excerpts from Christof Heyns and Magnus Killander, The African Regional Human Rights System in F. Gomez Isa and K. de Feyter (eds.), International Protection of Human Rights: Achievements and Challenges (2006).

University of British Columbia Law Review. Excerpts from Karl Klare, Legal Theory and Democratic Reconstruction, 25 University of British Columbia Law Review 69 (1991)

University of California Press. Excerpts from Pnina Lahav, Judgment in Jerusalem (1997).

University of Chicago Press. Excerpts from Sally Engle Merry, Human Rights and Gender Violence (2006).

University of Pennsylvania Press. Excerpts from Joan Fitzpatrick, Human Rights In Crisis: The International System for Protecting Rights During States of Emergency (1994); Makau Mutua, Human Rights and the African Fingerprint, in Mutua, Human Rights: A Political and Cultural Critique (2002); Makau Mutua, Human Rights, Religion, and Proselytism, in Mutua, Human Rights: A Political and Cultural Critique (2002).

Vanderbilt Journal of Transnational Law. Excerpts from Harold Hongju Koh, Foreign Official Immunity After Samantar: A United States Government Perspective, 44 Vanderbilt Journal of Transnational Law 1141 (Nov. 2011).

Vatican Radio. Excerpts from Statement by the Holy See Delegation (Archbishop Silvano M. Tomasi, Permanent Observer of the Holy See to the UN and Other International Organizations in Geneva) (9 March 2012).

Versa Books. Excerpts from Richard Rorty, Human Rights, Rationality and Sentimentality, in Obrad Saviç (ed.), The Politics of Human Rights (1999).

Virginia Journal of International Law. Excerpts from M. O. Chibundu, Making Customary International Law Through Municipal Adjudication: A Structural Inquiry 39 Virginia Journal of International Law 1069 (1999).

Wall Street Journal. Excerpts from Max Boot, When 'Justice' and 'Peace' Don't Mix (2 Oct. 2000).

The Washington Post. Excerpts from Richard Goldstone, Reconsidering the Goldstone Report on Israel and War Crimes (1 April 2011).

The Washington Quarterly. Excerpts from Timothy Savage, Europe and Islam: Crescent Waxing, Cultures Clashing, 27 The Washington Quarterly No. 3 (2004).

Western Australia. Excerpts from the Report of the Consultation Committee for a Proposed WA Human Rights Act, November 2007 ©State of Western Australia.

William Easterly. Excerpts from William Easterly, Poverty is Not a Human Rights Violation, Aid Watch blog (5 June 2009).

Wilton Park. Excerpts from Isobelle Jaques, Strengthening Democratic Governance: The Role of Civil Society, Report on Wilton Park Conference S06/10 (2006).

Wolters Kluwer Law & Business. Excerpts from Mohammed Bedjaoui, The Right to Development in M. Bedjaoui (ed.), International Law: Achievements and Prospects (1991).

World Bank. Excerpts from the World Development Report 2012, Gender Equality and Development; Siobhan McInerney-Lankford, Mac Darrow and Lavanya

Rajamani, Human Rights and Climate Change: A Review of the International Legal Dimensions (2011); Varun Gauri, Redressing Grievances and Complaints Regarding Basic Service Delivery, Policy Research Working Paper 5699, June 2011. The findings, interpretations, and conclusions expressed in this paper are entirely those of the authors. They do not necessarily represent the views of the International Bank for Reconstruction and Development/World Bank and its affiliated organizations, or those of the Executive Directors of the World Bank or the governments they represent.

World Health Organization. Excerpts from World Health Organization Fact Sheet No. 241 (2012).

World Peace Foundation. Excerpts from Henry Steiner, Introduction to Truth Commissions in Yael Tamir (ed.) Truth Commissions: A Comparative Assessment (1997).

W. W. Norton & Company. Excerpts from Kathryn Sikkink, The Justice Cascade (2011).

Yale Human Rights and Development Law Journal. Excerpts from Mac Darrow, Lies, Damned Lies, and the Millennium Development Goals: Human Rights Priorities for the Post-2015 Development Agenda, 15 Yale Hum. Rts. & Devt. L. J. (2012).

Yale Journal of International Law. Excerpts from José Alvarez, Crimes of States/ Crimes of Hate: Lessons from Rwanda, 24 Yale Journal of International Law 365 (1999).

Yale Law Journal. Excerpts from Oona A. Hathaway, Do Human Rights Treaties Make A Difference?, 111 Yale Law Journal 1935 (2002).

While every care has been taken to establish and acknowledge copyright, and contact the copyright owners, the publishers tender their apologies for any accidental infringement. They would be pleased to come to a suitable agreement with the rightful owners in each case.

Additional comments from Professor Amartya Sen

The following footnote from Professor Sen supplements the article 'More Than 100 Million Women are Missing' (cited on pp 168–70):

'My *New York Review* article on "missing women" was written in the early 1990s and it mainly used the empirical material that had emerged in the 1980s. At that time, the phenomenon of missing women was mainly due to discrimination against women — both young girls and adult women — in the attention that their health conditions received. Since that time there has emerged another increased source of discrimination — the use of sex-selective abortion aimed particularly at aborting female fetuses. Indeed, even as the mortality differential against females declined, exerting a downward influence on the ratio of missing women, the emergence and increased use of sex determination of fetuses, followed by selective abortion, had an upward influence on the proportion of missing women (due to what can be called "natality discrimination"). As a result the overall proportion of missing women have not declined — or declined only by a little for many countries, including China and India.

My 2003 editorial article in the *British Medical Journal*, called "'Missing Women' Revisited," discusses this changing pattern of discrimination against women. In India there is also a sharp divide between Northern and Western states, on one side, which had developed sizable anti-female bias by the time of 2001 census, and the states in the East and the South which did not indicate large use of selective abortion of female fetuses. This issue is discussed in greater detail in my joint book with Jean Dreze, *India: Development and Participation* (Oxford University Press, 2002). The census of 2011 broadly confirms the same regional division, with Northern and Western states of India showing clear — and in fact increased — evidence of sex-selective abortion of female fetuses, while nearly all the Southern and Eastern states record female-male ratios at, and following, birth that are still comparable to those in Europe and America.'

PART A

INTRODUCTORY NOTIONS AND BACKGROUND TO THE INTERNATIONAL HUMAN RIGHTS REGIME

This course book examines the world of contemporary human rights, including legal norms, political contexts and moral ideals. It takes us into diverse realms, including humanitarian laws of war, human rights discourse, state interests, international relations and institutions, governmental (state) and nongovernmental (non-state) actors, and economic development. The boundaries of the subject have steadily expanded as the human rights regime that emerged after the Second World War has become an indelible part of our legal, political and moral landscape. Given the breadth and complexity of the regime, including its engagement with law, politics, morals and radically different cultures, the course book necessarily includes materials from a range of disciplines.

Three principal themes — law, politics and morals — are interrelated, indeed inseparable, for an understanding of the regime. The political and moral aspects of international human rights are self-evident; it is the international legal aspect that is novel. The rules and standards of contemporary human rights are expressed not only through states' constitutions, laws and practices, but also through treaties and international custom, as well as the work products (decisions about action, forms of adjudication, studies, investigative reports, resolutions, recommendations) of diverse international institutions and organs.

Throughout, the materials underscore the youth of this regime, and the task of students and others committed to its ideals is to see themselves not as apprentices learning about an established, even static, framework of ideas and institutions, but rather as shapers and architects of the regime's ongoing development. The book's goal is then not only to train students to work effectively within existing structures and boundaries, but also to impart a broad as well as critical understanding, and to provoke ideas about the directions in which the regime may be or ought to be heading.

The Preface sets forth the book's pedagogical goals, conceptual structure and formal organization.

1

Human Rights Concepts and Discourse

This introductory chapter assumes no special knowledge about the foundations or content of rights, human rights and international human rights. Rather it is meant to spur thoughts about a range of issues that later chapters examine.

The two sections of the chapter explore some fundamental questions from complementary perspectives. Section A introduces human rights issues in the large, as they arise and become known. It is not attentive to courts, for in many of the situations it addresses, courts will play only a marginal role, if a role at all. The medium for looking at these issues is journalistic reporting.

Section B moves to an examination of the way that courts from different states address and argue about the alleged violations of rights that come before them. The common issue in Section B engaging these courts is the legality of capital punishment under illustrative state laws and under the developing international human rights law. At the same time, these materials examine the growing attention of national courts to foreign law, whether constitutional, or statutory or judicial decisions, to learn how other countries reason and decide about the permissibility of capital punishment (and many other issues). Those inquiries lead us to what many would describe as the 'special case' (or 'situation') of the United States with respect to human rights (and other fields), that involves so-called US exceptionalism or unilateralism.

A. GLOBAL SNAPSHOTS

The following media excerpts reflect the diverse human rights problems that the world confronts. When reading them, consider the following questions:

What is the source of the rules or standards under which governmental, inter-governmental and nongovernmental organizations evaluate and criticize a state?
What different roles do the types of organizations referred to in these articles seem to play?
How would you identify the alleged human rights violation in each story?
Are you clear in each story that (if the reported facts are true) there has been a violation?

Does all conduct that you believe may violate a right address only individuals' rights, or do rights of groups also seem relevant?

Are (international) human rights violations committed only by states, or are nongovernmental forces and individuals also accused of such violations?

What steps, if any, seem to be taken to bring an end to the violations?

MEDIA STORIES: WHAT HUMAN RIGHTS ISSUES ARE RAISED?

(1) Sri Lanka: A Child is Summarily Executed

by Callum Macrae, *The Independent*, 11 Mar. 2012

It is a chilling piece of footage that . . . dates from the final hours of the bloody 26-year civil war between the Sri Lankan government and the secessionist rebels of the Tamil Tigers, the LTTE.

A 12-year-old boy lies on the ground. He is stripped to the waist and has five neat bullet holes in his chest. His name is Balachandran Prabhakaran and he is the son of the LTTE leader, Velupillai Prabhakaran. He has been executed in cold blood. Beside him lie the bodies of five men, believed to be his bodyguards. There are strips of cloth on the ground indicating that they were tied and blindfolded before they were shot — further evidence suggesting that the Sri Lankan government forces had a systematic policy of executing many surrendering or captured LTTE fighters and leading figures, even if they were children.

. . .

Last year, a special panel of experts appointed by the UN Secretary-General, Ban Ki-moon, suggested that as many as 40,000 civilians died in the last few weeks of the war — the vast majority as a result of government shelling, much of which was targeted on so called "No Fire Zones" set up by the government itself. But as international concern grew over the emerging evidence of appalling crimes against civilians, the Sri Lankan government, headed by President Mahinda Rajapaksa, and his powerful brother, the Defence Minister, Gotabaya Rajapaksa, launched a counter-offensive. At its heart was a special inquiry appointed by the President, the Lessons Learnt and Reconciliation Commission (LLRC).

This, they insisted, would answer the international criticisms. When the LLRC finally reported last December, it did make important concessions — not least an admission that considerable numbers of civilians had died (a fact denied by the government until then). But it specifically denied that civilians had been targeted and rejected allegations of war crimes by the government. It thus failed entirely to deal with the evidence of blame pointing to the political and military leadership.

But still the criticisms have grown — and are likely to increase, following the new revelations in the Channel 4 film. In one incident, legally significant because it is well documented, two international UN workers leading the last UN overland food convoy became trapped near a temporary hospital in a village primary school in Uddiyakattu, in the first of the government's No Fire Zones.

With the help of other civilians they began to dig bunkers to provide some protection from incoming shellfire. As was standard practice, one of the UN workers, an Australian called Peter Mackay, took precise GPS co-ordinates of the site, and these were supplied to the government. But if that had any effect, it was certainly not the desired one. Over the next couple of days the camp was subjected to a massive, sustained barrage of incoming shellfire, much of it falling directly on or near to the UN bunker. Dozens were killed — and many more horrifically injured. It was all photographed by the UN workers.

In a sense, it was just one relatively small incident in the ongoing carnage of the war, but it is potentially significant because it provides specific evidence linking the Sri Lankan government's chain of command to knowledge of targeted attacks on civilians — attacks that appear to constitute war crimes.

...

(2) NAACP to Call on UN to Investigate Voter Disfranchisement in US
by Ed Pilkington, *The Guardian*, 9 Mar. 2012

The leaders of the National Association for the Advancement of Colored People, the NAACP, will travel to Geneva next week to tell the UN human rights council that a co-ordinated legislative attempt is being made by states across America to disfranchise millions of black and Latino voters in November's presidential election.

The delegation . . . [will] . . . call on the UN body to launch a formal investigation into the spread of restrictive electoral laws, particularly in southern states. The NAACP intends to invite a UN team to travel across America to see for itself the impact of the new laws, which it argues are consciously designed to suppress minority voting.

The UN has no power to intervene in the workings of individual American states. But [the NAACP President] told the Guardian that the UN had a powerful weapon in its armoury: shame.

"Shame alone is effective. The US, and individual states within the US that have introduced these laws, have a vested interest in maintaining the opinion that we are the world's leading democracy. That means something". . . .

...

A recent report by [NYU Law School's] Brennan Center for Justice estimated that since last year more than 5 million eligible voters had had their right to vote stripped from them.

There are already 19 new laws on the books in 14 different states. . . . Some laws involve a requirement to show photo identification in polling stations — disproportionately hitting black and elderly people, who often do not have such ID.

Other laws have cut back on early voting schemes, heavily used by ethnic minority and older people, and still others disfranchise former convicted prisoners, even in some cases years after their sentences were completed.

...

(3) Women Must Be Given Equal Rights in Decision-Making, Pillay Says

by Jennifer M. Freedman, Bloomberg, 7 Mar. 2012

Women remain under-represented in politics and business, and won't be recognized as equal partners in decision-making changes without institutional change, said the United Nations' top human-rights official.

"With too few women leaders in politics, and woefully insufficient numbers of women leaders in industry, women are not taking part in decisive discussions on how to respond to global crises," UN High Commissioner for Human Rights Navi Pillay said in a statement today. "Such exclusion is at our own peril –the refusal to embrace gender equality has led to many scourges, one tragic example being the ferocious spread of HIV/AIDS."

UN statistics show that women held only 19.3 percent of seats in single or lower houses of parliament worldwide as of last year and just 12 of the Fortune 500 companies have women at the helm. The European Union's justice chief Viviane Reding said in a March 5 interview she may impose quotas to compel EU companies to add more women to their boards.

Some 13.7 percent of board seats in the 27-nation EU are filled by women after a 1.9 percentage point increase between October 2010 and January 2012, the European Commission said in a March 5 report.

While women produce 60 percent to 80 percent of the food in developing countries, they rarely have rights to the land they cultivate. . . . [O]nly a fifth of landowners globally are women.

. . .

"Meaningful participation requires that women are able to access relevant information and are empowered, through education and political access, to make contributions," [Pillay] said. . ..

(4) UN Fears Public Health Disaster from Unhealthy Food

India Blooms News Service, 7 Mar. 2012

Globalized food systems and the spread of Western lifestyles has spawned an international public health disaster with over a billion people suffering from undernourishment while another billion remain overweight or obese, an independent United Nations expert warned on Tuesday.

"Our food systems create sick people," said Olivier De Schutter, the UN Special Rapporteur on the right to food. . . .

"The right to food means not only access to an adequate quantity of food, but also the ability to have a balanced and nutritious diet," he added. . . .

. . . De Schutter identified five priorities for putting nutrition back at the heart of food systems in both the developed and developing world. They are taxing unhealthy products; regulating foods high in saturated fats, salt and sugar; cracking down on junk food advertising; overhauling "wrong-headed" agricultural subsidies making unhealthy ingredients cheaper than others; and supporting local food production.

"Urbanization, supermarketization, and the global spread of Western lifestyles have shaken up traditional food habits. The result is a public health disaster," said the expert. "Governments have been focusing on increasing calorie availability, but they have often been indifferent to what kind of calories are on offer, at what prices, to whom they are accessible, and how they are marketed."

De Schutter pointed to the accessibility and abundance of highly-processed foods as a major factor in nutrition-related illnesses as they tend to be richer in saturated and trans-fatty acids, salt and sugars.

As a result, he argued, children frequently become addicted to the junk foods targeted at them. Also, it is the poorest population groups in wealthy countries that are most affected by processed foods, which are often more affordable than healthy diets. He further noted that the export of such Western dietary habits had brought diabetes and heart disease to the developing world.

"We have deferred to food companies the responsibility for ensuring that a good nutritional balance emerges. Voluntary guidelines and piecemeal nutrition initiatives have failed to create a system with the right signals, and the odds remain stacked against the achievement of a healthy, balanced diet," said De Schutter.

"Ambitious, targeted nutrition strategies can work," he added, "but only if the food systems underpinning them are put right."

(5) Women on the Back Foot in the Arab Spring

by Ines Bel Aiba, Agence France Presse, 5 Mar. 2012

They were on the front line during last year's Arab uprisings, but women now fear for their rights as Islamists reap the fruits of revolt, winning elections in Egypt and Tunisia and gaining influence in Libya.

In Tunisia, the dominant Islamist Ennahda party has said it wants to fortify the personal status code, which bans polygamy and grants Tunisian women unparalleled rights in the region, by making it a basic law.

Changing such a law requires two thirds of the votes in parliament.

But recent debates in the constituent assembly on the mention of sharia—Islamic law— in Tunisia's constitution have worried women and liberal parties who fear a decline in women's rights.

In Egypt, where Islamists dominated parliamentary and senate elections, female representation in parliament fell from 12 percent to just two percent, and a quota that gave women 64 seats was abandoned.

"Women are now confronting attempts to exclude them from public life, as well as acts of discrimination and violence, perpetrated with impunity by extremist groups and security forces," said a report by the International Federation for Human Rights.

In Tunisia, some teachers have been intimidated for not wearing the hijab, a head covering worn by devout women.

...

Kuwaiti women's rights activist Ebtehal al-Khatib said the rise of the Islamists in the aftermath of the Arab Spring revolutions will "first and foremost negatively affect the role of women" in the Arab world.

"When religious groups rise to positions of power . . . the first to be affected negatively are women . . . her issues and concerns and rights will be the first thing to be shelved" as Islamist-oriented parliaments take hold in the Middle East, she said.

In Egypt, the Muslim Brotherhood, whose Freedom and Justice Party dominates parliament, says a woman cannot become president of the country. "Any law that agrees with sharia is welcome. Those that do not aren't," Brotherhood spokesman Mahmud Ghozlan told AFP.

. . .

The day he declared Libya liberated [after the reign of Colonel Kadhafi], the head of the National Transitional Council Mustafa Abdel Jalil said sharia would be the main source of law and any law that violates sharia would be null, mentioning marriage and divorce laws.

A first draft of the electoral law in Libya reserved 10 percent of seats in the constituent assembly for women, but that was later abandoned, much to the outrage of women's rights advocates.

. . .

[T]he International Federation for Human Rights called on countries in the region to "enshrine in the constitution the principle of equality between men and women and the prohibition of all forms of discrimination against women."

(6) Guatemala Judge Denies ex-Dictator's Amnesty Claim

by Romina Ruiz-Goiriena, The Associated Press, 1 Mar. 2012

A former U.S.-backed dictator who presided over one of the bloodiest periods of Guatemala's civil war has no amnesty from charges he ordered the murder, torture and displacement of thousands of Mayan Indians, a judge ruled Thursday.

The decision to strip ex-Gen. Efrain Rios Montt of the pardon granted by his successor more than a quarter-century ago will be appealed to Guatemala's highest court, his defense said. That means any trial of the 85-year-old former strongman could be months or years away.

Nonetheless, human rights advocates said, Judge Miguel Angel Galvez's decision is an important symbolic victory for the victims of one of the most horrific of the conflicts that devastated Central America during the last decades of the Cold War.

Guatemala's leaders have been criticized for years for their inability or unwillingness to prosecute government forces and allied paramilitaries accused of marching into Mayan villages, carrying out rapes and torture, and slaughtering women, children and unarmed men in a "scorched earth" campaign aimed at eliminating the support for a left-wing guerrilla movement.

Despite a series of international inquiries finding him responsible for war crimes, Rios Montt served as a Guatemalan congressman for 15 years until he lost a re-election race late last year. He had held immunity from prosecution while a member of Congress and was put under house arrest after losing his post.

One of the highest priorities of the president who won last year's election, Otto Perez Molina, has been campaigning for the elimination of a U.S. ban on military aid to Guatemala, which is locked in a fight against heavily armed drug cartels that have taken over swathes of the country.

Among the conditions set by the U.S. Congress for restoring the aid is reforming Guatemala's justice system and putting an end to impunity.

. . .

Galvez ruled that a 1986 amnesty law passed by Gen. Oscar Mejia Victores, who ousted Rios Montt, was invalidated by an international treaty against genocide that Guatemala signed in 1949.

Rios Montt is accused of authorizing 1,400 human rights violations, the displacement of 29,000 indigenous Guatemalans and 1,771 killings, many under a program intended to completely eliminate an indigenous Mayan ethnic group known as the Ixil.

"There are crimes like genocide and crimes against humanity that have no statute of limitations, and for that reason there can be no amnesty decree," Galvez said.

. . .

(7) Nato Must Investigate Civilian Deaths in Libya, says Amnesty

***The Guardian*, 19 Mar. 2012**

Nato [the North Atlantic Treaty Organization] has failed to properly investigate or provide compensation for civilian deaths caused by its air strikes during the seven-month operation in Libya that helped bring about the overthrow of Muammar Gaddafi, Amnesty International has said.

Echoing similar criticisms aired this month by Russia, Amnesty said scores of Libyans who were not involved in the conflict had been killed or injured in Nato bombings but there had been no proper investigations into their deaths.

"Nato officials repeatedly stressed their commitment to protecting civilians," said Donatella Rovera, a senior crisis adviser at Amnesty. "They cannot now brush aside the deaths of scores of civilians with some vague statement of regret without properly investigating these deadly incidents."

Inquiries should determine whether any civilian casualties resulted from a breach of international law, and if so, those responsible should be brought to justice, Amnesty said.

The Nato military mission, authorised by the UN security council, began on 31 March [2011] with the aim of protecting civilians under attack or threat of attack.

Nato forces carried out about 26,000 sorties including 9,600 strike missions and destroyed about 5,900 targets before operations ended on 31 October.

Investigators for the UN human rights council concluded this month that Nato had caused civilian deaths but had taken extensive precautions to ensure civilians were not killed.

Amnesty agreed Nato had made significant efforts to minimise the risk of civilian casualties, through precision bombing and warning where strikes would occur.

However, the rights group said that did not absolve Nato from carrying out investigations into any deaths, or making reparations to victims or families of those killed.

Survivors and victims' relatives interviewed by Amnesty said they had never even been contacted by Nato.

Amnesty said Nato itself had documented 55 cases of civilians, including 16 children and 14 women, being killed in air strikes in Tripoli, Zlitan, Majer, Sirte and Brega, often in private homes with no clear evidence of any military purpose.

Another 34 people, including eight children, were killed in three separate attacks on two houses in Majer with no explanation for why they were targeted, Amnesty said.

Nato's most recent response to Amnesty stated it "deeply regretted any harm" its air strikes had caused but said it no longer had a mandate to carry out any activities in Libya.

...

(8) William Easterly, Poverty is Not a Human Rights Violation

Aid Watch, blog, 5 June 2009

The title of this blog will make many think I am callous, and yet I definitely agree that poverty is an EXTREMELY BAD THING. Perhaps some use the words "human rights violation" to be equivalent to "extremely bad thing," but why? There are many different "extremely bad things," and it helps if everybody discriminates between them.

The only useful definition of human rights is one where a human rights crusader could identify WHOSE rights are being violated and WHO is the violator. That is what historically has led to progress on human rights. The government officers of the slave-owning antebellum US and the slave-owners were violating the rights of slaves — leading to activism against such violators that eventually yielded the Emancipation Proclamation. The local southern government officers were violating the civil rights of southern blacks under Jim Crow [US laws providing for racial segregation], leading to activism against these violators that yielded the Civil Rights Act and the Voting Rights Act. The apartheid government officers in South Africa violated the rights of black South Africans, and activism against these violators brought the end of apartheid.

Poverty does not fit this definition of rights. Who is depriving the poor of their right to an adequate income? There are many theories of poverty, but few of them lead to a clear identification of the Violator of this right. Moreover, human rights are a clear dichotomy — someone violates your rights or they do not. But the line between poor and not-poor is arbitrary — it is different in different countries, and on a global scale, many still argue what is the right dividing line that constitutes poverty. So calling poverty a "human rights violation" does not point to any concrete actions that the "violator" must stop in order to restore rights to the "violated."

So it's disappointing that the 2009 report of Amnesty International is blurring its previous clear focus on human rights to a fuzzy vision that now includes poverty:

So many people are living in utter destitution . . . As the global economic outlook appears more and more gloomy, hope lies in the . . . determination of human rights defenders willing to challenge entrenched interests despite the risks they face. (p. 9)

Social and political progress arguably happens the same way as progress in science or as progress in business: somebody precisely defines a problem and somebody (possibly somebody else?) hits upon a way to solve that well-defined problem. To confuse poverty and human rights violations is to slow down the solutions to both.

...

(9) Wronged Women of Liberia Reluctant to Revisit Human Rights Abuses

by Tamasin Ford, *The Guardian*, 28 Feb. 2012

"Most of the women here were raped [during the war]," says Yarih Geebah, the speaker for Ganta Concerned Women. "But if you don't have money, nothing happens. [For] we, the poor people, we who don't know book... justice don't prevail."

Liberia went through a 14-year civil war in which people were forced to perform the most debased and cruel acts imaginable. [A] survey in 2004 estimated 40% of the country's women were subjected to sexual violence, although other estimates suggest the figure is higher.

One woman from the group spoke of how she was taken as a "rebel wife" and raped repeatedly. Eight years later, the boy she was "married to" — now a man, and also the father of her daughter — sells petrol in Ganta. She sees him every day.

In August 2003, when the Accra peace accord was signed, it was decided the best chance for Liberia to get some form of justice was through a Truth and Reconciliation Commission (TRC), as had been set up in countries such as South Africa and Rwanda. The commission's mandate was to document and investigate human rights abuses committed between January 1979 and October 2003 and then make recommendations to the Liberian government.

Geebah and many of her group testified in front of the TRC when it toured the country between 2007 and 2008. They were encouraged to speak of the trauma and horrors they endured, and also to name their perpetrators. Many who testified complain that they have seen no benefits from the process. No court cases, no reparations, no counselling and no justice. They also worry it has put them at risk. "We're in danger now," said Geebah. "We named those people who did the bad things."

No one has been tried for any crimes committed in Liberia. Former president Charles Taylor is currently awaiting a verdict after being tried for war crimes and crimes against humanity at The Hague, but the offences in question were committed in neighbouring Sierra Leone, not Liberia.

In June 2009, the TRC released its final report. Its findings were marred by controversy, mainly because of two recommendations: first, that a war crimes tribunal should be established; second, that President Johnson Sirleaf should be banned from political office for 30 years because of her ties to former warring factions. To date, the TRC report lies dormant.

However, the first annual message of Sirleaf's second term was dominated by words like reconciliation, unity and healing. "To claim the future, we must reflect and heal the past," she said. Sirleaf even went so far as to add: "We will advance the truth and reconciliation process by implementing all practical recommendations."

Presumably, she wasn't referring to the recommendation about her exclusion from political office.

Sirleaf also spoke about the national palava hut programme, which was one of the TRC's recommendations. Palava huts form a big part of Liberia's traditional justice system; people from the community gather inside an open-walled hut, discuss the crime and then together decide on the punishment.

In November, the president told a room of international reporters that the palava hut programme would start in the new year and, since she was among those named by the TRC, she would be the first person to appear.

Sirleaf said the government had allocated funds for the programme and named fellow Nobel peace laureate Leymah Gbowee as the person to spearhead it. She likened the plans to the Gacaca courts in Rwanda; people will be brought together, face the truth, and then seek forgiveness. Eminent members of the community will be there to witness the process, and those who still don't feel satisfied can pursue their case in court.

But for some of the women in Ganta, the idea of revisiting the past does not amount to reconciliation. "We don't want to explain it to anyone again," said Geebah. "We don't want the memory to come back." The things they need are jobs, education for their children, food on the table, and homes to live in — not another truth-seeking exercise. And they are not convinced they will get justice in a palava hut.

...

(10) UN Chief Urges Africa to Respect Gay Rights

by Peter Heinlein, Voice of America, 29 Jan. 2012

U.N. Secretary-General Ban Ki-moon has called on African leaders to respect gay rights, and to accept the jurisdiction of the International Criminal Court.

On a continent where homosexuality is outlawed in many places, the U.N. chief told Africa's leaders to end discrimination against gays and lesbians. He said laws against homosexuality violate the Universal Declaration of Human Rights.

"Let me mention one form of discrimination that has been ignored or even sanctioned by many states for far too long, discrimination based on sexual orientation or gender identity. This has prompted some governments to treat people as second-class citizens, or even criminals," he said. "Confronting this discrimination is a challenge. But we must live up to the ideals of the Universal Declaration."

The more than 30 African heads of state and government sat silently during Ban's speech. But more than one speaker at the opening summit session expressed irritation at what many perceive as outside interference in African affairs.

Homosexuals face severe discrimination in most African societies. Gays are often ostracized. South Africa is the only African country where gay rights are officially recognized.

An international AIDS conference in Addis Ababa last month was nearly derailed when the leaders of Ethiopia's main religious denominations scheduled a joint news conference to express outrage at a planned meeting of gay-rights activists.

The clergymen called off their protest only after the gay-rights meeting was moved from a local hotel to the United Nations compound.

Many of those same religious leaders met reporters in 2008 to urge passage of a constitutional amendment against homosexuality.

Secretary General Ban also used his speech to urge respect for the International Criminal Court. Several African leaders have accused the court of an anti-African bias.

Outgoing AU chairman, Equatorial Guinea's President Teodoro Obiang Nguema told the summit Africa should establish its own court to put an end to what he called "unjust and discriminatory actions" by international tribunals.

But Secretary General Ban pointed out the new chief prosecutor of the ICC is an African woman, Fatou Bensouda of Gambia

(11) David Cameron Calls for Reform of European Court of Human Rights

by Nicholas Watt, *The Guardian*, 24 Jan. 2012

[British Prime Minister] David Cameron is to warn that the European court of human rights is in danger of turning into a "small claims court" that fails to deal with serious violations of human rights, unless it embarks on reforms.

Amid anger in Britain at last week's decision of the court to block the deportation of the Islamist cleric Abu Qatada to Jordan, the prime minister will on Wednesday accuse the court of undermining its reputation by unnecessarily overturning judgments reached in credible national courts.

...

The court enforces the European convention on human rights, drafted in 1950 by the Council of Europe, which is designed to ensure universal human rights across Europe. The council has 47 members and is separate from the 27-strong EU.

The prime minister will say: "The court should be free to deal with the most serious violations of human rights; it should not be swamped with an endless backlog of cases. The court should ensure that the right to individual petition counts; it should not act as a small claims court. And the court should hold us all to account; it should not undermine its own reputation by going over national decisions where it does not need to. For the sake of the 800 million people the court serves, we need to reform it so that it is true to its original purpose."

...

The UK government privately believes the court should spend less time focusing on countries such as Britain, France and Germany, which have well-regarded legal systems and a strong record on human rights, and more time focusing on countries such as Russia and Ukraine with less impressive records. Russia accounts for 26.6% of the backlog at the court. Cameron contrasts Britain's record with other Council of Europe member states, which face cases over extrajudicial killings and torture.

The court found against Bulgaria after an inmate was forcibly placed in a psychiatric institution and held against their will for years. It found against Ukraine over the ill-treatment of prisoners in "training exercises" by special forces, and it found against Russia over the persecution of the children of Chechen dissidents.

The prime minister will make clear that the court should focus on such violations, and will say Britain has a long and exemplary record on human rights. "Human rights is a cause that runs deep in the British heart and long in British history."

…

(12) China Moves to Stop Transplants of Organs after Executions

by Keith Bradsher, *New York Times*, 23 Mar. 2012

China said on Friday that within three to five years it planned to end the practice of transplanting organs from executed prisoners, a step that would address what for decades has been one of the country's most criticized human rights issues.

A wide range of official news media outlets ran apparently coordinated articles describing the merits of voluntary organ donations by the public. …

[In a speech, the Vice-Minister of Health] Mr. Huang did not acknowledge any ethical issues involved in taking organs from prisoners. Instead, he raised a medical issue, saying that the rates of fungal and bacterial infection in organs taken from executed inmates were often high, which he said explained why the long-term survival rates of organ transplant recipients in China were consistently below those of other countries.

Nicholas Bequelin, a senior researcher in Hong Kong for Human Rights Watch, welcomed the policy announcement, which the rights group has campaigned for since 1994. …

…

For many years, China resisted even passing national legislation for organ donation or for establishing when brain death occurs. The worry was that in poorer areas of China or areas with lax or particularly corrupt law enforcement, doctors would be tempted to act prematurely in declaring people to be brain-dead in order to harvest their organs.

China's cabinet, the State Council, issued regulations in 2007 for voluntary organ donations. But it has struggled to popularize the practice. Chinese customs call for people to be buried or cremated with their organs intact.

People's Daily, the official newspaper of the Chinese Communist Party, said that China had 150 people who needed organ transplants for every organ that was donated voluntarily. The newspaper did not say how much of the difference was made up from executed prisoners.

…

The Dui Hua Foundation, a human rights group in San Francisco, estimated in December that China executed 4,000 people a year. …

…

Human rights groups have long criticized organ transplant procedures in mainland China for creating an incentive for prisons to execute prisoners and sell the organs. The groups have also assailed China for not following the World Health

Organization's recommendation that organs be taken only from people who are brain-dead. China allows organ harvests from people whose hearts have stopped.

. . .

Another concern has been whether prisoners and their families give informed consent, without inappropriate pressure from prison officials, for the use of organs. Families of executed prisoners sometimes complain that no one gave permission but that they were given back bodies that were sewn up after the removal of organs; Chinese prison officials have contended that these prisoners may have been the subject of autopsies.

. . .

(13) Hungary Pressed to Ease Judiciary and News Media Laws

by Palko Karasz & Melissa Eddy, *New York Times*, 21 Mar. 2012

The Council of Europe is pressing Hungary to make further statutory changes to protect the independence of the judiciary and the news media, saying that recent amendments, while welcome, are not enough.

Thorbjorn Jagland, the secretary general of the Council of Europe, met Wednesday in Budapest with Prime Minister Viktor Orban and members of his government over the disputed laws, which also tightened the rules for recognizing certain religious groups.

The Hungarian justice minister, Tibor Navracsics, said the . . . government had taken into consideration many of the suggestions made by the Venice Commission, a body that deals with constitutional affairs under the Council of Europe, which promotes democracy and human rights among its 47 member countries, including Hungary.

. . .

In a report on Hungary's judicial system issued this week, the Venice Commission said the new Constitution — which was drawn up by Mr. Orban's government and took effect on Jan. 1 — concentrated too much power, including the selection of judges, in the hands of a single person, the head of the newly created National Judicial Office, who is appointed for a nine-year term.

The new Constitution immediately raised concerns in the European Union, including worries about the independence of Hungary's central bank, and Mr. Orban responded by removing some of the powers from the judicial office.

"They have taken quite a big step regarding the independence of the judiciary," Mr. Jagland said in an interview before the meetings in Budapest. "But more has to be done."

. . .

(14) Mali Junta Announces Constitution as Pressure Mounts

by Thomas Morfin, Agence France Presse, 28 Mar. 2012

. . .

Five days after the internationally condemned military coup [in Mali] that toppled President Amadou Toumani Toure, the junta lifted its night-time curfew and reopened the borders in a bid to show the country was returning to normal.

. . .

In a statement read out by a soldier on Mali state television, the junta said the new constitution would guarantee the rule of law and basic human rights in "a pluralist democracy".

Under the terms of the constitution, no member of the junta, known as the National Committee for the Recovery of Democracy and the Restoration of the Rule, would be permitted to stand for office.

...

The rebel troops took power on March 22, blaming Toure and his government for not having adequately equipped them to tackle a rebellion by Tuareg desert warriors in the north of the country.

The international community was quick to shun the new regime. The European Union, the United States and other Western powers cut off hundreds of millions of dollars of support—except for emergency aid to drought-hit regions of the country suffering food shortages.

And at an emergency meeting Tuesday in Abidjan, Ivory Coast, the west African bloc ECOWAS renewed its call for the immediate restoration of constitutional order in Mali.

The group said it would send a delegation of six heads of state to Mali within 48 hours. It warned too that its regional troops were on standby and the bloc had not ruled out the use of force.

...

(15) Supreme Court Ruling Allows Strip Searches for Any Arrest

by Adam Liptak, *New York Times*, 2 Apr. 2012

The Supreme Court on Monday ruled by a 5-to-4 vote that officials may strip-search people arrested for any offense, however minor, before admitting them to jails even if the officials have no reason to suspect the presence of contraband.

Justice Anthony M. Kennedy, joined by the court's conservative wing, wrote that courts are in no position to second-guess the judgments of correctional officials who must consider not only the possibility of smuggled weapons and drugs, but also public health and information about gang affiliations.

"Every detainee who will be admitted to the general population may be required to undergo a close visual inspection while undressed," Justice Kennedy wrote, adding that about 13 million people are admitted each year to the nation's jails.

The procedures endorsed by the majority are forbidden by statute in at least 10 states and are at odds with the policies of federal authorities. According to a supporting brief filed by the American Bar Association, international human rights treaties also ban the procedures.

The federal appeals courts had been split on the question, though most of them prohibited strip searches unless they were based on a reasonable suspicion that contraband was present....

...

... Justice Breyer wrote that people have been subjected to "the humiliation of a visual strip search" after being arrested for driving with a noisy muffler, failing to use a turn signal and riding a bicycle without an audible bell.

A nun was strip-searched, he wrote, after an arrest for trespassing during an anti-war demonstration.

Justice Kennedy responded that "people detained for minor offenses can turn out to be the most devious and dangerous criminals."

The case [*Florence v. County of Burlington*] arose from the arrest of Albert W. Florence in New Jersey in 2005. Mr. Florence was in the passenger seat of his BMW when a state trooper pulled his wife, April, over for speeding. A records search revealed an outstanding warrant for Mr. Florence's arrest based on an unpaid fine. (The information was wrong; the fine had been paid.)

Mr. Florence was held for a week in jails in Burlington and Essex Counties, and he was strip-searched in each. [H]e was made to stand naked in front of a guard who required him to move intimate parts of his body.

. . .

QUESTIONS

Consider the human rights implications of these stories. Here are a few illustrations:

1. (Item No. 1) What international laws are at issue here? How feasible is it likely to be to get compelling evidence of governmental wrongdoing in such situations?

2. (Item No. 4) A UN expert on the right to food is understandably concerned about freedom from hunger, but should he also be taking issue with dietary patterns world-wide?

3. (Item No. 6) What factors do you think might have been important in bringing about the rejection in 2012 of an amnesty law passed by the Guatemalan congress in 1986? Are there any problems with such an approach?

4. (Item No. 11) Should international human rights bodies focus most of their attention on major violators and not devote very many resources to states whose overall record is good?

B. THE GLOBAL FRAMEWORK FOR CONTEMPORARY HUMAN RIGHTS DISCOURSE: CAPITAL PUNISHMENT, INTERACTIONS AMONG STATES, EXCEPTIONALISM

Section A drew on media accounts to illustrate the large range of issues that are implicated in human rights doctrine and discourse. In their descriptions of a number of problems, many of the articles found it necessary to include not only the specific violation that may have been involved, but also the broad political, social, economic or military context. They did not draw on the work of courts.

Section 1 below differs in several respects. It examines one broad issue, capital punishment, either in the large or with respect to a particular category of criminal defendants. And it examines a few illustrative judicial decisions to explore the argument of courts, and the evolving character of human rights discourse in the hands of courts, those most 'legal' of institutions. It is important to bear in mind that much of the invocation of rights and many of the arguments in these decisions are phenomena of the last half-century. The very institutions to which these courts refer simply did not previously exist.

Section 2 considers the degree to which these courts and other national and international organs (like a parliament, or a United Nations body) form part of a global framework of interaction and discourse. For example, do many national courts look to international law, or to the law in foreign states, whether judicial or legislative or constitutional in form, as part of their inquiry and research into a concrete human rights issue? Do they ask (even if not formally bound by a treaty or customary law): what does international law have to say about this, or what do other states have to say about this? In a broader sense, to what extent can we say that some form of world community is developing among the judiciaries or legislatures of many states with respect to human rights issues, at least with respect to interest in what other states are saying about common issues?

Section 3 takes a look at one such country, the United States, and at the critical and sceptical stance that it has taken in recent years towards international law and decisions of other states on controverted human rights issues. This stance goes by many terms that carry different shades of meaning — unilateralism, or exceptionalism, for example. Sections 1 and 2 provide pertinent background for the readings about and inquiry into these terms. Indeed, Section B in its entirety raises questions that reappear and continue to be troubling in later chapters of this book.

1. THE RAPIDLY CHANGING LAW ON CAPITAL PUNISHMENT

A 1965 UN report listed 25 abolitionist countries. By 1998, 35 countries were considered to have completely abolished the death penalty and 17 others had abandoned it for all peacetime crimes. One hundred and twenty-eight countries retained the death penalty for murder and sometimes other crimes, although 27 of them had not carried out an execution for at least ten years. Progress in the intervening period has been promoted by a series of international treaties requiring states to abolish the death penalty. They include the Second Optional Protocol to the International Covenant on Civil and Political Rights (74 states parties in May 2012), the Protocol to the American Convention on Human Rights to Abolish the Death Penalty (13 states); and Protocols 6 and 13 to the European Convention on Human Rights (46 and 43 states respectively).

AMNESTY INTERNATIONAL, DEATH SENTENCES AND EXECUTIONS 2011

(2012)

Global trend towards abolition

- The USA was the only country in the G8 to have carried out executions in 2011. Three countries in the G20 carried out executions in 2011: China, Saudi Arabia and the USA.
- The USA and Belarus were the only two of the 56 Member States of the Organization for Security and Cooperation in Europe to have carried out executions in 2011.
- Four of the 54 Member States of the African Union were known to have carried out judicial executions in 2011: Egypt, Somalia, Sudan and South Sudan. Thirty-eight Member States are abolitionist in law or practice.
- Two of the 54 Member States of the Commonwealth were known to have carried out executions in 2011: Bangladesh and Malaysia.
- Nine of 22 Member States of the League of Arab Nations carried out executions in 2011: Egypt, Iraq, Palestinian Authority, Saudi Arabia, Somalia, Sudan, Syria, United Arab Emirates and Yemen.
- Two of the 10 Member States of the Association of Southeast Asian Nations were believed to have carried out executions in 2011: Malaysia and Viet Nam.
- 175 of the 193 Member States of the United Nations were execution-free in 2011.

The death penalty in 2011: global numbers

At least 20 countries were known to have carried out executions in 2011. [In 2010 the number was 23 and in 2001 it was 31.]

Reported executions in 2011

Afghanistan (2), Bangladesh (5+), Belarus (2), China (+), Egypt (1+), Iran (360+), Iraq (68+), Malaysia (+), North Korea (30+), Palestinian Authority (3 in Gaza14), Saudi Arabia (82+), Somalia (10 . . .), South Sudan (5), Sudan (7+), Syria (+), Taiwan (5), United Arab Emirates (1), USA (43), Viet Nam (5+), Yemen (41+).

At least 676 executions were known to have been carried out worldwide in 2011, [up from 527 in 2010]. The increase is largely due to a significant increase in judicial killings in Iran, Iraq and Saudi Arabia. However, the 676 figure does not include the thousands of people who were believed to have been executed in China in 2011. Beginning in the 2009 report, Amnesty International ceased to publish its estimates on the use of the death penalty in China, where such figures are considered a state secret. Amnesty International renews its challenge to the Chinese authorities to publish figures. . . .

[C]redible reports . . . of unconfirmed or even secret executions in Iran, . . . would almost double the number of officially acknowledged executions.

Official figures on the use of the death penalty in 2011 were available only in a small number of countries. In Belarus, China, Mongolia and Viet Nam data on the use of the death penalty continued to be classified as a state secret. Little or no information was available for Egypt, Eritrea, Libya, Malaysia, North Korea and Singapore. In Belarus, Japan and Viet Nam prisoners were not informed of their forthcoming execution, nor were their families and lawyers. In Belarus and Viet Nam the bodies of the executed prisoners were not returned to their families for burial.

Reported death sentences in 2011

. . .

At least 1,923 people were known to have been sentenced to death in 63 countries in 2011. [In 2010 the figure was 2,024.]

At least 18,750 people were under sentence of death worldwide at the end of 2011.

. . .

. . .

There were no reports of judicial executions carried out by stoning, or any new sentences of death by stoning. However, public executions were known to have been carried out in Iran, North Korea, Saudi Arabia and Somalia.

Amnesty International remained concerned that, in the majority of countries where people were sentenced to death or executed, the death penalty was imposed after proceedings that did not meet international fair trial standards, often based on "confessions" that were allegedly extracted through torture or other duress. This was particularly the case in Belarus, China, Iran, Iraq, North Korea, and Saudi Arabia. . . .

The mandatory death penalty continued to be used in India, Iran, Malaysia, Pakistan, Singapore, Trinidad and Tobago and Zambia. Mandatory death sentences are inconsistent with human rights protections because they do not allow any possibility of taking into account the defendant's personal circumstances or the circumstances of the particular offence.

In 2011 people continued to be sentenced to death or executed for crimes that did not involve the intention to kill resulting in the loss of life, therefore not meeting the threshold of "most serious crimes" as prescribed by Article 6 of the ICCPR. The death penalty was known to have been used to punish drug-related offences in countries such as China, India, Indonesia, Iran, Malaysia, Pakistan, Saudi Arabia, Singapore, Thailand, United Arab Emirates and Yemen.

Adultery and sodomy (Iran), religious offences such as apostasy (Iran) and blasphemy (Pakistan), "sorcery" (Saudi Arabia), the trafficking of human bones (Republic of Congo) and economic crimes (China), as well as rape (Saudi Arabia) and forms of "aggravated" robbery (Kenya, Zambia), were also punished with death sentences in 2011. Finally, different forms of "treason", "acts against national security" and other "crimes against the state" (such as "moharebeh" — enmity against God — in Iran), whether or not they led to a loss of life, were punished with death sentences in 2011 (Gambia, Kuwait, Lebanon, North Korea, Palestinian Authority and Somalia). In North Korea death sentences are often imposed even though the alleged crime is not subject to a death sentence under domestic law.

...

NOTE

The Death Penalty in the United States

The following information comes from: Death Penalty Information Center, *Facts about the Death Penalty*, 16 March 2012. In the United States, 34 states retain the death penalty, 16 do not. Since 1976 there have been 1,286 executions, with a high of 98 executed in 1999 to a low of 37 in 2008 and 43 in 2011. The race of defendants executed was: White, 56 per cent; Black, 34 per cent; Hispanic, 8 per cent; Other, 2 per cent. In contrast, the race of victims in death penalty cases was: White, 76 per cent; Black, 15 per cent; Hispanic, 6 per cent; Other, 3 per cent. The report notes that in Louisiana, the odds of a death sentence were 97 per cent higher for those whose victim was white than for those whose victim was black. Since 1973, over 130 people have been released from death row, based on evidence of their innocence. Between 2000 and 2011, there was an average of five exonerations per year.

The maximum penalty for persons convicted of war crimes, crimes against humanity or genocide by the International Criminal Tribunals created by the UN Security Council for the Former Yugoslavia and for Rwanda, or by the International Criminal Court is life imprisonment. (See pp. 1282 and 1330, *infra*.) The Nuremberg and related trials after the Second World War imposed the death sentence on certain defendants.

Religious Views

'Preaching consistency in moral values, Pope John Paul II today urged America's Roman Catholics to extend the crusade to protect human life to include murderers on death row. "The new evangelization calls for followers of Christ who are unconditionally pro-life", the Pope preached to 100,000 people [in St Louis]. "Modern society has the means of protecting itself, without definitively denying criminals the chance to reform." He called the death penalty "cruel and unnecessary", and said it was so "even in the case of someone who has done great evil"', *New York Times*, 28 January 1999, p. A14.

'International law arguments may be less convincing in the Islamic world, where an entrenched and immutable religious doctrine insists upon the death penalty in certain cases. Perhaps there is a role for Islamic legal scholars who can demonstrate an alternative and more progressive view of religious law. The intransigence of Islamic States on the subject raises the whole issue of cultural relativism. If there is no universal agreement on the most fundamental of human rights, the right to life, how can anything more be expected in the rest of the catalogue of human rights?' William Schabas, *The Abolition of the Death Penalty in International Law* 377 (3rd edn. 2002).

Arguments about Justifications for Continuing or Abolishing the Death Penalty

For centuries, law enforcement agencies, defence counsel, criminologists, philosophers, religious figures and the general public have argued about this issue from many different perspectives. It has become an important factor in political campaigns in democracies. 'Many people still accept the principle of "an eye for an eye, a tooth for a tooth", particularly when atrocious crimes are involved', Schabas, p. 21, *supra*. The debate has intensified as the abolitionist movement has grown.

The South African judicial decision below, issued at the very start of the post-apartheid regime, states many of the leading contemporary arguments. Advocates and courts cast those arguments both in terms of justice and fairness, and in instrumental terms that take into account the effects/consequences of capital punishment on the incidence of crime and other matters. The arguments often fall within the broadly invoked categories of retribution, fairness (including the issue of discrimination) and deterrence.

STATE v. MAKWANYANE

Constitutional Court of the Republic of South Africa, 1995, Case No. CCT/3/94, [1995] 1 LRC 269

[The two appellants were convicted of murder, and sentenced to death by the Witwatersrand Local Division of the Supreme Court. The Appellate Division postponed hearing of the appeals against the death sentence until the new, post-apartheid Constitutional Court decided the question of its constitutionality under the transitional 1993 Constitution. The eleven individual opinions of the Justices of the Constitutional Court were unanimous in holding that the death sentence was unconstitutional. They focused, however, on different constitutional provisions and arguments or elements of the case. There appear below excerpts from the opinion of Justice Chaskalson, President of the Court.]

Relevant provisions of the Constitution

[7] The Constitution

> . . . provides a historic bridge between the past of a deeply divided society characterised by strife, conflict, untold suffering and injustice, and a future founded on the recognition of human rights, democracy and peaceful co-existence and development opportunities for all South Africans, irrespective of colour, race, class, belief or sex.

It is a transitional constitution but one which itself establishes a new order in South Africa; an order in which human rights and democracy are entrenched and in which the Constitution:

> . . . shall be the supreme law of the Republic and any law or act inconsistent with its provisions shall, unless otherwise provided expressly or by necessary

implication in this Constitution, be of no force and effect to the extent of the inconsistency.

[8] Chapter Three of the Constitution sets out the fundamental rights to which every person is entitled under the Constitution and also contains provisions dealing with the way in which the Chapter is to be interpreted by the Courts. It does not deal specifically with the death penalty, but in section 11(2), it prohibits 'cruel, inhuman or degrading treatment or punishment' ...

...

[10] ... [S]*ection* 11(2) of the Constitution must not be construed in isolation, but in its context, which includes the history and background to the adoption of the Constitution, other provisions of the Constitution itself and, in particular, the provisions of Chapter Three of which it is part. It must also be construed in a way which secures for 'individuals the full measure' of its protection. Rights with which *section* 11(2) is associated in Chapter Three of the Constitution, and which are of particular importance to a decision on the constitutionality of the death penalty are included in *section* 9, 'every person shall have the right to life', *section* 10, 'every person shall have the right to respect for and protection of his or her dignity', and *section* 8, 'every person shall have the right to equality before the law and to equal protection of the law'. Punishment must meet the requirements of *sections* 8, 9 and 10; and this is so, whether these sections are treated as giving meaning to *Section* 11(2) or as prescribing separate and independent standards with which all punishments must comply.

[11] Mr. Bizos, who represented the South African government at the hearing of this matter, informed us that the government accepts that the death penalty is a cruel, inhuman and degrading punishment and that it should be declared unconstitutional. The Attorney General of the Witwatersrand, whose office is independent of the government, took a different view, and contended that the death penalty is a necessary and acceptable form of punishment and that it is not cruel, inhuman or degrading within the meaning of section 11(2)....

...

[27] The principal arguments advanced by counsel for the accused in support of their contention that the imposition of the death penalty for murder is a 'cruel, inhuman or degrading punishment', were that the death sentence is an affront to human dignity, is inconsistent with the unqualified right to life entrenched in the Constitution, cannot be corrected in case of error or enforced in a manner that is not arbitrary, and that it negates the essential content of the right to life and the other rights that flow from it. The Attorney General argued that the death penalty is recognised as a legitimate form of punishment in many parts of the world, it is a deterrent to violent crime, it meets society's need for adequate retribution for heinous offences, and it is regarded by South African society as an acceptable form of punishment....

International and foreign comparative law

[33] ... The movement away from the death penalty gained momentum during the second half of the present century with the growth of the abolitionist movement.

In some countries it is now prohibited in all circumstances, in some it is prohibited save in times of war, and in most countries that have retained it as a penalty for crime, its use has been restricted to extreme cases. According to Amnesty International, 1,831 executions were carried out throughout the world in 1993 as a result of sentences of death, of which 1,419 were in China, which means that only 412 executions were carried out in the rest of the world in that year. Today, capital punishment has been abolished as a penalty for murder either specifically or in practice by almost half the countries of the world including the democracies of Europe and our neighbouring countries, Namibia, Mozambique and Angola....

[34] ... The international and foreign authorities are of value because they analyze arguments for and against the death sentence and show how courts of other jurisdictions have dealt with this vexed issue. For that reason alone they require our attention. They may also have to be considered because of their relevance to section 35(1) of the Constitution, which states:

> In interpreting the provisions of this Chapter a court of law shall promote the values which underlie an open and democratic society based on freedom and equality and shall, where applicable, have regard to public international law applicable to the protection of the rights entrenched in this Chapter, and may have regard to comparable foreign case law.

[35] ... In the context of *section* 35(1), public international law would include non-binding as well as binding law. They may both be used under the section as tools of interpretation. International agreements and customary international law accordingly provide a framework within which Chapter Three can be evaluated and understood, and for that purpose, decisions of tribunals dealing with comparable instruments, such as the United Nations Committee on Human Rights, the Inter-American Commission on Human Rights, the Inter-American Court of Human Rights, the European Commission on Human Rights, and the European Court of Human Rights, and in appropriate cases, reports of specialized agencies such as the International Labour Organization may provide guidance as to the correct interpretation of particular provisions of Chapter Three.

[36] Capital punishment is not prohibited by public international law, and this is a factor that has to be taken into account in deciding whether it is cruel, inhuman or degrading punishment within the meaning of *section* 11(2). International human rights agreements differ, however, from our Constitution in that where the right to life is expressed in unqualified terms they either deal specifically with the death sentence, or authorize exceptions to be made to the right to life by law....

...

[40] ... From the beginning, the United States Constitution recognized capital punishment as lawful. The Fifth Amendment (adopted in 1791) refers in specific terms to capital punishment and impliedly recognizes its validity. The Fourteenth Amendment (adopted in 1868) obliges the states, not to 'deprive any person of life, liberty, or property, without due process of law' and it too impliedly recognizes the right of the states to make laws for such purposes. The argument that capital punishment is unconstitutional was based on the Eighth Amendment,

which prohibits cruel and unusual punishment. . . . [In a brief discussion of US constitutional law, the Court noted that the federal constitutionality of capital punishment was affirmed, subject to conditions stated, in *Gregg v. Georgia*, 428 U.S. 153 (1976).]

. . .

[43] . . . Mr Trengove contended on behalf of the accused that the imprecise language of section 277, and the unbounded discretion vested by it in the Courts, make its provisions unconstitutional.

[44] Section 277 of the Criminal Procedure Act provides:

> (1) The sentence of death may be passed by a superior court only and only in the case of a conviction for—
> (a) murder;
> (b) treason committed when the Republic is in a state of war;
> (c) robbery or attempted robbery, if the court finds aggravating circumstances to have been present;
> (d) kidnapping;
> (e) child-stealing;
> (f) rape.
>
> (2) The sentence of death shall be imposed—
> (a) after the presiding judge conjointly with the assessors (if any) . . . has made a finding on the presence or absence of any mitigating or aggravating factors; and
> (b) if the presiding judge or court, as the case may be, with due regard to that finding, is satisfied that the sentence of death is the proper sentence.

. . .

[45] Under our court system questions of guilt and innocence, and the proper sentence to be imposed on those found guilty of crimes, are not decided by juries. In capital cases, where it is likely that the death sentence may be imposed, judges sit with two assessors who have an equal vote with the judge on the issue of guilt and on any mitigating or aggravating factors relevant to sentence; but sentencing is the prerogative of the judge alone. The Criminal Procedure Act allows a full right of appeal to persons sentenced to death, including a right to dispute the sentence without having to establish an irregularity or misdirection on the part of the trial judge. The Appellate Division is empowered to set the sentence aside if it would not have imposed such sentence itself, and it has laid down criteria for the exercise of this power by itself and other courts . . . .

[46] Mitigating and aggravating factors must be identified by the Court, bearing in mind that the onus is on the State to prove beyond reasonable doubt the existence of aggravating factors, and to negative beyond reasonable doubt the presence of any mitigating factors relied on by the accused. Due regard must be paid to the personal circumstances and subjective factors which might have influenced the accused person's conduct, and these factors must then be weighed up with the main objects of punishment, which have been held to be: deterrence, prevention, reformation, and retribution. In this process '[e]very relevant consideration should receive the most scrupulous care and reasoned attention', and the death sentence should only be

imposed in the most exceptional cases, where there is no reasonable prospect of reformation and the objects of punishment would not be properly achieved by any other sentence.

[47] There seems to me to be little difference between the guided discretion required for the death sentence in the United States, and the criteria laid down by the Appellate Division for the imposition of the death sentence....

[48] The argument that the imposition of the death sentence under *section* 277 is arbitrary and capricious does not, however, end there. It also focuses on what is alleged to be the arbitrariness inherent in the application of *section* 277 in practice. Of the thousands of persons put on trial for murder, only a very small percentage are sentenced to death by a trial court, and of those, a large number escape the ultimate penalty on appeal. At every stage of the process there is an element of chance. The outcome may be dependent upon factors such as the way the case is investigated by the police, the way the case is presented by the prosecutor, how effectively the accused is defended, the personality and particular attitude to capital punishment of the trial judge and, if the matter goes on appeal, the particular judges who are selected to hear the case. Race and poverty are also alleged to be factors.

[49] Most accused facing a possible death sentence are unable to afford legal assistance, and are defended under the *pro deo* system. The defending counsel is more often than not young and inexperienced, frequently of a different race to his or her client, and if this is the case, usually has to consult through an interpreter. *Pro deo* counsel are paid only a nominal fee for the defence, and generally lack the financial resources and the infrastructural support to undertake the necessary investigations and research, to employ expert witnesses to give advice, including advice on matters relevant to sentence, to assemble witnesses, to bargain with the prosecution, and generally to conduct an effective defence. Accused persons who have the money to do so, are able to retain experienced attorneys and counsel, who are paid to undertake the necessary investigations and research, and as a result they are less likely to be sentenced to death than persons similarly placed who are unable to pay for such services.

...

[54] The differences that exist between rich and poor, between good and bad prosecutions, between good and bad defence, between severe and lenient judges, between judges who favour capital punishment and those who do not, and the subjective attitudes that might be brought into play by factors such as race and class, may in similar ways affect any case that comes before the courts, and is almost certainly present to some degree in all court systems.... Imperfection inherent in criminal trials means that error cannot be excluded; it also means that persons similarly placed may not necessarily receive similar punishment. This needs to be acknowledged....

...

[56] ... The acceptance by a majority of the United States Supreme Court of the proposition that capital punishment is not per se unconstitutional, but that in certain circumstances it may be arbitrary, and thus unconstitutional, has led to endless litigation. Considerable expense and interminable delays result from the exceptionally-high standard of procedural fairness set by the United States courts

in attempting to avoid arbitrary decisions. The difficulties that have been experienced in following this path . . . persuade me that we should not follow this route.

The right to dignity

[57] Although the United States Constitution does not contain a specific guarantee of human dignity, it has been accepted by the United States Supreme Court that the concept of human dignity is at the core of the prohibition of 'cruel and unusual punishment' by the Eighth and Fourteenth Amendments . . . .

[58] Under our constitutional order the right to human dignity is specifically guaranteed. It can only be limited by legislation which passes the stringent test of being 'necessary' . . . .

[59] In Germany, the Federal Constitutional Court has stressed this aspect of punishment.

> Respect for human dignity especially requires the prohibition of cruel, inhuman, and degrading punishments. [The state] cannot turn the offender into an object of crime prevention to the detriment of his constitutionally protected right to social worth and respect.

[60] That capital punishment constitutes a serious impairment of human dignity has also been recognized by judgments of the Canadian Supreme Court. *Kindler v Canada* [(1992) 6 CRR (2d) SC 4] was concerned with the extradition from Canada to the United States of two fugitives, Kindler, who had been convicted of murder and sentenced to death in the United States, and Ng who was facing a murder charge there and a possible death sentence. Three of the seven judges who heard the cases expressed the opinion that the death penalty was cruel and unusual:

> It is the supreme indignity to the individual, the ultimate corporal punishment, the final and complete lobotomy and the absolute and irrevocable castration. [It is] the ultimate desecration of human dignity.
>
> . . .

[61] Three other judges were of the opinion that:

> [t]here is strong ground for believing, having regard to the limited extent to which the death penalty advances any valid penological objectives and the serious invasion of human dignity it engenders, that the death penalty cannot, except in exceptional circumstances, be justified in this country.

. . .

The International Covenant on Civil and Political Right

[63] *Ng* [another case, *Ng v. Canada*] and *Kindler* took their cases to the Human Rights Committee of the United Nations, contending that Canada had breached its obligations under the International Covenant on Civil and Political Rights. Once

again, there was a division of opinion within the tribunal. In Ng's case [*Ng v. Canada*, Communication No. 469/1991, 5 Nov. 1993] it was said:

> The Committee is aware that, by definition, every execution of a sentence of death may be considered to constitute cruel and inhuman treatment within the meaning of article 7 of the covenant.

[64] There was no dissent from that statement. But the International Covenant contains provisions permitting, with some qualifications, the imposition of capital punishment for the most serious crimes. [See Article 6 of the International Covenant.] In view of these provisions, the majority of the Committee were of the opinion that the extradition of fugitives to a country which enforces the death sentence in accordance with the requirements of the International Covenant, should not be regarded as a breach of the obligations of the extraditing country . . . .

. . .

[The opinion considered the decision by the European Court of Human Rights in *Soering v. United Kingdom* (1989) 11 EHRR 439, involving the question whether the United Kingdom would violate the provisions on inhuman and degrading treatment or punishment in Article 3 of the Convention, by extraditing a fugitive to the United States to face murder charges that were subject to capital punishment. In the circumstances, including the experience of 'death row' in the US prisons and possible extradition of the fugitive by the United Kingdom for trial in another country that had abolished the death sentence, the European Court concluded that extradition to the United States would violate Article 3.

The opinion next examined a 1980 decision of the Indian Supreme Court holding that capital punishment did not violate the Indian Constitution. It distinguished the Indian decision partly by emphasizing the different wording of relevant provisions in the Constitutions of the two countries].

The right to life

[80] The unqualified right to life vested in every person by *section 9* of our Constitution is another factor crucially relevant to the question whether the death sentence is cruel, inhuman or degrading punishment within the meaning of *section 11(2)* of our Constitution. In this respect our Constitution differs materially from the Constitutions of the United States and India. It also differs materially from the European Convention and the International Covenant. Yet in the cases decided under these constitutions and treaties there were judges who dissented and held that notwithstanding the specific language of the constitution or instrument concerned, capital punishment should not be permitted.

[81] In some instances the dissent focused on the right to life. In *Soering's* case before the European Court of Human Rights, Judge de Meyer, in a concurring opinion, said that capital punishment is 'not consistent with the present state of European civilisation' and for that reason alone, extradition to the United States would violate the fugitive's right to life.

[82] In a dissent in the United Nations Human Rights Committee in *Kindler's* case, Committee member B. Wennergren also stressed the importance of the right to life.

> The value of life is immeasurable for any human being, and the right to life enshrined in article 6 of the Covenant is the supreme human right. It is an obligation of States [P]arties to the Covenant to protect the lives of all human beings on their territory and under their jurisdiction …

[83] An individual's right to life has been described as '[t]he most fundamental of all human rights', and was dealt with in that way in the judgments of the Hungarian Constitutional Court declaring capital punishment to be unconstitutional. . . .
. . .

Public opinion

[87] . . . It was disputed whether public opinion, properly informed of the different considerations, would in fact favour the death penalty. I am, however, prepared to assume that it does and that the majority of South Africans agree that the death sentence should be imposed in extreme cases of murder. The question before us, however, is not what the majority of South Africans believe a proper sentence for murder should be. It is whether the Constitution allows the sentence.

[88] Public opinion may have some relevance to the enquiry, but in itself, it is no substitute for the duty vested in the Courts to interpret the Constitution and to uphold its provisions without fear or favour. If public opinion were to be decisive there would be no need for constitutional adjudication. The protection of rights could then be left to Parliament, which has a mandate from the public, and is answerable to the public for the way its mandate is exercised, but this would be a return to parliamentary sovereignty, and a retreat from the new legal order established by the 1993 Constitution. . . . The very reason for establishing the new legal order, and for vesting the power of judicial review of all legislation in the courts, was to protect the rights of minorities and others who cannot protect their rights adequately through the democratic process. Those who are entitled to claim this protection include the social outcasts and marginalized people of our society. It is only if there is a willingness to protect the worst and the weakest amongst us, that all of us can be secure that our own rights will be protected.
. . .

Cruel, inhuman and degrading punishment
. . .

[94] Proportionality is an ingredient to be taken into account in deciding whether a penalty is cruel, inhuman or degrading. No Court would today uphold the constitutionality of a statute that makes the death sentence a competent sentence for the cutting down of trees or the killing of deer, which were capital offences in England in the 18th Century. But murder is not to be equated with such 'offences'. The wilful taking of an innocent life calls for a severe penalty, and there are many countries which still retain the death penalty as a sentencing option

for such cases. Disparity between the crime and the penalty is not the only ingredient of proportionality; factors such as the enormity and irredeemable character of the death sentence in circumstances where neither error nor arbitrariness can be excluded, the expense and difficulty of addressing the disparities which exist in practice between accused persons facing similar charges, and which are due to factors such as race, poverty, and ignorance, and the other subjective factors which have been mentioned, are also factors that can and should be taken into account in dealing with this issue. It may possibly be that none alone would be sufficient under our Constitution to justify a finding that the death sentence is cruel, inhuman or degrading. But these factors are not to be evaluated in isolation. They must be taken together, and in order to decide whether the threshold set by *section* 11(2) has been crossed they must be evaluated with other relevant factors, including the two fundamental rights on which the accused rely, the right to dignity and the right to life.

[95] The carrying out of the death sentence destroys life, which is protected without reservation under *section* 9 of our Constitution, it annihilates human dignity which is protected under *section* 10, elements of arbitrariness are present in its enforcement and it is irremediable. Taking these factors into account, as well as the assumption that I have made in regard to public opinion in South Africa, and giving the words of *section* 11(2) the broader meaning to which they are entitled at this stage of the enquiry, rather than a narrow meaning, I am satisfied that in the context of our Constitution the death penalty is indeed a cruel, inhuman and degrading punishment.

. . .

Section 33 and limitation of rights

[98] *Section* 33(1) of the Constitution provides, in part, that:

> The rights entrenched in this Chapter may be limited by law of general application, provided that such limitation—
> (a) shall be permissible only to the extent that it is—
> (i) reasonable; and
> (ii) justifiable in an open and democratic society based on freedom and equality; and
> (b) shall not negate the essential content of the right in question.

[99] *Section* 33(1)(b) goes on to provide that the limitation of certain rights, including the rights referred to in *section* 10 and *section* 11 'shall, in addition to being reasonable as required in paragraph (a)(I), also be necessary'.

[100] Our Constitution deals with the limitation of rights through a general limitations clause. . . . [T]his calls for a 'two-stage' approach, in which a broad rather than a narrow interpretation is given to the fundamental rights enshrined in Chapter Three, and limitations have to be justified through the application of section 33. In this it differs from the Constitution of the United States, which does not contain a limitation clause, as a result of which courts in that country have been obliged to find limits to constitutional rights through a narrow interpretation of the rights

themselves. Although the 'two-stage' approach may often produce the same result as the 'one-stage' approach, this will not always be the case.

...

[102] Under our Constitution, ... [i]t is not whether the decision of the State has been shown to be clearly wrong; it is whether the decision of the State is justifiable according to the criteria prescribed by section 33. It is not whether the infliction of death as a punishment for murder 'is not without justification', it is whether the infliction of death as a punishment for murder has been shown to be both reasonable and necessary, and to be consistent with the other requirements of *section* 33 ....

...

[106] Although there is a rational connection between capital punishment and the purpose for which it is prescribed, the elements of arbitrariness, unfairness and irrationality in the imposition of the penalty, are factors that would have to be taken into account in the application of the first component of this test. As far as the second component is concerned, the fact that a severe punishment in the form of life imprisonment is available as an alternative sentence, would be relevant to the question whether the death sentence impairs the right as little as possible.

...

[109] The European Convention also has no general limitations clause, but makes certain rights subject to limitation according to specified criteria. The proportionality test of the European Court of Human Rights calls for a balancing of ends and means. The end must be a 'pressing social need' and the means used must be proportionate to the attainment of such an end. The limitation of certain rights is conditioned upon the limitation being 'necessary in a democratic society' for purposes defined in the relevant provisions of the Convention ....

...

Deterrence

[116] The Attorney General attached considerable weight to the need for a deterrent to violent crime. He argued that the countries which had abolished the death penalty were on the whole developed and peaceful countries in which other penalties might be sufficient deterrents. We had not reached that stage of development, he said. If in years to come we did so, we could do away with the death penalty. Parliament could decide when that time has come ....

[117] ... Without law, individuals in society have no rights. The level of violent crime in our country has reached alarming proportions. It poses a threat to the transition to democracy, and the creation of development opportunities for all, which are primary goals of the Constitution ....

...

[119] The cause of the high incidence of violent crime cannot simply be attributed to the failure to carry out the death sentences imposed by the courts. ... It was a progression that started before the moratorium [on executions] was announced. There are many factors that have to be taken into account in looking for the cause of this phenomenon ....

[120] Homelessness, unemployment, poverty and the frustration consequent upon such conditions are other causes of the crime wave. . . .

[121] We would be deluding ourselves if we were to believe that the execution of the few persons sentenced to death during this period, and of a comparatively few other people each year from now onwards will provide the solution to the unacceptably high rate of crime. . . .

[122] The greatest deterrent to crime is the likelihood that offenders will be apprehended, convicted and punished. It is that which is presently lacking in our criminal justice system; and it is at this level and through addressing the causes of crime that the State must seek to combat lawlessness.

. . .

[126] . . . [B]etween the amendment of the Criminal Procedure Act in 1990, and January 1995 . . . 243 death sentences were imposed, of which 143 were confirmed by the Appellate Division. Yet, according to statistics placed before us by the Commissioner of Police and the Attorney General, there were on average approximately 20,000 murders committed, and 9,000 murder cases brought to trial, each year during this period. Would the carrying out of the death sentence on these 143 persons have deterred the other murderers or saved any lives?

. . .

Retribution

[129] Retribution is one of the objects of punishment, but it carries less weight than deterrence. The righteous anger of family and friends of the murder victim, reinforced by the public abhorrence of vile crimes, is easily translated into a call for vengeance. But capital punishment is not the only way that society has of expressing its moral outrage at the crime that has been committed. We have long outgrown the literal application of the biblical injunction of 'an eye for an eye, and a tooth for a tooth'. Punishment must to some extent be commensurate with the offence, but there is no requirement that it be equivalent or identical to it. . . . A very long prison sentence is also a way of expressing outrage and visiting retribution upon the criminal.

. . .

Conclusion

[144] The rights to life and dignity are the most important of all human rights, and the source of all other personal rights in Chapter Three. By committing ourselves to a society founded on the recognition of human rights we are required to value these two rights above all others. And this must be demonstrated by the State in everything that it does, including the way it punishes criminals . . .

. . .

[146] . . . Taking [all the described] factors into account, as well as the elements of arbitrariness and the possibility of error in enforcing the death penalty, the clear and convincing case that is required to justify the death sentence as a penalty for murder, has not been made out. The requirements of section 33(1) have

accordingly not been satisfied, and it follows that the provisions of section 277(1)(a) of the Criminal Procedure Act, 1977 must be held to be inconsistent with section 11(2) of the Constitution. In the circumstances, it is not necessary for me to consider whether the section would also be inconsistent with sections 8, 9 or 10 of the Constitution if they had been dealt with separately and not treated together as giving meaning to section 11(2).

...

[150] The proper sentence to be imposed on the accused is a matter for the Appellate Division and not for us to decide....

...

QUESTIONS

1. Article 6 of the International Covenant on Civil and Political Rights has been much cited and drawn on by both proponents and opponents of capital punishment. In what ways could an abolitionist employ Article 6 to strengthen her position?

2. As an opponent, would you find it advantageous in argument before a court to rely primarily on 'the inherent right to life', as in Article 6(1) of the International Covenant, or on 'cruel, inhuman or degrading treatment or punishment' in Article 7 (compare 'cruel and unusual punishments' in the Eighth Amendment to the US Constitution)? What disadvantages would each have?

3. Would you describe Justice Chaskalson's opinion as ultimately relying on traditional arguments for and against capital punishment that could have been debated by courts anywhere, or relying at least equally on contextual factors that were, if not unique, at least highly specific to South African history and culture? What were the links between these two strands in the opinion?

4. Consider the following comments (reported in Schabas, p. 21, *supra*, at 285) made during a debate in the Parliamentary Assembly of the Council of Europe on the then proposed protocol to the European Convention on Human Rights that would abolish the death penalty. Would you agree or disagree with the speaker, and if the latter, how would you respond to him?

> A Turkish member of the Assembly, Aksoy, said that he supported the report and the recommendation 'in principle', but that it did not take sufficient account of the particular situation of certain member States. He suggested that because of differing economic, social and political structures it was not possible to apply identical sentences in all countries. Were he Swedish, Swiss, Norwegian, Austrian or German, he would most certainly support total abolition of the death penalty, said Aksoy. Yet it would be a grave error to recommend abolition in countries where political assassination and terrorism are organized on a systematic scale.

5. With reference to the preceding opinion, consider (a) the comparative, or horizontal, dimensions of the human rights regime — that is, the spread among states of abolition of capital punishment and the cross-referencing by states to each other's legislation or constitutional decisions on this issue. Consider also (b) the vertical dimension — that is, the bearing of treaties and decisions or resolutions of international organs on this issue on how states argue and what they decide to do. In what ways are the horizontal and vertical dimensions of human rights related to each other? Do they appear to constitute equal parts of an international movement in favour of human rights?

ADDITIONAL READING

R. Hood & C. Hoyle, *The Death Penalty: A World-Wide Perspective* (4th edn. 2008); N. Rodley & M. Pollard, *The Treatment of Prisoners under International Law* (3rd edn. 2009); W. Schabas, *The Abolition of the Death Penalty in International Law* (3rd edn. 2002); D. Garland et al. (eds.), *America's Death Penalty: Between Past and Present* (2011).

NOTE

The following opinion of the US Supreme Court, although concluding that the death penalty as applied to the category of defendant involved in the case was unconstitutional, makes clear how dramatically the US differs from most states. The opinion is relevant both for its holding and summary of US constitutional jurisprudence of the last few decades with respect to capital punishment, and for the argument among the Justices about the propriety of looking to the law in this field in other states and in international law, a theme to which Section 2 returns.

ROPER v. SIMMONS

Supreme Court of the United States, 543 U.S. 551 (2005)

OPINION OF JUSTICE KENNEDY FOR THE COURT:

This case requires us to address . . . whether it is permissible under the Eighth and Fourteenth Amendments to the Constitution of the United States to execute a juvenile offender who was older than 15 but younger than 18 when he committed a capital crime. In *Stanford* v. *Kentucky*, 492 U.S. 361 (1989), a divided Court rejected the proposition that the Constitution bars capital punishment for juvenile offenders in this age group. We reconsider the question.

[Simmons committed murder at age 17 when a junior (the penultimate year) in secondary school. He was sentenced to death when he was 18. The murder was callous and premeditated. At trial, the judge instructed the jury that it could consider Simmons's age as a mitigating factor in sentencing. The jury recommended the death penalty, which the trial judge imposed. The Missouri Supreme Court affirmed.]

After these proceedings in Simmons' case had run their course, this Court held that the Eighth and Fourteenth Amendments prohibit the execution of a mentally retarded person. *Atkins* v. *Virginia*, 536 U.S. 304 (2002). Simmons filed a new petition for state postconviction relief, arguing that the reasoning of *Atkins* established that the Constitution prohibits the execution of a juvenile who was under 18 when the crime was committed. [The Missouri Supreme Court agreed, and resentenced Simmons to 'life imprisonment without eligibility for probation, parole, or release except by act of the Governor'.]

The Eighth Amendment provides: "Excessive bail shall not be required, nor excessive fines imposed, nor cruel and unusual punishments inflicted." The provision is applicable to the States through the Fourteenth Amendment. As the Court explained in *Atkins*, the Eighth Amendment guarantees individuals the right not to be subjected to excessive sanctions. The right flows from the basic "precept of justice that punishment for crime should be graduated and proportioned to [the] offense." 536 U.S. at 311. By protecting even those convicted of heinous crimes, the Eighth Amendment reaffirms the duty of the government to respect the dignity of all persons.

The prohibition against "cruel and unusual punishments," like other expansive language in the Constitution, must be interpreted according to its text, by considering history, tradition, and precedent, and with due regard for its purpose and function in the constitutional design. To implement this framework we have established the propriety and affirmed the necessity of referring to "the evolving standards of decency that mark the progress of a maturing society" to determine which punishments are so disproportionate as to be cruel and unusual. *Trop* v. *Dulles*, 356 U.S. 86, 100–101 (1958) (plurality opinion).

In *Thompson* v. *Oklahoma*, 487 U.S. 815 (1988), a plurality of the Court determined that our standards of decency do not permit the execution of any offender under the age of 16 at the time of the crime. The plurality opinion explained that no death penalty State that had given express consideration to a minimum age for the death penalty had set the age lower than 16. The plurality also observed that "[t]he conclusion that it would offend civilized standards of decency to execute a person who was less than 16 years old at the time of his or her offense is consistent with the views that have been expressed by respected professional organizations, by other nations that share our Anglo-American heritage, and by the leading members of the Western European community." The opinion further noted that juries imposed the death penalty on offenders under 16 with exceeding rarity; the last execution of an offender for a crime committed under the age of 16 had been carried out in 1948, 40 years prior.

Bringing its independent judgment to bear on the permissibility of the death penalty for a 15-year-old offender, the *Thompson* plurality stressed that "[t]he reasons why juveniles are not trusted with the privileges and responsibilities of an adult also explain why their irresponsible conduct is not as morally reprehensible as that of an adult." According to the plurality, the lesser culpability of offenders under 16 made the death penalty inappropriate as a form of retribution, while the low likelihood that offenders under 16 engaged in "the kind of cost-benefit analysis that attaches any weight to the possibility of execution" made the death penalty ineffective as a means of deterrence....

The next year, in *Stanford* v. *Kentucky* [*supra*], the Court, over a dissenting opinion joined by four Justices, referred to contemporary standards of decency in this country and concluded the Eighth and Fourteenth Amendments did not proscribe the execution of juvenile offenders over 15 but under 18. The Court noted that 22 of the 37 death penalty States permitted the death penalty for 16-year-old offenders, and, among these 37 States, 25 permitted it for 17-year-old offenders. These numbers, in the Court's view, indicated there was no national consensus "sufficient to label a particular punishment cruel and unusual."...

The same day the Court decided *Stanford*, it held that the Eighth Amendment did not mandate a categorical exemption from the death penalty for the mentally retarded. *Penry* v. *Lynaugh*, 492 U.S. 302 (1989). In reaching this conclusion it stressed that only two States had enacted laws banning the imposition of the death penalty on a mentally retarded person convicted of a capital offense. According to the Court, "the two state statutes prohibiting execution of the mentally retarded, even when added to the 14 States that have rejected capital punishment completely, [did] not provide sufficient evidence at present of a national consensus."

Three Terms ago the subject was reconsidered in *Atkins*. We held that standards of decency have evolved since *Penry* and now demonstrate that the execution of the mentally retarded is cruel and unusual punishment. The Court noted objective indicia of society's standards, as expressed in legislative enactments and state practice with respect to executions of the mentally retarded. When *Atkins* was decided only a minority of States permitted the practice, and even in those States it was rare. On the basis of these indicia the Court determined that executing mentally retarded offenders "has become truly unusual, and it is fair to say that a national consensus has developed against it."

... The *Atkins* Court ... returned to the rule, established in decisions predating *Stanford*, that "the Constitution contemplates that in the end our own judgment will be brought to bear on the question of the acceptability of the death penalty under the Eighth Amendment." Mental retardation, the Court said, diminishes personal culpability even if the offender can distinguish right from wrong. The impairments of mentally retarded offenders make it less defensible to impose the death penalty as retribution for past crimes and less likely that the death penalty will have a real deterrent effect....

...

III

A

The evidence of national consensus against the death penalty for juveniles is similar, and in some respects parallel, to the evidence *Atkins* held sufficient to demonstrate a national consensus against the death penalty for the mentally retarded. When *Atkins* was decided, 30 States prohibited the death penalty for the mentally retarded. This number comprised 12 that had abandoned the death penalty altogether, and 18 that maintained it but excluded the mentally retarded from its reach. By a similar calculation in this case, 30 States prohibit the juvenile death penalty, comprising 12 that have rejected the death penalty altogether and 18 that maintain it but, by express provision or judicial interpretation, exclude juveniles from its reach. *Atkins* emphasized that even in the 20 States without formal prohibition, the practice of executing the mentally retarded was infrequent.... In the present case, too, even in the 20 States without a formal prohibition on executing juveniles, the practice is infrequent ....

... Impressive in *Atkins* was the rate of abolition of the death penalty for the mentally retarded. Sixteen States that permitted the execution of the mentally retarded at the time of Penry [*supra*] had prohibited the practice by the time we heard *Atkins*. By contrast, the rate of change in reducing the incidence of the juvenile death penalty, or in taking specific steps to abolish it, has been slower. Five States that allowed the juvenile death penalty at the time of *Stanford* have abandoned it in the intervening 15 years — four through legislative enactments and one through judicial decisions.

Though less dramatic ... we still consider the change from *Stanford* to this case to be significant.... [T]he same consistency of direction of change has been demonstrated ....

...

B

A majority of States have rejected the imposition of the death penalty on juvenile offenders under 18, and we now hold this is required by the Eighth Amendment.

Because the death penalty is the most severe punishment, the Eighth Amendment applies to it with special force.... Capital punishment must be limited to those offenders who commit "a narrow category of the most serious crimes" and whose extreme culpability makes them "the most deserving of execution." This principle is implemented throughout the capital sentencing process ....

Three general differences between juveniles under 18 and adults demonstrate that juvenile offenders cannot with reliability be classified among the worst offenders. First, as any parent knows and as the scientific and sociological studies respondent and his *amici* cite tend to confirm, "[a] lack of maturity and an underdeveloped sense of responsibility are found in youth more often than in adults and are more understandable among the young. These qualities often result in impetuous and ill-considered actions and decisions." ... It has been noted that "adolescents are overrepresented statistically in virtually every category of reckless behavior." ...

The second area of difference is that juveniles are more vulnerable or susceptible to negative influences and outside pressures, including peer pressure....

The third broad difference is that the character of a juvenile is not as well formed as that of an adult. The personality traits of juveniles are more transitory, less fixed.

. . . The reality that juveniles still struggle to define their identity means it is less supportable to conclude that even a heinous crime committed by a juvenile is evidence of irretrievably depraved character. From a moral standpoint it would be misguided to equate the failings of a minor with those of an adult, for a greater possibility exists that a minor's character deficiencies will be reformed . . . .

Once the diminished culpability of juveniles is recognized, it is evident that the penological justifications for the death penalty apply to them with lesser force than to adults . . . .

As for deterrence, it is unclear whether the death penalty has a significant or even measurable deterrent effect on juveniles, as counsel for the petitioner acknowledged at oral argument. . . . [I]t is worth noting that the punishment of life imprisonment without the possibility of parole is itself a severe sanction, in particular for a young person.

Drawing the line at 18 years of age is subject, of course, to the objections always raised against categorical rules. . . . The age of 18 is the point where society draws the line for many purposes between childhood and adulthood. It is, we conclude, the age at which the line for death eligibility ought to rest.

. . .

IV

Our determination that the death penalty is disproportionate punishment for offenders under 18 finds confirmation in the stark reality that the United States is the only country in the world that continues to give official sanction to the juvenile death penalty. This reality does not become controlling, for the task of interpreting the Eighth Amendment remains our responsibility. Yet at least from the time of the Court's decision in *Trop* [*supra*], the Court has referred to the laws of other countries and to international authorities as instructive for its interpretation of the Eighth Amendment's prohibition of "cruel and unusual punishments." 356 U.S., at 102–103 (plurality opinion) ("The civilized nations of the world are in virtual unanimity that statelessness is not to be imposed as punishment for crime"); see also *Atkins*, *supra*, at 317, n. 21 recognizing that "within the world community, the imposition of the death penalty for crimes committed by mentally retarded offenders is overwhelmingly disapproved"); . . .

. . . Article 37 of the United Nations Convention on the Rights of the Child, which every country in the world has ratified save for the United States and Somalia, contains an express prohibition on capital punishment for crimes committed by juveniles under 18. United Nations Convention on the Rights of the Child, Art. 37. . . . No ratifying country has entered a reservation to the provision prohibiting the execution of juvenile offenders. Parallel prohibitions are contained in other significant international covenants. See [International Covenant on Civil and Political Rights], Art. 6(5), 999 U.N.T.S., at 175 (prohibiting capital punishment for anyone under 18 at the time of offense) (signed and ratified by the United States subject to a reservation regarding Article 6(5) . . . .

. . . [O]nly seven countries other than the United States have executed juvenile offenders since 1990: Iran, Pakistan, Saudi Arabia, Yemen, Nigeria, the Democratic Republic of Congo, and China. Since then each of these countries has either abolished capital punishment for juveniles or made public disavowal of the practice. In sum, it is fair to say that the United States now stands alone in a world that has turned its face against the juvenile death penalty.

Though the international covenants prohibiting the juvenile death penalty are of more recent date, it is instructive to note that the United Kingdom abolished the juvenile death penalty before these covenants came into being. The United Kingdom's experience bears particular relevance here in light of the historic ties between our countries and in light of the Eighth Amendment's own origins. The Amendment was modeled on a parallel provision in the English Declaration of Rights of 1689, which provided: "[E]xcessive Bail ought not to be required nor excessive Fines imposed; nor cruel and unusuall Punishments inflicted." . . .

It is proper that we acknowledge the overwhelming weight of international opinion against the juvenile death penalty. . . . The opinion of the world community, while not controlling our outcome, does provide respected and significant confirmation for our own conclusions.

Over time, from one generation to the next, the Constitution has come to earn the high respect and even, as Madison dared to hope, the veneration of the American people. The document sets forth, and rests upon, innovative principles original to the American experience, such as federalism; a proven balance in political mechanisms through separation of powers; specific guarantees for the accused in criminal cases; and broad provisions to secure individual freedom and preserve human dignity. These doctrines and guarantees are central to the American experience and remain essential to our present-day self-definition and national identity. Not the least of the reasons we honor the Constitution, then, is because we know it to be our own. It does not lessen our fidelity to the Constitution or our pride in its origins to acknowledge that the express affirmation of certain fundamental rights by other nations and peoples simply underscores the centrality of those same rights within our own heritage of freedom.

[Appendix B and Appendix C to the Court's opinion listed state statutes establishing a minimum age to vote (the 26th Amendment to the Constitution provides that the right of citizens who are 18 or older to vote shall not be denied or abridged on account of age), establishing a minimum age for jury service and establishing a minimum age for marriage without parental consent. The statutes used overwhelmingly the age of 18.]

JUSTICE O'CONNOR (DISSENTING)

. . .

I turn, finally, to the Court's discussion of foreign and international law. . . . In short, the evidence of an international consensus does not alter my determination that the Eighth Amendment does not, at this time, forbid capital punishment of 17-year-old murderers in all cases.

Nevertheless, I disagree with Justice Scalia's contention that foreign and international law have no place in our Eighth Amendment jurisprudence. Over the course of nearly half a century, the Court has consistently referred to foreign and international law as relevant to its assessment of evolving standards of decency. This inquiry reflects the special character of the Eighth Amendment, which, as the Court has long held, draws its meaning directly from the maturing values of civilized society. . . . But this Nation's evolving understanding of human dignity certainly is neither wholly isolated from, nor inherently at odds with, the values prevailing in other countries. On the contrary, we should not be surprised to find congruence between domestic and international values, especially where the international community has reached clear agreement — expressed in international law or in the domestic laws of individual countries — that a particular form of punishment is inconsistent with fundamental human rights. At least, the existence of an international consensus of this nature can serve to confirm the reasonableness of a consonant and genuine American consensus. The instant case presents no such domestic consensus, however . . . .

. . .

JUSTICE SCALIA (WITH WHOM THE CHIEF JUSTICE AND JUSTICE THOMAS JOIN, DISSENTING)

. . .

Though the views of our own citizens are essentially irrelevant to the Court's decision today, the views of other countries and the so-called international community take center stage.

. . .

More fundamentally, however, the basic premise of the Court's argument — that American law should conform to the laws of the rest of the world — ought to be rejected out of hand. In fact the Court itself does not believe it. In many significant respects the laws of most other countries differ from our law — including not only such explicit provisions of our Constitution as the right to jury trial and grand jury indictment, but even many interpretations of the Constitution prescribed by this Court itself. The Court-pronounced exclusionary rule, for example, is distinctively American . . . .

. . .

. . . To begin with, I do not believe that approval by "other nations and peoples" should buttress our commitment to American principles any more than (what should logically follow) disapproval by "other nations and peoples" should weaken that commitment. More importantly, however, the Court's statement flatly misdescribes what is going on here. Foreign sources are cited today, *not* to underscore our "fidelity" to the Constitution, our "pride in its origins," and "our own [American] heritage." To the contrary, they are cited to *set aside* the centuries-old American practice — a practice still engaged in by a large majority of the relevant States — of letting a jury of 12 citizens decide whether, in the particular case, youth should be the basis for withholding the death penalty. What these foreign sources "affirm," rather than repudiate, is the Justices' own notion of how the world ought to be, and their diktat that it shall be so henceforth in America . . . .

. . .

[Eds: In the *Atkins* decision relied on in *Roper* by Justice Kennedy, holding that execution of mentally retarded criminals constitutes cruel and unusual punishment, Chief Justice Rehnquist argued in his dissenting opinion that courts should look only to state and federal legislation and to jury determinations about the death sentence to

> ascertain the contemporary American conceptions of decency for purposes of the Eighth Amendment. They are the only objective indicia of contemporary values firmly supported by our precedents. More importantly, however, they can be reconciled with the undeniable precepts that the democratic branches of government and individual sentencing juries are, by design, better suited than courts to evaluating and giving effect to the complex societal and moral considerations that inform the selection of publicly acceptable punishments.

He disapproved of the Court's opinion in *Atkins* for taking account of what other countries had done, for 'if it is evidence of a *national* consensus for which we are looking then the viewpoints of other countries simply are not relevant.']

NOTE

In *Graham v. Florida*, 130 S. Ct. 2011 (2010) the Supreme Court held that the sentence of life without parole for a non-homicide offense committed by a juvenile violated the Eighth Amendment's prohibition against cruel and unusual punishments. Justice Kennedy, for the majority, noted the 'global consensus against the sentencing practice in question', but underlined the fact that the laws and practices of other nations and international agreements were relevant

> . . . not because those norms are binding or controlling but because the judgment of the world's nations that a particular sentencing practice is inconsistent with basic principles of decency demonstrates that the Court's rationale has respected reasoning to support it.

QUESTIONS

1. Consider the fifth paragraph of the opinion discussing approaches to interpreting and applying the Eighth Amendment. What possible approach to interpretation does it not include? Would it include Justice Scalia's view of the appropriate approach to interpretation?

2. How do you react to the idea that finding 'consensus' is very helpful or indispensable to concluding that capital punishment is unconstitutional in a given context? Why are the 50 states the appropriate accounting units (as opposed, say, to the total population in states going one or the other way on the issue)? How large a majority (of states, population, etc.) constitutes a consensus? Is not a trend over a few decades more compelling than the 'consensus' at a given moment? Why should consensus be decisive for a justice who follows a different approach to the question of constitutionality?

3. How do you assess consensus as an approach by an international tribunal applying international law to concluding that, say, capital punishment as applied in a given context violates the ICCPR? Would the court simply count the number of states going one way or the other?

2. SHOULD NATIONAL COURTS LOOK TO FOREIGN DECISIONS AND INTERNATIONAL LAW ABOUT HUMAN RIGHTS ISSUES EVEN WHEN NOT FORMALLY BOUND?

Roper v. Simmons is but one of a number of prominent Supreme Court decisions in recent decades that have debated the appropriateness of looking to and citing foreign and international law, even though neither the judicial decision, statute nor treaty referred to may bind the state involved. Apart from its significance for the case at issue, the answer that judges and courts bring to this question sheds light on a country's degree of nationalism or internationalism — matters considered below in Section 3.

GANESH SITARAMAN, THE USE AND ABUSE OF FOREIGN LAW IN CONSTITUTIONAL INTERPRETATION

32 Harv. J. L. & Pub. Pol'y 653 (2009)

... There are many critiques of and justifications for the use of foreign law, but they can be loosely grouped into two categories: arguments about liberal democratic values and arguments about accuracy. The first category encompasses both the argument that liberal democracy is undermined when judges rely upon the decisions of foreign courts or statements of international bodies, and the corresponding counterargument that the existence of a democratic society depends on preconstitutional values in the form of basic human rights or conditions for democratic participation. The second category includes both the argument that considering foreign materials has innumerable methodological problems such as selective or shallow use of sources, and the corresponding counterargument that considering foreign law provides more information and thus better judicial decision making....

...

A. Unproblematic Uses of Foreign Law

Mode 1: Quoting Language

Judges might cite foreign law or international law because they like a particular turn of phrase....

Mode 2: Illustrating Contrasts

Sometimes courts use foreign law or practices to illustrate a contrast with domestic practices or law. In *Raines v. Byrd*, for example, Chief Justice Rehnquist found that members of Congress did not have standing to challenge the line item veto, but he noted that the opposite rule would not be irrational because some courts in Europe have such a regime. . . .

Illustrating contrasts does not gravely implicate any of the values at stake in the foreign law debate. Democratic or expressive values are actually strengthened because the court is affirming a distinctive constitutional approach that is unique to the national community. . . .

Mode 3: Logical Reinforcement

Professor Steven Calabresi and Stephanie Zimdahl have identified a set of cases as "logical reinforcement" cases, "in which the Court looks to foreign law and practice to demonstrate that its decisions are logical and supported by reason." The Court decisions themselves rely upon domestic sources, but the Court uses foreign sources to show that its interpretation is not unreasonable or peculiar. . . .

. . . In *Ker v. Illinois*, the Court held that it had jurisdiction over a criminal defendant even though the defendant was forcibly kidnapped from another country. . . . [T] o support his conclusion [Justice Miller] cited two British cases — "authorities of the highest respectability" — holding that forcible abduction was insufficient to limit a court's jurisdiction. . . .

Because logical reinforcement is predicated foremost on domestic sources, methodological concerns . . . are minimal. The foreign sources do very little "work" in these cases. What work they do is indirect. . . . as a matter of persuasive rhetoric, the logical reinforcement model signals to domestic readers that the decision is not ridiculous or unreasonable.

Mode 4: Factual Propositions

Judges can cite foreign [law] . . . to establish factual propositions about history, practices, structure, or anything else. [The Supreme Court in] *Muller v. Oregon* . . . upheld a maximum hours law for women working in a Laundromat. . . . In a footnote, Justice Brewer cited the Brandeis Brief's "very copious collection" of legislation, reports, and studies from the United States and from seven European countries. . . . He noted that these laws and studies were not, "technically speaking, authorities". . . . He noted . . . that they provided "general knowledge" of "woman's physical structure, and the functions she performs in consequence thereof." . . .

. . .

Aside from the accuracy concern facing non-legal facts, the citation of factual propositions is unlikely to be problematic. It does not offend democratic or expressive values because the citation is used to establish a fact from another country, not to provide persuasive or authoritative reasoning for a decision. . . .

B. Potentially Problematic Uses of Foreign Law

Mode 5: Empirical Consequences

[F]oreign law might be helpful for judges to identify what consequences a certain rule might have if adopted. In these cases, the judges seek to ascribe the occurrence or non-occurrence of an event to a certain legal norm.... [I]n *Washington v. Glucksberg* ... Chief Justice Rehnquist referred to the experience of the Netherlands to show that Washington State had a reasonable fear that allowing physician-assisted suicide might result in involuntary euthanasia.

... [T]he actual consequences of a legal rule in any country are difficult to evaluate. In the euthanasia case, it may be that other laws, national norms, traditions, or public or private regulations (or their absence) influence the practice of physician-assisted suicide....

... [W]hen a court, as in *Glucksberg*, seeks to establish that a certain consequence is merely *possible*—rather than likely, inevitable, or impossible—the court may be on firmer ground....

Mode 6: Direct Application

Sometimes foreign law should be applied directly. The constitutional text may require or suggest looking to foreign or international law for interpretation....

...

In *Juilliard v. Greenman*, one of the *Legal Tender Cases*, the Court upheld the issuance of paper money. The Court found that this power was "incident to the power of borrowing money and issuing bills or notes of the government for money borrowed" and was "universally understood to belong to sovereignty, in Europe and America, at the time of the framing and adoption of the Constitution of the United States."...

...

Perhaps the most debated example is the Eighth Amendment's prohibition on "cruel and unusual punishments." In *Trop v. Dulles*, ... Chief Justice Warren ... declared that the "civilized nations of the world" reject the idea that statelessness can be imposed as punishment...

...

In addition to those specific textual provisions which incorporate international ideas, constitutional interpretation may require the use of foreign law when two constitutions share "genetic" or "genealogical" relationships. Genetic relationships exist when one constitution influenced the framing of another, or when two constitutions were influenced by another. Genealogical relationships exist when one constitutional order literally springs from another....

...

Mode 7: Persuasive Reasoning

Justice Breyer has suggested that judges in all countries face the "same kinds of problems ... armed with the same kinds of legal instruments." ... Persuasive reasoning involves a judge considering the argumentation or logic of a foreign decision and using that argument in his decision. The foreign case is not authoritative, but merely provides an example of an intelligent person reasoning through a legal problem.... In other words, the substance of the reasoning and not the identity of the source provides the reason for adopting the argument.

Democratic or expressive values are not likely to be curtailed because the reasoning is persuasive, rather than authoritative. The court is merely searching for persuasive logical reasoning and it happens to discover that reasoning in a court case rather than a treatise or article.... But there is a significant difficulty: methodology.... [T]he court [must] consider the context surrounding the foreign case. The texts of the provisions interpreted might be different, the foreign country's core values might differ, and the politics of the foreign country may have been instrumental in shaping the outcome of the decision. So long as the court is careful, however, persuasive reasoning can be an effective way to use foreign law.

C. Troublesome Uses of Foreign Law

Mode 8: Authoritative Borrowing

The first of the problematic uses of foreign law, authoritative borrowing, involves a judge using a foreign law decision as binding precedent on his court....

Though the U.S. Supreme Court has not pursued authoritative borrowing, Argentina's Supreme Court has.... [T]he Constitution of 1853 was grounded in the American model... in *Ercolano v. Lanteri de Renshaw*, the Argentine Court upheld a rent-control scheme based on the U.S. Supreme Court case of *Block v. Hirsh*, despite the presence of a textual provision different from the U.S. Constitution and contrary Argentine precedent.

Authoritative borrowing... offends democratic values by directly implementing the law of a foreign country without judges considering domestic values and interpretive materials. It is methodologically problematic because it requires a considerable amount of knowledge about a foreign jurisdiction's law, culture, history, and tradition, one that judges are unlikely to possess.... Judges do not find that the people of their nation do or should adhere to such values; rather, they find that *another* people adheres to its own values. Authoritative borrowing, then, appears to be a clear abuse of foreign law.

...

Mode 9: Aggregation

The aggregated information approach collects jurisdictions that adhere to a particular position, aggregates them into a larger total, and uses numerical consensus to indicate the validity of the widely held position. Aggregation can sometimes be undertaken as a form of logical reinforcement with merely persuasive force (Mode 3), but the distinction between aggregation and logical reinforcement is that aggregation is justified under theories which give normative force and legitimacy to the numerical dominance of the particular position....

...

Aggregation of foreign law is most frequently defended under "many minds" arguments, which claim that the opinions of many will be better than those of just one, but there are many varieties of "many minds" arguments, each of which has different contours and risks. Professor Adrian Vermeule has recently outlined [different] types of "many minds" arguments . . . [1] The information aggregation approach is most closely associated with the Condorcet Jury Theorem. The theorem posits that if each person has a greater than fifty percent likelihood of being correct when choosing between two alternatives, the greater number of people, the more likely a majority vote of the people will result in the correct answer. The information aggregation approach requires first that individuals are competent (that is, more likely than not of getting the correct answer and, as a result, better than random) and second that their guesses are statistically independent such that any biases are uncorrelated. . . . [2] The evolutionary approach seeks to explain the development and maintenance of a specific practice or a general system over a period of time. In evolution, mutations come about randomly, but the survival of the mutant gene is based on its fitness. . . . [3] The final approach, arguments about deliberation, asserts that through communication and discussion, groups can come to better decisions. . . .

. . .

[A]ggregation raises serious questions regarding democracy and the expressive values of the nation. . . . It takes the consensus rule of many nations as itself reason for deciding in line with that rule — absent the justifications given in the particular jurisdictions. In cases when the expression of national values is at stake, such a policy would give weight to contrary foreign opinions even though they conflict with longstanding domestic traditions or national opinion.

. . .

Mode 10: No Usage

The final mode of foreign law usage is not using foreign law in constitutional interpretation. This approach would certainly not offend democratic values of self-governance because decisions made would be limited to using domestic materials that would have a place in the constitutional structure. Still, and perhaps counterintuitively, not citing foreign law does not entirely solve the problem of foreign law usage. If some rights are so important as to be pre-constitutional, then perhaps foreign law should be included to identify those rights and bring their normative influence to bear, despite the democratic concerns. This is the purpose of a countermajoritarian court in the political system. As importantly, not using foreign law might result in absurd and inaccurate results. As the sections describing Mode 4, factual propositions, and Mode 6, direct application, showed, there are many instances when foreign law must or certainly should be used in constitutional interpretation. . . .

QUESTIONS

1. Do you agree with Sitaraman's typology with respect to which modes of judicial borrowing are more or less problematic?

2. Which mode of judicial borrowing does Justice Kennedy adopt in *Roper v. Simmons*? Which modes would you guess are more or less prevalent in judicial practice around the world?

3. Is it possible to avoid judicial borrowing altogether? How do judges understand conceptions of 'sovereignty' or of 'a free and democratic country' without relying, implicitly or explicitly, on the practices of other nations?

4. Do you agree with Sitaraman's explanation of the ways in which countermajoritarian concerns relate to the acceptability of judicial borrowing? Are there occasions in which the national polity would want judges to resort to foreign sources and situations in which embracing or engaging with foreign materials would be an expression of 'national values'.

5. Don't most constitutions have a 'genetic relationship' as Sitaraman describes it? If so, should that affect the acceptability of judicial borrowing more generally?

3. EXCEPTIONALISM AND UNILATERALISM: RECENT US APPROACHES TO INTERNATIONAL LAW AND HUMAN RIGHTS

JED RUBENFELD, UNILATERALISM AND CONSTITUTIONALISM

79 NYU L. Rev. 1971 (2004), at 1973

Introduction

...

... The United States has been unilateralist since the country was founded — although, historically, U.S. unilateralism was often a device for avoiding war, not making it. Since 1945, however, America has spoken out of both sides of its mouth on international law, championing internationalism in one breath, rejecting it in the next.

...

World War II came to represent, for continental Europe, the horrors of nationalism and populism. As a result, in the war's aftermath, European elites were ready to embrace an antinationalist, antidemocratic international legal system. The United States was not. The war had a very different meaning here, which led to a very different understanding of the internationalist project pursued in its wake. Basically, the United States promoted the new internationalism as part of an ambition to Americanize as much of the world as it could, which meant both the export of American institutions, including constitutional law, and the strengthening of American global influence.

Whatever its motivations, this ambition created a contradiction at the heart of our post-war internationalist strategy. Because the point of the new international law was to Americanize, the United States, from its own perspective, did not really need international law (being already American). Accordingly, we would lead the world in creating a new international legal order to which we ourselves never fully acceded.... [I] n the ensuing decades, the United States frequently found itself championing international law for other countries, while rejecting or resisting it for itself.

...

American constitutional history has always displayed a commitment to democratic constitutionalism [according to which a constitution is, first and foremost, supposed to be the foundational law a particular polity has given itself through a special act of popular law-making]. [A] second, universalistic conception has undoubtedly and often prominently figured in American constitutionalism as well, but it has never displaced the commitment to the first. By contrast, European constitutional developments since the Second World War have been increasingly committed to the universalistic view, with a corresponding diminution in the importance attached to democratic constitutionalism. The universalistic picture of constitutional law strongly favors supranational legal and political institutions, because the most important legal and political principles, from this perspective, transcend national boundaries and indeed exist to check national governments. For this reason, I will refer to the second conception as "international constitutionalism."

The great new international charters and international institutions that emerged after the Second World War were built, to a large degree, on the premises of international constitutionalism. For example, these premises underlie the entire contemporary discourse of "international human rights," which is predicated on the idea that there exists an identifiable body of universal law, everywhere binding, requiring no democratic provenance. In this sense, contemporary international law is deeply antidemocratic. That is the true challenge that international law's supporters must meet today.

Part IV [of this article concludes] that the institutions and ideologies surrounding international law, at least in its present form, do in fact pose a significant threat to democracy — not by accident, but structurally and by design. To this extent, America does in fact have a good reason to resist international governance today.

U.S. Unilateralism

...

For Europeans, World War II, with its almost sixty million deaths, carried two fundamental lessons. First, it exemplified the horrors of nationalism. In Germany especially, the war left a deep antinationalist scar....

...

Second, and more specifically, the war demonstrated the potential horrors of democracy. We may prefer to forget it, but Hitler was elected, and Mussolini rose to power through parliamentary processes. . . . Unpleasant as it is to acknowledge, Nazism and Fascism were populist movements and in fact manifestations of popular sovereignty. From the postwar European perspective, the Allies' victory was a victory not only against nationalism, but against popular sovereignty, against democratic excess.

The American experience of victory could not have differed more starkly. For Americans, the Allies' triumph was a victory for nationalism — for our nation, our kind of nationalism. It was a victory for popular sovereignty (our popular sovereignty) and a victory for democracy (our democracy). . . . If Europe was to develop democratically, it would need American tutelage and assistance. If Europe was to overcome its nationalist pathologies, it might need to become a United States (of Europe) . . . .

...

. . . The United Nations, the European Union, and international law more generally are expressly understood in Europe as antinationalist; they are constraints on nationalism and national sovereignty, the catastrophic perils of which were made so plain by the Second World War. . . . Just as important, and for the same reasons, international law is also understood, although often more covertly, as a restraint on democracy, at least in the sense of placing increasing power in the hands of international experts — bureaucrats, technocrats, diplomats, and judges — at a considerable remove from popular politics and popular will.

...

Unilateralism and Constitutionalism

...

Here is one way constitutionalism can be understood: Constitutional rights are universal. They are rights people have by nature, by virtue of being persons, by reason of morality, or by reason of Reason itself. Constitutional principles — essentially the liberal principles of the Enlightenment — possess an authority superior to that of politics, including, of course, democratic politics. This special authority, residing in a normative domain higher than that of politics, is what allows constitutional law properly to displace the outcomes of political decisionmaking, including democratic decisionmaking.

On this view, constitutional principles and structures ought in principle to be supra-national. Constitutional rights transcend national boundaries. Constitutional principles are superior to claims of national sovereignty or self-determination . . . .

In this constitutionalism, a democratic ratification process, if pursued at all, is pursued primarily for reasons of expedience. Ratification of a new constitution may be instrumentally valuable — a means of procuring acquiescence — but, in principle, having a committee of expert jurists draw up a constitution is equally satisfactory . . . .

The alternative conception is democratic constitutionalism. . . . These commitments will include fundamental rights that stand against majority rule at any given moment, but these counter-majoritarian rights are not therefore counter-democratic. . . . The reason . . . is that they represent the nation's self-given law, enacted through a special, democratic, constitutional politics, subject to democratic amendment processes in the future . . . .

From this perspective, a democratic process of constitution-making, particularly when it comes to ratification, is crucial. But the work of drafting and ratification is only the beginning. Just as important, if not more so, is the work of constitutional interpretation, because constitutional law must somehow remain the nation's self-given law even as it is reworked through judicial interpretation and reinterpretation . . . .

. . . The US Constitution differed in one fundamental respect from any democratic constitution that any large state had ever had: It was enacted through a process of popular deliberation and consent . . . .

Americans at bottom tend to be highly skeptical about the claims of a nonpolitical, neutral constitutional law. They are well aware that judges' values invariably inform constitutional law. Europeans tend to have a different attitude, which is often expressed in the form of a more dogmatic insistence on the separateness of politics from law, including constitutional law . . . .

. . . European constitutionalism today invests courts with full jurisdiction over constitutional rights. . . . [W]hat makes the new European constitutionalism cohere — what gives European constitutional courts their claim to legitimacy — is the ideology of universal or "international human rights," which owe their validity to no particular nation's constitution, and which possess therefore a supranational and almost supraconstitutional character, making them close to unamendable and rendering them peculiarly fit for interpretation by international juridical experts . . . .

By contrast, in America, where judges still can decry the introduction of international precedents as if they were in the presence of the first spores of a new virus, it would be nothing short of scandalous to suggest that US constitutional questions be decided by an international tribunal, claiming supremacy over our legal system. . . . International law has never quite achieved higher-law status in America; it almost has lower-law status. In the American constitutional perspective, law gains no special authority by virtue of being international law, and courts obtain no special legitimacy by virtue of being international courts. On the contrary, from the American perspective, national constitutional courts, which remain embedded within the nation's democratic processes, are an essential feature of constitutionalism . . . .

Practical Contrast

. . .

On the European view, human rights transcend national politics. Therefore, at least ideally, human rights ought to be uniform throughout the world. By contrast, on the American view, democratic nations can differ at least on some matters of fundamental rights.

. . .

Is International Law Really Antidemocratic?

...

... [W]hile international law can of course be justiciable in national courts, the natural juridical destination of international law is an international tribunal, if for no reason other than that the interpretation of international law by national courts will always be vulnerable to charges of partisanship.

The shift from national courts to international tribunals has serious implications for democracy. These implications are not apparent to most internationalists, whose thinking runs as follows: Once an issue is taken to be a matter of law, particularly a matter of constitutional law, the issue has been removed from the political domain. And once this has been done — once an issue has been placed in the domain of law, rather than politics — then democratic principles have little to say about whether the court that decides the law is a national or international court. What counts is that the court gets the law right....

... Judges [from the American perspective] may, in one sense, be nonpolitical actors, but the judiciary is nevertheless a governmental institution, embedded within a larger political process, and it makes a great difference, democratically speaking, whether adjudication occurs in national or international courts....

... When the power of fundamental lawmaking inherent in judicial review is confided to an international tribunal, the aspirations of democratic constitutionalism have been left behind, replaced by those of international constitutionalism....

DAVID GARLAND, PECULIAR INSTITUTION: AMERICA'S DEATH PENALTY IN AN AGE OF ABOLITION

(2010)

Chapter 1: A peculiar institution

...

America today practices capital punishment in a peculiar form that is difficult to understand or to justify even for its committed supporters. American legislators continue to pass capital punishment statutes, American courts continue to sentence murderers to death, and on forty or fifty occasions each year, mostly in the Southern states, executions are authorized and convicted offenders are put to death. This is what people mean when they say America is a "retentionist" nation where capital punishment still exists. But most of the thirty-five states with the death penalty rarely carry out their threat to put capital murderers to death, and the vast majority of convicted killers end up serving a life-long prison sentence. Wherever capital proceedings are undertaken, the process is skirted round with procedural, evidentiary, and appellate rules that are much more elaborate than in noncapital cases. And even in the rare instance when a death sentence is imposed — which occurs in less than1 percent of homicides — the majority of these death sentences are never executed because the sentence is overturned, the prisoner is exonerated, or the authorities refrain from setting an execution date. The primary cause of death for capitally convicted murderers is not judicial execution: it is "natural causes."

. . .

[The death penalty in the United States is often explained as an instance of American Exceptionalism. In contrasting US retentionism with the abolitionism of other Western nations, the phenomenon is often explained in binary terms with explanations such as]: "Americans" are punitive and "Europeans" are not. Americans are Puritan, or vigilante, or racist or individualistic, and Europeans are not. These, of course, are the preferred simplicities of the system's critics. But supporters have simplicities of their own: for them, the explanation is that America is truly democratic and Europe is not, or that Americans continue to be God-fearing while Europeans have lost their faith.

Such oppositions are misleading, quite apart from the dubious explanations that they propose. By aggregating "America" and "Europe," they collapse important internal distinctions, for example, between states such as Michigan, Wisconsin, or Rhode Island, which have been abolitionist since the mid-nineteenth century, and others such as Texas, Oklahoma, or Virginia, which still regularly put offenders to death. Likewise, they fail to distinguish between European nations such as Portugal, which first abolished capital punishment for ordinary crimes in 1867, and others such as France and Britain, which did not repeal their death penalty laws until more than a century later.

The opposition between American retention and European abolition also collapses historical time, relying on a snapshot comparison at a particular moment that may be misleading. In 1972, for example, the U.S. Supreme Court ruled all existing capital statutes unconstitutional while the French authorities decapitated Claude Buffet and Roger Bontems in the courtyard of the Sante Prison. Or consider that "abolition" usually occurs, when it does, not as the abrupt cessation of an unquestioned policy of routine executions but instead as the final stage of a long-term historical process in which the death penalty is incrementally restricted and restrained and displaced by other sanctions such as banishment, galley slavery, transportation, or life imprisonment.

Major historical change usually takes the form of a process rather than an event. It is therefore a mistake to juxtapose "abolition" and, "retention" — a binary opposition better suited to moral argument than to historical analysis. . . .

American jurisdictions still permit the death penalty, and this is, of course, a significant moral and political fact that properly commands our attention and shapes our debates. But the actual execution of this penalty is comparatively infrequent; its use is subject to close regulation and restraint; and its existence is a matter of legal and political controversy. Such facts ought not to be ignored. . . .

[This is not to deny the distinctiveness of America's death penalty.] Other Western nations, most notably the United Kingdom, share much of the punitive trajectory and culture of control that emerged in late twentieth-century America, but no other

Western nation exhibits the harsh sentencing tariffs, mass imprisonment, or capital punishment that now characterize the United States. So America is different from other Western nations in important respects, and a central aim of current research is to explain these differences. . . .

. . .

Talk of American Exceptionalism usefully reminds us of the need for a comparative perspective and of the distinctive institutional structures and cultures of which the American polity consists. It reminds us that Americans often think of themselves as "exceptional" and care little for international opinion. But in their conventional usage, notions of "American Exceptionalism" can be unhelpful, particularly when the explanations they offer rely on undifferentiated, ahistorical conceptions of "American culture" or the "American condition." America is not a single place for penological purposes, any more than is "Europe" or "the West." There are major regional and state-level differences within the United States (including differences among the thirty-five so-called death penalty states) which make talk of "American" capital punishment somewhat misleading. . . .

. . .

American Exceptionalism is a theory developed to explain a long-term, widespread, and persistent phenomenon — classically, the weakness of the American labor movement and socialist parties — by reference to structural and cultural features of the American nation that are also long-term and persistent. An analytical framework of that kind cannot plausibly be applied to a phenomenon (America's retention of the death penalty following abolition in all other Western nations) that is less than forty years old, is unevenly distributed across the nation's states and regions, and may yet prove to be transient rather than persistent over the long term.

If we replace the conventional dichotomy (capital punishment retained and capital punishment abolished) with a more refined sense of variation along a continuum, then the causal picture alters accordingly. Instead of supposing that qualitatively different effects must have qualitatively different causes, we can think in terms of general causal processes producing varied outcomes in different settings and circumstances. We might then hypothesize that the reasons for death penalty abolition in Europe are much the same as those for death penalty reform in the United States — except that America's anti-death penalty movement, the social forces that propelled it, and the political processes that gave it legal expression were somehow weakened, countered, or constrained in their operation, particularly in the final stages of the movement toward abolition. Instead of thinking in conventional terms of an "exceptional" history and all that this entails, we ought to think of America as a specific variant within a general set: an outlier on some dimensions, in the central tendency on others, but not different in kind. This approach leads away from myopic talk about "exceptions" toward more detailed and more nuanced historical comparisons.

. . .

Epilogue

...

The American capital punishment system has not survived into the twenty-first century because death sentences are more necessary or more functional than in the United States than elsewhere. Capital punishment's capacity to serve the conventional ends of crime control and criminal justice is no greater here than it was elsewhere in the modern West — indeed, the convoluted, restricted, and restrained forms of today's American death penalty make it even less well adapted to these purposes. Its survival has little to do with its instrumental value for governmental or penal purposes and everything to do with the institutional difficulty of securing abolition in the face of majority public opinion. But having continued in existence in this peculiar configuration, the institution has been used by groups and actors who have seized the opportunities that it provides to advance their interests or meet their needs. These actors have taken the death penalty and made it work for them, using it sometimes to express their sense of justice, sometimes to enhance their power, their profit, and their casual pleasure.

If capital punishment's early-modern mode was shaped by the overriding state purpose of maintaining rule, and its modern mode by the rationalized state purpose of governing crime, the late-modern mode is shaped not by any grand state purpose but by the partisan interests of political actors and their constituents. The day-to-day uses of the American death penalty are grounded in the microphysics of local politics — of group relations and status competition, professional rivalry and ambition, and the venal give-and-take of political exchange — rather than being connected to the great ends of state. Petty functions have replaced grand ones, private uses have largely replaced public ones. In late-modern America, capital punishment has ceased to be an instrument of state rule or penal purpose and has become, instead, a resource for political exchange and cultural consumption.

...

The system of capital punishment that exists in America today is primarily a communication system. For the most part the system is not about executions, which, outside of Texas and a few Southern states, are relatively rare — more people are killed each year by lightning. It is about mounting campaigns, taking polls, passing laws, bringing charges, bargaining pleas, imposing sentences, and rehearing cases. It is about threats rather than deeds, anticipated deaths rather than actual executions. What gets performed, for the most part, is discourse and debate. From the point of view of the system, the discreet violence of the execution is a necessary underpinning, but not the thing itself. Capital punishment is like a credit system with a high volume of circulating value underwritten by a gold standard — actual executions — that enables all of the system's exchanges but is less often cashed out.

Capital punishment in America today operates primarily on the plane of the imaginary, and the great majority of its deaths are imagined ones. But the political and economic effects of these grim fantasies are no less real for being imagined. In American criminal sentencing, the availability of the death penalty permits very lengthy sentences of imprisonment, even life imprisonment without parole, to appear comparatively humane, thereby contributing to the nation's extraordinary rates of imprisonment. In the American political system and in the entertainment zone of popular culture, talk about death permits symbolic acts, exchanges, and representations that are used by groups and individuals in their pursuit of power, profit, and pleasure. That the death penalty is increasingly declaratory and discursive makes it no less powerful in its political, legal, and cultural effects. Nor is it any less lethal for the more than twelve hundred men and women who have been put to their deaths since executions resumed three decades ago.

DAVID S. LAW & MILA VERSTEEG, THE DECLINING INFLUENCE OF THE UNITED STATES CONSTITUTION

87 NYU L. Rev.3 (2012)

...

VIII. Conclusion: explaining the decline of American constitutional leadership

... [R]ather than leading the way for global constitutionalism, the U.S. Constitution appears instead to be losing its appeal as a model for constitutional drafters elsewhere. The idea of adopting a constitution may still trace its inspiration to the United States, but the manner in which constitutions are written increasingly does not.

If the U.S. Constitution is indeed losing popularity as a model for other countries, what — or who — is to blame? ... [F]our possible hypotheses suggest themselves: (1) the advent of a superior or more attractive competitor; (2) a general decline in American hegemony; (3) judicial parochialism; (4) constitutional obsolescence; and (5) a creed of American exceptionalism. With respect to the first hypothesis, there is little indication that the U.S. Constitution has been displaced by any specific competitor. Instead, the notion that a particular constitution can serve as a dominant model for other countries may itself be obsolete. There is an increasingly clear and broad consensus on the types of rights that a constitution should include, to the point that one can articulate the content of a generic bill of rights with considerable precision. Yet it is difficult to pinpoint a specific constitution — or regional or international human rights instrument — that is clearly the driving force behind this emerging paradigm. ... The result might be likened to a global language of constitutional rights, but one that has been collectively forged rather than modeled upon a specific constitution. Another possibility is that America's capacity for constitutional leadership is at least partly a function of American "soft power" more generally. . . . [A]ny erosion of the American brand may also diminish the appeal of the Constitution for reasons that have little or nothing to do with the Constitution itself. Likewise, a decline in

American constitutional influence of the type documented in this Article is potentially indicative of a broader decline in American soft power.

There are also factors specific to American constitutionalism that may be reducing its appeal to foreign audiences. Critics suggest that the Supreme Court has undermined the global appeal of its own jurisprudence by failing to acknowledge the relevant intellectual contributions of foreign courts on questions of common concern, and by pursuing interpretive approaches that lack acceptance elsewhere. On this view, the Court may bear some responsibility for the declining influence of not only its own jurisprudence, but also the actual U.S. Constitution: one might argue that the Court's approach to constitutional issues has undermined the appeal of American constitutionalism more generally, to the point that other countries have become unwilling to look either to American constitutional jurisprudence or to the U.S. Constitution itself for inspiration.

It is equally plausible, however, that responsibility for the declining appeal of American constitutionalism lies with the idiosyncrasies of the Constitution itself rather than the proclivities of the Supreme Court. As the oldest formal constitution still in force, and one of the most rarely amended constitutions in the world, the U.S. Constitution contains relatively few of the rights that have become popular in recent decades, while some of the provisions that it does contain may appear increasingly problematic, unnecessary, or even undesirable with the benefit of two hundred years of hindsight. It should therefore come as little surprise if the U.S. Constitution strikes those in other countries — or, indeed, members of the U.S. Supreme Court — as out of date and out of line with global practice. . . .

. . . [V]arious scholars have argued that the U.S. Constitution lies at the very heart of an "American creed of exceptionalism," which combines a belief that the United States occupies a unique position in the world with a commitment to the qualities that set the United States apart from other countries. From this perspective, the Supreme Court's reluctance to make use of foreign and international law in constitutional cases amounts not to parochialism, but rather to respect for the exceptional character of the nation and its constitution.

Unfortunately, it is clear that the reasons for the declining influence of American constitutionalism cannot be reduced to anything as simple or attractive as a long-standing American creed of exceptionalism. . . . A complete explanation of the declining influence of American constitutionalism in other countries must instead be sought in more recent history, such as the wave of constitution-making that followed the end of the Cold War. During this period, America's newfound position as lone superpower might have been expected to create opportunities for the spread of American constitutionalism. But this did not come to pass.

Once global constitutionalism is understood as the product of a polycentric evolutionary process, it is not difficult to see why the U.S. Constitution is playing an increasingly peripheral role in that process. No evolutionary process favors a specimen that is frozen in time. . . .

QUESTIONS

1. On 2 November 2010, voters approved a ballot initiative to amend the Oklahoma Constitution to prevent the state's courts from considering or using Sharia law (defined for the purposes as 'Islamic law . . . based on . . . the Koran and the teachings of Mohammed'). It provided that 'The courts shall not look to the legal precepts of other nations or cultures. Specifically, the courts shall not consider international or Sharia Law.'[1] Does this seem to be a reasonable translation into law of Rubenfeld's concerns? What arguments would you use to challenge the proposal?

2. One of Garland's themes is the need to view abolition as a function of change over time. China, which continues to have the highest number of executions in the world, has made gradual progress in recent years, in part by reducing the number of capital offences from a high of 71 in 1997 to 35 in 2011, and by mandating Supreme Court review of all capital sentences since 2007. The Chinese government has envisaged eventual abolition, and prominent Chinese scholars have proposed a 40-year phased programme leading to abolition in 2048.[2] How, in your view, should human rights proponents respond to such gradualist or evolutionary approaches?

3. In light of Law and Versteeg's analysis, should we conclude that it is 'the exceptional character of the nation and its constitution' that militates against US judges engaging with foreign law in the human rights field?

[1] See M. Davis & J. Kalb, *Oklahoma State Question 755 and An Analysis of Anti-International Law Initiatives* (2011) at www.acslaw.org/sites/default/files/davis_and_kalb_anti-international_law.pdf.

[2] Jianping Lu & Jian Guo, *Death Penalty in People's Republic of China: Quo Vadis?*, at www.penal.org/IMG/DeathpenaltyChinaLU.pdf.

2

The Human Rights Regime: Background and Birth

COMMENT ON INTERNATIONAL DIMENSION OF HUMAN RIGHTS REGIME

In its discussion of the legality of the death penalty and related issues, Chapter 1(B) concentrated on the law — often the constitutional law — of different states. The selected opinions of state courts devoted most of their analysis to their own and to foreign legal systems. International law figured through relevant treaty provisions, but in a subsidiary way. It was not at centre stage.

Chapters 2 to 4, on the other hand, concentrate on the international law aspects of the human rights regime. Why has this path been followed? After all, it is possible to study human rights issues not at the international level but in the detailed contexts of different states' histories, socio-economic and political structures, legal systems, religions, cultures and so on. With respect to its legal dimension, a human rights course that was so organized would stress the internal law of states as well as foreign and comparative law. It would engage in a contextual and comparative analysis of bodies of domestic law, perhaps devoting its full attention to states like China, Saudi Arabia, Italy, the United States or Guatemala. It could stress the recent trend in many states toward (at least as a formal matter) liberal constitutionalism. For such a study of human rights, international law could play a peripheral role, relevant only when it exerted some clear influence on the national scene or had a place in the basic logic of a judicial decision.

The attractiveness of such an approach becomes more apparent when one contrasts with international human rights many other international subjects where international law occupies, indeed *must* occupy, a central position. Imagine, for example, that this course book's interest was not human rights but the humanitarian law of war as applied to interstate conflicts, or the regulation of fisheries, or immunities of diplomats from arrest, or the regulation of trade barriers like tariffs. Each of those fields is inherently, intrinsically, *international* in character. Each involves relations *between* states or between citizens of one state and other states. We could not profitably examine any one of them without examining international custom and treaties, international institutions and processes.

Violations of human rights are different. Not only are they generally rooted within states rather than in interstate engagements, but they need not on their surface involve any international consequences whatsoever. (Of course, systemic and severe human rights violations that appear to be 'internal' matters — for example, recurrent violence against an ethnic minority — could well have international consequences, perhaps by leading to refugee flows abroad or by angering other states whose populations are related by ethnicity to the oppressed minority.) In typical instances of violations, the police of state X torture defendants to extract confessions; the government of X shuts the opposition press as elections approach; prisoners are raped by their guards; courts decide cases according to executive command; women or a minority group are barred from education or certain work. Each of these events could profitably be studied entirely within a state's (or region's, culture's) internal framework, just as law students in many countries traditionally concentrate on the internal legal–political system, including that system's provision for civil liberties and human rights.

Nonetheless, since the Second World War it would be inadequate or even misleading to develop a framework for the study of human rights in many countries without including as a major ingredient the international legal and political aspects of the field: laws, processes and institutions. In today's world, human rights is characteristically imagined as a movement involving international law and institutions, as well as a movement involving the spread of liberal constitutions among states. Internal developments in many states have been much influenced by international law and institutions, as well as by pressures from other states trying to enforce international law.

Internal or comparative approaches to human rights law and the truly international aspects of human rights are now broadly recognized to be complexly intertwined and reciprocally influential with respect to the growth of human rights norms, the causes and effects of their violations, the reactions and sanctions of intergovernmental bodies or other states, the transformations of internal orders and so on.

From another perspective as well it would be impossible to grasp the character of the human rights regime without a basic knowledge about international law and its contributions to it. The regime's aspirations to universal validity are necessarily rooted in that body of law. Many of the distinctive organizations intended to help to realize those aspirations are creations of international law.

For such reasons, this course book frequently examines but does not concentrate on the internal law and politics of states. It relates throughout this 'horizontal' strand of the human rights movement, as constitutionalism spreads among states, to the 'vertical' strand of the new international law that is meant to bind states and that is implemented by the new international institutions. Both the horizontal and vertical dimensions are vital to an understanding of the human rights regime. But the truly novel developments of the last half-century have involved primarily this second dimension.

Chapter 2 has several functions. It sketches the doctrines and principles in an older international law that served as background to and precedents for the human rights regime that took root and developed immediately after the Second World War. It then examines the early instruments — particularly the Universal Declaration of Human Rights and the International Covenant on Civil and Political Rights — that (together with the later-described International Covenant on Economic, Social and Cultural Rights) form the substantive core of the regime, an International Bill of Rights. The chapter uses national and international decisions of courts and other tribunals not only to present basic doctrines and principles, but also to convey an understanding of international law: its so-called 'sources', its processes of growth, particularly with respect to customary and treaty law. The two tasks are interrelated. By what means or methods have the international rules and standards of the human rights regime developed? By what processes are international legal rules made, elaborated, applied and changed?

Several of the opinions and scholarly writings in the chapter draw on Article 38 of the Statute of the International Court of Justice (ICJ), the judicial organ of the United Nations that was created by the UN Charter of 1945.[1] That article has long served as a traditional point of departure for examining questions about the 'sources' of international law. It repeats (largely in identical language) the similar provisions of the 1921 Statute of its predecessor court, the Permanent Court of International Justice that was linked to the League of Nations and effectively died during the Second World War. It reads:

> 1. The Court, whose function is to decide in accordance with international law such disputes as are submitted to it, shall apply:
>   a. international conventions, whether general or particular, establishing rules expressly recognized by the contesting states;
>   b. international custom, as evidence of a general practice accepted as law;
>   c. the general principles of law recognized by civilized nations;
>   d. subject to the provisions of Article 59 [stating that decisions of the Court have no binding force except between the parties to the case], judicial decisions and the teachings of the most highly qualified publicists of the various nations, as subsidiary means for the determination of rules of law.

Although Article 38 formally instructs this particular Court about the method of applying international law to resolve disputes, its influence has extended to other international tribunals, to national courts, and indeed generally to argument based on international law that is made in settings other than courts.

The Article takes a positivist perspective. It defines the task of the Court in terms of its *application* of an identifiable body of international law that in one or another sense, has been consented to ('expressly recognized', 'accepted as law', 'recognized') directly or indirectly by states. Its skeletal list expresses a formal conception of the judicial function that is radically different from that of, say, a legal realist. Consider the following comments on Article 38 by José Alvarez, *International Organizations as Law Makers*, at 46 (2005):

> Public international lawyers, through at least the greater part of the 20th century, have sought to define their field as relatively autonomous from either politics or

[1] The Court can only hear cases to which states are parties: Article 34 of the Statute. A state's consent is necessary for the Court to exercise jurisdiction over it. That consent generally refers to the Court's adjudicating all 'legal disputes' concerning the 'interpretation of a treaty', a 'question of international law', the existence of a fact which, if established 'would constitute a breach of an international obligation' and the reparation to be made for breach of an international obligation: Article 36. Statute of the International Court of Justice, T.S. No. 993 (at p. 25) (U.S.).

> morality. Their endeavor turned many, particularly in Europe and North America, towards legal positivism. . . .
>
> . . .
>
> Nothing embodies these central positivist tenets in international law as much as the doctrine of sources. For most international lawyers trained in the West, article 38 of the Statute of the International Court of Justice remains the "constitution" of the international community. Its enumerated sources of international law — treaties, custom, and general principles of law — remain, for most, the exclusive means for generating legal obligations on states. Through the doctrine of sources, international lawyers define (and defend) their field as characteristically legal. Thanks to sources doctrine, international lawyers argue that international law, like domestic law, also has a circumscribed set of sources and rules for interpreting them; thanks to article 38, international law is distinguished from morality or politics. Thanks to sources, international rules have a distinctive either/or quality, essential to distinguish mere wishful thinking (*lex ferenda*) from black letter obligation (*lex lata*): something either is or is not within one of the recognized sources of international law and someone with the requisite skill, like a judge, can do so. . . .
>
> . . . The doctrine of sources then, has a dual agenda: it tells the lawyer where to find the law in an objective fashion because it is ostensibly based in the concrete practice of states but it also seeks to provide a normatively constraining code for states. . . .

NOTE

The chapter has the following organization: Section A examines customary law, and illustrates its theme through a national court decision in a field now known as 'the law of armed conflict'. Section B examines aspects of general principles of law and natural law, in the context of an arbitral decision on the law of state responsibility for injury to aliens. Section C examines treaty law by drawing on a decision of the Permanent Court of International Justice on the minorities regime in Europe between the two world wars. Section D looks at the judgment at Nuremberg after the Second World War, at the very threshold of the human rights movement. Section E carries the historical narrative into the formation of the movement, stressing the Universal Declaration of Human Rights.

A. THE LAW OF ARMED CONFLICT AND CUSTOMARY INTERNATIONAL LAW

NOTE

The following decision in *The Paquete Habana* deals with an earlier period in the development of the law of armed conflict (also called international humanitarian law or the laws of war), here naval warfare, and with a theme that became central in the later treaty development of this field — the protection of noncombatant civilians and their property (here, civilian fishing vessels) against the ravages of war. Within the framework of the law of armed conflict, this case involves *jus in bello*, the ways in which war ought to be waged, the rules of war itself, rather than the related but distinct *jus ad bellum*, the determination of those conditions (if any) in which a *just* or justified war can be waged, conditions in which (under contemporary international law) going to war is legal.

In its analysis of the question before it, the US Supreme Court here illustrates a classical understanding of customary international law — an understanding that, we shall see, is today open to substantial challenge and reformation. In reading the opinion, keep in mind two questions. What method does the majority opinion employ to conclude that a relevant, indeed decisive, rule of customary international law has developed? Does the dissent differ as to the method itself or as to its application in this case?

THE PAQUETE HABANA

Supreme Court of the United States, 175 U.S. 677 (1900)

MR. JUSTICE GRAY DELIVERED THE OPINION OF THE COURT

These are two appeals from decrees of the district court of the United States for the southern district of Florida condemning two fishing vessels and their cargoes as prize of war.

Each vessel was a fishing smack, running in and out of Havana, and regularly engaged in fishing on the coast of Cuba; sailed under the Spanish flag; was owned by a Spanish subject of Cuban birth, living in the city of Havana; was commanded by a subject of Spain also residing in Havana; and her master and crew had no interest in the vessel, but were entitled to shares, amounting in all to two thirds, of her catch, the other third belonging to her owner. Her cargo consisted of fresh fish, caught by her crew from the sea, put on board as they were caught, and kept and sold alive. Until stopped by the blockading squadron she had no knowledge of the existence of the war or of any blockade. She had no arms or ammunition on board, and made no attempt to run the blockade after she knew of its existence, nor any resistance at the time of the capture.

...

Both the fishing vessels were brought by their captors into Key West. A libel for the condemnation of each vessel and her cargo as prize of war was there filed on April 27, 1898; a claim was interposed by her master on behalf of himself and the other members of the crew, and of her owner; evidence was taken, showing the facts above stated; and on May 30, 1898, a final decree of condemnation and sale was entered, 'the court not being satisfied that as a matter of law, without any ordinance, treaty, or proclamation, fishing vessels of this class are exempt from seizure'.

Each vessel was thereupon sold by auction; the Paquete Habana for the sum of $490; and the Lola for the sum of $800. There was no other evidence in the record of the value of either vessel or of her cargo. . . .

. . .

We are then brought to the consideration of the question whether, upon the facts appearing in these records, the fishing smacks were subject to capture by the armed vessels of the United States during the recent war with Spain.

By an ancient usage among civilized nations, beginning centuries ago, and gradually ripening into a rule of international law, coast fishing vessels, pursuing their vocation of catching and bringing in fresh fish, have been recognized as exempt, with their cargoes and crews, from capture as prize of war.

This doctrine, however, has been earnestly contested at the bar; and no complete collection of the instances illustrating it is to be found, so far as we are aware, in a single published work, although many are referred to and discussed by the writers on international law, notable in 2 Ortolan, *Règles Internationales et Diplomatie de la Mer* (4th ed.) lib. 3, chap. 2, pp. 51–56; in 4 Calvo, *Droit International* (5th ed.) 2367–2373; in De Boeck, *Propriété Privé Ennemie sous Pavillon Ennemie*, 191–196; and in Hall, *International Law* (4th ed.) 148. It is therefore worth the while to trace the history of the rule, from the earliest accessible sources, through the increasing recognition of it with occasional setbacks, to what we may now justly consider as its final establishment in our own country and generally throughout the civilized world.

The earliest acts of any government on the subject, mentioned in the books, either emanated from, or were approved by, a King of England.

In 1403 and 1406 Henry IV issued orders to his admirals and other officers, entitled 'Concerning Safety for Fishermen — *De Securitate pro Piscatoribus*'. By an order of October 26, 1403, reciting that it was made pursuant to a treaty between himself and the King of France; and for the greater safety of the fishermen of either country, and so that they could be, and carry on their industry, the more safely on the sea, and deal with each other in peace; and that the French King had consented that English fishermen should be treated likewise, — it was ordained that French fishermen might, during the then pending season for the herring fishery, safely fish for herrings and all other fish, from the harbor of Gravelines and the island of Thanet to the mouth of the Seine and the harbor of Hautoune. . . .

The same custom would seem to have prevailed in France until towards the end of the seventeenth century. For example, in 1675, Louis XIV and the States General of Holland by mutual agreement granted to Dutch and French fishermen the liberty, undisturbed by their vessels of war, of fishing along the coasts of France, Holland, and England. . . .

The doctrine which exempts coast fishermen, with their vessels and cargoes, from capture as prize of war, has been familiar to the United States from the time of the War of Independence.

. . .

In the treaty of 1785 between the United States and Prussia, article 23. . . . provided that, if war should arise between the contracting parties, 'all women and children, scholars of every faculty, cultivators of the earth, artisans, manufacturers, and fishermen, unarmed and inhabiting unfortified towns, villages, or places, and in general all others whose occupations are for the common subsistence and benefit of mankind, shall be allowed to continue their respective employments, and shall not be molested in their persons, nor shall their houses or goods be burnt or otherwise destroyed, nor their fields wasted by the armed force of the enemy, into whose power, by the events of war, they may happen to fall; but if anything is necessary to be taken from them for the use of such armed force, the same shall be paid for at a reasonable price'....

Since the United States became a nation, the only serious interruptions, so far as we are informed, of the general recognition of the exemption of coast fishing vessels from hostile capture, arose out of the mutual suspicions and recriminations of England and France during the wars of the French Revolution.

...

On January 24, 1798, the English government by express order instructed the commanders of its ships to seize French and Dutch fishermen with their boats.... After the promulgation of that order, Lord Stowell (then Sir William Scott) in the High Court of Admiralty of England condemned small Dutch fishing vessels as prize of war. In one case the capture was in April, 1798, and the decree was made November 13, 1798. *The Young Jacob and Johanna*,1 C.Rob.20....

On March 16, 1801, the Addington Ministry, having come into power in England, revoked the orders of its predecessors against the French fishermen; maintaining, however, that 'the freedom of fishing was nowise founded upon an agreement, but upon a simple concession', that 'this concession would be always subordinate to the convenience of the moment', and that 'it was never extended to the great fishery, or to commerce in oysters or in fish'. And the freedom of the coast fisheries was again allowed on both sides....

Lord Stowell's judgment in *The Young Jacob and Johanna*, 1 C.Rob. 20, above cited, was much relied on by the counsel for the United States, and deserves careful consideration.

The vessel there condemned is described in the report as 'a small Dutch fishing vessel taken April, 1798, on her return from the Dogger bank to Holland'; and Lord Stowell, in delivering judgment, said: 'In former wars it has not been usual to make captures of these small fishing vessels; but this rule was a rule of comity only, and not of legal decision; it has prevailed from views of mutual accommodation between neighbouring countries, and from tenderness to a poor and industrious order of people. In the present war there has, I presume, been sufficient reason for changing this mode of treatment; and as they are brought before me for my judgment they must be referred to the general principles of this court; they fall under the character and description of the last class of cases; that is, of ships constantly and exclusively employed in the enemy's trade'. And he added: 'it is a further satisfaction to me, in giving this judgment, to observe that the facts also bear strong marks of a false and fraudulent transaction'.

Both the capture and the condemnation were within a year after the order of the English government of January 24, 1798, instructing the commanders of its ships to seize French and Dutch fishing vessels, and before any revocation of that order. Lord Stowell's judgment shows that his decision was based upon the order of 1798, as well as upon strong evidence of fraud. Nothing more was adjudged in the case.

But some expressions in his opinion have been given so much weight by English writers that it may be well to examine them particularly. The opinion begins by admitting the known custom in former wars not to capture such vessels; adding, however, 'but this was a rule of comity only, and not of legal decision'. Assuming the phrase 'legal decision' to have been there used, in the sense in which courts are accustomed to use it, as equivalent to 'judicial decision', it is true that so far as appears, there had been no such decision on the point in England. The word 'comity' was apparently used by Lord Stowell as synonymous with courtesy or goodwill. But the period of a hundred years which has since elapsed is amply sufficient to have enabled what originally may have rested in custom or comity, courtesy or concession, to grow, by the general assent of civilized nations, into a settled rule of international law....

The French prize tribunals, both before and after Lord Stowell's decision, took a wholly different view of the general question....

The English government [by Orders in Council of 1806 and 1810] unqualifiedly prohibited the molestation of fishing vessels employed in catching and bringing to market fresh fish....

Wheaton, in his Digest of the Law of Maritime Captures and Prizes, published in 1815, wrote: 'It has been usual in maritime wars to exempt from capture fishing boats and their cargoes, both from views of mutual accommodation between neighboring countries, and from tenderness to a poor and industrious order of people. This custom, so honorable to the humanity of civilized nations, has fallen into disuse; and it is remarkable that both France and England mutually reproach each other with that breach of good faith which has finally abolished it'. Wheaton, Captures, chap. 2,18.

This statement clearly exhibits Wheaton's opinion that the custom had been a general one, as well as that it ought to remain so. His assumption that it had been abolished by the differences between France and England at the close of the last century was hardly justified by the state of things when he wrote, and has not since been borne out.

...

In the war with Mexico, in 1846, the United States recognized the exemption of coast fishing boats from capture....

In the treaty of peace between the United States and Mexico, in 1848, were inserted the very words of the earlier treaties with Prussia, already quoted, forbidding the hostile molestation or seizure in time of war of the persons, occupations, houses, or goods of fishermen. 9 Stat. at L. 939, 940.

...

France in the Crimean war in 1854, and in her wars with Italy in 1859 and with Germany in 1870, by general orders, forbade her cruisers to trouble the coast fisheries, or to seize any vessel or boat engaged therein, unless naval or military operations should make it necessary.

...

Since the English orders in council of 1806 and 1810... in favor of fishing vessels employed in catching and bringing to market fresh fish, no instance has been found in which the exemption from capture of private coast fishing vessels honestly pursuing their peaceful industry has been denied by England or by any other nation. And the Empire of Japan (the last state admitted into the rank of civilized nations), by an ordinance promulgated at the beginning of its war with China in August, 1894, established prize courts, and ordained that 'the following enemy's vessels are exempt from detention', including in the exemption 'boats engaged in coast fisheries', as well as 'ships engaged exclusively on a voyage of scientific discovery, philanthrophy, or religious mission'. Takahashi, International Law, 11, 178.

International law is part of our law, and must be ascertained and administered by the courts of justice of appropriate jurisdiction as often as questions of right depending upon it are duly presented for their determination. For this purpose, where there is no treaty and no controlling executive or legislative act or judicial decision, resort must be had to the customs and usages of civilized nations, and, as evidence of these, to the works of jurists and commentators who by years of labor, research, and experience have made themselves peculiarly well acquainted with the subjects of which they treat. Such works are resorted to by judicial tribunals, not for the speculations of their authors concerning what the law ought to be, but for trustworthy evidence of what the law really is. Hilton v. Guyot, 159 U.S. 113, 163, 164, 214, 215, 40 L.Ed. 95, 108, 125, 126, 16 Sup.Ct.Rep. 139.

...

Chancellor Kent says: 'In the absence of higher and more authoritative sanctions, the ordinances of foreign states, the opinions of eminent statesmen, and the writings of distinguished jurists, are regarded as of great consideration on questions not settled by conventional law. In cases where the principal jurists agree, the presumption will be very great in favor of the solidity of their maxims; and no civilized nation that does not arrogantly set all ordinary law and justice at defiance will venture to disregard the uniform sense of the established writers on international law'. 1 Kent, Com. 18.

It will be convenient, in the first place, to refer to some leading French treatises on international law, which deal with the question now before us, not as one of the law of France only, but as one determined by the general consent of civilized nations...

[Discussion of French treatises omitted.]

...

No international jurist of the present day has a wider or more deserved reputation than Calvo, who, though writing in French, is a citizen of the Argentine Republic, employed in its diplomatic service abroad. In the fifth edition of his great work on international law, published in 1896, he observes, in 2366, that the international authority of decisions in particular cases by the prize courts of France, of England, and of the United States is lessened by the fact that the principles on which they are based are largely derived from the internal legislation of each country; and yet the peculiar character of maritime wars, with other considerations, gives to prize jurisprudence a force and importance reaching beyond the limits of the country in which it has prevailed. He therefore proposes here to group together a number of particular cases proper to serve as precedents for the solution of grave questions of maritime law in regard to the capture of private property as prize of war. Immediately, in 2367, he goes on to say: 'Notwithstanding the hardships to which maritime wars subject private property, notwithstanding the extent of the recognized rights of belligerents, there are generally exempted, from seizure and capture, fishing vessels'....

The modern German books on international law, cited by the counsel for the appellants, treat the custom by which the vessels and implements of coast fishermen are exempt from seizure and capture as well established by the practice of nations. Heffter, 137; 2 Kalterborn, 237, p. 480; Bluntschli, 667; Perels, 37, p. 217.

...

Two recent English text-writers cited at the bar (influenced by what Lord Stowell said a century since) hesitate to recognize that the exemption of coast fishing vessels from capture has now become a settled rule of international law. Yet they both admit that there is little real difference in the views, or in the practice, of England and of other maritime nations; and that no civilized nation at the present day would molest coast fishing vessels so long as they were peaceably pursuing their calling and there was no danger that they or their crews might be of military use to the enemy....

But there are writers of various maritime countries, not yet cited, too important to be passed by without notice....

[The opinion quotes from writing from the Netherlands, Spain, Austria, Portugal and Italy.]

This review of the precedents and authorities on the subject appears to us abundantly to demonstrate that at the present day, by the general consent of the civilized nations of the world, and independently of any express treaty or other public act, it is an established rule of international law, founded on considerations of humanity to a poor and industrious order of men, and of the mutual convenience of belligerent states, that coast fishing vessels, with their implements and supplies, cargoes and crews, unarmed and honestly pursuing their peaceful calling of catching and bringing in fresh fish, are exempt from capture as prize of war....

...

This rule of international law is one which prize courts administering the law of nations are bound to take judicial notice of, and to give effect to, in the absence of any treaty or other public act of their own government in relation to the matter.

...

To this subject in more than one aspect are singularly applicable the words uttered by Mr. Justice Strong, speaking for this court: 'Undoubtedly no single nation can change the law of the sea. The law is of universal obligation and no statute of one or two nations can create obligations for the world. Like all the laws of nations, it rests upon the common consent of civilized communities. It is of force, not because it was prescribed by any superior power, but because it has been generally accepted as a rule of conduct. Whatever may have been its origin, whether in the usages of navigation, or in the ordinances of maritime states, or in both, it has become the law of the sea only by the concurrent sanction of those nations who may be said to constitute the commercial world....Of [these facts] we may take judicial notice.

Foreign municipal laws must indeed be proved as facts, but it is not so with the law of nations'. The Scotia, 14 Wall. 170, 187, 188, sub nom. Sears v. The Scotia, 20 L.Ed. 822, 825, 826.

The position taken by the United States during the recent war with Spain was quite in accord with the rule of international law, now generally recognized by civilized nations, in regard to coast fishing vessels.

On April 21, 1898, the Secretary of the Navy gave instructions to Admiral Sampson, commanding the North Atlantic Squadron, to 'immediately institute a blockade of the north coast of Cuba, extending from Cardenas on the east to Bahia Honda on the west'. Bureau of Navigation Report of 1898, appx. 175. The blockade was immediately instituted accordingly. On April 22 the President issued a proclamation declaring that the United States had instituted and would maintain that blockade, 'in pursuance of the laws of the United States, and the law of nations applicable to such cases'. 30 Stat. at L. 1769. And by the act of Congress of April 25, 1898, chap. 189, it was declared that the war between the United States and Spain existed on that day, and had existed since and including April 21. 30 Stat. at L. 364.

On April 26, 1898, the President issued another proclamation which, after reciting the existence of the war as declared by Congress, contained this further recital: 'It being desirable that such war should be conducted upon principles in harmony with the present views of nations and sanctioned by their recent practice'. This recital was followed by specific declarations of certain rules for the conduct of the war by sea, making no mention of fishing vessels. 30 Stat. at L. 1770. But the proclamation clearly manifests the general policy of the government to conduct the war in accordance with the principles of international law sanctioned by the recent practice of nations....

Upon the facts proved in either case, it is the duty of this court, sitting as the highest prize court of the United States, and administering the law of nations, to declare and adjudge that the capture was unlawful and without probable cause; and it is therefore, in each case, –

Ordered, that the decree of the District Court be reversed, and the proceeds of the sale of the vessel, together with the proceeds of any sale of her cargo, be restored to the claimant, with damages and costs.

MR. CHIEF JUSTICE FULLER, WITH WHOM CONCURRED MR. JUSTICE HARLAN AND MR. JUSTICE MEKENNA, DISSENTING

The district court held these vessels and their cargoes liable because not 'satisfied that as a matter of law, without any ordinance, treaty, or proclamation, fishing vessels of this class are exempt from seizure'.

This court holds otherwise, not because such exemption is to be found in any treaty, legislation, proclamation, or instruction granting it, but on the ground that the vessels were exempt by reason of an established rule of international law applicable to them, which it is the duty of the court to enforce.

I am unable to conclude that there is any such established international rule, or that this court can properly revise action which must be treated as having been taken in the ordinary exercise of discretion in the conduct of war.

…

This case involves the capture of enemy's property on the sea, and executive action, and if the position that the alleged rule *proprio vigore* limits the sovereign power in war be rejected, then I understand the contention to be that, by reason of the existence of the rule, the proclamation of April 26 must be read as if it contained the exemption in terms, or the exemption must be allowed because the capture of fishing vessels of this class was not specifically authorized.

The preamble to the proclamation stated, it is true, that it was desirable that the war 'should be conducted upon principles in harmony with the present views of nations and sanctioned by their recent practice', but the reference was to the intention of the government 'not to resort to privateering, but to adhere to the rules of the Declaration of Paris'; and the proclamation spoke for itself. The language of the preamble did not carry the exemption in terms, and the real question is whether it must be allowed because not affirmatively withheld, or, in other words, because such captures were not in terms directed.

…

It is impossible to concede that the Admiral ratified these captures in disregard of established international law and the proclamation, or that the President, if he had been of opinion that there was any infraction of law or proclamation, would not have intervened prior to condemnation.

In truth, the exemption of fishing craft is essentially an act of grace, and not a matter of right, and it is extended or denied as the exigency is believed to demand.

It is, said Sir William Scott, 'a rule of comity only, and not of legal decision'.

…

It is difficult to conceive of a law of the sea of universal obligation to which Great Britain has not acceded. And I am not aware of adequate foundation for imputing to this country the adoption of any other than the English rule.

…

It is needless to review the speculations and repetitions of the writers on international law. Ortolan, De Boeck, and others admit that the custom relied on as consecrating the immunity is not so general as to create an absolute international rule; Heffter, Calvo, and others are to the contrary. Their lucubrations may be persuasive, but not authoritative.

In my judgment, the rule is that exemption from the rigors of war is in the control of the Executive. He is bound by no immutable rule on the subject. It is for him to apply, or to modify, or to deny altogether such immunity as may have been usually extended.

…

COMMENT ON THE LAW OF ARMED CONFLICT

The opinion in *The Paquete Habana* has the aura of a humane world in which, if war occurs, the fighting should be as compassionate in spirit as possible. It rests the rule of exemption of coastal fishing vessels 'on considerations of humanity to a poor and industrious order of men, and [on] the mutual convenience of fishing vessels'. The opinion seems more than a mere 14 years distant from the savagery of the First World War, let alone that war's successors during the last century with their massive civilian casualties, atrocities and wanton destruction in engagements of close to total war by one or both sides.

The intricate body of international humanitarian law considered by the Supreme Court grew out of centuries of primarily customary law, although custom was supplemented, informed and indeed developed centuries ago by selective bilateral treaties. To this day, custom remains essential to argument about the law of armed conflict, including to the norms considered by international criminal tribunals examined in Chapter 14 and potentially to assessments of military conflict following 11 September examined in Chapter 5. Like many other areas of international law, this field is increasingly dominated by multilateral instruments that have both codified customary standards and rules and developed new ones. Multilateral declarations and treaties started to achieve prominence in the second half of the nineteenth century. The treaties now include the Hague Conventions concluded around the turn of the century, the four Geneva Conventions of 1949 (as well as two significant protocols of 1977 to those conventions), and several discrete treaties since the Second World War on matters like bans on particular weapons and protection of cultural property.

In Chapter 5, we introduce the law of armed conflict in greater depth. For now, it is important to know that the basic Geneva Conventions (which have now obtained universal ratification) and the two Protocols (Protocol I, 171 parties; Protocol II, 166 parties) cover a vast range of problems stemming from land, air and naval warfare, including the protection of wounded combatants, prisoners of war, civilian populations and civilian objects, and medical and religious personnel and buildings. As suggested by this list, the provisions of the four Conventions and the two Protocols constitute the principal contemporary regulation of *jus in bello*, that is, how war ought to be waged.

This entire corpus of custom and treaties has as its broad purpose, in the words of the landmark St. Petersburg Declaration of 1868, 'alleviating as much as possible the calamities of war'. Here lies the tension, even contradiction, within this body of law. Putting aside the question of a war's legality (an issue central to the Judgment of the International Military Tribunal at Nuremberg, p. 120, *infra*, and today governed by the UN Charter), a war fought in compliance with the standards and rules of the laws of war permits — one might say authorizes or legitimates — massive intentional killing or wounding and massive other destruction that, absent a war, would violate the most fundamental human rights norms.

Hence all these standards and rules stand at some perilous and problematic divide between brutality and destruction (1) that is permitted or privileged and (2) that is illegal and subject to sanction. Broad standards like 'proportionality' in choosing military means or like the avoidance of 'unnecessary suffering' are employed to help to draw the line. The powerful ideal of reducing human suffering that animates international humanitarian law thus is countered by the goal of state parties to a war — indeed, in the eyes of states, the paramount goal — of gaining military objectives and victory while reducing as much as possible the losses to one's own armed forces.

The generous mood of *The Paquete Habana* toward the civilian population and its food-gathering needs was reflected in the various Hague Conventions regulating land and naval warfare that were adopted during the ensuing decade. Note Article 3 of the Hague Convention of 1907 on Certain Restrictions with Regard to the Exercise of the Right to Capture in Naval War, 36 Stat. 2396, T.S. No. 544, which proclaimed in 1910: 'Vessels used exclusively for fishing along the coast... are exempt from capture ...'.

The efforts to protect civilian populations and their property took on renewed vigor after the Second World War through the Geneva Conventions of 1949 and the Protocols of 1977. Consider Article 48 of Protocol I to the Geneva Conventions. Article 48 enjoins the parties to a conflict to 'distinguish between the civilian population and combatants and between civilian objects and military objectives'. Military attacks are to be directed 'only against military objectives'. Article 52 defines military objectives to be 'objects which, by their nature, location, purposes or use make an effective contribution to military action and whose total or partial destruction, capture or neutralization, in the circumstances ruling at the time, offers a definite military advantage'. Article 54 is entitled, 'Protection of Objects Indispensable to the Survival of the Civilian Population'. It states that '[s]tarvation of civilians as a method of warfare is prohibited'. Specifically, parties are prohibited from attacking or removing 'objects indispensable to the survival of the civilian population, such as foodstuffs ... for the specific purpose of denying them for their sustenance value to the civilian population or to the adverse Party....' An exception is made for objects used by an adverse party as sustenance 'solely' for its armed forces or 'in direct support of military action'.

Consider some special characteristics of *The Paquete Habana*:

(1) Note the emphasis on the fact that the Supreme Court here sat as a *prize court* administering the law of nations, and note its references to the international character of the law maritime. Indeed, the Court almost assumed the role of an international tribunal, a consideration stressed in the excerpts from the scholar Calvo. Nonetheless, the Court's statement that 'international law is part of our law' and must be 'ascertained and administered by courts of justice' as often as 'questions of right' depending on it are presented for determination, has been drawn on in many later judicial decisions in the United States involving unrelated international law issues.

(2) An antiquarian aspect of the decision and period is that the naval personnel who captured the fishing vessels participated in the judicial proceedings, for at the time of the war captors were entitled to share in the proceeds of the sale of lawful prizes. That practice has ended and proceeds are now paid into the Treasury. 70A Stat. 475 (1956), 10 U.S.C.A. 7651–81.

(3) The Court looked to a relatively small number of countries for evidence of state practice, dominantly in Western Europe. It referred to Japan as 'the last state admitted into the rank of civilized nations'. Even at the start of

the twentieth century, the world community creating international law was a small and relatively cohesive one; today's total of almost 200 states offers a striking contrast. Consider the multinational and multicultural character of an assembly of states today drafting a convention on the laws of war or a human rights convention, and imagine the range of states to which references might be made in a contemporary judicial opinion considering the customary law of international human rights.

COMMENT ON THE ROLE OF CUSTOM

The Supreme Court decision in *The Paquete Habana* raises basic questions about custom, which has been referred to as the oldest and original source of international law. Customary law remains indispensable to an adequate understanding of human rights law. It figures in many fora, from scholarship about the content of human rights law, to the broad debates about human rights within the United Nations, to the arguments of counsel before an international or national tribunal. As this chapter later indicates, the character of such argument today differs in significant respects from the character a century ago at the time of this decision.

Customary law refers to conduct, or the conscious abstention from certain conduct, of states that becomes in some measure a part of international legal order. By virtue of a developing custom, particular conduct may be considered to be permitted or obligatory in legal terms, or abstention from particular conduct may come to be considered a legal duty.

Consider the 1950 statement of a noted scholar describing the character of the state practice that can build a customary rule of international law: (1) 'concordant practice' by a number of states relating to a particular situation; (2) continuation of that practice 'over a considerable period of time'; (3) a conception that the practice is required by or consistent with international law; and (4) general acquiescence in that practice by other states.[2] Other scholars have contested some of these observations, and today many authorities contend that custom has long been a less rigid, more flexible and dynamic force in law-making.

Clause (b) of Article 38(1) of the Statute of the ICJ states that the Court shall apply 'international custom, as evidence of a general practice accepted as law'. The phrase is as confusing as it is terse. Contemporary formulations of custom have overcome some difficulties in understanding it, but three of the terms there used remain contested and vexing: 'general', 'practice' and 'accepted as law'.

Section 102 of the *Restatement (Third), Foreign Relations Law of the United States*, presents a clearer formulation of customary law that draws broadly on scholarly, judicial and diplomatic sources. Many authorities on international law, certainly in the developed world and to varying degrees in the developing states as well, could accept that formulation as an accurate description and guide. After including custom as one of the sources of international law, the *Restatement* provides in clause

[2] M. Hudson, Working Paper on Article 24 of the Statute of the International Law Commission, UN Doc. A/CN.4/16, 3 Mar. 1950, at 5.

(2): 'Customary international law results from a general and consistent practice of states followed by them from a sense of legal obligation'.

Each of these terms — 'general', 'consistent', 'practice', 'followed' and 'sense of legal obligation' — is defined in a particular way. For example, the *Restatement*'s comments on section 102 say:

> state practice includes diplomatic acts and instructions, public measures, and official statements, whether unilateral or in combination with other states in international organizations;
>
> inaction may constitute state practice as when a state acquiesces in another state's conduct that affects its legal rights;
>
> the state practice necessary may be of 'comparatively short duration';
>
> a practice can be general even if not universally followed;
>
> there is no 'precise formula to indicate how widespread a practice must be, but it should reflect wide acceptance among the states particularly involved in the relevant activity'.

The *Restatement* also addresses the question of the sense of legal obligation, or *opinio juris* in the conventional Latin phrase. For example, to form a customary rule, 'it must appear that the states follow the practice from a sense of legal obligation' (*opinio juris sive necessitatis*); hence a practice generally followed 'but which states feel legally free to disregard' cannot form such a rule; *opinio juris* need not be verbal or in some other way explicit, but may be inferred from acts or omissions. The comments also note that a state that is created after a practice has ripened into a rule of international law 'is bound by that rule'.

The *Restatement* (in the Reporter's Notes to Section 102) notes some of the perplexities in the concept of customary law:

> Each element in attempted definitions has raised difficulties. There have been philosophical debates about the very basis of the definition: how can practice build law? Most troublesome conceptually has been the circularity in the suggestion that law is built by practice based on a sense of legal obligation: how, it is asked, can there be a sense of legal obligation before the law from which the legal obligation derives has matured? Such conceptual difficulties, however, have not prevented acceptance of customary law essentially as here defined.

Consider the need to evaluate state practice with respect to (1) *opinio juris* and (2) the reaction of other states to a given state's conduct. Suppose that what is at issue in a case is a state's 'abstention'— for example, state X neither arrests nor asserts judicial jurisdiction over a foreign ambassador, which is one aspect of the law of diplomatic immunities that developed as customary law long before it was subjected to treaty regulation. During the period when this customary law was being developed, it would have been relevant to inquire why states generally did not arrest or prosecute foreign ambassadors. For example, assume that X asserted that it was not legally barred from such conduct but merely exercised its discretion, as a matter of expediency or courtesy, not to arrest or prosecute. Abstention by X coupled with such an explanation would not as readily have contributed to the formation of a customary legal rule. On the other hand, assume that a decision by the executive or courts of X not to arrest or assert judicial jurisdiction over the ambassador rested explicitly on the belief that international law required such abstention. Such practice of X would then constitute classic evidence of *opinio juris*.

Consider a polar illustration, where X acts in a way that immediately and adversely affects the interests of other states rather than abstains from conduct. Suppose that X imprisons without trial the ambassador from state Y, or imprisons many local residents who are citizens of Y. Surely it has not acted out of a sense of an international law *duty*. If it considered international law to be relevant at all, it may have concluded that its conduct was not prohibited by customary law, that customary law was here permissive. Or it may have decided that even if imprisonment was prohibited, it would nonetheless violate international law.

In this type of situation, the conception of *opinio juris* is less relevant, indeed irrelevant, to the state's conduct. The state did not act out of duty. What does appear central to a determination of the legality of X's conduct is the *reaction* of other states — in this instance, particularly Y. That reaction of Y might be one of tacit acquiescence, thus tending to support the legality of X's conduct, or, more likely on the facts here given, Y might make a diplomatic protest or criticize X's action in other ways as a violation of international law. Action and reaction, acts by a state perhaps accompanied by claims of the act's legality, followed by reaction-responses by other states adversely affected by those acts, here constitute the critical components of the growth of a customary rule.

These simplified illustrations suggest some of the typical dynamics of traditional customary international law. What is common to both illustrations — abstention from arrest, and arrest — is that the interests of at least two states were directly involved: at least the acting state X, and state Y. Of course states other than Y may well have taken an interest in X's action; after all, those states also have ambassadors and citizens in foreign countries. All of these possibilities are relevant to understanding *The Paquete Habana*.

Relationships between Treaties and Custom

Thus far we have considered custom independently of treaties (whose elements are described at p. 113, *infra*). But these two 'sources' or law-making processes of international law are complexly interrelated. For example, the question often arises of the extent to which a treaty should be read in the light of pre-existing custom. A treaty norm of great generality may naturally be interpreted against the background of relevant state practice or policies. In such contexts, the question whether the treaty is intended to be 'declaratory' of pre-existing customary law or to change that law may become relevant.

Moreover, treaties may give birth to rules of customary law. Assume a succession of bilateral treaties among many states, each containing a provision giving indigent aliens who are citizens of the other state party, the right to counsel at the government's expense in a criminal prosecution. The question may arise whether these bilateral treaties create a custom that would bind a state not party to any of them. Polar arguments will likely be developed by parties to such a dispute, for example: (1) The nonparty state cannot be bound by those treaties since it has not consented. The series of bilateral treaties simply constitutes special exceptions to the traditional customary law that leaves the state's discretion unimpaired on this matter. Indeed, the necessity that many states saw for treaties underscores that no obligation existed under customary law. (2) A solution worked out among many states should be considered relevant or persuasive for the development of a customary law setting standards for all countries. Similarly, the network of treaties may have become dense enough, and state practice consistent with the treaty may have become general enough, to build a customary norm binding all states. Article 38 of the Vienna Convention on the Law of Treaties signals rather than resolves this issue by stating that nothing in its prior articles providing generally that a treaty does not create obligations for a third state precludes a rule set forth in a treaty from becoming binding on a third state 'as a customary rule of international law, recognized as such'.

In contemporary international law, broadly ratified multilateral treaties are more likely than a series of bilateral treaties to generate the argument that treaty rules have become customary law binding nonparties. Some of the principal human rights treaties, for example, have from around 150 to 190 states parties from all parts of the world. Of course, one must distinguish between substantive norms in multilateral treaties that are alleged to constitute customary law that binds nonparties, and institutional arrangements created by the treaties in which parties have agreed, for example, to submit reports or disputes to a treaty organ.

AKEHURST'S MODERN INTRODUCTION TO INTERNATIONAL LAW

Peter Malanczuk (7th edn. 1997), at 39

[The following excerpts develop some themes about custom in the preceding Comment.]

...

Where to Look for Evidence of Customary Law

The main evidence of customary law is to be found in the actual practice of states, and a rough idea of a state's practice can be gathered from published material — from newspaper reports of actions taken by states, and from statements made by government spokesmen to Parliament, to the press, at international conferences and at meetings of international organizations; and also from a state's laws and judicial decisions, because the legislature and the judiciary form part of a state just as much as the executive does. At times the Foreign Ministry of a state may publish extracts from its archives; for instance, when a state goes to war or becomes involved in a particular bitter dispute, it may publish documents to justify itself in the eyes of the world. But the vast majority of the material which would tend to throw light on a state's practice concerning questions of international law — correspondence with other states, and the advice which each state receives from its own legal advisers — is normally not published; or, to be more precise, it is only recently that efforts have been made to publish digests of the practice followed by different states....

...

The Problem of Repetition

It has sometimes been suggested that a single precedent is not enough to establish a customary rule, and that there must be a degree of repetition over a period of time....

In the *Nicaragua* case [*Nicaragua v. US (Merits)*, ICJ Rep. 1986, para. 186] the ICJ held:

> It is not to be expected that in the practice of States the application of the rules in question should have been perfect, in the sense that States should have refrained, with complete consistency, from the use of force or from intervention in each other's internal affairs. The Court does not consider that, for a rule to be established as customary, the corresponding practice must be in absolutely rigorous conformity with the rule. In order to deduce the existence of customary rules, the Court deems it sufficient that the conduct of States should, in general, be consistent with such rules, and that instances of State conduct inconsistent with a given rule should generally have been treated as breaches of that rule, not as indications of the recognition of a new rule.

In sum, *major* inconsistencies in the practice (that is, a large amount of practice which goes against the 'rule' in question) prevent the creation of a customary rule ...

There remains the question of what constitutes 'general' practice. This much depends on the circumstances of the case and on the rule at issue. 'General' practice is a relative concept and cannot be determined in the abstract. It should include the conduct of all states, which can participate in the formulation of the rule or the interests of which are specially affected. 'A practice can be general even if it is not universally accepted; there is no precise formula to indicate how widespread a practice must be, but it should reflect wide acceptance among the states particularly involved in the relevant activity'....

What is certain is that general practice does not require the unanimous practice of all states or other international subjects. This means that a state can be bound by the general practice of other states even against its wishes if it does not protest against the emergence of the rule and continues persistently to do so (persistent objector). Such instances are not frequent and the rule also requires that states are sufficiently aware of the emergence of the new practice and law...

...

The Psychological Element in the Formation of Customary Law (opinio iuris)

...

There is clearly something artificial about trying to analyse the psychology of collective entities such as states. Indeed, the modern tendency is not to look for direct evidence of a state's psychological convictions, but to infer *opinio iuris* indirectly from the actual behaviour of states. Thus, official statements are not required; *opinio iuris* may be gathered from acts or omissions....

...

Customary law has a built-in mechanism of change. If states are agreed that a rule should be changed, a new rule of customary international law based on the new practice of states can emerge very quickly; thus the law on outer space developed very quickly after the first artificial satellite was launched....

...

Universality and the Consensual Theory of International Law

... Can the opposition of a single state prevent the creation of a customary rule? If so, there would be very few rules, because state practice differs from state to state on many topics. On the other hand, to allow the majority to create a rule against the wishes of the minority would lead to insuperable difficulties. How large must the majority be? In counting the majority, must equal weight be given to the practice of Guatemala and that of the United States? If, on the other hand, some states are to be regarded as more important than others, on what criteria is importance to be based? Population? Area? Wealth? Military power?...

...

... The International Court of Justice has emphasized that a claimant state which seeks to rely on a customary rule must prove that the rule has become binding on the defendant state. The obvious way of doing this is to show that the defendant state has recognized the rule in its own state practice (although recognition for this purpose may amount to no more than failure to protest when other states have applied the rule in cases affecting the defendant's interests). But it may not be possible to find any evidence of the defendant's attitude towards the rule, and so there is a second — and more frequently used — way of proving that the rule is binding on the defendant: by showing that the rule is accepted by other states. In these circumstances the rule in question is binding on the defendant state, unless the defendant state can show that it has expressly and consistently rejected the rule since the earliest days of the rule's existence; dissent expressed after the rule has become well established is too late to prevent the rule binding the dissenting state....

The problem of the 'persistent objector', however, has recently attracted more attention in the literature. Can a disagreeing state ultimately and indefinitely remain outside of new law accepted by the large majority of states? Do emerging rules of *ius cogens* require criteria different to norms of lesser significance? Such questions are far from settled at this point in time....

...

Ius cogens [or Jus cogens]

Some of the early writers on international law said that a treaty would be void if it was contrary to morality or to certain (unspecified) basic principles of international law. The logical basis for this rule was that a treaty could not override natural law. With the decline of the theory of natural law, the rule was largely forgotten, although some writers continued to pay lip-service to it.

Recently there has been a tendency to revive the rule, although it is no longer based on natural law.... The technical name now given to the basic principles of international law, which states are not allowed to contract out of, is 'peremptory norms of general international law', otherwise known as *ius cogens.*

Article 53 of the Convention on the Law of Treaties provides as follows:

> A treaty is void if, at the time of its conclusion, it conflicts with a peremptory norm of general international law. For the purposes of the present Convention, a peremptory norm of general international law is a norm accepted and recognized by the international community of States as a whole as a norm from which no derogation is permitted and which can be modified only by a subsequent norm of general international law having the same character.

What is said about treaties being void would also probably apply equally to local custom....

Although cautiously expressed to apply only 'for the purposes of the present Convention', the definition of a 'peremptory norm' is probably valid for all purposes. The definition is more skilful than appears at first sight. A rule cannot become a peremptory norm unless it is 'accepted and recognized [as such] by the international community of states *as a whole*'.... It must find acceptance and recognition by the international community at large and cannot be imposed upon a significant minority of states. Thus, an overwhelming majority of states is required, cutting across cultural and ideological differences.

At present very few rules pass this test. Many rules have been suggested as candidates. Some writers suggest that there is considerable agreement on the prohibition of the use of force, of genocide, slavery, of gross violations of the right of people to self-determination, and of racial discrimination. Others would include the prohibition on torture....

MARTTI KOSKENNIEMI, THE PULL OF THE MAINSTREAM

88 Mich. L. Rev. 1946 (1990)

... [I]nternational lawyers have had difficulty accounting for rules of international law that do not emanate from the consent of the states against which they are applied. In fact, most modern lawyers have assumed that international law is not really binding unless it can be traced to an agreement or some other meeting of wills between two or more sovereign states. Once the idea of a natural law is discarded, it seems difficult to justify an obligation that is not voluntarily assumed.

...

The matter is particularly important in regard to norms intended to safeguard basic human rights and fundamental freedoms. If the only states bound to respect such rights and freedoms are the states that have formally become parties to the relevant instruments … then many important political values would seem to lack adequate protection. It is inherently difficult to accept the notion that states are legally bound not to engage in genocide, for example, only if they have ratified and not formally denounced the 1948 Genocide Convention. Some norms seem so basic, so important, that it is more than slightly artificial to argue that states are legally bound to comply with them simply because there exists an agreement between them to that effect, rather than because, in the words of the International Court of Justice (ICJ), noncompliance would 'shock[] the conscience of mankind' and be contrary to 'elementary considerations of humanity'.

…

… Although it seems clear that not all international law can be based upon agreement, it seems much less clear what else, then, it may be founded upon…. A Grotian lawyer would not, of course, perceive a great difficulty. He would simply say that some norms exist by force of natural reason or social necessity. Such an argument, however, is not open to a modern lawyer or court, much less an international court, established for the settlement of disputes between varying cultures, varying traditions, and varying conceptions of reason and justice. Such conceptions seem to be historically and contextually conditioned, so that imposing them on a nonconsenting state seems both political and unjustifiable as such.

It is, I believe, for this reason — the difficulty of justifying conceptions of natural justice in modern society — that lawyers have tended to relegate into 'custom' all those important norms that cannot be supported by treaties. In this way, they might avoid arguing from an essentially naturalistic — and thus suspect — position. 'Custom' may seem both less difficult to verify and more justifiable to apply than abstract maxims of international justice.

…

Professor Meron [an authority on humanitarian law whose book is here under review by Koskenniemi] follows this strategy. Although he accepts the category of 'general principles' as a valid way to argue about human rights and humanitarian norms, he does not use this argumentative tack. Nor does he examine whether, or to what extent, such norms might be valid as natural law. His reason for so doing is clearly stated: he wishes to 'utilize irreproachable legal methods' to enhance 'the credibility of the norms' for which he argues. The assumption here is that to argue in terms of general principles or natural justice is to engage in a political debate and to fall victim to bias and subjectivism. Following his rationalistic credo, Meron hopes to base human rights and humanitarian norms on something more tangible, something that jurists can look at through a distinct (objective, scientific) method and thus ground their conclusions in a more acceptable way — a way that would also better justify their application against nonconsenting states.

The starting point — hoping to argue nontreaty-based human rights and humanitarian norms as custom — however, does not fare too well in Professor Meron's careful analysis of pertinent case law and juristic opinion. He accepts the orthodox 'two-element theory' of custom (*i.e.*, for custom to exist, there must be both material practice to that effect and the practice must have been motivated by a belief that it is required by law (p. 3)), yet case law contains little to actually support such a theory, although passages paying lip service to it are abundant....

...

... [The rest of material practice and the *opinio juris*] is useless, first, because the interpretation of 'state behavior' or 'state will' is not an automatic operation but involves the choice and use of conceptual matrices that are controversial and that usually allow one to argue either way. But it is also, and more fundamentally, useless because ... it is really our certainty that genocide or torture is illegal that allows us to understand state behavior and to accept or reject its legal message, not state behavior itself that allows us to understand that these practices are prohibited by law. It seems to me that if we are uncertain of the latter fact, then there is really little in this world we can feel confident about.

In other words, finding juristic evidence (a precedent, a habitual behaviour, a legal doctrine) to support such a conclusion adds little or nothing to our reasons for adopting it. To the contrary, it contains the harmful implication that it is *only* because this evidence is available that we can justifiably reach our conclusion. It opens the door for disputing the conclusion by disputing the presence of the evidence, or for requiring the same evidence in support of some other equally compelling conclusion, when that evidence might not be so readily available.

It is, of course, true that people are uncertain about right and wrong. The past two hundred years since the Enlightenment and the victory of the principle of arbitrary value have done nothing to teach us about how to know these things or how to cope with our strong moral intuitions. But one should not pretend that this uncertainty will vanish if only one is methodologically 'rigorous'. If the development of the human sciences has taught us anything during its short history, it is that the effort to replace our loss of faith in theories about the right and the good with an absolute faith in our ability to understand human life as a matter of social 'facts' has been a failure. We remain just as unable to derive norms from the facts of state behavior as Hume was. And we are just as compelled to admit that everything we know about norms which are embedded in such behavior is conditioned by an anterior — though at least in some respects largely shared — criterion of what is right and good for human life.

...

QUESTIONS

1. Suppose that an international tribunal rather than US courts had heard the controversy in *The Paquete Habana*, and had sought to decide it within the framework of Article 38 of the Statute of the International Court of Justice. Assuming that this tribunal came to the same conclusion, are any observations in the Supreme Court's opinion likely to have been omitted or changed by such an international tribunal? Which observations? Suppose, for example, that the historical record was identical with that reported by the Supreme Court except for the fact that the United States had consistently objected to this rule of exemption and had often refused to follow it.

2. Does the method of the Court in 'ascertaining' the customary rule appear consistent with some of the observations about the nature of custom and the processes for its development in the preceding readings? Consider, for example, how the Supreme Court deals with:

(a) the issue of *opinio juris*, and its relation to comity, grace, concession or discretion;

(b) the relevance of treaties, as expressing a customary norm or as special rules (*lex specialis*) negating the existence of a custom; and

(c) the departure from the rule of exemption during the Napoleonic wars, as a temporary interruption of or as aborting an emerging custom.

About which of these three aspects of the opinion does the dissenting opinion differ? How would you have argued against the Court's resolution of these three aspects?

3. How do you assess Koskenniemi's argument about customary law and natural law? How would you make the argument that the decision in *The Paquete Habana* in fact supports Koskenniemi's view of what underlies argument about customary law and what indeed should be brought to the forefront of argument?

4. Advocates acting on behalf of prisoners sentenced to death have argued in a number of countries that the death penalty is now barred by customary international law. Based on the materials in Chapter 1(B), and in light of the preceding discussions of custom, how would you develop the argument that customary international law bars capital punishment? How would you make the opposing argument? In developing your arguments, take account of the evidence of state practice and of *opinio juris*, and of the major difference between (a) ascertaining customary law through interaction between two states or between citizens of one state and the government of another state in a case like *The Paquete Habana*, and (b) ascertaining customary international law in a death penalty case.

COMMENT ON THE CHANGING CHARACTER OF CUSTOMARY INTERNATIONAL LAW AND OF 'SOFT LAW'

A remarkable, almost anachronistic, feature of *The Paquete Habana* is the reliance on bilateral agreements rather than multilateral agreements and multilateral intergovernmental organizations (IGOs). Since the Second World War, the international legal arena has experienced an extraordinary growth of multilateral instruments, many of them creating IGOs. So many fields of international law — human rights, peacekeeping, the use of force, monetary and trade agreements, environmental treaties, criminal law — contributed to this significant trend from bilateral to multilateral agreements and institutions as the preferred means by which to address some of the problems of the day. Inevitably these treaties and organizations so changed the international law context and the relationships between states and international law as well as between each other as to influence some basic concepts and doctrines, including doctrinal understanding of the sources of international law.

As we will see in the following chapters, the Universal Declaration of Human Rights (UDHR) and the major human rights treaties suggest the importance of this phenomenon for the evolution of the human rights regime. Not only do the basic duties of the state run towards its internal social and political order and population, but other states — independently or as members of various international human rights organizations — become involved in the process of attempting to assure the observance by delinquent states of those duties. IGOs become to one or another degree independent actors working toward treaties' goals. Or at least the scheme so suggests, for this book's later materials explore how far shy of that 'assurance' the system has in fact progressed.

These and other phenomena, ranging from the development of national and international human rights nongovernmental organizations (NGOs) to globalization embracing multiple cultures, have influenced the very paths of 'making' international law. For example, even outside the world of states and IGOs, there are today so many more voices and places contributing statements, resolutions, declarations, draft codes and other types of instruments about the content of international law — what it 'is', what it 'ought to be'. The Universal Declaration of Human Rights, for example, has evolved from its early status as an aspirational statement to a body of norms in which many provisions are widely accepted as authoritative — as, for example, part of customary international law, or as an authoritative interpretation of the Charter's human rights provisions. Which individuals, which groups, which institutions, which states served as agents of this process? Do those who understand the UDHR, or important parts of it, as authoritative international law, as much so as a treaty, rely on the traditional criteria of customary law to support their understanding? Do UN General Assembly resolutions approved with large majorities occupy a special status? Are different criteria for the formation of custom developing, and becoming widely accepted? Such questions, addressed not only to global and regional IGOs but also to human rights NGOs, to international associations of lawyers and judges, and to a broad range of other non-state groups issuing proposals about human rights, have led to the concept of 'soft law', which is now another, often perplexing ingredient in the multi-faceted evolution of international law.

For these reasons, we turn to such questions at this point, for they become immediately relevant to an understanding of the elaboration and evolution of civil-political and economic-social rights. The following two articles develop these themes and questions.

ANTHEA ROBERTS, TRADITIONAL AND MODERN APPROACHES TO CUSTOMARY INTERNATIONAL LAW: A RECONCILIATION

95 Am. J. Int'l. L. 757 (2001)

... [C]ustom has become an increasingly significant source of law in important areas such as human rights obligations. Codification conventions, academic commentary, and the case law of the International Court of Justice (the Court) have also contributed to a contemporary resurrection of custom. These developments have resulted in two apparently opposing approaches, which I term "traditional custom" and "modern custom." ...

... Custom is generally considered to have two elements: state practice and *opinio juris*.... This distinction is problematic because it is difficult to determine what states believe as opposed to what they say. Whether treaties and declarations constitute state practice or *opinio juris* is also controversial. For the sake of clarity, this article adopts Anthony D'Amato's distinction between action (state practice) and statements (*opinio juris*). Thus, actions can form custom only if accompanied by an articulation of the legality of the action. *Opinio juris* concerns statements of belief rather than actual beliefs. Further, treaties and declarations represent *opinio juris* because they are statements about the legality of action, rather than examples of that action....

What I have termed traditional custom results from general and consistent practice followed by states from a sense of legal obligation. It focuses primarily on state practice in the form of interstate interaction and acquiescence. *Opinio juris* is a secondary consideration invoked to distinguish between legal and nonlegal obligations. Traditional custom is evolutionary and is identified through an *inductive* process in which a general custom is derived from specific instances of state practice....

By contrast, modern custom is derived by a *deductive* process that begins with general statements of rules rather than particular instances of practice. This approach emphasizes *opinio juris* rather than state practice because it relies primarily on statements rather than actions. Modern custom can develop quickly because it is deduced from multilateral treaties and declarations by international fora such as the General Assembly, which can declare existing customs, crystallize emerging customs, and generate new customs.... A good example of the deductive approach is the Merits decision in *Military and Paramilitary Activities in and against Nicaragua* [1986 ICJ Rep. 14]. The Court paid lip service to the traditional test for custom but derived customs of non-use of force and nonintervention from statements such as General Assembly resolutions. The Court did not make a serious inquiry into state practice, holding that it was sufficient for conduct to be generally consistent with statements of rules, provided that instances of inconsistent practice had been treated as breaches of the rule concerned rather than as generating a new rule....

H. L. A. Hart and R. M. Hare distinguish between *descriptive* and *prescriptive* statements and laws. Descriptive laws can be discovered by observation and reasoning because they are statements about what the practice *has been*. By contrast, prescriptive laws are not determined primarily by observations of fact because they state demands about what the practice *should or ought to be*. Legal rules are *always prescriptive* because they make demands about how people and states should behave. However, their prescriptive nature can be justified by what the practice has been and/or what the practice should be. A law is primarily *descriptive* if it conforms to the premise: the *law is* what the practice *has been*. A law is primarily *normative* if it is formulated on the assumption: the *law is* what the practice *ought to be*. What the law *is* (prescription) can be justified by what the practice *has been* (description) or what the practice *ought to be* (normativity). Thus, we should distinguish between what the practice has been, what the law is, and what the practice ought to be: "has/is/ought" (description/prescription/normativity)....

... Moving from *has* to *is* involves some level of law creation because it requires the formulation of an abstract rule from actual practice, despite the existence of silences, ambiguities, and contradictions in that practice. Determining what the law *is* from what the practice *has been* relies heavily on the choice of characteristics under which precedents are classified and the degree of abstraction employed....

...

Traditional custom is closely associated with descriptive accuracy because norms are constructed primarily from state practice — working from practice to theory. Reliance on state practice provides continuity with past actions and reliable predictions of future actions. It results in practical and achievable customs that can actually regulate state conduct. By contrast, modern custom demonstrates a predilection for substantive normativity rather than descriptive accuracy. Modern custom derives norms primarily from abstract statements of *opinio juris* — working from theory to practice. Whereas state practice is clearly descriptive, *opinio juris* is inherently ambiguous in nature because statements can represent *lex lata* (what the law is, a descriptive characteristic) or *lex ferenda* (what the law should be, a normative characteristic). The Court has held that only statements of *lex lata* can contribute to the formation of custom. However, modern custom seems to be based on normative statements of *lex ferenda* cloaked as *lex lata*, for three reasons.

...

[Third], treaties and resolutions often use mandatory language to prescribe a model of conduct and provide a catalyst for the development of modern custom. Treaties and declarations do not merely photograph or declare the current state of practice on moral issues. Rather, they often reflect a deliberate ambiguity between actual and desired practice, designed to develop the law and to stretch the consensus on the text as far as possible. For example, some rights set out in the Universal Declaration of Human Rights of 1948 are expressed in mandatory terms and have achieved customary status even though infringements are 'widespread, often gross and generally tolerated by the international community.' As a result, modern custom often represents progressive development of the law masked as codification by phrasing *lex ferenda* as *lex lata*.

...

The moral content of modern custom explains the strong tendency to discount the importance of contrary state practice in the modern approach. Irregularities in description can undermine a descriptive law, but a normative law may be broken and remain a law because it is not premised on descriptive accuracy. For example, *jus cogens* norms prohibit fundamentally immoral conduct and cannot be undermined by treaty arrangement or inconsistent state practice. Since the subject matter of modern customs is not morally neutral, the international community is not willing to accept any norm established by state practice. Modern custom involves an almost teleological approach, whereby some examples of state practice are used to justify a chosen norm, rather than deriving norms from state practice.... Thus, the importance of descriptive accuracy varies according to the facilitative or moral content of the rule involved.

...

A critique of modern custom.... Deriving customs primarily from treaties and declarations, rather than state practice, is potentially more democratic because it involves practically all states. Most states can participate in the negotiation and ratification of treaties and declarations of international fora, such as the United Nations General Assembly. The notion of sovereign equality (one state, one vote) helps to level the playing field between developed and developing countries. While formal equality cannot remedy all inequalities in power, international fora provide less powerful states with a cost-efficient means of expressing their views.... [V]otes in the General Assembly usually receive little media scrutiny and are generally not intended to make law. For example, the General Assembly resolution on torture was adopted unanimously, while a much smaller number of states ratified the Convention Against Torture and others entered significant reservations to it.

...

The greatest criticism of modern custom is that it is descriptively inaccurate because it reflects ideal, rather than actual, standards of conduct. The normative nature of modern custom leads to an enormous gap between asserted customs and state practice. For example, customary international law prohibits torture, yet torture is endemic. A similar criticism is made of the 'emptiness' of *jus cogens* norms, which are often flouted in practice. These laws lack efficacy because states have not internalized them as standards of behavior to guide their actions and judge the behavior of others. The regulatory function of modern custom is doubtful because it appears merely to set up aspirational aims rather than realistic requirements about action.... Some theorists characterize modern customs as 'soft laws' or sub-legal obligations that do not amount to law. Indeed, norms that are honored in the breach do not yield reliable predictions of future conduct and are likely to bring themselves, and possibly custom as a whole, into disrepute.

...

DINAH SHELTON, INTRODUCTION: LAW, NON-LAW AND THE PROBLEM OF 'SOFT LAW'

in Dinah Shelton (ed.), Commitment and Compliance: The Role of Non-Binding Norms in the International Legal System (2000), at 1

... The subject of compliance with non-binding norms [is] concerned with why states and other international actors choose to conclude non-binding rather than binding normative instruments and whether or to what extent that choice affects their consequent behavior.

...

The project to study compliance with international non-binding norms or 'soft law' began with a workshop.... In part, the meeting sought to test the hypothesis that countries sometimes comply with non-binding legal instruments as well as they do with binding ones. The term 'soft *law*' itself seems to contain a normative element leading to expectations of compliance.

...

... [A] decision was made to compare four subject areas: human rights, environment, arms control, and trade and finance. Each of the fields has particularities that result in different uses for non-binding norms and a different ratio of non-binding norms to 'hard' law. Human rights law has developed over the past fifty years into a broad code of behavior for states and state agents, not only in their relations with other states, but primarily as non-reciprocal, unilateral commitments towards all those within the jurisdiction of the state. Environmental law, in contrast, aims more at regulating non-state behavior: most environmental harm is caused by private entities and not by state agents....

...

... The project participants discussed at length whether or not to include norms adopted by non-state actors. Ultimately it was decided to include them because they are usually intended to impact on state behavior or to circumvent state policies. In addition, with increasing globalization, transnational entities that make their own rules prepare and enter into normative instruments that look much the same as state-adopted norms....

...

Throughout the project, participants debated whether binding instruments (law) and non-binding ones (soft law or non-law) are strictly alternative, or whether they are two ends on a continuum from legally binding to complete freedom of action. Recent inclusion of soft law commitments in hard law instruments suggests that both form and content are relevant to the sense of legal obligation. Some soft law instruments may have a specific normative content that is 'harder' than the soft commitments in treaties. Other non-binding instruments may never be intended to have normative effect, but are promotional, serving as a catalyst to further action. This appears to be the case with some of the concluding acts of international conferences....

...

... A question posed in this study is whether state behavior in adopting and complying with non-binding instruments evidences acceptance of new modes of lawmaking not reflected in the Statute of the Court. *Ab initio*, however, we take the view that international law is created through treaty and custom, and thus 'soft law' is not legally binding *per se*.

It has become commonplace to note that the international system has undergone tremendous recent changes. From a community of predominately western states, the global arena now contains more than four times the number of states that existed at the beginning of the last century. In addition, other communities have emerged to play important international roles: intergovernmental organizations, non-governmental organizations, professional associations, transnational corporations, and mixed entities comprised of members of different communities. They both contribute to the making of international norms and increasingly are bound by them....

The line between law and not-law may appear blurred. Treaty mechanisms are including more 'soft' obligations, such as undertakings to endeavor to strive to cooperate. Non-binding instruments in turn are incorporating supervisory mechanisms traditionally found in hard law texts. Both types of instrument may have compliance procedures that range from soft to hard. The result seems to be a dynamic interplay between soft and hard obligations similar to that which exists between international and national law. In fact, it is rare to find soft law standing in isolation; instead, it is used most frequently either as a precursor to hard law or as a supplement to a hard law instrument. Soft law instruments often serve to allow treaty parties to authoritatively resolve ambiguities in the text or fill in gaps. This is part of an increasingly complex international system with variations in forms of instruments, means, and standards of measurement that interact intensely and frequently, with the common purpose of regulating behavior within a rule of law framework....

... Some scholars have distinguished hard law and soft law by stating that breach of law gives rise to legal consequences while breach of a political norm gives rise to political consequences. Such a distinction is not always easy to make. Testing normativity based on consequences can be confusing, since breaches of law may give rise to consequences that may be politically motivated. A government that recalls its ambassador can either be expressing political disapproval of another state's policy on an issue, or sanctioning noncompliance with a legal norm. Terminating foreign assistance also may be characterized either way. Even binding UN Security Council resolutions based on a threat to the peace do not necessarily depend upon a violation of international law.

... If states expect compliance and in fact comply with rules and principles contained in soft law instruments as well as they do with norms contained in treaties and custom, then perhaps the concept of international law, or the list of sources of international law, requires expansion. Alternatively, it may have to be conceded that legal obligation is not as significant a factor in state behavior as some would think. A further possibility is that law remains important and states choose a soft law form for specific reasons related to the requirements of the problem being addressed and unrelated to the expectation of compliance....

... There are several possible reasons that could explain the choice of soft law over hard law....

(5) Legally binding norms may be inappropriate when the issue or the effective response is not yet clearly identified, due to scientific uncertainty or other causes, but there is an urgent requirement to take some action. Similarly, it may be necessary where diverse legal systems preclude legally binding norms. Thus, soft law may be increasingly utilized because it responds to the needs of the new international system. In national legal systems, law-creating methods have always varied, from constitution-writing, to legislation, executive decrees, administrative regulation, and private contract, as well as common law. International law-making itself has changed over time. Where it was once almost entirely customary in origin, treaty-making,

first bilateral, then multilateral, has come to be seen as the predominant form of law-making in the modern world.

(6) Soft law allows for more active participation of non-state actors. Where states once created and applied international norms through processes that lacked transparency, participation, and accountability, non-state actors have become a significant source of power alongside, if not outside, state control....

NOTE

As the above readings explain, the sources of international law have expanded to encompass areas of soft law. These readings focus in significant part on sources of international law relating to the conduct of states. The expansion of sources of international law has also come about through the rise and influence of non-state actors in global affairs. Indeed, non-state actors do not fit within the classic framework for determining customary international law. As a formal matter, customary international law requires establishing a general and consistent practice of states, and followed out of a sense of state-level actors' sense of their legal obligations. That conception of the law does not apply well to non-state actors. Indeed, the rules of customary international law generally developed to regulate a particular arena with particular sets of actors: a global public order composed of sovereign entities that have been fairly stable, limited in number, and able to express their views on the legality of their own and their counterparts' conduct. The international legal regime for defining the rights and responsibilities of non-state actors has accordingly not been limited to the classic sources of international law, or custom in particular. The regime relies more on areas of soft law for the derivation of its norms. These soft law standards are said to reflect social expectations of the international community or of stakeholders for whom and upon whom power is exercised.

Consider the example of corporations, which we discuss at length in Chapter 16. In 2011, John Ruggie the UN Secretary-General's Special Representative on Human Rights and Businesses issued a set of 'Guiding Principles', (see p. 1479, *infra*) which were then endorsed by the UN Human Rights Council. For present purposes, the Principles are instructive both in the sources from which they were derived and in their authority for helping to regulate transnational affairs. As to the former, a preceding report by the Special Representative explained: 'In addition to compliance with national laws, the baseline responsibility of companies is to respect human rights. Failure to meet this responsibility can subject companies to the courts of public opinion — comprising employees, communities, consumers, civil society, as well as investors — and occasionally to charges in actual courts. Whereas governments define the scope of legal compliance, the broader scope of the responsibility to respect is defined by social expectations — as part of what is sometimes called a company's social licence to operate.' And, as a specific example, in explaining corporate responsibility to exercise due diligence, the Special Representative explained, 'For the substantive content of the due diligence process, companies should look, at a minimum, to the international bill of human rights and the core conventions of the ILO, because the principles they embody comprise the benchmarks against which other social actors judge the human rights impacts of companies'. The 2011 report also suggests the understanding of the Special Representative and of the Human Rights Council with respect to the legal and normative force of the Principles: 'The Guiding Principles' normative contribution lies not in the creation of new international law obligations but in elaborating the implications of existing standards and practices for States and businesses'. Notably, human rights nongovernmental organizations did not criticize the content of the Guiding Principles (e.g., whether the Principles properly described a legal duty) as much as the lack of a mechanism to monitor and scrutinize their implementation.

Consider another example of non-state actors whose conduct does not easily fit the classic conception of customary international law: IGOs. There are currently between 2,000 and 3,000 IGOs operating worldwide and in diverse areas including the regulation of fisheries, water resources, pharmaceuticals and internet governance. A new unified field of theory and practice — Global Administrative Law (GAL) — has emerged, in part, to consider rules that do and should govern the practices of these organizations and how they effect individuals' lives. The principal theorists of GAL explain that 'the traditional mechanisms based on State consent as expressed through treaties or custom are simply no longer capable of accounting' for all these institutions (S. Cassese et al. 2008); 'Customary international law is still generally understood as being formed primarily by state action, and thus for the time being does not fully incorporate the relevant practice of non-state actors, such as global administrative bodies' (B. Kingsbury, N. Krisch and R. Stewart 2005). Standards that govern the conduct of IGOs — such as due process and participation rights — may thus also be derived from the past practices of the organizations, accepted standards and guidelines and general principles of public accountability and rule-making for international bodies. GAL is also specifically relevant to human rights in several respects. Some IGOs directly administer human rights or humanitarian mandates, some IGOs regulate areas that indirectly affect human rights (e.g., pharmaceutical innovation), some IGOs administer other areas but their decision-making process implicates procedural, and potentially political, rights, and some IGOs support or contract with third parties whose conduct might violate human rights (cf. B. Kingsbury and L. Casini 2009).

ADDITIONAL READING

E. Hafner-Burton, D. G. Victor & Y. Lupu, 'International Relations for International Law', 106 Am. J. Int'l. L. (2012); G. C. Shaffer & M. A. Pollack, 'Hard vs. Soft Law: Alternatives, Complements, and Antagonists in International Governance', 94 Minnesota L. Rev. 706 (2010); A. T. Guzman & T. L. Meyer, 'International Common Law: The Soft Law of International Tribunals', 9 Chicago J. Int'l. L. 515, 516 (2009); B. Kingsbury & L. Casini, 'Global Administrative Law Dimensions of International Organizations Law', 40 Int'l. Orgs. L. Rev. 319 (2009); S. Cassese et al., *Global Administrative Law: Cases, Materials, Issues* (2nd edn. 2008); B. Kingsbury,

N. Krisch & R. B. Stewart, 'The Emergence of Global Administrative Law', 68 Law & Contemp. Probs. 16 (2005); K. Raustiala, 'Form and Substance in International Agreements', 99 Am. J. Int'l. L. 581, 581–2 (2005); Barbara Koremenos, Charles Lipson & Duncan Snidal, 'The Rational Design of International Institutions', 55 Int'l. Org. 761 (2001); Martha Finnemore & Stephen J. Toope, 'Alternatives to "Legalization", Richer Views of Law and Politics', 55 Int'l. Org. 743 (2001); K. W. Abbott & D. Snidal, 'Hard and Soft Law in International Governance', 54 Int'l. Org. 421 (2000); S. Ratner & A.-M. Slaughter (eds.), 'Symposium on Method in International Law', 93 Am. J. Int. L. 291 (1999); A. Cassese, *International Law* (2nd edn. 2004), M. Shaw, *International Law* (5th edn. 2003); M. Koskenniemi, *Apology and Utopia* (1989, reissued 2006); C. Reus-Smit (ed.), *The Politics of International Law* (2004); J. Klabbers, 'The Redundancy of Soft Law', 65 Nordic J. Int'l. L. 167, 168 (1996); I. Shearer, *Starke's International Law* (11th edn. 1994); B. Simma et al. (eds.), *The Charter of the United Nations: A Commentary* (2nd edn. 2002); J. Klabbers, *An Introduction to International Institutional Law* (2002); J.-M. Henckaerts & L. Doswold-Beck (eds.), *Customary International Humanitarian Law* (3 vols. 2005).

B. STATE RESPONSIBILITY, GENERAL PRINCIPLES AND NATURAL LAW

COMMENT ON THE LAW OF STATE RESPONSIBILITY

The *Chattin* case described below was decided under a 1923 General Claims Convention between the United States and Mexico, 43 Stat. 1730, T.S. No. 678. That treaty provided that designated claims against Mexico of US citizens (and vice versa) for losses or damages suffered by persons or by their properties that (in the case of the US citizens) had been presented to the US Government for interposition with Mexico and that had remained unsettled 'shall be submitted to a Commission consisting of three members for decision in accordance with the principles of international law, justice and equity'. Each state was to appoint one member, and the presiding third commissioner was to be selected by mutual agreement (and by stipulated procedures failing agreement).

These arbitrations grew out of and further developed the law of state responsibility for injuries to aliens, a branch of international law that was among the important predecessors to contemporary human rights law. That body of law addressed only certain kinds of conflicts — not including, for example, conflicts originating in the first instance in a dispute between a claimant state (X) and a respondent state (Y). Thus it did not cover a dispute, say, based on a claim by X that Y had violated international law by its invasion of X's territory or by its imprisonment of X's ambassador.

Rather, the claims between states that were addressed by the law of state responsibility for injuries to aliens grew out of disputes arising in the first instance between a citizen-national of X and the government of Y. For example, respondent state Y allegedly imprisoned a citizen of claimant state X without hearing or trial, or seized property belonging to citizens of X — allegations which, if true, could show violations of international law. Note that these illustrations involve action leading to injury of X's citizens by governmental officials or organs (executive, legislative, judicial) of Y. The law of state responsibility required that the conduct complained of be that of the state or, in less clear and more complex situations, be ultimately attributable to the state.

In the normal case, the citizen of X would seek a remedy within Y, probably through its judiciary — release from jail, return of the seized property or compensation for it. Indeed, before invoking the aid of his own government, the citizen of X would generally be required under the relevant treaty to pursue such a path, to 'exhaust local remedies'. But that path could prove to be fruitless, because of lack of recourse to Y's judiciary, because that judiciary was corrupt, or because of Y's law adverse to the citizen of X that would certainly be applied by its judiciary. In such circumstances, the injured person may turn to his own government X for diplomatic protection.

The 1924 decision of the Permanent Court of International Justice in the *Mavrommatis Palestine Concessions (Jurisdiction)* case, P.C.I.J., Ser. A, No. 2, gave classic expression to such diplomatic protection. It pointed out that when a state took up the cause of one of its subjects (citizens-nationals) in a dispute originating between that subject and respondent state, the dispute:

> entered upon a new phase; it entered the domain of international law, and became a dispute between two States.... It is an elementary principle of international law that a State is entitled to protect its subjects, when injured by acts contrary to international law committed by another State, from whom they have been unable to obtain satisfaction through the ordinary channels. By taking up the case of one of its subjects and by resorting to diplomatic action or international judicial proceedings on his behalf, a State is in reality asserting its own rights — its right to ensure, in the person of its subjects, respect for the rules of international law.

Precisely what action to take, what form of diplomatic protection to extend, lay within the discretion of the claimant state. If it decided to intervene and thereby make the claim its own, it might espouse the claim through informal conversations with the respondent state, or make a formal diplomatic protest, or exert various economic and political pressures to encourage a settlement (extending at times to military intervention), or, if these strategies failed, have recourse to international tribunals. Such recourse was infrequent. International tribunals to whose jurisdiction states had consented for the resolution of disputes between them were rare. Moreover, states were reluctant to raise controversies between their citizens and foreign states to the level of interstate conflict before an international tribunal except where a clear national interest gave reason to do so.

An arbitral tribunal to which the claimant state turned may have been created by agreement between the disputing states to submit to it designated types of disputes. That agreement may have been part of a general arbitration treaty (which after the Second World War found scant use) covering a broad range of potential disputes between the two parties. Or it may have been a so-called 'compromissory clause' (*compromis*) in a treaty dealing with a specific subject that bound the parties to submit to arbitration disputes that might arise under that treaty. Of course, two states could always agree to submit specified disputes to arbitration, as in the 1923 General Claims Convention between the United States and Mexico under which *Chattin* was decided.

In 1921, ad hoc arbitral tribunals were first supplemented by an international court, the Permanent Court of International Justice provided for in the Covenant of the League of Nations. Again, problems of states' consent to jurisdiction and states' reluctance to start interstate litigation limited the role of that court (and indeed the role of its successor, the International Court of Justice created under the Charter of the United Nations) in developing the law of state responsibility (or, today, in developing the international law of human rights).

The growth in the nineteenth and twentieth centuries of the law of state responsibility for injury to aliens was the product of and evidenced by a range of state interactions — diplomatic protests and responses, negotiated settlements, arbitral decisions — and the writings of scholars. Before the Second World War, there was little attempt at formal codification or creative development of this body of law through treaties — that is, treaties spelling out the content of what international law required of a state in its treatment of aliens.

As it developed, the international law of state responsibility reflected the more intense identification of the individual with his state (or later, the identification of the corporation with the state of its incorporation, or of most of its shareholders) that accompanied the nationalistic trends of that era. This body of law would not have developed so vigorously but for Western colonialism and economic imperialism that reached their zenith during this period. Transnational business operations centred in Europe, and later in the United States as well, penetrated those regions now known as the Third World or developing countries. The protection afforded aliens under international law had obvious importance for the foreign operations of transnational corporations that were often directed by foreign nationals.

In such circumstances, given the links between the success and wealth of corporations in their foreign ventures and national wealth and power, the security of the person and property of a national or corporation operating in a foreign part of the world became a concern of his or its government. That concern manifested itself in the vigorous assertion of diplomatic protection and in the enhanced activity of arbitral tribunals. In the late nineteenth and early twentieth centuries, some such arbitrations occurred under the pressure of actual or threatened military force by the claimant states, particularly against Latin American governments.

A statement in an arbitral proceeding in 1924 by Max Huber, a Judge of the Permanent Court of International Justice, cogently expressed some basic principles of that era's consensus (among states of the developed world) about the law of state responsibility:[3]

> ... It is true that the large majority of writers have a marked tendency to limit the responsibility of the State. But their theories often have political inspiration

[3] Judge Huber delivered these remarks in his role as a Reporter (in effect, arbitrator) in a dispute between Great Britain and Spain. British Claims in the Spanish Zone of Morocco, 2 U.N.R.I.A.A. 615 (1924), at 639.

> and represent a natural reaction against unjustified interventions in the affairs of certain nations....
>
> ... The conflicting interest with respect to the problem of compensation of aliens are, on the one hand, the interest of a State in exercising its public power in its own territory without interference or control of any nature by foreign States and, on the other hand, the interest of the State in seeing the rights of its nationals established in foreign countries respected and well protected.
>
> Three principles are hardly debatable:
>
> ...
>
> (2) In general, a person established in a foreign country is subject to the territorial legislation for the protection of his person and his property, under the same conditions as nationals of that country.
>
> (3) A State whose national established in another State is deprived of his rights has a right to intervene if the injury constitutes a violation of international law....
>
> ... The territorial character of sovereignty is so essential a trait of contemporary public law that foreign intervention in relationships between a territorial State and individuals subject to its sovereignty can be allowed only in extraordinary cases....
>
> ... This right of intervention has been claimed by all States; only its limits are under discussion. By denying this right, one would arrive at intolerable results: international law would become helpless in the face of injustices tantamount to the negation of human personality, for that is the subject which every denial of justice touches.
>
> ... No police or other administration of justice is perfect, and it is doubtless necessary to accept, even in the best administered countries, a considerable margin of tolerance. However, the restrictions thus placed on the right of a State to intervene to protect its nationals assume that the general security in the country of residence does not fall below a certain standard....

How was it determined whether, in Huber's words, an 'injury' to an alien 'constitutes a violation of international law', or whether the administration of justice in a given country fell below 'a certain standard'? To what materials would, for example, an arbitral tribunal turn for help in defining the content of that standard? What types of argument and justifications would inform the development of this body of international law? Decisions in the many arbitrations, including the *Chattin* case below, shed light on these questions.

COMMENT ON THE *CHATTIN* CASE

The *Chattin* case[4] is among the more interesting of the arbitral decisions. Chattin, a US citizen, was a conductor on a railroad in Mexico from 1908 to 1910, when he

[4] *United States of America (B.E. Chattin) v. United Mexican States*, United States–Mexican Claims Commission, 1927. Opinions of Commissioners under the 1923 Convention between the United States and Mexico, 1927, at 422, 4 U.N.R.I.A.A. 282.

was arrested for embezzlement of fares. His trial was consolidated with those of several other Americans and Mexicans who had been arrested on similar charges. In February 1911 he was convicted and sentenced to two years' imprisonment. His appeal was rejected in July 1911. In the meantime the inhabitants of Mazatlán, during a political uprising, threw open the doors of the jail and Chattin escaped to the United States. In asserting Chattin's claims, the United States argued that the arrest was illegal, that Chattin was mistreated while in prison, that his trial was unreasonably delayed, and that there were irregularities in the trial. It claimed that Chattin suffered injuries worth $50,000 in compensation.

Of the three members of the Claims Commission, one came from the United States (Nielsen) and another from Mexico (MacGregor). Each wrote an opinion. Excerpts from the opinion of the third Commissioner follow:

COMMISSIONER VAN VOLLENHOVEN

This opinion examined a range of complaints about the conduct of the trial. The Commissioner gave particular attention to three such complaints.

(1) Chattin claimed that he had not been duly informed of the charges. The opinion concluded that this claim was 'proven by the record, and to a painful extent'. The principal complainant, an American manager of the railroad company, made full statements to the Court 'without ever being confronted with the accused and his colleagues', and indeed was 'allowed to submit to the Court a series of anonymous written accusations....It is not shown that the confrontation between Chattin and his accusers amounted to anything like an effort on the Judge's part to find out the truth'. Nonetheless Chattin was generally aware of the details of the investigation.

(2) Van Vollenhoven dismissed Chattin's charge that witnesses were not sworn as irrelevant, 'as Mexican law does not require an "oath" (it is satisfied with a solemn promise, *protesta*, to tell the truth), nor do international standards of civilization'.

(3) Van Vollenhoven found the charge that the hearings in open court lasted only five minutes was proven by the record. That hearing was 'a pure formality', in which written documents were confirmed and defence counsel said only a word or two. The opinion concludes that 'the whole of the proceedings discloses a most astonishing lack of seriousness on the part of the Court', and cites instances where the judge failed to follow leads or examine certain people. Excerpts follow:

> Neither during the investigations nor during the hearings in open court was any such thing as an oral examination or cross-examination of any importance attempted. It seems highly improbable that the accused have been given a real opportunity during the hearings in open court, freely to speak for themselves. It is not for the Commission to endeavor to reach from the record any conviction as to the innocence or guilt of Chattin and his colleagues; but even in case they were guilty, the Commission would render a bad service to the Government of Mexico if it failed to place the stamp of its disapproval and even indignation on a criminal procedure so far below international standards of civilization as the present one.

Nonetheless, the opinion found the record sufficient to warrant a conviction of Chattin and rejected a charge that the court was biased against American citizens, since four Mexicans were also convicted.

> ... Since this is a case of alleged responsibility of Mexico for injustice committed by its judiciary, it is necessary to inquire whether the treatment of Chattin amounts even to an outrage, to bad faith, to wilful neglect of duty, or to an insufficiency of governmental action recognizable by every unbiased man ... and the answer here again can only be in the affirmative.

Taking all these factors into account, the opinion allowed damages in the sum of $5,000.

COMMISSIONER NIELSEN (CONCURRING)

Nielsen observed that counsel for Mexico had stressed that during the period of investigation a Mexican judge was at liberty to receive anything placed before him, including anonymous accusations. Although European procedure allowed 'a similar measure of latitude' for judges, there was one essential difference: after proceedings before a judge of investigation, the case is taken over by another judge who conducts the actual trial. Thus, said Nielsen, under the French law of the period

> the preliminary examination does not serve as a foundation for the verdict of the judge who decided as to the guilt of the accused. The examination allows the examining judge to determine whether there is ground for formal charge, and in case there is, to decide upon the jurisdiction....[The trial of the accused] is before a judge whose functions are of a more judicial character than those of a judge of investigation employing inquisitorial methods in the nature of those used by a prosecutor....

Nielsen, 'having further in mind the peculiarly delicate character of an examination of judicial proceedings by an international tribunal, as well as the practical difficulties inherent in such examination', concluded that the Commission should render a small award based on the mistreatment of Chattin during the period of investigation.

COMMISSIONER MACGREGOR (DISSENTING)

In his dissent, Commissioner MacGregor referred to the charge that the trial proper lasted only five minutes, 'implying thereby that there was really no trial and that Chattin was convicted without being heard'. This was an 'erroneous criticism which arises from the difference between Anglo-Saxon procedure and that of other countries'. Mexican criminal procedure consisted of two parts: preliminary proceedings (sumario) and plenary proceedings (plenario). In the sumario, evidence is gathered, investigations occur, the judge or defendant can cross examine. When the judge concludes that there are sufficient facts to establish a case, the sumario ends as the record is given to all parties to be certain that they do not request more testimony and so that they can make final pleas. Then a public hearing (plenario) is held 'in which the parties very often do not have anything further to allege'. That hearing is formal, and serves little new function. Such occurred in the *Chattin* case.

> In view of the foregoing explanation, I believe that it becomes evident that the charge, that there was no trial proper, can not subsist, for, in Mexican procedure, it is not a question of a trial in the sense of Anglo-Saxon law, which requires that the case be always heard in plenary proceedings, before a jury, adducing all the circumstances and evidence of the cause, examining and cross-examining all the witnesses, and allowing the prosecuting attorney and counsel for the defense to make their respective allegations. International law insures that a defendant be judged openly and that he be permitted to defend himself, but in no manner does it oblige these things to be done in any fixed way, as they are matters of internal regulation and belong to the sovereignty of States....
>
> ...
>
> ... It is hardly of any use to proclaim in theory respect for the judiciary of a nation, if, in practice, it is attempted to call the judiciary to account for its minor acts. It is true that sometimes it is difficult to determine when a judicial act is internationally improper and when it is so from a domestic standpoint only. In my opinion the test which consists in ascertaining if the act implies damage, wilful neglect, or palpable deviation from the established customs becomes clearer by having in mind the damage which the claimant could have suffered. There are certain defects in procedure that can never cause damage which may be estimated separately, and that are blotted out or disappear, to put it thus, if the final decision is just. There are other defects which make it impossible for such decision to be just. The former, as a rule, do not engender international liability; the latter do so, since such liability arises from the decision which is iniquitous because of such defects. To prevent an accused from defending himself, either by refusing to inform him as to the facts imputed to him or by denying him a hearing and the use of remedies; to sentence him without evidence, or to impose on him disproportionate or unusual penalties, to treat him with cruelty and discrimination; are all acts which per se cause damage due to their rendering a just decision impossible. But to delay the proceedings somewhat, to lay aside some evidence, there existing other clear proofs, to fail to comply with the adjective law in its secondary provisions and other deficiencies of this kind, do not cause damage nor violate international law. Counsel for Mexico justly stated that to submit the decisions of a nation to revision in this respect was tantamount to submitting her to a régime of capitulations. All the criticism which has been made of these proceedings, I regret to say, appears to arise from lack of knowledge of the judicial system and practice of Mexico, and, what is more dangerous, from the application thereto of tests belonging to foreign systems of law. For example, in some of the latter the investigation of a crime is made only by the police magistrates and the trial proper is conducted by the Judge. Hence the reluctance in accepting that one same judge may have the two functions and that, therefore, he may have to receive in the preliminary investigation (instrucción) of the case all kinds of data, with the obligation, of course, of not taking them into account at the time of judgment, if they have no probative weight.... [T]he foreign-law procedure is used to understand what is a trial or open trial imagining at the same time that it must have the sacred forms of common-law and without remembering that the same goal is reached by many roads. And the same can be said when speaking of

> the manner of taking testimony of witnesses, of cross-examination, of holding confrontations, etc.... In view of the above considerations, I am of the opinion that this claim should be disallowed.

NOTE

The opinions of the Commissioners underscore the methodological problems in developing a minimum international standard of criminal procedure out of such diverse materials — a diversity that was restricted in *Chattin* to Europe and Latin America, hence far less perplexing than today's worldwide diversity of legal cultures and criminal processes. A treaty was relevant to *Chattin*, but as indicated above, it addressed the scope and structure of the arbitration between the United States and Mexico rather than the international norms of criminal procedure to be applied. The only reference of the General Claims Convention to applicable norms was the terse provision in Article 1 that claims should be submitted to the tripartite Commission 'for decision in accordance with the principles of international law, justice and equity'.

Today a dispute like that in *Chattin* could draw on a human rights treaty, the International Covenant on Civil and Political Rights to be discussed in Chapter 3 that (as of May 2012) had 167 state parties. Article 14 of that Covenant dealing with criminal trials provides in relevant part:

> 1. All persons shall be equal before the courts.... [E]veryone shall be entitled to a fair and public hearing by [an] impartial tribunal....
>
> 2. Everyone ... shall have the right to be presumed innocent until proved guilty according to law.
>
> 3. .... [E]veryone shall be entitled to the following minimum guarantees....
>
>   (d) To be tried in his presence and to defend himself in person or through legal assistance of his own choosing....
>
>   (e) To examine, or have examined, the witnesses against him and to obtain the attendance and examination of witnesses on his behalf....

QUESTIONS

1. Why is international law relevant to this decision? Were there any international factors in the trial and conviction and, if so, how do they compare with the international factors in *The Paquete Habana*?

2. How would you identify the most serious problem in the judicial process leading to Chattin's conviction — say, on the basis of a comparison with judicial processes in other legal systems?

3. How do the Commissioners approach the task of identifying an 'international standard of civilization' (or, within the terms of the 1923 Convention, the relevant 'international law, justice and equity') against which they are to test the legality of the conviction? Do they resort to customary international law?

4. Would the tribunal's task have been much simpler if there had been a treaty between the United States and Mexico regulating treatment of aliens that included Article 14 of the ICCPR? Would Article 14 have resolved the basic issues on its face?

NOTE

The issues considered in connection with the *Chattin* case illustrate one of the most important building blocks of the twenty-first century law of state responsibility. However, as codified in the International Law Commission's Draft Articles on Responsibility of States for Internationally Wrongful Acts (2001), that law now goes well beyond issues relating to the treatment of aliens. In broad terms, state responsibility today encapsulates a broad set of 'secondary' rules that determine such matters as when a state is responsible for an internationally wrongful act and the remedies for a state's breach of 'primary' or substantive rules of international law (such as the prohibition on genocide). For present purposes, we provide a rough sketch of these secondary rules. They include the following subjects:

1. *Attribution*: This set of rules determine when conduct consisting of the acts or omissions of state officials or other groups and individuals can be considered the responsibility of the state. These rules are relevant in the human rights context, for example, in determining the conditions under which a state is responsible for extraterritorial human rights violations by corporations and when a state is responsible for human rights violations committed by armed opposition groups that the state supports.
2. *Circumstances Precluding Wrongfulness*: This set of rules provide defences that preclude the wrongfulness of state conduct that is not in conformity with the state's international obligations. These rules include duress, force majeure, necessity and self-defence. In the human rights context, for example, necessity may allow a state to suspend obligations that implicate human rights but forecloses that defence if the state contributed to bringing about the condition of necessity.
3. *Consequences that follow when a state breaches an international obligation*: These rules set forth remedies that a state must provide for violation of an international obligation. The remedies include cessation, reparations, restitution, compensation, satisfaction and assurances of non-repetition. In the human rights context, these rules are relevant, for example, in determining what actions by a state are sufficient when it has subject a foreign

national to execution without access to their foreign consul in violation of an international agreement.

4. *Countermeasures*: These rules regulate the permissible range of responses to another state's breach of international law. In the human rights context, these rules may be important in determining whether and to what degree a state may employ sanctions in response to another state's human rights violations. Notably, these rules also preclude states from taking countermeasures in other contexts that would affect 'obligations for the protection of fundamental human rights' or 'obligations of a humanitarian character prohibiting reprisals' (Art. 50).[5]

It is important to note two additional features of this area of law. First, state responsibility exists side by side with treaty law, including those treaties governing human rights. However, when the latter constitute *lex specialis*, or special rules, they take priority if there is any inconsistency. Second, the articles of state responsibility are highly focused on state-to-state interactions. That feature limits their value for human rights law. Admittedly, Article 33 (pertaining to consequences of a breach) provides that the obligations set forth by these rules can be owed to another state 'or to the international community as a whole'; and Article 33 also provides that nothing in the rules should prejudice any rights arising from the international responsibility of a state that would 'accrue directly to any person'. Nevertheless, many of the rules are framed in terms of an injury to another state and the actions that states may take in response to being unlawfully injured.

OSCAR SCHACHTER, INTERNATIONAL LAW IN THEORY AND PRACTICE

(1991), at 50

Chapter IV: General Principles and Equity

...

The Broad Expanse of General Principles of Law

We can distinguish five categories of general principles that have been invoked and applied in international law discourse and cases. Each has a different basis for its authority and validity as law. They are:

(1) The principles of municipal law 'recognized by civilized nations'.

(2) General principles of law 'derived from the specific nature of the international community'.

5 See J. Crawford, *The International Law Commission's Articles on State Responsibility: Introduction, Text and Commentaries* (2002).

(3) Principles 'intrinsic to the idea of law and basic to all legal systems'.

(4) Principles 'valid through all kinds of societies in relationships of hierarchy and co-ordination'.

(5) Principles of justice founded on 'the very nature of man as a rational and social being'.

Although these five categories are analytically distinct, it is not unusual for a particular general principle to fall into more than one of the categories. For example, the principle that no one shall be a judge in his own cause or that a victim of a legal wrong is entitled to reparation are considered part of most if not all, systems of municipal law and as intrinsic to the basic idea of law.

Our first category, general principles of municipal law, has given rise to a considerable body of writing and much controversy. Article 38(1)*(c)* of the Statute of Court does not expressly refer to principles of national law but rather general principles 'recognized by civilized nations'.... Elihu Root, the American member of the drafting committee, prepared the text finally adopted and it seemed clear that his amendment was intended to refer to principles 'actually recognized and applied in national legal systems'. The fact that the subparagraph was distinct from those on treaty and custom indicated an intent to treat general principles as an independent source of law, and not as a subsidiary source. As an independent source, it did not appear to require any separate proof that such principles of national law had been 'received' into international law.

However, a significant minority of jurists holds that national law principles, even if generally found in most legal systems, cannot *ipso facto* be international law. One view is that they must receive the *imprimatur* of State consent through custom or treaty in order to become international law. The strict positivist school adheres to that view. A somewhat modified version is adopted by others to the effect that rules of municipal law cannot be considered as recognized by civilized nations unless there is evidence of the concurrence of States on their status as international law. Such concurrence may occur through treaty, custom or other evidence of recognition. This would allow for some principles, such as *res judicata*, which are not customary law but are generally accepted in international law....

...

... The most important limitation on the use of municipal law principles arises from the requirement that the principle be appropriate for application on the international level. Thus, the universally accepted common crimes — murder, theft, assault, incest — that apply to individuals are not crimes under international law by virtue of their ubiquity....

At the same time, I would suggest a somewhat more positive approach for the emergent international law concerned with the individual, business companies, environmental dangers and shared resources. In as much as these areas have become the concern of international law, national law principles will often be suitable for international application. This does not mean importing municipal rules 'lock, stock and barrel', but it suggests that domestic law rules applicable to such matters as individual rights, contractual remedies, liability for extra-hazardous activities, or restraints on use of common property, have now become pertinent for recruitment into international law. In these areas, we may look to representative legal systems not only for the highly abstract principles of the kind referred to earlier but to more specific rules that are sufficiently widespread as to be considered 'recognized by civilized nations'....

The second category of general principles included in our list comprises principles derived from the specific character of the international community. The most obvious candidates for this category of principles are ... the necessary principles of co-existence. They include the principles of *pacta sunt servanda*, non-intervention, territorial integrity, self-defence and the legal equality of States. Some of these principles are in the United Nations Charter and therefore part of treaty law, but others might appropriately be treated as principles required by the specific character of a society of sovereign independent members.

...

The foregoing comments are also pertinent to the next two categories of general principles. The idea of principles '*jus rationale*' 'valid through all kinds of human societies' ... is associated with traditional natural law doctrine. At the present time its theological links are mainly historical as far as international law is concerned, but its principal justification does not depart too far from the classic natural law emphasis on the nature of 'man', that is, on the human person as a rational and social creature.

The universalist implication of this theory — the idea of the unity of the human species — has had a powerful impetus in the present era. This is evidenced in at least three significant political and legal developments. The first is the global movements against discrimination on grounds of race, colour and sex. The second is the move toward general acceptance of human rights. The third is the increased fear of nuclear annihilation. These three developments strongly reinforce the universalistic values inherent in natural law doctrine. They have found expression in numerous international and constitutional law instruments as well as in popular movements throughout the world directed to humanitarian ends. Clearly, they are a 'material source' of much of the new international law manifested in treaties and customary rules.

In so far as they are recognized as general principles of law, many tend to fall within our fifth category — the principles of natural justice. This concept is well known in many municipal law systems (although identified in diverse ways). 'Natural justice' in its international legal manifestation has two aspects. One refers to the minimal standards of decency and respect for the individual human being that are largely spelled out in the human rights instruments. We can say that in this aspect, 'natural justice' has been largely subsumed as a source of general principles by the human rights instruments....

ADDITIONAL READING

J. Crawford, *The International Law Commission's Articles on State Responsibility: Introduction, Text and Commentaries* (2002); D. Bodansky & J. R. Crook, 'Symposium: The ILC's State Responsibility Articles', 96 Am. J. Int'l. L. 773 (2002); 'Symposium: State Responsibility', 10 Eur. J. Int'l. L. 339 (1999); H. P. Aust, *Complicity and the Law of State Responsibility* (2011); A. Bird, 'Third State Responsibility for Human Rights Violations', 21 Eur. J. Int'l. L. 883 (2010); A. Randelzhofer & C. Tomuschat (eds.), *State Responsibility and the Individual: Reparation in Instances of Grave Violations of Human Rights* (1999); J. Weiler, A. Cassese & M. Spinedi (eds.), *International Crimes of State: A Critical Analysis of the ILC's Draft Article 19 on State Responsibility*; Malgosia Fitzmaurice & Dan Sarooshi (eds.), *Issues of State Responsibility Before International Judicial Institutions* (2004); R. McCorquodale & P. Simons, 'Responsibility Beyond Borders: State Responsibility for Extraterritorial Violations by Corporations of International Human Rights Law', 70 Modern L. Rev. 598 (2007); E. A. Posner & A. O. Sykes, 'An Economic Analysis of State and Individual Responsibility Under International Law', 9 Am. L. Econ. Rev. 72 (2007).

C. INTERWAR MINORITIES REGIME AND THE ROLE OF TREATIES

COMMENT ON THE MINORITIES REGIME AFTER THE FIRST WORLD WAR

The *Minority Schools in Albania* opinion, which follows, illustrates treaties as a source and major expression of international law, and introduces another field of international law that influenced the growth of the human rights regime. This Comment provides some background to the opinion.

Treaties and other special regimes to protect minorities have a long history in international law dating from the emergence in the seventeenth century of the modern form of the political state, sovereign within its territorial boundaries. Within Europe, religious issues became a strong concern since states often included more than one religious denomination, and abuse by a state of a religious minority could lead to intervention by other states where that religion was dominant. Hence peace treaties sometimes included provisions on religious minorities. In the eighteenth and nineteenth centuries, the precarious situation of Christian minorities within the Ottoman Empire and of religious minorities in newly independent East European or Balkan states led to outbreaks of violence and to sporadic treaty regulation.

The First World War ushered in an era of heightened attention to problems of racial, religious or linguistic minorities. The collapse of the great Austro-Hungarian and Ottoman multinational empires, and the chaos as the Russian empire of the Romanoffs was succeeded by the Soviet Union, led to much redrawing of maps and the creation of new states. President Wilson's Fourteen Points, however compromised they became in the Versailles Treaty and later arrangements, nonetheless exerted influence on the postwar settlements. In it and other messages, Wilson stressed the ideals of the freeing of minorities and the related 'self-determination' of peoples or nationalities. That concept of self-determination, so politically powerful and open to such diverse interpretations, continues to this day to be much disputed and to have profound consequences. It not only appears in the UN Charter but is given a position of high prominence in the two principal human rights covenants.

From concepts like 'self-determination' and out of the legacy of nineteenth-century liberal nationalism that saw the development of nation-states like Germany and Italy, the principle of nationalities took on a new force. Here was another ambiguous and disputed concept — the 'nation' or 'nationality' as distinct from the political state, the nation (often identified with a 'people') defined in cultural or historical terms, often defined more concretely in racial, linguistic and religious terms. One goal in displacing the old empires with new or redrawn states was to identify the nation with the state — ideally, to give each 'nation' its own state. Membership in a 'nation' would ideally be equivalent to membership in a 'state' consisting only or principally of that nation.

Within the pure realization of this ideal, all 'Poles', for example, would be situated in Poland; there would be no 'Polish' national minority in other states, and other 'nationalities' would not be resident in Poland. Indeed, the detaching of Poland after the First World War from the empires and states that had absorbed different parts of it represented one of the few instances of relatively strict congruence between the 'nation' and 'state'. There were polar moves; for example, the creation of Yugoslavia as a multiethnic state that after 70 years has had such tragic consequences.

Of course the goal of total identification of state with nation — a goal itself disputed and in contradiction with other conceptions of the political state that did not emphasize cultural homogeneity or ethnic purity — could not be realized. Life and history were and remain too various and complex for such precise correlation. The nineteenth-century examples of Germany and Italy, for instance, were far from unitary; each had its national, ethnic, linguistic and religious minorities. National or ethnic homogeneity could be achieved in the vast majority of the world's states only by the compulsory and massive migrations of minority groups, migrations far more systematic and coercive than were some of the population movements and exchanges after the First World War. A 'nation' defined, say, in linguistic-religious terms would generally transcend national boundaries and be located in the territories of two or several sovereign states in the new world created by the postwar settlements. A Greek-speaking Christian minority would, for example, be present in the reconfigured Muslim Albania.

Bear in mind another confusing linguistic usage. The term 'national' is generally used in international law to signify the subjects or citizens of a state. Hence members of the 'German' nation (in the sense of a 'people' and' culture') living in Poland could be Polish 'nationals' in the sense of being citizens of Poland. Or they could possess only German citizenship and be alien residents in Poland. In the *Minority Schools in Albania* case that follows, members of the Greek-speaking Christian minority (part of a 'nation' in the cultural or ethnic sense) in Muslim Albania were 'nationals' (citizens) of Albania. One can imagine the ambiguity attending the frequent usage of the term 'national minorities', which could mean at least (1) a group in a state belonging in the cultural or ethnic sense to a 'nation' that constituted a minority in that state, or (2) all minorities in a state who were 'nationals' (citizens) of that state.

After the First World War, the victorious powers and the new League of Nations sought to address this situation. They confronted the impossibility, even if it were desirable, of creating ethnically homogeneous states. Hence they had to deal with the continuing presence in states of minorities which had frequently been abused in ways ranging from economic discrimination to pogroms and other violence that could implicate other states, spill across international boundaries and lead to war. The immediate trigger for the outbreak of the First World War in the tormented Balkans was fresh in memory.

President Wilson had proposed that the Covenant of the League of Nations include norms governing the protection of minorities that would have embraced all members of the League. The other major powers rejected this approach, preferring discrete international arrangements to handle discrete problems of minorities in particular states of Central-East Europe and the Balkans rather than a universal treaty system. This compromise led to the regime of the so-called 'Minorities Treaties' that were imposed on the new or reconfigured states of Central-East Europe and the Balkans.

For some states like Austria and Hungary, provisions for minority protection were included in the peace treaties. Other states like Poland or Greece signed minority protection treaties with the allied and associated powers. Some states like Albania and Lithuania made minority protection declarations as a condition for their membership in the League of Nations. There were also bilateral treaties protecting minorities such as one between Germany and Poland. Note that one of the features of this new regime was to insulate the victorious powers from international regulation of their treatment of their own citizens belonging to minorities.

Although there were significant variations among these treaties and declarations, many provisions were common. The 1919 Minorities Treaty between the Principal Allied and Associated Powers and Poland served as a model for later treaties and declarations. It provided for protection of life and liberty and religious freedom for all 'inhabitants of Poland'. All Polish nationals (citizens) were guaranteed equality before the law and the right to use their own language in private life and judicial proceedings. Members of racial, religious or linguistic minorities were guaranteed 'the same treatment and security in law and in fact' as other Polish nationals, and the right to establish and control at their expense their own religious, social and educational institutions. In areas of Poland where a 'considerable proportion' of Polish nationals belonged to minorities, an 'equitable share' of public funds would go to such minority groups for educational or religious purposes. In view of the particular history of oppression and violence, there were specific guarantees for Jews.

Jan Herman Burgers[6] has described the special regimes formed by the minority provisions as follows:

> ... [T]he regime consisted of three categories of obligations. Firstly, it guaranteed full and complete protection of life and liberty to all *inhabitants* of the country or region concerned, without distinction of birth, nationality, language, race or religion. Secondly, it guaranteed that all nationals would be equal before the law

[6] 'The Road to San Francisco: The Revival of the Human Rights Idea in the Twentieth Century', 14 Hum. Rts. Q. 447 (1992), at 450.

> and would enjoy the same civil and political rights, without distinction as to race, language or religion. Thirdly, it provided for a series of special guarantees for nationals belonging to minorities, for instance concerning the use of their language and the right to establish social and religious institutions.

Like other minority treaties and declarations, the Polish treaty's provisions were placed under the guarantee of the League of Nations to the extent that 'they affect persons belonging to' minority groups. The League developed procedures to implement its duties, including a right of petition to it by beleaguered minorities claiming that a treaty regime or declaration had been violated, and including a minorities committee given the task of seeking negotiated solutions to such disputes. As shown by the *Minority Schools in Albania* case, the Council of the League could invoke in accordance with its usual procedures the advisory opinion jurisdiction of the Permanent Court of International Justice (PCIJ), the first international court (supplementing ad hoc arbitral tribunals as in the *Chattin* case). The Court was created by the League in 1921, became dormant in the Second World War, and was then succeeded by the International Court of Justice created under the UN Charter.

MINORITY SCHOOLS IN ALBANIA

Advisory Opinion, Permanent Court of International Justice, 1935, Ser. A/B, No. 64

[In 1920, the Assembly of the League of Nations adopted a recommendation requesting that if Albania were admitted into the League, it 'should take the necessary measures to enforce the principles of the Minorities Treaties' and to arrange the 'details required to carry this object into effect' with the Council of the League. Albania was admitted to membership a few days later. In 1921 the Council included on its agenda the question of protection of minorities in Albania.

The Greek Government, in view of the presence of a substantial Christian minority of Greek origin in (dominantly Muslim) Albania, communicated to the League proposals for provisions going beyond the Minorities Treaties that were related to Christian worship and to education in the Greek language. The Council commissioned a report, and the reporter submitted to it a draft Declaration to be signed by Albania and formally communicated to the Council. The Declaration was signed by Albania and submitted to the Council in 1921, with basic similarities to but some differences from the typical clauses of the Minorities Treaties. The Council decided that the stipulations in the Declaration about minorities should be placed under the guarantee of the League from the date of the Declaration's ratification by Albania, which took place in 1922.

The first paragraph of Article 5 of the Declaration, at the core of the dispute that later developed, provided as follows:

> Albanian nationals who belong to racial, linguistic or religious minorities, will enjoy the same treatment and security in law and in fact as other Albanian

> nationals. In particular, they shall have an equal right to maintain, manage and control at their own expense or to establish in the future, charitable, religious and social institutions, schools and other educational establishments, with the right to use their own language and to exercise their religion freely therein.

Over the years, numerous changes in the laws and practices of the Albanian Government led to questions about compliance with the Declaration. In 1933, the Albanian National Assembly modified Articles 206 and 207 of the Constitution, which had provided that 'Albanian subjects may found private schools' subject to government regulation, to state:

> The instruction and education of Albanian subjects are reserved to the State and will be given in State schools. Primary education is compulsory for all Albanian nationals and will be given free of charge. Private schools of all categories at present in operation will be closed.

The new provisions affecting Greek-language and other private schools led to petitions and complaints to the League from groups including the Greek minority in Albania. Acting within its regular powers, the Council requested the Permanent Court of International Justice in 1935 to give an advisory opinion whether, in light of the 1921 Declaration as a whole, Albania was justified in its position that it had acted in conformity with 'the letter and the spirit' of Article 5 because (as Albania argued) its abolition of private schools was a general measure applicable to the majority as well as minority of Albanian nationals.

There follow excerpts from the opinion for the PCIJ and from a dissenting opinion. For present purposes, the Albanian Declaration can be understood as tantamount to a treaty. The opinions draw no relevant distinction between the two, and refer frequently to the Minorities Treaties to inform their interpretation of the Declaration.]

The contention of the Albanian Government is that the above-mentioned clause imposed no other obligation upon it, in educational matters, than to grant to its nationals belonging to racial, religious, or linguistic minorities a right equal to that possessed by other Albanian nationals. Once the latter have ceased to be entitled to have private schools, the former cannot claim to have them either. This conclusion, which is alleged to follow quite naturally from the wording of paragraph I of Article 5, would, it is contended, be in complete conformity with the meaning and spirit of the treaties for the protection of minorities, an essential characteristic of which is the full and complete equality of all nationals of the State, whether belonging to the majority or to the minority. On the other hand, it is argued, any interpretation which would compel Albania to respect the private minority schools would create a privilege in favour of the minority and run counter to the essential idea of the law governing minorities. Moreover, as the minority régime is an extraordinary régime constituting a derogation from the ordinary law, the text in question should, in case of doubt, be construed in the manner most favourable to the sovereignty of the Albanian State.

According to the explanations furnished to the Court by the Greek Government, the fundamental idea of Article 5 of the Declaration was on the contrary to guarantee freedom of education to the minorities by granting them the right to retain their existing schools and to establish others, if they desired; equality of treatment is, in the Greek Government's opinion, merely an adjunct to that right, and cannot impede the purpose in view, which is to ensure full and effectual liberty in matters of education. Moreover, the application of the same régime to a majority as to a minority, whose needs are quite different, would only create an apparent equality, whereas the Albanian Declaration, consistently with ordinary minority law, was designed to ensure a genuine and effective equality, not merely a formal equality.

...

As the Declaration of October 2nd, 1921, was designed to apply to Albania the general principles of the treaties for the protection of minorities, this is the point of view which, in the Court's opinion, must be adopted in construing paragraph 1 of Article 5 of the said Declaration.

The idea underlying the treaties for the protection of minorities is to secure for certain elements incorporated in a State, the population of which differs from them in race, language or religion, the possibility of living peaceably alongside that population and co-operating amicably with it, while at the same time preserving the characteristics which distinguish them from the majority, and satisfying the ensuing special needs.

In order to attain this object, two things were regarded as particularly necessary, and have formed the subject of provisions in these treaties.

The first is to ensure that nationals belonging to racial, religious or linguistic minorities shall be placed in every respect on a footing of perfect equality with the other nationals of the State.

The second is to ensure for the minority elements suitable means for the preservation of their racial peculiarities, their traditions and their national characteristics.

These two requirements are indeed closely interlocked, for there would be no true equality between a majority and a minority if the latter were deprived of its own institutions, and were consequently compelled to renounce that which constitutes the very essence of its being as a minority.

In common with the other treaties for the protection of minorities, and in particular with the Polish Treaty of June 28th, 1919, the text of which it follows, so far as concerns the question before the Court, very closely and almost literally, the Declaration of October 2nd, 1921, begins by laying down that no person shall be placed, in his relations with the Albanian authorities, in a position of inferiority by reason of his language, race or religion....

...

In all these cases, the Declaration provides for a régime of legal equality for all persons mentioned in the clause; in fact no standard of comparison was indicated, and none was necessary, for at the same time that it provides for equality of treatment the Declaration specifies the rights which are to be enjoyed equally by all.

...

It has already been remarked that paragraph 1 of Article 5 consists of two sentences, the second of which is linked to the first by the words *in particular*: for a right apprehension of the second part, it is therefore first necessary to determine the meaning and the scope of the first sentence. This sentence is worded as follows:

> Albanian nationals who belong to racial, linguistic or religious minorities, will enjoy the same treatment and security in law and in fact as other Albanian nationals.

The question that arises is what is meant by the *same treatment and security in law and in fact.*

It must be noted to begin with that the equality of all Albanian nationals before the law has already been stipulated in the widest terms in Article 4. As it is difficult to admit that Article 5 set out to repeat in different words what had already been said in Article 4, one is led to the conclusion that 'the same treatment and security in law and in fact' which is provided for in Article 5 is not the same notion as the equality before the law which is provided for in Article 4.

...

This special conception finds expression in the idea of an equality in fact which in Article 5 supplements equality in law. All Albanian nationals enjoy the equality in law stipulated in Article 4; on the other hand, the equality between members of the majority and of the minority must, according to the terms of Article 5, be an equality in law and in fact.

It is perhaps not easy to define the distinction between the notions of equality in fact and equality in law; nevertheless, it may be said that the former notion excludes the idea of a merely formal equality; that is indeed what the Court laid down in its Advisory Opinion of September 10th, 1923, concerning the case of the German settlers in Poland (Opinion No. 6), in which it said that:

> There must be equality in fact as well as ostensible legal equality in the sense of the absence of discrimination in the words of the law.

Equality in law precludes discrimination of any kind; whereas equality in fact may involve the necessity of different treatment in order to attain a result which establishes an equilibrium between different situations.

It is easy to imagine cases in which equality of treatment of the majority and of the minority, whose situation and requirements are different, would result in inequality in fact; treatment of this description would run counter to the first sentence of paragraph 1 of Article 5. The equality between members of the majority and of the minority must be an effective, genuine equality; that is the meaning of this provision.

The second sentence of this paragraph provides as follows:

> In particular they shall have an equal right to maintain, manage and control at their own expense or to establish in the future, charitable, religious and social institutions, schools and other educational establishments, with the right to use their own language and to exercise their religion freely therein.

This sentence of the paragraph being linked to the first by the words 'in particular', it is natural to conclude that it envisages a particularly important illustration of the application of the principle of identical treatment in law and in fact that is stipulated in the first sentence of the paragraph. For the institutions mentioned in the second sentence are indispensable to enable the minority to enjoy the same treatment as the majority, not only in law but also in fact. The abolition of these institutions, which alone can satisfy the special requirements of the minority groups, and their replacement by government institutions, would destroy this equality of treatment, for its effect would be to deprive the minority of the institutions appropriate to its needs, whereas the majority would continue to have them supplied in the institutions created by the State.

Far from creating a privilege in favour of the minority, as the Albanian Government avers, this stipulation ensures that the majority shall not be given a privileged situation as compared with the minority.

It may further be observed that, even disregarding the link between the two parts of paragraph 1 of Article 5, it seems difficult to maintain that the adjective 'equal', which qualifies the word 'right', has the effect of empowering the State to abolish the right, and thus to render the clause in question illusory; for, if so, the stipulation which confers so important a right on the members of the minority would not only add nothing to what has already been provided in Article 4, but it would become a weapon by which the State could deprive the minority régime of a great part of its practical value. It should be observed that in its Advisory Opinion of September 15th, 1923, concerning the question of the acquisition of Polish nationality (Opinion No. 7), the Court referred to the opinion which it had already expressed in Advisory Opinion No.6 to the effect that 'an interpretation which would deprive the Minorities Treaty of a great part of its value is inadmissible'.

...

The idea embodied in the expression 'equal right' is that the right thus conferred on the members of the minority cannot in any case be inferior to the corresponding right of other Albanian nationals. In other words, the members of the minority must always enjoy the right stipulated in the Declaration, and, in addition, any more extensive rights which the State may accord to other nationals....

The construction which the Court places on paragraph 1 of Article 5 is confirmed by the history of this provision.

[Analysis of the proposals of the Greek Government and replies of the Albanian Government during the period of drafting of the Declaration omitted.]

The Court, having thus established that paragraph 1 of Article 5 of the Declaration, both according to its letter and its spirit, confers on Albanian nationals of racial, religious or linguistic minorities the right that is stipulated in the second sentence of that paragraph, finds it unnecessary to examine the subsidiary argument adduced by the Albanian Government to the effect that the text in question should in case of doubt be interpreted in the sense that is most favourable to the sovereignty of the State.

...

For these reasons,

The Court is of opinion,

by eight votes to three,

that the plea of the Albanian Government that, as the abolition of private schools in Albania constitutes a general measure applicable to the majority as well as to the minority, it is in conformity with the letter and spirit of the stipulations laid down in Article 5, first paragraph, of the Declaration of October 2nd, 1921, is not well founded.

...

DISSENTING OPINION BY SIR CECIL HURST, COUNT ROSTWOROWSKI, AND MR. NEGULESCO

The undermentioned are unable to concur in the opinion rendered by the Court. They can see no adequate reason for holding that the suppression of the private schools effected in Albania in virtue of Articles 206 and 207 of the Constitution of 1933 is not in conformity with the Albanian Declaration of October 2nd, 1921.

...

The construction of the paragraph is clear and simple. The first sentence stipulates for the treatment and the security being the same for the members of the minority as for the other Albanian nationals. The second provides that as regards certain specified matters the members of the minority shall have an equal right. The two sentences are linked together by the words 'In particular' (*notamment*). These words show that the second sentence is a particular application of the principle enunciated in the first. If the rights of the two categories under the first sentence are to be the same, the equal right provided for in the second sentence must indicate equality between the same two categories, viz. the members of the minority and the other Albanian nationals. The second sentence is added because the general principle laid down in the first sentence mentions only 'treatment and security in law and in fact' — a phrase so indefinite that without further words of precision it would be doubtful whether it covered the right to establish and maintain charitable, religious and social institutions and schools and other educational establishments, but the particular application of the general principle of identity of treatment and security remains governed by the dominating element of equality as between the two categories.

The word 'equal' implies that the right so enjoyed must be equal in measure to the right enjoyed by somebody else. '*They shall have an equal right*' means that the right to be enjoyed by the people in question is to be equal in measure to that enjoyed by some other group. A right which is unconditional and independent of that enjoyed by other people cannot with accuracy be described as an 'equal right'. 'Equality' necessarily implies the existence of some extraneous criterion by reference to which the content is to be determined.

If the text of the first paragraph of Article 5 is considered alone, it does not seem that there could be any doubt as to its interpretation. It is, however, laid down in the Opinion from which the undersigned dissent that if the general purpose of the minority treaties is borne in mind and also the contents of the Albanian Declaration taken as a whole, it will be found that the 'equal right' provided for in the first paragraph of Article 5 cannot mean a right of which the extent is measured by that enjoyed by other Albanian nationals, and that it must imply an unconditional right, a right of which the members of the minority cannot be deprived.

. . .

As the opinion of the Court is based on the general purpose which the minorities treaties are presumed to have had in view and not on the text of Article 5, paragraph 1, of the Albanian Declaration, it involves to some extent a departure from the principles hitherto adopted by this Court in the interpretation of international instruments, that in presence of a clause which is reasonably clear the Court is bound to apply it as it stands without considering whether other provisions might with advantage have been added to it or substituted for it, and this even if the results following from it may in some particular hypothesis seem unsatisfactory.

. . .

Furthermore, the suppression of the private schools — even if it may prejudice to some appreciable extent the interests of a minority — does not oblige them to abandon an essential part of the characteristic life of a minority. In interpreting Article 5, the question whether the possession of particular institutions may or may not be *important* to the minority cannot constitute the decisive consideration. There is another consideration entitled to equal weight. That is the extent to which the monopoly of education may be of importance to the State. The two considerations cannot be weighed one against the other: Neither of them — in the absence of a clear stipulation to that effect — can provide an objective standard for determining which of them is to prevail.

International justice must proceed upon the footing of applying treaty stipulations impartially to the rights of the State and to the rights of the minority, and the method of doing so is to adhere to the terms of the treaty — as representing the common will of the parties — as closely as possible.

. . .

If the intention of the second sentence: 'In particular they [the minority] shall have an equal right . . .', had been that the right so given should be universal and unconditional, there is no reason why the draftsman should not have dealt with the right to establish institutions and schools in the earlier articles [of the Declaration that set up fixed and universal standards for all Albanians on matters like protection of life and free exercise of religion]. The draftsman should have dealt with the liberty to maintain schools and other institutions on lines similar to those governing the right to the free exercise of religion, which undoubtedly is conferred as a universal and unconditional right. Instead of doing so the right conferred upon the minority is an 'equal' right. . . .

. . .

COMMENT ON FURTHER ASPECTS OF THE MINORITY TREATIES

The *Minority Schools in Albania* opinions address many current issues that remain vexing. The discussions about the nature of 'equality' and assurances thereof, in particular about equality 'in law' and 'in fact', inform contemporary human rights law as well as constitutional and legislative debates in many states with respect to issues like equal protection and affirmative action. The question whether the Declaration and the Court's opinion recognized only the rights of individual members of a minority, or also the right of the minority itself as a collective or group, remains one that vexes the discussion of minority rights. Protection aiming at the cultural survival of minorities continues to raise the troubling issue of which types of minorities merit such protection, and whether assurance of equal protection (with the majority) is sufficient for the purpose.

But if the issues debated within the minorities regime remain, the regime itself has disappeared. Over the next two decades, its norms were roundly violated. Its international machinery within the League of Nations proved to be ineffectual, partly for the same lack of political will that led to other disastrous events in the interwar period. The failure of the regime was tragic in its consequences. Its noble purposes were distorted or blunted or ignored as Europe of the 1930s moved toward the horrors of the Second World War, the Holocaust and the brutalization and slaughter of so many other minorities. The settlements, norms and institutions after the Second World War designed to prevent further savagery against minorities stressed different principles and created radically different institutions, principally within the universal human rights system built in and around the United Nations.

Nonetheless, it is important to recognize the distinctive dilemmas and advances as well as the shortcomings of this minorities regime. Sovereignty in the sense of a state's (absolute) internal control over its own citizens was to some extent eroded. Treaties-declarations subjected aspects of the state's treatment of its own citizens to international law and international processes — that is, citizens who were members of a racial, religious or linguistic minority. Although the norms were expressed in bilateral treaties or declarations, the regime took on a multilateral aspect through its incorporation into the League as well as through the large number of nearly simultaneous treaties and declarations. The whole scheme was informed by multilateral planning, in contrast with the centuries-old examples of sporadic bilateral treaties protecting (usually religious) minorities. Minorities became a matter of formal international concern, the treaties-declarations fragmented the state into different sections of its citizens, and international law reached beyond the law of state responsibility to protect some of a state's own citizens.

The precise issue of the *Minority Schools in Albania* case is now addressed in the 1960 UNESCO Convention against Discrimination in Education. Article 5(1)(c) recognizes the 'right of members of national minorities to carry on their own educational activities, including the maintenance of schools and, depending on the educational policy of each State, the use or the teaching of their own language ...'. The article subjects this right to several provisos. For example, its exercise should not prevent minorities from understanding the culture and language of the larger community as well, or prejudice national sovereignty.

COMMENT ON TREATIES

Treaties have inevitably figured in this chapter's prior discussions — for example, the bilateral treaties whose relevance to custom was debated in *The Paquete Habana*, or the convention underlying the *Chattin* litigation. As noted above, the Albanian Declaration can be understood for present purposes as tantamount to a treaty, for the opinions do not distinguish between the two and refer to the Minorities Treaties to advance their interpretation of the Declaration. Hence this Comment, and particularly its sections on issues like interpretation, is relevant here.

In Article 38(1) of the Statute of the International Court of Justice, the Court is instructed in clause (a) to apply 'international conventions, whether general or particular, establishing rules expressly recognized by the contesting states'. Treaties thus head the list. They have become the primary expression of international law and, particularly when multilateral, the most effective if not the only path toward international regulation of many contemporary problems. Multilateral treaties have been the principal means for development of the human rights regime. One striking advantage of treaties over custom should be noted. Only treaties can create, and define the powers and jurisdiction of, international institutions in which state parties participate and to which they may owe duties.

The terminology for this voluminous and diverse body of international law varies. International agreements are referred to as pacts, protocols (generally supplemental to another agreement), covenants, conventions, charters, and exchanges of notes, as well as treaties — terms that are more or less interchangeable in legal significance. Within the internal law of some countries such as the United States, the term 'treaty' (as contrasted, say, with international executive agreement) has a particular constitutional significance.

Consider the different purposes that treaties serve. Some concerning vital national security interests have a basic political character: alliances, peace settlements, control of nuclear weapons. Others, outside the scope of national security, also involve relationships between governments and affect private parties only indirectly: agreements on foreign aid, cooperation in the provision of governmental services such as the mails. But treaties often have a direct and specific impact upon private parties. For many decades, tariff accords, income tax conventions, and treaties of friendship, commerce and navigation have determined the conditions under which the nationals or residents of one signatory can export to, or engage in business activities within, the other signatory's territory. Most significant for this book's purposes, human rights treaties have sought to extend protection to all persons against governmental abuse.

Domestic analogies to the treaty help to portray its distinctive character: contract and legislation. Some treaties settling particular disputes between states resemble an accord and satisfaction under contract law: an agreement over boundaries, an agreement to pay a stated sum as compensation for injury to the receiving nation or its nationals. Others are closer in character to private contracts of continuing significance or to domestic legislation because they regulate recurrent problems by defining rights and obligations of the parties and their nationals: agreements over rules of navigation, income taxation or the enforcement of foreign judgments. The term 'international legislation' to describe treaties has accordingly gained some currency particularly with respect to multilateral treaties such as human rights agreements that impose rules on states intended to regulate their conduct. The Albanian Declaration and the many bilateral treaties that formed part of the minorities regime of the period come within this description.

Nonetheless, domestic legislation differs in several critical respects from the typical treaty. A statute is generally enacted by the majority of a legislature and binds all members of the relevant society. Even changes in a constitution, which usually require approval by the legislature and other institutions or groups, can be accomplished over substantial dissent. The ordinary treaty, on the other hand, is a consensual arrangement. With few exceptions, such as Article 2(6) of the UN Charter, it purports to bind or benefit only parties. Alteration of its terms by one state party generally requires the consent of all.

Consider the institution of contract. Like the treaty, a contract can be said to make or create law between the parties: within the facilitative framework of governing law and subject to that law's mandatory norms and constraints, courts recognize and enforce contract-created duties. The treaty shares a contract's consensual basis, but treaty law lacks the breadth and relative inclusiveness of a national body of contract law. It has preserved a certain Roman law flavour ('*pacta sunt servanda*', '*rebus sic stantibus*') acquired during the long period from the Renaissance to the nineteenth century, when continental European scholars dominated the field. But treaty law often reflects the diversity of approaches to domestic contract law that lawyers bring to the topic, a diversity that is particularly striking on issues of treaty interpretation.

Duties Imposed by Treaty Law

Whatever its purpose or character, an international agreement is generally recognized from the perspective of international law as an authoritative starting point for legal reasoning about any dispute to which it is relevant. The maxim '*pacta sunt servanda*' is at the core of treaty law. It embodies a widespread recognition that commitments publicly, formally and (more or less) voluntarily made by a nation should be honoured. As stated in Article 26 of the Vienna Convention on the Law of Treaties: 'Every treaty in force is binding upon the parties to it and must be performed by them in good faith'.

Whatever the jurisprudential or philosophical basis for this norm, one can readily perceive the practical reasons for and the national interests served by adherence to the principle of *pacta sunt servanda*. The treaty represents one of the most effective means for bringing some order to relationships among states or their nationals, and for the systematic development of new principles responsive to the changing needs of the international community. It is the prime legal form through which that community can realize some degree of predictability and seek to institutionalize ideals like peaceful settlement of disputes and the protection of human rights. Often such goals can be achieved only through international organizations whose powers, structure, membership and purposes will be set forth in the treaties that bring them into existence. Treaties then are the basic instruments underlying much contemporary international regulation.

Acceptance of the primary role of the treaty does not, however, mean that a problem between two countries is adequately solved from the perspective of legal ordering simply by execution of a treaty with satisfactory provisions. A body of law has necessarily developed to deal with questions analogous to those addressed by domestic contract law — for example, formation of a treaty, its interpretation and performance, remedies for breach, and amendment or termination. But that body of law is often fragmentary and vague, reflecting the scarcity of decisions of international tribunals and the political tensions which some aspects of treaty law reflect.

There have been recurrent efforts to remedy this situation through more or less creative codification of the law of treaties. The contemporary authoritative text grows out of a United Nations Conference on the Law of Treaties that adopted in 1969 the Convention on the Law of Treaties. That Convention became effective in 1980 and (as of May 2012) had been ratified by 111 states. Excerpts from it appear in the Documents Supplement. For reasons stemming largely from tensions between the Executive and the Congress over authority over different types of international agreements, the United States has not ratified the Vienna Convention. Nonetheless, in its provisions on international agreements, the *Restatement (Third), Foreign Relations Law of the United States* (1987) 'accepts the Vienna Convention as, in general, constituting a codification of the customary international law governing international agreements, and therefore as foreign relations law of the United States ...'. All other major industrial countries have ratified the Convention. And the United States has signed it.

Treaty Formation

A treaty is formed by the express consent of its parties. Although there are no precise requirements for execution or form, certain procedures have become standard. By choice of the parties, or in order to comply with the internal rules of a signatory country that are considered in Chapter 12, it may be necessary to postpone the effectiveness of the agreement until a national legislative body has approved it and national executive authorities have ratified it. Instruments of ratification for bilateral agreements are then exchanged. In the case of multilateral treaties, such instruments are deposited with the national government or international organization that has been designated as the custodian of the authentic text and of all other instruments relating to the treaty, including subsequent adhesions by nations that were not among the original signatories. Thereafter a treaty will generally be proclaimed or promulgated by the executive in each country.

Consent

Given the established principle that treaties are consensual, what rules prevail as to the character of that consent? Do domestic law contract principles about the effect of duress carry over to the international field?

In a domestic legal system, a party cannot enforce a contract which was signed by a defendant at gunpoint. One could argue that victorious nations cannot assert rights under a peace treaty obtained by a whole army. It is not surprising that the large powers are reluctant to recognize that such forms of duress can invalidate a treaty. If duress were a defence, it would be critical to define its contours, for many treaties result from various forms of military, political or economic pressure. The paucity of and doubts about international institutions with authority to develop answers to such questions underscore the reluctance to open treaties to challenge on these grounds. Article 52 of the Vienna Convention states: 'A treaty is void if its conclusion has been procured by the threat or use of force in violation of the principles of international law embodied in the Charter of the United Nations'. Attempts at Vienna to broaden the scope of coercion to include economic duress failed, although they resulted in a declaration condemning the use of such practices.

Reservations

Problems of consent that have no precise parallel in national contract law arise in connection with reservations to treaties, i.e., unilateral statements made by a state accepting a treaty 'whereby it purports to exclude, or vary the legal effect of certain provisions of the treaty in their application to a state' (Art. 2(1)(d) of the Vienna Convention). With bilateral treaties, no conceptual difficulties arise: ratification with reservations amounts to a counteroffer; the other state may accept (or reject) explicitly or may be held to have tacitly accepted it by proceeding with its ratification process or with compliance with the treaty. With multilateral treaties the problems may be quite complex. The traditional rule held that acceptance by all parties was required. The expanding number of states has required more flexibility.

Given the increased number of reservations, some of great significance, that many states are attaching to their ratifications of basic human rights treaties, questions about those reservations' validity under general treaty law or under the terms of a specific treaty have become matters of high concern within the human rights regime. We discuss the issue of reservation at greater length in Chapter 12.

Violations of and Changes in Treaties

Violation of a treaty may lead to diplomatic protests and a claim before an international tribunal. But primarily because of the limited and qualified consent of states to the jurisdiction of international tribunals, the offended party will usually resort to other measures. In a national system of contract law, well-developed rules govern such measures. They may distinguish between a minor breach not authorizing the injured party to terminate its own performance, and a material breach providing justification for such a move. Article 60 of the Vienna Convention provides that a material breach (as defined) of a bilateral treaty entitles the other party to terminate the treaty or suspend its performance in whole or in part. These rules necessarily grow more complex for multilateral treaties, but they also entitle a party affected the material breach of another party to terminate or suspend its obligations under certain conditions. Article 60, however, explains that termination or suspension 'do[es] not apply to provisions relating to the protection of the human person contained in treaties of a humanitarian character'. That said, it might very well apply to treaties that only indirectly affect human rights (e.g., an agreement on pharmaceutical patents; a multilateral peace agreement).

Amendments raise additional problems. The treaty's contractual aspect suggests that the consent of all parties is necessary. Parties may however agree in advance (see Art. 108 of the UN Charter) to be bound with respect to certain matters by the vote of a specified number. Such provisions in a multilateral treaty bring it closer in character to national legislation. They may be limited to changes which do not impose new obligations upon a dissenting party, although a state antagonistic to an amendment could generally withdraw. Absent such provisions, a treaty might aggravate rather than resolve a fundamental problem of international law: how to achieve in a peaceful manner changes in existing arrangements that are needed to adapt them to developing political, social or economic conditions.

One of the most contentious issues in treaty law is whether the emergence of conditions that were unforeseeable or unforeseen at the time of the treaty's conclusion terminates or modifies a party's obligation to perform. This problem borders the subject of treaty interpretation, considered *infra*, since it is often described as a question whether an implied condition or an escape clause should be read into a treaty. Mature municipal legal systems have developed rules for handling situations where the performance of one party is rendered impossible or useless by intervening conditions. 'Impossibility', 'frustration', 'force majeure' and 'implied conditions' are the concepts used in Anglo-American law.

At the international level, possibilities of changes in conditions that upset assumptions underlying an agreement are enhanced by the long duration of many treaties, the difficulty in amending them and the rapid political, economic and social vicissitudes in modern times. Thus nations have occasionally used *rebus sic stantibus* as the basis for declaring treaties no longer effective. Article 62 of the Vienna Convention states that a 'fundamental change of circumstances' which was not foreseen by the parties may not be invoked as a ground for terminating a treaty unless 'the existence of those circumstances constituted an essential basis of the consent of the parties to transform the extent of obligations still to be performed under the treaty'; and 'the effect of the change is radically to transform the extent of obligations still to be performed under the treaty.'

Treaty Interpretation

There is no shortcut to a reliable sense of how a given treaty will be construed. Even immersion in a mass of diplomatic correspondence and cases would not develop such a skill. In view of the variety of treaties and of approaches to their interpretation, such learning would more likely shed light on the possibilities than provide a particular answer to any given question.

One obstacle to reliable generalization about treaty interpretation is the variety of purposes which treaties serve. Different approaches are advisable for treaties that lay down rules for a long or indefinite period, in contrast with those settling past or temporally limited disputes. The long-term treaty must rest upon a certain flexibility and room for development if it is to survive changes in circumstances and relations between the parties. Changes in conditions like those that make *rebus sic stantibus* an attractive doctrine may lead a court or executive official to interpret a treaty flexibly so as to give it a sensible application to new circumstances. The type of problem that a treaty addresses will influence the approach of an official charged with interpreting it. Certain categories, such as income tax conventions, lend themselves to a detailed draftsmanship that will often be impractical and undesirable in a constitutional document such as the UN Charter. Conventions such as those relating to human rights will, for some matters, necessarily use broad terms and standards like fairness or *ordre public*. As a formal matter, a general rule of interpretation holds that a treaty should be interpreted in light of 'its object and purpose'.

Maxims similar to those found in domestic fields exist for treaties as well. The Vienna Convention contains several. Article 31 provides that a 'treaty shall be interpreted in good faith in accordance with the ordinary meaning to be given to the terms of the treaty in their context'. Article 32 goes on to add that recourse may be had to supplementary means — including *travaux préparatoires* (literally, 'preparatory work', and analogous to legislative history) — if interpretation produces a meaning that is 'ambiguous or obscure' or an outcome 'manifestly absurd or unreasonable'. A standard form of interpretation also takes into account the subsequent practice of states in the application of the treaty.

One way to build a framework for construing treaties is to consider the continuum which lies between 'strict' interpretation according to the 'plain meaning' of the treaty, and interpretation according to the interpreter's view of the best means of implementing the purposes or realizing the principles expressed by the treaty. Of course, both extremes of the spectrum are untenanted. One cannot wholly ignore the treaty's words, nor can one always find an unambiguous and relevant text that resolves the immediate issue.

Part of the difficulty is that treaties may be drafted in several languages. If domestic courts deem it unwise to 'make a fortress out of the dictionary', it would seem particularly unwise when interpreters need to resort to dictionaries in several languages (and in different legal systems according different meanings to linguistically similar terms). Sometimes corresponding words in the different versions may shed more light on the intended meaning; at other times, they generate greater ambiguity.

Reliance upon literal construction or 'strict' interpretation may however be an attractive method or technique to an international tribunal that is sensitive to its weak political foundation. It may be tempted to take refuge in the position that its decision is the ineluctable outcome of the drafters' intention expressed in clear text, and not a choice arrived at on the basis of the tribunal's understanding of policy considerations or relevant principles that may resolve a dispute over interpretation. Reliance on *travaux préparatoires* can achieve the same result of placing responsibility on the drafters. The charge of 'judicial legislation' evokes strong reactions in some political and legal cultures; it inevitably influences judges of international tribunals and heightens the temptation to take refuge in the dictionary.

QUESTIONS

1. The types of protections or assurances given by treaty to a distinctive group within a larger polity can be categorized in various ways, including the following. The assurance can be *absolute* (fixed, unconditional) or *contingent* (dependent on some reference group). For example, treaties of commerce between two states may reciprocally grant to citizens of each state the right to reside (for business purposes) and do business (as aliens) in the other state. Some assurances in such treaties will be absolute — for example, citizens of each state are given the right to buy or lease real property for residential purposes in the other state. Other assurances will be contingent — for example, citizens of each state are given the right to organize a corporation and qualify to do business in the other state on the same terms as citizens of that other state (so called 'national treatment'). Within this framework, how would you characterize the rights given to members of a designated minority by the Albanian Declaration? Do the majority and dissenting opinions differ about how to characterize them?

2. If you were a member of the Greek-speaking Christian minority, would you have been content with a Declaration that contained no more than a general equal protection clause? If not, why not? How would you justify your argument for more protection?

3. Would Albania have been justified in imposing some control on the Greek schools, such as defining subjects to be taught and censoring teaching materials that, say, urged independence from Albania?

4. Why do the opinions refer to this minorities regime as 'extraordinary'? In what respects does it depart from classical conceptions of international law, or differ from the law of state responsibility?

5. Why do you suppose that Article 6(a) on crimes against peace (wars of aggression) has fallen into disuse with respect to individual criminal liability? What factors would make its return likely? The crime of aggression was omitted from the criminal provisions in the Statutes for the International Criminal Tribunals for the Former Yugoslavia and for Rwanda. Adopted in 1998, the Rome Treaty creating the International Criminal Court (ICC) states that the Court shall have jurisdiction over 'the crime of aggression once a provision is adopted [by the parties to the treaty] defining the crime'. No provision has been adopted. That said, in 2010 the ICC's Assembly of States Parties adopted a resolution that provides a definition and a set of extraordinary jurisdictional prerequisites for the Court to hear a case of aggression. The compromise document, however, essentially postpones the decision for several years. It requires the Assembly of States Parties to vote again to reaffirm the amendment after January 2017.

6. Consider how close to or distant from the minorities regime Article 27 of the International Covenant on Civil and Political Rights appears on its face to be. It provides:

> In those States in which ethnic, religious or linguistic minorities exist, persons belonging to such minorities shall not be denied the right, in community with the other members of their group, to enjoy their own culture, to profess and practice their own religion, or to use their own language.

ADDITIONAL READING

On the minorities regime, see B. Rechel (ed.), *Minority Rights in Central and Eastern Europe* (2009); T. Malloy, *National Minority Rights in Europe* (2005); G. Pentassuglia, *Minorities in International Law: An Introductory Study* (2002); M. Weller, *Universal Minority Rights: A Commentary on the Jurisprudence of International Courts and Treaty Bodies* (2007); S. Wheatley, *Democracy, Minorities and International Law* (2005); R. Letschert, *The Impact of Minority Rights Mechanisms* (2005); & P. de Azcarate, *The League of Nations and National Minorities* (1945). On treaty law, see E. Cannizzaro (ed.), *The Law of Treaties Beyond the Vienna Convention* (2011); A. Aust, *Modern Treaty Law and Practice* (2nd edn. 2007); B. Simma, 'Human Rights and General International Law: A Comparative Analysis', in 4 Collected Courses of the Academy of European Law 1 (1995); P. Reuter, *Introduction to the Law of Treaties* (3rd edn. 1995); D. Greig, *Invalidity and the Law of Treaties* (2006); S. Davidson, *The Law of Treaties* (2004); S. Scott, *The Political Interpretation of Multilateral Treaties* (2004); R. Gardiner, *Treaty Interpretation* (2007); O. Corten & P. Klein (eds.), *The Vienna Conventions on the Law of Treaties: A Commentary* (2011).

D. JUDGMENT AT NUREMBERG

COMMENT ON THE NUREMBERG TRIAL

The trial at Nuremberg in 1945–1946 of major war criminals among the Axis powers, dominantly Nazi party leaders and military officials, gave the nascent human rights movement a powerful impulse. The UN Charter that became effective in 1945 included a few broad human rights provisions. But they were more programmatic than operational, more a programme to be realized by states over time than a system in place for application to states. Nuremberg, on the other hand, was concrete and applied: prosecutions, convictions, punishment. The prosecution and the Judgment of the International Military Tribunal in this initial, weighty trial for massive crimes committed during the war years were based on concepts and norms, some of which had deep roots in international law and some of which represented a significant development of that law that opened the path toward the later formulation of fundamental human rights norms.

The striking aspect of Nuremberg was that the trial and Judgment applied international law doctrines and concepts to impose criminal punishment on individuals for their commission of any of the three types of crimes under international law that are described below. The notion of crimes against the law of nations for which violators bore an individual criminal responsibility was itself an older one, but it had operated in a restricted field. As customary international law developed from the time of Grotius, certain conduct came to be considered a violation of the law of nations — in effect, a universal crime. Piracy on the high seas was long the classic example of this limited category of crimes. Given the common interest of all nations in protecting navigation against interference on the high seas outside the territory of any state, it was considered appropriate for the state apprehending a pirate to prosecute in its own courts. Since there was no international criminal tribunal, prosecution in a state court was the only means of judicial enforcement. To the extent that the state courts sought to apply the customary international law defining the crime of piracy, either directly or as it had become absorbed into national legislation, the choice of forum became less significant, for state courts everywhere were in theory applying the same law.

One specialized field, the humanitarian laws of war, had long included rules regulating the conduct of war, the so-called '*jus in bello*'. This body of law imposed sanctions against combatants who committed serious violations of the restrictive rules. Such application of the laws of war, and its foundation in customary norms and in treaties, figure in the Judgment, *infra*. But the concept of individual criminal responsibility was not systematically developed. It achieved a new prominence and a clearer definition after the Nuremberg Judgment, primarily through the Geneva Conventions of 1949 and their 1977 Protocols. Gradually other types of conduct have been added to this small list of individual crimes under international law — for example, slave trading long prior to Nuremberg and genocide thereafter. Recent years have seen the creation of the International Criminal Tribunals for the former Yugoslavia and for Rwanda in the 1990s and the initiation of the International Criminal Court in 2002, all discussed in Chapter 14.

As the Second World War came to an end, the Allied Powers held several conferences to determine what policies they should follow towards the Germans responsible for the war and for the systematic barbarity and annihilation of the period. The wartime destruction and civilian losses were known. The nature and extent of the Holocaust were first becoming widely known. These conferences culminated in the (United States, USSR, Britain, France) London Agreement of 8 August 1945, 59 Stat. 1544, E.A.S. No. 472, in which the parties determined to constitute 'an International Military Tribunal for the trial of war criminals'. The Charter annexed to the Agreement provided for the composition and basic procedures of the Tribunal and stated the criminal provisions for the trials in its three critical articles:

> *Article 6.*
> The Tribunal established by the Agreement referred to in Article 1 hereof for the trial and punishment of the major war of the criminals European Axis countries shall have the power to try and punish persons who, acting in the interests of the European Axis countries, whether as individuals or as members of organizations, committed any of the following crimes.
>
> The following acts, or any of them, are crimes coming within the jurisdiction of the Tribunal for which there shall be individual responsibility:
>
> (a) *Crimes Against Peace*: namely, planning, preparation, initiation or waging of a war of aggression, or a war in violation of international treaties, agreements or assurances, or participation in a common plan or conspiracy for the accomplishment of any of the foregoing;
> (b) *War Crimes*: namely, violations of the laws or customs of war. Such violations shall include, but not be limited to, murder, ill-treatment or

deportation to slave labor or for any other purpose of civilian population of or in occupied territory, murder or ill-treatment of prisoners of war or persons on the seas, killing of hostages, plunder of public or private property, wanton destruction of cities, towns or villages, or devastation not justified by military necessity;

(c) *Crimes Against Humanity*: namely, murder, extermination, enslavement, deportation, and other inhumane acts committed against any civilian population, before or during the war, or persecutions on political, racial or religious grounds in execution of or in connection with any crime within the jurisdiction of the Tribunal, whether or not in violation of the domestic law of the country where perpetrated.

Leaders, organizers, instigators and accomplices participating in the formulation or execution of a common plan or conspiracy to commit any of the foregoing crimes are responsible for all acts performed by any persons in execution of such plan.

Article 7.

The official position of defendants, whether as Heads of State or responsible officials in Government Departments, shall not be considered as freeing them from responsibility or mitigating punishment.

Article 8.

The fact that the Defendant acted pursuant to order of his Government or of a superior shall not free him from responsibility, but may be considered in mitigation of punishment if the Tribunal determines that justice so requires.

Note the innovative character of these provisions. Although the Tribunal of four judges (one from each of the major Allied Powers) was restricted to the four victorious powers creating it, nonetheless the Tribunal had an international character in its formation and composition, and to that extent was radically different from the national military courts before which the laws of war had to that time generally been enforced. At the core of the Charter lay the concept of international crimes for which there would be 'individual responsibility', a sharp departure from the then-existing customary law or conventions which stressed the duties of (and sometimes sanctions against) states. Moreover, in defining crimes within the Tribunal's jurisdiction, the Charter went beyond the traditional 'war crimes' (para. (b) of Art. 6) in two ways.

First, the Charter included the war-related 'crimes against peace'—so-called '*jus ad bellum*', in contrast with the category of war crimes or *jus in bello*. International law had for a long time been innocent of such a concept. After a slow departure during the post-Reformation period from earlier distinctions of philosophers, theologians and writers on international law between 'just' and 'unjust' wars, the European nations moved towards a conception of war as an instrument of national policy, much like any other, to be legally regulated only with respect to *jus in bello*, the manner of its conduct. The Covenant of the League of Nations did not frontally challenge this principle, although it attempted to control aggression through collective decisions of the League. The interwar period witnessed some fortification of the principles later articulated in the Nuremberg Charter, primarily through the Kellogg-Briand Pact of 1927 that is referred to in the Judgment. Today the UN Charter requires members (Art. 2(4)) to 'refrain in their international relations from the threat or use of force' against other states, while providing (Art. 51) that nothing shall impair 'the inherent right of individual or collective self-defence if an armed attack occurs against a Member ...' When viewed in conjunction with the Nuremberg Charter, those provisions suggest the contemporary effort to distinguish not between 'just' and 'unjust' wars but between the permitted 'self-defence' and the forbidden 'aggression' — the word used in defining 'crimes against peace' in Article 6(a) of that Charter.

Second, Article 6(c) represented an important innovation. There were few precedents for use of the phrase 'crimes against humanity' as part of a description of international law, and its content was correspondingly indeterminate. On its face, paragraph (c) might have been read to include the entire programme of the Nazi government to exterminate Jews and other civilian groups, in and outside Germany, whether 'before or during the war', and thus to include not only the Holocaust but also the planning for and early persecution of Jews and other groups preceding the Holocaust. Moreover, that paragraph appeared to bring within its scope the persecution or annihilation by Germany of Jews who were German nationals as well as those who were aliens. This would represent a great advance on the international law of state responsibility to aliens as described at p. 90, *supra*. Note, however, how the Judgment of the Tribunal interpreted Article 6(c) with respect to these observations.

In other respects as well, the concept of 'crimes against humanity', even in this early formulation, developed the earlier international law. War crimes could cover discrete as well as systematic action by a combatant — an isolated murder of a civilian by a combatant as well a systematic policy of wanton destruction of towns. Crimes against humanity were directed primarily to planned conduct, to systematic conduct.

In defining the charges against the major Nazi leaders tried at Nuremberg and its successor tribunals, the Allied Powers took care to exclude those types of conduct which had not been understood to violate existing custom or conventions and in which they themselves had engaged — for example, the massive bombing of cities with necessarily high tolls of civilians that was indeed aimed at demoralization of the enemy.

JUDGMENT OF NUREMBERG TRIBUNAL

International Military Tribunal, Nuremberg (1946)

...

[The Law of the Charter]

The jurisdiction of the Tribunal is defined in the [London] Agreement and Charter, and the crimes coming within the jurisdiction of the Tribunal, for which there shall be individual responsibility, are set out in Article 6. The law of the Charter is decisive, and binding upon the Tribunal.

The making of the Charter was the exercise of the sovereign legislative power by the countries to which the German Reich unconditionally surrendered; and the undoubted right of these countries to legislate for the occupied territories has been recognized by the civilized world. The Charter is not an arbitrary exercise of power on the part of the victorious Nations, but in the view of the Tribunal, as will be shown, it is the expression of international law existing at the time of its creation; and to that extent is itself a contribution to international law.

The Signatory Powers created this Tribunal, defined the law it was to administer, and made regulations for the proper conduct of the Trial. In doing so, they have done together what any one of them might have done singly; for it is not to be doubted that any nation has the right thus to set up special courts to administer law. With regard to the constitution of the Court, all that the defendants are entitled to ask is to receive a fair trial on the facts and law.

The Charter makes the planning or waging of a war of aggression or a war in violation of international treaties a crime; and it is therefore not strictly necessary to consider whether and to what extent aggressive war was a crime before the execution of the London Agreement. But in view of the great importance of the questions of law involved, the Tribunal has heard full argument from the Prosecution and the Defence, and will express its view on the matter.

It was urged on behalf of the defendants that a fundamental principle of all law — international and domestic — is that there can be no punishment of crime without a pre-existing law. '*Nullum crimen sine lege, nulla poena sine lege.*' It was submitted that *ex post facto* punishment is abhorrent to the law of all civilized nations, that no sovereign power had made aggressive war a crime at the time that the alleged criminal acts were committed, that no statute had defined aggressive war, that no penalty had been fixed for its commission, and no court had been created to try and punish offenders.

In the first place, it is to be observed that the maxim *nullum crimen sine lege* is not a limitation of sovereignty, but is in general a principle of justice. To assert that it is unjust to punish those who in defiance of treaties and assurances have attacked neighboring states without warning is obviously untrue, for in such circumstances the attacker must know that he is doing wrong, and so far from it being unjust to punish him, it would be unjust if his wrong were allowed to go unpunished ...

This view is strongly reinforced by a consideration of the state of international law in 1939, so far as aggressive war is concerned. The General Treaty for the Renunciation of War of 27 August 1928, more generally known as the Pact of Paris or the Kellogg-Briand Pact, was binding on 63 nations, including Germany, Italy and Japan at the outbreak of war in 1939....

... The nations who signed the Pact or adhered to it unconditionally condemned recourse to war for the future as an instrument of policy, and expressly renounced it. After the signing of the Pact, any nation resorting to war as an instrument of national policy breaks the Pact. In the opinion of the Tribunal, the solemn renunciation of war as an instrument of national policy necessarily involves the proposition that such a war is illegal in international law; and that those who plan and wage such a war, with its inevitable and terrible consequences, are committing a crime in so doing. War for the solution of international controversies undertaken as an instrument of national policy certainly includes a war of aggression, and such a war is therefore outlawed by the Pact. . . .

. . . The Hague Convention of 1907 prohibited resort to certain methods of waging war. These included the inhumane treatment of prisoners, the employment of poisoned weapons, the improper use of flags of truce, and similar matters. Many of these prohibitions had been enforced long before the date of the Convention; but since 1907 they have certainly been crimes, punishable as offenses against the law of war; yet the Hague Convention nowhere designates such practices as criminal, nor is any sentence prescribed, nor any mention made of a court to try and punish offenders. For many years past, however, military tribunals have tried and punished individuals guilty of violating the rules of land warfare laid down by this Convention. In the opinion of the Tribunal, those who wage aggressive war are doing that which is equally illegal, and of much greater moment than a breach of one of the rules of the Hague Convention. . . . The law of war is to be found not only in treaties, but in the customs and practices of states which gradually obtained universal recognition, and from the general principles of justice applied by jurists and practised by military courts. This law is not static, but by continual adaptation follows the needs of a changing world. Indeed, in many cases treaties do no more than express and define for more accurate reference the principles of law already existing.

. . .

All these expressions of opinion, and others that could be cited, so solemnly made, reinforce the construction which the Tribunal placed upon the Pact of Paris, that resort to a war of aggression is not merely illegal, but is criminal. The prohibition of aggressive war demanded by the conscience of the world, finds its expression in the series of pacts and treaties to which the Tribunal has just referred.

. . .

. . . That international law imposes duties and liabilities upon individuals as well as upon States has long been recognized. . . .Crimes against international law are committed by men, not by abstract entities, and only by punishing individuals who commit such crimes can the provisions of international law be enforced.

. . .

The authors of these acts cannot shelter themselves behind their official position in order to be freed from punishment in appropriate proceedings. Article 7 of the Charter expressly declares:

> The official position of Defendants, whether as heads of State, or responsible officials in Government departments, shall not be considered as freeing them from responsibility, or mitigating punishment.

On the other hand the very essence of the Charter is that individuals have international duties which transcend the national obligations of obedience imposed by the individual state. He who violates the laws of war cannot obtain immunity while acting in pursuance of the authority of the state if the state in authorizing action moves outside its competence under international law.

It was also submitted on behalf of most of these defendants that in doing what they did they were acting under the orders of Hitler, and therefore cannot be held responsible for the acts committed by them in carrying out these orders. The Charter specifically provides in Article 8:

> The fact that the Defendant acted pursuant to order of his Government or of a superior shall not free him from responsibility, but may be considered in mitigation of punishment.

The provisions of this article are in conformity with the law of all nations. That a soldier was ordered to kill or torture in violation of the international law of war has never been recognized as a defense to such acts of brutality, though, as the Charter here provides, the order may be urged in mitigation of the punishment. The true test, which is found in varying degrees in the criminal law of most nations, is not the existence of the order, but whether moral choice was in fact possible.

...

War Crimes and Crimes against Humanity

... War Crimes were committed on a vast scale, never before seen in the history of war. They were perpetrated in all the countries occupied by Germany, and on the High Seas, and were attended by every conceivable circumstance of cruelty and horror. There can be no doubt that the majority of them arose from the Nazi conception of 'total war', with which the aggressive wars were waged. For in this conception of 'total war,' the moral ideas underlying the conventions which seek to make war more humane are no longer regarded as having force or validity. Everything is made subordinate to the overmastering dictates of war. Rules, regulations, assurances, and treaties all alike are of no moment; and so, freed from the restraining influence of international law, the aggressive war is conducted by the Nazi leaders in the most barbaric way. Accordingly, War Crimes were committed when and wherever the Führer and his close associates thought them to be advantageous. They were for the most part the result of cold and criminal calculation.

...

... Prisoners of war were ill-treated and tortured and murdered, not only in defiance of the well-established rules of international law, but in complete disregard of the elementary dictates of humanity. Civilian populations in occupied territories suffered the same fate. Whole populations were deported to Germany for the purposes of slave labor upon defense works, armament production, and similar tasks connected with the war effort. Hostages were taken in very large numbers from the civilian populations in all the occupied countries, and were shot as suited the German purposes. Public and private property was systematically plundered and pillaged in order to enlarge the resources of Germany at the expense of the rest of Europe. Cities and towns and villages were wantonly destroyed without military justification or necessity.

...

Murder and Ill-Treatment of Civilian Population

Article 6(b) of the Charter provides that 'ill-treatment ... of civilian population of or in occupied territory ... killing of hostages ... wanton destruction of cities, towns, or villages' shall be a war crime. In the main, these provisions are merely declaratory of the existing laws of war as expressed by the Hague Convention, Article 46....

...

One of the most notorious means of terrorizing the people in occupied territories was the use of concentration camps ... [which] became places of organized and systematic murder, where millions of people were destroyed.

In the administration of the occupied territories the concentration camps were used to destroy all opposition groups....

A certain number of the concentration camps were equipped with gas chambers for the wholesale destruction of the inmates, and with furnaces for the burning of the bodies. Some of them were in fact used for the extermination of Jews as part of the 'final solution' of the Jewish problem....

...

Slave Labor Policy

Article 6(b) of the Charter provides that the 'ill-treatment or deportation to slave labor or for any other purpose, of civilian population of or in occupied territory' shall be a War Crime. The laws relating to forced labor by the inhabitants of occupied territories are found in Article 52 of the Hague Convention.... The policy of the German occupation authorities was in flagrant violation of the terms of this convention.... [T]he German occupation authorities did succeed in forcing many of the inhabitants of the occupied territories to work for the German war effort, and in deporting at least 5,000,000 persons to Germany to serve German industry and agriculture.

...

Persecution of the Jews

The persecution of the Jews at the hands of the Nazi Government has been proved in the greatest detail before the Tribunal. It is a record of consistent and systematic inhumanity on the greatest scale. Ohlendorf, Chief of Amt III in the RSHA from 1939 to 1943, and who was in command of one of the Einsatz groups in the campaign against the Soviet Union testified as to the methods employed in the extermination of the Jews....

When the witness Bach Zelewski was asked how Ohlendorf could admit the murder of 90,000 people, he replied: 'I am of the opinion that when, for years, for decades, the doctrine is preached that the Slav race is an inferior race, and Jews not even human, then such an outcome is inevitable'.

...

... The Nazi Party preached these doctrines throughout its history, *Der Stürmer* and other publications were allowed to disseminate hatred of the Jews, and in the speeches and public declarations of the Nazi leaders, the Jews were held up to public ridicule and contempt.

... By the autumn of 1938, the Nazi policy towards the Jews had reached the stage where it was directed towards the complete exclusion of Jews from German life. Pogroms were organized, which included the burning and demolishing of synagogues, the looting of Jewish businesses, and the arrest of prominent Jewish business men....

It was contended for the Prosecution that certain aspects of this anti-Semitic policy were connected with the plans for aggressive war. The violent measures taken against the Jews in November 1938 were nominally in retaliation for the killing of an official of the German Embassy in Paris. But the decision to seize Austria and Czechoslovakia had been made a year before. The imposition of a fine of one billion marks was made, and the confiscation of the financial holdings of the Jews was decreed, at a time when German armament expenditure had put the German treasury in difficulties, and when the reduction of expenditure on armaments was being considered....

It was further said that the connection of the anti-Semitic policy with aggressive war was not limited to economic matters....

The Nazi persecution of Jews in Germany before the war, severe and repressive as it was, cannot compare, however, with the policy pursued during the war in the occupied territories.... In the summer of 1941, however, plans were made for the 'final solution' of the Jewish question in Europe. This 'final solution' meant the extermination of the Jews....

The plan for exterminating the Jews was developed shortly after the attack on the Soviet Union....

...

... Adolf Eichmann, who had been put in charge of this program by Hitler, has estimated that the policy pursued resulted in the killing of 6 million Jews, of which 4 million were killed in the extermination institutions.

The Law Relating to War Crimes and Crimes against Humanity

...

The Tribunal is of course bound by the Charter, in the definition which it gives both of War Crimes and Crimes against Humanity. With respect to War Crimes, however, as has already been pointed out, the crimes defined by Article 6, Section (b), of the Charter were already recognized as War Crimes under international law. They were covered by Articles 46, 50, 52, and 56 of the Hague Convention of 1907, and Articles 2, 3, 4, 46, and 51 of the Geneva Convention of 1929. That violation of these provisions constituted crimes for which the guilty individuals were punishable is too well settled to admit of argument.

But it is argued that the Hague Convention does not apply in this case, because of the 'general participation' clause in Article 2 of the Hague Convention of 1907. That clause provided:

> The provisions contained in the regulations (Rules of Land Warfare) referred to in Article 1 as well as in the present Convention do not apply except between contracting powers, and then only if all the belligerents are parties to the Convention.

Several of the belligerents in the recent war were not parties to this Convention.

In the opinion of the Tribunal it is not necessary to decide this question. The rules of land warfare expressed in the Convention undoubtedly represented an advance over existing international law at the time of their adoption. But the Convention expressly stated that it was an attempt 'to revise the general laws and customs of war', which it thus recognized to be then existing, but by 1939 these rules laid down in the Convention were recognized by all civilized nations, and were regarded as being declaratory of the laws and customs of war which are referred to in Article 6(b) of the Charter.

...

With regard to Crimes against Humanity there is no doubt whatever that political opponents were murdered in Germany before the war, and that many of them were kept in concentration camps in circumstances of great horror and cruelty. The policy of terror was certainly carried out on a vast scale, and in many cases was organized and systematic. The policy of persecution, repression, and murder of civilians in Germany before the war of 1939, who were likely to be hostile to the Government, was most ruthlessly carried out. The persecution of Jews during the same period is established beyond all doubt. To constitute Crimes against Humanity, the acts relied on before the outbreak of war must have been in execution of, or in connection with, any crime within the jurisdiction of the Tribunal. The Tribunal is of the opinion that revolting and horrible as many of these crimes were, it has not been satisfactorily proved that they were done in execution of, or in connection with, any such crime. The Tribunal therefore cannot make a general declaration that the acts before 1939 were Crimes against Humanity within the meaning of the Charter, but from the beginning of the war in 1939 War Crimes were committed on a vast scale, which were also Crimes against Humanity; and insofar as the inhumane acts charged in the Indictment, and committed after the beginning of the war, did not constitute War Crimes, they were all committed in execution of, or in connection with, the aggressive war, and therefore constituted Crimes against Humanity.

[The opinion considered individually each of the 22 defendants at this first trial of alleged war criminals. It found 19 of the defendants guilty of one or more counts of the indictment. It imposed 12 death sentences. Most convictions were for war crimes and Crimes Against Humanity, the majority of those convicted being found guilty of both crimes.]

NOTE

Note the following statement in Ian Brownlie, *Principles of Public International Law* (4th edn. 1990), at 562:

> But whatever the state of the law in 1945, Article 6 of the Nuremberg Charter has since come to represent general international law. The Agreement to which the

> Charter was annexed was signed by the United States, United Kingdom, France, and USSR, and nineteen other states subsequently adhered to it. In a resolution adopted unanimously on 11 December 1946, the General Assembly affirmed 'the principles of international law recognized by the Charter of the Nuremberg Tribunal and the judgment of the Tribunal'.

There has been considerable expansion in the definitions of two of the crimes defined in Article 6. The field of individual criminal responsibility for war crimes has been both broadened and clarified, through provisions of the Geneva Conventions of 1949 and of the 1998 Rome Statute for the International Criminal Court. Particularly relevant are the provisions for 'grave breaches' in these conventions, later discussed. The concept of crimes against humanity has expanded greatly in coverage and shed some limitations placed on it by the Judgment of the Tribunal. Such developments are described in the materials dealing with the current International Criminal Tribunals for the former Yugoslavia and for Rwanda and the International Criminal Court in Chapter 14. The notion of 'crimes against peace', however, has fallen into relative disuse.

The problem of *ex post facto* trials has received much commentary, some of which appears below. See in this connection Article 15 of the International Covenant on Civil and Political Rights.

Compare with the Nuremberg Judgment the following provisions of the Convention on the Prevention and Punishment of the Crime of Genocide (142 parties as of May 2012) bearing on personal responsibility. The treaty parties 'confirm' in Article I that genocide 'is a crime under international law which they undertake to prevent and to punish'. Article 2 defines genocide:

> In the present Convention, genocide means any of the following acts committed with intent to destroy, in whole or in part, a national, ethnical, racial or religious group, as such:
>
> (a) Killing members of the group;
> (b) Causing serious bodily or mental harm to members of the group;
> (c) Deliberately inflicting on the group conditions of life calculated to bring about its physical destruction in whole or in part;
> (d) Imposing measures intended to prevent births within the group;
> (e) Forcibly transferring children of the group to another group.

Persons committing acts of genocide 'shall be punished, whether they are constitutionally responsible rulers, public officials or private individuals' (Art. IV). The parties agree (Art. V) to enact the necessary legislation to give effect to the Convention and 'to provide effective penalties for persons guilty of genocide'. Under Article VI, persons charged with genocide are to be tried by a tribunal 'of the State in the territory of which the act was committed, or by such international penal tribunal as may have jurisdiction with respect to those Contracting Parties which shall have accepted its jurisdiction'. No international penal tribunal of general jurisdiction has been created.

VIEWS OF COMMENTATORS

There follow a number of authors' observations about the charges, the Judgment and the principles in the Nuremberg trials.

(1) In a review of a book by Sheldon Glueck entitled *The Nuremberg Trial and Aggressive War* (1946), the reviewer George Finch, 47 Am. J. Int'l. L. 334 (1947), makes the following arguments:

> As the title indicates, this book deals with the charges at Nuremberg based upon the planning and waging of aggressive war. The author has written it because in his previous volume he expressed the view that he did not think such acts could be regarded as 'international crimes'. He has now changed his mind and believes 'that for the purpose of conceiving aggressive war to be an international crime, the Pact of Paris may, together with other treaties and resolutions, be regarded as evidence of a sufficiently developed *custom* to be accepted as international law' (pp. 4–5)....
>
> The reviewer fully agrees with the author in regard to the place of custom in the development of international law. He regards as untenable, however, the argument not only of the author but of the prosecutors and judges at Nuremberg that custom can be judicially established by placing interpretations upon the words of treaties which are refuted by the acts of the signatories in practice, by citing unratified protocols or public and private resolutions of no legal effect, and by ignoring flagrant and repeated violations of non-aggression pacts by one of the prosecuting governments which, if properly weighed in the evidence, would nullify any judicial holding that a custom outlawing aggressive war had been accepted in international law....

(2) In his article, 'The Nurnberg Trial', 33 Va. L. Rev. 679 (1947), at 694, Francis Biddle, the American judge on the Tribunal, commented on the definition of 'crimes against humanity' in Article 6(c) of the Charter:

> ... The authors of the Charter evidently realized that the crimes enumerated were essentially domestic and hardly subject to the incidence of international law, unless partaking of the nature of war crimes. Their purpose was evidently to reach the terrible persecution of the Jews and liberals within Germany before the war. But the Tribunal held that 'revolting and horrible as many of these crimes were', it had not been established that they were done 'in execution of, or in connection with' any crime within its jurisdiction. After the beginning of the war, however, these inhumane acts were held to have been committed in execution of the war, and were therefore crimes against humanity.
>
> ...
>
> Crimes against humanity constitute a somewhat nebulous conception, although the expression is not unknown to the language of international law.... With one possible exception ... crimes against humanity were held [in the Judgment of the Tribunal] to have been committed only where the proof also fully established the commission of war crimes. Mr. Stimson suggested [that the

Tribunal eliminate from its jurisdiction matters related to pre-war persecution in Germany], which involved 'a reduction of the meaning of crimes against humanity to a point where they became practically synonymous with war crimes'. I agree. And I believe that this inelastic construction is justified by the language of the Charter and by the consideration that such a rigid interpretation is highly desirable in this stage of the development of international law.

(3) Professor Hans Kelsen, in 'Will the Judgment in the Nuremberg Trial Constitute a Precedent in International Law?', 1 Int'l. L. Q. 153 (1947), at 164, was critical of several aspects of the London Agreement and the Judgment. But with respect to the question of retroactivity of criminal punishment, he wrote:

> The objection most frequently put forward — although not the weightiest one — is that the law applied by the judgment of Nuremberg is an ex post facto law. There can be little doubt that the London Agreement provides individual punishment for acts which, at the time they were performed were not punishable, either under international law or under any national law.... However, this rule [against retroactive legislation] is not valid at all within international law, and is valid within national law only with important exceptions. [Kelsen notes several exceptions, including the rule's irrelevance to 'customary law and to law created by a precedent, for such law is necessarily retroactive in respect to the first case to which it is applied....']
>
> A retroactive law providing individual punishment for acts which were illegal though not criminal at the time they were committed, seems also to be an exception to the rule against ex post facto laws. The London Agreement is such a law. It is retroactive only in so far as it established individual criminal responsibility for acts which at the time they were committed constituted violations of existing international law, but for which this law has provided only collective responsibility.... Since the internationally illegal acts for which the London Agreement established individual criminal responsibility were certainly also morally most objectionable, and the persons who committed these acts were certainly aware of their immoral character, the retroactivity of the law applied to them can hardly be considered as absolutely incompatible with justice.

(4) In his biography entitled *Harlan Fiske Stone: Pillar of the Law* (1956), Alpheus Thomas Mason discussed Chief Justice Stone's views about the involvement of Justices of the US Supreme Court in extrajudicial assignments and, in particular, Stone's views about President Truman's appointment of Justice Robert Jackson to be American Prosecutor at the trials. The following excerpts (at 715) are all incorporations by Mason in his book of quotations of Chief Justice Stone's remarks:

> So far as the Nuremberg trial is an attempt to justify the application of the power of the victor to the vanquished because the vanquished made aggressive war,....I dislike extremely to see it dressed up with a false facade of legality. The best that can be said for it is that it is a political act of the victorious States which may be morally right.... It would not disturb me greatly.... if that power were openly and frankly used to punish the German leaders for being a bad lot, but it disturbs me some to have it dressed up in the habiliments of the common law and the Constitutional safeguards to those charged with crime.

> Jackson is away conducting his high-grade lynching party in Nuremberg.... I don't mind what he does to the Nazis, but I hate to see the pretense that he is running a court and proceeding according to common law. This is a little too sanctimonious a fraud to meet my old-fashioned ideas.

(5) Professor Herbert Wechsler, in 'The Issues of the Nuremberg Trial', 62 Pol. Sci. Q. 11 (1947), at 23 observed:

> ... [M]ost of those who mount the attack [on the Judgment on contentions including *ex post facto* law] hasten to assure us that their plea is not one of immunity for the defendants; they argue only that they should have been disposed of politically, that is, dispatched out of hand. This is a curious position indeed. A punitive enterprise launched on the basis of general rules, administered in an adversary proceeding under a separation of prosecutive and adjudicative powers is, in the name of law and justice, asserted to be less desirable than an ex parte execution list or a drumhead court-martial constituted in the immediate aftermath of the war.... Those who choose to do so may view the Nuremberg proceeding as 'political' rather than 'legal' — a program calling for the judicial application of principles of liability politically defined. They cannot view it as less civilized an institution than a program of organized violence against prisoners, whether directed from the respective capitals or by military commanders in the field.

(6) Mark Osiel, in *Mass Atrocity, Collective Memory, and the Law* (1997), comments on charges against the defeated states (at 122):

> For the Nuremberg and Tokyo courts, it mattered little to the validity of criminal proceedings against Axis leadership that Allied victors had committed vast war crimes of their own. Unlike the law of tort, criminal law has virtually no place for 'comparative fault', no doctrinal device for mitigating the wrongdoing or culpability of the accused in light of the accusers'.... For the public, however, ... it mattered *greatly* in gauging the legitimacy of the trials that they seemed tendentiously selective, aimed at focusing memory in partisan ways. It mattered for such listeners that the defendants ... had constituted only a single side to a two- or multi-sided conflict, one in which other parties had similarly committed unlawful acts on a large scale. This unsavory feature of the Nuremberg judgment has undermined its authority in the minds of many, weakening its normative weight.

(7) David Luban, in *Legal Modernism* (1994), describes what he sees as a confusion in the Nuremberg charges (at 336):

> This idea that Nuremberg was to be the Trial to End All Wars seems fantastic and naïve forty years (and 150 wars) later. It has also done much to vitiate the real achievements of the trial, in particular the condemnation of crimes against humanity. To end all war, the authors of the Nuremberg Charter were led to incorporate an intellectual confusion into it. The Charter criminalized aggression; and by criminalizing aggression, the Charter erected a wall around state sovereignty and committed itself to an old-European model of unbreachable nation-states.

> But crimes against humanity are often, even characteristically, carried out by states against their own subjects. The effect, and great moral and legal achievement, of criminalizing such acts and assigning personal liability to those who order them and carry them out is to pierce the veil of sovereignty. As a result, Article 6(a) pulls in the opposite direction from Articles 6(c), 7 and 8, leaving us ... with a legacy that is at best equivocal and at worst immoral.

(8) Thane Rosenbaum, in 'The Romance of Nuremberg and the Tease of Moral Justice', 27 Cardozo L. Rev. 1731 (2006), argues about legal and moral justice (at 1736):

> When it came to the Nazis, jurisdictional concerns, retroactive punishments, standard causation requirements, and freedom of association principles, were not going to impede moral justice and the development of international law. No one seemed to mind during Nuremberg that these constitutional principles were being upended, and that a strict adherence to constitutional safeguards seemingly did not make the trip to Germany. Given the enormity of the Nazis' crimes and the moral implications of acquitting them on procedural grounds, the Constitution, as a document, apparently was deemed not fit for travel and therefore was left behind. There was little ambivalence among the American prosecutors, including a sitting Supreme Court justice, about applying this new path to justice, one that looked legal but tilted in an entirely moral direction.

QUESTIONS

1. Recall clause (c) of Article 38(1) of the Statute of the ICJ, and the comments thereon of Oscar Schachter, at p. 99, *supra*. Should the Tribunal have relied on that clause to respond to charges of *ex post facto* application of Article 6(c) to individuals who were responsible for the murder of groups of Germans or aliens?

2. Do you agree with the Tribunal's restrictive interpretation of Article 6(c)? Consider the commentary above by Francis Biddle.

3. How do you evaluate the criticism by Finch of the Tribunal's use of treaties in deciding whether customary international law included a given norm? Recall the comments about the growth of customary law by Schachter.

4. How do you evaluate the criticism of the Nuremberg trial by Chief Justice Stone? By Osiel? By Luban? By Rosenbaum?

5. Why do you suppose that Article 6(a) on crimes against peace (wars of aggression) has fallen into disuse with respect to individual criminal liability? It was omitted from the criminal provisions in the Statutes for the International Criminal Tribunals for the former Yugoslavia and for Rwanda. The Rome Treaty creating the International Criminal Court states that the Court shall have jurisdiction over 'the crime of aggression once a provision is adopted [by the parties to the treaty] defining the crime ...' No such provision has been adopted.

6. How do you assess the significance and consequences of Nuremberg? Even if you agree with some or several of the criticisms above, do you nonetheless conclude that the trial and judgment were justified in their actual historical forms? If so, why?

ADDITIONAL READING

On Nuremberg see three books by Telford Taylor: *Nuremberg Trials: War Crimes and International Law* (1949); *Nuremberg and Vietnam: An American Tragedy* (1978) and *The Anatomy of the Nuremberg Trials: A Personal Memoir* (1992). See also Memorandum Submitted by the Secretary-General, *The Charter and Judgment of the Nürnberg Tribunal: History and Analysis,* UN Doc. A/CN.4/5 (1949); E. Schwelb, 'Crimes against Humanity', 23 Brit. Ybk. Int'l. L. 178 (1946); Symposium: 'The Nuremberg Trials: A Reappraisal and Their Legacy', 27 Cardozo L. Rev. 1549–738 (2006); Kevin John Heller, *The Nuremberg Military Tribunals and the Origins of International Criminal Law* (2011). More generally, see T. Meron, *War Crimes Law Comes of Age: Essays* (1998).

NOTE

This chapter has offered an illustrative survey of different forms or sources of international law (custom, general principles, treaties) and of several traditional international law topics (laws of war, state responsibility, minority-protection treaties, and international criminal law) as background to the study of the post-Second World War human rights regime. The following excerpts from lectures by Louis Henkin fill in a number of gaps in the history of ways in which pre-1945 international law had been concerned with protection of individuals. Like the earlier materials in this chapter, they too bring contemporary human rights to mind.

LOUIS HENKIN, INTERNATIONAL LAW: POLITICS, VALUES AND FUNCTIONS

216 Collected Courses of The Hague Academy of International Law (Vol. IV, 1989) 13, at 208

Chapter X:
State Values and Other Values: Human Rights

. . .

That until recently international law took no note of individual human beings may be surprising. Both international law and domestic legal norms in the Christian world had roots in an accepted morality and in natural law, and had common intellectual progenitors (including Grotius, Locke, Vattel). But for hundreds of years international law and the law governing individual life did not come together. International law, true to its name, was law only between States, governing only relations between States on the State level. What a State did inside its borders in relation to its own nationals remained its own affair, an element of its autonomy, a matter of its 'domestic jurisdiction'.

Antecedents of the International Law of Human Rights

In fact, neither the international political system nor international law ever closed out totally what went on inside a State and what happened to individuals within a State. Early, international law began to attend to internal matters that held special interest for other States, and those sometimes included concern for individual human beings, or at least redounded to the benefit of individual human beings. But what was in fact of interest to other States, and what was accepted as being of legitimate interest to other States (and therefore to the system and to law), were limited *a priori* by the character of the State system and its values. Of course, every State was legitimately concerned with what happened to its diplomats, to its diplomatic mission and to its property in the territory of another State. States were concerned, and the system developed norms to assure, that their nationals (and the property of their nationals) in the territory of another State be treated reasonably, 'fairly', and the system and the law early identified an international standard of justice by which a State must abide in its treatment of foreign nationals. States also entered into agreements, usually on a reciprocal basis, promising protection or privilege — freedom to reside, to conduct business, to worship — to persons with whom the other State party to the treaty identified because of common religion or ethnicity.

Concern for individual human welfare seeped into the international system in the eighteenth and nineteenth centuries in other discrete, specific respects. In the nineteenth century, European (and American) States abolished slavery and slave trade. Later, States began to pursue agreements to make war less inhumane, to outlaw some cruel weapons to safeguard prisoners of war, the wounded, civilian populations. It is noteworthy that, in these instances, even less-than-democratic States began to attend to human values, though humanitarian limitations on the conduct of war may have brought significant cost to the State's military interests.

Following the First World War, concern for individual human beings was reflected in several League of Nations programmes. Building on earlier precedents in the nineteenth century, the dominant States pressed selected other States to adhere to 'minorities treaties' guaranteed by the League, in which States Parties assumed obligations to respect rights of identified ethnic, national or religious minorities among their inhabitants.... The years following the First World War also saw a major development in international concern for individual welfare, a development that is often overlooked and commonly underestimated: the

International Labour Office (now the International Labour Organisation (ILO)) was established and it launched a variety of programmes including a series of conventions setting minimum standards for working conditions and related matters.

In general, the principles of customary international law that developed, and the special agreements that were concluded, addressed only what happened to *some* people inside a State, only in respects with which other States were in fact concerned, and only where such concern was considered their proper business in a system of autonomous States. One can only speculate as to why States accepted these norms and agreements, but it may be reasonable to doubt whether those developments authentically reflected sensitivity to human rights generally. States attended to what occurred inside another State when such happenings impinged on their political-economic interests. States were concerned, and were deemed legitimately concerned, for the freedoms, privileges, and immunities of their diplomats because an affront to the diplomat affronted his prince (or his State), and because interference with a diplomat interfered with his functions and disturbed orderly, friendly relations. Injury to a foreign national or to his or her property was also an affront to the State of his or her nationality, and powerful States exporting people, goods, and capital to other countries in the age of growing mercantilism insisted on law that would protect the State interests that these represented.

…

Humanitarian developments in the law of war reflected some concern by States to reduce the horrors of war for their own people and a willingness in exchange to reduce them for others. Powerful States promoted minorities treaties because mistreatment of minorities with which other States identified threatened international peace. Those treaties were imposed selectively, principally on nations defeated in war and on newly created or enlarged States; they did not establish general norms requiring respect for minorities by the big and the powerful as well; they did not require respect for individuals who were not members of identified minorities, or for members of the majority. …

Even the ILO conventions, perhaps, served some less-than-altruistic purposes. Improvement in the conditions of labour was capitalism's defence against the spectre of spreading socialism which had just established itself in the largest country in Europe. States, moreover, had a direct interest in the conditions of labour in countries with which they competed in a common international market: a State impelled to improve labour and social conditions at home could not readily do so unless other States did so, lest the increase in its costs of production render its products non-competitive.

I have stressed the possibly political-economic (rather than humanitarian) motivations for early norms and agreements, identifying a State's concern for the welfare of some of its nationals as an extension of its Statehood and perhaps reflecting principally concern for State interests and values. If some norms and agreements in fact were motivated by concern for a State's own people generally, they did not reflect interest in the welfare of those in other countries, or of human beings generally. State interests rather than individual human interests, or at best the interests of a State's own people rather than general human concerns, also inspired voluntary inter-State co-operation to promote reciprocal economic interests. . . .

I would not underestimate the influence of ideas of rights and constitutionalism in the seventeenth and eighteenth centuries, and of a growing and spreading enlightenment generally: Locke, Montesquieu, other Encyclopedists, Rousseau; the example of the Glorious Revolution in England and the establishment of constitutionalism in the United States; the influence of the French Declaration of the Rights of Man and of the Citizen. Such ideas and examples have influenced developments inside countries, but they did not easily enter the international political and legal system. Concern by one country for the welfare of individual human beings inside another country met many obstacles, not least the conception and implications of Statehood in a State system. The human condition in other countries and the treatment of individuals by other Governments were not commonly known abroad since they were not included in the information sources of the time. Information (and concern) were filtered through the State system and through diplomatic sources, and human values as such were not the business of diplomacy. For those reasons, and for other reasons flowing from the State system, other States took little note and expressed little concern for what a Government did to its own citizens. In general, the veil of Statehood was impermeable. If occasionally something particularly horrendous happened — a massacre, pogrom — and was communicated and made known by the available media of communication, it evoked from other States more-or-less polite diplomatic expressions of regret, not on grounds of law but of *noblesse oblige* or of common princely morality wrapped in Christian charity (whose violation gave princes and Christianity a bad name).

Even if the implications of Statehood had not been an obstacle, as regards any but the grossest violations of what we now call human rights, few if any States had moral sensitivity and moral standing to intercede. When a State invoked an international standard of justice on behalf of one of its nationals abroad, it may have been invoking a standard unknown and unheeded at home. Few States had constitutional protections and not many had effective legislative or common-law protections for individual rights. Torture and police brutality, denials of due process, arbitrary detention, perversions of law, were not wildly abnormal. Surely, few States recognized political freedom — freedom of speech, association and assembly, universal suffrage. Many States denied religious freedom to some, and few States granted complete religious toleration; full equality to members of other than the dominant religion was slow in coming anywhere. Women were subject to rampant and deep-rooted inequalities and domination, often to abuse and oppression. Even today such violations are not the stuff of dramatic television programmes and do not arouse international revulsion and reaction; in earlier times, surely, violations of what are today recognized as civil and political rights caused little stir outside the country. A State's failure to provide for the economic and social welfare of its inhabitants was wholly beyond the ken of other States. There were no alert media of information and few civil rights or other non-governmental organizations to sensitize and activate people and Governments.

. . .

QUESTION

Henkin sharply separates the prior era from the modern human rights regime. In particular, he emphasizes 'political–economic (rather than humanitarian) motivations' for early norms and antecedents of modern human rights law. Is his assessment correct or does he excessively depreciate the degree to which humanitarian values might have influenced the observed state practices? To what degree do 'political–economic (rather than humanitarian) motivations' characterize state promotion of international human rights law in the modern era?

E. BIRTH OF THE REGIME: THE UN CHARTER AND THE UDHR

The Nuremberg trial and several provisions of the United Nations Charter of 1945 held centre stage in the incipient human rights regime until 1948, when the UN General Assembly approved the Universal Declaration of Human Rights. For 28 years, the UDHR occupied centre stage. The two fundamental human rights treaties, the International Covenant on Civil and Political Rights and the International Covenant on Economic, Social and Cultural Rights, both became effective in 1976. (Note: only these two human rights treaties bear the solemn title of 'Covenant'.)

Together with the Declaration, the Covenants form the International Bill of Human Rights, which now stands at the core of the *universal* human rights system — universal in the sense that membership is open to states from all parts of the world. Chapter 11 examines three regional human rights systems, each open to members only from the designated part of the world: the European Convention for the Protection of Human Rights and Fundamental Freedoms (known as the 'European Convention on Human Rights'), the American Convention on Human Rights and the African Charter on Human and Peoples' Rights. Each of these treaties is supported and developed (in different ways) by an intergovernmental body that in most cases is created by the treaty itself. The central institutional participants in the human rights regime also include other intergovernmental bodies such as the International Labour Organization, national governments and human rights agencies, nongovernmental human rights organizations, and a range of nongovernmental (and often international) organizations such as labour unions and churches.

This section focuses on the Charter and Declaration, while the next two chapters examine respectively civil and political rights, and economic and social rights. The Declaration itself includes both categories. These categories are far from airtight. Many treaties declare rights that straddle the two, or that fall clearly within the domains of both of them. Many rights are hard to categorize. Nonetheless, at their core, the conventional distinctions are clear, whatever the relationships and interdependency between the two. Freedom from torture, equal protection, due process and the right to form political associations fall within the first category; the right to health or food or education come within the second.

COMMENT ON THE CHARTER, UDHR AND ORIGINS OF THE HUMAN RIGHTS REGIME

The human rights regime is not simply a systematic ordering, basically through treaties and customary law, of fundamental postulates, ideologies and norms (that is, 'oughts' in the form of rules, standards, principles). To the contrary, these basic elements are imbedded in institutions, some of them state and some international, some governmental or intergovernmental and some nongovernmental and in related international processes. It is impossible to grasp this regime adequately without an appreciation of its close relation to and reliance on international organizations. For example, the basic instruments of the universal system were drafted within the different organs of the United Nations and adopted by its General Assembly, before (in the case of the treaties) being submitted to states for ratification. UN organs play a major role in monitoring, officially commenting on, and applying sanctions to state behaviour.

The United Nations Charter itself first gave formal and authoritative expression to the human rights regime that began at the end of the Second World War. Since its birth in 1945, the UN has served as a vital institutional spur to the development of the regime, as well as serving as a major forum for many-sided debates about it. The purpose of the present comments is to call attention to aspects of the UN and its Charter that bear particularly on the human rights regime.

Readers should now become familiar with the provisions (in the Documents Supplement) of the Charter that are referred to below, and of the UDHR.

Charter Provisions

Consider first the Charter's radical transformation of the branch of the laws of war concerning *jus ad bellum*. Recall that for several centuries that body of law had addressed almost exclusively *jus in bello*, the rules regulating the conduct of warfare rather than the justice or legality of the waging of war. The International Military Tribunal at Nuremberg was empowered to adjudicate 'crimes against peace', part of *jus ad bellum* and the most disputed element of that Tribunal's mandate.

The Charter builds on the precedents to which the Nuremberg Judgment refers and states the UN's basic purpose of securing and maintaining peace. It does so by providing in Article 2(4) that UN members 'shall refrain in their international relations from the threat or use of force against the territorial integrity or political independence of any state', a rule qualified by Article 51's provision that nothing in the Charter 'shall impair the inherent right of individual or collective self-defence if an armed attack occurs' against a member.

The Charter's references to human rights are scattered, terse, even cryptic. The term 'human rights' appears infrequently. Note its occurrence in the following provisions: second paragraph of the Preamble, Article 1(3), Article 13(1)(b), Articles 55 and 56, Article 62(2) and Article 68.

Several striking characteristics of these provisions emerge. Many have a promotional or programmatic character, for they refer principally to the purposes or goals of the UN or to the competences of different UN organs: 'encouraging respect for human rights', 'assisting in the realization of human rights', 'promote . . . universal respect for, and observance of, human rights'. Not even a provision such as Article 56, which refers to action of the member states rather than of the UN, contains the language of obligation. It notes only that states 'pledge themselves' to action 'for the achievement' of purposes including the promotion of observance of human rights. Note that only one substantive human right, the right to equal protection, receives specific mention in the Charter (Arts. 1(3), 13(1)(b) and 55).

The Universal Declaration

Despite proposals to the contrary, the Charter stopped shy of incorporating a bill of rights. Instead, there were proposals for developing one through the work of a special commission that would give separate attention to the issue. That commission was contemplated by Charter Article 68, which provides that one of the UN organs, the Economic and Social Council (ECOSOC), 'shall set up commissions in economic and social fields and for the promotion of human rights'. In 1946, ECOSOC established the Commission on Human Rights (referred to in this book as the UN Commission), which evolved over the decades to become the world's single most important (and perhaps most disputed) human rights organ. At its inception, the new Commission was charged primarily with submitting reports and proposals on an international bill of rights. (The UN Commission was displaced by a newly created Human Rights Council in 2006. Chapter 9 examines the work of both the Commission and Council.)

The UN Commission first met in its present form early in 1947, its individual members (representatives of the states that were members of the Commission) including such distinguished founders of the human rights movement as René Cassin of France, Charles Malik of the Lebanon and Eleanor Roosevelt of the United States. Some representatives urged that the draft bill of rights under preparation should take the form of a declaration — that is, a recommendation by the General Assembly to Member States (see Charter Art. 13) that would exert a moral and political influence on states rather than constitute a legally binding instrument. Other representatives urged the Commission to prepare a draft convention containing a bill of rights that would, after adoption by the General Assembly, be submitted to states for their ratification.

The first path was followed. In 1948, the UN Commission adopted a draft Declaration, which in turn was adopted by the General Assembly that year as the Universal Declaration of Human Rights, with 48 states voting in favour and eight abstaining — Saudi Arabia, South Africa and the Soviet Union together with four East European states and a Soviet republic whose votes it controlled. (It is something of a jolt to realize today, in a decolonized and fragmented world of over 190 states, that UN membership in 1948 stood at 56 states.)

The Universal Declaration was meant to precede more detailed and comprehensive provisions in a single convention that would be approved by the General Assembly and submitted to states for ratification. After all, within the prevailing concepts of human rights at that time, the UDHR seemed to cover most of the field, including economic and social rights (see Arts. 22–26) as well as civil and political rights. But during the years of drafting — years in which the Cold War took harsher and more rigid form, and in which the United States strongly qualified the nature of its commitment to the universal human rights regime — these matters became more contentious. The human rights regime was buffeted by ideological conflict and the formal differences of approach in a polarized world. One consequence was the decision in 1952 to build on the UDHR by dividing its provisions between two treaties, one on civil and political rights, the other on economic, social and cultural rights.

The plan to use the Universal Declaration as a springboard to treaties triumphed, but not as quickly as anticipated. The two principal treaties — the ICCPR and the International Covenant on Economic, Social and Cultural Rights (ICESCR) — made their ways through the drafting and amendment processes in the Commission, the Third Committee and the General Assembly, where they were approved only in 1966. Another decade passed before the two Covenants achieved in 1976 the number of ratifications necessary to enter into force.

During the 28 years between 1948 and 1976, a number of specialized human rights treaties such as the Genocide Convention entered into force. But not until the two principal Covenants became effective did a treaty achieve as broad coverage of human rights topics as the Universal Declaration. It was partly for this reason that the UDHR became so broadly known and frequently invoked. During these intervening years, it was the only broad-based human rights instrument available. To this day, it:

> has retained its place of honor in the human rights movement. No other document has so caught the historical moment, achieved the same moral and rhetorical force, or exerted as much influence on the movement as a whole.... [T]he Declaration expressed in lean, eloquent language the hopes and idealism of a world released from the grip of World War II. However self-evident it may appear today, the Declaration bore a more radical message than many of its framers perhaps recognized. It proceeded to work its subversive path though many rooted doctrines of international law, forever changing the discourse of international relations on issues vital to human decency and peace.[7]

As a declaration voted in the General Assembly, the UDHR lacked the formal authority of a treaty that binds its parties under international law. Nonetheless, it remains in some sense the constitution of the entire regime, as well as the single most cited human rights instrument.

[7] H. Steiner, 'Securing Human Rights: The First Half-Century of the Universal Declaration, and Beyond', Harvard Magazine, Sept.–Oct. 1998, p. 45.

Other UN Organs Related to Human Rights

Together with the UN Commission, other UN organs have played major roles in developing universal human rights. Their full significance with respect to drafting and approving treaties or declarations, monitoring, censuring, and authorizing or ordering state action becomes apparent in later chapters. A brief description follows.

Chapter IV of the Charter sets forth the composition and powers of the General Assembly. Those powers are described in Articles 10–14 in terms such as 'initiate studies', 'recommend', 'promote', 'encourage' and 'discuss'. Particularly relevant are Articles 10 and 13. Article 10 authorizes the General Assembly to 'discuss any questions or any matters within the scope of the present Charter [and] ... make recommendations to the Members of the United Nations ... on any such questions or matters'. Article 13 authorizes the GA to 'make recommendations' for the purpose of, *inter alia*, 'assisting in the realization of human rights'. Throughout its history, the GA has been active in voting resolutions related to human rights issues.

Contrast the stronger and more closely defined powers of the Security Council under Chapter VII. Those powers range from making recommendations to states parties about ending a dispute, to the power to authorize and take military action 'to maintain or restore international peace and security' (Art. 42) after the Council 'determine[s] the existence of any threat to the peace, breach of the peace, or act of aggression' (Art. 39). Under Article 25, member states 'agree to accept and carry out' the Security Council's 'decisions' on these and other matters. No such formal obligation of states attaches to recommendations or resolutions of the General Assembly. As Chapter 9 indicates, the Security Council has in recent years used its powers to address situations involving major human rights violations.

Two of the seven Main Committees of the General Assembly — committees of the whole, for all UN members are entitled to be represented on them — have also participated in the drafting or other processes affecting human rights. The Social, Humanitarian and Cultural Committee (Third Committee) and the Legal Committee (Sixth Committee) have reviewed drafts of proposed declarations or conventions and often added their comments to the document submitted to the plenary General Assembly for its ultimate approval.

Historical Sequence and Typology of Instruments

That part of the universal human rights regime consisting of intergovernmental instruments — that is, excluding for present purposes both national laws and nongovernmental institutions forming part of the regime — can be imagined as a four-tiered normative edifice, the tiers described generally in the order of their chronological appearance.

(1) The UN Charter, at the pinnacle of the human rights system, has relatively little to say about the subject. But what it does say has been accorded great significance. Through interpretation and extrapolation, as well as frequent invocation, the sparse text has constituted a point of departure for inventive development of the entire regime.

(2) The UDHR, viewed by some as a further elaboration of the brief references to human rights in the Charter, occupies in important ways the primary position of constitution of the entire regime. Today many understand the UDHR — or more specifically, numbers of its provisions — to have gained formal legal force by becoming a part of customary international law.

(3) The two principal covenants, which alone among the universal treaties have broad coverage of human rights topics, develop in more detail the basic categories of rights that figure in the Universal Declaration, and include additional rights as well

(4) A host of multilateral human rights treaties (usually termed 'conventions', for there are only the two basic 'covenants'), as well as resolutions or declarations with a more limited or focused subject than the comprehensive International Bill of Rights, have grown out of the United Nations (drafting by UN organs, approval by the General Assembly) and (in the case of treaties) have been ratified by large numbers of states. They develop further the content of rights that are more tersely described in the two covenants or, in some cases, that escape mention in them. This fourth tier consists of a network of treaties, most but not all of which became effective after the two Covenants, including: the Convention on the Prevention and Punishment of the Crime of Genocide (142 states parties as of May 2012), the International Convention on the Elimination of all Forms of Racial Discrimination (175 parties), the Convention on the Elimination of all Forms of Discrimination against Women (187 parties), the Convention against Torture and other Cruel, Inhuman or Degrading Treatment or Punishment (147 parties), and the Convention on the Rights of the Child (193 parties). This book discusses to one or another degree most of these instruments.

QUESTION

Compare the premises to and character and provisions of the UDHR with the prior illustrations in Chapter 2 of certain premises and doctrines in international law that constitute 'background' to the postwar human rights regime. In what respects (putting aside its legal character as a declaration rather than a treaty) does the UDHR stand out as strikingly different, as resting on premises that were not simply alien to but close to heresies within the preceding international law?

NOTE

Consider the following observations in Louis Henkin, *International Law: Politics, Values and Functions*, 216 Collected Courses of The Hague Academy of International Law (Vol. IV, 1989), at 215:

> The United Nations Charter, a vehicle of radical political-legal change in several respects, did not claim authority for the new human rights commitment it

> projected other than in the present consent of States. Unlike the international standard of justice for foreign nationals, which derived from the age of natural law and clearly reflected common acceptance of some natural rights, the Charter is a 'positivist' instrument. It does not invoke natural rights or any other philosophical basis for human rights. (The principal Powers could not have agreed on any such basis.) The Charter Preamble links human rights with human dignity but treats that value as self-evident, without need for justification. Nor does the Charter define either term or give other guidance as to the human rights that human dignity requires. In fact, to help justify the radical penetration of the State monolith, the Charter in effect justifies human rights as a State value by linking it to peace and security.
>
> Perhaps because we now wish to, we tend to exaggerate what the Charter did for human rights. The Charter made the promotion of human rights a purpose of the United Nations; perhaps without full appreciation of the extent of the penetration of Statehood that was involved, it thereby recognized and established that relations between a State and its own inhabitants were a matter of international concern. But the Charter did not erode State autonomy and the requirement of State consent to new human rights law....
>
> ...
>
> In 1945, the principal Powers were not prepared to derogate from the established character of the international system by establishing law and legal obligation that would penetrate Statehood in that radical way; clearly, they themselves were not ready to submit to such law....

NOTE

From the start, the human rights regime had universal aspirations. It was not to address only the developed countries of the West/North but rather all regions and all states, whatever their form of government, socio-economic situation or religious–cultural traditions. After all, the key document at the very start of the regime was entitled the *Universal* Declaration of Human Rights. Its language, like that of many later human rights treaties, speaks abstractly of 'everyone', or 'no person'. It communicates no sense of differentiation among its subjects based on religion, gender, colour, ethnicity, national origin, wealth, region, education. To the contrary, the human rights texts fasten on equal protection as a cardinal concept.

Over the decades, the question of how 'universal' the postwar human rights are or should seek to become has assumed greater prominence. The 'universal' is often contrasted with the 'particular' or 'culturally specific', or 'cultural relativism'. The different meanings of these concepts and illustrations of their significance for a number of human rights topics figure as a central theme in Chapters 6 and 7. As a preface to those chapters, and as companion to this section's introduction to the UDHR, the excerpts below from Mary Ann Glendon's book on the making of the Declaration comment on the question of its universality and on the political and ethical traditions that inform it.

MARY ANN GLENDON, A WORLD MADE NEW (2001), at 221

Chapter 12: Universality under Siege

The problem of what universality might mean in a multicultural world haunted the United Nations human rights project from the beginning.... Earlier [in 1947] some of the world's best-known philosophers had been asked to ponder the question, "How is an agreement conceivable among men who come from the four corners of the earth and who belong not only to different cultures and civilizations, but to different spiritual families and antagonistic schools of thought?"

No one has yet improved on the answer of the UNESCO philosophers: Where basic human values are concerned, cultural diversity has been exaggerated. The group found, after consulting with Confucian, Hindu, Muslim and European thinkers, that a core of fundamental principles was widely shared in countries that had not yet adopted rights instruments and in cultures that had not embraced the language of rights. Their survey persuaded them that basic human rights rest on "common convictions," even though those convictions "are stated in terms of different philosophic principles and on the background of divergent political and economic systems?"....

...

The hopeful view of the UNESCO philosophers was challenged when a host of new nations appeared on the international stage in the 1950s. With sixteen new members joining the United Nations in 1955 alone and with many Latin American countries retreating from their pro-US positions, the balance of power in the General Assembly had shifted....

Over the years that mood was expressed in characterizations of the Declaration as an instrument of neocolonialism and in attacks on its universality in the name of cultural integrity, self-determination of peoples, or national sovereignty. In some cases the motivations are transparently self-serving. When leaders of authoritarian governments claim that the Declaration is aimed at imposing "foreign" values, their real concern is often domestic: the pressure for freedom building among their own citizens. That might have been the case, for example, when the Iranian representative at a ceremony commemorating the Declaration's fiftieth anniversary in 1998 charged that the document embodies a "Judeo-Christian" understanding of rights, unacceptable to Muslims. Or on the occasions when Singapore's Lee Kuan Yew attempted to justify the suppression of human rights in the name of economic development or national security.

... [M]any challenges to the Declaration's universality are made by individuals who are genuinely concerned about ideological imperialism.... University of Buffalo law professor Makau Mutua described the Declaration as an arrogant attempt to universalize a particular set of ideas and to impose them upon three-quarters of the world's population, most of whom were not represented at its creation. Kenya-born Mutua said, "Muslims, Hindus, Africans, non-Judeo-Christians, feminists, critical theorists, and other scholars of an inquiring bent of mind have exposed the Declaration's bias and exclusivity."

These accusations of cultural relativism and cultural imperialism need to be taken seriously. *Is* the Declaration a "Western" document in some meaningful sense, despite its aspiration to be universal? *Are* all rights relative to time and place? *Is* universality a cover for cultural imperialism? Let us examine the charges on their merits.

Those who label the Declaration "Western" base their claim mainly on two facts: 1) many peoples living in non-Western nations or under colonial rule, especially those in sub-Saharan Africa, were not represented in the United Nations in 1948; and 2) most of the Declaration's rights first appeared in the European and North or South American documents on which John Humphrey based the original draft. Those statements are accurate, but do they destroy the universality of the Declaration?

... It is true that much of the world's population was not represented in the UN in 1948: large parts of Africa and some Asian countries remained under colonial rule; and the defeated Axis powers — Japan, Germany, Italy, and their allies — were excluded as well. But Chang, Malik, Romulo, Mehta, and Santa Cruz were among the most influential, active, and independent members of the Human Rights Commission. And the members of the third committee, who discussed every line of the draft over two months in the fall of 1948, represented a wide variety of cultures.

... Before the whole two-year process from drafting and deliberation to adoption reached its end, literally hundreds of individuals from diverse backgrounds had participated. Thus Malik could fairly say, "The genesis of each article, and each part of each article, was a dynamic process in which many minds, interests, backgrounds, legal systems and ideological persuasions played their respective determining roles."

Proponents of the cultural-imperialism critique sometimes say that the educational backgrounds or professional experiences of men like Chang and Malik "westernized" them, but their performance in the Human Rights Commission suggests something rather different....

...

... On December 10, 1948, Brazil's Belarmino de Athayde summed up sentiments that had been expressed by many other third committee members when he told the General Assembly that the Declaration did not reflect the particular point of view of any one people or group of peoples or any particular political or philosophical system. The fact that it was the product of cooperation among so many nations, he said, gave it great moral authority.

...

The Declaration ... was far more influenced by the modern dignitarian rights tradition of continental Europe and Latin America than by the more individualistic documents of Anglo-American lineage. The fact is that the rights dialect that prevails in the Anglo-American orbit would have found little resonance in Asia or Africa. It implicitly confers its highest priority on individual freedom and typically formulates rights without explicit mention of their limits or their relation to other rights or to responsibilities. The predominant image of the rights bearer, heavily influenced by Hobbes, Locke, and John Stuart Mill, is that of a self-determining, self-sufficient individual.

Dignitarian rights instruments, with their emphasis on the family and their greater attention to duties, are more compatible with Asian and African traditions. In these documents, rights bearers tend to be envisioned within families and communities; rights are formulated so as to make clear their limits and their relation to one another as well as to the responsibilities that belong to citizens and the state ...

In the spirit of the latter vision, the Declaration's "Everyone" is an individual who is constituted, in important ways, by and through relationships with others. "Everyone" is envisioned as uniquely valuable in himself (there are three separate references to the free development of one's personality), but "Everyone" is expected to act toward others "in a spirit of brotherhood." "Everyone" is depicted as situated in a variety of specifically named, real-life relationships of mutual dependency: families, communities, religious groups, workplaces, associations, societies, cultures, nations, and an emerging international order. Though its main body is devoted to basic individual freedoms, the Declaration begins with an exhortation to act in "a spirit of brotherhood" and ends with community, order, and society.

Whatever else may be said of him or her, the Declaration's "Everyone" is not a lone bearer of rights.... [The] departure from classical individualism while rejecting collectivism is the hallmark of dignitarian rights instruments such as the Declaration.

In the years since its adoption, the Declaration's aspiration to universality has been reinforced by endorsements from most of the nations that were not present at its creation. Specific references to the Declaration were made in the immediate post-independence constitutions of [the author names 19 African and Asian states]....

... All in all, it has been estimated that the Declaration has inspired or served as a model for the rights provisions of some ninety constitutions.... And in 1993,... representatives of 171 countries at the Vienna Conference on Human Rights affirmed by consensus their "commitment to the purposes and principles contained in the Charter of the United Nations and the Universal Declaration of Human Rights."

...

It would be unwise, however, to minimize the danger of human rights imperialism. Today governments and interest groups increasingly deploy the language of human rights in the service of their own political, economic, or military ends. One of the twentieth century's most distinguished diplomats, George F. Kennan, expressed his misgivings about the United States' statements and demands concerning human rights in a 1993 memoir. He sensed in them, he said, "an implied assumption of superior understanding and superior virtue."

...

... Much confusion has been created in current debates by two assumptions that would have been foreign to the framers of the Declaration. Today both critics and supporters of universal rights tend to take for granted that the Declaration mandates a single approved model of human rights for the entire world. Both also tend to assume that the only alternative would be to accept that all rights are relative to the circumstances of time and place.

Nothing could be further from the views of the principal framers. They never envisioned that the document's "common standard of achievement" would or should produce completely uniform practices....

The Declaration's architects expected that its fertile principles could be brought to life in a legitimate variety of ways. Their idea was that each local tradition would be enriched as it put the Declaration's principles into practice and that all countries would benefit from the resulting accumulation of experiences....

There is little doubt about how the principal framers of the Universal Declaration would have responded to the charge of "Western-ness." What was crucial for them — indeed, what made universal human rights possible — was the *similarity* among all human beings. Their starting point was the simple fact of the common humanity shared by every man, woman, and child on earth, a fact that, for them, put linguistic, racial, religious. and other differences into their proper perspective.

NOTE

Makau Mutua, to whose ideas Glendon refers in the preceding excerpts, takes a fundamentally different position about the origin and character of the UDHR — a position examined in the materials on cultural relativism in Chapters 6 and 7. He states:[8]

> ... Non-Western philosophies and traditions particularly on the nature of man and the purposes of political society were either unrepresented or marginalized during the early formulation of human rights.... There is no doubt that the current human rights corpus is well meaning. But that is beside the point.... International human rights fall within the historical continuum of the European colonial project in which whites pose as the saviors of a benighted and savage non-European world. The white human rights zealot joins the unbroken chain that connects her to the colonial administrator, the Bible-wielding missionary, and the merchant of free enterprise.... Thus human rights reject the cross-fertilization of cultures and instead seek the transformation of non-Western cultures by Western cultures.

QUESTIONS

1. As a principle of interpretation, in what direction (if any) would Glendon's understanding of the UDHR'S 'dignitarian' tradition point with respect to, say, (a) a question of freedom of speech as applied to hate speech, (b) a question of individual liberty in relation to the right of others to an adequate standard of living, (c) a question of equal protection in relation to a claim for gay marriage?

[8] M. Mutua, 'The Complexity of Universalism in Human Rights', in András Sajó (ed.), *Human Rights with Modesty* (2004), at 51.

2. From a textual examination of the UDHR (that is, independent of locating the UDHR in a larger historical and philosophical context) are you persuaded by Glendon's more community-oriented account of its rights-based prescriptions or by a more individualistic account?

3. Based on Glendon's argument in these excerpts, how do you react to her position that the UDHR was at its origin and is now properly understood as having universal validity?

NOTE

Understandings of the Universal Declaration have inevitably changed over time. Appreciation of earlier ideas at the start of the human rights regime illuminates its general evolution as well as suggests how perceptions of it and, more broadly, international law have developed over the 60 years. There follow some excerpts from an influential book by a preeminent scholar of international law of his generation, Hersch Lauterpacht. At the time of the book's publication, the Declaration was two years old and untested as to its character and significance.

H. LAUTERPACHT, INTERNATIONAL LAW AND HUMAN RIGHTS

(1950), at 61

Chapter 4: The Subjects of the Law of Nations, the Function of International Law, and the Rights of Man

...

What have been the reasons which have prompted the changes in the matter of subjects of international law, with regard both to international rights and to international duties? These causes have been numerous and manifold. They have included, with reference to the recognition of the individual as a subject of international rights, the acknowledgment of the worth of human personality as the ultimate unit of all law; the realisation of the dangers besetting international peace as the result of the denial of fundamental human rights; and the increased attention paid to those already substantial developments in international law in which, notwithstanding the traditional dogma, the individual is in fact treated as a subject of international rights. Similarly, in the sphere of international duties there has been an enhanced realisation of the fact that the direct subjection of the individual to the rule of international law is an essential condition of the strengthening of the ethical basis of international law and of its effectiveness in a period of history in which the destructive potentialities of science and the power of the machinery of the State threaten the very existence of civilised life.

Above all, with regard to both international rights and international duties the decisive factor has been the change in the character and the function of modern international law. The international law of the past was to a large extent of a formal character. It was concerned mainly with the delimitation of the jurisdiction of States.... In traditional international law the individual played an inconspicuous part because the international interests of the individual and his contacts across the frontier were rudimentary. This is no longer the case....

...

... [I]t is in relation to State sovereignty that the question of subjects of international law has assumed a special significance. Critics of the traditional theory have treated it as an emanation of the doctrine of sovereignty. In their view it is State sovereignty — absolute, petty, and overbearing — which rejects, as incompatible with the dignity of States, the idea of individuals as units of that international order which they have monopolised and thwarted in its growth. It is the sovereign State, with its claim to exclusive allegiance and its pretensions to exclusive usefulness that interposes itself as an impenetrable barrier between the individual and the greater society of all humanity....

...

... [T]he recognition of the individual, by dint of the acknowledgment of his fundamental rights and freedoms, as the ultimate subject of international law, is a challenge to the doctrine which in reserving that quality exclusively to the State tends to a personification of the State as a being distinct from the individuals who compose it, with all that such personification implies. That recognition brings to mind the fact that, in the international as in the municipal sphere, the collective good is conditioned by the good of the individual human beings who comprise the collectivity. It denies, by cogent implication, that the corporate entity of the State is of a higher order than its component parts....

... International law, which has excelled in punctilious insistence on the respect owed by one sovereign State to another, henceforth acknowledges the sovereignty of man. For fundamental human rights are rights superior to the law of the sovereign State.... [T]he recognition of inalienable human rights and the recognition of the individual as a subject of international law are synonymous. To that vital extent they both signify the recognition of a higher, fundamental law not only on the part of States but also, through international law, on the part of the organized international community itself. That fundamental law, as expressed in the acknowledgment of the ultimate reality and the independent status of the individual, constitutes both the moral limit and the justification of the a international legal order....

Chapter 5: The Idea of Natural Rights in Legal and Political Thought

...

... The law of nature and natural rights can never be a true substitute for the positive enactments of the law of the society of States. When so treated they are inefficacious, deceptive and, in the long run, a brake upon progress.... The law of nature, even when conceived as an expression of mere ethical postulates, is an inarticulate but powerful element in the interpretation of existing law. Even after human rights and freedoms have become part of the positive fundamental law of mankind, the ideas of natural law and natural rights which underlie them will constitute that higher law which must forever remain the ultimate standard of fitness of all positive law, whether national or international....

[Lauterpacht then turns to historical antecedents of 'the notion and the doctrine of natural, inalienable rights of man pre-existent to and higher than the positive law of the State'. He observes that 'ideas of the law of nature date back to antiquity', and briefly describes such ideas and notions of natural right in Greek philosophy and the Greek state, in Roman thought, in the Middle Ages and in the Reformation and the period of Social Contract. Lauterpacht then addresses 'fundamental rights in modern constitutions'.]

In the nineteenth and twentieth centuries the recognition of the fundamental rights of man in the constitutions of States became, in a paraphrase of Article 38 of the Statute of the Permanent Court of International Justice, a general principle of the constitutional law of civilised States. It became part of the law of nearly all European States....

... [T]here is one objection to the notion of natural rights which, far from invalidating the essential idea of natural rights, is nevertheless in a sense unanswerable. It is a criticism which reveals a close and, indeed, inescapable connexion between the idea of fundamental rights on the one hand and the law of nature and the law of nations on the other. That criticism is to the effect that, in the last resort, such rights are subject to the will of the State: that they may—and must—be regulated, modified, and if need be taken away by legislation and, possibly, by judicial interpretation; that, therefore, these rights are in essence a revocable part of the positive law of a sanctity and permanence no higher than the constitution of the State either as enacted or as interpreted by courts and by subsequent legislation....

...

Chapter 17: The Universal Declaration of Human Rights

The Universal Declaration of Human Rights ... has been hailed as an historic event of profound significance and as one of the greatest achievements of the United Nations.... Mrs. Roosevelt, Chairman of the Commission on Human Rights and the principal representative of the United States on the Third Committee, said: 'It [the Declaration] might well become the international Magna Carta of all mankind.... Its proclamation by the General Assembly would be of importance comparable to the 1789 proclamation of the Declaration of the Rights of Man, the proclamation of the rights of man in the Declaration of Independence of the United States of America, and similar declarations made in other countries'....

...

The practical unanimity of the Members of the United Nations in stressing the importance of the Declaration was accompanied by an equally general repudiation of the idea that the Declaration imposed upon them a legal obligation to respect the human rights and fundamental freedoms which it proclaimed. The debates in the General Assembly and in the Third Committee did not reveal any sense of uneasiness on account of the incongruity between the proclamation of the universal character of the human rights forming the subject matter of the Declaration and the rejection of the legal duty to give effect to them. The delegates gloried in the profound significance of the achievement whereby the nations of the world agree as to what are the obvious and inalienable rights of man ... but they declined to acknowledge them as part of the law binding upon their States and Governments....

... [T]he representative of the United States, in the same statement before the General Assembly in which she extolled the virtues of the Declaration, said: 'In giving our approval to the declaration today, it is of primary importance that we keep clearly in mind the basic character of the document. It is not a treaty; it is not an international agreement. It is not and does not purport to be a statement of law or of legal obligation....'

...

... It is now necessary to consider the view, expressed in various forms, that, somehow, the Declaration may have an indirect legal effect.

In the first instance, it may be said — and has been said — that although the Declaration in itself may not be a legal document involving legal obligations, it is of legal value inasmuch as it contains an authoritative interpretation of the 'human rights and fundamental freedoms' which do constitute an obligation, however imperfect, binding upon the Members of the United Nations. It is unlikely that any tribunal or other authority administering international law would accept a suggestion of that kind. To maintain that a document contains an authoritative interpretation of a legally binding instrument is to assert that that former document itself is as legally binding and as important as the instrument which it is supposed to interpret....

... [T]here would seem to be no substance in the view that the provisions of the Declaration may somehow be of importance for the interpretation of the Charter as a formulation, in this field, of the 'general principles of law recognized by civilised nations'. The Declaration does not purport to embody what civilized nations generally recognize as law.... The Declaration gives expression to what, in the fullness of time, ought to become principles of law generally recognized and acted upon by States Members of the United Nations....

...

Undoubtedly the Declaration will occasionally be invoked by private and official bodies, including the organs of the United Nations. But it will not — and cannot — properly be invoked as a source of legal obligation....

Not being a legal instrument, the Declaration would appear to be outside international law. Its provisions cannot form the subject matter of legal interpretation. There is little meaning in attempting to elucidate, by reference to accepted canons of construction and to preparatory work, the extent of an obligation which is binding only in the sphere of conscience....

The fact that the Universal Declaration of Human Rights is not a legal instrument expressive of legally binding obligations is not in itself a measure of its importance. It is possible that, if divested of any pretence to legal authority, it may yet prove, by dint of a clear realisation of that very fact, a significant landmark in the evolution of a vital part of international law....

...

The moral authority and influence of an international pronouncement of this nature must be in direct proportion to the degree of the sacrifice of the sovereignty of States which it involves. Thus conceived, the fundamental issue in relation to the moral authority of the Declaration can be simply stated: That authority is a function of the degree to which States commit themselves to an effective recognition of these rights guaranteed by a will and an agency other than and superior to their own....

Its moral force cannot rest on the fact of its universality — or practical universality — as soon as it is realised that it has proved acceptable to all for the reason that it imposes obligations upon none....

... [C]ompare the Declaration of 1948 with that of [the French Declaration of] 1789 and similar constitutional pronouncements. These may not have been endowed, from the very inception, with all the remedies of judicial review and the formal apparatus of enforcement. But they became, from the outset, part of national law and an instrument of national action. They were not a mere philosophical pronouncement.... One of the governing principles of the Declaration — a principle which was repeatedly affirmed and which is a juridical heresy — is that it should proclaim rights of individuals while scrupulously refraining from laying down the duties of States. To do otherwise, it was asserted, would constitute the Declaration a legal instrument. But there are, in these matters, no rights of the individual except as a counterpart and a product of the duties of the State. There are no rights unless accompanied by remedies. That correlation is not only an inescapable principle of juridical logic. Its absence connotes a fundamental and decisive ethical flaw in the structure and conception of the Declaration.

...

QUESTION

Looked at from today's perspective, which of Lauterpacht's ideas or predictions about the UDHR and human rights would require substantial revision?

ADDITIONAL READING

J. Morsink, *The Universal Declaration of Human Rights: Origins, Drafting, and Intent* (1999); G. Alfredsson & A. Eide, *The Universal Declaration of Human Rights: A Common Standard of Achievement* (1999); B. van der Heijden & B. Tahzib-Lie (eds.), *Reflections on the Universal Declaration of Human Rights: A Fiftieth Anniversary Anthology* (1998); Y. Danieli, E. Stamatopoulou & C. J. Dias (eds.), *Universal Declaration of Human Rights: 50 Years and Beyond* (1999); and M. A. Glendon, *A World Made New* (2001).

PART B

NORMATIVE FOUNDATION OF INTERNATIONAL HUMAN RIGHTS

3

Civil and Political Rights

This chapter introduces basic ideas and instruments of the *universal* human rights regime that concern civil and political rights; the next chapter addresses economic and social rights. It picks up where Chapter 2(E) ended, after the UN Charter entered into force and the General Assembly adopted the Universal Declaration of Human Rights (UDHR). The chapter has four sections:

Section A begins with an examination of one of the two principal UN treaties: the International Covenant on Civil and Political Rights (ICCPR) (167 states parties as of May 2012).

Section B then turns to the Convention on the Elimination of All Forms of Discrimination against Women (CEDAW) (187 states parties) a major treaty that took form several decades after work on drafting the ICCPR began, and that reveals different concerns, goals and strategies of the human rights regime. Comparison of the ICCPR and CEDAW offers insight into the evolution and changing character of civil and political rights and their implementation.

In Section C we focus on efforts designed to prohibit discrimination on the grounds of sexual orientation and to protect the rights of gay, lesbian, bisexual and transgender persons in order to illustrate the evolution of new norms within the international system.

Section D makes for a contrast with Section C by looking at threats posed in recent years, primarily in the context of counter-terrorism activities, to the long-established and seemingly well-entrenched norm against torture.

A. THE INTERNATIONAL COVENANT ON CIVIL AND POLITICAL RIGHTS: INTRODUCTION

COMMENT ON RELATIONSHIPS BETWEEN THE UNIVERSAL DECLARATION AND THE ICCPR

You should now become familiar with the substantive part (Arts. 1–27) of the International Covenant on Civil and Political Rights. The comparisons below between the UDHR and the ICCPR assume that familiarity. One basic similarity informs all of the following discussion; each instrument aspires to universality.

The UDHR was supported by the great majority of states of its time; the ICCPR now includes the great majority of the world's states. This section's examination of the ICCPR is brief; Chapter 9 examines the Covenant more intensively through the work of the treaty body that it creates, the Human Rights Committee.

(1) Under international law, approval by the General Assembly of a declaration like the UDHR has a different consequence from a treaty that has become effective through the required number of ratifications. Of course the declaration will have solemn effects as the formal act of a deliberative body of global importance. Its subject matter, like that of the UDHR, may be of the greatest significance. But when approved or adopted, it is hortatory and aspirational, recommendatory rather than, in a formal sense, binding.

The Covenant, on the other hand, binds the states parties in accordance with its terms and with international law, subject to such formal matters as reservations and the kinds of exceptional circumstances described in the Comment on Treaties, p. 113, *supra*. Of course this statement of international law doctrine and its basic postulate, *pacta sunt servanda*, does not end discussion. The content of important provisions of a treaty may long remain in dispute among the states parties. Differences over interpretation will likely arise; some states will disagree with others as to what even basic provisions of the Covenant (such as, in the case of the ICCPR, the 'right to life') mean and require. What indeed is the 'commitment'? Absent a consensus over meaning, which state party or international institution can provide an interpretation that most parties will view as authoritative and decisive? Even if there is a widespread consensus, one must confront the question of whether states will honour this 'binding' commitment and, if not, whether the UN or some member states will apply pressure against violators sufficient to persuade them to comply. Does or should the probability of enforcement against violators have any bearing on the legally binding character of an international agreement?

In the case of the UDHR, the years have further blurred the threshold contrast between 'binding' and 'hortatory' instruments. The countless references to and invocations of the Declaration as the fountainhead or constitution or grand statement of the human rights regime has affected how it is viewed — perhaps as shy of 'binding', but somehow relevant to norm formation and influential with respect to state behaviour as so-called 'soft law'(see p. 81, *supra*). Moreover, broadly supported arguments have developed for viewing all or parts of this Declaration as legally binding, either as a matter of customary international law or as an authoritative interpretation of the UN Charter.

(2) A resolution of the General Assembly (such as that approving the Universal Declaration) with the formal status of a recommendation will not generally seek to create an international institution with defined membership, structure and powers. Neither can customary international law. A treaty can and often does. The Charter creates numerous organs, some organically part of the UN and some distinct from but related to it. The ICCPR creates an ongoing institution, a so-called 'treaty body': the Human Rights Committee. That organ gives institutional support to the Covenant's norms, for the Covenant imposes on states parties formal obligations (such as the submission of periodic reports) to the Committee. This Committee is

charged with the performance of the tasks defined both in the Covenant and in its Optional Protocol (114 states parties as of May 2012).

(3) Both the UDHR and ICCPR are terse about their derivations or foundations in moral and political thought. Such statements as are made that have the character of foundational assumptions, justifications or explanations appear in the preambles (with a few exceptions such as Article 21 of the UDHR and Article 25 of the ICCPR). But clearly these instruments differ radically from, say, a tax treaty that expresses a compromise and temporary convergence of interests among its states parties. They speak to matters deep, lasting, purportedly universal. What then are the intuitions that shape them, their sources in intellectual history or moral or religious thought, the important guides to their interpretation and evolution?

(4) Many rights declared in the Covenant closely resemble the provisions of the Universal Declaration, although they are stated in considerably greater detail. Compare, for example, the requirements for criminal trials in Articles 10 and 11 of the Declaration with the analogous provisions in Articles 14 and 15 of the Covenant.

(5) *Individual* rights characterize these instruments. Group or collective rights — that is, rights that pertain to and are exercised by the collectivity as such, perhaps by vote but more likely through representatives — are rare. In a few cases, they are either asserted or hinted at in the Covenant, most directly in Articles 1 (on self-determination of peoples) and 27 (on survival of cultures). The Universal Declaration lacks such provisions. Both the UDHR and the ICCPR refer to the family as the 'natural and fundamental group unit of society'. On the other hand, it should be kept in mind that rights cast in terms of the individual, such as the right to equal protection or the right to practice one's religion or participate in associations, have an inherent group character, either in the sense that the identity at issue in denials of equal protection is a group identity (race, ethnicity, gender, religion) or in the sense that the right is generally practised in community with others (as suggested by ICCPR Art. 27).

(6) In both instruments the idea of *rights* dominates with respect to individuals. Duties characteristically attach to the state. Article 29(1) of the Declaration does provide that everyone 'has duties to the community in which alone the free and full development of his personality is possible'. The Covenant contains no article referring to individuals' *duties*, though its Preamble has such a clause.

(7) Article 17 of the Declaration on the 'right to own property' and protection against arbitrary deprivation thereof does not figure among the rights declared in the Covenant. Ideological disputes between East and West, and disputes between the West and the South over the nationalization of industries and other resources made agreement on a consensus formulation impossible.

(8) The UDHR goes little beyond the bare declaration of rights to provide (Art. 8) that everyone has the 'right to an effective remedy by the competent national tribunals' for violations of fundamental rights. The remedial structure of the ICCPR reaches much further. In Article 2, states parties agree to 'ensure' to all persons within their territory the rights recognized by the Covenant, and to adopt such legislative or other measures as may be necessary to achieve that goal. Moreover, the parties undertake to 'ensure' that any person whose rights are violated 'shall have an effective remedy', and that 'the competent authorities shall enforce such

remedies when granted'. They undertake in particular 'to develop the possibilities of judicial remedy'.

(9) Two types of provisions in the ICCPR limit states' obligations thereunder:

(a) Under closely stated conditions and limits, Article 4 dealing with a public emergency ('which threatens the life of the nation and the existence of which is officially proclaimed') permits a *derogation*, in the sense of a temporary adjustment to or suspension of the operation of some of the rights declared by the Covenant. Thus states may consciously, purposively depart from such rights as those in Article 9 relating to arrest and detention. Note that under Article 4(2) certain rights are non-derogable. This issue of derogation becomes a major concern in Chapter 5, which deals with national security issues.

(b) Several articles include *limitation clauses*—that is, provisions indicating that a given right is not absolute but may be adapted to take account of a state's need to protect public safety, order, health or morals, or national security. See, for example, Articles 18 and 19. In Articles 21 and 22, the limitation clause is phrased in terms of permitting those restrictions on a right 'which are necessary in a democratic society'. Compare the broad provision of Article 29(2) of the UDHR, which is not linked to a specific right. Note that the limitation clauses may overlap with but are not identical with the common problem of resolving conflicts between *rights* (such as rights to speech and to privacy, as accommodated in the law of defamation) that also may lead to a 'limitation', in this case of one right to give space to the other.

(10) Article 5 of the UDHR bans 'cruel, inhuman or degrading' punishment, but that instrument does not refer to capital punishment as such. See Article 6(2) of the ICCPR. The Second Optional Protocol to the ICCPR, aiming at abolition of the death penalty, had 74 states parties as of May 2012. Article 1 provides that 'No one within the jurisdiction of a State Party to the present Protocol shall be executed.... Each State Party shall take all necessary measures to abolish the death penalty within its jurisdiction'. Recall the discussion about measures affecting capital punishment at pp. 17–55, *supra*.

One can organize or classify the rights declared in the Declaration and Covenant in various ways, depending on the purpose of the typology. Consider the adequacy of the following scheme that embraces most of the Covenant's rights, although it excludes such distinctive provisions as ICCPR Article 1 on the self-determination of peoples and Article 27 on the enjoyment by minorities of their own cultures:

(a) Protection of the individual's physical integrity, as in provisions on torture, arbitrary arrest and arbitrary deprivation of life;
(b) procedural fairness when government deprives an individual of liberty, as in provisions on arrest, trial procedure and conditions of imprisonment;
(c) equal protection norms defined in racial, religious, gender and other terms;
(d) freedoms of belief, speech and association, such as provisions on political advocacy, the practice of religion, press freedom, and the right to hold an assembly and form associations; and
(e) the right to political participation.

These five categories of rights can be imagined as on a spectrum. At one extreme lie killing or torture over which there exists a broad formal-verbal consensus among states (whatever the degree of ongoing violation of the relevant rights by many states). At the other extreme lie rights whose purposes, basic meanings and even validity are formally disputed. For example, few if any states (even those that practise it) formally justify torture (see pp. 238–276, *infra*). A good number of states, however, may justify some form of religious or gender discrimination stemming from religious belief or customary practices, and argue that such practices should be viewed as consistent with the goals of the human rights regime — perhaps because (the argument goes) in such circumstances, equal protection rights should not be viewed as 'universal' so as to bind local cultures or practices or traditions that differ. Or states that reject the core practices of political democracy may justify different forms of political organization ranging from hereditary or elite (say, 'vanguard') leadership to a theocracy.

Among the intergovernmental organs or institutions referred to in this Comment, some such as the UN Human Rights Council are mandated by the UN Charter, others such as the Human Rights Committee by distinct treaties (in this case, the ICCPR). As a matter of convenience, the first set is often referred to as 'Charter-based' organs/institutions, and the second set as 'treaty-based' organs/institutions or 'treaty bodies' (i.e., treaties other than the Charter).

But the human rights treaties adopted since the Charter are distinct from it only up to a point. Thus the ICCPR and other human rights treaties noted above all grew within the UN, from the time that they were first drafted in an organ like the UN Commission on Human Rights (now the Human Rights Council) to their final approval by the General Assembly and submission to states for ratification. Typically for such treaties, the ICCPR provides for a number of ongoing links to the UN. Article 45 indicates that the Annual Report of the ICCPR Committee should be submitted to the General Assembly. Note also the provisions for amendment of the ICCPR in Article 51. Moreover, each of these separate treaty regimes like the ICCPR depends for funding on the regular biennial budget adopted by the General Assembly.

QUESTIONS

1. Relying only on the preambles and texts of the UDHR and the ICCPR, how would you identify the reasons for those instruments, their justifications in moral and political thought, the moral and political traditions from which they derive? Why do you suppose there was such a sparse statement of reasons or justifications in these instruments?

2. Do you see in either of these instruments any departure from 'universal' premises, rights and related obligations of states? That is, are there concessions in any provisions to different cultures or regions that would allow those cultures or regions to privilege their own practices and traditions rather than follow these instruments' rules — for example, by inflicting certain severe modes of criminal punishment, or governing by theocracy or inherited rule, or imposing restrictions on minority religions or on activities of women?

3. Article 2 of the ICCPR includes states' undertakings 'to respect and to ensure to all individuals' the recognized rights. States parties must 'ensure' that persons whose rights are violated have an 'effective remedy'. Competent authorities 'shall enforce such remedies when granted'.

(a) Is it accurate to say that rights are borne by individuals, and duties are borne only by states since the ICCPR is concerned only with state violations? Who may violate, say, your right to bodily security? Who may violate your right to political participation under Article 25, or your right to procedural due process under Article 14?

(b) Is it accurate to say that the duties of the state are entirely 'negative', in the sense of requiring no more than that the state generally keep its 'hands off' individuals, and refrains from certain conduct such as torture, discrimination, or repression of hostile (to it) political opinion? Is it accurate to say that fulfilment by the state of its duties would then be cost-free?

NOTE

Note the following observations about the progressive or immediate character of the state's obligations under the ICCPR, in Dominic McGoldrick, *The Human Rights Committee* (1991), at 12:

> There were marked differences of opinion during the drafting on the matter of the obligations that would be incurred by a State party to the ICCPR. Some representatives argued that the obligations under the ICCPR were absolute and immediate and that, therefore, a State could only become a party to the ICCPR after, or simultaneously with, its taking the necessary measures to secure those rights. If there were disparities between the Covenant and national law they could best be met by reservations....
>
> Against this view it was argued that the prior adoption of the necessary measures in domestic law was not required by international law....
>
> ...
>
> Proposals to provide that the necessary measures be taken within a specified time limit or within a reasonable time were rejected as was a suggestion that each State fix its own time limit in its instrument of ratification. The only clear intentions of the [UN Commission on Human Rights] that emerged were those of avoiding excessive delays in the full implementation of the Covenant and of not introducing the general notion of progressiveness that was a feature of the obligations under the then draft [International Covenant on Economic, Social and Cultural Rights].
>
> The objections to the draft article 2(2) were again voiced in the Third Committee but the provision remained unchanged. The Committee's report stated that:
>
>> It represented the minimum compromise formula, the need for which, particularly in new States building up their body of legislation, was manifest. The notion of implementation at the earliest possible moment was implicit in article 2 as a whole. Moreover, the reporting requirement in article 49 (later article 40) would indeed serve as an effective curb on undue delay.

NOTE

It is frequently stated that all rights declared in the ICCPR are 'equal and interdependent'. Within that formulation, the right of an indigent person to be assigned legal assistance in a criminal case in Article 14(3) (c) is of the same rank as and interdependent with the right not to be tortured in Article 7. The following readings explore this issue of equality or hierarchy, and implicitly the notion of interdependence and indivisibility of all rights (terms that have come to describe the entire corpus of international human rights in more recent official documents). Note how the answer may change with the purpose for which the question is asked. These readings are concerned primarily with derogation during emergencies.

ANTONIO CASSESE, A PLEA FOR A GLOBAL COMMUNITY GROUNDED IN THE CORE OF HUMAN RIGHTS

in Realizing Utopia: The Future of International Law (2012), 137, at 139

We should first of all draw a distinction between (i) a core of fundamental values which must be common to all nations, states, and individuals and may not, therefore, be derogated from and (ii) other values, the application of which may need to take into account national conditions. The fundamental values of the world society are those enshrined in that core of rules that constitute the international *jus cogens*, a set of peremptory norms that may not be derogated from.

[I]n the 1960s for the first time in world history the notion was accepted that there should be a hierarchy in the body of rules of the international community and that some principles or norms should be at the summit of the legal system. States could not transgress or derogate from these principles inter se. . . .

With this new development came a clear understanding that *jus cogens* rules included norms concerning human rights: those banning genocide, slavery, racial discrimination, and forcible denial of self-determination. Over the years national or international bodies have suggested that other international rules also enjoy the status of peremptory norms: the ban on torture, the prohibition of the slave trade, the right to life, the right of access to justice, the right of any person arrested or detained to be brought promptly before a judge (the so-called habeas corpus right), the ban on *refoulement* (refusal of entry of refugees at the frontier), the prohibition of collective penalties, and the principle of personal responsibility in criminal matters. I would also add the right to a fair trial. Other norms are likely gradually to rise to the level of *jus cogens* through a process of accretion. This normative process unfolds through judicial decisions (be they national or international), pronouncements by collective bodies such as the UN General Assembly, and declarations of states and other international legal subjects. The formation of a norm possessed with *jus cogens* force results from the convergence of a wide number of factors, all expressing in different forms and to varying degrees the legal view (the *opinio juris*) that the international rule at issue enshrines values so fundamental that no deviation from it is admissible.

> ... [P]eremptory norms...can be considered as those which have universal scope and bearing. They must be obeyed by all nations, states, and individuals of the planet. Other values, consecrated instead in international rules deprived of the nature of *jus cogens*, although still important, can be restrained in their incidence and scope by individual states, or adjusted to some extent to national conditions — as long as, however, such interpretation or adjustment does not appear to be absolutely arbitrary or unwarranted to other states or the relevant international bodies.
>
> The existence of two different sets of values and corresponding international norms can make allowance for the coexistence of a core of indispensable and absolute values and a set of other, less imperative values. The gradual expansion over time of the first group of norms might eventually lead in the future to the formation of a global community where all the basic norms on human rights must be equally respected by everyone in any part of the planet.
>
> ...

NOTE

Compare Cassese's observations with those in Theodor Meron, *On a Hierarchy of International Human Rights*, 80 Am. J. Int'l. L. 1 (1986), at 21:

> ...Hierarchical terms constitute a warning sign that the international community will not accept any breach of those rights. Historically, the notions of 'basic rights of the human person' and 'fundamental rights' have helped establish the *erga omnes* principle, which is so crucial to ensuring respect for human rights. Eventually, they may contribute to the crystallization of some rights, through custom or treaties, into hierarchically superior norms, as in the more developed national legal systems.
>
> Yet the balance of pros and cons does not necessarily weigh clearly on the side of the pros. Resort to hierarchical terms has not been matched by careful consideration of their legal significance. Few criteria for distinguishing between ordinary rights and higher rights have been agreed upon. There is no accepted system by which higher rights can be identified and their content determined. Nor are the consequences of the distinction between higher and ordinary rights clear. Rights not accorded quality labels, i.e., the majority of human rights, are relegated to inferior, second-class, status. Moreover, rather than grapple with the harder questions of rationalizing human rights lawmaking and distinguishing between rights and claims, some commentators are resorting increasingly to superior rights in the hope that no state will dare — politically, morally and perhaps even legally — to ignore them. In these ways, hierarchical terms contribute to the unnecessary mystification of human rights, rather than to their greater clarity.
>
> Caution should therefore be exercised in resorting to a hierarchical terminology. Too liberal an invocation of superior rights such as 'fundamental rights' and 'basic rights,' as well as *jus cogens*, may adversely affect the credibility of human rights as a legal discipline.

NOTE

The issue arose in the 1990s of a state party's right to withdraw from the ICCPR, which unlike many treaties has no provision about termination of obligations. The Human Rights Committee issued its General Comment 26 (1997) on this question. Excerpts follow:

> 1. … [T]he possibility of termination, denunciation or withdrawal must be considered in the light of applicable rules of customary international law which are reflected in the Vienna Convention on the Law of Treaties….
>
> …
>
> 3. … [I]t is clear that the Covenant is not the type of treaty which, by its nature, implies a right of denunciation. Together with the simultaneously prepared and adopted International Covenant on Economic, Social and Cultural Rights, the Covenant codifies in treaty form the universal human rights enshrined in the Universal Declaration of Human Rights, the three instruments together often being referred to as the 'International Bill of Human Rights'. As such, the Covenant does not have a temporary character typical of treaties where a right of denunciation is deemed to be admitted, notwithstanding the absence of a specific provision to that effect.
>
> 4. The rights enshrined in the Covenant belong to the people living in the territory of the State party. The Human Rights Committee has consistently taken the view…that once the people are accorded the protection of the rights under the Covenant, such protection devolves with territory and continues to belong to them, notwithstanding change in government of the State party, including dismemberment in more than one State or State succession….
>
> 5. The Committee is therefore firmly of the view that international law does not permit a State which has ratified or acceded or succeeded to the Covenant to denounce it or withdraw from it….

QUESTIONS

1. Cassese suggests dividing human rights into two categories, one of which would be 'fundamental and intransgressible' and the other of which would be flexible and contingent. What are the arguments for and against such a development?

2. Does the list of non-derogable rights in Article 4 of the ICCPR necessarily express some abstract, general hierarchy of rights in terms of their 'fundamental' importance or some similar criterion? How do you compare the rights there listed with others that are derogable? Can you suggest another purpose and criterion for deciding on a list of non-derogable rights in Article 4?

3. Suppose that you are a director of an international nongovernmental human rights organization working on one specific right, such as torture, or food. Would you feel obliged to accord significant attention to the overall framework of human rights, in recognition of their interdependence, or would you adopt a narrow and specific focus on the particular right in question?

ADDITIONAL READING

L. Henkin (ed.), *The International Bill of Rights: The Covenant on Civil and Political Rights* (1981); W. Kälin & J. Künzli, *The Law of International Human Rights Protection* (2009); A. Clapham, *Human Rights: A Very Short Introduction* (2007); C. Tomuschat, *Human Rights: Between Idealism and Realism* (2nd edn. 2008); P. Lauren, *The Evolution of International Human Rights* (1999); M. Nowak, *UN Covenant on Civil and Political Rights: ICCPR Commentary* (2nd edn. 2005); S. Joseph, J. Schultz & M. Castan, *The International Covenant on Civil and Political Rights: Cases, Materials, and Commentary* (2nd edn. 2004); M. Nowak, *Introduction to the International Human Rights Regime* (2003); E. de Wet & J. Vidmar (eds.), *Human Rights and Hierarchy in International Law* (2012).

B. WOMEN'S RIGHTS AND CEDAW

The study of women's rights illustrates the increasing ambition, breadth and complexity of the human rights regime. We see a proliferation of instruments and institutions, but also growing conflicts about premises and goals within the women's movement itself. The feminist literature relevant to human rights assumptions, goals and strategies has moved adventurously in many directions, sometimes polar directions; its engagement with the human rights regime has enriched and deepened thought about the entire project. The complexity and different currents of advocacy and criticism, idealism and scepticism, views of sexuality and gender, and indeed views of equality are captured in an innovative and ambitious treaty, CEDAW (187 states parties as of May 2012).

Of the several blind spots in the early development of the human rights regime, none is as striking as the failure to give to violations of women's (human) rights the attention, and in some respects the priority, that they require. It is not only that these problems adversely affect half of the world's population. They affect everyone, for a deep change in women's circumstances and possibilities produces change throughout social, economic and political life. Even in a field where the human rights regime acted with vigour in setting standards, passing resolutions and at times imposing sanctions — for example, racial discrimination — it is often the case that progress in many countries has been measured or slight, and that problems of the most serious character not only survive but remain entrenched. Nonetheless, it is instructive to contrast the vigour of the regime in trying to 'eliminate' racial discrimination with its relative apathy until the last 15 years or so in responding to gender discrimination — and to explore why this is so.

The materials in Section B suggest the complexly interwoven socio-economic, legal, political and cultural strands to the problem of women's subordination and to the content of women's rights. Although a systematic study of economic and social rights must await Chapter 4, Section B demonstrates in many ways the interrelationships and functional interdependence of civil and political rights (CPR) and economic and social rights (ESR). The title to CEDAW incorporates a classic CPR issue — discrimination — but the content of this convention's rights and the work of its

Committee range more broadly. Moreover, when one focuses specifically on what appear to be women's issues, links between them and other aspects of social order (disorder) appear pervasive. All is interrelated. The problem is truly systemic.

You should bear in mind that this is our *first* look at women's rights. Some parts of Chapters 6 and 7 return to this theme, but stress different issues, particularly the tension between universalism and cultural relativism in the understanding of those rights, and the imbedded traditions, practices, attitudes and religiously-based understandings about women that may be broadly accepted (and not only by men) in some parts of the world while abhorred and criticized as violations of rights in other parts.

1. BACKGROUND TO CEDAW: SOCIO-ECONOMIC CONTEXT, DISCRIMINATION AND ABUSE

These introductory materials present reports about the situation of women in different parts of the world. They suggest the complex relationships among diverse phenomena that bear on women's rights. Several themes recur in the readings.

(1) Legal norms capture and reinforce deep cultural norms and community practices. They entrench ideas and help give them the sense of being natural, part of the inevitable order of things.

(2) Reformers and advocates of deep legal and cultural transformation insist that change is possible, so that what was seen as natural or inevitable comes to be understood as socially constructed and thus contingent, open to change.

(3) Property rights and economic dependence interact with patterns of authority within family and workplace, and with vital issues like education, health, and political participation.

(4) Major economic and political programmes, like a development or privatization scheme or structural adjustment requirements or a stress on market deregulation and trade, may impose particular and severe costs on women that are not apparent on the face of the programmes.

(5) The statistics created by bureaucracies or scholars structure and confine the imagination. They are often viewed as objective data, without awareness of the disputable methods and categories that determine their formulation (see also p. 1225, *infra*). What they record as well as what they do not record influence policies as well as perceptions. New methods and categories in the statistical tables prepared by such institutions as the United Nations Development Program introduce new criteria to judge women's (and other groups') circumstances and progress.

The status of women within the international human rights regime and the task of ensuring human rights for women are incomprehensible without taking into account the social and economic conditions that characterize women's lives around the world. Much information appears in later materials in this section addressing issues such as violence against women.

Later readings underscore the degree to which rights abuses are strongly correlated to victims' slight social and economic power, hence political power. Those who are most vulnerable to human rights abuses often lack the favour or protection of the state, as well as the power within their communities to protect and further their basic needs and interests.

According to virtually every indicator of social well-being and status — political participation, legal capacity, access to economic resources and employment, wage differentials, levels of education and health care — women fare significantly and sometimes dramatically worse than men. In developing regions, 96 girls were enrolled in primary and in secondary school for every 100 boys in 2009. In 1999, the ratios were 91 and 88, respectively. The global share of women in non-agricultural paid employment increased from 35 per cent in 1990 to almost 40 per cent in 2009. In 2011, women held only 19.3 per cent of seats in single or lower houses of parliament worldwide, although this was a big improvement from 1995 when the figure was 11.6 per cent. In 48 countries in 2011 women made up less than 10 per cent of the members, and nine countries had no women parliamentarians at all.[1]

Contrary to the expectations that many hold, economic reform and development is not an automatic route to the relative advancement of women within society. Economic globalization and restructuring (such as efforts to radically reduce public spending) may in fact worsen their situation, at least during the transition. Like structural adjustment programmes associated with the International Monetary Fund, such market-oriented strategies may involve serious reductions of welfare, social-safety-net programmes that particularly affect women.

Analysis of gender issues has come increasingly to stress cultural context, and has led scholars to surprising statistical reflections of discriminatory practices. Consider an article by Amartya Sen, 'More than 100 Million Women are Missing' (*N.Y. Review of Books*, 20 Dec. 1990), examining low ratios of women to men (0.94 or lower) in populations in South and West Asia and China, despite the fact that boys worldwide outnumber girls at birth by about 105 to 100. Indeed, in Europe, the United States and Japan, despite ongoing forms of gender discrimination, women outnumber men. Why the difference in regions? Sen stresses forms of discrimination that are less common in the West:

> The fate of women is quite different in most of Asia and North Africa. In these places the failure to give women medical care similar to what men get and to provide them with comparable food and social services results in fewer women surviving than would be the case if they had equal care. In India, for example, except in the period immediately following birth, the death rate is higher for women than for men fairly consistently in all age groups until the late thirties. This relates to higher rates of disease from which women suffer, and ultimately to the relative neglect of females, especially in health care and medical attention. Similar neglect of women vis-à-vis men can be seen also in many other parts of the world. The result is a lower proportion of women than would be the case if they had equal care — in most of Asia and North Africa, and to a lesser extent Latin America.

[1] United Nations, The Millennium Development Goals Report 2011, at 20.

> This pattern is not uniform in all parts of the third world, however. Sub-Saharan Africa, for example, ravaged as it is by extreme poverty, hunger, and famine, has a substantial excess rather than deficit of women, the ratio of women to men being around 1.02. The 'third world' in this matter is not a useful category, because it is so diverse.
>
> ...
>
> To get an idea of the numbers of people involved in the different ratios of women to men, we can estimate the number of 'missing women' in a country, say, China or India, by calculating the number of extra women who would have been in China or India if these countries had the same ratio of women to men as obtain in areas of the world in which they receive similar care. If we could expect equal populations of the two sexes, the low ratio of 0.94 women, to men in South Asia, West Asia, and China would indicate a 6 percent deficit of women; but since, in countries where men and women receive similar care, the ratio is about 1.05, the real shortfall is about 11 percent. In China alone this amounts to 50 million 'missing women', taking 1.05 as the benchmark ratio. When that number is added to those in South Asia, West Asia, and North Africa, a great many more than 100 million women are 'missing'. These numbers tell us, quietly, a terrible story of inequality and neglect leading to the excess mortality of women.

Sen discounts two 'simplistic explanations' for this phenomenon: Western civilization is less sexist than Eastern, and unequal nutrition and health care are consequences of underdevelopment. Rather, he suggests we must examine 'the complex ways in which economic, social, and cultural factors can influence the regional differences'. He discusses decision-making within the family as the pursuit of cooperation 'in which solutions for the conflicting aspects of family life are implicitly agreed on'. Analysis of these 'cooperative conflicts' in different regions and cultures can 'provide a useful way of understanding the influences that affect the "deal" that women get in the division of benefits within the family'. Perceptions of who is doing 'productive' work or contributing to the family's welfare can be very influential, and such social perceptions are 'of pervasive importance in gender inequality', particularly 'in sustaining female deprivation in many of the poorer countries'.

Division of a family's joint benefits are apt to be more favourable to women if (1) they earn outside income, (2) their work is recognized as productive, (3) they own some economic resources or hold economic rights, and (4) there is an understanding of ways in which women are deprived. 'Considerable empirical evidence' suggests that gainful employment such as working outside the home for a wage as opposed to unpaid housework 'can substantially enhance the deal that women get'. Not only access to funds but also women's status and standing in the family improve. Moreover, women bring home experience of the outside world, a form of education. Such factors can 'counter the relative neglect of girls as they grow up', as women are seen as economic producers.

Sen discusses the different situation in China, where other explanatory factors may be important, such as the strong measures to control the size of families in the framework of a strong cultural preference for boys:

> To ascribe importance to the influence of gainful employment on women's prospects for survival may superficially look like another attempt at a simple

economic explanation, but it would be a mistake to see it this way. The deeper question is why such outside employment is more prevalent in, say, sub-Saharan Africa than in North Africa, or in Southeast and Eastern Asia than in Western and Southern Asia. Here the cultural, including religious, backgrounds of the respective regions are surely important. Economic causes for women's deprivation have to be integrated with other — social and cultural — factors to give depth to the explanation.

Of course, gainful employment is not the only factor affecting women's chances of survival. Women's education and their economic rights — including property rights — may be crucial variables as well....

Since Sen wrote, the figures have changed little. In 2012 the World Bank reported that 3.9 million women below the age of 60 still go 'missing' each year. 'About two-fifths of them are never born, one-fifth goes missing in infancy and childhood, and the remaining two-fifths do so between the ages of 15 and 59' (World Bank, p. 173, *infra*, at p. 14).

In the following readings we examine the first report made to the CEDAW Committee by Guatemala. Although over 20 years old, it provides an excellent illustration of many of the themes of this chapter. Next, we look at a World Bank assessment of the challenges of achieving gender equality and at Sandra Fredman's argument that the promotion of women's rights requires more than a non-discrimination approach.

INITIAL REPORT OF GUATEMALA SUBMITTED TO THE CEDAW COMMITTEE

CEDAW/C/Gua/1–2, 2 April 1991

[CEDAW requires in Article 18 that states parties submit periodic reports on 'measures which they have adopted to give effect' to CEDAW's provisions. Those reports 'may indicate factors and difficulties affecting the degree of fulfillment of obligations' under CEDAW. The reports are to be submitted to the Committee created by Article 17 of CEDAW. In its introduction to this report, Guatemala noted the difficulty of assembling it, stressing that 'studies of this type are only a recent innovation'. The task of preparation 'has also been a positive exercise in thought, analysis and self-appraisal with respect to the position of women in Guatemala in 1983, and the changes made to date'. That work stimulated action to design 'strategies and targets... to improve the situation encountered in the short and medium term'.

This Guatemalan report offers an unusually graphic and complete picture of the situation of women with family and society. The following excerpts are taken from the report's sections addressing Articles 5 and 16 of the Convention.]

Article 5

46. Guatemala is a multi-ethnic, multi-cultural and multilingual country with traditional, cultural patterns that reinforce the subordination of women on the

social, cultural, economic and political planes. Extended Guatemalan families in the country and nuclear families in the city are governed by a patriarchal system in which decisions are taken by men (husband, father or eldest son), who are considered the heads of the household, a role assumed by women only in their absence.

47. In Guatemalan society the man is expected to be the breadwinner, the legal representative, the repository of authority; the one who must 'correct' the children, while the mother is relegated to their care and upbringing, to household tasks, and to 'waiting on' or looking after her husband or partner. These roles often have to be performed in addition to engaging in some profitable activity which generates earnings that are always regarded as 'complementary'.

48. For their childhood, little boys and girls are guided towards work considered 'masculine' or 'feminine'; for example, boys play at working outside the home as carpenters, mechanics, farmers or pilots, and in all those jobs that are considered 'tough' or that require physical strength. Girls, on the other hand, are taught to interest themselves in cooking, weaving, sewing, washing, ironing, or cleaning the house and, especially, caring for the children and helping the mother, as a responsibility and duty more than just a game.

49. Care of the children is strictly considered the responsibility of the mother, grandmother, and/or sister; and in the event of divorce, separation or dissolution of the marriage, custody of the children is generally awarded to the mother.

50. The aforementioned patterns vary slightly with the socio-economic stratum, which generally also determines the social class to which the women belong and which in addition is related to their level of education and knowledge.

51. Notwithstanding what has been said, the woman is the chief social agent in the majority of spheres of action. An empirical profile of a Guatemalan woman may cover the following characteristics.

52. She is responsible for family health and hygiene and for the supervision of the formal and informal upbringing of the children in the home; she organizes and maintains living and sanitary conditions and a supply of water for domestic use. She produces nutritional supplements for the family, including animal proteins (cattle, sheep and goats) and sources of vitamins (fruit and vegetables); she is the one in charge of the purchase, preparation, stocking and distribution of food within the home. In addition, she manages the family income, ensuring that payment in kind and in cash is used in such a way as to maximize the material well-being of the family.

53. She takes responsibility for generating additional income or for producing consumer goods when her partner's income does not cover the minimum family requirements.

54. In the case of an irresponsible father, the entire responsibility for the support of the children devolves upon her, reflected in particular by a considerable increase in her hours of work.

55. Her work is poorly paid or not paid at all and is generally of low productivity owing to lack of access to capital.

56. It is falsely assumed that the man is the one who makes the principal economic contributions to the family, for which reason he is the owner and beneficiary of all payments and services.

57. The educational level of the woman is low, which reflects on the effectiveness of her efforts to maintain and improve the health, feeding, housing and other living conditions of her family.

58. In the paid work that she does, her salary is inferior to a man's and her instability in the sense of a job is greater.

59. The man has traditionally been considered the 'head of the household'.

Article 16

184. Family relations in Guatemala, as regards the guardianship, wardship, trusteeship and adoption of children, the ownership of property, its disposition and enjoyment, etc. are governed by the Guatemalan Civil Code (Decree-Law No. 106).

...

190. The woman's rights and responsibilities in marriage are as follows:

...

(2) The husband owes his wife protection and assistance, and must provide her with all the means necessary to maintain the household, in accordance with his financial resources. The woman has a special right and duty to nurture and care for her children during their minority, and to take charge of domestic affairs.

...

(5) The woman may be employed or ply a trade, occupation, public office or business, where she is able to do so without endangering the interests and the care of her children, or other needs of her household.

...

197. Married women are restricted in representing the marriage and in administration of marital assets, roles which are assigned by law to the husband, and this constitutes a relative incapacity.

198. Parental authority is a right which is virtually forbidden to women, since it is assigned to the father. Women only come to exercise this right when the father is imprisoned or legally barred from such.

...

201. The legal context allows the husband to object to the wife engaging in activities outside the home, thus barring her from the right and freedom to work. The legal context restricts her right to personal fulfillment in areas outside her function as mother and housewife and restricts her personal liberty.

...

203. A judicial declaration of paternity in cases of rape, rape of juveniles and abduction is dependent on the conduct of the mother, based on what the law terms 'notoriously disorderly conduct', an express form of discrimination against women and the product of conception resulting from forced intercourse.

...

209. Adultery defined as an 'offence against honour' protects the legal right of filiation and 'the interests of the family', but makes a clear distinction concerning the gravity of the act, depending on whether it involves the man or the woman, providing a tougher sentence for the woman; the proof and the procedure are different in the two cases, so that in practice it is only applied to women.

210. Offences 'against life' in which women are most affected are defined as abortion, which is defined as criminal conduct by which the death of the foetus is caused deliberately, within the mother's womb or by its premature expulsion. Medical abortion to avoid danger to the health or death of the mother, or due to deformities of the foetus, is not punishable. This is not envisaged when it is the result of rape.

211. With regard to the offence of rape, the punishment is graded according to the age of the victim and the relationship of authority which may exist between the victim and the offender. Reference is made to the 'honourable woman', requiring that the offender has used seduction, promise of marriage or deceit and the woman is a virgin; this emphasizes the value of 'honour', defining it as an offence against honour rather than against personal integrity, as would be correct.

212. Maltreatment of women and children and domestic violence are not defined as offences against the person and in practice are lumped together with injuries, coercion and threats, causing serious difficulties with regard to proof and other procedural problems.

...

WORLD BANK, WORLD DEVELOPMENT REPORT 2012, GENDER EQUALITY AND DEVELOPMENT

p. 3

Overview

...

Misallocating women's skills and talent comes at a high (and rising) economic cost

... When women's labor is underused or misallocated — because they face discrimination in markets or societal institutions that prevents them from completing their education, entering certain occupations, and earning the same incomes as men — economic losses are the result. When women farmers lack security of land tenure... the result is lower access to credit and inputs and to inefficient land use, reducing yields. Discrimination in credit markets and other gender inequalities in access to productive inputs also make it more difficult for female-headed firms to be as productive and profitable as male-headed ones. And, when women are excluded from management positions, managers are less skilled on average, reducing the pace of innovation and technology adoption.

The direct payoff to correcting these failures, many rooted in how markets and institutions function, is large: ensuring that women farmers have the same access as men to fertilizer and other agricultural inputs would increase maize yields by 11 to 16 percent in Malawi and by 17 percent in Ghana. Improving women's property rights in Burkina Faso would increase total household agricultural production by about 6 percent.... The Food and Agriculture Organization (FAO) estimates that equalizing access to productive resources between female and male farmers could increase agricultural output in developing countries by as much as 2.5 to 4 percent. Eliminating barriers that prevent women from working in certain occupations or sectors would have similar positive effects, reducing the productivity gap between male and female workers by one-third to one-half and increasing output per worker by 3 to 25 percent across a range of countries. But achieving these gains will not occur automatically as countries get richer: multiple and sometimes reinforcing barriers to gender equality can get in the way.

... [G]ender inequality has become more costly for most countries in a world of open trade. Gender inequality diminishes a country's ability to compete internationally — particularly if the country specializes in exporting goods and services for which men and women workers are equally well suited. Industries that rely more on female labor expand more in countries where women are more equal. The relationship also goes the other way: countries with an advantage in making products that rely more on women's labor also have become more gender equal. And in countries and regions with rapidly aging populations... encouraging women to enter and remain in the labor force can help dampen the adverse impact of shrinking working-age populations. So, in a globalized world, countries that reduce gender-based inequalities, especially in secondary and tertiary education and in economic participation, will have a clear advantage over those that delay action.

Women's endowments, agency, and opportunities shape those of the next generation

Greater control over household resources by women leads to more investment in children's human capital, with dynamic positive effects on economic growth.... [I]ncreasing the share of household income controlled by women, either through their own earnings or cash transfers, changes spending in ways that benefit children....

Improvements in women's own education and health also have positive impacts on these and other outcomes for their children. Better nutritional status of mothers has been associated with better child health and survival. And women's education has been positively linked to a range of health benefits for children — from higher immunization rates to better nutrition to lower child mortality....

Medical research from developed countries has established a link between exposure to domestic violence as a child and health problems as an adult — men and women who experienced violence in the home as children are two to three times more likely to suffer from cancer, a stroke, or cardiovascular problems, and five to ten times more likely to use alcohol or illegal drugs than those who did not. Numerous studies also document how experiencing violence between parents as a child is a risk factor for women experiencing violence from their own partners as adults, and for men perpetrating violence against their partners.

...

Chapter 7: Public Action for Gender Equality

...

Enhancing women's voice within households

The muted voice of women within their households reflects the combined influence of their access to economic opportunities, the nature of social norms, the legal framework, and the enforcement of laws. Some of the policies aimed at increasing women's economic opportunities have been discussed earlier, and this section focuses more on the laws that affect households (including their enforcement) as well as on the societal norms that impinge on households. Of the two, the laws and their enforcement are more directly amenable to public action, and that is the main focus here. Although such legislative change will not by itself shift social norms, experience shows that removing or amending discriminatory laws is an essential part of that process over time. And changes in law have to be accompanied by other interventions to make them effective.

Reconciling multiple legal systems

Before discussing specific laws, it is important that the overall system function well even where, as in many countries, multiple legal systems exist. Customary law and religious law are sometimes part of the formal state-sanctioned legal framework, and, even where these are not officially recognized, they continue to matter in determining women's capacity to access and control assets. So, where there is a constitutional nondiscrimination clause (as in the majority of constitutions in the world), the first step is to make sure that all sources of law are governed by it. Nondiscrimination needs to be the benchmark for the validity for all laws, particularly those determining the control of resources within households and families. For example, Kenya recently removed the exemption from nondiscrimination that the constitution had previously granted to customary family and inheritance law.

Ensuring that all laws conform to the nondiscrimination clause will also enhance the ability of citizens to challenge laws as unconstitutional. Such challenges, initiated by alliances of women's groups and other stakeholders, have overturned statutory laws favoring male heirs in Nepal and Tanzania. A key is ensuring that the legal system provides for constitutional challenges and also increases women's access to the justice system.

In reconciling multiple legal systems, customary law should not be ignored. It is the everyday reality for many men and women, so recognizing its impact and potential for change is both pragmatic and constructive. Customary law is more familiar and accessible. It uses mediation rather than an adversarial model. And it offers greater legitimacy particularly in fragile, postconflict countries where the formal system is nonexistent or decimated. In Botswana, where customary law and customary courts are formally recognized, women have become tribal chiefs, making decisions and breaking centuries of tradition. Removing gender biases in the customary system through sensitization, encouraging greater participation by women, and promoting the system's values, such as the protection of women, should thus be encouraged. And forging links between the informal and formal systems can help bring about greater parity throughout the legal system.

Control over household resources

While greater economic opportunities can provide a vehicle for increasing women's resources and their control over these resources, laws are a direct way to ensure more control. Modifying aspects of family law that govern marriage, divorce, and provisions of land laws that are discriminatory should be a priority.

Laws over property within marriage

The main inequities in this arena are those that concern the rights of husbands and wives to decide on the use and disposition of matrimonial property. Despite recent reforms, many such laws remain on the books of countries, particularly in Sub-Saharan Africa and the Middle East and North Africa. Fifteen of the 47 countries in Sub-Saharan Africa, for example, still have laws that give husbands greater control over marital assets. Laws that vest control over marital property in the hands of the husband also remain in force in Chile.

...

Making rights effective — Increasing women's access to justice

Besides improving the substance of the law, measures also need to be taken not only to empower women to demand that their rights are effective but also to make justice systems more responsive to women's needs. Actions in three areas are needed.

First, women need to be better represented within the organizations charged with formulating, implementing, and enforcing these laws, and the voices of female clients and stakeholders must be better reflected in the justice system....

...

Second, women's rights can be made more effective when various parts of the justice system are made sensitive to the specific needs of women or target women clients explicitly....

...

Third, data have to be collected and made public so that the problems of women's access to justice are made more visible....

Increasing voice in fertility decisions

The availability of family planning services remains a constraint in some parts of the world. In some cases, the underserved population covers entire countries, but more often the underserved live in specific geographic areas within countries — for example, availability is more likely to be a problem in rural than urban areas. In addition, certain subpopulations such as the poor may also face limited access. For these groups, improved delivery of family planning services is a priority.

Control over fertility decisions — the number and spacing of children — goes beyond the provision of reproductive health services, however. Thus, two additional areas of policy are critical to increase women's control over fertility. The first involves boosting women's ability to exert bargaining power within the household, allowing them to act on their preferences about the number of children the couple has, and over time to change the social norms that help determine these preferences. The second policy focus involves improving the quality of family planning services to excluded groups.

...

SANDRA FREDMAN, ENGENDERING SOCIO-ECONOMIC RIGHTS

Oxford Legal Research Paper Series, Paper No. 54/2010 June 2010, at http://ssrn.com/abstract=1631765

...

II The Gendered Nature of Women's Disadvantage

The fact that women are disproportionately represented amongst the world's poorest has been frequently underlined. In 1995... of the 1.3 billion people living in absolute poverty, 70 per cent were women. Ten years later, these figures had not changed. But it is not simply the fact that women are living in poverty that matters. What is of real importance is the gendered nature of that poverty.... [G]ender inequality specifically shapes women's experience of poverty... in several ways. Foremost among them is the fact that women remain primarily responsible for childcare, elder-care and home work. At the same time, they are increasingly required to contribute to the income of the household through paid work. This has serious implications for women. Constraints on time and mobility mean that their opportunities in the job market are often limited. Women's market work is therefore disproportionately concentrated in part-time and precarious work. This has been exacerbated in recent years. With the growing movement towards 'flexibilisation' of labour markets... many firms are increasingly making use of sub-contracted women home workers at very low wages to replace core full-time workers....

...

Thus while paid work can bring with it a modicum of agency and independence, women are often in a position where they have no option but to accept precarious and exploitative working conditions and pay. With no economic value given to unpaid activities, women's contribution remains invisible, as does their role in facilitating men's ability to access work. This affects not just their actual income but also their ability to act as equal partners in most economic transactions such as purchasing property or their ability to offer collateral for bank loans. Moreover, because women are for the most part engaged in low-paid work in the small-scale retail sector, informal sector or small farming, they are particularly vulnerable to economic downturns, public spending cuts and privatisation of public utilities such as water and electricity. Yet poverty reduction strategies take little or no account of the fact that socially essential subsistence, reproductive, and community work performed predominantly by women are not market-oriented.

The fact that the traditional household division of labour has remained intact despite women's increased participation in paid work means that women work longer hours than men in nearly every country, and a significantly larger proportion of their working time is spent on unpaid activities than that of men....

...

A further way in which women experience gender-specific disadvantage is in the context of gender-based violence, both physical and psychological. . . .

Particularly important is the impact of gender on the power to control important decisions in one's life. As summarised by Sweetman poverty is 'as much about agency compromised by abuse, stress, fatigue and voicelessness as it is about lack of resources'. . . .

Women's ability to access socio-economic rights, such as housing, education and health, is also shaped by the gendered nature of social institutions, including legal, cultural, customary and traditional factors. . . .

. . .

III The relationship between socio-economic rights and gender inequality

. . .

One approach is to regard equality as simply extending socio-economic rights to women. While this has some benefits, it is . . . not sufficient. [I]t is not enough to treat women in the same way as men. Instead, a much more substantive approach to equality is required, which demands restructuring of institutions. A substantive approach to equality, in turn, entails a reconceptualisation of the rights themselves. Rather than regarding socio-economic rights as bundles of goods to be distributed in different ways, . . . engendered socio-economic rights should take into account the ways in which goods and opportunities can in fact be enjoyed in the context of the actual relationships in which women live. . . . [P]articular weight [should be given] to the values of caring and interdependence.

. . . Courts should consider how the values and purposes underpinning equality may be relevant and useful to that of socio-economic rights and vice versa. This allows courts to be responsive to the reality that the most severe forms of disadvantage are experienced as a result of an intersection between group-based discrimination and socio-economic marginalisation.

QUESTIONS

1. How typical do you thing Guatemala's 1991 CEDAW report might be? What factors might explain its strongly self-critical approach?

2. Part of the World Bank's report makes a strong pragmatic argument in favour of improving the status of women. Would it help to premise the report instead on an insistence that human rights norms must be upheld, whether or not they are supported by the economics of the matter?

3. Does Fredman's approach differ significantly from that reflected in the World Bank analysis?

2. CEDAW: PROVISIONS AND COMMITTEE

BACKGROUND TO CEDAW

In 1967 the UN General Assembly adopted a non-binding Declaration on the Elimination of Discrimination against Women. It took another 12 years for the declaration to be developed into a binding treaty. The CEDAW Convention of 1979 had 118 states parties in 1993 at the time of the Second World Conference on Human Rights, compared to 187 today.

COMMENT ON CEDAW'S SUBSTANTIVE PROVISIONS

The Convention is among the many that elaborate in one particular field the norms and ideals that are generally and tersely stated in the Universal Declaration, and stated somewhat more amply in the ICCPR. Its preamble suggests how far-reaching the issues are and that the norms of this Convention must be placed in a broader transformative context. It recognizes 'that a change in the traditional role of men as well as the role of women in society and in the family is needed to achieve full equality between men and women'.

The reader should be familiar with the provisions of the Convention, a few of which are addressed by the following comments.

Article 1: Note three vital characteristics of the definition of 'discrimination against women'. (a) The article refers to *effect* as well as *purpose*, thus directing attention to the consequences of governmental measures as well as the intentions underlying them. (b) The definition is not limited to discrimination through 'state action' or action by persons acting under colour of law, as are the definitions of many rights such as the definition of torture under the Convention against Torture. (c) The definition's range is further expanded by the concluding phrase, 'or any other field'.

Article 2: The goals stated in this article are to be pursued 'without delay'. Consider the possible meanings of the terms 'equality' in clause (a) and 'any act of discrimination' in clause (c). Note the breadth of clauses (e) and (f) with respect to the private, nongovernmental sectors of society, particularly in relation to the definition in Article 1. Note throughout the Convention the blurred lines between the private and public spheres of life, and the range of obligations on states to intervene in the private sector, to go beyond 'respect' in order to 'protect', 'ensure' and 'promote'.

Article 3: Note the grand goal set forth for states, to 'ensure the full development and advancement of women', and consider whether the other human rights instruments examined contain a similar conception for any group, or for people in general.

Article 4: This 'affirmative action' clause, duly qualified, appears as well in the Convention on the Elimination of all Forms of Racial Discrimination, but not in the ICCPR. Consider this article in relation to Article 2(e) and (f), and Article 11.

Article 5: The breadth and aspiration of this article can be described only as striking. Provisions such as Article 10(c) impose a similar obligation on states in defined contexts. Other human rights treaties lack a similar provision, although Article 2 of the Racial Discrimination Convention comes close. Consider how a state in good faith might decide on 'appropriate measures' under this article, bearing in mind the injunction in Article 2 to proceed 'without delay' as well as the claims of the Convention's other provisions.

Articles 6–16: These articles evidence how a treaty devoted to one set of problems — here, ending discrimination against women and achieving equality — makes possible discrete, disaggregated treatment of the different issues relevant to these problems. Clearly the variety and detail in these articles would have been out of place, indeed impossible, in a treaty of general scope like the ICCPR. Note the great range of verbs that are used throughout these articles to define states parties' duties, including: eliminate, provide, encourage, protect, introduce, accord, ensure.

Article 6 is typical of many provisions in requiring a state party to regulate specific nongovernmental activity.

Articles 7–9, to the contrary, deal with the traditional notion of state action, here barring discrimination by the state.

Article 10 concerns a particular field, education, and lists specific goals which, in their totality, take on a programmatic character. Note paragraph (h) on family planning and its relationship to three other provisions: Articles 12(1), 14(2)(b) and 16(e). The Convention does not address as such the question of abortion.

Article 12 together with a number of other provisions indicate the degree to which CEDAW involves and interrelates the classical categories of civil-political rights and economic-social rights. It imposes a limited duty to provide free health care.

Article 14 disaggregates women's problems in regional and functional terms. It underscores strategies for realizing goals that permeate the entire Convention, such as mobilization through functional grass roots groups and participation in local decision-making. CEDAW is not a convention in which solutions are to be provided only by the central authority of the state.

Article 16 orders the states to sweep away a large number of fundamental, traditional discriminations against and forms of subordination of women. Like several other articles, it could be understood as a complement to, as one specification of, the broad goals stated in Article 5. Compare its provisions with the Report of Guatemala, p. 170, *supra*.

NOTE

More states have entered reservations to their ratification of CEDAW than to any other human rights treaty. Some reservations seriously qualify a state's commitment, particularly those that base the reservation on conflicting principles or rules in a religion or culture. The Comment at p. 1082, *infra*, gives examples of reservations and examines them in the context of a discussion about universalism and cultural relativism.

COMMENT ON TYPES OF STATE DUTIES IMPOSED BY HUMAN RIGHTS TREATIES

To understand the significance and implications of the rights stated in the ICCPR, CEDAW and other human rights treaties, it is helpful to examine the related duties/ obligations of states — even though human rights conventions rarely talk of duties. Attention to such duties clarifies the significance and even content of the related rights. It also points to strategies to realize a right, as by persuading the state to change its behaviour in one or another respect. The effort, then, is to deconstruct a right into its related state duties, perhaps duties that an advocate seeks to have imposed on the state.

Some of these duties can fairly be called correlative (corresponding) to the right — for example, implying from your right not to be tortured the state's correlative duty not to torture you. These may be the duties that come most promptly and naturally to the mind of the rights-holder. As a practical matter and from a functional perspective, other duties may be necessary implications from the nature of a given right even if they are not spelled out in treaty text — for example, a state's duty to create and operate electoral institutions and processes if the citizen's right to vote is to be realized.

Different rights may point to different types of state duties. All depends on the nature of the right, on the problems that it was meant to overcome or to prevent. Some types of state duties described below are more prominent in the ICCPR, some in CEDAW, some in the International Covenant on Economic, Social and Cultural Rights discussed in Chapter 4, or in other human rights treaties. Identifying the multiple duties that may be relevant to any one right sharpens an understanding of what is distinctive to and necessary to realize that right.

Two points should be kept in mind as we examine different kinds of rights from the perspective of related variable state duties.

(1) At the start of the human rights regime, much weight was given to a distinction between so-called 'negative' and 'positive' rights. The negative rights basically imposed a duty of 'hands-off', a duty of a state not to interfere with, say, an individual's physical security. The illustration of torture noted above fits well here. Thus, the right not to be tortured was imagined to impose only such a negative duty — the state's correlative duty not to torture. Positive rights, on the other hand, imposed affirmative (positive) duties on the state — in the classic case, a duty to provide food (food stamps/subsidies and so on) if such provision was essential to satisfy the right to food. Thus economic and social rights such as the right to food were considered positive rights, which frequently required financial expenditures by the state, unlike the classic negative rights that were thought to require merely abstention from unjustified interference with another person. It will be important to consider how much of this negative-positive distinction remains valid in the light of the illustrations and analysis below, and whether it clarifies or confuses the issues before us.

Consider the following classic presentation of this distinction in Maurice Cranston, 'Are There Any Human Rights?', in 112/4 Daedalus 12 (1983):

> The traditional political and civil rights are not difficult to institute. For the most part, they require governments, and other people generally, to leave a man

> alone.... Do not injure, arrest, or imprison him. To respect a man's right to life, liberty, and property is not a very costly exercise. As Locke and others have explained, it requires a system of law that recognizes those rights to protect those rights. But rulers are not called upon to do anything that it is unreasonable to expect of them.... Political... rights can be secured by fairly simple legislation. Since those rights are largely rights against government interference, the greatest effort will be directed toward restraining the government's own executive arm. But this is no longer the case where economic and social rights are concerned....

(2) Rights are not static. They evolve. They broaden or contract over time. One way of understanding an expansion of the content of a given right (to speech, to food) is to examine the duties related to that right, and to inquire whether and how they have expanded. The argument for a broader construction of a given right often amounts to the claim that further duties ought to be imposed on the state in order to satisfy the right. Consider some examples. The right to speech implies at a minimum the government's correlative duty not to interfere with it. It should not enjoin or penalize the rights-holder who indeed speaks. A modest expansion of this 'hands off' right imposes the further duty on government to protect a speaker against deliberate interference by non-state actors. Your right to speak loses meaning if others are permitted to block you in various ways from publishing or orally communicating your ideas. An argument for further expansion can be based on the claim that government must facilitate speech by assuring access of political groups to the media (that is, to newspapers or electronic media whether or not owned or controlled by the state). Such arguments for expansion of the kinds of state duties can constitute a strategy of change. So attention to duties, how they differ among rights within a treaty and among treaties, and how they change over time is one vital way of examining and fostering change in the human rights regime as a whole.

The following scheme of five types of state duties derives from but modifies earlier writings, particularly Henry Shue, *Basic Rights* (2nd edn. 1996), and G. J. H. van Hoof, 'The Legal Nature of Economic, Social and Cultural Rights', in P. Alston and K. Tomasevski (eds.), *The Right to Food* (1984), at 97.

(1) Respect Rights of Others

This duty requires the state to treat persons equally, to respect their individual dignity and worth, and hence not to interfere with or impair their declared rights, whether they be physical security rights or rights to due process, equal protection, speech or political participation. This duty of respect has often been described as 'negative' in the sense of being a 'hands-off' duty. The broad idea is not to worsen an individual's situation by depriving that person of the enjoyment of a declared right.

Of course the observance by states of this duty of respect would itself, without the possibility of any further state duties, lead to a vast improvement in the human condition. In this sense, the duty of respect can be seen to lie at the core of the human rights regime. Compliance with it would avoid most of the worst calamities: genocides, massacres, torture. The duty of respect is in this sense allied to the 'antidisaster' element of the human rights regime — the notion that the human rights regime arose and developed to prevent recurrence of the massive abominations of the twentieth century that preceded it. But observance would achieve far more, such as realizing the basic conditions for a democratic society.

For many but not all rights declared in the treaties, the duty of respect reaches beyond states to obligate individuals and non-state entities. A person's right to bodily security or to vote imposes a correlative duty on all other persons to refrain from interfering with it. My right to bodily security mean little unless my neighbours are prohibited by the state from violating it. On the other hand, the other duties identified in categories (2) to (5) below are in most cases associated only with the state. Under the human rights treaties, individuals or non-state entities are generally not considered to bear direct duties to protect other individuals against physical attack or to provide housing for them. Such issues about the character and range of individual duties are considered elsewhere at pp. 509 and 517, *infra*. This Comment covers only state duties.

(2) Create Institutional Machinery Essential to Realization of Rights

Some rights may be impaired or effectively annulled not only by government's direct interference with them (torture, preventing a citizen from expressing ideas or voting), but also by its failure to put in place the institutional machinery essential for the realization or practice of the right. Political participation offers a simple illustration. A citizen's right to vote means little unless a government maintains fair electoral machinery that makes possible the act of voting, counting of ballots and so on. Voting rights are, then, hardly cost-free for government. It is not simply a matter of 'hands off'. Public funds must be expended to create the infrastructure on which the practical realization of the right depends. Public care must be taken to be certain the voting mechanisms function fairly and honestly. The negative–positive distinction, while having some utility, is inadequate to describe this duty, as well as the state's duty to institutionalize rights that is described in category (3) below.

(3) Protect Rights/Prevent Violations

Several human rights treaties make explicit the state's duty to protect against and to prevent violations of rights — for example, Article 2 of the ICCPR that gives victims of violations the right to a remedy. Again institutional machinery is required, in this instance to comply with a specific command of the treaties. In the case of the ICCPR, that command is expressed through the state's duty in Article 2 to 'ensure to all individuals' the recognized rights. States must then do the necessary to ensure. Surely they must provide a police force to protect people against violations of their rights (to physical security, or free speech, or property) either by state or non-state ('private') actors. They must create normative systems like tort or criminal law, as well as institutions like courts or jails, processes like civil suits or criminal prosecutions, in order to maintain a system of justice that provides remedies for violations and imposes sanctions on violators. This duty to protect has been vital to the development of CEDAW and women's rights.

As in category (2) above, the state's duty to protect/prevent involves state expenditures.

Again, the negative-positive rights distinction is not helpful. The classic 'negative' rights here demand the classic 'positive' protection. It is difficult to imagine a right for which this is not true. As Henry Shue, in *Basic Rights* (2nd edn. 1996) puts it:

> All these activities and institutions [of government, like police, courts, jails] are attempts at providing social guarantees for individuals' security so that they are not left to face alone forces that they cannot handle on their own. How much more than these expenditures one thinks would be necessary in order for people actually to be reasonably secure... depends on one's theory of violent crime, but it is not unreasonable to believe that it would involve extremely expensive, 'positive' programs.... A demand for physical security is not normally a demand simply to be left alone, but demand to be protected against harm. It is a demand for positive action....

Note that the concepts of protect and prevent, though linked in this category (3), can take on quite different meanings, depending on context. For example, promotion of cultural change (category (5) below) about, say, violence against women may help to prevent such violence. Prevention may then be realized in the long run through strategies well outside such everyday forces for protection as police.

(4) Provide Goods and Services to Satisfy Rights

The state's duty here is primarily to provide material resources to the rights-bearer, like housing or food or health care, matters associated with the International Covenant on Economic, Social and Cultural Rights. (Resources provided by the state may go directly from it to the individual rights-bearer, as by providing food stamps or subsidized public housing, *or* it may go indirectly to the ultimate beneficiary through, say, subsidies to construction firms that will then offer low-rent housing.) Unlike the duty of respect (do not worsen the situation of the rights-bearer), this duty to provide generally is meant to improve the situation of the rights-bearer.

It is most evident and explicit in this category (4) that the state must expend public funds to meet its duties. It is for this reason that state duties related to welfare rights have most frequently been described as affirmative (positive). Unlike categories (2) and (3) above, both of which also involve state expenditures, these expenditures are at the core of, are the very essence of, the individual right. They are not merely incidental to it, essential means to realize some other right, as for example state expenditures for police are essential to fulfil a duty to protect.

On the other hand, the realization of economic and social rights need not depend on 'direct' or 'indirect' provision by the state in the sense described above. Other, radically different policies may achieve the goal of satisfying a right to, say, food. For example, one way of overcoming poverty and malnutrition in rural areas might be to undertake a programme of expropriation and land reform that would increase employment and yield and thereby make more people self-sufficient with respect to food. Again, monetary or fiscal policy designed to lower unemployment and hence malnutrition and homelessness could reduce the need for direct provision of funds or goods. Such characteristic policies of the modern welfare state may then make the direct or indirect provision of funds or goods measures of last rather than first resort.

(5) Promote Rights

This state duty refers to bringing about changes in public consciousness or perception or understanding about a given problem or issue, with the purpose of alleviating the problem. In certain contexts, such promotion of rights may be a useful or indeed essential path towards their better recognition by non-state actors. Like the duty of protection, it generally requires the state to expend funds and create the institutions that are necessary to promoting acceptance of the right. Thus a state's duty to promote often involves public education — for example, school education or public campaigns meant to change attitudes about violence towards women or children. Promotion to achieve such types of cultural change plays a vital role in CEDAW.

Promotion underscores the point that these categories of duties are not discrete. They are often complexly interrelated, and indeed overlap. For example, fulfilment of a duty to promote may bear on the duty not only to provide but also to protect, as when the state promotes and disseminates knowledge about the evil consequences of discrimination that may reduce, say, racism or homophobic violence.

QUESTIONS

1. Consider CEDAW's stress on eliminating discrimination to achieve equality between men and women, as well as its means for realizing that equality. The phrase 'on the basis of equality of men and women' recurs in many of its articles. Compare the notion of equality in the ICCPR — say, in ICCPR Article 3 ('to ensure the equal rights of men and women to the enjoyment of all civil and political rights' in that covenant), or ICCPR Article 26 ('All persons are equal before the law and are entitled without any discrimination to the equal protection of the law'). Are the two treaties' conceptions of equality identical, similar, very different?

2. Do the provisions of CEDAW on their face make any concession to cultural relativism, to cultural diversity in regional, ethnic, religious or other terms? Or do they insist throughout on universal application of its norms without variation, no matter what the cultural context, history or circumstances of the state involved?

3. Under Article 2, states parties agree to pursue the required policies, 'by all appropriate means and without delay'. Contrast the description of state obligations in Article 2 of the Covenant on Economic, Social and Cultural Rights: 'achieving progressively the full realization' of the recognized rights. Is this textual contrast accurate with respect to CEDAW? How do you understand the question of CEDAW's 'time frame' in comparison, say, with the ICCPR?

4. Which provisions of CEDAW fall into which of the categories of state duties that are described in the preceding Comment? Does any one category appear to dominate? Which category represents the most significant change from the ICCPR?

COMMENT ON THE COMMITTEE ON THE ELIMINATION OF DISCRIMINATION AGAINST WOMEN

Two institutions within the universal human rights system are concerned exclusively with women's rights. The UN Commission on the Status of Women (CSW) was created in 1946 and is made up of governments. Women's welfare and their role in the overall development process dominated its agenda for many years. In the human rights arena it has clearly been less influential than the CEDAW Committee. The latter was set up in 1981, after the Convention came into force. It is a 'treaty organ' rather than a 'Charter organ' within the distinction made at p. 161, *supra*. Chapter 9 will examine the ICCPR Committee. You should now read Articles 17–21 of the Convention.

The UN General Assembly, in deciding on the appropriate type of supervisory body for CEDAW, drew on the model of the ICCPR Committee. Thus the CEDAW Committee was constituted as a body of independent experts — that is, not state officials or other persons representing the state or subject to its instructions — given the task of monitoring states' efforts to meet their obligations through review of periodic reports submitted by the states parties. Moreover, the Committee was authorized to issue General Recommendations to all states. Finally, pursuant to a later Optional Protocol to the Convention, the Committee gained authority to hear contentious cases before it based on alleged violations of CEDAW and to issue recommendatory 'views'. The Committee's importance has steadily increased over its life, partly as a consequence of the greater attention given women's rights on the world scene.

Committee members have had diverse backgrounds, from fields like sociology, medicine, international relations, education, political science, law and government. With only three exceptions, all Committee members have been women.[2]

This is perhaps no surprise, since the membership of treaty bodies reflects one national selection process multiplied many times, and in most countries there is likely to be a higher percentage of women than men working on issues relating to women's equality, thus making it more likely that a woman will be nominated. But a better balance would help to avoid the impression that all-female membership may create, namely that discrimination against women is a concern only of women, and not something that men should be concerned with. By the same token, there

[2] For a detailed analysis see A. Byrnes, 'The Committee on the Elimination of Discrimination against Women', in P. Alston & F. Mégret (eds.), *The UN and Human Rights* (2nd edn. 2013).

remains a significant imbalance in the predominantly male membership of most of the other treaty bodies.

The large question posed by the illustrations that follow of Concluding Comments, General Recommendations and Views concerns the effectiveness of the Committee's work in moving states towards the goal of equality of dignity and equal protection for women. It will immediately become apparent that the Committee itself lacks means of 'enforcing' its policies and understanding of CEDAW on states. How then can it influence state behaviour? How can it influence the course of law-making about women's rights, both national and international law, since it has no explicit power to legislate?

We start inquiry into the Committee by looking at its function of monitoring states parties with respect to their compliance with the Convention. It does so through its examination of the periodic reports on compliance that states parties are required to submit to the Committee. The Committee, like other treaty organs, has developed the practice of holding a meeting between Committee members and representatives of the state party to discuss the report and then publishing its concluding observations.

CONCLUDING OBSERVATIONS OF THE COMMITTEE ON THE ELIMINATION OF DISCRIMINATION AGAINST WOMEN BRAZIL

UN Doc. CEDAW/C/BRA/CO/7 (23 Feb. 2012)

A. Introduction

2. The Committee [regretted that Brazil's report had not taken account of its 2007 concluding observations on Brazil's previous report.] ...

...

B. Positive Aspects

4. The Committee welcomes the election of, Ms. Dilma Roussef, as the first female president of Brazil, in October 2010 and appreciates the appointment of 10 women ministers....

C. Principal areas of concern and recommendations

...

National machinery for the advancement of women

14. The Committee welcomes that the Secretariat for Women's Policies (SPM) has been integrated as one of the essential entities of the Office of the President of the Republic, and that it has extended its presence to 23 states and 400 municipalities. However, it expresses its concern with respect to existing inconsistencies

between the resources effectively released to the Secretariat, which are significantly lower, and the resource allocations foreseen in the Budget Law (LOA)....

15. The Committee... recommends that the State party:

a) Revise existing funding allocation policies...;

b) Strengthen the capacity of the Secretariat for Women's Policies, at the federal, state and municipal levels, by providing it with sufficient human, technical and financial resources, to increase its effectiveness...; and

c) Take further efforts to extend the setting up of women's policies and institutional mechanisms in all 27 states, the federal district and municipalities in order to ensure the effective implementation and coordination of policies aimed at achieving substantive gender equality.

Violence against Women

18. The Committee appreciates that the Supreme Court pronounced itself on the legal controversies around the constitutionality of the Maria da Penha Law on domestic and family violence against women (Law 11340). However, given the resistance from various sectors of the judiciary to apply this law as well as the Federal and decentralized configuration of the State party, the Committee is concerned about the compliance with both the verdicts of the Supreme Court and the Maria da Penha Law by judges at the local level. It is also concerned about the lack of expertise within the judiciary to deal with domestic and family violence cases. It is further concerned about the shortages in the collection of accurate and consistent data on violence against women....

19. The Committee urges the State party to:

a) Provide systematic training to judges, prosecutors and lawyers on women's rights and violence against women as well as on the Maria da Penha Law and on its constitutionality...;

b) Strengthen its judicial system to ensure that women, in particular disadvantaged groups have effective access to justice...;

...

d) Provide all entities which participate in the implementation of the National Plan to Combat Violence against Women with substantial human, technical and financial resources, including for the establishment of shelters for women victims of violence.

Trafficking and exploitation of prostitution

20. While taking note of the State party initiatives to address trafficking in persons such as the establishment, in March 2011, of a parliamentary inquiry commission (CPI) to investigate the causes and consequences of internal and international trafficking in Brazil and the preparation of a Second National Plan to Combat Human Trafficking, the Committee is concerned at the lack of information about the extent of the phenomenon of trafficking in women and girls. It is also concerned about the lack of a comprehensive and concerted approach to combat trafficking in persons.... It is particularly concerned at information received stating

that women and girls are exploited for the purposes of prostitution and employment in some regions where large development projects are being implemented and about the sexual exploitation of women and girls in touristic zones in the northeast of the country.

21. The Committee recommends that the State party:

a) Consider adopting a comprehensive law against trafficking in persons...;

b) ... [D]esign and implement a comprehensive strategy aimed at combating and preventing the exploitation of prostitution and sex tourism in the State party;

...

Participation in political and public life

22. The Committee takes note of the efforts of the State party aimed at increasing the participation in political and public life of women, such as the adoption of Law No. 12034/2009 which requires that political parties maintain a minimum of 30% and a maximum of 70% representation of women or men in their candidate lists and the launch of the permanent campaign "More Women in Power" in 2008. However, it regrets that the persistence of patriarchal attitudes and stereotypes as well as the lack of mechanisms to ensure the implementation of adopted temporary special measures, continue to impede women's participation in parliament and in decision-making positions at the state and municipal levels of the public administration. It is further concerned at the low representation of women in the highest instances of the Judiciary and in top managerial positions in the private sector, despite the increasing number of women with judicial careers as well as the increasing number of women who participate in the labour market.

23. The Committee calls upon the State party to:

a) Strengthen its efforts to amend or adopt legislation aiming at increasing the de facto participation of women in political life...;

b) Adopt and ensure the implementation of temporary special measures...in order to accelerate women's full and equal participation in public and political life, in particular with respect to disadvantaged groups of women, such as Afro-descendent and indigenous women, and women with disabilities; and

c) Carry out awareness-raising campaigns targeting both men and women aimed at eliminating patriarchal attitudes and stereotypes regarding roles for men and women and at highlighting the importance of women's full and equal participation in political and public life and in decision-making positions in the public and private sectors and in all fields.

...

Employment

26. The Committee [is] concerned that stereotypes related to gender and race contribute to the segregation of Afro-descendent and indigenous women into lower quality jobs. It is further concerned at the lack of information regarding measures to protect women from sexual harassment in the workplace as well as about the persistence of the exploitation of women and children as domestic workers.

27. The Committee recommends that the State party:

a) Prioritize the adoption of the Equality in the Workplace Bill (No. 6653/2009), which provides for the creation of mechanisms to prevent and prohibit discrimination against women in the field of employment;

b) Adopt effective measures in the formal labour market, including temporary special measures, to eliminate occupational segregation based on stereotypes related to gender, race and ethnicity; to narrow and close the wage gap between women and men; and to ensure the application of the principle of equal remuneration for work of equal value, and equal opportunities at work;

c) Include in its next periodic report legislative and other measures taken to protect women from sexual harassment in the workplace and to protect women's rights in the informal sector; and

...

Women in detention

...

33. The Committee urges the State party to:

a) Take measures to reduce the number of women in conflict with the law, including through targeted prevention programmes aimed at addressing the causes of women's criminality;

b) Address the situation of women and girls in detention through the development of comprehensive gender-sensitive policies, strategies and programmes, aimed at facilitating their access to justice and ensuring the respect of their fair trial guarantees, in particular for indigenous women; and providing educational, rehabilitative and resettlement programmes for women and girls; and

c) Improve the conditions of women's detention facilities according to international standards, to solve the overcrowding difficulties in the prisons, guarantee separate residence facilities for men and women inmates; and ensure the provision of adequate health facilities and services, in particular for pregnant women.

...

Dissemination

38. The Committee requests the wide dissemination in Brazil of the present concluding observations....

...

Follow-up to concluding observations

40. The Committee requests the State party to provide, within two years, written information on the steps undertaken to implement the recommendations contained in paragraphs 21 [on trafficking and prostitution] and 29 [omitted, and addressing maternal mortality and the criminalization of abortion] above.

...

QUESTIONS

1. Do the concluding observations reflect a balance between ESR and CPR issues?

2. Is the Committee sparing in its emphasis on affirmative action ('special measures')? Should it be?

3. What provisions of the Convention empower the Committee to be concerned about the exploitation of women and girls 'for the purposes of prostitution and employment'? Should the Committee go further and insist upon the criminalization of prostitution?

4. How gender-specific are the Committee's concerns about women in detention? If the issues are more generic would they not be more appropriately addressed by a committee whose mandate covers all prisoners?

5. In what ways, if any, could these concluding comments serve to put pressure on the Brazilian Government to act in accordance with the recommendations? How do you assess the utility or significance for realizing the goals of CEDAW of these periodic reports and reactions by the Committee?

3. THE PUBLIC/PRIVATE DIVIDE: 'PRIVATE' VIOLENCE AGAINST WOMEN

In classical terms human rights obligations are assumed by, or imposed upon, the state. The resulting duties are 'public' or governmental. Some treaties, such as the Torture Convention are exclusively state-centric, focusing only on actions taken 'by or at the instigation of or with the consent or acquiescence of a public official or other person acting in an official capacity'. CEDAW, on the other hand, is explicit in also addressing conduct attributable not to the state ('public' actors) but to non-state/nongovernmental ('private') actors. The resulting divide between what is public and what is private thus becomes an especially prominent theme in relation to women's rights, although it has important ramifications in other areas as well.[3]

The terms 'public' and 'private' can refer to either actors or contexts, and the divide is often not straightforward. Thus a government official might act in ways that are entirely outside her legitimate public functions, as a result of which her actions will be deemed private. Or conduct by a private individual might be characterized as public because the state was in some way complicit, as in the acts of death squads operating with governmental connivance. And, of particular importance in the present context, a government might become liable for the entirely private

[3] For example, the Convention on the Rights of Persons with Disabilities makes several explicit references to private actors.

acts of private individuals if it can be shown that it did not do all it could or should have to prevent such actions, or to investigate and punish them after the event.

This section examines some of the issues arising out of the public/private divide:

the practical, political and ideological significance of the divide;
the shifting boundary line between the two as conceptions of their significance and content change;
the degree to which human rights treaties should require states parties to regulate the relevant conduct of private (in the sense of non-state) actors; and
the degree to which human rights treaties should directly regulate the relevant conduct of such private actors and impose sanctions on such actors for violations of their duties within the regulatory scheme.

We use the fight to eliminate violence against women as the lens through which to explore these issues, while highlighting both the central role of CEDAW and the interaction among key institutional actors to achieve a crucial degree of normative and policy consensus around dealing with the problem.

As noted by the World Bank (see report cited on p. 173, *supra*, at p. 20):

> Women are at far greater risk of violence by an intimate partner or someone they know than from violence by other people. And women are more likely than men to be killed, seriously injured, or victims of sexual violence by intimate partners. The prevalence of domestic violence varies greatly across countries, with no clear relationship to incomes; while incidence tends to rise with socioeconomic deprivation, violence knows no boundaries. In some middle-income nations, such as Brazil (Sao Paolo and Pernambuco region) and Serbia (Belgrade), women report that the incidence of physical violence by intimate partners is as high as 25 percent. In Peru (Cusco), almost 50 percent of women are victims of severe physical violence during their lifetime, and in Ethiopia (Butajira), 54 percent of women reported being subject to physical or sexual abuse by an intimate partner in the past 12 months.

A particularly dramatic example of such violence is so-called 'honour killing', defined as '[t]he killing of a family member on suspicion of engagement in any actions deemed dishonorable, ranging from mere association with the opposite sex to sexual relations or running away from home' (UN Doc. A/HRC/11/2/Add.4 (6 May 2009) para. 63). The Human Rights Commission of Pakistan (an independent NGO) reported that in 2011:

> at least 943 women were killed in the name of honour, of which 93 were minors. The purported reasons given for this were illicit relations in 595 cases and the demand to marry of their own choice in 219 cases. [I]n 180 cases the murderer [was] a brother and in 226 cases... the husband of the victim. The majority of cases (557) were of married women. Before being killed, at least 19 women were raped, 12 of them gang raped....[4]

[4] Annual Report 2011 (2012), p. 167.

But the issue of violence against women remained largely 'invisible' prior to the 1979 adoption of the CEDAW Convention, which contains not a single reference to it. World Conferences on Women in 1980 and 1985 alluded to the problem, but the first serious steps in the UN context came with resolutions by the ECOSOC in 1984 and the General Assembly in 1985 (GA Res. 40/36 (29 Nov. 1985)). These led to a pathbreaking UN study on 'Violence against Women in the Family' (UN Doc. ST/CSDHA/2 (1989)), and a more detailed General Assembly resolution in 1990 (GA Res. 45/114). These developments occurred at the same time as the Inter-American Court of Human Rights adopted a judgment that was to become a classic in the field because of its clarification of a state's duties with respect to violence committed by non-state actors.

VELÁSQUEZ RODRÍGUEZ CASE

Inter-American Court of Human Rights, 1988, Ser. C, No. 4, 9 Hum. Rts. L. J. 212 (1988)

[A petition against Honduras was received by the Inter-American Commission of Human Rights, alleging that Velásquez Rodríguez was arrested without warrant by Honduran national security units. Knowledge of his whereabouts was consistently denied by police and security forces. Velásquez had disappeared. Petitioners argued that through this conduct, Honduras had violated several articles of the American Convention on Human Rights. After hearings and conclusions, the Commission referred the matter to the Inter-American Court of Human Rights, whose contentious jurisdiction had been recognized by Honduras. The Court concluded that Honduras had violated the Convention.

In the excerpts below, the Court addresses the issue of just what the obligations of Honduras were under the Convention? Was Honduras obligated only to 'respect' individual rights and not directly violate them, as by torture or illegal arrest? Or was Honduras obligated to take steps, within reasonable limits, to protect people like Velásquez from seizure even by non-state, private persons? In an earlier portion of the opinion (see p. 1004, *infra*), the Court had found that the Honduran state was implicated in the arrest and disappearance, and that the acts of those arresting Velásquez could be imputed to the state. In the present excerpts, the Court reviews that information, and considers what might be the responsibility of Honduras even if the seizure and disappearance of Velásquez were caused by private persons unconnected with the government.]

161. Article 1(1) of the Convention provides:

> 1. The States Parties to this Convention undertake to respect the rights and freedoms recognized herein and to ensure to all persons subject to their jurisdiction the free and full exercise of those rights and freedoms. . . .

. . .

164. Article 1(1) is essential in determining whether a violation of the human rights recognized by the Convention can be imputed to a State Party. In effect, that article charges the States Parties with the fundamental duty to respect and guarantee the rights recognized in the Convention. Any impairment of those rights which can be attributed under the rules of international law to the action or omission of any public authority constitutes an act imputable to the State, which assumes responsibility in the terms provided by the Convention itself.

165. The first obligation assumed by the States Parties under Article 1(1) is 'to respect the rights and freedoms' recognized by the Convention....

166. The second obligation of the States Parties is to ['ensure'] the free and full exercise of the rights recognized by the Convention to every person subject to its jurisdiction. This obligation implies the duty of the States Parties to organize the governmental apparatus and, in general, all the structures through which public power is exercised, so that they are capable of juridically ensuring the free and full enjoyment of human rights. As a consequence of this obligation, the States must prevent, investigate and punish any violation of the rights recognized by the Convention and, moreover, if possible attempt to restore the rights violated and provide compensation as warranted for damages resulting from the violation.

...

169. According to Article 1(1), any exercise of public power that violates the rights recognized by the Convention is illegal....

170. This conclusion is independent of whether the organ or official has contravened provisions of internal law or overstepped the limits of his authority. Under international law a State is responsible for the acts of its agents undertaken in their official capacity and for their omissions, even when those agents act outside the sphere of their authority or violate internal law.

...

172. Thus, in principle, any violation of rights recognized by the Convention carried out by an act of public authority or by persons who use their position of authority is imputable to the State. However, this does not define all the circumstances in which a State is obligated to prevent, investigate and punish human rights violations, nor all the cases in which the State might be found responsible for an infringement of those rights. An illegal act which violates human rights and which is initially not directly imputable to a State (for example, because it is the act of a private person or because the person responsible has not been identified) can lead to international responsibility of the State, not because of the act itself, but because of the lack of due diligence to prevent the violation or to respond to it as required by the Convention.

...

174. The State has a legal duty to take reasonable steps to prevent human rights violations and to use the means at its disposal to carry out a serious investigation of violations committed within its jurisdiction, to identify those responsible, impose the appropriate punishment and ensure the victim adequate compensation.

175. This duty to prevent includes all those means of a legal, political, administrative and cultural nature that promote the safeguard of human rights and ensure

that any violations are considered and treated as illegal acts, which, as such, may lead to the punishment of those responsible and the obligation to indemnify the victims for damages. It is not possible to make a detailed list of all such measures, as they vary with the law and the conditions of each State Party. Of course, while the State is obligated to prevent human rights abuses, the existence of a particular violation does not, in itself, prove the failure to take preventive measures....

...

177. In certain circumstances, it may be difficult to investigate acts that violate an individual's rights. The duty to investigate, like the duty to prevent, is not breached merely because the investigation does not produce a satisfactory result. Nevertheless, it must be undertaken in a serious manner.... Where the acts of private parties that violate the Convention are not seriously investigated, those parties are aided in a sense by the government, thereby making the State responsible on the international plane.

178. In the instant case, the evidence shows a complete inability of the procedures of the State of Honduras, which were theoretically adequate, to ensure the investigation of the disappearance of Manfredo Velásquez and the fulfillment of its duties to pay compensation and punish those responsible, as set out in Article 1(1) of the Convention.

179. As the Court has verified above, the failure of the judicial system to act upon the writs brought before various tribunals in the instant case has been proven. Not one writ of habeas corpus was processed. No judge had access to the places where Manfredo Velásquez might have been detained. The criminal complaint was dismissed.

180. Nor did the organs of the Executive Branch carry out a serious investigation to establish the fate of Manfredo Velásquez. There was no investigation of public allegations of a practice of disappearances nor a determination of whether Manfredo Velásquez had been a victim of that practice. The Commission's requests for information were ignored to the point that the Commission had to presume, under Article 42 of its Regulations, that the allegations were true....

...

182. The Court is convinced, and has so found, that the disappearance of Manfredo Velásquez was carried out by agents who acted under cover of public authority. However, even had that fact not been proven, the failure of the State apparatus to act, which is clearly proven, is a failure on the part of Honduras to fulfill the duties it assumed under Article 1(1) of the Convention, which obligated it to guarantee Manfredo Velásquez the free and full exercise of his human rights.

...

NOTE

In addition to its consideration of reports submitted by states parties, the CEDAW Committee has several techniques at its disposal, in addition to the reporting mechanism considered above, through which it can elaborate upon its understanding of the requirements of the Convention. One of these involves the adoption of General Recommendations through which it explains its understanding of a particular right or issue that arises under the Convention.

GENERAL RECOMMENDATION NO. 19 OF CEDAW (1992), VIOLENCE AGAINST WOMEN

UN Doc. A/47/38

6. . . . The definition of discrimination includes gender-based violence, that is, violence that is directed against a woman because she is a woman or that affects women disproportionately. It includes acts that inflict physical, mental or sexual harm or suffering, threats of such acts, coercion and other deprivations of liberty. Gender-based violence may breach specific provisions of the Convention, regardless of whether those provisions expressly mention violence.

7. Gender-based violence, which impairs or nullifies the enjoyment by women of human rights and fundamental freedoms under general international law or under human rights conventions, is discrimination within the meaning of article 1 of the Convention. [The rights violated by gender-based violence amounting to discrimination include the right to life, to liberty and security of the person, to equality in the family, to the highest standard attainable of physical and mental health, and to just and favourable conditions of work.]

. . .

9. It is emphasized, however, that discrimination under the Convention is not restricted to action by or on behalf of Governments (see articles 2(e), 2(f) and 5).... Under general international law and specific human rights covenants, States may also be responsible for private acts if they fail to act with due diligence to prevent violations of rights or to investigate and punish acts of violence, and for providing compensation.

. . .

11. Traditional attitudes by which women are regarded as subordinate to men or as having stereotyped roles perpetuate widespread practices involving violence or coercion, such as family violence and abuse, forced marriage, dowry deaths, acid attacks and female circumcision. Such prejudices and practices may justify gender-based violence as a form of protection or control of women. The effect of such violence on the physical and mental integrity of women is to deprive them of the equal enjoyment, exercise and knowledge of human rights and fundamental freedoms. While this comment addresses mainly actual or threatened violence, the underlying consequences of these forms of gender-based violence help to maintain women in subordinate roles and contribute to their low level of political participation and to their lower level of education, skills and work opportunities.

. . .

20. In some States there are traditional practices perpetuated by culture and tradition that are harmful to the health of women and children. These practices include dietary restrictions for pregnant women, preference for male children and female circumcision or genital mutilation.

...

23. Family violence is one of the most insidious forms of violence against women. It is prevalent in all societies....

[The Committee recommends that states parties should (among other measures) take a range of steps to 'overcome all forms of gender-based violence, whether by public or private act', provide adequate protective and support services for victims of family violence and provide gender-sensitive training to police and judges, take measures 'to ensure that the media respect and promote respect for women', take measures to eliminate prejudices and attitudes that lead to violence, and ensure that women need not resort to illegal abortion 'because of lack of appropriate services in regard to fertility control'.]

NOTE

CEDAW's 1992 General Recommendation was followed soon after by the UN General Assembly's adoption of the Declaration on the Elimination of Violence against Women (GA Res. 48/104 (20 Dec. 1993)) which, in practice, amounted to endorsement by governments of the Committee's approach. The Declaration, known as DEVAW, defined violence against women as meaning 'any act of gender-based violence that results in, or is likely to result in, physical, sexual or psychological harm or suffering to women, including threats of such acts, coercion or arbitrary deprivation of liberty, whether occurring in public or in private life' (Art. 1). The formally non-binding Declaration stated that 'States should condemn violence against women and should not invoke any custom, tradition or religious consideration to avoid their obligations with respect to its elimination. States should pursue by all appropriate means and without delay a policy of eliminating violence against women....' (Art. 4).

This in turn was followed by the UN Commission on Human Rights appointment of a Special Rapporteur 'on violence against women, its causes and consequences'. This expert was authorized to undertake field missions, seek information from governments and other sources, and submit analytical and other reports to the Commission. Radhika Coomaraswamy (1994–2003), Yakin Ertürk (2003–2009) and Rashida Manjoo (2009–) have undertaken detailed studies on a wide range of issues affecting women and report annually to the Human Rights Council on country missions and other activities that they have undertaken.

For its part, the CEDAW Committee, having played the crucial role of catalyst in developing the initial normative consensus, has continued to deepen the understanding of the issue and its implications through the use of two other techniques, in addition to state reporting and General Recommendations. They are the undertaking of 'inquiries' and the consideration of 'communications' (complaints). Both of these procedures are laid down in an Optional Protocol to CEDAW (the 'OP'), adopted in 1999. The OP is open to ratification only by parties to CEDAW itself, and is a way in which they can extend, or deepen, their commitments to cooperate with the Committee. As of May 2012, 104 states had agreed to the OP, compared with

187 parties to CEDAW itself. (Chapter 9, *infra*, on the Human Rights Committee created by the ICCPR examines in more detail the work of that Committee under a similar OP to the ICCPR which also enables it to examine complaints.)

The *inquiry procedure* under the OP begins with a submission to the Committee, most likely by an NGO, of 'reliable information indicating grave or systematic violations by a State Party of rights set forth in the Convention'. The government concerned is then asked to comment on the information before the Committee decides whether or not to 'designate one or more of its members to conduct an inquiry and to report urgently to the Committee.' The OP provides that '[w]here warranted and with the consent of the State Party, the inquiry may include a visit to its territory.' The inquiry is conducted confidentially, ideally with the government's cooperation at all stages. The resulting report, including recommendations, is sent to the government, which is invited to respond and the issues can subsequently be pursued under the Convention's regular reporting procedures. The first such inquiry was initiated in 2003 (Mexico) and the second in 2011 (Canada). Both relate to the murder and disappearances of women and girls.

Under the *complaints procedure*, states parties to the OP agree to recognize the competence of the Committee 'to receive and consider communications'. Individuals or 'groups of individuals' under the 'jurisdiction' of a state party may submit communications to the Committee, 'claiming to be victims of a violation [by the state] of any of the rights set forth in the Convention'. Communications must meet certain conditions and criteria to be judged admissible — for example, submission following exhaustion of domestic remedies. The Committee brings the communication confidentially to the attention of the state party involved. After finding the communication admissible and examining it, the Committee transmits its 'views' on the communication, 'together with its recommendations', to the concerned parties. The state party 'shall give due consideration' to the Committee's views and recommendations. Between 2003 and May 2012, 27 complaints were registered.

The following materials illustrate how these two procedures have been used in the Committee's work on violence against women.

REPORT ON MEXICO PRODUCED BY THE COMMITTEE ON THE ELIMINATION OF DISCRIMINATION AGAINST WOMEN UNDER ARTICLE 8 OF THE OPTIONAL PROTOCOL TO THE CONVENTION, AND REPLY FROM THE GOVERNMENT OF MEXICO

UN Doc. CEDAW/C/2005/OP.8/MEXICO (27 Jan. 2005)

I. Introduction

...

2. Mexico ratified the [OP] on 15 March 2002....
3. In a letter dated 2 October 2002, the non-governmental organizations Equality Now and Casa Amiga, located in [New York and Ciudad Juárez], respectively,

requested the Committee to conduct an inquiry…into the abduction, rape and murder of women in and around Ciudad Juárez….

[The Committee appointed two of its members to review submissions from the government and additional information from NGOs. On the basis of the report of these members, it decided, in July 2003 that it should undertake an inquiry to be carried out by the same two members. In August 2003 the government agreed to the visit, which took place from 18–26 October 2003.]

Different forms of gender violence — data, characteristics and initial reactions

…

36. According to [a widely-cited survey based on newspaper reports] a total of 321 women were murdered between January 1993 and July 2003 in Ciudad Juárez. [Other estimates ranged up to 370.] …

37. According to the authorities, the murders in Ciudad Juárez have different motives, including domestic and intra-family violence, drug trafficking, crimes of passion, quarrels, robbery, vengeance and sexual motives. And yet, a significant proportion of the murders — around one third — include a sexual violence component and similar characteristics….

…

40. The authorities' response to the murders, disappearances and other forms of violence against women has been extremely inadequate, especially during the early 1990s….

…

VII. Conclusions and recommendations

…

259. … [T]he Committee finds that the facts…constitute grave and systematic violations of the provisions of [CEDAW] as well as of Recommendation No. 19 of the [CEDAW] and [VEDAW].

260.… [These violations] have continued for over 10 years, and [the Committee] notes with consternation that it has not yet been possible to eradicate them, to punish the guilty and to provide the families of the victims with the necessary assistance.

…

A. General recommendations

…

264. [Recommendation:] Comply with all obligations assumed under [CEDAW]. Recall, in particular, that the obligation to eliminate discrimination against women refers not only to actions or omissions by the State at all levels, but also to the need to take all appropriate measures to eliminate discrimination against women by any person, organization or enterprise.

265. The Committee considers that at present, in response to growing national and international demands for urgent action, there has been a positive evolution

in the attitude of the Mexican authorities at the federal level....However, the Committee notes that these measures are still insufficient, and that the coordination among the three branches of Government that is required to implement these measures does not exist. Moreover, since the state and municipal authorities still tend to play down the importance and magnitude of the problem....

266. [Recommendation:] Strengthen coordination and participation at all levels of authority — federal, state and municipal....

267. ... [N]ot all actions and programmes have clearly incorporated a gender perspective, that is, that consideration has not been given to the impact of such policies on women and men, bearing in mind their socially constructed roles and the power relations between them....

268. [Recommendation:] Incorporate a gender perspective into all investigations, polices to prevent and combat violence, and programmes to restore the social fabric....

...

B. Recommendations concerning the investigation of the crimes and punishment of the perpetrators

271. The Committee is concerned that the majority of crimes against women, and in particular all crimes resulting from sexual violence, have not been solved by the relevant institutions....

272. [Recommendation:] Strengthen the coordination and cooperation between the federal and state authorities through the Joint Agency established in Ciudad Juárez in August 2003, in order to ensure that each case is handled jointly by both authorities and that the Public Prosecutor's Department continues to review each case and to compile systematic records of all available information. Propose that the federal Government examine the possibility of giving the federal authorities jurisdiction over all crimes of sexual violence that have not been solved in the past 10 years...

273. [T]here has been no serious and thorough investigation of each case and...complaints by relatives have even been ignored and evidence and proof destroyed. Impunity has prevailed for an entire decade, in which these crimes have been treated as common acts of violence belonging to the private sphere, and the existence of a pattern of discrimination, whose most brutal manifestation has been extreme violence against women, has been ignored. The Committee is also concerned at the inefficiency, negligence, and tolerance shown by the authorities charged with investigating the crimes, the evidence that false confessions have been obtained through torture, and the fact that cases are considered, and recorded, as having been concluded or solved when they are brought before the courts, even though the accused have neither been arrested nor punished....

274. [Recommendation:] Investigate thoroughly and punish the negligence and complicity of public authorities in, the disappearances and murders of women, and the fabrication of confessions under torture; investigate and punish public officials for their complicity in or tolerance of persecution, harassment or threats directed against victims' relatives, members of organizations representing them, and other persons involved in defending them.

275. The Committee is gravely concerned at the lack of due diligence shown by the state and municipal authorities in cases involving disappearances of women, the inconsistencies in their data, and... the lack of sufficient resources and staff trained to act on complaints, and the fact that days sometimes pass before an investigation is opened....

276. [Recommendation:] Establish early warning and emergency search mechanisms... [P]rovide the competent authorities with the training and the human and material resources needed to act with due diligence.

277. The Committee is concerned at the irregularities in the investigations, the apparent incompetence of the authorities, the strange conditions in which the victims are found, the irregularities in the forensic examinations, the number of victims who remain unidentified, and the apparent disarray in which case files are kept....

278. [Recommendation:] Adopt measures to ensure the total autonomy and independence of the forensic departments and experts in their investigation of the crimes, and provide the training and resources required for the effective, full, and prompt discharge of their duties and responsibilities.... The Committee also recommends the establishment of a national register of murdered and abducted women.

...

C. Preventing violence, guaranteeing security and promoting and protecting the human rights of women

287. ... [B]ecause what is involved is a structural situation and a social and cultural phenomenon deeply rooted in the consciousness and customs of the population, it requires a global and integrated response, a strategy aimed at transforming existing sociocultural patterns, especially with regard to eradicating the notion that gender violence is inevitable....

288. [Recommendation:] Organize — with the active participation, at each stage of the process, of civil society organizations, including men and boys — massive, immediate and ongoing campaigns to eradicate discrimination against women, promote equality between women and men and contribute to women's empowerment.... Promote training and capacity-building for public officials... and judges.... Heighten the mass media's awareness of gender violence and challenge them to take a positive and pedagogical approach to the issue....

...

NOTE

In 2007 Mexico enacted the General Law on Women's Access to a Life Free from Violence, strengthening federal/state coordination and cooperation and providing a framework for revising state penal codes, developing government policies and establishing multi-sectoral institutional arrangements. All 32 Mexican states subsequently adopted the law. In 2009, the Inter-American Court of Human Rights in *González et al. ('Cotton Field') v. Mexico* held that Mexico had violated a significant number of rights and ordered far-reaching reparations to be made (see p. 1023, *infra*).

We next examine the approach to the issue of violence that the CEDAW Committee has taken in exercising its complaints function under the OP.

MS. A. T. v. HUNGARY

Communication No. 2/2003, CEDAW Committee Views, Jan. 26, 2005, UN Doc. CEDAW/C/32/D/2/2003 (2005)

[The author stated that she had been subjected for four years 'to regular severe domestic violence and serious threats by her common law husband, L. F., father of her two children', one of whom was brain-damaged. L. F. threatened to kill the author and rape the children, but the author didn't go to a shelter 'because no shelter in the country is equipped to take on a fully disabled child together with his mother and sister.' Moreover, no protection orders or restraining orders are available under Hungarian law. Civil proceedings brought no relief. Ten medical certificates had been issued in connection with separate incidents of 'severe physical violence', even after L. F. left the family residence to live with another woman. At one stage, L. F. broke into the apartment when he no longer had a key. One beating required hospitalization and caused serious kidney injury. The author lives 'at serious risk' and 'in constant fear'. Criminal proceedings against L. F. were initiated but have come to no conclusion; 'no action has been taken by the Hungarian authorities to protect the author from [L. F.]'.]

3.1 The author alleges that she is a victim of violations by Hungary of articles 2 (a), (b) and (e), 5 (a) and 16 of the [CEDAW] for its failure to provide effective protection from her former common law husband. She claims that the State party passively neglected its "positive" obligations under the Convention and supported the continuation of a situation of domestic violence against her.

3.2 She claims that the irrationally lengthy criminal procedures against L. F., the lack of protection orders or restraining orders under current Hungarian law and the fact that L. F. has not spent any time in custody constitute violations of her rights under the Convention as well as violations of general recommendation 19 of the Committee. She maintains that these criminal procedures can hardly be considered effective and/or immediate protection.

...

3.4 The author is also seeking the Committee's intervention into the intolerable situation, which affects many women from all segments of Hungarian society. In particular, she calls for the (a) introduction of effective and immediate protection for victims of domestic violence into the legal system, (b) provision of training programmes on gender-sensitivity, the [CEDAW] and the Optional Protocol, including for judges, prosecutors, police and practising lawyers, and (c) provision of free legal aid to victims of gender-based violence, including domestic violence.

...

[The state's account of some of these events and descriptions differed, at times substantially, from the author's, generally presenting the civil and criminal proceedings in a more favourable light. Nonetheless, 'the State party admits that [such remedies as were provided] were not capable of providing immediate protection to the author . . .'. It had, however, instituted a comprehensive action programme against domestic violence in 2003, details of which it provided.]

6.9 The author requests that the Committee . . . decide on the merits that the rights under the Convention have been violated by the State party. She requests that the Committee recommend to the State party to urgently introduce effective laws and measures towards the prevention of and effective response to domestic violence, both in her specific case and in general. . . . The author believes that the most effective way would be to provide her with a safe home, where she could live in safety and peace with her children, without constant fear of her batterer's "lawful" return and/or substantial financial compensation.

. . .

Consideration of the merits

. . .

9.2 The Committee recalls its general recommendation No. 19 on violence against Women [p. 196, *supra*]. . . . "[U]nder general international law and specific human rights covenants, States may also be responsible for private acts if they fail to act with due diligence to prevent violations of rights or to investigate and punish acts of violence, and for providing compensation". [The issue] is whether the author of the communication is the victim of a violation of articles 2 (a), (b) and (e), 5 (a) and 16 of the Convention. . . .

9.3 With regard to article 2(a), (b), and (e), the Committee notes that the State party has admitted that the remedies pursued by the author were not capable of providing immediate protection to her against ill-treatment by her former partner and, furthermore, that legal and institutional arrangements in the State party are not yet ready to ensure the internationally expected, coordinated, comprehensive and effective protection and support for the victims of domestic violence. While appreciating the State party's efforts . . ., the Committee believes that these have yet to benefit the author and address her persistent situation of insecurity. The Committee further notes the State party's general assessment that domestic violence cases as such do not enjoy high priority in court proceedings. The Committee is of the opinion that the description provided of the proceedings resorted to in the present case, both the civil and criminal proceedings, coincides with this general assessment. Women's human rights to life and to physical and mental integrity cannot be superseded by other rights, including the right to property and the right to privacy. The Committee also takes note that the State party does not offer information as to the existence of alternative avenues that the author might have pursued that would have provided sufficient protection or security from the danger of continued violence. In this connection, the Committee recalls its concluding comments from August 2002 on the State party's combined fourth and fifth periodic report. . . . Bearing this in mind, the Committee concludes that the obligations of the State party set out in [CEDAW] remain unfulfilled and constitute a violation of the author's human rights and fundamental freedoms, particularly her right to security of person.

9.4 The Committee...has stated on many occasions that traditional attitudes by which women are regarded as subordinate to men contribute to violence against them. [The Committee restates the author's failed attempts to get relief from beatings and threats, and the absence of legal remedies.] None of these facts have been disputed by the State party and, considered together, they indicate that the rights of the author under articles 5 (a) and 16 of the Convention have been violated.

...

9.6 Acting under article 7, paragraph 3, of the Optional Protocol...[the Committee] makes the following recommendations to the State party:

I. Concerning the author of the communication

(a) Take immediate and effective measures to guarantee the physical and mental integrity of A. T. and her family;

(b) Ensure that A. T. is given a safe home in which to live with her children, receives appropriate child support and legal assistance as well as reparation proportionate to the physical and mental harm undergone and to the gravity of the violations of her rights;

II. General

[The general recommendations to the state included: respecting and promoting women's human 'right to be free from all forms of domestic violence'; taking measures for 'prevention and effective treatment of violence...promptly implemented and evaluated'; providing regular training of judges and law enforcement officials about CEDAW's requirements; seeking enactment of laws providing for 'protection and exclusion orders as well as support services, including shelters'; and providing offenders with rehabilitation programmes. The state was requested to publish and widely distribute the Committee's views 'in order to reach all relevant sectors of society'.]

NOTE

The efforts begun in the late 1980s to label and prohibit violence against women, and in which CEDAW played a major part, have since generated a rich array of new treaty provisions, especially at the regional level,[5] as well as domestic and international case law. In *Vishaka v. State of Rajasthan* (13 Aug. 1997) the Indian Supreme Court relied on constitutional gender equality norms interpreted in light of CEDAW General Recommendation No. 19 to fashion a right to freedom from sexual harassment at

[5] Inter-American Convention on the Prevention, Punishment and Eradication of Violence against Women, 1994; Protocol to the African Charter on Human and Peoples' Rights on the Rights of Women in Africa, 2003; and Council of Europe, Convention on Preventing and Combating Violence against Women and Domestic Violence, 2011.

work. In *Jessica Lenahan (Gonzales) v. United States* the Inter-American Commission on Human Rights (Report No. 80/11, 21 July 2011) held that the United States had failed to act with due diligence to protect Lenahan and her children from domestic violence, and failed to provide equal protection before the law. In *Opuz v. Turkey* (Application No. 33401/02, 9 June 2009), the European Court of Human Rights held that the failure, stretching over a number of years, to take action against the applicant's husband violated not only the right to life and the right to equal protection but also the right to be free from cruel and inhuman treatment.

QUESTIONS

1. Identify the important similarities and differences between the judgment in *Velásquez Rodríguez* and the views in *Ms. A. T. v. Hungary*, with respect to nature and functions of the forum, specificity and breadth of the conclusions, and character and effect of remedies. Is it accurate to say that the views are a direct and unproblematic application to women's rights of the ideas in the judgment?

2. What different objectives do you think the Committee's inquiry report on Mexico might have been designed to achieve?

3. 'The due diligence standard is a Trojan Horse designed to transform the clearly defined negative obligations that states have willingly accepted into expansive and open-ended positive obligations to undertake a very wide range of preventive and proactive measures. There is no natural boundary to such an obligation and thus no limit to what might be asked of states.' Comment.

4. AFFIRMATIVE ACTION AND QUOTAS

CEDAW explicitly endorses the need for affirmative action or what are termed 'temporary special measures'. This includes measure designed to enhance women's participation in the political process. The CEDAW Committee has adopted expansive interpretations of the relevant provisions in several General Recommendations.

CEDAW, GENERAL RECOMMENDATION NO. 25 (2004): TEMPORARY SPECIAL MEASURES

www2.ohchr.org/english/bodies/cedaw/comments.htm

...

3. The Convention is a dynamic instrument. [The Committee has] contributed through progressive thinking to the clarification and understanding of the substantive content of the Convention....

...

8. … [T]he Convention requires that women be given an equal start and that they be empowered by an enabling environment to achieve equality of results. It is not enough to guarantee women treatment that is identical to that of men. Rather, biological as well as socially and culturally constructed differences between women and men must be taken into account. Under certain circumstances, non-identical treatment of women and men will be required in order to address such differences….

…

10. … [M]easures [must be] adopted towards a real transformation of opportunities, institutions and systems so that they are no longer grounded in historically determined male paradigms of power and life patterns.

…

14. … [T]he application of temporary special measures in accordance with the Convention is one of the means to realize de facto or substantive equality for women, rather than an exception to the norms of nondiscrimination and equality.

18. … While the application of temporary special measures often remedies the effects of past discrimination against women, the obligation of States parties under the Convention to improve the position of women to one of de facto or substantive equality with men exists irrespective of any proof of past discrimination. The Committee considers that States parties that adopt and implement such measures under the Convention do not discriminate against men.

…

20. Article 4, paragraph 1, explicitly states the "temporary" nature of such special measures. Such measures should therefore not be deemed necessary forever, even though the meaning of "temporary" may, in fact, result in the application of such measures for a long period of time. The duration of a temporary special measure should be determined by its functional result in response to a concrete problem and not by a predetermined passage of time….

…

22. The term "measures" encompasses a wide variety of legislative, executive, administrative and other regulatory instruments, policies and practices, such as outreach or support programmes; allocation and/or reallocation of resources; preferential treatment; targeted recruitment, hiring and promotion; numerical goals connected with time frames; and quota systems….

23. … As temporary special measures aim at accelerating achievement of de facto or substantive equality, questions of qualification and merit, in particular in the area of employment in the public and private sectors, need to be reviewed carefully for gender bias as they are normatively and culturally determined. For appointment, selection or election to public and political office, factors other than qualification and merit, including the application of the principles of democratic fairness and electoral choice, may also have to play a role.

24. … Article 4, paragraph 1, read in conjunction with articles 1, 2, 3, 5 and 24, needs to be applied in relation to articles 6 to 16 which stipulate that States parties "shall take all appropriate measures". Consequently, the Committee considers that States parties are obliged to adopt and implement temporary special measures in relation to any of these articles if such measures can be shown to be necessary and

appropriate in order to accelerate the achievement of the overall, or a specific goal of, women's de facto or substantive equality.

...

37. The Committee reiterates its general recommendations Nos. 5, 8 and 23, wherein it recommended the application of temporary special measures in the fields of education, the economy, politics and employment, in the area of women representing their Governments at the international level and participating in the work of international organizations, and in the area of political and public life....

...

CEDAW, GENERAL RECOMMENDATION NO. 23 (1997): POLITICAL AND PUBLIC LIFE

www2.ohchr.org/english/bodies/cedaw/comments.htm

...

5. Article 7 obliges States parties to take all appropriate measures to eliminate discrimination against women in political and public life and to ensure that they enjoy equality with men in political and public life.... The political and public life of a country is a broad concept. It refers to the exercise of political power, in particular the exercise of legislative, judicial, executive and administrative powers. The term covers all aspects of public administration and the formulation and implementation of policy at the international, national, regional and local levels. The concept also includes many aspects of civil society, including public boards and local councils and the activities of organizations such as political parties, trade unions, professional or industry associations, women's organizations, community-based organizations and other organizations concerned with public and political life.

...

14. No political system has conferred on women both the right to and the benefit of full and equal participation. While democratic systems have improved women's opportunities for involvement in political life, the many economic, social and cultural barriers they continue to face have seriously limited their participation. Even historically stable democracies have failed to integrate fully and equally the opinions and interests of the female half of the population. Societies in which women are excluded from public life and decision-making cannot be described as democratic.... The examination of States parties' reports shows that where there is full and equal participation of women in public life and decision-making, the implementation of their rights and compliance with the Convention improves.

15. ... Under article 4, the Convention encourages the use of temporary special measures in order to give full effect to articles 7 and 8. Where countries have developed effective temporary strategies in an attempt to achieve equality of participation, a wide range of measures has been implemented, including recruiting, financially assisting and training women candidates, amending electoral

procedures, developing campaigns directed at equal participation, setting numerical goals and quotas and targeting women for appointment to public positions such as the judiciary or other professional groups that play an essential part in the everyday life of all societies....

16. ... Research demonstrates that if women's participation reaches 30 to 35 per cent (generally termed a "critical mass"), there is a real impact on political style and the content of decisions, and political life is revitalized.

...

22. The system of balloting, the distribution of seats in Parliament, the choice of district, all have a significant impact on the proportion of women elected to Parliament. Political parties must embrace the principles of equal opportunity and democracy and endeavour to balance the number of male and female candidates.

...

29. Measures that have been adopted by a number of States parties in order to ensure equal participation by women in senior cabinet and administrative positions and as members of government advisory bodies include: adoption of a rule whereby, when potential appointees are equally qualified, preference will be given to a woman nominee; the adoption of a rule that neither sex should constitute less than 40 per cent of the members of a public body; a quota for women members of cabinet and for appointment to public office; and consultation with women's organizations to ensure that qualified women are nominated for membership in public bodies and offices and the development and maintenance of registers of such women in order to facilitate the nomination of women for appointment to public bodies and posts....

...

31. Examination of the reports of States parties also demonstrates that in certain cases the law excludes women from exercising royal powers, from serving as judges in religious or traditional tribunals vested with jurisdiction on behalf of the State or from full participation in the military. These provisions discriminate against women, deny to society the advantages of their involvement and skills in these areas of the life of their communities and contravene the principles of the Convention.

32. ... Political parties should be encouraged to adopt effective measures to... ensure that women have an equal opportunity in practice to serve as party officials and to be nominated as candidates for election.

33. Measures that have been adopted by some political parties include setting aside for women a certain minimum number or percentage of positions on their executive bodies, ensuring that there is a balance between the number of male and female candidates nominated for election, and ensuring that women are not consistently assigned to less favourable constituencies or to the least advantageous positions on a party list....

34. Other organizations such as trade unions and political parties have an obligation to demonstrate their commitment to the principle of gender equality in their... memberships with gender-balanced representation on their executive boards so that these bodies may benefit from the full and equal participation of all sectors of society and from contributions made by both sexes....

...

39. The globalization of the contemporary world makes the inclusion of women and their participation in international organizations, on equal terms with men, increasingly important. The integration of a gender perspective and women's human rights into the agenda of all international bodies is a government imperative....

...

[The Committee's recommendations identify concrete measures to be implemented and specifies the details and statistical data on these issues to be provided in the periodic state reports.]

NOTE

Before the adoption of CEDAW in 1979, only a handful of countries had adopted quotas to promote women's representation in the political arena. Today, over 100 countries have such quotas. There are three main forms: (1) parliamentary seats reserved by law for women (20% of countries with quotas have this type — mostly in South Asia and Africa); (2) legal quotas requiring a percentage of political party nominees to be women (38%, mainly in Latin America and Africa); and (3) voluntary quotas adopted by the political parties themselves (61%, mainly in Western Europe). Quotas might apply at the local, regional or national levels; they might set a low or a high percentage; and they might be weakly or strongly enforced. The imposition of candidate quotas increased female parliamentary representation from 16 to 22.6% in Mexico and from 6.7 to 17.5% in Macedonia. Reserving seats resulted in an increase from 0.6 to 10.8% in Morocco and from 1.3 to 5.5% in Jordan.

But quotas are not without controversy. Krook points out that both feminist and non-feminist actors might promote quotas for 'distinct and even contradictory reasons', and she cites four concerns held by at least some feminists: 'that quotas further neoliberal projects, demobilize women's movements, result in the election of non-feminist women, promote a static view of "women" as a group, and decrease the effectiveness of women as political actors.'[6]

A different set of concerns centres around different standards for developing and developed countries. Developing countries have embraced quotas quite strongly. A recent study argues that this primarily reflects international rather than domestic pressures. Quotas 'are adopted by developing countries due to the direct influence of the international community in post-conflict societies and the indirect inducements of the international community in countries that are concerned with foreign aid, foreign investment, international reputation, and legitimacy.'[7] But the

[6] M. L. Krook, 'Quota Laws for Women in Politics: Implications for Feminist Practice', 15 Social Politics 345 (2008), at 360.

[7] S. Sunn Bush, 'International Politics and the Spread of Quotas for Women in Legislatures', 65 Int'l. Org. 103 (2011), at 131.

determined export of quota models to 'emerging democracies' by the industrialized democracies sits uneasily with the latter's domestic policies.

RUTH RUBIO MARIN, A NEW EUROPEAN PARITY-DEMOCRACY SEX EQUALITY MODEL AND WHY IT WON'T FLY IN THE UNITED STATES

60 Am. J. Comp. L. 99 (2012)

Gender inequalities in the United States and Europe are persisting. Only 59% of women in the United States are in the labor force. Women in the United States continue to earn less money than men for equal work, shoulder more childcare and household responsibilities and are more likely to live in poverty. Women are said to hold only 15% of [board] seats in Fortune 500 companies, chairing only 2% of the boards. [In 2011 women represent] only 16.80% in Congress and 17% in the Senate.... In spite of this, gender quotas in politics or in business are not a popular concept.

In Europe as well women continue to hold an unequal position in the employment domain. [In 2009], the employment rate of women was only 62.5%.... Women across the European Union still earned 17.5% less on average than men. [In 2010 women held only 24% of parliamentary seats, and only 27% of senior ministerial posts.] ... [O]nly 3% of the largest publicly quoted companies had a woman chairing the highest decision-making body.

Nevertheless, as opposed to the United States, over the last two decades the unequal distribution of roles, tasks and power between women and men has become a key issue in European democracies resulting in new approaches, including different types of gender quotas.... Europe is slowly departing from a narrowly conceived equal rights/opportunities (i.e., formal/substantive) sex equality framework in order to gradually embrace...a parity democracy equality model [designed to enable] both men and women to participate equally in all domains of citizenship.

...

V. Exporting Parity Citizenship to the United States: An Unlikely Venture?

...

A. Sexual Contract versus Racial Contract

One of the most striking differences between Europe and the United States seems to lie in the impossibility to discuss quotas for women in the United States without simultaneously addressing the political underrepresentation or disempowerment of blacks and other minorities. The European parity democracy model seems to rest on the assumption that the sexual contract is foundational to the modern state and needs to be disestablished, and that this distinguishes the political exclusion of women from that of other groups whose political exclusion is, so to say, not as foundational.

...

B. Women versus the Family

... [C]onservative forces in the United States, often mobilized by Christian religious fundamentalism, have historically succeeded in presenting every instance of affirmation of women's rights and fight for equality as a threat to the family. This applies to women's campaign for suffrage; for the Equal Rights Amendment; for reproductive rights; and for the ratification of CEDAW. It is therefore most likely that the parity democracy model would first be constructed as a fundamental threat to the family, and, to the extent that it stems from a nation-wide project, also to federalism notions locating the family within the sphere of state jurisdiction; it would then be resisted on the exact same grounds as all other women's rights initiatives. In other words, it would probably be perceived as social engineering forcing women out of and men into the house, thereby challenging a presumed natural order of things. Constitutionally, both gender neutral readings of the Equal Protection Clause and privacy notions derived from the Fourteenth Amendment would probably be alleged to claim non-interference with the family.

The irony is of course that the parity equality model purports to enhance the political and social recognition of the activities that so far mostly women perform in the so called private (family) domain. This is why resistance articulated precisely in the name of family values shows that what is truly at stake is the defense of an alleged natural order of things (i.e., preserving the sexual contract) and not the defense of care, human reproduction and interdependency.

In Europe, the parity measures have been defended as good for all (politics and corporations will be better off if the resources of both sexes are included, and society will be better off if both men and women can better reconcile family and work) or as a matter of justice to women whose equal rights and participation must define what democracy is fundamentally about. Thus, to the extent that the family has come into the discussion it is to claim the need for men's larger involvement in it or the likeliness that women's empowerment will translate into more family friendly policies.

C. Individualism, Autonomy, Meritocracy and the Unencumbered Market Forces

Underlying the U.S. rejection of strict and mandatory gender quotas is of course the critical understanding that quotas on the basis of sex violate formal equality and a gender neutral reading of the Equal Protection Clause.... [S]trict quotas are not uncontroversial in Europe either because despite the prevalent substantive equality model and the application of indirect discrimination as a constitutional doctrine, the formal equality principle still exists forcing a proportionality analysis. Such analysis is more likely to succeed with regard to measures that are less invasive than strict quotas and closer to the ideal of ensuring equal opportunities but not equal results....

The greater resistance towards the enactment of legislative measures to ensure women's access to positions of power in both the political and the economic domains is also related to the stronger U.S. individualist tradition and its faith in both autonomy and meritocracy as expressed through the free functioning of the market and of social forces, including capital and political parties, that constitutional provisions such as First Amendment associational rights of political parties help to protect. In Europe, the social or welfare state tradition with its post-World War II constitutional embedding has less difficulty advancing the notion that political and economic imbalances of powers may require positive corrections by the State to protect the more vulnerable. Also in harmony with this social state tradition is the conceptualization of positions of power in political office and corporate governance not only as highly paid and recognized positions for which individuals must freely compete, but also as positions of social responsibility that might justify interference of otherwise constitutionally protected spheres of autonomy (such as freedom of enterprise or the autonomy of political parties) for the sake of ensuring a more egalitarian system and a more perfect democracy....

D. Anti-essentialism and Anti-stereotyping

... In Europe, quotas have been defended both by those who believe that women can add a distinctive way of ruling (more collaborative, less competitive or ego driven) and those who sustain that this is ultimately irrelevant because the point is simply treating women as equal citizens. In contrast, in the United States, quotas would most likely be seen as rigid and essentializing, and the affirmation of the difference that women can make is likely to be controversial enough to prevent feminists of different strands from joining forces to support the initiative.

The reasons that account for this utmost concern with essentializing women are probably several. For one thing, the U.S. sex antidiscrimination doctrine has been mostly concerned with fighting gender stereotypes in general, and those that confine the women to the home, perpetuate the breadwinner role, and limit women's ability to act as full citizens in particular. This has prevented this doctrine from allowing the law to accommodate women's differences, even if they can be statistically proven (like women doing more housework than men) and even if they can be interpreted not as inherent differences (i.e., expressive of women's essential and distinctive nature) but rather as differences that result from masculine norms such as those enshrining the separate spheres ideology. Given that reactionary movements resisting women's rights have relied precisely on the defense of the family, it is not surprising that there has been resistance towards defending women's rights and equality on the grounds of "family-related" specificities of women, whether natural or constructed. Also, in a state that can only be minimally relied upon to limit the powers of employers, granting women-specific rights that reflect their roles in care and reproduction is inevitably a double-edge sword.

...

QUESTIONS

1. How do you react to the provisions in both General Recommendations on affirmative action, either by the state or by political parties? As a member of the Committee, which if any of these provisions would you oppose? Is it consistent with Article 25 of the ICCPR, guaranteeing the right to vote? How do you react to para. 31 of GR No. 23?

2. If the United States were to ratify CEDAW would it need to lodge a reservation in relation to Article 7 of the Convention?

3. Is it problematic that CEDAW norms affect states differentially, depending on whether the international community can exert pressure through development assistance and other forms of influence?

5. REPRODUCTIVE RIGHTS AND DEBATES OVER US RATIFICATION OF CEDAW

Ratification has been considered by the United States on several occasions. In 1994 the Senate Committee on Foreign Relations, after hearings, recommended ratification to the Senate, by a vote of 13–5, subject to various reservations, understandings and declarations, including the following:

> [T]he Constitution and laws of the United States establish extensive protections against discrimination, reaching all forms of governmental activity as well as significant areas of non-governmental activity. However, individual privacy and freedom from governmental interference in private conduct are also recognized as among the fundamental values of our free and democratic society. The United States understands that by its terms the Convention requires broad regulation of private conduct, in particular under Articles 2, 3 and 5. The United States does not accept any obligation under the Convention to enact legislation or to take any other action with respect to private conduct except as mandated by the Constitution and laws of the United States.[8]

The Committee also proposed reservations to the right to equal pay understood as comparable worth, the right to paid maternity leave, and any obligation under Articles 5, 7, 8 and 13 of the Convention that might restrict constitutional rights to speech, expression and association.

Five senators (a Republican minority) on the Committee objected to ratification. In their Minority Views they endorsed the goal of eliminating discrimination against women, but felt that CEDAW was not the best means of pursuing that objective. The Minority Views made the following points:

> (1) CEDAW may enable ratifying states to generate 'political capital', but is 'unlikely to convince governments to make policy changes they would otherwise avoid'.

[8] See S384–10, Exec. Rep. Sen. Comm. on For. Rel., 3 October 1994. The text of all proposed reservations is in 89 Am. J. Int'l. L. 102 (1995).

(2) Countries like the United States 'must guard against treaties that overreach', and must not promise 'more than we can deliver or we risk diluting the moral suasion that undergirds existing covenants'.

(3) More than 30 states, including Islamic states, had made significant and sometimes problematic reservations when ratifying CEDAW. The statement questioned 'whether such behavior does not, in fact, "cheapen the coin" of human rights treaties generally'. These reservations suggest that CEDAW 'may reach beyond the necessarily restrictive scope of an effective human rights treaty'.

(4) 'Improvement in the status of women in countries such as India, China, and Sudan will ultimately be made in those countries, not in the United States Senate'.

(5) Evolution of 'internationally accepted norms' on human rights must 'take place within an international system of sovereign nations with differing cultural, religious and political systems. Pushing a normative agenda beyond that system's ability to incorporate it leads, we believe, to what is represented by this convention....'

The Convention was not brought to a vote in the full Senate. Since 1994 there has been little action.[9] In 1998 President Clinton sought congressional support for gaining Senate consent to ratification. In 2002, the Senate Foreign Relations Committee held a brief hearing on CEDAW and voted 12–7 for ratification, subject to most of the earlier proposed reservations, understandings and declarations, plus two additional ones. Democratic Senator Biden, chairman of the Committee, sponsored an understanding to the effect that 'the CEDAW Committee has no authority to compel parties to follow its recommendations'.[10] Republican Senator Jesse Helms proposed an understanding that 'nothing in this Convention shall be construed to reflect or create any right to abortion and in no case should abortion be promoted as a method of family planning.' This issue has subsequently assumed greater significance in the US debate, as illustrated by the following analysis.

LUISA BLANCHFIELD, THE UN CONVENTION ON THE ELIMINATION OF ALL FORMS OF DISCRIMINATION AGAINST WOMEN (CEDAW): ISSUES IN THE US RATIFICATION DEBATE

Congressional Research Service, 28 June 2011

...

Abortion

... Many who support U.S. ratification hold that the treaty is abortion neutral because the word "abortion" is never mentioned in the Convention's text. [T]he Clinton Administration... declared the treaty abortion neutral in 1994. Supporters

[9] In 2010 the Senate Judiciary Committee's Subcommittee on Human Rights and the Law held CEDAW hearings, at which the Obama Administration expressed support for ratification.

[10] Congressional Research Service Report for Congress, The UN Convention on the Elimination of All Forms of Discrimination Against Women (CEDAW): Issues in the US Ratification Debate (26 June 2011).

also emphasize that many countries where abortion is regulated or illegal, including Burkina Faso, Colombia, and Ireland, ratified the Convention without associated reservations....

Many opponents of U.S. ratification argue that parts of the Convention text could be interpreted to undermine current U.S. abortion law. Specifically, some have taken issue with Article 12(1), which states that countries "shall take all appropriate measures to eliminate discrimination against women in the field of health care in order to ensure... access to health care services, including those related to family planning." Critics have also expressed concern regarding Article 16(1)(e), which requires that States Parties take all appropriate measures to ensure that women have the right to "decide freely and responsibly on the number and spacing of their children." Opponents suggest that such language could lead to the abolishment of state parental notification laws, require federal funding for abortions, or obligate the U.S. government to promote and provide access to abortion. Two States Parties to the Convention — Malta and Monaco — explicitly stated in their reservations to CEDAW that they do not interpret Article 16(1)(e) as imposing or forcing the legalization of abortion in their respective countries.

CEDAW supporters counter such criticisms by emphasizing that Articles 12 and 16 [leave] it up to States Parties to determine what actions are appropriate based on their domestic laws and policies. To support this view, some have cited the negotiating history of CEDAW....

CEDAW Committee Recommendations Related to Abortion

The CEDAW Committee's recommendations to States Parties regarding abortion are a particularly controversial aspect of the U.S. ratification debate. Many opponents of CEDAW, particularly pro-life advocates, are strongly critical of the Committee because, in their view, it calls on States Parties to support and encourage abortion despite the fact that it is never mentioned in the CEDAW text. As evidence of this, critics point to the Committee's General Recommendation 24, which elaborates on CEDAW Article 12(1) addressing women's equal access to health care, including family planning services. The Committee recommends that "when possible, legislation criminalizing abortion could be amended to remove punitive provisions imposed on women who undergo abortion." Opponents also criticize Committee recommendations to individual countries that appear to encourage the decriminalization or legalization of abortion and oppose conscientious objector policies. In... 2007, the Committee urged Poland "to ensure that women seeking legal abortion have access to it, and that their access is not limited by the use of the conscientious objection clause."... [S]ome critics have expressed concern with a May 2006 decision by the Constitutional Court of Colombia, which cited CEDAW when it determined that abortion should not be considered a crime in all circumstances (such as rape or incest and when the life of the mother is in danger).

... CEDAW supporters emphasize that the purpose of the Committee is to consider the progress of States Parties' implementation of the Convention. They point out that CEDAW has no established mechanism for non-compliance and that it relies primarily on States Parties to fulfill their treaty obligations. Further, proponents contend that many of the Committee recommendations to States Parties demonstrate its overall opposition to abortion as a method of family planning. In

2006, for example, the Committee expressed concern that in the Former Yugoslav Republic of Macedonia "abortion continues to be used as a method of birth control." Similarly, in 2007 the Committee noted with concern that in Greece "due to inadequate access to family planning and contraceptive methods, abortion is often used by women and adolescent girls as a method of birth control." Moreover, supporters maintain that the overall goal of the Committee is to encourage States Parties to reduce abortion rates through education and family planning....

NOTE

In *Szijjarto v. Hungary*, Communication No. 4/2004, Views of the CEDAW Committee, 29 August 2006, UN Doc. CEDAW/C/36/D/4/2004, the author, a Hungarian Roma woman, with three children, encountered serious problems in another pregnancy and was brought into a Hungarian hospital when in an emergency situation and in considerable pain and confusion and in a state of shock.

While on the operating table, the author was asked to sign a form consenting to the caesarean section. She signed this as well as a barely legible note that had been handwritten by the doctor and added to the bottom of the form, which read: 'Having knowledge of the death of the embryo inside my womb I firmly request my sterilization [a Latin term unknown to the author was used]. I do not intend to give birth again; neither do I wish to become pregnant.'

Within 17 minutes of the ambulance's arrival at the hospital, the caesarean section was performed and the author's fallopian tubes were tied. The author's narrative, accepted in large part by the Committee, made clear that she had no idea of what she had signed and in fact desired more children. The sterilization violated her Catholic beliefs and led to a depression and feeling of having violated the Roma culture in which she lived. Her civil action against the hospital for pecuniary and non-pecuniary damages failed at the trial and appellate level. In this case initiated before the CEDAW Committee under the Optional Protocol, the author claimed that she had been 'subjected to coerced sterilization by medical staff at a Hungarian hospital', and that Hungary thereby violated her rights under Articles 10(h), 12 and 16 (para. 1(e)) of CEDAW.

The Committee agreed. The 'recommendations' that it made to the state first referred to 'appropriate compensation' for the author 'commensurate with the gravity of the violations of her rights'. Its 'general' recommendations to the state included taking measures 'to ensure' that CEDAW's relevant provisions and some earlier general recommendations of the Committee 'are known and adhered to by all relevant personnel in public and private health centres'; reviewing legislation on informed consent 'to ensure its conformity with international human rights and medical standards'; and monitoring public and private health centres performing sterilization procedures 'so as to ensure that fully informed consent is being given... with appropriate sanctions in place in the event of a breach'.

In a later case, the Committee addressed the issue of abortion.

L. C. v. PERU

Communication No. 22/2009, CEDAW Committee Views, 17 October 2011, UN Doc. CEDAW/C/50/D/22/2009

...

2.1 [When L. C., the daughter of the author of the communication,] was 11 years old, she began to be sexually abused by J.C.R., a man about 34 years old. As a result, she became pregnant at the age of 13 and, in a state of depression, attempted suicide on 31 March 2007 by jumping from a building. She was taken to Daniel Alcides Carrión public hospital....

2.2 The damage to the spinal column, in addition to other medical problems, caused paraplegia of the lower and upper limbs requiring emergency surgery. The head of the Neurosurgery Department recommended surgery in order to prevent the injuries she suffered from worsening and leaving her disabled. As a result, the intervention was scheduled for 12 April 2007.

[When the hospital authorities discovered she was pregnant, the surgery was postponed.]

2.5 On 18 April 2007, the author, after consulting with her daughter, requested the hospital officials to carry out a legal termination of the pregnancy in accordance with article 119 of the Penal Code.[11] ...

2.6 Given the excessive delay by the hospital authorities [the author consulted an NGO which] brought the case to the attention of the office of the Deputy Defender for Women's Rights in the Public Defender's Office....

2.7 The Deputy Defender requested a medical report from the High-Level Commission on Reproductive Health of the Medical College of Peru. [Its opinion was that] 'if the pregnancy continues, there is grave risk to the girl's physical and mental health; a therapeutic abortion, if requested by the subject, would therefore be justified'.

2.8 On 7 June 2007, when L.C. was 16 weeks pregnant, the author submitted an appeal for a reconsideration of its opinion regarding the termination of the pregnancy to the hospital medical board, attaching the report of the Medical College and stressing the serious and immediate risk to both the physical and mental health of the minor, the sole requirements established under the Penal Code to allow the legal termination of pregnancy.

2.9 On 16 June 2007, L.C. miscarried spontaneously....

2.10 On 11 July 2007, L.C. had surgery for her spinal injuries....

2.11 L.C....is paralyzed from the neck down and has regained only partial movement in her hands....

2.12 According to the author, no administrative recourse exists in the State party to request the legal termination of a pregnancy. Nor is there a protocol for care that indicates the procedure for requesting a legal abortion....

[11] This provision states that 'abortion shall not be punishable if performed by a doctor with the consent of the pregnant woman or her legal representative, if any, when it is the only way to save the life of the mother or to avoid serious and permanent harm to her health'.

2.13 The previous Peruvian Health Code established as a requirement in order to perform a therapeutic abortion that it must be performed by a doctor and be supported by two other doctors. However, the General Health Act currently in force... repealed that standard and created a legal vacuum....

2.14 According to the author, there is no appropriate judicial mechanism allowing access to the courts to request termination of a pregnancy for therapeutic reasons, nor to provide full redress for a violation of this type....

...

Consideration on the merits

...

8.11 The Committee recalls the obligation of the State party under article 12.... It also recalls its general recommendation No. 24, which, as an authoritative interpretation tool in relation to article 12, states that "it is discriminatory for a State party to refuse to legally provide for the performance of certain reproductive health services for women" (para. 11)....

8.12 [The Committee notes that surgery was unquestionably necessary.]

...

8.15 [T]he Committee considers that, owing to her condition as a pregnant woman, L.C. did not have access to an effective and accessible procedure allowing her to establish her entitlement to the medical services that her physical and mental condition required. Those services included both the spinal surgery and the therapeutic abortion. This is even more serious considering that she was a minor and a victim of sexual abuse. The suicide attempt is a demonstration of the amount of mental suffering she had experienced as a result of the abuse. The Committee therefore considers that the facts as described constitute a violation of the rights of L.C. under article 12 of the Convention. The Committee also considers that the facts reveal a violation of article 5 of the Convention, as the decision to postpone the surgery due to the pregnancy was influenced by the stereotype that protection of the foetus should prevail over the health of the mother....

...

8.17 The Committee considers that, since the State party has legalized therapeutic abortion, it must establish an appropriate legal framework that allows women to exercise their right to it under conditions that guarantee the necessary legal security, both for those who have recourse to abortion and for the health professionals who must perform it. It is essential for this legal framework to include a mechanism for rapid decision-making, with a view to limiting to the extent possible risks to the health of the pregnant mother, that her opinion be taken into account, that the decision be well-founded and that there be a right to appeal.13 In the present case... an effective remedy was not available to L.C. and that the facts described give rise to a violation of article 2 (c) and (f) of the Convention.

8.18 The Committee notes that the failure of the State party to protect women's reproductive rights and establish legislation to recognize abortion on the grounds of sexual abuse and rape are facts that contributed to L.C.'s situation....

...

9 … The Committee therefore makes the following recommendations to the State party.

(a) Concerning L.C.: provide reparation that includes adequate compensation for material and moral damages and measures of rehabilitation…
(b) General:

(i) Review its laws with a view to establish a mechanism for effective access to therapeutic abortion under conditions that protect women's physical and mental health and prevent further occurrences in the future of violations similar to the ones in the present case;…

…

QUESTIONS

1. Which objections to ratification of CEDAW that were set forth in the Minority Views seem particular to CEDAW, and which could refer generally to many human rights treaties?

2. In what ways might the Committee's views in these two cases be invoked in the US ratification debate?

3. By 2005, 45 cities, 18 counties and 16 states within the United States had adopted formal statements to this effect, and in 1998 San Francisco adopted the provisions of CEDAW as part of its local law.[12] Might such initiatives encourage US ratification, or are they of largely rhetorical value?

ADDITIONAL READING

On women's rights generally see: UN Women, *Progress of the World's Women 2011–2012* (2011); World Economic Forum, *Global Gender Gap Report 2011* (2011); K. Askin & D. Koenig (eds.), *Women and International Human Rights Law* (3 vols. 1999–2000); F. Banda, *Women, Law and Human Rights: An African Perspective* (2005); D. Buss & A. Manji (eds.), *International Law: Modern Feminist Approaches* (2005); H. Charlesworth & C. Chinkin, *The Boundaries of International Law: A Feminist Analysis* (2000).

On CEDAW see: M. Freeman, C. Chinkin & B. Rudolf (eds.), *The UN Convention on the Elimination of All Forms of Discrimination Against Women: A Commentary* (2012); A. Byrnes & J. Connors, *The International Bill of Rights for Women: The*

[12] J. Resnik, 'Comparative (In)equalities: CEDAW, the Jurisdiction of Gender, and the Heterogeneity of Transnational Law Production', 10 Int'l. J. Const. L. 531 (2012).

Impact of the CEDAW Convention (2013); Australian Human Rights Commission, *Mechanisms for Advancing Women's Human Rights: A Guide to Using the Optional Protocol to CEDAW and Other International Complaint Mechanisms* (2011); M. L. Krook, *Quotas for Women in Politics: Gender and Candidate Selection Reform Worldwide* (2009); R. J. Cook & S. Cusack, *Gender Stereotyping: Transnational Legal Perspectives* (2010).

On issues of public and private and violence against women see: B. Meyersfeld, *Domestic Violence and International Law* (2010); S. Mullally, 'Domestic Violence Asylum Claims and Recent Developments in International Human Rights Law: A Progress Narrative?' 60 *ICLQ* 459 (2011); A. Clapham, *Human Rights Obligations of Non-State Actors* (2006); Law Commission of Canada, *New Perspectives on the Public-Private Divide* (2003); F. Olsen, 'Feminist Critiques of the Public/Private Distinction', in D. Dallmeyer (ed.), *Reconceiving Reality: Women and International Law* (1993), at 157.

C. EVOLUTION OF HUMAN RIGHTS: SEXUAL ORIENTATION DISCRIMINATION

In this section we turn to the evolution of new norms, and consider the particular case of lesbian, gay and bisexual (LGB) rights.[13] This brief consideration of LGB rights addresses important questions for the study and practice of international human rights law more generally. For example, how does a new human rights norm emerge? What relationship might it have to the existing legal framework? How does it overcome strong political resistance from different corners of the globe? How do like-minded states work strategically to promote the wider recognition of a new norm?

National and Transnational Social and Legal Change

At the international level, formal recognition of LGB rights by international authorities came about in the closing decades of the twentieth century (1980–1999). Many of the changes at the international level took place after fundamental social changes had occurred at the national level. It is, therefore, important to consider some of the developments in domestic society and politics before 1980.

Efforts to forge a new legal regime for LGB rights were galvanized, in particular, by two key developments in the United Kingdom and the United States. In England, a government-appointed commission, composed of eminent persons from the public and private sector, issued a report in 1957 (the Wolfenden Report),

[13] The social and legal history of transgender and intersex rights involves a related but also distinct set of issues. The discussion in this section focuses on the degree to which the international legal system has recognized LGB rights, as a tool for understanding how other dynamic human rights norms — including transgender and intersex rights — might follow a similar trajectory.

which concluded that 'homosexual behaviour between consenting adults in private should no longer be a criminal offence'. The ensuing public debate culminated in legal reforms and substantial (though incomplete) decriminalization of same-sex conduct in 1967. In the United States, a new social movement was launched around the same time. It started in part with an uprising among gay residents in New York City in response to systematic police harassment. A flashpoint occurred at a gay bar, the Stonewall Inn, in 1969. The following year on the anniversary of the 'Stonewall Riots', the first Gay Pride marches took place in major cities of the United States. These social changes were also emboldened by changes within the medical establishment, and especially the 1973 decision of the American Psychiatric Association no longer to classify homosexuality as a mental disorder which gave an important impetus to social change in the United States (and globally). Also in 1973, the American Civil Liberties Union created the Sexual Privacy Project (later renamed the Lesbian, Gay, Bisexual, Transgender and AIDS Project). And, in 1973, Lambda Legal Defense and Education Fund was established as the first legal organization dedicated to achieving equal rights for lesbian and gay people.

These social and legal changes soon acquired a transnational dimension. LGB organizations formed in multiple countries. And one of the primary legal objectives for the emergent transnational lesbian and gay rights movement was the decriminalization of same-sex conduct. Sociologist David John Frank provides the following description:[14]

> One indicator of the global diffusion of LGBT human rights appears in Figure 1. It depicts the total number of nation-state ties to (or memberships in) eleven LGBT international nongovernmental organizations between 1965 and 2005. Before 1980, there are no LGBT INGO memberships. By 2005, the total is more than 250, representing more than 100 different countries....

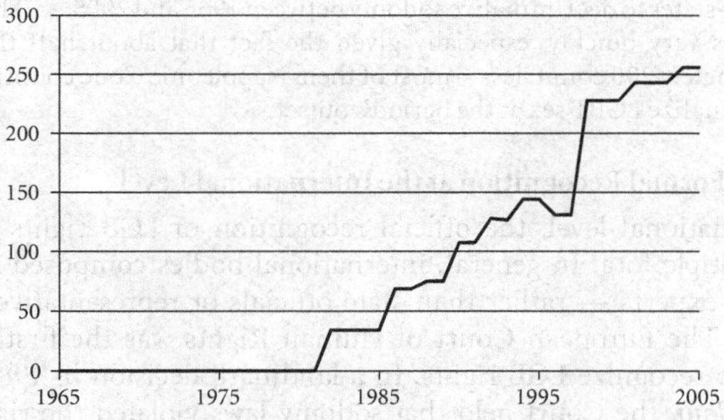

Figure 1 Country Ties to 11 LGBT INGOs, 1965–2005

> Naturally, nation-states are not equally well connected to LGBT international nongovernmental organizations. By 2005, for example, France and Germany

[14] David John Frank, 'Making Sense of LGBT Asylum Claim: Change and Variation in Institutional Contexts', 44 N.Y.U. J. Int'l. L. & Pol'y. 485 (2012).

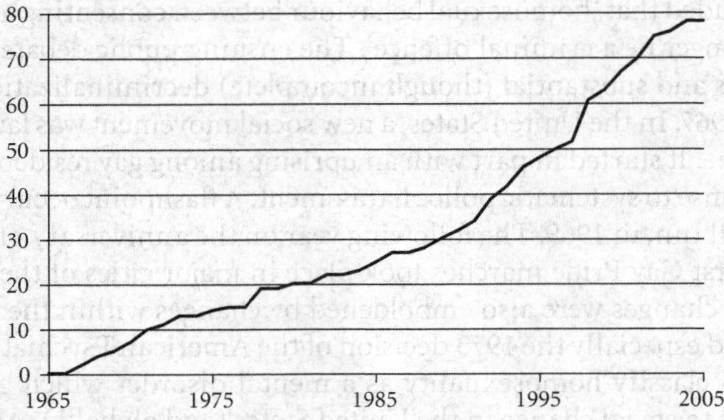

Figure 2 Cumulative Number of Countries to Decriminalize Sodomy, 1965–2005

> have representatives in ten of the eleven LGBT INGOs represented in Figure 1. Lebanon and Uruguay, meanwhile, have representatives in only one.

…

[T]he globalized, individualized, and human-rightsified world described above mobilized strongly, as a first order of business, against enduring criminal prohibitions against LGBT sex.

…

> It is thus critical to recognize that, in the recent period, decriminalization has happened rapidly on a worldwide basis. Figure 2 shows the cumulative number of nation-states to decriminalize sodomy between 1965 and 2005.... The number multiplies very quickly, especially given the fact that about half the world's approximately 200 countries — most of them Napoleonic Code countries — did not criminalize LGBT sex at the period's outset.

The Road to Formal Recognition at the International Level

At the international level, the official recognition of LGB rights has occurred through multiple fora. In general, international bodies composed of judges and independent experts — rather than state officials or representatives of states — led the way. The European Court of Human Rights was the first international institution to recognize LGB rights. In a landmark decision in 1981, *Dudgeon v. United Kingdom*, the Court held that sodomy laws violated the right to privacy under the European Convention.[15] And the Court subsequently reaffirmed its decision in cases arising out of Ireland in 1988 and Cyprus in 1993. Beginning in 1994, the United Nations High Commissioner for Refugees recognized that sexual orientation qualifies as a 'particular social group' eligible for protection under

[15] In contrast, the Inter-American Court of Human Rights decided its first case recognizing LGB rights in 2012.

international refugee law. Also in 1994, the UN Human Rights Committee, the supervisory body of the ICCPR, concluded that Tasmania's local sodomy law violated the universal covenant (*Toonen v. Australia*).[16] The Committee's reasoning rested primarily on the right to privacy. However, in an aside and without much explanation, the Committee also stated that discrimination on the basis of sexual orientation was regulated by the right to equality under the ICCPR. In the following year, the Committee reviewed the US record of compliance, and the Committee expressed its concern 'at the serious infringement of private life' due to US sodomy statutes. By 2001, four of the other five universal human rights treaties were interpreted by their respective supervisory organs to cover sexual orientation discrimination (CEDAW in 1999, CESCR in 2000, CRC in 2000 and CAT in 2001).

It is important to note that the Committee on the Elimination of Racial Discrimination was long absent from this practice — despite the fact that the Committee often addresses issues of 'double discrimination' against people who belong to both racial and other minorities. As Michael O'Flaherty and John Fisher explain, 'This gap is startling when one considers the authoritative evidence of such persons [LGBT people who belong to a racial minority] facing forms of "double discrimination", as reported, for instance, by the UN Human Rights Council's Special Rapporteur on contemporary forms of racism, racial discrimination, xenophobia and related intolerance' (O'Flaherty and John Fisher: 2008). Notably, the Convention on the Elimination of Racial Discrimination defines distinctions based on 'national origin' as a form of racial discrimination, and the Committee accordingly often reviews asylum and immigration practices. This is at least one domain in which significant forms of discrimination against LGB people occurs — yet the Committee remained silent. That said, the Committee may have recently aligned more closely with the other treaty bodies.[17]

In conjunction with the treaty bodies, in the 1990s independent experts working under a UN mandate — beginning with the Special Rapporteur on violence against women and the Special Rapporteur on extrajudicial, summary or arbitrary executions — took up the issue of discrimination based on sexual orientation as part of their respective mandates. They were followed, in the early 2000s, by several other mandate-holders and UN-appointed experts, including the Special

[16] Tasmania today has one of the most protective regimes for LBGT people in Australia. In 2010, its parliament was the first in the nation to pass legislation recognizing same-sex marriages performed in foreign jurisdictions. In 2011, its lower house of parliament became the first in the nation to vote in support of marriage for same-sex couples in Australia.

[17] In its 2007 Concluding Observations on the Czech Republic, the CERD Committee expressed 'concern that a condition under the Act on Registered Partnerships between Persons of the Same Sex, currently under debate in Parliament, may be that at least one of the persons be a Czech citizen' and explained that 'differential treatment based on citizenship constitutes discrimination if the criteria for such differentiation, judged in the light of the objectives and purposes of the Convention, are not applied pursuant to a legitimate aim, and are not proportional to the achievement of this aim'. In the oral proceedings, the Committee asked for an explanation why the requirement did not apply to heterosexual couples, and the government delegate acknowledged that the provision could constitute 'an inequality based on sexual orientation'. The Committee has also welcomed laws that prohibit discrimination on multiple grounds including sexual orientation (e.g., 2006 Concluding Obs.: Denmark, praising the fact that the criminal code 'introduced an aggravating circumstance for offences based on another's ethnic origin, faith, sexual orientation or the like'; 2009 Concluding Obs.: Greece; 2008 Concluding Obs.: Germany; 2006 Concluding Obs.: Lithuania).

Rapporteur on torture (2001); the Working Group on Arbitrary Detention (2001); the Special Representative on human rights defenders (2001); and the Special Rapporteur on the independence of judges and lawyers (2002). In the following years, several more mandate-holders would help consolidate this practice (e.g., Special Rapporteur on adequate housing (2010); Special Rapporteur on health (2009); Independent Expert on minority issues (2006)).

As the formal recognition of LGB rights at the global level was first led by independent institutions and office-holders, a second wave involved an increasingly large group of states and their representatives working within international fora. The first decade of concerted state effort — the 1990s — involved limited action and a mixed record. During that period, European institutions succeeded in establishing the most protective laws and policies concerning LGB rights. For example, in 1997, the Amsterdam Treaty (amending the Treaty of the European Union) became the first international agreement with an explicit aim to prohibit discrimination based on 'sexual orientation'. Also during this period, as part of EU expansion, preconditions for applicant states included decriminalization of homosexual conduct and the elimination of other laws violating LGB rights.

A key turning point — and a valuable set of lessons — in the struggle for equality occurred at the Fourth World Conference on Women held in Beijing in 1995. The conference adopted an important Declaration and Platform for Action. In the drafting process, a highly mobilized coalition of NGOs pressed for the inclusion of explicit references to sexual orientation. As is common with world conferences of this type, states convened regional preparatory meetings in the run up to Beijing. At the European preparatory meeting, member states voted to include references to sexual orientation in their region's proposed text. As a result, the draft text negotiated in Beijing included four references. Each reference was bracketed — a standard technique of international negotiations indicating parts of the draft where text is still contested and subject to review.[18] In the final hours of the Beijing conference (indeed, after 4 a.m.), the Chair of the Working Group holding discussions on these parts of the text announced that all references to sexual orientation would be eliminated due to significant opposition. A reference to women's freedom of sexuality remained in the text, but it was placed under a heading for health and reproductive rights. In addition, some states were concerned that the text's references to 'gender' could apply to sexual orientation. Those states obtained a concession that the President of the Conference would issue a statement accompanying the final report, which explained that 'the word "gender" had been commonly used and understood in its ordinary, generally accepted usage in numerous other United Nations forums and conferences' and 'there was no indication that any new meaning or connotation

[18] States supporting references to sexual orientation included: Australia, Barbados, Bolivia, Brazil, Canada, Chile, Colombia, Cook Islands, Cuba, European Union (15 states), Israel, Jamaica, Latvia, New Zealand, Norway, Slovenia, South Africa, Switzerland, and the United States. States that had expressed opposition included: Algeria, Bangladesh, Belize, Benin, Cote d'Ivoire, Egypt, Ghana, Guatemala, Honduras, Iran, Jordan, Kuwait, Libya, Nigeria, Senegal, Sudan, Syria, Uganda, United Arab Emirates, Venezuela and Yemen.

of the term, different from accepted prior usage, was intended in the Platform for Action'.[19]

Over 25 states reportedly registered an objection to the deletion of references to sexual orientation (Helfer and Miller, p. 226, *infra*). Several of these governments stated that they would nevertheless interpret particular parts of the final text to include sexual orientation (Canada, Israel, Jamaica, Latvia, New Zealand, Norway, Slovenia and South Africa). For example, they would interpret sexual orientation to be implicitly included in the phrase 'barriers to full equality...because of such factors as their race, age...and *other status*' as well as in the phrase referring to women's 'right to have control over and decide freely and responsibly on matters related to their *sexuality*'. Additionally, the United States issued an Interpretive Statement which provided: 'The United States Government has a firm policy of non-discrimination on the basis of sexual orientation and considers that the omission of this reference in paragraph 46 and elsewhere in the Platform for Action in no way justifies such discrimination in any country'.

Observers have expressed a range of views on whether the result at Beijing marked a step forward or backward in the recognition of LGB rights. Consider the following viewpoints among different human rights scholars:

> Any mention of women's problems arising from sexual orientation was expressly excluded, under threats by States to refuse to endorse the document. While the drafting histories (travaux préparatoires) of the leading human rights instruments are merely inconclusive on the drafters' intentions relevant to sexual orientation — not clearly alluding to it one way or the other — the Beijing Declaration now delivers affirmative evidence that sexual minorities are specifically meant to be excluded. With the Beijing Declaration, the international human rights movement does not merely give sexual minorities 'nothing'. It actively brands them as unsuitable for human rights protections.

E. Heinze, 'Sexual Orientation and International Law: A Study in the Manufacture of Cross-Cultural "Sensitivity"', 22 Mich. J. Int'l. L. 283 (2001).

> [L]esbian-specific scholarship and activism building on the women's human rights movement has become increasingly visible internationally. In particular, the Fourth World Conference on Women held in Beijing...brought lesbian human rights to new global prominence. Although the final Declaration and Platform for Action adopted at the Beijing Conference does not explicitly address sexual orientation, these documents do reflect the influence of lesbian advocacy efforts at the conference and may point the way for more significant advances in the future. [The authors contend that the sections of the Platform of Action referring to discrimination based on 'other status' and women's control over their sexuality 'can be construed to protect significant aspects of lesbian human rights'.]

[19] The 1998 Rome Statute for the International Criminal Court, building on the Beijing precedent, included a similar statement in the body of its treaty text. Article 7(3) provides: 'For the purposes of this Statute, it is understood that the term "gender" refers to the two sexes, male and female, within the context of society. The term "gender" does not indicate any meaning different from the above'.

L. R. Helfer and A. M. Miller, 'Sexual Orientation and Human Rights: Toward a United States and Transnational Jurisprudence', 9 Harv. Hum. Rts. J. 61 (1996).

> On the positive side, women's sexual orientation was firmly positioned as a central issue for public discussion during the entire Conference and, as a result, many delegates and NGO representatives rethought their views, although this was not enough to alter the outcome. Many now know that this is an issue in their country, when they had previously believed that it wasn't. A number of states argued strongly for international recognition of women's sexual diversity and can be expected to maintain that view into the future. On the negative side, it can now be argued that the issue should not be reopened in future global forums because it has been well-canvassed and a consensus position reached, This is a powerful argument in the international context. . . .
>
> . . .
>
> The importance of international forums like the [Beijing world conference] lies less in their specific legal outcomes than in their contestation of the dominant global discourse, including the 'truths' promoted by international law, and the shifts in power and new possibilities that emerge as a result. The Beijing discussion made important inroads into breaking the dominant codes of lesbian invisibility and in placing women's sexuality and sexual identities firmly onto the main agenda.

Dianne Otto, 'Lesbians? Not in My Country', 10 Alternative L. J. 288 (1995).

By the early 2000s, like-minded states worked together to have the United Nations officially recognize LGB rights. Countries taking leadership positions included Brazil, France, South Africa and eventually (by 2010) the United States. This initiative set its sights on three types of resolutions: an annual resolution of the UN Human Rights Commission on the death penalty; a biennial resolution of the General Assembly condemning extrajudicial, summary and arbitrary executions; and a potential new resolution recognizing the principle of equality and freedom from discrimination for LGB persons. The first two resolutions offered an easier target and a potential political wedge. It would be difficult for most states to endorse the death penalty for homosexual conduct or to support language suggesting that LGB individuals should not receive protection from extrajudicial killings. At the same time, opponents understood the symbolic and precedential significance of any UN resolution referring to sexual orientation or the rights of LGB people explicitly.

Death Penalty Resolutions

The first successful effort along these lines involved a UN resolution on the death penalty. Since the mid-1990s, the principal human rights organ of the UN General Assembly — the Commission for Human Rights (replaced by the Human Rights Council in 2006) — passed an annual resolution calling for strictly circumscribing, if not eventually abolishing, the death penalty. Once supporters secured a majority of states in favour of the resolution, subsequent meetings of the Commission included incremental expansion of the scope and demands of the resolution. In 2002, negotiators achieved another 'incremental' step. A section of the resolution calling on states to limit the death penalty to the 'most serious crimes' included a phrase also urging states to ensure 'the death penalty is not imposed for non-violent acts such as . . . sexual relations between consenting adults'. That text was retained in the death penalty resolutions that the Commission adopted over the following years.

Extrajudicial and Arbitrary Executions Resolutions

A parallel effort occurred in a series of resolutions adopted by the General Assembly on the topic of extrajudicial, summary or arbitrary executions. Starting in 1992, the Assembly adopted a resolution on this topic every two years. Arising from the General Assembly's Third Committee, these resolutions also became more expansive over time. Specifically, in 2002, the extrajudicial killing resolution became the first official text of the United Nations to acknowledge the obligation of member states to protect individuals on the basis of their 'sexual orientation'. The 2002 General Assembly Resolution '[r]eaffirms the obligation of Governments to ensure the protection of the right to life of all persons under their jurisdiction, and calls upon Governments concerned to investigate promptly and thoroughly . . . all killings committed for any discriminatory reason, including sexual orientation'. Each successive passage of the resolution included similar text.

This track record was at least temporarily unsettled in 2010. During the meeting of the Third Committee that year, a coalition of opposing states managed to pass an amendment removing the reference to sexual orientation. Uganda (on behalf of the OIC [Organization of Islamic Conference]) had proposed a similar amendment in the Third Committee in 2008, but that proposal was defeated by a vote of 59 (in favour of the amendment), 77 (against) and 25 (abstentions). In 2010, the amendment passed with 79 in favour, 70 against and 17 abstentions. The International Service for Human Rights, an organization that closely observes the UN human rights machinery, reported the following:

> Although discrimination on the basis of sexual orientation and gender identity remains one of the most sensitive topics under discussion in the UN human rights system, most States have been in favour of the reference remaining in the extrajudicial executions resolution because it focuses on the most egregious violations. However, this year the decision by the African Group, Arab Group and OIC to jointly (rather than individually) bring an amendment finally tipped the balance in the other direction. Ten African States that had abstained from the vote on the same issue in 2008 switched to vote in favour of the deletion this year, along with a handful of other States, mostly from the Caribbean.
>
> . . .
>
> All States that spoke in support of the amendment began by confirming their belief that human rights should be equally enjoyed by all, particularly the right to live free from discrimination and violence. . . . Benin [which had spoken on behalf of the African Group], Morocco [which had spoken on behalf of the Arab Group and OIC], Cuba and Jamaica argued that deleting the reference to sexual orientation was a 'non-selective' and 'non-controversial' way for the Third Committee to avoid this divisive issue, and at the same time, not exclude any group from protection by the State. St. Lucia echoed this point, adding that the co-sponsors' 'shopping list' approach was not only unwieldy, but would lead to 'misinterpretation and misuse'. Some groups were highlighted at the expense of others, when all people should enjoy equal protection under the law. Although no State advocated deleting any other part of the paragraph at this stage, Jamaica

suggested that in future, all that was needed was a 'general reference to all vulnerable groups, without distinction'.

As the main sponsor of the biennial resolution, Finland (on behalf of the Nordic Group)...[stated that] [n]one of the co-sponsors were claiming that any group was more important than another, rather the purpose of highlighting sexual orientation was to alert States that they needed to take steps to protect LGB communities from these killings. The general reference to States' obligation to prevent 'discrimination on any basis', would not, in the opinion of the co-sponsors, be sufficient to ensure all States understood that they needed to take targeted steps to protect LGB individuals.

Several Western States supported Finland and advocated the reference to sexual orientation be retained...Sweden warned that the deletion would suggest that the General Assembly was 'looking the other way' or 'condoning' discrimination on the basis of sexual orientation as a legitimate ground for carrying out an extrajudicial execution. This was at odds with the General Assembly's obligation to investigate and prosecute crimes against all persons. The UK added that impunity for any extrajudicial executions was completely unacceptable. Along with Sweden, the UK...argued the paragraph only referred to highly vulnerable groups that had been identified by the Special Rapporteur, and as such was consistent with the approach taken in other General Assembly resolutions. The US said the arguments put forward to support the amendment were 'without merit'. The reference to sexual orientation did not create new rights, but reaffirmed the right to life.

Latin American States, which have been strong advocates of the rights of LGB people in the General Assembly in recent years, were largely absent from the discussion. Brazil was the only one to make a statement, which was brief and rather muted in its support....

A new element in the discussions at the Third Committee was the suggestion that if the international community wanted to address the issue of sexual orientation, it should agree to do so in a direct and focused manner, rather than through divisive resolutions. It was notable that this suggestion came from Benin (on behalf of the African Group) and South Africa. Benin suggested that States would first need to agree on a format and framework for discussion. South Africa suggested that an open-ended intergovernmental discussion was required so that States could establish the parameters of sexual orientation under international law.

For proponents of LGB rights, the setback in the Third Committee mobilized important actors to restore the original text before a vote by the General Assembly the following month. UN Secretary-General Ban Ki-moon, who had acquired a reputation for soft-peddling human rights, adopted a strong and unequivocal stance. In an address on Human Rights Day 2010, he stated:

Today is Human Rights Day — a day we dedicate to defending freedoms and protections for all people.

We know how controversial the issues surrounding sexual orientation can be.

In the search for solutions, we recognize that there can be very different perspectives.

And yet, on one point we all agree — the sanctity of human rights.

As men and women of conscience, we reject discrimination in general, and in particular discrimination based on sexual orientation and gender identity.

When individuals are attacked, abused or imprisoned because of their sexual orientation, we must speak out.

We cannot stand by. We cannot be silent.

This is all the more true in cases of violence.

These are not merely assaults on individuals.

They are attacks on all of us.

...

Today, many nations have modern constitutions that guarantee essential rights and liberties.

And yet, homosexuality is considered a crime in more than 70 countries.

This is not right.

Yes, we recognize that social attitudes run deep.

Yes, social change often comes only with time.

Yet, let there be no confusion:

Where there is tension between cultural attitudes and universal human rights, universal human rights must carry the day.

Personal disapproval, even society's disapproval, is no excuse to arrest, detain, imprison, harass or torture anyone — ever.

...

In all these kinds of cases, I put myself on the line.

I take pains to find the right balance between public and private diplomacy to reach difficult solutions.

I will continue to do so.

I will continue to speak out, at every opportunity, wherever I go.

And I will do so because this is the right thing to do.

Because this cause is just.

...

Violence will end only when we confront prejudice.

Stigma and discrimination will end only when we agree to speak out.

That requires all of us to do our part.

To speak out — at home, at work, in our schools and communities.

To stand in solidarity.

...

People were not put on this planet to live in fear of their fellow human beings.

The watchwords of civilization have always been tolerance, understanding and mutual respect.

That is why we are here today.

And that is why we ask the nations and the peoples of the world to join us.

To join us in common cause in the name of justice and a better life for all.

The United States also took a leadership position in the effort to restore the text on sexual orientation. US Ambassador to the United Nations Susan Rice, during an LGB Core Group event marking Human Rights Day, said:

> I'm particularly honored that some of the brave activists on the front lines of that struggle are here with us today.... We're joined by determined and defiant men and women who have suffered persecution, harassment, and outright violence simply because of their sexual orientation or gender identity. You have shown great courage and conviction in the face of bigotry and intolerance, and I'm deeply moved to be here with you.
>
> The story of my country is, in part, a story of the expanding boundaries of rights and dignity — of the way that discrimination and prejudice have been countered by acceptance and equality. I feel this deeply and I feel it very personally. Even at a time of profound challenges at home and abroad, we dare not give up on the great causes of equality and fundamental rights. And that includes the pursuit of full and equal rights for the millions of people in this country and around the world who are gay, lesbian, bisexual, or transgender.
>
> ...
>
> Here at the United Nations, like many of you, I was incensed by the recent vote in the General Assembly's Third Committee, which eliminated any mention of lesbian, gay, bisexual, and transgender individuals from a resolution condemning extrajudicial killing of vulnerable people around the world. We fought hard for that reference when it came to a Committee vote, and we lost. But we're not done yet. The resolution now goes to the full General Assembly. For countries that voted in the Committee to keep the reference to sexual orientation, we thank you. For countries that haven't yet done so, we urge you to join us. And for countries that have supported this reference in the past but changed course this year, we urge you to stand again with us and with all vulnerable people around the world at risk of violence. We are going to fight to restore the reference to sexual orientation. We're going to stand firm on this basic principle. And we intend to win.

The United States sponsored a proposal to restore the reference to 'sexual orientation' in the text. The General Assembly voted 93 in favour, with 55 countries voting against and 27 abstaining.

Sexual Orientation-Specific Resolutions

States have also attempted to adopt a UN resolution specific to human rights and sexual orientation, an effort that finally succeeded in 2011. The first significant attempt occurred in 2003. Perhaps buoyed by the success of the 2002 resolutions on the death penalty and on extrajudicial killings, a group of states circulated a draft of the so-called 'Brazilian Resolution' at the 2003 meeting of the UN Human Rights Commission. Rather than insert a reference to LGB issues in a resolution dealing with another subject (such as the death penalty or extrajudicial executions), the Brazilian text recognized LGB rights directly. The draft expressed 'deep concern at the occurrence of violations of human rights in the world against persons on the grounds of their sexual orientation' and stressed that 'human rights and fundamental freedoms are the birthright of all human beings... and that the enjoyment of such rights and freedoms should not be hindered in any way on the grounds of sexual orientation'. Twenty states officially co-sponsored the Resolution; they were all European countries with the exception of Brazil and Canada. The Commission decided to postpone discussion of the resolution until the following year. In the intervening period, several Islamic states and the Vatican expressed stiff opposition to the proposed resolution. In the 2004 meeting of the Commission, Brazil withdrew its proposal citing a lack of support, and the government did not bring it back on the agenda in subsequent years.

Between 2005 and 2010, three important developments shaped the trajectory of state support for LGB rights. The first involved an effort by NGOs. In previous years, international NGOs—such as Amnesty International, Human Rights Watch and the International Gay and Lesbian Rights Commission—provided extensive documentation of human rights violations across the globe. Their reports covered a wide range of issues including criminal prohibitions, arbitrary denials of asylum, police abuse and extrajudicial killings. The work of these organizations also turned to an important standard-setting project to promote a legal framework for LGB rights. That initiative culminated in the 2006 Yogyakarta Principles on the Application of Human Rights Law in relation to Sexual Orientation and Gender Identity (the Yogyakarta Principles), which were drafted by a group of 29 international human rights experts. The Principles are intended to affirm binding international legal standards pertaining to LGBT rights. They contain a broad range of human rights standards including the rights to life, work, asylum, health, education and to found a family. Among other effects, the Principles helped to counter the argument of detractors that international law lacks any basis for rights relating to sexual orientation and gender identity. The 'Jurisprudential Annotations' to the Principles contain extensive citations to existing legal authority supporting each of the provisions in the final text.

The second development occurred within the Inter-American system. At the global level, state efforts to recognize LGB rights had previously been cast along a largely North-South (or developed v. developing country) divide. The predominance of European co-sponsors of the 'Brazilian Resolution' was one example. A groundbreaking decision by the Organization of American States unsettled that narrative. In June 2008, the OAS unanimously adopted a resolution entitled 'Human Rights, Sexual Orientation, and Gender'. The preamble reaffirmed the right to equality and freedom from discrimination, and an operative paragraph expressed concern about 'acts of violence and related human rights violations committed against individuals because of their sexual orientation and gender identity'. The measure was significant because it also marked a change (or nuance) in the position of individual states that had opposed other international efforts to recognize LGB rights.[20]

The third development between 2005 and 2010 involved diplomatic efforts within the United Nations. Following the withdrawal of the Brazilian text, in 2005 New Zealand issued a public statement supported by 32 countries calling for the Commission on Human Rights to address the issue of sexual orientation in the near

[20] For instance, at the Beijing conference in 1995, Belize, Guatemala, Honduras and Venezuela opposed references to sexual orientation. As another example, in 2004, Costa Rica voted to eliminate the reference to sexual orientation in the extrajudicial killing resolution. In the 2010 meetings of the Third Committee on the extrajudicial executions resolution, Bahamas, Haiti and Jamaica supported the amendment to remove the reference to sexual orientation, and Colombia abstained (Colombia had opposed such an amendment in 2008).

future. The Statement also read: 'Sexual orientation is a fundamental aspect of every individual's identity and an immutable part of self. It is contrary to human dignity to force an individual to change their sexual orientation, or to discriminate against them on this basis'. In 2006, a group of 54 states, led by Norway (and this time including the United States), issued a Joint Statement at the Human Rights Council calling for consideration of human rights abuses involving violence based on sexual orientation and gender identity. The statement also 'call[ed] upon all Special Procedures and treaty bodies to continue to integrate consideration of human rights violations based on sexual orientation and gender identity within their relevant mandates'. On 18 December 2008, a group of 66 states issued a joint statement at the General Assembly. The Statement was sponsored by France and accompanied by a covering letter signed by eight states including Argentina, Brazil, Croatia, Gabon and Japan. The Statement called for abolition of criminal penalties based on sexual orientation or gender identity and urged states 'to ensure that human rights violations based on sexual orientation or gender identity are investigated and perpetrators held accountable and brought to justice'. The United States refused to support the measure. A high-ranking US diplomat explained, 'We are opposed to any discrimination, legally or politically, but the nature of our federal system prevents us from undertaking commitments and engagements where federal authorities don't have jurisdiction'. (In 2009, within the first 100 days of the Obama Administration, the United States officially joined the Statement.) On the same day as the Joint Statement, a group of 57 states led by Syria issued a Response, which was also delivered at the General Assembly. The Response stated:

> [W]e are seriously concerned at the attempt to introduce to the United Nations some notions that have no legal foundations in any international human rights instrument. We are even more disturbed at the attempt to focus on certain persons on the grounds of their sexual interests and behaviors, while ignoring that intolerance and discrimination regrettably exist in various parts of the world, be it on the basis of color, race, gender, or religion to mention only a few.
>
> Our alarm does not merely stem from concern about the lack of legal grounds.... More importantly, it arises owing to the ominous usage of those two notions. The notion of orientation spans a wide range of personal choices that expand way beyond the individual's sexual interest in copulatory behavior with normal consenting adult human beings, thereby ushering in the social normalization and possibly the legitimization of many deplorable acts including pedophilia. The second is often suggested to attribute particular sexual interests or behaviors to genetic factors, a matter that has been scientifically rebuffed repeatedly.
>
> [W]e affirm that those two notions are not and should not be linked to existing international human rights instruments....
>
> We strongly deplore all forms of stereotyping, exclusion, stigmatization, prejudice, intolerance, discrimination and violence directed against peoples, communities and individuals on any ground whatsoever, wherever they occur.
>
> We also reaffirm Article 29 of the Universal Declaration of Human Rights and the right of Member States to enact laws that meet "just requirements of morality, public order, and the general welfare in a democratic society".
>
> ... We note with concern the attempts to create "new rights" or "new standards" by misinterpreting the Universal Declaration and international treaties

> to include such notions that were never articulated nor agreed by the general membership. These attempts... seriously jeopardize the entire international human rights framework.
>
> ...
>
> ... [W]e urge all Member States, the United Nations system, and non-governmental organizations to continue to devote special attention and resources to protect the family as "the natural and fundamental group unit of society" in accordance with article 16 of the Universal Declaration of Human Rights.
>
> To conclude, Mr. President, we also urge all States and relevant international human rights mechanisms to intensify their efforts to consolidate the commitment to the promotion and protection of human rights of everyone on an equal footing without exception.

At the Human Rights Council's June 2011 session, South Africa took the lead in sponsoring the UN's first ever resolution on 'human rights, sexual orientation and gender identity' (Res. A/HRC/17/19 of 17 June 2011). The Resolution narrowly passed with 23 in favour, 19 against and 3 abstentions. The White House called the Resolution 'a significant milestone' in the struggle for equal rights. The text took three steps: (1) it expressed 'grave concern at acts of violence and discrimination, in all regions of the world, committed against individuals because of their sexual orientation and gender identity'; (2) it asked the Office of the High Commissioner for Human Rights to conduct a study 'to document discriminatory laws and practices and acts of violence against individuals based on their sexual orientation and gender identity, in all regions of the world, and how international human rights law can be used to end violence and related human rights violations based on sexual orientation and gender identity'; and (3) it decided to convene a panel to discuss the report at a session of the Human Rights Council in 2012. In December 2011, the High Commissioner for Human Rights released its report (UN Doc. A/HRC/19/41). In February 2012, Pakistan, on behalf of the 57-member OIC, submitted a letter to the Council that reiterated many of the points raised in the Syria Statement in 2008. The letter concluded that 'the Member States of the OIC would like to place on record their opposition to the holding of this panel and will not accept its considerations and recommendations'. In 2012, the Human Rights Council held the unprecedented panel discussion. The panel opened with statements from the UN Secretary-General and the High Commissioner for Human Rights. As an official protest, most Arab and African nations walked out of the conference hall during the discussion. The following reading contains a summary record of a sample of views expressed by states explaining their vote on the resolution.

EXPLANATIONS OF VOTE ON 2011 HUMAN RIGHTS COUNCIL RESOLUTION ON HUMAN RIGHTS, SEXUAL ORIENTATION, AND GENDER IDENTITY

17 June 2011, at www.ohchr.org/EN/NewsEvents/Pages/DisplayNews.aspx?NewsID=11167&LangID=E

SOUTH AFRICA, introducing [the] draft resolution..., said that dialogue was an extremely powerful tool when dealing with a difficult subject matter.... The resolution did not seek to impose values on Member States but sought to initiate a dialogue which would contribute to ending discrimination and violence based on sexual orientation, gender identity or gender identity. In South African non-discrimination on the basis of sexual orientation and gender identity was constitutionally protected. Despite this there were still challenges relating to violence against such individuals. South Africa believed that intergovernmental dialogue could find ways to address this subject. Further, although South Africa was a predominantly Christian society, all religions were treated the same; and although South Africa was predominantly a black country, all racial groups enjoyed equal rights. It further noted in relation to apartheid that when some were imprisoned moral and political support was received from all sections of the world; South Africans never said that they could not accept support on the basis of gender identify. South Africa stressed that the United Nations was the common parliament for the international community and as such it should discuss complex and difficult issues. The resolution called for the UN Human Rights Council to offer an opportunity to the international community to have a factual based dialogue relating to discrimination against those who had different sexual orientation or gender identity....

...

NIGERIA, speaking in an explanation of the vote before the vote, said that African countries, and more than 90 per cent of the African people did not support this draft resolution. South Africa had referred to a declaration of African leaders indicating desires to deal with human rights in an objective and non-confrontational manner and accused the resolution of disregarding the universality of human rights and putting individual conduct above international instruments. Notions on sexual orientation should not be imposed on countries... Some issues of individual nature should not be under discussion at the Council. [NIGERIA later...] said the African Group remained committed to the principle of non-discrimination. Nigeria believed that no human being should be subjected to discrimination based on any particular behavior.... Nigeria said it was unacceptable that countries lacked the ability to have laws on sexual orientation and countries lacked the political will to subject themselves to a true picture of democracy. It went against all norms preached in the Human Rights Council, such as transparency, accountability and democracy. This was a signal that the Human Rights Council should be careful to not again go against its roots.

SAUDI ARABIA,... said the draft resolution was not in line with internationally agreed human rights principles. It was not appropriate to impose these values on other countries. Cultural and religious considerations should be taken into account. It was not appropriate to impose values without considering them as counter to Sharia in Islam, and other religions.

BAHRAIN,... condemned the attempt to make the Council deal with controversial issues such as gender identity. This was an attempt to create new standards and new human rights by misinterpreting the existing international human rights standards. These were issues based on personal decisions and were not fundamental human rights.

BANGLADESH, . . . supported all human rights, including the right to development and condemned violence against individual groups. There was no legal foundation for this draft resolution in human rights instruments. Bangladesh was disturbed by the focus on personal sexual interests while discrimination based on race, ethnicity, religion and other issues remained ignored. Bangladesh believed that rights included in the Universal Declaration of Human Rights had been coded into international instruments. By introducing notions not articulated in human rights instruments, these very instruments and the human rights framework were undermined.

. . .

MEXICO, . . . what was being discussed should be seen in relation to something else, not the imposition of values, not something linked to changing cultural practices or condemning or condoning individual cultural practice. It was a question of non-discrimination, not a new subject in the Council. Non-discrimination on grounds of race and religion and non-discrimination against women, the elderly and those with disabilities were values that stood fully recognized by all. Non-discrimination on grounds of sexual orientation was the same thing. Mexico did not share the views of colleagues that the Council would be imposing non-recognized rules. This was a human right. For that reason and with the utmost respect for other Member States, Mexico supported with complete conviction the draft resolution. . . .

. . .

UNITED STATES, . . . said the United States was thrilled to join South Africa and other Member States on this resolution. The Universal Declaration on Human Rights was the first full affirmation that all people should enjoy full rights and freedoms. An important step forward was made in recognizing that human rights were universal. Violence against any person on grounds of sexual orientation was a violation of human rights. The right to choose who to love was sacred. Each human deserved protection from violence. Moving forward with this resolution confirmed the aspiration to attain the best of human nature . . .

JORDAN, . . . said that the text before the Council had rendered it divided and prevented it from obtaining a joint position. Jordan regretted it could not join the consensus on this draft resolution.

MAURITANIA, . . . said . . . that the resolution did not promote the advancement of human rights but rather the dehumanisation of human beings.

STATEMENT BY THE HOLY SEE DELEGATION (THE VATICAN)

9 March 2012, at www.radiovaticana.org/EN1/Articolo.asp?c=569943

1. The Holy See Delegation has noted with careful attention the Report on "Discriminatory Laws and Practices and Acts of Violence against Individuals based on their Sexual Orientation and Gender Identity". The Holy See has condemned repeatedly violence against people because of their perceived sexual differences.

The Catechism of the Catholic Church, in fact, states: "Every sign of unjust discrimination in regard [of homosexual persons] should be avoided." The teaching of the Catholic Church on this issue was authoritatively set forth in a 1986 letter to all the Catholic bishops throughout the world, as follows: "It is deplorable that homosexual persons have been and are the object of violent malice in speech or in action. Such treatment deserves condemnation from the Church's pastors wherever it occurs. It reveals a kind of disregard for others which endangers the most fundamental principles of a healthy society. The intrinsic dignity of each person must always be respected in word, in action, and in law."

...

Mr. Chairman, it is the firm view of the Holy See that the grave problems of discrimination and violence toward the population upon which the Report focuses, or toward any other victimized groups or individuals, must be pursued on the basis of the principle of subsidiarity. Thus these problems should receive attention and effective action at the level of national and local governments, civil society, religious and cultural leaders. Such situations cannot be resolved by defining new categories, laws or policies that posit rights and privileges to special groups in society.

4. ... My Delegation, however, finds both confusing and misleading the High Commissioner's decision to further develop her argumentation with an exclusive focus on those persons subjected to discrimination and violence on the basis of their perceived sexual differences. The rights cited by the High Commissioner are rights that should and must be universally respected and enjoyed; thus efforts to particularize or to develop special rights for special groups of people could easily put at risk the universality of these rights.

5. Moreover, the Holy See Delegation wishes to raise serious concern with the insertion of terms such as "sexual orientation" and "gender identity" which do not enjoy mention in binding documents of the United Nations and which are ambiguous in nature since they lack specific definition in international Human Rights instruments. In fact, my Delegation believes that the use of the term "gender identity" was settled, in 1998, during the discussion leading up to the promulgation of the Statute of the International Criminal Court.... Any requirement for States to take such terms into account in their efforts to promote and implement fundamental human rights could result in serious uncertainty in the application of law and undermine the ability of States to enter into and enforce new and existing human rights conventions and standards.

6. In...her Report, the High Commissioner rightly asserts that "the Human Rights Committee has held that States are not required, under international law, to allow same-sex couples to marry." She immediately proposes, however, that Sates [sic] have an obligation to "ensure that unmarried same-sex couples are treated in the same way and entitled to the same benefits as unmarried opposite-sex couples." In this regard, the Holy See expresses grave concern that, under the guise of "protecting" people from discrimination and violence on the basis of perceived sexual differences, this Council may be running the risk of demeaning the sacred and time-honoured legal institution of marriage between man and woman, between husband and wife, which enjoyed special protection from time immemorial within legal, cultural, and religious traditions and within the modern human

rights instruments, starting with the Universal Declaration of Human Rights, and extending to numerous other covenants, treaties, and laws. Marriage contributes to society because it models the way in which women and men live interpedently and commit, for the whole of life, to seek the good of each other. The marital union also provides the best conditions for raising children; namely, the stable, loving relationship of a mother and a father; it is the foundation of the natural family, the basic cell of society. States confer legal recognition on the marital relationship between husband and wife because it makes a unique and essential contribution to the public good. If marriage were to be re-defined in a way that makes other relationships equivalent to it, as has occurred in some countries and as the High Commissioner seems to be encouraging in her Report, the institution of marriage, and consequently the natural family itself, will be both devalued and weakened.

...

QUESTIONS

1. In his Human Rights Day statement, the UN Secretary-General stated that 'homosexuality is considered a crime in more than 70 countries'. What is the proper role for the Secretary-General given that, on his own account, at least 70 UN member states presumably disagree with a core part of his normative position? Are there other issues on which a UN Secretary-General should express strong views in the face of direct opposition by many states? Are human rights issues different? Are LGB issues special in some way?

2. How important are biological and other explanations of sexual orientation for securing recognition of LGB rights? That is, how important are empirical assumptions about whether sexual orientation is innate, malleable, or immutable to these debates? Consider the 2005 New Zealand statement that sexual orientation 'is a fundamental aspect of every individual's identity and an immutable part of self'. And consider Syria's 2008 statement referring to conceptions that 'attribute particular sexual interests or behaviors to genetic factors, a matter that has been scientifically rebuffed repeatedly'. What is at stake for proponents and opponents of LGB rights in these disagreements about genetics, biology, immutability and the like? How might the arguments in this domain affect the support for rights related to gender identity? Do LGB proponents who invoke notions of immutability make it more difficult for the transgender community to secure recognition of their rights?

3. The United States claimed that references to sexual orientation in the extrajudicial executions resolution would not create new rights. And South Africa contended that the 2011 Resolution was designed only to open dialogue, not to impose a particular perspective. Are these correct representations of the intention of the drafters and the effect of such texts? Are the opponents correct that these resolutions help to build important legal (and political) authority for recognition of LGB rights more generally?

4. What are the strongest arguments made by the opponents of LGB rights? What are their weakest arguments?

5. Was the Beijing conference a step forward or backward for LGB rights? What are the main lessons that advocates of new or emergent human rights norms should draw from Beijing or from the success of LGB rights at the United Nations? What lessons do opponents of such rights probably draw from these experiences?

ADDITIONAL READING

S. Barclay, M. Bernstein & A.-M. Marshall (eds.), *Queer Mobilizations: LGBT Activists Confront the Law* (2009); M. O'Flaherty & J. Fisher, 'Sexual Orientation, Gender Identity and International Human Rights Law: Contextualising the Yogyakarta Principles', 8 Hum. Rts. L. Rev. 207 (2008); D. J. Frank, B. J. Camp & S. A. Boutcher, 'Worldwide Trends in the Criminal Regulation of Sex, 1945 to 2005', 75 Am. Soc. Rev. 867 (2010); D. Sanders, 'Human Rights and Sexual Orientation in International Law', 5 Nov. 2005, at http://ilga.org/ilga/en/article/577; I. Saiz, 'Bracketing Sexuality: Human Rights and Sexual Orientation: A Decade of Development and Denial at the UN', 7 Health and Human Rights 48 (2004); N. Gartner, 'Articulating Lesbian Human Rights', 14 UCLA Women's L. J. 61 (2005); D. J. Frank & E. H. McEneaney, 'The Individualization of Society and the Liberalization of State Policies on Same-Sex Sexual Relations, 1984–1995', 77 Soc. Forces 911 (1999); J. E. Halley, 'Sexual Orientation and the Politics of Biology: A Critique of the Argument from Immutability', 46 Stan. L. Rev. 503 (1994).

D. NORM REGRESSION: THE TORTURE PROHIBITION

If one were to ask a representative number of people committed to human rights values which if any right among, say, those declared in the UDHR had priority in importance, torture would surely rank high on the list. It could be said, 'If anything is a human right, then it's the right not to be tortured.' Consider its prominence in human rights texts. Article 5 of the UDHR states that no one shall be subject 'to torture or to cruel, inhuman or degrading treatment or punishment'. Article 7 of the ICCPR restates this language. An entire treaty — the Convention against Torture and other Cruel, Inhuman or Degrading Treatment or Punishment — addresses the problem of state-inflicted torture. As of 2012, that treaty had 150 states parties. The regional conventions reveal the same emphasis on the prohibition, in both general and torture-specific treaties.

Nonetheless, despite this broad normative consensus over prohibition of torture by states, its incidence remains significant and widespread, more in authoritarian than liberal regimes, more in the developing than developed worlds, but in developed and democratic countries as well. Some amount of torture by the state will stem from truly aberrational conduct by a state official violating state policy and possibly later sanctioned for such unlawful conduct. But torture by the state predominantly takes place because of state policies expressly allowing or requiring it or because of quiet toleration of violations of formal policy. Undoubtedly sheer venality — the satisfaction of sexual and sadistic desires or the desire to humiliate and exercise total physical dominion over another's body — has always played its role. It appears that periods of mass violence of horrific proportions, such as the Cambodian and Rwandan genocides, weaken inherent or acquired inhibitions against vile behaviour so as to make commonplace the torture of helpless civilian populations and prisoners. Such abominations, themselves often fostered by state propaganda to enlist the participation of non-state actors in the savaging of the target population, may constitute both a response to and heightening of the process of dehumanization that underlies mass violence, to the extreme of genocide.

Torture by state officials is then rarely gratuitous or attributable simply to aberrational conduct stemming from the dark side of our human nature. It generally serves an instrumental purpose as a means to some further goal, as in a broad sense dehumanization serves a genocidal programme. A state, for example, may systematically employ torture as a method for terrorizing a population and discouraging dissent or other behaviour condemned by the government. As Amnesty International has long said, torture can be understood as the 'price of dissent', a familiar instrument of terror of the repressive and ruthless authoritarian state to maintain a given structure or ideology and to assure those holding power of their position. Stalin's Soviet Union, Nazi Germany and Maoist China offer the most striking and tragic examples during a century rich in illustrations.

Torture as broadly understood today has figured in many cultures as a part of punishment itself after the criminal process has ended in a conviction. The historical punishments of being drawn and quartered, or placed on the rack, or burned at the stake, provide classic illustrations. Today few such formal institutions of punishment remain, though dispute continues over methods of capital punishment used in many countries, and over methods of punishment that may be religiously based such as amputation of limbs. Historically in the West, torture served for hundreds of years another related function that was largely abolished by the eighteenth century. It had long been routinely and deeply a formal, judicially sanctioned part of criminal procedure, used in many European states to investigate a suspect once some threshold of facts leading to suspicion had been uncovered, and used (subject to certain safeguards designed to heighten the credibility of what was revealed or confessed) both to extract incriminating information and to achieve a confession that, despite the coercion, was used by courts to establish guilt.

If then progress has been made, principally in normative terms but also in the diminishing incidence of torture as part of a broad system of investigation or punishment, the current resurgence of interest and concern of state use of torture suggests today that the human rights movement is not uni-directional, that prohibitions of state conduct once thought settled as a matter of normative consensus are again in contention. Not surprisingly, perhaps, the movement finds itself in new circumstances in which assumed foundational beliefs have been challenged and again figure in high-level and popular discussion. The question is with us not simply in terms of actual use but also in terms of normative justification for such use. Moreover, the question is centred in the West where such important progress seemed to have been achieved — in the United States and other Western democracies as they confront the perils of a post-9/11 world: weapons of mass destruction, non-state actors, terrorism, threats of massive killing. And it is centred on interrogation, on the effort to extract information from suspected terrorists that may destroy networks, bring mass killers to justice and prevent attacks from occurring that could cost thousands if not millions of lives. Such is the limited focus of this section: the question of state torture to obtain information in this new, threatening context.

INTERNATIONAL INSTRUMENTS PROHIBITING TORTURE

The following illustrations of prohibitions and (where the instrument provides) definitions of torture are drawn from major declarations and treaties on human rights and on humanitarian law. They are listed in chronological order.

Universal Declaration of Human Rights, 1948

Article 5. No one shall be subjected to torture or to cruel, inhuman or degrading treatment or punishment.

Geneva Conventions, 1949

[All four Geneva Conventions of 1949 prohibit torture. The term appears in a number of articles, including]

Common Article 3. In the case of armed conflict not of an international character occurring in the territory of one of the High Contracting Parties, each Party to the conflict shall be bound to apply, as a minimum, the following provisions:

(1) Persons taking no active part in the hostilities, including members of armed forces who have laid down their arms and those placed hors de combat by sickness, wounds, detention, or any other cause, shall in all circumstances be treated humanely....

To this end the following acts are and shall remain prohibited at any time and in any place whatsoever with respect to the above-mentioned persons:

(a) violence to life and person, in particular murder of all kinds, mutilation, cruel treatment and torture;...

[The term 'torture' also appears in the similarly worded provision of each convention on the definition and consequences of 'grave breaches'. The following illustration is drawn from the Third Geneva Convention Relative to the Treatment of Prisoners of War.]

Article 129. The High Contracting Parties undertake to enact any legislation necessary to provide effective penal sanctions for persons committing, or ordering to be committed, any of the grave breaches of the present Convention defined in the following Article.

...

Article 130. Grave breaches to which the preceding Article relates shall be those involving any of the following acts, if committed against persons or property protected by the Convention:... torture or inhuman treatment, including biological experiments, wilfully causing great suffering or serious injury to body or health....

...

European Convention for the Protection of Human Rights and Fundamental Freedoms, 1950

Article 3. No one shall be subjected to torture or to inhuman or degrading treatment or punishment.

International Covenant on Civil and Political Rights, 1966

Article 4. [This article concerns the conditions to derogations by parties from their obligations under the Covenant. Paragraph 2 provides that no derogation may be made from certain articles, including Article 7.]

Article 7. [Same text as Universal Declaration.]

UN Declaration on the Protection of All Persons from Being Subjected to Torture and Other Cruel, Inhuman or Degrading Treatment or Punishment, 1975

Article 1(1). For the purpose of this Declaration, torture means any act by which severe pain or suffering, whether physical or mental, is intentionally inflicted by or at the instigation of a public official on a person for such purposes as obtaining from him or a third person information or confession, punishing him for an act he has committed or is suspected of having committed, or intimidating him or other persons. It does not include pain or suffering arising only from, inherent in or incidental to, lawful sanctions to the extent consistent with the Standard Minimum Rules for the Treatment of Prisoners.

(2). Torture constitutes an aggravated and deliberate form of cruel, inhuman or degrading treatment or punishment.

African (Banjul) Charter on Human and Peoples' Rights, 1981

Article 5. Every individual shall have the right to the respect of the dignity inherent in a human being and to the recognition of his legal status. All forms of exploitation and degradation of man particularly slavery, slave trade, torture, cruel, inhuman or degrading punishment and treatment shall be prohibited.

Convention against Torture and Other Cruel, Inhuman or Degrading Treatment or Punishment, 1984

Article 1(1). For the purposes of this Convention, the term 'torture' means any act by which severe pain or suffering, whether physical or mental, is intentionally inflicted on a person for such purposes as obtaining from him or a third person information or a confession, punishing him for an act he or a third person has committed or is suspected of having committed, or intimidating or coercing him or a third person, or for any reason based on discrimination of any kind, when such pain or suffering is inflicted by or at the instigation of or with the consent or acquiescence of a public official or other person acting in an official capacity. It does not include pain or suffering arising only from, inherent in or incidental to lawful sanctions.

Article 2(2). No exceptional circumstances whatsoever, whether a state of war or a threat of war, internal political instability or any other public emergency, may be invoked as a justification of torture.

Article 4(1). Each State Party shall ensure that all acts of torture are offences under its criminal law....

Article 16. Each State Party shall undertake to prevent in any territory under its jurisdiction other acts of cruel, inhuman or degrading treatment or punishment which do not amount to torture as defined in article 1....

Inter-American Convention to Prevent and Punish Torture, 1985

Article 2. For the purposes of this Convention, torture shall be understood to be any act intentionally performed whereby physical or mental pain or suffering is inflicted on a person for purposes of criminal investigation, as a means of intimidation, as personal punishment, as a preventive measure, as a penalty, or for any other purpose. Torture shall also be understood to be the use of methods upon a person intended to obliterate the personality of the victim or to diminish his physical or mental capacities, even if they do not cause physical pain or mental anguish.

The concept of torture shall not include physical or mental pain or suffering that is inherent in or solely the consequence of lawful measures, provided that they do not include the performance of the acts or use of the methods referred to in this article.

...

Article 5(1). The existence of circumstances such as a state of war, threat of war, state of siege or of emergency, domestic disturbance or strife, suspension of constitutional guarantees, domestic political instability, or other public emergencies or disasters shall not be invoked or admitted as justification for the crime of torture.

Rome Statute for the International Criminal Court, 1998

Article 7. Crimes against humanity

1. For the purpose of this Statute, "crime against humanity" means any of the following acts when committed as part of a widespread or systematic attack directed against any civilian population, with knowledge of the attack:

...

(f) Torture;

...

2. For the purpose of paragraph 1:

...

(e) "Torture" means the intentional infliction of severe pain or suffering, whether physical or mental, upon a person in the custody or under the control of the accused; except that torture shall not include pain or suffering arising only from, inherent in or incidental to, lawful sanctions.

BENTHAM ON TORTURE

W. L. Twining & P. E. Twining (eds. and commentary), 24 N. Ireland Leg. Q. 305 (1973)

[These previously unpublished manuscripts of Jeremy Bentham, a principal and influential expounder of utilitarianism for modern Western thought, were written mid-1770s to 1780, almost two centuries before the birth of the international human rights movement. The excerpts below are taken from Bentham Manuscripts, University College, London, 46/56–70.]

...

Torture, as I understand it, is where a person is made to suffer any violent pain of body in order to compel him to do something or to desist from doing something which done or desisted from the penal application is immediately made to cease.

...

The very circumstance by which alone what is called Torture stands distinguished from what is commonly called punishment is a circumstance that operates in its favour. This circumstance is, that as soon as the purpose for which it is applied is answered, it can at any time be made to cease. With punishment it is necessarily otherwise. Of punishment, in order to make sure of applying as much as is necessary you must commonly run a risque of applying considerably more: of Torture there need never be a grain more applied than what is necessary.... Two men are caught setting a house on fire; one of them escapes: set the prisoner on the rack, ask him who his Accomplice is, the instant he has answered you may untie him. Torture then when not abused, Torture considered in itself is in this point of view less liable to exception than punishment is.

The great objection against Torture is, that it is so liable to abuse.... [O]f Torture a very great quantity may be employed and the purpose not answered....

...

There seem to be two Cases in which Torture may with propriety be applied.

1. The first is where the thing which a Man is required to do being a thing which the public has an interest in his doing, is a thing which for a certainty is in his power to do; and which therefore so long as he continues to suffer for not doing he is sure not to be innocent.

2. The second is where a man is required what probably though not certainly it is in his power to do; and for the not doing of which it is possible that he may suffer, although he be innocent; but which the public has so great an interest in his doing that the danger of what may ensue from his not doing it is a greater danger than even that of an innocent person's suffering the greatest degree of pain.... Are there in practice any cases that can be ranked under this head? If there be any, it is plain there can be but very few.

...It may now be time to... state in a more concise manner the Rules that seem requisite to be observed in order to prevent its being employed to an improper degree, or in improper Cases. With regard to the first of the two Cases in which it may be admitted, the following Rules may be proper to be observed.

Rule 1st

1. First then it ought not to be employed without good proof of its being in the power of the prisoner to do what is required of him.

Rule 2d

2. This proof ought to be as strong as that which is required to subject him to a punishment equal to the greatest degree of suffering to which he can in this way be exposed.

Rule 3d

3. It ought not to be employed but in cases which admit of no delay; in cases in which if the thing done were not done immediately there is a certainty, at least a great probability, that the doing it would not answer the purpose.

Rule 4

4. In cases which admit of delay a method of compulsion apparently less severe and therefore less unpopular ought to be employed in preference.

Rule 5

5. Even on occasions which admit not of delay, it ought not to be employed but in Cases where the benefit produced by the doing of the thing required is such as can warrant the employing of so extreme a remedy.

...

Rule 7

7. In order that as little misery may be incurred in waste as possible the torture employed should be of such a kind as appears to be the most acute for the time the dolorific application lasts, and of which the pain goes off the soonest after the application is at an end.

...

Next with regard to the remaining case of the two in which it may be admitted the following additional Rules seem proper to be observed.

Rule 1

Torture ought not to be employed but in Cases where the exigency will not wait for a less penal method of compulsion.

Rule 2

2. It ought not to be employed but where the safety of the whole state may be endangered for want of that intelligence which it is the object of it to procure.

Rule 3

3. The power of employing it ought not to be vested in any hands but such as from the business of their office are best qualified to judge of that necessity: and from the dignity of it perfectly responsible in case of their making an ill use of so terrible a power.

Rule 4

4. In whatever hands the power is reposed, as many and as efficacious checks ought to be applied to the exercise of it as can be made consistent with the purpose for which it is conferred.

. . .

Upon the whole therefore it appears, that provided the utmost of suffering that can be inflicted in this way be limited, there is no more danger in trusting a Judge to decide upon this question, whether it is in the power of the prisoner to give such or such a piece of information, than in trusting him to decide upon any other question, by the event of which a man may be subjected to punishment equally severe.

What reconciles me the better to it in the cases in which I have proposed it should be established, is that it may very well be established and answer all the purposes it is designed to answer, without ever being actually applied. In general Cases a man's knowing that it may be applied will be sufficient. In countries where Torture is absolutely forbidden a malefactor scarce ever betrays his accomplice; for why should he? . . . Establish Torture, and you give him the compleatest of all Excuses, irresistable Necessity.

. . .

Torture, by many of those who have sitten in judgement over it, seems to have been regarded in one single point of view, as if it were one single individual thing, applied constantly to one and the same purpose. Those who viewed it in this light which ever part they take, whether they approve it, or whether they condemn it, can not fail of being mistaken. On this subject as much as on most others it behoves us to be on our guard not to be led astray by words. There is no approving it in the lump, without militating against reason and humanity: nor condemning it without falling into absurdities and contradictions.

. . .

QUESTIONS

1. A number of discussions below employ the 'ticking bomb' hypothetical case. As you read ahead, ask: how would Bentham approach and resolve that issue?

2. With respect to interrogation, what if any safeguards for the detainee does Bentham propose?

3. Consider the final sentence in the preceding excerpts, arguing against approving or condemning torture 'in the lump'. What is its relevance to Bentham's larger scheme?

PUBLIC COMMITTEE AGAINST TORTURE IN ISRAEL v. GOVERNMENT OF ISRAEL

Supreme Court of Israel, 1999, H.C. 5100/94

[English translation: www.jewishvirtuallibrary.org/jsource/Politics/GSStext.html]

[The applications for relief brought before the Court concerned interrogation methods used by the General Security Service (GSS) to investigate individuals suspected of committing crimes against Israel's security. The Court noted the 'unceasing struggle' of Israel for its existence and security, in particular the combat against terrorist organizations committed to Israel's annihilation. Terrorist attacks that included suicide bombings against civilian and military targets led to 121 deaths and 707 injured people from 1996 to May 1998. For an in-depth description, the Court referred to the 1987 Report of the Commission of Inquiry Regarding the GSS' Interrogation Practices with Respect to Hostile Terrorist Activities, headed by (ret.) Supreme Court Justice M. Landau (the 'Commission of Inquiry Report'). The GSS is the main body charged with fighting terrorism. Its investigation and interrogation of suspects seek information 'for the purpose of thwarting and preventing [terrorists] from carrying out these attacks'. It used 'physical means' in the interrogations.

GSS investigators informed the Court of the physical means employed. Internal regulations of the GSS, approved by a special Ministerial Committee on GSS interrogations, provided when physical means were to be used in particular instances, and required permission from officials within the GSS hierarchy. The Court's opinion written by its then-President A. Barak explored the physical means at issue.]

Shaking

9. A number of applicants claimed that the shaking method was used against them. Among the investigation methods outlined in the GSS' interrogation regulations, shaking is considered the harshest. The method is defined as the forceful shaking of the suspect's upper torso, back and forth, repeatedly, in a manner which causes the neck and head to dangle and vacillate rapidly. According to an expert opinion submitted in one of the applications, the shaking method is likely to cause serious brain damage, harm the spinal cord, cause the suspect to lose consciousness, vomit and urinate uncontrollably and suffer serious headaches.

... To [the State's] contention, there is no danger to the life of the suspect inherent to shaking; ... In any event, they argue, doctors are present. ...

All agree that in one particular case the suspect in question expired after being shaken. ... [T]he State argues in its response that the shaking method is only resorted to in very particular cases, and only as a last resort. The interrogation directives define the appropriate circumstances for its application and the rank responsible for authorizing its use. The investigators ... must probe the severity of the danger that the interrogation is intending to prevent; consider the urgency of uncovering the information presumably possessed by the suspect in question; and seek an alternative means of preventing the danger.... According to the respondent, shaking is indispensable to fighting and winning the war on terrorism.... Its use in the past has lead to the thwarting of murderous attacks.

Waiting in the "Shabach" Position

10. ... [A] suspect investigated under the "Shabach" position has his hands tied behind his back. He is seated on a small and low chair, whose seat is tilted forward, towards the ground. One hand is tied behind the suspect, and placed inside the gap between the chair's seat and back support. His second hand is tied behind the chair, against its back support. The suspect's head is covered by an opaque sack, falling down to his shoulders. Powerfully loud music is played in the room.... [S]uspects are detained in this position for a prolonged period of time, awaiting interrogation at consecutive intervals.

The aforementioned affidavits claim that prolonged sitting in this position causes serious muscle pain in the arms, the neck and headaches. The State [submitted] that both crucial security considerations and the investigators' safety require tying up the suspect's hands as he is being interrogated. The head covering is intended to prevent contact between the suspect in question and other suspects. The powerfully loud music is played for the same reason.

[The opinion described three additional 'physical means' included in the applications: (1) the 'frog crouch', consecutive, periodical crouches on tip toes each crouch lasting five minutes, (2) excessive tightening of hand or leg cuffs, allegedly leading to serious injuries, and (3) sleep deprivation while being tied in the 'Shabach' position, involving long interrogations without breaks.]

Applicants' Arguments

14. ... [Applicants] argue that the physical means employed by GSS investigators not only infringe upon the human dignity of the suspect undergoing interrogation, but in fact constitute criminal offences. These methods, argue the applicants, are in violation of International Law as they constitute "Torture," which is expressly prohibited under International Law. Thus, the GSS investigators are not authorized to conduct these interrogations....

We asked the applicants' attorneys whether the "ticking time bomb" rationale was not sufficiently persuasive to justify the use of physical means, for instance, when a bomb is known to have been placed in a public area and will undoubtedly explode causing immeasurable human tragedy if its location is not revealed at once. This question elicited a variety of responses from the various applicants before the Court. There are those convinced that physical means are not to be used under any circumstances; the prohibition on such methods to their mind is absolute, whatever the consequences may be. On the other hand, there are others who argue that even if it is perhaps acceptable to employ physical means in most exceptional "ticking time bomb" circumstances, these methods are in practice used even in absence of the "ticking time bomb" conditions. The very fact that, in most cases, the use of such means is illegal provides sufficient justification for banning their use altogether, even if doing so would inevitably absorb those rare cases in which physical coercion may have been justified....

The State's Arguments

15.... With respect to the physical means employed by the GSS, the State argues that these do not violate International Law. Indeed, it is submitted that these methods cannot be qualified as "torture," "cruel and inhuman treatment" or "degrading treatment," that are strictly prohibited under International Law. Instead, the practices of the GSS do not cause pain and suffering, according to the State's position.

Moreover, the State argues that these means are equally legal under Israel's internal (domestic) law. This is due to the "necessity" defence outlined in article 34(11) of the Penal Law (1977). Hence, in the specific cases bearing the relevant conditions inherent to the "necessity" defence, GSS investigators are entitled to use "moderate physical pressure" as a last resort in order to prevent real injury to human life and well being. Such "moderate physical pressure" may include shaking, as the "necessity" defence provides in specific instances. Resorting to such means is legal, and does not constitute a criminal offence.... [E]ven in these rare cases [where physical means are allowed], the application of such methods is subject to the strictest of scrutiny and supervision, as per the conditions and restrictions set forth in the Commission of Inquiry's Report....

The Commission of Inquiry's Report

16.... [T]he Commission concluded that in cases where the saving of human lives necessarily requires obtaining certain information, the investigator is entitled to apply both psychological pressure and "a moderate degree of physical pressure." Thus, an investigator who, in the face of such danger, applies that specific degree of physical pressure, which does not constitute abuse or torture of the suspect, but is instead proportional to the danger to human life, can avail himself of the "necessity" defence, in the face of potential criminal liability. The Commission was convinced that its conclusions to this effect were not in conflict with International Law, but instead reflect an approach consistent with both the Rule of Law and the need to effectively safeguard the security of Israel and its citizens.

The Commission approved the use of "a moderate degree of physical pressure" with various stringent conditions including directives that were set out in the second (and secret) part of the Report, and for the supervision of various elements both internal and external to the GSS. The Commission's recommendations were duly approved by the government.

[The Court explored bases for the authority of the GSS to conduct interrogations and concluded that it was so authorized.]

The Means Employed for Interrogation Purposes

21. [The state] argued before this Court that some of the physical means employed by the GSS investigators are permitted by the "law of interrogation" itself....

22. ... Quite accurately, it was noted that:

> Any interrogation, be it the fairest and most reasonable of all, inevitably places the suspect in embarrassing situations, burdens him, intrudes his conscience,

penetrates the deepest crevices of his soul, while creating serious emotional pressure. (Y. Kedmi, *On Evidence*, Part A, 1991 at 25).

... In crystallizing the interrogation rules, two values or interests clash. *On the one hand*, lies the desire to uncover the truth, thereby fulfilling the public interest in exposing crime and preventing it. *On the other hand*, is the wish to protect the dignity and liberty of the individual being interrogated. This having been said, these interests and values are not absolute. A democratic, freedom-loving society does not accept that investigators use any means for the purpose of uncovering the truth.... At times, the price of truth is so high that a democratic society is not prepared to pay it. To the same extent however, a democratic society, desirous of liberty seeks to fight crime and to that end is prepared to accept that an interrogation may infringe upon the human dignity and liberty of a suspect provided it is done for a proper purpose and that the harm does not exceed that which is necessary....

Our concern, therefore, lies in the clash of values and the balancing of conflicting values. The balancing process results in the rules for a 'reasonable interrogation'. These rules are based, *on the one hand*, on preserving the "human image" of the suspect, and on preserving the "purity of arms" used during the interrogation. *On the other hand*, these rules take into consideration the need to fight the phenomenon of criminality in an effective manner generally, and terrorist attacks specifically. These rules reflect "a degree of reasonableness, straight thinking (right mindedness) and fairness". The rules pertaining to investigations are important to a democratic state. They reflect its character. An illegal investigation harms the suspect's human dignity. It equally harms society's fabric.

23. ... The "law of interrogation" by its very nature, is intrinsically linked to the circumstances of each case. This having been said, a number of general principles are nonetheless worth noting:

First, a reasonable investigation is necessarily one free of torture, free of cruel, inhuman treatment of the subject and free of any degrading handling whatsoever. There is a prohibition on the use of "brutal or inhuman means" in the course of an investigation. This conclusion is in perfect accord with (various) International Law treaties — to which Israel is a signatory — which prohibit the use of torture, "cruel, inhuman treatment" and "degrading treatment". These prohibitions are "absolute". There are no exceptions to them and there is no room for balancing. Indeed, violence directed at a suspect's body or spirit does not constitute a reasonable investigation practice. The use of violence during investigations can potentially lead to the investigator being held criminally liable. *Second*, a reasonable investigation is likely to cause discomfort; It may result in insufficient sleep; The conditions under which it is conducted risk being unpleasant.... In the end result, the legality of an investigation is deduced from the propriety of its purpose and from its methods. Thus, for instance, sleep deprivation for a prolonged period, or sleep deprivation at night when this is not necessary to the investigation time wise may be deemed a use of an investigation method which surpasses the least restrictive means.

From the General to the Particular

24. ... Plainly put, shaking is a prohibited investigation method. It harms the suspect's body. It violates his dignity. It is a violent method which does not form part of a legal investigation. It surpasses that which is necessary.... In any event, there is no doubt that shaking is not to be resorted to in cases outside the bounds of "necessity" or as part of an "ordinary" investigation.

25. ... [O]ne of the investigation methods employed consists of the suspect crouching on the tips of his toes for five minute intervals.... This is a prohibited investigation method. It does not serve any purpose inherent to an investigation. It is degrading and infringes upon an individual's human dignity.

26. The "Shabach" method is composed of a number of cumulative components: the cuffing of the suspect, seating him on a low chair, covering his head with an opaque sack (head covering) and playing powerfully loud music in the area. Are any of the above acts encompassed by the general power to investigate? Our point of departure is that there are actions which are inherent to the investigation power. Therefore, we accept that the suspect's cuffing, for the purpose of preserving the investigators' safety, is an action included in the general power to investigate.... Notwithstanding, the cuffing associated with the "Shabach" position is unlike routine cuffing.... This is a distorted and unnatural position. The investigators' safety does not require it.... The use of these methods is prohibited....

[The opinion explored further possible justifications for the 'Shabach' position and found them wanting. 'All these methods do not fall within the sphere of a "fair" interrogation. They are not reasonable. They impinge upon the suspect's dignity, his bodily integrity, and his basic rights in an excessive manner (or beyond what is necessary).' It examined the state's justifications for covering a suspect's head with an opaque sack. '... [L]ess harmful means must be employed [for example, to prevent communication with other suspects being interrogated] It degrades [the suspect].... It suffocates him.']

30. ... A similar—though not identical—combination of interrogation methods were discussed in the case of *Ireland v. United Kingdom* (1978) 2 EHRR 25....

31. The interrogation of a person is likely to be lengthy.... Indeed, a person undergoing interrogation cannot sleep as does one who is not being interrogated.... This is part of the "discomfort" inherent to an interrogation. This being the case, depriving the suspect of sleep is, in our opinion, included in the general authority of the investigator....

The above described situation is different from those in which sleep deprivation shifts from being a "side effect" inherent to the interrogation, to an end in itself. If the suspect is intentionally deprived of sleep for a prolonged period of time, for the purpose of tiring him out or "breaking" him — it shall not fall within the scope of a fair and reasonable investigation. Such means harm the rights and dignity of the suspect in a manner surpassing that which is required.

32. All that was stated regarding the exceptions pertinent to an interrogation, flowing from the requirement that an interrogation be fair and reasonable, is the accepted law with respect to a regular police interrogation. The power to interrogate given to the GSS investigator by law is the same interrogation powers the law bestows upon the ordinary police force investigator....

Physical Means and the "Necessity" Defence

33. … [A]n explicit authorization permitting GSS to employ physical means is not to be found in our law. An authorization of this nature can, in the State's opinion, be obtained in specific cases by virtue of the criminal law defense of "necessity", prescribed in [Article 34 (1) of] the Penal Law….

> A person will not bear criminal liability for committing any act immediately necessary for the purpose of saving the life, liberty, body or property, of either himself or his fellow person, from substantial danger of serious harm, imminent from the particular state of things [circumstances], at the requisite timing, and absent alternative means for avoiding the harm.

The State's position is that by virtue of this "defence" to criminal liability, GSS investigators are also authorized to apply physical means, such as shaking, in the appropriate circumstances, in order to prevent serious harm to human life or body, in the absence of other alternatives…. It is choosing the lesser evil. Not only is it legitimately permitted to engage in the fighting of terrorism, it is our moral duty to employ the necessary means for this purpose…. [T]here is no obstacle preventing the investigators' superiors from instructing and guiding them with regard to when the conditions of the "necessity" defence are fulfilled and the proper boundaries in those circumstances. From this flows the legality of the directives with respect to the use of physical means in GSS interrogations. In the course of their argument, the State's attorneys submitted the "ticking time bomb" argument…. Is a GSS investigator authorized to employ physical means in order to elicit information regarding the location of the bomb in such instances? The State's attorneys answer in the affirmative.

34. We are prepared to assume that — although this matter is open to debate — the "necessity" defence is open to all, particularly an investigator, acting in an organizational capacity of the State in interrogations of that nature. Likewise, we are prepared to accept — although this matter is equally contentious — that the "necessity" exception is likely to arise in instances of "ticking time bombs", and that the immediate need ("necessary in an immediate manner" for the preservation of human life) refers to the imminent nature of the act rather than that of the danger….

…

35. … This however, is not the issue before this Court. We are not dealing with the potential criminal liability of a GSS investigator…. Moreover, we are not addressing the issue of admissibility or probative value of evidence obtained as a result of a GSS investigator's application of physical means against a suspect…. The question before us is whether it is possible to infer the authority to, in advance, establish permanent directives setting out the physical interrogation means that may be used under conditions of "necessity"…. According to the State, it is possible to imply from the "necessity" defence, available (*post factum*) to an investigator indicted of a criminal offence, an advance legal authorization….

36. In the Court's opinion… [t]he "necessity" defence does not constitute a source of authority, allowing GSS investigators to make use of physical means

during the course of interrogations. [That defence]... deals with deciding those cases involving an individual reacting to a given set of facts; It is an ad hoc endeavour, in reaction to an event.... [T]he very nature of the defence does not allow it to serve as the source of a general administrative power. The administrative power is based on establishing general, forward looking criteria....

...

...The very fact that a particular act does not constitute a criminal act (due to the "necessity" defence) does not in itself authorize the administration to carry out this deed, and in doing so infringe upon human rights. The Rule of Law (both as a formal and substantive principle) requires that an infringement on a human right be prescribed by statute, authorizing the administration to this effect....

37. ... If the State wishes to enable GSS investigators to utilize physical means in interrogations, they must seek the enactment of legislation for this purpose. This authorization would also free the investigator applying the physical means from criminal liability. This release would flow not from the "necessity" defence but from the "justification" defense which states [Article 34(13) of the Penal Law]:

> A person shall not bear criminal liability for an act committed in one of the following cases:
>
> (1) He was obliged or authorized by law to commit it.

The defence to criminal liability by virtue of the "justification" is rooted in an area outside of the criminal law. This "external" law serves as a defence to criminal liability.... These questions and the corresponding answers must be determined by the Legislative branch. This is required by the principle of the Separation of Powers and the Rule of Law, under our very understanding of democracy.

38. Our conclusion is therefore the following: According to the existing state of the law, neither the government nor the heads of security services possess the authority to establish directives and bestow authorization regarding the use of liberty infringing physical means during the interrogation of suspects suspected of hostile terrorist activities, beyond the general directives which can be inferred from the very concept of an interrogation. Similarly, the individual GSS investigator — like any police officer — does not possess the authority to employ physical means which infringe upon a suspect's liberty during the interrogation, unless these means are inherently accessory to the very essence of an interrogation and are both fair and reasonable.

An investigator who insists on employing these methods, or does so routinely, is exceeding his authority. His responsibility shall be fixed according to law. His potential criminal liability shall be examined in the context of the "necessity" defence, and according to our assumptions, the investigator may find refuge under the "necessity" defence's wings (so to speak), provided this defence's conditions are met by the circumstances of the case....

A Final Word

39. This decision opens with a description of the difficult reality in which Israel finds herself security wise. We shall conclude this judgment by re-addressing that

harsh reality. We are aware that this decision does not ease dealing with that reality. This is the destiny of democracy, as not all means are acceptable to it, and not all practices employed by its enemies are open before it.... Preserving the Rule of Law and recognition of an individual's liberty constitutes an important component in its understanding of security. At the end of the day, they strengthen its spirit and its strength and allow it to overcome its difficulties.... If it will nonetheless be decided that it is appropriate for Israel, in light of its security difficulties to sanction physical means in interrogations..., this is an issue that must be decided by the legislative branch which represents the people. We do not take any stand on this matter at this time....It is there that the required legislation may be passed, provided, of course, that a law infringing upon a suspect's liberty "befitting the values of the State of Israel," is enacted for a proper purpose, and to an extent no greater than is required. (Article 8 to the Basic Law: Human Dignity and Liberty).

40. Deciding these applications weighed heavy on this Court. True, from the legal perspective, the road before us is smooth. We are, however, part of Israeli society. Its problems are known to us and we live its history. We are not isolated in an ivory tower. We live the life of this country. We are aware of the harsh reality of terrorism in which we are, at times, immersed. Our apprehension... that this decision will hamper the ability to properly deal with terrorists and terrorism, disturbs us. We are, however, judges. Our brethern require us to act according to the law....

...

Consequently... we declare that the GSS does not have the authority to "shake" a man, hold him in the "Shabach" position... force him into a "frog crouch" position and deprive him of sleep in a manner other than that which is inherently required by the interrogation....

[Seven Justices agreed with the opinion. Justice J'Kedmi accepted the opinion's conclusion but would have suspended the judgment's effectiveness for one year.]

QUESTIONS

1. Is allowing the defence of 'necessity' consistent with an 'absolute' view of protection against torture, such that exceptions and balancing are both forbidden (see para. 23)? How would you state the criteria for and the conditions to a 'necessity' defence?

2. What is the relationship between, on the one hand, a required standard of reasonableness and fairness in the policies and practices of the state during interrogations, and on the other hand, an absolute protection against torture? Would you expect a consensus among states about what kind of conduct in what circumstances would clearly violate an absolute ban, but might be viewed as permissible within the reasonableness standard?

3. Consider para. 31 and its terms like 'general authority', 'inherent' and an 'end in itself'. What if any actions can the state take that are intended to apply pressures on the detainee that may lead to useful information?

4. What is the effect of this opinion? Does it 'ban' torture (as defined or understood) in Israel? If not, what does it achieve? Is 'torture' indeed a category of analysis and definition in the opinion?

NOTE

Compare *A (FC) v. Secretary of State for the Home Department* [2005] UKHL 71. Under British legislation, the Secretary of State has authority to issue a certificate to the effect that he reasonably believes a named non-UK national to pose a national security risk and to be a terrorist. A person so certified can challenge the certification before the Special Immigration Appeals Commission (SIAC). Appellants brought their appeals to the House of Lords after losing a challenge before SIAC as well as their appeal to the Court of Appeals, which held that evidence that was (as claimed by appellants), or might have been, 'procured by torture inflicted by foreign officials without the complicity of the British authorities' was admissible before SIAC. Appellants argued before the House of Lords that the common law, as well as the European Convention on Human Rights, barred admission of such evidence.

The House of Lords unanimously held that evidence obtained by torture by officials of a foreign state without the participation of British authorities was not admissible before SIAC. Lord Bingham delivered the main judgment, stating that he was 'startled... at the suggestion... that this deeply-rooted tradition [abhorrence of torture] and an international obligation solemnly and explicitly undertaken [the Convention against Torture] can be overridden by a statute and a procedural rule which makes no mention of torture at all.... The issue is one of constitutional principle... irrespective of where, or by whom, or on whose authority the torture was inflicted'. The common law, as well as the European Convention, required exclusion of such evidence. Lord Bingham did observe that 'it would of course be within the power of a sovereign Parliament (in breach of international law) to confer power on SIAC to receive third party torture evidence.'

Importantly, the Law Lords drew a distinction between the use of evidence in judicial proceedings and the use of evidence by the executive branch in crime prevention. In the latter case, the judges stated that the executive can lawfully rely on 'foreign torture evidence' (information obtained from torture by a foreign government) for law enforcement purposes (e.g., to stop a future threat). Lord Bingham emphasized that the question involved torture committed by a foreign government: 'I am prepared to accept... that the Secretary of State does not act unlawfully if he certifies, arrests, searches and detains on the strength of what I shall for convenience call foreign torture evidence. But by the same token it is, in my view, questionable whether he would act unlawfully if he based similar action on intelligence obtained by officially-authorised British torture' (see also Lord Carswell, para. 149). Lord Nicholls stated that it would be 'absurd' to reject such information from foreign sources if it 'might save lives', 'ludicrous' to disregard it in the case of stopping 'a ticking time bomb', and permissible to take it into account in making an arrest. He stated in that in these cases 'the executive arm of the state is open to the charge that it is condoning the use of torture. So, in a sense, it is. The government is using information obtained by torture. But in cases such as these the government cannot be expected to close its eyes to this information at the price of endangering the lives of its own citizens. Moral repugnance to torture does not require this'. Lord Rodger squarely addressed the claim by human rights groups: 'Amnesty International and a number of other interveners, indicated that, in their view, it would be wrong for the Home Secretary to rely on such statements since it would be tantamount to condoning the torture by which the statements were obtained. That stance has the great virtue of coherence; but the coherence is bought at too dear a price. It would mean that the Home Secretary might have to fail in one of the first duties of government, to protect people in this country from potential attack'. More forcefully, Lord Brown stated the executive is 'not merely... *entitled* to make use of such information... it is *bound* to do so' to meet its 'prime responsibility to safeguard the security of the state' (emphasis in original).

Lord Hoffmann offered the following analysis:

> It is not the function of the courts to place limits upon the information available to the Secretary of State, particularly when he is concerned with national security. Provided that he acts lawfully, he may read whatever he likes. In his dealings with foreign governments, the type of information that he is willing to receive and the questions that he asks or refrains from asking are his own affair. As I have said, there may be cases in which he is required to act urgently and cannot afford to be too nice in judging the methods by which the information has been obtained, although I suspect that such cases are less common in practice than in seminars on moral philosophy.

But the 2001 Act makes the exercise by the Secretary of State of his extraordinary powers subject to judicial supervision. The function of SIAC under section 25 is not to decide whether the Secretary of State at some particular time, perhaps at a moment of emergency, acted reasonably in forming some suspicion or belief. It is to form its own opinion, after calm judicial process, as to whether it considers that there are reasonable grounds for such suspicion or belief. It is exercising a judicial, not an executive function. Indeed, the fact that the exercise of the draconian powers conferred by the Act was subject to review by the judiciary was obviously an important reason why Parliament was willing to confer such powers on the Secretary of State.

QUESTIONS

1. Should the distinct question relevant to this decision — the admissibility of evidence in a legal proceeding, rather than the criminality or permissibility of certain methods of interrogation — affect a legislature's or court's view of the nature or consequences of torture? Should it, for example, be relevant (a) whether the alleged

conduct constituted 'torture' or some other form of coercive interrogation such as 'cruel, inhuman or degrading' treatment, or (b) whether the torture leading to the evidence involved might be viewed as justified within a 'ticking bomb' scenario?

2. Evaluate the following criticisms of the House of Lords' conclusion that the executive branch can rely on information procured by torture committed by other states:

> The real question is whether it is permissible to use information acquired through torture to identify and apprehend the suspects. Lord Bingham says that it is, provided that it is 'foreign torture evidence', though quite why the nationality of the torturer or the place of the torture should make any difference in such circumstances is entirely unclear; it either is or is not appropriate to act on the basis of the information to hand, irrespective of its origins if the matter is approached from the perspective of human rights thinking.

M. D. Evans, '"All the Perfumes of Arabia"': The House of Lords and "Foreign Torture Evidence"', 19 Leiden J. Int'l. L. 1125 (2006).

> [A]lthough Lord Brown did indeed say that the executive is generally entitled and even bound to make use of all information it acquires, he also stressed that it must not enlist torturers to its aid. Since torture is encouraged by any reliance upon its fruits, seeking to draw a line between its promotion and the mere acquisition of information resulting from it is questionable. Drawing such a line is also likely to be difficult in practice, especially in the context of international collaboration against terrorism....

N. Grief, 'The Exclusion of Foreign Torture Evidence: A Qualified Victory for the Rule of Law', 2 Eur. H. R. L. Rev. 201 (2006).

3. Article 41 of the Articles of State Responsibility, see p. 98, *supra*, provides: 'No State shall recognize as lawful a situation created by a [gross or systematic failure to fulfill a *jus cogens* obligation], nor render aid or assistance in maintaining that situation'. How should such a principle apply to the executive's use of foreign torture evidence if, indeed, Lord Nicholls is correct that the executive branch 'is open to the charge that it is condoning the use of torture' and 'in a sense, it is'?[21]

4. Did the House of Lords reach the right result? Should the use of 'foreign torture evidence' be subject to a balancing test: evaluating the degree to which the executive practice encourages the use of torture versus the probability and scale of lives potentially saved? Is the case of terrorism a special category or should the use of such information be allowed for all types of crimes? Should it matter whether the foreign state is also a party to the European Convention on Human Rights?

[21] M. Pollard, 'Rotten Fruit: State Solicitation, Acceptance and the Use of Information Obtained through Torture by Another State', 23 Netherlands Q. H. R. 349 (2005), at 376–7.

SANFORD LEVINSON (ED.), TORTURE: A COLLECTION

(2004)

Sanford Levinson, Contemplating Torture: An Introduction, at 23

...

It turns out to be surprisingly hard to avoid granting some element of "legitimacy" to torture, unless one resolutely believes, in the face of all the evidence, that any and all known events of torture will be prosecuted with significant severity under a doctrine of what lawyers call "strict liability," that is, limiting the legal issue to whether the alleged activity occurred at all, accepting no possible arguments by the defendant that it was justifiable or even excusable... [F]ew theorists, and no legal systems, have endorsed such strict liability. Most telling, in a way, is that even Professor Shue, who insists that all acts of "torture ought to remain illegal," nonetheless added immediately that "anyone who sincerely believes such an act to be the least available evil" should be

> placed in the position of needing to justify his or her act morally in order to defend himself or herself legally.... Anyone who thinks an act of torture is justified should have no alternative but to convince a group of peers in a public trial that all necessary conditions for a morally permissible act were indeed satisfied.... If the situation approximates those in the imaginary examples in which torture seems possible to justify, *a judge can surely be expected to suspend the sentence.* (Emphasis added)

...

Few governments, including the United States, Great Britain, and Israel, among others that could no doubt be cited, appear eager, or even particularly willing, to prosecute as criminals agents of the state who engaged in violations of the relevant prohibitions. As John Conroy writes, "throughout the world torturers are rarely punished, and when they are, the punishment rarely corresponds to the severity of the crime." Miscreants, for example, sometimes lose their jobs, but they rarely go to jail.

Conroy's explanation for the infrequency of punishment is derived from the very title of his excellent book *Unspeakable Acts, Ordinary People.* Torturers cannot be reduced to the obvious "sadists" one would, for moral clarity's sake, like them to be. They view themselves as servants of a state — fighting a just war; indeed, as Osiel points out, they are often encouraged in their views by the clergy — in the case of Argentina, Catholic priests....

Jean Bethke Elshtain, Reflection on the Problem of 'Dirty Hands', at 77

...

A certain asceticism is required of those who may be required, in a dangerous and extreme situation, to temporarily override a general prohibition. They should not seek to legalize it. They shoulnot aim to normalize it. And they should not write elaborate justifications of it, as if there were a tick-list one can do down and, if a sufficient number of ticks appears, one is given leave to torture. The tabooed and forbidden, the extreme, nature of this mode of physical coercion must be preserved so that it never becomes routinized as just the way we do things around here.

...

... The position I have developed pushes in the following direction: there is no absolute prohibition to what some call torture. Once again, torture is not sufficiently disaggregated. Recall the possibilities: pulling out fingernails; grinding the teeth down or pulling teeth...; raping men or women; burning breasts, genitalia; hanging for hours from the arms; crucifying; torturing the spouse or children. There should be — and are — prohibitions against such practices. In an exceptional and truly extreme circumstance, would it be defendable to do any of these things? Everything in me says no and tells me that when we think of torture it is these sorts of extreme forms of physical torment we are thinking of. If torture is the inflicting of severe and devastating pain, as the dictionary defines it, the horrors I have listed are certainly torture.

But there are other options that also come under condemnation as torture. In a striking piece, "The Dark Art of Interrogation," Mark Bowden details some of these. They are called "torture lite:" and, Bowden tells us, some argue that such methods are not properly torture at all. This list includes

> sleep deprivation, exposure to heat or cold, the use of drugs to cause confusion, rough treatment (slapping, shoving or shaking), forcing a prisoner to stand for days at a time or sit in uncomfortable positions, and playing on his fears for himself and his family. Although excruciating for the victim, these tactics generally leave no permanent marks and do no lasting physical harm.

The Geneva Convention, however, makes no distinctions of any kind between these tactics and the horrific possibilities I noted earlier. Torture is torture, it says in effect.

... It seems to be the case, as Bowden documents it, that techniques like solitary confinement and sensory deprivation often suffice to induce a prisoner to give up sensitive information about terrorist operations. The skilled interrogator often finds that the fear that something may happen is "more effective than any drug, tactic, or torture device.... The threat of coercion usually weakens or destroys resistance more effectively than coercion itself." Forms of psychological pressure and the arts of deception and trickery — for example, telling a captive that others have capitulated so he might as well talk — are standard tools of the interrogator's trade, though some absolutists would forbid them, too....

Bowden concludes that few "moral imperatives make such sense on a large scale" — referring to the prohibition against torture — "but break down so dramatically in the particular."...It follows that when human rights groups label "unpleasant or disadvantageous treatment of any kind" torture, they...embrace a moralistic "code fetishism" that flies in the face of the harsh and dangerous realities of the world in which we find ourselves...;

... The ban on torture must remain. But "moderate physical pressure" to save innocent lives, "coercion" by contrast to "torture," is not only demanded in certain extreme circumstances, it is arguably the "least bad" thing to do....

...

Let's sum up this unhappy subject. Far greater moral guilt falls on a person in authority who permits the deaths of hundreds of innocents rather than choosing to "torture" one guilty or complicit person. One hopes and prays such occasions emerge only rarely. Were I the parent or grandparent of a child whose life might be spared, I confess, with regret, that I would want officials to rank their moral purity as far less important in the overall scheme of things than eliciting information that might spare my child or grandchild and all those other children and grandchildren. But I do not want a law to "cover" such cases, for, truly, hard cases do make bad laws. Instead, we work with a rough rule of thumb in circumstances in which we believe an informant might have information that would probably spare the lives of innocents. In a world of such probabilities, we should demur from Torture 1 — the extreme forms of physical torment. But Torture 2, for which we surely need a different name, like coercive interrogation, may, with regret, be used.... This is a distinction with a difference.

...

John Parry, Escalation and Necessity, at 145

...

International tribunals have given additional content to these definitions and to the distinctions between them. Thus, severe beatings that do not break bones or cause lesions but cause intense pain and swelling are "classic" forms of torture. Torture also includes the combination of being made to stand all day for days at a time, beatings, and withholding food; beatings and being buried alive; electric shocks, beatings, being hung with one's arms behind one's back, having one's head forced under water until nearly asphyxiated, and being made to stand for hours. Rape or threats of physical mutilation are torture as well.

Another series of cases has found that certain combinations of conduct are torture *and* cruel or inhuman treatment.... In a third group of cases, the European Commission of Human Rights found that beatings and one or more instances of electric shock, mock execution, or refusal of food and water were either torture *or* inhuman treatment.

...

The most significant case to examine the difference between torture and cruel or inhuman treatment is *Ireland v. United Kingdom* [*supra*]....

...

The Israeli situation presents the potential importance under the Convention for determining the difference between torture and the lesser — but still illegal — category of cruel, inhuman, or degrading treatment. The Convention [against Torture] bars torture absolutely.... By contrast, states that ratify the Convention must "undertake to prevent" cruel, inhuman, or degrading treatment, but the "no exceptional circumstances" provision does not apply. Thus, if conduct similar to Israel's former practices would not be torture under the Convention, an exceptional circumstances justification could be available....

...

... [T]he Senate's statement that the definition of cruel, inhuman, or degrading treatment or punishment must be tied to the Fifth, Eighth, and Fourteenth Amendments gives federal courts the ultimate power to define our international obligations. A series of cases assessing the voluntariness of confessions under the due process clause suggests that these obligations could be broad. But if the Court limits the applicability of these cases or changes course and determines that a particular practice is constitutional, then that practice is permitted under international law as well, at least as the United States understands it.

...

Oren Gross, The Prohibition on Torture and the Limits of Law, at 229

...

Absolutists — those who believe that an unconditional ban on torture ought to apply without exception regardless of circumstances — frequently base their position on deontological grounds, that is, they assess the intrinsic moral value of things independent of their consequences. For them, torture is inherently wrong. It is an evil that can never be justified or excused. It violates the physical and mental integrity of the person subjected to it, negates her autonomy and humanity, and deprives her of human dignity. It reduces her to a mere object, a body, from which information is to be exacted, while coercing her to act in a manner that may be contrary to her most fundamental beliefs, values, and interests. Torture is also wrong because of its depraving and corrupting effects on individual torturers as well as on society at large....

Others support an absolutist view of the ban on torture by arguing that social costs of permitting the use of torture, even in narrowly defined exceptional circumstances..., would always outweigh the social benefits that could be derived from applying torture....

It is easy to see why this uncompromising point of view is castigated by its opponents as utopian, naive, or even outright hypocritical. The case of the ticking bomb is used by those who advocate the position that use of coercive interrogation methods may be justified in certain — albeit exceptional and extraordinary — circumstances....

The most prevalent arguments in support of the conditionality of the prohibition on torture are consequentialist claims comparing costs and benefits on a case-by-case basis....

One attempt to escape both sets of criticisms calls for the use of what Charles Black coined "orders of magnitude" assessment. Thus, even if a straightforward cost-benefit analysis leads to the conclusion that, in a given case, the benefits from use of torture outweigh the costs involved, torture is not to be used unless the magnitude of the threat to society (which may be prevented or minimized as a result of resorting to torture) is of a particularly large scale (e.g., the "nuclear weapon in a suitcase in the middle of a major metropolis" scenario). Under this approach, the prohibition on torture sets out a strong presumption against the use of torture. That presumption is, however, rebuttable. Yet to refute it in any given case a showing must be made of the exceptional magnitude of the risk involved....

A third set of arguments put forward by the conditionalists suggests that the prohibition on torture cannot be defensible as a moral absolute.... Thus, for example, when the choice is between the physical integrity and dignity of a suspected terrorist, on the one hand, and the lives of a great many innocent persons (e.g., those who are highly likely to be killed or be seriously injured should the ticking bomb actually go off),on the other hand, an absolute ban on torture cannot be morally defensible.

...

In this article I defend an absolute prohibition on torture while at the same time arguing that the ticking-bomb case should not be brushed aside as merely hypothetical or as either morally or legally irrelevant.... [T]he proposal made herein focuses on the possibility that truly exceptional cases may give rise to official disobedience: public officials may step outside the legal framework, that is, act extralegally, and be ready to accept the legal ramifications of their actions. However, there is also the possibility that the extralegal actions undertaken by those officials will be legally (if not morally) excused ex post....

My focus is on what I call *preventive interrogational torture*.... By adding "preventive" I seek to limit the discussion to that use of torture whose aim is to gain information that would assist the authorities in foiling exceptionally grave future terrorist attacks. Hence, the aim is entirely forward-looking....

A second clarification concerns the scope of the term "torture".... [T]he argument I develop hereafter seeks to address instances where interrogation methods that clearly fall within the ambit of "torture" are used....

...

...To deny the use of preventive interrogational torture in [catastrophic] cases...is also hypocritical: as experience tells us, when faced with serious threats to the life of the nation, government will take whatever measures it deems necessary to abate the crisis....

... As a result, particular norms, and perhaps the legal system in general, may break down, as the ethos of obedience to law may be seriously shaken and challenges emerge with respect to the reasonableness of following these norms. Thus, legal rigidity in the face of severe crises is not merely hypocritical but is, in fact, detrimental to long-term notions of the rule of law.... It may also lead to more, rather than less, radical interference with individual rights and liberties....

...

...We want our leaders and our public officials to possess the highest moral character. But I do not believe we want them to be brazen Kantians.... [F]ew would want a leader who follows Kant's absolutist view to its extreme rather than act to save the lives of innocent civilians. As Judge Posner aptly put it, "if the stakes are high enough, torture is permissible. No one who doubts that this is the case should be in a position of responsibility."...

...

I peg my belief on the twin notions of *pragmatic absolutism* and *official disobedience*.… [T]he way to reconcile that absolute ban on torture with the necessities of the catastrophic case is not through any means of legal accommodation (such as recognizing an explicit legal exception to the ban on torture that applies to catastrophic cases) but rather through a mechanism of extralegal action that I would term *official disobedience:* in circumstances amounting to a catastrophic case, the appropriate method of tackling extremely grave national dangers and threats *may* entail going outside the legal order, at times even violating otherwise accepted constitutional principles.

Going completely outside the law in appropriate cases preserves, rather than undermines, the rule of law in a way that bending the law to accommodate for catastrophes does not.… [T]o say that governments are going to use preventive interrogational torture in the catastrophic case is not the same as saying that they should be authorized to do so through a priori, ex ante legal rules. It is extremely dangerous to provide for such eventualities and such awesome powers within the framework of the existing legal system because of the large risks of contamination and manipulation of that system and the deleterious message involved in legalizing such actions (e.g., constitutional protections are really designed only for ordinary times and are easily suspended precisely when they are needed the most).

Instead, my proposal calls on public officials having to deal with the catastrophic case to consider the possibility of acting outside the legal order while openly acknowledging their actions and the extralegal nature of such actions. Those officials must assume the risks involved in acting extralegally. State agents may regard strict obedience to legal authority (such as the absolute legal ban on torture) as irrational or immoral under circumstances of a true catastrophic case.… Society retains the role of making the final determination whether the actor ought to be punished and rebuked or rewarded and commended for her actions…

…[T]he acting official may…for example, need to resign her position, face criminal charges or civil suits, or be subjected to impeachment proceedings. Alternatively, the people may approve the actions and ratify them.… [L]egal modes of ratification may include exercising prosecutorial discretion not to bring criminal charges against persons accused of using torture, jury nullification where criminal charges are brought, executive pardoning or clemency where criminal proceedings result in conviction, or governmental indemnification of state agents who are found liable for damages to persons who were tortured.…

Alan Dershowitz, Tortured Reasoning, at 257

…

The Supreme Court of Israel [see p. 246, *supra*] left the security services a tiny window of opportunity in extreme cases. Borrowing from the Landau Commission, it cited the traditional common-law defense of necessity.… This leaves each individual member of the security services in the position of having to guess how a court would ultimately resolve his case. That is unfair to such investigators. It would have been far better, in my view, had the court required any investigator who believed that torture was necessary in order to save lives to apply to a judge, when feasible.

The judge would then be in a position either to authorize or refuse to authorize a "torture warrant." Such a procedure would require judges to dirty their hands by authorizing torture warrants or bear the responsibility for failing to do so....

In response to the decision of the Supreme Court of Israel, it was suggested that the Knesset — Israel's parliament — could create a procedure for advance judicial scrutiny, akin to the warrant requirement in the Fourth Amendment to the United States Constitution. It is a traditional role for judges to play, since it is the job of the judiciary to balance the needs for security against the imperatives of liberty. Interrogators from the security service are not trained to strike such a delicate balance. Their mission is single-minded: to prevent terrorism.... The essence of a democracy is placing responsibility for difficult choices in a visible and neutral institution like the judiciary.

...

...I sought a debate [after September 11]:...if torture would, *in fact* be employed by a democratic nation under the circumstances, would the rule of law and principles of accountability require that any use of torture be subject to some kind of judicial (or perhaps executive) oversight (or control)?...My answer, unlike that of the Supreme Court of Israel, is yes. To elaborate, I have argued that unless a democratic nation is prepared to have a proposed action governed by the rule of law, it should not undertake, or authorize, that action. As a corollary, if it needs to take the proposed action, then it must subject it to the rule of law. Suggesting that an after-the-fact "necessity defense" might be available in extreme cases is not an adequate substitute for explicit advance approval

...In explaining my preference for a warrant, I [earlier] wrote the following.

...

There is, of course, a downside: legitimating a horrible practice that we all want to see ended or minimized. Thus we have a triangular conflict unique to democratic societies: If these horrible practices continue to operate below the radar screen of accountability, there is no legitimation, but there is continuing and ever expanding *sub rosa* employment of the practice. If we try to control the practice by demanding some kind of accountability, then we add a degree of legitimation to it while perhaps reducing its frequency and severity. If we do nothing, and a preventable act of nuclear terrorism occurs, then the public will demand that we constrain liberty even more. There is no easy answer.

...

The strongest argument against my preference for candor and accountability is the claim that it is better for torture — or any other evil practice deemed necessary during emergencies — to be left to the low-visibility discretion of low-level functionaries than to be legitimated by high-level, accountable decision-makers. Posner makes this argument:

> Dershowitz believes that the occasions for the use of torture should be regularized — by requiring a judicial warrant for the needle treatment, for example. But he overlooks an argument for leaving such things to executive discretion. If rules are promulgated permitting torture in defined circumstances, some officials are bound to want to explore the outer bounds of the rules. Having been regularized,

the practice will become regular. Better to leave in place the formal and customary prohibitions, but with the understanding that they will not be enforced in extreme circumstances.

…

QUESTIONS

1. Which approach do you believe preferable: (a) the decision of the Israeli Supreme Court, or the argument of Dershowitz? (b) the proposals of Gross or Dershowitz? What considerations point you in one or the other direction in each case?

2. Is any one of these varied proposals more likely than others to avoid the danger signalled by Posner in the closing paragraph above?

3. Do any proposals in these materials respond to the risk that the probability of a given detainee's possessing information relevant to stopping a terrorist attack will be overstated, or in many cases be simply indeterminate? How would you respond to it?

4. Make a list of considerations that you believe relevant to a legislative debate about what limits if any to place on methods of interrogation by military or police personnel in cases posing national security concerns.

NOTE

In contrast to the conventions of the last three decades, the eighteenth-century US Constitution and its amendments do not refer to torture as such. The first ten amendments to the Constitution, effective two years after the Constitution itself, constitute the Bill of Rights. Two striking differences emerge between the Eighth Amendment and the postwar conventions. The former provides: 'Excessive bail shall not be required, nor excessive fines imposed, nor cruel and unusual punishments inflicted.' The phrase 'cruel and unusual', rather than torture, describes the limit imposed on state action. Moreover, the phrase refers only to 'punishments', whereas the ICCPR characteristically bars 'torture' and 'cruel, inhuman or degrading *treatment or punishment*' (emphasis added).[22]

Outside the context of punishment, then, the courts have had to resort to other constitutional provisions to determine whether, for example, incriminating evidence obtained coercively from a defendant could be admitted in evidence at

[22] *Roper v. Simmons*, p. 34, *supra*, illustrates the contemporary application by the Supreme Court of the Eighth (and Fourteenth) Amendments to decide if capital punishment of criminals who committed the crime when juveniles would be constitutional.

the criminal trial. The principal provisions that have been invoked are the 'due process' clauses of the Fifth and Fourteenth Amendments.

A decision of the US Supreme Court growing out of a California criminal case — *Rochin v. California*, 342 U.S. 165 (1952) — illustrates such due process jurisprudence. Police officers had information that defendant Rochin was selling narcotics. They illegally entered his home, and Rochin promptly swallowed two capsules seen by the police. The police took him to a hospital, where a doctor was ordered to insert into his stomach an emetic solution through a tube. Defendant therefore vomited and brought up the two capsules, which contained morphine. Primarily on that evidence, he was convicted of illegal possession of morphine. The US Supreme Court upset the conviction, concluding that the evidence obtained by coercion could not be admitted. The opinion stated (at p. 172):

> ... [W]e are compelled to conclude that the proceedings by which this conviction was obtained do more than offend some fastidious squeamishness or private sentimentalism about combating crime too energetically. This is conduct that shocks the conscience. Illegally breaking into the privacy of the petitioner, the struggle to open his mouth and remove what was there, the forcible extraction of his stomach's contents — this... is bound to offend even hardened sensibilities. They are methods too close to the rack and the screw to permit of constitutional differentiation.... [C]onvictions cannot be brought about by methods that offend 'a sense of justice.' Coerced confessions offend the community's sense of fair play and decency....

The State Department has argued that the constitutional protections noted above as well as several common crimes defined in federal and state statutes (such as the longstanding crimes of assault and battery) adequately cover the issue. See, e.g., Fourth Periodic Report of the United States of America to the United Nations Committee on Human Rights Concerning the ICCPR (2011), paras. 171–94.

COMMENT ON US LAW AND POLICY OF TORTURE AFTER 11 SEPTEMBER

The events of 11 September 2001 led the Administration at the time to develop and institutionalize a broad policy of counter-terrorism. It proposed, and Congress enacted, broad legislation like the Patriot Act. In important part, the Administration also proceeded through the Executive Branch, independently of Congress — for example, by interpretations of both domestic legislation and treaties that bore on vital matters including the question of prohibited methods of interrogation of persons detained on suspicion of participation in terrorism.

The issue of torture, and its regulation under US legislation as well as by the Convention against Torture and the Geneva Conventions, thereby became prominent within the Administration, in congressional debate and among the general public. The decisions reached, particularly those within the Executive Branch, provoked foreign criticism of US policy. The question of torture, once thought settled and closed as a normative matter (despite its ongoing practice in the world), became newly relevant in a domestic and international context.

As a background matter, it is important that the US had entered the following reservation to its ratification (in 1994) of the Convention against Torture:

> That the United States considers itself bound by the obligation under Article 16 to prevent "cruel, inhuman or degrading treatment or punishment," only insofar as the term "cruel, inhuman or degrading treatment or punishment" means the cruel, unusual and inhumane treatment or punishment prohibited by the Fifth, Eighth, and/or Fourteenth Amendments to the Constitution of the United States.

A similarly worded reservation to US ratification (in 1992) of the International Covenant on Civil and Political Rights was entered with respect to Article 7 of the Covenant.

The ratification of the Convention against Torture was also made subject to the following 'understanding' of the US:

> That with reference to Article 1, the United States understands that, in order to constitute torture, an act must be specifically intended to inflict severe physical or mental pain or suffering and that mental pain or suffering refers to prolonged mental harm caused by or resulting from: (1) the intentional infliction or threatened infliction of severe physical pain or suffering; (2) the administration or application, or threatened administration or application, of mind altering substances or other procedures calculated to disrupt profoundly the senses or the personality; (3) the threat of imminent death; or (4) the threat that another person will imminently be subjected to death, severe physical pain or suffering, or the administration or application of mind altering substances or other procedures calculated to disrupt profoundly the senses or personality.

The following readings include excerpts from a few memoranda by US officials holding important positions in the Department of Justice. They concern both the definition of torture and the broad issue of the heightened role and powers of the Executive Branch on national security matters in the age of modern terrorism.

US Department of Justice, Memorandum from Jay Bybee, Assistant Attorney General, to Alberto Gonzales, Counsel to the President, August 1, 2002

This memorandum concerned standards of conduct for interrogation of detainees outside the United States under the Torture Act, 18 U.S.C. §§2340–2340A implementing the Convention against Torture (CAT) and the provisions for grave breaches in the Geneva Conventions. It separately analysed the statute and treaty. Section 2340 reads in part:

> As used in this chapter –
>
> (1) 'torture' means an act committed by a person acting under the color of law specifically intended to inflict severe physical or mental pain or suffering

(other than pain or suffering incidental to lawful sanctions) upon another person within his custody or physical control;

(2) 'severe mental pain or suffering' means the prolonged mental harm caused by or resulting from –

(A) the intentional infliction or threatened infliction of severe physical pain or suffering;

(B) the administration or application, or threatened administration or application, of mind-altering substances or other procedures calculated to disrupt profoundly the senses or the personality;

(C) the threat of imminent death; or

(D) the threat that another person will imminently be subjected to death, severe physical pain or suffering, or the administration or application of mind-altering substances or other procedures calculated to disrupt profoundly the senses or personality. . . .

. . .

Section 2340A states in part:

> Whoever outside the United States commits or attempts to commit torture shall be fined under this title or imprisoned not more than 20 years, or both, and if death results to any person from conduct prohibited by this subsection, shall be punished by death or imprisoned for any term of years or for life.

The statute does not define the critical word 'severe'. Turning to dictionary definitions to identify the 'ordinary or natural meaning' of that term, the memo concludes that 'the pain or suffering must be of such a high level of intensity that the pain is difficult for the subject to endure'. Turning to other statutes using the term 'severe' such as those defining an emergency medical condition for the purpose of providing health care, Bybee understood them to suggest that 'severe' pain in Section 2340:

> must rise to a similarly high level — the level that would ordinarily be associated with a sufficiently serious physical condition or injury such as death, organ failure, or serious impairment of body functions — in order to constitute torture.

The memo then refers to the statute's four-part definition of severe 'mental' pain or suffering, and summarizes its views:

> Each component of the definition emphasizes that torture is not the mere infliction of pain or suffering on another, but is instead a step well removed. The victim must experience intense pain or suffering of the kind that is equivalent to the pain that would be associated with serious physical injury so severe that death, organ failure, or permanent damage resulting in a loss of significant body function will likely result. If that pain or suffering is psychological, that suffering must result from one of the acts set forth in the statute. In addition, these acts must cause long-term mental harm.

The memo understands the statutory requirement of 'prolonged mental harm' to mean that 'the acts giving rise to the harm must cause some lasting, though not necessarily permanent, damage... [T]he development of a mental disorder such as post-traumatic stress disorder, which can last months or even years, or even chronic depression, which also can last for a considerable period of time if untreated, might satisfy the prolonged harm requirement.' The memo states that it is not enough for the victim to suffer prolonged mental suffering. The perpetrator must also specifically intend, in other words purposefully aim to achieve, that result.

The memo then addressed treaties. It recalled that CAT distinguishes between 'torture' and 'cruel, inhuman or degrading treatment or punishment which does not amount to torture as defined in Article 1.' Recall the 'understanding' informing the US ratification of CAT, p. 266, *supra*, that later found its way into the definition of mental pain or suffering in Section 2340.

The Bybee memo referred to testimony at the time of the memo of an official from the Department of Justice stating that 'torture is understood to be that barbaric cruelty which lies at the top of the pyramid of human rights misconduct'. That testimony gave as examples 'the needle under the fingernail, the application of electrical shock to the genital area, the piercing of eyeballs, etc'. In conclusion, the memo argued that CAT's text, ratification history and negotiating history confirmed that torture 'is a step far-removed from other cruel, inhuman or degrading treatment or punishment'. CAT reaches only 'the most heinous acts'. Such an interpretation gave the Executive Branch more leeway in deciding on methods of interrogation seeking information from suspected terrorists that were shy of the ultimate prohibition of torture.

The memorandum also considers 'defenses', including that of 'necessity'. Such a defence could eliminate criminal liability even if the statutory definition of torture was found to have been violated. The memo stresses two factors: (1) The greater the certainty of government officials that the person under interrogation has information needed to prevent a serious attack, the more necessary the interrogation. (2) The greater the likelihood that a terrorist attack will occur, and the greater the damage expected from such an attack, the more the interrogation would be necessary. Much then depends on the knowledge of the government official conducting the interrogation. 'While every interrogation that might violate Section 2340A does not trigger a necessity defense, we can say that certain circumstances would support such a defense.'

US Department of Justice, Memorandum from Daniel Levin, Acting Assistant Attorney General, to James B. Comey, Deputy Attorney General, December 30, 2004

[The Bybee memorandum above provoked extensive debate and much criticism, much of which was directed to its very restrictive definition of torture. The memorandum below examined the legal standards applicable under 18 U.S.C. §§2340–2340A. Excerpts follow:]

> Torture is abhorrent both to American law and values and to international norms. This universal repudiation of torture is reflected in our criminal law...;

international agreements...; customary international law, centuries of Anglo-American law and the longstanding policy of the United States, repeatedly and recently reaffirmed by the President.

This Office interpreted the federal criminal prohibition against torture — codified at 18 U.S.C. §§ 2340–2340A — in [the August 2002 Memorandum appearing above, which] also addressed a number of issues beyond interpretation of those statutory provisions, including the President's Commander-in-Chief power.... Questions have since been raised, both by this Office and by others, about the appropriateness and relevance of the non-statutory discussion in the August 2002 Memorandum, and also about various aspects of the statutory analysis....

We decided to withdraw the August 2002 Memorandum.... This memorandum supersedes the August 2002 Memorandum in its entirety. Because the discussion in that memorandum concerning the President's Commander-in-Chief power... was — and remains — unnecessary, it has been eliminated from the analysis that follows. Consideration of the bounds of any such authority would be inconsistent with the President's unequivocal directive that United States personnel not engage in torture.

We have also modified in some important respects our analysis of the legal standards applicable under 18 U.S.C. §§ 2340–2340A. For example, we disagree with statements in the August 2002 Memorandum limiting "severe" pain under the statute to "excruciating and agonizing" pain, or to pain "equivalent in intensity to the pain accompanying serious physical injury, such as organ failure, impairment of bodily function, or even death."...

...

[The memo notes that the Senate attached an understanding to its advice and consent to ratification of the CAT that differs from the constituent elements of an act of torture set forth in the CAT. That understanding is generally tracked in §§2340–2340A.]

Although Congress defined "torture" under sections 2340–2340A to require conduct specifically intended to cause "severe" pain or suffering, we do not believe Congress intended to reach only conduct involving "excruciating and agonizing" pain or suffering.... We are not aware of any evidence suggesting that the standard was raised in the statute and we do not believe that it was.

...

(2) The meaning of 'severe physical pain or suffering.'

...Although we think the meaning of "severe physical pain" is relatively straightforward, the question remains whether Congress intended to prohibit a category of "severe physical suffering" distinct from "severe physical pain." We conclude that under some circumstances "severe physical suffering" may constitute torture even if it does not involve "severe physical pain." Accordingly, to the extent that the August 2002 Memorandum suggested that "severe physical suffering" under the statute could in no circumstances be distinct from "severe physical pain," we do not agree.

...

The memorandum's discussion about the meaning of 'severe mental pain or suffering' and 'specific intent' is omitted. In that discussion, it drew further distinctions between its understanding and that of the earlier, withdrawn August 2002 memorandum.

NOTE

Did the 2005 Memorandum alter US interrogation practices? The 2005 Memorandum included an important caveat suggesting that specific methods of interrogation previously approved by the Office of Legal Counsel would still be valid even under its more restrictive legal definitions. In a footnote, the 2005 Memorandum stated: 'While we have identified various disagreements with the August 2002 Memorandum, we have reviewed this Office's prior opinions addressing issues involving treatment of detainees and do not believe that any of their conclusions would be different under the standards set forth in this memorandum'. It was later revealed that another (Top Secret) 1 August 2002 Memorandum by Bybee had discussed and approved a wide range of specific techniques including 'waterboarding' — forcibly pouring water down the throat of a restrained individual to create the uncontrollable physiological sensation of drowning — sleep deprivation, throwing an individual against a flexible false wall, and confining the individual inside a box and introducing an insect into the box. In 2005, the Office of Legal Counsel issued an opinion stating explicitly — and explaining in detail — that these techniques were consistent with the 2004 Memorandum by Levin and thus did not constitute torture. As an example, it provided the following analysis of waterboarding:

> To the extent that in some applications the use of the waterboard could cause choking or similar physical — as opposed to mental — sensations, those physical sensations might well have an intensity approaching the degree contemplated by the statute. However, we understand that any such physical — as opposed to mental — sensations caused by the use of the waterboard end when the application ends. Given the time limits imposed, and the fact that any physical distress... would occur only during the actual application of water, the physical distress caused by the waterboard would not be expected to have the duration required to amount to severe physical suffering....
>
> ... The sensation of drowning that we understand accompanies the use of the waterboard arguably could qualify as a "threat of imminent death" within the meaning of section 2340(2)(C) and thus might constitute a predicate act of "severe mental pain or suffering" under the statute....
>
> Nevertheless, the statutory definition of "severe mental pain or suffering" also requires that the predicate act produce "prolonged mental harm." 18 U.S.C. § 2340(2).... [T]here is no medical basis to believe that the technique would produce any mental effect beyond the distress that directly accompanies its use and the prospect that it will be used again.

❁ ❁ ❁

Following the public debate over dissemination of pictures from the Abu Ghraib prison facility in Iraq, President Bush issued a statement in 2004 that said in part:

> Today, on United Nations International Day in Support of Victims of Torture, the United States reaffirms its commitment to the worldwide elimination of torture.... Freedom from torture is an inalienable human right, and we are committed to building a world where human rights are respected and protected by the rule of law.... We will investigate and prosecute all acts of torture and undertake to prevent other cruel and unusual punishment in all territory under our jurisdiction.... The United States also remains steadfastly committed to upholding the Geneva Conventions, which have been the bedrock of protection in armed conflict for more than 50 years.... We expect other nations to treat our service members and civilians in accordance with the Geneva Conventions.

During 2005 and 2006, intense debate continued about the treatment of prisoners with respect to a range of issues, including interrogation methods. Senator John McCain, a survivor of torture in the Vietnam War, introduced an amendment to legislation on the defence budget which bore his name. As enacted as part of the Detainee Treatment Act of 2005, it provided that (1) no one in the custody of the Department of Defense 'shall be subject to any treatment or technique of interrogation not authorized by and listed in the United States Army Field Manual on Intelligence Interrogation', and that (2) no one in the custody of the US Government, 'regardless of nationality or physical location, shall be subject to cruel, inhuman, or degrading treatment or punishment'. It did not refer to 'torture' as such, but stated that the term 'cruel, inhuman, or degrading treatment of punishment' means (as provided in the Reservations, Declarations and Understandings to the US ratifications of the ICCPR and CAT) such treatment or punishment prohibited by the Fifth, Eighth and Fourteenth Amendments to the Constitution. The McCain Amendment left open a number of key questions bearing on its consistency with the international standard for state-inflicted torture — for example, whether the due-process test employed (through the Fourteenth Amendment) in the *Rochin* case, p. 265, *supra*, to bar evidence would now permit national security considerations to be employed in a balancing test. Such a test might ask whether the harm inflicted in interrogation is worth the information gained.

In late 2006, the US Government passed the Military Commissions Act of 2006 (MCA). The Act followed the Supreme Court's decision in *Hamdan v. Rumsfeld*, which held that Common Article 3 of the Geneva Conventions applies to the conflict with Al Qaeda, see p. 475, *infra*. Among other things, the MCA amended the War Crimes Act of 1996 by specifically defining those violations of Common Article 3 that incur criminal liability. Several of the MCA provisions involve the definition of torture under US law.

Prior to the MCA, the War Crimes Act criminalized 'violation[s] of common article 3'. Common Article 3 prohibits 'violence to life and person, in particular murder of all kinds, mutilation, cruel treatment and torture' as well as 'outrages upon personal dignity, in particular, humiliation and degrading treatment'. The MCA designates only certain violations of Common Article 3 as a criminal offence under the War Crimes Act. Included in that category is torture, which the MCA defines as follows:

> TORTURE. — The act of a person who commits, or conspires or attempts to commit, an act specifically intended to inflict severe physical or mental pain or suffering (other than pain or suffering incidental to lawful sanctions) upon another person within his custody or physical control for the purpose of obtaining information or a confession, punishment, intimidation, coercion, or any reason based on discrimination of any kind.

The MCA also defines cruel or inhuman treatment as a criminal offence:

> CRUEL OR INHUMAN TREATMENT. — The act of a person who commits, or conspires or attempts to commit, an act intended to inflict severe or serious physical or mental pain or suffering (other than pain or suffering incidental to lawful sanctions), including serious physical abuse, upon another within his custody or control.

Under the MCA, the meaning of 'serious physical pain or suffering' is further defined as bodily injury that involves:

(i) a substantial risk of death;
(ii) extreme physical pain;
(iii) a burn or physical disfigurement of a serious nature (other than cuts, abrasions, or bruises); or
(iv) significant loss or impairment of the function of a bodily member, organ, or mental faculty.

Compare with this definition that used by the Department of Justice in the August 2002 memo to define 'severe pain' as requiring 'the level that would ordinarily be associated with a sufficiently serious physical condition or injury such as death, organ failure, or serious impairment of body functions'.

The definition of severe mental pain or suffering in 18 U.S.C. 2340A(2), discussed above, applies to the MCA's definition of serious mental pain or suffering, with one exception. For conduct occurring after the enactment of the MCA, the term 'prolonged mental harm' is replaced by the term 'serious and non-transitory mental harm (which need not be prolonged)'.

The MCA's definitions of torture and cruel or inhuman treatment apply only to the War Crimes Act's criminalization of Common Article 3 violations. It does not apply to other proscriptions on torture and coercive interrogation, including the McCain Amendment. Nor does it preclude other criminal offences, such as assault, which may exist in other statutes.

CONCLUSIONS AND RECOMMENDATIONS OF COMMITTEE AGAINST TORTURE RELATING TO REPORT SUBMITTED BY THE UNITED STATES

CAT/C/USA/CO/2, 25 July 2006

[The Committee against Torture created by the CAT serves several functions comparable to those of the CEDAW Committee discussed in Part C of this chapter. Those functions include receiving and reacting to reports about compliance with CAT that states parties are required to submit periodically to the Committee. In 2006, the Committee issued its conclusions and recommendations concerning a report submitted by the United States that year. The excerpts below include both expressions of 'concern' and formal recommendations.]

13. ... The Committee also regrets that, despite the occurrence of cases of extraterritorial torture of detainees, no prosecutions have been initiated under the extraterritorial criminal torture statute (arts. 1, 2, 4 and 5).

The Committee reiterates its previous recommendation that the State party should enact a federal crime of torture consistent with article 1 of the Convention.... The State party should ensure that acts of psychological torture, prohibited by the Convention, are not limited to "prolonged mental harm" as set out in the State party's understandings lodged at the time of ratification of the Convention, but constitute a wider category of acts, which cause severe mental suffering, irrespective of their prolongation or its duration....

14. The Committee regrets the State party's opinion that the Convention is not applicable in times and in the context of armed conflict, on the basis of the argument that the "law of armed conflict" is the exclusive *lex specialis* applicable, and that the Convention's application "would result in an overlap of the different treaties which would undermine the objective of eradicating torture".

The State party should recognize and ensure that the Convention applies at all times, whether in peace, war or armed conflict, in any territory under its jurisdiction and that the application of the Convention's provisions are without prejudice to the provisions of any other international instrument, pursuant to paragraph 2 of its articles 1 and 16.

15. ... The State party should recognize and ensure that the provisions of the Convention expressed as applicable to "territory under the State party's jurisdiction" apply to, and are fully enjoyed, by all persons under the effective control of its authorities, of whichever type, wherever located in the world.

16. The Committee notes with concern that the State party does not always register persons detained in territories under its jurisdiction outside the United States, depriving them of an effective safeguard against acts of torture (art. 2). The State party should register all persons it detains in any territory under its jurisdiction, as one measure to prevent acts of torture....

17. The Committee is concerned by allegations that the State party has established secret detention facilities, which are not accessible to the International Committee of the Red Cross. Detainees are allegedly deprived of fundamental legal

safeguards, including an oversight mechanism in regard to their treatment and review procedures with respect to their detention.

The Committee is also concerned by allegations that those detained in such facilities could be held for prolonged periods and face torture or cruel, inhuman or degrading treatment....

...

22. The Committee, noting that detaining persons indefinitely without charge constitutes per se a violation of the Convention, is concerned that detainees are held for protracted periods at Guantánamo Bay, without sufficient legal safeguards and without judicial assessment of the justification for their detention (arts. 2, 3 and 16).

The State party should cease to detain any person at Guantánamo Bay and close this detention facility, permit access by the detainees to judicial process or release them as soon as possible, ensuring that they are not returned to any State where they could face a real risk of being tortured, in order to comply with its obligations under the Convention.

...

24. ... The State party should rescind any interrogation technique, including methods involving sexual humiliation, "waterboarding", "short shackling" and using dogs to induce fear, that constitutes torture or cruel, inhuman or degrading treatment or punishment, in all places of detention under its de facto effective control, in order to comply with its obligations under the Convention.

...

27. The Committee is concerned that the Detainee Treatment Act of 2005 aims to withdraw the jurisdiction of the State party's federal courts with respect to habeas corpus petitions, or other claims by or on behalf of Guantánamo Bay detainees, except under limited circumstances....

The State party should ensure that independent, prompt and thorough procedures to review the circumstances of detention and the status of detainees are available to all detainees, as required by article 13 of the Convention.

...

NOTE

President Bush and other high officials of the Executive Branch, as well as a number of legislators, disputed the Committee's conclusions and recommendations and characterized them as seriously inaccurate in major respects.

Upon taking office, the President Barak Obama's Administration adopted a dual approach: (prospectively) banning any ongoing or future use of torture but (retrospectively) generally avoiding prosecutions or pursuit of individuals responsible for authorizing or engaging in torture in the past. The prospective policy included several actions. First, in his first week in office, President Obama signed an executive order subjecting all future interrogations — including by the CIA — to the lawful techniques long permitted by the Army Field Manual. The McCain Amendment had required the Defense Department — but not the CIA — to abide by the Army Field Manual. Second, President Obama revoked all legal opinions by the prior administration that had analysed the law governing interrogations. Third, the President ordered the closure of the CIA's secret overseas detention centres (black sites) where high-value detainees had been held incommunicado. On September 2006, President Bush announced that he had moved all detainees out of these sites and transferred those individuals to Guantánamo. However, after that announcement, the Bush Administration used CIA prisons to detain two al Qaeda operatives for several months each before being sent to Guantánamo. Hence, the Obama Administration's decision to foreclose that option marked a substantive change in policy. Fourth, President Obama and the Attorney General of the United States both stated unequivocally that waterboarding constitutes torture. And, finally, the President declassified and made publicly available thousands of pages of material detailing the CIA's interrogation practices, related CIA communications, and legal opinions adopted by the Bush Administration.

Retrospectively, the Administration took a very different path. The Attorney General announced that 'the Department would not prosecute anyone who acted in good faith and within the scope of the legal guidance given by the Office of Legal Counsel regarding the interrogation of detainees'. As a result, in 2011, the Justice Department announced that it would only conduct a criminal investigation for the death in custody of two individuals. Notably, in their respective memoirs published in 2010 and 2011, President George W. Bush and Vice President Dick Cheney admitted that they authorized waterboarding and stated that they had no regrets.

QUESTIONS

1. How do you assess US policy and legislation on torture since 11 September with respect to its consistency with international human rights?

2. Consider the following commentary by Tom Parker, Policy Director for Terrorism, Counterterrorism and Human Rights at Amnesty International USA:

> [In March 2012] the United States sponsored a resolution at United Nations Human Rights Council calling on Sri Lanka to investigate alleged human rights abuses that occurred in the final days of the country's struggle with the Liberation Tigers of Tamil Eelam.
>
> . . .
>
> However, welcome though the US-sponsored resolution is, it is greatly undermined by the embarrassing gap that exists between US rhetoric and US behavior. Critics have not been slow in pointing this out.
>
> Without any apparent trace of irony, the US resolution calls on Sri Lanka to:
>
> "Address serious allegations of violations of international law by initiating credible and independent investigations and prosecutions of those responsible for such violations."

This from the country whose President's mantra has been that he intends to "turn the page" on the abuses that occurred during the Bush administration and to "look forwards not backwards." ...

You can't have it both ways.

Hypocrisy acts like kryptonite on moral authority. The complete failure of the United States to address the deliberate use of torture as an integral part of the War on Terror hugely diminishes its ability to put pressure on other states to adhere to human rights standards that it itself has ignored.

And we are all the poorer for it.

... [A]ccountability is nothing to be afraid of. Indeed it can be a powerful force for good.

The US Army actually has a fairly impressive track record of holding its troops to account for their actions in combat. The Army prosecuted forty-four soldiers for murder or manslaughter of civilians in Iraq or Afghanistan from 2001 to 2011; Thirty soldiers have been convicted of some form of homicide. Six have been convicted of lesser offenses. Only eight have been acquitted.

We should also not forget that it was a Special Agent in the US Army's Criminal Investigation Command that initiated the investigation into the abuses that occurred in Abu Ghraib.

The US military's reputation has not been significantly tarnished by abuses that have occurred in Afghanistan and Iraq precisely because there has been a genuine measure of accountability. The Obama administration should learn from the military's example.

...

We need a strong US voice speaking out for human rights in the world, but that can't happen without real accountability at home.

ADDITIONAL READING

J. L. Goldsmith, *Power and Constraint: The Accountable Presidency After 9/11* (2102); F. de Londras & F. F. Davis, 'Controlling the Executive in Times of Terrorism: Competing Perspectives on Effective Oversight Mechanisms', 30 Oxford J. L. Stud. 19 (2010); Karen Greenberg, *The Least Worst Place: Guantanamo's First 100 Days* (2009); M. Nowak & E. McArthur, *The United Nations Convention against Torture: A Commentary* (2008); D. Rejali, *Torture and Democracy* (2007); M. D. Evans, '"All the Perfumes of Arabia"': The House of Lords and "Foreign Torture Evidence"', 19 Leiden J. Int'l. L. 1125 (2006); Karen Greenberg (ed.), *The Torture Debate in America* (2005); J. Langbein, *Torture and the Law of Proof: Europe and England in the Ancien Regime* (2006, first published 1976); S. Levinson (ed.), *Torture: A Collection* (2004); K. Roth, M. Worden & A. Bernstein, *Torture: Does It Make Us Safer? Is It Ever OK?: A Human Rights Perspective* (2005).

4

Economic and Social Rights

A. OVERVIEW

The Universal Declaration of Human Rights recognizes two sets of human rights: the 'traditional' civil and political rights, as well as economic, social and cultural rights. In transforming the Declaration's provisions into legally binding obligations, the United Nations adopted two separate International Covenants which, taken together, constitute the bedrock of the international normative regime for human rights. The issues raised in earlier chapters concentrated on civil and political rights. This chapter explores the International Covenant on Economic, Social and Cultural Rights (ICESCR).

The 'official' position, dating back to the Universal Declaration and reaffirmed in innumerable resolutions since that time, is that the two covenants and sets of rights are, in the words adopted by the 1993 second World Conference on Human Rights in Vienna, 'universal, indivisible and interdependent and interrelated. The international community must treat human rights globally in a fair and equal manner, on the same footing, and with the same emphasis' (Vienna Declaration, para. 5). But this formal consensus, although restated by the UN General Assembly in its 2005 resolution creating the Human Rights Council, masks a deep and enduring disagreement over the proper status of economic, social and cultural rights. At one extreme lies the view that these rights are superior to civil and political rights in terms of an appropriate value hierarchy and in chronological terms. Of what use is the right to free speech to those who are starving and illiterate? The homeless cannot register to vote, the illiterate cannot fully exercise their political rights. At the other extreme we find the view that economic and social rights (ESR) do not constitute rights (as properly understood) at all. Treating them as rights undermines the enjoyment of individual freedom, distorts the functioning of free markets by justifying large-scale state intervention in the economy, and provides an excuse to downgrade the importance of civil and political rights.

Although variations on these extremes have dominated both diplomatic and academic discourse, the majority of governments have taken some sort of intermediate position. For the most part that position has involved (1) support for the equal status and importance of ESR (as of June 2012, 160 states were parties to the ICESCR, compared with 167 parties to the ICCPR), together with (2) failure to take steps to entrench those rights constitutionally, to adopt legislative or administrative provisions based explicitly on the recognition of specific ESR as international human rights, or to provide effective means of redress to individuals or groups alleging violations of those rights. In recent years, however, an increasing number of states have moved to take such measures and ESR have clearly assumed greater importance in the domestic legal order of states than has ever been the case before.

Even before the final adoption of the UDHR, the debate over the relationship between the two sets of rights had become a casualty of the Cold War: the Communist countries abstained from voting on its adoption by the General Assembly on the grounds that the ESR provisions were inadequate, and the Western countries were insistent that there should be two Covenants rather than a single integrated one. Since the 1970s, the debate has also taken on important North-South dimensions. These include claims that developing countries should not be held to the same standards in some respects and that respect for rights by poorer states must be linked to international aid, and trade and other concessions. As a result, the debate carries a lot of ideological baggage. With the rejection of communism and the widespread embrace of free-market economic solutions within the ongoing processes of globalization, ESR are certain to remain among the most controversial issues in the years ahead and their status will have important implications for other aspects of human rights law.

In a statement to the Vienna World Conference in 1993, the UN Committee on Economic, Social and Cultural Rights (hereafter the ESCR Committee) drew attention to:

> [t]he shocking reality...that States and the international community as a whole continue to tolerate all too often breaches of economic, social and cultural rights which, if they occurred in relation to civil and political rights, would provoke expressions of horror and outrage and would lead to concerted calls for immediate remedial action. In effect, despite the rhetoric, violations of civil and political rights continue to be treated as though they were far more serious, and more patently intolerable, than massive and direct denials of economic, social and cultural rights....
>
> ... Statistical indicators of the extent of deprivation, or breaches, of economic, social and cultural rights have been cited so often that they have tended to lose their impact. The magnitude, severity and constancy of that deprivation have provoked attitudes of resignation, feelings of helplessness and compassion fatigue. Such muted responses are facilitated by a reluctance to characterize the problems that exist as gross and massive denials of economic, social and cultural rights. Yet it is difficult to understand how the situation can realistically be portrayed in any other way.[1]

COMMENT ON HISTORICAL ORIGINS OF ECONOMIC AND SOCIAL RIGHTS

The historical origins of the recognition of ESR are diffuse. Those rights have drawn strength from the injunctions expressed in different religious traditions to care for

[1] UN Doc. E/1993/22, Annex III, paras. 5 and 7.

those in need and those who cannot look after themselves. In Catholicism, papal encyclicals have long promoted the importance of the right to subsistence with dignity, while 'liberation theology' has sought to build upon this 'preferential option for the poor'. Virtually all of the major religions manifest comparable concern for the poor and oppressed (see p. 308, *infra*). Other sources include philosophical analyses and political theory from authors as diverse as Thomas Paine, Karl Marx, Immanuel Kant and John Rawls; the political programmes of the nineteenth-century Fabian socialists in Britain, Chancellor Bismarck in Germany (who introduced social insurance schemes in the 1880s) and the New Dealers in the United States; and constitutional precedents such as the Mexican Constitution of 1917, the first and subsequent Soviet Constitutions, and the 1919 Constitution of the Weimar Republic (embodying the *Wohlfahrtsstaat* concept).

This comment concentrates on the evolution of these ideas in international human rights law. The most appropriate starting point is the International Labour Organization (ILO). Established by the Treaty of Versailles in 1919 to abolish the 'injustice, hardship and privation' which workers suffered and to guarantee 'fair and humane conditions of labour', it was conceived as the response of Western countries to the ideologies of Bolshevism and Socialism arising out of the Russian Revolution.[2]

In the interwar years, the ILO adopted international minimum standards in relation to a wide range of matters which now fall under the rubric of ESR. They included, *inter alia*, conventions dealing with freedom of association and the right to organize trade unions, forced labour, minimum working age, hours of work, weekly rest, sickness protection, accident insurance, invalidity and old-age insurance, and freedom from discrimination in employment. The Great Depression of the early 1930s underscored the need for social protection of those who were unemployed and gave a strong impetus to full employment policies such as those advocated by Keynes in his *General Theory of Employment, Interest and Money* (1936).

Partly as a result of these developments, various proposals were made during the drafting of the UN Charter for the inclusion of provisions enshrining the maintenance of 'full employment' as a commitment to be undertaken by member states. The strongest version, known after its principal proponents as the 'Australian Pledge', committed UN members to take action to secure 'improved labour standards, economic advancement, social security, and employment for all who seek it'.[3]

Despite significant support, the United States opposed the proposal on the grounds that any such undertaking would involve interference in the domestic, economic and political affairs of states. Ultimately agreement was reached on Article 55(a) of the Charter, which simply states that the United Nations shall promote 'higher standards of living, full employment, and conditions of economic and social progress and development' but does not call for specific follow-up at the international level.

[2] J. T. Shotwell, 'The International Labor Organization as an Alternative to Violent Revolution', 166 Annals of the American Academy of Political and Social Science 18 (1933).

[3] See generally Ruth Russell & Jean Muther, *A History of the United Nations Charter: The Role of the United States 1940–1945* (1958), at 786.

US opposition in this context did not signify the rejection of ESR *per se*. Indeed, in 1941 President Roosevelt had nominated 'freedom from want' as one of the four freedoms that should characterize the future world order. He spelled out this vision in his 1944 State of the Union address.[4]

> We have come to a clear realization of the fact that true individual freedom cannot exist without economic security and independence. 'Necessitous men are not free men.' People who are out of a job are the stuff of which dictatorships are made.
>
> In our day these economic truths have become accepted as self-evident. We have accepted, so to speak, a second bill of rights, under which a new basis of security and prosperity can be established for all — regardless of station, race, or creed.
>
> Among these are:
>
> The right to a useful and remunerative job in the industries, or shops, or farms, or mines of the Nation;
>
> The right to earn enough to provide adequate food and clothing and recreation; The right of every farmer to raise and sell his products at a return which will give him and his family a decent living;
>
> The right of every businessman, large and small, to trade in an atmosphere of freedom from unfair competition and domination by monopolies at home or abroad;
>
> The right of every family to a decent home;
>
> The right to adequate medical care and the opportunity to achieve and enjoy good health;
>
> The right to adequate protection from the economic fears of old age, sickness, accident, and unemployment;
>
> The right to a good education.
>
> All of these rights spell security. And after this war is won we must be prepared to move forward, in the implementation of these rights, to new goals of human happiness and well-being.

This approach was subsequently reflected in a draft international Bill of Rights, completed in 1944, by a Committee appointed by the American Law Institute. In addition to listing the rights contained in the US Bill of Rights (the first ten amendments to the Constitution), the Institute's proposal advocated international recognition of a range of rights and acceptance of the correlative duties in relation to education, work, reasonable conditions of work, adequate food and housing, and social security.[5] In relation to each of the proposed rights, a Comment by the Committee drew attention to the fact that it had already been recognized in the 'current or recent constitutions' of many countries; e.g., 40 countries in the case of the right to education; 9 for the right to work; 11 for the right to adequate housing; 27 for the right to social security.

Although these proposals of the Committee were never formally endorsed by the American Law Institute, they were submitted to the United Nations and were to prove highly influential in the preparation of the first draft of the Universal

[4] Eleventh Annual Message to Congress (11 Jan. 1944), in J. Israel (ed.), *The State of the Union Messages of the Presidents* (1966), Vol. 3, at 2881. See generally Cass Sunstein, *The Second Bill of Rights: FDR's Unfinished Revolution and Why We Need It More than Ever* (2004).

[5] See Statement of Essential Human Rights, UN Doc. A/148 (1947), Arts. 11–15.

Declaration in 1947. In the drafting of Articles 22–28 of the UDHR, strong support for the inclusion of ESR came from the United States (a delegation led by Eleanor Roosevelt), Egypt, several Latin American countries (particularly Chile) and from the (Communist) countries of Eastern Europe. The United Kingdom opposed their inclusion,[6] as did South Africa which objected first that 'a condition of existence does not constitute a fundamental human right merely because it is eminently desirable for the fullest realization of all human potentialities' and secondly that if the proposed economic rights were to be taken seriously it would be 'necessary to resort to more or less totalitarian control of the economic life of the country'.[7]

After the adoption of the Universal Declaration in 1948, the next step was to translate the rights it recognized in Articles 22–28 into binding treaty obligations. This process took from 1949 to 1966. The delay was due to reasons including the Cold War, developing US opposition to the principle of international human rights treaties, and the scope and complexity of the proposed obligations. By 1955, the main lines of what was to become the ICESCR were agreed.

Between 1949 and 1951 the Commission on Human Rights worked on a single draft covenant dealing with both of the categories of rights. But in 1951 the General Assembly, under pressure from the Western-dominated Commission, agreed to draft two separate covenants. The following analysis of the drafting process, prepared by the United Nations, captures the main dilemmas and controversies relating to the inclusion of economic, social and cultural rights.[8]

> 6 ... [T]he goal was for the two covenants] to contain 'as many similar provisions as possible' and to be approved and opened for signature simultaneously, in order to emphasize the unity of purpose.
>
> ...
>
> 8. Those who were in favour of drafting a single covenant maintained that human rights could not be clearly divided into different categories, nor could they be so classified as to represent a hierarchy of values. All rights should be promoted and protected at the same time. Without economic, social and cultural rights, civil and political rights might be purely nominal in character; without civil and political rights, economic, social and cultural rights could not be long ensured....
>
> 9. Those in favour of drafting two separate covenants argued that civil and political rights were enforceable, or justiciable, or of an 'absolute' character, while economic, social and cultural rights were not or might not be; that the former were immediately applicable, while the latter were to be progressively implemented; and that, generally speaking, the former were rights of the individual 'against' the State, that is, against unlawful and unjust action of the State, while the latter were rights which the State would have to take positive action to promote. Since the nature of civil and political rights and that of economic, social and cultural rights, and the obligations of the State in respect thereof, were different, it was desirable that two separate instruments should be prepared.

[6] See B. Andreassen, 'Article 22' and A. & W. B. Eide, 'Article 25', in G. Alfredsson & A. Eide (eds.), *The Universal Declaration of Human Rights* (1999); and J. Morsink, *The Universal Declaration of Human Rights: Origins, Drafting and Intent* (1999) Chs. 5–6.

[7] UN Doc. E/CN.4/82/Add.4 (1948), at 11, 13.

[8] Annotations on the Text of the Draft International Covenants on Human Rights, UN Doc. A/2929 (1955), at 7.

10. The question of drafting one or two covenants was intimately related to the question of implementation. If no measures of implementation were to be formulated, it would make little difference whether one or two covenants were to be drafted. Generally speaking, civil and political rights were thought to be 'legal' rights and could best be implemented by the creation of a good offices committee, while economic, social and cultural rights were thought to be 'programme' rights and could best be implemented by the establishment of a system of periodic reports. Since the rights could be divided into two broad categories, which should be subject to different procedures of implementation, it would be both logical and convenient to formulate two separate covenants.

11. However, it was argued that not in all countries and territories were all civil and political rights 'legal' rights, nor all economic, social and cultural rights 'programme' rights. A civil or political right might well be a 'programme' right under one régime, an economic, social or cultural right a 'legal' right under another. A covenant could be drafted in such a manner as would enable States, upon ratification or accession, to announce, each in so far as it was concerned, which civil, political, economic, social and cultural rights were 'legal' rights, and which 'programme' rights, and by which procedures the rights would be implemented.

...

NOTE

The ICESCR was adopted by the General Assembly in Res. 2200A (XXI) of 16 December 1966 and entered into force on 3 January 1976. It is divided into five 'Parts'. Part I (like Part I of the ICCPR) recognizes the right of peoples to self-determination; Part II defines the general nature of states parties obligations; Part III enumerates the specific substantive rights; Part IV deals with international implementation; and Part V contains typical final provisions of a human rights treaty. In terms of substantive rights the right to property, although recognized in the Universal Declaration, was not included, primarily because of the inability of governments to agree on a formulation governing public takings and the compensation therefor.

Economic and social rights are not to be found only in the ICESCR. To the contrary, they figure in most of the other major treaties.

While it is essential to read the full text of the Covenant, the following excerpts from Parts II and III provide a flavour of some of the key issues. Later materials explore the meaning of Article 2.

EXCERPTS FROM THE ICESCR

...

PART II

Article 2

1. Each State Party to the present Covenant undertakes to take steps, individually and through international assistance and co-operation, especially economic

and technical, to the maximum of its available resources, with a view to achieving progressively the full realization of the rights recognized in the present Covenant by all appropriate means, including particularly the adoption of legislative measures....

PART III

Article 6

1. The States Parties to the present Covenant recognize the right to work, which includes the right of everyone to the opportunity to gain his living by work which he freely chooses or accepts, and will take appropriate steps to safeguard this right.

2. The steps to be taken by a State Party to the present Covenant to achieve the full realization of this right shall include technical and vocational guidance and training programmes, policies and techniques to achieve steady economic, social and cultural development and full and productive employment under conditions safeguarding fundamental political and economic freedoms to the individual.

Article 7

The States Parties to the present Covenant recognize the right of everyone to the enjoyment of just and favourable conditions of work which ensure, in particular:

(a) Remuneration which provides all workers, as a minimum, with:
   (i) Fair wages and equal remuneration for work of equal value...;
   (ii) A decent living for themselves and their families...;

(b) Safe and healthy working conditions;

...

(d) Rest, leisure and reasonable limitation of working hours and periodic holidays with pay, as well as remuneration for public holidays....

Article 9

The States Parties to the present Covenant recognize the right of everyone to social security, including social insurance.

...

Article 11

1. The States Parties to the present Covenant recognize the right of everyone to an adequate standard of living for himself and his family, including adequate food, clothing and housing, and to the continuous improvement of living conditions....

2. The States Parties to the present Covenant, recognizing the fundamental right of everyone to be free from hunger, shall take, individually and through international co-operation, the measures, including specific programmes, which are needed:

(a) To improve methods of production, conservation and distribution of food...;

...

Article 12

1. The States Parties to the present Covenant recognize the right of everyone to the enjoyment of the highest attainable standard of physical and mental health.

2. The steps to be taken by the States Parties to the present Covenant to achieve the full realization of this right shall include those necessary for:

(a) The provision for the reduction of the stillbirth-rate and of infant mortality and for the healthy development of the child;

(b) The improvement of all aspects of environmental and industrial hygiene;

(c) The prevention, treatment and control of epidemic, endemic, occupational and other diseases;

(d) The creation of conditions which would assure to all medical service and medical attention in the event of sickness.

Article 13

1. The States Parties to the present Covenant recognize the right of everyone to education....

2. The States Parties to the present Covenant recognize that, with a view to achieving the full realization of this right:

(a) Primary education shall be compulsory and available free to all;

(b) Secondary education... shall be made generally available and accessible to all by every appropriate means, and in particular by the progressive introduction of free education;

(c) Higher education shall be made equally accessible to all, on the basis of capacity, by every appropriate means, and in particular by the progressive introduction of free education;

...

COMMENT ON ASPECTS OF ICESCR

Differences Between the ICESCR and the ICCPR

The two Covenants use different terminology in relation to each right. Thus where the ICCPR contains terms such as 'everyone has the right to...' or 'no one shall be...', the ICESCR usually employs the formula 'States Parties recognize the right of everyone to...'. There are major differences in terms of the general obligations clause. Article 2(1) provides that these are subject to the availability of resources ('to the maximum of its available resources'), and that the obligation is one of progressive realization ('with a view to achieving progressively').

This language has been subject to conflicting critiques. On the one hand, it is often suggested that the nature of the obligation under the ICESCR is so onerous that virtually no government will be able to comply. Developing countries, in particular, are seen to be confronting an impossible challenge. On the other hand, it is argued that the relative open-endedness of the concept of progressive realization, particularly in light of the qualification about availability of resources, renders the obligation devoid of meaningful content. Governments can present themselves as defenders of ESR without international imposition of any precise constraints on their policies and behaviour. A related criticism is that the Covenant imposes only 'programmatic' obligations upon governments — that is, obligations to be fulfilled incrementally through the ongoing execution of a programme. It therefore becomes difficult if not impossible to determine when those obligations ought to be met or indeed have been met.

Interdependence of the Two Covenants

The interdependence of the two categories of rights has always been part of UN doctrine. The UDHR of 1948 included both categories without any sense of separateness or priority. The Preamble to the ICESCR, in terms mirroring those used in the ICCPR, states that 'in accordance with the Universal Declaration…, the ideal of free human beings enjoying freedom from fear and want can only be achieved if conditions are created whereby everyone may enjoy his economic, social and cultural rights, as well as his civil and political rights'.

The interdependence principle, apart from its use as a political compromise between advocates of one or two covenants, reflects the fact that the two sets of rights can neither logically nor practically be separated in watertight compartments. Civil and political rights may constitute the condition for and thus be implicit in ESR.

Similarly, a given right might fit equally well within either covenant, depending on the purpose for which it is declared. Some illustrations follow:

(1) The right to form trade unions is contained in the ICESCR, while the right to freedom of association is recognized in the ICCPR.

(2) The ICESCR recognizes various 'liberties' and 'freedoms' in relation to scientific research and creative activity.

(3) While the right to education and the parental liberty to choose a child's school are dealt with in the ICESCR (Art. 13), the liberty of parents to choose their child's religious and moral education is recognized in the ICCPR (Art. 18).

(4) The prohibition of discrimination in relation to the provision of, and access to, educational facilities and opportunities can be derived from both Article 2 of the ICESCR and Article 26 of the ICCPR.

(5) Even the European Convention on Human Rights, which is generally considered to cover only civil and political rights issues, states (in Art. 2 of Protocol 1) that 'no person shall be denied the right to education'.

Economic Rights, Social Rights, Cultural Rights

The ICESCR does not make explicit any distinction between economic, social or cultural rights. Commentators differ as to their characterization of one or the other of the declared rights,[9] or ignore the distinction. The original drafting rationale was an essentially bureaucratic one: the rights of concern to the ILO (Arts. 6–9) were assumed to be 'economic', those relevant to UN agencies such as the Food and Agriculture Organization and the World Health Organization (Arts. 10–12) were treated as 'social', and those that fell within the sphere of interest of UNESCO (Arts. 13–15) were designated as 'cultural'. In practice, however, most such distinctions are difficult to maintain. Education, for example, can arguably be classified as belonging to all of the relevant categories—economic, social and cultural, not to mention civil and political.

Although the title of the ICESCR expressly refers to 'cultural rights' and Article 15(1) recognizes 'the right of everyone...to take part in cultural life', such rights have attracted relatively little attention in this context. Rather, they have tended to be dealt with in relation to the ICCPR, whether under its non-discrimination clause (Art. 2(1)), the minorities provision (Art. 27) or specific rights such as freedoms of expression, religion and association and the right to 'take part in the conduct of public affairs'. The consequence has been a clear neglect of the specifically economic and social rights dimensions of cultural rights, with a few exceptions such as the focus on indigenous peoples' rights.

Implementation — The ESCR Committee

The greatest challenge is to identify effective approaches to implementation—i.e., to the means by which ESCR can be given effect and governments can be held accountable to fulfil their obligations. The Covenant says only that governments must use 'all appropriate means' to work towards the stated ends. Such means may be universally valid or relevant or may be quite specific to a particular culture or legal system. The Covenant gives no further pointers, beyond noting that 'appropriate means' includes 'particularly the adoption of legislative measures'. It is clear, however, that neither legislation nor effective remedies of a judicial nature, which are both central to the domestic implementation framework contained in the ICCPR (Art. 2), will play the same roles or *per se* be sufficient in relation to the ICESCR.

The principal UN body concerned with ESCR is the Committee on Economic, Social and Cultural Rights (the 'ESCR Committee'). The creation of the Committee was not foreseen in the text of the Covenant. It first met in 1987, having been established by a 1985 resolution of the Economic and Social Council after earlier monitoring arrangements had failed. The Committee has 18 independent expert members, elected for four-year terms on the basis of equitable geographic representation. In most respects it functions along the same lines as the ICCPR Committee, the work of which is analysed in detail in Chapter 9, *infra*, and the CEDAW Committee discussed in Chapter 3, *supra*. For that reason, little detail as to procedures is provided in the present context. Its task is to supervise compliance by states parties with their obligations under the ICESCR. It does this on the basis of regular reports submitted by states parties in accordance with its 'reporting guidelines'. An initial report by

[9] E.g. Henry Steiner, 'Social Rights and Economic Development: Converging Discourses?', 4 Buffalo Hum. Rts. L. Rev. 25 (1998), at 27.

each state party is due within two years, and subsequent reports are required at five-yearly intervals. The examination of a state's report by the Committee culminates in the adoption of the Committee's 'concluding observations', following the same sort of approach as we saw earlier in relation to the CEDAW Committee (p. 187, *supra*). In addition to its reporting function, there is a 2008 Optional Protocol that envisages a complaints procedure to be overseen by the Committee. The Protocol has not yet entered into force.[10] The Committee holds a 'day of general discussion' at most of its sessions to enable experts from civil society, academia, international agencies and elsewhere to discuss key issues relating to ESCR.

Finally, the Committee has also been active in producing General Comments,[11] a term that describes a function very similar to that performed by the CEDAW Committee's General Recommendations. The Committee's General Comment on the right to water illustrates the strengths as well as some of the problems inherent in this process. Recall that the ICESCR makes no reference to water, let alone a right thereto.

ESCR COMMITTEE, THE RIGHT TO WATER, GENERAL COMMENT NO. 15

UN Doc. E/C.12/2002/11 (2002)

1. … The human right to water is indispensable for leading a life in human dignity. It is a prerequisite for the realization of other human rights.…

2. The human right to water entitles everyone to sufficient, safe, acceptable, physically accessible and affordable water for personal and domestic uses. An adequate amount of safe water is necessary to prevent death from dehydration, to reduce the risk of water-related disease and to provide for consumption, cooking, personal and domestic hygienic requirements.

3. Article 11, paragraph 1, of the Covenant specifies a number of rights emanating from, and indispensable for, the realization of the right to an adequate standard of living 'including adequate food, clothing and housing'. The use of the word 'including' indicates that this catalogue of rights was not intended to be exhaustive. The right to water clearly falls within the category of guarantees essential for securing an adequate standard of living, particularly since it is one of the most fundamental conditions for survival.…

[10] GA Res. 63/117 (2008). The Optional Protocol requires ten ratifications to enter into force. As of May 2012 it had received eight: Argentina, Bolivia, Bosnia and Herzegovina, Ecuador, El Salvador, Mongolia, Slovakia and Spain.

[11] Between 1989 and March 2012 the ESCR Committee adopted 21 General Comments. They are: No. 1: Reporting by States parties (1989); No. 2: International technical assistance (1990); No. 3: The nature of States parties' obligations (1990); No. 4: Right to adequate housing (1991); No. 5: Persons with disabilities (1994); No. 6:ESCR of older persons (1995); No. 7: Forced evictions (1997); No. 8: Economic sanctions and ESCR (1997); No.9:Domestic application of the Covenant (1998); No. 10: National human rights institutions and ESCR (1998); No. 11: Plans of action for primary education (1999); No. 12: Right to adequate food (1999); No. 13: Right to education (1999); No. 14: Right to health (2000); No. 15: Right to water (2002); No.16: Equal right of men and women to ESCR (2005); No. 17: Authorial rights under Art. 15(1)(c); No. 18: Right to work (2005); No. 19: The right to social security (2008); No. 20: Non-discrimination in ESCR (2009); and No. 21: Right of everyone to take part in cultural life (2009).

...

10. The right to water contains both freedoms and entitlements. The freedoms include the right to maintain access to existing water supplies necessary for the right to water, and the right to be free from interference, such as the right to be free from arbitrary disconnections or contamination of water supplies. By contrast, the entitlements include the right to a system of water supply and management that provides equality of opportunity for people to enjoy the right to water.

11. The elements of the right to water must be *adequate* for human dignity, life and health.... The adequacy of water should not be interpreted narrowly, by mere reference to volumetric quantities and technologies. Water should be treated as a social and cultural good, and not primarily as an economic good....

12. While the adequacy of water required for the right to water may vary according to different conditions, the following factors apply in all circumstances:

Availability. The water supply for each person must be sufficient and continuous for personal and domestic uses...;

Quality. The water required for each personal or domestic use must be safe, therefore free from micro-organisms, chemical substances and radiological hazards that constitute a threat to a person's health. Furthermore, water should be of an acceptable colour, odour and taste for each personal or domestic use.

Accessibility. Water and water facilities and services have to be accessible to *everyone* without discrimination, within the jurisdiction of the State party....

...

International obligations

30. [ICESCR Articles 2(1), 11(1) and 23] require that States parties recognize the essential role of international cooperation and assistance and take joint and separate action to achieve the full realization of the right to water.

31. To comply with their international obligations in relation to the right to water, States parties have to respect the enjoyment of the right in other countries. International cooperation requires States parties to refrain from actions that interfere, directly or indirectly, with the enjoyment of the right to water in other countries. Any activities undertaken within the State party's jurisdiction should not deprive another country of the ability to realize the right to water for persons in its jurisdiction.

32. States parties should refrain at all times from imposing embargoes or similar measures,...

33. Steps should be taken by States parties to prevent their own citizens and companies from violating the right to water of individuals and communities in other countries....

34. Depending on the availability of resources, States should facilitate realization of the right to water in other countries, for example through provision of water resources, financial and technical assistance, and provide the necessary aid when required....

35. ... States parties should take steps to ensure that [any international agreements to which they are parties] do not adversely impact upon the right to water.

Agreements concerning trade liberalization should not curtail or inhibit a country's capacity to ensure the full realization of the right to water.

...

NOTE

In response to the General Comment, some governments expressed strong reservations. Canada, for example, argued that while governments owe a responsibility to their own people to provide access to water and sanitation, this did not translate into a human right. But other governments and many NGOs enthusiastically embraced the right. In 2004 the World Bank published a study on the issue[12] and efforts began to appoint a Special Rapporteur. But, in order to accommodate differences of opinion, while also facilitating further work on the subject, in 2008 the Human Rights Council appointed an 'Independent Expert on the issue of human rights obligations related to access to safe drinking water and sanitation'. The Expert, Catarina de Albuquerque, subsequently presented a series of reports that helped to persuade states of the importance and validity of the right and in 2010 the UN General Assembly (Res. 64/292 of 28 July 2010) recognized 'the right to safe and clean drinking water and sanitation as a human right that is essential for the full enjoyment of life and all human rights'.

The resolution was adopted with 122 votes in favour, 0 against and 41 abstentions. Among the latter were many Western governments, including the United States and the United Kingdom. The latter criticized the sponsors of the resolution for insisting on taking the issue directly to the General Assembly before the process involving the Independent Expert had fully played out. More importantly, the United Kingdom argued that 'there was no sufficient legal basis for declaring or recognizing water or sanitation as freestanding human rights, nor was there evidence that they existed in customary law.' Despite this reluctance on the part of 41 states, several months later the Council adopted a resolution, without a vote (i.e., with no formal objections) recalling the Assembly's resolution and affirming 'that the human right to safe drinking water and sanitation is derived from the right to an adequate standard of living and inextricably related to the right to the highest attainable standard of physical and mental health, as well as the right to life and human dignity' (HRC Res. 15/9 of 30 Sept. 2010). Six months later the Council voted to change the title of the Independent Expert to that of Special Rapporteur on the human right to safe drinking water and sanitation (Res. 16/2 of 24 Mar. 2011). The transformation from no mention in the ICESCR and strong opposition from key governments, to uncontested recognition of the right and the appointment of a Special Rapporteur to move it forward was thus complete.

The remaining question is whether there is a single right to water and sanitation or whether they are separate rights. The Expert defines sanitation as 'a system for the collection, transport, treatment and disposal or re-use of human excreta and associated hygiene'. In November 2010 the ESCR Committee adopted a Statement insisting that 'sanitation has distinct features which warrant its separate treatment from water', and

[12] S. Salman & S. McInerney-Lankford, *The Human Right to Water* (2004).

noting that '[a]lthough much of the world relies on waterborne sanitation, increasingly sanitation solutions which do not use water are being promoted and encouraged.' It thus called on states to recognize a freestanding right to sanitation.[13]

QUESTIONS

1. Is the ESCR Committee skating over important terminological issues when it claims that we tolerate 'breaches of economic, social and cultural rights which, if they occurred in relation to civil and political rights, would provoke expressions of horror and outrage'?

2. Consider the following issues in relation to the excerpts from the ICESCR: does the right to work amount to a guarantee of employment? Is Article 7 on working conditions utopian or relevant only to an advanced industrial economy? Is the much-derided 'right to holidays with pay' defensible? How could the right to social security be meaningful in a poor developing country? Why is the right to health not formulated in terms of a right of access to health care? Is the vision of the right to education in Article 13 outdated?

3. Craven has argued that a 'desire to conserve the status quo may involve occasionally reading an instrument such as the Covenant in a "teleological" or "evolutive" manner, just as a desire to transform or change social relations may involve reading it "literally".'[14] What interpretive strategy does the Committee use to justify its conclusion that there is a right to water, and how persuasive is it?

4. Mechlem has criticized the ESCR Committee for claiming, in its General Comment No. 12 on the Right to Food, that international organizations such as the FAO and the World Bank have 'international obligations' under the Covenant. She notes that there is no mention of any such obligations in the text and that these organizations cannot become parties to the treaty:

> Disconnected from any methodological basis, its conclusions seem to have been reached at random. Because statements rather than arguments are offered, it is also difficult to reconstruct the train of thought of the CESCR. . . .
>
> The CESCR pays a price for its endorsement of forward-looking human rights thinking. Because this endorsement cannot be based on a legally sound interpretation of the ICESCR, it undermines the credibility and legitimacy of its overall interpretation output.[15]

Is this a valid criticism? If so, what are the implications for the Committee's approach to the right to water? If not, what are the limits to the Committee's 'creativity' in proclaiming new norms and obligations?

[13] Statement on the Right to Sanitation, UN Doc. E/C.12/2010/1 (19 Nov. 2010).

[14] Matthew Craven, 'Some Thoughts on the Emergent Right to Water', in E. Riedel & P. Rothen (eds.), *The Human Right to Water* (2006) 37, at 39.

[15] Kerstin Mechlem, 'Treaty Bodies and the Interpretation of Human Rights', 42 Vand. J. Transnat'l. L. 905 (2009).

ADDITIONAL READING

S. Fredman, *Human Rights Transformed: Positive Rights and Positive Duties* (2008); P. Alston & G. Quinn, 'The Nature and Scope of States Parties' Obligations Under the International Covenant on Economic, Social and Cultural Rights', 9 Hum. Rts Q. 156 (1987); M. Craven, *The International Covenant on Economic, Social and Cultural Rights: A Perspective on its Development* (1995); M. Sepúlveda, *The Nature of the Obligations under the International Covenant on Economic, Social and Cultural Rights* (2003); Daphne Barak-Erez & Aeyal M. Gross, *Exploring Social Rights: Between Theory and Practice* (2007); C. Gearty & V. Mantouvalou, *Debating Social Rights* (2011); P. Alston, 'The United Nations' Specialized Agencies and Implementation of the International Covenant on Economic, Social and Cultural Rights', 18 Columbia J. Transnat'l. L. 79 (1979); M. Langford & J. King, 'Committee on Economic, Social and Cultural Rights', in M. Langford (ed.), *Social Rights Jurisprudence* (2008); Catarina de Albuquerque, 'The Coming into Life of the Optional Protocol to the International Covenant on Economic, Social and Cultural Rights — The Missing Piece of the International Bill of Human Rights', 32 Hum. Rts. Q. 144 (2010); F. Sultana & A. Loftus (eds.), *The Right to Water: Politics, Governance and Social Struggles* (2011); T. S. Bulto, 'The Emergence of the International Right to Water in International Human Rights Law: Invention or Discovery?', 12 Melb. J. Int'l. L. 290 (2011).

B. COMPETING PERSPECTIVES ON ESR

In the following materials we examine some of the philosophical, religious, economic and legal challenges that are frequently posed by the critics of ESR, both at the national and international levels. The materials tend to emphasize the US debate, partly because the United States still tends to be the key player on these issues in international fora and partly because US-style economic liberalism has been widely adopted elsewhere.

But before reviewing the various critiques it is important to note that there are many settings in which ESR are widely accepted in both theory and practice. The right to education, at least at primary school level, is almost universally accepted and has achieved extensive constitutional recognition. When people are forcibly evicted from their homes and have nowhere else to live, most legal systems recognize some dimensions of their right to shelter or housing. The deliberate denial of access to food — whether in relation to detainees, displaced persons, disfavoured ethnic or racial groups, or in the context of an embargo — is widely acknowledged to violate basic human rights norms. When states fail to establish and enforce basic minimal health and safety protections for workers the international community considers a violation of labour rights to have occurred. But despite such examples there remain many challenges to these rights, as the following readings indicate.

1. AMBIVALENCE TOWARDS ESR

Despite the widespread embrace of the doctrine that ESR are of equal importance with CPR (p. 277, *supra*) many governments and NGOs continue to be ambivalent towards ESR. Thus, for example, in terms of formal commitments:

- While all 47 member states of the Council of Europe are parties to the European Convention on Human Rights and thus to its complaints procedure (indeed its acceptance is a prerequisite to membership), less than one-third of them (14) have accepted the collective complaints system under the European Social Charter (which is the Convention's counterpart in the field of ESR).
- The Additional Protocol to the American Convention on Human Rights in the Area of Economic, Social and Cultural Rights, of 1988 (the 'Protocol of San Salvador'), has only been ratified by 16 countries, compared with the 25 parties to the Convention itself.

The only open hostility to this group of rights has come from the United States, whose attitude has varied considerably from one administration to another.[16] Eleanor Roosevelt, who represented the Truman Administration, was a strong proponent of ESR. The United States, under President Johnson, voted in the General Assembly in 1966 to adopt the Covenant. Although neither the Nixon nor Ford Administrations were opposed to these rights, neither actively promoted them. The Carter Administration adopted a different approach epitomized by Secretary of State Cyrus Vance's 'Law Day Speech' at the University of Georgia, in which he defined human rights as including:

> First,... the right to be free from governmental violation of the integrity of the person.... Second,... the right to the fulfilment of such vital needs as food, shelter, health care and education.... Third,... the right to enjoy civil and political liberties....[17]

In 1978, President Carter signed the Covenant and sent it to the Senate for its advice and consent with a view to ratification. At the time, however, no action was taken by the Senate, even in Committee. The Reagan and first Bush Administrations reversed official policy and opposed the concept of ESR on the grounds that while:

> the urgency and moral seriousness of the need to eliminate starvation and poverty from the world are unquestionable... the idea of economic and social rights is easily abused by repressive governments which claim that they promote human rights even though they deny their citizens the basic... civil and political rights.[18]

[16] P. Alston, 'Putting Economic, Social, and Cultural Rights Back on the Agenda of the United States', in William F. Shulz (ed.), *The Future of Human Rights: US Policy for a New Era* (2008), 120.

[17] 76 Dept. of State Bulletin 505 (1977).

[18] Introduction, US Dept. of State, Country Reports on Human Rights Practices for 1992, 5.

In 1993, the Clinton Administration committed to moving for ratification of the Covenant, but did not do so and continued to oppose the inclusion of all references to rights such as the right to adequate housing and the right to adequate food in international diplomatic settings. The Administration of George W. Bush remained unsympathetic but became open to formal acknowledgement of ESR while insisting that they were very different in nature. Thus it characterized the right to food as 'a goal or aspiration to be realized progressively' that translates into 'the opportunity to secure food; [and] not a guaranteed entitlement'.[19]

The Obama Administration announced a major policy shift in 2011. It rebutted the concerns of previous administrations that: (1) recognition of ESCR would obligate the United States to provide increased foreign assistance; (2) such rights might become justiciable; (3) states' rights and prerogatives would be threatened; and (4) recognition would play into the hands of those who use ESR to justify neglect of CPR. Assistant Secretary of State Michael Posner announced that the United States would henceforth 'work constructively with like-minded delegations to adopt fair and well-reasoned resolutions at the UN' on ESCR that 'are consistent with our own laws and policies'. Five considerations would be taken into account: (1) the rights concerned must be expressly set forth, or reasonably derived from', the UDHR and the ICESCR. As a signatory to the Covenant, the United States is 'committed to not defeating the object and purpose of the treaty'; (2) 'we will only endorse language that reaffirms the "progressive realization" of these rights and prohibits discrimination'; (3) 'language about enforcement must be compatible with our domestic and constitutional framework'; (4) 'we will highlight the U.S. policy of providing food, housing, medicine and other basic requirements to people in need'; and (5) 'we will emphasize the interdependence of all rights and recognize the need for accountability and transparency in their implementation, through the democratic participation of the people.'[20]

It is noteworthy, however, that the State Department's annual *Country Report on Human Rights Practices* continues not to address ESR, although it does include a range of labour rights (which are classified as ESR by UN instruments).

But the United States is not alone in its ambivalence. Although formal support for ESCR has been near universal, in practice no group of states has consistently followed up its rhetorical support at the international level with practical and sustained programmes of implementation. West European social democracies would seem best placed to promote the importance of these rights. But while being consistently supportive of initiatives they have been generally cautious, in part because the rights are often not accorded full constitutional or other recognition as rights *per se*, and in part because of the consistent calls within some states for a reduction in the scope of the European welfare state. Developing countries continue to be the most vocal proponents of these rights but they have made few concrete proposals beyond calling for more attention to be accorded to them. Cuba, for example, was

[19] See www.fao.org/DOCREP/MEETING/005/Y7106E/y7106e03.htm.

[20] Michael H. Posner, 'The Four Freedoms Turn 70: Ensuring Economic, Political, and National Security in the 21st Century', 24 Mar. 2011, at www.state.gov/j/drl/rls/rm/2011/159195.htm.

so reluctant to treat these rights as individually enforceable that it initially resisted the appointment of any special rapporteurs to investigate ESCR.[21]

A different form of reticence about ESR is illustrated by the position of China. In international fora it has been among the strongest proponents of ESR, but its support is nuanced. It continues to prioritize ESR, as indicated in its National Human Rights Action Plan of China (2009–2010) which states:

> By putting people first, the Chinese government makes sure the constitutional principle that 'the state respects and protects the human rights of its citizens' is implemented. While respecting the universal principles of human rights, the Chinese government in the light of the basic realities of China, gives priority to the protection of the people's rights to subsistence and development, and lawfully guarantees the rights of all members of society to equal participation and development on the basis of facilitating sound and rapid economic and social development. In the practice of governance, the Chinese government stands by the principle that development is for the people, by the people and with the people sharing its fruits, spares no effort to solve the most specific problems of the utmost and immediate concern to the people, promotes social equity and justice, and strives to ensure that all the people enjoy their rights to education, employment, medical and old-age care, and housing. The Chinese government persists in ensuring the people's position as masters of the country, expands citizens' orderly participation in political affairs at each level and in every field, improves the institutions for democracy, diversifies its forms and expands its channels, carries out democratic election, decision-making, administration and supervision in accordance with the law to guarantee people's rights to be informed, to participate, to be heard, and to oversee.[22]

In addition, although China has done very well on some ESR indicators in recent years, it has done little to ensure accountability for violations of ESR or to provide a significant role for the courts. Peerenboom has suggested that shortcomings in the relevant regulatory frameworks include 'the lack of specific and robust individual remedies in many laws, institutional design that limits the power of the judiciary within the Chinese constitutional structure, political limitations inherent in an effectively single-party social state, ideological conflicts between... advocates of socialist justice and... proponents of neoliberalism, and resource constraints...'.[23]

Finally, some of the most prominent NGOs have also been ambivalent towards ESR. Until 1993 Human Rights Watch (HRW) eschewed ESCR and Amnesty International effectively did so until 2001. Since then both organizations have sought to develop a coherent strategy in relation to these rights, with varying degrees of success. At the same time, a number of more specialized groups such as Physicians for Human Rights, ESCR-Net, the Center for Economic and Social Rights and the National Economic and Social Rights Initiative, along with the International

[21] UN Doc. E/CN.4/1998/25, para. 16.

[22] At http://news.xinhuanet.com/english/2009-04/13/content_11177126_1.htm.

[23] N. Randall Peerenboom, 'Economic and Social Rights: The Role of Courts in China', 12 San Diego Int'l. L.J. 303 (2011), at 329.

Commission of Jurists, have made important contributions to enhanced understanding of these rights.[24] One of the biggest challenges for mainstream NGOs is to determine whether they can apply the same 'methodologies' they have developed for CPR in relation to ESR. This is the subject of the following analysis by Kenneth Roth, Executive Director of HRW since 1993.

KENNETH ROTH, DEFENDING ECONOMIC, SOCIAL AND CULTURAL RIGHTS: PRACTICAL ISSUES FACED BY AN INTERNATIONAL HUMAN RIGHTS ORGANIZATION

26 Hum. Rts. Q. 63 (2004)

...

In my view, the most productive way for international human rights organizations, like Human Rights Watch, to address ESC rights is by building on the power of our methodology. The essence of that methodology ... is not the ability to mobilize people in the streets, to engage in litigation, to press for broad national plans, or to provide technical assistance. Rather, the core of our methodology is our ability to investigate, expose, and shame. We are at our most effective when we can hold governmental (or, in some cases, nongovernmental) conduct up to a disapproving public....

... [T]o shame a government effectively — to maximize the power of international human rights organizations like Human Rights Watch — clarity is needed around three issues: violation, violator, and remedy. We must be able to show persuasively that a particular state of affairs amounts to a violation of human rights standards, that a particular violator is principally or significantly responsible, and that a widely accepted remedy for the violation exists. If any of these three elements is missing, our capacity to shame is greatly diminished....

...

Broadly speaking, [these elements are] clearest when it is possible to identify arbitrary or discriminatory governmental conduct that causes or substantially contributes to an ESC rights violation. These three dimensions are less clear when the ESC shortcoming is largely a problem of distributive justice. If all an international human rights organization can do is argue that more money be spent to uphold an ESC right — that a fixed economic pie be divided differently — our voice is relatively weak. We can argue that money should be diverted from less acute needs to the fulfillment of more pressing ESC rights, but little reason exists for a government to give our voice greater weight than domestic voices. On the other hand, if we can show that the government (or other relevant actor) is contributing to the ESC

[24] See especially various interpretive guides adopted by civil society groups, such as (1) the Limburg Principles on the Implementation of the International Covenant on Economic, Social and Cultural Rights (1986), 9 Hum. Rts. Q. 122 (1987); (2) the Maastricht Guidelines on Violations of Economic, Social and Cultural Rights (1997), 20 Hum. Rts Q. 691 (1998); and (3) the Montréal Principles on Women's Economic, Social and Cultural Rights (2002), 26 Hum. Rts. Q. 760 (2004).

shortfall through arbitrary or discriminatory conduct, we are in a relatively powerful position to shame: we can show a violation (the rights shortfall), the violator (the government or other actor through its arbitrary or discriminatory conduct), and the remedy (reversing that conduct).

...

To conclude, let me offer a hypothesis about the conduct of international human rights organizations working on ESC rights. It has been clear for many years that the movement would like to do more in the ESC realm. Yet despite repeated professions of interest, its work in this area remains limited. Part of the reason, of course, is expertise; the movement must staff itself somewhat differently to document shortfalls in such matters as health or housing than to record instances of torture or political imprisonment. But much of the reason, I suspect, is a sense of futility. International human rights activists see how little impact they have in taking on matters of pure distributive justice so they have a hard time justifying devoting scarce institutional resources for such limited ends....

QUESTIONS

1. Given the reticence of many states, how would you explain the fact that ESR continue to occupy an important place within the international regime? What factors might lead any given government to be strongly supportive of the concept and practice of such rights? Why would the US Government be so keen to address labour rights in its annual reports?

2. If China has done so well in recent years in lifting vast numbers out of poverty, is there any reason to worry about the fact that it has few significant accountability mechanisms in place in relation to ESR?

3. Lee Kuan Yew, the former Prime Minister of Singapore, adopted an ESR policy which has been described in the following terms:

> [It is government policy] not to provide direct funds to individuals in its 'welfare' programs. Instead, much is spent on education, public housing, health care and infrastructure build-up as human capital investments to enable the individual and the nation as a whole to become economically competitive in a capitalist world.... For those who fall through the economic net...public assistance is marginal and difficult to obtain.... The government's position is that 'helping the needy' is a moral responsibility of the community itself and not just of the state. So construed, the recipients of the moral largesse of the community are to consider themselves privileged and bear the appropriate sense of gratitude.

Does such an approach give priority to ESR or does it instead put economic growth ahead of both sets of rights? If Singapore were to decide to become a party to the ICESCR, would it need to change such policies?

4. Are ESR matters of 'pure distributive justice', and if so, does this make them any less human rights than civil and political rights?

2. PHILOSOPHICAL PERSPECTIVES

Much of the literature on ESR tends to overlook the philosophical dimensions of the issue. But, in practice, those aspects are not far below the surface in most debates about ESR. It is thus necessary to have at least a general sense of philosophical arguments for and against ESR. In the readings that follow, Neier and Kelley argue that ESR should not properly be viewed as 'rights', while Griffin and Nickel outline different but related justifications for such rights. Sen responds to two major critiques of ESR.

ARYEH NEIER, SOCIAL AND ECONOMIC RIGHTS: A CRITIQUE[25]

13/2 Hum. Rts. Brief (2006)

... [L]et me first make clear that I favor a fairer distribution of the world's resources; [but] through the political process. For the most part,... it cannot take place through the assertion of rights.... Rights only have meaning if it is possible to enforce them. But there has to be some mechanism for that enforcement, and adjudication seems to be the mechanism that we have chosen. Therefore, from my standpoint, if one is to talk meaningfully of rights, one has to discuss what can be enforced through the judicial process.

... [A]lthough there certainly will be economic ramifications of efforts to enforce [civil and political rights such as access to counsel for accused persons, and decent prisons], they do not involve a broad redistribution of society's resources or its economic burdens. Therefore, I would distinguish the incidental costs of protecting civil and political rights from the much more substantial costs of economic redistribution.

Furthermore, there will always be, in unfair economic distribution, elements of invidious discrimination, discrimination on grounds of race or gender, or denials of due process. In these circumstances, I believe it is appropriate to invoke rights. For example, if a town provides roads and sewage collection, or water and electricity, to people of one race and not to those of another.... But I think of these matters in terms of race discrimination, which involves a denial of civil and political rights, and not economic redistribution. Finally, I want to make it clear that certain constitutions incorporate some things that could be called economic and social rights with a certain degree of legislative specificity. For example, a constitution may provide that every child shall be entitled to a free primary school or a free secondary school education. When a constitution provides that level of legislative specificity, I think it is certainly appropriate to use the judicial mechanism to enforce one's rights accordingly.

Social/economic rights and the democratic process

The concern I have with economic and social rights is when there are broad assertions... of a right to shelter or housing, a right to education, a right to social security, a right to a job, and a right to health care. There, I think, we get into territory that is

[25] Neier was founder of Human Rights Watch.

unmanageable through the judicial process and that intrudes fundamentally into an area where the democratic process ought to prevail.

In my view, the purpose of the democratic process is essentially to deal with two questions: public safety and the development and allocation of a society's resources.... Economic and security matters ought to be questions of public debate. To withdraw either of them from the democratic process is to carve the heart out of that process.

Everybody has an opinion on what should be done to protect the public's safety, and...as to what is appropriate in the allocation of a society's resources and its economic burdens.... These issues ought to be debated by everyone in the democratic process, with the legislature representing the public and with the public influencing the legislature in turn. To suggest otherwise undermines the very concept of democracy by stripping from it an essential part of its role.

Indeed, whenever you get to these broad assertions of shelter or housing or other economic resources, the question becomes: What shelter, employment, security, or level of education and health care is the person entitled to? It is only possible to deal with this question through the process of negotiation and compromise.... [A] court is not the place where it is possible to engage in [the necessary] sort of negotiation and compromise.... That is the heart of the political process....

Consider the question of health care.... If you are allocating the resources of a society, how do you deal with the person who says they need [a] kidney transplant or [a] bypass or...anti-retroviral drugs to save their life when the cost of these procedures may be equivalent to providing primary health care for a thousand children? Do you say the greater good for the greater number, a utilitarian principle, and exclude the person whose life is at stake if they do not get the health care that they require? I do not believe that is the kind of thing a court should do....

Consider next the question of education. What if a constitution talks about a right to an education but is silent as to the type of education people should be entitled to? A society may say that it needs a certain elite — scientists, engineers, and brain surgeons — as well as people who are going to able to work effectively in factories and service jobs. Does someone have a right to say they are entitled to an elite education...? Can you deal with these questions through the adjudicatory process? Again, I do not believe it is possible.

Finally, consider the question of jobs. Suppose that a decision is made through the legislative process that we have to spend a certain amount on building roads because we want peasants to be able to take their goods to market for sale. Suppose further that we have to build a port to export those goods.... Can the judicial process deal with the question of the short-term need for jobs and social security as opposed to that of long-term socio-economic growth?...

Civil and political rights

...I am a believer in very strong civil and political rights: the right to free speech, the right to assemble, the right not to be tortured, etc. Those rights have to mean exactly the same thing every place in the world. With social and economic "rights," however, it is inevitable that they are going to be applied differently in different places. That is, if you are talking about one country with extensive resources and one that is very poor, there is not going to be the same right to shelter or to health care....

But suppose that one takes that same idea — that different stages of development mean different things for each country — and applies it to the concept of civil and political rights. Suppose China or Zimbabwe says it is not a developed country and therefore cannot provide the same civil and political rights as a developed country....

Another way in which the idea of social and economic rights is dangerous is that you can only address economic and social distribution through compromise, but compromise should not enter into the adjudication of civil and political rights. I do not want a society to say that it cannot afford to give individuals the right to speak or publish freely, or the right not to be tortured....

...

DAVID KELLEY, A LIFE OF ONE'S OWN: INDIVIDUAL RIGHTS AND THE WELFARE STATE

(1998), at 1

In our personal lives, most of us realize that the world doesn't owe us a living....

Yet in our public lives we have accepted an obligation to provide food, shelter, jobs, education, pensions, medical care, child support, and other goods to every member of society. The premise of the welfare state — the sprawling network of programs for transferring wealth from taxpayers to recipients — is that the world *does* owe us a living. If someone is unable or unwilling to support himself, the government will provide food stamps, housing subsidies, and possibly cash assistance as well....

...

... [T]he welfare state is a specific historical phenomenon. In its modern form it is just over 100 years old. During the 1880s, Germany under Otto von Bismarck created social insurance programs for old age, job-related accidents, and other medical costs. Great Britain began building its welfare state, partly on Bismarck's model, in the early years of this century. In the United States,... the major welfare programs were created during the 1930s and 1960s....

... The welfare state... rests on an idea. The thinkers and activists who built it insisted that the social provision of goods be treated as a right possessed by all people as citizens, rather than as an act of charity or noblesse oblige, a gift from some to others....

...

[Ch.] 2. What is a Welfare Right?

... America remains unique in the role that rights play in the national culture. [The Declaration of Independence reflects the principles of Enlightenment individualism, including] the idea that the individual's primary need is for liberty: the freedom to act without interference, to be secure against assault on his person or property, to think and speak his mind freely, to keep the fruits of his labor. And while government is necessary to secure that freedom, it is also the greatest danger to it. Thus, the concept of rights served two functions in the political theory of the Enlightenment: to legitimate government and to control it....

It is against that background that we must understand the concept of welfare rights, a concept that reflects a more expansive view of the role of government than anything envisioned by the classical liberals of the Enlightenment. 'For Jefferson,...the poor had no right to be free from want', observes legal scholar Louis Henkin. 'The framers saw the purposes of government as being to police and safeguard, not to feed and clothe and house'.... They differ in what is being claimed as a right, in the obligations that they impose, and in the way they are implemented.

...

Welfare rights differ from the classical rights to life, liberty, and property in the nature of the claim that they embody....

The primary difference is one of content, a difference in what it is that people are said to have a right *to*. The classical rights are rights to freedom of action, whereas welfare rights are rights to goods. That distinction has often been described as the difference between 'freedom from' and 'freedom to'. The classical rights guarantee freedom from interference by others — and may thus be referred to as liberty rights — whereas welfare rights guarantee freedom to have various things that are regarded as necessities. What that means, in essence, is that the classical liberty rights are concerned with processes, whereas welfare rights are concerned with outcomes.

Liberty rights set conditions on the way in which individuals interact. Those rights say that we cannot harm, coerce, or steal from each other as we go about our business in life, but they do not guarantee that we will succeed in our business....

Welfare rights, by contrast, are intended to guarantee success, at least at a minimum level. They are conceived as entitlements to have certain goods, not merely to pursue them. They are rights to have the goods provided by others if one cannot (or will not) earn them oneself....

...

One person's right always involves corresponding obligations on the part of others to respect that right. The moral claim inherent in a right would be meaningless if no one were obliged to comply with it. [L]iberty rights impose on other people only the negative obligation not to interfere, not to restrian one forcibly from acting as he chooses....

But welfare rights impose positive obligations on others.... A welfare right is by nature a right to a postive outcome, not contingent on the success of one's own efforts. It must therefore impose on others the obligation to ensure that outcome.

On whom does the obligation fall [to provide what welfare rights require]? Here is another point of difference between liberty and welfare rights. One person's liberty rights impose on every other human being the obligation to respect them. I am obliged not to murder or steal from other individuals, even those I have never encountered and with whom I have no relationship. But am I obliged to respect their welfare rights? No advocate of welfare rights would say that a poor person has a right to appear at my door and demand food, or a place to sleep, or any of the other goods to which he is said to have a right. The obligation to supply those goods does not fall upon me as a particular individual; it falls upon all of us indifferently, as members of society.... Insofar as welfare rights are implemented through government programs, for example, the obligation is distributed among all taxpayers.

...

To implement the liberty rights of individuals, government must protect them against incursions by other individuals.... The laws involved are relatively simple; they essentially prohibit specific types of actions. The government apparatus required is relatively small, the 'night-watchman state' of classical liberalism. The only significant expense involved is that of the military, to protect against foreign aggression.

The implementation of welfare rights requires a much more activist form of government. The welfare state typically involves large-scale transfer programs... through which wealth is transferred from taxpayers to those on whom the state confers entitlements to various goods.

...

... [T]he administration of the transfer programs is enormously complex by contrast with the relatively simple prohibitions involved in protecting the rights to life, liberty, and property. The welfare state involves government in running large-scale business enterprises: pension plans, health insurance, and so on. A complex set of regulations... and a large bureaucracy [are] required to enforce those regulations.

...

Liberty and welfare rights differ, finally, in the level at which it is possible to implement them. The economic and technological development of a society affects the degree to which it can provide welfare rights to its members. A preindustrial society obviously cannot guarantee access to modern medical equipment and procedures. Even in a wealthy society, the potential demand for goods like health care or insurance against economic risks is open-ended. If individuals have rights to at least minimum levels of such goods, then the political process must decide what constitutes the minimum, the level that represents need rather than luxury. There is no universal and nonarbitrary standard for distinguishing need from luxury and thus for defining the content of welfare rights. It depends on the level of wealth in a given society.

The implementation of liberty rights, however, is not historically relative in the same way. The protection of an individual's liberty rights requires that other individuals, and the government itself, refrain from forcibly harming or constraining him or appropriating his property. The ability to forbear such actions is not a function of wealth....

...

In short, liberty rights reflect an individualist political philosophy that prizes freedom, welfare rights a communitarian or collectivist one that is willing to sacrifice freedom....

JAMES GRIFFIN, THE PRESIDENTIAL ADDRESS: DISCREPANCIES BETWEEN THE BEST PHILOSOPHICAL ACCOUNT OF HUMAN RIGHTS AND THE INTERNATIONAL LAW OF HUMAN RIGHTS

101 Proceedings of the Aristotelian Society 1–28 (2000)

...

According to my account, there are two grounds for human rights.... Personhood initially generates the rights; practicalities give them, where needed, a sufficiently determinate shape.

The way to understand personhood more fully is to distinguish the various strands of agency.... The first stage of agency is our taking our own decisions for ourselves, not being dominated or controlled by someone else (autonomy). To be more than empty tokens, our decisions must be informed; we must have basic education, access to information and to other people's views. And then, having formed a conception of a good life, we must be able to pursue it. So we need enough in the way of material provisions to support ourselves. And if we have all that, then we need others not to stop us (liberty). Whenever the word 'basic' appears here, it means the base needed not just to keep body and soul together but to live as an agent.

From this... we should be able to derive all human rights. We have a right to autonomy. In private life, this means... those in authority... must not make us, or keep us, submissive to their wills.... We have a right to life and to some form of security of person. We have a right not to be tortured.... We have rights to education, free expression, peaceful assembly. And we have various rights to basic material provision; these so-called welfare rights are much challenged, but for all my inclination to keep the class of human rights tight, it seems to me impossible to exclude them. So there must be a large range of rights to certain necessary conditions of agency.

Then, we must be free from interference in the pursuit of our major ends.... [T]here must be a large range of liberty rights, because liberty is the other essential component of agency.

This, of course, is the merest start of a list. There are many more human rights...

V

Twentieth century lists: economic, social, and cultural rights. [S]ome writers are deeply sceptical about the whole class of welfare rights.... What seems to me undeniable is that there is a human right to the minimum resources needed to live as an agent. That is more than the resources needed simply to keep body and soul together, but it is a good deal less than the lavish provision that many of the international documents have in mind. So I think that there are acceptable claims to (human) welfare rights in the major international documents. But, on my account, there is also a vast number of unacceptable and debatable claims, many more than in the case of civil and political rights.

(a) *Unacceptable Cases*: Some of the claims to welfare rights are hardly credible. Article 7c of the *Additional Protocol to the American Convention* asserts that there is a right of every worker to promotion or upward mobility in his employment. But some perfectly good jobs have no career structure....

...

... The *Universal Declaration* of 1948 proclaims... a right to work.... Yet on my account, there is no right to work. There is certainly a right to the resources needed to live as an agent, but those resources do not have to come from work. If in an advanced technological society there were not enough work for everyone, and those without it were adequately provided for, then, on the face of it, no one's human rights would be violated....

...

[Then in the ICESCR, there is] a right to 'the highest attainable standard of physical and mental health'. On my account, there is no such right. [This] is not even a reasonable social aim. Societies *could* mount crash programmes ... in the case of illnesses for which cures are attainable, but they often do not. They regard themselves as free to decide when they have spent enough on health, even if they are still short of the highest attainable standards, and may devote their inevitably limited resources to [other social goals]....

VI

The future of international lists of human rights. Suppose that I am right. How should we react to what would then be all the debatable and unacceptable items on the lists in international law?

...

The sensible answer, I think, is this: accept them as human rights. Their defect, such as it is, is that they cannot be seen as defending personhood. They cannot be brought under what I am proposing as the canonical heading 'protection of a component of human agency'. But very few words in our language are governed wholly by a canonical formula.... Their lack of essential properties does not matter; their having a settled use is enough for there to be criteria for determining whether or not they are used correctly.

...

JAMES W. NICKEL, POVERTY AND RIGHTS

55 The Philosophical Q. 385 (2005)

Human rights are not ideals of the good life for humans; rather they are concerned with ensuring the conditions, negative and positive, of a minimally good life....

Some philosophers have followed this line of thought to the conclusion that the main economic and social right is 'subsistence'. Henry Shue, John Rawls and Brian Orend[26] make subsistence the centrepiece of their concern for economic and social rights. Shue defines subsistence as 'unpolluted air, unpolluted water, adequate food, adequate clothing, adequate shelter, and minimal preventative health care'.... Rawls includes 'subsistence' on his very short list of human rights, treating it along with security as part of the right to life. He interprets 'subsistence' as including 'minimum economic security' or 'having general all-purpose economic means'.

The idea of subsistence alone offers too minimal a conception of economic and social rights. It neglects education, gives an extremely minimal account of health services, and generally gives too little attention to people's ability to be

[26] Eds.: see H. Shue, *Basic Rights* (2nd edn. 1996); B. Orend, *Human Rights: Concept and Context* (2002); and J. Rawls, *The Law of Peoples* (1999).

active participants and contributors. It covers the requirements of having a life, but neglects the conditions of being able to lead one's life.

If Shue, Rawls and Orend err by making economic and social rights too minimal, international human rights documents make them excessively grandiose....

... I advocate a conception [that] suggests that economic and social rights focus on survival, health and education. It requires governments to govern in such a way that the following questions can be answered affirmatively:

> 1. Subsistence: Do conditions allow all people to secure safe air, food and water as well as environmentally appropriate shelter and clothing if they engage in work and self-help in so far as they can, practise mutual aid through organizations such as families, neighbourhoods and churches, and procure help from available government assistance programmes? Do people enjoy access to productive opportunities that allow them to contribute to the well-being of themselves, their families and their communities?
>
> 2. Health: Do environmental conditions, public health measures and available health services give people excellent chances of surviving childhood and childbirth, achieving physical and mental competence and living a normal lifespan?
>
> 3. Education: Do available educational resources give people a good chance of learning the skills necessary for survival, health, functioning, citizenship and productivity?

...

II. The Justification of Economic and Social Rights

It is sometimes alleged that economic and social rights do not have the importance that civil and political rights have. If the objection is...that economic and social rights do not protect fundamental interests or are too burdensome to be justifiable, very plausible rebuttals are available.

...

[Contrary to Griffin's argument], autonomy by itself does not seem likely to be able to generate economic and social rights, due process rights, or rights to non-discrimination and equality before the law. To compensate, Griffin accordingly relies heavily on 'practicalities' in allowing these rights. The result is to make the justification of rights other than liberties appear shaky and derivative. This could have been avoided by introducing some other fundamental values or norms, particularly a requirement of fair treatment when very important interests are at stake.... A fairness norm would be no more controversial than autonomy as a starting-point for human rights, and it would allow due process rights to be as central and non-derivative as liberty rights.

[Nickel then proposes] a framework that suggests that people have secure, but abstract, moral claims on others in four areas:

- A secure claim to have a life
- A secure claim to lead one's life
- A secure claim against severely cruel or degrading treatment
- A secure claim against severely unfair treatment.

...

All four principles protect aspects of human dignity

The UDHR speaks of the 'inherent dignity... of all members of the human family', and declares that 'All human beings are born free and equal in dignity and rights. They are endowed with reason and conscience.' The four grounds of human rights that I have proposed provide an interpretation of these ideas. We respect a person's dignity when we protect his life and agency and when we prevent others from imposing treatment that is severely degrading or unfair.

...

AMARTYA SEN, THE IDEA OF JUSTICE

(2009), at 379

...

The Plausibility of Economic and Social Rights

...

Two of the most powerful rejections [of ESR by theorists and philosophers] have come from Maurice Cranston and Onora O'Neill....

There are... two specific lines of reproach, which I shall call the 'institutionalization critique' and the 'feasibility critique'. The institutionalization critique, which is aimed particularly at economic and social rights, relates to the belief that real rights must involve an exact correspondence with precisely formulated correlate duties. Such a correspondence, it is argued, would exist only when a right is institutionalized. Onora O'Neill has presented the following criticism with clarity and force:

> Unfortunately much writing and rhetoric on rights heedlessly proclaims universal rights to goods or services, and in particular 'welfare rights', as well as to [ESCR], without showing what connects each presumed right-holder to some specified obligation-bearer(s), which leaves the content of these supposed rights wholly obscure... Some advocates of universal economic, social and cultural rights go no further than to emphasize that they can be institutionalized, which is true. But the point of difference is that they must be institutionalized: if they are not there is no right.

In responding to this criticism, we have to invoke the understanding... that obligations can be both perfect and imperfect. Even the classical 'first-generation' rights, like freedom from assault, can be seen as imposing imperfect obligations on others

...

Indeed, the supportive activities of social organizations are often aimed precisely at institutional change, and the activities are plausibly seen as part of imperfect obligations that individuals and groups have in a society where basic human rights are violated.... To deny the ethical status of these claims would be to ignore the reasoning that fires these constructive activities, including working for institutional changes....

The 'feasibility critique'... proceeds from the argument that even with the best of efforts, it may not be feasible to realize many of the alleged economic and social rights for all.... Maurice Cranston puts the argument thus:

> The traditional political and civil rights are not difficult to institute. For the most part, they require governments, and other people generally, to leave a man alone... The problems posed by claims to economic and social rights, however, are of another order altogether. How can the governments of those parts of Asia, Africa, and South America, where industrialization has hardly begun, be reasonably called upon to provide social security and holidays with pay for millions of people who inhabit those places and multiply so swiftly?

Is this apparently plausible critique persuasive? I would argue that it is based on a confounding of the content of what an ethically acknowledged right must demand.... [H]uman rights advocates want the recognized human rights to be maximally realized. The viability of this approach does not crumble merely because further social changes may be needed at any point of time to make more and more of these acknowledged rights fully realizable and actually realized.

Indeed, if feasibility were a necessary condition for people to have any rights, then not just social and economic rights, but all rights — even the right to liberty — would be nonsensical, given the infeasibility of ensuring the life and liberty of all against transgression.... Non-realization does not, in itself, make a claimed right a non-right. Rather, it motivates further social action. The exclusion of all economic and social rights from the inner sanctum of human rights, keeping the space reserved only for liberty and other first-generation rights, attempts to draw a line in the sand that is hard to sustain.

...

IMMANUEL KANT, THE DOCTRINE OF VIRTUE

in The Metaphysics of Morals (1797, M. J. Gregor, trans. 1964), at 116

[24.] When we are speaking of laws of duty (not laws of nature) and, among these, of laws governing men's external relations with one another, we are considering a moral (intelligible) world where, by analogy with the physical world, attraction and repulsion bind together rational beings (on earth). The principle of mutual love admonishes men constantly to come nearer to each other; that of the respect which they owe each other, to keep themselves at a distance from one another. And should one of these great moral forces fail, 'then nothingness (immorality), with gaping throat, would drink the whole kingdom of (moral) beings like a drop of water'....

[25.] In this context, however, love is not to be taken as a feeling (aesthetic love), i.e. a pleasure in the perfection of other men; it does not mean emotional love (for others cannot oblige us to have feelings). It must rather be taken as a maxim of benevolence (practical love), which has beneficence as its consequence.

The same holds true of the respect to be shown to others: it is not to be taken merely as the feeling that comes from comparing one's own worth with another's (such as mere habit causes a child to feel toward his parents, a pupil toward his teacher, a subordinate in general toward his superior). Respect is rather to be taken in a practical sense (*observantia aliis praestanda*), as a maxim of limiting our self-esteem by the dignity of humanity in another person.

Moreover, the duty of free respect to others is really only a negative one (of not exalting oneself above others) and is thus analogous to the juridical duty of not encroaching on another's possessions. Hence, although respect is a mere duty of virtue, it is considered narrow in comparison with a duty of love, and it is the duty of love that is considered wide.

The duty of love for one's neighbour can also be expressed as the duty of making others' ends my own (in so far as these ends are only not immoral), The duty of respect for my neighbour is contained in the maxim of not abasing any other man to a mere means to my end (not demanding that the other degrade himself in order to slave for my end).

By the fact that I fulfill a duty of love to someone I obligate the other as well: I make him indebted to me. But in fulfilling a duty of respect I obligate only myself, contain myself within certain limits in order to detract nothing from the worth that the other, as a man, is entitled to posit in himself.

...

[30.] It is every man's duty to be beneficent — that is, to promote, according to his means, the happiness of others who are in need, and this without hope of gaining anything by it.

For every man who finds himself in need wishes to be helped by other men. But if he lets his maxim of not willing to help others in turn when they are in need become public, i.e. makes this a universal permissive law, then everyone would likewise deny him assistance when he needs it, or at least would be entitled to. Hence the maxim of self-interest contradicts itself when it is made universal law — that is, it is contrary to duty. Consequently the maxim of common interest — of beneficence toward the needy — is a universal duty of men, and indeed for this reason: that men are to be considered fellow-men — that is, rational beings with needs, united by nature in one dwelling place for the purpose of helping one another.

...

[Casuistical Questions]

...

The ability to practice beneficence, which depends on property, follows largely from the injustice of the government, which favours certain men and so introduces an inequality of wealth that makes others need help. This being the case, does the rich man's help to the needy, on which he so readily prides himself as something meritorious, really deserve to be called beneficence at all?

...

[38.] Every man has a rightful claim to respect from his fellow-men and is reciprocally obligated to show respect for every other man.

Humanity itself is a dignity; for man cannot be used merely as a means by any man (either by others or even by himself) but must always be treated at the same time as an end....

QUESTIONS

1. The position outlined by Neier seems to track existing United States approaches closely. Does this make it more or less convincing from a human rights perspective? Does he effectively exclude the recognition of all ESR?

2. Based on the preceding readings, how would you identify the salient distinctions between civil and political and ESR? How useful is it to think in terms of rights versus needs, negative versus positive, individual versus collective, determinate versus open textured, law versus policy?

3. Does Griffin's theory of agency provide a satisfactory basis for a theory of ESR? What about Nickel's reliance upon subsistence and human dignity?

4. 'If we were to make a rough analogy, Kant's duty of respect recalls the ICCPR, while the duty of beneficence recalls the ICESCR.' Do you agree or disagree, and why?

3. RELIGIOUS PERSPECTIVES

Isaiah, Ch. 58 (Holy Scriptures, Masoretic Text, 1917)

[The reference is to a fast of repentance.]

Behold, in the day of your fast ye pursue your business, and exact all your labours.

Behold, ye fast for strife and contention, and to smite with the fist of wickedness;

Ye fast not this day so as to make your voice to be heard on high.

Is such the fast that I have chosen? The day for a man to afflict his soul?

Is it to bow down his head as a bulrush, and to spread sackcloth and ashes under him?

Wilt thou call this a fast, and an acceptable day to the Lord?

Is not this the fast that I have chosen? To loose the fetters of wickedness, to undo the bands of the yoke,

And to let the oppressed go free, and that ye break every yoke?

Is it not to deal thy bread to the hungry, and that thou bring the poor that are cast out to thy house?

When thou seest the naked, that thou cover him, and that thou hide not thyself from thine own flesh?

…

And if thou draw out thy soul to the hungry, and satisfy the afflicted soul;

Then shall thy light rise in darkness, and thy gloom be as the noonday;

And the Lord will guide thee continually, and satisfy thy soul in drought, and make strong thy bones;

And thou shalt be like a watered garden, and like a spring of water, whose waters fail not.

Matthew, Ch.26 (Holy Bible, King James Version)

When the Son of man shall come in his glory, and all the holy angels with him, then shall he sit upon the throne of his glory;

…

Then shall the King say unto them on his right hand. Come, ye blessed of my Father, inherit the kingdom prepared for you from the foundation of the world.

For I was an hungered, and ye gave me meat; I was thirsty, and ye gave me drink; I was a stranger, and ye took me in;

Naked, and ye clothed me. I was sick, and ye visited me; I was in prison, and ye came unto me.

Then shall the righteous answer him, saying, Lord, when saw we thee an hungred, and fed thee, or thirsty, and gave thee drink?

…

And the King shall answer and say unto them. Verily I say unto you, Inasmuch as you have done it unto any of the least of these my brethren, ye have done it unto me.

Surah 63: Al Munafiqun, 9 and 10 (Holy Qur'an, Abdullah Yusuf' Ali trans. 1989)

O ye who believe!
Let not your riches
Or your children divert you
From the remembrance of Allah.
If any act thus,
The loss is their own.
And spend something (in charity)
Out of the substance
Which We have bestowed
On you

QUESTIONS

1. Compare as a group the verses from the Hebrew Bible, the Christian Bible and the Qur'an with Article 11 of the ICESCR. What similarities and what differences do you find

with respect to the invocation of rights and duties, and with respect to who bears what rights or duties?

2. An ESR critic might argue that these readings illustrate the necessary distinction between ethical or moral duties, and legal or human rights obligations. Would you agree?

ADDITIONAL READING

J. Griffin, *On Human Rights* (2008); C. Beitz, *The Idea of Human Rights* (2009); H. Shue, *Basic Rights: Subsistence, Affluence, and U.S. Foreign Policy* (2nd edn. 1996); A. Gewirth, *The Community of Rights* (1997); J. Nickel, *Making Sense of Human Rights* (2nd edn. 2007); C. R. Beitz & R. E. Goodin (eds.), *Global Basic Rights* (2009); R. Plant, *Modern Political Thought* (1991); Friedrich von Hayek, *Law, The Mirage of Social Justice* (1976); S. Holmes & C. Sunstein, *The Cost of Rights: Why Liberty Depends on Taxes* (1999); C. McCrudden, 'Human Dignity and Judicial Interpretation of Human Rights', 19 E.J.I.L. 655 (2008); T. Khaitan, 'Dignity as an Expressive Norm: Neither Vacuous Nor a Panacea', 32 Oxford J. Leg. Stud. 1 (2012); P. Vizard, S. Fukuda-Parr & D. Elson, 'Introduction: The Capability Approach and Human Rights', 12 J. Hum. Devt. & Capabilities 1 (2011).

C. THE RELATIONSHIP BETWEEN THE TWO SETS OF RIGHTS

The phrase first coined in 1950 and then adapted at the 1993 Vienna World Conference — that all rights are 'indivisible and interdependent and interrelated' — expresses the international community's attempt to resolve in the context of its discussions of human rights the longstanding debate over the relationship between freedom and equality. While the claim of indivisibility would be difficult to sustain as an empirical matter,[27] interdependence is more widely accepted, although that fact has not prevented regular claims that one set of rights or the other must in fact be accorded priority.

The relationship between the two sets of rights is a broad theme that runs through many of the materials in this book. Consider, for example, the relationship between upholding the norm of non-discrimination as a civil right and its potential for achieving full gender equality (see p. 177, *supra*), or the debate over the content of

[27] See James Nickel, 'Rethinking Indivisibility: Towards A Theory of Supporting Relations between Human Rights', 30 Hum. Rts Q. 984 (2008).

the right to development (see p. 1525, *infra*). In the materials that follow we look primarily at the relationship between democracy and ESR. Amartya Sen's pathbreaking work on famines emphasizes the importance of upholding a wide range of civil and political rights in order to ensure that potential famines are exposed and remedied in advance. But other commentators have been less optimistic about the extent to which a democratic society will inevitably provide adequate protection for ESR. Both Fredman and Drèze question the latter proposition and argue that democratic processes need to be supplemented.

AMARTYA SEN, FREEDOMS AND NEEDS

The New Republic (10 and 17 Jan. 1994) 31, at 32

...

... Do needs and rights represent a basic contradiction? Do the former really undermine the latter? I would argue that this is altogether the wrong way to understand, first, the force of economic needs and, second, the salience of political rights. The real issues that have to be addressed lie elsewhere, and they involve taking note of extensive interconnections between the enjoyment of political rights and the appreciation of economic needs. Political rights can have a major role in providing incentives and information toward the solution of economic privation. But the connections between rights and needs are not merely instrumental, they are also constitutive. For our conceptualization of economic needs depends on open public debates and discussions, and the guaranteeing of those debates and those discussions requires an insistence on political rights.

...

Consider the matter of famine. I have tried to argue elsewhere that the avoidance of such economic disasters as famines is made much easier by the existence, and the exercise, of various liberties and political rights, including the liberty of free expression.... But famines have never afflicted any country that is independent, that goes to elections regularly, that has opposition parties to voice criticisms, that permits newspapers to report freely and to question the wisdom of government policies without extensive censorship.

...

Why might we expect a general connection between democracy and the nonoccurrence of famines? The answer is not hard to seek. Famines kill millions of people in different countries in the world, but they do not kill the rulers. The kings and the presidents, the bureaucrats and the bosses, the military leaders and the commanders never starve. And if there are no elections, no opposition parties, no forums for uncensored public criticism, then those in authority do not have to suffer the political consequences of their failure to prevent famine. Democracy, by contrast, would spread the penalty of famine to the ruling groups and the political leadership.

There is, moreover, the issue of information. A free press, and more generally the practice of democracy, contributes greatly to bringing out the information that can have an enormous impact on policies for famine prevention, such as facts about the early effects of droughts and floods, and about the nature and the results of unemployment.... Indeed, I would argue that a free press and an active political opposition constitute the best 'early warning system' that a country threatened by famine can possess....

In making such arguments, of course, there is the danger of exaggerating the effectiveness of democracy. Political rights and liberties are permissive advantages, and their effectiveness depends on how they are exercised. Democracies have been particularly successful in preventing disasters that are easy to understand, in which sympathy can take an especially immediate form. Many other problems are not quite so accessible. Thus India's success in eradicating famine is not matched by a similar success in eliminating non-extreme hunger, or in curing persistent illiteracy or in relieving inequalities in gender relations. While the plight of famine victims is easy to politicize, these other deprivations call for deeper analysis, and for greater and more effective use of mass communication and political participation — in sum, for a fuller practice of democracy.

...

JEAN DRÈZE, DEMOCRACY AND THE RIGHT TO FOOD

in P. Alston & M. Robinson (eds.), Human Rights and Development: Towards Mutual Reinforcement (2005), at 45

...

1.3 Democracy and Social Rights

Perhaps the most startling aspect of the nutrition situation in India is that there is virtually no discussion of it, outside specialised circles. Chronic hunger rarely figures in public debates and electoral politics....

This neglect of social issues in general, and of chronic hunger in particular, is often attributed to "lack of political will". This...begs the question as to why there is no political will in the first place. In a democracy, political will is an outcome of democratic politics. Seen in this light, the deafening silence surrounding hunger and nutrition issues in India is an invitation to reflect on the nature and limitations of Indian democracy.

As far as democratic institutions are concerned, India is doing reasonably well in historical and international perspective. To illustrate, in comparison with the United States..., India fares much better in many respects. For instance, India has much higher voter turnout rates...; it has more extensive provisions for the political representation of socially disadvantaged groups; and it is less vulnerable to the influence of "big money" in electoral politics. There is also far greater pluralism in Indian than in US politics.... Even the quality of the Indian press is much higher, in many respects....

Having said this, Indian democracy has one minor flaw, namely that most people are unable to participate in it due to economic insecurity, lack of education, social discrimination and other forms of disempowerment. Voter turnout rates may be reasonably high (about 60 per cent for parliamentary elections), but informed participation in democratic institutions on a sustained basis is confined to a tiny minority. And even voting is a very limited form of democratic participation when most people are unable to distinguish clearly between the different political parties and their respective programmes.

In short, Indian democracy is trapped in a vicious circle of exclusion and elitism. Because underprivileged sections of the population are excluded from active participation in democratic politics, their aspirations and priorities are not reflected in public policy. The elitist orientation of public policy, in turn, perpetuates the deprivations (poverty, hunger, illiteracy, discrimination, etc.) that disempower people and prevent them from participating in democratic politics.

...

[The author cites Sen's famines thesis with approval.]

Outside the specific context of famine prevention (and other extreme circumstances, such as "starvation deaths"), democratic practice has delivered rather little, so far, in terms of holding the state accountable to its responsibility for protecting the right to food. However, this situation is not immutable. In fact, I would argue that there are vast possibilities of radical change in this field. These possibilities arise mainly from the growing participation of underprivileged groups in democratic politics, and the fact that food security is one of their main concerns. Another positive development in this context is that the tools of democratic participation are becoming more diverse over time.... [W]e have good grounds for enhanced confidence about the possibilities of public action outside the traditional arena of electoral politics. These possibilities have already been creatively harnessed for various causes, ranging from gender equality and Dalit liberation to war resistance and the defence of civil liberties. There is no reason why these initiatives should not be extended to the assertion of economic and social rights....

...

SANDRA FREDMAN, HUMAN RIGHTS TRANSFORMED: POSITIVE RIGHTS AND POSITIVE DUTIES

(2008), at 32

...

A. Positive Duties and Democracy

... [T]he dichotomy between positive human rights duties and democracy is misconceived. This is because human rights and particularly positive human rights duties are essential to achieve the participation which is at the core of all democratic theories.

...

(ii) 'We the people': participation and democracy

At first glance, the democratic argument against positive human rights duties seems self-evident. In a democracy, it is for the people to decide fundamental issues, without

human rights pre-commitments. This is particularly true for positive duties, which inevitably require the State to make distributive allocations. This presumes that the people actually do make such decisions. But in what sense can it be said that democracy means decision-making by the people? …
…

(iii) Enhancing democracy through positive duties

The above discussion has suggested that modern democracies are a complex amalgam of individual representation, interest group bargaining, and deliberative procedures. Against this background, it becomes clear that to counterpoise democracy with human rights is a false contradiction. Instead, positive human rights duties should be recognized as necessary to constitute democracy and ensure that it functions properly. As a start, positive duties are necessary to ensure that elections take place and individuals are free to vote. In addition, the State may need to take positive steps to protect individuals against other individuals' interference with the right. The existence of a universal suffrage does not mean that everyone can in fact exercise their rights.…

Even when blatant exclusionary practices are not in place, it is clear that, as Rawls acknowledged, social and economic inequalities in a modern democratic State are so large that those with greater wealth and position usually control political life and enact legislation and social policies that advance their interests. Even more to the point is TH Marshall's approach. For him, political citizenship is not sufficient. To ensure full and democratic citizenship, it is necessary to go beyond liberal and political rights, to the granting of social rights. These in turn enlist the positive contribution of the State. Nor is it sufficient to resort to collective organization, as the pluralists would have it. Interest group bargaining inevitably entrenches existing balances of power. Therefore, to the extent that decision-making is a result of interest bargaining among groups in society, democracy can only be sustained if there is a positive duty on the State to ensure that all are equally able to exercise their democratic rights and participate in society.

The same is true for deliberative democracy. To secure the conditions for effective exercise of deliberative democracy, participants must be both formally and substantively equal. This in turn means that the distribution of power and resources should not obstruct their chances to contribute to deliberation. All of these require positive input from the State to create the appropriate arenas for deliberation.…
…

NOTE

Varun Gauri offers the following observation related to electoral democracy:

> [E]mpowerment, participation, and information become critical because regular elections do not as a matter of routine lead to universal access to minimally decent health care and education.
>
> From the human rights perspective, the reason for this is that explicit legal discrimination, prolonged social exclusion, patterns of prejudice, and/or the internalization of low expectations lead to inadequate service utilization for some groups

and individuals. Problems such as these are acute in developing countries, where former colonial powers bequeathed varying group-based civil law for different ethnicities and religions, and where liberal constitutions are contemporaneous with feudal, clientelist, and patriarchal practices. The remedy requires correcting legal defects, as well as empowering citizens and the civil society organizations that act on their behalf to campaign against the informal cultural, social, and economic practices that sustain unfairness in access and utilization.

The economic approach is skeptical that electoral democracy by itself creates accountability in the health and education sectors for two reasons. Drawing on public choice theory, some economic analysts argue that interest groups, such as teachers unions, "capture" the institutions of service delivery for their own purposes. Using the principal findings of social choice theory, others contend that the preferences of service recipients are so heterogeneous that efforts to aggregate them, whether through democratic procedures or through market provision of jointly provided services like health care and education, are invariably bedeviled by impossibility, arbitrariness, and instability. Economic solutions to interest group capture entail strengthening the market and political position of recipients by giving consumers choices, exposing providers to competitive pressures, and, where services remain publicly provided, allowing service recipients more direct participation in decision making and monitoring. One solution to the aggregation problem involves group deliberation and the development of trust.[28]

QUESTIONS

1. In 1992 the ESCR Committee asserted that 'there is no basis whatsoever to assume that the realization of [ESCR] will necessarily result from the achievement of [CPR]', or that democracy can be a sufficient condition for their realization unless it is accompanied by targeted policies. Is Sen's analysis consistent with this approach and with the indivisibility thesis or does it give a clear priority to civil and political rights?

2. Consider Gearty's[29] critiques that proponents of judicially enforceable ESR downplay the deep systemic weaknesses that afflict the judicial system in most democracies while seeking to avoid the more legitimate goal of improving the responsiveness and legitimacy of the democratic system, rather than simply listing and accepting its shortcomings. For him, 'it is through politics rather than the law' that ESR are best promoted.

D. THE PROBLEM OF RESOURCES

Resources are at the heart of most of the challenges to ESR. Consider the following. The unique resource intensity of these rights gives them a fundamentally

[28] 'Social Rights and Economics: Claims to Health Care and Education in Developing Countries', in P. Alston & M. Robinson (eds.), *Human Rights and Development: Towards Mutual Reinforcement* (2005), at 65.

[29] Conor Geart, 'Against Judicial Enforcement', in C. Gearty & V. Mantouvalou, *Debating Social Rights* (2011) 1, at 71–84.

different character from CPR. Poor countries' governments simply cannot afford ESR. The complexity of identifying who should be liable, especially financially, for promoting their realization that makes the traditional naming and shaming approach adopted by NGOs virtually impossible to apply. And, the size of the funding required makes ESR inappropriate matters for judicial determination. A proponent of ESR must be able to provide coherent responses to these concerns and critiques by traditionalists.

An important related issue concerns how to measure compliance with ESR obligations. In recent years there has been a major move towards the use of various types of indicators for this purpose. They range from simple counts, through per capita and other type of ratios, to complex or composite indicators bringing together a range of different variables. Rather than being dealt with here, these approaches are considered in Chapter 14, *infra.*

This section begins with a review of different perspectives on the significance of the phrase 'available resources', which in turn holds the key to the possibilities for 'progressive realization'. It then explores the fiscal dimensions of ensuring that the 'maximum' amount of resources is available, such as through combating corruption and ensuring an adequate tax base.

1. 'AVAILABLE RESOURCES'

As already noted, one of the major distinctions between ESR and CPR is that obligations in relation to the former are limited to steps that can be taken within 'available resources'. No equivalent limitation is mentioned in the ICCPR, leading many experts to suggest that CPR are therefore not resource contingent. As a result, it is often argued that while wealthy industrialized countries may be able to afford policies designed to protect ESR, most developing countries cannot. For example, Maurice Cranston has written that: '[f]or a government to provide social security... it has to have access to great capital wealth.... The government of India, for example, simply cannot command the resources that would guarantee' each Indian an adequate standard of living.[30] A closely related issue concerns trade-offs. It is argued that more money on health inevitably means less for education, or water, or food etc. For many critics it follows that, in the absence of large-scale international aid or of rapid domestic economic growth (or both), the government's hands are tied and little can be expected of it in response to its obligations under the Covenant. (Note that the issue of international aid is considered in Chapter 17, *infra.*) Pressures to reduce the size of the public sector, to privatize various functions previously performed by governments, and to stimulate growth by reducing taxes, all render governments less able to accept responsibility for ESR.

Before focusing only on ESR, it is useful to reflect further on the resource dimensions of CPR. In principal, the issue does not arise because the relevant obligation

[30] 'Human Rights: Real and Supposed', in D. D. Raphael (ed.), *Political Theory and the Rights of Man* (1967) 43, at 51.

— to respect and ensure — is not made subject to any qualifications as to resources. But in reality, resources are always relevant in at least some respects. As noted earlier (p. 295, *supra*) Roth argues that ESR 'shortcomings [are] largely a problem of distributive justice', unless there is arbitrary or discriminatory government conduct. He cites a government's failure to provide universal primary education as a classic case, because 'there is not enough money to go around, so governments cannot provide education to all children.' But he also notes that:

> ... similar tradeoffs of scarce resources can arise in the realm of civil and political rights. Building prisons or creating a judicial system can be expensive. However, my experience has been that international human rights organizations implicitly recognize these tradeoffs by avoiding recommendations that are costly. For example, Human Rights Watch in its work on prison conditions routinely avoids recommending large infrastructure investments. Instead, we focus on improvements in the treatment of prisoners that would involve relatively inexpensive policy changes.[31]

These insights are confirmed in practice. Thus, for example, pursuing the death penalty costs the State of California an estimated $137 million per year, whereas a system with life without parole as the maximum sentence would cost $11.5 million annually.[32] Similarly, when California's prison population overflowed dramatically and the state concluded that it simply could not afford to house prisoners in conditions that would meet the required human rights standards, the US Supreme Court did not insist that more resources be mobilized but instead issued far-reaching orders requiring the state to find means to reduce the prison population drastically.[33]

But surely what Roth terms 'distributive justice' problems also arise in relation to CPR. Consider the question of how much funding to put into a judicial system, or a police service, or how elaborate and accessible arrangements for voting will be. Each of these can be funded more or less generously, and the decision will generally be made in light of the available resources, rather than being determined solely in light of an evaluation of the ideal level of supply.

The following readings survey a range of responses to this dilemma, with particular emphasis on the right to education. Weiner illustrates the fact that resource availability may not be the only problem. Sumner's research underscores the fact that most decisions about ESR are not made in contexts of absolute and unmovable resource constraints. The excerpt from the UNDP report suggests that there will always be room to adjust priorities in order to accommodate ESR if the political will is present. The section then concludes by looking at the various approaches to resources limitations adopted by the ESCR Committee.

[31] Kenneth Roth, 'Defending Economic, Social and Cultural Rights: Practical Issues Faced by an International Human Rights Organization', 26 Hum. Rts Q. 63 (2004), at 65–6.

[32] A. L. Alarcón & P. M. Mitchell, Executing the Will of the Voters?: A Roadmap to Mend or End the California Legislature's Multi-Billion-Dollar Death Penalty Debacle', 44 Loyola of Los Angeles L. Rev S41 (2011).

[33] *Brown v. Plata*, No. 09–1233, May 23, 2011.

MYRON WEINER, CHILD LABOUR IN DEVELOPING COUNTRIES: THE INDIAN CASE

2 Int. J. Children's Rts. 121 (1994)

Governments do not advocate child labour or oppose compulsory education.... Why, then, is child labour so widespread in developing countries? Why are so many children not in school?

The answers are well known and widely accepted. Governments in developing countries, it is said, lack the financial resources for universal compulsory primary school education; governments lack the administrative resources to enforce child labour laws; poor families need the labour and the income of their children; and children and their parents often find the schools in developing countries irrelevant to meet their needs.

By drawing upon examples from India, I will argue that these explanations are unsatisfactory. India is the world's largest producer of non-school going child workers; a review of the Indian experience will therefore help in understanding the reasons for the persistence of child labour not only in India but perhaps also in other developing states. I propose to develop three alternative explanations, firstly, that child labour is not simply an unfortunate feature of low income developing countries that cannot be eliminated until national incomes grow but is in fact sustained by government policies on primary education; secondly, that in India the establishment of compulsory primary education has not been in the interests of the middle classes who are concerned with the expansion of government expenditures on higher education; and finally, that child labour has become part of the government's industrial strategy to promote the small scale sector and to expand exports.

...

... [One] conclusion is that the establishment of compulsory education is a necessary condition for the reduction and abolition of child labour. Without compulsory education governments are unable to enforce child labour laws. In one country after another the phased extension of the age of compulsory education went hand in hand with a phased extension of restrictions on the employment of children. If the school-leaving age is lower than the age of admission to employment, children are likely to illegally seek employment, and the enforcement of child labour laws is rendered more difficult. It is administratively easier to monitor school attendance than to monitor children in the work place, and easier to force parents to send their children to school than to force employers not to hire children. No country has successfully ended child labour without first making education compulsory. So long as children are free not to attend school, they will enter the labour force.

India need not wait until incomes rise to make primary education universal and compulsory. The sooner India acts, the quicker will be the fall in the illiteracy rate, the more likely it is that child labour will be reduced, and the greater are the prospects for a reduction in fertility rates as children are no longer seen as financial assets to the family. But Indian policy makers continue to be mired in a set of views that preclude their taking the necessary steps to get children into school and out of the labour force and a set of industrial policies that promote the employment of children in the small scale sector. Moreover, these views are so widely shared in India that no political parties of the left or right, none of the trade unions, no religious organizations, and not even the educational establishment is pressing for policy changes. There is little indication of fundamental rethinking within the state or central governments. Even officials who recognize that regular school attendance is a solution to the problem of child labour continue to believe that the responsibility of sending children to school should be with parents, not with the state. Policy makers continue to believe that parents should be permitted to send their children into the labour force, and that child labour cannot be eliminated while there is poverty. Government policy is to work around the fringes of the problem: promote adult literacy campaigns, provide non-formal education to working children, and provide free school lunches to encourage children to remain in school. But neither the central nor the state governments have been willing to do what has been done historically by every developed and now by many developing countries: declare that all children ages six to twelve or fourteen *must* attend school, that parents, no matter how needy, will *not be* permitted to remove their children from school, that school attendance *will* be enforced by local authorities, and that the government *will* be obligated to locate a primary school within reasonable distance of all school age children. Only through such a policy will it be possible to end child labour in India, and within a generation raise India's literacy rate to that of other large developing countries.

NOTE

Research by Andy Sumner showed that in 1990, 93 per cent of the world's poor people lived in what the World Bank defines as low income countries (LICs — those with gross national income per capita less than $995). By 2007, three-quarters of the world's approximately 1.3 billion poor people lived in middle-income countries (MICs). The remaining quarter of the world's poor, estimated at around 370 million people, were in 39 LICs, most of which were in sub-Saharan Africa.[34]

The MICs include countries like Brazil, China and India, all of which manifest dramatic contrasts in terms of economic well-being. In India, for example, a 2009 report estimated that 37 per cent of Indians nationwide, or more than 400 million people, lived below the poverty line.[35] And in 2012 the Prime Minister released a detailed survey that concluded:

> Despite India's remarkable economic growth over the last decade, many children still struggle to meet their most basic needs, including access to sufficient food and health care. [Based on a 2005–2006 survey], 20 per cent of Indian children under five years old were wasted (acutely malnourished) and 48 per cent were stunted (chronically malnourished). Importantly, with 43 per cent of children underweight

[34] Andy Sumner, 'Global Poverty and the New Bottom Billion: What if Three-Quarters of the World's Poor Live in Middle-Income Countries?', Sept. 2010, at www.ids.ac.uk/files/dmfile/GlobalPovertyDataPaper1.pdf.

[35] Report of the Expert Group to Review the Methodology for Estimation of Poverty, at http://planningcommission.nic.in/reports/genrep/rep_pov.pdf.

(with a weight deficit for their age) rates of child underweight in India are twice higher than the average figure in sub-Saharan Africa (22 per cent).[36]

According to the report, hunger accounted for one-third to one-half of child deaths, caused widespread stunted physical growth and cognitive development that last a lifetime, and generated economic losses equivalent to 3 per cent of India's GDP.

Yet India's GDP grew at an average of 7.45 per cent between 2000 and 2011 and India now provides foreign aid to countries such as Afghanistan, Bangladesh and Sri Lanka. For its part, China has a much larger foreign aid budget. A 2011 White Paper on China's Foreign Aid indicates that it has assisted 123 developing countries. Thirty Asian and 51 African countries have received aid, accounting for 80 per cent of total Chinese aid.

In drawing conclusions from his study of the changing geography of poverty, Sumner observed that 'poverty is increasingly turning from an international to a national distribution problem, and that governance and domestic taxation and redistribution policies become of more importance than overseas development assistance.' Questions that arise include: 'If the poor live in stable MICs, do those countries need aid flows or are domestic resources available? Whose 'responsibility' are the poor in MICs — donors or governments or both? If most stable MICs don't need aid... should aid flows be redirected to LICs... and/or to global public goods?'

UN DEVELOPMENT PROGRAMME, HUMAN DEVELOPMENT REPORT

(1990), at 4

...

7. Developing countries are not too poor to pay for human development and take care of economic growth.

The view that human development can be promoted only at the expense of economic growth poses a false tradeoff. It misstates the purpose of development and underestimates the returns on investment in health and education. These returns can be high, indeed. Private returns to primary education are as high as 43% in Africa, 31% in Asia and 32% in Latin America. Social returns from female literacy are even higher — in terms of reduced fertility, reduced infant mortality, lower school dropout rates, improved family nutrition and lower population growth.

Most budgets can, moreover, accommodate additional spending on human development by reorienting national priorities. In many instances, more than half

[36] The HUNGaMA Survey Report — 2011, at www.naandi.org/CP/HungamaBKDec11LR.pdf ('Hungama' is a Hindi word meaning 'stir' or 'ruckus', and the report adapts it to reflect the initial letters of the words hunger and malnutrition).

the spending is swallowed by the military, debt repayments, inefficient parastatals, unnecessary government controls and mistargetted social subsidies. Since other resource possibilities remain limited, restructuring budget priorities to balance economic and social spending should move to the top of the policy agenda for development in the 1990s.

Special attention should go to reducing military spending in the Third World — it has risen three times as fast as that in the industrial nations in the last 30 years.... Developing countries as a group spend more on the military (5.5% of their combined GNP) than on education and health (5.3%).... There are eight times more soldiers than physicians in the Third World.

Governments can also do much to improve the efficiency of social spending by creating a policy and budgetary framework that would achieve a more desirable mix between various social expenditures, particularly by reallocating resources:

- from curative medical facilities to primary health care programmes,
- from highly trained doctors to paramedical personnel,
- from urban to rural services,
- from general to vocational education,
- from subsidising tertiary education to subsidising primary and secondary education,
- from expensive housing for the privileged groups to sites and services projects for the poor,
- from subsidies for vocal and powerful groups to subsidies for inarticulate and weaker groups and
- from the formal sector to the informal sector and the programmes for the unemployed and the underemployed.

Such a restructuring of budget priorities will require tremendous political courage. But the alternatives are limited, and the payoffs can be enormous.

...

NOTE

The debates over available resources and progressive realization have been central to much of the work of the Committee on ESCR. In 1990 it adopted a broad-ranging General Comment that laid the groundwork for its overall approach. This Comment has informed a significant number of subsequent judicial decisions in diverse jurisdictions (see, e.g., South Africa, p. 353, *infra*). In 1999, the Committee elaborated upon the steps that should be taken by a state in a situation in which available resources are clearly inadequate to enable implementation of the right to primary education. And in 2007 the Committee, called upon to reassure governments and others that it would adopt a measured approach to the question of available resources if a complaints procedure were to be adopted in the form of an Optional Protocol, laid out the factors that it would take into account.

COMMITTEE ON ECONOMIC, SOCIAL AND CULTURAL RIGHTS, GENERAL COMMENT NO. 3 (1990)

UN Doc. E/1991/23, Annex III

The nature of States parties obligations (article 2, paragraph 1)

1. Article 2 ... describes the nature of the general legal obligations undertaken by States parties to the Covenant. Those obligations include both what may be termed (following the work of the International Law Commission) obligations of conduct and obligations of result.... [W]hile the Covenant provides for progressive realization and acknowledges the constraints due to the limits of available resources, it also imposes various obligations which are of immediate effect. Of these, two are of particular importance in understanding the precise nature of States parties obligations. One of these,... is the 'undertaking to guarantee' that relevant rights 'will be exercised without discrimination ....'.

2. The other is the undertaking in article 2(1) 'to take steps', which in itself, is not qualified or limited by other considerations.... [W]hile the full realization of the relevant rights may be achieved progressively, steps towards that goal must be taken within a reasonably short time after the Covenant's entry into force for the States concerned. Such steps should be deliberate, concrete and targeted as clearly as possible towards meeting the obligations recognized in the Covenant.

3. The means which should be used in order to satisfy the obligation to take steps are stated in article 2(1) to be 'all appropriate means, including particularly the adoption of legislative measures'. The Committee recognizes that in many instances legislation is highly desirable and in some cases may even be indispensable. For example, it may be difficult to combat discrimination effectively in the absence of a sound legislative foundation for the necessary measures. In fields such as health, the protection of children and mothers, and education, as well as in respect of the matters dealt with in articles 6 to 9, legislation may also be an indispensable element for many purposes.

4. ... [H]owever, the adoption of legislative measures, as specifically foreseen by the Covenant, is by no means exhaustive of the obligations of States parties. Rather, the phrase 'by all appropriate means' must be given its full and natural meaning .... [T]he ultimate determination as to whether all appropriate measures have been taken remains for the Committee to make.

...

7. Other measures which may also be considered 'appropriate' for the purposes of article 2(1) include, but are not limited to, administrative, financial, educational and social measures.

...

9. ... The concept of progressive realization constitutes a recognition of the fact that full realization of all economic, social and cultural rights will generally not be able to be achieved in a short period of time. In this sense the obligation differs significantly from that contained in article 2 of the Covenant on Civil and Political Rights which embodies an immediate obligation to respect and ensure all of the relevant rights. Nevertheless, the fact that realization over time, or in other words progressively,

is foreseen under the Covenant should not be misinterpreted as depriving the obligation of all meaningful content. It is on the one hand a necessary flexibility device, reflecting the realities of the real world and the difficulties involved for any country in ensuring full realization of economic, social and cultural rights. On the other hand, the phrase must be read in the light of the overall objective, indeed the *raison d'être* of the Covenant which is to establish clear obligations for States parties in respect of the full realization of the rights in question. It thus imposes an obligation to move as expeditiously and effectively as possible towards that goal. Moreover, any deliberately retrogressive measures in that regard would require the most careful consideration and would need to be fully justified....

10. ... [T]he Committee is of the view that a minimum core obligation to ensure the satisfaction of, at the very least, minimum essential levels of each of the rights is incumbent upon every State party. Thus, for example, a State party in which any significant number of individuals is deprived of essential foodstuffs, of essential primary health care, of basic shelter and housing, or of the most basic forms of education is, prima facie, failing to discharge its obligations under the Covenant. If the Covenant were to be read in such a way as not to establish such a minimum core obligation, it would be largely deprived of its *raison d'être*. By the same token, it must be noted that any assessment as to whether a State has discharged its minimum core obligation must also take account of resource constraints applying within the country concerned. Article 2(1) obligates each State party to take the necessary steps 'to the maximum of its available resources'. In order for a State party to be able to attribute its failure to meet at least its minimum core obligations to a lack of available resources it must demonstrate that every effort has been made to use all resources that are at its disposition in an effort to satisfy, as a matter of priority, those minimum obligations.

11. ... [T]he obligations to monitor the extent of the realization, or more especially of the non-realization, of economic, social and cultural rights, and to devise strategies and programmes for their promotion, are not in any way eliminated as a result of resource constraints....

12. Similarly, the Committee underlines the fact that even in times of severe resource constraints whether caused by a process of adjustment, of economic recession, or by other factors, the vulnerable members of society can and indeed must be protected by the adoption of relatively low-cost targeted programmes.

...

COMMITTEE ON ECONOMIC, SOCIAL AND CULTURAL RIGHTS, GENERAL COMMENT NO. 11 (1999)

UN Doc. E/C.12/1999/4

Plans of action for primary education

1. Article 14 of the [ICESCR] requires each State party which has not been able to secure compulsory primary education, free of charge, to undertake within two years, to work out and adopt a detailed plan of action for the progressive

implementation, within a reasonable number of years, to be fixed in the plan, of the principle of compulsory primary education free of charge for all....

...

6. *Compulsory*. The element of compulsion serves to highlight the fact that neither parents, nor guardians, nor the State is entitled to treat as optional the decision as to whether the child should have access to primary education....

7. *Free of charge*. The nature of this requirement is unequivocal. The right is expressly formulated so as to ensure the availability of primary education without charge to the child, parents or guardians. Fees imposed by the Government, local authorities or the school, and other direct costs, constitute disincentives to the enjoyment of the right and may jeopardize its realization. They are also often highly regressive in effect. Their elimination is a matter which must be addressed by the required plan of action. Indirect costs, such as compulsory levies on parents (sometimes portrayed as being voluntary, when in fact they are not), or the obligation to wear a relatively expensive school uniform, can also fall into the same category. Other indirect costs may be permissible, subject to the Committee's examination on a case-by-base basis....

8. *Adoption of a detailed plan*. The State party is required to adopt a plan of action within two years....

9. *Obligations*. A State party cannot escape the unequivocal obligation to adopt a plan of action on the grounds that the necessary resources are not available. If the obligation could be avoided in this way, there would be no justification for the unique requirement contained in article 14 which applies, almost by definition, to situations characterized by inadequate financial resources. By the same token, and for the same reason, the references to 'international assistance and cooperation' in articles 2.1 and 23 of the Covenant are of particular relevance in this situation. Where a State party is clearly lacking in the financial resources and/or expertise required to 'work out and adopt' a detailed plan, the international community has a clear obligation to assist.

10. *Progressive implementation*.... Unlike the provision in article 2.1, however, article 14 specifies that the target date must be 'within a reasonable number of years' and moreover, that the time-frame must 'be fixed in the plan'. In other words, the plan must specifically set out a series of targeted implementation dates for each stage of the progressive implementation of the plan....

COMMITTEE ON ECONOMIC, SOCIAL AND CULTURAL RIGHTS, AN EVALUATION OF THE OBLIGATION TO TAKE STEPS TO THE 'MAXIMUM OF AVAILABLE RESOURCES' UNDER AN OPTIONAL PROTOCOL TO THE COVENANT: STATEMENT

UN Doc. E/C.12/2007/1 (21 Sept. 2007)

...

8. In considering a communication concerning an alleged failure of a State party to take steps to the maximum of available resources, the Committee will examine the measures that the State party has effectively taken, legislative or otherwise. In

assessing whether they are "adequate" or "reasonable", the Committee may take into account, inter alia, the following considerations:

(a) The extent to which the measures taken were deliberate, concrete and targeted towards the fulfilment of economic, social and cultural rights;
(b) Whether the State party exercised its discretion in a non-discriminatory and nonarbitrary manner;
(c) Whether the State party's decision (not) to allocate available resources was in accordance with international human rights standards;
(d) Where several policy options are available, whether the State party adopted the option that least restricts Covenant rights;
(e) The time frame in which the steps were taken;
(f) Whether the steps had taken into account the precarious situation of disadvantaged and marginalized individuals or groups and, whether they were nondiscriminatory, and whether they prioritized grave situations or situations of risk.

9. The Committee notes that in case of failure to take any steps or of the adoption of retrogressive steps, the burden of proof rests with the State party to show that such a course of action was based on the most careful consideration and can be justified by reference to the totality of the rights provided for in the Covenant and by the fact that full use was made of available resources.

10. Should a State party use "resource constraints" as an explanation for any retrogressive steps taken, the Committee would consider such information on a country-by-country basis in the light of objective criteria such as:

(a) The country's level of development;
(b) The severity of the alleged breach, in particular whether the situation concerned the enjoyment of the minimum core content of the Covenant;
(c) The country's current economic situation, in particular whether the country was undergoing a period of economic recession;
(d) The existence of other serious claims on the State party's limited resources; for example, resulting from a recent natural disaster or from recent internal or international armed conflict.
(e) Whether the State party had sought to identify low-cost options; and
(f) Whether the State party had sought cooperation and assistance or rejected offers of resources from the international community for the purposes of implementing the provisions of the Covenant without sufficient reason.

QUESTIONS

1. Could it reasonably be argued that virtually every country could afford to provide universal primary education and access to primary health care if it wished to do so?

2. Do the ESCR Committee's General Comments reflect a workable balance that resolves the objections of ESR critics to the effect that such rights are unaffordable if taken seriously and almost meaningless if the emphasis is placed on resources which will never be sufficiently 'available'? How workable are the criteria that the Committee proposes to apply in examining a complaint alleging that available resources have not been used to achieve respect for a given right?

3. Kenya's 2010 Constitution recognizes a wide range of ESR. What problems would you foresee with Article 20(5), excerpted at p. 339, *infra*.

2. THE FISCAL DIMENSION OF DETERMINING 'AVAILABLE RESOURCES'

Until very recently, human rights advocates paid only scant attention to fiscal policy, even though it is arguably the single most important element in determining 'available resources'. Consider the number of issues which fall under the rubric of fiscal policy in the following list of factors determining the resources available to a government:

- size and structure of the economy and its rate of growth
- structure of tax rates
- effectiveness of tax administration
- structure of user fees
- effectiveness of administration of user fees
- availability of other sources of revenue
- inflow of foreign aid
- government borrowing
- interest payments for domestic and foreign creditors
- underlying distribution of resources in the society.[37]

Schumpeter observed that 'nothing shows so clearly the character of a society and of a civilization as does the fiscal policy that its political sector adopts'.[38] And Murphy and Nagel have noted that while '[n]othing could be more mundane than taxes,...they provide a perfect setting for constant moral argument and possible moral progress.'[39] For them, taxation has two primary functions:

> (1) It determines how much of a society's resources will come under the control of government, for expenditure in accordance with some collective decision procedure, and how much will be left to the discretionary control of private individuals,

[37] D. Elson, *Budgeting for Women's Rights* (2006), at 15.
[38] J. Schumpeter, *History of Economic Analysis* (1954), at 769.
[39] Liam Murphy & Thomas Nagel, *The Myth of Ownership: Taxes and Justice* (2002), at 188.

> as their personal property.... (2) It plays a central role in determining how the social product is shared out among different individuals, both in the form of private property and in the form of publicly provided benefits.[40]

When we talk about fiscal policy we are talking about far more than transfers to the poor. Tax policy can reward the rich (for certain types of investments such as housing or capital stock), can exempt certain groups, and determines the overall pool of available resources.

> Budgets...entail moral claims and obligations, resting on social and political norms about willingness to pay taxes, and expectations of what kinds of social protection governments should provide (for instance, universal schemes which involve everyone or targeted schemes that reach only particular social groups). Thus Government budgets rest upon what has been described as a 'fiscal covenant': 'the basic socio-political agreement that legitimizes the role of the State and establishes the areas and scope of government responsibility in the economic and social spheres'....

Government budgets affect people in multiple ways: their primary impact is through distributing resources to people via expenditure and claiming resources from them via tax and other measures. They also have secondary impacts via their impacts on job creation, economic growth and inflation. Drawing up a budget entails consideration of how to balance the different claims and obligations; how to balance total expenditure, total revenue and government borrowing, so as to avoid high rates of inflation on the one hand and economic stagnation or recession on the other. This means setting priorities and considering costs; and trying to make the most effective use of resources. It is not possible to meet all the demands that citizens make about revenue and expenditures. Choices have to be made about which ones will be met in any given year. Budgets are always constrained by legal claims and obligations and by the moral claims and obligations inherent in the fiscal covenant.[41]

These issues are illustrated below in relation to both Guatemala and Brazil. In relation to the latter a UN Special Rapporteur criticized the 'highly regressive' tax structure: 'Tax rates are high for goods and services and low for income and property, bringing about very inequitable outcomes. According to one estimate, families with an income amounting to less than two minimum wages pay an average of 46 per cent of their income in indirect taxes, while families earning over 30 times the minimum wage pay around 16 per cent in indirect taxes.' Property taxes are also problematic. The 'rural territorial tax' collected in 2008 amounted to only 0.1 per cent of GDP. 'Given the very high level of land concentration and the large incomes generated by the agricultural sector, this is highly regressive. In contrast, taxes on goods and services, as well as social contributions to pensions and social security accounted for the lion's share of Government income: over 70 per cent in 2008.' He concluded that while Brazil's social programmes 'are impressive in scope, they are

[40] Ibid., at 76.

[41] D. Elson, *Budgeting for Women's Rights: Monitoring Government Budgets for Compliance with CEDAW* (UNIFEM, 2006), at 10.

essentially funded by the very persons whom they seek to benefit, as the regressive system of taxation seriously limits the redistributive impact of the programmes. Only by introducing a tax reform that would reverse the current situation could Brazil claim to be seeking to realize the right to adequate food by taking steps to the maximum of its available resources.'[42]

RIGHTS OR PRIVILEGES? FISCAL COMMITMENT TO THE RIGHTS TO HEALTH, EDUCATION AND FOOD IN GUATEMALA

Center for Economic and Social Rights and the Central American Institute for Fiscal Studies (2009)

Introduction

...

Almost 50 percent of boys and girls under five [in Guatemala] are severely stunted ...

... The country has the highest estimated maternal mortality rate in Latin America along with Bolivia; a Guatemalan woman is 20 times more likely to die from complications in childbirth or pregnancy than a woman in Costa Rica, for example. One in 20 Guatemalan children does not reach age five due to infectious and diarrheal diseases that are easily prevented and treatable. Two in three children do not complete primary school at the appropriate age and illiteracy levels are closer to the average in sub-Saharan Africa than that of Latin America.

The fact that Guatemala's development indicators lag so far behind those of other countries in the region is all the more surprising considering the country's income. Guatemala is a middle-income country with a gross domestic product (GDP) per capita comparable to that of Ecuador. However, more than half the population lives below the national poverty line and one in seven Guatemalans lives in conditions of extreme poverty. Despite being the largest economy in Central America, the country's social indicators are generally much lower than those of the poorest countries in the sub-region, such as Honduras and Nicaragua.

...

Guatemala stands out as much for its indicators of wealth as for the indicators of poverty... The country with the highest number of private airplanes and helicopters per head in Central America is also the country with the highest rate of women dying from unresolved complications in pregnancy due to lack of affordable transportation to a health center. While more than half the population (approximately 6.5 million people) earns less than US$2 per day, 0.003% of Guatemalans own 50 percent of the country's total bank deposits.

[42] Report of the Special Rapporteur on the right to food, Olivier De Schutter, Mission to Brazil, UN Doc. A/HRC/13/33/Add.6 (19 Feb. 2009), para. 36.

These stark contrasts suggest that the dismal state of economic and social rights in Guatemala cannot be attributed to a lack of state resources, but to the way in which they are distributed....

...

... Guatemala's poor performance in guaranteeing basic levels of economic and social rights for the entire population is due, in large part, to the lack of political will of successive governments to invest in these rights, using the maximum resources available in the most equitable way possible. For decades, Guatemala has been one of the countries in the region that invests the least amount of resources in social policies; the proportion of GDP devoted to social spending is among the lowest in Latin America. In turn, it is a country with one of the lowest levels of tax collection, curtailing the ability of the government to respond adequately to the needs of the population through the public budget process. Guatemala has one of the lowest tax burdens in Latin America, as well as one of the most generous regimes of exemptions and tax breaks.

Since the signing of the Peace Accords, tax reforms agreed with civil society participation have been repeatedly blocked by the sectors of the country's economy that most benefit from these tax privileges. Thus, a small but powerful economic elite has prevented the generation of the necessary resources to maintain a level of social spending consistent with the country's needs. It is not a question of the state's incapacity or inefficiency in gathering and reassigning public resources; it is, rather, the historical co-option of the state by socioeconomic elites which has ensured that public policymaking protects their privileges at the expense of the rights of the whole population.

...

Fiscal commitment to economic and social rights

The low level of social spending is... a result of the reduced size of the public budget, which is one of lowest in the region (15 percent of GDP, while the regional average is almost 27 percent)....

One the main reasons for Guatemala's limited social spending lies in a tax base that deprives the state of its capacity to generate the necessary revenue....

... Direct taxation (on income and assets) is very low. The tax structure consists primarily of indirect taxes on consumption, which affect the poorest sectors of the population disproportionately....

Moreover, the system is riddled with tax exemptions and privileges that undermine its effectiveness and equity. The country's most profitable business sectors enjoy significant tax incentives.... In 2008, the total amount of these tax breaks, deductions and exemptions was twice the amount the state expected to collect in income tax....

The tax system also lacks effective control mechanisms to prevent tax evasion, which benefits the rich disproportionately.... It has been estimated that in 2006, tax evasion and exemptions... cost the state approximately... 4.3% of GDP. This was more than the total amount invested by the State in the health and education of its citizens that year....

QUESTIONS

1. If a government decides to reduce tax rates dramatically, with the result that funding is no longer available for basic ESR programmes, how could it be argued that this is a violation of ESR obligations? What if the government responds that lower tax rates will mean higher growth which will greatly benefit all members of society, including the poorest?

2. To what extent should, or can, the ESCR Committee scrutinize a government's fiscal policies? What should it do in a situation such as that in Guatemala?

ADDITIONAL READING

K. G. Young, 'The Minimum Core of Economic and Social Rights: A Concept in Search of Content', 33 Yale J. Int'l. L. 113 (2008); A. Chapman & S. Russell (eds.), *Core Obligations: Building a Framework for Economic, Social and Cultural Rights* (2002); M. Dowell-Jones, *Contextualising the International Covenant on Economic, Social and Cultural Rights: Assessing the Economic Deficit* (2004); J. Tobin, *The Right to Health in International Law* (2012); S. Narula, 'The Right to Food: Holding Global Actors Accountable under International Law', 44 Colombia J. Transnat'l. L. 691 (2006); P. Alston & K. Tomaševski (eds.), *The Right To Food* (1984); A. Blyberg, 'The Case of the Mislaid Allocation: Economic and Social Rights and Budget Work', 6/11 Sur 123 (Dec. 2009); S. Hertel & L. Minkler (eds.), *Economic Rights: Conceptual, Measurement, and Policy Issues* (2007).

E. CONSTITUTIONS, COURTS AND ADMINISTRATIVE REMEDIES

In recent years ESR have assumed major constitutional significance in many countries through: (1) explicit constitutional recognition; (2) judicial interpretation of CPR to encompass at least some ESR; and (3) judicial willingness to treat previously non-justiciable ESR provisions as being justiciable. An increasingly rich case law has resulted. While this chapter looks at some of the key judicial decisions on ESR adopted in India, South Africa and the United States, a range of other jurisdictions could also have provided important examples.

The accountability of governments and other entities, as well as the availability of a remedy in cases of a violation, are indispensable elements of international human rights law. Under Article 8 of the UDHR '[e]veryone has the right to an effective remedy by the competent national tribunals for acts violating the fundamental rights granted him by the constitution or by law.' The Declaration recognizes ESR and there is nothing to indicate that this provision was intended to apply only to

CPR. There is, however, nothing in the ICESCR that is equivalent to the requirement in the ICCPR that states parties 'develop the possibilities of judicial remedy' (Art. 2(3)(b)). This lacuna seems to have encouraged many governments and commentators to assume that traditional legal remedies such as court actions are either inappropriate or at best impracticable for the vindication of ESR.

This section looks first at ESR in constitutions and then examines relevant administrative schemes and complaints mechanisms. It then turns to justiciability (i.e., the ability of courts to provide a remedy for aggrieved individuals claiming a violation of those rights) which many observers continue to see as the essential hallmark of a 'real' human right. In that context, we focus particularly on the case law emerging from the leading courts in South Africa and India. Before moving to those issues we consider the extent to which states are required by international law to provide constitutional recognition of ESR or specific types of remedies in relation to them.

COMMITTEE ON ECONOMIC, SOCIAL AND CULTURAL RIGHTS, GENERAL COMMENT NO. 9 (1998)

UN Doc. E/1999/22, Annex IV

Domestic Application of the Covenant

A. The duty to give effect to the Covenant in the domestic legal order

1. ... The central obligation in relation to the Covenant is for States parties to give effect to the rights recognized therein. By requiring governments to do so 'by all appropriate means', the Covenant adopts a broad and flexible approach which enables the particularities of the legal and administrative systems of each State, as well as other relevant considerations, to be taken into account.

2. But this flexibility co-exists with the obligation upon each State Party to use *all* the means at its disposal to give effect to the rights recognised in the Covenant. In this respect, the fundamental requirements of international human rights law must be borne in mind. Thus the norms themselves must be recognised in appropriate ways within the domestic legal order, appropriate means of redress, or remedies, must be available to any aggrieved individual or group, and appropriate means of ensuring governmental accountability must be put in place.

...

C. The role of legal remedies

Legal or judicial remedies?

9. The right to an effective remedy need not be interpreted as always requiring a judicial remedy. Administrative remedies will, in many cases, be adequate.... Any such administrative remedies should be accessible, affordable, timely, and effective.... [But] whenever a Covenant right cannot be made fully effective without some role for the judiciary, judicial remedies are necessary.

Justiciability

10. In relation to civil and political rights, it is generally taken for granted that judicial remedies for violations are essential. Regrettably, the contrary presumption is too often made in relation to economic, social and cultural rights. This discrepancy is not warranted either by the nature of the rights or by the relevant Covenant provisions. The Committee has already made clear that it considers many of the provisions in the Covenant to be capable of immediate implementation. Thus in General Comment No. 3 it cited, by way of example: articles 3, 7(a)(i), 8, 10(3), 13(2)(a), 13(3), 13(4) and 15(3).[43] It is important in this regard to distinguish between justiciability (which refers to those matters which are appropriately resolved by the courts) and norms which are self-executing (capable of being applied by courts without further elaboration). While the general approach of each legal system needs to be taken into account, there is no Covenant right which could not, in the great majority of systems, be considered to possess at least some significant justiciable dimensions. It is sometimes suggested that matters involving the allocation of resources should be left to the political authorities rather than the courts. While the respective competences of the different branches of government must be respected, it is appropriate to acknowledge that courts are generally already involved in a considerable range of matters which have important resource implications. The adoption of a rigid classification of economic, social and cultural rights which puts them, by definition, beyond the reach of the courts would thus be arbitrary and incompatible with the principle that the two sets of human rights are indivisible and interdependent. It would also drastically curtail the capacity of the courts to protect the rights of the most vulnerable and disadvantaged groups in society.

1. ESR IN CONSTITUTIONS

Before the end of the Cold War it was widely assumed that the only constitutions that gave prominent recognition to ESR were the façade constitutions of the Soviet Union and other Communist states. While this perception was incorrect, the past two decades have seen a much heightened awareness of these rights in the context of constitutional arrangements. A recent analysis suggested that there might even be an international legal obligation to give constitutional recognition to ESR, based on several principles:

- *Principle of good faith*: [This] supports the proposition that failure to incorporate the right to food...into domestic law, including constitutional law, could be viewed in theory as a violation of international law.
- *Effet utile*: [This principle] supports reading international treaties in a manner designed to give effect to their provisions.... Domestic procedures

[43] These refer respectively to: equal rights of men and women (Art. 3), equal pay for equal work (Art. 7(a)(i)), the right to form and join trade unions and the right to strike (Art. 8), the right of children to special protection (Art. 10(3)), the right to free, compulsory, primary education (Art. 13(2)(a)), the liberty to choose a non-public school (Art. 13(3)), the liberty to establish schools (Art. 13(4)), and the freedom for scientific research and creative activity (Art. 15(3)).

concerning the right to food could be deemed effective from an international human rights law perspective only if individuals are able to invoke the right as recognized internationally before domestic courts. ...

- *Effective right to remedy*: It is difficult to envisage how provisions on an effective right to remedy ('second order' right) can be met without first of all incorporating substantive primary rights ('first order' rights) into domestic law. ...[44]

The authors conclude by questioning 'whether constitutional law that fails to incorporate the right to food in a meaningful way can "ensure" future implementation, i.e., provide the human right to food with the necessary degree of security and protection from future legislative encroachment.'

In this section we first examine the arguments for and against constitutional recognition that have emerged in different contexts in recent years. In Australia, a National Human Rights Consultation was unsympathetic to the inclusion of ESR in any new legislative initiative. Ghai and Cottrell respond to some of the arguments often made in this regard. We then turn to examine the more specific question of how ESR might be protected if they are included in a bill of rights or equivalent instruments and conclude by examining the approach reflected in the Kenyan Constitution of 2010.

AUSTRALIA: NATIONAL HUMAN RIGHTS CONSULTATION, REPORT

September 2009, Ch. 15, at www.humanrightsconsultation.gov.au/

[Eds.: Australia's Constitution dates from 1900. It includes very few rights-related provisions and has rarely been amended. In 2008 the Federal Government appointed an expert group to undertake a community consultation on: (1) which human rights should be protected and promoted; (2) are these human rights currently sufficiently protected and promoted; and (3) how could Australia better protect and promote human rights? In its findings, the Committee addressed the first question in relation to ESR.]

For most Australians the main concern is the realisation of primary economic and social rights such as the rights to education, housing and the highest attainable standard of health. The Committee acknowledges that it would be very difficult, if not impossible, to make such rights matters for determination in the courts.

In our robust democracy these are the very rights that feature most often in political debate, especially at election time. They are the rights that are scrutinised by specialist parliamentary committees on health and ageing, education and training, family, community, housing and youth. They are the rights that demand large resource allocations by government. No matter what the level of public deliberation

[44] Lidija Knuth & Margret Vidar, 'Constitutional and Legal Protection of the Right to Food Around the World' (UN Food and Agriculture Organization, 2011).

in allocating scarce resources for securing these rights, there will always be some people who miss out....

...

[At a roundtable held in Mintabie, a remote town with a population of 250] the Committee was struck by the dilemma confronting any government trying to deliver services to small, remote communities. There, the decision had been made to close the health clinic, whereas the primary school was to be maintained. If it came to a choice between the maintenance of the clinic or the primary school, there would be no suitable criteria a judge could apply to make such a determination. If the residents had petitioned the court to maintain the clinic, the judge might not even be apprised of the fact that the school was being maintained.

The Committee endorses the observations of Professor Tom Campbell and Dr Nicholas Barry:

> Courts have a bias towards negative rights, which protect the individual from interference by the state. Because ensuring the protection of socioeconomic rights requires positive action by the state, it involves decisions about the allocation of state resources which courts do not have the expertise or information to make.

The Committee recommends that, if economic and social rights are listed in a federal Human Rights Act, those rights not be justiciable and that complaints be heard by the Australian Human Rights Commission....

YASH GHAI & JILL COTTRELL, THE MILLENNIUM DECLARATION, RIGHTS AND CONSTITUTIONS

(2011), at 71

...

Constitutions should not be changed at whim, but the supposed perpetuity of the constitution should not be made an article of faith.... [A] constitution should respond to the needs of the particular country and reflect what the citizens believe is important.

...

... The importance of the constitutionalization of [ESR] arises from the fact that the... future of human rights... depends substantially, even fundamentally, on protection and promotion at the national level.

... A principal argument against constitutionalization... is that the constitution should be value neutral.... The fact is that no constitution is neutral, even if it does not explicitly contain any values. A constitution which is restricted to rules on formation of, and decision-making within, the government is not neutral, but is directed towards the maintenance of the economic and social status quo.

It is also often argued that the sole purpose of the constitution is to limit and restrain the exercise of political power. This is also often an ideological position...so that those who are already dominant in society enjoy maximum freedom, with the state responsible only for maintaining law and order.

Some say that only provisions which are both clear and legally binding should be included in the constitution.... [B]ut...a constitution is also a political and social document. In truth, most constitutional provisions have a degree of ambiguity and the courts are asked all the time to interpret values or abstract terms, even if they are not labelled "principles" or "values".

A further objection would be that constitutions with values and aspirations are hard, if not impossible, to implement. This failure diminishes the legitimacy of the constitution and can give rise to the dangerous idea that the constitution need not be taken seriously or that some of its provisions can be ignored.... The first assumption of this position is that achievement of social goals is impossible. [That is often so] for the simple reason that little attempt is made to implement them. The criticism should be levelled at the government for want of effort, not at the constitution. The second assumption is that constitutions without values are, or can be fully implemented, but, as we have suggested, no constitution is really without values and in truth no constitution is fully implemented.

These criticisms are based on the preference for a particular kind of constitution, with minimalist scope.... [I]n many developing, formerly colonial, states[,] there are major problems of nation-building. Primary identities are attached to religious or ethnic communities, or certain pre-colonial historical traditions. Many find it hard to envisage citizenship as the basic unit of society and, so, there is little solidarity as a nation. Consequently, there is little sympathy for the poor and oppressed of other communities. Nation-building based on common citizenship is essential for many purposes, particularly a commitment to a wider sense of social justice.

The modern state itself is a relatively new concept in many of these societies, where there is little familiarity with the modalities and morals of State power, or the true significance of democracy for the organization of the State and society. Consequently, it is necessary to spell these out in a constitution, to guide the exercise of power and establish new institutions of accountability, since society is unable on its own to do this effectively. The full range of human rights, as a primary component of meaningful democracy, must be fully reflected in the constitution and the design of political organizations....

Furthermore, in most developing countries, there are large pockets of extreme poverty. To say that only a state with limited power is compatible with the constitution is to condemn the poor to perpetual poverty. The notion of the limited state is usually to imply that the state should have a restricted role in relation to the market. It is patent that the market, which is often the cause of poverty, cannot pull the poorest out of their condition. An activist state, with sufficient power to extract and distribute resources, is necessary to assist them to help themselves. Without this role, the very future of the state and society is imperiled... [ESR] are the principal instruments for this purpose.

...

REPORT OF THE CONSULTATION COMMITTEE FOR A PROPOSED WA [WESTERN AUSTRALIA] HUMAN RIGHTS ACT

(Nov. 2007), at www.gtcentre.unsw.edu.au/sites/gtcentre.unsw.edu.au/files/mdocs/WA_Human_Rights_Final_Report.pdf

[The Government of Western Australia proposed the adoption of a state Human Rights Act, containing only CPR. It then organized a community consultation process to consider its proposals. In its report it canvasses six different models that could be considered for protecting ESR.]

...

4.4 How should economic, social and cultural rights be protected by a WA Human Rights Act?

...

4.4.1 Model One: treat economic, social and cultural rights in the same way as civil and political rights

... [S]uch rights would be subject to limitations which are reasonable and demonstrably justifiable in a free and democratic society based on human dignity, equality and freedom....

4.4.2 Model Two: progressive implementation of economic, social and cultural rights

[ESC] rights would be treated in the same way as civil and political rights but a WA Human Rights Act would expressly recognise that such rights should be progressively implemented. [The Committee cited an approach proposed by the Australian Capital Territory Consultative Committee that would include the following provision in relation to the recognition of ESR:]

> Where the sole source of human rights is the ICESCR, it is acknowledged that those human rights are subject to progressive realisation. Accordingly, in any proceeding under this Act that raises the application and operation of those human rights, a court or tribunal must consider all relevant circumstances of the particular case including:
>
> (a) the nature of the benefit or detriment likely to accrue or be suffered by any person concerned; and
> (b) the financial circumstances and the estimated amount of expenditure required to be made by a public authority to act in a manner compatible with human rights
> (c) before determining that the provisions of any Territory law or that the acts or conduct of a public authority are incompatible with the Act.

...

4.4.3 Model Three: modify the operation of certain parts of the Act to economic, social and cultural rights

... [ESC] rights would be included as "human rights"... but some parts of the Act would not apply to those rights, or would have a modified application to those rights. There are a variety of options.... For example:

1. ... The breach of an ESC right would not be able to be the subject of a remedy in the courts, but could still be the subject of complaints and administrative remedies....

2. If informal avenues of complaint were available in relation to ESC rights, this approach would permit the gathering of information about future litigation that might arise if these rights were made enforceable in the courts. Consequently, informed decisions could be made as to how and when to take additional steps for the positive enforcement of ESC rights.

3. ... ESC rights "could be included in the Bill without being enforceable against the Government, but still be used to direct Parliament when enacting written laws."

...

4.4.4 Model Four: economic, social and cultural rights as non-binding principles or objectives

... [T]he Act would contain a statement to the effect that the Parliament and/or the government aspired to observe these rights, but that [the CPR-related implementation provisions] would not apply to such rights.

4.4.5 Model Five: pursue economic, social and cultural rights through different means

... [The] Act could establish a body with the power to conduct human rights audits of those government agencies responsible for services such as health care. That body could also be given the responsibility to monitor the implementation of recommendations made in relation to that government agency, and to report to the relevant Minister and Parliament....

...

4.4.6 Model Six: indirect protection for economic, social and cultural rights through the application of civil and political rights

... [I]n some jurisdictions, ESC rights have been advanced indirectly through the interpretation and application of civil and political rights (in particular, the right to equality and non-discrimination, and the right to due process (fair trial))....

The Committee... consider[s] it undesirable that the protection of ESC rights should depend upon the occurrence of a breach of a civil and political right in a context which also involves the enjoyment of an ESC right.

4.4.7 Conclusion — the preferable model for the implementation of ESC rights

It is the Committee's view that any of the options outlined above may be practically possible. Having said that, we accept that it is a political decision for the Government, and for the Parliament, as to whether to implement ESC rights in the same manner as civil and political rights, to implement such rights in a minimalist way, or to implement ESC rights through a staged approach and therefore to "make haste slowly". Our preference is for ... Model One....

...

NOTE

Despite the extent to which countries such as Australia, the United Kingdom and others continue to debate how best to reflect ESR in their national legal systems, many other states have already accorded constitutional recognition to them. A survey of the right to food outlined the extent to which three separate approaches have been embraced worldwide:

> [1] **Explicit and direct recognition of the right to food**
>
> ... 23 constitutions recognize the right to food explicitly as a human right. Of these, nine countries recognize the right as a separate and stand-alone right....
>
> Ten constitutions recognize the right to food of a specific segment of the population [such as children, indigenous children, and prisoners and detainees].
>
> An additional five countries recognize the right to food explicitly as part of a human right to an adequate standard of living, quality of life, or development....
>
> [2] **The right to food is implicit in a broader human right**
>
> There are 33 countries that recognize broader rights which are generally considered to include the right to food, such as the right to an adequate standard of living or similar rights. [These include the right to a decent standard of living (10 countries), the right to well-being (6), the right to be provided with a standard of living that is not below the subsistence level (4)].
>
> The right to the means necessary to live a dignified life is also recognized in eight countries....
>
> The right to development is recognized in five countries....
>
> [3] **Directive principle of state policy**
>
> ... 13 countries recognize the right to food or provide for state obligations related to food and nutrition security as a directive principle of state policy....[45]
>
> ...

CONSTITUTION OF KENYA

(27 Aug. 2010)

...

Chapter IV The Bill of Rights

Part I General Provisions Relating to the Bill of Rights

...

[45] Ibid.

Article 20 Application of Bill of Rights

(1) The Bill of Rights applies to all law and binds all State organs and all persons.

...

(3) In applying a provision of the Bill of Rights, a court must

(a) develop the law to the extent that it does not give effect to a right or fundamental freedom; and

(b) adopt the interpretation that most favours the enforcement of a right or fundamental freedom.

(4) In interpreting the Bill of Rights, a court, tribunal or other authority must promote

(a) the values that underlie an open and democratic society based on human dignity, equality, equity and freedom; and

(b) the spirit, purport and objects of the Bill of Rights.

(5) In applying any right under Article 43, if the State claims that it does not have the resources to implement the right, a court, tribunal or other authority must be guided by the following principles:

(a) it is the responsibility of the State to show that the resources are not available;

(b) in allocating resources, the State gives priority to ensuring the widest possible enjoyment of the right or fundamental freedom having regard to prevailing circumstances, including the vulnerability of particular groups or individuals; and

(c) the court, tribunal or other authority may not interfere with a decision by a State organ concerning the allocation of available resources, solely on the basis that it would have reached a different conclusion.

...

Article 22 Enforcement of Bill of Rights

(1) Every person has the right to institute court proceedings claiming that a right or fundamental freedom in the Bill of Rights has been denied, violated or infringed, or is threatened.

...

Part II Rights and Fundamental Freedoms

...

Article 43 Economic and social rights

(1) Every person has the right

(a) to the highest attainable standard of health, which includes the right to health care services, including reproductive health care;

(b) to accessible and adequate housing, and to reasonable standards of sanitation;

(c) to be free from hunger, and to have adequate food of acceptable quality;

(d) to clean and safe water in adequate quantities;

(e) to social security; and

(f) to education.

(2) A person may not be denied emergency medical treatment.

(3) The State provides appropriate social security to persons who are unable to support themselves and their dependants.

QUESTIONS

1. How compelling is the suggestion of an existing international legal obligation to accord ESR constitutional recognition?

2. Do you agree with Ghai and Cottrell that the argument for ESR constitutional recognition might be strongest in poorer, more fragile, polities?

3. What strengths and weaknesses do you see in the formula adopted by the Kenyan Constitution?

2. ADMINISTRATIVE APPROACHES TO ESR

Whether or not ESR are given constitutional status, there will be a strong need for appropriate administrative procedures to give them full effect. Gauri explores what these might look like.

VARUN GAURI, REDRESSING GRIEVANCES AND COMPLAINTS REGARDING BASIC SERVICE DELIVERY

World Bank, Policy Research Working Paper 5699 (June 2011)

...

II. What are redress procedures, and why are they important?

This paper defines redress procedures as ex post reviews of service delivery transactions with particular end users. Here, the term — transaction refers to omissions as well as actions, so that a review of the reasons for the non-receipt of a service that should have been provided, according to the end-user or her advocate, is also the potential subject of a redress procedure. This definition allows one to distinguish redress or complaints procedures from neighboring accountability-enhancing interventions. Budget monitoring and corruption reporting — whether based on new information technologies, public expenditure tracking, or another instrument — focus on the processes of service delivery governance rather than transactions with end users. Citizen scorecards…, sometimes ask end users to evaluate service transactions ex post, but their focus is aggregate performance rather than particular transactions; and they frequently focus on service delivery outcomes rather than the transactions themselves. Similarly, although social audits are ex post reviews, they tend to focus on governance processes rather than individual transactions. Information campaigns sometimes identify potential problems in specific transactions but do so ex ante. All of these related accountability-enhancing procedures share certain features and functions; in particular, they all have the potential to improve accountability relationships in the social sectors both by empowering clients and by providing information to policymakers. But redress procedures have a distinctive purpose, and these neighboring accountability-enhancing are not substitutes for them.

[R]edress procedures address basic fairness for particular individuals…in two ways.

First, claims that make use of redress procedures typically seek some form of compensation for a service delivery transaction that has harmed a particular user or group of users.…

Second, redress procedures support the rule of law, even a minimal understanding of which holds that like cases should be treated alike.…

…

… [R]edress procedures might function as — fire alarms for policy makers, allowing them to observe and effectively sanction the behavior of administrators and service providers who deviate from expected performance standards; as well as for politicians, who can use them to observe whether executive agency policy makers and administrators are properly implementing national legislation. For this to work, however, (i) the complaints procedures must be sufficiently utilized; (ii) they must be utilized for the kinds of transactions and kinds of users that the principal aims to monitor; and (iii) standard management processes need to incorporate information from the complaints process.…

…

[L]egal scholars have long recognized that a pre-condition for the institutionalization of legalized venues and judicial review is rights consciousness. In many settings, in developing and developed countries alike, it is not enough that a redress venue exists. Low levels of literacy and political/social marginalization mean that many individuals, including ethnic minorities, will not take advantage of redress procedures even if they are available. It is important, then, to pay attention not only to the supply of redress procedures but to the demand for them, and to support organizations that stimulate and aggregate demand for redress. This paper will consider two such demand-side organizations: the media and NGOs. Measures to stimulate demand can include support (or a supportive legal environment) for NGOs/CSOs, granting access to independent media, and publicizing extant redress procedures.

III. Basic design principles

Redress procedures can take a variety of forms.... How they are designed, and how they should be designed, depend significantly on historical factors, such as the authority of judges and the nature of the legal tradition (e.g. common law or civil law), the statutory authority of bureaucrats, and the extent of specialization in the service delivery agencies. It is important to build on the local legal and political culture, rather than importing an institutional form alien to the local landscape. Still, when designing a system of redress procedures, the following design principles are important to bear in mind.

Demand for redress. Effective redress procedures require i) an adequate venue in which complaints can be received and ii) sufficient demand. Weak or non-credible venues will undermine demand because service users will not bother to lodge complaints. In addition, many service users, particularly the most marginalized, will not believe they are entitled to complain, and as a result the sample of complaints received will bias — fire alarms monitoring. Consequently, active measures to promote demand for redress will be necessary, along with efforts to lower the costs of accessing redress procedures....

Cost and benefit. The more accessible that redress procedures are, the more likely that the benefits associated with them will be realized, including the monitoring of agents and the increase in information to policy makers. On the other hand, excessive time spent on redress procedures... can reduce the efficiency of service delivery....

As a general principle, it will be less costly to resolve complaints at the point of service delivery, where information about service practices is clearest and where transaction costs are lowest. Typically, access to redress procedures tends to become more costly as one moves from government agencies to external non-court entities and then to courts, and as one extends quasi-legal attributes to the resolution processes within frontline ministries....

...

Independent review. The possibility of independent review gives service users greater confidence in the objectivity and neutrality of the dispute resolution process. The institutional attributes of independent agencies typically include funding sources that are somewhat autonomous of political powers and some degree of insulation from politically, economically, and socially powerful individuals and groups....

Absent the expectation of a credible and effective response, service users may avoid grievance procedures altogether....

...

Legality. Redress procedures vary in the extent to which they exhibit legal attributes. These include standards for the kinds of evidence to be presented..., the public availability of both the complaints petitions themselves and the reasoning behind the dispute resolver's response, and the incorporation of other trial-like characteristics... into the procedures to be used.... Of course, as legal safeguards increase, so do the costs of providing the redress procedures.

Political economy concerns. [T]he realities of political and economic power often hinder the implementation and operation of [an ideal] system.... [A] casual review suggests that effective redress procedures seem to have emerged under broadly the same conditions that have facilitated the emergence of autonomous and effective courts: sufficient rights consciousness in the population, and the existence of a functioning democracy with relatively competitive electoral systems.

...

IV. The supply side

Redress procedures within government agencies

It is possible for line agencies to establish a variety of venues for the receipt of complaints and grievances, including dedicated mail boxes, email addresses, text messaging systems, telephone hotlines, interactive websites, office windows, and complaints handling officers....

...

Some of the most well-specified redress procedures within line agencies exist in developed countries, but these are feasible in low-income countries as well....

...

Independent redress institutions

External non-judicial redress procedures include tribunals, ombudsmen, public inquiries, a variety of sector-specific entities, such as labor relations boards, and civil society organizations. It is difficult to generalize about this heterogeneous collection of actors, but a few comments are possible. First, these entities typically exist outside the formal bureaucratic apparatus and sometimes possess little or no public authority to compel parties to accept their findings. Their judgments are often advisory only. Second, their authority typically rests somewhere between the line agency power to examine internal compliance with extant rules and the judicial function of reviewing the adequacy of extant rules, regulations, and even, in the case of constitutional courts, laws. Third, these are most useful when the incoming pathways from line agencies to them, as well as the outgoing pathways from them to courts, are well-publicized and widely known.

...

Courts

The extent to which courts hear and redress the failures of line agencies and providers to comply with their statutory and contractual obligations, versus the extent to which courts review the regulations that govern service delivery in light of the law and the law in light of the constitution, depends on local legal traditions, institutional configurations, and political circumstances....

...

V. The demand side

In general, low levels of literacy and political/social marginalization mean that many individuals, including ethnic minorities, will not take advantage of redress procedures even where they are well designed. It is important to stimulate demand. Measures to stimulate demand can include explicit financial support (or just a supportive legal environment) for NGOs/CSOs, granting access to independent media, and publicizing extant redress procedures.

...

NOTE

In India, the National Food Security Bill, introduced into Parliament in December 2011, and designed to 'to provide for food and nutritional security…, by ensuring access to adequate quantity of quality food at affordable prices to people to live a life with dignity' contains a number of administrative redress mechanisms. The Bill would establish National and State Food Commissions, each of which would be tasked with monitoring and evaluating the implementation of the act and inquiring into violations of entitlements either on its own initiative or on receipt of a complaint. District Grievance Redressal Officers would be appointed, and there would be a right of appeal to the State Commission against her decision.

The National Commission would advise the central government in creating synergies among existing schemes and framing new schemes, recommend steps for effective implementation of food and nutrition related schemes, issue guidelines for training, capacity building and performance management of officials, hear appeals against the orders of the state commission and prepare annual reports to Parliament on the implementation of the act.

The bill would require that all relevant records be open for public inspection, and that periodic social audits be conducted by the relevant authorities.

NOTE

The next three sections examine ESR cases in India, South Africa and the United States. When reading these materials, bear in mind several aspects of the question of justiciability that underlie some of the courts' discussion.

(1) Are ESR formulated in a manner that is sufficiently precise to enable judges to apply them in concrete cases?
(2) To the extent that such cases will involve decisions about public spending priorities, should such decisions remain the exclusive domain of the executive and legislature?
(3) Are judges well suited in terms of their expertise, social and political background and the facilities available to them to make such decisions?
(4) Are there creative approaches to remedies that courts could, and should, develop in relation to ESR?

Bear in mind also the suggestion that quite similar questions might well be posed, in theory at least, in relation to key civil and political rights norms such as the prohibition on cruel, inhuman or degrading treatment or punishment or the right to due process.

3. INDIA: PUBLIC INTEREST LITIGATION

In India the concept of 'directive principles of state policy' was originally developed in contra-distinction to that of 'fundamental rights'. They were considered to be distinct from, and usually inferior in status to, rights that appear in the constitution without the qualification 'directive'. They appear in different forms in diverse constitutions including those of Nigeria and Papua New Guinea. Various European constitutions, including those of Ireland and Spain, also contain long lists of judicially unenforceable social rights. The Indian experience holds the greatest interest for our purposes. The Indian Constitution of 1950 contains one chapter dealing with 'fundamental rights' which consists largely of civil and political rights enforceable in the courts, and another chapter dealing with 'directive principles of state policy'. Some illustrations from the Constitution follow.

Part III. Fundamental Rights

...

Article 21. No person shall be deprived of his life or personal liberty except according to procedure established by law.

...

Part IV. Directive Principles of State Policy

...

Article 37. The provisions contained in this Part shall not be enforced by any court, but the principles therein laid down are nevertheless fundamental in the governance of the country and it shall be the duty of the State to apply these principles in making laws.

Article 39. The State shall, in particular, direct its policy towards securing:

(a) that the citizens, men and women equally, have the right to an adequate means of livelihood;
(b) that the ownership and control of the material resources of the community are so distributed as best to subserve the common good;
(c) that the operation of the economic system does not result in the concentration of wealth and means of production to the common detriment;
(d) that there is equal pay for equal work for both men and women;
(e) that the health and strength of workers, men and women, and the tender age of children are not abused and that citizens are not forced by economic necessity to enter avocations unsuited to their age or strength;
(f) that children are given opportunities and facilities to develop in a healthy manner and in conditions of freedom and dignity and that childhood and youth are protected against exploitation and against moral and material abandonment.

...

Article 41. The State shall, within the limits of its economic capacity and development, make effective provision for securing the right to work, to education and to public assistance in cases of unemployment, old age, sickness and disablement, and in other cases of undeserved want.

...

Article 47. The State shall regard the raising of the level of nutrition and the standard of living of its people and the improvement of public health as among its primary duties....

Over the years the Indian courts have redefined the relationship between fundamental rights and directive principles by integrating the two categories so that the latter become effectively enforceable. The readings below start with a survey by the then Chief Justice of India of the origins of this expansive approach through the means of 'public interest litigation'. We then consider some of the landmark cases in this area.

KONAKUPPAKATIL GOPINATHAN BALAKRISHNAN, GROWTH OF PUBLIC INTEREST LITIGATION IN INDIA

21 Singapore Academy of Law J. 1 (2009)

...

3 Beginning with the first few instances in the late-1970s, the category of PIL has come to be associated with its own "people-friendly" procedure. The foremost change came in the form of the dilution of the requirement of "locus standi" for initiating proceedings. Since the intent was to ensure redressal to those who were otherwise too poor to move the courts or were unaware of their legal entitlements, the court allowed actions to be brought on their behalf by social activists and lawyers. In numerous instances, the court took *suo moto* cognisance of matters involving the abuse of prisoners, bonded labourers and inmates of mental institutions, through letters addressed to sitting judges. This practice of initiating proceedings on the basis of letters has now been streamlined and has come to be described as "epistolary jurisdiction".

4 ... [I]n most public interest related litigation, the judges take on a far more active role in terms of posing questions to the parties as well as exploring solutions.... [T]he orientation of the proceedings is usually more akin to collective problem-solving rather than an acrimonious contest between the counsels. Since these matters are filed straightaway at the level of the Supreme Court or the High Court, the parties do not have a meaningful opportunity to present evidence on record before the start of the court proceeding. To overcome this problem, our courts have developed the practice of appointing "factfinding commissions" on a case-by-case basis, which are deputed to inquire into the subject-matter of the case and report back to the court. These commissions usually consist of experts in the concerned fields or practising lawyers....

5 ... [T]he Indian courts have pushed the boundaries of constitutional remedies by evolving the concept of a "continuing mandamus" which involves the passing of regular directions and the monitoring of their implementation by executive agencies. In addition to designing remedies for ensuring that their orders are complied with, the courts have also resorted to private law remedies such as injunctions and "stay" orders in PIL matters.... [U]nder Art 141 of the Constitution of India, the

Supreme Court's rulings are considered to be the "law of the land" and become binding precedents for all courts and tribunals in the country's legal system....

6 The advent of PIL is one of the key components of the approach of "judicial activism" that is attributed to the higher Judiciary in India. The courts' interventions have played a pivotal role in advancing the protection of civil liberties ... and the guarantee of socio-economic entitlements.... This has not only strengthened the position of the Judiciary vis-à-vis the other wings of Government, but has also raised its prestige among the general populace. However, this activist disposition of the courts also has its critics.

7 [Critics suggest that the separation of powers principle has been undermined, that the ease of access has 'opened up the floodgates for frivolous cases', that the increased caseload imposes a heavy burden and impedes efficiency, and that there is no barrier to judicial populism.]

8 [By way of defence, the] main rationale for "judicial activism" in India lies in the highly unequal social profile of our population, where judges must take proactive steps to protect the interests of those who do not have a voice in the political system and do not have the means or information to move the courts. This places the Indian courts in a very different social role as compared to several developed nations where directions given by "unelected judges" are often viewed as unjustified restraints on the will of the majority. It is precisely this countermajoritarian function that needs to be robustly discharged by an independent and responsible Judiciary....

...

OLGA TELLIS V. BOMBAY MUNICIPAL CORPORATION

Supreme Court of India, 1985, AIR 1986 SC 18

CHANDRACHUD, C.

1. These Writ Petitions portray the plight of lakhs [hundreds of thousands] of persons who live on pavements and in slums in the city of Bombay. They constitute nearly half the population of the city.... Those who have made pavements their homes exist in the midst of filth and squalor, which has to be seen to be believed. Rabid dogs in search of stinking meat and cats in search of hungry rats keep them company....

It is these men and women who have come to this Court to ask for a judgment that they cannot be evicted from their squalid shelters without being offered alternative accommodation. They rely for their rights on Art. 21 of the Constitution which guarantees that no person shall be deprived of his life except according to procedure established by law. They do not contend that they have a right to live on the pavements. Their contention is that they have a right to live, a right which cannot be exercised without the means of livelihood....

...

32. ... For purposes of argument, we will assume the factual correctness of the premise that if the petitioners are evicted from their dwellings, they will be deprived of their livelihood. Upon that assumption, the question which we have to consider is whether the right to life includes the right to livelihood. We see only one answer to that question, namely, that it does. The sweep of the right to life conferred by Art. 21 is wide and far-reaching.... That, which alone makes it possible to live, leave aside what makes life livable, must be deemed to be an integral component of the right to life. Deprive a person of his right to livelihood and you shall have deprived him of his life. Indeed, that explains the massive migration of the rural population to big cities....

33. Article 39(a) of the Constitution, which is a Directive Principle of State Policy, provides that the State shall, in particular, direct its policy towards securing that the citizens, men and women equally, have the right to an adequate means of livelihood. [Reference is made to Arts. 41 and 37, see p. 345, *supra*] ... The Principles contained in Arts. 39(a) and 41 must be regarded as equally fundamental in the understanding and interpretation of the meaning and content of fundamental rights. If there is an obligation upon the State to secure to the citizens an adequate means of livelihood and the right to work, it would be sheer pedantry to exclude the right to livelihood from the content of the right to life....

...

35 ... It would be unrealistic on our part to reject the petitions on the ground that the petitioners have not adduced evidence to show that they will be rendered jobless if they are evicted from the slums and pavements. Commonsense, which is a cluster of life's experiences, is often more dependable than the rival facts presented by warring litigants.

...

37. Two conclusions emerge from this discussion: one, that the right to life which is conferred by Art. 21 includes the right to livelihood and two, that it is established that if the petitioners are evicted from their dwellings, they will be deprived of their livelihood. But the Constitution does not put an absolute embargo on the deprivation of life or personal liberty. By Art. 21, such deprivation has to be according to procedure established by law....

...

57. To summarise,... pavement dwellers who were censused or who happened to be censused in 1976 should be given, though not as a condition precedent to their removal, alternate [sites] at Malavani or at such other convenient place as the Government considers reasonable but not farther away in terms of distance; slum dwellers who were given identity cards and whose dwellings were numbered in the 1976 census must be given alternate sites for the resettlement: slums which have been in existence for a long time, say for twenty years or more, and which have been improved and developed will not be removed unless the land on which they stand or the appurtenant land, is required for a public purpose, in which case, alternate sites or accommodation will be provided to them.... In order to minimise the hardship

involved in any eviction, we direct that the slums, wherever situated, will not be removed until one month after the end of the current monsoon season....

NOTE

In subsequent cases the Court expanded its interpretation of Article 21 in relation to a wide range of social sectors, including health. In *Rakesh Chandra Narayan v. State Of Bihar* (1989 AIR 348) a PIL complaint alleged abusive conditions at a mental hospital in Bihar. At the Court's request, a Chief Judicial Magistrate, visited and reported that only nine out of 16 medical officers had been appointed, that there was an acute water shortage, none of the toilets functioned, there was no additional light or ventilation provided, there were 300 beds for 1,580 patients, that meals were wholly inadequate and medicines were in very short supply. In response the Court requested the Bihar authorities to put forth a 'definite scheme for improving the working of the Institution'. The Health Secretary of Bihar subsequently filed a report that the Court found to be entirely inadequate. It then ordered that a series of specific measures be taken. Eighteen months later it observed that the responses of the authorities 'have not given us the satisfaction of the touch of appropriate sincerity in action' and that they had been 'half-hearted'. It concluded that it could not, 'with any sense of confidence...leave the management to the Health Department of the State of Bihar'. While recognizing the difficulty involved in managing a hospital located 1,000 kilometres away, it nonetheless appointed a Committee of Management 'with full powers to look after all aspects of the institution', prescribed its exact composition, scheduled its meetings and kept the case open.

In *Consumer Education & Research Centre v. Union of India* ((1995) 3 SCC 42) the Court examined a PIL petition complaining of the hazards faced by workers in asbestos-related industries. The petition cited International Labour Organization standards and detailed the medical consequences of the exposure. The Court took the opportunity to expand its definition of the right to life and to make a detailed remedial order:

> 26. The right to health to a worker is an integral facet of meaningful right to life to have not only a meaningful existence but also robust health and vigour without which worker would lead life of misery....
>
> 27. Therefore, we hold that right to health, medical aid to protect the health and vigour to a worker while in service or post retirement is a fundamental right under Article 21, read with Articles 39(e), 41, 43, 48A and all related Articles and fundamental human rights to make the life of the workman meaningful and purposeful with dignity of person.
>
> ...
>
> 33. The writ petition is, therefore, allowed. All the industries are directed (1) To maintain and keep maintaining the health record of every worker up to a minimum period of 40 years...; (2) The Membrane Filter test, to detect asbestos fibre

> should be adopted by all the factories...; (3) All the factories...are directed to compulsorily insure health coverage to every worker; (4) The Union and the State Governments are directed to review the standards of permissible exposure...in tune with...international standards...; (6) [all the relevant workers shall be medically examined and, if found to be suffering from an occupational health hazards, shall be compensated 100,000 rupees.]

In *Paschim Banga Khet Mazdoor Samity v. State of West Bengal* ((1996) 4 SCC 37) the petitioner fell off a train and suffered serious head injuries. He was taken by ambulance to a succession of hospitals and turned away, either because the hospital did not have the necessary facilities, or because no free beds were available. He ended up at an expensive private hospital. The Court found a violation of Article 21:

> The Constitution envisages the establishment of a welfare state at the federal level as well as at the state level. In a welfare state the primary duty of the Government is to secure the welfare of the people [which includes providing] adequate medical facilities...by running hospitals and health centres.... Article 21 imposes an obligation on the State to safeguard the right to life of every person. Preservation of human life is thus of paramount importance. The Government hospitals run by the State and the medical officers employed therein are duty bound to extend medical assistance for preserving human life. Failure on the part of a Government hospital to provide timely medical treatment to a person in need of such treatment [violates] Article 21....

The Court ordered measures specific to the applicant, but also remedial measures designed to ensure that in future 'proper medical facilities are available for dealing with emergency cases'. They included ordering additional emergency facilities at Primary Health Centres, the upgrading of local hospitals, improved ambulance facilities and preparation to ensure that medical personnel 'are geared to deal with larger number of patients needing emergency treatment on account of higher risk of accidents on certain occasions and in certain seasons.' In considering the financial implications of these orders it stated:

> It is no doubt true that financial resources are needed for providing these facilities. But at the same time it cannot be ignored that it is the constitutional obligation of the State to provide adequate medical services to the people. Whatever is necessary for this purpose has to be done. In the context of the constitutional obligation to provide free legal aid to a poor accused this Court has held that the State cannot avoid its constitutional obligation in that regard on account of financial constraints....The said observations would apply with equal, if not greater, force in the matter of discharge of constitutional obligation of the State to provide medical aid to preserve human life. In the matter of allocation of funds for medical services the said constitutional obligation of the State has to be kept in view. It is necessary that a time-bound plan for providing these services should be chalked out...and steps should be taken to implement the same....

But the most dramatic illustration of the PIL approach is the ongoing litigation over the right to food.

LAUREN BIRCHFIELD & JESSICA CORSI, THE RIGHT TO LIFE IS THE RIGHT TO FOOD: PEOPLE'S UNION FOR CIVIL LIBERTIES V. UNION OF INDIA & OTHERS

Washington College of Law, American University, 17/3 Human Rights Brief 15 (2010)

...

Creating and Expanding a Constitutional Right to Food

India's ongoing effort to realize a constitutional right to food began with a petition brought in July 2001 on behalf of the poor in the state of Rajasthan who had not been receiving the required employment and food relief mandated by the Rajasthan Famine Code of 1962. Filed in response to the failure of the federal and state governments to address acute hunger and starvation deaths at a time when India was producing a grain surplus, the PUCL petition sought enforcement of a constitutional right to food under Article 21 of the Constitution of India. Ten years into the litigation, PUCL has been expanded to apply to all state governments and to address larger, more complex issues of hunger, unemployment, and food security. [The] litigation remains... one of the longest running mandamus cases of its kind.

While early interim orders in the litigation addressed mainly the public distribution of food grains to families and persons falling below the government-designated poverty line, the Supreme Court order of November 28, 2001 critically and expansively transformed PUCL by identifying which food schemes were to be considered legal entitlements under the constitutional right to food and determining in detail how those government schemes were to be implemented. Since this watershed order, PUCL's interim orders have sought to define gradually, but in increasing detail, India's constitutional right to food. Important developments to government schemes in recent years have included preservation of the Public Distribution System, through which grains are delivered to people of extreme poverty; the universalization of the Integrated Child Development Scheme (ICDS), which allows all children to access services provided at ICDS feeding centers; the mandated continuance of the Mid-Day Meal Scheme (MDMS) in schools; and the issuance of court directives prohibiting any modification or discontinuance of any food scheme covered in previous orders without prior permission of the Supreme Court.

...

From Court Orders to Measurable Results

... The Supreme Court's ruling that the right to food is a justiciable, reviewable, expandable, legally enforceable, constitutional — and thus inviolable — right opened up new avenues both for political discourse and for concrete action. Justiciability provides a vehicle for ordinary people to access and utilize the courts. Moreover, enshrining the right to food as a legal entitlement provides an extremely important tool for holding the state accountable and demanding change. This change may take the form of opening a specific ration shop, increasing government inputs for agricultural production, or raising the quality of the cooked food provided at school mid-day meals. As the last decade under PUCL has shown, when the right to food is protected as a legal, constitutional entitlement, the option for the government to rollback programs designated to fulfill the right to food disappears. The legal entitlement also provides a foothold for preserving and expanding existing right-to-food programs and for developing new programs to fight hunger, malnutrition, discrimination, and poverty.

Concrete examples of the PUCL case's marked, positive impact on the lives of India's poorest citizens abound. In perhaps an unprecedented move, the Supreme Court forced the government of India to increase its budget and spend millions of dollars on programs related to ensuring adequate food and nutrition.... The November 28, 2001 interim order commanded state governments and union territories "to implement the Mid-Day Meal Scheme by providing every child in every Government and Government assisted Primary Schools with a prepared mid-day meal with a minimum content of 300 calories and 8–12 grams of protein each day of school for a minimum of 200 days" and mandated that "those Governments providing dry rations instead of cooked meals must within three months start providing cooked meals in all Government and Government aided Primary Schools." A subsequent interim order, handed down on April 20, 2004, required that the Indian government allocate funds to cover the conversion cost for food-grains into cooked meals and absolutely prohibited the recovery of any portion of these costs from children or their parents.

The success of India's Mid-Day Meal Scheme is an excellent example of the power and utility of the PUCL case. The Supreme Court's 2001 interim orders galvanized the mandatory provision of cooked lunches at government-run schools throughout the country. While the MDMS was officially launched in 1995, prior to PUCL, it was poorly implemented, reaching only a handful of states throughout the country. Additionally, the original program only provided for uncooked grains as opposed to a nutritionally balanced cooked meal, which allowed for more "leakages" of food grains (i.e., the siphoning off of grains for personal use or sale on the black market). The activists drafting the original pleas asked the Supreme Court to mandate proper implementation of the MDMS. Right-to-food advocates knew that the states of Tamil Nadu and Gujarat were implementing the MDMS extremely well, and thus provided a successful model for how combining central-government and state-level resources could result in significant and measurable improvements in student enrollment and nutritional intake. The Supreme Court's interim orders, issued in response to this petition, set off a spark that completely reversed the non-implementation of the MDMS in other states.

One of the ways the Supreme Court orders galvanized the MDMS was by handing down specific instructions regarding operationalization of the program and designating the state governments of India as the entities responsible for the implementation of this scheme. Placing responsibility on state governments allowed the Court to ensure proper implementation by targeting more organized, powerful, and better-funded government entities. Moreover, requiring specific minimum calorie and protein contents and that the meals be cooked transformed the program into a scheme that is inherently more difficult to corrupt and, on its face, much more supportive of school attendance and child nutrition goals.

The reshaping of the MDMS gave the Right to Food Campaign, as well as concerned parents and community members, a foothold for further advocacy. The Campaign launched a "country-wide 'day of action on mid-day meals' in April 2002" and spent several years monitoring, reporting, organizing, lobbying, and campaigning on the issue.…

[The authors note that the National Food Security Bill, p. 344 *supra*, is an 'example of how the PUCL litigation has launched the right to food into both mainstream political discourse'.]

QUESTIONS

1. Does the Supreme Court's expansion of the scope of Article 21 and its transformation of the legal status of the directive principles go too far? In what respects? Against what criteria would you assess the success of the right to food case law?

2. In defending the Court's approach, the Chief Justice points to the specificity of the challenges facing Indian society. Similarly, Gauri argues that critiques based on separation of powers arguments tend to assume that only one model is appropriate rather than recognizing 'that courts may play a variety of roles in different settings.'[46] And Landau concludes that in a society such as India, 'more aggressive, unconventional enforcement strategies—especially the judicious use of structural injunctions — can more effectively target social rights interventions towards the poor' than 'weak-form' or dialogue-based approaches to judicial review.[47] What do you think makes India special in this regard, and does this mean that its experience is unhelpful for determining how other societies should approach ESR?

3. What approach has the Indian Court taken in determining the 'available resources'? It has been estimated that over 80 per cent of health care spending in India occurs in the private sector. Does this suggest that the Court is effectively imposing ever-more burdens on a sector that is already failing?

4. In 2012 the Indian Supreme Court held that there is a right to sleep.[48] It did so in a case in which over 1,000 police had forcibly evicted a group of more than 20,000 persons involved in what the police had deemed to be an unlawful assembly, protesting against government corruption. The police chose to act after midnight when all of the protesters had gone to sleep for the night. On what basis and under what circumstances do you think a right to sleep might reasonably be grounded in the Indian Constitution?

4. SOUTH AFRICA: A MODEL SOCIAL RIGHTS CONSTITUTION?

When South Africa's post-apartheid constitution was being debated, consideration was given to following the directive principles approach in relation to social rights. This was rejected, however, and full constitutional recognition was accorded to them. In the decade since, the South African jurisprudence has had a major impact on

[46] Varun Gauri, 'Fundamental Rights and Public Interest Litigation in India: Overreaching or Underachieving', 1 Indian J. of L. & Econ. 71 (2010).

[47] David Landau, 'The Reality of Social Rights Enforcement', 53 Harv. Int'l. L.J. 402 (2012), at 404.

[48] *In Re: Ramlila Maidan Incident Dt.4/5.06.2011 v. Home Secretary, Union of India & Ors*, Judgment of 23 Feb. 2012.

discussions of ESR globally, with many commentators arguing that the *Grootboom* and *TAC* cases in particular show the way forward for an effective and manageable approach to making these rights justiciable.[49] Some of the relevant provisions of the Constitution (1996) are provided below, followed by excerpts from four major cases.

Section 1

The Republic of South Africa is one sovereign democratic state founded on the following values:

(a) Human dignity, the achievement of equality and the advancement of human rights and freedoms.

...

Section 7

(1) This Bill of Rights is a cornerstone of democracy in South Africa. It enshrines the rights of all people in our country and affirms the democratic values of human dignity, equality and freedom.
(2) The state must respect, protect, promote and fulfil the rights in the Bill of Rights.
(3) The rights in the Bill of Rights are subject to the limitations contained or referred to in section 36, or elsewhere in the Bill.

...

Section 10

Everyone has inherent dignity and the right to have their dignity respected and protected.

Section 11

Everyone has the right to life.

...

Section 26

(1) Everyone has the right to have access to adequate housing.
(2) The state must take reasonable legislative and other measures, within its available resources, to achieve the progressive realisation of this right.
(3) No one may be evicted from their home, or have their home demolished, without an order of court made after considering all the relevant circumstances. No legislation may permit arbitrary evictions.

Section 27

(1) Everyone has the right to have access to –
  (a) health care services, including reproductive health care;
  (b) sufficient food and water; and
  (c) social security, including, if they are unable to support themselves and their dependants, appropriate social assistance.
(2) The state must take reasonable legislative and other measures, within its available resources, to achieve the progressive realisation of each of these rights.
(3) No one may be refused emergency medical treatment.

[49] Two other notable ESR cases are *Khosa v. Minister for Social Development* 2004 (6) BCLR 569 (social security for non-citizens) and *Port Elizabeth Municipality v. Various Occupiers* 2004 (12) BCLR 1268 (housing rights).

Section 28

(1) Every child has the right:

...

(b) to family care or parental care, or to appropriate alternative care when removed from the family environment;

(c) to basic nutrition, shelter, basic health care services and social services;

...

Section 39

(1) When interpreting the Bill of Rights, a court, tribunal or forum:

(a) must promote the values that underlie an open and democratic society based on human dignity, equality and freedom;

(b) must consider international law; and

(c) may consider foreign law.

(2) When interpreting any legislation, and when developing the common law or customary law, every court, tribunal or forum must promote the spirit, purport, and objects of the Bill of Rights.

SOOBRAMONEY V. MINISTER OF HEALTH (KWAZULU-NATAL)

Constitutional Court of South Africa, Case CCT 32/97, 27 Nov. 1997

CHASKALSON P.

[1] The appellant, a 41 year old unemployed man, is a diabetic who suffers from ischaemic heart disease and cerebro-vascular disease which caused him to have a stroke during 1996. In 1996 his kidneys also failed. Sadly his condition is irreversible and he is now in the final stages of chronic renal failure. His life could be prolonged by means of regular renal dialysis. He has sought such treatment from the renal unit of the Addington state hospital in Durban. The hospital can, however, only provide dialysis treatment to a limited number of patients. The renal unit has 20 dialysis machines available to it, and some of these machines are in poor condition.... Because of the limited facilities that are available for kidney dialysis the hospital has been unable to provide the appellant with the treatment he has requested.

[2] ... Additional dialysis machines and more trained nursing staff are required to enable it to do this, but the hospital budget does not make provision for such expenditure. The hospital would like to have its budget increased but it has been told by the provincial health department that funds are not available for this purpose.

[3] Because of the shortage of resources the hospital follows a set policy in regard to the use of the dialysis resources. Only patients who suffer from acute renal failure, which can be treated and remedied by renal dialysis are given automatic access to renal dialysis at the hospital. Those patients who, like the appellant, suffer from chronic renal failure which is irreversible are not admitted automatically to the renal programme. A set of guidelines has been drawn up and adopted to determine which applicants who have chronic renal failure will be given dialysis treatment....

[The opinion noted that the appellant did not qualify under the guidelines. He alleged that he could not afford treatment at private hospitals, and he sought a judicial order directing Addington Hospital to provide the necessary treatment.

His application was dismissed, and he then applied for leave to appeal to the Constitutional Court. His claim was based on sections 27(3) and 11 of the 1996 Constitution, *supra*. The Court stressed the great disparities in wealth in South Africa, and the deplorable conditions and poverty in which millions of people lived, including lack of access to adequate health facilities.]

...

[11] What is apparent from these provisions is that the obligations imposed on the state by sections 26 and 27 in regard to access to housing, health care, food, water and social security are dependent upon the resources available for such purposes, and that the corresponding rights themselves are limited by reason of the lack of resources. Given this lack of resources and the significant demands on them that have already been referred to, an unqualified obligation to meet these needs would not presently be capable of being fulfilled. This is the context within which section 27(3) must be construed.

[14] Counsel for the appellant argued that section 27(3) should be construed consistently with the right to life entrenched in section 11 of the Constitution and that everyone requiring life-saving treatment who is unable to pay for such treatment herself or himself is entitled to have the treatment provided at a state hospital without charge.

[15] This Court has dealt with the right to life in the context of capital punishment but it has not yet been called upon to decide upon the parameters of the right to life or its relevance to the positive obligations imposed on the state under various provisions of the bill of rights. In India the Supreme Court has developed a jurisprudence around the right to life so as to impose positive obligations on the state in respect of the basic needs of its inhabitants.... Unlike the Indian Constitution ours deals specifically in the bill of rights with certain positive obligations imposed on the state, and where it does so, it is our duty to apply the obligations as formulated in the Constitution and not to draw inferences that would be inconsistent therewith.

...

[17] The purposive approach [to constitutional interpretation] will often be one which calls for a generous interpretation to be given to a right to ensure that individuals secure the full protection of the bill of rights, but this is not always the case, and the context may indicate that in order to give effect to the purpose of a particular provision 'a narrower or specific meaning' should be given to it.

[18] In developing his argument on the right to life counsel for the appellant relied upon...*Paschim Banga Khet Mazdoor Samity and others v. State of West Bengal and another*...[See p. 350 *supra*. The Court drew a strong distinction between the two cases. It concluded that the circumstances in that case made it] precisely the sort of case which would fall within section 27(3). It is one in which emergency treatment was clearly necessary. The occurrence was sudden, the patient had no opportunity of making arrangements in advance for the treatment that was required, and there was urgency in securing the treatment in order to stabilize his condition. The treatment was available but denied.

[19] In our Constitution the right to medical treatment does not have to be inferred from the nature of the state established by the Constitution or from the right to life which it guarantees. It is dealt with directly in section 27. If section 27(3)

were to be construed in accordance with the appellant's contention it would make it substantially more difficult for the state to fulfill its primary obligations under sections 27(1) and (2) to provide health care services to ' everyone' within its available resources. It would also have the consequence of prioritising the treatment of terminal illnesses over other forms of medical care and would reduce the resources available to the state for [non-life threatening medical needs]. In my view much clearer language than that used in section 27(3) would be required to justify such a conclusion.

[20] Section 27(3) itself is couched in negative terms — it is a right not to be refused emergency treatment. The purpose of the right seems to be to ensure that treatment be given in an emergency, and is not frustrated by reason of bureaucratic requirements or other formalities.... What the section requires is that remedial treatment that is necessary and available be given immediately to avert that harm.

[21] The applicant suffers from chronic renal failure. To be kept alive by dialysis he would require such treatment two to three times a week. This is not an emergency which calls for immediate remedial treatment. It is an ongoing state of affairs resulting from a deterioration of the applicant's renal function which is incurable. In my view section 27(3) does not apply to these facts.

[22] The appellant's demand to receive dialysis treatment at a state hospital must be determined in accordance with the provisions of sections 27(1) and (2) and not section 27(3). These sections entitle everyone to have access to health care services provided by the state 'within its available resources'.

...

[24] At present the Department of Health in KwaZulu-Natal does not have sufficient funds to cover the cost of the services which are being provided to the public.... There are many more patients suffering from chronic renal failure than there are dialysis machines to treat such patients. This is a nation-wide problem and resources are stretched in all renal clinics throughout the land. Guidelines have therefore been established [and] ... were applied in the present case.

[25] By using the available dialysis machines in accordance with the guidelines more patients are benefited than would be the case if they were used to keep alive persons with chronic renal failure, and the outcome of the treatment is also likely to be more beneficial because it is directed to curing patients, and not simply to maintaining them in a chronically ill condition. It has not been suggested that these guidelines are unreasonable or that they were not applied fairly and rationally....

...

[28] ... It is estimated that the cost to the state of treating one chronically ill patient by means of renal dialysis provided twice a week at a state hospital is approximately R60,000 per annum. If all the persons in South Africa who suffer from chronic renal failure were to be provided with dialysis treatment ... the cost of doing so would make substantial inroads into the health budget. And if this principle were to be applied to all patients claiming access to expensive medical treatment or expensive drugs, the health budget would have to be dramatically increased to the prejudice of other needs which the state has to meet.

[29] The provincial administration which is responsible for health services in KwaZulu-Natal has to make decisions about [health care] funding.... These choices

involve difficult decisions to be taken at the political level in fixing the health budget, and at the functional level in deciding upon the priorities to be met. A court will be slow to interfere with rational decisions taken in good faith by the political organs and medical authorities whose responsibility it is to deal with such matters.

[30] ... The dilemma confronting health authorities faced with such cases was described by Sir Thomas Bingham MR in *R v. Cambridge Health Authority, ex parte B*:[50]

> ... health authorities of all kinds are constantly pressed to make ends meet.... Difficult and agonising judgments have to be made as to how a limited budget is best allocated to the maximum advantage of the maximum number of patients. That is not a judgment which the court can make.

[31] One cannot but have sympathy for the appellant and his family...[b]ut the state's resources are limited and the appellant does not meet the criteria for admission to the renal dialysis programme. Unfortunately, this is true not only of the appellant but of many others who need access to renal dialysis units or to other health services. There are also those who need access to housing, food and water, employment opportunities, and social security....

The state has to manage its limited resources in order to address all these claims. There will be times when this requires it to adopt a holistic approach to the larger needs of society rather than to focus on the specific needs of particular individuals within society.

[37] ... The appeal... is dismissed.

GOVERNMENT OF SOUTH AFRICA V. GROOTBOOM

Constitutional Court of South Africa, Case CCT 11/00, 4 Oct. 2000

[Irene Grootboom and most other respondents (390 adults and 510 children) lived in a squatter settlement called Wallacedene. Their living conditions were 'lamentable': very low income population, overcrowded shacks (95 per cent of which lacked electricity), no water or sewage or refuse removal services, the area partly waterlogged and dangerously close to a main thoroughfare. Many inhabitants who had applied for subsidized low-cost housing from the municipality had been on the waiting list up to seven years.

Facing the prospect of indefinitely long intolerable conditions, respondents began to move out of Wallacedene in September 1998, putting up shacks on vacant privately owned land (named 'New Rust') that was earmarked for eventual low-cost housing. Court proceedings brought by the owner resulted in an order of May 1999 instructing the sheriff to evict respondents and dismantle their shacks. The magistrate also ordered the parties and municipality to identify alternative land for permanent or temporary occupation by the New Rust residents. No mediation occurred, and respondents were evicted, their houses bulldozed and possessions

[50] [1995] 2 All ER 129 (CA) at 137d–f.

destroyed. They then took shelter on the Wallacedene sports fields under such temporary structures as were feasible, at the time when winter rains began.

Respondents' court-appointed attorney then applied to the Cape of Good Hope High Court for an order requiring the government to provide them with adequate basic housing until they obtained permanent accommodation. The High Court ordered the appellants to provide the respondents who were children and their parents with shelter. Its judgment stated that 'tents, portable latrines and a regular supply of water (albeit transported) would constitute the bare minimum.' The appellants, representing all spheres of government responsible for housing (central government, province of the Western Cape and municipality), brought the present appeal to challenge that order.]

JUSTICE YACOOB [FOR THE COURT]

[6] The cause of the acute housing shortage lies in apartheid.

[The High Court concluded that the respondents' challenge under section 26 failed, because the appellant had taken 'reasonable legislative measures and other measures within its available resources to achieve the progressive realisation of the right to have access to adequate housing.' The Constitutional Court interpreted section 26 to impose certain obligations in this case.

The following excerpts from Justice Yacoob's opinion concern only section 26.]

...

[20] ... Section 7(2) of the Constitution requires the state "to respect, protect, promote and fulfil the rights in the Bill of Rights" and the courts are constitutionally bound to ensure that they are protected and fulfilled. The question is therefore not whether socio-economic rights are justiciable under our Constitution, but how to enforce them in a given case....

...

ii) The relevant international law and its impact

[26] During argument, considerable weight was attached to the value of international law in interpreting section 26....

[The Court turned to a discussion of the ICESCR and the work of the UN Committee on ESCR. The opinion emphasized Art. 11 (the right of everyone to an adequate standard of living..., including adequate food, clothing and housing) and Art. 2 (States parties will take appropriate steps to ensure the realization of this right...to the maximum of available resources etc.). The opinion drew particular attention to para. 10 of General Comment No. 3 (at p. 322, *supra*) in relation to a minimum core obligation.]

[31] ... Each right has a "minimum essential level" that must be satisfied by the states parties.... Minimum core obligation is determined generally by having regard to the needs of the most vulnerable group that is entitled to the protection of the right in question. It is in this context that the concept of minimum core obligation must be understood in international law.

[32] It is not possible to determine the minimum threshold for the progressive realisation of the right of access to adequate housing without first identifying the needs and opportunities for the enjoyment of such a right. These will vary according to

factors such as income, unemployment, availability of land and poverty. The differences between city and rural communities will also determine the needs and opportunities for the enjoyment of this right. Variations ultimately depend on the economic and social history and circumstances of a country. All this illustrates the complexity of the task of determining a minimum core obligation for the progressive realisation of the right....

[33] ... [T]he real question in terms of our Constitution is whether the measures taken by the state to realise the right afforded by section 26 are reasonable. There may be cases where it may be possible and appropriate to have regard to the content of a minimum core obligation to determine whether the measures taken by the state are reasonable....

iii) Analysis of section 26

...

[34] ... Subsections (1) and (2) are related and must be read together.... Although the subsection does not expressly say so, there is, at the very least, a negative obligation placed upon the state and all other entities and persons to desist from preventing or impairing the right of access to adequate housing. The negative right is further spelt out in subsection (3) which prohibits arbitrary evictions. Access to housing could also be promoted if steps are taken to make the rural areas of our country more viable so as to limit the inexorable migration of people from rural to urban areas in search of jobs.

[35] ... A right of access to adequate housing also suggests that it is not only the state who is responsible for the provision of houses, but that other agents within our society, including individuals themselves, must be enabled by legislative and other measures to provide housing. The state must create the conditions for access to adequate housing for people at all economic levels of our society....

[36] ... For those who can afford to pay for adequate housing, the state's primary obligation lies in unlocking the system, providing access to housing stock and a legislative framework to facilitate self-built houses through planning laws and access to finance. Issues of development and social welfare are raised in respect of those who cannot afford to provide themselves with housing. State policy needs to address both these groups. The poor are particularly vulnerable and their needs require special attention. It is in this context that the relationship between sections 26 and 27 and the other socio-economic rights is most apparent. If under section 27 the state has in place programmes to provide adequate social assistance to those who are otherwise unable to support themselves and their dependants, that would be relevant to the state's obligations in respect of other socio-economic rights.

[37] The state's obligation to provide access to adequate housing depends on context, and may differ from province to province, from city to city, from rural to urban areas and from person to person. Some may need access to land and no more; some may need access to land and building materials; some may need access to finance; some may need access to services such as water, sewage, electricity and roads...

...

Reasonable legislative and other measures

[39] What constitutes reasonable legislative and other measures must be determined in the light of the fact that the Constitution creates different spheres of government: national government, provincial government and local government.... A reasonable programme therefore must clearly allocate responsibilities and tasks to the different spheres of government and ensure that the appropriate financial and human resources are available.

...

[41] The measures must establish a coherent public housing programme directed towards the progressive realisation of the right of access to adequate housing within the state's available means.... The precise contours and content of the measures to be adopted are primarily a matter for the legislature and the executive. They must, however, ensure that the measures they adopt are reasonable.... A court considering reasonableness will not enquire whether other more desirable or favourable measures could have been adopted, or whether public money could have been better spent. The question would be whether the measures that have been adopted are reasonable....

[42] ... Mere legislation is not enough....

...

[43] Those whose needs are the most urgent and whose ability to enjoy all rights therefore is most in peril, must not be ignored.... It may not be sufficient to meet the test of reasonableness to show that the measures are capable of achieving a statistical advance in the realisation of the right....

...

[46] ... Section 26 does not expect more of the state than is achievable within its available resources.... The measures must be calculated to attain the goal expeditiously and effectively but the availability of resources is an important factor in determining what is reasonable.

...

[52] ... [T]here is no express provision [in the national housing programme] to facilitate access to temporary relief for people who have no access to land, no roof over their heads, for people who are living in intolerable conditions and for people who are in crisis because of natural disasters such as floods and fires, or because their homes are under threat of demolition. These are people in desperate need. Their immediate need can be met by relief short of housing which fulfils the requisite standards of durability, habitability and stability encompassed by the definition of housing development in the [Housing] Act.

...

[66] ... The nationwide housing programme falls short of obligations imposed upon national government to the extent that it fails to recognise that the state must provide for relief for those in desperate need. They are not to be ignored in the interests of an overall programme focussed on medium and long-term objectives. It is essential that a reasonable part of the national housing budget be devoted to this, but the precise allocation is for national government to decide in the first instance.

...

[68] Effective implementation requires at least adequate budgetary support by national government. This, in turn, requires recognition of the obligation to meet immediate needs in the nationwide housing programme. Recognition of such needs in the nationwide housing programme requires it to plan, budget and monitor the fulfilment of immediate needs and the management of crises. This must ensure that a significant number of desperate people in need are afforded relief, though not all of them need receive it immediately....

[69] In conclusion...the programmes adopted by the state fell short of the requirements of section 26(2) in that no provision was made for relief to the categories of people in desperate need identified earlier....

...

H. Evaluation of the conduct of the appellants towards the respondents

...

[88] ... The state had an obligation to ensure, at the very least, that the eviction was humanely executed. However, the eviction was reminiscent of the past and inconsistent with the values of the Constitution. The respondents were evicted a day early and to make matters worse, their possessions and building materials were not merely removed, but destroyed and burnt....

...

[92] This judgment must not be understood as approving any practice of land invasion for the purpose of coercing a state structure into providing housing on a preferential basis to those who participate in any exercise of this kind. Land invasion is inimical to the systematic provision of adequate housing on a planned basis. It may well be that the decision of a state structure, faced with the difficulty of repeated land invasions, not to provide housing in response to those invasions, would be reasonable. Reasonableness must be determined on the facts of each case.

I. Summary and conclusion

...

[94] I am conscious that it is an extremely difficult task for the state to meet these obligations in the conditions that prevail in our country. This is recognised by the Constitution.... I stress however, that despite all these qualifications, these are rights, and the Constitution obliges the state to give effect to them. This is an obligation that courts can, and in appropriate circumstances, must enforce.

[95] ... [S]ection 26 does oblige the state to devise and implement a coherent, coordinated programme designed to meet its section 26 obligations. The programme that has been adopted...fell short of the obligations imposed....

...

J. The Order

[99] ... It is declared that:

...

2. (a) Section 26(2) of the Constitution requires the state to devise and implement within its available resources a comprehensive and coordinated programme progressively to realise the right of access to adequate housing.

(b) The programme must include reasonable measures…to provide relief for people who have no access to land, no roof over their heads, and who are living in intolerable conditions or crisis situations.

(c) [T]he state housing programme [at issue in this case] fell short of compliance with the requirements in paragraph (b)….

TREATMENT ACTION CAMPAIGN v. MINISTER OF HEALTH

Constitutional Court of South Africa, Case CCT 8/02, 5 July 2002

[The Treatment Action Campaign (TAC) was the lead applicant among various other civil society groups working on HIV/AIDS. The respondents were the national Minister of Health and the various provincial authorities. The Court noted that the applicants' affidavits addressed the issues raised 'from a variety of specialised perspectives, ranging from paediatrics, pharmacology and epidemiology to public health administration, economics and statistics'.]

The Issues

[19] … [As noted in the TAC affidavit] the Applicants' case is as follows:

"22.1 The HIV/AIDS epidemic…has reached catastrophic proportions.

22.2 One of the most common methods of transmission of HIV in children is from mother to child at and around birth. Government estimates are that since 1998, 70 000 children are infected in this manner every year.

…

22.4 The Medicines Control Council has registered Nevirapine for use to reduce the risk of mother-to-child transmission of HIV. This means that Nevirapine has been found to be suitable for this purpose, and that it is safe, of acceptable quality, and therapeutically efficacious.

22.5 The result is that doctors in the private profession can and do prescribe Nevirapine for their patients when, in their professional judgment, it is appropriate to do so.

22.6 In July 2000 the manufacturers of Nevirapine offered to make it available to the South African government free of charge for a period of five years….

22.7 The government has formally decided to make Nevirapine available only at a limited number of pilot sites, which number two per province.

22.8 The result is that doctors in the public sector, who do not work at one of those pilot sites, are unable to prescribe this drug….

22.9 The Applicants are aware of the desirability of a multiple-strategy approach to the prevention of mother-to-child transmission. However, they cannot and do not accept that this provides a rational or lawful basis for depriving patients at other sites of the undoubted benefits of Nevirapine….

22.10 ... Whether or not to prescribe Nevirapine is a matter of professional medical judgment, which can only be exercised on a case-by-case basis. It is not a matter which is capable of rational or appropriate decision on a blanket basis.

22.11 There is no rational or lawful basis for allowing doctors in the private sector to exercise their professional judgment in deciding when to prescribe Nevirapine, but effectively prohibiting doctors in the public sector from doing so.

22.12 ... [T]he government has failed over an extended period to implement a comprehensive programme for the prevention of mother-to-child transmission of HIV.

22.13 The result of this refusal and this failure is the mother-to-child transmission of HIV in situations where this was both predictable and avoidable.

22.14 This conduct of the government is irrational, in breach of the Bill of Rights, and contrary to the values and principles prescribed for public administration in section 195 of the Constitution. Furthermore, government conduct is in breach of its international obligations...."

...

[22] In their argument counsel for the government raised issues pertaining to the separation of powers. This may be relevant in two respects — (i) in the deference that courts should show to decisions taken by the executive concerning the formulation of its policies; and (ii) in the order to be made where a court finds that the executive has failed to comply with its constitutional obligations....

Enforcement of socio-economic rights

...

Minimum core

[26] [T]he first and second amici...contended that section 27(1) of the Constitution establishes an individual right vested in everyone. This right, so the contention went, has a minimum core to which every person in need is entitled. The concept of "minimum core" was developed by the United Nations Committee on [ESCR in its General Comment No. 3]....

...

[28] ...In the case of sections 26 and 27...rights and obligations are stated separately. There is accordingly a distinction between the self-standing rights in sections 26(1) and 27(1), to which everyone is entitled, and which in terms of section 7(2) of the Constitution "[t]he state must respect, protect, promote and fulfil", and the independent obligations imposed on the state by sections 26(2) and 27(2). This minimum core might not be easy to define, but includes at least the minimum decencies of life consistent with human dignity. No one should be condemned to a life below the basic level of dignified human existence. The very notion of individual rights presupposes that anyone in that position should be able to obtain relief from a court.

[29] In effect what the argument comes down to is that sections 26 and 27 must be construed as imposing two positive obligations on the state: one an obligation to give effect to the 26(1) and 27(1) rights; the other a limited obligation to do so progressively through "reasonable legislative and other measures, within its available resources". Implicit in that contention is that the content of the right in subsection

(1) differs from the content of the obligation in subsection (2). This argument fails to have regard to the way subsections (1) and (2) of both sections 26 and 27 are linked in the text of the Constitution itself, and to the way they have been interpreted by this Court in *Soobramoney* and *Grootboom*.

...

[34] Although Yacoob J [in *Grootboom*] indicated that evidence in a particular case may show that there is a minimum core of a particular service that should be taken into account in determining whether measures adopted by the state are reasonable, the socio-economic rights of the Constitution should not be construed as entitling everyone to demand that the minimum core be provided to them. Minimum core was thus treated as possibly being relevant to reasonableness under section 26(2), and not as a self-standing right conferred on everyone under section 26(1).

[35] A purposive reading of sections 26 and 27 does not lead to any other conclusion. It is impossible to give everyone access even to a "core" service immediately. All that is possible, and all that can be expected of the state, is that it act reasonably to provide access to the socio-economic rights identified in sections 26 and 27 on a progressive basis....

...

[37] It should be borne in mind that in dealing with such matters the courts are not institutionally equipped to make the wide-ranging factual and political enquiries necessary for determining what the minimum-core standards called for by the first and second amici should be, nor for deciding how public revenues should most effectively be spent. There are many pressing demands on the public purse....

[38] Courts are ill-suited to adjudicate upon issues where court orders could have multiple social and economic consequences for the community. The Constitution contemplates rather a restrained and focused role for the courts.... [D]eterminations of reasonableness may in fact have budgetary implications, but are not in themselves directed at rearranging budgets. In this way the judicial, legislative and executive functions achieve appropriate constitutional balance.

[39] We therefore conclude that section 27(1) of the Constitution does not give rise to a self-standing and independent positive right enforceable irrespective of the considerations mentioned in section 27(2). Sections 27(1) and 27(2) must be read together as defining the scope of the positive rights that everyone has and the corresponding obligations on the state to "respect, protect, promote and fulfil" such rights. The rights conferred by sections 26(1) and 27(1) are to have "access" to the services that the state is obliged to provide in terms of sections 26(2) and 27(2).

...

The applicants' contentions

[44] It is the applicants' case that the measures adopted by government...were deficient in two material respects: first, because they prohibited the administration of nevirapine at public hospitals and clinics outside the research and training sites; and second, because they failed to implement a comprehensive programme for the prevention of mother-to-child transmission of HIV.

…

The policy confining nevirapine to the research and training sites

…

[51–55] In substance four reasons were advanced in the affidavits for confining the administration of nevirapine to the research and training sites. [(1) Where the comprehensive package was unavailable the benefits of nevirapine would be counteracted by the transmission of HIV from mother to infant through breastfeeding. But delivery of that package is costly and problematic in some contexts. (2) The administration of nevirapine to the mother and her child might lead to the development of resistance to the efficacy of nevirapine and related antiretrovirals in later years. (3) In safety terms the hazards of using neviripine are unknown. (4) It is unclear if the public health system has the capacity to provide the package.]

…

[56] We deal with each of these issues in turn.

Efficacy

[57] … It is clear from the evidence that the provision of nevirapine will save the lives of a significant number of infants even if it is administered without the full package.…

[58] … [T]he wealth of scientific material produced by both sides makes plain that sero-conversion of HIV takes place in some, but not all, cases and that nevirapine thus remains to some extent efficacious in combating mother-to-child transmission even if the mother breastfeeds her baby.

Resistance

[59] … The prospects of the child surviving if infected are so slim and the nature of the suffering so grave that the risk of some resistance manifesting at some time in the future is well worth running.

Safety

[60] The evidence shows that safety is no more than a hypothetical issue.… That is why [nevirapine's] use is recommended without qualification for this purpose by the World Health Organization.…

Considerations relevant to reasonableness

[67] The policy of confining nevirapine to research and training sites… fails to distinguish between the evaluation of programmes for reducing mother-to-child transmission and the need to provide access to health care services required by those who do not have access to the sites.

[68] … A programme for the realisation of socio-economic rights must "be balanced and flexible and make appropriate provision for attention to… crises and to short, medium and long term needs. A programme that excludes a significant segment of society cannot be said to be reasonable." [*Grootboom*]

…

Children's rights

[77] While the primary obligation to provide basic health care services no doubt rests on those parents who can afford to pay for such services, it was made clear in *Grootboom* that "[t]his does not mean…that the State incurs no obligation in relation to children who are being cared for by their parents or families."

[78] The provision of a single dose of nevirapine to mother and child for the purpose of protecting the child against the transmission of HIV is, as far as the children are concerned, essential.… Their rights are "most in peril" as a result of the policy that has been adopted and are most affected by a rigid and inflexible policy that excludes them from having access to nevirapine.

[79] The state is obliged to ensure that children are accorded the protection contemplated by section 28 that arises when the implementation of the right to parental or family care is lacking. Here we are concerned with children born in public hospitals and clinics to mothers who are for the most part indigent and unable to gain access to private medical treatment which is beyond their means. They and their children are in the main dependent upon the state to make health care services available to them.

…

The powers of the courts

[96] Counsel for the government contended that even if this Court should find that government policies fall short of what the Constitution requires, the only competent order…that a court can make is to issue a declaration of rights to that effect. That leaves government free to pay heed to the declaration made and to adapt its policies in so far as this may be necessary to bring them into conformity with the court's judgment. This, so the argument went, is what the doctrine of separation of powers demands.

[97] In developing this argument counsel contended that under the separation of powers the making of policy is the prerogative of the executive and not the courts, and that courts cannot make orders that have the effect of requiring the executive to pursue a particular policy.

[98] This Court has made it clear on more than one occasion that although there are no bright lines that separate the roles of the legislature, the executive and the courts from one another, there are certain matters that are pre-eminently within the domain of one or other of the arms of government and not the others. All arms of government should be sensitive to and respect this separation. This does not mean, however, that courts cannot or should not make orders that have an impact on policy.…

[99] The primary duty of courts is to the Constitution and the law.… The Constitution requires the state to "respect, protect, promote, and fulfil the rights in the Bill of Rights". Where state policy is challenged as inconsistent with the Constitution, courts have to consider whether in formulating and implementing such policy the state has given effect to its constitutional obligations. If it should hold

in any given case that the state has failed to do so, it is obliged by the Constitution to say so. In so far as that constitutes an intrusion into the domain of the executive, that is an intrusion mandated by the Constitution itself. There is also no merit in the argument advanced on behalf of government that a distinction should be drawn between declaratory and mandatory orders against government. Even simple declaratory orders against government or organs of state can affect their policy and may well have budgetary implications. Government is constitutionally bound to give effect to such orders whether or not they affect its policy and has to find the resources to do so....

...

[102] ... Particularly in a country where so few have the means to enforce their rights through the courts, it is essential that on those occasions when the legal process does establish that an infringement of an entrenched right has occurred, it be effectively vindicated. The courts have a particular responsibility in this regard and are obliged to 'forge new tools' and shape innovative remedies, if needs be, to achieve this goal....

...

[106] We thus reject the argument that the only power that this Court has in the present case is to issue a declaratory order. Where a breach of any right has taken place, including a socio-economic right, a court is under a duty to ensure that effective relief is granted. The nature of the right infringed and the nature of the infringement will provide guidance as to the appropriate relief in a particular case....

...

[112] [After reviewing cases from the United States, India, Germany, Canada and the United Kingdom, the Court concludes] that in none of the jurisdictions surveyed is there any suggestion that the granting of injunctive relief breaches the separation of powers. The various courts adopt different attitudes to when such remedies should be granted, but all accept that within the separation of powers they have the power to make use of such remedies — particularly when the state's obligations are not performed diligently and without delay.

[114] A factor that needs to be kept in mind is that policy is and should be flexible. It may be changed at any time and the executive is always free to change policies where it considers it appropriate to do so. The only constraint is that policies must be consistent with the Constitution and the law. Court orders concerning policy choices made by the executive should therefore not be formulated in ways that preclude the executive from making such legitimate choices....

...

Orders

[135] ...

...

3. Government is ordered without delay to:

   a) Remove the restrictions that prevent nevirapine from being made available for the purpose of reducing the risk of mother-to-child transmission of HIV at public hospitals and clinics that are not research and training sites.

b) Permit and facilitate the use of nevirapine for the purpose of reducing the risk of mother-to-child transmission of HIV and to make it available for this purpose at hospitals and clinics when in the judgment of the attending medical practitioner acting in consultation with the medical superintendent of the facility concerned this is medically indicated, which shall if necessary include that the mother concerned has been appropriately tested and counselled.

c) Make provision if necessary for counsellors based at public hospitals and clinics other than the research and training sites to be trained for the counselling necessary for the use of nevirapine to reduce the risk of mother-to-child transmission of HIV.

d) Take reasonable measures to extend the testing and counselling facilities at hospitals and clinics throughout the public health sector to facilitate and expedite the use of nevirapine for the purpose of reducing the risk of mother-to-child transmission of HIV.

4. The orders made in paragraph 3 do not preclude government from adapting its policy in a manner consistent with the Constitution if equally appropriate or better methods become available to it for the prevention of mother-to-child transmission of HIV.
5. The government must pay the applicants' costs, including the costs of two counsel.

...

MAZIBUKO v. CITY OF JOHANNESBURG

Constitutional Court of South Africa, CCT 39/09 [2009] ZACC 28, 8 Oct. 2009

[Recall that Section 27 of the South African Constitution provides that 'everyone has the right to have access to . . . sufficient food and water . . . '. The new government adopted a highly innovative example of a rights-based water policy. The Water Services Act (1997) recognized everyone's 'right of access to basic water supply and basic sanitation' and required every water services institution to 'take reasonable measures to realise these rights'. It defined a 'basic water supply' as 'the prescribed minimum standard of water supply services necessary for the reliable supply of a sufficient quantity and quality of water to households, including informal households, to support life and personal hygiene.' It authorized the Minister to prescribe 'compulsory national standards'. Accordingly, Regulation 3 (2001) provides that:

> The minimum standard for basic water supply services is:
>
> ...
>
> (b) a minimum quantity of potable water of 25 litres per person per day or 6 kilolitres per household per month
>
> (i) at a minimum flow rate of not less than 10 litres per minute;
>
> (ii) within 200 metres of a household; and

(iii) with an effectiveness such that no consumer is without a supply for more than seven full days in any year.

In 1994, 12 million people did not have adequate access to water. By the end of 2006 the figure was down to 8 million, of whom 3.3 million had no access at all.

The applicants lived in Phiri, in Soweto, a township set up in the apartheid era. It was next to Johannesburg, a city with 3.2 million people living in about a million households, half of which are very poor and almost one-fifth of which are located in informal settlements. Almost 20 per cent of households have no access to basic sanitary services and 10 per cent have no access to a tap providing clean water within 200 metres of their home.

The respondents were the City of Johannesburg, Johannesburg Water (Pty) Ltd, and the national Minister for Water Affairs and Forestry. Since the water company was wholly owned by the City, no issue arose concerning the responsibilities of private actors.

The pipes to Soweto were badly corroded and extensive leakage occurred. Sowetan households consumed an average of 67 kilolitres per month, but were charged a flat rate based on a deemed consumption of 20 kilolitres. But less than 10 per cent of households actually paid their bills and the water company derived 1 per cent of its revenue from the one-quarter to one-third of its total water sales that went to Soweto. Seventy-five per cent of water pumped into Soweto was thus not accounted for.

The company introduced Operation *Gcin'amanzi* (to save water), initiated in Phiri. It abandoned the flat rate system of deemed consumption and introduced three service levels: (1) a tap within 200 metres of each dwelling; (2) a tap in the yard of a household with a water flow of only 6 kilolitres per month; and (3) a metered connection. Phiri residents had to choose between (2) and (3) with the latter involving a pre-paid meter.

In 2008 the High Court rejected the pre-paid meters as being unauthorized by the City's by-laws, procedurally unfair and racially discriminatory. It also held the free water allowance to be inadequate and ordered the provision of 50 litres per person per day. In 2009 the Supreme Court of Appeal gave the City two years to amend its by-laws and set the free water allocation at 42 litres.]

O'REGAN J. [FOR THE COURT]

...

The role of courts in determining the content of social and economic rights: the proper interpretation of section 27(1)(b) and 27(2) of the Constitution

...

[50] [Reading] section 27(1)(b) [together] with section 27(2), it is clear that the right does not require the state upon demand to provide every person with sufficient water without more; rather it requires the state to take reasonable legislative and other measures progressively to realise the achievement of the right of access to sufficient water, within available resources.

...

[56] The applicants' argument [is] that the Court should adopt a quantified standard determining the content of the right not merely its minimum content. The argument must fail for the same reasons that the minimum core argument failed in *Grootboom* and *Treatment Action Campaign No 2.*

[57] Those reasons are essentially twofold. [First, the Constitution] requires the state to take reasonable legislative and other measures progressively to achieve the right of access to sufficient water within available resources. It does not confer a right to claim "sufficient water" from the state immediately.

...

[59] ... Social and economic rights empower citizens to demand of the state that it acts reasonably and progressively to ensure that all enjoy the basic necessities of life. In so doing, the social and economic rights enable citizens to hold government to account for the manner in which it seeks to pursue the achievement of social and economic rights.

[60] Moreover, what the right requires will vary over time and context. Fixing a quantified content might, in a rigid and counter-productive manner, prevent an analysis of context. The concept of reasonableness places context at the centre of the enquiry and permits an assessment of context to determine whether a government programme is indeed reasonable.

[61] Secondly, ordinarily it is institutionally inappropriate for a court to determine precisely what the achievement of any particular social and economic right entails and what steps government should take to ensure the progressive realisation of the right. This is a matter, in the first place, for the legislature and executive, the institutions of government best placed to investigate social conditions in the light of available budgets and to determine what targets are achievable in relation to social and economic rights. Indeed, it is desirable as a matter of democratic accountability that they should do so for it is their programmes and promises that are subjected to democratic popular choice.

[62] ... [T]his case illustrates that the obligation in relation to the right of access to sufficient water will vary depending upon circumstance. As emerges from research by the World Health Organisation in 2003 ... the expert evidence on the record provides numerous different answers to the question of what constitutes "sufficient water". Courts are ill-placed to make these assessments for both institutional and democratic reasons.

...

[66] The Constitution envisages that legislative and other measures will be the primary instrument for the achievement of social and economic rights. ...

[67] Thus the positive obligations imposed upon government by the social and economic rights in our Constitution will be enforced by courts in at least the following ways. If government takes no steps to realise the rights, the courts will require government to take steps. If government's adopted measures are unreasonable, the courts will similarly require that they be reviewed so as to meet the constitutional standard of reasonableness. From *Grootboom,* it is clear that a measure will be unreasonable if it makes no provision for those most desperately in need. If government adopts a policy with unreasonable limitations or exclusions, as in *Treatment Action Campaign No* 2, the Court may order that those are removed. Finally, the obligation

of progressive realisation imposes a duty upon government continually to review its policies to ensure that the achievement of the right is progressively realised.

[68] These considerations were overlooked by the High Court and the Supreme Court of Appeal which...found it appropriate to quantify the content of the right,...they erred in this approach and the applicants' argument that the Court should set 50 litres per person per day as the content of the section 27(1)(b) right must fail.

The relevance of regulation 3(b) of the National Water Standards Regulations

[69] ...[The] minimum standard for basic water supply [contained in Regulation 3(b)] is the basis of the policy adopted by the City and Johannesburg Water.

National government should set the targets it wishes to achieve in respect of social and economic rights clearly....The minimum standard set by the Minister informs citizens of what government is seeking to achieve. In so doing, it enables citizens to monitor government's performance and to hold it accountable politically if the standard is not achieved. This also empowers citizens to hold government accountable through legal challenge if the standard set is unreasonable.

[71] A reasonableness challenge requires government to explain the choices it has made. To do so, it must provide the information it has considered and the process it has followed to determine its policy. This case provides an excellent example of government doing just that....If the process followed by government is flawed or the information gathered is obviously inadequate or incomplete, appropriate relief may be sought....

...

[76] [I]t will in most circumstances be difficult for an applicant who does not challenge the minimum standard set by the legislature or the executive for the achievement of social and economic rights to establish that a policy based on that prescribed standard is unreasonable....

The reasonableness of the City's Free Basic Water policy

[78] It will be useful here to set out the City's policy. [The Court then gives the details of the three service levels].

[79] ... Every consumer in the City, whether rich or poor, who has a metered connection services gets the first 6 kilolitres of water free per month and must pay for water used in excess of that amount.

[80] ... The tariff is determined according to a rising block tariff structure so that the more water used, the higher the per kilolitre tariff. The tariff structure also provides for credit meter users to be charged more than pre-paid meter users. The effect of the tariff structure is that heavy users of water cross-subsidise those who use less water.

[81] In addition to the 6 kilolitres monthly provided free of charge, accountholders whose households have a combined household income of less than twice the highest national government social grant plus R1 [one Rand] (R1 881)are entitled to register on the City's indigent register. To be registered, accountholders must accept the installation of pre-paid electricity and water meters in their homes

(where available). The effect of registration is that all arrears owed to the City are written off. From July 2007, those on the register were also entitled to an additional 4 free kilolitres of water monthly (making a total of 10 free kilolitres). However, at the time the answering affidavits were lodged in January 2007 only 118 000 households had registered as indigent households, despite at least 500 000 households apparently being eligible.... All households with pre-paid meters were eligible for a single allocation annually of 4 kilolitres of water for emergency use.

[82] The applicants argue that the policy is unreasonable....

Rich and Poor

[83] The first question is whether it is unreasonable for the City to provide the 6 kilolitres of free water to rich and poor alike.... First, [the City] asserts that the rising block tariff structure means that wealthier consumers, who tend to use more water, are charged more for their heavier water usage. The effect of this is that the original 6 kilolitres that is provided free is counterweighed by the extent to which heavy water users cross-subsidise the free allocation. Secondly, the City points to the difficulty of establishing a method to target those households who are deserving of free water. This is a matter to which I return [see paras. 98–102 below]. In my view, these reasons are persuasive and rebut the charge of unreasonableness on this ground.

Per household versus per person allowance

[84] Secondly, the applicants argue that the policy is unreasonable because it is formulated as 6 kilolitres per household (or accountholder) rather than as a per person allowance. Again the City presents cogent evidence that it is difficult to establish how many people are living on one stand at any given time; and that it is therefore unable to base the policy on a per person allocation. This evidence seems indisputable. The continual movement of people within the city means that it would be an enormous administrative burden, if possible at all, for the City to determine the number of people on any given stand sufficiently regularly to supply a per person daily allowance. The applicants' argument on this basis too must fail.

Policy based on a misconception

[85] The third argument, which the Supreme Court of Appeal upheld, is that the policy is unreasonable because the City considered that it was not under an obligation to provide a specified amount of free basic water. What is clear from the discussion above is that the City is not under a constitutional obligation to provide any *particular* amount of free water to citizens per month. It is under a duty to take reasonable measures progressively to realise the achievement of the right. This the City accepts.... The applicants' argument on this score must also fail.

Insufficient for large households

[86] The fourth argument is that the 6 kilolitres per month per household is not sufficient in that it does not provide 50 litres per person per day across the board. There is a welter of evidence on the record indicating that household sizes in Johannesburg vary markedly....

[87] The picture is further complicated, however, by the fact that there is often more than one household relying on one water connection. This is especially so in townships.... What emerges from the record, thus, is that although the average household size is quite low, the variation in the number of occupants per water connection is significant. There are many water connections where there is only one resident, but there are some with as many as 20.

[88] Where the household size is average, that is 3.2 people, the free basic water allowance will provide approximately 60 litres per person per day.... The difficulty is that many households are larger than the average.... Yet, to raise the free basic water allowance for all so that it would be sufficient to cover those stands with many residents would be expensive and inequitable, for it would disproportionately benefit stands with fewer residents.

> [89] Establishing a fixed amount per stand will inevitably result in unevenness because those stands with more inhabitants will have less water per person than those stands with fewer people. This is an unavoidable result of establishing a universal allocation. Yet it seems clear on the City's evidence that to establish a universal per person allowance would administratively be extremely burdensome and costly, if possible at all. The free basic water allowance established is generous in relation to the average household size in Johannesburg. Indeed, in relation to 80% of households (with four occupants or fewer), the allowance is adequate even on the applicants' case. In the light of this evidence, coupled with the fact that the amount provided by the City was based on the prescribed national standard for basic water supply, it cannot be said that the amount established by the City was unreasonable.

Inflexibility of the policy

[90] The final argument raised by the applicants is that the quantity selected by the City was inflexible in that it did not, at least originally, provide for any individualised variation to avoid the hardship that larger households or households with special needs might face in the light of the fixed free basic water allocation.

...

[93] ... On 6 December 2006, five months after the applicants launched their challenge, the City Mayoral Committee [decided that] registered indigent households would receive an additional 4 kilolitres of free water per month....

...

[95] ... If the City had not continued to review and refine its Free Basic Water policy after it was introduced in 2001, and had taken no steps to ensure that the poorest households were able to obtain an additional allocation, it may well have been concluded that the policy was inflexible and therefore unreasonable....However, the City has not set its policy in stone....

[96] It may well be, as the applicants urge, that the City's comprehensive and persistent engagement has been spurred by the litigation in this case. If that is so, it is not something to deplore....The litigation will in that event have attained at least some of what it sought to achieve.

...

Indigent registration policy

[98] The applicants also challenge the reasonableness of the City's indigent registration policy on two main grounds: the first is that it is demeaning for citizens to have to register as indigents; and the second is that because only approximately one-fifth of the households who are eligible to register are registered, the policy is unreasonable because it is under-inclusive.

...

[101] Although a means-tested policy requires citizens to apply for benefits and so disclose that they are poor, to hold a means-tested policy to be constitutionally impermissible would deprive government of a key methodology for ensuring that government services target those most in need. Indeed, nearly all social security benefits afforded by the national government are based on means-testing.... Means-testing may not be a perfect methodology [but] it seeks to ensure that those most in need benefit from government services. In their affidavits, the applicants proposed no third way as an alternative....

[102] ... The dilemma is not readily solved.... [I]t cannot be said that the policy as formulated...was unreasonable. The applicants' argument in this regard must fail.

...

Installation of pre-paid water meters

[Discussion omitted].

...

Litigating social and economic rights

[159] The outcome of the case is that the applicants have not persuaded this Court to specify what quantity of water is "sufficient water" within the meaning of section 27 of the Constitution. Nor have they persuaded the Court that the City's policy is unreasonable. The applicants submitted during argument that if this were to be the result, litigation in respect of the positive obligations imposed by social and economic rights would be futile. It is necessary to consider this submission.

[160] The purpose of litigation concerning the positive obligations imposed by social and economic rights should be to hold the democratic arms of government to account through litigation. In so doing, litigation of this sort fosters a form of participative democracy that holds government accountable and requires it to account between elections over specific aspects of government policy.

[161] When challenged as to its policies relating to social and economic rights, the government agency must explain why the policy is reasonable. Government must disclose what it has done to formulate the policy: its investigation and research, the alternatives considered, and the reasons why the option underlying the policy was selected. The Constitution does not require government to be held to an impossible standard of perfection. Nor does it require courts to take over the tasks that in a democracy should properly be reserved for the democratic arms of government....

...

LUCY A. WILLIAMS, THE ROLE OF COURTS IN THE QUANTITATIVE-IMPLEMENTATION OF SOCIAL AND ECONOMIC RIGHTS: A COMPARATIVE STUDY

3 Constitutional Court Review 2010 [South Africa] (2011) 141

[The author compares the approach of the German Federal Constitutional Court (FCC) in *Hartz IV* (2009)[51] and the South African Constitutional Court in *Mazibuko* (2009).]

...

In *Hartz IV* unemployed individuals and their dependents challenged the constitutionality of certain recently enacted legislation that reduced the level of basic subsistence grants. A central claim was that, because the benefit amounts determined by Parliament did not provide a subsistence minimum of income, they were in derogation of the dignity clause of the German Basic Law — Article 1. The FCC concluded that, in accord with separation of powers principles, courts should not establish the level of subsistence benefits in specific quantitative terms. At the same time, the FCC engaged in a searching examination of the method of calculation used by the legislature to set these amounts. The FCC held that the legislature's justification for determining benefit amounts must be based on a sound empirical basis and coherent methods rather than random estimates. As Parliament's calculations did not meet this standard, the FCC sent the matter back to the legislature for recalibration of the benefits using a constitutionally adequate procedure.

...

[T]he way in which the *Mazibuko* Court *operationalised* its review of the City's program brought a very different — much lower and more cursory — level of attention to the evidence regarding the City's calculations than was shown by the FCC in reviewing welfare benefits in *Hartz IV*. If the SACC interrogated the evidence regarding the government's statistics and calculation methods, the Court does not indicate this in the opinion, nor does it provide much guidance for future courts and litigants regarding how — operationally — reasonableness review is to be conducted in quantitative-implementation cases. In practice, if not in doctrine, the level of scrutiny O'Regan J applied to the City's water policy is much closer to American 'minimum rationality' than to South African 'reasonableness'.

I will give a few examples....

...

(1) The judgment ignored important, but contrary, evidence....

...

[Rather than examining the various expert affidavits or calculations] the Court stated: '[T]he expert evidence on the record provides numerous different answers to the question of what constitutes "sufficient water." Courts are ill-placed to make these assessments for both institutional and democratic reasons.' Perhaps the evidence was adequate to sustain the reasonableness of the City's calculations; perhaps

[51] Bundesverfassungsgericht, 1 BVL 1/09, 1 BVL 3/09, 1 BVL 4/09 of 9 Feb. 2010 (Hartz IV).

a court would overstep its rightful boundaries by insisting on local evidence. But the Court gave the parties and the public no reason or explanation as to *why* this is so.

(2) The judgment does not indicate that the Court reviewed the City's calculation methods with an eye toward determining whether they were minimally or reasonably accurate and coherent. . . .

. . .

. . . If it is enough for a court to give a cursory and conclusory assertion of rationality, future challenges are almost always destined to fail, litigation will not provide a tool to hold the government accountable in any meaningful way nor will it provide the public a means to render the government's calculation methods transparent, and civil society and litigants will not be in a position to play a meaningful role in the progressive achievement of social justice contemplated by the Constitution.

(3) In its treatment of the City's reliance on city-wide average household size and on the per account-holder (rather than per person) allocation of FBW supply, the judgment sustained as reasonable calculation methods used by the City which the Court itself acknowledges result in adverse racial and class consequences. No doubt the responsible City officials intended nothing of the kind. Yet despite the City's best efforts, its water program carries forward the legacy of apartheid.

. . . [T]he Court acknowledged that 'average household size' in a city such as Johannesburg is a statistic that glosses over the apartheid legacy of residential segregation. Despite the strides made since democratic transition in 1994, residential segregation by race remains an indelible feature of South African life. This will probably be true for at least a generation. In that setting, use of a city-wide average of household size as the basis for calculating FBW allocations treats the predominantly black and predominantly white zones equally, to the great disadvantage of the predominantly black zones such as Soweto.

. . . In a city with Johannesburg's history, a policy premised on calculations using city-wide average household size as a key indicator should have set off alarm bells for any reviewing court. . . .

. . .

[T]he judgment frequently views remedies in binary terms. In terms of quantitative implementation, for example, there seem to be only two possibilities: either courts must not determine constitutional sufficiency in quantitative terms at all, or courts have the power to determine a precise quantity for a socio-economic right, which will then be set in perpetuity. This latter possibility the Court views — appropriately — as counterproductive because it prevents the ongoing development of rights within context. However, the Court fails to explore the many other possibilities in quantitative implementation cases, such as using a specific number in the remedial phase of the case as a temporary or interim benchmark; referring the case back to the government to determine a plan for reaching that benchmark or returning with an alternate proposal of the maximum amount that the governmental entity believes it can achieve in an interim period; ordering that the more destitute receive a designated amount until the government's program can be placed on a constitutionally adequate basis, or using precise numbers to monitor and track the process of 'progressive realisation'.

. . .

Overall,... the judgment deployed an unnecessarily limiting concept of judicial deference, resulting in an outcome that was inconsistent with the aspirations reflected in the vision she articulated.

...

QUESTIONS

1. Compare the approaches taken by the Court in *Soobramoney*, *Grootboom* and *TAC*. Is the approach consistent or does the Court shift the goalposts significantly from one case to the next?

2. 'In the TAC case the Court rolls out all the classic statements of deference to the legislature before it engages in an aggressive demolition of the government's policy choices and replaces them with its own.' Comment.

3. 'In administrative law there is generally a detailed legislative standard to apply or interpret, whereas in constitutional law the provisions are, almost by definition, open-ended. By applying a reasonableness test that is shaped by administrative law notions in interpreting constitutional provisions the Court avoids the sort of deep inquiry that is essential if ESR are to be given substantive, as opposed to merely procedural, content.' Comment.

4. How persuasive is William's critique of *Mazibuko*? Is it for the Constitutional Court to undertake a probing technical evaluation of the evidence before it? How 'creative' should it be in fashioning remedies? Does it have anything to learn from the approach of the Indian Supreme Court?

5. THE UNITED STATES: EDUCATION RIGHTS

At least until very recently, the United States has generally opposed ESR initiatives at the international level (see p. 292, *supra*). The situation in terms of domestic law is, however, rather more complex. The right to education provides an interesting case study. It has been addressed, in different ways, in the constitutions of many of the 50 component states.[52] In 1954 in the landmark case of *Brown v. Board of Education*[53] a unanimous Court recognized 'education [as] perhaps the most important function of state and local governments' and declared it to be 'a right which must be made available to all on equal terms'. But, almost two decades later, in *San Antonio Independent School District v. Rodriguez*[54] the Court took a very different approach.

52 Allen Hubsch, 'Note: The Emerging Right to Education under State Constitutional Law', 65 Temple L. Rev. 1325 (1992); and Woods and Lewis, *Human Rights and the Global Marketplace: Economic, Social and Cultural Dimensions* (2005), at 901–11.

53 347 U.S. 483 (1954).

54 411 U.S. 1 (1973).

While much of the 5–4 majority decision was concerned with the finer points of US equal protection law, the Court also considered whether education was a constitutionally protected fundamental right. It insisted that such a right could not be derived from arguments about the 'relative societal significance of education' but only from the text of the Constitution. And it found that, despite dramatic differences in the funding provided for education from one district to another, there was no 'absolute denial of educational opportunities to any' children, and thus no right to education issue. In doing so it expressed concerns that a finding of a right to education might logically lead to findings relating to issues such as denials of 'decent food and shelter'. The majority decision indicated that it was enough for education reforms to 'take one step at a time', and was concerned about the federalism implications of intervening in state decisions. It also claimed the Court lacked the 'expertise and the familiarity with local problems' necessary to decide issues of local taxation. Finally, the Court attached importance to the view that better financing would not necessarily bring better education.

In reaction to *Rodriguez*, most subsequent action has been at the state level. Hershkoff and Loffredo note the extent to which ESR have been recognized in different state constitutions and Rebell makes the case in favour of interpreting such provisions as requiring the provision of meaningful educational opportunity.

HELEN HERSHKOFF & STEPHEN LOFFREDO, STATE COURTS AND CONSTITUTIONAL SOCIO-ECONOMIC RIGHTS: EXPLORING THE UNDERUTILIZATION THESIS

115 Penn State L. Rev 923, 929 (2011)

...

Positive-rights provisions in state constitutions reflect the diversity that is associated with the "states as laboratories" metaphor: they include so-called "progressive" rights that are associated in international circles with the promotion of human dignity — for example, rights to income support, to education, and to housing — as well as collective rights, such as achieving the goal of a healthy environment. But as one commentator observes, regarding state constitutional income-support provisions, "[n]o two constitutional provisions are exactly the same." In addition, some state constitutions include socio-economic provisions that are expected to run not simply against the government, but also against private actors. Commentators tend to equate the practice of extending constitutional norms to private relations — so-called "horizontality" — as a contemporary development, yet at least some of these state constitutional provisions date back to the nineteenth-century and reflect Progressive-era reforms aimed at protecting industrial workers from unfair labor practices and ensuring safe employment settings.

Socio-economic provisions play both a substantive and a structural role in state governance in the sense of defining individual rights and regulating inter-branch relations. The federal government operates under a theory of limited and enumerated powers, which confines federal action to the affirmative grants of authority in the national Constitution. By contrast, state governments build on a theory of plenary power, which presumes a background source of police power. The decision to include socio-economic provisions in a state constitution thus is understood as a mandate to the legislature that narrows the scope of political discretion. In some state constitutions, authority for carrying out particular socio-economic functions is delegated to constitutive units within the state. Finally, some positive rights in state constitutions are intended to alter the relation of the judiciary to the other branches of government, serving to expand or to contract the jurisdictional space in which courts review and assess political outputs.

…

MICHAEL A. REBELL, THE RIGHT TO COMPREHENSIVE EDUCATIONAL OPPORTUNITY

47 Harv. Civ. Rts-Civ. Liberties L. Rev 47 (2012)

…

III. The Right to Comprehensive Educational Opportunity under State Constitutional Educational Adequacy Provisions

A. General Overview of the Adequacy Litigations

Over the past thirty-five years, litigations challenging the constitutionality of state education finance systems have been filed in forty-five of the fifty states.… Overall, plaintiffs have prevailed in 60% of these state court litigations, and, in the more recent subset of "education adequacy" cases decided since 1989, plaintiffs have won twenty-two of thirty-three (67%) of the final constitutional decisions.

The … "adequacy" cases … are based on clauses in almost all of the state constitutions that guarantee all students some basic level of education, although they use different terms for doing so. The contemporary courts have, in essence, revived and given major significance to the long-dormant provisions that were originally incorporated into state constitutions as part of the common school movement of the mid-19th century.…

The state defendants in many of these cases have argued that the education clauses should be interpreted to guarantee students only a "minimal" level of education. Significantly, however, the state courts that have closely reviewed students' needs for education in contemporary society, by and large, have required the state school systems to provide substantially more than a minimum level of knowledge and skills. The cases often draw on the state's own strong commitment to standards based reforms, and essentially call upon the states to ensure that all students, including those from impoverished backgrounds, have sufficient resources to have a reasonable opportunity to meet those standards.

The courts have tended to insist that the states provide students an education that will equip them to obtain a decent job in our increasingly complex society and to carry out effectively their responsibilities as citizens in a modern democratic polity. Accordingly, many of the cases have specified that an adequate education must include, in addition to traditional reading and mathematical skills: knowledge of the physical sciences, "sufficient knowledge of economic, social and political systems to enable the student to make informed choices," "sufficient knowledge of governmental processes to enable the student to understand the issues that affect his or her community, state and nation," and "sufficient levels of academic or vocational skills to ... compete favorably ... in the job market."

One of the clearest rejections of a minimalist interpretation of a state constitution adequacy clause was the 2003 decision of the New York Court of Appeals, the state's highest court.... [I]t held that New York's schoolchildren were constitutionally entitled to the "opportunity for a meaningful high school education, one which prepares them to function productively as civic participants." ...

B. The Growing Focus on Comprehensive Services

[S]ome state courts have begun to recognize that students who come to school disadvantaged by the burdens of severe poverty need a broader set of services and resources in order to have a meaningful educational opportunity. Thus, the New Jersey Supreme Court ordered that students in the state's poorest urban districts be provided additional resources, beyond the level currently enjoyed by students in affluent suburbs, because:

> ... the ... needs of students in poorer urban districts ... go beyond educational needs; they include food, clothing and shelter, and extend to lack of close family and community ties and support, and lack of helpful role models....

In a later follow-up decision, the New Jersey Supreme Court required the state to provide low income and minority students a range of specific comprehensive services, including after-school and summer supplemental programs, school-based health and social services, and preschool services for children ages three and four.

...

QUESTIONS

1. Would the analysis and outcome in *Rodriguez* have been significantly different if the United States had been a party to the ICESCR? How and why?

2. The scholarly literature on these ESR provisions in state constitutions is relatively sparse and the decisions of state courts upholding such rights have not proven to be unusually controversial. How would you account for this, given the United States' long-standing opposition to ESR and the strong political resistance at the federal level to the right to health care?

ADDITIONAL READING

General: K. G. Young, *Constituting Economic and Social Rights* (2012); A. Ely Yamin & S. Gloppen (eds.), *Litigating Health Rights: Can Courts Bring More Justice to Health?* (2011); L. E. White & J. Perelman (eds.), *Stones of Hope: How African Activists Reclaim Human Rights to Challenge Global Poverty* (2011); V. Gauri & D. M. Brinks (eds.), *Courting Social Justice: Judicial Enforcement of Social and Economic Rights in the Developing World* (2008); M. Langford (ed.), *Social Rights Jurisprudence: Emerging Trends in International and Comparative Law* (2008); M. Tushnet, *Weak Courts, Strong Rights: Judicial Review and Social Welfare Rights in Comparative Constitutional Law* (2008) A. Nolan, *Children's Socio-Economic Rights, Democracy and the Courts* (2011); T. J. Melish, 'Maximum Feasible Participation of the Poor: New Governance, New Accountability, and a 21st Century War on the Sources of Poverty', 13 Yale H.R. & Dev. L.J. 1 (2010); Gerald Rosenberg, *The Hollow Hope: Can Courts Bring about Social Change?* (2nd edn. 2008).

South Africa: S. Liebenberg, *Socio-Economic Rights: Adjudicating Under a Transformative Constitution* (2010); S. Wilson & J. Dugard, 'Taking Poverty Seriously: The South African Constitutional Court and Socio-Economic Rights', 3 Stellenbosch L. Rev. 664 (2011); B. Ray, 'Proceduralisation's Triumph and Engagement's Promise in Socio-Economic Rights Litigation', 27 SAJHR 107 (2011); K. Klare & D. M. Davis, 'Transformative Constitutionalism and the Common & Customary Law', 26 South African J. Hum. Rts. 403 (2010).

India: L. Birchfield & J. Corsi, 'Between Starvation and Globalization: Realizing the Right to Food in India', 31 Mich. J. Int'l. L. 691 (2010); M. Khosla, 'Making Social Rights Conditional', 8 Int'l. J. Const. L. 739 (2010).

Colombia: A.E. Yamin & O. Parra-Vera, 'Judicial Protection of the Right to Health in Colombia: From Social Demands to Individual Claims to Public Debates', 33 Hastings Int'l. & Comp. L. Rev. 431 (2010); C. Rodriguez-Garavito, 'Beyond the Courtroom: The Impact of Judicial Activism on Socioeconomic Rights in Latin America', 89 Tex. L. Rev. 1669 (2011).

5

National Security, Terrorism and the Law of Armed Conflict

The intersection of national security and human rights has long troubled international law. This chapter explores the subject through the prism of counter-terrorism law and practice. In this specific domain, international legal institutions have gained considerable experience over several decades in dealing with situations involving terrorism, military insurgencies, and states of emergency. A rich body of legal rules and principles has developed in response to the interests and aspirations of various actors over time. As a result, significant insights can be drawn from past experiences, while appreciating that new threats — to security and to rights and freedoms — may require different responses than those previously adopted.

This chapter explores recent historical cases such as the response of Latin American governments to insurgencies in the late twentieth century and contemporary cases including Turkey's battle with Kurdish separatist movements and the UK and US confrontation with Al Qaeda. Each of these cases involved the resort to international tribunals, national courts or regional bodies. They accordingly raise important considerations about the distribution of interpretative and regulatory authority in times of public emergency. The selected cases also demonstrate the prospect of sweeping changes in response to modern terrorism. We have previously discussed some of these issues with respect to the law and practice of torture, see Chapter 3. The potential implications span not only civil and political rights, but also social and economic rights. This chapter explores this wider range of implications. In the world being remade after 11 September 2001, recurring questions include whether the proper balance is being struck between security and rights, and which rules and which institutions are best equipped to strike that balance. A threshold issue for such discussions, however, is the definition of terrorism itself.

A. TERRORISM AND HUMAN RIGHTS: DEFINITIONS AND RELATIONSHIPS

At the international level, states have long struggled to find a generally, if not universally, acceptable definition of terrorism. The adage that 'one person's terrorist is another person's freedom fighter' might reflect more of a political challenge than a legal or semantic challenge to achieving this goal. Competent lawyers are presumably capable of classifying specific acts as illicit under any circumstance and without regard to the motivation of fighting forces. Instead, at different points in history various states and other international actors have employed legal craft to create exceptions for their favoured political groups or ideological struggles.

Without a strong political consensus, states interested in outlawing terrorism through international treaties had to resign themselves for decades to codifying the definition and prohibition of specific acts — such as hostage taking and seizure of civilian aircraft. The UN began this piecemeal approach with the adoption of the 1963 Tokyo Convention on Offences and Certain Other Acts Committed on Board Aircraft. Eight conventions of a similar character were adopted in the 1970s and 1980s, and two more before 1999. A general definition of terrorism and a categorical outlawing of the practice remained politically elusive.

Over the latter half of the twentieth century, success on those fronts was stymied by divergent political interests. Some argued that any definition and accompanying regulatory regime ought to recognize the legitimacy of armed struggle by national liberation groups, such as the Palestine Liberation Organization and the African National Congress, and groups resisting colonial domination. In contrast, others argued that no definition of terrorism would be acceptable if it implied that attacks on civilians could be excused in the case of armed resistance or insurgencies waged for particular purposes. Another political impasse involved the regulation of 'state terrorism'. That is, some proposed definitions of terrorism faced stiff opposition because they focused on actions by non-state actors and failed to address violence that governments employed against civilians. Finally, a nagging legal question was whether crimes against humanity — a widespread or systematic attack against a civilian population — already covered significant acts of terrorism. That set of crimes, however, lacked codification and, in the view of many, it also lacked specificity.

More recently, states have taken significant steps towards a comprehensive definition of terrorism. Developments include the International Convention for the Suppression of the Financing of Terrorism, agreed to by the UN General Assembly near the close of the twentieth century. The Terrorism Financing Convention, adopted in December 1999, includes the first general definition of terrorism in an international treaty:

> Any other act intended to cause death or serious bodily injury to a civilian, or to any other person not taking an active part in the hostilities in a situation of armed conflict, when the purpose of such act, by its nature or context, is to intimidate a population, or to compel a Government or an international organization to do or to abstain from doing any act.

By mid 2001, only four states had ratified the Convention — far short of the 22 required for the treaty to enter into force. In the days following the attacks on 11 September, the Security Council called on states to become party to the Convention 'as soon as possible'. Within five years, 155 states had done so.

Another significant step towards achieving a universal definition was spurred by the Security Council. In August 2004, the government of Russia introduced

Resolution 1566 on terrorism. The previous month, Russia had experienced one of the worst hostage crises in its history. A Chechnyan armed group seized a Russian school in the town of Beslan, and the standoff ended in the deaths of over 300 civilians, most of them children. The resolution was intended, in part, to expand the work of a Security Council committee beyond its existing focus on Al Qaeda and the Taliban. The Council broke new ground with language that effectively provided a general definition of terrorism:

> The Security Council ... acting under Chapter VII ... [r]ecalls that criminal acts, including against civilians, committed with the intent to cause death or serious bodily injury, or taking of hostages, with the purpose to provoke a state of terror in the general public or in a group of persons or particular persons, intimidate a population or compel a government or an international organization to do or to abstain from doing any act, and all other acts which constitute offences within the scope of and as defined in the international conventions and protocols relating to terrorism, are under no circumstances justifiable by considerations of a political, philosophical, ideological, racial, ethnic, religious or other similar nature ....

The Security Council members adopted the resolution unanimously (Res. 1566).

These various developments, however, have not completely resolved the legal ambiguities and political controversy surrounding a definition. Upon ratifying the Terrorism Financing Convention, three states (Egypt, Jordan and Syria) submitted a reservation to the definition of terrorism. Jordan's reservation, for example, stated that its government 'does not consider acts of national armed struggle and fighting foreign occupation in the exercise of people's right to self-determination as terrorist acts within the context of paragraph 1(b) of Article 2 of the Convention.' Two dozen states formally objected to the reservation. Most of them contended that the reservation was incompatible with the object and purpose of the treaty.[1] None of the objections were made by an Islamic or African country.

Similar cleavages emerged with respect to Security Council Resolution 1566. In statements immediately before and after the Council vote, the governments of Turkey (on behalf of the 57-member Organization of the Islamic Conference), Algeria and Pakistan (both Security Council members at the time) claimed diplomatic victories. They reportedly obtained compromises during the negotiations that assured them the text would not undermine their position on liberation struggles. The resolution's definition, for example, arguably refers only to existing international conventions that outlaw specific terrorist acts. Additionally, a Security Council committee specifically targets and sanctions a list of individuals and groups associated with Al Qaeda and the Taliban. An early draft of Resolution 1566 would have added to the list individuals and groups involved in terrorist activities without an association with Al Qaeda or the Taliban. That language was dropped. 'It doesn't open any new doors', Pakistan's UN ambassador stated after passage of the resolution. 'We ought not, in our desire to confront terrorism, erode the principle of the legitimacy of national resistance that we have upheld for 50 years.'

[1] Argentina, Austria, Belgium, Canada, Czech Republic, Denmark, Estonia, Finland, France, Germany, Hungary, Ireland, Italy, Japan, Latvia, the Netherlands, Norway, Poland, Portugal, Russia, Spain, Sweden, United Kingdom, United States of America.

Given the persistent international disagreement, it may be helpful to try to understand how acts of terrorism become, expressly or tacitly, accepted by perpetrators and third parties. The discussion in Chapter 3 explored how absolute ethical proscriptions — against torture — erode under the pressure from extraordinary threats to national security. Analogously, proscriptions on attacking civilians may erode in the pursuit of certain ideological struggles, such as struggles to achieve national liberation. In *Through Our Enemies' Eyes: Osama Bin Laden, Radical Islam and the Future of America*, Michael Scheuer draws provocative comparisons between the 'idealistic' visions of Osama bin Laden, leaders of the American Revolution and the militant John Brown who helped inspire the abolitionist movement against American slavery. The goal for Scheuer, who served for 22 years in the CIA and headed the agency's Osama Bin Laden Unit, is not to justify Al Qaeda's actions, but to explain (and defeat) them. Social scientists and other experts on terrorism also discuss political and ideological objectives as a motivating force behind the resort to terrorist violence. Political scientist Martha Crenshaw, for example, has written that '[t]he first condition that can be considered a direct cause of terrorism is the existence of concrete grievances among an identifiable subgroup of a larger population, such as an ethnic minority discriminated against by the majority.'

A particular form of terrorism — suicidal terrorism — may provide special insights into socio-political or other conditions that give rise to extreme acts of violence. Suicidal terrorism, indeed, requires the suspension of profound moral and psychological constraints. It often depends upon a broader social system to encourage individuals to end their own lives and disregard or dehumanize the lives of civilians. In his book, *Dying to Win: The Strategic Logic of Suicidal Terrorism*, political scientist Robert Pape concludes that historical and contemporary cases demonstrate that the perceived foreign occupation of a group's homeland is a strong motivating factor for such extreme cases of terrorism. Pape considers not only the logic of individual terrorists and terrorist organizations; he also explores the support of the broader social community that is needed to sustain such campaigns. For terrorism more generally, the international political environment may also be shaped by such 'root causes' including the perceived legitimacy of the purpose of the struggle. That sense of legitimacy may involve not only quests for self-determination, which Pape emphasizes, but also quests for the primacy of a particular vision of society and the extermination of others. Indeed, other experts such as professor of political psychology and international affairs Jerrold Post argue that the primary determinants of terrorism are psychological and are reflected in the polarizing, intolerant and absolutist visions of terrorist group members.

These various explanations naturally do not exhaust theories of terrorism. Nevertheless, they help one to begin to appreciate the background against which human rights institutions must operate in addressing the scourge of terrorism — often adopted in the name of self-determination — and excessive governmental actions and reactions — often adopted in the name of self-defence. Exploring the possible explanations for terrorism may also help to understand why international political cleavages have impeded a universal definition and efforts at international cooperation.

While (and perhaps because) the international rules remain unsettled, national legal conceptions of terrorism vary significantly. Not only do diverse definitions of terrorism exist across nations, but even within a single state the domestic legal order may include multiple formulations. The definition of terrorism in the criminal code might be one among many. Different definitions of terrorism may be found in provisions for civil law suits, grounds for immigration exclusion and deportation, and standards for regulating nonprofit and charitable organizations. There may be logistical or administrative reasons to employ definitions of different scope in each of these domains. Maintaining vague or excessively broad definitions to control individuals' behaviour, however, raises rights-related concerns. The Inter-American Commission on Human Rights examined problems with vague statutes in the context of fair trial rights:

> 261 . . . [M]ost fundamental fair trial requirements cannot justifiably be suspended under either international human rights law or international humanitarian law. These protections therefore apply to the investigation, prosecution and punishment of crimes, including those relating to terrorism, regardless of whether such initiatives may be taken in time of peace or times of national emergency, including armed conflict, and include the following:
>
> (a) The right to respect for fundamental principles of criminal law, including the *non-bis-in-idem* principle, the *nullum crimen sine lege* and *nulla poena sine lege* principles, the presumption of innocence, and the right not to be convicted of an offense except on the basis of individual penal responsibility. Of particular pertinence in the context of terrorism, these principles demand that any laws that purport to proscribe conduct relating to terrorism be classified and described in precise and unambiguous language that narrowly defines the punishable offense, and accordingly require a clear definition of the criminalized conduct establishing its elements and the factors that distinguish it from behaviors that are not punishable or involve distinct forms of punishment. Ambiguities in laws proscribing terrorism not only undermine the propriety of criminal processes that enforce those laws, but may also have serious implications beyond criminal liability and punishment, such as the denial of refugee status.
>
> As indicated above, the Commission and the Court have previously found certain domestic anti-terrorism laws to violate the principle of legality because, for example, they have attempted to prescribe a comprehensive definition of terrorism that is inexorably overbroad and imprecise. . . .[2]

Concerns about vagueness relate not only to the definition of terrorism but also to the scope of direct and indirect responsibility ascribed to individuals and organizations. Resolution 1566, for example, also includes language calling on states to 'find, deny safe haven and bring to justice . . . any person who supports, facilitates, participates or attempts to participate in the financing, planning, preparation or commission of terrorist acts or provides safe havens.' Amnesty International criticized this construction on the grounds that the

> language casts the net so wide that people, including human rights advocates or peaceful political activists can easily and unintentionally fall victim to the measures

[2] Report on Terrorism and Human Rights, Inter-American Commission on Human Rights, 22 Oct. 2002, available at www.cidh.org/Terrorism/Eng/toc.htm.

advocated in the resolution. The resolution does not even require that acts contributing to 'terrorists acts' [sic], such as unknowingly providing lodging, have to be intentional or done with the knowledge that they will assist the crime. In resorting to such exceptionally broad language, the resolution would call for measures which do not even permit individuals to foresee whether their acts will be lawful or not, a basic requirement in criminal law....

B. 11 SEPTEMBER 2001: A TURNING POINT

The attacks on 11 September 2001 constituted a turning point in the relationships between international law, global institutions and terrorism. Why (and how much) did 11 September change the international legal and political landscape?

It was one of the deadliest days in American history, totalling more deaths — nearly 3,000 — than the attack on Pearl Harbor and rivalling, if not exceeding, the number of Americans killed on D-Day. Nineteen members of Al Qaeda hijacked four commercial jets, two of which crashed into the 110-story twin towers of the World Trade Center, one into the Pentagon and one in a field in Pennsylvania. Almost two hours passed between the first collision and the collapse of the second WTC tower, with the loss of life and panic televised around the world as the events unfolded. The near simultaneous attacks exposed major vulnerabilities in the security system of the world's superpower. Al Qaeda cells had resided within US territory. They had converted commercial transportation into catastrophic weapons. Their members' willingness to embrace (if not glory in) suicide represented a unique strategic threat, one less susceptible to traditional modes of deterrence. With the demonstrated willingness of Al Qaeda to massacre thousands of people, intelligence agencies in the United States and elsewhere began considering with special intensity the prospect of a terrorist organization acquiring and employing weapons of mass destruction.

International institutions responded in a swift and extraordinary manner. In a resolution passed on 12 September, the UN Security Council determined that the attacks constituted a 'threat to international peace and security' and also recognized the 'inherent right of individual or collective self-defence in accordance with the Charter' (Res. 1368). Accordingly, the resolution implicitly recognized that the acts of 11 September constituted an 'armed attack' under Article 51 of the UN Charter. Although the United States and other countries had experienced and responded to terrorist attacks with force in the past, the Council had never before issued such a finding. Also unprecedented, both the North Atlantic Treaty Organization and the Organization of American States formally considered 11 September an 'armed attack' and invoked the collective self-defence provisions of their respective treaties.

In late September, the Security Council, acting under its binding Chapter VII powers, required all states to take financial, penal and other regulatory measures against individuals and organizations involved in terrorist activities (Res. 1373). The Council also established the Counter-Terrorism Committee (CTC) to monitor implementation of the resolution. José Alvarez describes the special significance of the CTC:

> To date [the CTC] has received hundreds of reports from the UN's members purporting to explain how each has implemented the Council's edicts within their domestic law and practice.... In . . . prior instances, it could readily be assumed that the Council's enforcement action would cease when such specific situations were resolved. Resolution 1373, by contrast, has no express or implied time or geographic limitations. It is the closest thing we have in international institutional law to real 'law-making' as some define it. This is action that is binding, backed by the possibility of real coercive sanction, affecting all relevant actors, and capable of repeated application across time in comparable instances.[3]

The CTC has been criticized for not considering whether governmental actions reported to it or adopted pursuant to the Council's dictates comply with international human rights obligations. Indeed, one of the main concerns about the CTC has been the lack of safeguards in listing and de-listing individuals and organizations for targeted sanctions. The first Chair of the CTC expressed the Committee's policy in a briefing to the Security Council:

> Monitoring performance against other international conventions, including human rights law, is outside the scope of the Counter-Terrorism Committee's mandate. But we will remain aware of the interaction with human rights concerns, and we will keep ourselves briefed as appropriate. It is, of course, open to other organizations to study States' reports and take up their content in other forums.

In 2004, however, the Council adopted resolutions '[r]eminding States that they must ensure that any measures taken to combat terrorism comply with all their obligations under international law, and should adopt such measures in accordance with international law, in particular international human rights, refugee, and humanitarian law' (Res. 1535 and 1566). In a 'policy guidance' adopted in mid 2006, the CTC instructed its Executive Directorate to liaise with the Office of the High Commissioner for Human Rights and to 'advise the CTC on how to ensure that any measures States take to implement the provisions of [Security Council anti-terrorism mandates] comply with their obligations under international law, in particular international human rights law, refugee law, and humanitarian law'. One of the most recent reforms is the creation of an Office of the Ombudsperson (Res. 1904). Established in December 2009, this body can receive petitions directly from individuals and organizations that wish to challenge their designation and request removal from the Council's list of members and associates of terrorist organizations.

These reforms resulted in part from human rights concerns that had been raised by powerful actors. In 2008, a landmark decision by the European Court of Justice — *Kadi & Al Barakaat International Foundation v. Council and Commission* — annulled the implementation of the CTC's asset-freezing mandates on the ground that they violated the right to a fair process and property rights. The Human Rights Committee also concluded, in 2008, that Belgium violated its obligations under the Covenant on Civil and Political Rights by transmitting an individual's name to the CTC (*Vinck v. Belgium*, Comm. No. 1472/2006). That said, the reforms have not

[3] José E. Alvarez, *International Organizations as Law-Makers* (2005), 196–7.

satisfied many of the critics of the CTC. For example, in 2010, the lower body of the European Court of Justice — the General Court of the European Union — stated that these reforms remained inadequate. The Court stated:

> In essence, the Security Council has still not deemed it appropriate to establish an independent and impartial body responsible for hearing and determining, as regards matters of law and fact, actions against individual decisions taken by the Sanctions Committee. Furthermore, [none of the reforms] affects the principle that removal of a person from the Sanctions Committee's list requires consensus within the committee. Moreover, the evidence which may be disclosed to the person concerned continues to be a matter entirely at the discretion of the State which proposed that he be included on the Sanctions Committee's list and there is no mechanism to ensure that sufficient information be made available to the person concerned in order to allow him to defend himself effectively. . . .

The Security Council's strong push for states to combat terrorism may have also contributed to two trends across states. First, as some commentators argue, the actions of the Security Council have encouraged repressive states to exploit anti-terrorism discourse. As one commentator explains:

> Some States have deployed the international legitimacy conferred by Council authorization to define terrorism to repress or de-legitimize political opponents, and to conflate them with Al-Qaeda. Thus, China bluntly characterizes Uighur separatists in Xinjiang as terrorists; Russia asserts that Chechen rebels are terrorists, even though many are fighting in an internal conflict; and India seldom distinguishes militants from terrorists in Kashmir. In Indonesia, insurgencies in Aceh and West Papua have been described and combated as terrorism, as have a Maoist insurgency in Nepal and an Islamist movement in Morocco. Predictably, Israel has identified Palestinians with Al-Qaeda, with Ariel Sharon calling Arafat 'our Bin Laden'.[4]

After 11 September, the organization Human Rights Watch stated that 'many countries around the globe cynically attempted to take advantage of this struggle to intensify their own crackdowns on political opponents, separatists and religious groups, or to suggest they should be immune from criticism of their human rights practices.' A catalogue of such practices can be found on the organization's website.[5]

Second, the Security Council's actions, along with legislation adopted by especially influential countries, have propelled a cascade of standardized counter-terrorism laws. These laws often have similar structural features despite varying conditions within countries. Professor Kent Roach argues that, as a result, counter-terrorism legislation in a given country may not be tailored to combat security threats efficiently or to do so with human rights safeguards suited to the particular political context:

[4] B. Saul, 'Definition of "Terrorism" in the UN Security Council: 1985–2004', 4 Chinese J. Int'l L. 141 (2005).

[5] Human Rights Watch, 'Opportunism in the Face of Tragedy: Repression in the name of anti-terrorism', at www.hrw.org/campaigns/september11/opportunismwatch.htm.

> In the five years since the terrorist attacks on the United States, a staggering array of new anti-terrorism laws have been enacted throughout the world.... [I]nternational and domestic organizations often draft anti-terrorism initiatives on the fly, engaging in bricolage with what is at hand, but with limited information about the effects of various measures on security or human rights. The sources and process used to make anti-terrorism laws can reveal much about their substance. In particular, it can expose the contingent, questionable but not easily reversed choices that have been made with respect to both security and human rights.
>
> ... [T]hree influential sources for the anti-terrorism laws [are] found in a number of jurisdictions including Australia, Canada, South Africa, the United Kingdom and the United States. It is possible to focus on only a few sources in part because there has been a faddish aspect to post 9/11 anti-terrorism laws with a number of countries following trends established by a small number of influential international and domestic instruments.
>
> ...
>
> ... Many countries have followed the lead of the Security Council and used immigration law as anti-terrorism law. This has had adverse effects on various human rights because immigration proceedings typically offer less procedural protections for detainees than criminal proceedings and because a number of countries are re-evaluating the right not to be deported to torture. The focus on immigration law also has had adverse effects on security as it has encouraged some western states to focus anti-terrorism efforts on non-citizens even though, as the London bombings tragically confirm, citizens can also commit acts of terrorism.
>
> ... There is a need for continued critical evaluation of broad definitions of terrorism on both human rights and security. There is a danger that broad definitions of terrorism could facilitate the targeting of extremists in domestic protest movements as opposed to those who identify with al Qaeda. Broad definitions of terrorism could have adverse effects on security, as well as human rights, if they result in a misallocation of limited law enforcement and security intelligence resources.[6]

In assessing these accounts of post-11 September legislation, one should also consider the baseline against which these changes occurred. For example, do you think the *actions* of opportunistic states changed after 11 September or just their rhetoric? Does the international discourse surrounding terrorism mean that states will engage in a level of rights violations that they would otherwise refrain from committing? Separately, Professor Roach identifies inefficiencies in anti-terrorism legislation adopted around the world. Without the international impetus to enact counter-terrorism legislation, however, there might have been an 'undersupply' of laws focusing on this transnational security threat. Is it not better for more countries to adopt counterterrorism laws with some inefficiency than for them to adopt none at all? Finally, what motivates countries to adopt, in Professor Roach's words, 'faddish' counter-terrorism legislation? If all these accounts of the pitfalls and problems with the global spread of counter-terrorism law are accurate, what measures should be taken to counteract the negative effects while preserving the positive aspects?

[6] K. Roach, 'Sources and Trends in Post 9/11 Anti-Terrorism Laws', in B. Goold and L. Lazarus (eds.), *Security and Human Rights* (2007).

Finally, 11 September also represented a turning point in the strategic approach of the United States to terrorism and Al Qaeda in particular. The Bush Administration proclaimed a 'Global War on Terrorism' and, in more technical legal terms, contended that the United States was in an 'armed conflict' with Al Qaeda and its affiliates. This strategic posture entailed the adoption of a 'war model' in dealing with terrorism in contrast with an exclusively 'criminal law model'. A war model employs the instruments of warfare such as armed interventions, armed forces and military violence. A criminal law model employs the instruments of law enforcement, policing and prosecutions.

Choosing to adopt a war model may have a greater effect on political discourse and psychological frames than on rights and obligations under international human rights law. As will be discussed shortly, international human rights law adjusts state obligations regardless of whether a public emergency is designated a war or another type of threat to public order and national security. The nature of the threat — its gravity and probability — is the critical variable. That said, domestic legal questions, such as constitutional presidential powers, may turn on the classification of a situation as a war or something else. Furthermore, as discussed at length below, the existence of an armed conflict triggers the application of international humanitarian law (IHL). Whether IHL supplements, displaces or discounts human rights law raises a host of interesting and important questions.

QUESTIONS

1. Consider for the purpose of discussion the following statement:

[W]hether the global war on terrorism is truly a war is difficult to answer. On balance, the answer is affirmative. At the most abstract level, it is best understood as a politico-moral campaign against the abhorrent practice of targeting innocents for certain strategic ends. In this sense, the fight against terrorism is a war akin to the great campaigns against piracy and slavery earlier. All these struggles . . . involved military, diplomatic, economic, and ideological instruments of warfare. The current battle against terrorism, therefore, has a long and distinguished lineage. Viewed in this perspective, it is indeed appropriate . . . to conceive of the current struggle as a war against terrorism itself — terrorism now understood not as some abstract Platonic form that cannot be defeated at a world-historical level, but as an inhumane political practice that can be targeted and, more importantly, delegitimized, even if it cannot be totally eradicated. Given this objective, President Bush has been right all along: terrorism is, and ought to be, an unacceptable instrumentality because it sacrifices innocent life in the service of some political vision that, no matter how attractive or justifiable, subordinates means to ends and, accordingly, paves the way for a tyranny that obliterates the respect for persons that lies at the center of every good political order.[7]

[7] Ashley J. Tellis, 'Assessing America's War on Terror: Confronting Insurgency, Cementing Primacy', 15 NBR Analysis [National Bureau of Asian Research], no. 4, Dec. 2004, available at www.carnegieendowment.org/files/NBRAnalysis-Tellis_December2004.pdf.

2. Consider broader ramifications of the relationship between terrorism and human rights law beyond national security. The issue whether existing international law — including crimes against humanity — prohibits terrorism and the insistence that states bring terrorists to justice lends insights into the content of human rights law more generally. A fundamental issue is whether terrorism constitutes a human rights violation, and, if so, what legal consequences follow for state and non-state actors. As we explore in other chapters, some international human rights obligations may apply directly to non-state actors. Some obligations may also apply indirectly to non-state actors such that states have international duties to prevent private actors from interfering with individuals' rights. Terrorism obviously implicates the right to be free from the arbitrary deprivation of life. Several of the readings in this chapter accordingly refer to a state's obligation to combat terrorism. Does a deep understanding of such obligations in the context of terrorism inform prevailing notions of state responsibility for human rights protection more broadly? If one accepts the premise that states have a duty to combat terrorist threats to their citizenry, does it follow that states have similar obligations to prevent and redress violence against women, malnutrition, natural disasters, infectious disease? Has the law developed to confront terrorism but not these other cases, and, if so, why the imbalance?

ADDITIONAL READING

K. T. Huber & A. Rodiles, 'An Ombudsperson in the United Nations Security Council: A Paradigm Shift?', X Aniversario Anuario Mexicano de Derecho Internacional 107–42 (2012); G. de Búrca, 'The European Court of Justice and the International Legal Order After *Kadi*', 51 Harv. Int'l. L. J. 1 (2010); I. Johnstone, 'Legislation and Adjudication in the UN Security Council: Bringing Down the Deliberative Deficit', 102 Am. J. Int'l. L. 102 (2008); C. True-Frost, 'The Development of Individual Standing in International Security', 32 Cardozo L. Rev. 1183 (2011); K. Roach, 'The Post 9/11 Migration of Britain's Terrorism Act, 2000', in S. Choudhry (ed.), *The Migration of Constitutional Ideas* (2007); K. L. Scheppele, 'The Migration of Anti-Constitutional Ideas: The Post-9/11 Globalization of Public Law and the International State of Emergency', in S. Choudhry (ed.), *The Migration of Constitutional Ideas* (2007); C. A. MacKinnon, 'Women's September 11th: Rethinking the International Law of Conflict', 47 Harv. Int. L.J. 1 (2006); D. Jinks, 'September 11 and the Laws of War', 28 Yale J. Int'l. L. 1 (2003); D. Jinks, 'State Responsibility for the Acts of Private Armed Groups', 4 Chicago J. Int'l. L. 83 (2003); D. PoKempner, 'Terrorism and Human Rights: The Legal Framework', in M. Schmitt & G. L. Beruto (eds.), *Terrorism and International Law* (2003); A. P. Schmid & A. J. Jongman, *Political Terrorism: A New Guide to Actors, Authors, Concepts, Data Bases, Theories, and Literature* (1988).

C. THE LEGAL FRAMEWORK: PUBLIC EMERGENCIES, DEROGATIONS AND THE LAW OF ARMED CONFLICT

International law permits states to limit or suspend part of their legal obligations, and thus restrict some rights, under certain circumstances. To that end, the legal recourse available to states includes limitation clauses (discussed in the context of civil and political rights in Chapter 3 and economic, social and cultural rights in Chapter 4) and derogations systems codified in various treaties or available through norms of customary international law.

Limitation and derogation clauses in treaties have a similar function in the sense that both provide legal avenues for states to break free of obligations that would ordinarily constrain their actions. They are also similar in that neither permits states to ignore their human rights obligations altogether. However, one significant difference between the two is that derogations were designed to be applicable only in the exceptional case of a grave threat to the survival and security of a nation. The implication is that derogations were intended to be invoked as temporary measures. In contrast, limitation clauses apply across the spectrum, from everyday public order maintenance and policing strategies to national security and large-scale military actions.

In human rights instruments, limitation clauses are commonplace. The UDHR, as discussed in Chapter 3, contains a general limitation clause in Article 29. The ICESCR contains a general limitation clause in Article 4. It permits state parties to subject the rights contained in the Covenant 'only to such limitations as are determined by law only in so far as this may be compatible with the nature of these rights and solely for the purpose of promoting the general welfare.' The ICCPR, by contrast, does not contain a general limitation clause. Instead, limitation clauses are included in various rights provisions such as those pertaining to freedom of association (Art. 22), freedom of movement (Art. 12), expulsion of foreign nationals (Art. 13) and access of the press and public to criminal trials (Art. 14). Several provisions in the ICCPR, such as those prohibiting torture (Art. 7) and slavery (Art. 8), are subject to no limitation.

Article 4 of the ICCPR codifies the rules for states to derogate from obligations during a state of emergency. Specific conditions are attached to a state's exercise of this option. For example, governmental measures must generally be prescribed and determined by law, shown to be necessary and designed to protect particular public interests. These conditions and associated rules perform multiple functions. Most obviously, they are designed to strike a balance between security and human rights. In important respects, they are also designed to avoid balancing or, rather, do more than just balance. Some of the rules, for example, preclude any relaxation of obligations with respect to core rights. The prohibition on genocide is a prime example. The categorical prohibition on genocidal acts is subject to no qualification. In addition to balancing competing interests, the rules are also designed to ensure that governments do not restrict rights that have no rational or reasoned connection to meeting national concerns during a time of emergency.

The following readings examine the derogation system in contrast with the protections (and limitations) that ordinarily apply.

JOAN FITZPATRICK, HUMAN RIGHTS IN CRISIS: THE INTERNATIONAL SYSTEM FOR PROTECTING RIGHTS DURING STATES OF EMERGENCY

(1994)

Approaching [the law on derogations] chronologically, the first legally significant standard is Article 3 common to the four Geneva Conventions of 1949, also known as "Common Article 3." Applicable during periods of internal armed conflict, a frequent setting for the invocation of emergency powers in the past several decades, Common Article 3 prescribes a set of minimal protections that must be afforded even under these dire circumstances. The guarantees of Common Article 3 are further elaborated in Articles 4 to 6 of Protocol II [to the Geneva Conventions, adopted in 1977], particularly with respect to non-derogable fair trial standards. Indeed, the entire body of international humanitarian law, both customary and codified, is highly relevant to protection of human rights during states of emergency, especially in defining non-derogable rights. International humanitarian law by nature is designed to apply in full force during the subset of emergencies involving armed conflict, so in a sense it is all emergency law. And because situations of armed conflict tend to be among the direst of emergencies, protections available then should logically be available in any other emergency context.

Two crucial sets of treaty standards were also drafted at approximately the same time as Common Article 3. Article 15 of the European Convention was drafted primarily during early 1950 with the benefit of almost three years of discussion by drafters of the Covenant on Civil and Political Rights within the United Nations. The derogation article of the European Convention served as a focal point for the debate between two alternate approaches to treaty drafting, which might be called "general enumeration" and "precise definition." The proponents of general enumeration favored drafting a document with positive definitions of rights and no exceptions or restrictions other than a single general limitations clause, similar to Article 29 of the Universal Declaration. The proponents of precise definition, on the other hand, wanted not only specific limitations clauses in many provisions defining particular rights but also a derogation article for emergencies, arguing that these clauses would actually prevent abusive suspension or denial of rights. During the final stages of the drafting process, the attraction of entrenching a list of nonderogable rights swayed a majority to favor inclusion of the derogation article.

Whereas the drafting of the Covenant on Civil and Political Rights dragged on until 1966, debate on the advisability and specific terms of a derogation article occurred during the relatively compressed period between 1947 and 1952. Article 4 became the focus of the division of opinion between the general-enumeration and precise-definition camps, as had Article 15 in the case of the European Convention.

Another key division, leading to an awkward compromise, developed on the question whether the clause on non-derogable rights should include only those rights most important and central to human dignity and most at risk during typical emergencies, or should be expanded to include all rights that no reasonable government would need to limit substantially in any conceivable emergency.

The drafters of the American Convention on Human Rights, who began work in earnest in the 1960s, had the benefit of earlier-drafted human rights treaties as a model and began with an apparent consensus on the precise-definition approach .... The special interest developed within the OAS on protecting human rights during states of emergency may help explain the rather different form the derogation article takes in the American Convention, as compared to those in the European Convention and the Covenant.

A brief comparison of the three derogation articles in the human rights treaties to the relevant portions of the major humanitarian law instruments reveals some interesting similarities and differences, as well as "lacunae," that have attracted ongoing efforts to formulate additional, more complete standards. Discussion will be limited to the substantive aspects of these emergency provisions....

...

Along with the threshold of severity, the principle of proportionality is the most important and yet most elusive of the substantive limits imposed on the privilege of derogation.... The principle of proportionality embodied in the derogation clauses has its roots in the principle of necessity, which also forms one of the key pillars of international humanitarian law. The existence of competent active, and informed organs of supervision, both at the national as well as at the international level, is vital if the proportionality principle is to have meaning in practice. As the ensuing chapters will demonstrate both logistical (access to information and ability to act promptly) and attitudinal (deference to national authorities, e.g., by extension of a "margin of appreciation") factors affect the functioning of the various treaty implementation organs.

The Covenant and the American Convention include clauses specifying that derogation measures may not be imposed in a manner that discriminates on the grounds of race, color, sex, language, religion, or social origin....

Article 15 of the European Convention is silent on the issue of discrimination in the application of emergency measures.... The issue of discriminatory treatment of minorities in the application of emergency measures was touched on during the drafting of the European Convention, but it never achieved prominence in the discussions, and no concrete proposals for a nondiscrimination clause were made. Nevertheless, arbitrary discrimination against disfavored groups of various types would be difficult to justify as being "strictly required." Thus, there may be no substantive difference between the silence of the European Convention and the explicit non-discrimination clauses of the other two treaties, if only arbitrary distinctions are outlawed by the latter.

Draft non-discrimination provisos to the Covenant's derogation article were proposed by the United States (in 1948) and by France (in 1949), but adding the element of non-discrimination was not easily accomplished. The Commission on Human Rights voted in May 1950 on the basis of an oral amendment during debate to add Article 20, the non-discrimination article to the list of non-derogable rights in Article 4. Objections were immediately raised that disparate treatment of enemy aliens would be necessary during wartime, and the decision was reversed the following day. A way around this impasse was found in 1952 when a non-discrimination clause not including the classification of national origin was added to the draft derogation article.

The idea that only arbitrary discrimination is outlawed by Article 4(1) is underlined by the deliberate inclusion of the word "solely" in its text.[8] Even without this term, however, the reference to discrimination in Article 4 conveys the implication that only arbitrary and unjustifiable distinctions in the application of emergency measures would be outlawed. Thus, where an identifiable racial or religious group poses a distinct security threat not posed by other members of the community, presumably, emergency measures could be deliberately targeted against the group, despite the non-discrimination clause.

The absence of the word "solely" from the non-discrimination clause in Article 27(1) of the American Convention on Human Rights apparently has no intended significance. The word was included in the draft prepared by the IACHR but "disappeared from the final text, and the records of the conference provide no clue as to the reason." Thus, the three treaties would seem to impose a virtually identical nondiscrimination obligation, despite disparate phraseology.

The three treaties diverge dramatically with respect to defining absolute rights never subject to suspension. The process of defining non-derogable rights has been a markedly progressive one, with each later drafted instrument expanding the core of non-derogable rights. The European Convention begins with just four, sparely defined: the right to life, excepting deaths resulting from lawful acts of war (Article 2); the ban on torture or inhuman or degrading treatment or punishment (Article 3); the prohibition on slavery or servitude (Article 4(1)); and the prohibition on retroactive criminal penalties (Article 7).

HUMAN RIGHTS COMMITTEE, STATES OF EMERGENCY, GENERAL COMMENT 29 (ON ARTICLE 4)

(24 July 2001)

1. ... The restoration of a state of normalcy where full respect for the Covenant can again be secured must be the predominant objective of a State party derogating from the Covenant....

2. ... Before a state moves to invoke Article 4, two fundamental conditions must be met: the situation must amount to a public emergency that threatens the life of the nation, and the state party must have officially proclaimed a state of emergency.

[8] A separate vote was taken on the UK proposal to frame the clause in terms of discrimination 'solely' on one of the forbidden grounds. Support of the inclusion of 'solely' was premised on the notion that wartime measures aimed at a particular nationality, for example, might predominantly affect persons of a particular race without being race-based.

The latter requirement is essential for the maintenance of the principles of legality and rule of law at times when they are most needed. When proclaiming a state of emergency with consequences that could entail derogation from any provision of the Covenant, States must act within their constitutional and other provisions of law that govern such proclamation and the exercise of emergency powers; it is the task of the Committee to monitor the laws in question with respect to whether they enable and secure compliance with Article 4. In order that the Committee can perform its task, States parties to the Covenant should include in their reports submitted under Article 40 sufficient and precise information about their law and practice in the field of emergency powers.

3. Not every disturbance or catastrophe qualifies as a public emergency which threatens the life of the nation.... If States parties consider invoking Article 4 in other situations than an armed conflict, they should carefully consider the justification and why such a measure is necessary and legitimate in the circumstances. On a number of occasions the Committee has expressed its concern over States parties that appear to have derogated from rights protected by the Covenant, or whose domestic law appears to allow such derogation in situations not covered by Article 4. [The Committee cites to situations in Tanzania, the Dominican Republic, the United Kingdom, Peru, Bolivia, Colombia, Lebanon, Uruguay and Israel.]

4. ... [The requirement that derogation measures are limited to the extent strictly required by the exigencies of the situation] relates to the duration, geographical coverage and material scope of the state of emergency and any measures of derogation resorted to because of the emergency. Derogation from some Covenant obligations in emergency situations is clearly distinct from restrictions or limitations allowed even in normal times under several provisions of the Covenant. Nevertheless, the obligation to limit any derogations to those strictly required by the exigencies of the situation reflects the principle of proportionality which is common to derogation and limitation powers. Moreover, the mere fact that a permissible derogation from a specific provision may, of itself, be justified by the exigencies of the situation does not obviate the requirement that specific measures taken pursuant to the derogation must also be shown to be required by the exigencies of the situation. In practice, this will ensure that no provision of the Covenant, however validly derogated from will be entirely inapplicable to the behaviour of a State party....

5. The issues of when rights can be derogated from, and to what extent, cannot be separated from the provision in Article 4, paragraph 1, of the Covenant according to which any measures derogating from a State party's obligations under the Covenant must be limited 'to the extent strictly required by the exigencies of the situation'. This condition requires that States parties provide careful justification not only for their decision to proclaim a state of emergency but also for any specific measures based on such a proclamation. If States purport to invoke the right to derogate from the Covenant during, for instance, a natural catastrophe, a mass demonstration including instances of violence, or a major industrial accident, they must be able to justify not only that such a situation constitutes a threat to the life of the nation, but also that all their measures derogating from the Covenant are strictly required by the exigencies of the situation. In the opinion of the Committee, the possibility of restricting certain Covenant rights under the terms of, for instance,

freedom of movement (Article 12) or freedom of assembly (Article 21) is generally sufficient during such situations and no derogation from the provisions in question would be justified by the exigencies of the situation.

...

7. ... Conceptually, the qualification of a Covenant provision as a non-derogable one does not mean that no limitations or restrictions would ever be justified. The reference in Article 4, paragraph 2, to Article 18, a provision that includes a specific clause on restrictions in its paragraph 3, demonstrates that the permissibility of restrictions is independent of the issue of derogability. Even in times of most serious public emergencies, States that interfere with the freedom to manifest one's religion or belief must justify their actions by referring to the requirements specified in Article 18, paragraph 3....

8. According to Article 4, paragraph 1, one of the conditions for the justifiability of any derogation from the Covenant is that the measures taken do not involve discrimination solely on the ground of race, colour, sex, language, religion or social origin. Even though Article 26 or the other Covenant provisions related to nondiscrimination (Articles 2, 3, 14, paragraph 1, 23, paragraph 4, 24, paragraph 1, and 25) have not been listed among the non-derogable provisions in Article 4, paragraph 2, there are elements or dimensions of the right to non-discrimination that cannot be derogated from in any circumstances.

...

10. Although it is not the function of the Human Rights Committee to review the conduct of a State party under other treaties, in exercising its functions under the Covenant the Committee has the competence to take a State party's other international obligations into account when it considers whether the Covenant allows the State party to derogate from specific provisions of the Covenant. Therefore, when invoking Article 4, paragraph 1, or when reporting under Article 40 on the legal framework related to emergencies, States parties should present information on their other international obligations relevant for the protection of the rights in question, in particular those obligations that are applicable in times of emergency. In this respect, States parties should duly take into account the developments within international law as to human rights standards applicable in emergency situations.[9]

...

12. In assessing the scope of legitimate derogation from the Covenant, one criterion can be found in the definition of certain human rights violations as crimes against humanity. If action conducted under the authority of a State constitutes a basis for individual criminal responsibility for a crime against humanity by the persons involved in that action, Article 4 of the Covenant cannot be used as justification that a state of emergency exempted the State in question from its responsibility in relation to the same conduct. Therefore, the recent codification of crimes against

[9] [Eds.: In a footnote, the Committee refers to UN and other international initiatives involving the identification of fundamental standards of humanity applicable in all circumstances, and the report of the International Committee of the Red Cross on customary international humanitarian law.]

humanity, for jurisdictional purposes, in the Rome Statute of the International Criminal Court is of relevance in the interpretation of Article 4 of the Covenant.[10]

13. In those provisions of the Covenant that are not listed in Article 4, paragraph 2, there are elements that in the Committee's opinion cannot be made subject to lawful derogation under Article 4. Some illustrative examples are presented below.

(a) All persons deprived of their liberty shall be treated with humanity and with respect for the inherent dignity of the human person…a norm of general international law not subject to derogation.…
(b) The prohibitions against taking of hostages, abductions or unacknowledged detention . . . justified by their status as norms of general international law.
(c) …[T]he rights of persons belonging to minorities includes elements that must be respected in all circumstances.…
(d) … [D]eportation or forcible transfer of population without grounds permitted under international law.…
(e) No declaration . . . may be invoked as justification for a State party to engage itself, contrary to Article 20, in propaganda for war, or in advocacy of national, racial or religious hatred that would constitute incitement to discrimination, hostility or violence.

14. Article 2, paragraph 3, of the Covenant requires a State party to the Covenant to provide remedies for any violation of the provisions of the Covenant. This clause is not mentioned in the list of non-derogable provisions in Article 4, paragraph 2, but it constitutes a treaty obligation inherent in the Covenant as a whole. Even if a State party, during a state of emergency, and to the extent that such measures are strictly required by the exigencies of the situation, may introduce adjustments to the practical functioning of its procedures governing judicial or other remedies, the State party must comply with the fundamental obligation, under Article 2, paragraph 3, of the Covenant to provide a remedy that is effective.

15. It is inherent in the protection of rights explicitly recognized as non-derogable in Article 4, paragraph 2, that they must be secured by procedural guarantees, including, often, judicial guarantees. The provisions of the Covenant relating to procedural safeguards may never be made subject to measures that would circumvent the protection of non-derogable rights. Article 4 may not be resorted to in a way that would result in derogation from non-derogable rights. Thus, for example, as Article 6 of the Covenant is non-derogable in its entirety, any trial leading to the imposition of the death penalty during a state of emergency must conform to the provisions of the Covenant, including all the requirements of Articles 14 and 15.

16. Safeguards related to derogation, as embodied in Article 4 of the Covenant, are based on the principles of legality and the rule of law inherent in the Covenant

[10] [T]he category of crimes against humanity as defined in [the Rome Statute] covers . . . violations of some provisions of the Covenant that have not been mentioned in the said provision of the Covenant. For example, certain grave violations of Article 27 may at the same time constitute genocide under Article 6 [genocide] of the Rome Statute, and Article 7 [crimes against humanity], in turn, covers practices that are related to, besides Articles 6, 7 and 8 of the [ICCPR], also Articles 9, 12, 26 and 27.

as a whole. As certain elements of the right to a fair trial are explicitly guaranteed under international humanitarian law during armed conflict, the Committee finds no justification for derogation from these guarantees during other emergency situations. The Committee is of the opinion that the principles of legality and the rule of law require that fundamental requirements of fair trial must be respected during a state of emergency. Only a court of law may try and convict a person for a criminal offence. The presumption of innocence must be respected. In order to protect non-derogable rights, the right to take proceedings before a court to enable the court to decide without delay on the lawfulness of detention, must not be diminished by a State party's decision to derogate from the Covenant.[11]

17. In paragraph 3 of Article 4 . . . [s]uch notification is essential not only for the discharge of the Committee's functions, in particular in assessing whether the measures taken by the State party were strictly required by the exigencies of the situation, but also to permit other States parties to monitor compliance with the provisions of the Covenant. . . . Sometimes, the existence of a state of emergency and the question of whether a State party has derogated from provisions of the Covenant have come to the attention of the Committee only incidentally, in the course of the consideration of a State party's report. The Committee emphasizes the obligation of immediate international notification whenever a State party takes measures derogating from its obligations under the Covenant. The duty of the Committee to monitor the law and practice of a State party for compliance with Article 4 does not depend on whether that State party has submitted a notification.

NOTE

If the ICCPR contained no derogation clause, could states parties lawfully suspend particular treaty obligations in the event of a public emergency? Two areas of international law are relevant to answering this question: rules governing the suspension of treaties and rules governing circumstances precluding wrongfulness. As to the former, the Vienna Convention on the Law of Treaties sets forth default rules for treaty interpretation. Article 62 provides that a state can suspend its treaty obligations due to a 'fundamental change in circumstances'. The suspension may apply to the treaty as a whole or to a single clause or provision. See Vienna Convention, Article 44. In the

[11] See the Committee's concluding observations on Israel: 'The Committee considers the present application of administrative detention to be incompatible with Articles 7 and 16 of the Covenant, neither of which allows for derogation in times of public emergency. . . . The Committee stresses, however, that a State party may not depart from the requirement of effective judicial review of detention.' See also the recommendation by the Committee to the Sub-Commission on Prevention of Discrimination and Protection of Minorities concerning a draft third optional protocol to the Covenant: 'The Committee is satisfied that States parties generally understand that the right to habeas corpus and amparo should not be limited in situations of emergency. Furthermore, the Committee is of the view that the remedies provided in Article 9, paragraphs 3 and 4, read in conjunction with Article 2 are inherent to the Covenant as a whole.' [Eds.: The Human Rights Committee provided the latter comments in response to a proposal for a draft optional protocol to the ICCPR which would have added Art. 9 paras. 3 and 4 (arrest and detention) and Art. 14 (criminal procedure) to the list of nonderogable provisions under Art. 4(2). The Committee also commented that there was a 'considerable risk' that such an optional protocol 'might implicitly invite States parties to feel free to derogate from the provisions of article 9 of the Covenant during states of emergency if they do not ratify the proposed optional protocol' (UN Doc. A/49/40, paras. 22–5.)]

drafting process, states can elect to modify the default rules with respect to a specific treaty. For example, treaty drafters could narrow (or expand) the scope of conditions that permit a state to suspend its obligations. Likewise, treaty drafters could condition the ability to suspend a treaty obligation on the satisfaction of procedural criteria.

Second, the Articles on Responsibility of States for International Wrongful Acts drafted by the International Law Commission[12] describe rules for 'circumstances precluding wrongfulness'. The draft articles of state responsibility define conditions under which a state may justify its failure to perform an international legal obligation. In the preceding analysis of derogation clauses, Joan Fitzpatrick alludes to one such justification: necessity. According to the articles of state responsibility, '[n]ecessity may not be invoked by a State as a ground for precluding the wrongfulness of an act unless the act [i]s the only way for the State to safeguard an essential interest against a grave and imminent peril.'

Another justification that may be relevant is force majeure. This principle excuses a state from legal responsibility if 'the occurrence of an irresistible force or of an unforeseen event, beyond the control of the State, mak[es] it materially impossible in the circumstances to perform the obligation', according to the draft articles. The practice of the International Labour Organization, for example, suggests that states can derogate from ILO conventions in the event of an armed conflict by invoking force majeure — whether or not the convention contains an explicit suspension clause. These issues have begun to receive attention as part of a general study by the International Law Commission under the heading 'effects of armed conflicts on treaties'. The Law Commission's Special Rapporteur, Professor Ian Brownlie, issued a handful of insightful reports that serve as a useful resource on the topic.

In addition to the substantive scope of the right to derogate, consider the specific procedures a state is supposed to follow in derogating from its treaty obligations. Article 4 contains two procedural elements: official proclamation of a public emergency and notification to other states parties. In a landmark decision, *Silva v. Uruguay*, Communication No. 34/1978 (1981), the Human Rights Committee elaborated its views on the notification requirement:

> Although the sovereign right of a State party to declare a state of emergency is not questioned, yet, in the specific context of the present communication, the Human Rights Committee is of the opinion that a State, by merely invoking the existence of exceptional circumstances, cannot evade the obligations which it has undertaken by ratifying the Covenant. Although the substantive right to take derogation measures may not depend on a formal notification being made pursuant to Article 4(3) of the Covenant, the State party concerned is duty-bound to give a sufficiently detailed account of the relevant facts when it invokes Article 4(1) of the Covenant in proceedings under the Protocol. It is the function of the Human Rights Committee, acting under the Optional Protocol, to see to it that States parties live up to their commitments under the Covenant. In order to assess whether a situation of the kind described in Article 4(1) of the Covenant exists in the country concerned, it needs full and comprehensive information. If the respondent Government does

[12] The International Law Commission is a body of 34 independent experts created by the UN General Assembly with the purpose of helping to promote and codify international law.

not furnish the required justification itself, as it is required to do under Article 4(2) of the Optional Protocol and Article 4(3) of the Covenant, the Human Rights Committee cannot conclude that valid reasons exist to legitimize a departure from the normal legal regime prescribed by the Covenant.

QUESTIONS

1. Should a state's failure to satisfy the notification requirement forfeit its right to derogate from the ICCPR? In *Silva v. Uruguay*, the Committee clearly concludes no. Consider the other procedural element of Article 4 as well. General Comment 29 suggests that the proclamation of a public emergency constitutes one of two 'fundamental conditions' before a state can avail itself of Article 4. What purposes does such a condition serve? Should a government lose its right to adopt a derogation measure to address a serious security threat simply because it failed to proclaim an emergency?

2. All *jus cogens* norms are nonderogable under Article 4, but not all nonderogable rights under Article 4 are *jus cogens* norms. In other words, there is a residual category in Article 4: ICCPR provisions that do not reflect *jus cogens* norms but nevertheless may not be suspended due to a public emergency. What are the general features of such provisions? What is the logic behind their receiving this extraordinary protection if they do not implicate peremptory norms?

3. In General Comment 24, the Committee provides an expanded list of nonderogable rights beyond those explicitly enumerated in Article 4(2). Did the Committee go too far or not far enough? What would you exclude or include?

4. Do you agree with the Committee's reasoning that other international legal norms, such as those contained in the Rome Statute for the International Criminal Court, should be applied in interpreting the Covenant? These appear to be international instruments that directly relate to human rights, but what defines 'human rights' for this purpose and how direct does the relationship have to be? Are environmental treaties, peace agreements, or other instruments also relevant to assessing states' human rights obligations? Note that according to a general rule of treaty interpretation, sources to be consulted in interpreting a treaty include 'any relevant rules of international law applicable in the relations between the parties' (Vienna Convention, Art. 31).

ADDITIONAL READING

N.C. Lazar, *States of Emergency in Liberal Democracies* (2009); D. McGoldrick, 'The Interface Between Public Emergency Powers and International Law', 2 Int'l. J. Const. L. 380 (2004); A.-L. Svensson-McCarthy, *The International Law of Human Rights and States of Exception* (1998); O. Gross & F. N. Aoláin, *Law in Times of Crisis: Emergency Powers in Theory and Practice* (2006).

COMMENT ON RELATIONSHIPS BETWEEN INTERNATIONAL HUMAN RIGHTS AND THE LAW OF ARMED CONFLICT

International law protects the rights of individuals during wartime. A potential difficulty in securing such protection, however, is determining how two areas of international law — the law of armed conflict (also called 'international humanitarian law') and human rights law — interrelate. Also, which institutions should have the power to interpret and apply these bodies of law? For example, should human rights institutions have the authority and competence to interpret the law of armed conflict? For the moment we focus on the content of the law of armed conflict and the first set of concerns, namely, the relationship between the two legal regimes. Once we better understand those issues, we can consider questions about the appropriate role of various institutions in interpreting the law.

1. The Structure and Content of the Law of Armed Conflict

The law of armed conflict is certainly a specialized body of law. It regulates, often in exacting detail, the methods of conducting hostilities and the treatment of victims of warfare. At the outset, it is important to understand three parameters that define the scope of the regime's application. First, the regime applies only in situations of armed conflict and military occupation. Second, an important distinction involves the classification of a conflict as either international (i.e., between two or more states) or non-international (e.g., between a state and a non-state group; or between two non-state groups). In general, a broader and more demanding set of IHL rules applies to international armed conflict, and only a subset of those obligations applies to non-international armed conflict. A primary reason for that normative hierarchy is that the legal authority of the state is generally at its zenith in dealing with matters within its sovereign territory; and state authority is more constrained when acting abroad in direct confrontation with the sovereign interests of another state. Third, the obligations of IHL are meant to apply equally to all parties involved in a conflict. That is, the rights and responsibilities of actors do not change according to the purported justness of one side's cause. The rules are neither more stringent for a state that aggressively invades another state, nor more relaxed for a state acting in self-defence against an aggressor. In other words, the rules that apply to conduct during an armed conflict (*jus in bello*) are separate from the rules that apply to the initial reasons for going to war (*jus ad bellum*).

The law of armed conflict is governed by overarching principles and a set of specific rules. The former includes three general principles. First is the principle of necessity: an obligation to use only the amount of force needed to obtain a military objective. Second is the principle of distinction: an obligation to attack only legitimate military targets and never deliberately attack civilians or civilian objects. Third is the principle of proportionality: an obligation to ensure an acceptable relationship between the legitimate destructive effect and undesirable collateral effects of a military attack. The principle of proportionality may, alternatively, be formulated as an obligation to ensure any incidental loss or injury to civilian life is not excessive in relation to the military objective of an attack.

The law of armed conflict is often divided into two domains, though these boundaries have merged in more recent years. One domain concerns legal obligations related to the methods and means of warfare in the conduct of military operations. This domain has historically been called 'Hague Law' — due to the city in which the principal treaties on this subject were initially adopted. Its rules are codified, for example, in the Hague Conventions concluded in 1899 and 1907. And, customary international law currently plays a significant role in defining its content, as an International Court of Justice advisory opinion on the use of nuclear weapons demonstrates. Examples of Hague Law include prohibitions on specific weapons, on the infliction of superfluous injury and unnecessary suffering, on assassination and on perfidious conduct. Contemporary issues in this domain include the use of cluster bombs, the use of remote controlled drones, the tactics of cyber attacks and cyber warfare more generally, and the definition of acts of terrorism in the context of an armed conflict.

In contrast with Hague Law, the second domain of the law of armed conflict concerns the treatment of civilians and combatants who have laid down their arms and are subject to the effective authority of an opposing party to the conflict. This domain has historically been called 'Geneva Law' due as well to the treaty conferences that initially codified this area of law. The principal instruments are the four Geneva Conventions of 1949. The conventions were drafted in the aftermath of the Second World War, during the same period in which war crimes trials were taking place on the European continent and in East Asia. Collectively, the 1949 Conventions provide rules for the wounded, sick and shipwrecked (the First and Second Geneva Conventions), prisoners of war (the Third Geneva Convention) and civilians (the Fourth Geneva Convention). Contemporary controversies involving the application of Geneva Law include the definition of persons who are lawfully subject to detention and the composition of military trials in non-international armed conflict.

Most of the rules in the 1949 Conventions apply to international armed conflicts — war between two or more states. However, Article 3 common to all four Conventions, which has been called a 'convention in miniature', contains rules that apply to non-international conflicts such as civil wars. Common Article 3 imposes direct legal obligations on all parties to a conflict — including non-state actors. These obligations include the most basic rights of individuals such as freedom from torture, murder, mutilation and cruel treatment; the right to a fair trial, and the general right 'in all circumstances [to] be treated humanely'. The International Court of Justice famously referred to the rules in Common Article 3 as 'a minimum yardstick' for all armed conflicts because they reflect 'elementary considerations of humanity'.

In the midst of the Cold War, states reconvened in Geneva to negotiate two additional protocols to the 1949 Conventions. Finalized in 1977, the two Protocols involve a convergence of Hague Law and Geneva Law. That is, each Protocol contains rules pertaining to the two domains in a relatively undifferentiated organizational structure. Additional Protocol I elaborates the rules that apply in international armed conflicts. It also defines 'international armed conflict' to include national liberation and other armed struggles in exercise of the right of self-determination. Additional Protocol II contains a more modest set of rules for internal armed conflicts.

In terms of their status, the 1949 Geneva Conventions and the 1977 Protocols have secured widespread ratification. In 2006, the 1949 Conventions became the first treaties in modern history to achieve ratification by every state in the world. Their rules are also generally considered binding as a matter of customary international law. Currently (as of May 2012) 172 states are party to Protocol I, and many of its provisions are considered customary international law applicable in all armed conflicts. Recent adherents include France and the United Kingdom and, for a longer time, China and Russia. The United States is one of the few states not to ratify the Protocol (along with India, Indonesia, Iran, Iraq, Israel, Myanmar (Burma), Nepal, Pakistan, the Philippines, Sri Lanka and Turkey). The US Government, however, considers much of the Protocol binding customary international law. And, although the United Kingdom ratified the Protocol in 1998, the government also attached a reservation stating that 'the term "armed conflict" of itself and in its context denotes a situation of a kind which is not constituted by the commission of ordinary crimes including acts of terrorism whether concerted or in isolation.' Additional Protocol II has been ratified by 166 states. Its states parties include all permanent members of the Security Council except the United States, which has signed but not ratified the agreement.

The most recent international instrument to include a broad range of IHL prohibitions is the 1998 Rome Statute for the International Criminal Court. The drafters of the Rome Statute considered it their task to produce a treaty reflecting the existing IHL regime, not to develop new law. As a consequence, Article 8 is widely understood to codify customary IHL and thus serves as a useful reference point. The Rome Statute is, however, limited to rules that incur international criminal liability. State obligations under the law of armed conflict, of course, encompass far more than war crimes. In 2005, the International Committee of the Red Cross finalized a study on customary international humanitarian law. This vast set of materials provides the ICRC's views on the rules that have acquired the status of custom in international and non-international armed conflict. The study, however, was not completed without controversy. The US Government, for example, objected to parts of the methodology used to ascertain rules and some substantive conclusions of the study. See J. Bellinger III and W. J. Haynes II, 'A US Government Response to the International Committee of the Red Cross Study on Customary International Humanitarian Law', 89 Int'l. Rev. Red Cross 443 (2007); J.-M. Henckaerts, 'Customary International Humanitarian Law: A Response to US Comments', 89 Int'l. Rev. Red Cross 473 (2007).

2. The Relationship Between International Human Rights and the Law of Armed Conflict

A principle familiar to many legal systems, public international law included, is *lex specialis derogat legi generali*. That is, a specific or special rule should take precedence over a general rule. This principle raises an important challenge for the legal regulation of warfare: should the law of armed conflict supplant human rights law in defining the rights and obligations of individuals and states during an armed conflict?

In contrast with the law of armed conflict, international human rights law applies during peacetime and wartime. The first formal recognition of the application of human rights law to armed conflict is often dated back to the 1968 International Conference on Human Rights at Teheran. That world conference also spurred a series of annual UN General Assembly Resolutions entitled 'Respect for Human Rights in Armed Conflicts', and those resolutions were a prelude to the 1977 Geneva Protocols. The recognition of the interconnections between human rights law and armed conflict, however, was a growing trend that began before the Teheran conference. Human rights instruments, some finalized before 1968 and some after, clearly contemplate situations of warfare and military matters. The European Human Rights Convention (adopted in 1950) and the Inter-American Convention (adopted in 1969) both contain derogation clauses referring to 'time of war'. The European Convention also lists the right to life as nonderogable 'except in respect of deaths resulting from lawful acts of war'. The derogation clause in the ICCPR (adopted in 1966) uses the phrase 'public emergency which threatens the life of the nation' and is well understood to encompass armed conflicts. Article 2 of the Torture Convention (adopted in 1984) states: 'No exceptional circumstances whatsoever, whether a state of war or a threat of war . . . may be invoked as a justification of torture.' The Convention on the Rights of the Child (adopted in 1989) commits states to promoting the recovery and reintegration of 'child victim[s] of . . . armed conflicts' and prohibits the recruitment and use of child soldiers. Article 30 of the Declaration on the Rights of Indigenous Peoples, adopted by the UN Human Rights Council in 2006, places restrictions on 'military activities' in the lands and territories of indigenous peoples. And Article 43 of the 2006 Convention for the Protection of All Persons from Enforced Disappearance states that the 'Convention is without prejudice to the provisions of international humanitarian law'.

In corresponding fashion, conventions related to IHL indicate the applicability of human rights norms to situations of armed conflict. The 1949 Geneva Conventions might have referred to universal human rights in preambular language, but disputes over unrelated language culminated in dropping the idea of having a preamble. As the historian Geoffrey Best explains, 'What seems beyond doubt is that the human rights affiliation expressly claimed by the original, minimal preambles was in itself accepted by all parties to the 1949 diplomatic conference to the point even of being taken for granted.'[13] The most readily apparent influence of human rights norms is perhaps Common Article 3, which regulates practices within states' sovereign borders. According to the ICRC Commentaries, the article reflects 'the few essential rules of humanity which all civilized nations consider as valid everywhere and under all circumstances and as being above and outside war itself.'

The 1977 Additional Protocols to the Geneva Conventions continued this trend. For example, Article 72 of Additional Protocol I, which delineates some of the convention's field of application, acknowledges the relevance of human rights law: 'The provisions of this Section are additional to the rules concerning humanitarian

[13] G. Best, *War and Law Since 1945* (1994), 72.

protection of civilians and civilian objects in the power of a Party to the conflict contained in the Fourth Convention . . . as well as to other applicable rules of international law relating to the protection of fundamental human rights during international armed conflict.' Protocol II contains a preamble, which notes that 'international instruments relating to human rights offer a basic protection to the human person'. More fundamentally, the 1977 Protocols represented a significant shift toward the convergence of human rights and humanitarian law norms. One of the leading commentators on the subject, Professor Colonel G. I. A. D. Draper, voiced a series of cautions at the time. He cautioned that actors engaged in promoting such a fusion should consider the divergent interests and distinct structural concerns that animate the two domains of law. In a controversial essay that retains some influence, Draper explained his position:

> The law of armed conflicts purports to govern the hostile relations of states engaged in armed confrontation. It was, and is, part of the law of nations. Human-rights law purports to govern part of the relations between government and governed by setting limits to the intrusions by governments upon those areas of human freedom thought to be essential for the proper functioning of the human being in society and for his development therein. A war or 'emergency' situation impinges, within specified limits, upon those guaranteed rights and freedoms, in relation to the governed i.e. 'everyone within their jurisdiction', and not in relation to an enemy. These freedoms, when internationalized in human-rights instruments, are neither intended nor adequate to govern an armed conflict between two states in a condition of enmity. The relevance of war to a human-rights regime is that the regime determines what happens to those human rights in that event. The regime in no way purports to regulate the conduct of the war between two states even assuming that both were subject to that human-rights regime. Hostilities and government-governed relationships are different in kind, origin, purpose, and consequences. Accordingly, the law that relates to them, respectively, has the like differences. Human-rights regimes and the humanitarian law of war deal with different and distinct relationships. [T]he process whereby human-rights law ha[s] now been 'internationalized' has not changed the quality of the relationships to which that law applies. What has happened is that certain states, sharing a common civilization and ideas about the limits of government and the freedom of the individual in society, have entered into a system of binding mutual guarantees of specific human rights and freedoms, listed and defined, in their respective states, enforceable by international organs established by the convention concerned. It is not possible to have a regional law of war. It is possible to have a regional regime of human rights....
>
> ...
>
> The attempt to confuse the two regimes of law is insupportable in theory and inadequate in practice. The two regimes are not only distinct but are diametrically opposed....
>
> If there be a common base for the two regimes, it might be found in the shared base of the idea of humanity, but the conception is too vague to justify the confusion attempted by the UN in the application of the two regimes of law here considered. At the end of the day, the law of human rights seeks to reflect the cohesion and harmony in human society and must, from the nature of things, be a different

and opposed law to that which seeks to regulate the conduct of hostile relationships between states or other organized armed groups, and in internal rebellions. The humanitarian nature of the modern law of war neither justifies the confusion with, nor dispels the opposition to, human rights.[14]

More recently a different version, if not revision, of Draper's points has emerged: some commentators and a few states (the United States included) have argued that in addressing particular issues during an armed conflict, IHL should displace or supplant the application of human rights law.[15]

The International Court of Justice provided one of the most influential statements on this matter in an Advisory Opinion, *Legality of the Threat or Use of Nuclear Weapons*. The Court was faced with various opposing arguments. One argument maintained that the possession, threat or use of nuclear weapons violated the right to life under the ICCPR, a position supported by a General Comment of the Human Rights Committee in 1984. Another position held that the ICCPR protects human rights only in peacetime. And, some states (including the Netherlands, the United Kingdom and the United States) took the position that IHL provides a safe harbour for parties to an armed conflict: if deaths result from actions that comply with IHL, those actions cannot be considered 'arbitrary' deprivations of the right to life. The British Government, for example, stated, 'The only sensible construction which can be placed on the term "arbitrary" in this context is that it refers to whether or not the deliberate taking of life is unlawful under that part of the international law which was specifically designed to regulate the conduct of hostilities, that is the laws of armed conflict.'[16] In an oft-quoted passage, the ICJ stated:

[T]he protection of the International Covenant of Civil and Political Rights does not cease in times of war, except by operation of Article 4 of the Covenant whereby certain provisions may be derogated from in a time of national emergency. Respect for the right to life is not, however, such a provision. In principle, the right not arbitrarily to be deprived of one's life applies also in hostilities. The test of what is an arbitrary deprivation of life, however, then falls to be determined by the applicable *lex specialis*, namely, the law applicable in armed conflict which is designed to regulate the conduct of hostilities.

[14] G.I.A.D. Draper, 'Humanitarian Law and Human Rights', Acta Juridica 193 (1979).

[15] Notably, a contrary position may be reflected in a remarkable provision of the Rome Statute for the International Criminal Court. The Rome Statute covers crimes involving violations of both IHL and human rights law. Article 21 sets forth the 'applicable law' for the Court to employ such as the Statute itself and 'established principles of the international law of armed conflict'. Article 21(3) contains a notable rider: 'The application and interpretation of law pursuant to this Article must be consistent with internationally recognized human rights.' It appears that human rights law may obtain primacy under this framework. A.Pellet, 'Applicable Law', in J.R.W.D. Jones, P.Gaeta and A.Cassese (eds.), *The Rome Statute of the International Criminal Court: A Commentary* (2002), 1051.

[16] The Netherlands, like other states, also referred to the negotiating history of the ICCPR:

[T]he travaux preparatoires of Article 6 of the International Covenant make clear that, instead of listing the circumstances in which the deprivation of life would not be considered contrary to the right to life, the drafters decided to agree on the formulation that 'No one shall be arbitrarily deprived of his life.' One of the instances mentioned in this connection by the drafters as an example of a deprivation of life which is not arbitrary was 'the performance of lawful acts of war'.

As with many judicial opinions, the meaning of this statement has been subject to different, and sometimes conflicting, interpretations. Consider the following articulation of the Court's analysis and the rationale behind a broad application of the *lex specialis* doctrine:

> Confronted with two legal regimes — human rights law and humanitarian law — containing rules on the taking of lives, the ICJ resorted to the principle that *lex specialis derogat lex generali* to reconcile them, holding that the ICCPR provision on the right to life must be construed by making a *renvoi* to humanitarian law. *Lex specialis derogat lex generali*, or, the specific provision overcomes the general provision, is a canon of construction that is widely considered to be a general principle of law, as applicable in the international legal system as it is in national legal systems. Koskenniemi [in a 2003 paper] provides the principle's rationale: a 'special rule is more to the point ("approaches more nearly the subject in hand") than a general one and it regulates the matter more effectively ("are ordinarily more effective") than general rules do'. The thinking goes that because many of the same states have negotiated and acceded to the human rights law and humanitarian law treaties, we should presume that these treaties are consistent with one another. We should not think, for example, that it violates the right to liberty under the ICCPR or ECHR to hold a combatant as a prisoner of war until the end of active hostilities when, after all, the same states that negotiated the ICCPR and ECHR also negotiated an entire treaty on prisoners of war that allows exactly that. Because general rules ('No one shall be subjected to arbitrary arrest or detention.') may be interpreted in more than one way, we should interpret them in light of specific rules ('Prisoners of war shall be released and repatriated without delay after the cessation of hostilities.') rather than vice versa.[17]

The ICJ issued two more recent opinions involving the application of human rights in armed conflict and military occupation. The first, in 2004, concerned Israel's construction of a physical barrier in occupied Palestinian territory. The second, in 2006, involved an armed conflict between the Democratic Republic of the Congo and Uganda. On both occasions, the Court provided the following formulation:

> The protection offered by human rights conventions does not cease in case of armed conflict, save through the effect of provisions for derogation of the kind to be found in Article 4 of the International Covenant on Civil and Political Rights. As regards the relationship between international humanitarian law and human rights law, there are thus three possible situations: some rights may be exclusively matters of international humanitarian law; others may be exclusively matters of human rights law; yet others may be matters of both these branches of international law.

[17] W. Abresch, 'A Human Rights Law of Internal Armed Conflict: The European Court of Human Rights in Chechnya',16 Eur. J. Int'l. L. 741 (2005).

Some of the following commentaries predate this most recent statement by the ICJ. Consider, among other issues, how the ICJ's general formulation might affect the analysis in the following commentaries. Australian Navy Commander Dale Stephens, for example, argues that the *Nuclear Weapons* opinion suggests placing greater weight upon human rights commitments in interpreting and applying the law of armed conflict:

> While human rights proponents welcomed [the] ICJ's application of Article 6 of the ICCPR during times of armed conflict, the interpretation of its Opinion remains ambiguous. The Court did not determine that the law of armed conflict had been modified in any structural manner by the parallel application of non-derogable provisions of the ICCPR. Rather, the Opinion suggests that 'humanitarian law is to be used to actually interpret a human rights rule.' Such an interpretation suggests that the possible legal content of Article 6 completely assimilates into the applicable rules of the law of armed conflict. Indeed, according to one authoritative view, it suggests that 'in the context of the conduct of hostilities, human rights law cannot be interpreted differently from humanitarian law.'[18]

While this interpretation may be formalistically correct, it nonetheless is quite narrow. It is based upon an orthodox interpretation by acknowledging that the language of Article 6 is very general. In contrast, the plethora of rules governing the protection (and destruction) of life as contained within the law of armed conflict are quite detailed and therefore should, under common canons of interpretation, continue to be the exclusive governing regime. Those seeking to ensure specific separation of the two streams of international law have applauded this manner of interpretation. These commentators contend that the rules of the law of armed conflict were largely the product of strenuous and specific negotiation. Accordingly, the import of applying operative peacetime human rights concepts, such as the right to life, would undermine the integrity of the existing rules and only promote numerous reservations and declarations to current and future law of armed conflict regimes. While possibly representative of realpolitik, such views represent a narrow assessment of the import of the Court's approach to the issue.

> Though the Court formally maintained the priority of the law of armed conflict, it interpreted that law in terms of the underlying principles of humanity. This emphasis elevated the humanitarian aspects and priorities of the law of armed conflict and ensured that these 'weighted' humanitarian aspects must be considered when determining the legitimacy of military actions.... Hence, the Court develops its reasoning by re-interpreting the law of armed conflict with a newfound emphasis on promoting humanitarian considerations.[19]

[18] L. Doswald-Beck, 'International Humanitarian Law and the Advisory Opinion of the International Court of Justice on the Legality of the Threat or Use of Nuclear Weapons', 316 Int'l Rev. Red Cross 35 (1997), at 51.

[19] D. Stephens, 'Human Rights and Armed Conflict — The Advisory Opinion of the International Court of Justice in the Nuclear Weapons Case', 4 Yale H.R. & Development L. J. 1 (2001).

INTERNATIONAL COMMITTEE OF THE RED CROSS, INTERNATIONAL HUMANITARIAN LAW AND OTHER LEGAL REGIMES: INTERPLAY IN SITUATIONS OF VIOLENCE

(2003), at www.icrc.org/eng/assets/files/other/interplay_other_regimes_nov_2003.pdf

[In 2003, the International Committee of the Red Cross co-sponsored a gathering in which 200 governmental and nongovernmental experts participated. Following is the ICRC summary of the participants' views on the relationship between IHL and human rights law, including on the ICJ's *Nuclear Weapons* Opinion.]

... [A] consensus emerged that, even in this hypothesis of conflict, at least the non-derogable rules of human rights law continue to apply and to complement IHL.

...

... [T]he great majority of the participants simply recalled that IHL represented a special law in as much as it has been specifically framed to apply in a period of armed conflict. They noted that, in offering ground rules adapted to this particular context of violence, this body of law makes it possible — in many cases — to specify the precise content of the non-derogable human rights. In this regard, many references were made to the reasoning followed by the International Court of Justice in its advisory opinion rendered on 8 July 1996 in the matter of the *Legality of the Threat or Use of Nuclear Weapons.* In this case, the Court, having confirmed the nonderogable nature of the right to life, held in effect that it was appropriate to refer to IHL — framed as *lex specialis* — to determine what could be considered as an arbitrary deprivation of life.

However, several participants pointed out that this reasoning — though perfectly consistent for interpreting the precise content of the right to life — could not necessarily be generalised to all relations between IHL and human rights law. On the contrary, as human rights law is more precise than IHL in certain domains, the relation of interpretation must also be able to operate in the other direction. For example, Article 3(1)(d) common to the Geneva Conventions explicitly refers to the "judicial guarantees recognised as indispensable by civilised peoples" but without further specifying the meaning of this expression. It was suggested that . . . reference [can] be made to human rights law in order to deduce the substantive guarantees resulting from this general formula. The lively debate that ensued between the participants as to the extent to which IHL could be "supplemented" by human rights law did not come to any final conclusion.... [S]ome of the experts maintained that only the non-derogable human rights could be appropriate in this regard and that any other approach would lead to an extension of the scope of application of human rights law without any legal basis.

INTERNATIONAL LAW COMMISSION, REPORT OF THE STUDY GROUP FINALIZED BY MARTTI KOSKENNIEMI, FRAGMENTATION OF INTERNATIONAL LAW

Fifty-eighth session, 1 May–9 June and 3 July–11 August 2006, at http://untreaty.un.org/ilc/documentation/english/a_cn4_l682.pdf

[In 2002, the International Law Commission included the topic of 'Fragmentation of international law' in its programme of work and established a Study Group. Professor Martti Koskenniemi served as the Chair. Following is an extract of his 2006 report to the Commission.]

88. There are two ways in which law may take account of the relationship of a particular rule to general one. A particular rule may be considered an application of a general standard in a given circumstance. The special relates to the general as does administrative regulation to law in domestic legal order. Or it may be considered as a modification, overruling or a setting aside of the latter. The first case is sometimes seen as not a situation of normative conflict at all but is taken to involve the simultaneous application of the special and the general standard. Thus, only the latter is thought to involve the application of a genuine *lex specialis*.

...

91. . . . [T]he European Court of Human Rights has thought the *lex specialis* applicable even in the absence of direct conflict between two provisions and where it might be said that both apply concurrently. This is the proper approach. There are two reasons for why it is useful to consider the case of "application" in connection with the case where the *lex specialis* sets up an exception or involves a "setting aside". First, it follows from the definition of the *lex specialis* adopted above that this case is also included: the norm of application is more specific because it contains the general rule itself as one element in the definition of its scope of application. Second, and more important, though the distinction is analytically sound, it is in practice seldom clear-cut. It may often be difficult to say whether a rule "applies" a standard, "modifies" it or "derogates from" it. An "application" or "modification" involves also a degree of "derogation" and "setting aside"....

96. Or what to say of the place of *lex specialis* in the Legality of the Threat or Use of Nuclear Weapons case (1996)? Here the ICJ observed that both human rights law (namely the International Covenant on Civil and Political Rights) and the laws of armed conflict both applied "in times of war". Nevertheless, when it came to determine what was an "arbitrary deprivation of life" under Article 6 (1) of the Covenant, this fell "to be determined by the applicable *lex specialis*, namely the law applicable to armed conflict". In this respect, the two fields of law applied concurrently, or within each other. From another perspective, however, the law of armed conflict — and in particular its more relaxed standard of killing — set aside whatever standard might have been provided under the practice of the Covenant.

...

104. The example of the laws of war focuses on a case where the rule itself identifies the conditions in which it is to apply, namely the presence of an "armed conflict". Owing to that condition, the rule appears more "special" than if no such condition had been identified. To regard this as a situation of *lex specialis* draws attention to an important aspect of the operation of the principle. Even as it works so as to justify recourse to an exception, what is being set aside does not vanish altogether. The [ICJ] was careful to point out that human rights law continued to apply within armed conflict. The exception — humanitarian law — only affected one (albeit important) aspect of it, namely the relative assessment of "arbitrariness". Humanitarian law as *lex specialis* did not suggest that human rights were abolished in war. It did not function in a formal or absolute way but as an aspect of the pragmatics of the Court's reasoning.... Legality of Nuclear Weapons was a "hard case" to the extent that a choice had to be made by the Court between different sets of rules none of which could fully extinguish the others. *Lex specialis* did hardly more than indicate that though it might have been desirable to apply only human rights, such a solution would have been too idealistic, bearing in mind the speciality and persistence of armed conflict....

119. *Lex specialis derogat lege generali* refers to a standard technique of legal reasoning, operative in international law as in other fields of law understood as systems. Its power is entirely dependent on the normative considerations for which it provides articulation: sensitivity to context, capacity to reflect State will, concreteness, clarity, definiteness. Its functioning cannot be assessed independently of the role of considerations of the latter type in specific context of legal reasoning. How does a particular agreement relate to the general law around it? Does it implement or support the latter, or does it perhaps deviate from it? Is the deviation tolerable or not? No general, context-independent answers can be given to such questions. In this sense, the *lex specialis* maxim cannot be meaningfully codified.

120. The role of *lex specialis* cannot be dissociated from assessments about the nature and purposes of the general law that it proposes to modify, replace, update or deviate from. This highlights the systemic nature of the reasoning of which arguments from "special law" are an inextricable part. No rule, treaty, or custom, however special its subject-matter or limited the number of the States concerned by it, applies in a vacuum. Its normative environment includes ... not only whatever general law there may be on that very topic, but also principles that determine the relevant legal subjects, their basic rights and duties, and the forms through which those rights and duties may be supplemented, modified or extinguished.

D. REGULATING DETENTION

1. CASE STUDY: GUANTÁNAMO DETAINEES — PROCESS FOR DETERMINING STATUS AND GROUNDS FOR DETENTION

Following the 11 September attacks and the Security Council recognition of the US right to self-defence, US and British forces invaded Afghanistan on 7 October 2001. By January 2002, the United States began transporting alleged Taliban and Al Qaeda members to its military base at Guantánamo Bay, Cuba. Individuals linked to Al Qaeda were apprehended not only in Afghanistan, but in other countries as well including Bosnia-Herzegovina, Egypt, Gambia, Mauritania, Pakistan and Thailand, and then transferred to Guantánamo.

The US Government contended that all Taliban and Al Qaeda members were 'unlawful combatants' who, therefore, failed to qualify as prisoners of war (POW) under the Third Geneva Convention. What was at stake? As a legal matter, according detainees POW status would require the Government to guarantee specific trial rights not necessarily provided by US military commissions. POW status would also provide combatant immunity for membership in an enemy armed force (though no immunity applies to the commission of acts of terrorism, perfidy or other war crimes). POW status would also oblige the United States to provide for certain conditions of detention, though these conditions are not clearly far superior to conditions of detention required under the Civilians (Fourth Geneva) Convention.[20] As a more general matter, according POW status might accord a form of legitimacy to these organizations.

Article 4 of the Third Convention sets forth the requirements for POW status. Under Article 4(a), POWs include individuals who belong to any of the following categories:

(1) Members of the armed forces of a Party to the conflict, as well as members of militias or volunteer corps forming part of such armed forces.

(2) Members of other militias and members of other volunteer corps, including those of organized resistance movements, belonging to a Party to the conflict and operating in or outside their own territory, even if this territory is occupied, provided that such militias or volunteer corps, including such organized resistance movements, fulfil the following conditions:

(a) that of being commanded by a person responsible for his subordinates;

(b) that of having a fixed distinctive sign recognizable at a distance;

(c) that of carrying arms openly;

(d) that of conducting their operations in accordance with the laws and customs of war.

. . .

[20] Derek Jinks, 'The Declining Significance of POW Status', 45 Harv. Int'l. L. J. 367 (2004).

(4) Persons who accompany the armed forces without actually being members thereof, such as . . .supply contractors, members of labour units or of services responsible for the welfare of the armed forces . . . .

Article 5 of the POW Convention states that '[s]hould any doubt arise as to whether persons, having committed a belligerent act and having fallen into the hands of the enemy, belong to any of the categories enumerated in Article 4, such persons shall enjoy the protection of the present Convention until such time as their status has been determined by a competent tribunal.'

The United States declared that the Geneva Conventions applied to the international armed conflict with Afghanistan. The United States, however, contended that the Taliban and Al Qaeda failed to satisfy the criteria of Article 4(a)2; that the criteria of Article 4(a)2 apply to 4(a)1 groups that Al Qaeda as a non-state actor (and especially as a terrorist group) could not receive the protections of the Geneva Conventions in any case; and that no doubt about status existed and hence there was not need for a tribunal under Article 5 of the POW Convention.

Several international intergovernmental and nongovernmental organizations have opposed the US position including the European Parliament, the International Committee of the Red Cross, the UN High Commissioner for Human Rights, UN human rights special mechanisms such as the UN Working Group on Arbitrary Detention and a number of foreign governments.

In early 2002, a coalition of civil society groups (the Center for Constitutional Rights, the Human Rights Clinic at Columbia Law School and the Center for Justice and International Law) petitioned the Inter-American Commission on Human Rights. They argued, *inter alia*, that the United States violated the American Declaration on the Rights and Duties of Man in failing to comply with the procedures established under the Third Geneva Convention and in holding the individuals in prolonged detention without access to a court.

In March 2002, the Commission issued a decision requesting the United States to adopt precautionary measures — to 'take the urgent measures necessary to have the legal status of the detainees at Guantánamo Bay determined by a competent tribunal'. Over the following years, the US Government and petitioners submitted numerous briefs and participated in oral hearings before the Commission. Over this time, the Commission has issued multiple statements and decisions reiterating and amplifying its March 2002 communication. The Commission also recognized that some intervening developments, including US Supreme Court decisions and revisions in US Department of Defense policy, partially satisfied US obligations identified in the Commission's initial decision. Some commentators credit the cumulative effect of pressure from the Commission, alongside other international authorities and domestic groups, in helping to bring about those changes. That said, other actions by the United States — such as congressional legislation suspending *habeas corpus* — clashed with the legal norms propounded by the Commission and other international authorities.

Throughout its exchanges with the Commission, the US Government contended that the law of armed conflict has the status of *lex specialis* and displaces the application of human rights law. The United States also contended that the Commission lacked the jurisdictional competence to interpret and apply the laws of war. These and other arguments are explored in the following materials.

INTER-AMERICAN COMMISSION ON HUMAN RIGHTS ORGANIZATION OF AMERICAN STATES DETAINEES IN GUANTÁNAMO BAY, CUBA REQUEST FOR PRECAUTIONARY MEASURES

(13 Mar. 2002)

[The Organization of American States] charge[s] the Commission with supervising member states' observance of human rights in the Hemisphere. These rights include those prescribed under the American Declaration of the Rights and Duties of Man, which constitutes a source of legal obligation for all OAS member states in respect of persons subject to their authority and control....

... [W]hile its specific mandate is to secure the observance of international human rights protections in the Hemisphere, this Commission has in the past looked to and applied definitional standards and relevant rules of international humanitarian law in interpreting the American Declaration and other Inter-American human rights instruments in situations of armed conflict.

In taking this approach, the Commission has drawn upon certain basic principles that inform the interrelationship between international human rights and humanitarian law. It is well-recognized that international human rights law applies at all times, in peacetime and in situations of armed conflict. In contrast, international humanitarian law generally does not apply in peacetime and its principal purpose is to place restraints on the conduct of warfare in order to limit or contain the damaging effects of hostilities and to protect the victims of armed conflict, including civilians and combatants who have laid down their arms or have been placed hors de combat. Further, in situations of armed conflict, the protections under international human rights and humanitarian law may complement and reinforce one another, sharing as they do a common nucleus of non-derogable rights and a common purpose of promoting human life and dignity. In certain circumstances, however, the test for evaluating the observance of a particular right, such as the right to liberty, in a situation of armed conflict may be distinct from that applicable in time of peace. In such situations, international law, including the jurisprudence of this Commission, dictates that it may be necessary to deduce the applicable standard by reference to international humanitarian law as the applicable *lex specialis*.

Accordingly, where persons find themselves within the authority and control of a state and where a circumstance of armed conflict may be involved, their fundamental rights may be determined in part by reference to international humanitarian law as well as international human rights law. Where it may be considered that the protections of international humanitarian law do not apply, however, such persons remain the beneficiaries at least of the non-derogable protections under international human rights law. In short, no person under the authority and control of a state, regardless of his or her circumstances, is devoid of legal protection for his or her fundamental and non-derogable human rights.

This basic precept is reflected in the Martens clause common to numerous long-standing humanitarian law treaties, including the Hague Conventions of 1899 and 1907 respecting the laws and customs of war on land, according to which human persons who do not fall within the protection of those treaties or other international agreements remain under the protection of the principles of the law of nations, as they result from the usages established among civilized peoples, from the laws of humanity, and the dictates of the public conscience. And according to international norms applicable in peacetime and wartime, such as those reflected in Article 5 of the Third Geneva Convention and Article XVIII of the American Declaration of the Rights and Duties of Man, a competent court or tribunal, as opposed to a political authority, must be charged with ensuring respect for the legal status and rights of persons falling under the authority and control of a state.

Specifically with regard to the request for precautionary measures presently before it, the Commission observes that certain pertinent facts concerning the detainees at Guantánamo Bay are well-known and do not appear to be the subject of controversy. These include the fact that the government of the United States considers itself to be at war with an international network of terrorists, that the United States undertook a military operation in Afghanistan beginning in October 2001 in defending this war, and that most of the detainees in Guantánamo Bay were apprehended in connection with this military operation and remain wholly within the authority and control of the United States government.

It is also well-known that doubts exists [*sic*] as to the legal status of the detainees. This includes the question of whether and to what extent the Third Geneva Convention and/or other provisions of international humanitarian law apply to some or all of the detainees and what implications this may have for their international human rights protections. According to official statements from the United States government, its Executive Branch has most recently declined to extend prisoner of war status under the Third Geneva Convention to the detainees, without submitting the issue for determination by a competent tribunal or otherwise ascertaining the rights and protections to which the detainees are entitled under US domestic or international law. To the contrary, the information available suggests that the detainees remain entirely at the unfettered discretion of the United States government. Absent clarification of the legal status of the detainees, the Commission considers that the rights and protections to which they may be entitled under international or domestic law cannot be said to be the subject of effective legal protection by the State.

In light of the foregoing considerations, and without prejudging the possible application of international humanitarian law to the detainees at Guantánamo Bay, the Commission considers that precautionary measures are both appropriate and necessary in the present circumstances, in order to ensure that the legal status of each of the detainees is clarified and that they are afforded the legal protections commensurate with the status that they are found to possess, which may in no case fall below the minimum standards of non-derogable rights. On this basis, the Commission hereby requests that the United States take the urgent measures necessary to have the legal status of the detainees at Guantánamo Bay determined by a competent tribunal.

. . .

The Commission wishes to note in accordance with . . . the Commission's Rules of Procedure that the granting of these measures and their adoption by the State shall not constitute a prejudgment on the merits of a case.

RESPONSE OF THE UNITED STATES TO REQUEST FOR PRECAUTIONARY MEASURES, DETAINEES IN GUANTÁNAMO BAY, CUBA

(15 Apr. 2002)

. . . [T]he Commission's request for precautionary measures and the precautionary measures themselves are not premised on any rights set forth in the American Declaration. This case is not about the American Declaration. Rather, this case is about the detention of captured enemy combatants who took part in hostilities during an armed conflict.... It involves solely the interpretation and application of specific articles of the Geneva Convention and related customary international humanitarian law, neither of which lies within the scope of the Commission's competence. In order to request provisional measures in this case, the Commission necessarily has had to interpret and apply humanitarian law, specifically Article 5 and other provisions of the Geneva Convention — a body of law separate and distinct from the American Declaration and the body of human rights law.

. . .

Petitioners' . . . citation to international human rights law is misguided, in part because it rests on the assumption that human rights law is equally applicable during armed conflict and indeed takes precedence over international humanitarian law. In fact, international human rights law is not applicable to the conduct of hostilities or the capture and detention of enemy combatants, which are governed by the more specific laws of armed conflict.

. . .

. . . Furthermore, the detainees in this case . . . are not subject to the Fourth Geneva Convention on civilians. Rather they are unlawful enemy combatants who were captured while taking part in hostilities against the United States and its allies. . . .

. . .

Nor can Petitioners save the jurisdictional competence of the Commission by framing the issues in terms of human rights law, evidently ignoring the separate and distinct humanitarian law rules at issue. For example, the Petitioners assert that the United States has violated the detainees' human rights to be free from, *inter alia*, arbitrary and prolonged detention without, however, any reference to the separate and distinct rules of detention in international humanitarian law. Under international humanitarian law, states engaged in armed conflict have the right to capture and detain enemy combatants, whether or not the combatants are POWs.[21] In this case, active hostilities are ongoing. The United States is therefore fully entitled to hold the detainees.

...

Under the ICJ's methodology, the Commission would have to interpret the American Declaration in light of the *lex specialis*, i.e., international humanitarian law and the Geneva Convention. The ICJ explained in its Advisory Opinion on the Legality of the Threat or Use of Nuclear Weapons that, to the extent human rights law is applicable during armed conflict, it must be interpreted in light of relevant *lex specialis* as set forth in the body of humanitarian law.

Accordingly, the ICJ's analysis would require the Commission to take the following analytical steps in this case:

- First, the Commission would determine the generally applicable human rights norm. The generally applicable norm under the American Declaration, Article XVIII, provides that individuals may resort to the courts to protect their legal rights. American Declaration, Art. XVIII. Absent applicable *lex specialis*, therefore, detainees generally would have recourse to the courts to challenge their detentions.
- Second, the Commission would determine whether there is any applicable *lex specialis*. In this case, the *lex specialis* would be international humanitarian law because the detainees were captured in the context of an ongoing armed conflict.
- Third, the Commission would determine whether the *lex specialis* forms a separate and distinct rule altogether, or rather, merely refines the otherwise applicable concepts embodied in the American Declaration.
- Fourth, if the *lex specialis* forms a separate and distinct rule altogether, the Commission would determine whether it had competence to interpret the separate and distinct *lex specialis*. In this case, the Commission would recognize that the international humanitarian laws on detention are quite explicit, as well as separate and distinct from the human rights norms in the American Declaration. The Commission would recognize that it, unlike the ICJ, has a very limited jurisdictional competence which does not include international humanitarian law, for reason previously discussed. The Commission would then acknowledge that where it lacks the competence to interpret and apply the relevant law, it must decline to grant the Petitioners' request.

...

[21] The underlying principle that a state has the authority to detain combatants for the duration of hostilities certainly is not diminished by the mere fact that a combatant is acting unlawfully, as opposed to lawfully. Geneva Convention Art. 118, which sets forth release and repatriation obligations and conditions with respect to lawful combatants, i.e., POWs reflects the international humanitarian law principle that combatants may be detained for at least the duration of hostilities. The authority to detain unlawful combatants is at a minimum equal to that with respect to lawful combatants. To afford rights to unlawful combatants greater than those afforded to lawful combatants would be entirely inconsistent with the letter and spirit of the Geneva Convention, as well as customary international humanitarian law....

... [T]he *lex specialis* in this case is the body of international humanitarian law relating to detentions, which affords the detainees, as captured unlawful enemy combatants, no right of access to the detaining power's courts.

...

The Commission Letter states that "precautionary measures are both appropriate and necessary ... in order to ensure that the legal status of each of the detainees is clarified...." This statement assumes that the legal status of the detainees needs clarification. In fact, however, their legal status has been stated clearly and is widely known.

The United States has stated publicly that the detainees are not entitled to POW status because they are unlawful combatants. For example, the United States has said:

> Under Article 4 of the Geneva Convention, ... Taliban detainees are not entitled to POW status.... The Taliban have not effectively distinguished themselves from the civilian population of Afghanistan. Moreover, they have not conducted their operations in accordance with the laws and customs of war.... Al Qaeda is an international terrorist group and cannot be considered a state party to the Geneva Convention. Its members, therefore, are not covered by the Geneva Convention, and are not entitled to POW status under the treaty.

...

Thus, contrary to the Commission's assertion, the detainees' legal status is clear. The United States has made it a matter of public record that the detainees are not POWs because they do not meet the criteria applicable to lawful combatants....

In light of the fact that the status already has been clarified, precautionary measures are unnecessary.

INTER-AMERICAN COMMISSION ON HUMAN RIGHTS, REITERATION OF PRECAUTIONARY MEASURES REGARDING DETAINEES IN GUANTÁNAMO

(23 July 2002)

... The additional information provided by the Petitioners in their observations May 13, 2002, to which the United States chose not to respond in substance, have augmented the Commission's concerns. In particular, as indicated by the Petitioners and as reported in the media, the manner in which certain detainees at Guantánamo Bay were captured raises reasonable doubts concerning whether they belong to the enemy's armed forces or related groups. These detainees are alleged to include, for example, six Algerian citizens arrested by US authorities in Bosnia and ten Kuwaiti nationals arrested in Pakistan. Without more, this information raises further serious concerns regarding the legal status of each of the detainees at Guantánamo Bay and the international rights and protections to which they may be entitled.

INTER-AMERICAN COMMISSION ON HUMAN RIGHTS, DETAINEES IN GUANTÁNAMO BAY, CUBA, REITERATION AND FURTHER AMPLIFICATION OF PRECAUTIONARY MEASURES

(28 Oct. 2005)

[In 2004, the US Supreme Court decided two cases relevant to the proceedings before the Inter-American Commission. One case, *Rasul v. Bush*, is directly discussed in the following excerpt from the Commission. The other case, *Hamdi v. Rumsfeld*, is dealt with indirectly. *Hamdi* involved a US citizen alleged to have been a Taliban member and held in the United States without trial. The Supreme Court, in a plurality opinion, ruled that Hamdi was entitled, under the US Constitution, to a hearing to determine whether he was indeed a combatant who could consequently be detained until the cessation of hostilities. The Court also stated that the President's detention power, as provided by congressional authorization to use military force, should be construed in light of 'longstanding law-of-war principles'. Although Hamdi was a US citizen and held inside the US mainland, after the Supreme Court's ruling, the United States established Combatant Status Review Tribunals (CSRTs) for all foreign nationals held by the Defense Department at Guantánamo. CSRTs, composed of three military officers, are mandated to determine whether an individual is an 'enemy combatant'. The Order establishing CSRTs defines 'enemy combatant' as 'an individual who was part of or supporting Taliban or Al Qaeda forces, or associated forces that are engaged in hostilities against the United States or its coalition partners. This includes any person who has committed a belligerent act or has directly supported hostilities in aid of enemy armed forces.' The United States also established Administrative Review Boards to review periodically whether an enemy combatant should continue to be detained.]

... [T]he Commission observes that when it first adopted these precautionary measures in March 2002, the urgency of the matter arose from the fact that according to available information, the detainees at Guantánamo Bay remained entirely at the unfettered discretion of the United States government. As no person under the authority and control of a state, regardless of his or her circumstances, is devoid of legal protection for his or her fundamental and non-derogable human rights, the Commission considered that the rights and protections to which the detainees may be entitled under international or domestic law could not be said to be the subject of effective legal protection by the State absent clarification of the legal status of the detainees. Over two years later, the U.S. Supreme Court reached essentially the same conclusion in its judgment in the case of *Rasul v. Bush*, in which a majority of the Court held that United States courts have jurisdiction to consider challenges to the legality of detention of foreign nationals captured abroad in connection with hostilities and incarcerated at Guantánamo Bay. The Court's finding in this respect was based upon, inter alia, the longstanding and fundamental role that the writ of habeas corpus plays as a means of reviewing Executive detention. In this respect, Mr. Justice Stevens, writing for the majority, quoted Justice Jackson's statement from his dissenting opinion in the case of *Shaughnessey v. United States ex rel. Mezei*, that:

> Executive imprisonment has long been considered oppressive and lawless since John, at Runnymede, pledged that no free man should be imprisoned, dispossessed, outlawed, or exiled save by the judgment of his peers or by the law of the land. The judges of England developed the writ of habeas corpus largely to preserve these immunities from executive restraint.

Notwithstanding the Supreme Court's pronouncement, the information before the Commission indicates that over one year since the decision, nearly half of the detainees at Guantánamo Bay have not been given effective access to counsel or otherwise provided with a fair opportunity to pursue a habeas corpus proceeding in accordance with the Supreme Court's ruling, despite the fact that the purpose of habeas is intended to be a timely remedy aimed at guaranteeing personal liberty and humane treatment. Moreover, in those habeas petitions that have been filed, no final determinations have yet been reached as to the legal status of the detainees or the rights to which they are entitled under domestic or international law. While the State argues that the procedures before the Combatant Status Review Board and the Administrative Review Boards likewise satisfy the Commission's request, it remains entirely unclear from the outcome of those proceedings what the legal status of the detainees is or what rights they are entitled to under international or domestic law. The information available only indicates that 558 of the 596 detainees have been found by the Combatant Status Review Tribunal to be "enemy combatants not entitled to prisoner of war protections." Accordingly, the Commission does not consider that these procedures have adequately responded to the concerns at the base of the Commission's request for precautionary measures.

In these circumstances, the Commission considers that the urgent situation at Guantánamo Bay continues to exist and, moreover, has been exacerbated by the fact that some detainees have been subjected to additional processes and proceedings, including removal to third countries and trial by military commission, while their legal status remains unclear. Based upon these considerations, the Commission finds that the State has not complied with this aspect of the Commission's request for precautionary measures, that a serious and urgent situation of irreparable harm to persons remains at Guantánamo Bay, and therefore reiterates its request that the State take the immediate measures necessary to have the legal status of the detainees at Guantánamo Bay effectively determined by a competent tribunal.

INTER-AMERICAN COMMISSION ON HUMAN RIGHTS, RESOLUTION NO. 2/06 ON GUANTÁNAMO BAY PRECAUTIONARY MEASURES

(28 July 2006)

[In December 2005, the US Government passed the Detainee Treatment Act, which eliminated the federal courts' statutory jurisdiction over *habeas corpus* claims brought by individuals held at Guantánamo. In *Rasul v. Bush*, the Supreme Court had held only that Guantánamo detainees had a statutory right to *habeas corpus*. The Court did not reach the question whether the constitution guaranteed such a right. The Detainee Treatment Act thus nullified the Court's ruling in *Rasul*.

Separately, in 2006, the US Supreme Court decided *Hamdan v. Rumsfeld*, which concerned fair trial rights before military commissions. Salim Ahmed Hamdan, Osama bin Laden's driver, had been captured in Afghanistan, transferred to Guantánamo and selected for trial by military commission (see p. 475, *infra*). The Court ruled that Common Article 3 applied to the conflict between the United States and Al Qaeda, and that the creation of military commissions to prosecute Al Qaeda members violated Common Article 3. The Court expressly noted that it reserved judgment on whether Hamdan could qualify for POW status.]

On March 12, 2002 . . . the Inter-American Commission on Human Rights granted precautionary measures in favor of the detainees at Guantánamo Bay requesting that the United States take the "urgent measures necessary to have the legal status of the detainees at Guantánamo determined by a competent tribunal." The Commission considered that, without this determination, the fundamental and non-derogable rights of the detainees may not be recognized and guaranteed by the United States.

Since that time, the Commission has held three hearings on the precautionary measures and has reiterated the measures to the United States on four separate occasions. Moreover, the Commission amplified the measures in response to information indicating the possible torture or other cruel, inhuman or degrading treatment or punishment of detainees at Guantánamo Bay . . .

Notwithstanding this extensive procedural history, the Commission has not received information indicating that the United States has complied with the Commission's requests. The United States has stated, among other things, that the IACHR lacks jurisdiction due to the fact that international humanitarian law and not international human rights law is the applicable regime in this matter. Thus, over four years after the Commission's measures were issued, the legal status of the detainees remains unclear. . . .

The Commission is also aware of a report issued by five special mandate holders of the United Nations Human Rights Commission in February 2006 criticizing the situation at Guantánamo Bay and urging the United States to close the facility without further delay, as well as a report issued by the United Nations Committee Against Torture in May 2006 making similar recommendations.

Finally, the Commission takes note of the June 29, 2006, decision of the U.S. Supreme Court in the case of *Hamdan v. Rumsfeld* in which the Court struck down the military commissions that the United States proposed to use to try the detainees at Guantánamo Bay, based in part upon concerns that the commissions did not satisfy the minimum protections under Common Article 3 to the Geneva Conventions. The Commission is further aware of the follow up Memorandum from the Department of Defense of July 7, 2006 [instructions for all Defense Department operations to comply with Common Article 3 in the treatment of detainees in the conflict with Al Qaeda].

In view of the forgoing, the Inter-American Commission, resolves to:

INDICATE that the failure of the United States to give effect to the Commission's precautionary measures has resulted in irreparable prejudice to the fundamental rights of the detainees at Guantánamo Bay including their rights to liberty and to humane treatment.

URGE the United States to close the Guantánamo Bay facility without delay.

...

URGE the United States to comply with its obligation to investigate, prosecute and punish any instances of torture or other cruel, inhuman or degrading treatment or punishment that may have occurred at the facility, even in the event that Guantánamo Bay facility is closed.

INTER-AMERICAN COMMISSION ON HUMAN RIGHTS WELCOMES ORDER TO CLOSE GUANTÁNAMO DETENTION CENTER

Press Release No. 02/09 (27 Jan. 2009)

[In 2008, the Supreme Court, in *Boumediene v. Bush*, held that the US Constitution guarantees a right to *habeas corpus* for individuals detained at Guantánamo — overturning that part of the Detainee Treatment Act.]

The Inter-American Commission on Human Rights (IACHR) expresses its deep satisfaction over the decision by the President of the United States, Barack Obama, to close the detention center at the Guantánamo Bay Naval Base within a period of no later than one year and to prohibit cruel, inhuman, or degrading treatment in interrogations of detained individuals.

President Obama made these decisions on 22 January 2009, with the signing of the executive orders entitled "Review and Disposition of Individuals Detained at the Guantánamo Bay Naval Base and Closure of Detention Facilities" and "Ensuring Lawful Interrogations." These decisions order government officials to immediately review the status of all individuals detained at Guantánamo and to ensure that the conditions of detention comply with all applicable national and international laws, including the Geneva Conventions. The constitutional privilege of habeas corpus of all detained individuals is also recognized, and the detention center at Guantánamo is ordered to be closed within a period of no later than one year.

...

The IACHR will continue to monitor the situation of the Guantánamo detainees until the definitive closure of the detention center and the determination of their legal status.

…

INTER-AMERICAN COMMISSION ON HUMAN RIGHTS, RESOLUTION NO. 2/11 REGARDING THE SITUATION OF THE DETAINEES AT GUANTÁNAMO

(22 July 2011)

[In March 2009, the Obama Administration provided its first definition of individuals who could be detained in the conflict with Al Qaeda and the Taliban. The Administration included the following definition in a memorandum submitted to a federal district court: persons who 'planned, authorized, committed, or aided the terrorist attacks that occurred on 11 September 2001, and persons who harbored those responsible for those attacks,' and 'persons who were part of, or substantially supported, Taliban or al-Qaida forces or associated forces that are engaged in hostilities against the United States or its coalition partners, including any person who has committed a belligerent act, or has directly supported hostilities, in aid of such enemy armed forces.' The government also stated that the scope of the Executive's detention authority, which was pursuant to congressional authorization, would be governed according to the laws of war including customary international law.

In March 2011, the President issued Executive Order 13567, which requires periodic review of all detainees held at Guantánamo. The Order also establishes the 'standard for continued detention': 'if it is necessary to protect against a significant threat to the security of the United States'. The Order requires a 'file review' of each detainee to be held every six months, and a more substantial 'full review' on a triennial basis. Information presented during a file review can also trigger a full review. At a full review, detainees shall be assisted by a government representative who advocates on their behalf and can receive additional assistance from private counsel not at the expense of the US Government. The Order states: 'If a final determination is made that a detainee does not meet the standard [for continued detention], the Secretaries of State and Defense shall be responsible for ensuring that vigorous efforts are undertaken to identify a suitable transfer location for any such detainee, outside of the United States …']

According to information that the Commission has received since 2009, the United States has endeavored to determine the legal status of the detainees at Guantánamo Bay by means of a review process carried out by an executive task force and the review of habeas corpus petitions by the federal courts. With respect to the former, the Executive determined that of the 240 persons who were detained at Guantánamo Bay in 2009, 48 could be held indefinitely without criminal charges in light of the alleged threat that they present to U.S. national security. It was further determined that 30 nationals of Yemen were subject to an indeterminate period of "conditional detention" for similar reasons. While the Executive expressed its intent to prosecute 36 individuals detained at Guantánamo, the Commission observes that to date, reports indicate that only six cases have been resolved by military commissions and one prosecution has taken place in U.S. courts.

The Commission notes that the grounds for detaining the 78 aforementioned individuals will be subject to continuing review by both the U.S. courts and the Executive branch. However, it is troubled by the lack of clarity regarding the circumstances that will justify the release of the detainees. In particular, the Commission notes with concern that U.S. courts have held that their release will be appropriate when the political branches determine that hostilities have ceased.

. . .

The United States has recognized that the laws of war govern the detention and treatment of the detainees at Guantánamo Bay. [citing the government's Memorandum of 13 March 2009]. At the same time, while the law of war generally provides for a party to the conflict to deprive combatants of their liberty as a security measure for the duration of hostilities, the U.S. government contends that many of the features of traditional armed conflict do not apply to the conflict in which it is presently engaged. Its combat operations are reportedly in response to a series of terrorist acts perpetrated in countries throughout the world by purported members of transnational groups. In contrast to a traditional armed conflict, there is unlikely to be a definitive settlement of the present state of hostilities.

The Commission reminds the United States that in situations of armed conflict, both international human rights law and international humanitarian law apply. Although international humanitarian law is the *lex specialis* for determining states' obligations in these situations, in certain circumstances, its norms may not provide sufficient protection for the rights of the persons affected. It is important to recall that the relevant provisions of international human rights law were established to protect individuals from being deprived of their liberty for prolonged periods of time at the unfettered discretion of the Executive.

The Commission has emphasized the duty of states to protect the security of their citizens, and it has recognized that reasons of public security may justify the extension of normal periods of preventive or administrative detention. Nevertheless, it has also observed that extraordinary circumstances "cannot serve as a pretext for the indefinite detention of individuals, without any charge whatever. It is obvious that when these security measures are extended beyond a reasonable time they become true and serious violations of the right to freedom" [citing a 1976 Annual Report of the IACHR].

In the present case, the ongoing detention of at least 78 of the beneficiaries of the present precautionary measures appears to be based on their alleged prior links to terrorist organizations and the contention that their release anywhere in the world may result in future acts of violence against the United States. At the same time, the United States considers that there is insufficient evidence against them to secure a conviction in the courts of justice. Under these circumstances, the Commission considers that the detention of these individuals constitutes a violation of their fundamental rights.[22] As such, the Commission reiterates that the United States should

[22] [Eds.: The Commission here cited sources in addition to its own prior positions. These additional sources included the 2006 Report of five UN mandate-holders on the situation of detainees in Guantánamo, which stated: 'The persons held at Guantánamo Bay are entitled to challenge the legality of their detention before a judicial body in accordance with article 9 of ICCPR, and to obtain release if detention is found to lack a proper legal basis . . . . [T]he continuing detention of all persons held at Guantánamo Bay amounts to arbitrary detention in violation of article 9 of ICCPR.' The

close the Guantánamo Bay facility without delay and try or release the detainees through a process undertaken in full accordance with international human rights and humanitarian law.

...

In conclusion, the failure of the United States to give effect to the Commission's precautionary measures has resulted in irreparable harm to the fundamental rights of the detainees at Guantánamo Bay, as the Commission has stated on previous occasions. The United States has recognized the detainees' right to judicial review of the bases for their ongoing deprivation of liberty; however, the U.S. courts appear consistently to defer to the Executive in a manner that renders this right illusory. Once again, the Commission urges the United States to close the Guantánamo Bay facility without delay and arrange for the trial or release of the detainees.

...

INTER-AMERICAN COMMISSION ON HUMAN RIGHTS, PRESS RELEASE, 10 YEARS AFTER DETENTIONS IN GUANTÁNAMO BEGAN, THE IACHR REPEATS ITS CALL TO CLOSE THE DETENTION CENTER

(11 Jan. 2012)

[After months of debate, the United States passed the National Defense Authorization Act for Fiscal Year 2012, which included several provisions on detention in the conflict with the Taliban and Al Qaeda.

First, the Act *codifies the definition* of individuals subject to detention using the same formula that the Administration advanced in its 13 March 2009 memorandum. Second, under a heading referring to the 'disposition of a person under the law of war', the Act confirms the authority of the military to use the option of '*detention under the law of war without trial* until the end of the hostilities'. Other options include trial — by military commission or another court — and transfer to a foreign country. Third, the Act establishes *mandatory military detention* for certain individuals pending the disposition of their case, but the Act also allows the Executive to issue a waiver for national security purposes. The mandatory detention provision applies only to a subgroup of individuals: members of Al Qaeda and associated forces who specifically participated in planning or carrying out an attack against the United States. The mandatory detention provision also excludes US citizens. Fourth,

Commission also cited the Concluding Observations of the Committee Against Torture on the United States periodic report in 2006, which stated that '[t]he Committee, noting that detaining persons indefinitely without charge constitutes per se a violation of the Convention, is concerned that detainees are held for protracted periods at Guantánamo Bay, without sufficient legal safeguards and without judicial assessment of the justification for their detention (Arts. 2, 3 and 16). The State party should cease to detain any person at Guantánamo Bay and close this detention facility, permit access by the detainees to judicial process or release them as soon as possible ...' The Commission also cited the ECtHR Grand Chamber decision — *Al Jedda v. United Kingdom* (2011) — which held that Art. 5 of the European Convention prohibited UK forces in Iraq detaining an individual on the ground that he posed a future security threat.]

the Act requires a *military judge* to preside over proceedings for determining the status of 'any unprivileged enemy belligerent who will be held in long-term detention under the law of war' and for whom *habeas corpus* is not available (e.g., an alleged Taliban member captured and detained in Afghanistan). The Act also states that the individual can choose to be represented by military counsel during those proceedings. Fifth, the Act prohibits the use of funds for *transferring or releasing into the United States* any individual previously held in Guantánamo, and also precludes the use of funds for an alternative site for detention in the United States, its territories or possessions. Finally, the Act includes provisions relating to the periodic review for Guantánamo detainees established by Executive Order 13567. The Act states that the Secretary of Defense 'is responsible for any final decision to release or transfer an individual detained in military custody' and 'in making such a final decision, the Secretary shall consider the recommendation of a periodic review board ... but shall not be bound by any such recommendation.']

Ten years after the first detainee was transferred by the United States Government to the Naval Base in Guantánamo Bay, the Inter-American Commission on Human Rights (IACHR) urges the U.S. Government to close the detention facility without delay.

The IACHR reiterates that the Government of the United States of America must close down the detention center at the Naval Base in Guantánamo, Cuba, without further delay. Moreover, the IACHR reiterates that the United States must determine the legality of the deprivation of liberty of the persons detained in Guantánamo ... and allow the Inter-American Commission and the international protection bodies to conduct monitoring visits to the detention facilities.

...

The IACHR has held eight hearings related to the situation of the detainees at the Naval Base in Guantánamo, in the years 2002, 2003, 2005 (two), 2007, 2008 and 2010. Additionally, in 2007 and 2011 the IACHR requested authorization to carry out a visit to the Guantánamo detention center. In both instances, the Government replied that the only institution with the competence to be allowed access to the detainees was the International Red Cross, and that a visit by the IACHR would therefore have to be limited to a guided visit of the installations, without access to detainees. The IACHR expressed to the United States Government that these conditions were not acceptable and declined to conduct the visit under such circumstances. Doing so would have limited the functions of the Commission and implied a lack of recognition for its mandate as a principal organ of the Organization of American States charged with the observation and defense of human rights in the hemisphere.

...

Finally, the IACHR expresses its concern over new legislation in the United States that authorizes the indefinite detention of persons without trial. The provision is part of the National Defense Authorization Act for Fiscal Year 2012, approved by Congress and signed by the President.... In this regard, the American Declaration of the Rights and Duties of Man establishes that, "Every individual who has been deprived of his liberty has the right to have the legality of his detention ascertained without delay by a court, and the right to be tried without undue delay or, otherwise, to be released [. . .]." (Art. XXV). It further establishes that, "Every accused person is presumed to be innocent until proved guilty [. . .]." (Art. XXVI). Thus, under all circumstances, a judge must periodically review whether the personal circumstances of the detainee and the facts of the case still meet the conditions established by law to keep the person in custody. If these conditions no longer exist, the detainee must be released. Any deprivation of liberty must be strictly in accordance with the law on which it is based, with international human rights law and, when applicable, with international humanitarian law. Therefore, the IACHR reiterates that when the detention of persons without charge, even in extraordinary situations, extends beyond a reasonable time, it represents a serious violation of the right to personal liberty.

NOTE

Some commentators believe that the Obama Administration qualified the earlier US position on the relationship between international human rights law and the law of armed conflict. A key text in this regard is the US state party report submitted to the UN Human Rights Committee on 30 December 2011. The most relevant passages include the following:

> 506. With respect to the application of the Covenant and the international law of armed conflict (also referred to as international humanitarian law or "IHL"), the United States has not taken the position that the Covenant does not apply "in time of war." Indeed, a time of war does not suspend the operation of the Covenant to matters within its scope of application. To cite but two obvious examples from among many, a State Party's participation in a war would in no way excuse it from respecting and ensuring rights to have or adopt a religion or belief of one's choice or the right and opportunity of every citizen to vote and to be elected at genuine periodic elections.
>
> 507. More complex issues arise with respect to the relevant body of law that determines whether a State's actions in the actual conduct of an armed conflict comport with international law. Under the doctrine of *lex specialis*, the applicable rules for the protection of individuals and conduct of hostilities in armed conflict are typically found in international humanitarian law, including the Geneva Conventions of 1949, the Hague Regulations of 1907, and other international humanitarian law instruments, as well as in the customary international law of armed conflict. In this context, it is important to bear in mind that international human rights law and the law of armed conflict are in many respects complementary and mutually reinforcing. These two bodies of law contain many similar protections. For example prohibitions on torture and cruel treatment exist in both, and the drafters in each area have drawn from the other in developing aspects of new instruments; the Commentaries to Additional Protocol II to the Geneva Conventions make clear that a number of provisions in the Protocol were modeled on comparable provisions in the ICCPR. Determining the international law rule that applies to a particular action taken by a government in the context of an armed conflict is a fact-specific determination, which cannot be easily generalized,

and raises especially complex issues in the context of non-international armed conflicts occurring within a State's own territory.

508. . . . Along with other actions, on January 22, 2009, President Obama issued three Executive Orders relating to U.S. detention and interrogation policies broadly and the Guantánamo Bay detention facility specifically. For example, Executive Order 13491 on Ensuring Lawful Interrogations (2009), which was adopted, inter alia, "to ensure compliance with the treaty obligations of the United States, including the Geneva Conventions," provides that

> Consistent with the requirements of . . . the Convention Against Torture, Common Article 3, and other laws regulating the treatment and interrogation of individuals detained in any armed conflict, such persons shall in all circumstances be treated humanely and shall not be subjected to violence to life and person . . . whenever such individuals are in the custody or under the effective control of an officer, employee, or other agent of the United States Government or detained within a facility owned, operated, or controlled by a department or agency of the United States.

Id., Preamble and Sec. 3(a).

Executive Order 1356 (2011), concerning the periodic review of individuals detained at Guantánamo, also included a statement that the order 'shall be implemented . . . consistent with applicable law including: the Convention Against Torture; Common Article 3 of the Geneva Conventions; the Detainee Treatment Act of 2005; and other laws relating to the transfer, treatment, and interrogation of individuals detained in an armed conflict'.

QUESTIONS

1. Is the US Government's position on the relationship between the two bodies of law — IHL and human rights law — persuasive? Do human rights bodies, such as the Inter-American Commission, have the proper expertise and competence to interpret and apply IHL? What factors should determine the appropriate role for such an institution? Has the US Government's position on *lex specialis* changed fundamentally?

2. Should the administrative detention of suspected terrorists, or unlawful combatants in an armed conflict, be subject to review by a court? Human rights law says one thing, and IHL arguably says another. Articles XVIII and XXV of the Declaration on the Rights and Duties of Man contemplate 'resort to the courts' and 'legality of . . . detention ascertained . . . by a court'. So does a corresponding provision in the ICCPR: Article 9(4). Article 5 of the POW Convention, however, refers only to a 'competent tribunal', which most authorities conclude could be satisfied by an administrative body composed of military personnel. The ICRC Commentaries on a similar article in Protocol I state:

> This rule is more or less based on Article 5 of the Third Convention and the question which arises is obviously that of knowing what is meant by a 'competent tribunal'. This problem had already arisen for the drafters of Article 5 of the Third

> Convention.... The drafters finally agreed upon the expression 'competent tribunal', and the Rapporteur indicated in his report that 'as in the case of Article 5, such a tribunal may be administrative in nature', which includes, in particular, military commissions.

Can the principle of *lex specialis derogat legi generali* resolve this conflict? Or, should the *lex specialis* principle operate only in the case of a 'true conflict' of law — when one rule prohibits an action that another rule requires? Should Article 5 be interpreted differently in light of the evolution of human rights norms since 1949?

3. Does the nature of the conflict with Al Qaeda amplify or reduce the need for judicial review of detention decisions? Does the special threat posed by terrorism suggest that older, more protective rules are less applicable in this new context? Or is the nature of the conflict so vague and open-ended such that greater judicial safeguards are needed?

4. Have changes in US policy fulfilled the obligations expressed by the Inter-American Commission? Do aspects of US detention policy still violate those obligations? Does the Commission give the United States sufficient credit for changes that occurred in more recent years? Does the Commission fail to criticize US policy strongly enough? What might have motivated the United States to change or maintain some of these detention policies over time?

2. CASE STUDY: INDEFINITE DETENTION IN EUROPE

Prior to 11 September, the UK Parliament passed the Terrorism Act 2000. The law provides a general definition of terrorism, which serves as the backbone of British anti-terrorism laws and practices. Section 1 of the legislation reads:

1 Terrorism: interpretation

(1) In this Act 'terrorism' means the use or threat of action where –
  (a) the action falls within subsection (2),
  (b) the use or threat is designed to influence the government or to intimidate the public or a section of the public, and
  (c) the use or threat is made for the purpose of advancing a political, religious or ideological cause.

(2) Action falls within this subsection if it –
  (a) involves serious violence against a person,
  (b) involves serious damage to property,
  (c) endangers a person's life, other than that of the person committing the action,
  (d) creates a serious risk to the health or safety of the public or a section of the public, or
  (e) is designed seriously to interfere with or seriously to disrupt an electronic system.

(3) The use or threat of action falling within subsection (2) which involves the use of firearms or explosives is terrorism whether or not subsection (1)(b) is satisfied.

(4) In this section –

(a) 'action' includes action outside the United Kingdom,

(b) a reference to any person or to property is a reference to any person, or to property, wherever situated,

(c) a reference to the public includes a reference to the public of a country other than the United Kingdom, . . .

. . .

(5) In this Act a reference to action taken for the purposes of terrorism includes a reference to action taken for the benefit of a proscribed organisation.

In the aftermath of 11 September, the United Kingdom took two significant steps. First, Parliament passed the Anti-terrorism, Crime and Security Act 2001 (ATCSA). The Act provides broad powers to detain foreign nationals who cannot be deported, for example due to the threat of torture on their return or the lack of agreement with their home country. Section 23(1) states:

(1) A suspected international terrorist may be detained . . . despite the fact that his removal or departure from the United Kingdom is prevented (whether temporarily or indefinitely) by –

(a) a point of law which wholly or partly relates to an international agreement, or

(b) a practical consideration.

Second, the government submitted a detailed Derogation Order under the European Convention on Human Rights and the ICCPR in contemplation of the new detention rules.

Under the ATCSA, the UK Home Secretary certified a total of 17 foreign nationals as 'suspected international terrorists'. These individuals were detained without the prospect of a criminal trial. They were alleged by the Home Secretary to have engaged in various activities including maintaining 'extensive contacts to senior terrorists worldwide', being 'at the centre in the UK of terrorist activities associated with al-Qaeda', being an 'active supporter of various international terrorist groups, including those with links to Osama Bin Laden's terrorist network . . . [and engaging in] activities on their behalf include[ing] fund raising', and being 'an active supporter of the Tunisian Fighting Group, a terrorist organisation with close links to al-Qaeda . . . [and having] provided direct assistance to a number of active terrorists.'

In a case brought before the UK's highest court, the then House of Lords, the petitioners had been certified as suspected international terrorists between December 2001 and early 2002. They could not be deported to their home countries because they faced a risk of torture or inhuman or degrading treatment. The Home Secretary accordingly detained the petitioners pursuant to section 23(1) of the ATCSA. Two of the detainees exercised their right to leave the United Kingdom: one went to Morocco and the other to France. One detainee was released on bail on strict conditions in April 2004. The Home Secretary revoked the certification of another detainee in

September 2004. Due to the significance of the case, the House of Lords convened a panel of nine rather than the ordinary five judges, an action that had occurred only once since the Second World War. The court held that the detention measures were incompatible with the European Convention on Human Rights. Only one Law Lord dissented in the case.[23] On appeal to the European Court of Human Rights, a regular judicial chamber was assembled but that body quickly relinquished jurisdiction to the Grand Chamber of the Court. The decision of the Grand Chamber follows.

A AND OTHERS v. UNITED KINGDOM

European Court of Human Rights (Grand Chamber), 2009

10. The Government contended that the events of 11 September 2001 demonstrated that international terrorists, notably those associated with al'Qaeda, had the intention and capacity to mount attacks against civilian targets on an unprecedented scale.... In the Government's assessment, the United Kingdom, because of its close links with the United States, was a particular target. They considered that there was an emergency of a most serious kind threatening the life of the nation. Moreover, they considered that the threat came principally, but not exclusively, from a number of foreign nationals present in the United Kingdom, who were providing a support network for Islamist terrorist operations linked to al'Qaeda. A number of these foreign nationals could not be deported because of the risk that they would suffer treatment contrary to Article 3 of the Convention in their countries of origin.

11. On 11 November 2001 the Secretary of State made a Derogation Order . . . [and] lodged the derogation with the Secretary General of the Council of Europe. The derogation notice provided as follows:

...

> As a result of the public emergency, provision is made in the [ATCSA], inter alia, for an extended power to arrest and detain a foreign national which will apply where it is intended to remove or deport the person from the United Kingdom but where removal or deportation is not for the time being possible . . . The extended power to arrest and detain will apply where the Secretary of State issues a certificate indicating his belief that the person's presence in the United Kingdom is a risk to national security and that he suspects the person of being an international terrorist. That certificate will be subject to an appeal to the Special Immigration Appeals Commission ('SIAC').... In addition, the certificate will be reviewed by SIAC at regular intervals. SIAC will also be able to grant bail, where appropriate, subject to conditions. It will be open to a detainee to end his detention at any time by agreeing to leave the United Kingdom.

[23] Sangeeta Shah, 'The UK's Anti-Terror Legislation and the House of Lords: The First Skirmish', 6 Hum. Rts. L. R. 416 (2006).

> The extended power of arrest and detention … is a temporary provision which comes into force for an initial period of 15 months and then expires unless renewed by the Parliament. Thereafter, it is subject to annual renewal by Parliament. …
>
> …
>
> It is well established that Article 5(1)(f) permits the detention of a person with a view to deportation only in circumstances where 'action is being taken with a view to deportation' (*Chahal v United Kingdom* (1996) 23 EHRR 413 at paragraph 112). In that case the European Court of Human Rights indicated that detention will cease to be permissible under Article 5(1)(f) if deportation proceedings are not prosecuted with due diligence. … In some cases, where the intention remains to remove or deport a person on national security grounds, continued detention may not be consistent with Article 5(1)(f) as interpreted by the Court in the *Chahal* case. This may be the case, for example, if the person has established that removal to their own country might result in treatment contrary to Article 3 of the Convention. … If no alternative destination is immediately available then removal or deportation may not, for the time being, be possible even though the ultimate intention remains to remove or deport the person once satisfactory arrangements can be made. In addition, it may not be possible to prosecute the person for a criminal offence given the strict rules on the admissibility of evidence in the criminal justice system of the United Kingdom and the high standard of proof required.
>
> … To the extent, therefore, that the exercise of the extended power [to detain] may be inconsistent with the United Kingdom's obligations under Article 5(1), the Government has decided to avail itself of the right of derogation conferred by Article 15(1) of the Convention and will continue to do so until further notice.

…

i. The Court's approach

173. The Court recalls that it falls to each Contracting State, with its responsibility for "the life of [its] nation", to determine whether that life is threatened by a "public emergency" and, if so, how far it is necessary to go in attempting to overcome the emergency. By reason of their direct and continuous contact with the pressing needs of the moment, the national authorities are in principle better placed than the international judge to decide both on the presence of such an emergency and on the nature and scope of the derogations necessary to avert it. Accordingly, in this matter a wide margin of appreciation should be left to the national authorities.

Nonetheless, Contracting Parties do not enjoy an unlimited discretion. It is for the Court to rule whether, *inter alia*, the States have gone beyond the "extent strictly required by the exigencies" of the crisis. The domestic margin of appreciation is thus accompanied by a European supervision. In exercising this supervision, the Court must give appropriate weight to such relevant factors as the nature of the rights affected by the derogation and the circumstances leading to, and the duration of, the emergency situation (*Ireland v. the United Kingdom,* cited above, § 207; *Brannigan and McBride v. the United Kingdom,* judgment of 26 May 1993, § 43, Series A no. 258; *Aksoy*, cited above, § 68).

174. The object and purpose underlying the Convention, as set out in Article 1, is that the rights and freedoms should be secured by the Contracting State within its jurisdiction. It is fundamental to the machinery of protection established by the Convention that the national systems themselves provide redress for breaches of its provisions, with the Court exercising a supervisory role subject to the principle of subsidiarity (*Z. and Others v. the United Kingdom*, no. 29392/95, § 103, ECHR 2001-V). Moreover, the domestic courts are part of the "national authorities" to which the Court affords a wide margin of appreciation under Article 15. In the unusual circumstances of the present case, where the highest domestic court has examined the issues relating to the State's derogation and concluded that there was a public emergency threatening the life of the nation but that the measures taken in response were not strictly required by the exigencies of the situation, the Court considers that it would be justified in reaching a contrary conclusion only if satisfied that the national court had misinterpreted or misapplied Article 15 or the Court's jurisprudence under that Article or reached a conclusion which was manifestly unreasonable.

ii. Whether there was a "public emergency threatening the life of the nation"

175. The applicants argued that there had been no public emergency threatening the life of the British nation, for three main reasons: first, the emergency was neither actual nor imminent; secondly, it was not of a temporary nature; and, thirdly, the practice of other States, none of which had derogated from the Convention, together with the informed views of other national and international bodies, suggested that the existence of a public emergency had not been established.

176. The Court recalls that in *Lawless*, cited above, § 28, it held that in the context of Article 15 the natural and customary meaning of the words "other public emergency threatening the life of the nation" was sufficiently clear and that they referred to "an exceptional situation of crisis or emergency which affects the whole population and constitutes a threat to the organised life of the community of which the State is composed". In the *Greek Case* (1969) 12 YB 1, § 153, the Commission held that, in order to justify a derogation, the emergency should be actual or imminent; that it should affect the whole nation to the extent that the continuance of the organised life of the community was threatened; and that the crisis or danger should be exceptional, in that the normal measures or restrictions, permitted by the Convention for the maintenance of public safety, health and order, were plainly inadequate. In *Ireland v United Kingdom*, cited above, §§ 205 and 212, the parties were agreed, as were the Commission and the Court, that the Article 15 test was satisfied, since terrorism had for a number of years represented "a particularly far-reaching and acute danger for the territorial integrity of the United Kingdom, the institutions of the six counties and the lives of the province's inhabitants". The Court reached similar conclusions as regards the continuing security situation in Northern Ireland in *Brannigan and McBride*, cited above, and *Marshall v. the United Kingdom* (dec.), no. 41571/98, 10 July 2001. In *Aksoy*, cited above, it accepted that Kurdish separatist violence had given rise to a "public emergency" in Turkey.

177. Before the domestic courts, the Secretary of State adduced evidence to show the existence of a threat of serious terrorist attacks planned against the United

Kingdom. Additional closed evidence was adduced before SIAC. All the national judges accepted that the danger was credible (with the exception of Lord Hoffmann, who did not consider that it was of a nature to constitute "a threat to the life of the nation"). Although when the derogation was made no al'Qaeda attack had taken place within the territory of the United Kingdom, the Court does not consider that the national authorities can be criticised, in the light of the evidence available to them at the time, for fearing that such an attack was "imminent", in that an atrocity might be committed without warning at any time. The requirement of imminence cannot be interpreted so narrowly as to require a State to wait for disaster to strike before taking measures to deal with it. Moreover, the danger of a terrorist attack was, tragically, shown by the bombings and attempted bombings in London in July 2005 to have been very real. Since the purpose of Article 15 is to permit States to take derogating measures to protect their populations from future risks, the existence of the threat to the life of the nation must be assessed primarily with reference to those facts which were known at the time of the derogation. The Court is not precluded, however, from having regard to information which comes to light subsequently (see, *mutatis mutandis*, *Vilvarajah and others v. the United Kingdom*, judgment of 30 October 1991, § 107(2), Series A no. 215).

178. While the United Nations Human Rights Committee has observed that measures derogating from the provisions of the ICCPR must be of "an exceptional and temporary nature", the Court's case-law has never, to date, explicitly incorporated the requirement that the emergency be temporary, although the question of the proportionality of the response may be linked to the duration of the emergency. Indeed, the cases cited above, relating to the security situation in Northern Ireland, demonstrate that it is possible for a "public emergency" within the meaning of Article 15 to continue for many years. The Court does not consider that derogating measures put in place in the immediate aftermath of the al'Qaeda attacks in the United States of America, and reviewed on an annual basis by Parliament, can be said to be invalid on the ground that they were not "temporary".

179. The applicants' argument that the life of the nation was not threatened is principally founded on the dissenting opinion of Lord Hoffman, who interpreted the words as requiring a threat to the organised life of the community which went beyond a threat of serious physical damage and loss of life. It had, in his view, to threaten "our institutions of government or our existence as a civil community". However, the Court has in previous cases been prepared to take into account a much broader range of factors in determining the nature and degree of the actual or imminent threat to the "nation" and has in the past concluded that emergency situations have existed even though the institutions of the State did not appear to be imperilled to the extent envisaged by Lord Hoffman [sic].

180. As previously stated, the national authorities enjoy a wide margin of appreciation under Article 15 in assessing whether the life of their nation is threatened by a public emergency. While it is striking that the United Kingdom was the only Convention State to have lodged a derogation in response to the danger from al'Qaeda, although other States were also the subject of threats, the Court accepts that it was for each Government, as the guardian of their own people's safety, to make their own assessment on the basis of the facts known to them. Weight must,

therefore, attach to the judgment of the United Kingdom's executive and Parliament on this question. In addition, significant weight must be accorded to the views of the national courts, who were better placed to assess the evidence relating to the existence of an emergency.

181. On this first question, the Court accordingly shares the view of the majority of the House of Lords that there was a public emergency threatening the life of the nation.

iii. Whether the measures were strictly required by the exigencies of the situation

182. . . . As previously stated, the Court considers that it should in principle follow the judgment of the House of Lords on the question of the proportionality of the applicants' detention, unless it can be shown that the national court misinterpreted the Convention or the Court's case-law or reached a conclusion which was manifestly unreasonable. It will consider the Government's challenges to the House of Lords' judgment against this background.

183. The Government contended, first, that the majority of the House of Lords should have afforded a much wider margin of appreciation to the executive and Parliament to decide whether the applicants' detention was necessary. A similar argument was advanced before the House of Lords, where the Attorney General submitted that the assessment of what was needed to protect the public was a matter of political rather than judicial judgment.

184. When the Court comes to consider a derogation under Article 15, it allows the national authorities a wide margin of appreciation to decide on the nature and scope of the derogating measures necessary to avert the emergency. Nonetheless, it is ultimately for the Court to rule whether the measures were "strictly required". In particular, where a derogating measure encroaches upon a fundamental Convention right, such as the right to liberty, the Court must be satisfied that it was a genuine response to the emergency situation, that it was fully justified by the special circumstances of the emergency and that adequate safeguards were provided against abuse (see, for example, *Brannigan and McBride*, cited above, §§ 48–66; *Aksoy,* cited above, §§ 71–84; and the principles outlined in paragraph 173 above). The doctrine of the margin of appreciation has always been meant as a tool to define relations between the domestic authorities and the Court. It cannot have the same application to the relations between the organs of State at the domestic level. As the House of Lords held, the question of proportionality is ultimately a judicial decision, particularly in a case such as the present where the applicants were deprived of their fundamental right to liberty over a long period of time. In any event, having regard to the careful way in which the House of Lords approached the issues, it cannot be said that inadequate weight was given to the views of the executive or of Parliament.

. . .

186. The Government's third ground of challenge to the House of Lords' decision was directed principally at the approach taken towards the comparison between non-national and national suspected terrorists. The Court, however, considers that the House of Lords was correct in holding that the impugned powers were not to be seen as immigration measures, where a distinction between nationals and

non-nationals would be legitimate, but instead as concerned with national security. Part 4 of the 2001 Act was designed to avert a real and imminent threat of terrorist attack which, on the evidence, was posed by both nationals and non-nationals. The choice by the Government and Parliament of an immigration measure to address what was essentially a security issue had the result of failing adequately to address the problem, while imposing a disproportionate and discriminatory burden of indefinite detention on one group of suspected terrorists. As the House of Lords found, there was no significant difference in the potential adverse impact of detention without charge on a national or on a non-national who in practice could not leave the country because of fear of torture abroad.

187. Finally, the Government advanced two arguments which the applicants claimed had not been relied on before the national courts.... In these circumstances, even assuming that the principle of subsidiarity does not prevent the Court from examining new grounds, it would require persuasive evidence in support of them.

188. The first of the allegedly new arguments was that it was legitimate for the State, in confining the measures to non-nationals, to take into account the sensitivities of the British Muslim population in order to reduce the chances of recruitment among them by extremists. However, the Government has not placed before the Court any evidence to suggest that British Muslims were significantly more likely to react negatively to the detention without charge of national rather than foreign Muslims reasonably suspected of links to al'Qaeda. In this respect the Court notes that the system of control orders, put in place by the Prevention of Terrorism Act 2005, does not discriminate between national and non-national suspects.

189. The second allegedly new ground relied on by the Government was that the State could better respond to the terrorist threat if it were able to detain its most serious source, namely non-nationals. In this connection, again the Court has not been provided with any evidence which could persuade it to overturn the conclusion of the House of Lords that the difference in treatment was unjustified. Indeed, the Court notes that the national courts, including SIAC, which saw both the open and the closed material, were not convinced that the threat from non-nationals was more serious than that from nationals.

190. In conclusion, therefore, the Court, like the House of Lords, and contrary to the Government's contention, finds that the derogating measures were disproportionate in that they discriminated unjustifiably between nationals and non-nationals. It follows there has been a violation of Article 5 § 1....

...

252. The decision whether to award monetary compensation in this case and, if so, the amount of any such award, must take into account a number of factors. The applicants were detained for long periods, in breach of Article 5 § 1, and the Court has, in the past, awarded large sums in just satisfaction in respect of unlawful detention. The present case is, however, very different. In the aftermath of the al'Qaeda attacks on the United States of 11 September 2001, in a situation which the domestic courts and this Court have accepted was a public emergency threatening the life of the nation, the Government were under an obligation to protect the population of the United Kingdom from terrorist violence. The detention scheme in Part 4 of the 2001 Act was devised in good faith, as an attempt to reconcile the need

to prevent the commission of acts of terrorism with the obligation under Article 3 of the Convention not to remove or deport any person to a country where he could face a real risk of ill-treatment. Although the Court, like the House of Lords, has found that the derogating measures were disproportionate, the core part of that finding was that the legislation was discriminatory in targeting non-nationals only. Moreover, following the House of Lords' judgment, the detention scheme under the 2001 Act was replaced by a system of control orders under the Prevention of Terrorism Act 2005.[24] All the applicants in respect of whom the Court has found a violation of Article 5 § 1 became, immediately upon release in March 2005, the subject of control orders. It cannot therefore be assumed that, even if the violations in the present case had not occurred, the applicants would not have been subjected to some restriction on their liberty.

253. Against this background, the Court finds that the circumstances justify the making of an award substantially lower than that which it has had occasion to make in other cases of unlawful detention. It awards 3,900 euros (EUR) to the first, third and sixth applicants; EUR 3,400 to the fifth applicant; EUR 3,800 to the seventh applicant; EUR 2,800 to the eighth applicant; EUR 3,400 to the ninth applicant; EUR 2,500 to the tenth applicant; and EUR 1,700 to the eleventh applicant, together with any tax that may be chargeable.

COMMENT ON THE HOUSE OF LORDS JUDGMENT IN *A AND OTHERS*

As the Grand Chamber mentioned, the House of Lords similarly invalidated the detention measures on the ground that they were disproportionate. However, in its proportionality analysis, the House of Lords not only concluded that the law was under-inclusive because it failed to cover British nationals. They also concluded that the law was: (1) under-inclusive in the use of coercive power because it allowed foreign nationals to leave for another country; and (2) over-inclusive in its coverage

[24] Control orders are also referenced in para. of 188 of the Court's opinion. And they are referenced in a subsequent opinion by the European Court, *Othman (Abu Qatada) v. United Kingdom* (2012), which we discuss later in this chapter. Subsequent to the House of Lords' invalidation of the detention measures in *A and Others*, Parliament passed the Prevention of Terrorism Act 2005. The Act provided for 'control orders' to be imposed on individuals of any nationality (including British) who were suspected of being 'involved in terrorism-related activity'. Control orders were intended to apply when there was insufficient evidence to pursue criminal prosecution. The Act provided for two types of control orders: derogating control orders, which impose obligations on an individual that are incompatible with the right to liberty under Art. 5 of the European Convention and which require a specific order of derogation; and nonderogating control orders. Control orders have included various measures such as confinement to specific premises, electronic monitoring, restrictions on use of certain services or facilities, restrictions in respect of work or other occupation, prohibitions and restrictions on associations and communications and prohibitions on being at specified places or within specified areas during particular times of the day. The government phased out control orders and replaced them with Terrorism Prevention and Investigation Measures (TPIMS) in late 2011. The new regime retains many of the control order restrictions. However, it removes the ability of the government to relocate individuals within the country. And it potentially limits the restrictive measures to two years unless there is a finding of continued 'terrorism-related activity'.

because it extended beyond Al Qaeda to target terrorist groups that posed no threat to the United Kingdom. The House of Lords explained:

> [S]ections 21 and 23 [of the ATCSA] do permit a person certified and detained to leave the United Kingdom and go to any other country willing to receive him, as two of the appellants did when they left for Morocco and France respectively. Such freedom to leave is wholly explicable in terms of immigration control: if the British authorities wish to deport a foreign national but cannot deport him to country "A" because of *Chahal* their purpose is as well served by his voluntary departure for country "B". But allowing a suspected international terrorist to leave our shores and depart to another country, perhaps a country as close as France, there to pursue his criminal designs, is hard to reconcile with a belief in his capacity to inflict serious injury to the people and interests of this country. It seems clear from the language of section 21 of the 2001 Act, read with the definition of terrorism in section 1 of the 2000 Act, that section 21 is capable of covering those who have no link at all with Al-Qaeda (they might, for example, be members of the Basque separatist organisation ETA), or who, although supporting the general aims of Al-Qaeda, reject its cult of violence....

Some of these features of the 2001 Act were the subject of comment by the European Commissioner for Human Rights in his Opinion 1/2002 (28 Aug. 2002):

> The proportionality of the derogating measures is further brought into question by the definition of international terrorist organisations provided by section 21(3) of the Act. The section would appear to permit the indefinite detention of an individual suspected of having links with an international terrorist organisation irrespective of its presenting a direct threat to public security in the United Kingdom and perhaps, therefore, of no relation to the emergency originally requiring the legislation under which his Convention rights may be prejudiced.
>
> ...
>
> It would appear, therefore, that the derogating measures of the [ATCSA] allow both for the detention of those presenting no direct threat to the United Kingdom and for the release of those of whom it is alleged that they do. Such a paradoxical conclusion is hard to reconcile with the strict exigencies of the situation.

The House of Lords independently considered a claim of discrimination under Article 14 of the European Convention. The Grand Chamber decided not to reach that question on the ground that the Chamber's reasoning and conclusion in relation to Article 5 rendered that determination unnecessary. The House of Lords' opinion, however, is an important judicial landmark in analysing non-discrimination principles in the context of combating terrorism. An excerpt of the lead opinion by Lord Bingham follows:

> The appellants complained that in providing for the detention of suspected international terrorists who were not UK nationals but not for the detention of suspected international terrorists who were UK nationals, section 23 unlawfully discriminated against them as non-UK nationals in breach of Article 14 of the European Convention....

Jackson J reflected this belief in his well-known judgment in *Railway Express Agency Inc v New York* 336 US 106, 112–113 (1949), when he said:

> "I regard it as a salutary doctrine that cities, states and the Federal Government must exercise their powers so as not to discriminate between their inhabitants except upon some reasonable differentiation fairly related to the object of regulation. This equality is not merely abstract justice. The framers of the Constitution knew, and we should not forget today, that there is no more effective practical guaranty against arbitrary and unreasonable government than to require that the principles of law which officials would impose upon a minority must be imposed generally. Conversely, nothing opens the door to arbitrary action so effectively as to allow those officials to pick and choose only a few to whom they will apply legislation and thus to escape the political retribution that might be visited upon them if larger numbers were affected. Courts can take no better measure to assure that laws will be just than to require that laws be equal in operation."

...

The United Kingdom did not derogate from Article 14 of the European Convention (or from Article 26 of the ICCPR, which corresponds to it)....

...

... [T]he appellants' chosen comparators were suspected international terrorists who were UK nationals. The appellants pointed out that they shared with this group the important characteristics (a) of being suspected international terrorists and (b) of being irremovable from the United Kingdom. Since these were the relevant characteristics for purposes of the comparison, it was unlawfully discriminatory to detain non-UK nationals while leaving UK nationals at large.

Were suspected international terrorists who were UK nationals, the appellants' chosen comparators, in a relevantly analogous situation to the appellants? ... The Court of Appeal thought not because (per Lord Woolf, para 56) "the nationals have a right of abode in this jurisdiction but the aliens only have a right not to be removed". This is, however, to accept the correctness of the Secretary of State's choice of immigration control as a means to address the Al-Qaeda security problem, when the correctness of that choice is the issue to be resolved. In my opinion, the question demands an affirmative answer. Suspected international terrorists who are UK nationals are in a situation analogous with the appellants because, in the present context, they share the most relevant characteristics of the appellants.

... The undoubted aim of the relevant measure, section 23 of the 2001 Act, was to protect the UK against the risk of Al-Qaeda terrorism. As noted above that risk was thought to be presented mainly by non-UK nationals but also and to a significant extent by UK nationals also. The effect of the measure was to permit the former to be deprived of their liberty but not the latter. The appellants were treated differently because of their nationality or immigration status....

... In his discussion paper ... the Secretary of State said:

> ".... The Government believes it is defensible to distinguish between foreign nationals and our own citizens and reflects their different rights and responsibilities. Immigration powers and the possibility of deportation could not apply to British citizens. While it would be possible to seek other powers

to detain British citizens who may be involved in international terrorism it would be a very grave step. The Government believes that such draconian powers would be difficult to justify. Experience has demonstrated the dangers of such an approach and the damage it can do to community cohesion and thus to the support from all parts of the public that is so essential to countering the terrorist threat."

...

The Court of Appeal differed from SIAC on the discrimination issue: [2004] QB 335. Lord Woolf CJ referred to a tension between Article 15 and Article 14 of the European Convention. He held that it would be "surprising indeed" if Article 14 prevented the Secretary of State from restricting his power to detain to a smaller rather than a larger group....

I must respectfully differ from this analysis.... Any discriminatory measure inevitably affects a smaller rather than a larger group, but cannot be justified on the ground that more people would be adversely affected if the measure were applied generally. What has to be justified is not the measure in issue but the difference in treatment between one person or group and another. What cannot be justified here is the decision to detain one group of suspected international terrorists, defined by nationality or immigration status, and not another....

QUESTIONS

1. Is the definition of terrorism in the Terrorism Act 2000 excessively vague? Which provisions are most vulnerable to criticism along those lines? What purposes might be served by the use of ambiguity? Is this vagueness more acceptable in the context of administrative law (e.g., immigration and nationality law) than in other legal domains such as criminal law? For example, should the state retain greater power and discretion in the regulation of its borders? Are the interests in avoiding vagueness strongest for criminal defendants than for other subjects of the law?

2. The Grand Chamber announced a relaxed standard of review '[i]n the unusual circumstances ... where the highest domestic court has examined the issues relating to the State's derogation and concluded that there was a public emergency threatening the life of the nation but that the measures taken in response were not strictly required by the exigencies of the situation.' Do you agree with the logic behind this approach? Why should the European Court relax its scrutiny only when state action is invalidated, rather than upheld, by an apex court? Should this approach be limited to the situation of derogations?

3. Consider the proportionality analysis by the Grand Chamber. Are there other plausible reasons that could justify treating the class of individuals subject to detention differently than British nationals? The Court suggests that the level of threat posed by the two groups is essentially indistinguishable. Do you agree? Could British nationals generally pose a greater threat than foreign nationals? Are there other factors the Court should have used to compare the two classes of individuals? Is this decision compatible with the war model for combating terrorism discussed previously?

4. In the previous section of this chapter, p. 428, *supra*, we discussed legislation in the United States, the US National Defense Authorization Act for Fiscal Year 2012, which establishes mandatory military detention for Al Qaeda members but expressly excludes US citizens. The United States has also established military commissions to try members of Al Qaeda and associated forces, but the jurisdiction of those commissions is expressly limited to prosecuting 'alien unprivileged enemy belligerents'. Do such laws run afoul of the proportionality analysis articulated in the Grand Chamber opinion? Do such laws run afoul of the discrimination principles articulated in the House of Lords' judgment?

5. The Grand Chamber gives significant deference on the determination of a public emergency — the nature of the threat to the nation — and asserts a more active role for itself in determining the proportionality of a derogation measure. The latter, however, also includes factual inquiries into the source and extent of the national security threat (see para. 189 of the opinion). Do you agree with the Grand Chamber's approach to defining its role and the role of national authorities? What aspects of its approach turn on the level of authority involved — supranational versus national — and what aspects turn on the type of authority involved — judicial versus political?

6. Is the Grand Chamber's explanation of the reasons for reduced remedial compensation in this particular case (paras. 252–3 of the opinion) convincing?

7. Evaluate the following assessment of the House of Lords' opinion.

> The House of Lords demonstrated how antiquated the derogation system is when it comes to transnational terrorism in the twenty-first century. During the proceedings, the government invoked Security Council resolutions calling on states to fight transnational terrorism, and the UK Terrorism Act of 2000 accordingly applies to terrorist acts outside UK territory. Not only do the derogation rules fail to take such transnational concerns into account; acting on such concerns may discredit a state's position. Indeed, Lord Bingham considered the government's actions — to combat terrorist threats to other countries — evidence of a lack of proportionality. This reasoning is gravely mistaken. It does not give credit to the government's motivations, and it undercuts the type of international cooperation that is necessary to combat transnational terrorism. Human rights doctrine needs to be fundamentally updated, and that project can be achieved without introducing unwarranted loopholes into the law of derogations.

ADDITIONAL READING

Int'l. Rev. Red Cross No. 871 (2008) (issue on Human Rights and Humanitarian Law); N. K. Modirzadeh, *The Dark Sides of Convergence: A Pro-Civilian Critique of the Extraterritorial Application of Human Rights Law in Armed Conflict, 86 International Law Studies* (2010), at 349; R. Goodman, 'Controlling the Recourse to War by Modifying Jus in Bello', 53 Ybk Int'l. Humanitarian L. 53 (2009); P. Alston, J.

Morgan-Foster & W. Abresch, 'The Competence of the UN Human Rights Council and its Special Procedures in relation to Armed Conflicts: Extrajudicial Executions in the "War on Terror"', 19 Eur. J. Int'l. L. 183 (2008); P. Rowe, *The Impact of Human Rights Law on Armed Forces* (2006); A. Roberts, 'Transformative Military Occupation: Applying the Laws of War and Human Rights', 100 Am. J. Int'l. L. 580 (2006); M. J. Dennis, 'Application of Human Rights Treaties Extraterritorially in Times of Armed Conflict and Military Occupation', 99 Am. J. Int'l. L. 119 (2005); J. Pejic, 'The Right to Food in Situations of Armed Conflict: The Legal Framework', 844 Int'l. Rev. Red Cross 1097 (2001); P. Alston & G. Quinn, 'The Nature and Scope of States Parties' Obligations under the International Covenant on Economic, Social, and Cultural Rights', 9 Hum. R. Q. 156 (1987).

E. TORTURE AND DIPLOMATIC ASSURANCES

The potential tension between a state's need to protect its citizens from national security risks and to respect fundamental human rights is well illustrated by current controversies over the use of 'diplomatic assurances' in the context of deportation and transfer procedures. International human rights law prohibits states from sending a person to a country where he or she will be subject to torture. In light of that obligation, several governments have chosen to seek assurances from the receiving state that the individual will not be subject to ill treatment. This practice has received greater attention in recent years in cases arising out of terrorist threats and armed conflicts. Several states have attempted to use diplomatic assurances to remove individuals allegedly involved in terrorism to other countries, including Canada (to Sri Lanka), Germany (to Turkey), Italy (to Tunisia), Spain (to Russia), Sweden (to Egypt), the United States (to Tajikistan) and the United Kingdom (to Jordan). In the armed conflict in Afghanistan, Australian, British, Canadian and US forces have transferred hundreds of individuals into the hands of Afghan authorities where they have been subject to torture. A Canadian diplomatic who served 17 months in Afghanistan sent political shockwaves when he testified before Parliament in 2009 stating: 'According to our information, the likelihood is that all Afghans we handed over were tortured'; 'The most common forms of torture were beatings, whipping with power cables, and the use of electricity. Also common was sleep deprivation, use of temperature extremes, use of knives and open flames, and sexual abuse, that is, rape'; 'Some of these Afghans may have been foot soldiers or day fighters, but many were just local people, farmers, truck drivers, tailors, peasants, random human beings in the wrong place at the wrong time, young men in their fields and villages, who were completely innocent but were nevertheless rounded up'. In recent years, the Committee on the Convention Against Torture and the Special Rapporteur on Torture have reminded other members of the International Security Assistance Force in Afghanistan — such as Denmark, Norway and Sweden — of their international human rights obligations in transferring detainees within their effective custody to the custody of any other state.

The principal obligation is enshrined in Article 3 of the Convention Against Torture, which provides:

1. No State Party shall expel, return ('refouler') or extradite a person to another State where there are substantial grounds for believing that he would be in danger of being subjected to torture.
2. For the purpose of determining whether there are such grounds, the competent authorities shall take into account all relevant considerations including, where applicable, the existence in the State concerned of a consistent pattern of gross, flagrant or mass violations of human rights.

According to standard accounts of international human rights law, this obligation is considered a norm of customary international law subject neither to limitations for national security reasons nor to derogation in times of public emergency. Thus, while human rights law might allow some rights to be qualified in the face of national security concerns, the general nature of this particular obligation aligns completely with the rights-based interest. That said, the standard of proof — 'substantial grounds' — does provide states some freedom of action. In that respect, the rule might be understood to internalize a trade-off between the risk to the individual and competing state interests.

Notably, the principle of non-refoulement is also considered a cornerstone of international refugee law.[25] The 1951 Refugee Convention expresses the obligation *with* a significant proviso for national security concerns:

Article 33

1. No Contracting State shall expel or return ("refouler") a refugee in any manner whatsoever to the frontiers of territories where his life or freedom would be threatened on account of his race, religion, nationality, membership of a particular social group or political opinion.
2. The benefit of the present provision may not, however, be claimed by a refugee whom there are reasonable grounds for regarding as a danger to the security of the country in which he is, or who, having been convicted by a final judgement of a particularly serious crime, constitutes a danger to the community of that country.

In interpreting the national security proviso, the UN Office of the High Commissioner for Refugees (UNHCR) has stated:

- 'as Article 33 (2) is an exception to a principle, it is to be interpreted and implemented in a restrictive manner';
- 'given the seriousness of an expulsion for the refugee, such a decision should involve a careful examination of the question of proportionality between the danger to the security of the community or the gravity of the crime, and the persecution feared. The application of this exception must be the ultima ratio (the last recourse) to deal with a case reasonably';

[25] A corresponding obligation is contained in the law of armed conflict (POW Convention, Art. 12; Civilians Convention, Art. 45; Additional Protocol II, Art. 5).

- '[r]ead in conjunction with Articles 31 and 32 of the 1951 Convention,[26] a State should allow a refugee a reasonable period of time and all necessary facilities to obtain admission into another country, and initiate refoulement only when all efforts to obtain admission into another country have failed';[27]
- '[t]he provisions of Article 33(2) of the 1951 Convention do not affect the host State's non-refoulement obligations under international human rights law, which permit no exceptions. Thus, the host State would be barred from removing a refugee if this would result in exposing him or her, for example, to a substantial risk of torture'.[28]

With respect to the issue of diplomatic assurances, the UNHCR stated in a 2006 Note on Diplomatic Assurances and International Refugee Protection:

> Diplomatic assurances should be given no weight when a refugee who enjoys the protection of Article 33(1) of the 1951 Convention is being refouled, directly or indirectly, to the country of origin or former habitual residence. The reason for this is that the country of refuge has already made a determination in the individual case and has recognized the refugee to have a well-founded fear of being persecuted in the country of origin. Once the country of refuge has made this finding, it would be fundamentally inconsistent with the protection afforded by the 1951 Convention for the sending State to look to the very agent of persecution for assurance that the refugee will be well-treated upon refoulement.

International authorities that are focused on legal obligations that arise out of the global human rights regime have expressed a range of possible approaches with respect to the use of diplomatic assurances in cases of torture. For the purpose of clarification, we group these approaches according to the following five levels.

Level 1: Categorical and comprehensive approach: prohibits any use of diplomatic assurances to address torture.

Level 2: Categorical approach based on individual risk: prohibits use of diplomatic assurances when the person is likely to be subject to torture.

Level 3: Categorical approach based on country conditions: prohibits use of diplomatic assurances when torture is practiced systematically in the receiving state.

Level 4: Valid but not central factor: diplomatic assurances are a valid factor in considering, and reducing, the risk of torture but should never be a central factor.

Level 5: Unqualified, valid factor: diplomatic assurances are a valid factor in considering, and reducing, the risk of torture in all cases.

[26] Article 31(2), which addresses the issue of refugees unlawfully in the country of refuge, provides: 'The Contracting States shall allow such refugees a reasonable period and all the necessary facilities to obtain admission into another country'. And, Art. 3, which address the issue of expulsion, provides:

> 1. The Contracting States shall not expel a refugee lawfully in their territory save on grounds of national security or public order.
>
> . . .
>
> 3. The Contracting States shall allow such a refugee a reasonable period within which to seek legal admission into another country. . . .

[27] UN High Commissioner for Refugees, Note on the Principle of Non-Refoulement (1997).

[28] UN High Commissioner for Refugees, Advisory Opinion on the Extraterritorial Application of Non-Refoulement Obligations under the 1951 Convention relating to the Status of Refugees and its 1967 Protocol (2007).

Level 1

The strongest position — Level 1 — has been expressed most forcefully by the former High Commissioner for Human Rights (2004–2008) Louise Arbour. She stated that the existence of such bilateral arrangements has 'an acutely corrosive effect' on the global regime against torture and '[t]he fact that some governments conclude legally nonbinding agreements with other governments on a matter that is at the core of several legally binding UN instruments threatens to empty international human rights law of its content' (L. Arbour, 'No Exceptions to the Ban on Torture', *NY Times*, 6 Dec. 2005). She also provided one of the most extensive arguments against diplomatic assurances in a 2006 speech before the British Institute of International and Comparative Law and Chatham House:[29]

> Some have postulated that diplomatic assurances could work if effective post-return monitoring mechanisms were put in place. Based on the long experience of international monitoring bodies and experts, it is unlikely that a post-return monitoring mechanism set up explicitly to prevent torture and ill-treatment in a specific case would have the desired effect. These practices often occur in secret, with the perpetrators skilled at keeping such abuses from detection. The victims, fearing reprisal, are often reluctant to speak about their suffering, or are not believed if they do. Although efforts could be made to improve on the practice of seeking these assurances, in my view it is fundamentally flawed in several ways. First, we must acknowledge that diplomatic assurances would presumably only be sought after an assessment has been made that there is a risk of torture in the receiving State. Otherwise the demarche would be both useless and insulting.
>
> Secondly, . . . while receiving States are under binding legal obligations to respect and protect human rights, including the prohibition of torture, they often are far from fully implementing their obligations, resulting in widespread violations. It is difficult to make a case that if a Government does not comply with binding law it will respect legally non-binding bilateral agreements that are concluded on the basis of trust only, without enforcement or sanctions if violated.
>
> Thirdly, even though all persons are entitled to the equal protection of existing treaties, assurances basically create a two-class system amongst those transferred, attempting to provide special bilateral protection and monitoring for a selected few while ignoring the plight of many others in detention. By seeking assurances for a chosen few, sending Governments could in fact be seen as condoning torture and cruel, inhuman or degrading treatment by acknowledging that these practices exist in the receiving State but conveniently ignoring their systemic nature.
>
> In the end we are back to the same fundamental question: why are these people sent to countries where they face the risk of torture? They may be sent to face trial, or simply to be held in custody, possibly indefinitely, or to be interrogated with the hope that the interrogation abroad will yield more information than the methods that could be used at home. The last two scenarios involve, at best, legal avoidance: suspects will be transferred because what will be done to them abroad could not legally be done at home. I fail to see any justification for any State to be a party to such practice. If they are transferred to face trial, prudence would dictate

[29] L. Arbour, 'In Our Name and on Our Behalf', 55 Int'l. & Comp. L.Q. 511 (2006); see also A/HRC/4/88.

> that their transfer should not be tainted with illegality since in many countries this could lead to the courts declining to exercise jurisdiction.

Arbour's successor, Navanethem Pillay the current High Commissioner for Human Rights has also adopted a strong position against diplomatic assurances. She, however, has not elaborated her position. In a 2010 joint publication with the Asia Pacific Forum of National Human Rights Institutions (a regional membership organization of national human rights commissions) and the Association for the Prevention of Torture (an NGO), the High Commissioner stated:

> The principle of non-refoulement is an illustration of the absolute prohibition of torture and other forms of ill-treatment. It has been undermined in recent years by the practice of some States to seek diplomatic assurances when there are known risks that the person being returned may be subjected to torture or ill-treatment.... This practice is considered to violate the principle of non-refoulement and is not permissible.

(See also, OHCHR, Fact Sheet 32: Human Rights, Terrorism and Counter-terrorism Fact Sheet (2008), at 35.) This statement might be classified as a Level 1 or Level 2 standard.

Level 2

Other international authorities adopt as a standard that diplomatic assurances cannot be used to counteract the risk that a particular individual would be in danger of torture or ill-treatment (Level 2). In other words, if the antecedent condition is that the transfer would be proscribed by international human rights law — e.g., Article 3 of the Convention Against Torture — the sending state could not use a diplomatic assurance to overcome that prohibition. This legal standard closely approximates a categorical prohibition, because the standard eliminates the option of diplomatic assurance in the very cases in which a sending state would consider the measure most useful.

The office of the Special Rapporteur on Torture and Other Cruel, Inhuman or Degrading Treatment or Punishment has become the most influential authority for the Level 2 position. As early as 1996, the then-Special Rapporteur on Torture, Sir Nigel Rodley addressed the issue. The Special Rapporteur sent an urgent appeal on behalf of an Algerian national residing in Canada whose deportation to Algeria appeared imminent. The detainee was reportedly a member of a militant opposition group in Algeria and had previously been tortured by the Algerian police. The Special Rapporteur explained:

> In view of all the circumstances the Special Rapporteur appealed to the Government not to deport Saadi Bouslimani or, if he were to be deported, to seek, and take measures to ensure compliance with, assurances from the Government of Algeria that he would not be subjected to torture or any other ill-treatment.
>
> ... [T]he Government informed the Special Rapporteur that the case of Saadi Bouslimani had been analysed very carefully by the authorities, who had concluded

> ... that, should he return to Algeria, there was no objective risk that he would be subjected to torture.... [T]he Government [stated] that it would not be appropriate to seek assurances from the Algerian Government that Mr. Bouslimani would not be subjected to torture or ill-treatment, because to do so would amount to questioning the willingness of the Algerian Government to comply with the obligations it had assumed when it ratified the International Covenant on Civil and Political Rights and the Convention against Torture.... [T]he Special Rapporteur replied that in the case of an individual who is to be sent to a country where he fears torture and where the latter reportedly occurs, it is perfectly appropriate and not uncommon to seek relevant assurances from the Government in question. The intent in seeking such assurances was not to call into question the commitment of the receiving Government to fulfil its treaty obligations, but rather to make that Government aware of the concerns that have been expressed with respect to the case and thereby to reduce the potential risk to the deported person. Futhermore, the standard of proof demanded by the Government of Canada was that of a direct personal risk of torture to Mr. Bouslimani. If this standard were always to be applicable for obtaining assurances from a receiving Government, then there would never be a need to obtain assurances, since the level of risk would preclude the person concerned from being sent back in the first place.
>
> At a later date, the Special Rapporteur learned that Saadi Bouslimani had been deported to a third country.

The next Special Rapporteur on Torture (2002–2004) Theo van Boven explicitly set forth a Level 3 approach, which we discuss below. His successor as Special Rapporteur (2004–2010) Manfred Nowak, set forth a Level 2 standard over the course of several statements. One of Nowak's most important statements on the subject outlined a set of specific concerns about the validity and effectiveness of diplomatic assurances. In a presentation before the Council of Europe, he stated the following concerns:

> (a) The principle of non-refoulement (CAT, art. 3; ECHR, art. 3; (ICCPR), art. 7) is an absolute obligation deriving from the absolute and non-derogable nature of the prohibition of torture;
>
> (b) Diplomatic assurances are sought from countries with a proven record of systematic torture, i.e. the very fact that such diplomatic assurances are sought is an acknowledgement that the requested State, in the opinion of the requesting State, is practicing torture. In most cases, those individuals in relation to whom diplomatic assurances are being sought belong to a high-risk group ("Islamic fundamentalists");
>
> (c) It is often the case that the requesting and the requested States are parties to CAT, ICCPR and other treaties absolutely prohibiting torture. Rather than using all their diplomatic and legal powers as States parties to hold other States parties accountable for their violations, requesting States, by means of diplomatic assurances, seek only an exception from the practice of torture for a few individuals, which leads to double standards vis-à-vis other detainees in those countries;
>
> (d) Diplomatic assurances are not legally binding. It is therefore unclear why States that violate binding obligations under treaty and customary international law should comply with non-binding assurances. Another important

> question in this regard is whether the authority providing such diplomatic assurances has the power to enforce them vis-à-vis its own security forces;
> (e) Post-return monitoring mechanisms are no guarantee against torture — even the best monitoring mechanisms (e.g. ICRC and [European Committee for the Prevention of Torture]) are not 'watertight' safeguards against torture;
> (f) The individual concerned has no recourse if assurances are violated;
> (g) In most cases, diplomatic assurances do not contain any sanctions in case they are violated, i.e. there is no accountability of the requested or requesting State, and therefore the perpetrators of torture are not brought to justice;
> (h) Both States have a common interest in denying that returned persons were subjected to torture. Therefore, where States have identified independent organizations to undertake monitoring functions under the agreement, these interests may translate into undue political pressure upon these monitoring bodies, particularly where one is funded by the sending and/or receiving State.
>
> In conclusion, the Special Rapporteur stated that diplomatic assurances with regard to torture are nothing but attempts to circumvent the absolute prohibition of torture and refoulement....

Nowak's statements also indicate how closely the Level 2 standard approaches an absolute prohibition on diplomatic assurances (Level 1). As another example, in 2009, he stated:

> As [the Special Rapporteur] has pointed out on numerous occasions, diplomatic assurances with regard to torture are nothing but attempts to circumvent the absolute prohibition of torture and non-refoulement. Further, diplomatic assurances are unreliable and ineffective in protection against torture and ill-treatment. The Special Rapporteur is therefore of the opinion that States cannot resort to diplomatic assurances as a safeguard against torture and ill-treatment where there are substantial grounds for believing that a person would be in danger of being subjected to torture or ill-treatment upon return.

Nowak's position — that diplomatic assurances are never acceptable when there are substantial grounds for believing that a person would be in danger of being subjected to torture or ill-treatment upon return — has directly influenced other institutions. His conclusions have been explicitly followed, for example by the European Parliament (European Parliament Resolution 2006/2027(INI)) at para. 32 ('call[ing] on the Member States to reject altogether reliance on diplomatic assurances against torture, as recommended by Manfred Nowak') and by the UN Working Group on Arbitrary Detention (A/HRC/4/40).

The same standard has also been applied by other international authorities, including the Committee Against Torture, the Inter-American Commission for Human Rights and a group of UN human rights mandate-holders. In 2009, in response to Spain's position that the return of individuals to their home state on the basis of diplomatic assurances did not violate the Convention, the Committee stated: 'under no circumstances must diplomatic guarantees be used as a safeguard against torture or ill-treatment where there are substantial grounds for believing that a person would be in danger of being subjected to torture or ill-treatment upon return.' At the same time, the Committee outlined a set of reporting requirements in the event of the state party's use of diplomatic assurances that do not violate the Convention: 'If the State party resorts to diplomatic guarantees in any situation other than those excluded under article 3 of the Convention, it must provide in its next report to the Committee information on the number of cases of extradition or expulsion that have been subject to the receipt of diplomatic assurances or guarantees since the consideration of this report; the State party's minimum requirements for such assurances or guarantees; follow-up action taken subsequently in such cases; and the enforceability of the assurances or guarantees given.' The Committee has adopted the same language in reviewing the practices of other states parties (e.g., Australia in 2008; Germany in 2011). The Inter-American Commission has also adopted the same general standard in considering the US Government's transfers of individuals from Guantánamo. Also in the context of Guantánamo detainees, a group of five UN human rights mandate-holders — the Chair of the Working Group on Arbitrary Detention, the Special Rapporteur on the independence of judges and lawyers, the Special Rapporteur on torture (Nowak), the Special Rapporteur on freedom of religion or belief and the Special Rapporteur on the right to health — issued a joint statement (months after a more famous and lengthier report by the group), which adopted a standard on diplomatic assurances consistent with Level 2. The group stated: 'It is also of utmost importance that the detainees are not returned to countries where they are at risk of torture or other serious human rights violations, such as disappearance, summary executions or arbitrary detention, in accordance with the principle of non-refoulement. Where such a risk does exist, it cannot be overcome by seeking so-called "diplomatic assurances".' Finally, Nowak's successor, the current Special Rapporteur on Torture Juan Méndez has adopted a Level 2 standard that potentially expands its scope compared with prior iterations. Specifically, in 2011, Méndez stated: 'diplomatic assurance has been proven to be unreliable, and cannot be considered an effective safeguard against torture and ill-treatment, particularly in States where there are *reasonable grounds* to believe that a person would face the danger of being subjected to torture or ill-treatment. Like his predecessor, the Special Rapporteur regards the practice of diplomatic assurances "as an attempt to circumvent the absolute prohibition of torture and nonrefoulement"' (emphasis added).

Level 3

As mentioned above, the Special Rapporteur on Torture (2001–2004) Theo van Boven adopted a Level 3 standard. In a report to the General Assembly in 2004, he explained:

> The factors and circumstances contained in articles 3 and 20 of the Convention [Against Torture], in terms of a "consistent pattern of gross, flagrant or mass violations of human rights" and the "systematic practice of torture", cover common ground, although the former term is broader in scope and not clearly defined. Thanks to the efforts of the Committee against Torture, the latter term provides,

> for present purposes, more concrete guidance, encompassing torture both as a State policy and as a practice by public authorities over which a Government has no effective control. In circumstances where this definition of "systematic practice of torture" applies, the Special Rapporteur believes that the principle of non-refoulement must be strictly observed and diplomatic assurances should not be resorted to.

Notably in an interim report to the General Assembly two years earlier, van Boven appeared to set forth a Level 5 approach by referring to the need for diplomatic assurances in cases of transferring terrorist detainees and by discussing the modalities (e.g., the need for monitoring) of such assurances (A/57/173 2002). In his 2004 report, van Boven qualified his earlier position explaining that it applied to 'situations and cases where resort to diplomatic assurances should not be ruled out a prior'. Nowak also adopted a Level 3 standard (E/CN.4/2006/6), and he explained as well that the standard did not exclude the acceptance of assurances 'in respect of countries with no substantial risk of torture' and 'under the condition that they are not aimed at circumventing international obligations of non-refoulement' (Council of Europe, Steering Committee for Human Rights, Meeting Report, Strasbourg, DH-STER(2005)018, 7–9 Dec. 2005; Gillard 2008).

Most famously, the UN Committee for the Convention Against Torture adopted a Level 3 standard in its review of the United States periodic report. The Committee stated: 'When determining the applicability of its non-refoulement obligations under article 3 of the Convention, the State party *should only rely on "diplomatic assurances" in regard to States which do not systematically violate the Convention's provisions*, and after a thorough examination of the merits of each individual case. The State party should establish and implement clear procedures for obtaining such assurances, with adequate judicial mechanisms for review, and effective post-return monitoring arrangements' (emphasis added).

Other international authorities have also adopted a Level 3 approach but with less precision in the legal standard. Indeed, some of these instances include elements of a Level 1 standard by suggesting that diplomatic assurances would never be appropriate. For example, the Council of Europe Commissioner on Human Rights Thomas Hammarberg stated that diplomatic assurances 'are definitely not the answer to the dilemma of extradition or deportation to a country where torture has been practiced. . . . The governments concerned have already violated binding international norms and it is plain wrong to subject anyone to the risk of torture on the basis of an even less solemn undertaking to make an exception in an individual case. In short, the principle of non-refoulement should not be undermined by convenient, non-binding promises of such kinds', and that 'respect for such promises is very difficult to monitor. It is absolutely wrong to put individuals at risk through testing such dubious assurances' (2008). The previous Commissioner for Human Rights, Alvaro Gil-Robles, stated in 2004: 'The weakness inherent in the practice of diplomatic assurances lies in the fact that where there is a need for such assurances, there is clearly an acknowledged risk of torture and ill-treatment. Due to the absolute nature of the prohibition of torture or inhuman or degrading treatment, formal assurances cannot suffice where a risk nonetheless remains. As the UN Special Rapporteur on

Torture [Van Boven] has noted, such assurances must be unequivocal and a system to monitor such assurances must be in place. When assessing the reliability of diplomatic assurances, an essential criteria must be that the receiving state does not practice or condone torture or ill-treatment, and that it exercises effective control over the acts of non-state agents. In all other circumstances it is highly questionable whether assurances can be regarded as providing indisputable safeguards against torture and ill-treatment.'

Finally, the former UN Sub-Commission on the Promotion and Protection of Human Rights adopted a Level 3 standard in a resolution passed in 2005. An important feature of the resolution is that it also appears squarely to reject a Level 2 approach. The resolution states that the Sub-Commission:

> 4. *Confirms* that where torture or cruel, inhuman or degrading treatment is widespread or systematic in a particular State, especially where such practice has been determined to exist by a human rights treaty body or a special procedure of the Commission on Human Rights, there is presumption that any person subject to transfer would face a real risk of being subjected to such treatment and recommends that, in such circumstances, the presumption shall not be displaced by any assurance, undertaking or other commitment made by the authorities of the State to which the individual is to be transferred;
> 5. *Also confirms* that in other cases, where a real risk of torture is determined to exist in a particular case, in no circumstances shall a transfer of the individual be effected;
> 6. *Strongly recommends* that, in situations where there is a real risk of torture or cruel, inhuman or degrading treatment in a particular case, no transfer shall be carried out unless:
>   (*a*) The State authorities effecting the transfer seek and receive credible and effective assurances, undertakings or other binding commitments from the State to which the person is to be transferred that he or she will not be subjected to torture or cruel, inhuman or degrading treatment;
>   (*b*) Provision is made, in writing, for the authorities of the transferring State to be able to make regular visits to the person transferred in his/her normal place of detention, with the possibility of medical examination, and for the visits to include interviews in private during which the transferring authorities shall ascertain how the person who has been transferred is being treated;
>   (*c*) The authorities of the transferring State undertake, in writing, to make the regular visits referred to.

Level 4

The first UN Special Rapporteur on Human Rights and Counterterrorism, Martin Sheinin, adopted a weaker stance compared to his UN counterparts. He initially signaled a strong stance in 2005 report in which he referred to diplomatic assurances as an example of 'the most alarming "new trend" related to counter-terrorism measures [which] is the increased questioning or compromising of the absolute prohibition of torture and all forms of cruel, inhuman or degrading treatment.' In 2007, however, the Special Rapporteur explicitly endorsed a Level 4 approach:

> In the view of the Special Rapporteur diplomatic assurances can, at best, be taken into account as one of the several factors to be addressed in the individual assessment of the risk. Furthermore, such assessment must be subject to effective and independent, preferably judicial, safeguards. Mindful of the fact that diplomatic assurances against torture or inhuman treatment, even when accompanied by post-removal monitoring, tend not to work in practice, the Special Rapporteur discourages the creation of removal or resettlement mechanisms where such assurances would play a central role.

A year later, in a field mission to Spain, Sheinin alternated to a marginally stronger position stating: 'the Special Rapporteur recalls that there is widespread agreement that diplomatic assurances do not work in respect of the risk of torture or other ill-treatment, as has been stated in a number of individual cases considered by international human rights bodies.' (See also Joint Statement by UN Special Rapporteurs on Torture, Manfred Nowak, and on Human Rights and Counter-Terrorism, Martin Scheinin on Fate of Guantánamo Detainees, 21 July 2010.)

Level 5

According to some commentators, the Human Rights Committee has adopted a standard that regards diplomatic assurances as a valid consideration in all cases evaluating the risk of torture (e.g., Johnston 2011). The key text is a landmark determination by the Human Rights Committee in *Alzery v. Sweden* (Communication No. 1416/2005 (10 November 2006)). In that decision the Committee suggested that as a supervisory body it 'must consider all relevant elements' in a risk analysis including assurances. However, the committee also heavily scrutinized the substance of the assurances and determined that the government had erroneously relied on the arrangements. The issue involved a decision by the Government of Sweden to return an Egyptian national, Mohammed Alzery, to Egypt. Sweden had determined that Alzery, allegedly a leader of an organization implicated in terrorist activities in Egypt, could not be returned due to the likelihood that he would be tortured. Swedish authorities then arranged for diplomatic assurances with the Government of Egypt and returned Alzery on that basis. Once in Egyptian custody, Alzery was allegedly subject to weeks of harsh interrogation and torture including electric shocks applied to his genitals, nipples and ears. The Committee issued the following Views:

> 11.3 . . . In determining the risk of such treatment in the present case, the Committee must consider all relevant elements, including the general situation of human rights in a State. The existence of diplomatic assurances, their content and the existence and implementation of enforcement mechanisms are all factual elements relevant to the overall determination of whether, in fact, a real risk of proscribed ill-treatment exists.
>
> . . .
>
> 11.5 The Committee notes that the assurances procured contained no mechanism for monitoring of their enforcement. Nor were any arrangements made outside the text of the assurances themselves which would have provided for effective

> implementation. The visits by the State party's ambassador and staff commenced five weeks after the return, neglecting altogether a period of maximum exposure to risk of harm. The mechanics of the visits that did take place, moreover, failed to conform to key aspects of international good practice by not insisting on private access to the detainee and inclusion of appropriate medical and forensic expertise, even after substantial allegations of ill-treatment emerged. In light of these factors, the State party has not shown that the diplomatic assurances procured were in fact sufficient in the present case to eliminate the risk of ill-treatment to a level consistent with the requirements of article 7 of the Covenant. The author's expulsion thus amounted to a violation of article 7 of the Covenant.

Notably, the Human Rights Committee has separately suggested a sliding scale approach to evaluating diplomatic assurances, which could be compatible with a Level 3 analysis. In its 2006 review of the United States periodic report, the Committee recommended: 'The State party should exercise the utmost care in the use of diplomatic assurances, and adopt clear and transparent procedures with adequate judicial mechanisms for review before individuals are deported, as well as effective mechanisms to monitor scrupulously and rigorously the fate of the affected individuals. The State party should further recognize that the more systematic the practice of torture or cruel, inhuman or degrading treatment or punishment, the less likely it will be that a real risk of such treatment can be avoided by such assurances, however stringent any agreed follow-up procedures may be.' The Committee adopted the same framework in its review of Sweden's state party report in 2009 (but cf. Concluding Observations — Denmark 2008).

CASE OF OTHMAN (ABU QATADA) v. UNITED KINGDOM

European Court of Human Rights (2012)

[In 1993, Jordanian citizen Omar Othman, a.k.a. Abu Qatada, fled Jordan and arrived in the United Kingdom. He was granted asylum and leave to remain temporarily in the United Kingdom on the ground that Jordanian authorities had detained and tortured him on multiple occasions. During his stay in the United Kingdom, Jordanian courts convicted Othman *in absentia* for multiple acts of terrorism. During this time, Othman also became known in the British mainstream media as 'the hate preacher' and Al Qaeda's spiritual leader in Europe. In his sermons and other public statements, he reportedly sought to justify or call for the killing of Jews, including children, attacking Americans and killing Muslims who renounce their faith and to kill their families. In 2002, UK authorities arrested and detained Othman without charge under the ATCSA. After that Act was repealed, the government proceeded to hold Othman under a control order pursuant to the Prevention of Terrorism Act 2005.

The government then moved to deport Othman. The Foreign and Commonwealth Office had advised the British Government that Article 3 of the European Convention on Human Rights precluded the deportation of terrorist suspects to Jordan. As a result, the government decided to obtain diplomatic assurances from the Jordanian Government. A Memorandum of Understanding between the United Kingdom and Jordan on the transfer of detainees was signed on 10 August 2005. The next day, the Secretary of State served Othman a notice of intention to deport.

Othman filed suit claiming that he would be subject to torture on return to Jordan — in violation of Article 3 of the European Convention on Human Rights — and that he would be retried in Jordan on the basis of evidence obtained by torture of third persons — in violation of Article 6 of the Convention. In Britain, his case was heard by the Special Immigration Appeals Commission (SIAC), the Court of Appeal and ultimately the House of Lords, which upheld his deportation order. On appeal from the House of Lords, the European Court of Human Rights unanimously held for the government on the first claim (Art. 3) and for Othman on the second claim (Art. 6). As a result, even though the government would theoretically be able to deport Othman pursuant to the diplomatic assurances contained in the MOU, it could not lawfully deport him to Jordan where he would face trial. The following materials include excerpts of the UK-Jordanian MOU and parts of the ECtHR's analysis of Othman's Article 3 claim.]

Memorandum of Understanding Between the Governments of the United Kingdom and of Jordan Regulating the Provision of Undertakings in Respect of Specified Persons Prior to Deportation

Application and Scope

This arrangement will apply to any person accepted by the receiving state for admission to its territory following a written request by the sending state under the terms of this arrangement.

Such a request may be made in respect of any citizen of the receiving state who is to be returned to that country by the sending state on the grounds that he is not entitled, or is no longer entitled, to remain in the sending state according to the Immigration laws of that state.

...

Understandings

It is understood that the authorities of the United Kingdom and of Jordan will comply with their human rights obligations under International law regarding a person returned under this arrangement. Where someone has been accepted under the terms of this arrangement, the conditions set out in the following paragraphs (numbered 1–8) will apply, together with any further specific assurances provided by the receiving state.

1. If arrested, detained or imprisoned following his return, a returned person will be afforded adequate accommodation, nourishment, and medical treatment and will be treated in a humane and proper manner, in accordance with internationally accepted standards.

2. A returned person who is arrested or detained will be brought promptly before a judge or other officer authorised by law to exercise judicial power in order that the lawfulness of his detention may be decided.

3. A returned person who is arrested or detained will be informed promptly by the authorities of the receiving state of the reasons for his arrest or detention, and of any charge against him.

4. If the returned person is arrested, detained or imprisoned within 3 years of the date of his return, he will be entitled to contact, and then have prompt and regular visits from the representative of an independent body nominated jointly by the UK and Jordanian authorities. Such visits will be permitted at least once a fortnight, and whether or not the returned person has been convicted, and will include the opportunity for private interviews with the returned person. The nominated body will give a report of its visits to the authorities of the sending state.

5. Except where the returned person is arrested, detained or imprisoned, the receiving state will not impede, limit, restrict or otherwise prevent access by a returned person to the consular posts of the sending state during normal working hours. However, the receiving state is not obliged to facilitate such access by providing transport free of charge or at discounted rates.

6. A returned person will be allowed to follow his religious observance following his return, including while under arrest, or while detained or imprisoned.

7. A returned person who is charged with an offence following his return will receive a fair and public hearing without undue delay by a competent, independent and impartial tribunal established by law. Judgment will be pronounced publicly, but the press and public may be excluded from all or part of the trial in the interests of morals, public order or national security in a democratic society, where the interests of juveniles or the protection of the private life of the parties so require, or to the extent strictly necessary in the opinion of the court in special circumstances where publicity would prejudice the interests of justice.

8. A returned person who is charged with an offence following his return will be allowed adequate time and facilities to prepare his defence, and will be permitted to examine or have examined the witnesses against him and to call and have examined witnesses on his behalf. He will be allowed to defend himself in person or through legal assistance of his own choosing, or, if he has not sufficient means to pay for legal assistance, to be given it free when the interests of justice so require.

Withdrawal

Either government may withdraw from this arrangement by giving 6 months notice in writing to the Embassy of the other government.

Where one or other government withdraws from the arrangement, the terms of this arrangement will continue to apply to anyone who has been returned in accordance with its provisions.

[The unanimous opinion of the European Court of Human Rights follows.]

1. General principles

185. . . . [I]t is well-established that expulsion by a Contracting State may give rise to an issue under Article 3, and hence engage the responsibility of that State under the Convention, where substantial grounds have been shown for believing that the person concerned, if deported, faces a real risk of being subjected to treatment

contrary to Article 3. . . . Article 3 is absolute and it is not possible to weigh the risk of ill-treatment against the reasons put forward for the expulsion (*Saadi v. Italy* [GC], no. 37201/06, §§ 125 and 138, ECHR 2008).
186. . . . [T]he Court accepts that, as the materials provided by the applicant and the third party interveners show, there is widespread concern within the international community as to the practice of seeking assurances to allow for the deportation of those considered to be a threat to national security. However, it [sic] not for this Court to rule upon the propriety of seeking assurances, or to assess the long term consequences of doing so; its only task is to examine whether the assurances obtained in a particular case are sufficient to remove any real risk of ill-treatment. . . .

187. In any examination of whether an applicant faces a real risk of ill-treatment in the country to which he is to be removed, the Court will consider both the general human rights situation in that country and the particular characteristics of the applicant. In a case where assurances have been provided by the receiving State, those assurances constitute a further relevant factor which the Court will consider. . . . The weight to be given to assurances from the receiving State depends, in each case, on the circumstances prevailing at the material time.

188. . . . [T]he preliminary question is whether the general human rights situation in the receiving State excludes accepting any assurances whatsoever. However, it will only be in rare cases that the general situation in a country will mean that no weight at all can be given to assurances.

189. More usually, the Court will assess first, the quality of assurances given and, second, whether, in light of the receiving State's practices they can be relied upon. In doing so, the Court will have regard, *inter alia*, to the following factors:

(i) whether the terms of the assurances have been disclosed to the Court (*Ryabikin v. Russia*, no. 8320/04, § 119, 19 June 2008; *Muminov v. Russia*, no. 42502/06, § 97, 11 December 2008; see also *Pelit v. Azerbaijan*, cited above);
(ii) whether the assurances are specific or are general and vague (*Saadi*, cited above; *Klein v. Russia*, no. 24268/08, § 55, 1 April 2010; *Khaydarov v. Russia*, no. 21055/09, § 111, 20 May 2010);
(iii) who has given the assurances and whether that person can bind the receiving State (*Shamayev and Others v. Georgia and Russia*, no. 36378/02, § 344, ECHR 2005-III; *Kordian v. Turkey* (dec.), no. 6575/06, 4 July 2006; *Abu Salem v. Portugal* (dec.), no 26844/04, 9 May 2006; cf. *Ben Khemais v. Italy*, no. 246/07, § 59, ECHR 2009–. . . (extracts); *Garayev v. Azerbaijan*, no. 53688/08, § 74, 10 June 2010; *Baysakov and Others v. Ukraine*, no. 54131/08, § 51, 18 February 2010; *Soldatenko v. Ukraine*, no. 2440/07, § 73, 23 October 2008);
(iv) if the assurances have been issued by the central government of the receiving State, whether local authorities can be expected to abide by them (*Chahal*, cited above, §§ 105–107);
(v) whether the assurances concerns treatment which is legal or illegal in the receiving State (*Cipriani v. Italy* (dec.), no. 221142/07, 30 March 2010; *Youb Saoudi v. Spain* (dec.), no. 22871/06, 18 September 2006; *Ismaili v. Germany*, no. 58128/00, 15 March 2001; *Nivette v. France* (dec.),

no 44190/98, ECHR 2001 VII; *Einhorn v. France* (dec.), no 71555/01, ECHR 2001-XI; see also *Suresh* and *Lai Sing*, both cited above)

(vi) whether they have been given by a Contracting State (*Chentiev and Ibragimov v. Slovakia* (dec.), nos. 21022/08 and 51946/08, 14 September 2010; *Gasayev v. Spain* (dec.), no. 48514/06, 17 February 2009);

(vii) the length and strength of bilateral relations between the sending and receiving States, including the receiving State's record in abiding by similar assurances (*Babar Ahmad and Others*, cited above, §§ 107 and 108; *Al-Moayad v. Germany* (dec.), no. 35865/03, § 68, 20 February 2007);

(viii) whether compliance with the assurances can be objectively verified through diplomatic or other monitoring mechanisms, including providing unfettered access to the applicant's lawyers (*Chentiev and Ibragimov* and *Gasayev*, both cited above; cf. *Ben Khemais*, § 61 and *Ryabikin*, § 119, both cited above; *Kolesnik v. Russia*, no. 26876/08, § 73, 17 June 2010; see also *Agiza*, *Alzery* and *Pelit*, cited above);

(ix) whether there is an effective system of protection against torture in the receiving State, including whether it is willing to cooperate with international monitoring mechanisms (including international human rights NGOs), and whether it is willing to investigate allegations of torture and to punish those responsible (*Ben Khemais*, §§ 59 and 60; *Soldatenko*, § 73, both cited above; *Koktysh v. Ukraine*, no. 43707/07, § 63, 10 December 2009);

(x) whether the applicant has previously been ill-treated in the receiving State (*Koktysh*, § 64, cited above); and

(xi) whether the reliability of the assurances has been examined by the domestic courts of the sending/Contracting State (*Gasayev*; *Babar Ahmad and Others*, § 106; *Al-Moayad*, §§ 66–69).

2. The applicant's case

...

191. Turning therefore to the evidence before it, the Court first notes that the picture painted by the reports of United Nations bodies and NGOs of torture in Jordanian prisons is as consistent as it is disturbing. Whatever progress Jordan may have made, torture remains, in the words of the United Nations Committee Against Torture, "widespread and routine". The Committee's conclusions are confirmed by the other reports summarised . . . above, which demonstrate beyond any reasonable doubt that torture is perpetrated systematically by the General Intelligence Directorate, particularly against Islamist detainees. Torture is also practiced by the GID with impunity. This culture of impunity is, in the Court's view, unsurprising: the evidence shows that the Jordanian criminal justice system lacks many of the standard, internationally recognised safeguards to prevent torture and punish its perpetrators. As the Human Rights Committee observed in its concluding observations, there is an absence of a genuinely independent complaints mechanism, a low number of prosecutions, and the denial of prompt access to lawyers and independent medical examinations. The conclusions of the Committee Against Torture

(which are corroborated by the reports of Amnesty International, Human Rights Watch and the Jordanian National Centre for Human Rights) show that these problems are made worse by the GID's wide powers of detention and that, in state security cases, the proximity of the Public Prosecutor to the GID means the former provides no meaningful control over the latter. Finally, as the Special Rapporteur, Amnesty International and the NCHR [Jordan's National Centre for Human Rights] confirm, there is an absence of co-operation by the GID with eminent national and international monitors.

192. As a result of this evidence it is unremarkable that the parties accept that, without assurances from the Jordanian Government, there would be a real risk of ill-treatment of the present applicant if he were returned to Jordan. The Court agrees. It is clear that, as a high profile Islamist, the applicant is part of a category of prisoners who are frequently ill-treated in Jordan. It is also of some relevance that he claims to have previously been tortured in Jordan (see his asylum claim . . .). However, consistent with the general approach the Court has set out at paragraphs 187–189 above, the Court must also consider whether the assurances contained in the MOU, accompanied by monitoring by Adaleh [the Adaleh Centre for Human Rights Studies, a Jordanian NGO], remove any real risk of ill-treatment of the applicant.

193. In considering that issue, the Court observes that the applicant has advanced a number of general and specific concerns as to whether the assurances given by Jordan are sufficient to remove any real risk of ill-treatment of him. At the general level, he submits that, if Jordan cannot be relied on to abide by its legally binding, multilateral international obligations not to torture, it cannot be relied on to comply with non-binding bilateral assurances not to do so. He has also argued that assurances should never be relied on where there is a systematic problem of torture and ill-treatment and further argues that, even where there is evidence of isolated, non-systemic acts of torture, reliance should only be placed on assurances where those are supported by the independent monitoring of a body with a demonstrable track-record of effectiveness in practice. The Court does not consider that these general submissions are supported by its case-law on assurances. As the general principles set out at paragraphs 187–189 above indicate, the Court has never laid down an absolute rule that a State which does not comply with multilateral obligations cannot be relied on to comply with bilateral assurances; the extent to which a State has failed to comply with its multilateral obligations is, at most, a factor in determining whether its bilateral assurances are sufficient. Equally, there is no prohibition on seeking assurances when there is a systematic problem of torture and ill-treatment in the receiving State; otherwise, as Lord Phillips observed (see paragraph 57 above),[30] it would be paradoxical if the very fact of having to seek assurances meant one could not rely on them.

194. Moreover, the Court does not consider that the general human rights situation in Jordan excludes accepting any assurances whatsoever from the Jordanian

[30] In para. 58, the Court noted that, in the House of Lords decision below, Lord Philips 'referred to the "abundance" of international law material, which supported the proposition that assurances should be treated with scepticism if they are given by a country where inhuman treatment by State agents was endemic. However, for Lord Phillips this came "close to a 'Catch 22' proposition that if you need to ask for assurances you cannot rely on them"'.

Government. Instead, the Court considers the United Kingdom and Jordanian Governments have made genuine efforts to obtain and provide transparent and detailed assurances to ensure that the applicant will not be ill-treated upon return to Jordan. The product of those efforts, the MOU, is superior in both its detail and its formality to any assurances which the Court has previously examined. The MOU would also appear to be superior to any assurances examined by . . . the United Nations Human Rights Committee (see . . . Alzery . . .). The MOU is specific and comprehensive. It addresses directly the protection of the applicant's Convention rights in Jordan. The MOU is also unique in that it has withstood the extensive examination that has been carried out by an independent tribunal, SIAC, which had the benefit of receiving evidence adduced by both parties, including expert witnesses who were subject to extensive cross-examination.

195. . . . [T]he Court considers that there is sufficient evidence for it to conclude that the assurances were given in good faith by a Government whose bilateral relations with the United Kingdom have, historically, been very strong (see Babar Ahmad and Others and Al-Moayad, both cited at paragraph 189(vii) above). Moreover, they have been approved at the highest levels of the Jordanian Government, having the express approval and support of the King himself. Thus, it is clear that, whatever the status of the MOU in Jordanian law, the assurances have been given by officials who are capable of binding the Jordanian State. Just as importantly, the assurances have the approval and support of senior officials of the GID. In the Court's view, all of these factors make strict compliance with both the letter and spirit of the MOU more likely.

196. Similarly, although the applicant has argued that his high profile would place him at greater risk, the Court is unable to accept this argument, given the wider political context in which the MOU has been negotiated. It considers it more likely that the applicant's high profile will make the Jordanian authorities careful to ensure he is properly treated; the Jordanian Government is no doubt aware that not only would ill-treatment have serious consequences for its bilateral relationship with the United Kingdom, it would also cause international outrage. . . .

197. In addition to general concerns about the MOU, the Court notes that the applicant has relied on six specific areas of concern as to the meaning and operation of the assurances. He submits that the MOU is not clear as to: (i) what was meant by "judge" in respect of the guarantee that he would be "brought promptly before a judge"; (ii) whether he would have access to a lawyer during the interrogation period of his detention; . . .; (iv) whether, as a matter of Jordanian law, the assurances in the MOU were legal and enforceable . . . and (vi) [the Adaleh Center's] capacity to monitor the assurances. . . .

198. For the first, the Court considers that the MOU would have been considerably strengthened if it had contained a requirement that the applicant be brought within a short, defined period after his arrest before a civilian judge, as opposed to a military prosecutor. This is all the more so when experience has shown that the risk of ill-treatment of a detainee is greatest during the first hours or days of his or her detention. However, the Court notes that, although it is unusual for lawyers to accompany detainees to appearances before the Public Prosecutor, as a matter of Jordanian law, the applicant would be entitled as of right to have a lawyer present.

Given that the applicant's appearance before the Public Prosecutor within twenty-four hours of his return would be the first public opportunity for the Jordanian authorities to demonstrate their intention to comply with the assurances, the Court considers that it would be unlikely for the Public Prosecutor to refuse to allow a lawyer to be present. Moreover, the applicant's first appearance before the Public Prosecutor must be seen in the context of the other arrangements which are in place for his return. For instance, it is likely that the monitors who would travel with the applicant from the United Kingdom to Jordan would remain with him for at least part of the first day of detention in Jordan. This compares favourably with the delay of five weeks in obtaining access which the UN Human Rights Committee found to be deficient in Alzery and significantly diminishes any risk of ill-treatment that may have arisen from a lack of clarity in the MOU.

199. For the second concern, the absence of a lawyer during interrogation, SIAC found that it was unlikely that the applicant would have a lawyer present during questioning by the GID, that it was likely that he would have a lawyer present for any questioning by the Public Prosecutor and very likely that he would have such representation for any appearance before a judge. Denial of access to a lawyer to a detainee, particularly during interrogation is a matter of serious concern: the right of a detainee to have access to legal advice is a fundamental safeguard against ill-treatment. However, in the present case, that risk is substantially reduced by the other safeguards contained in the MOU and the monitoring arrangements.

. . .

201. Fourth, it may well be that as matter of Jordanian law the MOU is not legally binding. Certainly, as an assurance against illegal behaviour, it should be treated with more scepticism than in a case where the State undertakes not to do what is permitted under domestic law (see paragraph 189(v) above). . . . The Court shares SIAC's view, not merely that there would be a real and strong incentive in the present case for Jordan to avoid being seen to break its word but that the support for the MOU at the highest levels in Jordan would significantly reduce the risk that senior members of the GID, who had participated in the negotiation of the MOU, would tolerate non-compliance with its terms.

. . .

203. Sixth, it is clear that the Adaleh Centre does not have the same expertise or resources as leading international NGOs such as Amnesty International, Human Rights Watch or the International Committee of the Red Cross. Nor does it have the same reputation or status in Jordan as, for example, the Jordanian NCHR. However, in its determination SIAC recognised this weakness. It recognised the Centre's "relative inexperience and scale" but concluded that it was the very fact of monitoring visits which was important. The Court agrees with this conclusion. Moreover, the Court is persuaded that the capability of the Centre has significantly increased since SIAC's determination, even if it still has no direct experience of monitoring. . . . [I] t has been generously funded by the United Kingdom Government, which in itself provides a measure of independence for the Centre, at least from the Jordanian Government. Given the United Kingdom Government's broader interest in ensuring that the assurances are respected, it can be expected that this funding will continue. . . . Similarly, although Mr Rababa [the head of the Adaleh Centre] may well

have family ties the security services, as alleged by Ms Refahi in her second statement (see paragraph 92 above), there is no evidence that anyone close to him will be responsible for the applicant's detention. More importantly, the scrutiny the Centre can expect from Jordanian and international civil society as to how it carries out the monitoring must outweigh any remote risk of bias that might arise from Mr Rababa's family ties.

...

205. For the foregoing reasons the Court concludes that, on the basis of the evidence before it, the applicant's return to Jordan would not expose him to a real risk of ill-treatment.

QUESTIONS

1. In practice, if the British Government deported Othman to Jordan on the basis of the MOU, what would prevent the two governments from subsequently entering a side agreement modifying the terms of their understanding and qualifying the protections afforded Othman?

2. Which standard — Levels 1 to 5 — is most justified in addressing the use of diplomatic assurances? Are diplomatic assurances prohibited, under any circumstance, by customary international law? Bobby Chesney argues: 'The United States is far from alone in relying on diplomatic assurances to deflect fear-of-torture concerns. [A Human Rights Watch] report described previously relates examples of this practice also by Canada, Sweden, the United Kingdom, the Netherlands, Austria, and Turkey. This extensive state practice precludes any argument that there may be a customary international law norm against reliance on diplomatic assurances in the context of non-refoulement' (R. M. Chesney, 'Leaving Guantánamo: The Law of International Detainee Transfers', 40 U. Rich. L. Rev. 657, 697 n. 192 (2005–2006)).

3. If diplomatic assurances can be lawfully used to return a person to a state that systematically perpetrates torture, should that legal option extend to other arenas of international practice such as returning refugees to countries in which they would otherwise be persecuted?

4. The European Court of Human Rights (ECtHR) in *Othman* stated: 'it [is] not for this Court to rule upon the propriety of seeking assurances, or to assess the long term consequences of doing so; its only task is to examine whether the assurances obtained in a particular case are sufficient to remove any real risk of ill-treatment.' Do you agree that the role of the court — or any judicial body — is not to assess the long-term consequences of relying on diplomatic assurances and is only to assess the potential injury to an individual in a particular case? Recall that the former High Commissioner for Human Rights Louise Arbour opposed diplomatic assurances partly on the ground that acceptance of the practice would undercut the objectives of the global anti-torture regime. Should a court be able to consider such consequences?

5. Did the ECtHR reach the correct conclusion in *Othman*? Are the assurances provided in the MOU sufficient? If not, what alternative arrangements, if any, would suffice

to reduce the risk of torture and protect Othman's rights under Article 3 of the European Convention?

6. Did the ECtHR in *Othman* err in accepting the Adaleh Centre as an independent monitoring body? Should a human rights NGO be willing to perform such a role? Consider the following news report of Amnesty International's position:[31]

> Amnesty International said today it would refuse to work with the [British] government to monitor the treatment of foreign nationals deported from Britain under toughened anti-terrorist measures.
>
> The human rights group said it would not prioritise the human rights of individuals removed from the UK over those of other inmates....
>
> ...
>
> 'Clearly we would not want to prioritise the human rights concern of prisoner X over Y,' a spokesman said. 'Neither would we want to endorse a scheme in which people are going to be deported where diplomatic assurances are a big part of the arrangement.
>
> 'We are not going to see our job as being one where we are effectively endorsing or propping up the deportation route. That would not be something we are willing to take part in.'

Is Amnesty International correct to adopt such a position? Now that the ECtHR has approved the US-Jordanian model of a diplomatic assurance, would it be advisable for Amnesty International to change its position? If the Adaleh Centre requests their advice and training, should Amnesty International provide such support?

7. The *Othman* opinion is predicated on assumptions about the motivation and incentives of various state actors to comply with international norms. Are these assumptions correct? For example, the court references, as a 'given', 'the United Kingdom Government's broader interest in ensuring that the assurances are respected.' The Court states that the strength of the Jordanian and British bilateral relations is a factor that helps 'make strict compliance with both the letter and spirit of the MOU more likely'. And the Court states that Jordanian authorities are not likely to torture Othman because 'the Jordanian Government is no doubt aware that ... ill-treatment ... would also cause international outrage'.

ADDITIONAL READING

J. G. Johnston, 'The Risk of Torture as a Basis for Refusing Extradition and the Use of Diplomatic Assurances to Protect against Torture after 9/11', 11 Int'l. Crim. L. Rev. 1 (2011); E. Schmid, 'The End of the Road on Diplomatic Assurances: International Law and the Removal of Terror Suspects', 8 Essex Hum. Rts. Rev. 297 (2011); A.

[31] James Sturcke, 'Amnesty Refuses Involvement in UK Deportations', *The Guardian*, 26 Aug. 2005.

Duffy, 'Expulsion to Face Torture? Non-Refoulement in International Law', 20 Int'l. J. Ref. L. 373 (2008); E.-C. Gillard, 'There's No Place Like Home: States' Obligations in Relation to Transfers of Persons', 871 Int'l. Rev. Red Cross 703 (2008); C. Droege, 'Transfers of Detainees — Legal Framework, Non-Refoulement and Contemporary Challenges', 871 Int'l. Rev. Red Cross 669 (2008).

F. GUARANTEEING FAIR TRIALS

The right to a fair trial ranks among the most basic protections in humanitarian and human rights law. Three provisions of the 1949 Geneva Conventions and their Protocols deserve special mention. First, Common Article 3 outlaws 'the passing of sentences and the carrying out of executions without previous judgment pronounced by a regularly constituted court, affording all the judicial guarantees which are recognized as indispensable by civilized peoples.' The ICRC Commentaries explain that this provision calls for extension of the general law concerning fair trials to the arena of warfare: 'All civilized nations surround the administration of justice with safeguards aimed at eliminating the possibility of judicial errors. The Convention has rightly proclaimed that it is essential to do this even in time of war.' Second, the Civilians Convention contains a 'security proviso' permitting states to suspend treaty obligations when dealing with unlawful combatants such as spies and saboteurs; yet it too requires that 'such persons shall nevertheless be treated with humanity and, in case of trial, shall not be deprived of the rights of fair and regular trial prescribed by the present Convention.' Third, Article 75 (entitled 'Fundamental Guarantees') of Additional Protocol I is generally recognized, including by the United States, as binding customary law. It specifies elements of the right to a fair trial that are guaranteed to all individuals who do not benefit from more favourable treatment under the 1949 Conventions or the Additional Protocol. These three IHL provisions establish a floor of fair trial rights below which no state may pass. Recall that General Comment 29 relies on such fundamental protections in reasoning that if certain elements of a fair trial cannot be lawfully transgressed in war, they can never be subject to derogation under the ICCPR. A difficulty is defining the content of those core fair trial rights.

One of the most vexing issues in defining the right to a fair trial in the national security context involves military tribunals. Can a military tribunal provide a fair trial and, if so, under what conditions? The following readings address this set of concerns. A report by the Inter-American Commission on Human Rights sets the stage by discussing the broader legal and normative framework. The Inter-American Commission took up the general subject of human rights law and terrorism, and issued a lengthy report in 2002. The report provides, *inter alia*, one of the most comprehensive formal pronouncements on the content of derogable and nonderogable fair trial rights. The Commission developed these legal principles partly in response to the use of military courts by Latin American governments in the 1980s and early to mid 1990s. Governmental practices that sparked international criticism included

Colombia's use of 'faceless' prosecutors, judges, witnesses and attorneys in cases of terrorism and subversion; Peru's trials of civilians accused of treason and terrorism in closed proceedings before a military court and with defence counsel prohibited from accessing the government's evidence or questioning military and police witnesses; Guatemala's Special Courts for subversive activities which operated in secret locations, relied on confessions from the accused taken without counsel present and provided little time for the accused to prepare a defence; and Uruguay's secret hearings, materially ineffective appeals process for objecting to an indictment, and inadequate access of defence counsel to evidentiary files.

With respect to a specific issue — prosecution of civilians before military tribunals — the Inter-American Commission is among the international bodies that most strongly oppose such practices. A December 2001 resolution by the Commission states: 'According to the doctrine of the IACHR, military courts may not try civilians, except when no civilian courts exist or where trial by such courts is materially impossible.' The content of the 2002 Report, however, is arguably more qualified. Pay particular attention to the Commission's understanding of 'civilians' charged with involvement in terrorism and of 'unlawful combatants' in an armed conflict. Also, look closely at the Commission's concerns that might provide the basis for a categorical prohibition on prosecuting civilians before military tribunals. Is it, for example, the troubled history of military courts in the Americas that explains the Commission's position? If that is the case, the particular experience of summary proceedings might inspire a prophylactic rule against military trials. Such a rule might be advisable even if, theoretically, a government could establish a military court system that secures the rights of defendants. Otherwise, why not disallow particular procedures rather than deem military trials of civilians *per se* illegal? Alternatively, consider whether the concerns regarding military trials may have more to do with the institutional relationship of the military and the executive rather than specific trial procedures. The related readings that follow, from the Human Rights Committee and the European Court of Human Rights, provide other examples of approaches to regulating such courts.

INTER-AMERICAN COMMISSION ON HUMAN RIGHTS, REPORT ON TERRORISM AND HUMAN RIGHTS

(22 Oct. 2002)

Right to a Hearing by a Competent, Independent and Impartial Tribunal previously established by Law.

229. Underlying this aspect of the right to a fair hearing are the fundamental concepts of judicial independence and impartiality.... The requirement of independence in turn necessitates that courts be autonomous from the other branches of government, free from influence, threats or interference from any source and for any reason, and benefit from other characteristics necessary for ensuring the correct and independent performance of judicial functions, including tenure and

appropriate professional training.... These requirements in turn require that a judge or tribunal not harbor any actual bias in a particular case, and that the judge or tribunal not reasonably be perceived as being tainted with any bias.

230. In the context of these fundamental requirements, the jurisprudence of the inter-American system has long denounced the creation of special courts or tribunals that displace the jurisdiction belonging to the ordinary courts or judicial tribunals and that do not use the duly established procedures of the legal process. This has included in particular the use of ad hoc or special courts or military tribunals to prosecute civilians for security offenses in times of emergency, which practice has been condemned by this Commission, the Inter-American Court and other international authorities. The basis of this criticism has related in large part to the lack of independence of such tribunals from the Executive and the absence of minimal due process and fair trial guarantees in their processes.

231. It has been widely concluded in this regard that military tribunals by their very nature do not satisfy the requirements of independent and impartial courts applicable to the trial of civilians, because they are not a part of the independent civilian judiciary but rather are a part of the Executive branch, and because their fundamental purpose is to maintain order and discipline by punishing military offenses committed by members of the military establishment. In such instances, military officers assume the role of judges while at the same time remaining subordinate to their superiors in keeping with the established military hierarchy.

232. ... Military tribunals are also precluded from prosecuting civilians, although certain human rights supervisory bodies have found that in exceptional circumstances military tribunals or special courts might be used to try civilians but only where the minimum requirements of due process are guaranteed. During armed conflicts, a state's military courts may also try privileged and unprivileged combatants, provided that the minimum protections of due process are guaranteed. Article 84 of the Third Geneva Convention, for example, expressly provides that

> [a] prisoner of war shall be tried only by a military court, unless the existing laws of the Detaining Power expressly permit the civil courts to try a member of the armed forces of the Detaining Power in respect of the particular offense alleged to have been committed by the prisoner of war. In no circumstances whatever shall a prisoner of war be tried by a court of any kind which does not offer the essential guarantees of independence and impartiality as generally recognized, and, in particular, the procedure of which does not afford the accused the rights and means of defence provided for in Article 105....

Although the provisions of international humanitarian law applicable to unprivileged combatants, including Article 75 of Additional Protocol I, do not specifically address the susceptibility of such combatants to trial by military courts, there appears to be no reason to consider that a different standard would apply as between privileged and unprivileged combatants. In any event, the standards of due process to which unprivileged combatants are entitled may in no case fall below those under Article 75 of Additional Protocol I.

...

Fair Trial, Due Process of Law and Derogation

...

246. ... [N]o human rights supervisory body has yet found the exigencies of a genuine emergency situation sufficient to justify suspending even temporarily basic fair trial safeguards....

249. Without detracting from the above standards, prevailing norms suggest that there may be some limited aspects of the right to due process and to a fair trial from which derogation might in the most exceptional circumstances be permissible. Any such suspensions must, however, comply strictly with the principles of necessity, proportionality and non-discrimination, and must remain subject to oversight by supervisory organs under international law.

250. Due process and fair trial protections that might conceivably be subject to suspension include the right to a public trial where limitations on public access to proceedings are demonstrated to be strictly necessary in the interests of justice. Considerations in this regard might include matters of security, public order, the interests of juveniles, or where publicity might prejudice the interests of justice. Any such restrictions must, however, be strictly justified by the state concerned on a case by case basis and be subject to on-going judicial supervision.

251. The right of a defendant to examine or have examined witnesses presented against him or her could also be, in principle, the subject of restrictions in some limited instances. It must be recognized in this respect that efforts to investigate and prosecute crimes, including those relating to terrorism, may in certain instances render witnesses vulnerable to threats to their lives or integrity and thereby raise difficult issues concerning the extent to which those witnesses can be safely identified during the criminal process. Such considerations can never serve to compromise a defendant's non-derogable due process protections and each situation must be carefully evaluated on its own merits within the context of a particular justice system....

252. Similarly, the investigation and prosecution of terrorist crimes may render judges and other officials involved in the administration of justice vulnerable to threats. As noted above, states are obliged to take all necessary measures to prevent violence against such persons. Accordingly, states may be compelled by the exigencies of a particular situation to develop mechanisms to protect a judge's life, physical integrity and independence ... subject to such measures as are necessary to ensure a defendant's right to challenge the competence, independence or impartiality of his or her prosecuting tribunal....

...

International Humanitarian Law

...

256. As noted above, while international human rights law prohibits the trial of civilians by military tribunals, the use of military tribunals in the trial of prisoners of war is not prohibited ...

261. ... [M]ost fundamental fair trial requirements cannot justifiably be suspended under either international human rights law or international humanitarian law ... includ[ing] the following:

... The right to be tried by a competent, independent and impartial tribunal in conformity with applicable international standards. In respect of the prosecution of civilians, this requires trial by regularly constituted courts that are demonstrably independent from the other branches of government and comprised of judges with appropriate tenure and training, and generally prohibits the use of ad hoc, special, or military tribunals or commissions to try civilians. A state's military courts may prosecute members of its own military for crimes relating [to] the functions that the law assigns to military forces and, during international armed conflicts, may try privileged and unprivileged combatants, provided that the minimum requirements of due process are guaranteed.

...

HUMAN RIGHTS COMMITTEE, ARTICLE 14: RIGHT TO EQUALITY BEFORE COURTS AND TRIBUNALS AND TO A FAIR TRIAL, GENERAL COMMENT 32

(UN Doc. CCPR/C/GC/32 (2007))

... The Committee notes the existence, in many countries, of military or special courts which try civilians. While the Covenant does not prohibit the trial of civilians in military or special courts, it requires that such trials are in full conformity with the requirements of article 14 and that its guarantees cannot be limited or modified because of the military or special character of the court concerned. The Committee also notes that the trial of civilians in military or special courts may raise serious problems as far as the equitable, impartial and independent administration of justice is concerned. Therefore, it is important to take all necessary measures to ensure that such trials take place under conditions which genuinely afford the full guarantees stipulated in article 14. Trials of civilians by military or special courts should be exceptional, i.e. limited to cases where the State party can show that resorting to such trials is necessary and justified by objective and serious reasons, and where with regard to the specific class of individuals and offences at issue the regular civilian courts are unable to undertake the trials.

İNCAL v. TURKEY

European Court of Human Rights (Grand Chamber), 1998

[In Turkey's third largest city, İzmir, Mr İbrahim İncal served on the local executive committee of a pro-Kurdish political party (the People's Labour Party). The executive committee decided to distribute a leaflet criticizing the local government's restrictions on small-scale illegal trading and squatter camps. The leaflet stated that these restrictions were part of a larger campaign to drive Kurds back to their own regions; that 'passivity as a form of defence against this devastation has encouraged the State'; and that the Kurdish population should organize themselves into 'neighbourhood communities ... to assume their responsibilities and oppose this special war being waged.'

The public prosecutor instituted criminal proceedings in the İzmir National Security Court against İncal and other members of the People's Labour Party. The prosecutor accused them of attempting to incite hatred and hostility through racist words and asked the court to apply the Criminal Code, the Prevention of Terrorism Act and the Press Act. The National Security Court, composed of three judges, one of whom was a member of the military, refused to apply the Prevention of Terrorism Act but otherwise found the applicant guilty of the offences charged and sentenced him to nearly seven months' imprisonment and a fine of 55,555 Turkish lira. Following is the decision of the Grand Chamber of the ECtHR.]

63. [The Grand Chamber first analysed and decided that İncal's criminal conviction infringed his right to freedom of expression under the Convention. The Chamber then turned to the right to a fair trial under Article 6.] The Government submitted that the . . . arguments concerning these judges' responsibility towards their commanding officers and the rules governing their professional assessment were overstated; their duties as officers were limited to obeying military regulations and observing military courtesies. They were safe from any pressure from their hierarchical superiors, as such an attempt was punishable under the Military Criminal Code. The assessment system applied only to military judges' non-judicial duties. In addition, they had access to their assessment reports and could even challenge their content in the Supreme Military Administrative Court.

In the present case, neither the colleagues or hierarchical or disciplinary superiors of the military judge in question nor the public authorities who had appointed him had any connection with the parties to Mr İncal's trial or any interest whatsoever in the judgment to be delivered.

. . .

65. The Court reiterates that in order to establish whether a tribunal can be considered "independent" for the purposes of Article 6 § 1, regard must be had, *inter alia*, to the manner of appointment of its members and their term of office, the existence of safeguards against outside pressures and the question whether it presents an appearance of independence.

. . .

66. . . . National Security Courts . . . are composed of three judges, one of whom is a regular officer and member of the Military Legal Service.

As the independence and impartiality of the two civilian judges is not disputed, the Court must determine what the position was with regard to the military judge.

67. The Court notes that the status of military judges sitting as members of National Security Courts provides certain guarantees of independence and impartiality. For example, military judges undergo the same professional training as their civilian counterparts, which gives them the status of career members of the Military Legal Service. When sitting as members of National Security Courts, military judges enjoy constitutional safeguards identical to those of civilian judges; in addition, with certain exceptions, they may not be removed from office or made to retire early without their consent; as regular members of a National Security Court they sit as individuals; according to the Constitution, they must be independent and no public

authority may give them instructions concerning their judicial activities or influence them in the performance of their duties.

68. On the other hand, other aspects of these judges' status make it questionable. Firstly, they are servicemen who still belong to the army, which in turn takes its orders from the executive. Secondly, they remain subject to military discipline and assessment reports are compiled on them by the army for that purpose. Decisions pertaining to their appointment are to a great extent taken by the administrative authorities and the army. Lastly, their term of office as National Security Court judges is only four years and can be renewed.

...

70. At the hearing before the Court the Government submitted that the only justification for the presence of military judges in the National Security Courts was their undoubted competence and experience in the battle against organised crime, including that committed by illegal armed groups. For years the armed forces and the military judges — in whom, moreover, the people placed great trust — had acted, partly under martial law, as the guarantors of the democratic and secular Republic of Turkey, while assuming their social, cultural and moral responsibilities. For as long as the terrorist threat persisted, military judges would have to continue to lend their full support to these special courts, whose task was extremely difficult.

It is not for the Court — which is aware of the problems caused by terrorism — to pass judgment on these assertions. Its task is not to determine *in abstracto* whether it was necessary to set up such courts in a Contracting State or to review the relevant practice, but to ascertain whether the manner in which one of them functioned infringed the applicant's right to a fair trial.

71. In this respect even appearances may be of a certain importance. What is at stake is the confidence which the courts in a democratic society must inspire in the public and above all, as far as criminal proceedings are concerned, in the accused. In deciding whether there is a legitimate reason to fear that a particular court lacks independence or impartiality, the standpoint of the accused is important without being decisive. What is decisive is whether his doubts can be held to be objectively justified.

72. Mr İncal was convicted of disseminating separatist propaganda capable of inciting the people to resist the government and commit criminal offences, for participating in the decision to distribute the leaflet in issue.... As the acts which gave rise to the case were considered likely to endanger the founding principles of the Republic of Turkey, or to affect its security, they came *ipso jure* under the jurisdiction of the National Security Courts.

The Court notes, however, that in considering the question of compliance with Article 10 it did not discern anything in the leaflet which might be regarded as incitement of part of the population to violence, hostility or hatred between citizens. [The Court refers to the earlier section of the opinion holding that the government violated İncal's right to freedom of expression.] Moreover, the National Security Court refused to apply the Prevention of Terrorism Act (Law no. 3713). In addition, the Court attaches great importance to the fact that a civilian had to appear before a court composed, even if only in part, of members of the armed forces.

It follows that the applicant could legitimately fear that because one of the judges of the Izmir National Security Court was a military judge it might allow itself to be unduly influenced by considerations which had nothing to do with the nature of the case....

73. In conclusion, the applicant had legitimate cause to doubt the independence and impartiality of the İzmir National Security Court.

There has accordingly been a breach of Article 6 § 1.

JOINT PARTLY DISSENTING OPINION OF JUDGES THÓR VILHJÁLMSSON, GÖLCÜKLÜ, MATSCHER, FOIGHEL, SIR JOHN FREELAND, LOPES ROCHA, WILDHABER AND GOTCHEV

. . .

In a number of cases the Court has acknowledged that a special court whose members include "experts" may be a "tribunal" within the meaning of Article 6 § 1. The domestic legislation of the Council of Europe member States provides many examples of courts in which professional judges sit alongside specialists in a particular sphere whose knowledge is desirable and even necessary in deciding certain cases, provided that all the members of the court can offer the required guarantees of independence and impartiality.

As to military judges who are members of the National Security Courts, paragraph 67 of the judgment describes the constitutional safeguards they enjoy, and paragraph 68 goes on to say that certain aspects of their status make it questionable. We consider the conclusions the Court drew from these aspects . . . unconvincing.

In that connection we would observe that it is possible for ordinary judges too to be subject to assessment and to disciplinary rules and for decisions pertaining to their appointment to be taken by the administrative authorities, and that the Court has held even a three-year term of office to be sufficient. In addition, at the end of their term of office as National Security Court judges, where that term is not renewed, the judges in question remain military judges for the whole duration of their careers.

As to the argument that the composition of the court may have caused the applicant to harbour doubts about its impartiality and independence, from the point of view of "appearances", we consider that, in view of the constitutional safeguards enjoyed by military judges, doubts about their independence and impartiality cannot be regarded as objectively justified.

The logical consequence of asserting the contrary would be to cease to consider that even specialised courts can be "tribunals" for the purposes of Article 6 § 1, thus departing from the Court's well-established case-law.

COMMENT ON MILITARY JUDGES AND MILITARY COURTS AFTER İNCAL AND 11 SEPTEMBER

European Court of Human Rights: Öcalan v. Turkey Grand Chamber, App. No. 46221/99 (2005)

In a high-profile case and one of the first international court decisions following 11 September, the Grand Chamber reaffirmed its ruling in *İncal v. Turkey*. The case involved the capture and trial of Abdullah Öcalan, the leader of the militant separatist group, Kurdistan Workers Party. In early 1999, Turkish forces captured Öcalan in

Kenya and transferred him to Turkey where he was subject to prosecution before a State Security Court. A 139-page indictment accused him of founding an armed group to secede from Turkey's national territory and of instigating numerous terrorist acts.

Öcalan's trial before the Ankara State Security Court, composed of two civilian and one military judge, began in late March 1999. Following the *İncal* judgment, Turkey started to amend its Constitution and national legislation to permit only civilian judges to sit on state security courts. The legislative amendments passed on 22 June 1999 and went into immediate effect. The next day a civilian judge replaced the military judge in Öcalan's trial court. The replacement judge had been present throughout the proceedings and attended all the hearings of the State Security Court from the beginning of the trial. On 29 June, the security court found Öcalan guilty.

A majority of the Grand Chamber of the ECtHR held that the presence of the military judge violated Öcalan's right to be tried by an independent and impartial tribunal:[32]

> 113. It is understandable that the applicant — prosecuted in a State Security Court for serious offences relating to national security — should have been apprehensive about being tried by a bench which included a regular army officer belonging to the military legal service. On that account he could legitimately fear that the State Security Court might allow itself to be unduly influenced by considerations which had nothing to do with the nature of the case.
>
> 114. As to whether the military judge's replacement by a civilian judge in the course of the proceedings before the verdict was delivered remedied the situation, the Court considers, firstly, that the question whether a court is seen to be independent does not depend solely on its composition when it delivers its verdict. In order to comply with the requirements of Article 6 regarding independence, the court concerned must be seen to be independent of the executive and the legislature at each of the three stages of the proceedings, namely the investigation, the trial and the verdict (those being the three stages in Turkish criminal proceedings according to the Government).
>
> 116. In its previous judgments, the Court attached importance to the fact that a civilian had to appear before a court composed, even if only in part, of members of the armed forces (see, among other authorities, *İncal*). Such a situation seriously affects the confidence which the courts must inspire in a democratic society.

Then-President of the ECtHR, Judge Luzius Wildhaber together with five other judges issued a dissenting opinion disagreeing strongly with the majority's view on the independence and impartiality of the trial court. The dissenting opinion stated:

> 6. ... To say that the presence of a military judge, who was replaced under new rules (that were introduced to comply with the case-law of the European Court of Human Rights) made the State Security Court appear not to be independent and impartial is to take the "theory" of appearances very far. That, in our opinion at least, is neither realistic, nor even fair.

[32] The Court also held, *inter alia*, that the government violated the right of Öcalan to be brought promptly before a judge following his arrest, the right to initiate proceedings to determine the lawfulness of his detention and the right to legal assistance.

> ...
>
> 8. In addition, in Mr Öçalan's case [sic], and without departing from the principles established in the *İncal* judgment itself, it is hard to agree with what is said in paragraph 116 of the judgment. The applicant is there described as a civilian (or equated to a civilian). However, he was accused of instigating serious terrorist crimes leading to thousands of deaths, charges which he admitted at least in part. He could equally well be described as a warlord, which goes a long way to putting into perspective the fact that at the start of his trial one of the three members of the court before which he appeared was himself from the military.

United States: Hamdan v. Rumsfeld, 126 S. Ct. 2749 (2006) and the Military Commission Act

In June 2006, the US Supreme Court decided a case involving an alleged member of Al Qaeda who was held at Guantánamo Bay and designated for trial by military commission. The Court invalidated the President's military commissions on the ground that they were not properly authorized by Congress. The Court held that the commissions violated a congressional statute requiring the President to adhere to IHL. The Court thus left open the possibility that Congress could subsequently authorize such commissions.

A majority of the Court ruled that Common Article 3 applies to the conflict between the United States and Al Qaeda and that the military commissions violated the fair trial provisions of the article. The majority held that the US commissions did not constitute a 'regularly constituted court', because the government failed to justify setting up special ad hoc tribunals outside the existing courts martial system. The majority thus implicitly accepted that a courts martial — a standing US military tribunal — would constitute a regularly constituted court. A plurality of the Supreme Court went on to conclude that particular procedures of the military commission — precluding the defendant from seeing classified evidence — failed to 'afford[] all the judicial guarantees which are recognized as indispensable by civilized peoples'. Following are excerpts from *Hamdan*:

> ... While the term "regularly constituted court" is not specifically defined in either Common Article 3 or its accompanying commentary, other sources disclose its core meaning. The commentary accompanying a provision of the Fourth Geneva Convention, for example, defines "'regularly constituted'" tribunals to include "ordinary military courts" and "definitely exclud[e] all special tribunals." GCIV Commentary 340 (defining the term "properly constituted" in Article 66, which the commentary treats as identical to "regularly constituted"); see also *Yamashita*, 327 U.S., at 44, 66 S. Ct. 340 (Rutledge, J., dissenting) (describing military commission as a court "specially constituted for a particular trial"). And one of the Red Cross' own treatises defines "regularly constituted court" as used in Common Article 3 to mean "established and organized in accordance with the laws and procedures already in force in a country." Int'l. Comm. of Red Cross, 1 Customary International Humanitarian Law 355 (2005); see also GCIV Commentary 340 (observing that "ordinary military courts" will "be set up in accordance with the recognized principles governing the administration of justice").

> ... At a minimum, a military commission "can be 'regularly constituted' by the standards of our military justice system only if some practical need explains deviations from court-martial practice."[33] ...
>
> [A plurality of the Court continued.]
>
> Inextricably intertwined with the question of regular constitution is the evaluation of the procedures governing the tribunal and whether they afford "all the judicial guarantees which are recognized as indispensable by civilized peoples." Like the phrase "regularly constituted court," this phrase is not defined in the text of the Geneva Conventions. But it must be understood to incorporate at least the barest of those trial protections that have been recognized by customary international law. Many of these are described in Article 75 of [Protocol I]. Although the United States declined to ratify Protocol I, its objections were not to Article 75 thereof. Indeed, it appears that the Government "regard[s] the provisions of Article 75 as an articulation of safeguards to which all persons in the hands of an enemy are entitled." Taft, The Law of Armed Conflict After 9/11: Some Salient Features, 28 Yale J. Int'l. L. 319, 322 (2003). Among the rights set forth in Article 75 is the "right to be tried in [one's] presence." Protocol I, Art. 75(4)(e).[34]
>
> ... [V]arious provisions of Commission Order No. 1 dispense with the principles, articulated in Article 75 and indisputably part of the customary international law, that an accused must, absent disruptive conduct or consent, be present for his trial and must be privy to the evidence against him. That the Government has a compelling interest in denying Hamdan access to certain sensitive information is not doubted. But, at least absent express statutory provision to the contrary, information used to convict a person of a crime must be disclosed to him.

Subsequent to the Supreme Court decision, Congress passed the Military Commission Acts of 2006 and 2009. Notably the statute expressly embraces the application of Common Article 3 to the conflict between the United States and Al Qaeda. It authorizes the President to prosecute 'unprivileged enemy belligerent' before military commissions. The Obama Administration initially suspended military missions. In 2011, however, the Administration resumed military commissions after Congress cut off funding to transfer any detainee from Guantánamo to the United States for trial or any other purpose.

QUESTIONS

1. What aspect, if any, of the European Court of Human Rights' analysis in *Incal* turns on the status of the defendant (civilian versus military) or on the nature of the offence?

[33] Further evidence of this tribunal's irregular constitution is the fact that its rules and procedures are subject to change mid trial, at the whim of the Executive. See Commission Order No. 1, ß 11 (providing that the Secretary of Defense may change the governing rules 'from time to time').

[34] Other international instruments to which the United States is a signatory include the same basic protections set forth in Art. 75. See, e.g., ICCPR, Art. 143(*d*), 23 Mar. 1976, 999 U.N.T.S. 171 (setting forth the right of an accused '[t]o be tried in his presence, and to defend himself in person or through legal assistance of his own choosing'). Following the Second World War, several defendants were tried and convicted by military commission for violations of the law of war in their failure to afford captives fair trials before imposition and execution of sentence. In two such trials, the prosecutors argued that the defendants' failure to apprise accused individuals of all evidence against them constituted violations of the law of war. See 5 UN War Crimes Commission 30 (trial of Sergeant-Major Shigeru Ohashi), 75 (trial of General Tanaka Hisakasu).

Do those distinctions explain the source of disagreement between the majority and dissenting opinions? Why should the test for an independent and impartial tribunal turn on such considerations? Should it matter whether a conflict is between a government and an internal separatist movement, a state and a transnational terrorist organization, or two states?

2. Does the classification of the US struggle with Al Qaeda as an armed conflict pose a threat to human rights? Consider the following statement:

> The United States is at war with Al Qaeda. The sooner we agree on that fact the more the conflict will be regulated by a more rights-protective regime. The Supreme Court's decision in *Hamdan* is exhibit A. The Court held that the situation constitutes an armed conflict under Common Article 3. By extension, Common Article's fair trial rights govern military commissions and the Article's prohibition on torture, cruel, humiliating, and degrading treatment regulates interrogations. Were the situation not an armed conflict, rights protections would not be so obvious, US courts may not be bound to apply international treaties, derogation clauses would risk overprotecting state interests, and the moral force of the Geneva Conventions would be absent.

3. Why does the Inter-American Commission suggest that any trial of a civilian by a military court is categorically prohibited? Should that rule apply as well in international and transnational armed conflicts? Consider the following commentary:

> The disapproval of military tribunals seems understandable in the context of alleged internal subversion, where judicial independence provides an important protection for domestic political opponents. The Court appears to strike a balance, creating a prophylactic, institutionally justified rule that avoids the need for case-by-case inquiry and reduces the risk of unfair trial. As dissenting judges have sometimes warned, however, the limits of its reasoning are unclear, and it would potentially call into question all forms of military justice....
>
> The Court's prophylactic rule is not necessarily appropriate for international armed conflict, or conflict with a foreign terrorist organization. In international armed conflicts, military jurisdiction over regular forces of the enemy is not only traditional, but is specifically sanctioned by the Third Geneva Convention. [Articles 84 of the Third Convention states: '[a] prisoner of war shall be tried only by a military court, unless the existing laws of the Detaining Power expressly permit the civil courts to try a member of the armed forces of the Detaining Power in respect of the particular offense....' And Article 102 states: 'A prisoner of war can be validly sentenced only if the sentence has been pronounced by the same courts according to the same procedure as in the case of members of the armed forces of the Detaining Power'.] Arguably, in war, civilians may be as biased, or more biased, against the enemy than military professionals. Moreover, military judges may interpret the laws of war with the knowledge that their own forces will be bound by their interpretations, and may be less inclined to use adjudication as a vehicle for the progressive development of international humanitarian law than civilian judges. These considerations may have lesser force in the asymmetrical context of conflict between a state and a non-state actor. But military trials, with compensating procedural guarantees that both international humanitarian law and human rights law require, can be a legitimate consequence of the shift to the military model.[35]

[35] G. Neuman, 'Counter-Terrorist Operations and the Rule of Law', 15 E. J. Int'l. L. 1019 (2004).

4. In *İncal*, the Court found that the participation of a military judge violates the guarantee of an independent and impartial tribunal partly because military judges 'are servicemen who still belong to the army, which in turn takes its orders from the executive'. Does the logical extension of the Court's analysis invalidate courts-martial and military tribunals in which the entire judicial panel or jury are comprised of service members answerable ultimately to the executive? Does the Court's analysis turn on the specific structural position of the military judges in Turkey's system or on the mere fact that they are members of a military? How would US military commissions — which consist of a military judge and at least five military officers with jurisdiction to try 'unprivileged enemy belligerents' — fare under this analysis?

5. Should the presence of a single military judge on a three-judge panel be a sufficient reason to invalidate the proceedings? Does the presence of civilian judges help counteract potential bias? How might military judges be different from other 'expert' judges that the dissenters in *İncal* suggest are permitted under the Court's case law? Would modifying other aspects of the proceedings — a different number and ratio of civilian and military judges, weighted voting rules, or appellate review — make the presence of military judges acceptable in your view? Chapter 14 returns to a similar set of questions about the composition and biases of judges in the case of hybrid tribunals such as the Special Court for Sierra Leone. In that context, panels were composed of international and national judges, and the latter were often criticized for being too closely connected to the conflict.

6. Could problems associated with holding war crimes and terrorism trials be averted by suspending prosecutions at least until the conclusion of the conflict? Wouldn't the political atmosphere, for example, generally be more conducive to ensuring the fairness of proceedings after a state of emergency? Consider the following text from ICRC Commentaries to the Geneva Conventions:

> Proceedings in respect of war crimes may not be brought against prisoners of war in conditions and at a time when any normal defence of the prisoners' interests is impossible. As long as hostilities continue, a prisoner of war accused of such offences will usually be unable to adduce the proof or evidence which might absolve him of responsibility or reduce that responsibility. It seems necessary that, except in special cases, prisoners of war accused of war crimes should not be tried until after the end of hostilities, that is to say when communications have been re-established between the belligerent countries and the prisoner is in a position to procure the necessary documents for his defence and to call witnesses.
>
> If prisoners of war were nevertheless tried while hostilities were still in progress, in conditions which would not afford them a proper defence, they would in fact be deprived of the regular trial to which they are entitled under Article 99. A trial conducted in such circumstances could then constitute a grave breach of the Convention, as covered by Article 130.

Consider also the following argument by Professors Jack Goldsmith and Eric Posner:

> [The authors start by asking why the US Government plans to prosecute only a small fraction of the Guantánamo detainees.] Because it is difficult to try terrorists in this

war. For most detainees, the government lacks evidence of overt crimes such as murder. It can prosecute these detainees only for the vague and problematic crime of conspiracy to commit a terrorist act based on membership in and training with al-Qaeda or the Taliban. Beyond this problem, witnesses are scattered around the globe, and much of the evidence is in a foreign language, or classified, or hearsay — in many cases all of these things.

Even if these obstacles are overcome, . . .trials of political enemies are more difficult, more time-consuming and, in the end, more circuslike than an ordinary criminal trial. The defendant or his lawyers will use a trial not to contest guilt but rather to rally followers and demoralize foes.

. . .

There is a better and easier way to deal with captured terrorists. The Supreme Court has made clear that the conflicts with al-Qaeda and the Taliban are governed by the laws of war, and the laws of war permit detention of enemy soldiers without charge or trial until hostilities end. . . .

The main concern with military detentions is that the war will last a long time, perhaps indefinitely. If so, detention could mean a life sentence. We don't yet know whether this concern is warranted. But there are several ways to assure Americans and the world that the system is as fair and humane as circumstances permit.

. . .

When hostilities in the war against al-Qaeda and its affiliates cease, of course, the detention rationale will dissipate and detainees must be released or (if they have committed law-of-war violations) tried. For such people, if there are any, regular criminal trial procedures should be adequate. If hostilities are really over, the risk that a former terrorist might walk free as a result of insufficient evidence is no more troublesome than it is for trials of ordinary criminals. . . .[36]

COMMENT ON NATIONAL SECURITY AND SOCIO-ECONOMIC RIGHTS

Discussions about potential relationships between national security and human rights law commonly focus on civil and political rights. It is important, however, to consider relationships between national security and economic and social rights. One set of issues concerns whether the national security landscape post-11 September will (and should) affect rights protections within this domain. Does the mantra that the full range of human rights are 'indivisible, interdependent and interrelated' suggest that accommodations for national security concerns in the civil and political rights realm will (and should) translate into accommodations across the human rights system? More generally, what economic and social rights protections might national security interests directly or indirectly affect? Should these rights protections, just like civil and political rights guarantees, regulate the acts of belligerents in

[36] J. Goldsmith & E. A. Posner, 'Op-Ed, A Better Way on Detainees', *Washington Post*, 4 Aug. 2006, A17.

times of war, or does the programmatic nature of economic and social rights necessitate alternative ways of thinking about the rights–security relationship?

On the face of it, the Covenant on Economic, Social and Cultural Rights suggests little direct connection with national security concerns. The Covenant explicitly references 'national security' only in an article dealing with trade union rights (a corollary to rights of association). In contrast, the International Covenant on Civil and Political Rights references 'national security' in the limitations clauses of six separate articles. And, Article 4 of the ICCPR contains a derogation mechanism for public emergencies. The ICESCR has no such device.[37]

Nevertheless, situations involving armed conflict, militarization and terrorism can directly implicate economic and social rights. And various international human rights mechanisms have begun to address such matters. The UN supervisory committee that monitors and evaluates implementation of the ICESCR, for example, denounced the housing, health and nutritional conditions of civilians displaced in the Sri Lankan civil war and criticized the government's failure to implement a peace plan to devolve power to regional authorities. That Committee has also reviewed the record of Israel on multiple occasions. In its more recent evaluations, the Committee stated that it was

> gravely concerned about the deplorable living conditions of the Palestinians in the occupied territories, who — as a result of the continuing occupation and subsequent measures of closures, extended curfews, roadblocks and security checkpoints — suffer from impingement of their enjoyment of economic, social and cultural rights enshrined in the Covenant, in particular access to work, land, water, health care, education and food.

In its 2011 concluding observations, the Committee also included international humanitarian law in its analysis and adopted a more rigorous test in the context of cultural rights: the Committee recommended Israel 'take measures to ensure that Palestinians living in the Occupied Palestinian Territory can exercise their right to take part in cultural and religious life, without restrictions other than those that are strictly proportionate to security considerations and are non-discriminatory in their application, in accordance with international humanitarian law.' The Committee also called for the state to 'ensure timely and unfettered access by the humanitarian organizations operating in the Occupied Palestinian Territory to the Palestinian population, including in all areas affected by the Wall and its associated regime.' Other examples include the Committee's review of Russia concerning conditions in Chechnya, Colombia concerning displacement of Afro-Colombian communities and street children affected by the armed conflict, Afghanistan concerning recruitment of child soldiers, and Algeria concerning the impact of the protracted state of emergency. Notably, the International Court of Justice relied heavily on the Covenant on Economic, Social and Cultural Rights in its Advisory Opinion concerning the

[37] The Additional Protocol to the American Convention on Human Rights in the Area of Economic, Social and Cultural Rights ('Protocol of San Salvador') contains no derogation clause. The African Charter on Human and Peoples' Rights recognizes both civil and political rights and economic and social rights, but it does not contain a derogation clause for either.

Israeli 'barrier', or 'wall', and in evaluating the effects on the Palestinian people living in occupied territories.

In 2007, the Office of the High Commissioner for Human Rights published a 'Fact Sheet on Human Rights, Terrorism and Counter-terrorism', which included concerns for economic, social and cultural rights:

> Targeted sanctions which result in freezing assets, imposing travel bans and other restrictions may also have serious consequences for the ability of the affected individuals and their families to enjoy economic and social rights, as their access to education and employment may be severely restricted. The effective use of humanitarian exemptions may be one important means for limiting the negative impact of targeted sanctions on the enjoyment of economic, social and cultural rights. Similarly, repressive security measures (such as control orders and the construction of physical barriers to limit the movement of certain individuals and groups), adopted with a view to countering terrorism, have severely restricted the ability of certain individuals and populations to work, and their rights to education, health services and a family life.

The Special Rapporteur on Human Rights and Counterterrorism also issued an important report dedicated largely to economic and social rights (A/HRC/6/17).

The European Committee on Social Rights, a similar body responsible for monitoring and evaluating implementation of a regional treaty, has also issued opinions addressing national security. The European Committee is aided by the fact that its governing treaty, the revised European Social Charter, explicitly contemplates such questions. The Charter includes a general limitation clause permitting governments to restrict economic and social rights when such measures are 'prescribed by law and are necessary in a democratic society for the protection of . . . national security'. The Charter also includes a general derogation provision modelled on provisions in civil and political rights treaties. It permits a state to suspend treaty obligations 'in time of war or other public emergency threatening the life of the nation'. No economic and social rights are listed as nonderogable.

Under this framework, the European Committee has rendered decisions delineating which economic and public sectors are sufficiently related to national security. Those determinations affect whether particular areas of the workforce are subject to exceptional government powers such as prohibiting strikes, prohibiting collective action or excluding foreign nationals from employment. The European Committee has also decided whether specific governmental measures are proportionate to meeting national security objectives. Measures subject to such an inquiry have included blanket prohibitions on the right to strike, an exceptionally lengthy period of compulsory service for military officers and disparate periods of governmental service for conscientious objectors.

UN officials whose mandate covers economic and social rights have increasingly addressed violations occurring in situations of armed conflict.[38] In 2001 and 2002, the UN Special Rapporteur on the Right to Food reported on the use of food as 'a method of warfare against insurgents and civilian populations' by the Government of Myanmar including 'the deliberate destruction by government armed forces of staple crops and

[38] We introduce the general responsibilities and practices of these offices in Chapter 9.

confiscation of food from civilians'. The Special Rapporteur also reported on situations in Afghanistan and occupied Palestinian territories. The Special Rapporteur on the Right to Adequate Housing criticized house demolitions in occupied Palestinian territory in 2003, forced evictions in Afghanistan in 2004 and displacement of civilian populations in Sudan in 2005. The Special Rapporteur on the Right to Health, on one occasion, urged the Coalition Provisional Authority in Iraq to inquire into the health of the civilian population in the city of Falluja following massive military operations by US-led forces and, on another occasion, sent an urgent appeal following the bombing of a field clinic by Iraqi and multinational forces.

Many of the state obligations might seem relatively straightforward in these contexts. The cases generally do not involve positive obligations requiring a state to *protect* individuals from the depredations of private actors, nor do they involve obligations to take affirmative steps to promote and *fulfil* economic and social well-being. Rather, the cases generally involve the obligation to *respect* economic and social rights. They refer to acts of commission not omission, and they concern direct governmental intrusions that interfere with and undermine human welfare. Governmental actions in many of these instances also clearly contravene the principle of non-regression. Along all these dimensions, the analysis of state obligations appears to rest on politically and philosophically less controversial ground than other situations involving economic and social rights.

These cases are, at the same time, deceptively simple. Indeed, national security cases reveal the significant difficulties that can arise in determining whether the obligation of a state to respect economic and social rights is lawfully discharged. When economic and social rights conflict with national security and military imperatives, which interests should prevail? What constitutes a proportional loss of health, housing or livelihood, for example, in the face of a proffered national security or military justification? What function should courts—international or domestic—perform in addressing such questions? How should judicial and other authorities frame an analysis that decides when such economic and social interests trump national security objectives proffered by state officials?

Another important dimension of the relationship between national security and economic and social rights is the significance of international humanitarian law. Recall our discussion of debates about *lex specialis* earlier in this chapter. Are there special reasons for having international humanitarian law displace (or supplement) human rights law in the area of economic and social rights? When reading the following commentary by Louise Doswald-Beck and Sylvain Vité consider the advantages and disadvantages of an international humanitarian law framework in regulating practices that implicate economic and social welfare of civilians during armed conflict. Also consider whether international human rights standards would unduly complicate or reduce obligations of parties to a conflict by introducing imprecision to international humanitarian law or by providing broad justifications for restricting rights that would not otherwise exist under international humanitarian law. In an issue of the International Review of the Red Cross, Doswald-Beck and Vité analyse distinctions between the IHL and human rights regimes:

> [T]here is a phenomenon in human rights law which is quite alien to humanitarian law, namely . . . the fact that most of these treaties make a distinction between so-called "civil and political rights" and "economic, social and cultural" rights. The

legal difference between these treaties is that the "civil and political" ones require instant respect for the rights enumerated therein, whereas the "economic, social and cultural" ones require the State to take appropriate measures in order to achieve a progressive realization of these rights....

...

... [I]t is a fact that the implementation of most of the economic rights does necessitate some resources and thought as to the best economic arrangement in order to achieve the best standard of living possible. The genuine difficulty thus created in giving a proper interpretation to the ESC Covenant in the particular circumstances of each State has a direct effect on the nature of the individual's economic rights....

[T]he major difficulty of applying human rights law as enunciated in the treaties is the very general nature of the treaty language. Even outside armed conflict situations, we see that the documents attempt to deal with the relationship between the individual and society by the use of limitation clauses. Thus the manner in which the rights may be applied in practice must be interpreted by the organs instituted to implement the treaty in question. Although the United Nations Human Rights Committee, created by the [ICCPR], has made some general statements on the meaning of certain articles, the normal method of interpretation by both the United Nations and regional systems has been through a decision or an opinion on whether a particular set of facts constitutes a violation of the article in question.... The major legal difference is that humanitarian law is not formulated as a series of rights, but rather as a series of duties that combatants have to obey. This does have one very definite advantage from the legal theory point of view, in that humanitarian law is not subject to the kind of arguments that continue to plague the implementation of economic and social rights.

...

[T]he Protocol protects life in a way that goes beyond the traditional civil right to life. First, it prohibits the starvation of civilians as a method of warfare and consequently the destruction of their means of survival (which is an improvement on earlier customary law).[39] Secondly, it offers means for improving their chance of survival by, for example, providing for the declaration of special zones that contain no military objectives and consequently may not be attacked. Thirdly, there are various stipulations in the Geneva Conventions and their Additional Protocols that the wounded must be collected and given the medical care that they need. In human rights treaties this would fall into the category of "economic and social rights". Fourthly, the Geneva Conventions and their Protocols specify in considerable detail the physical conditions that are needed in order to sustain life in as reasonable a condition as possible in an armed conflict. Thus, for example, the living conditions required for prisoners of war are described in the Third Geneva Convention and similar requirements are also laid down for civilian persons interned in an occupied territory. With regard to the general population, an

[39] Article 54 of Additional Protocol I provides in part:

1. Starvation of civilians as a method of warfare is prohibited.
2. It is prohibited to attack, destroy, remove or render useless objects indispensable to the survival of the civilian population, such as food-stuffs, agricultural areas for the production of food-stuffs, crops, livestock, drinking water installations and supplies and irrigation works, for the specific purpose of denying them for their sustenance value to the civilian population or to the adverse Party, whatever the motive, whether in order to starve out civilians, to cause them to move away, or for any other motive.

occupying power is required to ensure that the people as a whole have the necessary means of survival and to accept outside relief shipments if necessary to achieve this purpose.[40] There are also provisions for relief for the Parties' own populations, but they are not as absolute as those that apply in occupied territory. Once again, these kinds of provisions would be categorized by a human rights lawyer as "economic and social".[41]

QUESTIONS

1. Does international humanitarian law offer a framework superior to human rights law for regulating violations of economic and social rights in times of war? Do you agree with Doswald-Beck and Vité's comparisons?

2. Are the international humanitarian law rules precise but too narrow? Does Article 54 of Additional Protocol I, for example, outlaw actions taken only with a specific intent — e.g., purposefully depriving civilians of sustenance rather than knowingly or negligently engaging in such acts? Does this feature demonstrate that international humanitarian law cannot adequately address the full range of human rights concerns in armed conflicts?

3. In 2002, the ICESCR Committee issued General Comment No. 15 on the right to water. Consider the following excerpt from that Comment:

> The Committee notes that during armed conflicts, emergency situations and natural disasters, the right to water embraces those obligations by which States parties are bound under international humanitarian law.[42] This includes protection of objects indispensable for survival of the civilian population, including drinking water installations and supplies and irrigation works, protection of the natural environment against widespread, long-term and severe damage and ensuring that civilians, internees and prisoners have access to adequate water.

[40] Article 55 of the Civilians Convention provides: 'To the fullest extent of the means available to it, the Occupying Power has the duty of ensuring the food and medical supplies of the population; it should, in particular, bring in the necessary foodstuffs, medical stores and other articles if the resources of the occupied territory are inadequate.'

Article 56 of the Convention provides: 'To the fullest extent of the means available to it, the Occupying Power has the duty of ensuring and maintaining, with the cooperation of national and local authorities, the medical and hospital establishments and services, public health and hygiene in the occupied territory, with particular reference to the adoption and application of the prophylactic and preventive measures necessary to combat the spread of contagious diseases and epidemics. Medical personnel of all categories shall be allowed to carry out their duties.'

Article 69 of Additional Protocol I states: 'In addition to the duties specified in Article 55 of the [Civilians] Convention concerning food and medical supplies, the Occupying Power shall, to the fullest extent of the means available to it and without any adverse distinction, also ensure the provision of clothing, bedding, means of shelter, other supplies essential to the survival of the civilian population of the occupied territory…'

[41] L. Doswald-Beck & S. Vité, 'International Humanitarian Law and Human Rights Law', 293 Int'l. Rev. Red Cross 94–119 (1993).

[42] For the interrelationship of human rights law and humanitarian law, the Committee notes the conclusions of the International Court of Justice in *Legality of the Threat or Use of Nuclear Weapons (Request by the General Assembly)*, ICJ Rep. 1996, p. 226, para. 25.

In a detailed analysis of the subject, the Special Rapporteur on the Right to Food adopted a similar position: 'The right to food must be protected in times of peace, but also in times of war. This section looks at the right to food in situations of armed conflict in which international humanitarian law comes into effect and is the more appropriate way to protect people suffering from hunger and malnutrition.'

Should international humanitarian law standards completely substitute for human rights law during armed conflict as the Committee's and Rapporteur's analysis might suggest? The Committee references the *Nuclear Weapons* Advisory Opinion of the International Court of Justice which we discuss earlier in the chapter. The ICJ stated: 'The test of what is an arbitrary deprivation of life, however, then falls to be determined by the applicable *lex specialis*, namely, the law applicable in armed conflict which is designed to regulate the conduct of hostilities.' If IHL serves as the test for arbitrary deprivations of life, does it necessarily follow that this body of law should serve as the test for unlawful deprivations of economic and social rights in armed conflict as well

PART C

RIGHTS, DUTIES AND DILEMMAS OF UNIVERSALISM

The preceding chapters conveyed no sense of a uniform, coherent, uncontested human rights regime. From the controversies over capital punishment in Chapter 1, the dispute over permitted methods for interrogating prisoners in Chapter 3, the implementation of economic and social rights in Chapter 4 and the issues of national security in Chapter 5, we have seen major differences in understandings of human rights both among legal orders of different states and within states. Such contests and struggles within and about the human rights regime can be contrasted with conduct (police brutality, summary executions, racial discrimination, sham trials, coerced religious practice) that the vast majority of states throughout the world view as violations of universally accepted human rights norms.

Part C concentrates on notions of rights and of contests and disputes about them, exploring the very idea of rights more systematically than did the prior materials. Chapter 6 examines the nature of rights and rights discourse, and the character and consequences of duty-oriented rather than rights-oriented social systems. Chapter 7 begins with exploration of the opposition between universalism and cultural relativism in understanding the character of the human rights regime. Theoretical writings introduce these notions, followed by illustrative case studies.

6

Rights or Duties as Organizing Concepts

Thus far the materials have described but barely commented on the fundamental characteristic of the UDHR and ICCPR, their foundation in the rhetoric and concept of rights. Many view that rhetoric as unproblematic, as the central and inevitable component of a universal discourse about human dignity and humane treatment of individuals by governments. Others, to the contrary, view a discourse about rights as alien and harmful to their states or cultures, disruptive of traditional social structures, subversive of authority. Consider the following queries:

(1) Why does the language of rights dominate the texts of the declarations and treaties as well as many new constitutions and even the slogans and polemics of political debate?

(2) Is that language intrinsically superior to other possible ones — for example, the language of duties that might lead to a Universal Declaration of Human Duties, or the language and methods of utility? Is rights language essential to the values and goals of the human rights regime? Or is the currency of that language a matter of historical contingency, in that the postwar movement to protect human dignity found its roots in liberal political cultures in which rights had long ago taken root.

(3) Does a particular substantive content necessarily attach to the language of rights? For example, do 'rights' necessarily express the principles of the liberal political tradition, as with respect to non-discrimination, or fair procedures, or freedom of religion or speech? Are the same questions as relevant to the language of duties? Are either rights or duties empty receptacles that are open to many different types of values and ideas, some of which might be antagonistic to the liberal tradition?

(4) Universality informs the discourse and content of rights in the UDHR and the basic treaties. But why should we accept that the stated norms are universal? Are arguments about their universal character accepted worldwide? Or do some parts of the world view many important provisions in the basic human rights instruments as particular to the Western liberal tradition, hence inapplicable to radically different states and cultures? Would the same criticism be as applicable to a duty-based Universal Declaration?

A. IDEAS ABOUT RIGHTS AND THE EFFECTS OF RIGHTS RHETORIC

We here consider different understandings, historical and contemporary, of the notion of 'rights' and inquire whether rights have inherent implications for a society's moral, political and socio-economic order. For example, does rights rhetoric in a constitution and statutes, or in a dominant moral and political theory, point to an individualistic, communitarian, or other type of society? Does it necessarily assume certain institutional arrangements for government, such as a constitutional separation of powers and an independent judiciary?

The readings begin with a brief description of the evolution from earlier concepts of natural law and natural rights to contemporary notions of rights in domestic and international contexts.

BURNS H. WESTON, HUMAN RIGHTS

Britannica, Academic Edition (2012), www.britannica.com/ EBchecked/topic/275840/human-rights/%20rights

...

The expression "human rights" is relatively new, having come into everyday parlance only since World War II, the founding of the United Nations in 1945, and the adoption by the UN General Assembly of the Universal Declaration of Human Rights in 1948. It replaced the phrase "natural rights," which fell into disfavour in part because the concept of natural law (to which it was intimately linked) had become a matter of great controversy; and it replaced as well the later phrase "the rights of Man"....

...

The modern conception of natural law as meaning or implying natural rights was elaborated primarily by thinkers of the 17th and 18th centuries. The intellectual — and especially the scientific — achievements of the 17th century... encouraged a belief in natural law and universal order; and during the 18th century, the so-called Age of Enlightenment, a growing confidence in human reason and in the perfectibility of human affairs led to the more comprehensive expression of this belief. Particularly important were the writings of John Locke, arguably the most important natural-law theorist of modern times, and the works of the 18th-century philosophers centred mainly in Paris, including Montesquieu, Voltaire, and Jean-Jacques Rousseau. Locke argued in detail, mainly in writings associated with the English Glorious Revolution (1688), that certain rights self-evidently pertain to individuals as human beings (because these rights existed in "the state of nature" before humankind entered civil society); that chief among them are the rights to life, liberty (freedom from arbitrary rule), and property; that, upon entering civil society, humankind surrendered to the state — pursuant to a "social contract" — only the right to enforce these natural rights and not the rights themselves; and that the state's failure to secure these rights gives rise to a right to responsible, popular revolution. The philosophes, building on Locke and others and embracing many and varied currents of thought with a common supreme faith in reason, vigorously attacked religious and scientific dogmatism, intolerance, censorship, and social and economic restraints. They sought to discover and act upon universally valid principles governing nature, humanity, and society, including the inalienable "rights of Man," which they treated as a fundamental ethical and social gospel.

Not surprisingly, this liberal intellectual ferment exerted a profound influence in the Western world of the late 18th and early 19th centuries. Together with the Glorious Revolution in England and the resulting Bill of Rights, it provided the rationale for the wave of revolutionary agitation that swept the West, most notably in North America and France. Thomas Jefferson, who had studied Locke and Montesquieu, gave poetic eloquence to the plain prose of the 17th century in the Declaration of Independence, proclaimed by the 13 American colonies on July 4, 1776: "We hold these truths to be self-evident, that all men are created equal, that they are endowed by their Creator with certain unalienable Rights, that among these are Life, Liberty and the Pursuit of Happiness." Similarly, the marquis de Lafayette...imitated the pronouncements of the English and American revolutions in the Declaration of the Rights of Man and of the Citizen of August 26, 1789, proclaiming that "men are born and remain free and equal in rights" and that "the aim of every political association is the preservation of the natural and imprescriptible rights of man."

In sum, the idea of human rights, though known by another name, played a key role in late 18th- and early 19th-century struggles against political absolutism. It was, indeed, the failure of rulers to respect the principles of freedom and equality that was responsible for this development.

... [B]ecause they were conceived in essentially absolutist terms, natural rights were increasingly considered to conflict with one another. Most importantly, the doctrine of natural rights came under powerful philosophical and political attack from both the right and the left.

In England, for example, conservative political thinkers such as Edmund Burke and David Hume united with liberals such as Jeremy Bentham to condemn the doctrine, the former out of fear that public affirmation of natural rights would lead to social upheaval, the latter out of concern lest declarations and proclamations of natural rights substitute for effective legislation. In his Reflections on the Revolution in France (1790), Burke — a believer in natural law who nonetheless denied that the "rights of Man" could be derived from it — criticized the drafters of the Declaration of the Rights of Man and of the Citizen for proclaiming the "monstrous fiction" of human equality, which, he argued, serves but to inspire "false ideas and vain expectations in men destined to travel in the obscure walk of laborious life." Bentham, one of the founders of Utilitarianism, was no less scornful. "Rights," he wrote, "is the child of law; from real law come real rights; but from imaginary laws, from 'law of nature,' come imaginary rights....Natural rights is simple nonsense; natural and imprescriptible rights (an American phrase)...[is] rhetorical nonsense, nonsense upon stilts." Agreeing with Bentham, Hume insisted that natural law and natural rights are unreal metaphysical phenomena.

This assault upon natural law and natural rights intensified and broadened during the 19th and early 20th centuries. John Stuart Mill, despite his vigorous defense of liberty, proclaimed that rights ultimately are founded on utility. The German jurist Friedrich Karl von Savigny, England's Sir Henry Maine, and other "historicalist" legal thinkers emphasized that rights are a function of cultural and environmental variables unique to particular communities. The English jurist John Austin argued that the only law is "the command of the sovereign" (a phrase of Hobbes). And the logical positivists of the early 20th century insisted that the only truth is that which can be established by verifiable experience and that therefore ethical pronouncements are not cognitively significant. By World War I, there were scarcely any theorists who would defend the "rights of Man" along the lines of natural law....

...

Although the heyday of natural rights proved short, the idea of rights nonetheless endured. The abolition of slavery, the implementation of factory legislation, the rise of popular education and trade unionism, the universal suffrage movement — these and other examples of 19th-century reformist impulses afford ample evidence that the idea was not to be extinguished, even if its priori derivation had become a matter of general skepticism. But it was not until the rise and fall of Nazi Germany that the idea of human rights truly came into its own....

...

To say that there is widespread acceptance of the principle of human rights is not to say that there is complete agreement about the nature and scope of such rights — which is to say, their definition. Among the basic questions that have yet to receive conclusive answers are the following: whether human rights are to be viewed as divine, moral, or legal entitlements; whether they are to be validated by intuition, culture, custom, social contract, principles of distributive justice, or as prerequisites for happiness; whether they are to be understood as irrevocable or partially revocable; and whether they are to be broad or limited in number and content.

...

NOTE

In 'Contemporary Reinterpretations of the Concept of Human Rights' (in David Sidorsky (ed.), *Essays on Human Rights* (1979)), Sidorsky observes:

> ... [A] major characterization of natural rights derived from [the] belief that rights are the properties of persons capable of exercising rational choice. For, when men asserted their natural rights they were expressing their autonomy as individuals. Hence, the model or pattern for the exercise of natural rights became the protection of the sphere of the autonomous individual from arbitrary incursion by the state or other coercive association. The listing of the right to life, for example, did not involve a commitment to the extension or universalization of health care or to actions for shaping a safer environment but to a rule of law that would restrain arbitrary acts of violence, especially those of governmental authorities, against individuals. Similarly, the natural right to liberty did not refer to support of policies

> that would enhance self-realization through the universalization of education, but it did require the legal protection of individuals against arbitrary imprisonment.

Sidorsky illustrates his remarks by referring to health care and education, and seems to be broadly contrasting civil-political and economic-social rights. Recall that from the start, the canonical texts of the international human rights regime gave these two bodies of rights a formal equal significance.

The following readings describe their authors' understandings of basic characteristics of rights in contemporary legal and political discourse and argument. The brief excerpt from Eugene Kamenka distinguishes claims of rights from other types of claims, taking a positivist position about rights. Duncan Kennedy analyses rights discourse as it has evolved in a liberal political culture such as the United States. He is thus more attentive to the role of rights in adjudication than are most of the materials in this course book, which examine rights discourse in the framework not only of judicial opinions but also of broader political processes — advocacy and speeches, UN resolutions, committee reports, investigative missions, scholarly writings and so on. Nonetheless, the analysis and critique of rights in Kennedy's book inform rights discourse throughout the international human rights regime as well. In two readings that follow, Cass Sunstein and Karl Klare respond in different ways to aspects of the broad 'critique of rights' that schools of thought and groups throughout the world have developed over recent decades. David Kennedy raises underlying questions about contradictions within the human rights regime, the socio-economic and political consequences of rights-based advocacy, and arguments for and against a rights-based strategy for achieving reform.

Ideas in these readings are central to grasping the special characteristics, strengths and weaknesses of a movement based on rights, whether rights language figures in broad political debates or in the opinions of courts. They bear importantly on the discussion of cultural relativism in Chapter 7.

EUGENE KAMENKA, HUMAN RIGHTS, PEOPLES' RIGHTS

in James Crawford (ed.), The Rights of Peoples (1988), at 127

Rights are claims that have achieved a special kind of endorsement or success: legal rights by a legal system; human rights by widespread sentiment or an international order. All rights arise in specific historical circumstances. They are claims made, conceded or granted by people who are themselves historically and socially shaped. They are asserted by people on their own behalf or as perceived and endorsed implications of specific historical traditions, institutions and arrangements or of a historically conditioned theory of human needs and human aspirations, or of a human conception of a Divine plan and purpose. In objective fact as opposed to (some) subjective feeling, they are neither eternal nor inalienable, neither prior to society or societies nor independent of them. Some such rights can be singled out, and they often are singled out, as social ideals, as goals to strive toward. But even as such, they cannot be divorced from social content and context.

Claims presented as rights are claims that are often, perhaps usually, presented as having a special kind of importance, urgency, universality, or endorsement that makes them more than disparate or simply subjective demands. Their success is dependent on such endorsement — by a government or a legal system that has power to grant and protect such rights, by a tradition or institution whose authority is accepted in those circles that recognize these claims as rights, by widespread social sentiment, regionally, nationally, or internationally.

Claims, whether presented as rights or not, conflict. So do the traditions, institutions and authorities that endorse the claim as a right. They conflict both with each other and, often, in their internal structure, implications and working out....

The concept of human rights is no longer tied to belief in God or natural law in its classical sense. But it still seeks or claims a form of endorsement that transcends or pretends to transcend specific historical institutions and traditions, legal systems, governments, or national and even regional communities. Like moral claims more generally, it asserts in its own behalf moral and sometimes even logical priority — connection with the very concept (treated as morally loaded) of what it means to be a human being or a person, or of what it means to behave morally. These are questions on which moral philosophers do have a certain expertise, at least in seeing where the difficulties lie, and on which they, like ordinary people throughout the world, have long disagreed and continue to disagree.

NOTE

Compare the following remarks of Norberto Bobbio, in *The Age of Rights* (trans. Allan Cameron) (1996), at 18:

> My theoretical approach has always been...that human rights however fundamental are historical rights and therefore arise from specific conditions characterized by the embattled defence of new freedoms against old powers.... Religious freedom resulted from the religious wars, civil liberties from the parliamentarian struggles against absolutism, and political and social freedoms from the birth, growth and experience of movements representing workers, landless peasants and smallholders....
>
> ...
>
> ...The expression rights of man is certain emphatic, and even if that emphasis is expedient, it can be misleading because it implies that there are rights belonging to an abstract man and thus removed from the historical context, and that by contemplating this essential and eternal man we can arrive at the certain knowledge of his rights and duties. Today we know that the so-called human rights are the product of human civilization and not nature, because historical rights are changeable and therefore susceptible to transformation and growth. It is sufficient to look at the writings of the early advocates of natural law to realize how the list of rights

> has been getting longer and longer. Indeed Hobbes only recognized one right, the right to life.... If someone had told Locke, the champion of the rights to liberty, that all citizens should have the right to participate in politics, or even worse that they had the right to paid employment, he would have called it madness....
>
> The rights listed in the [Universal] Declaration...are the rights of a historical man as perceived by those who drew up the Declaration following the tragedy of the Second World War, in an époque which commenced with the French Revolution and included the Soviet Revolution....

DUNCAN KENNEDY, A CRITIQUE OF ADJUDICATION (1997), at 305

[Kennedy, a leading scholar in the critical legal studies movement that started in the United States and spread to other countries, devotes part of his book to the examination and critique of rights. He is not directly concerned with the substance of rights — for example, whether a right to free speech should have broader or narrower boundaries — but rather with the discourse of rights itself, with the way in which advocates and courts argue and reason about rights. Thus Kennedy examines matters such as the assumptions made by courts and advocates about rights, the distinctive characteristics of rights rhetoric and the types of reasoning (legal and other) that are explicitly or implicitly involved in the interpretation, elaboration and application of rights to given cases or contexts.

These ideas, although rooted in this book in the American experience, bear directly on rights discourse in the international human rights regime. The ideas below figure in the responses by Karl Klare and Cass Sunstein to criticism of rights and rights rhetoric that appear in the next following materials.

Kennedy notes that rights 'play a central role in the American mode of political discourse'. He describes rights as 'mediators' between two elements or domains in that discourse: *value judgements*, which he describes as matters of preference, related to subjectivity of views and to 'philosophical' premises; and *factual judgements* (also referred to as *factoid*) that represent the domain of the scientific, the empirical, objective judgements.

Excerpts from the chapters on rights follow.]

... [I]t seems to me that in American political discourse [the ways of understanding the nature of rights] all presuppose a basic distinction between rights argument and other kinds of normative argument. The point of an appeal to a right, the reason for making it, is that it *can't be reduced* to a mere 'value judgment' that one outcome is better than another. Yet it is possible to make rights arguments about matters that fall outside the domain commonly understood as factual, that is, about political or policy questions of how the government ought to act. In other words, rights are mediators between the domain of pure value judgments and the domain of factual judgments.

The word 'mediation' here means that reasoning from the right is understood to have properties from both sides of the divide: 'value' as in value judgment, but 'reasoning' as in 'logic', with the possibility of correctness. Rights reasoning, in short, allows you to be right about your value judgments, rather than just stating 'preferences', as in 'I prefer chocolate to vanilla ice cream'. The mediation is possible because rights are understood to have two crucial properties.

First, they are 'universal' in the sense that they derive from needs or values or preferences that every person shares or ought to share. For this reason, everyone does or ought to agree that they are desirable. This is the first aspect of rights as mediators: they follow from values but are neither arbitrary nor subjective because they are universal.

Second, they are 'factoid', in the sense that 'once you acknowledge the existence of the right, then you have to agree that its observance *requires x, y*, and *z*'. For example, everyone recognizes that the statement 'be good' is too vague to help resolve concrete conflicts, even though it is universal. But once we have derived a *right* from universal needs or values, it is understood to be possible to have a relatively objective, rational, determinate discussion of how it ought to be instantiated in social or legal rules.

...

I pointed out [earlier] that rights occupy an ambiguous status with respect to the distinction between rules and reasons for rules. 'Congress shall make no law abridging the freedom of speech' is an enacted rule of the legal system, but 'protecting freedom of speech' is a reason for adopting a rule, or for choosing one interpretation of a rule over another. In this second usage, the right is understood to be something that is outside and preexists legal reasoning.

The outside right is something that a person has even if the legal order doesn't recognize it and even if 'exercising' it is illegal. 'I have the right to engage in homosexual intercourse, even if it is forbidden by the sodomy statutes of every government in the universe'. Or 'slavery denies the right to personal freedom, which exists in spite of and above the law of slave states'.

The Constitution, and state and federal statutes, legalize some highly abstract outside rights, such as the right of free speech in the First Amendment or of property in the Fourteenth. Positive law also legalizes less abstract rights that are understood to derive from more abstract, but not enacted, outside rights....

...

[Kennedy observes that these 'outside' rights, which pre-exist any incorporation of them into law (e.g., the right not to be tortured by state officials exists whether or not the formal legal system incorporates it and thus makes it a 'legal' right), can be analogized to 'natural rights' in classical liberal political theory.

When a party to litigation makes a legal claim of right, other factors come into play, such as the 'duty of interpretive fidelity' of judges who are bound by the legal formulation of the right and have a duty to be faithful to it in their interpretation and application. The adjudication of constitutional rights brings all these problems together. When incorporated in a constitution, such as the First Amendment to the US Constitution, constitutional rights 'are both legal rights embedded in and formed by legal argumentative practice (legal rules) and entities that "exist" prior to and outside the constitution'. Thus argument based on constitutional rights involves both 'legal argument (under a duty of interpretive fidelity) and legislative argument (appealing to the political values of the community).' By 'legislative argument',

Kennedy refers to the broad range of arguments based on preferences, values and policies that are characteristically advanced by opposing parties and interests within the legislative political process.

Kennedy then discusses legal rights in legal reasoning. He notes that rights arguments 'are open to the same analysis of open texture of indeterminacy as legal argument in general'. He describes one of the ways in which the critique of legal rights collapses the distinction between rights-based argument and policy argument in general. For example, suppose that a claimant appeals to the right to free speech to urge a court to interpret some rule in a way that protects free speech. The court will frequently 'balance' the conflicting claims, perhaps the right to free speech and (with respect to sexually abusive speech in the workplace) the other party's right to a non-abusive workplace. What determines the balance struck by the court is not any logical chain of reasoning from the asserted right, or from two asserted conflicting rights, but the court's 'considering obviously open-textured arguments from morality, social welfare, expectations, and institutional competence and administrability'.]

The upshot, when both sides are well represented, is that the advocates confront the judge with two plausible but contradictory chains of rights reasoning, one proceeding from the plaintiff's rights and the other from the defendant's. Yes, the employer has property rights, but the picketers have free-speech rights. Yes, the harasser has free-speech rights, but the harassed has a right to be free of sex discrimination in the workplace. Yes, the landowner has the right to do whatever he wants on his land, but his neighbor has a right to be free from unreasonable interference. And each chain is open to an internal critique.

Sometimes the judge more or less arbitrarily endorses one side over the other; sometimes she throws in the towel and balances. The lesson of practice for the doubter is that the question involved cannot be resolved without resort to policy, which in turn makes the resolution open to ideological influence. The critique of legal rights reasoning becomes just a special case of the general critique of policy argument: once it is shown that the case requires a balancing of conflicting rights claims, it is implausible that it is the rights themselves, rather than the 'subjective' or 'political' commitments of the judges, that are deciding the outcome.

...

People sometimes say, 'A critique of rights? But if you got rid of rights, then the state could do anything it wanted to you! What about the right of privacy? We wouldn't have any way to object to state intrusion!' They are just missing the point!

In the Western democracies, rights 'exist' in the sense that there are legal rules limiting what people can do to one another and limiting the executive and the legislature. The critique of rights recognizes the reality of rule-making, rule-following, and rule-enforcing behavior. It is about faith in the rational procedures through which legislators, adjudicators, or enforcers elaborate gaps, conflicts, and ambiguities in the 'text' of inside or outside rights.

There is nothing in the critique that might suggest a reduction in the rights of citizens vis-à-vis their governments. Having lost one's faith in rights discourse is perfectly consistent with, indeed often associated with, a passionate belief in radical expansion of citizen rights against the state. Moreover, loss of faith is consistent with advocacy of greatly increased tenant rights in dealings with landlords, as well as with the reverse, just as it is consistent with favoring more or less government control over abortion decisions. It is not about the question of how we ought to define rights but rather about how we should *feel about the discourse in which we claim them.*

…

CASS R. SUNSTEIN, RIGHTS AND THEIR CRITICS

70 Notre Dame L. Rev. 727 (1995), at 730

[This article, though written with respect to ongoing debate about rights in the United States, bears also on the international discourse of rights. The author develops six different categories of charges against rights drawn from judicial opinions and from critics. Excerpts follow.]

B. The Rigidity of Rights

Other critics charge that rights have a strident and absolutist character, and that for this reason they impoverish political discourse. Rights do not admit of compromise. They do not allow room for competing considerations. For this reason, they impair and even foreclose deliberation over complex issues not realistically soluble by simple formulas.

Rooted in nineteenth-century ideas of absolute sovereignty over property, rights are said to be ill-adapted to what we usually need, that is, a careful discussion of trade-offs and competing concerns. If rights are (in Ronald Dworkin's suggestive and influential phrase, criticized below) 'trumps', they are for that very reason harmful to the difficult process of accommodating different goals and considerations in resolving such thorny problems as abortion, the environment, and plant closings.

C. Indeterminacy

In one of his greatest aphorisms, Justice Holmes wrote that '[g]eneral propositions do not decide concrete cases'. Rights, of course, take the form of general propositions. For this reason they are said to be indeterminate and thus unhelpful.

If we know that there is a right to private property, we do not know whether an occupational safety and health law or a law requiring beach access is permissible. In fact, we know relatively little. Standing by itself, the constitutional protection against government 'takings' tells us very little about how to handle particular problems. This is true of rights generally. To say that there is a right to equal protection of the law is not to say, for example, that affirmative action programs are acceptable, mandatory, or prohibited. In fact, the right to equal protection of the law requires a great deal of supplemental work to decide cases. The right must be specified in order to have concrete meaning. The specification will depend on premises not contained within the announcement of the right itself. Rights purport to solve problems, but when stated abstractly — it is claimed — they are at most the beginning of a discussion.

Perhaps the area of free speech is the most vivid illustration. Everyone agrees that such a right exists; but without supplemental work, we cannot know how to handle the hard questions raised by commercial speech, libel, obscenity, or campaign finance restrictions. A serious problem with modern free speech discussions is that the term 'free speech' tends to be used as if it handled the hard questions by itself.

D. Excessive Individualism

A different objection is that rights are unduly individualistic and associated with highly undesirable characteristics, including selfishness and indifference to others. Rights miss the 'dimension of sociality'; they posit selfish, isolated individuals who assert what is theirs, rather than participating in communal life. Rights, it is said, neglect the moral and social dimensions of important problems.

The important and contested right of privacy, for example, is said to have emerged as an unduly individual right, rooted in the 'property paradigm' and loosened from connections to others. Critics urge that this conception of the issues involved in the so-called privacy cases misses crucial aspects of the relevant problems — abortion, family living arrangements, and the asserted right to die. Such issues do not involve simple privacy; they call up a range of issues about networks of relationships, between individuals and the state, between individuals and families, between individuals and localities. ...

...

F. Rights Versus Responsibilities

A final and especially prominent objection is that the emphasis on rights tends to crowd out the issue of responsibility. In American law and in American public discourse, some critics complain, it is too rare to find the idea that people owe duties to each other, or that civic virtue is to be cultivated, prized, and lived. Rights, and especially new protections of rights since the 1960s, are said to be a major problem here.

In a simple formulation: People who insist on their rights too infrequently explore what it is right to do. Or they become dependent on the official institutions charged with safeguarding rights, rather than doing things for themselves. The controversy over whether rights turn women or blacks into a 'dependent class' is in part about this issue. People who insist that their status as victims entitles them to enforce their legal rights may not conceive of themselves in ways that engender equality and equal citizenship.

...

[The author then turns to clarification of some conceptual issues raised by the criticism, and concludes that the critique, while embodying some limited and important truths, 'does not by any means support a general challenge to rights'. He starts by noting the position advanced by many rights advocates — Ronald Dworkin comes immediately to mind — that rights refer to important human interests 'that operate as "trumps", in the sense that they cannot be compromised by reference to collective policies or goals.' He doubts that this conception is helpful.]

... The first problem is that almost every right is defeasible at some point, and defeasible just because the collective interest is very strong. In American law, no right is absolute. If, for example, the rest of the human race will be eliminated because of the protection of a right, the right will certainly be redefined or legitimately infringed, probably under some version of the 'compelling interest' test. The real question then becomes when rights are defeasible because of collective justifications — under what conditions and for what reasons. The formula of 'trumps' is misleading for this reason. We need to know what sorts of reasons are admissible and how weighty they must be; these are the key questions in the exploration of rights.

Rights characteristically limit the kinds of arguments that can be used by way of justification, and they characteristically require justification of special weight. Above all, rights exclude certain otherwise admissible reasons for action. But ideas of this kind do not support the 'trumps' metaphor and indeed lead in quite different directions.

The second problem is that many conceptual puzzles are raised by the understanding of right as interests operating 'against' the collectivity. Often rights are something that the collectivity recognizes and protects in order to protect its interests. If this is so, there is no easy opposition between rights and the collectivity.... Rights are collectively conferred and designed to promote collective interests. They are protected by social institutions for social reasons....

[Sunstein turns his attention to what he describes as 'truths and partial truths' in the 'highly eclectic' views of the critics of rights. He observes:]

It is also important to point out that references to rights can make for unduly rigid understandings of complex problems and can sometimes stop discussion in its tracks before analysis has even started. Claims of right often have the vices of rules. Even worse, rights can be conclusions masquerading as reasons. In thinking about claims of right, it is often necessary to be detailed and concrete about the social consequences of competing courses of action. The invocation of 'rights' can be a serious obstacle to this process. Consider, for example, the current debates over regulation of the electronic media, violent pornography, hate speech at universities, or advertising for cigarettes. To say that any restriction on these forms of expression violates the 'right to free speech' may in the end be correct; but this requires a long and complex argument, not a shorthand phrase. The claim of a 'right to free speech' is far too general and abstract to support the argument. Here it does seem important and true to say that rights, stated abstractedly, do not solve concrete cases. They are indeterminate until they are specified.

As they operate in law, rights generally *are* specified. Hence the rights protected by the Constitution and the common law are far from indeterminate, however hard it is to know what they are when stated abstractly. The claim of indeterminacy is for this reason far too broad. The problem, to which the critics have correctly drawn attention, lies in the use of general claims of right to resolve cases in which the specification has not yet occurred.

It is also true that efforts to think about many social and economic problems in terms or rights can obscure those problems. A claimed right to clean air and water or to safe products and workplaces makes little sense in light of the need for close assessment, in particular cases, of the advantages of greater environmental protection or more safety, as compared with the possible accompanying disadvantages — higher prices, lower wages, less employment, and more poverty. Perhaps the legal system will create rights of a kind after it has undertaken this assessment. But to the extent that the regulatory programs of the 1970s were billed as simple vindications of 'rights', they severely impaired political deliberation about their content and about the necessity for trade-offs.

…

D. Confusions and Misconceptions

Despite the various partial truths in the attack on rights, there is a pervasive problem in that attack: Rights need not have the functions or consequences that they are alleged to have. The challenge to rights is properly directed against certain kinds of rights, not against rights in general. At most, the challenge to rights creates a contingent, partial warning about the appropriate content of rights and about the possibly harmful role of certain social institutions safeguarding rights….

…

… Often critics write as if rights and responsibilities are opposed, or as if those who favor the former are completely different from these who favor the latter. As they see it, rights are individual, atomistic, selfish, crude, licentious, antisocial, and associated with the Warren Court. Responsibilities, on the other hand, are seen as collective, social, altruistic, nuanced, and associated with appropriate or traditional values. But this understanding is quite inadequate, for some rights lack the characteristics claimed for them, and other rights have the features associated with responsibilities.

For example, the right to freedom of speech may be owned by individuals, but it is a precondition for a highly social process, that of democratic deliberation. That right keeps open the channels of communication; it is emphatically communal in character. It ensures a sine qua non of sociality, an opportunity for people to speak with one other. Indeed, everyone who owns a speech right does so partly so as to contribute to the collectivity; it is this fact that explains the government's inability to 'buy' speech rights even when a speaker would like to sell. So too, the right to associational freedom is hardly individualistic. It is meant precisely to protect collective action and sociality.

…

… Moreover, a principal characteristic of totalitarian states is the endless cataloguing of responsibilities owed by citizens to the state. The Soviet Constitution was an ignoble example. For example, that Constitution created a duty 'to make thrifty use of the people's wealth', 'to preserve and protect socialist property', to 'work conscientiously', and 'to concern themselves with the upbringing of children'. The Soviet Constitution offers a cautionary note against enthusiasm for responsibilities…

…

KARL KLARE, LEGAL THEORY AND DEMOCRATIC RECONSTRUCTION

25 U. of Brit. Colum. L. Rev. 69 (1991), at 97

[The author discusses the appropriate place of 'rights' in the formal legal structures and guarantees and in the legal-political discourse of the post-Communist states of Central-Eastern Europe. He concludes that 'it seems obvious that post-communist law should be founded upon an explicit charter of human rights guarantees. How could there be any doubt of the central place of rights in democratic legal reconstruction?' Nonetheless, Klare notes, recent debates among Western legal scholars have developed a serious 'critique of rights', and he undertakes to summarize 'some of the major lines of criticism advanced by the rights skeptics'. The following excerpts deal with two aspects of this critique and Klare's responses thereto.]

A second branch of rights skepticism concerns the efficacy and limitations of the rights tradition in relationship to social change. [T]he skeptics call attention to certain self-imposed limitations internal to rights discourse stemming from its embrace of the public/private distinction. Rights thinking has predominantly concerned the relationship between the individual and the state. As traditionally understood, the human rights project is to erect barriers between the individual and the state, so as to protect human autonomy and self-determination from being violated or crushed by governmental power.

Unquestionably, a just society requires such protections, but human freedom can also be invaded or denied by nongovernmental forms of power, by domination in the so-called 'private sphere'. Human dignity is denied by *de jure* racial segregation, but it is also denied by employers who discriminate on the basis of race.... Rights charters almost invariably concern restrictions on state power and therefore leave intact many forms of 'private' domination, including hierarchies of class, race, gender and sexual preference....

Given the injustices committed by the Stalinist regimes, it is understandable that the first priority of postcommunist lawyers is to guard against the abuse of state power.... Granting this, the argument goes, to realize freedom in all aspects of life, to establish arrangements in all social contexts that will be committed to human dignity, self-realization and equality, requires a deep transformation, in both East and West, not only of governmental but also of non-state institutions and practices that are left untouched by conventional human rights doctrine. A strong version of rights skepticism suggests that the fixation on the individual/state relationship in the rights tradition actually diverts intellectual and political resources from other, needed approaches to social justice....

This brings us to a third aspect of contemporary rights skepticism, the so-called 'indeterminacy critique'....

... Because human rights concepts tend to be very elastic and open-ended, they are capable of being given a wide range of meanings, including inconsistent meanings. Take freedom of speech, for example. One meaning is the right to dissent and to criticize the powers that be. Yet the right to free speech can also be given quite a different meaning, as, e.g., in the American cases barring government from trying to prevent the distortion of the electoral process by corporate campaign contributions. In the former interpretation, free speech permits individuals to unfreeze hierarchy and open up political debate, whereas in the latter case, the right to free speech is mobilized to reinforce domination by entrenched power....

Thus, rights concepts are sufficiently elastic so that they can mean different things to different people. People who seek to reinforce hierarchy and perpetuate domination can speak the language of rights, often with sincerity. But there is an even deeper problem. Even those who would consistently invoke rights in the service of self-determination, autonomy and equality find that rights concepts are internally contradictory. That is because, like all of legal discourse, rights theory is an arena of conflicting conceptions of justice and human freedom.... Proponents of democracy have advanced conceptions of rights to freedom of association and also conceptions of rights of excluded minorities to insist on membership in important groups....

...

The problem is that rights discourse itself does not provide neutral decision procedures with which to make such choices.

...

... My point here is that, by itself, rights discourse does not and probably cannot provide us with the criteria for deciding between conflicting claims of right. In order to resolve rights conflicts, it is necessary to step outside the discourse. One must appeal to more concrete and therefore more controversial analyses of the relevant social and institutional contexts than rights discourse offers; and one must develop and elaborate conceptions of and intuitions about human freedom and self-determination by reference to which one seeks to assess rights claims and resolve rights conflicts.

If the processes of concretizing rights concepts and of resolving rights conflicts extend beyond the traditional discourse of rights onto the terrain of social theory and political philosophy, it follows that rights rhetoric must be politicized in order to serve as a foundation for legal reconstruction.... Surely it is insufficient to think of human rights practice in terms of obtaining the correct list of rights and then enacting them into a code. Rather, postcommunist lawyers must think of rights discourse and rights charters as relatively open media in which to advance visions of socially desirable institutions and practices. That is, the rights foundation of legal reconstruction is an invitation to make political philosophy, not only in promulgating the initial charters, but at every step along the way of articulating and interpreting rights concepts and filling them with concrete legal and institutional meaning. But this revised, 'politicized' conception of human rights discourse and practice in postcommunist legal reconstruction sits uneasily with the idea of an autonomous rule of law that is ostensibly the basis of the whole enterprise.

...

NOTE

A number of different understandings about rights — their derivation, nature, content and consequences — appear in the readings in Chapters 3–5 and the immediately preceding readings. Consider the following lists: (1) setting forth in the left column assertions or understandings about rights that derive from natural rights or related deep premises about the nature of human beings or divine law, and typify much (surely not all) rights discourse within liberal societies, in opposition to a list (2) setting forth in the right column very different understandings that, for example, (a) inform arguments in favour of cultural relativism that Chapter 7(A) discusses, and (b) inform utilitarian or policy-oriented argument as opposed to argument derived from natural rights or related deep premises about the nature of human beings or divine law.

inalienable	as opposed to	socially constructed, given and taken
absolute		qualified, contingent, content dependent on context
universal		particular, culturally specific
eternal, ahistorical		historicist, evolving, open to change
based on equal human dignity		based on utility, power

Note that — as Duncan Kennedy and Cass Sunstein's articles make clear — the same 'content' of a right may be argued toward and justified starting with the assumptions in lists in the left or right columns. Indeed, the same result may be reached whether argument to justify a given rule or its interpretation is rights-based at all or rather uses the different language and methodology associated with utilitarian-consequentialist-cost/benefit thought. Often both modes of justification may be at issue, and may be seen as complementary and mutually supportive. For example: (1) free speech may be justified as a right inhering in human personality, a mode of self-realization, a recognition of equal human dignity. Or it may be justified as contributing to the 'marketplace of ideas', offering many competitive ideas from which rational conclusions and the 'best' regulation of speech may be more readily devised. (2) A rule excluding from court proceedings any evidence that the police illegally seize may be understood as resting on notions of right and fairness and basic relations between individual and state, or as a method of disciplining the police not to act illegally for their evidence cannot be used in trial. (3) Torture may be viewed as a violation of human dignity and personality, a violation of a basic and eternal human right, or it may be viewed as illegal because it is often an unreliable path towards procuring accurate and reliable evidence. Recall the arguments of Bentham and other authors in Chapter 3(D).

DAVID KENNEDY, THE DARK SIDE OF VIRTUE

(2004), at 3

Chapter One: The International Human Rights Movement: Part of the Problem?

... Among well-meaning legal professionals in the United States and Europe — humanitarian, internationalist, liberal, compassionate in all the best senses of these terms — the human rights movement has become a central object of devotion.

But are there also dark sides? This chapter develops a short list of hypotheses about the possible risks, costs, and unanticipated consequences of human rights activism.... [I]n the end, one cannot think pragmatically about human rights work without some such list of possible costs in mind.

...

A checklist of possible downsides is not a general critique of human rights. Benefits and harms must be analyzed in particular cases, under specific conditions, at particular times. The cases and conditions may be extremely specific (pursuing this petition will make this magistrate less likely to grant this other petition) or quite general (articulating social welfare needs as individual "rights" makes people everywhere more passive and isolated)....

... Ultimately, we must also compare whatever assessment we make of the human rights vocabulary against the costs and benefits of *other* emancipatory vocabularies which might be used to the same ends.

In the end, of course, different observers will weigh the costs and benefits of human rights activism in different ways....

...

... [F]or me, nothing goes in the "costs" column until the human rights movement has a bad *effect.* A bad effect means influencing someone to act (or fail to act) or to think in a way which counts as a cost (again, ethically, politically, philosophically, aesthetically) for the person making the argument....

...

Here is my short list of pragmatic worries.

Human Rights Occupies the Field of Emancipatory Possibility

[The author here discusses the 'hegemony' of human rights as resource allocation, criticism and distortion.]

The claim here is that this institutional and political hegemony makes other valuable, often more valuable, emancipatory strategies less available. This argument is stronger, of course, when one can say something about what those alternatives are — or might be. But there may be something to the claim that human rights has so dominated the imaginative space of emancipation that alternatives can now be thought only, perhaps unhelpfully, as negations of what human rights asserts — passion to its reason, local to its global.... This is easiest to see when human rights attracts institutional energy and resources which would otherwise flow elsewhere. But this is not only a matter of scarce resources.

Human rights also occupies the field by implicit or explicit delegitimation of other emancipatory strategies.... Where this is so, pursuing a human rights initiative or promoting the use of human rights vocabulary may have fully unintended negative consequences for other existing emancipatory projects, including those relying on more religious, national, or local energies....

To the extent emancipatory projects must be expressed in the vocabulary of "rights" to be heard, good policies which are not framed that way go unattended. This also distorts the way projects are imagined and framed for international consideration. For example, it is often asserted that the international human rights movement makes an end run around local institutions and strategies which would often be better — ethically, politically, philosophically, aesthetically.... A "universal" idea of what counts as a problem and what works as a solution snuffs out all sorts of promising local political and social initiatives to contest local conditions in other terms. But there are other lost vocabularies which are equally global — vocabularies of duty, of responsibility, of collective commitment. Encouraging people concerned about environmental harm to rethink their concerns as a human rights violation will have bad consequences if it would have turned out to be more animating, for example, to say there is a duty to work for the environment, rather than a right to a clean environment.

The "right to development" is a classic — and well-known — example. Once concerns about global poverty are raised in these terms, energy and resources are drawn to developing a literature and an institutional practice of a particular sort at the international level. Efforts which cannot be articulated in these terms seem less legitimate, less practical, less worth the effort. Increasingly, people of goodwill concerned about poverty are drawn into debate about a series of ultimately impossible legal quandaries — rights of whom, against whom, remediable how — and into institutional projects of codification and reporting familiar from other human rights efforts, without evaluating how these might compare with other deployments of talent and resources. . . .

. . .

Human Rights Views the Problem and the Solution too Narrowly

People have made many different claims about the narrowness of human rights. Here are some: the human rights movement foregrounds harms done explicitly by *governments* to individuals or groups — leaving potentially more severe harms brought about by private groups or indirect governmental action largely unaddressed and more legitimate by contrast. Even when addressing private harms, human rights focuses attention on *public* remedies — explicit rights formalized and implemented by the state. One criticizes the *state* and seeks *public* law remedies, but leaves unattended or enhanced the powers and felt entitlements of private actors. . . .

When combined, these ideas about human rights often define problems and solutions in ways unlikely to change the economy. Human rights foregrounds problems of *participation* and *procedure*, at the expense of distribution. As a result, existing distributions of wealth, status, and power can seem more legitimate after rights have been legislated, formal participation in government achieved, and institutional remedies for violations provided. However useful saying "that's my right" is in extracting things from the state, it is not good for extracting things from the economy, unless you are a property holder. Indeed, a practice of rights claims against the state may actively weaken the capacity of people to challenge economic arrangements.

. . . [T]he imbalance between civil/political and social/economic rights is neither an accident of politics nor a matter which could be remedied by more intensive commitment. It runs deep in the philosophy of human rights, and seems central to the conditions of political possibility that make human rights an emancipatory strategy in the first place, and to the institutional character of the movement.

The strong attachment of the human rights movement to the legal formalization of rights and the establishment of legal machinery for their implementation makes the achievement of these forms an end in itself. . . . These are the traditional problems of form: form can hamper peaceful adjustment and necessary change, can be overinclusive or underinclusive. Is the right to vote a floor — or can it become a ceiling?

The emphasis on human rights can leave unattended the wide array of laws that do not explicitly condone violations, but that certainly affect their frequency and may in fact be doing more harm than the absence of rights. These background laws, left with clean hands, can seem more legitimate....

Even very broad social movements of emancipation — for women, for minorities, for the poor — have their vision bunkered by the promise of recognition in the vocabulary and institutional apparatus of human rights. They will be led away from the economy and toward the state, away from political and social conditions and toward forms of legal recognition....

...

Human Rights is Limited by its Relationship to Western Liberalism

...

Human rights encourages people to seek emancipation in the vocabularies of reason rather than faith, in public rather than private life, in law rather than politics, in politics rather than economics. The human rights vocabulary helps draw the lines between these spheres. In each case, it underestimates what it takes as the natural base and overestimates our ability to instrumentalize what it takes as the artificial domain of emancipation. Moreover, human rights is too quick to conclude that emancipation *means* progress forward from the natural passions of politics into the civilized reason of law. The urgent need to develop a more vigorous human politics is sidelined by the effort to throw thin but plausible nets of legal articulation across the globe. Work to develop law comes to be seen as an emancipatory end in itself, leaving the human rights movement too ready to articulate problems in political terms and solutions in legal terms.

The posture of human rights as an emancipatory political project which extends and operates within a domain above or outside politics — a political project repackaged as a form of knowledge — delegitimates other political voices and makes less visible the local, cultural, and political dimensions of the human rights movement itself....

...

[T]he human rights movement contributes to the framing of political choices in the third world as oppositions between "local/traditional" and "international/modern" forms of government and modes of life. This effect is strengthened by the presentation of human rights as part of belonging to the modern world, but coming from some place outside political choice, from the universal, the rational, the civilized. By strengthening the articulation of third world politics as a choice between tradition and modernity, the human rights movement impoverishes local political discourse, often strengthening the hand of self-styled "traditionalists" who are offered a commonsense and powerful alternative to modernization for whatever politics they may espouse.

...

Human Rights Promotion Can Be Bad Politics in Particular Contexts

It may be that this is all one can say — promoting human rights can sometimes have bad consequences. All of the first nine types of criticism suggested that human rights suffered from one or another design defect—as if these defects would emerge, these costs would be incurred, regardless of context. Perhaps this is so. But so long as none of these criticisms has been proven in such a general way (and it is hard to see just how they could be), it may be that all we have is a list of possible downsides, open risks, bad results which have sometimes occurred, which might well occur. In some context, for example, it might turn out that pursuing emancipation as entitlement could reduce the capacity and propensity for collective action. Something like this seems to have happened in the United States in the last twenty years—the transformation of political questions into legal questions, and then into questions of legal "rights," has made other forms of collective emancipatory politics less available. But it is hard to see that this is always and everywhere the destiny of human rights initiatives....

...

QUESTIONS

1. How damaging to a rights-oriented international movement are the criticisms about rights discourse and argument that are developed (and in some cases, responded to) in the preceding articles? To which of them are the UDHR, treaties and other materials examined in Chapters 3–5 most vulnerable?

2. Duncan Kennedy and Klare both stress that, at a given point, rights-based assertions give out, and a claimant or judge or other decision-maker must resort to (Kennedy) 'open-textured arguments from morality, social welfare, expectations, and institutional competence and administrability'. Klare stresses that 'choices must be made in elaborating any structure of human rights guarantees...and the choices bear socially and politically significant consequences. The problem is that rights discourse itself does not provide neutral decision procedures with which to make such choices.... In order to resolve rights conflicts, it is necessary to step outside the discourse.'

Apply these observations to a conception as basic as the 'right to life'. What 'choices' about the meaning of this conception are before treaty-makers, legislatures, courts or advocates elaborating this right, and through what methods or processes can those choices be resolved? What different issues are posed by, say, a 'right to health care'?

3. Duncan Kennedy, Klare and Sunstein all stress the significance of the indeterminacy of rights-based argument, including the problem of conflicting rights. Kennedy notes that these features of 'open texture or indeterminacy' are open to the same analysis 'as legal argument in general'. That is, they are not particular to rights. Give some examples, other than those stated in the preceding writings, of pressing and difficult issues raised by the ICCPR, CEDAW or the ICESCR that stem from the indeterminacy of the texts or contradictions among rights? How would you go about resolving a concrete issue about the content and reach of a right that involves indeterminacy or contradiction (say, the right to speech or privacy)? Bear in mind that for many international human rights issues and in many states, it will be impractical or impossible to invoke the jurisdiction of a court that could issue a 'binding' precedent.

4. Do you understand David Kennedy's 'dark side' of human rights to advance significantly different criticism of rights, rights rhetoric and rights-based advocacy and strategy than do the three articles preceding it? In what respects? To the extent that these three earlier (in time) articles address in different ways some of Kennedy's concerns, how do you assess their arguments?

5. With respect to David Kennedy's arguments, consider: (a) What illustrations could you offer of situations where reliance on rights rhetoric to advance popular claims crowded out other 'emancipatory vocabularies' and strategies—for example, mass political action—that could possibly or even likely have achieved more? Consider, for example, earlier materials examining the struggles for 'women's rights', the arguments against torture, and arguments in favour of economic/social rights like health care or housing. Is mass political action — electoral campaigns, marches by protestors to a capital city, boycotts — necessarily independent of rights rhetoric embedded in such action? (b) Suppose that a human rights advocate argued to a minister of education in a developing country that giving schoolgirls equal educational opportunities would improve talent, energy, productivity and the level of economic well-being within the family and the country — that is, benefits will far exceed costs. Is the 'hegemony' of rights rhetoric apt to block such argument? Could both modes of argument be used together? What of using simultaneously several different modes of argument — utilitarian, fairness-based, rights-based — with respect to environmental degradation? (c) Do this book's earlier materials support the author's argument that human rights directs so much attention to the public sector (that is, the state as the only identified violator of human rights in the conventions and in human rights discourse) that many violations occurring in the non-state sector (employment discrimination, family violence) are apt to remain hidden and untouched? (d) The author several times characterizes human rights as claims and arguments based on reason, whereas other emancipatory languages and strategies rely on faith and passion. Do you agree with this distinction, which tends to characterize 'rights' as cerebral and abstract, while other languages/strategies are more basic, emotional, appealing, stimulating to people?

B. DUTY-BASED SOCIAL ORDERS

COMMENT ON DUTIES

The following readings describe and analyse duty-oriented rather than rights-oriented social ordering through law and cultural tradition. Robert Cover comments on the legal culture of Judaism with its stress on obligations imposed by God rather than on rights. He suggests historical reasons why Western states and Judaism developed in these different ways. Jomo Kenyatta describes aspects of the education of the young in the Gikuyu people in Kenya, particularly the inculcation of elements of social obligations and duty. Although the cultural and religious contexts and the content of the duties referred to are radically different in these readings, they both suggest important consequences of an orientation towards duty/obligation and the gap between such an orientation and the liberal political culture that influenced the human rights regime.

Note that the duties/obligations referred to in these readings are *not* the same as duties within a *scheme of rights* that are correlative to the described rights. For example, the individual's basic right to be free from torture imposes a correlative (corresponding) duty on the state not to torture. The following readings talk of duties imposed on *individuals* rather than on the state or some other collective entity. That is, they are not correlative duties to others' rights, but initially imposed on the individual. Article 29(1) of the UDHR offers an analogy to such use of duties, as does the preamble to the ICCPR. But explicit language of individual duty to other individuals (other than the implied, traditional correlative duties), to society, or to the state in the universal human rights system is rare. A closer analogy to the present readings, particularly the excerpts from Kenyatta, is provided by the African Charter on Human and Peoples' Rights, examined at p. 517, *infra*.

ROBERT COVER, OBLIGATION: A JEWISH JURISPRUDENCE OF THE SOCIAL ORDER

5 J. of L. and Relig. 65 (1987)

I. Fundamental Words

Every legal culture has its fundamental words. When we define our subject this weekend as human rights, we also locate ourselves in a normative universe at a particular place. The word 'rights' is a highly evocative one for those of us who have grown up in the post-enlightenment secular society of the West....

Judaism is, itself, a legal culture of great antiquity. It has hardly led a wholly autonomous existence these past three millennia. Yet, I suppose it can lay as much claim as any of the other great legal cultures to have an integrity to its basic categories. When I am asked to reflect upon Judaism and human rights, therefore, the first thought that comes to mind is that the categories are wrong. I do not mean, of course, that basic ideas of human dignity and worth are not powerfully expressed in the Jewish legal and literary traditions. Rather, I mean that because it is a legal tradition Judaism has its own categories for expressing through law the worth and dignity of each human being. And the categories are not closely analogous to 'human rights'. The principal word in Jewish law, which occupies a place equivalent in evocative force to the American legal system's 'rights', is the word 'mitzvah' which literally means commandment but has a general meaning closer to 'incumbent obligation'.

Before I begin an analysis of the differing implications of these two rather different key words, I should like to put the two words in a context — the contexts of their respective myths. For both of us these words are connected to fundamental stories and receive their force from those stories as much as from the denotative meaning of the words themselves. The story behind the term 'rights' is the story of social contract. The myth postulates free and independent if highly vulnerable beings who voluntarily trade a portion of their autonomy for a measure of collective security. The myth makes the collective arrangement the product of individual choice and thus secondary to the individual. 'Rights' are the fundamental category because it is the normative category which most nearly approximates that which is the source of the legitimacy of everything else. Rights are traded for collective security. But some rights are retained and, in some theories, some rights are inalienable. In any event the first and fundamental unit is the individual and 'rights' locate him as an individual separate and apart from every other individual.

I must stress that I do not mean to suggest that all or even most theories that are founded upon rights are 'individualistic' or 'atomistic'. Nor would I suggest for a moment that with a starting point of 'rights' and social contract one must get to a certain end. Hobbes as well as Locke is part of this tradition. And, of course, so is Rousseau. Collective solutions as well as individualistic ones are possible but, it is the case that even the collective solutions are solutions which arrive at their destination by way of a theory which derives the authority of the collective from the individual....

The basic word of Judaism is obligation or mitzvah. It, too, is intrinsically bound up in a myth — the myth of Sinai. Just as the myth of social contract is essentially a myth of autonomy, so the myth of Sinai is essentially a myth of heteronomy. Sinai is a collective — indeed, a corporate — experience. The experience at Sinai is not chosen. The event gives forth the words which are commandments. In all Rabbinic and post Rabbinic embellishment upon the Biblical account of Sinai this event is the Code for all Law. All law was given at Sinai and therefore all law is related back to the ultimate heteronomous event in which we were chosen-passive voice.

...

What have these stories to do with the ways in which the law languages of these respective legal cultures are spoken? Social movements in the United States organize around rights. When there is some urgently felt need to change the law or keep it in one way or another a 'Rights' movement is started. Civil rights, the right to life, welfare rights, etc. The premium that is to be put upon an entitlement is so coded. When we 'take rights seriously' we understand them to be trumps in the legal game. In Jewish law, an entitlement without an obligation is a sad, almost pathetic thing.

...

Indeed, to be one who acts out of obligation is the closest thing there is to a Jewish definition of completion as a person within the community. A child does not become emancipated or 'free' when he or she reaches maturity. Nor does she/he become *sui juris*. No, the child becomes bar or bat mitzvah, literally one who is of the obligations. Traditionally, the parent at that time says a blessing. Blessed is He that has exonerated me from the punishment of this child. The primary legal distinction between Jew and non-Jew is that the non-Jew is only obligated to the 7 Noachide commandments....

The Uses of Rights and Obligations

The Jewish legal system has evolved for the past 1900 years without a state and largely without much in the way of coercive powers to be exercised upon the adherents of the faith. I do not mean to idealize the situation. The Jewish communities over the millennia have wielded power. Communal sanctions of banning and shunning have been regularly and occasionally cruelly imposed on individuals or groups. Less frequently, but frequently enough, Jewish communities granted quasi-autonomy by gentile rulers, have used the power of the gentile state to discipline dissidents and deviants. Nonetheless, there remains a difference between wielding a power which draws on but also depends on pre-existing social solidarity, and, wielding one which depends on violence....

In a situation in which there is no centralized power and little in the way of coercive violence, it is critical that the mythic center of the Law reinforce the bonds of solidarity. Common, mutual, reciprocal obligation is necessary. The myth of divine commandment creates that web.... It was a myth that created legitimacy for a radically diffuse and coordinate system of authority. But while it created room for the diffusion of authority it did not have a place for individualism. One might have independent and divergent understandings of the obligations imposed by God through his chosen people, but one could not have a world view which denied the obligations.

The jurisprudence of rights, on the other hand, has gained ascendance in the Western world together with the rise of the national state with its almost unique mastery of violence over extensive territories. Certainly, it may be argued, it has been essential to counterbalance the development of the state with a myth which a) establishes the State as legitimate only in so far as it can be derived from the autonomous creatures who trade in their rights for security — i.e., one must tell a story about the State's utility or service to us, and b) potentially justifies individual and communal resistance to the Behemoth. It may be true as Bentham so aptly pointed out that natural rights may be used either apologetically or in revolutionary fashion, and there is nothing in the concept powerful enough analytically to constrain which use it shall be put to. Nevertheless, it is the case that natural right apologies are of a sort that in their articulation they limit the most far-reaching claims of the State, and the revolutionary ideology that can be generated is also of a sort which is particularly effective in countering organic statist claims.

Thus, there is a sense in which the ideology of rights has been a useful counter to the centrifugal forces of the western nation state while the ideology of mitzvoth or obligation has been equally useful as a counter to the centripetal forces that have beset Judaism over the centuries.

...

... [T]he Maimonides system contrasts the normative world of mitzvoth with the world of vanity — hebel. It seems that Maimonides, in this respect, as in so many others has hit the mark. A world centered upon obligation is not, really cannot be, an empty or vain world. Rights, as an organizing principle, are indifferent to the vanity of varying ends. But mitzvoths because they so strongly bind and locate the individual must make a strong claim for the substantive content of that which they dictate. The system, if its content be vain, can hardly claim to be a system. The rights system is indifferent to ends and in its indifference can claim systemic coherence without making any strong claims about the fullness or vanity of the ends it permits.

...

JOMO KENYATTA, FACING MOUNT KENYA: THE TRIBAL LIFE OF THE GIKUYU (1965), at 109

[These excerpts are taken from a description by Kenyatta, who later became the first post-colonial president of Kenya, of the Gikuyu people (often rendered in English as 'Kikuyu') in that country. The excerpts stress elements of duty inculcated in Gikuyu children, and appear in Chapter 5, 'System of Education.']

[The children] are also taught definitely at circumcision the theory, as it were, of respect to their parents and kinsfolk. Under all circumstances they must stay with them and share in their joys and sorrows. It will never do to leave them and go off to see the world whenever they take the notion, especially when their parents are in their old age. They must give them clothes, look after their garden, herd their cattle, sheep and goats, build their grain stores and houses. It thus becomes a part of their outlook on life that their parents shall not suffer want nor continue to labour strenuously in their old age while their children can lend a hand and do things to give them comfort.

This respect and duty to parents is further emphasised by the fact that the youth or girl cannot advance from one stage to another without the parent's will and active assistance. The satisfaction of all a boy's longings and ambitions depends on the father's and family's consent. . . .

. . .

The teaching of social obligations is again emphasised by the classification of age-groups to which we have already referred. This binds together those of the same status in ties of closest loyalty and devotion. Men circumcised at the same time stand in the very closest relationship to each other. When a man of the same age-group injures another it is a serious magico-religious offence. They are like blood brothers; they must not do any wrong to each other. It ranks with an injury done to a member of one's own family. The age-group (*riika*) is thus a powerful instrument for securing conformity with tribal usage. The selfish or reckless youth is taught by the opinion of his gang that it does not pay to incur displeasure. He will not be called to eat with the others when food is going. He may be put out of their dances, fined, or even ostracised for a time. If he does not change his ways he will find his old companions have deserted him.

. . . The age-groups do more than bind men of equal standing together. They further emphasise the social grades of junior and senior, inferior and superior. We see the same principle in evidence all through the various grades. . . .

Owing to the strength and numbers of the social ties existing between members of the same family, clan and age-group, and between different families and clans through which the tribe is unified and solidified as one organic whole, the community can be mobilised very easily for corporate activity. House-building, cultivation, harvesting, digging trap-pits, putting up fences around cultivated fields, and building bridges, are usually done by the group; hence the Gikuyu saying: '*Kamoinge koyaga ndere*', which means collective activities make heavy tasks easier. In the old days sacrifices were offered and wars were waged by the tribe as a whole or by the clan. Marriage contracts and ceremonies are the affairs of families and not of individuals. Sometimes even cattle are bought by joint effort. Thus the individual boy or girl soon learns to work with and for other people. An old man who has no children of his own is helped by his neighbour's children in almost everything. His hut is built, his garden dug, firewood is cut and water is fetched for him. If his cattle, sheep or goats are lost or in difficulties the children of his neighbour will help to bring them back, at great pains and often at considerable risk. The old man reciprocates by treating the children as though they were his own. Children learn this habit of communal work like others, not by verbal exhortations so much as by joining with older people in such social services.... All help given in this way is voluntary, and kinsfolk are proud to help one another. There is no payment or expectation of payment. They are well feasted, of course. This is not regarded as payment, but as hospitality. The whole thing rests on the principle of reciprocal obligations. It is taken for granted that the neighbour whom you assist in difficulty or whose house you help to build will do the same for you when in similar need. Those who do not reciprocate these sentiments of neighbourliness are not in favour....

...

The selfish or self-regarding man has no name or reputation in the Gikuyu community. An individualist is looked upon with suspicion and is given a nickname of *mwebongia*, one who works only for himself and is likely to end up as a wizard. He may lack assistance when he needs it....

In the Gikuyu community there is no really individual affair, for every thing has a moral and social reference. The habit of corporate effort is but the other side of corporate ownership; and corporate responsibility is illustrated in corporate work no less than in corporate sacrifice and prayer.

In spite of the foreign elements which work against many of the Gikuyu institutions and the desire to implant the system of wholesale Westernisation, this system of mutual help and the tribal solidarity in social services, political and economic activities are still maintained by the large majority of the Gikuyu people. It is less practised among those Gikuyu who have been Europeanised or detribalised. The rest of the community look upon these people as mischief-makers and breakers of the tribal traditions, and the general disgusted cry is heard: '*Mothongo ne athogonjire-borori*', i.e. the white man had spoiled and disgraced our country.

...

The striking thing in the Gikuyu system of education, and the feature which most sharply distinguishes it from the European system of education, is the primary place given to personal relations. Each official statement of educational policy repeats this well-worn declaration that the aim of education must be the building of character and not the mere acquisition of knowledge....

...

QUESTIONS

1. 'A duty-based social order seems inherently less subject to universalization (with respect to the duties imposed on individuals) than a rights-based social order (with respect to the rights attributed to individuals). That is, the content of duties (obligations toward elders, toward the community, toward God) seems to be very particular and bound to a given context, a product of a given religion or political or social culture or history, whereas individuals' rights seem to be more divorced from a particular context and can therefore be stated more abstractly.' Do you agree? Any examples?

2. '"Individual rights" necessarily imply equality among all rights holders, which is to say among all members of society. This in fact is what the contemporary human rights instruments declare. To the contrary, duties can be (and frequently are) defined so as to impose hierarchy, status, and discrimination in a given social order.' Do you agree? Any examples?

3. 'Different from a regime of rights, a regime of duties intrinsically exerts an inward, centripetal force. It draws individual duty-bearers into the society, connects them intricately with other individuals and the community in a variety of ways, blurs the separate identity of the individual from society, and leads to a more communal and collective structure of life.' Do you agree?

4. Note that Article 2(3) of the ICCPR requires states to provide all persons whose rights have been violated with 'an effective remedy', and to develop particularly the possibilities of 'judicial remedy'. Do rights imply a preference for or even require individual (judicial or other) remedies against the state, whereas a regime of individual duties is less likely to provide such remedies?

COMMENT ON DUTY PROVISIONS OF NATIONAL CONSTITUTIONS

In modern constitutions, as in human rights treaties, provisions conferring rights on individuals far outnumber those imposing duties. There appear below English translations of articles in a number of state constitutions that, as of recent dates, expressed such duties. Presented here in isolation from the context of the constitutions and political societies in which they take meaning, these articles serve merely to illustrate the range of such duties. Within their national contexts, they may be understood or interpreted to impose slight or significant duties, which moreover may be viewed merely as hortatory or may be subject to enforcement by civil or criminal actions brought by the state or by non-state parties.

Belarus

Article 53: Everyone shall respect the dignity, rights, liberties, and legitimate interests of others.

Article 55: It shall be the duty of everyone to protect the environment.

Cambodia

Article 47: Parents shall have the duty to take care of and educate their children to become good citizens. Children shall have the duty to take good care of their elderly mother and father according to Khmer traditions.

China

Article 42: (3) Work is the glorious duty of every able-bodied citizen. All working people in state enterprises and in urban and rural economic collectives should perform their tasks with an attitude consonant with their status as masters of the country. ...

Article 49: (2) Both husband and wife have the duty to practice family planning. (3) Parents have the duty to rear and educate their minor children, and children who have come of age have the duty to support and assist their parents.

Article 54: It is the duty of citizens of the People's Republic of China to safeguard the security, honour, and interests of the motherland; they must not commit acts detrimental to the security, honour and interests of the motherland.

India

Article 51A: It shall be the duty of every citizen of India ... (b) to cherish and follow the noble ideals which inspired our national struggle for freedom; ... (e) to promote harmony and the spirit of common brotherhood amongst all the people of India transcending religious, linguistic and regional or sectional diversities; to renounce practices derogatory to the dignity of women; ... (g) to protect and improve the natural environment ... and to have compassion for living creatures. ...

Italy

Article 4: The Republic recognizes the right of all citizens to work and promotes such conditions as will make this right effective. (2) Every citizen shall undertake, according to his possibilities and his own choice, an activity or a function contributing to the material and moral progress of society.

Poland

Article 86: Everyone shall care for the quality of the environment and shall be held responsible for causing its degradation. The principles of such responsibility shall be specified by statute.

Saudi Arabia

Article 12: The consolidation of national unity is a duty, and the state will prevent anything that may lead to disunity, sedition and separation.

Spain

Article 45: (1) Everyone has the right to enjoy an environment suitable for the development of the person as well as the duty to preserve it.

Thailand

Article 68: Every person shall have a duty to exercise his or her right to vote at an election. The person who fails to attend an election for voting without notifying the appropriate cause of such failure shall lose his or her right to vote as provided by law.

Uganda

Article 39: The exercise and enjoyment of rights and freedoms is inseparable from the performance of duties and obligations, and accordingly, it shall be the duty of every citizen . . . (c) to foster national unity and live in harmony with others; (d) to engage in gainful employment for the good of himself, the family, the common good and to contribute to the national development; . . . (f) to contribute to the well-being of the community where the citizen lives; (g) to protect and safeguard the environment; and (h) to promote democracy and the rule of law.

QUESTIONS

1. Which if any of the preceding provisions are inconsistent with, or indeed threaten, the human rights declared by the leading international instruments? Which if any do you view as implicitly incorporated in those instruments?

2. How do you understand, and would you support for inclusion in your own country's constitution, the provisions relating to work, to environment and to voting?

COMMENT ON COMPARISONS BETWEEN RIGHTS AND DUTIES IN THE AFRICAN CHARTER AND IN OTHER HUMAN RIGHTS INSTRUMENTS

The newest, the least developed or effective (in relation to the European and Inter-American regimes), the most distinctive and the most controversial of the three established regional human rights regimes involves African states. In 1981 the Assembly of Heads of States and Government of the Organization of African Unity adopted the African Charter on Human and Peoples' Rights (see the Documents Supplement). It entered into force in 1986. The OAU was succeeded in 2002 by the African Union, which as of May 2012 had 54 member states. All such states are parties to the African Charter.

The present discussion of the Charter emphasizes the distinctive attention that the African system gives to duties as well as rights. This distinctive emphasis is obvious on the face of the African Charter, even before one considers any elaboration or application of the provisions on duties by the African Commission. You should now become familiar with the provisions of the Charter. Other aspects of the Charter, and of the role of the Commission created by it, are discussed at pp. 1025–44, *infra*.

The Charter's Preamble itself suggests some of the striking differences from other human rights instruments, universal and regional. Its key theme is regional cultural distinctiveness, as when it refers to '[t]aking into consideration the virtues of [African states'] historical tradition and the values of African civilization'.

Rights

Consider first Chapter 1 of Part I, dealing with 'human and peoples' rights'.

1. Compare the important opening provisions (Arts. 1 and 2) of the Charter on the obligations of states with the analogous provisions in Article 2 of the ICCPR.
2. Several of the rights are expressed in ways that differ in wording from equivalent provisions in other instruments but that amount in the large to a similar conception. See, for example, Article 4.
3. Many rights are expressed in significantly different ways from the equivalent provisions in, say, the ICCPR. Compare, for example, Article 7 of the Charter on criminal procedure with Articles 14 and 15 of the ICCPR; and Article 13 of the Charter on political participation with Article 25 of the ICCPR. Note the respects in which Article 25 is more specific.
4. The protection of the property right in Article 14 recalls Article 17 of the UDHR but finds no equivalent in the ICCPR. The European Convention as first drafted included no such provision, but its First Protocol extends protection to the property right.
5. Some provisions state familiar norms, but illustrate them or make them specific in ways that recall Africa's experience with the Western slave trade and with colonization. They bear out the phrase in the Preamble quoted above. See, for example, Articles 5, 19 and 20. Other provisions refer to abuses in Africa's own post-colonial history, such as Article 12(5) that recalls Uganda's expulsion of its citizens of Asian descent.
6. A number of provisions draw attention to the attempts of the states to reconcile humane treatment of individuals with their interests in territorial integrity and security. See, for example, Article 23(2).
7. Compare the characteristic limitations on rights in the Charter with those in the ICCPR. See, for example, Articles 18(3) and 22(2) of the ICCPR. Compare with them Article 6 of the Charter, assuring the right to liberty 'except for reasons and conditions previously laid down by law'; Article 8 providing that freedom of conscience and religion are 'subject to law and order'; and Article 10 declaring the right to free association 'provided that [the individual] abides by the law'. See also Articles 11 and 12(2).
8. Note that the Charter has no provision for derogation of rights in situations of national emergency, equivalent to Article 4 of the ICCPR.

9. The Charter includes economic-social rights as in Articles 15 and 16, but does not qualify these rights with respect to their progressive realization and with respect to resource constraints to which the rights are subject, as does Article 1 of the International Covenant on Economic, Social and Cultural Rights.

10. The Charter includes several collective or peoples' rights, sometimes referred to as 'third-generation' human rights, in provisions like those in Articles 23 and 24 dealing with peoples' rights 'to national and international peace and security' and 'to a generally satisfactory environment favourable to their development'. The Charter's title itself signals the importance of this feature.

Duties

Consider now the distinctive Chapter 2 of Part I, on 'duties'. As prior materials in this chapter stress, references to 'duties' are not alien to human rights instruments: Article 29 of the UDHR, the preamble to the ICCPR, indeed the preamble to the UN Charter itself.

Nonetheless, the Charter is the first human rights treaty to include an enumeration of, to give forceful attention to, individuals' duties. In this respect, it goes well beyond the conventional notion that duties may be correlative to rights, such as the obvious duties of states that are correlative (corresponding) to individual rights — for example, states' duties not to torture or to provide a structure for voting in political elections. The Charter also goes beyond correlative duties of individuals that many human rights instruments explicitly or implicitly impose — for example, an individual's right to bodily security imposes a duty on other individuals not to invade that right. The Charter differs by defining duties that are not simply the 'other side' of individual rights, and that run from individuals to the state as well as to other groups and individuals. Hence the Charter directly raises the issues of universalism and cultural relativism that are addressed in Chapter 7.

Depending on their interpretation and their possible application within the African human rights regime, the duties declared in the Charter could constitute part of the deep structure of the society contemplated by that instrument. For example, they could determine in basic ways the relationships between the individual on the one hand, and society and state on the other. They could resolve in specific ways the tension between the individual and the collective. They could contradict some provisions in the Charter's preceding elaboration of rights.

Note some of the vital phrases in Articles 27–29. Article 27 refers to duties towards one's 'family and society, the State and other legally recognized communities and the international community'. Rights are to be exercised with 'due regard to the rights of others, collective security, morality and common interest'.

The language of Article 29 is striking. Note such phrases as the 'harmonious development of the family', 'cohesion and respect', 'serve the national community', 'not to compromise the security of the state', 'strengthen social and national solidarity', 'strengthen positive African cultural values in [one's] relations with other members of the society', and 'contribute to the best of [one's] abilities . . . to the promotion and achievement of African unity'.

This theme of solidarity appears also in the African Charter's definitions of rights. Article 10(2) protects individuals against being compelled 'to join an association', but '[s]ubject to the obligation of solidarity provided for in Article 29'. Article 25 provides that states must 'promote and ensure through teaching, education and publication' respect for the rights declared and to assure that such rights 'as well as corresponding obligations and duties are understood'.

That is, depending on their interpretation and application, duties and ideals of solidarity may impinge in clear and serious ways on the Charter's definitions of rights themselves. Moreover, the Charter imposes individual duties not only on the state but also on different groups or communities within (or perhaps transcending) that state.

Consider some of the problems raised by these provisions about individual duties:

1. Sometimes what appear to be conventional terms of reference may bear plural meanings that affect the nature of the duty. For example, what definition applies to the word 'family' in Article 27 — the nuclear or extended family? In the African context, one might think of the extended family. Nonetheless, the only specific reference to family relationships in the three articles on duties deals with parents and children (Art. 29(1)).

Or how are we to understand 'society' in Article 27 — as referring to the nation-state, or to prevailing social and cultural structures within the state? It is striking that the article does not mention or seem to include ethnic groups, for they are frequently not 'legally' recognized.

2. As in the other two articles on duties, the requirements put on the individual by Article 28 raise the question of whether, and by whom, these duties are to be enforced. Who or what institution is to give meaning and application to them, or even provide general guidance for their performance? To the present, the African Commission has taken no steps towards interpretation or general elaboration of the provisions on duties. The question remains open whether the three articles are to constitute in some sense 'binding' and enforceable obligations.

3. The duties are of such breadth and so ambiguous in their connotations that a regime of serious enforcement without some degree of prior elaboration is difficult to imagine. Consider, for example, Article 28's provision that non-discrimination is not simply a duty of the state, but individuals also must not discriminate against other individuals. The article does not list any forbidden grounds for discrimination. Nor does it on its face distinguish between discrimination in the so-called private and public spheres — that is, discrimination in personal social relationships, and in employment or housing.

4. Article 29 raises a host of such issues, none more salient than the question whether it imposes on individuals a duty to uphold extant, traditional structures ranging from the family to the government. The critical terms seem to be 'harmonious', 'cohesion', 'community', 'security', 'social and national solidarity', 'territorial integrity', 'positive African cultural values', 'moral well-being of society' and, last but not least, 'African unity'. How are these injunctions to be reconciled with the rights earlier declared?

Consider the following analysis of duties and their relationships both to rights and to African tradition and culture.

MAKAU MUTUA, HUMAN RIGHTS AND THE AFRICAN FINGERPRINT

in Mutua, Human Rights: A Political and Cultural Critique (2002), at 71

...

... [M]uch of the criticism of the Charter has been directed at its inclusion of duties on individuals.... This criticism ... should [lead us to] examine the concept of duty in precolonial African societies and demonstrate its validity in conceptualizing a unitary, integrated conception of human rights in which the extreme individualism of current human rights norms is tempered by the individual's obligation to the society.

Capturing the view of many Africans, B. Obinna Okere has written that the 'African conception of man is not that of an isolated and abstract individual, but an integral member of a group animated by a spirit of solidarity.' ...

...

In practical terms, this philosophy of the group-centered individual evolves through a series of carefully taught rights and responsibilities. At the root were structures of social and political organization, informed by gender and age, which served to enhance solidarity and ensure the existence of the community into perpetuity.... Relationships, rights, and obligations flowed from these organizational structures, giving the community cohesion and viability. Certain obligations, such as the duty to defend the community and *its* territory, attached by virtue of birth and group membership....

...

Defense of the community, a state-type right exacted on those who came under its protection, was probably the most serious positive public obligation borne by young men.... [M]ost individual duties attached at the family and kinship levels ....

...

This conception, that of the individual as a moral being endowed with rights but also bounded by duties, proactively uniting his needs with the needs of others, was the quintessence of the formulation of rights in precolonial societies. It radically differs from the liberal conception of the individual as the state's primary antagonist.... Moreover, it provides those concerned with the universal conception of human rights with a basis for imagining another dialectic: the harmonization of duties and rights.... This African worldview, [Cobbah] writes, "is for all intents and purposes as valid as the European theories of individualism and the social contract." Any concept of human rights with pretensions of universality cannot avoid mediating between these two seemingly contradictory notions.

The Duty/Rights Conception

... [T]he African Charter is the first human rights document to articulate the concept [of duty] in any meaningful way....

... Perhaps at no other time in the history of the continent have Africans needed each other more than they do today. Although there is halting progress toward democratization in some African countries, the continent is generally on a steady track to political and economic collapse. Now in the fifth decade of postcolonialism, African states have largely failed to forge viable, free, and prosperous countries.... The new African states have failed to inspire loyalty in the citizenry; to produce a political class with integrity and a national interest; to inculcate in the military, the police, and the security forces their proper roles in society; to build a nation from different linguistic and cultural groups; and to fashion economically viable policies.

...

...

Ironically, colonialism, though a divisive factor, created a sense of brotherhood or unity among different African nations within the same colonial state, because they saw themselves as common victims of an alien, racist. and oppressive structure. Nevertheless, as the fissures of the modern African state amply demonstrate, the unity born out of anticolonialism has not sufficed to create an enduring identity of nationhood in the context of the postcolonial state....

This difficult social and political transformation from self-governing ethnocultural units to the multilingual, multicultural modern state — the disconnection between the two Africas: one precolonial, the other post-colonial — lies at the root of the current crisis....

...

... While acknowledging that it is impossible to recapture and reinstitute precolonial forms of social and political organization, this chapter nonetheless asserts that Africa must partially look inward, to its precolonial past, for possible solutions. Certain ideals in precolonial African philosophy, particularly the conception of humanity, and the interface of rights and duties in a communal context as provided for in the African Charter, should form part of that process of reconstruction....

...

The series of explicit duties spelled out in articles 27 through 29 of the African Charter could be read as intended to recreate the bonds of the precolonial era among individuals and between individuals and the state. They represent a rejection of the individual "who is utterly free and utterly irresponsible and opposed to society." In a proper reflection of the nuanced nature of societal obligations in the precolonial era, the African Charter explicitly provides for two types of duties: direct and indirect. A direct duty is contained, for example, in article 29(4) of the Charter which requires the individual to "preserve and strengthen social and national solidarity, particularly when the latter is threatened." There is nothing inherently sinister about this provision; it merely repeats a duty formerly imposed on members of precolonial communities. If anything, there exists a heightened need today, more than at any other time in recent history, to fortify communal relations and defend national solidarity....

The African Charter provides an example of an indirect duty in article 27(2), which states that "The rights and freedoms of each individual shall be exercised with due regard to the rights of others, collective security, morality and common interest." This duty is in fact a limitation on the enjoyment of certain individual rights. It merely recognizes the practical reality that in African societies, as elsewhere in the world, individual rights are not absolute. Individuals are asked to reflect on how the exercise of their rights in certain circumstances might adversely affect other individuals or the community. …

Duties are also grouped according to whether they are owed to individuals or to larger units such as the family, society, or the state. Parents, for example, are owed a duty of respect and maintenance by their children. Crippling economic problems do not allow African states to contemplate some of the programs of the welfare state. The care of the aged and needy falls squarely on family and community members. This requirement — a necessity today — has its roots in the past: it was unthinkable to abandon a parent or relative in need. …

Some duties are owed by the individual to the state. These are not distinctive to African states; many of them are standard obligations that any modern state places on its citizens. … Such duties are rights that the community or the state, defined as all persons within it, holds against the individual. …

The duties that require the individual to strengthen and defend national independence, security, and the territorial integrity of the state are inspired by the continent's history of domination and occupation by outside powers over the centuries. The duties represent an extension of the principle of self-determination, used in the external sense, as a shield against foreign occupation. … Likewise, the duty to place one's intellectual abilities at the service of the state is a legitimate state interest, for the "brain drain" has robbed Africa of massive intellect. In recognition of the need for the strength of diversity, rather than its power to divide, the Charter asks individuals to promote African unity, an especially critical role given arbitrary balkanization by the colonial powers and the ethnic animosities fostered within and between the imposed states.

… [T]he Charter also requires the state to protect the family, which it terms "the natural unit and basis of society," and the "custodian of morals and traditional values." There is an enormous potential for advocates of equality rights to be concerned that these provisions could be used to support the patriarchy and other repressive practices of precolonial social ordering. It is now generally accepted that one of the strikes against the precolonial regime was its strict separation of gender roles and, in many cases, the limitation on, or exclusion of, women from political participation.

…

However, these are not the practices that the Charter condones when it requires states to assist families as the "custodians of morals and traditional values." Such an interpretation would be a cynical misreading of the Charter. The reference is to those traditional values which enhanced the dignity of the individual and emphasized the dignity of motherhood and the importance of the female as the central link in the reproductive chain; women were highly valued as equals in the process of the regeneration of life. The Charter guarantees, unambiguously and without equivocation, the equal rights of women in its gender equality provision by requiring states to "eliminate every discrimination against women" and to protect women's rights in international human rights instruments." …

…

The most damaging criticism of the language of duties in Africa sees them as "little more than the formulation, entrenchment, and legitimation of state rights and privileges against individuals and peoples." However, critics who question the value of including duties in the Charter point only to the theoretical danger that states might capitalize on the duty concept to violate other guaranteed rights. The fear is frequently expressed that emphasis on duties may lead to the "tramping" of individual rights if the two are in opposition....

...

... It should be the duty of the African Commission in its jurisprudence to clarify which, if any, of these duties are moral or legal obligations, and what the scope of their application ought to be. The Commission could lead the way in suggesting how some of the duties — on the individual as well as the state — might be implemented. The concept of national service, for example, could utilize traditional notions in addressing famine, public works, and community self-help projects. The care of parents and the needy could be formalized in family/state burden-sharing. The Commission should also indicate how, and in what forum, the state would respond to the breach of individual duties. It might suggest the establishment of community arbitration centers to work out certain types of disputes....

...

This chapter was not intended to dismiss concerns about the potential *for* the misuse of the duty/rights conception by political elites to achieve narrow, personal ends. However, any notions are subject to abuse by power-hungry elites. There is no basis for concluding that the duty/rights conception is unique in this respect... Is it possible to introduce in the modern African state grassroots democracy, deepening it in neighborhood communities and villages in the tradition of the precolonial council of elders? Can the family reclaim its status as the basic organizational political unit in this redemocratization process? Is it possible to create a state of laws — where elected officials are bound by checks and balances — as in the days of old, where rulers were held accountable, at times through destooling?

...

QUESTIONS

1. Does Mutua's article (a) explain and seek to justify in terms of African history and culture the relevant provisions of the Charter, or (b) seek to reconcile those provisions with the human rights regime, or (c) both? Do you believe that he succeeds in the second task? Does he suggest that the West and Africa should in some respects go their separate ways, or that Africa has indeed much to teach the West about the directions of its own rights-oriented thought?

2. Does the Charter protect an advocate of radical reform who seeks significant changes in her state with respect to gender relationships or the character of the family? How, for example, would you reconcile the provisions of Article 29 with Article 18, to the effect that the state should 'ensure the elimination of every discrimination against women'? How would you state your argument for the supremacy of Article 18? Are you persuaded by Mutua's argument?

3. What effect might Articles 27–29 have on the Charter's provisions for speech and association, which are the very conditions of effective political participation? Are Mutua's views here helpful?

4. 'Whatever the African Charter says, African states like all states are subject to the universal human rights system of the UDHR and the two basic Covenants. If there is a conflict, if this regional regime requires or permits state conduct that universal norms prohibit, those norms must prevail. Or else the "universal" human rights movement collapses into regional anarchy.' Comment.

NOTE

As prior readings underscore, rights as a fundamental language of law, politics and morals grew within and are associated with the Western liberal tradition. This is not, however, to say that the claims, interests, values and ideals expressed through rights language in the basic human rights instruments are exclusive to the Western liberal tradition. Many of them, as we have seen, may be expressed through other languages as well — for example, the language of duty and responsibility of the state, government and individuals. The final reading in this section outlines some of the main notions implicit in the liberal political tradition.

To place the basic instruments in historical context, and as background for the discussion of cultural relativism in Chapter 7, it will be helpful to have in mind some notions about liberal political thought and the liberal state. The following Comment sketches basic characteristics.

HENRY STEINER, SOME CHARACTERISTICS OF THE LIBERAL POLITICAL TRADITION

in H. Steiner & P. Alston, International Human Rights in Context (1996), at 187

Observers from different regions and cultures can agree that the human rights movement, with respect to its language of rights and the civil and political rights that it declares, stems principally from the liberal tradition of Western political and legal thought. That observation lies at the core of argument by states from non-Western parts of the world that some basic provisions in instruments like the UDHR or ICCPR are inappropriate and inapplicable to their circumstances. Those instruments, the argument goes, purport to give a genuinely universal expression to certain tenets of liberal political culture, and advocates basing their criticism of counties in the developing world on the human rights movement are effectively advancing a contemporary form of imperialism. Thus liberal thought and practices inform much contemporary debate examined in Chapter 7 about the meaning and relevance of cultural relativism.

For the purpose of facilitating some comparisons between liberalism and the human rights movement, this Comment sketches characteristics that observers would associate with the different expressions of the liberal tradition during the twentieth century. The Comment has a limited historical scope. It does not reach back to the origins of liberal thought in the seventeenth century and Age of Enlightenment, or to changes in that body of thought in the nineteenth century.

The liberal political tradition has never been and surely is not today a monolithic body of thought requiring one and only one form of government. The very term 'liberal' has assumed different meanings, from the liberal economics associated with the *laissez faire* school of the nineteenth century to contemporary associations of liberalism in a country like the United States with a more active and engaged state concerned with the general welfare of the population and with regulation of the market and nongovernmental actors — the modern regulatory and welfare state so familiar to Western states.

The contemporary expressions of liberal thought by theorists like Dworkin or Rawls depart significantly from the writings of the classical theorists influencing its development, like Bentham, Kant, Locke, Mill, Rousseau and Tocqueville. The differences among such classical writers are reflected in the distinct versions of liberal ideology and the varied structures and practices of self-styled liberal democracies. This variety and ongoing transformation suggest caution in making inclusive and dogmatic comparisons between, say, liberalism and the human rights movement, which has during the last six decades generated its own internal conflicts and has itself undergone significant change.

No characteristic of the liberal tradition is more striking than its emphasis on the individual. Liberal political theory and the constitutive instruments of many liberal states frequently employ basic concepts or premises like the dignity and autonomy of the individual, and the respect that is due to all individuals. The vital concept of equality informs these terms: the equal dignity of all human beings, the equal respect to which individuals are entitled, the equal right for self-realization. It is not then surprising that equal protection and equal opportunities without repressive discrimination constitute so cardinal a value of contemporary liberalism. In general, the protection of members of minorities against invidious discrimination continues to be a central concern for the liberal state.

Such stress on the individual informs basic justifications for the state. The liberal state rests on, its very legitimacy stems from, the consent of the people within it. Within liberal theory, that consent is both hypothetical, as in the notion of a social contract among the inhabitants of a state of nature to create the political state, and institutionalized through typical practices such as periodic elections. Such ideas are explicit in the basic human rights instruments. Note Article 21 of the UDHR ('The will of the people shall be the basis of the authority of government') and Article 25 of the ICCPR (the importance of elections 'guaranteeing the free expression of the will of the electors').

From the start, liberal theory has been attentive to the risk of abuse of the individual by the state. The rights language that is found in constitutional bills of rights, statutory provisions for basic rights, political traditions not expressed in positive law and writings of theorists and advocates respond to this need for protection against the state. The rights with which the individual is endowed limit governmental power — the right not to be tortured, not to be discriminated against on stated grounds. Until the early twentieth century, liberal theory and the liberal state were far less attentive to violations of rights by non-state actors, corporations or individuals, but heightened regulation of the non-state (private) sector and the growth of international human rights have brought significant change, particularly since World War II.

Historically the protection of the property right against interference by the state and others played a major role in liberal theory. Indeed, questions of the relationships between liberalism and free enterprise or capitalism have long been debated. They take on a particular pungency in the post Cold-War world of spreading markets, spreading democracy and globalization.

Sometimes the types of rights just referred to are described as 'negative': the hands-off or non-interference rights (don't touch), or the right to be interfered with (as by arrest, imprisonment) only pursuant to stated processes. It is partly the prominence of the rights related to notions of individual liberty, autonomy and choice and the right related to property protection that produces the sharp division in much liberal thought between the state and individual, between government and nongovernmental sectors, between what are often referred to as the public and private realms or spheres of action.

This conception of negative rights, and of negative freedom as the absence of external constraints, together with the historical alliance of political liberalism with conceptions of a free market and *laissez faire*, led to liberalism's early emphasis on sharply limited government. The tension between that early ideology and background, and the growing emphasis over more than a century on the welfare and regulatory functions of the modern liberal state, remain central to much political and moral debate today.

That debate is related to an opposition that has developed in liberal thought between *negative* rights or negative liberty (freedom), and *positive* or *affirmative* rights or liberty (freedom). Those terms have acquired different meanings, to be explored in this and later chapters. For example, 'positive rights' have been described as entitlements of individuals to the effect that the state should not simply respect the 'private' sphere of inviolability of the individual (the negative rights),but should also 'act' in particular ways to benefit the individual, perhaps by providing education or health care. In this sense, the 'positive rights' of individuals such as the right to education or health care impose duties on the state to provide the necessary institutions or resources. [Compare the Comment on state duties at p. 181, *supra.*]

In a different and more ample sense, *positive liberty* has been described as 'liberty to' as opposed to 'liberty from' — for example, the liberty to realize oneself, to satisfy one's real interests, to achieve individual self-determination. One form of such positive liberty facilitated by the state would be governmental policies and institutions fostering the active political participation of citizens in electoral and other processes that help to determine the exercise of public power. Through such positive liberty, the individual can participate in the creation and recreation of self and state. The state readily and naturally becomes involved in this search of individuals for positive liberty, characteristically by creating the conditions that make the individual quest more likely to succeed, but at the dangerous authoritarian extreme by attempting to define the content of genuine self-realization and by coercing individuals to achieve it.

What an individual should seek in life, what idea of the good in life that individual holds, how the individual seeks self-realization, remain in the liberal state matters of individual choice to which both negative and positive conceptions of rights and freedom are relevant. That state must be open to a variety of ends, a variety of conceptions of the good, that individuals will express. The liberal state must then be a pluralist state. Its structure of rights, going beyond the rights to personal security and equal protection to include rights of conscience and speech and association, facilitates and protects the many types of diversity within pluralism, as well as ongoing argument in the public arena about the forms and goals of social and political life.

Precisely what governmental structures best realize such liberal principles is among the disputed features of the liberal tradition. The liberal state is closely associated with the ideal of the rule of law, hence with some minimum of separation of government powers such as an independent judiciary that can protect individual rights against executive abuse. The fear of tyranny of the majority lies at the foundation of the argument for restrictions on governmental power through a constitutional bill of rights limiting or putting conditions on what government can do. How to enforce that bill of rights against the executive and legislature has never achieved a consensus among liberal states. They vary in the degree to which they subject legislative action to judicial review, hence in the degree to which governmental power, even if supported by a freely voting majority of the population, can abridge or transform or abolish rights. The trend among liberal democracies over the last few decades has been toward judicial review of legislative as well as executive action.

The liberal tradition continues to be subjected to deep challenges from within and without, and thus continues its process of evolutionary change. During and particularly after the Cold War, its interaction with states of the developing world posed complex issues in relation to efforts of some of those states to develop new forms of government and economy. For example, the relationships in the former Communist states of Central and East Europe between liberalism, privatization and property rights, markets and regulation thereof, and the provision of welfare remain ambiguous and in flux. More generally, questions of the relationship between liberalism and a market economy, or liberalism and ethnic nationalism, have assumed heightened prominence. In a Western country such as the United States, liberalism responds to challenges from diverse perspectives such as communitarian ideas, civic republicanism, and multiculturalism (cultural particularism).

Some of these contemporary challenges underscore a continuing debate within liberalism, the two sides to which can lead to significantly different political and social orders: *individual* or *group* identity as primary. The group may be — to use the conventional porous and overlapping terms — national, linguistic, religious, cultural, ethnic. At the extreme, it is not compatible with a liberal creed for a governing order to subordinate individuals fully to the demands of such kinds of groups. With respect to the core values of liberalism, individual rights remain lexically prior to the demands of a culture or group, to the claims of any collective identity or group solidarity.

Nonetheless, the liberal state is hardly hostile to groups as such. It is not blind to the influence of groups (religious, cultural, ethnic) or of group and cultural identity in shaping the individual. Indeed, the political life of modern liberal democracies is largely constituted by the interaction, lobbying and other political participation of groups, some of which are natural in their defining characteristic (race, sex, elderly citizens), and some formed out of shared interests (labour unions, business associations, environmental groups). The liberal state, by definition committed to pluralism, must accommodate different types of groups, and maintain the framework of rights in which they can struggle for recognition, power and survival.

Such issues indicate how much is open and debated within liberalism about the significance of the priority of the individual in the contemporary liberal state — or different types of liberal states. Should we, for example, understand the 'individual' *abstractly*, as similar in vital respects everywhere, both within the same state and universally? Or do we understand the individual *contextually*, as influenced or even determined by ethnic, cultural, national, religious and other traditions and communities? Should we even phrase the question in such dramatic contrasts, or should we rather assume that the answers are too complex for any clear choice between them?

Since the birth of the human rights movement, and particularly since the collapse of the Soviet Union, such issues about the individual and the collective have taken on great pungency in the contradictions bred, on the one hand, by the spread of both liberal ideology with its emphasis on the individual and of market ideology with its stress on private initiative, and on the other hand, by the often savage bursts of ethnic nationalism in many parts of the world with their stress on collective rather than individual identity.

The emphasis in both liberalism and the human rights movement on individual 'rights' leads to one final observation related to several of this chapter's readings. Rights are no more determinate in meaning, no less susceptible to varying interpretations and disputes among states, than any other moral, political or legal conception — for example, 'property', or 'sovereignty', or 'consent', or 'national security'. Within liberal states, different institutional solutions have been brought to the question of who should determine and develop the content of rights, and who should resolve the many and puzzling conflicts among rights. In the international arena, this problem becomes all the more complex. What mechanisms, what institutional framework, what allocation or separation of powers, what blend of overtly political and judicial resolution of these issues, will we find in the international human rights movement?

ADDITIONAL READING

F. Mégret, 'Where Does the Critique of International Human Rights Law Stand? An Exploration in 18 Vignettes', in D. Kennedy & J. Beneyto (eds.), *New Approaches to International Law: Lessons from the European Experience* (2012); W. Edmundson, *An Introduction to Rights* (2nd edn. 2012); M. Freeman, *Human Rights: An Interdisciplinary Approach* (2011); J. Nickel, *Making Sense of Human Rights* (2nd edn.

2007); J. Griffin, *On Human Rights* (2009); A. Clapham, *Human Rights: A Very Short Introduction* (2007); C. Gearty, *Can Human Rights Survive?* (2006); C. Beitz, *The Idea of Human Rights* (2009); S. Moyn, *The Last Utopia: Human Rights in History* (2010); C. Douzinas, *Human Rights and Empire: The Political Philosophy of Cosmopolitanism* (2007); M. Ignatieff, 'Human Rights as Idolatry', in A. Gutmann (ed.), *Human Rights as Politics and Idolatry* (2003); R. Dickinson et al. (eds.), *Examining Critical Perspectives on Human Rights* (2012); J. Waldron (ed.), *Theories of Rights* (1984); C. Nino (ed.), *Rights* (1992).

7

Conflict in Culture, Tradition and Practices: Challenges to Universalism

A. UNIVERSALISM AND CULTURAL RELATIVISM

The question of the 'universal' or 'relative' character of human rights has been a source of debate and contention from the outset. These understandings of the character of human rights have sometimes been cast as alternatives, as polar visions with no neutral ground between them, and sometimes as allowing for a more complex view that understands some norms as universal, some as relative to context and culture. The generally antagonistic positions have borne a number of descriptions — for example, 'absolute' rights (compare 'universal') as opposed to 'contingent' rights (compare 'relative'), or imperialism in imposing rights (compare 'universal') as opposed to self-determination of peoples (compare 'relative'). The contest between these positions took on renewed vigour as the human rights regime slowly developed, and in important respects weakened, earlier more robust understandings of the scope of national sovereignty and of domestic jurisdiction. Indeed, significant links have developed over the decades between some of the claims associated with cultural relativism and claims of sovereign autonomy for a state to follow its own path.

Put simply, the partisans of universality claim that international human rights like rights to equal protection, physical security, fair trials, free speech, freedom of religion and free association, are and must be the same everywhere. This claim applies at least to the rights' general content, for advocates of the position that rights are universal or course recognize that many basic rights (such as the right to a fair criminal trial) allow for historically and culturally influenced forms of implementation or realization (i.e., states are not required to use the Anglo-American jury to assure a fair trial; states need not follow any one particular voting system to meet the requirement of a government that represents the will of the people).

Advocates of cultural relativism claim that (most, some) rights and rules about morality are encoded in and thus depend on cultural context, the term 'culture' often being used in a broad and diffuse way that reaches beyond indigenous traditions and customary practices to include political and religious ideologies and institutional structures. Hence notions of right (and wrong) and moral rules based on them necessarily differ throughout the world because the cultures in which they take root and inhere themselves differ. This relativist position can then be understood simply to assert as an empirical matter that the world contains an impressive diversity in views about right and wrong that is linked to the diverse underlying cultures.

But the strong relativist position goes beyond arguing that there is — as a matter of fact, empirically — an impressive diversity. It attaches an important consequence to this diversity: that no transcendent or transcultural ideas of right can be found or agreed on, and hence that no culture or state (whether or not in the guise of enforcing international human rights) is justified in attempting to impose on other cultures or states what must be understood to be ideas associated particularly with it. In this strong form, cultural relativism necessarily contradicts a basic premise of the human rights regime. Its strong values are respect for diversity and the related local autonomy.

On their face, human rights instruments (which in their treaty form mean to impose legal obligations, to convert moral rules into legal rules) are surely on the 'universalist' side of this debate. The landmark instrument is the *Universal* Declaration of Human Rights, parts of which have clearly become customary international law. The two Covenants, with states parties from all the world's regions, also speak in universal terms: 'everyone' has the right to liberty, 'all persons' are entitled to equal protection, 'no one' shall be subjected to torture, 'everyone' has the right to an adequate standard of living. Neither in the definitions of rights nor in the limitation clauses (such as limitations of rights because of public order or policy or public health) does the text of these basic instruments make any explicit concession to cultural variation. (The regional instruments examined in Chapter 11, and particularly the aspects of the African Charter on Human and Peoples' Rights examined at p. 517, *supra*, do express an important degree of cultural variation.)

To the relativist, these instruments and their pretension to universality may suggest primarily the arrogance or 'cultural imperialism' of the West, given the West's traditional urge — expressed, for example, in political ideology (liberalism) and in religious faith (Christianity) — to view its own forms and beliefs as universal, and to attempt to universalize them. Moreover, the push to universalization of norms is said by some relativists to destroy diversity of cultures and hence to amount to another path towards cultural homogenization in the modern world — itself a contradiction of the value of cultural survival stressed in Article 27, for example, of the ICCPR. But the debate between these two positions follows no simple route. It is open to a range of views and strategies that the materials in Part A explore at a general and theoretical level — and that the case studies in Part B further probe.

During the Cold War, such debates (sometimes no more than highly politicized accusations, routine polemics) were dominantly between the Communist world (and its sympathizers) and the Western democracies. The Western democracies charged the Communist world with violating many basic rights, particularly those of a civil and political character. That world replied both by charging the West with violations of the more important economic and social rights, and by asserting that the political and ideological structures of Communist states pointed towards a different understanding of rights.

That debate died more-or-less together with the Soviet Union, though some of its themes survive in different form. Today the universal-relative debate takes place primarily in a North-South (or West-East) framework between developed and less developed countries, or in a religious (West-Islam) framework. It also includes non-state actors such as indigenous peoples.

NOTE

The principle of universalism of human rights norms that permeates the universal instruments starting with the Universal Declaration rests on a few basic postulates, beliefs and assumptions. Perhaps the fundamental postulate, one that embraces all human beings, is equal human dignity. Denial of that principle, at least with respect to the regulation of action and behaviour, itself shatters universalism in the sense of the human rights corpus, without even reaching the divisive issues posed by cultural relativism. That denial has been a commonplace in world history, strikingly evident in the history of the twentieth century. Consider the following observations of a philosopher, Richard Rorty, in 'Human Rights, Rationality and Sentimentality', in Obrad Savić (ed.), *The Politics of Human Rights* (1999) 67, at 74:

> ... [E]verything turns on who counts as a fellow human being, as a rational agent in the only relevant sense — the sense in which rational agency is synonymous with membership in *our* moral community.
>
> For most white people, until very recently, most Black people did not so count. For most Christians, up until the seventeenth century or so, most heathens did not so count. For the Nazis, Jews did not so count. For most males in countries in which the average annual income is under four thousand dollars, most females still do not so count. Whenever tribal and national rivalries become important, members of rival tribes and nations will not so count. Kant's account of the respect due to rational agents tells you that you should extend the respect you feel for people like yourself to all featherless bipeds. This is an excellent suggestion, a good formula for secularizing the Christian doctrine of the brotherhood of man. But it has never been backed up by an argument based on neutral premises, and it never will be. Outside the circle of post-Enlightenment European culture...most people are simply unable to understand why membership in a biological species is supposed to suffice for membership in a moral community. This is not because they are insufficiently rational. It is, typically, because they live in a world in which it would be just too risky — indeed, would often be insanely dangerous — to let one's sense of moral community stretch beyond one's family, clan, or tribe.
>
> To get whites to be nicer to Blacks, males to females, Serbs to Muslims, or straights to gays, to help our species link up into what Rabossi calls a 'planetary community' dominated by a culture of human rights, it is of no use whatever to say, with Kant: notice that what you have in common, your humanity, is more important than these trivial differences. For the people we are trying to convince will rejoin that they notice nothing of the sort. Such people are *morally* offended by the suggestion that they should treat someone who is not kin as if he were a

> brother.... They are offended by the suggestion that they treat people whom they do not think of as human as if they were human....
>
> This rejoinder is not just a rhetorical device, nor is it in any way irrational. It is heartfelt. The identity of these people, the people whom we should like to convince to join our Eurocentric human rights culture, is bound up with their sense of who they are *not*. Most people — especially people relatively untouched by the European Enlightenment — simply do not think of themselves as, first and foremost, human beings. Instead, they think of themselves as being a certain *good* sort of human being — a sort defined by explicit opposition to a particularly bad sort. It is crucial for their sense of who they are that they are *not* an infidel, not a queer, not a woman, *not* an untouchable. Just in so far as they are impoverished, and as their lives are perpetually at risk, they have little else than pride in not being what they are not to sustain their self-respect....

NOTE

The three introductory readings below come out of the rich anthropological literature on culture and cultural relativism. Anthropologists have long had to wrestle with these issues, in the context of their ethnographic writings about diverse cultures whose practices and values depart radically from the West. Often those practices would be subject to serious moral criticism from the perspectives of Western thought. The anthropological writings have sought primarily to describe, explain and understand the alien culture, within the framework of one or another theoretical perspective or methodology. They have not historically sought to pass judgement on the practices involved, to condemn or praise even as they describe.

Thus the role of the anthropologist has traditionally been very different from that of the human rights investigator who monitors and reports and the human rights advocate who works to arrest the described violations. To be sure, investigators and advocates may also seek to understand and to describe the cultural contexts in which they are working. But those working with the large international human rights organizations characteristically combine their description with moral and legal assessment of a given state's conduct against international human rights standards. They will in appropriate cases condemn the state's conduct and urge the state or others to take corrective or coercive measures. Their work is inherently judgmental, normatively based. They seek to vindicate and advance respect for human rights.

As noted in the readings, the traditional anthropologists' approach to these questions has come under recurrent challenge. Questions have been raised about the appropriate stance of the anthropologist towards practices and values that are offensive from a Western viewpoint. Ought she be critical of them, or on the contrary be tolerant and accepting, or simply be distant and neutral while in the role of observer and explainer. If critical, under what standards would she criticize?

The 1948 Statement on Human Rights, p. 542, *infra*, was a response to the drafting of the UDHR but it was not until much later that a sustained debate emerged on these issues. When reading the following excerpts bear in mind that the human rights regime addresses primarily states — and primarily individuals' rights against the state — whereas ethnographic writings involve primarily peoples or tribes or societies, which may be non-state (often sub-state) entities or which in any event are objects of study distinct from the political organization and political acts of the state itself.

ELVIN HATCH, CULTURE AND MORALITY: THE RELATIVITY OF VALUES IN ANTHROPOLOGY

(1983), at 8

... Herskovits [the author of the 1948 Statement] wrote that cultural relativism developed because of

> the problem of finding valid cross-cultural norms. In every case where criteria to evaluate the ways of different peoples have been proposed, in no matter what aspect of culture, the question has at once posed itself: 'Whose standards?' ... [T]he need for a cultural relativistic point of view has become apparent because of the realization that there is no way to play this game of making judgments across cultures except with loaded dice.

Ethical relativism is generally conceived as standing at the opposite pole from absolutism, which is the position that there is a set of moral principles that are universally valid as standards of judgment. One absolutist ethical theory is the traditional Christian view that right and wrong are God-given, and that all people may be judged according to Christian values. A wide range of purely secular ethical theories have also developed....

It is the *content* of moral principles, not their existence, that is variable among human beings. It seems that all societies have some form of moral system, for people everywhere evaluate the actions of kinsmen, neighbors, and acquaintances as virtuous, estimable, praiseworthy, and honorable, or as unworthy, shameful, and despicable. These evaluations take objective form as sanctions, such as open praise or rebuke; and in extreme cases, violence and execution. The ubiquity of the moral evaluation of behavior apparently is a feature which sets humanity apart from other organisms....

...

Chapter 4: The Call for Tolerance

... By and large ethical relativists have been anthropologists and not philosophers, and it is chiefly in the anthropological literature that we find arguments in its favor. Two people in particular have stood out as its proponents in the United States, Melville Herskovits and Ruth Benedict, both of whom were students of Boas. Almost without exception, the philosophers are disapproving, for usually they mention ethical relativism only to criticize it while in the course of arguing some other ethical theory.

At least two very different versions of ethical relativism have been advanced by anthropologists, and these need to be distinguished since they have their own faults and virtues. The first is sometimes classified (erroneously, as we shall see) as a form of skepticism, and I will call it the Boasian version of ethical relativism.... Skepticism in ethics is the view that nothing is really either right or wrong, or that there are no moral principles with a reasonable claim to legitimacy. It has been suggested that the Boasian position differs from this on one main point: Boasian relativism implies that principles of right and wrong do have some validity, but a very limited one, for they are legitimate only for the members of the society in which they are found. The values of the American middle class are valid for middle-class Americans, but not for the Trobriand Islanders, and vice versa.

Philosophers have presented a wide range of arguments against Boasian ethical relativism...According to this argument, Boasian relativism is in essence a moral theory that gives a central place to one particular value.... It contains a more or less implicit value judgment in its call for tolerance: it asserts that we *ought* to respect other ways of life....

...The call for tolerance was an appeal to the liberal philosophy regarding human rights and self-determinism. It expressed the principle that others ought to be able to conduct their affairs as they see fit, which includes living their lives according to the cultural values and beliefs of their society. Put simply, what was at issue was human freedom.

The call for tolerance (or for the freedom of foreign peoples to live as they choose) was a matter of immediate, practical importance in light of the pattern of Western expansion. As Western Europeans established colonies and assumed power over more and more of the globe, they typically wanted both to Christianize and civilize the indigenous peoples. Christian rituals were fostered or imposed, and 'pagan' practices were prohibited, sometimes with force. The practice of plural marriage was condemned as a barbaric custom, and Western standards of modesty were enforced in an attempt to improve morals by covering the body. In the Southwest of North America, Indians who traditionally had lived in scattered encampments were made to settle in proper villages like 'civilized' people. The treatment of non-Western societies by the expanding nations of the West is a very large blot on our history, and had the Boasian call for tolerance — and for the freedom of others to define 'civilization' for themselves — been heard two or three centuries earlier, this blot might not loom so large today.

...

To develop a moral theory around the principle of tolerance raises the need to justify that principle: what reasons or grounds can be given to make the case that cultural differences ought to be respected?...The relativists make the error of deriving an 'ought' statement from an 'is' statement. To say that values vary from culture to culture is to describe (accurately or not) an empirical state of affairs in the real world, whereas the call for tolerance is a value judgment of what ought to be, and it is logically impossible to derive the one from the other. The fact of moral diversity no more compels our approval of other ways of life than the existence of cancer compels us to value ill-health.

...

Chapter 5: The Limits of Tolerance

The Boasian version of ethical relativism is subject to even harsher criticism... in its commitment to the status quo. The approval it enjoins seems to be absolute, leaving no room for judgment....

...

The moral principle of tolerance that is proposed by Boasian relativism carries the obligation that one cannot be indifferent toward other ways of life — it obligates us to approve what others do. So if missionaries or government officials were to interfere in Yanomamo affairs for the purpose of reducing violence, the relativist would be obligated to oppose these moves in word if not action. Similarly, by the strict logic of relativism, Chagnon was wrong to insist that the mother feed her emaciated child. The Boasian relativist is placed in the morally awkward position of endorsing the infant's starvation, the rape of abducted women, the massacre of whole villages....

Chapter 6: A Growing Disaffection

...

We can now understand why ethical relativism has fallen on such hard times in spite of the resurgence of pessimism during the 1960s and later. First, it has been the experience of most anthropologists that non-Western peoples (and especially Third World nations) want change, at least to some extent: second, it is clear that they are often disadvantaged if it does not come; third, anthropologists by and large have altered their thinking about the relativity of material interests and improvement: most today consider these to be general values that can be applied throughout the world.

Not only has relativism fallen on hard times, it has become the subject of angry criticism, much of it from the Third World, which tends to conceive anthropologists as conservative in their attitudes toward change and therefore as promoting the subservience of the underdeveloped nations....

...

Whatever the cause, according to the radical critique, relativism has played directly into the hands of the oppressors throughout the world by its tacit support of the status quo. The relativists have not recognized that the exotic cultures to which they grant equal validity are poverty-stricken, powerless, and oppressed. William Willis comments that the relativist 'avoids the distress and misery' of foreign peoples who are 'cringing and cursing at the aggressive cruelty' of the Western nations. This avoidance of the matter of oppression 'helps explain the lack of outrage that has prevailed in anthropology until recent years'. Willis writes: 'Since relativism is applied only to 'aboriginal' customs, it advises colored peoples to preserve those customs that contributed to initial defeat and subsequent exploitation.... Hence, relativism defines the good life for colored peoples differently than for white people, and the good colored man is the man of the bush'. Instead of leaving cultures as they are, as museum pieces, we should help to bring about change — or, better, we should help the oppressed to bring about change.

...

SALLY ENGLE MERRY, HUMAN RIGHTS AND GENDER VIOLENCE

(2006), at 2

Chapter 1: Culture and Transnationalism

...

... Human rights ideas, embedded in cultural assumptions about the nature of the person, the community, and the state, do not translate easily from one setting to another. If human rights ideas are to have an impact, they need to become part of the consciousness of ordinary people around the world. Considerable research on law and everyday social life shows that law's power to shape society depends not on punishment alone but on becoming embedded in everyday social practices, shaping the rules people carry in their heads. Yet, there is a great distance between the global sites where these ideas are formulated and the specific situations in which they are deployed. We know relatively little about how individuals in various social and cultural contexts come to see themselves in terms of human rights.

Nor do ideas and approaches move readily the other way from local to global settings. Global sites are a *bricolage* of issues and ideas brought to the table by national actors. But transnational actors, and even some national elites, are often uninterested in local social practices or too busy to understand them in their complicated contexts.... Transnational reformers must adhere to a set of standards that apply to all societies if they are to gain legitimacy....

The division between transnational elites and local actors is based less on culture or tradition than on tensions between a transnational community that envisions a unified modernity and national and local actors for whom particular histories and contexts are important. Intermediaries such as NGO and social movement activists play a critical role in interpreting the cultural world of transnational modernity for local claimants.... [T]hey take local stories and frame them in...human rights language....

...[H]uman rights create a political space for reform using a language legitimated by a global consensus on standards. But this political space comes with a price. Human rights promote ideas of individual autonomy, equality, choice, and secularism even when these ideas differ from prevailing cultural norms and practices. Human rights ideas displace alternative visions of social justice that are less individualistic and more focused on communities and responsibilities, possibly contributing to the cultural homogenization of local communities....

...

There are several conundrums in applying human rights to local places. First, human rights law is committed to setting universal standards using legal rationality, yet this stance impedes adapting those standards to the particulars of local context. This perspective explains why local conditions often seem irrelevant to global debates. Second, human rights ideas are more readily adopted if they are packaged in familiar terms, but they are more transformative if they challenge existing assumptions about power and relationships. Activists who use human rights for local social movements face a paradox. Rights need to be presented in local cultural terms in order to be persuasive, but they must challenge existing relations of power in order to be effective. Third, to have local impact, human rights ideas need to be framed in terms of local values and images, but in order to receive funding, a wider audience, and international legitimacy, they have to be framed in terms of transnational rights principles....

Theorizing the Global-Local Interface

The global-local divide is often conceptualized as the opposition between rights and culture, or even civilization and culture. Those who resist human rights often claim to be defending culture. For example, male lineage heads in the rural New Territories of Hong Kong claimed that giving women rights to inherit land would destroy the social fabric.... [T]hese arguments depend on a very narrow understanding of culture and the political misuse of this concept....

Even as anthropologists and others have repudiated the idea of culture as a consensual, interconnected system of beliefs and values, the idea has taken on new life in the public sphere, particularly with reference to the global South....

...

Seeing culture as contested and as a mode of legitimating claims to power and authority dramatically shifts the way we understand the universalism-relativism debate. It undermines those who resist changes that would benefit weaker groups in the name of preserving "culture," and it encourages human rights activists to pay attention to local cultural practices. This view of culture emphasizes that culture is hybrid and porous and that the pervasive struggles over cultural values within local communities are competitions over power. More recent anthropological scholarship explores processes by which human rights ideas are mobilized locally, adapted, and transformed and, in turn, how they shape local political struggles. As Cowan, Dembour, and Wilson point out, "Rather than seeing universalism and cultural relativism as alternatives which one must choose, once and for all, one should see the tension between the positions as part of the continuous process of negotiating ever-changing and interrelated global and local norms". Culture in this sense does not serve as a barrier to human rights mobilization but as a context that defines relationships and meanings and constructs the possibilities of action.

...

Deconstructing Culture

Although culture is a term on everyone's lips, people rarely talk about what they mean by it. The term has many meanings in the contemporary world. It is often seen as the basis of national, ethnic, or religious identities. Culture is sometimes romanticized as the opposite of globalization, resolutely local and distinct.... In international human rights meetings, culture often refers to traditions and customs: ways of doing things that are justified by their roots in the past. There is a whiff of the notion of the primitive about this usage of the term culture. It is not what modern urbanites do but what governs life in the countryside.... Culture was often juxtaposed to civilization during the civilizing mission of imperialism, and this history has left a legacy in contemporary thinking.

...

There is a critical need for conceptual clarification of culture in human rights practice. Insofar as human rights relies on an essentialized model of culture, it does not take advantage of the potential of local cultural practices for change....

... Cultures consist of repertoires of ideas and practices that are not homogeneous but continually changing because of contradictions among them or because new ideas and institutions are adopted by members. They typically incorporate contested values and practices. Cultures are not contained within stable borders but are open to new ideas and permeable to influences from other cultural systems, although not all borders are equally porous. Cultural discourses legitimate or challenge authority and justify relations of power.

Of the myriad ways culture is imagined in transnational human rights discussions, two of the most common ones reflect an essentialized concept of culture....

[1] Culture as Tradition

Within the discourse of human rights activism, culture is often used as a synonym for tradition. Labeling a culture as traditional evokes an evolutionary vision of change from a primitive form to something like civilization.... So-called traditional societies are at an earlier evolutionary stage than modern ones, which are more evolved and more civilized. Culture in this sense is not used to describe the affluent countries of the global North but the poor countries of the global South, particularly isolated and rural areas....

Although some human rights activists refer to "good" cultural practices and "harmful" cultural practices and a few feminist scholars examine cultural practices that protect women from violence, many who write about women's right to protection from violence identify culture and tradition as the source of the problem.... [T] he human rights process seeks to replace cultural practices that are discriminatory with other cultural practices rooted in modern ideas of gender equality. Thus, like the colonial state, they seek to move ethnically defined subjects into the realm of rights-bearing modernity. This effort sometimes demonizes culture as it seeks to save individuals from its oppressive effects.

Female genital cutting (also called female genital mutilation) is the poster child for this understanding of culture....

...

[2] Culture as National Essence

A second common understanding of culture is as national essence or identity This concept of culture grows out of the German romantic tradition of the nineteenth century. Confronted with the claims to universal civilization of England and France, Germans began to draw a distinction between the external trappings of civilization and the inward, spiritual reality of culture. German romantics asserted the importance of a distinct culture, or *Kultur*, which formed the spiritual essence of their society. Each people, or *Volk*, has its own history and culture that expresses its genius. This includes its language, its laws, and its religion. The cosmopolitan elite corrupts it, while foreign technological and material values undermine it....

Culture as national essence is fundamental to claims to indigenous sovereignty and ethnonationalism, often in resistance to human rights. In 1993, when Lee Kuan Yew of Singapore claimed that human rights failed to incorporate Asian values, he drew on this understanding of culture. With support from several other Asian leaders, he argued that Asian values differed from Western conceptions of human rights. In some ways, the Asian values argument replays the German romantic resistance to French and English claims to civilization. Indeed, one critic of the Asian values argument notes that it falls into Orientalist notions of a communitarian East, with communal values, and an individualistic West.

Although the Asian values argument is less often articulated now, it represents one of many ways that leaders assert that human rights violate the fundamental cultural principles of a nation or a religion and therefore cannot be adopted. Women's rights are often opposed by those who claim to defend culture....

Culture as Contentious

... Over the last two decades, anthropology has elaborated a conception of culture as unbounded, contested, and connected to relations of power, as the product of historical influences rather than evolutionary change. Cultural practices must be understood in context, so that their meaning and impact change as their context shifts.... [Cultures] include institutional arrangements, political structures, and legal regulations. As institutions such as laws and policing change, so do beliefs, values, and practices. Cultures are not homogeneous and "pure" but produced through hybridization or creolization.

... These different perspectives on culture affect policies concerning women. For example, in Uruguay's country report to the committee monitoring the Women's Convention, the government expressed regret that more women were not involved in politics but blamed cultural traditions, women's involvement in domestic tasks, and the differences in wages by gender. In contrast, facing the same absence of women politicians, Denmark offered funds to offset babysitting expenses when women attended meetings. In the first case, the barrier to change is theorized as cultural tradition; in the second case, as institutional arrangements of child care. The first model sees culture as fixed; the second assumes that the meanings of gender will change as institutional and legal arrangements change.

...

... [C]ulture is as important in shaping human rights conferences as it is in structuring village mortuary rituals. Thinking of those peoples formerly labeled "backward" as the only bearers of culture neglects the centrality of culture to the practice of human rights. UN meetings are deeply shaped by a culture of transnational modernity, one that specifies procedures for collaborative decision-making, conceptions of global social justice, and definitions of gender roles. Human rights law is itself primarily a cultural system. Its limited enforcement mechanisms mean that the impact of human rights law is a matter of persuasion rather than force, of cultural transformation rather than coercive change. Its documents create new cultural frameworks for conceptualizing social justice. It is ironic that the human rights system tends to promote its new cultural vision through a critique of culture.

...

AMERICAN ANTHROPOLOGICAL ASSOCIATION, STATEMENT ON HUMAN RIGHTS

49 Amer. Anthropologist No. 4, 539 (1947)

[In 1947, the UN Commission on Human Rights had begun drafting what ultimately became the Universal Declaration of Human Rights, approved by the UN General Assembly in 1948. To contribute to the international debate the Statement below was submitted in 1947 by the Executive Board of the American Anthropological Association. It uses several designations to refer to the pending document that became the UDHR.]

The problem faced by the Commission on Human Rights of the United Nations in preparing its Declaration on the Rights of Man must be approached from two points of view. The first, in terms of which the Declaration is ordinarily conceived, concerns the respect for the personality of the individual as such and his right to its fullest development as a member of his society. In a world order, however, respect for the cultures of differing human groups is equally important.

These are two facets of the same problem, since it is a truism that groups are composed of individuals, and human beings do not function outside the societies of which they form a part. The problem is thus to formulate a statement of human rights that will do more than just phrase respect for the individual as an individual. It must also take into full account the individual as a member of the social group of which he is a part, whose sanctioned modes of life shape his behavior, and with whose fate his own is thus inextricably bound.

... How can the proposed Declaration be applicable to all human beings and not be a statement of rights conceived only in terms of the values prevalent in the countries of Western Europe and America? ...

If we begin, as we must, with the individual, we find that from the moment of his birth not only his behavior, but his very thought, his hopes, aspirations, the moral values which direct his action and justify and give meaning to his life in his own eyes and those of his fellows, are shaped by the body of custom of the group of which he becomes a member.... [I]f the essence of the Declaration is to be, as it must, a statement in which the right of the individual to develop his personality to the fullest is to be stressed, then this must be based on a recognition of the fact that the personality of the individual can develop only in terms of the culture of his society.

...

... Doctrines of the 'white man's burden' have been employed to implement economic exploitation and to deny the right to control their own affairs to millions of peoples over the world, where the expansion of Europe and America has not meant the literal extermination of whole populations. Rationalized in terms of ascribing cultural inferiority to these peoples, or in conceptions of their backwardness in development of their 'primitive mentality', that justified their being held in the tutelage of their superiors, the history of the expansion of the western world has been marked by demoralization of human personality and the disintegration of human rights among the peoples over whom hegemony has been established.

The values of the ways of life of these peoples have been consistently misunderstood and decried. Religious beliefs that for untold ages have carried conviction and permitted adjustment to the Universe have been attacked as superstitious, immoral, untrue. And, since power carries its own conviction, this has furthered the process of demoralization begun by economic exploitation and the loss of political autonomy....

We thus come to the first proposition that the study of human psychology and culture dictates as essential in drawing up a Bill of Human Rights in terms of existing knowledge:

1. The individual realizes his personality through his culture, hence respect for individual differences entails a respect for cultural differences.

There can be no individual freedom, that is, when the group with which the individual identifies himself is not free. There can be no full development of the individual personality as long as the individual is told, by men who have the power to enforce their commands, that the way of life of his group is inferior to that of those who wield the power.

...

2. Respect for differences between cultures is validated by the scientific fact that no technique of qualitatively evaluating cultures has been discovered.

This principle leads us to a further one, namely that the aims that guide the life of every people are self-evident in their significance to that people....

3. Standards and values are relative to the culture from which they derive so that any attempt to formulate postulates that grow out of the beliefs or moral codes of one culture must to that extent detract from the applicability of any Declaration of Human Rights to mankind as a whole.

Ideas of right and wrong, good and evil, are found in all societies, though they differ in their expression among different peoples. What is held to be a human right in one society may be regarded as anti-social by another people, or by the same people in a different period of their history. The saint of one epoch would at a later time be confined as a man not fitted to cope with reality. Even the nature of the physical world, the colors we see, the sounds we hear, are conditioned by the language we speak, which is part of the culture into which we are born.

The problem of drawing up a Declaration of Human Rights was relatively simple in the eighteenth century, because it was not a matter of *human* rights, but of the rights of men within the framework of the sanctions laid by a single society....

Today the problem is complicated by the fact that the Declaration must be of worldwide applicability. It must embrace and recognize the validity of many different ways of life. It will not be convincing to the Indonesian, the African, the Indian, the Chinese, if it lies on the same plane as like documents of an earlier period....

...

NOTE

In 1999, the American Anthropological Association adopted a Declaration on Anthropology and Human Rights:

> As a professional organization of anthropologists, the AAA has long been, and should continue to be, concerned whenever human difference is made the basis for a denial of basic human rights, where "human" is understood in its full range of cultural, social, linguistic, psychological, and biological senses.
>
> [The AAA in its working definition of principles of respect for difference "builds on" the UDHR and the basic human rights covenants and conventions.] The AAA definition thus reflects a commitment to human rights consistent with international principles but not limited by them. Human rights is not a static concept. Our understanding of human rights is constantly evolving as we come to know more about the human condition. It is therefore incumbent on anthropologists to be involved in the debate on enlarging our understanding of human rights on the basis of anthropological knowledge and research.[1]

The excerpts from Merry's book engage briefly in the deconstruction of culture. The human rights discourse of the last half-century often raises the question of what the different proponents in the ongoing debate mean by culture, or cultural tradition or identity. What is being asserted by the claim that a given state or region must be free to follow its own 'cultural tradition', even if thereby violating norms in universal treaties? Many meanings of the term appear and disappear in this debate; often 'culture' as a justification for difference is not referred to as such but is implicit in a state's argument. Or that broad term is disaggregated into some of its complex components, such as language, religion, traditions, rituals and other practices.

Meanings of culture may also differ across the divides of different languages. Consider some definitions for 'culture' in the *American Heritage Dictionary of the English Language* (1969):

> … 4. Intellectual and social formation. 5. The totality of socially transmitted behavior patterns, arts, beliefs, characteristic of a community or population. 6. A style of social and artistic expression peculiar to a society or class. 7. Intellectual and artistic activity.

Consider:

BRITANNUS (*shocked*):
Caesar, this is not proper.

THEODOTUS (*outraged*):
How?

CAESAR (*recovering his self-possession*):
Pardon him Theodotus: he is a barbarian, and thinks that the customs of his tribe and island are the laws of nature.

George Bernard Shaw, *Caesar and Cleopatra*, Act II

[1] www.aaanet.org/stmts/humanrts.htm.

The following article explores cultural relativism from the perspective of Islam. An-Na'im looks at the 'Muslim world'. Committed to international human rights and of the Islamic faith, he argues that 'human rights advocates in the Muslim world must work within the framework of Islam to be effective ... [and] should struggle to have their interpretations of the relevant [Islamic] texts adopted as the new Islamic scriptural imperatives for the contemporary world.' Those interpretations would be broadly consistent with the norms of international human rights. An-Na'im is then attentive to the relation between the international system and a given religious tradition, and to the possibility of reconciliation through reinterpretation of the tradition, rather than through identification of cross-cultural values among different systems that in some sense transcend or trump aspects of the religious tradition that defy or are otherwise inconsistent with them.

ABDULLAHI AHMED AN-NA'IM, HUMAN RIGHTS IN THE MUSLIM WORLD

3 Harv. Hum. Rts. J. 13 (1990)

Introduction

Historical formulations of Islamic religious law, commonly known as Shari'a, include a universal system of law and ethics and purport to regulate every aspect of public and private life. The power of Shari'a to regulate the behavior of Muslims derives from its moral and religious authority as well as the formal enforcement of its legal norms. As such, Shari'a influences individual and collective behavior in Muslim countries through its role in the socialization processes of such nations regardless of its status in their formal legal systems. For example, the status and rights of women in the Muslim world have always been significantly influenced by Shari'a, regardless of the degree of Islamization in public life. Of course, Shari'a is not the sole determinant of human behavior nor the only formative force behind social and political institutions in Muslim countries.

...

I conclude that human rights advocates in the Muslim world must work within the framework of Islam to be effective. They need not be confined, however, to the particular historical interpretations of Islam known as Shari'a. Muslims are obliged, as a matter of faith, to conduct their private and public affairs in accordance with the dictates of Islam, but there is room for legitimate disagreement over the precise nature of these dictates in the modern context. Religious texts, like all other texts, are open to a variety of interpretations. Human rights advocates in the Muslim world should struggle to have their interpretations of the relevant texts adopted as the new Islamic scriptural imperatives for the contemporary world.

A. Cultural Legitimacy for Human Rights

The basic premise of my approach is that human rights violations reflect the lack or weakness of cultural legitimacy of international standards in a society. Insofar as these standards are perceived to be alien to or at variance with the values and institutions of a people, they are unlikely to elicit commitment or compliance. While cultural legitimacy may not be the sole or even primary determinant of compliance with human rights standards, it is, in my view, an extremely significant one. Thus, the underlying causes of any lack or weakness of legitimacy of human rights standards must be addressed in order to enhance the promotion and protection of human rights in that society.

... This cultural illegitimacy, it is argued, derives from the historical conditions surrounding the creation of the particular human rights instruments. Most African and Asian countries did not participate in the formulation of the Universal Declaration of Human Rights because, as victims of colonization, they were not members of the United Nations. When they did participate in the formulation of subsequent instruments, they did so on the basis of an established framework and philosophical assumptions adopted in their absence. For example, the pre-existing framework and assumptions favored individual civil and political rights over collective solidarity rights, such as a right to development, an outcome which remains problematic today. Some authors have gone so far as to argue that inherent differences exist between the Western notion of human rights as reflected in the international instruments and non-Western notions of human dignity. In the Muslim world, for instance, there are obvious conflicts between Shari'a and certain human rights, especially of women and non-Muslims.

... In this discussion, I focus on the principles of legal equality and nondiscrimination contained in many human rights instruments. These principles relating to gender and religion are particularly problematic in the Muslim world.

...

II. Islam, Shari'a and Human Rights

...

A. The Development and Current Application of Shari'a

To the over nine hundred million Muslims of the world, the Qur'an is the literal and final word of God and Muhammad is the final Prophet. During his mission, from 610 A.D. to his death in 632 A.D., the Prophet elaborated on the meaning of the Qur'an and supplemented its rulings through his statements and actions. This body of information came to be known as Sunna. He also established the first Islamic state in Medina around 622 A.D. which emerged later as the ideal model of an Islamic state....

While the Qur'an was collected and recorded soon after the Prophet Muhammad's death, it took almost two centuries to collect, verify, and record the Sunna. Because it remained an oral tradition for a long time during a period of exceptional turmoil in Muslim history, some Sunna reports are still controversial in terms of both their authenticity and relationship to the Qur'an.

Because Shari'a is derived from Sunna as well as the Qur'an, its development as a comprehensive legal and ethical system had to await the collection and authentication of Sunna. Shari'a was not developed until the second and third centuries of Islam....

...

Shari'a is not a formally enacted legal code. It consists of a vast body of jurisprudence in which individual jurists express their views on the meaning of the Qur'an and Sunna and the legal implications of those views. Although most Muslims believe Shari'a to be a single logical whole, there is significant diversity of opinion not only among the various schools of thought, but also among the different jurists of a particular school....

Furthermore, Muslim jurists were primarily concerned with the formulation of principles of Shari'a in terms of moral duties sanctioned by religious consequences rather than with legal obligations and rights and specific temporal remedies. They categorized all fields of human activity as permissible or impermissible and recommended or reprehensible. In other words, Shari'a addresses the conscience of the individual Muslim, whether in a private, or public and official, capacity, and not the institutions and corporate entities of society and the state.

...

Whatever may have been the historical status of Shari'a as the legal system of Muslim countries, the scope of its application in the public domain has diminished significantly since the middle of the nineteenth century. Due to both internal factors and external influence, Shari'a principles had been replaced by European law governing commercial, criminal, and constitutional matters in almost all Muslim countries. Only family law and inheritance continued to be governed by Shari'a....

Recently, many Muslims have challenged the gradual weakening of Shari'a as the basis for their formal legal systems. Most Muslim countries have experienced mounting demands for the immediate application of Shari'a as the sole, or at least primary, legal system of the land. These movements have either succeeded in gaining complete control, as in Iran, or achieved significant success in having aspects of Shari'a introduced into the legal system, as in Pakistan and the Sudan. Governments of Muslim countries generally find it difficult to resist these demands out of fear of being condemned by their own populations as anti-Islamic. Therefore, it is likely that this so-called Islamic fundamentalism will achieve further successes in other Muslim countries.

The possibility of further Islamization may convince more people of the urgency of understanding and discussing the relationship between Shari'a and human rights, because Shari'a would have a direct impact on a wider range of human rights issues if it became the formal legal system of any country....

I believe that a modern version of Islamic law can and should be developed. Such a modern 'Shari'a' could be, in my view, entirely consistent with current standards of human rights. These views, however, are appreciated by only a tiny minority of contemporary Muslims. To the overwhelming majority of Muslims today, Shari'a is the sole valid interpretation of Islam, and as such *ought* to prevail over any human law or policy.

B. Shari'a and Human Rights

In this part, I illustrate with specific examples how Shari'a conflicts with international human rights standards....

...

The second example is the Shari'a law of apostasy. According to Shari'a, a Muslim who repudiates his faith in Islam, whether directly or indirectly, is guilty of a capital offense punishable by death. This aspect of Shari'a is in complete conflict with the fundamental human right of freedom of religion and conscience. The apostasy of a Muslim may be inferred by the court from the person's views or actions deemed by the court to contravene the basic tenets of Islam and therefore be tantamount to apostasy, regardless of the accused's personal belief that he or she is a Muslim.

The Shari'a law of apostasy can be used to restrict other human rights such as freedom of expression. A person may be liable to the death penalty for expressing views held by the authorities to contravene the official view of the tenets of Islam. Far from being an historical practice or a purely theoretical danger, this interpretation of the law of apostasy was applied in the Sudan as recently as 1985, when a Sudanese Muslim reformer was executed because the authorities deemed his views to be contrary to Islam.[2]

A third and final example of conflict between Shari'a and human rights relates to the status and rights of non-Muslims. Shari'a classifies the subjects of an Islamic state in terms of their religious beliefs: Muslims, *ahl al-Kitab* or believers in a divinely revealed scripture (mainly Christian and Jews), and unbelievers. In modern terms, Muslims are the only full citizens of an Islamic state, enjoying all the rights and freedoms granted by Shari'a and subject only to the limitations and restrictions imposed on women. *Ahl al-Kitab* are entitled to the status of *dhimma*, a special compact with the Muslim state which guarantees them security of persons and property and a degree of communal autonomy to practice their own religion and conduct their private affairs in accordance with their customs and laws. In exchange for these limited rights, *dhimmis* undertake to pay *jizya* or poll tax and submit to Muslim sovereignty and authority in all public affairs....

According to this scheme, non-Muslim subjects of an Islamic state can aspire only to the status of *dhimma*, under which they would suffer serious violations of their human rights. *Dhimmis* are not entitled to equality with Muslims. [Economic and family law illustrations omitted.]

...

IV. A Case Study: The Islamic Dimension of the Status of Women

...

[2] ... The Salman Rushdie affair illustrates the serious negative implications of the law of apostasy to literary and artistic expression. Mr Rushdie, a British national of Muslim background, published a novel entitled *The Satanic Verses*, in which irreverent reference is made to the Prophet of Islam, his wives, and leading companions. Many Muslim governments banned the book because their populations found the author's style and connotations extremely offensive. The late Imam Khomeini of Iran sentenced Rushdie to death *in absentia* without charge or trial....

The present focus on Muslim violations of the human rights of women does not mean that these are peculiar to the Muslim world.[3] As a Muslim, however, I am particularly concerned with the situation in the Muslim world and wish to contribute to its improvement.

The following discussion is organized in terms of the status and rights of Muslim women in the private sphere, particularly within the family, and in public fora, in relation to access to work and participation in public affairs. This classification is recommended for the Muslim context because the personal law aspects of Shari'a, family law and inheritance, have been applied much more consistently than the public law doctrines.[4] The status and rights of women in private life have always been significantly influenced by Shari'a regardless of the extent of Islamization of the public debate.

A. *Shari'a and the Human Rights of Women*

... The most important general principle of Shari'a influencing the status and rights of women is the notion of *qawama*. *Qawama* has its origin in verse 4:34 of the Qur'an: 'Men have *qawama* [guardianship and authority] over women because of the advantage they [men] have over them [women] and because they [men] spend their property in supporting them [women]'. According to Shari'a interpretations of this verse, men as a group are the guardians of and superior to women as a group, and the men of a particular family are the guardians of and superior to the women of that family.

... For example, Shari'a provides that women are disqualified from holding general public office, which involves the exercise of authority over men, because, in keeping with the verse 4:34 of the Qur'an, men are entitled to exercise authority over women and not the reverse.

Another general principle of Shari'a that has broad implications for the status and rights of Muslim women is the notion of *al-hijab*, the veil. This means more than requiring women to cover their bodies and faces in public. According to Shari' a interpretations of verses 24:31, 33:33,[5] 33:53, and 33:59[6] of the Qur'an, women are supposed to stay at home and not leave it except when required to by urgent necessity.

[3] It is difficult to distinguish between Islamic, or rather Shari'a, factors and extra-Shari'a actors affecting the status and rights of women. The fact that women's human rights are violated in all parts of the world suggests that there are universal social, economic, and political factors contributing to the persistence of this state of affairs. Nevertheless, the articulation and operation of these factors varies from one culture or context to the next. In particular, the rationalization of discrimination against the denial of equality for women is based on the values and customs of the particular society. In the Muslim world, these values and customs are supposed to be Islamic or at least consistent with the dictates of Islam. It is therefore useful to discuss the Islamic dimension of the status and rights of women.

[4] The private/public dichotomy, however, is an artificial distinction. The two spheres of life overlap and interact. The socialization and treatment of both men and women at home affect their role in public life and vice versa. While this classification can be used for analysis in the Muslim context, its limitations should be noted. It is advisable to look for both the private and public dimensions of a given Shari'a principle or rule rather than assume that it has only private or public implications.

[5] [O Consorts of the Prophet ...] And stay quietly in your houses, and make not a dazzling display, like that of the former Times of Ignorance; and establish regular prayer, and give regular charity; and obey God and His Apostle. And God only wishes to remove all abomination from you, ye Members of the Family, and to make you pure and spotless.

[6] O Prophet! Tell thy wives and daughters, and the believing women, that they should cast their outer garments over their persons (when abroad): that is most convenient, that they should be known (as such) and not molested. And God is Oft-Forgiving, Most Merciful.

When they are permitted to venture beyond the home, they must do so with their bodies and faces covered. *Al-hijab* tends to reinforce women's inability to hold public office and restricts their access to public life. They are not supposed to participate in public life, because they must not mix with men even in public places.

… In family law for example, men have the right to marry up to four wives and the power to exercise complete control over them during marriage, to the extent of punishing them for disobedience if the men deem that to be necessary.[7] In contrast, the co-wives are supposed to submit to their husband's will and endure his punishments. While a husband is entitled to divorce any of his wives at will, a wife is not entitled to a divorce, except by judicial order on very specific and limited grounds. Another private law feature of discrimination is found in the law of inheritance, where the general rule is that women are entitled to half the share of men.

In addition to their general inferiority under the principle of *qawama* and lack of access to public life as a consequence of the notion of *al-hijab*, women are subjected to further specific limitations in the public domain. For instance, in the administration of justice, Shari'a holds women to be incompetent witnesses in serious criminal cases, regardless of their individual character and knowledge of the facts. In civil cases where a woman's testimony is accepted, it takes two women to make a single witness. *Diya*, monetary compensation to be paid to victims of violent crimes or to their surviving kin, is less for female victims than it is for male victims.

… These overlapping and interacting principles and rules play an extremely significant role in the socialization of both women and men. Notions of women's inferiority are deeply embedded in the character and attitudes of both women and men from early childhood.

…

C. Muslim Women in Public Life

A similar and perhaps more drastic conflict exists between reformist and conservative trends in relation to the status and rights of women in the public domain. Unlike personal law matters, where Shari'a was never displaced by secular law, in most Muslim countries, constitutional, criminal, and other public law matters have come to be based on secular, mainly Western, legal concepts and institutions. Consequently, the struggle over Islamization of public law has been concerned with the re-establishment of Shari'a where it has been absent for decades, or at least since the creation of the modern Muslim nation states in the first half of the twentieth century. In terms of women's rights, the struggle shall determine whether women can keep the degree of equality and rights in public life they have achieved under secular constitutions and laws.

…

… Educated women and other modernist segments of society may not be able to articulate their vision of an Islamic state in terms of Shari'a, because aspects of Shari'a are incompatible with certain concepts and institutions which these groups

[7] Polygamy is based on verse 4:3 of the Qur'an. The husband's power to chastise his wife to the extent of beating her is based on verse 4:34 of the Qur'an.

take for granted, including the protection of all human rights. To the extent that efforts for the protection and promotion of human rights in the Muslim world must take into account the Islamic dimension of the political and sociological situation in Muslim countries, a modernist conception of Islam is needed.

V. Islamic Reform and Human Rights

...

Islamic reform needs must be based on the Qur'an and Sunna, the primary sources of Islam. Although Muslims believe that the Qur'an is the literal and final word of God, and Sunna are the traditions of his final Prophet, they also appreciate that these sources have to be understood and applied through human interpretation and action....

A. An Adequate Reform Methodology

... The basic premise of my position, based on the work of the late Sudanese Muslim reformer *Ustadh* Mahmoud Mohamed Taha, is that the Shari'a reflects a historically-conditioned interpretation of Islamic scriptures in the sense that the founding jurists had to understand those sources in accordance with their own social, economic, and political circumstances. In relation to the status and rights of women, for example, equality between men and women in the eighth and ninth centuries in the Middle East, or anywhere else at the time, would have been inconceivable and impracticable. It was therefore natural and indeed inevitable that Muslim jurists would understand the relevant texts of the Qur'an and Sunna as confirming rather than repudiating the realities of the day.

In interpreting the primary sources of Islam in their historical context, the founding jurists of Shari'a tended not only to understand the Qur'an and Sunna as confirming existing social attitudes and institutions, but also to emphasize certain texts and 'enact' them into Shari'a while de-emphasizing other texts or interpreting them in ways consistent with what they believed to be the intent and purpose of the sources. Working with the same primary sources, modern Muslim jurists might shift emphasis from one class of texts to the other, and interpret the previously enacted texts in ways consistent with a new understanding of what is believed to be the intent and purpose of the sources. This new understanding would be informed by contemporary social, economic, and political circumstances in the same way that the 'old' understanding on which Shari'a jurists acted was informed by the then prevailing circumstances. The new understanding would qualify for Islamic legitimacy, in my view, if it is based on specific texts in opposing the application of other texts, and can be shown to be in accordance with the Qur'an and Sunna as a whole.

For example, the general principle of *qawama*, the guardianship and authority of men over women under Shari'a, is based on verse 4:34 of the Qur'an.

... This verse presents *qawama* as a consequence of two conditions: men's advantage over and financial support of women. The fact that men are generally physically stronger than most women is not relevant in modern times where the rule of law prevails over physical might. Moreover, modern circumstances are making the economic independence of women from men more readily realized and appreciated. In other words, neither of the conditions — advantages of physical might or earning power — set by verse 4:34 as the justification for the *qawama* of men over women is tenable today.

The fundamental position of the modern human rights movement is that all human beings are equal in worth and dignity, regardless of gender, religion, or race. This position can be substantiated by the Qur'an and other Islamic sources as understood under the radically transformed circumstances of today. For example, in numerous verses the Qur'an speaks of honor and dignity for 'humankind' and 'children of Adam', without distinction as to race, color, gender, or religion. By drawing on those sources and being willing to set aside archaic and dated interpretations of other sources, such as the one previously given to verse 4:34 of the Qur'an, we can provide Islamic legitimacy for the full range of human rights for women.

Similarly, numerous verses of the Qur'an provide for freedom of choice and non-compulsion in religious belief and conscience.[8] These verses have been either de-emphasized as having been 'overruled' by other verses which were understood to legitimize coercion, or 'interpreted' in ways which permitted such coercion. For example, verse 9:29 of the Qur'an was taken as the foundation of the whole system of *dhimma*, and its consequent discrimination against non-Muslims. Relying on those verses which extoll freedom of religion rather than those that legitimize religious coercion, one can argue now that the *dhimma* system should no longer be part of Islamic law and that complete equality should be assured regardless of religion or belief. The same argument can be used to abolish all negative legal consequences of apostasy as inconsistent with the Islamic principle of freedom of religion. [Discussion omitted of mechanisms and methods within Islam for development and reform.]

... The ultimate test of legitimacy and efficacy is, of course, acceptance and implementation by Muslims throughout the world.

B. *Prospects for Acceptance and Likely Impact of the Proposed Reform*

...

... Governments of Muslim countries, like many other governments, formally subscribe to international human rights instruments because, in my view, they find the human rights idea an important legitimizing force both at home and abroad ...

Nevertheless, the proposed reform will probably be resisted because it challenges the vested interests of powerful forces in the Muslim world and may upset male-dominated traditional political and social institutions. These forces probably will try to restrict opportunities for a genuine consideration of this reform methodology....

Consequently, the acceptance and implementation of this reform methodology will involve a political struggle within Muslim nations as part of a larger general struggle for human rights. I would recommend this proposal to participants in that struggle who champion the cause of justice and equality for women and

[8] See, for example, verse 2:256 of the Qur'an which provides: 'Let there be no compulsion in religion: Truth stands out clear from error ...' In verse 18:29 God instructs the Prophet: 'Say, the Truth is from your Lord. Let him who will, believe, and let him who will, reject [it]'.

non-Muslims, and freedom of belief and expression in the Muslim world. Given the extreme importance of Islamic legitimacy in Muslim societies, I urge human rights advocates to claim the Islamic platform and not concede it to the traditionalist and fundamentalist forces in their societies. I would also invite outside supporters of Muslim human rights advocates to express their support with due sensitivity and genuine concern for Islamic legitimacy in the Muslim world.

...

WOMEN AND ISLAM: A DEBATE WITH HUMAN RIGHTS WATCH

New York Review of Books, 22 Mar. 2012

To Kenneth Roth:

In your Introduction to Human Rights Watch's World Report 2012, "Time to Abandon the Autocrats and Embrace Rights," you urge support for the newly elected governments that have brought the Muslim Brotherhood to power in Tunisia and Egypt....

You say, "It is important to nurture the rights-respecting elements of political Islam while standing firm against repression in its name," but you fail to call for the most basic guarantee of rights — the separation of religion from the state. Salafi mobs have caned women in Tunisian cafes and Egyptian shops; attacked churches in Egypt; taken over whole villages in Tunisia and shut down Manouba University for two months in an effort to exert social pressure on veiling. And while "moderate Islamist" leaders say they will protect the rights of women (if not gays), they have done very little to bring these mobs under control. You, however, are so unconcerned with the rights of women, gays, and religious minorities that you mention them only once, as follows: "Many Islamic parties have indeed embraced disturbing positions that would subjugate the rights of women and restrict religious, personal, and political freedoms. But so have many of the autocratic regimes that the West props up." Are we really going to set the bar that low? This is the voice of an apologist, not a senior human rights advocate.

Nor do you point to the one of the clearest threats to rights — particularly to women and religious and sexual minorities — the threat to introduce so-called "shari'a law." It is simply not good enough to say we do not know what kind of Islamic law, if any, will result, when it is already clear that freedom of expression and freedom of religion — not to mention the choice not to veil — are under threat.... [R] ather than examine the record of Muslim fundamentalists in the West, you keep demanding that Western governments "engage."

...

Like you, we support calls to dismantle the security state and to promote the rule of law. But we do not see that one set of autocratic structures should be replaced by another which claims divine sanction. And while the overthrow of repressive governments was a victory and free elections are, in principle, a step towards democracy, shouldn't the leader of a prominent human rights organization be supporting popular calls to prevent backlash and safeguard fundamental rights? In other words, rather than advocating strategic support for parties who may use elections to halt the call for continuing change and attack basic rights, shouldn't you support the voices for both liberty and equality that are arguing that the revolutions must continue?

...

[Signed]

Meredith Tax, Centre for Secular Space; Sultana Kamal, Ain O Salish Kendra, Bangladesh; Fatou Sow, Women Living Under Muslim Laws; Faizun Zackariya, Muslim Women's Research and Action Front, Sri Lanka; and thirteen other women's rights organizations around the world....

Human Rights Watch replies:

In the [report] Kenneth Roth wrote that Western governments cannot credibly maintain a commitment to democracy if they reject electoral results when an Islamic party does well. That was the hypocritical stance of the West when, for example, it acquiesced in the Algerian military's interruption of free elections that the Islamist Salvation Front was poised to win..., or when President George W. Bush cut short his "democracy agenda" after Hamas won Palestinian elections in 2006 and the Muslim Brotherhood did better than expected in Egyptian parliamentary elections in 2005.

Western governments should reject this inconsistent and unprincipled approach to democracy [and] come to terms with the rise of Islamic political parties and press them to respect rights. As rights activists, we are acutely aware of the possible tension between the right to choose one's leaders and the rights of potentially disfavored groups such as women, gays and lesbians, and religious minorities. Anyone familiar with the history of Iran or Afghanistan knows the serious risks involved. However, in the two Arab Spring nations that have had free and fair elections so far, a solid majority voted for socially conservative political parties in Egypt, and a solid plurality did so in Tunisia. The sole democratic option is to accept the results of those elections and to press the governments that emerge to respect the rights of all rather than to ostracize these governments from the outset. As Roth wrote:

> ... It is important to nurture the rights-respecting elements of political Islam while standing firm against repression in its name. So long as freely elected governments respect basic rights, they merit presumptive international support, regardless of their political or religious complexion.

...

The people who signed the above letter... insist on "separation of religion from the state," presented as "the most basic guarantee of rights." But that is obviously not what the people of Egypt and Tunisia, when given a choice, voted for. So what exactly do the letter writers propose? A military coup should not be recommended lightly. Taking the position that adherence to democratic principles can be achieved only when non-Islamic parties prevail, as Bush did, is a disaster for those principles.

Promoting tolerance of women and gays by way of intolerance for Islam... does not seem a productive approach.

Of course, any electoral choice must be constrained by international human rights law, but there is no internationally recognized right to separate religion from the state—a separation mandated by certain national constitutions, such as those of the United States or France, but not others, such as Norway or the United Kingdom.

QUESTIONS

1. Cowan argues that while the foremost task of anthropologists is essentially descriptive, the empirical can only be grasped 'through the terms of a prior social theory'. In addition, anthropologists have a 'pronounced ethical streak' reflecting their 'collective self-image as advocates of the less powerful, [their] egalitarian commitments, and the political vision implicit in any critical analytical approach.'[9] What conclusions would you draw as to the appropriate relationship between anthropologists and the human rights regime?

2. An-Na'im suggests an approach to the questions of how to understand divergences among cultures with respect to human rights issues and how to go about finding common ground. How would you describe that approach? Exogenous, endogenous, some mix? Does it appear helpful in resolving contemporary disputes over, say, gender discrimination or capital punishment? Do Merry's observations about culture and modes of cultural change support or call into question An-Na'im's project?

3. After reading the exchange between Human Rights Watch and the Centre for Secular Space, how would you respond to proposals to support a coalition government in Afghanistan involving the Taliban, a group that had an abysmal record on women's rights when it was in power prior to 2002?

NOTE

Consider the following observations on cultural relativism in the human rights context:

Rosalyn Higgins, *Problems and Process: International Law and How We Use It* (1994), at 96:

> It is sometimes suggested that there can be no fully universal concept of human rights, for it is necessary to take into account the diverse cultures and political systems of the world. In my view this is a point advanced mostly by states, and by liberal scholars anxious not to impose the Western view of things on others. It is rarely advanced by the oppressed, who are only too anxious to benefit from perceived universal standards. The non-universal, relativist view of human rights is in fact a very state-centred view and loses sight of the fact that human rights are

[9] J. F. Cowan, 'Culture and Rights after *Culture and Rights*', 108 Am. Anthropologist 9 (2006), at 11.

human rights and not dependent on the fact that states, or groupings of states, may behave differently from each other so far as their politics, economic policy, and culture are concerned. I believe, profoundly, in the universality of the human spirit. Individuals everywhere want the same essential things: to have sufficient food and shelter; to be able to speak freely; to practise their own religion or to abstain from religious belief; to feel that their person is not threatened by the state; to know that they will not be tortured, or detained without charge, and that, if charged, they will have a fair trial. I believe there is nothing in these aspirations that is dependent upon culture, or religion, or stage of development. They are as keenly felt by the African tribesman as by the European city-dweller, by the inhabitant of a Latin American shanty-town as by the resident of a Manhattan apartment.

Louise Arbour, UN High Commissioner for Human Rights, statement to the UN Commission on Human Rights, 14 March 2005:

I am ... concerned that we have unduly embroiled our normative discourse in unnecessary clashes of vision, creating competing images, each incomplete and ineffective without the addition of the other. Are human rights universal or culturally specific? Are they collectively or individually held? Should we promote them, or protect them? Which is the more effective: technical cooperation or naming and shaming; country analysis or thematic debates? Which comes first: peace or justice; economic, social and cultural rights, or civil and political rights; development or democracy?

Such questions serve, in practice, as little more than a series of diversions to the real task in hand. They become the theoretical playground within which we demonstrate our irrelevance and justify our inaction, whether than inaction is borne of indifference, shrewd calculation, or despair.

Judge Bonello, Concurring Opinion in *Al-Skeini v. United Kingdom* (Eur. Ct. of Hum. Rts., Application No. 55721/07, Grand Chamber, 7 July 2011, p. 914, *infra*), which concerned the issue of whether UK obligations under the European Convention on Human Rights applied to certain actions of its troops in Iraq:

37. I confess to be quite unimpressed by the pleadings of the United Kingdom Government to the effect that exporting the European Convention on Human Rights to Iraq would have amounted to "human rights imperialism". It ill behoves a State that imposed its military imperialism over another sovereign State without the frailest imprimatur from the international community, to resent the charge of having exported human rights imperialism to the vanquished enemy. It is like wearing with conceit your badge of international law banditry, but then recoiling in shock at being suspected of human rights promotion.

38. Personally, I would have respected better these virginal blushes of some statesmen had they worn them the other way round. Being bountiful with military imperialism but bashful of the stigma of human rights imperialism, sounds to me like not resisting sufficiently the urge to frequent the lower neighbourhoods of political inconstancy. For my part, I believe that those who export war ought to see to the parallel export of guarantees against the atrocities of war. And then, if necessary, bear with some fortitude the opprobrium of being labelled human rights imperialists.

ADDITIONAL READING

A.-B. Preis, 'Human Rights as Cultural Practice: An Anthropological Critique', 18 Hum. Rts. Q. 286 (1996); M. Goodale, *Surrendering to Utopia: An Anthropology of Human Rights* (2009); M. Goodale & S. Engle Merry (eds.), *The Practice of Human Rights: Tracking Law Between the Global and the Local* (2007); E. Cotran & A. Sherif (eds.), *Democracy, The Rule of Law and Islam* (1999); S. Waltz, 'Universal Human Rights: The Contribution of Muslim States', 26 Hum. Rts. Q. 799 (2004); A. Sajó (ed.), *Human Rights with Modesty: The Problem of Universalism* (2004); W. Twining, *General Jurisprudence: Understanding Law from a Global Perspective* (2009).

B. DISSONANCE AND CONFLICT: ILLUSTRATIONS

Against the background of Chapters 6 and 7(A), with their examination of rights discourse and presentation of different perspectives on universalism and cultural relativism, this Part explores four topics that are among the human rights issues now in contention and active debate among and within countries.

In the illustrations below, two different phenomena become central to the debate. (1) The asserted universal norm itself may be challenged, perhaps on the ground that it lacks universal validity, or that it conflicts with ultimate religious commands, or that it violates long-standing tradition that assures cultural integrity and survival. That is, the legitimacy or validity of the human rights norm is itself challenged. In such respects, this chapter's illustrations further develop the theme of cultural relativism. (2) Sometimes related to cultural relativism and sometimes distinct, the second phenomenon involves a conflict among rights that are all recognized to some extent in the leading human rights instruments. The dispute is formally internal to the human rights corpus. What, for example, are the respective boundaries of rights that in given contexts squarely conflict with each other? Freedom of religious belief and practice may conflict with non-discrimination norms; freedom of speech may conflict with the protection of minority groups. As materials in Chapter 6(A) made clear, such types of conflict are endemic to rights discourse, as they are to law in general.

In several of the following studies, the issues have to do with family, gender and religion — interrelated topics that have characterized much discussion of the last decade about cultural relativism and that often involve conflicting rights. Thus the studies examine gender and family in relation to a state's or ethnic group's internal custom, or in relation to religion.

The problems discussed in this chapter have become acute within many developing countries. In recent decades, such countries experienced strong external and internal pressures to rethink and revise, sometimes radically, their traditional beliefs and practices. The relentless assault of the developed world on other cultures, the penetration of those cultures by trade, investment, high-tech media and tourism, as well as the universalization of ideas and values like human rights, have launched transformative processes that are often referred to under the broad rubric of globalization. The challenge to a state or region's traditional ways and to other state practices that depart from the universal human rights instruments increasingly comes from internal groups as well as from international advocates and organizations. The upheavals in Arab countries following the Arab Spring provide but one striking illustration in that regard. Women played an important part in the demonstrations that brought down the Mubarak government, but it has been estimated that 90 per cent of married women in Egypt have been subjected to female genital mutilation. Virginity tests were applied to women arrested in the pro-democracy demonstrations, and the Egyptian Criminal Code (Section 60) states that 'no punitive damages can be obtained if the woman has been beaten by her husband with good intentions'.[10]

1. GENDER

The potential for conflict in a large number of states between the objectives of several human rights treaties, on the one hand, and customary laws and practices as well as religious beliefs, on the other, has become a salient contemporary concern. Gender-related issues are here prominent, for many traditional norms and much local custom that retain power and influence today impose different roles and duties on men and women. To some extent, such problems stem from the increasing power and prominence in recent years of fundamentalist religious groups, many of which actively oppose the transformative impetus of human rights with respect to traditional gender roles.

Customary laws and practices may conflict with prohibitions in the text of the ICCPR and CEDAW or in the action taken by the bodies created by these treaties. Recall Articles 2(f) and 5(a) of CEDAW that require states to take all appropriate measures to modify or abolish customs, practices and social and cultural patterns of conduct that constitute discrimination or that are based on the idea of inferiority or on stereotyped roles for women.

This section begins with a reading that explores some problems in developing a feminist perspective on human rights related to gender, problems that bear on the following case studies. It then explores a practice that is variously referred to, with strikingly different political and moral innuendo and sometimes agendas, as female circumcision *or* female genital mutilation.

TRACY HIGGINS, ANTI-ESSENTIALISM, RELATIVISM, AND HUMAN RIGHTS

19 Harvard Women's L. J. 89 (1996)

During the Fourth United Nations World Conference on Women [in 1995], cultural differences among women presented a series of practical and theoretical problems.

[10] M. Eltahawy, 'Why Do They Hate Us?', Foreign Policy, May/June 2012.

The practical problems arose out of the enormous task of negotiating among a large group of people a single, albeit complex, document that would set an agenda for addressing the problems of women globally. Differences in culture, language, religion, and education presented complications at every stage of the process. As a theoretical matter, such differences presented a less immediate but in some ways more difficult and persistent problem: In the face of profound cultural differences among women, how can feminists maintain a global political movement yet avoid charges of cultural imperialism?

This theoretical dilemma has become a serious political hurdle for global feminism as the challenge of cultural relativism permeates the politics of any discussion of women's rights on the international stage. For example, at the 1994 United Nations Population Conference in Cairo, the Vatican joined with several Muslim governments to condemn what they viewed as the imposition of Western norms of sexual license and individual autonomy on the rest of the world....

Feminist responses to this charge are complicated and sometimes conflicting. On the one hand, feminists note that culture and religion are often cited as justifications for denying women a range of basic rights, including the right to travel, rights in marriage and divorce, the right to own property, even the right to be protected by the criminal law on an equal basis with men. Women have much to lose, therefore, in any movement away from a universal standard of human rights in favor of deference to culture. On the other hand, feminists acknowledge that feminism itself is grounded in the importance of participation, of listening to and accounting for the particular experiences of women, especially those on the margins of power. Indeed, much feminist criticism of traditional human rights approaches has focused on the tendency of international policymakers to exclude women's experiences and women's voices. Thus, the claim that Western concepts of women's equality are exclusionary or imperialist strikes at the heart of one of feminism's central commitments — respect for difference.

In short, both the move to expand universal human rights to include those rights central to women's condition and the move toward a relativist view of human rights are consistent with and informed by feminist theory. Indeed, the tension between them reflects a tension within feminism itself, between describing women's experience collectively as a basis for political action and respecting differences among women. Addressing this tension, this Article endeavors to sort out the degree to which feminism, by virtue of its own commitments, must take cultural defenses seriously, particularly when articulated by women themselves.

...

Despite the general consensus [over the universality of human rights that was reflected in the Universal Declaration], differences have persisted over the scope and priorities of the international human rights agenda, differences that are translated with surprising frequency into the rhetoric of universality versus cultural relativism, imperialism versus self-determination. Notwithstanding the language of universality, the question remains: To what extent may a state depart from international norms in the name of culture? ...

...

The influence of the universalist/relativist divide on the politics of human rights is perhaps nowhere more evident than in debates over women's rights as human rights. Cultural relativists have targeted feminism itself as a product of Western ideology and global feminism as a form of Western imperialism. Ironically, cultural relativists have accused feminist human rights activists of imposing Western standards on non-Western cultures in much the same way that feminists have criticized states for imposing male-defined norms on women. The complexity of this debate has sown confusion among feminist human rights activists, undermining the effectiveness of the global feminist movement...

[Higgins considers the criticism of some feminists that the movement in general has been characterized by 'essentialism' — that is, the belief that many categories (like gender) or groups (like women) have a real, true essence, and thus fixed properties that define what they are. Essentialism in this sense is likely to be linked to a universalist position.]

Much incisive and insightful criticism, particularly by feminists of color, has revealed that treating gender difference as the primary concern of feminism has had the effect of reinforcing gendered categories and collapsing differences among women. These critics have argued convincingly that early feminist descriptions of women's experience focused on white, middle-class, educated, heterosexual women. Consequently, the political priorities of the women's movement in the West (e.g., equal access to education and employment, abortion rights) have reflected the most urgent concerns of a relatively more powerful group of women...Accused of essentialism, feminists who theorized a commonality among women were criticized for committing the dual sin of reinforcing patriarchal assumptions about women as a group and marginalizing some women along the lines of race, class, and sexual orientation.

Despite its theoretical and political vulnerabilities, the practical appeal of essentialism, like the appeal of universalism, persists. Essentialist assumptions offer the promise of uniting women in a way that transcends or precedes politics...

Much feminist activism on the international level has been premised on two assumptions, both of which may be characterized as essentialist: first, that women share types of experiences and are oppressed in particular ways as women; and second, that these experiences are often different than those of men...[F]eminist progress in reshaping the scope of the international human rights agenda stands as an important example of the power of organizing around assumptions of commonality.

...

[Higgins explores two views about culture and coercion that are relevant to a response by feminists who are committed to universalism to the criticisms and challenge of cultural relativists and anti-essentialists. The first view has to do with the tendency in some strands of cultural relativism to 'essentialize' the local culture itself and in the process to obscure coercion.]

Feminists have questioned arguments based on a simple assertion of cultural integrity for several reasons. First, cultural relativists may inadequately attend to the degree to which power relationships within the culture itself constrain the ability of individuals to renegotiate cultural norms. Yet, this inattention is inconsistent with a concern about coercion. The relativist cannot criticize Western imperialism and at the same time ignore non-Western states' selective use of the defense of culture in the service of state power. The risk of such intra-cultural coercion seems especially great when that selective invocation of culture has differential effects on groups within the state such as minority ethnic or racial groups or women.

Second, cultural relativist arguments may oversimplify the complexity and fluidity of culture by treating culture as monolithic and moral norms within a particular culture as readily ascertainable. Yet, a single, inward glance at Western culture reveals the absurdity of this assumption. The multiplicity of beliefs in the United States (or even within a single community or family) about the legitimacy of abortion or the role of women in the family illustrates the complexity of translating imperfectly shared assumptions into evaluative standards. Such oversimplification seems inconsistent with the very premises of cultural relativism. Indeed, cultural relativists' tendency to describe differences in terms of simple opposition — Western versus non-Western — without exploring how specific cultural practices are constituted and justified 'essentializes' culture itself.

Treating culture as monolithic fails to respect relevant intra-cultural differences just as the assumption of the universality of human rights standards fails to respect cross-cultural differences. Cultural differences that may be relevant to assessing human rights claims are neither uniform nor static. Rather, they are constantly created, challenged, and renegotiated by individuals living within inevitably overlapping cultural communities.

This oversimplification of culture may lead relativists to accept too readily a cultural defense articulated by state actors or other elites on the international level, actors that tend not to be women. Yet, it seems unlikely that a cultural defense offered by the state will adequately reflect the dynamic, evolving, and possibly conflicting cultural concerns of its citizens.

Given the complexity and multiplicity of culture, the ability or inclination of heads of state to identify and translate cultural practices into specific defenses against the imposition of Western human rights norms is questionable. Feminists in particular have cited example after example in which culture has been selectively and perhaps cynically invoked to justify oppressive practices.

...

[The second view about culture and coercion raises the question of the role of private ordering in coercion.]

In contrast to cultural relativists and liberal pluralists, feminist anti-essentialists are centrally concerned with the interplay between culture and self, exploring ways in which culture constructs gendered individuals.... [F]eminism emphasizes the role of private power. The most important premise of this feminist view is that the sex/gender system is substantially a product of culture rather than divine will, human biology or natural selection. Implicit in this assumption is the claim that cultural norms — language, law, myth, custom — are not merely products of human will and action but also define and limit the possibilities for human identity.

Connected with this view of cultural limitations on human subjectivity is the notion that cultural norms function as a source of power and control within modern society. Consistent with this recognition, many feminists have rejected a theory of power that posits monolithic control held by a coherent or unified sovereign. Yet, it is precisely this model of power that traditional human rights standards are designed to regulate and to which cultural relativists often defer when exercised within cultural boundaries. In contrast, feminists... have emphasized the degree to which power is exercised both from above, by sovereigns, and within concrete social interactions and relationships — in short, through culture. For feminists, culture itself becomes a source of control and a site of resistance, a form of power that feminist human rights activists must engage directly along with more traditional public and private forms.

...

Conclusion

Confronted with the challenge of cultural relativism, feminism faces divergent paths, neither of which seems to lead out of the woods of patriarchy. The first path, leading to simple tolerance of cultural difference, is too broad. To follow it would require feminists to ignore pervasive limits on women's freedom in the name of an autonomy that exists for women in theory only.

The other path, leading to objective condemnation of cultural practices, is too narrow. To follow it would require feminists to dismiss the culturally distinct experiences of women as false consciousness. Yet to forge an alternative path is difficult, requiring feminists to confront the risks inherent in global strategies for change.

Building upon women's shared experiences inevitably entails a risk of misdescription, or worse, cooptation but contains the promise of transforming and radicalizing women's understanding of their own condition. Emphasizing difference threatens to splinter women politically, undermining hard-won progress, but may simultaneously uncover new possibilities for re-creating gender relations. Forging a combined strategy that respects both commonality and difference requires feminists to acknowledge that we cannot eliminate the risk of coercion altogether, but the risk of inaction is also ever present.

VIEWS OF COMMENTATORS ABOUT FEMALE GENITAL MUTILATION

World Health Organization, Fact Sheet No. 241 (2012)

...

Female genital mutilation (FGM) comprises all procedures that involve partial or total removal of the external female genitalia, or other injury to the female genital organs for non-medical reasons.

The practice is mostly carried out by traditional circumcisers, who often play other central roles in communities, such as attending childbirths. However, more than 18% of all FGM is performed by health care providers, and this trend is increasing.

FGM is recognized internationally as a violation of the human rights of girls and women. It reflects deep-rooted inequality between the sexes, and constitutes an extreme form of discrimination against women. It is nearly always carried out on minors and is a violation of the rights of children. The practice also violates a person's rights to health, security and physical integrity, the right to be free from torture and cruel, inhuman or degrading treatment, and the right to life when the procedure results in death.

Procedures

Female genital mutilation is classified into four major types.

1. Clitoridectomy: partial or total removal of the clitoris... and, in very rare cases, only the prepuce....
2. Excision: partial or total removal of the clitoris and the labia minora, with or without excision of the labia majora....
3. Infibulation: narrowing of the vaginal opening through the creation of a covering seal....
4. Other: all other harmful procedures to the female genitalia for non-medical purposes, e.g. pricking, piercing, incising, scraping and cauterizing the genital area.

No health benefits, only harm

FGM has no health benefits, and it harms girls and women in many ways. It involves removing and damaging healthy and normal female genital tissue, and interferes with the natural functions of girls' and women's bodies.

Immediate complications can include severe pain, shock, haemorrhage (bleeding), tetanus or sepsis (bacterial infection), urine retention, open sores in the genital region and injury to nearby genital tissue.

Long-term consequences can include:

- recurrent bladder and urinary tract infections;
- cysts;
- infertility;
- an increased risk of childbirth complications and newborn deaths;
- the need for later surgeries. For example, the FGM procedure that seals or narrows a vaginal opening (type 3 above) needs to be cut open later to allow for sexual intercourse and childbirth. Sometimes it is stitched again several times, including after childbirth, hence the woman goes through repeated opening and closing procedures, further increasing and repeated both immediate and long-term risks.

Who is at risk?

Procedures are mostly carried out on young girls sometime between infancy and age 15, and occasionally on adult women. In Africa, about three million girls are at risk for FGM annually.

About 140 million girls and women worldwide are living with the consequences of FGM. In Africa, about 92 million girls age 10 years and above are estimated to have undergone FGM.

The practice is most common in the western, eastern, and north-eastern regions of Africa, in some countries in Asia and the Middle East, and among migrants from these areas.

Cultural, religious and social causes

The causes of female genital mutilation include a mix of cultural, religious and social factors within families and communities.

- Where FGM is a social convention, the social pressure to conform to what others do and have been doing is a strong motivation to perpetuate the practice.
- FGM is often considered a necessary part of raising a girl properly, and a way to prepare her for adulthood and marriage.
- FGM is often motivated by beliefs about what is considered proper sexual behaviour, linking procedures to premarital virginity and marital fidelity.
- FGM is in many communities believed to reduce a woman's libido and therefore believed to help her resist "illicit" sexual acts. When a vaginal opening is covered or narrowed (type 3 above), the fear of the pain of opening it, and the fear that this will be found out, is expected to further discourage "illicit" sexual intercourse among women with this type of FGM.
- FGM is associated with cultural ideals of femininity and modesty, which include the notion that girls are "clean" and "beautiful" after removal of body parts that are considered "male" or "unclean".
- Though no religious scripts prescribe the practice, practitioners often believe the practice has religious support.
- Religious leaders take varying positions with regard to FGM: some promote it, some consider it irrelevant to religion, and others contribute to its elimination.
- Local structures of power and authority, such as community leaders, religious leaders, circumcisers, and even some medical personnel can contribute to upholding the practice.
- In most societies, FGM is considered a cultural tradition, which is often used as an argument for its continuation.
- In some societies, recent adoption of the practice is linked to copying the traditions of neighbouring groups. Sometimes it has started as part of a wider religious or traditional revival movement.
- In some societies, FGM is practised by new groups when they move into areas where the local population practice FGM.

...

PLAN, Tradition and Rights: Female Genital Cutting in West Africa (2006), at www.crin.org/resources/infodetail.asp?id=11060

...

Laws against Female Genital Cutting in West Africa

In November 2005, the Republic of Togo became the 15th Member State of the African Union to ratify the 2003 Protocol to the African Charter on Human and Peoples' Rights on the Rights of Women in Africa, commonly known as the Maputo Protocol. This means that the Protocol is now in force, and all African countries are obliged to pass legislation prohibiting excision. Legislation prohibiting female genital cutting already exists in most West African countries.... However, with the exception of Burkina Faso, prosecutions under the laws are rare. In Guinea, for example, almost all girls are excised, yet there has never been a court case.

...

The practice of excision is severely sanctioned in Burkina Faso since 1996.... The law against female genital cutting is applied rigorously. Between 1996 and 2005 more than 400 convictions have been recorded. However, the application of the law is not the only strategy pursued by the State. The Government has conducted public information campaigns about excision. Members of the police and the army have been trained to intervene in support of the law. The topic of excision is integrated in school curricula. Women suffering from complications of female genital cutting are treated free of charge in public health care facilities. A telephone hotline has been set up to help the denunciation of planned excisions. It receives approximately 150 calls a year. The Government and civil society actions against excision appear to be effective. The number of girls being excised is falling rapidly....

The Complex Dynamics of Female Genital Cutting

... The underlying dynamics of excision in West Africa are complex. They are linked to social, cultural, political and developmental issues in the region.

... [A] large proportion of the population practicing excision is illiterate and lives below the line of poverty. National public education campaigns rarely reach these people, and when they do they are not understood....

Talking about genital organs is a sensitive and uncomfortable subject in all cultures. In addition, the subject of female genital cutting is considered taboo in many West African societies. It is only discussed under specific circumstances by selected members of the community.... [I]n communities where the practice of excision is strongly supported by local opinion leaders, campaigners against female genital cutting may be afraid to speak out, fearing for their reputation or even their lives.

The most commonly heard argument in favour of continuing the practice of female genital cutting is: "It is a tradition that we have found with our ancestors". What is hiding behind this statement?...Excision is often associated with ethnic identity in West Africa. The practice is a heritage of the ancestors and a source of pride. It is understandable that communities react with hostility when outsiders criticise practices linked to their ethnic identity. Traditions are maintained to preserve values. These values allow the individual to be socially accepted. They stand for dignity, security, and a source of identity within the community....

Campaigners against female genital cutting cannot ignore the conflict between human rights and societal norms. Clearly, girls have the right to be protected from harm and the right to have an intact body. But they also have a need to get married and to be accepted members of their community. This conflict needs to be resolved before there can be progress towards the abandonment of female genital cutting.

…

PLAN'S Work on Female Genital Cutting in West Africa

For the communities who practice excision, the Government and the international organisations are external actors. Engagement of foreign anti-excision activists has often done more harm than good. In some communities it has created the prejudice that the abandonment of excision is a "project of white people", an attempt to destroy African culture….

…

An acceptable and frequently used door opener is to start a discussion about the health risks and long-term reproductive health complications of excision. This information is usually of interest to all community members. It is, however, important not to become stuck in the discussion at this point. Information about the risks does not prevent people from excising their daughters. It may lead to an increasing medicalisation of the practice. But tradition and social conformism are much stronger behavioural motivators than information about adverse health outcomes….

…

The abandonment of female genital cutting is not a priority for communities; it is a priority for development agencies. Community members become easily annoyed when a development organisation appears to have no concern for their daily problems and insists to speak only about excision…. In order to be effective, efforts to promote the abandonment of excision have to be integrated into a development program that is consistent with the needs and demands articulated by the community. This can be an education program, a micro-finance program, a health program or any other program that is seen as a priority….

…

Men are intimately involved in the issue of female genital cutting. In many communities they play a major role in preserving the practice. But the PLAN field studies also found that sometimes men are most interested in abandoning excision because of the burden of having to pay for the ceremony. This points to a common error of anti-excision activists to "feminise" the issue. Female genital cutting is not a "women's problem", it is a gender and a child protection issue that affects the whole community.

…

UNICEF, Female Genital Mutilation/Cutting: A Statistical Exploration (2005)

…

VIII. Conclusions and Recommendations

In its many and complex cultural meanings, FGM/C is a long-standing tradition that has become inseparable from ethnic and social identity among many groups.

As stated by the International Conference on Population and Development, "For women it is not only a painful ordeal but a means of social bargaining and negotiation; for societies it is a collective identity marker — a status symbol in the fullest sense — as well as a creator of cohesion."

The following summarizes five essential points resulting from this statistical analysis.

FGM/C prevalence rates are slowly declining in some countries. Evidence of change can be obtained by comparing the experiences of different age cohorts within a given country. The most recent survey data indicate consistently, for all countries, that women aged 15–19 are less likely to have been circumcised than women in the older age groups. In countries with high prevalence rates (particularly in Egypt, Guinea, Mali and Sudan), the difference between the 15–19 and 20–24 age cohorts is less than 1 per cent. Nevertheless, it is believed to indicate the beginning of change.

Attitudes towards FGM/C are slowly changing as more and more women oppose its continuation. In almost all countries that have conducted more than one survey during the past decade, data indicate that opposition to the practice is increasing. These results are reinforced by the fact that support for the discontinuation of the practice is particularly high among younger women. As FGM/C is deeply ingrained in the social fabric, and in most countries has been practised for a very long time, any increase in opposition, even a small one, represents a significant indication of change....

Strategies to end FGM/C must be accompanied by holistic, community-based education and awareness-raising. As a social behaviour, the practice of FGM/C derives its roots from a complex set of belief systems.... In many ways, bringing an end to FGM/C requires changing community norms and societal attitudes that discriminate against women and subjugate their rights to those of men.... [T]his study shows the close link between women's ability to exercise control over their lives and their belief that FGM/C should be ended. Programmatic interventions must aim to promote the empowerment of women and girls through awareness-raising campaigns and increasing their access to education, as well as their access to and control of economic resources....

Programmes must be country specific and adapted to reflect regional, ethnic and socioeconomic variances.... [T]he practice of FGM/C differs significantly between and within countries. Any strategy to end FGM/C must address the specific situation for each country and reflect regional and ethnic differences.... Furthermore, as the section on attitudes illustrates, FGM/C is practised for a wide variety of cultural reasons. For some communities, it is related to rites of passage. In others, it is considered aesthetically pleasing. Some practise it for reasons related to morality and sexuality. Research into why and how FGM/C is practised among a given group or region is essential for the design of culturally appropriate, effective programmatic interventions.

Detailed segregation of data by socio-economic variables can significantly enhance and strengthen advocacy efforts at the country level. Advocacy efforts are instrumental in influencing behaviour change and awareness. In many situations, however, advocacy can be severely hampered by the lack of systematic and accurate data. In the field of FGM/C, the link between advocacy efforts and accurate data is particularly strong due to the availability of such instruments.... Programmatic interventions to end FGM/C should continue to draw upon the available measurement tools and use data to better tailor their advocacy messages. By examining the different factors and variables that surround the practice, this study attempts to identify girls most at risk and thus take the first step towards ensuring their protection. FGM/C is no longer a cultural practice alone, removed from the scrutiny of international attention and human rights concerns. Rather, it has become a phenomenon that cannot be independently evaluated without looking at the social and economic injustices surrounding women and girls. Any approach that aims to end FGM/C must incorporate a holistic strategy that addresses the multitude of factors that perpetuate it.

Bettina Shell-Duncan, From Health to Human Rights: Female Genital Cutting and the Politics of Intervention

110 American Anthropologist 225 (2008)

...

Previous Frameworks for Opposing FGC [Female Genital Cutting]

...

The initial phase of the global campaign framed opposition to FGC as a health problem... [and] centered on a community-based education approach of delivering a message on the adverse health effects, which assumed that as people were made aware of the risks, they would be motivated to abandon the practice.... [These] programs have, however, gradually fallen from favor for several reasons.

First, although these efforts succeeded in raising awareness [they] failed to motivate large-scale behavior change. In circumcising communities, people are often already aware of many, if not most, of the potential adverse health outcomes but feel that the risk is worth taking in light of the social and cultural importance of the practice....

Additionally, health information delivered in anticircumcision campaigns is often drawn from medical case studies of infibulation with extreme complications, resulting in perceived, and often real, exaggerations of health risks....

Another problem is that closer scrutiny of scientific evidence on health problems associated with FGC shows that it is indeed difficult to establish the medical "facts"....

In June 2006, the WHO released [a study showing] "that women who have had [FGM] are significantly more likely to experience difficulties during childbirth and that their babies are more likely to die as a result of the practice".... [But, in fact, the overall magnitude of risk is modest.] As Ronán M. Conroy notes, "for women with WHO type III mutilations (the most severe) there was a relative risk of 1.3 for both caesarean section and infant resuscitations, and 1.6 for stillbirth or early neonatal death, and there was not increased risk for the 32% of women who had WHO type I mutilation".... [He] notes that, in comparing risk factors in pregnancy, this places FGC somewhere behind maternal smoking.... For this study, as well as others, the real issue comes down to interpretation of existing data and the contention between contested evaluations of what constitutes "acceptable risk" or "nontrivial harm" (see Obermeyer 1999, 2003, and Mackie 2003 for an extended debate on this issue).

A final [problem]... is that the emphasis on health risks is believed by anti-circumcision advocates to have inadvertently promoted the conceptualization of FGC as a health issue amenable to treatment through medical care....

Reframing as Rights

Since the early 1990s, the global anti-FGM campaign has actively attempted to distance itself from the health approach, largely adopting instead an alternative human rights framework for justifying opposition to FGC....

...

... Major rights-based claims include the following: the rights of the child, the rights of women, the right to freedom from torture, and the right to health and bodily integrity.

The Rights of the Child

... [Children's] vulnerability provides a potentially compelling basis for denouncing the practice of FGC [but] there are several problems with this approach. Parents who... view genital cutting as being in the best interest of the child's mental, moral, and spiritual development... would be classified as "incompetent and abusive [parents]".... Additionally, by focusing on physical harm to the exclusion of social acceptance, this approach overlooks the fact that in societies with a high prevalence of FGC, a child's right to develop "normally" includes being circumcised.

The Rights of Women

... Moreover, the fact that the decision to perform FGC is often firmly in the control of women weakens the claim of gender discrimination.

Freedom from Torture

[FGC may be characterized as a form of torture, but state involvement is often only indirect and] consent makes the process of defining the practice as torture difficult. Moreover, Breitung... argues that applying the label of "torture" to a social custom valued by most practitioners may be viewed as an attack on culture and may be more likely to cause resistance than to help end the practice.

The Right to Health and Bodily Integrity

... [T]his approach... is less judgmental and more politically acceptable than other rights claims [but there are still] numerous problems with it. For instance, a narrow focus on health complications does not exclude various forms of medicalization as solutions. In addition,... a preventive health approach is not economically feasible in countries battling more acute health problems.... Nonetheless, most scholars conclude that the health angle is the least problematic approach for calling for the elimination of FGC.

Therefore, in the end, attempts to divorce health and human rights concepts have been unsuccessful, and the alliance, no matter how fragile or contradictory, persists.

...

...

Perils and Pitfalls

In recent years, a number of commentators have warned against viewing the human rights movement as a panacea for prevention of harm....

[The author then explores the claim that legal strategies in isolation will be ineffective and the critique that human rights is an imposed Western construct.]

...

Undermining Women's Agency

A third potential problem with applying a human rights framework involves questions of undermining women's agency....Although acknowledging significant gains in protection of women's rights, several commentators...argue that the VAW [violence against women] movement has transformed the image of Third World women to one of powerless victims incapable of self-determination, self-expression, and reasoned decision making.

...

... Corinne Kratz has charged that many writings on FGC fail to recognize differences in African women based on nationality, class, ethnicity, education, or age. Instead, what emerges is the image of a homogenized, essentialized African woman who is "powerless, constrained by tradition defined by men, unable to think clearly, and [has] only problems and needs, not choices"....

...

Unresolved Questions Concerning Consent

As noted above, since the early 1990s an increasing number of countries have passed legislation banning the practice of FGC. The level of restrictiveness, however, varies.

...

In cases of minors, debates center on whether parents and guardians have decision-making authority regarding FGC for their minor daughters.... Alison Slack (1988) has drawn as an analogy the example of consent for medical treatment...and argues that "it seems unjust that the decision to have an operation performed on a baby girl — one that could risk her life or health, one that will permanently change her physical characteristics and may even harm her future children — would be made without her understanding or consent"....

...

The case of FGC appears to be held to exceptionally strict standards when compared to other body modifications such as piercing, scarring, tattooing, and, as several commentators note, male circumcision....Shweder and colleagues question whether "unequal treatment of male and female circumcision demonstrate[s] hypocrisy, ethnocentricism, or unjustifiable limits to the tolerance granted ethnic minority groups in the United States and European nations?".... Furthermore, only rarely in comparative analyses is the type of FGC considered. Should the same standards for consent apply to symbolic or nicking forms of FGC as to infibulations?

The issue of consent is contested not only for minor girls but also for adult women. Opponents of FGC have argued that it is impossible for adult women to provide informed consent because only someone who was "coerced, manipulated or highly irrational will agree to undergo female genital mutilation" (Sheldon and Wilkinson 1998:271). Such opponents of FGC therefore argue that the practice should be banned overall, irrespective of age....

...

Sheldon and Wilkinson (1998) point to perplexing and disturbing contradictions that arise in the United Kingdom when legislation banning FGC is applied to adult African women but not applied to cosmetic surgeries on Western women.... The irony of differential treatment of FGC and cosmetic surgeries has become magnified with the growing popularity in Europe and the United States of female genital cosmetic surgeries (FGCS). Such surgeries include labia reduction, labia remodeling, clitoral reductions, and vaginal "tucks"..., procedures that are referred to by some as "designer vaginas" rather than FGM.... The arrogance of the implication that Western, but not African, women can rise above the pressure of societal norms of ideal physical form to provide valid consent is disturbing....

...

CEDAW, Female Circumcision

General Recommendation No. 14, 9th Sess., 1990

[As we have seen (p. 186, *supra*), the Committee on the Elimination of Discrimination against Women, adopts General Recommendations expounding upon its understanding of the Convention.]

Recommends that States parties:

(a) Take appropriate and effective measures with a view to eradicating the practice of female circumcision. Such measures could include:

(i) The collection and dissemination by universities, medical or nursing associations, national women's organizations or other bodies of basic data about such traditional practices;

(ii) The support of women's organizations at the national and local levels working for the elimination of female circumcision and other practices harmful to women;

(iii) The encouragement of politicians, professionals, religious and community leaders at all levels, including the media and the arts, to co-operate in influencing attitudes towards the eradication of female circumcision;

(iv) The introduction of appropriate educational and training programmes and seminars based on research findings about the problems arising from female circumcision;

(b) Include in their national health policies appropriate strategies aimed at eradicating female circumcision in public health care. Such strategies could include the special responsibility of health personnel, including traditional birth attendants, to explain the harmful effects of female circumcision;

(c) Invite assistance, information and advice from the appropriate organizations of the United Nations system to support and assist efforts being deployed to eliminate harmful traditional practices;

(d) Include in their reports to the Committee under articles 10 and 12...information about measures taken to eliminate female circumcision.

USA: Female Genital Mutilation, 18 U.S.C.A. §116

Section 116 of this federal criminal statute was enacted in 1996. It reads:

(a) Except as provided in subsection (b), whoever knowingly circumcises, excises, or infibulates the whole or any part of the labia majora or labia minora or clitoris of another person who has not attained the age of 18 years shall be fined under this title or imprisoned not more than 5 years, or both.

(b) A surgical operation is not a violation of this section if the operation is — [Clauses (1) and (2) refer to the operation's being necessary for health/medical purposes and being performed by a licensed medical practitioner.]

(c) In applying subsection (b)(1), no account shall be taken of the effect on the person on whom the operation is to be performed of any belief on the part of that person, or any other person, that the operation is required as a matter of custom or ritual.

Ireland: Criminal Justice (Female Genital Mutilation) Act 2012, Sec. 2 (2)

[No offence under the Act is committed if:]

(a) the act concerned is a surgical operation performed by a registered medical practitioner on the girl or woman concerned, which is necessary for the protection of her physical or mental health,

(b) the act [is] for purposes connected with the labour or birth,

(c) the person is the girl or woman on whom the act of female genital mutilation is done, or

(d) the act concerned is done to a woman who is not less than 18 years of age and there is no resultant permanent bodily harm.

AAWORD, A Statement on Genital Mutilation

Miranda Davies (ed.), Third World-Second Sex: Women's Struggles and National Liberation (1983), at 217

[The Association of African Women for Research and Development (AAWORD) is a group of African women researchers dedicated to doing women's research from an African perspective. They are based in Dakar, Senegal, where their first official meeting was held in December 1977.]

...

This new crusade of the West has been led out of the moral and cultural prejudices of Judeo-Christian Western society: aggressiveness, ignorance or even contempt, paternalism and activism are the elements which have infuriated and then shocked many people of good will. In trying to reach their own public, the new crusaders have fallen back on sensationalism, and have become insensitive to the dignity of the very women they want to 'save'. They are totally unconscious of the latent racism which such a campaign evokes in countries where ethnocentric prejudice is so deep-rooted. And in their conviction that this is a 'just cause', they have forgotten that these women from a different race and a different culture are also *human beings*, and that solidarity can only exist alongside self-affirmation and mutual respect.

...

AAWORD, whose aim is to carry out research which leads to the liberation of African people and women in particular, *firmly condemns* genital mutilation and all other practices — traditional or modern — which oppress women and justify exploiting them economically or socially, as a serious violation of the fundamental rights of women.

...

However, as far as AAWORD is concerned, the fight against genital mutilation, although necessary, should not take on such proportions that the wood cannot be seen for the trees....

... [T]o fight against genital mutilation without placing it in the context of ignorance, obscurantism, exploitation, poverty, etc., without questioning the structures and social relations which perpetuate this situation, is like 'refusing to see the sun in the middle of the day'. This, however, is precisely the approach taken by many Westerners, and is highly suspect, especially since Westerners necessarily profit from the exploitation of the peoples and women of Africa, whether directly or indirectly.

Feminists from developed countries — at least those who are sincerely concerned about this situation rather than those who use it only for their personal prestige — should understand this other aspect of the problem. They must accept that it is a problem for *African women*, and that no change is possible without the conscious participation of African women....

...

Yael Tamir, Hands off Clitoridectomy

31 Boston Review 21 (Summer 1996)

...

Clitoridectomy is obviously a deplorable practice. It is, among other things, an extremely painful, traumatizing mutilation of young girls that leaves them permanently disfigured and deprived of sexual enjoyment. We should express no sympathy toward those who practice it, and support those who struggle to end it.

But we also should be suspicious about the role of clitoridectomy in current political debate. Despite their liberal appearance, references to clitoridectomy commonly reveal a patronizing attitude toward women, suggesting that they are primarily sexual beings. Moreover, those references involve a certain degree of dishonesty. They intentionally widen the gap between our culture and those in which clitoridectomy is practiced, thus presenting those other cultures as incommensurable with ours. The effect of this distancing is to disconnect criticism of their practices from criticism of our own, and turn reflection on other cultures into yet another occasion for celebrating our special virtues. We should resist such self-congratulation. And if we do, the debate about clitoridectomy takes on an entirely different cast.

...

Moreover, we are all aware of painful practices of body piercing, tattooing, and abnormal elongation of lips, ear lobes, and necks. National Geographic runs cover photos of women and men who have undergone such severe malformations, not in protest but as a neutral representation of other ways of life with their different conceptions of beauty. So hostility to clitoridectomy is not driven principally by concerns about physical suffering. Those who object to it would be no less hostile if it were performed in hygienic conditions under anesthesia.

It might be said that these examples are all irrelevant as they do not include the mutilation of the body. But when is the body improved and when is it mutilated? Are parents who force their children to wear braces mutilating their children's teeth or improving them? In most cases, the answer depends on one's conception of beauty.... To be sure, parents say (sincerely) that these treatments will improve their children's life chances, self-image, and social standing. But parents who perform clitoridectomy on their daughters invoke precisely the same arguments.

Furthermore, it seems clear that Western conceptions of female beauty encourage women to undergo a wide range of painful, medically unnecessary, and potentially damaging processes — extreme diets, depilation, face lifts, fat pumping, silicone implants. Of course, adult women do these things to their own bodies, and, it is said, their decisions are freely made. But would our gut reaction to female circumcision be very different if it were performed on consenting adults? It is not unlikely that girls at the age of 13 or 14, who are considered in traditional societies as adults mature enough to wed and bear children, would 'consent' to the mutilation of their bodies if they were convinced that marriage and children were contingent on so doing. Many women who followed the tradition of Sati seemed to do it as a matter of choice. Did their 'consent' make this tradition defensible? Women 'consent' to such practices because the alternative is even more painful — a life of solitude, humiliation, and deprivation.

...

Perhaps, then, we object to clitoridectomy because it is performed on minors. But think of the parents in our culture who foster in their daughters bad eating habits that might destroy their teeth or their vital organs, or, in more tragic cases, lead to life-threatening eating disorders. Are we ready to judge these parents as harshly as we judge parents who require clitoridectomies?

In both cases, parents sincerely believe that they are serving the interests of their children and allowing them to live what is, according to their conception of the good, a meaningful life. Both cases may thus be taken to demonstrate that parents are not the most trustworthy guardians of their children, but why should one case be more harshly judged than the other?

...

The common answer is that clitoridectomy damages women's sexual organs, thus depriving them of sexual enjoyment — a basic need, perhaps even a right. One may wonder, however, when precisely our society became so deeply committed to women's sexual enjoyment.

...

Sexual enjoyment has acquired a mythical status in our society, advocated both as the most sublime and most corruptive pleasure. Advocates of clitoridectomy see the corruption: Performing clitoridectomy will restrict the sexual desires of women, thereby turning them into more chaste and righteous wives and mothers. They believe that the pursuit of sexual pleasures may lead a person astray, and that women are more likely to be influenced by such desires and act unscrupulously.

Both assumptions are also well grounded in the Western tradition. The failure to control the pursuit of sexual pleasures was seen by religious thinkers, as well as by many secular liberals, as undermining virtue, fostering bad habits and pernicious behavior, and hindering the possibility of true love (either of God or of other human beings). In the Christian tradition celibacy was affirmed as the highest ideal, and 'sex within marriage was regarded as an evil necessary for the continuation of the species'.

...

... Societies discriminate, dominate, and abuse their members in various ways, but there is something common to all expressions of oppression. We should place this core aspect, repeated in all traditions in different forms, at the center of our criticism. In the cases discussed here, it is not a particular practice but a set of ill-motivated efforts to control the sexuality of women and to restrict their ability to compete for social and political resources that we should find reprehensible.

Does the overwhelming disgust at clitoridectomy signal an emerging social commitment to structural change — to ensuring equal social, economic, and political status for women? I'm afraid not. Of course, the absence of such commitment is no justification for clitoridectomy. My purpose, however, is not to justify clitoridectomy, but to expose the roots of the deep hostility to it — to reveal the smug, unjustified self-satisfaction lurking behind the current condemnation of clitoridectomy. Referring to clitoridectomy, and emphasizing the distance of the practice from our own conventions, allows us to condemn them for what they do to their women, support the struggle of their women against their primitive, inhuman culture, and remain silent on the status of women in our society.

...

Multicultural exchanges raise acute concerns not because they point to the incommensurability of cultures, or the impossibility of cross-cultural conversation, but because they confront us with our own deficiencies....

[This article of Yael Tamir was followed by several commentators on the article. One such commentator, Martha Nussbaum, wrote:]

> I am prepared to agree with Tamir to this extent. The attention given FGM seems to me somewhat disproportionate, among the many gross abuses the world practices against women — lack of equality under the law, lack of equal access to educa-

> tion, sex-selective infanticide and feticide, domestic violence, marital rape, rape in police custody, and many more.... [T]he reason for this focus is not a fascination with sex but the relative tractability of FGM as a practical problem, given the fact that it is already widely resisted and indeed illegal; how much harder to grapple with women's legal inequality before Islamic courts, their pervasive danger, their illiteracy.... Surely Tamir is right that we should not focus on this one abuse while relaxing our determination to make structural changes that would bring women closer to full equality worldwide.

NOTE

As comments in the preceding readings make clear, the practice of female genital mutilation raises the distinctive question of who (if anyone), which party or actor, is violating international human rights. Apparently no state enforces the practice, or instructs or advocates through its affiliated religious or educational institutions that the practice be continued.

The practice then raises the question addressed in the discussions of the ICCPR and CEDAW in Chapter 3: the degree to which the human rights regime regulates directly or indirectly the conduct of non-state — and in this sense, private — actors. Again we consider the reach of the regime to 'private' actors and to actions that cannot readily be attributed directly to the 'public' state, another instance of the public–private question that recurs throughout the course book.

Note that this question also points towards the serious obstacles to practical implementation of human rights norms, even by states that are hostile to and seek to curb the challenged practice. A government may find it difficult to disregard the sentiments of politically powerful groups or segments of society that wish to maintain religious or customary law. Moreover, a state's motivation to bring about change will depend on that change's relation to other state objectives and on the depth of the socio-cultural roots of the practices. Indeed, the state might not possess the necessary influence or power to proceed. Authority may be divided among the central government and regional or ethnic leaders. The supervision and enforcement of some customary laws may rest not with the state but with another body, such as a religious court or officials. And as the preceding materials have indicated, secular remedies, even if available, may have limited utility or not even be the best route to follow for critics of the practice.

QUESTIONS

1. African state X is a party to the ICCPR and CEDAW. Its government takes no formal, legal position on female genital mutilation, which is undergone by a substantial number of girls in X in the different ways described in the readings. No law, no subsidy, no official policy, requires or facilitates or prohibits the practice. Suppose that you are a member of a nongovernmental human rights organization in X criticizing this widespread practice

before an international human rights body such as the committees created by the ICCPR (see Chapter 9) and CEDAW, on the ground that it violates those treaties.

(a) Precisely what is the violation, and whom would you charge with committing it? The state? Why? If not the state, are any non-state actors subject to duties under these instruments?

(b) On what provisions of these treaties would you rely for your claim of a human rights violation? What arguments would you make based on them?

2. 'It's no wonder that challenges to female circumcision have generated so much controversy in states where it is practised. Could the line-up be worse from the perspective of getting things done? It's West vs. the rest, the uneducated and backward rest. It's whites vs. non-whites. It's science vs. culture.' Comment. If you agree, how would you attempt to change this line-up?

3. In 2010 the American Academy of Pediatrics adopted a Policy Statement on 'Ritual Genital Cutting of Female Minors'. While opposing all types of FGC that pose risks of physical or psychological harm, the statement also observed that 'the ritual nick suggested by some pediatricians is not physically harmful and is much less extensive than routine newborn male genital cutting. There is reason to believe that offering such a compromise may build trust between hospitals and immigrant communities, save some girls from undergoing disfiguring and life threatening procedures in their native countries, and play a role in the eventual eradication of FGC. It might be more effective if federal and state laws enabled pediatricians to reach out to families by offering a ritual nick as a possible compromise to avoid greater harm.' An alternative approach, proposed by Norway's Children's Ombudsman in 2011 is to set a minimum age of 15 or 16 for ritual male circumcision in order to respect 'children's best interests and their right to self-determination on religious and health matters'. A leader of the Norwegian Jewish community was highly critical of the proposal. Comment on these proposals in light of the materials above.

4. Are the articles by Merry and An-Na'im in Part A of this chapter helpful in devising a strategy to reduce the incidence of FGM in countries or regions where it now prevails?

NOTE

Consider the remarks of Yakin Ertürk, Special Rapporteur of the UN Commission on Human Rights on Violence against Women, in her Report on Integration of the Human Rights of Women and the Gender Perspective (E/CN.4/2004/66), at 13:

> ... [CEDAW] draws attention to the contradictions that may arise in the intersectionality of collective rights and the human rights of women. This paradox begs the question, "Does the right to cultural difference and specificity, as embedded in the freedom of religion and belief, contradict the universality of human rights of women?" Alternatively, the question can be turned around as follows; "Is control over the regulation of women the only means by which cultural specificity

and tradition can be sustained?" "Is it culture, or authoritarian patriarchal coercion and the interests of hegemonic masculinity that violates the human rights of women everywhere?" "When a man beats his wife, is he exercising his right in the name of culture? If so, are culture, tradition and religion the property of men alone?"

Universal human rights norms are clear on these questions. The Declaration [on the Elimination of Violence against Women, UN Doc. A/48/629, Art. 4] stresses that States "should not invoke any custom, tradition or religious consideration to avoid their obligations with respect to [the elimination of violence against women]."

RADHIKA COOMARASWAMY, REPORT ON CULTURAL PRACTICES IN THE FAMILY THAT ARE VIOLENT TOWARDS WOMEN

Commission on Human Rights, E/CN.4/2002/83 (2002)

[Radhika Coomaraswamy submitted this Report to the Commission on Human Rights, in her capacity as Special Rapporteur on Violence against Women.]

I. Introduction

1. Throughout the world, there are practices in the family that are violent towards women and harmful to their health ... but have avoided national and international scrutiny because they are seen as cultural practices that deserve tolerance and respect.... Cultural relativism is therefore often an excuse to allow for inhumane and discriminatory practices against women in the community....

...

5. Despite these international norms and standards, the tension between universal human rights and cultural relativism is played out in the everyday lives of millions of women throughout the globe. The situation is made more complex by the fact that women also identify with their culture and are offended by the arrogant gaze of outsiders who criticize their way of doing things. Since their sense of identity is integrally linked to the general attitude towards their community, their sense of dignity and self-respect often comes from being members of the larger community. In minority communities and third world communities that already suffer from discrimination, this sense of identity poses major problems for women. Some women have told the Special Rapporteur that they do not mind wearing the veil because they see the veil as subversive against imperialism. Cultural markers and cultural identity that allow a group to stand united against the oppression and discrimination of a more powerful ethnic or political majority often entail restrictions on the rights of women.... For this reason, the issue of cultural relativism requires a measure of sensitivity. Women's rights must be vindicated but women should win those rights in a manner that allows them to be full participants in a community of their choosing ...

6. Nevertheless, many of the practices enumerated in the next section are unconscionable and challenge the very concept of universal human rights. Many of them involve "severe pain and suffering" and may be considered "torture like" in their manifestation.... [T]hose cultural practices that involve "severe pain and suffering" for the woman or the girl child, those that do not respect the physical integrity of the female body, must receive maximum international scrutiny and agitation....

...

II. Cultural Practices in the Family that Violate Women's Rights

11. There are many cultural practices throughout the world that are violent toward women. In this section some of the more disturbing violations are described, in order to highlight the nature of the problem.

[The Report describes a number of practices omitted from these excerpts, including female genital mutilation, witch hunting, caste, honour killings, parentally determined marriage, practices violating reproductive rights, required dress in public and incest.]

H. Son Preference

70. Son preference, the preference of parents for male children, often manifests itself in neglect, deprivation or discriminatory treatment of girls to the detriment of their physical and mental health. It is generally recognized to exist in most African and Asian countries, but varies in intensity and expression from one country to another.

71. In many regions of the world, entrenched patriarchal systems perpetuate bias and discrimination against females from the time they are conceived and even before they are born. But economic considerations such as the traditional role of men with regard to agriculture and as property owners underlie this type of discrimination against women. This is seen in practices such as prenatal sex selection, female infanticide and gender differences in nutrition, health and education....

72. ... [W]ith modern technology such as amniocentesis or sonograms, it is easier to determine the sex of the unborn child. This advancement of science and technology is exploited to select the sex of the child through aborting the unwanted child instead of merely monitoring the health of the foetus Most often, it is the female foetus that is considered unwanted. UNICEF has provided the following statistics:

> A study of 10,000 abortions following gender tests by amniocentesis in Bombay, India revealed that 9,999 of the foetuses were female; A recent official survey in China revealed that 12 per cent of all female foetuses were aborted or otherwise unaccounted for, mainly the result of ultrasound screening throughout the country to determine the sex of unborn children; In one survey in Bangladesh, 96 per cent of women said that they wanted their next child to be a boy. Only 3 per cent wanted a girl.

73. In India, where there is a strong societal preference for sons, many sex identification clinics have started up. Sex identification before birth was made unlawful many years ago but is commonly practised throughout India. It is argued that a girl will be a financial burden that will only increase as she grows. A modern

saying in India, "Better 500 rupees now than 5,000 rupees later", compares the cost of sex selective technology and the future dowry.

74. In many cultures, the revulsion towards the birth of a daughter is so strong that female infanticide is accepted as a necessary evil. A baby girl may be deprived of food and water in the hope that she will die or she may even be killed.... In China, many families prefer that the one child they are allowed under the Sate one-child policy should be a son, for various reasons. Many baby girls are put in dying rooms and left to die without food or water. This wilful neglect of girls is common throughout their lives. Given the number of men in India and China at present, there should today be 30 million more women in India and 38 million more women in China than there are.

75. ... In Taiwan, daughters are commonly referred to by epithets such as "goods on which one loses" and "water spilled on the ground". In Arabic, the term *Abubanat*, meaning the father of daughters, is an insult.... Such terms are never used with reference to a boy even as a joke. These are some of the countless ways women learn how little they are valued.

76. ... UNICEF estimates that more than 1 million female babies die each year from malnutrition and abuse who would have lived if they were boys. Many mothers stop breastfeeding a girl child early in order to try and get pregnant with a male.... If there are shortages of money and food, sons have priority treatment over the daughters. Daughters are trained to wait patiently while their father and brothers finish their meal, and eat what is remaining....

77. Traditionally, females are not taken to hospital or to other medical providers until their illness reaches a critical stage. They are more often treated at home or taken to a traditional healer. More boys are immunized and treated by hospitals than girls.... A boy is more carefully taken care of to ensure that he will grow into a strong man to provide for the family.

78. ... It is thought that boys need a better education to look after their families when they grow up. In societies where girls are married off at a young age, they are withdrawn from school, even primary school....

...

80. There are various cultural, religious and economic reasons for the above-mentioned practices. In many societies, male children carry on the family lineage.... Among many communities in Asia and Africa, men perform most religious ceremonies and sons perform burial rites for parents.... In agricultural societies, the need for a strong labour force is a factor which perpetuates son preference.... The deprived economic status of women and the low esteem attached to women's economic contribution result in the preference for sons.

81. This is illustrated in a saying common in societies where son preference is prevalent: "To have a son is good economics and good politics, whereas bringing up a girl is like watering the neighbour's garden".

III. Ideologies that Perpetuate Cultural Practices that are Violent towards Women

98. Violence against women in the family in the name of culture is often sanctioned by dominant ideologies and structures within societies. These ideologies and

structures emerged in a different era but continue to dominate public opinion and individual lifestyles, thus preventing the eradication of practices that are harmful to women.

A. The regulation of female sexuality

99. Many of the cultural practices discussed above are often based on a society's belief that the freedom of a woman, especially with regard to her sexual identity should be curtailed and regulated....

100. In many cases, female sexuality is regulated by physical violence and force. Honour killings... are the most obvious examples. Women who fall in love, commit adultery, request divorce, or choose their own husbands are seen as transgressors of the boundaries of appropriate sexual behaviour. As a result, they are subject to direct violence of the most horrific kind. The killing of women with impunity for these transgressions is perhaps the most overt example of the brutal control of female sexuality.

...

B. Masculinity and violence

105. In recent times, anthropologists and scholars have pointed out that, in certain contexts and in certain societies, being "masculine" in an ideal sense involves a tolerance of violence. In many societies, the ideal of heroic masculinity requires acceptance of the notion of honour and the violent regulation of female sexuality ... . Heroic men in these societies use violence as a means of furthering justice and the social good, but they also use violence to ensure that women behave and are subordinate to their will.

...

QUESTION

In light of the Report of the Special Rapporteur, what strategies might you urge as a member of the CEDAW Committee or of an international human rights NGO to reduce or eliminate prevalent practices in a given country or region such as honour killings, denial of equal health care to girls, or abortion of female fetuses after determination of sex? In planning a strategy, what specific information would you want to know about the country or region involved?

ADDITIONAL READING

E. Doggett & M. Fahnestock, *Policy and Advocacy Initiatives to Support the Elimination of Female Genital Cutting in Mali* (2010); S. Mullally & T. ní Mhuirthile, 'Reforming Laws on Female Genital Mutilation in Ireland: Responding to Gaps in Protection', 17 Dublin U. L. Rev. 243 (2010); Y. Hernlund & B. Shell-Duncan (eds.), *Transcultural Bodies: Female Genital Cutting in Global Context* (2007); K. Askin & D. Koenig (eds.), *Women and International Human Rights Law* (1999); K. Knop (ed.),

Gender and Human Rights (2004); C. MacKinnon, *Are Women Human?: And Other International Dialogues* (2007).

2. RELIGION

No topic generates more controversy — or indeed more complex ideas — than relationships between (1) institutionalization of religion in the state or religious belief or practice and (2) human rights norms. From one perspective, religious beliefs and human rights are complementary expressions of similar ideas, even though religious texts invoke the language of duties rather than rights. Important aspects of the major religious traditions — canonical text, scholarly exegesis, ministries — provide the foundation or justification for, or reinforce, many basic human rights. Evident examples include rights to bodily security, or to economic and social provision for the needy. From another perspective, religious traditions may impinge on human rights, and religious leaders may assert the primacy of those traditions over rights. Recall the illustrations in An-Na'im's article, *Human Rights in the Muslim World*, p. 545, *supra*. The banner of cultural relativism may here be held high. If notions of state sovereignty represent one powerful concept and a force that challenges and seeks to limit the reach of the international human rights movement, religion can then represent another.

The topics in this section explore selected issues within this large theme. They involve the distinction sketched by some scholars between freedom *of* religion, and freedom *from* religion. The first freedom is threatened primarily by state conduct that prohibits public expression of religious belief and sharply restricts religious practice or ritual. Such conduct may stem from an ideologically secular state (such as the Peoples' Republic of China) that seeks to limit the role of organized religions, or at the other extreme from fundamentalist states that will not tolerate other forms of religious expression. The second freedom *from* again is threatened primarily by the state, which may impose the beliefs or practices of an official or dominant religion on all citizens, whatever their religious community (if any, for some citizens will be secular or atheist). In such circumstances, human rights additional to the right to freedom of religion may also be implicated. Forms of gender discrimination enforced by the state may find roots in sacred religious text. The state may repress certain speech that is widely viewed as offensive to the dominant religion. And so on.

These issues do not involve a simple dichotomy of the 'state' and 'citizens'. As the materials in Chapters 6 and 7 have illustrated, religion-based restraints or obligations may be rooted in a broad religious culture that is both closely related to and distinct from the state, and that may be insisted on or enforced by a range of non-state actors. Religion and society will often be as apt a framework for discussion as religion and state. The state itself may adopt many attitudes and pursue many policies, ranging from support of the religious culture, to a pose of neutrality, to active opposition to a religion's teachings and demands.

The following materials start with a comparative survey of questions of religion and state and freedom of religion. These comparisons among states highlight a vital issue that permeates this section: what are the links between religious communities, or one religious community, and the state? The spectrum is large, from notions of separation that are strong in the United States (the 'establishment' clause of the First Amendment to the Constitution, the metaphor much used by courts of the 'wall of separation' between church and state), to the pervasive interrelationships in several countries between Islam and the state.

This section continues with analyses of ways in which the international human rights instruments address the broad array of issues sketched in the preceding paragraphs.

a. COMPARATIVE PERSPECTIVES AMONG STATES

COLE DURHAM, PERSPECTIVES ON RELIGIOUS LIBERTY: A COMPARATIVE FRAMEWORK

in Johan van der Vyver & John Witte (eds.), Religious Human Rights in Global Perspective (1996), at 12

...

Up to this point, we have identified various cultural tensions that make religion potentially divisive and the countervailing considerations that have helped moderns since Locke to understand how respect for religion and its potential divisiveness can result in stabilization rather than disintegration of a society and its political institutions. We turn now to an effort to provide a comparative framework for possible configurations of religious and state institutions and resulting patterns of religious freedom.

...

The Relationship between Religious Freedom Rights and Church-State Separation

... The degree of religious liberty in a particular society can be assessed along two dimensions — one involving the degree to which state action burdens religious belief and conduct and another involving the degree of identification between government and religious institutions. In the United States, because of the wording of the religion clause of the First Amendment of the U.S. Constitution, these two dimensions are thought of respectively as the 'free exercise' and 'establishment' aspects of religious liberty. But for comparative purposes, it is useful to think more broadly in terms of varying degrees of religious freedom and church-state identification.

At least in lay thought, there is a tendency to assume that there is a straightforward linear correlation between these two values that could be represented as shown in Figure 1.

This picture considerably over simplifies matters. The primary difficulties arise in connection with the church-state identification gradient and its correlation to the religious freedom continuum. Few religious establishments have ever been so totalistic as to achieve complete identification of church and state. To the extent that extreme situation is reached or approached, there is clearly an absence of religious freedom. This is obviously true for adherents of minority religions, and even the majority religion is likely to suffer because of extensive state involvement in or regulation of its affairs or due to the enervation that results from excessive dependence of religious institutions on the state.

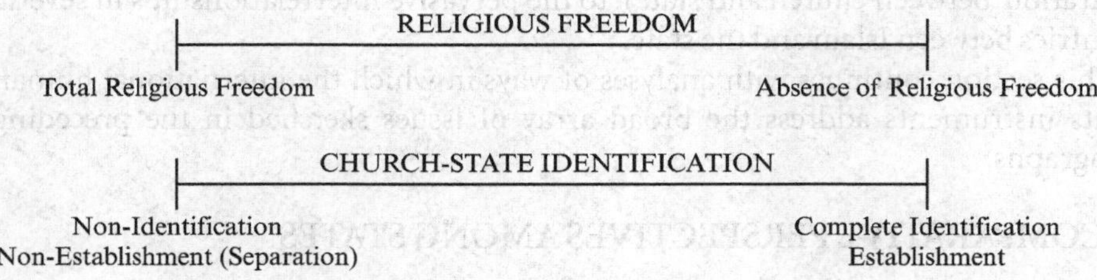

Figure 1

At the other end of the church-state identification continuum, things seem more confused. The mere fact that a state does not have a formally established church does not necessarily mean that it has a separationist regime characterized by rigorous non-identification with religion. Moreover, there is considerable disagreement about the exact configuration of relationships between church and state that maximizes religious liberty, and it may well be that the optimal configuration for one culture may be different than that for another. Further, it is not clear whether 'non-identification' accurately marks the end of this particular continuum. Non-establishment and separation may mark intermediate points along a longer continuum that actually ends with 'negative' identification: i.e., overt hostility or persecution. But if persecution lies at both ends of the church-state identification continuum, it is not at all clear how this continuum correlates with the religious liberty continuum.

[The author draws on an article by George Ryskamp, 'The Spanish Experience in Church-State Relations: A Comparative Study of the Interrelationship between Church-State Identification and Religious Liberty', 1980 Brigham Young Univ. L. Rev. 616, including that article's diagram using the same two continua as in Figure 1 above. But countries in Ryskamp's diagram appear at different points of the two continua; there is no precise correlation. The author challenges Ryskamp's location of several countries on these continua, but asks generally 'why states located at opposite ends of the identification gradient should be located so close to each other on the religious freedom gradient'.]

The answer to this seeming puzzle lies in reconceptualizing the church-state identification continuum as a loop that correlates with the religious freedom continuum as shown in Figure 3.

This model accurately reflects the fact that both strong positive and strong negative identification of church and state correlate with low levels of religious freedom. In both situations, the state adopts a sharply defined attitude toward one or more religions, leaving little room for dissenting views.

...

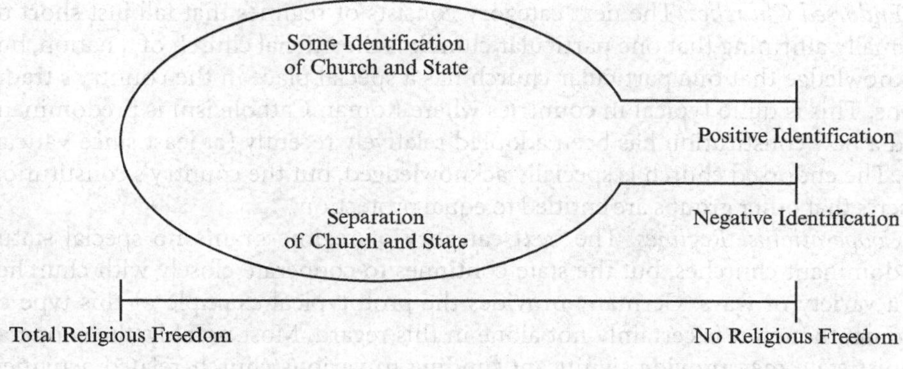

Figure 3

Another significant aspect of religious liberty clarified by the model is that one cannot simply assume that the more rigidly one separates church and state, the more religious liberty will be enhanced. At some point, aggressive separationism becomes hostility toward religion. Mechanical insistence on separation at all costs may accordingly push a system toward inadvertent insensitivity and ultimately intentional persecution. Stalinist constitutions generally had very strong church-state separation provisions, but these can hardly be said to have maximized religious liberty. Rather, they were construed as a demand that religion should be excluded from any domain where the state was present. But in a totalitarian state, this became a demand in practice that religion be marginalized to the vanishing point....

...

Turning first to the identification continuum, one can conceive it as a representation of a series of types of church-state regimes. Beginning at the positive identification end of the continuum, one first encounters *absolute theocracies* of the type one associates with stereotypical views of Islamic fundamentalism. In fact, a range of regimes is possible in Muslim theory, depending on the scope given to internal Muslim beliefs about toleration and also depending on the extent to which flexible interpretation of Shari'a law creates normative space for modernization.

Established Churches. The notion of an 'established church' is vague, and can in fact cover a range of possible church-state configurations with very different implications for the religious freedom of minority groups. At one extreme, a regime with an established church that is granted a strictly enforced monopoly in religious affairs is closely related to one with theocratic rule. Spain or Italy at some periods are classical exemplars. The next position is held by countries that have an established religion that tolerates a restricted set of divergent beliefs. An Islamic country that tolerates 'people of the Book'(but not others) would be one example; a country with an established Christian church that tolerates a number of major faiths, but disparages others would be another. The next position is a country that maintains an established church, but guarantees equal treatment for all other religious beliefs. Great Britain would be a fitting example.

Endorsed Churches. The next category consists of regimes that fall just short of formally affirming that one particular church is the official church of a nation, but acknowledge that one particular church has a special place in the country's traditions. This is quite typical in countries where Roman Catholicism is predominant and a new constitution has been adopted relatively recently (at least since Vatican II). The endorsed church is specially acknowledged, but the country's constitution asserts that other groups are entitled to equal protection....

Cooperationist Regimes. The next category of regime grants no special status to dominant churches, but the state continues to cooperate closely with churches in a variety of ways. Germany provides the prototypical example of this type of regime, though it is certainly not alone in this regard. Most notably, the cooperationist state may provide significant funding to various church-related activities, such as religious education or maintenance of churches, payment of clergy, and so forth. Very often in such regimes, relations with churches are managed through special agreements, concordats, and the like. Spain, Italy and Poland as well as several Latin American countries follow this pattern. The state may also cooperate in helping with the gathering of contributions (e.g., the withholding of 'church tax' in Germany). Cooperationist countries frequently have patterns of aid or assistance that benefit larger denominations in particular. However, they do not specifically endorse any religion, and they are committed to affording equal treatment to all religious organizations....

...

Accommodationist Regimes. A regime may insist on separation of church and state, yet retain a posture of benevolent neutrality toward religion. Accommodationism might be thought of as cooperationism without the provision of any direct financial subsidies to religion or religious education. An accommodationist regime would have no qualms about recognizing the importance of religion as part of national or local culture, accommodating religious symbols in public settings, allowing tax, dietary, holiday, Sabbath, and other kinds of exemptions, and so forth. Many scholars in the United States argue that the United States religion clause should be construed to allow a more accommodationist approach to religious liberty. Note that the growth of the state intensifies the need for accommodation. As state influence becomes more pervasive and regulatory burdens expand, refusal to exempt or accommodate shades into hostility.

Separationist Regimes. As suggested by the earlier comments on Stalinist church-state separation, the slogan 'separation of church and state' can be used to cover a fairly broad and diverse range of regimes. At the benign end, separationism differs relatively little from accommodationism. The major difference is that separationism, as its name suggests, insists on more rigid separation of church and state. Any suggestion of public support for religion is deemed inappropriate. Religious symbols in public displays such as Christmas creches are not allowed. Even indirect subsidies to religion through tax deductions or tax exemptions are either suspect or proscribed. Granting religiously-based exemptions from general public laws is viewed as impermissible favoritism for religion. No religious teaching or indoctrination of any kind is permitted in public schools (although some teaching about religions from an objective standpoint may be permitted). The mere reliance on religious premises in public argument is deemed to run afoul of the church-state separation principle. Members of the clergy are not permitted to hold public office.

More extreme forms of separationism make stronger attempts to cordon off religion from public life. One form this can take is through tightening the state monopoly on certain forms of educational or social services. In the educational realm, the state can ban home schooling altogether, can proscribe private schools, or can submit either of the foregoing to such extensive accreditation requirements that it is virtually impossible for independent religious education to function. Different regimes make differing judgments about the extent to which religious marriages will be recognized. A range of social or charitable services (including health care) may be regulated in ways that make it difficult for religious organizations to carry out their perceived ministries in this area. 'Separation' in its most objectionable guise demands that religion retreat from any domain that the state desires to occupy, but is untroubled by intrusive state regulation and intervention in religious affairs.

...

Hostility and Overt Persecution. The test in this area is how smaller religious groups are treated. Government officials seldom persecute larger religious groups (though this was certainly not unheard of in communist lands). Persecution can take the form of imprisonment of those who insist on acting in accordance with divergent religious beliefs. In its most egregious forms, it involves 'ethnic cleansing' or most extreme, genocide. More typical problems involve less dramatic forms of bureaucratic roadblocks which cumulatively have the effect of significantly impairing religious liberty. These can take the form of denying or delaying registration (granting entity status) and obstructing land use approvals.

With the foregoing categories in mind, the relationship between the more refined identification gradient and the religious freedom gradient can be modeled as shown in Figure 4.

There is some room for argument about which type of regime should be displayed as the type most likely to maximize religious liberty. My contention is that accommodationist regimes have the best claim to this position. Historical experience suggests that maximal religious liberty tends to be achieved when church-state identification is in the accommodation or non-hostile separation mode. Of course, substantial religious liberty can also exist in cooperationist or endorsed church regimes, at least where genuine religious equality is present. However, there is always a sense in such regimes that smaller religious communities have a kind of second-class status, and to the extent that public funds are directly supporting programs of major churches, there is a sense that members of religious minorities are being coerced to support religious programs with which they do not agree. As between separationist and accommodationist regimes, accommodationism has the edge in contemporary settings where the modern secular 'performance state' has emerged with its welfare and regulatory dimensions. As state action or influence pervades more and more of social life, wooden insistence on separation too easily slips into marginalization of religion. Moreover, as regulations proliferate, there is increased demand for exceptions that can sensitively accommodate religious needs. In the last analysis, if accommodation can be achieved without undue difficulty, a regime which fails to accommodate manifests a lesser degree of religious liberty.

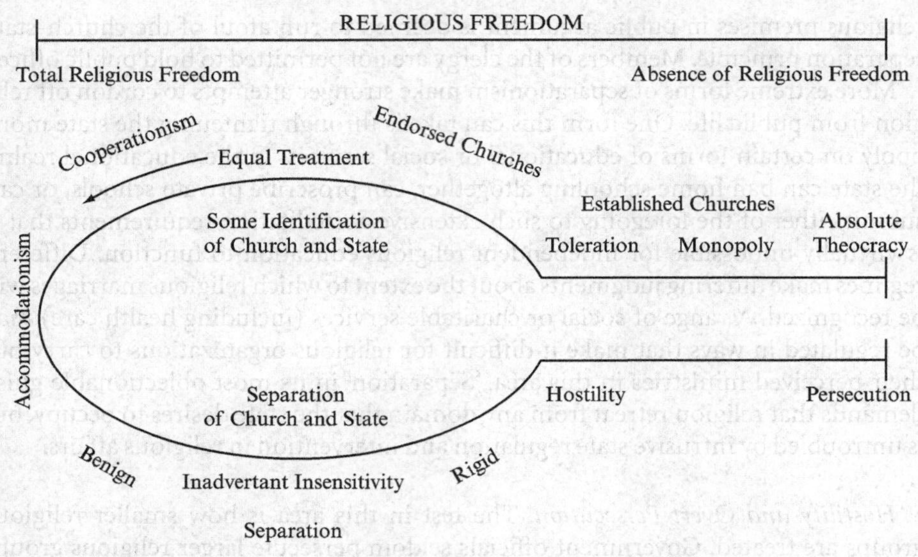

Figure 4

…

The church-state identification loop is useful not only in comparing types of institutional configurations, but also in keeping institutional issues in perspective. It is useful to note, for example, that the often highly polarized constitutional debates in the United States are in fact debates about which of a fairly narrow range of institutional options is optimal. . . .

…

DINAH SHELTON & ALEXANDRE KISS, A DRAFT MODEL LAW ON FREEDOM OF RELIGION

in Johan van der Vyver & John Witte, Jr. (eds.), Religious Human Rights in Global Perspective (1996), at 572

…

The freedom to have a religion means that the government does not prescribe orthodoxy or prohibit particular religions or beliefs. In practice, this is not always the case. Among the examples that may be cited, Indonesia bans the Jehovah's Witness religion because of 'its aggressive manner in propagating its teachings, trying to convert other adherents to this faith'. According to the government, 'misleading cults' are banned in order to maintain peace and harmony between and among adherents of the various religions. 'Without the Government's handling in the matter, the activities of "cults" (including Jehovah's Witnesses and Baha'is) may create disturbances and disrupt the existing religious tolerance'. Similar justifications are put forward by other states that ban specific religions. In some countries, coercion is employed to force renunciation of banned religions.

Short of banning, laws may severely interfere with minority religions. In Pakistan, the Ahmadis are prevented by law from calling themselves Muslims and using Muslim practices in worship or in the public manifestations of their faith.

...

The constitutions of some states establish the primacy of a religion over the state, granting privileges that are incompatible with religious liberty and non-discrimination. Even in states with excellent human rights records, links between religion and state pose problems. In Norway, the king and a majority of the cabinet are required to be members of the state church. Christianity is still a mandatory subject in the Norwegian public schools. Nonconformists have been permitted to teach it since 1969 as long as they do so in accordance with evangelical Lutheran doctrine. Only in 1964 was the constitution amended to guarantee all inhabitants the free exercise of religion. A 1969 Law Concerning Religious Denominations extends the right to form denominations and stipulates that groups registered with the Department of Justice may receive financial aid from both the national and municipal governments on the same basis as parishes of the state church in proportion to their membership statistics. The majority remains opposed to disestablishment of the state church. It is seen as 'a public institution in which membership does not require a commitment of faith and which presently has approximately equal numbers of atheists and "personal Christians" on its rolls'.

In England, the Anglican Church remains at the center of public policy and has substantial support from the state. Prime ministers appoint bishops and the House of Lords contains 26 Anglican bishops who are the lords spiritual. The Parliament can rule on doctrinal and liturgical matters — most recently on the issue of ordination of women. Although there may be little real intervention in the internal affairs of the church, its strongly privileged position can be seen to discriminate against minority religions.

State budgets provide for some religious denominations in Spain, Italy, Greece, Belgium, and Luxembourg. Religious taxes exist in Austria, Switzerland, Denmark, Germany, Norway, and Finland. Indirect support is provided in France, Great Britain, the Netherlands, and Sweden.

Established religions exist in all parts of the world. In Africa, the constitutions of the Comoros, Mauritania, Libya, and Somalia proclaim Islam as the religion of the state. Libya also declares that 'the Holy Koran is the constitution of the Socialist People's Libyan Arab Jamahiriya'. In the Sudan, all legislation must conform to Islamic prescriptions. The head of state must be a Muslim, and non-Muslims are incompetent to testify against Muslims. Propagation of heretical beliefs is a crime. In contrast, the constitution of Botswana specifically recognizes the individual's right to propagate his religion. Proselytizing or converting others is permissible.

...

Mexico's constitution contains some of the more restrictive provisions. Its articles provide that no minister of any faith may be a candidate for elected office. Article

130 provides that ministers cannot form associations for political purposes or rally in favor of or against any candidate, political party or association.... It is also forbidden to hold political meetings in the churches....

...

NOTE

The two preceding articles provide rich illustrations of different types of relationships between religion and state throughout the world. The First Amendment to the US Constitution, prohibiting Congress from making laws 'respecting an establishment of religion, or prohibiting the free exercise thereof', would appear to stand at the end of a spectrum with respect to establishment, although as Durham demonstrates, it is problematic to place the United States at the extreme, for all depends on how the spectrum is defined. For example, the United States and Iran (excerpts from the Iranian Constitution appear below) do represent extremes with respect to involvement of religion in the state, and the state in religion. But the United States would be located on a different point in a spectrum if states like Iran were at one end, and states hostile to and suppressing all religious belief and practice (which of course would be non-establishment states) were at the other.

Although there continues to be extensive constitutional litigation in the United States with respect to both the 'establishment' and 'free exercise' clauses, it is important to bear in mind that, relative to most of the countries discussed below, 'the often highly polarized constitutional debates in the United States are in fact debates about which of a fairly narrow range of institutional options is optimal.' Durham, *supra*. We here introduce some illustrations of these observations, starting with a well-known US Supreme Court decision that explores aspects of the establishment clause, and continuing with illustrations from societies and states that depart substantially or radically from the underlying assumptions, constitutional doctrine, and practice in the United States.

LYNCH v. DONNELLY

Supreme Court of the United States, 465 U.S. 669, 104 S. Ct. 1355 (1984)

[For at least 40 years during the Christmas season, the city of Pawtucket, R.I. had erected a display within a park owned by a nonprofit organization that was located in the heart of the shopping district. The display consisted of several objects owned by the city, including a Christmas tree, a banner reading 'Seasons Greetings' and a creche or scene of the Nativity that included the traditional figures of the Infant Jesus, Mary and Joseph, and angels. The city's expenses in installing and repairing objects in the creche were negligible.

Respondents in this case had brought an action in the Federal District Court challenging the city's inclusion of the creche in the display by contending that it violated the Establishment Clause as made applicable to states by the Fourteenth Amendment. The District Court upheld the challenge, enjoining the city from including the creche in the display, and the Court of Appeals affirmed. There follow excerpts from the opinion for the Court by Chief Justice Burger that reversed the Court of Appeals by a 5–4 decision.]

... The concept of a "wall" of separation [between church and state] is a useful figure of speech [serving] as a reminder that the Establishment Clause forbids an established church or anything approaching it. But the metaphor itself is not a wholly accurate description of the practical aspects of the relationship that in fact exists between church and state.

...

Executive Orders and other official announcements of Presidents and of the Congress have proclaimed both Christmas and Thanksgiving National Holidays in religious terms. And, by Acts of Congress, it has long been the practice that federal employees are released from duties on these National Holidays, while being paid from the same public revenues that provide the compensation of the Chaplains of the Senate and the House and the military services....

Other examples of reference to our religious heritage are found in the statutorily prescribed national motto "In God We Trust," which Congress and the President mandated for our currency, and in the language "One nation under God," as part of the Pledge of Allegiance to the American flag.

...

Rather than mechanically invalidating all governmental conduct or statutes that confer benefits or give special recognition to religion in general or to one faith — as an absolutist approach would dictate — the Court has scrutinized challenged legislation or official conduct to determine whether, in reality, it establishes a religion or religious faith, or tends to do so....

... The line between permissible relationships and those barred by the Clause can no more be straight and unwavering than due process can be defined in a single stroke or phrase or test. The Clause erects a "blurred, indistinct, and variable barrier depending on all the circumstances of a particular relationship."

In the line-drawing process we have often found it useful to inquire whether the challenged law or conduct has a secular purpose, whether its principal or primary effect is to advance or inhibit religion, and whether it creates an excessive entanglement of government with religion....

...

... The District Court inferred from the religious nature of the creche that the city has no secular purpose for the display.... When viewed in the proper context of the Christmas Holiday season, it is apparent that, on this record, there is insufficient evidence to establish that the inclusion of the creche is a purposeful or surreptitious effort to express some kind of subtle governmental advocacy of a particular religious message. In a pluralistic society a variety of motives and purposes are implicated. The city, like the Congresses and Presidents, however, has principally taken note of a significant historical religious event long celebrated in the Western World.

The creche in the display depicts the historical origins of this traditional event long recognized as a National Holiday.

The narrow question is whether there is a secular purpose for Pawtucket's display of the creche. The display is sponsored by the city to celebrate the Holiday and to depict the origins of that Holiday. These are legitimate secular purposes. The District Court's inference, drawn from the religious nature of the creche, that the city has no secular purpose was, on this record, clearly erroneous.

...

The dissent asserts some observers may perceive that the city has aligned itself with the Christian faith by including a Christian symbol in its display and that this serves to advance religion. We can assume, *arguendo*, that the display advances religion in a sense; but our precedents plainly contemplate that on occasion some advancement of religion will result from governmental action. The Court has made it abundantly clear, however, that "not every law that confers an 'indirect,' 'remote,' or 'incidental' benefit upon [religion] is, for that reason alone, constitutionally invalid." Here...display of the creche is no more an advancement or endorsement of religion than the Congressional and Executive recognition of the origins of the Holiday itself as "Christ's Mass," or the exhibition of literally hundreds of religious paintings in governmentally supported museums.

...

... This case does not involve a direct subsidy to church-sponsored schools or colleges, or other religious institutions, and hence no inquiry into potential political divisiveness is even called for. In any event, apart from this litigation there is no evidence of political friction or divisiveness over the creche in the 40-year history of Pawtucket's Christmas celebration....

...

Of course the creche is identified with one religious faith but no more so than the examples we have set out from prior cases in which we found no conflict with the Establishment Clause.... To forbid the use of this one passive symbol — the creche — at the very time people are taking note of the season with Christmas hymns and carols in public schools and other public places, and while the Congress and legislatures open sessions with prayers by paid chaplains, would be a stilted overreaction contrary to our history and to our holdings. If the presence of the creche in this display violates the Establishment Clause, a host of other forms of taking official note of Christmas, and of our religious heritage, are equally offensive to the Constitution.

The Court has acknowledged that the "fears and political problems" that gave rise to the Religion Clauses in the 18th century are of far less concern today. We are unable to perceive the Archbishop of Canterbury, the Bishop of Rome, or other powerful religious leaders behind every public acknowledgment of the religious heritage long officially recognized by the three constitutional branches of government. Any notion that these symbols pose a real danger of establishment of a state church is farfetched indeed.

...

JUSTICE O'CONNOR, CONCURRING

...

The Establishment Clause prohibits government from making adherence to a religion relevant in any way to a person's standing in the political community. Government can run afoul of that prohibition in two principal ways. One is excessive entanglement with religious institutions, which may interfere with the independence of the institutions, give the institutions access to government or governmental powers not fully shared by nonadherents of the religion, and foster the creation of political constituencies defined along religious lines. The second and more direct infringement is government endorsement or disapproval of religion. Endorsement sends a message to nonadherents that they are outsiders, not full members of the political community, and an accompanying message to adherents that they are insiders, favored members of the political community. Disapproval sends the opposite message.

...

... I would find that Pawtucket did not intend to convey any message of endorsement of Christianity or disapproval of non-Christian religions. The evident purpose of including the creche in the larger display was not promotion of the religious content of the creche but celebration of the public holiday through its traditional symbols. Celebration of public holidays, which have cultural significance even if they also have religious aspects, is a legitimate secular purpose.

...

... The display celebrates a public holiday, and no one contends that declaration of that holiday is understood to be an endorsement of religion. The holiday itself has very strong secular components and traditions. Government celebration of the holiday, which is extremely common, generally is not understood to endorse the religious content of the holiday, just as government celebration of Thanksgiving is not so understood....

...

These features combine to make the government's display of the creche in this particular physical setting no more an endorsement of religion than such governmental "acknowledgments" of religion as legislative prayers... government declaration of Thanksgiving as a public holiday, printing of "In God We Trust" on coins, and opening court sessions with "God save the United States and this honorable court." Those government acknowledgments of religion serve, in the only ways reasonably possible in our culture, the legitimate secular purposes of solemnizing public occasions, expressing confidence in the future, and encouraging the recognition of what is worthy of appreciation in society. For that reason, and because of their history and ubiquity, those practices are not understood as conveying government approval of particular religious beliefs....

...

JUSTICE BRENNAN, WITH WHOM JUSTICE MARSHALL, JUSTICE BLACKMUN, AND JUSTICE STEVENS JOIN, DISSENTING

...

... [O]ur precedents in my view compel the holding that Pawtucket's inclusion of a life-sized display depicting the biblical description of the birth of Christ as part of its annual Christmas celebration is unconstitutional. Nothing in the history of such practices or the setting in which the city's creche is presented obscures or diminishes the plain fact that Pawtucket's action amounts to an impermissible governmental endorsement of a particular faith.

...

... [A]ll of Pawtucket's "valid secular objectives can be readily accomplished by other means." Plainly, the city's interest in celebrating the holiday and in promoting both retail sales and goodwill are fully served by the elaborate display of Santa Claus, reindeer, and wishing wells that are already a part of Pawtucket's annual Christmas display. More importantly, the nativity scene, unlike every other element of the Hodgson Park display, reflects a sectarian exclusivity that the avowed purposes of celebrating the holiday season and promoting retail commerce simply do not encompass.... The inclusion of a distinctively religious element like the creche, however, demonstrates that a narrower sectarian purpose lay behind the decision to include a nativity scene....

... The effect on minority religious groups, as well as on those who may reject all religion, is to convey the message that their views are not similarly worthy of public recognition nor entitled to public support. It was precisely this sort of religious chauvinism that the Establishment Clause was intended forever to prohibit....

Finally, it is evident that Pawtucket's inclusion of a creche as part of its annual Christmas display does pose a significant threat of fostering "excessive entanglement."... Jews and other non-Christian groups, prompted perhaps by the Mayor's remark that he will include a Menorah in future displays, can be expected to press government for inclusion of their symbols, and faced with such requests, government will have to become involved in accommodating the various demands....

...

Finally, and most importantly, even in the context of Pawtucket's seasonal celebration, the creche retains a specifically Christian religious meaning. I refuse to accept the notion implicit in today's decision that non-Christians would find that the religious content of the creche is eliminated by the fact that it appears as part of the city's otherwise secular celebration of the Christmas holiday. The nativity scene is clearly distinct in its purpose and effect from the rest of the Hodgson Park display for the simple reason that it is the only one rooted in a biblical account of Christ's birth. It is the chief symbol of the characteristically Christian belief that a divine Savior was brought into the world and that the purpose of this miraculous birth was to illuminate a path toward salvation and redemption. For Christians, that path is exclusive, precious, and holy. But for those who do not share these beliefs, the symbolic reenactment of the birth of a divine being who has been miraculously incarnated as a man stands as a dramatic reminder of their differences with Christian faith ...

...

... While I remain uncertain about these questions, I would suggest that such practices as the designation of "In God We Trust" as our national motto, or the references to God contained in the Pledge of Allegiance to the flag can best be understood, in Dean Rostow's apt phrase, as a form a "ceremonial deism," protected from Establishment Clause scrutiny chiefly because they have lost through rote repetition any significant religious content.... The practices by which the government has long acknowledged religion are therefore probably necessary to serve certain secular functions, and that necessity, coupled with their long history, gives those practices an essentially secular meaning.

...

Under our constitutional scheme, the role of safeguarding our "religious heritage" and of promoting religious beliefs is reserved as the exclusive prerogative of our Nation's churches, religious institutions, and spiritual leaders.... [T]he city's action should be recognized for what it is: a coercive, though perhaps small, step toward establishing the sectarian preferences of the majority at the expense of the minority, accomplished by placing public facilities and funds in support of the religious symbolism and theological tidings that the creche conveys....

...

QUESTIONS

1. Based on the preceding excerpts from *Lynch v. Donnelly*, how would you describe the major purposes in the United States of the establishment clause? Does one or do several of those purposes appear essential to the character of the United States as a liberal democratic country protecting freedoms of conscience, speech, assembly, association and religion?

2. What do you understand to be the relationship, if any, between the establishment clause and the free exercise clause? For example, is the first relevant to the second? Essential to the second?

3. 'I don't understand why the question posed in *Lynch v. Donnelly* is thought to raise a constitutional issue. Most Americans are Christian — simply a fact. Non-Christian Americans — whether Jews or Muslims or Hindus or any other of the many religions observed in the United States — are therefore minorities. Many aspects of a state's practices stem from the majority culture and beliefs — the Christmas holiday, for example. Minorities rarely feel completely at home in a country in which the large majority of the population is different — whether the factor making them minorities is race, ethnicity, cultural practices, or religion. They may feel excluded, left out, uncomfortably different. There's nothing "wrong" with that from a legal or moral point of view. It's inevitable.' Comment.

EDMUND ANDREWS, GERMAN CHURCHES, EVER GIVING, ASK TO RECEIVE

New York Times, 6 Jan. 1998, p. A8

...

Under an unusual century-old system, religious institutions in Germany get almost all their revenue from a 9 percent church surtax imposed on the income tax of every registered Catholic, Protestant and Jew. Taxpayers are asked to declare their religion on their income tax returns, and churchgoers are pressed to register their religion with the Government. Those who are not members of the religions covered by the tax do not pay it, nor do those who have taken the bureaucratic step of revoking their registration.

Church taxes totaled about $11 billion in 1996, almost as much as the sin tax on cigarettes. In striking contrast to the United States, with its separation of church and state, Germany uses its religion taxes for the salaries of priests and rabbis, the construction of churches and a sprawling array of church-run social programs, from Christian day-care centers and kindergartens to drug-counseling clinics and hospitals.

But now the church-state partnership is cracking. With 4.3 million Germans, or more than 11 percent of the work force, unemployed, and thus paying no taxes, church revenue fell about 4 percent in 1996. It could have plunged as much as 10 percent in 1997. That would represent a combined drop in revenues for all religions of more than $1 billion.

...

Germany's church tax supports three main religious groups: the Evangelical Churches, an umbrella organization of Protestants that oversees the Lutheran, Reform and United Protestant branches; Roman Catholicism, and Judaism. Protestants, most of them Lutherans, account for 45 percent of the German population, with Roman Catholics at 37 percent. Jews represent only a small percentage. Muslims and others are not part of the tax structure.

Much like German industry, German religion is now preaching the need to cut costs, become more efficient and refocus priorities. In Munich, Protestant leaders even got a free strategic analysis from the management consultants McKinsey & Company. And they are talking about trying to wean themselves, at least partly, from the tax system.

In early November, Protestant leaders in Hesse announced plans to cut 25 percent of spending on 19 programs, like psychological counseling and adult education. Pastors will also be sent into retirement as soon as they turn 60, while new seminarians will be kept out. In addition, the church will sharply reduce its extensive support for kindergartens and cut the number of religion teachers it sends to public schools.

...

The financial crunch is causing religious people at all levels to rethink their partnership with the Government. It began when the state took it upon itself to tax people who went to church and to funnel that money back to the denominations. In exchange, the churches assumed a range of nonreligious responsibilities in areas like adult education and social work as well as providing religious instruction in public schools.

...

Meanwhile, churches have begun to pull away from responsibilities not directly related to church life. In the case of kindergartens, Protestant officials want to force either the state or parents to pay more. Under the budget plan here in Hesse, the church's contribution to kindergarten costs would drop to 15 percent, from 40 percent in some schools. And children who do not belong to the church will have to pay extra.

...

CONSTITUTION OF IRAN

1979 (as amended)

[Events of the last few years underscore the severe tensions and at times outright conflict between the forces for religious or secular rule in Iran, which became an Islamic republic in 1979 when the ruling monarchy was overthrown. In the process, the implications and very meaning of the 1979 revolution against the Shah led by Ayatollah Khomeini (Khumayni), and the Constitution that it spawned, are brought into public debate. The paradoxes and indeed contradictions of Iran's complex governmental structure (religious leader, institutionalization of Islamic principles, elected president and assembly) are reflected in the excerpts below from the Constitution.[11]]

Chapter I: General Principles

Article 1 [Form of Government]

The form of government of Iran is that of an Islamic Republic, endorsed by the people of Iran on the basis of their longstanding belief in the sovereignty of truth and Koranic justice, in the referendum of 29 and 30 March 1979, through the affirmative vote of a majority of 98.2% of eligible voters, held after the victorious Islamic Revolution led by Imam Khumayni.

Article 2 [Foundational Principles]

The Islamic Republic is a system based on belief in:

(1) the One God (as stated in the phrase 'There is no god except Allah'), His exclusive sovereignty and right to legislate, and the necessity of submission to his commands;

(2) Divine revelation and its fundamental role in setting forth the laws;

...

(6) the exalted dignity and value of man, and his freedom coupled with responsibility before God; in which equity, justice, political, economic, social, and cultural independence, and national solidarity are secured by recourse to: (a) continuous leadership of the holy persons, possessing necessary qualifications, exercised on the basis of the Koran and the Sunnah, upon all of whom be peace; ...

[11] Original text is based on a translation provided by the Iranian Embassy in London. It has been extensively changed in 1994 and 1995.

Article 3 [State Goals]

In order to attain the objectives specified in Article 2, the government of the Islamic Republic of Iran has the duty of directing all its resources to the following goals:

(1) the creation of a favorable environment for the growth of moral virtues based on faith and piety and the struggle against all forms of vice and corruption;

(2) raising the level of public awareness in all areas, through the proper use of the press, mass media, and other means;

...

(6) the elimination of all forms of despotism and autocracy and all attempts to monopolize power;

(7) ensuring political and social freedoms within the framework of the law;

(8) the participation of the entire people in determining their political, economic, social, and cultural destiny;

...

(16) framing the foreign policy of the country on the basis of Islamic criteria, fraternal commitment to all Muslims, and unsparing support to the freedom fighters of the world.

Article 4 [Islamic Principle]

All civil, penal financial, economic, administrative, cultural, military, political, and other laws and regulations must be based on Islamic criteria. This principle applies absolutely and generally to all articles of the Constitution as well as to all other laws and regulations, and the wise persons of the Guardian Council are judges in this matter.

...

Article 6 [Administration of Affairs]

In the Islamic Republic of Iran, the affairs of the country must be administered on the basis of public opinion expressed by the means of elections, including the election of the President, the representatives of the Islamic Consultative Assembly, and the members of councils, or by means of referenda in matters specified in other articles of this Constitution.

...

Article 8 [Community Principle]

In the Islamic Republic of Iran, 'al-'amr bilma'ruf wa al-nahy 'an al-munkar' is a universal and reciprocal duty that must be fulfilled by the people with respect to one another, by the government with respect to the people, and by the people with respect to the government. The conditions, limits, and nature of this duty will be specified by law. (This is in accordance with the Koranic verse 'The believers, men and women, are guardians of one another; they enjoin the good and forbid the evil'. [9:71])

...

Article 12 [Official Religion]

The official religion of Iran is Islam and the Twelver Ja'fari school, and this principle will remain eternally immutable. Other Islamic schools are to be accorded full respect, and their followers are free to act in accordance with their own jurisprudence in performing their religious rites. These schools enjoy official status in matters pertaining to religious education, affairs of personal status (marriage, divorce, inheritance, and wills) and related litigation in courts of law. In regions of the country where Muslims following any one of these schools constitute the majority, local regulations, within the bounds of the jurisdiction of local councils, are to be in accordance with the respective school, without infringing upon the rights of the followers of other schools.

Article 13 [Recognized Religious Minorities]

Zoroastrian, Jewish, and Christian Iranians are the only recognized religious minorities, who, within the limits of the law, are free to perform their religious rites and ceremonies, and to act according to their own canon in matters of personal affairs and religious education.

Article 14 [Non-Muslims' Rights]

In accordance with the sacred verse 'God does not forbid you to deal kindly and justly with those who have not fought against you because of your religion and who have not expelled you from your homes' [60:8], the government of the Islamic Republic of Iran and all Muslims are duty-bound to treat non-Muslims in conformity with ethical norms and the principles of Islamic justice and equity, and to respect their human rights. This principle applies to all who refrain from engaging in conspiracy or activity against Islam and the Islamic Republic of Iran.

…

Chapter III: The Rights of the People

Article 19 [No Discrimination, No Privileges]

All people of Iran, whatever the ethnic group or tribe to which they belong, enjoy equal rights; color, race, language, and the like, do not bestow any privilege.

Article 20 [Equality Before Law]

All citizens of the country, both men and women, equally enjoy the protection of the law and enjoy all human, political, economic, social, and cultural rights, in conformity with Islamic criteria.

Article 21 [Women's Rights]

The government must ensure the rights of women in all respects, in conformity with Islamic criteria, and accomplish the following goals:

(1) create a favorable environment for the growth of woman's personality and the restoration of her rights, both the material and intellectual;

…

Article 22 [Human Dignity and Rights]

The dignity, life, property, rights, residence, and occupation of the individual are inviolate, except in cases sanctioned by law.

Article 23 [Freedom of Belief]

The investigation of individuals' beliefs is forbidden, and no one may be molested or taken to task simply for holding a certain belief.

Article 24 [Freedom of the Press]

Publications and the press have freedom of expression except when it is detrimental to the fundamental principles of Islam or the rights of the public. The details of this exception will be specified by law.

...

Article 26 [Freedom of Association]

The formation of parties, societies, political or professional associations, as well as religious societies, whether Islamic or pertaining to one of the recognized religious minorities, is permitted provided they do not violate the principles of independence, freedom, national unity, the criteria of Islam, or the basis of the Islamic Republic....
[Sections of economic and social rights are omitted.]

Chapter V: The Rights of National Sovereignty
Article 57 [Separation of Powers]

The powers of government in the Islamic Republic are vested in the legislature, the judiciary, and the executive powers, functioning under the supervision of the absolute religious Leader and the Leadership of the Ummah, in accordance with the forthcoming articles of this Constitution. These powers are independent of each other.

Article 58 [Legislature]

The functions of the legislature are to be exercised through the Islamic Consultative Assembly, consisting of the elected representatives of the people. Legislation approved by this body, after going through the stages specified in the articles below, is communicated to the executive and the judiciary for implementation.

...

Article 60 [Executive]

The functions of the executive, except in the matters that are directly placed under the jurisdiction of the Leadership by the Constitution, are to be exercised by the President and the Ministers.

Article 61 [Judiciary]

The functions of the judiciary are to be performed by courts of justice, which are to be formed in accordance with the criteria of Islam, and are vested with the authority to examine and settle lawsuits, protect the rights of the public, dispense and enact justice, and implement the Divine limits.

Chapter VI: The Legislative Power

Article 62 [Election]

(1) The Islamic Consultative Assembly is constituted by the representatives of the people elected directly and by secret ballot.

(2) The qualifications of voters and candidates, as well as the nature of election, will be specified by law.

...

Article 64 [270 Members, Religious Representatives]

(1) There are to be two hundred seventy members of the Islamic Consultative Assembly....

(2) The Zoroastrians and Jews will each elect one representative; Assyrian and Chaldean Christians will jointly elect one representative; and Armenian Christians in the north and those in the south of the country will each elect one representative.

(3) The delimitation of the election constituencies and the number of representatives will be determined by law.

...

Article 72 [Limits]

The Islamic Consultative Assembly cannot enact laws contrary to the official religion of the country or to the Constitution. It is the duty of the Guardian Council to determine whether a violation has occurred, in accordance with Article 96.

Article 89 [Interpellation]

...

(2) In the event at least one-third of the members of the Islamic Consultative Assembly interpellate the President [formally question about government policy] concerning his executive responsibilities in relation with the Executive Power and the executive affairs of the country the President must be present in the Assembly within one month after the tabling of the interpellation in order to give adequate explanations in regard to the matters raised. In the event, after hearing the statements of the opposing and favoring members and the reply of the President, two-thirds of the members of the Assembly declare a vote of no confidence, the same will be communicated to the Leadership for information and implementation of Article 110(10).

...

Article 91 [Guardian Council]

With a view to safeguard the Islamic ordinances and the Constitution, in order to examine the compatibility of the legislation passed by the Islamic Consultative

Assembly with Islam, a council to be known as the Guardian Council is to be constituted with the following composition:

1. six religious men, conscious of the present needs and the issues of the day, to be selected by the Leader, and

2. six jurists, specializing in different areas of law, to be elected by the Islamic Consultative Assembly from among the Muslim jurists nominated by the Head of the Judicial Power.

...

Article 94 [Review of Legislation]

All legislation passed by the Islamic Consultative Assembly must be sent to the Guardian Council. The Guardian Council must review it within a maximum of ten days from its receipt with a view to ensuring its compatibility with the criteria of Islam and the Constitution. If it finds the legislation incompatible, it will return it to the Assembly for review. Otherwise the legislation will be deemed enforceable.

...

Article 98 [Authoritative Interpretation]

The authority of the interpretation of the Constitution is vested with the Guardian Council, which is to be done with the consent of three-fourths of its members.

...

Chapter VIII: The Leader or Leadership Council

Article 107 [Religious Leader]

(1) After the demise of Imam Khumayni, the task of appointing the Leader shall be vested with the experts elected by the people. The experts will review and consult among themselves concerning all the religious men possessing the qualifications specified in Articles 5 and 109.... The Leader thus elected by the Assembly of Experts shall assume all the powers of the religious leader and all the responsibilities arising therefrom.

...

Article 109 [Leadership Qualifications]

(1) Following are the essential qualifications and conditions for the Leader:
  a. Scholarship, as required for performing the functions of religious leader in different fields.
  b. Justice and piety, as required for the leadership of the Islamic Ummah.
  c. Right political and social perspicacity, prudence, courage, administrative facilities, and adequate capability for leadership.

...

Article 110 [Leadership Duties and Powers]

(1) Following are the duties and powers of the Leadership:
  1. Delineation of the general policies of the Islamic Republic of Iran after consultation with the Nation's Exigency Council.

2. Supervision over the proper execution of the general policies of the system.
3. Issuing decrees for national referenda.
4. Assuming supreme command of the Armed Forces.
5. Declaration of war and peace and the mobilization of the Armed Forces.
6. Appointment, dismissal, and resignation of:
   a. the religious men on the Guardian Council,
   b. the supreme judicial authority of the country,
   c. the head of the radio and television network of the Islamic Republic of Iran,
   d. the chief of the joint staff,
   e. the chief commander of the Islamic Revolution Guards Corps, and
   f. the supreme commanders of the Armed Forces.
7. Resolving differences between the three wings of the Armed Forces and regulation of their relations.
8. Resolving the problems which cannot be solved by conventional methods, through the Nation's Exigency Council.
9. Signing the decree formalizing the election of the President of the Republic by the people. The suitability of candidates for the Presidency of the Republic, with respect to the qualifications specified in the Constitution, must be confirmed before elections take place by the Guardian Council, and, in the case of the first term of a President, by the Leadership.
10. Dismissal of the President of the Republic, with due regard for the interests of the country, after the Supreme Court holds him guilty of the violation of his constitutional duties, or after a vote of the Islamic Consultative Assembly testifying to his incompetence on the basis of Article 89.

...

[Selected Provisions]

Article 144 [Islamic Army]

The Army of the Islamic Republic of Iran must be an Islamic Army, i.e., committed to Islamic ideology and the people, and must recruit into its service individuals who have faith in the objectives of the Islamic Revolution and are devoted to the cause of realizing its goals.

...

Article 167 [Rule of Law for Judiciary]

The judge is bound to endeavor to judge each case on the basis of the codified law. In case of the absence of any such law, he has to deliver his judgment on the basis of authoritative Islamic sources and authentic fatawa....

QUESTIONS

1. What similarities with and differences from Iran would you stress in comparing the Western states noted above with respect to relationships between religion and state?

2. What do you believe to be the likely implications of a close (or closer than the United States) relationship between religion and state for non-discrimination among religions or their adherents?

3. Does the state's 'entanglement' with churches in Germany appear to violate the US establishment clause? Does it seem to impair freedom of religion? How would you answer the same questions with respect to Iran?

b. INTERNATIONAL LAW PERSPECTIVES

Here we turn to the universal human rights instruments. Note the limited degree to which those instruments have developed ideas about religion and state or religion and human rights, at least in relation to their far greater development of human rights ideas in fields like race, gender or democratic participation. A purpose of this section is to explore why this should be the case.

A starting point is Article 18 of the International Covenant on Civil and Political Rights (ICCPR):

1. Everyone shall have the right to freedom of thought, conscience and religion. This right shall include freedom to have or to adopt a religion or belief of his choice, and freedom, either individually or in community with others and in public or private, to manifest his religion or belief in worship, observance, practice and teaching.

2. No one shall be subject to coercion which would impair his freedom to have or to adopt a religion or belief of his choice.

3. Freedom to manifest one's religion or beliefs may be subject only to such limitations as are prescribed by law and are necessary to protect public safety, order, health, or morals or the fundamental rights and freedoms of others.

4. The States Parties to the present Covenant undertake to have respect for the liberty of parents and, when applicable, legal guardians to ensure the religious and moral education of their children in conformity with their own convictions.

HUMAN RIGHTS COMMITTEE, GENERAL COMMENT NO. 22: THE RIGHT TO FREEDOM OF THOUGHT, CONSCIENCE AND RELIGION

(1993)

[The Human Rights Committee, established under the ICCPR, has authority to issue 'general comments', effectively used by the Committee to issue interpretive comments on the Covenant's provisions. See pp. 791–808, *infra*, for a discussion of the Committee's General Comments and their effects.]

...

2. Article 18 protects theistic, non-theistic and atheistic beliefs, as well as the right not to profess any religion or belief. The terms 'belief' and 'religion' are to be

broadly construed. Article 18 is not limited in its application to traditional religions or to religions and beliefs with institutional characteristics or practices analogous to those of traditional religions....

3. Article 18 distinguishes the freedom of thought, conscience, religion or belief from the freedom to manifest religion or belief. It does not permit any limitations whatsoever on the freedom of thought and conscience or on the freedom to have or adopt a religion or belief of one's choice. These freedoms are protected unconditionally....

4. The freedom to manifest religion or belief may be exercised 'either individually or in community with others and in public or private'. The freedom to manifest religion or belief in worship, observance, practice and teaching encompasses a broad range of acts. The concept of worship extends to ritual and ceremonial acts giving direct expression to belief, as well as various practices integral to such acts, including the building of places of worship, the use of ritual formulae and objects, the display of symbols, and the observance of holidays and days of rest. The observance and practice of religion or belief may include not only ceremonial acts but also such customs as the observance of dietary regulations, the wearing of distinctive clothing or head coverings, participation in rituals associated with certain stages of life, and the use of a particular language customarily spoken by a group. In addition, the practice and teaching of religion or belief includes acts integral to the conduct by religious groups of their basic affairs, such as the freedom to choose their religious leaders, priests and teachers, the freedom to establish seminaries or religious schools and the freedom to prepare and distribute religious texts or publications.

5. The Committee observes that the freedom to 'have or to adopt' a religion or belief necessarily entails the freedom to choose a religion or belief, including the right to replace one's current religion or belief with another or to adopt atheistic views, as well as the right to retain one's religion or belief. Article 18.2 bars coercion that would impair the right to have or adopt a religion or belief, including the use of threat of physical force or penal sanctions to compel believers or non-believers to adhere to their religious beliefs and congregations, to recant their religion or belief or to convert....

6. The Committee is of the view that article 18.4 permits public school instruction in subjects such as the general history of religions and ethics if it is given in a neutral and objective way.... The Committee notes that public education that includes instruction in a particular religion or belief is inconsistent with article 18.4 unless provision is made for non-discriminatory exemptions or alternatives that would accommodate the wishes of parents and guardians.

7. In accordance with article 20, no manifestation of religion or belief may amount to propaganda for war or advocacy of national, racial or religious hatred that constitutes incitement to discrimination, hostility or violence....

8. Article 18.3 permits restrictions on the freedom to manifest religion or belief only if limitations are prescribed by law and are necessary to protect public safety, order, health or morals, or the fundamental rights and freedoms of others. The freedom from coercion to have or to adopt a religion or belief and the liberty of parents and guardians to ensure religious and moral education cannot be restricted. In interpreting the scope of permissible limitation clauses...limitations may be

applied only for those purposes for which they were prescribed and must be directly related and proportionate to the specific need on which they are predicated....

9. The fact that a religion is recognized as a state religion or that it is established as official or traditional or that its followers comprise the majority of the population, shall not result in any impairment of the enjoyment of any of the rights under the Covenant, including articles 18 and 27, nor in any discrimination against adherents to other religions or non-believers. In particular, certain measures discriminating against the latter, such as measures restricting eligibility for government service to members of the predominant religion or giving economic privileges to them or imposing special restrictions on the practice of other faiths, are not in accordance with the prohibition of discrimination based on religion or belief and the guarantee of equal protection under article 26....

10. If a set of beliefs is treated as official ideology in constitutions, statutes, proclamations of ruling parties, etc., or in actual practice, this shall not result in any impairment of the freedoms under article 18 or any other rights recognized under the Covenant nor in any discrimination against persons who do not accept the official ideology or who oppose it.

...

DECLARATION ON THE ELIMINATION OF ALL FORMS OF INTOLERANCE AND OF DISCRIMINATION BASED ON RELIGION OR BELIEF

GA Res. 36/55 (1981)

The General Assembly

...

Considering that the disregard and infringement of human rights and fundamental freedoms, in particular of the right to freedom of thought, conscience, religion or whatever belief, have brought, directly or indirectly, wars and great suffering to mankind, especially where they serve as a means of foreign interference in the internal affairs of other States and amount to kindling hatred between peoples and nations,

Considering that religion or belief, for anyone who professes either, is one of the fundamental elements in his conception of life and that freedom of religion or belief should be fully respected and guaranteed,

Considering that it is essential to promote understanding, tolerance and respect in matters relating to freedom of religion and belief...,

...

Proclaims this Declaration on the Elimination of All Forms of Intolerance and of Discrimination Based on Religion or Belief:

Article 1

1. Everyone shall have the right to freedom of thought, conscience and religion. This right shall include freedom to have a religion or whatever belief of his choice,

and freedom, either individually or in community with others and in public or private, to manifest his religion or belief in worship, observance, practice and teaching.

2. No one shall be subject to coercion which would impair his freedom to have a religion or belief of his choice.

3. Freedom to manifest one's religion or belief may be subject only to such limitations as are prescribed by law and are necessary to protect public safety, order, health or morals or the fundamental rights and freedoms of others.

Article 2

1. No one shall be subject to discrimination by any State, institution, group of persons, or person on the grounds of religion or other belief.

2. For the purposes of the present Declaration, the expression 'intolerance and discrimination based on religion or belief' means any distinction, exclusion, restriction or preference based on religion or belief and having as its purpose or as its effect nullification or impairment of the recognition, enjoyment or exercise of human rights and fundamental freedoms on an equal basis.

Article 3

Discrimination between human being on the grounds of religion or belief constitutes an affront to human dignity and a disavowal of the principles of the Charter of the United Nations, and shall be condemned as a violation of the human rights and fundamental freedoms proclaimed in the Universal Declaration of Human Rights and enunciated in detail in the International Covenants on Human Rights, and as an obstacle to friendly and peaceful relations between nations.

Article 4

1. All States shall take effective measures to prevent and eliminate discrimination on the grounds of religion or belief in the recognition, exercise and enjoyment of human rights and fundamental freedoms in all fields of civil, economic, political, social and cultural life.

2. All States shall make all efforts to enact or rescind legislation where necessary to prohibit any such discrimination, and to take all appropriate measures to combat intolerance on the grounds of religion or other beliefs in this matter.

Article 5

1. The parents or, as the case may be, the legal guardians of the child have the right to organize the life within the family in accordance with their religion or belief and bearing in mind the moral education in which they believe the child should be brought up.

2. Every child shall enjoy the right to have access to education in the matter of religion or belief in accordance with the wishes of his parents or, as the case may be, legal guardians, and shall not be compelled to receive teaching on religion or belief against the wishes of his parents or legal guardians, the best interests of the child being the guiding principle.

...

Article 6

In accordance with article 1 of the present Declaration, and subject to the provisions of article 1, paragraph 3, the right to freedom of thought, conscience, religion or belief shall include, inter alia, the following freedoms:

...

(d) To write, issue and disseminate relevant publications in these areas;
(e) To teach a religion or belief in places suitable for these purposes;
(f) To solicit and receive voluntary financial and other contributions from individuals and institutions;
(g) To train, appoint, elect or designate by succession appropriate leaders called for by the requirements and standards of any religion or belief;
(h) To observe days of rest and to celebrate holidays and ceremonies in accordance with the precepts of one's religion or belief;
(i) To establish and maintain communications with individuals and communities in matters of religion and belief at the national and international levels.

Article 7

The rights and freedoms set forth in the present Declaration shall be accorded in national legislation in such a manner that everyone shall be able to avail himself of such rights and freedoms in practice.

...

Article 8

Nothing in the present Declaration shall be construed as restricting or derogating from any right defined in the Universal Declaration of Human Rights and the International Covenants on Human Rights.

DONNA SULLIVAN, ADVANCING THE FREEDOM OF RELIGION OR BELIEF THROUGH THE UN DECLARATION ON THE ELIMINATION OF RELIGIOUS INTOLERANCE AND DISCRIMINATION

82 Am. J. Int. L. 487 (1988)

[The General Assembly adopted this Declaration in 1981 by consensus, 19 years after efforts began in the UN system to develop protections for religious freedom that went beyond the provisions of what became Article 18 of the ICCPR. As the author notes, this long delay in producing a Declaration — not a Convention — may be attributed partly 'to the potential for controversy inherent in the subject matter itself'. The excerpts below discuss a few of the Declaration's provisions.]

Although it lacks, of course, the nature of an international agreement, the Declaration is 'regarded throughout the world as articulating the fundamental rights of freedom of religion and belief'. The Declaration gives specific content to the general statements of the rights to freedom of religion or belief and freedom from discrimination based on religion or belief contained in the major human rights instruments.... That the United Nations General Assembly intended that it be normative and not merely hortatory is apparent from its Articles 4 and 7.... There is no consensus on whether the prohibition of discrimination on grounds of religion or belief already constitutes a norm of customary law. As the Declaration acquires concrete material content through its implementation, it will contribute to the acceptance of the customary law status of this important principle.

...

I. Preliminary Observations

The norms stated in the Declaration hold a striking potential for conflict with other rights.... Two general features of the Declaration are likely to affect the resolution of such conflicts. First, it is directed primarily toward actions taken by governments, or by individuals who do not subscribe to a given religion or belief, against individuals who do hold and practice that belief. Interactions among members of the same religious groups are therefore not easily analyzed under the Declaration. Second, application of the Declaration is most straightforward when the belief or practice under consideration corresponds to a typically Western model of religion, in which religious institutions and authority are structurally separable from political and other social institutions.... [T]he protections offered in the Declaration are not premised upon the separation of church and state and are clearly distinguished in this regard from First Amendment rights under the United States Constitution.

...

II. The Scope of Article 1

...

[Coercion]

Coercive forms of persuasion, which attack the intellectual and psychological aspects of belief, should be encompassed by the prohibited forms of coercion. In two common situations, such 'moral' coercion generates conflict between principles stated in the Declaration itself. Proselytizing activities, the first of these, by their very nature attempt moral compulsion to some degree. [Such activities are examined at pp. 613–27, *infra*.]

A desire to avoid the implicit approval of proselytizing was one of the considerations underlying the omission from the Declaration of an explicit reference to the freedom to change one's religion or belief....

The right of individuals to maintain their own beliefs is central to the concerns that motivated the drafting of the Declaration itself. This principle necessarily entails not only the right to retain a belief, but also the freedom to choose a belief without coercion, including the right to reject one's current belief and accept another. Although explicit reference to the right to change beliefs was dropped from the Declaration, that right remains implicit in the right to have a religion or belief. Moreover, Article 8, the savings clause of the Declaration, preserves the standards set forth in the Universal Declaration of Human Rights and the International Covenants on Human Rights.... The Universal Declaration affirms the freedom to change beliefs and the Political Covenant refers to the freedom to adopt a religion or belief.

Nonetheless, the parameters of the right to change one's religion or belief remain uncertain, as illustrated by the difficulty of evaluating the treatment to be accorded apostates and heretics under the Declaration, a second area implicated by the prohibition of coercion.... History is replete with examples of religious persecution perpetrated in the guise of punishment for heresy....

...

[Boundary Between Religion and Politics]

...

Governments do have a legitimate interest in controlling violence against the state or disruptions of public order, and may do so by using methods consistent with other human rights obligations. Nonetheless, governmental violations of religious freedoms and persecution of religious leaders and groups under the pretense of restraining impermissible political activity are far more prevalent than is the use of a religious identity to camouflage actions motivated by purely partisan political concerns....

... [T]he distinction between religious and political activities may be artificial. For example, pacifist religious convictions may prompt an individual to participate in public protest, to refuse to pay taxes used for military expenses and to attempt to influence decisions made by political leaders. Religious beliefs inevitably assume political significance in such circumstances.

... Moreover, the structural separation of secular and religious authority is obviously not a universal feature of societies, as demonstrated by Iran. Finally, political beliefs are presumably subsumed within the general category of 'beliefs' to which the Declaration extends and are protected under that rubric....

...

III. The Scope of the Prohibition of Discrimination and Intolerance

...

[Intolerance]

... Two general views have been taken of the meaning of 'intolerance' and its significance in the Declaration....

... The view that intolerance describes the emotional, psychological, philosophical and religious attitudes that may prompt acts of discrimination or violations of religious freedoms is persuasive. Where intolerance fuels such conduct as killing or the destruction of property, these acts constitute violations of substantive international human rights, such as the right to life, and, in most cases, violations of national law. If intolerance motivates deprivations of the freedom to manifest religion or belief, these acts again constitute violations of substantive rights protected by the Declaration itself.

...

... [E]ducational measures to eradicate intolerance are of vital significance. Educational activities obviously lie within the scope of the 'appropriate' measures contemplated by Article 4(2), although no express reference to such activities appears in the Declaration. Efforts to promote and implement the Declaration should compensate for the omission of a provision explicitly calling for educational measures by emphasizing the importance of such activities.

A second approach to combating intolerance, which was proposed during drafting but rejected, is to prohibit the expression of ideas based on religious hatred and the incitement of hatred and discrimination based on religion or belief. [See Article 20 of the ICCPR.] ...

[Religious Law and Human Rights Law]

Although the rights to establish religious courts and administer religious law are not stated in the Declaration, religious tribunals and the implementation of religious law are manifestations of religious belief to which the protections of Article 1 should apply. Nevertheless, the extent to which religious law may be administered without restrictions by the state or without limitations derived from other human rights obligations may vary with the substantive content of the law itself, and with the scope of the subject matter and personal jurisdiction vested in the religious courts.

...

QUESTIONS

1. In what respects does the General Comment of the Human Rights Committee appear to go beyond Article 18 itself with respect to notions of religious freedom, and beyond the 1981 Declaration? What implications have Article 18 and the 1981 Declaration for the issue of 'establishment'?

2. Does the Declaration reach beyond action by the state to cover conduct (that is, to require or prohibit certain conduct) by private (non-state) actors? If so, under what provisions and with respect to what kinds of conduct?

3. How would you resolve apparent conflicts between the Declaration and other human rights instruments — for example, requirements of non-discrimination in employment under CEDAW and a religiously based belief that women should not be given certain kinds of employment? Do the savings clauses — Article 8 of the Declaration and Article 23 of CEDAW — provide an answer?

4. Under the Declaration, what are the state's duties with respect to religious intolerance that expresses itself in interactions among individuals and non-state entities but that state organs or officials do not themselves urge or actively reinforce? The same as a state's duties under CEDAW?

5. Assess the consistency of the provisions of the Iranian Constitution with (a) Article 18 of the ICCPR, and (b) the 1981 Declaration, assuming (contrary in some instances

to fact) that all religious faiths including Sunni Moslems, Christians of all sects, Jews, Baha'is, and others are allowed freely to hold and observe their religious beliefs and to practise their religious commandments in groups and in houses of worship. How likely is it that a state committed to a constitution similar to Iran's will afford freedom of religion to all faiths?

NOTE

Consider the following comments in Malcolm Evans, *Religious Liberty and International Law in Europe* (1997), at 257. The author speculates about prospects for a convention on religious freedom and discrimination, and notes that the complexity and variety of views on religious issues suggests how arduous the legal and political paths would be towards agreement on its provisions. He notes that there have been suggestions for such a treaty in the UN Commission on Human Rights and the Sub-Commission, and that reports examining this possibility have been prepared. Evans states that these reports highlight one factor among the many that need to be addressed in preparing such a treaty — namely, 'the intolerant attitude of believers themselves. This is seen as a handicap which can be overcome with copious doses of education concerning human rights.' He quotes from one such report, which observed that:

> the reservations concerning religious freedom that have been expressed...should be dealt with patiently and deliberately, through further dialogue. Such dialogue should take into account the factors, be based on internationally established principles...and set a long-term course without any concessions.... The only way to make progress in promoting religious freedom is to avoid categorical, inflexible attitudes....

Reacting to these observations and to similar ones in other reports, Evans states:

> If this means anything, it means that the freedom of religion does not include the right to adhere to a religion which is intolerant of the beliefs of others. On this view, 'Human Rights' has itself become a 'religion or belief 'which is itself as intolerant of other forms of value systems which may stand in opposition to its own central tenets as any of those it seeks to address.

Evans also refers to a recommendation of the Parliamentary Assembly of the Council of Europe that described the current 'crisis of values' in society, and the inadequacy of a market society to meet needs for (quoting from the recommendation) 'individual well-being and social responsibility. The recourse to religion as an alternative has, however, to be reconciled with the principles of democracy and human rights.' Evans expresses his opinion about these assertions:

> In seeking to assert itself in this fashion, the international community risks becoming the oppressor of the believer, rather than the protector of the persecuted. Clearly the time is not yet ripe for a convention: not because of the unwillingness of States to

adopt such an instrument, but because of the reluctance of the international community to accept that in the religious beliefs of others the dogmas of human rights are met with an equally powerful force which must be respected, not overcome.

QUESTIONS

1. Do you agree with the views of Evans about resolution of the tension between 'religious beliefs of others and the dogmas of human rights'? In what directions would his views point, for example, with respect to dealing with gender discrimination based on religion?

2. Do you agree that the time is not ripe for a convention? Given all the problems, what kind of changes from the terms of the 1981 Declaration would you advocate in such a convention, and what strategies would you follow in working towards agreement among diverse states and religions on the proposed terms?

ADDITIONAL READING

J. Witte Jr. & M. C. Green (eds.), *Religion and Human Rights: An Introduction* (2012); T. S. Shah et al. (eds.), *Rethinking Religion and World Affairs* (2012); M. D. Evans, *Religious Liberty and International Law in Europe* (2008); T. Lindholm et al. (eds.), *Facilitating Freedom of Religion or Belief* (2004); C. Evans, *Freedom of Religion Under the European Convention on Human Rights* (2001); M. Janis & C. Evans, *Religion and International Law* (1999).

c. PROSELYTISM

KOKKINAKIS v. GREECE

European Court of Human Rights, 1993, Ser. A, No. 260-A

[Minos Kokkinakis, a Greek national, was born in 1919 into an Orthodox Christian family. In 1936, he became a Jehovah's Witnesses, a Christian sect originating in the nineteenth century, and known for intense door-to-door canvassing by its members. He was arrested more than 60 times for proselytism, and on several occasions imprisoned for a period of months. In 1986, he and his wife called at the home of a Mrs Kyriakaki to engage her in discussion about religion. Her husband, cantor at a local Orthodox church, informed the police who arrested him. Kokkinakis was convicted under Law No. 1363/1938 of the crime of engaging in proselytism and was sentenced to four months' imprisonment. The Court of Appeal upheld the conviction. The Court of Cassation dismissed an appeal, rejecting the plea that the Law violated Article 13 of the Greek Constitution and hence could not be applied.

Kokkinakis then brought a case against Greece before the European Commission of Human Rights, claiming that his conviction violated provisions of the European

Convention on Human Rights. Greece, a party to that Convention, had accepted the jurisdiction of the Commission to hear individual complaints. The Commission found that Greece had violated Article 9 of the Convention. It then referred the case to the European Court of Human Rights, whose jurisdiction Greece had also accepted. (The jurisdiction and work of this Court are examined at p. 906, *infra.*)

Section 4 of Law No.1363/1938, as later amended, made 'engaging in proselytism' a crime, and further provided:

> 2. By 'proselytism' is meant, in particular, any direct or indirect attempt to intrude on the religious beliefs of a person of a different religious persuasion, with the aim of undermining those beliefs, either by any kind of inducement or promise of an inducement or moral support or material assistance, or by fraudulent means or by taking advantage of his inexperience, trust, need, low intellect or naïvety.

The Greek Constitution of 1975 stated in Article 3 that the 'dominant religion in Greece is that of the Christian Eastern Orthodox Church'....

Article 13 of the Constitution provided:

> 1. Freedom of conscience in religious matters is inviolable. The enjoyment of personal and political rights shall not depend on an individual's religious beliefs.
> 2. There shall be freedom to practise any known religion; individuals shall be free to perform their rites of worship without hindrance and under the protection of the law. The performance of rites of worship must not prejudice public order or public morals. Proselytism is prohibited.

Several accounts appeared in the opinions of the Greek courts of the interaction between Kokkinakis and Kryiakaki. The trial court stated that the defendant:

> attempted to proselytise and, directly or indirectly, to intrude on the religious beliefs of Orthodox Christians, with the intention of undermining those beliefs, by taking advantage of their inexperience, their low intellect and their naïvety. In particular, they went to the home of [Mrs Kyriakaki] ... and told her that they brought good news; by insisting in a pressing manner, they gained admittance to the house and began to read from a book on the Scriptures which they interpreted with reference to a king of heaven, to events which had not yet occurred but would occur, etc., encouraging her by means of their judicious, skilful explanations ... to change her Orthodox Christian beliefs.

The Court of Appeal repeated this account, and added that Kokkinakis began to read out passages from Holy Scripture, which he:

> skillfully analysed in a manner that the Christian woman, for want of adequate grounding in doctrine, could not challenge, and at the same time offered her various similar books and importunately tried, directly and indirectly, to undermine her religious beliefs. He must consequently be declared guilty of the above-mentioned offence.

One appeal judge dissented, asserting that no evidence showed that Kyriakaki was particularly inexperienced in Orthodox Christian belief or was of particularly low intellect or naïve.

There follow excerpts from the opinion of the European Court:]

[A 1953 judgment of the Greek Supreme Administrative Court had stated with respect to the meaning of the prohibition of proselytism that the Constitutional ban]

> means that purely spiritual teaching does not amount to proselytism, even if it demonstrates the errors of other religions and entices possible disciples away from them, who abandon their original religions of their own free will; this is because spiritual teaching is in the nature of a rite of worship performed freely and without hindrance. Outside such spiritual teaching, which may be freely given, any determined, importunate attempt to entice disciples away from the dominant religion by means that are unlawful or morally reprehensible constitutes proselytism as prohibited by the aforementioned provision of the Constitution.

18. The Greek courts have held that persons were guilty of proselytism who...offered a scholarship for study abroad; ... distributed 'so-called religious' books and booklets free to 'illiterate peasants' or to 'young schoolchildren'; or promised a young seamstress an improvement in her position if she left the Orthodox Church, whose priests were alleged to be 'exploiters of society'.

[The opinion noted that the Jehovah's Witnesses movement had been present in Greece for about a century, and that its membership in Greece was estimated to be between 25,000 and 70,000. Between 1975 and 1992, 4,400 members had been arrested, 1,233 committed to trial and 208 convicted, some for other offences than proselytism. It then turned to Kokinnakis's claim that Article 9 of the European Convention had been violated.]

28. The applicant's complaints mainly concerned a restriction on the exercise of his freedom of religion. The Court will accordingly begin by looking at the issues relating to Article 9, which provides:

> 1. Everyone has the right to freedom of thought, conscience and religion; this right includes freedom to change his religion or belief and freedom, either alone or in community with others and in public or private, to manifest his religion or belief, in worship, teaching, practice and observance.
> 2. Freedom to manifest one's religion or beliefs shall be subject only to such limitations as are prescribed by law and are necessary in a democratic society in the interests of public safety, for the protection of public order, health or morals, or for the protection of the rights and freedoms of others.

29. The applicant did not only challenge what he claimed to be the wrongful application to him of section 4 of Law no. 1363/1938. His submission concentrated on the broader problem of whether that enactment was compatible with the right enshrined in Article 9 of the Convention...He pointed to the logical and legal difficulty of drawing any even remotely clear dividing-line between proselytism and freedom to change one's religion or belief and, either alone or in community with others, in public and in private, to manifest it, which encompassed all forms of teaching, publication and preaching between people.

...

Mr Kokkinakis complained, lastly, of the selective application of this Law by the administrative and judicial authorities; it would surpass 'even the wildest academic hypothesis' to imagine, for example, the possibility...that an Orthodox Christian would be prosecuted for proselytising on behalf of the 'dominant religion'.

...

31. ...According to Article 9, freedom to manifest one's religion is not only exercisable in community with others, 'in public' and within the circle of those whose faith one shares, but can also be asserted 'alone' and 'in private'; furthermore, it includes in principle the right to try to convince one's neighbour, for example through 'teaching', failing which, moreover, 'freedom to change [one's] religion or belief', enshrined in Article 9,would be likely to remain a dead letter.

...

33. ... [The limitations clause in Article 9(2)] refers only to 'freedom to manifest one's religion or belief'. In so doing, it recognises that in democratic societies, in which several religions coexist within one and the same population, it may be necessary to place restrictions on this freedom in order to reconcile the interests of the various groups and ensure that everyone's beliefs are respected.

...

36. The sentence passed by the [criminal court and the court of appeal] amounts to an interference with the exercise of Mr Kokkinakis's right to 'freedom to manifest [his] religion or belief'. Such an interference is contrary to Article 9 unless it is 'prescribed by law', directed at one or more of the legitimate aims in paragraph 2 and 'necessary in a democratic society' for achieving them.

...

[Kokkinakis claimed that the requirement that a prohibition be 'prescribed by law' had not been met by Section 4 of the Greek Law; and that the definition of proselytism had no 'objective' base, perhaps a deliberate decision 'to make it possible for any kind of religious conversation or communication to be caught by the provision'. He referred to the risk of extension 'by the police and often by the courts too of the vague terms of the section, such as..."indirect attempt" to intrude on the religious beliefs of others.' And he added that '[p]unishing a non-Orthodox Christian even when he was offering "moral support or material assistance" was tantamount to punishing an act that any religion would prescribe and that the Criminal Code required in certain emergencies.'

The Court noted that it was essential to avoid 'excessive rigidity' in legislation in order to keep pace with changing circumstances. Many criminal statutes 'to a greater or lesser extent are vague'. Practice under the proselytism statute and a 'body of settled national case-law' interpreting the Law were such as to 'enable Mr. Kokkinakis to regulate his conduct in the matter'. Hence the Law was 'prescribed by law' within the meaning of Article 9(2).

The Court next inquired into whether there had been a 'legitimate aim' for the Law within the meaning of Article 9(2).]

43. In the applicant's submission, religion was part of the 'constantly renewable flow of human thought' and it was impossible to conceive of its being excluded from public debate. A fair balance of personal rights made it necessary to accept that others' thought should be subject to a minimum of influence, otherwise the result would be a 'strange society of silent animals that [would] think but...not

express themselves, that [would] talk but…not communicate, and that [would] exist but…not coexist'.

44. Having regard to the circumstances of the case and the actual terms of the relevant courts' decisions, the Court considers that the impugned measure was in pursuit of a legitimate aim under Article 9 para. 2, namely the protection of the rights and freedoms of others, relied on by the Government.

[The Court turned to the requirement that a restrictive measure be 'necessary in a democratic society.']

45. Mr Kokkinakis did not consider it necessary in a democratic society to prohibit a fellow citizen's right to speak when he came to discuss religion with his neighbour. He was curious to know how a discourse delivered with conviction and based on holy books common to all Christians could infringe the rights of others. Mrs Kyriakaki was an experienced adult woman with intellectual abilities; it was not possible, without flouting fundamental human rights, to make it a criminal offence for a Jehovah's Witness to have a conversation with a cantor's wife. Moreover, the Crete Court of Appeal, although the facts before it were precise and absolutely clear, had not managed to determine the direct or indirect nature of the applicant's attempt to intrude on the complainant's religious beliefs; its reasoning showed that it had convicted the applicant 'not for something he had done but for what he was'.

…

46. The Government…pointed out that if the State remained indifferent to attacks on freedom of religious belief, major unrest would be caused that would probably disturb the social peace.

47. The Court has consistently held that a certain margin of appreciation is to be left to the Contracting States in assessing the existence and extent of the necessity of an interference, but this margin is subject to European supervision, embracing both the legislation and the decisions applying it, even those given by an independent court. The Court's task is to determine whether the measures taken at national level were justified in principle and proportionate.

…

48. First of all, a distinction has to be made between bearing Christian witness and improper proselytism. The former corresponds to true evangelism, which a report drawn up in 1956 under the auspices of the World Council of Churches describes as an essential mission and a responsibility of every Christian and every Church. The latter represents a corruption or deformation of it. It may, according to the same report, take the form of activities offering material or social advantages with a view to gaining new members for a Church or exerting improper pressure on people in distress or in need; it may even entail the use of violence or brainwashing; more generally, it is not compatible with respect for the freedom of thought, conscience and religion of others.

Scrutiny of section 4 of Law no. 1363/1938 shows that the relevant criteria adopted by the Greek legislature are reconcilable with the foregoing if and in so far as they are designed only to punish improper proselytism, which the Court does not have to define in the abstract in the present case.

49. The Court notes, however, that in their reasoning the Greek courts established the applicant's liability by merely reproducing the wording of section 4 and

did not sufficiently specify in what way the accused had attempted to convince his neighbour by improper means. None of the facts they set out warrants that finding.

That being so, it has not been shown that the applicant's conviction was justified in the circumstances of the case by a pressing social need. The contested measure therefore does not appear to have been proportionate to the legitimate aim pursued or, consequently, 'necessary in a democratic society... for the protection of the rights and freedoms of others'.

50. In conclusion, there has been a breach of Article 9 of the Convention.

...

PARTLY CONCURRING OPINION OF JUDGE PETTITI:

I was in the majority which voted that there had been a breach of Article 9 but I considered that the reasoning given in the judgment could usefully have been expanded.

Furthermore, I parted company with the majority in that I also took the view that the current criminal legislation in Greece on proselytism was in itself contrary to Article 9.

...

In the first place, I take the view that what contravenes Article 9 is the Law.... [T] he definition is such as to make it possible at any moment to punish the slightest attempt by anyone to convince a person he is addressing.

... [T]he mere threat of applying a provision, even one that has fallen into disuse, is sufficient to constitute a breach.

The expression "proselytism that is not respectable", which is a criterion used by the Greek courts when applying the Law, is sufficient for the enactment and the case-law applying it to be regarded as contrary to Article 9.

...

... [T]he haziness of the definition leaves too wide a margin of interpretation for determining criminal penalties.

...

Proselytism is linked to freedom of religion; a believer must be able to communicate his faith and his beliefs in the religious sphere as in the philosophical sphere. Freedom of religion and conscience is a fundamental right and this freedom must be able to be exercised for the benefit of all religions and not for the benefit of a single Church, even if this has traditionally been the established Church or 'dominant religion'.

Freedom of religion and conscience certainly entails accepting proselytism, even where it is 'not respectable'. Believers and agnostic philosophers have a right to expound their beliefs, to try to get other people to share them and even to try to convert those whom they are addressing.

The only limits on the exercise of this right are those dictated by respect for the rights of others where there is an attempt to coerce the person into consenting or to use manipulative techniques.

The other types of unacceptable behaviour — such as brainwashing, breaches of labour law, endangering of public health and incitement to immorality, which are found in the practices of certain pseudo-religious groups — must be punished in positive law as ordinary criminal offences. Proselytism cannot be forbidden under cover of punishing such activities.

...

... Non-criminal proselytism remains the main expression of freedom of religion. Attempting to make converts is not in itself an attack on the freedom and beliefs of others or an infringement of their rights.

...

Spiritual, religious and philosophical convictions belong to the private sphere of beliefs and call into play the right to express and manifest them. Setting up a system of criminal prosecution and punishment without safeguards is a perilous undertaking, and the authoritarian regimes which, while proclaiming freedom of religion in their Constitutions, have restricted it by means of criminal offences of parasitism, subversion or proselytism have given rise to abuses....

The wording adopted by the majority of the Court in finding a breach, namely that the applicant's conviction was not justified in the circumstances of the case, leaves too much room for a repressive interpretation by the Greek courts in the future, whereas public prosecution must likewise be monitored. In my view, it would have been possible to define impropriety, coercion and duress more clearly and to describe more satisfactorily, in the abstract, the full scope of religious freedom and bearing witness.

...

DISSENTING OPINION OF JUDGE VALTICOS:

...

Let us look now at the facts of the case. On the one hand, we have a militant Jehovah's Witness, a hardbitten adept of proselytism, a specialist in conversion, a martyr of the criminal courts whose earlier convictions have served only to harden him in his militancy, and, on the other hand, the ideal victim, a naïve woman, the wife of a cantor in the Orthodox Church (if he manages to convert her, what a triumph!). He swoops on her, trumpets that he has good news for her (the play on words is obvious, but no doubt not to her), manages to get himself let in and, as an experienced commercial traveller and cunning purveyor of a faith he wants to spread, expounds to her his intellectual wares cunningly wrapped up in a mantle of universal peace and radiant happiness. Who, indeed, would not like peace and happiness? But is this the mere exposition of Mr Kokkinakis's beliefs or is it not rather an attempt to beguile the simple soul of the cantor's wife? Does the Convention afford its protection to such undertakings? Certainly not.

...

I should certainly be inclined to recommend the Government to give instructions that prosecutions should be avoided where harmless conversations are involved, but not in the case of systematic, persistent campaigns entailing actions bordering on unlawful entry.

That having been said, I do not consider in any way that there has been a breach of the Convention.

...

NOTE

Kokkinakis remains the landmark judgment for the European human rights regime. The framework it set forth — especially paragraph 48 — has been criticized as too ambiguous and insufficient a protection of the right to engage in proselytism. In a recent analysis of this area of human rights law, one commentator explains:[12]

> This particular statement [para. 48] has been much criticized for its uncertainty, especially since it was invoked in *Kokkinakis* merely to construct a rationale for a finding of violation on the narrowest possible grounds. This was in keeping with a practice, for which the European Court has more generally been reprehended in academic literature, of developing principles which allow wide discretion to states in the use of limitation provisions, both through permitting a wide margin of appreciation, or range of discretion, to states, and in its almost automatic acceptance of claims by states pursuing a "legitimate aim." For example, in *Kokkinakis*, the Court accepted that the aim of laws might be designed to punish extreme or "improper" proselytism when that sort of proselytism was never at issue. This distinctively European approach in permitting states broad latitude represents a marked departure from UN jurisprudence, even though it is clear that conventional proselytism is unequivocally treated as a legitimate form of manifestation.

In light of the above concerns, consider the following 2006 report by the UN Special Rapporteur on freedom of religion or belief on her visit to Sri Lanka:

> [A] draft [bill], entitled "Prohibition of forcible conversion of religion"... was designed to "protect and foster the Buddha Sasana" which is "the foremost religion professed and practised by the majority of people of Sri Lanka"... [A]rticle 2 provides that "No person shall convert or attempt to convert, either directly or otherwise, any person from one religion to another by the use of force or by allurement or by any fraudulent means nor shall any person aid or abet any such conversions." [Penalties include imprisonment and fines, which are] 'increased... if the victim of the attempted conversion is a woman, a minor, or a person listed in the first schedule to the Bill. The proceedings can be instituted by a great variety of persons. The police may take action upon complaint by any "person who has reasons to believe that the provisions of the act have been violated" or by "a person aggrieved by the offence".
>
> [The] Bill also provides that those who have converted to another religion as well as those who have converted another person should report the conversion to the authorities.
>
> ...
>
> The... Bill was challenged before the Supreme Court.... [T]he Supreme Court held that the provision... requiring a person who is converting... to report to the authorities [violated] article 10 [freedom of religion] of the Constitution. In terms of institution of the proceedings, the Court recommended that they should be

[12] P. M. Taylor, 'Religion and Freedom of Choice', in J. Witte and M. C. Green (eds.), *Religion and Human Rights* (2011).

initiated according to the Criminal Procedure Code Act subject to the written permission of the Attorney-General. Finally, the Court suggested a minor amendment to the definitions of "allurement", "force" and "fraudulent means" as they appear in the draft.

…

Supporters of the "unethical" conversions bills were confident that the text of the bills had been carefully drafted and did not violate or contravene international law, including the right to freedom of religion or belief. They often referred to the findings of the European Court of Human Rights in the case *Kokkinakis v. Greece*, and in particular its paragraph 48 …

…

In commenting on the determination of the Supreme Court, the Rapporteur on Religious Intolerance of the Human Rights Commission of Sri Lanka observed that the Court had relied on *Kokkinakis* case, "albeit mistakenly". … The Rapporteur concluded that in all three determinations made by the Supreme Court around the issue of conversion, its decisions were "in the realm of conjecture or speculation that the disadvantaged or vulnerable would be subject to improper conversion. What material was submitted to the Court to back this impression is not clear".

… [T]he [UN] Special Rapporteur is of the opinion that the supporters of the draft laws have disregarded the context of the *Kokkinakis* case. She recalls that the European Court eventually found a violation of the right to freedom of religion or belief of those who wanted to propagate their religion. The Court also held that [the Report quotes from para. 31 of the ECtHR judgment].

… The Special Rapporteur's role is indeed to ensure that individuals are both protected against acts aimed at forced conversions and that their freedom to adopt a religion of their choice or to change religion is safeguarded. In its general comment No. 22, the Human Rights Committee clearly held that "the freedom to 'have or to adopt' a religion or belief necessarily entails the freedom to choose a religion or belief, including the right to replace one's current religion or belief with another or to adopt atheistic views, as well as the right to retain one's religion or belief".

Moreover, the draft laws challenge an aspect of the right to manifest one's religion because they would criminalize certain acts that, according to how restrictively the laws are interpreted, may be part of the right to manifest one's religion. According to the Human Rights Committee,

"The freedom to manifest religion or belief in worship, observance, practice and teaching encompasses a broad range of acts. … [T]he practice and teaching of religion or belief includes acts integral to the conduct by religious groups of their basic affairs, such as the freedom to choose their religious leaders, priests and teachers, the freedom to establish seminaries or religious schools and the freedom to prepare and distribute religious texts or publications".

…

… Moreover, it is very difficult to assess the genuineness of a conversion. While it may be easy to prove that a person has received a gift, it would not be easy to demonstrate that the person has converted because of the gift. Under international law, freedom of conscience is absolute and cannot be subject to any limitation. A mechanism designed to monitor conversions and thus the reasons and purposes behind them could constitute a limitation on freedom of conscience.

> The wording of the draft laws is also too vague. It allows too great a margin of interpretation, which could be a source of possible abuse and could potentially transform the law into a tool of persecution by those who are genuinely opposed to religious tolerance.... The bill[] allow[s] anyone to complain even if the victim may be unwilling to do so. It thus leaves the door wide open for overzealous people to create further polarisation and to generate an atmosphere of fear among religious minorities.

MAKAU MUTUA, HUMAN RIGHTS, RELIGION, AND PROSELYTISM

in Mutua, Human Rights: A Political and Cultural Critique (2002), at 94

... This chapter is an exploration of the historical experience of religious penetration and advocacy in a very specific context and a quest to demonstrate the possibilities of conflict between certain forms of evangelistic advocacy and certain human rights norms. With the African theater as the basic laboratory, I intend to unpack the meaning of religious freedom at the point of contact between the messianic faiths and African religions and illustrate how that meeting resulted in a phenomenon akin to cultural genocide. The main purpose here is not merely to defend forms of religion or belief but rather to problematize the concept of the right to the free exercise of messianic faiths, which includes the right to proselytize in the marketplace of religions. In societies such as those in Africa where religion is woven into virtually every aspect of life, its delegitimation can eventually lead to the collapse of social norms and cultural identities. The result, as has been the case in most of sub-Saharan Africa, is a culturally disconnected people, neither themselves nor the outsiders in Europe, North America, and the Arab world that they seek to imitate. In other words, I argue that imperial religions have necessarily violated the individual conscience and the communal expressions of Africans and their communities by subverting African religions. In so doing, they have robbed Africans of essential elements of their humanity....

Since the right to religious freedom includes the right to be left alone — to choose freely whether to believe and what to believe in — the rights regime by requiring that African religions compete in the marketplace of ideas incorrectly assumes a level playing field. The rights corpus not only forcibly imposes on African religions the obligation to compete — a task for which as nonproselytizing, noncompetitive creeds they are not historically fashioned — but also protects evangelizing religions in their march toward universalization. In the context of religious freedom, the privileging by the rights regime of the competition of ideas over the right against cultural invasion, in a skewed contest, amounts to condoning the dismantling of African religions.

I also argue that the playing field, the one crucial and necessary ingredient in a fair fight, is heavily weighted against Africans. Messianic religions have been forcibly imposed or their introduction was accomplished as part of the cultural package borne by colonialism. Missionaries did not simply offer Jesus Christ as the savior of benighted souls, his salvation was frequently a precondition for services in education and health, which were quite often the exclusive domain of the Church and the colonial state.... [I]n most cases, the embrace of indigenous societies by the European imperial powers was so violent and total that conformity was the only immediate option. In making this argument, I also rely on notions of human rights law which, as I seek to show, suggest that indigenous beliefs have a right to be respected and left alone by more dominant external traditions.

...

A discussion about limitations on religious rights at first blush appears to frustrate some of the major ideals of the human rights movement. It raises the question about the tension between the restriction of the right to evangelize or advocate a point of view and one of the central ideals of the human rights movement, the promotion of diversity and the right to advocate ideas or creeds. An exploration of the manner in which the human rights corpus ought to view religious rights—whether to further limit or to expand the protections they currently enjoy—raises a fundamental tension: how does a body of principles that promotes diversity and difference protect the establishment and manifestation of religious orders that seek to destroy difference and forcibly impose an orthodoxy in Africa—as both Christianity and Islam, the two major proselytizing religions, attempted, and in many cases successfully did? Precisely because of the ethos of universalization common to both, the messianic faiths sought to eradicate, with the help of the state, all other forms of religious expression and belief and close off any avenues through which other competing faiths could be introduced or sustained....

...

The challenge for the human rights movement is to move beyond the singular obsession with wrongs committed directly by the state—although it remains the most important obligee of the discourse—and confront nonstate actors in order to contain and control human rights violations in the private sphere. To do so, the movement has to take on powerful private institutions in the private realm, including established religion. It is my argument that although religious human rights must be defined, secured, and protected, there is a correlative duty on the part of religions to respect the human rights of nonbelievers and adherents of other religions or faiths and not to seek their coerced conversion either directly or through the manipulation and destruction of other cultures.

...

The two most geographically diverse religions—Christianity and Islam—are also the most imperial; they are proselytizing and universalist in their attempts to convert into their faith the entire human race. Although these religions are not spread through physical violence today, they have historically been forcibly introduced. They have also been negatively competitive against each other as well as other creeds as they have fought over the souls of both different religious groups and individuals. But central to them is the belief in the racial superiority of the proselytizers... It does not require a profound knowledge of history to prove that both Arab and European perceptions of Africa have been decidedly racist over the centuries....

...

The UDHR and the ICCPR do not specially recognize indigenous religions in relation to dominant faiths or cultures; they do not even refer to them. Article 18 [of the ICCPR] ... prohibits the use of force to make converts as was the case in early European crusades in Africa and the conquest of parts of the continent by Arab Muslims. It would also appear to disallow using state resources — such as educational, health, and other services — to disadvantage particular faiths. Missionaries who worked against other religions with the help of colonial regimes would seem to be in violation of this provision.

While no authoritative human rights body has issued a definitive interpretation of such construction, the Human Rights Committee has adopted a General Comment on article 27 of the ICCPR, providing that states are under an obligation to protect the cultural, linguistic, and religious rights of minorities. It said, in part:

> Although the rights protected under Article 27 are individual rights, they depend in turn on the ability of the minority group to maintain its culture, language or religion. Accordingly, positive measures by States may also be necessary to protect the identity of a minority and the rights of its members to enjoy and develop their culture and language and to practice their religion, in community with other members of the group.

...

... The emphasis placed on the importance of creating and maintaining a diverse society is one of the most striking characteristics of human rights law. Diversity is encouraged, though not required, by the rights corpus in cultural, religious, political, and other endeavors and pursuits. Through this emphasis, human rights law "evidences throughout its hostility to imposed uniformity."

...

Although human rights law amply protects the right to proselytize through the principles of free speech, assembly, and association, the pecking order of rights problematizes the right to evangelize where the result is the destruction of other cultures or the closure of avenues for other religions. It is my argument that the most fundamental of all human rights is that of self-determination and that no other right overrides it. Without this fundamental group or individual right, no other human right could be secured, since the group would be unable to determine for its individual members under what political, social, cultural, economic, and legal order they would live. Any right which directly conflicts with this right ought to be void to the extent of that conflict.

Traditionally, the self-determination principle has been employed to advance the cause of decolonization or to overcome other forms of external occupation. The principle was indispensable to the decolonization process. This usage of the principle — as a tool for advancing demands for external self-determination — could be expanded to disallow cultural and religious imperialism or imposition by external agencies through acculturation, especially where the express intent of the invading culture or religion, as was the case in Africa, is to destroy its indigenous counterparts and seal off the entry or growth of other traditions. Furthermore, the principle could also be read to empower internal self-determination, that is, the right of a people to "cultural survival." ...

...

. . . Although many of the rights enumerated in human rights law attach to individuals, they only make sense in a collective, social perspective. This is the case because the creation or development of a culture or a religion are societal, not individual, endeavors. I make this point to underline the importance of culture or religion to individuals and groups. An individual's morals, attitudes toward life and death, and identity come from this collective construction of reality through history.

No one culture or religion is sovereign in relationship to any other culture or religion. Proper human rights ought to assume that all cultures are equal. This view rejects the notion that there is a hierarchy of cultures or religions; that some cultures are superior to others even though they may more technologically advanced. Belief in the contrary has led to military invasions to "civilize," colonize, and enslave, as was the case with Christianity in Africa. Cultures, however, have always interacted throughout history; there are no pure cultures, as such, although many traditions retain their distinctive personality. In many cases, the voluntary, unforced commingling of cultures has led to a more vital and creative existence. Several lessons can be drawn from this premise. The human rights movement should encourage the crossbreeding of cultures and tolerance for diversity. But it should frown upon homogenization and the imposition of uniformity.

...

Perhaps there is nothing that can be done today to reverse the negative effects of forced or coerced religious proselytization during the era of colonialism in Africa. Nor is it possible to reclaim wholly the African past as though history has stood still. This does not mean, however, that we should simply forget the past and go on as if nothing happened. The anguish and deprivation caused by that historical experience is with me and millions of other Africans today. We bear the marks of that terrible period. For those Africans who choose not to be Christians or Muslims, the past is not really an option: it was so effectively destroyed and delegitimized that it is practically impossible to retrieve as a coherent scheme of values. It is this loss that I mourn and for which I blame Christianity and Islam. The human rights corpus should outlaw those forms of proselytization used in Africa, because their purpose and effect have been the dehumanization of an entire race of people. It could do so by elaborating a treaty that addresses religious human rights but provides for the protection and mechanisms of redress for forms of proselytization that seek to unfairly assimilate or impose dominant cultures on indigenous religions.

ALESSANDRA STANLEY, POPE TELLS INDIA HIS CHURCH HAS RIGHT TO EVANGELIZE

***New York Times*, 8 Nov. 1999, p. A3**

Summoning all his moral authority, Pope John Paul II tried today to persuade leaders of other religions here that interfaith understanding should lead them to recognize the Roman Catholic Church's right to evangelize. 'Religious freedom constitutes the very heart of human rights', the pope, on a three-day visit to India, said at a interreligious gathering that included Hindus, Muslims, Sikhs, Jews and representatives of several other faiths. 'Its inviolability is such that individuals must be recognized as having the right even to change their religion, if their conscience so demands.'

But that is an argument that many religious leaders in India accept only with difficulty. Christian conversions are at the heart of a political and religious dispute that has made the 79-year-old pope's visit a tense one. Christian proselytizing is fuel for Muslim fundamentalists, but it is also a source of uneasiness between the pope and some of his more moderate and like-minded religious peers.

'Conversions are a fundamental right,' Samdhong Rinpoche, a Buddhist monk who is the speaker of the Tibetan Parliament in exile, said after leaving the podium he shared with the pope. 'But what we fear is that between indoctrination and anybody's inner-consciousness to choose his religion, there is a clean line.' 'Any kind of action to encourage, or to persuade or to motivate in favor of any particular religion, that is a form of conversion that we as Buddhists cannot recommend,' the monk said.

...

... Shankaracharya Madhavananda Saraswati, a moderate Hindu leader who has criticized fundamentalist protests against the visit... also expressed private misgivings about Christian evangelization....

The pope, who came to India to close a synod of Asian bishops, has declared the evangelization of Asia, where Catholics remain a tiny minority, to be one of the church's top priorities for the next millennium. He said it was a 'mystery' why Christ is largely unknown on the continent and added, 'The peoples of Asia need Jesus Christ and his Gospel'.

In India, however, Hindu fundamentalists accuse Christian missionaries, who are most active in poor rural and tribal areas, of preying on the most susceptible in society — buying their souls with education, medical aid and economic assistance.

Anti-Christian attacks by Hindu fundamentalists, often encouraged by political extremists, have increased dramatically in the last two years, with more than 150 recorded incidents of church lootings, beatings, rapes and killings....

The pope came to India with two agendas: He preached ardently for religious tolerance for all faiths, but also instructed his own to convert new followers. To even the mildest leaders of other religions, the two messages do not easily blend.

'Religious people are more busy with increasing the number of their followers rather than paying attention to the challenges that beset religion,' Acharya Mahapragya, head of the Jain faith, said at the podium. Speaking through a lavender-colored surgical mask — Jains are Hindus who revere all forms of life and veil their speech to prevent their breath from destroying living micro-organisms — he was the only leader, besides the pope, to address the issue of conversions publicly.

In the current climate, some Indian Catholics say, their simplest acts of charity are misunderstood. 'We help people with scholarships and medical aid,' said Bartholomew Abraham, 40, a businessman who traveled almost 1,500 miles by train to see the pope. 'If we were really bribing converts, after 2,000 years we wouldn't still only be 2 percent of the population'.

The pope wants church leaders to adapt their pastoral style to suit the culture and customs of their native lands, and he showed the way today by presiding over a colorful sitar Mass for 40,000 worshipers in Nehru Stadium. The Mass coincided with the most important Hindu celebration of the year, Diwali, the festival of light, which was noisily celebrated all over New Delhi with fireworks. At the Mass, under a huge abstract poster of Mother Teresa of Calcutta, women in brown and gold saris danced before the altar while a choir of sitar-players performed Indian-style hymns.

...

QUESTIONS

1. How do you assess the *Kokkinakis* opinion? Do you find justification for any restriction on proselytizing other than those related to coercion, undue imposition on the listener, and similar matters?

2. How do you assess Mutua's views? Can they be limited to matters or religion, or would his arguments apply equally to other attributes of a culture, such as discrimination, or extreme forms of punishment, or authoritarian rule by priests or by elders of a community? How would you seek to resolve the tensions that Mutua underscores, such as through arguments in favour of cultural variety and survival as opposed to arguments for universal norms?

3. 'The human rights instruments are very attentive to the rights of parents to persuade their children to particular beliefs, including religious beliefs and related practices. For example, Article 18(4) of the ICCPR commits the states parties "to have respect for the liberty of parents...to ensure the religious and moral education of their children in conformity with their own convictions". Religious belief is of fundamental importance to a human being. Why should parents be given this authority, and states then be permitted to prohibit efforts of others to persuade adults to a different belief?' Respond.

3. DRESS AND SYMBOLS, MIGRATION AND MULTICULTURALISM

The larger flows of immigrants in recent decades from developing countries to Europe and the United States have led to more complex and sometimes abrasive cultural mixes. Migrants carry cultural and religious beliefs and practices with them; many immigrants continue to adhere to those beliefs and seek to continue the practices accompanying them as well as the beliefs' manifestations in routine daily behaviour. Sometimes, as in the case of female genital mutilation, the practices grow out of deeply rooted culture and traditions. Sometimes, as in the issue of headscarves that is discussed below, they have at least in part a religious foundation. In either case, in the increasingly multicultural states of the developed world, newcomers' practices and routine behaviour — one or another form of dress is frequently at issue — stir discomfort, concern and even intense hostility in the host state. That concern and hostility will often continue after the immigrants or their children have become citizens. The issue is starkly posed whether the immigrants or new citizens should be allowed to continue their practices or whether they should be required to follow laws and practices of the developed country that effectively require their abolition. Severe sanctions, including expulsion from schools and criminal proceedings, may await those who refuse to surrender their beliefs and ways.

Of course, such conflicts raise serious human rights issues. Such is the concern of this section. The opening materials concern immigrant communities, while the later materials examine similar issues that arise in national settings among groups of citizens.

BARBARA CROSSETTE, TESTING THE LIMITS OF TOLERANCE AS CULTURES MIX

New York Times, 6 Mar. 1999, p. B9

In Maine, a refugee from Afghanistan was seen kissing the penis of his baby boy, a traditional expression of love by this father. To his neighbors and the police, it was child abuse, and his son was taken away. In Seattle, a hospital tried to invent a harmless female circumcision procedure to satisfy conservative Somali parents wanting to keep an African practice alive in their community. The idea got buried in criticism from an outraged public.

How do democratic, pluralistic societies like the United States, based on religious and cultural tolerance, respond to customs and rituals that may be repellent to the majority? As new groups of immigrants from Asia and Africa are added to the demographic mix in the United States, Canada and Europe, balancing cultural variety with mainstream values is becoming more and more tricky.

Many Americans confront the issue of whether any branch of government should have the power to intervene in the most intimate details of family life.

'I think we are torn,' said Richard A. Shweder, an anthropologist at the University of Chicago and a leading advocate of the broadest tolerance for cultural differences. 'It's a great dilemma right now that's coming up again about how we're going to deal with diversity in the United States and what it means to be an American.'

Anthropologists have waded deeply into this debate, which is increasingly engaging scholars across academia, as well as social workers, lawyers and judges who deal with new cultural dimensions in immigration and asylum. Some, like Mr. Shweder, argue for fundamental changes in American laws, if necessary, to accommodate almost any practice accepted as valid in a radically different society if it can be demonstrated to have some social or cultural good.

For example, although Mr. Shweder and others would strongly oppose importing such practices as India's immolation of widows, they defend other controversial practices, including the common African ritual that opponents call female genital mutilation, which usually involves removing the clitoris at a minimum. They say that it is no more harmful than male circumcision and should be accommodated, not deemed criminal, as it now is in the United States and several European countries. At the Harvard Law School, Martha Minow, a professor who specializes in family and school issues, said that intolerance often arises when the behavior of immigrants seems to be 'nonmodern, nonscientific and nonrational'. She cites as an example the practice of 'coining' among Cambodians, where hot objects may be pressed on a child's forehead or back as cures for various maladies, leaving alarming welts that for teachers and social workers set off warnings of child abuse.

Americans are more than happy to accept new immigrants when their traditions seem to reinforce mainstream ideals. There are few cultural critics of the family values, work ethic or dedication to education found among many East Asians, for example.

But going more than halfway to tolerate what look like disturbing cultural practices unsettles some historians, aid experts, economists and others with experience in developing societies. Such relativism, they say, undermines the very notion of progress. What's more, it raises the question of how far acceptance can go before there is no core American culture, no shared values, left.

Many years of living in a variety of cultures, said Urban Jonsson, a Swede who directs the United Nations Children's Fund, UNICEF, in sub-Saharan Africa, has led him to conclude that there is 'a global moral minimum', which he has heard articulated by Asian Buddhists and African thinkers as well as by Western human rights advocates.

'There is a nonethnocentric global morality,' he said, and scholars would be better occupied looking for it rather than denying it. 'I am upset by the anthropological interest in mystifying what we have already demystified. All cultures have their bad and good things.'

...

Scholars like Mr. Shweder are wary of attempts to catalogue 'good' and 'bad' societies or practices... [H]e helped form a group of about 15 legal and cultural experts to investigate how American law affects ethnic customs among African, Asian, Caribbean and Latin American immigrants.

...

'Despite our pluralistic ideals, something very much like a cultural un-American activities list seems to have begun circulating among powerful representatives and enforcers of mainstream culture', the group says in its statement. 'Among the ethnic minority activities at risk of being dubbed "un-American" are the use of disciplinary techniques such as shaming and physical punishment, parent/child co-sleeping arrangements, rituals of group identity and ceremonies of initiation involving scarification, piercing and genital alterations, arranged marriage, polygamy, the segregation of gender roles, bilingualism and foreign language use and many more'.

Some sociologists and anthropologists on this behavioral frontier argue that American laws and welfare services have often left immigrants terrified of the intrusive power of government. The Afghan father in Maine who lost his son to the social services, backed by a lower court, did not prevail until the matter reached the state Supreme Court, which researched the family's cultural heritage and decided in its favor — while making clear that this was an exceptional case, not a precedent.

Spanking, puberty rites, animal sacrifices, enforced dress codes, leaving children unattended at home and sometimes the use of narcotics have all been portrayed as acceptable cultural practices. But who can claim to be culturally beyond the prevailing laws and why?

…

Paradoxically, while some Americans want judgment-free considerations of immigrants' practices and traditional rituals in the countries they come from, asylum seekers from those same countries are turning up at American airports begging to escape from tribal rites in the name of human rights. Immigration lawyers and judges are thus drawn into a debate that is less and less theoretical.

Mr. Jonsson of UNICEF…labels those who would condemn many in the third world to practices they may desperately want to avoid as 'immoral and unscientific.' In their academic towers, Mr. Jonsson said, cultural relativists become 'partners of the tormentors'.

Jessica Neuwirth, an international lawyer who is director of Equality Now, a New York-based organization aiding women's groups in the developing world and immigrant women in this country, asks why the practices that cultural relativists want to condone so often involve women: how they dress, what they own, where they go, how their bodies can be used.

'Culture is male-patrolled in the way that it is created and transmitted,' she said. 'People who control culture tend to be the people in power, and who constitutes that group is important. Until we can break through that, we can't take the measure of what is really representative'.

…

TIMOTHY SAVAGE, EUROPE AND ISLAM: CRESCENT WAXING, CULTURES CLASHING

27 The Washington Quarterly No. 3, p. 25 (2004)

[Although written some years ago, this work remains highly relevant to modern-day Europe. It also lays the foundation for the court cases that follow, which involved disputes arising out of the large societal changes that the author describes.]

… Internally, Europe must integrate a ghettoized but rapidly growing Muslim minority that many Europeans view as encroaching upon the collective identity and public values of European society…

…

More than 23 million Muslims reside in Europe, comprising nearly 5 percent of the population….

…

Currently, the waves of immigrants and asylum seekers from the Middle East and North Africa (MENA) — the region with the world's second-highest fertility rate — have had more to do with the worsening conditions in the MENA countries than with labor shortages in Europe, the region with the world's lowest fertility rate.

As the MENA population doubles in the next three decades and Europe's shrinks, increased migratory flows from south to north appear unavoidable — a trend augmented by Europe's graying population, as opposed to the youthful MENA average. In 2000 the UN projected that, to counterbalance their increasingly graying populations, EU states annually would need 949,000 migrants to maintain their 1995 populations; 1,588,000 migrants to maintain their 1995 working-age populations; or 13,480,000 migrants to maintain their population support ratios (the ratio of people aged 15–64 to those aged 65 and older). Furthermore, rather than help alleviate the problem, demographics of the 10 new EU member states increase these gaps. Whichever goal is pursued, most of these individuals will be Muslims.

...

The growing Muslim presence in Europe has tended to cluster geographically within individual states, particularly in industrialized, urban areas within clearly defined, if not self-encapsulated, poorer neighborhoods such as Berlin's Kreuzberg district, London's Tower Hamlets, and the *banlieues* (suburbs) of major French cities, further augmenting its visibility and impact yet circumscribing day-to-day contact with the general population....

...

The nature of the Muslim presence in Europe is also changing. No longer "temporary guest workers," Muslims are now a permanent part of western European national landscapes, as they have been for centuries in southeastern Europe. The institutionalization of Islam in Europe has begun, as has a "re-Islamization" of Muslims in Europe.

... Like European Christians and Jews, European Muslims are not a monolithic group. Nonetheless, Muslims increasingly identify first with Islam rather than with either their family's country of origin or the European country in which they now reside. Moreover, this phenomenon is significantly more pronounced among younger Muslims.

... The current generation is also modernizing and acculturating to aspects of contemporary European society at a faster rate than the first waves of Muslim immigrants did. Younger Muslims are adopting attributes of the European societies in which they were born and raised, such as language; socialization through schooling; and, in many cases, some of the secular perspectives of the country in which they reside. Yet, generally they do not feel part of the larger society nor that they have a stake in it. Conversely, even though they may be third-generation citizens, they often are not viewed as fellow citizens by the general public but are still identified as foreigners and immigrants instead.

...

Despite these trends in citizenship, younger Muslims are resisting assimilation into secular European societies even more steadfastly than the older generation did. Europe's Muslims, including the younger generation, are willing to integrate and respect national norms and institutions as long as they can, at the same time, maintain their distinct Islamic identity and practices. They fear that assimilation, that is, total immersion into European society, will strip them of this identity. Yet, this is the price many Muslims increasingly see European governments and publics demanding: to have Europe become a melting pot without accommodation by or modifications of the existing culture. Studies in France and Germany find that second- and particularly third-generation Muslims are less integrated into European societies than their parents or grandparents were. The recent headscarf affairs in France and Germany underscore and further exacerbate this basic clash.

Perceived discrimination in European societies affecting employment, education, housing, and religious practices is compelling many second- and third-generation Muslims to embrace Islam as their badge of identity. Indeed, the unemployment rate among Muslims is generally double that of non-Muslims, and it is worse than that of non-Muslim immigrants. Educational achievement and skill levels are relatively low, participation by Muslim women in the workforce is minimal, opportunities for advancement are limited, and biases against Muslims are strong. Such factors contribute to the isolation — and self-encapsulation — of Muslim communities in Europe....

...

The rapidly growing Muslim populations seem to be overwhelming the ability of European governments to draw the lines of tolerance rationally, consistently, and convincingly. Europeans see Muslims as a direct challenge to the collective identity, traditional values, and public policies of their societies, as demonstrated by the heated controversies over the hijab [scarf], Muslim food (*halal*), the construction of mosques, the teaching of Islam in schools, and Muslim burial rites. This attitude is also reflected in intense debates over women's rights, church-state relations, and Islam's compatibility with democracy. Politicians, pundits, and ordinary citizens are all seized with the "Islamic challenge."

... The threat is framed in terms of security (terrorism) and economics (jobs); yet, the core issue is identity and the perceived cultural threat Islam poses to the European way of life. Europeans have even coined a name for it: Islamophobia. Conversely, this tendency to see Muslims as a monolith has its reverse image in Muslim allegiance to the umma, which transcends other loyalties; tends to reinforce the "we/them" perspective; and is part of the reason why Muslims resist assimilation — the total loss of identity-related indicators of existing differences from European societies — and insist on integration — a reconstituted identity that stresses remaining differences — or, in some cases, recommunalization — a physical presence in Europe but no accommodation with European society....

[T]he challenge for Europe seems more daunting [than that of the United States with respect to racial hostility and tolerance] because it involves not only integration and tolerance but also redefining both parties' identities. Each side will have to change and move toward the other. Europe's Muslims will need to accept the norms, customs, and cultures of the states in which they live and reject efforts to establish a parallel society, while the general European population will need to broaden its horizons to embrace and accommodate diversity, accepting integration and not just complete assimilation as a valid relationship to society.

...

For their part, Muslims in Europe, who must confront poverty, bigotry, de facto segregation, and limited social mobility, are likely to find it difficult to embrace Europe's liberal democratic views on gender equality; sexual liberalization; and the principles of compromise, egalitarianism, and identification with the state. These are all issues that challenge the traditional views not only of Muslims but also of individuals with an Arab, Turkish, or South Asian heritage, as the vast majority of Europe's Muslims are. These cultural backgrounds have not included the Enlightenment as a central pillar, and the idea of a secular society is for the most part alien. Moreover, as Mustafa Malik notes, in these societies, "[Resistance] to liberalism was heightened by hatred for European colonialists, who represented liberal values." Lack of organization and political standing, diversity of views and interests, economic weakness, and the absence of clear leadership pose major complicating hurdles, all of which Europe's Muslims will need to address if they are to contribute their part to Europe's transformation.

…

Although the situation in Europe is not quite there, the tipping point may be closer than is generally realized. As intolerance toward Muslim communities grows in Europe, European Muslims are growing more self-confident but also more dissatisfied, particularly as Europe's economy continues to sputter. The percentage of Muslims in France is rapidly approaching that of African-Americans in the United States in 1950 (10 percent), and the percentage of Muslims in Europe as a whole will pass that benchmark within the next decade....

…

Conversely, however, a success in dealing with the building clash of cultures and identities, which results in a shift of both Muslim and non-Muslim European mind-sets, and crafts a societal framework that encourages integration and respects individual as well as national identities would negate Huntington's thesis of the inevitable incompatibility of Islam and the West. It would require change in European society, to be sure. As with all change, there would be winners and losers. Yet, success holds out the hope of reinvigorating and redefining Europe, proffering a possible corrective to its projected political, economic, and demographic decline as well as moving European integration to a new level and giving it new meaning.

…

NOTE

Following this Note is the European Court of Human Rights (ECtHR) judgment in *Şahin v. Turkey*, which involved a Muslim female student attending university in Turkey. Four years earlier than the *Şahin* decision, the ECtHR decided *Dahlab v. Switzerland*, Application No. 42393/98 (2001). (These two decisions of the European Court of Human Rights, like the *Kokkinakis* decision at p. 613, *supra*, anticipate the systematic examination of that Court in Chapter 11.) In *Dahlab*, the applicant, a Catholic woman, was a primary school teacher in the secular public school system in Geneva. She converted to Islam and soon began to 'observe a precept laid down in the Koran whereby women were enjoined to draw their veils over themselves in the presence of men.' She refused the request of the Director General of Primary Education to stop wearing a headscarf to class, and was soon dismissed. She was not given relief by the Swiss authorities, and thus brought an action before the European

Court on the ground that the prohibition of the headscarf infringed her freedom to manifest her religion pursuant to Article 9 of the European Convention. The Court agreed with the conclusions of the Swiss administrative and judicial authorities and declared the application inadmissible. It stated in part:

> The Court accepts that it is very difficult to assess the impact that a powerful external symbol such as the wearing of a headscarf may have on the freedom of conscience and religion of very young children [between 4 and 8].... [T]he wearing of a headscarf might have some kind of proselytizing effect, seeing that it appears to be imposed on women by a precept which is laid down in the Koran and which...is hard to square with the principle of gender equality. It therefore appears difficult to reconcile the wearing of an Islamic headscarf with the message of tolerance, respect for others and, above all, equality and non-discrimination that all teachers in a democratic society must convey to their pupils.... [H]aving regard, above all, to the tender age of the children for whom the applicant was responsible as a representative of the State, the Geneva authorities did not exceed their margin of appreciation and...the measure they took was therefore not unreasonable.

In the year before the Grand Chamber decision, a French law came into force effectively banning from state primary and secondary schools the headscarf worn by many Muslim girls as well as 'conspicuous', or 'overtly manifest', clothing or symbols of other religions such as large crosses for Christians and large skullcaps for Jewish boys. In an unusual step, the US Government openly criticized the French law. Discussing the French legislation at a press conference, the US Ambassador-at-Large for International Religious Freedom stated: 'A fundamental principle of religious freedom that we work for in many countries of the world, including on this very issue of headscarves, is that all persons should be able to practice their religion and their beliefs peacefully, without government interference, as long as they are doing so without provocation and intimidation of others in society', and, he added, 'Where people are wearing these with no provocation simply as a manifestation of their own heartfelt beliefs, we don't see where this causes divisions among peoples.' The French law, however, may have simply been the most salient at the time. Other states in Europe allowed schools to prohibit headscarves in certain cases. These developments across the European landscape were understood by the Grand Chamber of the European Court of Human Rights when it issued its judgment in *Şahin v. Turkey*.

ŞAHIN v. TURKEY

European Court of Human Rights (Grand Chamber), 2005

[The applicant, a Turkish citizen, came from a traditional family of practising Muslims, and considered it her religious duty to wear the Islamic headscarf. She did so during her four years studying medicine in a Turkish university. She then transferred to Istanbul University to continue her studies. In a series of episodes beginning in 1998 she was censured by university authorities for refusing to comply with university circulars based on legislation banning students wearing headscarves from lectures and courses. After being denied enrolment and admission to lectures, she sought relief from Turkish courts, but was unsuccessful. Ultimately, the applicant abandoned her studies in Turkey and pursued her medical education at Vienna University. After failing to secure judicial relief in Turkey, she initiated proceedings against Turkey under the European Convention on Human Rights. In a 2004 judgment, a Chamber of the European Court of Human Rights held unanimously that there had been no violation of the Convention. The applicant's request that the case be referred to the Court's Grand Chamber was accepted. In its 2005 judgment, the Grand Chamber also ruled against the applicant. Excerpts from that opinion and a dissenting opinion follow.]

30. The Turkish Republic was founded on the principle that the State should be secular (*laik*). Before and after the proclamation of the Republic on 29 October 1923, the public and religious spheres were separated through a series of revolutionary reforms....

31. The principle of secularism was inspired by developments in Ottoman society in the period between the nineteenth century and the proclamation of the Republic.... Significant advances in women's rights were made during this period (equality of treatment in education, the introduction of a ban on polygamy in 1914, the transfer of jurisdiction in matrimonial cases to the secular courts that had been established in the nineteenth century).

32. The defining feature of the Republican ideal was the presence of women in public life and their active participation in society. Consequently, the ideas that women should be freed from religious constraints and that society should be modernised had a common origin.... [W]omen obtained equal political rights with men.

...

35. In Turkey wearing the Islamic headscarf to school and university is a recent phenomenon which only really began to emerge in the 1980s.... Those in favour of the headscarf see wearing it as a duty and/or a form of expression linked to religious identity. However, the supporters of secularism ... see the Islamic headscarf as a symbol of a political Islam ...

[In the Turkish Constitutional Court's opinion that upheld the university's position, the judges stated that secularism had achieved so important a position among constitutional values because of the country's historical experience and the particularities of Islam compared to other religions; secularism was an essential condition for democracy and acted as a guarantor of freedom of religion and of equality before the law. Students must be allowed to work in a tolerant atmosphere without being deflected from their goals by signs of religious affiliation such as the headscarf.

The ECtHR opinion included a comparative survey about laws about headscarves across different European countries. The survey indicated that state legislation varied on many details — for example, how, if at all, the headscarf was regulated, and the level of school/university that was covered by any regulation.]

I. ALLEGED VIOLATION OF ARTICLE 9 OF THE CONVENTION

70. The applicant submitted that the ban on wearing the Islamic headscarf in institutions of higher education constituted an unjustified interference with her right to freedom of religion, in particular, her right to manifest her religion. She relied on Article 9 of the Convention, which provides:

> 1. Everyone has the right to freedom of thought, conscience and religion; this right includes freedom to change his religion or belief and freedom, either alone or in community with others and in public or private, to manifest his religion or belief, in worship, teaching, practice and observance.
> 2. Freedom to manifest one's religion or beliefs shall be subject only to such limitations as are prescribed by law and are necessary in a democratic society in the interests of public safety, for the protection of public order, health or morals, or for the protection of the rights and freedoms of others.

...

104. The Court reiterates that as enshrined in Article 9, freedom of thought, conscience and religion is one of the foundations of a "democratic society" within the meaning of the Convention. This freedom is, in its religious dimension, one of the most vital elements that go to make up the identity of believers and their conception of life, but it is also a precious asset for atheists, agnostics, sceptics and the unconcerned. The pluralism indissociable from a democratic society, which has been dearly won over the centuries, depends on it. That freedom entails, *inter alia*, freedom to hold or not to hold religious beliefs and to practise or not to practise a religion.

105. While religious freedom is primarily a matter of individual conscience, it also implies, *inter alia*, freedom to manifest one's religion, alone and in private, or in community with others, in public and within the circle of those whose faith one shares. Article 9 lists the various forms which manifestation of one's religion or belief may take, namely worship, teaching, practice and observance....

106. In democratic societies, in which several religions coexist within one and the same population, it may be necessary to place restrictions on freedom to manifest one's religion or belief in order to reconcile the interests of the various groups and ensure that everyone's beliefs are respected....

107. The Court...also considers that the State's duty of neutrality and impartiality is incompatible with any power on the State's part to assess the legitimacy of religious beliefs or the ways in which those beliefs are expressed ...

...

109. Where questions concerning the relationship between State and religions are at stake, on which opinion in a democratic society may reasonably differ widely, the role of the national decision-making body must be given special importance. This will notably be the case when it comes to regulating the wearing of religious symbols in educational institutions, especially in view of the diversity of the approaches taken by national authorities on the issue. It is not possible to discern throughout Europe a uniform conception of the significance of religion in society and the meaning or impact of the public expression of a religious belief will differ according to time and

context. Rules in this sphere will consequently vary from one country to another according to national traditions and the requirements imposed by the need to protect the rights and freedoms of others and to maintain public order....

110. This margin of appreciation goes hand in hand with a European supervision embracing both the law and the decisions applying it. The Court's task is to determine whether the measures taken at national level were justified in principle and proportionate. In delimiting the extent of the margin of appreciation in the present case the Court must have regard to what is at stake, namely the need to protect the rights and freedoms of others, to preserve public order and to secure civil peace and true religious pluralism, which is vital to the survival of a democratic society....

...

115. After examining the parties' arguments, the Grand Chamber sees no good reason to depart from the approach taken by the Chamber as follows [Eds.: Indented paragraphs are quotations from the 2004 judgment of the Chamber]:

> ... The Court... notes the emphasis placed in the Turkish constitutional system on the protection of the rights of women... Gender equality — recognised by the European Court as one of the key principles underlying the Convention and a goal to be achieved by member States of the Council of Europe — was also found by the Turkish Constitutional Court to be a principle implicit in the values underlying the Constitution...
>
> ... In addition, like the Constitutional Court ..., the Court considers that, when examining the question of the Islamic headscarf in the Turkish context, there must be borne in mind the impact which wearing such a symbol, which is presented or perceived as a compulsory religious duty, may have on those who choose not to wear it. As has already been noted, the issues at stake include the protection of the "rights and freedoms of others" and the "maintenance of public order" in a country in which the majority of the population, while professing a strong attachment to the rights of women and a secular way of life, adhere to the Islamic faith. Imposing limitations on freedom in this sphere may, therefore, be regarded as meeting a pressing social need by seeking to achieve those two legitimate aims, especially since, as the Turkish courts stated..., this religious symbol has taken on political significance in Turkey in recent years.
>
> ... The Court does not lose sight of the fact that there are extremist political movements in Turkey which seek to impose on society as a whole their religious symbols and conception of a society founded on religious precepts... It has previously said that each Contracting State may, in accordance with the Convention provisions, take a stance against such political movements, based on its historical experience. The regulations concerned have to be viewed in that context and constitute a measure intended to achieve the legitimate aims referred to above and thereby to preserve pluralism in the university.

...

117. The Court must now determine whether in the instant case there was a reasonable relationship of proportionality between the means employed and the legitimate objectives pursued by the interference.

118. Like the Chamber..., the Grand Chamber notes at the outset that it is common ground that practising Muslim students in Turkish universities are free, within the limits imposed by educational organisational constraints, to manifest their

religion in accordance with habitual forms of Muslim observance. In addition, the resolution adopted by Istanbul University on 9 July 1998 shows that various other forms of religious attire are also forbidden on the university premises.

…

121. … By reason of their direct and continuous contact with the education community, the university authorities are in principle better placed than an international court to evaluate local needs and conditions or the requirements of a particular course.…

122. In the light of the foregoing and having regard to the Contracting States' margin of appreciation in this sphere, the Court finds that the interference in issue was justified in principle and proportionate to the aim pursued.

123. Consequently, there has been no breach of Article 9 of the Convention.

II. ALLEGED VIOLATION OF ARTICLE 2 OF PROTOCOL NO. 1

[Applicant also argued that Article 2 of Protocol No. 1 of the European Convention should be interpreted to uphold her right to wear a headscarf while attending the university. That article provides:

> No person shall be denied the right to education. In the exercise of any functions which it assumes in relation to education and to teaching, the State shall respect the right of parents to ensure such education and teaching in conformity with their own religious and philosophical convictions.

The Grand Chamber relied heavily on its reasoning with respect to freedom of religion in concluding that there had been no violation of Article 2 of Protocol No. 1. It said in part:]

157. … [T]he Court is able to accept that the regulations on the basis of which the applicant was refused access to various lectures and examinations for wearing the Islamic headscarf constituted a restriction on her right to education, notwithstanding the fact that she had had access to the University and been able to read the subject of her choice in accordance with the results she had achieved in the university entrance examination. However, an analysis of the case by reference to the right to education cannot in this instance be divorced from the conclusion reached by the Court with respect to Article 9.…

158. … The obvious purpose of the restriction was to preserve the secular character of educational institutions.

159. As regards the principle of proportionality, the Court found in paragraphs 118 to 121 above that there was a reasonable relationship of proportionality between the means used and the aim pursued. In so finding, it relied in particular on the following factors which are clearly relevant here. Firstly, the measures in question manifestly did not hinder the students in performing the duties imposed by the habitual forms of religious observance. Secondly, the decision-making process for applying the internal regulations satisfied, so far as was possible, the requirement to weigh up the various interests at stake. The university authorities judiciously sought a means whereby they could avoid having to turn away students wearing the headscarf and at

the same time honour their obligation to protect the rights of others and the interests of the education system. Lastly, the process also appears to have been accompanied by safeguards — the rule requiring conformity with statute and judicial review — that were apt to protect the students' interests.

...

161. Consequently, the restriction in question did not impair the very essence of the applicant's right to education....

[By 16 votes to 1, the Court concluded that there had been no violation of Article 9 or of the first sentence of Article 2 of Protocol No. 2.]

DISSENTING OPINION OF JUDGE TULKENS

...

2. ... Underlying the majority's approach is the *margin of appreciation* which the national authorities are recognised as possessing and which reflects, *inter alia*, the notion that they are "better placed" to decide how best to discharge their Convention obligations in what is a sensitive area. The Court's jurisdiction is, of course, subsidiary and its role is not to impose uniform solutions, especially "with regard to establishment of the delicate relations between the Churches and the State"....

3. I would perhaps have been able to follow the margin-of-appreciation approach had not two factors drastically reduced its relevance in the instant case. The first concerns the argument the majority use to justify the width of the margin, namely the diversity of practice between the States on the issue of regulating the wearing of religious symbols in educational institutions and, thus, the lack of a European consensus in this sphere. The comparative-law materials do not allow of such a conclusion, as in none of the member States has the ban on wearing religious symbols extended to university education, which is intended for young adults, who are less amenable to pressure. The second factor concerns the European supervision that must accompany the margin of appreciation.... [O]ther than in connection with Turkey's specific historical background, European supervision seems quite simply to be absent from the judgment. However, the issue raised in the application, whose significance to the right to freedom of religion guaranteed by the Convention is evident, is not merely a "local" issue, but one of importance to all the member States. European supervision cannot, therefore, be escaped simply by invoking the margin of appreciation.

4. On what grounds was the interference with the applicant's right to freedom of religion through the ban on wearing the headscarf based? In the present case, relying exclusively on the reasons cited by the national authorities and courts, the majority put forward, in general and abstract terms, two main arguments: secularism and equality.... In a democratic society, I believe that it is necessary to seek to harmonise the principles of secularism, equality and liberty, not to weigh one against the other.

5. As regards, firstly, *secularism*...: Religious freedom is, however, also a founding principle of democratic societies. Accordingly, the fact that the Grand Chamber recognised the force of the principle of secularism did not release it from its obligation to establish that the ban...met a "pressing social need".... [W]here there has been interference with a fundamental right, the Court's case-law clearly establishes that mere affirmations do not suffice: they must be supported by concrete examples....

6. Under Article 9 of the Convention, the freedom with which this case is concerned is not freedom to have a religion (the internal conviction) but to manifest one's religion (the expression of that conviction). If the Court has been very protective (perhaps over-protective) of religious sentiment…it has shown itself less willing to intervene in cases concerning religious practices…which only appear to receive a subsidiary form of protection.

…

7. … The majority thus consider that wearing the headscarf contravenes the principle of secularism. In so doing, they take up position on an issue that has been the subject of much debate….

In the present case, a generalised assessment of that type gives rise to at least three difficulties. Firstly, the judgment does not address the applicant's argument — which the Government did not dispute — that she had no intention of calling the principle of secularism, a principle with which she agreed, into doubt. Secondly, there is no evidence to show that the applicant, through her attitude, conduct or acts, contravened that principle…. Lastly, the judgment makes no distinction between teachers and students, whereas in the *Dahlab v. Switzerland* decision of 15 February 2001, which concerned a teacher, the Court expressly noted the role-model aspect which the teacher's wearing the headscarf had…. [T]he position of pupils and students seems to me to be different.

8. Freedom to manifest a religion entails everyone being allowed to exercise that right, whether individually or collectively, in public or in private, subject to the dual condition that they do not infringe the rights and freedoms of others and do not prejudice public order.

As regards the first condition, this could have been satisfied if the headscarf the applicant wore as a religious symbol had been ostentatious or aggressive or was used to exert pressure, to provoke a reaction, to proselytise or to spread propaganda and undermined — or was liable to undermine — the convictions of others. However, the Government did not argue that this was the case and there was no evidence before the Court to suggest that Ms Şahin had any such intention. As to the second condition, it has been neither suggested nor demonstrated that there was any disruption in teaching or in everyday life at the University….

9. … [T]he possible effect which wearing the headscarf, which is presented as a symbol, may have on those who do not wear it does not appear to me, in the light of the Court's case-law, to satisfy the requirement of a pressing social need….

10. In fact, it is the threat posed by "extremist political movements" seeking to "impose on society as a whole their religious symbols and conception of a society founded on religious precepts" which, in the Court's view, serves to justify the regulations in issue, which constitute "a measure intended…to preserve pluralism in the university"….

While everyone agrees on the need to prevent radical Islamism, a serious objection may nevertheless be made to such reasoning. Merely wearing the headscarf cannot be associated with fundamentalism and it is vital to distinguish between those who wear the headscarf and "extremists" who seek to impose the headscarf as they do other religious symbols. Not all women who wear the headscarf are fundamentalists and there is nothing to suggest that the applicant held fundamentalist views.... [T]he judgment fails to provide any concrete example of the type of pressure concerned....

11. Turning to *equality*, the majority focus on the protection of women's rights and the principle of sexual equality.... By converse implication, wearing the headscarf is considered synonymous with the alienation of women. The ban on wearing the headscarf is therefore seen as promoting equality between men and women. However, what, in fact, is the connection between the ban and sexual equality? The judgment does not say.... [W]earing the headscarf has no single meaning; it is a practise that is engaged in for a variety of reasons. It does not necessarily symbolise the submission of women to men and there are those who maintain that, in certain cases, it can even be a means of emancipating women. What is lacking in this debate is the opinion of women, both those who wear the headscarf and those who choose not to.

12. On this issue, the Grand Chamber refers in its judgment to the *Dahlab v. Switzerland*... citing what to my mind is the most questionable part of the reasoning in that decision, namely that wearing the headscarf represents a "powerful external symbol", which "appeared to be imposed on women by a religious precept that was hard to reconcile with the principle of gender equality" and that the practice could not easily be "reconciled with the message of tolerance, respect for others and, above all, equality and non-discrimination that all teachers in a democratic society should convey to their pupils".

... The applicant, a young adult university student, said — and there is nothing to suggest that she was not telling the truth — that she wore the headscarf of her own free will. In this connection, I fail to see how the principle of sexual equality can justify prohibiting a woman from following a practice which, in the absence of proof to the contrary, she must be taken to have freely adopted....

13. ... In these circumstances, there has been a violation of the applicant's right to freedom of religion, as guaranteed by the Convention.

...

[The dissenting opinion also disagreed on several grounds with the majority's disposition of applicant's claim based on Article 2 of Protocol No. 1.]

20. I end by noting that all these issues must also be considered in the light of the observations set out in the annual activity report published in June 2005 of the European Commission against Racism and Intolerance, which expresses concern about the climate of hostility existing against persons who are or are believed to be Muslim and considers that the situation requires attention and action in the future. Above all, the message that needs to be repeated over and over again is that the best means of preventing and combating fanaticism and extremism is to uphold human rights.

NOTE

In 2008, under the leadership of Prime Minister Recep Tayyip Erdoğan and his Justice and Development Party (the *Adalet ve Kalkınma Partisi*), Turkey's Parliament passed a constitutional amendment, by an overwhelming majority, allowing women to wear headscarves on university campuses. The amendment was challenged in a case brought before the Constitutional Court. The Court invalidated the measure reasoning, in part, that it violated the Turkish Constitution's foundational commitment to secularism.

In 2010, the ruling party won sweeping changes to the constitution through a national referendum. The political triumph emboldened the ruling party to revisit the headscarf issue. Within a few months, the Higher Education Council eased restrictions on headscarves at state universities by announcing that instructors could no longer adopt disciplinary action such as removing an individual from class for an infraction of the dress code. Headscarves bans remained unaltered in secondary schools. However, in mid 2012, the Ministry of Education announced that an educational reform bill would allow female students in secondary school to wear headscarves during elective courses on religion.

COMMENT ON PROHIBITION OF HEADSCARVES IN FRANCE

As discussed, p. 634, *supra*, France enacted a national law in 2004 categorically prohibiting any student attending an elementary or secondary state school from wearing 'conspicuous' religious garb and symbols, including the headscarf. Prior to passage of that Act, French law provided state schools the discretion to prohibit Muslim girls from wearing the headscarf under certain conditions. Those conditions included a determination by school authorities that 'inherently, in the circumstances in which [religious signs] are worn, individually or collectively, or conspicuously or as a means of protest, might constitute a form of pressure, provocation, proselytism or propaganda, undermine the dignity or freedom of the pupil or other members of the educational community, compromise their health or safety, disrupt the conduct of teaching activities and the educational role of the teachers, or, lastly, interfere with order in the school or the normal functioning of the public service.' The law also designated local disciplinary authorities to determine whether an individual's breach of a dress code would result in suspension from school.

In 2008, a chamber of the European Court of Human Rights issued a judgment addressing the pre-2004 French legal regime. The case, *Dogru v. France* (Application No. 27058/05), involved an 11-year-old Muslim girl who was expelled from a state school due to her failure to obey a school rule prohibiting headscarves in physical education classes. The Court applied the Grand Chamber's framework in *Sahin* and concluded that the school's actions were consistent with the Convention. The Court explained:

> 29.... [T]he Conseil d'Etat [France's highest administrative court] has... annulled the internal rules of schools that have imposed a strict ban on the wearing of any distinctive religious sign in classes or on the school premises on the grounds that the terms used were too general [citing decisions in 1992 and 1994]. Likewise, penalties for merely wearing a headscarf in a school cannot be upheld if it is not established that the behaviour of the pupil in question amounted to an act of pressure

or proselytism or interfered with public order in the school [citing decisions in 1996 and 1997].

64.... [T]he State may limit the freedom to manifest a religion, for example by wearing an Islamic headscarf, if the exercise of that freedom clashes with the aim of protecting the rights and freedoms of others, public order and public safety. Accordingly, compelling a motorcyclist, who was a practising Sikh wearing a turban, to wear a helmet was a safety measure and any resulting interference with the exercise of his freedom of religion was justified on grounds of the protection of health (see *X v. the United Kingdom*, Commission decision (1978)). Likewise, security checks enforced at airports (see *Phull v. France* (2005) or at the entrance to consulates (see *El Morsli v. France* (2008)) and consisting in ordering the removal of a turban or a veil in order to submit to such checks do not constitute disproportionate interferences with the exercise of the right to religious freedom. Nor does the regulation of student dress or the refusal to provide administrative services, such as issuing a diploma, constitute a disproportionate interference where the individual concerned fails to comply with the rules (in the case in point requiring a student wearing the Islamic headscarf to appear with her head uncovered on a passport photo), regard being had to the requirements of the secular university system (see *Karaduman v. Turkey* (1993)). [The Court also reiterated its holding in *Dahlab*].

...

68. ... [In] the present case, the Court observes that the domestic authorities justified the ban on wearing the headscarf during physical education classes on grounds of compliance with the school rules on health, safety and assiduity which were applicable to all pupils without distinction....

69. The Court also observes, more generally, that the purpose of that restriction on manifesting a religious conviction was to adhere to the requirements of secularism in state schools....

70. The Court next notes that it transpires from these various sources that the wearing of religious signs was not inherently incompatible with the principle of secularism in schools, but became so according to the conditions in which they were worn and the consequences that the wearing of a sign might have.

71. In that connection the Court refers to its earlier judgments in which it held that it was for the national authorities, in the exercise of their margin of appreciation, to take great care to ensure that, in keeping with the principle of respect for pluralism and the freedom of others, the manifestation by pupils of their religious beliefs on school premises did not take on the nature of an ostentatious act that would constitute a source of pressure and exclusion (see *Köse and Others* (2006)). In the Court's view, that concern does indeed appear to have been answered by the French secular model.

72. The Court also notes that in France, as in Turkey or Switzerland, secularism is a constitutional principle, and a founding principle of the Republic, to which the entire population adheres and the protection of which appears to be of prime importance, in particular in schools. The Court reiterates that an attitude which fails to respect that principle will not necessarily be accepted as being covered by the freedom to manifest one's religion and will not enjoy the protection of Article 9 of the Convention....

73. In the present case the Court considers that the conclusion reached by the national authorities that the wearing of a veil, such as the Islamic headscarf, was

incompatible with sports classes for reasons of health or safety is not unreasonable....

74. The Court also notes that the disciplinary proceedings against the applicant fully satisfied the duty to undertake a balancing exercise of the various interests at stake.... [T]he authorities concerned made many unsuccessful attempts over a long period of time to enter into dialogue with the applicant and a period of reflection was granted her and subsequently extended. Furthermore, the ban was limited to the physical education class, so cannot be regarded as a ban in the strict sense of the term (see *Köse and Others*). Moreover, it can be seen from the circumstances of the case that these events had led to a general atmosphere of tension within the school....

...

76. The Court considers, having regard to the foregoing, that the penalty of expulsion does not appear disproportionate, and notes that the applicant was able to continue her schooling by correspondence classes...

Following the judgment by the ECtHR, France enacted new legislation which came into force in 2011. The law specifically addresses full-face coverings such as burqas and niqabs.[13] Women are forbidden from wearing such garments in public spaces, defined very broadly to include streets, markets, private stores, government buildings, train stations and public transit. Belgium adopted a very similar prohibition which also came into force in 2011. Unlike the French law, Belgium's includes the possibility of imprisonment (up to seven days) for women who violate the law. Some municipalities in other European countries (e.g., Italy and Spain) have also enacted laws prohibiting burqas and niqabs in public institutions or have interpreted existing law to effectuate such a prohibition.

QUESTIONS

1. Turkey's situation showed some similarities to the French situation and some dramatic differences. Do you believe that as a matter of policy or law that the ban of headscarves in public educational institutions was equally justified or unjustified in France and Turkey or more justified in one country than the other?

2. Is the *Dahlab* decision an easier or more difficult decision than *Şahin* to justify under the European Convention?

3. In her dissenting opinion in *Şahin*, Judge Tulkens emphasizes that the individual in the case at hand did not intend to persuade others to adopt a form of religion by wearing her headscarf and that she chose to wear a headscarf of her own free will. Are these relevant factors for assessing the legality of the government's policy?

[13] The burqa is a full-body garment that hides a woman's face by a mesh screen. The niqab is a garment that includes a veil covering the entirety of a woman's hair and face except for her eyes.

4. What arguments would you make under the ICCPR (France is a state party) to challenge the legality of the French ban on headscarves for girls in public schools? Would exactly the same arguments apply if you were challenging the law's ban on 'large' crosses for Christian children or 'large' skullcaps for Jewish boys?

5. Putting challenges to the law's legality to the side, what is your view of the appropriateness or likely effectiveness (with respect to what French goals?) of the law, given the context that it addresses? Should the Government have pursued other policies? Which?

6. In *Dogru v. France*, the ECtHR referenced the fact that the regulations on religious dress involved determinations by local authorities with regard to the specific circumstances in a school. How would France's 2004 law categorically prohibiting headscarves across all state schools fare under the ECtHR framework? Is France's 2011 law on burqas and niqabs consistent with the Convention?

CRUCIFIXES IN ITALIAN CLASSROOMS

In a major controversy involving religious symbolism, the ECtHR decided *Lautsi v. Italy*, which concerned the presence of crucifixes in state school classrooms in Italy. In a unanimous opinion, a chamber of seven judges held that the practice was incompatible with the freedom of religion. Relying in part on *Dahlab*, the Court reasoned:

> Ms Lautsi's convictions also concern the impact of the display of the crucifix on her children, who at the material time were aged 11 and 13. The Court acknowledges that, as submitted, it is impossible not to notice crucifixes in the classrooms. In the context of public education they are necessarily perceived as an integral part of the school environment and may therefore be considered "powerful external symbols" (see *Dahlab v. Switzerland* (2001)).
>
> The presence of the crucifix may easily be interpreted by pupils of all ages as a religious sign, and they will feel that they have been brought up in a school environment marked by a particular religion. What may be encouraging for some religious pupils may be emotionally disturbing for pupils of other religions or those who profess no religion. That risk is particularly strong among pupils belonging to religious minorities. Negative freedom of religion...extends to practices and symbols expressing, in particular or in general, a belief, a religion or atheism. That negative right deserves special protection if it is the State which expresses a belief and dissenters are placed in a situation from which they cannot extract themselves if not by making disproportionate efforts and acts of sacrifice.

A close observer of the Court wrote, 'The political response to the Chamber's judgment in *Lautsi* is without precedent in European human rights terms'...'The Chamber's judgment was reported to have "caused the most widespread opposition in the history of the European Court of Human Rights: 20 countries are officially opposed and have joined Italy in the defence of the crucifix"' (McGoldrick 2011).

Lautsi v. Italy

European Court of Human Rights, 2011, Judgment of Grand Chamber, Application No. 30814/06

[T]he second sentence of Article 2 of Protocol No. 1 does not prevent States from imparting through teaching or education information or knowledge of a directly or indirectly religious or philosophical kind....

... [I]t requires the State, in exercising its functions with regard to education and teaching, to take care that information or knowledge included in the curriculum is conveyed in an objective, critical and pluralistic manner, enabling pupils to develop a critical mind particularly with regard to religion in a calm atmosphere free of any proselytism. The State is forbidden to pursue an aim of indoctrination that might be considered as not respecting parents' religious and philosophical convictions. That is the limit that the States must not exceed.

...

There is no evidence before the Court that the display of a religious symbol on classroom walls may have an influence on pupils and so it cannot reasonably be asserted that it does or does not have an effect on young persons whose convictions are still in the process of being formed.

However, it is understandable that the first applicant might see in the display of crucifixes in the classrooms of the State school formerly attended by her children a lack of respect on the State's part for her right to ensure their education and teaching in conformity with her own philosophical convictions. Be that as it may, the applicant's subjective perception is not in itself sufficient to establish a breach of Article 2 of Protocol No. 1.

The Government, for their part, explained that the presence of crucifixes in State-school classrooms, being the result of Italy's historical development, a fact which gave it not only a religious connotation but also an identity-linked one, now corresponded to a tradition which they considered it important to perpetuate. They added that, beyond its religious meaning, the crucifix symbolised the principles and values which formed the foundation of democracy and western civilisation, and that its presence in classrooms was justifiable on that account.

The Court takes the view that the decision whether or not to perpetuate a tradition falls in principle within the margin of appreciation of the respondent State. The Court must moreover take into account the fact that Europe is marked by a great diversity between the States of which it is composed, particularly in the sphere of cultural and historical development. It emphasises, however, that the reference to a tradition cannot relieve a Contracting State of its obligation to respect the rights and freedoms enshrined in the Convention and its Protocols.

...

The Court concludes in the present case that the decision whether crucifixes should be present in State-school classrooms is, in principle, a matter falling within the margin of appreciation of the respondent State. Moreover, the fact that there is no European consensus on the question of the presence of religious symbols in State schools speaks in favour of that approach.

This margin of appreciation, however, goes hand in hand with European supervision . . .

In that connection, it is true that by prescribing the presence of crucifixes in State-school classrooms — a sign which, whether or not it is accorded in addition a secular symbolic value, undoubtedly refers to Christianity — the regulations confer on the country's majority religion preponderant visibility in the school environment.

That is not in itself sufficient, however, to denote a process of indoctrination. . . .

. . .

. . . [A] crucifix on a wall is an essentially passive symbol and this point is of importance in the Court's view, particularly having regard to the principle of neutrality. It cannot be deemed to have an influence on pupils comparable to that of didactic speech or participation in religious activities.

[The Grand Chamber next describes the passages of the ECtHR's lower chamber opinion (which we reproduced above) relying on *Dahlab*.]

The Grand Chamber . . . considers that [*Dahlab*] cannot serve as a basis in this case because the facts of the two cases are entirely different.

It points out that the case of *Dahlab* concerned the measure prohibiting the applicant from wearing the Islamic headscarf while teaching, which was intended to protect the religious beliefs of the pupils and their parents and to apply the principle of denominational neutrality in schools enshrined in domestic law. After observing that the authorities had duly weighed the competing interests involved, the Court held, having regard above all to the tender age of the children for whom the applicant was responsible, that the authorities had not exceeded their margin of appreciation.

Moreover, the effects of the greater visibility which the presence of the crucifix gives to Christianity in schools needs to be further placed in perspective by consideration of the following points. Firstly, the presence of crucifixes is not associated with compulsory teaching about Christianity. Secondly, according to the indications provided by the Government, Italy opens up the school environment in parallel to other religions. The Government indicated in this connection that it was not forbidden for pupils to wear Islamic headscarves or other symbols or apparel having a religious connotation; alternative arrangements were possible to help schooling fit in with non-majority religious practices; the beginning and end of Ramadan were "often celebrated" in schools; and optional religious education could be organised in schools for "all recognised religious creeds". Moreover, there was nothing to suggest that the authorities were intolerant of pupils who believed in other religions, were non-believers or who held non-religious philosophical convictions. In addition, the applicants did not assert that the presence of the crucifix in classrooms had encouraged the development of teaching practices with a proselytising tendency. . . .

J. H. H. Weiler, Editorial, State and Nation; Church, Mosque and Synagogue — The Trailer

8 Int'l. J. Con. L. 157 (2010)

[Joseph Weiler, who represented a group of eight intervening states on the appeal to the Grand Chamber, wrote the following commentary subsequent to the oral pleadings before the Grand Chamber.]

...

I want to offer a somewhat novel, surely contestable, way of framing the issues as they manifest themselves today....

...

Consider France and the United Kingdom, good examples because both are founding members of the European Convention of Human Rights and, with the usual imperfections, are both considered robust liberal democracies in good standing.

France, in its very Constitution, defines itself as laïque — usually understood as a political doctrine which does not allow the State any endorsement or support of religion and would, say, consider the display of religious symbols by the State or the funding of religious schools, as, well, anathema....

Laïcité is to be contrasted with an opposing doctrine, which is also very common in Europe and which has no accepted name. "Theocracy"...would not be an appropriate label to describe a state like the modern UK or Denmark. For convenience let us refer to 'non-laïque' states. Like France, like everyone else, the non-laïque are both committed to, and obligated by, an imperative of assuring individual freedom of and from religion, but see no wrong in a religious, or religiously rooted, self-understanding of nation and state, and in a public space more or less replete with state-endorsed religious symbology. In England, part of the UK, the Monarch is both the Head of State but also the Titular head of the Anglican Faith and its institutional manifestation in the Church of England: the "Established Church" of the Nation and State. Many state functions have a religious character: clergy sit (or sat) ex-ufficio as part of the legislature, the flag carries the Cross (of St. George) and the national anthem is a Prayer to God.

...

... [T]here is a deep contestation about the most suitable way to regulate the symbolic and iconographic entanglement of Church and State. The laïque position is surely not "neutral" about that contestation: It is as much a polar position as is the 'non-laïque' position. It does not simply choose a side. It is a side.

...

... There are those who truly believe that laïcité is a primordial condition — sine-qua-non for a good liberal democracy and that, at least implicitly, the non-laïque position is sub-optimal at best and aberrational at worst. Consequently, it is morally imperative for good democrats and liberal pluralists to attempt to clip the wings of religious manifestations of the non-laïque state as far as possible — a principled and consistent position.

There are others (myself included) who hold the view that, even more in today's world than before, the European version of the non-laïque state is hugely important in the lesson of tolerance it forces on such states and its citizens towards those who do not share the "official" religions and in the example it gives the rest of the world of a principled mediation between a collective self-understanding rooted in a religious sensibility, or religious history, or religiously-inspired values and the imperative exigencies of liberal democracy. That there is something inspiring and optimistic by the fact that even though the Queen is the Titular Head of the Church of England, the many Catholics, Muslims and Jews, not to mention the majority of atheists and agnostics, can genuinely consider her as "their Queen" too, and equal citizens of England and the UK. I think there is intrinsic value of incalculable worth in the European pluralism which validates both a France and UK as acceptable models in which the individual right to and from religion may take place.

...

... [S]urely Freedom FROM Religion is not absolute, and its vindication has to be so balanced, and the principle collective good against which it should be balanced would, in my view, be the aforementioned collective freedom of a self-understanding, self-definition and determination of the collective self as having some measure of religious reference. Freedom OF Religion surely requires that no school kid be obligated to chant God's name, even in, say, God Save the Queen. But does Freedom FROM Religion entitle such to demand that others not so chant, to have another national anthem? How does one negotiate the individual and the collective rights at issue here?

... [B]oth to understand the new debates and to arrive at meaningful, ethical, deontological, identitarian and pragmatic results may profit by this reframing.

...

Stanley Fish, Crucifixes and Diversity: The Odd Couple

New York Times, 28 Mar. 2011

The question is not what can a crucifix possibly mean in all the settings the world might offer, but what does it in mean in this setting, hanging on the wall of every classroom with a state imprimatur? What is a non-Christian student likely to think —"Aha, a symbol of pluralism and universal acceptance" or "I get it; this is a Catholic space and I'm here on sufferance?"...

...

Exclusion would be the result, we are told, if the students had been the objects of indoctrination, but because the crucifixes just hang there without saying anything, they were not: "[A] crucifix on a wall is an essentially passive symbol" and "it cannot be deemed to have an influence on pupils comparable to that of didactic speech." Judge Bonello [in concurrence] glosses and drives home the point: "The mere display of a voiceless testimonial of a historical symbol...in no away amounts to teaching." Actually, it does: the lesson (of official authority) is enhanced by not being voiced; the absence of didactic speech itself says "you don't have to be told what this means; you know." The effect is the one produced in a country where a king or leader-for-life has his picture hung everywhere. Nothing need be said.

Dominic McGoldrick, Religion in the European Public Square and in European Public Life: Crucifixes in the Classroom?

11 Hum. Rts. L. Rev. 451 (2011)

There was no evidence before the GC [Grand Chamber] that the display of a religious symbol on classroom walls might have an influence on pupils....The GC's reliance on the lack of evidence is particularly interesting. In previous religious clothing cases the Court either ignored evidence that the wearing had not actually caused any problems or made its own assertions about their possible effects (*Dahlab*, *Şahin*).

...

Even engaging in a relative approach to the assessment of symbols was inevitably going to leave the GC open to criticism. Islamic headscarves, worn by a minority, may be powerful external symbols that challenge neutrality. However, Christian crucifixes, a symbol of the majority religion, are somehow merely passive and do not challenge neutrality. It may have been better for the GC to have simply accepted that the assessment of the meaning and effect of religious symbols was complex and would be left to the national authorities to assess within the normal bounds of the margin of appreciation.

...

As noted, the GC's view was that the decision whether or not to perpetuate a tradition fell in principle within the margin of appreciation of the State. Historically, those traditions have been dominated by Christianity. The inevitable consequence is that non-dominant traditions (i.e. minority, non-Christian ones) will not be equally represented or perpetuated in the public reasoning and public visual squares. Added to that, the ECtHR has accepted that, in the defence of a secular order, a state can prohibit the wearing of Islamic headscarves in schools, and even in universities....

It has been suggested that Christianity and Christian values have been defended even at the expense of trampling on fundamental individual freedoms, because the ECtHR does not perceive them as conflicting with the core values of the Convention system. Islam, on the other hand, even when it is the vast majority's religion (as with Turkey), has been restrictively regulated on the ground that it threatens the democratic basis of the State. Assessing the value of the ECHR to Muslims is a complex task. However, the problem is also one of public and political perception.... It has been argued that the GC's decision in Lautsi, 'confirms the Christian-centric outlook of European institutions and it will confirm many Turks' perceptions that as Muslims, they are inevitably viewed with suspicion'.

QUESTIONS

1. Is the logic of the ECtHR ruling in *Dahlab* consistent with the Chamber's or the Grand Chamber's decision in *Lautsi*?

2. Does the presence of the crucifix in Italian classrooms constitute in itself an injury to minority groups that is incompatible with the freedom of religion or is the real threat the prospective risk of a slippery slope?

3. Are you persuaded by Weiler that all citizens of England see the Queen as 'their Queen'? Weiler also framed that claim in the following terms:

> [I]t is this special combination of private and public liberties, reflecting a particular spirit of tolerance, which explains how in countries such as, say, Britain or Denmark

to give but two examples, where there is an established state church no less — Anglican and Lutheran, respectively — Catholics, Jews, Muslims and, of course, the many citizens who profess no religious faith, can be entirely 'at home,' play a full role in public life including the holding of the highest office, and feel it is 'their country' no less than those belonging to the established church.

Do you agree with this set of claims? How much of Weiler's overall argument depends on the persuasiveness of this claim?

4. McGoldrick states that the Grand Chamber perhaps should have 'simply accepted that the assessment of the meaning and effect of religious symbols was complex and would be left to the national authorities to assess within the normal bounds of the margin of appreciation.' Would his criticism result in a different outcome in the *Lautsi* case or simply a different rationale for the same holding?

ADDITIONAL READING

D. W. Cole, R. Torfs, D. M. Kirkham, & C. Scott (eds.), *Islam, Europe and Emerging Legal Issues* (2012); M. Richards et al., 'Voluntary Codes of Conduct for Religious Persuasion: Effective Tools for Balancing Human Rights and Resolving Conflicts?', 6 Religion & Hum. Rts. 151 (2011); Article XIX, *Bans on the Full Face Veil and Human Rights A Freedom of Expression Perspective* (2010); I. Rorive, 'Religious Symbols in the Public Space: In Search of a European Answer', 30 Cardozo L. Rev. 2669 (2009); P. G. Danchin, 'Islam in the Secular Nomos of the European Court of Human Rights', 32 Mich. J. Int'l. L. 663 (2011); Z. R. Calo, 'Pluralism: Secularism and the European Court of Human Rights', 26 J. L. & Religion 261 (2010–11); P. G. Danchin, 'Of Prophets and Proselytes: Freedom of Religion and the Conflict of Rights in International Law', 49 Harv. Int'l. L. J. 249 (2008); N. Lerner, *Religion, Secular Beliefs and Human Rights: 25 Years after the 1981 Declaration* (2006); P. M. Taylor, *Freedom of Religion: UN and European Human Rights Law and Practice* (2006).

4. FREEDOM OF SPEECH

Freedom of speech forms one of the obvious boundary lines between relatively open and closed societies, between liberal democracies and different types of authoritarian states like China, Iran, North Korea or Zimbabwe. Whatever the form of authoritarian regime, a liberal value like speech and its related rights such as assembly and association will bow to one or another degree to censorship and other repressive controls. In some instances, the explanations for different understandings of this human right would stress factors like an authoritarian regime's guiding ideology and its rulers' concern about resistance or subversion. Relatively free speech may pose too great a danger for the survival of the existing political system. In other cases, different conceptions of free speech and its relation to other rights and state interests may reflect religious beliefs, cultural patterns or long-standing traditions and practices.

Section 4 examines such different conceptions of free speech and its limitations. Some of these differences exist among states within the world of liberal democracies, whereas others involve liberal democracies and authoritarian states in such diverse regions as Europe and the Middle East. The topics selected to explore these issues concern 'hate speech' and blasphemy (ranging from offensive texts to cartoons).

COMMENT ON HATE SPEECH

The view of the ICCPR Committee under that Convention's Optional Protocol that appears below, the *Faurisson* case, involves a so-called 'Holocaust-denial law' that has a close affinity with laws making 'hate speech' a criminal offence (that may also be subject to civil sanctions). This Comment provides background on the general issue of hate speech, several definitions of which appear in the official texts below. The fundamental idea covers abusive, denigrating, harassing speech based on a group or individual's national, religious, racial or ethnic identity. In some but not all definitions, such speech must incite violence or discrimination.

The laws imposing criminal and other sanctions on hate speech clearly impinge on freedom of speech, a core value of the human rights movement that is protected under the major universal and regional human rights instruments. Consider the universal instruments, which at once proclaim and limit this freedom:

> *Article 19, UDHR*: Everyone has the right to freedom of opinion and expression; this right includes freedom to ... impart information and ideas through any media and regardless of frontiers.
>
> *Article 19, ICCPR*: ...
>
> (2) Everyone shall have the right to freedom of expression; this right shall include freedom to...impart information and ideas of all kinds, regardless of frontiers....
>
> (3) The exercise of the right provided for in paragraph 2 of this article carries with it special duties and responsibilities. It may therefore be subject to certain restrictions, but these shall only be such as are provided by law and are necessary:
>
> (a) For respect of the rights or reputations of others;
>
> (b) For the protection of national security or of public order (*ordre public*), or of public health or morals.

Note also the following ICCPR articles, each of which has a comparable UDHR article: (1) the equal protection clause in Article 26; (2) the provision in ICCPR Article 5 that nothing in the Covenant should be interpreted as implying 'for any group or person any right to engage in any activity...aimed at the destruction of any of the rights and freedom recognized herein....'; and (3) the provision in Article 17 that no one shall be subject to 'arbitrary or unlawful interference with his privacy...nor to unlawful attacks on his honour and reputation'.

The arguments in favour of free speech are broadly familiar, for example: the full realization of the individual human personality, the challenge to existing beliefs (the 'marketplace of ideas') and the related stimulus to inquiry and debate and development of knowledge, the relation to principles of democratic government and pluralism, and its close functional association with other human rights like freedoms of belief, religion and association. But are these arguments sufficient to justify the protection of hate speech directed to particular racial, ethnic, religious, gender or other groups or their members? Such speech itself attacks basic premises of the human rights system, premises as deep as equal human dignity, respect for others and equal protection. It may deny that the targeted group is entitled to benefit together with the rest of the population from human rights protections. It may advocate, indeed passionately urge, discriminatory or even violent action against members of the targeted group. It may pose threats of a greater or lesser immediacy of such violence.

The quoted provisions above of the ICCPR include qualifications to free speech that bear generally on these types of restrictive laws. Several human rights instruments are more explicit on these issues — for example, Article 20(2) of the ICCPR: 'Any advocacy of national, racial or religious hatred that constitutes incitement to discrimination, hostility or violence shall be prohibited by law.' Manfred Nowak, in his *U.N. Covenant on Civil and Political Rights: CCPR Commentary* (2nd edn. 2005), observes (pp. 474–5) that the 'legal formulation of this provision is not entirely clear'. The wording of paragraph (2):

> literally means that incitement to discrimination without violence must also be prohibited. ... Particularly inexplicable is the insertion of the word 'discrimination'. . . .
>
> . . . It is most difficult to conceive of an advocacy of national, racial or religious hatred that does not simultaneously incite discrimination. . . . Art. 20(2) . . . may be sensibly interpreted only in light of its object and purpose, i.e., taking into consideration its *responsive character* with regard to the Nazi racial hatred campaigns. . . . Thus, despite its unclear formulation, Art 20(2) does not require States parties to prohibit advocacy of hatred in private that instigates non-violent acts of racial or religious discrimination. What the delegates . . . had in mind was to . . . prevent the public incitement of racial hatred and violence within a State or against other States and peoples.

Some states have forbidden political groups or parties that are based on racism, and hence that employ hate speech, from participating in elections. In Israel, for example, a system of proportional representation works by having a candidates' list from different parties or political formations presented to the electorate, which votes for a list as a whole. Amendment No. 9 to the Basic Law on the Knesset (Parliament) provides: 'A candidate's list shall not participate in elections to the Knesset if its objects or actions, expressly or by implication, include one of the following: . . . (3) incitement to racism'.

The *Jersild* Decision

Consider the approach of the European Court of Human Rights in *Jersild v. Denmark*, (Application No. 15890/89) (1994). The question posed was whether Jersild, a Danish journalist, was criminally liable for aiding and abetting three youths who made racist remarks on interviews conducted by Jersild on a television programme on matters of public interest. The three young men were members of a group, the Greenjackets, that engaged in hate speech against particular groups — in this case people, particularly Danish residents, of African descent. In the course of the interview conducted by Jersild after he had located the men, and which had been sharply edited by Jersild from an initial length of hours to a few minutes, the men made numerous ugly and denigrating remarks about blacks. There was no allegation in the criminal charge that Jersild or the broadcasting station shared those views. On the other hand, since the point of the programme was to convey information to the Danish public about atypical, small racist groups, there was no effort by Jersild or the broadcasting station to challenge or oppose the racist views expressed.

A Danish penal statute, responsive to obligations of Denmark under the Convention on the Elimination of All Forms of Racial Discrimination, imposed a fine or imprisonment on '[a]ny person who, publicly or with the intention of disseminating it to a wide circle of people, makes a statement, or other communication, threatening insulting or degrading a group of persons on account of their race, colour, national or ethnic origin or belief ....' The three youths were found guilty of violating the statute, and did not appeal. Jersild was found guilty of aiding and abetting the three youths. His conviction was affirmed by the Danish appellate courts, and he then instituted proceedings before the European Commission on Human Rights, which ultimately referred the case to the European Court of Human Rights.

The Court decided that the conviction — that is, not the hate-speech statute abstractly, but the statute as here applied to Jersild for aiding and abetting — violated the free expression provisions (including freedom of media) of Article 10 of the European Convention on Human Rights. Its opinion stressed the need to protect freedom of the press, and that news reporting through interviews was an important means of informing the public. Conviction of a journalist in these circumstances could hamper discussion of matters of public interest. It concluded that the limitation on Jersild's freedom of expression was not 'necessary in a democratic society', a requirement of Article 10. The prosecution and conviction were disproportionate to the state's interest, also expressed in Article 10, of protecting the reputation or rights of others.

One of the dissenting opinions observed:

> ... The applicant has cut the entire interview down to a few minutes, probably with the consequence or even the intention of retaining the most crude remarks. That being so, it was absolutely necessary to add at least a clear statement of disapproval. The majority of the Court sees such disapproval in the context of the interview, but this is an interpretation of cryptic remarks. Nobody can exclude that certain parts of the public found in the television spot support for their racist prejudices.
>
> And what must be the feelings of those whose human dignity has been attacked, or even denied, by the Greenjackets? Can they get the impression that seen in context the television broadcast contributes to their protection? A journalist's good intentions are not enough in such a situation, especially in a case in which he has himself provoked the racist statements.

Another dissenting opinion noted:

While appreciating that some judges attach particular importance to freedom of expression, the more so as their countries have largely been deprived of it in quite recent times, we cannot accept that this freedom should extend to encouraging racial hatred, contempt for races other than the one to which we belong, and defending violence against those who belong to the races in question. It has been sought to defend the broadcast on the ground that it would provoke a healthy reaction of rejection among the viewers. That is to display an optimism, which to say the least, is belied by experience. Large numbers of young people today, and even of the population at large, finding themselves overwhelmed by the difficulties of life, unemployment and poverty, are only too willing to seek scapegoats who are held up to them without any real word of caution; for — and this is an important point — the journalist responsible for the broadcast in question made no real attempt to challenge the points of view he was presenting, which was necessary if their impact was to be counterbalanced, at least for the viewers.

Sexual Orientation Hate Speech

In *Vejdeland & Ors v. Sweden* (Application No. 1813/07) (2012) the four applicants were convicted for distributing some 100 leaflets left in or on pupils' lockers in an upper secondary school. They contained anti-homosexual messages that the Swedish Supreme Court found to constitute agitation against a national or ethnic group, defined at the time to include contempt for a group of people with reference to their sexual orientation.

Having found that the convictions did interfere with the applicants Article 10(1) freedom of expression, the Court examined whether that interference was 'necessary in a democratic society', in terms of Article 10(2). It reiterated its long-standing jurisprudence according to which freedom of expression protects ideas, even if they offend, shock or disturb, but that necessary restrictions can be imposed.

> 54. The Court notes that the applicants distributed the leaflets with the aim of starting a debate about the lack of objectivity of education in Swedish schools.... [E]ven if this is an acceptable purpose, regard must be paid to the wording of the leaflets. [A]ccording to the leaflets, homosexuality was "a deviant sexual proclivity" that had "a morally destructive effect on the substance of society" [and] was one of the main reasons why HIV and AIDS had gained a foothold and that the "homosexual lobby" tried to play down paedophilia. In the Court's opinion, although these statements did not directly recommend individuals to commit hateful acts, they are serious and prejudicial allegations.
>
> 55. [I]nciting to hatred does not necessarily entail a call for an act of violence, or other criminal acts. Attacks on persons committed by insulting, holding up to ridicule or slandering specific groups of the population can be sufficient for the authorities to favour combating racist speech in the face of freedom of expression exercised in an irresponsible manner.... [D]iscrimination based on sexual orientation is as serious as discrimination based on "race, origin or colour"....
>
> 56. The Court also takes into consideration that the leaflets were left in the lockers of young people who were at an impressionable and sensitive age and who had no possibility to decline to accept them.... Moreover, the distribution of the leaflets took place at a school which none of the applicants attended and to which they did not have free access.

57. In considering the approach of the domestic courts when deciding whether a "pressing social need" existed, and the reasons the authorities adduced to justify the interference, the Court observes the following. The Supreme Court acknowledged the applicants' right to express their ideas while at the same time stressing that along with freedoms and rights people also have obligations; one such obligation being, as far as possible, to avoid statements that are unwarrantably offensive to others, constituting an assault on their rights. The Supreme Court thereafter found that the statements in the leaflets had been unnecessarily offensive. It also emphasised that the applicants had left the leaflets in or on the pupils' lockers, thereby imposing them on the pupils. Having balanced the relevant considerations, the Supreme Court found no reason not to apply the relevant Article of the Penal Code.

58. Finally, an important factor to be taken into account when assessing the proportionality of an interference with freedom of expression is the nature and severity of the penalties imposed.... The Court notes that the applicants were not sentenced to imprisonment, although the crime of which they were convicted carries a penalty of up to two years' imprisonment. Instead, three of them were given suspended sentences combined with fines ranging from approximately EUR 200 to EUR 2,000, and the fourth applicant was sentenced to probation. The Court does not find these penalties excessive in the circumstances.

59. Having regard to the foregoing, the Court considers that the conviction of the applicants and the sentences imposed on them were not disproportionate to the legitimate aim pursued and that the reasons given by the Supreme Court in justification of those measures were relevant and sufficient. The interference with the applicants' exercise of their right to freedom of expression could therefore reasonably be regarded by the national authorities as necessary in a democratic society for the protection of the reputation and rights of others.

60.... [T]he application does not reveal a violation of Article 10 of the Convention.

CONCURRING OPINION OF JUDGE SPIELMANN
JOINED BY JUDGE NUSSBERGER

1. I have to confess that it is with the greatest hesitation that I voted in favour of finding no violation of Article 10 of the Convention.

2. As my colleague, Judge András Sajó, pointed out in his dissenting opinion joined to the *Féret v. Belgium* judgment [Application No. 15615/07, 16 July 2009]:

> "Content regulation and content-based restrictions on speech are based on the assumption that certain expressions go "against the spirit" of the Convention. But "spirits" do not offer clear standards and are open to abuse. Humans, including judges, are inclined to label positions with which they disagree as palpably unacceptable and therefore beyond the realm of protected expression. However, it is precisely where we face ideas that we abhor or despise that we have to be most careful in our judgment, as our personal convictions can influence our ideas about what is actually dangerous."

...

4.... [The Swedish Supreme Court] justified the interference by acknowledging the applicant's right to express his ideas, while at the same time stressing that freedoms and rights went hand in hand with obligations; one of which was "to avoid, as far as possible, statements that are unwarrantably offensive to others, constituting an assault on their rights"....

5. It is submitted that this is a rather vague test which seems to me to be inconsistent with the traditional and well-established case-law of our Court....

6. Still, I agreed, albeit very reluctantly, to find no violation because the distribution of the leaflets took place at a school which none of the applicants attended and to which they did not have free access.... [T]he factual circumstances of the distribution have an impact regarding the scope of the margin of appreciation in a case where... the penalties were not excessive or disproportionate. [T]he leaflets were in the lockers of young people who were at an impressionable and sensitive age and who had no possibility to decline to accept the leaflets. [Members of the LGBT community face deeply rooted prejudices, hostility and widespread discrimination all over Europe....] ...

7. It should also not been forgotten that a real problem of homophobic and transphobic bullying and discrimination in educational settings may justify a restriction of freedom of expression under [Article 10(2)]....

8. It is against this background that I am satisfied, on balance, that the conviction... did not violate Article 10 of the Convention.

CONCURRING OPINION OF JUDGE BOŠTJAN M. ZUPANČIČ

1. It was with some hesitation that I voted for no violation of Article 10....

...

3. [T]he American Supreme Court takes a very liberal position concerning the contents of the controversial messages. That the statement is arguably of inappropriate or controversial character "... *is irrelevant to the question of whether it deals with a matter of public concern*"... "*Speech on public issues occupies the highest rank of the hierarchy of First Amendment values, and is entitled to special protection*".

4. Moreover, the American Supreme Court has set a higher standard for the applicable law in such cases to be facially constitutional. First, it must avoid *content* discrimination (i.e., the State cannot forbid or prosecute inflammatory speech only on *some* "disfavoured" subjects) and, second, it must avoid *viewpoint* discrimination (i.e., forbidding or prosecuting inflammatory speech that expresses one particular view on the subject).... [I]f this American double test were applied to the present case, the [Swedish law] would not pass muster on either count, especially the second: had the applicants defended homosexuality and railed against "wicked homophobes" in their leaflets, they would probably not have been convicted.

5. In our case we have relied on a different kind of logic as did the Swedish Supreme Court, among others (although divided three to two), which considered the relatively inoffensive language of the leaflets to be a cause for *criminal* prosecution and eventually for conviction and punishment.

[The judgment highlights the fact that the pupils could be characterized as a captive audience.]

9.... School grounds [are] a non-public place, requiring an intrusion in order to distribute any information of whatever kind that has not been previously approved by the school's authorities. Coming back to the Supreme Court of the United States, it has held that "*the undoubted freedom to advocate unpopular and controversial views in schools and classrooms must be balanced against the society's countervailing interest in teaching students the boundaries of socially appropriate behaviour*".

10. [Because the pupils can be considered a captive audience in this sense] I maintain that I would be in perfect agreement with the judgment were it based solely (or at least predominantly) on the considerations contained in paragraph 56 of the judgment.

...

12. Nevertheless, we seem to go too far in the present case — on the grounds of proportionality and considerations of hate speech — in limiting freedom of speech by over-estimating the importance of what is being said. In other words, if exactly the same words and phrases were to be used in public newspapers..., they would probably not be considered as a matter for criminal prosecution and condemnation.

Hate Speech in Former Yugoslavia and Rwanda

The effect of years of intense Serbian-nationalist rhetoric under the rule of Milosević on the internal and international wars in the Former Yugoslavia is well known. A news article reported in 1999 that the United States and its Western allies in the Bosnia peacekeeping operation were creating a tribunal with power to close radio and television stations and punish newspapers that issued propaganda undermining peace efforts. Western officials described the broadcasts that they wished to arrest as 'poisonous propaganda'. Groups of journalists and civil liberties groups expressed their concern about these efforts by democratic states to place restraints on the media. The Western officials avoided use of the term censorship, and explained that they 'had no other option, given the venomous propaganda that they said often masquerades as news coverage in Bosnia and that can threaten the safety of the American-led NATO peacekeeping force there.' One spokesman said, 'Basically, there's a tradition here of propaganda in the class of Goebbels'. A State Department official said: 'There are obvious free-speech concerns, but we need to put in place something to deal with the abuses of the media — the hate, the racial epithets and ethnic slurs': *New York Times*, 24 Apr. 1998, p. A8.

NOTE

Recall the 1946 Judgment of the International Military Tribunal at Nuremberg, which makes sparse reference to the Holocaust but includes the following observation, p. 127, *supra*:

> The persecution of the Jews at the hands of the Nazi Government has been proved in the greatest detail before the Tribunal. It is a record of consistent and systematic inhumanity on the greatest scale. Ohlendorf, Chief of Amt III in the RSHA from 1939 to 1943, and who was in command of one of the Einsatz groups in the campaign against the Soviet Union testified as to the methods employed in the extermination of the Jews.... When the witness Bach Zelewski was asked how Ohlendorf could admit the murder of 90,000 people, he replied: 'I am of the opinion that when, for years, for decades, the doctrine is preached that the Slav race is an inferior race, and Jews not even human, then such an outcome is inevitable'.... The Nazi Party preached these doctrines throughout its history, *Der Stürmer* and

other publications were allowed to disseminate hatred of the Jews, and in the speeches and public declarations of the Nazi leaders, the Jews were held up to public ridicule and contempt....

... In the summer of 1941, however, plans were made for the 'final solution' of the Jewish question in Europe. This 'final solution' meant the extermination of the Jews.... Adolf Eichmann, who had been put in charge of this program by Hitler, has estimated that the policy pursued resulted in the killing of 6 million Jews, of which 4 million were killed in the extermination institutions.

Consider the following observations about Rwanda by Bill Berkeley, 'Radio in Rwanda: The Sounds of Silence', *San Diego Union-Tribune*, 18 Aug. 1994:

...

... Human rights groups, the United Nations and even, reluctantly, the U.S. State Department have described this systematic slaughter [in Rwanda] as 'genocide', yet no one has explained how thousands of peasants who say they had never killed before could have been lured, incited or coerced into participating in mass murder on par with this century's worst massacres. One answer, according to captive killers like Kiruhura and other moderate Hutus who were targeted by death squads but managed to escape, lies in the sinister propaganda broadcast by radio stations affiliated with the now-deposed Rwandan government. This was the match that started the fire, they say.

...

... The Tutsis were demonized ... Radio Rwanda and a station owned by members of [the former Hutu President] Habyarimana's inner circle, Radio Milles Collines, had been terrorizing the Hutus with warnings about the evil Tutsi-led RPF and Hutu oppositionists, who were labeled 'enemies' or 'traitors' and who 'deserved to die'. Endless speeches, songs and slogans demonized the Tutsis....

Throughout the terror, Radio Rwanda and Radio Milles Collines have systematically blurred the distinction between rebel soldiers and Tutsi civilians. On May 23, for example, Radio Rwanda warned its listeners of what it called the 'means and clues that the Inyenzi [cockroaches] use to infiltrate in a given zone'. It said RPF soldiers 'change their clothing appearance most of the time, trying to be confused with ordinary people who till the soil and go to the market'.

Hutus were urged to 'guard seriously the roadblock', a reference to the checkpoints where Tutsis were selected for slaughter. On June 1 Radio Milles Collines described the rebels as 'criminals' responsible for a series of harrowing massacres, a fact it claimed had been 'confirmed by international sources'.... [T]he broadcast concluded: 'This is the real face of the RPF. These people are not Rwandans, they are revengeful Ugandans. We hate them; we are disgusted with them, and nobody will accept that they take power....'

...

'All the Westerners who come here ask us this question', says Sixbert Musangamfura, a Hutu journalist. 'They forget the evil of Hitler's propaganda. The propaganda heard here resembles the propaganda made by Joseph Goebbels. People received this propaganda all day long. It is the propaganda that is at the base of this tragedy.' ...

❁ ❁ ❁

The *Faurisson* opinion that follows deals with 'Holocaust denial laws' that have been enacted by several states including Austria, Belgium, France, Germany, Israel, Lithuania, Spain and Switzerland. As noted in McGoldrick and O'Donnell, 'Hate-Speech Laws: Consistency with National and International Human Rights Law', 18 Leg. Stud. 453 (1997), at 457, these laws vary a great deal:

> The essential feature of the laws which attracts the label of holocaust denial is that they make it a criminal offence to deny certain things in a certain way.... [F]or the French law it is 'crimes against humanity as defined by the Nuremberg International Military Tribunal'. The German law is wider, as it refers to 'persecution under National Socialism or any other form of despotism or tyranny'. The Israeli law is even wider again: 'acts committed in the period of the Nazi regime, which are crimes against the Jewish people or crimes against humanity'. The Austrian law extends to denial of the 'nationalist socialist genocide or other national socialist crimes against humanity'. The Austrian law extends to cover the gross trivialisation, approval or justification of the same. The German law is similar.

The following excerpts from Frederick Schauer, 'The Exceptional First Amendment', in Michael Ignatieff, *American Exceptionalism and Human Rights* (2005), at 32, underscore the breadth of the concept.

> ... Although the label "hate speech" tends to be applied capaciously, the phrase can be understood as encompassing four distinct but interrelated freedom of speech issues. First, there is the question of the legitimacy of prohibiting various racial, ethnic, and religious epithets — *nigger, wog, kike, paki, kaffir*, and the like — words whose use, except as ironic self-reference by members of those groups, is invariably intended to harm, to offend, and to marginalize. Second, the question of hate speech sometimes involves the issue of restrictions on circulating certain demonstrably false factual propositions about various racial or religious groups, with prohibitions on Holocaust denial being the most common example. A third hate speech issue arises with respect to laws prohibiting the advocacy of or incitement to racial or religious intolerance, hatred, or violence, as with explicit calls to race-based violence, explicit appeals for racial exclusion, and explicit calls for repatriation of members of racial or religious minorities to the countries of their ancestry. Finally, hate speech questions are presented, especially in the context of gender when it is argued that epithets, and occasionally pictures, create a hostile, and therefore marginalizing or excluding, workplace or educational or cultural environment.
>
> ... The precise form of attempting to control hate speech by law varies considerably among the nations of the world. Germany and Israel, among other countries, ban the Nazi Party and its descendants, as well as prohibiting other political parties whose programs include racial hatred, racial separation, and racial superiority.' ... Germany, Israel, and France are among the nations that prohibit the sale and distribution of various Nazi items, including swastikas, Nazi flags, and, on occasion, images of Adolph Hitler and copies of *Mein Kampf*.... Canada, Germany, and France, along with others, permit sanctions against those who would deny the existence of the Holocaust.'... France imposes fines with some frequency on public utterances espousing the racial or religious inferiority of various groups, or advocating the exclusion of people from France on the basis of their race, their religion, their

> ethnicity, or their national origin. The Netherlands outlaws public insults based on race, religion, or sexual preference."...And South Africa, New Zealand, Australia, Canada, the United Kingdom, and all of the Scandinavian countries, among many others, follow the mandates of Article 20(2) of the International Covenant on Civil and Political Rights, and Articles 4(a) and 4(b) of the Convention on the Elimination of all Forms of Racial Discrimination, by making it a crime to engage in the incitement to racial, religious, or ethnic hatred or hostility.

FAURISSON v. FRANCE

Communication No. 550/1993, Human Rights Committee
Views of Committee, 8 Nov. 8, 1996, UN Doc. A/52/40 (1999), Vol. II, at 84

[Robert Faurisson, author of the communication and a former professor of literature, was removed from his university chair in 1991. He had expressed doubt about or denial of the accuracy of conventional accounts of the Holocaust, including (1) his conviction that there were no homicidal gas chambers for the extermination of Jews in Nazi concentration camps, (2) his doubts over the number of people killed, and (3i) his disbelief in the records and evidence of the Nuremberg trial that were used to convict Nazis.

In 1990, the French legislature passed the so-called 'Gayssot Act'. It amended the 1881 law on Freedom of the Press by adding Article 24 *bis*, which made it an offence to contest (*contestation*) the existence of the category of crimes against humanity as defined in the London Charter of 1945, on the basis of which Nazi leaders were convicted by the International Military Tribunal at Nuremberg in 1945–1946. For the relevant provision of the Charter and excerpts from the Nuremberg judgment, see pp. 121–29, *supra*.

Faurisson attacked the 1990 law as a threat to academic freedom, including freedom of research and expression. He claimed that the Gayssot Act raised to the rank of infallible dogma the proceedings and verdict at Nuremberg, and endorsed forever the orthodox Jewish version of the Second World War. Arguing that the Nuremberg records could not be treated as infallible, he cited examples of historical revision such as the Katyn massacre in Poland of Polish army officers that was initially attributed to Germans but that was later shown to be of Soviet responsibility. Faurisson described as 'exorbitant' the 'privilege of censorship' from which the representatives of the Jewish community in France benefitted.

The state party noted that anti-racism legislation adopted by France in the 1980s was considered insufficient to bring legal action against the trivialization of Nazi crimes. There was governmental concern over 'revisionism' by individuals justifying their writing through their status as historians. The French Government viewed these revisionist theses as a 'subtle form of contemporary anti-semitism'. The Gayssot Act was meant to fill a legal vacuum while defining the new criminal conduct as precisely as possible.

Associations of French resistance fighters and of deportees to German concentration camps filed a private criminal action against Faurisson, who was convicted in

1991 of violating the Gayssot Act. The Court of Appeal of Paris upheld the conviction and imposed a fine. Faurisson took the position that further appeal to the Court of Cassation would be futile and filed the present communication. He argued that the Act violated the ICCPR, although his communication did not invoke specific provisions.

The ICCPR Committee concluded in an earlier proceeding that the communication was admissible and that it raised issues under Article 19 of the Covenant. This proceeding led to the views of the Committee under Article 5(4) of the Optional Protocol, as well as five individual opinions signed by seven Committee members. Excerpts from the views of the Committee and several individual opinions follow.]

9.3 Although it does not contest that the application of the terms of the Gayssot Act... may lead, under different conditions than the facts of the instant case, to decisions or measures incompatible with the Covenant, the Committee is not called upon to criticize in the abstract laws enacted by States parties. The task of the Committee under the Optional Protocol is to ascertain whether the conditions of the restrictions imposed on the right to freedom of expression are met in the communications which are brought before it.

9.4 Any restriction on the right to freedom of expression must cumulatively meet the following conditions: it must be provided by law, it must address one of the aims set out in paragraph 3(a) and (b) of article 19, and must be necessary to achieve a legitimate purpose.

9.5 ... [T]he Committee concludes... that the finding of the author's guilt [in the French proceedings] was based on his following two statements: '... I have excellent reasons not to believe in the policy of extermination of Jews or in the magic gas chambers... I wish to see that 100 per cent of the French citizens realize that the myth of the gas chambers is a dishonest fabrication'. His conviction therefore did not encroach upon his right to hold and express an opinion in general. Rather the court convicted Mr. Faurisson for having violated the rights and reputation of others. For these reasons the Committee is satisfied that the Gayssot Act, as read, interpreted and applied to the author's case by the French courts, is in compliance with the provisions of the Covenant.

9.6 To assess whether the restrictions placed on the author's freedom of expression by his criminal conviction were applied for the purposes provided for by the Covenant, the Committee begins by noting... that the rights for the protection of which restrictions on the freedom of expression are permitted by article 19, paragraph 3, may relate to the interests of other persons or to those of the community as a whole. Since the statements made by the author, read in their full context, were of a nature as to raise or strengthen anti-semitic feelings, the restriction served [sic] the respect of the Jewish community to live free from fear of an atmosphere of anti-semitism. The Committee therefore concludes that the restriction of the author's freedom of expression was permissible under article 19, paragraph 3 (a), of the Covenant.

9.7 Lastly the Committee needs to consider whether the restriction of the author's freedom of expression was necessary. The Committee noted the State party's argument contending that the introduction of the Gayssot Act was intended to serve the struggle against racism and anti-semitism. It also noted the statement of a member of the French Government, the then Minister of Justice, which characterized the denial of the existence of the Holocaust as the principal vehicle for anti-semitism.... [T]he Committee is satisfied that the restriction of Mr. Faurisson's freedom of expression was necessary within the meaning of article 19, paragraph 3, of the Covenant.

10. [The Committee found there had been no violation by France of Article 19(3).]

Statement of Thomas Buergenthal

As a survivor of the concentration camps of Auschwitz and Sachsenhausen whose father, maternal grandparents and many other family members were killed in the Nazi Holocaust, I have no choice but to recuse myself from participating in the decision of this case.

INDIVIDUAL OPINION BY NISUKE ANDO (CONCURRING)

... In my view the term 'negation' ('contestation'), if loosely interpreted, could comprise various forms of expression of opinions and thus has a possibility of threatening or encroaching the right to freedom of expression, which constitutes an indispensable prerequisite for the proper functioning of a democratic society. In order to eliminate this possibility it would probably be better to replace the Act with a specific legislation prohibiting well-defined acts of anti-semitism or with a provision of the criminal code protecting the rights or reputations of others in general.

INDIVIDUAL OPINION BY ELIZABETH EVATT AND DAVID KRETZMER, CO-SIGNED BY ECKART KLEIN (CONCURRING)

...

2. ... The main issue is whether the restriction has been shown by the State party to be necessary, in terms of article 19, paragraph 3 (a), for respect of the rights or reputations of others.

3. ... While we entertain no doubt whatsoever that the author's statements are highly offensive both to Holocaust survivors and to descendants of Holocaust victims (as well as to many others), the question under the Covenant is whether a restriction on freedom of expression in order to achieve this purpose may be regarded as a restriction necessary for the respect of the rights of others.

4. Every individual has the right to be free not only from discrimination on grounds of race, religion and national origins, but also from incitement to such discrimination. This is stated expressly in article 7 of the Universal Declaration of Human Rights. It is implicit in the obligation placed on States parties under article 20, paragraph 2, of the Covenant to prohibit by law any advocacy of national, racial or religious hatred that constitutes incitement to discrimination, hostility or violence. The crime for which the author was convicted under the Gayssot Act does not expressly include the element of incitement, nor do the statements which served as the basis for the conviction fall clearly within the boundaries of incitement, which the State party was bound to prohibit, in accordance with article 20, paragraph 2. However, there may be circumstances in which the right of a person to be free from

incitement to discrimination on grounds of race, religion or national origins cannot be fully protected by a narrow, explicit law on incitement that falls precisely within the boundaries of article 20, paragraph 2. This is the case where, in a particular social and historical context, statements that do not meet the strict legal criteria of incitement can be shown to constitute part of a pattern of incitement against a given racial, religious or national group, or where those interested in spreading hostility and hatred adopt sophisticated forms of speech that are not punishable under the law against racial incitement, even though their effect may be as pernicious as explicit incitement, if not more so.

...

6. The notion that in the conditions of present-day France, Holocaust denial may constitute a form of incitement to anti-semitism cannot be dismissed....

7. The Committee correctly points out, as it did in its General Comment 10, that the right for the protection of which restrictions on freedom of expression are permitted by article 19, paragraph 3, may relate to the interests of a community as a whole. This is especially the case in which the right protected is the right to be free from racial, national or religious incitement.... It appears...that the restriction on the author's freedom of expression served to protect the right of the Jewish community in France to live free from fear of incitement to anti-semitism....

8. The power given to States parties under article 19, paragraph 3, to place restrictions on freedom of expression, must not be interpreted as license to prohibit unpopular speech, or speech which some sections of the population find offensive. Much offensive speech may be regarded as speech that impinges on one of the values mentioned in article 19, paragraph 3(a) or (b) (the rights or reputations of others, national security, ordre public, public health or morals). The Covenant therefore stipulates that the purpose of protecting one of those values is not, of itself, sufficient reason to restrict expression. The restriction must be necessary to protect the given value. This requirement of necessity implies an element of proportionality. The scope of the restriction imposed on freedom of expression must be proportional to the value which the restriction serves to protect....

9. The Gayssot Act is phrased in the widest language and would seem to prohibit publication of bona fide research connected with matters decided by the Nuremburg Tribunal. Even if the purpose of this prohibition is to protect the right to be free from incitement to anti-semitism, the restrictions imposed do not meet the proportionality test. They do not link liability to the intent of the author, nor to the tendency of the publication to incite to anti-semitism. Furthermore, the legitimate object of the law could certainly have been achieved by a less drastic provision that would not imply that the State party had attempted to turn historical truths and experiences into legislative dogma that may not be challenged, no matter what the object behind that challenge, nor its likely consequences. In the present case we are not concerned, however, with the Gayssot Act, in abstracto, but only with the restriction placed on the freedom of expression of the author by his conviction for his statements in the interview in Le Choc du Mois. Does this restriction meet the proportionality test?

10. The French courts examined the author's statements in great detail. Their decisions, and the interview itself, refute the author's argument that he is only

driven by his interest in historical research. In the interview the author demanded that historians 'particularly Jewish historians' who agree that some of the findings of the Nuremburg Tribunal were mistaken be prosecuted. The author referred to the 'magic gas chamber' ('la magique chambre à gaz') and to 'the myth of the gas chambers' ('le mythe des chambres à gaz'), that was a 'dirty trick' ('une gredinerie') endorsed by the victors in Nuremburg. The author has, in these statements, singled out Jewish historians over others, and has clearly implied that the Jews, the victims of the Nazis, concocted the story of gas chambers for their own purposes. While there is every reason to maintain protection of bona fide historical research against restriction, even when it challenges accepted historical truths and by so doing offends people, anti-semitic allegations of the sort made by the author, which violate the rights of others in the way described, do not have the same claim to protection against restriction. The restrictions placed on the author did not curb the core of his right to freedom of expression, nor did they in any way affect his freedom of research.... It is for these reasons that we joined the Committee....

INDIVIDUAL OPINION BY RAJSOOMER LALLAH (CONCURRING)

...

11. I conclude, therefore, that the creation of the offence provided for in the Gayssot Act, as it has been applied by the Courts to the author's case, falls more appropriately, in my view, within the powers of France under article 20, paragraph 2, of the Covenant. The result is that there has, for this reason, been no violation by France under the Covenant....

13. Recourse to restrictions that are, in principle, permissible under article 19, paragraph 3, bristles with difficulties, tending to destroy the very existence of the right sought to be restricted. The right to freedom of opinion and expression is a most valuable right and may turn out to be too fragile for survival in the face of the too frequently professed necessity for its restriction in the wide range of areas envisaged under paragraphs (a) and (b) of article 19, paragraph 3.

...

NOTE

Consider the following views of Christopher Caldwell, in 'Historical Truth Speaks for Itself', *Financial Times*, 18 Feb. 2006:

> Madeleine Reberioux, the late leftist historian, warned of the biggest danger of the Gayssot law as soon as it was passed. "One day", she wrote, "it's going to lead into other areas besides the genocide against the Jews — other genocides and other assaults on what will be called 'historical truth'." She was right. A law declaring the Turkish killings of Armenians early last century to be a "genocide" was passed in 2001; later that year, another law defined the slave trade as a "crime against humanity"; a year ago, legislation mandated that teachers stress the "positive role" of the French presence in North Africa. Each new officialisation of remembrance calls

into being more "moral lobbies", which press their claims with ever more insistence in ever more obscure corners of political life and with ever more legal clout.

...

Mr Dworkin's case [*infra*] for abolishing laws against Holocaust denial on grounds of political legitimacy is the right one. Of course, no one should be under the illusion that being able to go out and deny the Holocaust will add much to any "debate". The official truth of western governments about the Holocaust happens to be the truth. Allowing delusions or anti-Semitic propaganda to masquerade as "opinions" will not change that. So those western countries with laws against Holocaust denial are now in a tricky position. They must undo laws that have proved unworkable and counterproductive — and at a moment when some of those laws' most vocal detractors are violent people of ill will.

QUESTIONS

1. Two of the concurring opinions in *Vejdeland* acknowledge hesitation in agreeing with the Court's opinion. How convincing do you find the Court's analysis? Is it a major victory in terms of sexual orientation or a slippery slope for inroads against freedom of expression in relation to contested issues?

2. As a legislator, would you have voted for the Gayssot Act? How would you have reacted to the following argument in general, or as applied to the passage of that Act?

> Freedom of expression is indeed a fundamental right. While its protection may sometimes be an end in itself, its exercise may not disturb the fundamental goals underlying human rights law. One of the most fundamental of those goals is achieving equality and non-discrimination. In fact, if there is any right which enjoys primacy among rights, it is arguably the principle of equality and non-discrimination.... The goal of hate mongers is to convince others that the members of the target group are not entitled to equal protection of the law; the hate mongers seek a society of discrimination.... They should not be entitled to claim protection under the right to freedom of expression for their abuse of speech rights to achieve that goal.[14]

3. Suppose that an author's statements leading to a prosecution under the Gayssot Act appeared in a periodical article that was the only writing by the author on the subject. The author concludes that the Nuremberg judgment, later judicial decisions describing the Holocaust, and 'official' accounts of the Holocaust were part of a conscious conspiracy among the victorious Allies to spur feelings of guilt by Germans and hatred of others toward them.

4. Would a conviction by French courts be likely to be upheld under the opinion above for the Committee? Under the concurring opinion by Elizabeth Evatt and David Kretzmer? How do these opinions differ, and which do you view as the better one? How

[14] Stephanie Farrior, 'Moulding the Matrix: The Historical and Theoretical Foundations of International Law Concerning Hate Speech', 14 Berkeley J. Int'l. L. 1 (1996), at 6, 98.

would you reconcile the Committee's majority approach with its statement 15 years later, in General Comment No. 34 (2011) that '[l]aws that penalize the expression of opinions about historical facts are incompatible with the obligations that the Covenant imposes on States parties in relation to the respect for freedom of opinion and expression. The Covenant does not permit general prohibition of expressions of an erroneous opinion or an incorrect interpretation of past events. Restrictions on the right of freedom of opinion should never be imposed and, with regard to freedom of expression, they should not go beyond what is permitted in paragraph 3 or required under article 20'?

5. Should the opinions have referred to arguments in favour of freedom of speech, or to the criteria in Article 19 for limiting speech, such as 'public order' or 'public morals'? What could have been the bases or events in France and French history for relying on such criteria to uphold the statute and affirm the conviction? Would comparable bases have been available in the United States to justify legislation similar to the Gayssot Act?

6. Do you think that the opinions as a whole succeed in illuminating the relevant aspects of the ICCPR, or indeed of human rights in general? Do they advance understanding of the value and limitations of free speech, and of the dilemmas of resolving conflicts among rights within the human rights instruments?

NOTE

The United States ratified the ICCPR in 1992. In giving its consent to ratification, and acting consistently with proposals made to it by the Bush Administration (see p. 1092, *infra*), the Senate entered a reservation to Article 20 that then qualified the US ratification. It reads: 'Article 20 does not authorize or require legislation or other action by the United States that would restrict the right to free speech and association protected by the Constitution and laws of the United States.'

Compare with Article 20 an equivalent provision, Article 4 of the Convention on the Elimination of All Forms of Racial Discrimination. In that article, the states parties 'condemn all propaganda . . . based on ideas or theories of superiority of one race or group of persons or one colour or ethnic origin'. They undertake to declare a punishable offence 'all dissemination of ideas based on racial superiority or hatred, incitement of racial discrimination, as well as all acts of violence' against such a race or group. Article 1 defines 'racial discrimination' to mean any distinction based on 'race, colour, descent, or national or ethnic origin' that has the purpose or effect of impairing equal enjoyment of rights 'in the political, economic, social, cultural or any other field of public life'. When the United States ratified the Racial Convention, it reserved as to Article 4.

The primary constitutional provision referred to in these two reservations by the United States is the First Amendment: 'Congress shall make no law . . . abridging the freedom of speech. . . .'

FREDRICK SCHAUER, THE EXCEPTIONAL FIRST AMENDMENT

in Michael Ignatieff (ed.), American Exceptionalism and Human Rights (2005), at 29

... [A]lthough a constitutional or quasi-constitutional right to freedom of expression is the international norm, the contours of that right vary widely even among the liberal democracies that understand the value of the right and the importance of enforcing it seriously. And among the most interesting manifestations of that variety among liberal democracies is the way in which the American First Amendment, as authoritatively interpreted, remains a recalcitrant outlier to a growing international understanding of what the freedom of expression entails. In numerous dimensions, the American approach is *exceptional*.... [P]rotection of freedom of expression is generally stronger than that represented by an emerging multinational consensus — but stronger in ways that may also reflect an exceptional though not necessarily correct understanding of the relationship between freedom of expression and other goals, other interests, and other rights.

...

... [The effects of the US reservations in several treaties like the ICCPR on hate-speech issues] are important in their own right but also reflect a deeper division between the United States and the rest of the world on freedom of expression issues; for as a matter of formal legal doctrine and significantly as a matter of public opinion as well, the American understanding is that principles of freedom of speech do not permit government to distinguish protected from unprotected speech on the basis of the point of view espoused. Specifically, this prohibition on what is technically called "viewpoint discrimination" extends to the point of view that certain races or religions are inferior, to the point of view that hatred of members of minority races and religions is desirable, and to the point of view that violent or otherwise illegal action is justified against people because of their race, their ethnicity, or their religious beliefs. If government may not under the First Amendment distinguish between Republicans and Communists, or prohibit the speeches of the flat-earthers because of the patent falsity of their beliefs, then the government may not, so American First Amendment doctrine insists, distinguish between espousals of racial equality and espousals of racial hatred, nor may the government prohibit public denials of the factuality of the Holocaust just because of the demonstrable falsity of that proposition and the harm that would ensue from its public articulation.

Some of the American aversion to discriminating against speech because of its point of view, including racist points of view, was spawned when the Supreme Court in 1969 established the still-prevailing test distinguishing permitted advocacy from regulable incitement. Advocacy even of illegal conduct, the Court held, was protected by the First Amendment, and only if that advocacy was explicitly directed to urging "imminent" lawless acts in a context in which such imminent lawless acts were "likely" — essentially standing in front of an angry mob and verbally leading them to immediate violence — could the constraints of the First Amendment be overridden. This doctrine applies to the full range of public political or ideological utterances, but for our purposes what is most important is that the doctrine was created in the context of a case [*Brandenburg v. Ohio*, 395 U.S. 444 (1969)] in which Clarence Brandenburg, a local leader of the Ku Klux Klan in southern Ohio, had called for acts of "revengance" against African Americans and Jews. But because Brandenburg's advocacy fell short of explicitly urging "imminent" unlawful acts in a context in which those unlawful acts were "likely," his speech was held to be constitutionally immune from criminal (and, almost certainly, civil as well) punishment. In the context of hate speech, therefore, *Brandenburg* stands for the proposition that in the United States restrictions on the incitement of racial hatred can be countenanced under the First Amendment only when they are incitements to *violent* racial hatred, and even then only under the rare circumstances in which the incitements unmistakably call for immediate violent action, and even then only under the more rare still circumstances in which members of the listening audience are in fact likely immediately to act upon the speaker's suggestion.... Jean Le Pen could not be sanctioned in the United States, as he was in France, for accusing Jews of exaggerating the Holocaust, nor could Brigitte Bardot be fined in the United States, as she was in France, for crusading against Islam and urging the deportation of those of Arab ethnicity. Ernst Zundel and James Keegstra can be charged with crimes in Canada for denying the Holocaust, but not in the United States.

The distinction between American practice and that in other liberal democracies, exists not only with respect to incitement, but also with respect to racial epithets and insults intended not to rally or motivate the speaker's allies but rather to cause psychic harm and mental distress to those to whom the words are directed. When Frank Cohn, then the leader of the American Nazi Party, proposed in 1977 to march with his followers, in full Nazi regalia, in Skokie, Illinois, a community disproportionately populated by survivors of the Holocaust, both the state and federal courts made clear that under the First Amendment there was no plausible cause for prohibiting the march. More recent cases involving racial intimidation, membership in racist groups, and restrictions on racist speech on university campuses have all emphasized that this form of "hate speech" will not be treated differently under the First Amendment...from any other viewpoint or any other form of public offensiveness.... In much of the developed world one uses racial epithets at one's legal peril, one displays Nazi regalia and the other trappings of ethnic hatred at significant legal risk, and one urges discrimination against religious minorities under threat of fine or imprisonment, but in the United States all such speech remains constitutionally protected.

The divergence between American and international approaches to freedom of expression is hardly unique to the issue of hate speech. A similar divergence, for example, exists between American and non-American free speech and free press understandings with respect to defamation law — the law of libel (written) and slander (spoken). Traditionally, the United States shared with the rest of the common law world an English law heritage in which defamation was treated as a strict liability tort. In order to win a lawsuit and recover money damages, a person suing for libel or slander needed only to prove by a bare preponderance of the evidence (the normal burden of proof in civil, as opposed to criminal, cases) that the defendant had uttered (or, more commonly, published) words tending to injure the alleged victim's reputation. The plaintiff/victim was not required to prove that the defendant/publisher was negligent or in any other way at fault, and indeed the plaintiff did not even have to prove that the imputation was false. The defendant could, to be sure, prevent recovery by asserting an affirmative defense and showing that the words were true...but the fact that the burden of proof was on the publisher to demonstrate truth rather than on the target to demonstrate falsity underscores the way in which the common law of defamation traditionally embodied the view that one published at one's peril....

The United States departed dramatically from this tradition in 1964. In *New York Times* Co. *v. Sullivan* [376 U.S. 264 (1964)], the Supreme Court, in the name of the First Amendment, constitutionalized what had previously been the constitutionally untouched common law of defamation, concluding that actions for libel and slander brought by public officials could succeed only upon proof by clear and convincing evidence (and not merely by a preponderance of the evidence, as would be the case in other civil actions) of *intentional* falsity, a burden of proof almost impossible to meet. To the Supreme Court, the traditional common law approach imposed all of the risk of falsity upon the publisher, making publishers wary of publishing even those charges that turned out to be true. This phenomenon, now widely labeled "the chilling effect," was to the Court inconsistent with a First Amendment part of whose goal was to encourage exposing and thus checking the abuses of those in power. Although requiring intentional falsity to sustain liability would undoubtedly increase the amount of published falsehood, this error, the Court implicitly concluded, was far less grave than the opposite error of inhibiting the publication of political truth. And even if some of what would be published under the new rule turned out to be vituperative and uncivil, this was only to be expected, for the common law approach was inconsistent with a First Amendment centered on the importance of "uninhibited," "robust," and "wide-open" public debate.

In the ensuing years, the Supreme Court has refused to back away from the *Sullivan* approach and has indeed substantially extended it. A few years after *Sullivan* it applied its basic holding to candidates for public office as well as to office holders, and, more surprisingly and more significantly, to public figures as well as to public officials, even to those public figures — pop stars, television chefs, and professional athletes, for example — who have little to no involvement in or effect on public policy or political debates. The Court then required that even private individuals prove negligence in order to prevail, and thus by 1975 the constitutionalization of American defamation law was complete.... For all practical purposes the availability in the United States of defamation remedies for public officials and public figures, even in cases of provable falsity, has come to an end.

Largely through the efforts of journalists, newspapers, and their lawyers, there has been an active effort to persuade other countries to adopt the American approach, and to conclude that the harm of unpublished truth about public officials and public figures is far greater than the harm of unsanctioned falsity. Yet although these efforts have been successful in moving most common law countries slightly away from the strictest version of the common law model, and in securing some modifications of analogous remedies even in civil law countries, the overwhelming reaction of the rest of the world to the American approach has been negative. In Australia, New

Zealand, Canada, the United Kingdom, and a number of other countries, the unalloyed American approach has been rejected....

... In disputes over the persistent and inevitable conflict between freedom of the press to report on criminal prosecutions and the right of the accused to a fair trial uninfluenced by potentially inflammatory pretrial and midtrial publicity, the United States favors the former over the latter to a degree unmatched in the world. In much of the rest of the world, press restrictions, often under the label of sanctions for "contempt," are acceptable as means to preserve the sanctity of the trial process, but in the United States considerable interference with that sanctity is tolerated so that trials, no less than other governmental processes, are open for all that is best and worst about press coverage and public scrutiny. In the same vein, disputes between the interest in privacy of victims of crimes and the interest of the press in reporting on criminal proceedings are typically resolved in favor of the press and against the victim's privacy.

...

... Where in the rest of the world freedom of expression appears to be understood as an important value to be considered along with other important values of fairness, equality, dignity, health, privacy, safety and respect, among others, in the United States the freedom of expression occupies pride of place, prevailing with remarkable consistency in its conflicts with even the most profound of other values and the most important of other interests.

QUESTION

What historical and other factors come to mind that could help to explain the significant differences between European (and other) countries and the United States with respect to defining the boundaries of free speech in relation to competing interests and concerns?

COMMENT ON BLASPHEMY CASES

In *Otto-Preminger-Institut v. Austria*, Ser. A, 295-A, 1994, the European Court of Human Rights decided by 6 votes to 3 that the seizure and forfeiture of a blasphemous film did not violate the freedom of expression guaranteed by Article 10 of the European Convention. The applicant association had advertised the screening of the film, *Das Liebeskonzil*, based on an 1894 play, which:

> ... portrays the God of the Jewish religion, the Christian religion and the Islamic religion as an apparently senile old man prostrating himself before the devil with whom he exchanges a deep kiss and calling the devil his friend.... Other scenes show the Virgin Mary permitting an obscene story to be read to her and the manifestation of a degree of erotic tension between the Virgin Mary and the devil. The adult Jesus Christ is portrayed as a low grade mental defective and in one scene is shown lasciviously attempting to fondle and kiss his mother's breasts, which she is shown as permitting.

The film was presented by the association as a 'satirical tragedy'. 'Trivial imagery and absurdities of the Christian creed are targeted in a caricatural mode and the relationship between religious beliefs and worldly mechanisms of oppression is investigated.' The Innsbruck Regional Court in Austria ordered seizure and forfeiture of the film under Section 188 of the Austrian Penal Code for the criminal offence of 'disparaging religious precepts'. The criminal proceedings against the association were eventually dropped.

Since there was no dispute that the seizure constituted an interference with the association's freedom of expression, the European Court considered whether the seizure was permissible under the conditions set by of Article 10, paragraph 2. The Court concluded that the interference had the 'legitimate aim' of protecting the rights of others to freedom of religion. Interpreting Article 9 of the Convention to include the right to respect for one's religious feelings, the Court found that such considerations outweighed the film's contribution to public debate. The Court reasoned:

> The respect for the religious feelings of believers as guaranteed in Article 9 can legitimately thought to have been violated by provocative portrayals of objects of religious veneration; and such portrayals can be regarded as malicious violation of the spirit of tolerance, which must also be a feature of democratic society. The Convention is to be read as a whole and therefore the interpretation and application of Article 10 in the present case must be in harmony with the logic of the Convention.... [T]he Court accepts that the impugned measures pursued a legitimate aim under Article 10 para. 2, namely 'the protection of the rights of others'.

The Court stressed that freedom of expression applies not only to ideas that are favourably received, but also to those 'that shock, offend or disturb the State or any sector of the population. Such are the demands of that pluralism, tolerance and broadmindedness without which there is no "democratic society."' Nonetheless, people exercising their rights under Article 10 were subject to duties, among which could legitimately be included 'an obligation to avoid as far as possible expressions that are gratuitously offensive to others and thus an infringement of their rights, and which therefore do not contribute to any form of public debate capable of further progress in human affairs'.

The Court determined that the seizure could be considered 'necessary in a democratic society'. There was no 'uniform conception of the significance of religion in society' throughout Europe, 'even within a single country'. A 'certain margin of appreciation is therefore to be left to the national authorities in assessing the existence and extent of the necessity of such interference'. It is 'for the national authorities, who are better placed than the international judge, to assess the need for such a measure in the light of the situation obtaining locally'. Given that the Tyrolean population was 87 per cent Roman Catholic, the Court found that the Austrian authorities had acted within their margin of appreciation 'to ensure religious peace in that region and to prevent that some people should feel the object of attacks on their religious beliefs in an unwarranted and offensive manner.'

Three judges dissented. Given the precautions against offence to viewers taken by the association through a warning announcement, the showing of the film to a paid audience only, and the restriction of viewing to those over 17 years of age, the dissent found the seizure and forfeiture to be disproportionate to the aim pursued, and thus not necessary in a democratic society.

In *Wingrove v. United Kingdom*, European Court of Human Rights, 1996, Rep. 1996-V, fasc. 23, a film director who was a British national brought a complaint before the European Commission alleging that the United Kingdom had violated Article 10 by interfering with the director's freedom of expression through refusing to grant a distribution certificate for the director's 18-minute video work, *Visions of Ecstasy*. The video work involved visions of St Teresa about the crucified Christ, and in the view of the British Board of Film Classification, drew Christ graphically into the erotic desire of St Teresa. The refusal to grant the certificate was based on the Board's conclusion that the video constituted blasphemy, defined in a recent case as 'any contemptuous, reviling, scurrilous or ludicrous matter related to God, Jesus Christ or the Bible'. The decision was upheld by the Video Appeals Committee.

The European Commission expressed the opinion in a 14–2 vote that there had been a violation of Article 10. The Commission and the United Kingdom brought the case before the European Court, which concluded by a 7–2 vote that there had been no violation of Article 10. Some of its observations about the requirement in Article 10 that a restriction be 'necessary in a democratic society' follow:

> 57. The Court observes that the refusal to grant Visions of Ecstasy a distribution certificate was intended to protect 'the rights of others', and more specifically to provide protection against seriously offensive attacks on matters regarded as sacred by Christians....
>
> ... [B]lasphemy legislation is still in force in various European countries. It is true that the application of these laws has become increasingly rare and that several States have recently repealed them altogether.... Strong arguments have been advanced in favour of the abolition of blasphemy laws, for example, that such laws may discriminate against different faiths or denominations.... However, the fact remains that there is as yet not sufficient common ground in the legal and social orders of the member States of the Council of Europe to conclude that a system whereby a State can impose restrictions on the propagation of material on the basis that it is blasphemous is, in itself, unnecessary in a democratic society and thus incompatible with the Convention....
>
> 58. Whereas there is little scope under Article 10 para. 2 of the Convention for restrictions on political speech or on debate of questions of public interest,...a wider margin of appreciation is generally available to the Contracting States when regulating freedom of expression in relation to matters liable to offend intimate personal convictions within the sphere of morals or, especially, religion. Moreover, as in the field of morals, and perhaps to an even greater degree, there is no uniform European conception of the requirements of 'the protection of the rights of others' in relation to attacks on their religious convictions. What is likely to cause substantial offence to persons of a particular religious persuasion will vary significantly from time to time and from place to place, especially in an era characterised by an ever growing array of faiths and denominations. By reason of their direct and

> continuous contact with the vital forces of their countries, State authorities are in principle in a better position than the international judge to give an opinion on the exact content of these requirements with regard to the rights of others as well as on the 'necessity' of a 'restriction' intended to protect from such material those whose deepest feelings and convictions would be seriously offended....
>
> This does not of course exclude final European supervision. Such supervision is all the more necessary given the breadth and open-endedness of the notion of blasphemy and the risks of arbitrary or excessive interferences with freedom of expression under the guise of action taken against allegedly blasphemous material.... Moreover the fact that the present case involves prior restraint calls for special scrutiny by the Court....

The Court (para. 50) also considered the fact that the English law of blasphemy 'only extends to the Christian faith'. It was not, however, for the European Court 'to rule *in abstracto*' about the compatibility of British law with the Convention. 'The extent to which English law protects other beliefs is not in issue before the Court which must confine its attention to the case before it.... The uncontested fact that the law of blasphemy does not treat on an equal footing the different religions practised in the United Kingdom does not detract from the legitimacy of the aim pursued in the present context.' A concurring opinion of Judge Pettiti observed that the Convention left 'scope for review under Article 14. In the present case no complaint had been made to the European Court under that article.'

A dissenting opinion of Judge Lohmus noted that the law of blasphemy 'only protects the Christian religion and, more specifically, the established Church of England.... This in itself raises the question whether the interference was (in the language of Article 10) "necessary in a democratic society".'

QUESTIONS

1. Do these opinions resolve the question of who in the liberal state must show tolerance to whom? Must the majority put up with the minority's views and modes of expression (at least where those views and expressions are not 'forced' on the majority through unavoidable public acts)? Or is it the minority that must take account of the majority's sensibility and refrain from offending it?

2. During the colonial period, the British colonial government in India enacted several laws as part of the Indian Penal Code that defined offences including 'defiling a place of worship', 'acts insulting religion or religious beliefs', 'disturbing a religious assembly', 'trespassing on burial grounds' and 'utterances wounding religious feelings'. Punishments were a maximum of two years' imprisonment, a fine or both.

These laws were amended or supplemented by the Government of Pakistan. Section 295-B of the Pakistan Penal Code, added in 1982, provided:

> Whoever willfully defiles, damages or desecrates a copy of the Holy Quran or an extract therefrom or uses it in any derogatory manner or for any unlawful purpose shall be punishable with imprisonment for life.

Section 295-C was enacted in 1986. It stated:

> Whoever by words, either spoken or written, or by any visible representation, or by any imputation, innuendo, or insinuation, directly or indirectly, defiles the sacred name of the Holy Prophet Mohammed (peace be upon him) shall be punished with death, or imprisonment for life and shall also be liable to fine.

Compare the Pakistani statutes with the laws and action described in the *Otto-Preminger-Institut* and *Wingrove* cases. What are the salient differences? How would the Pakistani statutes be judged under the European Convention?

NOTE

In 2005, a Danish newspaper named *Jyllands-Posten* published cartoons that proved to be offensive to many Muslims. They consisted of unflattering and mocking notions about Muslims and caricatures of the Prophet Mohammed, including a cartoon portraying Mohammed wearing a turban in the shape of a bomb ready to explode — an obvious reference to terrorist acts committed in the name of Islam. The controversy led to widespread protests and riots, the severing of diplomatic relations between an Arab state and Denmark, death threats against the cartoonists and others involved and far-reaching trade boycotts by some states of Danish goods. The cartoons were republished by newspapers in several European countries, including France, Germany, Italy, the Netherlands, Spain and Switzerland. By contrast, most major newspapers in the United States, Canada and the United Kingdom refrained from republication, although the cartoons were rapidly available on the internet.

The protests were the stronger because many Muslims understand that Islam bans any image, let alone caricatures, of the Prophet; such images are often viewed as blasphemous. As Professor Ruti Teitel noted at the time:

> Many people saw the cartoons as…exhibiting intolerance toward those whose religion is Islam…. To understand why so many Muslims were so gravely offended, it is important to see that the cartoons don't stand alone, but rather were published against a backdrop of political and legislative action that, to many Muslims, reflects a repeated pattern of disparagement of Islam in the public sphere. At present, Europe is struggling with issues of identity…. The crisis arises because of new demographics, at the same time as new regionalism. Many Muslims feel they are being relegated to second-class citizenship in Europe. And they relate the publication of the cartoons — by a newspaper they feel would not consider publishing anti-Christian or anti-Jewish cartoons — to this wrongful sense that they are not full citizens.[15]

[15] 'No Laughing Matter', Findlaw, 15 Feb. 2006, at http://writ.news.findlaw.com/ commentary/20060215_teitel.html.

In the wake of the diplomatic outcry the Danish Prime Minister refused to meet with a group of 11 ambassadors from Muslim-majority countries. The government responded that 'freedom of expression has a wide scope and the Danish government has no means of influencing the press.' It added that blasphemy was, however, prohibited under Danish law and that offended parties could bring suit if they wished. A subsequent complaint was dismissed by the public prosecutor. The Egyptian Minister of Foreign Affairs called for 'an official Danish statement underlining the need for and the obligation of respecting all religions and desisting from offending their devotees to prevent an escalation which would have serious and far-reaching consequences.' No such statement was forthcoming. The following year, the Organization of the Islamic Conference (OIC), representing 57 states with significant Muslim populations, established an OIC Observatory on Islamophobia. It tracked developments worldwide including, for example, the 2008 movie, *Fitna*, in which a Dutch politician, Geert Wilders, interspersed excerpts from the Qur'an with media images of acts of hatred or violence attributed to Muslims, and the March 2011 burning by a Florida pastor of a Qur'an. The Observatory's 2011 report stated that '[t]he scourge of Islamophobia continued unabated, despite all efforts to raise awareness of its dangers and the need to contain it' and concluded that 'Islamophobia remains a matter of transcendental priority for the OIC.'

The OIC's principal response to the problem at the international level took the form of a campaign begun in 1999 to combat the 'defamation of religions'. Over a number of years, resolutions were adopted by contested votes in the UN Human Rights Council and the General Assembly. GA Resolution 62/154 (18 Dec. 2007), adopted by a vote of 108 in favour, 51 against and 25 abstentions, is representative:

The General Assembly,

...

2. Expresses its deep concern about the negative stereotyping of religions and manifestations of intolerance and discrimination in matters of religion or belief still in evidence in the world;

3. Strongly deplores physical attacks and assaults on businesses, cultural centres and places of worship of all religions as well as targeting of religious symbols;

4. Expresses its deep concern about programmes and agendas pursued by extremist organizations and groups aimed at the defamation of religions and incitement to religious hatred, in particular when condoned by Governments;

5. Also expresses its deep concern that Islam is frequently and wrongly associated with human rights violations and terrorism;

6. Notes with deep concern the intensification of the campaign of defamation of religions and the ethnic and religious profiling of Muslim minorities in the aftermath of the tragic events of 11 September 2001;

7. Recognizes that, in the context of the fight against terrorism and the reaction to counter-terrorism measures, defamation of religions and incitement to religious hatred becomes an aggravating factor that contributes to the denial of fundamental rights and freedoms of members of target groups, as well as their economic and social exclusion;

8. Deplores the use of the print, audio-visual and electronic media, including the Internet, and any other means to incite acts of violence, xenophobia or related

intolerance and discrimination against Islam or any other religion, as well as targeting of religious symbols;

9. Stresses the need to effectively combat defamation of all religions and incitement to religious hatred, against Islam and Muslims in particular;

10. Emphasizes that everyone has the right to hold opinions without interference and the right to freedom of expression, and that the exercise of these rights carries with it special duties and responsibilities and may therefore be subject to limitations as are provided for by law and are necessary for respect of the rights or reputations of others, protection of national security or of public order, public health or morals and respect for religions and beliefs;

11. Urges States to take action to prohibit the advocacy of national, racial or religious hatred that constitutes incitement to discrimination, hostility or violence;

12. Also urges States to provide, within their respective legal and constitutional systems, adequate protection against acts of hatred, discrimination, intimidation and coercion resulting from defamation of religions, to take all possible measures to promote tolerance and respect for all religions and beliefs and the understanding of their value systems and to complement legal systems with intellectual and moral strategies to combat religious hatred and intolerance;

13. Urges all States to ensure that all public officials, including members of law enforcement bodies, the military, civil servants and educators, in the course of their official duties, respect people regardless of their different religions and beliefs and do not discriminate against persons on the grounds of their religion or belief, and that any necessary and appropriate education or training is provided;

14. Underscores the need to combat defamation of religions and incitement to religious hatred by strategizing and harmonizing actions at the local, national, regional and international levels through education and awareness-raising;...

The concept that a religion could be defamed was subsequently hotly debated in various UN fora. In April 2009, for example, three UN Special Rapporteurs (dealing with racism, freedom of religion and freedom of expression) issued a joint statement:

We have repeated time and again that all human rights are universal, indivisible and interdependent and interrelated. Yet nowhere is this interdependence more obvious than in the discussion of freedom of expression and incitement to racial or religious hatred. The right to freedom of expression constitutes an essential aspect of the right to freedom of religion or belief and therefore needs to be adequately protected in domestic legislation. Freedom of expression is essential to creating an environment in which a critical discussion about religion can be held. While the exercise of freedom of expression could in some extreme cases affect the right to manifest the religion or belief of certain identified individuals, it is conceptually inaccurate to present "defamation of religions" in abstracto as a conflict between the right to freedom of religion or belief and the right to freedom of opinion or expression.

In recent years, there have been challenges with regard to the dissemination of expressions which offend certain believers.... [A] clear distinction shall be made between three types of expression: (1) expressions that constitute an offence under international law; (2) expressions that are not criminally punishable but may justify a civil suit; and (3) expressions that do not give rise to criminal or civil sanctions but still raise a concern in terms of tolerance, civility and respect for the religion or beliefs of others.…

Whereas the debate concerning the dissemination of expressions which may offend certain believers has throughout the last ten years evolved around the notion of "defamation of religions", we welcome the fact that the debate seems to be shifting to the concept of "incitement to racial or religious hatred", sometimes also referred to as "hate speech".

Indeed, the difficulties in providing an objective definition of the term "defamation of religions" at the international level make the whole concept open to abuse. At the national level, domestic blasphemy laws can prove counter-productive, since this could result in the de facto censure of all inter-religious and intra-religious criticism. Many of these laws afford different levels of protection to different religions and have often proved to be applied in a discriminatory manner. There are numerous examples of persecution of religious minorities or dissenters, but also of atheists and non-theists, as a result of legislation on religious offences or overzealous application of laws that are fairly neutral.

Whereas some have argued that "defamation of religions" could be equated to racism, we would like to caution against confusion between a racist statement and an act of "defamation of religion". We fully concur with the affirmation from the ICERD that any doctrine of superiority based on racial differentiation is scientifically false, morally condemnable, socially unjust and dangerous. However, there is not necessarily an analogy to be drawn with regard to religious issues. Indeed, several religions are characterized by truth claims — or even by superiority claims — which have been traditionally accepted as part of their theological grounds. Consequently, the elements that constitute a racist statement may not be the same as those that constitute a statement "defaming a religion" as such. To this extent, the legal measures, and in particular the criminal measures, adopted by national legal systems to fight racism may not necessarily be applicable to "defamation of religions".…[16]

In her 2010 report the Special Rapporteur on freedom of religion welcomed the fact that the United Kingdom had recently abolished the offences of blasphemy and blasphemous libel, but also noted that the Indonesian Constitutional Court had upheld an anti-blasphemy law 'which imposes criminal penalties of up to five years imprisonment on individuals who deviate from the basic teachings of the official religions.'[17]

In 2011 the UN Human Rights Committee adopted General Comment No. 34 on Article 19: Freedoms of opinion and expression, in which it observed (in para. 48) that:

Prohibitions of displays of lack of respect for a religion or other belief system, including blasphemy laws, are incompatible with the Covenant, except in the specific circumstances envisaged in article 20, paragraph 2, of the Covenant. Such prohibitions must also comply with the strict requirements of article 19, paragraph 3, as well as such articles as 2, 5, 17, 18 and 26. Thus, for instance, it would be impermissible for any such laws to discriminate in favour of or against one or certain

[16] http://www2.ohchr.org/english/issues/racism/rapporteur/docs/Joint_Statement_SRs.pdf.

[17] UN Doc. A/65/207 (29 July 2010), para. 44.

> religions or belief systems, or their adherents over another, or religious believers over non-believers. Nor would it be permissible for such prohibitions to be used to prevent or punish criticism of religious leaders or commentary on religious doctrine and tenets of faith.

In response to these debates, in 2011 the UN Human Rights Council adopted by consensus a resolution (Res. 16/18 of 24 Mar. 2011) that omitted all references to defamation and drew directly upon proposals put forward by the OIC. It called on states 'to foster a domestic environment of religious tolerance, peace and respect, by':

> (a) Encouraging the creation of collaborative networks to build mutual understanding, promoting dialogue and inspiring constructive action towards shared policy goals and the pursuit of tangible outcomes...;
> (b) Creating an appropriate mechanism within Governments to, inter alia, identify and address potential areas of tension between members of different religious communities, and assisting with conflict prevention and mediation;
> (c) Encouraging training of Government officials in effective outreach strategies;
> (d) Encouraging the efforts of leaders to discuss within their communities the causes of discrimination, and evolving strategies to counter these causes;
> (e) Speaking out against intolerance, including advocacy of religious hatred that constitutes incitement to discrimination, hostility or violence;
> (f) Adopting measures to criminalize incitement to imminent violence based on religion or belief;
> (g) Understanding the need to combat denigration and negative religious stereotyping of persons, as well as incitement to religious hatred, by strategizing and harmonizing actions at the local, national, regional and international levels through, inter alia, education and awareness-building;
> (h) Recognizing that the open, constructive and respectful debate of ideas, as well as interfaith and intercultural dialogue at the local, national and international levels, can play a positive role in combating religious hatred, incitement and violence;
> ...

RONALD DWORKIN, EVEN BIGOTS AND HOLOCAUST DENIERS MUST HAVE THEIR SAY

The Guardian, 14 Feb. 2006

The British media were right, on balance, not to republish the Danish cartoons that millions of furious Muslims protested against in violent and terrible destruction around the world. Reprinting would very likely have meant more people killed and more property destroyed. It would have caused many British Muslims great pain.... [T]he public does not have a right to read or see whatever it wants no matter what the cost, and the cartoons are in any case widely available on the internet.

There is a real danger, however, that the decision of British media not to publish, though wise, will be wrongly taken as an endorsement of the widely held opinion that freedom of speech has limits, that it must be balanced against the virtues of multiculturalism, and that the government was right after all to propose that it be made a crime to publish anything "abusive or insulting" to a religious group. Freedom of speech is not just a special and distinctive emblem of western culture that might be generously abridged or qualified as a measure of respect for other cultures that reject it, the way a crescent or menorah might be added to a Christian religious display. Free speech is a condition of legitimate government. Laws and policies are not legitimate unless they have been adopted through a democratic process, and a process is not democratic if government has prevented anyone from expressing his convictions about what those laws and policies should be. Ridicule is a distinct kind of expression; its substance cannot be repackaged in a less offensive rhetorical form without expressing something very different from what was intended. That is why cartoons and other forms of ridicule have for centuries, even when illegal, been among the most important weapons of both noble and wicked political movements.

So in a democracy no one, however powerful or impotent, can have a right not to be insulted or offended. That principle is of particular importance in a nation that strives for racial and ethnic fairness. If weak or unpopular minorities wish to be protected from economic or legal discrimination by law — if they wish laws enacted that prohibit discrimination against them in employment, for instance — then they must be willing to tolerate whatever insults or ridicule people who oppose such legislation wish to offer to their fellow voters, because only a community that permits such insult may legitimately adopt such laws. If we expect bigots to accept the verdict of the majority once the majority has spoken, then we must permit them to express their bigotry in the process whose verdict we ask them to respect. Whatever multiculturalism means — whatever it means to call for increased "respect" for all citizens and groups — these virtues would be self-defeating if they were thought to justify official censorship.

Muslims who are outraged by the Danish cartoons point out that in several European countries it is a crime publicly to deny, as the president of Iran has denied, that the Holocaust ever took place. They say that western concern for free speech is therefore only self-serving hypocrisy, and they have a point. But of course the remedy is not to make the compromise of democratic legitimacy even greater than it already is but to work toward a new understanding of the European convention on human rights that would strike down the Holocaust-denial law and similar laws across Europe for what they are: violations of the freedom of speech that that convention demands.

It is often said that religion is special, because people's religious convictions are so central to their personalities that they should not be asked to tolerate ridicule in that dimension, and because they might feel a religious duty to strike back at what they take to be sacrilege. Britain has apparently embraced that view because it retains the crime of blasphemy, though only for insults to Christianity. But we cannot make an exception for religious insult if we want to use law to protect the free exercise of religion in other ways. If we want to forbid the police from profiling people who look or dress like Muslims for special searches, for example, we cannot also forbid people from opposing that policy by claiming, in cartoons or otherwise, that Islam is committed to terrorism, however silly we think that opinion is. Religion must be tailored to democracy, not the other way around. No religion can be permitted to legislate for everyone about what can or cannot be drawn any more than it can legislate about what may or may not be eaten. No one's religious convictions can be thought to trump the freedom that makes democracy possible.

QUESTIONS

1. What provisions of the ICCPR could you have relied on to seek relief for the publication in a European country of the cartoons? Would it be relevant if you were a resident Muslim in such a country or were a national and resident of a Middle Eastern country?

2. Blitt suggests that the Human Rights Council's 2011 change of direction 'represents merely a cynical and strategic decision to continue the campaign to legitimize a ban on defamation of religion by other means'.[18] How do you evaluate the evolution of approaches within the UN to respond to allegations of Islamophobia?

3. Do you agree with the views expressed by Dworkin?

ADDITIONAL READING

L. Hennebel & T. Hochmann (eds.), *Genocide Denials and the Law* (2011); L. Leo et al., 'Protecting Religions from "Defamation": A Threat to Universal Human Rights Standards', 34 Harv. J. L & Pub. Pol'y 769 (2011); C. Evans, 'Religion and Freedom of Expression', in J. Witte Jr. & M. C. Green (eds.), *Religion and Human Rights: An Introduction* (2012), 188; P. Thornberry, 'Forms of Hate Speech and the Convention on the Elimination of all Forms of Racial Discrimination', 5 Religion & Hum. Rts. 97 (2010); J. Bowen, *Why the French Don't Like Headscarves* (2006); S. Coliver (ed.), *Striking a Balance: Hate Speech, Freedom of Expression and Non-Discrimination* (1992); K. Greenawalt, *Fighting Words: Individuals, Communities, and Liberties of Speech* (1995); S. Douglas-Scott, 'The Hatefulness of Protected Speech: A Comparison of the American and European Approaches', 7 Wm. & Mary Bill of Rts. J. 305 (1999); M. Rosenfeld, 'Hate Speech in Comparative Perspective', 24 Cardozo L. Rev. 1523 (2003).

[18] R. C. Blitt, Defamation of Religion: Rumors of Its Death are Greatly Exaggerated, 2–3 (2012) at http://ssrn.com/abstract=2040812.

PART D

INTERNATIONAL HUMAN RIGHTS ORGANIZATIONS

8

The United Nations Human Rights System

This chapter explores the complex and often confusing set of institutional arrangements that make up the United Nations human rights system. It places particular emphasis on the role played by the UN Human Rights Council, set up in 2006 as the direct successor to the UN Commission on Human Rights which first met in 1946. Other UN organs of major importance include the Security Council and the General Assembly. Individual office-holders, such as the UN Secretary-General and the UN High Commissioner for Human Rights, have also come to play increasingly central roles.

The chapter starts with a brief overview of the different UN organs and then moves to explore the crucial role of 'fact-finding' in responding to violations of human rights. It then looks in-depth at the Human Rights Council and its different functions: responding to violations, setting human rights standards, dealing with complaints against states and monitoring states' compliance with their obligations. The chapter also looks at the role of the High Commissioner and the human rights-related work of the Security Council, including the concept of the Responsibility to Protect, that posits an obligation on the part of states to respond under certain circumstances to mass atrocities.

In considering the work of these institutions, it is necessary to keep in mind two crucial sets of issues that are implicated, in different ways, at almost every turn. The doctrinal issues concern the relationship between notions of state sovereignty and human rights, and the closely related challenge of determining the extent of a state's domestic jurisdiction. The policy-related issues concern the extent to which we would like to see the international community 'enforcing' human rights in concrete situations.

COMMENT ON SOVEREIGNTY AND DOMESTIC JURISDICTION

The complex and unresolved relationship between the sovereignty of states and their obligations to respect human rights is nowhere better exemplified than in the UN Charter. Article 1(3) lists one of the purposes of the UN as being 'to achieve international cooperation...in promoting and encouraging respect for human rights'. And Article 55(c) tasks the UN with promoting 'universal respect for, and observance of, human rights'. Article 2(7), on the other hand, reassures governments that nothing in the Charter 'shall authorize the United Nations to intervene in matters which are essentially within the domestic jurisdiction of any State', with the sole exception of binding measures prescribed by the Security Council. While the two sets of provisions are not directly contradictory, they clearly raise and leave unresolved the question of how far the UN and other states can go in insisting upon respect for human rights, while respecting sovereignty and not interfering in the internal affairs of a state. According to Emmanuelle Jouannet, this 'initial dilemma remains intact' today. She observes that progress in resolving the relevant tensions and contradictions can only be made 'on a case by case basis'.[1] In contrast, other scholars, and certainly some governments, consider that there has already been a dramatic tilt towards the human rights side of the equation. They see the doctrine of the 'responsibility to protect' as a logical and appropriate outcome of this development, because it elevates an understanding of 'popular sovereignty', defined in human rights terms, over more traditional notions of state sovereignty.

These issues arise throughout the book. The introduction to international law (Chapter 2) considered the clash between international regulation and national governments' internal control of their polity — cases like *Chattin* or *Minority Schools in Albania*, for example. States' arguments based on sovereignty provided a counterpoint in Chapter 3 to the description of the growth of the human rights regime. States' claims based on notions of cultural relativism in Chapters 6 and 7 often spoke the language of autonomy and sovereign independence. And subsequent chapters, whether addressing the limits of the reach of the European Court of Human Rights, or the international community's response to massive tragedies, also raise the same themes.

Consider at the outset brief comments of several scholars about the meaning of this notion in contemporary international law and argument.

Malanczuk[2] notes that the origin of the modern theory lies in internal analyses of state structure, analyses that reach to writings of theorists like Machiavelli, Bodin and Hobbes. Originally used to describe the commands of a sovereign within a state (internal sovereignty), sovereignty later came to be used to describe as well the relationship of the ruler towards other rulers or states (external sovereignty, a continuing deep concern of international law). He suggests that the word 'sovereignty' should be replaced by 'independence'. 'In so far as "sovereignty" means anything in addition to "independence", it is not a legal term with any fixed meaning but a wholly emotive term. Everyone knows that states are powerful, but the emphasis on sovereignty exaggerates their power and encourages them to abuse it ...'.

Brownlie[3] states that:

> [s]overeignty and equality of states represent the basic constitutional doctrine of the law of nations, which governs a community consisting primarily of states having a uniform legal personality. If international law exists, then the dynamics of state sovereignty can be expressed in terms of law, and, as states are equal and have

[1] E. Jouannet, *The Liberal-Welfarist Law of Nations: A History of International Law* (2012), 227.

[2] Peter Malanczuk, *Akehurst's Modern Introduction to International Law* (7th edn. 1997), 17–18.

[3] Ian Brownlie, *Principles of Public International Law* (4th edn. 1990), Ch. XIII, 287.

> legal personality, sovereignty is in a major aspect a relation to other states (and to organizations of states) defined by law.

He describes the principal corollaries of states' sovereignty and equality as:

> (1) a jurisdiction, prima facie exclusive, over a territory and the permanent population living there; (2) a duty of non-intervention in the area of exclusive jurisdiction of other states; and (3) the dependence of obligations arising from customary law and treaties on the consent of the obligor.

Koskenniemi[4] observes that it is 'notoriously difficult to pin down the meaning of sovereignty', but that nonetheless the literature characteristically starts with a definition. Usually the concept is connected with ideas of independence (external sovereignty) and self-determination (internal sovereignty). He quotes a classic definition in an arbitral decision to the effect that sovereignty 'in the relations between States signifies independence: independence in regard to a portion of the globe is the right to exercise therein, to the exclusion of any other States, the functions of a State.' Sovereignty thus implies freedom of action by a state.

If, argues Koskenniemi, this or any agreed-on definition of sovereignty had a clear, ascertainable meaning, then 'whether an act falls within the State's legitimate sphere of action could always be solved by simply applying [that definition] to the case'. But '[t]here simply is no fixed meaning, no natural extent to sovereignty at all'. Thus in disputes between two states, each may base its argument on its own sovereignty. Assuming that 'sovereignty had a fixed content would entail accepting that there is an antecedent material rule which determines the boundaries of State liberty regardless of the subjective will or interest of any particular State.' Such material boundaries not stemming from the free choice of the state 'will appear as unjustified coercion'. It is indeed 'impossible to define "sovereignty" in such a manner as to contain our present perception of the State's full subjective freedom and that of its objective submission to restraints to such freedom.'

Keck and Sikkink, in *Activists Beyond Borders: Advocacy Networks in International Politics* 215(1998), on the other hand, see sovereignty much more in political terms and as having a strong North-South dimension:

> ... Northerners within networks usually see third world leaders' claims about sovereignty as the self-serving positions of authoritarian or, in any case, elite actors. They consider that a weaker sovereignty might actually improve the political clout of the most marginalized people in developing countries.
>
> In the south, however, many activists take quite a different view. Rather than seeing sovereignty as a stone wall blocking the spread of desired principles and norms, they recognize its fragility and worry about weakening it further. The doctrines of sovereignty and nonintervention remain the main line of defense against foreign efforts to limit domestic and international choices that third world states (and their citizens) can make.

[4] Martti Koskenniemi, *From Apology to Utopia: The Structure of International Legal Argument* (1989), Ch. 4.

They also note that the sovereignty, for third world activists, is closely related to the issue of structural inequality. In a similar vein, Benedict Kingsbury has warned that 'discarding sovereignty in favour of a functional approach will intensify inequality, weakening restraints on coercive intervention, diminishing critical roles of the state as a locus of identity and an autonomous zone of politics and redividing the world into zones.'[5]

While doctrines seeking to justify intervention, such as the responsibility to protect, might raise these concerns, most commentators do not see human rights obligations *per se* as posing any serious challenge to sovereignty. James Crawford notes that while the human rights movement has clearly eroded the domestic domain, sovereignty 'is not exhausted by the concession or recognition of rights'. 'Human rights standards qualify, but do not displace, the sovereignty of states. Indeed in subtle ways they reinforce it: the more we look to the state for human rights compliance, the more we seem to concede to a state domain.'[6]

Within the UN context, these theoretical debates about the status of sovereignty and its relationship to the human rights agenda have played out largely in relation to Article 2(7) of the Charter which safeguards the 'domestic jurisdiction' of states. The main questions are what constitutes a domestic matter for this purpose and who decides.

Some critics have stressed that the Charter did not give any UN organ the power to make authoritative interpretations of these or any other provisions. In Watson's view, 'as a result, the power of autointerpretation still remains with individual states'.[7] Each state, when addressed by a UN organ (other than the Security Council acting under explicit powers), would then decide for itself whether or not the matter raised was part of its *domaine reservé* (domestic jurisdiction) and thus off limits to the UN under Article 2(7). The overwhelming majority of commentators have rejected this analysis, and have instead argued that (1) the General Assembly must have the power to interpret its own mandate, including the implications of Article 2(7); (2) a teleological approach should be applied in interpreting Article 2(7) in light of the (developing) purposes of the Organization (Art. 1); (3) the resolutions of the UN and other bodies have made clear that a narrow interpretation is to be given to Article 2(7); and (4) as legitimate matters of international concern, human rights cannot reasonably be characterized as being exclusively an internal matter.

Over the course of more than 60 years, UN organs have systematically reduced the scope claimed for the domestic jurisdiction 'defence'. The early case of South Africa was critical. A special Commission on the Racial Situation in the Union of South Africa appointed by the General Assembly in 1952 concluded that Article 2(7) prohibited only 'dictatorial interference', a phrase interpreted as implying 'a peremptory demand for positive conduct or abstention — a demand which, if not complied with, involves a threat of or recourse to compulsion....' Article 2(7) referred 'only to direct intervention in the domestic economy, social structure, or cultural arrangements of the State concerned but does not in any way preclude recommendations,

[5] B. Kingsbury, 'Sovereignty and Inequality', 9 Eur. J. Int'l. L. 599 (1998).

[6] J. Crawford, 'Sovereignty as a Legal Value', in J. Crawford & M. Koskenniemi (eds.), *The Cambridge Companion to International Law* (2012), 117, at 122.

[7] J. Watson, *Theory and Reality in the International Protection of Human Rights* (1999), at 205.

or even inquiries conducted outside the territory of such State.'[8] The Commission's report gave rise to extensive debate, in which South Africa took the position that the General Assembly could not even discuss the subject of race relations in that country. Only rarely today does one hear even distant echoes of that extreme position.

The domestic jurisdiction defence was regularly invoked in the 1970s and 1980s, but never really prevailed.[9] Even China, which was a strong proponent for many years, now relies primarily on a call for consensus and constructive dialogue rather than placing much reliance on sovereignty arguments.

The end of the Cold War brought the adoption of the following statement in 1991 by the Conference on Security and Co-operation in Europe (see p. 971, *infra*):

> The participating States emphasize that issues relating to human rights, fundamental freedoms, democracy and the rule of law are of international concern.... They categorically and irrevocably declare that the commitments undertaken in the field of the human dimension of the CSCE are matters of direct and legitimate concern to all participating States and do not belong exclusively to the internal affairs of the State concerned.[10]

Today the issue of domestic jurisdiction is rarely raised in other than a perfunctory manner in UN fora, but that does not mean that there are no limits to the extent to which other states or international organizations are entitled to challenge domestic decisions by states.

COMMENT ON CONCEPTIONS OF ENFORCEMENT

Most observers would assume that the effectiveness of the UN human rights system should generally be judged by its ability to 'enforce' respect for the legal norms that originated within it. But, for many governments, the very concept of international 'enforcement' is controversial, leading some to oppose it overtly, and others to invoke more subtle arguments to preclude or undermine such measures. It is therefore not surprising that the UN's efforts to establish institutions and procedures capable of securing enforcement have been more controversial than its work in setting human rights standards, upon which all states — at least in theory — often agree.

Evaluating the UN's performance will largely depend on the observer's starting point or perspective on world order. For example:

(1) Do we assume that the 'globalization' of issues such as human rights is desirable, even unavoidable, so that a nation's treatment of its own nationals is a legitimate concern of all others (an *erga omnes* approach)? Or do we hold to a more traditional

[8] UN Doc. A/2505 (1953), 16–22.

[9] M. Kamminga, *Inter-State Accountability for Violations of Human Rights* (1992).

[10] 30 Int'l. Leg. Mat. 1670 (1991), at 1672.

image of the sovereign state that emphasizes the inviolability of national boundaries for at least most human rights issues as well as many other purposes?

(2) Even if the former, do we envisage a world in which an effective multilateral organization such as the UN should be able to act against the will of the government(s) concerned to enforce universal norms? Or do we believe that despite the pressures towards globalization of standards, the actual implementation by individual governments of human rights norms, each in its own way, remains the most effective, desirable or realistic approach? Or is the solution to create a World Human Rights Court, the jurisdiction of which states will be asked voluntarily to accept?

(3) Are we prepared to accept that the measures that we would happily support against another country might, in a different context, be applied against our own? Do we assume that international enforcement actions must be applied equally to powerful nations and to smaller states, so that we should only adopt policies that can be applied across the board, consistently? Or are there legitimate differences in the ways in which the international community should respond to human rights violations in different types of states (democratic/non-democratic, large/small, developed/developing, etc.)?

The answers to such questions depend partly on the definition of enforcement. Should it be defined only to include peacekeeping, policing or military action that involves the presence in a state of UN or other foreign forces? The only use of the term 'enforcement' in the UN Charter occurs in relation to the enforcement under Chapter VII of decisions of the Security Council (Art. 45). This has led some international lawyers to equate enforcement with the use of, or threat to use, economic or other sanctions or armed force. Although most dictionary definitions of enforcement include an element of coercion, it is nonetheless true that coercion may be moral as well as physical. It is also true that the use of force for human rights purposes has won increasing support in recent years, starting with Kosovo and East Timor in the early 1990s through to Guinea and Libya in 2011, but this is surely not what is meant by calls for the UN to 'enforce', routinely, universal human rights norms.

At the other extreme from the use of sanctions or armed force, enforcement has been defined as 'comprising all measures intended and proper to induce respect for human rights'.[11] That definition could extend to the other extreme of UN action, the frequent debates or recommendatory resolutions of the Human Rights Council or the General Assembly. But such a definition is so open-ended that it provides no criteria against which to evaluate the UN's performance. It puts the emphasis on intentions rather than on results achieved, and suggests that 'enforcement' measures might be confined to the adoption of resolutions and other such hortatory activities of the UN.

[11] R. Bernhardt, 'General Report', in Bernhardt & Jolowicz (eds.), *International Enforcement of Human Rights* (1985), at 5.

QUESTION

Is the term 'enforcement' the right term to use to describe what you would like the UN to be able to do in response to its findings that major human rights violations, or perhaps mass atrocities, are taking place or are likely to take place? Are there other powers, stopping short of this sense of 'enforcement', that you would wish to vest in the UN or any other international organization to respond to gross violations?

A. OVERVIEW OF THE UN HUMAN RIGHTS MACHINERY

The UN's human rights regime reflects a 'two-track' approach:

(1) *UN Charter-based bodies* including those (a) whose creation is directly mandated by the UN Charter, such as the General Assembly and the Human Rights Council (as the successor to the Commission on Human Rights), (b) subsidiary bodies created by one of the principal organs, such as the Commission on the Status of Women or the Human Rights Council Advisory Committee, and (c) groups or individuals accorded specific mandates by those organs to monitor, draft standards or for other purposes.

(2) *Treaty-based bodies* such as the Human Rights Committee established under the ICCPR, to monitor compliance by states with their obligations under those treaties. Such treaty bodies include the CEDAW Committee (dealt with in Chapter 3), the ESCR Committee (Chapter 4) and the ICCPR Committee (Chapter 9).

The focus of this chapter is on Charter-based bodies. While the Human Rights Council is of particular importance, other UN organs also play significant roles. The UN Charter of 1945 establishes several 'principal organs': the Security Council, the General Assembly, the Economic and Social Council, the Trusteeship Council, the Secretariat and the International Court of Justice. One of these organs is now virtually defunct — the highly successful postwar decolonization processes overseen by the UN rendered the *Trusteeship Council* superfluous and it suspended its work in 1994. Although the *Economic and Social Council* (ECOSOC) once played a major role as an intermediary between the Assembly and the Commission on Human Rights, and still has a theoretically important role of coordination within an increasingly disparate UN system, its substantive contributions to the human rights debate since the 1970s have been extremely limited and its coordination efforts have had little practical impact. One of the aims of creating the Human Rights Council in 2006 was to bypass the role of ECOSOC and enable the new Council to report directly to the General Assembly. As a result the main human rights-relevant role played today by ECOSOC concerns the granting of 'consultative status' with the UN to nongovernmental organizations.

We turn now to the organs whose work is examined in this chapter. Until the mid 1990s, the *Security Council* was extremely reluctant to become involved in human rights matters. Since that time, its role in the field has become significant in a variety of ways. Similarly, the *International Court of Justice* (ICJ) exerted a relatively marginal influence over the understanding and interpretation of international human rights law until the mid 1990s, despite its consideration of a handful of important cases focusing on issues such as self-determination and genocide. Over the past decade, however, the ICJ has adopted a series of judgments of major importance in terms of their contribution to an understanding of aspects of the international human rights regime.

The *Secretariat* is led by the *Secretary-General*, who is appointed for five years by the General Assembly on the recommendation of the Security Council. A nominee may thus be vetoed by any of the five permanent members of the Council (China, France, Russia, the United Kingdom and the United States). The Secretary-General is the chief administrative officer of the UN and also exerts important moral authority within the wider international system. For decades successive Secretaries-General were very reluctant to embrace human rights concerns actively for fear of offending governments and jeopardizing their wider role in the promotion of international peace and security. Two examples illustrate this reluctance. In the 1950s Dag Hammarskjöld (Sweden) was said to have directed that the UN human rights programme should cruise at no more than 'minimum flying speed'. In 1993 the proposal that led to the creation of the post of High Commissioner for Human Rights in December 1993 was strongly opposed by then Secretary-General Boutros Boutros-Ghali (Egypt). In contrast, Kofi Annan (Ghana), Secretary-General from 1997 to 2006, took a much more active human rights stance than any of his predecessors and appointed a series of strong High Commissioners. He also oversaw a process of 'mainstreaming' human rights throughout the organization which meant that bodies dealing with issues such as development, peacekeeping and environment were encouraged to address systematically the human rights dimensions of their work. His successor, Ban Ki-moon (South Korea) took office in 2007 and has been elected to a second term until 2016. His approach has very often favoured 'quiet diplomacy', but he has taken a strong stand on issues such as sexual orientation and the Responsibility to Protect.

Under the Secretary-General, the *High Commissioner for Human Rights* (HCHR) is the UN official with principal responsibility for human rights. In formal terms she is subject to the direction and authority of the Secretary-General and acts within the mandate given to her by the policy organs. In practice she and her Office (the OHCHR) are increasingly viewed as central players in their own right (see p. 742, *infra*).

The *General Assembly* is empowered by the UN Charter to 'discuss any questions or any matters within the scope of the... Charter' (Art. 10) and to 'initiate studies and make recommendations for the purpose of... [*inter alia*] assisting in the realization of human rights' (Art. 13). The Assembly's principal significance derives from the fact that it is composed of all UN member states, each of which has one vote regardless of population, wealth or other factors. While most issues are decided by a simple majority vote, decisions on important questions, such as those on peace and security, admission of new members and budgetary matters, require a two-thirds majority. Nevertheless, much of its work is carried out on a consensus basis, thus avoiding the need for a vote. The Assembly meets intensively from September to December each year and at other times as required. Its resolutions are not *per se* legally binding but they are an important reflection of the will of the world community. Much of the debate and drafting occurs in six Main Committees, three of which are of particular relevance to human rights: the Third (Social, Humanitarian and Cultural issues); the Fifth (Administrative and Budgetary issues); and the Sixth (Legal issues).

In 2006 the *Human Rights Council* replaced the *Commission on Human Rights* which had functioned since 1946. We examine these two bodies in some depth in Section B *infra*.

One other body that warrants a mention here is the *Commission on the Status of Women*. It was established in 1946 and reports to ECOSOC in relation to policies to promote women's rights in the political, economic, civil, social and educational fields. It consists of 45 governmental representatives, and meets for only ten days each year. It drafted many of the key treaties dealing with women's rights ranging from the 1952 Convention on the Political Rights of Women to the 1979 Convention on the Elimination of All Forms of Discrimination against Women. Its mandate includes follow-up to the four UN Women's Conferences held since 1975, and especially that held in Beijing in 1995. Its importance has been enhanced by the creation in 2010 of the UN Entity for Gender Equality and the Empowerment of Women, known as 'UN Women', one of whose roles is to assist the Commission in formulating relevant policies, global standards and norms.

In contrast with the treaty-based bodies discussed earlier, most of the Charter-based bodies are political organs which have a much broader mandate to promote awareness, to foster respect and to respond to violations. They derive their legitimacy and their mandate, in the broadest sense, from the human rights provisions of the Charter. Consider the following contrasts between the two types of organs.

Treaty-based organs are distinguished by: a limited clientele consisting only of states parties to the treaty in question; a limited mandate reflecting the terms of the treaty; a limited range of procedural options for responding to violations; consensus-based decision-making as far as possible; a preference for a non-adversarial relationship with states parties (particularly with respect to state reports) based on the concept of a 'constructive dialogue'; and a particular concern with addressing issues in ways that contribute to developing the normative understanding of the relevant rights.

By contrast, the political organs such as the General Assembly and the Human Rights Council generally: focus on a diverse range of issues; insist that every state is an actual or potential client (or respondent), regardless of its specific treaty obligations; work on the basis of a flexible and expanding mandate designed to respond to crises as they emerge; engage, as a last resort, in adversarial actions vis-à-vis states; rely more heavily upon NGO inputs and public opinion generally to ensure the effectiveness of their work; take decisions by often strongly contested majority voting; pay less attention to normative issues *per se*; and are very wary about establishing specific procedural frameworks within which to work, preferring a more ad hoc approach in most situations.

B. THE UN HUMAN RIGHTS COUNCIL

Rather than including an international bill of rights in the UN Charter in 1945, it was agreed instead to create a Commission on Human Rights whose primary function would be to draft such a bill. In late 1945 the UN appointed a Preparatory Commission to make provisional arrangements for institutional competences. It envisaged a Commission directed towards:

a) formulation of an international bill of rights;
b) formulation of recommendations for an international declaration or convention on such matters as civil liberties, status of women, freedom of information;
c) protection of minorities;
d) prevention of discrimination on grounds of race, sex, language, or religion; and
e) any matters within the field of human rights considered likely to impair the general welfare or friendly relations among nations.[12]

It was, however, set up as a subsidiary body of ECOSOC. The Council deleted paragraph (e) from the terms of reference it gave to the so-called Nuclear Commission which was to make detailed suggestions for the shape of the new Commission. The Nuclear Commission's nine members, chaired by Eleanor Roosevelt, proposed a body consisting solely of independent experts with an open-ended mandate including the role of aiding 'the Security Council in the task entrusted to it by Article 39 of the Charter, by pointing to cases where a violation of human rights committed in one country may, by its gravity, its frequency, or its systematic nature, constitute a threat to the peace' (E/38/Rev.1 (1946), p. 7). But this conception was rejected by ECOSOC which insisted that the Commission would be an intergovernmental rather than an expert body and would focus primarily on standards, studies and recommendations. It did, however, insert a new paragraph (e), giving the Commission a role with respect to 'any other matter concerning human rights not covered by items (a) (b) (c) and (d)'. In its later years the Commission was able to build upon this open-ended provision to expand its range of activities.

For the first 20 years of its existence the Commission devoted itself largely to standard-setting, and particularly to the drafting of the UDHR and the two Covenants. Meanwhile, the Cold War and the decolonization movement dominated much of the action in the General Assembly and the Security Council, and most of the 'real' action on human rights took place in the Assembly.

The Commission's response to violations went through three distinct phases. The first (1946–1966) began with a statement that the Commission had 'no power to take any action in regard to any complaints concerning human rights' (ESC Res. 75 (V) (1947)). UN officials warned at the time that this approach would 'lower the prestige and the authority' of both the Commission and the UN as a whole. Hersch Lauterpacht called it an 'extraordinary...abdication' of the UN's proper functions. During a second phase (1967–1978) the Commission's composition was

[12] *Report of the Preparatory Commission of the United Nations* (1945), PC/20, Ch. III, Sec. 4, paras. 14–16.

changed dramatically as a result of decolonization and the new members demanded responses to the problems associated with racism and colonialism. New procedures were adopted (the so-called 1235 and 1503 Procedures, named after ECOSOC's authorizing resolutions) and strong measures were taken against apartheid in particular (see p. 746, *infra*). At the same time it failed to act in response to horrendous violations in Pol Pot's Democratic Kampuchea (Cambodia), Amin's Uganda, Bokassa's Central African Empire, Macias's Equatorial Guinea, the military's Argentina and Uruguay and several other situations. As the human rights movement grew, public opinion began to assert itself, and the Carter Administration became more activist, the Commission entered a third phase (1979–2005) in which it evolved more effective procedures and tackled a growing range of state violators. All of these procedures were effectively passed on to the new Council in 2006.

While the Commission's achievements were actually considerable, its demise resulted from the disenchantment of all of its key constituencies, often for directly contradictory reasons. The United States was mostly frustrated in its efforts to condemn China's violations in the wake of the Tiananmen Square uprising of 1989, and irked by the active role of Cuba, Libya, Sudan and others. Its failure to win re-election in 2001 was the last straw. China, on the other hand, led a large number of developing countries in criticizing the Commission as a forum in which the North put countries of the South in the dock. They called instead for dialogue and consensus. And human rights NGOs considered the Commission to be unresponsive on key issues. By the end, all groups were accusing it of being 'politicized', albeit in very different ways. The resolution creating its successor body was a compromise among strongly competing visions.

GENERAL ASSEMBLY RESOLUTION 60/251

(2006)

The General Assembly,

...

Reaffirming further that all human rights are universal, indivisible, interrelated, interdependent and mutually reinforcing, and that all human rights must be treated in a fair and equal manner, on the same footing and with the same emphasis,

Reaffirming that, while the significance of national and regional particularities and various historical, cultural and religious backgrounds must be borne in mind, all States, regardless of their political, economic and cultural systems, have the duty to promote and protect all human rights and fundamental freedoms,

...

Affirming the need for all States to continue international efforts to enhance dialogue and broaden understanding among civilizations, cultures and religions,...

...

1. *Decides* to establish the Human Rights Council...as a subsidiary organ of the General Assembly...;

2. *Decides* that the Council shall be responsible for promoting universal respect for the protection of all human rights and fundamental freedoms for all, without distinction of any kind and in a fair and equal manner;

3. *Decides also* that the Council should address situations of violations of human rights, including gross and systematic violations, and make recommendations thereon. It should also promote the effective coordination and the mainstreaming of human rights within the United Nations system;

4. *Decides further* that the work of the Council shall be guided by the principles of universality, impartiality, objectivity and non-selectivity, constructive international dialogue and cooperation...;

5. *Decides* that the Council shall, inter alia:

(*a*) Promote human rights education and learning as well as advisory services, technical assistance and capacity-building...;
(*b*) Serve as a forum for dialogue on thematic issues on all human rights;
(*c*) Make recommendations to the General Assembly for the further development of international law in the field of human rights;
(*d*) Promote the full implementation of human rights obligations undertaken by States...;
(*e*) Undertake a universal periodic review [see p. 737, *infra*]...;
(*f*) Contribute, through dialogue and cooperation, towards the prevention of human rights violations and respond promptly to human rights emergencies;
(*g*) Assume the role and responsibilities of the Commission on Human Rights relating to the work of the Office of the [OHCHR];
(*h*) Work in close cooperation...with Governments, regional organizations, national human rights institutions and civil society;
(*i*) Make recommendations with regard to the promotion and protection of human rights;
(*j*) Submit an annual report to the General Assembly;

...

12. *Decides also* that the methods of work of the Council shall be transparent, fair and impartial and shall enable genuine dialogue, be results oriented, allow for subsequent follow-up discussions to recommendations and their implementation and also allow for substantive interaction with special procedures and mechanisms;

...

NOTE

Membership: Where the Commission on Human Rights (CHR) had 54 members, the Council has 47. General Assembly Resolution 60/251 diluted the proportion of European states and maintained the strong emphasis on regional blocs that had dogged the Commission. The Council thus consists of 13 states from Africa, 13 from

Asia, six from Eastern Europe, eight from Latin American and the Caribbean, and seven from Western Europe and Other states (which includes the United States, Australia, Canada, New Zealand and Israel).

Term: States are elected for three-year terms and are not eligible for immediate re-election after two consecutive terms. The big powers, such as the United States and the USSR/Russia, had served almost continuously on the CHR. A state that commits gross and systematic human rights violations may be suspended from the rights of membership by a two-thirds majority vote in the General Assembly. An important precedent was set when Libya was suspended in 2011. It was readmitted in 2012.

Elections: One of the major issues that led to the disbanding of the Commission was the criticism that its members included governments which were major violators of human rights. As the US Ambassador put it in 2005, the members of the Commission 'must be the firefighters of the world, not the arsonists'. The United States had previously urged that only democratic and human rights-respecting states should be elected to the Commission. In 2003 Human Rights Watch put forward a much modified set of criteria proposing that potential members 'should have ratified core human rights treaties, complied with their reporting obligations, issued open invitations to U.N. human rights experts and not have been condemned recently by the Commission for human rights violations.' But all too few states, the United States included, could meet such criteria.[13] The innovation in relation to the Council was to urge that those voting for states 'shall take into account the contribution of candidates to the promotion and protection of human rights and their voluntary pledges and commitments'. Once elected a state 'shall uphold the highest [human rights] standards'. In the first round of elections many states took the pledge seriously; few have done so subsequently.[14] NGOs have, however, succeeded in dissuading some states from nominating, and have contributed to the defeat of some candidacies.

Sessions: The CHR met for a single six-week annual session, with very occasional special (emergency sessions). The Council meets for at least ten weeks (four in March, three in June and three in September). Special sessions 'to address human rights violations and emergencies' can be convened upon the request of one-third of the Council's members.

Presidency: The Council's presidency rotates annually among the regional groups, but the office is considerably more powerful than was the case under the CHR. The President now has a full-time personal staff of three to provide 'support...and to enhance efficiency and institutional memory' (HRC Dec. 17/118 (17 June 2011)).

In 2011 a full review by the General Assembly of the Council's first five years resulted in only minor adjustments. In particular, proposals to enhance the Council's responsiveness to violations were rejected by China, Russia and many states from the South.

[13] P. Alston, 'Promoting the Accountability of Members of the New UN Human Rights Council', 15 J. Transnat'l. L. & Pol'y. 49 (2005).

[14] The OHCHR suggested the elements that should be addressed in the pledges. See www2.ohchr.org/english/bodies/hrcouncil/docs/pledges.pdf.

Apart from states — both members and non-members — the main actors in the Council are the High Commissioner and the OHCHR, independent experts, NGOs and national human rights institutions (NHRIs).

OHCHR: We consider the role of the High Commissioner (HC) below (p. 742, *infra*). One of the HC's principal roles is to direct the OHCHR which provides the secretariat to the Council and is charged with implementing the great majority of the Council's decisions. In the formal institutional hierarchy, however, the HC is answerable to the General Assembly rather than the Council. It is the Assembly's Fifth Committee that exercises direct oversight of the Office's budget and administration. In 2010 Cuba and allied states proposed that the HC would answer first to the Council, but this was strongly resisted by the HC and the majority of states. Under a compromise contained in a Presidential Statement (PRST 18/2 of 30 Sept. 2011) the HC was 'invited' to include in her annual report to the Council a detailed breakdown of budgetary sources and allocations.

Experts: The Commission and the Council have both accorded important and diverse roles to 'independent experts', although their efforts remain almost entirely advisory rather than determinative. The most important group are those holding specific 'mandates' under the Special Procedures system which we examine in the Comment below. In addition, the following expert bodies report to the Council:

(1) The *Human Rights Council Advisory Committee*, consisting of 18 independent experts, is officially described as the Council's 'think-tank' and 'work[s] at its direction' rather than on its own initiative. It generates studies and 'research-based advice' and meets in two sessions for a total of ten days per year. It replaced the *Sub-Commission on the Promotion and Protection of Human Rights* that advised the Commission on Human Rights from 1947 to 2006 and produced some 73 studies, starting in 1956, on issues such as the rights of indigenous populations, contemporary forms of slavery, minorities, transnational corporations, the administration of justice and the right to food. Whereas the Sub-Commission adopted resolutions on a wide range of issues, including violations in specific countries, the Advisory Committee is prohibited from doing so and must limit itself to providing 'advice' on thematic issues. As of 2012, its main areas of study have been a draft Declaration on Human Rights Education and Training, the right to food, missing persons, leprosy-related discrimination and the right to peace.

(2) The *Expert Mechanism on the Rights of Indigenous Peoples* was established in 2007 and consists of five experts who meet annually in July. It advises the Council, through research studies, on its work in relation to indigenous peoples. Studies have focused on the rights to education, participation and language and culture. It is separate from the Council's Special Rapporteur on the rights of indigenous peoples and ECOSOC's Permanent Forum on Indigenous Issues. The latter consists of 16 independent experts, half of whom are nominated by governments and half by indigenous organizations. It meets annually in New York for two weeks.

(3) The *Forum on Minority Issues* meets for two days and bring together experts to advise the Council's Independent Expert on minority issues in relation to national, ethnic, religious and linguistic minorities.
(4) The *Social Forum* meets for three days annually and brings together civil society, experts and governments to discuss pressing social issues.

NGOs and NHRIs: NGOs and the representatives of those NHRIs that are accredited by the International Coordinating Committee of National Institutions for the Promotion and Protection of Human Rights (ICC) are entitled to attend Council meetings, to submit written statements and to speak in debates. The 'space' that is in fact made available to these groups is a matter of significant contention, with many governments being more committed in theory than in practice to supporting such participation. By way of illustration, at the Council's eighteenth session, in September 2011, 187 NGOs were registered and together presented 91 written statements, many of which had multiple signatories.

COMMENT ON THE SPECIAL PROCEDURES SYSTEM

In 2006 former UN Secretary-General Kofi Annan described the special procedures as 'the crown jewel of the [UN human rights] system'. Those procedures consist of mandates focused solely on a specific country and a range of 'thematic procedures' devoted to a theme rather than a state or region and thus with a potentially global scope. The first such mechanism was the Working Group on Disappearances, established by the Commission in 1980. Its origins lay in efforts to respond to the massive 'disappearances' that took place during the 1970s in Argentina's 'dirty war' against leftist and other forces opposed to the military government. The government's strategy was effective in avoiding condemnation by international human rights fora until 1978 when the Inter-American Commission on Human Rights issued a damning indictment. Despite this precedent, within the UN context many governments were reluctant to 'name' Argentina, for a variety of reasons ranging from trade interests to fear that they themselves might be next on the list.

To get around this opposition the UN Commission opted to avoid a country-specific inquiry and instead established the first 'thematic' mechanism. Argentina hoped that the thematic approach would not single out any one country, would demonstrate that it was only one of many countries that had problems and would give a significant number of governments a strong incentive to ensure that the new mechanism would be kept under careful political control and thus remain ineffectual. But in the first few years of its existence, the Disappearances Working Group played an important role in developing techniques which were subsequently to serve as a model for a growing range of mechanisms dealing with other themes.

Number and Scope

Rapporteurs focused on specific countries are dealt with below (see p. 704). While the number of country rapporteurs has remained relatively stable, the thematic mechanisms have grown almost exponentially. In 1985 there were three, there were six in 1990, 14 in 1995, 21 in 2000, 28 in 2007 and by May 2012 there were 36. Of these, six were working groups: on disappearances, arbitrary detention, mercenaries, people of African descent, discrimination against women, and business. In 2010, by way of example, these mechanisms submitted 156 reports to the Council, including 58 country visit reports. The same year, 604 communications were sent to 110 governments concerning 1,407 individual cases. These figures were down from 1,300 communications sent to 142 governments concerning 4,448 individual cases in 2004.

The 36 mandates deal with: (1) disappearances; (2) extrajudicial executions; (3) torture; (4) freedom of religion or belief; (5) the sale of children, child prostitution and child pornography; (6) arbitrary detention; (7) freedom of opinion and expression; (8) contemporary forms of racism; (9) independence of judges and lawyers; (10) violence against women; (11) hazardous substances and waste; (12) extreme poverty; (13) migrants; (14) foreign debt; (15) the right to education; (16) the right to food; (17) the right to housing; (18) human rights defenders; (19) indigenous peoples; (20) people of African descent; (21) the right to health; (22) internally displaced persons; (23) trafficking in persons; (24) mercenaries; (25) terrorism; (26) international solidarity; (27) business; (28) minority issues; (29) contemporary forms of slavery; (30) right to water and sanitation; (31) cultural rights; (32) freedom of assembly and association; (33) discrimination against women; (34) a democratic and equitable international order; (35) truth and justice; and (36) environment. Thus, in the 32 years since the creation of the first mechanism, more than one new mechanism has been created on average every year.

The terminology used for the different mechanisms is confusing — 'Working Group', 'Special Rapporteur', 'Independent Expert', 'Representative' or 'Special Representative' of the Secretary-General — but relatively little significance attaches to it in practice. A few are appointed by the Secretary-General or the HCHR but most are appointed by the Chairperson of the Council who is expected to 'consult' with the regional groups before making an appointment. Those selected are generally prominent personalities from human rights-related backgrounds, including academics, lawyers, economists and NGO leaders. The first female expert was not appointed until 1994, but by 2012 thematic mandate-holders were evenly split between men and women. Interestingly, not one of the ten country rapporteurs was a woman. The experts receive no financial reward for their work, although their expenses are covered. They rely upon the OHCHR for secretariat services, but they have long complained of the gross inadequacy of the assistance available to them as a result of chronic financial and staff shortages within that Office.

Mandate-holders may be nominated by governments or NGOs. A Consultative Group, consisting of five government representatives who consult with all stakeholders, then makes prioritized recommendations to the President. If the latter decides not to follow the Group's suggestions she is required to give reasons for the divergence. 'Individuals holding decision-making positions in governments or in any other organization or entity which could represent a conflict of interest with the responsibilities arising from the mandate' are not eligible. A mandate-holder may be renewed once for a three-year term. The resolution establishing the Council envisaged that the Council might 'streamline, merge or eventually dismantle' some mandates. While country mandates have regularly been terminated, no thematic mandates have been.

Functions

The functions undertaken by the Special Procedures (with variations according to whether it is a country or a thematic mandate, and the nature of the issues involved) include the following:

- Take action on alleged violations, usually by means of correspondence with the government concerned or occasionally by a public statement.
- Undertake fact-finding missions to specific countries to examine the situation and make recommendations to the government and the Council.
- Undertake studies of a particular right or issue with a view to enhancing understanding and perhaps contributing to the process of developing jurisprudence.
- Report annually to the Council and, in some cases, also the General Assembly.

QUESTION

A major debate in establishing the Council concerned its optimum size. The Commission had 53 members and the United States proposed that the Council should have only 20, or a maximum of 30. After an examination of the issue a High-Level Panel reporting to the UN Secretary-General in December 2004 concluded that efforts to identify membership criteria would have little chance of changing the negative dynamics in the Commission and only risked 'further politicizing the issue'. The Panel thus advocated universal membership of a revamped Council, thereby opening the way for the full participation of all 193 UN member states.[15] The compromise chosen was 47. What are the arguments for and against a universal or a very selective membership for the Council?

We turn now to considering each of the Council's principal functions: standard-setting, country reporting, examining complaints and carrying out the Universal Periodic Review.

1. STANDARD-SETTING

In historical terms it might well be considered that the single most important contribution made by the Charter-based bodies, and especially by the Commission and

[15] High-Level Panel on Threats, Challenges and Change, *A More Secure World– Our Shared Responsibility*, UN Doc. A/59/565 (2004), 282–91.

now the Council which have frequently played the lead role, has been through the elaboration of an ever-growing body of standards designed to flesh out the meaning and implications of the relatively bare norms enunciated in the Universal Declaration. Although the Commission's 1946 terms of reference included a general mandate to address any human rights matter, it spent most of its first 20 years engaged almost exclusively in standard-setting. This included the preparation of the first draft of the UDHR and the two Covenants, as well as a range of other instruments.

But, at least since the entry into force of the two Covenants in 1976, the need for additional standards has often been questioned. Even when new treaties on discrimination against women, or torture, or the rights of the child were first mooted there were those who observed that the issues were already dealt with in the Covenants and who urged that the focus should instead be on better implementing existing standards and developing their content through interpretation. Such suggestions, as we know, proved unpersuasive. When the Human Rights Council was created, there were again suggestions that new standards were not a high priority. A 2006 NGO report by the International Council on Human Rights Policy (ICHRP) reflected the arguments in favour of at least slowing down such activities:

> [International human rights standards have had a transformative impact.] At the same time, the proliferation of standards has created new challenges. Some overlap and duplicate one another....
>
> The system developed to monitor their implementation and handle complaints is also under stress. States find it burdensome to submit so many reports and the United Nations committees that monitor human rights treaties and deal with complaints have accumulated a backlog of work. As a result, even cooperative states have become more reluctant to adopt new monitoring mechanisms, without which legal standards risk becoming ineffective.
>
> In addition, much more needs to be done to improve implementation of standards that exist. There is little point in elaborating standards if they are not implemented....
>
> The slowness of standard-setting processes is a further deterrent. Even if there are exceptions to every rule, most recent negotiations have been cumbersome and long-winded.... Some texts have been watered down, others have been abandoned. The creation of new standards is so time-consuming that many states have become reluctant to discuss new initiatives, while [NGOs] are starting to question whether they should engage in protracted negotiations that might result in weak texts.
>
> As a result of these challenges, some fear that efforts to create new standards may weaken rather than strengthen protection of rights, or even undermine the entire system. On this basis, it is sometimes argued that governments and human rights advocates should broaden the application of existing standards, in order to extend protection as required, rather than create new ones.
>
> Yet there are limits to the extension of existing standards: new standards will continue to be needed in the future. Society is continually changing and human rights laws must also change when gaps in protection appear....
>
> Nor should the influence of new standards be underestimated. Especially when supported by public advocacy, they can promote reform of domestic law and practices, and they provide objective benchmarks by which to measure the per-

> formance of state institutions. They can therefore improve accountability and the redress available to victims.[16]

Other commentators have drawn attention to what they perceive as a marked imbalance between North and South in this area. Makau Mutua, for example, warns of a 'participation deficit' in the context of standard-setting:

> Numerically, the South dominates the UN General Assembly, but ... [s]tates from the North still dominate the UN human rights norm making bodies. There are several reasons for this state of affairs. First, and perhaps most important, donor or capital exporting states have a disproportionate voice in international organizations. ...
>
> Such asymmetry of power allows states from the North to exert their will over IGOs and have their concerns addressed. ...
>
> ... The delegations of most states in the South lack adequate expertise in human rights, international law and related fields. This is not only a direct result of their poor economies, but also a function of bad governance and an absence of coherent foreign policies, among other factors. The combination of these factors lead to ill-prepared delegations, unable or unwilling to advocate effectively for their positions. Instead, most delegations from the South engage in high but empty rhetoric, devoid of serious analysis and development of the issues into law-like formulations. Moreover, many states in the South are suspicious of human rights NGOs and do not have cordial relations with them, unlike their counterparts in the North. This hostility extends to both domestic NGOs and INGOs. Nor do states in the South usually consult human rights scholars [or NGOs] for advice. ... This places them at a considerable disadvantage to states in the North whose skilled technocrats normally accord NGOs more open access, so they can tap into their expertise and advice. Delegations from the North are also adept at using academics and think-tanks as resources to keep them abreast of cutting-edge thinking and recent developments. ...
>
> ...
>
> INGOs are adept at lobbying for human rights standards and their implementation. Amnesty International and Human Rights Watch have in particular been key leaders in the work of standard setting within IGOs. Although NGOs from the South have become increasingly active in IGO circles, they remain "outsiders." ...[17]

Yet, since 2006, the Council has adopted the International Convention for the Protection of All Persons from Enforced Disappearances, the Declaration on the Rights of Indigenous Peoples, optional complaints protocols for the ICESCR and the CRC and has established an Ad Hoc Committee to explore the need for 'complementary standards' on racism, racial discrimination, xenophobia and related intolerance. In addition, the work of many of the Special Procedures is directed towards the interpretation of existing standards and in some cases the elaboration of new standards. Important examples of the latter are the Guiding Principles on Business

[16] ICHRP, Human Rights Standards: Learning from Experience (2006), 2 (available at www.ichrp.org/files/reports/31/120b_report_en.pdf).

[17] M. Mutua, 'Standard Setting in Human Rights: Critique and Prognosis', 29 Hum. Rts. Q. 547 (2007), at 606.

and Human Rights (see p. 1479, *infra*) and the Guiding Principles on Internal Displacement,[18] both of which originated from the work of experts reporting to the Council.

QUESTIONS

1. In 1986 the General Assembly (Res. 41/120) adopted 'guidelines' for future human rights standard-setting. It suggested that proposed instruments should, *inter alia*:

(a) be consistent with the existing body of international human rights law;

(b) be of fundamental character and derive from the inherent dignity and worth of the human person;

(c) be sufficiently precise to give rise to identifiable and practicable rights and obligations;

(d) provide, where appropriate, realistic and effective implementation machinery, including reporting systems;

(e) attract broad international support.

Are these guidelines likely to exclude very many proposals? What factors do you consider might be the most crucial in deciding whether to embark upon a new standard-setting exercise?

2. In 2012, the Human Rights Council adopted Res. 19/9 on the importance of birth registration and the right of everyone to recognition everywhere as a person before the law. While the CRC (Art. 7) requires that every child 'be registered immediately after birth', large numbers continue not to be and this creates huge problems for them later in life. Should a new treaty or protocol be adopted to spell out what needs to be done in such an area? If not, why not?

3. The ICHRP report (p. 702, *supra*) suggests that 'standard-setting may take new forms in the future, and those involved may need to organise in new ways'. What might those new forms and methods consist of?

2. COUNTRY REPORTS

Reporting on the human rights situation in individual countries constitutes an important part of the work of the Council, although it remains controversial and contested. Country reports are prepared by country rapporteurs, thematic rapporteurs and ad hoc commissions of inquiry, all of which are dealt with in this chapter. It bears emphasizing that the focus on violations is only one part of the Council's

[18] www.idpguidingprinciples.org/. See generally S. Bagshaw, *Developing a Normative Framework for the Protection of Internally Displaced Persons* (2005).

overall work. The present chapter does not address the issue of fact-finding methodologies, which are dealt with indepth in Chapter 10.

(1) Country Rapporteurs

As of May 2012 the following ten country situations were being examined under separate 'country mandates' by the Human Rights Council: Cambodia, Côte'Ivoire, Democratic People's Republic of Korea, Haiti, Islamic Republic of Iran, Myanmar, Palestinian Territories occupied since 1967, Somalia, Sudan and the Syrian Arab Republic. Until 2011, the dominant groups within the Council were pushing to eliminate most of the individual country mandates, except for that dealing with the Occupied Palestinian territories (see p. 720, *infra*). The influence of the Arab Spring led to a change of approach and the addition of three new mandates in 2011. In reading the materials below on the Democratic People's Republic of Korea (the DPRK or North Korea) and Cambodia, consider what the goals of such mechanisms might be and how they might become more effective.

(i) North Korea

The situation in North Korea has been summarized in the following terms:

> [North Korea] is a dictatorship.... [It] has an estimated population of 23.5 million.... National elections held in March 2009 were not free or fair. Security forces did not report to civilian authorities.
>
> Citizens did not have the right to change their government. The government subjected citizens to rigid controls over many aspects of their lives. There continued to be reports of extrajudicial killings, disappearances, arbitrary detention, arrests of political prisoners, harsh and life-threatening prison conditions, and torture. There continued to be reports that pregnant female prisoners underwent forced abortions in some cases, and in other cases babies were killed upon birth in prisons. The judiciary was not independent and did not provide fair trials. Citizens were denied freedom of speech, press, assembly, and association, and the government attempted to control all information. The government restricted freedom of religion, citizens' movement, and worker rights. There continued to be reports of severe punishment of some repatriated refugees and their family members. There were widespread reports of trafficking in women and girls....[19]

A 2012 NGO report by the Committee for Human Rights in North Korea notes the government's claim in the Universal Periodic Review process (see p. 737, *infra*) that it holds no political prisoners. However, based on extensive interviews with some of the 23,000 North Korean refugees recently arrived in South Korea, the report estimates that between 150,000 and 200,000 persons are incarcerated in prison labour camps, only some of whom are common criminals. It describes the political prisoners, many of whom are held for life, as 'real, suspected or imagined wrong-doers and wrong-thinkers, or persons with wrong-knowledge and/or wrong-associations who

[19] US Department of State, '2010 Country Reports on Human Rights Practices', 8 Apr. 2011.

have been deemed to be irremediably counter-revolutionary and pre-emptively purged from North Korean society.' It concludes that this system, which has been in operation for some 50 years, 'constitutes a clear and massive crime against humanity' that violates ten of the eleven actions proscribed in Article 7 of the Rome Statute of the International Criminal Court.[20]

The UN Commission on Human Rights adopted a resolution in 2003 in which it:

> 1. Expresses its deep concern about reports of systemic, widespread and grave violations of human rights in the [DPRK], including:
>   (a) Torture and other cruel, inhuman or degrading treatment or punishment, public executions, imposition of the death penalty for political reasons, the existence of a large number of prison camps and the extensive use of forced labour, and lack of respect for the rights of persons deprived of their liberty;
>   (b) All-pervasive and severe restrictions on the freedoms of thought, conscience, religion, opinion and expression, peaceful assembly and association and on access of everyone to information, and limitations imposed on every person who wishes to move freely within the country and travel abroad;
>   (c) The mistreatment of and discrimination against disabled children…;
>   (d) Continued violation of the human rights and fundamental freedoms of women;
> 2. Notes with regret that the authorities of the [DPRK] have not created the necessary conditions to permit the international community to verify these reports in an independent manner and calls upon the Government to respond to these reports and these concerns urgently….

Having received no response, the Commission appointed a country rapporteur, an office held by Vitit Muntarbhorn (Thailand) 2004–2010, and then Marzuki Darusman since 2010. Neither has been permitted to visit the country, but they have visited neighbouring states to speak with refugees, officials and others with knowledge of the situation. The rapporteur reports each year to both the Human Rights Council and the General Assembly. In his final report, Muntarbhorn characterized the DPRK as being a *sui generis* case involving 'violations which are both harrowing and horrific' (UN Doc. A/HRC/13/47 (17 Feb. 2010)).

Darusman, in his first report, focused on issues such as family separation, abductions, the right to food, legal reforms and freedom of expression. In relation to detention and correctional facilities he offered the following analysis:

> 53. [H]uman rights violations are committed in all correctional centres. Correctional officers sometimes beat inmates, but it is understood that more often it is the inmates who would beat up other inmates upon instruction from the officers. It is further claimed that human rights abuses, including deaths, are rampant inside correctional centres. [There are] reports of dire living conditions inside

[20] D. Hawk, *The Hidden Gulag: The Lives and Voices of 'Those who are Sent to the Mountains'* (2nd edn. 2012).

these correctional centres.... These ... serious allegations ... need to be investigated and rectified immediately.

54. ... North Korea is reported to have been operating a number of "political concentration camps", collection centres and labour training camps. Political prisoners are incarcerated in ... facilities ... called "control districts" or "special district for dictatorial control".

55. References to such labour training camps can be found in [national law].... This reinforces the Special Rapporteur's view that reforms need to take place both to end the use of such labour training camps and amend legislation to ensure it is aligned with international standards.

56. While in Japan and the Republic of Korea, the Special Rapporteur heard some graphic stories of the conditions and treatment of the detainees.... Under the revised Penal Code of 2004, those being punished as a political prisoner include anyone involved in conspiracy to topple the State, treason against the State, espionage, terrorism, anti-State propaganda and agitation, destruction and murder, armed intervention, and agitation to serve foreign relations and hostile actions against foreigners. Although the Penal Code is less vague on who a political prisoner is, what needs to be borne in mind is that — irrespective of the nature of crime — administering torture, cruel inhuman or degrading treatment can never be justified. Similarly, it is of paramount importance that due process of law be followed by the State at all times for all trials.

57. [T]he Special Rapporteur's [reporting] ... will continue to focus on correctional centres ... with the hope that this will ultimately prompt the [DPRK] ... to improve the situation....[21]

Darusman's second report adopted a slightly different approach, and did not repeat or update the analysis of the correctional facilities. He submitted the following 'Conclusions and Recommendations' to the Council:

52. [The DPRK needs] to ensure the overall protection and promotion of human rights in the country, as provided under international human rights instruments.

53. The Special Rapporteur calls on the Government ... to cooperate with the various United Nations human rights mechanisms....

54. The Special Rapporteur urges the Government to repeal provisions in its legislation that are counter to the international standards....

55. The Special Rapporteur recognizes the paramount importance of resuming inter-Korean dialogue [between North and South Korea]....

...

58. While calling on the [DPRK] to invest more resources in its agriculture sector and to take corrective measures to increase food production in the country, the Special Rapporteur stresses the need for the revival of effective humanitarian assistance by the international community to the people of the [DPRK]. Provisions of such humanitarian aid, including food and medicine, while subject to "no access, no aid" policies, should not be made contingent upon any political requirements.

[21] UN Doc. A/HRC/16/58 (21 Feb. 2011).

> 59. ... [T]he Special Rapporteur calls on other neighbouring countries to protect and treat all people fleeing the [DPRK] humanely and to respect the principle of non-refoulement, as provided for under the Convention relating to the Status of Refugees.[22]

In response, the Council (Res. 19/13 (22 Mar. 2012)) expressed 'its very serious concern at the ongoing grave, widespread and systematic human rights violations', commended the rapporteur for his efforts, extended his mandate and urged the DPRK to cooperate with him in the future and 'to ensure full, rapid and unimpeded access of humanitarian assistance'.

For the first time, the resolution was adopted without a vote, because no country insisted upon a counting of heads. In 2010, when the General Assembly acted in relation to the DPRK the vote was 100 in favour, 18 against and 60 abstaining. Those against included Algeria, Belarus, China, Cuba, Egypt, Guinea, Iran, Libya, Malaysia, Myanmar, Oman, Russian Federation, Somalia, Sudan, Syria, Uzbekistan, Venezuela, Vietnam and Zimbabwe. Most Asian countries abstained. As China explained: 'politicizing human rights issues and exerting pressure would only provoke unnecessary confrontation'. Note that neither the report nor the resulting resolutions are translated into Korean by the UN.

(ii) Cambodia

In 1993 the Commission on Human Rights established the post of Special Representative of the Secretary-General on Cambodia. The first Special Representative (1993–1996) was Michael Kirby (Australia). In the reading below, Hilary Charlesworth analyses the experience of Kirby and his three successors. She notes that the reports were robust and critical and that the Cambodian Government often expressed its displeasure with the Special Representatives (SRs). Prime Minister Hun Sen referred to one SR, Yash Ghai (Kenya), as 'deranged', a 'short term tourist' and 'lazy'. She concludes that '[a]lmost all the issues Michael Kirby addressed [as SR]...remain problems today in Cambodia....From a human rights perspective, there has been a great deal of human rights talk in Cambodia but very little actual progress....'

HILARY CHARLESWORTH, SWIMMING TO CAMBODIA: JUSTICE AND RITUAL IN HUMAN RIGHTS AFTER CONFLICT

[2011] ALRS 4, at www.austlii.edu.au/au/journals/ALRS/2011/4.html

...

Human Rights Ritualism

...

Regulation of behaviour through human rights standards is complex. The UN human rights mission in Cambodia illustrates the intricate politics of the

[22] UN Doc. A/HRC/19/65 (13 Feb. 2012).

international human rights system. For example, in some international quarters there has been a sense that Cambodian culture is inhospitable to ideas of human rights and that the Cambodians are at a primitive stage in developing human rights ideas. This has promoted the view that the role of the international community is to guide the Cambodians to better human rights protection. The effect of this approach has been to prevent the development of local human rights expertise and remove human rights questions from local debates. Caroline Hughes has argued that the international community's promotion of human rights in post-conflict Cambodia can be best understood as ritualism in the sense that ideas of rights lost their radical political potential and become a more technical exercise of creating 'responsible citizens' in an efficiently run state mainly through the mechanism of education. Even this more modest goal has not been achieved, according to Hughes....

How can we understand the weakness of the international human rights system in achieving political and social change in post-conflict societies such as Cambodia? I want to suggest that the idea of regulatory ritualism can be helpful in this context, drawing on the work of... John Braithwaite, Valerie Braithwaite and Toni Makkai. Ritualism is one of the five types of adaptation to a normative or cultural order identified by sociologist Robert Merton. Merton's four other types of adaptation are conformity (acceptance of both normative goals and the institutionalised means to achieve them), innovation (acceptance of normative goals but supporting alternative (perhaps even perverse) means to fulfill them, retreatism (resistance to both normative goals and their formal institutions) and rebellion (replacing normative goals and their institutions with new ones). Ritualism occurs when there is no acceptance of particular normative goals, but great deference is paid to the formal institutions that support them. It can be defined as 'acceptance of institutionalized means for securing regulatory goals while losing all focus on achieving the goals or outcomes themselves.'

...

[I]n the field of human rights, rights ritualism is a more common response than an outright rejection of human rights standards and institutions. Rights ritualism can be understood as a way of embracing the language of human rights precisely to deflect real human rights scrutiny and to avoid accountability for human rights abuses. Countries are often willing to accept human rights treaty commitments to earn international approval, but they resist the changes that the treaty obligations require.

...

As we have seen, rights ritualism in Cambodia has sometimes edged closer to disengagement at various points.... Overall, however, the strategy of rights ritualism seems to have been successful for Cambodia....

...

... Participation in international human rights processes and institutions is imbued with symbols and rituals. Cambodia illustrates Murray Edelman's observation that concentrated interests (in this case the Cambodian government) receive tangible rewards (such as international aid funds and political power) while diffuse interests (for example local human rights NGOs) get symbolic rewards (such as statements about the importance of human rights) rather than rewards that can make a difference or challenge the distribution of political power.

MICHAEL KIRBY, UNITED NATIONS PROCEDURES: A RESPONSE TO PROFESSOR HILARY CHARLESWORTH

29 Australian Year Book of International Law (2010)

...

Because of the many defects in the system of special procedures..., an inevitable question is posed: whether the system has so many faults that it risks unduly raising false expectations. In short, does it clothe the United Nations with a deceptive veneer of vigilance in guarding human rights on vulnerable issues and in vulnerable countries? Do the flawed procedures... run the risk of lulling the UN organs, the watching public, and even perhaps the Special Representatives and Special Rapporteurs themselves, into a false assessment of their own achievements?

...

... [W]ould it be better to fold up the tent of special procedures and work towards eventual machinery that would be more principled and effective rather than persisting with procedures that are ultimately highly (or even entirely) dependent upon the cooperation of unlovely autocrats? Why should the UN continue to cloak such people with the appearance of respectability in the field of human rights, by submitting themselves to UN monitoring when the reality is that they only respond to criticism when it pleases them and they ignore it, most of the time, because it does not?

...

Inherent weakness of the system:

...

[Given the troubled history of human rights enforcement efforts within the UN, realism] suggests that the UN procedures must be measured not against an ideal criterion, which presently appears unattainable, but by the standards of the institutions that are in place or likely to be attained, at least in the foreseeable future. In judging the United Nations, we should not lose our faculty of critical, even sceptical, assessment. But neither should we lose our sense of realism and practicality, given the geopolitical realities of the world whose nation states make up the membership of the United Nations.

Particular difficulties:...

... [By 1996, the] refusal of the Prime Ministers to meet me during my missions, the public insults and broadsheet attacks on me... produced a very difficult situation. To this was added the actual danger resulting from death threats launched against me, broadcast by the Khmer Rouge clandestine radio.

...

Each of the succeeding [SRSGs] was, in turn, treated to the same regime of non-co-operation; calumny; and demand for replacement....

On the face of things, this sorry chronicle appears to lend support to [Charlesworth's thesis].... If [special] procedures are ignored with impunity, their proponents insulted and left unsupported by the UN, a point will be reached when it will be preferable to discontinue them....

...

The Utility and Improvement of Special Procedures

... [M]y experience suggests that the existence of the office of SR was useful in the support, and defence of human rights in Cambodia in a number of respects:

- In reminding the government and people of Cambodia, in a repeated and very public way, of the existence and content of universal human rights...;
- In the support given to [NGOs] in Cambodia...;
- ... The SR and the [UN's Office of Human Rights] also provided support to and, to some extent, international protection for, the minority voices in the society of Cambodia;
- In the likelihood that many particular issues would not have been raised, or raised effectively, without the appointment of the SR...;

...

Additionally, the reports of the SR... represented not only a voice to the people of Cambodia themselves, but also to the foreign missions, UN agencies and international donor agencies....

... On some issues (such as press freedom and the defence of political speech), the government of Cambodia was intolerant and excessively sensitive of criticism. Yet on other issues (such as land mine clearance, preservation of cultural treasures and pursuing HIV strategies), the government was willing to listen. In my experience, it was even anxious for technical assistance which the SR could sometimes help to procure.

No doubt the foregoing list, measured against the acknowledged defects, will be seen as a mixed bag of success and failure. It would be wrong, however, to assume that it was an unrelieved story of ineffectiveness and failure....

...

An Evolving Institution

...

Viewing the advance of universal human rights and the role of the United Nations and its "special procedures"..., it is natural to be impatient with the emerging institutional weaknesses, inefficiencies and more than occasional instances of institutional and individual hypocrisy, duplicity and incompetence. Nonetheless, I remain convinced that the world has made important progress [since 1948].

When seen from the perspective of the urgent needs that exist in the world and the terrible sufferings of millions in war and genocide in the last century, the imperfections of the Organisation are all too obvious. But when measured against the neglect of the preceding centuries and the difficulty of securing any agreement and action, the achievements have been notable and incontestably valuable....

... The challenge before the UN itself, its SRs, and the global community is to continuously reduce the imperfections and to increase and expand the achievements.

Healthy self-criticism, appropriate candour and realistic scepticism are essential. So is courage, flexibility, and imagination. But despair and abandonment are not the way to improve global human rights in practice.

QUESTIONS

1. The human rights situation in the DPRK is clearly appalling. What do you make of the approach adopted by the different actors? What are the alternatives?

2. What would be the consequences in a situation such as that described in Cambodia of a decision by the Council to abort the role of the SRSG as a result of the government's non-cooperation? At what point does 'human rights ritualism' do serious damage to the system as a whole?

3. Is Kirby's emphasis on the need for a long-term perspective in evaluating impact persuasive?

(2) Country Reports by Thematic Special Rapporteurs

Thematic mandate-holders generally undertake two or three country missions annually. The purpose of these missions is explained below in the Manual prepared by the mandate-holders to guide their own activities. We then look at a controversial report looking at extrajudicial executions in Kenya, and the government's response.

MANUAL OF OPERATIONS OF THE SPECIAL PROCEDURES OF THE HUMAN RIGHTS COUNCIL

(2007), p. 16 at www2.ohchr.org/english/bodies/chr/special/docs/Manual_August_2008.doc

...

52. Country visits are an essential means to obtain direct and first-hand information on human rights violations. They allow for direct observation of the human rights situation and facilitate an intensive dialogue with all relevant state authorities, including those in the executive, legislative and judicial branches. They also allow for contact with and information gathering from victims, relatives of victims, witnesses, national human rights institutions, international and local NGOs and other members of civil society, the academic community, and officials of international agencies present in the country concerned.

53. Country visits generally last between one and two weeks but can be shorter or longer if the circumstances so require. The visit occurs at the invitation of a State.

...

54. Country visits...enhance awareness...of the specific problems...inter alia, through meetings, briefings, press coverage of the visit and dissemination of the report.

...

56. When a State does not respond to requests for an invitation to visit, it is appropriate for a mandate-holder to remind the Government concerned, to draw the attention of the Council to the outstanding request, and to take other appropriate measures....

57. Considerations which might lead a mandate-holder to request to visit a country include, inter alia, human rights developments at the national level (whether positive or negative), the availability of reliable information regarding human rights violations falling within the mandate, or a wish to pursue a particular thematic interest. Other factors...might include considerations of geographical balance, the expected impact of the visit and the willingness of national actors to cooperate with the mandate-holder, the likelihood of follow-up on any recommendations made, the recent adoption by one or more treaty bodies of relevant concluding observations, the upcoming examination of the situation by one or more treaty bodies, recent or proposed visits by other Special Procedure mandate-holders, the list of countries scheduled for consideration under the Council's Universal Periodic Review (UPR) mechanism, follow up to the recommendations and conclusions of the UPR mechanism, and the priorities reflected in OHCHR's country engagement strategy.

...

REPORT OF THE SPECIAL RAPPORTEUR ON EXTRAJUDICIAL, SUMMARY OR ARBITRARY EXECUTIONS, PHILIP ALSTON, MISSION TO KENYA

UN Doc. A/HRC/11/2/Add.6 (26 May 2009)

...

II. EXTRAJUDICIAL EXECUTIONS BY POLICE

5. Killings by the police are widespread. Some killings are opportunistic, reckless or personal. Many others are carefully planned. It is impossible to estimate reliably how many killings occur, because the police do not keep a centralized database. But police shootings are reported nearly every day of the week by the press and the total number is certainly unacceptably high. In just a five month period in 2007, the Kenya National Commission on Human Rights (KNCHR) documented approximately 500 people killed or disappeared.

6. There are six primary factors which account for the frequency with which police can kill at will in Kenya: (i) official sanctioned targeted killings of suspected criminals; (ii) a dysfunctional criminal justice system incentivizes police to counter crime by killing suspected criminals, rather than arresting them; (iii) internal and external police accountability mechanisms are virtually non-existent; there is little check on, and virtually no independent investigations of, alleged police abuses;

(iv) use of force laws are contradictory and overly permissive; (v) witnesses to abuse are often intimidated, and fear reporting or testifying; and (vi) the police force lacks sufficient training, discipline and professionalism.

A. Context

7. Kenyans are subjected to significant levels of both indiscriminate and organized violent criminality. Armed robbery, carjacking, and violent street crime are all common. . . .

8. There are many such criminal groups, but the Mungiki have become particularly prominent. . . . In the early 1990s, the Mungiki, initially a cultural-religious movement, began providing security and basic services in slums. While many of these activities were originally appreciated by slum residents, as the Mungiki grew, so did its level of control, and ruthless tactics were employed to preserve it. Today, the Mungiki are responsible for a large number of crimes, including murder . . .

B. Evidence of widespread killings by police

9. The Government has a clear obligation to protect citizens from Mungiki and other criminal violence, while respecting human rights, including the right to life. Suspects should be arrested, charged, tried and punished accordingly. In a context of violent criminality, police will inevitably be required to use force on occasion, and sometimes lethal force in order to protect life. The police, including the Police Commissioner, assured me that there have been no unlawful police killings. However, as I detail below, the evidence is compelling that the police respond — frequently — with unlawful force: murdering, rather than arresting suspects. Further, investigations by police are so deficient and compromised that claims by the police that all killings are lawful are inherently unreliable and unsustainable.

10. During my mission, I received compelling evidence that death squads — including one called *Kwekwe* — exist within the police force in Kenya, and that these squads were set-up to eliminate the Mungiki and other high-profile suspected criminals, upon the orders of senior police officials. Detailed evidence was provided by civil society investigations, witnesses to the squad's activities, survivors of attempted killings, family members of deceased or disappeared victims, and victim autopsy reports indicating shots at close range and back entry wounds. A further key component of this evidence is the now public testimony of a police whistleblower, who recorded his statement in July 2008, before he was murdered while in hiding in October 2008. His account provides, in precise and often excruciating, detail the composition and operations of the death squad in which he was a part, and the circumstances of the murder of 67 persons between February 2007 and July 2008. Together, this evidence implicates the Commissioner of Police, and senior police officials from the Criminal Investigation Division, Special Crime Unit, and the Criminal Intelligence Unit. From this large amount of testimony, it is possible to set-out in detail the operations of the death squads [details omitted].

. . .

11. Evidence presented to me indicates that these targeted and planned death squad killings are only the tip of the iceberg of police killings in Kenya. In addition

to the death squad killings described above, I received detailed information on a wide range of circumstances in which unlawful killings have taken place. . . .

12. Lethal force is also commonly used in legitimate law enforcement operations in which the police could have readily made an arrest. . . .

C. Official response to allegations

13. Some Government officials stated that if killings occurred, they were committed infrequently and by "rogue" officers. To their credit, a small number of Government officials did acknowledge the magnitude of the killings. But senior police officials were unwilling to acknowledge the problem at all: in essence, their response was one of denial, stone-walling, and obfuscation. . . . Senior police flatly denied to me any knowledge of the *Kwekwe* death squad. And yet its existence was confirmed in Parliament by the Minister of State. . . .

. . .

16. . . . [T]he police response to my visit has consisted of continued denials of all wrongdoing, ad hominem attacks against me, and apparent police involvement in the broad daylight assassination of two human rights defenders with whom I met. Rather than in any way addressing the substance of the allegations contained in my initial statement, some police officials have sought to structure public debate so that criticisms of police actions are equated with condoning criminal activity. In this way, the police have tried to position civil society — and also my own reporting — as aligned with the interests of criminal organizations. This in turn sets up the police to launch further attacks against the Mungiki and others, while failing to take any steps to address the real issues. Efforts to monitor and reform policing so that it is carried out with respect for human rights do not mean being "soft" on crime. Security policies only truly provide security if the rights of all — victims, the general public, police, and criminals — are respected. The violent police response to crime has done nothing to promote security. Innocent bystanders have been shot by police, the public has lost faith that the police force can protect them, and the police have undertaken few if any measures to investigate and prosecute those Mungiki and other criminals who continue to terrorize and extort private citizens.

17. . . . [M]embers of criminal organisations — because of their regular intimidation of residents — are easily identifiable. This was repeatedly noted by witnesses. . . . If the police were serious about crime control, they would be able to locate and arrest suspects. Unfortunately, in many Mungiki controlled areas, police profit from criminal control by accepting bribes to permit continued Mungiki control. . . .

D. Removal of the Police Commissioner

. . .

19. . . . [T]here is abundant evidence linking [the Police Commissioner] to a central role in devising and overseeing the policy of extrajudicially executing large numbers of "suspected criminals". He flatly refuses to acknowledge that any unlawful killings are taking place, derides detailed and compelling reports to the contrary, blocks investigations, and prevents all transparency.

20. Most importantly in terms of the interests of the Kenyan population, he has utterly failed to devise any law enforcement strategy worthy of the name for dealing with Mungiki and other forms of criminality. Widespread killings of suspects and innocents alike, combined with a failure to rein in rampant corruption on the part of key officials, do not add up to a strategy for policing.

...

E. Accountability and the criminal justice system

22. Failures in the criminal justice system, and in internal and external police accountability mechanisms, encourage the commission of unlawful killings by police.

23. The criminal justice system as a whole was widely described as "terrible". Investigation, prosecution, and judicial processes are slow and corrupt. Predictably, this leads to widespread distrust of the system, and impunity for criminals (particularly for those with power and money). It also acts as an incentive for police to kill, rather than arrest suspects: because of the low probability of securing convictions, many police think it is easier and more effective to take "justice" into their own hands. And, significantly, police themselves also benefit from the systemic faults—they are rarely held to account for the abuses they commit.

...

1. Police investigations

25. Police investigations of murders are generally inadequate, due in large part to resource, training, and capacity constraints. But investigations are especially poor when the police themselves are implicated in a death....

...

2. Prosecutions

...

29. The Attorney-General has security of tenure, for life, and has been in office since 1991. He has overseen, for nearly two decades, a system that clearly does not work. The Attorney-General has the constitutional power to "require" the Police Commissioner to investigate any matter relating to an alleged offence. As documents provided by the Attorney-General clearly indicate, he is all too aware of the grave deficiencies in police investigations. But instead of using his constitutional powers to force individual investigations, and to promote essential institutional reforms, letters simply go back and forth for years, with cases neither investigated sufficiently, nor prosecuted. In addition, the repeated failure to prosecute *any* senior officials for their role in large-scale election violence over a period of many years...has led to a complete loss of faith in the commitment of his office to prosecute those in Government with responsibility for crimes.

30.... [The Attorney-General's] unrelenting failure to prosecute any senior officials implicated in extrajudicial executions renders him not just complicit in, but absolutely indispensable to, a system which has institutionalized impunity in Kenya. In order to restore the integrity of the office, the current Attorney-General should resign or be required to leave office....

...

X. RECOMMENDATIONS

A. Killings by police

85. The President should publicly acknowledge his commitment to ending unlawful killings by the police. To this end:

(a) The Police Commissioner should be replaced immediately;
(b) Unambiguous public orders should be issued that under no circumstances will unlawful killings by the security forces be tolerated.

86. Police death squad killings should be prevented, investigated, and punished:

(a) The Minister for Internal Security should order the disbandment of all death squads, and report to Parliament on the measures [taken];
(b) The Government should establish an independent inquiry into the operation of police death squads. To secure the inquiry's integrity and independence, Kenya should invite foreign police investigators (such as the FBI, or Scotland Yard) to assist....;
(c) All individuals under investigation for their involvement in police death squads should be removed from active duty during that period.

87. A review of the use of force provisions in the Constitution of Kenya, the Police Act, and the Standing Force Orders should be undertaken to bring them into line with Kenya's obligations under international law.

...

89.... All police stations should be required to report [police killings] to headquarters within 24 hours. The complete statistics of police killings should be made public... on a monthly basis....

B. Killings by the Mungiki

90. The Mungiki should immediately cease their harassment, abuse, and murder of Kenyans.

91. The Mungiki political leadership should publicly condemn killings and other abuses by their members, and take action to prevent all such crimes.

C. Accountability for police killings

92. Internal and external accountability for police should be improved through [suggested] institutional reforms....

D. Criminal justice system

93. The Attorney-General should resign. This is necessary to restore public trust in the office, and to end its role in promoting impunity.

94. Political control over prosecutions should be eliminated and the prosecutorial powers currently held by the Attorney-General should be vested in an independent Department of Public Prosecutions.

95. To reduce corruption and incompetence in the judiciary:

(a) Radical surgery needs to be undertaken to terminate the tenure of the majority of the existing judges and replace them with competent and non-corrupt appointees;
(b) Judicial appointment procedures should be made more transparent, and all appointments made following a merits-based review of the appointee;

…

GOVERNMENT OF KENYA RESPONSE, PHILIP ALSTON'S REPORT PATERNALISTIC, UNHELPFUL AND UNCALLED FOR

at www.communication.go.ke/documents/ KenyaGovernmentsResponseToAlstonReport.pdf

INTRODUCTION

The Government of Kenya expresses its deep displeasure with the report of Prof. Philip Alston.…

His approach, conduct and method of work were contrary to the Code of Conduct for the Special Procedures Mandate-holders [see HRC Res. 5/2 (June 18, 2007), *infra*].…

The Government expresses grave concern regarding the allegations contained in the report by the Special Rapporteur. His questioning of the very basis of the Kenyan State and in particular its institutions is totally unacceptable, and impinges on Kenya's sovereignty. The Rapporteur's call for the removal of constitutional office holders in key Government institutions is paternalistic, unhelpful and uncalled for. The Government outrightly rejects this call. He failed to understand the country's peculiarities, recent political problems and the challenges it faces in its healing and reconciliation process after the post-election violence. The Government expected to have an interactive engagement on Kenya's capacity needs and the expectation was that the Rapporteur's work would compliment ongoing systemic reforms.

Kenya remains fully committed to fulfilling all her human rights obligations.

…

NOTE

After the presentation of the report on Kenya, the African Group in the Council made an official statement characterizing the 'call of the rapporteur for the removal of constitutional officials in Kenya is not only unprecedented but also illegal', and called for the termination of the rapporteur's mandate. No action was taken, however, after the Prime Minister of Kenya indicated that his country 'recognised that extrajudicial killings were a serious problem in our country, and accepted most of Prof Alston's recommendations on how to put an end to this terrible scourge.'[23]

[23] Raila Odinga, 'Africans Must Lead the Global Struggle against Impunity', *Daily Nation*, 17 June 2009.

QUESTIONS

1. What potential audiences should a Special Rapporteur seek to reach? What difficulties might arise in trying to reach multiple audiences?

2. Recommendations by a Special Rapporteur can range from unhelpful generalities to detailed prescriptions. What balance should be struck and what factors should influence the determination. Does the Kenya report go beyond what is appropriate, or at least what is prudent?

(3) Special Sessions of the Council

The Commission decided in 1992 to hold special sessions when needed, but only five were called in the following 13 years (two focused on the former Yugoslavia in 1992, and one each on Rwanda in 1994, East Timor in 1999 and the Palestinian territories in 2000). The Council has made much more extensive use of the technique, having held 18 sessions between 2006 and 2012. They have dealt with: (1) Occupied Palestinian Territory (OPT) — 2006; (2) Lebanon — 2006; (3) OPT — 2006; (4) Darfur — 2006; (5) Myanmar — 2007; (6) OPT — 2008; (7) world food crisis — 2008; (8) Democratic Republic of the Congo — 2008; (9) OPT — 2009; (10) global financial crisis — 2009; (11) Sri Lanka — 2009; (12) OPT — 2009; (13) Haiti earthquake — 2010; (14) Côte d'Ivoire — 2010; (15) Libya — 2011; (16), (17) and (18) Syria — 2011.

The goal of these sessions is 'to address human rights violations and emergencies', with the implication that the Council would take prompt and effective action when it is most needed. But the mechanism achieved little through 2010, and fuelled allegations of double standards in relation to Israel which was the focus of six of the first 12 special sessions (see note on Israel *infra*). The low point during this period was the 2009 session on Sri Lanka. The government was strongly supported by the member states of the Non-Aligned Movement and tabled its own draft resolution. Amendments proposed by the European Union were blocked procedurally. The resolution adopted by a vote of 29–12–6 (HRC Res. S-11/1 of 27 May 2009) commended the government for its actions, welcomed its various assurances and urged the international community to provide more financial resources. The Secretary-General's decision one year later to appoint his own Panel of Experts (p. 848, *infra*) was widely viewed as a response to the Council's failure. It also laid the groundwork for the Council effectively to reverse itself three years later by requesting Sri Lanka to present the Council with a 'comprehensive action plan' detailing its steps to implement the recommendations of a domestic inquiry and to 'address alleged violations of international law' (HRC Res. 19/2 of 22 Mar. 2012 adopted by a vote of 24–15–8).

The latter initiative reflected the much more fluid and responsive approach of the Council post-2010. As a result, special sessions have led to the High Commissioner being requested in 2010 to report on violations in Côte d'Ivoire, and commissions of inquiry being established in 2011 in relation to both Libya and Syria. Subsequent debates in the Security Council relied significantly on the data contained in these reports.

COMMENT ON ISRAEL

The Council's programme of work is divided into ten different 'items'. Under item 4 — 'human rights situations that require the Council's attention' — violations anywhere in the world can be debated. A separate item 7 concerns the 'human rights situation in Palestine and other occupied Arab territories'. No other country situation is accorded a separate item. The Organization of the Islamic Conference and other blocs within the Council argue that this is justified because the situation is unique by virtue of the ongoing occupation. The Western Group and others consider the separate item to be discriminatory and evidence of a double standard that singles out Israel and downplays other situations of grave concern. In December 2006 the UN Secretary-General expressed his concern at the Council's 'disproportionate focus on violations by Israel. Not that Israel should be given a free pass. Absolutely not. But the Council should give the same attention to grave violations committed by other states as well.'

The Council has launched a series of high-profile inquiries, the most controversial of which was the Fact Finding Mission on the Gaza Conflict, which was requested 'to investigate all violations of international human rights law and international humanitarian law that might have been committed at any time in the context of the military operations that were conducted in Gaza during the period from 27 December 2008 and 18 January 2009, whether before, during or after.' The Gaza authorities facilitated a visit by the Commission, but Israel refused all cooperation. The 452-page report (UN Doc. A/HRC/12/48 of 25 Sept. 2009), commonly called the 'Goldstone Report' after the Chairman of the group, concluded that grave violations of international human rights and humanitarian law and possible war crimes and crimes against humanity had been committed by both the Israel Defence Forces and the Palestinian armed groups. It recommended follow-up action by the Security Council, as well as by the Human Rights Council and the General Assembly. Consider the following sampling of reactions.

Israel Ministry of Foreign Affairs, Initial Response to Report of the Fact Finding Mission on Gaza
(24 Sept. 2009)

1. The [Goldstone Report] was instigated as part of a political campaign, and itself represents a political assault directed against Israel and against every State forced to confront terrorist threats.

…

3. [T]he Report advances a narrative which ignores the threats to Israeli civilians, as well as Israel's extensive diplomatic and political efforts to avoid the outbreak of hostilities. In this narrative self defense finds no place.…

4. … [T]he Report engages in creative editing, misrepresentations of facts and law, and repeatedly adopts evidentiary double standards, attributing credibility to every anti-Israel allegation, and invariably dismissing evidence that indicates any wrongdoing by Hamas.

5. The Report repeatedly downplays or ignores the reality of terrorist threats, and the complexity of the military challenges in urban warfare. It also goes far beyond its mandate as a fact-finding mission, making legal and judicial determinations of criminal wrongdoing, even in the absence of crucial information.

6. The Report dismisses the Israeli legal system and its extensive investigation process of allegations of misconduct by Israeli armed forces. In so doing, the Report effectively calls into question the internal investigation procedures of the armed forces of most democratic states since Israel's system is similar to, and in many cases more stringent than, those of many other countries.

...

Conclusion

31. In the final analysis, the true test of such a Report can only be whether in future armed conflicts it will have the effect of increasing or decreasing respect for the rule of law by the parties. Regrettably a one-sided report of this nature, claiming to represent international law but in fact perverting it to serve a political agenda, can only weaken the standing of international law in future conflicts.

...

The Public Committee Against Torture in Israel (PCATI), No Second Thoughts: The Changes in the Israeli Defense Forces' Combat Doctrine in Light of 'Operation Cast Lead'

(2009), at 4

Since March 2009, various organizations, including Amnesty International, Human Rights Watch and the [Goldstone Committee] have produced reports on the entire operation or specific aspects of it. In addition, Israeli human rights organizations, both in joint statements and in individual publications such as those by B'Tselem and Gisha, have also related in a critical manner to the IDF's (Israeli Defense Forces) actions during the operation. All these publications have arrived at the general conclusion that was expressed in [the Amnesty International] report:

> "Much of the destruction was wanton and resulted from direct attacks on civilian objects as well as indiscriminate attacks that failed to distinguish between legitimate military targets and civilian objects. Such attacks violated fundamental provisions of international humanitarian law, notably the prohibition on direct attacks on civilians and civilian objects (the principle of distinction), the prohibition on indiscriminate or disproportionate attacks, and the prohibition on collective punishment."

Alan Dershowitz, The Case Against the Goldstone Report: A Study in Evidentiary Bias

(2010), at www.alandershowitz.com/goldstone.pdf

The Goldstone Report, when read in full and in context, is much worse than most of its detractors (and supporters) believe. It is far more accusatory of Israel, far less balanced in its criticism of Hamas, far less honest in its evaluation of the evidence, far less responsible in drawing its conclusion, far more biased against Israeli than Palestinian witnesses, and far more willing to draw adverse inferences of intentionality from Israeli conduct and statements than from comparable Palestinian conduct and statements. It is worse than any report previously prepared by any other United Nations agency or human rights group. As Major General Avichai Mandelblit, the advocate general of the Israeli Defense Forces, aptly put it:

> 'I have read every report, from Human Rights Watch, Amnesty International, the Arab League. We ourselves set up investigations into 140 complaints. It is when you read these other reports and complaints that you realize how truly vicious the Goldstone report is. He made it look like we set out to go after the economic infrastructure and civilians, that it was intentional: It's a vicious lie.'

The Goldstone report is, to any fair reader, a shoddy piece of work, unworthy of serious consideration by people of good will, committed to the truth.

Most of the criticism and praise of the report has been based on its highly publicized and controversial conclusions, rather than on its methodology, analysis and substantive findings....

... There are 1223 footnotes, though many of its most critical statements are not well sourced.... It is laden with internal inconsistencies, shoddy citations of authority, and overall poor craftsmanship....

...

Dinah PoKempner [General Counsel, Human Rights Watch], Valuing the Goldstone Report

16 Global Governance 144 (2010)

The Goldstone Report had a politicized and emotional reception that has colored its evaluation to date. There have been so many attacks on the report...that the campaign took on a life and logic of its own. Most of the attacks allege bias in some way without seriously contesting the actual findings of the report.... [T]hese attacks are ill-founded at best and sometimes just efforts to change the subject. But calls of bias strongly resonate, given Israel's sense of continual siege and the mission's sponsorship by the UN Human Rights Council, hardly a neutral broker in the conflict....

...

As an example of UN fact-finding, the mission followed the best UN efforts, and its findings are consistent with that of other independent analysts. Although it might have been more explicit as to the evidentiary standards it employed, the mission did consider facts on each side and explained how it discounted or credited evidence. Its legal analysis follows current international legal interpretation while opening new questions to debate and development. The report provided a detailed template against which to judge progress in investigation and accountability.

However, action by the Security Council on the report remains blocked, and Israel has so far rejected an independent commission of inquiry....

...

The Report's Impact

...

[D]oes the report do what it is supposed to do — impel the parties to investigate violations and hold perpetrators responsible? Its immediate history is discouraging. The United States kept silent for a few days following the report's release, and then pronounced it "unfair" without contesting its findings, leaving the impression of a political decision, not a legal or intelligence assessment. The US House of Representatives passed a [one-sided] resolution condemning the report.... The Human Rights Council [and General Assembly both endorsed the report] and called on both sides to mount credible investigations. The Security Council ... is not expected to make a resolution, given US determination....

...

The depressing assessment on impunity so far must be counterbalanced by the useful impact of the report in giving a standard against which both Israel and Hamas will be measured by the world in the years to come. The delegitimation campaign almost, but not quite, obscured the huge coverage and debate that the report caused globally. The report seems to have goaded further IDF efforts to investigate, as well as a pledge from Hamas that it too would examine the report's allegations....

There are no perfect fact-finding exercises, and this one operated under heavy constraints due to Israel's noncooperation. Many of the report's shortcomings derive from this, but the mission cannot be faulted for setting forth conclusions from an incomplete picture. To empower noncooperating parties would be to defeat international fact-finding entirely....

Richard Goldstone, Reconsidering the Goldstone Report on Israel and War Crimes

***Washington Post*, 1 Apr. 2011**

We know a lot more today about what happened in the Gaza war of 2008–09 than we did when [the Goldstone Report was written]. If I had known then what I know now, the Goldstone Report would have been a different document.

The final report by the U.N. committee of independent experts — chaired by former New York judge Mary McGowan Davis — that followed up on the recommendations of the Goldstone Report has found that "Israel has dedicated significant resources to investigate over 400 allegations of operational misconduct in Gaza" while "the de facto authorities (i.e., Hamas) have not conducted any investigations into the launching of rocket and mortar attacks against Israel."

Our report found evidence of potential war crimes and "possibly crimes against humanity" by both Israel and Hamas. That the crimes allegedly committed by Hamas were intentional goes without saying — its rockets were purposefully and indiscriminately aimed at civilian targets.

The allegations of intentionality by Israel were based on the deaths of and injuries to civilians in situations where our fact-finding mission had no evidence on which to draw any other reasonable conclusion. While the investigations published by the Israeli military and recognized in the U.N. committee's report have established the validity of some incidents that we investigated in cases involving individual soldiers, they also indicate that civilians were not intentionally targeted as a matter of policy.

For example, the most serious attack the Goldstone Report focused on was the killing of some 29 members of the al-Simouni family in their home. The shelling of the home was apparently the consequence of an Israeli commander's erroneous interpretation of a drone image, and an Israeli officer is under investigation for having ordered the attack. While the length of this investigation is frustrating, it appears that an appropriate process is underway, and I am confident that if the officer is found to have been negligent, Israel will respond accordingly. The purpose of these investigations, as I have always said, is to ensure accountability for improper actions, not to second-guess, with the benefit of hindsight, commanders making difficult battlefield decisions.

While I welcome Israel's investigations into allegations, I share the concerns reflected in the McGowan Davis report that few of Israel's inquiries have been concluded and believe that the proceedings should have been held in a public forum. Although the Israeli evidence that has emerged since publication of our report doesn't negate the tragic loss of civilian life, I regret that our fact-finding mission did not have such evidence explaining the circumstances in which we said civilians in Gaza were targeted, because it probably would have influenced our findings about intentionality and war crimes.

…

John Dugard, Where Now for the Goldstone Report?

The New Statesman, 6 Apr. 2011

In short, there are no new facts that could possibly have led Richard Goldstone to change his mind about the UN-backed investigation into Israel and the conflict in Gaza.

…

The op-ed [above] makes strange reading.

It states that the Goldstone report would have been a different document "had I known then what I know now", but fails to disclose any information that seriously challenges the findings of the Goldstone Report.

It claims that investigations published by the Israeli military and recognised by a follow-up UN committee report chaired by Judge Mary McGowan Davis, which appeared in March, "indicate that civilians were not intentionally targeted as a matter of policy". But the McGowan Davis report contains absolutely no such "indication" and instead seriously questions Israel's investigations, finding them to be lacking in impartiality, promptness and transparency.

Goldstone expresses "confidence" that the officer responsible for perhaps the gravest atrocity of Operation Cast Lead (Israel's code name for its assault on Gaza) — the killing of 29 members of the al-Samouni family — will be punished properly by Israel, even though the McGowan Davis report provides a critical assessment of Israel's handling of the investigation into this killing.

Finally he claims that the McGowan Davis report finds that Israel has carried out investigations "to a significant degree", but in fact this report paints a very different picture of Israel's investigations of 400 incidents, which have resulted in two convictions, one for theft of a credit card, resulting in a sentence of seven months' imprisonment, and another for using a Palestinian child as a human shield, which resulted in a suspended sentence of three months.

...

MAG Legal Opinion: Al-Samouni Family Incident

(1 May 2012), at www.law.idf.il/163-5080-en/Patzar.aspx

... [T]he MAG [Military Advocate General of the Israeli Defence Forces] found that the Criminal Investigation [into the al-Samouni incident, which is the focus of Goldstone's Op Ed, above] comprehensively refuted the serious allegations cast against the IDF, according to which the strikes were directly and intentionally aimed at civilians not taking a direct part in the hostilities, or alternatively were carried out in a reckless manner with respect to the possibility that such civilians may be harmed as a result thereof. The investigation also found that there were no grounds to the allegation that IDF forces directed civilians to gather in the house which was later struck. As a result, the MAG concluded that there are no grounds for the allegation that the Incident involved the commission of war crimes, which according to international law require a mental element constituting criminal intent.

In addition, the MAG found that with respect to the strikes in which civilians not taking a direct part in hostilities were harmed and that were the subject of the allegations filed with the MAG Corps, none of the persons involved — including the Brigade Commander — acted negligently in a manner giving rise to criminal responsibility under the circumstances. Notwithstanding the fact that a number of decisions made by the Brigade Commander during the Incident were found to be deficient, and that he was expected to act otherwise, the MAG found that the decisions taken during the Incident did not deviate from the boundaries of discretion that a "reasonable military commander" operating in similar circumstances possesses.

...

In light of the above, the MAG found that there were no grounds for employing criminal or disciplinary measures against any of those involved in the Incident, and instructed that the file be closed....

The military's response does not detail the findings of the investigation, nor does it provide the reasons behind the decision to close the file or any new information about the circumstances.

Jessica Montell, No Closure in Killing of 21 Gaza Family Members

B'Tselem (8 May 2012), at www.btselem.org/gaza_strip/20120508_samuni_op_ed

On 4 January 2009, at the start of the ground phase of operation Cast Lead, about 100 members of the extended a-Samuni family were huddled inside one house in the a-Zeitun neighborhood of Gaza City. The next morning, an Israeli airstrike killed 21 people inside the house, including 9 children and 10 women, and injured dozens of other family members. During the next two days, the army refused access to medical teams, in spite of being informed of the terrible outcome by family members who managed to escape the bombed home and human rights and humanitarian organizations, including B'Tselem. When medics managed to get to site, they found four small children next to their dead mothers in one of the houses, and evacuated several wounded people. The army refused permission to evacuate the bodies and they remained in the rubble for a further two weeks.

[The MAG statement, above] does not detail the findings of the investigation, nor does it provide the reasons behind the decision to close the file....

...

... B'Tselem never alleged that this was a case of willful killing, but this is far from the only standard against which to judge our military's behavior. The military is also obligated to take all feasible precautions to avoid harm to the civilian population. Was this the case in the a-Samuni incident? Such is the implication of the MAG's response — yet it is a very difficult conclusion to reconcile with all the facts of the case. The lack of accountability for the a-Samuni family is no aberration. Some fifty military police investigations were opened into harm to Palestinian civilians in Operation Cast Lead, yet the overwhelming majority appear to be gathering dust. The MAG Corps has created a haze around these investigations, preventing any possibility of examining their effectiveness. It appears that three indictments have been filed against soldiers who took part in Cast Lead: [the two cited by Dugard], and for "manslaughter of an anonymous person." In three other cases, disciplinary action alone was taken. The fate of the rest of the cases is entirely unclear.

There has never been an investigation meeting international standards into the suspicions raised by B'Tselem and other organizations regarding breaches of international humanitarian law by the military during the operation....

Another important element in the overall equation is that the Security Council has been effectively unable to take action in relation to most proposed resolutions concerning Israel. Since 2001, a total of 21 vetoes have been cast by the five Permanent Members. Of those, ten have been cast by the United States in relation to issues affecting Israel: (1) appointment of UN observer force in OPT (2001, 9 votes in favour, 1 against); (2) condemning acts of terror and proposing observers (2001, 12–1); (3) killing of UN employees and destruction of World Food Programme warehouse (2002, 12–1); (4) calling on Israel not to expel Palestinian leader (2003, 11–1); (5) calling on Israel not to extend the wall (2003, 10–1); (6) condemning Israel for targeted assassination of Sheik Yassin and six others (2004, 11–1); (7) calling for an end to military activities in Gaza (2004, 11–1); (8) calling on Israel to release Palestinian cabinet ministers and cease shelling of Gaza (2006, 10–1); (9) calling for Gaza force withdrawal and inquiry into attack on Beit Hanoun (2006, 10–1); and (10) calling for a halt to new settlements (2011; 14–1).[24]

[24] The details of the resolutions are available at www.jewishvirtuallibrary.org/jsource/UN/usvetoes.html.

It should be noted that the Council's very heavy focus on Israel has not, however, involved an examination of the human rights situation within Israel itself. Rather it has been concerned with the consequences of occupation, and the inevitably fraught situation arising in such a context (the OPT), and in the use of force in another country (Lebanon).

In terms of Israel's domestic human rights situation, the relationship with the relevant UN treaty bodies has been consistently positive. Israel reported to the CERD Committee in 2012, the CEDAW and ICESCR Committees in 2011, the Committee on the Rights of the Child in 2010 and the Committee against Torture in 2009.

Nevertheless, the Council maintains its preoccupation with Israel. In March 2012, it adopted 39 resolutions, 15 of which were country-specific. Five, or one-third of the total, related to Israel. All of those were adopted with only one opposing vote (that of the United States). They were: Res. 19/4: Human rights in the occupied Syrian Golan; 19/15: Right of the Palestinian people to self-determination; 19/16 Human rights situation in the Occupied Palestinian Territory, including East Jerusalem; 19/18: Follow-up to the report of the UN Independent International Fact-Finding Mission on the Gaza Conflict; and 19/17 (adopted by 36 votes, 1 against (the United States) and 10 abstentions), the text of which follows:

HRC Res. 19/17: Israeli settlements in the Occupied Palestinian Territory, including East Jerusalem, and in the Occupied Syrian Golan

(22 Mar. 2012)

The Human Rights Council

...

Expressing its concern at the failure of the Government of Israel to cooperate fully with the relevant United Nations mechanisms, in particular the Special Rapporteur on the situation of human rights in the Palestinian Territories occupied since 1967,

1. Welcomes the Council of the European Union['s statement calling] upon the government of Israel to immediately end all settlement activities...;

...

4. Expresses its grave concern at:

    (a) The continuing Israeli settlement and related activities, in violation of international law, including the expansion of settlements, the expropriation of land, the demolition of houses, the confiscation and destruction of property, the expulsion of Palestinians and the construction of bypass roads, which change the physical character and demographic composition of the occupied territories...and constitute a violation of the fourth Geneva Convention...;

    ...

5. Urges Israel, the occupying Power:

    (a) To reverse the settlement policy...;

…

9. Decides to dispatch an independent international fact-finding mission, to be appointed by the President of the Human Rights Council, to investigate the implications of the Israeli settlements on the civil, political, economic, social and cultural rights of the Palestinian people throughout the Occupied Palestinian Territory, including East Jerusalem, with a mandate ending on submission of a report to the Council, and calls upon Israel, the occupying Power, not to obstruct the process of investigation and to cooperate fully with the mission;

…

QUESTIONS

1. 'The Council's pre-occupation with Israel reflects the state of international relations in general rather than the Council's shortcomings. In any event, the optimal course is not for a reduced focus on violations such as those of which Israel is accused, but a more systematic targeting of this type focusing on a wide range of countries and organizations involved in systematic violations.' Comment.

2. After the adoption of HRC Res. 19/17 (*supra*) Israel announced that it would no longer have anything to do with the Council and would not cooperate with any requests it might make. How should the Council, and other states, respond?

3. Many observers suggest that the Goldstone report process was 'politicized'. What might that mean in practice and what techniques could be used to reduce such problems?

3. THEMATIC REPORTS OF SPECIAL RAPPORTEURS

Each Special Rapporteur presents an annual report to the Council and many of them use that opportunity to develop themes that have arisen in their country-specific work or to offer interpretations of relevant standards. We encountered prominent examples in Chapter 3 in relation to violence against women and LGB rights (see pp. 191 and 220, *supra*). The overall quality of the analyses varies, but some have had a major impact when judged by the amount of media coverage garnered, the uptake of their ideas by judges, governments, human rights groups, scholars and other potential users of the information, and the strong reactions of governments. Thematic studies can also play an important role in informal agenda-setting within the Council. The example below takes a principle that has been widely recognized but poorly defined and seeks to spell out its implications.

REPORT OF THE SPECIAL RAPPORTEUR ON THE SITUATION OF HUMAN RIGHTS AND FUNDAMENTAL FREEDOMS OF INDIGENOUS PEOPLES, JAMES ANAYA

UN Doc. A/HRC/12/34 (15 July 2009)

...

II. A Core Issue: The Duty to Consult

A. The normative grounding and general character of the duty to consult

38. [T]he duty of States to consult with indigenous peoples on decisions affecting them finds prominent expression in the United Nations Declaration on the Rights of Indigenous Peoples, and is firmly rooted in international human rights law. This duty is referenced throughout the Declaration in relation to particular concerns ..., and it is affirmed as an overarching principle in article 19, which provides: "States shall consult and cooperate in good faith with the indigenous peoples concerned through their own representative institutions in order to obtain their free, prior and informed consent before adopting and implementing legislative or administrative measures that may affect them."

[The Rapporteur notes that ILO Convention No. 169 requires States to consult with indigenous peoples in good faith, and observes that the ILO's jurisprudence 'draws out some of the contours of the duty to consult'. He also notes other relevant international and regional treaty provisions and the approaches adopted by the relevant supervisory organs.]

42. As a general matter, decisions of the State should be made through democratic processes in which the public's interests are adequately represented.... However, special, differentiated consultation procedures are called for when State decisions affect indigenous peoples' particular interests. Such special procedures are justified because of the nature of those particular interests, arising as they do from indigenous peoples' distinctive cultural patterns and histories, and because the normal democratic and representative processes usually do not work adequately to address the concerns that are particular to indigenous peoples, who are typically marginalized in the political sphere....

B. Situations in which the duty to consult applies

43. ... [T]he duty to consult...applies whenever a State decision may affect indigenous peoples in ways not felt by others in society. Such a differentiated effect occurs when the interests or conditions of indigenous peoples that are particular to them are implicated in the decision, even when the decision may have a broader impact....

44. The duty...arises whenever [indigenous peoples'] particular interests are at stake, even when those interests do not correspond to a recognized right to land or other legal entitlement...

...

C. The requirement that consultations be in good faith, with the objective of achieving agreement or consent

46. The character of the consultation procedure and its object are also shaped by the nature of the right or interest at stake...and the anticipated impact.... [Article 19] should not be regarded as according indigenous peoples a general "veto power" over decisions that may affect them, but rather as establishing consent as the objective of consultations....

47. Necessarily, the strength or importance of the objective of achieving consent varies according to the circumstances and the indigenous interests involved. A significant, direct impact on indigenous peoples' lives or territories establishes a strong presumption that the proposed measure should not go forward without indigenous peoples' consent. In certain contexts, that presumption may harden into a prohibition of the measure or project in the absence of indigenous consent. The Declaration recognizes two [such] situations[:] when the project will result in the relocation of a group from its traditional lands, and in cases involving the storage or disposal of toxic waste within indigenous lands....

48. ... The Special Rapporteur regrets that in many situations the discussion[s] over the duty to consult...have been framed in terms of whether or not indigenous peoples hold a veto power.... The Special Rapporteur considers that focusing the debate in this way is not in line with the spirit or character of the principles of consultation and consent as they have developed in international human rights law....

49. These principles are designed to build dialogue in which both States and indigenous peoples are to work in good faith towards consensus and try in earnest to arrive at a mutually satisfactory agreement.... [They] are aimed at avoiding the imposition of the will of one party over the other, and at instead striving for mutual understanding and consensual decision-making.

D. Elements of confidence-building conducive to consensus

50. ... The creation of a climate of confidence is particularly important in relation to indigenous peoples, "given their lack of trust in State institutions and their feeling of marginalization ...".

...

52. The building of confidence and the possibility of genuine consensus also depends on a consultation procedure in which indigenous peoples' own institutions of representation and decision-making are fully respected.... [T]he failure of indigenous groups to clarify their representative organization structures can confuse and slow down the consultation process.... [T]he Declaration recalls that the functioning of indigenous institutions should be "in accordance with international human rights standards" (art. 34) and calls for particular attention "to the rights and special needs of indigenous elders, women, youth, children and persons with disabilities"....

53. In cases involving natural resource exploitation or development projects affecting indigenous lands,...it is necessary that [indigenous peoples] are provided with full and objective information about all aspects of the project that will affect them, including the impact of the project on their lives and environment.... [I]t is

essential for the State to carry out environmental and social impact studies [which] must be presented to the indigenous groups concerned at the early stages of the consultation, allowing them time to understand the results of the impact studies and to present their observations and receive information addressing any concerns. Further, a consensus-driven consultation process in such contexts should not only address measures to mitigate or compensate for adverse impacts of the project, but also explore and arrive at means of equitable benefit-sharing in a spirit of true partnership.

E. The duty to consult and private company responsibility

54. Frequently, issues of consultation arise when Governments grant concessions to private companies to extract natural resources, build dams, or pursue other development projects within or in close proximity to indigenous lands. In this connection, the State itself has the responsibility to carry out or ensure adequate consultation, even when a private company, as a practical matter, is the one promoting or carrying out the activities that may affect indigenous peoples' rights and lands. . . .

. . .

QUESTION

Does the Special Rapporteur's explanation of the duty to consult assist governments in understanding their obligations? Does it seem well grounded in established law? If not, what weight should be accorded to his views?

4. HANDLING COMPLAINTS

(1) The Council's Confidential Procedure

Ever since the Magna Carta, a right to petition has been an important aspect of human rights, although it was not included in the UDHR. As noted earlier, the Commission was deprived almost from the outset of the ability to examine the many petitions that poured in from all over the world. This changed only in 1970 when ECOSOC Resolution 1503 (XLVIII) established a confidential process for examining communications which appeared 'to reveal a consistent pattern of gross and reliably attested violations of human rights'. It involved a cumbersome procedure and yielded very few known results. It nevertheless had its supporters among those who felt that any procedure that put governments under pressure to account must be a step forward.

When the Council replaced the Commission it effectively 'inherited' the 1503 procedure. HRC Res. 5/1 of 18 June 2007 established two bodies to manage the procedure. The Working Group on Communications (WGC) consists of five independent expert members of the Council's Advisory Committee. It determines whether complaints are admissible and forwards those, along with its recommendations, to the Council's Working Group on Situations (WGS) which consists of one state representative designated by each of the five regional groups. The latter makes recommendations to the Council, which may or may not decide to take any action. Because the procedure is confidential, almost nothing is known about its impact. A well-informed observer has reported, however, that in March 2009 the WGC 'had before it 40 files of communications relating to 23 countries. National governments had presented replies to 33 out of the 40 files; a reply rate of 87.5%.' All but two of those 40 were either kept pending, postponed or expressly discontinued. Unsurprisingly, the same observer suggested that, unless substantially reformed, the procedure should be consigned 'to the drawers of history'.[25]

(2) Special Procedures and Complaints

The great majority of special procedures mandates envisage a process of 'communicating' with governments about alleged human rights violations either through 'allegation letters' seeking an official response to alleged violations or through 'urgent action' letters which allege imminent harm unless a government acts immediately. This system seeks to: raise international awareness of allegedly significant violations; give states an opportunity to set the record straight and justify their actions; generate a record of abuses alleged against states over time; enable the mandate-holder to offer an interpretation of the applicable law; and provide an incentive for governments to act to rectify any violations.

The most sophisticated of the Special Procedures communications processes is that developed by the five-member Working Group on Arbitrary Detention, established in 1991. The Group receives cases from any relevant source, transmits the allegations to governments with a request for a reply within 90 days and then adopts an 'opinion' on the case. It was previously termed a 'decision', but this characterization was resisted by governments. An example follows.

WORKING GROUP ON ARBITRARY DETENTION, OPINION NO. 31/2006 (IRAQ AND UNITED STATES OF AMERICA), 1 SEPTEMBER 2006

UN Doc. A/HRC/4/40/Add. 1 (2007), p. 103

Communication addressed to the Governments on 3 May 2005 concerning: Mr. Saddam Hussein Al-Tikriti

[The Working Group is responding to a communication submitted on behalf of Saddam Hussein Al-Tikriti, the former President of Iraq. The allegations were transmitted to the United States and Iraq for comments and the United States replied on 30 August 2006.]

[25] M. Schmidt, 'Is the United Nations Human Rights Council Living up to the International Community's Expectations?', in A. Eide et al. (eds.), *Making Peoples Heard* (2011), 99, at 110.

9. A first set of allegations and arguments presented by the source regard the composition of the SICT [Supreme Iraqi Criminal Tribunal]. In January 2006 the presiding judge of the Dujail trial, Rizar Amin, resigned. His resignation followed public criticism of his handling of the trial by senior Iraqi government officials and was, according to the source, due to pressure by a high level member of a Shi'a party in the Interim Legislature. His successor as presiding judge of the Dujail trial chamber, Saeed al-Hameesh, was transferred to a different chamber of the SICT after being accused of being a former member of the Baath party. On 24 January 2006, a new judge, Raouf Rasheed Abdel-Rahman, was nominated to preside the Dujail trial. The source expresses serious doubts regarding his impartiality, since he was born in Halabja, the Kurdish town which was attacked with poison gas by the Iraqi armed forces in 1988, and reportedly lost several family members in the attack. Moreover, judge Abdel-Rahman made statements indicating that the guilt of Saddam Hussein is a foregone conclusion [and that] Saddam Hussein should be executed without trial....

10. The source further reports that the identity of the judges sitting on Saddam Hussein's trial in the Dujail case is not disclosed, with the exception of the presiding judge. It argues that as a consequence of the judges' "facelessness", the defense cannot verify whether they meet the requirements for judicial office and are impartial and independent.

11. A second set of allegations and arguments presented by the source concern restrictions of Saddam Hussein's rights to be represented by lawyers of his own choosing and to communicate with his lawyers. Most fundamentally, the source states that the lawyers were not allowed to meet the defendant in private, all meetings taking place in the presence of United States officials. Moreover, the source reports numerous instances of obstruction of the lawyers' work....

...

13. According to the source, the failure of the authorities to take steps to protect the life and physical integrity of defense lawyers further contributed to undermining the fairness of proceedings. As publicly reported, defense lawyers have been the object of several attacks which resulted in the death of three of them....

14. The third set of allegations and arguments presented by the source relates to the right to present the defense case in conditions of equality with the prosecution. In this respect, the source states that evidence was reportedly read into the record on the basis of affidavits of which the defense counsel had no adequate prior notice, and which they therefore could not meaningfully question. Moreover, the defense was not provided with copies of the statements of prosecution witnesses.

[Neither the United States nor Iraq replied substantively to the allegations.]

22. [Based on the allegations in paragraph 9 above], the Working Group finds that Saddam Hussein did not enjoy the right to be tried by an independent and impartial tribunal as required by Article 14(1) ICCPR....

23. Saddam Hussein did not "have adequate time and facilities for the preparation of his defence", as required by Article 14(3)(b) ICCPR....

24. Finally, Saddam Hussein did not enjoy the possibility "to obtain the attendance and examination of witnesses on his behalf under the same conditions as witnesses against him", as required by Article 14(3)(e) ICCPR....

25. It is because the Working Group is deeply committed to the principle that serious violations of human rights, whether committed by political leaders or others, must be inquired into and redressed by putting the perpetrators to justice, that it considers that procedures to hold the perpetrators of gross human rights violations accountable must scrupulously respect the rules and standards elaborated and accepted by the international community to guarantee a fair trial to any person charged with a criminal offence. This is all the more necessary when the death penalty could be imposed.

26. The Working Group believes that also from the perspective of the victims, who under international law enjoy the right to reparation, truth and justice, it is particularly important that the investigation of the gross violation of human rights and the trial of their alleged perpetrators are conducted in a legitimate and transparent legal process. For them as well, it is essential that justice is not only fair but also be seen to be fair.

27. In the light of the foregoing, the Working Group renders the following opinion:

> The deprivation of liberty of Mr. Saddam Hussein is arbitrary [because it contravenes Article 24 of the ICCPR].

28. [T]he Working Group requests the Governments of Iraq and the United States...to remedy the situation of Mr. Saddam Hussein.... In this context, the Working Group invites the Government of Iraq to give serious consideration to the question whether a trial of the former Head of State in conformity with international law is at all possible before an Iraqi tribunal in the current situation in the country, or whether the case should not be referred to an international tribunal.

QUESTIONS

1. Under what circumstances is a government likely to be responsive to the views of a Working Group or Special Rapporteur in the context of a communications procedure? When might a confidential procedure be effective?

2. Asian and other governments have called for an exhaustion of domestic remedies rule in relation to communications sent by the special procedures. Amnesty International opposes the suggestion: 'For the Special Procedures system, which is neither quasi-judicial, nor treaty-based, or accusatory, the introduction of a threshold requiring exhaustion of domestic remedies before mandate-holders can act would stifle the responsiveness of the Special Procedures that has been so important in saving lives and preventing violations. As former rapporteur Prof Peter Kooijmans commented: "...humanitarian intervention asks for speed and effectiveness rather than for proper procedures connected with the concept of State responsibility".'[26] What do you consider to be the arguments for and against such a rule in this context?

[26] Amnesty International, *United Nations Special Procedures: Building on a Cornerstone of Human Rights Protection* (2005), p. 12.

3. In the Saddam Hussein case, the Working Group bases itself entirely on the allegations received and on unspecified press reports. It is now clear that a number of the allegations were incorrect. Is this a problem? How convincing is the Group's 'opinion', and does the Group effectively justify its conclusion that the United States shared some responsibility in the situation?

5. EVALUATING THE SPECIAL PROCEDURES

Efforts to evaluate the impact of specific human rights mechanisms remain all too rare, despite the recent scholarly interest in overall evaluations of the human rights regime, as discussed in Chapter 14. A major Brookings Institution study is a notable exception:

TED PICCONE, CATALYSTS FOR RIGHTS: THE UNIQUE CONTRIBUTION OF THE U.N.'S INDEPENDENT EXPERTS ON HUMAN RIGHTS, FINAL REPORT OF THE BROOKINGS RESEARCH PROJECT ON STRENGTHENING U.N. SPECIAL PROCEDURES

(Oct. 2010)

Summary of Findings

1. Our research found that the U.N.'s independent experts have played a valuable and, in some cases, decisive role in drawing attention to chronic and emerging human rights issues and in catalyzing improvements in respect for human rights on the ground, including direct support to victims.

2. At the same time, state cooperation with the Special Procedures is highly uneven and generally disappointing, with some notable exceptions. Cooperation by states ranges from regularly accepting country visits by multiple independent experts along with high response rates to their communications, to virtually zero recognition or dialogue with the rapporteurs. . . .

3. The Special Procedures are also hobbled by a host of other challenges, including inadequate training and resources, insufficient understanding of the local context for their work, and the lack of a systematic process for following up their recommendations. Despite these obstacles, the Special Procedures mechanism represents one of the most effective tools of the international human rights system and deserves further strengthening and support.

. . .

Effects on State Behavior

17. In general, states have made modest but important progress toward implementing the recommendations a Special Procedure makes after a country visit. . . . In

many cases, an SP's country visit serves as an important tool for elevating human rights issues to senior levels of government and generating action to remedy the problem....

...

20. Typically, however, a direct connection between an SP's recommendation and government action is hard to prove. In part this is due to the fact that the relevant national authorities are not inclined to give credit to a U.N. mechanism for their actions or are motivated by other domestic political factors.

...

Key Factors to Explain Impact of Country Visits

22....

a. *The credibility of the United Nations* in the country concerned.... The moral power of the U.N.... and the public attention a U.N. expert commands often... generate positive state action.

b. *The timing of the visit* as it relates to a country's political and human rights situation. Countries in transition, moving away from conflict or authoritarian rule and toward a more open, peaceful and democratic society, tend to offer more opportunities for external influence....

c. *The quality and specificity of the SP's research, analysis and recommendations* and the level of preparation before a visit.... The language, tone and style a rapporteur uses matters almost as much as the content of what he or she has to say. Positive words acknowledging progress where it exists can go a long way toward helping government officials accept the more critical findings of a rapporteur's report....

d. *The willingness of the relevant government to cooperate* with the SP's visit. For example, a well-placed, sympathetic official or leading parliamentarian can often make a difference....

e. The ability of local and international NGOs and victims' groups to communicate their grievances in a timely and effective manner and to engage in follow-up advocacy....

f. The level of freedom of the media to report on an SP's activities....

g. The capacity of and attention paid by the U.N. country team and other relevant U.N. agencies like the U.N. High Commissioner for Refugees and the U.N. Development Program. The potential contribution of these U.N. actors to the success of a country visit is great but in practice has varied.... Some U.N. country teams prefer to remain at arms length from the SPs due to the sensitive topics they raise. Others admit that the rapporteurs can say tough things that need to be said....

NOTE

Alston poses the question as to why states acting rationally would agree to delegate authority to experts whose stance on a particular issue is often going to be very difficult to predict with any certainty, given the vagueness of the norms, the difference of approach adopted by different SRs and the extensive room for discretion contained in most mandates. He responds:

> ... One [reason] is that a given state might value an exposé of the shortcomings of other states more than it worries about the possibility of exposing itself to such criticism.... Linked to this is the proposition that a mandate-holder can give voice to criticisms of the practices of a given state which, if expressed by another state would immediately be dismissed as biased and unreliable.... SRs can gain access to sources and places which other states cannot, and they bring a reputation for expertise and impartiality that far exceeds anything another government can match. This, in turn, will make cooperation more likely. Another common motivation for delegation in the human rights area is to constrain successor governments [or to expose previous governments]....
>
> ... The system as a whole enables states to demonstrate their commitment to respecting human rights, and to do so at what is anticipated to be a very low cost. Linked to this is the function of seeking to impose some costs on states that are flouting the established norms, thus enhancing the credibility of the commitments given by all states. Given the empirically demonstrated reticence of states to take formal action to condemn other states' human rights records, the system also helps to overcome a collective action problem by empowering individual experts to expose and criticize such violations. Another benefit relates to the pooling of information, thus forming a knowledge base which might otherwise not exist in relation to specific issues, policies, and empirical practices. This function can also lead to a reduction in the transaction costs of international cooperation, by facilitating standard-setting and other cooperative approaches to shared human rights challenges.[27]

6. THE UNIVERSAL PERIODIC REVIEW

The Universal Periodic Review (UPR), established in 2006, requires all UN member states to report to the Council once every 4–5 years on their human rights record. The primary significance of the innovation was to ensure that every state, and not only those accused of serious violations, would need to account to the Council. It is a peer mechanism in the sense that the review is undertaken by states, rather than experts, and the reporting state retains significant control over the outcome.

The review is carried out by all 47 Council members acting as a Working Group. Three states, chosen by lottery (the 'troika'), act as Rapporteurs in the review of a given state's report. Two other reports are considered: (1) a compilation by the OHCHR of information from treaty bodies, special procedures and other UN sources; and (2) a summary of information submitted by NGOs, researchers, national human rights institutions and others.

The 'constructive dialogue' between the state and Working Group members lasts for three hours. NGOs may observe but not pose questions. The troika then prepares

[27] Philip Alston, 'Hobbling the Monitors: Should U.N. Human Rights Monitors be Accountable?', 52 Harv. Int'l. L. J. 561 (2011), at 579.

a review of issues raised and the government concerned indicates which recommendations it accepts or rejects. The final outcome of the review is adopted by consensus. The first round of the UPR was completed in 2012 and the second round will run from 2012 to 2016. Some examples of the outcomes follow.

Thailand

In 2011, in the wake of a series of prosecutions and long prison sentences, the Special Rapporteur on freedom of expression urged the Thai Government to amend its laws on *lèse majesté*. The Thai penal code (Sec. 112) provides that 'whoever defames, insults or threatens the King, the Queen, the Heir to the throne or the Regent shall be punished with imprisonment of three to fifteen years.' During Thailand's UPR dialogue several states recommended a review or reconsideration of the laws. Thailand explained why it did not support those recommendations:

- 89.51. The lèse-majesté law is a highly sensitive issue that concerns the security and unity of the nation. This matter is regarded as part of our domestic affairs, for which the Thai people will find an appropriate approach.
- ...
- 89.58. The existence of the lèse-majesté law is indispensable for Thailand as it aims to protect the King as the Head of State, which is normal practice for any country under constitutional monarchy. Thailand is therefore unable to accept such recommendation to repeal the law.

In response to recommendations to ratify various major human rights treaties, Thailand responded that it sees 'merit in studying the possibility of becoming a Party to those instruments' but noted that its 'final position on each instrument will depend on the outcome of the related study'.

In response to recommendations by ten states concerning the death penalty, the government replied that it is 'embarking on a process of studying the possibility of abolishing the death penalty', but nothing could be done until that process is completed.[28]

Swaziland

In 2012 Human Rights Watch reported that:

> the Kingdom of Swaziland, ruled by King Mswati III since 1986, is in the midst of a serious crisis of governance. Years of extravagant expenditure by the royal family, fiscal indiscipline, and government corruption have left the country on the brink of economic disaster.
>
> Under Swazi law and custom, all powers are vested in the king. Although Swaziland has a prime minister who is supposed to exercise executive authority, in reality, King Mswati holds supreme executive powers and control over the judiciary and legislature.... Political parties have been banned in the country since 1973.[29]

[28] UN Doc. A/HRC/19/8/Add.1 (6 Mar. 2012).

[29] www.hrw.org/world-report-2012/world-report-2012-swaziland.

Related issues were taken up by various states in the UPR process. States suggested that it should:

- Consider allowing the registration and operation of political parties, including greater political freedoms through free, fair, transparent democratic elections;
- Remove all legislative and practical restrictions impeding the free exercise of civil and political rights, in particular those related to freedom of association and expression, with a view, to allow the creation of political parties and respect for trade unions; and
- Enact legislative measures to facilitate the existence of political parties.

Swaziland's response to each of these was: 'Not acceptable. The country is not yet ready to accept this recommendation.'

On the other hand, it deemed 'acceptable' the following recommendations:

- To ratify the Convention on Disappearances, the Rome Statute of the International Criminal, and the Optional Protocol to the Convention Against Torture;
- To establish a national mechanism for prevention of torture, abrogate the provisions of a 2008 anti-terrorism law which could allow police to use torture, and criminalize and sanction torture; and
- Abrogate laws and regulations that discriminate against women, adopt new gender equality laws, and repeal laws and practices that discriminate against women, including in respect of property, land ownership and marriage.[30]

Syria

Rather than indicating which specific recommendations it accepted and which ones it did not, Syria provided a general response in which it affirmed its commitment to human rights and the UPR process. It objected, however, to the comments made by certain states:

> [P]osing as the guardians of human rights...they prevented the mechanism from serving as a forum for exchanges of views aimed at producing positive outcomes.... They preferred to proceed with their customary dissemination of toxic material and to provoke tensions.... They pervert such forums in order to advance their own agendas, which consist in establishing global hegemony and turning the world into their back garden, so that they may violate human rights with impunity....
>
> The Syrian Arab Republic rejected the recommendations made by such States.... Such conduct amounts to brazen interference in the internal affairs of an independent and sovereign State which is neither a banana republic nor a sheikhdom that they can activate as they wish and whose human rights violations they conceal....

[30] UN Doc. A/HRC/19/6/Add.1 (6 Mar. 2012).

> The Syrian Arab Republic welcomed the constructive comments and recommendations made by other States that were motivated by the aim of promoting and protecting human rights, and it has actually begun implementing the recommendations....[31]

NOTE

Both supporters and detractors of the UPR acknowledge that a full accounting must await the completion of the second cycle (by 2016), which will provide the opportunity to evaluate whether states have taken affirmative steps in response to the outcome of the first cycle. Consider the case for viewing the UPR as transformative in nature:

> [T]he mechanism has steadily gained credence among member states and in the wider international community for being a forum to raise awareness of a country's human rights performance. During the national consultations, many NGOs, civil society groups and national governmental agencies have provided testimony, written reports or other information that has been incorporated into national reports or submitted independently to the OHCHR as part of the UPR process. The interactive dialogue of the UPR has become both a public expression of human rights values and a forum for expressly admonishing or congratulating countries on specific human rights accomplishments. In the final reports, the UPR has given specific guidance to each country under review regarding what should be done to bring national policy into compliance with international standards. Additionally, individual nations have, of their own initiative and free will, undertaken to provide interim reports to the UPR regarding implementation of the recommendations in their final reports.[32]

A less positive assessment follows.

OLIVIER DE FROUVILLE, BUILDING A UNIVERSAL SYSTEM FOR THE PROTECTION OF HUMAN RIGHTS: THE WAY FORWARD

in M. Cherif Bassiouni & W. Schabas (eds.), New Challenges for the UN Human Rights Machinery: What Future for the UN Treaty Body System and the Human Rights Council Procedures? (2011), 241, at 250

Is the UPR of Real Added Value to the System?

[The author notes that some see the UPR as the Council's most visible innovation, but he argues that it has failed to live up to expectations.]

[31] UN Doc. A/HRC/19/11/Add.1 (6 Mar. 2012).

[32] C. de la Vega & T. Lewis, 'Peer Review in the Mix: How the UPR Transforms Human Rights Discourse', in M. Cherif Bassiouni & W. Schabas (eds.), *New Challenges for the UN Human Rights Machinery: What Future for the UN Treaty Body System and the Human Rights Council Procedures?* (2011), 353, at 385.

a) ... There is no real complementarity because there is no real interaction between the UPR and the other mechanisms for the protection of human rights. For sure, one of the three reports used as a basis for the review is [the compilation by the Office of information from treaty bodies, special procedures etc, but this is] a brief and sometimes selective summary [as a result of which] the hard work [done] by the treaty bodies and the special procedures is totally simplified, summarized, diluted.

... [F]ar from being complementary, the UPR is overshadowing the work of the treaty bodies and of the special procedures... through the media and the general public, who now tend to identify the UN human rights system with the UPR. [The author contrasts the highly favourable outcome of Tunisia's UPR report before the revolution, with the almost simultaneous examination of Tunisia by the Human Rights Committee, which yielded a far more critical assessment.]

... Retrospectively, watching the UPR of Libya is surrealistic..., with a series of statements congratulating [it] for its progress in the field of human rights! Is it really the image that the United Nations wants to give of itself? ...

...

The UPR is also materially overshadowing the other mechanisms.... [Translations for documents used by the Special Procedures have been greatly delayed because of the demands of the UPR.] ...

b) The global efficiency of the mechanism is wholly dependent upon the good will of the state under review. In that sense the UPR is not as [egalitarian] as it pretends to be....

... [T]he States who take it the most seriously and who are the most honest are also those who may carry the most heavy burden in terms of obligations and who may get the more criticized in the end. Debating with civil society, committing itself to implement recommendations at the national level, setting up some specific mechanisms to this regard is costly. On the opposite the dishonest state whose firm intention from the very beginning is only to "look as if" might get a bit stressed before the working group's debate, but will shortly be reassured when all [its] "friends" will take the floor to congratulate it on its achievements (expecting they will get the same treatment in return). [T]he honest state is punished while the dishonest state is rewarded....

c) ... It is a "political" process [driven by states].... There is nothing bad in this: again, the UN is an intergovernmental organization and, as such, aside the Secretariat, is composed of political organs, and it is quite logical that political debates are held in those political organs. However, human rights are legal norms and [it] is obviously very difficult for a political entity to address legal norms, as the interpretation it will give of those norms will always be oriented by extra-legal considerations and in particular, as far as states are concerned, by their national interest.

QUESTION

Is the UPR a good example of 'ritualism', or are there additional elements that might make it more effective?

C. THE ROLE OF THE HIGH COMMISSIONER FOR HUMAN RIGHTS

Proposals to create a post of UN High Commissioner for Human Rights emerged as early as 1947. The Soviet Union and its allies were strongly opposed, most developing countries were very wary, and even the West was ambivalent. The breakthrough came at the Vienna World Conference on Human Rights in 1993. A combination of factors were at play: the demise of the Socialist bloc and associated post-Cold War optimism, the election of the Clinton Administration in the United States which was keen to find new ideas in the human rights area, and, the determination of the UN Secretary-General to keep the appointee under a tight rein.

GENERAL ASSEMBLY RESOLUTION 48/141: HIGH COMMISSIONER FOR THE PROMOTION AND PROTECTION OF ALL HUMAN RIGHTS

(1993)

The General Assembly,

...

1. Decides to create the post of the High Commissioner for Human Rights;
2. Decides that the High Commissioner for Human Rights shall:

   (a) Be a person of high moral standing and personal integrity and shall possess expertise, including in the field of human rights, and the general knowledge and understanding of diverse cultures necessary for impartial, objective, non-selective and effective performance of the duties of the High Commissioner;

   (b) Be appointed by the Secretary-General of the United Nations and approved by the General Assembly, with due regard to geographical rotation, and have a fixed term of four years with a possibility of one renewal for another fixed term of four years;

...

3. Decides that the High Commissioner for Human Rights shall:

   (a) Function within the framework of the Charter of the United Nations, the Universal Declaration of Human Rights, other international instruments of human rights and international law, including the obligations, within this framework, to respect the sovereignty, territorial integrity and domestic jurisdiction of States and to promote the universal respect for and observance of all human rights, in the recognition that, in the framework of the purposes and principles of the Charter, the promotion and protection of all human rights is a legitimate concern of the international community;

(b) Be guided by the recognition that all human rights — civil, cultural, economic, political and social — are universal, indivisible, interdependent and interrelated and that, while the significance of national and regional particularities and various historical, cultural and religious backgrounds must be borne in mind, it is the duty of States, regardless of their political, economic and cultural systems, to promote and protect all human rights and fundamental freedoms;

(c) Recognize the importance of promoting a balanced and sustainable development for all people and of ensuring realization of the right to development, as established in the Declaration on the Right to Development;

4. Decides that the High Commissioner for Human Rights shall be the United Nations official with principal responsibility for United Nations human rights activities under the direction and authority of the Secretary-General; within the framework of the overall competence, authority and decisions of the General Assembly, the Economic and Social Council and the Commission on Human Rights, the High Commissioner's responsibilities shall be:

(a) To promote and protect the effective enjoyment by all of all civil, cultural, economic, political and social rights;

(b) To carry out the tasks assigned to him/her by the competent bodies of the United Nations system in the field of human rights and to make recommendations to them with a view to improving the promotion and protection of all human rights;

...

(e) To coordinate relevant United Nations education and public information programmes in the field of human rights;

(f) To play an active role in removing the current obstacles and in meeting the challenges to the full realization of all human rights and in preventing the continuation of human rights violations throughout the world, as reflected in the Vienna Declaration and Programme of Action;

(g) To engage in a dialogue with all Governments in the implementation of his/her mandate with a view to securing respect for all human rights;

...

(j) To rationalize, adapt, strengthen and streamline the United Nations machinery in the field of human rights with a view to improving its efficiency and effectiveness;

...

NOTE

The following individuals have served as High Commissioner (HC): José Ayala-Lasso (Ecuador) 1994–1997, Mary Robinson (Ireland) 1997–2002, Sergio Vieira de Mello (Brazil) 2002–2003, B. G. Ramcharan, acting-HC (Guyana) 2003–2004, Louise Arbour (Canada) 2004–2008, and Navanethem Pillay (South Africa) 2008–2014.

The roles of both the HC and the Office have evolved dramatically since 1993. The first HC had almost no resources at his disposal and answered to a Secretary-General who was keen that he should maintain a low profile. But the power and influence of the HC has been steadily expanded under the direction of his forceful successors. By 2011, OHCHR employed 1,108 staff, half of whom were based in Geneva. There were an additional 884 human rights officers serving in 15 UN peace missions and 18 human rights advisers working with UN Country Teams at the national level. In addition, there were 12 country offices and 13 regional offices. The proposed budget for the 2012–2013 biennium is US$448.1 million, an increase of 10 per cent over the previous biennium. Thirty-five per cent will come from the UN's regular budget and 65 per cent will be solicited from donors (mainly states). Forty-six per cent of the budget goes to field operations, 12 per cent to research, 12 per cent to support the Human Rights Council and its special procedures and 7 per cent to support the treaty bodies. (Source: OHCHR Management Plan 2012–2013.)

But these statistics do not reveal the extent to which the HC today speaks out on virtually any significant human rights issue around the world, from the killing of a teenager in Florida, in alleged self-defence, to the atrocities in Syria, or the flogging of women in the Maldives in punishment for extra-marital relations. Whereas her predecessors were largely restricted to giving informal briefings to the Security Council, Navi Pillay has regularly briefed the Council on situations such as Libya and Syria, while also criticizing it for its inaction in the latter case.

In addition, the various field offices and representatives play a key role in pressuring governments in relation to a wide range of practices. In Afghanistan, for example, OHCHR and the UN Assistance Mission in Afghanistan (UNAMA) reported in October 2011 that 125 of 273 detainees (46 per cent) whom it interviewed had 'experienced interrogation techniques at the hands of NDS [National Directorate of Security] officials that constituted torture, and that torture is practiced systematically in a number of NDS detention facilities throughout Afghanistan.'[33] The Afghan Ministry of Foreign Affairs responded that:

> respect for human munificence is among the fundamental Islamic and Human principles.... Hence to follow up on the claims and to prevent the publication of such lies an inter-ministerial mechanism is due to be established.[34]

The report did, however, lead to a temporary cessation of cooperation between the NDS and the international forces in Afghanistan and strong pressures to undertake meaningful reforms.

QUESTIONS

1. The role of the HCHR has evolved considerably since 1993. Much depends on the office-holder and on her relationship with governments and the Secretary-General.

[33] http://unama.unmissions.org/Portals/UNAMA/Documents/October10_%202011_UNAMA_Detention_Full-Report_ENG.pdf.

[34] http://mfa.gov.af/en/news/8242.

The question of her accountability is a vexed one. If she is seen to be accountable to the Secretary-General for every decision then her role as an independent voice is at risk, since the Secretary-General is likely to come under regular pressure from powerful states to 'rein in' the High Commissioner. If she is subject to the direction of the Human Rights Council then her office becomes a mere secretariat. How then is she to be held to account?

2. In 2005 the HC, Louise Arbour, criticized US use of secret prisons and reliance on diplomatic assurances that detainees would not be tortured when rendered to countries with poor human rights records. In response, the US Ambassador to the UN replied that it was 'inappropriate and illegitimate for an international civil servant to second-guess the conduct that we're engaged in [within] the war on terror, with nothing more as evidence than what she reads in the newspapers.' Do you agree?

D. THE SECURITY COUNCIL AND THE RESPONSIBILITY TO PROTECT

COMMENT ON EARLIER WORK OF SECURITY COUNCIL

For more than four decades, the Security Council exercised a remarkably limited role in human rights matters. With the end of the Cold War, however, the Council's role expanded significantly and many of the issues coming before it have since involved human rights dimensions. The Council has, for example, played an important role in ensuring the inclusion of human rights provisions in peace agreements, in efforts to eliminate the use of child soldiers, and in considering the role of human rights protections in the work of its own Counter-Terrorism Committee established in the wake of the 9/11 attacks on the United States. Its biggest challenge, however, has involved the authorization of forcible measures, including military intervention, to stop massive human rights violations in member states.

The Security Council consists of 15 members, five of which are permanent — China, France, Russia, the United Kingdom and the United States. Ten others are elected by the General Assembly for two-year terms. Each member has one vote. Substantive decisions require nine votes out of the 15, and must include the concurring votes (defined by the Council to include abstentions) of all five permanent members. This is the so-called 'veto' power. The Council is able to be convened at any time and non-members may be invited to participate, but without a vote, when their interests are affected.

The Council is given 'primary responsibility' for the maintenance of international peace and security under the collective security system provided for in the UN Charter (Art. 24), and member states are obligated to carry out its decisions (Art. 25). It can act under *Chapter VI* of the Charter (Arts. 33–8) to achieve the pacific settlement of 'any dispute, the continuance of which is likely to endanger the maintenance of international peace and security'. It is empowered to investigate any such dispute and to recommend 'appropriate procedures or methods of adjustment'. It can act under *Chapter VII* (Arts. 39–51) whenever it determines 'the existence of any threat to the peace, breach of the peace, or act of aggression'. In such situations, the Council can call on states to apply sanctions of various kinds (Art. 41) or to take such military action 'as may be necessary to restore international peace and security' (Art. 42). Since all states are obligated by Article 2(4) of the Charter to 'refrain in their international relations from the threat or use of force against the territorial integrity or political independence of any state', except in the exercise of the right of self-defence against an armed attack (Art. 51), the Council enjoys a legal monopoly over the use of force in all other circumstances. This monopoly extends to Article 53(1) which authorizes the Council to make use of 'regional arrangements or agencies for enforcement action under its authority'. But the latter are not permitted to act without the Council's authorization.

Precedents Set in the Struggle Against Apartheid

Many procedures and techniques which were eventually developed by the General Assembly and the Security Council to deal with human rights were hammered out on the anvil of the South African apartheid system. The issue was first brought to the Assembly in 1946 by India which complained of the discriminatory treatment of persons of Indian origin. Very early on, India suggested that such conduct could be seen as a threat to international peace and thus as requiring the attention of the Council. South Africa replied that most of those concerned were its nationals and that, in any event, the issue was exclusively a domestic affair.

The battle lines were thus set for a struggle continuing until today to clarify two key issues: (1) the relationship between the human rights provisions of the UN Charter and the domestic jurisdiction clause in Article 2(7) of the Charter (considered at p. 688, *supra*); and (2) the circumstances under which gross human rights violations can be considered to threaten international peace and security and thus warrant Security Council measures under Chapter VII. While South Africa was the main focus of these debates, the situations in Southern Rhodesia (Zimbabwe) and the Portuguese colonies in southern Africa (Angola and Mozambique) also figured.

With the influx of newly independent states into the United Nations from the late 1950s onwards, the South African case pitted a Security Council, dominated by Western governments that were reluctant to act, against a General Assembly which was increasingly frustrated at the intransigence of the racist governments in southern Africa and the failure of the Assembly's barrage of resolutions to make any difference. In 1962 the Assembly tested the limits of its division of labour with the Security Council by itself calling upon member states to break off diplomatic relations with South Africa, to refuse entry to its ships and aircraft, to boycott its goods and to impose an arms embargo. In 1963 the Council characterized the South African situation as 'seriously disturbing international peace and security' and called for, but did not mandatorily impose, an arms embargo. The Assembly raised the stakes again in 1966 by condemning apartheid as 'a crime against humanity', an approach which was taken further by its adoption in 1973 of the Convention on the Suppression and Punishment of the Crime of Apartheid (GA Res. 3068 (XXVIII)). Three years later, the Assembly concluded that 'the continued brutal repression, including indiscriminate mass killings' by the apartheid regime left 'no alternative to the oppressed people of South Africa but to resort to armed struggle to achieve their legitimate rights', thus giving its imprimatur to the national liberation struggle.

It was not until 1977 that the Council (Res. 418) imposed a mandatory arms embargo under Chapter VII. In 1984, the Council rejected a new constitution that had been adopted by an exclusively white electorate as contrary to UN principles and thus 'null and void'. With the end of apartheid and the transition to democracy the Council terminated the arms embargo and all other restrictions in May 1994.

From Humanitarian Intervention to the 'Responsibility to Protect'

It has long been claimed that, despite the prohibition on the use of force contained in Article 2(4) of the UN Charter, there is a humanitarian exception of some sort which would justify the use of force by a state to protect individuals in another state from egregious violations of human rights. With the end of the Cold War, the 1990s brought a distinctly greater willingness on the part of some states, including the United States, to intervene for such reasons. Somalia, Haiti and the former Yugoslavia were key examples. But the failure to intervene in the face of genocide in Rwanda and to stop a genocidal massacre in Bosnia traumatized the UN and other actors and led to extensive soul-searching as to the nature of any principle of intervention for humanitarian reasons. A UN-commissioned report on Rwanda characterized the 1994 genocide in which 800,000 people were killed in about 100 days as 'one of the most abhorrent events of the twentieth century'. It condemned the failure to 'prevent, and subsequently, to stop the genocide in Rwanda' as a failure by the UN system as a whole. 'The fundamental failure was the lack of resources and political commitment devoted to developments in Rwanda and to the United Nations presence there. There was a persistent lack of political will by Member States to act, or to act with enough assertiveness....' It called upon the 'Security Council and troop contributing countries... to act to prevent acts of genocide or gross violations of human rights wherever they may take place.'[35] The UN also published a critical report of its failure to stop massacres in Bosnia.

In the same year as the UN published these strongly self-critical reviews a crisis erupted in Kosovo, then a province of Serbia. Since 1993 reports to the UN Commission on Human Rights had documented serious human rights abuses by Serbia against the Kosovo Albanians who made up 90 per cent of the province's population. In 1998 the Security Council, acting under Chapter VII, imposed an arms embargo (Res. 1160) and subsequently determined that there was 'a threat to peace and security in the region' (Res. 1199). Russia and China, however, made clear that they would veto any Council resolution authorizing the use of force. After a grave deterioration of the situation, and the failure of talks among the relevant parties held in Rambouillet, the North Atlantic Treaty Organization (NATO) launched military action against Serbia for non-compliance with the Council resolutions and

[35] Report of the Independent Inquiry into the Actions of the United Nations During the 1994 Genocide in Rwanda, UN Doc. S/1999. For a detailed inquiry into failings of the UN in Bosnia, see 'The Fall of Srebrenica', UN Doc. A/54/549 (1999).

in the name of 'humanitarian intervention'. It was estimated that 90 per cent of the Kosovo Albanian population — some 1.45 million people — had been displaced by the conflict by the time it ended.[36]

VIEWS ON THE RESPONSIBILITY TO PROTECT

Kofi Annan, Implications of International Response to Events in Rwanda, Kosovo Examined by Secretary-General

UN Press Release GA/9595 (20 Sept. 1999)

[This is a report of a speech to the General Assembly by the UN Secretary-General, Kofi Annan.]

'While the genocide in Rwanda will define for our generation the consequences of inaction in the face of mass murder, the more recent conflict in Kosovo had prompted important questions about the consequences of action in the absence of unity on the part of the international community', he said. In the case of Kosovo, the inability of that community to reconcile the question of the legitimacy of an action taken by a regional organization without a United Nations mandate, on one side, and the universally accepted imperative of effectively halting gross and systematic violations of human rights, on the other, could only be viewed as a tragedy. It had revealed the core challenge to the Security Council and the United Nations in the next century: To forge unity behind the principle that massive, systematic violations of human rights — wherever they might take place — should not be allowed to stand.

He said that, to those for whom the greatest threat to the future of international order was the use of force in the absence of a Council mandate, one might ask — not in the context of Kosovo, but in the context of Rwanda — if a coalition of States had been prepared to act in defence of the Tutsi population, but had not received prompt Council authorization, should such a coalition have stood aside and allowed the horror to unfold? To those for whom the Kosovo action heralded a new era when States and groups of States could take military action outside the established mechanisms for enforcing international law, one might ask: Was there not a danger of such intervention undermining the imperfect, yet resilient, security system created after the Second World War, and of setting dangerous precedents for future interventions?

...

... [I]n the Charter's own words, 'armed force shall not be used, save in the common interest'...

...

... In [Rwanda and Kosovo] Member States of the United Nations should have been able to find common ground in upholding the principles of the Charter, and

[36] OSCE, 'Kosovo/Kosova: As Seen, As Told', Dec. 1999, at www.asylumlaw.org/docs/kosovo/osce99_kosovo_asseenastold.pdf.

acting in defence of 'our common heritage'. The Charter required the Council to be the defender of the 'common interest'. Unless it was seen to be so, there was a danger that others could seek to take its place.

The Responsibility to Protect Report

(2001)

In order to address systematically the policy issues emerging from situations such as Rwanda and Kosovo the Canadian Government established an International Commission on Intervention and State Sovereignty which reported in 2001. Its Report, entitled *The Responsibility to Protect* put forward a series of 'core principles' premised on the argument that while the notion of state sovereignty could not be brushed aside in the name of intervention, it should be interpreted as implying that 'the primary responsibility for the protection of its people lies with the state itself'. But where a state is 'unwilling or unable' to halt or avert serious harm to its own population, 'the principle of non-intervention yields to the international responsibility to protect'.[37] A similar approach was subsequently endorsed by a 'High-Level Panel' appointed by the UN Secretary-General.

A More Secure World: Our Shared Responsibility, Report of the High-Level Panel on Threats, Challenges and Change

(2004), at www.un.org/secureworld/report3.pdf

...

201. The successive humanitarian disasters in Somalia, Bosnia and Herzegovina, Rwanda, Kosovo and now Darfur, Sudan, have concentrated attention not on the immunities of sovereign Governments but their responsibilities, both to their own people and to the wider international community. There is a growing recognition that the issue is not the "right to intervene" of any State, but the "responsibility to protect" of *every* State when it comes to people suffering from avoidable catastrophe — mass murder and rape, ethnic cleansing by forcible expulsion and terror, and deliberate starvation and exposure to disease. And there is a growing acceptance that while sovereign Governments have the primary responsibility to protect their own citizens from such catastrophes, when they are unable or unwilling to do so that responsibility should be taken up by the wider international community — with it spanning a continuum involving prevention, response to violence, if necessary, and rebuilding shattered societies. The primary focus should be on assisting the cessation of violence through mediation and other tools and the protection of people through such measures as the dispatch of humanitarian, human rights and police missions. Force, if it needs to be used, should be deployed as a last resort.

202. The Security Council so far has been neither very consistent nor very effective in dealing with these cases, very often acting too late, too hesitantly or not at all.

[37] http://responsibilitytoprotect.org/ICISS%20Report.pdf.

But step by step, the Council and the wider international community have come to accept that, under Chapter VII and in pursuit of the emerging norm of a collective international responsibility to protect, it can always authorize military action to redress catastrophic internal wrongs if it is prepared to declare that the situation is a "threat to international peace and security", not especially difficult when breaches of international law are involved.

203. We endorse the emerging norm that there is a collective international responsibility to protect, exercisable by the Security Council authorizing military intervention as a last resort, in the event of genocide and other large-scale killing, ethnic cleansing or serious violations of international humanitarian law which sovereign Governments have proved powerless or unwilling to prevent.

B. The question of legitimacy

...

207. In considering whether to authorize or endorse the use of military force, the Security Council should always address — whatever other considerations it may take into account — at least the following five basic criteria of legitimacy:

(a) *Seriousness of threat.* Is the threatened harm to State or human security of a kind, and sufficiently clear and serious, to justify *prima facie* the use of military force? In the case of internal threats, does it involve genocide and other large-scale killing, ethnic cleansing or serious violations of international humanitarian law, actual or imminently apprehended?

(b) *Proper purpose.* Is it clear that the primary purpose of the proposed military action is to halt or avert the threat in question, whatever other purposes or motives may be involved?

(c) *Last resort.* Has every non-military option for meeting the threat in question been explored, with reasonable grounds for believing that other measures will not succeed?

(d) *Proportional means.* Are the scale, duration and intensity of the proposed military action the minimum necessary to meet the threat in question?

(e) *Balance of consequences.* Is there a reasonable chance of the military action being successful in meeting the threat in question, with the consequences of action not likely to be worse than the consequences of inaction?

2005 World Summit Outcome, General Assembly Res. 60/1

...

138. Each individual State has the responsibility to protect its populations from genocide, war crimes, ethnic cleansing and crimes against humanity. This responsibility entails the prevention of such crimes, including their incitement, through appropriate and necessary means. We accept that responsibility and will act in accordance with it. The international community should, as appropriate, encourage and help States to exercise this responsibility and support the United Nations in establishing an early warning capability.

139. The international community, through the United Nations, also has the responsibility to use appropriate diplomatic, humanitarian and other peaceful means, in accordance with Chapters VI and VIII of the Charter, to help to protect populations from genocide, war crimes, ethnic cleansing and crimes against humanity. In this context, we are prepared to take collective action, in a timely and decisive manner, through the Security Council, in accordance with the Charter, including Chapter VII, on a case-by-case basis and in cooperation with relevant regional organizations as appropriate, should peaceful means be inadequate and national authorities are manifestly failing to protect their populations from genocide, war crimes, ethnic cleansing and crimes against humanity. We stress the need for the General Assembly to continue consideration of the responsibility to protect populations from genocide, war crimes, ethnic cleansing and crimes against humanity and its implications, bearing in mind the principles of the Charter and international law. We also intend to commit ourselves, as necessary and appropriate, to helping States build capacity to protect their populations from genocide, war crimes, ethnic cleansing and crimes against humanity and to assisting those which are under stress before crises and conflicts break out.

COMMENT ON SECURITY COUNCIL ACTION AND INACTION ON LIBYA AND SYRIA

In the wave of democratic and popular uprisings across the Arabian world that began in late 2010, large numbers of people in Libya and Syria also took to the streets. The result was a brutal crackdown, including summary killings of peaceful protestors, by the Qaddafi and Assad regimes. In both countries, some citizens calling for fundamental political reform also turned to armed opposition. The Security Council, however, responded differently to the two situations.

In March 2011, the Security Council adopted Resolution 1973 establishing a no-fly zone over Libya and authorizing military action to stop the bloodshed by Libyan forces. The resolution was adopted by a vote of 10 in favour and 5 abstentions. Russia and China agreed not to exercise their veto power; and other important countries such as Brazil and India, who had seats on the Council at the time, also abstained. As a diplomatic compromise, the resolution placed limits on the use of force. It specifically authorized military force only for the purpose 'to protect civilians and civilian populated areas under threat of attack', and it excluded 'a foreign occupation force of any form on any part of Libyan territory'.

Many argued that the ensuing NATO-led military campaign exceeded Resolution 1973's limits by helping the rebels to defeat the Libyan Government's forces and oust Gaddafi from power. For example, after the NATO campaign began, South African President Jacob Zuma, whose government had voted for the resolution, stated that NATO had 'misuse[d]' the authorization to use force: 'The continuing bombing by NATO and its allies is a concern that has been raised by our committee and by the AU Assembly, because the intention of Resolution 1973 was to protect the Libyan people and facilitate the humanitarian effort.... The intention was not to authorise a campaign for regime change or political assassination.' India's Ambassador to the UN remarked that 'the Libyan case has already given R2P [responsibility to protect] a bad name'.

In contrast with Libya, Security Council action on Syria was stymied by Russia and China. In February 2012, an important draft resolution on Syria (S/2012/77) failed by a vote of 13–2 with Russia and China both exercising their veto. The draft resolution had been supported by the Arab League (as well as India and South Africa). The proposed resolution (1) 'condemn[ed]...widespread and gross violations of human rights and fundamental freedoms by the Syrian authorities'; (2) demanded that Syria implement 'without delay' a Plan of Action issued by the League of Arab States which required the government to 'withdraw all Syrian military and armed forces from cities and towns, and return them to their original home barracks', 'guarantee the freedom of peaceful demonstrations' and 'allow full and unhindered access and movement for all relevant League of Arab States' institutions and Arab and international media in all parts of Syria'; (3) 'fully support[ed]...the League of Arab States' 22 January 2012 decision to facilitate a Syrian-led political transition to a democratic, plural political system...in accordance with the timetable set out by the League of Arab States'; and (4) decided 'to review implementation of this resolution within 21 days and, in the event of non-compliance, to consider further measures'. The League of Arab States 22 January decision called on Assad to step aside in favour of a government of national unity to be established within two months.

A news report summarized Russia's response:[38]

> Russia in particular has been vocal in proclaiming that it felt tricked by UNSC Resolution 1973 on Libya, which led to a sustained NATO bombing campaign in support of the uprising against Muammar Qaddafi. Russia says...that the armed and coordinated support from NATO for the rebels...went far beyond the UN mandate. Determined to not allow that to happen again and concerned about the precedent that such actions set, Russia insisted that it would only support a resolution that explicitly ruled out regime change or eventual armed intervention....

The US Ambassador to the UN stated that her governments was 'disgusted' by the Russian and Chinese opposition, and added that 'this intransigence is even more shameful when you consider that at least one of these members continues to deliver weapons to Assad.' US Secretary of State Hillary Clinton called the double veto 'despicable'. Pakistan's Ambassador said that the two vetoes brought to mind 'Pontius Pilate washing his hands and saying "I have nothing to do with this,"' when Jesus was sentenced to death. France's Ambassador stated that Russia and China 'made themselves complicit in a policy of repression', and the British Ambassador stated that his country was 'appalled' and that '[t]hose that blocked the action must ask themselves how many more deaths they are prepared to tolerate. Russia and China have taken a choice to turn their backs on the Arab world and to support tyranny.'

[38] Dan Murphy, 'After Massacre in Syria, Russia and China Veto UN Resolution', CS Monitor, 4 Feb. 2012.

The Security Council's action and inaction on Libya and Syria raise important questions, including:

(1) Did the NATO-led military campaign in Libya exceed the scope of the Security Council resolution and the scope of the R2P principle?
(2) Did the Libyan experience undermine Russia and China's support for a more forceful resolution on Syria?
(3) What lasting impact could the Libyan and Syrian situations have on the Security Council's legitimacy and the status of R2P?

The following excerpts provide a range of perspectives on these questions.

Scott Horton, Up in Smoke: Did the Idea of a Legal War Die Along with Muammar al-Qaddafi?

Foreign Policy, 25 Oct. 2011

Compared with the cost and doubtful outcomes in both Iraq and Afghanistan, the Libya campaign looks — for now, at least — like a stroke of genius.

But seen through the lens of the law, the victory is a distinctly Pyrrhic one. ...

...

... [A]ttacks fairly early in the conflict targeted command-and-control centers of the Qaddafi regime. Such steps would be routine in wartime and would plainly be authorized under the laws of armed conflict. But it's not so clear that they were authorized by Resolution 1973, the authority of which rested on the doctrine of "responsibility to protect".... After all, strikes were mounted against military positions far away from the attacks on civilians and with no apparent linkage to them. Moreover, as the war progressed, the posture of the fading Qaddafi regime became increasingly defensive. The final weeks of the campaign put this in sharpest perspective, as Qaddafi and his final core group of retainers withdrew to his hometown of Sirte, ultimately fleeing in a convoy that was fired upon by NATO aircraft and an American Predator drone, destroying two vehicles.... [T]he role played by NATO in his final moments points to the near perfect inversion of the mission. Instead of protecting civilians from attack by Qaddafi and his forces, they were attacking a fleeing and clearly finished Qaddafi.

At this point, some members of the Security Council clearly feel they got suckered. They voted for a resolution to protect the people of Benghazi from slaughter and saw their authority invoked to depose Qaddafi and install a new government. That will have consequences for future humanitarian crises. Russia and China have now blocked Security Council resolutions targeting Syria....

NATO's operations in Libya began as a valid demonstration of the use of military force to protect civilians. But they evolved quickly into an exercise in regime change. In the wake of Libya, the Security Council is unlikely to embrace another R2P operation anytime soon. And that is bad news for the people of Damascus and Hama, as well as for advocates of the responsibility to protect.

Mehrdad Payandeh, The UN, Military Intervention, and Regime Change in Libya

52 Va. J. Int'l. L. 355 (2012)

... While Resolution 1973 specifies the goal of the authorization — that is, the protection of civilians and civilian populated areas — it does not elaborate on the admissible means that may be employed in order to implement and achieve this goal. This distinction allows for the argument that while regime change may not have been a legitimate *goal* to be pursued on the basis of Resolution 1973, it might have been a legitimate *means* to pursue the objective of the Security Council mandate, namely the protection of civilians. This argument is supported by the fact that, as the conflict in Libya continued, it became more and more clear that the safety of the civilians and of the opposition could not be guaranteed as long as Gadhafi was in power.... While ceasefire and political dialogue could have been achieved, regime change was not strictly necessary for the protection of the civilian population. When it turned out that such a dialogue and all other peaceful means to settle the dispute were futile, this evaluation changed, and states began to consider regime change a necessary prerequisite for the protection of civilians and civilian populated areas in Libya.

...

... On the one hand,... [t]he legality of forceful regime change should not be easily presumed, and authorizations of the Security Council to use force should not be interpreted extensively. On the other hand, the Security Council deliberately authorized military measures knowing that this action would be aimed primarily against the Gadhafi regime and would contribute to the opposition movement. Measures necessary for the protection of civilians and civilian-populated areas might at the same time have promoted regime change in Libya.... The mere fact that the intervening states were at the same time also contributing to the overthrow of Gadhafi or even acting with the political intention of achieving this goal does not render their attacks illegal. For the evaluation of the legality of a certain act under international law, the intention of the acting state is irrelevant.

Measures that cannot convincingly be understood as necessary for the protection of civilians or civilian-populated areas, on the other hand, were impermissible under the Security Council resolution....

Eric Voeten, How Libya Did and Did Not Affect the Security Council Vote on Syria

(7 Feb. 2012)

What is not credible... is that the Russians couldn't have foreseen that resolution 1973 essentially authorized regime change.... [R]esolution 1973 actively takes sides and condemns the Libyan regime. It allows France, the UK, and the US to use force to protect civilian populated areas under threat of attack, specifically mentioning Benghazi where the uprising was at its most intense. This is clearly a resolution that was designed to aid the Libyan rebels in their struggle against the government. There is no credible legal or other mechanism to hold states accountable for exceeding the restrictions of the resolution. These resolutions only matter to the extent that they make the intervention appear more legitimate in the eyes of domestic and foreign publics and governments. Why would you authorize such a resolution if your objective is to prevent actively encouraging regime change?

... Russian foreign minister Sergei Lavrov was that country's UN permanent representative for a decade. He has been part of many deals where the Russians and Chinese were perfectly willing to set aside their rhetorical commitment to non-intervention in domestic affairs. There is no way he didn't understand what he was authorizing. Just as Obama's insistence that this was not about regime change should have been taken with a heavy grain of salt, so should Lavrov's later cries of foul play. This is business as usual in international politics: you strike deals that your constituents don't like or that are inconsistent with past rhetoric, ask the other side to cloak it in terms that are acceptable, and then feign outrage when things happen that you knew would happen when you struck the deal.

What is much more plausible is that Libya didn't pan out in the way the Russians and Chinese hoped. Recent UN authorized interventions have actually been pretty good for Russian and Chinese interests. They left the West bogged down in costly conflicts and didn't affect their commercial interests very much. By contrast, Libya was cheap for the West and left the Russians and the Chinese on the outside....

Then there are the domestic consequences, where protesters in both China and Russia appeared to gather strength from the Arab Spring revolutions.... Before they thought it might be expedient to cautiously be on the side of the Arab League. Now firm resistance seems like the better policy option to protect their interests....

Jonathan Eyal, The Responsibility to Protect: A Chance Missed

in A. Johnson & S. Mueen (eds.), Short War, Long Shadow The Political and Military Legacies of the 2011 Libya Campaign Royal United Services Institute (2012)

... R2P was ideally suited to the Libyan situation, as it initially presented itself. A rebellion against a tyrannical regime... spontaneous and not encouraged from outside; indeed, Western governments were initially accused of preferring the survival of the Qadhafi regime....

...

... The real errors were... in the way Resolution 1973 was subsequently applied.

...

... [T]he authority given by Resolution 1973 was 'to protect civilians and civilian populated areas under threat of attack'. Can this be interpreted to mean that Western forces should have continued the operations long after the immediate threat to Benghazi's residents was lifted and when the pro-Qadhafi forces were in full retreat? ...

But probably the most evident departure from the spirit of Resolution 1973 — if not its letter — was the decision of the Western powers to allow the supply of weapons and training to the Libyan rebels. The Resolution built upon... Security Council Resolution 1970, which imposed an arms embargo on Libya. Resolution 1973 toughened these provisions further, by creating an enforcement mechanism for the implementation of the arms embargo.... In short, when the NATO-led operation began, the legal position was clear: the military intervention was designed to save people, rather than tilt the balance in favour of one side or another in the internal conflict in Libya.... However, Cathy Adams, Legal Counsellor at the [UK] Foreign Office,... [i] n her own testimony to the House of Commons Defence Committee... [stated] that Resolution 1973...also mentioned that this was 'notwithstanding paragraph 9 of resolution 1970', which was the arms embargo provision. Adams alleged that the effect of this mention is to create an 'expressed derogation'; in effect, Resolution 1973 set aside the arms embargo. Yet, as Adams must or should have known, this is nothing more than just another legal sophistry. The 'notwithstanding' expression in Resolution 1973 was included in order to underline that, whatever military action was being undertaken in Libya should not be hampered by the arms embargo.... And, if the derogation was so extensive, then why did the British government consider it important to make a distinction between 'offensive' weapons, whose delivery it believed to be banned, and 'defensive' ones which, supposedly, were not?

...

... [The] important priority — that of anchoring the Responsibility to Protect concept in a more predictable setting — was missed, yet again.

Michael Emerson, The Responsibility to Protect and Regime Change

Centre for European Policy Studies (Dec. 2011)

Libya 2011 has now become the most famous instance of R2P being operationalised through Resolution 1973.... The passing of Resolution 1973 of the Security Council was greatly helped by the resolutions adopted by the African Union and Arab League....

...

... What has been going on in Syria has become unbearable for its Arab neighbours to stand by and watch (excepting Lebanon and Iraq who abstained, but did not block the Arab League action). It bears some similarities with how the EU viewed the humanitarian atrocities that came with the break-up of Yugoslavia. Military intervention is still not expected in Syria, although France's foreign minister has now floated the idea of a 'humanitarian corridor' into Syria, without saying whether this should be militarily protected. But the key point is that the Arab League and the West have moved closer together. Both are interested in advancing democratic freedoms, albeit some faster than others, both are prepared to act across state borders to protect the people in their close neighbourhood, both are prepared to advocate regime change explicitly in extreme cases (Libya, Syria, Yemen). This marks a certain recovery of the R2P doctrine after the critique of the Libyan campaign by Russia and China. It not so clearly now the West versus the Rest.

Zack Beauchamp, Syria's Crisis and the Future of R2P

Foreign Policy, 16 Mar. 2012

... Military intervention in Syria would not only be a misapplication of R2P, but would radically weaken the doctrine's role in building both a better Middle East and a better world. Our responsibility to protect both Syrians and the R2P doctrine itself demands that we stay out of it.

…

Understanding the limits of military force in the Syrian case is critical to R2P's viability as an international norm. A failed intervention — which would almost certainly involve the death of international troops — would taint the idea among emerging powers like Brazil and India who are crucial to making it a widely accepted part of state practice in the 21st century. Such states, while open to R2P as a doctrine, are wary of its use to justify humanitarian intervention. …

… Expanding the R2P's power, at the moment, requires persuading states to get on-board with the doctrine. Since Russia and China are likely to be incorrigible R2P foes for the foreseeable future, a wider group of states must be brought on board to create a "critical mass" for enshrining R2P as a binding international norm. If you believe R2P could be the foundation for a more just international order, pushing influential actors away from the doctrine just as it is beginning to really influence the international debate on human rights and mass atrocities would be a terrible error.

Yun Sun, Syria: What China Has Learned From its Libya Experience

152 Asia Pacific Bulletin (Feb. 2012)

Beijing's perception of gaining nothing while losing everything in Libya after abstaining on UNSCR 1973 significantly contributed to its decision to veto the Syria resolution. …

… [A]lthough China sees its acquiescence as directly contributing to the fall of Muammar Qaddafi, it was rather disappointed with the payoff. First of all, at home and abroad, the abstention was seen as Beijing's short-sighted compliance to the West. It raised speculation about whether China was abandoning its long held non-interference principle, tarnishing the very image that Beijing takes great pride in. …

Meanwhile, China's perceived compromise did not bring the desired outcome. …

… China found its acquiescence as having little influence in securing favorable considerations for its economic interests in Libya. …

A similar vote on Syria would have fared no better. … While Beijing saw little to lose, it saw much to gain by vetoing the Syria resolution. China's veto saved Moscow from international isolation — the joint veto was a powerful demonstration of Sino-Russia diplomatic cooperation — a favor that Russia now has to return. … Furthermore, the veto prevented a double precedent to legitimize UN military intervention as a method to remove a sovereign government in conflict with democratic oppositions supported by the West, a scenario that Beijing has to consider through the lens of its own domestic politics. …

Walter Russell Mead, Russia's Syrian Bet Explained

The American Interest, 5 Feb. 2012

[W]hat Russia thought it expected and deserved in return for its abstention on the Libya vote was due consideration for its commercial interests in Libya. France,

Britain and Qatar seem to be dividing that pie enthusiastically among themselves and nobody is thinking about Russia's share and Russia's price. From that point of view, Russia has no choice but to bring the hammer down and make as much trouble as possible in Syria. That the western powers exceeded the limits of the resolution and did exactly what they wanted in Libya could be endured — if they had paid Moscow's fair price. But they didn't, and if Russia doesn't respond, no one will ever respect its interests.

NOTE

In March 2012, the Security Council unanimously agreed to a Presidential Statement supporting a peace plan brokered by former UN Secretary-General Kofi Annan. The Presidential Statement also used language similar to the failed February 2012 draft resolution by stating that '[t]he Security Council expresses its full support for the efforts of the Envoy to . . . facilitate a Syrian-led political transition to a democratic, plural political system.' However, the Statement made no reference to the League of Arab States' plan or to any other demand for Assad to step down. 'We are very pleased,' Russia's Ambassador to the UN stated, 'The Security Council has finally chosen to take a pragmatic look at the situation in Syria'. An article in China's Xinhua news agency stated:

> Unlike the two blocked draft resolutions, the new presidential statement does not contain any words implying the forced regime change in Syria, the one-sided pressure on the Syrian government, and sanctions or the threat of sanctions on Damascus . . . The new presidential statement reflects a softened Western stance on Syria, compared with the one contained in the two killed drafts at the Security Council.

The following month, the Security Council unanimously authorized the establishment of the United Nations Supervision Mission in Syria. Resolution 2043 stated that the mission would be composed of 'up to 300 unarmed military observers as well as an appropriate civilian component as required by the Mission to fulfil its mandate' and that 'the mandate of the Mission shall be to monitor a cessation of armed violence in all its forms by all parties and to monitor and support the full implementation' of the Annan ceasefire and peace plan.

QUESTIONS

1. Are the criteria identified by the High-level Panel likely to be very helpful in resolving a concrete situation that comes before the Security Council? If not, why not?

2. How far does the General Assembly's 2005 resolution go towards resolving the problems that arise when the Security Council is unable to act in a given crisis situation because of the threat of a veto by one of the Permanent Members?

3. Did NATO exceed the authority provided by Resolution 1973 and what implications does the military campaign have for the future of R2P? What impact does the Security Council response to Syria have on the future of R2P?

E. A WORLD COURT FOR HUMAN RIGHTS?

As early as 1947, Australia called for the creation of an international human rights court, and the United Kingdom responded by suggesting that the International Court of Justice could be authorized to give advisory opinions on human rights. Neither proposal was successful, but the idea has continued to surface periodically. In recent years, several NGO-led, but government-supported, initiatives have put forward elaborate proposals for such a world human rights court. Note that the International Criminal Court already has jurisdiction over crimes against humanity, thus enabling it to adjudicate on a significant range of human rights violations. The most developed proposal for a new court has been put forward by Julia Kozma, Manfred Nowak and Martin Scheinin in *A World Court of Human Rights: Consolidated Statute and Commentary* (2010). Nowak summarizes the proposed initiative.

MANFRED NOWAK, IT'S TIME FOR A WORLD COURT OF HUMAN RIGHTS

in M. Cherif Bassiouni & W. Schabas (eds.), New Challenges for the UN Human Rights Machinery: What Future for the UN Treaty Body System and the Human Rights Council Procedures? (2011), 17, at 29

...

The Main Features of the Consolidated Draft Statute for a World Court of Human Rights

...

The Court shall be a permanent institution with international legal personality based in Geneva. It shall have the power to decide in a final and legally binding manner on all complaints about alleged human rights violations brought before it in accordance with the statute. In exercising its jurisdiction, it shall be guided by the principles of the international law of State responsibility, of universality, interdependence and indivisibility of all human rights, by general international law, general principles of law and by the jurisprudence of other international and regional courts (Article 6). The Court shall consist of 21 judges elected by a meeting of the Assembly of States Parties, who shall serve as full-time members (Article 20). The Court shall sit as a plenary court and, similar to the European Court of Human Rights, in three chambers of seven judges and six committees of three judges each (Articles 26 and 27). The judges shall have established competence in the law of human rights and extensive experience in a professional legal capacity (Article 21) [and] shall be independent (Article 31)....

The jurisdiction of the Court shall apply to States parties and "Entities", i.e. intergovernmental organizations and non-State actors, such as transnational corporations, organized opposition movements and autonomous communities exercising a degree of public power and factual control over a territory (Article 4 and commentary). The Court decides on individual complaints from any person, non-governmental organization or group of individuals claiming to be the victim of a violation of any human right provided for in any of the UN human rights treaties explicitly listed in Article 5. This list goes beyond the core human rights treaties and covers most UN treaties in the field of human rights. States accept the jurisdiction of the Court...only in relation to treaties to which they are parties....States may, at the time of ratification or accession, declare that they do not recognize the jurisdiction of the Court in relation to certain human rights treaties or certain provisions thereof.... The ratification of, or accession to the statute shall be treated as a notification by a State of the suspension of the operation of complaint procedures accepted by the State in question under the human rights treaties covered by the Court's jurisdiction (Article 7(3))...."Entities" recognize the competence of the Court by means of special declarations in accordance with Article 51. When making such a declaration, the "Entity" may also specify which human rights treaties and which provisions thereof (e.g. freedom of association, prohibition of forced labour or child labour) shall be subject to the jurisdiction of the Court (Article 51(2)). In addition to its contentious jurisdiction, the Court shall also issue advisory opinions on the request of UN member States, the Secretary General and the High Commissioner for Human Rights (Article 8).

The procedure concerning individual complaints by and large follows that applied by existing regional human rights courts and UN treaty monitoring bodies. [The authors then discuss exhaustion of domestic remedies, non-duplication of international procedures, third party intervention arrangements, fact-finding missions, friendly settlements, public hearings, etc.] The judgments of the Court shall be final and binding. If the Court finds a human rights violation, it shall order the respondent party to afford the victim adequate reparation for the harm suffered.... States and "Entities" are bound to abide by the judgments of the Court, and States parties shall enact special laws for the implementation of their obligations under the Statute (Articles 41 and 42). The implementation of the judgments and binding interim measures (Article 19) shall be supervised by the High Commissioner for Human Rights (Article 18(4)). If the High Commissioner concludes that a State or "Entity" fails to abide by or enforce any judgment, he or she shall seize the Human Rights Council or even the Security Council with a request to take the necessary measures that will bring about the enforcement of the judgment (Article 18(5)).

The Assembly of States Parties is responsible for electing the judges, deciding the budget for the Court and salaries of judges.... The Statute of the World Court shall enter into force as soon as 30 States have become parties to it (Article 49).

QUESTION

What arguments do you see for and against the creation of a World Court as proposed above? Writing in 2004, Stefan Trechsel noted: 'If one imagines an ideal world, certainly a WCHR is desirable.... If one looks at the world today, one will have very serious doubts. The conflicts which we read about every day are not of a kind that could be solved by judicial proceedings.' He concluded that such a Court is 'neither desirable, nor necessary, nor probable'.[39]

ADDITIONAL READING

H. Morsink, *The Universal Declaration of Human Rights: Origins, Drafting and Intent* (1999); International Service for Human Rights, *Human Rights Monitor* (1989–present); P. Alston & F. Mégret, *The UN and Human Rights* (2nd edn. 2013); W. Kälin & J. Künzli, *The Law of International Human Rights Protection* (2009); Geneva Academy of International Humanitarian Law and Human Rights, *Expertise in the Human Rights Council* (2010); S. Subedi, 'The UN Human Rights Mandate in Cambodia', 15 Int'l. J. Hum. Rts. 249 (2011); T. Baldwin-Pask & P. Scannella, 'The Unfinished Business of a Special Procedures System', in M. Cherif Bassiouni & W. Schabas (eds.), *New Challenges for the UN Human Rights Machinery: What Future for the UN Treaty Body System and the Human Rights Council Procedures?* (2011), at 405; V. Chetail, 'The Human Rights Council and the Challenges of the United Nations System on Human Rights: Towards a Cultural Revolution?', in L. Boisson de Chazournes & M. Kohen (eds.), *International Law and the Quest for its Implementation* (2010), at 193.

[39] S. Trechsel, 'A World Court for Human Rights?', 1 NW U.. J. Int'l Hum. Rts. 3 (2004).

9

Treaty Bodies: The ICCPR Human Rights Committee

This chapter continues the inquiry into the structure, roles, functions and processes of international human rights bodies. We continue to emphasize the relationships among human rights norms, institutions and processes, as well as the reasons and techniques for 'institutionalization' of norms.

The Human Rights Council, created under the UN Charter (thus a 'Charter organ'), which was examined in Chapter 8, remains the most complex and politically charged of the specifically human rights organs with universal reach. It differs markedly in organization, functions and powers, as well as notoriety, from the ten 'treaty bodies' established to monitor implementation of the key UN treaties (dealing respectively with civil and political rights, economic, social and cultural rights, racial discrimination, gender discrimination, torture (a committee and a separate sub-committee), children's rights, migrant workers' rights, persons with disabilities and enforced disappearances. Each of the treaty bodies is distinctive in some respects; each has functions only with respect to the treaty creating it; each such treaty regime is now to some extent 'monitored' or 'implemented' or 'developed' by that body.

Chapter 9 provides a systematic study of one such treaty body, the Human Rights Committee created by and functioning within one of the UN's two principal human rights treaties, the International Covenant on Civil and Political Rights. As of May 2012, 167 states are party to the ICCPR. We continue to use the abbreviation 'ICCPR Committee' to distinguish it from the 'Human Rights Council'.

Previous chapters have introduced the work of other treaty bodies, including the CEDAW Committee and the CAT Committee (Chapter 3) as well as the ICESCR Committee (Chapter 4). The emphasis of the present chapter is on institutional structure, functions, powers and efficacy. Why has the ICCPR Committee assumed the character, structure and functions that it has? After 35 years in existence, is it now time for a significant overhaul? But this chapter also addresses important substantive issues, albeit through the lens of the work of the Committee.

Two thoughts should be kept in mind: (1) the ICCPR Committee forms part of a complex system of universal bodies concentrating on human rights issues, both Charter and treaty bodies. Should it then be understood and evaluated not only as an isolated organ functioning under and within the ICCPR, but also as part of this larger complex? If so, it becomes relevant to assess the Committee's work in relation to that of the Human Rights Council, and of other actors such as NGOs. (2) Even when we examine the Committee's work only within the ICCPR, can we understand each of its basic functions in isolation from the others, or should each discrete function be seen as part of an overall ICCPR system?

A. POWERS, FUNCTIONS AND PERFORMANCE OF THE ICCPR COMMITTEE

1. INTRODUCTION

COMMENT ON THE FORMAL ORGANIZATION OF THE ICCPR COMMITTEE

Based on Articles 40 and 41 of the Covenant, and on the first Optional Protocol to the ICCPR, the Committee has four main functions: (1) the consideration of states' reports; (2) the adoption of 'general comments'; (3) the examination of 'communications' (i.e. complaints) from individuals claiming to be victims of violations by states parties of the Covenant; and (4) an interstate complaints procedure (Art. 21). While the latter was considered to be potentially important when the Covenant was drafted, it has never been used by states. Governments apparently prefer to resolve such matters on a bilateral basis, or through the political organs of international or regional organizations.

Before considering the first three of these functions we consider the organizational arrangements reflected in the ICCPR.

Article 28

1. There shall be established a Human Rights Committee.... It shall consist of eighteen members and shall carry out the functions hereinafter provided.

2. The Committee shall be composed of nationals of the States Parties to the present Covenant who shall be persons of high moral character and recognized competence in the field of human rights, consideration being given to the usefulness of the participation of some persons having legal experience.

3. The members of the Committee shall be elected and shall serve in their personal capacity.

...

Article 31

1. The Committee may not include more than one national of the same State.

2. In the election of the Committee, consideration shall be given to equitable geographical distribution of membership and to the representation of the different forms of civilization and of the principal legal systems.

...

Article 38

Every member of the Committee shall, before taking up his duties, make a solemn declaration in open committee that he will perform his functions impartially and conscientiously.

...

Article 39

... (2)(b) Decisions of the Committee shall be made by a majority vote of the members present.

The professional background of Committee members has varied considerably and includes judges, university teachers, public interest lawyers, former diplomats and former government officials. In general, members have demonstrated a high level of competence. Because Article 31(2) does not actually set regional quotas, the group of experts elected to the Committee has not always reflected the 'equitable geographical' balance called for. As of May 2012, the 18 Committee members came from Algeria, Argentina, Colombia, Egypt, France, Ireland, Japan, Kazakhstan, Mauritius, the Netherlands, Romania, South Africa, Suriname, Sweden, Switzerland, the United Kingdom, the United States (and one vacancy).

Under Article 28(3), all members are to be 'elected and shall serve in their personal capacity'. The UN term for such members is 'experts', as opposed to the 'representatives' of states who sit on the UN Human Rights Council. The inference is that Committee members are to act independently of the governments of their states.

Generally this aspiration appears to have been realized, but in many contexts 'independence' in the sense identified has been a relative rather than absolute concept. Since membership on the Committee is a part-time activity, a minority of members have continued to hold government (diplomatic and other) posts, thus qualifying the degree of possible independence from their governments' positions on given issues. But even determinedly independent individuals have to be in sufficiently good standing with their own governments in order to gain nomination in the first place. Consider the following 'Guidelines' adopted by the Committee:

1. The independence of members of the Committee is essential. The principle of independence requires that the members are not removable during their term of office and are not subject to direction or influence of any kind, or to pressure from the State or its agencies in regard to the performance of their duties....

2. In their work...members...should not only be impartial, but should also appear to be so.

3. ... [I]t is important that the election of one of its nationals to the Committee should not result in, or be thought to result in, either more favourable or less favourable treatment for the nominating State.

...

> 4. It is the practice of the Committee that a member does not participate in the examination of the reports presented by his or her country....
>
> ...
>
> 6. ... [A] member [should] take no part whatsoever, formally or informally, in the discussion of communications from his or her own country....
>
> ...
>
> 8. It is desirable for a member of the Committee to abstain from being on the Board of Directors or the Executive Committee of an international nongovernmental organization which regularly submits reports and information to the Committee, so as to avoid the appearance of any conflict in their respective capacities.
>
> ...
>
> 9. ... Members should abstain from participation in any political body of the United Nations or of any other intergovernmental organization concerned with human rights. They should also abstain from acting as experts, consultants or counsels for any Government in a matter that might come up for consideration before the Committee.[1]

The Committee meets for three sessions annually, each three weeks long, twice in Geneva and once in New York. There is some inter-sessional work by individual members in the context of working groups, which meet for one week prior to the start of each session. Living and travel expenses are paid by the UN but since 2002 an annual honorarium of $3,000 previously paid to members has been reduced to a token $1, in order to save money. The work is part time, members hold 'regular', often full-time, jobs, and must fit the Committee's work into already busy schedules. Most meetings (other than those considering 'communications' under the Optional Protocol) are public. Public attendance is usually rather limited, although reports from certain countries can attract a 'full house' in a small conference room.

Decisions of the Committee are, in theory, by majority vote pursuant to Article 39(2). In fact, all decisions to date have been taken by consensus, although as a formal matter any member could demand a vote on any issue. This unbroken practice of reaching decisions by consensus (e.g., on decisions about the Committee's concluding observations on a state's report, p. 770, *infra*, or about the text of a General Comment, p. 793, *infra*) meets with varying reactions from Committee members. Its advantages in avoiding the factional battles that have dominated much of the life of the UN political organs and in permitting the Committee to move ahead as a unit are obvious. Its undoubted, if indeterminate, historical effects on the action taken by the Committee are as obvious: compromise, the blunting of positions, the failure to take the bolder step.

Committee members have said that the practice has had the general effect of not permitting an individual member to hold out for a different position from the large majority, but also has generated a lot of give and take while encouraging members

[1] Report of the Human Rights Committee, UN Doc. A/53/40 (1998), p. 89, Annex III.

holding minority views to go along with a clear trend or dominant opinion. In relation to one activity, the writing of 'Views' about communications discussed at p. 832, *infra*, Committee practice has allowed individual members to write concurring or dissenting opinions.

As with the Council, the ICCPR Committee has witnessed vast changes in global politics since it first met in 1977. The disputes and compromises over the Committee's basic structure and functions that marked the drafting of the Covenant and the Optional Protocol have left a strong imprint on the Committee today. History's traces are indeed everywhere in the Committee's activities, as part of Section 3 below on General Comments seeks to illustrate.

NOTE

Consider the following brief summaries by two authors of the nature of the earlier disputes and their continuing influence. The first is taken from Dominic McGoldrick, *The Human Rights Committee* (1991), at 13–14:

> 1.18 There was general agreement during the drafting that the primary obligation under the ICCPR would be implementation at the national level by States. There was continuing disagreement, however, on the question whether there should also be international measures of implementation. A minority of States, principally the Soviet bloc, insisted that there should be provisions to ensure implementation but that there should be no international measures of implementation. It was argued that such measures were a system of international pressure intended to force States to take particular steps connected with the execution of obligations under the Covenant. They were, therefore, contrary to the principle of domestic jurisdiction in article 2(7) of the United Nations Charter, would undermine the sovereignty and independence of States and would upset the balance of powers established by the UN Charter. Moreover, the establishment of petitions systems would transform complaints into international disputes with consequent effects upon peaceful international relations.
>
> 1.19 Against these views it was argued that the undertaking of international measures of implementation was an exercise of domestic jurisdiction and not an interference with it. International measures were essential to the effective observance of human rights, which were matters of international concern. However, even within those States that agreed that international measures were essential, there were significant differences of opinion as to the appropriate types of measures. The proposals included an International Court of Human Rights empowered to settle disputes concerning the Covenant; settlement by diplomatic negotiation and, in default, by *ad hoc* fact-finding Committees; the establishment of an Office of High Commissioner (or Attorney-General) for Human Rights; the establishment of reporting procedures covering some or all of the provisions in the Covenant; empowering the proposed Human Rights Committee to collect information on all matters relevant to the observance and enforcement of human rights and to initiate an inquiry if it thought one necessary.
>
> . . .

1.21 The lengthy drafting process of the ICCPR largely coincided with the depths of cold war confrontation, the explosive development of notions of self-determination and independence, the accompanying political tensions of large scale decolonization, and the consequential effects of a rapidly altering balance of diplomatic power within the United Nations. In retrospect then it must be acknowledged that it was much more difficult to agree on the text of a Covenant containing binding legal obligations and limited measures of international implementation than it had been to agree upon the statement of political principles in the Universal Declaration in 1948....

The second summary is by Torkel Opsahl, 'The Human Rights Committee', in Philip Alston (ed.), *The United Nations and Human Rights* (1992), at 371:

... The draft Covenant prepared in 1954 by the Commission envisioned a quasi-judicial Human Rights Committee quite different in its powers and functions from that which actually came into existence. It was another twelve years before the General Assembly's Third Committee debated the proposed implementation provisions, at which time they were drastically altered. The majority was opposed to making obligatory the procedure for interstate communications....

All of the various positions, except that of dispensing with the Committee altogether, were taken into account by a formula worked out by the Afro-Asian group. According to this version, the Committee's only compulsory role would be to study and comment generally upon the reports of States Parties, a function originally intended for the Commission on Human Rights. Many of the details of this proposal were amended, which later caused doubts and disagreements about the proper role of the Committee in the reporting system. The functions relating to communications were made entirely optional, and arrangements providing for the consideration of individual complaints of violations were separated from the Covenant and put in the Optional Protocol. In other words, the result was a compromise between those States which favoured strong international measures and those which emphasized the primacy of national sovereignty and responsibility. As is inevitably the case with such compromises, many specific issues were left unresolved, perhaps intentionally. As a result the subsequent evolution of the arrangements has had to be shaped by a continuing give-and-take within the Committee over many years.

QUESTIONS

1. Some commentators would like to characterize the ICCPR Committee as a 'quasi-judicial' body. How is this affected by the part-time, unpaid basis of the work, the very limited conflict of interest provisions contained in the Guidelines and the fact that the Committee generally works by consensus? What changes would be desirable if the Committee were to seek to resemble more closely a quasi-judicial model?

2. The Guatemalan report to the ICCPR Committee in 2012 was presented by a delegation headed by a member of the Committee on the Elimination of Racial Discrimination. Does such linkage compromise independence?

2. STATE REPORTING
COMMENT ON REPORTS OF STATES

Submission by states of reports to a human rights treaty body about their implementation of that treaty has become a familiar requirement. But consider how revolutionary a practice this must have appeared at the time of the first proposals about 60 years ago. To many, it would have seemed nearly inconceivable that most of the world's states would periodically submit a report to an international body about their internal matters involving many politically sensitive aspects of relations between government and citizens, and then participate in a discussion about that report with members of that body drawn from all over the world.

The relevant provision is Article 40:

> 1. The States Parties to the present Covenant undertake to submit reports on the measures they have adopted which give effect to the rights recognized herein and on the progress made in the enjoyment of those rights:
>
> (*a*) Within one year of the entry into force of the present Covenant for the States Parties concerned;
>
> (*b*) Thereafter whenever the Committee so requests.
>
> 2. …Reports shall indicate the factors and difficulties, if any, affecting the implementation of the present Covenant.
>
> …
>
> 4. The Committee shall study the reports…[and shall submit them], and such general comments as it may consider appropriate, to the States Parties….
>
> 5. The States Parties to the present Covenant may submit to the Committee observations on any comments that may be made in accordance with paragraph 4 of this article.

Discussions of reports are public proceedings, with attendance varying considerably depending on the country concerned, and the vibrancy of the domestic NGO community and of the national media. The proceedings amount less to a systematic 'study' (to use the term of Art. 40) than to an examination of the report with members speaking individually, making comments and posing questions. The representative of the state responds to comments and questions. Reports are generally presented by a state party every five years or at other intervals determined by the Committee in its Concluding Observations. A practice of requesting 'emergency reports', pioneered by the Committee in 1992 in relation to Iraq, Rwanda and the former Yugoslavia, has not since been reactivated in this form.

The Covenant makes no provision about the form of reports, but the Committee has issued general guidelines (UN Doc. CCPR/C/2009/1 (22 Nov. 2010)). The initial report, due within one year after the Covenant enters into force for that state, is required to be comprehensive. Subsequent ('periodic') reports are due every 4–6 years and are expected to address primarily the issues of concern identified by the Committee in its consideration of the previous report. As with other treaty bodies, the Committee has encountered various problems in the reports submitted to it: incomplete coverage, abstraction and formality that lead states to stress their formal constitutional or statutory provisions rather than to offer a realistic description of practices; and great delays in filing reports. This led to a new initiative in 2010 which encourages states to adopt a different approach in all future periodic reporting. This LOIPR procedure ('list of issues prior to reporting') envisages that the Secretariat will prepare a comprehensive 'country file', containing all relevant data about that country. The Committee will then draw up a list of issues and the state will, for the most part, only be required to report on those issues. This should generate a more focused and streamlined procedure.

As noted by the ICCPR Committee's sister treaty body, the ESCR Committee, much of the value of the reporting process lies at the domestic rather than the international level:

> The process of reporting provides an opportunity for an individual State party to conduct a comprehensive review of the measures it has taken to bring its national law and policy into line with the provisions of the treaties to which it is a party. The preparation of reports provides a platform for national dialogue on human rights amongst the various stakeholders in a State party. The report itself provides the Government and others, including civil society, with a baseline for the elaboration of clearly stated and targeted policies, which include priorities consistent with the provisions of the treaties. The process of reporting also encourages and facilitates public scrutiny at the national level of Government approaches to implementation and stimulates constructive discussion with civil society of ways to advance the enjoyment by all of the rights laid down in the various conventions. Consideration of the reports by the Committee, through constructive dialogue with States parties, allows individual States and States as a whole to exchange experience on the problems faced in implementation of the instruments, and good practices that facilitate enhanced implementation. It also allows for international scrutiny, which underlines States' responsibility and accountability for human rights protection.[2]

The reporting process generally garners little publicity. In 2008 the Committee acknowledged that its work needed to become better known and it thus adopted 'A Strategic Approach to Public Relations' (UN Doc. CCPR/C/94/3). In 2012 the UN began live webcasting of the Committee's sessions. Some states include civil society groups in the preparation of their report or in considering the Committee's reaction to the report. The most participatory dimension of the official UN process involves the submission of 'shadow reports' by such groups. These are posted on the Committee's website and serve both to critique the governmental report and to flag other issues to be considered. When accurate, detailed and concise such reports can have a major impact.

It has been suggested that the effectiveness of reporting will depend on:

> the willingness and capacity of States to report regularly, use the process as an opportunity for a frank and comprehensive assessment of implementation of

[2] 'Concept Paper on the High Commissioner's Committee on Economic, Social and Cultural Rights, proposal for a unified standing treaty body', UN Doc. General Comment 1 (1989): Reporting by States Parties, HRI/MC/2006/2 (2006) summarizing the approach of UN Doc. HRI/GEN/1/Rev.8, p. 9, para. 8.

> international obligations, and engage in a dialogue with national stakeholders before and after the consideration of reports by the Committee. It also depends on the awareness and knowledge of national constituencies and their interest in participating in the process and using it to assess progress in implementation and raise issues, including obstacles to implementation, at the national and international levels. In addition, it depends on the lapse of time between submission and consideration of a report, the quality and fairness of the dialogue, concluding observations and recommendations and any follow-up action that may occur.[3]

Diverse and accurate information is essential to the Committee's work. For the first decade or so of its existence the Committee was pressured by a majority of its members not to rely upon any information other than that presented by states. Information from intergovernmental organizations, let alone from NGOs, was strongly contested. In the course of the 1990s these self-imposed restrictions gradually evaporated and the Committee now receives regular briefings from UN agencies, and holds 30-minute official meetings and additional informal lunch-time gatherings at which it is briefed by NGOs on the situation in the countries whose reports it is about to consider. In 2012 the Committee adopted a policy paper designed to enhance its interactions on various fronts with NGOs.

The formal procedure for examining reports consists of several steps. The first is the appointment of a 'country report task force' of 4–6 members. They have the main responsibility for the conduct of the debate on the report. One of these members will also be designated as the 'country rapporteur'. He or she takes the lead in preparing a list of issues to be sent to the state party which is requested to provide written replies of not more than 30 pages in length. This will change considerably as the LOIPR procedure replaces previous practice.

During the 'constructive dialogue' with the representatives of the state party, the country rapporteur and other task force members take the lead in posing questions, with other members free to join in thereafter. The task force then drafts the concluding observations, which are debated in private, adopted and usually released at the end of the relevant session. The Committee normally deals with no more than 5–6 reports at each of its three-week sessions. Governments are requested to inform it of the measures taken in response to the observations, and the Committee often asks governments to report back on selected issues one year later. It has a Special Rapporteur on follow-up to concluding observations and has had lengthy discussions on the type of steps it might take to obtain more consistent results.

One final problem concerns the failure of states to report at all, or to delay greatly the submission of reports. This is a problem which the ICCPR Committee shares with most of the other treaty bodies. In relation to the ICCPR, some states are as much as 20 years behind in their submission of reports. For example, in its 2011 Annual Report the Committee listed Gambia (26 years overdue), Equatorial Guinea (22), Somalia (20), Côte d'Ivoire (18), along with others such as Romania (13), Nigeria (11) and South Africa (11). The reports overdue by five years or more also included 22 initial reports, meaning that states had ratified the Covenant but not

[3] Ibid., para. 10.

bothered to submit even an initial report. Because this frustrates 'a major objective of the Covenant', the Committee has adopted a procedure for examining the situation in non-reporting states, if necessary in the absence of a report and even a delegation from the country concerned. As of 2012, the procedure has been initiated 13 times and in almost every instance the state concerned eventually responded either by submitting a report or by commenting on Committee assessments.[4]

In the next section of the chapter we consider three case studies in reporting. The most detailed is that of the United States, and the others concern the Islamic Republic of Iran and the UN Interim Administration Mission in Kosovo.

CASE STUDY: REPORT OF THE USA TO THE ICCPR COMMITTEE

(July 2006)

The United States ratified the ICCPR in 1992 and submitted its initial report on time in September 1993. It was examined by the Committee in July 1994. Its second and third periodic reports were submitted together in November 2005. In March 2006 the Committee sent a six-page list of issues to the US Government, and received a 102-page reply. Almost 50 NGOs made detailed submissions.[5] Excerpts from one follow. We then look at excerpts from the dialogue between the Committee and the government, followed by the conclusions drawn by the Committee.

Memorandum to Members of the U.N. Human Rights Committee from Human Rights Watch

(10 Jan. 2006), at www2.ohchr.org/english/bodies/hrc/87ngos_info.htm

(1) The Cloak of Federalism: ... [T]he United States' system of federalism is used to justify the failures to abide by its treaty obligations.

The United States has consistently failed to develop, monitor, or enforce any national standards for law enforcement personnel and treatment of prisoners and detained persons within the United States. The national government has consistently left such practices up to the individual states and localities, with little to no guidance or monitoring.

This failure is reflected in the report itself. Whereas the report cites a long list of court cases and statutes, it fails to provide any description of the reality on the ground; i.e. how these statutes are being implemented and any how violations of the Convention are monitored. The report does not contain such a description because the federal government does not know — it has not established mechanisms to acquire the necessary information. Moreover, the report heavily emphasizes federal statutes and federal standards, while stating little about the state statutes, standards

[4] Report of the Human Rights Committee, UN Doc. A/66/40 (Vol. I) (2011), pp. 24–30.

[5] All these documents are available at www2.ohchr.org/english/bodies/hrc/87ngo_info.htm.

and enforcement mechanisms — even though law enforcement personnel are almost all state or local, and most prisoners are in state or local facilities.

HRW urges the committee to ask the United States questions about law enforcement and corrections policies and practices within the states, in particular the policies and practices with regard to the treatment of juveniles in the criminal justice system, use of force (including restraint devices and electronic stun devices) by law, sexual abuse of prisoners, the operation of super maximum prisons, and the treatment of the mentally ill in prison.

(2) Article 2 — Effective Remedies: Courts provide the primary vehicle by which individuals in the United States can seek redress of violations of their rights. Over the last ten years the U.S. government has increasingly restricted access to courts for persons who believe public officials have violated their rights to liberty, due process or to be free from torture or other cruel, inhuman or degrading treatment. Of particular concern are the limitations on prisoners, immigrants, and "enemy combatant" detainees' access to the courts, as highlighted in the coalition's submission under Article 2.

HRW urges the committee to question the United States about the availability of judicial and other effective remedies available to certain groups of persons, including prisoners, immigrants, and detainees in the so-called "war on terror."

DIALOGUE BETWEEN THE HUMAN RIGHTS COMMITTEE AND THE DELEGATION OF THE USA

Second and third periodic reports of the United States of America, 18 July 2006)

UN Doc. CCPR/C/SR.2380 (27 July 2006)

2. *Mr. WAXMAN* (United States of America) said that his Government did not consider questions concerning the war on terrorism, and detention and interrogation outside United States territory to fall within the scope of the Covenant. However, his delegation would use the opportunity to exchange views and share information with the Committee and NGOs. He agreed that measures taken to combat terrorism should not compromise human rights principles. The Al-Qaida attacks on the United States constituted a global threat that did not correspond to existing legal categories....

3. The Government drew a clear distinction between the global threat posed by transnational terrorism and the legal status of his country's armed conflict with Al-Qaida, and its affiliates and supporters. While the Covenant continued to apply to the treatment of prisoners in domestic United States prisons, the law of armed conflict governed United States detention operations in Guantánamo Bay, Afghanistan and Iraq....

4. In accordance with the traditional rule of warfare, enemy fighters could be held until the end of the conflict in order to prevent them from returning to the battlefield. Given the unique nature of the current war, however, his Government

had made significant efforts to develop individualized administrative procedures to review each case in Guantánamo and elsewhere. Once the Government was convinced that detainees would have adequate security and humane treatment on returning to their home countries, they were released or returned to those countries.

5. *Mr. HARRIS* (United States of America) said that his Government regretted the delay in submitting its second and third periodic reports.... The Covenant was well known in his country and had been cited in many legal cases. All reports were published on the State Department and other websites. The legislative branch of government was familiar with the Covenant thanks to the ratification process, which had included extensive public discussion. Several training programmes on international treaty obligations for federal judges covered the Covenant.

6. The Government had taken measures to engage individual states in the preparation of the report. Given that United States civil rights protections were enforced through federal and state legal processes, and that the Constitution was applicable to both, the absence of detailed reporting did not, however, indicate a failure to implement the Covenant at state level. Should the Committee have concerns regarding a particular state, it would be helpful if it could inform the Government prior to preparation of the fourth periodic report.

7. His Government had not entered a derogation under article 4 of the Covenant because no actions in his country had derogated from the obligations under the Covenant....

8. [In relation to the scope of Article 2 (1) of the Covenant], his delegation found it difficult to accept that the conjunction in the phrase "within its territory and subject to its jurisdiction" could be interpreted as meaning "and/or". That was particularly implausible given that the Covenant negotiators had rejected the proposal to substitute the word "or" for "and". In general, only the parties to a treaty were empowered to give a binding interpretation of its provisions unless the treaty provided otherwise. That was not the case in the Covenant, nor did it authorize the International Court of Justice to issue legally binding interpretations of its provisions....

10. His Government respectfully disagreed with the Committee's conclusion that article 7 of the Covenant contained a non-refoulement obligation[6] with respect to torture and cruel, inhuman or degrading treatment or punishment. That conclusion went well beyond the language of article 7 and the scope of the non-refoulement provision contained in article 3 of the Convention against Torture and Other Cruel, Inhuman or Degrading Treatment or Punishment. His Government did not accept that the obligations of a State party under a treaty were affected by non-binding general comments or individual complaints procedures that the State had not accepted....

11. *Ms. HODGKINSON* (United States of America) said that detainees were being held in Guantánamo in order to remove them to a location safe from the continuing battle, while keeping dangerous terrorists from the proximity of the

[6] This is an obligation not to return a person to a country in which there is a possibility he will be tortured.

American public. Guantánamo had been the best option as a military base with existing facilities.

…

19. His [sic] country did not transfer detainees to States where it was "more likely than not" that they would be tortured, and did not transport any individual to a third country to be tortured. In accordance with domestic legislation and policy, his delegation would not discuss specific intelligence activities. Nevertheless, many countries, including the United States, had used renditions for decades to transport individuals between countries for law enforcement purposes. Where appropriate, the United States negotiated diplomatic assurances to ensure that individuals transferred from Guantánamo would not be tortured on return to their countries, and that they did not pose a significant threat to the United States or its allies. Diplomatic assurances were not, however, deemed a substitute for a thorough review of whether it was "more likely than not" that a person would be tortured. Rather, they were one of many components considered when analysing each situation.

…

21. *Mr. KIM* (United States of America) said that several laws safeguarded the constitutional rights of all prisoners, including women. The Civil Rights Division of the Department of Justice investigated and prosecuted prison officials found guilty of violating inmates' and detainees' constitutional rights. Between 2001 and 2005, 334 police and prison officials had been charged with misconduct. The Department of Justice also monitored conditions in state local prisons and juvenile detention facilities. Since 2001, it had concluded formal investigations of 42 jails, prisons and juvenile facilities to ensure that constitutional rights were protected. It was currently monitoring agreements involving 97 such institutions and would remain vigilant in protecting the rights of women in custody.

…

27. On the question of surveillance, in some instances it was necessary to gather evidence of an ongoing crime, and alerting the criminal to the fact that the evidence being gathered was not practicable. Nevertheless, numerous safeguards ensured that delayed-notice search warrants were used appropriately….

28. Protection against racial profiling was provided by the Fourteenth Amendment, which prohibited law enforcement actions motivated solely by race or national origin. The current Government had further prohibited the use of racial profiling in federal law enforcement….

…

37. *Mr. TIMOFEYEV* (United States of America) said that his country strongly supported the United Nations Guiding Principles on Internal Displacement. His Government's response to the internal displacement caused by Hurricane Katrina had included providing relief assistance to all victims as quickly as possible without discrimination…. Despite the extensive displacement caused by the hurricane, the situation did not come within the challenges that the Guiding Principles were designed to address.

…

46. [*Mr. KIM* (United States of America)]...said that the federal maximum security facility...was used only for offenders who were hardened and dangerous criminals. Inmates in the facility had access to a broad range of classes, programmes and services, regular access to the prison chaplain, and five hours of out-of-cell recreation per week. On prison rape, he said that the rape of an inmate was a serious crime, which was vigorously prosecuted.... It was not general policy or practice to shackle women giving birth in detention. Inmates were only restrained during labour and delivery in the unlikely event that they posed a threat to themselves, their babies or others around them. Although the use of shackles was not prohibited, allegations of their misuse in federal or state prisons were investigated by the Department of Justice.

47. The Prison Litigation Reform Act contained provisions to curtail frivolous lawsuits by prison inmates (question 22). Civil action for damages could not be brought by a prisoner for mental or emotional injury suffered in custody, without a prior showing of physical injury. A civil action could, however, be brought by a prisoner to redress torture or cruel, inhuman or degrading treatment or punishment. A wide range of alternative avenues was open, through which prisoners could file complaints and express grievances.

...

49. Persons under the age of 18 in the United States could be sentenced to life in prison without the possibility of parole (question 24). Lengthy sentences had been imposed on persons who, despite their youth, were hardened criminals who had been convicted of extremely serious crimes and constituted an extreme danger to society. Each state handled the prosecution, rehabilitation, treatment and imprisonment of young offenders pursuant to its own statutes....

...

52. *Mr. O'FLAHERTY* [Committee member] reminded the delegation that some of the Committee's questions had remained unanswered. In some instances, the delegation had failed to acknowledge situations of fact and to analyse the effectiveness of government responses to those situations. A mere statement of how much money had been allocated to addressing a certain situation did not constitute an explanation or justification of government activities....

53. ... Any programme that increased the risk of infection or death raised issues under the Covenant. Research had shown that abstinence programmes increased the risk of contracting HIV, falling pregnant, undergoing unsafe abortions and death. He wished to know what measures were being taken to reduce those risks. The Committee had been informed that 49 per cent of pregnancies in the United States were unplanned. He wished to know if that figure was correct.

...

55. *Mr. LALLAH* [Committee member]...Although legislative guarantees were in place to protect all prisoners from cruel, inhuman or degrading treatment or punishment, the Committee had been informed that the provisions of that legislation were not always implemented effectively. He wondered what the results had been of the adoption of the Prison Rape Elimination Act, and whether there was any monitoring of the implementation of that legislation.... He asked what efforts were

being made to improve conditions for women in prison, and in particular to review the procedure of shackling women detainees during childbirth.

56. *Mr. KÄLIN* [Committee member] said that although the delegation's responses had been clear and enlightening, he regretted its minimalist approach to some issues and its tendency merely to insist that the United States had not violated the Covenant. The examination of a State party's report was not a quasi-judicial procedure. States were required under article 2 not only to respect the Covenant but also to ensure that all individuals enjoyed Covenant rights. The purpose of the Committee's review of periodic reports was to explore with each State how it could move beyond the current stage of implementation of the Covenant, on the understanding that there was always room for improvement when it came to protecting human rights.

57. With regard to continuing differences between the State party and the Committee on how to interpret important parts of the Covenant, he agreed that there was no binding procedure for determining the correct interpretation. However, that did not bar the International Court of Justice (ICJ) from ruling on any questions of law that arose.... Moreover, the Committee was mandated by article 40 to make general comments on the Covenant, so that its findings, though not legally binding, had considerable authoritative status.

58. Several States parties had informed the Committee that they accepted the principle of extraterritorial applicability of the Covenant. Some were even training their armed forces in Covenant rights since they might be stationed abroad not only in combat situations but also as part of a peacekeeping mission to which international humanitarian law no longer applied. It would be very odd if no human rights protection was available under such circumstances and troops were free to behave as they wished.

59. He had taken note of the delegation's statement that there was no rendition to a place where it was "more likely than not" that a person would be tortured. It must therefore unfortunately be inferred that persons could be rendered to a place where the risk of torture was as great as 49 per cent. [O]ther common law jurisdictions...had concluded that it could not be considered an appropriate standard under international law or even under common law.

...

62. He agreed that the Covenant did not rule out the possibility of excluding criminals from the right to vote. However, it was a matter of concern that such exclusions had led in the United States to the disenfranchisement of millions of voters. In Florida alone an estimated 600,000 people of voting age had been prevented from casting their vote in the last two presidential elections.... The right to vote had a collective dimension — the right to have at least some chance of securing a majority.

...

64. *Sir Nigel RODLEY* [Committee member] said that some of the delegation's responses had been dogged reaffirmations of positions already stated in the report.

...

...

69. The Committee had been assured that persons in prolonged incommunicado detention were humanely treated in accordance with the prohibition of torture and cruel, inhuman or degrading treatment or punishment.... [According to resolutions of the Commission on Human Rights] prolonged incommunicado detention could violate that prohibition. As the United States had invariably joined in the consensus on that resolution, it was unclear how consistent its current interpretation of the scope of article 7 was with its earlier position.

...

77. The United States had incarcerated some 2,270,000 people out of a population of approximately 280 million, which was equivalent to 757 per 100,000 members of the population, a ratio that was between 500 and 1,000 per cent higher than for any other developed country. He wondered why such high levels of incarceration were necessary.

...

79. *Mr. WIERUSZEWSKI* [Committee member]...asked whether the State party had taken any steps to ratify the Convention on the Rights of the Child. The fact that the United States was one of only two States that had failed to ratify the Convention was an unfortunate example of exceptionalism and an impediment to universality.

...

83. *Mr. SHEARER* [Committee member] noted with dismay the increasingly strident rejection of the relevance of international law and standard-setting by significant public figures in the United States such as judges and government officials.

...

105. *Mr. HARRIS* (United States of America) said that his delegation's views on the scope of certain provisions of the Covenant differed from the views held by the Committee. Each Government had the sovereign right to decide which obligations to assume under international treaty law. When acceding to a treaty, his Government reviewed all of its provisions carefully to determine which of the resulting obligations could be implemented at both the State and federal levels. Reservations were entered in respect of those provisions whose implementation was considered unfeasible. As a result, the country became bound by a set of obligations set forth in the treaty. It was not for the Committee to change his country's obligations flowing from the Covenant or to issue authoritative guidance in that respect. His Government did not agree with all opinions adopted and jurisprudence developed by the Committee over time.

106. The way in which questions were raised during his delegation's dialogue with the Committee at times appeared to suggest that the United States acted in violation of its obligations, which, in turn, sparked a perhaps overly defensive reaction on the part of the delegation. He hoped that the clarification concerning his Government's approach to its treaty obligations might dispel certain misconceptions and tensions pervading his delegation's dialogue with the Committee and facilitate a more constructive dialogue in the future.

...

CONCLUDING OBSERVATIONS OF THE HUMAN RIGHTS COMMITTEE, UNITED STATES OF AMERICA

UN Doc. A/61/40 (Vol. I) (2006), p. 60[7]

[Eds.: The Committee's document alternates between diagnosis, in regular font, and prescriptions, in bold font.]

Introduction

...

3. The Committee regrets that the State party has not integrated into its report information on the implementation of the Covenant with respect to individuals under its jurisdiction and outside its territory. The Committee notes however that the State party has provided additional material "out of courtesy". The Committee further regrets that the State party, invoking grounds of non-applicability of the Covenant or intelligence operations, refused to address certain serious allegations of violations of the rights protected under the Covenant.

4. The Committee regrets that only limited information was provided on the implementation of the Covenant at the State level.

B. Positive aspects

5–9. The Committee welcomes [various Supreme Court decisions including *Hamdan v. Rumsfeld* (2006) establishing the applicability of Common Article 3 of the Geneva Conventions; *Roper v. Simmons* (2005), prohibiting the juvenile death penalty; *Atkins v. Virginia* (2002), prohibiting the execution of mentally retarded criminals; and *Lawrence et al. v. Texas* (2003), declaring unconstitutional legislation criminalizing homosexual relations between consenting adults. It also welcomes the National Detention Standards (2000), establishing minimum standards for detention facilities holding Department of Homeland Security detainees.]

C. Principal subjects of concern and recommendations

10. The Committee notes with concern the restrictive interpretation made by the State party of its obligations under the Covenant, as a result in particular of (a) its position that the Covenant does not apply with respect to individuals under its jurisdiction but outside its territory, nor in time of war, despite the contrary opinions and established jurisprudence of the Committee and the International Court of Justice; (b) its failure to take fully into consideration its obligation under the Covenant not only to respect, but also to ensure the rights prescribed by the Covenant; and (c) its restrictive approach to some substantive provisions of the Covenant, which is not in conformity with the interpretation made by the Committee before and after the State party's ratification of the Covenant.

The State party should review its approach and interpret the Covenant in good faith, in accordance with the ordinary meaning to be given to its terms in their context, including subsequent practice, and in the light of its object and purpose....

[7] As amended by UN Doc. A/61/40 (Vol.1)/Corr.1 (2006).

11. The Committee expresses its concern about the potentially overbroad reach of the definitions of terrorism under domestic law….

The State party should ensure that its counter-terrorism measures are in full conformity with the Covenant….

12. … The State party should immediately cease its practice of secret detention and close all secret detention facilities. It should also grant the International Committee of the Red Cross prompt access to any person detained in connection with an armed conflict. The State party should also ensure that detainees, regardless of their place of detention, always benefit from the full protection of the law.

13. The Committee is concerned with the fact that the State party has authorized for some time the use of enhanced interrogation techniques, such as prolonged stress positions and isolation, sensory deprivation, hooding, exposure to cold or heat, sleep and dietary adjustments, 20-hour interrogations, removal of clothing and deprivation of all comfort and religious items, forced grooming, and exploitation of detainees' individual phobias. Although the Committee welcomes the assurance that, according to the Detainee Treatment Act of 2005, such interrogation techniques are prohibited by the present Army Field Manual on Intelligence Interrogation, the Committee remains concerned that (a) the State party refuses to acknowledge that such techniques,…violate…article 7 of the Covenant; (b) no sentence has been pronounced against an officer, employee, member of the Armed Forces, or other agent of the United States Government for using harsh interrogation techniques that had been approved; (c) these interrogation techniques may still be authorized or used by other agencies, including intelligence agencies and "private contractors"; and (d) the State party has provided no information to the fact that oversight systems of such agencies have been established to ensure compliance with article 7….

14. … The State party should conduct prompt and independent investigations into all allegations concerning suspicious deaths, torture or cruel, inhuman or degrading treatment or punishment inflicted by its personnel (including commanders) as well as contract employees, in detention facilities in Guantanamo Bay, Afghanistan, Iraq and other overseas locations. The State party should ensure that those responsible are prosecuted and punished in accordance with the gravity of the crime. The State party should adopt all necessary measures to prevent the recurrence of such behaviors, …

…

16. The Committee notes with concern the State party's restrictive interpretation of article 7 of the Covenant according to which it understands (a) that the obligation not to subject anyone to treatment prohibited by article 7 of the Covenant does not include an obligation not to expose them to such treatment by means of transfer, rendition, extradition, expulsion or refoulement; (b) that in any case, it is not under any other obligation not to deport an individual who may undergo cruel, inhuman or degrading treatment or punishment other than torture, as the State party understands the term; and (c) that it is not under any international obligation to respect a non-refoulement rule in relation to persons it detains outside its territory…. Its concern is deepened by the so far successful invocation of State secrecy in cases where the victims of [renditions] have sought a remedy before the State party's courts (e.g. the cases of *Maher Arar v. Ashcroft* (2006) and *Khaled Al-Masri v. Tenet* (2006)).

The State party should review its position, in accordance with the Committee's general comments No. 20 [and No. 31]…. The State party should exercise the utmost care in the use of diplomatic assurances and adopt clear and transparent procedures with adequate judicial mechanisms for review before individuals are deported, as well as effective mechanisms to monitor scrupulously and vigorously the fate of the affected individuals. The State party should further recognize that the more systematic the practice of torture or cruel, inhuman or degrading treatment or punishment, the less likely it will be that a real risk of such treatment can be avoided by such assurances, however stringent any agreed follow-up procedures may be.

17. The Committee is concerned that the Patriot Act and the 2005 REAL ID Act of 2005 may bar from asylum and withholding of removal any person who has provided "material support" to a "terrorist organization", whether voluntarily or under duress. It regrets having received no response on this matter from the State party.

…

18. … The State party should ensure, in accordance with article 9 (4) of the Covenant, that persons detained in Guantanamo Bay are entitled to proceedings before a court to decide, without delay, on the lawfulness of their detention or order their release. Due process, independence of the reviewing courts from the executive branch and the army, access of detainees to counsel of their choice and to all proceedings and evidence, should be guaranteed in this regard.

19. The Committee…is concerned by reports that, following the September 11 attacks, many non-U.S. citizens, suspected to have committed terrorism-related offences have been detained for long periods pursuant to immigration laws with fewer guarantees than in the context of criminal procedures, or on the basis of the Material Witness Statute only. The Committee is also concerned with the compatibility of the Statute with the Covenant since it may be applied for up-coming trials but also to investigations or proposed investigations.

…

21. The Committee…notes that section 213 of the Patriot Act, expanding the possibility of delayed notification of home and office searches; section 215 regarding access to individuals' personal records and belongings; and section 505, relating to the issuance of national security letters, still raise issues of concern in relation to article 17 of the Covenant. In particular, the Committee is concerned about the restricted possibilities for the concerned persons to be informed about such measures and to effectively challenge them. Furthermore, the Committee is concerned that the State Party, including through the National Security Agency (NSA), has monitored and still monitors phone, email, and fax communications of individuals both within and outside the U.S., without any judicial or other independent oversight.

… The State party should ensure that any infringement on individual's rights to privacy is strictly necessary and duly authorized by law, and that the rights of individuals to follow suit in this regard are respected.

22. The Committee is concerned with reports that some 50% of homeless people are African American although they constitute only 12% of the United States population.

The State party should take measures, including adequate and adequately implemented policies, to bring an end to such de facto and historically generated racial discrimination.

23. The Committee notes with concern reports of de facto racial segregation in public schools, reportedly caused by discrepancies between the racial and ethnic composition of large urban districts and their surrounding suburbs, and the manner in which schools districts are created, funded and regulated. The Committee is concerned that the State party, despite measures adopted, has not succeeded in eliminating racial discrimination such as regarding the wide disparities in the quality of education across school districts in metropolitan areas, to the detriment of minority students. It also notes with concern the State party's position that federal government authorities cannot take legal action if there is no indication of discriminatory intent by state or local authorities.

... The State party should conduct in-depth investigations into the de facto segregation described above and take remedial steps, in consultation with the affected communities.

24. ... The State party should continue and intensify its efforts to put an end to racial profiling used by federal as well as state law enforcement officials. The Committee wishes to receive more detailed information about the extent to which such practices still persist, as well as statistical data on complaints, prosecutions and sentences in such matters.

25. The Committee notes with concern allegations of widespread incidence of violent crime perpetrated against persons of minority sexual orientation, including by law enforcement officials. It notes with concern the failure to address such crime in the legislation on hate crime adopted at the federal level and in many states. It notes with concern the failure to outlaw employment discrimination on the basis of sexual orientation in many states....

26. ... In the aftermath of Hurricane Katrina, the State party should increase its efforts to ensure that the rights of the poor, and in particular African-Americans, are fully taken into consideration in the reconstruction plans with regard to access to housing, education and healthcare....

27. The Committee regrets that it has not received sufficient information on the measures the State party considers adopting in relation to the reportedly nine million undocumented migrants now in the United States.... [T]he Committee remains concerned about the increased level of militarization on the southwest border with Mexico.

...

28. The Committee regrets that many federal laws which address sex-discrimination are limited in scope and restricted in implementation. The Committee is especially concerned about the reported persistence of employment discrimination against women. (articles 3 and 26)

The State party should take all steps necessary, including at state level, to ensure the equality of women before the law and equal protection of the law, as well as effective protection against discrimination on the ground of sex, in particular in the area of employment.

29. ... The State party should review federal and state legislation with a view to restricting the number of offences carrying the death penalty. The State party should also assess the extent to which death penalty is disproportionately imposed

on ethnic minorities and on low-income population groups.... In the meantime, the State party should place a moratorium on capital sentences, bearing in mind the desirability of abolishing death penalty.

30. The Committee reiterates its concern about reports of police brutality and excessive use of force by law enforcement officials....

...

32. The Committee reiterates its concern that conditions in some maximum security prisons are incompatible with the obligation contained in article 10 (1) of the Covenant to treat detainees with humanity and respect for the inherent dignity of the human person. It is particularly concerned by the practice in some such institutions to hold detainees in prolonged cellular confinement, and to allow them out-of-cell recreation for only five hours per week, in general conditions of strict regimentation in a depersonalized environment....

...

33. ... The Committee reiterates its recommendation that male officers should not be granted access to women's quarters, or at least be accompanied by women officers. The Committee also recommends the State party to prohibit the shackling of detained women during childbirth.

34. The Committee notes with concern reports that forty-two states and the Federal government have laws allowing persons under the age of eighteen at the time the offence was committed, to receive life sentences, without parole, and that about 2,225 youth offenders are currently serving life sentences in United States prisons.... The Committee is of the view that sentencing children to life sentence without parole is of itself not in compliance with article 24 (1) of the Covenant.

...

35. The Committee is concerned that about five million citizens cannot vote due to a felony conviction, and that this practice has significant racial implications. The Committee also notes with concern that the recommendation made in 2001 by the National Commission on Federal Election Reform that all states restore voting rights to citizens who have fully served their sentences has not been endorsed by all states. The Committee is of the view that general deprivation of the right to vote for persons who have received a felony conviction, and in particular those who are no longer deprived of liberty, do not meet the requirements of articles 25 or 26 of the Covenant, nor serves the rehabilitation goals of article 10 (3).

...

38. The Committee...requests that the State party's [report] and the present concluding observations be published and widely disseminated in the State party, to the general public as well as to the judicial, legislative and administrative authorities....

...

NOTE

The US Government submitted its fourth periodic report on 30 December 2011. It was 188 pages long and addressed many of the issues raised in the preceding dialogue. The report is scheduled for consideration by the Committee in March 2013 and the results of that dialogue will be published at www2.ohchr.org/english/bodies/hrc/hrcs107.htm.

FOURTH PERIODIC REPORT, UNITED STATES OF AMERICA

UN Doc. CCPR/C/USA/4 (2012)

Introduction

...

2. Treaty reporting is a way in which the [US] Government...can inform its citizens and the international community of its efforts to ensure the implementation of those obligations it has assumed, while at the same time holding itself to the public scrutiny of the international community and civil society....

...

4. In this report, the United States has considered carefully the views expressed by the Committee....

...

[Shackling]

231. Shackling of pregnant female prisoners during transportation, labor, and delivery. The DOJ Bureau of Prisons (DOJ/BOP) announced in October 2008 that it would no longer engage in [this] practice..., except in the most extreme circumstances. DHS/ICE has also adopted policies substantially limiting the use of restraints on pregnant women in immigration detention.

232. States are also increasingly adopting similar rules....

...

458. Felony disenfranchisement is a matter of continuing debate in the states.... It has been criticized as weakening our democracy by depriving citizens of the vote, and also for its disproportionate affects [sic] on racial minorities....

459. Since the submission of the [2005 Report], modification of state laws and procedures has continued. For example, in 2005, the Governor of Iowa issued an executive order eliminating lifetime disenfranchisement for persons convicted of an "infamous crime" and making restoration of voting rights automatic for persons completing their sentences. This order, however, was revoked by a successor Governor in 2011. Also in 2005, the legislature in Nebraska repealed its lifetime ban on voting for all felons and replaced it with a 2-year post-sentence ban....Florida, however, toughened its laws in March 2011, banning automatic restoration of voting rights for all convicted felons. Currently 48 states restrict voting by persons convicted of felonies in some manner....

...

III. Committee Concluding Observations

...

[This part responds to paragraph 10 of the Concluding Observations (p. 778, *supra*)].

(a) Territorial Scope

...

505. The United States in its prior appearances before the Committee has articulated the position that article 2(1) would apply only to individuals who were both within the territory of a State Party and within that State Party's jurisdiction. The United States is mindful that in General Comment 31 (2004) the Committee presented [a different view].... The United States is also aware of the jurisprudence of the International Court of Justice ("ICJ"), which has found the ICCPR "applicable in respect of acts done by a State in the exercise of its jurisdiction outside its own territory," as well as positions taken by other States Parties.

(b) Applicable Law

506. With respect to the application of the Covenant and [IHL], the United States has not taken the position that the Covenant does not apply "in time of war."...

507. More complex issues arise with respect to the relevant body of law that determines whether a State's actions in the actual conduct of an armed conflict comport with international law. Under the doctrine of lex specialis, the applicable rules for the protection of individuals and conduct of hostilities in armed conflict are typically found in [IHL].... [I]t is important to bear in mind that international human rights law and the law of armed conflict are in many respects complementary and mutually reinforcing.... Determining the international law rule that applies... is a fact-specific determination, which cannot be easily generalized, and raises especially complex issues in the context of non-international armed conflicts occurring within a State's own territory.

...

508. The United States understands... that there have been concerns about a lack of adequate international legal protections for those the United States engages with overseas, particularly in armed conflict situations. In part to address these concerns, President Obama has taken a number of actions [including issuing] three Executive Orders relating to U.S. detention and interrogation policies broadly and the Guantanamo Bay detention facility specifically....

...

(c) Coordination with the Committee

510. The United States appreciates its ongoing dialogue with the Committee with respect to the interpretation and application of the Covenant, considers the Committee's views in good faith, and looks forward to further discussions....

...

[International transfers]

554. In Executive Order 13491, President Obama ordered the establishment of the Special Interagency Task Force on Interrogations and Transfer Policy Issues to ensure that U.S. transfer practices comply with the domestic laws, U.S. international obligations, and policies of the United States and do not result in the transfer of individuals who would be more likely than not to be tortured....

555. … The Task Force made several recommendations aimed at clarifying and strengthening U.S. procedures for obtaining and evaluating diplomatic assurances from receiving countries for those transfers in which such assurances are obtained. These included a recommendation that the State Department be involved in evaluating all diplomatic assurances, and … recommendations aimed at improving the United States' monitoring of the treatment of individuals transferred to other countries. …

…

[Life without parole for juveniles]

678. This is an issue that has been raised by civil society in the United States as an issue of particular concern. Under a May 17, 2010, Supreme Court decision [*Graham v. Florida*], persons under the age of 18 at the time of the crime may not be sentenced to life in prison without the possibility of parole in the United States unless they have been convicted of homicide offenses. …

CONCLUDING OBSERVATIONS OF THE HUMAN RIGHTS COMMITTEE, ISLAMIC REPUBLIC OF IRAN

UN Doc. CCPR/C/IRN/CO/3 (29 Nov. 2011)

[Eds.: This is Iran's first report to the Committee since 1993. The report was submitted in 2010 (UN Doc. CCPR/C/IRN/3 (31 May 2010)). Iran's 18-person delegation included two Members of Parliament, and representatives of the Ministry of Foreign Affairs, the High Council for Human Rights, the Judicial Division of the Administrative Justice Tribunal, the Legal Division of the Judiciary, the Ministry of the Interior, the Office for Treaties, the Directorate for Human Rights, the Ministry of Culture and Islamic Guidance, the General Directorate for Foreign Media and the Iranian Permanent Mission in Geneva. The document alternates between diagnosis, in regular font, and prescriptions, in bold font.]

…

B. Positive aspects

4. The Committee welcomes:

[ratification of and accession to several human rights treaties].

C. Principal matters of concern and recommendations

5. The Committee notes with concern that reference is made in the State party's system to certain religious tenets as primary norms.

The State party should ensure that all the obligations of the Covenant are fully respected and that the provisions of its internal norms are not invoked as justification for its failure to fulfil its obligations under the Covenant.

…

7. …

The State party should consider establishing a national human rights institution with a broad human rights mandate, and provide it with adequate financial and human resources, in line with the Paris Principles.

...

9. The Committee is concerned about the continuing inequality of women with regard to marriage, family and inheritance matters (arts. 2 and 26).

The State party should amend the Civil Code and further amend the draft Family Protection Law, to (a) abolish the requirement for a father's or paternal grandfather's approval to legalize a marriage; (b) grant women equal rights to divorce; (c) award equal custody rights to the mother, including after a child reaches the age of seven or if she remarries; (d) award guardianship of a child to the mother in the case of the father's death; (e) grant women the same inheritance rights as men; (f) remove the legal obligation for a woman to be obedient to her husband; (g) remove the requirement for a husband's approval when a woman intends to leave the country; (h) prohibit polygamy; and (i) remove the power of a man to prohibit his wife from entering employment. The State party should also adopt legislation giving Iranian women the right to transmit their nationality to their children.

...

12. The Committee continues to be deeply concerned about the extremely high and increasing number of death sentences pronounced and carried out in the State party, the wide range and often vague definition of offences for which the death penalty is applied, and the large number of capital crimes and execution methods. The Committee is also concerned about the continued use of public executions, as well as stoning, as a method of execution. It also notes with concern the high rate of State executions in ethnic minority areas (arts. 6 and 7).

...

13. The Committee is gravely concerned about the continued execution of minors and the imposition of the death penalty for persons who were found to have committed a crime while under 18 years of age, which is prohibited by...the Covenant (art. 6).

...

16. The Committee is concerned about the continued imposition of corporal punishment by judicial and administrative authorities, in particular amputations and flogging for a range of crimes, including theft, enmity against God (*mohareb*) and certain sexual acts. It is also concerned that corporal punishment of children is lawful in the home, as a sentence of the courts and in alternative care settings (art. 7).

The State party should amend the Penal Code to abolish the imposition of corporal punishment by judicial and administrative authorities. The State party should also explicitly prohibit all forms of corporal punishment in child-rearing and education,...

...

19. ...

The State party should take immediate steps to establish a system of regular and genuinely independent monitoring of places of detention, and ensure that conditions of detention conform to articles 7 and 10 of the Covenant, and to the United Nations Standard Minimum Rules for Treatment of Prisoners....

20. The Committee is concerned about the persistent trafficking in women and children, particularly young girls from rural areas, often facilitated by temporary marriages (*siqeh*) (art. 8).

The State party should take steps to combat and prevent the trafficking and sale of persons under 18 years of age. The State party is also requested to provide the Committee in its next periodic report with statistics, on an annual basis, on the number of arrests and convictions under the 2004 law to combat trafficking.

21. The Committee is deeply concerned about the frequent violations of fair trial guarantees provided for under the Covenant, especially in the Revolutionary Courts and the Evin Prison Court....

...

22. The Committee is concerned that the independence of the judiciary is not fully guaranteed and is compromised by undue pressure from the Executive power, including the Office for Supervision and Evaluation of Judges, as well as senior clerics and high-ranking Government officials ahead of trials. The Committee is also concerned that judges have used Shari'a law and fatwas to reach a verdict that was in contravention of the rights and principles as laid down in the Covenant (art. 14).

...

26. The Committee is concerned that the right to freedom of assembly and association is severely limited, and notes that the holding of public gatherings and marches as well as the establishment of associations are conditional upon compliance with "principles of Islam", which are not defined under national legislation. The Committee is also concerned about continuing reports of harassment or intimidation, prohibition and forceful breaking up of demonstrations, and arrests and arbitrary detentions of human rights defenders. It notes with concern that human rights defenders and defence lawyers often serve prison sentences based on vaguely formulated crimes such as mohareb or the spreading of propaganda against the establishment. The Committee also notes in particular the large number of women's rights activists who have been arrested and detained, including volunteers and members of the One Million Signatures Campaign (arts. 19, 21 and 22).

The State party should ensure that the right to freedom of assembly and association is guaranteed to all individuals without discrimination, and release immediately and unconditionally anyone held solely for the peaceful exercise of this right....

...

REPORT ON KOSOVO (REPUBLIC OF SERBIA) SUBMITTED BY THE UNITED NATIONS INTERIM ADMINISTRATION MISSION IN KOSOVO (UNMIK)

UN Doc. A/61/40 (2006), Vol. I, p. 68

A. Introduction

2. The Committee welcomes the submission by [UNMIK] of a report on the human rights situation in Kosovo since 1999, pursuant to a request formulated by

the Committee in its concluding observations on the initial report of Serbia and Montenegro in 2004. The Committee notes with appreciation that UNMIK, on the basis of its obligations under Security Council resolution 1244 to protect and promote human rights in Kosovo, prepared its report in general conformity with the harmonized guidelines....

3. The Committee regrets the lack of statistical data and of information on the practical implementation of the Covenant in Kosovo since 1999. It appreciates the dialogue with the UNMIK delegation. The Committee acknowledges with appreciation the efforts undertaken by the Republic of Serbia to facilitate this dialogue....

...

B. Positive aspects

5. The Committee notes that the Covenant was made part of the applicable law in Kosovo,...binding on all persons undertaking public duties or holding public office in Kosovo, and that it was subsequently included in the Constitutional Framework for the Provisional Institutions of Self-Government, promulgated by UNMIK Regulation 2001/9.

...

C. Principal subjects of concern and recommendations

9. The Committee expresses its concern that, despite the establishment of various advisory bodies on human rights, as well as of human rights units within the Ministries, human rights concerns are often not sufficiently attended to in the programmes of UNMIK and the PISG [Provisional Institutions of Self-Government].

UNMIK, in cooperation with the PISG, should ensure that institutional structures and capacities are in place and actually utilized to fully integrate human rights in their programmes.

...

11. The Committee is concerned about the persistence of male-dominated attitudes within Kosovar society, low representation of women in the Ministries and central institutions of Kosovo, under-reporting of incidents of domestic violence, low numbers of convictions related to domestic violence, limited capacity of victim assistance programmes, and the absence of a comprehensive evaluation of the effectiveness of measures to combat domestic violence.

UNMIK, in cooperation with the PISG, should take prompt and effective measures with the goal of achieving equal representation of women in public offices and intensify training for judges, prosecutors and law enforcement officers on the application of existing laws and other instruments to combat gender discrimination and domestic violence. It should further facilitate the reporting of gender-related crimes, the obtaining of protection orders against perpetrators, enhance victim assistance programmes, and ensure effective remedies.

...

18. The Committee is concerned about the very low number of minority returns and the inability of displaced persons to recover their real property, including agricultural lands (art. 12).

UNMIK, in cooperation with PISG, should intensify efforts to ensure safe conditions for sustainable returns of displaced persons, in particular those belonging to minorities. In particular, it should ensure that they may recover their property, receive compensation for damage done and benefit from rental schemes for property temporarily administered by the Kosovo Property Agency.

...

23. The Committee requests that the text of the present report and these concluding observations be made public and broadly disseminated throughout Kosovo, and that the next periodic report be made available by relevant authorities to civil society and to non-governmental organizations operating in Kosovo.

NOTE

Since 2003, and with increasing emphasis in recent years, the Committee has sought to follow-up on its concluding observations by requesting states to provide the additional information or explanations sought. In 2009 it introduced five categories for evaluating states' follow-up information: (1) largely satisfactory; (2) cooperative but incomplete; (3) recommendation(s) not implemented; (4) receipt acknowledged (i.e., no substantive information); and (5) no response. The Committee's Special Rapporteur on follow-up sends reminders to states, seeks meetings with representatives and reports back to the Committee.[8] In some cases, this has yielded strong positive results, but in many instances it has resulted in a long and protracted correspondence. The Committee's experience with UNMIK has not been atypical in this respect. The Committee's follow-up action in response to some of its recommendations, such as paragraph 18 above, was requested to be provided by 1 January 2007. The Committee's 2011 report recounts the sending of various reminders, the receipt of incomplete replies and various meetings. It ends with the following entries:

> *28 September 2010* While taking note of the cooperativeness of UNMIK, the Committee sent a letter in which it noted the measures taken but indicated that none of the recommendations has been fully implemented.
>
> ...
>
> *20 July 2011* The [Committee's Special Rapporteur on follow-up] met with [an UNMIK official] who indicated that the supplementary information... would be forwarded before the October 2011 session.

Continuing discussions about how to render follow-up more effective across the system of treaty bodies have identified techniques such as the adoption of more detailed procedural guidelines for follow-up, enhancing the visibility of the process and considering in situ visits to countries.

[8] For an overview, see 'Follow-up procedures of human rights treaty bodies on concluding observations, inquiries and visits', UN Doc. HRI/ICM/WGFU/2011/2 (18 Nov. 2010).

QUESTIONS

1. What does the Committee's use of soft terminology such as 'regrets' or 'is concerned' say about the underlying assumptions of the process of 'constructive dialogue' and of the system's aspirations in terms of 'compelling' change at the domestic level?

2. The Committee's concluding observations on the United States run to 12 single-line-spaced pages, with no indication of priorities among the many concerns identified. Should the Committee indicate priority concerns? This would facilitate follow-up and make it easier for others, including domestic actors, to generate pressure for change in relation to the state concerned. Would it, however, undermine the principle of indivisibility of all rights? Would it be likely to lead to the downgrading of certain concerns — such as those relating to women, children and minorities — which might be less likely than anti-terrorism policies and torture to feature among the top concerns identified in relation to most countries?

3. What options are available to the various actors where the Committee and a government clearly disagree on legal interpretation as illustrated by the US position disputing the Committee's view that Article 7 obliges non-refoulement or prohibits renditions, or that Article 2 means the Covenant can apply to US activities 'outside its territory'. Consider the following statement by Prof. José Alvarez, President of the American Society of International Law, in 2006:

> A panoply of UN experts and assorted others — from human rights treaty bodies to the special rapporteur on torture — now routinely make ever more specific legal pronouncements — about such things as the propriety or consequences of "invalid" treaty reservations, specific interrogation techniques, or states' reliance on diplomatic assurances when engaging in the foreign rendition of suspects. While our Executive contests many of these pronouncements, even the 100 plus lawyers of the U.S. State Department are no match for the sheer quantity and variety of this institutionalized output, which, as amplified by the voice of organizations like Human Rights Watch, may achieve a legitimacy greater than the views of any single nation, including our own.[9]

4. How could the Committee seek to resolve factual disagreements, such as those that result when the US Government simply denies problems described in detail in reports submitted by Human Rights Watch and other groups to the Committee on issues such as prison rape, or the shackling of female prisoners when giving birth?

5. Do you see any differences in the positions taken by the United States between the 2006 process and its 2012 report?

6. In 2001, Jack Goldsmith warned against the incorporation of the ICCPR in US domestic law:

> [A] domesticated ICCPR would generate enormous litigation and uncertainty, potentially changing domestic civil rights law in manifold ways. Human rights

[9] José E. Alvarez, 'The Internationalization of U.S. Law' (28 Oct. 2006), at www.asil.org/aboutasil/documents/ILAweekend061102.pdf.

protections in the United States are not remotely so deficient as to warrant these costs. Although there is much debate around the edges of domestic civil and political rights law, there is a broad consensus about the appropriate content and scope of this law. This consensus has built up slowly over the past century. It is the product of years of judicial interpretation of domestic statutory and constitutional law, various democratic processes, lengthy and varied experimentation, and a great deal of practical local experience. Domestic incorporation of the ICCPR would threaten to upset this balance. It would constitute a massive, largely standardless delegation of power to federal courts to rethink the content and scope of nearly every aspect of domestic human rights law.[10]

Comment in light of the Committee's 2006 examination of the US report.

7. Iran is not a party to the CEDAW Convention. In response to questions, the delegation observed that women were treated differently due to 'physiological differences'. Did the Committee exceed its ICCPR mandate by virtue of the scope and specificity of its observations on women's rights?

8. What is the significance of the fact that the UN Mission (UNMIK) is presenting a report to the Committee which, in turn, addresses its concerns and recommendations to the Mission?

3. GENERAL COMMENTS

The text of the ICCPR is characteristically terse and ambiguous about what is intended by 'general comments'. Article 40, after setting forth the undertaking of states to submit periodic reports to the Committee, provides in paragraph 4 that the Committee 'shall study the reports' submitted by states and 'shall transmit its reports, and such *general comments* as it may consider appropriate' to the states (emphasis added). Under paragraph 5, states 'may submit to the Committee observations on any [such] comments'.

Many options existed for the interpretation of this opaque text, depending on how the Committee answered questions such as: Should the general comments be directed only to states' reports? Should they vary with the report, addressing concretely this or that problem of this or that state? Alternatively, should they remain truly 'general' in the sense that they do not pertain exclusively to one state but rather address issues of general relevance to all or many states? Should they deal only with the processes of reporting or also with substantive provisions of the Covenant? Should they elaborate upon those substantive provisions?

The following materials focus on such questions of institutional and systemic policy, as well as on a selection of the substantive issues addressed by the Committee in its General Comments.

[10] Jack Goldsmith, 'Should International Human Rights Law Trump US Domestic Law?', 1 Chi. J. Int'l. L. 327 (2000), at 332.

PHILIP ALSTON, THE HISTORICAL ORIGINS OF THE CONCEPT OF 'GENERAL COMMENTS' IN HUMAN RIGHTS LAW

in L. Boisson de Chazournes & V. Gowlland-Debbas (eds.), The International Legal System in Quest of Equity and Universality: Liber Amicorum Georges Abi-Saab (2001), at 763

It would be difficult to imagine a more oddly and even misleadingly named instrument than a 'General Comment'. What, after all, could be the jurisprudential value of a mere 'comment', and an explicitly 'general' one at that? Yet the adoption of such a statement is today one of the potentially most significant and influential tools available to each of the [then] six United Nations human rights treaty bodies....

...

The potential significance of General Comments derives from the fact that a great many international human rights norms are notoriously, but unavoidably, vague or open-ended. As Beccaria reminded us, terms such as 'rights' and 'obligations' are, in some respects at least, "abbreviated symbols of a rational argument" rather than ideas in themselves. It is thus hardly surprising that the governments, courts and administrators who are supposed to be applying them can invoke that vagueness, sometimes with conviction, sometimes not, sometimes creatively and other times brazenly, in ways which effectively avoid the 'risk' that the norms might have any significant practical impact....

[The author then recounts what he terms the 'improbable origins' of the concept of General Comments. The adoption of the phrase in 1966 followed extensive debate over whether any comments resulting from the Committee's examination of reports should be general or specific in nature. Neither side ever spelled out precisely what might have been envisaged by their respective formulae. It was thus left to the Committee, once the Covenant had entered into force over a decade later, to decide what to do. West European members of the Committee wanted country-specific and violations-focused comments to emerge from the reporting process. In contrast, the East Europeans rejected both specificity and appraisal and insisted that, since the Covenant was not a 'control mechanism', General Comments should be directed to all states parties rather than one. A compromise was adopted in 1980 under which such comments would be designed to 'promote co-operation' and 'stimulate activities' by states and would focus on procedural issues as well as 'questions related to the application and the content of individual articles of the Covenant'. It would not be until 1992 that the Committee would begin to adopt 'concluding observations' on states' reports.]

In many ways the evolution of General Comments from a concept of unclear and contested meaning to a tool of fundamental importance in the armoury of those seeking to promote international human rights law provides a classic case study of the techniques and processes which are so familiar to international lawyers, yet so puzzling and even dubious to many outsiders. The process has several steps. The first is the articulation of a series of clearly incompatible positions or perspectives in the context of diplomatic negotiations over the relevant treaty provisions. These provisions are then 'accommodated' within a draft text on which a compromise is able to be reached based on the incorporation of language which has already been used elsewhere and partly on the inherent open-endedness of the formulation adopted. While the proponents of each of the different starting positions insist that the outcome reflects, or at least fully compatible with, their preferred approach, all recognise implicitly that the key points of contention remain unresolved and that they will need to be addressed again in due course. A different group is then entrusted with the task of determining which interpretation will be adopted. That group (the Human Rights Committee, in this case) undertakes its own debate against a very different background and has a very different make-up. While arguments made in the original debate are cited in defence of the different positions put forward, the outcome actually reflects a significantly changed set of considerations....

COMMENT ON EVOLUTION OF GENERAL COMMENTS

Between 1981 and 2012 the ICCPR Committee adopted 34 General Comments. While most are devoted to specific rights or articles, there are also a number of wide-ranging General Comments which deal with broader issues such as reservations, emergencies, gender equality and states' obligations in general.[11]

A close reading of these Comments and of the evolution in style and substance reflected therein reveals that the Committee's record might usefully be understood by distinguishing four somewhat, but not entirely, separate phases in its approach to General Comments. They are: (1) consolidation of procedures — 1981–1983; (2) tentative first substantive steps — 1984–1988; (3) the post-Cold War period in which agreement could be reached on expansive interpretations of key substantive rights; and (4) since 2000 when the Committee has adopted an important set of umbrella comments designed to consolidate its understanding of the system as a whole.

The output in the first of these phases has been described as 'laconic', 'hesitant', 'bland and uninspiring'.[12] Judged by today's standards this is fair, but in fact the General Comments adopted during this phase played a very important

[11] The subjects and dates of adoption are as follows: No. 1 Reporting obligations (1981); No. 2 Reporting guidelines (1981); No. 3 Implementation at the national level (1981); No. 4 Equal right of men and women (1981); No. 5 Derogations; No. 6 Right to life (1982); No 7. Prohibition of torture or cruel, inhuman or degrading treatment or punishment (1982); No 8. Right to liberty and security of persons (1982); No 9. Article 10 (Humane treatment of persons deprived of their liberty (1982); No. 10 Freedom of opinion (1983); No. 11 Article 20 (propaganda for war and advocacy of hatred) (1983); No. 12 Right to self-determination (1984); No. 13 Administration of justice (1984); No. 14 Right to life (1984); No. 15 The position of aliens under the Covenant (1986); No. 16 Right to privacy (1998); No. 17 Rights of the child (1989); No. 18 Non-discrimination (1989); No. 19 The family (1990); No. 20 Prohibition of torture, or other cruel, inhuman or degrading treatment or punishment (1992); No. 21 Humane treatment of persons deprived of their liberty (1992); No. 22 Freedom of thought, conscience religion (1993); No. 23 Rights of minorities (1994); No. 24 Reservations (1994); No 25. Participation in public affairs and the right to vote (1996); No. 26 Continuity of obligations (1997); No. 27 Freedom of movement (1999); No. 28 The equality of rights between men and women (2000); No. 29 Derogations during a state of emergency (2001); No. 30 Reporting obligations (2002); No. 31 The Nature of the General Legal Obligation Imposed on States Parties to the Covenant (2004); No. 32 Right to a Fair Trial (2007); No. 33 Obligations of States Parties under the Optional Protocol (2008); No. 34 Freedom of opinion and expression (2011).

[12] T. Buergenthal, 'The Human Rights Committee', 5 Max Planck Yearbook of United Nations Law 341 (2001), at 387.

role in consolidating various procedural and organizational innovations in the Committee's working methods which, up until that point, might have been reversible. These included, for example, the 'requirement' that states' representatives make an oral presentation and respond to questions, and the need for states' reports to follow the Committee's reporting guidelines. Neither practice is specifically authorized by the terms of the Covenant. The caution of this phase was also justified by the need to ensure that states would acquiesce in the development of the notion of General Comments.

The second phase saw the adoption of only three Comments but they were considerably longer, more detailed and reflected more sophisticated legal analysis. The constraints imposed by political factors were nevertheless evident, both in the Comments that were adopted and those that were not (e.g., a long-term effort to adopt a draft on the rights of minorities had to be abandoned)[13] and the jurisprudential innovations were rather limited.

The third phase, after 1989, showed a Committee which had freed itself from most of the limitations that flowed from competing socialist and liberal perceptions both of the nature of human rights and of the appropriate role of treaty bodies and from the constraints that flowed from the early understandings of the limited functions of General Comments. It adopted expansive Comments on the rights of the child, non-discrimination and the family, and it marked a definitive break with the past by adopting revised Comments on Articles 7 and 10 of the Covenant which replaced the very tentative efforts it had made during the first phase with much longer and more assertive texts. The end of the influence of the Cold War was also strongly underlined by the range of topics on which detailed and progressive Comments were adopted after 1992. In particular, the Comments on freedom of expression (1993), minorities (1994), the right to vote and take part in government (1996) and freedom of movement (1999) could never have been agreed during the earlier phases and each contains very important jurisprudential elements.

The fourth phase, since 2000, has seen the Committee consolidate its views on the system as a whole with detailed and expansive statements on gender equality, rights in emergency contexts, reporting obligations, the legal nature of states' obligations and freedom of expression.

ILLUSTRATIONS OF GENERAL COMMENTS

In reading the sampling of General Comments (GCs) that follows you should re-read the relevant articles of the Covenant.[14] Consider: the functions played by GCs, what their evolution reflects in terms of the changing roles of the Covenant and of the Committee, what they reveal about the Committee's understanding of

[13] For the record of debates over an aborted draft, see UN Docs. CCPR/C/SR 590, 607, 618, 633 (1985).

[14] In addition to those excerpted below, other GCs feature elsewhere in the book. See e.g.: (1) GC No. 26 at p. 165, *supra*, on a state's withdrawal from the Covenant; (2) GC No. 22 at p. 604, *supra*, on freedom of religion; (3) GC No. 24 at p. 1097, *infra*, on reservations to the ICCPR; (4) GC No. 29 at p. 397, *supra*, on states of emergency; and (5) GC No. 32 at p. 470, *supra*, on the right to a fair trial.

the Covenant, the significance of GCs in expanding the interpretive reach of the Covenant and its norms and the relevance of GCs in relation to the human rights regime in general.

(1) Phase 1 (1981–1983)

> The purpose of [the Committee's] general comments is to make this experience available for the benefit of all States parties in order to promote their further implementation of the Covenant; to draw their attention to insufficiencies disclosed by a large number of reports; to suggest improvements in the reporting procedure and to stimulate the activities of these States and international organizations in the promotion and protection of human rights....[15]

GC No. 2, 'Reporting Guidelines' (1981):

> 3. The Committee considers that the reporting obligation embraces not only the relevant laws and other norms relating to the obligations under the Covenant but also the practices and decisions of courts and other organs of the State party....

GC No. 3, 'Implementation at the National Level' (1981):

> 1. The Committee notes that article 2 of the Covenant generally leaves it to the States parties concerned to choose their method of implementation in their territories within the framework set out in that article. It recognizes, in particular, that the implementation does not depend solely on constitutional or legislative enactments, which in themselves are often not per se sufficient.... [T]he obligation under the Covenant is not confined to the respect of human rights, but that States parties have also undertaken to ensure the enjoyment of these rights to all individuals under their jurisdiction. This aspect calls for specific activities by the States parties to enable individuals to enjoy their rights. [I]n principle this undertaking relates to all rights set forth in the Covenant.
>
> 2. In this connection, it is very important that individuals should know what their rights under the Covenant (and the Optional Protocol, as the case may be) are and also that all administrative and judicial authorities should be aware of the obligations which the State party has assumed under the Covenant. To this end, the Covenant should be publicized in all official languages of the State and steps should be taken to familiarize the authorities concerned with its contents as part of their training. It is desirable also to give publicity to the State party's cooperation with the Committee.

(2) Phase 2 (1984–1988)

GC No. 14, 'Article 6' (1984) builds on *GC No. 6, 'Article 6'* (1982). Both address the right to life, and their orientation reflects the revived influence of Cold War concerns, as well as efforts to explore how the ICCPR Covenant might relate to economic and social rights-type concerns. The Committee did not take up either of

[15] UN Doc. HRI/GEN/1/Rev.8 (2006).

these issues systematically in its later work. Consider the following excerpt from *GC No. 6*:

> 1. The right to life enunciated in article 6 of the Covenant has been dealt with in all State reports. It is the supreme right from which no derogation is permitted even in time of public emergency which threatens the life of the nation (art. 4). However, the Committee has noted that quite often the information given concerning article 6 was limited to only one or other aspect of this right. It is a right which should not be interpreted narrowly.
>
> ...
>
> 5. Moreover, the Committee has noted that the right to life has been too often narrowly interpreted. The expression 'inherent right to life' cannot properly be understood in a restrictive manner, and the protection of this right requires that States adopt positive measures. In this connection, the Committee considers that it would be desirable for States parties to take all possible measures to reduce infant mortality and to increase life expectancy, especially in adopting measures to eliminate malnutrition and epidemics.

Compare these provisions from the earlier GC with *GC No. 14*, two years later:

> 3. While remaining deeply concerned by the toll of human life taken by conventional weapons in armed conflicts, the Committee has noted that, during successive sessions of the General Assembly, representatives from all geographical regions have expressed their growing concern at the development and proliferation of increasingly awesome weapons of mass destruction, which not only threaten human life but also absorb resources that could otherwise be used for vital economic and social purposes, particularly for the benefit of developing countries, and thereby for promoting and securing the enjoyment of human rights for all.
>
> 4. The Committee associates itself with this concern. It is evident that the designing, testing, manufacture, possession and deployment of nuclear weapons are among the greatest threats to the right to life which confront mankind today. This threat is compounded by the danger that the actual use of such weapons may be brought about, not only in the event of war, but even through human or mechanical error or failure.
>
> ...
>
> 6. The production, testing, possession, deployment and use of nuclear weapons should be prohibited and recognized as crimes against humanity.
>
> 7. The Committee accordingly, in the interest of mankind, calls upon all States, whether Parties to the Covenant or not, to take urgent steps, unilaterally and by agreement, to rid the world of this menace.

GC No. 16, 'Article 17' (1988) (p. 21) elaborates the article's reference to interference with privacy. The following excerpt illustrates the Committee's preparedness to go into substantive issues in more depth and to read more into the terms of the Covenant than it had been prepared to do at the outset:

> 10. The gathering and holding of personal information on computers, databanks and other devices, whether by public authorities or private individuals or bodies,

must be regulated by law. Effective measures have to be taken by States to ensure that information concerning a person's private life does not reach the hands of persons who are not authorized by law to receive, process and use it, and is never used for purposes incompatible with the Covenant. In order to have the most effective protection of his private life, every individual should have the right to ascertain in an intelligible form, whether, and if so, what personal data is stored in automatic data files, and for what purposes. Every individual should also be able to ascertain which public authorities or private individuals or bodies control or may control their files. If such files contain incorrect personal data or have been collected or processed contrary to the provisions of the law, every individual should have the right to request rectification or elimination.

(3) Phase 3 (1989–1999)

GC No. 18, 'Non-discrimination' (1989) deals with several provisions of the Covenant — Articles 2, 3 and 26 among others — that state the principle of non-discrimination. Compare it with GC No. 28 on equality, adopted during the fourth phase.

7. ... [T]he Committee believes that the term 'discrimination' as used in the Covenant should be understood to imply any distinction, exclusion, restriction or preference which is based on any ground such as race, colour, sex, language, religion, political or other opinion, national or social origin, property, birth or other status, and which has the purpose or effect of nullifying or impairing the recognition, enjoyment or exercise by all persons, on an equal footing, of all rights and freedoms.

...

10. The Committee also wishes to point out that the principle of equality sometimes requires States parties to take affirmative action in order to diminish or eliminate conditions which cause or help to perpetuate discrimination prohibited by the Covenant. For example, in a State where the general conditions of a certain part of the population prevent or impair their enjoyment of human rights, the State should take specific action to correct those conditions. Such action may involve granting for a time to the part of the population concerned certain preferential treatment in specific matters as compared with the rest of the population. However, as long as such action is needed to correct discrimination in fact, it is a case of legitimate differentiation under the Covenant....

...

12. ... [A]rticle 26 does not merely duplicate the guarantee already provided for in article 2 but provides in itself an autonomous right.... [T]he application of the principle of non-discrimination contained in article 26 is not limited to those rights which are provided for in the Covenant.

13. [N]ot every differentiation of treatment will constitute discrimination, if the criteria for such differentiation are reasonable and objective and if the aim is to achieve a purpose which is legitimate under the Covenant.

GC No. 20, 'Article 7' (1992) concerns torture and cruel or degrading treatment or punishment. Note the detail in the following provisions that bear on implementation:

11. ... To guarantee the effective protection of detained persons, provisions should be made for detainees to be held in places officially recognized as places of detention and for their names and places of detention, as well as for the names of persons responsible for their detention, to be kept in registers readily available and accessible to those concerned, including relatives and friends. To the same effect, the time and place of all interrogations should be recorded, together with the names of all those present and this information should also be available for purposes of judicial or administrative proceedings. Provisions should also be made against incommunicado detention. In that connection, States parties should ensure that any places of detention be free from any equipment liable to be used for inflicting torture or ill-treatment. The protection of the detainee also requires that prompt and regular access be given to doctors and lawyers and, under appropriate supervision when the investigation so requires, to family members.

12. It is important for the discouragement of violations under article 7 that the law must prohibit the use of admissibility in judicial proceedings of statements or confessions obtained through torture or other prohibited treatment.

...

15. The Committee has noted that some States have granted amnesty in respect of acts of torture. Amnesties are generally incompatible with the duty of States to investigate such acts; to guarantee freedom from such acts within their jurisdiction; and to ensure that they do not occur in the future. States may not deprive individuals of the right to an effective remedy, including compensation and such full rehabilitation as may be possible.

(4) Phase 4 (2000–present)

Today, the Committee adopts a complete draft and then invites comments from all stakeholders. Thus, for example, in drafting GC No. 34 (*infra*) 18 states, a UN body, a regional organization, 4 national human rights institutions, 21 NGOs and 4 academics made submissions. Another important innovation in this phase is the inclusion of footnote references either to a set of concluding observations or of final views adopted by the Committee in response to a communication in order to establish or reinforce many of the propositions put forward, or to justify the examples given. GC No. 34, for example, consists of 15 pages including 117 footnotes.

GC No. 28, 'Equality of rights between men and women' (2000):

3. The obligation to ensure to all individuals the rights recognized in the Covenant, established in articles 2 and 3 of the Covenant, requires that States parties take all necessary steps to enable every person to enjoy those rights. These steps include the removal of obstacles to the equal enjoyment of such rights, the education of the population and of State officials in human rights, and the adjustment of domestic legislation so as to give effect to the undertakings set forth in the Covenant. The State party must not only adopt measures of protection, but also positive measures in all areas so as to achieve the effective and equal empowerment of women....

4. States parties are responsible for ensuring the equal enjoyment of rights without any discrimination. Articles 2 and 3 mandate States parties to take all steps necessary, including the prohibition of discrimination on the ground of sex,

to put an end to discriminatory actions, both in the public and the private sector, which impair the equal enjoyment of rights.

5. Inequality in the enjoyment of rights by women throughout the world is deeply embedded in tradition, history and culture, including religious attitudes. The subordinate role of women in some countries is illustrated by the high incidence of prenatal sex selection and abortion of female foetuses. States parties should ensure that traditional, historical, religious or cultural attitudes are not used to justify violations of women's right to equality before the law and to equal enjoyment of all Covenant rights....

GC No. 31, 'Nature of the General Legal Obligation' (2004):

2. While article 2 is couched in terms of the obligations of State parties towards individuals as the right-holders under the Covenant, every State party has a legal interest in the performance by every other State party of its obligations. This follows from the fact that the "rules concerning the basic rights of the human person" are *erga omnes* obligations.... [The Committee then urges States parties to make use of the so far moribund interstate complaints procedure provided for in Article 41.] To draw attention to possible breaches of Covenant obligations by other States parties and to call on them to comply with their Covenant obligations should, far from being regarded as an unfriendly act, be considered as a reflection of legitimate community interest.

...

4. The obligations of the Covenant in general and article 2 in particular are binding on every State party as a whole. All branches of government (executive, legislative and judicial), and other public or governmental authorities, at whatever level (national, regional or local) are in a position to engage the responsibility of the State party. The executive branch that usually represents the State party internationally, including before the Committee, may not point to the fact that an action incompatible with the provisions of the Covenant was carried out by another branch of government as a means of seeking to relieve the State party from responsibility for the action and consequent incompatibility....

...

13. Article 2, paragraph 2, requires that States parties take the necessary steps to give effect to the Covenant rights in the domestic order....Article 2 allows a State party to pursue this in accordance with its own domestic constitutional structure and accordingly does not require that the Covenant be directly applicable in the courts, by incorporation of the Covenant into national law. The Committee takes the view, however, that Covenant guarantees may receive enhanced protection in those States where the Covenant is automatically or through specific incorporation part of the domestic legal order....

14. The requirement under article 2, paragraph 2, to take steps to give effect to the Covenant rights is unqualified and of immediate effect. A failure to comply with this obligation cannot be justified by reference to political, social, cultural or economic considerations within the State.

15. Article 2, paragraph 3, requires that in addition to effective protection of Covenant rights States parties must ensure that individuals also have accessible and effective remedies to vindicate those rights. Such remedies should be appropriately adapted so as to take account of the special vulnerability of certain categories

of person, including in particular children. The Committee attaches importance to States parties' establishing appropriate judicial and administrative mechanisms for addressing claims of rights violations under domestic law.... National human rights institutions, endowed with appropriate powers, can contribute to this end. A failure by a State party to investigate allegations of violations could in and of itself give rise to a separate breach of the Covenant. Cessation of an ongoing violation is an essential element of the right to an effective remedy.

16. Article 2, paragraph 3, requires that States parties make reparation to individuals whose Covenant rights have been violated.... [T]he Covenant generally entails appropriate compensation. The Committee notes that, where appropriate, reparation can involve restitution, rehabilitation and measures of satisfaction, such as public apologies, public memorials, guarantees of non-repetition and changes in relevant laws and practices, as well as bringing to justice the perpetrators of human rights violations.

17. In general, the purposes of the Covenant would be defeated without an obligation integral to article 2 to take measures to prevent a recurrence of a violation of the Covenant....

18. ... [W]here public officials or State agents have committed violations of the Covenant rights referred to in [Articles 6, 7 or 9], the States parties concerned may not relieve perpetrators from personal responsibility, as has occurred with certain amnesties (see general comment No. 20 (44)) and prior legal immunities and indemnities. Furthermore, no official status justifies persons who may be accused of responsibility for such violations being held immune from legal responsibility. Other impediments to the establishment of legal responsibility should also be removed, such as the defence of obedience to superior orders or unreasonably short periods of statutory limitation in cases where such limitations are applicable. States parties should also assist each other to bring to justice persons suspected of having committed acts in violation of the Covenant that are punishable under domestic or international law.

...

GC No. 34, 'Article 19: Freedoms of opinion and expression' (2011):

...

Freedom of expression

11. Paragraph 2 requires States parties to guarantee the right to freedom of expression, including the right to seek, receive and impart information and ideas of all kinds regardless of frontiers. This right includes the expression and receipt of communications of every form of idea and opinion capable of transmission to others, subject to the provisions in article 19, paragraph 3, and article 20. It includes political discourse, commentary on one's own and on public affairs, canvassing, discussion of human rights, journalism, cultural and artistic expression, teaching, and religious discourse. It may also include commercial advertising. The scope of paragraph 2 embraces even expression that may be regarded as deeply offensive, although such expression may be restricted in accordance with the provisions of article 19, paragraph 3 and article 20.

12. Paragraph 2 protects all forms of expression and the means of their dissemination. Such forms include spoken, written and sign language and such non-verbal expression as images and objects of art. Means of expression include books, newspapers, pamphlets, posters, banners, dress and legal submissions. They

include all forms of audio-visual as well as electronic and internet-based modes of expression.

Freedom of expression and the media

13. A free, uncensored and unhindered press or other media is essential in any society to ensure freedom of opinion and expression and the enjoyment of other Covenant rights. It constitutes one of the cornerstones of a democratic society....

...

Right of access to information

18. Article 19, paragraph 2 embraces a right of access to information held by public bodies. Such information includes records held by a public body, regardless of the form in which the information is stored, its source and the date of production....

...

Limitative scope of restrictions on freedom of expression in certain specific areas

37. Among restrictions on political discourse that have given the Committee cause for concern are the prohibition of door-to-door canvassing, restrictions on the number and type of written materials that may be distributed during election campaigns, blocking access during election periods to sources, including local and international media, of political commentary, and limiting access of opposition parties and politicians to media outlets. Every restriction should be compatible with paragraph 3. However, it may be legitimate for a State party to restrict political polling imminently preceding an election in order to maintain the integrity of the electoral process.

38. ... [T]he mere fact that forms of expression are considered to be insulting to a public figure is not sufficient to justify the imposition of penalties, albeit public figures may also benefit from the provisions of the Covenant. Moreover, all public figures, including those exercising the highest political authority such as heads of state and government, are legitimately subject to criticism and political opposition. Accordingly, the Committee expresses concern regarding laws on such matters as, *lese majeste*, *desacato*, disrespect for authority, disrespect for flags and symbols, defamation of the head of state and the protection of the honour of public officials, and laws should not provide for more severe penalties solely on the basis of the identity of the person that may have been impugned. States parties should not prohibit criticism of institutions, such as the army or the administration.

...

48. Prohibitions of displays of lack of respect for a religion or other belief system, including blasphemy laws, are incompatible with the Covenant, except in the specific circumstances envisaged in article 20, paragraph 2, of the Covenant. Such prohibitions must also comply with the strict requirements of article 19, paragraph 3, as well as such articles as 2, 5, 17, 18 and 26. Thus, for instance, it would be impermissible for any such laws to discriminate in favour of or against one or certain religions or belief systems, or their adherents over another, or religious believers over non-believers. Nor would it be permissible for such prohibitions to be used to prevent or punish criticism of religious leaders or commentary on religious doctrine and tenets of faith.

...

NOTE

Consider the following suggested ideal approach to GCs in the future. It is put forward on the basis of a lengthy analysis of current practice, and reflects legitimacy-based criteria identified by Helen Keller and Leena Grover, 'General Comments of the Human Rights Committee and their Legitimacy', in H. Keller & G. Ulfstein (eds.), *UN Human Rights Treaty Bodies: Law and Legitimacy* (2012), 116, at 193:

> Structurally, the General Comment would contain a statement of purpose and headings that distinguish between its legal analytical, policy recommendation and practice direction functions. Permissive (e.g. 'may') and mandatory language (e.g. 'shall') would be used in accordance with a practice direction that the Committee applies to the drafting of all General Comments. For example, mandatory language would be used in the legal analytical portion of all General Comments and permissive language in the policy recommendation section. If defining a Covenant right, interpretive findings would respect the wording of the Covenant. These findings would either be supported by footnotes citing to past Views of the Committee that adhere to secondary rules of interpretation, or else by such interpretive reasoning in the General Comment itself. The scope of the relevant right would be defined in the following ways, if possible: to whom it applies, who owes corresponding duties, where it applies, what activities and/or objects are protected, when the right and corresponding duties are triggered and how the right relates to other rights in the Covenant. Limitations to the right would be explained, its derogability indicated and legal tests and factors included for determining its violation provided. Interpretive aids would be cited and include relevant hard and soft international laws with a view to harmonisation where appropriate. Where the General Comment tries to fill a legal gap in the Covenant, applicable law would be invoked in a manner that respects the secondary rules on sources of international law.
>
> The process for selecting the topic for the General Comment, for selecting the principal drafter, and for drafting and adopting the General Comment would be the same for all General Comments and provided for in the Committee's Rules of Procedure, as would rules about how state and non-state actors may submit observations to the Committee during this drafting process. All of these rules would be accessible on the website of the OHCHR. The first draft of the General Comment would also have been made available to the public on this website, and debates on it within the Committee live streamed and archived. Relevant documents influencing these debates, including submissions by state and non-state actors on the content of the draft General Comment would also be on the OHCHR website....

QUESTIONS

1. GCs are often characterized as authoritative interpretations of the Covenant, yet Keller and Grover conclude that 'General Comments are not legally binding', a position that they say is borne out by the views expressed by governments and judges. They describe them instead as '"secondary soft law instruments", meaning sources of

non-binding norms that interpret and add detail to the [relevant] rights and obligations.'[16] On what grounds might it be argued that they are binding?

2. How do you react to the suggestions made by Keller and Grover? Would the template they propose change the nature of GCs for better or for worse? In terms of the transparency of the process, live streaming of the public sessions of treaty bodies began in 2012, but comments by states and others on draft GCs are still not made publicly available by the Committee. Should they be, and why do you think they are currently not available?

3. In paragraph 14 of GC No. 31, the Committee says the requirement in Article 2(2) to 'take the necessary steps ... to adopt such legislative or other measures as may be necessary to give effect to the rights' is 'unqualified and of immediate effect'. It goes on to state that 'failure to comply with this obligation cannot be justified by reference to ... economic considerations within the State'. What do you think this means in practice? The prevention of torture as a technique of policing, for example, usually requires careful training of law enforcement personnel, the creation of effective monitoring and complaints mechanisms and the existence of a vigilant and independent judiciary. How do Sweden's obligations differ from Swaziland's?

4. The Executive Director of Human Rights Watch has stated that, in its work on prison conditions, his organization 'routinely avoids recommending large infrastructure investments' and instead 'focus[es] on improvements in the treatment of prisoners that would involve relatively inexpensive policy changes. Similarly, our advocacy of due process in places such as Rwanda with weak and impoverished judicial systems implicitly takes account of the practical limitations facing the country leading us to be more tolerant of prosecutorial compromises such as *gacaca* courts than we would be in a richer country.'[17] Is this approach consistent with GC No. 31?

COMMENT ON SOME CONTROVERSIES ADDRESSED IN GCs

In some important instances GCs have been the Committee's chosen vehicle for propounding far-reaching and often controversial, interpretations of the Covenant. Consider the following examples relating to reservations, succession and jurisdiction.

(1) Reservations: GC No. 24 (1994)[18]

> 8. ... [P]rovisions in the Covenant that represent customary international law (and a fortiori when they have the character of peremptory norms) may not be the subject of reservations. Accordingly, a State may not reserve the right to engage in slavery, to torture, to subject persons to cruel, inhuman or degrading treatment or

[16] Keller & Grover, p. 802, *supra*, at 129.

[17] Kenneth Roth, 'Defending Economic, Social and Cultural Rights: Practical Issues Faced by an International Human Rights Organization', 26 Hum. Rts. Q. 63 (2004).

[18] Note that more detailed excerpts from this GC appear at p. 1097, *infra*.

punishment, to arbitrarily deprive persons of their lives, to arbitrarily arrest and detain persons, to deny freedom of thought, conscience and religion, to presume a person guilty unless he proves his innocence, to execute pregnant women or children, to permit the advocacy of national, racial or religious hatred, to deny to persons of marriageable age the right to marry, or to deny to minorities the right to enjoy their own culture, profess their own religion, or use their own language. And while reservations to particular clauses of article 14 may be acceptable, a general reservation to the right to a fair trial would not be.

...

18. It necessarily falls to the Committee to determine whether a specific reservation is compatible with the object and purpose of the Covenant. This is in part because, as indicated above, it is an inappropriate task for States parties in relation to human rights treaties, and in part because it is a task that the Committee cannot avoid in the performance of its functions. In order to know the scope of its duty to examine a State's compliance under article 40 or a communication under the first Optional Protocol, the Committee has necessarily to take a view on the compatibility of a reservation with the object and purpose of the Covenant and with general international law. Because of the special character of a human rights treaty, the compatibility of a reservation with the object and purpose of the Covenant must be established objectively, by reference to legal principles, and the Committee is particularly well placed to perform this task....

Nowak notes that, prior to the adoption of GC No. 24, several members of the Committee had expressed the view that it was not authorized to review the validity of reservations. He notes that several governments — in particular France, the United States, and the United Kingdom — expressly objected to some of the conclusions reached in the GC, and that some academic commentators have also been critical.[19] Nowak characterizes GC No. 24 as 'one of the most important legal documents ever adopted on the controversial question of reservations to human rights treaties'. While supportive of the Committee's conclusions as to its own competence, he questions the broad range of reasons given to justify the incompatibility:

First of all, the Committee made no clear distinction between customary international law and peremptory norms (ius cogens).... Secondly, the list of provisions regarded as representing customary law seems far too broad.... [Since rights relating to self-determination, marriage, minorities and incitement to hatred] have in fact been the subject of reservations by a considerable number of States, it is not surprising that Governments objected to this comprehensive list which, according to the Committee, may not be the subject of reservations.[20]

In written comments, submitted in 1995, France rejected the 'entire analysis' contained in paragraph 18 and stated that:

As for the opinion that the Committee is particularly well placed to take decisions on the compatibility of a reservation with the object and purpose of the Covenant,

[19] Nowak, *UN Covenant on Civil and Political Rights: ICCPR Commentary* (2nd edn. 2005), pp. xxxi–xxxiii.

[20] See n. 19.

France points out that the Committee, like any other treaty body or similar body established by agreement, owes its existence exclusively to the treaty and has no powers other than those conferred on it by the States parties; it is therefore for the latter, and for them alone, unless the treaty states otherwise, to decide whether a reservation is incompatible with the object and purpose of the treaty.[21]

(2) Succession and denunciation: GC No. 26 (1997)

Two very important issues in relation to treaty law concern whether: (1) a successor state is automatically bound by the international human rights treaty obligations of its predecessor; and (2) whether a state which is a party to the ICCPR can denounce it, and is thus no longer bound by its provisions. The text of the Covenant is silent on both issues, although Article 12 of the First Optional Protocol to the ICCPR explicitly provides for a state to denounce the Protocol.

GC No. 26, Continuity of obligations (1997):

1. [The Committee observes that the issue is governed by customary law as reflected in the Vienna Convention on the Law of Treaties]. On this basis, the Covenant is not subject to denunciation or withdrawal unless it is established that the parties intended to admit the possibility of denunciation or withdrawal or a right to do so is implied from the nature of the treaty.

2. [The Committee notes that denunciation is specifically provided for in relation to (i) the interstate procedure under Article 41(2); (ii) the First Optional Protocol to the ICCPR; and (iii) the International Convention on the Elimination of All Forms of Racial Discrimination, adopted before the ICCPR.] It can therefore be concluded that the drafters of the Covenant deliberately intended to exclude the possibility of denunciation. The same conclusion applies to the Second Optional Protocol in the drafting of which a denunciation clause was deliberately omitted.

3. Furthermore, it is clear that the Covenant is not the type of treaty which, by its nature, implies a right of denunciation. Together with the simultaneously prepared and adopted [ICESCR], the Covenant codifies in treaty form the universal human rights enshrined in the [UDHR], the three instruments together often being referred to as the "International Bill of Human Rights". As such, the Covenant does not have a temporary character typical of treaties where a right of denunciation is deemed to be admitted, notwithstanding the absence of a specific provision to that effect.

4. The rights enshrined in the Covenant belong to the people living in the territory of the State party. The Human Rights Committee has consistently taken the view, as evidenced by its long-standing practice, that once the people are accorded the protection of the rights under the Covenant, such protection devolves with territory and continues to belong to them, notwithstanding change in government of the State party, including dismemberment in more than one State or State succession or any subsequent action of the State party designed to divest them of the rights guaranteed by the Covenant.

5. The Committee is therefore firmly of the view that international law does not permit a State which has ratified or acceded or succeeded to the Covenant to denounce it or withdraw from it.

[21] UN Doc. CCPR A/51/40 (1995), Annex VI, para. 14.

The succession issue arose in relation to some of the successor states to the former Soviet Union and Hong Kong and Macau. While most of the former group accepted the continuing applicability of the ICCPR obligations, they nonetheless deposited instruments of succession, rather than assuming the automaticity of the process.[22] Kazakhstan was the exception, but the Committee continued to treat it as a state party and requested reports. Eventually, in 2006, Kazakhstan ratified the Covenant. When China resumed its control of Hong Kong and Macau in 1997 it also agreed to succeed to the pertinent ICCPR obligations of the United Kingdom (in relation to Hong Kong) and Portugal (Macau), and has since presented a report to the ICCPR Committee on compliance with the Covenant in those two territories.

Denunciation was more complex. The GC was adopted in October 1997 in direct response to North Korea's purported denunciation of the ICCPR, lodged with the UN in August 1997. North Korea did not pursue it plans, and subsequently presented a report to the Committee. But other states had also previously contemplated denunciation. Thus, for example, the Netherlands considered withdrawal after decisions of the ICCPR Committee on non-discrimination in relation to social security law which had major financial implications.[23]

(3) Jurisdiction

Consider the following extracts from GC No. 31 on the 'Nature of the General Legal Obligation' (2004) in light of the objections raised by the United States in its reporting to the Committee, excerpted above.[24]

> 10. States parties are required by article 2, paragraph 1, to respect and to ensure the Covenant rights to all persons who may be within their territory and to all persons subject to their jurisdiction. This means that a State party must respect and ensure the rights laid down in the Covenant to anyone within the power or effective control of that State party, even if not situated within the territory of the State party.... This principle also applies to those within the power or effective control of the forces of a State party acting outside its territory, regardless of the circumstances in which such power or effective control was obtained, such as forces constituting a national contingent of a State party assigned to an international peacekeeping or peace-enforcement operation.
>
> 11. As implied in general comment No. 29, the Covenant applies also in situations of armed conflict to which the rules of international humanitarian law are applicable. While, in respect of certain Covenant rights, more specific rules of international humanitarian law may be especially relevant for the purposes of the interpretation of Covenant rights, both spheres of law are complementary, not mutually exclusive.
>
> 12. Moreover, the article 2 obligation requiring that States parties respect and ensure the Covenant rights for all persons in their territory and all persons under their control entails an obligation not to extradite, deport, expel or otherwise remove a person from their territory, where there are substantial grounds for

[22] One Committee member subsequently indicated in remarks under an Optional Protocol case that he agreed with para. 4 of GC No. 26 'as a matter of policy, but I cannot agree with it as a statement of a rule of customary international law' (Mr Ando in *Kuok Koi v. Portugal*, No. 925/00).

[23] See *Broeks v. The Netherlands*, No. 172/1984; and generally Nowak, n. 20 *supra*, p. xxxvi.

[24] See p. 773, *supra*.

believing that there is a real risk of irreparable harm, such as that contemplated by articles 6 and 7 of the Covenant, either in the country to which removal is to be effected or in any country to which the person may subsequently be removed.

Consider the following defence of the Committee's position by Nowak:

> States are basically responsible only for the legal security of persons who are located on their territory and subject to their sovereign authority. This means, on the one hand, that States parties are not responsible for violations of the Covenant by persons who are on their territory but not subject to their jurisdiction (e.g., for actions by international organizations against their officials or for actions by occupation troops). On the other hand, this means that States are not responsible for violations against persons over whom they have personal jurisdiction (in particular, nationals), when such violations take place on foreign territory and are attributable to some other sovereign. The motive behind the formulation of Art. 2(1) was to preclude this responsibility of States parties.
>
> When States parties, however, take *actions on foreign territory* that violate the rights of persons subject to their sovereign authority, it would be contrary to the purpose of the Covenant if they could not be held responsible. It is irrelevant whether these actions are permissible under general international law (e.g., sovereign act by diplomatic or consular representatives, or in border traffic or by border officials in customs-free zones; actions by occupation forces in accordance with the rules of the law of war) or constitute illegal interference, such as the kidnapping of persons by secret service agents.
>
> Departing from earlier views in the literature, which had adhered to a literal reading of Art. 2(1), the Committee has sought to correct the wording of this provision by developing case law oriented along the object and purpose of the Covenant and affording increased legal protection. In the first place, it has made it clear that persons who have fled abroad are not prevented by Art. 2(1) from submitting individual communications. Second, in the so-called *Passport cases* concerning Uruguay, it held that States parties are also responsible for violations of the Covenant (at least of Art. 12) by foreign diplomatic representatives. Third, it has considered communications by persons who had been kidnapped by Uruguayan agents in neighbouring States to be admissible, reasoning that States parties are responsible for the actions of their agents on foreign territory.[25]

QUESTIONS

1. In its 1987 Restatement (Third), the American Law Institute lists the following customary law prohibitions: genocide, slavery, murder, disappearance, torture etc., prolonged arbitrary detention, systematic racial discrimination, or a consistent pattern of gross violations of internationally recognized human rights. Compare this with the Committee's list in GC No. 24.

2. What are the characteristics of the ICCPR which make it the type of treaty which is not susceptible to denunciation? How potentially far-reaching are the implications of the Committee's reasoning, especially in paragraph 3 of GC No. 26?

[25] Nowak, n. 19 *supra*, at pp. 43–4.

3. Is the Committee's reasoning persuasive in defence of its interpretation of Article 2(1) as covering persons who are subject to a state's jurisdiction, even when they are not within its territory?

4. INDIVIDUAL COMMUNICATIONS[26]

COMMENT ON COMMUNICATIONS

As of May 2012, 114 of the 167 states parties to the ICCPR were also parties to the First Optional Protocol, which allows for individuals to submit 'communications' (complaints). Note some of its critical provisions. The communications must be 'from individuals...who claim to be victims of a violation' by a state party to the Protocol 'of any of the rights set forth in the Covenant'. After being notified of the communication, the state party shall 'submit to the Committee written explanations or statements clarifying the matter ...'. The Committee considers communications 'in the light of all written information made available to it by the individual and by the State Party concerned.' It will not consider a communication before ascertaining that the matter is 'not being examined under another procedure of international investigation or settlement'. Examination of the communications takes place at 'closed meetings'. The Committee is to forward 'its views' to the individual and state concerned. The goals of the procedure are said to be to: (1) enable the Committee 'to identify steps that States should take to comply with their international legal obligations in the context of concrete individual situations'; (2) to 'offer individual relief to victims of human rights violations'; and (3) to 'stimulate general legal, policy and programme change'.[27]

The historical background to the adoption of the Optional Protocol highlights two aspects: (1) the deep disagreement over whether such a procedure was appropriate; and (2) the extremely vague understanding of how such a procedure should work which emerged from the hurried drafting process. Consider the following description:

> [A complaints procedure] was intensely discussed in the early stages of the [Human Rights Commission's] deliberations [in drafting the Covenant]. In 1950, the [General Assembly] called upon the [Human Rights Commission] 'to proceed with the consideration of provisions, to be inserted in the draft covenant or in separate protocols, for the receipt and examination of petitions from individuals and organizations with respect to alleged violations of the covenant.' However, all the [relevant drafts] were either withdrawn or defeated, usually by narrow majorities.[28]

[26] All but one of the main UN human right treaties provide for communications procedures, although not all have yet entered into force. The ICCPR Committee, however, is the oldest of them all and has received and examined far more complaints than the others put together. See Table 9.1 at p. 840, *infra*.

[27] UN Doc. HRI/MC/2006/2 (2006), para. 9.

[28] Nowak, 'Historical Background to the OP', in *UN Covenant on Civil and Political Rights: ICCPR Commentary* (2nd edn. 2005), at 821.

> Since the [Human Rights Commission] was dominated by proponents of State sovereignty, the draft adopted in 1954 contained no provision for an individual communication.
>
> Twelve years passed before the [General Assembly] once again took up this issue. In 1966 the Netherlands [proposed] an optional right of communication on the part of individuals and groups; in a supplementary motion, Jamaica even sought to make this procedure obligatory.... But opposition persisted from a variety of States, particularly Socialist countries, all of whom viewed the individual communication as a violation of State sovereignty, a threat to international relations and a departure from the principle that individuals are not subjects of international law. On account of this, France introduced a compromise that sought to limit the function of the Committee to the mere acknowledgement of and confidential reply to communications by individuals and groups. The three drafts were ultimately withdrawn in favour of a proposal introduced by 10 States from all geopolitical regions with the exception of Eastern Europe. [In response to warnings by the Socialist states] that the adoption of this proposal in the text of the Covenant would threaten its chances for ratification, [it was proposed to make the protocol separate and optional]....
>
> Time began to run out for the concrete drafting of the OP. The text finally adopted is based on a Nigerian proposal, which was clearly oriented along the "10 State Draft".... This motion was then discussed quite superficially, which means that the *travaux préparatoires* are of only limited assistance for the interpretation of the various provisions of the OP. The time pressure under which these provisions were drafted led to a rather rudimentary description of the procedure, to systematic absurdities and to lack of clarity at points. It is thus not incorrect to assume that the Committee had been provided with quite wide discretion...to work out the details of the procedure....

The resulting provisions led to the adoption of a rather barebones procedure. Note the following characteristics:

1. The proceedings are in no sense a continuation of, or appeal from, judicial proceedings (if there were any) in the state in which the dispute originated. They are fresh, distinct proceedings that may involve the same two parties to prior proceedings, or different parties.
2. Unlike some complaints procedures, communications to the ICCPR Committee need not allege that the violation complained of is systemic — that is, involves a consistent pattern of violations reaching a certain level of gravity. Thus, an isolated, atypical violation can suffice to found a communication.
3. There are no provisions for oral hearings, let alone direct confrontation between the parties, or for independent fact-finding (such as examination of the parties or witnesses or independent experts, or on-site visits) by the Committee. The Optional Protocol refers only to written proceedings. This contrasts with both the CERD Committee and the CAT Committee which can meet with the petitioner or her representative.
4. There are no public hearings or debates by the Committee about how to deal with a particular communication.

5. There is no provision setting forth the precise legal effect of Views, and certainly no provision in the text to indicate that the Views are binding. Nor does the text set forth what follow-up should take place if the Committee's Views indicating that a state should take particular action (such as payment of compensation or release of a prisoner) are ignored by that state.

But the procedures described in these provisions have evolved significantly through the practice of the Committee. This evolving practice sets the scene for the main challenge in evaluating the work of the Committee under the Optional Protocol: how to reconcile the paucity of powers and resources given to the Committee for this purpose as a reflection of the determinedly modest original vision of the drafters, with the substantial subsequent evolution of the Committee's, and more generally the human rights regime's, aspirations in relation to such procedures. The questions to focus upon in reading the following materials are: (1) the extent to which the ICCPR Committee is using rather primitive tools to achieve increasingly sophisticated goals; and (2) whether such an approach is sustainable without major procedural innovations designed to create a better equilibrium between the tools used and the goals sought.

The Committee's Caseload

Between 1977 and 2011 the Committee registered 2,076 communications concerning 85 states parties. Of those, 882 led to the adoption of Views, including 731 in which violations of the Covenant were found. There were 569 declared inadmissible, 302 which were discontinued or withdrawn and 323 were pending. Of 151 cases reported as having been decided in the year 2010–2011, five involved governments that failed to cooperate at all with the Committee (Belarus, Kyrgyzstan, Libya, South Africa and Tajikistan).

The Committee's Working Methods

Complaints which are submitted to the UN Secretary-General and which allege a violation of the ICCPR by a state party to the Optional Protocol are sent on to the Committee's Special Rapporteur on New Communications, who may decide to register them and send them on to states for a response. In appropriate circumstances he or she might also request interim measures (see p. 832, *infra*). The Working Group on Communications meets for one week prior to each of the Committee's sessions, and can declare some communications to be inadmissible without needing to refer them to the government concerned. While the Protocol envisages two separate stages in the examination of a communication — the first considering its admissibility and the second examining the merits of a complaint once it has been declared admissible — the Committee's practice now generally involves consideration of both issues at the same time. The bulk of the Committee's work on any particular communication is carried out by the Special Rapporteur and the Working Group, and the Committee as a whole will generally only examine a communication once in light of the recommendations of the Working Group.

This description of the formalities does little to capture the key challenges confronting members of the Committee in their work on communications. Consider the following comment by a former Committee member:

> ... When dealing with communications, members...listen to each other, learn from each other, adjust their own prejudices and assumptions and try to reach an agreed position. But it is not always possible to agree. In the past few years, there has been a tendency...to adopt individual opinions.... Some decisions of the Committee appear rather obscure or brief because of amendments and deletions carried out in order to arrive at consensus. While consensus is desirable and maintains the collegial approach and the anonymity of decisions, in some cases the price of consensus is too high.... In those cases it is better for different shades of opinion to be separately presented rather than to undermine or truncate the reasoning of the majority.[29]

Findings of Fact

One of the biggest challenges for the Committee is its inability to undertake independent fact-finding when confronted with contradictory evidence offered by a complainant and a state party. Consider, for example, the following response by the Committee to a claim that an individual on death row in Guyana had been tortured:

> 5.1 ... In the current case, the Committee notes that the testimony of 3 doctors at the trial, that Mr. Deolall displayed injuries,...as well as Mr. Deolall's own statement, would prima facie support the allegation that such ill-treatment indeed occurred during the police interrogations, prior to his signing of the confession statement....
>
> 5.2 The Committee maintains its position that it is generally not in the position to evaluate facts and evidence presented before a domestic court. In the current case, however, the Committee takes the view that the instructions to the jury raise an issue under article 14 of the Covenant, as the defendant had managed to present prima facie evidence of being mistreated, and the Court did not alert the jury that the prosecution must prove that the confession was made without duress. This error constituted a violation of Mr. Deolall's right to a fair trial as required by the Covenant, as well as his right not to be compelled to testify against himself or confess guilt....[30]

In dealing with cases in which clearly conflicting evidence is presented, it has been observed that:

> The HRC's Views often give little information regarding what evidence it considered and why it accorded the evidence the value it did....
>
> ...

[29] E. Evatt, 'Reflecting on the Role of International Communications in Implementing Human Rights', 5(2) Australian J. of Hum. Rts. 20 (1999).

[30] *Deolall v. Guyana*, Communication No. 912/2000, UN Doc. CCPR/C/82/D/912/2000 (28 Jan. 2005).

> The HRC appears to rely frequently on circumstantial evidence, including evidence of a consistent pattern of conduct.... The use of inference can be highly prejudicial to a state party as it is a very small shift in logic to conclude from the existence of a general pattern that this person, the author, suffered from the alleged violation. It therefore becomes particularly important that the HRC identify the circumstantial evidence, such as patterns of conduct, that it is using to raise an inference or a rebuttable presumption.[31]

The same author suggests that there are ways in which the Committee could transform the process if it wished to do so. In particular she advocates the use of oral proceedings and, based on the Committee's willingness to adopt innovative procedures in so many other respects, rejects the argument that it does not have competence to initiate such an approach. In her view:

> The Committee's refusal...is probably more motivated by logistics: oral proceedings would increase the HRC's workload when it already lacks adequate means to deal with its current burden....
>
> The HRC's fact-finding could also be enhanced if it were enabled to go beyond the materials provided by the parties.... This would not necessarily entail embarking on on-site missions or extensive research in every case. In some cases, the HRC could simply charge its Secretariat with using material obtained through other treaty or U.N. bodies that would confirm the author's allegations. In addition, there are many NGOs that could be invited to provide evidence in support of allegations, such as corroborative testimony or relevant statistics.
>
> The HRC is in no way barred from sending missions to a state party where that state party has consented....[32]

QUESTION

How feasible do you consider these various proposals to be? Would they transform the role of the Committee in problematic ways, such as moving it from a relatively light and non-costly procedure into a judicial model which would require fundamental reforms and challenge many of the assumptions on the basis of which the procedure was established and has been operating? Or is the Committee moving inexorably in this direction?

CASE STUDIES

We now consider four diverse examples of communications. In the Algerian disappearances case below, note the importance of the principle of exhaustion of domestic remedies. The Australian sexual orientation case is distinguished by the fact that the respondent government was actually opposed to the laws in force in one of its

[31] K. A. Young, *The Law and Process of the U.N. Human Rights Committee* (2002), at 299–300.

[32] Ibid.

states and thus encouraged the Committee to take a strong stand. In the Algerian case, and the Korean conscientious objection cases, the Committee finds itself dealing with many similar cases. In the latter it decides to consider 100 cases together, while in the former it keeps each case separate, although the Algerian Government still suggests that it might be an abuse of procedure to consider a series of complaints all focusing on the same historical events. In both of those cases, the Committee is confronted with strong arguments that it should take account of overriding security concerns. The Canadian deportation case highlights the challenge of weighing individual rights against legitimate state interests.

Aouabdia v. Algeria

Communication No. 1780/2008, Views adopted 22 Mar. 2011, UN Doc. CCPR/C/101/D/1780/2008

...

The facts as submitted by the author

2.1 The author claims that her husband, Brahim Aouabdia, was arrested at his workplace on 30 May 1994 at 9 a.m. by police officers in uniform.... These police officers did not present an arrest warrant and did not inform him of the reasons for the arrest. Many other people, including members of local councils, representatives elected in the latest cancelled parliamentary elections, militants and supporters of the Front Islamique du Salut (Islamic Salvation Front) (FIS), a banned political party, [were arrested at the same time]....

[The author then describes her sustained efforts to ascertain the whereabouts of her husband, involving various conflicting stories being given to her by the authorities, none of which led anywhere.]

...

The complaint

3.1 The author claims that the facts supporting her petition demonstrate that her husband has been a victim of enforced disappearance.... Noting that in this particular case the State party has not made any effort to shed light on his fate, and with reference to the Committee's general comment on article 6, the author claims that Brahim Aouabdia was the victim of a violation of article 6 of the Covenant, read alone and in conjunction with article 2, paragraph 3.

[The author claims various other violations of the ICCPR:

- Article 7, both for the stress and suffering caused to her husband, and separately to herself and her children.
- Article 9, because of her husband's arrest without warrant, his subsequent arbitrary detention, the failure to notify him of any charges and the subsequent trial in absentia that found him guilty.
- Article 10(1), because, in detention, her husband had not been treated with humanity or respect for his inherent dignity.

- Article 16, because her husband had been treated as a 'non-person' before the law.
- Article 2(3), because the state failed to conduct 'a thorough and diligent investigation' and because 'a total and general amnesty has been declared guaranteeing impunity to the individuals responsible for violations.']

3.9 Concerning the issue of exhaustion of domestic remedies, the author stresses that after 13 years, all her efforts have been in vain: the authorities have never conducted an investigation.... The letters she has sent regularly since 1994 to the highest levels of State authority have prompted no action. [In 2005, a Charter for Peace and National Reconciliation was adopted by referendum, and subsequently implemented through Ordinance No. 06-01 (2006). The author maintains that the latter] prohibits under penalty of imprisonment the pursuit of legal remedies to shed light on the most serious crimes such as enforced disappearances.... The author therefore maintains that she is no longer obliged to keep pursuing her efforts at the domestic level....

State party's observations on the admissibility of the communication

4.1 On 3 March 2009 the State party contested the admissibility of the present communication and 10 other[s].... [It] is of the view that communications incriminating public officials, or persons acting on behalf of public authorities, in enforced disappearances during the period in question, namely, from 1993 to 1998, must be considered in the wider domestic socio-political and security context that prevailed during a period in which the Government was struggling to fight terrorism.

4.2 During that period...it was difficult for civilians to distinguish between the actions of terrorist groups and those of the security forces, to whom civilians often attributed enforced disappearances. Thus there are numerous cases of enforced disappearance but, according to the State party, they cannot be blamed on the Government....

...

4.4 The State party further argues that not all domestic remedies have been exhausted.... [While the complainants have used political and administrative avenues, they] have not actually initiated legal proceedings and seen them through to their conclusion.... [T]he Code of Criminal Procedure authorizes [victims and their beneficiaries] to sue for damages by filing a complaint with the investigating judge.... This remedy...was not used....

...

4.6 ... [Ordinance No. 06-01] prescribes legal measures for the discontinuance of criminal proceedings and the commutation or remission of sentences for any person who is found guilty of acts of terrorism or who benefits from the provisions of the legislation on civil dissent, except for persons who have committed or been accomplices in mass killings, rapes or bombings in public places. This ordinance also helps to address the issue of disappearances by introducing a procedure for filing an official finding of presumed death, which entitles beneficiaries to receive compensation as victims of the national tragedy....

4.7 In addition to establishing funds to compensate all victims of the national tragedy, the sovereign people of Algeria have, according to the State party, agreed to a process of national reconciliation as the only way to heal the wounds inflicted. The State party insists that the [Charter] reflects a desire to avoid confrontation in the courts, media outpourings and the settling of political scores. The State party is therefore of the view that the authors' allegations are covered by the comprehensive domestic settlement mechanism provided for in the Charter.

...

Additional observations by the State party on the admissibility of the communication

5.1 [T]he State party [also] raises the question of whether the submission of a series of individual communications to the Committee might not actually be an abuse of procedure aimed at bringing before the Committee a broad historical issue involving causes and circumstances of which the Committee is unaware. The [communications focus] solely on the actions of the security forces and never [mention] those of the various armed groups that used criminal concealment techniques to incriminate the armed forces.

...

Issues and proceedings before the Committee

Consideration of admissibility

...

6.2 [The Committee is not authorized to look into a matter that is being examined under another procedure of international investigation or settlement. But the case of Brahim Aouabdia was reported to the Human Rights Council's Working Group on Enforced or Involuntary Disappearances. However, the Committee recalls that such extra-conventional procedures,] whose mandates are to examine and report publicly on human rights situations in specific countries or territories, or cases of widespread human rights violations worldwide, do not generally constitute an international procedure of investigation or settlement [for the purposes of Article 5(2)(a) of the Optional Protocol]....

6.3 ... The Committee recalls its jurisprudence to the effect that authors must avail themselves of all legal remedies in order to fulfil the requirement of exhaustion of all available domestic remedies, insofar as such remedies appear to be effective in the given case and are de facto available to the author. Under the circumstances, the Committee considers that bringing a civil action for offences as serious as those alleged in the present case cannot be considered a substitute for the proceedings that should have been brought by the public prosecutor, especially given that the author had filed a criminal complaint with the prosecutor regarding her husband's disappearance....

...

Consideration of the merits

...

7.2 [In response to the state party's invocation of the Charter for Peace and National Reconciliation, the Committee recalls that in 2007 it had adopted concluding observations on Algeria's ICCPR report which characterized Ordinance No. 06-01 as promoting impunity and infringing the right to an effective remedy and thus incompatible with the Covenant....]

7.3 The Committee... notes that the State party has provided no response to the author's allegations on the merits. It further reaffirms that the burden of proof cannot rest on the author of a communication alone, especially since an author and a State party do not always have equal access to the evidence, and that it is frequently the case that the State party alone has the relevant information. It is implicit in article 4, paragraph 2, of the Optional Protocol that the State party has the duty to investigate in good faith all allegations of violation of the Covenant made against it and its authorities and to furnish to the Committee the information available to it.

[The Committee then examines each of the alleged violations identified by the author of the communication, before summarizing its findings.]

8. The Human Rights Committee... is of the view that the facts before it disclose violations by the State party of article 6, read in conjunction with article 2, paragraph 3; article 7; article 9; article 10, paragraph 1; and article 16 of the Covenant with regard to Brahim Aouabdia. Moreover, the facts reveal a violation of article 7 alone and read in conjunction with article 2, paragraph 3, with regard to the author (the victim's wife) and their six children.

9. In accordance with article 2, paragraph 3, of the Covenant, the State party is under an obligation to provide the author with an effective remedy, including by (i) conducting a thorough and effective investigation into the disappearance of Brahim Aouabdia; (ii) providing his family with detailed information about the results of the investigation; (iii) freeing him immediately if he is still being detained incommunicado; (iv) if he is dead, handing over his remains to his family; (v) prosecuting, trying and punishing those responsible for the violations committed; and (vi) providing adequate compensation for the author and her children for the violations suffered, and for Brahim Aouabdia if he is alive. The State party is also under an obligation to take steps to prevent similar violations in the future.

10. ... [T]he Committee wishes to receive from the State party, within 180 days, information about the measures taken to give effect to its Views. The State party is also requested to publish the present Views.

Toonen v. Australia

Communication No. 488/1992, Views adopted 31 Mar. 1994, UN Doc. CCPR/C/50/D/488/1992

[The author of this communication was an Australian citizen resident in the state of Tasmania, and a leading member of the Tasmanian Gay Law Reform Group. He claimed that he was a victim of violations by Australia of Articles 2(1), 17 and 26 of the ICCPR. He challenged two provisions of the Tasmanian Criminal Code which criminalized 'various forms of sexual conduct between men, including all forms of sexual contacts between consenting adult homosexual men in private'. The Tasmanian police had not charged anyone with violations of these statutes, such as 'intercourse against nature', but there remained a threat of enforcement. Moreover, the author alleged that the criminalization of homosexuality had nourished prejudice and 'created the conditions for discrimination in employment, constant stigmatization, vilification, threats of physical violence and the violation of basic democratic rights.' Tasmania, alone among Australian jurisdictions, continued to have such laws in effect, and the Federal Government's position before the Human Rights Committee was critical of those laws.]

...

6.5 The state party does not accept the argument of the Tasmanian authorities that the retention of the challenged provisions is partly motivated by a concern to protect Tasmania from the spread of HIV/AIDS, and that the laws are justified on public health and moral grounds. This assessment in fact goes against the Australian Government's National HIV/AIDS Strategy, which emphasizes that laws criminalizing homosexual activity obstruct public health programmes promoting safer sex. The State party further disagrees with the Tasmanian authorities' contention that the laws are justified on moral grounds, noting that moral issues were not at issue when article 17 of the Covenant was drafted.

6.6 Nonetheless, the State party cautions that the formulation of article 17 allows for *some* infringement of the right to privacy if there are reasonable grounds, and that domestic social mores may be relevant to the reasonableness of an interference with privacy. The State party observes that while laws penalizing homosexual activity existed in the past in other Australian states, they have since been repealed with the exception of Tasmania. Furthermore, discrimination on the basis of homosexuality or sexuality is unlawful in three of six Australian states and the two self-governing internal Australian territories. The Federal Government has declared sexual preference to be a ground of discrimination that may be invoked under ILO Convention No. 111 (Discrimination in Employment or Occupation Convention), and created a mechanism through which complaints about discrimination in employment on the basis of sexual preference may be considered by the Australian Human Rights and Equal Opportunity Commission.

6.7 On the basis of the above, the State party contends that there is now a general Australian acceptance that no individual should be disadvantaged on the basis of his or her sexual orientation. Given the legal and social situation in all of Australia except Tasmania, the State party acknowledges that a complete prohibition on sexual activity between men is unnecessary to sustain the moral fabric of Australian society. On balance, the State party 'does not seek to claim that the challenged laws are based on reasonable and objective criteria'.

...

Examination of the merits:

...

8.2 Inasmuch as article 17 is concerned, it is undisputed that adult consensual sexual activity in private is covered by the concept of 'privacy', and that Mr. Toonen is actually and currently affected by the continued existence of the Tasmanian laws.

…

8.3 The prohibition against private homosexual behaviour is provided for by law.... As to whether it may be deemed arbitrary, the Committee recalls that pursuant to its General Comment 16 on article 17, the 'introduction of the concept of arbitrariness is intended to guarantee that even interference provided for by the law should be in accordance with the provisions, aims and objectives of the Covenant and should be, in any event, reasonable in the circumstances'. The Committee interprets the requirement of reasonableness to imply that any interference with privacy must be proportional to the end sought and be necessary in the circumstances of any given case.

…

8.5 ... [T]he Committee notes that the criminalization of homosexual practices cannot be considered a reasonable means or proportionate measure to achieve the aim of preventing the spread of AIDS/HIV....

8.6 The Committee cannot accept either that for the purposes of article 17 of the Covenant, moral issues are exclusively a matter of domestic concern, as this would open the door to withdrawing from the Committee's scrutiny a potentially large number of statutes interfering with privacy. It further notes that with the exception of Tasmania, all laws criminalizing homosexuality have been repealed throughout Australia and that, even in Tasmania,...there is no consensus.... Considering further that these provisions are not currently enforced, which implies that they are not deemed essential to the protection of morals in Tasmania, the Committee concludes that the provisions do not meet the 'reasonableness' test in the circumstances of the case, and that they arbitrarily interfere with Mr. Toonen's right under article 17, paragraph 1.

8.7 The State party has sought the Committee's guidance as to whether sexual orientation may be considered an 'other status' for the purposes of article 26. The same issue could arise under article 2, paragraph 1, of the Covenant. The Committee confines itself to noting, however, that in its view the reference to 'sex' in articles 2, paragraph 1, and 26 is to be taken as including sexual orientation.

9. The [Committee] is of the view that the facts before it reveal a violation of articles 17, paragraph 1, *juncto* 2, paragraph 1, of the Covenant.

10. ... In the opinion of the Committee, an effective remedy would be the repeal of Sections 122 (a), (c) and 123 of the Tasmanian Criminal Code.

11. Since the Committee has found a violation of Mr. Toonen's rights under articles 17(1) and 2(1) of the Covenant requiring the repeal of the offending law, the Committee does not consider it necessary to consider whether there has also been a violation of article 26 of the Covenant.

…

Warsame v. Canada

Communication No. 1959/2010, Views adopted 21 July 2011, UN Doc. CCPR/C/102/D/1959/2010

[The author was born in 1984 in Saudi Arabia but never obtained Saudi citizenship. He is of Somali descent, however he has never resided in or visited Somalia. He came to Canada in 1998, aged 4 and was granted permanent resident status. After a string of convictions, including a two-year sentence for possession of cocaine for the purposes of trafficking, he received a deportation order for 'serious criminality'. His appeal was rejected but a Pre-Removal Risk Assessment (PRRA) resulted in a finding that his life would be at risk if he was returned to Somalia. The Ministry of Public Safety disputed this finding and classified him as a danger to the public in Canada. On 21 July 2010 he was notified that he would be deported to Bossasso in Somalia nine days later. The author and the government made detailed submissions to the Committee in relation to the risks that might be involved in deportation.]

…

Consideration of merits

…

[Articles 6(1) and 7]

8.2 The Committee notes the author's claim that his removal from Canada to Somalia would expose him to a risk of irreparable harm in violation of articles 6, paragraph 1 and 7, of the Covenant. It also notes his arguments that his risk is personalized and distinct of [sic] that faced by the general population in Somalia, in light of the fact that he was born outside of Somalia and never resided there, he has limited language skills, he doesn't have any family in the area of Puntland, he lacks clan support, he is at risk of forced recruitment by pirate or Islamist militia groups and he would be exposed to generalized violence. The Committee also notes the observations of the State party, according to which the author has not provided prima facie basis for believing that he himself faces a personal risk of death, torture, or cruel, inhuman or degrading treatment and that his alleged complete lack of clan membership is unsupported….

…

8.3 The Committee recalls its General Comment No. 31, in which it refers to the obligation of States parties not to extradite, deport, expel or otherwise remove a person from their territory where there are substantial grounds for believing that there is a real risk of irreparable harm….The Committee…concludes that the author's deportation to Somalia would, if implemented, constitute a violation of articles 6, paragraph 1 and 7, of the Covenant.

[Article 12(4)]

8.4 … [T]he Committee must first consider whether Canada is indeed the author's "own country" for purposes of this provision and then decide whether his deprivation of the right to enter that country would be arbitrary. On the first issue, the Committee recalls its General Comment No. 27 on freedom of movement where it has considered that the scope of "his own country" is broader than the concept "country of his nationality". It is not limited to nationality in a formal sense, that is, nationality acquired at birth or by conferral; it embraces, at the very least, an individual who, because of his or her special ties to or claims in relation to a given country, cannot be considered to be a mere alien….The words "his own country" invite consideration of such matters as long standing residence, close personal and family ties and intentions to remain, as well as to the absence of such ties elsewhere.

8.5 ... [The author's nuclear family lives in Canada... [and he] has lived almost all his conscious life in Canada, [and] received his entire education in Canada.... [T]he Committee considers that the author has established that Canada was his own country within the meaning of article 12[(4)], in the light of the strong ties connecting him to Canada, the presence of his family in Canada, the language he speaks, the duration of his stay in the country and the lack of any other ties than at best formal nationality with Somalia.

8.6 As to the alleged arbitrariness of the author's deportation, the Committee recalls its General Comment No. 27 on freedom of movement where it has stated that even interference provided for by law should be in accordance with the provisions, aims and objectives of the Covenant and should be, in any event, reasonable in the particular circumstances. The Committee considers that there are few, if any, circumstances in which deprivation of the right to enter one's own country could be reasonable.... [A] deportation of the author to Somalia would render his return to Canada de facto impossible due to Canadian immigration regulations. The Committee therefore considers that the author's deportation to Somalia impeding his return to his own country would be disproportionate to the legitimate aim of preventing the commission of further crimes and therefore arbitrary. [It would thus violate article 12(4).]

[Articles 17 and 23(1)]

8.7 [Under the Committee's jurisprudence, the expulsion of a family member could constitute arbitrary interference with the family if the separation and its effects were disproportionate to the objectives of the removal.]

8.8 [Since the deportation will interfere with family relations, the question is whether it is either arbitrary or unlawful.] ... The Committee notes the State party's observation that the authorities acted neither unlawfully nor arbitrary and that the minimal disruption to the author's family life was outweighed by the gravity of his crimes....

...

8.10 ... The Committee notes that the intensity of the author's family ties with his mother and sisters remains disputed.... Nevertheless,...the author's family ties would be irreparably severed if he were to be deported to Somalia, as his family could not visit him there and the means to keep up a regular correspondence between the author and his family in Canada are limited. In addition to that, for a significant lapse of time, it would be impossible for the author to apply for a visitor's visa to Canada to visit his family. The Committee also notes that due to the de facto unavailability of judicial remedies, the author could not raise his claims before the domestic courts. The Committee, therefore, concludes that the interference with the author's family life, which would lead to irreparably severing his ties with his mother and sisters in Canada would be disproportionate to the legitimate aim of preventing the commission of further crimes. [Deportation would thus violate Articles 17 and 23(1) alone and in conjunction with Article 2(3).]

10. ... [T]he State party is under an obligation to provide the author with an effective remedy, including by refraining from deporting him to Somalia.

[Several members of the Committee appended individual dissenting opinions on a variety of grounds.]

Min-Kyu Jeong et al. v. Republic of Korea
Communication Nos. 1642–1741/2007, Views adopted 24 Mar. 2011, UN Doc. CCPR/C/101/D/1642-1714/2007

1.2 ... [T]he Committee decided to join the 100 communications for decision in view of their substantial factual and legal similarity.

The facts as presented by the authors

2.1 All 100 authors are Jehovah's Witnesses, who have been sentenced to one and a half years of imprisonment for refusing to be drafted for military service, based on their religious belief. None of the authors appealed their cases to higher courts [since these have previously] decided that conscientious objectors must serve in the army or face prison terms....

State party's observations on admissibility and merits

...

4.3 ... The State party submits that its painful history of war constitutes one of the reasons why its government places such emphasis on national security as the most significant priority in its national policy agenda....

4.4 ... [The state party] fears that alternative military service would jeopardize national security. It highlights that 70% of the Korean Peninsula is mountainous, making it all the more necessary to be equipped with enough ground forces to face guerrilla warfare. However, the number of soldiers in the State party remains at around 680,000, only 58% of that of the DPRK, which amounts to about 1,170,000, and between 2000 and 2005 there has been a significant decrease in the number of male soldiers between 15 and 25 years. This trend is expected to continue in the future and makes it even more difficult to accept cases of exception from conscription.

4.5 According to the State party, there have always been those who are intent on "evading" conscription due to the relatively challenging conditions often required in the military, or concern over the effect such an interruption will have on one's academic or professional career. Thus, it is even more necessary to maintain its current system of a no-exception policy in mandatory military service to ensure sufficient ground forces. It submits that if it were to accept claims of exemption from military service, in the absence of public consensus on the matter, it would be impeded from securing sufficient military manpower required for national security by weakening the public's trust in the fairness of the system, leading the public to question its necessity and legitimacy....

4.6 [In response to previous communications on this issue the Committee stated] that, "respect on the part of the State for conscientious beliefs and manifestations thereof is itself an important factor in ensuring cohesive and stable pluralism in society", [but] the State party is of the view that as a unique security environment prevails, fair and faithful implementation of mandatory military service is a determining factor to secure social cohesion.... Public opinion polls conducted in July 2005 and in September 2006 show that 72.3% and 60.5% respectively expressed opposition to the recognition of alternative service arrangements for conscientious objectors. In the States party's view, the introduction of such an arrangement at a premature stage within a relatively short period of time, without public consensus, would intensify social tensions rather than contribute to social cohesion.

...

4.8 The State party regrets that upon its accession to the Optional Protocol to the Covenant on 10 April 1990, the Committee had not provided a clear position on [this issue and only did so in GC No. 22 of 1993]....

...

Issues and proceedings before the Committee

...

Consideration of the merits

7.3...Although the Covenant does not explicitly refer to a right of conscientious objection, the Committee believes that such a right derives from article 18, inasmuch as the obligation to be involved in the use of lethal force may seriously conflict with the freedom of conscience. The right to conscientious objection to military service inheres in the right to freedom of thought, conscience and religion. It entitles any individual to an exemption from compulsory military service if this cannot be reconciled with that individual's religion or beliefs. The right must not be impaired by coercion. A State may, if it wishes, compel the objector to undertake a civilian alternative to military service, outside the military sphere and not under military command. The alternative service must not be of a punitive nature. It must be a real service to the community and compatible with respect for human rights.

7.4 In the present cases, the Committee considers that the authors' refusal to be drafted for compulsory military service derives from their religious beliefs which, it is uncontested, were genuinely held and that the authors' subsequent conviction and sentence amounted to an infringement of their freedom of conscience, in breach of article 18, paragraph 1 of the Covenant....

QUESTIONS

1. On the basis of these cases, how would you characterize the Committee's approach to the domestic remedies rule?

2. Do you think the Committee is justified in finding a violation of Article 6 (the right to life) in *Aouabdia*?

3. How do you understand and assess paragraph 8.2 in *Toonen*? As a Committee member, would you have supported or opposed inclusion of this paragraph in its present form, or in any form? Was it necessary? What distinct issues are raised by inclusion of sexual orientation in the term 'sex' in Articles 2(1) and 26?

4. How do you assess the Committee's argument relating to Article 17? Would you have taken a different approach? What differences do you see between the Committee expressing its understanding of Articles 17 and 2(1) in relation to homosexual acts through a view such as *Toonen*, or through a GC expressing the same ideas? Which route would you favour?

5. Do you think the Committee in *Warsame* placed too much emphasis on the rights of the individual at the expense of the interests of the overall community? How important are the specific facts? Note that the Committee adopted an almost identical approach in a case involving Australia's efforts to deport a repeat offender to Sweden (*Nystrom et al. v Australia*, CCPR/C/102/D/1557/2007 (1 Sept. 2011)).

COMMENT ON INTERIM MEASURES

One of the most controversial aspects of the remedies that might be sought by the Committee concerns 'interim measures' which call upon the state to suspend any action while the communication is being considered. While the Committee itself provided for these in its Rules of Procedure (Rule 92) it did not spell out the status of any such measures. In its GC No. 33 of 2008 it explained the approach that it had evolved:

> 19. Measures may be requested by an author, or decided by the Committee on its own initiative, when an action taken or threatened by the State party would appear likely to cause irreparable harm to the author or the victim unless withdrawn or suspended pending full consideration of the communication by the Committee. Examples include the imposition of the death penalty and violation of the duty of non-refoulement.... Failure to implement [requests by the Committee for] interim or provisional measures is incompatible with the obligation to respect in good faith the procedure of individual communication established under the Optional Protocol.

Consider the following examples.

Piandiong et al. v. The Philippines

Communication No. 869/1999, Views adopted 19 Oct. 2000, UN Doc. CCPR/C/70/D/869/1999

1.1 The authors of the communication...claim [to be] victims of violations of articles 6, 7 and 14 of the [ICCPR]....

1.2 On 7 November 1994, [they] were convicted of robbery with homicide and sentenced to death by the Regional Trial Court of Caloocan City. The Supreme Court denied the appeal, and confirmed both conviction and sentence.... [A subsequent request for clemency by the President was denied. The Committee invoked its rule on interim measures and requested the Philippines not to execute the petitioners while their case was under consideration by the Committee. Shortly thereafter the men were executed.]

…

3.5 In respect to counsel's request to the Committee for interim measures of protection as a matter of urgency, the State party notes that counsel found no need to address the Committee during the year that his clients were on death row after all domestic remedies had been exhausted. Even after the President granted a 90 day reprieve, counsel waited until the end of that period to present a communication to the Committee. The State party argues that in doing so counsel makes a mockery of the Philippine justice system and of the constitutional process.

3.6 The State party assures the Committee of its commitment to the Covenant and states that its action was not intended to frustrate the Committee….

…

5.1 By adhering to the Optional Protocol, a State party to the Covenant recognizes the competence of the Human Rights Committee to receive and consider communications…. Implicit in a State's adherence to the Protocol is an undertaking to cooperate with the Committee in good faith…. It is incompatible with these obligations for a State party to take any action that would prevent or frustrate the Committee in its consideration and examination of the communication, and in the expression of its Views.

5.2 … [A] State party commits grave breaches of its obligations under the Optional Protocol if it acts to prevent or frustrate consideration by the Committee of a communication alleging a violation of the Covenant, or to render examination by the Committee moot and the expression of its Views nugatory and futile. [In this case]…the State party breaches its obligations under the Protocol, if it proceeds to execute the alleged victims before the Committee concludes its [work]. It is particularly inexcusable for the State to do so after the Committee has [requested] that the State party refrain from doing so.

5.3 … There is nothing in the Optional Protocol that restricts the right of an alleged victim of a violation of his or her rights under the Covenant from submitting a communication after a request for clemency or pardon has been rejected, and the State party may not unilaterally impose such a condition that limits both the competence of the Committee and the right of alleged victims to submit communications. Furthermore, the State party has not shown that by acceding to the Committee's request for interim measures the course of justice would have been obstructed.

5.4 Interim measures…are essential to the Committee's role under the Protocol. Flouting of the Rule, especially by irreversible measures such as the execution of the alleged victim or his/her deportation from the country, undermines the protection of Covenant rights through the Optional Protocol.

…

Mansour Ahani v. Canada

Communication No. 1051/2002, Views adopted 29 Mar. 2004, UN Doc. CCPR/C/80/D/1051/2002

1.1 [The author of the communication, dated 10 January 2002, is Mansour Ahani, an Iranian citizen, detained in Canada] pending conclusion of legal proceedings in the Supreme Court of Canada concerning his deportation. He claims to be a victim of violations by Canada of articles 2, 6, 7, 9, 13 and 14 of the [ICCPR]....

1.2 On 11 January 2002, the Committee... requested the State party, in the event that the Supreme Court's decision expected the same day would permit the author's deportation, "to refrain from deportation until the Committee has had an opportunity to consider the allegations, in particular those that relate to torture, other inhuman treatment or even death as a consequence of the deportation".... On 10 June 2002, the State party deported the author to Iran.

...

2.1 ... On 1 April 1992, the Immigration and Refugee Board determined that the author was a Convention refugee based on his political opinion and membership in a particular social group.

2.2 On 17 June 1993, the Solicitor-General of Canada and the Minister of Employment & Immigration, having considered security intelligence reports stating that the author was trained to be an assassin by the Iranian Ministry of Intelligence and Security ("MIS"), both certified... [under the relevant Act that] there were reasonable grounds to believe that he would engage in terrorism, that he was a member of an organization that would engage in terrorism and that he had engaged in terrorism. On the same date,... he was taken into mandatory detention, where he remained until his deportation nine years later.

...

2.10 ... On 15 January 2002, the Ontario Superior Court (Dambrot J) rejected the author's argument that the principles of fundamental justice, protected by the Charter, prevented his removal prior to the [Human Rights] Committee's consideration of the case. On 8 May 2002, the Court of Appeal for Ontario upheld the decision, holding that the request for interim measures was not binding upon the State party. On 16 May 2002, the Supreme Court, by a majority, dismissed the author's application for leave to appeal (without giving reasons). On 10 June 2002, the author was deported to Iran.

...

5.2 By submissions dated 5 December 2002, the State party, in response to the Committee's request for explanation, argued that it fully supported the important role mandated to the Committee and would always do its utmost to co-operate with the Committee. It contended that it took its obligations under the Covenant and the Optional Protocol very seriously and that it was in full compliance with them. The State party points out that alongside its human rights obligations it also has a duty to protect the safety of the Canadian public and to ensure that it does not become a safe haven for terrorists.

5.3 The State party noted that neither the Covenant nor the Optional Protocol provide for interim measures requests and argues that such requests are recommendatory, rather than binding. Nonetheless, the State party usually responded favourably to such requests. As in other cases, the State party considered the instant request seriously, before concluding in the circumstances of the case, including the finding (upheld by the courts) that he faced a minimum risk of harm in the event of return, that it was unable to delay the deportation. The State party pointed out that usually it responds favourably to requests[;] its decision to do so was determined to be legal and consistent with the Charter up to the highest judicial level. The State party argues that interim measures in the immigration context raise "some particular difficulties" where, on occasion, other considerations may take precedence over a request for interim measures. The particular circumstances of the case should thus not be construed as a diminution of the State party's commitment to human rights or the Committee.

...

8.1 The Committee finds, in the circumstances of the case, that the State party breached its obligations under the Optional Protocol, by deporting the author before the Committee could address the author's allegation of irreparable harm to his Covenant rights. The Committee observes that torture is, alongside the imposition of the death penalty, the most grave and irreparable of possible consequences to an individual of measures taken by the State party. Accordingly, action by the State party giving rise to a risk of such harm, as indicated a priori by the Committee's request for interim measures, must be scrutinized in the strictest light.

8.2 Interim measures... are essential to the Committee's role under the Protocol. Flouting of the Rule, especially by irreversible measures such as the execution of the alleged victim or his/her deportation from a State party to face torture or death in another country, undermines the protection of Covenant rights through the Optional Protocol....

NOTE

In recent years the Committee has issued an average of 16 interim measures orders annually. Many have been respected, including by Canada and a range of other countries. In March 2010 the Committee issued this public statement:

> The Human Rights Committee has recently received information indicating that two individuals under sentence of death, whose cases are currently pending before the Committee, and who alleged that they did not receive, in particular, a fair trial, have been executed in Belarus, despite the fact that requests for interim measures of protection had been issued by the Committee.
>
> ...
>
> [Having received no reply from Belarus to its inquiries, the Committee] expressed its dismay and indignation at the apparent execution of the two individuals, and its concern at the State party's failure to cooperate in a good faith with the Committee.... The Committee also reiterated that executing individuals whose cases are pending before the Committee amounts to a grave breach of the Optional Protocol, in particular where a request for interim protection... has been issued.

The European Court of Human Rights — which developed interim measures orders long before the Committee — has a detailed 'Practice Direction' which requires interim measures applications to be fully reasoned, supported by all key documents from domestic courts and sent as soon as possible after the domestic decision has been taken.[33]

QUESTIONS

1. One commentator, reflecting on the Committee's Views in *Piandiong*, suggests that the 'Committee's reasoned justification for its conclusion, [consistent] with the "dynamic and evolutive" approach to human rights treaties, must be considered correct, if only on the utilitarian ground of seeking to ensure maximum protection for people at risk.'[34] What other factors might reasonably be taken into account in evaluating whether the Committee's approach to interim measures is justified?

2. What do you make of the fact that the governments of both the Philippines and Canada insist on their respect for the interim measures procedure in principle but reject it in the case at hand? What would be the consequences from the Committee's perspective of accepting the Canadian view that interim measures 'requests are recommendatory, rather than binding'?

3. Do you agree that '[a] State that has accepted the right of individual petition…has bound itself to support that process by complying with any interim measures ordered. It would be incompatible with the obligations voluntarily undertaken by the State for the State to act or refrain from acting in a way that frustrates the consideration of an individual petition.'[35]

COMMENT ON NATIONAL LEVEL FOLLOW-UP

The Optional Protocol procedure is premised on the assumption that the Views reached will be taken seriously at the national level. While there are many options available to the governments concerned, one of the most important issues concerns the response of the national courts whose earlier decisions are often impugned in communications. Consider the Committee's Views in a Sri Lankan case, followed by the reaction of the Sri Lankan Supreme Court.

Singarasa v. Sri Lanka
Communication No. 1033/2001, UN Doc. CCPR/C/81/D/1033/2001 (23 Aug. 2004)

…

[33] ECtHR, Practice Direction: Request for Interim Measures, as amended, 7 July 2011.

[34] Gino Naldi, 'Interim Measures in the UN Human Rights Committee', 53 Int'l. & Comp. L.Q. 445 (2004), at 454.

[35] Jo M. Pasqualucci, 'Interim Measures in International Human Rights: Evolution and Harmonization', 38 Vand. J. Transnat'l. L. 1 (2005), at 48.

Facts as submitted by the author

2.1 On 16 July 1993...the author was arrested, by Sri Lankan security forces...and accused of supporting the Liberation Tigers of Tamil Eelam (known as "the LTTE")....

2.2 ... He was detained pursuant to...the Prevention of Terrorism Act No. 48 of 1979....

2.3 [Between July and September 1993 he was interrogated, held incommunicado and denied legal representation and medical assistance. For two days he claims to have been tortured.]

...

2.5 [During his interrogation, since] the author could not speak Sinhalese, the PC [Police Constable] interpreted between Tamil and Sinhalese. The author was then requested to sign a statement, which had been translated and typed in Sinhalese by the PC. The author refused to sign as he could not understand it. He alleges that the ASP then forcibly put his thumbprint on the typed statement. The prosecution later produced this statement as evidence of the author's alleged confession....

...

2.9 On 12 January 1995, in an application to the High Court, defence counsel submitted that there were visible marks of assault on the author's body, and moved for a medical report to be obtained. On the Court's order, a Judicial Medical Officer then examined him. According to the author, the medical report stated that the author displayed scars on his back and...a corneal scar on his left eye...[and] that 'injuries to the lower part of the left back of the chest and eye were caused by a blunt weapon while that to the mid back of the chest was probably due to application of sharp force'.

2.10 On 2 June 1995, the author's alleged confession was the subject of a voir dire hearing by the High Court, at which the ASP, PC and author gave evidence, and the medical report was considered. The High Court concluded that the confession was admissible...[based on] Section 16(2) of the PTA [that] put the burden of proof that any such statement is irrelevant on the accused. The Court did not find the confession irrelevant, despite defence counsel's motion to exclude it on the grounds that it was extracted from the author under threat.

2.11 According to the author, the High Court gave no reasons for rejecting the medical report.... In holding that the confession was voluntary, the High Court relied upon the author's failure to complain to anyone at any time about the beatings....

2.12 On 29 September 1995, the High Court convicted the author on all five counts, and on 4 October 1995, sentenced him to 50 years imprisonment. The conviction was based solely on the alleged confession....

...

The State party's submissions on admissibility and merits

...

4.8 On the claim of torture, the State party submits that the trial court and the Court of Appeal made clear and unequivocal findings that these allegations were inconsistent with the medical report adduced in evidence, and that the author had failed to make such allegations to the Magistrate or to the police, prior to the trial.

4.9 ... On the issue of a violation of article 14, paragraph 5, it notes that the author was afforded every opportunity to have his conviction and sentence reviewed by a tribunal according to law, and that he merely seeks to question the findings of fact made by the domestic courts before the Committee....

...

Issues and proceedings before the Committee

Consideration of the Merits

...

7.2 ... [A]s clearly appears from the court proceedings, the confession took place in the sole presence of the two investigating officers.... The Committee concludes that the author was denied a fair trial in accordance with article 14, paragraph 1, of the Covenant by solely relying on a confession obtained in such circumstances.

...

7.4 ... The Committee considers that it is implicit in [Article 14(3)(g) of the Covenant] that the prosecution prove that the confession was made without duress.... [T]he Committee also notes that the burden of proving whether the confession was voluntary was on the accused.... Even if, as argued by the State party, the threshold of proof is "placed very low" and "a mere possibility of involuntariness" would suffice to sway the court in favour of the accused, it remains that the burden was on the author. The Committee notes in this respect that the willingness of the courts at all stages to dismiss the complaints of torture and ill-treatment on the basis of the inconclusiveness of the medical certificate (especially one obtained over a year after the interrogation and ensuing confession) suggests that this threshold was not complied with. Further, insofar as the courts were prepared to infer that the author's allegations lacked credibility by virtue of his failing to complain of ill-treatment before its Magistrate, the Committee finds that inference to be manifestly unsustainable in the light of his expected return to police detention. Nor did this treatment of the complaint by its courts satisfactorily discharge the State party's obligation to investigate effectively complaints of violations of article 7....

...

7.6 [T]he State party is under an obligation to provide the author with an effective and appropriate remedy, including release or retrial and compensation. The State party is under an obligation to avoid similar violations in the future and should ensure that the impugned sections of the PTA are made compatible with the provisions of the Covenant.

...

Subsequent to this set of Views adopted by the Committee, Singarasa requested the Sri Lankan Supreme Court to revise its earlier decision taking into consideration the views of the Committee. *Singarasa* was the sixth case against Sri Lanka in which the Committee had found violations. The Chief Justice was involved in several of those, including the *Singarasa* case.

Nallaratnam Singarasa v. Attorney-General
Supreme Court of the Democratic Socialist Republic of Sri Lanka, 15 Sept. 2006, S.C. Spl (LA) No. 182/99
SARATH N. SILVA, C.J.

...

(i) [T]he alternative remedies specified by the Committee [see para. 7.6, *supra*] cannot be comprehended in the context of our court procedure. A release and compensation (to be sought in a separate civil action) predicate a baseless mala fide prosecution. Whereas a retrial is ordered when there is sufficient evidence but the conviction is flawed by a serious procedural illegality. The High Court convicted the Petitioner on the basis of his confession after a full *voir dire* inquiry as to its voluntariness. If the confession is adequate to base a conviction, a retrial (as contemplated by the Committee) would be a superfluous re-enactment of the same process.

(ii) The Petitioner has been convicted with [sic] having conspired with others to overthrow the lawfully elected Government of Sri Lanka and for that purpose attacked several Army camps. The offences are directly linked to the Sovereignty of the People of Sri Lanka, and the Committee at Geneva, not linked with the Sovereignty of the People, has purported to set aside the orders made at all three levels of Courts that exercise the judicial power of the People of Sri Lanka.

...

The resulting position is that the Petitioner cannot seek to "vindicate and enforce" his rights through the Human Rights Committee at Geneva, which is not reposed with judicial power under our Constitution. A fortiori it is submitted that this Court being "the highest and final Superior Court of record in the Republic" in terms of Article 118 of the Constitution cannot set aside or vary its order as pleaded by the Petitioner on the basis of the findings of the Human Rights Committee in Geneva which is not reposed with any judicial power under or in terms of the Constitution.

...

... [W]here the President enters into a treaty or accedes to a Covenant the content of which is "inconsistent with the provisions of the Constitution or written law" it would be a transgression of the limitation in Article 33(f) [of the Constitution] and ultra vires. Such act of the President would not bind the Republic qua state....

...

[Recognition of the role of the ICCPR Committee to receive and consider communications] is a purported conferment of a judicial power on the Human Rights Committee at Geneva....

Therefore the accession to the Optional Protocol in 1997 by the then President and Declaration made under Article 1 is inconsistent with the provisions of the Constitution specified above and is in excess of the power of the President as contained in Article 33(f) of the Constitution. The accession and declaration does not bind the Republic qua state and has no legal effect within the Republic.

...

In these circumstances the Petitioner cannot plead a legitimate expectation to have the findings of the Human Rights Committee enforced or given effect to by an order of this Court.

NOTE

In reflecting on these developments, Nigel Rodley, a member of the Committee suggested that the case 'seems to be an example of judicial waywardness', giving rise to this question: 'when does the inevitable elasticity that must be acknowledged to inhere in the judicial process of textual interpretation snap and leave us with the uncontrolled application of judicial caprice?' He argues that because the Committee's Views do not create binding obligations, and are thus not *per se* justiciable domestically, 'the suggestion that the Committee has been invited to intrude on the judicial monopoly that may be given to a state's courts is preposterous.'[36]

The Committee now undertakes an increasingly robust follow-up to its Views under the Optional Protocol, but it reported in 2009 merely that a follow-up dialogue was 'ongoing' (UN Doc. A/64/40, p. 155). More generally, it has been calculated that the Committee received only 54 'satisfactory responses' from states out of 474 findings of violations.[37]

In addition, the particularities of *Singarasa* should not lead us to dismiss the important question of how national courts are expected to deal with Views of the Committee that recommend the revision or setting aside of the judgment of a national court. It has been observed that there is a clear tension between 'the argument that states should give full effect to their international obligations as interpreted or formulated by treaty bodies [and] the requirements of the rule of law.' The result is that 'individuals who, according to the [Committee], are entitled to a retrial are often left empty-handed within their national legal order.'[38] The straightforward solution — national legislation prescribing a way in which the Views can be effectively implemented — has not generally proved attractive to states.

QUESTIONS

1. Are the Committee's procedures adequate to enable it to deal with a case such as *Singarasa*? How could its procedures in such cases be improved?

2. What, in your view, would be the ideal approach for a government to adopt in order to underscore in advance that it will pay appropriate deference to the Committee's Views? Is there an intermediate position between agreeing to be bound and leaving the response entirely to the vagaries of the political system?

[36] N. Rodley, 'The Singarasa Case: Quis Custodiet…? A Test for the Bangalore Principles of Judicial Conduct', 41 Israel L. Rev. 500 (2008), at 501 and 506.

[37] G. Ulfstein, 'Individual Complaints', in Keller & Ulfstein, p. 802, *supra*, 73, at 104-5.

[38] R. van Alebeek & A. Nollkaemper, 'The Legal Status of Decisions by Human Rights Treaty Bodies in National Law', in ibid., 356, at 378.

COMMENT ON OUTCOME OF THE COMMUNICATIONS PROCEDURES

(1) Remedies

In its early years the Committee was reluctant to recommend specific remedies and instead relied upon the standard phrase, still used at the end of every set of Views, that calls upon the state party to adopt 'measures... to give effect to the Committee's Views'. But, over time, the Committee has become increasingly specific as to the measures it believes states should take. They include: (1) undertaking a public investigation to establish the facts; (2) bringing the perpetrators to justice; (3) providing compensation; (4) ensuring that the violation will not be repeated; (5) amending the law; (6) providing restitution of liberty, employment or property; (7) providing medical care and treatment; (8) permitting the victim to leave the country; or (9) enjoining an imminent violation.[39] Complainants have often urged the Committee to quantify the compensation recommended, but it has so far refrained from doing so.

(2) Follow-Up and Compliance

A recent UN survey of implementation observes with what seems to be studied imprecision that 'there have been around 20 to 25 amendments to legislation to which decisions of [the Committee] have contributed'. But it goes on to note:

> While there have been many cases which could be considered as 'success stories', it is clear that a large number of States fail to apply the remedies as recommended. This obviously has an adverse effect on the credibility and authority of the complaints procedure. The reasons why States parties often fail to implement these decisions have often been suggested to relate to, inter alia: a lack of understanding by States parties of their obligations under the respective treaties; unwillingness, on the part of certain States parties to abide by their obligations; the 'non-legally binding' nature of decisions; the divergent views between States and the Committees on the interpretation of treaty provisions; weak decisions often resulting from consensus decision-making; insufficient follow-up by the Committees themselves; lack of political support (unlike ECHR — where implementation is monitored by the Council of Ministers, i.e. the States themselves); lack of expertise within States parties and lack of assistance to them on how to better implement; and failure to adopt enabling legislation.[40]

Although lamentably few empirical studies have been undertaken, Australia provides a useful case study. It is the state with the third highest number of registered cases. Between December 1991 and May 2012 the Committee adopted decisions in

[39] Dinah Shelton, *Remedies in International Human Rights Law* (2nd edn. 2005), 184–5.
[40] 'Follow-up procedures on individual complaints', UN Doc. HRI/ICM/WGFU/2011/3 (16 Dec. 2010), p. 5.

response to 59 cases concerning Australia (of a total of 124 cases registered). It found violations in 21 of the 27 cases in which it adopted Views. Part of the explanation is that Australia does not have a constitutional bill of rights.[41] In 2006 Australia assured the Committee that human rights were well protected because Australia

> already has a robust constitutional structure, an extensive framework of legislation protecting human rights and prohibiting discrimination, and an independent human rights institution, the [Human Rights and Equal Opportunity] Commission. The latter mechanism holds the legislative branch and Australian Government accountable against human rights standards and thereby substantively achieves the same outcome in this respect as would legislation that directly implements the Covenant. Australia adds that human rights are also protected and promoted by Australia's strong democratic institutions.[42]

In 2008, the Committee asked Australia to indicate if there were any further developments in relation to a range of Views in response to which the government had earlier replied either that 'further dialogue on the matter would not be fruitful' or that it did not accept the Committee's views and recommendations. It listed seven such cases by way of example.[43] In its Concluding Observations in 2009, the Committee expressed 'once again its concern at the State party's restrictive interpretation of, and failure to fulfill its obligations under the [Protocol and the Covenant], and at the fact that victims have not received reparation.' It called upon Australia to 'review its position... and establish appropriate procedures to implement' the Committee's Views.[44] In its 2011 Annual Report, the Committee lists 24 cases with violations and classifies seven of the responses received from Australia as 'unsatisfactory', while 17 are listed as involving ongoing dialogue.[45]

This overview illustrates some of the ways in which the Committee seeks to implement a systematic follow-up policy, overseen by a 'Special Rapporteur for follow-up on Views'.

Thus, letters are sent requesting information, the Special Rapporteur meets with the state's representatives, the matter is discussed in a public meeting, all replies and non-replies are recorded in detail in the Annual Report and in some cases the Special Rapporteur has requested a country visit. Only once has such a visit occurred, when a mission was undertaken to Jamaica in 1995 to discuss a large number of outstanding communications against a background of rapidly growing governmental dissatisfaction with the procedure. In addition to proposing more frequent use of follow-up missions, a former member of the Committee called upon it to use the internet to publicize 'case opinions and [indicate] the compliance or non-compliance' of states, to 'find ways to speak to States and to parliaments directly, without,

[41] See A. Byrnes, H. Charlesworth & G. McKinnon, *Bills of Rights in Australia: History, Politics and Law* (2009).

[42] Response to Views in Faure, 1036/2001, Human Rights Committee Annual Report 2006, UN Doc. A/61/40, Vol. II.

[43] 'List of issues to be taken up in connection with the consideration of the fifth periodic report of Australia', UN Doc. CCPR/C/AUS/Q/5 (24 Nov. 2008), para. 3.

[44] UN Doc. CCPR/C/AUS/CO/5 (2 Apr. 2009), para. 10.

[45] UN Doc. A/66/40 (Vol. II, Part Two), pp. 88–9.

of course, evading diplomatic channels' and to seek 'to increase the influence and didactic effectiveness of its jurisprudence'.[46]

(3) The Legal Status of Views

The legal status of the Committee's Views is important. If they are legally binding, then their relative neglect by many states is deeply problematic. If they are merely advisory, it would hardly be surprising if states downplayed their significance. The views of commentators vary.

Manfred Nowak argues that the Committee 'cannot be termed a court in the strict sense of the word' because of 'the relatively brief term of office of its members and the lack of internationally binding effect of its decisions', as well as its designation as a 'Committee'. He concludes that it is a 'quasi-judicial organ',[47] and has suggested that the Views enjoy a 'quasi-binding nature'.[48]

A former member of the Committee, Martin Scheinin, argues that its Views are, in effect, binding:

> [I]t would be wrong to categorize the Committee's views as mere 'recommendations'. They are the end result of a quasi-judicial adversarial international body established and elected by the States Parties for the purpose of interpreting the provisions of the Covenant and monitoring compliance with them. It would be incompatible with these preconditions of the procedure if a state that voluntarily has subjected itself to such a procedure, would, after first being one of the two parties in a case, then after receiving the Committee's views, simply replaces the Committee's position with its own interpretation as to whether there has been a violation of the Covenant or not. If a state wishes to question the correctness of a legal interpretation by the Committee, it should at least resort to some other procedure before an international court or independent expert body. As this is not likely to happen in practice, the presumption should be that the Committee's views in Optional Protocol cases are treated as the authoritative interpretation of the Covenant under international law.[49]

In contrast, Walter Kälin, also a Committee member, considers the Views to be 'legally non-binding', but adds that they 'possess considerable authority because they stem from a body entrusted and empowered by states parties to determine authoritatively whether human rights have been violated in specific cases. Thus, the principle of good faith requires that states at least weigh the reasons why they are not ready to implement a finding of a violation.'[50] Christian Tomuschat agrees but goes a little further by concluding that '[i]f a state disagrees with the views expressed on a given case, it must present detailed observations specifying its counter-arguments.'[51]

The Committee's position, in the midst of these competing perspectives, follows.

46 UN Doc. CCPR/C/SR.2412 (2006), para. 52.

47 Nowak, n. 19 *supra*, pp. 668–9.

48 M. Nowak & E. McArthur, *The United Nations Convention against Torture: A Commentary* (2008), pp.77-8.

49 R. Hanski & M. Scheinin (eds.), *Leading Cases of the Human Rights Committee* (2003), at 22.

50 W. Kälin & J. Künzli, *The Law of International Human Rights Protection* (2009), at 225.

51 C. Tomuschat, *Human Rights: Between Idealism and Realism* (2nd edn. 2008), at 220.

HUMAN RIGHTS COMMITTEE, GENERAL COMMENT NO. 33: THE OBLIGATIONS OF STATES PARTIES UNDER THE OPTIONAL PROTOCOL TO THE [ICCPR]

UN Doc. CCPR/C/GC/33 (5 Nov. 2008)

...

11. While the function of the...Committee in considering individual communications is not, as such, that of a judicial body, [its Views] exhibit some important characteristics of a judicial decision. They are arrived at in a judicial spirit, including the impartiality and independence of Committee members, the considered interpretation of the language of the Covenant, and the determinative character of the decisions.

...

13. The views of the Committee...represent an authoritative determination by the organ established under the Covenant itself charged with the interpretation of that instrument. These views derive their character, and the importance which attaches to them, from the integral role of the Committee under both the Covenant and the Optional Protocol.

14. [Where a violation has been found, the Committee consistently uses this wording in issuing its Views:]

> "In accordance with article 2, paragraph 3(a) of the Covenant, the State party is required to provide the author with an effective remedy. By becoming a party to the Optional Protocol the State party has recognized the competence of the Committee to determine whether there has been a violation of the Covenant or not and that, pursuant to article 2 of the Covenant, the State party has undertaken to ensure to all individuals within its territory or subject to its jurisdiction the rights recognized in the Covenant and to provide an effective and enforceable remedy in case a violation has been established. In this respect, the Committee wishes to receive from the State party, within 180 days, information about the measures taken to give effect to the Committee's views."

15. The character of the views of the Committee is further determined by the obligation of States parties to act in good faith, both in their participation in the procedures under the Optional Protocol and in relation to the Covenant itself. A duty to cooperate with the Committee arises from an application of the principle of good faith to the observance of all treaty obligations.

...

18. Some States...have failed to accept the Committee's views, in whole or in part, or have attempted to re-open the case. In a number of those cases [the state has simply not responded]. In other cases, rejection of the Committee's views, in whole or in part, has come after the State party has participated in the procedure and where its arguments have been fully considered by the Committee. In all such cases, the Committee regards dialogue between the Committee and the State party as ongoing with a view to implementation....

...

(4) Redefining the Committee's Role under the Optional Protocol

Steiner has argued that the Committee cannot realistically serve the basic dispute-resolution function that informs adjudication by courts in many national legal systems. Nor can it effectively do justice in the individual case within the limits of its jurisdiction and to that extent vindicate the rule of law. Nor can it effectively protect rights under the ICCPR through deterrence. What remains is the function of 'expounding (elucidating, interpreting and explaining) the Covenant so as to engage the Committee in an ongoing, fruitful dialogue' with all relevant actors.

HENRY STEINER, INDIVIDUAL CLAIMS IN A WORLD OF MASSIVE VIOLATIONS: WHAT ROLE FOR THE HUMAN RIGHTS COMMITTEE?

in P. Alston & J. Crawford (eds.), The Future of UN Human Rights Treaty Monitoring (2000), 15, at 38

Despite its stark differences from courts, the Committee could contribute to the international adjudicatory processes that elaborate human rights law in the same manner as do opinions of the European and Inter-American Courts of Human Rights....

Two significant changes in the Committee's mode of functioning under the Protocol would be necessary for realising these proposals: breaking with the historical pattern and style of writing views, and moving from a mandatory to a discretionary jurisdiction.

[In developing his first point, Steiner criticizes the 'formulaic presentations' of the great majority of the Committee's views, particularly because of their lack of readability and the frequent terse, unelaborated statement of the Committee's conclusions following an exhaustive presentation of the parties' arguments. He notes that 'the very effort to reach consensus has sapped the views of strength.... The upshot is that views...hardly summon the human rights community to debate and dialogue. They fail to educate their readership....']

The writing of views that possess the suggested characteristics requires that the Committee husband its energies under the Protocol, to allow more time to research and reflect on an issue, and to write. The Committee would have to allocate time to cases meriting exploration for the development of the Covenant, rather than depend on the flow of registered communications. These requirements would be difficult to satisfy in light of the overload of cases before the Committee and the prospects for its increase.

What then can be done to enable the Committee to establish some control over its caseload and the allocation of its time?...

Achieving [the necessary reduction in caseload] could then require amending the Protocol to make the jurisdiction of the Committee (in whole or in substantial part) discretionary rather than mandatory....

Operating under a discretionary jurisdiction, the Committee might be able to issue 20 to 30 views a year, an ample number for making significant contributions to the understanding and development of the Covenant, and for stimulating thought and dialogue with diverse actors. In so different a system, the Committee would necessarily develop criteria for selection of communications. Such criteria might, for example, lead to rejection of cases where the case turned on controverted matters of fact that the Committee was not in a good position to resolve. They could disfavour cases raising issues that had been settled in prior views or that were not of general significance. The criteria might give priority to emergent issues affecting many states. The Committee might decide to handle a group of related problems, such as issues of criminal procedure or free speech, over several sessions.

... The Judicial Code of the United States gives the United States Supreme Court (with minor exceptions) discretion whether to review any case decided below by a federal or state court — even cases of the highest significance, involving the constitutionality of federal or state statutes, that had previously been subject to mandatory jurisdiction. The Court's criteria for exercising discretion in favour of review include a decision by a state or federal court on 'an important question of federal law that has not been, but should be, settled by this Court'.

...

QUESTIONS

1. Do you consider states to be 'bound' by the Views? If so, on the basis of what theory of obligation? Is it desirable for the communications procedure to have a binding outcome? What techniques do you think the Committee should use to promote compliance with its Views?

2. An earlier draft of GC No. 33 portrayed the Committee as an 'authentic interpreter', stated that states parties were obliged to 'respect' the Committee's Views, stated that rejection of the Views would be 'inconsistent' with treaty obligations and described the Views as an 'essential element' of the states' undertaking to provide a remedy.[52] Does the GC, as adopted, suggest that the Views are binding or not?

3. Why do you suppose Steiner rejects certain functions as impractical or unrealistic for the Committee, such as (1) a general dispute resolution for the states parties, (2) vindication of the rule of law by achieving justice in the individual case, and (3) acting as a deterrent to violations of the ICCPR? Do you agree?

4. How do you assess Steiner's proposal? What guidelines would you suggest for determining whether to hear on the merits a given communication?

[52] G. Ulfstein, 'The Legal Status of Views Adopted by the Human Rights Committee: From Genesis to Adoption of General Comment No. 33', in A. Eide & J. T. Moller (eds.), *Making Peoples Heard* (2011), at 159.

5. 'Each of the Committee's three functions can be found inadequate from different perspectives. But if we look at the Committee as a totality, and examine these functions not discretely but as complementary approaches, we reach a far more favourable judgment about the significance of the Committee's contribution to the human rights regime.' Do you agree?

B. COMMENT ON THE OVERALL UN HUMAN RIGHTS TREATY BODY SYSTEM

While this chapter has focused on the ICCPR, many of the techniques used are followed by the other treaty bodies operating within the UN human rights regime. Until 2003 there were six 'core' treaties in force, each with its own monitoring body. In 2012 there are ten:

- *ICCPR: Human Rights Committee*;
- *ICESCR*: Committee on Economic, Social and Cultural Rights (ICESCR — see Chapter 4);
- *CERD*: Committee on the Elimination of Racial Discrimination (International Convention on the Elimination of All Forms of Racial Discrimination);
- *CEDAW*: Committee on the Elimination of Discrimination against Women (CEDAW Convention — see Chapter 3);
- *CAT*: Committee against Torture (Convention against Torture and Other Cruel, Inhuman or Degrading Treatment or Punishment);
- *SPT*: Subcommittee on Prevention of Torture (Optional Protocol to the CAT Convention);
- *CRC*: Committee on the Rights of the Child (Convention on the Rights of the Child);
- *CMW*: Committee on Migrant Workers (Convention on the Protection of All Migrant Workers and Members of Their Families);
- *CRPD*: Committee on the Rights of Persons with Disabilities (Convention on the Rights of Persons with Disabilities);
- *CED*: Committee on Enforced Disappearances (International Convention for the Protection of All Persons from Enforced Disappearance).

The precise details as to dates, composition, functions, number of cases, etc., are too complex to warrant detailed analysis here. Instead Table 9.1 provides the salient facts. This final section takes note of proposals to streamline or reform the treaty body system as a whole that have been around since at least 1988 and have taken on new life in 2012.

Even when there were only six treaty bodies, and many fewer states parties to the key treaties than is now the case, concerns had been raised about the sustainability of a system which is fragmented, complex and under-resourced. Critics identified shortcomings in all aspects of the reporting process. They noted widespread non-reporting and significant tardiness in reporting by states, and that reports are often superficial. Governments are reluctant to facilitate domestic debate around the reports. In relation to the committees themselves, the level of expertise and independence of members has been questioned, the Concluding Observations on states reports are often excessively general, the approach adopted to reports by different states by a single treaty body is not always consistent and there is inadequate follow-up to recommendations made to governments.

Another pressing issue concerns the duplication of reporting obligations under the different treaty regimes. As originally conceived, the system was designed to enable a state to become a party to one treaty, even if it had no interest in any of the others. Now that a great many states have ratified most of the treaties, the overlapping reporting burden and the uncoordinated responses by the different committees are increasingly being challenged by governments. And identical reports might elicit different responses from different committees. NGOs with sparse resources must deal with the difficulties of monitoring states' compliance with each of these treaties and seek to give adequate publicity to the work of each.

A snapshot of the system's expansion illustrates the nature of the challenge. Between 2000 and 2012 the system grew:

- in number of treaty bodies (from 6 to 10 treaty bodies);
- in overall number of sessions (from 11 to 24);
- in overall number of weeks in session (from 44 to 73);
- in the number of treaty body experts (from 97 to 172);
- in the quantity of final decisions taken on individual complaints (from 51 final decisions taken by the three treaty bodies having an active petitions procedure in 2000 to 120 decisions in 2010 by four treaty bodies);
- in the quantity of State party reports under annual review (from 105 State party reports in 2000 to 120 State party reports in 2011);
- in the number of ratifications (currently at 1536 ratifications under the 9 core conventions and two Optional Protocols with reporting obligations, in contrast to 927 in 2000); and
- in the number and type of service requests (list of issues prior to reporting, follow-up procedures etc.) placed on the [Secretariat].[53]

In commenting on these developments, the High Commissioner for Human Rights observes that:

> This growth has not been matched by financial and human resources. [The system's] potential coherence is also challenged by the multiplication of treaty bodies as many treaty bodies are now dealing with cross-treaty themes. Resources and coherence are therefore the main two challenges....
>
> [Backlogs also threaten the system]: 250 States parties reports and 470 individual communications (averages for 2011) are pending consideration, though at the same time over 600 States parties reports are overdue (only one-third of States parties submit their reports on time). The reporting process is already close to

[53] The High Commissioner's Treaty Body Strengthening Initiative, Information Note, 26 Jan. 2012.

Table 9.1 UN Human Rights Treaties

Treaty	ICCPR	ICESCR	ICERD	CEDAW	CAT	OPCAT	CRC	CMW	CRPD	ICED
Adopted in	1966	1966	1965	1979	1984	–	1989	1990	2006	2006
Entry into force	1976	1976	1969	1981	1987	–	1990	2003	2008	2010
States parties (as at 5/2012)	167	160	175	187	150	–	193	45	112	32
OPs adopted/in force	1:1966/1976	1: 2008/not yet in force	–	1: 1999/2000	1: 2002/2006 (OPCAT—see next column)	2002/2006	1:2000/2002 (armed conflict)	–	1: 2006/2008	–
	2:1989/1991	–	–	–	–	–	2:2000/2002 (sale of children)	–	67	–
	–	–	–	–	–	–	3: 2011/not yet in force (communications procedure)	–	–	–
States parties to OPs	1: 114	1: 8 (needs 10 to enter into force)	–	1: 104	1: 63	63	1: 147	–	–	–
	2: 73	–	–	–	–	–	2: 157	–	–	–
	–	–	–	–	–	–	3: 0	–	–	–
Treaty Body	HR C'ee	ESCR C'ee	CERD C'ee	CEDAW C'ee	C'ee agst Torture	Subc'ee on Prevention of Torture	C'eeRC	C'ee MW	C'ee RPD	C'eeED
C'ee Members	18	18	18	23	10	25	18	14	18	10

Reporting periodicity: initial/periodic	1 yr/whenever the C'ee so requests	2/5 yrs	1/2 yrs	1/4 yrs	1/4 yrs	No reporting facility – visits	2/5 yrs	1/5 yrs	2/4 yrs	2 yrs/whenever the C'ee so requests
Weeks of mtgs per year	9	6	6	9	8	3	9	3	2	2
No of reports examined per year	14 in 2011	20 in 2011	21 in 2011	23 in 2011	17 in 2011	3 countries visited in 2011	20 in 2011	4 in 2011	5 in 2011	None yet
Interstate complaint procedure?	Yes	No	Yes	Yes (OP)	Yes	No	No	No	Yes (OP)	Yes
Individual complaints procedure?	Yes	Not yet (OP)	Yes	Yes	Yes	No	No (OP)	Yes (not yet operative)	Yes	Yes
Total cases registered (as at last annual report)	2,076	–	48	20	462	–	–	–	0	–
Cases decided (during last annual reporting period)	151	–	1	6	17	–	–	–	0	–
On-site inquiry visits	No	No	No	Yes (OP)	Yes (in CAT & OP)	Yes	No	No	No	Yes
No. of GCs	34	21	34	28	2	–	13	1	0	0
Day of General Discussion?	No	Yes	Yes	No	No	–	Yes	Yes	Yes	No

> becoming meaningless under some treaties, as the backlog results in States reports to be considered years after their submissions: six to seven years for CRPD..., three to four years for CESCR and the CRC and usually two to three years for other treaty bodies (with a reporting periodicity established in treaties of 4–5 years). Equally, for those treaty bodies considering individual communications, the increasing number of petitions has led to important delays. For instance, for the Human Rights Committee, with 360 pending cases, the average delay between registration and a final decision on a case is around three and a half years. The average delay for the Committee against Torture, which has 100 cases pending, is two and a half years. This has a negative impact not only for the petitioners who have to wait a long time for their case to be decided, but equally on States parties who are often faced with a Committee's request for interim measures over a prolonged period of time.[54]

Proposals to reform the system have been on the table for over two decades. Beginning in 1989, the issues were analysed in three reports by Philip Alston, appointed by the UN Secretary-General to suggest long-term options for the system. He proposed: (1) reducing the number of treaty bodies and hence the number of reports required; (2) encouraging states to produce a single 'global' report to be submitted to all relevant treaty bodies; and (3) replacing the requirement of comprehensive periodic reports with specifically tailored reports.[55] Governments responses to these proposals were mixed,[56] but a new impetus to reform came from reports by the UN Secretary-General in 2002 and 2005.[57]

In 2006, Louise Arbour as High Commissioner, put forward a far-reaching proposal to replace the then seven treaty bodies with a single full-time body.[58] The proposal envisaged that '[t]he specificities of each treaty must be preserved and their focus on specific rights...should not be diminished.' The goal was to highlight 'the interdependent and indivisible nature of the obligations set out in the treaties', while strengthening implementation without requiring the renegotiation of existing substantive obligations of states parties. The proposal warned that unless the overall system 'functions and is perceived as a unified, single entity responsible for monitoring the implementation of all international human rights obligations, with a single, accessible entry point for rights-holders, the lack of visibility, authority and access which affects the current system will persist.'

The proposal suggested the following advantages of such a body: it could adopt a holistic approach; its procedures could be more flexible and creative; its relative simplicity would facilitate the work of NGOs, national human rights institutions and other stakeholders; the interpretation of comparable provisions of different treaties would be consistent; General Comments would be consistent and clear; pending

[54] Ibid.

[55] P. Alston, 'Final Report on Enhancing the Long- Term Effectiveness of the United Nations Human Rights Treaty System', UN Doc. E/CN.4/1997/74. Earlier reports were published as UN Doc. A/44/668 (1989) and UN Doc. A/CONF.157/PC/62/Add.11/ Rev.1 (1993).

[56] See UN Docs. E/CN.4/1998/85 and E/CN.4/ 2000/98.

[57] An Agenda for Further Change, UN Doc. A/57/387 (2002); and In Larger Freedom, UN Doc. A/59/2005/Add.3 (2005).

[58] Concept Paper on the High Commissioner's Proposal for a Unified Standing Treaty Body, UN Doc. HRI/MC/2006/2.

individual complaints would be adjudicated expeditiously, which would make the system more effective and attractive; follow-up capacity would be enhanced; it could be flexible in terms of the timing and venue of its sessions; it could take on the supervision of new treaty standards if necessary; and it could work more closely with other human rights bodies, such as the special procedures or regional human rights bodies. Perhaps, most importantly, it 'would inevitably be more visible than the existing treaty bodies, and would be able to make its procedures, recommendations and decisions better known at the national level.'

The report acknowledges that a unified body could adopt various modes of operation including: (1) a single body with no chambers; (2) chambers operating in parallel; (3) chambers along functional lines; (4) chambers along treaty lines; (5) chambers along thematic lines; and (6) chambers along regional lines. In terms of the legal challenge of introducing such a system the report notes: 'At a minimum, a simplified ratification procedure, or the provisional application of the new monitoring regime pending the entry into force of the amendments... could be envisaged.'

The proposal met with strong resistance, both from states and especially from treaty body members. Various states and NGOs subsequently convened meetings designed to come up with proposals to reform and enhance the system. These included conferences in Dublin (2009), Marrakech (2010), Poznan (2010) and Sion (2011) (the outcome documents are available at www.ishr.ch/treaty-body-reform).

In 2012, the General Assembly (Res. 66/254 of 23 Feb. 2012) authorized 'an open-ended intergovernmental process... to conduct open, transparent and inclusive negotiations on how to strengthen and enhance the effective functioning of the human rights treaty body system.' The resolution was not considered by the Assembly's Third Committee, as would normally be the case, and was adopted by a vote of 85 for, 0 against and 66 abstentions. The proposal's sponsors were Belarus, Bolivia, China, Cuba, Indonesia, Iran, Nicaragua, Pakistan, Russia, Syria, Tajikistan, Venezuela and Zimbabwe. The states that had previously been most actively involved in reform discussions dissociated themselves from the initiative, but did not vote against it.

QUESTION

What do you see as the principal disadvantages of a unified treaty body? Could these be overcome through creative arrangements in establishing the new body, or would too much of the appeal of the existing system be lost?

ADDITIONAL READING

H. Keller & G. Ulfstein (eds.), *UN Human Rights Treaty Bodies: Law and Legitimacy* (2012); M. Cherif Bassiouni & W. Schabas (eds.), *New Challenges for the UN Human Rights Machinery: What Future for the UN Treaty Body System and the Human Rights Council Procedures?* (2011); S. Egan, *The UN Human Rights Treaty System:*

Law and Procedure (2011); M. O'Flaherty, 'The Concluding Observations of United Nations Human Rights Treaty Bodies', 27 Hum. Rts. L. Rev. 27 (2006); M. Nowak, *UN Covenant on Civil and Political Rights: ICCPR Commentary* (2nd edn. 2005); P. Alston & J. Crawford (eds.), *The Future of UN Human Rights Treaty Monitoring* (2000); C. Heyns & F. Viljoen, *The Impact of the United Nations Human Rights Treaties on the Domestic Law* (2002); A. Bayefsky, *The UN Human Rights Treaty System: Universality at the Crossroads* (2001). The best website for UN treaty body documents is www.bayefsky.com and the best for reporting and analysis is that of the International Service for Human Rights: www.ishr.ch.

10

International Human Rights Fact-Finding

Fact-finding is at the core of most human rights advocacy. In recent years there has been a huge increase in the number and variety of fact-finding missions undertaken by intergovernmental bodies, international NGOs and a range of other actors. There is, however, no clear definition of the term 'fact-finding'. Indeed, on its face, the notion that an investigator will simply find the 'facts' of a complex and contested situation or incident is problematic at various levels. Nevertheless, fact-finding has become a term of art in the human rights field and it generally involves: (1) seeking to ascertain the facts about alleged human rights abuses, ideally through on-site visits, (2) determining state responsibility and perhaps also individual responsibility for violations of human rights, and (3) making recommendations as to reforms and reparations.

International law has long made use of the technique of establishing fact-finding mechanisms in the form of commissions of inquiry in order to resolve disputes among states. The 1899 Hague Convention (I) for the Pacific Settlement of International Disputes contained an entire chapter on such international inquiries. States unable to resolve a dispute diplomatically were urged to 'institute an International Commission of Inquiry, to facilitate a solution of these differences by elucidating the facts by means of an impartial and conscientious investigation.' Important protections were, however, built in. The provisions did not apply to disputes involving 'honor [or] vital interests', and reports were 'limited to a statement of facts', thus leaving 'the conflicting Powers entire freedom as to the effect to be given to this statement'. Subsequently both the League of Nations Covenant of 1919 (Art. 12) and the UN Charter (Art. 33(1)) called for the use of international inquiries as one of the measures that should be considered in seeking to resolve disputes endangering international peace and security.

In the human rights area, the 1919 Constitution of the International Labour Organization (Art. 26) provided for the creation of a commission of inquiry in cases of persistent violations of labour rights. Although only used 12 times — most recently in relation to Myanmar (1998), Belarus (2004) and Zimbabwe (2010) — the procedure has been developed in a systematic and relatively rigorous manner. As a result, much of the early literature on human rights fact-finding drew significantly on the ILO's procedures and practice.

By far the largest volume of fact-finding undertaken in the human rights area is carried out by nongovernmental organizations. Amnesty International began country missions in 1962, and Human Rights Watch (then Helsinki Watch) in the early 1980s. HRW's later approach to reporting has been widely imitated. Many other groups, such as the International Commission of Jurists, the International Crisis Group, the International Federation of Human Rights and diverse specialist groups — focused on issues such as the death penalty, torture, housing rights, health and racial, gender and religious discrimination — now generate hundreds of fact-finding reports every year. In addition, much reporting occurs at the national level, either by local NGOs, national human rights institutions or sector-specific groups. While the focus of the present chapter is primarily on fact-finding by intergovernmental organizations such as the UN, the principles discussed are broadly applicable to these other actors as well.

The international dimension of fact-finding is increasingly central. Given that, by definition, human rights violations usually imply governmental wrongdoing, the governments in question are often unlikely to undertake meaningful domestic investigations. International involvement thus becomes a means to break through the domestic stalemate. Today, serious human rights violations are increasingly likely to attract sustained international attention and lead to insistent calls for some form of international monitoring or other involvement. Perhaps the commonest response is to establish an international fact-finding mechanism. This is well illustrated by the plethora of inquiries that came out of the 'Arab Spring' uprisings that began in January 2011, with major UN Human Rights Council-mandated investigations in relation to Libya and Syria, an independent international commission report on Bahrain and a range of fact-finding and assessment reports by the OHCHR on various countries, including Egypt, Libya, Tunisia and Yemen.

At the domestic level, governments might seek to head off international involvement by authorizing a fresh investigation into previously rejected allegations, urging a re-trial in a controversial case, permitting scrutiny by an independent actor of the police and the judiciary's performance or perhaps even creating a national commission of inquiry with a fact-finding mandate. But most such initiatives can be effectively captured, diverted or muzzled if the government concerned chooses to do so. International involvement in fact-finding thus becomes a way to transcend obstacles that might otherwise seem insurmountable.

Some of this fact-finding activity has become relatively routinized, such as the monitoring and reporting carried out by a large number of Special Rapporteurs in the name of the UN Human Rights Council (p. 699, *supra*), by the Council of Europe's Human Rights Commissioner (p. 986, *infra*) and by the Inter-American Commission on Human Rights (p. 991, *infra*). In addition, new fact-finding procedures are also now being activated under the auspices of various UN human rights treaty bodies (p. 840, *supra*). But a great deal of fact-finding is relatively ad hoc. It takes the form of diverse types of inquiries established by a range of intergovernmental bodies, both international and regional, inquiries that are set-up on a one-time only basis in response to a particularly serious or politicized incident or pattern of abuses. These fact-finding bodies are differently composed, are given varying mandates, use widely differing methodologies and tend to serve a broad range of objectives.

Unsurprisingly, and indeed perhaps appropriately, some of the more routinized fact-finding has proven to be very controversial, and there has been extensive criticism by governments of such activities (see Kenya, p. 718, *supra*). But it is the ad hoc, or one-time only, inquiries that have often proven to be the most contentious. Some of them have generated immense international attention, as well as criticism, as illustrated by the reactions to the September 2009 report to the Human Rights Council by the Goldstone Commission on alleged violations of human rights and international humanitarian law during the Gaza conflict in 2008–2009 (see p. 720, *supra*).

This proliferation of major inquiries across a wide range of situations challenges the common wisdom which portrays the emergence of the various international and mixed criminal courts and tribunals over the past two decades as the most significant development in the human rights field. It could reasonably be argued that the explosion of international fact-finding activities has been a development of comparable significance, but while the criminal courts and tribunals have generated a veritable industry and a vast literature, fact-finding has been largely neglected as an area for sustained exploration, critique and refinement.

At its best, fact-finding is comparatively cost-effective, is very flexible in design, can be mobilized rapidly, can transform public and governmental understanding of a situation and has the potential to promote wide-ranging political or institutional reform. It can also play a crucial role in attributing criminal responsibility and laying the groundwork for subsequent prosecutions.

This chapter begins with a case study of Sri Lanka by looking at the norms governing accountability and the ways in which these obligations might or might not be effectively discharged at the national level. It then introduces two further case studies — of the Darfur region in the Sudan, and the Democratic Republic of the Congo — in order to illustrate some of the most critical issues that must be confronted in such fact-finding. These include the mandate of the inquiry, the law to be applied, the judicial or other character of the inquiry, the nature of the state's obligation to cooperate, the investigative methodology, the reliability of witness testimony, the due process rights of governments, whether criminal responsibility should be established and whether standardized guidelines for international fact-finding should be adopted. The chapter concludes by looking at a typology of governmental responses to fact-finding and considers the potential impact on fact-finding of new information and communication technologies.

A. THE RELATIONSHIP BETWEEN NATIONAL AND INTERNATIONAL LEVEL FACT-FINDING

Because the primary responsibility for responding to human rights violations lies at the national level, international fact-finding should ideally only be a subsidiary or complementary undertaking. This Part explores the relationship between these two levels through a case study of Sri Lanka's response to allegations of serious violations of human rights and international humanitarian law in the final months of its 30-year-long conflict with a rebel group, the Liberation Tigers of Tamil Eelam (the LTTE or 'Tamil Tigers'). As government forces finally gained the decisive upper hand, large numbers of primarily Tamil civilians and combatants were trapped within an increasingly small enclave in the northeast of the island. What actually happened between September 2008 and May 2009 is heavily contested, but commentators have estimated that as many as 40,000 civilians might have been killed.

Many foreign governments and other actors called for an independent inquiry into the events. These efforts were rejected by a majority in the UN Human Rights Council in May 2009, but international pressure for an investigation remained strong. In May 2010, the President of Sri Lanka appointed an eight-member national-level *Lessons Learnt and Reconciliation Commission* (LLRC), and the following month the UN Secretary-General appointed an international *Panel of Experts* consisting of Marzuki Darusman, a former Indonesian Attorney-General, Steven Ratner, a US law professor, and Yasmin Sooka, a member of both the South African and Sierra Leonean Truth and Reconciliation Commissions. The Panel, which reported in March 2011, was not given access to the country. The LLRC reported in November 2011.

The UN report begins with a summary of its findings, followed by an analysis of the applicable principles of accountability, and a brief review of the LLRC's terms of reference and composition. The materials then reproduce some of the most contentious findings of the LLRC.

REPORT OF THE SECRETARY-GENERAL'S PANEL OF EXPERTS ON ACCOUNTABILITY IN SRI LANKA

(31 Mar. 2011)

Executive Summary

...

Allegations found credible by the Panel

The Panel's determination of credible allegations reveals a very different version of the final stages of the war than that maintained to this day by the Government of Sri Lanka. The Government says it pursued a "humanitarian rescue operation" with a policy of "zero civilian casualties." ...

... Between September 2008 and 19 May 2009, the Sri Lanka Army advanced its military campaign into the Vanni [the Northern Province] using large-scale and widespread shelling, causing large numbers of civilian deaths. This campaign constituted persecution of the population of the Vanni. Around 330,000 civilians were trapped into an ever decreasing area, fleeing the shelling but kept hostage by the LTTE. The Government sought to intimidate and silence the media and other critics of the war through a variety of threats and actions, including the use of white vans to abduct and to make people disappear.

The Government shelled on a large scale in three consecutive No Fire Zones, where it had encouraged the civilian population to concentrate, even after indicating that it would cease the use of heavy weapons. It shelled the United Nations hub, food distribution lines and near the International Committee of the Red Cross

(ICRC) ships that were coming to pick up the wounded and their relatives from the beaches. It shelled in spite of its knowledge of the impact, provided by its own intelligence systems and though notification by the United Nations, the ICRC and others. Most civilian casualties in the final phases of the war were caused by Government shelling.

The Government systematically shelled hospitals on the frontlines [and] systematically deprived people in the conflict zone of humanitarian aid.... Tens of thousands lost their lives from January to May 2009....

The Government subjected victims and survivors of the conflict to further deprivation and suffering after they left the conflict zone....

...

[I]n conclusion, the Panel found credible allegations that comprise five core categories of potential serious violations committed by the Government of Sri Lanka: (i) killing of civilians through widespread shelling; (ii) shelling of hospitals and humanitarian objects; (iii) denial of humanitarian assistance; (iv) human rights violations suffered by victims and survivors of the conflict, including both IDPs and suspected LTTE cadre; and (v) human rights violations outside the conflict zone, including against the media and other critics of the Government.

The Panel's determination of credible allegations against the LTTE associated with the final stages of the war reveal six core categories of potential serious violations: (i) using civilians as a human buffer; (ii) killing civilians attempting to flee LTTE control; (iii) using military equipment in the proximity of civilians; (iv) forced recruitment of children; (v) forced labour; and (vi) killing of civilians through suicide attacks.

Accountability

Accountability for serious violations of international humanitarian or human rights law is not a matter of choice or policy; it is a duty under domestic and international law. These credibly alleged violations demand a serious investigation and the prosecution of those responsible. If proven, those most responsible, including Sri Lanka Army commanders and senior Government officials, as well as military and civilian LTTE leaders, would bear criminal liability for international crimes.

At the same time, accountability goes beyond the investigation and prosecution of serious crimes that have been committed; rather it is a broad process that addresses the political, legal and moral responsibility of individuals and institutions for past violations of human rights and dignity....

...

V. A. Applicable international standards and comparative experiences

262. [Based on experience in diverse conflicts world-wide, the Panel identifies] a set of global expectations that have found their expression in international standards [of accountability and] a range of diverse practical approaches for addressing such crimes....

263. Several human rights treaties...contain obligations regarding investigation. Article 2(3) of the ICCPR requires the State to provide an effective remedy to victims of human rights violations. That treaty provision has been interpreted by

the United Nations Human Rights Committee to require States to investigate all violations of the Covenant and, in the case of gross violations or those constituting international crimes, to bring the alleged perpetrator to justice. In addition, Article 12 of the Convention against Torture... requires States to investigate and prosecute (or extradite to another State seeking to prosecute) all persons alleged to have committed the international crime of torture.

264. [Such investigations should comply with international legal standards relating to:] *independence, impartiality, thoroughness, effectiveness* and *promptness*.

265. Apart from the obligations arising from these treaties, the duty to investigate derives from several other international bodies and resolutions [such as the] *Basic Principles and Guidelines on the Right to a Remedy and Reparations for Victims of Violations of International Human Rights and Humanitarian Law* [GA Res. 60/147 (2006)]. The Security Council too has frequently reiterated the importance of eliminating impunity for serious abuses of human dignity, including through prosecutions of war crimes and crimes against humanity....

266. In addition, various United Nations processes have formulated important standards and frameworks regarding accountability. Of particular significance is the 2005 *Set of Principles for the Protection and Promotion of Hunan Rights through Action to Combat Impunity* [which] lays out the core understanding that victims of crimes under international law have three basic rights: the right to the truth, the right to justice and the right to reparations, including through institutional guarantees of non-recurrence.

267. ... States have increasingly refrained from amnesties for genocide, war crimes and crimes against humanity, or have used judicial or legislative measures to overturn earlier amnesties; international courts have similarly ruled that amnesties for such crimes are impermissible. This is also the policy position of the United Nations. The Government of Sri Lanka has also said that "it is our considered view that amnesties intrinsically encourage a culture of impunity and are therefore inappropriate."

268. With respect to violations of international humanitarian law in internal armed conflict, there is now strong support in international practice and judicial precedent for a legal duty upon States to investigate and, if the evidence warrants, prosecute serious violations. In particular, an interpretation that accepts a duty to investigate such violations in international armed conflicts but not in an internal armed conflict is no longer sustainable....

269. The legal duties and standards elaborated above are now buttressed by a generation of state practice....

270. The concept of transitional justice as an inter-related set of measures required to address legacies of violations has gained global acceptance....

...

272. [It] is a useful lens through which Sri Lanka can focus its approach to accountability. It is applicable in any post-conflict setting'.... Sri Lanka should seek to guarantee the rights of victims to *truth*, *justice* and *reparations*, all of which are based on international standards and should form an essential part of a transitional justice approach.

...

B. The Government of Sri Lanka's position on accountability

278. … Sri Lanka's approach to accountability should, thus, be assessed against international standards and comparative experiences to discern how effectively it enables victims of the war to realize their rights to truth, justice and reparations.

279. … Sri Lanka is seeking to balance accountability and reconciliation through … (1) judicial proceedings against some members of the LTTE, and (2) political responsibility of successive Governments for their failure to discharge their constitutional obligation to protect Sri Lanka's people and territory against the LTTE. [According to the Government]:

> … what happened in the past must be relegated to history, by all communities inclusive of the majority community. This must be accompanied by a manifestation of contrition on part of the wrong doer as a recognition of the supremacy of the rule of law within a democratic process.

280. The Government of Sri Lanka told the Panel that the LLRC … is not focused on individual accountability, but on a wider notion of political responsibility. …

281. Missing from the Government's two-pronged conception is any notion of accountability for its own conduct in the prosecution of the war, especially during the final stages. …

…

285. … A de facto decision not to hold accountable those who committed serious crimes on behalf of the State during the final stages of the war is a clear violation of Sri Lanka's international obligations and is not a permissible transitional justice option. While there is some flexibility on the forms of punishment under international law, investigations and trials are not optional, and the creation of a commission such as the LLRC does not in itself fulfill the State's duty in this case.

286. In relation to … "restorative justice" … Sri Lanka recognizes the non-applicability of amnesties, but it is not taking action on the accountability of its military and political leaders. …

287. Further, the suggestion that there is a choice between "restorative" and "retributive" justice is based upon a false dichotomy, since international standards require that States both ensure justice, by investigating violations and prosecuting crimes, and implement other measures for victims, including truth and reparations. Equating criminal justice with retributive justice is simply not accurate, as criminal justice has many goals beyond retribution. …

…

C. Lessons Learnt and Reconciliation Commission

…

292. The Government of Sri Lanka has repeatedly referred to the LLRC as the essential mechanism of its domestic response to issues arising from the armed conflict. …

…

1. Mandate of the LLRC

...

303. [T]he LLRC's temporal mandate explicitly ends on 19 May 2009, an end-point that necessarily precludes consideration by the LLRC of credible violations that occurred in the aftermath of the armed conflict, after that date.

304. [T]he LLRC's mandate does not satisfy international standards for clarity in the mandate of an accountability mechanism, which should explicitly refer to the power to investigate violations of international humanitarian or human rights law, committed by any party in a conflict, including the State or its agents.

2. Independence and impartiality of the Commission

305. International law requires a body investigating alleged violations of humanitarian and human rights law to be independent, impartial and competent. Independence comprises both actual independence and the public perception thereof.

306. In the case of the LLRC, at least three of its members have serious conflicts of interest that both directly compromise their ability to function with independence and impartiality, and undermine public perception of them as independent. The Chair [was previously] Attorney-General.... A second member was Sri Lanka's Permanent Representative to the United Nations during the final stages of the armed conflict, representing and defending the Government's views on the evolving military and humanitarian situation. A third member was...legal advisor...and then advisor on international legal affairs [to the Ministry of Foreign Affairs during the period covered by the Commission.]

...

REPORT OF THE COMMISSION OF INQUIRY ON LESSONS LEARNT AND RECONCILIATION

(Nov. 2011), at p. 328

...

Chapter Four: Observations and Recommendations IHL Issues relevant to the final phase of the conflict

Measures to safeguard civilians and avoid civilian casualties

9.4 [T]he Commission is satisfied that the military strategy that was adopted to secure the LTTE held areas was one that was carefully conceived, in which the protection of the civilian population was given the highest priority....

9.5 [P]rotection of civilian life was a key factor in the formulation of a policy for carrying out military operations. They militate against any proposition that deliberate targeting of civilians was part and parcel of a policy, although specific episodes...warrant further investigation....

No Fire Zones (NFZs)

9.6 [T]he Commission concludes that the Security Forces had not deliberately targeted the civilians in the NFZs, although civilian casualties had in fact occurred in the course of crossfire....

9.7 ... [Was] the action of the Security Forces of returning fire into the NFZs...excessive in the context of the Principle of Proportionality. Given the complexity of the situation [the Commission considers] that the Security Forces were confronted with an unprecedented situation when no other choice was possible and all "feasible precautions" that were practicable in the circumstances had been taken.

...

Specific Instances of Death or Injury to Civilians

9.9 The Commission is faced with similar difficulties in attempting a re-construction of certain incidents involving the loss of civilian lives.... [Material presented] points towards possible implication of the Security Forces for the resulting death or injury to civilians, even though this may not have been with an intent to cause harm. In these circumstances the Commission stresses that there is a duty on the part of the State to ascertain more fully, the circumstances under which such incidents could have occurred, and if such investigations disclose wrongful conduct, to prosecute and punish the wrong doers....

Hospitals/Makeshift Hospitals

9.10 [In relation to the shelling of hospitals, the material] points to a somewhat confused picture as to the precise nature of events, from the perspective of time, exact location and direction of fire.

9.11 In this backdrop, the challenge faced by the Commission is the determination of responsibility for the acts in question, on the basis of concrete evidence.

9.12 In making its determination, the difficulty faced by the Commission is twofold;

> a.... [N]o immediate investigation in the nature of a crater analysis had been undertaken, presumably given the intensity of the conflict, in the areas in question.
>
> b. None of the persons making representations was able to state with certainty that they were in a position to definitely confirm that the shells which fell on the hospitals, originated exclusively from the side of the Sri Lanka Army or from the LTTE....

9.13 Thus the Commission's task of reaching a definite conclusion as to who was responsible...is made extremely difficult by the non-availability of primary evidence of a technical nature and also the fact that supportive civilian evidence is equivocal in nature....

9.14 ... [Nevertheless,] consideration should be given to the expeditious grant of appropriate redress to those affected...as a humanitarian gesture....

...

Medical Supplies

...

9.22 [G]iven the inconclusive nature of the material before it, the issue of medical supplies to civilians in the conflict areas during the final days of the conflict is a matter that requires further examination....

Alleged disappearances after surrender/arrest

9.23 ... [A] number of people...stated that they had directly witnessed certain persons surrendering to the custody of the Army[;] it is the clear duty of the State to cause necessary investigations into such specific allegations.... [T]he launching of a full investigation into these incidents and where necessary instituting prosecutions is an imperative also to clear the good name of the Army who have by and large conducted themselves in an exemplary manner....

...

Observations on the IHL Regime in its application to Internal Conflicts

9.27 [The Commission describes IHL applicable to non-state groups in internal armed conflicts as 'rudimentary' and cites the example of the 'cynical disregard' by such groups for the well-being of civilians as exemplified by the 'integration of "Safety Zones" into combat strategy and the use of civilians as human shields'. These practices result in 'grey areas' in the law.]

...

9.31 The careful construction of a legal framework governing conflicts between States and non state armed groups...could provide the answer in ensuring greater compliance with IHL principles by the non state armed groups. These complex issues [demand] the immediate attention of...States and...the UN and the ICRC...to fill the existing lacunae in IHL....

...

Observations and Recommendations on the issue of Casualties

9.33 Based on the firsthand accounts and other material placed before it by the affected civilians and detainees, it was clear to the Commission that despite the efforts by the Security Forces to avoid harm to people, there have been instances of exchanges of fire over the civilian areas including NFZs causing death and injury to civilians.

9.34 The Commission recognizes the complex challenge faced by the Security Forces in neutralizing a suicide cult based terrorist group seeking security behind a human shield. It also appreciates that the priority, and indeed the natural instinct, of the security forces and other authorities was to 'save lives rather than count bodies.' The Commission however notes with regret that there is no official record or a post conflict estimate of civilian casualties either by the civilian administrative authorities in the area or by the defense authorities. Whilst the Security Forces had their own casualty figures and an estimate of the LTTE casualties, the absence of authoritative civilian casualty records, with the exception of the limited data from the Ministry of Health, has led to widely varying figures of civilian casualty estimates by different entities, media organizations and authorities.

9.35 The fact that there was no proper verification process, either by the civilian administration or by the military has contributed to the unverified sweeping generalizations, of a highly speculative nature as regards casualty figures.

9.36 It is the considered view of the Commission however, that eye witness accounts and other material available to it indicate that considerable civilian casualties had in fact occurred during the final phase of the conflict. This appears to be due to cross fire, the LTTE's targeted and deliberate firing at civilians, as well as due to the dynamics of the conflict situation, the perils of the geographical terrain, the LTTE using civilians as human shields and the LTTE's refusal to let the hostages get out of harm's way.

9.37 The Commission therefore recommends [the investigation of several specific incidents and the undertaking of a] household survey covering all affected families in all parts of the island to ascertain firsthand the scale and the circumstances of death and injury to civilians, as well as damage to property during the period of the conflict.

...

NOTE

In response to the LLRC report, the International Crisis Group (ICG) commended the Commission for 'its sensible recommendations on governance, land issues and the need for a political solution', but criticized its failure to undertake an independent investigation of alleged violations. In particular, it criticized the conclusions excerpted above on several grounds. First, the Commission 'considered only the materials the government chose to place before it' and made 'no independent assessment of the full scope of information in the government's possession — including all communications with the UN, ICRC and sources in the conflict zone, as well as other evidence from government and international sources, such as uncensored satellite images and footage from the military's unmanned drones.' Second, it criticized the Commission for drawing 'conclusions ruling out unlawful attacks when there are thousands of witnesses who did not come forward, partly because of the lack of witness protection, and when there is no indication that the LLRC had physical access to the final war zone', an area that has 'been off limits to everyone but the military since the end of hostilities'. Third, it criticized the Commission for fundamentally misstating or misapplying the relevant principles of international law, including its failure to present a fair exposition of the principle of distinction under international humanitarian law. Fourth, the LLRC failed to engage the UN Panel's 'legal or factual analysis in any meaningful way'.

The ICG also noted that 'numerous witnesses who testified to the commission about government violations have since been questioned and harassed by the military and the police.' It noted that the 'LLRC's request that the government conduct a series of further, limited inquiries into some of these issues is far from an adequate response. The Sri Lankan government's past three years of denial, dissimulation and intimidation of critics has proven it is neither willing nor able to carry out impartial and effective investigations.' As a result, it concluded that the 'responsibility now falls on the international community to take up the task of ensuring post-war accountability'.[1]

QUESTIONS

1. Should all current or former government officials be excluded from appointment to a commission of inquiry? Would the same reason preclude the appointment of someone with a human rights NGO background?

2. Having received the LLRC report, what steps could the government take to demonstrate its commitment to international standards for accountability?

3. In light of the competing perspectives reflected in the UN and LLRC reports, what approach should the international community adopt?

4. How would you evaluate the approach adopted by the Commission in paras. 9.34–9.37? What alternative approaches might it have adopted?

NATIONAL COMMISSIONS OF INQUIRY

The creation of a national level commission of inquiry is a technique that has long been used in a great many countries in response to serious violations of human rights. An analysis of the outcomes of nine such inquiries in Sri Lanka between 1977 and 2001 concluded, *inter alia*, that: (1) some of the inquiries had been 'used by governments to expose the abuses of a previous political regime for partisan reasons or, conversely...to escape accountability'; (2) the commissions' recommendations had a negligible impact in terms of prosecutions and legal accountability; (3) the state had failed to amend or reform its laws and regulations in response to the commissions' recommendations; and (4) the judicial system had generally failed the victims; even where judicial orders had been made they had remained unimplemented by successive governments.[2]

Sri Lanka is not, however, alone in setting up commissions of inquiry that end up achieving very little in terms of respect for human rights. Consider the following survey, based on a large number of inquiries held in countries throughout the world.

[1] International Crisis Group, *Statement on the Report of Sri Lanka's Lessons Learnt and Reconciliation Commission*, 22 Dec. 2011.

[2] Kishali Pinto-Jayawardena, *Post-War Justice in Sri Lanka: Rule of Law, the Criminal Justice System, and Commissions of Inquiry* (2010), 16–17.

REPORT OF THE SPECIAL RAPPORTEUR ON EXTRAJUDICIAL, SUMMARY OR ARBITRARY EXECUTIONS, PHILIP ALSTON

UN Doc. A/HRC/8/3 (2 May 2008), at p. 6

...

1. Reasons to establish inquiries

16. [The regular criminal justice system will often fail in response to major human rights violations]. First, the police may lack the necessary investigative capacities.... Second, those charged with investigating the events might themselves be suspected, or closely connected to suspects.... Third, victims, relatives and witnesses might lack confidence in the police or other investigating authorities and be unprepared to cooperate with them. Fourth, political interference at the local, State or federal levels might be hindering an effective investigation. Fifth, the killings might be part of a phenomenon which needs to be investigated more broadly and not confined to a criminal investigation. Sixth, a solution to the problem, including the punishment of those responsible, might require the mobilization of a degree of public pressure and political will which require more than a regular investigation.

...

2. Positive role of commissions of inquiry in addressing impunity

22. In principle, commissions of inquiry can play an important role in combating impunity. First, the commission [might] provide an independent investigation where the criminal justice institutions are seen to be biased or incompetent. This is often the case where ... the police or military, are themselves involved in abuses.... It is also the case where there is long history of repeated abuses that police fail to investigate, public prosecutors fail to prosecute, or courts fail to punish due to incompetence, bias, or lack of expertise. A commission may also be seen as desirable where one incident is particularly complex and significant....

23. Second, a commission can provide informed advice to the Government on the institutional reforms necessary to prevent similar incidents from occurring in the future. It can perform an essential function that is generally unsuitable to police, prosecutors or courts, and explain the underlying causes.... [W]here it appears that the regular institutions are incapable of combating impunity, a commission can propose structural or long-term reforms to address criminal justice institutional deficiencies....

...

3. Guiding principles for a national commission of inquiry

25. In order for a commission to address impunity, it must be independent, impartial and competent. The commission's mandate should [empower it] to obtain all information necessary to the inquiry but it should not suggest a predetermined outcome. Commission members must have the requisite expertise and competence to effectively investigate the matter and be independent from suspected

perpetrators and from institutions with an interest in the outcome of the inquiry. Commissions should be provided transparent funding and sufficient resources to carry out their mandate. Effective protection from intimidation and violence needs to be provided to witnesses and commission members. When it establishes the commission, the Government should undertake to give due consideration to the commission's recommendations; when the report is completed, the Government should reply publicly to the commission's report or indicate what it intends to do in response to the report. The commission's report should be made public in full and disseminated widely.

…

5. Lessons learned from 26 years of reporting on commissions of inquiry

50. … Far too many of the commissions dealt with by the Special Rapporteur over the past 26 years have resulted in de facto impunity for all those implicated.

51. In essence, the problem is that commissions can be used very effectively by Governments for the wrong purposes: to defuse a crisis, to purport to be upholding notions of accountability and to promote impunity.… Because a commission creates the appearance of government action, its announcement often prevents or delays international and civil society advocacy around the human rights abuses alleged. Moreover, an ineffective commission can be more than just a waste of time and resources; it can contribute to impunity by deterring other initiatives, monopolizing available resources and making subsequent endeavours to prosecute difficult or impossible.

B. CHALLENGES OF FACT-FINDING

Fact-finding is, of course, infinitely more complex than its name suggests. 'Facts' are not simply waiting to be 'found'. Faced with the prospect of an international inquiry, governments will often be hostile or at least reluctant. In the next readings, a former senior official of the International Labour Organization, Nicolas Valticos, seeks to balance the importance of achieving some sort of due process with the need for flexibility. An excerpt from the State Department's annual Country Report on Human Rights Practices emphasizes the difficulty of getting to the truth of the matter, and Diane Orentlicher explores some of the practical challenges confronting fact-finders.

NICOLAS VALTICOS, FOREWORD

in B. G. Ramcharan (ed.), International Law and Fact-Finding in the Field of Human Rights (1982), at vii

… [How can fact-finding be designed] to meet the requirements of the international community while taking account of the susceptibilities of the State involved?

...

... [F]act-finding in the field of human rights has a special importance, and also encounters special difficulties, both because of the subject-matter and because of the importance attached to it by public opinion, which regards it as the acid test of the effectiveness of international organisations. [It] is however all the more difficult, because it frequently concerns the action and essential interests, if not indeed the very structure, of the States involved, who are therefore less inclined to accept international intervention in such matters. The issues often have political aspects and are the subject of discussion in political bodies, a factor which necessarily complicates their examination....

...

... [As] we are on the frequently unstable terrain of international law, it is necessary ... not to confine oneself within unduly rigid categories or rules. In international law, functions intertwine — at times, indeed, too much — and judicial aspects cannot always be distinguished clearly from non-judicial ones. It is therefore not always possible, in international fact-finding, to transpose internal judicial procedures in full. Nor is it always possible — or even desirable — to establish unduly detailed rules which may turn out not to be applicable in practice. If procedures are too formal and judicial and rules too detailed, they may prove not to be adapted to the great variety of situations, to the susceptibilities and objections of the States concerned, or to practical needs.

One conclusion to be drawn from this is that it is necessary to have available a variety of procedures suited to different situations, ranging from quasi-judicial inquiries to methods involving a minimum of formality....

...

The principles must be such that, having regard to the procedure followed and the persons entrusted with it, the fact-finding process enjoys the confidence of the international community as well as of the State concerned. It thus becomes possible more readily to obtain the co-operation of the latter, while not leaving the international community in any doubt about the integrity and reliability of the findings.

These principles must naturally be based on the principal concepts of due process of law in domestic procedures ..., but they must also make allowance for the special features of this kind of international action. Thus, in the event of on-the-spot visits, it will not normally be possible for a representative of the complainant to be present, nor will it be appropriate for a representative of the party complained against to take part in interviews with private individuals. The latter party should, however, be given an opportunity to comment on allegations received in the course of such visits. Similarly, precautions have sometimes to be taken to ensure the safety of witnesses and to protect them against intimidation or reprisals (or the mere fear of reprisals)....

A process as difficult as human rights fact-finding calls not only for procedural safeguards. In a divided and distrustful world, and on questions where there exist profound differences of views, fact-finding itself and the conclusions and recommendations emanating from it are more likely to find acceptance if it is entrusted to independent and impartial persons. Not only logic, but also several decades of experience lead to that conclusion.

US DEPARTMENT OF STATE, 2010 COUNTRY REPORTS ON HUMAN RIGHTS PRACTICES

(2011)

Introduction

2010 marks the 35th year that the State Department has produced [these reports]. What began as the response to a Congressional mandate to report on the human rights situation in those countries that were receiving U.S. assistance in the mid 1970s has blossomed into a detailed analysis of human rights conditions in all countries that are members of the United Nations.…

… [T]hese reports are used throughout the U.S. government and by many foreign governments. And, importantly, they are increasingly being used by individual citizens and NGOs as critical sources of information on what is happening in the world.… [R]eports are translated into over 50 languages and made available online.

The U.S. government compiles the human rights report because we believe it is imperative for countries, including our own, to ensure that respect for human rights is an integral component of foreign policy. We provide these reports as a form of comprehensive review and analysis.

…

… These 194 country reports are comprehensive, if not exhaustive. Their production is a Herculean endeavor requiring extra-ordinary efforts by a team of talented and committed human rights officers at U.S. Embassies around the world, and by their counterparts in Washington, D.C.… Each country team collects, analyzes, and synthesizes information from a variety of sources, including domestic and international human rights organizations, other governments, multilateral organizations, and members of civil society. Once the reports are drafted, they are rigorously edited, reviewed, and fact-checked, to ensure accuracy and objectivity.

…

Appendix A — Notes on Preparation of Report

The annual Country Reports on Human Rights Practices are based on information available from a wide variety of sources, including U.S. and foreign government officials, victims of human rights abuse, academic and congressional studies, and reports from the press, international organizations, and nongovernmental organizations (NGOs) concerned with human rights. We find particularly helpful, and make reference in the reports to, the role of NGOs, ranging from groups within a single country to those that concern themselves with human rights worldwide. While much of the information that we use is already public, information on particular abuses frequently cannot be attributed, for obvious reasons, to specific sources. This report reflects the Department of State's assessments and concerns with respect to the human rights situation around the world. The Department of States does not use sources or information it believes lack credibility.

… The Country Reports cover respect for human rights in foreign countries and territories worldwide; they do not purport to assess any human rights implications of actions by the United States Government or its representatives, nor do they consider human rights implications of actions by the United States Government or of coalition forces in Iraq or Afghanistan. . . .

We have attempted to make the reports as comprehensive, objective, and uniform as possible in both scope and quality of coverage. We have paid particular attention to attaining a high standard of consistency in the reports despite the multiplicity of sources and the problems associated with varying degrees of access to information, structural differences in political, legal, and social systems.

Evaluating the credibility of reports of human rights abuses is often difficult. Most governments and opposition groups deny that they commit human rights abuses and sometimes go to great lengths to conceal any evidence of such acts. There are often few eyewitnesses to specific abuses, and they frequently are intimidated or otherwise prevented from reporting what they know. On the other hand, individuals and groups opposed to a government sometimes have powerful incentives to exaggerate or fabricate abuses, and some governments similarly distort or exaggerate abuses attributed to opposition groups. We have made every effort to identify those groups (for example, government forces) or individuals who are believed, based on all the evidence available, to have committed human rights or other related abuses. Many governments that profess to oppose human rights abuses in fact secretly order or tacitly condone them or simply lack the will or the ability to control those responsible for them. Consequently, in judging a government's policy, the reports look beyond statements of policy or intent and examine what a government has done to prevent human rights abuses, including the extent to which it investigates, brings to trial, and appropriately punishes those who commit such abuses.

DIANE F. ORENTLICHER, BEARING WITNESS: THE ART AND SCIENCE OF HUMAN RIGHTS FACT-FINDING

3 Harv. Hum. Rts J. 83 (1990), at 109

. . .

A. Direct Evidence

The leading international NGOs generally regard direct evidence—testimony of victims or eyewitnesses—as highly probative; such evidence forms the bedrock of the prototypical NGO report on human rights conditions in a country. Some human rights professionals will not, as a matter of principle, use hearsay accounts of human rights violations. Eyewitness and victim testimony is not, however, persuasive in itself; the probative value of direct testimony turns largely upon the circumstances and manner in which it is obtained, including the process used to "select" witnesses, the conditions under which they are interviewed, and the corroboration obtained.

1. Identifying Potential Witnesses

Several overarching goals, each designed to maximize the evidentiary value of direct testimony, guide human rights investigators in identifying interviewees who can furnish direct evidence of violations.

a. Avoiding Politically-Biased Selection Criteria
First, NGOs seek to ensure that the selection process does not produce testimony that is politically motivated or otherwise biased. . . .

Sometimes, however, the richest sources of information about potential witnesses and the best witnesses themselves may be — or may appear to be — politically biased. Because repressive governments persecute in particular their perceived or actual opponents, human rights organizations would lose the benefit of much victim testimony if they excluded as interview subjects persons who appeared to be politically biased against their government. . . .

b. Obtaining Representative Testimony
Second, human rights investigators seek to avoid selection procedures that produce a skewed picture of overall patterns of violations in a country. When possible, NGOs draw upon a broad range of sources to help identify potential witnesses. Input from multiple sources helps minimize distortions that might be built into any particular source's contribution.
. . .

c. Time Period Covered
Third, NGOs generally seek witnesses who can provide testimony about recent practices. . . .

. . . Generally, NGOs tend to focus on the year preceding publication of their reports, concentrating on the latter half of the year. Because, however, it is relatively difficult to obtain and corroborate recent direct testimony about abuses in a closed country, reports on such countries often cover a longer period, perhaps reaching back several years. . . .
. . .

In many contexts, 'watershed' developments — a change in government, the lifting of martial law, the beginning of a ceasefire coupled with implementation of a political amnesty — are presumed or thought likely to affect the state of human rights observance in a country. In these situations a country report released after the benchmark event has occurred may be discounted. . . .

d. Size of Sample Group
Fourth, human rights investigators seek to obtain a large enough sample of direct testimony on the subject of their inquiry to enable them to reach judgments about overall patterns of abuse and to support their final conclusions. . . .
. . .

2. Circumstances of Interviews

. . . [C]ircumstances surrounding an interview can play an important role in ensuring the reliability of direct testimony. Many human rights professionals conduct all interviews of victims and eyewitnesses outside the presence of third persons to ensure that the witness' testimony is not inhibited or otherwise influenced by others. This approach also enables the interviewer to attempt to corroborate a witness' allegations by separately interviewing other witnesses to the same incident.

Despite the general benefits associated with private interviews, many NGOs have avoided adopting an inflexible rule in this regard. At times, the presence of a third person during an interview can be helpful; a traumatized victim of torture may, for example, be more comfortable speaking to a stranger if a familiar, trusted intermediary is present.

Even if conducted in private, an interview can be compromised by the nearby presence of others. This risk often arises when a fact-finding delegation seeks to interview residents of refugee settlements....

3. The Interview

Testimony of eyewitnesses and victims is more valuable than hearsay allegations because the finder of fact has an opportunity to test and, through direct observation, to assess the credibility of persons who purport to have direct knowledge of critical facts. Also, the interviewer is able to elicit, through highly specific questions, the sort of detailed information necessary to a credible inquiry....

At the outset, the way an interviewer presents himself and the nature of the organization he represents can affect a witness' inclination to be forthcoming and honest.... [I]nformation presented by an interviewer respecting his purpose in speaking to the witness, the use that will be made of the testimony, and conditions of confidentiality may have a significant effect on the witness' disposition to cooperate.

Early on, the interviewer should make clear that the final product of the interview will be a public report. At some point, the interviewer must ask the witness if she is willing to allow her testimony to be used and, if so, whether she is willing to be identified by name in the report.

...

The interviewer's questions should generally be open-ended, and in other respects (including the use of a nonjudgmental tone of voice) should avoid suggesting that a particular answer to a question is the "right" one. Still, an interviewer must at times ask highly specific questions to elicit detailed information about alleged violations.

...

...

Relentless follow-up questions also help a researcher bridge cultural or other gaps in communication. Human rights investigators travel throughout the world, and interview people whose concepts of time, space, and other factors may differ from those of the investigators. While these differences cannot be overcome entirely, their potentially distorting effects can be substantially minimized through extensive, detailed questioning.

...

4. Corroborating Direct Testimony

Human rights investigators use a broad range of techniques to corroborate testimony of victims and eyewitnesses. Highly persuasive forms of corroboration, such as autopsy reports concluding that torture inflicted during detention was the cause of death, are simply unavailable in many situations investigated by NGOs. In these circumstances, investigators turn to other means of corroboration that, while not conclusive standing alone, contribute to a broader process of verification.

Under any circumstances a skilled interviewer can test a witness' testimony during the interview itself. One important test is the internal consistency and coherence of the testimony. …

…

In evaluating credibility, it is always relevant to assess the personal motivations of witnesses. Testimony is, of course, most persuasive when the witness has no apparent personal interest in the allegations, or when her statements actually run counter to her personal interest. Sometimes, however, the most direct evidence available comes from unquestionably partisan sources. While partisan interest does not render witnesses incapable of being truthful, it does signal the need to obtain corroborating evidence strong enough to rebut presumptions that the witnesses' testimony is unreliable.

In many cases, elements of a witness' testimony can be corroborated from sources external to the interview [such as] through a visual inspection of the site of an alleged incident. Sometimes, portions of a witness' testimony can be corroborated by reference to court records, police logs, medical, or inquest records. …

The testimony of other witnesses to the same alleged incident can provide strong corroboration. …

In these circumstances, skilled interviewers often attempt to elicit seemingly irrelevant details, like the weather conditions at the time of an alleged military attack, as well as the central facts of the reported violations. This information can be a useful basis for assessing the credibility of accounts, since witnesses are unlikely to coordinate a fabricated account to the extent of agreeing on such details.

A human rights investigator should not, however, expect to find perfect concordance with respect to every detail from one account to the next. Human perceptions and memory are imperfect at best, and the most reliable accounts of eyewitnesses may vary with respect to such details as the estimated time of an event. Experienced fact-finders develop the ability to detect which discrepancies cast doubt upon witnesses' allegations, and which ones merely reflect the level of ambiguity that surrounds any recalled event.

…

QUESTIONS

1. When President Obama was pressed in 2009 to agree to a commission to investigate the use of torture and renditions by the administration of his predecessor, he responded that he was 'more interested in looking forward than I am in looking backwards'. Under what circumstances might a government agree to set up a truly independent inquiry into alleged human rights violations of its own or of a predecessor?

2. Is the account by Valticos convincing in terms of the feasibility of combining respect for due process with the sort of flexibility and adaptability that he says is essential?

3. To what extent can a government agency such as the US State Department present an 'objective' report on human rights around the world? Is the credibility of the

exercise affected by the omission of any reference to the actions of the United States and the unexplained exemption of actions by international, including US, forces in Iraq and Afghanistan?

4. Based on Orentlicher's analysis, how much of an 'art' or a 'science' is fact-finding? Should extensive training be required for any individual who participates in a fact-finding mission?

C. FACT-FINDING METHODOLOGIES: CASE STUDIES

The challenges of ascertaining what really happened, and of devising the best possible strategy to achieve justice for both the victims and the perpetrators, can best be understood through the lens of actual case studies. In considering two of the most important recent international fact-finding missions — to Darfur and the DRC — our focus is on the methodology used. Following excerpts from the two very lengthy reports, the materials explore some of the key issues that need to be addressed in designing such inquiries.

1. Darfur

The Darfur region in the west of Sudan has long been in crisis. A 2009 report by the African Union's High-Level Panel on Darfur noted that the roots of the crisis 'lie in a history of neglect of the Sudanese peripheries, dating from colonial times and continuing during the years of Sudan's independence.' The report characterizes the current situation as 'a manifestation of Sudan's inequitable distribution of wealth and power', and suggests that it 'consists of different levels of conflict, including local disputes over resources and administrative authority, conflict between Darfur and the centre of power in Khartoum, and an internationalised conflict between Sudan and Chad.'[3] Other observers have offered significantly different explanations for the crisis. HRW traces the present phase back to early 2003 when Sudanese Government forces and ethnic militia known as 'Janjaweed' became involved in an armed conflict with two rebel groups — the Sudanese Liberation Army/Movement and the Justice and Equality Movement. According to HRW, government forces responded to the rebels by waging 'a systematic campaign of "ethnic cleansing" against the civilian population who are members of the same ethnic groups as the rebels. Sudanese government forces and the Janjaweed militias burned and destroyed hundreds of villages....' Informed estimates of the numbers who died range as high as 300,000. Thousands of women and girls were raped or assaulted,

[3] Darfur: The Quest for Peace, Justice and Reconciliation, Report of the African Union High-Level Panel on Darfur (AUPD), Oct. 2009, AU Doc. No. PSC/AHG/2(CCVII), paras. 2–3.

well over two million people were displaced and perhaps two million others have required 'some form of food assistance because the conflict has destroyed the local economy, markets, and trade in Darfur'.[4] But the precise magnitude of the problem remains a matter of contention among the parties and outside observers.

By mid 2004 international concern was high and there was considerable pressure on international organizations to respond decisively. The Security Council (Res. 1564 of 18 Sept. 2004) expressed its 'grave concern at the lack of progress with regard to security and the protection of civilians, disarmament of the Janjaweed militias and identification and bringing to justice of the Janjaweed leaders responsible for human rights and international humanitarian law violations in Darfur'; recalled 'that the Sudanese Government bears the primary responsibility to protect its population [and] to respect human rights' and noted 'that all parties are obliged to respect international humanitarian law' (preambular paras.). Invoking its powers under Chapter VII of the UN Charter, it:

> 12. *Requests* that the Secretary-General rapidly establish an international commission of inquiry in order immediately to investigate reports of violations of international humanitarian law and human rights law in Darfur by all parties, to determine also whether or not acts of genocide have occurred, and to identify the perpetrators of such violations with a view to ensuring that those responsible are held accountable, *calls on* all parties to cooperate fully with such a commission....

REPORT OF THE INTERNATIONAL COMMISSION OF INQUIRY ON DARFUR TO THE UNITED NATIONS SECRETARY-GENERAL

Geneva (25 Jan. 2005)

...

1. Establishment of the Commission

1. [In October 2004] the Secretary-General appointed a five member body (Mr. Antonio Cassese, from Italy; Mr. Mohammed Fayek, from Egypt; Ms Hina Jilani, from Pakistan; Mr. Dumisa Ntsebeza, from South Africa, and Ms Theresa Striggner-Scott, from Ghana), and designated Mr. Cassese as its Chairman. The Secretary-General decided that the Commission's staff should be provided by the Office of the High Commissioner for Human Rights.... The Secretary-General requested the Commission to report to him within three months, i.e. by 25 January 2005.

2. Terms of reference

...

3. The first [task assigned by the Security Council] implies that the Commission, rather than investigating alleged violations, must investigate "reports" of such

[4] Human Rights Watch, Q & A: Crisis in Darfur, Dec. 2006.

violations committed by "all parties".... In this respect the Commission must act as a fact-finding body, beginning with an assessment of information contained in the various reports made by other bodies including Governments, United Nations bodies, organs of other intergovernmental organizations, as well as NGOs.

4. It also falls to the Commission to characterize, from the viewpoint of international criminal law, the violations of international human rights law and humanitarian law it may establish. This legal characterization is implicitly required by the [Council's mandate]....

5. The second task... is that of legally characterizing the reported violations with a view to ascertaining whether they amount to genocide.

6. The third task is that of "identifying the perpetrators of violations" "with a view to ensuring that those responsible are held accountable". This requires the Commission... also to suggest possible mechanisms for holding those perpetrators accountable. The Commission therefore must collect a reliable body of material that indicate which individuals may be responsible for violations committed in Darfur and who should therefore be brought to trial with a view to determining their liability. The Commission has not been endowed with the powers proper to a prosecutor (in particular, it may not subpoena witnesses, or order searches or seizures, nor may it request a judge to issue arrest warrants against suspects). It may rely only upon the obligation of the Government of the Sudan and the rebels to cooperate....

7. ... [T]he Commission has to interpret the word "perpetrators" as covering the executioners or material authors of international crimes, as well as... those who may be held responsible for international crimes, under the notion of superior responsibility, because they failed to prevent or repress the commission of such crimes although they a) had (or should have had) knowledge of their commission, and b) wielded control over the persons who perpetrated them. This interpretation is justified by basic principles of international criminal law....

8. ... [T]he tasks of the Commission include that of "ensuring that *those responsible* are held accountable".... [If the Security Council] aimed at putting an end to atrocities, why should the Commission confine itself to the material perpetrators, given that those who bear the greatest responsibility normally are the persons who are in command, and who either plan or order crimes, or knowingly condone or acquiesce in their perpetration?

...

10. The fourth task [is to ensure] that "those responsible are held accountable". To this effect, the Commission intends to propose measures for ensuring that those responsible for international crimes in Darfur are brought to justice.

...

3. Working methods

12. [The Commission started by writing to member states, intergovernmental organizations and nongovernmental organizations], providing information about its mandate and seeking relevant information....

13. The Commission agreed at the outset that it would discharge its mission in strict confidentiality. In particular, it would limit its contacts with the media to

providing factual information about its visits to the Sudan. The Commission also agreed that its working methods should be devised to suit each of its different tasks.

14. Thus, with regard to its first and second tasks, the Commission decided to examine existing reports on violations of international human rights and humanitarian law in Darfur, and to verify the veracity of these reports through its own findings, as well as to establish further facts. Although clearly it is not a judicial body, in classifying the facts according to international criminal law, the Commission adopted an approach proper to a judicial body. It therefore collected all material necessary for such a legal analysis.

15. The third task, that of "identifying perpetrators", posed the greatest challenge. The Commission discussed the question of the standard of proof that it would apply in its investigations. In view of the limitations inherent in its powers, the Commission decided that it could not comply with the standards normally adopted by criminal courts (proof of facts beyond a reasonable doubt), or with that used by international prosecutors and judges for the purpose of confirming indictments (that there must be a prima facie case). It concluded that the most appropriate standard was that requiring a reliable body of material consistent with other verified circumstances, which tends to show that a person may reasonably be suspected of being involved in the commission of a crime. The Commission would obviously not make final judgments as to criminal guilt; rather, it would make an assessment of possible suspects that would pave the way for future investigations, and possible indictments, by a prosecutor.

16. The Commission also agreed that, for the purpose of "identifying the perpetrators", it would interview witnesses, officials and other persons occupying positions of authority, as well as persons in police custody or detained in prison; examine documents; and visit places (in particular, villages or camps for IDPs, as well as mass grave sites) where reportedly crimes were perpetrated.

17. For the fulfilment of the fourth task the Commission deemed it necessary to make a preliminary assessment of the degree to which the Sudanese criminal justice system has been able and willing to prosecute and bring to trial alleged authors of international crimes perpetrated in Darfur, and then consider the various existing international mechanisms available. It is in the light of these evaluations that it has made recommendations on the most suitable measures.

4. Principal constraints under which the Commission has operated

18–19. [The Commission identifies two major constraints: (i) the time limit of three months that required it 'to work intensely and under heavy time pressure'; and (ii) its limited budget that provided for only 13 staff members: a Chief Investigator and four other investigators, two female investigators specializing in gender violence, four forensic experts and two military analysts.] ...

5. Brief account of the Commission's visits to the Sudan

20. The Commission first visited the Sudan from 8 to 20 November 2004. It met with a number of high level officials including the First Vice-President, the [Ministers of Justice, Foreign Affairs, Interior, Defence and Federal Affairs], the

Deputy Chief Justice, the Speaker of Parliament, the Deputy Head of the National Security and Intelligence Service, and members of the Rape Committees. It met with representatives of non-governmental organizations, political parties,...interested foreign government representatives, [and UN representatives in the Sudan]....

21. From 11 to 17 November 2004, the Commission visited Darfur. It divided itself into three teams, each focusing on one of the three states of Darfur. Each team met with the State Governor (*Wali*) and senior officials, visited camps of internally displaced persons, and spoke with witnesses and to the tribal leaders....

...

24. A second visit to the Sudan took place between 9 and 16 January 2005....

...

6. Cooperation of the Sudanese authorities and the rebels

...

27. [The resolution creating the Commission, adopted under Chapter VII of the UN Charter] "*calls on* all parties to cooperate fully with such a commission". The Commission considers that, by the very nature of the Commission and its mandate, both the Government of the Sudan and the rebels are under a *bona fide obligation* to cooperate with it in the discharge of its various functions. In any event, both the Government of the Sudan and the rebel groups have willingly accepted to cooperate with the Commission.

(i.) Criteria for appraising cooperation

28. The Commission set forth the following criteria for evaluating the degree of cooperation of both the Government and the rebels: (i) freedom of movement throughout the territory of the Sudan; (ii) unhindered access to all places and establishments, and freedom to meet and interview representatives of governmental and local authorities, military authorities, community leaders, non-governmental organizations and other institutions, and any such person whose testimony is considered necessary for the fulfilment of its mandate; (iii) free access to all sources of information, including documentary material and physical evidence; (iv) appropriate security arrangements for the personnel and documents of the Commission; (v) protection of victims and witnesses and all those who appear before the Commission in connection with the inquiry and, in particular, guarantee that no such person would, as a result of such appearance, suffer harassment, threats, acts of intimidation, ill-treatment and reprisals; and (vi) privileges, immunities and facilities necessary for the independent conduct of the inquiry. A letter was sent to the Government outlining these criteria.

(ii.) Cooperation of the Government

...

30. Generally speaking the attitude of the Government authorities towards the Commission has been cooperative....

31. ... [O]n 12 November 2004...the Minister of Justice provided the following assurances...: a) the Government would accept the report of the Commission,

whatever its findings; b) witnesses of incidents would not be subjected to maltreatment; and c) following strict instruction from the President, Omer Hassan Al-Bashir, no Sudanese officials would obstruct the Commission's investigations.

32. Furthermore, the Government did not impede the conduct of the Commission's work in the Sudan.... [On two occasions when access to detainees or places of detention was refused by mid-level officials, the Commission successfully appealed to higher authorities.]

33. ... [In response to a specific request the Commission was assured] that it would be able to have access to and examine the minutes of the meetings of the Security Committees in the three States of Darfur and their various localities. However, when requested to produce those minutes, each of the Governors of the three States asserted that no such minutes existed and instead produced a selected list of final decisions on general issues. According to reliable sources, minutes and reports of such meetings are in fact produced [but] the Commission did not see copies of these documents.

34. ... [T]he Commission requested access to records of the deployment of military aircraft and helicopter gunships in Darfur since February 2003. Again, the Commission undertook to treat such records confidentially. The Minister of Defence agreed to comply with the request.... [While some records were provided] a complete set of the records requests was never provided to the Commission.

35. The Commission also wishes to stress that there have been episodes indicative of pressure put by some regional or local authorities on prospective witnesses, or on witnesses already interviewed by the Commission....

36. In other instances, local authorities refused to allow the Commission's investigative team entry into a camp to interview witnesses. However these cases were settled in due course, after negotiations with the authorities.

(iii.) Cooperation of the Rebels

37. The Commission was in contact only with the two main rebel movements, the JEM and the SLM/A, and generally considers that both groups cooperated with the Commission. The Commission met with representatives and members of the two groups on a number of occasions in the Sudan, as well as outside the country.... Discussions were open and frank....

...

39. The Commission was never refused access to areas under the control of the rebels and was able to move freely in these areas. The rebel groups did not interfere with the Commission's investigations of reported incidents involving the rebels.

VI. Violations of International Human Rights and Humanitarian Law — The Commission's Factual and Legal Findings.

...

4. The task of the Commission

222. Taking... into account [reports from 'other bodies', the Government of Sudan and 'the rebel groups'] the Commission conducted independent investigations to

establish the facts. The conclusions of the Commission are based on the evaluation of the facts gathered or verified through these investigations. However, reports from other sources are relied upon for analysis where the facts reported are consistent with the results of the Commission's own inquiry.

223. It was not possible for the Commission to investigate all of the many hundreds of individually documented incidents reported by other sources. The Commission, therefore, selected incidents and areas that were most representative of acts, trends and patterns relevant to the determination of violations of international human rights and humanitarian law and with greater possibilities of effective fact-finding. In making this selection, access to the sites of incidents, protection of witnesses and the potential for gathering the necessary evidence were, amongst others, of major consideration.

...

Section III

Identification of the Possible Perpetrators of International Crimes

I. General

523. The Commission has satisfied itself, on the basis of credible probative information which it has collected or has been rendered to it, and which is consistent with reports from various reliable sources, that a number of persons may be suspected to bear responsibility for crimes committed in Darfur....

...

525. The Commission has however decided to withhold the names of these persons from the public domain. It will instead list them in a sealed file that will be placed in the custody of the United Nations Secretary-General. The Commission recommends that this file be handed over to a competent Prosecutor (the ICC Prosecutor, according to the Commission's recommendations), who will use that material as he or she deems fit for his or her investigations. A distinct and voluminous sealed file, containing all the evidentiary material collected by the Commission, will be handed over to the High Commissioner for Human Rights. This file should be delivered to a competent Prosecutor.

526. The decision to keep confidential the names...is based on three main grounds. First, it would be contrary to elementary principles of due process or fair trial to make the names of these individuals public. In this connection, it bears emphasizing Article 14 of the ICCPR and Article 55 (2) of the ICC Statute, which concern the rights of persons under investigation and which may be reasonably held to codify customary international law. These rights include the right to be informed that there are grounds to believe that the person has committed a crime, the right to remain silent and to have legal assistance. The publication of the names would be done without granting the possible perpetrators the fundamental rights that any suspect must enjoy.

...

528. The second [ground is that] the Commission has not been vested with prosecutorial or investigative functions proper. It has therefore confined itself to collecting reliable information about the persons that might be suspected to be responsible

for crimes in Darfur. Most of the persons the Commission has interviewed took part on the basis of assurances of confidentiality. The Commission therefore did not take signed witness statements, but rather made careful accounts of the testimony given by witnesses. In addition to witness accounts, it collected police reports, judicial decisions, hospital records, etc. It also made crime scene verification (checking for consistency with witness version, photographing and mapping, and assessing located grave sites).... However, the information it has gathered would be misused if names were to be published, as this could lead to premature judgements about criminal guilt that would not only be unfair to the suspect, but would also jeopardize the entire process undertaken to fight impunity.

529. The third ground for confidentiality is the need to protect witnesses heard by the Commission (as well as prospective witnesses)....

...

531. The Commission notes at the outset that it has identified ten (10) high-ranking central Government officials, seventeen (17) Government officials operating at the local level in Darfur, fourteen (14) members of the Janjaweed, as well as seven (7) members of the different rebel groups and three (3) officers of a foreign army (who participated in their individual capacity in the conflict), who may be suspected of bearing individual criminal responsibility for the crimes committed in Darfur.

532. The Commission's mention of the number of individuals it has identified should not however be taken as an indication that the list is exhaustive....

2. The Democratic Republic of the Congo

The DRC has 71 million people, and 250 distinct ethnic groups, spread across a landmass the size of Western Europe. In the early 1960s, after a stormy road to independence from Belgium, Colonel Mobutu seized power and re-named the country Zaire. By late 1994 the war in neighbouring Rwanda had spilled over into the DRC and in 1997 Mobutu was forced into exile by Laurent-Desire Kabila, acting with Rwandan assistance. But President Kabila soon fell out with his former allies and the country disintegrated into regions controlled by Kabila, Rwanda and Uganda respectively. Kabila was assassinated in 2001 and was succeeded by his son, Joseph Kabila. Although elections were held in 2006 and 2011, widespread violence has continued, especially in the eastern part of the country. One widely reported estimate (by the International Rescue Committee) was that some 5.4 million people died in the DRC between 1998 and 2007 as a result of the war, mostly as a result of disease and starvation, as well as from violence.[5] An effort in 1997–1998 by the UN to document human rights violations had to be abandoned. After mass graves were discovered in 2005 in North Kivu, the effort was renewed and led to Security Council support and the DRC Government's agreement. The following report reflects the work of over 20 human rights officers.

[5] In a perfect example of the challenges of fact-finding, the calculations upon which this estimate is based have been strongly contested. See *The Shrinking Costs of War: Human Security Report* (2009), Ch. 3.

OFFICE OF THE HIGH COMMISSIONER FOR HUMAN RIGHTS DEMOCRATIC REPUBLIC OF THE CONGO, 1993–2003: REPORT OF THE MAPPING EXERCISE

(Aug. 2010)

89. [The terms of reference, approved by the Secretary-General, were to:]

- Conduct a mapping exercise of the most serious violations of human rights and international humanitarian law committed within the territory of the DRC between March 1993 and June 2003.
- Assess the existing capacities within the national justice system to deal appropriately with such human rights violations that may be uncovered.
- Formulate a series of options aimed at assisting the Government of the DRC in identifying appropriate transitional justice mechanisms to deal with the legacy of these violations, in terms of truth, justice, reparation and reform....

90. It was decided that OHCHR would lead the Mapping Exercise and the project was funded by the voluntary contributions of ten interested partners....

91. ... By contributing significantly to the documentation on the most serious violations of human rights and international humanitarian law committed in the DRC during this time of conflict, this report aims to assist the Congolese authorities and civil society in defining and implementing a strategy that will enable the many victims to obtain justice and thereby fight the widespread impunity. This should also enable the mobilisation of other international resources to address the principal challenges faced by the DRC with regard to justice and reconciliation.

92. [The Mapping Exercise took ten months in total, from the arrival of the Team leader in the DRC to the submission of the final report to the HCHR.] ...

93. [The government of the DRC was invited to comment on any factual inaccuracies in the report, while the governments of other named countries were also invited to provide feedback. The comments received would be made public when the report was released.]

Methodology

94. A "mapping exercise" is based on a number of methodological premises. A mapping exercise itself should be concerned not only with the violations themselves but also with the context(s) in which they were committed.... Such an exercise may include various activities, such as the collection, analysis and assessment of information, surveys and witness interviews, and consultation with field experts and consultants, among others. This type of project...functions perfectly as a preliminary step prior to the formulation of transitional justice mechanisms, whether they be judicial or not, to enable the identification of challenges, the assessment of needs and better targeting of interventions....Among the recent examples of mapping exercises, some have been based solely on documents in the public domain (Afghanistan) and others on interviews with thousands of witnesses (Sierra Leone).

95. One of the major premises is that mapping remains a preliminary exercise that does not seek to gather evidence that would be admissible in court, but rather to "provide the basis for the formulation of initial hypotheses of investigation by giving a sense of the scale of violations, detecting patterns and identifying potential leads or sources of evidence". With regard to human rights and international humanitarian law violations, the Mapping Exercise should provide a description of the violation(s), their nature and location in time and space, the victim(s) and their approximate number and the — often armed — group(s) to which the perpetrators belong(ed), among others. As a result, the findings of such an operation should be very useful for all transitional justice mechanisms, whether they be judicial or not.

96. ... [The limited time frame] imposed certain constraints in terms of the methodology to be used. It did not foresee in-depth investigations, but rather the gathering of basic information on the most serious incidents, chronologically and province by province. The collection, analysis and use of any existing information sources on the violations committed during the period under examination was also established as a starting point for the Exercise, in particular "the outcome of past United Nations missions to the country". The subsequent six-month deployment of five in-field mobile Teams allowed for this information to be verified and either corroborated or invalidated in accordance with the standards set out herein with the aid of independent sources, while also enabling the reporting of previously undocumented violations.

97. ... It was important that the methodology adopted for the Mapping Exercise [outlined below] catered for the requirements and constraints of the ToR, in particular the necessity to cover the entire Congolese territory as well as the period from 1993 to 2003, to report only the "most serious" violations of human rights and international humanitarian law and to ensure that the security of witnesses was not compromised and that information was kept confidential.

Gravity threshold

98. The expression "serious violations of human rights and international humanitarian law"... is non-specific and open to interpretation. Generally speaking, it is intended to apply to violations of the right to life and the right to physical integrity. It may also cover violations of other fundamental human rights, in particular where such violations are systematic and motivated by forms of discrimination forbidden under international law. In international humanitarian law, violations are considered serious when they endanger protected persons and property, or when they violate important values.

99. Given the scale of the violations committed in the ten years of conflict over a very vast territory, it was necessary to select from the most serious crimes. Each recorded incident demonstrates the commission of one or several serious violations of human rights and international humanitarian law localised to a given date and location. Occasionally, a wave of individual violations (e.g. arbitrary arrests and detentions, summary executions, etc.) is considered as one incident.

100. [To identify the most serious incidents the report uses the following four sets of criteria applied cumulatively:]

- Nature of the crimes and violations linked to a given incident: Each recorded incident points to the commission of one or more crimes under international law, be they war crimes, crimes against humanity, genocide or other crimes constituting serious human rights violations. All of these crimes can be classified on the basis of the objective gravity threshold, where violations of the right to life are considered most serious (murder, massacre, summary execution, etc.), followed by violations of the right to physical and mental integrity (sexual violence, torture, mutilation, injury to body, etc.), the right to liberty and security of person (arbitrary arrest and detention, forced displacement, slavery, recruitment and use of child soldiers, etc.), the right to equality before the law and equal protection of the law without any discrimination (persecution) and, lastly, violations relating to the right to own property (destruction of civilian property, pillage, etc.).
- Scale (number) of crimes and violations linked to an incident: Each recorded incident points to the commission of numerous crimes resulting in many victims. The number of crimes committed and the number of victims is taken into consideration when establishing the gravity of an incident.
- How the crimes and violations were committed: Crimes and violations of a widespread and systematic nature, crimes targeting a specific group (vulnerable groups, ethnic groups, political groups, etc.), and indiscriminate/disproportionate attacks with many civilian victims are all elements that will contribute to raising the gravity level of an incident.
- Impact of the crimes and violations committed: Aside from the number of victims of the crimes revealed, some incidents may have a devastating impact in the context, either by triggering conflict, threatening existing peace efforts, or preventing humanitarian relief efforts and the return of refugees or displaced persons, etc. The regional impact of an incident or its legacy for a specific community, and its particular significance for certain ethnic, political, religious or other groups may also contribute to raising its gravity level.

Standard of evidence

101. Since the primary objective of the Mapping Exercise is to "gather basic information on incidents uncovered", the level of evidence required is naturally lesser than would normally be expected in a case brought before a criminal court. It is not a question, therefore, of being satisfied beyond all reasonable doubt that a crime was committed, but rather having reasonable suspicion that the incident did occur; a level of evidence decidedly lower than that required to secure a criminal conviction. Reasonable suspicion is defined as "a reliable body of material consistent with other verified circumstances tending to show that an incident or event did happen"....

Assessing the reliability of information

102. Assessing the reliability of the information obtained was a two-stage process involving evaluation of the reliability and credibility of the source, and then the pertinence and truth of the information itself. This method is known as the admiralty scale. Reliability of the source is determined using several factors, including the

nature, objectivity and professionalism of the organisation providing the information, the methodology used and the quality of prior information obtained from the same source. The validity and authenticity of the information is assessed by comparing it to other available data relating to the same incidents to ensure that it tallies with already verified elements and circumstances. In other words, the process involves cross-checking the originally obtained information by ensuring that the corroborating elements do in fact come from a different source than the primary source that provided the information in the first place. . . .

Identification of individual and group perpetrators

. . .

104. . . . Although the primary objective of the Mapping Exercise is not to identify the alleged perpetrators or people who should be held accountable for their actions, it was nevertheless necessary to gather basic information relating to the identity of alleged individual or group perpetrators. Given the level of evidence used in this Exercise, however, it would be imprudent, and unjust, to seek to ascribe criminal responsibility to certain individuals. Such a conclusion should be dependent on legal proceedings pursued on the basis of an appropriate level of evidence. However, it seems essential to identify the groups involved in order to classify these serious violations of international humanitarian law. Finally, the identities of the alleged perpetrators of some of the crimes listed will not appear in this report but are held in the confidential project database submitted to the United Nations High Commissioner for Human Rights, who will determine the conditions for its access. However, the identities of perpetrators under warrant of arrest and those already sentenced for crimes listed in the report have been disclosed. It should also be noted that where political officials have assumed public positions encouraging or provoking the violations listed, their names have been cited in the sections relating to the political context.

Other aspects accounted for in the methodology

. . .

106. In this report, each incident verified in accordance with this methodology is reported in a separate paragraph. . . . [For each one] figures relating to the number of victims have been provided as a means of assessing the scale of violations and are in no way intended to be definitive. As a general rule, the Mapping Exercise has used the lowest and most realistic assessment of victim numbers indicated by the various sources and has sometimes resorted to estimates. In light of its mandate, it was not the responsibility of the Mapping Exercise to ascertain the total number of victims of violations of human rights and international humanitarian law in the DRC during the period in question, given that precise victim counts are not essential to determining the legal classification of violations. Each paragraph describing an incident is followed by a footnote identifying the primary and secondary sources of the information reported. Incidents not corroborated by a second independent source have not been included in this report, even in cases where the information came from a reliable source. Such incidents are, however, recorded in the database.

ISSUES AND QUESTIONS

A careful reading of the excerpts above from the fact-finding reports on Darfur and the DRC raises a number of challenging questions relating to the methodologies of international human rights fact-finding.

(a) Selection of situations

The decision to create a fact-finding mechanism remains largely in the hands of political bodies such as the Human Rights Council and the Security Council. As a result there are no consistent criteria applied and double-standards prevail. Should the High Commissioner for Human Rights be given delegated responsibility to set up such inquiries when she deems it appropriate, based on established criteria? Or should the decision remain a quintessentially political one?

(b) Composition

How should the composition of fact-finding missions be determined? Should the chairperson always be a lawyer? Should diplomats be involved? Should there always be a mix of professional backgrounds and expertise? Should a majority of the members be from the region in which the situation has arisen? Is a regional response (such as the monitoring mission sent by the Arab League to Syria in 2012) the best approach?

(c) The mandate and its interpretation

Should the mandate be open-ended to allow for flexibility and adaptation or should it be determined with some precision in advance in order to provide for some degree of predictability? The Darfur Commission interpreted its mandate to cover not only those directly responsible, but also those who planned, ordered or condoned the actions. Should all fact-finding missions adopt such an approach and, if so, what might be the consequences?

Consider the approach taken by a Panel of Inquiry appointed by the UN Secretary-General in response to an incident involving the boarding by Israeli forces of a 'flotilla' which was seeking to break a blockade to bring humanitarian supplies to Gaza in May 2010. Nine civilians were killed and many wounded. The Panel of four (Geoffrey Palmer, former New Zealand Prime Minister, Alvaro Uribe, former Colombian President, and an appointee of each of the states involved — Israel and Turkey) was asked to '(a) examine and identify the facts, circumstances and context of the incident; and (b) consider and recommend ways of avoiding similar incidents in the future'. Its July 2011 report stated:

> 5. … [T]his Panel is unique. Its methods of inquiry are similarly unique. The Panel is not a court. It was not asked to make determinations of the legal issues or to adjudicate on liability.
>
> …
>
> 14. … [T]he legal issues at large in this matter have not been authoritatively determined by the two States involved and neither can they be by the Panel.
>
> 15. The Panel will not add value for the United Nations by attempting to determine contested facts or by arguing endlessly about the applicable law. Too much

> legal analysis threatens to produce political paralysis. Whether what occurred here was legally defensible is important but in diplomatic terms it is not dispositive of what has become an important irritant not only in the relationship between two important nations but also in the Middle East generally.[6]

Compare this approach with that of the Sri Lanka Panel. What role should law play in such inquiries?

(d) Separating facts and law

Article 90 of Additional Protocol I to the Geneva Conventions establishes an International Humanitarian Fact-Finding Commission (IHFFC) which may be activated by the parties to a conflict to ascertain whether or not serious violations of international humanitarian law have occurred. It has been suggested that 'it is only concerned with facts, and essentially has no competence to proceed to a legal assessment'.[7] Can facts and law be separated in this way? Should a fact-finding commission be tasked just to compile facts and not to render any evaluation as to the legal consequences of those facts?[8]

(e) The character of the inquiry

The IHFFC is explicitly stated not to be a judicial body. In contrast, ILO commissions of inquiry characterize themselves as judicial in nature, and adopt detailed rules of procedure to guide their work.[9] The Darfur Commission claims to have 'adopted an approach proper to a judicial body'. Should such inquiries adopt a 'judicial' approach, and if so, what might that imply?

(f) The time frame

Compare the approach taken in each of the two reports in defining the time frame to be covered by the report. To what extent should a fact-finding report incorporate detailed historical materials in order to contextualize the issues? Can this be determined on a case by case basis without vesting undue discretion in the fact-finders to either circumscribe or open up the nature of the inquiry in ways that will have a major impact on the outcome of the report?

(g) Defining cooperation

If an inquiry is set up under Chapter VII of the UN Charter, there is an international legal obligation upon the government to cooperate. This still leaves open the

[6] www.un.org/News/dh/infocus/middle_east/Gaza_Flotilla_Panel_Report.pdf.

[7] Yves Sandoz et al. (eds.), *Commentary on the Additional Protocols of 8 June 1977 to the Geneva Conventions of 12 August 1949* (1987), 1041.

[8] A 2009 US State Department report on Sri Lanka indicated that it had 'compile[d] alleged incidents…which may constitute violations.… The report does not reach legal conclusions as to whether the incidents described herein actually constitute violations of…international law. Nor does it reach conclusions concerning whether the alleged incidents detailed herein actually occurred.' US Department of State, *Report to Congress on Incidents during the Recent Conflict in Sri Lanka* (2009), 3.

[9] See ILO, *Truth, reconciliation and justice in Zimbabwe* (2009), 19.

question of what is encompassed by such an obligation. The Darfur Commission specifies its criteria in para. 28 (p. 869, *supra*), and they closely resemble a list of terms relied upon by Special Rapporteurs appointed by the Human Rights Council.[10]

In 2006, the UN Special Rapporteur on Torture complained that a number of governments had balked at his request to have unhindered access to places of detention. He explained that what was required was:

> ... unimpeded access, with or without prior notice, to any place where persons may be deprived of their liberty (e.g. police lock-up, pretrial, prison, juvenile, administrative, psychiatric or other facilities, as well as detention facilities within military installations); not being subject to arbitrary time limits for carrying out his work (e.g. visiting hours, working hours of daytime prison staff, etc.); free movement within the facility and access to any room in order to gather information, including by use of electronic means, such as photography; having access to any detainee or staff, and the possibility of conducting confidential and private interviews, unsupervised by government officials, in places either chosen by the Special Rapporteur or in cooperation with the detainee....[11]

Are these demands excessive? If they exceed the powers of most domestic officials, is it reasonable for an international fact-finder to insist upon them? Or are they merely the minimum conditions required to ensure that the facts are not concealed or manipulated under the guise of upholding an outdated notion of sovereignty? At what point should fact-finders refuse to undertake a mission if all of their pre-conditions are not met? The United States agreed to permit UN Special Rapporteurs to visit the Guantánamo Bay prison camp, but refused access to the prisoners. Should the experts have cancelled the visit, as they decided to do?

Governments are expected to guarantee that witnesses and others who cooperate with an international mission will not be threatened, harassed or punished as a result. There have, however, been cases in which reprisals have been systematic and where witnesses have subsequently been killed. What could fact-finders do in response to such incidents and how should they structure their activities in situations where such threats are present?

(h) *Dealing with non-cooperation*

Governments often refuse access to an intergovernmental fact-finding mission. Iran, Israel and North Korea have consistently done so, as did Syria in 2011. How should the mission respond? The Human Rights Council's mission to Syria expressed its deep regret at not being given access, but went ahead on the basis of interviews with 223 victims and/or witnesses, including security force defectors (UN Doc. A/HRC/S-17/2/Add.1 (2011)). As a governmental advisor, when would you propose non-cooperation and how would you weigh the costs and benefits?

[10] Terms of Reference for Fact-Finding Missions by Special Rapporteurs/Representatives of the Commission on Human Rights, UN Doc. E/CN.4/1998/45, appendix V.

[11] UN Doc. E/CN.4/2006/6, para. 23.

(i) Witness testimony

Writing in 1990, Orentlicher suggested that victim or eyewitness testimony should be considered to be 'highly probative'. Consider, however, the conclusions reached by Combs in a very detailed 2009 study of the reliability of witness testimony before international criminal tribunals:

> [Based on] a large-scale review of transcripts from the [International Criminal Court for Rwanda, the Special Court for Sierra Leone, and the Special Panels in the Dili District Court in East Timor] I conclude that much eyewitness testimony at the international tribunals is of highly questionable reliability. In particular, many international witnesses are unable to convey the information that court personnel expect — and need — to receive, if they are to have confidence in the factual determinations they make. Sometimes, witnesses claim not to know the sought-after information, while in other instances, the communication breaks down as a result of the questioning process. Moreover, what clear information is provided during witness testimony often is inconsistent with the information that the witness previously provided in a pre-trial statement.... [M]any witnesses lack the education and life experiences to be able to read maps, tell time, or answer questions concerning distances and dates. Cultural norms and taboos create additional communication difficulties, as some witnesses are reluctant to speak directly or at all about certain events and as international judges may inappropriately assess witnesses' demeanor and willingness to answer questions by Western norms. The need for language interpretation for virtually every fact witness — sometimes through multiple interpreters — and the unfamiliarity of most witnesses with the predominantly adversarial trial procedures in use at the international tribunals only compound these problems.
>
> ...
>
> ... [M]any of the testimonial difficulties canvassed in [the study]...could also stem from a witness's desire to evade. Although every criminal justice system in the world has its share of lying witnesses, [the] ICTR and the SCSL have more than their share. The group-based loyalty and ethnic divisions that gave rise to the international crimes in the first place can create powerful incentives to put enemies in prison, whether they belong there or not, and the international tribunals provide additional incentives — perhaps unwittingly — through the financial assistance that they provide to testifying witnesses....[12]

Are the concerns that Combs notes in relation to international prosecutions less problematic in the context of international human rights fact-finding reports? If so, would this explain the difference in perspective between Orentlicher and Combs, or are we just more aware of the problems of witness testimony now than was the case 20 years earlier?

(j) The standard of proof

The standard of proof applied varies greatly from body to body and from one mandate to another. One author has identified a spectrum of commonly used standards:

[12] Nancy Amoury Combs, 'Testimonial Deficiencies and Evidentiary Uncertainties in International Criminal Trials', 14 UCLA J. Int'l. L. & For. Aff. 235 (2009), at 239.

(1) on the balance of probability or a preponderance of evidence; (2) evidence 'capable of establishing the truth of the allegations in a convincing manner' (used by the Inter-American Court of Human Rights); and (3) the criminal law standard of proof, beyond a reasonable doubt.[13] Where does the 'reasonable suspicion' standard used by both the Darfur and DRC reports fit on that spectrum? Given the potential impact on the reputations of governments and officials of some fact-finding exercises, is reasonable suspicion a sufficiently demanding standard? The International Court of Justice, in ruling on claims against states, applies a sliding scale according to which grave charges must be proved by fully conclusive evidence, but less serious allegations might be proven where there is a preponderance of the evidence. Should international fact-finding missions adopt a comparably scaled approach depending on the severity of the allegations?

(k) *Practical constraints: timing, resources and expertise*

The Darfur Commission complained about too tight a time schedule, insufficient resources and a lack of access to necessary expertise. Yet it had three months, a sizeable staff and diverse expertise available to it. Many UN Special Rapporteurs undertake such missions in the space of ten days on the ground, with perhaps one staff person and no additional expert assistance. Should there be minimum standards in terms of these aspects of missions and, if so, how would they be determined?

(l) *Meetings with rebels*

Some fact-finders insist on meeting with relevant rebel groups, even if the governments concerned object. Others steer clear of such actors whether for fear of legitimating them, offending the government or being unlikely to obtain much assistance from them. Such groups are often indispensable in peace-making contexts, but commentators have suggested that they should only be invited to participate if their activities comply with a code of minimum humanitarian standards.[14] Should there be such standards in relation to fact-finding, or will every situation be different? If a state, such as Israel, demands as a condition for admitting a fact-finding team that it not talk with a group such as Hamas that the Israeli Government considers to be terrorists, should the fact-finders acquiesce in such a demand?

(m) *Identifying individual perpetrators*

NGOs are generally loath to identify individual perpetrators, on the grounds that it is not the job of a human rights group to conduct criminal investigations and that their inquiry methods are not designed or suitable for such purposes. At the end of the day, such groups collect a lot of information, but not necessarily a lot of evidence. With the advent of the International Criminal Court and the greater likelihood of criminal prosecutions in domestic and other settings, should the largest human rights NGOs consider changing their methodologies in order to provide

[13] Sylvain Vité, cited in Théo Boutruche, 'Credible Fact-Finding and Allegations of International Humanitarian Law Violations: Challenges in Theory and Practice', 16 J. Conflict & Security L. 1, 9 (2011).

[14] Zoe Salzman, Armed Groups in Peace Processes: Who Gets a Seat at the Negotiating Table?, IILJ Emerging Scholars Paper 10(2008), at www.iilj.org/publications/documents/Salzman.ESP10-08.pdf.

more useful inputs into eventual criminal prosecutions? Some of the issues you might consider in responding to this question are: (1) how would the group reconcile the assurances of confidentiality given to witnesses with the prospect that any such information might one day be disclosed in a criminal trial?; (2) what would be the implications for the security of those who provided information?; (3) would the group have to worry about being sued for defamation if names are cited; and (4) would the naming of those alleged to have committed crimes have an adverse impact upon the NGO's ability to continue working in the country in question and, if so, should that be a concern?

Inquiries established by an intergovernmental organization increasingly include a mandate such as that given to the Darfur Commission. What are the arguments for and against such fact-finding commissions being directed to name perpetrators?

(n) Due process

Valticos calls for respect for due process of law in fact-finding. Others have also argued that fairness and credibility can be achieved only through 'universally applicable minimum standards of due process to control both the way the facts are established and what is done with them afterwards.'[15] In 2006 the Security Council acknowledged that although its appointed sanctions-monitoring mechanisms were non-judicial in nature, their findings might be used by judicial authorities, and thus 'their methodological standards may affect the [UN's] credibility'. Accordingly it called for, but did not set, common methodological standards and noted that monitoring mechanisms should, *inter alia*:

> ... identify the sources of information contained in their reports, ensure that such information is as transparent and verifiable as possible to protect the credibility of findings and the integrity of the process, and check and corroborate all citations and facts.
>
> ... rely on verified documents and, wherever possible, on first-hand, on-site observations by the experts themselves, including photographs.
>
> ... endeavour to ensure that their assertions are corroborated by solid information and that their findings are substantiated by credible sources.
>
> ... take particular care when analysing the reliability of confidential information... In all cases, efforts should be made to ensure the veracity of information gained in confidence against independent and verifiable sources.[16]

Do the case studies above comply with these standards? Is human rights fact-finding so context-specific that it makes little sense to insist upon fixed 'due process' standards?

[15] Thomas M. Franck & H. Scott Fairley, 'Procedural Due Process in Human Rights Fact-Finding by International Agencies', 74 Am. J. Int'l. L. 308 (1980), at 309.

[16] UN Sanctions Committee Guidelines, in Note by the President of the Security Council, UN Doc. S/2006/997 (22 Dec. 2006).

(o) Should there be standardized guidelines for fact-finding?

One of the most experienced international fact-finders, Cherif Bassiouni, has lamented the absence of standard operating procedure for fact-finding missions.

> [N]o manual exists to describe how an investigation should be conducted and there is no standard, though adaptable, computer program to input collected data. Worst of all, there is no continuity. In short, there is nothing to guide, instruct, or assist the heads and appointees to these missions of how to better carry out their mandates. It strains one's belief that in fifty years the most elementary aspects of standardized organization, planning, documentation, and reporting have not been developed. Thus, each mission has to reinvent the wheel.... The results are usually poor or mediocre performance, except where particularly competent persons are appointed to these missions.... [T]here is little consistency and predictability as to the methods and outcomes....
>
> The lack of standardized methods, particularly as to empirical research and field investigation, means that there is no basis to test the validity of the research in order to assess the plausibility of the conclusions. It is safe to say that no scientific research methodology would consider the above-described approach as anything but selective, insufficient, unreliable, and, at best, anecdotal.[17]

Antonio Cassese's solution is to adopt regulations outlining 'the structure, powers and functioning of fact-finding commissions, so that, once the need arises to investigate a situation, all the relevant rules are already in place.'[18] What are the arguments for and against such an approach? Is it possible to develop meaningful guidelines to govern such a broad array of circumstances and challenges? Are existing guidelines so general as to provide little real guidance? Or are the interests of human rights better served by avoiding the constraining effects of excessive professionalization and leaving maximum room for creativity and innovation?

(p) New technologies

Twitter and Facebook have played key roles in recent anti-government movements in many states. In what ways might the development of new information and communication technologies transform fact-finding, both for better and worse?

D. GOVERNMENT RESPONSES TO FACT-FINDING

Governments rarely welcome critical reporting by fact-finders. Human rights proponents might assume that this is inevitable and disregard it. After all, such reports are directed at a variety of audiences or constituencies and their impact is not

[17] M. Cherif Bassiouni, 'Appraising UN Justice-Related Fact-Finding Missions', 5 Wash. U. J. L. & Pol'y. 35 (2001).

[18] Antonio Cassese, 'How to Ensure Increased Compliance with International Standards: Monitoring and Institutional Fact-Finding', in A. Cassese (ed.), *Realizing Utopia: The Future of International Law* (2012), 303. Cf. a set of guidelines developed for NGO fact-finding: Lund-London Guidelines on International Human Rights Fact-Finding Visits and Reports adopted by the Raoul Wallenberg Institute and the International Bar Association (2009).

dependent upon the nature of the relevant government's public response. But there is good reason to seek to understand such responses. Before looking at the response by Rwanda to the DRC Mapping Report, consider Cohen's survey of the types of responses that fact-finding reports traditionally elicit from governments.

STANLEY COHEN, GOVERNMENT RESPONSES TO HUMAN RIGHTS REPORTS: CLAIMS, DENIALS AND COUNTERCLAIMS

18 Hum. Rts. Q. 517 (1996)

...

A. The Classic Discourse of Official Denial

Three forms of denial appear in the discourse of official responses to allegations about human rights violations....

...

1. "Nothing is Happening": Literal Denial

Literal denials assert simply that "nothing happened" or "nothing is happening": There was no massacre, no one was tortured, there are no political prisoners in our country....

...

There are no limits to the astonishing methods that are used to deny, cover-up, explain away, or lie about the most obvious realities. This is clear in the well-known episodes of historical denial: the intense efforts by the Turkish government to deny the genocide of the Armenians, the Holocaust denial movement, the Soviet denials of the atrocities against its own citizens. As soon as events become assigned to "history," powerful denial techniques become available: it happened too long ago, memory is unreliable, the records have been lost, no one will ever know what took place....

[In response] to visual evidence...journalists may be accused of slanting their reports, selecting pictures to fit an already predicted scenario, or — more dramatically — staging the incident in collusion with the victims. Or the event is conceded, but knowledge about it denied....Or responsibility is displaced onto third parties ("unknown forces")...."Maximum deniability" is often built into the judicial system.

The most common [approach] is to attack the reliability, objectivity, and credibility of the observer. Victims are lying and cannot be believed because they have a political interest in discrediting the government. Witnesses are untrustworthy or drawn from the political opposition. Journalists and human rights organization are selective, biased, working from a hidden political agenda or else naive, gullible, and easily manipulated. If the source of the evidence can be shown to be suspect in any of these ways, then the violations obviously did not take place or are being exaggerated.

...

... Literal denial to foreign audiences often seems credible: the sources of information can be discredited easily, the situation is too complicated for an outsider to understand, patron governments can participate in the cover-up. In the domestic setting, though, it is harder to get away with such denial. Everybody knows what is happening. The essence of state terror is that everyone should know.

2. "What is Happening is Really Something Else": Interpretive Denial

...

The most common alternative is to admit the "raw" facts — yes, something did happen: people were killed, injured, or detained without trial — but to deny the interpretive framework that is placed on these events. No, what happened was not really torture, genocide, or extra-judicial killing, but something else. The harmful behavior is cognitively reframed and then reallocated to a different, less pejorative class of events.

This strategy is complex and subtle to study, precisely because the process of interpretation is inherent in the naming of all social events. Many current forms of radical social constructionism or epistemological relativism would assert, of course, that there can be no objective, universally agreed definition of any social event. However, the human rights ethos assumes that such definitions can be made in good faith and with some degree of consensus. Without some idea of what constitutes torture, a fair trial, or freedom of speech, human rights work becomes impossible. A human rights report must be able to assign a mutually acceptable definition to an event. This definition might have some ambiguities, but it should be able to exclude those official reinterpretations that are deliberate evasions not made in good faith.

Such evasions are deployed because some categorizations are so pejorative, stigmatic, and universally condemned that they cannot be openly admitted or defended.... [N]o government will concede publicly that it is responsible for systematic torture, political massacres, and genocide.... They have to reframe and rename....

This process, of course, is often entirely plausible. There is an arena of legitimate controversy — claims and counterclaims — between human rights organizations and governments. These definitional disputes arise not because of the sociological truism that all actions are interpreted, but because the dominant language of interpretation is legal....

The resulting disputes become legitimate because law is a "plastic medium of discourse," capable of varied, though certainly not infinite, interpretations.... Without these legalistic games of truth, the institutions of international human rights enforcement would collapse and return to the older moralistic language that they replaced.

Reinterpretation is a compromise form of response.... The following four techniques tend to be used in combination:

a. *Euphemism*: ... These are everyday devices for masking, sanitizing, and conferring respectability by using palliative terms that deny or misrepresent cruelty or harm, giving them neutral or respectable status.

[George] Orwell's original...examples have become only too banal: "pacification," "transfer of population," "elimination of unreliable elements." In each instance, "[s]uch phraseology is needed if one wants to name things without calling up mental pictures of them." ...

The area of torture is a rich source of euphemisms: ["intensive interrogations," "special procedures," "moderate physical pressure"].

b. *Legalism*: ...

... [One] strategy is the legalistic claim that while the event in question took place, it does not fit the appropriate category (right, law, article, convention). Yes, this demonstrator was arrested, but this was not a violation of freedom of expression. A second strategy denies that the provisions of a particular prohibition or convention are applicable in the circumstances in question....

A third strategy is...to respond to an allegation by "proving" that it could not possibly have the meaning imputed to it, because this type of action is illegal in the country....

Such defenses are more difficult for human rights organizations to counter than crude denials of fact. They are plausible precisely because they appear to recognize the legitimacy of human rights concerns....Instead of countering patent lies or evasions, the task of human rights reporting becomes more subtle and looks more polemical: to expose the gap between noble rhetoric and actual reality.

c. *Denial of Responsibility*:...One use [of denial] is as a justification that deflects ultimate responsibility onto the victim. [The author then lists three other variations: (i) the act occurred, but responsibility is attributed to other forces — named or unknown; (ii) the claim that no responsibility can be found anywhere because lines of political authority have collapsed; and (iii) using the 'agentless passive form' to create the impression that atrocities just happen, without involving human agency.]

d. *Isolation*: [This involves denial of] the systematic, routine, or repeated quality attributed to the act. This was an "isolated incident"....

3. *"What's Happening is Justified": Implicatory Denial*

...

[Typical official justifications include:]

...

a. *Righteousness*:...One claim is that there are no such universal values at all and, therefore, any society can act according to its own morality. The other claim asserts that there are alternative sets of values that under certain circumstances (or in regard to certain people) take precedence over any universals....

b. *Necessity*:..."[W]e had to do it," "there was no alternative."...The claim is that the government, reluctantly, had to act out of necessity: self-defense, national survival, prevention of greater harm, anticipation of danger, protection of its citizens.

...

A more ideological version of the necessity/security defense might appear in the notion of a Darwinian struggle for survival: The conflict has gone on for centuries, only one side can win, no compromises are possible, it's either them or us.

c. *Denial of the Victim*: There are complex ways of displacing blame onto those who are harmed....

The most common forms of victim blaming are variations on the themes of "they started it," or "they got what they deserved." ...

Other forms of "denial of the victim"... include: First, *dehumanization*: disparagement of the victim groups by repudiating their humanity.... Violence is "the only language they understand." Second, *condescension*: the other is regarded not so much as evil or subhuman but is to be patronized as inferior, childlike, uncivilized, and irrational. Third, *distancing*: the dominant group ceases to feel the presence of others; they virtually do not exist. Because their very presence is not acknowledged, they cannot be seen as victims.

... [Fourth:] double standards — a different set of moral rule and obligation applies to different categories of people. We would never behave like this to our own people.

... [Fifth:] expanding the target — the "legitimate" enemy is redefined to include a wider category of "sympathizers" or "passive supporters." ...

...

d. *Contextualization and Uniqueness*:...

A strong form of contextualization is to assert that the particular circumstances in which this country finds itself are so special that normal standards of judgement cannot apply. There are unique features of the situation — the military threat, the methods used by terrorists, the balance of forces — that make it wholly specific....

Another... is to assert that a level of violence is normal, acceptable, and ordinary in this particular situation. What is happening may look bad elsewhere, but here everyone is used to it....

e. *Advantageous Comparisons*:... the self-righteous comparison of your own record with that of your critics....

...

f. *Rejection of Universal Standards*: The "higher loyalty" defense appeals to an ideology that temporarily or permanently supersedes universal human rights standards; the "specificity" defense depicts a situation so unique that universal values do not apply. A more radical version of these justifications — worth separate attention because of its current prominence in the human rights debate — is the principled rejection of any universality.

...

NOTE

The Government of the DRC called the Mapping Report detailed and credible. The Rwandan Government, however, reacted strongly. While it attacked the report as a whole, its outrage was primarily caused by the report's openness to considering that some of the systematic, methodical and premeditated attacks by Tutsi forces in the DRC could have been motivated 'to destroy the Hutu ethnic group in the DRC in part', which would meet the criteria for the crime of genocide. Although the report also acknowledged that 'countervailing factors... could lead a court to find that the requisite intent was lacking, and hence that the crime of genocide was not committed', Rwanda, at one point, threatened to pull its 3,000 peacekeepers out of the African Union-UN peacekeeping mission in Darfur in response to the report.

OFFICIAL GOVERNMENT OF RWANDA COMMENTS ON THE DRAFT UN MAPPING REPORT ON THE DRC

Kigali (30 Sept. 2010)

Executive Summary of Comments

... Rwanda categorically states that The Draft Mapping Report is unacceptable. Rwanda's concerns relate to the entire report, and are not limited to narrow definitional issues or specific allegations. These serious concerns include:

1. The manipulation of UN processes by organizations and individuals — both inside and outside the UN — for purposes of rewriting history, improperly apportioning blame for the genocide that occurred in Rwanda, and reignite the conflict in Rwanda and the region.
2. The omission of the historical context, especially the immediate and serious threat posed by armed and ideologically charged refugees positioned right at the border of Rwanda and Zaire, as well as the nature of the conflict within Zaire at the time. This is despite the UN's knowledge of the situation and its blatant inaction.
3. The contradiction between the report and contemporaneous accounts of the situation from the UN Security Council, NGOs and many other eyewitnesses in the region who confirmed that genocidal forces, often posing as civilian refugees, were operating under the cover of UN refugee camps.
4. The flawed methodology and application of the lowest imaginable evidentiary standard.
5. The overreliance on the use of anonymous sources, hearsay assertions, unnamed, un-vetted and unidentified investigators and witnesses, who lack credibility; and allegation of the existence of victims with uncertain identity.
6. Failure to address the glaring inconsistency that claims of genocide are directly contradicted by Rwanda's extensive and coordinated efforts to repatriate, resettle and reintegrate 3.2 million Hutu refugees; efforts that were supported by the UN.
7. The dangerous and irresponsible attempt by the Report to undermine the peace and stability attained in the Great Lakes region, which directly contradicts the very mission of the [UN].

QUESTIONS

1. Cohen refers to theories that posit that there can be no objective, agreed definition of any social event. How feasible and credible does the overall human rights fact-finding enterprise seem to you on the basis of the materials studied in this chapter?

2. In light of the excerpts from the Mapping Report (p. 873, *supra*), and of Cohen's analysis, how would you respond to Rwanda's critique if you were the person responsible for the Report?

11

Regional Arrangements

In the realm of human rights, regional intergovernmental systems have played a major role. The European and Inter-American systems have innovative institutions and processes; the African system has distinctive norms; and Arab and Asian initiatives are at an embryonic point. These arrangements add in important ways to an understanding of the full range of techniques available for protecting and promoting human rights.

This chapter concentrates on one distinctive aspect of each system. The remarkable feature of the European system is its productive and effective Court; the materials illustrate its work and the dilemmas of supranational adjudication through its decisions on the right to life and on political democracy, and its response to the admission of new members with complex and often problematic human rights records such as Russia. In the Inter-American system, the materials look briefly at its Court but concentrate on its Commission on Human Rights, a powerful organ with tasks and functions not found in the European system. The African system is developing gradually in institutional terms and we look primarily at the complaints system that it has created.

The relationship between 'universal' (meaning, in this context, UN-sponsored) and regional human rights arrangements is a complex one. Chapter VIII of the UN Charter makes provision for regional arrangements in relation to peace and security, but it is silent as to human rights. Nevertheless, the Council of Europe moved as early as 1950 to adopt the European Convention on Human Rights and various proposals were made in the early 1950s to include human rights in the frameworks that eventually led to the European Union.[1] It was not until 1969 that the analogous American Convention was adopted. In the meantime, at least until the mid 1960s, the UN remained at best ambivalent about such developments. As Vasak has noted, 'there was often a tendency to regard it as the expression of a breakaway movement, calling the universality of human rights into question.'[2] But he suggests that there was less suspicion of regionalism once the two UN Covenants were adopted in 1966. By the time they had entered into force, in 1977, the UN General Assembly was sufficiently convinced as to appeal 'to States in areas where regional arrangements in the field of human rights do not yet exist to consider agreements with a view to the establishment within their respective regions of suitable regional machinery for the

[1] G. de Búrca, 'The Road Not Taken: The European Union as a Global Human Rights Actor', 105 Am. J. Int'l. L. 649 (2011).

[2] In K. Vasak & P. Alston (eds.), *The International Dimensions of Human Rights* (Vol. 2, 1982), at 451.

promotion and protection of human rights' (GA Res. 32/127 (1977)). Four years later, the African Charter of Human and Peoples' Rights was adopted. Throughout this period the Communist states of Eastern Europe were strongly opposed to regional arrangements, and the Asian and Pacific countries generally argued that their region was much too heterogeneous to permit the creation of a regional mechanism.

In subsequent years, various sub-regional initiatives have been launched, but few have had any staying power.[3] For example, the states from the former Soviet Union adopted a Commonwealth of Independent States Convention on Human Rights in Minsk in 1995, but it has amounted to little in practice.[4] In contrast, the transformation of the Organization for Security and Co-operation in Europe (OSCE) from an East-West debating forum into an organization designed to promote respect for a broadly defined range of human rights, has added another important dimension to regional human rights cooperation.

Some sub-regional initiatives have also had significant human rights components. In Africa, for example, the Community Court of Justice of the Economic Community of West African States (ECOWAS) has developed an impressive record in the human rights area since 2005. Similarly the East African Court of Justice has delivered some important judgments in this area and the Southern African Development Community Tribunal was essentially aborted after it delivered a strong judgment against Zimbabwe in relation to human rights violations.[5]

There are strong arguments for a regional approach to human rights, although in some respects the counter-arguments might be almost as strong. One study listed the following factors favouring regionalism: (1) the existence of geographic, historical, and cultural bonds among states of a particular region; (2) the fact that recommendations of a regional organization may meet with less resistance than those of a global body; (3) the likelihood that publicity about human rights will be wider and more effective; and (4) the fact that there is less possibility of 'general, compromise formulae', which in global bodies are more likely to be based on 'considerations of a political nature'.[6]

Inis Claude pointed to some of the downsides. He observed, for example, that '[i]ntraregional affinities may be offset by historically rooted intraregional animosities, and geographical proximity may pose dangers which states wish to diminish by escaping into universalism.' He suggested that a regional organization might sometimes 'be too small, in that it may represent a dangerous form of confinement for local rivalries. Global stretching, in short, may be no worse than regional cramping.'[7]

[3] See M. Evans, 'The Future(s) of Regional Courts on Human Rights', in A. Cassese (ed.), *Realizing Utopia: The Future of International Law* (2012), 261.

[4] See text in 17 Hum. Rts. L. J. 159 (1996) and critiques in ibid., 164 and 181.

[5] An excellent database tracking many of these sub-regional courts is www.worldcourts.com/. On ECOWAS see K. Alter, 'The Global Spread of European Style International Courts', 35 W. Eur. Pol.135 (2012).

[6] Regional Promotion and Protection of Human Rights: Twenty-Eighth Report of the Commission to Study the Organization of Peace (1980), 15.

[7] I. Claude, *Swords into Plowshares* (4th edn. 1984), 102.

Some commentators, however, are strongly optimistic about the role of regionalism in the human rights regime. Dinah Shelton, for example, has argued that the interactions between the principal regional systems and the universal one has led to 'converging norms and procedures in an overarching interdependent and dynamic system. In many respects they are thinking globally and acting regionally. Each uses the jurisprudence of the other systems and amends and strengthens its procedures with reference to the experience of the others. In general, their mutual influence is highly progressive, both in normative development and institutional reform.'[8]

Before we examine the principal regional systems, note the flexibility of conceptions of the term 'region'. For a range of purposes, such as caucuses among state representatives in the UN Human Rights Council, the UN divides the world into five geopolitical regions: Asia, Africa, Eastern Europe, Latin America, and Western Europe and Others (including the United States). But that classification need bear no relation to appropriate definitions of regions for the purposes of setting up a regional or sub-regional human rights regime. Take Asia and the Pacific by way of example. Consideration might be given to sub-regional initiatives covering the Pacific region (with or excluding Australia and New Zealand), South Asia, West Asia, and Southeast Asia.

We turn now to explore the oldest and most developed of the regional systems.

A. THE EUROPEAN CONVENTION SYSTEM

1. INTRODUCTION AND OVERVIEW

The European Convention for the Protection of Human Rights and Fundamental Freedoms (ECHR) was signed in 1950 and entered into force in 1953. The ECHR is of particular importance within the context of international human rights for several reasons: it was the first comprehensive treaty in the world in this field; it established the first international complaints procedure and the first international court for the determination of human rights matters; it remains the most judicially developed of all the human rights systems; it has generated a more extensive jurisprudence than any other part of the international system; and it now applies to almost 25 per cent of the nations in the world. Our principal concern in this selective examination of the European Convention is with its evolving institutional architecture, particularly with the European Court of Human Rights and the manner in which it has performed the judicial function.

The impetus for the adoption of a European Convention came from three factors. It was first a regional response to the atrocities committed in Europe during the Second World War and an affirmation of the belief that governments respecting human rights are less likely to wage war on their neighbours. Second, both

[8] Dinah Shelton, 'The Promise of Regional Human Rights Systems', in B. Weston & S. Marks (eds.), *The Future of International Human Rights* (1999), 351, at 356.

the Council of Europe, which was set up in 1949 (and under whose auspices the Convention was adopted), and the European Union (previously the European Community or Communities, the first of which was established in 1952) were partly based on the assumption that the best way to ensure that Germany would be a force for peace, in partnership with France, the United Kingdom, and other West European states, was through regional integration and the institutionalization of common values. This strategy contrasted strongly with the punitive, reparations-based, approach embodied in the 1919 Versailles Treaty after the First World War.

Thus, the Preamble to the European Convention refers (perhaps somewhat optimistically at the time) to the 'European countries which are likeminded and have a common heritage of political traditions, ideals, freedom and the rule of law . . . '. But this statement also points to the third major impetus towards a Convention — the desire to bring the non-Communist countries of Europe together within a common ideological framework and to consolidate their unity in the face of the Communist threat. 'Genuine democracy' (to which the Statute of the Council of Europe commits its members) or the 'effective political democracy' to which the Preamble of the Convention refers, had to be clearly distinguished from the 'people's democracy' which was promoted by the Soviet Union and its allies.

The European Convention's transformation of abstract human rights ideals into a concrete legal framework followed a path which has characterized virtually all subsequent attempts. The initial enthusiasm was soon tempered by concerns over sovereignty and a reluctance to take the concept of a state's accountability too far. Thus, a call by the Congress of Europe in 1948 for the adoption of a Charter of Human Rights to be enforced by a Court of Justice 'with adequate sanctions for the implementation of this Charter' went further than West European governments were prepared to go. Instead, the final version of the Convention acknowledges in the Preamble that it constitutes only 'the first steps for the collective enforcement of certain of the Rights stated in the Universal Declaration'.

Both during the drafting of the Convention and in the years after its adoption there was considerable reluctance on the part of key states in relation to many of its key provisions. In this regard the most detailed historical analyses have been undertaken in relation to the United Kingdom and it is an instructive example.[9] During the Second World War, Prime Minister Churchill often returned to the theme that the war was being fought 'to establish, on impregnable rocks, the rights of the individual', and commentators such as Hersch Lauterpacht insisted that the war was, in large part, about 'the enthronement of the rights of man' and the correlative limitation of state sovereignty.[10] But when victory brought the opportunity to draft a human rights treaty, British diplomats and politicians raised a host of objections, as the following excerpt shows.

[9] See A. W. B. Simpson, *Human Rights and the End of Empire: Britain and the Genesis of the European Convention* (2004); and G. Marston, 'The United Kingdom's Part in the Preparation of the European Convention on Human Rights, 1950', Int'l. & Comp. L. Q. 796 (1993).

[10] See M. Mazower, *Dark Continent: Europe's Twentieth Century* (1998), 193–4.

ANDREW MORAVCSIK, THE ORIGINS OF HUMAN RIGHTS REGIMES: DEMOCRATIC DELEGATION IN POSTWAR EUROPE

54 Int. Org. 217 (2000), at 238

The British . . . supported international declaratory norms but firmly opposed any attempt to establish binding legal obligations, centralized institutions, individual petition, or compulsory jurisdiction. As W. E. Beckett, legal advisor to the Foreign Office and the initiator of the British government's participation [in the drafting of the ECHR], put it, "We attach the greatest importance to a well-drafted Convention of Human Rights but we are dead against anything like an international court to which individuals who think they are aggrieved in this way could go." . . .

What issues were raised in confidential British deliberations? The secondary literature on British human rights policy makes much of two British concerns: the fear that residents of British colonies and dependencies might invoke the ECHR, and aversion to European federalism. To judge from confidential discussions, however, neither appears to have been a dominant concern. . . .

. . .

Instead British officials and politicians — most notably in Cabinet discussions — dwelled primarily on the fear that the convention would threaten idiosyncratic (but not unambiguously undemocratic) political practices and institutions in the United Kingdom. . . .

The defense of British institutional idiosyncrasy elicited the most violent rhetoric from British politicians and officials. Lord Chancellor Jowitt's official paper criticized the draft convention . . . as:

> so vague and woolly that it may mean almost anything. Our unhappy legal experts . . . have had to take their share in drawing up a code compared to which . . . the Ten Commandments . . . are comparatively insignificant. . . . It completely passes the wit of man to guess what results would be arrived at by a tribunal composed of elected persons who need not even be lawyers, drawn from various European states possessing completely different systems of law, and whose deliberations take place behind closed doors. . . . Any student of our legal institutions must recoil from this document with a feeling of horror.

A common complaint was that judicial review would undermine parliamentary sovereignty. Beckett wrote: "It seems inconceivable that any Government, when faced with the realities of this proposal, would take the risk of entrusting these unprecedented powers to an international court, legislative powers which Parliament would never agree to entrust to the courts of this country which are known and which command the confidence and admiration of the world." "Our whole constitution," a government document intoned, "is based on the principle that it is for the Parliament to enact the laws and for the judges to interpret the laws." . . .

The specific issue cited most often by the government's legal authorities was the British policy toward political extremists. A ministerial brief referred to a "blank cheque" that would "allow the Governments to become the object of such potentially vague charges by individuals as to invite Communists, crooks, and cranks of every type to bring actions."... Lord Chancellor Jowitt's complaint was that "the Convention would prevent a future British government from detaining people without trial during a period of emergency... or judges sending litigants to prison for throwing eggs at them; or the Home Secretary from banning Communist or Fascist demonstrations."

...

What blunted British opposition to any postwar European human rights regime was, above all, the fear of resurgent totalitarianism abroad that might pose an eventual military threat to the United Kingdom — precisely as republican liberal theory predicts. This fear reflected not just a concern with a resurgence of Fascism, but also a turnaround in British foreign policy in 1948 in response to the perceived rise of the Communist threat in Western Europe. The West, the government argued, needed not only to maintain the military balance but also to strengthen continental democracies....

In the minds of British officials, however, the primacy of domestic sovereignty over collective defense of the democratic peace remained unchallenged. The cabinet mandated efforts to water down the force of any agreement in Britain. British representatives sought to limit the potential risk of open-ended jurisprudence by calling for the careful enumeration and definition of human rights before agreeing on any enforcement mechanism. The expectation was that governments would not be able to agree on a list both extensive and precise. Acting on Prime Minister Clement Attlee's direct instruction, the British delegation successfully pressed to place the right of individual petition and the jurisdiction of the court into optional clauses. Foreign Minister Ernest Bevin himself instructed British negotiators to veto any mandatory right of individual petition "even if it [means] being in a minority of one."...

Having secured these concessions, which essentially rendered the convention unenforceable in Britain, the cabinet unanimously accepted the desirability of signing it....

COMMENT ON ADMISSION TO MEMBERSHIP AND CONTENT OF RIGHTS

This historical review seems a long way from the world of the twenty-first century in which the UK Human Rights Act 1998, however distinctly formulated, made all of the rights recognized in the Convention an integral part of domestic law. More generally, major reforms of institutional provisions of the Convention have helped to move the system closer to that envisaged by the maximalists of the early 1950s. As with most systems for the protection of human rights, progress has required the gradual growth of popular expectations and an accumulation of experience in the functioning of the procedures that has served to assuage the worst fears of governments.

An Overview of the ECHR System

The Council of Europe was established in 1949 by a group of ten states, primarily to promote democracy, the rule of law, and greater unity among the nations of Western Europe. It represented both a principled commitment of its members to these values and an ideological stance against Communism. Over the years its activities have included the promotion of cooperation in relation to social, cultural, sporting, and a range of other matters. Until 1990, the Council had 23 members, all from Western Europe. Post-Cold War developments, however, had a major impact upon the Council and by 2012 it had more than double that number (47).[11]

The conditions for the admission of a state to the Council of Europe are laid down in Article 3 of its Statute. The state must be a genuine democracy that respects the rule of law and human rights and must 'collaborate sincerely and effectively' with the Council in these domains. In practice, such collaboration involves becoming a party to the European Convention on Human Rights. An applicant state must satisfy the Council's Committee of Ministers that its legal order conforms with the requirements of Article 3. The opinion of the Parliamentary Assembly is sought and the Assembly in turn will appoint an expert group to advise it.

The opinion of the experts is based upon an on-site visit. A 1994 report on Russia concluded that the requirements were not met. The report noted 'important shortcomings with regard to the rights to liberty and security of person and to fair trial' as well as the absence of the rule of law in view of the fact that the 'activities of public authorities are mainly decided upon according to general policy choices, personal allegiance and the effective power structure.'[12] Russia was admitted, nevertheless, in 1996. This decision by the Council's Parliamentary Assembly, and another to admit Croatia, were strongly criticized at the time by some human rights advocates.

The importance attached by the states of Central and Eastern Europe to membership of the Council reflected not only a commitment to human rights but a determination to gain respectability within Europe and, perhaps most importantly, to qualify for certain membership benefits as well as for admission to the European Union. Although the process of becoming a party to the Convention is not required to be completed prior to obtaining membership in the Council, it is generally assumed that the domestic legislative and other measures required to enable the state to ratify or accede will be completed within two years.

The Rights Recognized in the ECHR

Although the initial moves to create a European Convention pre-dated the UN's adoption of the Universal Declaration, the text of the latter was available to those

[11] Albania, Andorra, Armenia, Austria, Azerbaijan, Belgium, Bosnia and Herzegovina, Bulgaria, Croatia, Cyprus, Czech Republic, Denmark, Estonia, Finland, France, Georgia, Germany, Greece, Hungary, Iceland, Ireland, Italy, Latvia, Liechtenstein, Lithuania, Luxembourg, Malta, Moldova, Monaco, Montenegro, Netherlands, Norway, Poland, Portugal, Romania, Russian Federation, San Marino, Serbia, Slovakia, Slovenia, Spain, Sweden, Switzerland, the Former Yugoslav Republic of Macedonia, Turkey, Ukraine, and the United Kingdom.

[12] R. Bernhardt et al., 'Report on the Conformity of the Legal Order of the Russian Federation with Council of Europe Standards' (7 Oct. 1994).

responsible for the final drafting of the Convention. Eventually the drafters defined rights in terms similar to the early version of the draft ICCPR. (You should now read Articles 2–12 and 14 of the Convention.) Since the Covenant went through numerous changes before adoption, the formulations used in the two treaties sometimes differ significantly. Several weighty provisions appear in only one or the other. For example, the European Convention contains no provision relating to self-determination or to the rights of members of minority groups (Arts. 1 and 27 of the ICCPR). Each treaty limits freedoms of expression, association, and religion in similar ways (e.g., criteria of public safety or national security), but the European Convention consistently requires that a limitation be 'necessary in a democratic society' (Arts. 8–11). The derogation clauses (Art. 4 of the ICCPR, Art. 15 of the European Convention) differ with respect to the list of non-derogable provisions.

Article 1 requires the parties to 'secure [these rights] to everyone within their jurisdiction', while Article 13 requires the state to provide 'an effective remedy before a national authority' for everyone whose rights are violated. Compare the more demanding Article 2 of the ICCPR, which refers to states' duty to adopt legislative and other measures to give effect to the recognized rights and to 'develop the possibilities of judicial remedy'.

When the Convention was adopted in 1950, there were several outstanding proposals on which final agreement could not be reached. It was therefore agreed to adopt Protocols containing additional provisions. Since 1952, 11 protocols have been adopted. While the majority are devoted to procedural matters, others have recognized the following additional rights: the right to property ('the peaceful enjoyment of [one's] possessions'), the right to education, and the obligation to hold free elections (Protocol 1 of 1952); freedom from imprisonment for civil debts, freedom of movement and residence, freedom to leave any country, freedom from exile, the right to enter the country of which one is a national, and no collective expulsion of aliens (Protocol 4 of 1963); abolition of the death penalty (Protocol 6 of 1983); the right of an alien not to be expelled without due process, the right to appeal in criminal cases, the right to compensation for a miscarriage of justice, immunity of double prosecution for the same offence, and equality of rights and responsibility of spouses (Protocol 7 of 1984); the general prohibition of discrimination (Protocol 12 of 2000); and abolition of the death penalty, in all circumstances (Protocol 13 of 2002). Acceptance of each of the Protocols is optional.

By May 2012, all 47 member states of the Council of Europe were parties to the European Convention, and to Protocol Nos. 2, 3, 5, 8, 11, and 14. Ratifications for the other Protocols were: No. 1, 45; No. 4, 43; No. 6, 46; No. 7, 43; No. 9, 24; No. 10, 25; No. 12, 18; and No. 13, 43.[13]

[13] Source: http://conventions.coe.int/Treaty/Commun/ListeTraites.asp?CM=8&CL=ENG.

2. THE EUROPEAN COURT AND ITS PROCEDURES

The ECHR provides for both individual petitions (Art. 34) and interstate complaints (Art. 33). The latter are rare, but the opportunity continues to be significant. In contrast, the former, which may be brought by individuals, legal persons (such as corporations), groups of individuals, or nongovernmental organizations, have grown exponentially in numerical terms.

The Convention makes clear that the primary responsibility for implementation rests with the member states themselves. The implementation machinery of the Convention comes into play only after domestic remedies are considered to have been exhausted. The great majority of complaints submitted are deemed inadmissible, frequently on the ground that domestic law provides an effective remedy for any violation that may have taken place. Recall the obligations of member states under Articles 1 and 13 of the Convention to 'secure to everyone' the Convention's rights and to provide 'an effective remedy before a national authority' for violations of those rights. This preference for domestic resolution is also reinforced by the requirement to seek a 'friendly settlement' wherever possible and by the procedures for full government consultation in the examination of complaints.

The remedy given by a domestic court may be pursuant to provisions of domestic law that stand relatively independently of the Convention, although perhaps influenced by it, such as a human rights Act, a code of criminal procedure, or a constitutional provision that are consistent with the Convention. Or a remedy may be given as a result of the incorporation of the Convention into domestic law, which may be achieved as an automatic consequence of ratification or through the adoption of special legislation. See generally pp. 1047–80, *infra*.

COMMENT ON THE DRAMATIC EVOLUTION OF THE ECHR SYSTEM

The system of considering individual complaints is the hallmark of the ECHR regime. Its evolution from a tentative and optional procedure which was used relatively sparingly to one which is now compulsory and extremely widely used has compelled the Contracting States (or states parties, to use UN terminology) to undertake a series of fundamental reforms. Driven by a flood of applications and the ever-present risk that the system will collapse from overload, the Court has been forced to consider very far-reaching and controversial changes and, in the process, to reflect carefully on what exactly it aspires to achieve. Much of the latter debate has taken place under the rubric of whether the ECHR is, or should be, a 'constitutional court'.

When originally devised in the 1950s, and for several decades thereafter, the petition procedure was optional. Only three of the original ten members accepted it from the outset, while many of the rest made clear that they wanted no part of it. For example, it was not until 1981 that France accepted the right of individual complaint for its citizens. And during the 1970s the British Government regularly raised the prospect that it might withdraw its acceptance of the procedure. Until the late 1990s the procedures used were much less 'judicial' than they are today, and were surrounded by safeguards aimed at providing reassurances to governments that they need not fear too much encroachment on their national sovereignty.

In terms of institutions, all complaints were first considered by the European Commission on Human Rights ('the Commission'). It initially considered whether a complaint was admissible. If it was, an effort was made to broker a 'friendly settlement', as provided for in the Convention. In the absence of such a settlement the Commission reported on the facts and expressed its opinion on the merits of the case. That report went to the Committee of Ministers, a political body, which could endorse or reject it. In instances where the state concerned had opted to accept the compulsory jurisdiction of the Court, either the Commission or that state could refer the case to the Court for a final, binding adjudication including, where appropriate, an award of compensation. The Court was thus dependent on the Commission or the state concerned in order to be able to consider a case. When cases did not go to the Court but to the Committee of Ministers, which found there had been a violation of the Convention, it might award 'just satisfaction' to the victim.

Over time, more and more states accepted the compulsory jurisdiction of the Court and acceptance of the complaints procedure itself had become unanimous by 1990. A major reform introduced in 1994 (when Protocol No. 9 entered into force) allowed applicants to submit their case to a screening panel composed of three judges, which decided whether the Court should take up the case. As the Court's workload grew, and an increasing number of states from Central and Eastern Europe joined the ECHR, the need for even more major reforms became irresistible.

There have since been three waves of reform, resulting in Protocol No. 11 of 1994 which took effect in 1998, Protocol No. 14, adopted in 2004 but which did not enter into force until June 2010, and an ongoing discussion of the need for major reforms in the years ahead. Those debates are considered at p. 962, *infra*.

The entire system was streamlined by Protocol No. 11. The right of individual petition became compulsory, the Commission ceased to exist (as of October 1999), the Court became full time and assumed all the relevant functions of the Commission, individuals gained direct access to the Court, and the political (and too often problematic) role played by the Committee of Ministers is now limited to matters of enforcement.

The System

Proceedings under the individual petitions procedure of Article 34 begin with a complaint by an individual, group or NGO against a state party. To be declared admissible a petition must not be anonymous, manifestly ill-founded, or constitute an abuse of the right of petition. Domestic remedies must have been exhausted, it must be presented within six months of the final decision in the domestic forum, and it must not concern a matter which is substantially the same as one which has already been examined under the ECHR or submitted to another procedure of international investigation or settlement.

The Court is organized as follows:

> 11. ...The Court is composed of a number of judges equal to that of the Contracting States [47]. Judges are elected by the Parliamentary Assembly of the Council of Europe, which votes on a shortlist of three candidates put forward by the States. Beginning in 2011, each State's shortlist is submitted in advance to an advisory panel of eminent national and European judges, who consider whether each of the candidates meets the criteria set down in the Convention. Judges serve a single term of office of nine years, with a mandatory retirement age of 70....
>
> 12. Judges sit on the Court in their individual capacity and do not represent any State. They cannot engage in any activity which is incompatible with their independence or impartiality, or with the demands of full-time office....
>
> 13. The Plenary Court... elects... the President, the two Vice-Presidents (who also preside over a Section) and the three other Section Presidents. In each case, the term of office is three years. The Plenary Court also elects the Registrar and Deputy Registrar for a term of office of five years. The Rules of Court are adopted and amended by the Plenary Court. It also determines the composition of the Sections, and may request the Committee of Ministers to reduce the size of Chambers from seven judges to five for a fixed period.
>
> 14. [E]very judge is assigned to one of the five Sections, whose composition is geographically and gender balanced and takes account of the different legal systems of the Contracting States. The composition of the Sections is changed every three years.
>
> 15. Chambers are composed within each Section. The Section President and the judge elected in respect of the State concerned sit in each case....
>
> 16. Committees of three judges are set up within each Section for twelve-month periods. Their principal function is to deal with cases covered by well-established case-law. Committees retain a residual competence as regards filtering, and are called on occasionally to deal with cases referred to them by a single judge for decision.
>
> 17. It is the single-judge formation that is now mainly responsible for filtering clearly inadmissible or ill-founded applications, these accounting for some 90% of all applications decided by the Court. [Twenty judges are designated each year for this purpose.] They are assisted in their role by some sixty experienced Registry lawyers, designated by the President to act as rapporteurs, and acting under his authority. These judges continue to carry out their usual work on Chamber and Grand Chamber cases.
>
> 18. The Grand Chamber of the Court is composed of seventeen judges, [including] the President, Vice- Presidents and Section Presidents. The Grand Chamber deals with cases that raise a serious question of interpretation or application of the Convention, or a serious issue of general importance. A Chamber may relinquish jurisdiction in a case to the Grand Chamber at any stage in the procedure before judgment, as long as both parties consent. Where judgment has been delivered in a case, either party may, within a period of three months, request referral of the case to the Grand Chamber. Such requests are considered by a panel of five judges, which includes the President of the Court. Where a request is granted, the whole case is reheard.[14]

In 2011, the five-member panel received requests relating to 239 cases, 108 of which were submitted by the respective governments. Of those, only 11 cases were accepted for hearing by the Grand Chamber.

[14] European Court of Human Rights, Annual Report 2011 (2012), at 13.

NOTE

The procedures followed by the European Court of Human Rights (ECtHR) are, especially since the entry into force of Protocol No. 11 and in response to its very heavy workload, complex and not easy to follow. The rather dry description that follows illustrates both the key rules and the resulting complexity.

EUROPEAN COURT OF HUMAN RIGHTS, ANNUAL REPORT 2011

(2012), at 17

...

D. Procedure before the Court

1. General

19. Any Contracting State . . . or individual claiming to be a victim of a violation of the Convention [may directly lodge an application with the Court].

20. The procedure before the Court is adversarial and public. It is largely a written procedure. Hearings, which are held only in a very small minority of cases, are public, unless the Chamber/Grand Chamber decides otherwise on account of exceptional circumstances. Memorials and other documents filed with the Court's Registry by the parties are, in principle, accessible to the public.

21. Individual applicants may present their own case, but they should be legally represented once the application has been communicated to the respondent State. The Council of Europe has set up a legal aid scheme for applicants who do not have sufficient means.

22. The official languages of the Court are English and French, but applications may be submitted in one of the official languages of the Contracting States. Once the application has been formally communicated to the respondent State, one of the Court's official languages must be used, unless the President of the Chamber/Grand Chamber authorises the continued use of the language of the application.

2. The handling of applications

23. All new applications are initially sifted by Registry lawyers who refer them to the appropriate judicial formation. An individual application that clearly fails to meet one of the admissibility criteria is referred to a single judge, who . . . [may reject it or] refer it instead to a Committee or to a Chamber for examination.

24. In a case that can be dealt with by applying well-established case-law, the judgment may be delivered by a three-judge Committee. . . . Committee judgments require unanimity; where this is not achieved, the case will be referred to a Chamber. A Committee judgment is final and binding. . . .

25. Cases not assigned to either of the above formations will be dealt with by a Chamber, one of whose members will be designated as the judge rapporteur for the

case. The judge elected in respect of the respondent State is automatically included in the Chamber. Where that judge is unable to take part in the examination of the case, an ad hoc judge will be appointed by the presiding judge. The procedure involves communicating the case to the Government to obtain its observations on the admissibility and merits of the application. The Government is normally given sixteen weeks to reply, with shorter time-limits applying to the later stages of the procedure. The Government's pleadings will be sent to the applicant for comment, and the applicant will also be requested to make his or her claim for just satisfaction at that stage. The applicant's comments and claims will be forwarded to the Government for its final observations, following which the judge rapporteur will present the case to the Chamber for decision. Where it finds a violation of one or more Convention rights, the Chamber will generally award compensation.... It may also ... provide guidance to the State regarding any structural problem giving rise to a finding of a violation and the steps that might be taken to resolve it....

26. At any stage of the proceedings the Court may, through its Registry, propose a friendly settlement of the case to the parties. Typically this involves some recognition on the part of the State of the merits of the applicant's complaints along with an undertaking to pay compensation or to take certain measures in favour of the applicant. Where the parties reach an agreement that the Court deems acceptable, this will be recorded in a decision striking the application out. Where the parties fail to agree, the Government may then submit a unilateral declaration to the Court admitting that there has been a violation of the Convention and affording compensation to the applicant. This too, if accepted, will lead to the application being struck out by a Court decision. Both means of dealing with applications, the first being reflected in the text of the Convention, the second being based on practice, have become increasingly common in recent years.

27. All final judgments of the Court are binding on the respondent States concerned. Responsibility for supervising the execution of judgments, as well as of decisions relating to friendly settlements, lies with the Committee of Ministers of the Council of Europe. The Committee of Ministers verifies whether the State in respect of which a violation of the Convention has been found has taken adequate remedial measures.... [The Committee] may ask the Court to clarify the meaning of a judgment [or] to determine whether a State has adequately executed a judgment against it.

QUESTION

There is a judge on the Court from every one of the contracting states and if that judge cannot serve on a case involving her home state, an ad hoc judge of that nationality is nominated. Commentators have argued that the nationality link for international judges is 'contrary to standard conceptions of independence and impartiality', as well as 'anachronistic and self-defeating'.[15] What are the consequences in terms of professionalism and judicial independence of retaining the nationality link?

[15] T. Dannenbaum, 'Nationality and the International Judge: The Nationalist Presumption Governing the International Judiciary and Why it Must Be Reversed', 45 Cornell Int'l. L. J. 77 (2012), at 183.

3. THE INTERSTATE PROCEDURE: ARTICLE 33

Article 33 of the revised Convention contains a procedure by which one or more states may allege breaches of the Convention by another state party. Unlike the traditional approach to such cases under the international law of state responsibility for injury to aliens, p. 90, *supra* it is not necessary for an applicant state to allege that the rights of its own nationals have been violated.

This procedure has generally been used very sparingly. In relation to the member states of the European Union this sparing use is likely to be reinforced by Article 7 of the EU Treaty which provides for a suspension procedure whereby the voting and other rights of any of its currently 27 member states (almost 60 per cent of the states parties to the ECHR) accused of a serious and persistent violation of fundamental rights may be suspended. The EU procedure is both a more immediate one and one with more serious consequences. But the ECHR interstate procedure will continue to be the only option in relation to disputes between non-EU member states.

In general, states are reluctant to set in motion a formal condemnation procedure when they do not have a direct stake in the matter or when they perceive a serious risk of antagonizing the target state through what will be seen as a hostile act. One predictable result of such litigation would be the filing of a counter-suit. The reluctance to use the ECHR's interstate procedure is consistent with the fact that a comparable procedure involving the Human Rights Committee under Articles 41–3 of the ICCPR has also never been invoked.

Between 1956 and 1999, the former Commission considered 17 interstate applications, the most significant of which addressed only seven different situations: (1) *Greece v. United Kingdom* (1956, 1957) relating to the declaration of a state of exception in Cyprus (then a British colony); (2) *Austria v. Italy* (1960) concerning the murder trial of six members of the German-speaking minority in the South Tyrol; (3) *Denmark, Netherlands, Norway and Sweden v. Greece* (1967, 1970) relating to the coup d'état carried out by the Greek colonels in 1967. The Commission's response in that case has been described as a model 'for demonstrating both the possibilities and the political limitations of the international protection of human rights'.[16] The case also provided an early illustration of a model of international fact-finding, undertaken by a sub-commission of the former Commission, which was pathbreaking at the time, although it has since become commonplace; (4) *Ireland v. United Kingdom* (1971, 1972) relating to the state of emergency in Northern Ireland; (5) *Cyprus v. Turkey* (1974, 1975, 1977, 1996) cases arising out of the Turkish armed intervention in Cyprus; (6) *Denmark, France, the Netherlands, Norway and Sweden v. Turkey* (1982), alleging violations, including torture, by the military government. Under the settlement approved by the Commission, the Turkish Government gave a number of vague undertakings such as a commitment to instruct 'the State Supervisory Council . . . to have special regard to the observance by all public

[16] Francis Jacobs, *The European Convention on Human Rights* (3rd edn. 1993), *European Rights* (1975), at 27.

authorities' of the Convention's prohibition against torture. The settlement was widely criticized on the ground that it was not based on the respect for human rights required by the Convention; and (7) *Denmark v. Turkey* (1997) alleging torture of a Danish citizen during detention by Turkish authorities, and resulting in a friendly settlement.

Since 1959, the Court has delivered judgment in only three interstate cases — *Ireland v. United Kingdom* (1978), *Denmark v. Turkey* (2000), and *Cyprus v. Turkey* (2001) — but three applications were made by Georgia against Russia between 2007 and 2009. One was subsequently withdrawn. In the first interstate case, Ireland claimed that interrogation techniques used by the British violated Article 3 of the Convention. In a controversial decision the Court found that they amounted to 'inhuman and degrading treatment', but not torture. The case was also noteworthy for the fact that the Court rejected a British submission that the case should effectively be considered moot on the grounds that the United Kingdom had not contested the finding by the Commission of a violation of Article 3, that the practices in question had been renounced and a solemn undertaking not to reintroduce them had been given, and that individuals had been punished for the acts in question. The Court held, however, that:

> [T]he responsibilities assigned to it within the framework of the system under the Convention extend to pronouncing on the non-contested allegations of violation of Article 3. The Court's judgments in fact serve not only to decide those cases brought before the Court but, more generally, to elucidate, safeguard and develop the rules instituted by the Convention, thereby contributing to the observance by the States of the engagements undertaken by them as Contracting Parties.[17]

The case brought by Georgia accuses the Russian Federation of a wide range of ECHR violations in the context of its response to an incident in September 2006 in which four Russian officers were arrested in Tbilisi, Georgia, on spying charges. Subsequently Russia deported hundreds of Georgians, cut off mail and transport links with Tbilisi, and cracked down on Georgian businesses alleged to have been operating illegally in Russia. Georgia alleged that the resulting harassment of the Georgian immigrant population in the Russian Federation led to 'interferences with the respect for private and family life, home and correspondence, the peaceful enjoyment of possessions and the right to education together with widespread arrests and detention generating a generalized threat to security of the person and multiple interferences with the right to liberty on arbitrary grounds.' The Georgian Government also complained of the conditions in which 'at least 2,380 Georgians' had been detained. The case was declared admissible in 2009 but was subsequently relinquished by the chamber for hearing by the Grand Chamber, to take place in 2012.

[17] *Ireland v. United Kingdom* (Application No. 5310/71, 18 Jan. 1978), para. 154.

Finally, we turn to the case of *Cyprus v. Turkey* which illustrates the potentially very complex nature of interstate cases.

FRANK HOFFMEISTER, CASE NOTE: CYPRUS v. TURKEY[18]

96 Am. J. Int'l. L. 445 (2002)

In the first interstate case after the reform of 1998, the European Court of Human Rights, sitting as a grand chamber of seventeen judges, rendered the longest judgment in its history. It ruled . . . that Turkey was responsible for various breaches of the [ECHR] in the "Turkish Republic of Northern Cyprus" (TRNC). . . .

. . . Cyprus alleged that, with respect to the situation that has existed in Cyprus since the start of Turkey's military operations in northern Cyprus in July 1974, Turkey was in breach of the entire set of human rights guaranteed by the Convention (Articles 1–11, 13, 14, and 17), with the exception of the right to marry (Article 12). . . .

. . . [T]he Court rejected Turkey's contention that only the TRNC had jurisdiction in northern Cyprus. The Court concluded that "having effective overall control over northern Cyprus, [Turkey's] responsibility cannot be confined to the acts of its own soldiers or officials in northern Cyprus but must also be engaged by virtue of the acts of the local administration which survives by virtue of Turkish military and other support." It would frustrate the purpose of the Convention as an instrument of European public order if Cyprus's continuing inability to exercise its Convention obligations in northern Cyprus was allowed to result in a vacuum in human rights protection in that territory, now under the effective control of Turkey.

With respect to the requirement of exhaustion of local remedies. . . . Cyprus argued that local judicial authorities of the TRNC could not be expected to "issue effective decisions against persons exercising authority with the backing of the [Turkish] army in order to remedy violations of human rights committed in furtherance of the general policies of the regime." Turkey maintained, however, that the local judiciary was fully developed and independent. . . . Referring to the need to avoid a vacuum in the protection of human rights in northern Cyprus, the European Court thus found that the absence of TRNC courts would work to the detriment of the people living there. Therefore, the judicial organs of the TRNC could not be simply disregarded. The Court concluded that the inhabitants of the territory were required to exhaust local remedies unless the absence or ineffectiveness of such remedies can be proved — a question that needs to be settled on a case-by-case basis.

Turning to the merits, the Court first examined the matter of Greek Cypriot missing persons. It noted that there was no proof that any of the missing persons had been unlawfully killed by Turkish troops in 1974. In any case, the six-month period for bringing a claim under the Convention was long past, and the relevant events did not come within the scope *ratione temporis* of the application. Nevertheless, the

[18] (Application No. 25781/94, 10 May 2001).

Court also determined that it could examine the matter of the missing persons from the perspective of a contracting state's procedural obligation under Article 2 to protect the right to life — an obligation that arises upon "proof of an arguable claim" that a person, last seen in the custody of state agents, subsequently disappeared in a context that could be considered life-threatening.

In addressing this question, the Court observed that many persons now missing were detained either by Turkish or Turkish Cypriot forces at a time when the conduct of military operations was accompanied by arrests and killings on a large scale. The Court rejected Turkey's claim that its cooperation with the UN Committee on Missing Persons (CMP) satisfied the need to inquire into the whereabouts of the missing persons. As the Court noted, the CMP's task was to determine only whether any of the missing persons on the list were dead or alive; it was not empowered to make findings either on the cause of death or on the issue of responsibility for any deaths. The Court therefore concluded that the CMP's investigations could not be regarded as effective. It found, moreover, a continuing violation of the right to life because no effective investigation has ever been undertaken into the whereabouts and fate of Greek Cypriot missing persons who disappeared in 1974 under life-threatening circumstances. The Court added that it was incumbent on the authorities to account for the whereabouts of given individuals after they had assumed control over them. By virtue of the failure of Turkish authorities to do so, there was also, according to the Court, a continuing violation of the right to liberty under Article 5 of the Convention. The Court held, moreover, that the silence of the Turkish authorities in the face of the legitimate concerns of the missing persons' relatives was inhuman treatment within the meaning of Article 3 of the Convention.

The second substantive matter addressed by the Court related to the rights of displaced persons with respect to their homes and property. . . .

. . . As regards property rights, the Court repeated its finding in the *Loizidou* judgment that Article 159 of the 1985 TRNC Constitution, which provides that abandoned property devolves to the TRNC, is deemed to be invalid for the purposes of the Convention. Hence, the Greek Cypriots remained the owners of their property lying in the north. . . .

The third substantive matter addressed by the Court concerned the living conditions of the remaining 429 Greek Cypriots in the Karpas region of northern Cyprus. It found that their freedom of religion was infringed since TRNC authorities prevented them from traveling outside their villages to attend religious ceremonies. Furthermore, the censorship regime imposed upon Greek-language schoolbooks violated the freedom of expression (Article 10 of the Convention), and the absence of appropriate secondary-school facilities for Greek Cypriots violated the right to education (Article 2 of Protocol No. 1). . . .

. . .

Finally, the Court decided that the question of the possible application of Article 41 of the Convention — under which it can grant just satisfaction if the internal law of the respondent state allows only partial reparation to be made for the consequences of the violations found — was "not ready for decision"; the Court therefore "adjourn[ed] consideration" of the Article 41 request.

QUESTIONS

1. Some of the largest European countries, including the United Kingdom, Germany, and Spain, have never lodged an interstate complaint against another European government. Does this mean that this procedure is only likely to be invoked by small countries with limited political clout? If so, would that indicate a fundamental weakness of the procedure?

2. Under what circumstances might the lodging of an interstate complaint be most productive and when might it be considered counter-productive?

3. In the Cyprus case, six dissenting judges criticized the proposition that the TRNC courts should be considered to provide appropriate 'domestic remedies' that needed to be exhausted before appealing to the ECHR. They cited an 'obvious and justifiable lack of confidence' in those courts. What do you see as the reasons for, and the implications of, the Court's finding in this regard?

4. THE COURT'S JURISDICTION

The ECtHR cannot consider an application unless it ascertains that it has jurisdiction over the case. If an event occurred prior to the state becoming a party to the ECHR and has no continuing dimension, if the state whose conduct is complained about is not a party to the Convention, and so on, the Court will have no jurisdiction. One of the most controversial and complex issues currently giving cause for concern is the extent to which the Court has jurisdiction over events which occur beyond the territory of a Contracting Party. The issue of extraterritorial jurisdiction arises in connection with situations which have become increasingly common. They include, to take the examples dealt with below, situations in which a military strike is launched from within the legal space (*l'éspace juridique*) of the Council of Europe but results in damage outside that area, actions taken by armed forces of one state operating in the territory of another which may or may not be a member of the Council of Europe, and the responsibility of a state contributing troops to a UN or other multilateral peacekeeping force under the auspices of the UN Security Council.

These issues highlight the challenge of evolving approaches in response to challenges that were not foreseen at the time of drafting the ECHR. The Court has often affirmed the importance of a dynamic, evolutive or teleological approach to interpretation, but in relation to territorial jurisdiction it seems surprisingly reticent to adopt such an approach. The challenges discussed below also underscore the impact of globalization and the extent to which it remains possible to defend the notion that the Convention is essentially designed to uphold the human rights of those within the *éspace juridique*. As boundaries become ever more porous and European states deepen their involvement in complex ways in neighbouring countries and beyond, such a restrictive notion will be increasingly challenged.

The most contentious of the cases below is *Banković*, in which forces operating under the control of the North Atlantic Treaty Organization (NATO) fired a missile which killed and injured civilians in the course of an air strike on a television station. The Court's rejection of jurisdiction in that case seems to have been qualified in the *Issa* case which follows, which concerns the acts of Turkish Government troops in neighbouring Iraq which resulted in the killing of a number of individuals. Finally, after extensive litigation in the British courts, the ECtHR was called upon in *Al-Skeini and Others v. United Kingdom* to determine whether six individuals killed by UK forces as the occupying power in an area of Iraq in 2003 could be considered to fall under the UK's ECHR jurisdiction.

Note that the excerpts below omit the many cross-references to its own jurisprudence that the Court tends to include in the text of its judgments.

BANKOVIĆ AND OTHERS v. BELGIUM AND OTHERS

European Court of Human Rights, Application No. 52207/99 (Grand Chamber), 12 Dec. 2001

[On 23 April 1999 a missile launched from a NATO forces' aircraft hit the building in Belgrade which housed the master control room of RTS which operated three television channels and four radio stations. In total 24 targets were hit in the FRY on the same night, including three in Belgrade. The applicants in the case included one person injured and five relatives of some of the 16 persons killed in the RTS attack. The respondent governments were all NATO members who were party to the ECHR: Belgium, the Czech Republic, Denmark, France, Germany, Greece, Hungary, Iceland, Italy, Luxembourg, the Netherlands, Norway, Poland, Portugal, Spain, Turkey, and the United Kingdom.

After considering a range of issues the Court concluded that 'the essential question to be examined therefore is whether the applicants and their deceased relatives were, as a result of that extra-territorial act [of firing a missile], capable of falling within the jurisdiction of the respondent States.' Before addressing the jurisdiction issue the Court noted the applicable rules of interpretation. The framework is that reflected in the rules set out in the Vienna Convention on the Law of Treaties (VCLT) and involves ascertaining the 'ordinary meaning to be given to the phrase "within their jurisdiction" in its context and in the light of the object and purpose of the Convention', and taking account of any additional applicable rules of international law. The Court also noted that 'it must remain mindful of the Convention's special character as a human rights treaty', as well as interpreting it 'as far as possible in harmony with other principles of international law of which it forms part'. In addition, the *travaux préparatoires* can be consulted with a view to confirming the ordinary meaning of a provision or when such an approach to interpretation 'leaves the meaning "ambiguous or obscure" or leads to a result which is "manifestly absurd or unreasonable"' (Arts. 31–2 of the VCLT).]

(b) The meaning of the words "within their jurisdiction"

59. As to the "ordinary meaning" of the relevant term in Article 1 of the Convention, the Court is satisfied that, from the standpoint of public international law, the jurisdictional competence of a State is primarily territorial. While international law does not exclude a State's exercise of jurisdiction extra-territorially, the suggested bases of such jurisdiction (including nationality, flag, diplomatic and consular relations, effect, protection, passive personality and universality) are, as a general rule, defined and limited by the sovereign territorial rights of the other relevant States.

60. Accordingly, for example, a State's competence to exercise jurisdiction over its own nationals abroad is subordinate to that State's and other States' territorial competence. In addition, a State may not actually exercise jurisdiction on the territory of another without the latter's consent, invitation or acquiescence, unless the former is an occupying State in which case it can be found to exercise jurisdiction in that territory, at least in certain respects.

61. The Court is of the view, therefore, that Article 1 of the Convention must be considered to reflect this ordinary and essentially territorial notion of jurisdiction, other bases of jurisdiction being exceptional and requiring special justification in the particular circumstances of each case.

62. ... [In terms of state practice] no State has indicated a belief that its extraterritorial actions involved an exercise of jurisdiction within the meaning of Article 1 of the Convention by making a derogation pursuant to Article 15 of the Convention...

63. Finally, the Court finds clear confirmation of this essentially territorial notion of jurisdiction in the *travaux préparatoires* which demonstrate that the Expert Intergovernmental Committee replaced the words "all persons residing within their territories" with a reference to persons "within their jurisdiction" with a view to expanding the Convention's application to others who may not reside, in a legal sense, but who are, nevertheless, on the territory of the Contracting States.

64. It is true that the notion of the Convention being a living instrument to be interpreted in light of present-day conditions is firmly rooted in the Court's case-law. The Court has applied that approach not only to the Convention's substantive provisions... but more relevantly to its interpretation of former Articles 25 and 46 concerning the recognition by a Contracting State of the competence of the Convention organs....

65. However, the scope of Article 1, at issue in the present case, is determinative of the very scope of the Contracting Parties' positive obligations and, as such, of the scope and reach of the entire Convention system of human rights' protection as opposed to the question, under discussion in the *Loizidou* case (*preliminary objections*), of the competence of the Convention organs to examine a case. In any event, the extracts from the *travaux préparatoires* detailed above constitute a clear indication of the intended meaning of Article 1 of the Convention which cannot be ignored. The Court would emphasise that it is not interpreting Article 1 "solely" in accordance with the *travaux préparatoires* or finding those *travaux* "decisive"; rather this preparatory material constitutes clear confirmatory evidence of the ordinary meaning of Article 1 of the Convention as already identified by the Court (Article 32 of the Vienna Convention 1969).

66. Accordingly, and as the Court stated in the *Soering* case:

> "Article 1 sets a limit, notably territorial, on the reach of the Convention. In particular, the engagement undertaken by a Contracting State is confined to 'securing' ('*reconnaître*' in the French text) the listed rights and freedoms to persons within its own 'jurisdiction'. Further, the Convention does not govern the actions of States not Parties to it, nor does it purport to be a means of requiring the Contracting States to impose Convention standards on other States."

(c) Extra-territorial acts recognised as constituting an exercise of jurisdiction

67. In keeping with the essentially territorial notion of jurisdiction, the Court has accepted only in exceptional cases that acts of the Contracting States performed, or producing effects, outside their territories can constitute an exercise of jurisdiction by them within the meaning of Article 1 of the Convention.

68. Reference has been made in the Court's case-law, as an example of jurisdiction "not restricted to the national territory" of the respondent State (the *Loizidou* judgment (*preliminary objections*), at § 62), to situations where the extradition or expulsion of a person by a Contracting State may give rise to an issue under Articles 2 and/or 3 (or, exceptionally, under Articles 5 and or 6) and hence engage the responsibility of that State under the Convention.

However, the Court notes that liability is incurred in such cases by an action of the respondent State concerning a person while he or she is on its territory, clearly within its jurisdiction, and that such cases do not concern the actual exercise of a State's competence or jurisdiction abroad.

...

70. Moreover, in that first *Loizidou* judgment (*preliminary objections*), the Court found that, bearing in mind the object and purpose of the Convention, the responsibility of a Contracting Party was capable of being engaged when as a consequence of military action (lawful or unlawful) it exercised effective control of an area outside its national territory. The obligation to secure, in such an area, the Convention rights and freedoms was found to derive from the fact of such control whether it was exercised directly, through the respondent State's armed forces, or through a subordinate local administration. The Court concluded that the acts of which the applicant complained were capable of falling within Turkish jurisdiction within the meaning of Article 1 of the Convention.

...

In its subsequent *Cyprus v. Turkey* judgment, the Court added that since Turkey had such "effective control", its responsibility could not be confined to the acts of its own agents therein but was engaged by the acts of the local administration which survived by virtue of Turkish support. Turkey's "jurisdiction" under Article 1 was therefore considered to extend to securing the entire range of substantive Convention rights in northern Cyprus.

71. In sum, the case-law of the Court demonstrates that its recognition of the exercise of extra-territorial jurisdiction by a Contracting State is exceptional: it has done so when the respondent State, through the effective control of the relevant territory and its inhabitants abroad as a consequence of military occupation or through

the consent, invitation or acquiescence of the Government of that territory, exercises all or some of the public powers normally to be exercised by that Government. . . .

73. Additionally, the Court notes that other recognised instances of the extraterritorial exercise of jurisdiction by a State include cases involving the activities of its diplomatic or consular agents abroad and on board craft and vessels registered in, or flying the flag of, that State. In these specific situations, customary international law and treaty provisions have recognised the extra-territorial exercise of jurisdiction by the relevant State.

(d) Were the present applicants therefore capable of coming within the "jurisdiction" of the respondent States?

74. The applicants maintain that the bombing of RTS by the respondent States constitutes yet a further example of an extra-territorial act which can be accommodated by the notion of "jurisdiction" in Article 1 of the Convention, and are thereby proposing a further specification of the ordinary meaning of the term "jurisdiction" in Article 1 of the Convention. The Court must be satisfied that equally exceptional circumstances exist in the present case which could amount to the extra-territorial exercise of jurisdiction by a Contracting State.

75. In the first place, the applicants suggest a specific application of the "effective control" criteria developed in the northern Cyprus cases. . . . The Court considers that the applicants' submission is tantamount to arguing that anyone adversely affected by an act imputable to a Contracting State, wherever in the world that act may have been committed or its consequences felt, is thereby brought within the jurisdiction of that State for the purpose of Article 1 of the Convention.

The Court is inclined to agree with the Governments' submission that the text of Article 1 does not accommodate such an approach to "jurisdiction". Admittedly, the applicants accept that jurisdiction, and any consequent State Convention responsibility, would be limited in the circumstances to the commission and consequences of that particular act. However, the Court is of the view that the wording of Article 1 does not provide any support for the applicants' suggestion that the positive obligation in Article 1 to secure "the rights and freedoms defined in Section I of this Convention" can be divided and tailored in accordance with the particular circumstances of the extra-territorial act in question and, it considers its view in this respect supported by the text of Article 19 of the Convention. Indeed the applicants' approach does not explain the application of the words "within their jurisdiction" in Article 1 and it even goes so far as to render those words superfluous and devoid of any purpose. Had the drafters of the Convention wished to ensure jurisdiction as extensive as that advocated by the applicants, they could have adopted a text the same as or similar to the contemporaneous Articles 1 of the four Geneva Conventions of 1949.

Furthermore, the applicants' notion of jurisdiction equates the determination of whether an individual falls within the jurisdiction of a Contracting State with the question of whether that person can be considered to be a victim of a violation of rights guaranteed by the Convention. These are separate and distinct admissibility conditions, each of which has to be satisfied in the afore-mentioned order, before an individual can invoke the Convention provisions against a Contracting State.

76. Secondly, the applicants' alternative suggestion is that the limited scope of the airspace control only circumscribed the scope of the respondent States' positive obligation to protect the applicants and did not exclude it. The Court finds this to be essentially the same argument as their principal proposition and rejects it for the same reasons.

...

78. Fourthly, the Court does not find it necessary to pronounce on the specific meaning to be attributed in various contexts to the allegedly similar jurisdiction provisions in the international instruments to which the applicants refer because it is not convinced by the applicants' specific submissions in these respects.... [A]s to Article 2 § 1 the CCPR 1966, as early as 1950 the drafters had definitively and specifically confined its territorial scope and it is difficult to suggest that exceptional recognition by the Human Rights Committee of certain instances of extra-territorial jurisdiction (and the applicants give one example only) displaces in any way the territorial jurisdiction expressly conferred by that Article of the CCPR 1966 or explains the precise meaning of "jurisdiction" in Article 1 of its Optional Protocol 1966....

79. Fifthly and more generally, the applicants maintain that any failure to accept that they fell within the jurisdiction of the respondent States would defeat the *ordre public* mission of the Convention and leave a regrettable vacuum in the Convention system of human rights' protection.

80. The Court's obligation, in this respect, is to have regard to the special character of the Convention as a constitutional instrument of *European* public order for the protection of individual human beings and its role, as set out in Article 19 of the Convention, is to ensure the observance of *the engagements undertaken* by the Contracting Parties (the above-cited *Loizidou* judgment (*preliminary objections*), at § 93). It is therefore difficult to contend that a failure to accept the extra-territorial jurisdiction of the respondent States would fall foul of the Convention's *ordre public* objective, which itself underlines the essentially regional vocation of the Convention system, or of Article 19 of the Convention which does not shed any particular light on the territorial ambit of that system.

It is true that, in its above-cited *Cyprus v. Turkey* judgment (at § 78), the Court was conscious of the need to avoid "a regrettable vacuum in the system of human-rights protection" in northern Cyprus. However, and as noted by the Governments, that comment related to an entirely different situation to the present: the inhabitants of northern Cyprus would have found themselves excluded from the benefits of the Convention safeguards and system which they had previously enjoyed, by Turkey's "effective control" of the territory and by the accompanying inability of the Cypriot Government, as a Contracting State, to fulfil the obligations it had undertaken under the Convention.

In short, the Convention is a multi-lateral treaty operating, subject to Article 56 of the Convention, in an essentially regional context and notably in the legal space (*espace juridique*) of the Contracting States. The FRY clearly does not fall within this legal space. The Convention was not designed to be applied throughout the world, even in respect of the conduct of Contracting States. Accordingly, the desirability of avoiding a gap or vacuum in human rights' protection has so far been relied on by the Court in favour of establishing jurisdiction only when the territory in question was one that, but for the specific circumstances, would normally be covered by the Convention.

...

4. The Court's conclusion

82. The Court is not therefore persuaded that there was any jurisdictional link between the persons who were victims of the act complained of and the respondent States. Accordingly, it is not satisfied that the applicants and their deceased relatives were capable of coming within the jurisdiction of the respondent States on account of the extra-territorial act in question.

...

ISSA AND OTHERS v. TURKEY

European Court of Human Rights, Application No. 31821/96, 16 Nov. 2004

[The case was brought by six Iraqi nationals, who earn their living by shepherding sheep, and who complained of the alleged unlawful arrest, detention, ill-treatment, and subsequent killing of their relatives in the course of a military operation conducted by the Turkish army in northern Iraq in April 1995. The Turkish Government responded that while a military operation had taken place in this region at the relevant time, its forces had not been within ten kilometres of the area where the alleged violations occurred.]

II. Whether the applicants' relatives came within the jurisdiction of Turkey

...

B. The Court's assessment

...

67. The established case-law in this area indicates that the concept of "jurisdiction" for the purposes of Article 1 of the Convention must be considered to reflect the term's meaning in public international law.

From the standpoint of public international law, the words "within their jurisdiction" in Article 1 of the Convention must be understood to mean that a State's jurisdictional competence is primarily territorial, but also that jurisdiction is presumed to be exercised normally throughout the State's territory.

68. However, the concept of "jurisdiction" within the meaning of Article 1 of the Convention is not necessarily restricted to the national territory of the High Contracting Parties. In exceptional circumstances the acts of Contracting States performed outside their territory or which produce effects there ("extra-territorial act") may amount to exercise by them of their jurisdiction within the meaning of Article 1 of the Convention.

69. According to the relevant principles of international law, a State's responsibility may be engaged where, as a consequence of military action — whether lawful or unlawful — that State in practice exercises effective control of an area situated outside its national territory. The obligation to secure, in such an area, the rights and freedoms set out in the Convention derives from the fact of such control, whether it be exercised directly, through its armed forces, or through a subordinate local administration.

70. It is not necessary to determine whether a Contracting Party actually exercises detailed control over the policies and actions of the authorities in the area situated outside its national territory, since even overall control of the area may engage the responsibility of the Contracting Party concerned.

71. Moreover, a State may also be held accountable for violation of the Convention rights and freedoms of persons who are in the territory of another State but who are found to be under the former State's authority and control through its agents operating — whether lawfully or unlawfully — in the latter State.... Accountability in such situations stems from the fact that Article 1 of the Convention cannot be interpreted so as to allow a State party to perpetrate violations of the Convention on the territory of another State, which it could not perpetrate on its own territory.

2. Application of the above principles

72. In the light of the above principles the Court must ascertain whether the applicants' relatives were under the authority and/or effective control, and therefore within the jurisdiction, of the respondent State as a result of the latter's extra-territorial acts.

73. In this connection, the Court notes that it is undisputed between the parties that the Turkish armed forces carried out military operations in [the relevant area at the time]....

74. The Court does not exclude the possibility that, as a consequence of this military action, the respondent State could be considered to have exercised, temporarily, effective overall control of a particular portion of the territory of northern Iraq. Accordingly, if there is a sufficient factual basis for holding that, at the relevant time, the victims were within that specific area, it would follow logically that they were within the jurisdiction of Turkey (and not that of Iraq, which is not a Contracting State and clearly does not fall within the legal space (*espace juridique*) of the Contracting States).

75. However, notwithstanding the large number of troops involved in the aforementioned military operations, it does not appear that Turkey exercised effective overall control of the entire area of northern Iraq....

76. The essential question to be examined in the instant case is whether at the relevant time Turkish troops conducted operations in the area where the killings took place. The fate of the applicants' complaints in respect of the killing of their relatives depends on the prior establishment of that premise. The Government have vigorously denied that their troops were active in or around Azadi village in the Spna area. The reasonableness of that assertion must be tested in the light of the documentary and other evidence which the parties have submitted to the Court, having regard to the standard of proof which it habitually employs when ascertaining whether there

is a basis in fact for an allegation of unlawful killing, namely proof "beyond reasonable doubt", it being understood that such proof may follow from the coexistence of sufficiently strong, clear and concordant inferences or of similar unrebutted presumptions of fact.

...

81. On the basis of all the material in its possession, the Court considers that it has not been established to the required standard of proof that the Turkish armed forces conducted operations in the area in question, and, more precisely, in the hills above the village of Azadi where, according to the applicants' statements, the victims were at that time.

3. The Court's conclusion

82. In the light of the above, the Court is not satisfied that the applicants' relatives were within the "jurisdiction" of the respondent State for the purposes of Article 1 of the Convention....

AL-SKEINI AND OTHERS v. UNITED KINGDOM

European Court of Human Rights, Application No. 55721/07 (Grand Chamber), 7 July 2011

[Following the invasion of Iraq in March 2003 by the United States, the United Kingdom, and other coalition members, the United States and the United Kingdom became occupying powers in May 2003. The United Kingdom was put in charge of the South East, including the province of Al-Basrah, with responsibility for maintaining security and supporting the civil administration. This case was brought by the relatives of six persons killed during that period. Three of the victims were shot dead by British soldiers; one was fatally wounded in an exchange of fire between a British patrol and unknown gunmen; one was beaten by British soldiers and forced into a river, where he drowned; and one, Baha Mousa, died of asphyxiation at a British military base, with 93 separate bodily injuries. The two principal issues before the Court were (1) whether it had jurisdiction over events in Iraq, as a non-party to the Convention and (2) whether the UK Government had fulfilled its Article 2 obligation to carry out an effective investigation into the killings. In relation to the latter, it held that there had been a violation, although it tailored the test to the circumstances ('the authorities must take the reasonable steps available to them'). The following excerpt concerns only the jurisdiction issue.

In the United Kingdom, the then House of Lords[19] held that the death of Baha Mousa was within the UK's jurisdiction by analogizing a prison 'with the extra-territorial exception made for embassies'. In relation to the other five victims, killed by UK soldiers on patrol, the House of Lords followed *Banković* in concluding that they were not within the UK's jurisdiction.]

...

[19] [2007] UKHL 26.

1. Jurisdiction

...

(b) The Court's assessment

(i) General principles relevant to jurisdiction under Article 1 of the Convention

...

(α) The territorial principle

131. A State's jurisdictional competence under Article 1 is primarily territorial.... Conversely, acts of the Contracting States performed, or producing effects, outside their territories can constitute an exercise of jurisdiction within the meaning of Article . only in exceptional cases.

132. To date, the Court in its case-law has recognised a number of exceptional circumstances capable of giving rise to the exercise of jurisdiction by a Contracting State outside its own territorial boundaries. [E]ach case ... must be determined with reference to the particular facts.

(β) State agent authority and control

133. The Court has recognised in its case-law that, as an exception to the principle of territoriality, a Contracting State's jurisdiction under Article 1 may extend to acts of its authorities which produce effects outside its own territory.... It is necessary to examine the Court's case-law to identify the defining principles.

134. First, it is clear that the acts of diplomatic and consular agents, who are present on foreign territory in accordance with provisions of international law, may amount to an exercise of jurisdiction when these agents exert authority and control over others.

135. Secondly, the Court has recognised the exercise of extra-territorial jurisdiction by a Contracting State when, through the consent, invitation or acquiescence of the Government of that territory, it exercises all or some of the public powers normally to be exercised by that Government....

136. In addition, the Court's case-law demonstrates that, in certain circumstances, the use of force by a State's agents operating outside its territory may bring the individual thereby brought under the control of the State's authorities into the State's Article 1 jurisdiction. This principle has been applied where an individual is taken into the custody of State agents abroad. For example, in *Öcalan v. Turkey* [GC], no. 46221/99, § 91, ECHR 2005-IV, the Court held that "directly after being handed over to the Turkish officials by the Kenyan officials, the applicant was effectively under Turkish authority and therefore within the 'jurisdiction' of that State for the purposes of Article 1 of the Convention, even though in this instance Turkey exercised its authority outside its territory". In *Issa and Others v. Turkey*, no. 31821/96, 16 November 2004, the Court indicated that, had it been established that Turkish soldiers had taken the applicants' relatives into custody in Northern Iraq, taken them to a nearby cave and executed them, the deceased would have been within Turkish jurisdiction by virtue of the soldiers' authority and control over them. In *Al-Saadoon*

and Mufdhi v. the United Kingdom (dec.), no. 61498/08, §§ 86–89, 30 June 2009, the Court held that two Iraqi nationals detained in British-controlled military prisons in Iraq fell within the jurisdiction of the United Kingdom, since the United Kingdom exercised total and exclusive control over the prisons and the individuals detained in them. Finally, in *Medvedyev and Others v. France* [GC], no. 3394/03, §67, ECHR 2010-. . . , the Court held that the applicants were within French jurisdiction by virtue of the exercise by French agents of full and exclusive control over a ship and its crew from the time of its interception in international waters. The Court does not consider that jurisdiction in the above cases arose solely from the control exercised by the Contracting State over the buildings, aircraft or ship in which the individuals were held. What is decisive in such cases is the exercise of physical power and control over the person in question.

137. It is clear that, whenever the State through its agents exercises control and authority over an individual, and thus jurisdiction, the State is under an obligation under Article 1 to secure to that individual the rights and freedoms under Section 1 of the Convention that are relevant to the situation of that individual. In this sense, therefore, the Convention rights can be "divided and tailored".

(γ) Effective control over an area

138. Another exception to the principle that jurisdiction under Article . is limited to a State's own territory occurs when, as a consequence of lawful or unlawful military action, a Contracting State exercises effective control of an area outside that national territory. The obligation to secure, in such an area, the rights and freedoms set out in the Convention, derives from the fact of such control, whether it be exercised directly, through the Contracting State's own armed forces, or through a subordinate local administration. Where the fact of such domination over the territory is established, it is not necessary to determine whether the Contracting State exercises detailed control over the policies and actions of the subordinate local administration. The fact that the local administration survives as a result of the Contracting State's military and other support entails that State's responsibility for its policies and actions. The controlling State has the responsibility under Article 1 to secure, within the area under its control, the entire range of substantive rights set out in the Convention and those additional Protocols which it has ratified. It will be liable for any violations of those rights.

139. It is a question of fact whether a Contracting State exercises effective control over an area outside its own territory. In determining whether effective control exists, the Court will primarily have reference to the strength of the State's military presence in the area. Other indicators may also be relevant, such as the extent to which its military, economic and political support for the local subordinate administration provides it with influence and control over the region.

. . .

(δ) The Convention legal space ("espace juridique")

141. The Convention is a constitutional instrument of European public order (see *Loizidou v. Turkey* (preliminary objections), cited above, § 75). It does not govern the actions of States not Parties to it, nor does it purport to be a means of

requiring the Contracting States to impose Convention standards on other States (see *Soering*, cited above, § 86).

142. The Court has emphasised that, where the territory of one Convention State is occupied by the armed forces of another, the occupying State should in principle be held accountable under the Convention for breaches of human rights within the occupied territory, because to hold otherwise would be to deprive the population of that territory of the rights and freedoms hitherto enjoyed and would result in a "vacuum" of protection within the "Convention legal space". However, the importance of establishing the occupying State's jurisdiction in such cases does not imply, *a contrario*, that jurisdiction under Article 1 of the Convention can never exist outside the territory covered by the Council of Europe Member States. The Court has not in its case-law applied any such restriction.

. . .

(iii) Conclusion as regards jurisdiction

149. [F]ollowing the removal from power of the Ba'ath regime and until the accession of the Interim Government, the United Kingdom (together with the United States) assumed in Iraq the exercise of some of the public powers normally to be exercised by a sovereign government. In particular, the United Kingdom assumed authority and responsibility for the maintenance of security in South East Iraq. In these exceptional circumstances, the Court considers that the United Kingdom, through its soldiers engaged in security operations in Basrah during the period in question, exercised authority and control over individuals killed in the course of such security operations, so as to establish a jurisdictional link between the deceased and the United Kingdom for the purposes of Article 1 of the Convention.

. . .

II. APPLICATION OF ARTICLE 41 OF THE CONVENTION

. . .

A. Damage

179. [Applicants 1–4] asked the Court to order the Government to carry out an Article 2-compliant investigation into their relatives' deaths. They also claimed GBP 15,000 each in compensation for the distress they had suffered. . . .

. . .

182. [T]he Court recalls that it is not its role under Article 41 to function akin to a domestic tort mechanism court in apportioning fault and compensatory damages between civil parties. Its guiding principle is equity, which above all involves flexibility and an objective consideration of what is just, fair and reasonable in all the circumstances of the case, including not only the position of the applicant but the overall context in which the breach occurred. Its non-pecuniary awards serve to give recognition to the fact that moral damage occurred as a result of a breach of a fundamental human right and reflect in the broadest of terms the severity of the damage. In the light of all the circumstances of the present case, the Court considers that, to compensate each of the first five applicants for the distress caused by the lack

of a fully independent investigation into the deaths of their relatives, it would be just and equitable to award the full amount claimed. . . .

. . .

FOR THESE REASONS, THE COURT UNANIMOUSLY

. . .

4. *Holds* that the applicants' deceased relatives fell within the jurisdiction of the respondent State and *dismisses* the Government's preliminary objection as regards jurisdiction;

5. *Holds* that the sixth applicant can no longer claim to be a victim of a violation of the procedural obligation under Article 2 of the Convention [because an independent judicial investigation was under way at the national level;[20]

. . .

CONCURRING OPINION OF JUDGE BONELLO

. . .

5. Up until now, the Court has, in matters concerning the extra-territorial jurisdiction of Contracting Parties, spawned a number of "leading" judgments based on a need-to-decide basis, patchwork case-law at best. Inevitably, the doctrines established seem to go too far to some, and not far enough to others. As the Court has, in these cases, always tailored its tenets to sets of specific facts, it is hardly surprising that those tenets then seem to limp when applied to sets of different facts. . . .

. . .

7. . . . [T]he judicial decision-making process in Strasbourg has, so far, squandered more energy in attempting to reconcile the barely reconcilable than in trying to erect intellectual constructs of more universal application. A considerable number of different approaches to extra-territorial jurisdiction have so far been experimented with by the Court on a case-by-case basis, some not completely exempt from internal contradiction.

8. My guileless plea is to return to the drawing board. To stop fashioning doctrines which somehow seem to accommodate the facts, but rather, to appraise the facts against the immutable principles which underlie the fundamental functions of the Convention.

. . .

16. In my view, the one honest test, in *all* circumstances (including extra-territoriality), is the following: did it depend on the agents of the State whether the alleged violation would be committed or would not be committed? Was it within the power of the State to punish the perpetrators and to compensate the victims? If the answer is yes, self-evidently the facts fall squarely within the jurisdiction of the State. All the rest seems to me clumsy, self-serving alibi hunting, unworthy of any State that has grandiosely undertaken to secure the "universal" observance of human rights whenever and wherever it is within its power to secure them, and, may I add, of courts whose only *raison d'etre* should be to ensure that those

[20] See the Report of the Baha Mousa Inquiry (93 vols., 2011), at www.bahamousainquiry.org/report/index.htm.

obligations are not avoided or evaded. The Court has, in the present judgment, thankfully placed a sanitary cordon between itself and some of these approaches.
...

NOTE

A related issue, addressed by the Court in a judgment issued on the same day as *Al-Skeini*, is whether actions taken by national forces in furtherance of a binding UN Security Council resolution could be evaluated for compliance with the ECHR. In *Al-Jedda v. United Kingdom* (Application No. 27021/08 (Grand Chamber), judgment of 7 July 2011) the Court unanimously rejected the government's claim that the internment action impugned in the application was attributable to the UN and not to the United Kingdom.

> The Court... noted that, at the time of the invasion in March 2003, there was no UN Security Council (UNSC) resolution providing for the allocation of roles in Iraq if the existing regime was displaced. In May 2003 the US and the UK, having displaced the previous regime, assumed control over the provision of security in Iraq; the UN was allocated a role in providing humanitarian relief, supporting the reconstruction of Iraq and helping in the formation of an Iraqi interim government, but had no role as regards security. The Court did not consider that subsequent UNSC Resolutions altered that position. As the UNSC had neither effective control nor ultimate authority and control over the acts and omissions of troops within the Multi-National Force, Mr Al-Jedda's internment was not attributable to the UN. It took place within a detention facility in Basrah City, controlled exclusively by British forces. He was therefore within the authority and control of the UK throughout....[21]

Following the *Al-Skeini* judgment most commentators have assumed that the Court's *Banković* line of jurisprudence is far from settled. In addition to involving the powerful NATO alliance, *Banković* was decided in the immediate shadow of 11 September 2001. Subsequent judgments of the Court had already been difficult to reconcile with it. For example, in *Mansur Pad and Others v. Turkey* (Application No. 60167/00, 28 June 2007), action was brought on behalf of seven Iranians who were killed close to the border by Turkish helicopter gunships. It was disputed whether the killings took place on Turkish or Iranian soil. The Chamber reasoned that it was 'not required to determine the exact location of the impugned events, given that [Turkey] had already admitted that the fire discharged from the helicopters had caused the killing of the applicants' relatives, who had been suspected of being terrorists' (paras. 53–4). Applying a personal, rather than a territorial, model of jurisdiction, it held Turkey liable because the victims had been under its 'authority and control through its agents operating — whether lawfully or unlawfully', regardless of the side of the border on which they were located.

[21] ECtHR, Factsheet on Extra-territorial Jurisdiction of ECHR States (Dec. 2011). p. 4.

But even in *Al-Skeini*, there was no acknowledgement by the Court that it had in any way overruled *Banković*.

QUESTIONS

1. Marko Milanovic[22] has suggested that after *Al-Skeini* several issues remain unresolved or unclear:

(a) [What will the] Court will do when it has to decide the case brought against Russia by the family of Alexander Litvinenko, assassinated in London in 2006 by radioactive poison, ostensibly at the orders of or with the collusion of the Kremlin. Russia could hardly be said to have exercised 'public powers' on British soil. And what of the Court's judgments in *Issa*... or *Pad*?

(b) And what of various extraterritorial complicity scenarios, say if a UK agent were to feed questions to a coercive interrogation of a terrorist suspect in Pakistan? Would that person be within the UK's 'authority and control' and does the UK exercise some kind of 'public powers'?

(c) The scope of positive obligations is likewise unclear. Would, for example, the UK have had the positive obligation to protect the right to life of the applicants in *Al-Skeini* even from purely private violence, as it would have on its own territory, and as it arguable would have under the spatial conception of jurisdiction, i.e., if it had effective overall control over Basra? Similarly, would it have had the procedural positive obligation to investigate if one of the killings was purely private in nature, i.e., if there was no involvement by UK soldiers?

2. Milanovic also raises the question of how the ECtHR would deal with a British case decided in conformity with *Banković* one year before *Al-Skeini*. In *R (Smith) v. Secretary of State for Defence*,[23] Private Jason Smith had died of hyperthermia in Iraq in 2003, after requests for medical assistance had gone unheeded. A 6–3 majority of the UK Supreme Court held that he was only within the UK's jurisdiction when he was 'within premises under the effective control of the army'. The Court was not prepared to find that this extended to the athletics stadium 12 kilometres from base where he was working when he died, and noted that it would be for the ECtHR to clarify such an issue. Following *Al-Skeini*, would the United Kingdom be exercising 'public powers' over its troops wherever they are located?

5. THE EUROPEAN COURT IN ACTION: SOME ILLUSTRATIVE CASES

The role of the European Court is of particular importance for several reasons. First, in quantitative terms, is the fact that it now has the final say in relation to the

[22] M. Milanovic, 'Al-Skeini and Al-Jedda in Strasbourg', 23 E.J.I.L. 121 (2012), at 132–3.
[23] [2010] UKSC 29.

interpretation of the human rights standards applicable in relation to 47 different nations and covering over 800 million people. Second, its caseload has expanded exponentially over the past decade or so and this has important consequences in terms of the quantity and range of case law or jurisprudence being generated. Thus, in 1999 the ECtHR handed down 177 judgments (a number far exceeding that of any other international human rights tribunal). By 2009 that number had increased to 1,625. By 2011 it had reduced to 1,157, but there were 151,624 applications pending. The challenges posed by this potentially overwhelming caseload are considered at pp. 962–70, *infra*. Another consequence of this judicial output is the extent to which the ECtHR's jurisprudence is likely to influence, or be taken into account, in the work of the other leading human rights adjudicatory organs such as the Inter-American Court and the ICCPR Committee.

Third, in qualitative terms, the jurisdiction of the Court now spans a diverse array of cultural contexts, political systems, social perspectives, and levels of economic development. As a result, where once it might have been portrayed as a Court whose docket covered only a rather limited range of issues, and often not necessarily those which were seen to be the most pressing, today it is confronted on a daily basis with virtually the full range of human rights challenges of the utmost importance within the societies concerned. A fourth reason for its importance is the crucial role it now plays both as a constitutional court in its own right, and in relation to national constitutional courts, across the whole of Europe. While it does not enjoy formal hierarchical superiority vis-à-vis the highest court in the EU, the European Court of Justice, that Court is now showing a growing degree of deference to the normative pronouncements of the ECtHR and the EU's proposed accession to the Convention will increase the pressure in that direction.

The decisions below explore some of the characteristic problems that arise when international tribunals decide human rights issues that may deeply affect the internal order of states. They involve issues ranging from the right to life, broadly defined, to electoral democracy, and the voting rights of convicted persons.

The differences between the handling of complaints within the UN system by a body such as the ICCPR Human Rights Committee and the European Court are striking. Of course, deep and often disputed moral and political premises inform the work of both types of body and sometimes enter into explicit debate. But the Court's opinions take the traditional forms of the law — the facts of the dispute, argument about the interpretation of the text and related argument about the policies or principles involved, reflection on the institutional role of the Court in relation to national political orders, the ultimate decision applying the Convention in a decision binding the states parties, and possible recourse to a political body if a state does not comply with the Court's decision. From this point of view, a study of the European Court's decisions best illustrates the promise of an international (regional) *legal* order brought to bear on national human rights issues.

The question inevitably arises of how transferable this experience of the European human rights system may be — whether, for example, an equally effective judicial system aspiring to such a high record of compliance by states could function under a universal human rights treaty such as the ICCPR, or in a different kind of regional regime such as the Americas or Africa.

An important jurisprudential and political theme that is unique in the ECHR system is the doctrine of margin of appreciation, critical to an understanding of the dilemmas before this international court and the ways in which it tries to come to terms with them.

(1) The Right to Life

Article 2 of the Convention states:

> 1. Everyone's right to life shall be protected by law. No one shall be deprived of his life intentionally save in the execution of a sentence of a court following his conviction of a crime for which this penalty is provided by law.
>
> 2. Deprivation of life shall not be regarded as inflicted in contravention of this Article [Art. 2] when it results from the use of force which is no more than absolutely necessary:
>
> (a) in defence of any person from unlawful violence;
> (b) in order to effect a lawful arrest or to prevent the escape of a person lawfully detained;
> (c) in action lawfully taken for the purpose of quelling a riot or insurrection.

The cases that follow serve to highlight just a few of the very complex issues that have arisen in relation to the right to life. Recall that in Chapter 4 we saw the Indian Supreme Court relying heavily on this right in order to render a range of economic and social rights justiciable, and in Chapter 9 we saw the ICCPR Committee proposing an expansive approach to the right to life in a couple of its General Comments. Although the ECHR recognizes no social rights (other than the right to education in Protocol No. 1), and the ECtHR has been rather conservative in relation to such matters, it has also developed jurisprudence under Article 2 that would support a much more robust notion of positive obligations in certain areas. Compare the ways in which it has approached the right to life in four representative cases.

McCANN AND OTHERS v. UNITED KINGDOM

European Court of Human Rights, Application No. 18984/91 (Grand Chamber), 27 Sept. 1995

[Three members of the Provisional IRA [Irish Republican Army] were shot dead on 6 March 1988 in Gibraltar by the British Army's 'special forces', the Special Air Service (SAS). The UK, Spanish, and Gibraltar authorities had been alerted to a planned terrorist attack, and were tracking the members of the group with a view to arresting them at the appropriate time. One of the group was seen parking a car and then joined the other two. It was decided to arrest them and the SAS soldiers on the scene were alerted. Fearing that they would be armed and were trying to detonate remote control devices, the soldiers shot them at close range. No weapons or detonator devices were found on the bodies of the suspects; nor did the car that had been observed contain any explosive device, although another car did. A Gibraltar jury returned verdicts of lawful killing, and judicial review was refused. The applicants claimed a violation of ECHR Article 2. The Court rejected as unsubstantiated the contention that the killings had been premeditated either by the soldiers or their superior officers.]

...

200. The Court accepts that the soldiers honestly believed, in the light of the information that they had been given, ... that it was necessary to shoot the suspects in order to prevent them from detonating a bomb and causing serious loss of life. The actions which they took, in obedience to superior orders, were thus perceived by them as absolutely necessary in order to safeguard innocent lives.

It considers that the use of force by agents of the State in pursuit of one of the aims delineated in [Article 2(2)] of the Convention may be justified under this provision where it is based on an honest belief which is perceived, for good reasons, to be valid at the time but which subsequently turns out to be mistaken. To hold otherwise would be to impose an unrealistic burden on the State and its law-enforcement personnel in the execution of their duty, perhaps to the detriment of their lives and those of others.

It follows that, having regard to the dilemma confronting the authorities in the circumstances of the case, the actions of the soldiers do not, in themselves, give rise to a violation of this provision.

201. The question arises, however, whether the anti-terrorist operation as a whole was controlled and organised in a manner which respected the requirements of Article 2 and whether the information and instructions given to the soldiers which, in effect, rendered inevitable the use of lethal force, took adequately into consideration the right to life of the three suspects.

(3) Control and organisation of the operation

202. ... [I]t had been the intention of the authorities to arrest the suspects at an appropriate stage....

203. It may be questioned why the three suspects were not arrested at the border immediately on their arrival in Gibraltar ... if they were believed to be on a bombing mission. Having had advance warning of the terrorists' intentions it would certainly have been possible for the authorities to have mounted an arrest operation....

204. [T]he Government submitted that at that moment there might not have been sufficient evidence to warrant the detention and trial of the suspects. Moreover, to release them, having alerted them to the authorities' state of awareness but leaving them or others free to try again, would obviously increase the risks. Nor could the authorities be sure that those three were the only terrorists they had to deal with or of the manner in which it was proposed to carry out the bombing.

205. The Court [observes] that the danger to the population of Gibraltar — which is at the heart of the Government's submissions in this case — in not preventing their entry must be considered to outweigh the possible consequences of having insufficient evidence to warrant their detention and trial. In its view, either the authorities knew that there was no bomb in the car — which the Court has already discounted — or there was a serious miscalculation by those responsible for controlling the operation. As a result, the scene was set in which the fatal shooting,

given the intelligence assessments which had been made, was a foreseeable possibility if not a likelihood. . . .

206. The Court notes that at the briefing on 5 March attended by Soldiers A, B, C, and D it was considered likely that the attack would be by way of a large car bomb. A number of key assessments were made. In particular, it was thought that the terrorists would not use a blocking car; that the bomb would be detonated by a radio-control device; that the detonation could be effected by the pressing of a button; that it was likely that the suspects would detonate the bomb if challenged; that they would be armed and would be likely to use their arms if confronted.

207. In the event, all of these crucial assumptions, apart from the terrorists' intentions to carry out an attack, turned out to be erroneous [although] they were all possible hypotheses in a situation where the true facts were unknown and where the authorities operated on the basis of limited intelligence information.

208. In fact, insufficient allowances appear to have been made for other assumptions. For example, since the bombing was not expected until 8 March when the changing of the guard ceremony was to take place, there was equally the possibility that the three terrorists were on a reconnaissance mission. While this was a factor which was briefly considered, it does not appear to have been regarded as a serious possibility.

In addition, at the briefings or after the suspects had been spotted, it might have been thought unlikely that they would have been prepared to explode the bomb, thereby killing many civilians, as Mr McCann and Ms Farrell strolled towards the border area since this would have increased the risk of detection and capture. It might also have been thought improbable that at that point they would have set up the transmitter in anticipation to enable them to detonate the supposed bomb immediately if confronted.

Moreover, even if allowances are made for the technological skills of the IRA, the description of the detonation device as a "button job" without the qualifications subsequently described by the experts at the inquest, of which the competent authorities must have been aware, over-simplifies the true nature of these devices.

209. It is further disquieting in this context that the assessment made by Soldier G, after a cursory external examination of the car, that there was a "suspect car bomb" was conveyed to the soldiers, according to their own testimony, as a definite identification that there was such a bomb. It is recalled that while Soldier G had experience in car bombs, it transpired that he was not an expert in radio communications or explosives. . . .

210. In the absence of sufficient allowances being made for alternative possibilities, and the definite reporting of the existence of a car bomb which, according to the assessments that had been made, could be detonated at the press of a button, a series of working hypotheses were conveyed to Soldiers A, B, C and D as certainties, thereby making the use of lethal force almost unavoidable.

211. However, the failure to make provision for a margin of error must also be considered in combination with the training of the soldiers to continue shooting once they opened fire until the suspect was dead. [A]ll four soldiers shot to kill the suspects. . . . Against this background, the authorities were bound by their obligation to respect the right to life of the suspects to exercise the greatest of care in evaluating

the information at their disposal before transmitting it to soldiers whose use of firearms automatically involved shooting to kill.

212. . . . [I]t is not clear whether [the soldiers] had been trained or instructed to assess whether the use of firearms to wound their targets may have been warranted by the specific circumstances that confronted them at the moment of arrest.

Their reflex action in this vital respect lacks the degree of caution in the use of firearms to be expected from law enforcement personnel in a democratic society, even when dealing with dangerous terrorist suspects, and stands in marked contrast to the standard of care reflected in the instructions in the use of firearms by the police which had been drawn to their attention and which emphasised the legal responsibilities of the individual officer in the light of conditions prevailing at the moment of engagement.

This failure by the authorities also suggests a lack of appropriate care in the control and organisation of the arrest operation.

213. In sum, having regard to the decision not to prevent the suspects from travelling into Gibraltar, to the failure of the authorities to make sufficient allowances for the possibility that their intelligence assessments might, in some respects at least, be erroneous and to the automatic recourse to lethal force when the soldiers opened fire, the Court is not persuaded that the killing of the three terrorists constituted the use of force which was no more than absolutely necessary in defence of persons from unlawful violence within the meaning of Article 2[a]. . . .

. . .

FOR THESE REASONS, THE COURT

Holds by *ten votes to nine* that there has been a violation of Article 2 of the Convention;

. . .

FINOGENOV AND OTHERS v. RUSSIA

European Court of Human Rights, Applications Nos. 18299/03 and 27311/03 (Chamber Judgment), 20 Dec. 2011

[On 23 October 2002, 40 Chechen separatists seized over 900 people in a Moscow theatre and held them hostage for three days. The theatre was also booby-trapped and 18 suicide bombers were positioned among the hostages. The terrorists demanded, *inter alia*, the withdrawal of Russian troops from Chechnya. The Federal Security Service (FSB) set up a 'crisis cell' to negotiate and free the hostages. Although several hostages were released, others were killed. The applicants believed that further negotiations were possible, but the authorities felt that all hostages might be killed. At around 5 a.m. on 26 October security forces pumped an unknown narcotic gas into the building and then stormed it. All the terrorists were killed and the majority of the hostages were freed. But 125 of them died either on the spot or in hospital. The applicants claimed that the rescue operation was chaotic in almost every respect.

Subsequently, the Moscow City Prosecution Office (MPO) opened a criminal investigation. An accomplice to the terrorists was convicted but the MPO repeatedly refused to investigate the actions of the authorities during the crisis. The investigation concluded that the 125 hostages had died from a combination of individual weaknesses and chronic illnesses, exacerbated by the stress of three days of captivity, and that the gas used had at best had an 'indirect effect' on their demise. The death of the hostages was therefore attributed to 'natural' factors and not the use of the gas by the FSB.]

I. ALLEGED VIOLATION OF ARTICLE 2 OF THE CONVENTION

...

C. The Court's assessment

...

1. Whether the case falls within the ambit of Article 2 of the Convention

...

201. ... [T]he general conclusion of the expert report ... is difficult to accept. It is unthinkable that 125 people of different ages and physical conditions died almost simultaneously and in the same place because of various pre-existing health problems....

202. ... [I]t is safe to conclude that the gas remained a primary cause of the death of a large number of the victims.

203. In sum, the present case is about the use of a dangerous substance (no matter how it is described) by the authorities within a rescue operation which resulted in the death of many of those whom the authorities were trying to liberate and in mortal danger for many others. The situation is thus covered by Article 2.... The Court has now to examine whether the use of force was compatible with the requirements of this provision.

...

4. Standard of scrutiny to be applied

...

212. The Court is acutely conscious of the difficulties faced by States in protecting their populations from terrorist violence, and recognises the complexity of this problem [as well as the particular problems faced by Russia].

213. ... The hostage-taking came as a surprise for the authorities.... so the military preparations for the storming had to be made very quickly and in full secrecy. It should be noted that the authorities were not in control of the situation inside the building. In such a situation the Court accepts that difficult and agonising decisions had to be made by the domestic authorities. It is prepared to grant them a margin of appreciation, at least in so far as the military and technical aspects of the situation are concerned, even if now, with hindsight, some of the decisions taken by the authorities may appear open to doubt.

214. In contrast, the subsequent phases of the operation may require a closer scrutiny by the Court; this is especially true in respect of such phases where no serious time constraints existed and the authorities were in control of the situation.

...

5. The use of force

(a) Decision to storm

...

219. The question is whether [the Government's] aims could have been attained by other, less drastic, means....

220. [G]enerally speaking, there is no necessity to use lethal force "where it is known that the person to be arrested poses no threat to life or limb and is not suspected of having committed a violent offence".... [T]he situation in the present case was quite different: the threat posed by the terrorists was real and very serious. The authorities knew that many of the terrorists... were well-trained, well-armed and dedicated to their cause...; that the explosion of the devices installed in the main auditorium would probably have killed all of the hostages; and that the terrorists were prepared to detonate those devices if their demands were not met.

...

226. In sum, the situation appeared very alarming. Heavily armed separatists dedicated to their cause had taken hostages and put forward unrealistic demands. The first days of negotiations did not bring any visible success; in addition, the humanitarian situation (the hostages' physical and psychological condition) had been worsening and made the hostages even more vulnerable. The Court concludes that there existed a real, serious and immediate risk of mass human losses and that the authorities had every reason to believe that a forced intervention was the "lesser evil" in the circumstances. Therefore, the authorities' decision to end the negotiations and storm the building in the circumstances did not run counter to Article 2 of the Convention.

(b) Decision to use the gas

...

228. [The Court's case law and relevant UN Principles] indicate that laws and regulations on the use of force should be sufficiently detailed and should prescribe, inter alia, the types of arms and ammunition permitted.

229. The legislative framework for the use of the gas in the present case remains unclear.... The exact formula of the gas was not revealed by the authorities; consequently, it is impossible for the Court to establish whether or not the gas was a "conventional weapon", and to identify the rules for its use. In the circumstances the Court is prepared to admit that the gas was an ad hoc solution, not described in the regulations and manuals for law-enforcement officials.

230. ... [But the] general vagueness of the Russian anti-terrorism law does not necessarily mean that in every particular case the authorities failed to respect the applicants' right to life. Even if necessary regulations did exist, they probably would be of limited use in the situation at hand, which was totally unpredictable, exceptional and required a tailor-made response...

231. The Court will now move to the applicants' main argument. They claimed that the gas had been a lethal weapon which was used indiscriminately against both

terrorists and innocent hostages. That claim deserves the most serious consideration, since "the massive use of indiscriminate weapons... cannot be considered compatible with the standard of care prerequisite to an operation involving use of lethal force by state agents". The Court observes that the German Constitutional Court in a judgment of 15 February 2006 found incompatible with the right to life, as guaranteed by the German Constitution, a law authorising the use of force to shoot down a hijacked aircraft believed to be intended for a terrorist attack. It found, inter alia, that the use of lethal force against the persons on board who were not participants in the crime would be incompatible with their right to life and human dignity....

232. In the present case, however, the gas used by the Russian security forces, while dangerous, was not supposed to kill.... [A]lthough the gas was dangerous and even potentially lethal, it was not used "indiscriminately" as it left the hostages a high chance of survival, which depended on the efficiency of the authorities' rescue effort. The hostages in the present case were not in the same desperate situation as all the passengers of a hijacked airplane.

...

235. Another of the applicants' argument was that the concentration of the gas had been grossly miscalculated, and that the risks to the hostages' life and limb associated with its use outweighed the benefits.... The Government claimed that the gas dosage had been calculated on the basis of an "average person's reaction". The Court notes that even that dose turned out to be insufficient to send everybody to sleep.... In any event, the Court is not in a position to evaluate the issue of the dosage of the gas....

236. In sum, the Court concludes that the use of gas during the storming was not in the circumstances a disproportionate measure, and, as such, did not breach Article 2 of the Convention.

6. Rescue and evacuation operation

237. ... [Was the operation] planned and implemented in compliance with the authorities' positive obligations under Article 2 of the Convention, namely whether the authorities took all necessary precautions to minimise the effects of the gas on the hostages, to evacuate them quickly and to provide them with necessary medical assistance....

...

265. In other words, many important factual details in this case are missing. That being said, the Court stresses that its role is not to establish the individual liability of those involved in the planning and coordination of the rescue operation. The Court is called upon to decide whether the State as a whole complied with its international obligations under the Convention, namely its obligation to "take all feasible precautions in the choice of means and methods of a security operation mounted against an opposing group with a view to avoiding and, in any event, minimising, incidental loss of civilian life".

266. The Court acknowledges that in such situations some measure of disorder is unavoidable. It also recognises the need to keep certain aspects of security

operations secret. However, in the circumstances the rescue operation of 26 October 2002 was not sufficiently prepared, in particular because of the inadequate information exchange between various services, belated beginning of the evacuation, limited on-the-field coordination of various services, lack of appropriate medical treatment and equipment on the spot, and inadequate logistics. The Court concludes that the State breached its positive obligations under Article 2 of the Convention.

7. Effectiveness of the investigation

. . .

i. Whether the official investigation was "effective"

273. The present case clearly falls into the category of cases where the authorities must investigate the circumstances of the victims' deaths. . . . [T]he events in issue "lay wholly, or in large part, within the exclusive knowledge of the authorities" in the sense that it was virtually impossible for the applicants to obtain any evidence independently from the authorities. In such circumstances the authorities were under an obligation to carry out an effective official investigation in order to provide a "satisfactory and convincing" explanation of the victims' deaths and the degree of the authorities' responsibility for it.

274. The Court stresses that it is not concerned with the investigation into the terrorist act itself. In this part the investigation appeared to be quite ample and successful. . . . The question is whether the investigation was equally successful in examining the authorities' own actions during the hostage crisis.

275. The Court notes that the investigation was opened and continued under Articles 205 ("Terrorist acts") and 206 ("Hostage-taking") of the Criminal Code. Negligence by the authorities cannot be characterised under either of those two provisions. . . .

276. Although the investigation is not yet formally completed, the prosecution repeatedly decided that, as regards the authorities' alleged negligence, there was no case to answer. The first decision in that sense was taken . . . slightly over one month after the events. . . .

277. [While the investigation did address some relevant questions] in some other respects [it] was manifestly incomplete. First and foremost, the formula of the gas has never been revealed by the FSB to the domestic investigative authorities, despite the latter's request to that end, although the investigative team included FSB officers and most of the experts in the case were also from the FSB, and thus, at least in theory, could have been trusted.

. . .

279. The Court is surprised by the fact that . . . all of the crisis cell's working papers were destroyed. In the Court's opinion those papers could have been an essential source of information about the planning and conduct of the rescue operation. . . . The Government did not explain when those papers were destroyed, why, on whose authority and on what legal basis. . . . Even assuming that some of them

might have contained sensitive information, indiscriminate destruction of all documents ... was not justified.

280. Amongst others, the investigators did not try to establish certain facts which, in the Court's opinion, were relevant and even crucial for addressing the question of the authorities' alleged negligence....

281. Lastly, the investigative team was not independent.... [T]he members of the investigative team and the experts whose conclusions were heavily relied on by the lead investigator had conflicts of interests, so manifest that in themselves those conflicts could have undermined the effectiveness of the investigation and the reliability of its conclusions.

282. Other elements of the investigative process are probably also worthy of attention (such as the limited access to the materials of the case by the victims' relatives, and their inability to formulate questions to the officially appointed experts and examine witnesses). However, the Court does not need to examine these aspects of the proceedings separately. It has sufficient evidence to conclude that the investigation into the authorities' alleged negligence in this case was neither thorough nor independent, and, therefore, not "effective". The Court concludes that there was a breach of the State's positive obligation under Article 2 of the Convention on this account.

OSMAN v. UNITED KINGDOM

European Court of Human Rights, Application No. 87/1997/871/1083, 28 Oct. 1998

[A schoolteacher named Paul Paget-Lewis developed an obsession with Ahmet Osman, a teenage schoolboy. After a long series of incidents in which Paget-Lewis was suspected but never charged, he shot and wounded Ahmet and killed his father Ali Osman. Ahmet's mother and the wife of Ali complained that the authorities had failed to appreciate and act on a series of clear warning signs that Paget-Lewis represented a serious threat to the family's physical safety.]

I. ALLEGED VIOLATION OF ARTICLE 2 OF THE CONVENTION

B. The Court's assessment

...

2. As to the alleged failure of the authorities to protect the rights to life of Ali and Ahmet Osman

115. The Court notes that the first sentence of Article 2 § 1 enjoins the State not only to refrain from the intentional and unlawful taking of life, but also to take appropriate steps to safeguard the lives of those within its jurisdiction. It is common ground that the State's obligation in this respect extends beyond its primary duty to secure the right to life by putting in place effective criminal-law provisions to deter the commission of offences against the person backed up by

law-enforcement machinery for the prevention, suppression and sanctioning of breaches of such provisions. It is thus accepted by those appearing before the Court that Article 2 of the Convention may also imply in certain well-defined circumstances a positive obligation on the authorities to take preventive operational measures to protect an individual whose life is at risk from the criminal acts of another individual. The scope of this obligation is a matter of dispute between the parties.

116. For the Court, and bearing in mind the difficulties involved in policing modern societies, the unpredictability of human conduct and the operational choices which must be made in terms of priorities and resources, such an obligation must be interpreted in a way which does not impose an impossible or disproportionate burden on the authorities. Accordingly, not every claimed risk to life can entail for the authorities a Convention requirement to take operational measures to prevent that risk from materialising. Another relevant consideration is the need to ensure that the police exercise their powers to control and prevent crime in a manner which fully respects the due process and other guarantees which legitimately place restraints on the scope of their action to investigate crime and bring offenders to justice....

[Where the authorities are alleged to have violated their positive obligations] it must be established to [the Court's] satisfaction that the authorities knew or ought to have known at the time of the existence of a real and immediate risk to the life of an identified individual or individuals from the criminal acts of a third party and that they failed to take measures within the scope of their powers which, judged reasonably, might have been expected to avoid that risk. The Court does not accept the Government's view that the failure to perceive the risk to life in the circumstances known at the time or to take preventive measures to avoid that risk must be tantamount to gross negligence or wilful disregard of the duty to protect life. Such a rigid standard must be considered to be incompatible with the requirements of Article 1 of the Convention and the obligations of Contracting States under that Article to secure the practical and effective protection of the rights and freedoms laid down therein, including Article 2.... [I]t is sufficient for an applicant to show that the authorities did not do all that could be reasonably expected of them to avoid a real and immediate risk to life of which they have or ought to have knowledge. This is a question which can only be answered in the light of all the circumstances of any particular case.

On the above understanding the Court will examine the particular circumstances of this case.

...

121. In the view of the Court the applicants have failed to point to any decisive stage in the sequence of the events leading up to the tragic shooting when it could be said that the police knew or ought to have known that the lives of the Osman family were at real and immediate risk from Paget-Lewis.... [The police] cannot be criticised for attaching weight to the presumption of innocence or failing to use powers of arrest, search and seizure having regard to their reasonably held view that they lacked at relevant times the required standard of suspicion to use those powers or that any action taken would in fact have produced concrete results.

122. For the above reasons, the Court concludes that there has been no violation of Article 2 of the Convention in this case.
...

ÖNERYILDIZ v. TURKEY

European Court of Human Rights, Application No. 48939/99 (Grand Chamber), 30 Nov. 2004

[A methane explosion in a rubbish tip run by the municipal authorities resulted in the deaths of 39 persons and the destruction of ten homes in an illegal settlement. Two years previously, an expert report had warned of the danger of such an explosion because of the absence of an appropriate ventilation system. The complainants thus alleged that the authorities had failed to do all that could have been expected of them to prevent the deaths occurring.]

71. ... Article 2 does not solely concern deaths resulting from the use of force by agents of the State but also ... lays down a positive obligation on States to take appropriate steps to safeguard the lives of those within their jurisdiction.

The Court considers that this obligation must be construed as applying in the context of any activity, whether public or not, in which the right to life may be at stake, and *a fortiori* in the case of industrial activities, which by their very nature are dangerous, such as the operation of waste-collection sites.
...

107. The Court acknowledges that it is not its task to substitute for the views of the local authorities its own view of the best policy to adopt in dealing with the social, economic and urban problems in this part of Istanbul. It therefore accepts the Government's argument that in this respect an impossible or disproportionate burden must not be imposed on the authorities without consideration being given, in particular, to the operational choices which they must make in terms of priorities and resources; this results from the wide margin of appreciation States enjoy, as the Court has previously held, in difficult social and technical spheres....

However, even when seen from this perspective, the Court does not find the Government's arguments convincing. The preventive measures required by the positive obligation in question fall precisely within the powers conferred on the authorities and may reasonably be regarded as a suitable means of averting the risk brought to their attention. The Court considers that the timely installation of a gas-extraction system at the Ümraniye tip before the situation became fatal could have been an effective measure without diverting the State's resources to an excessive degree ... or giving rise to policy problems to the extent alleged by the Government. Such a measure would not only have complied with Turkish regulations and general practice in the area, but would also have been a much better reflection of the humanitarian considerations the Government relied on before the Court.
...

[The Grand Chamber examined the adequacy of the judicial response to the explosion.]

117. Accordingly, it cannot be said that the manner in which the Turkish criminal justice system operated in response to the tragedy secured the full accountability of State officials or authorities for their role in it and the effective implementation of provisions of domestic law guaranteeing respect for the right to life, in particular the deterrent function of the criminal law.

118. In short, it must be concluded in the instant case that there has also been a violation of Article 2 of the Convention in its procedural aspect, on account of the lack, in connection with a fatal accident provoked by the operation of a dangerous activity, of adequate protection "by law" safeguarding the right to life and deterring similar life-endangering conduct in future.

...

QUESTIONS

1. The *McCann* case was decided in 1995, at a time when only a handful of European states were experiencing terrorist violence. Do the changed international environment since 11 September 2001 and the much stronger emphasis on counter-terrorism measures, warrant a revisiting by the Court of its approach in *McCann*?

2. How would you compare the Court's deference to governmental judgments in the *McCann* and *Finogenov* judgments?

3. 'While the outcome in the *Osman* case is entirely acceptable, the doctrine enunciated by the Court towards the end of paragraph 116 places an undue burden on public authorities.' Do you agree?

4. Does the *Öneryildiz* obligation to take preventive measures raise the prospect that the Court might be prepared to take an active role in relation to a wide range of environmental and public health risks?

(b) Democracy and Political Participation

The following materials address the links between political participation, elections, and democratic government. They focus on two of a significant number of cases decided by the European Court since 1998 involving the banning or dissolution of political parties in Turkey.

The literature in this area often distinguishes between 'procedural' and 'militant' democracy. The former are comparatively permissive and do not seek to limit the political rights even of those seeking to undermine or overthrow the constitutional order. They will, of course, use the criminal law in individual cases of transgression but will not ban political parties. Militant democracy, on the other hand, refers to an approach which seeks to place certain core foundational values beyond the reach of the democratic process. Those who seek to trespass upon those values will face the risk of being excluded from the political process. The German Constitution adopted after the Second World War is a classic example of the latter approach. The dilemma is simple:

> Must a democratic system stand idly by and watch antidemocratic forces gather strength? Must liberal constitutions, because they support tolerance and openness, function as suicide pacts, preventing effective self-defense? . . .
>
> The correct answer is "no". Constitutional democracies can and do act preemptively; for instance, by banning extremist parties while they are still relatively weak. Endangered democracies can curtail freedom of speech, freedom of association, and associated political rights to vote and compete for office and still remain recognizably liberal and democratic. To be sure, honest debate remains possible about the most effective and least restrictive ways of defending democracy against its most virulent enemies. And there is another important question that remains unanswered: What constitutional obstacles can be put in place to prevent political incumbents from opportunistically invoking the defense of democracy against antidemocratic forces as a justification for cracking down on perfectly legitimate political rivals?[24]

It might be thought that the issues arising in the cases that follow concerning Turkey and Latvia would be unlikely to arise in the context of the established democracies that make up the core of the 'old' Council of Europe. But this would be a mistake. Consider, for example, the 2004 banning by the Belgian High Court of the Vlaams Blok, a Flemish independence party focusing strongly on 'nationalist' issues such as immigration and crime. The Court found its programme to be racist and soon after it was dissolved. Its leadership, however, started another party with an appropriately toned-down platform.

In the United Kingdom, then Prime Minister Tony Blair responded to the July 2005 bombings of the London Underground railway by, *inter alia*, proposing to ban an Islamic political party, Hizb-ut-Tahrir, which had campaigned for the introduction of Sharia law in all countries. After extensive domestic controversy, and on the basis of legal and police advice, the proposal was eventually dropped in December 2006. In 2009 the ECtHR upheld the dissolution of two political parties linked to the banned Basque separatist group ETA (*Herri Batasuna and Batasuna v. Spain*, Application Nos. 25803/04 and 25817/04, 30 June 2009) and also upheld the exclusion of other political groups from presenting candidates in municipal, regional, and autonomous community elections (*Etxeberría and Others v. Spain*, Application Nos. 35579/03, 35613/03, 35626/03 and 35634/03, 30 June 2009; and *Herritarren Zerrenda v. Spain*, Application No. 43518/04, 30 June 2009). In *Sejdić and Finci v. Bosnia and Herzegovina* (Application Nos. 27996/06 and 34836/06, 22 Dec. 2009) the Grand Chamber held the Constitution of the state to be in violation of the ECHR as a result of the power-sharing arrangements between the three 'constituent peoples' of the state that had been agreed by the international community in the Dayton Peace Accords. Members of other groups, such as Jews or Roma, were thus excluded from election to the House of Peoples and the Presidency.[25]

[24] Stephen Holmes, Book Review, 4 Int'l. J. Const. L. 586 (2006).

[25] For a critique see S. Wheatley, 'The Construction of the Constitutional Essentials of Democratic Politics by the European Court of Human Rights following *Sejdić and Finci*', in R. Dickinson et al. (eds.), *Examining Critical Perspectives on Human Rights* (2012), 153.

UNITED COMMUNIST PARTY OF TURKEY v. TURKEY

European Court of Human Rights, Application No. 133/1996/752/951 (Grand Chamber), 30 Jan. 1998

...

7. The United Communist Party of Turkey ('the TBKP'), the first applicant, was a political party that was dissolved by the Constitutional Court. Mr Nihat Sargin and Mr Nabi Yagci, the second and third applicants, were respectively Chairman and General Secretary of the TBKP. They live in Istanbul.

8. The TBKP was formed on 4 June 1990. On the same day, its constitution and programme were submitted to the office of Principal State Counsel at the Court of Cassation for assessment of their compatibility with the Constitution and Law no. 2820 on the regulation of political parties.

9. On 14 June 1990, when the TBKP was preparing to participate in a general election, Principal State Counsel at the Court of Cassation ('Principal State Counsel') applied to the Constitutional Court for an order dissolving the TBKP. He accused the party of having sought to establish the domination of one social class over the others ... of having incorporated the word 'communist' into its name ... of having carried on activities likely to undermine the territorial integrity of the State and the unity of the nation ... and of having declared itself to be the successor to a previously dissolved political party, the Turkish Workers' Party....

[The following excerpts from the opinion concern almost exclusively the principal charge of undermining the unity of the nation. In omitted portions, the opinion found the other three grounds inadequate to justify interference with the right of association under Article 11.]

In support of his application Principal State Counsel relied in particular on passages from the TBKP's programme, mainly taken from a chapter entitled 'Towards a peaceful, democratic and fair solution for the Kurdish problem'; that chapter read as follows:

...

The TBKP will strive for a peaceful, democratic and fair solution of the Kurdish problem, so that the Kurdish and Turkish peoples may live together of their free will within the borders of the Turkish Republic, on the basis of equal rights and with a view to democratic restructuring founded on their common interests.

...

10. On 16 July 1991 the Constitutional Court made an order dissolving the TBKP, [resulting in the liquidation of the party, the transfer of its assets to the Treasury, and the banning of its founders and managers from holding similar office in any other political body].

...

As to the allegation that the TBKP's constitution and programme contained statements likely to undermine the territorial integrity of the State and the unity of the nation, the Constitutional Court noted, inter alia, that those documents referred to two nations: the Kurdish nation and the Turkish nation. But it could not be accepted that there were two nations within the Republic of Turkey, whose citizens, whatever their ethnic origin, had Turkish nationality. In reality the proposals in the party constitution covering support for non-Turkish languages and cultures were intended to create minorities, to the detriment of the unity of the Turkish nation.

Reiterating that self-determination and regional autonomy were prohibited by the Constitution, the Constitutional Court said that the State was unitary, the country indivisible and that there was only one nation....

...

AS TO THE LAW

I. Alleged Violation of Article 11 of the Convention[26]

...

25. ... [P]olitical parties are a form of association essential to the proper functioning of democracy. In view of the importance of democracy in the Convention system, there can be no doubt that political parties come within the scope of Article 11.

...

27. ... [A]n association, including a political party, is not excluded from the protection afforded by the Convention simply because its activities are regarded by the national authorities as undermining the constitutional structures of the State....

[W]hile it is in principle open to the national authorities to take such action as they consider necessary to respect the rule of law or to give effect to constitutional rights, they must do so in a manner which is compatible with their obligations under the Convention and subject to review by the Convention institutions.

28. The Preamble to the Convention refers to the 'common heritage of political traditions, ideals, freedom and the rule of law', of which national constitutions are in fact often the first embodiment....

...

30. The political and institutional organization of the member States must accordingly respect the rights and principles enshrined in the Convention. It matters little in this context whether the provisions in issue are constitutional or merely legislative....

...

32. It does not, however, follow that the authorities of a State in which an association, through its activities, jeopardizes that State's institutions are deprived of the right to protect those institutions. In this connection, the Court points out that it has previously held that some compromise between the requirements of defending democratic society and individual rights is inherent in the system of the Convention. For there to be a compromise of that sort any intervention by the authorities must be in accordance with paragraph 2 of Article 11, which the Court considers below....

...

[26] Eds.: Article 11 provides:

1. Everyone has the right to freedom of ... association with others, including the right to form and to join trade unions....
2. No restrictions shall be placed on the exercise of these rights other than such as are prescribed by law and are necessary in a democratic society in the interests of national security ... or for the protection of the rights and freedoms of others.]

37. Such an interference [by Turkey with Article 11] will constitute a breach of Article 11 unless it was 'prescribed by law', pursued one or more legitimate aims under paragraph 2 and was 'necessary in a democratic society' for the achievement of those aims.

...

(b) Legitimate aim

...

41. [T]he Court considers that the dissolution of the TBKP pursued at least one of the 'legitimate aims' set out in Article 11: the protection of 'national security'.

(c) 'Necessary in a democratic society'

42. The Court reiterates that notwithstanding its autonomous role and particular sphere of application, Article 11 must also be considered in the light of Article 10. The protection of opinions and the freedom to express them is one of the objectives of the freedoms of assembly and association as enshrined in Article 11.

43. That applies all the more in relation to political parties in view of their essential role in ensuring pluralism and the proper functioning of democracy.

As the Court has said many times, there can be no democracy without pluralism....

...

45. Democracy is without doubt a fundamental feature of the European public order.... The Court has... pointed out several times that the Convention was designed to maintain and promote the ideals and values of a democratic society.

...The only type of necessity capable of justifying an interference with any of those rights is, therefore, one which may claim to spring from 'democratic society'. Democracy thus appears to be the only political model contemplated by the Convention and, accordingly, the only one compatible with it....

46. Consequently,... only convincing and compelling reasons can justify restrictions on such parties' freedom of association. In determining whether a necessity within the meaning of Article 11(2) exists, the Contracting States have only a limited margin of appreciation, which goes hand in hand with rigorous European supervision embracing both the law and the decisions applying it, including those given by independent courts....

47. When the Court carries out its scrutiny, [it does not have] to confine itself to ascertaining whether the respondent State exercised its discretion reasonably, carefully and in good faith; it must look at the interference complained of in the light of the case as a whole and determine whether it was 'proportionate to the legitimate aim pursued' and whether the reasons adduced by the national authorities to justify it are 'relevant and sufficient'....

2. Application of the principles to the present case

...

49. The Government pointed out that... faced with a challenge to the fundamental interests of the national community, such as national security and territorial

integrity, the Turkish authorities had not in any way exceeded the margin of appreciation conferred on them by the Convention.

...

51. The Court notes at the outset that the TBKP was dissolved even before it had been able to start its activities and that the dissolution was therefore ordered solely on the basis of the TBKP's constitution and programme, which ... contain nothing to suggest that they did not reflect the party's true objectives and its leaders' true intentions. Like the national authorities, the Court will therefore take those documents as a basis for assessing whether the interference in question was necessary.

...

55. The second submission accepted by the Constitutional Court was that the TBKP sought to promote separatism and the division of the Turkish nation....

56. The Court notes that although the TBKP refers in its programme to the Kurdish 'people' and 'nation' and Kurdish 'citizens', it neither describes them as a 'minority' nor makes any claim — other than for recognition of their existence — for them to enjoy special treatment or rights, still less a right to secede from the rest of the Turkish population. On the contrary, the programme states: 'The TBKP will strive for a peaceful, democratic and fair solution of the Kurdish problem, so that the Kurdish and Turkish peoples may live together of their free will within the borders of the Turkish Republic, on the basis of equal rights and with a view to democratic restructuring founded on their common interests'. With regard to the right to self-determination, the TBKP does no more in its programme than deplore the fact that because of the use of violence, it was not 'exercised jointly, but separately and unilaterally', adding that 'the remedy for this problem is political' and that '[i]f the oppression of the Kurdish people and discrimination against them are to end, Turks and Kurds must unite'.

...

57. The Court considers one of the principal characteristics of democracy to be the possibility it offers of resolving a country's problems through dialogue, without recourse to violence, even when they are irksome. Democracy thrives on freedom of expression. From that point of view, there can be no justification for hindering a political group solely because it seeks to debate in public the situation of part of the State's population and to take part in the nation's political life in order to find, according to democratic rules, solutions capable of satisfying everyone concerned....

...

59. The Court is also prepared to take into account the background of cases before it, in particular the difficulties associated with the fight against terrorism....

60. Nor is there any need to bring Article 17 into play as nothing in the constitution and programme of the TBKP warrants the conclusion that it relied on the Convention to engage in activity or perform acts aimed at the destruction of any of the rights and freedoms set forth in it.

61. Regard being had to all the above, a measure as drastic as the immediate and permanent dissolution of the TBKP, ordered before its activities had even started and coupled with a ban barring its leaders from discharging any other political responsibility, is disproportionate to the aim pursued and consequently

unnecessary in a democratic society. It follows that the measure infringed Article 11 of the Convention.

...

REFAH PARTİSİ (THE WELFARE PARTY) AND OTHERS v. TURKEY

European Court of Human Rights, Application Nos. 41340/98, 41342/98, 41343/98 and 41344/98 (Grand Chamber), 13 Feb. 2003

[Four applications were submitted by the Turkish Welfare Party (Refah) and three of its members in May 1998. They alleged that the dissolution of Refah by the Turkish Constitutional Court and the suspension of certain political rights of the party leaders breached Articles 9, 10, 11, 14, 17, and 18 of the ECHR and Articles 1 and 3 of Protocol No. 1. The case was first heard by a Chamber. In July 2001 it held by a vote of four to three that there had been no violation of Article 11 and that it was unnecessary to examine the other alleged breaches. In December 2001, after a request by the applicants, the case was referred to the Grand Chamber.]

THE FACTS

...

11. Refah took part in a number of general and local elections. In the local elections in March 1989 Refah obtained about 10% of the votes ...

Ultimately, Refah obtained approximately 22% of the votes in the general election of 24 December 1995 and about 35% of the votes in the local elections of 3 November 1996.

The results of the 1995 general election made Refah the largest political party in Turkey.... On 28 June 1996 Refah came to power by forming a coalition government with the centre-right.... According to an opinion poll carried out in January 1997,... Refah might obtain 67% of the votes in the general election to be held roughly four years later.

B. Proceedings in the Constitutional Court

...

12. On 21 May 1997 Principal State Counsel at the Court of Cassation applied to the Turkish Constitutional Court to have Refah dissolved on the grounds that it was a "centre" (*mihrak*) of activities contrary to the principles of secularism. In support of his application, he referred to the following acts and remarks by certain leaders and members of Refah.

– Whenever they spoke in public Refah's chairman and other leaders advocated the wearing of Islamic headscarves in State schools and buildings occupied by public administrative authorities, whereas the Constitutional Court had already ruled that this infringed the principle of secularism enshrined in the Constitution.

– At a meeting on constitutional reform Refah's chairman, Mr Necmettin Erbakan, had made proposals tending towards the abolition of secularism in Turkey.

He had suggested that the adherents of each religious movement should obey their own rules rather than the rules of Turkish law.

– On 13 April 1994 Mr Necmettin Erbakan had asked Refah's representatives in the Grand National Assembly to consider whether the change in the social order which the party sought would be "peaceful or violent" and would be achieved "harmoniously or by bloodshed".

– At a seminar held in January 1991 in Sivas, Mr Necmettin Erbakan had called on Muslims to join Refah, saying that only his party could establish the supremacy of the Koran through a holy war (jihad) and that Muslims should therefore make donations to Refah rather than distributing alms to third parties.

...

– Several members of Refah, including some in high office, had made speeches calling for the secular political system to be replaced by a theocratic system. These persons had also advocated the elimination of the opponents of this policy, if necessary by force. Refah, by refusing to open disciplinary proceedings against the members concerned and even, in certain cases, facilitating the dissemination of their speeches, had tacitly approved the views expressed.

– On 8 May 1997 a Refah MP, Mr Ibrahim Halil Çelik, had said in front of journalists in the corridors of the parliament building that blood would flow if an attempt was made to close the "*Imam-Hatip*" theological colleges....

...

THE LAW

I. Alleged Violation of Article 11 of the Convention

[The Court considered whether the interference had been 'prescribed by law' and had been in pursuance of a 'legitimate aim'. It responded affirmatively on both issues.]

...

3. "Necessary in a democratic society"

...

98. [T]he Court considers that a political party may promote a change in the law or the legal and constitutional structures of the State on two conditions: firstly, the means used to that end must be legal and democratic; secondly, the change proposed must itself be compatible with fundamental democratic principles. It necessarily follows that a political party whose leaders incite to violence or put forward a policy which fails to respect democracy or which is aimed at the destruction of democracy and the flouting of the rights and freedoms recognised in a democracy cannot lay claim to the Convention's protection against penalties imposed on those grounds....

99. The possibility cannot be excluded that a political party, in pleading the rights enshrined in Article 11 and also in Articles 9 and 10 of the Convention, might attempt to derive therefrom the right to conduct what amounts in practice to activities intended to destroy the rights or freedoms set forth in the Convention and thus bring about the destruction of democracy (see *Communist Party (KPD) v. Germany*,

no. 250/57, Commission decision of 20 July 1957, Yearbook 1, p. 222). In view of the very clear link between the Convention and democracy, no one must be authorised to rely on the Convention's provisions in order to weaken or destroy the ideals and values of a democratic society. Pluralism and democracy are based on a compromise that requires various concessions by individuals or groups of individuals, who must sometimes agree to limit some of the freedoms they enjoy in order to guarantee greater stability of the country as a whole.

In that context, the Court considers that it is not at all improbable that totalitarian movements, organised in the form of political parties, might do away with democracy, after prospering under the democratic regime, there being examples of this in modern European history.

100. The Court reiterates, however, that the exceptions set out in Article 11 are, where political parties are concerned, to be construed strictly; only convincing and compelling reasons can justify restrictions on such parties' freedom of association. In determining whether a necessity within the meaning of Article 11 § 2 exists, the Contracting States have only a limited margin of appreciation. Although it is not for the Court to take the place of the national authorities, which are better placed than an international court to decide, for example, the appropriate timing for interference, it must exercise rigorous supervision embracing both the law and the decisions applying it, including those given by independent courts. Drastic measures, such as the dissolution of an entire political party and a disability barring its leaders from carrying on any similar activity for a specified period, may be taken only in the most serious cases.... Provided that it satisfies the conditions set out in paragraph 98 above, a political party animated by the moral values imposed by a religion cannot be regarded as intrinsically inimical to the fundamental principles of democracy, as set forth in the Convention.

...

(ε) The appropriate timing for dissolution

102. In addition, the Court considers that a State cannot be required to wait, before intervening, until a political party has seized power and begun to take concrete steps to implement a policy incompatible with the standards of the Convention and democracy, even though the danger of that policy for democracy is sufficiently established and imminent. The Court accepts that where the presence of such a danger has been established by the national courts, after detailed scrutiny subjected to rigorous European supervision, a State may "reasonably forestall the execution of such a policy, which is incompatible with the Convention's provisions, before an attempt is made to implement it through concrete steps that might prejudice civil peace and the country's democratic regime" (see the Chamber's judgment, § 81).

103. ...A Contracting State may be justified under its positive obligations in imposing on political parties, which are bodies whose *raison d'être* is to accede to power and direct the work of a considerable portion of the State apparatus, the duty to respect and safeguard the rights and freedoms guaranteed by the Convention and the obligation not to put forward a political programme in contradiction with the fundamental principles of democracy.

(ζ) Overall examination

104. In the light of the above considerations, the Court's overall examination … must concentrate on the following points: (i) whether there was plausible evidence that the risk to democracy, supposing it had been proved to exist, was sufficiently imminent; (ii) whether the acts and speeches of the leaders and members of the political party concerned were imputable to the party as a whole; and (iii) whether the acts and speeches imputable to the political party formed a whole which gave a clear picture of a model of society conceived and advocated by the party which was incompatible with the concept of a "democratic society".

105. … [T]he Court must [also] take account of the historical context in which the dissolution of the party concerned took place and the general interest in preserving the principle of secularism in that context in the country concerned to ensure the proper functioning of "democratic society".

(ii) Application of the above principles to the present case

…

(α) Pressing social need

The appropriate timing for dissolution

…

108. The Court … considers that at the time of its dissolution Refah had the real potential to seize political power without being restricted by the compromises inherent in a coalition. If Refah had proposed a programme contrary to democratic principles, its monopoly of political power would have enabled it to establish the model of society envisaged in that programme.

…

110. While it can be considered, in the present case, that Refah's policies were dangerous for the rights and freedoms guaranteed by the Convention, the real chances that Refah would implement its programme after gaining power made that danger more tangible and more immediate. …

In short, the Court considers that in electing to intervene at the time when they did in the present case the national authorities did not go beyond the margin of appreciation left to them under the Convention.

…

The main grounds for dissolution cited by the Constitutional Court

116. The Court considers on this point that among the arguments for dissolution pleaded by Principal State Counsel at the Court of Cassation those cited by the Constitutional Court as grounds for its finding that Refah had become a centre of anti-constitutional activities can be classified into three main groups: (i) the arguments that Refah intended to set up a plurality of legal systems, leading to discrimination based on religious beliefs; (ii) the arguments that Refah intended to apply sharia to the internal or external relations of the Muslim community within the context of this plurality of legal systems; and (iii) the arguments based on the

references made by Refah members to the possibility of recourse to force as a political method. The Court must therefore limit its examination to those three groups of arguments cited by the Constitutional Court.

(a) The plan to set up a plurality of legal systems

...

119. The Court sees no reason to depart from the Chamber's conclusion that a plurality of legal systems, as proposed by Refah, cannot be considered to be compatible with the Convention system. In its judgment, the Chamber gave the following reasoning:

> "70. . . . the Court considers that Refah's proposal that there should be a plurality of legal systems would introduce into all legal relationships a distinction between individuals grounded on religion, would categorise everyone according to his religious beliefs and would allow him rights and freedoms not as an individual but according to his allegiance to a religious movement.
>
> The Court takes the view that such a societal model cannot be considered compatible with the Convention system, for two reasons.
>
> Firstly, it would do away with the State's role as the guarantor of individual rights and freedoms. . . .
>
> Secondly, such a system would undeniably infringe the principle of non discrimination between individuals as regards their enjoyment of public freedoms. . . ."

(b) Sharia

122. . . . [After examining the various comments attributed to Refah leaders the Court accepted] the Constitutional Court's conclusion that these remarks and stances of Refah's leaders formed a whole and gave a clear picture of a model conceived and proposed by the party of a State and society organised according to religious rules.

123. The Court concurs in the Chamber's view that sharia is incompatible with the fundamental principles of democracy, as set forth in the Convention:

> "72. Like the Constitutional Court, the Court considers that sharia, which faithfully reflects the dogmas and divine rules laid down by religion, is stable and invariable. Principles such as pluralism in the political sphere or the constant evolution of public freedoms have no place in it. The Court notes that, when read together, the offending statements, which contain explicit references to the introduction of sharia, are difficult to reconcile with the fundamental principles of democracy, as conceived in the Convention taken as a whole. It is difficult to declare one's respect for democracy and human rights while at the same time supporting a regime based on sharia, which clearly diverges from Convention values, particularly with regard to its criminal law and criminal procedure, its rules on the legal status of women and the way it intervenes in all spheres of private and public life in accordance with religious precepts. . . . In the Court's view, a political party whose actions seem to be aimed at introducing sharia in a State party to the Convention can hardly be regarded as an association complying with the democratic ideal that underlies the whole of the Convention."

124. The Court must not lose sight of the fact that in the past political movements based on religious fundamentalism have been able to seize political power in certain States and have had the opportunity to set up the model of society which they had in mind. It considers that, in accordance with the Convention's provisions, each Contracting State may oppose such political movements in the light of its historical experience.

125. The Court further observes that there was already an Islamic theocratic regime under Ottoman law. When the former theocratic regime was dismantled and the republican regime was being set up, Turkey opted for a form of secularism which confined Islam and other religions to the sphere of private religious practice. Mindful of the importance for survival of the democratic regime of ensuring respect for the principle of secularism in Turkey, the Court considers that the Constitutional Court was justified in holding that Refah's policy of establishing sharia was incompatible with democracy.

...

(d) The possibility of recourse to force

...

130. The Court considers that, whatever meaning is ascribed to the term "jihad" used in most of the speeches mentioned above (whose primary meaning is holy war and the struggle to be waged until the total domination of Islam in society is achieved), there was ambiguity in the terminology used to refer to the method to be employed to gain political power. In all of these speeches the possibility was mentioned of resorting "legitimately" to force in order to overcome various obstacles Refah expected to meet in the political route by which it intended to gain and retain power.

131. Furthermore, the Court endorses the following finding of the Chamber:

> "74.... While it is true that [Refah's] leaders did not, in government documents, call for the use of force and violence as a political weapon, they did not take prompt practical steps to distance themselves from those members of [Refah] who had publicly referred with approval to the possibility of using force against politicians who opposed them. Consequently, Refah's leaders did not dispel the ambiguity of these statements about the possibility of having recourse to violent methods in order to gain power and retain it."

Overall examination of "pressing social need"

132.... [Taking account of the factors above the Court concluded that the dissolution order] may reasonably be considered to have met a "pressing social need".

Proportionality of the measure complained of

133. After considering the parties' arguments, the Court sees no good reason to depart from the following considerations in the Chamber's judgment:

> "82.... [A]fter [Refah's] dissolution only five of its MPs (including the applicants) temporarily forfeited their parliamentary office and their role as leaders of a political party. The 152 remaining MPs continued to sit in Parliament and pursued their political careers normally.... The Court considers in that connection that the nature and severity of the interference are also factors to be taken into account when assessing its proportionality...."

4. The Court's conclusion regarding Article 11 of the Convention

135. Consequently, following a rigorous review to verify that there were convincing and compelling reasons justifying Refah's dissolution and the temporary forfeiture of certain political rights imposed on the other applicants, the Court considers that those interferences met a "pressing social need" and were "proportionate to the aims pursued". It follows that Refah's dissolution may be regarded as "necessary in a democratic society" within the meaning of Article 11 § 2.

136. Accordingly, there has been no violation of Article 11 of the Convention. [The Court therefore concluded that there was no need to examine the same issues in relation to the other provisions of the Convention cited by the applicants.]

...

CONCURRING OPINION OF JUDGE KOVLER

...

[The judge agrees that there is no violation of Article 11.] What bothers me about some of the Court's findings is that in places they are unmodulated, especially as regards the extremely sensitive issues raised by religion and its values. I would prefer an international court to avoid terms borrowed from politico-ideological discourse, such as "Islamic fundamentalism"..., "totalitarian movements"..., "threat to the democratic regime"..., etc., whose connotations, in the context of the present case, might be too forceful.

I also regret that the Court, in reproducing the Chamber's conclusions (paragraph 119 of the judgment), missed the opportunity to analyse in more detail the concept of a plurality of legal systems, which is linked to that of legal pluralism and is well-established in ancient and modern legal theory and practice.... Not only legal anthropology but also modern constitutional law accepts that under certain conditions members of minorities of all kinds may have more than one type of personal status.... Admittedly, this pluralism, which impinges mainly on an individual's private and family life, is limited by the requirements of the general interest. But it is of course more difficult in practice to find a compromise between the interests of the communities concerned and civil society as a whole than to reject the very idea of such a compromise from the outset.

This general remark also applies to the assessment to be made of sharia, the legal expression of a religion whose traditions go back more than a thousand years, and which has its fixed points of reference and its excesses, like any other complex system....

QUESTIONS

1. Commenting upon the *Refah* case Issacharof stated that 'On first impression, the opinion jars many democratic sensibilities, particularly those formed in the free speech environment of the United States.... [T]he use of a deferential "reasonableness" standard for the political exclusion of a party with broad popular support gives a great deal of latitude to national determinations that are necessarily problematic.'[27] Do you think the

[27] Samuel Issacharoff, 'Fragile Democracies', 120 Harv. L. Rev 1405 (2007), at 1446.

Court went too far in this case? What other options might have been available to the government or the Court to deal with such perceived threats to democracy without going so far as to dissolve an entire political party?

2. Consider the following response by Frédéric Mégret to *Refah*. He observes that the human rights regime is remarkably tolerant of pluralism at the international level but intolerant of it within the national order. 'Why', he asks, 'should legal differentiation be the unique privilege of sovereigns?' His answer lies in 'the deep but often neglected statism of international human rights law'. But this internal legal monism remains problematic because it will sometimes be both undemocratic and do violence to a variety of individual and group legal aspirations.

> ... [N]ot only has international human rights law by and large failed to take the principled position in favour of legal pluralism that its ethos might suggest, but it has ironically used states' very margin of appreciation (itself a broad recognition of international legal pluralism) to condone sovereign attacks on domestic legal pluralism.... The opening up of the rights project to a great diversity of domestic legal orders, of course, requires a commensurate opening up of these legal orders to the human rights project. In that respect, however, the demand of minority law is not necessarily to either supplant state law or set itself as beyond the scrutiny of human rights, but merely to be judged by the same human rights standards that are supposed to govern the substance and administration of all law, including that of the state.[28]

3. After reviewing the European Court's political party dissolution cases, Mersel argues that the Court should also pay attention to the internal structures of political parties to ensure that they too meet appropriate criteria of democracy.[29] Where they are not democratically structured they might reasonably be banned. In your view, would this be an appropriate extension of the Court's existing jurisprudence?

(3) Prisoners' Right to Vote

One of the most contentious issues before the Court in recent years concerns the right of convicted persons to vote. The major cases have come from the United Kingdom and Italy. In addition to their inherent interest, these cases serve to illustrate several important aspects of the ECHR system. They are (1) the 'margin of appreciation', a doctrine that allows a degree of deference to national preferences; (2) the 'pilot judgment' technique that allows the Court to deal with systemic problems; and (3) the politics of implementation and enforcement.

The margin of appreciation

The margin of appreciation doctrine has been widely relied upon by the Court in relation to many provisions and is likely soon to be enshrined in the actual text of

[28] F. Mégret, 'Is There Ever a 'Right to One's Own Law? An Exploration of Possible Rights Foundations for Legal Pluralism', 45 Israel L. Rev. 3 (2012), at 33.

[29] Yigal Mersel, 'The Dissolution of Political Parties: The Problem of Internal Democracy', 4 Int'l. J. Const. L. 84 (2006).

the Convention (p. 969, *infra*). Its precise nature and function remain contested, however. It is closely linked to the Court's quest to find a 'European consensus' in the sense of a common ground in the law and practice of the member states.

> Generally speaking, the existence of similar patterns of practice or regulation across the different Member States will legitimize a wider margin of appreciation for the State that stays within that framework and delegitimize attempts to part ways with them. Against this background, the non-existence of a European consensus on the subject-matter will be normally accompanied by a wider margin of appreciation accorded to the State in question.[30]

The extent of the margin of appreciation will thus generally depend on 'the weight the Court attaches to the following factors: the European consensus, the nature of the right and the aim pursued by the contested measure.'[31]

Former President Wildhaber has noted that it:

> ...embraces an element of deference to decisions taken by democratic institutions, a deference deriving from the primordial place of democracy within the Convention system. It is not the role of the European Court systematically to second guess democratic legislatures. What it has to do is to exercise an international supervision in specific cases to ensure that the solutions found do not impose an excessive or unacceptable burden on one sector of society or individuals. The democratically elected legislature must be free to take measures in the general interest even where they interfere with a given category of individual interests. The balancing exercise between such competing interests is most appropriately carried out by the national authorities. There must however be a balancing exercise, and this implies the existence of procedures which make such an exercise possible. Moreover the result must be that the measure taken in the general interest bears a reasonable relationship of proportionality both to the aim pursued and the effect of the individual interest concerned. In that sense the area of discretion accorded to the States, the margin of appreciation, will never be unlimited and the rights of individuals will ultimately be protected against the excesses of majority rule. The margin of appreciation recognizes that where appropriate procedures are in place a range of solutions compatible with human rights may be available to the national authorities. The Convention does not purport to impose uniform approaches to the myriad different interests which arise in the broad field of fundamental rights protection; it seeks to establish common minimum standards to provide an Europe-wide framework for domestic human rights protection.[32]

But the way in which the Court evaluates the existence or otherwise of such a consensus has itself been the subject of considerable criticism. George Letsas, for example, has called for a distinction to be drawn between substantive and structural versions of the doctrine. The former involves the relationship between

[30] Council of Europe, Lisbon Network, 2008, 'The Margin of Appreciation', p. 5, at www.coe.int/t/dghl/cooperation/lisbonnetwork/themis/ECHR/Paper2_en.asp.

[31] Ibid., p. 15.

[32] Luzius Wildhaber, 'A Constitutional Future for the European Court of Human Rights?', 23 Hum. Rts. L. J. 161 (2002), at 162.

individual freedoms and collective goals and illustrates the 'limitability or non-absoluteness of the Convention rights'. The latter involves deference to the judgment of national authorities and recognition of the subsidiarity principle. He attributes 'much of the confusion and controversy surrounding' the concept 'to the Court's failure to distinguish between these two ideas in its case law'. It uses the same term

> both for saying that the applicant did not, as a matter of human rights, have the right he or she claimed, and for saying that it will not substantively review the decision of national authorities as to whether there has been a violation. This explains why the doctrine is described as 'the other side of the principle of proportionality' by some and as enabling 'the Court to balance the sovereignty of Contracting Parties with their obligations under the Convention' by others.[33]

Pilot judgments

The pilot judgment procedure emerged from a cluster of cases involving property rights in Poland (*Broniowski v. Poland*, Application No. 31443/96, 22 June 2004). It is a method for dealing with repetitive cases that are considered to derive from a recurring dysfunction at the national level. It has been applied, for example, in relation to prison conditions in Russia, the non-enforcement of judgments relating to social housing in Moldova, the excessive length of proceedings in administrative courts in Germany, Greece, and Turkey, and in prisoners' voting rights cases.

The procedure was codified in Rule 61 of the ECtHR's Rules of Court (21 Feb. 2011). The Court can adopt such a procedure in situations involving 'the existence of a structural or systemic problem or other similar dysfunction' giving rise to multiple similar applications. It first seeks the views of the parties to determine the suitability of this approach in the circumstances, and gives priority attention to all applications included under the umbrella of the pilot judgment. In it judgment the Court identifies the nature of the systemic problems and the type of remedial measures that must be taken. It can prescribe a time limit for this purpose. The Court may adjourn its examination of all similar applications pending the adoption of the prescribed remedial measures, but may resume its examination at any time 'where the interests of the proper administration of justice so require'. Ideally, the outcome of the procedure is as follows:

> Where the parties to the pilot case reach a friendly-settlement agreement, such agreement shall comprise a declaration by the respondent Government on the implementation of the general measures identified in the pilot judgment as well as the redress to be afforded to other actual or potential applicants. [Rule 61(7)]

The cases below illustrate these aspects of the Court's work, including the political milieu in which it must function.

[33] G. Letsas, *A Theory of Interpretation of the European Convention on Human Rights* (2007), 80–1.

HIRST v. UNITED KINGDOM (NO. 2)

European Court of Human Rights, Application No. 74025/01 (Grand Chamber), 6 Oct. 2005

[John Hirst is a British national who, in 1980, was given a life sentence for manslaughter. As a convicted person he was thus subject during the period of his detention to a ban on voting in any parliamentary or local elections, pursuant to the Representation of the People Act 1983. In a Chamber judgment of 30 March 2004 the Court found a violation of Article 3 of ECHR Protocol No. 1 which provides:

> The High Contracting Parties undertake to hold free elections at reasonable intervals by secret ballot, under conditions which will ensure the free expression of the opinion of the people in the choice of the legislature.]

I. ALLEGED VIOLATION OF ARTICLE 3 OF PROTOCOL No. 1

...

A. The Chamber judgment

41. The Chamber found that the exclusion from voting imposed on convicted prisoners in detention was disproportionate. It had regard to the fact that it stripped a large group of people of the vote; that it applied automatically irrespective of the length of the sentence or the gravity of the offence; and that the results were arbitrary and anomalous, depending on the timing of elections.... It concluded at paragraph 51:

> "The Court accepts that this is an area in which a wide margin of appreciation should be granted to the national legislature in determining whether restrictions on prisoners' right to vote can still be justified in modern times and if so how a fair balance is to be struck. In particular, it should be for the legislature to decide whether any restriction on the right to vote should be tailored to particular offences, or offences of a particular gravity or whether, for instance, the sentencing court should be left with an overriding discretion to deprive a convicted person of his right to vote. The Court would observe that there is no evidence that the legislature in the United Kingdom has ever sought to weigh the competing interests or to assess the proportionality of the ban as it affects convicted prisoners. It cannot accept however that an absolute bar on voting by any serving prisoner in any circumstances falls within an acceptable margin of appreciation...."

...

B. The Court's assessment

[Having concluded that the overall aim of the legislation was legitimate, the Court examined whether it was proportionate.]

...

(b) Proportionality

...

78. The breadth of the margin of appreciation has been emphasised by the Government....

79. As to the weight to be attached to the position adopted by the legislature and judiciary in the United Kingdom, there is no evidence that Parliament has ever sought to weigh the competing interests or to assess the proportionality of a blanket ban on the right of a convicted prisoner to vote. It is true that the question was considered by the multi-party Speaker's Conference on Electoral Law in 1968 which unanimously recommended that a convicted prisoner should not be entitled to vote....

...

81. As regards the existence or not of any consensus among Contracting States ... the fact remains that it is a minority of Contracting States in which a blanket restriction on the right of convicted prisoners to vote is imposed or in which there is no provision allowing prisoners to vote....

82. Therefore, while the Court reiterates that the margin of appreciation is wide, it is not all-embracing. [The Court then reiterates the concerns noted by the Chamber, in para 41 above.] Such a general, automatic and indiscriminate restriction on a vitally important Convention right must be seen as falling outside any acceptable margin of appreciation, however wide that margin might be, and as being incompatible with Article 3 of Protocol No. 1.

83. Turning to the Government's comments concerning the lack of guidance from the Chamber as to what, if any, restrictions on the right of convicted prisoners to vote would be compatible with the Convention, the Court notes that its function is in principle to rule on the compatibility with the Convention of the existing measures. It is primarily for the State concerned to choose, subject to supervision by the Committee of Ministers, the means to be used in its domestic legal order in order to discharge its obligation under Article 46 of the Convention.... In cases where a systemic violation has been found the Court has, with a view to assisting the respondent State in fulfilling its obligations under Article 46, indicated the type of measure that might be taken to put an end to the situation found to exist (see, for example, *Broniowski v. Poland* [GC], no. 31443/96 ...). In other exceptional cases, the nature of the violation found may be such as to leave no real choice as to the measures required....

84. In a case such as the present one, where Contracting States have adopted a number of different ways of addressing the question of the right of convicted prisoners to vote, the Court must confine itself to determining whether the restriction affecting all convicted prisoners in custody exceeds any acceptable margin of appreciation, leaving it to the legislature to decide on the choice of means for securing the rights guaranteed by Article 3 of Protocol No. 1....

85. The Court concludes that there has been a violation of Article 3 of Protocol No. 1.

...

NOTE

Reaction to the judgment in the United Kingdom was generally very negative. A leading Conservative Party spokesman said it was 'an outrageous decision and a perfect example of how Europe is intruding in areas of our national life where it has no business.' Nevertheless, in April 2006, the UK Government submitted an action plan to the Council of Europe's Committee of Ministers in response to *Hirst*. It envisaged legislative reform by 2007 preceded by a national-level consultation. The latter began in December 2006 and concluded in September 2009, a delay characterized by the UK Parliament's Joint Committee on Human Rights as being 'disproportionate'. No reform was introduced prior to the 2010 General Election, leading the Committee of Ministers to express its 'profound regret' that nothing had happened despite its 'repeated calls'.

The powerful British tabloid press was highly critical of the outcome in *Hirst*. A 2011 study produced for a group of conservative Members of Parliament suggested that between 1966, when the United Kingdom first accepted the Court's jurisdiction, and 2010, 'the UK faced over 350 rulings from the judges in Strasbourg on whether or not it had violated an ECHR right. In about three-quarters of these judgments the Court ruled that the UK had breached a Convention right.' The study concluded that the UK Parliament should be empowered to 'overturn' ECtHR judgments in order to 'ensure the Strasbourg Court did not impose on the British people interpretations of human rights that offended their common understanding of those rights.' Acknowledging that this was unlikely since it would require revision of the entire Convention system, the study urged UK withdrawal from the ECHR so that it 'would be free democratically to determine its laws and policies, with respect for human rights, without the European Court of Human Rights imposing its own — often strange and damaging — ideas on this country.'[34] The study hit its target and the *Daily Mail* newspaper (12 Jan. 2012) ran a headline 'Europe's war on British justice: UK loses three out of four human rights cases, damning report reveals'. The campaign against *Hirst* rapidly transcended political divisions as both the Government and the Opposition expressed their disagreement with the judgment.

Commentators were quick to point out that the figures cited had ignored the fact that 97 per cent of complaints lodged against the United Kingdom had been deemed inadmissible by the Court, thus yielding a figure of less than 2 per cent of cases in which a violation had been found.[35]

In January 2012, the UK Prime Minister, addressing the Council of Europe, warned that the concept of human rights was being 'distorted' and 'discredited' as a result of some ECtHR judgments. He said that *Hirst* had caused 'credible democratic anxiety' and argued that 'where an issue like this has been subjected to proper, reasoned democratic debate and has also met with detailed scrutiny by national courts in line with the convention, the decision made at a national level should be treated with respect.' In a newspaper article published just before the Prime Minister's

[34] R. Broadhurst, *Human Rights: Making Them Work for the People of the UK* (2011).

[35] A. Tickell, 'Is the European Court of Human Rights obsessively interventionist?', UK Human Rights Blog, 22 Jan. 2012.

speech, the President of the Court (who happened also to be British) said it was unfortunate that the prisoner voting issue had 'been used as the springboard for a sustained attack on the court' and expressed his disappointment at hearing 'senior British politicians lending their voices to criticisms more frequently heard in the popular press, often based on a misunderstanding of the court's role and history, and of the legal issues at stake.'[36]

In the meantime, the Court received 2,500 new applications challenging the government's failure to act. In *Greens and M.T. v. United Kingdom* (Application Nos. 60041/08 and 60054/08, 23 Nov. 2010) the Court activated its pilot judgment procedure and gave the United Kingdom six months from 11 April 2011, the date on which the judgment became final, to remedy the situation. The United Kingdom sought, and was granted, a new deadline of six months after the Grand Chamber's judgment in the following case.

SCOPPOLA v. ITALY (NO. 3)

European Court of Human Rights, Application No. 126/05 (Grand Chamber), 22 May 2012

[The applicant, Franco Scoppola, is an Italian national who was convicted in 2002 of killing his wife and wounding his son in a violent family argument. Under the Italian Criminal Code his life sentence entailed a lifetime ban from holding any public office, which in turn meant the permanent forfeiture of his right to vote. He appealed to the ECtHR and a Chamber found a violation of Article 3 of Protocol No. 1 because of the automatic and indiscriminate nature of the ban. The Italian Government requested referral of the case to the Grand Chamber. In those proceedings the UK Government asserted the role of 'third party intervener' and participated actively in argument before the Court.]

...

c) Proportionality

(i) Whether the principles set forth in the Hirst judgment should be confirmed

93. In its observations, the third-party intervener affirmed that the Grand Chamber's findings in the *Hirst (no. 2)* case were wrong and asked the Court to revisit the judgment. It argued in particular that whether or not to deprive a group of people — convicted prisoners serving sentences — of the right to vote fell within the margin of appreciation afforded to the member States in the matter....

94. The Court reiterates that while it is not formally bound to follow its previous judgments, "it is in the interests of legal certainty, foreseeability and equality before the law that it should not depart, without good reason, from precedents laid down in previous cases. However, since the Convention is first and foremost a system for the protection of human rights, the Court must have regard to the changing conditions

[36] Nicolas Bratza, 'Britain should be Defending European Justice, Not Attacking It', *The Independent*, 24 Jan. 2012.

within the respondent State and within Contracting States generally and respond, for example, to any evolving convergence as to the standards to be achieved".…

95. It does not appear, however, that anything has occurred or changed at the European and Convention levels since the *Hirst (no. 2)* judgment that might lend support to the suggestion that the principles set forth in that case should be re-examined. On the contrary, analysis of the relevant international and European documents…and comparative-law information…reveals the opposite trend, if anything—towards fewer restrictions on convicted prisoners' voting rights.

96. The Court accordingly reaffirms the principles set out by the Grand Chamber in the Hirst judgment…, in particular the fact that when disenfranchisement affects a group of people generally, automatically and indiscriminately, based solely on the fact that they are serving a prison sentence, irrespective of the length of the sentence and irrespective of the nature or gravity of their offence and their individual circumstances, it is not compatible with Article 3 of Protocol No. 1 (ibid., § 82).

(ii) Whether the decision to deprive convicted prisoners of the right to vote should be taken by a court

97. The Court observes that the Chamber found a violation of Article 3 of Protocol No. 1 in the instant case, noting the lack "of any examination by the trial court of the nature and gravity of the offence" (see paragraph 62 above). In so doing it based itself, inter alia, on the Court's findings in the *Frodl* judgment.… [In *Frodl v. Austria* (Application No. 20201/04, 8 Apr. 2010) the Court held that Austrian legislation was not in conformity with the Convention because 'the decision on disenfranchisement should be taken by a judge', and should be accompanied by specific reasoning 'explaining why in the circumstances of the specific case disenfranchisement was necessary'.]

…

99. That reasoning takes a broad view of the principles set out in *Hirst*, which the Grand Chamber does not fully share. The Grand Chamber points out that the *Hirst* judgment makes no explicit mention of the intervention of a judge among the essential criteria for determining the proportionality of a disenfranchisement measure. The relevant criteria relate solely to whether the measure is applicable generally, automatically and indiscriminately within the meaning indicated by the Court.… While the intervention of a judge is in principle likely to guarantee the proportionality of restrictions on prisoners' voting rights, such restrictions will not necessarily be automatic, general and indiscriminate simply because they were not ordered by a judge. Indeed, the circumstances in which the right to vote is forfeited may be detailed in the law, making its application conditional on such factors as the nature or the gravity of the offence committed.

100. It is true that in answering certain of the arguments put forward by the United Kingdom Government in the *Hirst (no. 2)* case the Court noted that "when sentencing, the criminal courts in England and Wales make no reference to disenfranchisement and it is not apparent, beyond the fact that a court considered it appropriate to impose a sentence of imprisonment, that there is any direct link between the facts of any individual case and the removal of the right to vote".… But these are considerations of a general nature: they did not concern the applicant's

particular situation and, unlike the arguments based on the general, automatic and indiscriminate nature of the disenfranchisement, they are not reiterated in paragraph 82 of the *Hirst* judgment, where the criteria for assessing the proportionality of the impugned measure are set out.

101. In addition, according to the comparative-law data in the Court's possession . . ., arrangements for restricting the right of convicted prisoners to vote vary considerably from one national legal system to another, particularly as to the need for such restrictions to be ordered by a court. Only nineteen of the States examined impose no restrictions on the voting rights of convicted prisoners. Of the remaining twenty-four States, which do apply restrictions to varying degrees, eleven require a decision of the criminal court on a case-by-case basis. . . .

102. This information underlines the importance of the principle that each State is free to adopt legislation in the matter in accordance with "historical development, cultural diversity and political thought within Europe, which it is for each Contracting State to mould into their own democratic vision". . . . In particular, with a view to securing the rights guaranteed by Article 3 of Protocol No.. . . ., the Contracting States may decide either to leave it to the courts to determine the proportionality of a measure restricting convicted prisoners' voting rights, or to incorporate provisions into their laws defining the circumstances in which such a measure should be applied. In this latter case, it will be for the legislature itself to balance the competing interests in order to avoid any general, automatic and indiscriminate restriction. It will then be the role of the Court to examine whether, in a given case, this result was achieved and whether the wording of the law, or the judicial decision, was in compliance with Article 3 of Protocol No. 1.

(iii) Whether the right enshrined in Article 3 of Protocol No. 1 was respected in the applicant's case

103. Looking at the circumstances of the instant case, the Court observes first of all that the matter of the applicant's permanent disenfranchisement was not examined by the trial court. . . .

104. However, . . . removal of the right to vote without any ad hoc judicial decision does not, in itself, give rise to a violation of Article 3 of Protocol No. 1. The impugned measure must also be found to be disproportionate. . . .

105. As to the legal framework, it should be noted that in the Italian system the measure is applied to individuals convicted of a series of specific offences for which express provision is made by law, irrespective of the duration of the sentence imposed . . ., or to people sentenced to certain terms of imprisonment specified by law. In this latter case, prisoners sentenced by the courts to three years' imprisonment or more forfeit the right to vote temporarily, for five years, while those sentenced to five years or more, or to life imprisonment, permanently forfeit the right to vote. . . .

106. In the Court's opinion the legal provisions in Italy defining the circumstances in which individuals may be deprived of the right to vote show the legislature's concern to adjust the application of the measure to the particular circumstances of the case in hand, taking into account such factors as the gravity of the offence committed and the conduct of the offender. . . .

. . .

108. [Given the seriousness of the crimes committed] the Court cannot conclude that the Italian system has the general, automatic and indiscriminate character that led it, in the *Hirst (no. 2)* case, to find a violation of Article 3 of Protocol No. 1. In Italy there is no disenfranchisement in connection with minor offences or those which, although more serious in principle, do not attract sentences of three years' imprisonment or more, regard being had to the circumstances in which they were committed and to the offender's personal situation. The Court of Cassation rightly pointed this out (see paragraph 28 above). As a result, a large number of convicted prisoners are not deprived of the right to vote in parliamentary elections.

109. Furthermore, the Court cannot underestimate the fact that under Italian law it is possible for a convicted person who has been permanently deprived of the right to vote to recover that right. Three years after having finished serving his sentence, he can apply for rehabilitation [and potentially recover the right to vote].... In the Court's opinion this possibility shows that the Italian system is not excessively rigid.

3. Conclusion

110. Taking the above considerations into account, the Court finds that, in the circumstances of the present case, the restrictions imposed on the applicant's right to vote did not "thwart the free expression of the people in the choice of the legislature", and maintained "the integrity and effectiveness of an electoral procedure aimed at identifying the will of the people through universal suffrage".... The margin of appreciation afforded to the respondent Government in this sphere has therefore not been overstepped.

Accordingly, there has been no violation of Article 3 of Protocol No. 1.

...

QUESTIONS

1. In the sole dissent in the *Scoppola* case, Judge Björgvinsson argues that the factual differences between *Hirst* and *Scoppola* were inconsequential and that the Italian legislation should have been struck down in accordance with *Hirst*. Do you agree?

2. Voting rights issues are increasingly controversial in the United States and elsewhere.[37] Do you agree with this characterization of the merits of prisoner disenfranchisement:

> Section 3 of the Representation of the People Act 1983 is surely right; convicted prisoners should lose their right to vote while in custody. By committing an offence warranting prison, these people have shown a serious contempt for democracy, by flouting important provisions of the law as democratically decided. Why, for the duration of their sentence of imprisonment, should they have a say in making the law that governs us all, when they have shown they are prepared to ignore key aspects of it?[38]

[37] R. Ziegler, 'Legal Outlier, Again? U.S. Felon Suffrage: Comparative and International Human Rights Perspectives', 29 Boston U. Int'l' L. J. 197 (2011).

[38] Broadhurst, n 34 *supra*, at 24.

6. THE CONVENTION AND THE COURT AT THE NATIONAL LEVEL

For all the importance of streamlining the Court's procedures and trying to make the system as a whole more efficient and more readily able to cope with the ever increasing caseload, there are two closely related challenges which hold the key to almost everything else. Both concern what happens or does not happen at the national level. The first is to ensure that the Convention, or at least its normative provisions, are as fully integrated as possible into the domestic legal system. Alec Stone Sweet describes below both the extraordinary progress that has been made in this respect and provides insights into the dynamics that have driven reform in key Contracting States.

The second challenge is to ensure that states provide effective domestic remedies in response to the judgments of the Court, and excerpts below from reports by the Council of Europe's Parliamentary Assembly illustrate some of the political efforts to pressure states to comply with judgments.

ALEC STONE SWEET, A COSMOPOLITAN LEGAL ORDER: CONSTITUTIONAL PLURALISM AND RIGHTS ADJUDICATION IN EUROPE

1 J. Global Constitutionalism 53 (2012), at 65

...

The domestification of the Convention

In 1950, when the ECHR was signed, Ireland was the only member of the Council of Europe with any meaningful experience with rights review. The constitutions of Belgium, France, Luxembourg, The Netherlands, and the UK did not include a charter of rights and/or prohibited the judicial review of statutes.... The German and the Italian constitutional courts were still being designed. Not surprisingly, a majority of states rejected proposals to grant individuals a right of petition, and to accept the compulsory jurisdiction of the European Court (which began operation only in 1959). With Protocol No. 11 (1998), states embraced a robust legal regime. Two factors were crucial. First, the development of EU law gave national officials, including judges, a chance to adjust to new forms of judicial power under constitutional pluralism.... Second, the Soviet bloc collapsed. In the 1990s, with constitutional reconstruction in full swing, the EU and the Council of Europe offered admission to post-Communist states on the basis of certain conditions, including a commitment to rights protection. Locking them into the ECHR, and placing them under the supervision of its Court, was an obvious means of securing that commitment.

...

... [D]omestification of the Convention proceeded via different routes: express constitutional provision (Austria, many post-Communist states); judicial interpretation of constitutional provisions related to treaty law generally (most states in Western Europe); or special statutes (UK, Ireland, and Scandinavian states). With incorporation, all national courts in the system are capable of enforcing the Convention: individuals can plead the ECHR at national bar against any act of public authority; judges are under a duty to identify statutes that conflict with Convention rights, and to interpret statutes in lights of the ECHR to avoid conflicts whenever possible; and virtually all courts may refuse to apply statutes that conflict with Convention rights, with the notable exception of those in the UK and Ireland.

Incorporation is an inherently constitutional process: it subverted centralized sovereignty at the national level, while provoking dynamics of systemic construction at the transnational level. The Convention quickly developed into a 'shadow' or 'surrogate' constitution in every state that did not possess its own judicially-enforceable charter of rights (including original signatories, Belgium, France, The Netherlands, Switzerland, and the UK). In the 1990s, Finland, Norway, and Sweden enacted new Bills of Rights, closely modeled on (and invoking) the ECHR, in order to fill gaps in their own constitutions.

In those states that possess, at least on paper, relatively complete systems of constitutional justice, incorporation provides supplementary protection. We find this situation in Germany, Greece, Ireland, Italy, Portugal, Spain, Turkey, and in the post-Communist states. The Spanish Constitutional Tribunal, for example, enforces the ECHR as quasi-constitutional norms. The Tribunal will strike down statutes that violate the Convention as per se unconstitutional; it interprets Spanish constitutional rights in light of the ECHR, wherever possible; and it has ordered the ordinary courts to abide by the Strasbourg Court's jurisprudence as a matter of constitutional obligation, including case law generated by litigation not involving Spain. If the judiciary ignores the Court's jurisprudence, individuals can appeal directly to the Tribunal for redress. Nonetheless, the Tribunal insists that in the event of an irreconcilable conflict between the ECHR and the Spanish Constitution, the latter will prevail — a common position among constitutional courts. In many post-Communist states, as well, constitutional judges invoke the Strasbourg Court's jurisprudence as authority, in order to enhance the status of fundamental rights — and hence their own positions — in the domestic context.

Strikingly, some states give the Convention constitutional rank (e.g., Albania, Austria, Slovenia); and, in The Netherlands, the ECHR enjoys supra-constitutional status. In Belgium, the Constitutional Court has determined that the ECHR possesses supra-legislative but infra-constitutional rank, while the Supreme Court holds that the ECHR possesses supra-constitutional status, thereby enhancing its autonomy vis-à-vis the Constitutional Court.

...The incorporation of the ECHR generated constitutional pluralism and inter-judicial competition within the national order; it destroyed doctrines that underpinned centralized sovereignty (e.g., legislative supremacy, the monopoly of constitutional courts over the domain of rights protection); and it enhanced judicial power with respect to legislative and executive power.

Transformation

Constitutional pluralism expands the discretionary authority of courts. Many judges will now refuse to apply law that conflicts with the Convention; at the same time, they are rapidly abandoning traditional methods of statutory interpretation. Instead of seeking to discern legislative intent, judges increasingly favor the purposive construction of statutes in light of fundamental rights jurisprudence. In systems in which multiple, functionally-differentiated, high courts co-exist (the majority of states), pluralism means that the supreme courts of ordinary jurisdiction may assume the mantle of de facto constitutional courts whenever they review the Conventionality of statutes. France, which for two centuries famously embraced and propagated the dogmas of the General Will (legislative sovereignty and the prohibition of judicial review), is now a robust example of pluralism. From the point of view of the rights claimant, the Supreme Civil Court (Cour de Cassation) and the Council of State (the supreme administrative court) function as the 'real' constitutional courts; and litigants and judges treat the Convention as the 'real' charter of rights. The outcome is dictated by the fact that individuals have no direct access to the Constitutional Council; and it is the European Court, not the Constitutional Council, that supervises the rights-protecting activities of the civil and administrative courts. Today, three autonomous high courts protect fundamental rights on an ongoing basis; and there is no formal means of coordinating rights doctrine, or of resolving conflicts, among these courts. Without revising the constitution or exiting the ECHR, French officials are now locked into a pluralist system of rights protection.

Some of the most powerful states in Western Europe have had the greatest difficulty incorporating the ECHR to permit judges to enforce it against statute. In legal terms, the structural problem concerns the fact that in so-called 'dualist' systems — including original signatories, Germany, Ireland, Italy, Sweden, Norway, and the UK — constitutions confer upon treaty law the same rank as statute. In such systems, conflicts between statutes and treaty provisions are expected to be resolved according to the rule, *lex posterior derogat legi priori*. The rule is anathema to a CLO [Cosmopolitan Legal Order], since legislation adopted after the transposition of the ECHR into national law would normally be immune from review under the Convention. What is critical for the emergence of the CLO is that, in these states, the rule has been relaxed or overridden altogether.

In Italy, at least until the late 1960s, 'Italian courts refused to apply the Convention considering its provisions to be merely programmatic'. In the past decade, courts incorporated the Convention, destroying the *lex posterior* rule and producing a pluralist order. In 2004, the Supreme Court (Cassazione) began treating the Convention as directly applicable, while in 2007, the Italian Constitutional Court (ICC) struck down a statute (concerning expropriation) as unconstitutional on the grounds that it violated property rights under the Convention. In its decision, the ICC held that Italian judges are required to interpret national law in light of the ECHR and, where a conflict is unavoidable, to refer the matter to the ICC. Some judges have chosen to ignore this jurisprudence. In 2008, for example, a court of appeal decided on its own authority to refuse to apply a controlling statute on grounds that it was incompatible with the Convention. The situation has given rise to a fierce debate: does the ECHR enjoy supra-legislative but infra-constitutional rank (the ICC's position) or constitutional status (the position of some civil courts and scholars)? This is yet another example of constitutional pluralism in action.

...

In two states — Ireland and the UK — the lex posterior rule has also been relaxed, although no judge is authorized to set aside legislation conflicting with the Convention. Pursuant to the ECHR Act (2003), Irish officials are under a duty to respect and enforce the Convention, and individuals can plead it against all acts of public authority, except those of Parliament and the courts. Under the UK Human Rights Act ([effective] 2000), individuals may challenge all acts, including Parliamentary legislation; if a Parliamentary statute is found to be incompatible with the ECHR, the high courts are obligated to issue a ruling of incompatibility — but they may not set aside the offending legislative provisions. Declarations of incompatibility are addressed to the Parliament, which must indicate what remedial legislation, if any, will be proposed. In Ireland, the high courts may also issue rulings of incompatibility, although Parliament is not obliged to respond to them....

... [T]he ECHR has played a crucial role in democratic transitions after 1989. New bills of rights were modeled on the ECHR, with an eye towards future membership in the EU and the Council of Europe; and some states even signed the ECHR prior to ratifying new constitutions (including Albania, Armenia, Azerbaijan, Georgia, Poland, Slovakia, and Ukraine). For the core states of Western Europe, folding the post-Communist states into the ECHR also fulfilled important strategic interests....

...

Beyond minimalism

The Court routinely generates new rights and expands the scope of existing ones, placing even powerful states out of compliance with the Convention. This outcome has not influenced the philosophical discourse on rights, which remains dominated by minimalist precepts, and there are good reasons for wonderment. Most of the original signatories of the Convention assumed that the treaty enshrined minimalism, thereby affording substantial latitude in how states would balance public interests and rights. One might also suppose that a transnational court would have weaker political legitimacy in comparison with national courts.... The transnational judge's gaze ... is an alien presence. Why has this situation not led to a jurisprudence of rights minimalism?

The answer lies in how decentralized sovereignty operates. Three factors deserve emphasis. First, the Court expends great resources to convince its audience that it fully understands the richness and particularity of the dispute, as well as variation in the relevant national law across the regime. In its rulings, the Court carefully traces the process through which individuals exhausted remedies, and it dwells on the arguments briefed by the defendant state and others filing as amici. Findings of violation may not convince states, but it is not plausible to argue that the Court has ignored domestic law and context....

Second, the Court has developed a doctrinal framework — proportionality analysis (PA) — to adjudicate virtually all Convention rights, and it insists that all national courts use it as well.... What is common across the national systems ... is not a list of norms defined in a lowest-common denominator manner, but a mode of argumentation, and justification: the proportionality framework.

The Court uses PA, in part, to determine how much discretion — the 'margin of appreciation' in the jargon — states should have in infringing a right for public purposes. In practice, the Court combines PA with a simple comparative method for determining when the scope of a Convention right has expanded. Typically, the Court will raise the standard of protection in a given domain of law when a sufficient number of states have withdrawn public interest justifications for restricting the right. The margin of appreciation thus shrinks as consensus on higher standards of rights protection emerges within the regime, shifting the balance in favor of future applicants. The move will always put some states out of compliance. Nonetheless, the Court can claim that there is an external, 'objective' means of determining the weights to be given to the values in conflict, and the Court's supporters can usually assert that the Court's bias is majoritarian, transnational, and pro-rights. A state that chooses not to comply is left to defend a lower standard of rights protection, on idiosyncratic or nationalistic grounds. Although states may balk when it comes to implementing controversial judgments, they eventually comply in the vast majority of cases.

...

Beyond individual justice

...

... [There are] myriad ways in which ECHR membership bolsters weak domestic systems. Even the worst 'problem' states, such as Russia and the Ukraine, Turkey and Greece, and many other post-Communist states, have undergone massive legal reforms, major progress that would not have been made without ECHR membership and incorporation.... As Buyse and Hamilton put it: 'Through its jurisprudence and its ripple effects, the Court fosters the values of democracy, plurality, openness and the rule of law. In doing so, it maps the transitional goals to be pursued and helps [post-Communist] societies, through the interplay with national institutions and civil society actors, [to address] current and future threats to democracy and human rights.'

States boasting robust systems of domestic rights protection (e.g., Germany, Ireland, and Spain) generate important cases in areas in which the protection offered lags behind that of other important systems. The perception of a differential in relative standards across jurisdictions not only attracts applications; it also animates the Court's majoritarian activism and the dynamic of inter-judicial competition.... Perhaps counter-intuitively, the Court's oracular, law-making function is most prominently exercised when it deals with high-standard states....

...

IMPLEMENTATION OF JUDGMENTS OF THE EUROPEAN COURT OF HUMAN RIGHTS

Parliamentary Assembly of the Council of Europe, Resolution 1787 (2011)

...

5. The Assembly notes with grave concern the continuing existence of major systemic deficiencies which cause large numbers of repetitive findings of violations of

the Convention and which seriously undermine the rule of law in the states concerned. These problems relate in particular to:

5.1. excessive length of judicial proceedings leading to ineffective protection of a wide range of substantial rights (endemic notably in Italy);

5.2. chronic non-enforcement of domestic judicial decisions (widespread, in particular, in the Russian Federation and Ukraine);

5.3. ill-treatment by law-enforcement officials — sometimes causing death — and a lack of effective investigations thereof (particularly apparent in the Russian Federation and Moldova);

5.4. unlawful detention and excessive length of detention on remand (in Moldova, Poland, the Russian Federation and Ukraine).

. . .

7. The Assembly, in particular, urges the following states to give priority to specific problems:

. . .

7.7. the Russian Federation must tackle pressing issues, in particular:

7.7.1. relating to the functioning of the administration of justice and the prison system: the authorities must ensure that the reform adopted in May 2010 to address the non-enforcement of domestic judicial court decisions (see the Court's pilot judgment in *Burdov v. Russia (No. 2)* of 15 January 2009) is finally implemented and is effective, seven years after the original *Burdov v. Russia* judgment of 7 May 2002. . . . Continuing efforts to solve the major issues of poor conditions and overcrowding in remand centres, ill-treatment in police custody, excessive length of detention on remand and several procedural deficiencies related to the latter, are insufficient . . .;

7.7.2. related to the action of security forces in the Chechen Republic: the greatest concern relates to repetitive grave human rights violations in this region. Regrettably, the alleged recent structural improvements of domestic investigation procedures have not as yet led to any tangible results . . .;

7.7.3. related to the numerous judgments of the Court finding grave and repeated violations of human rights in the North Caucasus region: the Assembly reiterates that the Russian Federation must, just like the other States Parties to the Convention, implement the individual measures required to put an end to the violations found, address their consequences, and take the necessary general measures to effectively prevent similar violations in the future;

. . .

10. [T]he Assembly:

10.1. strongly urges national parliaments which have not yet done so to introduce specific mechanisms and procedures for effective parliamentary oversight of the implementation of the Court's judgments;

10.2. calls upon the member states to set up, either by legislation or otherwise, effective domestic mechanisms . . . for rapid execution of judgments of the [ECtHR], and ensure that a decision-making body at the highest political level takes full responsibility for the co-ordination of all aspects of the domestic implementation process;

. . .

QUESTIONS

1. 'Getting 46 States, with such a vast array of legal systems and ongoing human rights challenges to adopt the measures necessary to ensure effective domestic implementation and avoid acts of intimidation against those who would submit claims to Strasbourg is surely wishful thinking.' Do you agree?

2. Can you think of any objections to the pilot judgment scheme in light of the aims of the Convention? And how easy will it be to apply it to rights other than the right to property?

3. Are there analogues to the ECtHR's friendly settlement procedure in the domestic law of most states, or does this represent an unusual conciliation procedure for a court to be overseeing?

7. THE CONTINUING NEED FOR REFORM

Despite the effectiveness of earlier waves of reform, the Court is currently facing considerable pressure to change its approach in a variety of ways. Many observers see the problems as flowing primarily from the great success of the system and see the solutions consisting largely of administrative reforms and enhanced political will. They point to the relatively small budget and staffing of the system and to states' reluctance to augment the resources significantly as the workload has grown exponentially. They also argue that if states in general, and especially the handful of states against which the majority of judgments finding violations have been rendered, were more responsive the number of cases would drop substantially and problems would be resolved domestically without needing to go to Strasbourg. But despite the centrality of these problems, there is also a deeper political problem in the sense that some states feel that the system has become too intrusive and that it is starting to 'bite' in ways that they are not willing to accept. In some states, such as the United Kingdom as illustrated in the *Hirst* case, there has also been a populist dimension to this resentment at being 'dictated to by Strasbourg'. We turn now to examine some of the statistics and then to review the types of reform that have been proposed.

Statistics[39]

Between 1959 and 2011 the Court delivered more than 15,000 judgments, 91 per cent of which came from 1998 onwards. Nearly half of the total concerned four states: Turkey (2,747), Italy (2,166), Russia (1,212), and Poland (945).

The main subjects dealt with have been: right to a fair trial — Art. 6 (45.01 per cent), protection of property — Protocol 1 (13.35 per cent), right to liberty and

[39] See ECHR, Annual Report 2011 (2012) and ECHR Overview 1959–2011 (2012) both at www.echr.coe.int.

security — Art. 5 (11.46 per cent), right to an effective remedy — Art. 13 (8.1 per cent), prohibition of torture and inhuman or degrading treatment — Art. 3 (7.5 per cent), right to life — Art. 2 (4.15 per cent), and other violations (10.43 per cent).

As of 31 December 2011, the backlog of cases was 151,624. These came from Russia (26.6 per cent), Turkey (10.5 per cent), Italy (9.1 per cent), Romania (8.1 per cent), Ukraine (6.8 per cent), Serbia (4.5 per cent), Poland (4.2 per cent), Moldova (2.8 per cent), Bulgaria (2.7 per cent), the United Kingdom (2.4 per cent), and 37 other states (22.4 per cent). Thus 61 per cent of the total are from only six states. In 2011 the Court rejected 50,677 applications as being inadmissible, but received 64,500 new applications in the meantime.

Of the existing caseload, about 6,000 concern issues to which the Court gives 'priority' such as the right to life, personal freedom and security, and violations involving children or family life. It has taken steps to enable it to keep up with these cases. There are 19,000 cases listed as 'non-priority' involving issues such as free speech and property rights, and 34,000 are non-priority 'repetitive' cases that have been admitted and will be considered in conjunction with other cases under pilot judgment and related procedures. The remaining 90,000 cases await a determination as to whether they will be held admissible, and the Court estimates that 90 per cent of those will be inadmissible.

To deal with this workload, in 2011 the Court had, in addition to its 47 judges, 658 staff in its registry (lawyers, administrative and technical staff, and translators) and operated on a budget of €59 million (US$73 million).

In 2012 the states parties to the Convention met in Brighton, United Kingdom, to discuss and decide on proposed reforms. In the lead up to the conference, all of the key stakeholders made suggestions. The most influential of these came from the Steering Committee for Human Rights, known as the CDDH after its French acronym. It is composed of representatives of the 47 states, at a 'working' level and focuses primarily on identifying procedural reforms that would enhance the system. The following document reflects its analysis of the issues to be considered by the politicians in Brighton. The excerpts from its report below feature primarily options that were not, in the final outcome, endorsed in the Brighton Declaration. They are followed by the most relevant provisions of that Declaration.

STEERING COMMITTEE FOR HUMAN RIGHTS (CDDH) FINAL REPORT ON MEASURES REQUIRING AMENDMENT OF THE EUROPEAN CONVENTION ON HUMAN RIGHTS

Doc. CDDH(2012)R74 Addendum I (15 Feb. 2012)

...

B. THE REFORM PROPOSALS

...

I. Measures to regulate access to the Court

7. The following proposals would regulate access to the Court. They all share a principal aim of addressing the problem of the very large number of clearly inadmissible, and even futile or abusive applications.

Fees for applicants to the Court

[These comments address the 'practicality and utility' of fees, rather than the principles involved.]

9. [There are at least three possible purposes or visions in relation to fees]: a system intended as a deterrent to discourage clearly inadmissible applications; a system intended as a penalty for those introducing clearly inadmissible applications; and a system intended to reflect the fact that many member States' highest courts themselves require applicants to pay a fee.

...

12. The introduction of any system of fees involves reconciling tensions between competing interests.

a. First, between minimising administrative and budgetary consequences, on the one hand, and minimising possible discriminatory effects, on the other.
b. Second, between the competing interests of maximising deterrent effect against clearly inadmissible applications, on the one hand, and avoiding discriminatory deterrence of well-founded applications, on the other.

...

Compulsory legal representation

15. It has been suggested that making representation by a lawyer compulsory from the outset could be an effective and appropriate means of ensuring applicants receive proper legal advice before filing an application and would increase the quality of drafting of applications. It would be consistent with the principle of subsidiarity in so far as it links directly into the national legal system. The suggestion was made on condition that any introduction of compulsory representation should be subject to the setting-up of appropriate legal aid facilities for applicants at national level.

16. The CDDH considers that this proposal . . . could present disadvantages . . . : without provision of legal aid for persons of insufficient means, it would impact the right of individual application. It was not certain that lawyers succeeded in dissuading clients from making clearly inadmissible applications, nor did the Court's statistics show that applications brought by legally represented persons were proportionally less likely to be clearly inadmissible than those brought by unrepresented persons. Requiring legal aid in simple cases would unnecessarily add to procedural costs.

17. As to the issue of legal aid, the CDDH notes the substantial budgetary implications for those member States that do not currently provide legal aid to applicants. . . .

...

A sanction in futile cases

19. The proposal would be to impose a pecuniary sanction in "futile" cases, where an applicant has repeatedly submitted applications that are clearly inadmissible and lacking in substance. Although the Court would be unable directly to enforce payment of the sanction, the applicant would be informed that no further applications would be processed until the sanction had been paid [unless] the further application concerned "core rights" . . . (e.g. Articles 2, 3 and 4). . . .

20. [S]uch a sanction would . . . have an educative effect on the applicant concerned and a disciplining influence on the behaviour of others. . . .

21. The following arguments were raised against the proposal. A sanctions system would not be in conformity with the purpose, spirit and even the letter of the Convention. It was not established that many people engaged in abusive litigation before the Court. Those that did, did not necessarily only engage in such litigation. Such applications were in any case already dealt with simply and were not a major case-processing problem. . . . There would inevitably be a cost in terms of financial and human resources, along with a heavy discretionary burden on the Court when deciding who or what case to sanction. The sanction would create inequality between applicants of different financial means.

. . .

Introduction of a new admissibility criterion relating to cases properly considered by national courts

28. The proposal to introduce a new admissibility criterion relating to cases properly considered by national courts is intended to address not only the problem of the very large number of cases pending before Chambers, but also the issue of relations between the Court and national courts, which should respect the principle of subsidiarity. An application would be inadmissible if it were substantially the same as a matter that had already been examined by a domestic tribunal applying Convention rights, unless that tribunal had manifestly erred in its interpretation or application of the Convention rights or the application raised a serious question affecting interpretation or application of the Convention. The proposal could have special relevance with regard to Convention rights such as those contained in Articles 8 to 11.

. . .

30. Arguments against were that the proposal would place unacceptable restrictions on access to the Court and undermine the right of individual petition, without decreasing the Court's workload. It would limit the jurisdiction of the Court and its ability to address gaps in protection of Convention rights. The substantive application of the Convention by domestic courts is an issue which should be considered at the merits, rather than the admissibility stage. By limiting the scope of review to correction of manifest error, the criterion could jeopardise maintenance of uniform Convention interpretation. The notion of "manifest error" will be difficult to apply in practice. A finding of "manifest error" in a domestic court decision could undermine relations between the Court and the national judiciary concerned. There would be generalised focus on the overall quality of the domestic legal system, instead of on its treatment of the applicant's case.

. . .

II. Measures to address the number of applications pending before the Court

33. The following measures would address in various ways the problems of the very large numbers of cases pending. . . .

. . .

The "sunset clause" for applications not addressed within a reasonable time

43. The proposal is based on the premise that it is not realistic to expect the Court, using current resources and working methods, to be able to give a prompt, reasoned judicial decision to every application. Under the proposal, an application could be automatically struck off the Court's list of cases a set period of time after it was first made, unless during that period the Court had notified the case to the Government and invited it to submit observations.

44. It has been argued that the proposal would work in harmony with the Court's prioritisation policy, which, with a large backlog of applications, would mean that large numbers of applications would remain pending before the Court with no realistic prospect of being resolved either within a reasonable time or at all. The proposal is intended to cover those cases that fall into the lowest priority categories, releasing the Court from having to issue individual decisions on each application and thereby freeing resources to deal with more serious complaints. Applicants would be informed of the outcome of their case more quickly than at present.

45. Arguments raised against the proposal are that an automatic strike-out of cases without any judicial examination would be incompatible with the idea of access to justice and the right of individual petition. There would be no guarantee that only lowest priority category cases would be affected; well-founded applications could also be affected. Decisions giving no reason for why an application is ill-founded would fail to deter future ill-founded applications. There would be no relief of the Registry since it would remain responsible for triage. A sunset clause could harm the Court's authority. The proposal could have adverse effects, in that it could induce the Court to devote more of its capacity to adjudicating less important cases. . . .

. . .

Conferring on the Court a discretion to decide which cases to consider

47. Under this proposal, an application would not be considered unless the Court made a positive decision to deal with the case.

48. In its favour, it has been argued that it would make the Court's judicial task more manageable and allow all applications to be processed to a conclusion in a reasonable, foreseeable time. By allowing the Court to focus on highest priority cases, it would contribute to ensuring high-quality, consistent case-law. It would formalize the Court's existing prioritisation policy, without necessarily excluding the right of individual petition. It is uncertain that other proposals alone would suffice and unlikely that they would without additional resources.

49. Arguments expressed against include that it would radically change the Convention system and significantly restrict the right of individual application by

removing the requirement that decisions be taken by a judge. It offers a solution with respect to new applications, when other solutions might suffice, but none for the existing backlog. . . .

. . .

III. Measures to enhance relations between the Court and national courts

Extending the Court's jurisdiction to give advisory opinions[40]

51. A proposal has been made to extend the Court's jurisdiction to give advisory opinions, which would aim at reducing the backlog of applications pending before Committees, enhancing relations between the Court and national courts and reinforcing subsidiarity. The proposal features the following characteristics:

a. A request for an advisory opinion could only be made in cases revealing a potential systemic or structural problem (an alternative proposal would limit requests to cases concerning the compatibility of domestic law with the Convention).
b. A request could only be made by a national court against whose decision there is no judicial remedy under national law.
c. It should always be optional for the national court to make a request.
d. The Court should enjoy full discretion to refuse to deal with a request, without giving reasons.
e. All States Parties to the Convention should have the opportunity to submit written submissions to the Court on the relevant legal issues.
f. Requests should be given priority by the Court.
g. An advisory opinion should not be binding for the State Party whose national court has requested it.
h. The fact of the Court having given an advisory opinion on a matter should not in any way restrict the right of an individual to bring the same question before the Court under Art. 34 of the Convention.
i. Extension of the Court's jurisdiction in this respect would be based in the Convention.

52. General arguments in favour of the proposal include that it could contribute to decreasing the Court's work-load in the medium- and long-term; allow the Court to give clear guidance on numerous potential cases bringing forward the same question; allow for a clarification of the law at an earlier stage, increasing the chances of the issue being settled at national level by providing national courts with a solid legal base for deciding the case; and could reinforce the principle of subsidiarity by underlining the primary responsibility of the national court, enhancing the authority of the Court and its case-law in the member States whilst fostering dialogue between the Convention mechanism and domestic legal orders.

[40] [Under Article 47 the Court can give Advisory Opinions in response to] requests from the Committee of Ministers on legal questions concerning the interpretation of the Convention and the Protocols thereto, excluding questions relating to the scope of the rights [or] freedoms contained therein. . . .

53. Arguments against the proposal include that it lacks clarity and may be unsuitable to the specificities of the Convention mechanism; would increase the Court's workload by creating a new group of cases which the Court may have difficulty in absorbing satisfactorily; is unnecessary, since the Court already has many cases revealing potential systemic or structural problems; would cause additional work for national courts and introduce a delay into national proceedings; would put the Court's authority in question if the opinion were not followed; and may create conflicts of competence between national constitutional courts and the Court.

...

55. If this proposal is retained in principle, some aspects on which there is no broad agreement would have to be clarified further, notably: the extent to which the Court should take account of the factual circumstances giving rise to the request for an advisory opinion; whether the Court should have discretion to refuse requests; whether it should give reasons for any refusal; whether other interested actors, including other States Parties, should be able to intervene; the effects of the advisory opinion in the relationship between the Court and the requesting national authority, including whether or not it be binding on the latter; and whether there should be limitations on the right of an individual to bring the same legal issue before the Court under Article 34 of the Convention.

...

HIGH LEVEL CONFERENCE ON THE FUTURE OF THE EUROPEAN COURT OF HUMAN RIGHTS

Brighton Declaration (20 April 2012), at www.coe.int/en/20120419-brighton-declaration

1. The States Parties to the Convention ... reaffirm their deep and abiding commitment to the Convention....

...

A. Implementation of the Convention at national level

7. The full implementation of the Convention at national level requires States Parties to take effective measures to prevent violations. All laws and policies should be formulated, and all State officials should discharge their responsibilities, in a way that gives full effect to the Convention. States Parties must also provide means by which remedies may be sought for alleged violations of the Convention. National courts and tribunals should take into account the Convention and the case law of the Court. Collectively, these measures should reduce the number of violations of the Convention. They would also reduce the number of well-founded applications presented to the Court, thereby helping to ease its workload.

...

B. Interaction between the Court and national authorities

...

11. The jurisprudence of the Court makes clear that the States Parties enjoy a margin of appreciation in how they apply and implement the Convention, depending on the circumstances of the case and the rights and freedoms engaged. This reflects that the Convention system is subsidiary to the safeguarding of human rights at national level and that national authorities are in principle better placed than an international court to evaluate local needs and conditions. The margin of appreciation goes hand in hand with supervision under the Convention system. In this respect, the role of the Court is to review whether decisions taken by national authorities are compatible with the Convention, having due regard to the State's margin of appreciation.

12. The Conference therefore:

a) Welcomes the development by the Court in its case law of principles such as subsidiarity and the margin of appreciation, and encourages the Court to give great prominence to and apply consistently these principles in its judgments;
b) Concludes that, for reasons of transparency and accessibility, a reference to the principle of subsidiarity and the doctrine of the margin of appreciation as developed in the Court's case law should be included in the Preamble [thus necessitating an amendment to the Convention] ...;
c) Welcomes and encourages open dialogues between the Court and States Parties as a means of developing an enhanced understanding of their respective roles ...

...

d) Notes that the interaction between the Court and national authorities could be strengthened by the introduction into the Convention of a further power of the Court, which States Parties could optionally accept, to deliver advisory opinions upon request on the interpretation of the Convention in the context of a specific case at domestic level, without prejudice to the non-binding character of the opinions for the other States Parties....

...

C. Applications to the Court

13. The right of individual application is a cornerstone of the Convention system. The right to present an application to the Court should be practically realisable, and States Parties must ensure that they do not hinder in any way the effective exercise of this right.

...

15. The Conference therefore:

a) Welcomes the Court's suggestion that the time limit under Article 35(1) of the Convention within which an application must be made to the Court could be shortened; [and] concludes that a time limit of four months is appropriate;...

...

d) Affirms that an application should be regarded as manifestly ill-founded within the meaning of Article 35(3)(a), inter alia, to the extent that the Court considers that the application raises a complaint that has been duly considered by a domestic court applying the rights guaranteed by the Convention in light of well-established case law of the Court including on the margin of appreciation as appropriate, unless the Court finds that the application raises a serious question affecting the interpretation or application of the Convention; and encourages the Court to have regard to the need to take a strict and consistent approach in declaring such applications inadmissible, clarifying its case law to this effect as necessary;

...

g) Invites the Court to develop its case law on the exhaustion of domestic remedies so as to require an applicant, where a domestic remedy was available to them, to have argued before the national courts or tribunals the alleged violation of the Convention rights or an equivalent provision of domestic law, thereby allowing the national courts an opportunity to apply the Convention in light of the case law of the Court.

...

G. Longer-term future of the Convention system and the Court

...

32. Effective implementation of the Convention at national level will permit the Court in the longer term to take on a more focused and targeted role. The Convention system must support States in fulfilling their primary responsibility to implement the Convention at national level.

33. In response to more effective implementation at the national level, the Court should be in a position to focus its efforts on serious or widespread violations, systemic and structural problems, and important questions of interpretation and application of the Convention, and hence would need to remedy fewer violations itself and consequently deliver fewer judgments.

...

QUESTIONS

1. What do you think are the goals of paragraph 15(d) of the Brighton Declaration and how might it work in practice?

2. Paragraph 12(b) of the Declaration envisages an amendment to the Convention to include in its Preamble 'a reference to the principle of subsidiarity and the doctrine of the margin of appreciation'. What do you see as the significance of this proposal? Can

such an initiative be reconciled with Benvenisti's view that the 'margin of appreciation, with its principled recognition of moral relativism, is at odds with the concept of the universality of human rights. If applied liberally, this doctrine can undermine seriously the promise of international enforcement of human rights that overcomes national policies.'[41]

3. In recent years it has been argued that the Court should limit itself to a 'constitutional' role, reviewing only those individual applications that apply generally and contribute to the establishment of a European public order based upon human rights, democracy and the rule of law. However, [many stakeholders] are opposed to limiting individual access to the Court, arguing that such a reform would serve to undermine the legitimacy and fundamental purpose of the Convention, the crucial link between the individual and the Convention system.[42]

Consider that statement in light of the challenges of reform.

4. By comparison with most other human rights institutions which run on a shoestring, the ECtHR is not cheap. Its budget for 2011 was €59 million (US$73 million), which covers judges' remuneration, staff salaries, and operational expenditure, but not building and infrastructure. This was considerably less than the budget for the US Supreme Court. But, given that the ECtHR has more than five times as many judges, huge language translations costs, and a clientele almost three times as large as that of the US Supreme Court (in terms of population), is there an argument that European states are seeking to get justice at bargain-basement rates rather than investing the amount of money which would be justified in such a vital enterprise?

8. THE BROADER EUROPEAN INSTITUTIONAL CONTEXT: THE EU AND THE OSCE

The European Union

The origins of the European Union lie in the Treaty of Paris of 1952 establishing the European Coal and Steel Community (ECSC) and subsequently in the two Treaties of Rome of 1957 creating the European Economic Community (EEC) and the European Atomic Energy Community. Upon the entry into force in 1993 of the Treaty on Economic Union these communities became the European Union, and the Treaty of Paris expired in 2002. From six founding members in 1957 the EU has grown to 27 in 2012.

The impetus for the first step of creating the ECSC came essentially from a desire to ensure that the heavy industries of the Ruhr, which had underpinned Germany's

[41] Eyal Benvenisti, 'Margin of Appreciation, Consensus, and Universal Standards', 31 NYU J. Int'l. L. & Pol'y. 843 (1999), at 844.

[42] Committee on Legal Affairs and Human Rights, Parliamentary Assembly of the Council of Europe, Report: Guaranteeing the authority and effectiveness of the European Convention on Human Rights, Doc. 12811 (3 Jan. 2012), para. 9.

military might in two World Wars, would be 'contained' within an intergovernmental structure bringing together West Germany and its former antagonists. The expansion into an EEC in 1957 was an attempt to promote closer economic integration within Europe for both federalist and economic reasons. While the adoption of a bill of rights based on the ECHR had been proposed in the early 1950s, none of the subsequent treaties contained such a bill or a list of enumerated rights. The 1957 treaties were more concerned with the freedom of the marketplace than the rights of individuals. The latter were seen to be appropriately protected at the national level.

Despite the absence of a bill of rights, the European Court of Justice (the judicial organ of the EU) began in 1969 to evolve a specific doctrine of human rights, the original motivation for which probably owed more to a desire to protect the primacy of EC law over national law than to any concern to provide extended protection to individuals. Over the years during which the human rights doctrine has evolved, the Court has identified several different normative underpinnings for 'the general principles of EC law' of which human rights (referred to by the European Court of Justice as 'fundamental rights') were one category. These normative underpinnings include certain provisions of the Treaty of Rome, the constitutional traditions of the member states, and international treaties accepted by member states. The European Court of Justice has applied this concept of human rights to the actions of the Community itself, and, with certain qualifications, to the actions of the member states.[43] The Court's jurisprudence was subsequently reflected in the Treaty on European Union (TEU or 'Lisbon Treaty'), which entered into force in 2009. Relevant provisions include:

Article 2

> The Union is founded on the values of respect for human dignity, freedom, democracy, equality, the rule of law and respect for human rights, including the rights of persons belonging to minorities. These values are common to the Member States in a society in which pluralism, non-discrimination, tolerance, justice, solidarity and equality between women and men prevail.

Article 3

> . . .
>
> 5. In its relations with the wider world, the Union shall uphold and promote its values and interests and contribute to the protection of its citizens. It shall contribute to . . . the protection of human rights, in particular the rights of the child, as well as to the strict observance and the development of international law, including respect for the principles of the United Nations Charter.

Article 6

> . . .
>
> 2. The Union shall accede to the [ECHR]. Such accession shall not affect the Union's competences as defined in the Treaties.

[43] See P. Alston, M. Bustelo, & J. Heenan (eds.), *The EU and Human Rights* (1999).

> 3. Fundamental rights, as guaranteed by the [ECHR] and as they result from the constitutional traditions common to the Member States, shall constitute general principles of the Union's law.

The resulting state of the law has been summarized thus:

> ii. At least three formal sources for EU human rights law are today listed in Article 6 TEU. The first is the EU Charter of Fundamental Rights which was proclaimed in 2000, and upgraded to the same binding legal status as the Treaties by the Lisbon Treaty in 2009. The second is the ECHR, which has long been treated by the ECJ as a 'special source of inspiration' for EU human rights principles, and which will become formally binding on the EU when the EU accedes to the ECHR, as Article 6(2) TEU now mandates it to do. The third is the 'general principles of EU law', a body of legal principles, including human rights, which have been articulated and developed by the ECJ over the years, drawing from national constitutional traditions, the ECHR and other international treaties signed by the Member States. These three sources overlap, since many provisions of the EU Charter are based on the ECHR, creating a certain amount of legal confusion. Other international sources of human rights law have only rarely been invoked. The ECJ has recently made clear that it views the Charter as 'the principal basis' on which the EU Courts will ensure that human rights are observed. However, the UK, Poland, and the Czech Republic negotiated a protocol to the Lisbon Treaty which purports to limit the impact of the Charter in those states.
>
> iii. EU human rights standards are binding on the EU and its institutions and bodies in all of their activities, and on the Member States when they are acting within the scope of EU law. Questions continue to arise about what Member State action falls 'within the scope of EU law' for these purposes.
>
> iv. The EU has gradually integrated human rights concerns into a range of its policies. The main internally-oriented policy of this kind is the body of anti-discrimination law, which has expanded significantly in recent years, and also the developing field of data-protection and privacy. In EU external relations, human rights have featured more prominently. The EU actively promotes its 'human rights and democratization' policy in many countries around the world, and uses human rights clauses in its international trade and development policies. It has imposed a human rights-based 'political conditionality' on candidate Member States, and claims to integrate human rights concerns throughout its common foreign and security policy. In 2009 the EU for the first time concluded a major international human rights treaty, the UN Convention on the Rights of Persons with Disabilities, which has both internal and external policy implications.[44]

The TEU also provides (Art. 7) for the suspension of certain EU membership rights if 'a serious and persistent breach' of human rights is deemed to exist within a member state. But the EU has been reluctant even to take much lesser measures. In 2012 Human Rights Watch noted that 'The European Commission failed to pursue vigorously its duty to enforce fundamental rights, dropping proceedings against Hungary over its media law and France over Roma expulsions, and suspending proceedings against Greece on its dysfunctional asylum and migration system despite

[44] P. Craig and G. de Búrca, *EU Law: Text, Cases, and Materials* (5th edn. 2011), 362–3.

continuing problems. The commission's first annual report on rights inside the EU shied away from criticizing members states.... '[45] This is consistent with a broader ambivalence:

> It seems fair to say that the approach of Member States to developing the EU's legal powers in the field of human rights is equivocal. Whenever a potentially expansive new power, institution, or legal norm is agreed upon, such as the anti-discrimination competence in Article 19 TEU, the adoption of the Charter of Fundamental Rights, or the establishment of the Fundamental Rights Agency, there seems to be a countervailing restrictive move on the part of key political actors, particularly the Member States' governments. Examples of this are ... the attempt to narrow the scope of application of the Charter to Member States ..., and the refusal to allow the Fundamental Rights Agency to monitor Member States for the purposes of Article 7 TEU....[46]

The next major step will be the accession of the EU to the ECHR. A complex and detailed draft agreement was reached between the EU and the Council of Europe in October 2011, but as of May 2012 final action by the two sides was still awaited.[47]

The Organization for Security and Co-operation in Europe (OSCE)

The Conference on Security and Co-operation in Europe (CSCE) opened in 1973 and concluded in August 1975 with the signing of the Final Act of Helsinki (known as the Helsinki Accord) by the 35 participating states (including all European states except Albania, plus Canada and the United States). The Soviet Union was motivated mainly by a desire to obtain formal recognition of its European frontiers, while the West took advantage of a period of East-West détente to obtain concessions primarily in relation to security matters. Human rights were of only secondary concern.

The CSCE process continued in the form of conferences designed to follow up and elaborate on the obligations contained in the Helsinki Accord. These agreements are reflected in various 'Concluding Documents', the most important of which in the human rights field ('the human dimension of the CSCE') are those adopted in Vienna and Paris in 1989, Copenhagen in 1990, Moscow in 1991, and Geneva in 1992.

Several characteristics distinguish the work of the CSCE from that of other entities in the human rights field. Its standards are all formally non-binding (in the sense that they are solemn undertakings, but are not in treaty form and thus not ratified or acceded to by states). Second, its membership is far broader than that of the European Union or even the Council of Europe. By 2012, it had grown to 56 states. Third, until 1991 it had no more than a token institutional structure designed only to arrange its periodic meetings. It performed no operational tasks.

The non-binding diplomatic nature of the Helsinki Process led many observers to question its utility. Whatever contribution the process ultimately made to the demise of Communism, it clearly played an important role, especially in the second half of

[45] World Report 2012, p. 441.

[46] Craig and de Búrca, n 44 *supra*, at 393.

[47] CDDH, 'Report to the Committee of Ministers on the elaboration of legal instruments for the accession of the European Union to the European Convention on Human Rights', Doc. CDDH(2011)009.

the 1980s and early 1990s, in legitimating human rights discourse within Eastern Europe, providing a focus for nongovernmental activities at both the domestic and international levels, and developing standards in relation to democracy, the rule of law, 'human contacts', national minorities, and freedom of expression which went beyond those already in existence in other contexts such as the Council of Europe and the UN. To a large extent, its formally non-binding nature enabled the CSCE standard-setting process to yield more detailed and innovative standards than those adopted by its counterparts.

In 1995 the CSCE was officially transformed into the Organization for Security and Co-operation in Europe. Its official organs include the Parliamentary Assembly of the OSCE, the Ministerial Council (Foreign Ministers), the Permanent Council (which meets weekly), the 'Chairman-in-Office' which is a rotating post held by each member state Foreign Minister in turn, and Summit Meetings of heads of state or government. In 2011, the OSCE had over 2,800 staff and an annual budget of €151 million.

The OSCE's basic priorities today are: the consolidation of democratic institutions, civil society and the rule of law, conflict prevention and resolution, and the promotion of a cooperative security system. Its principal institutions are its Secretariat in Vienna, the Office for Democratic Institutions and Human Rights (ODIHR) based in Warsaw, a Representative on Freedom of the Media based in Vienna, and a High Commissioner on National Minorities based in The Hague. His role is to identify and resolve ethnic tensions that threaten peace and stability. OSCE organs or the country concerned may request a mission, but the decision whether to make an on-site visit is his own. His recommendations address both short-term policy towards minorities and longer term measures to encourage a continuing dialogue between the government and minority members.

The OSCE has played an important role in the field in a wide range of situations, and has been especially active in electoral observation.

QUESTION

How would you characterize the division of labour in relation to human rights among the Council of Europe, the EU, and the OSCE? Is there too much overlap, or does each organization make a very distinctive contribution?

9. OTHER HUMAN RIGHTS CONVENTIONS ADOPTED BY THE COUNCIL OF EUROPE

COMMENT ON THREE CONVENTIONS

The European Social Charter

Although economic and social rights were reflected in the post-Second World War constitutions of France, Germany, and Italy, they were not included in the European

Convention. One of the key drafters, Pierre-Henri Teitgen, explained this decision in 1949 on the grounds that it was first necessary 'to guarantee political democracy in the European Union and then to co-ordinate our economies, before undertaking the generalisation of social democracy.' These rights were subsequently recognized in the European Social Charter of 1961.

The ESC system consists of: (1) the original Charter of 1961 (ratified by 43 states, as of May 2012); (2) an Additional Protocol of 1988 extending some of the rights (ratified by 13); (3) an amending Protocol of 1991 which revises some of the original monitoring arrangements (ratified by 23 states); (4) a revised (consolidated) Charter of 1996 which brings the earlier documents up to date and adds some new rights (ratified by 32 states); and (5) a further Additional Protocol of 1995 which provides for a system of collective complaints (ratified by 13 states). All but the 1991 Protocol have entered into force. The resulting picture is heavily fragmented since different states are governed by different regimes depending on which parts of the system they have ratified.

The Charter and its Additional Protocol of 1988 guarantee a series of 'rights and principles' with respect to employment conditions and 'social cohesion'. The former relate to: non-discrimination, prohibition of forced labour, trade union rights, decent working conditions, equal pay for equal work, prohibition of child labour, and maternity protection. Among the latter are: health protection, social security, and certain rights for children, families, migrant workers, and the elderly. These rights are not legally binding *per se*. The legal obligations designed to ensure their effective exercise are contained in Part II, which details the specific measures to be taken in relation to each of the rights. Part III reflects the principle of progressive implementation tailored to suit the circumstances of individual states. Each contracting party must agree to be bound by at least five of seven rights which are considered to be of central importance. It must also accept at least five of the other rights as listed in Part II.

Part IV provides for a monitoring system based on the submission of regular reports by contracting parties. The reports are examined by the European Committee of Social Rights whose assessments of compliance and non-compliance are then considered by the Parliamentary Assembly and a Governmental Committee. Finally, on the basis of all these views, the Committee of Ministers may make specific recommendations to the state concerned. The Additional Protocol providing for collective complaints entered into force in July 1998, although as of May 2012 only 82 complaints had been registered. Decisions had been adopted in relation to issues such as the right to strike in Bulgaria, housing rights for the Roma in Italy and in Bulgaria, the right to collective bargaining in Belgium, corporal punishment in several states, and discrimination against autism sufferers in France.

The European Convention for the Prevention of Torture

In 1987 the Council of Europe adopted the European Convention for the Prevention of Torture and Inhuman or Degrading Treatment or Punishment (ECPT) which places a particular emphasis on prevention. As of May 2012 the ECPT had been ratified by 47 states. It is also open to non-Council of Europe states by invitation.

The Convention establishes a Committee for the Prevention of Torture (CPT) which is composed of independent experts. Its function is 'to examine the treatment of persons deprived of their liberty with a view to strengthening, if necessary, the protection of such persons' from torture, inhuman or degrading treatment (Art. 1). The Convention is not concerned solely with prisoners but with any 'persons deprived of their liberty by a public authority'. Each state party is required to permit the Committee to visit any such place within the state's jurisdiction (Art. 2), unless there are exceptional circumstances (which will rarely be the case). Most visits are routine and scheduled well in advance, but there is also provision for ad hoc visits with little advance notice (Art. 7).

As of May 2012 the CPT had made 193 periodic, and 126 ad hoc visits. It meets *in camera* and its visits and discussions are confidential as, in principle, are its reports. The latter, however, may be released, either at the request of the state concerned or if a state refuses to cooperate and the Committee decides by a two-thirds majority to make a public statement. This occurred in 1992 when the Committee concluded after three visits to Turkey that the government had failed to respond to its recommendations. Since then, virtually all states have voluntarily agreed to the release of the Committee's report and 258 have been published.

Framework Convention for the Protection of National Minorities

Despite the importance of national minorities within Europe and discussions about appropriate measures since 1949, the issue proved too controversial and complex for the Council of Europe to adopt specific standards until 1994, when the Framework Convention was adopted. In part, the impetus was the adoption of the 1992 UN Declaration on Rights of Persons Belonging to Minorities, and the development of non-binding standards and promotional activities in this field by the CSCE. The Council sought to avoid longstanding controversies by, among other things, confining the Convention to programmatic obligations that are not directly applicable and that leave considerable discretion about implementation to the state concerned. International supervision is undertaken by the Committee of Ministers of the Council based upon periodic reports to be submitted by states parties. The Convention entered into force in February 1998 and as of May 2012 had been ratified by 39 states.

ADDITIONAL READING

ECHR: E. Bates, *The Evolution of the European Convention on Human Rights* (2010); D. Harris et al., *Law of the European Convention on Human Rights* (2nd edn. 2009); ECHR Factsheets, at www.echr.coe.int/ECHR/en/Header/Press/Information+sheets/Factsheets/; H. Keller & A. Stone Sweet (eds.), *A Europe of Rights: The Impact of the ECHR on National Legal Systems* (2008); P. Van Dijk et al. (eds.), *Theory and Practice of the European Convention on Human Rights* (4th edn. 2006); S. Greer, *The European Convention on Human Rights: Achievements, Problems* *and Prospects* (2006); A. W. B. Simpson, *Human Rights and the End of Empire: Britain and the Genesis of the European Convention* (2004); R. Blackburn & J. Polakiewicz (eds.), *The European Convention on Human Rights 1950–2000* (2000); E. Bjorge, 'National Supreme Courts and the Development of ECHR Rights', 9 Int'l. J. Const'l. L. 5 (2011).

ECtHR: J. Christoffersen & M. R. Madsen (eds.), *The European Court of Human Rights between Law and Politics* (2011); A. Buyse & M. Hamilton (eds.), *Transitional Jurisprudence and the ECHR: Justice, Politics and Rights* (2011); Leonard L. Hammer & F. Emmert (eds.), *The European Convention on Human Rights and Fundamental Freedoms in Central and Eastern Europe* (2012); L. Helfer & E. Voeten, 'Do European Court of Human Rights Judgments Promote Legal and Policy Change?' (2011) at http://papers.ssrn.com/sol3/papers.cfm?abstract_id=1850526; H. Keller et al., *Friendly Settlements Before the European Court of Human Rights: Theory and Practice* (2010); P. Leach, *Taking a Case to the European Court of Human Rights* (2nd edn. 2005); M. D. Goldhaber, *A People's History of the European Court of Human Rights* (2007); A. Sajó (ed.), *Militant Democracy* (2004); P. Macklem, 'Guarding the Perimeter: Militant Democracy and Religious Freedom in Europe' (2010), at http://papers.ssrn.com/sol3/papers.cfm?abstract_id=1660649; R. Macdonald, 'The Margin of Appreciation', in R. Macdonald et al. (eds.), *The European System for the Protection of Human Rights* (1993), 122; J. Sweeney, 'Margins of Appreciation: Cultural Relativity and the European Court of Human Rights in the Post-Cold War Era', 54 Int'l. & Comp. L. Q. 459 (2005).

General: G. de Beco (ed.), *Human Rights Monitoring Mechanisms of the Council of Europe* (2012); W. Korey, *The Promises We Keep: Human Rights, the Helsinki Process, and American Foreign Policy* (1993).

The EU: P. Alston, M. Bustelo, & J. Heenan (eds.), *The EU and Human Rights* (1999); Marc Weller (ed.), *The Rights of Minorities in Europe: A Commentary on the European Framework Convention for the Protection of National Minorities* (2006); G. de Búrca and B. de Witte (eds.), *Social Rights* (2005); L. Betten & D. MacDevitt (eds.), *The Protection of Fundamental Social Rights in the European Union* (1996); P. Alston & O. de Schutter (eds.), *Monitoring Fundamental Rights in the EU: The Contribution of the Fundamental Rights Agency* (2005); S. Wheatley, *Democracy, Minorities and International Law* (2005).

B. THE INTER-AMERICAN SYSTEM

Section B illustrates the work of the Inter-American system, both the Inter-American Commission on Human Rights (IACHR) and the Inter-American Court of Human Rights (IACtHR). The applicable standards in the Inter-American system consist of the originally non-binding American Declaration on the Rights and Duties of Man (1948) and the American Convention on Human Rights (1969). The relationship between the two is comparable in some ways to that between the UDHR and the two International Covenants. Similarly, many of the techniques that are used by the Commission and Court will be familiar from our study of the UN and ECHR systems.

By the same token, the Inter-American system is distinctive in many ways. The issues it has been forced to address are often quite different from those that have preoccupied the ECtHR, for example. Disappearances, killings, the death penalty, amnesty laws, and related issues have been on the agenda of the Commission since the 1970s and of the Court since the 1980s. The Commission has undergone a significant evolution over time and now engages, albeit on a very limited budget, in a diverse range of activities. We focus below on the system of country reporting that it has developed. In relation to the Court, particular attention is given to judgments dealing with one of its early landmark cases dealing with responsibility for disappearances, and two representative cases dealing with the rights of indigenous peoples and the response to prison riots.

1. BACKGROUND AND INSTITUTIONS

COMMENT ON DEVELOPMENT OF THE INTER-AMERICAN SYSTEM

In May 1948 the ninth Inter-American Conference, held in Bogotá, established the Organization of American States (OAS). Its predecessor organizations date back to the International Union of American Republics of 1890. The 1948 Charter entered into force in December 1951 and has since been amended by the Protocol of Buenos Aires of 1967, the Protocol of Cartagena de Indias of 1985, the Protocol of Washington of 1992, and the Protocol of Managua of 1993. The purposes of the OAS are:

> to strengthen the peace and security of the continent; to promote and consolidate representative democracy, with due respect for the principle of nonintervention; to prevent possible causes of difficulties and to ensure the pacific settlement of disputes that may arise among the member states; to provide for common action on the part of those States in the event of aggression; to seek the solution of political, juridical and economic problems that may arise among them; to promote by cooperative action, their economic, social and cultural development, and to achieve an effective limitation of conventional weapons that will make it possible to devote the largest amount of resources to the economic and social development of the member states.[48]

Its principal organs are the General Assembly that meets annually and in additional special sessions if required, the Meeting of Consultation of Ministers of Foreign Affairs that considers urgent matters, the Permanent Council, and the General Secretariat. The latter two organs are based in Washington DC.

[48] *Annual Report of the Inter-American Commission on Human Rights 1994* (1995), at 347.

The Bogotá Conference of 1948 also adopted the American Declaration of the Rights and Duties of Man. The inter-American system thus had a human rights declaration seven months before the United Nations had adopted the Universal Declaration and two-and-a-half years before the European Convention was adopted. Nevertheless, the development of a regional treaty monitored by an effective supervisory machinery was to take considerably longer. The Inter-American Commission on Human Rights was created in 1959 and the American Convention on Human Rights was adopted in 1969. It entered into force in 1978.

The development of the inter-American system followed a different path from that of its European counterpart. Although the institutional structure is superficially very similar and the normative provisions are in most respects very similar, the conditions under which the two systems developed were radically different. Within the Council of Europe, military and other authoritarian governments have been rare and short-lived, while in Latin America they were close to being the norm until the changes that started in the 1980s.

On 11 September 2001, the OAS adopted the Inter-American Democratic Charter which recognized that 'The peoples of the Americas have a right to democracy and their governments have an obligation to promote and defend it' (Art. 1), declared the 'effective exercise of representative democracy [to be] the basis for the rule of law' (Art. 2) and defined representative democracy to include essential elements such as 'respect for human rights and fundamental freedoms, access to and the exercise of power in accordance with the rule of law, the holding of periodic, free, and fair elections..., the pluralistic system of political parties and organizations, and the separation of powers and independence of the branches of government' (Art. 3). The Charter also lays down various procedures to be followed when democracy is threatened. Thus, for example, 'In the event of an unconstitutional alteration of the constitutional regime that seriously impairs the democratic order in a member state' the OAS Permanent Council may be convoked and may initiate diplomatic initiatives. If necessary, the General Assembly can also act and can suspend the membership rights of the state concerned, although this does not affect that state's human rights obligations (Arts. 20–1).

In contrast to the type of cases and issues that have preoccupied the ECHR regime, states of emergency have been common in Latin America, the domestic judiciary has often been extremely weak or corrupt, and large-scale practices involving torture, disappearances, and executions have not been uncommon. Many of the governments with which the Inter-American Commission and Court have had to work have been ambivalent towards those institutions at best and hostile at worst.

In May 2012 there were 35 member states of the OAS, of which 24 were parties to the American Convention on Human Rights (Trinidad and Tobago had ratified in 1991 but registered a denunciation in 1998 over disagreement on the death penalty). Twenty-two states have recognized the jurisdiction of the Court. Although the United States signed the Convention in 1978, it has yet to ratify. Cuba remains, technically, a member of the OAS, but the Communist Government has been excluded from participation in its work since 1962. As we shall see below, these facts have not prevented the Inter-American Commission from scrutinizing the human rights records of those two states.

COMMENT ON RIGHTS RECOGNIZED IN THE AMERICAN DECLARATION AND CONVENTION

You should now become familiar with these two instruments, excerpts from which appear in the Document Annex.

In terms of rights, the American Declaration on the Rights and Duties of Man is similar in content to the Universal Declaration, including the economic and social rights therein. What distinguishes it are ten articles setting out the duties of the citizen: the duty 'so to conduct himself in relation to others that each and every one may fully form and develop his personality'; to 'aid support, educate and protect his minor children'; to 'acquire at least an elementary education'; to vote in popular elections; to 'obey the law and other legitimate commands of the authorities'; to 'render whatever civil and military service his country may require for its defence and preservation'; to cooperate with the state with respect to social security and welfare; to pay taxes; and to work.

The process of drafting an inter-American treaty began in 1959. The result was the American Convention on Human Rights of 1969 (also known as the Pact of San José, Costa Rica) which contains 26 rights and freedoms, 21 of which are formulated in similar terms to the provisions of the ICCPR. Consider some comparisons:

(1) Article 27 of the ICCPR, which recognizes the rights of members of minority groups, has no counterpart in the American Convention.
(2) The five provisions which are in that Convention but not in the ICCPR are the right of reply (Art. 14), the right to property (Art. 21), freedom from exile (Art. 22(5)), the right to asylum (Art. 22(7)), and prohibition of 'the collective expulsion of aliens' (Art. 21(9)).
(3) Some provisions in the American Convention express the same general idea as in other human rights treaties but give it a distinctive specification — for example, Article 4 on the right to life that provides in paragraph 1 that the right 'shall be protected by law and, in general, from the moment of conception'.
(4) Article 23 on participation in government, which figures in the later materials, contains the same rights and requirements as the analogous Article 21 of the UDHR and Article 25 of the ICCPR.

When the Convention was adopted in 1969 it was decided not to have a separate treaty relating to economic, social, and cultural rights but rather to include a general provision (Art. 26) in the following terms:

> The States Parties undertake to adopt measures, both internally and through international cooperation, especially those of an economic and technical nature, with a view to achieving progressively by legislation or other means, the full realization of the rights implicit in the economic, social, educational, scientific and cultural standards set forth in the Charter of the Organization of American States as amended by the Protocol of Buenos Aires.

The OAS Charter, as amended, sets up an Inter-American Council for Education, Science and Culture, as well as an Economic and Social Council, both of which are supposed to set standards, consider reports made by states, and make recommendations. That machinery has, however, achieved very little indeed in relation to economic, social, and cultural rights. In 1988 the OAS adopted an Additional Protocol to the American Convention on Human Rights in the Area of Economic, Social and Cultural Rights (known as the Protocol of San Salvador). It obliges parties to adopt measures, 'to the extent allowed by their available resources, and taking into account their degree of development', for the progressive achievement of the rights listed. The Protocol became effective in 1999 and had, as of May 2012, 16 states parties.

The rights recognized in the Protocol are similar to those in the International Covenant on Economic, Social and Cultural Rights, although the formulations differ significantly. The Protocol does not recognize the rights to adequate clothing and housing or to an adequate standard of living (Art. 11 of the ICESCR), but it does include the right to a healthy environment, the right to special protection in old age, and the rights of persons with disabilities, none of which are explicitly recognized in the ICESCR.

NOTE

Compare the individual duties expressed in the American Declaration with the ICCPR, in which duties are only referred to in the preamble that paraphrases Article 29(1) of the Universal Declaration ('Everyone has duties to the community in which alone the free and full development of his personality is possible'). The conception and nature of the duties expressed in the African Charter on Human and Peoples' Rights, p. 517, *supra*, is radically different.

JAMES CAVALLARO & STEPHANIE BREWER, REEVALUATING REGIONAL HUMAN RIGHTS LITIGATION IN THE TWENTY-FIRST CENTURY: THE CASE OF THE INTER-AMERICAN COURT

102 Am. J. Int'l. L. 678 (2008), at 778

...

II. OVERVIEW OF THE INTER-AMERICAN SYSTEM

... The quasi-judicial Commission acts as the first instance for victims of human rights violations who wish to bring cases before the system. Aside from its role in processing these individual petitions, the Commission undertakes a range of monitoring and promotional activities. The Court, on the other hand, is an exclusively judicial body that issues binding decisions in cases of human rights violations submitted to it by the Commission. In addition, the Court issues advisory opinions and grants provisional measures for the protection of individuals in imminent danger of rights violations.

Litigation before the inter-American system occurs within the legal framework of the main human rights instruments adopted by the OAS: the American Declaration of the Rights and Duties of Man and the American Convention on Human Rights. The Declaration lacks the binding status of a treaty, although the Inter-American Court has held that it applies to all member states of the OAS as the authoritative interpretation of human rights commitments contained in the OAS Charter. The Convention is a legally binding treaty ratified by most Latin American states. Both instruments set forth a range of fundamental rights; they are complemented by numerous specialized instruments focusing on specific issues such as torture and forced disappearance. States parties to the Convention have the option to recognize the jurisdiction of the Inter-American Court to hear contentious cases against them, and the majority of states parties (twenty-one states) has done so.

The result of this arrangement is that supranational human rights litigation before the system consists of two possible phases. Individuals alleging violations of protected rights by any OAS member state may file a petition before the Inter-American Commission. If the Commission finds the state responsible for the alleged violations, it may issue recommendations to that state concerning reparations and measures to be undertaken to prevent future violations. If, however, the state fails to implement these recommendations, and if it has recognized the contentious jurisdiction of the Inter-American Court, generally or for a particular case, the Commission may forward the case to the Court for a legally binding judgment.

The Inter-American Commission

Created in 1959, the Inter-American Commission is composed of seven independent members who meet during sessions held several times annually for approximately two weeks each, most often at the Commission's headquarters in Washington, D.C. The Commission also carries out on-site visits to evaluate the general human rights situation in member countries; publishes country and thematic reports; organizes human rights seminars, conferences, and meetings; and maintains rapporteurships on various human rights issues.

The Commission has multiple roles in relation to the Inter-American Court. Like member states of the OAS, it has standing to request advisory opinions [and] provisional measures.... [T]he Commission receives petitions from individuals alleging violations of rights protected in the system's human rights instruments. The number of complaints received by the Commission has increased significantly [see statistics at p. 992, *infra*]. Yet the Commission resolves only a small fraction of the matters before it each year....

[The Commission devotes some time at each session] to public hearings on the admissibility or merits of individual cases under consideration. It should be emphasized that even when such hearings are granted (which is by no means the rule), they ordinarily last one hour and are not dedicated primarily to taking live evidence from witnesses. When witnesses do appear, they ordinarily give a brief statement and are not subject to examination or cross-examination. Thus, as currently structured, the

Commission's fact-finding process in individual cases cannot be termed judicial. While one might imagine enhancing the procedures of the Commission to enable it to become the authoritative judicial fact-finder of the system, doing so would require significant changes that we do not foresee in the near future.

For cases in which it reaches a merits determination in favor of the petitioners, the Commission transmits its recommendations for remedying the violation in question to the state concerned. However, member states may ignore or otherwise fail to implement these recommendations, in which case the Commission may submit the matter to the Court.

Until 2001, the Commission exercised full discretionary control over whether to submit matters to the Court. For more than two decades, the Commission employed that discretion in few instances, forwarding a growing, but comparatively small number of cases to the Court. Since the entry into force of new Rules of Procedure for the Commission in 2001, the Commission's default procedure has now become to submit cases to the Court. These procedural reforms have more than doubled the number of cases sent to the Court each year, so that from 2004 to 2007 the Commission has forwarded an average of more than one dozen cases to the Court annually. This signifies a dramatic increase in workload for the Court....

The Inter-American Court

The... Court came into being...in 1979. Composed of seven judges, the Court holds sessions several times annually for approximately one to two weeks at a time, usually at its seat in San José, Costa Rica, but also, more recently, in various member states that offer to host its sessions. In addition to its jurisdiction over contentious cases, the Court exercises authority to prescribe provisional measures. It may also issue advisory opinions at the request of the Commission, OAS member states, and other organs of the OAS.

For roughly the first decade of its existence, the Court issued only advisory opinions, as the Commission failed to submit a single contentious case to it until 1986. Then, in 1988, the Court issued a landmark judgment on the merits of its first contentious case, *Velásquez Rodríguez v. Honduras*, concerning forced disappearances. During the next decade, the Court addressed first one and then three to four cases annually.

Like the Commission, the Court will not exercise jurisdiction over the merits of a case until it has satisfied itself that certain admissibility requirements have been met. Therefore, litigation before the Court has traditionally consisted of several phases, beginning with consideration of any preliminary objections to admissibility. If admitted, cases have continued to the merits phase, followed by a reparations stage (each phase routinely resulted in a separate decision, although this practice has changed in recent years). In any phase, the Court has the power to convene a public hearing and to receive the testimony of live witnesses.

When the Court determines that a state is responsible for human rights violations, it publishes a judgment setting forth the violations found and orders the state to carry out reparations measures. On the basis of its own interpretation of its mandate, the Court retains jurisdiction to monitor compliance with its judgments and issues periodic compliance orders. [It] faces considerable difficulties with respect to compliance with certain elements of its judgments. While states generally pay monetary damages, there are very few cases of full compliance, which is notably lacking as regards the obligation to bring perpetrators of violations to justice.

The working methods of the Court have evolved.... [O]riginally petitioners did not participate directly in the proceedings. Rather, once the Commission forwarded a case to the Court, it changed roles from neutral arbiter to litigant, representing the petitioners as the sole party opposing the state. In successive reforms to its Rules of Procedure, however, the Court gradually authorized greater participation of petitioners in its proceedings. As a result, today petitioners engage in Court proceedings alongside the Commission, adding a layer of complexity to the Court's work.

... [T]he Commission's procedural reforms of 2001 ... forced [the Court] roughly to triple its own rate of case resolution.

To keep pace with this remarkable increase in work, the Court has changed its procedures with a view to greatly shortening the amount of time spent on each case. In addition to combining the various phases of each case (preliminary objections, merits, reparations) into a single judgment, the Court has reduced the average number of days of public hearings devoted to each case and the average number of witnesses appearing in each case before it....

Although the Court now resolves a significantly increased number of cases each year, we emphasize that it remains an organ of extremely limited access for the vast majority of victims of human rights violations.... [The statistics reflect] an average of less than one case per year for each country that has recognized its contentious jurisdiction. Recalling that the Inter-American Commission receives more than thirteen hundred complaints each year — which already represent only a fraction of total victims of rights abuses — it is clear that the fourteen or so cases resolved by the Court each year make up a tiny percentage of the potential cases that would progress through the system if every victim of human rights violations had his or her proverbial day in court.

... [T]he Court contends with external constraints on its power. Namely, as an organ of the OAS, the Court depends on that organization's commitment to carry out its mandate. Yet throughout its existence, the Court has received relatively meager financial and political support from the OAS.

...

As of 2008, the Court's annual budget was U.S.$1,756,300, or 2 percent of the annual budget of the OAS; but this amount would suffice to fund only a portion of the Court's present activities. To continue operating at its current level, the Court depends for a large percentage of its funding on international institutions. For instance, in 2006 the European Union was [its] main financier....

...

[Another indicator of the lack of] strong political backing from the OAS [is that the latter has not] responded to repeated calls by the Court to appoint a permanent working group to monitor compliance with Court judgments and provide reports to facilitate discussion of this topic by the OAS General Assembly....

...

COMMENT ON THE INTER-AMERICAN AND EUROPEAN SYSTEMS

The experience under the European system was always part of the backdrop as the inter-American system evolved. But there have also always been significant differences. The European system was based from the start upon treaty obligations, whereas the inter-American system relied entirely upon the non-binding Declaration until 1979, and still relies on it in part. The European machinery has been more generously funded and staffed than its counterpart.

Although the European system originally had a Commission, there was no provision for regular *in-loco* visits by the Commission, whereas this became a crucial part of the activity of the Inter-American Commission. But the distinction is no longer quite so stark since given the Court's activities[49] and most importantly the Council of Europe's establishment in 1999 of the post of Commissioner for Human Rights. Especially in recent years, the Commissioner has undertaken extensive *in-loco* visits, resulting in detailed reports and recommendations to the government concerned and an ensuing dialogue.

Commentators have traditionally made much of two key distinguishing characteristics between the two systems in terms of the character of the governments involved and the nature of the most problematic violations. They have noted that where almost all parties to the ECHR were solidly democratic, many of those in the Americas were much less so. With the gradual consolidation of democracy in the Americas, and the expansion of the ECHR regime to include many former Communist states, this distinction is no longer of such importance. Similarly, commentators pointed to the fact that the inter-American institutions were more likely to be dealing with grave problems such as extrajudicial executions, enforced disappearances, torture, and arbitrary detention rather than the more standard fare that occupied the European institutions such as matters relating to sexuality, freedom of expression, and timely access to justice. But this too has been changing as the Europeans have had to confront a much broader range of violations and the inter-American system has become more familiar with the more complex types of issue that need to be adjudicated in the context of more established democratic societies. Of course, many differences remain in other respects. Where minority rights and religious freedom issues have been very important in Europe, the Americas have been more concerned with the rights of indigenous peoples, issues relating to land, and reparations for past injustices.

In terms of functions, the Inter-American Court's advisory jurisdiction is much broader than that of the ECtHR. Similarly, in its contentious jurisdiction the former is authorized to interpret not only the American Convention but also other human rights treaties ratified by OAS member states. Since 2009, another important difference is that the Inter-American Court no longer permits a state against whom a case is brought to have its own national or an ad hoc judge sitting in the case. This was

[49] P. Leach et al., *International Human Rights and Fact-Finding: An Analysis of the Fact-finding Missions Conducted by the European Commission and Court of Human Rights* (2009).

decided by the Court in an Advisory Opinion[50] that reversed previous practice and marks a meaningful difference from the ECtHR's approach.

2. THE STANDARDS TO BE APPLIED TO DIFFERENT STATES

The American Convention applies to each of the 25 states that have ratified it. But the Commission and the Court have had to confront complex issues in relation to some of the remaining ten states, especially Cuba and the United States, which have not ratified the Convention. In relation to Cuba, the Commission has adopted a series of reports ever since the Communist Government came to power in 1959. In relation to the United States, the debate turns around the status of the American Declaration. The United States has signed the American Convention but not ratified it. Its official position is that the American Declaration is clearly non-binding. It is a 'noble statement of human rights aspirations' which 'lacks the precision necessary to resolve complex legal questions'. 'It would seriously undermine the process of international lawmaking . . . to impose legal obligations on states through a process of "reinterpretation" or "inference" from a non-binding statement of principles.' It is hardly surprising then, given (1) the willingness of the United States to apply to other nations the Universal Declaration of Human Rights, the status of which is very similar, and (2) the enthusiasm of the United States for holding its Latin American neighbours to their human rights obligations, that other states within the inter-American system were keen to clarify the status of the American Declaration. The Advisory Opinion below does not mention the United States in any way, but its target is fairly clear.

In its 2006 Annual Report the IACHR restates the rationale for its endeavours to hold Cuba to account and indicates the outlines of its analysis:

> 54. Cuba is a member state of the Organization of American States since July 16, 1952. . . . The Commission has maintained that the Cuban State "is juridically answerable to the Inter-American Commission in matters that concern human rights" inasmuch as it "is party to the first international instruments established in the American hemisphere to protect human rights" and because "Resolution VI of the Eighth Meeting of Consultation excluded the Government of Cuba, not the State, from participating in the intra-American system." In this connection the IACHR stated: . . . it was not the intention of the Organization of American States to leave the Cuban people without protection. That Government's exclusion from the regional system in no way means that it is no longer bound by its international human rights obligations.
>
> 56. . . . [The following analysis refers] specifically to the need for ending economic and commercial sanctions against the Government of Cuba, inasmuch as they tend to aggravate restrictions on the actual exercise of economic, social and cultural rights by the Cuban people.

[50] Advisory Opinion, OC-20/2009, Inter-Am. Ct. H.R. (Ser. A) No. 20, P 34 (8 Sept. 2009).

57. Restrictions on political rights, freedom of expression and dissemination of ideas have amounted for decades to a permanent and systematic violation of the fundamental rights of Cuban citizens, a situation that is made worse, in particular, by the lack of independence of the judiciary.

58. The Commission finds it necessary to reiterate that the absence of free and fair elections based on universal secret suffrage as the sovereign expression of the people violates the right to political participation . . .

INTER-AMERICAN COURT OF HUMAN RIGHTS, ADVISORY OPINION OC-10/89, 14 JULY 1989

Interpretation of the American Declaration of the Rights and Duties of Man within the Framework of Article 64 of the American Convention on Human Rights: Requested by the Government of the Republic of Colombia

. . .

2. [In February 1988, the Government of Colombia sought an advisory opinion on] the following question:

Does Article 64 authorize the Inter-American Court of Human Rights to render advisory opinions at the request of a member state or one of the organs of the OAS, regarding the interpretation of the American Declaration of the Rights and Duties of Man, adopted by the Ninth International Conference of American States in Bogotá in 1948?

. . .

17. [At the public hearing the] representatives of the United States of America said that:

> It is the position of the United States that the American Declaration is not a treaty, and that therefore the Court does not have jurisdiction under Article 64 to interpret it or determine its normative status within the inter-American human rights system.
>
> . . .
>
> Because the Declaration is not and never has been a treaty, the United States believes that the Court has no jurisdiction to consider the present request, and should therefore dismiss it.
>
> . . .
>
> In the event that the Court does reach the issues of the normative status of the Declaration, the United States' view is that the Declaration remains for all member states of the O. A. S. what it was when it was adopted: an agreed statement of non-binding general human rights principles.
>
> . . .
>
> The United States must state, with all due respect, that it would seriously undermine the established international law of treaties to say that the Declaration is legally binding.
>
> . . .

IV

29. The Court will now address the merits of the question before it.

30. Article 64(1) of the Convention authorizes the Court to render advisory opinions "regarding the interpretation of this Convention or of other treaties concerning the protection of human rights in the American states." . . .

. . .

33. In attempting to define the word "treaty" as the term is employed in Article 64(1), it is sufficient for now to say that a "treaty" is, at the very least, an international instrument of the type that is governed by the two Vienna Conventions [on the law of treaties]. . . . [It is clear] that the Declaration is not a treaty as defined by the Vienna Conventions because it was not approved as such, and that, consequently, it is also not a treaty within the meaning of Article 64(1).

34. Here it must be recalled that the American Declaration was adopted by the Ninth International Conference of American States (Bogotá, 1948) through a resolution adopted by the Conference itself. It was neither conceived nor drafted as a treaty. . . .

. . .

[As noted] on September 26, 1949, by the Inter-American Committee of Jurisconsults . . .:

> It is evident that the Declaration of Bogotá does not create a contractual juridical obligation, but it is also clear that it demonstrates a well-defined orientation toward the international protection of the fundamental rights of the human person. . . .

35. The mere fact that the Declaration is not a treaty does not necessarily compel the conclusion that the Court lacks the power to render an advisory opinion containing an interpretation of the American Declaration.

36. In fact, the American Convention refers to the Declaration in paragraph three of its Preamble which reads as follows:

> *Considering* that these principles have been set forth in the Charter of the Organization of the American States, in the American Declaration of the Rights and Duties of Man, and in the Universal Declaration of Human Rights, and that they have been reaffirmed and refined in other international instruments, worldwide as well as regional in scope.

And in Article 29(d) which indicates:

> . . .
>
> No provision of this convention shall be interpreted as:
>
> . . .
>
> d. excluding or limiting the effect that the American Declaration of the Rights and Duties of Man and other international acts of the same nature may have.

From the foregoing, it follows that, in interpreting the Convention in the exercise of its advisory jurisdiction, the Court may have to interpret the Declaration.

37. ... [T]o determine the legal status of the American Declaration it is appropriate to look to the inter-American system of today in the light of the evolution it has undergone since the adoption of the Declaration, rather than to examine the normative value and significance which that instrument was believed to have had in 1948.

38. The evolution of the here relevant "inter-American law" mirrors on the regional level the developments in contemporary international law and specially in human rights law, which distinguished that law from classical international law to a significant extent. That is the case, for example, with the duty to respect certain essential human rights, which is today considered to be an *erga omnes* obligation....

39. The Charter of the Organization refers to the fundamental rights of man in [various provisions] ... but it does not list or define them. The member states of the Organization have, through its diverse organs, given specificity to the human rights mentioned in the Charter and to which the Declaration refers.

40. This is the case of Article 112 of the Charter ...:

> There shall be an Inter-American Commission on Human Rights, whose principal function shall be to promote the observance and protection of human rights and to serve as a consultative organ of the Organization in these matters.
>
> An inter-American convention on human rights shall determine the structure, competence, and procedure of this Commission, as well as those of other organs responsible for these matters.

Article 150 of the Charter provides as follows:

> Until the inter-American convention on human rights, referred to in Chapter XVIII (Chapter XVI of the Charter as amended by the Protocol of Cartagena de Indias), enters into force, the present Inter-American Commission on Human Rights shall keep vigilance over the observance of human rights.

41. These norms authorize the Inter-American Commission to protect human rights. These rights are none other than those enunciated and defined in the American Declaration. That conclusion results from Article 1 of the Commission's Statute ... [adopted in 1979]:

> 1. The Inter-American Commission on Human Rights is an organ of the Organization of the American States, created to promote the observance and defense of human rights and to serve as consultative organ of the Organization in this matter.
> 2. For the purposes of the present Statute, human rights are understood to be:
>   a. The rights set forth in the American Convention on Human Rights, in relation to the States Parties thereto;
>   b. The rights set forth in the American Declaration of the Rights and Duties of Man, in relation to the other member states.

Articles 18, 19 and 20 of the Statute enumerate these functions.

42. The General Assembly of the Organization has also repeatedly recognized that the American Declaration is a source of international obligations for the member states of the OAS. . . .

43. Hence it may be said that by means of an authoritative interpretation, the member states of the Organization have signaled their agreement that the Declaration contains and defines the fundamental human rights referred to in the Charter. Thus the Charter of the Organization cannot be interpreted and applied as far as human rights are concerned without relating its norms, consistent with the practice of the organs of the OAS, to the corresponding provisions of the Declaration.

44. In view of the fact that the Charter of the Organization and the American Convention are treaties with respect to which the Court has advisory jurisdiction by virtue of Article 64(1), it follows that the Court is authorized, within the framework and limits of its competence, to interpret the American Declaration and to render an advisory opinion relating to it whenever it is necessary to do so in interpreting those instruments.

QUESTIONS

1. Is the Commission's rationale for continuing to examine the human rights situation in Cuba convincing?

2. On the basis of the Court's Advisory Opinion, what is the legal status of the American Declaration, and how would you compare it in that respect with the Universal Declaration, discussed at pp. 14, *supra*?

3. THE COMMISSION AT WORK

Over the years, the Inter-American Commission has evolved significantly in terms of its techniques. As a former Commission President, Tom Farer, has noted, the original mandate provided to the Commission was vague and open-ended and the Commission could have decided in the 1970s to concentrate its efforts on individual cases. In Farer's view, this would have involved 'futilely but respectably pursuing an endless paper trail of victims' complaints and official denials'. But it opted for a different path:

> Instead, focusing upon the investigation of the facts and the preparation of country reports on the actual conditions that it found, the Commission converted itself into an accusatory agency, a kind of Hemispheric Grand Jury, storming around Latin America to vacuum up evidence of high crimes and misdemeanors and marshaling it into bills of indictment in the form of country reports for delivery to the political organs of the OAS and the court of public opinion.[51]

[51] T. Farer, 'The Rise of the Inter-American Human Rights Regime: No Longer a Unicorn, not Yet an Ox', in D. Harris & S. Livingstone (eds.), *The Inter-American System of Human Rights* (1998), 32.

The Commission's early success with *in-loco* visits to countries experiencing significant human rights problems contributed greatly to enhancing its stature. Its reports on Argentina at the height of the problem of disappearances, in 1978, remain a classic in terms of effective fact-finding and follow-up. But over the years the balance of its activities has shifted significantly. Today it processes a relatively large number of individual complaints, but undertakes rather fewer country visits. It has also developed a system of rapporteurs that adds a new dimension to its work. The following provides a statistical overview of its activities in 2011:

> [T]he Commission received over 1600 new petitions, held three periods of sessions, managed over 8,500 pending matters and, in connection to these, issued 67 Reports on Admissibility, 11 on Inadmissibility, eight Reports on Friendly Settlement, 54 Reports on Archiving, 25 Reports on the Merits. The Commission further published five Reports on the Merits and presented 23 cases to the consideration of the Inter-American Court, took cognizance of over 400 urgent requests for precautionary measures, held 91 hearings and 54 Working Meetings, carried out over 30 Working Visits led by its Members as Country or Thematic Rapporteurs; . . . issued 138 Press Releases and conducted 5 Seminars and Training Sessions.[52]

We now consider briefly each of the main functions it currently performs.

The Individual Complaints System

The materials in Chapter 5 (see pp. 415–32, *supra*) relating to the treatment of detainees in Guantánamo, provide an instructive example of the Inter-American Commission's complaints procedures at work.

The number of complaints received by the Commission has grown steadily. In 1997 there were 435, in 2001 there were 885, and by 2011 there were 1,658. Of the latter, only 25 per cent were accepted for processing, of which 65 came from Colombia, 40 from Argentina, 33 from Peru, 23 each from Chile and Mexico, 15 from Costa Rica, 14 from Ecuador, and 11 from the United States. The Commission nevertheless had a troubling backlog of 6,134 complaints pending evaluation. One of the most significant but also controversial activities of the Commission is the issuance of precautionary measures. These are the inter-American system's equivalent of the interim measures adopted by the ICCPR Committee and considered above (p. 763). In 2011, the Commission received 422 requests for precautionary measures, and granted 57. In the following excerpt, we see the Commission's explanation of the origins of its powers in this domain and how it exercises them as well as its explanation of the measures ordered in relation to the building of a dam in Brazil.

[52] Inter-American Commission on Human Rights, Position Document on the Process of Strengthening of the Inter American System for the Protection of Human Rights, OEA/Ser.L/V/II, Doc. 68 (8 Apr. 2012), no. 29.

ANNUAL REPORT OF THE INTER-AMERICAN COMMISSION ON HUMAN RIGHTS 2011 (2012)

CHAPTER III

...

C. Petitions and cases before the Inter-American Commission on Human Rights

1. Precautionary measures granted by the IACHR in 2011

6. The inter-American human rights system has used precautionary measures for over three decades.... The IACHR's authority to request urgent measures or order precautionary measures is reflective of a common practice in international human rights law.... The Commission has thus been performing its assigned mandate under Article 106 of the OAS Charter, which is "to promote the observance and protection of human rights"....

The history and legal framework of precautionary measures

7. [The Commission, in adopting its own Rules of Procedure in 1980, included Article 26 stating] that "provisional measures" were called for "[i]n urgent cases, when it becomes necessary to avoid irreparable damage to persons." [This step, along with the mechanism's] gradual development through application in practice fit the pattern by which the inter-American human rights system has traditionally cultivated its mechanisms of protection. This article follows from the IACHR's duty to ensure compliance with the commitments undertaken by the states parties, a duty set forth in Article 18 of the Commission's Statute and Article 41 of the American Convention, and is based on the states' general obligation to respect human rights and to ensure their free and full exercise to all persons subject to their jurisdiction (Article 1 of the American Convention), to adopt legislative and other measures necessary to give effect to those rights (Article 2), and to comply in good faith with the obligations undertaken in the Convention and the OAS Charter. The states themselves have frequently acknowledged how vital precautionary measures have been to ensuring the effective observance of human rights in very serious and urgent circumstances.

8. Recognizing the intrinsic value of the work that the Inter-American Commission performs, the OAS General Assembly has encouraged the member states to follow up on the Commission's recommendations and precautionary measures. When the General Assembly adopted the Inter-American Convention on Forced Disappearance of Persons in 1994, the member states acknowledged how effective precautionary measures were for purposes of examining allegations of this nature.

9. The system of precautionary measures has been a feature of the Commission's Rules of Procedure for over 30 years. The most recent amendment of the Rules of Procedure took effect on December 31, 2009. Article 25 describes the procedure for precautionary measures and how a precautionary measure may be related to the subject matter of a petition or case (Article 25.1); the adoption of precautionary

measures independently of any pending petition or case (Article 25.2); the individual or collective nature of precautionary measures (Article 25.3); the fact that the IACHR is to request relevant information from the state concerned, unless the urgency of the situation is such that the immediate granting of the measures is warranted (Article 25.5); the procedures for seeking withdrawal of the request for precautionary measures and the grounds for the Commission to withdraw its request for precautionary measures (Articles 25.7 and 25.8), and other points. In the amendment process, the Commission gave extensive consideration to the comments and criticisms submitted by many OAS member states, civil society organizations, academics and private citizens from across the hemisphere, in response to the consultations instituted concerning the text of the preliminary draft amendment.

Precautionary measures: their use as a means of ensuring observance of fundamental rights and preventing irreparable harm

10. In the last 30 years, precautionary measures have been invoked to protect thousands of persons or groups of persons at risk by virtue of their work or affiliation. They include human rights defenders, journalists, trade unionists, vulnerable groups such as women, children, Afro-descendant communities, indigenous peoples, displaced persons, LGTBI communities and persons deprived of their liberty. They have also been used to protect witnesses, officers of the court, persons about to be deported to a country where they might be subjected to torture or other forms of cruel and inhuman treatment, persons sentenced to the death penalty, and others. [And they have been used] to protect the right to health and the right of the family . . . and in situations involving the environment, where the life or health of persons or the way of life of indigenous peoples in their ancestral territory may be imperiled, and in other situations.

. . .

14. When it examines a request seeking precautionary measures, the Commission looks for three essential preconditions: i) gravity; ii) urgency, and iii) the risk of irreparable harm to persons.

15. The Commission's examination of requests seeking precautionary measures looks at the specifics of each situation. Hence, the Commission's analysis cannot be governed by strict criteria that must apply to each and every case; instead, it has to look at the nature of the risk and the harm that the precautionary measure seeks to avert. With this clarification, the following are some examples of the factors that the Commission has weighed when considering requests. . . . [The list is not exhaustive.]

16. As for [urgency] the risk or threat involved must be imminent. . . .

. . .

19. On the matter of irreparable harm, the events that warrant the request must suggest that there is a reasonable probability that the harm will materialize; the request must not rely on legal rights or interests that can be remedied.

. . .

21. Before arriving at a final decision as to whether to grant or reject the request seeking precautionary measures, the IACHR may request additional information from the person applying for precautionary measures or from the State concerned, or from both. Much of what the Commission does is to follow up requests for information from the State and from the petitioners. The failure of the State or of the

party requesting precautionary measures to reply to the Commission's request for information is a factor that the IACHR will consider when deciding whether or not to grant the requested measure.

. . .

23. In compliance with their international obligations, States must provide effective protection to prevent the risk from materializing. The parties are in the best position to know what type of tangible or other measures are called for to address the situation and prevent further danger.

24. The IACHR has various tools at its disposal for follow-up and monitoring of precautionary measures: exchanges of communications; working meetings or hearings convened during the IACHR's sessions; follow-up meetings during in loco or working visits by the Commission or the country rapporteurs; press releases, thematic reports or country reports.

25. The Commission welcomes the States' positive response to the precautionary measures. In carrying out the Commission's requests for precautionary measures, the States have ordered specific protection measures for beneficiaries (for example, bodyguards, security at office buildings, direct lines of communication with the authorities, protection of ancestral territory, and others), taking into account the opinion of the beneficiary and the beneficiary's representative; their active participation by supplying information requested by the IACHR or participating in working meetings or hearings held to follow up on precautionary measures; creating inter-institutional working groups to implement the protection measures requested by the inter-American system; and introducing compliance with precautionary measures into their case law and legislation.

Precautionary measures granted in 2011

26. Below is an overview of the precautionary measures granted in 2011. . . .

. . .

BRAZIL

PM 382/10 — Indigenous Communities of the Xingu River Basin, Pará, Brazil

32. On April 1, 2011, the IACHR granted precautionary measures for the members of [11 specified] indigenous communities. . . . The request for precautionary measure alleges that the life and physical integrity of the beneficiaries is at risk due to the impact of the construction of the Belo Monte hydroelectric power plant. The [Commission requested that Brazil] immediately suspend the licensing process for the [plant] and stop any construction work from moving forward until certain minimum conditions are met. The State must (1) conduct consultation processes, in fulfillment of its international obligations — meaning prior consultations that are free, informed, of good faith, culturally appropriate, and with the aim of reaching an agreement — in relation to each of the affected indigenous communities that are beneficiaries of these precautionary measures; (2) guarantee that, in order for this to be an informed consultation process, the indigenous communities have access beforehand to the project's Social and Environmental Impact Study, in an accessible format, including translation into the respective indigenous languages; (3) adopt measures to protect the life and physical integrity of the members of the indigenous

peoples in voluntary isolation of the Xingu Basin, and to prevent the spread of diseases and epidemics....

[In response to the Commission's request, Brazil called the proposed measures 'precipitous and unwarranted', severed formal relations with the Commission, recalled its OAS ambassador, and froze its annual $800,000 contribution to the IACHR. A key Senator called the request 'absurd' and added that it 'even threatens Brazilian sovereignty'. Critics of the project noted that it had been controversial since 1975, would flood nearly 200 square miles in the Amazon and displace 50,000 people, and lead to the disappearance of 1,000 species of plants and animals. Protests had been led by FUNAI (the National Indian Foundation of Brazil), Amazon Watch, the vocalist Sting' and movie director James Cameron. For its part, the Brazilian Government claimed that it would be the world's third largest dam, provide thousands of construction jobs, supply electricity to 23 million homes, and be a source of clean and renewable energy. It is said to be the first of as many as 70 dams scheduled for construction in the region.[53]]

33. On July 29, 2011,... based on information submitted by the State and the petitioners, [the Commission] modified the aim of the measure. [It focused especially on item (3) in paragraph 32 above and also requested the state to guarantee] that the processes still pending to regularize the ancestral lands of the Xingu Basin indigenous peoples will be finalized soon, and [to] adopt effective measures to protect those ancestral lands against intrusion and occupation by non-indigenous people and against the exploitation or deterioration of their natural resources. Moreover, the IACHR decided that the debate between the parties on prior consultation and informed consent with regard to the Belo Monte project has turned into a discussion on the merits of the matter, which goes beyond the scope of precautionary measures.

NOTE

In the course of 2011–2012 discussions about 'strengthening' the inter-American human rights system, OAS states proposed reforms designed to 'give greater clarity to the system of precautionary measures'. They called for: 'more precise objective criteria for granting, reviewing,... or lifting precautionary measures'; 'objective criteria or parameters for determining "serious and urgent situations" and the imminence of the harm'; the provision of 'reasons for the legal and factual elements' in the Commission's orders, including disclosure of all evidence available to it; and the provision of 'a reasonable amount of time for states to implement precautionary measures'.[54] In a conference to discuss these and other reforms, the OAS Secretary General said:

> the Inter-American Commission is not a court.... [W]hy can't [its representative] go to countries to promote solutions? [For example,] if there is a problem with a

[53] See generally L. Birns & K. Soltis, 'Controversy in the Amazon: Brazil Disregards the Inter-American Commission on Human Rights at Potentially Great Cost, Council on Hemispheric Affairs', 9 June 2011, at www.coha.org/controversy-in-the-amazon/.

[54] Report of the Special Working Group to Reflect on the Workings of the Inter-American Commission on Human Rights with a View to Strengthening the Inter-American Human Rights System for Consideration by the Permanent Council, OEA/Ser.G, GT/SIDH-13/11 rev. 2 (13 Dec. 2011), pp. 10–11.

> dam somewhere, why will not the . . . commission . . . say 'we have a problem'? Why don't we find some way to address it before having to [order measures]? Why must we communicate only by letter with governments or by making statements without listening [to them].[55]

The controversy over precautionary measures is also part of a larger debate over how to ensure more effective compliance with the Commission's recommendations. In evaluating compliance, the Commission uses three categories: (1) total compliance; (2) partial compliance; and (3) compliance pending (covering cases in which no steps have been taken, or the state has explicitly indicated that it will not comply, or the state has not reported to the IACHR and the latter has no information from other sources that would suggest compliance). In its 2011 report the Commission tracks the status of its recommendations contained in the reports on individual cases since 2002 — a total of 154 cases. Of these, it found 25 to be in total compliance, 97 to be in partial compliance, and compliance was pending in 32 cases. By comparison, in 2006 it had found total compliance in only one case out of 86.

In a Strategic Plan drawn up by the Commission in 2011, the main challenges confronting it are to achieve universal adherence to all inter-American human rights instruments, to improve the access of victims to the system, to enhance compliance with its recommendations, and to expand the available resources. Its budget in 2011 was almost $9.5 million, of which 54 per cent came from contributions outside the OAS budget (almost half of which came from European countries). In the plan, it sets itself a goal of increasing this to $35 million by 2016,[56] although it is unclear where these funds will come from unless member states show a dramatic change of heart.

QUESTIONS

1. What does the Commission mean when it says that its approach to precautionary measures fits the pattern by which the system has 'traditionally cultivated its mechanisms of protection' (para. 7)?

2. To what extent did the Commission back down in its confrontation with Brazil over precautionary measures? Would the reforms proposed by states improve the functioning of the system? And how should the Commission respond to the suggestion made by the OAS Secretary-General?

Interstate Complaints

The American Convention establishes an optional interstate complaints procedure (Arts. 45–51). As in the United Nations setting, such procedures have been rarely used. Assuming the states in question have recognized the Commission's competence for

[55] OAS Press Release, 30 May 2012, at www.oas.org/en/media_center/press_release.asp?sCodigo=E-194/12.

[56] Inter-American Commission on Human Rights, Strategic Plan 2011–2015, p. 150, at www.oas.org/en/iachr/docs/pdf/IACHRStrategicPlan20112015.pdf.

this purpose, and if the complaint is deemed admissible, the Commission will seek to reach a friendly settlement (Art. 48). If a settlement is not reached, the Commission shall report and may 'make such proposals and recommendations as it sees fit' (Art. 50). In March 2007 the Commission presented its first report on such a complaint.[57] It concerned allegations of systematic discrimination against Nicaraguan citizens resident in Costa Rica. The complaint was deemed inadmissible by virtue of the complainant's failure to submit the complaint within six months of its having been notified of a final decision being handed down in Costa Rica. Nonetheless, the Commission took the opportunity, in a 69-page judgment, to explore the applicable procedures, develop its jurisprudence on admissibility in such cases, exculpate Costa Rica in relation to some of the most serious charges, acknowledge Costa Rica's admission of the existence of discrimination and xenophobia in its territory, and to conclude by condemning 'all acts of discrimination or xenophobia against migrant persons of any origin' and recalling the 'obligation of states to protect individuals against discrimination, whether this occurs within the public sphere or among private parties'.

In October 2010, the Commission declared an application by Ecuador against Colombia to be admissible, alleging several violations of the American Convention on Human Rights. Ecuador commenced the interstate petition in June 2009 on behalf of one of its nationals killed during a military operation by Colombian forces on Ecuadorian territory to fight guerrilla fighters belonging to the Revolutionary Armed Forces of Colombia (also known as FARC). In March 2008, Colombia, without Ecuador's prior knowledge or approval, attacked a camp occupied by members of FARC inside Ecuadorian territory, killing 25. One of the bodies taken back to Colombia turned out to be that of an Ecuadorian, whose connection to FARC was contested. Despite requests to do so, Colombia failed to investigate fully the circumstances of his death. Ecuador alleged violations of the rights to life, humane treatment, judicial guarantees, and judicial protection. The Commission rejected Colombia's claims that international humanitarian law should apply and that domestic remedies had not been exhausted.[58]

Country Visits

As noted earlier, very few country visits are today undertaken by the Commission as a whole. In most cases, a single Commissioner undertakes a 'working visit' and issues a detailed press release at the end of the visit which outlines the major problems he or she has identified. The thematic reports, noted below, also play an important role in reporting on relevant practices at the national level.

In addition, Chapter IV of the Commission's Annual Report is focused on 'Human Rights Developments in the Region'. The stated aim is to provide the OAS with updated information on the human rights situation in countries that have 'been the subject of the Commission's special attention' or where an emerging problem is seen. Inclusion in the Chapter is an unwelcome 'honour' for any state. Since 1997,

[57] Report No. 11/07, Interstate Case 01/06, *Nicaragua v. Costa Rica* (8 Mar. 2007).

[58] Report No. 112/10, Inter-State Petition IP-02, Admissibility, Franklin Guillermo Aisalla Molina, Ecuador — Colombia, OEA/Ser.L/V/II.140, Doc. 10 (21 Oct. 2010).

the Commission has sought to apply five criteria in selecting countries for this purpose: (1) states ruled by governments that have not come to power through secret, genuine, periodic, and free elections; (2) states in which human rights 'have been, in effect, suspended totally or in part, by virtue of the imposition of exceptional measures'; (3) states which commit 'massive and grave violations'; (4) 'states that are in a process of transition from any of the above three situations'; and (5) where 'temporary or structural situations', such as major institutional crises, 'seriously affect the enjoyment of fundamental rights'. Based on these criteria, the Commission's 2011 report focused on four states: Colombia, Cuba, Honduras, and Venezuela. These states were sent the respective drafts in advance, but only Colombia and Honduras responded with observations. The section on Venezuela, which follows, provides an example of the approach used in a situation in which the Commission has been unable to gain access to the country concerned.

ANNUAL REPORT OF THE INTER-AMERICAN COMMISSION ON HUMAN RIGHTS 2011

(2012)

CHAPTER IV

...

VENEZUELA

I. INTRODUCTION

394. ...The IACHR based its analysis on information compiled during its hearings and information available from other public sources, as well as information compiled through the mechanisms for petitions, cases and precautionary measures....

...

397. [The Commission last visited Venezuela in 2002. While it has continued to monitor the situation, requests to visit have been denied.]

...

II. ANALYSIS OF THE SITUATION REGARDING CIVIL AND POLITICAL RIGHTS

A. Government actions to guarantee the right to life and personal integrity and democratic citizen security

400. The Commission has indicated on multiple occasions that States must take steps not only to protect their citizens from human rights violations committed by State agents, but also to prevent and punish acts of violence among private citizens....

[The report then relies significantly on Venezuela's report under the UN Human Rights Council's Universal Periodic Review procedure, and reports by NGOs and others in the same context.]

405. ... [During 2011] the Commission continued to receive information on citizen insecurity as well as specific actions against the population by police forces.

406. A case in point that the IACHR has been following closely involves the Barrios family. Between 1998 and 2010, six members of the Barrios family were killed.... [Two] were extrajudicially executed by the police of Aragua, and in processing this case the IACHR determined that there would be sufficient evidence to conclude that the same thing happened to [three other family members].

407. The Commission submitted the case of the Barrios family to the Inter-American Court of Human Rights in the first half of 2010. In January 2011, [another family member who was an eyewitness to one of the extrajudicial executions], suffered an attack on his life, which was condemned by the Commission. Subsequently, on May 28, 2011 [another family member], aged 28, was murdered by two persons dressed in black who shot him several times. [The latter] was the beneficiary of provisional measures issued by the Inter-American Court of Human Rights. The Commission condemned the murder and pointed out that

> The IACHR and the IA Court have followed this situation through all available mechanisms, including requests for information, precautionary and provisional measures, Commission reports on admissibility and the merits, and submission of an application to the Inter-American Court. However, the Venezuelan State has not adopted the necessary measures to protect the life of the members of this family, who continue to be targets of assassination, detentions, raids, threats and harassment. Moreover, the State has not ordered an effective investigation of these crimes, which remain in impunity.

The Barrios family is being eliminated while the State stands by, ignoring the calls, decisions, recommendations and orders of the two bodies of the Inter-American System on Human Rights.

B. Respect and guarantee of political rights

412. On December 17, 2010 a special session of the National Assembly enacted the "Law authorizing the President of the Republic to issue decrees with the rank, value and force of law, on the subject matters delegated to him," known as the "Enabling Law." ... [I]t was reported that starting on December 16, 2010, the National Assembly began an 18-day period of special sessions during which it enacted and amended more than 11 laws that would be incompatible with the Convention. These laws increased the power and control of the Executive Branch over various areas of society.... In addition, the National Assembly's Internal Rules of Procedure and Debate were amended to limit the number of sessions that can be held by new deputies in the Assembly, as well as their participation....

...

D. Guarantees for legal due process and effective access to justice

...

3. Situation of alleged political prisoners

476. … [The Commission received allegations about political prisoners, including] persons publicly known for their critical personal opinions or who have carried out public functions in which they have acted in ways displeasing to the Executive Branch.

477. It was reported that in most cases, the initial arrest was arbitrary and illegal, based on raids conducted without proper judicial guarantee. … [There is alleged to be] a "programmed and concerted effort among the organs of justice to criminalize and punish those citizens, using political prosecution for the most serious crimes established in the legal system."

III. ANALYSIS OF THE SITUATION OF ECONOMIC, SOCIAL AND CULTURAL RIGHTS

…

480. In its [July 2011 UPR report to the UN] Venezuela reported that its achievements in terms of eradicating poverty include reducing the number of households living in extreme poverty, which fell from 21% in 1998 to 7.1% in 2010 … [and] that it is the country with the least inequality in Latin America. …

…

485. Based on the information received, the Commission acknowledges and appreciates the progress made in [this area] … The priority that the State assigns to these measures is essential in guaranteeing a decent life for the Venezuelan population and an important basis for preserving democratic stability.

[The report then notes widespread expropriations of private property in order to expand the availability of public housing.]

490. … [T]he Commission recalls the need to establish a balance between the State's duty to guarantee the right to housing and the right to private property enshrined in Article 21 of the American Convention.

…

V. RECOMMENDATIONS

1. Guarantee the full exercise of political rights to all individuals. …
2. Refrain from taking reprisals or using the punitive power of the State to intimidate or sanction individuals based on their political opinions, and guarantee the plurality of opportunities and arenas for democratic activity. …
3. Effectively guarantee the separation and independence of the branches of government. …

…

6. Adopt the necessary measures to protect the life and personal integrity of all persons. …

…

8. Urgently adopt the measures necessary to correct the procedural delays and the high percentage of persons deprived of liberty without a final verdict, thereby avoiding the excessive, unnecessary and disproportionate reliance on preventive detention or detention pending trial. …

9. Step up efforts so as to gradually give full effect to economic, social and cultural rights while ensuring that this does not come at the cost of the people's other basic rights....

DOUG CASSEL, WILL CHAVEZ REMOVE VENEZUELA FROM THE INTER-AMERICAN COMMISSION?

Opinio Juris (blog), 11 May 2012, at http://opiniojuris.org/2012/05/11/chavez-removes-venezuela-from-iachr/

Venezuelan President Hugo Chavez on April 30 directed his Council of State (a policy advisory body) to study Venezuela's "withdrawal" from the [IACHR].... This is the latest move in the Bolivarian Republic's long record of denouncing the Commission and the [Court] as tools of US imperialism....

...

Withdrawing from the Commission, however, is not so simple. The Commission has a dual status, both as a treaty body under the American Convention on Human Rights, and as a body established by the Charter of the Organization of American States (OAS). Under the Convention, the Commission monitors human rights and receives complaints of violations by states parties, such as Venezuela. If States (such as Venezuela) which accept the contentious jurisdiction of the Inter-American Court fail to comply with Commission recommendations, the Commission can refer the case to the Court for a legally binding judgment.

Venezuela cannot exit merely from the Commission or from the Court. When Peruvian strongman Alberto Fujimori tried to withdraw from the Court in the 1990s, the Court ruled that countries cannot withdraw from its jurisdiction while remaining in the Convention. Their only exit route is to withdraw from the Convention entirely.

But denouncing the Convention requires a year's advance notice, during which countries remain bound by the Convention. During that year, any new violations may be brought before the Commission and eventually — even after the expiration of the year — may be referred by the Commission to the Court.

Even denouncing the Convention and waiting a year would not free Venezuela from the Commission. For States not party to the Convention, the Commission as an OAS Charter body receives complaints and assesses human rights violations by the standards of the American Declaration on the Rights and Duties of Man. Only by withdrawing from the OAS altogether could Chavez "withdraw" from the Commission as a Charter body.

...

Even governments which generally support the Inter-American Human Rights system have grievances against the Commission, and have supported "reforms" which could weaken it. Although the Commission has made mistakes, most of this tension is inherent in a system in which the Commission is called upon to police the human rights conduct of governments.

It does not help that the US and Canada — the principal funders of the OAS, and thus of the Commission's regular budget — have not joined the Convention. . . .

The system of rapporteurs

Starting in 1990, the Inter-American Commission began creating thematic rapporteurships in order to devote attention to certain groups, communities, and peoples that are particularly at risk. To date there are nine such initiatives: Rapporteurship on the Rights of Indigenous Peoples (created in 1990); Rapporteurship on the Rights of Women (1994); Rapporteurship on the Rights of Migrant Workers and Their Families (1996); Special Rapporteurship for Freedom of Expression (1997); Rapporteurship on the Rights of the Child (1998); Rapporteurship on Human Rights Defenders (2001); Rapporteurship on the Rights of Persons Deprived of Liberty (2004); Rapporteurship on the Rights of Afro-Descendants and against Racial Discrimination (2005); Unit on the Rights of Lesbian, Gay, Trans, Bisexual and Intersex Persons (2011). Many of the rapporteurs produce very detailed analytical studies which are published by the Commission and make an important contribution to the understanding of the legal and policy issues involved.[59]

QUESTIONS

1. How would you explain the fact that the Inter-American Commission receives fewer than 2,000 cases per year, in contrast to the tens of thousands received by the ECtHR?

2. How effective can the Commission's reporting be in the absence of a visit to the country?

3. What factors might deter a country like Venezuela from withdrawing from the entire system?

4. THE COURT IN ACTION

In the inter-American system, the Court plays a more restricted role than does its equivalent in the European system. Its governing provisions bear a close relationship to those of the ECtHR, although there are also key differences.

Initially the Court and the Commission saw each other as rivals. The Commission, established over two decades earlier, was very reluctant to refer contentious cases to the Court. The situation changed only in the late 1980s, beginning with the referral of three cases involving enforced disappearances in Honduras. The principal case, *Velásquez Rodríguez*, appears below. It was the first contentious case initiated by an

[59] E.g. Report on the Human Rights of Persons Deprived of Liberty in the Americas, OEA/Ser.L/V/II, Doc. 64 (31 Dec. 2011).

individual that involved systemic state violence. Outside as well as inside the inter-American system, it has proved to be one of the most influential and cited decisions of an international human rights tribunal.

VELÁSQUEZ RODRÍGUEZ CASE

Inter-American Court of Human Rights, 1988, Ser. C, No. 4

[This case arose out of a period of political turbulence, violence, and repression in Honduras. It originated in a petition against Honduras received by the Inter-American Commission on Human Rights in 1981. The thrust of the petition was that Angel Manfredo Velásquez Rodríguez was arrested without warrant in 1981 by members of the National Office of Investigations (DNI) and the G-2 of the Armed Forces. The 'arrest' was a seizure by seven armed men dressed in civilian clothes who abducted him in an unlicensed car. The petition referred to eyewitnesses reporting his later detention, 'harsh interrogation and cruel torture'. Police and security forces continued to deny the arrest and detention. Velásquez had disappeared. The petition alleged that through this conduct, Honduras violated several articles of the American Convention on Human Rights.

In 1986, Velásquez was still missing, and the Commission concluded that the Government of Honduras 'had not offered convincing proof that would allow the Commission to determine that the allegations are not true'. Honduras had recognized the contentious jurisdiction of the Inter-American Court of Human Rights, to which the Commission referred the matter. The Court held closed and open hearings, called witnesses, and requested the production of evidence and documents. The statement of facts below is taken from the Court's opinion and consists both of its independent findings and its affirmation of some findings of the Commission.

The Commission presented witnesses to testify whether 'between the years 1981 and 1984 (the period in which Manfredo Velásquez disappeared) there were numerous cases of persons who were kidnapped and who then disappeared, these actions being imputable to the Armed Forces of Honduras and enjoying the acquiescence of the Government of Honduras', and whether in those years there were effective domestic remedies to protect such kidnapped persons. Several witnesses testified that they were kidnapped, imprisoned in clandestine jails, and tortured by members of the Armed Forces. Explicit testimony described the severity of the torture — including beatings, electric shocks, hanging, burning, drugs, and sexual abuse — to which witnesses had been subjected. Several witnesses indicated how they knew that their captors and torturers were connected with the military. The Court received testimony indicating that 'somewhere between 112 and 130 individuals were disappeared from 1981 to 1984'.

According to testimony, the kidnapping followed a pattern, such as use of cars with tinted glass, with false licence plates and with disguised kidnappers. A witness who was President of the Committee for the Defense of Human Rights in Honduras testified about the existence of a unit in the Armed Forces that carried out the disappearance, giving details about its organization and commanding personnel. A former member of the Armed Forces testified that he had belonged to the battalion carrying out the kidnapping. He confirmed parts of the testimony of witnesses, claiming that he had been told of the kidnapping and later torture and killing of Velásquez, whose body was dismembered and buried in different places. All such testimony was denied by military officers and the Director of Honduran Intelligence.

The Commission also presented evidence showing that from 1981–1984 domestic judicial remedies in Honduras were inadequate to protect human rights. Courts were slow and judges were often ignored by police. Authorities denied detentions. Judges charged with executing the writs of *habeas corpus* were threatened and on several occasions imprisoned. Law professors and lawyers defending political prisoners were pressured not to act; one of the two lawyers to bring a writ of *habeas corpus* was arrested. In no case was the writ effective in relation to a disappeared person.

In view of threats against witnesses it had called, the Commission asked the Court to take provisional measures contemplated by the Convention. Soon thereafter, the Commission reported the death of a Honduran summoned by the Court to appear as a witness, killed 'on a public thoroughfare [in the capital city] by a group of armed men who . . . fled in a vehicle'. Four days later the Court was informed of two more assassinations, one victim being a man who had testified before the Court as a witness hostile to the government. After a public hearing, the Court decided on 'additional provisional measures' requiring Honduras to report within two weeks: (1) on measures that it adopted to protect persons connected with the case; (2) on its judicial investigations of threats against such persons; and (3) on its investigations of the assassinations.

The Court's opinion refers to several articles of the American Convention. *Article 4* gives every person 'the right to have his life respected. . . . No one shall be arbitrarily deprived of his life.' *Article 5* provides that no one 'shall be subjected to torture or to cruel, inhuman, or degrading punishment or treatment'. *Article 7* gives every person 'the right to personal liberty and security', prohibits 'arbitrary arrest or imprisonment', and provides for such procedural rights as notification of charges, recourse of the detained person to a competent court, and trial within a reasonable time or release pending trial. There follow excerpts from the opinion. (Other excerpts at p. 193, *supra*, discuss the liability of Honduras for the disappearance, whether the actual abductors were state or non-state actors.)]

[VII]

. . .

123. Because the Commission is accusing the Government of the disappearance of Manfredo Velásquez, it, in principle, should bear the burden of proving the facts underlying its petition.

124. The Commission's argument relies upon the proposition that the policy of disappearances, supported or tolerated by the Government, is designed to conceal and destroy evidence of disappearances. When the existence of such a policy or practice has been shown, the disappearance of a particular individual may be proved through circumstantial or indirect evidence or by logical inference. Otherwise, it would be impossible to prove that an individual has been disappeared. . . .

126. . . . If it can be shown that there was an official practice of disappearances in Honduras, carried out by the Government or at least tolerated by it, and

if the disappearance of Manfredo Velásquez can be linked to that practice, the Commission's allegations will have been proven to the Court's satisfaction, so long as the evidence presented on both points meets the standard of proof required in cases such as this.

127. The Court must determine what the standards of proof should be in the instant case. Neither the Convention, the Statute of the Court, nor its Rules of Procedure speak to this matter. Nevertheless, international jurisprudence has recognized the power of the courts to weigh the evidence freely, although it has always avoided a rigid rule regarding the amount of proof necessary to support the judgment.

...

130. The practice of international and domestic courts shows that direct evidence, whether testimonial or documentary, is not the only type of evidence that may be legitimately considered in reaching a decision. Circumstantial evidence, indicia, and presumptions may be considered, so long as they lead to conclusions consistent with the facts.

131. Circumstantial or presumptive evidence is especially important in allegations of disappearances, because this type of repression is characterized by an attempt to suppress any information about the kidnapping or the whereabouts and fate of the victim.

...

134. The international protection of human rights should not be confused with criminal justice. States do not appear before the Court as defendants in a criminal action. The objective of international human rights law is not to punish those individuals who are guilty of violations, but rather to protect the victims and to provide for the reparation of damages resulting from the acts of the States responsible.

135. In contrast to domestic criminal law, in proceedings to determine human rights violations the State cannot rely on the defense that the complainant has failed to present evidence when it cannot be obtained without the State's cooperation.

136. The State controls the means to verify acts occurring within its territory. Although the Commission has investigatory powers, it cannot exercise them within a State's jurisdiction unless it has the cooperation of that State.

...

138. The manner in which the Government conducted its defense would have sufficed to prove many of the Commission's allegations by virtue of the principle that the silence of the accused or elusive or ambiguous answers on its part may be interpreted as an acknowledgment of the truth of the allegations, so long as the contrary is not indicated by the record or is not compelled as a matter of law. This result would not hold under criminal law, which does not apply in the instant case...

...

[IX]

147. The Court now turns to the relevant facts that it finds to have been proven. They are as follows:

a. During the period 1981 to 1984, 100 to 150 persons disappeared in the Republic of Honduras, and many were never heard from again....

b. Those disappearances followed a similar pattern....

c. It was public and notorious knowledge in Honduras that the kidnappings were carried out by military personnel, police or persons acting under their orders....

d. The disappearances were carried out in a systematic manner, regarding which the Court considers the following circumstances particularly relevant:

i. The victims were usually persons whom Honduran officials considered dangerous to State security.... [Omitted paragraphs deal with arms used, details of the kidnappings and interrogations, denials by officials of any knowledge about the disappeared person, and the failure of any investigative committees to produce results.]

e. On September 12, 1981, between 4:30 and 5:00 p. m., several heavily armed men in civilian clothes driving a white Ford without license plates kidnapped Manfredo Velásquez from a parking lot in downtown Tegucigalpa. Today, nearly seven years later, he remains disappeared, which creates a reasonable presumption that he is dead....

f. Persons connected with the Armed Forces or under its direction carried out that kidnapping....

g. The kidnapping and disappearance of Manfredo Velásquez falls within the systematic practice of disappearances referred to by the facts deemed proved in paragraphs a–d.

...

[X]

149. Disappearances are not new in the history of human rights violations. However, their systematic and repeated nature and their use, not only for causing certain individuals to disappear, either briefly or permanently, but also as a means of creating a general state of anguish, insecurity and fear, is a recent phenomenon. Although this practice exists virtually worldwide, it has occurred with exceptional intensity in Latin America in the last few years.

150. The phenomenon of disappearances is a complex form of human rights violation that must be understood and confronted in an integral fashion.

151. The establishment of a Working Group on Enforced or Involuntary Disappearances of the United Nations Commission on Human Rights by Resolution 20(XXXVI) of February 29, 1980, is a clear demonstration of general censure and repudiation of the practice of disappearances.... The reports of the rapporteurs or special envoys of the Commission on Human Rights show concern that the practice of disappearances be stopped, the victims reappear and that those responsible be punished.

152. Within the inter-American system, the General Assembly of the Organization of American States (OAS) and the Commission have repeatedly referred to the practice of disappearances and have urged that disappearances be investigated and that the practice be stopped....

153. International practice and doctrine have often categorized disappearances as a crime against humanity, although there is no treaty in force which is applicable to the States Parties to the Convention and which uses this terminology....

...

155. The forced disappearance of human beings is a multiple and continuous violation of many rights under the Convention that the States Parties are obligated to respect and guarantee. The kidnapping of a person is an arbitrary deprivation of liberty, an infringement of a detainee's right to be taken without delay before a judge and to invoke the appropriate procedures to review the legality of the arrest, all in violation of Article 7 of the Convention....

156. Moreover, prolonged isolation and deprivation of communication are in themselves cruel and inhuman treatment, harmful to the psychological and moral integrity of the person and a violation of the right of any detainee to respect for his inherent dignity as a human being. Such treatment, therefore, violates Article 5 of the Convention....

157. The practice of disappearances often involves secret execution without trial, followed by concealment of the body to eliminate any material evidence of the crime and to ensure the impunity of those responsible. This is a flagrant violation of the right to life, recognized in Article 4 of the Convention....

158. The practice of disappearances, in addition to directly violating many provisions of the Convention, such as those noted above, constitutes a radical breach of that treaty in that it implies a crass abandonment of the values which emanate from the concept of human dignity and of the most basic principles of the inter-American system and the Convention....

...

[The part of the Court's opinion examining the obligation of a state not only to respect individual rights (such as by not 'disappearing' the government's opponents), but also to ensure free exercise of rights (such as by protecting those expressing political opinions against violence by private, nongovernmental actors), appears at p. 193, *supra*.]

[XII]

189. Article 63(1) of the Convention provides:

> If the Court finds that there has been a violation of a right or freedom protected by this Convention, the Court shall rule that the injured party be ensured the enjoyment of his right or freedom that was violated. It shall also rule, if appropriate, that the consequences of the measure or situation that constituted the breach of such rights or freedom be remedied and that fair compensation be paid to the injured party.

Clearly, in the instant case the Court cannot order that the victim be guaranteed the enjoyment of the right or liberty violated. The Court, however, can rule that the consequences of the breach of the rights be remedied and rule that just compensation be paid.

190. During this proceeding, the Commission requested the payment of compensation, but did not offer evidence regarding the amount of damages or the manner of payment. Nor did the parties discuss these matters.

191. The Court believes that the parties can agree on the damages. If an agreement cannot be reached, the Court shall award an amount. The case shall, therefore,

remain open for that purpose. The Court reserves the right to approve the agreement and, in the event no agreement is reached, to set the amount and order the manner of payment.

[In the concluding paragraphs, the Court unanimously declared that Honduras violated Articles 4, 5, and 7 of the Convention, all three read in conjunction with Article 1(1); and unanimously decided that Honduras was required to pay fair compensation to the victim's next of kin.]

QUESTIONS

1. The facts are contested. What method does the Court employ to resolve them? Does it employ such traditional notions of the law of evidence in systems of national law as burdens of proof (burdens of persuasion) or presumptions? For example:

(a) What is the relevance to the Court's finding of Honduran responsibility of the Court's use of terms like (the Honduran) 'practice' or 'policy', or the characterization of disappearances as 'systemic'?

(b) What is the significance of the Court's observation that the state 'controls the means to verify acts occurring within its territory'? Is the Court threatening the state with an adverse finding if it fails to make that effort?

2. 'It is wrong to argue that contentious cases before the Court can effectively address only individual situations and violations, while the Commission must expose structural and systemic violations of human rights through its state reports. The *Velásquez Rodríguez* case shows that the two tasks can be accomplished effectively at the same time. The Court is an adequate alternative to the Commission.' Comment.

NOTE

Among the significant contributions made by the Inter-American Court to human rights jurisprudence in general have been its defence of the rights of indigenous peoples and its emphasis on the provision of extensive and carefully tailored reparations by states found to have violated their human rights obligations. Cassel has suggested that there are six factors which have contributed to the expansive approach taken by the Court in relation to reparations: (1) it has been pushed to do so by the Commission and by victims; (2) substantial compliance by states with its reparations orders has encouraged a continued emphasis in this regard; (3) the increasing acceptance of the Court within Latin America; (4) its experience with political violence and impunity has encouraged more sweeping remedies; (5) doctrinal evolution on the issue; and (6) the influence of the approach of some 'particularly creative jurists on the Court'.[60]

[60] Douglas Cassel, 'The Expanding Scope and Impact of Reparations Awarded by the Inter-American Court of Human Rights', in K. de Feyter et al. (eds.), *Out of the Ashes: Reparation for Victims of Gross and Systematic Human Rights Violations* (2005), 191, at 211.

SAWHOYAMAXA INDIGENOUS COMMUNITY v. PARAGUAY

Inter-American Court of Human Rights, Judgment of 29 March 2006

...

73. Having assessed [all the evidence]. . . . the Court finds the following facts to be proven:

a) The Sawhoyamaxa Indigenous Community and the traditional occupation of the lands claimed

73(1) Towards the end of the 19th century vast stretches of land in the Paraguayan Chaco were acquired by British businessmen through the London Stock Exchange as a consequence of the debt owed by Paraguay after the so-called War of the Triple Alliance. The division and sale of such territories were made while their inhabitants, who, at the time, were exclusively Indians, were kept in full ignorance of the facts.

...

73(2) The economy of the indigenous peoples in the Chaco was mainly based on hunting, fishing, and gathering, and therefore, they had to roam their lands to make use of nature. . . .

73(3) Over the years, and particularly after the Chaco War between Bolivia and Paraguay (1933–1936), the non-indigenous occupation of the Northern Chaco which had started by the end of the 19th century was extended. The estates that started settling in the area used the Indians who had traditionally lived there as workers, who thus became farmhands and employees of new owners. Although the indigenous peoples continued occupying their traditional lands, the effect of the market economy activities into which they were incorporated turned out to be the restriction of their mobility, whereby they ended by becoming sedentary.

73(4) Since then, the lands of the Paraguayan Chaco have been transferred to private owners and gradually divided. This increased the restrictions for the indigenous population to access their traditional lands, thus bringing about significant changes in its subsistence activities. . . .

73(5) The Sawhoyamaxa ("from the place where coconuts have run out") Community is an indigenous community, typical of those traditionally living in the Paraguayan Chaco that has become sedentary. . . .

...

73(7) At present most members of the Sawhoyamaxa Indigenous Community live in the settlements known as "Santa Elisa" and "KM 16." "Santa Elisa" [both lying alongside roads. . . .

73(8) [In 2006], the Community has 407 members, grouped in approximately eighty-three dwelling places.

73(9) The lands claimed . . . are within the lands which they have traditionally occupied and which are part of their traditional habitat.

73(10) The lands claimed are suitable for the Indigenous Community members to continue with their current subsistence activities and to ensure their short and mid-term survival, as well as the beginning of a long-term process of development of alternative activities which will allow their subsistence to become sustainable.

[The Court considered several issues including whether the plea of non-exhaustion of domestic remedies could be invoked at this late stage, whether the existing indigenous land-claim administrative procedure was effective, and whether the time taken to consider claims had been reasonable. It reached negative conclusions on each issue.]

[Right to property — Article 21]

...

116. Article 21 of the American Convention declares that:

1. Everyone has the right to the use and enjoyment of his property. The law may subordinate such use and enjoyment to the interest of society.
2. No one shall be deprived of his property except upon payment of just compensation, for reasons of public utility or social interest, and in the cases and according to the forms established by law.
3. Usury and any other form of exploitation of man by man shall be prohibited by law.

117. In analyzing [Article 21] in relation to the communal property of the members of indigenous communities, the Court has taken into account Convention No. 169 of the ILO in the light of the general interpretation rules established under Article 29 of the Convention, in order to construe ... Article 21 in accordance with the evolution of the Inter-American system.... The State ratified Convention No. 169 and incorporated its provisions to domestic legislation by Law No. 234/93.

118. ... [T]he close ties the members of indigenous communities have with their traditional lands and the natural resources associated with their culture ..., must be secured under Article 21 of the American Convention. The culture of the members of indigenous communities reflects a particular way of life, of being, seeing and acting in the world, the starting point of which is their close relation with their traditional lands and natural resources, not only because they are their main means of survival, but also because they form part of their worldview, of their religiousness, and consequently, of their cultural identity.

119. [Article 13 of Convention No. 169 requires states to] respect "the special importance for the cultures and spiritual values of the peoples concerned of their relationship with the lands or territories, or both as applicable, which they occupy or otherwise use, and in particular the collective aspects of this relationship."

120. Likewise, this Court considers that indigenous communities might have a collective understanding of the concepts of property and possession, in the sense that ownership of the land "is not centered on an individual but rather on the group and its community." This notion of ownership and possession of land does not necessarily conform to the classic concept of property, but deserves equal protection under Article 21.... Disregard for specific versions of use and enjoyment of property, springing from the culture, uses, customs, and beliefs of each people, would be tantamount to holding that there is only one way of using and disposing of property, which, in turn, would render protection under Article 21 ... illusory for millions of persons.

121. Consequently, the close ties of indigenous peoples with their traditional lands and the native natural resources thereof, associated with their culture, as well as any incorporeal element deriving therefrom, must be secured under Article 21.... [In the Court's jurisprudence] "property" as used in Article 21, includes "material things which can be possessed, as well as any right which may be part of a person's patrimony; that concept includes all movable and immovable, corporeal and incorporeal elements and any other intangible object capable of having value".

122. The Paraguayan Constitution recognizes the existence of indigenous peoples as groups which have preceded the formation of the State, as well as their cultural identity, the relation with their respective habitat and their communal characteristics of their land-tenure system, and further grants them a series of specific rights which serve as basis for the Court to define the scope of Article 21 of the Convention.

123. On the other hand, Article 3 of Law No. 43/89 points out that settlements of indigenous communities are "constituted by a physical area made up of a core of houses, natural resources, crops, plantations, and their environs, linked insofar as possible to their cultural tradition....]"

...

125. The State has pointed out that it "does not deny its obligation to restore rights to these peoples," but the members of the Sawhoyamaxa Community "claim title to a piece of real estate based exclusively on an anthropologic report that, worthy as it is, collides with a property title which has been registered and has been conveyed from one owner to another for a long time." Likewise, the State fears that, would [the] claim by the Community be granted, "it would be convicted for the 'sins' committed during the [C]onquest" (inner quotation marks as used in the original text), and that this could lead to the "absurd situation in which the whole country could be claimed by indigenous peoples, for they are the primitive inhabitants of the stretch of territory that is nowadays called Paraguay."

126. Consequently, in order to address the issues in the instant case, the Court will proceed to examine, in the first place, whether possession of the lands by the indigenous people is a requisite for official recognition of property title thereto. In the event that possession not be a requisite for restitution rights, the Court will analyze, in the second place, whether enforcement of said rights is time-restricted. Finally, the Court will address the actions that the State must take to enforce indigenous communal property rights.

i) The possession of the lands

127. Acting within the scope of its adjudicatory jurisdiction, the Court has had the opportunity to decide on indigenous land possession in three different situations. On the one hand, in the *Case of the Mayagna (Sumo) Awas Tingni Community*, the Court pointed out [in 2001] that possession of the land should suffice for indigenous communities lacking real title to property of the land to obtain official recognition of that property, and for consequent registration. On the other hand, in the *Case of the Moiwana Community*, the Court considered [in 2005] that the members of the N'djuka people were the "legitimate owners of their traditional lands" although they did not have possession thereof, because they left them as a result of

the acts of violence perpetrated against them. In this case, the traditional lands have not been occupied by third parties. Finally, in the *Case of the Indigenous Community Yakye Axa*, the court [in 2005] considered that the members of the Community were empowered, even under domestic law, to file claims for traditional lands and ordered the State, as measure of reparation, to individualize those lands and transfer them on a for no consideration basis.

128. The following conclusions are drawn from the foregoing: 1) traditional possession of their lands by indigenous people has equivalent effects to those of a state-granted full property title; 2) traditional possession entitles indigenous people to demand official recognition and registration of property title; 3) the members of indigenous peoples who have unwillingly left their traditional lands, or lost possession therof, maintain property rights thereto, even though they lack legal title, unless the lands have been lawfully transferred to third parties in good faith; and 4) the members of indigenous peoples who have unwillingly lost possession of their lands, when those lands have been lawfully transferred to innocent third parties, are entitled to restitution thereof or to obtain other lands of equal extension and quality. Consequently, possession is not a requisite conditioning the existence of indigenous land restitution rights. The instant case is categorized under this last conclusion.

129. Paraguay acknowledges the right of indigenous peoples to claim restitution of their lost traditional lands. . . .

. . .

iii) Actions to enforce the rights of the community members over their traditional lands

135. Once it has been proved that land restitution rights are still current, the State must take the necessary actions to return them to the members of the indigenous people claiming them. However, as the Court has pointed out, when a State is unable, on objective and reasoned grounds, to adopt measures aimed at returning traditional lands and communal resources to indigenous populations, it must surrender alternative lands of equal extension and quality, which will be chosen by agreement with the members of the indigenous peoples, according to their own consultation and decision procedures.

136. Nevertheless, the Court can not . . . decide that Sawhoyamaxa Community's property rights to traditional lands prevail over the right to property of private owners or *vice versa*, since the Court is not a domestic judicial authority with jurisdiction to decide disputes among private parties. This power is vested exclusively in the Paraguayan State. Nevertheless, the Court has competence to analyze whether the State ensured the human rights of the members of the Sawhoyamaxa Community.

137. [The Court rejects three] arguments put forth by the State to justify nonenforcement of the indigenous people's property rights have not sufficed to release it from international responsibility. . . .

138. [First] . . . the fact that the claimed lands are privately held by third parties is not in itself an "objective and reasoned" ground for dismissing *prima facie* the claims by the indigenous people. Otherwise, restitution rights become meaningless and would not entail an actual possibility of recovering traditional lands, as it would be exclusively limited to an expectation on the will of the current holders, forcing indigenous communities to accept alternative lands or economic compensations.

In this respect, the Court has pointed out that, when there be conflicting interests in indigenous claims, it must assess in each case the legality, necessity, proportionality and fulfillment of a lawful purpose in a democratic society (public purposes and public benefit), to impose restrictions on the right to property, on the one hand, or the right to traditional lands, on the other....

139. [The same rationale applies to the second argument which suggests] that indigenous communities are not entitled, under any circumstances, to claim traditional lands the when they are exploited and fully productive, viewing the indigenous issue exclusively from the standpoint of land productivity and agrarian law, something which is insufficient for it fails to address the distinctive characteristics of such peoples.

140. [The third argument is that the owner's right is protected under a bilateral agreement between Paraguay and Germany which, because of its treaty status, has become part of the law of the land.] ... [T]he Court has not been furnished with the aforementioned treaty [but it is said to allow] ... for capital investments made by a contracting party to be condemned or nationalized for a "public purpose or interest", which could justify land restitution to indigenous people.... [The] enforcement [of such bilateral treaties] should always be compatible with the American Convention, which is a multilateral treaty on human rights that stands in a class of its own and that generates rights for individual human beings and does not depend entirely on reciprocity among States.

141. Based on the foregoing, the Court dismisses the three arguments of the State described above and finds them insufficient to justify non-enforcement of the right to property of the Sawhoyamaxa Community.

142. Finally, it is worth recalling that, under Article 1(1) of the Convention, the State is under the obligation to respect the rights recognized therein and to organize public authority in such a way as to ensure to all persons under its jurisdiction the free and full exercise of human rights.

143. Even though the right to communal property of the lands and of the natural resources of indigenous people is recognized in Paraguayan laws, such merely abstract or legal recognition becomes meaningless in practice if the lands have not been physically delimited and surrendered because the adequate domestic measures necessary to secure effective use and enjoyment of said right by the members of the Sawhoyamaxa Community are lacking. The free development and transmission of their culture and traditional rites have thus been threatened.

144. For the aforementioned reasons, the Court concludes that the State violated Article 21 of the American Convention, to the detriment of the members of the Sawhoyamaxa Community, in relation to Articles 1(1) and 2 therein.

[Right to life — Article 4]

...

155. It is clear for the Court that a State cannot be responsible for all situations in which the right to life is at risk. Taking into account the difficulties involved in the planning and adoption of public policies and the operative choices that have to be made in view of the priorities and the resources available, the positive obligations of the State must be interpreted so that an impossible or disproportionate burden

is not imposed upon the authorities. In order for this positive obligation to arise, it must be determined that at the moment of the occurrence of the events, the authorities knew or should have known about the existence of a situation posing an immediate and certain risk to the life of an individual or of a group of individuals, and that the necessary measures were not adopted within the scope of their authority which could be reasonably expected to prevent or avoid such risk.

. . .

163. The Court acknowledges the criterion of the State in the sense that it has not induced or encouraged the members of the Community to move and settle by the side of the road. However, the Court considers that there were powerful reasons for the members of the Community to abandon the estates where they lived and worked, due to the extremely hard physical and labor conditions they had to endure. Likewise, this argument is not enough for the State to disregard its duty to protect and guarantee the right to life of the alleged victims. It is necessary that the State proves that it carried out all necessary actions [to] take the indigenous peoples from the roadside, and in the meantime, to adopt all necessary measures to reduce the risk that they were facing.

164. In that respect, the Court notes that the principal means available for the State to get the members of the Community out of the side of the road was to give them their traditional lands. . . .

. . .

166. Consequently, this Court considers that the State has not adopted the necessary measures for the members of the Community to leave the roadside, and thus, abandon the inadequate conditions that endangered, and continue endangering, their right to life.

. . .

170. . . . Presidential Order No 3789 [of 1999 declared] the Sawhoyamaxa Community in a state of emergency. However, the measures adopted by the State in compliance with such order cannot be considered sufficient and adequate. Indeed, for six years after the effective date of the order, the State only delivered food to the alleged victims on ten opportunities, and medicine and educational material on two opportunities, with long intervals between each delivery. . . . [A]fter the emergency Presidential Order became effective, at least 19 persons died.

171. . . . [M]ost of the Community members that died were boys and girls under 3 years of age, and the causes of their deaths range from *enterocolitis*, dehydration, cachexia, tetanus, measles, and respiratory illnesses, such as pneumonia and bronchitis; all of them are reasonably foreseeable diseases that can be prevented and treated at a low cost.

. . .

173. The Court does not accept the State argument regarding the joint responsibility of the ill persons to go to the medical centers to receive treatment, and of the Community leaders to take them to such centers or to communicate the situation to the health authorities. From the issuance of the emergency Order, [the Government authorities] had the duty to take "the actions that might be necessary to immediately provide food and medical care to the families that form part of [the Sawhoyamaxa Community] . . .). Therefore, the provision of goods and health services did no

longer specifically depend on the individual financial capacity of the alleged victims, and therefore, the State should have taken action contributing to the provision of such goods and services. . . .

. . .

178. Considering the aforesaid, the Court finds that the State violated Article 4(1) . . . since it has not adopted the necessary positive measures within its powers, which could reasonably be expected to prevent or avoid risking the right to life of the members of the Sawhoyamaxa Community. . . .

[Right to juridical personality—Article 3]

. . .

187. In the instant case, neither the Commission nor the representatives have alleged the violation of Article 3 of the American Convention. However, from the facts of the case, it . . . appears that there has been no registration or official documentation of the existence of several members of the indigenous Sawhoyamaxa Community. The Court considers that the parties have had the opportunity of addressing such situation [sic], thus, it is pertinent to examine the obligations stemming from Article 3 of the American Convention which provides as follows:

> "Every person has the right to recognition as a person before the law."

. . .

192. The above mentioned members of the Community have remained in a legal limbo in which, though they have been born and have died in Paraguay, their existence and identity were never legally recognized, that is to say, they did not have personality before the law. Indeed, the State, in the instant proceeding before the Court, has intended to use this situation for its own benefit. In fact, at the time of referring to the right to life, the State alleged:

> If neither the existence of these persons nor even their death has even been proved, it is not possible to claim liability from anyone, lest [sic] the State, where are their birth and death certificates?

. . .

194. On the basis of the above considerations, and notwithstanding the fact that other members of the Community may be in the same situation, the Court finds that the State violated the right to personality before the law enshrined in Article 3. . . .

[Reparations]

. . . Article 63(1) of the American Convention states the following:

> If the Court finds that there has been a violation of a right or freedom protected by this Convention, the Court shall rule that the injured party be ensured the enjoyment of his right or freedom that was violated. It shall also rule, if appropriate, that the consequences of the measure or situation that constituted the breach of such right or freedom be remedied and that fair compensation be paid to the injured party.

. . .

198. The reparations, as the term itself indicates, consist of measures tending to eliminate the effects of the breaches perpetrated. Their nature and amount depend on both the pecuniary and non-pecuniary damages caused. The reparations cannot imply enrichment or detriment for the victims or their successors.

. . .

210. . . . [T]he Court orders that the State shall adopt all legislative, administrative or other type of measures necessary to guarantee the members of the Community ownership rights over their traditional lands, and consequently the right to use and enjoy those lands.

211. . . . [R]estitution of such lands to the Community is barred, since these lands are currently privately owned.

212. . . . [T]he State must consider the possibility of purchasing these lands or the lawfulness, need and proportionality of condemning these lands in order to achieve a lawful purpose in a democratic society. . . . If restitution of ancestral lands . . . is not possible on objective and sufficient grounds, the State shall make over alternative lands, selected upon agreement with the aforementioned Indigenous Community, in accordance with the community's own decision-making and consultation procedures, values, practices and customs. In either case, the extension and quality of the lands must be sufficient to guarantee the preservation and development of the Community's own way of life.

. . .

215. The State shall, within three years . . . formally and physically grant tenure [of] the lands to the victims, irrespective of whether they be acquired by purchase or by condemnation, or whether alternative lands are selected. The State shall guarantee all the necessary funds for the purpose.

. . .

219. Non-pecuniary damage may include distress and suffering caused directly to the victims or their relatives, tampering with individual core values, and changes of a non pecuniary nature in the living conditions of the victims or their families. . . . [S]aid damage may only be compensated in one of two ways. Firstly, . . . by paying an amount of money or delivering property or services. . . . And secondly, . . . through public actions or works, such as the publication of an official message repudiating the human rights violations at stake and committing to prevent further similar violations . . .

. . .

221. This Court finds that the non enforcement of the right to hold title . . . and the detrimental living conditions imposed upon them . . . must be taken into account. . . .

222. Similarly, the Court finds that the special meaning that these lands have for indigenous peoples, in general, and for the members of the Sawhoyamaxa Community, in particular, implies that the denial of those rights over land involves a detriment to values that are highly significant to the members of those communities, who are at risk of losing or suffering irreparable damage to their lives and identities, and to the cultural heritage of future generations.

224. . . . The State shall allocate the amount of US$ 1,000,000.00 (one million United States Dollars) to [a community development] fund, which will be used

to implement educational, housing, agricultural and health projects, as well as to provide drinking water and to build sanitation infrastructure, for the benefit of the members of the Community. These projects must be established by an implementation committee, as described below, and must be completed within two years as from delivery of the lands to the members of the Indigenous Community.

...

226. ... [T]he Court ... orders the State to pay compensation in the amount of US$ 20,000.00 ... to each of the 17 members of the Community who died as a result of the events in the instant case. That amount must be distributed among the next of kin of the victims pursuant to the cultural practices of the Sawhoyamaxa Community. ...

...

230. ... [T]he Court orders that, while the members of the Community remain landless, the State shall immediately, regularly and permanently adopt measures to: a) supply sufficient drinking water. ... b) provide medical check-ups, tests and care ...; c) deliver sufficient quantity and quality of food; d) set up latrines. ... and e) provide the school of the "Santa Elisa" settlement with all necessary material and human resources ...

...

235. ... [T]he State shall, within a reasonable time, enact into its domestic legislation, as per Article 2 of the American Convention, the legislative, administrative and other measures necessary to provide an efficient mechanism to claim the ancestral lands of indigenous peoples enforcing their property rights and taking into consideration their customary law, values, practices and customs.

...

236. As ordered in prior cases, the Court finds that, as a measure of satisfaction, the State shall publish ... in the Official Gazette and in another national daily newspaper, [parts of the judgment, and shall finance the radio broadcasting of key paragraphs] in the language indicated by the members of the Community, in a radio station accessible to them. Said radio broadcasting shall be made at least four times in two-week intervals. ...

...

248 The Court shall monitor full compliance with this Judgment and shall consider the instant case closed upon full compliance by the State with the provisions therein. Within a year ... the State shall submit to the Court a report on the measures adopted to comply herewith. ...

THE MIGUEL CASTRO CASTRO PRISON v. PERU

Inter-American Court of Human Rights, Judgment of 25 November 2006

...

197(1) During the period that goes from the beginning of the eighties until the end of the year 2000, Peru lived a conflict between armed groups and agents of the police force and the military. This conflict got worse in the midst of a systematic practice of violations to human rights, among them extrajudicial killings and forced disappearances of people suspected of belonging to armed groups that existed on the fringe of the law, such as Sendero Luminoso (hereinafter SL) and the Revolutionary Movement Tupac Amarú (hereinafter MRTA), all practices carried out by state agents following orders given by military and police leaders.

. . .

197(8) In the final report issued [in 2003] by the CVR [the Commission for Truth and Reconciliation] it established that "during the years of political violence, [the prisons] were not only areas for the imprisonment of those accused or convicted for crimes of terrorism, but scenarios in which the Communist Party of Peru [PCP-Sendero Luminoso] and, in less measure, the Revolutionary Movement Túpac Amaru, extended the armed conflict."

197(9) [From April 1992,] in order to fight subversive and terrorist groups, the State implemented in the prisons practices not compatible with the effective protection of the right to life and other rights, such as extrajudicial killings and cruel and inhuman treatments, as well as the disproportionate use of force in critical circumstances.

. . .

197(11) The national press [warned] that Sendero Luminoso was exercising territorial control within the Miguel Castro Castro Prison, that from within said center it was planning several attacks and that they had turned their pavilions "into teaching centers."

Miguel Castro Castro Prison

. . .

197(13) In the time in which the events occurred, pavilion 1A of the Miguel Castro Castro Prison was occupied by around 135 female inmates and 50 male, and pavilion 4B was occupied by approximately 400 male inmates. The inmates of pavilions 1A and 4B were accused or convicted for the crimes of terrorism or treason, and they were allegedly members of the Sendero Luminoso. Many of them had been accused and were awaiting conviction, and in some cases they were acquitted.

. . .

197(15) Law Decree No. 25421 of April 6, 1992 ordered the reorganization of the National Penitentiary Institute (INPE) and put the National Police of Peru in charge of the control of security at the penitentiaries. It was within the framework of this stipulation that "Operative Transfer 1" was planned and executed. The official version was that said "operative" consisted in the transfer of the women that were imprisoned in pavilion 1A of the Miguel Castro Castro Prison, to the maximum security prison for women in Chorrillos. The state authorities did not inform the Director of the criminal center, the prisoners, their next of kin or attorneys of the mentioned transfer.

197(16) The real objective of the "operative" was. . . premeditated attack . . . designed to attack the life and integrity of the prisoners located in pavilions 1A and 4B of the Miguel Castro Castro Prison. . . .

. . .

197(20) At [4am on May 6 the security forces] knocked down part of the external wall of the yard of pavilion 1A using explosives. . . .

197(21) The state, police, and military agents used war weapons, explosives, tear gas, vomiting, and paralyzing bombs against the inmates, from the start of the operation. The bullets and grenades used would fragment upon impact with the walls, injuring many inmates with splinters. Snipers were located on the roofs and windows of the other pavilions. . . .

197(22) [O]n May 6th the National Police introduced grenades, white phosphorous gas bombs, and tear gas bombs in pavilion 1A, which produced asphyxia, and a burning feeling in the respiratory system, eyes, and skin of the inmates. . . .

. . .

197(30) [On 7 May the President and the authorities took action] . . . [T]he presence of human rights organizations in the surrounding areas of the criminal center was forbidden, the supply of electricity, water, and food to inmates was cut off, and the attacks with fire weapons and explosives was increased.

197(31) In the afternoon, police officers and members of the Armed Forces intensified the attacks against pavilion 4B, using grenades, machine guns, and tear gas bombs.

197(32) On May 8, 1992, the third day of the "operative", the police and military officials continued the attack with rockets fired from helicopters, mortar fire, and grenades.

. . .

197(37) [On 9 May] the inmates announced to the state agents that they were coming out and they asked them to stop shooting. Groups of unarmed inmates, made up mainly by people labeled as members of the head of Sendero Luminoso, exited the pavilion, when they were reached by bursts of bullets fired by state agents. The majority of those inmates died. Later, a large number of inmates exited pavilion 4B, at a fast pace. The security agents of the State shot at them indiscriminately and in different parts of their bodies, even when they were injured on the floor. . . .

197(38) When the inmates were under the control of state agents, some were separated from the group and killed by state agents. One of the bodies presented mutilations and signs of torture.

197(39) The majority of the inmates that were killed presented between 3 and 12 bullet wounds to the head and thorax.

197(40) During the events of May 6 to 9, 1992 a police officer died, as a consequence of having received bullet wounds in the head and thorax; and approximately 9 police officers were injured.

[In total, it was estimated by the Inter-American Commission that at least 42 inmates died, 175 were injured, and 322 were subjected to cruel, inhuman, and degrading treatment. The Court determined that there was no justification for the legitimate use of force by the authorities under the circumstances. Based in part on acknowledgements of responsibility by the state, the Court concluded that the state was responsible for violations of Articles 4, 5, 8(1), and 25 of the American Convention, and of violations of the provisions of the Inter-American Convention to Prevent, Punish and Eradicate Violence Against Women, and of the Inter-American Convention to Prevent and Punish Torture.]

413. . . . The Court has established, on several occasions, that all violation of an international obligation that has produced damage involves the duty to adequately repair it. To these effects, Article 63(1) of the American Convention states that:

> [i]f the Court finds that there has been a violation of a right or freedom protected by [this] Convention, the Court shall rule that the injured party be ensured the enjoyment of his right or freedom that was violated. It shall also rule, if appropriate, that the consequences of the measure or situation that constituted the breach of such right or freedom be remedied and that fair compensation be paid to the injured party.

414. As previously stated by the Court, Article 63(1) of the American Convention constitutes a rule of customary law that enshrines one of the fundamental principles in contemporary international law on state responsibility. Thus, when an illicit act is imputed to the State, its international responsibility arises for the violation of the corresponding international norm, together with the subsequent duty of reparation and to put an end to the consequences of said violation. Said international responsibility is different to the responsibility in domestic legislation.

415. The reparation of the damage caused by a violation of an international obligation requires, whenever possible, full restitution. . . . When this is not possible, the international court will determine a series of measures to guarantee the rights violated, repair the consequences caused by the infractions, and establish payment of an indemnity as compensation for the harm caused or other means of satisfaction. The obligation to repair, regulated in all its aspects (scope, nature, modalities, and determination of the beneficiaries) by International Law, may not be modified or ignored by the State obliged, by invoking stipulations of its domestic law.

416. Reparations, as indicated by the term itself, consist in those measures necessary to make the effects of the committed violations disappear. Their nature and amount depend on the harm caused at both material and moral levels. Reparations cannot entail either enrichment or impoverishment of the victim or his successors. [The Court then considered and awarded various forms of pecuniary and non-pecuniary damages.]

D) Other forms of reparation

(Measures of Satisfaction and Non-Repetition Guarantees)

. . .

435. In this section the Tribunal will determine those measures of satisfaction that seek to repair non-pecuniary damages, that do not have a pecuniary scope, and it will establish measures of a public scope or repercussion. In cases such as the present that are characterized by extreme seriousness these measures acquire a special relevance.

. . .

441. [T]he State must, within a reasonable period of time, effectively carry out the ongoing criminal proceedings and the ones that may be opened, and it must adopt all measures necessary to elucidate all the facts of the present case and not only those that resulted in the death of the victims, in order to determine the intellectual and material responsibility of those who participated in the violations. The results

of these proceedings must be publicly diffused by the State, so that the Peruvian society may know the truth regarding the facts of the present case.

442. Likewise, as a guarantee of non-repetition, the Court rules that the State must, within a reasonable period of time, establish the necessary means in order to ensure that the information and documentation related to police investigations regarding facts as serious as those of the present case be conserved in a manner such that they do not obstruct the corresponding investigations.

. . .

445. [I]t is necessary, in order to repair the damage caused to the victims and their next of kin, and to avoid that facts like those of the present case repeat themselves, that the State carry out a public act of acknowledgment of its international responsibility in relation to the violations declared in this Judgments in amends to the victims and for the satisfaction of their next of kin. This act must be carried out in a public ceremony, with the presence of high State authorities and of the victims and their next of kin. The State must transmit said act through the media, including the transmission on radio and television. For this, the State has one year, as of the notification of the present Judgment.

. . .

451. The violations attributable to the State in the present case were perpetrated by police, and army personnel, as well as special security forces. . . .

452. Therefore, the State must design and implement, within a reasonable period of time, human rights education programs, addressed to agents of the Peruvian police force, on the international standards applicable to matters regarding treatment of inmates in situations of alterations of public order in penitentiary centers.

453. Regarding the measures requested by the Commission and the intervener, on the construction of monuments and the creation of a park in "the area of Canto Grande", the State argued that "a monument (called the Eye that Cries) has already been erected in a public place of the capital of the Republic in favor of all the victims of the conflict, and that it is the subject of continuous memorial and commemoration acts."

454. In this sense, the Court values the existence of the monument and public area called "The Eye that Cries", created upon the request of civil society and with the collaboration of state authorities, which constitutes an important public acknowledgment to the victims of violence in Peru. However, the Tribunal considers that, within a one-year period, the State must ensure that all the people declared as deceased victims in the present Judgment be represented in said monument. For this, it must coordinate with the next of kin of the deceased victims an act, in which they may include an inscription with the name of the victim as corresponds according to the monument's characteristics.

. . .

NOTE

Reporting on this judgment, the *New York Times* noted that the 'verdict set off a wave of anger in Peru over what many see as honoring terrorists and killers'. It added that the judgment had 'reopened scars of a rebellion that raged from 1980 to 1998' and reported that the congressional leader of the governing party 'said after meeting with President Alan García ... that the authorities were mulling Peru's withdrawal from the Inter-American Court of Human Rights ...'.[61]

The next major step in the Court's reparations jurisprudence came in *González et al. ('Cotton Field') v. Mexico*[62] which examined Mexico's responsibility in relation to the killings in Ciudad Juárez, documented in the CEDAW Committee's 2005 report (p. 198, *supra*). The Court laid down criteria for assessing proposed reparations that went beyond the standard objectives. Thus, reparation should also be 'designed to identify and eliminate the factors that cause discrimination [and be] adopted from a gender perspective, bearing in mind the different impact that violence has on men and on women.' Thus, for example, the state was ordered to:

> continue implementing permanent education and training programs and courses for public officials on human rights and gender, and on a gender perspective to ensure due diligence in conducting preliminary inquiries and judicial proceedings concerning gender-based discrimination, abuse and murder of women, and to overcome stereotyping about the role of women in society.... Every year, for three years, the State shall report on the implementation of the courses and training sessions.[63]

NOTE

Consider the following assessment by Cavallaro and Brewer (p. 982, *supra*, at 785–6):

> Our review of the compliance orders of the Court reveals a clear (though not universal) pattern in states' reactions to its judgments.... [S]tates generally pay some or all of the monetary damages awarded by the Court. In addition, states may comply with symbolic reparations, including those concerning public ceremonies. However, when it comes to more far-reaching measures to reduce impunity and advance human rights (such as prosecuting past violations or changing laws and practices), compliance is considerably less likely. Most salient, virtually no compliance decision records that a state has effectively investigated and punished the perpetrators of a human rights violation forming the basis of a Court decision. Even when states report taking some steps toward a full investigation of the case or having prosecuted some of the alleged perpetrators, they often do not progress to investigating fully or prosecuting all the parties involved, weakening the impact of those legal processes in combating impunity. States also frequently fail even to

[61] 'Ruling on Shining Path Rebels Angers Peru', *New York Times*, 11 Jan. 2007, p. 1.

[62] Inter-Am. Ct. H.R. (Ser. C) No. 205 (16 Nov. 2009).

[63] For a critique see R. Rubio-Marín & C. Sandoval, 'Engendering the Reparations Jurisprudence of the Inter-American Court of Human Rights: The Promise of the Cotton Field Judgment', 33 Hum. Rts. Q. 1062 (2011).

provide the Court with the data necessary to determine whether the state is complying with a judgment or not. In 2003 Panama challenged the principle that the Court even has the authority to monitor compliance with its orders. As of 2007, the Court reported full compliance in only 11.57 percent of resolved cases.

QUESTIONS

1. How compelling is the Court's justification for providing privileged treatment for the indigenous peoples in the Sawhoyamaxa Community?

2. 'The Court has gone too far in developing innovative remedies. It has turned itself into a dispenser of transitional justice and the righter of all wrongs. It would be better off confining itself to individual remedies and avoiding sweeping structural remedies.' Discuss.

3. What factors might explain the apparently low rates of compliance with the Court's judgments? What conclusions, if any, should the Court itself draw from this record?

ADDITIONAL READING

T. Antkowiak & L. Hennebel (eds.), *The American Convention on Human Rights: A Commentary* (2012); L. Burgorgue-Larsen & A. Ubeda de Torres, *The Inter-American Court of Human Rights: Case-Law and Commentary* (2011); A. Huneeus, 'Courts Resisting Courts: Lessons from the Inter-American Court's Struggle to Enforce Human Rights', 44 Cornell Int'l. L. J. 493 (2011); L. Hennebel, 'The Inter-American Court of Human Rights: The Ambassador of Universalism' [2011] Quebec J. Int'l. L. 57; C. Binder, 'The Prohibition of Amnesties by the Inter-American Court of Human Rights', 12 German L. J. 1203 (2011); G. L. Neuman, 'Import, Export, and Regional Consent in the Inter-American Court of Human Rights', 19 E.J.I.L. 101 (2008); T. Antkowiak, 'Remedial Approaches to Human Rights Violations: The Inter-American Court of Human Rights and Beyond', 46 Colum. J. Transnat'l. L. 351 (2008); T. Melish, 'The Inter-American Court of Human Rights: Beyond Progressivity', in M. Langford (ed.), *Social Rights Jurisprudence* (2008); ibid., 'The Inter-American Commission on Human Rights', in Langford, ibid (2008); J. Pasqualucci, *The Practice and Procedure of the Inter-American Court of Human Rights* (2003); J. Cavallaro & E. Schaffer, 'Less as More: Rethinking Supranational Litigation of Economic and Social Rights in the Americas', 56 Hastings L. J. 217; (2004) T. Melish, 'Rethinking the "Less as More" Thesis: Supranational Litigation of Economic Social, and Cultural Rights in the Americas', 39 NYU J. Int'l. L. & Pol'y. 171 (2007); D. Harris & S. Livingstone (eds.), *The Inter-American System of Human Rights* (1998); S. Davidson, *The Inter-American Human Rights System* (1996).

C. THE AFRICAN SYSTEM

The youngest, least well-resourced, and so far least developed of the regional systems is the African one. In 1981 the Assembly of Heads of States and Government of the Organization of African Unity adopted the African Charter on Human and Peoples' Rights. It entered into force in 1986. As of May 2012, 54 African states were parties.

In Chapter 6's discussion of rights and duties, at p. 572, *supra*, the Charter itself served as an important illustration of a human rights regime that was more duty-oriented than the universal human rights system or the two other regional systems. Section C focuses primarily on the institutional aspects of the African system, and especially on the work of the African Commission on Human and Peoples' Rights. The examination is relatively brief, because although the overall system has become increasingly elaborate, the lack of resources and the limited political will of governments have served to limit its achievements. Although the Commission has been in existence for a quarter of a century, its workload has expanded only gradually and it has been cautious in exercising its limited powers or creatively interpreting and developing them. The judges of the African Court of Human and Peoples' Rights were elected only in 2006, and the Court delivered its first judgment in 2009. Moreover, the basic structure and tasks of the Commission and the Court do not introduce novel themes to Section C's examination of the architecture of intergovernmental human rights institutions.

It follows that the African system has not yet yielded anywhere near the same amount of information and 'output' of recommendations or decisions — state reports and reactions thereto, communications (complaints) from individuals about state conduct, studies of 'situations' or investigations of particular violations — as have the other systems. In comparison with those systems, the states parties and Commission have taken only a few forceful or persuasive actions within the structure of the Charter to attempt to curb serious human rights violations, although recent years have shown promise of a more insistent and active stance.

This examination of institutional aspects of the African system begins with a brief description of the African Union. You should be familiar with the provisions of the African Charter.

COMMENT ON THE AFRICAN UNION

In 1963 the Organization of African Unity was established as the official regional body of African states. It was inspired by the anti-colonial struggles of the late 1950s, and was primarily dedicated to the eradication of colonialism. The emergent African states created through it a political bloc to facilitate intra-African relations and to forge a regional approach to Africa's relationships with external powers. In 2001 the OAU was replaced by the African Union (AU). Today, 54 of the 55 African states are members of the AU. The exception is Morocco which withdrew from the OAU in 1984 after the organization recognized Western Sahara.

For a variety of reasons, especially its experience of colonialism, the OAU Charter attached major importance to 'unity and solidarity' among African states, and defence of 'their sovereignty, their territorial integrity and independence'. Thus, the inviolability of territorial borders, expressed through the principle of non-interference in the internal affairs of member states, was one of the OAU's central creeds. But concern at the OAU's failure to react to various gross violations of human rights committed by dictators like Idi Amin in Uganda, Jean-Bédel Bokassa in the then Central African Empire, and Francisco Macias Nguema in Equatorial Guinea, combined with a growing recognition of the importance of human rights led the OAU to adopt, in 1981, the African Charter on Human and Peoples' Rights.

This development, in addition to the rapid expansion in national constitutions within Africa which contained detailed provisions relating to human rights, facilitated the inclusion of a wide range of human rights objectives and principles in the AU Charter. By comparison, the OAU Charter had said very little. Thus, among the objectives of the AU, listed in Article 3, are to '(e) encourage international cooperation, taking due account of the Charter of the United Nations and the Universal Declaration of Human Rights' and to '(h) promote and protect human and peoples' rights in accordance with the African Charter on Human and Peoples' Rights and other relevant human rights instruments'. Similarly, Article 4 lists the following principles in accordance with which the Union is to function:

> (g) non-interference by any Member State in the internal affairs of another;
> (h) the right of the Union to intervene in a Member State pursuant to a decision of the Assembly in respect of grave circumstances, namely: war crimes, genocide and crimes against humanity;
> ...
> (j) the right of Member States to request intervention from the Union in order to restore peace and security;
> ...
> (l) promotion of gender equality;
> (m) respect for democratic principles, human rights, the rule of law and good governance;
> (n) promotion of social justice to ensure balanced economic development;
> (o) respect for the sanctity of human life, condemnation and rejection of impunity and political assassination, acts of terrorism and subversive activities;
> (p) condemnation and rejection of unconstitutional changes of governments.

While the AU Charter does not contain any human rights requirements relating to admission to the Union, it does provide for the possible suspension of certain rights or the imposition of sanctions upon states that fail to comply with AU decisions and policies (Art. 23(2)). In addition, governments that 'come to power through unconstitutional means shall not be allowed to participate' in AU activities (Art. 30).

In addition to the African Charter, the OAU adopted two other important instruments addressing specifically the rights of women and of children. The African Charter on the Rights and Welfare of the Child was adopted in 1990 and entered into force in 1999. As of May 2012 it had 45 ratifications.

The Protocol to the African Charter on Human and Peoples' Rights on the Rights of Women in Africa was adopted in 2003 and entered into force in November 2005. As of May 2012 it had 28 ratifications. Activists welcomed the Protocol as an antidote to what is seen as the African Charter's relative neglect of women's issues. The Protocol is far-reaching, especially in certain areas. It defines 'discrimination against women' to include 'any distinction, exclusion or restriction or any differential treatment based on sex and whose objectives or effects compromise or destroy the recognition, enjoyment or the exercise by women, regardless of their marital status, of human rights and fundamental freedoms in all spheres of life.' It has detailed provisions dealing, *inter alia*, with 'harmful practices' ('all behaviour, attitudes and/or practices which negatively affect the fundamental rights of women and girls, such as their right to life, health, dignity, education and physical integrity' (Art. 5)), violence against women (Art. 4), equality in and after marriage (Arts. 6 and 7), the right to political participation (Art. 9), protection of women in armed conflicts (Art. 11), health and reproductive rights (Art. 14), and widow's rights (Art. 20). Its implementation is to be overseen in the same way as the African Charter.

COMMENT ON INSTITUTIONAL IMPLEMENTATION: THE AFRICAN COMMISSION

The 11 members of the Commission, elected by secret ballot by the Assembly of Heads of State and Government from a list of persons nominated by parties to the Charter, are to serve (Art. 31) 'in their personal capacity'. Article 45 defines the mandate or functions of the Commission to be: (1) to 'promote Human and Peoples' Rights'; (2) to 'ensure the protection of human and peoples' rights' under conditions set by the Charter; (3) to 'interpret all the provisions of the Charter' when so requested by states or OAU institutions; and (4) to perform other tasks that may be committed to it by the Assembly. So the three dominant functions appear to be promotion, ensuring protection, and interpretation.

The Commission's task of 'promotion' includes (Art. 45) undertaking 'studies and researches on African problems in the field of human and peoples' rights', as well as organizing seminars and conferences, disseminating information, encouraging 'local institutions concerned with human and peoples' rights', giving its views or making recommendations to governments, and formulating principles and rules 'aimed at solving legal problems related to human and peoples' rights... upon which African Governments may base their legislation.' Article 46 states tersely that the Commission 'may resort to any appropriate method of investigation'. In general, the 'Charter gives pre-eminence to the promotion of human rights and vests a wide range of responsibility on the Commission. In this regard, it has functions that are not directly vested in the ... American Commission.'[64] Several steps have been taken to implement the task of promotion — for example, resolutions by the Commission

[64] U. O. Umozurike, 'The African Commission on Human and Peoples' Rights', 1 Rev. Afr. Comm. Hum. & Peoples' Rts. 5 (1991), at 8.

to the effect that states should include the teaching of human rights at all levels of the educational curricula, should integrate the Charter's provisions into national laws, and should establish committees on human rights.

Communications (complaints) and state reports are the most significant functions or processes involving the Commission that are identified in the Charter. Thus far, the procedures in the Charter involving communications by a state party concerning another state party have not been used. Individuals and national and international institutions can also send communications to the Commission, as provided in Articles 55–9.

The Charter refers tersely to reports. Under Article 62, each party 'shall undertake to submit every two years.... report on the legislative or other measures taken with a view to giving effect to the rights' under the Charter. Compare the more elaborate provisions in Article 40 of the ICCPR about the role of the ICCPR Committee in reviewing states' reports under that Covenant.

Although there is some irony in the observation that the Commission, addressing a continent rife with state-imposed abuses, should have promotion as its primary function, that concentration of energy makes some sense in view of Africa's large uneducated population that is ignorant of its rights or lacks organization and capacity for mobilization to vindicate them. Creating 'rights awareness' could understandably be considered to be a primary function.

But in the long run, promotion alone will not be sufficient. This human rights regime covers some states that have committed rampant violations, and that lack experience in and institutions for curbing the abuse of governmental power. Such a regime must be able to generate significant protective measures if it is to be an effective catalyst of long-term change. The African system — in part through the work of the Commission — must raise the costs to states of violations through one or another of the sanctions with which other human rights regimes are familiar.

CHRISTOF HEYNS & MAGNUS KILLANDER, THE AFRICAN REGIONAL HUMAN RIGHTS SYSTEM

in F. Gomez Isa & K. de Feyter (eds.), International Protection of Human Rights: Achievements and Challenges (2006), at 524

5. 2. The African Commission on Human and Peoples' Rights

... The Commission is not formally an organ of the AU, as it was created by a separate treaty.

5. 2. 1. The Commissioners

The African Commission consists of 11 commissioners, who serve in their individual capacities. The Commission meets twice a year in regular sessions for a period of up to two weeks. They are nominated by state parties to the Charter and elected by the Assembly. The Secretariat of the Commission is based in Banjul, The Gambia. The Commission alternates its meetings between Banjul and other African capitals. The Commission has a protective as well as a promotional mandate.

Although the Charter provides that the Commissioners should be independent there have been many instances where the independence of individual Commissioners has been questioned. The fact that many Commissioners have been serving civil servants or ambassadors has received criticism.... [But, starting in April 2005,] the AU Commission provided guidelines that excluded senior civil servants and diplomatic representatives....

5. 2. 2. The Complaints Procedure

Both states and individuals may bring complaints to the African Commission alleging violations of the African Charter by state parties.

The procedure by which one state brings a complaint about an alleged human rights violation by another state is not often used. Currently one such case is pending before the Commission, between the Democratic Republic of Congo and three neighbouring countries.

The so-called individual communication or complaints procedure is not [c] learly provided for in the African Charter. One reading of the Charter is that communications could be considered only where "serious or massive violations" are at stake, which then triggers the rather futile Article 58 procedure, described below. However, the African Commission has accepted from the start that it has the power to deal with complaints about any human rights violations under the Charter even if "serious or massive" violations are not at stake, provided the admissibility criteria are met.

The Charter is silent on the question who can bring such complaints, but the Commission practice is that complaints from individuals as well as NGOs are accepted. From the case law of the Commission it is clear that the complainant does not need to be a victim or a family member of a victim....

The individual complaints procedure is [not used] ... as frequently as one would have expected on a continent with the kind of human rights problems that Africa has. This could to some extent be attributed to a lack of awareness about the system, but even where there is awareness, there is often not much faith that the system can make a difference. [The authors then cite the study by Viljoen and Louw excerpted below.]

As with other complaints systems, the African Charter poses certain admissibility criteria before the Commission may entertain complaints. The criteria include the requirement of exhausting local remedies. The Commission may be approached only once the matter has been pursued in the highest court in the country in question, without success, or a reasonable prospect of success.

The Commission has stated that for a case not to be admissible local remedies must be available, effective, sufficient and not unduly prolonged. In *Purohit and Moore v the Gambia*, a case dealing with detention in a mental health institution, the Commission gave a potentially far-reaching decision on the exhaustion of local remedies when it held that:

> the category of people being represented in the present communication are likely to be people picked up from the streets or people from poor backgrounds and as such it cannot be said that the remedies available in terms of the Constitution are realistic remedies for them in the absence of legal aid services.

The Charter also has a requirement that the communications are "not written in disparaging or insulting language directed against the state concerned and in institutions or to the Organization of African Unity".

When a complaint is lodged, the state in question is asked to respond to the allegations against it. If the state does not respond, the Commission proceeds on the basis of the facts as provided by the complainant. If the decision of the Commission is that there has indeed been a violation or violations of the Charter, the Commission sometimes also makes recommendations that continuing violations should stop (e. g. prisoners be released); or specific laws be changed, but often the recommendations are rather vague, and the state party is merely urged to "take all necessary steps to comply with its obligations under the Charter." Sometimes there is no provision at all as to remedies, while in other cases the remedies provided are elaborate. Recently the Commission required some states to report on measures taken to comply with the recommendations in their state reports to the Commission.

Article 58 provides that "special cases which reveal the existence of serious or massive violations of human and peoples' rights" must be referred by the Commission to the Assembly, which "may then request the Commission to undertake an in-depth study of these cases". Where the Commission has followed this route, the Assembly has failed to respond, but the Commission has nevertheless made findings that such massive violations have occurred. Today, the Commission does not seem to refer cases anymore to the Assembly in terms of Article 58.

The Charter does not contain a provision in terms of which the Commission has the power to take provisional or interim measures requesting state parties to abstain from causing irreparable harm. However, the Rules of Procedure of the Commission grants the Commission the power to do so. The Commission has used these provisional or interim measures in a number of cases....

5. 2. 3. Consideration of State Reports

Each state party is required to submit a report every two years on its efforts to comply with the African Charter. Although it is not provided for in the African Charter [these reports are now, with the approval of the Assembly, reviewed by the Commission]. NGOs are allowed to submit shadow or alternative reports, but the impact of this avenue is diminished by the lack of access of NGOs to the state reports to which they are supposed to respond. The reports are considered by the Commission in public sessions....

Reporting under the Charter, as in other systems, is aimed at facilitating both introspection and inspection. "Introspection" refers to the process when the state, in writing its report, measures itself against the norms of the Charter. "Inspection" refers to the process when the Commission measures the performance of the state in question against the Charter. The objective is to facilitate a "constructive dialogue" between the Commission and the states.

Reporting has been very tardy, and 18 of the 53 state parties to the African Charter have never submitted any report. In 2001 the Commission started to issue concluding observations in respect of reports considered. Their usefulness is diminished by the fact that neither the state reports nor the concluding observations are published by the Commission.

5. 2. 4. Special Rapporteurs and Working Groups

The Commission has appointed a number of special rapporteurs, with varying degrees of success. There is no obvious legal basis for the appointment of the special rapporteurs in the Charter. . . .

There has been widespread criticism of the lack of effective action on the part of the Special Rapporteur on Summary, Arbitrary and Extrajudicial Executions, while the same is true of at least the first incumbent of the position of Special Rapporteur on the Conditions of Women in Africa. In contrast, the Special Rapporteur on Prisons and Conditions of Detention in Africa has set the standards for years to come.

The Commission has recently appointed special rapporteurs on freedom of expression; refugees and internally displaced persons; and human rights defenders [as well as a committee to monitor guidelines on torture and Working Groups on Indigenous People or Communities and on Economic, Social and Cultural Rights]. Some of the members of these working groups are not members of the Commission.

5. 2. 5. On-Site Visits

The Commission has since 1995 conducted a number of on-site visits. These involve a range of activities, from fact finding to good offices and general promotional visits. Many mission reports have never been published.

5. 2. 6. Resolutions

The Commission has adopted resolutions on a number of human rights issues in Africa. . . .

5. 2. 7. Relationship with NGOs

NGOs have a special relationship with the Commission. Large numbers have registered for observer status. NGOs are often instrumental in bringing cases to the Commission; they sometimes submit shadow reports; propose agenda items at the outset of Commission sessions; and provide logistical and other support to the Commission, for example by placing interns at the Commission and providing support to the special rapporteurs and missions of the Commission. NGOs often organize special NGO workshops just prior to Commission sessions, and participate actively in the public sessions of the Commission. NGOs also collaborate with the Commission in developing normative resolutions and new protocols to the African Charter.

5. 2. 8. Interaction with AU Political Bodies

The Annual Activity Reports of the Commission . . . are submitted each year for permission to publish to the meetings of the Assembly. . . . [The task has since been delegated to the Executive Council.] . . .

In practice the Assembly has served as a rubber stamp for the publication of the report by the Commission containing its decisions, but the principle that the very people in charge of the institutions whose human rights practices are at stake — the Heads of State- should take the final decision on publicity undermines the legitimacy of the system. . . .

. . .

NOTE

Against this background, the materials that follow look at examples of: (1) a Commission fact-finding mission; (2) the work of special rapporteurs and working groups; (3) the Commission's approach to communications; and (4) the Commission's use of resolutions.

(1) Country Missions

The Commission has undertaken mainly 'promotional' rather than fact-finding country missions in recent years. The following is an illustration of the latter.

REPORT OF THE FACT-FINDING MISSION TO ZIMBABWE, 24–28 JUNE 2002

Executive Summary, in Seventeenth Annual Activity Report of the African Commission on Human and Peoples' Rights 2003–2004, Annex II, at 13

Following widespread reports of human rights violations in Zimbabwe, the African Commission [decided in May 2001] . . . to undertake a fact-finding mission to the Republic of Zimbabwe from 24th to 28th June 2002. . . .

FINDINGS

1. The Mission observed that Zimbabwean society is highly polarised. It is a divided society with deeply entrenched positions. The land question is not in itself the cause of division. It appears that at heart is a society in search of the means for change and divided about how best to achieve change after two decades of dominance by a political party that carried the hopes and aspirations of the people of Zimbabwe through the liberation struggle into independence.

2. There is no doubt that from the perspective of the fact-finding team, the land question is critical . . . [but recent legal and other developments mean] that land reform and land distribution can now take place in a lawful and orderly fashion.

3. There was enough evidence placed before the Mission to suggest that, at the very least during the period under review, human rights violations occurred in Zimbabwe. The Mission was presented with testimony from witnesses who were victims of political violence and others victims of torture while in police custody. There was evidence that the system of arbitrary arrests took place. . . .

4. There were allegations that the human rights violations that occurred were in many instances at the hands of ZANU PF [the ruling Zimbabwe African National Union — Patriotic Front] party activists. The Mission is however not able to find definitively that this was part of an orchestrated policy of the government of the Republic of Zimbabwe. . . .

5. The Mission is prepared and able to rule, that the Government cannot wash its hands from responsibility for all these happenings. It is evident that a highly charged

atmosphere has been prevailing, many land activists undertook their illegal actions in the expectation that government was understanding and that police would not act against them — many of them, the War Veterans, purported to act as party veterans and activists. Some of the political leaders denounced the opposition activists and expressed understanding for some of the actions of ZANU (PF) loyalists. Government did not act soon enough and firmly enough against those guilty of gross criminal acts. By its statements and political rhetoric, and by its failure at critical moments to uphold the rule of law, the government failed to chart a path that signalled a commitment to the rule of law.

(2) Special Rapporteurs and Working Groups

The Commission has set up close to 20 special mechanisms, including the following:

> *Special Rapporteurs* on: Extra-judicial Execution, Freedom of Expression and Access to Information, Prisons and Conditions of Detention, Human Rights Defenders, Refugees, Asylum Seekers, Migrants and Internally Displaced Persons, and Rights of Women.
>
> *Committees* for: the Prevention of Torture in Africa, and the Protection of the Rights of People Living With HIV.
>
> *Working Groups* on: Economic, Social and Cultural Rights; Death Penalty; Indigenous Populations/Communities in Africa; Specific Issues Related to the work of the African Commission, Rights of Older Persons and People with Disabilities, Extractive Industries, Environment and Human Rights Violations; and Fair Trial.
>
> In addition there is a Study Group on Freedom of Association, an Advisory Committee on Budgetary and Staff Matters, and a Working Group on Communications.

Some of the mechanisms are very active; others are much less so. For example, in 2012 the Working Group on the Death Penalty in Africa produced a major study examining the prospects for abolishing the death penalty in Africa. It identified the following challenges: 'public support for the death penalty, a support driven by ignorance and exacerbated by illiteracy; absence of effective policing in many countries; the influence of tradition and religion; and the perception by some African governments that abolition is yet another Euro-centric imposition.' It called upon those African states that still retain the death penalty to: 'impose a moratorium on sentencing to death; impose a moratorium on executions and commute all death sentences already passed into fixed-term or life sentences, depending on the gravity of the circumstances of the offence; and refrain from resuming executions once a moratorium is in place.'[65]

But the biggest problem facing the Commission's special mechanisms is their lack of resources. Writing in 2006, Heyns and Killander (p. 1028, *supra*) praised the work

[65] See www.achpr.org/files/news/2012/04/d46/study_question_deathpenalty_africa_2012_eng.pdf.

done by the Special Rapporteur on Prisons and Conditions of Detention in Africa. Yet in 2012 the then current office-holder made the following report to the Commission:

> 1. [Between May 2009 and 2012 the] Special Rapporteur undertook no prison inspection visits. Owing to resource constraints, ambitious projects and programmes which should have included a documentary on best practices have had to be deferred....
>
> 2. I continued to receive reports of poor prison administration in various prisons across the continent. Overcrowding, inadequate food rations, ill treatment of prisoners including torture, neglect of diseases like diarrhoea, tuberculosis, HIV/AIDs amongst inmates, long periods of detention of awaiting trial prisoners arising from slow, tardy prosecution processes, lack of uniforms, failure to confine young offenders to reformatory schools away from main stream prisons, lack of recreation facilities and reform programmes, inadequate sanitary amenities for female prisoners, poor arrangements for babies of prisoners etc., continue to afflict many prisons in Africa. In the absence verifiable data on particular prisons in various countries it would be presumptuous to attempt to engage governments on information received by the Commission through unofficial sources.
>
> 3. The true position, however, is that the majority of African prisons do not meet the Minimum Rules for the Treatment of Prisoners and the African Commission's Ouagadougou Declaration and Plan of Action on Accelerating Prison and Penal Reforms in Africa....

(3) Communications

LAWYERS FOR HUMAN RIGHTS v. SWAZILAND

African Commission on Human and Peoples' Rights, Application 251/2002 (May 2005)

[A Swaziland NGO, Lawyers for Human Rights, lodged a complaint on 3 June 2002 alleging that King Sobhuza I vested all legislative, executive, and judicial power in himself through a Proclamation of 12 April 1973. It also repealed the 1968 democratic Constitution of Swaziland which enshrined democratic principles such as the supremacy of the Constitution, separation of powers, amendment procedures, and a Bill of Rights.]

...

Law

...

Decision on the merits

...

40. The complainant prays the African Commission to:

- find the King's Proclamation of 12 April, 1973 to be in violation of the African Charter on Human and Peoples' Rights; and

- recommend and mandate strongly the Kingdom of Swaziland to take constitutional measures forthwith to give effect to all the provisions of the African Charter, specifically Articles 1, 7, 10, 11, 13 and 26 thereof.

Commission's decision on the merits

41. ... The decision on the merits was taken without any response from the State.... Under such circumstances, the Commission is left with no other option than to take a decision based on the information at its disposal.

42. It must be stated however that, by relying on the information provided by the complainant, the Commission did not rush into making a decision. The Commission analyzed each allegation made and established the veracity thereof.

...

51. In the opinion of the Commission, by ratifying the Charter without at the same time taking appropriate measures to bring domestic laws in conformity with it, the Respondent State's action defeated the very object and spirit of the Charter and thus violating [sic] Article 1 thereof.

52. The complainant also alleges violation of Article 7 of the Charter stating that the Proclamation vests all powers of State to the King, including judicial powers and the authority to appoint and remove judges and Decree No. 3/2001 which ousts the Courts' jurisdiction to grant bail on matters listed in the Schedule. According to the complainant this illustrates that Courts are not independent.

53. Article 7 of the African Charter provides for fair trial guarantees — safeguards to ensure that any person accused of an offence is given a fair hearing....

54. [T]he Proclamation of 1973 and the Decree of 2001 vested judicial power in the King and ousted the jurisdiction of the court on certain matters.... [These acts] not only constitute a violation of the right to fair trial.... but also tend to undermine the independence of the judiciary.

55. Article 26 of the Charter provides that States Parties shall have the duty to guarantee the independence of the courts. [The Commission then invokes provisions of the UN Basic Principles on the Independence of the Judiciary and of the International Bar Association (IBA)'s Minimum Standards of Judicial Independence.]

56. By entrusting all judicial powers to the Head of State with powers to remove judges, the Proclamation of 1973 seriously undermines the independence of the judiciary in Swaziland....

57. In its Resolution on the Respect and the Strengthening on the Independence of the Judiciary adopted [in 1996] ... the African Commission "recognised the need for African countries to have a strong and independent judiciary enjoying the confidence of the people for sustainable democracy and development"....

58. Clearly, retaining a law which vest all judicial powers in the Head of State with possibility of hiring and firing judges directly threatens the independence and security of judges and the judiciary as a whole. The Proclamation of 1973, to the extent that it allows the Head of State to dismiss judges and exercise judicial power is in violation of Article 26 of the African Charter.

59. With regards allegation of violation of Articles 10 and 11, the complainant submits that the Proclamation of 1973 abolishes and prohibits the existence and

the formation of political parties or organisations of a similar nature and that the Proclamation also violates Article 11 — right to assemble peacefully as the right to associate cannot be divorced from the right to assembly freely and peacefully.

...

61. ... By ratifying the Charter without taking appropriate steps to bring its laws in line with the same, the African Commission is of the opinion that the State has not complied with its obligations under Article 1.... The Commission therefore finds the State to have violated these two articles by virtue of the 1973 proclamation.

62. The complainant also alleges violation of Article 13 of the African Charter claiming that the King's Proclamation of 1973 restricted participation of citizens ... in issues of governance only within [local government] structures....

63. ... By prohibiting the formation of political parties, the King's Proclamation seriously undermined the ability of the Swaziland people to participate in the government of their country and thus violated Article 13 of the Charter.

From the above reasoning, the African Commission is of the view that the Kingdom of Swaziland by its Proclamation of 1973 and the subsequent Decree NO. 3 of 2001 violated Articles 1, 7, 10, 11, 13 and 26 of the African Charter.

The Commission hereby recommends as follows:

- that the Proclamation and the Decree be brought in conformity with the provisions of the African Charter;
- that the State engages with other stakeholders, including members of civil society in the conception and drafting of the New Constitution; and
- that the Kingdom of Swaziland should inform the African Commission in writing within six months on the measures it has taken to implement the above recommendations.

EGYPTIAN INITIATIVE FOR PERSONAL RIGHTS AND INTERIGHTS v. ARAB REPUBLIC OF EGYPT

African Commission on Human and Peoples' Rights, Communication 334/06 (Mar. 2011)

...

The African Commission's Analysis on the Merits

157. [T]he African Commission is called upon to determine whether the arrest, pre-trial detention, trial and sentencing of the [three men — referred to as 'the Victims' — who were sentenced to death by Egypt] following their alleged involvement in a bomb attack on 6 October 2004, in the Taba and Noueiba resorts of the Sinai Peninsula which led to the death of 34 and the injury of 105 Egyptian, Israeli and other foreigners, violates the victims' rights guaranteed under Articles 4, 5, 7(1) (a) (c) and 26 of the African Charter as alleged by the Complainants....

...

158. The Commission will accordingly proceed to analyze each of the Articles of the Charter alleged to have been violated by the Respondent State.

Alleged Violation of Article 5

159. The Complainants submit that the Respondent State violated Article 5 in that, the Victims were held incommunicado and denied access to their families, lawyers and medical care by SSI agents. They State that they were beaten, tortured, blindfolded and occasionally hung from the ceiling by their arms and legs in painful positions by SSI agents who applied electrical shocks to several parts of their bodies.

...

165. The Respondent State on the other hand submit that the investigations carried out by the Public Prosecutor established that it has conducted external check on the accused persons immediately when they were brought before it and that it was confirmed that they were free from any external injuries. The question therefore that would follow is, who then inflicted the injuries that were subsequently found on the Victims?

166. The Victims' allegation is also consistent with the forensic reports [although undertaken nine months after the injuries were sustained, found "dark discolorations" on parts of the victims' bodies.] ... [I]n both cases the government examiners concluded that the long time lapse between being examined and the injuries made it impossible to determine with certainty the reason, manner or time of such injuries.

167. The question therefore that begs the mind is who then is responsible for the dark colorations found on the bodies of the Victims? Certainly this could not have been inflicted by the Victims themselves, especially when it has been established that during all this time they were under the custody of the Respondent State's agents.

168. It is a well established principle of international human rights law, that when a person is injured in detention or while under the control of security forces, there is a strong presumption that the person was subjected to torture or ill-treatment. ...

...

170. In the present case, the Respondent State has made no attempt to give a satisfactory explanation of how the injuries were sustained, or to take any steps to investigate and address the surrounding circumstances. The trial court did nothing to follow up on questions raised in the FMA reports or the Victims' testimonies.

171. In the light of the above the African Commission concludes that the marks on the victims evidencing the use of torture could only have been inflicted by the Respondent State.

...

Alleged Violations of Article 7 and 26

191. The Complainants contend that the victims right to fair trial were violated in that;

- they were tried by a Court that was not independent and impartial and whose decisions cannot be appealed;
- their right to a counsel was not fully respected;
- confessions made under torture or ill-treatment were used by the Court; and

- they were denied the right of appeal.

…

200. [T]he African Commission is of the view that the degree of control which the President of the Republic exercises over the composition, conduct and outcome of proceedings before the State Security Court is antithetical to the notion of an independent and impartial judicial process. The law itself provides, for example, for the President to exercise the following powers:

- The President may suspend a case before it is submitted to Supreme State Security Emergency Court. …
- Decisions of the … Emergency Court are final only when they're approved by the President of the Republic, and cannot thereafter be challenged before any other court in Egypt.
- The President of the Republic may commute, change, suspend or cancel such decisions. …

201. [The] Emergency Court is not part of the regular criminal court structure in Egypt. …

…

207. The African Commission is of the view that the degree of control which the President exercises over the composition, conduct and outcome of proceedings before the State Security Court does not guarantee an independent and impartial judicial process. … [The verdict of the Court] did not offer guarantees of independence, impartiality and equity and therefore constitutes a violation of the Article 7 of the African Charter.

208. In any event, it was the responsibility of the Respondent State to adduce sufficient evidence to rebut the arguments that the court in its composition was independent and was capable of giving an impartial ruling, and this the Respondent State has not done. …

…

231. … Having held that the trial of the applicants offended Article 7 of the African Charter, it follows that any implementation of the death sentence imposed on the applicants by the Supreme State Security Emergency courts will therefore amount to an arbitrary deprivation of life.

…

233. For these reasons, the African Commission holds as follows:

(a) That the Respondent State — Republic of Egypt has violated the provisions of Articles 5, 7 (1) (a), (d) and 26 of the African Charter;

…

The African Commission therefore calls on the Respondent State;

I. Not to implement the death sentences;

II. Calls on the Respondent State to adequately compensate the victims in line with international standard;

III. Reform the composition of the State Security Emergency Courts and ensure their independence;

IV. Take measures to ensure that its law enforcement organs particularly the police respect the rights of suspects detained in line with article 5 of the Charter;

V. Calls on the Respondent State to harmonize the State Security Emergency Laws with a view to bringing it in conformity with the Charter and other international legislations and regional norms and standards

VI. Calls on the Respondent State to release the victims;

VII. Calls on the Respondent State to submit the African Commission within 180 days from the date of receipt of this decision ... on the measures taken to give effect to these recommendations.

[On 13 February 2012 Egypt's interim government announced the repeal of the death sentences.]

(4) Resolutions

The Commission has made increasing use of its power to adopt resolutions. Sometimes these are used to follow up on recommendations and sometimes to address entirely new situations.

Resolution 216 (2 May 2012): Human Rights Situation in the Kingdom of Swaziland

[The Commission expresses its 'alarm' at Swaziland's failure to implement the Commission's decision in its 2002 case (p. 1034, *supra*) and recommendations in a 2006 report by the Commission following a promotional mission to the country. The Commission:]

i. Calls on the Government of the Kingdom of Swaziland to respect, protect and fulfil the rights to freedom of expression, freedom of association, and freedom of assembly ...;

ii. Calls on the Government ... to implement the [Commission's] decision ... and submit a report on the status of implementation;

...

Resolution 214 (2 May 2012): Human Rights Situation in Federal Republic of Nigeria

[The Commission addressed itself to un-named non-state actors by 'condemning' attacks on newspaper offices in Abuja and Kaduna and places of worship in Kano and Maidiguri, killing and injuring dozens of people. It:]

3. Calls on the authors of such indefensible acts of violence to immediately stop their attacks against civilians;

4. Urges the Government ... to take all necessary measures to ensure the protection of its civilians in accordance with its regional and international human rights obligations; ...

Resolution 213 (2 May 2012): Unconstitutional Change of Governments

[The Commission] ...

...

Deeply concerned by the recent military takeovers in Mali on 22 March 2012 and in Guinea-Bissau on 12 April 2012 by military juntas, acts that are in violation of the right to participate freely in the government of one's country . . . ;

Further concerned by the serious humanitarian consequences and human rights violations, in particular the killings and arbitrary arrests which are as a result of the unconstitutional change of governments;

Strongly condemns the attempts at instituting autocratic regimes and the unconstitutional change of governments on the continent, acts which it considers to be a serious threat to stability, peace, security and development;

. . .

Calls on African Governments to engage [in] political and social dialogue with a view to promoting democratic practices and consolidating the culture of democracy and peace on the continent;

Urges the African Union and the international community to ensure that democratic governance is respected on the continent;

. . .

Resolution 217 (2 May 2012): Situation of the North of the Republic Mali

[The Commission] . . .

. . .

i. Condemns the unilateral declaration of the independence of Azawad by the MNLA [National Movement for the Liberation of Azawad];

ii. Condemns the attacks carried out by the MNLA, Ansardine, AQMI and Boko Haram against civilian populations and military camps in the north of Mali;

iii. Condemns the continued conflict which is forcing the displacement of thousands of Malians living in the north of Mali;

iv. Further condemns the illegal occupation of Kidal, Gao and Timbuktu by the various armed groups, and attempts at the balkanization of Mali which undermine the country's territorial integrity, national unity and social cohesion;

. . .

viii. Urges the Government of Mali to take all necessary measures to put an end to the conflict and acts of terrorism, and to ensure the security of the civilian population;

ix. Calls on the ECOWAS, African Union and the international community at large to lend their support to the people of Mali in their struggle to preserve the achievements of democracy, national security and the territorial integrity of Mali.

Resolution 218 (2 May 2012): Human Rights Situation in the Democratic Republic of Ethiopia

[The Commission] . . .

. . .

Deeply Concerned at the frequent allegations of the use of torture in pre-trial detention in Ethiopia, particularly in the Federal Police Crime Investigation and Forensic Department of Maikelawi in Addis Ababa . . . ;

Further Concerned with the difficulties encountered by independent monitors, legal representatives and family members to visit prisoners and to access places of detention . . . ;

Deeply concerned at the reported use of unofficial and ungazetted places of detention in Ethiopia, including military camps and private buildings, wherein torture is reported to take place . . . ;

Gravely alarmed by the arrests and prosecutions of journalists and political opposition members, charged with terrorism and other offences including treason, for exercising their peaceful and legitimate rights to freedom of expression and freedom of association;

Condemning the excessive restrictions placed on human rights work by the Charities and Societies Proclamation, denying human rights organizations access to essential funding, endowing the Charities and Societies Agency with excessive powers of interference in human rights organizations, further endangering victims of human rights violations by contravening principles of confidentiality;

[The Commission then calls on the government to address the various problems identified.]

NOTE

In a study of compliance with the Commission's decisions Frans Viljoen and Lirrette Louw[66] note that:

> [T]he attempt to chart compliance empirically and analytically is fraught with methodological difficulties. The most important of these is the Commission's failure to enunciate clear and specific remedies, leaving an unreliable yardstick for measuring compliance. Even when the yardstick is clearer, linking the steps toward compliance to the required remedial action often remains a matter of causal conjecture.
>
> Our analysis of cases of full and clear noncompliance suggests that the most important factors predictive of compliance are political, rather than legal. The only factor relating to the treaty body itself that shows a significant link to improved compliance is its follow-up activities. This finding lends support to arguments for a fully developed and effectively functional follow-up mechanism in the secretariat of the Commission, the consistent integration of follow-up activities into the Commission's mandate, and the appointment of a Special Rapporteur on follow-up. . . .
>
> [T]he Commission in November 2006 [called upon states parties to the Charter] . . . to report on compliance within ninety days of being notified of decisions against them [and] decided to include a report on "the compliance with its recommendations" in future activity reports.
>
> . . . [O]ur study suggests that the mere fact that the [African] Court will provide legally binding and specific remedies and better formulated judgments will not in

[66] F. Viljoen Y L. Louw, 'State Compliance with the Recommendations of the African Commission on Human and Peoples' Rights, 1994–2004', 101 Am. J. Int'l. L. 1 (2007), at 32.

> itself guarantee improved state compliance. The advent of the Court may coincide with a gradual hardening of human rights commitments and lead to improved human rights adherence, but it would then be on the strength of a stronger domestic and regional political commitment, increased publicity, and greater involvement of civil society.
>
> Inadequate political commitment at the regional level is an important factor underlying the lack of state compliance....
>
> ...[During the OAU period, the] absence of debate or the imposition of sanctions on states found in violation of the Charter translated into a lack of political pressure within the regional system to comply with the Commission's recommendations....

The authors conclude that while the AU Charter has brought significant improvements in institutional arrangements, it still remains to be seen whether the AU will take effective action based on the opportunities available to it.

COMMENT ON THE AFRICAN COURT ON HUMAN AND PEOPLES' RIGHTS

When the African Charter was adopted in 1981 a clear decision was taken to opt for a Commission rather than a Court as the principal institutional arrangement. Negotiations to establish a Court continued, however, and in 1998 the OAU Assembly adopted a Protocol to the African Charter on Human and Peoples' Rights to establish an African Court on Human and Peoples' Rights. The Protocol entered into force in 2004, after 15 states parties to the Charter had ratified it. As of May 2012 there were 26 parties.

The Court, based in Arusha, Tanzania, consists of 11 judges 'elected in an individual capacity'; no two judges may be nationals of the same state (Art. 11). Its membership is to include 'representation of the main regions of Africa and of their principal legal traditions', and in the election of judges the Assembly 'shall ensure that there is adequate gender representation' (Art. 14). Judicial independence is to be fully ensured (Art. 17). All judges must be from Africa and a judge must not sit in a case concerning his or her own state of nationality. The President of the Court works full time, while the other ten judges work on a part-time basis.

The Court's jurisdiction extends to cases and disputes 'concerning the interpretation and application' of the Charter, Protocol, 'and any other relevant human rights instrument ratified by the States concerned' (Art. 3). At the request of a member state of the OAU or the AU, the Court may give its advisory opinion 'on any legal matter related to the Charter or any other relevant human rights instruments', provided that the matter is not then being examined by the Commission (Art. 4).

To invoke the Court's contentious jurisdiction, the Commission, a state party that has brought a complaint before the Commission or against whom a complaint has been brought, a state party whose citizen is a victim of a violation, and African intergovernmental organizations can submit a case to the Court (Art. 5). On the other hand, the capacity of individuals and NGOs to bring a complaint against a state depends both on a special declaration by the state and on the discretion of the Court (Arts. 5 and 34). This double barrier represents a sharp contrast with the access of individuals to the other two regional courts. As of May 2012 only five states (Burkina Faso, Ghana, Malawi, Mali, and Tanzania) had made the Article 5 declaration.

The Commission continues to play an important role under the Protocol. The provisions on admissibility provide that the Court 'may consider cases or transfer them to the Commission' (Art. 6). The Court's Rules of Procedure are to state the conditions under which the Court shall consider cases, 'bearing in mind the complementarity between the Commission and the Court' (Art. 8). The communications procedure itself of the Commission is not reconciled with the new Court; it remains unclear when one or the other path should be followed by an institution or individual intending to submit a complaint against a state. Thus, the two organs appear to be in competition with each other, without any clear hierarchy, posing a large risk of duplication of effort.

If the Court finds a violation, 'it shall make appropriate orders to remedy the violation' (Art. 27). States parties to the Protocol 'undertake to comply with the judgment in any case to which they are parties... and to guarantee its execution' (Art. 30). The OAU Council of Ministers is to 'monitor' a judgment's execution (Art. 29).

The Court's first judgment, in *Yogogombaye v. Republic of Senegal* (Application No. 001/2008), was issued on 15 December 2009. The application, seeking the suspension of proceedings instituted in Senegal against Hissen Habre, former President of the Republic of Chad, was declared inadmissible since Senegal had not made the Article 5 declaration.

In March 2011, in *African Commission on Human and Peoples' Rights v. Great Socialist People's Libyan Arab Jamahiriya* (Application No. 004/2011), the Court examined alleged grave violations of human rights by the Libyan Government of Colonel Gaddafi. It considered that the circumstances in Libya and the imminent risks involved 'made it difficult' to serve the application on the government and to arrange a hearing, and thus opted to forego both written pleadings and oral hearings. In ordering provisional measures it called upon the government to 'immediately refrain from any action that would result in loss of life or violation of physical integrity of persons, which could be in breach' of its human rights obligations. It noted that these provisional measures were without prejudice to any findings it might subsequently make on jurisdiction, admissibility, or merits.

QUESTIONS

1. Does the Commission's decision in the Egyptian case set any important precedents that might be used any time soon in relation to other countries of the region?

2. What aspects of the resolutions adopted by the Commission in 2012 appear to be noteworthy? The range of issues dealt with, the entities addressed, the degree of detail provided, the language used, and the recommendations made?

3. Should the Commission in the Swaziland case have undertaken an analysis more along the lines of the ECtHR to assess whether the King might have been justified in taking some of the measures contained in the Proclamation complained of?

4. Do the provisional measures issued by the Court in the Libyan case represent a good precedent?

ADDITIONAL READING

F. Viljoen, *International Human Rights Law in Africa* (2nd edn. 2012); K. O. Kufuor, *The African Human Rights System: Origin and Evolution* (2010); O. C. Okafor, *The African Human Rights System, Activist Forces and International Institutions* (2010) M. Evans & R. Murray, *The African Charter on Human and Peoples' Rights: The System in Practice 1986–2006* (2nd edn. 2008); H. Abbas (ed.), *Africa's Long Road to Rights: Reflections on the 20th Anniversary of the African Commission on Human and Peoples' Rights* (2007); G. W. Mugwanya, *Human Rights in Africa* (2003); R. Murray, *Human Rights in Africa: From the OAU to the African Union* (2004); P. T. Zeleza & P. McConnaughay (eds.), *Human Rights, The Rule of Law, and Development in Africa* (2004); *Compendium of Key Human Rights Documents of the African Union* (2005); C. Heyns, 'The African Regional Human Rights System: The African Charter', 108 Penn. St. L. Rev. 679 (2004); F. Ougergouz, *The African Charter of Human and People's Rights: A Comprehensive Agenda for Human Dignity And Sustainable Democracy In Africa* (2003).

PART E

STATES AS PROTECTORS AND ENFORCERS OF HUMAN RIGHTS

Part E completes the basic structure of this course book. We first examined in Parts A–C the processes for the creation of international human rights norms and the basic categories of civil, political, economic and social rights. Our attention then turned in Part D to the relations between norms and institutions, particularly to the significance of international institutions and processes for the development and enforcement of norms.

Those parts gave primary attention to the international dimensions of the human rights regime. Of course, states — the creators of the norms, the designers and members of the institutions, the participants in the processes, as well as the primary duty-bearers under international human rights law — figured prominently in these earlier materials. They appeared frequently as the violators, the defendants, the entities being monitored, investigated and reported on by intergovernmental and nongovernmental organizations.

Part E shifts focus. Here we observe primarily the internal processes of the states themselves, particularly the decisions and acts of governments bearing on human rights issues. Our perspective is that of the state rather than the international community. For the most part, we examine executive, legislative and judicial decisions concerning the protection of human rights, rather than state action violating rights. In short, we here imagine states — and public institutions that compose the state — as the first-line enforcers of the international human rights system that they have created.

Part E has two chapters, both of which involve the interpenetration of national legal-political orders and the international system. Chapter 12 examines ways in which states observe and protect human rights. Chapter 13 examines the ways in which a state acts abroad as an enforcer of human rights norms against violator states.

In both chapters, as in the entire course book, the materials view the state primarily *in its relationships* to the international system. That is, these chapters do not examine state politics, history or culture *independently* of that system. Within this framework, states are meant to draw from and work to increase the efficacy of the international standards. The chapters discuss variations of state practice across several countries and types of legal systems.

12

Vertical Interpenetration: International Human Rights Law Within States' Legal and Political Orders

Ultimately, effective protection of human rights must come from within the state. The international system generally seeks to compel states to fulfil their obligations through one or another method — either observing national law (constitutional or statutory) that is consistent with the international norms, or making the international norms themselves part of the national legal and political order. Such is the focus of Chapter 12, which falls into two sections. Section A studies how states generally 'internalize' treaties and customary international law — that is, how states absorb international human rights norms within their domestic legal and political systems so that international human rights obligations can be implemented and enforced by state authorities. Section B addresses the specific topic of ratification of treaties, including the state practice of attaching reservations to opt out of particular obligations imposed by the treaty regime.

A. DOMESTIC INTERNALIZATION OF INTERNATIONAL LAW

Part A begins by focusing on the incorporation of international instruments, specifically human rights treaties, in domestic legal and political systems. It examines the interpenetration of the international and national systems, and the significance of treaties within states. Our discussion then expands to include relationships between customary international law and national systems. The broad questions explored are: how do these international norms influence the national legal and political systems of states? Are they automatically absorbed into a state legal system, or reproduced in state legislation, and with what effects on the different branches of government such as the executive and judiciary? Or do they remain distinct from the state system, 'above' it as part of international law? The readings draw on the techniques and experiences of a range of countries in this excursion into comparative constitutional and foreign affairs law.

COMMITTEE ON ECONOMIC, SOCIAL AND CULTURAL RIGHTS, GENERAL COMMENT NO. 9

Domestic Application of the Covenant, UN Doc. E/1999/22, Annex IV, 1998

A. The duty to give effect to the Covenant in the domestic legal order

...

2. [The Covenant requires] each State Party to use all the means at its disposal to give effect to the rights recognized in the Covenant.... Thus the norms themselves must be recognised in appropriate ways within the domestic legal order, appropriate means of redress, or remedies, must be available to any aggrieved individual or group, and appropriate means of ensuring governmental accountability must be put in place.

...

B. The status of the Covenant in the domestic legal order

4. In general, legally binding international human rights standards should operate directly and immediately within the domestic legal system of each State party, thereby enabling individuals concerned to seek enforcement of their rights before national courts and tribunals. The rule requiring the exhaustion of domestic remedies reinforces the primacy of national remedies in this respect....

5. The Covenant itself does not stipulate the specific means by which its terms are to be implemented in the national legal order. And there is no provision obligating its comprehensive incorporation or requiring it to be accorded any specific type of status in national law. Although the precise method by which Covenant rights are given effect in national law is a matter for each State Party to decide, the means used should be appropriate in the sense of producing results which are consistent with the full discharge of its obligations by the State Party. The means chosen are also subject to review as part of the Committee's examination of the State Party's compliance with its Covenant obligations.

...

C. The role of legal remedies

...

11. The Covenant itself does not negate the possibility that the rights may be considered self-executing in systems where that option is provided for. Indeed, when it was being drafted, attempts to include a specific provision in the Covenant providing that it be considered 'non-self-executing' were strongly rejected. In most States the determination of whether or not a treaty provision is self-executing will be a matter for the courts, not the executive or the legislature. In order to perform that function effectively the relevant courts and tribunals must be made aware of

the nature and implications of the Covenant and of the important role of judicial remedies in its implementation.... [W]hen Governments are involved in court proceedings, they should promote interpretations of domestic laws which give effect to their Covenant obligations....

...

D. The treatment of the Covenant in domestic courts

...

13. ... [S]ome courts have applied the provisions of the Covenant either directly or as interpretive standards. Other courts are willing to acknowledge, in principle, the relevance of the Covenant for interpreting domestic law, but in practice, the impact of the Covenant on the reasoning or outcome of cases is very limited. Still other courts have refused to give any degree of legal effect to the Covenant in cases in which individuals have sought to rely on it....

14. Within the limits of the appropriate exercise of their functions of judicial review, courts should take account of Covenant rights where this is necessary to ensure that the State's conduct is consistent with its obligations under the Covenant. Neglect by the courts of this responsibility is incompatible with the principle of the Rule of Law which must always be taken to include respect for international human rights obligations.

...

CHRISTOF HEYNS & FRANS VILJOEN, THE IMPACT OF THE UNITED NATIONS HUMAN RIGHTS TREATIES ON THE DOMESTIC LEVEL

(2002)

[The following presents the findings of a study initiated in collaboration with the Office of the High Commissioner for Human Rights. The study examines the effectiveness of the UN human rights treaty system across a variety of states.]

...

[T]he position in the following countries was investigated:

African region: Egypt, Senegal, South Africa, Zambia
Asian region: India, Iran, Japan, the Philippines
Eastern European region: the Czech Republic, Estonia, Romania, the Russian Federation (Russia)
Latin American and Caribbean region: Brazil, Colombia, Jamaica, Mexico
Western Europe and Other (WEOG) region: Australia, Canada, Finland, Spain

...

Compatibility studies comparing the treaties with domestic legislation prior to ratification or accession were done in respect of all six treaties in Brazil, Canada, Egypt, Japan and South Africa. Compatibility studies were done only in respect of some of the treaties, or were done to a limited extent only, in Australia, Finland, India, Iran, Jamaica, Romania, Senegal, Spain and Zambia. (In Senegal a study comparing the treaties and the Senegalese Constitution, but not ordinary legislation, was undertaken.)...

Compatibility studies have sometimes resulted in legislative amendments as part of the process of ratification or accession. Finland amended its Penal Code before ratifying CERD.

Compatibility studies have also culminated in the entering of reservations upon ratification (eg Australia (CERD), Finland, India, Japan). As mentioned above, a compatibility study in respect of CEDAW resulted in Iran not ratifying that Convention. In respect of CRC it led to a controversial reservation.

...

IMPACT OF THE TREATIES

...

i Level of awareness of the treaties

The younger generation of urbanised lawyers, government officials (mostly from departments of foreign affairs) and academics who deal with the treaties, and NGOs with a specific focus on an area covered by the treaties are the groups most likely to be familiar with the treaties throughout the world.

CERD is well known in some countries where race (ethnicity or religion) is an issue (eg Australia (especially in respect of indigenous peoples' issues), the Czech Republic, but not in Egypt, Finland (this is changing), Jamaica, Japan, the Philippines, Zambia). If one has to generalise, there seems to be a higher level of awareness in a number of countries of CEDAW and CRC than of other treaties (eg Canada, Japan, Mexico (especially CRC), South Africa, Spain, Zambia). NGOs are mobilised around these special treaties (eg Senegal). CESCR seems not to be well known in a number of countries (eg India, Japan, Mexico, Philippines), although in other countries (eg Romania, South Africa) NGOs are mobilised around this Covenant. CCPR has attracted special attention in a number of societies (eg Finland). In Iran CRC, in respect of which the controversial reservation cited above was made, ironically seems to be the only treaty of which there is some awareness. Knowledge of CAT is largely confined to those responsible for its implementation (eg Japan, Mexico).

...

Through a systematic newspaper search, less than 10 articles directly referring to the treaties were found in Brazil, Colombia, the Philippines and South Africa. Only Australia, Canada and Finland revealed a significant number of articles. (Over 800 are reported from Australia; over 100 from Canada; and from Finland the number of articles about two controversial cases before the HRC is estimated to exceed "several dozens".)

ii Constitutional recognition of treaty norms

The treaty norms form the basis of, or at least coincide with, most of the constitutional human rights provisions, such as the bills and charters of rights, of the 20 countries reviewed. This method of internalising treaty norms into the domestic legal system, especially where the constitutional human rights provisions are justiciable, constitutes one of the most powerful ways in which treaty norms could be enforced on the local level.

...In some instances...the treaties have impacted on the bills of rights even when they had not been ratified at the time (eg CRC in Brazil, CESCR in South Africa)....

The impact of the treaties on the constitutional human rights provisions in respect of which they have played a role may be categorised as follows:

- The treaties played an identifiable and significant role in the drafting process of constitutional human rights provisions

  To this category belong South Africa's 1993 and 1996 Constitutions (the greatest impact on the bill of rights recorded in the study); Brazil (most of the treaties, especially CESCR; also CRC even before it was ratified); Canada (especially CCPR was used as the basis of the 1982 Charter); Finland (when the bill of rights was changed in 1995, the treaties were clearly influential in the drafting, to the extent that the specific wording was followed).
- Many of the treaty norms are mirrored in bills of rights, and there is some (but not a very clear) causal link between the treaties and the constitutional human rights provisions

  This applies to Colombia (CESCR, CCPR were relied on by delegates in the Constitutional Convention who redrafted the constitution in 1991); the Czech Republic (CECSR is linked to the inclusion of socio-economic rights; CCPR also mirrored); Estonia (although the European Convention was more influential in the 1992 redraft); the Philippines (the 1987 Bill of Rights reflects the rights in CESCR and CCPR); Romania (the 1991 Constitution includes most of the rights in CESCR and CCPR, and some of those in the other treaties); Russia (a government report indicates that only one provision in the two Covenants is not affirmed in the Russian Constitution); and Spain (the 1978 Bill of Rights was drafted one year after the ratification of CCPR and CESCR, but there was little influence).
- Only some norms are reflected in constitutional human rights provisions, and there is no clear link between them.

  Egypt, Iran

iii Legislative reform

Numerous instances of legislative reform that were prompted by the treaties have been identified. Some of this reform took place as a result of compatibility studies, other in response to concluding observations, and some in the course of ordinary legislative review. A sample of only that legislation in which explicit reference was made to the treaties is given below:

Australia: Human Rights and Equal Opportunities Commission Act 1986 (CERD, CCPR and CRC); Native Titles Act of 1993 (CERD and CESCR); Aboriginal and Torres Strait Islander Commission Act of 1989 (CERD and CESCR); Workplace Relations Act 1996 (CESCR and CEDAW); Industrial Relations Reform Act 1993 (CESCR and CEDAW); Commonwealth and NSW Evidence Act of 1995 (CCPR); Sex Discrimination Act of 1984 (CEDAW); Various extradition legislation refers to CAT; the Australian Law Reform Commission often refers to CCPR in its law reform activities.

Brazil: Children's and Adolescents' Statute (CRC).

Canada: Canadian Multiculturalism Act (CERD and CCPR); Emergencies Act (CCPR).

Finland: Amendment of the Penal Code (CERD); enactment of the Equality Act and amendments to other laws (CEDAW); amendments to the Aliens Act, Act on Military Discipline and Act on Public Meetings (CCPR).

India: The Protection of Human Rights Act 1993, which created the National Human Rights Commission, defines "human rights" with reference to the Covenants.

Japan: The explanatory note of the Alien Registration Act cites the Covenants. (Especially CEDAW prompted dramatic changes in the laws of Japan.)

Mexico: The government of the Federal District (Mexico City) has incorporated the definition of discrimination as contained in CERD in its legislation; the Law for Minor lnfractors (CRC).

Philippines: Inter Country Adoption Act 1995, Family Courts Act 1997, Domestic Adoption Act 1998 (CRC).

Senegal: Amendment of the Criminal Code (CRC and CEDAW).

South Africa: Equality Bill (CERD and CEDAW); Domestic Violence Act (CEDAW and CRC); Maintenance Act (CRC and CEDAW).

Spain: The Penal Code was amended in accordance with CAT.

Zambia: Affiliation and Maintenance of Children Act (CRC).

There is ample evidence of the impact of the treaties on legislation in Finland (where they have been incorporated into national law) and Russia. They have played a very limited role in Colombia.

iv Judicial decisions

In some isolated instances, treaties have been used as an independent basis on which the substantive outcome of cases in domestic courts has hinged. Much more frequently, however, courts have used the treaties as interpretative guides to clarify legislative provisions, such as those of the national bills of rights.

Treaties have been used as the basis for substantive outcomes in Estonia (CRC) and Japan (CCPR was held to be self-executing). The Colombian Constitutional Court has an exceptional record of reference to the treaties, and has in 129 cases between 1992 and 1998 based their decisions on CCPR. CCPR has also played a significant role in the high courts in India.

Based purely on the number of references to the treaties as a tool of interpretation in decided cases traced in the course of this study, the following categories may be identified:

- Frequent use of treaties as an interpretative tool
  Australia (844 instances in which reference was made to at least one of the six treaties on the basis of a Lexis database case search); Canada (169 references); Finland (more than 36 references); South Africa (at least 28 references); Spain (at least 28 references)
- Infrequent use of treaties as an interpretative tool
  The Philippines (at least 8 references); the Czech Republic (at least 6 references)
- Very limited reference to treaties
  India (about 14 references), Romania (at least 7 references), Russia (a "very limited number of cases"), Egypt (at least 1 case), Zambia (one reference). In respect of Jamaica the only reference was in a decision of the Privy Council.
- No reference whatsoever to treaties found
  Iran, Mexico, Senegal

v Development of policy, etc.

In a number of countries national action plans on human rights in general, or plans that focus on particular interest groups that were largely inspired by the treaties have been developed....

National human rights institutions (or similar institutions) often make use of the treaties (eg in Colombia, Finland, India). The South African Human Rights Commission has a special mandate to monitor socio-economic rights, in respect of which CESCR (and to some extent the concomitant jurisprudence such as the General Comments of the CESCR Committee) plays a significant role. The Parliamentary Ombudsman in Finland and the Colombian Human Rights Ombudsman often make use of the treaties.

...

vi Use by NGOs

NGOs use specific treaties as focal points for lobbying activities (eg in Australia, Canada, India, the Philippines, Romania, Russia, Senegal). In Iran and Zambia this has happened in respect of children's and women's rights. Women's NGOs in Japan rally around CEDAW....

vii Academic publications

References to the treaties in academic publications (largely legal journals or books) are found in most of the countries reviewed. However, as systematic searches were not performed in each case, conclusive figures are not available.

The Australian, Canadian and South African reports cited the most references to the treaties, while Brazil, Colombia, Mexico, the Philippines and Senegal cited the least.

...

LIMITING AND ENHANCING FACTORS

...

Factors limiting the impact of the treaties

- There is ample evidence in the study that because governments guard their sovereignty jealously, they resist international supervision and are reluctant to implement recommendations and views.
- In many instances, however, conscious resistance is not necessary. The widespread ignorance of the treaty system in government circles, among lawyers and in civil societies around the world, effectively blocks any impact which the treaties may otherwise have had....
- The absence of a domestic human rights culture is another obvious factor that limits the impact of the UN treaties in many societies. A low level of domestic implementation of human rights norms in a particular country makes international supervision more important, but in practice the system is less likely to have an effect under such circumstances (Egypt, Iran, Zambia). In order for international human rights treaties to have an impact, an enabling domestic environment is required. The Japanese report mentions that the treaties need "domestic constituencies". An inactive civil society is also reflected in the absence of a strong domestic NGO sector....
- In some countries there is a shortage of journalists with human rights training (eg Czech Republic, Senegal)....
- Socio-economic factors often have a negative influence on the potential impact of the treaties. Illiteracy of the population is an important factor in this regard (eg Egypt, Senegal, Zambia)....

  ...
- In some instances treaties are associated with unpopular political causes (such as the abolition of the death penalty and restraints on the police in Jamaica; the fate of migrants and gypsies in Spain, secessionist movements in Senegal and India) and as such they are more readily discounted by governments and civil society, and human rights groups become reluctant to rely on these treaties. (At the same time the relevance of human rights to these causes inevitably enhances their legitimacy in the eyes of those who support them.).

  ...
- In some instances the progressive and effective protection of human rights on the domestic level could render the international system redundant. The South African Bill of Rights, for example, has incorporated most of the international norms, and in some cases provides a higher level of protection than the treaties (also Finland (CEDAW)).

- There is a lack of co-ordination within governments (between departments on the national level, and between national and local levels), between NGOs and between governments and NGOs. Making a treaty the exclusive responsibility of a certain government department limits its reach (eg CEDAW in Spain), although it is seen as necessary for one department to co-ordinate the others (eg CRC in Spain).
- The treaties cover six separate areas of human rights, but government departments are not organised in that way. The international and national systems are not synchronised. For example, normally a single government body is not responsible for children's rights. This makes it difficult in practice to pinpoint responsibility on the domestic level (Canada).
- Reporting is widely seen as an ad hoc activity, a once-off burden which the state has to deal with every few years, and not a continuous effort which involves an ongoing cycle of reporting....

  ...From the Russian perspective the reporting cycles are regarded as too long. Successive administrations are given the chance effectively to deny responsibility for what happened before the previous elections.
- Federal states find it more difficult to report (Canada) and at times also to take decisions to ratify treaties (Australia). In any event, awareness and impact is least at the lower levels of government, such as in the local government sphere (eg in South Africa).

...

- Correspondents report a widespread preference for regional systems above the UN system....According to the report on Estonia, the Council of Europe supports its human rights system better than the UN, by means of seminars, financial assistance and help with compatibility studies....

...

Best practices

The following practices that were encountered are among those that seem to have the potential to enhance the impact of the system:

- Interdepartmental institutions have been created to co-ordinate reporting on a continuous scale in a number of countries.
- In Finland public hearings are held on the basis of draft reports prior to their submission to the UN.

...

- In Estonia the state translated the concluding observations into Estonian and distributed them. It then took the initiative to have these published in privately owned newspapers. The concluding observations also were tabled in cabinet.
- A "tripartite follow-up" of politicians, government officials and NGOs was convened in respect of the concluding observations of the HRC in respect of the CCPR report in Japan, although it did not reach its full potential.
- In Colombia and Finland there are special procedures for the enforcement of the views of the treaty bodies.

...

- The Australian Law Reform Commission is required by statute to take international human rights treaties (and particularly CCPR) into account.

...

- In Japan the Prime Minister has been questioned in parliament on the implementation of concluding observations of the HRC....
- In South Africa the new constitution was tested by the Constitutional Court to establish whether it gave recognition to all internationally recognised human rights before it became law. The constitution states that courts must consider international law in interpreting the bill of rights.
- The Indian Supreme Court has overruled a reservation that India has entered in respect of CCPR, to the effect that victims of unlawful detention would not have a right to claim compensation.
- In Finland the Bill of Rights Drafting Commission that drafted the 1995 constitutional changes started their work by drawing up a comparative chart of those human rights contained in treaties ratified by Finland.
- In Australia country reports are tabled in parliament.

...

PROPOSALS

...

National human rights institutions (or similar institutions) are found in an increasing number of countries around the world today. It is proposed that they should be involved more prominently in mediating the interface between the UN and the relevant role players in the various states (civil servants as well as members of civil society). In particular, they should be encouraged to do their own follow-up of UN procedures, both as regards concluding observations and individual complaints, and to keep track of what has been done by governments in this respect. This information should be included in the yearly reports of national human rights institutions....

...

AFTERWORD

When one compares the world as it is with what it would have been without the treaties, treaties have made a huge difference. But when one considers their potential impact, much still remains to be done.

VIRGINIA LEARY, INTERNATIONAL LABOUR CONVENTIONS AND NATIONAL LAW

(1982), at 1

[The efficacy of human rights treaties] depends essentially on the incorporation of their provisions in national law....

...

International law determines the validity of treaties in the international legal system, i.e., when and how a treaty becomes binding upon a state as regards other State Parties. It also determines the remedies available on the international plane for its breach. But it is the national legal system which determines the status or force of law which will be given to a treaty within that legal system, i.e., whether national judges and administrators will apply the norms of a treaty in a specific case.... When the treaty norms become domestic law, national judges and administrators apply them, and individuals in the ratifying states may receive rights as a result of the treaty provisions. Thus, developed municipal legal systems supplement the more limited enforcement system of international law.

While the international legal system does not reach *directly* into the national systems to enforce its norms it attempts to do so *indirectly.* States are required under international law to bring their domestic laws into conformity with their validly contracted international commitments. Failure to do so, however, results in an international delinquency but does not change the situation within the national legal systems where judges and administrators may continue to apply national law rather than international law in such cases....

The status of treaties in national law is determined by two different constitutional techniques referred to in this study as 'legislative incorporation' and 'automatic incorporation'. In some states the provisions of ratified treaties do not become national law unless they have been enacted as legislation by the normal method. The legislative act creating the norms as domestic law is an act entirely distinct from the act of ratification of the treaty. The legislative bodies may refuse to enact legislation implementing the treaty. In this case the provisions of the treaty do not become national law. This method, referred to as 'legislative incorporation', is used, inter alia, in the United Kingdom, Commonwealth countries and Scandinavian countries. In other states, which have a different system, ratified treaties become domestic law by virtue of ratification. This method is referred to as 'automatic incorporation' and is the method adopted, inter alia, by France, Switzerland, the Netherlands...and many Latin American countries and some African and Asian countries.... Even in such states, however, some treaty provisions require implementing legislation before they will be applied by the courts. Such provisions are categorized as 'non-self-executing'.

...

International law does not dictate that one or the other of the methods of legislative or automatic incorporation must be used. Either is satisfactory assuming that the norms of treaties effectively become part of national law. Conversely, neither method is *ipso facto* satisfactory under international law, if, in practice, the norms of ratified treaties are not applied by national judges and administrators. The method by which treaties become national law is a matter in principle to be determined by the constitutional law of the ratifying state and not a matter ordained by international law. The international community, lacking more effective means of enforcement, is often dependent on the constitutional system of particular states for the effective application of treaties intended for internal application.

Some national constitutions provide for automatic incorporation of treaty provisions. In other states, judicial decisions have determined that treaties are to be automatically incorporated. A correlation appears to exist between legislative consent to ratification and automatic incorporation. In states with the system of automatic incorporation, legislative consent by at least one house of the legislature is generally required before the executive may ratify treaties. In states with the system of legislative incorporation, ratification of treaties is frequently a purely executive act not requiring prior approbation of the legislature. In the United Kingdom, and other common law countries which have followed UK precedent in this regard, parliamentary consent to ratification is normally not required and express legislative enactment of treaty provisions is necessary before they become domestic law.

...

An individual may invoke the provisions of a treaty before national courts in automatic incorporation states in the absence of implementing legislation only when its provisions are considered to be self-executing and when he has standing to do so.... [I]n general, treaty provisions are considered by national courts and administrators as self-executing when they lend themselves to judicial or administrative application without further legislative implementation....

...

COMMENT ON MONISM AND DUALISM

Comparative analyses of different constitutional approaches to incorporating international law often refer to 'monist' and 'dualist' theories concerning the relationship between international and national law. Monist theories imagine a unitary world legal system in which national and international law have 'comparable, equivalent, or identical subjects, sources, and substantive contents'.[1] Monists argue for the supremacy of international law in relation to national law. In its classical formulation, monism asserts that all activity of states is regulated by the superior international law. Thus the so-called 'domestic affairs' of a state are not affairs unregulated by international law, but rather affairs which a state has exclusive competence to regulate pursuant to and under international law.

Dualist theories distinguish between the system or public order of international law and of national law. Each has 'its own distinguishable subjects, distinguishable structures and processes of authority, and distinguishable substantive content'. Thus the subjects of international law are only states, its sources lie only in treaties and custom made by states, and its content involves only relations between states. Neither international law nor national law can *per se* create or invalidate the other. Of course, a state may by its own custom or national law adopt rules of international law as the law of the land, through practices and theories of incorporation, transformation, adoption and so on.

[1] All quotations in this Note are taken from Myres McDougal, 'The Impact of International Law upon National Law: A Policy-Oriented Perspective', 4 S. Dak. L. Rev. 25 (1959), at 27–31.

Hans Kelsen has stressed the different perspectives on institutions, world values and order that these two theories express:

> ...It may be that our choice...is guided by ethical or political preferences. A person whose political attitude is that of nationalism and imperialism may be inclined to accept as a hypothesis the basic norm of his own national law. A person whose sympathy is for internationalism and pacifism may be inclined to accept as a hypothesis the basic norm of international law and thus proceed from the primacy of international law. From the point of view of the science of law, it is irrelevant which hypothesis one chooses. But from the point of view of politics, the choice [between dualism and monism] may be important since it is tied up with the ideology of sovereignty.[2]

The monist theory is illustrated by the Dutch Constitution of 1983, discussed in the following excerpts:[3]

> ...Art. 93 of the Constitution provides that provisions of treaties and decisions of international organisations, the contents of which may be binding on everyone, shall have this binding effect as from the time of publication. The words 'the contents of which may be binding on everyone' are generally understood to refer to the self-executing character which is required for their application by Dutch Courts. The rights contained in the ECHR are considered self-executing by the courts and are therefore directly applicable.
>
> ...
>
> ...[Pursuant to Article 94 of the Dutch Constitution, Dutch courts must] give precedence to self-executing treaty provisions over domestic law that is not in conformity therewith, be it antecedent or posterior, statutory or constitutional law....But the courts have no competence to nullify, repeal or amend the legislation in question. The provision remains in force, but will not be applied.
>
> ...
>
> 3. *Case-law*
>
> ...
>
> [The earlier] reticent attitude of Dutch courts towards the ECHR has changed quite dramatically during the 1980s. The statistical survey recently given by Van Dijk shows a considerable increase of references to the ECHR. The percentage of cases, however, in which the Supreme Court has found a violation of the Convention remains small (an average of 9%). When confronted with a conflict between a provision of the ECHR and a provision of Dutch law, the Supreme Court tends to circumvent it by giving to the latter an interpretation or scope different from its original meaning and from the anterior legal practice, or by inserting a new principle into Dutch law derived from the treaty provision....

Dualist theories are illustrated in the practice and constitutional norms of several of the states described below.

[2] *Principles of International Law* (1952), at 446, quoted in McDougal, *supra* n.1.

[3] Jörg Polakiewicz and V. Jacob-Foltzer, 'The European Human Rights Convention in Domestic Law', 12 Hum. Rts. L. J. 65 (1991), at 125.

NOTE

As the discussion of monism and dualism suggests, understanding the relationship between international law and national legal systems must include customary international law as well as treaty obligations. An edited volume on the effects of treaties in domestic legal systems concludes with a capstone chapter by Michael P. Van Alstine. Although the volume focuses primarily on treaty law, consider Alystine's following observations:[4]

> One of the interesting results from the chapters in this work is the contrast between the force of international treaties — which are subject to individualized consent — and the treatment of customary international law. Almost irrespective of the general approach to the domestic law effect of treaties — whether traditional dualist or hybrid monist — a number of the country chapters report that domestic courts afford some form of direct effect for the rules of customary international law without any required sanction by domestic lawmaking institutions.
>
> ...
>
> In states that follow the common law tradition (e.g., Australia, Canada, India, the United Kingdom, the United States), the direct effect of customary international law has come about through the role of the courts in developing the common law. Interestingly, this is true even in the particularly purist states of the dualist tradition such as Australia and the United Kingdom.
>
> The Supreme Court of India has a particularly well-developed jurisprudence on this score. The India chapter reports that, under the Court's doctrine of incorporation, the customary rules of international law automatically apply in domestic courts, provided that they do not conflict with express statutory provisions: "The comity of nations," the Indian Supreme Court has explained, "requires that rules of international law may be accommodated in the municipal law even without express legislative sanction, provided they do not run into conflict with Acts of Parliament."
>
> As the latter clause of this quotation reflects, however, a common approach among the states studied in this work is that the rules of customary international law must yield to domestic law norms generated through legislative sanction. The same approach obtains even in international-law-friendly the Netherlands. The Supreme Court there has concluded based on the drafting history of the Constitution that the preeminence of treaties over domestic law does not extend to "the enforcement of unwritten international law if that clash[es] with national statutes".

COMMENT ON THE PRESUMPTION OF COMPATIBILITY

Courts across many nations employ a canon of construction that favours interpreting domestic law to be consistent with international law — whether enshrined in

[4] Michael P. Van Alstine, 'The Role of Domestic Courts in Treaty Enforcement', in D. Sloss, ed., Treaty Enforcement: A Comparative Study (2009).

treaty or customary international law obligations. This interpretive approach reappears in various readings in this chapter. It is most commonly adopted in the interpretation of national statutes. The following discusses existing practice:[5]

> Courts in both monist and dualist States frequently apply an interpretive presumption that statutes should be construed in conformity with the nation's international legal obligations, including obligations derived from both treaties and customary international law. This interpretive presumption is sometimes called a 'presumption of conformity' or a 'presumption of compatibility'. In the United States, the presumption is referred to as the 'Charming Betsy canon'. [See *Murray v. Schooner Charming Betsy*, 6 U.S. 64, 118 (1804) ("[A]n act of [C]ongress ought never to be construed to violate the law of nations if any other possible construction remains....")]. Labels aside, the presumption of conformity is probably the most widely used transnationalist tool. Courts in Australia, Canada, Germany, India, Israel, the Netherlands, Poland, South Africa, the United Kingdom, and the United States, among other countries, have applied the presumption in cases involving vertical treaty provisions to help ensure that government conduct conforms to the nation's international treaty obligations.

One recurring issue concerns the threshold conditions necessary to trigger application of the presumption. There is broad agreement that courts may apply the presumption in cases where the statute is facially ambiguous. The Supreme Court of Canada has gone further, holding that 'it is reasonable to make reference to an international agreement at the very outset of the inquiry to determine if there is any ambiguity, even latent, in the domestic legislation.' Justice Kirby advocated a similar approach in Australia.... However, the majority of the Australian High Court has rejected this approach, refusing 'to endorse a wider role for treaties in statutory interpretation other than where the legislature has clearly envisaged such a role or where there exists a clear ambiguity on the face of the statute.'

Should this canon of construction apply to interpreting the text of a national constitution as well as a parliamentary statute? Consider the following account of discrepancies between constitutional and statutory interpretation:[6]

...Many domestic legal systems...apply a rule of interpretation prescribing that ordinary legislation be construed, as far as possible, in harmony with the international obligations of the state. This presumption is often presented as reflective of a hypothetical parliamentary intent — that, barring contrary evidence, judges must assume that legislators had not intended to compromise their state's international obligations via legislation.

> However, courts in most of the surveyed legal systems do not apply this canon of interpretation to their [constitutional law], even when they are prepared to seek guidance from international law sources. Instead, references to IHR

[5] David Sloss, Domestic Application of Treaties, in D. Hollis ed., The Oxford Guide to Treaties (forthcoming 2012).

[6] Yuval Shany, 'How Supreme is the Supreme Law of the Land? Comparative Analysis of the Influence of International Human Rights Treaties upon the Interpretation of Constitutional Texts by Domestic Courts', 31 Brook. J. Int'l. L.341 (2006).

> treaties often seem to be based on a weaker, comparative law framework of analysis, based upon the inherent persuasiveness of IHR law (whether binding or not upon the relevant jurisdiction), and not on a recognized duty to incorporate it into [constitutional law]. Under this interpretive model, courts retain considerable discretion on whether or not to harmonize [constitutional law] and IHR treaties. For example, in the rare cases where IHR instruments and their treaty bodies' case law were invoked by U.S. Supreme Court justices, they were addressed within a weak interpretive framework alluding to the informative value of comparative law or non-binding international law, and not within the stronger Charming Betsy canon. [The author elsewhere explains, 'The doctrine has also been referred to as the "presumption of compatibility," "presumption of compliance".']

Some of the readings that follow raise the question whether courts should also apply the 'presumption of compatibility' in interpreting federal laws as well as provincial and local laws and in interpreting parliamentary legislation as well as executive and administrative acts. Also, should the presumption apply regardless of the source of the international norm — whether it is derived from a treaty, customary international law, 'soft law' or the common practices of other states?

QUESTIONS

1. To what extent does the Economic, Social and Cultural Rights Committee's General Comment go beyond the position about international law's requirements for state incorporation described by Leary at p. 1056, *supra*? How would you justify its position?

2. It has often been observed that respect for human rights begins and ends at home and that international organizations have little more than a catalytic or intermediary role. On the basis of the preceding descriptions of states' relationships to international human rights norms, how satisfactory have the efforts of each of the states been to ensure that its legal order respects the relevant norms?

3. Is the *de facto* preference for applying domestic constitutional rather than international human rights norms desirable, neutral or dangerous from the perspective of realizing international human rights?

4. Should future international human rights treaties require ratifying states to guarantee the full incorporation in and enforcement by domestic law of their provisions?

MICHAEL KIRBY, THE ROLE OF INTERNATIONAL STANDARDS IN AUSTRALIAN COURTS

in P. Alston and M. Chiam (eds.), Treaty-Making and Australia: Globalization versus Sovereignty (1995), at 82

The Bangalore Principles

The traditional view of most common law countries has been that international law is not part of domestic law. Blackstone in his Commentaries, suggested that:

> The law of nations (whenever any question arises which is properly the object of its jurisdiction) is here [in England] adopted in its full extent by the common law, and is held to be part of the law of the land.

Save for the United States, where Blackstone had a profound influence, this view came to be regarded, virtually universally, as being 'without foundation'....

More recently, however, a new recognition has come about of the use that may be made by judges of international human rights principles and their exposition by the courts, tribunals and other bodies established to give them content and effect. This reflects both the growing body of international human rights law and the instruments, both regional and international, which give effect to that law. It furthermore recognizes the importance of the content of those laws. An expression that seems to encapsulate the modern approach was given [at a meeting among jurists from many states] in February 1988 in Bangalore, India in the so-called *Bangalore Principles.*

The Bangalore Principles state, in effect, that:

(1) International law, whether human rights norms or otherwise, is not, as such, part of domestic law in most common law countries;
(2) Such law does not become part of domestic law until Parliament so enacts or the judges, as another source of law-making, declare the norms thereby established to be part of domestic law;
(3) The judges will not do so automatically, simply because the norm is part of international law or is mentioned in a treaty, even one ratified by their own country;
(4) But if an issue of uncertainty arises, as by a lacuna in the common law, obscurity in its meaning or ambiguity in a relevant statute, a judge may seek guidance in the general principles of international law, as accepted by the community of nations; and
(5) From this source material, the judge may ascertain and declare what the relevant rule of domestic law is. It is the action of the judge, incorporating the rule into domestic law, which makes it part of domestic law.

...

[S]ince Bangalore…something of a sea change has come over the approach of courts in Australia, as well as in New Zealand and England.

The clearest indication of the change in Australia can be found…in *Mabo v Queensland (No 2)* [1992]. In the course of explaining why a discriminatory doctrine, such as that of *terra nullius* (which refused to recognize the rights and interests in land of the indigenous inhabitants of a settled colony such as Australia) could no longer be accepted as part of the law of Australia, Brennan J said:

> The expectations of the international community accord in this respect with the contemporary values of the Australian people. The opening up of the international remedies to individuals pursuant to Australia's accession to the *Optional Protocol* to the [ICCPR] brings to bear on the common law the powerful influence of the *Covenant* and the international standards it imports. The common law does not necessarily conform with international law, but international law is a legitimate and important influence on the development of the common law, especially when international law declares the existence of universal human rights.

…

NOTE

Justice Kirby has commented further on the developments noted in his preceding article:[7]

> Critics of [these] developments…list a number of considerations which need to be kept in mind by judges as they venture upon this new source of principle for judicial law-making. The expressed concerns include:
>
> 1. Treaties are typically negotiated by the executive government. They may, or may not, reflect the will of the people as expressed in parliament.…
>
> …
>
> 3. In federal countries, such as Australia, Canada, Malaysia, and others, special concern may be expressed that the ratification of international treaties could be used as a means to undermine the constitutional distribution of powers.…
> 4. Judicial introduction of human rights norms may sometimes divert the community from the more open, principled and democratic adoption of such norms in constitutional or statutory amendments which have the legitimacy of popular endorsement.
> 5. Some commentators have also expressed scepticism about the international courts, tribunals and committees which pronounce upon human rights.

7 'Domestic Implementation of Human Rights Norms', 5 Aust. J. Hum. Rts. 109 (1999), at 119.

They argue that often they are composed of persons from legal regimes very different from our own.

6. ... [T]he broad generality of the expression of the provisions contained in international human rights instruments ... means that those who use them may be tempted to read into their broad language what they hope, expect or want to see. Whilst the judge of the common law tradition has a creative role, such creativity must be in the minor key... He or she must not undermine the primacy of democratic law-making by the organs of government directly or indirectly accountable to the people.

...

[Justice Kirby then outlines factors in support of the *Bangalore Principles*, including: The Principles apply only when national law-making bodies leave 'a gap in the common law or . . . an ambiguity of national legislation. Far from being a negation of sovereignty, this is an application of it'; The modern concept of democracy 'involves not merely the reflection in law-making of the will of the majority, intermittently expressed at elections. The legitimacy of democratic governance is now seen as depending upon the respect by the majority for the fundamental rights of minorities'; The increasing judicial use of the Principles 'may have the beneficial consequence of discouraging ratification by the executive where there is no serious intention to accept, for the nation, the obligations contained in a treaty'.]

MINISTER OF STATE FOR IMMIGRATION AND ETHNIC AFFAIRS v. AH HIN TEOH

High Court of Australia, 1995 183 CLR 273

[Mr Teoh, a Malaysian citizen, entered Australia in May 1988 on a temporary entry permit. In July he married an Australian citizen who had been the *de facto* spouse of his deceased brother. In November 1990 he was convicted on charges of heroin importation and possession and sentenced to six years' imprisonment. The offences were clearly related to Mrs Teoh's heroin addiction. In 1991 Teoh was ordered to be deported on the ground that he had committed a serious crime. At that time Mrs Teoh had six of her children living with her, all under ten years old, and three of them had been fathered by Teoh. The deportation order was appealed to the Federal Court, which upheld the appeal partly on the ground that the requirement in the Convention on the Rights of the Child, that the child's best interests be considered in such matters, had not been taken into account. The Minister appealed that decision to the High Court.]

MASON CJ AND DEANE J:

...

25. It is well established that the provisions of an international treaty to which Australia is a party do not form part of Australian law unless those provisions have been validly incorporated into our municipal law by statute....

26. But the fact that the Convention [on the Rights of the Child] has not been incorporated into Australian law does not mean that its ratification holds no significance

for Australian law. Where a statute or subordinate legislation is ambiguous, the courts should favour that construction which accords with Australia's obligations under a treaty or international convention to which Australia is a party, at least in those cases in which the legislation is enacted after, or in contemplation of, entry into, or ratification of, the relevant international instrument. That is because Parliament, *prima facie*, intends to give effect to Australia's obligations under international law.

27. ... If the language of the legislation is susceptible of a construction which is consistent with the terms of the international instrument and the obligations which it imposes on Australia, then that construction should prevail. So expressed, the principle is no more than a canon of construction and does not import the terms of the treaty or convention into our municipal law as a source of individual rights and obligations.

28. Apart from influencing the construction of a statute or subordinate legislation, an international convention may play a part in the development by the courts of the common law. The provisions of an international convention to which Australia is a party, especially one which declares universal fundamental rights, may be used by the courts as a legitimate guide in developing the common law. But the courts should act in this fashion with due circumspection when the Parliament itself has not seen fit to incorporate the provisions of a convention into our domestic law. Judicial development of the common law must not be seen as a backdoor means of importing an unincorporated convention into Australian law. A cautious approach... would be consistent with the approach which the courts have hitherto adopted....

...

34. ... [R]atification by Australia of an international convention... is a positive statement by the executive government of this country to the world and to the Australian people that the executive government and its agencies will act in accordance with the Convention. That positive statement is an adequate foundation for a legitimate expectation, absent statutory or executive indications to the contrary, that administrative decision-makers will act in conformity with the Convention and treat the best interests of the children as 'a primary consideration'....

...

36. ... To regard a legitimate expectation as requiring the decision-maker to act in a particular way is tantamount to treating it as a rule of law. It incorporates the provisions of the unincorporated convention into our municipal law by the back door....

37. But, if a decision-maker proposes to make a decision inconsistent with a legitimate expectation, procedural fairness requires that the persons affected should be given notice and an adequate opportunity of presenting a case against the taking of such a course.

...

TOOHEY J:

...

27. In *Reg. v. Home Secretary; Ex parte Brind* the House of Lords rejected the broad proposition that the Secretary of State should exercise a statutory discretion

in accordance with the terms of the [ECHR], which was not part of English domestic law. That decision was considered by the New Zealand Court of Appeal in *Tavita v. Minister of Immigration* where a deportee argued that those concerned with ordering his deportation were bound to take into account the Convention and the [ICCPR], both of which had been ratified by New Zealand. In the end the Court did not have to determine the point. But it said of the contrary proposition: 'That is an unattractive argument, apparently implying that New Zealand's adherence to the international instruments has been at least partly window-dressing...there must at least be hesitation about accepting it'.

...

MCHUGH J:

...

37. ...The people of Australia may note the commitments of Australia in international law, but, by ratifying the Convention, the Executive government does not give undertakings to its citizens or residents. The undertakings in the Convention are given to the other parties to the Convention. How, when or where those undertakings will be given force in Australia is a matter for the federal Parliament....

38. If the result of ratifying an international convention was to give rise to a legitimate expectation that that convention would be applied in Australia, the Executive...would have effectively amended the law of this country....The consequences for administrative decision-making in this country would be enormous....Australia is a party to about 900 treaties. Only a small percentage of them has been enacted into law. Administrative decision-makers would have to ensure that their decision-making complied with every relevant convention or inform a person affected that they would not be complying with those conventions.

39. I do not think that it is reasonable to expect that public officials will comply with the terms of conventions which they have no obligation to apply or consider merely because the federal government has ratified them....Total compliance with the terms of a convention may require many years of effort, education and expenditure of resources. For these and similar reasons, the parties to a convention will often regard its provisions as goals to be implemented over a period of time rather than mandates calling for immediate compliance....

NOTE

In a more recent decision, *Re Minister for Immigration and Multicultural Affairs: Ex parte Lam* (2003) 214 C.L.R. 1, various Justices on the Australian High Court indicated that they were inclined to overrule *Teoh.* Justices McHugh and Gummow stated, 'An aspect of the rule of law under the Constitution is that the role or function of [Chapter] III courts does not extend to the performance of the legislative function of translating policy into statutory form or the executive function of administration....If *Teoh* is to have continued significance at a general level for the principles which inform the relationship between international obligations and the domestic constitutional structure, then further attention will be required to the basis upon which *Teoh* rests.' Justice Callinan stated, '[T]he view is open that for the Court to give the effect to the Convention that it did, was to elevate the Executive above the parliament. This in my opinion is the important question rather than whether the Executive act of ratification is, or is not to be described as platitudinous or ineffectual. Whatever may be the current utility or status of the doctrine of "legitimate expectation", I agree with McHugh and Gummow JJ, for the reasons that their Honours give, that on no view can it give rise to substantive rights rather than to procedural rights.' Justice Hayne helped explain the context of *Teoh*:

> Legitimate expectation is a phrase which, although used in administrative law for more than 30 years...
>
> [L]ater, however, the phrase legitimate expectation has come to be used in very different ways. Instead of being used to describe why procedural fairness should be afforded to a person it has sometimes been used to refer to what matters the decision-maker should take into account in making a decision or, in England, to what decision the decision-maker should reach. This last development, said to engage concepts of abuse of power, directs attention to whether a person has a legitimate expectation of a benefit which is substantive rather than merely procedural and to whether to frustrate that expectation is unfair.
>
> It was not suggested that principles of this last-mentioned kind had any application in this case....I mention this use of the phrase legitimate expectation in connection with substantive rather than procedural benefits only to emphasise the dangers of using the phrase without careful articulation of the content of the principle which is said to be engaged in the particular case.
>
> ...[In *Teoh*, the] legitimate expectation identified was an expectation about what would be taken into account in reaching a decision.

PHILIP SALES & JOANNE CLEMENT, INTERNATIONAL LAW IN DOMESTIC COURTS: THE DEVELOPING FRAMEWORK

124 L. Q. Rev. 388 (2008)

...Following the decision of the High Court of Australia in *Minister of State for Immigration v Teoh*, arguments about legitimate expectation and unincorporated treaties in the English courts were given renewed vigour....

Arguments based on *Teoh* were considered by the Court of Appeal in England in *Behluli v Secretary of State for the Home Department*. The Court of Appeal expressly declined to follow *Teoh*....

However, two months later, a different division of the Court of Appeal indicated a willingness to adopt and follow *Teoh* in relation to decisions taken under the royal prerogative....

...The decision of the Court of Appeal in *Behluli*, declining to follow *Teoh* in English law, should be preferred.

...First, the concept of a legitimate expectation is inapt to apply in the context of English public law to the assumption of obligations under a treaty by the United Kingdom.... Ratification of a treaty involves the acceptance by one state of obligations on the plane of international law. However, ratification is not intended to operate other than on that plane. When and how those undertakings will be given effect in the United Kingdom is essentially a matter for Parliament. Precisely because under English law it is established that a treaty has no force in domestic law and is incapable of operating as a direct source of rights or obligations, ratification does not constitute a representation or undertaking operating on the plane of domestic law to perform obligations under the treaty...

Secondly, if ratification of an international treaty were to give rise to a legitimate expectation that the treaty would be applied in the United Kingdom, the executive would have effectively amended the law of this country, contrary to constitutional principle.... [I]t would be tantamount to the indirect enforcement in domestic law of an unincorporated treaty....

These points are not confined to claims for substantive legitimate expectations. A procedural legitimate expectation also creates binding obligations for the decision-maker in question, and on orthodox analysis in England the making of an unincorporated treaty should not change domestic law in any way.

Thirdly...it is not feasible to translate the obligation undertaken by the United Kingdom on the plane of international law into an obligation in domestic law...in relation to the conduct of a particular decision-maker. Statements or promises made by one public body cannot create any binding legitimate expectation in relation to another decision-making public authority, unless made with the latter's actual or (possibly) ostensible authority.... But the Crown does not enter into treaties on the basis of any actual or ostensible authority provided by other decision-makers.... The basic reason why discretions are conferred by Parliament upon decision-makers is to ensure that there should be flexibility in the decision-making system, whereby decision-makers can adjust their responses to take account of unforeseen circumstances or to allow scope for different evaluations to be made of how to act. Statutory discretionary powers are conferred upon a particular decision-making body because Parliament intends that body to exercise its own judgment in the light of the particular circumstances of a case....

SANJAY PATEL, FOUNDING LEGITIMATE EXPECTATIONS ON UNINCORPORATED TREATIES

15 Jud. Rev. 74 (2010)

...Philip Sales and Joanne Clement, in an important recent article on the role of international law in English courts, have criticised the decision in *Teoh*...[by contending, first, that]...individuals ought not to be able to found legitimate expectations on treaties as only sovereign states can claim to have an expectation that the UK executive will perform in accordance with the treaty provisions.

The English courts have repeatedly conceptualised treaties as transactions that exclusively concern sovereign states....

However, the English courts have acknowledged in more recent cases that this analysis is not accurate in all circumstances. In *Occidental Exploration v Republic of Ecuador* [2005] EWCA Civ 1116, Mance LJ (as he then was) recognised that domestic legal persons were able to derive rights from bilateral investment treaties as it was clear on construction of this type of treaty that they were intended to confer freestanding rights on investors. The mere fact that the Convention was an agreement between states did not preclude domestic legal persons from deriving rights from them....Once it is accepted that individuals can in principle derive rights from treaties, it is for the courts to decide on a case-by-case basis whether or not a particular provision merely confers rights on an inter-state level or is a binding commitment made to the world at large that confers rights on individuals in domestic courts.

Sales and Clement have argued that the result in *Teoh* gave the treaty excessive legal effect as the minister's decision was "curtailed" by the treaty. However, this conclusion downplays the importance of the High Court's decision only to provide procedural protection for the legitimate expectation created by the treaty provisions. *Teoh* merely contemplates that the decision to adopt a policy in conflict with treaty provisions triggers a modest procedural requirement compelling the executive to allow individuals the opportunity to give reasons for why such a policy should not be taken. Therefore, the imposition of a legitimate expectation in these circumstances does not substantively limit the discretion of the minister, as he is still free to act incompatibly with the treaty so long as he jumps through the relevant procedural hoops.

Furthermore, legitimate expectations will only fetter a minister's discretion where it would be consistent with public policy for the court to bind him by the content of his undertaking on the facts of the particular case. For example, where a minister is compelled to act in contravention of a treaty norm in the interests of national security, the countervailing public interest would take precedence and the decision of the minister could not be impugned. This flexibility in the application is unique to the law of legitimate expectation and is in contrast to the normative quality of rules of law, which cannot be applied and disapplied depending on context.

...

[Finally, with respect to whether treaty ratification can bind other ministers ...] It would be...inappropriate to put the powers, duties and responsibilities of the Foreign Secretary, when advising on whether or not to ratify an international instrument, into a separate box from those of the Secretary of State responsible for the UK's compliance with the substance of the treaty. The Foreign Secretary does not act alone when deciding to ratify a treaty, but as a matter of convention will only take a decision having consulted with relevant government departments. Consequently, the ratification is not a personal undertaking by the Foreign Secretary but the result of a consensus within the executive....

...

...While it is not for the courts to transform executive undertakings into hard-edged rules of law, it is equally undesirable for those upon whom the executive confers rights on the international plane to find that such rights are in fact illusory when the time comes for them to be enforced. The advantage of the application of the law of legitimate expectation to treaties is that it ensures that treaty ratification is an act of real legal value.

...The *Teoh* approach strikes the correct balance between leaving constitutional fundamentals intact without allowing the executive to ignore its own undertakings with impunity.

MICHAEL P. VAN ALSTINE, THE ROLE OF DOMESTIC COURTS IN TREATY ENFORCEMENT

in D. Sloss (ed.), Treaty Enforcement: A Comparative Study (2009), at 608–12

...

The Surprising Influence of Unimplemented Treaties

Given the fundamental importance of legislative implementation for the traditional dualist states, among the most remarkable conclusions from the country reports is that domestic courts have accorded broad influence even to treaties that have not been so implemented in domestic law. We have already seen one such meta-rule of interpretation above. As...explained, a broad presumption applies in traditional dualist states as well that courts should interpret domestic law wherever possible to advance conformity with their state's treaty obligations under international law. This presumption also applies to treaties that, although ratified by the executive, have not been implemented in domestic law by the legislature. In other words, even formally unimplemented treaties may have a significant influence in domestic law. Indeed, in Canada even legislative inaction may result in the implementation of a treaty through the doctrine of implied incorporation.

But as we shall see here, the effect of unimplemented treaties may extend beyond the basic interpretive presumption of conformity with international law. Courts in traditional dualist states also have relied on such treaties to limit the discretion of administrative bodies and even to recognize individual rights not otherwise established in domestic law. Curiously, the discussion of these issues has not been as robust in hybrid monist states.

A. Quasi-incorporation, implied incorporation, and constraints on administrative discretion. Among the more interesting results from the chapter reports is that some courts in traditional dualist states have afforded influence to unimplemented treaties (as well as customary international law) in a variety of functionally significant ways beyond the interpretive principles and presumptions previously described.... Prominent among these is a recognition that unimplemented treaties may function to limit the discretion delegated by the legislature to executive or administrative agencies. The chapters for Australia, India, and the United Kingdom each report some form of this proposition. The Israel chapter also notes a continuing debate on the subject (Interestingly, the chapter for hybrid-monist South Africa describes a similar principle with reference to otherwise-unenforceable treaties that the legislature has not implemented in a dualist fashion.)

The most notable example of this is the *Teoh* doctrine in Australia.... [T]he Canada chapter states that this principle has not (yet) received a warm reception by the courts there.

The Australia chapter also reports on a doctrine of "quasi-incorporation" of international treaty obligations. This actually involves three distinct, yet related mechanisms by which legislation indirectly or informally empowers courts to measure rights or obligations against international treaties otherwise not formally incorporated into domestic law. The first is where domestic statutes are "based, either substantially or partly, on international instruments and are clearly designed to give effect to international obligations." The second is where "government departments and administrative decision makers are given directions to take into account the provisions of" international treaties. Finally, legislation may "indicate[] that it is to operate subject to international obligations under international law." The Australia chapter concludes that this practice of "quasi-incorporation" (or "partial incorporation") will have a significant, although in some respects uncertain, impact on the power of the judiciary to enforce international treaties in the country.

Interestingly, the notion of "quasi-incorporation" parallels developments in other traditional dualist states examined above. Prominent among these is the jurisprudence of the Supreme Court of Canada on "implied incorporation," by which a formally unincorporated treaty may obtain domestic law effect through parliamentary inaction on related legislation. In the same vein is the possibility recognized by the United Kingdom report that implied treaty rights may arise by interpretive deduction even where legislation does not expressly refer to the treaty.

B. The influence of unimplemented treaties for new common law rights. Domestic courts in traditional dualist states also have recognized an indirect influence of unimplemented treaties with respect to the rights and remedies of individuals. Interestingly, but not surprisingly, the five states in this group emerged not only from the British constitutional tradition but also from its common law tradition. This judge-made common law has presented a vehicle for domestic courts to recognize individual rights or remedies even for treaties that have not yet been implemented in domestic law by the legislature.

To be sure, the level of enthusiasm for this use of the common law differs. The Israel chapter, for example, broadly states that "in discussing principles of Israel's common law, the courts regularly refer to conventions that have not been incorporated in domestic law." The Supreme Court of India likewise declared in a maritime case that, because certain relevant treaties "embody principles of law recognized by the generality of maritime States," they "can therefore be regarded as part of our common law." Significantly, the Court endorsed this principle even though India had not formally implemented the treaties at issue. The chapter for Australia also suggests that its courts "have become more open" to use of unimplemented treaties in this way.

The U.K. chapter, in contrast, reports a more tepid judicial reaction, observing only that a domestic court "might possibly consider" an unimplemented treaty in recognizing common law rights. The courts of Canada likewise have not yet expressly embraced the proposition, but the Canada chapter elsewhere notes in broader fashion that the particularly powerful presumption of conformity there has "further erod[ed] support for the proposition that treaties always require legislative implementation before taking effect in domestic law."

QUESTIONS

1. How would you respond to the concerns enumerated by Justice Kirby about the approach reflected in the Bangalore Principles?

2. Do the political and administrative consequences of the *Teoh* decision go beyond what can reasonably be expected of a state party to a human rights treaty? What should be the implications of the government's subsequent 'Joint Statement'?

ADDITIONAL READING

M. Groves, 'Treaties and Legitimate Expectations: The Rise and Fall of *Teoh* in Australia', J. Rev. 323 (2010); T. Webster, 'International Human Rights Law in Japan: The View at Thirty', 23 Colum. J. Asian L. 241 (2010); C. Tomuschat, 'The Effects of the Judgments of the European Court of Human Rights According to the German Constitutional Court', 11 German L. J. 513 (2010); T. Ginsburg, 'Locking in Democracy: Constitutions, Commitment, and International Law', 38 N.Y.U. J. Int'l. L. & Pol'y. 707 (2006); M. E. Adjami, 'African Courts, International Law, and Comparative Case Law: Chimera or Emerging Human Rights Jurisprudence?', 24 Mich. J. Int'l. L. 103 (2002); H. Knop, 'Here and There: International Law in Domestic Courts', 32 N.Y.U. J. Int'l. L. & Pol'y. 501 (2000); P. Alston (ed.), *Promoting Human Rights Through Bills of Rights* (1999).

COMMENT ON TREATIES IN THE UNITED STATES

Read the references to 'treaties' in the following provisions of the US Constitution: Article I, Section 10; Article II, Section 2; Article III, Section 2; and Article VI. The term 'treaty' has a special constitutional significance in the United States. The following materials speak of *treaties* in this constitutional sense, as opposed to another form of international agreement (so-called 'executive agreements') into which the United States enters. The information below complements the Comment on Treaties at p. 113, *supra*, which describes treaties from an international law rather than national perspective.

The conclusion of a treaty binding on the United States normally involves three stages. (1) Negotiation of the treaty is usually conducted by an agent of the Executive, although members of the Senate have occasionally been brought into the process at an early stage as observers and advisors. (2) The President submits the treaty to the Senate for the advice and consent required by Article II, Section 2. If the treaty fails to receive the required two-thirds vote of those present, no further action may be taken on it. If it receives the supermajority's support, the President may ratify it. (3) Ratification takes place by an exchange of instruments or, in the case of multilateral agreements, by deposit with a designated depositary. The President then proclaims the treaty, making it a matter of public notice and often effective as of that time.

Of course, the United States has had to resolve the same issues as other countries about the internal status and effect of treaties. Constitutional decisions have brought reasonably clear answers to some basic questions. For example, treaties that have become part of the internal legal order have the same domestic effect as federal statutes. A treaty thus supersedes earlier inconsistent legislation. Just as a statute can be superseded by a later inconsistent statute, so can a treaty be superseded, although maxims of interpretation encourage a judicial effort to construe the later-in-time statute so as not to violate the treaty. If that effort fails, the legislative rule prevails domestically, although as a matter of international law the United States has broken its obligations to the other treaty partners.

Perhaps one of the most important questions about a treaty effective as domestic law is its status vis-à-vis the Constitution. Will a treaty provision — perhaps one requiring a government to ban certain types of 'hate' speech — be given effect domestically even if legislation to the same effect that was independent of any treaty commitment (i.e., an ordinary congressional statute) would be judged to be unconstitutional? In *Reid v. Covert*, the US Supreme Court rejected such a proposition. The Court held that civilian dependants of members of the armed forces overseas could not constitutionally be tried by a court-martial in time of peace for capital offences. The Fifth and Sixth Amendments, according to the Court, prohibited these military trials. At the time, an agreement between the United States and the United Kingdom permitted the trials. Justice Black stated emphatically, 'It would be manifestly contrary to the objectives of those who created the Constitution, as well as those who were responsible for the Bill of Rights — let alone alien to our entire constitutional history and tradition — to construe Article VI as permitting the United States to exercise power under an international agreement without observing constitutional prohibitions.... This Court has regularly and uniformly recognized the supremacy of the Constitution over a treaty.'

Self-Executing Treaties

A question that frequently arises in the United States, as in the European states earlier examined, is whether a treaty is 'self-executing', in the sense that it creates rights and obligations for individuals that are enforceable in the courts without legislative implementation of the treaty. The concept of 'self-executing' is close to the concept of 'automatic incorporation' in the excerpts from Virginia Leary, p. 1056, *supra*.

Each country here faces distinct problems. In the United States, the answer to the question posed is bound up in constitutional text and in the allocation of powers over treaties among the Executive Branch, the Senate and the Congress as a whole. For example, note the status of 'supreme law' that is accorded the treaty under Article VI of the Constitution (the Supremacy Clause), and the relationship of that clause to the self-executing character of treaties.

Consider the following excerpts from Section 111 of the *Restatement (Third), Foreign Relations Law of the United States* (1987):

> (3) Courts in the United States are bound to give effect to international law and to international agreements of the United States, except that a 'non-self-executing' agreement will not be given effect as law in the absence of necessary implementation.
> (4) An international agreement of the United States is 'non-self-executing' (a) if the agreement manifests an intention that it shall not become effective as domestic law without the enactment of implementing legislation, (b) if the Senate in giving consent to a treaty, or Congress by resolution, requires implementing legislation, or (c) if implementing legislation is constitutionally required.

Comment (h) to Section 111 provides:

> In the absence of special agreement, it is ordinarily for the United States to provide how it will carry out its international obligations. Accordingly, the intention of the United States determines whether an agreement is to be self-executing in the United States or should await implementation by legislation or by appropriate executive or administrative action. If the international agreement is silent as to its self-executing character and the intention of the United States is unclear, account must be taken of ... any expression by the Senate or by Congress in dealing with the agreement.

... Whether an agreement is to be given effect without further legislation is an issue that a court must decide when a party seeks to invoke the agreement as law.... Some provisions of an international agreement may be self-executing and others non-self-executing. If an international agreement or one of its provisions is non self-executing, the United States is under an international obligation to adjust its laws and institutions as may be necessary to give effect to the agreement.

Certain types of treaties have traditionally been understood to be self-executing and have been applied by courts without any implementing legislation. Consider bilateral treaties giving (reciprocally) rights to nationals of each party to establish residence for certain purposes in the territory of the other party, establish corporations, conduct business there and so on, frequently on national-treatment terms. Courts have long entertained actions by nationals of a treaty party seeking to enforce one or another of the rights provided for in the treaty.

Under US law (as developed through constitutional decisions of the courts), certain types of treaties cannot be self-executing but require implementing legislation to have domestic effects. Note Section 111(4)(c) above of the *Restatement*.

For example, a treaty obligating the United States to make certain conduct criminal, even if it closely defined that conduct and stated its penalty, would nonetheless require such legislation. A treaty obligating the United States to pay funds to another state may require an appropriation of funds by the Congress.

Generally it is not relevant from an international law perspective whether a treaty is self-executing, since a state is obligated under international law to do whatever may be required under its internal law (such as legislative enactment) to fulfil its treaty commitments. The state can follow either path.

The question of the attributes of a self-executing treaty has assumed a new prominence in recent years through a number of human rights treaties ratified by the United States — the ICCPR, for example — that were approved by the Senate and ratified subject to a declaration that the treaties were not self-executing. The terms of the declaration have varied among treaties. The precise effect of some of these declarations on courts remains a matter of dispute — for example, whether the treaty could be invoked defensively by a defendant in a prosecution, even if it could not be used by a plaintiff as the foundation for an action. See p. 1091, *infra*.

QUESTIONS

1. What advantages or disadvantages do you see in the US system (self-executing treaties) for giving treaty provisions internal effect? If you were drafting the US Constitution anew, which of the constitutional arrangements in the prior readings for giving treaties internal effect would you select?

2. What relation do you see between the conception of self-executing treaties in the United States and the provision of Article VI of the Constitution that treaties consistent with the Constitution form part of the 'supreme law' of the land?

3. Consider the following statement:

> The path of self-executing treaty can frustrate fundamental democratic principles. It would be satisfactory if the House of Representatives, the more popular and representative House in Congress, participated in giving consent to ratification, but only the Senate does. If two-thirds of that body will go along with treaty provisions that might bring about deep internal change in U.S. law, the treaty has the force of "supreme law". But there has been no full legislative process and debate, and that's not how laws should be made in the U.S.

Can you give realistic illustrations for the argument made? Are they likely to be common in treaty-making?

ADDITIONAL READING

L. Henkin, *Foreign Affairs and the United States Constitution* (2nd edn. 1996); H. Koh, 'Why Do Nations Obey International Law?', 106 Yale L. J. 2599 (1997);

J. L. Goldsmith & C. Bradley, 'Customary International Law as Federal Common Law: A Critique of the Modern Position', 110 Harv. L. Rev. 815 (1997); D. Sloss, 'The Domestication of International Human Rights', 24 Yale J. Int'l. L. 129 (1999); N. H. Kaufman, *Human Rights Treaties and the Senate* (1990).

COMMENT ON NATIONAL HUMAN RIGHTS INSTITUTIONS

An important development over the last two decades is the emergence of national human rights institutions (NHRIs). NHRIs include governmental bodies such as national human rights commissions and human rights ombudsmen. These institutions are generally tasked with addressing a range of human rights issues — including civil and political as well as economic and social rights. In 1991, the UN convened an international conference in Paris to review existing NHRIs, with an eye towards establishing normative standards on the role, composition, status and function of these bodies. The resulting standards, the so-called 'Paris Principles', were adopted by the General Assembly in 1993 (A/RES/48/134). The Office of the High Commissioner for Human Rights played an instrumental role in helping establish NHRIs over the course of the next several years.

In the last 25 years, more than one hundred NHRIs have been established in such diverse countries as Argentina, Australia, India, Indonesia, Ireland, Kenya, Mexico, Morocco, Nepal, Nigeria, the Philippines, Poland and South Africa. One commentator describes the recognition and spread of NHRIs:[8]

> The fact that the Paris Principles have become widely known in the past ten years and are now accepted as a benchmark for governmental human rights bodies implies that the concept of national human rights institutions has become something of a "norm". To use theoretical terms, the critical threshold of acceptance, which was reached already...in 1993, has gradually led to such a broad acceptance of the concept of national institutions that, by the late 1990s, such institutions are almost taken for granted. As one observer concludes, "[t]he creation of National Human Rights Institutions is viewed as an important governmental step in becoming a legitimate member of the international community". It could be argued that the influence of the concept of national institution has been particularly strong on post-authoritarian and emerging democracies, which have modified their national structures in accordance with international values and principles in the 1990s and have therefore often resorted to external sources for appropriate institutional models.

The formal responsibilities of NHRIs can include a range of powers such as receiving and adjudicating individual complaints, conducting national inquiries on broad thematic issues, auditing proposed legislation, training public officials,

[8] Anna-Elina Pohjolainen, *The Evolution of National Human Rights Institution* (The Danish Institute for Human Rights 2006), at 12–13, www.nhri.net/pdf/Evolution_of_NHRIs.pdf.

undertaking education campaigns and encouraging ratification of treaties. These institutions are often uniquely situated. They work at the boundary of international and domestic legal orders and operate in the space between governments and civil society. In other words, these institutions can often contribute to the reception of global human rights norms into domestic legal and cultural systems. NHRIs, however, require sufficient political and financial support as well as confidence of the public to be effective.

RYAN GOODMAN & THOMAS PEGRAM, NATIONAL HUMAN RIGHTS INSTITUTIONS, STATE CONFORMITY, AND SOCIAL CHANGE

in R. Goodman & T. Pegram (eds.), Human Rights, State Compliance, and Social Change: Assessing National Human Rights Institutions (2012), at 2–3, 16–19

The relationship between NHRIs and the global order is multidimensional. NHRIs first gained recognition as potentially important links in the transmission of human rights norms from the international to the domestic level. And the activities of NHRIs along that track have accelerated in recent years. The Universal Periodic Review of state practices by the UN Human Rights Council routinely involves governments' encouraging other governments to establish an NHRI if such an institution does not yet exist in the country. Two of the twenty-first century's first human rights treaties — the Optional Protocol to the Torture Convention and the Convention on the Rights of Persons with Disabilities — create an unprecedented role for NHRIs in monitoring and implementing multilateral treaty obligations. In addition, the UN human rights treaty bodies have begun to rely increasingly on the work of NHRIs in reviewing state reports of compliance, and UN officials increasingly call on NHRIs to address specific subject matters such as multinational corporations and economic and social rights. In short, NHRIs are becoming instrumental in the transmission of human rights norms into domestic systems and ensuring national compliance with global standards.

NHRIs have also emerged as important actors in shaping human rights norms at the international level — both global and regional. Organized as a unified coalition in treaty negotiations, NHRIs from across the world played a significant role in drafting the Disability Rights Convention. They were also directly involved in the negotiations of the UN Declaration on the Rights of Indigenous People (Chris Sidoti, this volume). NHRIs have a formal seat at the table of the UN Human Rights Council, providing them with an opportunity to contribute to standard setting and the development of human rights norms at the global level. And NHRIs, organized in regional associations, have also begun to shape international standards. Consider, for example, pathbreaking work on sexual orientation and gender identity by the Asia Pacific Forum of National Human Rights Institutions. Indeed, acting as a group, these institutions may be more willing to push the frontiers of human rights norms than acting separately or alone.

...

Beyond Enforcement Measures and Material Inducements

[We] embrace[]a broad conception of the powers that NHRIs might employ to effectuate compliance with human rights standards. In existing international relations scholarship on compliance, changes in state behavior are often predicated (ultimately) on enforcement by formal institutions or material inducements such as threats to the tenure of public authorities. Several contributors to this volume, however, adopt a more nuanced conceptualization of the institution of an NHRI and its ability to foster social change and compliance. They focus instead on channels of influence that exist outside formal enforcement authority and material inducements.

Perhaps most notable in this regard are the chapters by Peruzzotti and Uggla. Building on new scholarship in the social sciences on opportunity structures and accountability theory, Peruzzotti contends that the involvement of the Argentinean NHRI in a dispute involving massive environmental contamination constituted a "turning point" in the social struggle. The NHRI, according to this case study, helped to legitimate the claims of social actors and helped to forge accountability across public authorities. In his study of Bolivia, Uggla argues that the NHRI effectuated compliance not by building relationships with external civil society actors but by building relationships of trust with state authorities and mobilizing other mechanisms of influence such as peer pressure. Regardless of whether Peruzzoti's or Uggla's findings are generalizable or replicated elsewhere, the important point is for analysts to consider such diverse mechanisms of influence in encouraging states to align their behavior with existing human rights standards.

Social Mobilization and Activism

National human rights institutions may exert their most powerful influence in fostering — or hindering — social mobilization. This volume gives special attention to such effects. David Meyer, for example, draws directly on social science scholarship that studies the conditions under which civil society actors mobilize to secure rights guarantees. A strong determinant of social mobilization, according to this area of research, is whether political institutions signal to social actors that new structural opportunities exist. Meyer accordingly examines how NHRIs, which sit uniquely at the intersection of the state and civil society, can create and signal such political openings.

Other contributions complement Meyer's account. For example, Obiora Okafor shows how African NHRIs may achieve their greatest effects by creating platforms for NGOs to engage the state system. And Thomas Pegram's research on Latin America suggests that a virtuous circle can unfold: while NHRIs further the prospect and legitimacy of social mobilization, the mobilizing forces can, in turn, provide NHRIs a "crucial ballast against hostile state actors." Indeed, as Okafor's and Pegram's work demonstrates, in some circumstances social actors may consider NHRIs allies within the corridors of power. And the existence of such allies is another important variable in the political structure that can induce social actors to mobilize.

The creation and operation of an NHRI may also have a demobilizing effect in some circumstances. Indeed, this book sheds light on potential perverse effects of inserting an NHRI into existing institutional arrangements within government and civil society. That is, NHRIs occupy an institutional space that can discourage or displace other actors who would otherwise help to advance human rights. Reflecting on various contributions in this volume, Meyer asks the key question: "Is the creation of NHRIs a step toward protecting and promoting human rights or a way of containing and insulating the pressure to do so?" Indeed, some of these effects may be intentional: states may deliberately use an NHRI to ward off international pressure to comply with human rights. And other consequences may be unintentional. The professionalization of human rights work through the offices of the NHRI, for instance, may help convince members of society that mobilization is unnecessary (Meyer chapter). Rosenblum, in his survey of the volume's contributions, also raises concerns that the insertion of NHRIs may redirect resources (including donor support) from other human rights organizations. Pegram suggests that "crowding out of social actors is a concern, with Defensorias ('human rights ombudsmen') potentially diverting international funding away from civil society actors as well as enticing highly qualified personnel away from the human rights sector." A systematic study of the prevalence of these effects and the success of efforts to overcome them does not appear in this volume. The contributions to the volume, however, identify the potential casual mechanisms and significance of these interactions. The research presented here thus provides strong reason for future studies to document such countervailing effects and to develop institutional designs to mitigate them.

Origin Matters

Finally, an empirical puzzle in the study of NHRIs is how specific institutions might escape their past or, more specifically, their origins. Most striking are cases of NHRIs born in inhospitable political conditions — brought to life, for example, by an autocratic or illiberal government — yet able to develop into an independent force that ultimately challenges the state's human rights practices. Such a path was followed by prototype NHRIs such as the Indonesian Commission on Human Rights, which subverted the intentions of its designers and helped legitimate the democracy movement that toppled Suharto....

...although NHRIs may escape their fate, the durability of this outcome is far from assured, and deteriorating political conditions and lapses in individual judgment within the organization can result in significant backsliding (Catherine Renshaw and Kieren Fitzpatrick chapter).

B. CONDITIONING CONSENT: RATIFICATION WITH RESERVATIONS

Article 2(1)(d) of the Vienna Convention on the Law of Treaties defines a reservation as 'a unilateral statement' made by a state when ratifying a treaty 'whereby it purports to exclude or to modify the legal effect of certain provisions of the treaty in their application to that State'. Article 19 provides that a state ratifying a treaty may make a reservation unless it is 'prohibited by the treaty' or 'is incompatible with the object and purpose of the treaty'. Section 313 of the *Restatement (Third), Foreign Relations Law of the United States* (1987), is to the same effect. Comment (g) to Section 313 refers to the terms *declaration* and *understanding*.

> When signing or adhering to an international agreement, a state may make a unilateral declaration that does not purport to be a reservation. Whatever it is called, it constitutes a reservation in fact if it purports to exclude, limit, or modify the state's legal obligation. Sometimes, however, a declaration purports to be an 'understanding', an interpretation of the agreement in a particular respect. Such an interpretive declaration is not a reservation if it reflects the accepted view of the agreement. But another contracting party may challenge the expressed understanding, treating it as a reservation which it is not prepared to accept.

The International Court of Justice addressed the question of the effect of reservations to a multilateral human rights treaty in its 1951 Advisory Opinion on *Reservations to the Genocide Convention*,[9] which influenced the Vienna Convention's provisions above. The principal questions put to the ICJ by the UN General Assembly were whether a reserving state could be regarded as a party to the Genocide Convention if its reservation was objected to by one or more existing parties but not by others, and, if so, what effect the reservation then had between the reserving state and the accepting or rejecting parties.

In responding to those questions,[10] the Court addressed the 'traditional concept... that no reservation was valid unless it was accepted by all the contracting parties without exception....' In the context of the Genocide Convention, the Court found it 'proper' to take into account circumstances leading to 'a more flexible application of this principle'. It emphasized the universal character and aspiration of multilateral human rights treaties. Widespread ratifications had 'already given rise to greater flexibility in the international practice' concerning them.

After concluding that the Genocide Convention (whose provisions were silent on the issue of reservations) permitted a state to enter a reservation, the Court considered 'what kind of reservations may be made and what kind of objections may be taken to them'. It underscored the special character of the Convention, which was 'manifestly adopted for a purely humanitarian and civilizing purpose. 'In such a convention the contracting states have a common interest in the 'accomplishment of those high purposes which are the *raison d'être* of the convention'. In such circumstances, one cannot 'speak of individual advantages or disadvantages to States, or of the maintenance of a perfect contractual balance between rights and duties'. Permitting any one state that objected to another state's reservation

[9] Advisory Opinion, 1951 I.C.J. 15.

[10] The Court concluded (1) that a state whose reservation has been objected to by one or more parties but not by others can be regarded as a party to the Convention 'if the reservation is compatible with the object and purposes of the Convention', and (2) that a state party objecting to a reservation that it views as incompatible with the Convention can consider the reserving state not to be a party.

to block adherence to the convention by the reserving state would frustrate the Convention's goal of universal membership.

On the other hand, the Court could not accept the argument that 'any State entitled to become a party to the Genocide Convention may do so while making any reservation it chooses by virtue of its sovereignty.' It followed that 'it is the compatibility of a reservation with the object and purpose of the Convention that must furnish the criterion for the attitude of a State in making the reservation on accession as well as for the appraisal by a State in objecting to the reservation.'

COMMENT ON RESERVATIONS TO CEDAW

The high number of reservations that have accompanied ratification of CEDAW have become a regrettably notorious feature of the Convention, which is in this respect first among the human rights treaties. In contrast, few states have entered reservations to the Convention on Racial Discrimination. Moreover, many of the CEDAW reservations are directed to fundamental provisions.

Unlike the ICCPR, which is silent on the issue, CEDAW addresses reservations in Article 28(2), which prohibits those incompatible with the 'object and purpose' of the Convention. Tolerance of reservations has been urged on various grounds—for example, the desirability of securing widespread participation in treaties serving a 'purely humanitarian and civilizing purpose' (in the words of the *Genocide Convention* Advisory Opinion), and hence the reluctance to view a ratification as invalid because of reservations. A commentator suggests another ground:[11]

> Most states are apprehensive about the possible consequences of accepting a human rights treaty, not least because such treaties may have a dynamic force and interpretation of their scope and impact is less certain than that of commercial treaties.... Reservations are seen to offer an assurance that the state can protect its interest to the fullest extent possible.

Other commentators have considered reservations to Article 2 of CEDAW to be 'manifestly incompatible' with the object and purpose of the Convention.[12] As noted below, several states parties have objected to these reservations on the ground that they threaten the integrity of the Convention and the human rights regime in general. Reservations that purport to be consistent with Article 28(2) of CEDAW raise issues of religious intolerance and of cultural relativism. The net result, claims one commentator, has been the diffuse and widespread view that international obligations assumed through the ratification of CEDAW are somehow 'separate and distinct' from and less binding than those of other human rights treaties.[13]

[11] Rebecca Cook, 'Reservations to the Convention on the Elimination of All Forms of Discrimination against Women', 30 Va. J. Int'l. L. 643 (1990), at 650.

[12] Belinda Clark, 'The Vienna Convention Reservations Regime and the Convention on Discrimination against Women', 85 Am J. Int. L. 281 (1991).

[13] Ibid.

Consider the following suggestions of Rebecca Cook about criteria for distinguishing between reservations that are compatible and incompatible with the Convention:[14]

> The thesis of this article is that the object and purpose of the Women's Convention are that states parties shall move progressively towards elimination of all forms of discrimination against women and ensure equality between men and women. Further, states parties have an obligation to provide the means to move progressively toward[s] this result. Although the Women's Convention envisions that states parties shall move progressively towards elimination of all forms of discrimination against women and ensure equality between men and women, reservations to the Convention's substantive provisions pose a threat to the achievement of this goal…Accordingly, reservations that contemplate the provision of means towards the pursuit of this goal will be regarded as compatible with 'the object and purpose of the treaty' as provided by article 28(2) of the Women's Convention and article 19(c) of the Vienna Convention. Similarly, any reservation that contemplates enduring inconsistency between state law or practice and the obligations of the Women's Convention is incompatible with the treaty's object and purpose.

Recall the reservations recommended by the US Senate Foreign Relations Committee with respect to the potential US ratification of CEDAW, p. 213, *supra*. As of mid 2012, 62 state parties had entered reservations or declarations to the Convention (though some of these reservations were simply to Article 29 providing for arbitration and adjudication by the ICJ). Twenty states had registered objections to one or more states' reservations. Selected illustrations follow.

Austria

Austria reserves its right to apply the provision of article 7(b) as far as service in the armed forces is concerned, and the provision of article 11 as far as night work of women and special protection of working women is concerned, within the limits established by national legislation.

Bangladesh (subsequently withdrawn with respect to Articles 13(a); 16(1)(c) and (f))

The Government of the People's Republic of Bangladesh does not consider as binding upon itself the provisions of articles 2, 13(a) and 16(1)(c) and (f) as they conflict with Shariah law based on Holy Koran and Sunna.

Belgium (subsequently withdrawn)

The application of article 7 shall not affect the validity of the provisions of the Constitution…which reserves for men the exercise of royal powers…

[14] Rebecca Cook, n. 11, *supra*, at 648.

Brazil (subsequently withdrawn)

The Government of the Federative Republic of Brazil hereby expresses its reservations to article 15, paragraph 4, and to article 16, paragraph 1(a), (c), (g) and (f)....

Egypt

Reservation to the text of article 9, paragraph 2, concerning the granting to women of equal rights with men with respect to the nationality of their children, without prejudice to the acquisition by a child born of a marriage of the nationality of his father.... It is clear that the child's acquisition of his father's nationality is the procedure most suitable for the child and that this does not infringe upon the principle of equality between men and women, since it is customary for a woman to agree, upon marrying an alien, that her children shall be of the father's nationality.

Reservation to the text of article 16 concerning the equality of men and women in all matters relating to marriage and family relations during the marriage and upon its dissolution, without prejudice to the Islamic Shariah provisions whereby women are accorded rights equivalent to those of their spouses so as to ensure a just balance between them. This is out of respect for the sacrosanct nature of the firm religious beliefs which govern marital relations in Egypt and which may not be called in question and in view of the fact that one of the most important bases of these relations is an equivalency of rights and duties so as to ensure complementarity which guarantees true equality between the spouses, not a quasi-equality that renders the marriage a burden on the wife.... The provisions of the Shariah lay down that the husband shall pay bridal money to the wife and maintain her fully and shall also make a payment to her upon divorce, whereas the wife retains full rights over her property and is not obliged to spend anything on her keep. The Shariah therefore restricts the wife's rights to divorce by making it contingent on a judge's ruling, whereas no such restriction is laid down in the case of the husband.

The Arab Republic of Egypt is willing to comply with the content of [Article 2], provided that such compliance does not run counter to the Islamic Shariah.

France

The Government of the French Republic declares that no provision of the Convention must be interpreted as prevailing over provisions of French legislation which are more favourable to women than to men.

Ireland

[Re Article 16(1)(d) and (f)] Ireland is of the view that the attainment in Ireland of the objectives of the Convention does not necessitate the extension to men of rights identical to those accorded to women in respect of the guardianship, adoption and custody of children born out of wedlock and reserves the right to implement the Convention subject to that understanding.

Malta

The Government of Malta does not consider itself bound by subparagraph (e) of Article 16, insofar as the same may be interpreted as imposing an obligation on Malta to legalize abortion.

Oman

Reservations:

1. All provisions of the Convention not in accordance with the provisions of the Islamic sharia and legislation in force in the Sultanate of Oman;
2. Article 9, paragraph 2, which provides that States Parties shall grant women equal rights with men with respect to the nationality of their children;
3. Article 15, paragraph 4, which provides that States Parties shall accord to men and women the same rights with regard to the law relating to the movement of persons and the freedom to choose their residence and domicile;
4. Article 16, regarding the equality of men and women, and in particular subparagraphs (a), (c), and (f) (regarding adoption).

...

Singapore

In the context of Singapore's multi-racial and multi-religious society and the need to respect the freedom of minorities to practise their religious and personal laws, the Republic of Singapore reserves the right not to apply the provisions of articles 2 and 16 where compliance with these provisions would be contrary to their religious or personal laws.

Singapore interprets article 11, paragraph 1, in the light of the provisions of article 4, paragraph 2 as not precluding prohibitions, restrictions or conditions on the employment of women in certain areas, or on work done by them where this is considered necessary or desirable to protect the health and safety of women or the human foetus....

Turkey

The Government of the Republic of Turkey [makes reservations] with regard to the articles of the Convention dealing with family relations which are not completely compatible with the provisions of the Turkish Civil Code....

Objections

Germany

The Federal Republic of Germany considers that the reservations made by Egypt regarding article 2, article 9, paragraph 2, and article 16, by Bangladesh regarding article 2, article 13 (*a*) and article 16, paragraph 1 (*c*) and (*f*), by Brazil regarding article 15, paragraph 4, and article 16, paragraph 1 (*a*), (*c*), (*g*) and (*h*), by Jamaica regarding article 9, paragraph 2, by the Republic of Korea regarding article 9 and article 16, paragraph 1 (*c*), (*d*), (*f*) and (*g*), and by Mauritius regarding article 11, paragraph 1 (*b*) and (*d*), and article 16, paragraph 1 (*g*), are incompatible with the object and purpose of the Convention (article 28, paragraph 2) and therefore objects to them. In relation to the Federal Republic of Germany, they may not be invoked in support of a legal practice which does not pay due regard to the legal status afforded to women and children in the Federal Republic of Germany in conformity with the above-mentioned articles of the Convention.

This objection shall not preclude the entry into force of the Convention as between Egypt, Bangladesh, Brazil, Jamaica, the Republic of Korea, Mauritius and the Federal Republic of Germany.

QUESTIONS

1. Which of the preceding reservations do you view as objectionable within the criteria of the Vienna Convention? Consider the reservations of Egypt. What arguments would you make for the validity of its reservations under the criteria stated in the Vienna Convention and CEDAW?

2. Which of the reservations raise issues of cultural relativism? Only those based on a state's local custom or religion?

3. How do you assess the criteria suggested by Cook? Would you judge any of the reservations above differently under her criteria?

4. Why do you suppose that CEDAW has attracted more reservations by states than other human rights treaties?

NOTE

In comparison with other democratic states, and even with many one-party and authoritarian states that are persistent and cruel violators of basic human rights, the United States has a modest record of ratification of human rights treaties. That comparison cuts both ways. One might say that the United States has a lesser commitment to and concern with developing international human rights than do many (say, European and Commonwealth) states of a roughly similar political and economic character. As the world's leading power, its lesser commitment necessarily weakens the human rights movement. Alternatively, one might say that the United States does not engage in the hypocrisy of many states in ratifying and then ignoring treaties. If it ratifies, it means to comply, and hence will take a careful look to be certain that full compliance is possible.

One can be certain that neither of these 'pure' explanations captures the complexity of the arguments within the Executive Branch and the Senate about ratification of these treaties. This section examines aspects of the ratification process of the ICCPR to illustrate that complexity.

As background to the materials on the ICCPR, the introductory readings below describe earlier attitudes within the United States about involvement in the international human rights system, and indicate the reasons why the United States effectively withdrew from participation in human rights treaties in the early 1950s. Recall the significant role played by the United States just a few years earlier in helping to launch the International Bill of Rights through the drafting of the Universal Declaration.

LOUIS SOHN & THOMAS BUERGENTHAL, INTERNATIONAL PROTECTION OF HUMAN RIGHTS

(1973), at 961

1. In 1945, during the Senate Foreign Relations Committee's hearings on the U. N. Charter, a principal Department of State expert on the Charter, Dr. Leo Pasvolsky, was questioned extensively on the relationship between Article 2(7) and the human rights provisions of the Charter. The following is an excerpt from his testimony:

> Senator Millikin. I notice several reiterations of the thought of the Charter that the Organization shall not interfere with domestic affairs of any country. How can you get into these social questions and economic questions without conducting investigations and making inquiries in the various countries?
>
> Mr. Pasvolsky. Senator, the Charter provides that the Assembly shall have the right to initiate or make studies in all of these economic or social fields....
>
> Senator Millikin. Might the activities of the Organization concern themselves with, for example, wage rates and working conditions in different countries?
>
> Mr. Pasvolsky. The question of what matters the Organization would be concerned with would depend upon whether or not they had international repercussions. This Organization is concerned with international problems. International problems may arise out of all sorts of circumstances....
>
> Senator Millikin. Could such an Organization concern itself with various forms of discrimination which countries maintain for themselves, bloc currency, subsidies to merchant marine, and things of that kind?
>
> Mr Pasvolsky. I should think that the Organization would wish to discuss and consider them. It might even make recommendations on any matters which affect international economic or social relations. The League of Nations did. The International Labor Office has done that. This new Organization being created will be doing a great deal of that....
>
> Senator Millikin. Would the investigation of racial discriminations be within the jurisdiction of this body?
>
> Mr. Pasvolsky. Insofar, I imagine, as the Organization takes over the function of making studies and recommendations on human rights, it may wish to make studies in those fields and make pronouncements.
>
> Senator Vandenberg. At that point I wish you would reemphasize what you read from the Commission Report specifically applying the exemption of domestic matters to the Social and Economic Council.

Mr. Pasvolsky. I will read that paragraph again.

Senator Vandenberg. Yes, please.

Mr. Pasvolsky. (reading): The members of Committee 3 of Commission II are in full agreement that nothing contained in chapter IX can be construed as giving authority to the Organization to intervene in the domestic affairs of Member states…

Senator Millikin. Is there any other international aspect to a labor problem or a racial problem or a religious problem that does not originate domestically?…

Mr. Pasvolsky. Well, Senator, I suppose we can say that there is no such thing as an international problem that is not related to national problems, because the word 'international' itself means that there are nations involved. What domestic jurisdiction relates to here, I should say, as it does in all of these matters, is that there are certain matters which are handled internally by nations which do not affect other nations or may not affect other nations. On the other hand, there are certainly many matters handled internally which do affect other nations and which by international law are considered to be of concern to other nations.

Senator Millikin. For example, let me ask you if this would be true. It is conceivable that there are racial questions on the southern shores of the Mediterranean that might have very explosive effects under some circumstances; but they originate locally, do they not, Doctor?

Mr Pasvolsky. Yes.

Senator Millikin. And because they might have explosive effects, this Organization might concern itself with them; is that correct?

Mr. Pasvolsky. It might, if somebody brings them to the attention of the Organization.

Senator Millikin. And by the same token, am I correct in this, that in any racial matter, any of these matters we are talking about, that originates in one country domestically and that has the possibility of making international trouble, might be subject to the investigation and recommendations of the Organization?

Mr. Pasvolsky. I should think so, because the Organization is created for that.

2. A number of different versions of a proposal to amend the treaty making power under the U.S. Constitution were considered by the Congress in the course of the so-called 'Bricker Amendment' debate, which lasted roughly from 1952 to 1957.[15]

…

4. It is generally acknowledged that the defeat of the proposed constitutional amendment was due in large measure to the vigorous lobbying by the Eisenhower Administration and its concomitant undertaking, articulated in the above-quoted testimony by Secretary of State John Foster Dulles, not to adhere to human rights treaties. This undertaking was also embodied in a policy statement

[15] [Eds.: The Bricker Amendment, a series a proposals for constitutional amendments, would have significantly limited executive power over treaties and correspondingly increased the power of the Senate or the Congress as a whole. Different versions of the amendments would have curtailed the use of self-executing treaties rather than treaties followed by legislation, and redrawn the boundary line between treaties and executive agreements so as to require larger Senate participation.]

issued by Mr. Dulles in the form of a letter addressed to Mrs. Oswald B. Lord, the United States Representative on the United Nations Commission on Human Rights. 28 DSB 579–80 (1953); 13 M. M. Whiteman, Digest of International Law 667–68 (Washington, D.C., 1970). This letter read in part:

> In the light of our national, and recently, international experience in the matter of human rights, the opening of a new session of the Commission on Human Rights appears an appropriate occasion for a fresh appraisal of the methods through which we may realize the human rights goals of the United Nations. These goals have a high place in the Charter as drafted at San Francisco and were articulated in greater detail in the Universal Declaration of Human Rights....
>
> Since the establishment of these goals, much time and effort has been expended on the drafting of treaties, that is, Covenants on Human Rights, in which it was sought to frame, in mutually acceptable legal form, the obligations to be assumed by national states in regard to human rights. We have found that such drafts of Covenants as had a reasonable chance of acceptance in some respects established standards lower than those now observed in a number of countries.
>
> While the adoption of the Covenants would not compromise higher standards already in force, it seems wiser to press ahead in the United Nations for the achievement of the standards set forth in the Universal Declaration of Human Rights through ways other than the proposed Covenants on Human Rights. This is particularly important in view of the likelihood that the Covenants will not be as widely accepted by United Nations members as initially anticipated. Nor can we overlook the fact that the areas where human rights are being persistently and flagrantly violated are those where the Covenants would most likely be ignored.
>
> In these circumstances, there is a grave question whether the completion, signing and ratification of the Covenants at this time is the most desirable method of contributing to human betterment particularly in areas of greatest need. Furthermore, experience to date strongly suggests that even if it be assumed that this is a proper area for treaty action, a wider general acceptance of human rights goals must be attained before it seems useful to codify standards of human rights as binding international legal obligations in the Covenants.
>
> With all these considerations in mind, the United States Government asks you to present to the Commission on Human Rights at its forthcoming session a statement of American goals and policies in this field; to point out the need for reexamining the approach of the Human Rights Covenants as the method for furthering at this time the objectives of the Universal Declaration of Human Rights; and to put forward other suggestions of method, based on American experience, for developing throughout the world a human rights conscience which will bring nearer the goals stated in the Charter....
>
> ...By reason of the considerations referred to above, the United States Government has reached the conclusion that we should not at this time become a party to any multilateral treaty such as those contemplated in the draft Covenants on Human Rights, and that we should now work toward the objectives of the Declaration by other means. While the Commission continues, under the General Assembly's instructions, with the drafting of the Covenants, you are, of course, expected to participate. This would be incumbent on the United States as a loyal Member of the United Nations.

NOTE

A 1953 memorandum prepared within the State Department[16] listed the pros and cons of US support for the then draft international covenants. The arguments noted in the memorandum for changing the present policy of support included: (1) It was doubtful that a covenant on civil and political rights could gain the necessary Senate consent. (2) It was 'by no means clear' that many countries ratifying the covenants would 'actually give effect to their provisions'. (3) The Covenants:

> could work to the disadvantage of United States interests, whether this country becomes a party or not. The Covenants would be a source of propaganda attack on positions taken by the United States and on conditions within this country. The Covenants might contain provisions on economic self-determination and the right of nationalization which would be detrimental to United States interests in certain areas abroad.

(4) US support appeared to some critics as 'inconsistent with the Administration's policy on civil rights in the United States, where the emphasis is now on persuasion as against any new federal civil rights legislation.'

COMMENT ON BACKGROUND TO SUBMISSION OF ICCPR TO SENATE

In the years following the decision to withdraw from participation in the two major Covenants, the United States did ratify a few human rights treaties, including the Slavery Convention, the Protocol Relating to the Status of Refugees, the Convention on the Political Rights of Women and the four Geneva Conventions on the laws of war. But it was not until the Carter Administration in the late 1970s that a President sought the Senate's consent for ratification of a number of major treaties (including the two Covenants).

In recent years, the record of the United States has substantially improved. The United States has become a party not only to the ICCPR but also to the Genocide Convention, the Convention against Torture and CERD. But there has never been sustained debate in the Senate or broader political debate in the country about participation in four major and widely ratified treaties: CEDAW, the American Convention on Human Rights, the CESCR or the CRC.

The following materials deal with aspects of the ratification process of the ICCPR. Given the similarities between the provisions of that Covenant and the US tradition of liberal constitutionalism and a Bill of Rights, no opponents of ratification then expressed doubt about the broad consistency between the principles of the Covenant and the US Constitution. There were statements from civil liberties

[16] United States Policy Regarding Draft International Covenants on Human Rights, Foreign Relations of the United States 1952–1954, Vol. III (1979), p. 1550.

groups stressing significant if more limited ways in which the United States, were it to become a party without making numerous legislative and policy changes, would be in violation of several ICCPR provisions.[17]

One of the recurrent issues before the Executive Branch and the Senate in deciding whether the United States should become a party was whether the Covenant, or salient parts of it, should be understood to be self-executing. Note that the ICCPR itself makes no reference to its self-executing or non-self-executing character but provides in Article 2(2):

> Where not already provided for by existing legislation or other measures, each State Party to the present Covenant undertakes to take the necessary steps, in accordance with its constitutional processes and with the provisions of the present Covenant, to adopt such legislative or other measures as may be necessary to give effect to the rights recognized in the present Covenant.

Article 2(3) bears out this obligation by stating the further undertaking to 'ensure that any persons whose rights... are violated shall have an effective remedy', and to 'ensure that any person claiming such a remedy shall have his right thereto determined by competent judicial, administrative or legislative authorities... and to develop the possibilities of judicial remedy.' How the states fulfil these obligations lies within their discretion; they are not obligated to incorporate the treaty *as such* within their domestic legal order, whether through automatic incorporation (self-executing treaty) or legislative incorporation. Consider the following comments on the ICCPR:[18]

> In its examination of individual communications and State reports, the [ICCPR Human Rights Committee] has originally confirmed that the States Parties may implement the Covenant domestically as they see fit. On the other hand, however, from the beginning there was a certain tendency of the Committee to promote the *direct applicability* of the Covenant.... In practice, a growing number of States parties are in fact enhancing the status of the Covenant in domestic law.... Of those countries in which the Covenant forms part of domestic law, only the United States has declared the operative articles (1 to 27) to be non-self-executing.

President George H. W. Bush sent a letter to the Senate Foreign Relations Committee in 1991,[19] urging the Senate to give its advice and consent to ratification of the ICCPR. It stated in part:

> The end of the Cold War offers great opportunities for the forces of democracy and the rule of law throughout the world. I believe the United States has a special responsibility to assist those in other countries who are now working to make the transition to pluralist democracies....

[17] See, e.g., Human Rights Watch and American Civil Liberties Union, *Human Rights Violations in the United States: A Report on U.S. Compliance with the International Covenant on Civil and Political Rights* (1993).

[18] Manfred Nowak, *UN Covenant on Civil and Political Rights: CCPR Commentary* (2nd edn. 2005), at 58.

[19] Rep. of S. Comm. for For. Rel. to Accompany Exec. E, 95–2 (1992), at 25.

> United States ratification of the Covenant on Civil and Political Rights at this moment in history would underscore our natural commitment to fostering democratic values through international law.... Subject to a few essential reservations and understandings, it is entirely consonant with the fundamental principles incorporated in our own Bill of Rights. U.S. ratification would also strengthen our ability to influence the development of appropriate human rights principles in the international community....

In 1978, the Carter Administration proposed a list of reservations, understandings and declarations (RUDs) when it submitted four human rights treaties to the Senate. The treaties were the ICCPR, CESCR, CERD and the American Convention on Human Rights. The Senate approved none of them. In 1991, when the Bush Administration revived the ICCPR alone among the four treaties, it submitted a revised list to the Senate Foreign Relations Committee. The following excerpt from this 1991 submission sets forth the Bush Administration's reasons for proposing several of the RUDs

PROPOSALS BY BUSH ADMINISTRATION OF RESERVATIONS TO INTERNATIONAL COVENANT ON CIVIL AND POLITICAL RIGHTS

Rep. of S. Comm. For. Rel. to Accompany Exec. E, 95–2 (1992), at 10

General Comments

In general, the substantive provisions of the Covenant are consistent with the letter and spirit of the United States Constitution and laws, both state and federal....

In a few instances, however, it is necessary to subject U.S. ratification to reservations, understandings or declarations in order to ensure that the United States can fulfill its obligations under the Covenant in a manner consistent with the United States Constitution, including instances where the Constitution affords greater rights and liberties to individuals than does the Covenant. Additionally, a few provisions of the Covenant articulate legal rules which differ from U.S. law and which, upon careful consideration, the Administration declines to accept in preference to existing law....

Formal Reservations

1. Free Speech (Article 20)

Although Article 19 of the Covenant specifically protects freedom of expression and opinion, Article 20 directly conflicts with the First Amendment by requiring the prohibition of certain forms of speech and expression which are protected under the First Amendment to the U.S. Constitution (i.e., propaganda for war and advocacy of national, racial or religious hatred that constitutes incitement to discrimination, hostility or violence). The United States cannot accept such an obligation.

Accordingly, the following reservation is recommended:

> Article 20 does not authorize or require legislation or other action by the United States that would restrict the right of free speech and association protected by the Constitution and laws of the United States.

...

2. Article 6 (capital punishment)

Article 6, paragraph 5 of the Covenant prohibits imposition of the death sentence for crimes committed by persons below 18 years of age and on pregnant women. In 1978, a broad reservation to this article was proposed in order to retain the right to impose capital punishment on any person duly convicted under existing or future laws permitting the imposition of capital punishment. The Administration is now prepared to accept the prohibition against execution of pregnant women. However, in light of the recent reaffirmation of U.S. policy towards capital punishment generally, and in particular the Supreme Court's decisions upholding state laws permitting the death penalty for crimes committed by juveniles aged 16 and 17, the prohibition against imposition of capital punishment for crimes committed by minors is not acceptable. Given the sharply differing view taken by many of our future treaty partners on the issue of the death penalty (including what constitutes 'serious crimes' under Article 6(2)), it is advisable to state our position clearly.

Accordingly, we recommend the following reservation to Article 6:

> The United States reserves the right, subject to its Constitutional constraints, to impose capital punishment on any person (other than a pregnant woman) duly convicted under existing or future laws permitting the imposition of capital punishment, including such punishment for crime committed by persons below eighteen years of age.

3. Article 7 (torture/punishment)

...

[We discuss the US reservation to Article 7 at p. 266, *supra*.]

4. Article 15(1) (post-offense reductions in penalty)

Article 15, paragraph 1... [provides]: 'If, subsequent to the commission of the offense, provision is made by law for the imposition of the lighter penalty, the offender shall benefit thereby.' Current federal law, as well as the law of most states, does not require such relief and in fact contains a contrary presumption that the penalty in force at the time the offense is committed will be imposed, although post-sentence reductions are permitted... and are often granted in practice when there have been subsequent statutory changes. Upon consideration, there is no disposition to require a change in U.S. law to conform to the Covenant. [A reservation was proposed.]

Understandings

1. Article 2(1), 4(1) and 26 (non-discrimination)

The very broad anti-discrimination provisions contained in the above articles do not precisely comport with long-standing Supreme Court doctrine in the equal protection field. In particular, Articles 2(1) and 26 prohibit discrimination not only on the bases of 'race, colour, sex, language, religion, political or other opinion, national or social origin, property, birth' but also on any 'other status.' Current U.S. civil rights law is not so open-ended: discrimination is only prohibited for specific statuses, and there are exceptions which allow for discrimination. For example, under the Age Discrimination Act of 1975, age may be taken into account in certain circumstances. In addition, U.S. law permits additional distinctions, for example between citizens and non-citizens and between different categories of non-citizens, especially in the context of the immigration laws.

...

Notwithstanding the very extensive protections already provided under U.S. law and the Committee's interpretive approach to the issue, we recommend [an understanding that expresses the preceding concerns.] [Eds.: The text of that understanding is here omitted.]

4. Article 14 (right to counsel, compelled witness, and double jeopardy)

In a few particular aspects, this Article could be read as going beyond existing U.S. domestic law.... Under the Constitution, double jeopardy attaches only to multiple prosecutions by the same sovereign and does not prohibit trial of the same defendant for the same crime in, for example, state and federal courts or in the courts of two states. See *Burton v. Maryland*, 395 U.S. 784 (1969).

To clarify our reading of the Covenant with respect to these issues, we recommend the following understanding, similar to the one proposed in 1978:

...The United States understands the prohibition upon double jeopardy in paragraph 7 to apply only when the judgment of acquittal has been rendered by a court of the same governmental unit, whether the Federal Government or a constituent unit, as is seeking a new trial for the same cause.

Declarations

1. Non-self-executing Treaty

For reasons of prudence, we recommend including a declaration that the substantive provisions of the Covenant are not self-executing. The intent is to clarify that the Covenant will not create a private cause of action in U.S. courts. As was the case with the Torture Convention, existing U.S. law generally complies with the Covenant; hence, implementing legislation is not contemplated.

We recommend the following declaration...

> The United States declares that the provisions of Articles 1 through 27 of the Covenant are not self-executing.

...

3. Article 41 (state-to-state complaints)

Under Article 41, States Party to the Covenant may accept the competence of the Human Rights Committee to consider state-to-state complaints by means of a formal declaration to that effect....

Accordingly, we recommend informing the Senate of our intent, subject to its approval, to make an appropriate declaration under Article 41 at the time of ratification, as follows:

> The United States declares that it accepts the competence of the Human Rights Committee to receive and consider communications under Article 41 in which a State Party claims another State Party is not fulfilling its obligations under the Covenant.

...

QUESTIONS

1. Several NGOs participating in the Senate hearings on ratification of the ICCPR opposed the proposed (and later adopted) non-self-executing declaration. Note the following comments in a joint report by the largest domestic civil liberties organization and the largest US-based international human rights organization in the United States:[20]

> ...Americans would have been able to enforce the treaty in U.S. courts either if it had been declared to be self-executing or if implementing legislation had been enacted to create causes of action under the treaty. The Bush administration rejected both routes. The result was that ratification became an empty act for Americans: the endorsement of the most important treaty for the protection of civil rights yielded not a single additional enforceable right to citizens and residents of the United States.
>
> We issue this report to demonstrate the inaccuracy of the view that Americans do not need the protection of the ICCPR. As we show, the Bush administration was wrong in its assessment that the United States is already complying with all the treaty's obligations, even after the administration nullified some of the rights through its reservations, declarations and understandings. In the areas of racial and gender discrimination, prison conditions, immigrants' rights, language discrimination, the death penalty, police brutality, freedom of expression and religious freedom, we show that the United States is now violating the treaty in important respects. As a result, the Clinton administration is under an immediate legal obligation to remedy these human rights violations at home, through specific steps that we outline.

[20] Human Rights Watch and American Civil Liberties Union, *Human Rights Violations in the United States: A Report on U.S. Compliance with the International Covenant on Civil and Political Rights* (1993), at 2.

Moreover, to ensure that these remedies are sufficient, we believe the U.S. government is obligated to grant Americans the right to invoke the protections of the treaty in U.S. courts, at least through specific legislation enabling them to do so, but preferably through a formal declaration that the treaty is self-executing, and thus invocable in U.S. courts without further legislation....

Do you agree with these observations about the need for a self-executing Covenant? What arguments would you make against this position?

2. Ratification by the United States of the ICCPR Optional Protocol does not seem to have been discussed. No such proposal was put to the Senate. (a) Why do you suppose this to have been the case? (b) As a member of the State Department, would you have argued for or against joining the Optional Protocol? (c) 'Ratification of the Optional Protocol would have been the correct solution, preferable to making the ICCPR self-executing.' Comment.

COMMENT ON EFFECTS OF RESERVATIONS WITH RESPECT TO OTHER STATES PARTIES

Upon the US ratification the ICCR, a number of states parties objected to one or more of the US reservations. Several states — including Belgium, Denmark, Finland, France, Germany, Italy, the Netherlands, Norway, Portugal, Spain and Sweden — objected to the reservation regarding Article 6, paragraph 5, prohibiting the imposition of the death sentence for crimes committed by persons below 18 years of age, and found that reservation incompatible with the object and purpose of the Covenant. Most of these states also objected to other reservations (or to understandings), particularly the one relating to Article 7. The objections, however, stressed that (to take one illustration) the state's position on the relevant reservations 'does not constitute an obstacle to the entry into force of the Covenant between the Kingdom of Spain and the United States of America'. Compare in this respect Articles 20–21 of the Vienna Convention on the Law of Treaties.

In objecting to three reservations and three understandings, Sweden observed that under international treaty law, the name 'assigned to a statement' that excluded or modified the effect of certain treaty provisions:

> does not determine its status as a reservation to the treaty. Thus, the Government considers that some of the understandings made by the United States in substance constitute reservations to the Covenant.
>
> A reservation by which a State modifies or excludes the application of the most fundamental provisions of the Covenant, or limits its responsibilities under that treaty by invoking general principles of national law, may cast doubts upon the commitment of the reserving State to the object and purpose of the Covenant. The reservations made by the United States of America include both reservations to essential and non-derogable provisions, and general references to national

legislation. Reservations of this nature contribute to undermining the basis of international treaty law. All States parties share a common interest in the respect for the object and purpose of the treaty to which they have chosen to become parties.

HUMAN RIGHTS COMMITTEE, GENERAL COMMENT NO. 24

CCPR/C/21/Rev. 1/Add. 6 (2 Nov. 1994)

[In 1994, the ICCPR Committee adopted General Comment No. 24 'on issues relating to reservations made upon ratification of accession to the Covenant or the Optional Protocols thereto, or in relation to declarations under article 41 of the Covenant.' This GC was adopted after the ratification of the ICCPR by the United States described above, and preceded the Committee's consideration of the first periodic report submitted by the United States in 1995. The GC refers to the provisions of the Vienna Convention on the Law of Treaties described at p. 1080, *supra*.

The GC notes that as of its date, 46 of the 127 states parties to the ICCPR had entered a total of 150 reservations, ranging from exclusion of the duty to provide particular rights, to insistence on the 'paramountcy of certain domestic legal provisions' and to limitations on the competence of the Committee. Those reservations 'tend to weaken respect' for obligations and 'may undermine the effective implementation of the Covenant'. The Committee felt compelled to act, partly under the necessity of clarifying for states parties just what obligations had been undertaken, a clarification that would require the Committee to determine 'the acceptability and effects' of reservations.

The GC observed that the ICCPR itself makes no reference to reservations (as is true also for the First Optional Protocol; the Second Optional Protocol limits reservations), and that the matter of reservations is governed by international law. It found in Article 19(3) of the Vienna Convention on the Law of Treaties 'relevant guidance'. Therefore, that article's 'object and purpose test... governs the matter of interpretation and acceptability of reservations'. The GC continues:]

8. Reservations that offend peremptory norms would not be compatible with the object and purpose of the Covenant. Although treaties that are mere exchanges of obligations between States allow them to reserve *inter se* application of rules of general international law, it is otherwise in human rights treaties, which are for the benefit of persons within their jurisdiction. Accordingly, provisions in the Covenant that represent customary international law (and *a fortiori* when they have the character of peremptory norms) may not be the subject of reservations. Accordingly, a State may not reserve the right to engage in slavery, to torture, to subject persons to cruel, inhuman or degrading treatment or punishment, to arbitrarily deprive persons of their lives, to arbitrarily arrest and detain persons, to deny freedom of thought, conscience and religion, to presume a person guilty unless he proves his innocence, to execute pregnant women or children, to permit the advocacy of national, racial or religious hatred, to deny to persons of marriageable age the right to marry, or to deny to minorities the right to enjoy their own culture, profess their own religion, or use their own language. And while reservations to

particular clauses of Article 14 may be acceptable, a general reservation to the right to a fair trial would not be.

9. Applying more generally the object and purpose test to the Covenant, the Committee notes that, for example,... a State [may not] reserve an entitlement not to take the necessary steps at the domestic level to give effect to the rights of the Covenant (Article 2(2)).

10. ... [I]t falls for consideration as to whether reservations to the non-derogable provisions of the Covenant are compatible with its object and purpose.... One reason for certain rights being made non-derogable is because their suspension is irrelevant to the legitimate control of the state of national emergency (for example, no imprisonment for debt, in article 11).... At the same time, some provisions are non-derogable exactly because without them there would be no rule of law. A reservation to the provisions of article 4 itself, which precisely stipulates the balance to be struck between the interests of the State and the rights of the individual in times of emergency, would fall in this category. And some non-derogable rights, which in any event cannot be reserved because of their status as peremptory norms, are also of this character [e.g., torture].... While there is no automatic correlation between reservations to non-derogable provisions, and reservations which offend against the object and purpose of the Covenant, a State has a heavy onus to justify such a reservation.

11. ... The Committee's role under the Covenant, whether under article 40 or under the Optional Protocols, necessarily entails interpreting the provisions of the Covenant and the development of a jurisprudence. Accordingly, a reservation that rejects the Committee's competence to interpret the requirements of any provisions of the Covenant would also be contrary to the object and purpose of that treaty.

12. ... Domestic laws may need to be altered properly to reflect the requirements of the Covenant; and mechanisms at the domestic level will be needed to allow the Covenant rights to be enforceable at the local level. Reservations often reveal a tendency of States not to want to change a particular law. And sometimes that tendency is elevated to a general policy. Of particular concern are widely formulated reservations which essentially render ineffective all Covenant rights which would require any change in national law to ensure compliance with Covenant obligations. No real international rights or obligations have thus been accepted. And when there is an absence of provisions to ensure that Covenant rights may be sued on in domestic courts, and, further, a failure to allow individual complaints to be brought to the Committee under the first Optional Protocol, all the essential elements of the Covenant guarantees have been removed.

...

17. ... [Human rights] treaties, and the Covenant specifically, are not a web of inter-State exchanges of mutual obligations.... Because the operation of the classic rules on reservations is so inadequate for the Covenant, States have often not seen any legal interest in or need to object to reservations. The absence of protest by States cannot imply that a reservation is either compatible or incompatible with the object and purpose of the Covenant....

18. It necessarily falls to the Committee to determine whether a specific reservation is compatible with the object and purpose of the Covenant.... Because of the

special character of a human rights treaty, the compatibility of a reservation with the object and purpose of the Covenant must be established objectively, by reference to legal principles, and the Committee is particularly well placed to perform this task. The normal consequence of an unacceptable reservation is not that the Covenant will not be in effect at all for a reserving party. Rather, such a reservation will generally be severable, in the sense that the Covenant will be operative for the reserving party without benefit of the reservation.

19. Reservations must be specific.... States should not enter so many reservations that they are in effect accepting a limited number of human rights obligations, and not the Covenant as such. So that reservations do not lead to a perpetual non-attainment of international human rights standards, reservations should not systematically reduce the obligations undertaken only to the presently existing in less demanding standards of domestic law. Nor should interpretative declarations or reservations seek to remove an autonomous meaning to Covenant obligations, by pronouncing them to be identical, or to be accepted only insofar as they are identical, with existing provisions of domestic law.

...

INTERNATIONAL LAW COMMISSION'S GUIDE TO PRACTICE ON RESERVATIONS TO TREATIES: PERMISSIBILITY OF RESERVATIONS AND AUTHORITY TO DECIDE

[In 2011, the International Law Commission (ILC), see p. 402, *supra*, adopted the Guide to Practice on Reservations to Treaties. The Guide reflected the culmination of 17 years of work under the leadership of Special Rapporteur and Commission member Alain Pellet. As with other ILC documents of its kind, early drafts of the guidelines were scrutinized annually by the UN General Assembly's Sixth Committee, a body of governmental representatives, which gave states an opportunity to express their views on the general endeavour and specific details. Through this process of governmental review and continued refinement of the text, the Guide increased its legitimacy and support among states. Accompanying the publication of the Guide, the Commission also published a lengthy (nearly 600 pages) set of Commentaries. The following excerpts of the Guide and Commentaries include sections that are relevant to important areas of international human rights law and practice. You should notice, as you read, several points of agreement and disagreement between the ILC and the Human Rights Committee.]

3.1.5 Incompatibility of a reservation with the object and purpose of the treaty

A reservation is incompatible with the object and purpose of the treaty if it affects an essential element of the treaty that is necessary to its general tenour, in such a way that the reservation impairs the *raison d'être* of the treaty.

Commentary

[N]either the object — defined as the actual content of the treaty — still less the purpose — the outcome sought — remain immutable over time, as the theory of emergent purpose advanced by Sir Gerald Fitzmaurice clearly demonstrates: 'The notion of object and purpose is itself not a fixed and static one, but is liable to change, or rather develop as experience is gained in the operation and working of the convention.'...

...

...[I]n an endeavour to avoid too high a 'threshold', the Commission chose the adjective 'necessary' in preference to the stronger term 'indispensable', and decided on the verb 'impair' (rather than 'deprive') to apply to the *'raison d'être'* of the treaty, it being understood... that the question could even arise of whether the *raison d'être* might change over time.

3.1.5.2 Vague or general reservations

A reservation shall be worded in such a way as to allow its meaning to be understood, in order to assess in particular its compatibility with the object and purpose of the treaty.

Commentary

Since, under article 19 (c) of the Vienna Conventions,... a reservation must be compatible with the object and purpose of the treaty, and since other States are required, under article 20, to take a position on this compatibility, it must be possible for them to do so. This will not be the case if the reservation in question is worded in such a way as to preclude any determination of its scope, in other words, if it is vague or general.... This is not, strictly speaking, a case in which the reservation is incompatible with the object and purpose of the treaty: it is rather a hypothetical situation in which it is impossible to assess this compatibility. This shortcoming seemed sufficiently serious to the Commission for it to come up with particularly strong wording: 'shall be worded' rather than 'should be worded' or 'is worded'. Furthermore, use of the term 'worded' highlights the fact that this is a requirement of substance and not merely one of form.

In any event, the requirement for precision in the wording of reservations is implicit in their very definition. It is clear from article 2, paragraph 1 (d), of the Vienna Conventions... that the object of reservations is to exclude or to modify 'the legal effect of certain provisions of the treaty in their application' to their authors.... [A]lthough 'across-the-board' reservations are common practice, they are, as specified in guideline 1.1.1, paragraph 2, valid only if they purport 'to exclude or modify the legal effect ... of the treaty as a whole with respect to certain specific aspects ...'.

...

[The 'text of the reservation does not allow its meaning to be understood'] often happens when a reservation invokes the internal law of the State that has formulated it without identifying the provisions in question or specifying whether they are to be found in its constitution or its civil or criminal code. In such cases, it is not the reference to the domestic law of the reserving State *per se* that is the problem, but rather the frequent vagueness and generality of the reservations referring to domestic law, which make it impossible for the other States parties to take a position on them. . . .

. . .

The same applies when a State reserves the general right to have its constitution prevail over a treaty, as for instance in the reservation by the United States of America to the Convention on the Prevention and Punishment of the Crime of Genocide: '. . . nothing in the Convention requires or authorizes legislation or other action by the United States of America prohibited by the Constitution of the United States as interpreted by the United States.'

Some of the so-called 'sharia reservations' give rise to the same objection, a case in point being the reservation by which Mauritania approved the 1979 Convention on the Elimination of All Forms of Discrimination against Women 'in each and every one of its parts which are not contrary to Islamic sharia'. Here again, the problem lies not in the fact that Mauritania is invoking a law of religious origin which it applies, but, rather that, as Denmark noted, 'the general reservations with reference to the provisions of Islamic law are of unlimited scope and undefined character'. Thus, as the United Kingdom put it, such a reservation 'which consists of a general reference to national law without specifying its contents does not clearly define for the other States Parties to the Convention the extent to which the reserving State has accepted the obligations of the Convention'. Basically, it is the impossibility of assessing the compatibility of such reservations with the object and purpose of the treaty, and not the certainty that they are incompatible, which makes them fall within the purview of article 19 (c) of the Vienna Convention on the Law of Treaties. . . .

. . .

Although the present Commentary may not be the right place for a discussion of the effects of vague or general reservations, it must still be noted that they raise particular problems. It would seem difficult, *a priori*, to maintain that they are invalid *ipso jure*: the main criticism that can be levelled against them is that they make it impossible to assess whether or not they satisfy the conditions for permissibility. . . .

3.1.5.3 Reservations to a provision reflecting a customary rule

The fact that a treaty provision reflects a rule of customary international law does not in itself constitute an obstacle to the formulation of a reservation to that provision.

Commentary

. . . Guideline 3.1.5.3 therefore sets out the principle that a reservation to a treaty rule which reflects a customary rule is not *ipso jure* incompatible with the object and purpose of the treaty, even if due account must be taken of that element in assessing such compatibility.

On occasion States parties to a treaty have objected to reservations and challenged their compatibility with its object and purpose on the pretext that they were contrary to well established customary rules. Thus, Austria declared, in cautious terms, that it was '...of the view that the Guatemalan reservations [to the 1969 Vienna Convention on the Law of Treaties] refer almost exclusively to general rules of [the said Convention] many of which are solidly based on international customary law. The reservations could call into question well-established and universally accepted norms. Austria is of the view that the reservations also raise doubts as to their compatibility with the object and purpose of the [said Convention] ...'

...

Moreover, although this principle is sometimes challenged, it is recognized in the preponderance of the literature, and rightly so:

- Customary rules are binding on States, independently of their expression of consent to a treaty rule but, unlike the case of peremptory norms, States may opt out by agreement inter se; it is not clear why they could not do so through a reservation...;
- A reservation concerns only the expression of the rule in the context of the treaty, not its existence as a customary rule, even if, in some cases, it may cast doubt on the rule's general acceptance 'as law'; as the United Kingdom remarked in its observations on general comment No. 24 of the Human Rights Committee, 'there is a clear distinction between choosing not to enter into treaty obligations and trying to opt out of customary international law';
- If the customary nature of the rule is well-established, States remain bound by it, independently of the treaty;
- Despite appearances, States may have a rationale for their action — for example, the desire to avoid placing the obligations in question within the purview of the monitoring or dispute settlement mechanisms envisaged in the treaty or to limit the role of domestic judges, who may have different competences with respect to treaty rules, on the one hand, and customary rules, on the other;

...

- And, lastly, a reservation may be the means by which a 'persistent objector' manifests the persistence of its objection; the objector may certainly reject the application, through a treaty, of a rule which cannot be invoked against it under general international law.

The question has been raised, however, whether this solution can be transposed to the field of human rights.... [The Commission finds no reason to make a distinction on this basis.]

...

The Commission did not consider it necessary to draft a specific guideline on reservations to a treaty provision reflecting a peremptory norm of general international law (*jus cogens*). Such a norm is, in almost all cases, customary in nature. It follows that the reasoning applicable to reservations to treaty provisions reflecting 'normal' customary rules can be transposed to reservations to provisions reflecting *jus cogens* norms.

...

3.1.5.4 Reservations to provisions concerning rights from which no derogation is permissible under any circumstances

A State or an international organization may not formulate a reservation to a treaty provision concerning rights from which no derogation is permissible under any circumstances [Eds.: e.g., Article 5 of the ICCPR], unless the reservation in question is compatible with the essential rights and obligations arising out of that treaty. In assessing that compatibility, account shall be taken of the importance which the parties have conferred upon the rights at issue by making them non-derogable.

3.1.5.7 Reservations to treaty provisions concerning dispute settlement or the monitoring of the implementation of the treaty

A reservation to a treaty provision concerning dispute settlement or the monitoring of the implementation of the treaty is not, in itself, incompatible with the object and purpose of the treaty, unless:

(i) the reservation purports to exclude or modify the legal effect of a provision of the treaty essential to its *raison d'être*

...

3.2 Assessment of the permissibility of reservations

The following may assess, within their respective competences, the permissibility of reservations to a treaty formulated by a State or an international organization:

- contracting States or contracting organizations;
- dispute settlement bodies;
- treaty monitoring bodies.

Commentary

In the first place... it must be acknowledged that the treaty bodies could not carry out their mandated functions if they could not be sure of the exact extent of their jurisdiction vis-à-vis the States concerned, whether in their consideration of complaints by States or individuals or of periodic reports, or in their exercise of an advisory function; it is therefore part of their functions to assess the permissibility of reservations.... Secondly, in so doing, they have neither more nor less authority than in any other area: the Human Rights Committee and the other international human rights treaty bodies which do not have decision-making power do not acquire it in the area of reservations... [T]hirdly... they may not substitute their own judgement for the State's consent to be bound by the treaty. It goes without saying that the powers of the treaty bodies do not affect the power of States or organizations to accept reservations or object to them, as established and regulated under articles 20, 21 and 23 of the Vienna Conventions.

...

It is clear that the multiplicity of possibilities for assessment presents certain disadvantages, not least of which is the risk of conflict between the positions different parties might take on the same reservation (or on two identical reservations of different States). In fact, however, this risk is inherent in any assessment system — over time, any given body may take conflicting decisions — and it is probably better to have too much assessment than no assessment at all.

...

3.2.3 Consideration of the assessments of treaty monitoring bodies

States and international organizations that have formulated reservations to a treaty establishing a treaty monitoring body shall give consideration to that body's assessment of the permissibility of the reservations.

Commentary

[T]here is no question but that [treaty bodies] may assess the permissibility of reservations to treaties whose observance they are required to monitor. On the other hand, they may not... [t]ake the place of the author of the reservation, in any case, in determining the consequences to be drawn from the impermissibility of a reservation....

QUESTIONS

1. Why was there near unanimity among the states parties to the ICCPR that objected to the reservations by the United States about the particular reservation concerning Article 6, paragraph 5 (death sentence)? Did that reservation raise a special problem under the Covenant? On the other hand, was there special reason for the United States to reserve as to that provision?

2. In light of General Comment No. 24, if you were a Senator committed to US ratification of the major human rights instruments, would you have voted for any reservation? Did any one of the reservations have a special justification?

3. Is General Comment No. 24 consistent with the spirit of the *Genocide Convention* Advisory Opinion described above, p. 1081, *supra*? Using that opinion, how would you argue that the reservations of the United States should be accepted in their entirety as valid under international law?

4. Do you agree with the ILC's reasons for concluding that it is permissible for a state to make reservations to treaty provisions that reflect customary international law (3.1.5.3)? Or do you agree, instead, with General Comment No. 24? The ILC relies largely on the proposition that reservations do not affect the customary international law status of the substantive obligation. Is that claim correct? And is it consistent with the ILC's other claim that such reservations 'may be the means by which a "persistent objector" manifests the persistence of its objection'? Should any distinction be made for reservations to treaty provisions that reflect *jus cogens* norms? Finally, consider the following concern (which the ILC raised but ultimately rejected):

On the more general issue of codifying conventions, it might be wondered whether reservations to them are not incompatible with their object and purpose. There is no doubt that the desire to codify is normally accompanied by a concern to preserve the rule being affirmed. If it were possible to formulate a reservation to a provision of customary origin in the context of a codification treaty [designed for this specific purpose], the codification treaty would fail in its objectives to the point that reservations and, at all events, multiple reservations, have been viewed as the very negation of the work of codification.[21]

5. The ILC Commentary admits that if every treaty body and various other institutions all have the authority to assess the permissibility of a reservation, multiple conflicting decisions may result. Nevertheless, the Commentary concludes that 'it is probably better to have too much assessment than no assessment at all' (Commentary to 3.2). Do you agree? Is the comparison to 'no assessment at all' the correct one? Is there a point — and if so, what is it — whereby the costs of multiple venues of assessment would undermine the goals of the human rights regime?

6. The Vienna Convention on the Law of Treaties does not include an express prohibition on 'vague' or 'general' reservations. Did the ILC Commentary go too far in developing this doctrine and in describing the reservations that it would discredit or does this section of the Commentary seem well tethered to existing law and practice?

COMMENT ON SEVERABILITY

France, the United Kingdom and the United States submitted observations to the ICCPR Committee on General Comment No. 24. The US Government stated that the GC 'appears to go much too far' and that the ICCPR does not 'impose on States Parties an obligation to give effect to the Committee's interpretations or confer on the Committee the power to render definitive interpretations of the Covenant.' The observations stated that paragraphs 16–20 of the GC 'appear to reject the established rules of interpretation of treaties' in the Vienna Convention and in customary international law. It criticized the GC's condemnation of the types of reservations that the United States had entered.

The observations were particularly critical of paragraph 18, which stated that in the indicated circumstances, 'the Covenant will be operative for the reserving party without benefit of the reservations'. This conclusion is 'completely at odds with established legal practice and principles....' If it were determined that any one or more of the US reservations were ineffective, the consequence would be that the ratification as a whole could thereby be nullified, and the United States

[21] See ILC Commentary to 3.1.5.3 at (10).

would not be party to the Covenant. France and the United Kingdom submitted similar observations. On the severability question, France 'reject[ed] this entire analysis.... [I]f these reservations are deemed incompatible with the purpose and object of the treaty, the only course open is to declare that this consent is not valid and decide that these States cannot be considered parties to the instrument in question.' On this point of law, the UK Government stated similar concerns and added a pragmatic one: 'questions of principle aside, an approach as outlined in ... the General Comment would risk discouraging States from ratifying human rights conventions (since they would not be in a position to reassure their national Parliaments as to the status of treaty provisions on which it was felt necessary to reserve).'

Despite these responses, other treaty bodies subsequently endorsed General Comment No. 24, and the Human Rights Committee employed its severability approach. In a communication submitted to the ILC, the chairpersons of the treaty bodies stated: 'The Chairpersons express[] their firm support for the approach reflected in General Comment No. 24 of the Human Rights Committee and they urge[] that the conclusions proposed by the International Law Commission should be adjusted accordingly to reflect that approach.' Shortly thereafter, the Human Rights Committee applied its severability approach in a First Optional Protocol proceeding involving a death row inmate from Trinidad and Tobago.

KENNEDY v. TRINIDAD AND TOBAGO

Communication No 845/1999, Human Rights Committee, 31 Dec. 1999, UN Doc. CCPR/C/67/D/845/1999

1. The author of the communication is Mr. Rawle Kennedy, a citizen of Trinidad and Tobago, awaiting execution in the State prison in Port of Spain....

3.3 The author claims to be a victim of violations of [various articles of the ICCPR on grounds of the mandatory nature of the death penalty for murder in Trinidad and Tobago, the imposition of the death penalty without consideration of mitigating circumstances in his particular situation as a secondary party to the killing, the lack of a fair hearing for the prerogative of mercy, torture prior to trial, inhumane conditions of detention on death row and] that carrying out his death sentence in such circumstances would constitute a violation of his rights under articles 6 and 7. Reference is made to the Judicial Committee of the Privy Council's judgment in *Pratt and Morgan v. The Attorney General of Jamaica* (1994) 2 AC1, in which it held that prolonged detention under sentence of death would violate, in that case, Jamaica's constitutional prohibition on inhuman and degrading treatment....

4.1 ... [T]he State party makes reference to its instrument of accession to the Optional Protocol of 26 May 1998, which included the following reservation:

> "... Trinidad and Tobago re-accedes to the Optional Protocol to the International Covenant on Civil and Political Rights with a Reservation to article 1 thereof to

> the effect that the Human Rights Committee shall not be competent to receive and consider communications relating to any prisoner who is under sentence of death in respect of any matter relating to his prosecution, his detention, his trial, his conviction, his sentence or the carrying out of the death sentence on him and any matter connected therewith."

6.2 On 26 May 1998, the Government of Trinidad and Tobago denounced the first Optional Protocol to the International Covenant on Civil and Political Rights. On the same day, it reacceded, including in its instrument of reaccession the reservation set out in paragraph 4. 1 above.

6.3 To explain why such measures were taken, the State party makes reference to the decision of the Judicial Committee of the Privy Council in *Pratt and Morgan v. the Attorney General for Jamaica*, in which it was held that "in any case in which execution is to take place more than five years after sentence there will be strong grounds for believing that the delay is such as to constitute 'inhuman or degrading punishment or other treatment'" in violation of section 17 of the Jamaican Constitution. The effect of the decision for Trinidad and Tobago is that inordinate delays in carrying out the death penalty would contravene . . . the Constitution of Trinidad and Tobago, which contains a provision similar to that in section 17 of the Jamaican Constitution. The State party explains that as the decision of the Judicial Committee of the Privy Council represents the constitutional standard for Trinidad and Tobago, the Government is mandated to ensure that the appellate process is expedited by the elimination of delays within the system in order that capital sentences imposed pursuant to the laws of Trinidad and Tobago can be enforced. Thus, the State party chose to denounce the Optional Protocol:

> "In the circumstances, and wishing to uphold its domestic law to subject no one to inhuman and degrading punishment or treatment and thereby observe its obligations under article 7 of the International Covenant on Civil and Political Rights, the Government of Trinidad and Tobago felt compelled to denounce the Optional Protocol. Before doing so, however, it held consultations on 31 March 1998, with the Chairperson and the Bureau of the Human Rights Committee with a view to seeking assurances that the death penalty cases would be dealt with expeditiously and completed within 8 months of registration. For reasons which the Government of Trinidad and Tobago respects, no assurance could be given that these cases would be completed within the timeframe sought."

6.6 In its General Comment No. 24, the Committee expressed the view that a reservation aimed at excluding the competence of the Committee under the Optional Protocol with regard to certain provisions of the Covenant could not be considered to meet th[e] test [whether or not the reservation by the state party can be considered to be compatible with the object and purpose of the Optional Protocol.]

6.7 The present reservation, which was entered after the publication of General Comment No. 24, does not purport to exclude the competence of the Committee under the Optional Protocol with regard to any specific provision of the Covenant, but rather to the entire Covenant for one particular group of complainants, namely prisoners under sentence of death. This does not, however, make it compatible with the object and purpose of the Optional Protocol. On the contrary, the Committee cannot accept a reservation which singles out a certain group of individuals for lesser procedural protection than that which is enjoyed by the rest of the population. In the view of the Committee, this constitutes a discrimination which runs counter to some of the basic principles embodied in the Covenant and its Protocols, and for this reason the reservation cannot be deemed compatible with the object and purpose of the Optional Protocol. The consequence is that the Committee is not precluded from considering the present communication under the Optional Protocol.

6.8 The Committee, noting that the State party has not challenged the admissibility of any of the author's claims on any other ground than its reservation, considers that the author's claims are sufficiently substantiated to be considered on the merits.

7. The Human Rights Committee therefore decides...the State party shall be requested to submit to the Committee, within six months of the date of transmittal to it of this decision, written explanations or statements clarifying the matter and the measures, if any, that may have been taken....[22]

INDIVIDUAL, DISSENTING, OPINION OF COMMITTEE MEMBERS NISUKE ANDO, PRAFULACHANDRA N. BHAGWATI, ECKART KLEIN AND DAVID KRETZMER

6. ...If a State party is free either to accept or not accept an international monitoring mechanism, it is difficult to see why it should not be free to accept this mechanism only with regard to some rights or situations, provided the treaty itself does not exclude this possibility. All or nothing is not a reasonable maxim in human rights law.

8. It goes without saying that a State party could not submit a reservation that offends peremptory rules of international law. Thus, for example, a reservation to the Optional Protocol that discriminated between persons on grounds of race, religion or sex, would be invalid. However, this certainly does not mean that every distinction between categories of potential victims of violations by the State party is unacceptable. All depends on the distinction itself and the objective reasons for that distinction.

9. ...As we are talking about a reservation to the Optional Protocol, and not to the Covenant itself, this requires us to examine not whether there should be any difference in the substantive rights of persons under sentence of death and those of other persons, but whether there is any difference between communications submitted by people under sentence of death and communications submitted by all other persons....

22 [Eds.: In response to the Committee's conclusion, Trinidad and Tobago denounced and withdrew from the Optional Protocol in 2000.]

10. The grounds for the denunciation of the Optional Protocol by the State party are set out in paragraph 6. 3 of the Committee's views and there is no need to rehearse them here. What is clear is that the difference between communications submitted by persons under sentence of death and others is that they have different results....

16. It is not our intention within the framework of the present case to reopen the whole issue dealt with in General Comment no. 24. Suffice it to say that even in dealing with reservations to the Covenant itself the Committee did not take the view that in every case an unacceptable reservation will fall aside, leaving the reserving state to become a party to the Covenant without benefit of the reservation. As can be seen from the section of General Comment no. 24 quoted above, the Committee merely stated that this would normally be the case. The normal assumption will be that the ratification or accession is not dependent on the acceptability of the reservation and that the unacceptability of the reservation will not vitiate the reserving state's agreement to be a party to the Covenant. However, this assumption cannot apply when it is abundantly clear that the reserving state's agreement to becoming a party to the Covenant is dependent on the acceptability of the reservation. The same applies with reservations to the Optional Protocol.

17. ... [I]f we had accepted the Committee's view that the reservation is invalid we would have had to hold that Trinidad and Tobago is not a party to the Optional Protocol....

18. ... [W]e wish to stress that we share the Committee's view that the reservation submitted by the State party is unfortunate.... [T]he reservation is wider than required in order to cater to the constitutional constraints of the State party, as it disallows communications by persons under sentence of death even if the time limit set by the Privy Council has already been exceeded (as would seem to be the case in the present communication). We understand that since the State party's denunciation and reaccession there have been developments in the jurisprudence of the Privy Council that may make the reservation unnecessary. These factors do not affect the question of the compatibility of the reservation with the object and purpose of the Optional Protocol. However, we do see fit to express the hope that the State party will reconsider the need for the reservation and withdraw it....

RYAN GOODMAN, HUMAN RIGHTS TREATIES, INVALID RESERVATIONS, AND STATE CONSENT

96 Am. J. Int. L. 531 (2002)

[The theory that] an invalid reservation can be severed...has recently encountered strong opposition. According to...the anti-severability (AS) position, international law [does not permit the option of severing an invalid reservation].... Proponents of the AS position ground their argument on a foundational precept of international law: the principle of state consent....

...I argue that reservations to human rights treaties should be presumed to be severable unless for a specific treaty there is evidence of a ratifying state's intent to the contrary. This argument has two parts: the first part contends that severability should be an option for a third-party institution (e.g., a domestic court, a national human rights commission, a regional court, the International Court of Justice (ICJ), a treaty body) to invoke after having found a reservation invalid; the second part contends that severance should be presumed to be the optimal remedy....

This approach better reflects and protects state consent than the AS position....

...

...[A] state may include more reservations than required to obtain its consent. Whether counting on other states not to object to its reservations or discounting the cost of such objections, a state may include supererogatory conditions in its package of reservations. Although some reservations are essential — integral to the state's consent to the treaty — others may be described as what Judge Armand-Ugon, in a related context, called "an accessory stipulation."

In various multilateral agreements, especially those without a juridical supervisory organ, states may incur little cost for submitting accessory reservations....

...

Newly established democracies. The greatest potential cost of an AS regime would be to newly established democracies. Andrew Moravcsik...argues that...the accession by newly democratic states to binding human rights agreements: "...is a tactic used by governments to 'lock in' and consolidate democratic institutions, thereby enhancing their credibility and stability vis-à-vis nondemocratic political threats." That is, these regimes attempt to entrench certain political choices in fear, or anticipation, that a future illiberal regime will roll back liberal gains....

...Under an AS regime, newly established democracies could not rely on the treaties for the purposes they desire. Without severance as a remedial option, they might more easily lose their membership in human rights treaties at some point in the future. This level of prospective uncertainty is not what these states want, nor is it the ground on which their consent to the treaty was built.

...

Established democracies....Moravcsik explains that established democracies perceive little domestic gain in agreeing to such international commitments and a significant sovereignty cost in doing so....In terms of the lack of domestic benefits, these states operate with a high baseline of strong democratic traditions and civil rights protections....Moravcsik concludes that the factor that ultimately encouraged the United Kingdom to ratify the [European Convention on Human Rights] was the perception that a regional human rights regime would help stave off the threat of totalitarianism in Western Europe, a concern well within the security interests of the British government....

...

The breadth of U.S. objectives in joining human rights treaties should suggest that in some circumstances those interests would outweigh the interests served by a particular reservation. If the government were faced with the choice of (1) the complete loss of membership in a treaty or (2) the loss of the application or effect of a particular reservation, in some circumstances the government would prefer the latter. Certain features of the American political system suggest that the number of times when that choice would prevail is not trivial. In her extended analysis of the subject, Natalie Kaufman discusses institutional relationships between executive agencies, the president, and the Senate that lead to "attachments [that] are unnecessary." According to Kaufman, wounds left by the debates on the Bricker Amendment in the 1950s often lead the executive branch to overcompensate in submitting its package of reservations to the Senate as a means of securing approval. Kaufman explains that this attitude frequently results in reservations that sweep much more broadly than required for passage...

...

Although the above discussion relies partly on Moravcsik's empirical work, his findings do not suffice for our purposes.... [S]everal established democracies, such as the Netherlands and Belgium, follow a consistent standard with regard to international human rights law. They evince a deep commitment to incorporating human rights treaties in their domestic law and to promoting international human rights abroad: hence, they can be characterized as consistent, rather than double, standard states....

...Because their domestic systems are closely tied to international regimes, they also potentially incur significant costs and benefits from developments in the law of treaties. All of these states have submitted reservations to the ICCPR. If a reservation were found invalid — by a domestic court or by another third-party institution — the determination whether the government was still bound to the treaty would have considerable ramifications.

...

A strict AS rule would release the government from this self-constraint, and suspend a panoply of civil and political rights protections in a manner the system would have a difficult time withstanding....

The double- and consistent-standard states analyzed above constitute opposite ends of a spectrum. Between the two lies an intermediate category of established democracies (such as Australia, Canada, Switzerland, and arguably India). In contrast to the double-standard democracies, these states evince genuine interest in incorporating human rights treaties in domestic law and in maintaining membership in them by dint of domestic political interests, not simply external foreign policy goals. However, their domestic systems of governance are not reliant on, or committed to, these treaties for the same ideational and pragmatic purposes as the consistent-standard states. The intermediate states, like all states, have an incentive to enter both essential and accessory reservations when ratifying multilateral agreements....

...

Nondemocratic states.... International relations scholars have recently begun to use sociological tools to understand the processes by which states pass from illiberal to liberal regimes....

Most significant for our purposes is the critical step in the socialization process from a phase of "tactical concessions" to one of "prescriptive status." These are the moments when we can expect states to ratify human rights treaties, and thus the political context in which the value the government attaches to a reservation would be indicated. In the "tactical concession" phase, such governments make cosmetic changes to placate domestic and international pressure groups. For example, a government may release some political prisoners, exercise greater permissiveness toward political demonstrations, or pass relatively superficial legislation. These concessions can propel certain causal mechanisms, resulting in further dynamic changes that potentially lead to the phase of "prescriptive status."...

...At first glance, the minimal use of reservations by nondemocratic states might suggest that the concern about where to place such states in a severability model is marginal. While the small number of reservations does diminish the concern, this phenomenon should also prompt heightened attention when nondemocratic states actually use reservations.

...[A] nondemocratic state that ratifies a treaty with reservations has begun to accept the prescriptive legitimacy of international rules. In these contexts, a state may be genuinely balancing competing goals so that a particular reservation may not be an essential condition of its accession to the treaty.

...

...[I]n some cases, honoring a state's initial act of ratification and the expression of political pressures reflected in that decision may require treating a reservation as dispensable. This result would reflect the nondemocratic state's consent.

A treaty regime that respects the choice of nondemocratic states' consent in the same manner that it respects the consent of other states may raise some normative concerns.... [I]t is worth emphasizing two aspects of the impact of a severability regime on the human rights practices of nondemocratic states. First, a severability regime provides a meaningful opportunity to keep a state bound to a human rights treaty despite an invalid reservation. In sharp contrast, an AS regime would consistently nullify a state's ratification without ever inquiring into the severability question....

...

[Second, a regime that permits severability] facilitates progressive movement through the phases [of socialization]...

...

...[Thomas] Risse argues that inducing nondemocratic governments to engage openly in the discourse of international legal norms, including juridical justifications to defend their actions, helps to facilitate progressive change. A severability regime — especially one that applies the default rule proposed [below] — includes an information-forcing mechanism that stimulates discourse by the nondemocratic state in international legal terms....

The above analysis of state treaty practice not only demonstrates the need for severing invalid reservations in particular circumstances, but also points toward the way to structure a regime that distinguishes between those circumstances and ones in which severance is inappropriate. A central problem in designing or administering such a regime concerns what an adjudicator should do in the face of silence or ambiguity.... When the text is silent or ambiguous, however, a default rule or interpretive presumption is required to determine the outcome. Such a rule will also be required for cases in which states have already acceded to a treaty without knowing to specify their intent at the time; for existing human rights treaties, that retrospective tail will be exceptionally long.

... [A]djudicators should assume an invalid reservation is not an essential condition of a state's decision to ratify a treaty unless evidence to the contrary is provided. A significant factor in setting the appropriate presumption involves reducing error costs. For example, if the adjudicator misjudges the state's intent, is it better for the error to fall in the domain of underinclusiveness or overinclusiveness?

The record of state treaty practice strongly suggests that error costs derived from a nonseverance presumption exceed those from a presumption favoring severance.... An adjudicator's erroneous expulsion of a state from a treaty risks significant costs along two dimensions: international (e.g., a sovereignty impact from the state's expulsion against its will, reputational costs to the state's international standing, loss of a leadership or participatory role in the regime) and domestic (e.g., the unhinging of a wide array of judicially enforceable civil and political rights protections, facilitation of illiberal rollbacks). The result would probably involve significant transaction costs in the process of re-ratifying the agreement.

...

A presumption favoring nonseverance risks more harmful outcomes than the severance presumption. Perhaps most important is the corrective action that states can adopt: re-ratification (in response to an erroneous decision not to sever) and withdrawal (in response to an erroneous decision to sever). The corrective action is far more difficult in the former case than in the latter.

INTERNATIONAL LAW COMMISSION'S GUIDE TO PRACTICE ON RESERVATIONS TO TREATIES: THE QUESTION OF SEVERABILITY

4.5.3 Status of the author of an invalid reservation in relation to the treaty

1. The status of the author of an invalid reservation in relation to a treaty depends on the intention expressed by the reserving State or international organization on whether it intends to be bound by the treaty without the benefit of the reservation or whether it considers that it is not bound by the treaty.

2. Unless the author of the invalid reservation has expressed a contrary intention or such an intention is otherwise established, it is considered a contracting State or a contracting organization without the benefit of the reservation.

3. Notwithstanding paragraphs 1 and 2, the author of the invalid reservation may express at any time its intention not to be bound by the treaty without the benefit of the reservation.

4. If a treaty monitoring body expresses the view that a reservation is invalid and the reserving State or international organization intends not to be bound by the treaty without the benefit of the reservation, it should express its intention to that effect within a period of twelve months from the date at which the treaty monitoring body made its assessment.

Commentary

...

[In discussions with UN members,] States were divided into two or [sic] more or less equal groups, one in favour and one opposed to the positive presumption retained provisionally by the Commission and to the principle of severability of the invalid reservation from the rest of the treaty. All agreed, however, that the intention of the author of the reservation was the key criterion for determining whether the author was bound by the treaty or not, and that the author of the reservation was best placed to specify what that intention was. This led some States to suggest a compromise solution, giving greater weight to the role of the intention; thus, Austria and the United Kingdom proposed to retain the positive presumption... but to allow authors of reservations to have the last word, by granting them the possibility of expressing a contrary intention. Guideline 4.5.3 is closely based on these proposals.

...

In 2006, the working group on reservations established to examine the practice of human rights treaty bodies, in that regard, noted that there were several potential consequences of a reservation that had been ruled invalid. It ultimately proposed the following recommendation No. 7:

> "The consequence that applies in a particular situation depends on the intention of the State at the time it enters its reservation. This intention must be identified during a serious examination of the available information, with the rebuttable presumption that the State would prefer to remain a party to the treaty without the benefit of the reservation, rather than being excluded."

According to the revised recommendation No. 7 of 2007 submitted by the working group on reservations established to examine the practice of human rights treaty bodies, which the sixth inter-committee meeting of the human rights treaty bodies endorsed the same year:

> "As to the consequences of invalidity, the Working Group agrees with the proposal of the Special Rapporteur of the International Law Commission according to which an invalid reservation is to be considered null and void. It follows that a State will not be able to rely on such a reservation and, *unless its contrary intention is incontrovertibly established*, will remain a party to the treaty without the benefit of the reservation" (emphasis added).

The deciding factor is still clearly the intention of the State that is the author of the invalid reservation. This is the principle set forth in paragraph 1 of guideline 4.5.3 (although the Commission has intentionally omitted the adverb "incontrovertibly", which appeared to impose a criterion that was too strict): the intention of the contracting State or contracting organization is the criteria on which its status as a party to the treaty must be assessed. Paragraph 3 clarifies that this intention can be expressed at any time.

...

The expression "or such an intention is otherwise established", which appears in paragraph 2 of guideline 4.5.3, reflects the limits of this positive presumption.... If a contrary intention can be established, by any means whatsoever, the presumption falls away.

...

...Since the starting presumption is rebuttable, however, it is vital to establish whether the author of the reservation would knowingly have ratified the treaty without the reservation or whether, on the contrary, it would have refrained from doing so.

...

When such an intention is not clearly expressed, other elements can provide guidance....

[The Commentary suggests the following methods, among others, for assessing the reserving state's intent:

(1) 'the author's failure to respond to the negative reactions [to the reservation] may, in certain circumstances, help to establish its intention to be bound by the treaty';

(2) 'one could also take into consideration the author's subsequent conduct with respect to the treaty';

(3) 'it is certainly not out of the question to refer to the prior attitude of the reserving State with regard to provisions [of other treaties] similar to those to which the reservation relates.]

NOTE

In 2010, Pakistan ratified the ICCPR along with reservations to several provisions of the Covenant. Consider two of these reservations:

> [The] Islamic Republic of Pakistan declares that the provisions of Articles 3, 6, 7, 18 and 19 shall be so applied to the extent that they are not repugnant to the Provisions of the Constitution of Pakistan and the Sharia laws.
>
> The Government of the Islamic Republic of Pakistan hereby declares that it does not recognize the competence of the Committee provided for in Article 40 of the Covenant.

Twenty states submitted objections on the ground that a number of the reservations were invalid or incompatible with the object and purpose of the ICCPR. Notably, some of these objections suggested that the reservations would be severed, that is, Pakistan would remain bound to the ICCPR without the reservations having any legal effect. That action has come to be called an objection with 'super-maximum' effect (or intent). For example, the Czech Republic stated: 'The Czech Republic, therefore, objects to the aforesaid reservations made by Pakistan to the Covenant....The Covenant enters into force in its entirety between the Czech Republic and Pakistan, without Pakistan benefiting from its reservation.'

In March 2011, the Human Rights Committee issued the following statement:

> ...Article 40 gives the Human Rights Committee the competence to consider and study reports submitted by the States Parties. This competence is of critical importance for the performance of the Committee's monitoring functions and essential to the raison d'être of the Covenant. Under rule 70 of its rules of procedure, the Committee can examine a State party's actions under the Covenant in the absence of a report. The initial report of the Islamic Republic of Pakistan is due, according to article 40, paragraph 1 (a) of the Covenant, by 23 September 2011.

Subsequently, the Secretary-General announced that Pakistan submitted a notification 'that it had decided to partially withdraw the reservations, made upon ratification, to articles 3, 6, 7, 12 13, 18, 19, 25 and 40 of the Convention'.

QUESTIONS

1. In *Kennedy v. Trinidad and Tobago*, the dissenting members of the Committee noted that application of the reservation in the present case 'is wider than required in order to cater to the constitutional constraints of the State party'. In such circumstances, should the Committee take a minimalist approach: refuse to apply a particular aspect of a reservation and not sever the reservation as whole? Is that approach better suited to institutions such as national courts?

2. The UK Government raised a significant pragmatic concern about General Comment No. 24 — that the Committee's severability approach 'would risk discouraging States from ratifying human rights conventions (since they would not be in a position to reassure their national Parliaments as to the status of treaty provisions on which it was felt necessary to reserve)', see p. 804, *supra*. How do you evaluate these concerns in light of the article by Goodman? Would different types of states respond the same way to a severability rule? Does it depend on a state's purposes in joining a human rights treaty regime? Would you anticipate the same effects for CEDAW, ICESCR or CERD?

3. The ILC Commentary suggests different options for designing a presumption favouring or disfavouring severability. Should the inquiry consider the intent of the reserving state 'at any time' or only 'the intention of the State at the time it enters its reservation'? Should the intention of the state be 'incontrovertibly established' or 'by any means whatsoever'?

4. Consider the case of the Pakistani reservation to Article 40. Did the Committee implicitly sever the state's reservation, and, if so, was that the correct approach? In General Comment No. 24, the Committee states that 'a reservation that rejects the Committee's competence to interpret the requirements of *any provisions* of the Covenant would also be contrary to the object and purpose of that treaty' (emphasis added). What should be the legal consequence if Pakistan's reservation restricted the competence of the Committee with respect to only one substantive obligation (e.g., Article 7) under the Covenant?

13

Horizontal Interpenetration: Transnational Influence and Enforcement of Human Rights

Chapter 12 offered the promise or ideal that states will take the necessary measures to assure internal compliance with international human rights. In many states, their own constitutions, whether predating or instituted during the human rights movement, will achieve broad compliance. In other contexts, states will internalize the international norms so that their courts apply those norms directly.

Our concern, of course, is with states that fall short of this ideal, sometimes far short. We have seen principally in Chapters 9 and 10, but also in the regional systems of Chapter 11, the efforts of intergovernmental institutions and their organs to secure compliance by violator states. Such modes of enforcement can be understood as vertical, in the sense that pressures are exerted and perhaps sanctions applied by international organs 'above' the state. Such organs apply international law. From the perspective of that law, those international bodies exercise authority over all member states in accordance with the terms of the treaties creating them.

Of course, international organizations' decision-making about what action, if any, to take is not divorced from the decisions of their member states. To the contrary, the international bodies attempting to ensure, or at least to heighten the probability of, compliance are often 'intergovernmental' in two senses. First, the treaties creating them were ratified by their member states. Second, within the UN Charter system (apart from the International Court of Justice), the decision-making bodies for compliance and enforcement measures are composed of representatives of such states. Their decisions are not then 'divorced' from these states' separate decisions, for each member of a given body must decide how to vote — say, within the Human Rights Council or General Assembly or Security Council. Nonetheless, the organ's vote (say, to pass a resolution, make an investigation, authorize or order sanctions or intervention or to refuse to take any of these actions) is a collective vote, an organizational decision, which may in the end impose obligations on many states individually. The organization, however influenced in its decision it may be by a few member states, is in a formal and vital sense the acting party.

Here, in Chapter 13, we consider entirely *horizontal* modes of implementing and enforcing human rights. Nations are increasingly providing formal mechanisms for victims seeking to redress human rights violations committed in foreign countries. This chapter focuses principally on judicial means of norm enunciation and enforcement. Indeed, both criminal prosecutors and civil courts are increasingly engaged with cases seeking to establish the wrongdoing of individuals for violations committed abroad. Such cases constitute a bridge between Chapters 12 and 13. Although they are decided by domestic institutions and domestic law plays a vital role, they may impose liability for activities occurring in other countries that involved citizens of those countries and did not involve citizens of the forum, and their decrees may impose remedies which affect officials or other citizens of those countries. Of course, these vehicles for redress may complement or interfere with other governmental approaches to influencing the human rights practices in other states. Those interactions are considered along with the cases studied in this chapter.

As a matter of international law, a threshold question is whether a national body has legal authority to exercise jurisdiction. Should courts, for example, be presumed to have such power unless international law expressly prohibits it? Or should courts be presumed not to have such power unless international law affirmatively authorizes it? Also consider different classes of defendants. That is, in addition to those thorny jurisdictional issues, should high state officials be immune from criminal and civil proceedings in foreign courts? In particular, should standard forms of diplomatic and sovereign immunity protect individuals who have allegedly engaged in crimes against humanity and other gross human rights violations? What is the proper balance between the need to protect sovereign prerogatives and the need to redress human rights abuses in these contexts? What principles should be developed to strike the correct balance and who should decide? These are some of the issues we explore in the sections that follow.

These issues variously concern the lawful authority and desirability of different forms of influence over foreign human rights practices. They demand answers to questions about the proper allocation of power between private individuals and public authorities. They also invite an exploration of the vices and virtues of criminal prosecution and civil litigation and the impact on foreign policy relationships in taking such cases to court.

The focus of Chapter 13 falls into three sections. Section A examines jurisdictional principles. It attends foremost to human rights enforcement by national bodies in cases having no direct nexus to the forum state. Section B turns to state judiciaries providing remedies to victims of human rights violations that occurred in other countries. It stresses the role of legislation in the United States, the Alien Tort Statute, and judicial doctrines regulating the power provided by that law. Finally, Section C considers sovereign and official immunity. It discusses the prospect of achieving justice in light of these defences and examines the competing interests at stake.

COMMENT ON INTERSTATE SANCTIONS

In this chapter, we consider horizontal modes of implementing and enforcing human rights between countries. Acting singly or as part of a consortium, states may apply a range of pressures to punish a violator state or to prevent violations from occurring. One of the softer forms of coercive power includes immigration and travel restrictions. In contrast, one of the most severe forms is the use of armed force. In Chapter 8, we discussed NATO's intervention in Kosovo in 1999 as a defining moment for 'humanitarian intervention' conducted without the authority of the Security Council, p. 747–8, *supra*. Historical examples of unilateral humanitarian intervention post 1945 might include India's invasion of East Pakistan, Tanzania's invasion of Uganda (to oust Idi Amin's regime) and Vietnam's invasion of Cambodia (to oust Pol Pot's regime). After the Cold War, examples of humanitarian intervention without prior Security Council approval include the Economic Community of West African States' intervention in Liberia; safe havens and no fly zones in northern and southern Iraq established by British, French and US forces following the 1991 Iraq War; and the Economic Community of West African States' intervention in Sierra Leone. After the 1999 NATO campaign, the Independent International Commission on Kosovo was established on the initiative of Sweden's Prime Minister and co-chaired by Justice Richard Goldstone and Mr Carl Tham. The Commission issued a report which concluded that NATO's intervention was 'illegal but legitimate'. The Commission explained: 'It was illegal because it did not receive prior approval from the United Nations Security Council. However,...the intervention was justified because all diplomatic avenues had been exhausted and because the intervention had the effect of liberating the majority population of Kosovo from a long period of oppression under Serbian rule.' The Responsibility to Protect, discussed in Chapter 8, drew in part from the Kosovo experience. Although unilateral military force is seldom employed to promote human rights, it is worth contemplating as a reference point on the spectrum of interstate sanctions.

One of the primary and more common tools of interstate sanctions involves the use of economic incentives. The range of such measures includes both carrots and sticks. These measures may rely on damaging the reputation of the state involved — 'shaming', to use a term commonly invoked as one of a range of strategies. Such efforts may impose boycotts or embargoes, suspend trade or encourage disinvestment. They may impose conditions on security assistance, development aid or trade advantages — conditions that require the targeted state to comply with fundamental human rights norms. Within such a 'horizontal' (state-to-state) application of inducements and pressures, the state imposing human rights conditions — so-called 'conditionality' — as part of its foreign policy becomes part of a multi-layered system of enforcement of international human rights.

A specific category of human rights inducements involves preferential trade agreements (PTAs). The following excerpt from an article on the topic describes some illustrative agreements as well as the empirical assumptions that underpin such mechanisms for influencing state behaviour:[1]

> PTAs [preferential trade agreements] are a rapidly growing class of international institutions that govern market access between member states of an economic region. Semi-autonomous from the global structure of the World Trade Organization (WTO), PTAs frequently regulate spheres of social governance that increasingly

[1] Emilie M. Hafner-Burton, 'Trading Human Rights: How Preferential Trade Agreements Influence Government Repression', 59(3) Int'l. Org. 593–629 (2005).

include human rights standards. Some, such as the Euro-Mediterranean Association Agreements, supply "hard" standards that tie agreement benefits to member compliance with specific human rights principles. Others, such as the West African Economic and Monetary Union, supply "soft" standards that are only vaguely tied to market access and unconditional on member states' actions.

....

[Some] PTAs provide member governments with "harder" institutional channels to manage and enforce their policy commitments (that is, benefits that are in some way conditional on member states' actions). These PTAs do so by placing the language of human rights in an enforceable incentive structure designed to provide members with the economic and political benefits of various forms of market access. These benefits are supplied under conditions of compliance with the protection of human rights principles or laws identified in the agreement. Behavioral change is a side payment for market gains, enforced through threat (direct or tacit) to disrupt integration or exchange unless a trade partner complies with their human rights commitments specified in the contract....

The Lomé and Cotonou Agreements are strong examples of these types of PTAs. Cotonou provides the new institutional structure for the European Community's largest financial and political framework for cooperation, offering nonreciprocal trade benefits for certain African, Caribbean, and Pacific states, including nearly unlimited entry to the EC market for a wide range of goods. The agreement, which replaced successive Lomé Agreements, commits "Parties [to] undertake to promote and protect all fundamental freedoms and human rights, be they civil and political, or economic, social and cultural." These principles are supported through a political dialogue designed to share information, to cultivate mutual understanding, and to facilitate the formation of shared priorities, including those concerning the respect for human rights. Obligations are binding on recipients. They are supported by a review mechanism established in the consultation procedures of Article 96, which require habitual assessments of national developments concerning human rights. Alongside the agreement are conditional financial protocols allocating resources available to eligible countries through the European Development Fund. When members are perceived to violate agreement terms, a variety of different actions can be taken to influence behavior. These include the threat or act of withdrawal of membership or financial protocols, as well as the enforcement of economic or political sanctions. Cotonou thus supplies strong elements of both coercion and persuasion.

...PTAs with hard standards can, under certain conditions, influence through coercion by changing repressive actors' costs and benefits of actualizing their preferences for repression. Consider again the abusive elite with strong preferences for repression. Where persuasion alone is likely to fail, hard standards can influence the problem of compliance without changing actors' preferences. They provide an economic motivation to promote human rights policy reforms that would not otherwise be implemented, and they do so in a relatively short time horizon. When institutionalized PTAs create new and valuable gains, hard agreements can also commit future elites with preferences for liberalization to human rights reforms they would not otherwise select. While influence through persuasion requires leveling a campaign to change a new leader's preferences for repression, influence through coercion requires only that the leader value the gains of integration more than the gains of repression.

The debate within the United States about the relevance of human rights to foreign economic policy has been active and contentious for decades. A centrepiece in this regard is the US Foreign Assistance Act, which is designed to restrict foreign aid to states 'engag[ing] in a consistent pattern of gross violations of internationally recognized human rights'. US foreign policy measures have also ranged from security assistance and development aid to trade and foreign investment. The contexts in which political controversies have arisen include US involvement with global 'hot spots' since the early 1970s — for example, US security or economic aid to, investment in, or trade with regimes in Burma, Chile, China, Cuba, Nicaragua, South Africa and others. The economic importance of aid and trade has concerned major sectors of the US economy — defence industries anxious to export their products, manufacturing and service-oriented firms fearful of losing foreign markets in retaliation for elimination by the United States of other states' advantages in trade, consumer groups fearful of losing cheaper imported products and so on. Such strong consequences raise the stakes for a politics of conditionality.

Of course, overall US foreign policy also has a 'carrot' side, or range of positive inducements. That is, the US Government offers help to states that are willing to attempt certain changes, such as a move towards democratic government or the rule of law. Launched in 2004, the Millennium Challenge Account (MCA) is one of the latest manifestations in this regard. The MCA is stylized as a 'reward' programme. It increases US development assistance to countries that demonstrate a willingness to meet certain performance indicators such as civil and political rights protections and investments in health care and education. More broadly, for decades various US or US-funded agencies have provided foreign states with a range of assistance — such as expert consultants and training government branches (particularly the judiciary) to observe basic principles of the rule of law. Such aid programmes, stressing relationships between democracy and the rule of law on the one hand, and market economies and free trade on the other, form part of the current globalization debate, discussed in Chapter 17.

The United States is not alone in these efforts. The European Union employs 'restrictive measures' to promote human rights. According to the EU, the range of measures includes:

diplomatic sanctions (expulsion of diplomats, severing of diplomatic ties, suspension of official visits);
suspension of cooperation with a third country;
boycotts of sport or cultural events;
trade sanctions (general or specific trade sanctions, arms embargoes);
financial sanctions (freezing of funds or economic resources, prohibition on financial transactions, restrictions on export credits or investment);
flight bans; and
restrictions on admission.

The list of countries in which governmental entities or individuals have been subject to EU measures has recently included Belarus, Burma, Côte d'Ivoire, Egypt, North Korea, Serbia and Montenegro, Sudan, Syria and Zimbabwe. Additionally, the European Community and Council of Development Ministers, in particular, promote human rights through project aid under such titles as 'governance and civil society' and 'social infrastructure projects in education and training'. Other countries have also followed suit, at least in their formal commitments. For instance, at the end of the Cold War, Japan adopted the Official Development Assistance Charter, which includes a commitment to condition foreign aid to promote human rights. In 2003, the government revised the Charter and maintained the commitment to consider human rights, among other factors, in its foreign aid programmes. Whether the government has implemented this principle in practice is subject to debate.

Some of the 'case studies' in the balance of this chapter explore the potential interactions between economic sanctions, foreign policy more generally and judicial cognizance of foreign human rights violations. Regardless of those relationships, economic sanctions should be recognized, in their own right, as alternative measures for state-to-state influence on human rights norms.

ADDITIONAL READING

J. Peters (ed.), *The European Union and the Arab Spring: Promoting Democracy and Human Rights in the Middle East* (2012); J. Lebovic & E. Voeten, 'The Cost of Shame: International Organizations, Foreign Aid, and Human Rights Norms Enforcement', 46 J. Peace Res. 79 (2009); B. Barratt, *Human Rights and Foreign Aid: For Love or Money?* (2008); F. Furuoka, 'Human Rights Conditionality and Aid Allocation: Case Study of Japanese Foreign Aid Policy', *Perspectives on Global Development and Technology* Vol. 4 (2005); S. H. Cleveland, 'Norm Internalization and U.S. Economic Sanctions', 1 Yale J. Int'l. L. 1 (2001); A. Addis, 'Economic Sanctions and the Problem of Evil', 25 Hum. Rts. Q. 573 (2003); D. Nogueras & L. Hinojosa, 'Human Rights Conditionality in the External Trade of the European Union', 7 Colum. J. Eur. L. 307 (2001); K. Tomaševski, *Between Sanctions and Elections: Aid Donors and their Human Rights Performance* (1997); D. Price & J. Hannah, 'The Constitutionality of United States State and Local Sanctions', 39 Harv. Int'l. L. J. 443 (1998); S. Poe et al., 'Human Rights and US Foreign Aid Revisited: The Latin American Region', 16 Hum. Rts. Q. 539 (1994); K. Arts, *Integrating Human Rights into Development Cooperation: The Case of the Lomé Convention* (2000); P. Alston (ed.), *The EU and Human Rights* (1999).

A. UNIVERSAL JURISDICTION

The principle of universal jurisdiction emerged primarily in the context of criminal prosecutions and subsequently extended to areas of civil litigation. It is accordingly helpful to review basic jurisdictional principles on which states prescribe (make law), particularly laws imposing individual criminal responsibility, and the basic jurisdictional principles on which a state's courts hear civil and criminal cases.

Criminal litigation, unlike civil litigation, ordinarily requires that the state whose courts are trying a case have custody of the defendant. Holding criminal trials *in absentia* is rare. Choice of law, so vital an element of many civil cases, generally does not figure in criminal litigation; the court applies only the law of the state from which it derives its authority, almost always the one in which it sits, even if the conduct occurred or the effects were felt in other states. The principle of universal jurisdiction examined below, constitutes a major exception to this generalization.

The bases on which states enact the criminal laws to which their courts look therefore becomes a critical issue. There are certain conventional categories, some of which are more broadly accepted internationally than others. Several of these categories appear in the following description, based on the American Law Institute, *Restatement (Third), Foreign Relations Law of the United States* (1987), section 402.

> (1) *Territorial principle*, or prescribing with respect to conduct taking place within a state's territory. This principle is surely the most common and the most readily accepted throughout the world. (2) *Effects principle*, prescribing with respect to conduct outside the territory that has effects within it. (3) *Nationality principle*, prescribing with respect to acts, interests or relations of a state's nationals within and outside its territory. (4) *Protective principle*, prescribing with respect to certain conduct of non-nationals outside a state's territory that is directed against the security of the state or against a limited class of state interests that threaten the integrity of governmental functions (such as counterfeiting). (5) *Passive personality principle*, or prescribing with respect to acts committed outside a state by a non-national where the victim was a national. This principle is surely the least recognized among states as a valid basis for criminal legislation.

These principles are bounded by a number of qualifications and competing considerations, some of which are sketched in section 403 of the *Restatement*. Consider the following discussion in the *Restatement on universal jurisdiction*.

> 404. Universal jurisdiction to Define and Punish Certain Offenses
> A state has jurisdiction to define and prescribe punishment for certain offenses recognized by the community of nations as of universal concern, such as piracy, slave trade, attacks on or hijacking of aircraft, genocide, war crimes, and perhaps certain acts of terrorism....
>
> COMMENT:
>
> *a. Expanding class of universal offenses*... [I]nternational law permits any state to apply its laws to punish certain offenses although the state has no links of territory with the offense, or of nationality with the offender (or even the victim). Universal jurisdiction over the specified offenses is a result of universal condemnation of those activities and general interest in cooperating to suppress them, as reflected in widely-accepted international agreements and resolutions of international organizations. These offenses are subject to universal jurisdiction as a matter of customary law. Universal jurisdiction for additional offenses is provided by international agreements, but it remains to be determined whether universal jurisdiction over a particular offense has become customary law for states not party to such an agreement....
>
> ...

REPORTERS' NOTES

1. *Offenses subject to universal jurisdiction.* Piracy has sometimes been described as 'an offense against the law of nations' — an international crime. Since there is no international penal tribunal, the punishment of piracy is left to any state that seizes the offender.... Whether piracy is an international crime, or is rather a matter of international concern as to which international law accepts the jurisdiction of all states, may not make an important difference.

...

That genocide and war crimes are subject to universal jurisdiction was accepted after the Second World War....

The [Genocide] Convention provides for trial by the territorial state or by an international penal tribunal to be established, but no international penal tribunal with jurisdiction over the crime of genocide has been established. Universal jurisdiction to punish genocide is widely accepted as a principle of customary law....

International agreements have provided for general jurisdiction for additional offenses, e.g., the Hague Convention for the Suppression of Unlawful Seizure of Aircraft...and the International Convention against the Taking of Hostages...These agreements include an obligation on the parties to punish or extradite offenders, even when the offense was not committed within their territory or by a national....An international crime is presumably subject to universal jurisdiction.

COMMENT ON THE EICHMANN TRIAL

The *Eichmann* trial and conviction in 1961 illustrate issues concerning the application of universal jurisdiction at an early stage of the post-Nuremberg evolution of human rights law.

Adolf Eichmann, operationally in charge of the mass murder of Jews in Germany and German-occupied countries, fled Germany after the war. He was abducted from Argentina by Israelis, and brought to trial in Israel under the Nazi and Nazi Collaborators (Punishment) Law, enacted after Israel became a state. Section 1(a) of the Law provided:

> A person who has committed one of the following offences — (1) did, during the period of the Nazi regime, in a hostile country, an act constituting a crime against the Jewish people; (2) did, during the period of the Nazi regime, in a hostile country, an act constituting a crime against humanity; (3) did, during the period of the Second World War, in a hostile country, an act constituting a war crime; is liable to the death penalty.

The Law defined 'crimes against the Jewish people' to consist principally of acts intended to bring about physical destruction. The other two crimes were defined similarly to the like charges at Nuremberg. The 15 counts against Eichmann involved all three crimes. The charges stressed Eichmann's active and significant participation in the 'final solution to the Jewish problem' developed and administered by Nazi officials. Eichmann was convicted in 1961 and later executed. There appear below summaries of portions of the opinions of the trial and appellate courts.

The Attorney-General of the Government of Israel v. Eichmann[2]

Eichmann argued that the prosecution violated international law by inflicting punishment (1) upon persons who were not Israeli citizens (2) for acts done by them outside Israel and before its establishment, (3) in the course of duty and (4) on behalf of a foreign country. In reply, the Court noted that, in the event of a conflict between an Israeli statute and principles of international law, it would be bound to apply the statute. However, it then concluded that 'the law in question conforms to the best traditions of the law of nations. The power of the State of Israel to enact the law in question or Israel's "right to punish" is based... from the point of view of international law, on a dual foundation: The universal character of the crimes in question and their specific character as being designed to exterminate the Jewish people.'

Thus the Court relied primarily on the universality and protective principles to justify its assertion of jurisdiction to try the crimes defined in the Law. It held such crimes to be offences against the law of nations, much as was the traditional crime of piracy. It compared the conduct made criminal under the Israeli statute (particularly the 'crime against the Jewish people') and the crime of genocide, as defined in Article 1 of the Convention for the Prevention and Punishment of Genocide.

> The Contracting Parties confirm that genocide, whether committed in time of peace or in time of war, is a crime under international law which they undertake to prevent and to punish.[3]

The Court also stressed the relationship between the Law's definition of 'war crime' and the pattern of crimes defined in the Nuremberg Charter. It rejected arguments of Eichmann based upon the retroactive application of the legislation, and stated that 'all the reasons justifying the Nuremberg judgments justify *eo ipse* the retroactive legislation of the Israeli legislator'.

The Court then discussed another 'foundation' for the prosecution — the offence specifically aimed at the Jewish people.

> [This foundation] of penal jurisdiction conforms, according to [the] acknowledged terminology, to the protective principle.... The 'crime against the Jewish people,' as defined in the Law, constitutes in effect an attempt to exterminate the Jewish people.... If there is an effective link (and not necessarily an identity) between the State of Israel and the Jewish people, then a crime intended to exterminate the Jewish people has a very striking connection with the State of Israel.... The connection between the State of Israel and the Jewish people needs no explanation.

[2] District Court of Jerusalem, Judgment of 11 December 1961. This summary and the selective quotations are drawn from 56 Am. J. Int'l. L. 805 (1962) (unofficial translation).

[3] Article 6 of the Convention, the meaning and implications of which were viewed differently by the parties, states: 'Persons charged with genocide or any of the other acts enumerated in Article III shall be tried by a competent tribunal of the State in the territory of which the act was committed, or by such international penal tribunal as may have jurisdiction with respect to those Contracting Parties which shall have accepted its jurisdiction.'

Eichmann v. The Attorney-General of the Government of Israel[4]

After stating that it fully concurred in the holding and reasoning of the district court, the Supreme Court proceeded to develop arguments in different directions. It stressed that Eichmann could not claim to have been unaware at the time of his conduct that he was violating deeply rooted and universal moral principles. Particularly in its relatively underdeveloped criminal side, international law could be analogized to the early common law, which would be similarly open to charges of retroactive law-making. Because the international legal system lacked adjudicatory or executive institutions, it authorized, for the time being, national officials to punish individuals for violations of its principles, either directly under international law or by virtue of municipal legislation adopting those principles.

Moreover, in this case Israel was the most appropriate jurisdiction for trial, a *forum conveniens* where witnesses were readily available. It was relevant that there had been no requests for extradition of Eichmann to other states for trial, or indeed protests by other states against a trial in Israel.

The Court affirmed the holding of the district court that each charge could be sustained. It noted, however, much overlap among the charges, and that all could be grouped within the inclusive category of 'crimes against humanity'.

PNINA LAHAV, JUDGMENT IN JERUSALEM (1997), at 150

[In this portion of her biography of Simon Agranat, Justice and later Chief Justice of the Israeli Supreme Court, Lahav analyses his role in the Supreme Court's affirmance of Eichmann's conviction and death sentence. The Court delivered its judgment in a *per curiam* opinion. Justice Agranat had prepared the section of that opinion dealing with jurisdictional challenges to the trial.]

Agranat also understood that more than appearance was at stake: the soul of the Zionist project was reshaped by the brutal confrontation with the Holocaust. The old tension within Zionism between universalism and particularism now tilted in favor of particularism. Israelis were perceiving themselves as special: a special target for genocide and special in their right to ignore international norms in pursuit of justice. Popular hubris was growing, nurturing a victim mentality, a sense of self-righteousness and excessive nationalism, threatening to weaken the already shaky foundations of universalism in Israeli political culture.

...

Agranat understood that the legal reasoning he chose would affect the resolution of the tension between particularism and universalism. The Supreme Court could either let the conviction stand on the basis of crimes against the Jewish people, thereby lending force to the contention that Israel operated by its own rules,

[4] Supreme Court sitting as Court of Criminal Appeals, 29 May 1962. This summary is based on an English translation of the decision appearing in 36 Int'l. L. Rep. 14–17, 277 (1968).

impervious to the laws developed by the community of nations, or it could try to show that Eichmann's trial was compatible with international norms of justice and fairness.

Most of the legal arguments advanced by Eichmann were designed to prove that Israel lacked jurisdiction to try him. Two of these arguments received extensive attention from the international community. The first was that the 1950 Israeli Law against the Nazis and Nazi Collaborators, which vested jurisdiction in the Israeli courts, was an ex post facto criminal law and as such could not apply to foreign nationals; the second was that, because the crimes were 'extra-territorial offenses' committed by a foreign national, Israel could not prosecute Eichmann according to the territoriality principle of international law.

In rejecting these arguments, the district court stressed the superiority of Israeli law in the sovereign state of Israel. The Law against the Nazis and Nazi Collaborators, the district court held, was a part of Israeli positive law and, as such, was binding on the courts of the land. It did hold that the law agreed with international norms, but emphasized the impact of the Holocaust on the evolution of the law of nations. This holding contained a symbolic message: Jewish national pride and self-assertion ruled the day. There was poetic justice in this interpretation. If the Final Solution was about the lawless murder of Jews, the *Eichmann* case was about the subjection of the perpetrators to Jewish justice, conceived and applied by the very heirs of those murdered.

There was ambivalence in Agranat's handling of this theme. On one hand, he endorsed the district court's analysis; on the other, his own reasoning went in a different direction. He sought to prove that the validity of the Law against the Nazis and Nazi Collaborators stemmed not from its superiority to the law of nations but from its compatibility with international law. Jewish justice was thereby not different from or superior to the law of nations; rather, it was a part of it.

...

...Citing scholarly works and judicial opinions, he asserted that international law did not prohibit ex post facto laws and was not dogmatic about the territoriality principle. Thus Israel's decision to prosecute, far from being a violation of international law, was simply a perfectly legitimate reluctance to recognize principles not fully endorsed by the community of nations....He wanted to show that Israel's law was not an aberration but an affirmation of the law of nations.

The Law against the Nazis and Nazi Collaborators created a new category of crimes: crimes against the Jewish people. As such, it was a unique ex post facto law. The crime was specific to Jews and created a category hitherto unknown in any legal system. It was precisely for this reason that the crime formed a coherent part of Zionism....Zionism portrayed the Holocaust less as the vile fruit of totalitarianism and more as the culmination of two millennia of anti-Semitism. The Jews had been defenseless because they did not possess political power. Even in Nuremberg the Allies refused to recognize that the Jews as a nation were especially targeted by the Nazis. The offense, 'crimes against the Jewish people', was designed to correct that myopia and to assert, ex post facto and forever, the Jewish point of view....

Speaking for the Supreme Court, Agranat raised a different voice. He reviewed the four categories of the indictment, and he concluded that they had a common denominator, a 'special universal characteristic'. About 'crimes against the Jewish people' he had this to say: 'Thus, the category of "crimes against the Jewish people" is nothing but…"the gravest crime against humanity". It is true that there are certain differences between them…but these are not differences material to our case'. Therefore, he concluded, in order to determine whether international law recognized Israeli jurisdiction stemming from this ex post facto statute, the Court could simply collapse the entire indictment into 'the inclusive category of "crimes against humanity"'. This 'simple' technique enabled Agranat to devote the bulk of his opinion to the universal aspects of the *Eichmann* case.

QUESTIONS

1. Consider the alternatives to trial of Eichmann by the Israeli court. Would any international tribunal have been competent? What would have been involved in an effort to establish another ad hoc international criminal tribunal like Nuremberg, and would that effort have been likely to succeed? Would trial before the courts of another state have been preferable? Which state?

2. What problems, if any, do you see in reliance on 'crimes against the Jewish people'? How would you distinguish it from, for example, legislation by an African state defining 'crimes against the black people' that could reach persons in Western or other states who are accused of violence against black people? Are both types of statutes good ideas?

COMMENT ON EX PARTE PINOCHET AND UNIVERSAL JURISDICTION

General Augusto Pinochet resigned as head of state of Chile in 1990 and became a 'Senator for life'. In 1998, he travelled to the United Kingdom for medical treatment. Judicial authorities in Spain sought to extradite him to stand criminal trial in Spain on several charges, including torture, related to the right-wing military overthrow of President Allende on 11 September 1973 and the subsequent political repression during Pinochet's term as head of state. An international warrant for his arrest was issued in Spain, and a British magistrate issued a provisional warrant under the UK Extradition Act 1989. None of the conduct alleged by the Spanish authorities was committed against UK citizens or in the United Kingdom. Seeking to return to Chile, Pinochet initiated proceedings for habeas corpus and for judicial review of the warrant.

On appeal, the House of Lords decided the case, but this judgment was set aside due to a conflict of interest involving one of the Law Lords. A differently constituted seven-member panel reheard the appeal in 1999. Six of the seven Law Lords upheld the extradition process, but (in the majority of their opinions) only with respect to a small number of the charges. Extradition was appropriate only for charges satisfying the 'double criminality' principle, which requires the conduct in question to have been criminal in both Spain and the United Kingdom at the time it was committed. A majority of the Law Lords concluded that because a section of the Criminal Justice Act 1988, incorporating the United Kingdom's obligations under the Convention Against Torture, had created a new domestic crime for torture committed outside the country, only the charges of torture committed after the Act's entry into force could proceed.[5]

Lord Browne-Wilkinson discussed the foundation for universal jurisdiction over torture:

> I have no doubt that long before the Torture Convention of 1984 state torture was an international crime in the highest sense.
>
> But there was no tribunal or court to punish international crimes of torture. Local courts could take jurisdiction: see ... *Attorney-General of Israel v. Eichmann*. But the objective was to ensure a general jurisdiction so that the torturer was not safe wherever he went.... The Torture Convention was agreed not in order to create an international crime which had not previously existed but to provide an international system under which the international criminal — the torturer — could find no safe haven....
>
> ...
>
> Under Article 5(2) a state party has to take jurisdiction over any alleged offender who is found within its territory.
>
> ...
>
> [I]n my judgment the Torture Convention did provide what was missing: a worldwide universal jurisdiction.

Other Law Lords expressed a range of opinions concerning universal jurisdiction. Consider, for example, Lord Millett's opinion:

> ... [C]rimes prohibited by international law attract universal jurisdiction under customary international law if two criteria are satisfied. First, they must be contrary to a peremptory norm of international law so as to infringe a jus cogens. Secondly, they must be so serious and on such a scale that they can justly be regarded as an attack on the international legal order. Isolated offences, even if committed by public officials, would not satisfy these criteria....
>
> ...
>
> ... Customary international law is part of the common law, and accordingly I consider that the English courts have and always have had extra-territorial criminal jurisdiction in respect of crimes of universal jurisdiction under customary international law.
>
> In my opinion, the systematic use of torture on a large scale and as an instrument of state policy had joined piracy, war crimes and crimes against peace as an international crime of universal jurisdiction well before 1984. I consider that it had done so by 1973. For my own part, therefore, I would hold that the courts of this country already possessed extra-territorial jurisdiction in respect of torture

[5] We discuss below analogous US domestic legislation implementing the Torture Convention, see p. 1177, *infra*.

> and conspiracy to torture on the scale of the charges in the present case and did not require the authority of statute to exercise it....
>
> ...
>
> Whereas the international community had condemned the widespread and systematic use of torture as an instrument of state policy, the Convention extended the offence to cover isolated and individual instances of torture provided that they were committed by a public official. I do not consider that offences of this kind were previously regarded as international crimes attracting universal jurisdiction....Whereas previously states were entitled to take jurisdiction in respect of the offence wherever it was committed, they were now placed under an obligation to do so.

In contrast, Lord Phillips remarked:

> I believe that it is still an open question whether international law recognises universal jurisdiction in respect of international crimes — that is the right, under international law, of the courts of any state to prosecute for such crimes wherever they occur. In relation to war crimes, such a jurisdiction has been asserted by the State of Israel, notably in the prosecution of Adolf Eichmann, but this assertion of jurisdiction does not reflect any general state practice in relation to international crimes. Rather, states have tended to agree, or to attempt to agree, on the creation of international tribunals to try international crimes. They have however, on occasion, agreed by conventions, that their national courts should enjoy jurisdiction to prosecute for a particular category of international crime wherever occurring.

After the decision, the extradition case continued while Pinochet remained under house arrest. France, Belgium and Switzerland also made extradition requests. In 2000, the British Home Secretary stated that medical examinations of Pinochet led him to conclude that the 84-year-old general was incapable of standing trial and should be released to return to Chile. Later that year, Pinochet was permitted to fly home, to a radically different political context in which he was an isolated, far less influential and potent figure. Judicial steps were underway towards intense investigation into Pinochet's connection with the killings and torture. The Chilean Supreme Court stripped Pinochet of immunity, and several charges were brought against him. However, on 10 December 2006, Pinochet died before any prosecution was brought.

CASE CONCERNING THE ARREST WARRANT OF 11 APRIL 2000 (DEMOCRATIC REPUBLIC OF THE CONGO v. BELGIUM)

International Court of Justice (2002)

[A leading treatment of the scope and viability of universal jurisdiction arose in proceedings before the International Court of Justice (ICJ). The case involved Belgium's 'universal jurisdiction' law, which has since been modified. At the time, the law permitted Belgian judicial authorities to prosecute violations of international humanitarian law regardless of where the acts were committed and regardless of the nationality of the perpetrators and victims. In late 1998, 12 individuals lodged a complaint with a Belgian investigating judge at the Brussels Court of First Instance. Of the 12 complainants, five were of Belgian nationality, seven were of Congolese nationality and all were resident in Belgium. The complaint concerned events that had taken place in the Democratic Republic of the Congo (DRC).

In mid 2000, the Belgian judge issued an arrest warrant *in absentia* against Mr Abdulaye Yerodia Ndombasi, who was the DRC's Minister for Foreign Affairs at the time. The warrant accused Mr Yerodia of committing war crimes and crimes against humanity before serving in his ministerial post. The complaint alleged that he made public speeches that incited the massacre of several hundred people, mainly of Tutsi origin, in the DRC. The Government of the DRC initiated proceedings against the Government of Belgium before the ICJ claiming that the issuance and international distribution of the arrest warrant unlawfully infringed the foreign minister's immunity and violated international rules on jurisdiction. A majority of the ICJ did not reach the issue of universal jurisdiction, holding instead that the promulgation and circulation of the arrest warrant violated Mr Yerodia's official immunity as Foreign Minister. A separate opinion joined by Judges Rosalyn Higgins, Peter Kooijmans and Thomas Buergenthal squarely addressed the issue of universal jurisdiction in one of the most extensive treatments of the subject to date. We return to the majority's assessment of the official immunity claim later in this chapter, p. 1211, *infra*. Excerpts of the joint separate opinion follow.]

JOINT SEPARATE OPINION OF JUDGES HIGGINS, KOOIJMANS AND BUERGENTHAL

19. We...turn to the question whether States are entitled to exercise jurisdiction over persons having no connection with the forum State when the accused is not present in the State's territory....

20. Our analysis may begin with national legislation, to see if it evidences a State practice.... [N]ational legislation, whether in fulfilment of international treaty obligations to make certain international crimes offences also in national law, or otherwise, does not suggest a universal jurisdiction over these offences. Various examples typify the more qualified practice. The Australian War Crimes Act of 1945, as amended in 1988, provides for the prosecution in Australia of crimes committed between 1 September 1939 and 8 May 1945 by persons who were Australian citizens or residents at the times of being charged with the offences. The United Kingdom War Crimes Act of 1991 enables proceedings to be brought for murder, manslaughter or culpable homicide, committed between 1 September 1935 and 5 June 1945, in a place that was part of Germany or under German occupation, and in circumstances where the accused was at the time, or has become, a British citizen or resident of the United Kingdom....

The Criminal Code of Canada 1985 allows the execution of jurisdiction when at the time of the act or omission the accused was a Canadian citizen or "employed by Canada in a civilian or military capacity;" or the "victim is a Canadian citizen or a citizen of a State that is allied with Canada in an armed conflict," or when "at the time of the act or omission Canada could, in conformity with international law, exercise jurisdiction over the person on the basis of the person's presence in Canada".

21. All of these illustrate the trend to provide for the trial and punishment under international law of certain crimes that have been committed extraterritorially. But none of them, nor the many others that have been studied by the Court, represent a classical assertion of a universal jurisdiction over particular offences committed elsewhere by persons having no relationship or connection with the forum State.

22. The case law under these provisions has largely been cautious so far as reliance on universal jurisdiction is concerned. In the Pinochet case in the English courts, the jurisdictional basis was clearly treaty based, with the double criminality rule required for extradition being met by English legislation in September 1988, after which date torture committed abroad was a crime in the United Kingdom as it already was in Spain....

...

26. In some of the literature on the subject it is asserted that the great international treaties on crimes and offences evidence universality as a ground for the exercise of jurisdiction recognized in international law. This is doubtful.

27. Article VI of the Convention on the Prevention and Punishment of the Crime of Genocide, 9 December 1948, provides:

> "Persons charged with genocide or any of the other acts enumerated in Article III shall be tried by a competent tribunal of the State in the territory of which the act was committed, or by such international penal tribunal as may have jurisdiction with respect to those Contracting Parties which shall have accepted its jurisdiction."

This is an obligation to assert territorial jurisdiction, though the travaux preparatoires do reveal an understanding that this obligation was not intended to affect the right of a State to exercise criminal jurisdiction on its own nationals for acts committed outside the State (A/C 6/SR, 134; p. 5). Article VI also provides a potential grant of non-territorial competence to a possible future international tribunal — even this not being automatic under the Genocide Convention but being restricted to those Contracting Parties which would accept its jurisdiction. In recent years it has been suggested in the literature that Article VI does not prevent a State from exercising universal jurisdiction in a genocide case. (And see, more generally, Restatement (Third) of the Foreign Relations Law of the United States (1987), § 404.)

28. Article 49 of the First Geneva Convention, Article 50 of the Second Geneva Convention, Article 129 of the Third Geneva Convention and Article 146 of the Fourth Geneva Convention, all of 12 August 1949, provide:

> "Each High Contracting Party shall be under the obligation to search for persons alleged to have committed, or to have ordered to be committed,...grave breaches, and shall bring such persons, regardless of their nationality, before its own courts. It may also, if it prefers, and in accordance with the provisions of its own legislation, hand such persons over for trial to another High Contracting Party concerned, provided such High Contracting Party has made out a prima facie case."

29. Article 85, paragraph 1, of the First Additional Protocol to the 1949 Geneva Convention incorporates this provision by reference.

30. The stated purpose of the provision was that the offences would not be left unpunished (the extradition provisions playing their role in this objective). It may immediately be noted that this is an early form of the aut dedere aut prosequi to be seen in later conventions. But the obligation to prosecute is primary, making it even stronger.

31. No territorial or nationality linkage is envisaged, suggesting a true universality principle. But a different interpretation is given in the authoritative Pictet Commentary: Geneva Convention for the Amelioration of the Condition of the Wounded and Sick in Armed Forces in the Field (1952), which contends that this obligation was understood as being an obligation upon States parties to search for offenders who may be on their territory. Is it a true example of universality, if the obligation to search is restricted to the own territory? Does the obligation to search imply a permission to prosecute in absentia, if the search had no result?

...

35. The Hague Convention for the Suppression of Unlawful Seizure of Aircraft, 16 December 1970, making preambular reference to the "urgent need" to make such acts "punishable as an offence and to provide for appropriate measures with respect to prosecution and extradition of offenders," provided in Article 4(1) for an obligation to take such measures as may be necessary to establish jurisdiction over these offences and other acts of violence against passengers or crew:

"(a) when the offence is committed on board an aircraft registered in that State;
(b) when the aircraft on board which the offence is committed lands in its territory with the alleged offender still on board;
(c) when the offence is committed on board an aircraft leased without crew to a lessee who has his principal place of business or, if the lessee has no such place of business, his permanent residence, in that State."

Article 4(2) provided for a comparable obligation to establish jurisdiction where the alleged offender was present in the territory and if he was not extradited pursuant to Article 8 by the territory. Thus here too was a treaty provision for aut dedere aut prosequi, of which the limb was in turn based on the principle of "primary universal repression." The jurisdictional bases provided for in Articles 4(1)(b) and 4(2), requiring no territorial connection beyond the landing of the aircraft or the presence of the accused, were adopted only after prolonged discussion. The travaux preparatoires show States for whom mere presence was an insufficient ground for jurisdiction beginning reluctantly to support this particular type of formula because of the gravity of the offence. Thus the representative of the United Kingdom stated that his country "would see great difficulty in assuming jurisdiction merely on the ground that an aircraft carrying a hijacker had landed in United Kingdom territory." Further, "normally his country did not accept the principle that the mere presence of an alleged offender within the jurisdiction of a State entitled that State to try him. In view, however, of the gravity of the offence... he was prepared to support... [the proposal on mandatory jurisdiction on the part of the State where a hijacker is found]." (Hague Conference, p. 75, para. 18.)

36. It is also to be noted that Article 4, paragraphs 1 and 2, provides for the mandatory exercise of jurisdiction in the absence of extradition; but does not preclude criminal jurisdiction exercised on alternative grounds of jurisdiction in accordance with national law (though those possibilities are not made compulsory under the Convention).

37. Comparable jurisdictional provisions are to be found in Articles 5 and 8 of the International Convention against the Taking of Hostages of 17 December 1979. The obligation enunciated in Article 8 whereby a State party shall "without exception whatsoever and whether or not the offence was committed in its territory," submit the case for prosecution if it does not extradite the alleged offender, was again regarded as necessary by the majority, given the nature of the crimes (Summary Record, Ad Hoc Committee on the Drafting of an International Convention Against the Taking of Hostages (A/AC. 188/SR. 5, 7, 8, 11, 14, 15, 16, 17, 23, 24 and 35)). The United Kingdom cautioned against moving to universal criminal jurisdiction (ibid., A/AC. 188/SR. 24, para. 27) while others (Poland, para. 18; Mexico, para. 11) felt the introduction of the principle of universal jurisdiction to be essential. The USSR observed that no State could exercise jurisdiction over crimes committed in another State by nationals of that State without contravening Article 2, paragraph 7, of the Charter. The Convention provisions were in its view to apply only to hostage taking that was a manifestation of international terrorism — another example of initial and understandable positions on jurisdiction being modified in the face of the exceptional gravity of the offence.

38. The Convention against Torture, of 10 December 1984, establishes in Article 5 an obligation to establish jurisdiction

> "(a) When the offences are committed in any territory under its jurisdiction or on board a ship or aircraft registered in that State;
> (b) When the alleged offender is a national of that State;
> (c) When the victim is a national of that State if that State considers it appropriate."

If the person alleged to have committed the offence is found in the territory of a State party and is not extradited, submission of the case to the prosecuting authorities shall follow (Art. 7). Other grounds of criminal jurisdiction exercised in accordance with the relevant national law are not excluded (Art. 5, para. 3), making clear that Article 5, paragraphs 1 and 2, must not be interpreted a contrario. (See J. H. Burgers and H. Danelius, The United Nations Convention against Torture, 1988, p. 133.)

39. The passage of time changes perceptions. The jurisdictional ground that in 1961 had been referred to as the principle of "primary universal repression" came now to be widely referred to by delegates as "universal jurisdiction" — moreover, a universal jurisdiction thought appropriate, since torture, like piracy, could be considered an "offence against the law of nations." (United States: E/CN.4/1367, 1980). Australia, France, the Netherlands and the United Kingdom eventually dropped their objection that "universal jurisdiction" over torture would create problems under their domestic legal systems. (See E/CN. 4/1984/72.)

40. This short historical survey may be summarized as follows.

41. The parties to these treaties agreed both to grounds of jurisdiction and as to the obligation to take the measures necessary to establish such jurisdiction. The specified grounds relied on links of nationality of the offender, or the ship or aircraft concerned, or of the victim. See, for example, Article 4(1) Hague Convention; Article 3(1) Tokyo Convention; Article 5, Hostages Convention; Article 5, Torture Convention. These may properly be described as treaty-based broad extraterritorial jurisdiction. But in addition to these were the parallel provisions whereby a State party in whose jurisdiction the alleged perpetrator of such offences is found, shall prosecute him or extradite him. By the loose use of language the latter has come to be referred to as "universal jurisdiction," though this is really an obligatory territorial jurisdiction over persons, albeit in relation to acts committed elsewhere.

42. Whether this obligation (whether described as the duty to establish universal jurisdiction, or, more accurately, the jurisdiction to establish a territorial jurisdiction over persons for extraterritorial events) is an obligation only of treaty law, inter partes or, whether it is now, at least as regards the offences articulated in the treaties, an obligation of customary international law was pleaded by the Parties in this case but not addressed in any great detail.

...

44. However, we note that the inaccurately termed "universal jurisdiction principle" in these treaties is a principle of obligation, while the question in this case is whether Belgium had the right to issue and circulate the arrest warrant if it so chose....

45. That there is no established practice in which States exercise universal jurisdiction, properly so called, is undeniable. As we have seen, virtually all national legislation envisages links of some sort to the forum State; and no case law exists in which pure universal jurisdiction has formed the basis of jurisdiction. This does not necessarily indicate, however, that such an exercise would be unlawful. In the first place, national legislation reflects the circumstances in which a State provides in its own law the ability to exercise jurisdiction. But a State is not required to legislate up to the full scope of the jurisdiction allowed by international law. The war crimes legislation of Australia and the United Kingdom afford examples of countries making more confined choices for the exercise of jurisdiction.... Moreover, while none of the national case law to which we have referred happens to be based on the exercise of a universal jurisdiction properly so called, there is equally nothing in this case law which evidences an opinio juris on the illegality of such a jurisdiction. In short, national legislation and case law, — that is, State practice — is neutral as to exercise of universal jurisdiction.

46. There are, moreover, certain indications that a universal criminal jurisdiction for certain international crimes is clearly not regarded as unlawful. The duty to prosecute under those treaties which contain the aut dedere aut prosequi provisions opens the door to a jurisdiction based on the heinous nature of the crime rather than on links of territoriality or nationality (whether as perpetrator or victim). The 1949 Geneva Conventions lend support to this possibility, and are widely regarded as today reflecting customary international law.

47. The contemporary trends, reflecting international relations as they stand at the beginning of the new century, are striking. The movement is towards bases of jurisdiction other than territoriality. "Effects" or "impact" jurisdiction is embraced both by the United States and, with certain qualifications, by the European Union. Passive personality jurisdiction, for so long regarded as controversial, is now reflected not only in the legislation of various countries (the United States, Ch. 113A, 1986 Omnibus Diplomatic and Antiterrorism Act; France, Art. 689, Code of Criminal Procedure, 1975), and today meets with relatively little opposition, at least so far as a particular category of offences is concerned.

48. In civil matters we already see the beginnings of a very broad form of extraterritorial jurisdiction. Under the Alien Torts Claim Act, the United States, basing itself on a law of 1789, has asserted a jurisdiction both over human rights violations and over major violations of international law, perpetrated by non-nationals overseas. Such jurisdiction, with the possibility of ordering payment of damages, has been exercised with respect to torture committed in a variety of countries (Paraguay, Chile, Argentina, Guatemala), and with respect to other major human rights violations in yet other countries. While this unilateral exercise of the function of guardian of international values has been much commented on, it has not attracted the approbation of States generally.

...

53. This brings us once more to the particular point that divides the Parties in this case: is it a precondition of the assertion of universal jurisdiction that the accused be within the territory?

54. Considerable confusion surrounds this topic, not helped by the fact that legislators, courts and writers alike frequently fail to specify the precise temporal moment at which any such requirement is said to be in play. Is the presence of the accused within the jurisdiction said to be required at the time the offence was committed? At the time the arrest warrant is issued? Or at the time of the trial itself?...The only prohibitive rule...is that criminal jurisdiction should not be exercised, without permission, within the territory of another State. The Belgian arrest warrant envisaged the arrest of Mr. Yerodia in Belgium, or the possibility of his arrest in third States at the discretion of the States concerned. This would in principle seem to violate no existing prohibiting rule of international law.

...

58. If the underlying purpose of designating certain acts as international crimes is to authorize a wide jurisdiction to be asserted over persons committing them, there is no rule of international law (and certainly not the aut dedere principle) which makes illegal co-operative overt acts designed to secure their presence within a State wishing to exercise jurisdiction.

59. If, as we believe to be the case, a State may choose to exercise a universal criminal jurisdiction in absentia, it must also ensure that certain safeguards are in place. They are absolutely essential to prevent abuse and to ensure that the rejection of impunity does not jeopardize stable relations between States.

No exercise of criminal jurisdiction may occur which fails to respect the inviolability or infringes the immunities of the person concerned. We return below to certain aspects of this facet, but will say at this juncture that commencing an investigation on the basis of which an arrest warrant may later be issued does not of itself violate those principles. The function served by the international law of immunities does not require that States fail to keep themselves informed.

A State contemplating bringing criminal charges based on universal jurisdiction must first offer to the national State of the prospective accused person the opportunity itself to act upon the charges concerned. The Court makes reference to these elements in the context of this case at paragraph 16 of its Judgment.

Further, such charges may only be laid by a prosecutor or juge d'instruction who acts in full independence, without links to or control by the government of that State. Moreover, the desired equilibrium between the battle against impunity and the promotion of good inter-State relations will only be maintained if there are some special circumstances that do require the exercise of an international criminal jurisdiction and if this has been brought to the attention of the prosecutor or juge d'instruction. For example, persons related to the victims of the case will have requested the commencement of legal proceedings.

60. It is equally necessary that universal criminal jurisdiction be exercised only over those crimes regarded as the most heinous by the international community.

...

64. The arrest warrant issued against Mr. Yerodia accuses him both of war crimes and of crimes against humanity. As regards the latter, charges of incitement to racial hatred, which are said to have led to murders and lynchings, were specified. Fitting of this charge within the generally understood substantive context of crimes against humanity is not without its problems. "Racial hatred" would need to be assimilated to "persecution on racial grounds," or, on the particular facts, to mass murder and extermination. [The opinion analyses whether incitement is an acceptable form of liability under international criminal law, and concludes that it is.]

65. It would seem (without in any way pronouncing upon whether Mr. Yerodia did or did not perform the acts with which he is charged in the warrant) that the acts alleged do fall within the concept of "crimes against humanity" and would be within that small category in respect of which an exercise of universal jurisdiction is not precluded under international law.

QUESTIONS

1. What does the Joint Separate Opinion mean by 'pure universal jurisdiction'? Are the distinctions between universal jurisdiction and forms of extraterritorial jurisdiction analytically coherent?

2. States can consent through a treaty to forms of jurisdiction that otherwise would not be permitted under international law. Should the existence of a treaty provision allowing broad-based jurisdiction such as a 'prosecute or extradite' provision support — or undermine — the proposition that substantive offences contained in that treaty are subject to universal jurisdiction as a matter of customary international law?

3. Assuming the Joint Separate Opinion correctly states prevailing international law, could Belgium pass a law authorizing the prosecution of individuals who become Belgian citizens or residents for acts committed before they become naturalized citizens or lawful residents? How about for acts committed by a foreign national visiting Belgium if the acts took place before her date of entry? Must these acts in question constitute universal crimes? Should international law be fashioned such that a line is drawn between citizens and foreign national residents? Between long-term residents and temporary visitors?

4. Does the exercise of universal jurisdiction interfere unjustifiably with the domestic affairs of another country? What about situations in which the relevant acts could not be prosecuted due to an amnesty passed in the foreign state (such as in South Africa)? In such situations, a strong argument could be made that criminal prosecutions would trample on the prerogatives of a democratic country deciding how best to deal with its past. Should the balance tip in favour of exercising jurisdiction when victims-complainants are nationals of the prosecuting state? Should the presence of a single Belgian victim (or a single Belgian perpetrator) change the calculus of whether to override a foreign state's approach to dealing with the past?

5. Does the Joint Separate Opinion strike the correct balance between the interests of the international community in punishing the commission of universal crimes and the interests of states in conducting diplomatic affairs?

6. The Joint Separate Opinion suggests that Belgium's exercise of jurisdiction is lawful unless an international rule clearly prohibits it. As a law clerk to one of the judges in the case would you have advised supporting such a presumption? Why or why not?

COMMENT ON DISCUSSIONS OF UNIVERSAL JURISDICTION AT THE UNITED NATIONS

In 2009, the African Union (AU) made a submission to the United Nations calling for a formal inquiry into the scope and application of universal jurisdiction. In its submission, the AU stated that it 'fully subscribes to and supports the principle of universal jurisdiction', but expressed concern that universal jurisdiction had been used selectively (in an 'ad hoc and arbitrary' manner) particularly against African defendants. The AU accordingly called for UN discussions with a 'view to establishing regulatory provisions' to govern the exercise of universal jurisdiction. That topic has since been part of the annual agenda of the General Assembly's Sixth (Legal) Committee. Those discussions have focused on criminal jurisdiction. And although the definition of universal jurisdiction has not been consistent across all states, governments generally agree that it includes cases in which a court adjudicates a case regardless of the nationality of the victims and offenders and the location of the offence. Some states include cases in which the alleged offender is present in the forum state (the United States); other states do not. Following three years of discussions, the General Assembly voted to establish a Working Group on universal jurisdiction to be formed in 2012.

Despite the AU's stated acceptance of universal jurisdiction, during the meetings of the Sixth Committee, several states have questioned the status of universal jurisdiction or suggested that it should apply to a very narrow range of offences. China, for example, stated that 'universal jurisdiction exists only with regard to dealing with acts of piracy'. Similar statements were made by Iran. Perhaps more surprisingly, the United Kingdom stated that 'universal jurisdiction in its true sense is only clearly established for a small number of specific crimes: piracy and war crimes'; and that its government 'acknowledges that there is a further limited group of crimes which some States consider to attract universal jurisdiction, including genocide and crimes against humanity, but there is a lack of international consensus on the issue.'

Nevertheless, dozens of states explained that various provisions within their domestic legal codes provide for universal jurisdiction and expressed support for the importance of universal jurisdiction in the human rights regime. The strongest proponents were largely clustered in Latin America, North America and Europe. They included Australia, Brazil, Canada, Chile, Colombia, Costa Rica, France, Germany, Mexico (speaking for the Rio Group), Norway, the Philippines and South Korea. Some states that expressed the greatest concerns about the scope or application of universal jurisdiction, also provided qualified support for the general principle of universal jurisdiction. Zambia, for example, stated that 'the principle of universal jurisdiction, used in good faith, was a powerful tool for the preservation of the international community's fundamental values, for the protection and promotion of the rule of law and human rights, and for the advancement of the fight against impunity' (quotation from UN summary records). Egypt stated: 'the principle of universal jurisdiction, deriving from international conventions relating to genocide, war crimes, crimes against humanity, slavery and torture, was an important means of ensuring that those who committed such heinous crimes were brought to justice. Their exceptional gravity made the suppression of such crimes a matter of concern to all members of the international community. It was a well-established principle that primary responsibility for investigation and prosecution of the crime rested with the State where the crime was committed. However, universal jurisdiction helped to cover jurisdictional gaps and could act as a deterrent' (UN summary record). Algeria stated: 'To combat impunity was a moral and legal obligation of States, and addressing it involved national and international jurisdictions. In this regard, universal jurisdiction "must be a last recourse" when other principles were impossible to apply in prosecution' (UN summary record). In addition, a major study by Amnesty International, which was prepared for the purpose of these Sixth Committee discussions, finds that a large majority of states have adopted universal jurisdiction for at least one serious human rights or humanitarian law violation. The study presents the following statistics:

> 145 (approximately 75.1%) states have provided universal jurisdiction over one or more of these crimes [war crimes, genocide, crimes against humanity, torture] and 91 (approximately 47.1%) states have provided universal jurisdiction over ordinary crimes, even when the conduct does not involve conduct amounting to a crime under international law, in most instances permitting their courts in certain

> circumstances to exercise universal jurisdiction over some conduct that amounts to a crime under international law.[6]

Two other aspects of these discussions deserve emphasis. First, with respect to the threshold question of the legal status of universal jurisdiction, states expressed different perspectives on the relevance of *aut dedere aut judicare* (extradite or prosecute) obligations under international treaties. The Report of the UN Secretary-General outlines two broad schools of thought:

> 20.... [D]ivergent conclusions were drawn in the comments. On the one hand, the point was made that, on a closer examination of relevant treaties, it was misleading to assert that universal jurisdiction was established by treaty in all instances, in particular for offences such as terrorism and drug trafficking, where there was an obligation to extradite or prosecute. State parties to such treaties were under a mandatory duty, as a treaty obligation, to establish criminal jurisdiction.... The obligation to extradite or prosecute could be established in a treaty for any type of crime, without such crimes necessarily being subject to universal jurisdiction. Thus, although, under the relevant treaty, there was an obligation on a State party where an offender was found to prosecute or extradite an offender, the jurisdictional basis arose from the obligation to criminalize the treaty offences and establish jurisdiction on the basis of established grounds as specified in the treaty. The principle of aut dedere aut judicare did not in itself establish universal jurisdiction for that particular treaty-based offence.
>
> 21. On the other hand, it was noted that the obligation to prosecute or extradite was inextricably linked to universal jurisdiction, particularly when the latter is understood in its conditional or limited sense, as quasi-universal. While universal jurisdiction was a legal principle, it could also be an obligation as a result of a treaty.... Moreover, by being party to a treaty incorporating *aut dedere aut judicare*, a State may exercise jurisdiction, as appropriate, even if it was entirely unconnected to the crime itself. Depending on the facts of the case, if the State was not in a position to extradite such individual, the right to exercise jurisdiction could become an obligation as a result of the *aut dedere aut judicare* provision, since as State party, it would be under obligation to prosecute.... [I]t was also considered useful to note that most of the universal counter-terrorism conventions excluded from their scope offences committed exclusively within a single State, where the offender and the victims were nationals of that State, the alleged offender was found in the territory of that State, and no other traditional basis for another State to assert jurisdiction would apply.

Second, states have advocated several safeguards to assure the principled application of universal jurisdiction in criminal proceedings. Such proposals include:

1. a principle of subsidiarity whereby the exercise of universal jurisdiction occurs only if no other state with stronger jurisdictional connections is willing or able to adjudicate the case (e.g., Argentina, Australia, Canada, New Zealand, Qatar);

[6] Amnesty International, 'Universal Jurisdiction: A Preliminary Survey of Legislation Around the World', Oct. 2011.

2. a principle of double jeopardy whereby universal jurisdiction is rejected if the accused has been convicted or acquitted by a foreign court (e.g., Ethiopia, Paraguay, Slovenia, Spain);
3. respect for immunities of state officials (e.g., Egypt, Iran, Kenya on behalf of the Africa Group, Qatar, Sri Lanka);
4. presence of the accused in the forum state (e.g., Egypt, France, South Africa, Spain, United Kingdom, United States);
5. preauthorization by a public official or agency before the initiation of criminal proceedings (e.g., Belgium, Finland, Israel, United Kingdom);
6. agreement by treaty such that a state's competence to exercise jurisdiction must be established in a broadly accepted international convention (e.g., Chile, Indonesia).

Other states disagreed with some of these measures. With respect to immunities of state officials, for example, Norway stated 'there were three reasons to refrain from discussing it under this agenda item: first, immunity as an obstacle to a court considering a case on its merits could arise only after jurisdiction had been established; second, questions of immunity could arise with regard to the exercise of any type of jurisdiction; and third, discussion of immunity for State officials might prejudice consideration of the topic, which had also been dealt with by the International Law Commission' (summary record; see also joint statement by Australia and Canada). Greece took an even stronger position stating that 'the granting of immunity and amnesties by Governments had "stood so far in the way of making this principle an effective tool in the fight against impunity"' (summary record). Also, some states such as Finland do not apply the principle of double jeopardy if the offence constitutes an international crime.

Compare the above list of 'safeguards' with a list of 'obstacles' that Amnesty International states should be eliminated. The latter list includes:

- presence requirements in order to open an investigation or to seek extradition;
- limiting universal jurisdiction to persons who are residents or who subsequently become residents or nationals;
- statutes of limitation;
- requirements of double criminality;
- recognition of claims by current or former foreign officials to immunities
- *ne bis in idem* (double jeopardy) bars, even when the foreign proceeding was a sham or unfair;
- political control over decisions to investigate, prosecute or extradite.[7]

Finally, it is important to consider a central, animating concern of some of the opponents of universal jurisdiction — the issue of selectivity. In a survey of all universal jurisdiction cases since the *Eichmann* trial, Maximo Langer concludes that the

[7] Ibid.

experience of universal jurisdiction has involved a significant degree of selectivity, but not against African defendants (Langer 2011). He states:

> African leaders have recently manifested their dissatisfaction with universal jurisdiction.... Universal jurisdiction's selectivity regarding African leaders could certainly be a possible scenario since African states tend to have relatively low leverage over other states. But, as the survey data indicate, universal jurisdiction trials have not concentrated on African leaders but on even lower cost defendants — those for whom their states of nationality have not been willing to exercise their leverage, and especially those on whose prosecution the international community has broadly agreed.

Langer emphasizes the following finding: 'Of the 32 defendants who have been brought to trial, 24 — amounting to three-quarters of all defendants tried under universal jurisdiction — have been Rwandans [11 cases], former Yugoslavs [8 cases], and Nazis [5 cases].' The other eight cases were four Afghan, one Argentinian, one Congolese, one Mauritanian and one Tunisian. The study also found that 1,051 complaints or cases considered by public authorities on their own motion — essentially criminal proceedings short of a trial — had occurred under universal jurisdiction. Of those proceedings, 92 per cent of defendants were Rwandans (359 cases), former Yugoslavs (185 cases), Argentinians (121 cases), Nazis (87 cases), US (55 cases), Chinese (44 cases), Israeli (44 cases), Chilean (16 cases), Moroccan (15 cases), Cameroonian (12 cases), Salvadoran (12 cases) and Uzbek (12 cases). Langer concludes that the political branches of states that have pursued universal jurisdiction cases 'concentrate on defendants who impose low international relations costs because it is only in these cases that the political benefits of universal jurisdiction prosecutions and trials tend to outweigh the costs.'

QUESTIONS

1. In its endorsement of the principle of universal jurisdiction, the African Union provides the following explanation:

> The principle of universal jurisdiction is well established in international law. Universal jurisdiction does not apply to all international crimes, but rather to a very limited category of offences. It allows a State to exercise its domestic jurisdiction to indict and prosecute perpetrators of serious offences such as piracy, slavery, torture, genocide, war crimes and crimes against humanity occurring outside its territory irrespective of the nationality of the perpetrators. The African Union respects this principle, which is enshrined in article 4(h) of the Constitutive Act.

Does Article 4(h) of the Constitutive Act enshrine universal jurisdiction? It allows the African Union to intervene in a member state in the event of war crimes, genocide or crimes against humanity. Is that the same as universal jurisdiction or is it just a consensual arrangement afforded by a treaty — effectively a form of waiver by state parties?

2. Which side is correct in the debates about aut dedere aut judicare? China, for example, stated that:

> clear differences exist in content, scope of application and conditions between this kind of 'aut dedere aut judicare' obligation and its corresponding jurisdiction, and the universal jurisdiction aimed at piracy;...the implementation of 'aut dedere aut judicare' rules...are applicable only with reference to crimes stipulated under the corresponding international treaties, and the rights and obligations entailed are limited to the States Parties to the corresponding treaties.

Is that analysis correct? What if a treaty obligates a member state to establish jurisdiction where an alleged offender is present in its territory even when the offender and victims are not nationals of any state party and the alleged conduct did not occur in the territory of any state party? Consider Article 5(2) of the Torture Convention, which resembles a provision found in many counterterrorism treaties.

3. In its tally of the number of states that have established universal jurisdiction, Amnesty International includes the following methodological note with respect to the Rome Statute for the International Criminal Court:

> In some instances, the state has defined a crime under international law, such as genocide, as a crime in national law and provided that its courts have jurisdiction over crimes in treaties it has ratified (some provisions do not specify that the treaty has to have been ratified). In those instances, the state would have jurisdiction not only over crimes in aut dedere aut judicare treaties, but treaties like...the Rome Statute of the International Criminal Court (Rome Statute) that do not contain an express obligation to exercise universal jurisdiction, although they may contain an implied obligation to do so. [The report accordingly records that the state has jurisdiction over the relevant crimes].

Is this analysis legally correct? Does the Rome Statute impose an (implicit) obligation on state-parties to establish universal jurisdiction over its core crimes?

4. Do the statistics in Amnesty International's survey reflect strong support for universal jurisdiction, or is the evidence relatively weak? Does the large number of states that provide universal jurisdiction for ordinary crimes undermine the value of these state practices? That is, 91 states have laws providing universal jurisdiction for ordinary offences that do not amount to serious international human rights violations. Accordingly, those laws are presumably not motivated by the seriousness or international character of the offence. Do these instances of what we might call 'universal jurisdiction for non-universal crimes' suggest that states may enact universal jurisdiction laws without adequate consideration of *opinio juris*?

5. In a submission to the UN, the US Government stated:

> [T]here are often prudential or other reasons why the United States refrains from exercising jurisdiction. For example, the United States may appropriately defer asserting jurisdiction in favor of a state on whose territory the crime was committed, as such crimes that injure the community where they have been perpetrated in particular,

...and prosecution within the territorial state may contribute to the strengthening of rule of law institutions in that state.

Do you agree with the empirical claim suggested by the United States, namely, that the exercise of universal jurisdiction often deprives the territorial state of an opportunity to strengthen its domestic institutions? Could the exercise of jurisdiction in the United States, on the contrary, help foster support for the rule of law in the territorial state, for example by demonstrating the importance of combating impunity while maintaining robust fair trial rights?

6. How does Amnesty International's list of 'obstacles' to the effective exercise of universal jurisdiction compare with the list of 'safeguards' advocated by various states? How would adoption of the latter list by courts around the world address the issue of selectivity, which is the stated core concern of the African Union?

ADDITIONAL READING

M. Langer, 'The Diplomacy of Universal Jurisdiction', 105 Am. J. Int'l. L. 1 (2011); Luc Reydams, 'The Rise and Fall of Universal Jurisdiction', in W. A. Schabas & N. Bernaz (eds.), *Handbook of International Criminal Law* (2011); D. F. Donovan & A. Roberts, 'The Emerging Recognition of Universal Civil Jurisdiction', 100 Am. J. Int'l. L. 142 (2006); N. Roht-Arriaza, *The Pinochet Effect: Transnational Justice in the Age of Human Rights* (2005); S. Macedo (ed.), *Universal Jurisdiction: National Courts and the Prosecution of Serious Crimes under International Law* (2004).

B. US CIVIL LITIGATION AND GLOBAL COMPARISONS

Within the realm of judicial enforcement of human rights violations committed in foreign countries, one of the most important lines of cases involves the US Alien Tort Statute (ATS). The ATS is a statutory provision enacted by the US Congress in 1789, but given new life by a decision of the Court of Appeals for the Second Circuit in 1980. Codified at 28 U. S. C. 1350, the ATS states in full: 'The district courts shall have original jurisdiction of any civil action by an alien for a tort only, committed in violation of the law of nations or a treaty of the United States.' In *Filártiga v. Peña-Irala*, the Court of Appeals for the Second Circuit permitted two Paraguayan citizens, Dr Joel Filaártiga and his daughter, to file an ATS suit against a Paraguayan official for allegedly torturing to death Dr Filártiga's teenage son. That decision has since been cited, for various propositions, in well over two hundred US federal court cases. Other federal courts subsequently permitted suits to be brought under the ATS for international law violations including genocide, slavery, disappearances and war crimes. Congressional passage of the US Torture Victim Protection

Act of 1991, which we discuss below (p. 1173, *infra*), added another dimension to the opportunities afforded by the ATS for human rights litigation in US courts. In addition, courts in other countries have expanded opportunities for private suits as well as criminal prosecution as a means of redress for human rights violations. One result is that the central concerns of private international law (jurisdiction, including *forum non conveniens*[8] and state immunity; choice of law; 'act of state' determinations; and enforcement of judgments) are now increasingly relevant to litigation based on human rights law. Another result may be the increased willingness of institutions within the countries in which violations were committed to undertake efforts to address injustices.

ELLEN LUTZ & KATHRYN SIKKINK, THE JUSTICE CASCADE: THE EVOLUTION AND IMPACT OF FOREIGN HUMAN RIGHTS TRIALS IN LATIN AMERICA

2 Chi. J. Int'l. L. 1 (2001)

[T]he British government arrested Chilean General and former President Augusto Pinochet on a Spanish extradition warrant for torture and other human rights crimes.... British courts assiduously considered the jurisdictional issues posed by the Spanish request and determined that the Spanish courts had jurisdiction to try Pinochet for crimes committed in Chile over a decade before. Although British authorities ultimately allowed Pinochet to return to Chile, finding that he was too incapacitated to stand trial, the events in Europe had important political repercussions in Chile that are now rippling across Latin America and the rest of the world....

...This Article examines what changed...that made Pinochet's arrest in Britain possible. We address two main questions: (1) why, in the last two decades of the 20th century, was there a major international norms shift towards using foreign or international judicial processes to hold individuals accountable for human rights crimes; and (2) what difference have foreign judicial processes made for human rights practices in the countries whose governments were responsible for those crimes.

...

...Because most of the work on norms cascades has been done by legal theorists interested in domestic norms, there have not been efforts to model what an international norms cascade would look like....

...

The justice norms cascade is being operationalized through a series of norm-affirming events including the decisions of foreign courts to try cases involving violations of international human rights, the active participation of non-governmental

[8] A common law doctrine which allows, or may even require, courts to decide not to take jurisdiction over a case because another country's court system is better suited to hear the case.

organizations ("NGOs") and governments in the process of establishing the ICC, and the willingness of states to ratify the ICC treaty. Even cases like Pinochet, in which a foreign court recognized the legitimacy of a third country's jurisdiction but ultimately did not take steps to ensure the trial of the perpetrator, can be seen as norm-affirming events.

The transnational justice network operates by enabling individuals whose access to justice is blocked in their home country to go outside their state and seek justice abroad. This dynamic is similar to the primary mechanism of other transnational advocacy networks. Foreign court rulings against rights-abusing defendants have the effect of putting pressure "from above" on the state where the rights abuses occurred. Increasingly, this pressure serves to open previously blocked domestic avenues for pursuing justice. Looking at other advocacy networks, Keck and Sikkink have called this dynamic a "boomerang pattern" — domestic activists bypass their states and directly search out international allies to bring outside pressure on their states....

...

A. The US Cases

The practice of "borrowing" foreign judicial systems to seek justice for past human rights abuses began in the United States in 1979 with the path-breaking *Filartiga v Peña-Irala*, and the family of cases that followed. The US cases differed from the later Spanish cases in that they were civil instead of criminal, and they required as a basis for jurisdiction that the defendant be physically present in the United States....

...

The success of *Filartiga* provided US human rights lawyers with a new avenue for striking back at perpetrators of human rights abuses and the means to offer some satisfaction to individuals who had suffered. A network of US lawyers mobilized to take on these cases and before long the nuances of the legal theories first raised in *Filartiga* were being tested in the courts. Many of the lawsuits involved victims and perpetrators of human rights abuses from Latin America....

...

B. The European Cases

Latin American human rights advocates also collaborated with their counterparts in Europe to apply outside pressure on their governments to bring rights violators to justice.... This was possible for two reasons. First, many European countries, unlike the United States, recognize the passive personality basis for criminal jurisdiction in which a state may exercise criminal jurisdiction over anyone who injures one of their nationals, no matter where the crime occurred. Second, the Southern Cone countries were populated by Spaniards, Italians, and others of European descent, and many of these European countries recognize as nationals their children and even subsequent generations. As a result, transnational justice network lawyers were able to convince European judges that they had jurisdiction to criminally try Latin

American perpetrators of rights abuses for the torture, disappearance, or murder of their nationals.

...

The impact of the European cases turned out to be more significant. The turning point was *Pinochet.* Although most of those indicted or charged with human rights crimes have, until now, evaded punishment, momentum for such trials has built and more and more cases are moving forward. The Argentine and Chilean cases before Judge Garzón, though initially brought on behalf of only a handful of victims, have swelled to include hundreds, and international arrest warrants have been issued for dozens of former junta members and military officers from those two countries.

...

In Chile, the arrest of Pinochet appears to have lifted psychological, political, and juridical barriers to justice by weakening the powerful forces blocking such trials in Chile since the return to democracy....

Since Pinochet's arrest, twenty-five Chilean officers have been arrested on charges of murder, torture, and kidnapping. In an interview, Defense Minister Edmundo Perez Yoma discussed a "new attitude" emerging among the military high command: "You deal with it or it will never go away. You have to confront it — that's the changed attitude." In July 1999, Chile's Supreme Court upheld a lower court decision that the amnesty law was no longer applicable to cases in which people had disappeared....

...

The European cases against the Argentine military officers had the unanticipated effect of spurring change in Argentina's willingness to try human rights cases. The decision by the Argentine government to imprison Admiral Massera and General Videla pending trial apparently was a preemptive measure in response to the Spanish judge's international arrest warrants....

...

Meanwhile, Pinochet and the efforts of Menchu to bring former Guatemalan dictators to account in Spain have contributed to an aura of contrition among Guatemala's senior policymakers. In August 2000, Guatemalan President Alfonso Portillo admitted government responsibility for atrocities committed during the country's thirty-six-year civil war and pledged to investigate massacres, prosecute those responsible, and compensate the victims. Moreover, in a show of good faith, President Portillo signed an agreement with the Inter-American Human Rights Commission ("IACHR") that affirms Guatemala's institutional responsibility for war crimes and empowers the IACHR to monitor the actions of the Guatemalan government in light of its new promises to redress those past wrongs. In December 2000, the Inter-American Court found that the Guatemalan government had killed Efrain Bamaca Velasquez, a rebel leader, and the husband of human rights activist Jennifer Harbury....

...

Latin American countries also have enthusiastically supported efforts to establish the ICC....

...

Conclusion

We have argued that a justice cascade is underway in Latin America today. This norms cascade was the result of the concerted efforts of a transnational justice advocacy network, made up of connected groups of activist lawyers with expertise in international and domestic human rights law....

...

...With respect to the perpetrators, even if they never face punishment, or even trial, they are finding themselves "landlocked." Even where their own government is willing to protect them from the reach of foreign courts, they dare not travel abroad for fear that the country they travel to will extradite them to a country seeking to try them....

The much bigger casualty seems to be the amnesty decrees that past Latin American dictators gave themselves before leaving office, or post-dictatorship democratic regimes gave their predecessors in exchange for their allowing democracy to flourish by not seizing power again. Old amnesties are not bearing up well against current national sovereignty concerns....No Latin American country, particularly those with rapidly consolidating democracies, wants to foster the perception that its courts lack the competence, capacity, or independence necessary to effectively try its own nationals....

Still, there is plenty of evidence that in Latin America the justice cascade is far from complete. In countries that have not yet faced the possibility that foreign judiciaries will try their nationals, policy-makers have had far less enthusiasm for trials even though they find the Pinochet precedent worrisome. Thus Uruguay has taken steps to restrict the foreign travel of its nationals who were implicated in past abuses of human rights, while at the same time stepping up other initiatives, such as the establishment of a national commission to investigate the disappearances of Uruguayan nationals....Even in countries where internalization of the justice cascade is more advanced, it is far from fully realized. Thus in Argentina, where there has been substantial progress with respect to conducting trials, there is far less movement when it comes to executing judgments for civil damages in human rights trials that occurred abroad....

We conclude that in Latin America, while the justice cascade is in progress, the extent of its realization in each country depends on numerous factors including: (1) the degree of consolidation of that country's democracy and legal system, (2) whether that country has directly faced the possibility that one of its former senior political figures would be tried abroad, (3) the amount of publicity and support foreign judicial processes have received, (4) the intensity of the determination of domestic human rights advocates and victims, amply supported by their international counterparts, to pressure their government to realize justice for past wrongs, (5) the degree to which each country feels it will bear some embarrassment or other international consequence for not conducting trials that is not outweighed by domestic political pressures exerted by the supporters of those it would try, and (6) the extent to which those now in power have internalized the justice norm and believe that trying past perpetrators is the right thing to do.

...

BETH STEPHENS, INDIVIDUALS ENFORCING INTERNATIONAL LAW: THE COMPARATIVE AND HISTORICAL CONTEXT

52 DePaul L. Rev. 433 (2002)[9]

Analysis of U.S. human rights litigation often assumes that in permitting such claims the United States is out on a limb, unsupported by the practices of any other nation. In fact, the U.S. line of cases bears important similarities to legal approaches that are underway in several nations and developing just as rapidly as the U.S. precedents.

First, civil lawsuits have been filed in several common law legal systems challenging corporate abuses committed by domestic corporations in their operations abroad. One case filed in England, for example, charged that a British asbestos corporation had permitted its foreign subsidiary in South Africa to operate in a way that endangered the health of black workers and their families. The plaintiffs alleged that the company forced black workers into the most dangerous jobs, without health care, while white workers were protected from the asbestos dust and received proper health care. A similar case filed against a British chemical company, Thor Chemical Holdings, resulted in a series of settlements that compensated South African workers poisoned by mercury....

Although properly styled as violations of domestic law, these lawsuits share the goals of much human rights litigation: holding accountable those who violate the fundamental rights of individuals around the world. Claims in the United States that might be styled as international law violations have been filed as negligence claims in England, Canada, and Australia. This litigation strategy may be necessitated by the absence of domestic statutory authorization such as that provided by the Alien Tort Claims Act.

Second, civil lawsuits in the United States have much in common with privately initiated criminal prosecutions in civil law legal systems. These similarities are often overlooked because of a tendency among domestic lawyers to assume that the lines dividing the categories of criminal and civil are fixed and definable and are constant across different legal systems. In fact, such lines are difficult to pin down even within a single legal system and do not transfer automatically from one system to another.

It is not surprising that these distinctions would vary across national lines. Even within legal systems, they are hard to define. In the United States, the civil/criminal divide has important constitutional consequences: defendants in criminal proceedings have the right to a panoply of constitutional protections that are not afforded to civil litigants. Despite repeated efforts, however, the U.S. Supreme Court has not been able to draw a clear line. The European regional system has confronted similar difficulties in applying criminal law protections to procedures that originate in diverse domestic legal systems. Rather than rely upon the domestic label, the European Court of Human Rights conducts an independent inquiry to determine the proper classification of legal actions. In deciding whether a proceeding

[9] See also Beth Stephens, 'Translating Filártiga: A Comparative and International Law Analysis of Domestic Remedies for International Human Rights Violations', 27 Yale J. Int'l. L. 1 (2002).

is properly classified as criminal rather than civil, the court considers whether the purpose of the proceedings is "deterrent and punitive" and whether the sanction imposed is "in its nature and degree" appropriate "to the 'criminal' sphere."

...

One commonly identified distinction between civil actions and criminal prosecutions is a difference in the purpose of a judgment: civil actions are said to be designed to compensate the injured party, without any attendant moral condemnation of the offender, while criminal actions aim to punish the guilty party for morally blameworthy conduct. United States tort actions, however, particularly those that include punitive damages, are designed to deter and punish as well as to compensate, and entail moral condemnation....

On the other hand, criminal prosecutions in many countries include the possibility of monetary compensation to those injured by the criminal acts. In some systems, compensation is an automatic feature of a criminal prosecution. In others, compensation is obtained by means of a coordinated civil suit, attached to the criminal prosecution and relying on the facts developed at the criminal trial. In such systems, if acts are subject to criminal prosecution, it may not be necessary for a private person to undertake an independent civil action for compensation.

Another traditional distinction between criminal and civil actions focuses on the party in charge of the proceeding: public prosecutors handle criminal prosecutions while private parties litigate torts....But comparative analysis also blurs the public/private distinction. In many civil law legal systems, private parties can file and even prosecute criminal proceedings. Moreover, criminal prosecutions in many systems rely upon an inquiry conducted by an investigating magistrate; those magistrates may operate with a great deal of independence from the executive branch of their governments. The Spanish prosecution of Augusto Pinochet, which led to the attempt to extradite him from England, illustrates both of these strands of independence: the prosecution was initiated by private parties over the objection of the public prosecutors, and the investigation was conducted by a magistrate despite the opposition of the country's executive branch.

Examples of such privately initiated, magistrate-driven prosecutions for human rights violations are common across Europe; in addition, one is underway in Paraguay, while another was filed but later dismissed in Senegal. As with the Pinochet case, the potential for embarrassment of the political branches of the government is high. A criminal case filed against Ariel Sharon in Belgium, for example, charges him with responsibility for the massacre of hundreds of Palestinians in refuge camps in Lebanon. Approximately thirty similar private criminal complaints have been filed in Belgium, under a broad criminal jurisdiction statute that permitted criminal prosecutions for universal crimes committed anywhere in the world, even where the defendant was not present in Belgium at the time the complaint was filed.

Private criminal prosecutions may also be filed against corporations. A new, non-profit organization in France was formed for the sole purpose of pursuing criminal human rights prosecutions against corporations. Its first prosecution was filed in March 2002 against a French corporation, alleging illegal plundering of resources in Cameroon. Criminal investigations have also been initiated in Belgium against an oil company for activities in Burma.

...

Civil human rights litigation in the United States bears a strong resemblance to actions termed criminal in other nations. These examples indicate that private parties are engaged in the enforcement of international human rights norms in the domestic courts of many nations. In the United States, such efforts are limited to civil lawsuits. In many countries, they are more likely to entail privately initiated criminal prosecutions, requests to magistrates to open investigations, or civil claims attached to criminal prosecutions.

These varied approaches reflect the diversity and strength of national legal systems as a means to enforce international law. All of these actions are part of the expanding international movement toward accountability for violations of international law. In each, the individual plays a key role as an enforcer of international norms. Each domestic legal system implements the international norms in a manner consistent with its local procedures.... Despite our unique line of civil litigation, the United States has significant company in this growing trend towards private enforcement of international law in domestic courts.

SOSA v. ALVAREZ-MACHAIN

Supreme Court of the United States, 542 U.S. 692 (2004)

[Beginning with *Filártiga* in 1980, the first wave of human rights litigation in US courts confronted the question whether the Alien Tort Statute provided a cause of action for violations of contemporary international human rights law. In 2004, the US Supreme Court finally addressed the issue and, at the same time, provided guidance for judicial management of future ATS litigation. Excerpts of the opinion follow.]

In 1985, an agent of the Drug Enforcement Administration (DEA), Enrique Camarena-Salazar, was captured on assignment in Mexico and taken to a house in Guadalajara, where he was tortured over the course of a 2-day interrogation, then murdered. Based in part on eyewitness testimony, DEA officials in the United States came to believe that respondent Humberto Alvarez-Machain (Alvarez), a Mexican physician, was present at the house and acted to prolong the agent's life in order to extend the interrogation and torture.

In 1990, a federal grand jury indicted Alvarez for the torture and murder of Camarena-Salazar, and the United States District Court for the Central District of California issued a warrant for his arrest. The DEA asked the Mexican Government for help in getting Alvarez into the United States, but when the requests and negotiations proved fruitless, the DEA approved a plan to hire Mexican nationals to seize Alvarez and bring him to the United States for trial. As so planned, a group of Mexicans, including petitioner Jose Francisco Sosa, abducted Alvarez from his house, held him overnight in a motel, and brought him by private plane to El Paso, Texas, where he was arrested by federal officers.

...

The case was tried in 1992, and ended at the close of the Government's case, when the District Court granted Alvarez's motion for a judgment of acquittal.

...

So far as it matters here, Alvarez sought damages...from Sosa under the ATS [Alien Tort Statute], for a violation of the law of nations.

...

A divided en banc court...relied upon what it called the "clear and universally recognized norm prohibiting arbitrary arrest and detention," to support the conclusion that Alvarez's arrest amounted to a tort in violation of international law....

We granted certiorari...to clarify the scope of...the ATS.

...

...Sosa...argues (as does the United States supporting him) that there is no relief under the ATS because the statute does no more than vest federal courts with jurisdiction, neither creating nor authorizing the courts to recognize any particular right of action without further congressional action. Although we agree the statute is in terms only jurisdictional, we think that at the time of enactment the jurisdiction enabled federal courts to hear claims in a very limited category defined by the law of nations and recognized at common law. We do not believe, however, that the limited, implicit sanction to entertain the handful of international law cum common law claims understood in 1789 should be taken as authority to recognize the right of action asserted by Alvarez here.

Judge Friendly called the ATS a "legal Lohengrin," *IIT v. Vencap, Ltd.*, 519 F. 2d 1001 (C. A. 2 1975); "no one seems to know whence it came," and for over 170 years after its enactment it provided jurisdiction in only one case. The first Congress passed it as part of the Judiciary Act of 1789....

The parties and amici here advance radically different historical interpretations of this terse provision. Alvarez says that the ATS was intended not simply as a jurisdictional grant, but as authority for the creation of a new cause of action for torts in violation of international law. We think that reading is implausible.... [W]e think the statute was intended as jurisdictional in the sense of addressing the power of the courts to entertain cases concerned with a certain subject.

But holding the ATS jurisdictional raises a new question, this one about the interaction between the ATS at the time of its enactment and the ambient law of the era. Sosa would have it that the ATS was stillborn because there could be no claim for relief without a further statute expressly authorizing adoption of causes of action. Amici professors of federal jurisdiction and legal history take a different tack, that federal courts could entertain claims once the jurisdictional grant was on the books, because torts in violation of the law of nations would have been recognized within the common law of the time. We think history and practice give the edge to this latter position.

"When the United States declared their independence, they were bound to receive the law of nations, in its modern state of purity and refinement. "*Ware v. Hylton*, 3 Dall. 199 (1796) (Wilson, J.). In the years of the early Republic, this law of nations comprised two principal elements, the first covering the general norms governing the behavior of national states with each other....

The law of nations included a second, more pedestrian element, however, that did fall within the judicial sphere, as a body of judge-made law regulating the conduct of individuals situated outside domestic boundaries and consequently carrying an international savor. To Blackstone, the law of nations in this sense was implicated "in mercantile questions, such as bills of exchange and the like; in all marine causes, relating to freight, average, demurrage, insurances, bottomry.... [and] in all disputes relating to prizes, to shipwrecks, to hostages, and ransom bills." The law merchant emerged from the customary practices of international traders and admiralty required its own transnational regulation. And it was the law of nations in this sense that our precursors spoke about when the Court explained the status of coast fishing vessels in wartime grew from "ancient usage among civilized nations, beginning centuries ago, and gradually ripening into a rule of international law...." *The Paquete Habana*, 175 U. S. 677 (1900).

There was, finally, a sphere in which these rules binding individuals for the benefit of other individuals overlapped with the norms of state relationships. Blackstone referred to it when he mentioned three specific offenses against the law of nations addressed by the criminal law of England: violation of safe conducts, infringement of the rights of ambassadors, and piracy. An assault against an ambassador, for example, impinged upon the sovereignty of the foreign nation and if not adequately redressed could rise to an issue of war. It was this narrow set of violations of the law of nations, admitting of a judicial remedy and at the same time threatening serious consequences in international affairs, that was probably on minds of the men who drafted the ATS with its reference to tort.

Before there was any ATS, a distinctly American preoccupation with these hybrid international norms had taken shape owing to the distribution of political power from independence through the period of confederation. The Continental Congress was hamstrung by its inability to" cause infractions of treaties, or of the law of nations to be punished, "J. Madison, Journal of the Constitutional Convention 60 (E. Scott ed. 1893), and in 1781 the Congress implored the States to vindicate rights under the law of nations....

Appreciation of the Continental Congress's incapacity to deal with this class of cases was intensified by the so-called Marbois incident of May 1784, in which a French adventurer, Longchamps, verbally and physically assaulted the Secretary of the French Legion in Philadelphia. See *Respublica v. De Longchamps*, 1 Dall. 111, 1 L. Ed. 59 (O. T. Phila. 1784). Congress called again for state legislation addressing such matters, and concern over the inadequate vindication of the law of nations persisted through the time of the constitutional convention....

...

...There is no record of congressional discussion about private actions that might be subject to the jurisdictional provision, or about any need for further legislation to create private remedies; there is no record even of debate on the section.... Still, the history does tend to support... [the proposition] that Congress intended the ATS to furnish jurisdiction for a relatively modest set of actions alleging violations of the law of nations. Uppermost in the legislative mind appears to have been offenses against ambassadors; violations of safe conduct were probably understood to be actionable, and individual actions arising out of prize captures and piracy may well have also been contemplated. But the common law appears to have understood only those three of the hybrid variety as definite and actionable, or at any rate, to have assumed only a very limited set of claims.

...

In sum, although the ATS is a jurisdictional statute creating no new causes of action, the reasonable inference from the historical materials is that the statute was intended to have practical effect the moment it became law. The jurisdictional grant is best read as having been enacted on the understanding that the common law would provide a cause of action for the modest number of international law violations with a potential for personal liability at the time.

We think it is correct, then, to assume that the First Congress understood that the district courts would recognize private causes of action for certain torts in violation of the law of nations.... We assume, too, that no development in the two centuries from the enactment of § 1350 to the birth of the modern line of cases beginning with *Filartiga v. Pena-Irala*, has categorically precluded federal courts from recognizing a claim under the law of nations as an element of common law; Congress has not in any relevant way amended § 1350 or limited civil common law power by another statute. Still, there are good reasons for a restrained conception of the discretion a federal court should exercise in considering a new cause of action of this kind. Accordingly, we think courts should require any claim based on the present-day law of nations to rest on a norm of international character accepted by the civilized world and defined with a specificity comparable to the features of the 18th-century paradigms we have recognized. This requirement is fatal to Alvarez's claim.

A series of reasons argue for judicial caution when considering the kinds of individual claims that might implement the jurisdiction conferred by the early statute. First, the prevailing conception of the common law has changed since 1789 in a way that counsels restraint in judicially applying internationally generated norms. When § 1350 was enacted, the accepted conception was of the common law as "a transcendental body of law outside of any particular State but obligatory within it unless and until changed by statute." *Black and White Taxicab & Transfer Co. v. Brown and Yellow Taxicab & Transfer Co.*, 276 U. S. 518 (1928) (Holmes, J., dissenting). Now, however, in most cases where a court is asked to state or formulate a common law principle in a new context, there is a general understanding that the law is not so much found or discovered as it is either made or created....

Second, along with, and in part driven by, that conceptual development in understanding common law has come an equally significant rethinking of the role of the federal courts in making it. *Erie R. Co. v. Tompkins*, 304 U. S. 64 (1938), was the watershed in which we denied the existence of any federal "general" common law, which largely withdrew to havens of specialty, some of them defined by express congressional authorization to devise a body of law directly, e.g., *Textile Workers v. Lincoln Mills of Ala.*, 353 U. S. 448 (1957) (interpretation of collective-bargaining agreements); Fed. Rule Evid. 501 (evidentiary privileges in federal-question cases). Elsewhere, this Court has thought it was in order to create federal common law rules in interstitial areas of particular federal interest.... the general practice has been to look for legislative guidance before exercising innovative authority over substantive law. It would be remarkable to take a more aggressive role in exercising a jurisdiction that remained largely in shadow for much of the prior two centuries.

Third, this Court has recently and repeatedly said that a decision to create a private right of action is one better left to legislative judgment in the great majority of cases. The creation of a private right of action raises issues beyond the mere consideration whether underlying primary conduct should be allowed or not, entailing, for example, a decision to permit enforcement without the check imposed by prosecutorial discretion. Accordingly, even when Congress has made it clear by statute that a rule applies to purely domestic conduct, we are reluctant to infer intent to provide a private cause of action where the statute does not supply one expressly. While the absence of congressional action addressing private rights of action under an international norm is more equivocal than its failure to provide such a right when it creates a statute, the possible collateral consequences of making international rules privately actionable argue for judicial caution.

Fourth, the subject of those collateral consequences is itself a reason for a high bar to new private causes of action for violating international law, for the potential implications for the foreign relations of the United States of recognizing such causes should make courts particularly wary of impinging on the discretion of the Legislative and Executive Branches in managing foreign affairs. It is one thing for American courts to enforce constitutional limits on our own State and Federal Governments' power, but quite another to consider suits under rules that would go so far as to claim a limit on the power of foreign governments over their own citizens, and to hold that a foreign government or its agent has transgressed those limits. Cf. *Banco Nacional de Cuba v. Sabbatino*, 376 U. S. 398, 431–432 (1964).... Since many attempts by federal courts to craft remedies for the violation of new norms of international law would raise risks of adverse foreign policy consequences, they should be undertaken, if at all, with great caution....

The fifth reason is particularly important in light of the first four. We have no congressional mandate to seek out and define new and debatable violations of the law of nations, and modern indications of congressional understanding of the judicial role in the field have not affirmatively encouraged greater judicial creativity. It is true that a clear mandate appears in the Torture Victim Protection Act of 1991, providing authority that "establish[es] an unambiguous and modern basis for" federal claims of torture and extrajudicial killing, H. R. Rep. No. 102–367, pt. 1, p. 3 (1991). But that affirmative authority is confined to specific subject matter, and although the legislative history includes the remark that § 1350 should "remain intact to permit suits based on other norms that already exist or may ripen in the future into rules of customary international law," id., at 4, Congress as a body has done nothing to promote such suits. Several times, indeed, the Senate has expressly declined to give the federal courts the task of interpreting and applying international human rights law, as when its ratification of the International Covenant on Civil and Political Rights declared that the substantive provisions of the document were not self-executing. 138 Cong. Rec. 8071 (1992).

...

Whereas Justice Scalia sees these developments as sufficient to close the door to further independent judicial recognition of actionable international norms, other considerations persuade us that the judicial power should be exercised on the understanding that the door is still ajar subject to vigilant doorkeeping, and thus open to a narrow class of international norms today. *Erie* did not in terms bar any judicial recognition of new substantive rules, no matter what the circumstances, and post-Erie understanding has identified limited enclaves in which federal courts may derive some substantive law in a common law way. For two centuries we have affirmed that the domestic law of the United States recognizes the law of nations. See, e. g., *Sabbatino*, 376 U. S., at 423 ("[I]t is, of course, true that United States courts apply international law as a part of our own in appropriate circumstances"); The *Paquete Habana*, 175 US., at 700 ("International law is part of our law, and must be ascertained and administered by the courts of justice of appropriate jurisdiction, as often as questions of right depending upon it are duly presented for their determination"); *The Nereide*, 9 Cranch 388, 423 (1815) (Marshall, C. J.) ("[T]he Court is bound by the law of nations which is a part of the law of the land"). It would take some explaining to say now that federal courts must avert their gaze entirely from any international norm intended to protect individuals.

...The First Congress, which reflected the understanding of the framing generation and included some of the Framers, assumed that federal courts could properly identify some international norms as enforceable in the exercise of § 1350 jurisdiction. We think it would be unreasonable to assume that the First Congress would have expected federal courts to lose all capacity to recognize enforceable international norms simply because the common law might lose some metaphysical cachet on the road to modern realism. Later Congresses seem to have shared our view. The position we take today has been assumed by some federal courts for 24 years, ever since the Second Circuit decided *Filartiga v. Pena-Irala*...Congress, however, has not only expressed no disagreement with our view of the proper exercise of the judicial power, but has responded to its most notable instance by enacting legislation supplementing the judicial determination in some detail. See supra (discussing the Torture Victim Protection Act).

...

...Whatever the ultimate criteria for accepting a cause of action subject to jurisdiction under § 1350, we are persuaded that federal courts should not recognize private claims under federal common law for violations of any international law norm with less definite content and acceptance among civilized nations than the historical paradigms familiar when § 1350 was enacted....This limit upon judicial recognition is generally consistent with the reasoning of many of the courts and judges who faced the issue before it reached this Court. See *Filartiga*, *supra*, at 890 ("[F]or purposes of civil liability, the torturer has become — like the pirate and slave trader before him — hostis humani generis, an enemy of all mankind"); *Tel-Oren v. Libyan Arab Republic*, 726 F. 2d 774, 781 (C. A. D. C. 1984) (Edwards, J., concurring) (suggesting that the "limits of section 1350's reach" be defined by "a handful of heinous actions — each of which violates definable, universal and obligatory norms"); see also *In re Estate of Marcos Human Rights Litigation*, 25 F. 3d 1467, 1475 (C. A. 9 1994) ("Actionable violations of international law must be of a norm that is specific, universal, and obligatory"). And the determination whether a norm is sufficiently definite to support a cause of action[10] should (and, indeed, inevitably must)

[10] A related consideration is whether international law extends the scope of liability for a violation of a given norm to the perpetrator being sued, if the defendant is a private actor such as a corporation or individual. Compare *Tel-Oren*

involve an element of judgment about the practical consequences of making that cause available to litigants in the federal courts.[11]

...

To begin with, Alvarez cites two well-known international agreements that, despite their moral authority, have little utility under the standard set out in this opinion. He says that his abduction by Sosa was an "arbitrary arrest" within the meaning of the Universal Declaration of Human Rights. And he traces the rule against arbitrary arrest not only to the Declaration, but also to article nine of the International Covenant on Civil and Political Rights to which the United States is a party, and to various other conventions to which it is not. But the Declaration does not of its own force impose obligations as a matter of international law. And, although the Covenant does bind the United States as a matter of international law, the United States ratified the Covenant on the express understanding that it was not self-executing and so did not itself create obligations enforceable in the federal courts. Accordingly, Alvarez cannot say that the Declaration and Covenant themselves establish the relevant and applicable rule of international law. He instead attempts to show that prohibition of arbitrary arrest has attained the status of binding customary international law.

Here, it is useful to examine Alvarez's complaint in greater detail. As he presently argues it, the claim does not rest on the cross-border feature of his abduction....[I]t relied on the conclusion that the law of the United States did not authorize Alvarez's arrest, because the DEA lacked extraterritorial authority under 21 U. S. C. § 878, and because Federal Rule of Criminal Procedure 4(d)(2) limited the warrant for Alvarez's arrest to "the jurisdiction of the United States." It is this position that Alvarez takes now: that his arrest was arbitrary and as such forbidden by international law not because it infringed the prerogatives of Mexico, but because no applicable law authorized it.

v. Libyan Arab Republic, 726 F.2d 774, 791–795 (C.A.D.C.1984) (Edwards, J., concurring) (insufficient consensus in 1984 that torture by private actors violates international law), with *Kadic v. Karadzic*, 70 F.3d 232, 239–241 (C.A.2 1995) (sufficient consensus in 1995 that genocide by private actors violates international law).

[11] This requirement of clear definition is not meant to be the only principle limiting the availability of relief in the federal courts for violations of customary international law, though it disposes of this case. For example, the European Commission argues as amicus curiae that basic principles of international law require that before asserting a claim in a foreign forum, the claimant must have exhausted any remedies available in the domestic legal system, and perhaps in other fora such as international claims tribunals. See Brief for European Commission as Amicus Curiae 24, n. 54 (citing I. Brownlie, Principles of Public International Law 472–481 (6th ed.2003)); cf. Torture Victim Protection Act of 1991, ß 2(b),106 Stat.73 (exhaustion requirement). We would certainly consider this requirement in an appropriate case.

Another possible limitation that we need not apply here is a policy of case-specific deference to the political branches. For example, there are now pending in federal district court several class actions seeking damages from various corporations alleged to have participated in, or abetted, the regime of apartheid that formerly controlled South Africa. See *In re South African Apartheid Litigation*, 238 F.Supp.2d 1379 (JPML 2002) (granting a motion to transfer the cases to the Southern District of New York). The Government of South Africa has said that these cases interfere with the policy embodied by its Truth and Reconciliation Commission, which "deliberately avoided a 'victors' justice' approach to the crimes of apartheid and chose instead one based on confession and absolution, informed by the principles of reconciliation, reconstruction, reparation and goodwill." Declaration of Penuell Mpapa Maduna, Minister of Justice and Constitutional Development, Republic of South Africa, reprinted in App. to Brief for Government of Commonwealth of Australia *et al.* as Amici Curiae (emphasis deleted). The United States has agreed. See Letter of William H. Taft IV, Legal Adviser, Dept. of State, to Shannen W. Coffin, Deputy Asst. Atty. Gen., Oct. 27, 2003, reprinted in id., at 2a. In such cases, there is a strong argument that federal courts should give serious weight to the Executive Branch's view of the case's impact on foreign policy. Cf. *Republic of Austria v. Altmann*, 541 U.S. 677 (2004) (discussing the State Department's use of statements of interest in cases involving the Foreign Sovereign Immunities Act of1976).

Alvarez thus invokes a general prohibition of "arbitrary" detention defined as officially sanctioned action exceeding positive authorization to detain under the domestic law of some government, regardless of the circumstances. Whether or not this is an accurate reading of the Covenant, Alvarez cites little authority that a rule so broad has the status of a binding customary norm today.[12] He certainly cites nothing to justify the federal courts in taking his broad rule as the predicate for a federal lawsuit, for its implications would be breathtaking. His rule would support a cause of action in federal court for any arrest, anywhere in the world, unauthorized by the law of the jurisdiction in which it took place, and would create a cause of action for any seizure of an alien in violation of the Fourth Amendment, supplanting the actions under Rev. Stat. § 1979, 42 U. S. C. § 1983 and Bivens v. Six Unknown Fed. Narcotics Agents, 403 U. S. 388 (1971), that now provide damages remedies for such violations. It would create an action in federal court for arrests by state officers who simply exceed their authority; and for the violation of any limit that the law of any country might place on the authority of its own officers to arrest. And all of this assumes that Alvarez could establish that Sosa was acting on behalf of a government when he made the arrest, for otherwise he would need a rule broader still.

Alvarez's failure to marshal support for his proposed rule is underscored by the Restatement (Third) of Foreign Relations Law of the United States (1987), which says in its discussion of customary international human rights law that a "state violates international law if, as a matter of state policy, it practices, encourages, or condones...prolonged arbitrary detention." Although the Restatement does not explain its requirements of a "state policy" and of "prolonged" detention, the implication is clear. Any credible invocation of a principle against arbitrary detention that the civilized world accepts as binding customary international law requires a factual basis beyond relatively brief detention in excess of positive authority. Even the Restatement's limits are only the beginning of the enquiry, because although it is easy to say that some policies of prolonged arbitrary detentions are so bad that those who enforce them become enemies of the human race, it may be harder to say which policies cross that line with the certainty afforded by Blackstone's three common law offenses. In any event, the label would never fit the reckless policeman who botches his warrant, even though that same officer might pay damages under municipal law.

Whatever may be said for the broad principle Alvarez advances, in the present, imperfect world, it expresses an aspiration that exceeds any binding customary rule having the specificity we require.[13] Creating a private cause of action to further that

[12] Specifically, he relies on a survey of national constitutions, Bassiouni, Human Rights in the Context of Criminal Justice: Identifying International Procedural Protections and Equivalent Protections in National Constitutions, 3 Duke J. Comp. & Int'l L. 235, 260–261 (1993); a case from the International Court of Justice, *United States v.Iran*,1980 I. C. J. 3, 42; and some authority drawn from the federal courts, see Brief for Respondent Alvarez-Machain 49, n. 50. None of these suffice. The Bassiouni survey does show that many nations recognize a norm against arbitrary detention, but that consensus is at a high level of generality....

[13] It is not that violations of a rule logically foreclose the existence of that rule as international law. Cf. *Filartiga v. Pena-Irala*, 630 F.2d 876, 884, n.15 (C.A. 2 1980) ("The fact that the prohibition of torture is often honored in the breach does not diminish its binding effect as a norm of international law"). Nevertheless, that a rule as stated is as far from full realization as the one Alvarez urges is evidence against its status as binding law; and an even clearer point against the creation by judges of a private cause of action to enforce the aspiration behind the rule claimed.

aspiration would go beyond any residual common law discretion we think it appropriate to exercise.[14] It is enough to hold that a single illegal detention of less than a day, followed by the transfer of custody to lawful authorities and a prompt arraignment, violates no norm of customary international law so well defined as to support the creation of a federal remedy.

...

JUSTICE BREYER, CONCURRING IN PART AND CONCURRING IN THE JUDGMENT

...

I would add one further consideration. Since enforcement of an international norm by one nation's courts implies that other nations' courts may do the same, I would ask whether the exercise of jurisdiction under the ATS is consistent with those notions of comity that lead each nation to respect the sovereign rights of other nations by limiting the reach of its laws and their enforcement. In applying those principles, courts help ensure that "the potentially conflicting laws of different nations" will "work together in harmony," a matter of increasing importance in an ever more interdependent world....

...

Since different courts in different nations will not necessarily apply even similar substantive laws similarly, workable harmony, in practice, depends upon more than substantive uniformity among the laws of those nations. That is to say, substantive uniformity does not automatically mean that universal jurisdiction is appropriate. Thus, in the 18th century, nations reached consensus not only on the substantive principle that acts of piracy were universally wrong but also on the jurisdictional principle that any nation that found a pirate could prosecute him....

Today international law will sometimes similarly reflect not only substantive agreement as to certain universally condemned behavior but also procedural agreement that universal jurisdiction exists to prosecute a subset of that behavior. That subset includes torture, genocide, crimes against humanity, and war crimes.

The fact that this procedural consensus exists suggests that recognition of universal jurisdiction in respect to a limited set of norms is consistent with principles of international comity....That consensus concerns criminal jurisdiction, but consensus as to universal criminal jurisdiction itself suggests that universal tort jurisdiction would be no more threatening. That is because the criminal courts of many nations combine civil and criminal proceedings, allowing those injured by criminal conduct to be represented, and to recover damages, in the criminal proceeding itself....Thus, universal criminal jurisdiction necessarily contemplates a significant degree of civil tort recovery as well.

[14] Alvarez also cites, Brief for Respondent Alvarez-Machain 49–50, a finding by a United Nations working group that his detention was arbitrary under the Declaration, the Covenant, and customary international law. See Report of the United Nations Working Group on Arbitrary Detention, U.N. Doc. E/CN.4/1994/27, pp.139–140 (Dec.17, 1993). That finding is not addressed, however, to our demanding standard of definition, which must be met to raise even the possibility of a private cause of action. If Alvarez wishes to seek compensation on the basis of the working group's finding, he must address his request to Congress.

JUSTICE SCALIA, WITH WHOM CHIEF JUSTICE REHNQUIST AND JUSTICE THOMAS JOIN, CONCURRING IN PART AND CONCURRING IN THE JUDGMENT

...

The analysis in the Court's opinion departs from my own in this respect: After concluding in Part III that "the ATS is a jurisdictional statute creating no new causes of action," the Court addresses at length in Part IV the "good reasons for a restrained conception of the *discretion* a federal court should exercise in considering a new cause of action" under the ATS. (emphasis added). By framing the issue as one of "discretion," the Court skips over the antecedent question of authority. This neglects the "lesson of *Erie*," that "grants of jurisdiction alone" (which the Court has acknowledged the ATS to be) "are not themselves grants of law-making authority." Meltzer, supra, at 541. On this point, the Court observes only that no development between the enactment of the ATS (in 1789) and the birth of modern international human rights litigation under that statute (in 1980) "has categorically *precluded* federal courts from recognizing a claim under the law of nations as an element of common law." (emphasis added). This turns our jurisprudence regarding federal common law on its head. The question is not what case or congressional action prevents federal courts from applying the law of nations as part of the general common law; it is what authorizes that peculiar exception from *Erie*'s fundamental holding that a general common law does not exist.

...

The Court recognizes that *Erie* was a "watershed" decision heralding an avulsive change, wrought by "conceptual development in understanding common law... [and accompanied by an] equally significant rethinking of the role of the federal courts in making it." The Court's analysis, however, does not follow through on this insight, interchangeably using the unadorned phrase "common law" in Parts III and IV to refer to pre-*Erie* general common law and post-*Erie* federal common law. This lapse is crucial, because the creation of post-*Erie* federal common law is rooted in a positivist mindset utterly foreign to the American common-law tradition of the late 18th century. Post-*Erie* federal common lawmaking (all that is left to the federal courts) is so far removed from that general-common-law adjudication which applied the "law of nations" that it would be anachronistic to find authorization to do the former in a statutory grant of jurisdiction that was thought to enable the latter. Yet that is precisely what the discretion-only analysis in Part IV suggests.

...

...In holding open the possibility that judges may create rights where Congress has not authorized them to do so, the Court countenances judicial occupation of a domain that belongs to the people's representatives. One does not need a crystal ball to predict that this occupation will not be long in coming, since the Court endorses the reasoning of "many of the courts and judges who faced the issue before it reached this Court," including the Second and Ninth Circuits.

The Ninth Circuit brought us the judgment that the Court reverses today. Perhaps its decision in this particular case, like the decisions of other lower federal courts that receive passing attention in the Court's opinion, "reflects a more assertive view of federal judicial discretion over claims based on customary international law than the position we take today." But the verbal formula it applied is the same verbal formula that the Court explicitly endorses. Compare ante (quoting *In re Estate of Marcos Human Rights Litigation*, 25 F. 3d 1467, 1475 (C. A. 9 1994), for the proposition that actionable norms must be "'specific, universal, and obligatory'"), with 331 F. 3d 604, 621 (C. A. 9 2003) (en banc) (finding the norm against arbitrary arrest and detention in this case to be "universal, obligatory, and specific"); id., at 619 ("[A]n actionable claim under the [ATS] requires the showing of a violation of the law of nations that is specific, universal, and obligatory" (internal quotation marks omitted)). Endorsing the very formula that led the Ninth Circuit to its result in this case hardly seems to be a recipe for restraint in the future.

...

Though it is not necessary to resolution of the present case, one further consideration deserves mention: Despite the avulsive change of *Erie*, the Framers who included reference to "the Law of Nations" in Article I, § 8, cl. 10, of the Constitution would be entirely content with the post-Erie system I have described, and quite terrified by the "discretion" endorsed by the Court. That portion of the general common law known as the law of nations was understood to refer to the accepted practices of nations in their dealings with one another (treatment of ambassadors, immunity of foreign sovereigns from suit, etc.) and with actors on the high seas hostile to all nations and beyond all their territorial jurisdictions (pirates). Those accepted practices have for the most part, if not in their entirety, been enacted into United States statutory law, so that insofar as they are concerned the demise of the general common law is inconsequential. The notion that a law of nations, redefined to mean the consensus of states on any subject, can be used by a private citizen to control a sovereign's treatment of its own citizens within its own territory is a 20th-century invention of internationalist law professors and human-rights advocates. See generally Bradley and Goldsmith, Critique of the Modern Position, 110 Harv. L. Rev., at 831–837. The Framers would, I am confident, be appalled by the proposition that, for example, the American peoples' democratic adoption of the death penalty, see, e.g., Tex. Penal Code Ann. § 12.31 (2003), could be judicially nullified because of the disapproving views of foreigners.

We Americans have a method for making the laws that are over us. We elect representatives to two Houses of Congress, each of which must enact the new law and present it for the approval of a President, whom we also elect. For over two decades now, unelected federal judges have been usurping this lawmaking power by converting what they regard as norms of international law into American law. Today's opinion approves that process in principle, though urging the lower courts to be more restrained.

This Court seems incapable of admitting that some matters — any matters — are none of its business. See, e. g., *Rasul v. Bush*, 124 S. Ct. 2686 (2004); *INS v. St. Cyr*, 533 U. S. 289 (2001). In today's latest victory for its Never Say Never Jurisprudence, the Court ignores its own conclusion that the ATS provides only jurisdiction, wags a finger at the lower courts for going too far, and then — repeating the same formula the ambitious lower courts themselves have used — invites them to try again.

It would be bad enough if there were some assurance that future conversions of perceived international norms into American law would be approved by this Court itself. (Though we know ourselves to be eminently reasonable, self-awareness of eminent reasonableness is not really a substitute for democratic election.) But in this illegitimate lawmaking endeavor, the lower federal courts will be the principal actors; we review but a tiny fraction of their decisions. And no one thinks that all of them are eminently reasonable.

…

QUESTIONS

1. Consider how the *Sosa* Court analysed various sources of international law. Did the Court's analysis depart from conventional approaches in determining the content of customary international law? Consider the following commentary:[15]

> [M]any pre-*Sosa* lower court decisions downplayed the traditional state practice requirement for CIL [customary international law] and emphasized instead state acceptance as reflected in instruments like General Assembly resolutions, multilateral treaties, national constitutions, and official pronouncements of international bodies. *Sosa* appears to render some of these sources irrelevant, minimize the significance of others, and reemphasize the importance of looking to state practice in ATS cases.
>
> …
>
> …[T]he Court in *Sosa* gave little weight to both the Universal Declaration of Human Rights and the ICCPR, narrowed the relevance of national constitutions and the Restatement, and reduced the allowable gap between a CIL norm's aspiration and the actual practice of states. It is no surprise, in this light, that the Court in *Sosa* envisioned that, under its approach, only a modest number of claims would be recognized under the ATS.
>
> It remains unclear, however, precisely how far *Sosa* went in this regard. The lack of clarity results from the Court's favorable citation to prior lower court opinions that had embraced the very methods and sources of CIL identification that the Court in *Sosa* appeared to discount….
>
> …
>
> In recent years, the Supreme Court has cited and relied on international and foreign materials in the course of interpreting provisions of the US Constitution….
>
> …
>
> …The Court has been much less rigorous with respect to foreign and international materials in its constitutional interpretation cases than it was with respect to these sources in the context of the ATS in *Sosa*. In *Roper v. Simmons*, for example, in which the Court held that the execution of juvenile offenders violates the Eighth Amendment, the Court cited, among other things, the Convention on the Rights of the Child, a treaty that had not been ratified by the United States, and the ICCPR, which the U.S. had ratified with a reservation declining to agree to the ban in that treaty on the juvenile death penalty. By contrast, in *Sosa*, as we discussed earlier, the Court described the ICCPR as having "little utility" in its analysis, even though,

[15] Curtis A. Bradley, Jack L. Goldsmith & David H. Moore, 'Sosa, Customary International Law, and the Continuing Relevance of Erie', 120 Harv. L. Rev. 869 (2007).

unlike in *Roper*, there was no relevant reservation with respect to the issue before the Court.

It is difficult to know what to make of the Supreme Court's differing treatment of foreign and international sources in the constitutional and ATS contexts....

2. The ATS provides jurisdiction for injuries 'committed in violation of the law of nations or a treaty of the United States'. After *Sosa*, is there any hope of successfully bringing a claim solely under the ICCPR? What if the self-executing declaration accompanying the US ratification of the ICCPR is incompatible with the object and the purpose of the treaty?

3. Do you agree with Justice Breyer that 'consensus as to universal criminal jurisdiction itself suggests that universal tort jurisdiction would be no more threatening'? Could civil jurisdiction be more threatening to a foreign state than a system of criminal jurisdiction?

4. How should US reservations, understandings or declarations to a treaty affect the interpretation of custom under the 'law of nations' prong of the ATS? Consider the following discussion in a lower federal court opinion:[16]

> Without diminishing the mistreatment allegedly suffered by Plaintiffs... their treatment pales in comparison to the acts which have been found by various courts and international authorities to constituted cruel, inhuman or degrading treatment....
>
> ...The Plaintiffs urge that finding cruel, inhuman or degrading treatment could be consistent with the Senate's ratifications of both the CAT and the ICCPR which reflects its intent to incorporate the constitutional test for cruel and unusual treatment or punishment prohibited by the Firth [sic], Eighth, or Fourteenth Amendment....The conduct alleged by Plaintiffs...would appear to establish a *prima facie* due process violation applicable to pretrial detainees....
>
> However, in ratifying the ICCPR, the Senate's expressed reservation states that "Art. 7 [prohibiting cruel, inhuman, or degrading treatment] shall not extend beyond protections of the 5th, 8th and 14th Amendments of the U.S. Constitution." (citation omitted). Thus, it would appear that the Senate intended that U.S. constitutional standards set the outermost limit to the interpretation of the ICCRP and not necessarily state its equivalent.
>
> In any event, irrespective of the Senate's interpretation, the constitutional standards of one nation is not necessarily determinative of standards to be followed by the international community as a whole. While one nation's practices may inform the question as to the existence of an internationally accepted standard, only those domestic standards rising to the level of customary usage and practice of the international community can constitute "the law of nations" under the ATCA.

Does this logic also apply in reverse? That is, if a court concludes that a defendant's conduct would not constitute a prima facie due process violation of the US Constitution could the court nevertheless hold that the conduct violates international standards of cruel, inhuman or degrading treatment?

[16] *Doe v. Qi*, 349 F.Supp.2d 1258, 1324 n. 44 (N.D. Cal. 2004).

Additionally, after *Sosa*, what weight should courts assign treaties such as the ICCPR, to which the United States has attached a non-self-executing declaration? Consider the following answer to that question by the Court of Appeals for the Second Circuit:[17]

> While adoption of a self-executing treaty or the execution of a treaty that is not self-executing may provide the best evidence of a particular country's custom or practice of recognizing a norm, the existence of a norm of customary international law is one determined, in part, by reference to the custom or practices of many States, and the broad acceptance of that norm by the international community. Agreements that are not self-executing or that have not been executed by [US] federal legislation, including the ICCPR, are appropriately considered evidence of the current state of customary international law. See *Khulumani*, 504 F.3d at 284 (Katzmann, J., concurring) (noting that "[w]hether a treaty that embodies [a norm of customary international law] is self-executing is relevant to, but is not determinative of, [the] question" of whether the norm permits ATS jurisdiction).
>
> ...
>
> The international community's recognition in the ICCPR of its obligation to protect humans against nonconsensual medical experimentation, regardless of the source of the action, is powerful evidence of the prohibition's place in customary international law.
>
> It is clear that, as the court mentioned in Sosa, the Universal Declaration of Human Rights and the ICCPR themselves could not establish the relevant, applicable rule of international law in that case. Nonetheless, the ICCPR, when viewed as a reaffirmation of the norm as articulated in the Nuremberg Code, is potent authority for the universal acceptance of the prohibition on nonconsensual medical experimentation. As we discuss below,[18] the fact that the prohibition on medical experimentation on humans without consent has been consciously embedded by Congress in our law and reaffirmed on numerous occasions by the [Food and Drug Administration] demonstrates that the United States government views the norm as the source of a binding legal obligation even though the United States has not ratified the ICCPR in full.

Does the court's analysis of the role of the Universal Declaration of Human Rights and the ICCPR effectively resolve the interpretive questions raised by the commentators in Question 1? The court refers to congressional legislation and actions by a federal agency as evidence, notwithstanding a RUD, that the United States considers the specific norm a binding legal obligation. Are you convinced?

5. Should the 'law of nations' prong of the ATS apply only to customary international law norms? Would it be appropriate for a court to consider an international norm derived from general principles of law? Does *Sosa* foreclose that legal avenue?

[17] *Abdullahi v. Pfizer, Inc.*, 562 F.3d 163 (2d Cir. 2009).

[18] The court subsequently stated that 'the sources on which our government relied in outlawing non-consensual human medical experimentation were the Nuremberg Code and the Declaration of Helsinki, which suggests the government conceived of these sources' articulation of the norm as a binding legal obligation. M. Cheriff Bassiouni et al., An Appraisal of Human Experimentation in International Law and Practice: The Need for International Regulation of Human Experimentation, 72 J. Crim. L. & Criminology 1597 (1981) (citing 21 C.F.R. § 310.102(h) (1980)).'

COMMENT ON ATS CLAIMS AFTER SOSA

Which human rights norms satisfy the test set forth in *Sosa*? Indeed, what are the elements of that test? After *Sosa*, should only *jus cogens* norms, in effect, be able to succeed? The following discussion considers cases that have grappled with those legal boundaries.

Substantive Causes of Action: Questions of Precision, Obligation and Content

Economic and social rights. Could economic and social rights ever satisfy the *Sosa* test? Consider the following statement by the Court of the Appeals for the Second Circuit involving a case in which Peruvian citizens sued a mining company alleging that 'egregious' pollution caused severe lung disease and deaths among the local population:[19]

> [W]e hold that the asserted "right to life" and "right to health" are insufficiently definite to constitute rules of customary international law.... [I]n order to state a claim under the ATCA, we have required that a plaintiff allege a violation of a "clear and unambiguous" rule of customary international law....
>
> Far from being "clear and unambiguous," the statements relied on by plaintiffs to define the rights to life and health are vague and amorphous. For example, the statements that plaintiffs rely on to define the rights to life and health include the following:
>
> > Everyone has the right to a standard of living adequate for the health and well-being of himself and of his family.... Universal Declaration of Human Rights, Art. 25.
> >
> > The States Parties to the present Covenant recognize the right of everyone to the enjoyment of the highest attainable standard of physical and mental health. International Covenant on Economic, Social, and Cultural Rights, Art. 12.
> >
> > Human beings are...entitled to a healthy and productive life in harmony with nature.
> >
> > Rio Declaration on Environment and Development ("Rio Declaration"), United Nations Conference on Environment and Development, Rio de Janeiro, Brazil, June 13, 1992, Principle 1.
>
> These principles are boundless and indeterminate. They express virtuous goals understandably expressed at a level of abstraction needed to secure the adherence of States that disagree on many of the particulars regarding how actually to achieve them. But in the words of a sister circuit, they "state abstract rights and liberties devoid of articulable or discernable standards and regulations." *Beanal v. Freeport-McMoran, Inc.*, 197 F. 3d 161 (5th Cir. 1999). The precept that "[h]uman beings are...entitled to a healthy and productive life in harmony with nature," for example, utterly fails to specify what conduct would fall within or outside of the law. Similarly, the exhortation that all people are entitled to the "highest attainable standard of physical and mental health" proclaims only nebulous notions that are infinitely malleable.

[19] *Flores v. Southern Peru Copper Corp.*, 414 F.3d 233 (2d Cir. 2003).

> In support of plaintiffs' argument that the statements and instruments discussed above are part of customary international law, plaintiffs attempt to underscore the universality of the principles asserted by pointing out that they "contain *no limitations as to how or by whom these rights may be violated.*" Pls. Br. at 10 (emphasis added). However, this assertion proves too much; because of the conceded absence of any "limitations" on these "rights," they do not meet the requirement of our law that rules of customary international law be clear, definite, and unambiguous.

Consider the fate of ATS claims involving child labour. In the following case, 23 Liberian children, whose ages ranged from 6 to 16, brought an action against the Firestone corporation alleging that the company used hazardous child labour on an 118,000-acre rubber plantation in Liberia. Judge Richard Posner, writing for the court, rejected the complaint on the basis of insufficient support for the norm in international law. He also included a cost-benefit analysis of child labour suggesting that such an inquiry follows from *Sosa*'s admonition to lower courts to exercise caution in considering new causes of action:[20]

> More promising for the plaintiffs is the International Labor Organization's Convention 182: The Worst Forms of Child Labor, which . . . is the one the United States has ratified. It provides, so far as bears on this case, that the worst forms of child labor include "work which, by its nature or the circumstances in which it is carried out, is likely to harm the health, safety or morals of children." Id., art. 3(d). This is still pretty vague, in part because no threshold of actionable harm is specified, in part because of the inherent vagueness of the words "safety" and "morals." And it is weakened by the further statement that "the types of work referred to under Article 3(d) shall be determined by national laws or regulations or by the competent authority." Art. 4(1). That sounds like forswearing the creation of an international legal norm.
>
> The Convention's Recommendation 190 adds some stiffening detail; it explains that Article 3(d) encompasses "work in an unhealthy environment which may, for example, expose children to hazardous substances, agents or processes, or to temperatures, noise levels, or vibrations damaging to their health," and "work under particularly difficult conditions such as work for long hours." But a "Recommendation" creates no enforceable obligations. . . .
>
> Given the diversity of economic conditions in the world, it's impossible to distill a crisp rule from the three conventions [the United Nations Convention on the Rights of the Child; ILO Minimum Age Convention 138; ILO Convention 182: The Worst Forms of Child Labor]. We would like to think that working conditions of children below the age of 13 that significantly reduce longevity or create a high risk (or actuality) of significant permanent physical or psychological impairment would be deemed to violate customary international law, but we cannot be certain even of that. The plaintiffs have furnished no "concrete evidence of the customs and practices of States" to show that states feel themselves under a legal obligation to impose liability on employers of child labor in our hypothetical case. Such evidence is readily available for the other types of child labor listed in ILO Convention 182,

[20] *Flomo v. Firestone Nat. Rubber Co.*, 643 F.3d 1013 (7th Cir. 2011); but see *Doe v. Nestle, S.A.*, 748 F.Supp.2d 1057 (C.D. Cal. 2010).

such as sexual exploitation of children and forced child labor. But not for the child labor in our example; and anyway the working conditions at the Firestone plantation, while bad, are not that bad — more precisely, the plaintiffs haven't presented evidence that would create a triable issue of whether they're that bad.

...

... Firestone doesn't employ children; the argument rather is that by imposing tough quotas it induces its employees to enlist their children as helpers. The plaintiffs' basic objection seems therefore to be to the quotas. This implies that courts must in a case such as this determine on an employer-by-employer basis what level of production quotas violates customary international law by encouraging oppressive child labor.

We also — and this is the biggest objection to this lawsuit — don't know the situation of Liberian children who don't live on the Firestone plantation. Conceivably, because the fathers of the children on the plantation are well paid by Liberian standards, even the children who help their fathers with the work are, on balance, better off than the average Liberian child, and would be worse off if their fathers, unable to fill their daily quotas, lost their jobs or had to pay adult helpers, thus reducing the family's income. There is a tradeoff between family income and child labor; children are helped by the former and hurt by the latter; we don't know the net effect on their welfare of working on the plantation.

In short, we have not been given an adequate basis for inferring a violation of customary international law, bearing in mind the Supreme Court's insistence on caution in recognizing new norms of customary international law in litigation under the Alien Tort Statute.

Crimes Against Humanity. In his concurring opinion in *Sosa*, Justice Breyer listed at least four actions that would presumably meet the requirements for the exercise of jurisdiction: torture, genocide, war crimes and crimes against humanity. Federal courts have generally embraced the first three, but have expressed reservations about the precise boundaries of the fourth. Consider two recent cases. First, in *Sarei v. Rio Tinto*, an *en banc* panel of the Ninth Circuit held that a food and medicine blockade of a civilian population did not constitute a crime against humanity:[21]

The complaint alleges crimes against humanity arising from a food and medical blockade. Under customary international law, primarily defined through the international criminal tribunals at Nuremberg and elsewhere, crimes against humanity require (1) a widespread or systematic attack directed against a civilian population; and (2) a prohibited act.

Assuming, without deciding, that Plaintiffs allege the blockade was a widespread and systematic attack, then whether Plaintiffs' blockade allegation would establish a violation of the law of nations giving rise to an ATS claim under Sosa depends upon whether the blockade constitutes a prohibited act. The articles defining crimes against humanity in each of the relevant international statutes include a list of specific acts constituting crimes against humanity, as well as a more general "other inhumane acts" provision.

[21] *Sarei v. Rio Tinto*, 2011 WL 5041927 (9th Cir. 2011) (*en banc*). Other courts have embraced crimes against humanity as a cause of action under the ATS without expressing such reservations. See, e.g., *Presbyterian Church of Sudan v. Talisman Energy, Inc.*, 582 F.3d 244 (2d Cir. 2009).

All statutes list "extermination" as a prohibited act amounting to a crime against humanity. Rome Statute, art. 7(1)(b); ICTY Statute, art. 5(b); ICTR Statute art. 3(b). Their definitions of what constitutes extermination, however, differ. Only the Rome Statute refers to the denial of access to the necessities of life. Its definition of "extermination" states that the term "includes the intentional infliction of conditions of life, inter alia the deprivation of access to food and medicine, calculated to bring about the destruction of part of a population...." Notably, the Rome Statute does not mention a blockade. Moreover, the deprivation of access to necessities is not necessarily synonymous with a blockade, because such deprivation can be effected without the imposition of a blockade.

The ICTR and the ICTY do not refer to deprivation of food and medicine. The ICTR "requires proof that the accused participated in a widespread or systematic killing or in subjecting a widespread number of people or systematically subjecting a number of people to conditions of living that would inevitably lead to death...." Gacumbitsi v. Prosecutor, Case No. ICTR–2001–64–A, Judgment, (2006). The ICTY requires the "intent to kill on a massive scale." Prosecutor v. Brdjanin, ICTY, Case No. IT–99–36–A (2007).

Since none of the statutes explicitly include a blockade in their definition of extermination, Plaintiffs' claim for crimes against humanity can come within the statutes only if the blockade constitutes "other inhumane acts." A food and medical blockade may well be an "other inhumane act[ ]" constituting a crime against humanity....

To meet the Sosa test, however, the blockade must be a violation of a recognized specific norm. The statutes do not create such a norm. There is no source of recognized international law that yet identifies a food and medical blockade as an "other inhumane act[ ]" or otherwise qualifies it as a crime against humanity....

...We note that Plaintiffs' claim for genocide is also pled as a crime against humanity, and as we have explained, the genocide claim does satisfy the Sosa requirements.

The court's favourable holding on the genocide claim rested, in part, on the court's acceptance of the fact that the Rio Tinto company engaged in 'the deliberate infliction of conditions of starvation "for the purpose of starving the bastards out"'—the words allegedly spoken by a top Rio Tinto manager encouraging government officials to continue the blockade (*Sarei*, at 21). How can the court's acceptance of the genocide claim on those grounds be reconciled with its rejection of the crimes against humanity claim? Do the same actions that constitute genocide not, *a fortiori*, establish a crime against humanity?

The Court of Appeals for the Eleventh Circuit rejected a crimes against humanity claim in a case involving alleged killings by government forces during an uprising in Bolivia. The court explained that its decision turned, in part, on the ambiguity of the content of the norm:[22]

The scope of what is, for example, widespread enough to be a crime against humanity is hard to know given the current state of the law.

...According to plaintiffs, the toll—one arising from a significant civil disturbance—was fewer than 70 killed and about 400 injured to some degree, over about two months. The alleged toll is sufficient to cause concern and distress. Nevertheless, especially given the mass demonstrations, as well as the threat to the capital city and

[22] *Mamani v. Berzain*, 654 F.3d 1148 (11th Cir. 2011).

> to public safety, we cannot conclude that the scale of this loss of life and of these injuries is sufficiently widespread — or that wrongs were sufficiently systematic, as opposed to isolated events (even if a series of them) — to amount definitely to a crime against humanity under already established international law.
>
> Allowing plaintiffs' claims to go forward would substantially broaden, in fact, the kinds of circumstances from which claims may properly be brought under the ATS. As we understand the established international law that can give rise to federal jurisdiction under the ATS, crimes against humanity exhibit especially wicked conduct that is carried out in an extensive, organized, and deliberate way, and that is plainly unjustified. It is this kind of hateful conduct that might make someone a common enemy of all mankind. But given international law as it is now established, the conduct described in the bare factual allegations of the Complaint is not sufficient to be a crime against humanity under the ATS.

As indicated in the final sentence, the court was also concerned about the manner in which the plaintiffs had alleged the facts in the case. Nevertheless, the court's view on the scope of crimes against humanity also drove its reasoning. Do you agree with the court's analysis in that regard? For a system of civil liability, should a set of practices be considered a crime against humanity only if the underlying conduct is extremely wicked, deliberate and hateful? Or are such factors more relevant for international criminal liability? As a separate matter, do you agree with the court's conclusion that 70 deaths and 400 injuries could not amount to a crime against humanity under the circumstances? Should the plaintiffs have refrained from making this argument? That is, should allegations of crimes against humanity be saved for more egregious cases?

Cruel, inhuman or degrading treatment. Is the prohibition on cruel, inhuman or degrading treatment (CIDT) sufficiently precise to be cognizable under the ATS? Federal courts have disagreed on this issue. Prior to *Sosa*, the Federal District Court for the Northern District of California concluded that a plaintiff 'failed to establish that there is any international consensus as to what conduct falls within the category of "cruel, inhuman or degrading treatment." Absent such consensus as to the content of this alleged tort, it is not cognizable under the Alien Tort Statute' (*Forti v. Suarez-Mason*, 694 F.Supp. 707, 712 (N.D. Cal. 1988)). Subsequent to *Sosa*, the Court of Appeals for the Eleventh Circuit overturned previous lower court decisions that had found CIDT actionable. The court stated: 'those courts relied on the International Covenant on Civil and Political Rights... [and] *Sosa* explains that the International Covenant did not "create obligations enforceable in the federal courts"' (*Aldana v. Del Monte Fresh Produce*, 416 F.3d 1242, 1247 (11th Cir. 2005)).[23]

Subsequent to *Sosa*, the Federal District Court for the Northern District of California took a different approach. Falun Gong practitioners sued local government officials of the People's Republic of China under the ATS. The court's analysis of the CIDT claim follows:[24]

> [T]he court in *Xuncax v. Gramajo*, 886 F.Supp. 162 (D. Mass. 1995), while acknowledging the complex definitional problem of this tort, reasoned that "[i]t is not

[23] Judge Barkett issued a dissent from the decision not to rehear the case *en banc* because she concluded the CIDT ruling constituted a 'precedent-setting error of exceptional importance'. *Aldana v. Del Monte Fresh Produce, N. A., Inc.*, 452 F.3d 1284 (11th Cir. 2006).

[24] *Doe v. Qi*, 349 F.Supp.2d 1258, 1321 (N.D. Cal. 2004).

necessary for every aspect of what might comprise a standard...be fully defined and universally agreed before a given action meriting the label is clearly proscribed under international law..." The focus, under *Xuncax*, is on the specific conduct at issue, and the question under the ATCA is whether that conduct is universally condemned as cruel, inhuman, or degrading....

This Court is persuaded that the *Xuncax* approach is correct....Moreover, subsequent to *Forti*, the United States ratified the International Covenant of Civil and Political Rights which prohibits, inter alia, "cruel, inhuman or degrading treatment or punishment." The fact that there may be doubt at the margins — a fact that inheres in any definition — does not negate the essence and application of that definition in clear cases.

This approach is entirely consistent with *Sosa*. The Court in *Sosa* acknowledged that the prohibition under international law of prolonged and arbitrary detention entailed a gray area at which it may be "hard [ ] to say which policies cross that line with the certainty" sufficient to state a common law claim under the ATCA; yet there are "some policies of prolonged arbitrary detentions [which] are so bad that those who enforce them become enemies of the human race." The inquiry turns on the specific facts of each case and is not precluded simply because there are questions at the margins.

...As previously noted, Plaintiffs Larsson, Lemish, and Odar allege that they were subjected to one day of incarceration and interrogation during which they were pushed, shoved, hit, and placed in a chokehold. Plaintiff Petit alleges that a police office[r] attempted to force his hand into her vagina while several other officers pinned her down.

The allegations of specific conduct must be compared with existing authorities on international law to determine whether the specific conduct alleged violated universally established norms. [The court examines several decisions by the Human Rights Committee, Committee Against Torture, the Inter-American Commission on Human Rights, the European Court of Human Rights and the African Commission on Human and Peoples' Rights.] Without diminishing the mistreatment allegedly suffered by Plaintiffs Larsson, Lemish, and Odar, their treatment pales in comparison to the acts which have been found by various courts and international authorities to constituted cruel, inhuman or degrading treatment. Simply put, a review of the authorities discussed above does not establish that the specific conduct alleged by these plaintiffs is universally prohibited by the international community as a whole. On the other hand, the sexual abuse suffered by Plaintiff Petit is different. The United Nations Committee Against Torture's Initial Report specifically lists sexual abuse as a cruel act....Plaintiff Petit has stated a claim for cruel, inhuman or degrading treatment in violation of the ATCA. Plaintiffs Larsson, Lemish, and Odar have not.

In *Mujica v. Occidental Petroleum Corp.*, 381 F. Supp. 2d 1164 (C.D. Cal. 2005), *remanded on other grnds by* 564 F.3d 1190 (9th Cir. 2009), another federal district court cited the Falun Gong case in distinguishing between different types of CIDT claims:

Plaintiffs' claims of cruel, inhuman, and degrading treatment allege that Defendant's acts resulted in gross humiliation, fear, and anguish. These actions caused Plaintiffs to fear for their lives and forced them to flee their homes. It would be impractical

> to recognize these allegations as constituting an ATS claim because it would allow foreign plaintiffs to litigate claims in U.S. courts that bear a strong resemblance to intentional infliction of emotional distress. While the Court [holds] that there is an international norm against cruel, inhuman, and degrading treatment, the broad swaths of conduct that could result in extreme fear and anguish counsel against recognizing such a claim. However, this should be taken to indicate that claims of cruel, inhuman, and degrading treatment should not be recognized when they arise out of more severe situations such as those involving sexual abuse.

The *Mujica* court explained that it was heeding *Sosa*'s admonition to consider the 'practical consequences' of expanding the causes of action under the ATS. *Mujica* noted that *Sosa* 'observed that the implications of recognizing a cause of action for arbitrary detention "would be breathtaking"'.

Is it desirable for courts, including the Supreme Court, to consider such 'practical consequences'? Should the political branches, instead of the judiciary, rein in the scope of such claims? Why is the consequence of exercising jurisdiction over acts of arbitrary detention 'breathtaking', but doing so for a single instance of torture or a single instance of sexual abuse is not? Have the courts drawn a sensible boundary?

Rationales for Limiting Causes of Action: Foreign Policy Implications

The *Sosa* opinion encourages courts to exercise 'great caution' before recognizing new violations of international law. The court explains that such 'adverse foreign policy consequences' constitute another 'reason for a high bar to new private causes of action for violating international law'. Consider the underlying assumption of the relationship between new causes of action and US foreign policy. Does the risk to US foreign policy operate only in that one direction? That is, under some circumstances, can such judicial restraint — and courts' rejection of an international norm — not also undermine US interests and the legislative and executive branches' management of foreign affairs?

Based on *Sosa*'s admonition to exercise caution, federal district courts have held that 'a claim for terrorism in general, or material support thereof, is not based on a sufficiently accepted, established, or defined norm of customary international law to constitute a violation of the law of nations'. See, e.g., *In re Chiquita Brands Intern., Inc. Alien Tort Statute and Shareholder Derivative Litigation*, 792 F.Supp.2d 1301 (S.D. Fla. 2011); *Saperstein v. Palestinian Authority*, No. 04–20225, 2006 WL 3804718 (S.D. Fla. 2006) *aff'd on other grnds* 611 F.3d 1350 (11th Cir. 2011). Similarly, in another case, plaintiffs alleged that an informant for the Israeli Government had been tortured by Palestinian forces over several months in the West Bank. Relying on *Sosa* for guidance, the Court of Appeals held that Common Article 3 of the Geneva Conventions did not apply because the torture occurred in the West Bank rather than the territory of Israel:[25]

> Article 3 applies "[i]n the case of an armed conflict not of an international character occurring in the territory of one of the High Contracting Parties."...The...difficulty

[25] *Ali Shafi v. Palestinian Authority*, 642 F.3d 1088 (D.C. Cir. 2011).

> with the Shafis' claim is that it is not obvious that Common Article 3 applies under the circumstances they have alleged.... Although Israel is a High Contracting Party to the Geneva Conventions, the PLO is not, and the status of the PLO and the nature of Israeli relations with the territory wherein the alleged torture took place, are subjects of continuing dispute. These claims fit well within the reasons provided by the Sosa Court for the cautious approach.

Note that the court's opinion might be interpreted to mean not that the judges doubted the clarity of the norm or scope of Common Article 3, but that they doubted underlying factual conditions and ancillary legal issues such as the status of the PLO. Do the reasons for *Sosa*'s cautious approach apply to such factual and legal questions as well?

In a different case involving the alleged killing of a civilian by Palestinian forces, the Court of Appeals for the Eleventh Circuit adopted a very different approach.[26] The court stated: 'there can be little doubt that the ATS permits federal courts to assert jurisdiction over hot-button matters of international law'. The court, however, took the foreign policy considerations in another direction. The court announced that ATS claims are reserved only for those causes of action that 'raise serious consequences in international affairs'. According to that criterion, the court held that 'a single murder committed by private actors... in the course of an ongoing armed conflict' does not give rise to subject matter jurisdiction under the ATS.[27] Does the court's criterion follow from *Sosa*'s explanation of the history and rationale of the ATS? Consider the Eleventh Circuit's analysis on this point:

> The Supreme Court has directed us to compare any proposed cause of action under the ATS to the three torts contemplated at the time of its passage — offenses against ambassadors, violations of safe conduct, and piracy. Violations of this "narrow set" of international norms "threaten[ed] serious consequences in international affairs," *Sosa*, 542 U.S. at 715; we cannot say the same of the murder of Ahuva Amergi.
>
> For one, the violent crime here was not committed by a state, or in concert with a state. Although state action is not required, again, its presence is powerful evidence that the crime may be one that affects "the affairs of a nation, acting in its national capacity, in relations with another nation." (citation omitted)....
>
> ...
>
> Moreover, this case differs significantly from cases in which the ATS has provided subject matter jurisdiction.... While we do not "doubt for a moment that the attack" on Ahuva Amergi and Moshe Saperstein, as alleged, "amounts to barbarity in naked and unforgivable form," *Tel-Oren*, 726 F.2d at 823 (Robb, J., concurring), it does not compare to the allegations in *Kadic*, allegations which, "if proved, would violate the most fundamental norms of the law of war," 70 F.3d at 243.

[26] *Estate of Amergi ex rel. Amergi v. Palestinian Authority*, 611 F.3d 1350 (11th Cir. 2010).

[27] This proposition is arguably dicta, because the court already concluded that (1) the plaintiffs failed to establish the existence of an armed conflict; and (2) murder (or torture) by a non-state actor would need to be committed in conjunction with other war crimes (the equivalent of a war crime nexus, not simply a war nexus).

> And in *Filartiga v. Pena-Irala*, 630 F.2d 876 (2d Cir. 1980), the Second Circuit...recognizing "the universal condemnation of torture in numerous international agreements, and the renunciation of torture as an instrument of official policy by virtually all of the nations of the world (in principle if not in practice)," held that state-sponsored torture supports jurisdiction under the ATS. Yet there is no state action in the case before this Court, and there are no international agreements, let alone numerous ones, compelling the conclusion that Ahuva Amergi's murder was a violation of the law of nations.
>
> ...
>
> Article 3 of the Geneva Conventions, which is also common to all four Conventions ("Common Article 3"), governs this conflict, and we will assume that the murder of Ahuva Amergi was a violation of Common Article 3.... [D]emonstrating a violation of the Geneva Conventions does not establish a violation of the law of nations, which is required to maintain jurisdiction under the ATS. A plaintiff must also show the violation of a norm of international law that, if left unredressed, would "threaten[ ] serious consequences in international affairs." *Sosa*, 542 U.S. at 715....
>
> A single murder, even of the most brutal sort, has never been accorded the status of a violation of the law of nations, and wrongs of this kind assuredly were not "on [the] minds of the men who drafted the ATS with its reference to tort." *Sosa*, 542 U.S. at 715. We take seriously our responsibility to guard federal jurisdiction under the ATS vigilantly, and we do that again today.

Even if the Eleventh Circuit's analysis is not necessitated by *Sosa*'s framework, does the opinion provide a principled limit on the types of actions pursued under the ATS?

TORTURE VICTIM PROTECTION ACT

106 Stat. 73 (1992), 28 U.S.C.A. 1350 Notes

...

Section 2. Establishment of Civil Action

(a) LIABILITY. — An individual who, under actual or apparent authority, or color of law, of any foreign nation –

 (1) subjects an individual to torture shall, in a civil action, be liable for damages to that individual; or

 (2) subjects an individual to extrajudicial killing shall, in a civil action, be liable for damages to the individual's legal representative, or to any person who may be a claimant in an action for wrongful death.

(b) EXHAUSTION OF REMEDIES. — A court shall decline to hear a claim under this section if the claimant has not exhausted adequate and available remedies in the place in which the conduct giving rise to the claim occurred.

(c) STATUTE OF LIMITATIONS. — No action shall be maintained under this section unless it is commenced within 10 years after the cause of action arose.

Section 3. Definitions

(a) EXTRAJUDICIAL KILLING. — For the purposes of this Act, the term 'extrajudicial killing' means a deliberated killing not authorized by a previous judgment pronounced by a regularly constituted court affording all the judicial guarantees which are recognized as indispensable by civilized peoples. Such term, however, does not include any such killing that, under international law, is lawfully carried out under the authority of a foreign nation.

(b) TORTURE. — For the purposes of this Act –

(1) the term 'torture' means any act, directed against an individual in the offender's custody or physical control, by which severe pain or suffering (other than pain or suffering arising only from or inherent in; or incidental to; lawful sanctions), whether physical, or mental, is intentionally inflicted on that individual for such purposes as obtaining from that individual or a third person information or a confession, punishing that individual for an act that individual or a third person has committed or is suspected of having committed, intimidating or coercing that individual or a third person, or for any reason based on discrimination of any kind; and

(2) mental pain or suffering refers to prolonged mental harm caused by or resulting from –

(A) the intentional infliction or threatened infliction of severe physical pain or suffering;

(B) the administration or application, or threatened administration or application, of mind altering substances or other procedures calculated to disrupt profoundly the senses or the personality;

(C) the threat of imminent death; or

(D) the threat that another individual will imminently be subjected to death, severe physical pain or suffering, or the administration or application of mind altering substances or other procedures calculated to disrupt profoundly the senses or personality.

SENATE REPORT ON THE TORTURE VICTIM PROTECTION ACT

S. Rep. 102–249, Committee on the Judiciary, 102nd Cong., 1st Sess., 1991

... This legislation will carry out the intent of the Convention against Torture and Other Cruel, Inhuman or Degrading Treatment or Punishment, which was ratified by the U.S. Senate on October 27, 1990. The convention obligates state parties to adopt measures to ensure that torturers within their territories are held legally accountable for their acts. This legislation will do precisely that — by making sure that torturers and death squads will no longer have a safe haven in the United States.

…

The TVPA would establish an unambiguous basis for a cause of action that has been successfully maintained under an existing law, section 1350 of title 28 of the U.S. Code….

…

The TVPA would…enhance the remedy already available under section 1350 in an important respect: while the Alien Tort Claims Act provides a remedy to aliens only, the TVPA would extend a civil remedy also to U.S. citizens who may have been tortured abroad.

…

IV. Analysis of Legislation

…

D. Who can be sued

First and foremost, only defendants over which a court in the United States has personal jurisdiction may be sued. In order for a Federal court to obtain personal jurisdiction over a defendant, the individual must have "minimum contacts" with the forum state, for example through residency here or current travel. Thus, this legislation will not turn the U.S. courts into tribunals for torts having no connection to the United States whatsoever.

The legislation uses the term "individual" to make crystal clear that foreign states or their entities cannot be sued under this bill under any circumstances: only individuals may be sued. Consequently, the TVPA is not meant to override the Foreign Sovereign Immunities Act (FSIA) of 1976, which renders foreign governments immune from suits in U.S. courts, except in certain instances.

The TVPA is not intended to override traditional diplomatic immunities which prevent the exercise of jurisdiction by U.S. courts over foreign diplomats. The United States is a party to the Vienna Convention on Diplomatic Relations, under which diplomats are immune from civil lawsuits except with regard to certain commercial activities.

Nor should visiting heads of state be subject to suit under the TVPA. Article 2(1) of the United Nations Convention on Special Missions provides that, when one state sends an official mission to another, the visiting head of state "shall enjoy in the receiving State or in a third State the facilities, privileges and immunities accorded by international law to Heads of State on an official visit."

However, the committee does not intend these immunities to provide former officials with a defense to a lawsuit brought under this legislation. To avoid liability by invoking the FSIA, a former official would have to prove an agency relationship to a state, which would require that the state "admit some knowledge or authorization of relevant acts." 28 U. S. C. 1603(b). Because all states are officially opposed to torture and extrajudicial killing, however, the FSIA should normally provide no defense to an action taken under the TVPA against a former official.

Similarly, the committee does not intend the "act of state" doctrine to provide a shield from lawsuit for former officials. In *Banco Nacional de Cuba v. Sabbatino*, 376 U. S. 398 (1964), the Supreme Court held that the "act of state" doctrine is meant to prevent U.S. courts from sitting in judgment of the official public acts of a sovereign foreign government. Since this doctrine applies only to "public" acts, and no state commits torture as a matter of public policy, this doctrine cannot shield former officials from liability under this legislation.

E. Scope of liability

In order for a defendant to be liable, the torture or extrajudicial killing must have been taken "under actual or apparent authority or under color of law of a foreign nation." Consequently, this legislation does not cover purely private criminal acts by individuals or nongovernmental organizations. However, because no state officially condones torture or extrajudicial killings, few such acts, if any, would fall under the rubric of "official actions" taken in the course of an official's duties. Consequently, the phrase "actual or apparent authority or under color of law" is used to denote torture and extrajudicial killings committed by officials both within and outside the scope of their authority. Courts should look to principles of liability under U.S. civil rights laws, in particular section 1983 of title 42 of the United States Code, in construing "under color of law" as well as interpretations of "actual or apparent authority" derived from agency theory in order to give the fullest coverage possible.

The legislation is limited to lawsuits against persons who ordered, abetted, or assisted in the torture. It will not permit a lawsuit against a former leader of a country merely because an isolated act of torture occurred somewhere in that country. However, a higher official need not have personally performed or ordered the abuses in order to be held liable. Under international law, responsibility for torture, summary execution, or disappearances extends beyond the person or persons who actually committed those acts — anyone with higher authority who authorized, tolerated or knowingly ignored those acts is liable for them....

...

F. Exhaustion of remedies

...Cases involving torture abroad which have been filed under the Alien Tort Claims Act show that torture victims bring suits in the United States against their alleged torturers only as a last resort. Usually, the alleged torturer has more substantial assets outside the United States and the jurisdictional nexus is easier to prove outside the United States. Therefore, as a general matter, the committee recognizes that in most instances the initiation of litigation under this legislation will be virtually prima facie evidence that the claimant has exhausted his or her remedies in the jurisdiction in which the torture occurred. The committee believes that courts should approach cases brought under the proposed legislation with this assumption.

More specifically, as this legislation involves international matters and judgments regarding the adequacy of procedures in foreign courts, the interpretation of section

2(b), like the other provisions of this act, should be informed by general principles of international law. The procedural practice of international human rights tribunals generally holds that the respondent has the burden of raising the nonexhaustion of remedies as an affirmative defense and must show that domestic remedies exist that the claimant did not use....

VII. Minority Views of Messrs. Simpson and Grassley

...

The executive branch, through the Department of Justice, has expressed a most serious concern with S. 313, which we share. Senate bill 313 could create difficulties in the management of foreign policy. For example, under this bill, individual aliens could determine the timing and manner of the making of allegations in a U.S. court about a foreign country's alleged abuses of human rights.

There is no more complex and sensitive issue between countries than human rights. The risk that would be run if an alien could have a foreign country judged by a U.S. court is too great. Judges of U.S. courts would, in a sense, conduct some of our Nation's foreign policy. The executive branch is and should remain, we believe, left with substantial foreign policy control.

In addition the Justice Department properly notes that our passage of this bill could encourage hostile foreign countries to retaliate by trying to assert jurisdiction for acts committed in the United States by the U.S. Government against U.S. citizens. For example, if this bill's principles were adopted abroad, Saddam Hussein could try a United States citizen police officer who happened to be present in Iraq, in an Iraqi court, for alleged human rights abuses against any United States citizen that the policeman happened to arrest while performing his duties in the United States.

...

COMMENT ON CRIMINAL PROSECUTION UNDER THE TORTURE CONVENTION AND FOR OTHER HUMAN RIGHTS VIOLATIONS

Although the preceding Senate Report states that the TVPA 'will carry out the intent' of the Torture Convention, it does so only with respect to civil liability. Article 14 of that Convention provides that each State Party 'shall ensure in its legal system that the victim of an act of torture obtains redress and has an enforceable right to fair and adequate compensation...'.

Compare the provisions for criminal prosecution under Article 1 of the Convention, which applies (with respect to torture, as there defined) to pain and suffering that is 'inflicted by or at the instigation of or with the consent or acquiescence of a public official or other person acting in an official capacity'. Article 2 provides that States Parties 'shall take effective...measures to prevent acts of torture' in their territory. But the Convention reaches beyond this traditional territorial base for a state's criminal jurisdiction. Under Article 4, each State Party 'shall ensure that all acts of torture are offences under its criminal law', and 'shall make these offences punishable by appropriate penalties'. Article 5 provides the grounds for establishing jurisdiction:

1. Each State Party shall take such measures as may be necessary to establish its jurisdiction over the offences referred to in article 4 in the following cases:
   (i) When the offences are committed in any territory under its jurisdiction or on board a ship or aircraft registered in that State;
   (ii) When the alleged offender is a national of that State;
   (iii) When the victim was a national of that State if that State considers it appropriate.
2. Each State Party shall likewise take such measures as may be necessary to establish its jurisdiction over such offences in cases where the alleged offender is present in any territory under its jurisdiction and it does not extradite him... to any of the States mentioned in Paragraph 1 of this article.

In 1990, the Senate Committee on Foreign Relations reported favourably on the Convention and recommended that the Senate give its consent to ratification. With respect to Section (1) of Article 5, the Committee report states:[28]

> A major concern in drafting Article 5... was whether the Convention should provide for possible prosecution by any State in which the alleged offender is found — so-called universal jurisdiction.[29] The United States strongly supported the provision for universal jurisdiction, on the grounds that torture, like hijacking, sabotage, hostage-taking, and attacks on internationally protected persons, is an offense of special international concern, and should have similarly broad, universal recognition as a crime against humanity, with appropriate jurisdictional consequences. Provision for 'universal jurisdiction' was also deemed important in view of the fact that the government of the country where official torture actually occurs may seldom be relied on to take action.... [E]xisting federal and state law appears sufficient to establish jurisdiction when the offense has allegedly been committed in any territory under U.S. jurisdiction.... Implementing legislation is therefore needed only to establish Article 5(1)(b) jurisdiction over offenses committed by U.S. nationals outside the United States, and to establish Article 5(2) jurisdiction over foreign offenders committing torture abroad who are later found in territory under U.S. jurisdiction.... Similar legislation has already been enacted to implement comparable provisions of the Conventions on Hijacking, Sabotage, Hostages, and Protection of Diplomats.

[28] Sen. Comm. For. Relations, Report on Convention against Torture, 100th Cong., 2d Sess. (1990).

[29] [Eds.: A discussion and illustrations of general bases for jurisdiction including universal jurisdiction appear at p. 1123, *supra*.]

In 1990, the Senate consented to ratification of the Convention, provided that the criminal legislation required by the Convention first be enacted by Congress. The Torture Convention Implementing Legislation was enacted in 1994, 18 U.S.C.A. 2340–2340B. Section 2340A gives courts jurisdiction for torture (as defined) committed 'outside the United States' where the alleged offender is a US national or 'is present in the United States, irrespective of the nationality of the victim or alleged offender'. The United States then ratified the Convention.

It was not until December 2006 that the US Government launched its first prosecution for the crime of torture. The US attorneys charged US citizen Charles McArther Emmanuel, alias 'Chuckie' Taylor, son of former Liberian President Charles Taylor, for multiple acts of torture committed in Liberia. President Taylor placed his 20-year-old son in charge of the Liberian Antiterrorist Unit (also known in Liberia as the 'Demon Forces'). At the time of the incidents, the defendant was commander of the unit. He was charged for multiple acts of torture including burning victims' flesh with a hot iron, molten plastic, lit cigarettes and scalding water; repeatedly electrically shocking a victim's genitalia and other body parts; severely beating victims with firearms; and cutting and stabbing victims. He was convicted and sentenced to 97 years in prison. He lost his appeal in 2010. Notably, in a submission to the UN in 2010, the US Government stated 'the US law would have permitted prosecution based solely on the principle of universality and the offender's presence in the United States', but there was an 'alternative bas[i]s for jurisdiction' in this particular case.

In 2009, the Department of Justice established the Human Rights and Special Prosecutions Section, which, among other activities, took over responsibility for the prosecution of Chuckie Taylor. That section has also prosecuted cases involving other serious human rights violations. In some cases, the government has not directly charged individuals with the underlying crime — as it did in the *Taylor* case — due to a lack of jurisdiction. Instead, prosecutions include charges such as unlawfully procuring US citizenship, visa fraud or making a false statement to a federal agency by concealing information (about such matters as prior membership in a foreign military group or the commission of a crime for which the person had not been arrested). For example, the Department of Justice prosecuted Gilberto Jordan for lying on his application for US citizenship by concealing his involvement in a well-known massacre in the village of Dos Erres, Guatemala in 1982. In 2010, Jordan plead guilty and was sentenced to the statutory maximum of 10 years in prison and stripped of his citizenship.

Other US statutes provide criminal jurisdiction for human rights violations committed by a non-US national against a non-US national in a foreign country — as long as the perpetrator is present in the United States. These statutes include the following offences: genocide, war crimes and the recruitment and use of child soldiers. Similar statutes provide jurisdiction for acts of terrorism, hostage-taking and attacks against internationally protected persons (which includes members of intergovernmental organizations such as UN human rights officials). It is also a federal offence for an foreign national who is a permanent resident in the United States (as well as for US citizens) to travel abroad to engage in sexual conduct with a minor (child sex trafficking).

SANDRA COLIVER, JENNIE GREEN & PAUL HOFFMAN, HOLDING HUMAN RIGHTS VIOLATORS ACCOUNTABLE BY USING INTERNATIONAL LAW IN US COURTS: ADVOCACY EFFORTS AND COMPLEMENTARY STRATEGIES

19 Emory Int'l. L. Rev. 169 (2005)

[The authors are among the leading litigators who have helped to bring many of the ATS and TVPA cases. They are respectively Executive Director, the Center for Justice & Accountability; Senior Attorney, Center for Constitutional Rights; Partner, Schonbrun, DeSimone, Seplow, Harris & Hoffman, LLP.]

Since 1980, at least sixteen human rights perpetrators (including Pena-Irala, the defendant in the landmark *Filartiga* case) have been sued successfully.[30] One of those was a current high-ranking government official: the Bosnian Serb leader Radovan Karadzic. Seven were former high-ranking civilian or military officials who continued to exercise considerable influence in their countries. All were found to have had substantial responsibility for egregious human rights violations, to be subject to the personal jurisdiction of the court, and not to be entitled to immunity from suit (sovereign, diplomatic, or otherwise). In all cases, the plaintiffs satisfied the requirements of standing and the statute of limitations, and demonstrated that they had exhausted any available and effective remedies in their home countries. In several cases the courts expressly found that the cases did not pose a significant interference to U.S. foreign policy or that the act of state doctrine applied.

...

1. Ensuring that the U.S. Does Not Remain a Safe Haven for Human Rights Abusers

The Center for Justice and Accountability ("CJA") estimates that several hundred human rights abusers now live in the United States with substantial responsibility for heinous atrocities, and that several dozen high-level perpetrators visit every year. These figures are supported by estimates from the U.S. Bureau of Immigration and Customs Enforcement (ICE). They have come from more than seventy countries, including Bosnia, Cambodia, Chile, El Salvador, Ethiopia, Guatemala, Haiti, Honduras, India, Liberia, Pakistan, Peru, Rwanda, Sierra Leone, Somalia, Sri Lanka, and Vietnam. Only a few dozen human rights abusers have been deported, in addition to the approximately ninety who were denaturalized, deported, or extradited for Naziera crimes. Most of the non-Nazis have been deported since 2000. Most of them are low-level abusers and nearly half are Haitian. The majority of them are identified in the asylum process when they declare that their fear of persecution

[30] [Eds.: The authors list numerous federal court decisions and defendants including a Paraguayan police chief, Argentinian general, Bosnian Serb leader, Guatemalan former defence minister, Bolivian corporation and civilian, Ghanaian security officer, former President of the Philippines, Rwandan radio station owner and political party leader, Indonesian general, former Haitian military ruler, Bosnian Serb paramilitary member, Ethiopian former municipal official, Chilean former member of military death squad, Salvadoran key organizer of Archbishop Romero assassination, Beijing Mayor and former Salvadoran generals and ministers of defence.]

is based on the fact that they were part of a unit that participated in human rights atrocities....

...Of the sixteen individuals who have been successfully sued using the ATS, one was deported based on information uncovered by the plaintiffs, one was extradited, one died, and ten left the country never to return (as far as we know), including five who had moved to the United States to settle. Only three of the sixteen remain in the United States and, of those, one has been denaturalized and is in detention while he awaits deportation; the other two are subject to deportation investigations based in large part on evidence uncovered during the course of the ATS cases.

These sixteen cases appear to have deterred numerous human rights perpetrators from coming to the United States. Following the ATS case against Paraguayan police chief Pena-Irala, the U.S. consulate in Paraguay reported a decrease in visas to visit the United States requested by Paraguayan officials and military officers. The Shah of Iran was the last major human rights abuser to seek medical treatment openly in the United States.... Salvadorans who have been watching for the entry of Salvadoran military officers who used to travel regularly to Miami and southern California report that they are no longer coming here. Immigration agents have confirmed that certain named human rights abusers from Central America stopped coming to the States after mid-2002, after two Salvadoran former defense ministers were found liable by a Florida jury and ordered to pay $54 million to the plaintiffs.

2. *Holding Perpetrators Accountable*

...Although the punishment does not fit the severity of the crimes, these civil cases are generally the only remedies available to survivors. The cases expose what the perpetrators have done and cause embarrassment to the perpetrators. In some cases, being sued under the ATS or TVPA may limit the careers of foreign officials if their advancement depends on their ability to travel to the United States without controversy. The lawsuits prevent foreign human rights violators from visiting or resettling in the United States with impunity.... In addition, lawyers continue to pursue the collection of assets in past judgments and increasingly are pursuing defendants with assets that may be reachable by U.S. courts.

Hector Gramajo, a Guatemalan ex-general, was one of those who fled the United States after being served with an ATS complaint in 1991. He had been grooming himself to run for the presidency of his country and had come to the United States to obtain a degree from the Kennedy School at Harvard. On his graduation day, he was served with the lawsuit. He immediately returned to Guatemala, his U.S. visa was revoked, and his party decided not to choose him as its presidential candidate. His inability to travel to the United States without embarrassment was a liability. Gramajo's political ambitions were harmed by the lawsuit and the public exposure surrounding it.

...

Kelbessa Negewo, held responsible by a federal court in Atlanta for acts of torture during the "Red Terror" in Ethiopia, lost several jobs as a result of the civil judgment and was denaturalized largely based on evidence produced at the civil trial....

The collection of ATS monetary judgments, however, has been difficult. It is believed that there has been money collected in only three of the individual defendant cases: a little more than $1 million from the estate of Philippine President Ferdinand Marcos,[31] and approximately $1,000 each from General Suarez-Mason and Kelbessa Negewo. In 2003, $270, 000 was collected from one of the defendants in the Romagoza case.[32]

…

3. Official Acknowledgment and Reparation for the Human Rights Victims and Survivors

These cases often help survivors experience a sense of justice, a sense of meaning in their survival, and tremendous satisfaction in knowing that they have brought dignity to the memories of those who were killed or tortured.… [T]he cases can serve as a kind of mini-truth commission.…

For instance, Juan Romagoza, a Salvadoran torture survivor, stated:

> When I testified, a strength came over me. I felt like I was in the prow of a boat and that there were many, many people rowing behind. I felt that if I looked back, I'd weep because I'd see them again: wounded, tortured, raped, naked, torn, bleeding. So, I didn't look back, but I felt their support, their strength, their energy. Being involved in this case, confronting the generals with these terrible facts — that's the best possible therapy a torture survivor could have.

7. Contributing to Transitional Justice

ATS cases can serve as a catalyst for the process of transitional justice in the home country.… By demonstrating that impunity can be challenged, ATS cases can stimulate discussion about the crimes of the past and build support for bringing perpetrators to justice in their own domestic courts. For instance, the Abebe-Jira case had an effect on public opinion in Ethiopia and on the commitment of the Ethiopian government to move forward with trials of former officials of the Dergue.[33]

…

The Romagoza case also stimulated witnesses to come forward with evidence against two more Salvadoran perpetrators who have lived in the United States for more than fifteen years: one of the organizers of the 1980 assassination of Archbishop Oscar Romero and Colonel Carranza, Head of the Hacienda (Treasury) Police, who was forced out of the military in 1985 as a result of his responsibility for

[31] A $150 million settlement was approved in the Marcos case but the Philippine courts blocked the transfer of Marcos's assets after the Philippine government intervened to claim the assets for itself.…Of course, all of the Holocaust Assets cases included ATS claims and billions of dollars in settlements have been achieved in those cases. Lawyers involved in these suits…have credited the foundation of ATS jurisprudence as being crucial in their efforts to obtain justice for victims of the Holocaust. See, e.g., Burt Neuborne, Preliminary Reflections on Aspects of Holocaust-Era Litigation in American Courts, 80 Wash. U. L.Q.795 nn.29–30 (2002).

[32] However, unless the reversal of this judgment is overturned, the funds collected will have to be returned. CJA has put special focus on collecting the assets of the individual defendants it sues and on taking cases where such collection is possible.…

[33] Plaintiffs' counsel was invited to give a nationally televised address during a visit to Ethiopia after the trial in March 1994. The case received substantial publicity within Ethiopia and within Ethiopian communities outside the country.

atrocities which endangered the continuation of U.S. military aid to El Salvador. Following the issuance of the verdict in the Romero case in September 2004, key representatives of the Catholic Church in El Salvador for the first time called for revisions to the amnesty law and a reopening of the criminal investigation into the assassination. The Archbishop of San Salvador stated that the verdict should help to establish Archbishop Romero's martyrdom, by having proved who was involved in the assassination plot.

M. O. CHIBUNDU, MAKING CUSTOMARY INTERNATIONAL LAW THROUGH MUNICIPAL ADJUDICATION: A STRUCTURAL INQUIRY

39 Va. J. Int'l. L. 1069 (1999)

... Even when one accepts the underlying norms of individual rights..., the proposition that these rights should be enforced in the domestic courts of any country without regard to the traditional concerns over sovereignty is flawed for numerous reasons, not the least of which are the paradoxes that are embedded in the claim.

The most obvious but telling paradox is that these "individual rights" claims invariably seem to arise from the most contested political conflicts in the Third World. Indeed, a recent survey of the litigation of "international human rights claims" in U.S. courts might easily have substituted as a current affairs topics primer of the trouble-spots of the non-Western world.... [T]he persistent and unilaterally-arrived-at decision by the courts of one nation to sit in judgment over political cases that consistently touch on the raw nerves of the internal conflicts of other societies surely push right up against (if it does not cross) well-tested norms in international law such as those of self-determination.

And here is to be found another paradox. One significant effect of "individual rights" litigation in courts purporting to apply "universal" law may be to deprive the local courts in strife-ridden countries the opportunity to develop and internalize those very same norms.... The losing elites in the political turbulences of the Third World, aided and abetted by the contingent interest groups that invariably emerge in the West — sometimes in response to the pull of social affinities like race, religion, ethnicity and national origin, and other times to the push of ideology or visual journalism — will invoke the well-developed, efficient and potentially remunerative Western judiciary to continue "by other means" the wars lost at home. Meanwhile, their local judiciaries atrophy. Individual rights are ignored in the home country, and the success of the local victors will continue to depend less on the judicial fashioning and enforcement of "individual rights" than on the extrajudicial mauling of opponents. Thus, even if one accepts that "human rights" are "universal" and "individual," the process by which the norm is actualized makes a good deal of difference.... To deprive turbulent societies of this necessary process under the guise of international humanism is no less imperial — and with about the same likely consequences — as were the European colonial "civilizing missions" of the nineteenth and early twentieth centuries.... [W]hatever its benefits may be to specific individuals in the short run, its effect is to contribute mightily to deprive the "backward societies" of the opportunity for nurture from within and the internalization of the necessary experiences without which those very cherished Western seeds of "democratic pluralism" and "individual rights" will not flourish.

...

...Interest groups in the United States, for example, purporting to act on behalf of individuals and groups living under such acknowledged repressive regimes as that of Ferdinand Marcos in the Philippines, Sani Abacha in Nigeria, and Suharto in Indonesia, have not limited their claims to core human rights claims such as torture, arbitrary arrests, unexplained disappearances or even "extrajudicial" killings — as substantial as such claims may be — but have asserted as remediable in U.S. courts alleged economic wrongs such as the uncompensated taking of the property of a local national by that local government, or the unregulated pollution of the local environment as a result of ill-advised policies by those governments. Nor have such actions been limited to miscreant government officials whose future conduct is sought to be deterred. Rather, these *Filartiga*-type actions have been read to embrace conduct by commercial concerns integrally involved in structuring the national economy, as well as by rebel movements in conflicts that are essentially about the internal self-determination and alignment of political power within these countries. In short, such proponents of the "universal jurisdiction" of U.S. courts in human rights cases assert, under the aegis of the ATCA and U.S. law, the imperial right to judicially impose wholesale structural reforms — political, social and economic — on societies whose human rights practices are deemed to be backward. Perhaps the societies would benefit from such changes, but it is surely questionable whether it is within the province of a judicial proceeding to undertake such systemic reconfiguration of a foreign society.

...

When one factors in such other considerations as the non-contemporaneity of the interests that are weighed (that is, power, interests, burdens and benefit are all dynamic and will have different weights over time), it becomes all too clear why civil judicial relief by the courts of a political system far removed from the events that it seeks to regulate is not only a blunt tool, but is entirely inadequate for the task....

...

...Although fashionable, it is a mistake to equate "justice" with "punishment." What is important is that the experience of trying to come to grips with the interplay of criminality and politics within the particular society is one that shapes the structures and institutions of that society, not the least of which are the judiciary and related institutions. Whether South Africa's Truth and Reconciliation Commission works or fails, the one certainty is that South Africans will learn from it, and cannot shift the responsibility for its failure (or for that matter allot the credit for its success) to others. Similarly, but of no small consequence, Westerners will not always saddle themselves with the guilt of failure, or, as is more likely the case, invariably take credit for the "new South Africa," effectively minimizing the role of the local population in its self-actualization.

...

As appealing as it may thus appear at first blush, the arrogation by a municipal court of the unbridled power to punish wrongdoing under the guise of enforcing international law should be resisted not only on account of its effectiveness, but more fundamentally because of what it says about the social distribution of power within the international community....Just as colonial outposts were incidental objects of metropolitan politics in late nineteenth and early twentieth centuries' European politics, so also is the fixation today on the undoubted atrocities taking place in some developing societies. Consider, for example, how much knowledge of these developing societies is possessed by those who, at the drop of a hat, are only too willing to brandish summons and complaints of human rights violations in those societies? Is the television camera any less superficial as a recorder of history than the yellow rags of the late nineteenth century?

...If the international community of jurists is to create an enduring jurisprudence of international human rights law, it will be because those norms converge from adjudications in multiple jurisdictions each reflecting the socio-political structures of its constitution, while seeking to conform local practices to evolving international standards.

QUESTIONS

1. Are you persuaded by Professor Chibundu's critique of ATS litigation? How much, if any, of his argument hinges on the notion that ATS cases will be used to vindicate norms far in excess of *jus cogens* violations (e.g., property violations)? If courts do not actually accept such attempts to stretch the doctrine, is his general argument substantially weakened?

2. Professor Chibundu's admonitions might apply not only to courts, but also directly to the organizations litigating these cases. What recommendations, if any, would you suggest to such an organization in light of his critiques?

3. Does ATS and TVPA litigation 'deprive the local courts in strife-ridden countries the opportunity to develop and internalize those very same norms'? Consider also the US Government's position on universal jurisdiction which raises similar concerns, p. 1143, *supra*. Can US federal courts develop and apply legal doctrines to address such concerns while still fully vindicating human rights? Consider, for example, the requirement that plaintiffs exhaust domestic remedies, which is referenced in *Sosa* and codified in the TVPA, p. 1173, *supra*. How might Lutz and Sikkink's article relate to this set of questions? Consider the following application of Lutz and Sikkink's work by the Court of Appeals for the Ninth Circuit—a remarkable reference to political science scholarship by a federal court:[34]

> [T]he argument that requiring exhaustion will improve compliance with international human rights law in other countries because it provides an incentive for those

[34] *Sarei v. Rio Tinto, PLC.*, 487 F.3d 1193 (9th Cir. 2007) *aff'd in part, rev'd in part by* 550 F.3d 822 (9th Cir. 2008) (*en banc*).

countries to improve their legal systems appears plausible on its face. (See Dissent at 1239–41.) Although advanced with some frequency, however, this argument remains fairly speculative and most often lacks any empirical data showing improvements in the quality or accessibility of local remedies as a result of the application of the local remedies rule at the international level.... An alternative and perhaps equally plausible hypothesis is that "[f]oreign court rulings against rights-abusing defendants have the effect of putting pressure 'from above' on the state where the rights abuses occurred." Ellen Lutz & Kathryn Sikkink, The Justice Cascade: The Evolution and Impact of Human Rights Trials in Latin America, 2 Chi. J. Int'l L. 1, 4 (2001); see also id. at 24–25, 30 (discussing the possibility that the arrest and near trial of General Pinochet in Europe and European court cases against Argentine military officers were catalysts in Chile and Argentina, respectively, for more aggressive pursuit of human rights suits in those countries). If this alternative hypothesis were true, the absence of the exhaustion rule, not its presence, would contribute to the development of effective remedies for human rights abuses.

[The majority analysis responds, in part, to the following passages from Judge Jay Bybee in dissent.]

By accepting jurisdiction over foreign suits that can be appropriately handled locally, the federal courts embroil the nation in a kind of judicial "imperialism"...

...The principle in international practice is "not to submit [the claimant] to a mere judicial exercise," but is "intended to afford the territorial government an opportunity actually to repair the injury sustained." The exhaustion rule is part of a concerted international effort to encourage countries to provide effective local remedies.

This consideration provides perhaps the most important practical consideration for the adoption of an exhaustion requirement in ATCA. If litigants are allowed to seek refuge in U.S. courts before pursuing available remedies at home, we will have facilitated parties — including politically-minded parties — who wish to circumvent the creation and refinement of local remedies.

...

Moreover, litigation is not always the best vehicle for resolving difficult internal matters. Exhaustion may thus encourage creative political solutions beyond our ken. The exhaustion requirement 'acknowledges that a sovereign is not only in the best position to succeed, particularly when acting within its own territory, but that a sovereign is also most familiar with the situation and best able to fashion a remedy appropriate to local circumstances.' Richard D. Glick, Environmental Justice in the United States: Implications of the International Covenant on Civil and Political Rights, 19 Harv. Envt'l. L. Rev. 69, 99 (1995).

COMMENT ON FOREIGN POLICY IMPACT

In *Sosa*, the court stated that there were other considerations to take into account before exercising jurisdiction in addition to the status of the human rights norm. The court explained that 'another possible limitation that we need not apply here is a policy of case-specific deference to the political branches'. When is such deference, if ever, appropriate? The court, in a remarkable step, referred to ongoing ATS litigation (against corporations that allegedly supported South Africa's apartheid regime). The court added, '[i]n such cases, there is a strong argument that federal courts should give serious weight to the Executive Branch's view of the case's impact on foreign policy.' Importantly, this consideration supplements the foreign policy considerations we discussed earlier. In the latter context, the court was concerned about the content of the human rights norm. The policy of case-specific deference to the political branches, however, could apply even if the status of the human rights norm is well settled. For instance, courts could defer to an Executive Branch determination that adjudication of widespread torture in a particular country would have a substantial negative impact on foreign policy.

Subsequent to *Sosa*, several federal courts have grappled with this consideration. A starting point in their analyses is often the political question doctrine. Under that doctrine, courts may decline to exercise jurisdiction over a case if the controversy is determined to involve a political question. According to the leading Supreme Court decision, *Baker v. Carr*, 369 U.S. 186 (1962), such a determination involves six factors:

> Prominent on the surface of any case held to involve a political question is found [1] a textually demonstrable constitutional commitment of the issue to a coordinate political department; or [2] a lack of judicially discoverable and manageable standards for resolving it; or [3] the impossibility of deciding without an initial policy determination of a kind clearly for nonjudicial discretion; or [4] the impossibility of a court's undertaking independent resolution without expressing lack of the respect due coordinate branches of government; or [5] an unusual need for unquestioning adherence to a political decision already made; or [6] the potentiality of embarrassment from multifarious pronouncements by various departments on one question.

The US Government submitted Statements of Interest (SOI) in multiple cases decided subsequent to *Sosa*. Courts generally responded by closely parsing the text of the Statement to determine the nature and strength of the government's concern and by analysing whether the exercise of jurisdiction would interfere with existing US policy. In short, they engaged in case-by-case analyses. Consider the following examples.

Doe v. Exxon Mobil I & II

473 F.3d 345 (Court of Appeals for the District of Columbia 2007) and 654 F.3d 11 (Court of Appeals for the District of Columbia 2011)

[Eleven Indonesian villagers alleged that Exxon's security forces, comprised exclusively of members of the Indonesian military and serving under the 'direction and control' of Exxon, committed murder, torture, sexual assault, battery, false imprisonment and other torts. The defendants asked the Court of Appeals to halt the lower court proceedings by issuing a writ of mandamus. Such an interlocutory motion would, according to the court's judgment in 2007, need to satisfy an especially high standard, that is, the appellate court would 'have to hold that the district court "clearly and indisputabl[y]" exceeded its jurisdiction by refusing to dismiss this case under the political question doctrine.' On that basis, the Court of Appeals proceeded to analyse Exxon's petition.]

Doe v. Exxon Mobil I (2007)

At the outset, we note that the district court has taken several steps to limit the scope of this litigation. For example, the court dismissed the plaintiffs' claims against a natural gas company that was partially owned by the Indonesian government because including this entity as a party would "create a significant risk of interfering in Indonesian affairs and thus U.S. foreign policy concerns." Likewise, the district court has greatly curtailed discovery in this case; for example, Exxon will not be required to produce documents from its Indonesian operations unless it receives all "necessary authorizations" from the Indonesian government. The district court imposed this limitation to ensure that there would be no discovery of documents that the Indonesian government deems classified or confidential.

We disagree with Exxon's contention that there is a conflict between the views of the State Department and those of the district court. In a letter... the Legal Adviser of the State Department noted that adjudication of the plaintiffs' claims would "risk a potentially serious adverse impact on significant interests of the United States." However, the letter also contained several important qualifications. It noted that the effects of this suit on U.S. foreign policy interests "cannot be determined with certainty." Moreover, the letter stated that its assessment of the litigation was "necessarily predictive and contingent on how the case might unfold in the course of litigation." Most importantly, the State Department emphasized that whether this case would adversely affect U.S. foreign policy depends upon "the nature, extent, and intrusiveness of discovery." We interpret the State Department's letter not as an unqualified opinion that this suit must be dismissed, but rather as a word of caution to the district court alerting it to the State Department's concerns. Indeed, the fact that the letter refers to "how the case might unfold in the course of the litigation" shows that the State Department did not necessarily expect the district court to immediately dismiss the case in its entirety. Thus, we need not decide what level of deference would be owed to a letter from the State Department that unambiguously requests that the district court dismiss a case as a non-justiciable political question. See *Sosa v. Alvarez-Machain*, 542 U. S. 692, 733 n. 21 (2004). Of course, if we have misinterpreted this letter, or if the State Department has additional concerns about this litigation, it is free to file further letters or briefs with the district court expressing its views....

But given the letter before us in the record, we cannot say it is "indisputable" that the district court erroneously failed to dismiss the plaintiffs' claims under the political question doctrine, no matter what level of deference is owed to the State Department's letter.

Doe v. Exxon Mobil II (2011)

The interlocutory appeal decided only that Exxon lacked a "clear and indisputable" right to a writ of mandamus ordering appellants' common law tort claims to be dismissed under the political question doctrine. Now this court reviews *de novo* the district court's decision to dismiss those claims. Subsequent events persuade us that the considered analysis by this court in *Doe I* is correct. The Supreme Court denied Exxon's petition for a writ of *certiorari*, which the United States opposed. The United States stated that "[t]he district court carefully considered concerns identified by the United States in its submissions to that court," noting dismissal of the federal law claims, "all claims against a defendant indirectly owned by the Indonesian government," and the "limit[ ] [on] discovery in a manner intended to avoid offending Indonesia's sovereign interests." Brief for the United States as Amicus Curiae, Exxon Mobil Corp. v. Doe I, 554 U.S. 909 (2008) (No. 07–81), 2008 WL 2095734, at *8. Further, that "[i]n light of that procedural history and *the absence of a request by the United States that the case be dismissed in its entirety*, the court of appeals reasonably regarded petitioners' interlocutory appeal as one from the denial of a motion to dismiss state-law tort claims based on an assertion by private defendants, *not by the Executive*, that the litigation itself would have adverse consequences for the Nation's foreign policy interests and thus raised separation-of-powers concerns." Id., 2008 WL 2095734, at *8–9 (emphasis added). Appellants also cite an *amicus* brief filed by the United States before the Second Circuit, emphasizing that the "requirement of an *explicit* request for dismissal on foreign policy grounds by the Executive Branch is, in our view, critical." Brief for the United States as Amicus Curiae at 11, *Balintulo v. Daimler AG*, No. 09–2778–cv (2d Cir. Nov. 30, 2009) (emphasis in original). The Executive Branch has made no such request in the instant cases.

...Currently the court has no occasion to "decide what level of deference would be owed to a letter from the State Department that *unambiguously* requests that the district court dismiss a case as a non-justiciable political question." *Doe I*, 473 F.3d at 354 (emphasis in original). Before this court are only: (1) an ambiguous statement of interest by the State Department in 2002 regarding the plaintiffs' litigation, respecting both the federal statutory and non-federal tort claims; (2) an *amicus* brief filed by the Solicitor General and the State Department's Legal Advisor emphasizing that the statement of interest did not constitute an explicit request for dismissal and affirming that the district court had mitigated the concerns of the United States regarding discovery; (3) silence from the United States in the years since the United States' statement as *amicus* to the Supreme Court, notwithstanding this court's invitation in *Doe I* to file a further statement of interest; and (4) an *amicus* brief filed by the United States in another circuit emphasizing that the United States will make an explicit request for dismissal when appropriate. Also lodged but not filed in this court is a letter of January 24, 2011 from the Indonesian Embassy expressing continuing objection to plaintiffs' lawsuits. Given the United States' subsequent filings — and subsequent silence — the court concludes that it did not misinterpret the Legal Advisor's 2002 statement of interest.

Nonetheless, insofar as the court is reviving appellants' ATS claims...the court recognizes the United States had previously expressed concern. Although the court lacks a sufficiently unambiguous and recent statement from the United States expressing concern as would justify dismissal of the ATS claims on justiciability grounds, if the State Department were to reassert concerns, as it has been invited to do, this court or, upon remand, the district court in the first instance, must assess whether they provide grounds for dismissing the complaints or a part thereof, particularly with regard to the ATS claims....

Joo v. Japan

413 F. 3d 45 (Court of Appeals for the District of Columbia 2005)

[Fifteen former 'comfort women', from China, the Philippines, South Korea and Taiwan, brought an ATS action against Japan. The plaintiffs alleged that they were abducted, forced into sexual slavery and routinely subject to rape, torture and mutilation by the Japanese Army during the Second World War. The defendant argued that their claims were foreclosed by a series of peace agreements between Japan and the plaintiffs' governments. Relying on *Sosa* and *Baker*, the Court of Appeals held that the court was an inappropriate forum to resolve such issues.]

As we explained in our previous opinion, Article 14 of the 1951 Treaty of Peace between Japan and the Allied Powers "expressly waives…'all claims of the Allied Powers and their nationals arising out of any actions taken by Japan and its nationals in the course of the prosecution of the war."'

The appellants from China, Taiwan, and South Korea argue that because their governments were not parties to the 1951 Treaty, the waiver of claims provision in Article 14 did not extinguish their claims.…Although the appellants acknowledge that "it may seem anomalous that aliens may sue where similar claims of U.S. nationals are waived," they argue "that is precisely the result contemplated by…the [Alien Tort Statute"].

"Anomalous" is an understatement. See Statement of Interest of the United States ("it manifestly was not the intent of the President and Congress to preclude Americans from bringing their war-related claims against Japan…while allowing federal or state courts to serve as a venue for the litigation of similar claims by non-US nationals"). Even if we assume, however, as the appellants contend, that the 1951 Treaty does not of its own force deprive the courts of the United States of jurisdiction over their claims, it is pellucidly clear the Allied Powers intended that all war-related claims against Japan be resolved through government-to-government negotiations rather than through private tort suits. Indeed, Article 26 of the Treaty obligated Japan to enter "bilateral" peace treaties with non-Allied states "on the same or substantially the same terms as are provided for in the present treaty".…

…

As evidenced by the 1951 Treaty itself, when negotiating peace treaties,

> governments have dealt with…private claims as their own, treating them as national assets, and as counters, 'chips', in international bargaining. Settlement agreements have lumped, or linked, claims deriving from private debts with others that were intergovernmental in origin, and concessions in regard to one category of claims might be set off against concessions in the other, or against larger political considerations unrelated to debts.

Louis Henkin, Foreign Affairs and the Constitution 300 (2nd edn. 1996)

…Indeed, Professor Henkin reports that "except as an agreement might provide otherwise, international claim settlements generally wipe out the underlying private debt, terminating any recourse under domestic law as well."…

…

...In order to adjudicate the plaintiffs' claims, the court would have to resolve their dispute with Japan over the meaning of the treaties between Japan and Taiwan, South Korea, and China, which, as the State Department notes...would require the court to determine "the effects of those agreements on the rights of their citizens with respect to events occurring outside the United States."

The question whether the war-related claims of foreign nationals were extinguished when the governments of their countries entered into peace treaties with Japan is one that concerns the United States only with respect to her foreign relations, the authority for which is demonstrably committed by our Constitution not to the courts but to the political branches, with "the President [having] the 'lead role."' *Garamendi*, 539 U. S. at 423 n. 12. And with respect to that question, the history of management by the political branches, *Baker*, 369 U. S. at 211, is clear and consistent: Since the conclusion of World War II, it has been the foreign policy of the United States "to effect as complete and lasting a peace with Japan as possible by closing the door on the litigation of war-related claims, and instead effecting the resolution of those claims through political means."...

...

...[T]he United States is not a party to the treaties the meaning of which is in dispute, and the Executive does not urge us to adopt a particular interpretation of those treaties. Rather, the Executive has persuasively demonstrated that adjudication by a domestic court not only "would undo" a settled foreign policy of state-to-state negotiation with Japan, but also could disrupt Japan's "delicate" relations with China and Korea, thereby creating "serious implications for stability in the region."...Is it the province of a court in the United States to decide whether Korea's or Japan's reading of the treaty between them is correct, when the Executive has determined that choosing between the interests of two foreign states in order to adjudicate a private claim against one of them would adversely affect the foreign relations of the United States? Decidedly not. The Executive's judgment that adjudication by a domestic court would be inimical to the foreign policy interests of the United States is compelling and renders this case nonjusticiable under the political question doctrine.

...[W]e defer to "the considered judgment of the Executive on [this] particular question of foreign policy." *Republic of Austria v. Altmann*, 541 U. S. at 702. For the court to disregard that judgment, to which the Executive has consistently adhered, and which it persuasively articulated in this case, would be imprudent to a degree beyond our power.

Sarei v. Rio Tinto

456 F. 3d 1069 (Court of Appeals for the Ninth Circuit 2006) *aff'd* 2011 WL 5041927 (2011) (*en banc*)

[Current and former residents of Bougainville, an island province of Papua New Guinea (PNG), sued Rio Tinto, an international mining company headquartered in London. Rio Tinto, with the assistance of the PNG Government, allegedly engaged in war crimes involving aerial bombardment of civilian targets, burning of villages and rape. In November 2001, the US Department of State filed an SOI in response to a request by the US federal district court. The opinion of the Court of Appeals follows.[35]]

After noting that the district court had not asked the United States to comment on the act of state and political question doctrines, the State Department reported that "in our judgment, continued adjudication of the claims . . . would risk a potentially serious adverse impact on the peace process, and hence on the conduct of our foreign relations," and that PNG, a "friendly foreign state, "had" perceive[d] the potential impact of this litigation on U.S.-PNG relations, and wider regional interests, to be 'very grave." Attached to the SOI was the PNG government's communique stating that the case "has potentially very serious social, economic, legal, political and security implications for" PNG, including adverse effects on PNG's international relations, "especially its relations with the United States."

...

We first observe that without the SOI, there would be little reason to dismiss this case on political question grounds, and therefore that the SOI must carry the primary burden of establishing a political question. There is no independent reason why the claims presented to us raise any warning flags as infringing on the prerogatives of our Executive Branch. As such, these claims can be distinguished from cases in which the claims by their very nature present political questions requiring dismissal. See, e. g., *Alperin v. Vatican Bank*, 410 F. 3d 532, 562 (9th Cir. 2005) (identifying nonjusticiable political question presented by claims regarding alleged war crimes of an enemy of the United States committed during World War II). The Supreme Court has been clear that "it is error to suppose that every case or controversy which touches foreign relations lies beyond judicial cognizance," and that the doctrine "is one of 'political questions,' not of 'political cases". *Baker*, 369 U. S. at 211, 217. Without the SOI, this case presents claims that relate to a foreign conflict in which the United States had little involvement (so far as the record demonstrates), and therefore that merely "touch[ ] foreign relations." Id. at 211.

When we take the SOI into consideration and give it "serious weight," we still conclude that a political question is not presented. Even if the continued adjudication of this case does present some risk to the Bougainville peace process, that is not sufficient to implicate the final three *Baker* factors. . . . The State Department explicitly did not request that we dismiss this suit on political question grounds, and we are confident that proceeding does not express any disrespect for the executive, even if it would prefer that the suit disappear. Nor do we see any "unusual need for unquestioning adherence" to the SOI's nonspecific invocations of risks to the peace process. And finally, given the guarded nature of the SOI, we see no "embarrassment" that would follow from fulfilling our independent duty to determine whether the case should proceed. We are mindful of *Sosa*'s instruction to give "serious weight" to the

[35] Following the panel decision in 2006, the US Government changed its position. The government informed the court that it no longer believed foreign policy concerns were material in the case and expressly stated that it was not 'seeking dismissal of the litigation based on purely case-specific foreign policy concerns'. The issue thus became moot by the time the case was decided by an *en banc* panel of the Ninth Circuit in 2011. *Sarei v. Rio Tinto*, 2011 WL 5041927 (2011) (*en banc*).

views of the executive, but we cannot uphold the dismissal of this lawsuit solely on the basis of the SOI.[36]

Our holding today is consistent with our recent dismissal of ATCA war crimes claims in *Vatican Bank*... There, a proposed class of Holocaust survivors sued the Vatican Bank (a financial institution connected to the Vatican) for its complicity in various war crimes of the Nazi-sympathizing Ustasha puppet regime in Croatia, including Vatican Bank's profiting from the Ustasha regime's theft of the class's property. We concluded that... "the broad allegations tied to the Vatican Bank's alleged assistance to the war objectives of the Ustasha, including the slave labor claims, which essentially call on us to make a retroactive political judgment as to the conduct of the war... are, by nature, political questions."...

We do not understand *Vatican Bank* as foreclosing the plaintiffs' claims that relate to the PNG regime's alleged war crimes, but instead read its holding to apply only to the narrower category of war crimes committed by enemies of the United States. Considering such claims would necessarily require us to review the acts of an enemy of the United States, which would risk creating a conflict with the steps the United States actually chose to take in prosecuting that war. See id. at 560 (expressing unwillingness to "intrude unduly on certain policy choices and value judgments that are constitutionally committed to the political branches... for we do not and cannot know why the Allies made the policy choice not to prosecute the Ustasha and the Vatican Bank.").

Reading *Vatican Bank* to preclude any ATCA war crimes claims would work a major, and inadvisable, shift in our ATCA jurisprudence.... [I]t would contradict *Sosa*,... when it stated that "[f]or two centuries we have affirmed that the domestic law of the United States recognizes the law of nations. It would take some explaining to say now that federal courts must avert their gaze entirely from any international norm intended to protect individuals."

[36] The plaintiffs have submitted recent letters from members of PNG's government urging that the suit will not harm or affect the ongoing Bouagainville peace process. The Chief Secretary to the Government of PNG, Joseph Kalinoe, wrote to the United States Ambassador to PNG on 30 March 2005 that "the [PNG Government] does not see the case presently before the U.S. courts in the U.S. affecting diplomatic and bilateral relations between our two countries nor does it see it affecting the peace process on the island of Bougainville." And on January 8, 2005, John Momis, the Interim Bougainville Provincial Governor, wrote to the State Department's legal advisor under whose name the SOI was written, "urg[ing] the Government of the United States to support the Prime Minister's position to permit the case to proceed in the courts of America, and to explain that the people of Bougainville strongly desire the case to proceed in America,..." Momis' letter includes detail about the current state of the Bougainville peace process, and about how "the litigation has not hindered or in any way adversely affected the peace negotiations." Indeed, the letter adds that "the *Sarei* litigation has helped facilitate the process as it is viewed as another source of rectifying the historic injustices perpetrated against the people of Bougainville." Finally, the letter asserts that "the only way that the litigation will impact [US/PNG] foreign relations is if the litigation is discontinued."

Whether these letters are properly authenticated is in dispute. But if they are authentic and their authors accurately describe the current state of affairs in PNG, that would seriously undercut the State Department's concerns expressed in its November 5, 2001 SOI-which itself depended on assessments by local government officials, including Joseph Kalinoe's predecessor as Chief Secretary to the Government of PNG. For whatever reason, the State Department has declined to update the SOI. Under these circumstances, we do not rely on the letters' substantive representations. But the letters, by suggesting there exists today a different reality in PNG from that portrayed in the SOI, illustrate why it is inappropriate to give the SOI final and conclusive weight as establishing a political question under *Baker*.

QUESTIONS

1. Should a court be more or less reluctant to exercise jurisdiction if a case involves actions that have no direct connection to the United States? If greater deference to the Executive Branch is due in cases that directly impact the United States, do the facts in *Joo v. Japan* constitute a sufficiently direct link?

2. Could *Sosa*'s directing courts to give 'serious weight to the Executive Branch's view of the case's impact on foreign policy' place the Executive in a difficult position? Are there situations in which the Executive Branch would prefer not to be asked its views concerning a case's potential impact on foreign policy? Consider the following commentary concerning a related context:

> [P]roblems...occurred under the pre-FSIA [Foreign Sovereign Immunity Act] regime of executive suggestion. Under that regime, the State Department established an informal administrative process to 'pre-adjudicate' immunity claims, the results of which were binding on courts. This process became heavily politicized, and had the effect of offending foreign nations more than when determinations were made by courts alone applying legal standards. There are ways to avoid this conundrum, including making the administrative determination of susceptibility to suit subject to strict legal standards. This latter approach may capture both rule of law benefits and expertise benefits in a manner akin to modern administrative agencies.[37]

Could a similar solution work with respect to evaluating a case's impact on foreign policy? Is such an inquiry amenable to strict legal standards? To any legal standards? Is a better solution to discard universal civil jurisdiction in favour of a system of universal criminal jurisdiction? In the criminal law context, public officials would be able to control assessments of foreign policy ramifications and perhaps do so without publicly exposing the nature of those internal decisions. Is transparency a desirable institutional feature given the foreign relations implications of such cases?

C. SOVEREIGN AND OFFICIAL IMMUNITY

Civil suits, especially those pursued under the ATS and TVPA, often end in default judgments and generally do not result in actual payment of damages. Several obstacles thwart the attainment of financial compensation. Individual defendants often do not have deep pockets. In contrast with criminal cases, defendants may also freely leave the country. Also, foreign enforcement of judgments is usually difficult if not practically impossible. Suits against two types of defendants — corporations and governments — do not pose such obstacles. This part considers obstacles that uniquely affect suits against states and state officials, the type of cases in which plaintiffs might have a real prospect of achieving compensation but principles of

[37] Jack Goldsmith & Ryan Goodman, 'U.S. Civil Litigation and International Terrorism', in John Norton Moore (ed.), *Civil Litigation and International Terrorism* (2004), 109, at 154.

immunity can close off such avenues. Indeed, questions of immunity have frequently arisen in cases under the ATS. These cases concern the ability of plaintiffs to sue a foreign state directly. They also concern the ability of plaintiffs to sue particular individuals in their official or personal capacity when those individuals claim to be protected by immunity.

The Foreign Sovereign Immunities Act of 1976 (FSIA), codified principally at 22 U.S.C.A. 1602–11, provides a comprehensive legislative framework for claims of immunity by foreign state defendants. Foreign states, including 'an agency or instrumentality' thereof, are immune from judicial jurisdiction, subject to enumerated exceptions. Those exceptions include court actions growing out of a foreign state's commercial activities that cause a direct effect in the United States; personal injury or death occurring in the United States and caused by a foreign state or its officials or employees acting within the scope of their office or employment; and actions in which the foreign state has 'waived its immunity either explicitly or by implication'.

Argentine Republic v. Amerada Hess Shipping Corp., 488 U.S. 428 (1989), involved an ATS action growing out of the Falklands (Malvinas) war between the United Kingdom and Argentina. It was based on damage to the plaintiff's ship by an attack of Argentinian aircraft. The Supreme Court refused to find an exception to the rule of immunity for suits under the ATS because of Argentina's alleged violation of international law. The Court held that the FSIA is 'the sole basis for obtaining jurisdiction over a foreign state in our courts'. It drew from the FSIA 'the plain implication that immunity is granted in those cases involving alleged violations of international law that do not come within one of the FSIA's exceptions.' Plaintiffs were accordingly required as a threshold matter to satisfy one of the conditions under the FSIA for suspending sovereign immunity.

Saudi Arabia v. Nelson, 507 U.S. 349 (1993), involved tort claims based on alleged human rights violations. The Supreme Court held that alleged conduct of the defendant state did not fall within the FSIA exception for 'commercial activity'. The plaintiff, a US citizen employee at a Saudi state hospital, claimed that Saudi Government agents subjected him to unlawful detention and torture as retaliation for his persistence in reporting hospital safety violations. The Supreme Court concluded that '[t]he conduct [complained of by plaintiff] boils down to abuse of the power of its police by the Saudi Government, and however monstrous such abuse undoubtedly may be, a foreign state's exercise of the power of its police has long been understood...as peculiarly sovereign in nature.' Sovereign immunity was granted to Saudi Arabia.

In *Siderman de Blake v. Republic of Argentina*, 965 F.2d 699 (9th Cir. 1992), the Court of Appeals agreed with the plaintiff's argument that official acts of torture attributed to Argentina constituted a violation of a *jus cogens* norm of the 'highest status within international law'. Nonetheless, taking its lesson from the *Amareda Hess* decision in which the Supreme Court was so specific, the court concluded that it was Congress that would have to make any further exceptions to sovereign immunity. 'The fact that there has been a violation of *jus cogens* does not confer jurisdiction under the FSIA.' See also *Sampson v. Federal Republic of Germany*, 250 F.3d 1145 (7th Cir. 2001); *Smith v. Socialist People's Libyan Arab Jamahiriya*, 101 F.3d

239 (2d Cir. 1996); *Princz v. Federal Republic of Germany*, 26 F.3d 1166 (D.C. Cir. 1994).

In view of the FSIA and the case law described above, US plaintiffs in section 1350 actions have also sought to avoid the issue of sovereign immunity by suing not the state itself but individual perpetrators — as indeed occurred in *Filártiga*. Courts required to sort out the relevance of sovereign immunity when individual defendants are before it have taken different approaches in characterizing the relationship between the individual and the state.

Consider *In re Estate of Ferdinand Marcos*, 25 F.3d 1467 (9th Cir. 1994). The court held that the FSIA did not bar jurisdiction under section 1350 over the estate of former President Ferdinand Marcos for alleged acts of torture and wrongful death, since those were not official acts perpetrated within the scope of his official authority in the Philippines but rather acts outside the scope of his authority as President. Quoting from a prior related case, the court stated that '[o]ur courts have had no difficulty in distinguishing the legal acts of a deposed ruler from his acts for personal profit that lack a basis in law'. At the same time, the requirement of state action under the definition of official torture could still be met by an official acting under colour of authority, though not within an official mandate. That is, such an official could violate international law for purposes of the ATS.

In *Jones v. Saudi Arabia* (2006), the UK House of Lords adopted a very different approach. Plaintiffs brought claims of torture against various defendants including the head of the Ministry of the Interior, a captain and a lieutenant in the Saudi Arabian police force, and a colonel in the Ministry of Interior and deputy governor of a prison facility. The court held that government officials should be equated with the state for the purpose of sovereign immunity. In an unusual line of reasoning, the court explained, in part, that because states are liable for actions of governmental officials (including actions in excess of authority or contravention of instructions) under international principles of state responsibility, it follows that civil suits against governmental officials activate sovereign immunity. Lord Bingham stated:

> It is certainly true that in *Pinochet* (No 1) and *Pinochet* (No 3) certain members of the House held that acts of torture could not be functions of a head of state or governmental or official acts. But the case was categorically different from the present, since it concerned criminal proceedings falling squarely within the universal criminal jurisdiction mandated by the Torture Convention.... The essential ratio of the decision, as I understand it, was that international law could not without absurdity require criminal jurisdiction to be assumed and exercised where the Torture Convention conditions were satisfied and, at the same time, require immunity to be granted to those properly charged.[38] The Torture Convention was the mainspring of the decision, and certain members of the House expressly accepted that the grant of immunity in civil proceedings was unaffected. It is, I think, difficult to accept that torture cannot be a governmental or official act, since under article 1 of

[38] [Eds.: In a concurring opinion, Lord Hoffmann added: 'To produce a conflict with state immunity, it is therefore necessary to show that the prohibition on torture has generated an ancillary procedural rule which, by way of exception to state immunity, entitles or perhaps requires states to assume civil jurisdiction over other states in cases in which torture is alleged.']

> the Torture Convention torture must, to qualify as such, be inflicted by or with the connivance of a public official or other person acting in an official capacity. The claimants' argument encounters the difficulty that it is founded on the Torture Convention; but to bring themselves within the Torture Convention they must show that the torture was (to paraphrase the definition) official; yet they argue that the conduct was not official in order to defeat the claim to immunity.
>
> ...
>
> ...A state is not criminally responsible in international or English law, and therefore cannot be directly impleaded in criminal proceedings. The prosecution of a servant or agent for an act of torture within article 1 of the Torture Convention is founded on an express exception from the general rule of immunity. It is, however, clear that a civil action against individual torturers based on acts of official torture does indirectly implead the state since their acts are attributable to it. Were these claims against the individual defendants to proceed and be upheld, the interests of the Kingdom would be obviously affected, even though it is not a named party.

Compare the logic of *Jones v. Saudi Arabia* with the Senate Report on the Torture Victim Protection Act, p. 1175, *supra*.

COMMENT ON SAMANTAR v. YOUSUF

In 2009, the US Supreme Court decided a case concerning the official immunity of a senior government official of Somalia for alleged acts of torture and extrajudicial killings. In the main, the decision involved a narrow question of statutory construction: whether the FSIA provisions on immunity applied to an individual sued for conduct undertaken in his official capacity. The Court held that the statute did not apply to such individuals. The Court, however, explained that officials could potentially receive immunity as a matter of federal common law. And, even if they were not immune, sovereign immunity might still preclude the exercise of jurisdiction:

> [N]ot every suit can successfully be pleaded against an individual official alone. Even when a plaintiff names only a foreign official, it may be the case that the foreign state itself, its political subdivision, or an agency or instrumentality is a required party, because that party has "an interest relating to the subject of the action" and "disposing of the action in the person's absence may...as a practical matter impair or impede the person's ability to protect the interest." Fed. Rule Civ. Proc. 19(a)(1)(B). If this is the case, and the entity is immune from suit under the FSIA, the district court may have to dismiss the suit, regardless of whether the official is immune or not under the common law. See *Republic of Philippines* v. *Pimentel*, 553 U. S. 851, 867 (2008) ("[W]here sovereign immunity is asserted, and the claims of the sovereign are not frivolous, dismissal of the action must be ordered where there is a potential for injury to the interests of the absent sovereign"). Or it may be the case that some actions against an official in his official capacity should be treated as actions against the foreign state itself, as the state is the real party in interest. Cf. *Kentucky* v. *Graham*, 473 U. S. 159, 166 (1985) ("[A]n official-capacity suit is, in all respects other than name, to be treated as a

suit against the entity. It is *not* a suit against the official personally, for the real party in interest is the entity" (citation omitted)).

Following the Supreme Court's decision, federal district courts have turned to the Department of State to determine whether a defendant should receive official immunity under the common law. In the suit against Samantar on remand from the Supreme Court, the State Department submitted to the district court that the defendant was not entitled to immunity. Harold Koh, Legal Adviser of the Department of State, has since discussed the US Government's position and practices following the Court's opinion in *Samantar*:[39]

> I am delighted to speak here… regarding the U.S. Government's perspective on Foreign Official Immunity after *Samantar v. Yousuf*.
>
> …
>
> …As a practical matter, based on historical experience, unless Congress passes legislation to govern official immunity, as it did with respect to foreign state immunity in the FSIA, we expect courts will again look to the State Department for authoritative guidance as to whether a foreign official enjoys immunity.
>
> …
>
> …In the same way that the law of foreign state immunity eventually took into account the global commercial revolution, official immunity law will need to take into account the human rights revolution. Just as the Tate Letter[40] acknowledged an important watershed in state practice — the increasing entry of governments into international commercial markets — changes in international human rights norms, as reflected in treaties ratified by the United States, new U.S. statutes, and U.S. judicial doctrines, have given rise to new views about the boundaries of official action appropriately subject to immunity, and call for review of the standards governing personal accountability for gross human rights abuses.[41]
>
> …
>
> [T]here is a historical distinction between status immunities (immunities *ratione personae*) — i.e., immunities that apply to individual officials because of their current status, which are designed to protect their ability to carry out current functions (diplomatic, head of state, special missions) — and conduct immunities (immunities *ratione materiae*), which derive from the nature of those individuals' conduct and protect centrally against inappropriate judicial oversight of foreign government conduct. Thus, certain foreign officials — such as sitting heads of state, diplomats, and members of qualifying special missions — are entitled to immunities by virtue of their status, during the time they hold that status. Thereafter, as former officials, they are entitled only to those conduct immunities

[39] Harold Hongju Koh, 'Foreign Official Immunity After *Samantar*: A United States Government Perspective', 44 Vand. J. Transnat'l. L. 1141 (Nov. 2011).

[40] In 1952, Acting Legal Adviser of the Department of State, Jack Tate, issued a famous letter announcing that the US government would adhere to the 'restrictive theory' of sovereign immunity which holds that foreign sovereign immunity is inapplicable with respect to a state's commercial activity.

[41] In an accompanying footnote, Koh stated: 'Current common law doctrine, statutes, treaties, and customary international law may impose obligations to hold accountable those who commit gross violations of human rights that did not exist when the Executive Branch and courts first addressed the immunity of foreign government officials'.

> that attach to challenged acts that can be deemed official in nature, which may depend upon the nature of their former office. Obviously, whether an act may be considered "official" for conduct immunity purposes also depends upon on the nature of the act alleged. A government official's legitimate authority has not generally been thought to encompass a right to commit "official acts" that violate both international and domestic law.

In an accompanying footnote to the latter paragraph, Koh wrote:

> Pre-*Samantar* case law treated acts in violation of international and domestic law as falling outside the scope of "official acts." *See, e.g.*, Enahoro v. Abubakar, 408 F.3d 877, 893 (7th Cir. 2005) (noting that "officials receive no immunity for acts that violate international *jus cogens* human rights norms (which by definition are not legally authorized acts)"); Hilao v. Estate of Marcos, 25 F.3d 1467, 1472 (9th Cir.1994) (noting that Marcos's "acts of torture, execution, and disappearance were clearly acts outside of his authority as President"); *see also* Torture Victim Protection Act of 1991, S. REP. NO. 102-249, at 8 (1991) ("[B]ecause no state officially condones torture or extrajudicial killings, few such acts, if any, would fall under the rubric of 'official actions' taken in the course of an official's duties.").

And another passage in Koh's article suggests that the nature of the alleged human rights violation can affect the State Department's determination whether an individual is entitled to official immunity. That is, Koh explained that in the case of *Ahmed v. Magan*, No. 2:10-CV-34 (S.D. Ohio 2011),

> the State Department recently determined that [a former Somali official] was not entitled to immunity in a suit brought by a Somali plaintiff in the U.S. District Court for the Southern District of Ohio under the TVPA and ATCA for alleged responsibility for torture, cruel, inhuman or degrading treatment, and arbitrary detention. The U.S. Government's filing noted, *inter alia*, that: (1) Magan is a former, not sitting, official of a state with no current government formally recognized by the United States who generally would enjoy only residual immunity, unless waived, and even then only for acts that may properly be considered authorized by the foreign state; (2) plaintiff had alleged that while in office, Magan "directed and participated in the interrogation and torture of Plaintiff and other civilians perceived as opponents of the Barre regime"; and (3) Magan resides in the United States, and basic principles of sovereignty provide that a state generally has a right to exercise jurisdiction over its residents.

COMMENT ON EX PARTE PINOCHET AND IMMUNITY

We previously discussed the case involving General Augusto Pinochet before the UK House of Lords, see p. 1128, *supra*. In addition to holding that the United Kingdom had jurisdiction over acts of torture allegedly committed by Pinochet after the Torture Convention had been incorporated into UK law, six of the seven Law Lords concluded that Pinochet did not enjoy state immunity from prosecution for these acts.

Lord Saville reasoned that the Torture Convention necessarily eliminated Pinochet's official immunity for the crime of torture:

> A former head of state who it is alleged resorted to torture for state purposes falls in my view fairly and squarely within those terms [of the Torture Convention] and on the face of it should be dealt with in accordance with them.
>
> ...
>
> To my mind these terms demonstrate that the states who have become parties have clearly and unambiguously agreed that official torture should now be dealt with in a way which would otherwise amount to an interference in their sovereignty.

Lord Browne-Wilkinson wrote:

> Can it be said that the commission of a crime which is an international crime against humanity and jus cogens is an act done in an official capacity on behalf of the state? I believe there to be strong ground for saying that the implementation of torture as defined by the Torture Convention cannot be a state function.
>
> ...
>
> I have doubts whether, before the coming into force of the Torture Convention, the existence of the international crime of torture as jus cogens was enough to justify the conclusion that the organisation of state torture could not rank for immunity purposes as performance of an official function. At that stage there was no international tribunal to punish torture and no general jurisdiction to permit or require its punishment in domestic courts. Not until there was some form of universal jurisdiction for the punishment of the crime of torture could it really be talked about as a fully constituted international crime.

Lord Hope of Craighead added:

> ...[T]here remains the question whether the immunity can survive Chile's agreement to the Torture Convention if the torture which is alleged was of such a kind or on such a scale as to amount to an international crime....
>
> ...
>
> Despite the difficulties which I have mentioned, I think that there are sufficient signs that the necessary developments in international law were in place by [29 September 1998, the date of entry into force of the Criminal Justice Act].
>
> ...
>
> I would not regard this as a case of waiver. Nor would I accept that it was an implied term of the Torture Convention that former heads of state were to be deprived of their immunity ratione materiae with respect to all acts of official torture as defined in article 1. It is just that the obligations which were recognised by customary international law in the case of such serious international crimes by the date when Chile ratified the Convention are so strong as to override any objection by it on the ground of immunity ratione materiae to the exercise of the

jurisdiction over crimes committed after that date which the United Kingdom had made available.

A handful of recent decisions by international courts have directly addressed the question of sovereign and official immunity. We consider first a decision by the Grand Chamber of the European Court of Human Rights involving a civil action against a foreign state.

AL-ADSANI v. UNITED KINGDOM

European Court of Human Rights (Grand Chamber), 21 Nov. 2001 Application No. 35763/97

[Mr Sulaiman Al-Adsani, a dual British-Kuwaiti national, initiated civil proceedings in the United Kingdom against the Government of Kuwait and individual Kuwaitis for his alleged torture in Kuwait. Mr Al-Adsani's specific allegations involved being beaten over several days, having his head held underwater in a swimming pool containing corpses and being severely burnt. The UK appellate court permitted Mr Al-Adsani to proceed against the individual Kuwaitis but held that UK law on state immunity barred suit against the Government of Kuwait.

Mr Al-Adsani appealed to the European Court of Human Rights, claiming in significant part that the application of state immunity denied him access to a court in violation of Article 6 of the European Convention for the Protection of Human Rights and Fundamental Freedoms. The Grand Chamber heard the appeal and, by a slim majority (9 votes to 8), rejected his claim. Parts of the majority and dissenting opinions follow.]

Relevant Legal Materials

[The State Immunity Act 1978]

21. The relevant parts of the State Immunity Act 1978 provide:

> "1. (1) A State is immune from the jurisdiction of the courts of the United Kingdom except as provided in the following provisions of this Part of this Act.
>
> …
>
> 5. A State is not immune as regards proceedings in respect of –
> (a) death or personal injury;
>
> …
>
> caused by an act or omission in the United Kingdom…"

[The Basle Convention]

22. The above provision (section 5 of the 1978 Act) was enacted to implement the 1972 European Convention on State Immunity ("the Basle Convention"), a Council

of Europe instrument, which entered into force on 11 June 1976....Article 11 of the Convention provides:

> "A Contracting State cannot claim immunity from the jurisdiction of a court of another Contracting State in proceedings which relate to redress for injury to the person or damage to tangible property, if the facts which occasioned the injury or damage occurred in the territory of the State of forum, and if the author of the injury or damage was present in that territory at the time when those facts occurred."

Article 15 of the Basle Convention provides that a Contracting State shall be entitled to immunity if the proceedings do not fall within the stated exceptions.

[State immunity in respect of civil proceedings for torture]

23. In its Report on Jurisdictional Immunities of States and their Property (1999), the working group of the International Law Commission (ILC) found that over the preceding decade a number of civil claims had been brought in municipal courts, particularly in the United States and United Kingdom, against foreign governments, arising out of acts of torture committed not in the territory of the forum State but in the territory of the defendant and other States. The working group of the ILC found that national courts had in some cases shown sympathy for the argument that States are not entitled to plead immunity where there has been a violation of human rights norms with the character of jus cogens, although in most cases the plea of sovereign immunity had succeeded....

24. The working group of the ILC did, however, note two recent developments which it considered gave support to the argument that a State could not plead immunity in respect of gross human rights violations. One of these was the House of Lords' judgment in *ex parte Pinochet* (No. 3) (see paragraph 34 below). The other was the amendment by the United States of its Foreign Sovereign Immunities Act (FSIA) to include a new exception to immunity. This exception,... applies in respect of a claim for damages for personal injury or death caused by an act of torture, extra-judicial killing, aircraft sabotage or hostage-taking, against a State designated by the Secretary of State as a sponsor of terrorism, where the claimant or victim was a national of the United States at the time the act occurred.

...

30. In its judgment in *Prosecutor v. Furundzija*, the International Criminal Tribunal for the Former Yugoslavia observed as follows:

> 144. ...the prohibition on torture is a peremptory norm or jus cogens....This prohibition is so extensive that States are even barred by international law from expelling, returning or extraditing a person to another State where there are substantial grounds for believing that the person would be in danger of being subjected to torture.
>
> 145. ...all States parties to the relevant treaties have been granted, and are obliged to exercise, jurisdiction to investigate, prosecute and punish offenders....
>
> 146. The existence of this corpus of general and treaty rules proscribing torture shows that the international community, aware of the importance of outlawing

> this heinous phenomenon, has decided to suppress any manifestation of torture by operating both at the interstate level and at the level of individuals. No legal loopholes have been left.
>
> ...
>
> 153. ...Because of the importance of the values it protects, this principle has evolved into a peremptory norm or jus cogens,...The most conspicuous consequence of this higher rank is that the principle at issue cannot be derogated from by States through international treaties or local or special or even general customary rules not endowed with the same normative force.
>
> ...

31. Similar statements were made in *Prosecutor v. Delacic and Others* and in *Prosecutor v. Kunarac.*

[Criminal jurisdiction of the United Kingdom over acts of torture]

32. The United Kingdom ratified the UN Convention with effect from 8 December 1988.

...

34. In its *Regina v. Bow Street Metropolitan Stipendiary Magistrate and Others, ex parte Pinochet Ugarte* (No. 3), judgment of 24 March 1999 [2000] Appeal Cases 147, the House of Lords held that the former President of Chile, Senator Pinochet, could be extradited to Spain in respect of charges which concerned conduct that was criminal in the United Kingdom at the time when it was allegedly committed. The majority of the Law Lords considered that extraterritorial torture did not become a crime in the United Kingdom until section 134 of the Criminal Justice Act 1988 came into effect. The majority considered that although under Part II of the State Immunity Act 1978 a former head of State enjoyed immunity from the criminal jurisdiction of the United Kingdom for acts done in his official capacity, torture was an international crime and prohibited by jus cogens (peremptory norms of international law). The coming into force of the UN Convention had created a universal criminal jurisdiction in all the Contracting States in respect of acts of torture by public officials, and the States Parties could not have intended that an immunity for ex-heads of State for official acts of torture would survive their ratification of the UN Convention. The House of Lords (and, in particular, Lord Millett, at p. 278) made clear that their findings as to immunity ratione materiae from criminal jurisdiction did not affect the immunity ratione personae of foreign sovereign States from civil jurisdiction in respect of acts of torture.

The Law

I. Alleged Violation of Article 3 of the Convention

[The Court rejected a separate claim, raised by Al-Adsani, that the United Kingdom violated an obligation to secure to everyone within its jurisdiction the freedom from torture and the right to an effective remedy. The Court unanimously concluded: 'The applicant does not contend that the alleged torture took place within the jurisdiction of the United Kingdom or that the United Kingdom authorities had any causal connection with its occurrence. In these circumstances, it cannot be said that the High Contracting Party was under a duty to provide a civil remedy to the applicant in respect of torture allegedly carried out by the Kuwaiti authorities.']

II. Alleged Violation of Article 6 § 1 of the Convention

42. The applicant alleged that he was denied access to a court in the determination of his claim against the State of Kuwait and that this constituted a violation of Article 6 § 1 of the Convention, which provides in its first sentence:

> "In the determination of his civil rights and obligations or of any criminal charge against him, everyone is entitled to a fair and public hearing within a reasonable time by an independent and impartial tribunal established by law."

...

47. Whether a person has an actionable domestic claim may depend not only on the substantive content, properly speaking, of the relevant civil right as defined under national law but also on the existence of procedural bars preventing or limiting the possibilities of bringing potential claims to court. In the latter kind of case Article 6 § 1 may be applicable. Certainly the Convention enforcement bodies may not create by way of interpretation of Article 6 § 1 a substantive civil right which has no legal basis in the State concerned. However, it would not be consistent with the rule of law in a democratic society or with the basic principle underlying Article 6 § 1 — namely that civil claims must be capable of being submitted to a judge for adjudication — if, for example, a State could, without restraint or control by the Convention enforcement bodies, remove from the jurisdiction of the courts a whole range of civil claims or confer immunities from civil liability on large groups or categories of persons (see *Fayed v. the United Kingdom*, judgment of 21 September 1994, Series A no. 294-B, pp. 49–50, § 65).

48. The proceedings which the applicant intended to pursue were for damages for personal injury, a cause of action well known to English law. The Court does not accept the Government's submission that the applicant's claim had no legal basis in domestic law since any substantive right which might have existed was extinguished by operation of the doctrine of State immunity. It notes that an action against a State is not barred in limine: if the defendant State waives immunity, the action will proceed to a hearing and judgment. The grant of immunity is to be seen not as qualifying a substantive right but as a procedural bar on the national courts' power to determine the right.

49. The Court is accordingly satisfied that there existed a serious and genuine dispute over civil rights. It follows that Article 6 § 1 was applicable to the proceedings in question.

Compliance with Article 6 § 1

1. Submissions of the parties

50. The Government contended that the restriction imposed on the applicant's right of access to a court pursued a legitimate aim and was proportionate.

The 1978 Act reflected the provisions of the Basle Convention (see paragraph 22 above), which in turn gave expression to universally applicable principles of public international law…Article 6 § 1 of the Convention could not be interpreted so as to compel a Contracting State to deny immunity to and assert jurisdiction over a non-Contracting State. Such a conclusion would be contrary to international law and would impose irreconcilable obligations on the States that had ratified both the Convention and the Basle Convention.

There were other, traditional means of redress for wrongs of this kind available to the applicant, namely diplomatic representations or an inter-State claim.

51. The applicant submitted that the restriction on his right of access to a court did not serve a legitimate aim and was disproportionate. The House of Lords in *ex parte Pinochet* (No. 3) (see paragraph 34 above) had accepted that the prohibition of torture had acquired the status of a jus cogens norm in international law and that torture had become an international crime. In these circumstances there could be no rational basis for allowing sovereign immunity in a civil action when immunity would not be a defence in criminal proceedings arising from the same facts.

Other than civil proceedings against the State of Kuwait, he complained that there was no effective means of redress available to him. He had attempted to make use of diplomatic channels but the Government refused to assist him….

2. The Court's assessment

53. The right of access to a court is not…absolute, but may be subject to limitations; these are permitted by implication since the right of access by its very nature calls for regulation by the State. In this respect, the Contracting States enjoy a certain margin of appreciation, although the final decision as to the observance of the Convention's requirements rests with the Court. It must be satisfied that the limitations applied do not restrict or reduce the access left to the individual in such a way or to such an extent that the very essence of the right is impaired. Furthermore, a limitation will not be compatible with Article 6 § 1 if it does not pursue a legitimate aim and if there is no reasonable relationship of proportionality between the means employed and the aim sought to be achieved (see *Waite and Kennedy v. Germany* [GC], no. 26083/94, § 59, ECHR 1999-I).

54. The Court must first examine whether the limitation pursued a legitimate aim. It notes in this connection that sovereign immunity is a concept of international law, developed out of the principle par in parem non habet imperium, by virtue of which one State shall not be subject to the jurisdiction of another State. The Court considers that the grant of sovereign immunity to a State in civil proceedings pursues the legitimate aim of complying with international law to promote comity and good relations between States through the respect of another State's sovereignty.

55. The Court must next assess whether the restriction was proportionate to the aim pursued….

56. It follows that measures taken by a High Contracting Party which reflect generally recognised rules of public international law on State immunity cannot in principle be regarded as imposing a disproportionate restriction on the right of access to a court as embodied in Article 6 § 1. Just as the right of access to a court is an inherent part of the fair trial guarantee in that Article, so some restrictions on access

must likewise be regarded as inherent, an example being those limitations generally accepted by the community of nations as part of the doctrine of State immunity.

57. The Court notes that the 1978 Act, applied by the English courts so as to afford immunity to Kuwait, complies with the relevant provisions of the 1972 Basle Convention, which, while placing a number of limitations on the scope of State immunity as it was traditionally understood, preserves it in respect of civil proceedings for damages for personal injury unless the injury was caused in the territory of the forum State. Except insofar as it affects claims for damages for torture, the applicant does not deny that the above provision reflects a generally accepted rule of international law. He asserts, however, that his claim related to torture, and contends that the prohibition of torture has acquired the status of a jus cogens norm in international law, taking precedence over treaty law and other rules of international law.

...

61. While the Court accepts, on the basis of these authorities, that the prohibition of torture has achieved the status of a peremptory norm in international law, it observes that the present case concerns not, as in *Furundzija* and *Pinochet*, the criminal liability of an individual for alleged acts of torture, but the immunity of a State in a civil suit for damages in respect of acts of torture within the territory of that State. Notwithstanding the special character of the prohibition of torture in international law, the Court is unable to discern in the international instruments, judicial authorities or other materials before it any firm basis for concluding that, as a matter of international law, a State no longer enjoys immunity from civil suit in the courts of another State where acts of torture are alleged. In particular, the Court observes that none of the primary international instruments referred to (Article 5 of the Universal Declaration of Human Rights, Article 7 of the International Covenant on Civil and Political Rights and Articles 2 and 4 of the UN Convention) relates to civil proceedings or to State immunity.

...

65. As to the *ex parte Pinochet* (No. 3) judgment, the Court notes that the majority of the House of Lords held that, after the UN Convention and even before, the international prohibition against official torture had the character of jus cogens or a peremptory norm and that no immunity was enjoyed by a torturer from one Torture Convention State from the criminal jurisdiction of another. But, as the working group of the ILC itself acknowledged, that case concerned the immunity ratione materiae from criminal jurisdiction of a former head of State, who was at the material time physically within the United Kingdom. As the judgments in the case made clear, the conclusion of the House of Lords did not in any way affect the immunity ratione personae of foreign sovereign States from the civil jurisdiction in respect of such acts (see in particular, the judgment of Lord Millett, mentioned in paragraph 34 above). In so holding, the House of Lords cited with approval the judgments of the Court of Appeal in *Al-Adsani* itself.

66. The Court, while noting the growing recognition of the overriding importance of the prohibition of torture, does not accordingly find it established that there is yet acceptance in international law of the proposition that States are not entitled to immunity in respect of civil claims for damages for alleged torture committed

outside the forum State. The 1978 Act, which grants immunity to States in respect of personal injury claims unless the damage was caused within the United Kingdom, is not inconsistent with those limitations generally accepted by the community of nations as part of the doctrine of State immunity.

67. In these circumstances, the application by the English courts of the provisions of the 1978 Act to uphold Kuwait's claim to immunity cannot be said to have amounted to an unjustified restriction on the applicant's access to a court.

It follows that there has been no violation of Article 6 § 1 of the Convention in this case.

For these reasons, the Court

1. Holds unanimously that there has been no violation of Article 3 of the Convention;

2. Holds by nine votes to eight that there has been no violation of Article 6 § 1 of the Convention.

CONCURRING OPINION OF JUDGE PELLONPÄÄ JOINED BY JUDGE SIR NICOLAS BRATZA

...

The acceptance of the applicant's argument concerning access to a court would thus have required a possibility of having judgments — probably often default judgments — delivered in torture cases executed against respondent States. This in turn would raise the question whether the traditionally strong immunity of public property from execution would also have had to be regarded as incompatible with Article 6. It would seem that this indeed would have been the inevitable consequence of the acceptance of the minority's line. If immunity from jurisdiction were to be regarded as incompatible with Article 6 because of the jus cogens nature of the prohibition of torture, which prevails over all other international obligations not having that same hierarchical status, it presumably would also have to prevail over rules concerning immunity from execution. Consequently, the Contracting States would have had to allow attachment and execution against public property of respondent States if the effectiveness of access to a court could not otherwise be guaranteed.

The acceptance of the applicant's argument indeed would have opened the door to much more far-reaching consequences than did the amendment to the United States Foreign Sovereign Immunities Act.... As appears from the plaintiff 's futile efforts of execution in *Flatow v. the Islamic Republic of Iran* [*Flatow v. Islamic Republic of Iran* (999 F.Supp. 1 (D.D.C. 1998)); *Flatow v. the Islamic Republic of Iran and Others* (76 F.Supp.2d 16, 18 (D.D.C. 1999))], this narrowly limited statutory amendment did not affect the immunity of a foreign State's public property from attachment and execution, causing the District Court Judge Royce C. Lamberth to characterise the plaintiff's original judgment against Iran as an epitome of the phrase "Pyrrhic victory."

...

... [I]n order not to contradict itself the Court would have been forced to hold that the prohibition of torture must also prevail over immunity of a foreign State's public property, such as bank accounts intended for public purposes, real estate used for a foreign State's cultural institutes and other establishments abroad (including even, it would appear, embassy buildings), etc., since it has not been suggested that immunity of such public property from execution belongs to the corps of jus cogens. Although giving absolute priority to the prohibition of torture may at first sight seem very "progressive", a more careful consideration tends to confirm that such a step would also run the risk of proving a sort of "Pyrrhic victory". International cooperation, including cooperation with a view to eradicating the vice of torture, presupposes the continuing existence of certain elements of a basic framework for the conduct of international relations. Principles concerning State immunity belong to that regulatory framework, and I believe it is more conducive to orderly international cooperation to leave this framework intact than to follow another course.

...

JOINT DISSENTING OPINION OF JUDGES ROZAKIS AND CAFLISCH JOINED BY JUDGES WILDHABER, COSTA, CABRAL BARRETO AND VAJIN

...

In our opinion, the distinction made by the majority and their conclusions are defective on two grounds.

Firstly, the English courts, when dealing with the applicant's claim, never resorted to the distinction made by the majority. They never invoked any difference between criminal charges or civil claims, between criminal and civil proceedings, in so far as the legal force of the rules on State immunity or the applicability of the 1978 Act was concerned. The basic position of the Court of Appeal — the last court which dealt with the matter in its essence — is expressed by the observations of Lord Justice Stuart-Smith who simply denied that the prohibition of torture was a jus cogens rule. In reading the Lord Justice's observations, one even forms the impression that if the Court of Appeal had been convinced that the rule of prohibition of torture was a norm of jus cogens, they could grudgingly have admitted that the procedural bar of State immunity did not apply in the circumstances of the case.

Secondly, the distinction made by the majority between civil and criminal proceedings, concerning the effect of the rule of the prohibition of torture, is not consonant with the very essence of the operation of the jus cogens rules. It is not the nature of the proceedings which determines the effects that a jus cogens rule has upon another rule of international law, but the character of the rule as a peremptory norm and its interaction with a hierarchically lower rule. The prohibition of torture, being a rule of jus cogens, acts in the international sphere and deprives the rule of sovereign immunity of all its legal effects in that sphere. The criminal or civil nature of the domestic proceedings is immaterial. The jurisdictional bar is lifted by the very interaction of the international rules involved, and the national judge cannot admit a plea of immunity raised by the defendant State as an element preventing him from entering into the merits of the case and from dealing with the claim of the applicant for the alleged damages inflicted upon him.

...

COMMENT ON GERMANY v. ITALY BEFORE THE INTERNATIONAL COURT OF JUSTICE (2012)

In 2012, the International Court of Justice (ICJ) issued a judgment on the relationship between *jus cogens* and state immunity that arose out of civil suits against the state of Germany. The dispute principally involved the commission of war crimes by the German military against Italian nationals during Germany's occupation of parts of Italy in the final years of the Second World War. In a series of decisions from 2004 to 2011, the Italian Court of Cassation held that Germany could be sued for compensation in Italian courts on the ground that immunity does not apply when the alleged conduct constitutes an international crime such as deportation to slave labour and massacres of civilians.

The ICJ held that the decision of the Court of Cassation was in violation of Italy's obligation to respect Germany's immunity under customary international law. The ICJ explained that sovereign immunity is firmly established in customary international law and grounded upon 'one of the fundamental principles of the international legal order' — the sovereign equality of states. That principle had to be 'viewed together with the principle that each State possesses sovereignty over its own territory and that there flows from that sovereignty the jurisdiction of the State over events and persons within that territory.' The Court suggested that an exception to immunity may exist for torts committed in the territory of the forum state (i.e., acts committed by German agents inside Italy). However, that exception, the Court decided, does not apply to acts committed by foreign military forces in a state's territory during an armed conflict. The Court explained that Article 31 of the European Convention on State Immunity, for example, reflects this customary international law exemption for military forces.[42]

The ICJ then turned to the question whether the fact that the alleged violations constituted *jus cogens* offences would supersede the immunity that applies to foreign military forces in a state's territory. The Court provided the following analysis:

> 92. [T]he second strand in Italy's argument...rests on the premise that there is a conflict between jus cogens rules forming part of the law of armed conflict and according immunity to Germany. Since jus cogens rules always prevail over any inconsistent rule of international law, whether contained in a treaty or in customary international law, so the argument runs, and since the rule which accords one State immunity before the courts of another does not have the status of jus cogens, the rule of immunity must give way.
>
> 93. ...Assuming for this purpose that the rules of the law of armed conflict which prohibit the murder of civilians in occupied territory, the deportation of civilian inhabitants to slave labour and the deportation of prisoners of war to slave labour are rules of jus cogens, there is no conflict between those rules

[42] Article 31 of the European Convention on State Immunity provides: 'Nothing in this Convention shall affect any immunities or privileges enjoyed by a Contracting State in respect of anything done or omitted to be done by, or in relation to, its armed forces when on the territory of another Contracting State.'

and the rules on State immunity. The two sets of rules address different matters. The rules of State immunity are procedural in character and are confined to determining whether or not the courts of one State may exercise jurisdiction in respect of another State. They do not bear upon the question whether or not the conduct in respect of which the proceedings are brought was lawful or unlawful.... For the same reason, recognizing the immunity of a foreign State in accordance with customary international law does not amount to recognizing as lawful a situation created by the breach of a jus cogens rule, or rendering aid and assistance in maintaining that situation, and so cannot contravene the principle in Article 41 of the International Law Commission's Articles on State Responsibility.[43]

94. ...Nor is the argument strengthened by focusing upon the duty of the wrongdoing State to make reparation, rather than upon the original wrongful act. The duty to make reparation is a rule which exists independently of those rules which concern the means by which it is to be effected. The law of State immunity concerns only the latter; a decision that a foreign State is immune no more conflicts with the duty to make reparation than it does with the rule prohibiting the original wrongful act. Moreover, against the background of a century of practice in which almost every peace treaty or post-war settlement has involved either a decision not to require the payment of reparations or the use of lump sum settlements and set-offs, it is difficult to see that international law contains a rule requiring the payment of full compensation to each and every individual victim as a rule accepted by the international community of States as a whole as one from which no derogation is permitted.

95. To the extent that it is argued that no rule which is not of the status of jus cogens may be applied if to do so would hinder the enforcement of a jus cogens rule, even in the absence of a direct conflict, the Court sees no basis for such a proposition.... [T]he rules which determine the scope and extent of jurisdiction and when that jurisdiction may be exercised do not derogate from those substantive rules which possess jus cogens status, nor is there anything inherent in the concept of jus cogens which would require their modification or would displace their application. The Court has taken that approach in two cases, notwithstanding that the effect was that a means by which a jus cogens rule might be enforced was rendered unavailable. In Armed Activities, it held that the fact that a rule has the status of jus cogens does not confer upon the Court a jurisdiction which it would not otherwise possess (Armed Activities on the Territory of the Congo (New Application: 2002), Judgment, I.C.J. Reports 2006, p. 6, paras. 64 and 125). In Arrest Warrant, the Court held, albeit without express reference to the concept of jus cogens, that the fact that a Minister for Foreign Affairs was accused of criminal violations of rules which undoubtedly possess the character of jus cogens did not deprive the Democratic Republic of the Congo of the entitlement which it possessed as a matter of customary international law to demand immunity on his behalf (Arrest Warrant of 11 April 2000 (Democratic Republic of Congo v. Belgium), Judgment, I.C.J. Reports 2002, p. 3, paras. 58 and

[43] [Eds.: Article 41(2) of the Draft Articles of State Responsibility provides: '(1) States shall cooperate to bring to an end through lawful means any serious breach [of an obligation arising under a peremptory norm] ; (2) No State shall recognize as lawful a situation created by a serious breach [of an obligation arising under a peremptory norm], nor render aid or assistance in maintaining that situation.']

78). The Court considers that the same reasoning is applicable to the application of the customary international law regarding the immunity of one State from proceedings in the courts of another.

...

108. ...The question whether Germany still has a responsibility towards Italy, or individual Italians, in respect of war crimes and crimes against humanity committed by it during the Second World War does not affect Germany's entitlement to immunity. Similarly, the Court's ruling on the issue of immunity can have no effect on whatever responsibility Germany may have.

CASE CONCERNING THE ARREST WARRANT OF 11 APRIL 2000 (DEMOCRATIC REPUBLIC OF THE CONGO v. BELGIUM)

International Court of Justice (2002)

[The background to these proceedings are discussed earlier in the chapter, p. 1130–1, *supra*. The following excerpts of the majority's opinion concern the issue of immunity raised by the Congolese Government.]

47. The Congo maintains that... no criminal prosecution may be brought against a Minister for Foreign Affairs in a foreign court as long as he or she remains in office, and that any finding of criminal responsibility a domestic court in a foreign country, or any act of investigation undertaken with a view to bringing him or her to court, would contravene the principle of immunity from jurisdiction...

...

49. Belgium maintains for its part that, while Ministers for Foreign Affairs in office generally enjoy an immunity from jurisdiction before the courts of a foreign State, such immunity applies only to acts carried out in the course of their official functions, and cannot protect such persons in respect of private acts or when they are acting otherwise than in the performance of their official functions.

50. Belgium further states that, in the circumstances of the present case, Mr. Yerodia enjoyed no immunity at the time when he is alleged to have committed the acts of which he is accused, and that there is no evidence that he was then acting in any official capacity. It observes that the arrest warrant was issued against Mr. Yerodia personally.

51. The Court would observe at the outset that in international law it is firmly established that, as also diplomatic and consular agents, certain holders of high-ranking office in a State, such as the Head of State, Head of Government and Minister for Foreign Affairs, enjoy immunities from jurisdiction in other States, both civil and criminal. For the purposes of the present case, it is only the immunity from criminal jurisdiction and the inviolability of an incumbent Minister for Foreign Affairs that fall for the Court to consider.

52. A certain number of treaty instruments were cited by the Parties in this regard...

…

These conventions provide useful guidance on certain aspects of the question of immunities. They do not, however, contain any provision specifically defining the immunities enjoyed by Ministers for Foreign Affairs. It is consequently on the basis of customary international law that the Court must decide the questions relating to the immunities of such Ministers raised in the present case.

53. In customary international law, the immunities accorded to Ministers for Foreign Affairs are not granted for their personal benefit, but to ensure the effective performance of their functions on behalf of their respective States. In order to determine the extent of these immunities, the Court therefore first consider the nature of the functions exercised by a Minister for Foreign Affairs. He or she is in charge of his or her Government's diplomatic activities and generally acts as its representative in international negotiations and intergovernmental meetings.… In the performance of these functions, he or she frequently required to travel internationally, and thus must be in a position freely to do so whenever the need should arise. He or she must also be in constant communication with the Government, and with its diplomatic missions around the world, and be capable at any time of communicating with representatives of other States. The Court further observes that a Minister for Foreign Affairs, responsible for the conduct of his or her State's relations with all other States, occupies a position such that, like the Head of State or the Head of Government, he or she is recognized under international law as representative of the State solely by virtue of his or her office.…

54. The Court accordingly concludes that the functions of a Minister for Foreign Affairs are such that, throughout the duration of his or her office, he or she when abroad enjoys full immunity from criminal jurisdiction and inviolability. That immunity and that inviolability protect the individual concerned against any act of authority of another State which would hinder him or her in the performance of his or her duties.

55. In this respect, no distinction can be drawn between acts performed by a Minister for Foreign Affairs in an "official" capacity, and those claimed to have been performed in a "private capacity", or, for that matter, between acts performed before the person concerned assumed office as Minister for Foreign Affairs and acts committed during the period of office, Thus, if a Minister for Foreign Affairs is arrested in another State on a criminal charge, he or she is clearly thereby prevented from exercising the functions of his or her office.… Furthermore, even the mere risk that, by travelling to or transiting another State a Minister for Foreign Affairs might be exposing himself or herself to legal proceedings could deter the Minister from travelling internationally when required to do so for the purposes of the performance of his or her official functions.

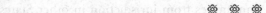

56. The Court will now address Belgium's argument that immunities accorded to incumbent Ministers for Foreign Affairs can in no case protect them where they are suspected of having committed war crimes or crimes against humanity.…

Belgium begins by pointing out that certain provisions of the instruments creating international criminal tribunals state expressly that the official capacity of a person shall not be a bar to the exercise by such tribunals of their jurisdiction.

Belgium also places emphasis on certain decisions of national courts, and in particular on the judgments rendered on 24 March 1999 by the House of Lords in the United Kingdom and on 13 March 2001 by the Court of Cassation in France in the *Pinochet* and *Qaddafi* cases respectively, in which it contends that an exception to the immunity rule was accepted in the case of serious crimes under international law. Thus, according to Belgium, the *Pinochet* decision recognizes an exception to the immunity rule when Lord Millett stated that "[i]nternational law cannot be supposed to have established a crime having the character of a jus cogens and at the same time to have provided an immunity which is co-extensive with the obligation it seeks to impose", or when Lord Phillips of Worth Matravers said that "no established rule of international law requires state immunity *rationae materiae* to be accorded in respect of prosecution for an international crime"....

57. The Congo, for its part, states that, under international law as it currently stands, there is no basis for asserting that there is any exception to the principle of absolute immunity from criminal process of an incumbent Minister for Foreign Affairs where he or she is accused of having committed crimes under international law.

In support of this contention, the Congo refers to State practice, giving particular consideration in this regard to the *Pinochet* and *Qaddafi* cases, and concluding that such practice does not correspond to that which Belgium claims but, on the contrary, confirms the absolute nature of the immunity from criminal process of Heads of State and Ministers for Foreign Affairs. Thus, in the *Pinochet* case, the Congo cites Lord Browne-Wilkinson's statement that "[t]his immunity enjoyed by a head of state in power and an ambassador in post is a complete immunity attached to the person of the head of state or ambassador and rendering him immune from all actions or prosecutions . . . "....

As regards the instruments creating international criminal tribunals and the latter's jurisprudence, these, in the Congo's view, concern only those tribunals, and no inference can be drawn from them in regard to criminal proceedings before national courts against persons enjoying immunity under international law.

58. The Court has carefully examined State practice, including national legislation and those few decisions of national higher courts, such as the House of Lords or the French Court of Cassation. It has been unable to deduce from this practice that there exists under customary international law any form of exception to the rule according immunity from criminal jurisdiction and inviolability to incumbent Ministers for Foreign Affairs, where they are suspected of having committed war crimes or crimes against humanity.

The Court has also examined the rules concerning the immunity or criminal responsibility of persons having an official capacity contained in the legal instruments creating international criminal tribunals, and which are specifically applicable to the latter (see Charter of the International Military Tribunal of Nuremberg, Art. 7; Charter of the International Military Tribunal of Tokyo, Art. 6; Statute of the International Criminal Tribunal for the former Yugoslavia, Art. 7, para. 2; Statute of the International Criminal Tribunal for Rwanda, Art. 6, para. 2; Statute of the International Criminal Court, Art. 27). It finds that these rules likewise do not enable it to conclude that any such an exception exists in customary international law in regard to national courts.

Finally, none of the decisions of the Nuremberg and Tokyo international military tribunals, or of the International Criminal Tribunal for the former Yugoslavia, cited by Belgium deal with the question of the immunities of incumbent Ministers for Foreign Affairs before national courts where they are accused of having committed war crimes or crimes against humanity. The Court accordingly notes that those decisions are in no way at variance with the findings it has reached above.

In view of the foregoing, the Court accordingly cannot accept Belgium's argument in this regard.

…

60. The Court emphasizes, however, that the immunity from jurisdiction enjoyed by incumbent Ministers for Foreign Affairs does not mean that they enjoy impunity in respect of any crimes they might have committed, irrespective of their gravity. Immunity from criminal jurisdiction and individual criminal responsibility are quite separate concepts. While jurisdictional immunity is procedural in nature, criminal responsibility is a question of substantive law. Jurisdictional immunity may well bar prosecution for a certain period or for certain offences; it cannot exonerate the person to whom it applies from all criminal responsibility.

61. Accordingly, the immunities enjoyed under international law by an incumbent or former Minister for Foreign Affairs do not represent a bar to criminal prosecution in certain circumstances.

First, such persons enjoy no criminal immunity under international law in their own countries, and may thus be tried by those countries' courts in accordance with the relevant rules of domestic law.

Secondly, they will cease to enjoy immunity from foreign jurisdiction if the State which they represent or have represented decides to waive that immunity.

Thirdly, after a person ceases to hold the office of Minister for Foreign Affairs, he or she will no longer enjoy all of the immunities accorded by international law in other States. Provided that it has jurisdiction under international law, a court of one State may try a former Minister for Foreign Affairs of another State in respect of acts committed prior or subsequent to his or her period of office, as well as in respect of acts committed during that period of office in a private capacity.

Fourthly, an incumbent or former Minister for Foreign Affairs may be subject to criminal proceedings before certain international criminal courts, where they have jurisdiction. Examples include the International Criminal Tribunal for the former Yugoslavia, and the International Criminal Tribunal for Rwanda, established pursuant to Security Council resolutions under Chapter VII of the United Nations Charter, and the future International Criminal Court created by the 1998 Rome Convention. The latter's Statute expressly provides, in Article 27, paragraph 2, that "[i]mmunities or special procedural rules which may attach to the official capacity of a person, whether under national or international law, shall not bar the Court from exercising its jurisdiction over such a person".

…

PROSECUTOR v. CHARLES TAYLOR, SPECIAL COURT FOR SIERRA LEONE (DECISION ON IMMUNITY FROM JURISDICTION)

(31 May 2004)

[What institutions qualify as an 'international criminal court' according to the ICJ in *Congo v. Belgium*? Does the International Military Tribunal of Nuremberg qualify even though it was established by four states (France, the Soviet Union, the United Kingdom and the United States)? How about the International Military Tribunal of Tokyo, which was established by a military order of General MacArthur and included the participation of 11 states?[44] Why should international criminal courts, in contrast with national courts, be permitted to suspend sovereign immunities?

These issues arose in a case decided by the Special Court for Sierra Leone involving Charles Taylor, the former President of Liberia. In the 1990s, Sierra Leone was ravaged by a civil war that claimed over 75,000 lives and displaced a third of the population. In June 2000, the President of Sierra Leone formally requested the UN Secretary-General to assist in prosecuting perpetrators of atrocities committed during the civil war. In response, the Security Council authorized the Secretary-General to negotiate an agreement between the UN and the Government of Sierra Leone to establish a criminal tribunal. The subsequent agreement, which was signed in January 2002, created the legal framework for the Special Court for Sierra Leone. The Special Court is seated in the capital Freetown. The Court is composed of international and domestic judges, prosecutors and administrative staff. The jurisdiction of the Court includes international and domestic crimes.]

1. This is an application by Mr. Charles Taylor, the former President of the Republic of Liberia, to quash his Indictment and to set aside the warrant for his arrest on the grounds that he is immune from any exercise of the jurisdiction of this court. The Indictment and arrest warrant were approved . . . on 7 March 2003, when Mr. Taylor was Head of State of Liberia.

. . .

5. The Indictment against Mr. Taylor contains seventeen counts. It accuses him of the commission of crimes against humanity and grave breaches of the Geneva Conventions, with intent "to obtain access to the mineral wealth of the Republic of Sierra Leone, in particular the diamond wealth of Sierra Leone, and to destabilize the state". It is alleged that he "provided financial support, military training, personnel, arms, ammunition and other support and encouragement" to rebel factions throughout the armed conflict in Sierra Leone. The counts variously accuse him of responsibility for "terrorizing the civilian population and ordering collective punishment", sexual and physical violence against civilians, use of child soldiers, abductions and forced labour, widespread looting and burning of civilian property, and attacks on and abductions of [UN] peacekeepers and humanitarian assistance workers. In short, the prosecution maintains that from an early stage and acting

[44] The states taking part in the prosecution and judgment were Australia, Canada, China, France, India, the Netherlands, New Zealand, the Philippines, the Soviet Union, the United Kingdom and the United States.

in a private rather than an official capacity he resourced and directed rebel forces, encouraging them in campaigns of terror, torture and mass murder, in order to enrich himself from a share in the diamond mines that were captured by the rebel forces.

...

6. The Applicant argues first that:

a) Citing the judgment of the International Court of Justice ("ICJ") in the case between the *Democratic Republic of Congo v. Belgium* ("*Yerodia* case"), as an incumbent Head of State at the time of his indictment, Charles Taylor enjoyed absolute immunity from criminal prosecution;
b) Exceptions from diplomatic immunities can only derive from other rules of international law such as Security Council resolutions under Chapter VII of the United Nations Charter ("UN Charter");
c) The Special Court does not have Chapter VII powers, therefore judicial orders from the Special Court have the quality of judicial orders from a national court;

...

38. Much issue had been made of the absence of Chapter VII powers in the Special Court. A proper understanding of those powers shows that the absence of the so-called Chapter VII powers does not by itself define the legal status of the Special Court.... Where the Security Council decides to establish a court as a measure to maintain or restore international peace and security it may or may not, at the same time, contemporaneously, call upon the members of the United Nations to lend their cooperation to such court as a matter of obligation.... It is to be observed that in carrying out its duties under its responsibility for the maintenance of international peace and security, the Security Council acts on behalf of the members of the United Nations. The Agreement between the United Nations and Sierra Leone is thus an agreement between *all* members of the United Nations and Sierra Leone. This fact makes the Agreement an expression of the will of the international community. The Special Court established in such circumstances is truly international.

39. By reaffirming in the preamble to Resolution 1315 'that persons who commit or authorize serious violations of international humanitarian law are individually responsible and accountable for those violations and that the international community will exert every effort to bring those responsible to justice in accordance with international standards of justice, fairness and due process of law', it has been made clear that the Special Court was established to fulfill an international mandate and is part of the machinery of international justice.

...

51. A reason for the distinction, in this regard, between national courts and international courts, though not immediately evident, would appear due to the fact that the principle that one sovereign state does not adjudicate on the conduct of another state; the principle of state immunity derives from the equality of sovereign states and therefore has no relevance to international criminal tribunals which are not organs of a state but derive their mandate from the international community.

Another reason is as put by Professor Orentlicher in her amicus brief that: states have considered the collective judgment of the international community to provide a vital safeguard against the potential destabilizing effect of unilateral judgment in this area.

52. Be that as it may, the principle seems now established that the sovereign equality of states does not prevent a Head of State from being prosecuted before an international criminal tribunal or court. We accept the view expressed by Lord Slynn of Hadley that 'there is . . . no doubt that states have been moving towards the recognition of some crimes as those which should not be covered by claims of state or Head of State or other official or diplomatic immunity when charges are brought before international tribunals.'

53. In this result the Appeals Chamber finds that Article 6(2) of the Statute is not in conflict with any peremptory norm of general international law and its provisions must be given effect by this court. . . .

59. Before this matter is concluded, it is apt to observe that the Applicant had at the time the Preliminary Motion was heard ceased to be a Head of State. The immunity *ratione personae* which he claimed had ceased to attach to him. Even if he had succeeded in his application the consequence would have been to compel the Prosecutor to issue a fresh warrant.

QUESTIONS

1. If the UK Government can espouse Al-Adsani's claims directly with the Kuwaiti Government, why can't (or shouldn't) the United Kingdom have Al-Adsani first submit his claims before a national tribunal before taking them up with the foreign government? Would the inclusion of court proceedings not provide a greater degree of independence and impartiality in evaluating private actors' claims?

2. Should the ICJ opinion in *Germany v. Italy* be narrowly construed to apply to a special set of facts in the case? Are there unique reasons to accord immunity for acts committed in the forum state if the conduct involved military forces during an armed conflict? In a concurring opinion, Justice Keith stated:

> At the international level, claims in respect of war damages and losses against former belligerents are in practice dealt with by inter-State negotiations and agreements, as shown in the present case by the treaties of 1947 and 1961; such agreements deal with the claims of loss on a general footing, often on a reciprocal basis and not by way of individual claims, whether based on fault or not. That international practice recognizes consequences of the widespread devastation and destruction that follow major armed conflicts. That destruction, along with the overwhelming need for former belligerent States to reconstruct their societies and their economies, as recognized in that practice, makes completely impracticable, as best as I understand the matter, the Italian proposition in these terms:
>
> > "States (both the State of the victims and the State which is responsible for the violations) when negotiating . . . agreements [for war damages] must ensure that (a) all categories of (if not all individual) victims of war crimes are covered;

> (b) there be sufficient financial means to make the reparation more than symbolic; (c) there be appropriate mechanisms for ensuring that the reparation is made to the victims. Thus, it would not be sufficient for a State just to say that the counterpart agreed to waive all claims in exchange for a sum of money. There must be certainty that the sum of money is sufficient and appropriate; there must be criteria for the identification of victims and for its distribution to victims." (Counter-Memorial of Italy)
>
> How could the stated requirements (a) and (b) possibly be satisfied in Europe following six years of unrelenting warfare? In practice any reparation received has often, and understandably, been used by States for general recovery purposes. And (c) is not an obligation recognized in law or always in fact.

Without state immunity for civil suits in such cases, would the peaceful settlement of armed conflicts be considerably more difficult to obtain? Is that a legitimate factor for an international court to consider?

3. Do you agree with the following statement, also excerpted above, on the part of the ICJ in *Germany v. Italy*?:

> [R]ecognizing the immunity of a foreign State in accordance with customary international law does not amount to recognizing as lawful a situation created by the breach of a jus cogens rule, or rendering aid and assistance in maintaining that situation, and so cannot contravene the principle in Article 41 of the International Law Commission's Articles on State Responsibility.

In the initial case that gave rise to the dispute between Germany and Italy, the Italian Court of Cassation had relied, in part, on Article 41 of the Articles of State Responsibility in denying sovereign immunity (*Ferrini v. Federal Republic of Germany*, Court of Cassation, Decision No. 5044/2004, 11 Mar. 2004). Consider the Court's reasoning:

> [S]uch rights are deemed to be inviolable[;] and it is recognized that all States are permitted to suppress their breach, irrespective of where such breach is committed, in accordance with the principles of universal jurisdiction (see the *Furundzija* judgment at pp. 15–16): in some cases it is even considered that States are obliged to suppress their breach (see especially Article 146 of 1949 Geneva Convention IV Relative to the Protection of Civilian Persons in Time of War). For this reason there is no doubt that the principle of universal jurisdiction also applies to civil actions which trace their origins to such crimes.
>
> This conclusion strengthens the conviction that such grave violations entail, even in respect of States, a response which, in qualitative terms, is different and more severe than that reserved for other illegal acts. In line with this tendency, it is affirmed in the *Furundzija* judgment that those States not involved in the illegal act are under a duty not to recognize the legitimacy of those circumstances which gave rise to its commission. In the same context, the Draft Declaration on the International Responsibility of States referred to above "forbids" States from helping to perpetuate situations which lead to violations and "obliges" them to use all legitimate means to bring an end to illegal activities (Article 41).
>
> The recognition of immunity from jurisdiction for States responsible for such misdeeds stands in stark contrast to the above normative analysis, in that such

recognition does not assist, but rather impedes, the protection of those norms and principles which are considered by the community of nations to be so essential as to justify mandatory measures in response to serious violations.

4. What factors, if any, distinguish the *Al-Adsani* and *Germany v. Italy* opinions from the *Arrest Warrant* opinion? Would (and should) the holding in the *Arrest Warrant* decision apply as well to a civil suit against Mr Yerodia?

5. Should official immunity of the sort ascribed to the Congolese Foreign Minister extend to acts committed by a defendant outside her own country? For example, imagine a Belgian judge proceeding against a foreign minister for an extrajudicial killing committed in Belgium.

6. Do you agree with the reasoning of the Special Court for Sierra Leone? Should the lack of Chapter VII authority have any bearing on whether a defendant enjoys immunity before such a judicial body?

DECISION ON THE FAILURE BY THE REPUBLIC OF MALAWI TO COMPLY WITH THE COOPERATION REQUESTS ISSUED BY THE COURT WITH RESPECT TO THE ARREST AND SURRENDER OF PRESIDENT OMAR AL BASHIR

International Criminal Court, Pre-Trial Chamber I (12 Dec. 2011)

[In 2005, the Security Council passed a Resolution, under Chapter VII of the UN Charter, referring the Situation of Darfur to the International Criminal Court (ICC), see p. 1341, *infra*. Upon an application by the Prosecutor, the Court subsequently issued an international arrest warrant for the Sudanese President Omar Al Bashir charging him with war crimes, crimes against humanity and genocide. Alongside the arrest warrant, the Court issued a request to all states parties to the ICC for the arrest and surrender of President Bashir. At the time, the defendant was the incumbent Head of State of Sudan, which was not a state party to the ICC.

The African Union (AU) requested the UN Security Council to defer the indictment for a year, which the Council has the power to do under Article 16 of the ICC Statute. (See the Documents Supplement in the Online Resource Centre.) The AU submitted that a deferral would provide an opportunity for peaceful settlement of the Darfur conflict. The Council did not act upon the request, and AU members suggested that the Council failed even to acknowledge their request for a long period of time.

Two articles of the ICC Statute suggest that states parties to the ICC are compelled to arrest President Bashir if he sets foot in their country, and a third article suggests the contrary. Article 89(1) requires states parties to cooperate with a request by the Court for the arrest and surrender of individuals located in their territory. It states: 'The Court may transmit a request for the arrest and surrender of a person...to any State on the territory of which that person may be found and shall request the cooperation of that State in the arrest and surrender of such a person. States Parties shall, in accordance with the provisions of this Part and the procedure under their national law, comply with requests for arrest and surrender.'

Additionally, Article 27 (entitled 'irrelevance of official capacity') provides in full:

1. This Statute shall apply equally to all persons without any distinction based on official capacity. In particular, official capacity as a Head of State or Government, a member of a Government or parliament, an elected representative or a government official shall in no case exempt a person from criminal responsibility under this Statute, nor shall it, in and of itself, constitute a ground for reduction of sentence.
2. Immunities or special procedural rules which may attach to the official capacity of a person, whether under national or international law, shall not bar the Court from exercising its jurisdiction over such a person.

However, another article of the ICC Treaty suggests that states parties may not be compelled to surrender an official of a non-state party who is protected by immunities under international law. Article 98(1) states: 'The Court may not proceed with a request for surrender or assistance which would require the requested State to act inconsistently with its obligations under international law with respect to the State or diplomatic immunity of a person or property of a third State, unless the Court can first obtain the cooperation of that third State for the waiver of the immunity.'

The question thus arose whether President Bashir, as the sitting head of state of a non-state party, was immune from arrest and transfer to the ICC. In 2009, the AU issued a Decision stating that 'in view of the fact that the request by the African Union [to the Security Council to defer the proceedings against President Bashir] has never been acted upon, the AU Member States shall not cooperate pursuant to the provisions of Article 98 of the Rome Statute of the ICC relating to immunities, for the arrest and surrender of President Omar El Bashir of The Sudan' (Doc. Assembly/AU/13(XIII), Assembly/AU/Dec.245(XIII), 3 July 2009). At the same time, the Decision could be read to accept that the Court constituted the proper authority to decide upon the relevant legal obligations. That is, the Decision also 'takes note that any party affected by the indictment has the right of legal recourse to the processes provided for in the Rome Statute regarding the appeal process and the issue of immunity.' Additionally, the AU Decision did not reflect a unified position. The Government of South Africa, for example, subsequently stated, 'South Africa...prides itself as a country that respects the rule of law, including international law and the struggle for a rules based international system. Furthermore, South Africa's constitution is based on the values of "human dignity, the achievement of equality and the advancement of human rights and freedoms". Ascension to the AU Assembly Decision will signal non-adherence to the above, which will negatively impact on our international reputation and stature as observed during South Africa's non-permanent membership to the UNSC.' In 2010, the AU issued a follow-up Decision which reiterated its position of noncooperation. The 2010 Decision also added a statement 'request[ing] Member States to balance, where applicable, their obligations to the AU with their obligations to the ICC'. That proviso was reportedly included at the insistence of states such as South Africa.

In a demonstration of opposition to the Court's international arrest warrant, President Bashir travelled to several states including parties and nonparties to the ICC. His visits to states parties included Chad, Djibouti, Kenya and Malawi. The state authorities in those countries made no attempt to arrest President Bashir — which brought the ICC's assertion of power and the proposed head of state immunity into direct confrontation. A Pre-Trial Chamber squarely addressed the legal dispute in a judgment issued in December 2011, parts of which are excerpted below.

Notably, in the months and weeks prior to the judgment, other developments raised the stakes for all sides to the dispute. First, in mid 2011, the AU reiterated its position of noncooperation with respect to President Bashir's arrest warrant. The AU also expanded its position of noncooperation to include the situation in Libya. By that point, the Security Council had also referred the Libyan conflict to the ICC, and the Court had issued an international arrest warrant for Libya's sitting Head of State Muammar Gaddafi (see pp. 1344 and 1333, *infra*). The AU Decision requested the Security Council to issue a deferral for Libya as well, and 'decide[d] that [AU] Member States shall not cooperate in the execution of [Gadaffi's] arrest warrant'. Second, in November 2011, a national body, the Court of Appeal of Kenya, held that Kenyan state authorities violated the state's obligations under the ICC Treaty by failing to arrest President Bashir when he was in the country. In response to that decision, the Chair of the AU Commission reiterated the organization's call for non-cooperation. Days later the ICC's Pre-Trial Chamber handed down its judgment, which follows.]

1. ...[T]he United Nations Security Council issued Resolution 1593 (2005), whereby it referred the situation in Darfur to the Court and 'urge[d] all States and concerned regional and other international organizations to cooperate fully' with the Court.

...

22. The Chamber will now assess whether, under international law, either former or sitting heads of States enjoy immunity in respect of proceedings before international courts....

23. The Chamber notes that as early as March 1919, in the aftermath of the First World War, the Commission on the Responsibility of the Authors of the War and on Enforcement of Penalties recommended the establishment of a High Tribunal rejecting the idea of immunities even for Heads of States...

...

34. The ICJ in the "Arrest Warrant Case" is concerned solely with immunity across national jurisdictions....The ICJ majority discussion of customary international law immunity is therefore distinct from the present circumstances, as here an international court is seeking arrest for international crimes. This distinction is meaningful because, as argued by Antonio Cassese, the rationale for foreign state officials being entitled to raise personal immunity before national courts is that otherwise national authorities might use prosecutions to unduly impede or limit a foreign state's ability to engage in international action. Cassese emphasised that

this danger does not arise with international courts and tribunals, which are "totally independent of states and subject to strict rules of impartiality".

35. [The Pre-Trial Chamber discusses the decision by the Special Court for Sierra Leone in the *Charles Taylor* case, including that Court's explanation that 'the fact that the principle that one sovereign state does not adjudicate on the conduct of another state; the principle of state immunity derives from the equality of sovereign states and therefore has no relevance to international criminal tribunals which are not organs of a state but derive their mandate from the international community."]

36. Therefore, the Chamber finds that the principle in international law is that immunity of either former or sitting Heads of State can not be invoked to oppose a prosecution by an international court. This is equally applicable to former or sitting Heads of States not Parties to the Statute whenever the Court may exercise jurisdiction. In this particular case, the Chamber notes that it is exercising jurisdiction following a referral by the United Nations Security Council made under Chapter VII of the United Nations Charter, in accordance with article 13(b) of the [ICC] Statute.

37. The Chamber notes that there is an inherent tension between articles 27(2) and 98(1) of the Statute and the role immunity plays when the Court seeks cooperation regarding the arrest of a Head of State. The Chamber considers that Malawi, and by extension the African Union, are not entitled to rely on article 98(1) of the Statute to justify refusing to comply with the Cooperation Requests.

38. First, as described above, immunity for Heads of State before international courts has been rejected time and time again dating all the way back to World War I.

39. Second, there has been an increase in Head of State prosecutions by international courts in the last decade. Only one international prosecution of a Head of State had been initiated when the judgment in the "Arrest Warrant Case" was rendered; this trial (Slobodan Milosevic) began only two days before this judgment was issued and its existence is not even referenced by the ICJ majority. Subsequent to 14 February 2002 [the date of the ICJ decision], international prosecutions against Charles Taylor, Muammar Gaddafi, Laurent Gbagbo and the present case show that initiating international prosecutions against Heads of State have gained widespread recognition as accepted practice.

40. Third, the Statute now has reached 120 States Parties in its 9 plus years of existence, all of whom have accepted having any immunity they had under international law stripped from their top officials. All of these states have renounced any claim to immunity by ratifying the language of article 27(2).... Even some States which have not joined the Court have twice allowed for situations to be referred to the Court by United Nations Security Council Resolutions,[45] undoubtedly in the knowledge that these referrals might involve prosecution of Heads of State who might ordinarily have immunity from domestic prosecution.

41. Fourth, all the States referenced above have ratified this Statute and/or entrusted this Court with exercising "its jurisdiction over persons for the most

45 [Eds.: The Pre-Trial Chamber's reference here is to the members of the Security Council who voted for the Council to refer the Darfur and Libyan situations to the ICC.]

serious crimes of international concern". It is facially inconsistent for Malawi to entrust the Court with this mandate and then refuse to surrender a Head of State prosecuted for orchestrating genocide, war crimes and crimes against humanity....

42. The Chamber considers that the international community's commitment to rejecting immunity in circumstances where international courts seek arrest for international crimes has reached a critical mass. If it ever was appropriate to say so, it is certainly no longer appropriate to say that customary international law immunity applies in the present context.

43. For the above reasons and the jurisprudence cited earlier in this decision, the Chamber finds that customary international law creates an exception to Head of State immunity when international courts seek a Head of State's arrest for the commission of international crimes. There is no conflict between Malawi's obligations towards the Court and its obligations under customary international law; therefore, article 98(1) of the Statute does not apply.

44. Furthermore, the Chamber is of the view that the unavailability of immunities with respect to prosecutions by international courts applies to any act of cooperation by States which forms an integral part of those prosecutions.

45. Indeed, the cooperation regime between the Court and States Parties, as established in Part IX of the Statute, can not in any way be equated with the inter-state cooperation regime which exists between sovereign States. This is evidenced by the Statute itself which refers in article 91 of the Statute to the "distinct nature of the Court", and in article 102 of the Statute which makes a clear distinction between "surrender", meaning the delivering up of a person by a State to the Court, and "extradition", meaning the delivering up of a person by one State to another as provided by treaty, convention or national legislation.

46. Indeed, it is the view of the Chamber that when cooperating with this Court and therefore acting on its behalf, States Parties are instruments for the enforcement of the *jus puniendi* of the international community whose exercise has been entrusted to this Court when States have failed to prosecute those responsible for the crimes within its jurisdiction.

...

QUESTIONS

1. Does the Pre-Trial Chamber's ruling on head of state immunity turn on the fact that the Darfur situation was referred by the Security Council under Chapter VII? Would the same ruling apply equally to other situations, for example for crimes committed on the territory of a state party (e.g., Afghanistan) when the alleged defendant is the head of state of a non-state party (e.g., Pakistan or the United States)? Notably, the Darfur Resolution, p. 1341, *infra*, did not compel states (other than Sudan) to cooperate with the ICC. Accordingly, the first paragraph of the Pre-Trial Chamber's opinion drew on relatively weak language in the resolution where the Council 'urge[d]' states to cooperate with the Court. Should the Pre-Trial Chamber have relied more (or less) on the fact that the case involved a referral by the Security Council?

2. The Pre-Trial Chamber states that 'the international community's commitment to rejecting immunity in circumstances where international courts seek arrest for international crimes has reached a critical mass.' Does the record discussed in the opinion support this proposition? What might the Chamber mean by 'a critical mass', and is it a potentially useful concept?

3. In criticizing the Pre-Trial Chamber's opinion, Professor Dapo Akande writes:

> The basic argument for a lack of immunity in international tribunals is that the international law immunity of foreign heads of States from national authorities is necessary to prevent national interference in the ability of a foreign State to engage in international action but that this danger does not arise with international courts since they are independent of States and act impartially. This argument is adopted by the Pre-Trial Chamber, which cites Antonio Cassese on this point (para. 34). This is quite an odd argument to make given that international courts are often created by States. The basic distinction being made between international and national courts fails to stand up to scrutiny as it would appear that what a State cannot do individually, it can do by agreement with one other State (two other States, ten other States?)
>
> ...
>
> Towards the end of its decision, the Chamber makes the grandiose statement (para. 46) that
>
> > 'it is the view of the Chamber that when cooperating with this Court and therefore acting on its behalf, States Parties are instruments for the enforcement of the *jus puniendi* of the international community whose exercise has been entrusted to this Court when States have failed to prosecute those responsible for the crimes within its jurisdiction.'
>
> This is somewhat true but the Chamber should also recall that is not the entire international community that has entrusted jurisdiction to the Court, less than two thirds of the States of the world have done so. The other one third cannot simply be ignored.[46]

Do you agree with Professor Akande's criticism?

[46] D. Akande, 'ICC Issues Detailed Decision on Bashir's Immunity (…At Long Last…) But Gets the Law Wrong', EJIL Talk!, 15 Dec. 2011, at www.ejiltalk.org/icc-issues-detailed-decision-on-bashir%E2%80%99s-immunity-at-long-last-but-gets-the-law-wrong/.

14

Measuring and Evaluating Human Rights Performance

How effective has the international human rights regime been in improving state practices around the world? And how do we measure effectiveness? This chapter is divided into two sections. Section A considers the measurement of human rights performance through the use of quantitative and qualitative indicators. We examine recent efforts by international organizations to develop metrics for assessing human rights performance. The readings discuss not only the accuracy and reliability of such indicators, but also the politics of their generation and deployment by various actors. The readings also raise important questions about potential differences between civil and political rights (CPR) and economic, social and cultural rights (ESCR) in this domain.

Section B considers interdisciplinary research on the empirical effects of international human rights law on state practice. Building on materials in earlier chapters, this section analyses the conditions under which states have been more or less likely to comply with the norms of the international human rights regime, and the motivations for compliance with (or defiance of) international standards. The research that is foregrounded in this section also considers the effects of international law beyond strict compliance with formal rules such as the broader effects of international law on mobilizing civil society actors. These readings ultimately raise questions about how to improve the design of the international regime to effectuate better human rights practices on the ground.

A. INDICATORS: THE CHALLENGE OF MEASURING HUMAN RIGHTS

Over the past five years, the Office of the High Commissioner for Human Rights (OHCHR) has engaged in a project to promote the creation and use of indicators to measure human rights performance. This project comes at a time when major intergovernmental organizations (e.g., the World Bank), nongovernmental organizations (e.g., Freedom House) and academic research programmes have also expanded the use of empirical measures of human rights-related practices across the world. Despite the institutional support for these efforts, they have also met with criticism from some academics and practitioners. In this section, we examine a wide range of perspectives on the ability and desirability of developing human rights indicators for both CPR and ESCR.

REPORT ON INDICATORS FOR PROMOTING AND MONITORING THE IMPLEMENTATION OF HUMAN RIGHTS

UN Doc. HRI/MC/2008/3 (6 June 2008)

...

14. Events-based data consists mainly of data on alleged or reported cases of human rights violations, identified victims and perpetrators. Indicators, such as alleged incidence of arbitrary deprivations of life, enforced or involuntary disappearances, arbitrary detention and torture, are usually reported by NGOs and are or can be processed in a standardized manner by, for instance, national human rights institutions and special procedures of the United Nations. In general, such data may underestimate the incidence of violations and may even prevent valid comparisons over time or across regions, yet it could provide some indication to the treaty bodies in undertaking their assessment of human rights situation in a given country. Though recent attempts have shown that this method can also be applied for monitoring the protection of economic, social and cultural rights, it has been mainly and most effectively used for monitoring the violation of civil and political rights only.

...

16. The contextual relevance of indicators is a key consideration in the acceptability and use of indicators among potential users. Countries and regions within countries differ in terms of their level of development and realization of human rights. These differences are reflected in the nature of institutions, the policies and the priorities of the State. Therefore, it may not be possible to have a set of universal indicators to assess the realization of human rights. Having said that, it is also true that certain human rights indicators, for example those capturing realization of some civil and political rights, may well be relevant across all countries and their regions, whereas others that capture realization of economic or social rights, such as the rights to health or adequate housing, may have to be customized to be of relevance in different countries. But even in the latter case, it would be relevant to monitor the minimum core content of the rights universally. Thus, in designing a set of human rights indicators, like any other set of indicators, there is a need to strike a balance between universally relevant indicators and contextually specific indicators, as both kinds of indicators are needed.

Structural indicators

18. Structural indicators reflect the ratification and adoption of legal instruments and existence of basic institutional mechanisms deemed necessary for facilitating realization of a human right. They capture commitments or the intent of the State in undertaking measures for the realization of the concerned human right. Structural indicators have to focus foremost on the nature of domestic law as relevant to the concerned right — whether it incorporates the international standards — and the institutional mechanisms that promote and protect the standards.... A national policy statement on a subject is an instrument that is expected to outline a Government's objectives, policy framework, strategy and/or a concrete plan of action to address issues under that subject. While providing an indication on the commitment of the Government to address the concerned subject, it may also provide relevant benchmarks for holding the Government accountable for its acts of commission or omission concerning that subject. Moreover, a policy statement is a means to translate the human rights obligations of a State party into an implementable programme of action that helps in the realization of the human rights. Thus, while identifying structural indicators on different rights and their attributes, an attempt was made to highlight the importance of having specific policy statements on issues of direct relevance to that human right attribute....

Process indicators

19. Process indicators relate State policy instruments with milestones that cumulate into outcome indicators, which in turn can be more directly related to the realization of human rights. State policy instruments refers to all such measures including public programmes and specific interventions that a State is willing to take in order to give effect to its intent/commitments to attain outcomes identified with the realization of a given human right. By defining the process indicators in terms of a concrete "cause-and-effect relationship", the accountability of the State to its obligations can be better assessed. At the same time, these indicators help in directly monitoring the progressive fulfilment of the right or the process of protecting the right, as the case may be for the realization of the concerned right. Process indicators are more sensitive to changes than outcome indicators and hence are better at capturing progressive realization of the right or in reflecting the efforts of the State parties in protecting the rights.

20. Two considerations guided the selection and formulation of process indicators. The first was to ensure that the articulation of process indicators reflected a causal relationship with the relevant structural as well as outcome indicator. Thus, for instance, a process indicator of the right to health — proportion of school-going children educated on health and nutrition issues — was chosen so that it could be related to the corresponding structural indicator, namely "time frame and coverage of national policy on child health and nutrition", as well as with the outcome indicator "proportion of underweight children under 5 years of age". The second

consideration in giving shape to a process indicator was to bringing out explicitly some measure of an effort being undertaken by the duty-holder in implementing its obligation. Thus, indicators such as "proportion of requests for social security benefits reviewed and met in the reporting period" or "proportion of the population that was extended access to improved sanitation in the reporting period" were included in the category of process indicators....

Outcome indicators

21. Outcome indicators capture attainments, individual and collective, that reflect the status of realization of human rights in a given context. It is not only a more direct measure of the realization of a human right but it also reflects the importance of the measure in the enjoyment of the right. Since it consolidates over time the impact of various underlying processes (that can be captured by one or more process indicators), an outcome indicator is often a slow-moving indicator, less sensitive to capturing momentary changes than a process indicator would be. For example, life expectancy or mortality indicators could be a function of immunization of the population, education or public health awareness, as well as of availability of, and access of individuals to, adequate nutrition....

[The report includes the following explanation in an accompanying footnote.] There is some similarity in process and outcome indicators which comes from the fact that any process can either be measured in terms of the inputs going into a process or alternately in terms of the immediate outputs or outcomes that the process generates. Thus, a process indicator on the coverage of immunization among children can be measured in terms of the public resources or expenditure going into immunization programme (which is the input variant) or in terms of the proportion of children covered under the programme (which is an outcome or impact variant). In terms of the definition outlined in this note, both these indicators are process indicators. They contribute to lowering child mortality, which is an outcome indicator as it captures the consolidated impact of the immunization programme over a period of time and it can be more directly related to the realisation of the right to health attribute on the child mortality and health care. It is desirable that the process indicator be measured in terms of the physical milestone that it generates rather than in terms of the resources that go into the concerned process. This is because experience across countries and across regions within the same country reveals that there is no monotonic relationship between public expenditure and the physical outcome that such expenditure generates. The physical outcome is a function of resources and other institutional and non-institutional factors that vary from place to place and thereby make it difficult to interpret indicators on public expenditure. For instance, it is possible that a lower per capita public expenditure produces better outcomes in one region in comparison to another region within the same country.

[The following tables are included in an Annex to the Report. They are intended to illustrate the approach proposed by the OHCHR.]

List of illustrative indicators on the right to adequate food (UDHR, Art. 25) (* MDG related indicators)

	Nutrition	Food Safety and Consumer Protection	Food Availability	Food Accessibility
Structural	• International human rights treaties, relevant to the right to adequate food, ratified by the State • Date of entry into force and coverage of the right to adequate food in the Constitution or other forms of superior law • Date of entry into force and coverage of domestic laws for implementing the right to adequate food • Number of registered and/or active non-governmental organizations (per 100,000 persons) involved in the promotion and protection of the right to adequate food			
	• Time frame and coverage of national policy on nutrition and nutrition adequacy norms	• Time frame and coverage of national policy on food safety and consumer protection • Number of registered and/or active civil society organisations working in the area of food safety and consumer protection	• Time frame and coverage of national policy on agricultural production and food availability • Time frame and coverage of national policy on drought, crop failure and disaster management	
Process	• Proportion of received complaints on the right to adequate food investigated and adjudicated by the national human rights institution, human rights ombudsperson or other mechanisms and the proportion of these responded to effectively by the government • Net official development assistance (ODA) for food security received or provided as a proportion of public expenditure on food security or Gross National Income			
	• Proportion of targeted population that was brought above the minimum level of dietary energy consumption* in the reporting period • Proportion of targeted population covered under public nutrition supplement programmes • Coverage of targeted population under public programmes on nutrition education and awareness • Proportion of targeted population that was extended access to an improved drinking water source* in the reporting period	• Disposal rate or average time to adjudicate a case registered in a consumer court • Share of public social sector budget spent on food safety and consumer protection advocacy, education, research and implementation of law and regulations relevant to the right • Proportion of food producing and distributing establishments inspected for food quality standards and frequency of inspections • Proportion of cases adjudicated under food safety and consumer protection law in the reporting period	• Proportion of female headed households or targeted population with legal title to agricultural land • Arable irrigated land per person • Proportion of farmers availing extension services • Share of public budget spent on strengthening domestic agricultural production (e.g. agriculture-extension, irrigation, credit, marketing) • Proportion of per capita availability of major food items sourced through domestic production, import & food-aid • Cereal import dependency ratio in the reporting period	• Share of household consumption of major food items for targeted population group met through publicly assisted programmes • Unemployment rate or average wage rate of targeted segments of labour force • Proportion of targeted population that was brought above the poverty line in the reporting period • Work participation rates, by sex and target groups • Estimated access of women and girls to adequate food within household • Coverage of programmes to secure access to productive resources for target groups

	Nutrition	Food Safety and Consumer Protection	Food Availability	Food Accessibility
Outcome	• Prevalence of underweight and stunting children under-five years of age* • Proportion of adults with body-mass index (BMI) <18.5	• Number of recorded deaths and incidence of food poisoning related to adulterated food	• Per capita availability of major food items of local consumption	• Proportion of population below minimum level of dietary energy consumption* / proportion of undernourished population • Average household expenditure on food for the bottom three deciles of population or targeted population
	• Death rates, including infant and under-five mortality rates, associated with and prevalence of malnutrition (including under-, overnutrition and inadequate intake of nutrients)			
24.4.08	***All indicators should be disaggregated by prohibited grounds of discrimination, as applicable and reflected in metasheets***			

List of illustrative indicators on the right to liberty and security of person (UDHR, Art. 3)

	Arrest and detention based on criminal charges	Administrative deprivation of liberty	Effective review by court	Security from crime and abuse by law enforcement officials
Structural	• International human rights treaties, relevant to the right to liberty and security of person, ratified by the State • Date of entry into force and coverage of the right to liberty and security of person in the Constitution or other forms of superior law • Date of entry into force and coverage of domestic laws for implementing the right to liberty and security of person • Time frame and coverage of policy and administrative framework against any arbitrary deprivations of liberty, whether based on criminal charges, sentences or decisions by a court or administrative grounds (e.g. immigration, mental illness, educational purposes, vagrancy) • Type of accreditation of National Human Rights Institutions by the rules of procedure of the International Coordinating Committee of National Institutions			
	• Legal time limits for an arrested or detained person before being informed of the reasons for the arrest or detention; before being brought to or having the case reviewed by an authority exercising judicial power; and for the trial duration of a person in detention			• Time frame and coverage of policy and administrative framework on security, handling of criminality and abuses by law enforcement officials
Process	• Proportion of received complaints on the right to liberty and security of person investigated and adjudicated by the national human rights institution, human rights ombudsperson or other mechanisms and the proportion of these responded to effectively by the government • Proportion of communications sent by the UN Working Group on Arbitrary Detention responded to effectively by the government • Proportion of law enforcement officials (including police, military and State security force) trained in rules of conduct concerning proportional use of force, arrest, detention, interrogation or punishment			
	• Number/proportion of arrests or entries into detention (pre- and pending trial) on the basis of a court order or due to action taken directly by executive authorities in the reporting period • Number/proportion of defendants released from pre- and trial detentions in exchange for bail or due to non-filing of charges in the reporting period	• Number/proportion of arrests or entries into detention under national administrative provisions (e.g. security, immigration control, mental illness and other medical grounds, educational purposes, drug addiction, financial obligations) in the reporting period • Number/proportion of releases from administrative detentions in the reporting period	• Proportion of cases where the time for arrested or detained persons before being informed of the reasons of arrest; before receiving notice of the charge (in a legal sense); or before being informed of the reasons of administrative detention exceeded the respective legally stipulated time limit • Number of *habeas corpus* and similar petitions filed in courts in the reporting period • Proportion of bail applications accepted by the court in the reporting period • Proportion of arrested or detained persons provided with access to a counsellor or legal aid	• Proportion of law enforcement officials formally investigated for physical and non-physical abuse or crime, including arbitrary arrest and detention (based on criminal or administrative grounds) in the reporting period • Proportion of formal investigations of law enforcement officials resulting in disciplinary actions or prosecution in the reporting period • Number of persons arrested, adjudicated, convicted or serving sentence for violent crime (including homicide, rape, assault) per 100,000 population in the reporting period

	Arrest and detention based on criminal charges	Administrative deprivation of liberty	Effective review by court	Security from crime and abuse by law enforcement officials
			• Proportion of cases subject to review by a higher court or appellate body • Reported cases where pre- and trial detentions exceeded the legally stipulated time limit in the reporting period	• Proportion of law enforcement officials killed in line of duty in the reporting period • Firearms owners per 100,000 population / Number of firearms licences withdrawn in the reporting period • Proportion of violent crimes with the use of firearms • Proportion of violent crimes reported to the police (victimisation survey) in the reporting period
Outcome	• Number of detentions per 100,000 population, on the basis of a court order or due to action by executive authorities at the end of the reporting period • Reported cases of arbitrary detentions, including post-trial detentions (e.g. as reported to the UN Working Group on Arbitrary Detention) in the reporting period		• Proportion of arrests and detentions declared unlawful by national courts • Proportion of victims released and compensated after arrests or detentions declared unlawful by judicial authority	• Proportion of population feeling 'unsafe', (e.g. walking alone in area after dark or alone at home at night) • Incidence and prevalence of physical and non-physical abuse or crime, including by law enforcement officials in line of duty, per 100,000 population, in the reporting period
24.04.08	***All indicators should be disaggregated by prohibited grounds of discrimination, as applicable and reflected in metasheets***			

NOTE

The World Bank notes that the measurement and analysis of poverty, inequality and vulnerability are crucial for cognitive, analytical, policymaking, and monitoring and evaluation purposes. The Bank emphasizes three key concepts. (1) *Poverty* which focuses on whether households or individuals possess enough resources or abilities to meet their current needs. Individuals' income, consumption, education or other attributes that are below a defined threshold are considered poor in that respect. (2) *Inequality*, especially in income distribution or consumption, is based on the premise that the relative position of individuals or households in society is an important aspect of their welfare. In addition, the overall level of inequality, in monetary and nonmonetary terms, is an important summary indicator of the relevant group's welfare. (3) *Vulnerability*, defined as the probability or risk today of being in poverty — or falling deeper into poverty — in the future.[1]

But measuring the extent of poverty and related phenomena is not the same as measuring the fulfilment of economic and social rights (ESR) obligations contained in international treaties. The specific nature of those obligations (including progressive realization and resource availability) as well as cross-cutting themes such as equality and non-discrimination, and an ultimate focus on individual well-being should all be taken into account in measuring ESR. The 1993 Vienna World Conference on Human Rights called for a 'system of indicators to measure progress in the realization' of ESR, and international monitoring bodies such as the UN Committee on ESCR, the African Commission on Human and Peoples' Rights and the Inter-American Commission on Human Rights[2] have all called upon states and other actors to develop indicators for this purpose. In particular, the UN Committee's reporting guidelines request states to provide '[s]tatistical data on the enjoyment of each Covenant right, disaggregated by age, gender, ethnic origin, urban/rural population and other relevant status, on an annual comparative basis over the past five years' (UN Doc. E/C.12/2008/2 (24 Mar. 2009)) and over half of the Committee's General Comments call for the use of indicators. Partly as a result, the OHCHR has developed 'a conceptual and methodological framework on indicators', aspects of which are summarized in the following report.

THE USE OF INDICATORS IN REALIZING ESCR, REPORT OF THE HIGH COMMISSIONER FOR HUMAN RIGHTS

UN Doc. E/2011/90 (13 May 2011)

II. Notion of human rights indicators

2. [T]he term "human rights indicators" refers to specific information on the state of an object, event, activity or an outcome that can be related to human rights

[1] See Aline Coudouel et al, *Poverty Measurement and Analysis* (2002), 29.

[2] Inter-American Commission on Human Rights, Guidelines for Preparation of Progress Indicators in the Area of Economic, Social and Cultural Rights, OEA/Ser.L/V/II.132, Doc. 14 rev.1, 19 July 2008.

norms and standards; that addresses and reflects human rights principles and concerns; and that can be used to assess and monitor the promotion and implementation of human rights....

3. Indicators can be of a quantitative or qualitative nature. [Q]uantitative indicators are those expressed primarily as numbers, percentages or indices. Qualitative indicators cover information articulated foremost in narrative or categorical forms....

III. Rationale for the use of indicators for implementing and monitoring economic, social and cultural rights

...

B. Needs and opportunities for the use of indicators for implementing and monitoring economic, social and cultural rights

8. In addition to normative requirements, there are more practical needs and opportunities for the use of human rights indicators. First, the use of indicators has been sought as a tool to strengthen systematic measurement of changes made over time in the enjoyment of human rights....

9. Second, the human rights community has been seeking ways to move beyond traditional, generic analysis of "economic and social situations" that fail to articulate a clear linkage with the human rights framework. In this context, methodologies which link statistical and other data to human rights standards are needed....

10. Lastly, the use of human rights indicators helps facilitate the operationalization of human rights in public policies....

IV. Considerations for the effective use of human rights indicators

...

A. Selection of indicators and collection of data

12. First, [there must be] a clear link to the applicable international and national human rights framework....

13. Second, it is essential to disaggregate indicators in order to capture existing or potential patterns of discrimination....

14. Third, it is important to strike a balance between contextually specific indicators and universally relevant indicators....

15. Fourth, to be practical, indicators should be: relevant, valid and realizable; simple, timely and few in number; based on objective, reliable and independent data-generating mechanisms; suitable for comparison over time and territory; in line with relevant international statistical standards; and possible to disaggregate by prohibited grounds of discrimination.

16. Fifth, the process of the production, processing and dissemination of data should also comply with legal, ethical and human rights safeguards, including the right to privacy, data protection and confidentiality, self-identification and participation....

17. Last, data should be sought from a variety of reliable and objective sources, including Governments (such as national statistical bureaus), international organizations (such as United Nations agencies), civil society organizations and national and international human rights mechanisms....

...

V. Role of indicators in implementing and monitoring economic, social and cultural rights

22. Combined with normative analysis, indicators and benchmarks can be useful to: (a) substantiate normative analysis in human rights assessments; (b) set clearer steps for implementing public policies and programmes; (c) set objective criteria for monitoring progress made towards full realization of rights; and (d) support claims on duty-bearers, such as governmental authorities, in courts and other redress mechanisms....

...

NOTE

Merry (p. 1238, *infra*) has divided indicators into three orders. 'As numerical representations, indicators range from simple counts of events or people to ratios to composites with greater interpretive depth and theoretical elaboration.' For her, first order numbers are 'counts, as in population censuses or counts of unemployed workers or racial minorities'. Second order numbers are 'ratios or percentages, such as maternal mortality, years of expected schooling per person, GDP per capita', and third order numbers are 'composites made up of multiple data sources blended together and weighted to produce a single number or rank'. These third order, or composite, indexes, are common in relation to CPR issues. Examples include Freedom House's annual rankings of Freedom in the World, *The Economist*'s Democracy Index, the UN's Rule of Law Indicators Project, the World Justice Project's Rule of Law Index and the World Bank's Worldwide Governance Indicators.

In recent years, important endeavours have been made to construct comparable approaches to ESR. One of these is the Social and Economic Rights Fulfillment (SERF) Index which measures states' compliance with their obligations for progressive realization of ESR, 'focusing on outcomes reflected in enjoyment of rights by people and adjusted for state capacity'. It takes account of the six principal rights listed in the International Covenant on Economic, Social and Cultural Rights (ICESCR) (the rights to food, education, health, housing, work and social security). To ensure that the indicators used are '(i) based on reliable data; (ii) measured with objective methods; (iii) legitimately comparable across countries and over time; and (iv) publicly accessible', the Index relies upon databases maintained by international organizations. In selecting specific indicators it also takes into account '(i) data availability and country coverage; (ii) frequency of data collection; and (iii) the extent of variation amongst countries.' Indicators were chosen with a view to reflecting 'the challenges most relevant to fulfilling a given right, rather than to encompass all aspects' of the right. Because no appropriate data are available for the right to social security, the 'Core SERF Index' (applicable to all except high-income OECD countries) uses the following indicators:

Food:	% children (under 5) not stunted
Education:	Primary school completion rate
	Combined school enrollment rate (gross)
Health:	Contraceptive use rate
	Child (under 5) survival rate
	Age 65 survival rate
Housing:	% rural population with access to improved water source
	% population with access to improved sanitation
Decent Work:	% with income >$2 (2005 PPP$) per day

The authors note that, because of the absence of appropriate data, the Index 'does not attempt to assess the extent to which States ensured the procedural rights of non-discrimination, participation and accountability.' In order to assess the element of 'progressive realization', the Index uses the concept of Achievement Possibility Frontiers (APFs) that set a benchmark for each country's obligation with regard to each indicator. The purpose is to 'reflect what is feasible to achieve when a country allocates the maximum of available resources to fulfilling [ESR] and uses those resources effectively. The frontiers are constructed so as to be stable over the medium term thus enabling inter-temporal comparison.' The overall Index reflects a weighted average of the substantive rights indices.[3]

A different approach to ESR monitoring involves a three-part 'toolkit' proposed by Eitan Felner. Rather than seeking to provide a comprehensive picture, his approach is designed to flag concerns to be taken up by other monitoring methods or bodies.

EITAN FELNER, CLOSING THE 'ESCAPE HATCH': A TOOLKIT TO MONITOR THE PROGRESSIVE REALIZATION OF ECONOMIC, SOCIAL, AND CULTURAL RIGHTS

1 J. Hum. Rts Practice (2009) 402, at 415

…

Step 1: Comparing Social Indicators with GDP Per Capita

This first step enables one to measure human rights progress over time according to the level of a country's development. The simplest method is to compare a social indicator over time, such as primary school completion rates or child malnutrition

[3] S. Fukuda-Parr, T. Lawson-Remer & S. Randolph, SERF Index Methodology: Version 2011.1, Technical Note, at www.serfindex.org/wp-content/uploads/2011/02/Data-Technical-Note.pdf. See also S. Randolph, S. Fukuda-Parr & T. Lawson-Remer, 'Economic and Social Rights Fulfillment Index: Country Scores and Rankings', 9 J. Hum. Rts. 230 (2010).

(as a proxy for the enjoyment of some aspects of a specific right) with GDP per capita (as a proxy for available resources). This method is helpful in cases where a country experiences a reversal in a social indicator during a period of significant economic growth.... In these circumstances, such reversals would indicate, prima facie, a state is not complying with its obligation to progressively realize key rights according to available resources.

...

Step 2: Analysis of Resource Allocations

...

Analysing the magnitude, composition, and distribution of resources allocated to social sectors (e.g. the educational or health systems) is crucial for assessing whether a state is devoting the maximum of its available resources to the progressive realization of ESC rights.

...

First of all, a snapshot of the extent of a state's commitment to a particular economic and social right can be obtained by looking at the proportion of the GDP of that state allocated to the relevant social sector. [For example, assume that the Step 1 analysis reveals lower primary education completion rates] than those observed in other countries of the same region with similar or lower levels of GDP per capita. In such a case, if this country has a lower primary education expenditure ratio than other countries in the same region with similar needs and overall income, this would suggest that the focus country is failing to comply with its obligation to devote the maximum of available resources to the progressive achievement of the right to education — since it is devoting a smaller proportion of GDP to primary education than these other countries, despite having a larger proportion of its children that do not enjoy this basic right.

In turn, the level of public spending on basic social services is determined by a set of policy decisions, ranging from fiscal policies to the distribution of resources within a specific social sector. Three key policy decisions are particularly relevant: (1) the level of aggregate public expenditure (as a proportion of GDP); (2) the fiscal priority assigned to the relevant social sector (e.g. the education or health sector); and (3) the priority of basic social services within total social sector expenditure.

...

Step 3: Analysis of Expenditure Per Capita

An analysis of the overall resources allocated by a state to specific social sectors has to be complemented by an analysis of the expenditure per capita on those sectors. [This depends not only on] government policies and priorities... but also on the level of economic growth (or contraction) and the size of the population — two factors over which any government has, at best, only partial control. Therefore, since states only commit violations of ESC rights when their actions or omissions reflect an unwillingness to comply with their human rights obligations, and not when they are unable to carry them out, the level of expenditure per capita... cannot in itself serve as an indicator of compliance....

Nevertheless, the analysis of per capita expenditure is still crucial for monitoring purposes. Such an analysis can help identify common policy problems that may hinder the progressive achievement of these rights. It can also help to determine the types of policy strategies a government should adopt to address these problems.

NOTE

The trend in international organizations to accord an important role to indicators — for CPR and ESCR — has not gone unchallenged. In the readings below, Merry questions the capacity of the UN treaty-monitoring bodies to deal effectively with indicators, and Rosga and Satterthwaite are concerned about the potential for indicators to reduce the space available for democratic contestation.

SALLY ENGLE MERRY, THE PROBLEM OF HUMAN RIGHTS INDICATORS

(unpublished manuscript, 2012), at www.law.uvic.ca/demcon/2012%20readings/Chapter%203%20Problem%20of%20HR%20indicators.pdf

...

Indicators as a technology of knowledge production do not fit easily into human rights monitoring. In many ways, treaty body monitoring is a tantalizing but difficult site for indicator use. Although treaty bodies use indicators to control more powerful states, states resist this control. They fail to provide indicators or offer ones that are not adequately disaggregated. Indicators provide a technology of power but not one divorced from other relations of power. Governance by indicators is more difficult when a weaker party mobilizes them to control a stronger party than when a stronger party uses them to control a weaker one. It is less effective when the monitor cannot itself connect the data to the indicator to produce charts and ranks.

...

The power of the treaty body vis-à-vis any state varies with the state's vulnerability to international pressures such as aid and trade and domestic pressures within a country that might use a treaty body's report to mobilize opinion. The international setting can provide a space for NGOs to challenge their governments, and may exert pressure on some states, particularly those with active civil society, but the treaty body's ability to exert power over states is highly indirect and contingent....

Moreover,...those produced by a single institution tend to be more coherent and usable than those produced by a collection of actors or institutions. The treaty bodies cannot easily produce uniform indicators for all treaties since each one prizes its autonomy and is committed to the particular terms of its treaty....

...

Three Orders of Indicators

...

Treaty bodies use first and second order numbers — counts and ratios — widely, but rarely employ composites....

...

In practice, the human rights system is torn between reliance on two forms of information: decentralized, complex and contextual information and highly focused, standardized, and quantitative information. On one side is the human rights system's strong commitment to a holistic perspective on human rights and its insistence on the inextricable connections between civil and political rights and social, economic, and cultural rights. Issues of inequality and discrimination are understood as the result of larger social structures. Treaty bodies consider states one at a time, probing state performance in light of a state's economic condition, political and legal structure, population characteristics, and history. They resist ranking and comparing states, while states themselves do not want such comparisons made. As central actors in a system of law, the treaty bodies delineate the legal duties of ratifying states and assess to what extent state performance fulfills these duties. Most treaty bodies have issued general comments or recommendations that seek to clarify and specify the more abstract obligations of the treaties. They seek to make broad obligations, such as providing adequate housing, more specific. A composite human rights indicator offers a general picture of state performance but sacrifices the specificity necessary for legal action against perpetrators (Landman 2004: 923). On the other side, there are clearly ways that the increased use of indicators is attractive to those seeking to improve state accountability and enhance human rights compliance.

The tradeoff between a simple, commensurable indicator and a comprehensive, contextualized picture of human rights performance is a major sticking point. Any single indicator of human rights compliance will inevitably neglect issues that human rights proponents view as important....

...

[The author then examines the background to and the approach of the OHCHR indicators project described above and comments on the lists of illustrative indicators, such as the one on the right to food at p. 1229, *supra*.]

...

Are these good indicators? From the perspective of presenting simplified data that will enable the public to master complex ideas, the answer is no. What makes indicators successful is their capacity to synthesize complex situations and present simplified accounts based on numerical data. They depend on a clear theory embedded in the indicator. These indicators lack a theory beyond the presumption that passing certain laws and enacting particular government programs will lead to specific impacts. The proponents refuse to rank and compare. The refusal to simplify and score represents a moral high ground but does not produce the most powerful indicator regime. There is a continuum between simplification and uptake, so that by retaining such a complicated structure and so many indicators, uptake is inhibited. What makes indicators useful and popular is the simplification and decontextualization and comparison that these human rights activists and academics are trying to avoid. While avoiding these pitfalls, the indicator project has produced tables that are not very effective in streamlining monitoring or bringing issues to public attention.

On the other hand, these indicators are more collaborative, multi-national, and multi-disciplinary than more simplified indicators. They were born from a more negotiative process than many others and resist simplification, highly targeted goals, and superficial assessments of complex situations. Ironically, it is their effort to be more true to the nature of human rights thinking that has made them less accessible as indicators that produce knowledge of human rights performance. Perhaps as public disillusion with composite indicators builds, more complex metrics such as these will gain in popularity. It depends what happens to indicator culture: whether public faith in its claims to make a complex world knowable through technical rationality, a pragmatic approach to measurement, and the magic of numbers grows along with enthusiasm for evidence-based governance and skepticism about political debate. If so, the human rights indicators may yet grow in popularity and power.

...

ANNJANETTE ROSGA & MARGARET L. SATTERTHWAITE, MEASURING HUMAN RIGHTS: U.N. INDICATORS IN CRITICAL PERSPECTIVE

in K. Davis, A. Fisher, B. Kingsbury & S. Merry (eds.), Governance by Indicators: Global Power through Quantification and Rankings (2012)

Introduction

...Quantitative data has been forwarded as a central tool in the drive for better methods of assessment, monitoring, and advocacy.... [Human rights indicators] are understood to have a variety of advantages: they render complex data simple and easy to understand; they can be designed to demonstrate compliance with obligations, fulfillment of rights, and government efforts toward these goals; and they are capable of capturing progress over time and across countries.... [I]t is not surprising that NGOs, inter-governmental bodies, and governments have all begun to develop human rights indicators.

...[T]hey are situated at the nexus of international human rights law, quantitative social science methodologies, administrative and regulatory apparatuses, advocacy projects, and the transnational spread of expert knowledges mobilized in the service of 'standardization'.

...A convergence of social, political, and economic forces and their accompanying epistemological shifts has dramatically increased demands for indicators without equal attention to their limitations. These demands arise not only from the perceived need within international human rights circles for better tools to hold governments to account, but also from the replication of verification and monitoring techniques used in a wide variety of business, non-profit, and governmental management contexts....

Increasing demands for 'indicators' are thus inextricable from the privileging of abstract, quantifiable, and putatively transferable data bits. As such, indicators partake of both the strengths and weaknesses of auditing practices....

[A discussion of the approach to indicators by the OHCHR and by the UN Committee on ESCR is omitted.]

...

Section II: Audit, distance and the problem with trusting indicators

...

The problems with trusting indicators

...

Numbers, statistics, and the language of quantification generally are seen as uniquely capable of reducing or eliminating subjectivity....

...

No one in the human rights field pretends that indicators can ever really be apolitical, but the need for information that is as accurate, reliable, and meaningful as possible is pressing. Unfortunately, discussions of criteria for good indicators tend not to specify which form of objectivity is at work. Wendy Lesser identifies two different senses of objectivity: the first sense of objectivity is the 'sense that an objective report is disinterested, honest, reliable, impartial.' The second sense of the term suggests that 'only something which is not subjective — which does not partake of the individual human viewpoint — can be fully objective, neutrally conveying things and events that are out in the world without the distorting coloration of human consciousness.' Lesser points out that only a machine (her example is a television camera) can ever hope to approach the second sense: 'And even that possibility seems remote...'

But humans, with human judgment and interpretation, she reminds us, are necessary for the first sense.

...

Discussions of 'objective' indicators are vulnerable to two tendencies: first, to conflate these two senses of objectivity (with the result that ultimately those indicators requiring obvious human interpretation, such as qualitative assessments, are valued less highly), and secondly, to privilege those (generally numerical) indicators whose interpretive work is invisible.

The tendency for measures to become targets

...Indicators are said ideally to allow comparisons between nations at similar levels of economic development, and over time within a given nation.

Yet even to the degree indicators 'can be made to look similar and... compared at an abstract level', across geographical space, they tend to lose their efficacy as accurate and adequate measures over time....

...[T]o the extent that governments do actively try to meet benchmarks and standards set in relation to international human rights treaties, the incentive to demonstrate success — or, say, 'progressive realization' — according to given indicators may become greater than any incentive to substantively ensure the fulfillment and/or enjoyment of human rights themselves....

...

Section IV: Human rights indicators as technologies of global governance

...

[C]ompliance indicators [have the capacity] to close down spaces for democratic contestation. In carrying out its human rights obligations, [a State] must continually make difficult prioritization choices, especially in the context of economic and social rights. Which rights should receive the State's most concentrated attention — the right to potable drinking water or the ability to access childhood vaccinations? Gender equality in higher education or ensuring non-discriminatory employment conditions? How should government authorities make such determinations? Who should decide and by what means? And most relevant to our purposes, what does human rights law have to say about these challenging questions, and how might indicators measure State efforts to answer them?

In many respects, human rights law has very little to say of a concrete nature in answer to these questions. Prioritization challenges are often answered with the demand that all rights receive equal attention and priority....In practice this is seldom, if ever, possible at the level of everyday policy — especially in resource-poor countries.... [W]hile there may not be clear answers to the question of prioritization, a good deal of work has been done to establish more concrete standards to guide governments' choices concerning competing rights demands.

...

[The minimum core concept and the principles of non-discrimination, equality and non-retrogression] provide a good deal of guidance to States seeking to uphold their human rights obligations, and in some scenarios, States may rely upon them to prioritize activities. However, the principles will often fail to provide the answers to questions about prioritization and emphasis in implementation. Only rarely will they provide a rule of decision for policy-makers choosing among options for actions that can improve human rights. This gap — between international norm and domestic implementation — is both normal and desirable. It opens space for States — and more importantly, for national populations within States — to determine how best to carry out their duties. Within this space, democratic contestation and participation by those most directly affected can take place. Without such a gap, human rights law would perversely short-cut democratic processes by imposing specific policy choices on States.

Indicators may threaten to close this fruitful gap...by, for example, targeting-through-measurement the outcomes of certain policies, or even turning specific policy choices themselves into indicators....

Further, given the problems of measurability and availability of data, there may be a tendency to choose indicators that capture the outcomes of the most easily — or the most consistently — measurable policies or programs....

...[T]he development and use of compliance indicators may have the tendency to artificially close the gap between international law and domestic policy, thus shrinking the required spaces for participation. If indicators are designed and imposed uniformly across countries, and if they are not capable of calibration according to national priorities and deliberation, they could backfire as accountability mechanisms.

[But the indicators project is not without some redeeming features.]

...

We believe that...the power of indicators, when harnessed by human rights advocates, may be fruitfully turned on the State by those the State has failed to serve, or even harmed. Indeed, we believe that human rights indicators — if designed with these valences of power in mind — can be used to monitor whether governments have arrived at effective human rights policies and actions through democratic processes. In other words, instead of disappearing politics, indicators should be designed to allow for the monitoring of governmental processes to ensure they are participatory and open to deliberation and debate.

Discussions of indicators need not be technical conversations devoid of political contestation. Nor must they be conversations in which participants are seeking to submerge difficult questions of judgment in the abstract language of numbers. They should be conversations in which engaged social actors are grappling with the very phenomena we have been describing — actors who are fully aware of both the power and the limits that statistics possess.

Conclusion

The value of indicators as a social technology cannot be determined in advance, nor on the basis that they draw on the power of quantitative language. While it may be true that quantitative methods, in their very abstraction and stripping away of contextualizing information have particular — and especially high — risks for misuse by those with the power to mobilize them, they are tools like any other. All tools can be misused; all social actors with power can misuse that power. The key lies in knowing where — and how — human judgment and political contestation should enter. Rather than trusting in numbers too quickly, those using human rights compliance indicators should [find] ways to utilize human rights indicators as a tool of global governance that allow the governed to form strategic political alliances with global bodies in the task of holding their governors to account.

QUESTIONS

1. Are indicators as important in relation to CPR as they are in relation to ESR? If not, why not?

2. What do you see as the main advantages and disadvantages of composite indicators in relation to ESR?

3. Does the inability of the SERF Index to capture issues such as discrimination and accountability undermine its utility?

4. Are the critiques of Rosga and Satterthwaite and Merry sufficient to convince you that we are better off avoiding the use of indicators in monitoring human rights?

5. The availability of reliable and up-to-date statistics varies hugely from one poor country to another. Their design, collection and presentation are also subject to strong political manipulation.[4] How should the human rights treaty bodies respond to such problems?

B. COMPLIANCE AND EFFECTIVENESS: ASSESSING THE EMPIRICAL RECORD

In this section we examine state-of-the-art research on the effectiveness of the international human rights regime. Various readings in previous chapters have touched upon this subject more or less directly. Recall, for example, the study of the impact of UN human rights treaties by Heyns & Viljoen in Chapter 12, p. 1049, *supra*; the debate among social scientists — Kathryn Sikkink, Jack Snyder & Leslie Vinjamuri — about the empirical effects of criminal trials on peace and rights protections, Chapter 15, pp. 1394 and 1399, *infra*; Ellen Lutz & Kathryn Sikkink's research on the cascade effects of ATS lawsuits across Latin America, Chapter 13, p. 1145, *supra*; David Kennedy's critique suggesting that the human rights regime has had unintended negative consequences for human welfare, Chapter 6, p. 504, *supra*; and Kenneth Roth's argument about the ineffectiveness of international NGOs to promote certain forms of economic and social rights, Chapter 4, p. 295, *supra*. It is important to reflect on those contributions in light of the issues addressed in this chapter.

The following readings directly engage questions about the definition of compliance, the reasons that states might comply with international human rights law and the conditions under which compliance is most likely to be achieved. The readings also examine, more broadly, the effects that the international human rights regime may produce (beyond mere rule-compliance) in changing the behaviour of states and other actors.

THOMAS RISSE & KATHRYN SIKKINK, CONCLUSION

in T. Risse, S. Ropp & K. Sikkink (eds.), From Commitment To Compliance: The Persistent Power of Human Rights (forthcoming 2013)

...The definition and operationalization of compliance is crucial....[A]s Dai reminds us, the compliance gap is not only an objective measure of behavioral

[4] Shanta Devarajan, 'Africa's Statistical Tragedy', 6 Oct. 2011, at http://blogs.worldbank.org/africacan/africa-s-statistical-tragedy.

change, but a "subjective benchmark" by which behavior ought to be evaluated. This benchmark has been increasing over the years.... So, for example, much of what we consider as problems of human rights compliance in this volume, such as compliance by transnational corporations, insurgent groups, private actors enacting gender violence, and the state's inability to combat human rights violations by non-state actors in areas of limited statehood, would simply not have been considered human rights violations two decades ago. In other words, the human rights bar has been moving ever higher, and so states (and now increasingly) non-state actors, have to jump higher to clear the bar.

Moreover, there is also much more information available about human rights violations in the world, including new understandings of what constitutes a human rights violations [sic].... [which] carries some potential problems for measuring changing levels of compliance with human rights....

The Role of Enforcement

...

...R2P is an important backdrop...providing a doctrinal justification for the wide range of tools the human rights community uses to promote human rights, as well as the distant possibility of coercive enforcement in a small subset of extreme cases.

A second important human rights trend that forms a backdrop...is the rise of individual criminal accountability for human rights violations. This increase in criminal accountability, not only through international tribunals like the International Criminal Court...and the [ICTY], but also through an increase in foreign and domestic criminal prosecutions for human rights violations is an important new type of enforcement for human rights norms...

...

Some scholars, however, have argued that human rights trials will not deter future violations and that, in some circumstances, they will actually lead to an increase in repression or to humanitarian atrocities (Snyder and Vinjamuri 2004, Goldsmith and Krasner 2003). For example, they contend that the threat of prosecution could cause powerful dictators or insurgents to entrench themselves in power rather than negotiate a transition from authoritarian regimes and/or civil war. Goodman and Jinks likewise argue in this volume that material sanctions could "crowd out" other motivations and actually be counterproductive for human rights compliance.

But analysis based on new datasets (Kim and Sikkink 2010; Olsen, Payne, and Reiter, 2010) confirm [sic] that enforcement in the form of human rights prosecutions can have a positive effect on compliance with human rights norms. Such research shows, for example, that transitional countries in which human rights prosecutions have taken place are less repressive than countries without prosecutions, holding other factors constant. Contrary to the arguments made by the trial skeptics, transitional human rights prosecutions have not tended to exacerbate human rights violations....

Human rights prosecutions, however, are not only instances of punishment or enforcement, but also high profile symbolic events that communicate and dramatize norms and socialize actors to accept those norms. It is thus difficult to separate out the enforcement or punishment effects of trials from their communicative or social dimension...

Persuasion and Discourse

Brysk's chapter on gender violence provides evidence for the power of persuasion and institutionalization, especially in the case of the decision to include gender violence as a criteria for Canadian asylum policy. Brysk argues that "male elites face no incentives or coercion to change gendered patterns of subjugation".... Compliance is more likely in cases, such as that of Canadian asylum policy, where the compliance decision is centralized and the state directly controls compliance. Where compliance decisions are radically decentralized, and not under state control, such as family decisions about female genital mutilation, compliance will be more difficult....

...

...Clark's chapter in this volume provides one of the first quantitative tests of the discursive mechanisms.... She shows that exposure to public naming and shaming by the UN Human Rights Commission resulted in significantly better compliance by states that had ratified the Anti-Torture Convention (CAT) as compared to those which either had not committed to the CAT or had not been exposed to public criticism....

...[I]t seems to be helpful to distinguish between what Jeffrey Checkel has called Type 1 as compared to Type 2 socialization. Type 1 socialization involves role-playing: [a]ctors know what is socially expected from them and behave accordingly, irrespective of whether they believe in the normative validity of the rule or not. In contrast, Type 2 socialization requires normative persuasion: actors are convinced that complying with a particular norm — human rights in our case — is the "right thing to do." Both types of socialization constitute variants of the logic of appropriateness (March and Olsen 1998), but Type 1 socialization does not require deep attitudinal change. [Our prior work] did not distinguish between these two variants and implicitly assumed that sustained compliance with human rights norms requires deep socialization and internalization. While it is certainly the case that compliance should be the more likely, the more actors are actually convinced of the normative validity of human rights, we now suggest that Type 1 socialization is sufficient for compliance....

...

Capacity Building

..."[I]nvoluntary non-compliance" needs to be addressed, too. If non-compliance results from limited statehood, i.e. weakness of state institutions to enforce the law, neither enforcement nor sanctions, positive incentives, or persuasion will result in human rights improvements.

...

Scope Conditions

The main theoretical contribution of this volume... is that we identified scope conditions under which compliance with human rights becomes more or less likely. In the introduction, we provided an overview of the four main scope conditions: regime type, degrees of statehood, centralization of rule implementation, and material and social vulnerability....

A schematic way to conceive of the scope conditions and the ways in which they interact is to build off the two dimensions of target characteristics: rule target *ability* to bring about change, and rule target *willingness* to bring about change. We can conceive of two of our scope conditions (state capacity and issue centralization) as being fundamentally about the *ability* of the rule target to bring about change. States with large areas of limited statehood lack the capacity, or ability to bring about compliance, even if they would wish to do so. But the degree of centralization of the compliance decision also influences the ability of states... to comply with norms.

Figure [1] Target Ability to Comply

		State Capacity	
		High	Low
Centralization of Compliance Decision	High	High probability	Mid level probability
	Low	Mid level probability	Low probability

Second, actor *willingness* to comply is related to the remaining two scope conditions, regime type and target vulnerability. Democratic states tend to be more willing to comply with human rights norms, but target vulnerability also makes targets more or less willing to comply. States that have social vulnerability are more willing to comply because they have identities that make them more sensitive to pressure; states that have material vulnerability are more willing to comply to gain material benefits or stop sanctions. We can use these two main characteristic to create a representation summarizing some of the ways in which the scope conditions might interact to provide a greater or lesser likelihood for compliance.

Figure [2]: Target Willingness to Comply

		Regime Type	
		Democratic	Authoritarian
Material and/or Social Vulnerability	High	High probability	Mid level probability
	Low	Mid level probability	Low probability

This way of organizing the scope conditions discussed... helps us think about the possibility of human rights change on a particular issue with a particular target. So, for example, if we wanted to think about the possibility of ending FGM in an authoritarian state with low capacity, and low vulnerability, we should be very pessimistic about change, because it would fall in the worst possibility of change category on both ability and willingness for change. But if we wondered about changing the use of the death penalty in democratic state with low capacity but higher vulnerability, we might be somewhat more optimistic....

Scope Conditions Primarily Influencing Target Willingness to Comply

Regime Type

The single most important factor for sustained state willingness to comply with human rights norms is regime type....

In her survey of the quantitative human rights literature, Simmons states that this literature has largely confirmed the argument in PoHR that liberalization and democratization are essential for sustained human rights improvements, so much so that political liberalization should now be considered a necessary (but not sufficient) condition for sustained human rights compliance (Apodaca 2001; Landman 2005; Neumayer 2005; Poe, Tate, and Keith 1999)....

...As to stable democracies, they are both less likely to violate rights, *and* more resilient to resisting external human rights pressures. Because democracies have greater legitimacy, they may be less socially vulnerable to outside pressures, as the cases of the U.S. under George W. Bush or of Israel suggest (see chapter by Sikkink; Liese 2006). While we can depend on rule of law institutions in some democracies to protect rights, electoral mechanisms are only useful for protecting the rights of certain constituencies. It is possible that democracies are more prone to "crowding out effects"....

Material and Social Vulnerability

...[A]s the examples of North Korea or Zimbabwe demonstrate, even materially extremely vulnerable states are able to fight off material pressures by the international community for a long time, as long as the regime is capable of suppressing any substantial internal opposition and/or as long as the regime does not care at all about its international reputation. North Korea and Zimbabwe are, therefore, examples of regimes that have been able to compensate for their material vulnerability because they lack social vulnerability.

These cases suggest that it is more interesting to look at the interaction effects between material and social vulnerability than to investigate these two factors in isolation....Clark's chapter suggests that commitment (treaty ratification) combined with reputational sanctions, short of enforcement, can lead to improvements in compliance. The more target countries want to become (or remain) members of the international community "in good standing," the more they are socially vulnerable to these reputational sanctions.

...

The U.S. case also illustrates the role that power can play in limiting/stopping efforts at sanctions, enforcement, or even incentives...Both China and the United States have shown themselves willing to use counter-sanctions and incentives to block human rights pressures...

...[T]he U.S. represents an interesting case of both material power and lack of social vulnerability....

The ability to use counter-discourses effectively to deflect criticism is not limited to key actors within powerful states....The Mubarak regime in Egypt also used a counter-discourse of the loyal reliable moderate ally in the Middle East to effectively block both social and material vulnerability. As a result, it was not subject to external material pressures for human rights change and only changed [in 2011] as a result of bottom up pressure for transition.

...

Policy Conclusions

...Liberalizing and democratizing states which have committed to human rights, but are unable to implement them because of limited statehood, should be the prime candidates for capacity building measures. This suggests, for example, that Tunisia, Egypt, and Libya are at present prime candidates for such mechanisms following the "Arab spring". On the other hand, strengthening state institutions alone might lead to adverse consequences in cases of semi-authoritarian regimes with areas of limited statehood. In such cases, capacity-building might lead to more, not less human rights violations (see e.g. Börzel and Pamuk, 2012). Capacity building rather than sanctions and enforcement is a more appropriate policy response mainly in democratic regime with low degrees of statehood.

...

...[T]here are some countries and issues where it will be harder to bring about change than in others and thus more persistence will be required. Because they are harder cases also does not mean they should not be chosen as targets for advocacy. It simply suggests that advocates, both internal and external, should have realistic assumptions about the speed and likelihood of change.

ROBERT HOWSE & RUTI TEITEL, BEYOND COMPLIANCE: RETHINKING WHY INTERNATIONAL LAW REALLY MATTERS

1 Global Policy 127 (2010)

...

...[T]he conceptual, and more recently empirical, study of compliance has become a central preoccupation, and perhaps the fastest growing subfield, in international legal scholarship...

...Looking at the aspirations of international law through the lens of rule compliance leads to inadequate scrutiny and understanding of the diverse complex purposes and projects that multiple actors impose and transpose on international legality, and especially a tendency to oversimplify if not distort the relation of international law to politics.

...

One reason that compliance is often seen as a central problem for international legal scholarship is the challenge (by realists and some but not all positivists) that law is only really law when accompanied by authoritative interpretation and enforcement (see Morgenthau, 1948). A focus on compliance, or more adequately perhaps obedience (see Henkin, 1968), aims to deflect such a claim by asserting that there is a range of considerations including reputational effects/long-term self-interest that lead to compliance with international law, regardless of the absence of authoritative interpretation and enforcement in most instances.

Such a response at once proves too much and too little....

... It is worth noting however that one of the most sophisticated positivist accounts of law, that of H. L. A. Hart, rejects the notion that legal obligation implies effective coercive sanctions, specifically informed by a consideration of international law. According to Hart,

> To argue that international law is not binding because of its lack of organized sanctions is tacitly to accept the analysis of obligation contained in the theory that law is essentially a matter of orders backed by threats. This theory, as we have seen, identifies 'having an obligation' or 'being bound' with 'likely to suffer the sanction or punishment threatened for disobedience'. Yet, as we have argued, this identification distorts the role played in all legal thought and discourse of the ideas of obligation and duty (Hart, 1961, pp. 217–218).

...

The following are some of the possible effects of international law that are not captured by the notion of behavioral 'compliance' with a 'rule' of law...

International law (norms and/or institutions such as courts and tribunals) may shift in whole or in part decision-making, interpretative and/or legitimating power from one set of elite actors to another (for example from diplomats, foreign policy analysts and military planners to legal professionals such as judges, lawyers and law professors). This effect is autonomous from that of compliance: in some cases, legal professionalization may lead to more compliance, and in some cases less. In others, it could even lead to 'ultracompliance': effects which go beyond what is desired from the perspective of the objectives of the legal regime, and which may even be perverse.

...

International law can affect the way that policy makers view international problems and conflicts (for example in terms of clashes of rights as opposed to balancing of political or economic interests) and their perception of the constituencies to whom they are accountable in addressing such problems and conflicts. In the Balkans, resolving the conflict, and building post-conflict societies, somehow became identified with the prosecution of crimes against humanity at the International Criminal Tribunal for the former Yugoslavia (ICTY). The role that international criminal law could play in achieving these goals was arguably exaggerated, leading to a relative neglect of other processes, such as local truth commissions, the building of grassroots democratic institutions and the reconstruction of civil society.

...

Consider what compliance might mean in the context of the International Criminal Court (ICC).... The normative and positive law innovations triggered by the establishment of and commitment to the ICC might... lead to prosecutions of a kind never contemplated by the jurisdiction of the Court itself, such as for crimes committed in the distant past. This is a clear instance of ultracompliance....

... [There is] an internal difficulty within the 'compliance' perspective. Goldsmith and Posner, for example, maintain that unlike ratification of human rights treaties, 'democracy, peace and economic development' have been shown to enhance human rights protection; however, this contrast assumes that democracy, peace and economic development occur entirely exogenously of the effects of international human rights law. If, as just suggested, international human rights law helps to lock in transitions to peaceful democratic conditions, then it may ultimately lead to what is usually conceived of as compliance, but only through a normative effect that is caught in the first instances by focusing on something other than rule compliance.

...

While Eric Posner, an international legal scholar heavily focused on compliance, tends to dismiss the influence of the International Court of Justice (ICJ), based on the number of judgments it has emitted and their purportedly distant effects on the controversies decided (Posner, 2004), the jurisprudential acquis of the ICJ on such essential questions as state responsibility, countermeasures and treaty interpretation has been repeatedly invoked, in for example, investor–state arbitrations, characterized by compulsory jurisdiction and a 'hard law' remedy, that is, monetary damages that can be enforced in domestic court. Along similar lines, sources such as the European Convention on Human Rights and its interpretation by the European Court of Human Rights have been used by investor–state tribunals.

...

Rather obviously legal agents bargain in the shadow of the law.... States, instead of simply 'complying' with international legal rules may bargain in light of them, and around them....

[In the context of] the international legal duty to punish crimes against humanity, recently reaffirmed by the ICJ in the *Bosnia* v. *Serbia* case, the increasing likelihood of such prosecutions given the creation of an inter-national criminal court may well affect peace or regime transition bargains between parties to a conflict, for instance making it more difficult or less plausible to use amnesties as a bargaining chip for acceptance of a peaceful, negotiated transition. On the other hand, with the ICC in the background now, and its ability to enforce international criminal law during an ongoing conflict, more cautious or restrained behavior by some of the participants in the conflict may result, and this could actually make a transitional bargain easier.... [T]hese effects do not even come into focus if one centers the analysis on effects on 'compliance' with the duty to prosecute and/or the duty to cooperate with the ICC for instance.

OONA A. HATHAWAY, DO HUMAN RIGHTS TREATIES MAKE A DIFFERENCE?

111 Yale L. J. 1935 (2002)

...

This Article undertakes [a] test with a large-scale quantitative analysis of the relationship between human rights treaties and countries' human rights practices. The analysis relies on a database encompassing the experiences of 166 nations over a nearly forty-year period in five areas of human rights law: genocide, torture, fair and public trials, civil liberties, and political representation of women. This data set is the empirical window through which I examine two separate but intimately related questions. First, do countries comply with or adhere to the requirements of the human rights treaties they have joined? Second, do these human rights treaties appear to be effective in improving countries' human rights practices — that is, are countries more likely to comply with a treaty's requirements if they have joined the treaty than would otherwise be expected?

...

From the standpoint of leading perspectives on international law, the results of my research are counterintuitive. Although the ratings of human rights practices of countries that have ratified international human rights treaties are generally better than those of countries that have not, noncompliance with treaty obligations appears to be common. More paradoxically, when I take into account the influence of a range of other factors that affect countries' practices, I find that treaty ratification is not infrequently associated with worse human rights ratings than otherwise expected. I do, however, find evidence suggesting that ratification of human rights treaties by fully democratic nations is associated with better human rights practices. These findings are not fully consistent with either the classic interest-based or the norm-based views of international law. If treaties are simply window-dressing for the self-interested pursuit of national goals, then there should be no consistent relationship between ratification and state behavior, positive or negative. If, by contrast, they have a powerful normative hold, then ratification of human rights treaties should be associated with better practices — not only by fully democratic nations — and should never be associated with worse practices.

My findings do not necessarily tell us that treaties lead to worse human rights practices. Countries with worse practices may be more inclined to ratify treaties, or we may simply know more about violations committed by countries that sign human rights treaties, making countries that ratify look worse than they are. Yet given that I find not a single treaty for which ratification seems to be reliably associated with better human rights practices and several for which it appears to be associated with worse practices, it would be premature to dismiss the possibility that human rights treaties may sometimes lead to poorer human rights practices within the countries that ratify them.

...

...External pressure on countries to demonstrate a commitment to human rights norms creates strong incentives for countries to engage in favorable expressive behavior by ratifying human rights treaties. But because human rights treaties are generally only minimally monitored and enforced, there is little incentive for ratifying countries to make the costly changes in actual policy that would be necessary to meet their treaty commitments. Given this, it is perhaps not so surprising that we find the patterns we do in the empirical analysis. Ratifying a human rights treaty can relieve pressure for change imposed by international actors, who may rely more heavily on positions than effects in evaluating countries' records. This reduction in pressure may in turn lead a country that ratifies to improve its practices less than it otherwise might....

...Although countries that ratify human rights treaties on the whole appear not to have better human rights practices than would otherwise be expected, treaties may have broader positive effects not captured by the analysis. Treaties may lead to more aggressive enforcement by UN Charter-based bodies, which may take action against ratifiers and nonratifiers alike. And human rights treaties and the process that surrounds their creation and maintenance may have a widespread effect on the practices of *all* nations by changing the discourse about and expectations regarding those rights.... [T]he collective expression of a series of countries may have genuine effect. Indeed, when a treaty gains a sufficient following, it is generally viewed as expressing what conduct is and is not acceptable to the community of nations. The treaty can thus influence individual countries' perceptions of what constitutes acceptable behavior.

What is important to note — and the reason that this effect would not be detected in the empirical analysis — is that this influence can be felt by countries regardless of whether they ratify the treaty or not....

...

The findings of this study may also give reason to reassess the current policy of the United Nations of promoting universal ratification of the major human rights treaties. Although universal ratification of a treaty can make a strong statement to the international community that the activity covered by the treaty is unacceptable, pressure to ratify, if not followed by strong enforcement and monitoring of treaty commitments, may be counterproductive. Indeed, it may be worthwhile to develop, consider, and debate more radical approaches to improving human rights through the use of new types of treaty membership policies. If countries gain some expressive benefit from ratifying human rights treaties, perhaps this benefit ought to be less easily obtained. Countries might, for example, be required to demonstrate compliance with certain human rights standards before being allowed to join a human rights treaty. This would ensure that only those countries that deserved an expressive benefit from treaty membership would obtain it. Or membership in a treaty regime could be tiered, with a probationary period during the early years of membership followed by a comprehensive assessment of country practices for promotion to full membership. Or treaties could include provisions for removing countries that are habitually found in violation of the terms of the treaty from membership in the treaty regime.

BETH A. SIMMONS, MOBILIZING FOR HUMAN RIGHTS: INTERNATIONAL LAW IN DOMESTIC POLITICS

(2009)

...

Fair Trials

...

Figure 5.2 illustrates the worldwide average of the fair trial score each year from 1982 to 2002. We only have data since 1982, but the trends are toward a slight

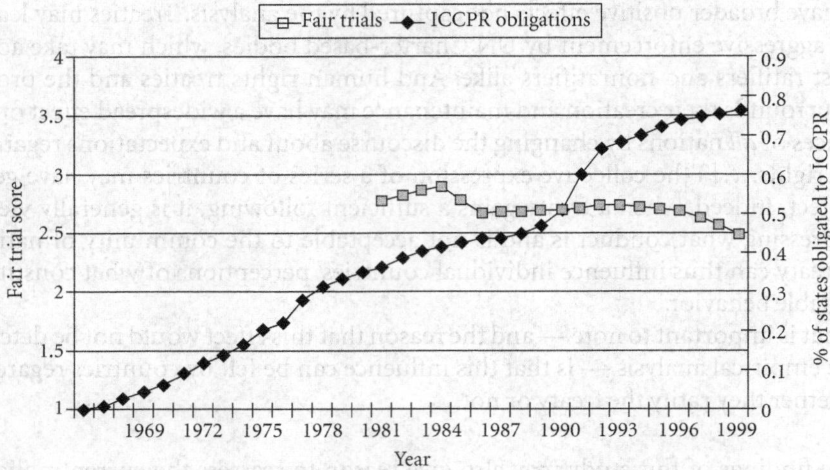

Figure 5.2. ICCPR Ratifications and Fair Trials. *Note:* Includes ratifications and accessions. *Source*: fair trial score: Hathway 2002 (updated, interpolated, and inverted so that high values represent better practices).

deterioration in the mid-1980s and again in the late 1990s. On the face of it, it would appear that there is very little relationship between average global ratification of the ICCPR and the average on this scale, in contrast to the broader civil liberties measure examined previously. Of course, many factors influence the will and capacity to provide individuals accused of a crime with a fair trial. What, if anything, does ratification contribute?

Oona Hathaway pioneered research in this area and found that ratification of the ICCPR had little effect on state practices with respect to a fair trial. Quite the contrary: Some analyses of her evidence suggest that rights practices worsen once a treaty commitment has been made. However, I am interested not only in the aggregate effects of the ICCPR with respect to fair trials, but also in *the conditions under which we might expect ratification to have its strongest impact.* Theoretically, there are strong reasons to suspect that fair trials are already provided in stable democracies, and there is little reason for ratification of the ICCPR to stimulate new political demands in that regard. Nor should we expect the ICCPR to make much difference in stable autocracies, where potential demanders can anticipate costly state resistance. Ratification should matter most where local groups have both the motive and the means to demand compliance. This is the case in countries characterized by some degree of regime transition....

Ratification of the ICCPR appears to have no discernible effects in countries that were never democratic during the post-World War II period or in stable democracies over those years. But if we run a similar test for countries that had had some experience with democratic politics — transitional countries in the sense that they had passed a moderately high democratic threshold at some point in the postwar years — ratification of the ICCPR is quite likely to be associated with fairer domestic trials from year to year, at least in the short run. When we look for the impact five years after ratification, the ICCPR effect becomes swamped by other factors. Nevertheless, there is some evidence that for the 55 countries coded as transitional, ratification has contributed to better practices — fairer trials for individuals than would have been the case had the treaty not been ratified at all.

Ratification of the ICCPR is, of course, not the only influence on fair trials, and the control variables tested here reveal some important influences on legal practices. The usually strongly positive lagged dependent variable indicates that countries with poor ratings were likely to have poor ratings in the next period, indicating that the fairness of trials is marked by a high degree of institutional inertia. The most consistent external influence across all categories of countries is the nature of the practices in the region in which the country is situated. Across all subgroups and the sample as a whole, fair trial practices in the region were a strong predictor of fair trial practices in a specific country. This effect appears to be the strongest among the moderately democratic and transitional countries, though it is statistically significant in every model. This pattern could be explained by shared cultural patterns or even regional socialization or mimicry. Another external influence that is strongest in transitional countries is the positive influence of overseas development assistance. But it is important to note that the effects of the ICCPR are noticeable among the transitional countries even when controlling for their regional context and foreign development aid.

One of the most important influences on fair trial practices is the nature of the domestic political regime, but the results hold some surprises in this regard. A country's extent of democracy at the time of observation does not have the positive effect on fair trials one might expect (except among those countries that have been stable democracies since World War II). Even more surprising, democratic change tends to lead to worse fair trial practices in the following year, and this result is especially robust for the 55 transitional countries. What these results suggest is that in practice, fair trials do not improve in lockstep with democracy and democratic improvements. Protecting the legal rights of the accused requires something more than encouraging participatory democracy.... There is also some evidence that governments especially committed to exposing the crimes and abuses of earlier regimes through the use of truth commissions also improve their trials in the following year....

There is little evidence that fair trial practices are driven by what might broadly be considered developmental or local social factors. While it undoubtedly takes resources to hold fair trials — providing the defense with qualified attorneys and educating independent judges are not low-cost options — it is not the case that wealthier countries conduct fairer trials, all else equal. In fact, there is some suggestion that the opposite is true, at least for the more authoritarian regimes. Countries that are more varied in terms of religion, language, and ethnic groups may tend to have somewhat better practices as well, but this result seems to be driven by the stable democracies, such as Belgium. A burgeoning population may contribute to deteriorating practices if social and other problems worsen, though in this case the effects seem to be concentrated in the stable autocracies. Overall, however, it is hard to say that there is a clear social or developmental country profile associated with fair trials.

Far clearer is the role that violent conflict plays in the administration of justice for the accused. The expectation that violent periods of "national emergency" are often used as reasons to short-circuit normal rights protections in the name of national security is borne out in these tests.... Overall, the influence of ICCPR ratification on fair trials is highly conditioned by the nature of the regime. There is a mild positive but statistically insignificant association across all countries, but the analysis of subgroups indicates that the positive effects are concentrated largely in neither the stable democracies nor the stable autocracies, but rather in those polities that have had some experience with democratic government, however fleeting. The statistical strength of the relationship is not very strong — we can only be 91–92 percent confident that the relationship is not due to chance alone — but it does offer some evidence that ratification is associated under the right political circumstances with actual improvements in fair trials, as required by the ICCPR.

...

Humane Treatment: The Prevalence and Prevention of Torture

...

The dependent variable is a five-category measure that captures the pervasiveness of the practice of torture by government officials. The worst cases (Category 1) are those in which torture (including severe beatings) was considered "prevalent" and "widespread." The next category (Category 2) includes cases in which torture was considered "common," there were widespread reports of beatings to death, or other beatings and other forms of abusive treatment were quite routine. The third category involves those cases in which there was some reference (without specified frequency) to maltreatment, or common beatings or isolated reports of severe beatings (e.g., to death). The fourth category includes those cases in which abuses were occasional or there were possible cases of beatings (though never to death). And finally, the fifth category involves the best cases, those in which serious abuses were never reported, though isolated cases of a less serious nature were on rare occasions reported and responded to with disciplinary action....

...

A series of control variables are included in all specifications to reduce the possibility of erroneously attributing causal significance to ratification of the CAT. Certainly, the basic causal explanations for the prevalence of torture are not likely to be an international legal commitment, but rather institutional and social features of each country, as well as each government's perceived threats to national security or to its hold on political power. No one should expect international law to overcome these basic conditions; rather, the question is, once we control for these conditions, does a treaty commitment make any difference to the prevalence of torture on the margins?

...

The tests reported in Table 7.2 [Eds. not reproduced here] suggest that the CAT may indeed have an important impact on the severity of torture practices for countries with only moderately accountable institutions. Table 7.2 shows there is practically no influence of ratifying the CAT in stable democracies...and countries that have never been democratic The results for countries in transition provide a sharp contrast. For these countries, it is fairly clear that those that ratify the CAT are much more likely to improve their practices (reduce their incidence of torture) than transitional countries that do not. Statistically speaking, we can be fairly confident (about 94 percent confident) that among transitional countries, CAT ratifiers' practices become much better than those of nonratifiers. Ratification of the CAT is associated with almost a 40 percent increase in the likelihood that a country will improve by one category on the torture scale. Among the control variables, the only consistent explanation appears to be the importance of information, as indicated by the strong positive effect of a relatively free press. The use of truth commissions may also be associated with future reductions in the use of torture, increasing the chances of moving from one category on the scale by about 15 percent. Surprisingly, neither international nor civil wars mattered significantly in these specifications for the transition countries. Nor did any of the UN mechanisms [visits by Special Rapporteur, 1503 procedures and UN country resolutions] have much impact in these countries.

...

Conclusion

...

...The best way to bias our thinking against the power of international law to protect human rights is to pick up the newspaper.

Perhaps this is why the prevailing sentiment among those who have given the issue much thought is that international law has done very little to improve the rights chances of people around the world. This sentiment has largely developed in an evidentiary vacuum. Anecdotes of noncompliance are typically held up as clear evidence that international law is meaningless for or even dangerous to the realization of human dignity. But even the most horrific anecdotes of international human rights law violations no more prove the absence of effective international law than do headlines about murder on the streets of Boston or Los Angeles prove the absence of effective law here at home. The key question is not whether crime exists — that is an indubitable point. It is, what and how has international law contributed to the chances that human beings will enjoy their rights more fully than would have been the case in the absence of the major human rights treaties? We should resist the understandable tendency to answer this question by drawing exclusively on the most dramatic rights tragedies of our time. After all, no one believes that international law is the only tool that can or should be used to address these kinds of abuses. But it is crucial to understand also that international law contains powerful norms that can inspire and be effectively wielded by stakeholders, at least under some circumstances. The evidence accumulated in this book suggests that we may have a much more powerful tool in our hands than we may have realized.

The claims in this book should not be misunderstood. International law is not a panacea for all ills. It will not eliminate ruthless dictators, end racial or gender discrimination for all time, or raise all humans to an acceptable standard of living. These international legal commitments are not magic bullets. They have helped but not cured the rights deficit the world so clearly faced and tried to address in 1947.

...The root causes of rights violations — structural inequities, social and psychological dynamics of violence and domination — cannot be directly addressed by these treaties. They are merely a set of principles that individuals should enjoy basic guarantees, but principles of an especially potent nature....

...

...I advocate a theoretical focus on how human rights treaties and their ratification interact with and influence domestic politics. I do not argue that transnational actors have not been crucial to the question of compliance, but they are too often presented as the "white knights" that make demands for those who are not often credited with the ability to speak, strategize, litigate, and mobilize for themselves and their society. Stakeholder agency is drastically underplayed in most accounts of compliance with human rights treaties....

And so, it is important to theorize how and why stakeholders and their allies use treaties to strengthen their rights claims. I have argued that treaties assist in the process of political mobilization of groups who stand to gain from their provisions. In many countries — especially those that are at least partially democratic and are based on the rule of law — ratified treaties provide highly legitimate focal points that help to clarify reasonable demands, support the legitimacy of those demands, and contribute to the political and legal resources stakeholders can bring to bear in the quest to realize treaty rights.

The evidence that treaties may have an effect on outcomes is surprisingly strong. Four treaties that vary significantly in their nature and content were shown by a broad range of tests to have contributed to the rights performance of governments around the world. The ICCPR, for example, has inspired religious groups to seek a greater arena of religious thought and practice, free from the interference of their government. Ratification of the ICCPR has supported these demands. The evidence suggests that governments that ratify are much more likely than those that do not to follow up that legal action by reducing their interference in the free practice of religion within their polity.

Quite clearly, though, the politics of rights differ by the nature of the right, the range of potential violators, and the nature of individuals who might benefit from the right in question. The norms and treaties analyzed in this book interact with domestic politics, and the way in which they interact varies significantly across the kind of right under consideration. From a mobilization perspective, it is easy to understand why an international commitment on freedom of religious practice differs systematically from one on fair trials. The former has a built-in pressure group — organized religious minorities — who are prepositioned to press governments for compliance. For a number of reasons, the mobilization mechanism is bound to be weaker in the case of fair trials. Most obviously, alleged criminals or other kinds of suspects typically are not well positioned to mobilize to demand better treatment by law enforcement authorities and the local court system. With the exception of the case of a well-organized political opposition, the most immediate stakeholders are often isolated individuals who stand accused of criminal activity. Moreover, alleged criminals do not enjoy the natural sympathy of a broad segment of most societies. In fact, it is easy to frame the issue of fair trials as being "soft on crime" or "soft on terrorism" and thereby convince people otherwise sympathetic to strong legal protections to back off from taking a stand for speedy, fair, and public trials....

The contrast with children's issues is stark. If there is any group around whom most societies can mobilize to protect, it is children. Children themselves represent practically no threat to any political regime or to national security. True, they can be used as a tool by rebels and governments to ratchet up civil war violence as child soldiers, but the recruitment of young children into the army typically does much more to change the social than the military dynamics of most conflicts. Thus, as we have seen, the more protective measures for children are fairly uncontroversial in principle. Protection from exploitation in the form of harsh and extensive work — especially when it competes with school — is increasingly viewed even in developing countries as bad for the full development of children. The CRC has helped activists to focus on this issue, and its ratification is strongly associated with reductions in rates of child labor, even when controlling for the economic, developmental, and demographic factors usually associated with the widespread use of children in the workforce. The employment of children has not nearly approached zero — nor should it, for many of the reasons discussed in Chapter 8 — but the awareness of the issues brought into focus most recently by the CRC and the processes of state reporting, justification, and counterjustification by children's activists have assisted in the exposure and reduction of the economic exploitation of children. Human rights issues vary in other important ways as well. For example, they vary considerably in the extent to which each right can effectively be observed and monitored. Governments are much less likely to violate rights that are centrally administered and easy to observe than rights that are highly decentralized.

...

Moreover, the evidence that international law has mattered for many rights and under certain circumstances is not redundant to broader trends in democratization. Many of the rights examined in this study — the right to not be executed by the government, the right of girls to access education in numbers equal to those of boys, the right of children not to be drafted into the military — simply do not correlate strongly with improvements within countries in participatory democracy. In the statistical tests, the effect of the treaty was forced to compete in most models with yearly democracy trends in each country. In fact, democratization was included in both the selection and the output equations; that is, it was systematically accounted for in the explanation for participation in the treaty regime and treaty compliance thereafter. In many cases, ratification of the human rights treaty has had a significant influence on rights practices, even controlling for changes in democracy within countries from one year to the next. Governments might have improved their human rights anyway because they were on the road to democracy, but treaties have made these improvements even more likely on the margin.

What is especially interesting and very important for understanding the nature of international law's contribution to human rights is the consistently important role it has played in polities in which institutions are changing, evolving, and in flux. In these cases, stakeholders, officials, and/or activists are searching for the right kinds of persuasive examples and focal points to influence the development of their own futures. Colombian women, for example, sought to influence the future institutions of their country by advocating the principles contained in the CEDAW during discussions of constitutional reform. The Chilean opposition insisted on the inclusion of international law's explicit constitutional status during debates over the nature of Chile's governing institutions into the future. The treaties discussed here have had an especially central role when the design of basic institutions in domestic governance was at stake. It is under these conditions that publics have had the motive to mobilize to advocate their vision of the future, and ratified treaties have provided crucial focal points for clarifying their position and making their voices heard.

The importance of an opportunity to influence a country's rights future is supported by the finding that ratified treaties have their strongest effects in countries that are neither stable democracies nor stable autocracies. . . . Even more striking, only in these partially democratic or transitioning countries did the ICCPR have any effect on provisions for a civil liberty as important as fair trials. Similarly, the CAT has had a significantly bigger positive impact in countries in which democracy has had a tenuous foothold. In all of these cases, this category includes countries that have transitioned to democracy, away from democracy, and have fluctuated somewhere in the middle. In fact, it is a conclusion that holds on average for all countries except those that have been stable democracies or stable autocracies since World War II. It is impossible to put exact numbers on this finding, but it means that for a broad swathe of human-kind, the CAT has been associated with a lower chance of being tortured when in government detention than would otherwise have been the case.

The theoretical reason for expecting the most powerful treaty effects in this middle group of countries goes beyond this particular measure of regime type. I have argued that mobilization to demand observance of a human rights obligation can be thought of as a combination of motive and means. On the one hand, if stakeholders and their allies have a motive to organize to demand observance but have no realistic chance of influencing government policy or outcomes, they are unlikely to pay the price to do so. On the other hand, if stakeholders and allies have a realistic chance of influencing government policy but have little motive to do so because they already enjoy a secure package of rights, they are also unlikely to organize to demand treaty compliance. The expected value of mobilization is maximized in polities where people have both the motive and the means to make clear their human rights demands. Treaties are useful because they can convince locals that they may indeed be entitled to think of themselves as rights holders, and because they provide additional political and legal resources for those who are motivated to pursue their rights.

. . .

Yet, it is quite likely that treaties have effects unrelated to ratification per se. First, a treaty could have existential effects. Its very existence could change global conceptions of what constitutes appropriate behavior of a government toward its own citizens. Governments could become socialized to the norms contained in a specific treaty, yet for a number of reasons — some of which have been discussed . . . — find it difficult to ratify a specific agreement. Second, a treaty could have anticipatory effects. Many governments specifically aim to come into compliance with a treaty before ratification. There is pretty clear evidence, for example, that governments abolish the death penalty prior to ratification of the OPDP to the ICCPR. Anticipatory effects can vary by the type of right in question. Since capital punishment is an especially easy-to-monitor practice, governments are encouraged to end it before formally being obligated in international law to do so. Third, treaties can mobilize international assistance to support compliance. The norms contained in certain treaties — for example, the health and education provisions of the CRC — are a delight to the governments of some developing countries, which are encouraged to believe that they have a strong basis to expect technical and infrastructural assistance from international agencies such as ECOSOC, the World Health Organization, and even private donors. . . .

All of this contributes to an important point: By focusing on treaty ratification, I have quite likely *underestimated* the influence of international law on human rights practices. Estimates of the influence of ratification are diminished by countries that internalize treaty norms but fail to ratify. They are also diminished by countries that insist on complying sometimes years prior to ratification. Nor do my results pick up the indirect effects of treaty ratification on various forms of mobilization of international society, whether for purposes of improving states' capacity to deliver the goods or shaming them into refraining from outright abuses, independent of their ratification decisions. Customary international law might also encourage governments to comply prior to ratification. The evidence presented in this study is therefore a *conservative* estimate of international law's overall effect on governments' behavior.

. . .

Governments everywhere should also be encouraged to ratify. But this research has shown that there is no particular payoff to pressuring stable, highly repressive regimes to do so; at least this should not be a high priority. Attention should instead be focused on supporting ratification in those countries in which the agreements are likely eventually to matter the most. To know which countries these are, it is crucial to understand their history, governing institutions, and culture. Where these are solidly opposed to the rights contained in (multilateral) treaties, ratification pressures are unlikely to help and could even be counterproductive. This policy implication runs counter to the goals of some organizations that advocate universal ratification of all treaties. This study suggests that resources should be focused instead on ratification in countries with some history of or prospect for liberalization. These are the crucial rights battle grounds in the medium term.

ERIC POSNER, SOME SKEPTICAL COMMENTS ON BETH SIMMONS'S MOBILIZING FOR HUMAN RIGHTS

44 NYU J. Int'l. L. & Pol'y. 819 (2012)

. . .

The mobilization mechanism . . . suffers from circularity. People who care about, say, stopping torture might be governed by leaders who share their view, who do not share their view, or who are divided. If the leaders oppose torture as well, then they will stop torture whether or not a treaty exists. If the leaders are divided about torture, then surely domestic anti-torture groups will know this, and those groups will not learn anything about the leaders' views about torture from the ratification of the Convention Against Torture (CAT). If the leaders approve of torture, but nonetheless ratify the CAT, it is possible that the domestic anti-torture groups will falsely believe that in fact the leaders reject torture, and mobilize, possibly producing some positive effect. It is only in this last case that the mobilization theory makes any logical sense, but is it plausible? Don't domestic groups know about the torture (that is why they form in the first place) and won't they believe that the leaders have no intention of complying with the treaty?

...Most anti-torture groups harbor few illusions about their government's motivations.

...In older debates about human rights treaties, discussions centered around the question of compliance. Do states that enter human rights treaties comply with them?...Simmons asks a different question: whether ratification of a human rights treaty has a causal effect on a state's human rights outcomes. The question is then whether human rights outcomes after ratification exceed human rights outcomes prior to ratification, all else equal.

...

Let us consider a human rights treaty. If a country enters the CAT, and the number of people tortured goes down from 100,000 per year to 50,000 per year, there is (arguable) causation, but not compliance. This counts as success in Simmons's empirics, not as failure. Which is the right perspective? It depends on what you care about. If the question is whether international law and human rights treaties in particular ever affect behavior, then all we care about is causation. If the question is whether states comply with human rights treaties, then we must make a judgment about what level of causation counts as compliance. That is a difficult judgment, which will depend a great deal on context...

...

...Simmons finds that at a statistically significant level, countries with an ICCPR commitment have more religious freedom. The coefficient is .08, which means that when a country ratifies the ICCPR, the probability that religious freedom will increase from 0 to 1 is eight percent. How should we understand this coefficient? Does religious freedom increase significantly or trivially when a state ratifies the ICCPR?

There are two problems with answering this question. The first is that religious freedom is a continuous phenomenon, which cannot be captured fully in a dichotomous variable. It is possible that the states that move from 0 to 1 when they ratify the treaty are states that barely fall short of receiving a 1 before they ratify the treaty and barely deserve a 1 after they ratify the treaty. Thus, their improvement is marginal....

...

...One concern is that she was drawn to provisions that require agencies to produce human rights outcomes that are easily measurable so as to facilitate empirical analysis, which requires measurable outcomes....The problem with this approach is that countries may well be less likely to comply with provisions that do not require easily measurable outcomes — precisely because observers cannot easily tell whether the state has complied with the treaty term....Indeed, there is an even worse possibility: that states that enter human rights treaties improve their behavior along measurable dimensions while worsening their behavior along unmeasurable dimensions, so that overall human rights outcomes stay the same or even decline.

... [T]he only way to address this problem is to test treaty provisions that require states to produce unmeasurable human rights outcomes, but of course if the outcomes are unmeasurable, then an empirical test cannot be performed.

...

But the main problem with Simmons's normative argument relates back to my comments at various points about the magnitudes of the coefficients in her regressions. Recall that Simmons does not show compliance but causation, and the degree of causation turns out to be limited. If the question is whether "we" or states or other entities should invest in encouraging other states to enter and comply with human rights treaties, Simmons's empirical results provide a pessimistic answer. We all have limited resources, and if the result of all this effort is that it becomes a few percentage points more likely that a state will improve human rights outcomes, we should ask whether our resources might be better used in some other way — for example, through the provision of foreign aid. And if states do not improve their overall human rights outcomes, but merely switch from more measurable abuses to less measurable abuses, then our resources are being wasted.

EDWARD T. SWAINE, ERSATZ TREATIES

44 NYU J. Int'l. L. & Pol'y. 833 (2012)

... For a book that winds up attributing unmistakable significance to human rights treaties, and will quite reasonably be embraced by many in the human rights field, Simmons's perspective on human rights may be surprising. The core of her argument eschews the conventional mechanisms typically invoked by international relations theorists and, even more, by international lawyers.... [S]he pointedly downplays expectations for international influences.... [T]he dominant argument is that ratification is mediated through the opportunities it creates for local actors.

The domestic concentration of this analysis thus revives, indirectly, the perennial question: precisely what function is performed by the *international law* aspects of human rights treaties? That is, what does the catalytic force of human rights treaties have to do with their character as treaties? Consider three alternative mechanisms for expressing and establishing fundamental norms of the kind presently captured by a human rights treaty:

(1) home-grown statutory or constitutional provisions;
(2) transplanted statutory or constitutional provisions borrowed from another state or derived from a trans-national process;
(3) statutory or constitutional provisions that track the substantive content of an international human rights treaty, but without the state assuming any international obligations.

...First, to what extent do such mechanisms achieve the advantages attributed to international human rights treaties, and which serve as predictors of their success? Second, are these other mechanisms competitive or complementary to international human rights treaties, and is their order of adoption significant?

...My objective...is to consider how the ersatz treaties fare on the causal pathways that the book identifies, to determine whether they might, under the right conditions, supply an alternative explanation for progress — perhaps warranting consideration by uncommitted states — or whether they hint that there is more to human rights treaties than meets the (domestic) eye.

...When it comes to rights, maybe the more the merrier...Even if, as is sometimes alleged, rights proliferation risks conflicts among entitlements, or inhibits other objectives, like economic development, redundancy in terms of the same rights — relating to their density rather than their breadth — likely sidesteps these objections....

Even so, there is cause to pause....It is plausible, for example, that ratifying a human rights treaty begets replication and alternative versions of those rights, but also that ratification of a treaty will diminish the appetite for constitutionalizing (or otherwise cementing domestically) those rights. It is unclear, in other words, whether alternative forms of fundamental norms are substitutes or complements.

We can be reasonably confident that when states already secure liberties through adequate domestic structures, their need for human rights treaties decreases — albeit without necessarily decreasing their appetite for ratification. From the standpoint of compliance, such states are a potential second set of "false positives"...it would be mistaken to attribute their high satisfaction of human rights objectives to treaties *per se*. We expect, too, that such states may well ratify at a high rate....

ROBERT HOWSE & RUTI TEITEL, BETH SIMMONS'S MOBILIZING FOR HUMAN RIGHTS: A 'BEYOND COMPLIANCE' PERSPECTIVE

44 NYU J. Int'l. L. & Pol'y. 813 (2012)

...[*Mobilizing for Human Rights*] is a leading example of a perspective on the way international law works that we call "beyond compliance."...

Simmons clearly looks at the effects of international law through a broader lens than that of state compliance with rules....

The significance of this approach, however, seems to be muted or understated as Simmons herself never does break with the language of "compliance" in the way in which she articulates the effects of international law. To some extent, this is a matter of semantics, of course. But it is not merely so. For is it really conceptually adequate to describe effects never intended or expected by the authors of the rules in question as "compliance"? Can one properly describe as "compliance" the effect of human rights treaties in empowering non-state actors to militate for domestic social and political change?...Another set of reflections concerns interpretation and the sense that the norms themselves are dynamic in the hands of the actors in question. If one were to take Simmons's project a step further, one would need to investigate cases where the relevant agents have taken ratified treaty norms and succeeded in using those as a basis for creating new normative and institutional structures for human rights....

...

[T]he Inter-American Court [has] craft[ed] a teleological or purposive interpretation of the human rights norms in question, in light of the challenges posed by recent history in Latin America. Nowhere were the specific duties of prevention, investigation, and punishment obvious from the text of the American Convention. Though of course there is a provision committing to provision of remedies. Instead, the Court relied on an expansive view of the right to life and security of the person — rights provided for in the Convention. Thus, the domestic effects identified by Simmons ultimately depended on a broader normative universe that supported, or sustained the legitimacy of, a certain *reading* of the treaty text.... Ultimately the question of compliance cannot be properly understood without attention to the problem of interpretation. The application of treaty rules through interpretation makes the norms themselves dynamic and results in the construction of new meanings. The dynamism in question is constituted by constant motion back and forth between domestic, international and transnational sites of interpretation.

BETH A. SIMMONS, REFLECTIONS ON MOBILIZING FOR HUMAN RIGHTS

44 NYU J. Int'l. L. & Pol'y. 729 (2012)

...*Mobilizing for Human Rights* was in many ways a conservative piece of research. It focused on traditional interpretations of specific treaty provisions, and looked for "obvious" effects in ratifying countries. Many of the participants in the Symposium noted that this is quite a limited test of the impact of international law on human rights. For example, Catharine MacKinnon noted that gender crime fits the book's frame-work, but cuts across treaties....

...More could be done, Catharine MacKinnon noted, to explore the effect of international law on perceptions of "legitimate" behavior. While the data are hard to come by and a different method would be necessary (ethnography, in the style of Sally Merry's persuasive work) this is an important way forward for understanding international law's more dynamic effects.

...In surveys administered between 2005 and 2011 in both the United States and Colombia, I have sought to determine whether there is any evidence that people hold governments accountable for their treaty commitments. I asked a sample of people I would consider well-informed opinion leaders the following question:

> There is currently a debate about whether the United States [Colombia] should tighten rules for interrogating detainees limiting psychological forms of abuse.

These forms of abuse are outlawed by the Convention Against Torture, which the U.S. [Columbia] has ratified. Do you think the U.S. [Colombia] should follow rules limiting psychological forms of detainee abuse, even if it makes it more difficult to collect intelligence information from them? Please circle one: Yes, Possibly, No, Don't Know.

Half of each survey sample randomly received the entire question, and half received the question with the bolded italicized sentence removed. Thus, we can think of exposure to information about the fact and nature of the United States [Colombian] commitment under international law as the "treatment" in this experiment.

The results suggest that when people are aware of the existence of an international legal commitment, they hold their governments accountable to these commitments. While the answers of the Colombians appear to be a bit more tolerant of torture, in both countries the suggestion of an international legal commitment increases by between 11–13% for the United States and Colombia, respectively, the share of people who think that their country should follow torture norms, even if they help to glean useful intelligence. This suggests — of course, it does not prove — that people care about the nature of the international legal commitments their government makes....

...

Some international law scholars remain puzzled about why a state would want to use international law to improve rights, when they have the autonomous ability to create rules to protect rights. Edward Swaine makes this point at great length... Joel Trachtman's contribution to this volume also puzzles over this question...

... Redundancy is simply not a puzzle, least of all for actors interested in developing a robust legal system. Scholars of public administration regard redundancy as "a powerful device for the suppression of error." Sociologists of the law interpret redundancy as a legal strength; it permits the communication about norms and expectations in a complementary yet consistent manner, ultimately contributing to system durability in the case of competing, contradictory demands....

... Constitutions, statutes and court cases can also affect domestic political debates in crucial ways. These are not alternatives, but often the mechanisms through which the norms contained in treaties become enmeshed in domestic settings. *Mobilizing for Human Rights* looked at direct treaty effects in the quantitative tests. The qualitative tests looked explicitly at the inspiration ratified treaties have provided for statutory change and domestic constitutional development. These changes in domestic law then become crucial in supporting human rights demands.

In follow up work with Tom Ginsburg and Zachary Elkins, we looked carefully at the relationship between treaty ratification and the contents of national constitutions. Based on their impressive database of constitutional provisions, we have found that states that have ratified the ICCPR for example are much more likely to contain similar provisions than those that have not ratified....

... [C]ountries that ratified the ICCPR had new constitutions that were much more similar to the ICCPR than they had before ratification, and more than was the case for countries who did not ratify.

...We found that, indeed, there are three distinct channels for improved human rights outcomes: treaty ratification, constitutional provisions, and treaty ratification mediated by constitutional provisions...

...Adoption of a norm at both levels increases the probability that the norm will actually be enforced, because it provides multiple monitors and alternative forums in which to challenge government behavior.

RYAN GOODMAN & DEREK JINKS, SOCIALIZING STATES: PROMOTING HUMAN RIGHTS THROUGH INTERNATIONAL LAW (forthcoming 2013)

Chapter 1: Introduction

...

First-generation scholarship in international human rights law, in our view, provides an indispensable but plainly incomplete framework. Prevailing approaches suggest that law changes human rights practices either by materially inducing states (and individuals) or by persuading states (and individuals) of the validity and legitimacy of human rights law. In our view, the former approach fails to grasp the complexity of the social environment within which states act, and the latter fails to account for many ways in which the diffusion of social and legal norms occurs. Indeed, a rich cluster of empirical studies in interdisciplinary scholarship documents particular processes that socialize states in the absence of material inducement or persuasion. These studies conclude that the power of social influence can be harnessed even if: (1) collective action problems and political constraints that inhibit effective material inducements are not overcome and (2) the complete internalization sought through persuasion is not achieved....

Our aim is to provide a more complete conceptual framework by identifying a third mechanism by which international law might change state behavior — what we call *acculturation*....We do not suggest that international legal scholarship has completely failed to identify aspects of this process. Rather, we maintain that the mechanism is underemphasized, insufficiently specified, and poorly understood, and that it is often conflated or confused with other constructivist mechanisms such as persuasion....

Chapter 2: Three Mechanisms of Social Influence

...

A. Material inducement

The first and most obvious social mechanism is material inducement — whereby states and institutions influence the behavior of other states by increasing the benefits of conformity or the costs of nonconformity through material rewards and punishments.

B. Persuasion

Persuasion is a mechanism of social influence documented principally by psychologists and sociologists — and applied by others to the spread of norms across states. Persuasion theory suggests that the practices of actors are influenced through processes of social "learning" and other forms of information conveyance that occur in exchanges within international organizations and transnational networks. Persuasion "requires argument and deliberation in an effort to change the minds of others." Persuaded actors "internalize" new norms and rules of appropriate behavior and redefine their interests and identities accordingly.... The touchstone of the overall process is that actors are consciously convinced of the truth, validity, or appropriateness of a norm, belief, or practice. That is, persuasion occurs when actors actively assess the content of a particular message — a norm, practice, or belief — and change their minds on the basis of the norms congruence with their existing beliefs and values.

Consider two microprocesses through which the content of a message may succeed in changing a target actor's views: "framing" and "cuing." In terms of the former, the persuasive appeal of a counterattitudinal message increases if the issue is restructured to resonate with already accepted norms....

C. Acculturation

Another important mechanism of social influence, in our view, is acculturation. In using the term acculturation, we intend to group together a set of related social processes identified by a growing interdisciplinary literature. Whereas persuasion emphasizes the *content* of a norm, acculturation emphasizes the *relationship* of the actor to a reference group or wider cultural environment.... Accordingly, acculturation encompasses processes such as mimicry and status maximization. The general mechanism induces behavioral changes through pressures to conform. Individual behavior (and community-level behavioral regularity) is in part a function of social structure — the relations between individual actors and some reference group. Actors are impelled to adopt the behavioral practices and attitudes of similar actors in their surrounding social environment.

The touchstone of acculturation is that varying degrees of identification with a reference group generate varying degrees of cognitive and social pressures to conform. The operation of this mechanism is best understood by reference to well-documented individual-level phenomena. One of the central insights of social psychology is that individual behavior and cognition reflect substantial social influence. Actors, in an important sense, are influenced by their environment; indeed, this generalized influence is one important way that "culture" is transmitted and reproduced. Although culture is typically understood as "learned behavior," much of what actors absorb from their social environment is not simply "informational social influence." Social influence is a rich process — one that also includes "normative social influence" whereby actors are impelled to adopt appropriate attitudes and behaviors. An actor need not be unaware of these influences — these processes can be subconscious or fully apparent....

...

Despite the obvious similarities, acculturation differs from persuasion in important respects. First, persuasion requires acceptance of the validity or legitimacy of a belief, practice, or norm — acculturation requires only that an actor perceive that an important reference group harbors the belief, engages in the practice, or subscribes to the norm. Accordingly, persuasion involves complete internalization. Acculturation can involve complete or incomplete internalization. Second, persuasion requires active assessment of the merits of a belief. Acculturation processes, in contrast, frequently (though not invariably) operate tacitly; it is often the very act of conforming that garners social approval and alleviates cognitive discomfort. Persuasion involves assessment of the content of the message (even if only indirectly); acculturation involves assessment of the social relation (the degree of identification) between the target audience and some group (and of the importance of the issue to the group). Acculturation occurs not as a result of the content of the relevant rule or norm but rather as a function of social structure. Acculturation depends less on the properties of the rule than on the properties of the relationship of the actor to the community. Because the acculturation process does not involve actually agreeing with the merits of a group's position, it may (but does not necessarily) result in outward conformity with a social convention without private acceptance or corresponding changes in private practices.

...

Chapter 4: Acculturation of States: The Empirical Record

...

With respect to human rights in particular, extensive empirical research indicates the force of acculturation in fundamental areas of governance....

1. Constitutional design

...

...Nearly every constitution adopted since the Universal Declaration of Human Rights (1948) has contained some set of rights provisions. By 1991, 97 percent of all states had a national constitution with substantial human rights provisions. A global shift has occurred from many constitutional protections of rights in the preamble (such as the constitutions of the Fourth and Fifth French Republics) to operative provisions of the constitution.

As to the content of constitutional rights, John Boli's leading study of the text of every constitution over a hundred-year period (1870–1970) finds states adopt constitutional forms that correlate, in a striking manner, with rights contained in other national constitutions written at the time. Boli also finds a worldwide shift overtime from inalienable rights to alienable rights. And he finds that particular economic and social rights "appeared in virtually no constitution before 1930 and then spread rapidly. By 1970, approximately 40 percent of all constitutions enumerated these rights of citizens." Other research documents the continued spread of economic and social rights in subsequent decades.

Notably, particular constitutional forms are directly related to the degree of national incorporation into the world structure. Boli's study, for example, finds that integration in world society is directly associated with the level of constitutional elaboration of state authority. He measures state authority by coding constitutional provisions conferring governmental power over specific areas of social life (56 possible items) and creating mechanisms to implement governmental power (45 possible items). Boli explains that two nations with similar levels of economic and technical development will likely have constitutions with substantially different levels of "state authority" if one nation is highly integrated into world society and the other is not. Additionally, integration in world society has more explanatory power than an "internal-development perspective," which posits that domestic factors best explain constitutional construction.

Boli also finds that integration is directly associated with citizen rights provisions. Those results, however, are somewhat perplexing. States with greater integration in world society are less likely to have constitutions that delineate citizen rights. His measure for "citizen rights," however, includes duties citizens owe to society or the government. That variable could explain the relationship — more highly integrated states, for example, may be less likely to emphasize citizen duties. Regardless, the fact that a direct association exists — between integration and level of constitutional rights elaboration — is itself significant for our present purposes.

Consider also contagion effects from global and regional cultural exemplars. Much has been written about the influence of the U.S. Constitution abroad... Professor Mohamed Yamin one of the framers of the 1945 Constitution of Indonesia invoked the U.S. model by explaining, "Before me is the structure of the Republic of the United States of America, which time and again has been used for several constitutions in the world." The U.S. model has also spread through the adoption by culturally important regional actors. For example, India copied rights provisions of the U.S. constitution, and other states have in turn been influenced by the Indian constitution.

Such "circuits of influence" also characterize the influence of non-US models. For example, the European Convention on Human Rights [and Fundamental] Freedoms was especially attractive to Nigeria because it reflected the "influence of a document forged by a transnational organization" encompassing numerous states. Sociologist Julian Go suggests the adoption by Nigeria then produced a cascade effect.

> The European Convention served as a model for rights provisions in the independence constitutions of many other African countries also, either through direct influence or indirectly through the Nigerian constitution serving as a precedent. These include, in chronological order after Nigeria, Sierra Leone, Uganda, Kenya, Malawi, Gambia, Botswana, Lesotho, Mauritius, Swaziland, the Seychelles, and Zimbabwe. There seems to have been a strong diffusion effect: once Nigeria adopted the European Convention as a model, so too did many others. As Smith has put it, "the trickle became a cascade."
>
> ...

Significant decoupling exists with constitutional rights guarantees.... [T]he near universal embrace of constitutional rights guarantees provides a good example of transnational [homogeneity] despite radically different internal social structures:

surprisingly all states codify constitutional rights despite variations in military-civilian relations and enormous cultural diversity across nations....

Another pattern of decoupling involves formal rights guarantees with a striking lack of capacity to implement them....At the very least, the formal reach of these constitutions exceeds their grasp, which is an "unstable equilibrium" that one would expect constitutional systems try to avoid.

The persistence of these constitutional forms despite such inefficiencies suggests that the adoption of such provisions serves other goals. Recall that "organizations are evaluated in terms of their 'social fitness' as well as their performance: legitimacy and accountability are as important as, if not more so than, reliability and efficiency." In this context, social fitness or legitimacy may be measured by the degree to which a national constitution meets certain standardized international expectations of rights guarantees. That explanation would at least involve a rational, stable equilibrium which these constitutions do potentially meet. Indeed, one study concludes that "[n]ational constitutions do not simply reflect processes of internal development," but rather "reflect legitimating ideas dominant in the world system at the time of their creation."

2. Substantive rights protections: Children's rights and women's rights

Consider particular substantive domains of human rights, beginning with children's rights. The number of constitutions that include provisions committed to the state management of childhood and children's rights has increased dramatically. A study of every national constitution in effect from 1870–1970 shows that the adoption of such constitutional provisions over time does not correlate with local forms of social organization (such as urbanization and national wealth) or with technical capacities of the relevant states. Moreover, each group of newly established states shows a significantly higher probability of adopting such constitutional provisions than the preceding group of entrants. According to these researchers, the overall findings suggest that "[n]ational constitutions do not simply reflect processes of internal development," but rather "reflect legitimating ideas dominant in the world system at the time of their creation."

Consider, also, state convergence with respect to women's rights. A leading study uses sophisticated analytic techniques to examine state definitions of political citizenship over a hundred-year period. According to the study, once universal suffrage became a legitimating principle associated with the modern nation-state, adoption of women's suffrage followed a pattern anticipated by theories of acculturation. After an initial stage of early adopters, the number of states providing women the right to vote increased steeply and included most states before the rate of adoption tapered off; the likelihood that a state would adopt women's suffrage correlated with world trend lines; and adoption correlated far less with domestic political conditions once significant cross-national [homogenization] took hold. Additionally, an important finding indicates a contagion effect: once the norm was institutionalized, a strong predictor for whether an individual state would enact women's suffrage was whether other states in its region had done so in the past five years. The overall findings suggest that, compared with local conditions such as the strength of domestic women's rights groups, "[c]ountries apparently are affected much less strongly by internal factors and much more strongly by shifts in the international logic of political citizenship."

These results are consistent with studies concerning other areas of women's rights. For example, a separate study of states in the western hemisphere examines how those governments made roughly contemporaneous commitments to eradicate violence against women. Within a relatively short time span, "[n]early all American states... created national women's councils that include[d] domestic violence problems among their priorities,... approved legal changes that define[d] domestic violence as a crime,... launched educational campaigns to combat the problem, and... created social services for victims." States also made these advances uniformly; no state substantially exceeded, or distinguished itself from, the average set of commitments. The extent of this homogeneity despite wide variations in national-level political, cultural, and social conditions is remarkable. Specifically, once the obligation to address domestic violence was institutionalized at the regional level, states joined the bandwagon despite dramatic differences in women's political power or access to economic resources at the national level. Indeed, the study concludes that, at this stage of institutionalization, "international socialization is more important than domestic politics" in getting "nonconformist states to change their policies to meet the standards of new international norms."

...

3. Network effects and human rights

Finally, consider evidence of diffusion of human rights scripts through social networks of states. Some studies that we discussed earlier overlook network effects. In particular, some of the studies that demonstrate an integration correlation — the greater degree to which a state is tied to international organizations, the greater likelihood or speed by which the state will adopt a global norm — fail to consider the network ties that connect states to other members of those organizations and the relative position of a state in the overall network....

Human rights research that focuses on network structures also provides strong evidence of acculturation. For example, Brian Greenhill employs network analysis to examine state violations of rights to physical integrity. He finds that states tend to conform their practices over time to the average human rights performance of states with which they share overlapping IGO memberships. The findings are especially remarkable because the convergence is associated with joint membership in IGOs that have no direct connection to human rights issues. Those IGOs are thus not designed for persuasive opportunities to discuss human rights issues, nor to deliver material inducements on the basis of human rights performance. The socialization effects presumably result instead from the organization of relationships formed by the IGO network. Greenhill concludes: "[T]he specific make up of IGOs — in terms of the human rights records of their member states — is much more important than the nature of the IGOs themselves.... One consequence of this is that when it comes to evaluating the ability of different international organizations to promote human rights, we should perhaps... shift our attention to the human rights records of their existing member states. In other words, we should think of states' human rights behavior as being defined to a large extent by the company they keep."

As another example, Magnus Torfason and Paul Ingram study whether network relationships result in states becoming more similar to one another in their democratic structures (implicating the rights to political participation and representation). Their research design involves a network autoregression model which measures the extent to which adjacent nodes in a network become more similar over time than would otherwise be expected. The study finds that "states that share IGO membership with countries with different levels of democracy tend to become more similar to their co-members in terms of democracy levels." The authors also present "evidence of mimetic isomorphism of rich countries by the poor, and coercive isomorphism whereby the militarily powerful influence the weak," … [and] mimesis has greater explanatory power in the contemporary period.

Notably, the spread of anti-democratic norms through the acculturation of network ties tends to be a powerful force, independent of the persuasive appeal of the norm. Torfason and Ingram admit that they mistakenly anticipated the persuasive content of the democratic norm — whether it resonates with existing values and norms within a society — would mediate the diffusion of democratic structures such that democratic states would not tend to become less democratic as a result of increased network ties to nondemocracies. According to this hypothesis, "The democracy-enhancing influence of more democratic countries ['positive influence'] through the IGO network will have a larger effect than the democracy-reducing influence of less democratic countries ['negative influence']." The data, however, demonstrate that the acculturation effects were not conditioned on such constraints. …

4. Regional/"neighborhood" effects

…

[C]onsider the spread of fair trials across a region. Simmons concludes that social influence within a region is central to an explanation of fair trial practices:

> The most consistent external influence across all categories of countries is the nature of the practices in the region in which the country is situated. Across all subgroups and the sample as a whole, fair trial practices in the region were a strong predictor of fair trial practices in a specific country. This effect appears to be the strongest among the moderately democratic and transitional countries, though it is statistically significant in every model. This pattern could be explained by shared cultural patterns or even regional socialization or mimicry.

The explanatory power of fair trial practices in the region is generally stronger than other important variables. And those other variables include factors of such significance as the ratification of the ICCPR, civil wars, international wars, and military government.

… Simmons documents similar patterns concerning the right to sex equality. The right to education for women and girls, for instance, is strongly influenced by enrollment levels in other states. Based on the data, Simmons reports:

> Regional enrollment ratios seem to exert a positive impact overall, but this external effect seems to be highly concentrated in the low rule of law countries and, to

much lesser extent, the transition countries. Surprisingly, these regional effects tell more consistent and statistically significant story than the national level developmental indicators.

With respect to reproductive rights, the data show similar results. Most importantly, average regional availability of family planning is a strong and highly statistically significant predictor of a government's policy with respect to family planning access.

...

... [T]hese findings are consistent with other studies on the diffusion of human rights practices through acculturation. Recall that the research on female suffrage demonstrated a contagion effect at the regional level: once the norm was institutionalized, a strong predictor for whether an individual state would enact women's suffrage was whether other states in its region had done so in the past five years. Other research demonstrates the diffusion of policy scripts to eradicate domestic violence within Latin America. Torfason and Igram's study of the diffusion of democracy also finds significant regional network effects. Wotipka and Ramirez also find regional effects in the ratification rates of the Convention on the Elimination of Discrimination Against Women. And these regional patterns are consistent with studies outside the human rights realm that also show acculturation through regional pathways. ...

KATERINA LINOS, DIFFUSION THROUGH DEMOCRACY

55 Am. J. Pol. Sci. 678 (2011)

...

Do voters' positions shift when they are informed about international models? ... A representative sample of 1,291 U.S. adults was used. Respondents were randomly assigned to one of five groups. Respondents in the first, baseline group were asked: "To what extent do you agree or disagree with the following statement: 'The United States should increase taxes in order to provide mothers of newborn children with paid leave from work.'" Response options were "Strongly Agree," "Somewhat Agree," "Somewhat Disagree," and "Strongly Disagree."

Respondents in Groups 2 through 5 received the same baseline question, prefaced by different introductions. For Group 2, the preface was "Canada provides mothers of newborn children with paid leave from work." For Group 3, the preface was "Most Western countries provide mothers of newborn children with paid leave from work." For Group 4, the preface was "The United Nations recommends that all countries should provide mothers of newborn children with paid leave from work." For Group 5, the preface was "American family policy experts recommend that the United States should provide mothers of newborn children with paid leave from work."

Table 1 presents the basic results of this experiment. Each row represents an experimental group. The columns give the percentage of respondents who expressed agreement ("Strongly Agree" and "Somewhat Agree") and disagreement ("Strongly Disagree" and "Somewhat Disagree"). Ninety-five percent confidence intervals appear in parentheses. Aggregate support for a tax increase to introduce paid maternity leave increases by about 20 percentage points when it is presented as the policy choice of Canada, the policy choice of most Western countries, or as the recommendation of U.S. experts. Aggregate support increases even more — by 28 percentage points — when the policy is introduced as a UN recommendation. The differences between each of the introductions and the baseline are statistically significant at the 0.10 level at least, as is the difference between the UN recommendation, on the one hand, and any of the other introductions, on the other.

Table 1. Support for a Tax Increase to Introduce Paid Maternity Leave

[Eds.: Some statistics have been omitted for purposes of simplification.]		
	Agree (%)	**Disagree (%)**
No Introduction	20	80
Canada Introduction	40	60
Most Western Countries Introduction	40	60
UN Recommendation Introduction	48	52
American Experts Introduction	41	59

How different groups respond to information about foreign models can shed light on what explains these effects. The theoretical discussion offers two possible pathways: the informational pathway, according to which voters gain information about the likely domestic consequences of a particular proposal, and the conformity pathway, according to which voters prefer that their country conform to international norms. To investigate the informational pathway, all respondents were asked how familiar they were with social policy issues. Specifically, they were asked: "Employers and employees pay taxes and fees for benefit programs such as health insurance, pensions, and childcare. In general, how well informed are you about the costs and benefits of such programs? Would you say you are very well informed, fairly well informed, not too well informed, or not at all informed?" Forty-eight percent of respondents answered that they were either very or fairly well informed, while 52% replied that they were either not too well or not at all informed. This indicates that some voters face substantial informational limitations in evaluating social policy proposals, in support of Proposition 1.

...To examine the conformity mechanism, respondents receiving information about an international norm (Groups 3 and 4), as well as respondents in the baseline group (Group 1), were also asked: "Do you have a very favorable, somewhat favorable, somewhat unfavorable or very unfavorable opinion of the United Nations?" Fifty-six percent responded that they had a very or somewhat favorable opinion of the UN, while 44% responded that they had a very or a somewhat unfavorable view. These data track the 2007 Pew Survey....

Figure 1 below shows how prior information about social policies influences responses to each of the prompts,...holding demographic variables at their means. For example, the far left column shows that when told that Canada provided

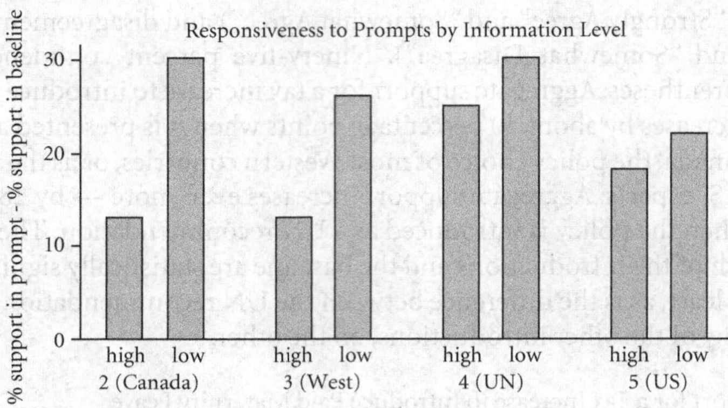

Figure 1 Responsiveness to Prompts by Respondent's Information Level

maternity leaves, respondents who rated themselves as well informed increased their support for maternity leave by 13 percentage points. The second column from the left shows that the effect was much larger among respondents who believed they had limited prior information about social policy — their support increased by 30 percentage points These findings are consistent with the claim that information is a key pathway through which foreign models influence public opinion.

Simulations..., holding demographic variables at their means, show that people who have favorable views of the UN respond significantly more to the UN recommendation than people who have unfavorable views of the UN; attitudes change by 36 percentage points. In contrast, responsiveness to the prompt about the practices of most Western countries does not depend on attitudes towards the UN. The finding that UN supporters respond more to the UN prompt is consistent both with the conformity and with the information mechanisms. People who hold favorable views of the UN may prefer that the United States conform to international norms because this is intrinsically desirable, or they may consider the UN to be a credible source of information about which policies work domestically. The strongest evidence for a conformity effect is the fact that responsiveness to a UN recommendation is in aggregate stronger than responsiveness to any of the other prompts, and that large shifts in attitudes occur even among persons who consider themselves well informed about social policy.

This experiment yields several additional surprises that could spark further research. First, even persons with negative views of the UN responded positively to the UN recommendation, although the effect was much smaller than for people with positive views of the UN. Perhaps the standard Pew survey question about attitudes to the UN, replicated here, conflates two dimensions: beliefs about the UN's goals and beliefs about the UN's efficacy. Perhaps some people with unfavorable views towards the UN are supportive of its goals, and thus swayed by its recommendations, but skeptical of its institutional capabilities to carry out these goals. Another surprising finding is that while attitudes towards the UN condition responsiveness to the UN recommendation, they do not influence responsiveness to the prompt concerning policy adoption by foreign countries. The fact that people with positive and negative views of the UN are equally likely to be influenced by foreign country policies suggests that no coherent "pro-international" attitude exists. Attitudes towards foreign endorsements may be nuanced; it is worth investigating responsiveness to particular foreign sources. Also surprising is that the adoption of a practice by Canada triggers just as large a response as the adoption of a practice by many Western countries.

How much are such effects likely to matter outside of the experimental setting, given that a large literature on political communication shows that voters respond differently to public opinion polls that raise different considerations?... Prior research suggests that the magnitude of these effects will likely decrease when voters are presented with competing information, but that the endorsement effects will not disappear entirely. Another important caveat concerns the information differential reported above: while less informed voters might be more likely to change their views if they get new information, they might also be less likely to receive this information if they are generally inattentive to politics. Ultimately, public opinion data as such cannot show how much endorsements will influence voters outside a controlled setting, and to what extent politicians will deviate from policies they would otherwise pursue, in order to increase voter support by gaining credible endorsements....

QUESTIONS

1. How would you define 'compliance' with international human rights law? Do you agree with Howse and Teitel's critique of the focus on compliance?

2. Has the overall record of state compliance with human rights law been, on average, a positive one? Is Posner correct that the marginal benefits to human rights treaty ratification are not worth the effort in many if not most cases?

3. What conditions are more or less conducive to compliance with international human rights law? Are democracies more or less likely to be influenced by the dictates of international law? What might be missing from the list of 'scope conditions' that Risse and Sikkink present? Do you agree with Simmons's analysis that different rights (e.g., women's rights versus the right to health) are more or less likely to improve as a result of treaty ratification due to their potential to mobilize domestic stakeholders? Do you agree that fair trial rights have much less potential in this regard and child rights have a much greater potential?

4. In the surveys conducted by Simmons on the CAT (2013) and by Linos on maternity leave policies, what do you think best explains the positive reaction by survey participants? Were these survey results surprising?

5. Do you agree with the policy recommendations proffered by Risse and Sikkink, Hathaway, and Simmons at the end of their respective analyses? Consider the following criticism of one of these approaches:[5]

> ...Because Hathaway's policy analysis is geared to solve one problem ('costless' ratification), she fails to account for the impact her proposals would have on other potentially positive effects of treaty ratification (effects not captured by her empirical or theoretical model)....[B]y reducing the opportunities for 'shallow' ratification by problem countries, Hathaway's approach would undermine the considerable constitutive effects of these treaties.
>
> ...[B]road ratification of human rights treaties plays an important role in the process of building national human rights cultures (and a transnational human rights culture). It is important to note that, even on Hathaway's view, states attempt to realize the signalling benefits of human rights treaty ratification precisely because the norms embodied in these treaties enjoy widespread (international) acceptance. As previously discussed, treaty regimes help foster this acceptance domestically by increasing the salience and legitimacy of human rights norms. In addition, universal (or broad-based) ratification furthers these objectives on the global plane by increasing the salience and legitimacy of these norms in the international community. In this sense, human rights treaties serve both a (global) expressive function and a (domestic) constitutive function. In terms of expressive significance. Hathaway acknowledges that 'treaties may have broader positive effects not captured by the analysis'. That is, even if ratifications are directly associated with negligible or deleterious effects in particular states, on the whole such treaties can have 'a widespread effect on the practices of all nations by changing the discourse about and expectations regarding those rights'....Despite these two types of effects — global and domestic — Hathaway asserts that we must remedy the short-term, negative effects on individual ratifying countries by raising the costs of ratification. Such a scheme, however, may well disrupt the gradual process of constructing a global normative order (a necessary step in the further legalization of international human rights regimes).

Is this criticism correct? Does the criticism apply to Simmons' policy recommendations as well?

6. In light of Swaine's analysis, which form of legalization would you propose pursuing in a given country instead of treaty ratification? What factors within the country would affect your choice?

7. If Goodman and Jinks are correct about the forms of influence on state human rights practices, how might that understanding change the ways in which NGOs build transnational human rights campaigns or the ways in which global human rights institutions are designed?

[5] R. Goodman & D. Jinks, 'Measuring the Effects of Human Rights Treaties', 14 Eur. J. Int'l. L. 171 (2003).

PART F

CURRENT TOPICS

Drawing on the framework created by Parts A–E, the chapters in Part F examine three broad topics of great significance for the human rights movement — three among the larger number of current and vital human rights themes that could as well have been selected. Chapters 14 and 15 examine consequences of massive human rights tragedies, particularly individual criminal prosecutions and truth commissions; Chapter 16 examines the growing role of non-state actors and Chapter 17 relationships between development, climate change and human rights.

15

Massive Human Rights Tragedies: Prosecutions and Truth Commissions

The topics and documents in this chapter grow out of massive human rights tragedies. The illustrations below include Libya, Rwanda, Sierra Leone, South Africa and the former Yugoslavia. Most of these tragedies were stimulated by an oppressor state, but some not. The theme of the chapter can be stated simply: What have been the nature and effects of two types of institutional reactions to such human rights violations — prosecutions before criminal tribunals and truth commissions? How do we understand these institutional responses, how do we assess them and in what directions do or should they now point?

To approach such questions, the chapter explores a number of related subjects: international crimes and individual culpability, the ad hoc international criminal tribunals for the former Yugoslavia and for Rwanda, the International Criminal Court, hybrid tribunals such as the Special Court for Sierra Leone, alternative national approaches such as gacaca courts in Rwanda and truth commissions, particularly in South Africa and Sierra Leone. With some exceptions, the emphasis in the earlier sections is on prosecutions before international tribunals, and in the concluding sections on other tribunals and truth commissions.

Several of the chapter's illustrations of systemic violations grow out of contexts of armed conflict, whether principally international in character or principally internal to a state. Others occurred in periods of severe internal repression that, despite its violence, stopped shy of internal armed conflict. For the first category, the *humanitarian laws of war* become particularly relevant. Hence the chapter builds on the earlier discussions of the law of war in connection with sources and foundations of international law, p. 69, *supra* (Comment on the Law of Armed Conflict), p. 120, *supra* (concerning the Nuremberg Judgment) and in connection with national security and terrorism, p. 404, *supra* (Comment on Relationships between International Human Rights and the Law of Armed Conflict). In cases like Augusto Pinochet's Chile and much (though not all) of the South African experience, the principal source of criticism and judgment has been mainstream *international human rights law* which has developed over the past six decades.

Nonetheless, the trends in both bodies of law over this period have brought them into a closer, intertwined relationship — a relationship vividly illustrated by the statutes of the international criminal tribunals, the judgments of such tribunals and the resolutions of the Security Council. Each field retains a near-exclusive interest in a large number of important issues — the laws of war, say, with respect to aspects of *jus in bello* such as military necessity in the waging of war; human rights law, say, with respect to free speech, gender equality or political participation. But on numerous issues that are germane to the international crimes and criminal prosecutions described below, the boundary lines are blurring.

The post-Nuremberg growth of the laws of war — particularly through the Geneva Conventions and their two Additional Protocols, and the statutes and judicial decisions of international criminal tribunals — as well as the striking success in standard-setting of the human rights movement, have greatly expanded the number of crimes defined by international law that are based on those bodies of law and that impose individual responsibility. Today's international crimes are both conventional and customary in character. Issues of punishment, impunity or immunity, amnesty and pardon of those involved in the most serious violations of human rights have become a feature of today's major conflicts.

A. INTERNATIONAL CRIMINAL TRIBUNALS FOR THE FORMER YUGOSLAVIA AND RWANDA

MARTHA MINOW, BETWEEN VENGEANCE AND FORGIVENESS

(1998), at 25

To respond to mass atrocity with legal prosecutions is to embrace the rule of law. This common phrase combines several elements. First, there is a commitment to redress harms with the application of general, preexisting norms. Second, the rule of law calls for administration by a formal system itself committed to fairness and opportunities for individuals to be heard both in accusation and in defense. Further, a government proceeding under the rule of law aims to treat each individual person in light of particular, demonstrated evidence. In the Western liberal legal tradition, the rule of law also entails the presumption of innocence, litigation under the adversary system, and the ideal of a government by laws, rather than by persons. No one is above or outside the law, and no one should be legally condemned or sanctioned outside legal procedures....

A trial in the aftermath of mass atrocity, then, should mark an effort between vengeance and forgiveness. It transfers the individuals' desires for revenge to the state or official bodies. The transfer cools vengeance into retribution, slows judgment with procedure, and interrupts, with documents, cross-examination, and the presumption of innocence, the vicious cycle of blame and feud. The trial itself steers clear of forgiveness, however. It announces a demand not only for accountability and acknowledgment of harms done, but also for unflinching punishment. At the end of the trial process, after facts are found and convictions are secured, there might be forgiveness of a legal sort: a suspended sentence, or executive pardon, or clemency in light of humanitarian concerns. Even then, the process has exacted time and agony from, and rendered a kind of punishment for defendants, while also accomplishing change in their relationships to prosecutors, witnesses, and viewing public. Reconciliation is not the goal of criminal trials except in the most abstract sense. We reconcile with the murderer by imagining he or she is responsible to the same rules and commands that govern all of us; we agree to sit in the same room and accord the defendant a chance to speak, and a chance to fight for his or her life. But reconstruction of a relationship, seeking to heal the accused, or indeed, healing the rest of the community, are not the goals in any direct sense.... Justice Jackson's own defense of the prosecutorial effort at Nuremberg was more modest than the assertion of deterrence offered by others since. He called for modest aspirations especially because wars are usually started only in the confidence that they can be won. Therefore, he acknowledged, '[p]ersonal punishment, to be suffered only in the event the war is lost, is probably not to be a sufficient deterrent to prevent a war where the war-makers feel the chances of defeat to be negligible'. Does the risk of punishment for human rights violations make the leaders of authoritarian regimes reluctant to surrender power in the first place? Individuals who commit atrocities on the scale of genocide are unlikely to behave as 'rational actors', deterred by the risk of punishment. Even if they were, it is not irrational to ignore the improbable prospect of punishment given the track record of international law thus far. A tribunal can be but one step in a process seeking to ensure peace, to make those in power responsible to law, and to condemn aggression....

MARTTI KOSKENNIEMI, BETWEEN IMPUNITY AND SHOW TRIALS

6 Max Planck Y.B. U.N. L. 1 (2002)

... Surely, as many of those involved in the process that led to the signature of the Statute for the International Criminal Court in 1998 seem to have assumed, the value of the new court lies in its deterrent message, the way in which it serves to prevent future atrocities. The force of this argument is, however, doubtful. In the first place, if crimes against humanity really emerge from what Kant labelled "radical evil", an evil that exceeds the bounds of instrumental rationality, that seeks no objective beyond itself, then by definition, calculations about the likelihood of future punishment do not enter the picture. Indeed, there is no calculation in the first place. But even if one remained suspicious about the metaphysics of "radical evil"... the deterrence argument would still fail to convince inasmuch as the atrocities of the 20th century have not emerged from criminal intent but as offshoots from a desire to do good. This is most evident in regard to the crimes of communism, the Gulag, the Ukraine famine, liquidation of the "Kulaks". But even the worst Nazi nightmares were connected to a project to create a better world.... But if the acts do not evidence criminal intent, and instead come about as aspects of ideological programmes that strive for the good life, however far in future, or to save the world from a present danger, then the deterrence argument seems beside the point.

In such case, criminal law itself will come to seem a part of the world which must be set aside, an aspect of the "evil" that the ideology seeks to eradicate.

As criminal lawyers know well, fitting crimes against humanity or other massive human rights violations into the deterrence frame requires some rather implausible psychological generalisations. Either the crimes are aspects of political normality — Arendt's "banality of evil" — in which case there is no mens rea, or they take place in exceptional situations of massive destruction and personal danger when there is little liberty of action. This is not to say that in such cases, people act as automatons, losing capacity for independent judgement. Many studies have elucidated the way individuals react to pressure created by either normality or exceptionality, and are sometimes able to resist. But it is implausible to believe that criminal law is able to teach people to become heroes, not least because what "heroism" might mean in particular situations is often at the heart of the confrontation between the political values underlying the criminal justice system (perhaps seen as victor's justice) and the system that is on trial.

...

How to understand the actions of the leaders of the Yugoslav communities — whether they were "criminal" or not — depends on which framework of interpretation one accepts.

...

...Focusing on the individual abstracts the political context, that is to say, describes it in terms of the actions and intentions of particular, well-situated individuals. Indeed, this is precisely what the Prosecutor in the Milosevic trial, Carla del Ponte, said she was doing in The Hague in February 2002. The (Serb) nation was not on trial, only an individual was. But the truth is not necessarily served by an individual focus. On the contrary, the meaning of historical events often exceeds the intentions or actions of particular individuals and can be grasped only by attention to structural causes, such as economic or functional necessities, or a broad institutional logic through which the actions by individuals create social effects. Typically, among historians, the "intentionist" explanations of the destruction of European Jewry are opposed by "functional" explanations that point to the material and structural causes that finally at the Wannsee conference of 1942 — but not until then — turned Nazi policy towards full-scale extermination. When Arendt and others were criticising the Eichmann trial, they pointed to the inability of an individual focus to provide an understanding of the way the Shoah did not come about as a series of actions by deviant individuals with a criminal mind but through Schreibtisch acts by obedient servants of a criminal State.

This is why individualisation is not neutral in its effects. Use of terms such as "Hitlerism" or "Stalinism" leaves the political, moral and organisational structures intact that are the necessary condition of the crime. To focus on individual leaders may even serve as an alibi for the population at large to relieve itself from responsibility...

...

The point here is not to try to settle the epistemological controversy about whether the individual or the contextual (functional, structural) focus provides the better truth but, rather, that neither can a priori override the other and that in some situations it is proper to focus individuals while in other cases — such as Nazi criminality, and perhaps in taking stock of Stasi collaboration in the GDR — the context provides the better frame of interpretation. But if that is so, then there is no guarantee that a criminal process a priori oriented towards individual guilt such as the Milosevic trial necessarily enacts a lesson of historical truth. On the contrary, it may rather obstruct this process by exonerating from responsibility those larger (political, economic, even legal) structures within which the conditions for individual criminality have been created — within which the social normality of a criminal society emerges.

As the German historian Martin Broszat has pointed out, the "one-sided personalisation" and rigid conceptualisation of criminal categories may lead not only to a different kind of truth but also a different way of distributing accountability.

...

But in the end, individualisation is also impossible. After all, the defences available to the accused refer precisely to the context in which his acts were undertaken. Was there an acceptable motive or an alternative course of action? Did the victim contribute to the action?... What was the chain of command that led to the Omarska camp or the Srebrenica massacre?... To create that chain will, in the absence of written orders, have to involve broad interpretations and assumptions about the political and administrative culture in the territory, including personal links and expectations between the various protagonists. In this way, even focus on individuals presumes a larger context in which particular individuals rise to key positions and in which their choices and preferences are formulated and come to seem either as "normal" or "deviant". The acts of former Nazis or the Communist Party Politburo — or perhaps more mundanely, Stasi agents or members of apartheid hit-squads — were not anti-social in the way of regular criminality but part of the political "normality" of criminal societies. This is precisely why Milosevic is able to reveal the hypocrisy in the Prosecutor's position: the trial is a trial of the Serbian nation inasmuch as his acts were part of (and not a deviation from) the social normality of Serbia's recent past.

It is at this point that the strategy chosen by Milosevic receives its full significance, and tends to demonstrate the limits of the criminal trial as an instrument of material truth and political reconciliation...

...

...[T]he West should not be allowed to remain confident that its version of the recent history of the Yugoslavian populations will be automatically vindicated. A trial that "automatically" vindicates the position of the Prosecutor is a show trial in the precise Stalinist sense of that expression.... To avoid looking like Vyshinsky, the judges not only must allow Milosevic to speak, but take what he says seriously. They will have to accept being directed by Milosevic into the context within which he will construct his defence in terms of patriotic anti-imperialism. As the political and historical "truth" of the Balkans becomes one aspect of the trial, then the West must accept that some — perhaps quite a bit — of responsibility will be assigned to its weak and contradictory policy. The bombing of Serbia in the spring of 1999 that caused around 500 civilian casualties will become one of the relevant factors. The Tribunal cannot ignore the question of whether that was a reasonable price to pay for flying at high altitudes so as to avert danger to NATO pilots. But who can tell how far in the past the chain of political causality leads, and what will turn up as Milosevic will reveal his interpretation of why the West rejected him as an acceptable interlocutor?

In the course of the trial Milosevic has conducted his defence less in order to save himself than in order to get his version of truth across to the public in Serbia, as well as to "history" by and large...

...

Having finally moved away from the Scylla of impunity — however incoherently and in response to external pressure — the West is now heading either towards a lesson in history and politics in which its own guilt will have to be assessed, or to the Charybdis of show trials.

SECURITY COUNCIL RESOLUTIONS ON ESTABLISHMENT OF AN INTERNATIONAL TRIBUNAL FOR THE FORMER YUGOSLAVIA

S.C. Res 808 (22 Feb. 1993)

...

Recalling paragraph 10 of its resolution 764 (1992) of 13 July 1992, in which it reaffirmed that all parties are bound to comply with the obligations under international humanitarian law and in particular the Geneva Conventions of 12 August 1949, and that persons who commit or order the commission of grave breaches of the Conventions are individually responsible in respect of such breaches...

Expressing once again its grave alarm at continuing reports of widespread violations of international humanitarian law occurring within the territory of the former Yugoslavia, including reports of mass killings and the continuance of the practice of 'ethnic cleansing',

Determining that this situation constitutes a threat to international peace and security,

Determined to put an end to such crimes and to take effective measures to bring to justice the persons who are responsible for them,

Convinced that in the particular circumstances of the former Yugoslavia the establishment of an international tribunal would enable this aim to be achieved and would contribute to the restoration and maintenance of peace.

...

1. *Decides* that an international tribunal shall be established for the prosecution of persons responsible for serious violations of international humanitarian law committed in the territory of the former Yugoslavia since 1991;

2. *Requests* the Secretary-General to submit for consideration by the Council... a report on all aspects of this matter, including specific proposals and where appropriate options for the effective and expeditious implementation of the decision contained in paragraph 1 above, taking into account suggestions put forward in this regard by Member States;

...

Resolution 827, 25 May 1993

...

Acting under Chapter VII of the Charter of the United Nations,

1. Approves the report of the Secretary-General;

2. Decides hereby to establish an international tribunal for the sole purpose of prosecuting persons responsible for serious violations of international humanitarian law committed in the territory of the former Yugoslavia between 1 January 1991 and a date to be determined by the Security Council upon the restoration of peace and to this end to adopt the Statute of the International Tribunal annexed to the above-mentioned report...

...

4. Decides that all States shall cooperate fully with the International Tribunal and its organs in accordance with the present resolution and the Statute of the International Tribunal and that consequently all States shall take any measures necessary under their domestic law to implement the provisions of the present resolution and the Statute, including the obligation of States to comply with requests for assistance or orders issued by a Trial Chamber under Article 29 of the Statute;...

...

7. Decides also that the work of the International Tribunal shall be carried out without prejudice to the right of the victims to seek, through appropriate means, compensation for damages incurred as a result of violations of international humanitarian law;

...

REPORT OF THE SECRETARY-GENERAL UNDER SECURITY COUNCIL RESOLUTION 808

UN Doc. S/2504 (3 May 1993)

...

I. The Legal Basis for the Establishment of the International Tribunal

...

18. Security Council resolution 808... [does not] indicate how such an international tribunal is to be established or on what legal basis.

19. The approach which, in the normal course of events, would be followed in establishing an international tribunal would be the conclusion of a treaty by which the States parties would establish a tribunal and approve its statute. This treaty would be drawn up and adopted by an appropriate international body (e.g., the General Assembly or a specially convened conference), following which it would be opened for signature and ratification. Such an approach...would allow the States participating in the negotiation and conclusion of the treaty fully to

exercise their sovereign will, in particular whether they wish to become parties to the treaty or not.

20. ... [T]he treaty approach incurs the disadvantage of requiring considerable time to establish an instrument and then to achieve the required number of ratifications for entry into force. Even then, there could be no guarantee that ratifications will be received from those States which should be parties to the treaty if it is to be truly effective.

21. ... The involvement of the General Assembly in the drafting or the review of the statute of the International Tribunal would not be reconcilable with the urgency expressed by the Security Council in resolution 808 (1993). The Secretary-General believes that there are other ways of involving the authority and prestige of the General Assembly in the establishment of the International Tribunal.

22. In the light of the disadvantages of the treaty approach in this particular case... the Secretary-General believes that the International Tribunal should be established by a decision of the Security Council on the basis of Chapter VII of the Charter of the United Nations. Such a decision would constitute a measure to maintain or restore international peace and security, following the requisite determination of the existence of a threat to the peace, breach of the peace or act of aggression.

23. This approach would have the advantage of being expeditious and of being immediately effective as all States would be under a binding obligation to take whatever action is required to carry out a decision taken as an enforcement measure under Chapter VII...

...

28. In this particular case, the Security Council would be establishing, as an enforcement measure under Chapter VII, a subsidiary organ within the terms of Article 29 of the Charter, but one of a judicial nature. This organ would, of course, have to perform its functions independently of political considerations; it would not be subject to the authority or control of the Security Council with regard to the performance of its judicial functions. As an enforcement measure under Chapter VII, however, the life span of the international tribunal would be linked to the restoration and maintenance of international peace and security in the territory of the former Yugoslavia, and Security Council decisions related thereto.

29. It should be pointed out that, in assigning to the International Tribunal the task of prosecuting persons responsible for serious violations of international humanitarian law, the Security Council would not be creating or purporting to 'legislate' that law. Rather, the International Tribunal would have the task of applying existing international humanitarian law.

...

II. Competence of the International Tribunal

...

33. According to paragraph 1 of resolution 808 (1993), the international tribunal shall prosecute persons responsible for serious violations of international humanitarian law committed in the territory of the former Yugoslavia since 1991.

This body of law exists in the form of both conventional law and customary law. While there is international customary law which is not laid down in conventions, some of the major conventional humanitarian law has become part of customary international law.

34. In the view of the Secretary-General, the application of the principle *nullum crimen sine lege* requires that the international tribunal should apply rules of international humanitarian law which are beyond any doubt part of customary law so that the problem of adherence of some but not all States to specific conventions does not arise. This would appear to be particularly important in the context of an international tribunal prosecuting persons responsible for serious violations of international humanitarian law.

35. The part of conventional international humanitarian law which has beyond doubt become part of international customary law is the law applicable in armed conflict as embodied in: the Geneva Conventions of 12 August 1949 for the Protection of War Victims; the Hague Convention (IV) Respecting the Laws and Customs of War on Land and the Regulations annexed thereto of 18 October 1907; the Convention on the Prevention and Punishment of the Crime of Genocide of 9 December 1948; and the Charter of the International Military Tribunal of 8 August 1945....

STATUTE OF THE INTERNATIONAL TRIBUNAL FOR THE FORMER YUGOSLAVIA

Article 1 — Competence of the International Tribunal

The International Tribunal shall have the power to prosecute persons responsible for serious violations of international humanitarian law committed in the territory of the former Yugoslavia since 1991 in accordance with the provisions of the present Statute.

Article 2 — Grave breaches of the Geneva Conventions of 1949

The International Tribunal shall have the power to prosecute persons committing or ordering to be committed grave breaches of the Geneva Conventions of 12 August 1949, namely the following acts against persons or property protected under the provisions of the relevant Geneva Convention:

(a) wilful killing;
(b) torture or inhuman treatment, including biological experiments;
(c) wilfully causing great suffering or serious injury to body or health;
(d) extensive destruction and appropriation of property, not justified by military necessity and carried out unlawfully and wantonly;
(e) compelling a prisoner of war or a civilian to serve in the forces of a hostile power;
(f) wilfully depriving a prisoner of war or a civilian of the rights of fair and regular trial;

(g) unlawful deportation or transfer or unlawful confinement of a civilian;
(h) taking civilians as hostages.

Article 3 — Violations of the laws or customs of war

The International Tribunal shall have the power to prosecute persons violating the laws or customs of war. Such violations shall include, but not be limited to:

(a) employment of poisonous weapons or other weapons calculated to cause unnecessary suffering;
(b) wanton destruction of cities, towns or villages, or devastation not justified by military necessity;
(c) attack, or bombardment, by whatever means, of undefended towns, villages, dwellings, or buildings;
(d) seizure of, destruction or wilful damage done to institutions dedicated to religion, charity and education, the arts and sciences, historic monuments and works of art and science;
(e) plunder of public or private property.

Article 4 — Genocide

1. The International Tribunal shall have the power to prosecute persons committing genocide as defined in paragraph 2 of this article or of committing any of the other acts enumerated in paragraph 3 of this article.

2. Genocide means any of the following acts committed with intent to destroy, in whole or in part, a national, ethnical, racial or religious group, as such:

(a) killing members of the group;
(b) causing serious bodily or mental harm to members of the group;
(c) deliberately inflicting on the group conditions of life calculated to bring about its physical destruction in whole or in part;
(d) imposing measures intended to prevent births within the group;
(e) forcibly transferring children of the group to another group.

3. The following acts shall be punishable:

(a) genocide;
(b) conspiracy to commit genocide;
(c) direct and public incitement to commit genocide;
(d) attempt to commit genocide;
(e) complicity in genocide.

Article 5 — Crimes against humanity

The International Tribunal shall have the power to prosecute persons responsible for the following crimes when committed in armed conflict, whether international or internal in character, and directed against any civilian population:

(a) murder;
(b) extermination;
(c) enslavement;

(d) deportation;
(e) imprisonment;
(f) torture;
(g) rape;
(h) persecutions on political, racial and religious grounds;
(i) other inhumane acts....

Article 7 — Individual criminal responsibility

1. A person who planned, instigated, ordered, committed or otherwise aided and abetted in the planning, preparation or execution of a crime referred to in articles 2 to 5 of the present Statute, shall be individually responsible for the crime.

2. The official position of any accused person, whether as Head of State or Government or as responsible Government official, shall not relieve such person of criminal responsibility nor mitigate punishment.

3. The fact that any of the acts referred to in articles 2 to 5 of the present Statute was committed by a subordinate does not relieve his superior of criminal responsibility if he knows or had reason to know that the subordinate was about to commit such acts or had done so and the superior failed to take the necessary and reasonable measures to prevent such acts or to punish the perpetrators thereof.

4. The fact that an accused person acted pursuant to an order of a Government or of a superior shall not relieve him of criminal responsibility, but may be considered in mitigation of punishment if the International Tribunal determines that justice so requires....

Article 10 — Non-bis-in-idem

1. No person shall be tried before a national court for acts constituting serious violations of international humanitarian law under the present Statute, for which he or she has already been tried by the International Tribunal.

2. A person who has been tried by a national court for acts constituting serious violations of international humanitarian law may be subsequently tried by the International Tribunal only if:

(a) the act for which he or she was tried was characterized as an ordinary crime; or
(b) the national court proceedings were not impartial or independent, were designed to shield the accused from international criminal responsibility, or the case was not diligently prosecuted....

Article 20 — Commencement and conduct of trial proceedings

1. The Trial Chambers shall ensure that a trial is fair and expeditious and that proceedings are conducted in accordance with the rules of procedure and evidence, with full respect for the rights of the accused and due regard for the protection of victims and witnesses....

4. The hearings shall be public unless the Trial Chamber decides to close the proceedings in accordance with its rules of procedure and evidence.

Article 21 — Rights of the accused

1. All persons shall be equal before the International Tribunal.

2. In the determination of charges against him, the accused shall be entitled to a fair and public hearing. . . .

3. The accused shall be presumed innocent until proved guilty according to the provisions of the present Statute.

4. In the determination of any charge against the accused pursuant to the present Statute, the accused shall be entitled to the following minimum guarantees, in full equality: [provisions for a fair trial omitted]

Article 22 — Protection of victims and witnesses

The International Tribunal shall provide in its rules of procedure and evidence for the protection of victims and witnesses. Such protection measures shall include, but shall not be limited to, the conduct of *in camera* proceedings and the protection of the victim's identity.

. . .

Article 24 — Penalties

1. The penalty imposed by the Trial Chamber shall be limited to imprisonment. In determining the terms of imprisonment, the Trial Chambers shall have recourse to the general practice regarding prison sentences in the courts of the former Yugoslavia.

. . .

Article 29 — Cooperation and judicial assistance

1. States shall cooperate with the International Tribunal in the investigation and prosecution of persons accused of committing serious violations of international humanitarian law.

2. States shall comply without undue delay with any request for assistance or an order issued by a Trial Chamber, including, but not limited to:

(a) the identification and location of persons;
(b) the taking of testimony and the production of evidence;
(c) the service of documents;
(d) the arrest or detention of persons;
(e) the surrender or the transfer of the accused to the International Tribunal. . . .

Article 32 — Expenses of the International Tribunal

The expenses of the International Tribunal shall be borne by the regular budget of the United Nations in accordance with Article 17 of the Charter of the United Nations.

. . .

NOTE

The establishment of the International Criminal Tribunal for the former Yugoslavia (ICTY) — the first such tribunal since the International Military Tribunal at Nuremberg, whose membership was indeed limited to the four major victorious powers — was an historic event holding considerable promise and unavoidable risk. Consider several aspects of the ICTY and its work.

1. Observers have read different motivations into the Security Council's decision to establish the Tribunal. Some understand the ICTY to be an essential response by the Council to the public outcry after exposure by the media of the outrages in the conflict — a minimum response, an effort to do 'something' that could prove to be significant and that was politically manageable (unlike the failures in efforts at negotiation or in discussions of types of intervention). Others understand the Tribunal as an attempt to salve the conscience of the West, a way of responding to ethnic cleansing and the accompanying brutality without taking effective action.

2. The ICTY is in a radically different situation from a court in a state observing fundamental principles of the rule of law in the sense that the state's executive and legislative branches comply with and execute court judgments. The Security Council has created an independent organ, as must be the case. Nonetheless, the ICTY remains dependent on an uncertain and changing political context; it lacks the relative autonomy of a court in a state with a strong tradition of an independent judiciary. The Tribunal depends for funds on a UN General Assembly whose members hold different views about it and who may judge its work differently. It must receive support from states and from the Security Council with respect to such basic matters as putting pressure on states to comply with its orders. There is no equivalent to a 'national tradition' for the Tribunal to draw on.

3. Beyond its fundamental mission of bringing a sense of justice and reconciliation to the combatants and civilians in the area, the ICTY (and the ICT for Rwanda, *infra*) possess an exceptional opportunity to develop international law in the field of individual criminal responsibility in an authoritative way. The Prosecutor and judges have confronted and will continue to confront numerous vexing issues, some of ancient lineage and some bred by the developments over the last half-century in international humanitarian law including the crimes defined at Nuremberg.

QUESTIONS

1. In what respects does the Statute on its face reveal changes in the definitions of war crimes and crimes against humanity from the Nuremberg Charter? What is the direction of those changes?

2. Why do you suppose the Statute lacks a provision for crimes against peace similar to that at Nuremberg?

COMMENT ON BACKGROUND TO THE TADIC LITIGATION BEFORE THE INTERNATIONAL CRIMINAL TRIBUNAL FOR THE FORMER YUGOSLAVIA

The Broad Context

The 1997 Opinion of a Trial Chamber of the ICTY in *Prosecutor v. Tadic*, *infra*, was the first determination of individual guilt or innocence in connection with serious violations of international humanitarian law by this tribunal. This Comment sketches the context in which this and similar cases arose. For this sketch, it draws on the opinion of the Trial Chamber, which relied on expert witnesses called by the Prosecution and Defence. Where conflict emerged between witnesses, the Trial Chamber sought to resolve it 'by adopting appropriately neutral language'. It did not turn to any other sources. The area stressed by the opinion was northwestern Bosnia and Herzegovina (hereafter Bosnia), particularly Prijedor Opstina (the Prijedor district).

For centuries the population of Bosnia, more than any other republic of the former Yugoslavia, had been multi-ethnic: Serbs (Eastern Orthodox), Bosnian Muslims and Croats (Roman Catholic); all indeed Slav peoples within a broader conception of ethnicity. In the nineteenth century, a concept of a state of the south Slavs, with a common language and ethnic origin, had developed, together with the growth among Serbs of the concept of a Greater Serbia including within its borders all ethnic Serbs. The collapse of the Ottoman Empire (it withdrew from the former Yugoslavia by 1912) and the Austro-Hungarian Empire after the First World War led to the creation of such a state of the south Slavs: Yugoslavia. The Axis occupation of Yugoslavia during the Second World War left bitter memories: Croatia's status as a puppet state of the Axis powers, the massacres it committed against Serbs and others, the fighting that occurred between the various Serb factions including the partisans under Marshal Tito (as he became later known), the retaliations after the war ended. Much of the fighting and many atrocities against civilians took place in Bosnia.

Nonetheless until about 1991, the different ethnic groups in Bosnia lived 'happily enough together', though particularly in rural areas such as those in the outlying parts of the Prijedor district the three populations tended to live separately. As the Opinion stated:

> Many witnesses speak of good inter-communal relations, of friendships across ethnic and coincident religious divides, of intermarriages and of generally harmonious relations. It is only subsequent events that may suggest that beneath that apparent harmony always lay buried bitter discord, which skilful propaganda readily brought to the surface, with terrible results.

Tito and his Communist regime acted sternly to suppress nationalist tendencies. The country consisted of six republics: Serbia (with its autonomous regions, Vojvodina and Kosovo), Slovenia, Croatia, Bosnia, Macedonia and Montenegro. Bosnia alone had no single majority ethnic grouping. During the latter part of Tito's rule from the mid 1960s on, there was a trend towards devolution of power to the republics, a trend which after Tito's death became useful to the overt resurgence of nationalist sentiment.

Economic and political crises developed simultaneously in the late 1980s. Slowly Yugoslavia fell apart as secessionist sentiment grew. A 1990 plebiscite in Slovenia voted overwhelmingly for independence from Yugoslavia, as did one in 1991 in Croatia. Slovenia effectively withdrew from Yugoslavia after brief fighting, but fierce hostilities broke out in Croatia. Both declared their independence, which was ultimately recognized by the European Union. The Bosnian Parliament declared Bosnia sovereign in 1991, and following a 1992 referendum, Bosnia declared itself independent. The United States and EU states recognized the independence of the three new states in 1992.

With the encouragement and direction of Slobodan Milosević, the Serbian president, the Serbian media stirred up nationalist feelings. With the break-up of Yugoslavia, the objectives of Serbia, including the Serbian-controlled JNA (Yugoslav People's Army) became the creation of a Serb-dominated western extension of Serbia to include Serb-dominated portions of Croatia and Bosnia, so as to form a new Yugoslavia with a substantially Serb population. But the large Muslim and Croat populations stood in the way. Hence it was deemed necessary to adopt the practice of ethnic cleansing. The media propaganda intensified and began to accuse non-Serbs of plotting genocide against Serbs. Serbs were told that they had to protect themselves against a fundamentalist Muslim threat. The message from the Government of Serbia was, as the Tribunal's Opinion put it, 'relentless', 'cogent and potent'.

By the end of 1991, Serb autonomous regions in Bosnia had been formed. Serb leadership, the JNA and paramilitary organizations, and special police units began to establish physical and political control over municipalities, sometimes by rigged plebiscites. In March 1992, a Serb Republic of Bosnia (Republika Srpska) was formed as a distinct political entity. The JNA, once a multi-ethnic national army although with a disproportionately Serb officer corps, became the instrument of policy of the new rump Federal Republic of Yugoslavia (consisting of Serbia and Montenegro). Gradually only ethnic Serbs were recruited into the armed forces. In late 1991, military units were formed in Serb-populated villages in Bosnia and supplied with weapons. Bosnian Serbs joined such distinct units as well as the JNA. More reliance came to be put on Serb paramilitary forces recruited in Serbia and Montenegro, and used to control non-Serb communities in Bosnia. Such forces acted in conjunction with the JNA.

By mid 1992 there were substantial international demands, including a Security Council resolution, that the JNA quit Bosnia. Serbia responded by ordering all non-Bosnian Serbs in the JNA to serve elsewhere, and by directing to Bosnia all Bosnian Serbs who served in the JNA. The eventual new army of Republika Srpska retained close contacts with and received weapons and funding from the JNA and its successor in the Former Yugoslavia, the VJ (Vojska Jugoslavije, Armed Forces of Yugoslavia).

As the Serb takeover of Serb-dominated areas continued, shelling and round-ups of non-Serbs intensified, leading to many civilian deaths and the flight of non-Serbs, who were forced to meet in stated assembly areas for expulsion from the area. The Prijedor district was important because of its location as part of a land corridor between Serb-dominated areas. Before the fighting and expulsions, Bosnian Muslims were a slight majority in the area. Careful Serbian planning preceded the takeover of the town of Prijedor, and the joining of Prijedor to a Serb region that was part of Republika Srpska. An attack on the nearby town of Kozarac, also in Prijedor municipality and with a concentrated Muslim population, led to great destruction and many deaths. The non-Serb population was effectively expelled. Severe restrictions were imposed on the movement of non-Serbs throughout the region, and forms of economic discrimination were instituted. Massive destruction of Muslim religious and cultural sites began. The population of Bosnian Muslims in the Prijedor district fell from about 50,000 to 6,000.

Thousands of Muslim and Croat civilians were confined to camps in Omarska, a former mining complex near Prijedor, as well as other locations, and were subjected to severe mistreatment. The Trial Chamber heard testimony from about 30 witnesses who survived the brutality, and who reported the frequent killings and torture. Up to 3,000 prisoners were at Omarska at any one time. They were held in very confined space and forced to live in filth and stifling heat. They received one inadequate meal a day, if that. There was rampant sickness. Frequent interrogations included severe beatings and injuries. Prisoners were summoned to be attacked with sticks and iron bars with nails. Bodies were slashed with knives. Many prisoners who were summoned never returned. Women were routinely summoned at night and raped. Dead bodies were a frequent sight. Prisoners heard bursts of machine-gun fire in one situation, and were called the next morning to load over 150 bodies on a truck.

Tadic

Doško Tadic was born in 1955 in Kozarac, to a prominent Serb family. He joined the Serb nationalist party in 1990. After the ethnic cleansing of Kozarac was completed, he became a political leader of the town. The military tried several times to enlist him, and he was indeed arrested or threatened with arrest several times by the military police. In June 1993 he was mobilized and posted to the war zone. He managed to escape several times, and ultimately fled to Germany, where he was arrested by German authorities in 1994 on suspicion of having committed offences at the Omarska camp that constituted crimes under German law. The ICTY then issued a formal request to Germany (as contemplated by the Statute and Rules of the ICTY) for deferral of its intended prosecution and surrender of Tadic to the tribunal. Germany enacted the necessary legislation for his surrender (distinct from normal extradition to another state), and Tadic was transferred in 1995 to a UN detention unit in the Hague.

The indictment by the Prosecutor against Tadic and a co-accused charged them with 132 counts involving grave breaches of the Geneva Conventions, violations of the laws or customs of war, and crimes against humanity.

Findings of Fact

The Trial Chamber considered separately each count of the indictment. It discussed the events alleged, the role of Tadic in those events, and the case for the defence. It then made findings of fact, leaving legal issues such as interpretation of the relevant articles of the Tribunal's Statute for the end of the Opinion.

Paragraph 7 of the indictment, for example, concerned events in Omarska prison camp. The cruel conduct alleged in some of the many counts in this paragraph included:

> A prisoner was frequently summoned for severe beatings. On one occasion, he was made to go on a hangar floor 'and there for up to half an hour was kicked and beaten by a group of soldiers armed with metal rods and metal cables. Then he was suspended upside down from an overhead gantry for some minutes.' As a result he suffered head fractures, a wasted hand, an injured spine and damage to his kidneys.
>
> A prisoner was struck as he entered the hangar floor. Another prisoner saw him being slashed with a knife and having black liquid poured over him. A third witness saw him being beaten with an iron bar and falling to the floor. This prisoner was never seen again.
>
> Two prisoners were forced to jump into an inspection pit with a third prisoner who was naked and bloody from beatings. One prisoner was ordered 'to suck his penis and then to bite his testicles. Meanwhile a group of men in uniform stood around the inspection pit watching and shouting to bite harder'. One prisoner was made to bite the other's testicles until he bit one testicle off and spat it out. He was then told that he was free to leave.

The Opinion reviewed in detail the testimony of each of the witnesses. The defence of the accused to these counts was principally by way of alibi. Tadic said that he never visited the Omarska camp and on the day in question was living in Prijedor and working as a traffic policeman.

In its findings of fact, the tribunal considered all elements of the defence position, and pointed out where prosecution witnesses were vague or seriously inconsistent with each other. Nevertheless, there was 'much evidence from many witnesses' that Tadic was indeed in the Omarska camp on the relevant day. The Trial Chamber was 'satisfied beyond reasonable doubt' that Tadic was among the group beating several of the named prisoners, and that he attacked another prisoner with a knife; and that Tadic was present on the hangar floor on the occasion of the sexual assault on and mutilation of prisoners. The Trial Chamber was 'not satisfied that [Tadic] took any active part' in those assaults and mutilation. However, Tadic's lack of active participation did not preclude the Trial Chamber from finding that he knowingly encouraged or supported the acts and holding that Tadic was liable for having 'intentionally assisted directly and substantially in the common purpose of inflicting physical suffering upon them and thereby aided and abetted in the commission of the crimes.'

Paragraph 4 of the indictment covered events at different locations in the Prijedor district. Several counts alleged that Serb forces including Tadic destroyed and plundered Muslim and Croat residential areas, imprisoned thousands under brutal conditions, and deported or expelled the majority of Muslim and Croat residents of the district. Muslims and Croats inside and outside the camp were subjected to a 'campaign of terror which included killings, torture, sexual assaults, and other physical and psychological abuse'. There was abundant testimony of systematic rape, often repetitive rape of the same victim, attended by great humiliation and cruelty, and sometimes followed by killing.

The Trial Chamber found beyond reasonable doubt that Tadic had participated in many of these events, and that he killed two Muslim policemen in Kozarac. All these events occurred 'within the context of an armed conflict'. Again the legal issues were reserved.

The Trial Chamber described the policy of discrimination instituted against non-Serbs, of which the camps were the most striking illustration. Those remaining were often required to wear white armbands and were continuously subject to beatings and terror tactics. Derogatory, denigrating curse words were common, and non-Serbs were forced to sing Serb nationalist songs. On various counts, the Trial Chamber found beyond a reasonable doubt that Tadic committed acts falling within this pattern of discrimination on religious and political grounds.

Legal Issues Relating to the Offences Charged

The Trial Chamber addressed several legal issues concerning Tadic's acts. Two of the most important issues concerned grave breaches of the Geneva Conventions and the mens rea required for crimes against humanity.

Article 2. The Opinion referred to the view of the Appeals Chamber that the Statute restricted prosecution of grave breaches to those committed against 'persons...protected under the provisions of the relevant Geneva Conventions'. The Fourth Geneva Convention dealing with civilian populations was directly on point. Under Article 4(1) of the Civilians Convention, protected persons are 'those who, at a given moment and in any manner whatsoever, find themselves, in case of a conflict or occupation, in the hands of a Party to the conflict or Occupying Power of which they are not nationals.' That requirement led the Trial Chamber to inquire whether the armed Serbian groups in Bosnia were under such control from the Federal Republic of Yugoslavia (FRY) that acts of such groups could be imputed to Yugoslavia's government. That the JNA played a role of 'vital importance' in establishing, supplying, maintaining and staffing local Serbian military groups was in itself 'not enough'. It was necessary to show that the FRY Government continued to 'exercise effective control' over the operations of such groups.

The Trial Chamber concluded that there was 'no evidence' on which it could state that the armed forces of the Republika Srpska 'were anything more than mere allies, albeit highly dependent allies', of the FRY Government. Hence the non-Serb civilian population of Bosnia, although it enjoyed the protection of prohibitions contained in Common Article 3 of the Geneva Conventions applicable to all armed conflict, did not benefit from the grave breaches regime of Article 2. It could not be said that the civilian victims 'were at any relevant time in the hands of a party to the conflict of which they were not nationals'. Hence the Trial Chamber found Tadic not guilty with respect to all charges based on grave breaches of the Geneva Conventions.

Article 5. The Opinion traced the development of the concept of crimes against humanity from Nuremberg to the present, and underscored such crimes' status as part of customary law. It repeated the statement in an earlier decision of the Appeals Chamber that it was now a 'settled rule of customary international law that crimes against humanity do not require a connection to international armed conflict'. The Trial Chamber stated, 'it is the occurrence of the act within the context of a widespread or systematic attack on a civilian population that makes the act a crime against humanity as opposed to simply a war crime or crime against national penal legislation, thus adding an additional element, and therefore in addition to the intent to commit the underlying offence the perpetrator must know of the broader context in which his act occurs.' The Opinion stated that, to constitute a crime against humanity, the perpetrator 'does not commit his act for purely personal motives completely unrelated to the attack on the civilian population.' At another point the Opinion stated, 'the act must not be taken for purely personal reasons unrelated to the armed conflict'. However, the Trial Chamber found that Tadic did not act for personal motives, and found him guilty of crimes against humanity beyond a reasonable doubt.

After analysing other components of the charges, the Trial Chamber found Tadic guilty on numerous counts including Article 5, but not guilty with respect to charges under Article 2 and with respect to several other counts.

The Appeals Chamber in its Judgment of 15 July 1999 reversed several holdings of the Trial Chamber. The Opinion of the Appeals Chamber follows.

PROSECUTOR v. TADIC

Appeals Chamber, International Criminal Tribunal for the Former Yugoslavia, Case No. IT-94–1-AR72, 15 July 1999

[Before reaching legal questions involving the definition of protected persons, the Appeals Chamber held that the armed forces of the Republika Srpska constituted a *de facto* organ of the FRY. The Appeals Chamber explained that the Trial Chamber applied an excessively strict test of state responsibility. The Appeals Chamber held that the appropriate test required the FRY to possess only 'overall control' of the Bosnian Serb forces. Under this more lenient standard, the acts of the armed forces of Republika Srpska could be attributed to the FRY.]

IV. [Whether the Victims Were 'Protected Persons' under Article 2 of the Statute]

5. The Status of the Victims

163. Having established that in the circumstances of the case the first of the two requirements set out in Article 2 of the Statute for the grave breaches provisions to be applicable, namely, that the armed conflict be international, was fulfilled, the Appeals Chamber now turns to the second requirement, that is, whether the victims of the alleged offences were "protected persons".

(a) The Relevant Rules

164. Article 4(1) of Geneva Convention IV (protection of civilians), applicable to the case at issue, defines "protected persons" — hence possible victims of grave breaches — as those "in the hands of a Party to the conflict or Occupying Power of

which they are not nationals". In other words, subject to the provisions of Article 4(2),[1] the Convention intends to protect civilians (in enemy territory, occupied territory or the combat zone) who do not have the nationality of the belligerent in whose hands they find themselves, or who are stateless persons. In addition, as is apparent from the preparatory work, the Convention also intends to protect those civilians in occupied territory who, while having the nationality of the Party to the conflict in whose hands they find themselves, are refugees and thus no longer owe allegiance to this Party and no longer enjoy its diplomatic protection (consider, for instance, a situation similar to that of German Jews who had fled to France before 1940, and thereafter found themselves in the hands of German forces occupying French territory).

165. Thus already in 1949 the legal bond of nationality was not regarded as crucial and allowance was made for special cases. In the aforementioned case of refugees, the lack of both allegiance to a State and diplomatic protection by this State was regarded as more important than the formal link of nationality.[2] In the cases provided for in Article 4(2), in addition to nationality, account was taken of the existence or non-existence of diplomatic protection: nationals of a neutral State or a co-belligerent State are not treated as "protected persons" unless they are deprived of or do not enjoy diplomatic protection. In other words, those nationals are not "protected persons" as long as they benefit from the normal diplomatic protection of their State; when they lose it or in any event do not enjoy it, the Convention automatically grants them the status of "protected persons".

166. This legal approach, hinging on substantial relations more than on formal bonds, becomes all the more important in present-day international armed conflicts. While previously wars were primarily between well-established States, in modern inter-ethnic armed conflicts such as that in the former Yugoslavia, new States are often created during the conflict and ethnicity rather than nationality may become the grounds for allegiance. Or, put another way, ethnicity may become determinative of national allegiance. Under these conditions, the requirement of nationality is even less adequate to define protected persons. In such conflicts, not only the text and the drafting history of the Convention but also, and more importantly, the Convention's object and purpose suggest that allegiance to a Party to the

[1] Article 4(2) of the Civilians Convention provides:

"Nationals of a State which is not bound by the Convention are not protected by it. Nationals of a neutral State who find themselves in the territory of a belligerent State, and nationals of a co-belligerent State, shall not be regarded as protected persons while the State of which they are nationals has normal diplomatic representation in the State in whose hands they are."

[2] In a corresponding footnote, the Appeals Chamber reproduced Articles 44 and 70(2) of the Civilians Convention. Article 44 provides:

"In applying the measures of control mentioned in the present Convention, the Detaining Power shall not treat as enemy aliens exclusively on the basis of their nationality de jure of an enemy State, refugees who do not, in fact, enjoy the protection of any government."

Article 70(2) provides:

"Nationals of the Occupying Power who, before the outbreak of hostilities, have sought refuge in the territory of the occupied State, shall not be arrested, prosecuted, convicted or deported from the occupied territory, except for the offences committed after the outbreak of hostilities, or for offences under common law committed before the outbreak of hostilities which, according to the law of the occupied State, would have justified extradition in time of peace."

conflict and, correspondingly, control by this Party over persons in a given territory, may be regarded as the crucial test.

(b) Factual Findings

167. In the instant case the Bosnian Serbs, including the Appellant, arguably had the same nationality as the victims, that is, they were nationals of Bosnia and Herzegovina. However, it has been shown above that the Bosnian Serb forces acted as de facto organs of another State, namely, the FRY. Thus the requirements set out in Article 4 of Geneva Convention IV are met: the victims were "protected persons" as they found themselves in the hands of armed forces of a State of which they were not nationals.

168. It might be argued that before 6 October 1992, when a "Citizenship Act" was passed in Bosnia and Herzegovina, the nationals of the FRY had the same nationality as the citizens of Bosnia and Herzegovina, namely the nationality of the Socialist Federal Republic of Yugoslavia. Even assuming that this proposition is correct, the position would not alter from a legal point of view. As the Appeals Chamber has stated above, Article 4 of Geneva Convention IV, if interpreted in the light of its object and purpose, is directed to the protection of civilians to the maximum extent possible. It therefore does not make its applicability dependent on formal bonds and purely legal relations. Its primary purpose is to ensure the safeguards afforded by the Convention to those civilians who do not enjoy the diplomatic protection, and correlatively are not subject to the allegiance and control, of the State in whose hands they may find themselves. In granting its protection, Article 4 intends to look to the substance of relations, not to their legal characterisation as such.

169. Hence, even if in the circumstances of the case the perpetrators and the victims were to be regarded as possessing the same nationality, Article 4 would still be applicable. Indeed, the victims did not owe allegiance to (and did not receive the diplomatic protection of) the State (the FRY) on whose behalf the Bosnian Serb armed forces had been fighting.

C. Conclusion

170. It follows from the above that the Trial Chamber erred in so far as it acquitted the Appellant on the sole ground that the grave breaches regime of the Geneva Conventions of 1949 did not apply.

...

VI. [Whether Crimes Against Humanity can be Committed for Purely Personal Motives]

...

A. Submissions of the Parties

1. The Prosecution Case

240. The Prosecution submits that there is nothing in Article 5 of the Statute which suggests that it contains a requirement that crimes against humanity cannot

be committed for purely personal motives. In the submission of the Prosecution, no such requirement can be inferred from the requirement that the crime must have a nexus to the armed conflict. In fact, to read the armed conflict requirement as requiring that the perpetrator's motives not be purely personal "would [...] transform this merely jurisdictional limitation under Article 5 into a substantive element of the mens rea of crimes against humanity".

...

242. The Prosecution argues that the weight of authority supports the proposition that crimes against humanity can be committed for purely personal reasons and that... [s]ubsequent decisions of the United States military tribunals under Control Council Law No. 10 and of national courts are also consistent with the view that a perpetrator of crimes against humanity may act out of purely personal motives.

243. Finally, the Prosecution contends that the object and purpose of the Tribunal's Statute support the interpretation that crimes against humanity may be committed for purely personal reasons, arguing that the objective of the Statute in providing a broad scope for humanitarian law would be defeated by a narrow interpretation of the category of offences falling within the ambit of Article 5. Furthermore, if proof of a non-personal motive was required, many perpetrators of crimes against humanity could evade conviction by the International Tribunal simply by invoking purely personal motives in defence of their conduct.

2. The Defence Case

...

245. The Defence contests the interpretation given to the applicable case law by the Prosecution, arguing that in all the cases cited, the defendants were linked to the system of extermination which formed the underlying predicate of crimes against humanity, and therefore did not commit their crimes for purely personal motives. In other words, the activities of the defendants were linked to the general activities comprising the pogroms against the Jews and thus the Defence submits that the acts of the defendants were not acts committed for purely personal reasons.

246. The Defence also contests the Prosecution's submissions regarding the object and purpose of the Statute of the International Tribunal, arguing, to the contrary, that policy suggests that it would be unjust if a perpetrator of a criminal act guided solely by personal motives was instead to be prosecuted for a crime against humanity.

B. Discussion

247. Neither Party asserts that the Trial Chamber's finding that crimes against humanity cannot be committed for purely personal motives had a bearing on the verdict.... Nevertheless this is a matter of general significance for the Tribunal's jurisprudence. It is therefore appropriate for the Appeals Chamber to set forth its views on this matter.

1. Article 5 of the Statute

248. The Appeals Chamber agrees with the Prosecution that there is nothing in Article 5 to suggest that it contains a requirement that crimes against humanity cannot be committed for purely personal motives. The Appeals Chamber agrees that it may be inferred from the words "directed against any civilian population" in Article 5 of the Statute that the acts of the accused must comprise part of a pattern of widespread or systematic crimes directed against a civilian population and that the accused must have known that his acts fit into such a pattern. There is nothing in the Statute, however, which mandates the imposition of a further condition that the acts in question must not be committed for purely personal reasons, except to the extent that this condition is a consequence or a re-statement of the other two conditions mentioned.

249. The Appeals Chamber would also agree with the Prosecution that the words "committed in armed conflict" in Article 5 of the Statute require nothing more than the existence of an armed conflict at the relevant time and place. The Prosecution is, moreover, correct in asserting that the armed conflict requirement is a jurisdictional element, not "a substantive element of the mens rea of crimes against humanity" (i.e., not a legal ingredient of the subjective element of the crime).

250. This distinction is important because, as stated above, if the exclusion of "purely personal" behaviour is understood simply as a re-statement of the two-fold requirement that the acts of the accused form part of a context of mass crimes and that the accused be aware of this fact, then there is nothing objectionable about it; indeed it is a correct statement of the law. It is only if this phrase is understood as requiring that the motives of the accused ("personal reasons", in the terminology of the Trial Chamber) not be unrelated to the armed conflict that it is erroneous. Similarly, that phrase is unsound if it is taken to require proof of the accused's motives, as distinct from the intent to commit the crime and the knowledge of the context into which the crime fits.

251. As to what the Trial Chamber understood by the phrase "purely personal motives", it is clear that it conflated two interpretations of the phrase: first, that the act is unrelated to the armed conflict, and, secondly, that the act is unrelated to the attack on the civilian population. In this regard, paragraph 659 of the Judgement held:

> 659. Thus if the perpetrator has knowledge, either actual or constructive, that these acts were occurring on a widespread or systematic basis and does not commit his act for purely personal motives completely unrelated to the attack on the civilian population, that is sufficient to hold him liable for crimes against humanity. Therefore the perpetrator must know that there is an attack on the civilian population, know that his act fits in with the attack and the act must not be taken for purely personal reasons unrelated to the armed conflict. (emphasis added)

Thus the "attack on the civilian population" is here equated to "the armed conflict". The two concepts cannot, however, be identical because then crimes against humanity would, by definition, always take place in armed conflict, whereas under customary international law these crimes may also be committed in times of peace.

So the two — the "attack on the civilian population" and "the armed conflict" — must be separate notions, although of course under Article 5 of the Statute the attack on "any civilian population" may be part of an "armed conflict". A nexus with the accused's acts is required, however, only for the attack on "any civilian population". A nexus between the accused's acts and the armed conflict is not required, as is instead suggested by the Judgement. The armed conflict requirement is satisfied by proof that there was an armed conflict; that is all that the Statute requires, and in so doing, it requires more than does customary international law.

...

2. The Object and Purpose of the Statute

253. The Prosecution has submitted that "the object and purpose of the Statute support the interpretation that crimes against humanity can be committed for purely personal reasons". The Prosecution cites the Tadic Decision on Jurisdiction, to the effect that "the 'primary purpose' of the establishment of the International Tribunal 'is not to leave unpunished any person guilty of [a] serious violation [of international humanitarian law], whatever the context within which it may have been committed'". This begs the question, however, whether a crime committed for purely personal reasons is a crime against humanity, and therefore a serious violation of international humanitarian law under Article 5 of the Statute.

254. The Appeals Chamber would also reject the Prosecution's submission concerning the onerous evidentiary burden which would be imposed on it in having to prove that the accused did not act from personal motives, as equally question-begging and inapposite. It is question-begging because if, arguendo, under international criminal law, the fact that the accused did not act from purely personal motives was a requirement of crimes against humanity, then the Prosecution would have to prove that element, whether it was onerous for it to do so or not. The question is simply whether or not there is such a requirement under international criminal law.

3. Case-law as Evidence of Customary International Law

255. Turning to the further submission of the Prosecution, the Appeals Chamber agrees that the weight of authority supports the proposition that crimes against humanity can be committed for purely personal reasons....

256. In this regard, it is necessary to review the case-law... to establish whether this case-law is indicative of the emergence of a norm of customary international law on this matter.

257. The Prosecution is correct in stating that the 1948 case cited by the Trial Chamber supports rather than negates the proposition that crimes against humanity may be committed for purely personal motives, provided that the acts in question were knowingly committed as "part and parcel of all the mass crimes committed during the persecution of the Jews". As the Supreme Court for the British Zone stated, "in cases of crimes against humanity taking the form of political denunciations, only the perpetrator's consciousness and intent to deliver his victim through denunciation to the forces of arbitrariness or terror are required".

...

259. The Prosecution's submission finds further support in other so-called denunciation cases rendered after the Second World War by the Supreme Court for the British Zone and by German national courts, in which private individuals who denounced others, albeit for personal reasons, were nevertheless convicted of crimes against humanity.

260. In *Sch.*, the accused had denounced her landlord solely "out of revenge and for the purpose of rendering him harmless" after tensions in their tenancy had arisen. The denunciation led to investigation proceedings by the Gestapo which ended with the landlord's conviction and execution. The Court of First Instance convicted Sch. and sentenced her to three years' imprisonment for crimes against humanity. The accused appealed against the decision, arguing that "crimes against humanity were limited to participation in mass crimes and... did not include all those cases in which someone took action against a single person for personal reasons". The Supreme Court dismissed the appeal, holding that neither the Nuremberg Judgement nor the statements of the Prosecutor before the International Military Tribunal indicated that Control Council Law No. 10 had to be interpreted in such a restrictive way. The Supreme Court stated:

> [T]he International Military Tribunal and the Supreme Court considered that a crime against humanity as defined in CCL 10 Article II 1 (c) is committed whenever the victim suffers prejudice as a result of the National Socialist rule of violence and tyranny ("Gewalt-oder Willkürherrschaft") to such an extent that mankind itself was affected thereby. Such prejudice can also arise from an attack committed against an individual victim for personal reasons. However, this is only the case if the victim was not only harmed by the perpetrator — this would not be a matter which concerned mankind as such — but if the character, duration or extent of the prejudice were determined by the National Socialist rule of violence and tyranny or if a link between them existed. If the victim was harmed in his or her human dignity, the incident was no longer an event that did not concern mankind as such. If an individual's attack against an individual victim for personal reasons is connected to the National Socialist rule of violence and tyranny and if the attack harms the victim in the aforementioned way, it, too, becomes one link in the chain of the measures which under the National Socialist rule were intended to persecute large groups among the population. There is no apparent reason to exonerate the accused only because he acted against an individual victim for personal reasons.

261. This view was upheld in a later decision of the Supreme Court in the case of *H.* H. denounced his father-in-law, V. F., for listening to a foreign broadcasting station, allegedly because V. F., who was of aristocratic origin, incessantly mocked H. for his low birth and tyrannised the family with his relentlessly scornful behaviour. The family members supposedly considered a denunciation to be the only solution to their family problems. Upon the denunciation, V. F. was sentenced by the Nazi authorities to three years in prison. V. F., who suffered from an intestinal illness, died in prison. Despite the fact that H.'s denunciation was motivated by personal reasons, the Court of First Instance sentenced H. for a crime against humanity,

stating that "it can be left open as to whether [...] H. was motivated by political, personal or other reasons". Referring to the established jurisprudence of the Supreme Court for the British Zone, the Court of First Instance held that "the motives ('Beweggründe') prompting a denunciation are not decisive (nicht entscheidend)".

…

263. Turning to the decisions of the United States military tribunals under Control Council Law No. 10 cited by the Prosecution, it must be noted that they appear to be less pertinent. These cases involve Nazi officials of various ranks whose acts were, therefore, by that token, already readily identifiable with the Nazi regime of terror. The question whether they acted "for personal reasons" would, therefore, not arise in a direct manner, since their acts were carried out in an official capacity, negating any possible "personal" defence which has as its premise "non-official acts". The question whether an accused acted for purely personal reasons can only arise where the accused can claim to have acted as a private individual in a private or nonofficial capacity. This is why the issue arises mainly in denunciation cases, where one neighbour or relative denounces another. This paradigm is, however, inapplicable to trials of Nazi ministers, judges or other officials of the State, particularly where they have not raised such a defence by admitting the acts in question whilst claiming that they acted for personal reasons. Any plea that an act was done for "purely personal" motives and that it therefore cannot constitute a crime against humanity is preeminently for the defence to raise and one would not expect the court to rule on the issue proprio motu and as obiter dictum.

…

268. … The Appeals Chamber believes, however, that a further reason why this was not in issue is precisely because motive is generally irrelevant in criminal law, as the Prosecution pointed out in the hearing of 20 April 1999:

> For example, it doesn't matter whether or not an accused steals money in order to buy Christmas presents for his poor children or to support a heroin habit. All we're concerned with is that he stole and he intended to steal, and what we're concerned with … here is the same sort of thing. There's no requirement for non-personal motive beyond knowledge of the context of a widespread or systematic act into which an accused's act fits. The Prosecutor is submitting that, as a general proposition and one which is applicable here, motives are simply irrelevant in criminal law.

269. The Appeals Chamber approves this submission, subject to the caveat that motive becomes relevant at the sentencing stage in mitigation or aggravation of the sentence (for example, the above mentioned thief might be dealt with more leniently if he stole to give presents to his children than if he were stealing to support a heroin habit). Indeed the inscrutability of motives in criminal law is revealed by the following reductio ad absurdum. Imagine a high-ranking SS official who claims that he participated in the genocide of the Jews and Gypsies for the "purely personal" reason that he had a deep-seated hatred of Jews and Gypsies and wished to exterminate them, and for no other reason. Despite this quintessentially genocidal frame of mind, the accused would have to be acquitted of crimes against humanity

because he acted for "purely personal" reasons. Similarly, if the same man said that he participated in the genocide only for the "purely personal" reason that he feared losing his job, he would also be entitled to an acquittal. Thus, individuals at both ends of the spectrum would be acquitted. In the final analysis, any accused that played a role in mass murder purely out of self-interest would be acquitted. This shows the meaninglessness of any analysis requiring proof of "non-personal" motives.

...

271. The Trial Chamber correctly recognised that crimes which are unrelated to widespread or systematic attacks on a civilian population should not be prosecuted as crimes against humanity. Crimes against humanity are crimes of a special nature to which a greater degree of moral turpitude attaches than to an ordinary crime. Thus to convict an accused of crimes against humanity, it must be proved that the crimes were related to the attack on a civilian population (occurring during an armed conflict) and that the accused knew that his crimes were so related.

272. For the above reasons, however,...the requirement that an act must not have been carried out for the purely personal motives of the perpetrator does not form part of the prerequisites necessary for conduct to fall within the definition of a crime against humanity under Article 5 of the Tribunal's Statute.

COMMENT ON SIGNIFICANCE OF NATIONALITY

[The nationality test for protected persons received further elaboration in a subsequent decision of the Appeals Chamber, *Prosecutor v. Delalic & Others*, Judgment, Case No. IT-96–21-A (2001) (Celebici camp case). The case involved a prison camp, which held Bosnian Serb detainees near the town of Celebici in central Bosnia and Herzegovina. The defendants included a Bosnian Muslim commander, a deputy commander and a guard who all served at the camp. The defendants urged the Appeals Chamber to revisit its analysis in *Tadic* on the grounds that they shared the same Bosnian nationality as the alleged victims and that the alleged acts occurred completely within Bosnia and Herzegovina. They contended that the nationality requirement in the Fourth Geneva Convention was specifically intended to preclude application of the grave breaches regime to such internal situations. The Trial Chamber had rejected the defendants' claims, stating, *inter alia*, that a more flexible interpretation of the nationality requirement 'is fully in accordance with the development of the human rights doctrine which has been increasing in force since the middle of this century. It would be incongruous with the whole concept of human rights, which protect individuals from the excesses of their own governments, to rigidly apply the nationality requirement of article 4, that was apparently inserted to prevent interference in a State's relations with its own nationals.' Excerpts of the Appeals Chamber Opinion follow.]

...

11. The appellants submit that "the traditional rules of treaty interpretation" should be applied to interpret strictly the nationality requirement set out

in Article 4 of Geneva Convention IV. The word "national" should therefore be interpreted according to its natural and ordinary meaning. The appellants submit in addition that if the Geneva Conventions are now obsolete and need to be updated to take into consideration a "new reality", a diplomatic conference should be convened to revise them.

12. The Prosecution on the other hand contends that the Vienna Convention on the Law of Treaties of 1969 provides that the ordinary meaning is the meaning to be given to the terms of the treaty in their context and in the light of their object and purpose. It is submitted that the Appeals Chamber in *Tadic* found that the legal bond of nationality was not regarded as crucial in 1949, i.e., that there was no intention at the time to determine that nationality was the sole criteria. In addition, adopting the appellants' position would result in the removal of protections from the Geneva Conventions contrary to their very object and purpose.

13. The argument of the appellants relates to the interpretative approach to be applied to the concept of nationality in Geneva Convention IV. The appellants and the Prosecution both rely on the Vienna Convention in support of their contentions. The Appeals Chamber agrees with the parties that it is appropriate to refer to the Vienna Convention as the applicable rules of interpretation, and to Article 31 in particular, which sets forth the general rule for the interpretation of treaties. The Appeals Chamber notes that it is generally accepted that these provisions reflect customary rules. The relevant part of Article 31 reads as follows:

> A treaty shall be interpreted in good faith in accordance with the ordinary meaning to be given to the terms of the treaty in their context and in the light of its object and purpose.

14. The Vienna Convention in effect adopted a textual, contextual and a teleological approach of interpretation, allowing for an interpretation of the natural and ordinary meaning of the terms of a treaty in their context, while having regard to the object and purpose of the treaty.

...

24. Relying on the ICRC Commentary to Article 4 of Geneva Convention IV, the appellants further argue that international law cannot interfere in a State's relations with its own nationals, except in cases of genocide and crimes against humanity. In the appellants' view, in the situation of an internationalised armed conflict where the victims and the perpetrators are of the same nationality, the victims are only protected by their national laws.

25. The purpose of Geneva Convention IV in providing for universal jurisdiction only in relation to the grave breaches provisions was to avoid interference by domestic courts of other States in situations which concern only the relationship between a State and its own nationals. The ICRC Commentary (GC IV), referred to by the appellants, thus stated that Geneva Convention IV is "faithful to a recognised principle of international law: it does not interfere in a State's relations with its own nationals". The Commentary did not envisage the situation of an internationalised conflict where a foreign State supports one of the parties to the conflict, and where the victims are detained because of their ethnicity, and because they

are regarded by their captors as operating on behalf of the enemy. In these circumstances, the formal national link with Bosnia and Herzegovina cannot be raised before an international tribunal to deny the victims the protection of humanitarian law. It may be added that the government of Bosnia and Herzegovina itself did not oppose the prosecution of Bosnian nationals for acts of violence against other Bosnians based upon the grave breaches regime.

26. It is noteworthy that, although the appellants emphasised that the "nationality" referred to in Geneva Convention IV is to be understood as referring to the legal citizenship under domestic law, they accepted at the hearing that in the former Yugoslavia "nationality", in everyday conversation, refers to ethnicity.

27. The Appeals Chamber agrees with the Prosecution that depriving victims, who arguably are of the same nationality under domestic law as their captors, of the protection of the Geneva Conventions solely based on that national law would not be consistent with the object and purpose of the Conventions. Their very object could indeed be defeated if undue emphasis were placed on formal legal bonds, which could also be altered by governments to shield their nationals from prosecution based on the grave breaches provisions of the Geneva Conventions. A more purposive and realistic approach is particularly apposite in circumstances of the dissolution of Yugoslavia, and in the emerging State of Bosnia and Herzegovina where various parties were engaged in fighting, and the government was opposed to a partition based on ethnicity, which would have resulted in movements of population, and where, ultimately, the issue at stake was the final shape of the State and of the new emerging entities.

28. In *Tadic*, the Appeals Chamber, relying on a teleological approach, concluded that formal nationality may not be regarded as determinative in this context, whereas ethnicity may reflect more appropriately the reality of the bonds....

29. As found in previous Appeals Chamber jurisprudence, Article 4 of Geneva Convention IV is to be interpreted as intending to protect civilians who find themselves in the midst of an international, or internationalised, conflict to the maximum extent possible. The nationality requirement of Article 4 should therefore be ascertained upon a review of "the substance of relations" and not based on the legal characterisation under domestic legislation. In today's ethnic conflicts, the victims may be "assimilated" to the external State involved in the conflict, even if they formally have the same nationality as their captors, for the purposes of the application of humanitarian law, and of Article 4 of Geneva Convention IV specifically....

30. ...The nationality of the victims for the purpose of the application of Geneva Convention IV should not be determined on the basis of formal national characterisations, but rather upon an analysis of the substantial relations, taking into consideration the different ethnicity of the victims and the perpetrators, and their bonds with the foreign intervening State.

...

43. ...As submitted by the Prosecution, the Trial Chamber correctly sought to establish whether the victims could be regarded as belonging to the opposing side of the conflict.

44. The Appeals Chamber particularly agrees with the Trial Chamber's finding that the Bosnian Serb victims should be regarded as protected persons for the

purposes of Geneva Convention IV because they "were arrested and detained mainly on the basis of their Serb identity" and "they were clearly regarded by the Bosnian authorities as belonging to the opposing party in an armed conflict and as posing a threat to the Bosnian State".

...

NOTE

The Court engages in a dynamic form of interpretation in defining the nationality requirement for 'protected persons'. Is it appropriate for the ICTY to depend on the purported object and purpose of the Geneva Conventions to secure 'the protection of civilians to the maximum extent possible'? What are the perils of this interpretive approach? What are the advantages?

The US Office of Legal Counsel under the George W. Bush Administration issued several controversial memos involving the conflict with Al Qaeda. In a memo titled '"Protected Person" Status in Occupied Iraq under the Fourth Geneva Convention', the Office of Legal Counsel refers to the *Tadic* Opinion at length. The memo describes the form of interpretation and understanding of the object and purpose of the Geneva Conventions in *Tadic.* The memo asserts that this same interpretive framework supports the conclusion that members of terrorist organizations that reject the Geneva Conventions should be denied status as protected persons. The memo explains:

> One object and purpose of the Geneva Conventions is to exclude from coverage those who engage in transnational armed conflict, even in occupied territory, if their representatives have rejected the burdens of the Geneva Convention system.

This "benefits-burdens" principle finds several expressions in the text of GC....

...

> ...Adherence to article 4's State-centric presuppositions in this context would violate GC's fundamental principle that warring entities cannot receive the benefits of GC if they reject Geneva Convention duties. Al Qaeda has pointedly declined to accept or apply GC or any other principle of the law of armed conflict. If nationals of a rogue State that refused to be bound by the Geneva Conventions engaged in unlawful belligerency on behalf of that rogue State, they would be denied "protected person" status everywhere in the world, including occupied Iraq. See GC art. 4(2) ("Nationals of a State which is not bound by the Convention are not protected by it."). It would run sharply contrary to the object and purpose of GC to give al Qaeda operatives a more elevated status than such individuals....
>
> ...
>
> ...In short, *Tadic* looked behind GC art. 4's nationality criterion to find a criterion that better served GC's object and purpose when applied to unforeseen circumstances.

In determining whether al Qaeda operatives warrant "protected person" status in occupied Iraq, it is at least as appropriate as in [*Tadic*]..., if not more so, to look to the fundamental principles underlying GC to determine how a genuine textual ambiguity in article 4 should be resolved in a context wholly outside the contemplation of GC's drafters. Our recourse to these fundamental principles supports the conclusion that, with the caveat addressed in Section D below [concluding that citizens and permanent residents of Iraq are protected persons even if members of terrorist organizations], al Qaeda operatives captured in occupied Iraq lack "protected person" status under GC.

...

QUESTIONS

1. 'It is clear that Tadic, a mere foot soldier in these sordid events, was selected for prosecution because the Tribunal did not have custody of a higher ranking, more significant figure. There were hundreds or thousands of people like Tadic, starting with his close companions in perpetrating the horrors described in the Opinion. What is the point of convicting one among them in what seems to be a mere lottery?' Comment.

2. 'It is wrong to imagine the prosecution of Tadic as serving the goal of individualizing guilt, so as to overcome notions of collective guilt and allow peoples like the Serbs to get on with their lives after the war. Tadic is part of a system. His guilt is deeply linked to the guilt of the larger bloody scheme in which he played a role. The Opinion indicts an entire leadership and those who executed its plans. These are not the isolated, deviant crimes of murder or torture or rape that occur within all countries and that are sensibly punished as such.' Comment. Also specifically consider this statement in light of the essay by Martti Koskenniemi. Does the prosecution of individuals like Tadic constitute a 'way of distributing accountability' that obscures the systemic causes of atrocities committed during such a conflict?

3. Should individuals who act for purely personal motives be liable for crimes against humanity? Do they deserve the same condemnation, under international criminal law, accorded to perpetrators who are primarily motivated by an interest in advancing the overall attack against the civilian population? Should the definition of elements of the crime be altered if proving the lack of personal motives would impose a highly onerous burden on the prosecution?

4. Observers have described the aims of the international criminal tribunals in ways that evoke traditional notions of the aims of the criminal law generally, but that also address specific characteristics of this conflict. Consider:

(a) *Deterrence*. Whom is the Tribunal attempting to deter: the present leaders in this conflict, or those who might instigate and commit crimes in future conflicts? Should different strategies be at work to achieve one or the other goal? Who indeed can be deterred in an ethnic conflict stirring such deep hatreds and cruel actions — only the leaders, or also the foot soldiers who commit many of the atrocities? Is a court the most effective instrument of deterrence, or does the Tribunal play this role because of failure of other means of addressing the conflict?

(b) *Punishment-retribution*. How can the Tribunal best serve this function? Is symbolic justice through the conviction and imprisonment of a small number of people (in relation to the number of people committing the international crimes defined by the Statute) sufficient to create a broad sense of justice among the conflict's victims? What other means (shy of forceful intervention) are available to help to build this sense of justice?

(c) *Reconciliation, long-term peace and stability.* Can reconciliation and a 'true' lasting peace be achieved partly through the work of the Tribunal? What role are convictions and imprisonment likely to play in this process of reconciliation in comparison with, for example, a Serbian-Bosnian settlement on issues like territorial control and resettlement or an international agreement on compensation of victims that may permit them to get on with their lives?

5. How do you understand the extreme cruelty shown by the Serbian captors to their prisoners? (The same question can be put to many parties to ethnic and other conflicts, such as the Rwandan conflict, as well as to members of majority or powerful groups that behave in physically cruel ways to the despised and dehumanized minority or powerless groups.) Is encouragement or condoning of such behaviour by those in charge meant to serve a purpose, like ethnic cleansing? Meant to humiliate? Does the context of weapons, force, and killing encourage release of this base side of human nature, in the sense that violence dissolves all bonds and restraints? Is such mass conduct in the context of mass violence deterrable?

NOTE

By Resolution 955 (1994), the Security Council established the International Criminal Tribunal for Rwanda (ICTR) to prosecute persons 'responsible for genocide and other serious violations of international humanitarian law' committed principally in that country in 1994. The new tribunal has the same appeals chamber as the ICTY, but separate trial chambers. The ICTR and ICTY also shared the same chief prosecutor until September 2003, at which point the Security Council appointed separate prosecutors for the two tribunals.

The preamble to Resolution 955 stated that the Council was convinced that prosecution of those responsible for serious violations 'would contribute to the process of national reconciliation and to the restoration and maintenance of peace', and would contribute to 'ensuring that such violations... are halted and effectively redressed'.

The Council, 'acting under Chapter VII of the Charter', adopted the annexed Statute of the ICTR, excerpts from which appear below.

STATUTE OF THE INTERNATIONAL TRIBUNAL FOR RWANDA

Article 1 — Competence of the International Tribunal for Rwanda

The International Tribunal for Rwanda shall have the power to prosecute persons responsible for serious violations of international humanitarian law committed in the territory of Rwanda and Rwandan citizens responsible for such violations committed in the territory of neighbouring States between 1 January 1994 and 31 December 1994. . . .

Article 2 — Genocide

[The definition of genocide is identical to Article 4 of the ICTY Statute, p. 1290, *supra*.]

Article 3 — Crimes against Humanity

The International Tribunal for Rwanda shall have the power to prosecute persons responsible for the following crimes when committed as part of a widespread or systematic attack against any civilian population on national, political, ethnic, racial or religious grounds:

(a) Murder;
(b) Extermination;
(c) Enslavement;
(d) Deportation;
(e) Imprisonment;
(f) Torture;
(g) Rape;
(h) Persecutions on political, racial and religious grounds;
(i) Other inhumane acts.

Article 4 — Violations of Article 3 common to the Geneva Conventions and of Additional Protocol II

The International Tribunal for Rwanda shall have the power to prosecute persons committing or ordering to be committed serious violations of Article 3 common to the Geneva Conventions of 12 August 1949 for the Protection of War Victims, and of Additional Protocol II thereto of 8 June 1977. These violations shall include, but shall not be limited to:

(a) Violence to life, health and physical or mental well-being of persons, in particular murder as well as cruel treatment such as torture, mutilation or any form of corporal punishment;
(b) Collective punishments;
(c) Taking of hostages;
(d) Acts of terrorism;
(e) Outrages upon personal dignity, in particular humiliating and degrading treatment, rape, enforced prostitution and any form of indecent assault;
(f) Pillage;
(g) The passing of sentences and the carrying out of executions without previous judgment pronounced by a regularly constituted court, affording all the judicial guarantees which are recognized as indispensable by civilized peoples;
(h) Threats to commit any of the foregoing acts.

Article 6: Individual Criminal Responsibility

1. A person who planned, instigated, ordered, committed or otherwise aided and abetted in the planning, preparation or execution of a crime referred to in Articles 2 to 4 of the present Statute, shall be individually responsible for the crime.

. . .

3. The fact that any of the acts referred to in Articles 2 to 4 of the present Statute was committed by a subordinate does not relieve his or her superior of criminal responsibility if he or she knew or had reason to know that the subordinate was about to commit such acts or had done so and the superior failed to take the necessary and reasonable measures to prevent such acts or to punish the perpetrators thereof.

. . .

[Many articles in the ICTR Statute are identical to the equivalent articles in the ICTY Statute, p. 1289, *supra*, including articles on personal jurisdiction, individual criminal responsibility, concurrent jurisdiction, *non-bis-in-idem*, investigation and preparation of indictment, review of the indictment, commencement and conduct of trial proceedings, rights of the accused, protection of victims and witnesses, judgment, penalties, appellate proceedings, enforcement of sentences, cooperation and judicial assistance and expenses of the tribunal.]

NOTE

One of the novel features of the indictments and Opinions of the ICTY and ICTR has been the strong attention to sexual crimes, particularly systematic sexual violence against women. Mass rape and other organized forms of sexual violence and humiliation have been frequent, and often used as instruments of fear, shame and ethnic cleansing. Rape itself, long unmentioned in definitions of crimes in the humanitarian law of war, is included in the definition of several crimes in the two statutes. Note the attention to sexual violence against women in the *Akayesu* Opinion below.

PROSECUTOR v. AKAYESU

Trial Chamber, International Criminal Tribunal for Rwanda, 1998
Case No. ICTR-96-4-T (2 Sept. 1998)

[The trial of Jean-Paul Akayesu resulted in the first conviction for genocide by an international court. The indictment charged Akayesu, a Hutu, with genocide, crimes against humanity and violations of Article 3 common to the Geneva Conventions, punishable under Articles 2–4 of the ICTR Statute. All alleged acts took place in Rwanda during 1994. The country is divided into 11 prefectures, which are subdivided into communes placed under the authority of bourgmestres (mayors). From April 1993 to June 1994, Akayesu served as bourgmestre of the Taba commune.

There were 15 counts in the indictment. Some illustrative charges follow: (1) at least 2, 000 Tutsis were killed in Taba from April to June 1994. Killings were so open and widespread that the defendant 'must have known about them', but despite his authority and responsibility, he never attempted to prevent the killings. (2) Hundreds of displaced Tutsi civilians sought refuge at the bureau communal. Females among them were regularly taken by the armed local militia and subjected to sexual violence, including multiple rapes. Civilians were frequently murdered on or near the communal premises. Akayesu knew of these events and at times was present during their commission. That presence and his failure to attempt to prevent 'encouraged these activities'. (3) At meetings, Akayesu 'urged the population to eliminate accomplices of the RPF, which was understood by those present to mean Tutsis.... The killing of Tutsis in Taba began shortly after the meeting. 'He also 'named at least three prominent Tutsis...who had to be killed because of their alleged relationships with the RPF.' Two of them were soon killed. (4) Akayesu ordered and participated in the killing of three brothers, and took eight detained men from the bureau communal and ordered militia members to kill them. (5) He ordered local people to kill intellectuals and influential people. On his instructions, five secondary school teachers were killed.

The Trial Chamber found it 'necessary to say, however briefly, something about the history of Rwanda, beginning from the pre-colonial period up to 1994'. Prior to and during colonial rule (first under Germany, and from 1917 until independence under Belgium), Rwanda was an advanced monarchy ruled by the monarch's representatives drawn from the Tutsi nobility. The Trial Chamber further explained:

> In those days, the distinction between the Hutu and Tutsi was based on lineage rather than ethnicity. Indeed, the demarcation line was blurred: one could move from one status to another, as one became rich or poor, or even through marriage.
>
> Both German and Belgian colonial authorities, if only at the outset as far as the latter are concerned, relied on an elite essentially composed of people who referred to themselves as Tutsi, a choice which, according to Dr. Alison Desforges, was born of racial or even racist considerations. In the minds of the colonizers, the Tutsi looked more like them, because of their height and colour, and were, therefore, more intelligent and better equipped to govern.
>
> In the early 1930s, Belgian authorities introduced a permanent distinction by dividing the population into three groups which they called ethnic groups, with the Hutu representing about 84% of the population, while the Tutsi (about 15%) and Twa (about 1%) accounted for the rest. In line with this division, it became mandatory for every Rwandan to carry an identity card mentioning his or her ethnicity. The Chamber notes that the reference to ethnic background on identity cards was maintained, even after Rwanda's independence and was, at last, abolished only after the tragic events the country experienced in 1994.

The Chamber explained that the Tutsi were more willing to be converted to Christianity; hence the church too supported their monopoly of power. The Trial Chamber also quoted the following testimony from Dr Alison Desforges, an expert witness:

> The primary criterion for [defining] an ethnic group is the sense of belonging to that ethnic group. It is a sense which can shift over time.... But, if you fix any

> given moment in time, and you say, how does this population divide itself, then you will see which ethnic groups are in existence in the minds of the participants at that time.... [R]eality is an interplay between the actual conditions and peoples' subjective perception of those conditions. In Rwanda, the reality was shaped by the colonial experience which imposed a categorization which was probably more fixed, and not completely appropriate to the scene.... The categorisation imposed at that time [by the Belgians] is what people of the current generation have grown up with. They have always thought in terms of these categories, even if they did not in their daily lives have to take cognizance of that.... [T]his division into three ethnic groups became an absolute reality.

When the Tutsi led campaigns for independence, the allegiance of the colonizer shifted to the Hutu. In the 1950s, elections were held and political parties were formed. The Hutu held a clear majority in voting power. Violence broke out between Hutu and Tutsi. Independence was attained in 1962. In 1975, a one-party system was instituted under (Hutu) President Habyarimana, whose policies became increasingly anti-Tutsi through discriminatory quota systems and other methods. In 1991, following violence and growing pressures, Habyarimana accepted a multi-party system.

Many Tutsi in exile formed a political organization and a military wing, the Rwandan Patriotic Army (RPA). Their aim was to return to Rwanda. Violence, negotiations and accords led to the participation of the Tutsi political organization (RPF) in the government institutions. Hard-line Hutu formed a radical political party, more extremist than Habyarimana. There were growing extremist calls for elimination of the Tutsi.

The Arusha accords between the government and the RPF in 1993 brought temporary relief from the threat of war. The climate worsened with assassinations, and the accords were denounced. Habyarimana died in an air crash, of unknown cause, in April 1994. The Rwandan army, Presidential Guard and militia immediately started killing Tutsi, as well as Hutu who were sympathetic to the Arusha accords and to power-sharing between Tutsi and Hutu. Belgian soldiers and a small UN peacekeeping force were withdrawn from the country. RPF troops resumed open war against Rwandan armed forces. The killing campaign against the Tutsi reached its zenith in a matter of weeks, and continued to July. The estimated dead in the conflict at that time, overwhelmingly Tutsi, ranged from 500,000 to 1,000,000.]

112. As regards the massacres which took place in Rwanda between April and July 1994, as detailed above in the chapter on the historical background to the Rwandan tragedy, the question before this Chamber is whether they constitute genocide. Indeed, it was felt in some quarters that the tragic events which took place in Rwanda were only part of the war between the Rwandan Armed Forces (the RAF) and the Rwandan Patriotic Front (RPF)...

...

118. In the opinion of the Chamber, there is no doubt that considering their undeniable scale, their systematic nature and their atrociousness, the massacres

were aimed at exterminating the group that was targeted.... In this connection, Alison Desforges, an expert witness, in her testimony before this Chamber... stated as follows: "on the basis of the statements made by certain political leaders, on the basis of songs and slogans popular among the Interahamwe, I believe that these people had the intention of completely wiping out the Tutsi from Rwanda so that— as they said on certain occasions—their children, later on, would not know what a Tutsi looked like, unless they referred to history books"....

119. ...Dr. Zachariah also testified that the Achilles' tendons of many wounded persons were cut to prevent them from fleeing. In the opinion of the Chamber, this demonstrates the resolve of the perpetrators of these massacres not to spare any Tutsi....

120. Dr. Alison Desforges testified that many Tutsi bodies were often systematically thrown into the Nyabarongo river, a tributary of the Nile. Indeed, this has been corroborated by several images shown to the Chamber throughout the trial....

121. ...even newborn babies were not spared. Even pregnant women, including those of Hutu origin, were killed on the grounds that the foetuses in their wombs were fathered by Tutsi men, for in a patrilineal society like Rwanda, the child belongs to the father's group of origin....

122. In light of the foregoing, it is now appropriate for the Chamber to consider the issue of specific intent that is required for genocide (mens rea or dolus specialis). In other words, it should be established that the above-mentioned acts were targeted at a particular group as such. In this respect also, many consistent and reliable testimonies... agree on the fact that it was the Tutsi as members of an ethnic group... who were targeted during the massacres.

123. ...the propaganda campaign conducted before and during the tragedy by the audiovisual media,... or the print media, like the Kangura newspaper... overtly called for the killing of Tutsi, who were considered as the accomplices of the RPF and accused of plotting to take over the power lost during the revolution of 1959...

...

126. Consequently, the Chamber concludes from all the foregoing that genocide was, indeed, committed in Rwanda in 1994 against the Tutsi as a group....

127. ...as to whether the tragic events that took place in Rwanda in 1994 occurred solely within the context of the conflict between the RAF and the RPF, the Chamber replies in the negative, since it holds that the genocide did indeed take place against the Tutsi group, alongside the conflict. The execution of this genocide was probably facilitated by the conflict, in the sense that the fighting against the RPF forces was used as a pretext for the propaganda inciting genocide against the Tutsi...

128. ...The accused himself stated during his initial appearance before the Chamber, when recounting a conversation he had with one RAF officer and...a leader of the Interahamwe, that the acts perpetrated by the Interahamwe against Tutsi civilians were not considered by the RAF officer to be of a nature to help the government armed forces in the conflict with the RPF.... The Chamber's opinion is that the genocide was organized and planned not only by members of the RAF, but also by the political forces who were behind the "Hutu-power", that it was executed

essentially by civilians including the armed militia and even ordinary citizens, and above all, that the majority of the Tutsi victims were non-combatants, including thousands of women and children, even foetuses....

5. Factual Findings

[The Chamber noted that in addition to testimony of witnesses, it would take 'judicial notice' of UN reports extensively documenting the massacres of 1994. Its listing included reports of a Commission of Experts established by a Security Council resolution, of a special rapporteur of the Secretary-General and of the High Commissioner for Human Rights. Note that the 'factual findings' *infra* are relevant to determining whether the conditions stated in several articles of the ICTR Statute were met.]

...

178. The Chamber now considers paragraph 12 of the Indictment, which alleges the responsibility of the Accused, his knowledge of the killings which took place in Taba between 7 April and the end of June 1994, and his failure to attempt to prevent these killings or to call for assistance from regional or national authorities.

...

184. There is a substantial amount of evidence establishing that before 18 April 1994 the Accused did attempt to prevent violence from taking place in the commune of Taba. Many witnesses testified to the efforts of the Accused to maintain peace in the commune and that he opposed by force the Interahamwe's attempted incursions into the commune to ensure that the killings which had started in Kigali on 7 April 1994 did not spread to Taba. Witness W testified that on the order of the Accused to the population that they must resist these incursions, members of the Interahamwe were killed. Witness K testified that Taba commune was calm during the period when Akayesu wanted that there be calm. She said he would gather the population in a meeting and tell them that they had to be against the acts of violence in the commune....

185. The Accused testified that he asked for three gendarmes at the meeting with the Prime Minister in Gitarama on 18 April 1994, to help him maintain order and security and to stop the killing of Tutsi.... Given the accused's testimony on this point, and its corroboration in part by the sole prosecution witness who was present at the Murambi meeting, the accused's version of events — that he did call for assistance from the national and regional authorities — must be credited.

186. Moreover, Defence witness DAAX, the former prefect of Gitarama supports the accused's account. Witness DAAX testified that he convened three meetings of bourgmestres between 6 April 1994 and 18 April 1994.... At this third meeting, the prefect testified, the accused took the floor and complained of the problems of security in his commune, in common with the Prefect and other bourgmestres. Witness DAAX's testimony agrees with that of the accused that the Prime Minister did not reply directly to the bourgmestre's expressions of concern about security in their Communes, but that he rather read parts of a prepared policy speech and threatened the complaining bourgmestres with dismissal. Witness DAAX further testified that at least one bourgmestre, the bourgmestre of Mugina, was killed shortly

after the meeting as a result. Witness DAAX also testified that the accused had to flee his commune due to pressure from the Interahamwe at some point between 6 April 1994 and 18 April 1994.... Witness DAAX said the Accused never officially requested gendarmes from him, unlike the bourgmestre of Mugina....

187. A substantial amount of evidence has been presented indicating that the conduct of the Accused did, however, change significantly after the meeting on 18 April 1994, and many witnesses... testified to the collaboration of the Accused with the Interahamwe in Taba after this date. Witness A testified that he was surprised to see that the Accused had become a friend of the Interahamwe. The Accused contends that he was overwhelmed. Witness DAX and Witness DBB, both witnesses for the Defence, testified that the Interahamwe threatened to kill the Accused if he did not cooperate with them. The Accused testified that he was coerced by the Interahamwe....

188. The Chamber recognises the difficulties a bourgmestre encountered in attempting to save lives of Tutsi in the period in question. Prosecution witness R, who was the bourgmestre of another commune... averred that a bourgmestre could do nothing openly to combat the killings after that date or he would risk being killed; what little he could do had to be done clandestinely. The Defence case is that this is precisely what the Accused did.

189. Defence witnesses, DAAX, DAX, DCX, DBB and DCC confirm that the Accused failed to prevent killings after 18 April 1994 and expressed the opinion that it was not possible for him to do anything with ten communal policemen at his disposal against more than a hundred Interahamwe.

190. The Defence contends that, despite pressure from the Interahamwe, the Accused continued to save lives after 18 April 1994. There is some evidence on this matter...

191. There is also evidence indicating that after 18 April 1994, there were people that came to the Accused for help, and he turned them away, and there is evidence that the Accused witnessed, participated in, supervised, and even ordered killings in Taba. Witness JJ testified that after her arrival at the bureau communal, where she came to seek refuge, she went to the Accused on behalf of a group of refugees, begging him to kill them with bullets so that they would not be hacked to death with machetes. She said he asked his police officers to chase them away and said that even if there were bullets he would not waste them on the refugees.

192. The Chamber finds that the allegations set forth in paragraph 12 cannot be fully established. The Accused did take action between 7 April and 18 April to protect the citizens of his commune. It appears that he did also request assistance from national authorities at the meeting on 18 April 1994....

193. Nevertheless, the Chamber finds beyond a reasonable doubt that the conduct of the Accused changed after 18 April 1994 and that after this date the Accused did not attempt to prevent the killing of Tutsi in the commune of Taba. In fact, there is evidence that he not only knew of and witnessed killings, but that he participated in and even ordered killings.... The Accused contends that he was subject to coercion, but the Chamber finds this contention greatly inconsistent with a substantial amount of concordant testimony from other witnesses. It is also inconsistent

with his own pre-trial written statement. Witness C testified to having heard the Accused say to an Interahamwe "I do not think that what we are doing is proper. We are going to have to pay for this blood that is being shed...", a statement which indicates the Accused's knowledge of the wrongfulness of his acts and his awareness of the consequences of his deeds. For these reasons, the Chamber does not accept the testimony of the Accused regarding his conduct after 18 April, and finds beyond a reasonable doubt that he did not attempt to prevent killings of Tutsi after this date. Whether he had the power to do so is not at issue, as he never even tried and as there is evidence establishing beyond a reasonable doubt that he consciously chose the course of collaboration with violence against Tutsi rather than shielding them from it.

...

[The Chamber continued in its examination of each count of the indictment and, after presenting testimony of witnesses, made findings of fact. Several counts dealt with sexual violence. Some of the Chamber's findings follow.]

499. ...Chamber finds that there is sufficient credible evidence to establish beyond a reasonable doubt that during the events of 1994, Tutsi girls and women were subjected to sexual violence, beaten and killed on or near the bureau communal premises, as well as elsewhere in the commune of Taba.... Hundreds of Tutsi, mostly women and children, sought refuge at the bureau communal during this period and many rapes took place on or near the premises of the bureau communal... Witness JJ was also raped repeatedly on two separate occasions in the cultural center on the premises of the bureau communal, once in a group of fifteen girls and women and once in a group of ten girls and women.... The Chamber notes that much of the sexual violence took place in front of large numbers of people, and that all of it was directed against Tutsi women.

450. ...There is no suggestion in any of the evidence that the Accused or any communal policemen perpetrated rape....

...

452. On the basis of the evidence set forth herein, the Chamber finds beyond a reasonable doubt that the Accused had reason to know and in fact knew that sexual violence was taking place on or near the premises of the bureau communal, and that women were being taken away from the bureau communal and sexually violated. There is no evidence that the Accused took any measures to prevent acts of sexual violence or to punish the perpetrators of sexual violence. In fact there is evidence that the Accused ordered, instigated and otherwise aided and abetted sexual violence.... On the two occasions Witness JJ was brought to the cultural center of the bureau communal to be raped, she and the group of girls and women with her were taken past the Accused, on the way. On the first occasion he was looking at them, and on the second occasion he was standing at the entrance to the cultural center. On this second occasion, he said, "Never ask me again what a Tutsi woman tastes like." Witness JJ described the Accused in making these statements as "talking as if someone were encouraging a player." More generally she stated that the Accused was the one "supervising" the acts of rape.

...

6. The Law

...

471. The Accused is charged under Article 6(1) of the Statute of the Tribunal with individual criminal responsibility for the crimes alleged in the Indictment.

With regard to Counts... on sexual violence, the Accused is charged additionally, or alternatively, under Article 6(3).... Article 6(1) sets forth the basic principles of individual criminal liability, which are undoubtedly common to most national criminal jurisdictions. Article 6(3), by contrast, constitutes something of an exception to the principles articulated in Article 6(1), as it derives from military law, namely the principle of the liability of a commander for the acts of his subordinates or "command responsibility".

...

488. There are varying views regarding the mens rea required for command responsibility.

...

489. ...it is certainly proper to ensure that there has been malicious intent, or, at least, ensure that negligence was so serious as to be tantamount to acquiescence or even malicious intent.

490. As to whether the form of individual criminal responsibility referred to Article 6 (3) of the Statute applies to persons in positions of both military and civilian authority, it should be noted that during the Tokyo trials, certain civilian authorities were convicted of war crimes under this principle. Hirota, former Foreign Minister of Japan, was convicted of atrocities — including mass rape — committed in the "rape of Nanking", under a count which charged that he had "recklessly disregarded their legal duty by virtue of their offices to take adequate steps to secure the observance and prevent breaches of the law and customs of war"....

It should, however, be noted that Judge Röling strongly dissented... and held that Hirota should have been acquitted. Concerning the principle of command responsibility as applied to a civilian leader, Judge Röling stated that:

> "Generally speaking, a Tribunal should be very careful in holding civil government officials responsible for the behaviour of the army in the field. Moreover, the Tribunal is here to apply the general principles of law as they exist with relation to the responsibility for omissions'. Considerations of both law and policy, of both justice and expediency, indicate that this responsibility should only be recognized in a very restricted sense".

491. The Chamber therefore finds that in the case of civilians, the application of the principle of individual criminal responsibility, enshrined in Article 6(3), to civilians remains contentious. Against this background, the Chamber holds that it is appropriate to assess on a case by case basis the power of authority actually devolved upon the Accused in order to determine whether or not he had the power to take all necessary and reasonable measures to prevent the commission of the alleged crimes or to punish the perpetrators thereof.

Genocide

498. Genocide is distinct from other crimes inasmuch as it embodies a special intent or dolus specialis. Special intent of a crime is the specific intention, required as a constitutive element of the crime, which demands that the perpetrator clearly seeks to produce the act charged. Thus, the special intent in the crime of genocide lies in "the intent to destroy, in whole or in part, a national, ethnical, racial or religious group, as such".

...

523. On the issue of determining the offender's specific intent, the Chamber considers that intent is a mental factor which is difficult, even impossible, to determine. This is the reason why, in the absence of a confession from the accused, his intent can be inferred from a certain number of presumptions of fact. The Chamber considers that it is possible to deduce the genocidal intent inherent in a particular act charged from the general context of the perpetration of other culpable acts systematically directed against that same group, whether these acts were committed by the same offender or by others. Other factors, such as the scale of atrocities committed, their general nature, in a region or a country, or furthermore, the fact of deliberately and systematically targeting victims on account of their membership of a particular group, while excluding the members of other groups, can enable the Chamber to infer the genocidal intent of a particular act.

524. Trial Chamber I of the International Criminal Tribunal for the former Yugoslavia also stated that the specific intent of the crime of genocide

> "may be inferred from a number of facts such as the general political doctrine which gave rise to the acts possibly covered by the definition in Article 4, or the repetition of destructive and discriminatory acts. The intent may also be inferred from the perpetration of acts which violate, or which the perpetrators themselves consider to violate the very foundation of the group — acts which are not in themselves covered by the list in Article 4(2) but which are committed as part of the same pattern of conduct"....

Complicity in Genocide

525. Under Article 2(3)(e) of the Statute, the Chamber shall have the power to prosecute persons who have committed complicity in genocide....

527. The Chamber notes that complicity is viewed as a form of criminal participation by all criminal law systems, notably, under the Anglo-Saxon system (or Common Law) and the Roman-Continental system (or Civil Law). Since the accomplice to an offence may be defined as someone who associates himself in an offence committed by another, complicity necessarily implies the existence of a principal offence.

528. According to one school of thought, complicity is borrowed criminality' (criminalité d'emprunt). In other words, the accomplice borrows the criminality of the principal perpetrator. By borrowed criminality, it should be understood that the physical act which constitutes the act of complicity does not have its own inherent criminality, but rather it borrows the criminality of the act committed by the principal perpetrator of the criminal enterprise. Thus, the conduct of the

accomplice emerges as a crime when the crime has been consummated by the principal perpetrator. The accomplice has not committed an autonomous crime, but has merely facilitated the criminal enterprise committed by another.

…

530. Consequently, the Chamber is of the opinion that in order for an accused to be found guilty of complicity in genocide, it must, first of all, be proven beyond a reasonable doubt that the crime of genocide has, indeed, been committed.

…

538. The intent or mental element of complicity implies in general that, at the moment he acted, the accomplice knew of the assistance he was providing in the commission of the principal offence. In other words, the accomplice must have acted knowingly.

539. Moreover, as in all criminal Civil law systems, under Common law, notably English law, generally, the accomplice need not even wish that the principal offence be committed. In the case of *National Coal Board v. Gamble*, Justice Devlin stated:

> "an indifference to the result of the crime does not of itself negate abetting. If one man deliberately sells to another a gun to be used for murdering a third, he may be indifferent about whether the third lives or dies and interested only the cash profit to be made out of the sale, but he can still be an aider and abettor."

In 1975, the English House of Lords also upheld this definition of complicity, when it held that willingness to participate in the principal offence did not have to be established. As a result, anyone who knowing of another's criminal purpose, voluntarily aids him or her in it, can be convicted of complicity even though he regretted the outcome of the offence.

…

547. Consequently, where a person is accused of aiding and abetting, planning, preparing or executing genocide, it must be proven that such a person acted with specific genocidal intent, i.e. the intent to destroy, in whole or in part, a national, ethnical, racial or religious group as such, whereas, as stated above, there is no such requirement to establish accomplice liability in genocide.

…

[Crimes against Humanity — Rape and other inhumane acts]

…

691. The Tribunal has found that the Accused had reason to know and in fact knew that acts of sexual violence were occurring on or near the premises of the bureau communal and that he took no measures to prevent these acts or punish the perpetrators of them. The Tribunal notes that it is only in consideration of Counts 13, 14 and 15 that the Accused is charged with individual criminal responsibility under Section 6(3) of its Statute.… Although the evidence supports a finding that a superior/subordinate relationship existed between the Accused and the Interahamwe who were at the bureau communal, the Tribunal notes that there is no allegation in the Indictment that the Interahamwe, who are referred to as "armed local militia," were subordinates of the Accused. This relationship is a fundamental

element of the criminal offence set forth in Article 6(3). The amendment of the Indictment with additional charges pursuant to Article 6(3) could arguably be interpreted as implying an allegation of the command responsibility required by Article 6(3). In fairness to the Accused, the Tribunal will not make this inference. Therefore, the Tribunal finds that it cannot consider the criminal responsibility of the Accused under Article 6(3).

...

694. The Tribunal finds, under Article 6(1) of its Statute, that the Accused, having had reason to know that sexual violence was occurring, aided and abetted... acts of sexual violence, by allowing them to take place on or near the premises of the bureau communal and by facilitating the commission of such sexual violence through his words of encouragement in other acts of sexual violence which, by virtue of his authority, sent a clear signal of official tolerance for sexual violence, without which these acts would not have taken place....

...

7.8. [Genocide and Complicity in Genocide]

...

704. The Chamber finds that, as pertains to the acts alleged in paragraph 12, it has been established that, throughout the period covered in the Indictment, Akayesu, in his capacity as bourgmestre, was responsible for maintaining law and public order in the commune of Taba and that he had effective authority over the communal police. Moreover, as "leader" of Taba commune, of which he was one of the most prominent figures, the inhabitants respected him and followed his orders. Akayesu himself admitted before the Chamber that he had the power to assemble the population and that they obeyed his instructions. It has also been proven that a very large number of Tutsi were killed in Taba between 7 April and the end of June 1994, while Akayesu was bourgmestre of the Commune. Knowing of such killings, he opposed them and attempted to prevent them only until 18 April 1994, date after which he not only stopped trying to maintain law and order in his commune, but was also present during the acts of violence and killings, and sometimes even gave orders himself for bodily or mental harm to be caused to certain Tutsi, and endorsed and even ordered the killing of several Tutsi.

705. In the opinion of the Chamber, the said acts indeed incur the individual criminal responsibility of Akayesu for having ordered, committed, or otherwise aided and abetted in the preparation or execution of the killing of and causing serious bodily or mental harm to members of the Tutsi group. Indeed, the Chamber holds that the fact that Akayesu, as a local authority, failed to oppose such killings and serious bodily or mental harm constituted a form of tacit encouragement, which was compounded by being present to such criminal acts.

...

728. ...The Chamber is of the opinion that it is possible to infer the genocidal intention that presided over the commission of a particular act, inter alia, from all acts or utterances of the accused, or from the general context in which other culpable acts were perpetrated systematically against the same group, regardless of

whether such other acts were committed by the same perpetrator or even by other perpetrators.

729. First of all, regarding Akayesu's acts and utterances during the period relating to the acts alleged in the Indictment, the Chamber is satisfied beyond reasonable doubt, on the basis of all evidence brought to its attention during the trial, that on several occasions the accused made speeches calling, more or less explicitly, for the commission of genocide.[3]...

730. ...Owing to the very high number of atrocities committed against the Tutsi, their widespread nature not only in the commune of Taba, but also throughout Rwanda, and to the fact that the victims were systematically and deliberately selected because they belonged to the Tutsi group, with persons belonging to other groups being excluded, the Chamber is also able to infer, beyond reasonable doubt, the genocidal intent of the accused in the commission of the above-mentioned crimes.

731. With regard, particularly, to...rape and sexual violence, the Chamber wishes to underscore the fact that in its opinion, they constitute genocide in the same way as any other act as long as they were committed with the specific intent to destroy, in whole or in part, a particular group, targeted as such. Indeed, rape and sexual violence certainly constitute infliction of serious bodily and mental harm on the victims and are even, according to the Chamber, one of the worst ways of inflict harm on the victim as he or she suffers both bodily and mental harm. In light of all the evidence before it, the Chamber is satisfied that the acts of rape and sexual violence described above, were committed solely against Tutsi women, many of whom were subjected to the worst public humiliation, mutilated, and raped several times, often in public, in the Bureau Communal premises or in other public places, and often by more than one assailant. These rapes resulted in physical and psychological destruction of Tutsi women, their families and their communities. Sexual violence was an integral part of the process of destruction, specifically targeting Tutsi women and specifically contributing to their destruction and to the destruction of the Tutsi group as a whole.

732. The rape of Tutsi women was systematic and was perpetrated against all Tutsi women and solely against them. A Tutsi woman, married to a Hutu, testified before the Chamber that she was not raped because her ethnic background was unknown. As part of the propaganda campaign geared to mobilizing the Hutu against the Tutsi, the Tutsi women were presented as sexual objects. Indeed, the Chamber was told, for an example, that before being raped and killed, Alexia, who was the wife of the Professor, Ntereye, and her two nieces, were forced by the Interahamwe to undress and ordered to run and do exercises "in order to display the thighs of Tutsi women". The Interahamwe who raped Alexia said, as he threw

[3] [Eds.: Earlier in the opinion, the Trial Chamber stated that, in a speech delivered on 19 Apr. 1994, Akayesu 'clearly urged the population to unite in order to eliminate what he termed the sole enemy: the accomplices of the Inkotanyi [described by the ICTR as a term for the RPF in its basic meaning and had a number of extended meanings including RPF sympathizer and potentially Tutsi as an ethnic group]' and that 'on the basis of consistent testimonies heard throughout the proceedings and the evidence of...[an] expert witness on linguistic matters, the Chamber is satisfied beyond a reasonable doubt that the population understood Akayesu's call as one to kill the Tutsi. Akayesu himself was fully aware of the impact of his speech on the crowd and of the fact that his call to fight against the accomplices of the Inkotanyi would be construed as a call to kill the Tutsi in general.']

her on the ground and got on top of her, "let us now see what the vagina of a Tutsi woman tastes like". As stated above, Akayesu himself, speaking to the Interahamwe who were committing the rapes, said to them: "don't ever ask again what a Tutsi woman tastes like". This sexualized representation of ethnic identity graphically illustrates that Tutsi women were subjected to sexual violence because they were Tutsi. Sexual violence was a step in the process of destruction of the Tutsi group—destruction of the spirit, of the will to live, and of life itself.

733. On the basis of the substantial testimonies brought before it, the Chamber finds that in most cases, the rapes of Tutsi women in Taba, were accompanied with the intent to kill those women. Many rapes were perpetrated near mass graves where the women were taken to be killed. A victim testified that Tutsi women caught could be taken away by peasants and men with the promise that they would be collected later to be executed. Following an act of gang rape, a witness heard Akayesu say "tomorrow they will be killed" and they were actually killed. In this respect, it appears clearly to the Chamber that the acts of rape and sexual violence, as other acts of serious bodily and mental harm committed against the Tutsi, reflected the determination to make Tutsi women suffer and to mutilate them even before killing them, the intent being to destroy the Tutsi group while inflicting acute suffering on its members in the process.

734. In light of the foregoing, the Chamber finds firstly that the acts described supra are indeed acts as enumerated in Article 2(2) of the Statute, which constitute the factual elements of the crime of genocide, namely the killings of Tutsi or the serious bodily and mental harm inflicted on the Tutsi. The Chamber is further satisfied beyond reasonable doubt that these various acts were committed by Akayesu with the specific intent to destroy the Tutsi group, as such.

[Akayesu appealed the Trial Chamber decision, though primarily on evidentiary and procedural grounds. In a decision issued in 2001, the Appeals Chamber affirmed the guilty verdict on all counts.]

QUESTIONS

1. Consider, as applied to the ICTR and the *Akayesu* Decision, question 4 at p. 1311, *supra*.

2. The Trial Chamber discussed superior responsibility contained in Article 6(3) of the Statute. What are the requirements for establishing such responsibility? Does the tribunal's analysis go too far in suggesting Akayesu could have been found guilty under this rationale? Should a different standard apply to civilian, as opposed to military, leaders? Compare Article 28 of the Rome Statute of the International Criminal Court.

3. Does the *Akayesu* Opinion (as presented in these excerpts) broaden the crimes defined in the Statute to any considerable degree? How? In particular, how does the ICTR respond to the sexual cruelty to which Tutsi women were subjected? Does the record of systematic rape described in the Opinion satisfy the elements of the crime of genocide? If not, should the definition of genocide be changed accordingly?

4. The ICTR concludes 'if the accused knowingly aided and abetted in the commission of... a murder while he knew or had reason to know that the principal was acting with genocidal intent, the accused would be an accomplice to genocide, even though he did not share the murderer's intent to destroy the group.' Does this rule seem appropriate? Does it relax the threshold of liability too far? Would it be more appropriate to require the accused possess specific genocidal intent? Should the individual at least know — not just have reason to know — that the principle is acting with genocidal intent? Do these questions raise concerns similar to the concerns raised in question 3 following the *Celebici* Opinion, p. 1311, *supra*, with respect to acts committed for purely personal motives as part of a crime against humanity?

BARBARA CROSSETTE, INQUIRY SAYS UN INERTIA IN '94 WORSENED GENOCIDE IN RWANDA

***New York Times*, 17 Dec. 1999, at A1**

A strongly worded report issued today by an international panel of experts holds both the United Nations and leading member countries, primarily the United States, responsible for failing to prevent or end the genocide in Rwanda in 1994, which cost hundreds of thousands of lives.

The report, commissioned by Secretary General Kofi Annan, who was then head of the peacekeeping department, spares no one, naming those in the highest reaches of the United Nations who were running the operation in Rwanda, including Mr. Annan and his predecessor, Secretary General Boutros Boutros-Ghali.

Mr. Annan and others in his department made weak and equivocal decisions in the face of mounting disaster, the panel found. At the same time the Clinton administration... persistently played down the problem, setting the tone for a Security Council generally lacking the political will for a tougher response.

Both the United Nations and the United States sent the wrong message to militias bent on genocide, the report concluded. Today Mr. Annan called the report 'thorough and objective.' 'On behalf of the United Nations, I acknowledge this failure and express my deep remorse,' he said, calling the events in Rwanda 'genocide in its purest and most evil form'....

... [T]he leader of the investigation, Ingvar Carlsson, a former Swedish prime minister, said it would 'always be difficult to explain' why the Security Council — managed by the world's major powers and not the United Nations bureaucracy — drastically cut the peacekeeping force in Rwanda, reducing it to a few hundred from 2,500 when the genocide began, and then increasing it to 5,500 when the weeks of massacres were over. The United States,... effectively blocked the Security Council in 1993 and 1994 from authorizing significant action in Rwanda....

Today Mr. Carlsson repeated the Clinton administration's explanation that the loss of 18 American Rangers in Somalia in 1993 had scared the United States off peacekeeping, particularly in Africa, for domestic political reasons.... On a trip to Rwanda last year, President Clinton apologized for Washington's inaction.... The

Rwanda report follows by several weeks the release of an internal United Nations inquiry into problems in the Bosnia peacekeeping operation that led to thousands of deaths in Serbian attacks on Bosnian Muslims in Srebrenica and other towns. That report also found fault with both the organization and Security Council members.

The report issued today shows a pattern of ignored warnings and missed signs of the genocide to come in Rwanda.... 'Information received by a United Nations mission that plans are being made to exterminate any group of people requires an immediate and determined response', the panel said.... In the bloody melee that followed [the very first steps in the genocide], groups of United Nations peacekeepers were rounded up by Rwandan Hutu troops and 10 Belgians were executed. The remaining Belgians, the best-qualified soldiers among the peacekeepers, were then abruptly withdrawn.

In the report, Belgium was criticized for this and for abandoning 2,000 civilians hiding in a technical school after telling them they would be protected. They were savagely attacked. The Belgian withdrawal prompted others to pull out, an action supported by the United States, the panel said....

JOSÉ ALVAREZ, CRIMES OF STATES/CRIMES OF HATE: LESSONS FROM RWANDA

24 Yale J. Int'l. L. 365 (1999), at 400

... [T]he West's complicity in the 1994 killings in Rwanda is a discomforting fact. The scale and seriousness of that complicity take various forms. At one level, certain European powers, namely the colonizers of Rwanda who imported their racist notions of 'superior races' to Rwanda, need to accept their responsibility for creating the 'tribalism without tribes' that helped make genocide possible and continues to characterize Rwanda today. Much greater blame can be attributed to those, like the French, who, in the 1990s and through the 1994 killings themselves, continued to befriend and arm the Habyarimana [Hutu] government. But the circle of blame extends much wider and includes Kofi Annan, who ignored warnings of the impeding genocide; all members of the U.N., and particularly the Security Council, who, in the wake of the fiasco of Somalia, failed to send the 5000 troops that, it is estimated, might have prevented the vast majority of the killings; and the international community as a whole, which, in the wake of the emergence of a new government in Rwanda after the genocide, ignored that new government's pleas for assistance but came to the aid of the Hutu killers in exile while failing to prevent their ongoing incursions into Rwanda to continue the genocide.

For all their attention to the attribution of individual blame for these crimes, international lawyers have not been attentive to these wider circles of guilt. In surreal fashion, international lawyers have argued that judges from some of the very countries that are regarded as partly 'to blame' for these crimes will be readily accepted as neutral arbitrators simply because they do not come from Rwanda. Blind to the colonial-era racism that helped to make the Rwandan genocide possible, and equally blind to the continuing insensitivities of the U.N. and its patrons since the genocide, international lawyers pin their hopes for verdicts that will be accepted as impartial on a U.N.-approved bench, simply because it does not contain a Hutu or a Tutsi. This seems a slim reed on which to rely. To the extent that the U.N., as an organization, was itself derelict in enforcing international humanitarian law, that fact is surely detrimental to the credibility of the ICTR's judgments.

...Knowledge of what led to the Rwandan killings as well as who is to blame in this wider sense strengthens the very premise that individuals must be held responsible. In addition, sensitivity to colonial-era racism and what has occurred in its wake prompts scrutiny of the policies now being touted by the U.N.'s Security Council with respect to Rwanda....Those who were blind once to the important consequences of acting on the basis of ethnic prejudices could be wrong a second time when they insist that international trials should proceed as if the prejudices they helped to instill can be ignored.

...Knowledge of the West's complicity should make us skeptical of a scheme that would deny to the Rwandan government what each Western state has for centuries enjoyed, namely the right to try its own war criminals.

QUESTIONS

1. Accepting the report of the panel appointed by Kofi Annan and Alvarez's analysis, what follows from them? Do they lessen, or strengthen, the argument for individual punishment of those committing the genocide on the ground? Should they lead to criminal liability under international law of non-Rwandans who are implicated in some other way in the genocide? Against whom, and under what charges?

2. Does this analysis delegitimate the ICTR and its judgments if a panel of the Trial Chamber or the Appeal Chamber consists predominantly of non-African judges, particularly judges from the states that are alleged to bear responsibility? Does it point to resorting to the Rwandan judiciary rather than to an international tribunal — a small judiciary in a country where tens of thousands of prisoners have been long awaiting trial for the genocide? Would analogous problems to those described by Alvarez arise in constituting a judicial bench in state criminal proceedings in countries that have suffered massive tragedies in civil conflict or severe repression? Does the fact that a conflict or political repression has a strong ethnic dimension in addition to its deep political divisions complicate such issues?

ADDITIONAL READING

D. Scheffer, *All the Missing Souls: A Personal History of the War Crimes Tribunals* (2012); R. Goodman et. al., 'Psychic Numbing and Mass Atrocity', in E. Shafir (ed.), *The Behavioral Foundations of Policy* (2012); A. K. Woods, 'Moral Judgments and International Crimes', 52 Virginia. J. Int'l. L. (2012); T. Meron, *The Making* of *International Criminal Justice: The View from the Bench* (2011); M. Osiel, *Making Sense of Mass Atrocity* (2011); Kevin Jon Heller, *The Nuremberg Military Tribunals and the Origins of International Criminal Law* (2011); Larry May, *Genocide: A Normative Account* (2010); W. Schabas, *Genocide in International Law* (2nd edn. 2009); B. Van Schaack, 'Crimen Sine Lege: Judicial Lawmaking at the Intersection of Law and Morals', 97 Georgetown L. J. 119 (2008); M. A. Drumbl, *Atrocity, Punishment, and International Law* (2007); E. Stover, *The Witnesses: War Crimes and the Promise of Justice in The Hague* (2005); Larry May, *Crimes Against Humanity: A Normative* Account (2004); G. J. Bass, *Stay the Hand of Vengeance: the Politics of War Crimes Tribunals* (2000); T. Meron, *War Crimes Law Comes of Age* (1998); S. Power, *A Problem from Hell: America and the Age of Genocide* (2002); R. A. Dallaire, *Shake Hands with the Devil: The Failure of Humanity in Rwanda* (2004); M. Scharf, *Balkan Justice: The Story Behind the First International War Crimes Tribunal since Nuremberg* (1997); M. C. Othman, *Accountability for International Humanitarian Law Violations: The Case of Rwanda and East Timor* (2005); V. Morris & M. Scharf, *The International Criminal Tribunal for Rwanda* (1998); S. Ratner, 'New Democracies: Old Atrocities; An Inquiry in International Law', 87 Georgetown L. J. 707 (1999); M. Cherif Bassiouni, 'Strengthening the Norms of International Humanitarian Law to Combat Impunity', in B. Weston & S. Marks (eds.), *The Future of International Human Rights* (1999); Symposium, 'Genocide, War Crimes, and Crimes against Humanity', 23 Fordham Int'l. L. J. 275–488 (1999); C. Eboe-Osuji, '"Complicity in Genocide" Versus "Aiding And Abetting Genocide": Construing the Difference in the ICTR and ICTY', 3 J. Int'l. Crim. Just. 56 (2005).

B. THE INTERNATIONAL CRIMINAL COURT

The idea of a permanent international criminal court has been a part of the human rights movement since 1948, when the General Assembly instructed the International Law Commission to study the possibility of establishing one. That initiative was rejuvenated following the end of the Cold War. In 1992, the General Assembly requested the Commission to draft a statute for a permanent criminal court. Those efforts led to a conference held in Rome in 1998, resulting in the adoption of the Statute for the International Criminal Court (ICC). In 2002, the ICC treaty came into force. As of May 2012, 120 states had ratified the treaty, including 27 of the 29 members of NATO (the two exceptions are Turkey and the United States). Other states parties include Afghanistan, Australia, Colombia, Central African Republic, Democratic Republic of the Congo, Georgia, Peru and Uganda. States that have not ratified the treaty include China, Egypt, India, Indonesia, Iran, Israel, Libya, Pakistan, Russia, Rwanda, Sudan, Syria and Zimbabwe.

Subject to other jurisdictional limitations which we discuss below, the ICC is empowered to investigate 'situations' involving genocide, crimes against humanity and war crimes. The ICC currently has seven situations on its docket. All of them arise out of countries in Africa — a regional focus that became a contentious issue during the tenure of the first Chief Prosecutor, Luis Moreno Ocampo. The first three situations taken up by the Court were the Democratic Republic of Congo (2004), Uganda (2004) and the Central African Republic (2005). The latter two were referred by the governments themselves. Although the DRC situation is often described as another instance of a self-referral, the record reveals a more complicated process. The DRC situation was initiated, at least informally, by the Prosecutor. According to an ICC Press Statement, 'In September 2003 the Chief Prosecutor informed the States Parties that he was ready to request authorization from the Pre-Trial Chamber to use his own powers to start an investigation, but that a referral and active support from the DRC would assist his work. In a letter in November 2003 the government of the DRC welcomed the involvement of the ICC and in March 2004 the DRC referred the situation in the country to the Court.' In 2005, the UN Security Council referred the fourth situation — Darfur — to the ICC. In 2010, the Prosecutor launched a *proprio motu* investigation concerning Kenya, which became the fifth situation on the docket. And the Prosecutor decided to pursue an investigation in Côte d'Ivoire in 2011 after that country had issued a voluntary referral under a provision of the ICC Statute available for states that are not party to the ICC (see Art. 12(3)). In 2011, the Security Council referred the seventh situation — Libya.

The Office of the Prosecutor (OTP) has also developed a practice of formally opening 'preliminary examinations', which the OTP describes as a process of 'proactively monitor[ing] information on crimes potentially falling within the jurisdiction of the Court'. The OTP has initiated such proceedings in a range of situations including Afghanistan, Colombia, Georgia, Guinea, Honduras, Nigeria, the Occupied Palestinian Territories and South Korea. The OTP has also published its conclusions to dismiss further inquiry into crimes allegedly committed in Iraq (by invading and occupying forces) and in Venezuela. The OTP issued the 2010 Draft Policy Paper on Preliminary Examinations describing and justifying this practice. In an implicit reference to the OTP's cases from Africa, the draft Policy Paper states, 'Factors such as geographical or regional balance are not relevant criterion [sic] for a determination that a situation warrants investigation under the Statute.' It also states that 'the Office's preliminary examination activities will be conducted in the same manner irrespective of whether the Office receives a referral from a State Party or the Security Council or acts on the basis of information of crimes obtained pursuant to article 15.'

As of early 2012, with seven situations under consideration, the Court had a handful of defendants in custody. The defendants included the following individuals.

(1) From the Sudan:
The Prosecutor brought charges against three leaders of a rebel group that had been fighting against the Sudanese Government in Darfur. The charges involved crimes committed in connection with an attack on an African Union peacekeeping mission. Two of the defendants (Abdallah Banda Abakaer Nourain and Saleh Mohammed Jerbo Jamus) are currently held in custody. A Pre-Trial Chamber dismissed the charges against

the third defendant (Bahar Idriss Abu Garda), who had appeared voluntarily in The Hague to contest the charges against him.

(2) From the DRC:
A former leader of a militia group, Patriotic Forces for the Liberation of Congo (FPLC), Thomas Lubanga Dyilo is being tried for allegedly enlisting and conscripting children under the age of 15 and using them to participate in hostilities.
Germain Katanga, allegedly the highest ranking commander of a rebel group, and Mathieu Ngudjolo Chui, an alleged leader of an associated rebel group, for individually and jointly committing crimes including the murder of civilians, sexual enslavement of women and girls, and the use of child soldiers.
Callixte Mbarushimana was held in custody, but, in December 2011, he became the first suspect ordered to be released from detention by a ruling of the Pre-Trial Chamber. The Prosecutor had alleged that Mbarushimana was a leader of the FPLC and principally responsible for an international media campaign to conceal the commission of mass atrocity crimes by the FPLC forces in the DRC. The Pre-Trial Chamber found there was insufficient evidence to confirm the charges.

(3) From Côte d'Ivoire:
Former President Laurent Gbagbo is allegedly responsible for committing crimes against humanity, including deliberately killing civilians, in the aftermath of presidential elections in Côte d'Ivoire.

(4) From the Central African Republic:
Former Vice-President of the DRC and commander-in-chief of the Movement for the Liberation of Congo, Jean-Pierre Bemba Gombo, is alleged to have command responsibility for war crimes and crimes against humanity committed by MLC forces operating inside CAR.

In addition to the above cases, the Court issued summons for six suspects from Kenya, including high-level state officials, to appear before the Pre-Trial Chamber in a preliminary hearing. All six appeared in The Hague, but were not held in custody.

The Court also has several outstanding warrants for arrest. These include:

(1) From the Sudan:
The sitting President of the Sudan, Omar Al Bashir;[4] Sudanese Defence Minister Abdelrahim Mohamed Hussein; the incumbent Minister for Humanitarian Affairs (formerly Minister of State for the Interior), Ahmad Harun; and a leader of the Janjaweed militia group, Ali Kushayb.

[4] See p. 1219, *supra* discussing ICC Pre-Trial Chamber judgment on Head of State immunity for President Bashir.

(2) From the DRC:
Deputy Chief of the General Staff of the FPLC, Bosco Ntaganda.

(3) From Uganda:
Joseph Kony and four other leaders of the Lord's Resistance Army, a rebel group fighting in Northern Uganda.

(4) From Libya:
Son of Muammar Gaddafi and allegedly former de facto Prime Minister, Saif Al-Islam Gaddafi; and former head of Military Intelligence, Abdullah Al-Senussi.

The Court had also issued an arrest warrant for Libya's sitting head of state, Muammar Gaddafi. That case was closed after opposition forces killed Gaddafi.

The excerpts of the ICC Statute in the Online Resource Centre include crimes that are within the substantive jurisdiction of the Court, procedural requirements for the exercise of jurisdiction and standards of liability. As you will see, Article 5(2) of the Statute includes a placeholder for the crime of aggression (e.g., the unlawful use of armed force against a state). In 2010, the Assembly of States Parties held a Review Conference in Kampala, Uganda, in part to determine whether a consensus could be reached on the crime of aggression. The result was a tentative compromise that provides a definition and a set of extraordinary jurisdictional prerequisites for the Court to hear a case of aggression. The compromise document, however, essentially postpones the decision for several years. It requires the Assembly of States Parties to vote again to reaffirm the amendment after January 2017. At Kampala, the Assembly of States Parties also adopted an amendment to the Statute extending the scope of war crimes to cover the use of specific types of weapons in non-international armed conflicts — they were previously considered war crimes only in an international armed conflict. Finally, South Africa on behalf of the African Union proposed an amendment to counteract what they considered a bias against African states in the Prosecutor's caseload. Under the proposal, the UN General Assembly would have the same power as the Security Council to defer investigations and prosecutions — but only when the Security Council failed to decide whether to exercise that power itself.[5] The proposal did not gain significant political traction in Kampala.

[5] The amendment would have replaced Art. 16 with the following text:

1) No investigation or prosecution may be commenced or proceeded with under this Statute for a period of 12 months after the Security Council, in a resolution adopted under the Chapter VII of the Charter of the United Nations, has requested the Court to that effect, that request may be renewed by the Council under the same conditions.

2) A State with jurisdiction over a situation before the Court may request the UN Security Council to defer the matter before the Court as provided for in (1) above.

3) Where the UN Security Council fails to decide on the request by the state concerned within six (6) months of receipt of the request, the requesting Party may request the UN General Assembly to assume the Security Council's responsibility under paragraph 1 consistent with Resolution 377 (v) of the UN General Assembly.

KENNETH ROTH, THE COURT THE US DOESN'T WANT

N.Y. Rev. Books, 19 Nov. 1998, at 45

. . . In favor of the [International Criminal] [C]ourt were most of America's closest allies, including Britain, Canada, and Germany. But the United States was isolated in opposition, along with such dictatorships and enemies of human rights as Iran, Iraq, China, Libya, Algeria, and Sudan. . . .

The Clinton administration's opposition to the ICC stemmed in part from its fear, a plausible one, that hostile states like Cuba, Libya, or Iraq might try to convince the court to launch a frivolous or politically motivated prosecution of US soldiers or commanding officers. The Rome delegates adopted several safeguards against this possibility, most importantly the so-called principle of complementarity. This gives the ICC jurisdiction over a case only if national authorities are 'unwilling or unable' to carry out a genuine investigation and, if appropriate, prosecution. The complementarity principle also reflects the widely shared view that systems of national justice should remain the front-line defense against serious human rights abuse, with the ICC serving only as a backstop.. . .

According to the principle of complementarity, if an American soldier were to commit a serious war crime — say, by deliberately massacring civilians — he could be brought before the ICC only if the US government failed to pursue his case. Indeed, even a national decision not to prosecute must be respected so long as it is not a bad faith effort to shield a criminal from justice. Because of the strength of the US judicial system, an ICC prosecutor would have a hard time dismissing a US investigation or prosecution as a sham. And, under the treaty, any effort to override a nation's decision not to prosecute would be subject to challenge before one panel of international judges and appeal before another.

Much would still depend on the character and professionalism of the ICC prosecutor and judges. The record of the International Criminal Tribunals for Rwanda and the former Yugoslavia suggests that faith in them would be well placed. . . .

There is every reason to believe that the ICC will be run by jurists of comparable stature. . . .

But the Pentagon and its congressional allies were not satisfied with the principle of complementarity as protection against unjustified prosecutions. . . .

Efforts by the US to exempt its nationals from the ICC's jurisdiction contributed to four points in contention during the Rome conference. . . . The resulting concessions [by other states] weakened the court significantly. . . .

The first controversy concerned whether and, if so, how the UN Security Council should be permitted to halt an ICC prosecution. The US proposed that before the ICC could even begin an investigation the Security Council would have to expressly authorize it. Because the United States, as a permanent Council member, could single-handedly block Council approval by exercising its veto, this proposal would have allowed Washington to prevent any investigation, including of its own soldiers and those of its allies. The other four permanent Council members — Britain, France, China, and Russia — would necessarily have had the same veto power. As a result, only criminals from a handful of pariah states would have been likely to face prosecution. . . .

Singapore offered a compromise to the veto problem which ultimately prevailed. It granted the Security Council the power to halt an ICC prosecution for a one-year period, which could be renewed. But the Security Council would act in its usual manner — by the vote of nine of its fifteen members and the acquiescence of all five permanent members. Therefore no single permanent Council member could use its veto to prevent a prosecution from being initiated.... The third major controversy involved what restrictions should be placed on the ICC's definition of war crimes.... Of special concern was the so-called rule of proportionality under international law, which prohibits a military attack causing an incidental loss of civilian life that is 'excessive' compared to the military advantage gained. This less precise rule could implicate activity that US military commanders consider lawful but the ICC might not. For example, the Gulf War bombing of Iraq's electrical grid was claimed to have killed a disproportionate number of civilians, including the thousands said to have died because of the resulting loss of refrigeration, water purification, and other necessities of modern life. What if the ICC had been in existence and had found such claims well founded?...

To avoid prosecution in such borderline situations, US negotiators successfully redefined the proportionality rule to prohibit attacks that injure civilians only when such injury is 'clearly excessive' in relation to the military advantage....

The United States, joined by France, also proposed that governments be allowed to join the ICC while specifying that their citizens would be exempted from war crimes prosecutions.... [A]s a compromise, the treaty allows governments to exempt their citizens from the court's war crimes jurisdiction for a period of seven years. That would allow a hesitant government to reassure itself about the court's treatment of war crimes without permanently denying the court jurisdiction over its citizens....

The most divisive issue delegates faced was deciding how — once the ICC treaty was ratified by sixty countries — the court would get jurisdiction over a case that was referred by an individual government or initiated by the prosecutor. (This issue does not arise when the Security Council refers a matter for prosecution, since the Council has the power to impose jurisdiction.)... South Korea put forward a more limited proposal which gained broad support. It would have granted the ICC jurisdiction when any one of four governments concerned with a crime had ratified the ICC treaty or accepted the court's jurisdiction over the crime. These were: (1) the government of the suspect's nationality; (2) the government of the victims' nationality; (3) the government on whose territory the crime took place; or (4) the government that gained custody of the suspect. In any given case, some and perhaps all of these governments would be the same, but each separate category increases the possibility that the court could pursue a particular suspect.

Speaking for the Clinton administration, Ambassador Scheffer vehemently insisted that the court should be empowered to act only if the government of the suspect's nationality had accepted its jurisdiction....

Clinton administration officials were not mollified by the fact that, under the doctrine of universal jurisdiction, American soldiers are already vulnerable to prosecution in foreign courts. The US government has many ways of dissuading governments from attempting to try an American — from diplomatic and economic pressure to the use of military force. But the administration fears such dissuasion would be less effective against the ICC. After all, the Pentagon could hardly threaten to bomb The Hague.

...Facing these extraordinary threats [from the United States], the Rome delegates gave in, but only partially. They got rid of two of Korea's proposed conditions for ICC jurisdiction: that the treaty would have to be ratified by the state of the victim's nationality or it would have to be ratified by the state that gained custody of the suspect.

This concession was damaging. Because a state could not give the ICC jurisdiction just by arresting a suspect, a leader who commits atrocities against his own country's citizens, such as a future Pol Pot or Idi Amin, could travel widely without being brought before the ICC — so long as his own government had not ratified the treaty (and assuming the Security Council does not act)....And if the victims' nationality cannot be used as grounds for ICC jurisdiction, then the ICC could not take action against the leader of a nonratifying government that slaughters refugees from a ratifying state who seek shelter on its territory (again, assuming the Security Council fails to act)....

But the Rome delegates did not accept the Clinton administration's demands entirely. They retained two grounds for the ICC's jurisdiction: not only that the government of the suspect's nationality had ratified the treaty (the only ground acceptable to the US) but also that the government on whose territory the crime took place had ratified it. In the case of a tyrant who commits crimes at home, these two governments would be the same....The United States, however, feared that the territorial hook might catch American troops, or their commanders, for alleged crimes committed while they were abroad. If the country where US troops are present has ratified the treaty, the ICC could pursue a case against them even though the United States had not joined the court....

NOTE

On 31 December 2000, President Clinton signed the Rome Treaty. In signing, he reiterated 'our concerns about significant flaws in the Treaty' and concluded that 'given these concerns, I will not, and do not recommend that my successor submit the Treaty to the Senate for advice and consent until our fundamental concerns are satisfied.' President Clinton also stated, 'Signature will enhance our ability to further protect U.S. officials from unfounded charges and to achieve the human rights and accountability objectives of the ICC. In fact, in negotiations following the Rome Conference, we have worked effectively to develop procedures that limit the likelihood of politicized prosecutions.'

On 6 May 2002, President Bush 'unsigned' the Rome Treaty by informing the UN Secretary-General that 'the United States does not intend to become a party to the treaty. Accordingly, the United States has no legal obligations arising from its signature.... The United States requests that its intention not to become a party, as expressed in this letter, be reflected in the depositary's status lists relating to this treaty.' The Obama Administration has not reversed this position, and in the US Senate there would presumably not be sufficient votes for ratification.

The US Undersecretary for Political Affairs issued the following statement on the day of President Bush's action. Consider his remarks in comparison with Kenneth Roth's commentary above.

MARC GROSSMAN, UNDERSECRETARY FOR POLITICAL AFFAIRS, AMERICAN FOREIGN POLICY AND THE INTERNATIONAL CRIMINAL COURT

Remarks to the Center for Strategic and International Studies, Washington, DC (6 May 2002)

President Bush has come to the conclusion that the United States can no longer be a party to this process. In order to make our objections clear, both in principle and philosophy, and so as not to create unwarranted expectations of U.S. involvement in the Court, the President believes that he has no choice but to inform the United Nations, as depository of the treaty, of our intention not to become a party.... These actions are consistent with the Vienna Convention on the Law of Treaties.

The decision to take this rare but not unprecedented act was not arrived at lightly. But after years of working to fix this flawed statute, and having our constructive proposals rebuffed, it is our only alternative.

Historical Perspective

Like many of the nations that gathered in Rome in 1998 for the negotiations to create a permanent International Criminal Court, the United States arrived with the firm belief that those who perpetrate genocide, crimes against humanity, and war crimes must be held accountable — and that horrendous deeds must not go unpunished.

The United States has been a world leader in promoting the rule of law. From our pioneering leadership in the creation of tribunals in Nuremberg, the Far East, and the International Criminal Tribunals for the former Yugoslavia and Rwanda, the United States has been in the forefront of promoting international justice. We believed that a properly created court could be a useful tool in promoting human rights and holding the perpetrators of the worst violations accountable before the world — and perhaps one day such a court will come into being.

A Flawed Outcome

...

First, we believe the ICC is an institution of unchecked power. In the United States, our system of government is founded on the principle that, in the words of John Adams, "power must never be trusted without a check." Unchecked power, our founders understood, is open to abuse, even with the good intentions of those who establish it.

But in the rush to create a powerful and independent court in Rome, there was a refusal to constrain the Court's powers in any meaningful way. . . .

Take one example: the role of the UN Security Council. Under the UN Charter, the UN Security Council has primary responsibility for maintaining international peace and security. But the Rome Treaty removes this existing system of checks and balances, and places enormous unchecked power in the hands of the ICC prosecutor and judges. The treaty created a self-initiating prosecutor, answerable to no state or institution other than the Court itself.

In Rome, the United States said that placing this kind of unchecked power in the hands of the prosecutor would lead to controversy, politicized prosecutions, and confusion . . .

. . .

Third, the treaty threatens the sovereignty of the United States. The Court, as constituted today, claims the authority to detain and try American citizens, even though our democratically-elected representatives have not agreed to be bound by the treaty. While sovereign nations have the authority to try non-citizens who have committed crimes against their citizens or in their territory, the United States has never recognized the right of an international organization to do so absent consent or a UN Security Council mandate.

Fourth, the current structure of the International Criminal Court undermines the democratic rights of our people and could erode the fundamental elements of the United Nations Charter, specifically the right to self defense.

With the ICC prosecutor and judges presuming to sit in judgment of the security decisions of States without their assent, the ICC could have a chilling effect on the willingness of States to project power in defense of their moral and security interests.

This power must sometimes be projected. The principled projection of force by the world's democracies is critical to protecting human rights — to stopping genocide or changing regimes like the Taliban, which abuse their people and promote terror against the world.

. . .

The United States has a unique role and responsibility to help preserve international peace and security. At any given time, U.S. forces are located in close to 100 nations around the world conducting peacekeeping and humanitarian operations and fighting inhumanity.

We must ensure that our soldiers and government officials are not exposed to the prospect of politicized prosecutions and investigations. Our President is committed to a robust American engagement in the world to defend freedom and defeat terror; we cannot permit the ICC to disrupt that vital mission.

. . .

Our Philosophy

While we oppose the ICC we share a common goal with its supporters — the promotion of the rule of law. Our differences are in approach and philosophy. In order for the rule of law to have true meaning, societies must accept their responsibilities and be able to direct their future and come to terms with their past. An unchecked international body should not be able to interfere in this delicate process.

For example: When a society makes the transition from oppression to democracy, their new government must face their collective past. The state should be allowed to choose the method. The government should decide whether to prosecute or seek national reconciliation. This decision should not be made by the ICC.

If the state chooses as a result of a democratic and legal process not to prosecute fully, and instead to grant conditional amnesty, as was done in difficult case of South Africa, this democratic decision should be respected.

Whenever a state accepts the challenges and responsibilities associated with enforcing the rule of law, the rule of law is strengthened and a barrier to impunity is erected. It is this barrier that will create the lasting goals the ICC seeks to attain. This responsibility should not be taken away from states.

International practice should promote domestic accountability and encourage sovereign states to seek reconciliation where feasible.

The existence of credible domestic legal systems is vital to ensuring conditions do not deteriorate to the point that the international community is required to intercede.

In situations where violations are grave and the political will of the sovereign state is weak, we should work, using any influence we have, to strengthen that will. In situations where violations are so grave as to amount to a breach of international peace and security, and the political will to address these violations is non-existent, the international community may, and if necessary should, intercede through the UN Security Council as we did in Bosnia and Rwanda.

...

We Will Continue To Lead

...

The existence of a functioning ICC will not cause the United States to retreat from its leadership role in the promotion of international justice and the rule of law.

The United States will:

...

- Continue our longstanding role as an advocate for the principle that there must be accountability for war crimes and other serious violations of international humanitarian law.

...

- The armed forces of the United States will obey the law of war, while our international policies are and will remain completely consistent with these norms.
- Continue to discipline our own when appropriate.
- We will remain committed to promoting the rule of law and helping to bring violators of humanitarian law to justice, wherever the violations may occur.

- We will support politically, financially, technically, and logistically any post-conflict state that seeks to credibly pursue domestic humanitarian law.
- We will support creative ad-hoc mechanisms such as the hybrid process in Sierra Leone — where there is a division of labor between the sovereign state and the international community — as well as alternative justice mechanisms such as truth and reconciliation commissions.

…

- We will seek to create a pool of experienced judges and prosecutors who would be willing to work on these projects on short-notice.
- We will take steps to ensure that gaps in United States' law do not allow persons wanted or indicted for genocide, war crimes, or crimes against humanity to seek safe haven on our soil in hopes of evading justice.

And when violations occur that are so grave and that they breach international peace and security, the United States will use its position in the UN Security Council to act in support of justice.

We believe that there is common ground, and ask those nations who have decided to join the Rome Treaty to meet us there. Encouraging states to come to face the past while moving into the future is a goal that no one can dispute. Enhancing the capacity of domestic judiciaries is an aim to which we can all agree.... Because, in the end, the best way to prevent genocide, crimes against humanity, and war crimes is through the spread of democracy, transparency and rule of law. Nations with accountable, democratic governments do not abuse their own people or wage wars of conquest and terror. A world of self-governing democracies is our best hope for a world without inhumanity.

QUESTIONS

1. Is the US Government correct that the ICC fails to provide sufficient safeguards against politically motivated prosecutions? Is the US Government's real concern that the Court will apply too much law (i.e., let legal standards determine which situations to investigate and who to prosecute) rather than too much politics? Is it a valid concern that the Court is not subject to sufficient political control?

2. Marc Grossman states that 'the ICC could have a chilling effect on the willingness of States to project power in defense of their moral and security interests.... The principled projection of force by the world's democracies is critical to protecting human rights ...' Ken Roth notes the Clinton Administration made a similar claim. Is it likely that powerful states would be deterred by the prospect of a few or more individual prosecutions? Don't decisions to engage in military campaigns routinely involve much greater risks to an intervening state's armed forces? Will the International Criminal Court reduce the likelihood that states engage in humanitarian interventions? If so, is that consequence worth the benefits of having the Court?

SECURITY COUNCIL RESOLUTION ON SITUATION IN SUDAN AND EXPLANATIONS OF VOTE

S.C. Res. 1593 (31 Mar. 2005)

The Security Council,

Taking note of the report of the International Commission of Inquiry on violations of international humanitarian law and human rights law in Darfur (S/2005/60),

Recalling article 16 of the Rome Statute under which no investigation or prosecution may be commenced or proceeded with by the International Criminal Court for a period of 12 months after a Security Council request to that effect,

Also recalling articles 75 and 79 of the Rome Statute and encouraging States to contribute to the ICC Trust Fund for Victims,

Taking note of the existence of agreements referred to in Article 98-2 of the Rome Statute,

Determining that the situation in Sudan continues to constitute a threat to international peace and security,

Acting under Chapter VII of the Charter of the United Nations,

1. Decides to refer the situation in Darfur since 1 July 2002 to the Prosecutor of the International Criminal Court;

2. Decides that the Government of Sudan and all other parties to the conflict in Darfur shall cooperate fully with and provide any necessary assistance to the Court and the Prosecutor pursuant to this resolution and, while recognizing that States not party to the Rome Statute have no obligation under the Statute, urges all States and concerned regional and other international organizations to cooperate fully;

...

5. Also emphasizes the need to promote healing and reconciliation and encourages in this respect the creation of institutions, involving all sectors of Sudanese society, such as truth and/or reconciliation commissions, in order to complement judicial processes and thereby reinforce the efforts to restore long-lasting peace, with African Union and international support as necessary;

6. Decides that nationals, current or former officials or personnel from a contributing State outside Sudan which is not a party to the Rome Statute of the International Criminal Court shall be subject to the exclusive jurisdiction of that contributing State for all alleged acts or omissions arising out of or related to operations in Sudan established or authorized by the Council or the African Union, unless such exclusive jurisdiction has been expressly waived by that contributing State;

7. Recognizes that none of the expenses incurred in connection with the referral, including expenses related to investigations or prosecutions in connection with that referral, shall be borne by the United Nations and that such costs shall be borne by the parties to the Rome Statute and those States that wish to contribute voluntarily;

The draft resolution was adopted by a vote of 11 in favour with 4 abstentions (Algeria, Brazil, China, United States).[6]

Following the vote, ANNE WOODS PATTERSON (United States) said her country strongly supported bringing to justice those responsible for the crimes and atrocities that had occurred in Darfur and ending the climate of impunity there....

While the United States believed that a better mechanism would have been a hybrid tribunal in Africa, it was important that the international community spoke with one voice in order to help promote effective accountability. The United States continued to fundamentally object to the view that the Court should be able to exercise jurisdiction over the nationals, including government officials, of States not party to the Rome Statute. Because it did not agree to a Council referral of the situation in Darfur to the Court, her country had abstained on the vote. She decided not to oppose the resolution because of the need for the international community to work together in order to end the climate of impunity in the Sudan, and because the resolution provided protection from investigation or prosecution for United States nationals and members of the armed forces of non-State parties.

The United States was and would be an important contributor to the peacekeeping and related humanitarian efforts in the Sudan, she said. The language providing protection for the United States and other contributing States was precedent-setting, as it clearly acknowledged the concerns of States not party to the Rome Statute and recognized that persons from those States should not be vulnerable to investigation or prosecution by the Court, absent consent by those States or a referral by the Council. In the future, she believed that, absent consent of the State involved, any investigations or prosecutions of nationals of non-party States should come only pursuant to a decision by the Council.

Although her delegation had abstained on the Council referral to the Court, it had not dropped, and indeed continued to maintain, its long-standing and firm objections and concerns regarding the Court, she continued. The Rome Statute was flawed and did not have sufficient protection from the possibility of politicized prosecutions. Non-parties had no obligations in connection with that treaty, unless otherwise decided by the Council, upon which members of the Organization had conferred primary responsibility for the maintenance of international peace and security.

She was pleased that the resolution recognized that none of the expenses incurred in connection with the referral would be borne by the United Nations, and that instead such costs would be borne by the parties to the Rome Statute and those that contributed voluntarily. That principle was extremely important. Any effort to retrench on that principle by the United Nations or other organizations to which the United States contributed could result in its withholding funding or taking other action in response.

The Council included, at her country's request, a provision that exempted persons of non-party States in the Sudan from the ICC prosecution. Persons from countries not party who were supporting the United Nations' or African Union's

[6] [Eds.: The following governmental statements are excerpted from UN Press Release SC/8351.]

efforts should not be placed in jeopardy. The resolution provided clear protection for United States persons. No United States person supporting operations in the Sudan would be subject to investigation or prosecution because of this resolution. That did not mean that there would be immunity for American citizens that acted in violation of the law. The United States would continue to discipline its own people when appropriate.

ELLEN MARGRETHE LØJ (Denmark) said that it had been two months since the Council had received the report of the Commission of Inquiry, which had strongly recommended referring the situation in Darfur to the ICC....

Denmark had only been able to support the text after some alterations were made, she said. Regarding the formulation on existing agreements referred to in article 98-2 of the Rome Statute, she noted that that reference was purely factual and referred to the existence of such agreements. Thus, the reference was in no way impinging on the Rome Statute. The result was a valid compromise leading to the first referral of a situation to the ICC....

CÉSAR MAYORAL (Argentina) said he had voted in support of the resolution on the basis of the report to the Council by the High Commissioner for Human Rights, who stated clearly what had been crimes against humanity in Darfur....

He noted that it was the first time the Council had referred to the Court a situation involving crimes over which the Court had jurisdiction. It was a crucial precedent. The letter and spirit of the Rome Statute must be respected, taking into account the legitimate concerns of States. Accordingly, he regretted that the Council had to adopt a text that provided an exemption to the Court, and hoped that that would not become normal practice. The exemption referred to in operative paragraph 6 only applied to those States not party to the Rome Statute.

JEAN-MARC DE LA SABLIERE (France) said the events in Darfur were deeply troubling, and the greatest concern was the plight of the people there. The Secretary-General's reports had provided a detailed picture of those atrocities. The Council had a duty to take action....

ADAMANTIOS TH. VASSILAKIS (Greece) stressed that impunity must not be allowed to go unpunished and that was why his country had turned to the International Criminal Court. It would have preferred a text that did not make exceptions, but it was better than one that allowed violations to go unpunished. The text strengthened the Council's authority, as well as that of the International Criminal Court, which would have the possibility of showing its competence....

Council President RONALDO MOTA SARDENBERG (Brazil), speaking in his national capacity, said his country was in favour of the resolution, but had been unable to join those who had voted in favour. However, Brazil was ready to cooperate fully with the International Criminal Court whenever necessary. The Court provided all the necessary checks and balances to prevent politically motivated prosecutions, and any fears to the contrary were both unwarranted and unhelpful.

However, there were limits to the responsibilities of the Council vis-à-vis international instruments, and Brazil had consistently maintained that position since the negotiations on the Rome Statute. But the Court remained the only suitable institution to deal with the violations in the Sudan. Brazil had been unable to support operative paragraph 6, which recognized exclusive jurisdiction. It would not strengthen the role of the International Criminal Court.

ELFATIH MOHAMED AHMED ERWA (Sudan) said that, once more, the Council had persisted in adopting unwise decisions against his country, which only served to further complicate the situation on the ground. The positions over the ICC were well known. The Darfur question had been exploited in light of those positions. It was a paradox that the language in which the resolution was negotiated was the same language that had buffeted the Council before on another African question. The resolution adopted was full of exemptions. He reminded the Council that the Sudan was also not party to the ICC, making implementation of the resolution fraught with procedural impediments. As long as the Council believed that the scales of justice were based on exceptions and exploitation of crises in developing countries and bargaining among major Powers, it did not settle the question of accountability in Darfur, but exposed the fact that the ICC was intended for developing and weak countries and was a tool to exercise cultural superiority.

The Council, by adopting the resolution, had once again ridden roughshod over the African position, he said. The initiative by Nigeria, as chair of the African Union, had not even been the subject of consideration. Also, the Council had adopted the resolution at a time when the Sudanese judiciary had gone a long way in holding trials, and was capable of ensuring accountability. Some here wanted to activate the ICC and exploit the situation in Darfur. Accountability was a long process that could not be achieved overnight. The Council was continuing to use a policy of double standards, and sending the message that exemptions were only for major Powers....

SECURITY COUNCIL RESOLUTION LIBYA

S.C. Res. 1970 (26 Feb. 2011)

The Security Council,

Expressing grave concern at the situation in the Libyan Arab Jamahiriya and condemning the violence and use of force against civilians,

Deploring the gross and systematic violation of human rights, including the repression of peaceful demonstrators, expressing deep concern at the deaths of civilians, and rejecting unequivocally the incitement to hostility and violence against the civilian population made from the highest level of the Libyan government,

Welcoming the condemnation by the Arab League, the African Union, and the Secretary General of the Organization of the Islamic Conference of the serious violations of human rights and international humanitarian law that are being committed in the Libyan Arab Jamahiriya,

Taking note of the letter to the President of the Security Council from the Permanent Representative of the Libyan Arab Jamahiriya dated 26 February 2011,

Welcoming the Human Rights Council resolution A/HRC/RES/S-15/1 of 25 February 2011, including the decision to urgently dispatch an independent international commission of inquiry to investigate all alleged violations of international human rights law in the Libyan Arab Jamahiriya, to establish the facts and circumstances of such violations and of the crimes perpetrated, and where possible identify those responsible,

Considering that the widespread and systematic attacks currently taking place in the Libyan Arab Jamahiriya against the civilian population may amount to crimes against humanity,

...

Recalling article 16 of the Rome Statute under which no investigation or prosecution may be commenced or proceeded with by the International Criminal Court for a period of 12 months after a Security Council request to that effect,

...

Acting under Chapter VII of the Charter of the United Nations, and taking measures under its Article 41,

...

4. Decides to refer the situation in the Libyan Arab Jamahiriya since 15 February 2011 to the Prosecutor of the International Criminal Court;

5. Decides that the Libyan authorities shall cooperate fully with and provide any necessary assistance to the Court and the Prosecutor pursuant to this resolution and, while recognizing that States not party to the Rome Statute have no obligation under the Statute, urges all States and concerned regional and other international organizations to cooperate fully with the Court and the Prosecutor;

6. Decides that nationals, current or former officials or personnel from a State outside the Libyan Arab Jamahiriya which is not a party to the Rome Statute of the International Criminal Court shall be subject to the exclusive jurisdiction of that State for all alleged acts or omissions arising out of or related to operations in the Libyan Arab Jamahiriya established or authorized by the Council, unless such exclusive jurisdiction has been expressly waived by the State;

7. Invites the Prosecutor to address the Security Council within two months of the adoption of this resolution and every six months thereafter on actions taken pursuant to this resolution;

8. Recognizes that none of the expenses incurred in connection with the referral, including expenses related to investigations or prosecutions in connection with that referral, shall be borne by the United Nations and that such costs shall be borne by the parties to the Rome Statute and those States that wish to contribute voluntarily

...

[The resolution was adopted with unanimous support, including from non-permanent members Bosnia and Herzegovina, Brazil, Colombia, Gabon, Germany, India, Lebanon, Nigeria, Portugal and South Africa. Unlike the resolution on Darfur, the Libya Resolution contained no reference to Article 98(2) of the ICC Statute.]

COMMENT ON IMMUNITY BEFORE THE ICC: WHO IS EXEMPT FROM INTERNATIONAL JUSTICE?

(1) Referrals of 'Situations' with *Ratione Personae* Exclusions

Look back at paragraph 6 of the Security Council resolution referring the Darfur situation to the ICC. In its referral of the Libyan situation, the Security Council inserted similar language precluding the Court from exercising jurisdiction over individuals from ICC non-state parties for any acts arising out of UN established or authorized operations. (S.C. Res. 1497, para. 6). The Statute for the Special Court of Sierra Leone, which was created pursuant to a Security Council resolution, contains a similar provision with respect to that tribunal (Art. 1(2)).[7] The Council has also adopted similar provisions, not in the context of creating or employing a tribunal, but in the course of authorizing peacekeeping operations. In 2002 and 2003, the Council passed resolutions of a general character: they excluded ICC jurisdiction over all personnel of states not party to the ICC for conduct arising out of any UN established or authorized operation.[8] The resolutions explicitly included text stating that such provisions were adopted 'consistent with the provisions of Article 16 of the Rome Statute' and limited to a 12-month period (S.C. Res. 1422 and S.C. Res. 1487). In terms of its structural relationship with the ICC, the Council 'request[ed]' the ICC to abide by these exemptions. In contrast, the Council 'decide[d]' that all UN member states shall take no action inconsistent with the exemptions. The 2002 and 2003 peacekeeping resolutions were adopted primarily in response to pressure from the US Government, which threatened to veto peacekeeping operations including the renewal of the UN mission in Bosnia and Herzegovina without such assurances. At the time, the US Ambassador to the United Nations John Negroponte stated:

> We will not permit... the imposition on our citizens of a novel legal system they have never accepted or approved, and which their government has explicitly rejected. We will never permit Americans to be jailed because judges of the ICC, chosen without the participation of those over whom they claim jurisdiction, so decide. We cannot allow that Americans who have been acquitted of accusations against them in the United States shall be subject to prosecution for the same acts if an ICC prosecutor or judge concludes that the American legal proceedings were somehow inadequate. We know that prosecutors who are responsible to no one constitute a danger, and we will not expose our citizens to such a danger.

The United States was unable to secure enough votes to renew these resolutions in 2004 following the revelation of abuses at the hands of US personnel in the Abu Ghraib facility in Iraq.

Despite the exemption for non-ICC states in the Libya referral, the Chief Prosecutor announced in a briefing before the Council, 'There are allegations of crimes committed by NATO forces.... These allegations will be examined impartially and independently by the Office.' Could the Prosecutor pursue cases involving NATO members who are not party to the ICC — i.e., Turkey and the United

[7] For another example of restricted *ratione personae* jurisdiction in past practice, see the Statute for the ICTR. The Statute provides the tribunal jurisdiction over any individual regardless of nationality for crimes committed in the territory of Rwanda. For crimes committed in the territory of neighbouring states, the Statute extends jurisdiction only to Rwandan citizens.

[8] The Council also adopted similar language in a resolution establishing the Multinational Force and UN Stabilization Force in Liberia (S.C. Res. 1497, para. 7 (2003)).

States? Could the Prosecutor argue that the exemption is legally ineffective — and thus continue to pursue such investigations? It is worth considering two legal grounds that might suggest such exclusions are legally ineffective, along with the practical implications of such an approach.

First, the Prosecutor might argue that NATO operations exceeded the authorization of the Security Council. In Resolution 1973, the Security Council effectively authorized NATO to use limited military force 'to protect civilians and civilian populated areas under threat of attack'. Some commentators argued that NATO's military campaign exceeded the limit of protecting civilians from attack. Once NATO's campaign began, South African President Jacob Zuma, whose government had voted for the resolution, stated that NATO had 'misuse[d]' the authorization to use force: 'The continuing bombing by NATO and its allies is a concern that has been raised by our committee and by the AU Assembly, because the intention of Resolution 1973 was to protect the Libyan people and facilitate the humanitarian effort.... The intention was not to authorise a campaign for regime change or political assassination.' Could the ICC decide that US military personnel were involved in actions that were not authorized by the Security Council and thus not covered by the exemption in paragraph 6?

Second, the Prosecutor might argue that the exemption is legally invalid.[9] Does Article 13 of the ICC Statute allow the Security Council to refer a 'situation' while exempting particular sets of individuals from jurisdiction? Note that some commentaries contend that the term 'situation' was meant to apply to all actors responsible for the commission of ICC crimes on every side of a given social or military conflict. (See, e.g., S. A. Williams and W. A. Schabas, 'Exercise of Jurisdiction', in O. Triffterer (ed.), *Commentary on the Rome Statute of the International Criminal Court: Observers' Notes, Article by Article* (2nd edn. 2008), at 571–2; R. Cryer, 'Sudan, Resolution 1593, and International Criminal Justice', 19 Leiden J. Int'l. L. 195 (2006).) On this view, a state or the Security Council cannot lawfully refer a matter to the ICC and limit the situation to crimes committed only by armed opposition groups and not by governmental forces. And, by way of illustration, if Israel's military actions were ever taken up by the Court, so would the actions of armed opposition groups be considered by the Prosecutor as part of the same situation. Concerned about the politicization of the Court, some commentators (see, e.g., José Alvarez's commentary below) argue that the ICC is based on a principle of impartiality, and referrals with such *ratione personae* restrictions would violate that foundational commitment. Writing specifically about the Libya referral, Kevin John Heller writes, 'Referrals are limited to situations for a reason: because they prevent the referring party (whether Security Council, State Party, or Prosecutor) from using the referral as a weapon against its political opponents. The Prosecutor must be able to prosecute any crime committed by any party to a conflict for the

[9] If these exemptions are legally impermissible, could a defendant — including a Sudanese or former Libyan official — argue that the resolution as a whole is void because a fundamental condition of the referral is invalid? As an analogue, compare Art. 44 of the Vienna Convention on the Law of Treaties for rules about severability for those types of legal instrument.

Court to be seen as legitimate. Paragraph 6 of the Security Council resolution referring the situation in Libya, if accepted by the ICC, would undermine that basic principle.' Other commentators, however, suggest that the ICC Statute is more ambiguous in terms of the definition of a 'situation' and in terms of the power of the Security Council to tailor its referrals. (P. Kirsch, QC & D. Robinson, 'Referral by State Parties', in A. Cassese, P. Gaeta & J. R. W. D. Jones (eds.), *The Rome Statute of the International Criminal Court: A Commentary* (2002), L. Condorelli & S. Villalpando, 'Referral and Deferral by the Security Council', in ibid., at 619, 625, 627; D. J. Scheffer, 'Staying the Course With the International Criminal Court', 35 Cornell Int'l. L J. 47 (2001–02), at 90.) For example, former Ambassador David J. Scheffer, who headed the US delegation on the ICC treaty negotiations, writes:

> The Chapter VII resolution would define the parameters of the Court's investigations in the particular situation. The Security Council also could use the power of referral to insulate domestic amnesty arrangements from the reach of the ICC by specifying in a referral, for example, that those individuals who have received or will receive amnesty in accordance with domestic procedures fall outside the scope of the referral. This may be particularly relevant for amnesties of low and mid-level personnel who normally would be of little interest to an ICC Prosecutor anyway. But the power of the Security Council to shape the referral could facilitate peace-making while still upholding a significant role for the ICC to play in achieving international justice in any particular situation.

If the ICC Statute allows the Security Council to tailor its referrals, should individual state referrals (under Art. 14) be able to include similar exemptions?[10] What differences might distinguish the two types of referrals? Note that the Security Council, under the terms of the ICC Statute, has legal powers associated with the referral and deferral of cases that state parties do not possess. For example, the Council can refer crimes committed by and on the territory of states that are not party to the Statute. That is, the Council is not bound by the jurisdictional preconditions in Article 12 of the Statute. Also note that for state referrals pursuant to Article 14, the debate about 'partial referrals' may be semantic: in practice, the Office of the Prosecutor can correct for such exclusions or limitations. If a state party to the ICC attempted to refer only particular groups within its territory, for example, the Prosecutor could exercise her *proprio motu* powers to address other actors and incidents on the territory of the state party including crimes committed by government officials. The same institutional correction does not exist for Security Council referrals involving conduct committed on the territory of a non-state party where the Prosecutor does not have an independent basis to pursue other cases.

If the Security Council is permitted to make the above type of exemptions, could the Council also lawfully exempt nationals from states that are parties to the ICC? For example, could the Security Council have referred the Libyan situation but

[10] Notably, the Government of Uganda apparently attempted a one-sided referral to cover crimes committed only by the Lord's Resistance Army. The office of the Prosecutor, however, elected to consider crimes committed on all sides of the conflict.

exempted members of the British and French forces? In considering these questions, note that all of the past Security Council exemptions from the ICC—including the Darfur and Libya referrals, the Liberia resolution and the 2002 and 2003 peacekeeping resolutions — exclude not only *nationals* of states that are not party to the ICC, but more generally 'current or former officials or personnel' of those states.[11]

How would states behave if these exemptions could not be assured? Would the United States be more reluctant to support Security Council referrals of mass atrocities to the ICC? On the other hand, if the Council were permitted to make such exemptions for UN-authorized actions, would states be more willing to resort to the Council to authorize the use of force (and gain the benefit of such exemptions) rather than exercising the use of force unilaterally? How might states behave if such exemptions could be assured for state referrals under Article 14? Wouldn't more states be willing to bring cases to the ICC under Article 14, and, if so, would that be an overall desirable result?

(2) US Bilateral Agreements

Kenneth Roth's commentary refers to bilateral treaties (sometimes called 'immunity agreements', 'Article 98 agreements' or 'bilateral non-surrender agreements') that the United States has crafted to ensure that US nationals and employees are not transferred to the Court. By the end of the George W. Bush Administration, the United States reportedly finalized over 100 agreements and over 50 states had publicly refused to enter such agreements.[12] The Obama Administration did not seek additional agreements. These treaties are not, however, a matter simply for historians to consider. Although the Obama Administration discontinued the policy of seeking new agreements, it did not adopt a policy of annulling existing ones. And US forces continued potentially to benefit from the background assurance provided by such agreements in places such as Afghanistan.

Are these agreements legally valid for parties to the ICC? Do these agreements defeat the object and purpose of the Rome Statute or are they consistent with Article 98 of the Statute? Note that a debate exists as to whether the term 'sending state' in Article 98 refers only to specific relationships, such as when US military and civilian personnel are sent to a receiving state under a Status of Forces or Status of Mission agreement. Compare the wording in Article 1 of the Statute of the Special Court for Sierra Leone, p. 1360, *infra*.

Article 18 of the Vienna Convention on the Law of Treaties requires states not to defeat the object and purpose of a treaty that they have signed but not yet ratified. According to Article 18 of the Vienna Convention, the obligation not to defeat the object and purpose exists 'until [the state] shall have made its intention clear not to become a party to the treaty'. Grossman (p. 1337, *supra*) states that the US Administration's announcement constituted 'actions [that] are consistent with the

[11] These resolutions are similar to US bilateral (Art. 98) agreements (see following subsection), which are also not restricted to US nationals. The agreements refer broadly to 'current or former Government officials, employees (including contractors), or military personnel or nationals'.

[12] See www.coalitionfortheicc.org/documents/CICCFS_BIAstatus_current.pdf.

Vienna Convention on the Law of Treaties'. The act of 'un-signing', on this view, constitutes notification of intent under Article 18 and thus released the United States from any obligation to support the Court. However, what about the obligations of states that are parties to the ICC and have a bilateral agreement with the United States? At some future date, the Court may have to decide whether to consider such agreements legally valid.

(3) Head of State Immunity

Refer to our discussion of immunity in Chapter 13, including our examination of the ICC Pre-Trial Chamber decision, in December 2011, holding that a sitting Head of State of a non-state party lacks immunity before the ICC.

JOSÉ ALVAREZ, OPENING REMARKS, HOW BEST TO ASSURE THE INDEPENDENCE OF THE ICC PROSECUTOR

Conference, NYU School of Law (11 Nov. 2011)

[T]hose who negotiated the Rome Statute for the ICC succeeded beyond all expectations in establishing a relatively independent prosecutor. They successfully defeated a strong push from the US, among others, that would have made both court and prosecutor subject to the whims of that political body par excellence, the UN Security Council....

...

[T]o the surprise of many, the SC has now referred two situations to the Court: the cases of Darfur (Resolution 1593) and Libya (Resolution 1970). Many have praised these actions — and especially the unanimous vote in favor of 1970 — as demonstrating that the Court has now achieved a certain legitimacy even among the members of the SC that are not parties to the Rome Statute. It *is* remarkable that non-parties to the Rome Statute like the US, Russia, China, and India all voted in favor of sending the Libya situation to the ICC. These resolutions suggest that the ICC has now become part of the SC's regular toolbox to deal with threats to the peace. But that is precisely the problem. These resolutions are a mixed blessing for the Court's and the prosecutor's perceived and real independence. These referrals might be seen as turning the Court — and its prosecutor — into a "mere" tool of diplomacy. Consider what the Council did in these instances:

It referred complex situations of on-going conflict within two African states to the Court in instances where the countries involved had not freely consented to the Rome Statute, where the situations were likely to require politically risky, and expensive investigations as well as extremely controversial high level indictments (including of then sitting presidents).

...

The Council referred these situations subject to time restrictions — in the case of Libya, for crimes committed only since Feb. 15, 2011. This limited time frame precludes the fuller inquiry needed to achieve the wider truth-seeking goals of international justice.

It referred these situations without any follow-up enforcement actions by the SC to date; that is, without any positive responses to the prosecutor's subsequent requests for assistance on securing arrests or evidence. Indeed, the very referrals to the Court specifically indicate that non-Rome party states incur no obligation to cooperate with the Court or the Prosecutor; and in both cases, the SC referrals specifically excluded the possibility that non-Rome party nationals could be prosecuted by the ICC, even for crimes committed in the Sudan or Libya by their own nationals during the relevant period.

These referrals are hardly unadorned endorsements of the Court or expressions of faith in the independent criminal process. With friends like the SC dumping selective cases on the Court without paying for them, who needs enemies? In both instances, the SC may have misused the Court if its goal was merely to put political pressure on the regimes in the Sudan and in Libya — without, in either case, really supporting the possibility that high level perpetrators would be arrested and actually tried by the Court. The fact that at one point the Council even considered deferring the situation in the Sudan under Art. 16 once its immediate goals for South Sudan were achieved also suggests that the SC sees the ICC as yet another political tool that can be traded away if politically expedient. And the Libyan referral was perhaps only a tool to delegitimize a regime that some members of the SC wanted to take down — even if this exceeded the formal "humanitarian" mandate of SC Res. 1973 authorizing the limited use of force in Libya. For some, the Feb. 15th temporal limits on the Court's jurisdiction in the Libya case is a transparent ploy to preclude inquiries into periods when certain members of the P-5 were implicated in the most noxious aspects of Qaddafi's regime. Transposed to the national level, this would seem a clear instance of political intrusion into prosecutorial discretion. The SC's arguably cynical misuse of the Court exacerbates the perception that the Court unduly focuses on African cases, does not adjudicate crimes by nationals of certain members of the SC itself, and does not constitute an impartial application of international criminal law. The fact that all of these flaws are due to the actions of the SC, and not the Court or its prosecutor, is likely to be lost on critics of international criminal justice who see it as prone to political selectivity.

...

The states that are parties to the Rome Statute can do much individually either to undermine or to promote prosecutorial independence. They undermine the Court to the extent they nominate — as they sometimes have — judges with no law degrees, for example. They undermine the Court's independence to the extent they defy it — as by failing to cooperate with judicial requests for cooperation and assistance. A state that hands someone indicted by the ICC the keys of the city instead of an arrest warrant undermines the independence of the prosecutor.... More counter-intuitively, the independence of the prosecutor and the Court can be undermined if states decide to refer politically troublesome cases to it even when they can conduct trials themselves. An institution designed to be the *last resort* under complementarity is undermined if used as a convenient dumping ground for hot potato cases — while being denied the resources to do a credible job with respect to serious crimes committed in places that can genuinely do nothing to try those responsible.

Of course the Court's independence is undermined when the UN itself — or its officials — conduct business as usual with ICC indictees or suggest, even casually, that ICC prosecutions can be side-lined when necessary to "promote the cause of peace."

COMMENT ON TRANSPORTING JUSTICE TO THE HAGUE: SHOULD STATES BE LIMITED IN THEIR RESORT TO THE ICC?

Many commentators laud the ICC for establishing its initial caseload on the basis of self-referrals by state parties under Article 14. The OTP's reliance on self-referrals is widely considered a more legitimate and politically pragmatic exercise of power — especially for such a young judicial body. However, some scholars contend that self-referrals have often undermined the Court and undercut valuable national institutions. Indeed, some of those scholars contend that a self-referral should be accepted by the Court only if a situation meets the preconditions of complementarity in Article 17. On this view, the complementarity regime is not designed simply to protect the primacy of states in conducting bona fide investigations and trials without undue interference. The complementarity regime also favours national institutions when state authorities possess an underlying will and capacity to investigate and prosecute mass crimes — for example, when a state would pursue such cases in the absence of an ICC referral.

In 2009, the ICC Appeals Chamber settled the legal question whether the complementarity requirements — the unwilling or unable tests in Article 17(1)(a) and (b) of the Statute — apply to self-referrals. In *Prosecutor v. Katanga (DRC)*, the defendant argued that 'if States are granted an unconditional right not to prosecute, this would seriously jeopardize any encouragement of States to prosecute domestically and thereby endanger the correct application of the principle of complementarity' and 'would negate th[e] ... primary responsibility for states to prosecute international crimes'. The Appeals Chamber held that a situation involving a state choosing not to investigate or prosecute a person in its own courts does not come under Article 17(1)(a) and (b). Those complementarity rules, according to the Court, apply only to situations in which the states have pursued an investigation or prosecution; they do not apply when those procedures are 'inactive' including situations in which a state decides to close all judicial proceedings against a suspect in an effort to facilitate her surrender to the ICC. In accordance with this interpretation, states may have the primary responsibility to prosecute international crimes, but they can fulfil that responsibility by transferring cases to the international court.

This construction of the ICC Statute, if left unchecked by other institutional safeguards, may raise two sets of concerns. The first set involves the impact on the Court itself. Some argue that unfettered self-referrals have previously allowed states to divert the ICC away from its core objectives. The purpose of the ICC, on this view, is to operate as a forum of last resort — when the national judiciary is hopeless — and not as a reserve for states to rid themselves of politically sensitive or noxious cases. Consider, for instance, Alvarez's statement: '[T]he independence of the prosecutor and the Court can be undermined if states decide to refer politically troublesome cases to it even when they can conduct trials themselves. An institution designed to be the *last resort* under complementarity is undermined if used as a convenient dumping ground for hot potato cases....' Indeed, these concerns are amplified if states, as a practical matter, decide to provide extraordinary assistance to the Court in investigating and prosecuting opponents of their regime, while providing the bare minimum or paltry assistance for crimes committed by their own members. Other commentators, such as Nidal Jurdi, also raise concerns that 'unrestricted referrals' may overburden the limited resources of the Court.[13]

A second set of concerns involves the effects of self-referrals on national institutions. Some commentators argue that the practice of states to refer cases to the ICC — especially when it becomes more common across a single region (Africa) — can result in the abdication of national responsibilities and the deterioration of local institutions. Consider the following comments by Owen Fiss:[14]

> The pursuit of justice is a moral obligation. The practical burdens facing national tribunals may make them capable of realizing only partial justice, but that does not, as a moral matter, excuse or justify a regime's failure to seek justice. Nor do these practical considerations justify the overwhelming tendency toward internationalization that now dominates the African continent. The pursuit of justice is also a political obligation, for it defines the foundational commitments of a given regime. The willingness of a regime to punish human rights abuses reveals — to its own citizens and to all the world — its true character. A regime's commitment to human rights is all the more powerful when justice is sought in the face of great practical obstacles.
>
> ... To lessen the burden, the nation-state may seek technical assistance or financial contributions from others, but never in a way that compromises its control of the process and thus its responsibility for the quality of justice achieved.
>
> ... Of course, in some cases an international tribunal may be more likely to achieve justice, but delegating responsibility to such a tribunal qualifies the commitment of the nation-state to human rights and lessens the meaning of the trial that eventually takes place....
>
> ... As a court of last resort, the ICC is governed by the principle of complementarity and pursues cases only upon determining that national courts are incapable or unwilling to prosecute crimes within their jurisdiction In fact, however, the ICC has assumed jurisdiction in some cases when national courts may well have been an option. This is not true of the Sudan.... No such justification exists in the other cases — the Congo, Uganda, and now CAR. The failure represented by these cases

[13] N. N. Jurdi, *The International Criminal Court and National Courts: A Contentious Relationship* (2011), at 181, 183.
[14] O. Fiss, 'Within Reach of the State: Prosecuting Atrocities in Africa', 31 H. R. Qtly. 59 (2009).

> belongs not only to the nation states for leaving it to — or getting — others to discharge their responsibilities but also to the ICC for acceding to their requests.

In a similar vein, Joseph Kaifala writes:[15]

> [T]he more African countries continue to send their war criminals and those accused of crimes against humanity to the ICC, the lesser the sense of justice or deterrence transmitted to ordinary African victims far removed from the Court.
>
> . . .
>
> While it is legitimate to argue that many of the accused come from countries with broken institutions, this is not always the case. These countries of origin have the advantages of being close to witnesses, evidence, and the relevant issues of confrontation and general deterrence. Democracy also requires that the people see the judiciary, the third branch of government, having an equal role in the restoration of society after periods of disruption. Justice at home may also serve as deterrence for other aspiring African leaders who follow proceedings close to home rather than in a foreign land and among foreign prosecutors.

What are the arguments in favour of the ICC's ruling and the practice of states to refer politically vexing cases to the Court? The Appeals Chamber answered that question in part by basing its holding on a 'purposive interpretation' of the Statute which entailed the 'aim of the Rome Statute to "put an end to impunity"' and to seek punishment for the most serious crimes. According to the Appeals Chamber: thousands of victims would be denied justice if the Court denied jurisdiction 'as long as the state is theoretically willing and able to investigate and prosecute the case'. Other commentators argue that the vision of the Court as an institution of last resort is overly restrictive. In defence of the *Kasanga* ruling, Payam Akhavan outlines three scenarios in which he contends a self-referral is consistent with the object and purpose of the Statute and the interests of justice within countries:[16]

> One potential scenario is where in a deeply divided nation, the perceived impartiality and fairness of the ICC can help avoid politicization of post-conflict justice and thus contribute to national reconciliation. In Uganda for instance, although the judiciary is among the best in Africa, any trials of LRA leaders before national courts may be perceived as biased in view of deep suspicions of the Government by elements of the Acholi population in the north. . . . Leaving aside the debate about the relative merits of local rather than global justice, prosecutions in The Hague are more likely to be perceived as fair trials whereas national proceedings may be portrayed with suspicion as biased or politically motivated.

[15] J. Kaifala, 'The Problems With Sending African Leaders To The Hague', Dec. 2011 available at www.policymic.com.

[16] P. Akhavan, 'Self-Referrals Before the International Criminal Court: Are States the Villains or the Victims of Atrocities?', 21 Crim. L. Forum (2010), at 103–20.

> A second scenario where relinquishment of jurisdiction may be warranted is where there is a volatile security situation. This could include for instance the prosecution of a powerful leader before national courts in a delicate post-conflict transitional situation. It is not inconceivable that such trials could destabilize a government or even result in the resumption of violence.... Where the only alternative to national trials is the ICC, security considerations may justify self-referrals, and the remoteness and safety of The Hague may be a distinctive advantage.
>
> A third scenario is where the conduct of a particularly complex trial in conformity with international standards entails exorbitant costs that cannot be managed within the limited resources of a State, especially those in the developing world.... Notwithstanding the desirability of domestic capacity-building, in some circumstances, the expeditious option of a self-referral to the ICC may be preferable to a potentially time-consuming and lengthy process of transferring resources to national courts.
>
> When considering these potential scenarios, it must be remembered that ultimately, a State cannot unilaterally oblige the Prosecutor or the Court to initiate proceedings following a self-referral. There are effective safeguards under the Statute against abuse of this right and the consequent politicization of the Court [such as Article 53].

What does the future hold for the 'inactivity test' announced by the Appeals Chamber? With respect to self-referrals, the Court's ruling will presumably discourage states from investigating or prosecuting suspects concurrent with a referral to the ICC. With respect to cases that do not arise from a self-referral, the inactivity test may provide a mechanism for the Court to bypass the complementarity rules in Article 17(1)(a)–(b) by declaring national proceedings inactive. In both situations, these types of cases may turn on how broadly the Court interprets the overlap between a case before it and relevant national proceedings. Pre-Trial and Trial Chambers have already suggested that such inquiries will turn on whether the same person and the same conduct are the subject of national proceedings. For example, the Pre-Trial Chamber in *Prosecutor v. Lubanga (Uganda)* held that the ICC case concerning child soldiers did not involve the same conduct as national proceedings against the defendant concerning crimes against humanity, genocide, murder, illegal detention and torture. (See S. A. Williams & W. A. Schabas, 'Issues of Admissibility', in O. Triffterer (ed.), *Commentary on the Rome Statute of the International Criminal Court: Observers' Notes, Article by Article* (2nd edn. 2008), at 605, 615–16.)

Finally, it is important to note that the questions raised in this comment are not limited to the ICC. They arise in other contexts in which states have consented to the 'internationalization of justice' in response to mass atrocities within their own territory. Another target of Fiss's criticisms, for example, is the structure of the Special Court for Sierra Leone. And, as we will discuss in the following section, the decision of that court to transfer former Liberian President Charles Taylor to The Hague raised challenges similar to the ones faced by the ICC with respect to self-referrals.

QUESTIONS

1. Does the US decision not to veto the Darfur Resolution and to vote for the Libya Resolution represent a significant change in the posture of the United States towards the Court? Does the US acceptance of the competence of the ICC in this case weaken the persuasive appeal of US concerns about the Court? Note that the US has officially taken the position that it will now cooperate with the ICC in the 'prosecution of those cases that advance U.S. interests and values' (US Nat'l. Security Strategy (2010)) such as the situation involving crimes committed by the Lord's Resistance Army in Uganda. And, the United States began attending meetings of the Assembly of States Parties starting with the Review Conference in Kampala.

2. What concessions were made to the US Government in the text of these two resolutions? The US representative takes the position — also suggested in Marc Grossman's statement and in Ambassador Negroponte's statement on the UN peacekeeping resolution — that nationals of a state not party to the Rome Statute should generally not be vulnerable to investigation or prosecution by the Court without that state's consent. Does the resolution strengthen the US position or, on the contrary, demonstrate that exemptions from the ICC require affirmative Security Council action? See also the Note following these Questions.

3. Do you agree with Alvarez that self-referrals under Article 14 of the ICC Statute can, in some circumstances, undermine the independence of the Court and Prosecutor? Are Fiss and Kaifala correct that states should often be discouraged from resorting to the Court and implored to rely instead on their own judicial institutions? If a state selects a few suspects to send to the Court and pursues its own prosecution of other suspects doesn't that suggest the state is both willing and able to investigate and prosecute all such cases? If you helped to design the statute for an international criminal court, would you suggest allowing/encouraging or prohibiting/discouraging the practice of selective referrals?

NOTE

One of the major criticisms of the ICC raised by the US Government concerns the jurisdiction of the Court over nationals of non-state parties. In 2008, the American Society of International Law (ASIL), a nonprofit educational membership organization, convened a blue ribbon Task Force on US Policy Toward the ICC. The Task Force members included, among others, former Judge and President of the ICJ Stephen Schwebel; former US Supreme Court Justice Sandra Day O'Connor, former Judge of the US Court of Appeals for the District of Columbia and of the ICTY Patricia Wald; and former Legal Adviser to the Department of State during the George W. Bush Administration, William Howard Taft IV. The Task Force issued its Final Report in 2010, and, among other topics, considered the US Government's criticisms of the scope of the Court's jurisdiction. Recall our discussion of universal and territorial jurisdiction in Chapter 13, and consider the following analysis in the ASIL Task Force's Final Report:

> The traditional international law rule is that a treaty "does not create either obligations or rights for a third State without its consent." (Vienna Convention on the Law of Treaties art. 34) As a technical matter, it should be observed that the ICC, as a criminal court, claims jurisdiction over individuals, not States. Thus, the Rome Statute, in establishing jurisdiction over nationals of non-Parties, does not bind the non-party State....
>
> ...
>
> The concern has been raised that, on "hearing cases in the official-acts category, [the ICC's] function will resemble less that of a municipal criminal court than that of an international court for the adjudication of interstate legal disputes," and thus the traditional treaty-based ban on non-consensual jurisdiction applies, if a State does not consent to jurisdiction over its nationals. The Task Force does not subscribe to this contention, which blurs the distinction between the State and its nationals. The Task Force agrees with the Nuremberg Tribunal's conclusion fifty years ago that "[c]rimes against international law are committed by men, not by abstract entities, and only by punishing individuals who commit such crimes can the provisions of international law be enforced."
>
> The Rome Statute encompasses crimes already proscribed by international treaty or customary law and most of these can be prosecuted under applicable national laws and/or the principle of territorial or treaty-based jurisdiction in any national court. And, as the United States is party to most of those treaties, U.S. nationals are already subject to the prohibitions and the possibility of extra-territorial prosecution for crimes over which the ICC has jurisdiction. In the exercise of its jurisdiction, the ICC does not rely on universal jurisdiction but the consent of either the State on whose territory the crime occurred or the State of nationality of the accused, unless the situation is referred by the Security Council.
>
> ...
>
> It is, however, contended that exercise of jurisdiction by a national court is different from having a State's national turned over to an international institution, the ICC, in which it chose not to participate.[17] The issue is 'whether the international community may exercise jurisdiction in lieu of the territorial State.' Yet this issue is not new. At Nuremberg, such international jurisdiction was accepted, recognizing that States had 'done together what any one of them might have done singly'.[18] For those who remain concerned about ICC jurisdiction over third-party

[17] Ruth Wedgwood, 'The Irresolution of Rome', 64 L.aw & Contemp. Probs. 193, 199 (2001) (pointing out that there is "no ordinary precedent for delegating national criminal jurisdiction to another tribunal, international or national, without consent of the affected states, except in the aftermath of international belligerency"). See also David Scheffer, Ambassador-at-Large for War Crimes Issues, U.S. Department of State, 'Deterrence of War Crimes in the 21st Century', Speech at the Twelfth Annual U.S. Pacific Command, International Military Operations and Law Conference, Honolulu, HI (Feb. 23, 1999) (asserting that it contravened "fundamental principles of treaty law" for a treaty to provide a basis for jurisdiction with respect to nationals of States that are not party to that treaty), available at http://www.iccnow.org/documents/USScheffer23Feb99.pdf. [Eds.: Notably, Wedgwood served as a member of the ASIL Task Force.]

[18] [International Military Tribunal, Nuremberg 1946.] See also Michael Scharf, 'The ICC's Jurisdiction Over the Nationals of Non-party States: A Critique of the U.S. Position', 64 Law & Contemp. Probs. 67 (2001), at 103–111 (discussing the precedents of Nuremberg and the International Criminal Tribunals of the Former Yugoslavia and Rwanda). 'States may choose to combine their jurisdictions under the universality principle and vest this combined jurisdiction in an international tribunal. The Nuremberg International Military Tribunal may be said to have derived its jurisdiction from such a combination of national jurisdiction of the States parties to the London Agreement setting

nationals, the complementarity principle is intended to protect affected sovereign interests. To address doubt on this point, it is also important to note that under the Rome Statute, the exercise of complementarity can be undertaken by any State whose nationals are involved — not just the State where the arrest was effected. Thus, if the national of a non-party State were arrested abroad, the non-party State could offer to investigate and prosecute the matter itself. A *bona fide* investigation and prosecutorial decision by the State of nationality would satisfy the test of complementarity and preclude ICC prosecution. In light of these considerations, the Task Force does not consider the ICC's jurisdiction over nationals of non-party States to be in conflict with principles of international law.

QUESTIONS

1. Is the ASIL Task Force correct that the US Government's criticism erroneously 'blurs the distinction' between acts of individual officials and the sovereign state? In answering that question, consider the potential relevance of the UK House of Lords decision in *Jones v. Saudi Arabia*, p. 1196, *supra*. In *Jones*, the court ruled that foreign officials could not be subject to civil suit because adjudication of the dispute would necessarily impugn the state. The court's reasoning was based, in part, on the claim that a state would be liable for actions of its officials under the international law of state responsibility. Does the *Jones* ruling provide important support for the US Government's position? Or, is the *Jones* reasoning itself flawed, and thus evinces further errors in the US position?

2. Is the Task Force correct to rely on the IMT ruling and on the Independent Commission of Experts for the former Yugoslavia (n. 18)? How well do the statements by those sources correspond to the jurisdictional issue concerning the ICC? Review the opening paragraphs of the IMT Opinion, pp. 123–4, *supra*, which provides the context for the statement excerpted by the Task Force. The IMT therein predicated its jurisdiction on the prerogative of belligerents to establish a court in occupied territory. It stated: 'The making of the Charter was the exercise of the sovereign legislative power by the countries to which the German Reich unconditionally surrendered; and the undoubted right of these countries to legislate for the occupied territories has been recognized by the civilized world.' And consider whether the quoted text from the Independent Commission of Experts employs a contestable theory of universal jurisdiction. Even if these two sources do not provide strong or direct support, is the Task Force nevertheless correct in its ultimate conclusions?

ADDITIONAL READING

N. N. Jurdi, *The International Criminal Court and National Courts: A Contentious Relationship* (2011); W. Schabas, *An Introduction to the International Criminal Court*

up that Tribunal'. Interim Report of the Independent Commission of Experts [for the former Yugoslavia] Established Pursuant to Security Council Resolution 780 (1992), P 73, U.N. Doc. S/25274 (1993), cited in Scharf, supra, at 105.

(4th edn. 2011); Kevin Jon Heller, 'A Sentence-Based Theory of Complementarity', 53 Harv. Int'l. L.J. (2012); C. C. Jalloh, D. Akande & M. du Plessis, 'Assessing the African Union Concerns about Article 16 of the Rome Statute of the International Criminal Court', 4 African J. L. Stud. 5 (2011); W. Schabas, *The International Criminal Court: A Commentary on the Rome Statute* (2010); P. Akhavan, 'Self-Referrals Before the International Criminal Court: Are States the Villains or the Victims of Atrocities?', 21 Crim. L. Forum (2010); B. Simmons & A. Danner, 'Credible Commitments and the International Criminal Court', 64 Int'l. Org. 225 (2010); O. Fiss, 'Within Reach of the State: Prosecuting Atrocities in Africa', 31 H. R. Qtly. 59 (2009); O. Triffterer (ed.), *Commentary on the Rome Statute of the International Criminal Court: Observers' Notes, Article by Article* (2nd edn. 2008); D. Scheffer, 'The United States and the International Criminal Court', 93 Am. J. Int'l. L. 12 (1999); M. Arsanjani, 'The Rome Statute of the International Criminal Court', 93 Am. J. Int'l. L. 22 (1999); D. Robinson, 'Defining "Crimes against Humanity" at the Rome Conference', 93 Am. J. Int'l. L. 43 (1999); C. Kress, '"Self-Referrals" and "Waivers of Complementarity"', 2 J. Int'l. Crim. J. 944 (2004); A. M. Danner, 'Enhancing the Legitimacy and Accountability of Prosecutorial Discretion at the International Criminal Court', 97 Am. J. Int'l. L. 510 (2003); J. Goldsmith, 'The Self-Defeating International Criminal Court', 70 U. Chi. L. Rev. 89 (2003); A. Cassese, P. Gaeta & J. R. W. D. Jones (eds.), *The Rome Statute of the International Criminal Court: A Commentary* (2002); M. Cherif Bassiouni, *The Statute of the International Criminal Court: A Documentary History* (1998); Roy Lee (ed.), *The International Criminal Court: The Making of the Rome Statute* (1999).

C. HYBRID TRIBUNALS: THE CASE OF SIERRA LEONE

Since the establishment of the ad hoc tribunals for the former Yugoslavia and Rwanda and the finalization of the Rome Statute, 'hybrid tribunals' — institutions whose structure is part international, part national — have been created to prosecute human rights and humanitarian law violations in Sierra Leone, East Timor, Kosovo and Cambodia. The first hybrid tribunal was the Special Court for Sierra Leone. That tribunal has been heralded as 'the model' for similar institutions. Its record of successes and failures thus carries special weight.

In the 1990s, Sierra Leone was ravaged by a civil war that claimed over 75,000 lives and displaced a third of the population. In mid 1999, the national government and the Revolutionary United Front (RUF) rebel group negotiated a comprehensive peace agreement at Lomé, Togo. The Lomé Peace Agreement mandated the establishment of a Truth and Reconciliation Commission. However, it did not effectively resolve all outstanding issues of accountability. In June 2000, the President of Sierra Leone asked the UN Secretary-General for assistance in prosecuting individuals who perpetrated atrocities during the civil war. In response, the Security Council authorized the Secretary-General to negotiate an agreement between the UN and the Government of Sierra Leone to establish a criminal tribunal. The subsequent agreement, signed in 2002, created the legal framework for the Special Court for Sierra Leone. The Special Court is notably located in the country in which the crimes were committed, and seated in the capital Freetown. The Court is composed of international and domestic judges, prosecutors and administrative staff. The jurisdiction of the Court includes international and domestic crimes. These and other features are reflected in the following provisions.

STATUTE OF THE SPECIAL COURT FOR SIERRA LEONE

Article 1: Competence of the Special Court

1. The Special Court shall, except as provided in subparagraph (2), have the power to prosecute persons who bear the greatest responsibility for serious violations of international humanitarian law and Sierra Leonean law...

2. Any transgressions by peacekeepers and related personnel present in Sierra Leone pursuant to the Status of Mission Agreement in force between the United Nations and the Government of Sierra Leone or agreements between Sierra Leone and other Governments or regional organizations, or, in the absence of such agreement, provided that the peacekeeping operations were undertaken with the consent of the Government of Sierra Leone, shall be within the primary jurisdiction of the sending State....

Article 2: Crimes against humanity...

Article 3: Violations of Article 3 common to the Geneva Conventions and of Additional Protocol II...

Article 4: Other serious violations of international humanitarian law

The Special Court shall have the power to prosecute persons who committed the following serious violations of international humanitarian law:

a. Intentionally directing attacks against the civilian population as such or against individual civilians not taking direct part in hostilities;

...

c. Conscripting or enlisting children under the age of 15 years into armed forces or groups or using them to participate actively in hostilities.

Article 5: Crimes under Sierra Leonean law

The Special Court shall have the power to prosecute persons who have committed the following crimes under Sierra Leonean law:

a. Offences relating to the abuse of girls under the Prevention of Cruelty to Children Act...

b. Offences relating to the wanton destruction of property under the Malicious Damage Act, 1861:
   i. Setting fire to dwelling — houses, any person being therein...;
   ii. Setting fire to public buildings...;
   iii. Setting fire to other buildings...

...

Article 12: Composition of the Chambers

1. The Chambers shall be composed of not less than eight (8) or more than eleven (11) independent judges, who shall serve as follows:

a. Three judges shall serve in the Trial Chamber, of whom one shall be a judge appointed by the Government of Sierra Leone, and two judges appointed by the Secretary-General of the United Nations (hereinafter "the Secretary-General").
b. Five judges shall serve in the Appeals Chamber, of whom two shall be judges appointed by the Government of Sierra Leone, and three judges appointed by the Secretary-General....

Article 13: Qualification and appointment of judges

1. The judges shall be persons of high moral character, impartiality and integrity who possess the qualifications required in their respective countries for appointment to the highest judicial offices. They shall be independent in the performance of their functions, and shall not accept or seek instructions from any Government or any other source...

...

3. The judges shall be appointed for a three-year period and shall be eligible for reappointment....

Article 15: The Prosecutor

1. ...The Prosecutor shall act independently as a separate organ of the Special Court. He or she shall not seek or receive instructions from any Government or from any other source.

2. The Office of the Prosecutor shall have the power to question suspects, victims and witnesses, to collect evidence and to conduct on-site investigations. In carrying out these tasks, the Prosecutor shall, as appropriate, be assisted by the Sierra Leonean authorities concerned.

3. The Prosecutor shall be appointed by the Secretary-General for a three-year term and shall be eligible for re-appointment....

4. The Prosecutor shall be assisted by a Sierra Leonean Deputy Prosecutor, and by such other Sierra Leonean and international staff as may be required to perform the functions assigned to him or her effectively and efficiently. Given the nature of the crimes committed and the particular sensitivities of girls, young women and children victims of rape, sexual assault, abduction and slavery of all kinds, due consideration should be given in the appointment of staff to the employment of

prosecutors and investigators experienced in gender-related crimes and juvenile justice.

. . .

Article 16: The Registry

1. The Registry shall be responsible for the administration and servicing of the Special Court.

3. The Registrar shall be appointed by the Secretary-General after consultation with the President of the Special Court and shall be a staff member of the United Nations. He or she shall serve for a three-year term and be eligible for reappointment.

4. The Registrar shall set up a Victims and Witnesses Unit within the Registry. . . .

. . .

Article 20: Appellate proceedings

. . .

3. The judges of the Appeals Chamber of the Special Court shall be guided by the decisions of the Appeals Chamber of the International Tribunals for the former Yugoslavia and for Rwanda. In the interpretation and application of the laws of Sierra Leone, they shall be guided by the decisions of the Supreme Court of Sierra Leone.

. . .

Article 22: Enforcement of sentences

1. Imprisonment shall be served in Sierra Leone. If circumstances so require, imprisonment may also be served in any of the States which have concluded with the International Criminal Tribunal for Rwanda or the International Criminal Tribunal for the former Yugoslavia an agreement for the enforcement of sentences, and which have indicated to the Registrar of the Special Court their willingness to accept convicted persons. The Special Court may conclude similar agreements for the enforcement of sentences with other States.

2. Conditions of imprisonment, whether in Sierra Leone or in a third State, shall be governed by the law of the State of enforcement subject to the supervision of the Special Court. . . .

Article 23: Pardon or commutation of sentences

If, pursuant to the applicable law of the State in which the convicted person is imprisoned, he or she is eligible for pardon or commutation of sentence, the State concerned shall notify the Special Court accordingly. There shall only be pardon or commutation of sentence if the President of the Special Court, in consultation with the judges, so decides on the basis of the interests of justice and the general principles of law. . . .

INTERNATIONAL CENTER FOR TRANSITIONAL JUSTICE, THE SPECIAL COURT FOR SIERRA LEONE: THE FIRST EIGHTEEN MONTHS

(Mar. 2004)

...

The Special Court for Sierra Leone is a tribunal established to try [individuals] for serious violations of international humanitarian law and certain provisions of Sierra Leonean domestic law since November 30, 1996.[19] ... From its outset, the jurisdiction of the Special Court was restricted to "those who bear the greatest responsibility." Clearly, this was intended to prevent the Special Court from expanding in size and expense as a result of an unwieldy prosecutorial policy, as some diplomats had characterized the ICTY and ICTR....

...

Another unique element of prosecutorial strategy in Sierra Leone has been the use of public statements on prosecutorial strategy to reassure the public. For example, the Prosecutor... declar[ed] that he did not intend to indict anyone for crimes committed while under the age of 18. He also declared that he would not seek information from the TRC. It is unusual for a Prosecutor to declare his prosecutorial plans or policies in advance, but on both these issues, his announcements have been positively received.

...Especially during the Court's start-up period, most of the key posts in the Office of the Prosecutor were filled by U.S. nationals, which attracted some criticism. By April 2003, 25 percent of the prosecutorial staff comprised Americans, including the Chiefs of Investigations, Prosecutions, and Operations (although two of these posts have been turned over to non-Americans).... As a consequence... some have perceived the Special Court as under undue American influence.

Comparing the Special Court to the Ad Hoc Tribunals

...Both [the ICTY and ICTR] tribunals have been criticized for their slow pace, prosecution strategies, high operational costs, and lack of connection to the societies where crimes were committed. This report mainly uses the ICTR as the reference point against which the Court is assessed.

A. An On-Site Court

The first major difference between the Special Court and the ICTR is geography. The ICTR is located 600 miles from where the crimes were committed. This has contributed to one of the major criticisms against the two ad hoc tribunals: their lack of connection to the people in the countries that suffered the violence.

[19] This limitation on the temporal jurisdiction of the war, based on the date of the failed Abidjan Accord, was intended to keep the budget down in comparison to the other international criminal tribunals.

Ten years after it began to function and seven years after it started trials, the ICTR is criticized as having very little impact on Rwanda's citizens and judiciary. According to some accounts, Rwandans have no sense of ownership of the ICTR and do not necessarily perceive the tribunal to be for them. This is exacerbated by the fact that many ICTR staff members have not even visited Rwanda, with the exception of those who have worked for the Office of the Prosecutor on investigations.

Against this background, there was strong pressure for the Special Court for Sierra Leone to be set up in Freetown, instead of in a neighboring country. In addition, having the Court on site allows for greater analysis of its impact on the Sierra Leonean people and judiciary.

From early on, the Court has demonstrated considerable concern about how it is perceived and understood in Sierra Leone. Between September 2002 and February 2003, the Chief Prosecutor and the Registrar held a series of "town hall meetings" in all 12 districts to explain the Court's work to the population in the provinces and receive feedback. The ad hoc tribunals did not do similar outreach at the outset (although each eventually established such a program).

By April 2003, the Registry had put into place an Outreach Unit that would eventually comprise 17 people, with small offices spread throughout the country in a District Grassroots Network. Through the Network, the Outreach Unit has built the capacity to get information to and from every district in the country within a 36-hour period, despite lack of phone coverage and poor road infrastructure. By September 2003, the Outreach Unit had conducted a number of activities — including targeted outreach among the military and a booklet explaining the Court to schoolchildren — and had developed detailed plans for the future, including the creation of a forum to interface between civil society and the Court (Special Court Interactive Forum). The Special Court has prioritized an outreach policy as part of its regular budget. . . .

Security is the main hazard of housing the Court inside Sierra Leone; the Special Court has faced challenges that the ICTR and ICTY have been spared. Hinga Norman's case [Minister of Internal Affairs and former leader of pro-government militia groups] is the most significant demonstration. . . . [S]everal unprecedented measures were taken following Norman's arrest, such as holding his initial appearance in closed session and seeking to negotiate his detention outside of the country.[20] A balance will have to be struck between security measures and the public nature of the trial (and the Court's ability to have an impact on public debate).

B. A Hybrid Court

A key difference between the Special Court and the ICTR is that the Special Court has both national and international staff members in all organs of the Court,

[20] Immediately after his arrest, authorities explored the option of flying Hinga Norman to The Hague (or Arusha), where he would be detained until the start of his trial, but it proved difficult to obtain the requisite permission from the various domestic authorities and ICTY/ICTR.

including the Chambers. By April 2003, 23 percent of the Court's professional staff members were Sierra Leoneans, and 56 percent of all employees were nationals. Even though internationals hold most key decision-making positions, the influence of Sierra Leonean staff within the structure is significant. There is a wide consensus that the presence and expertise of Sierra Leoneans has made the process more relevant and efficient....

Incorporating nationals helps the Court to carry out its work in an efficient manner that is sensitive to the country's conditions and to maintain its focus and sense of mandate. Furthermore, a major risk in tipping the balance of a hybrid composition in favor of internationals is that the institution will be seen as detached and will have less legitimacy among Sierra Leoneans. However, Sierra Leonean views on this inevitably vary, and while Freetown residents have often urged more inclusion of Sierra Leoneans at senior levels, many of those outside Freetown distrust the Freetown "elites" and prefer to have internationals in key positions.

Whether most Sierra Leoneans perceive the Special Court as mainly international or domestic is still open to debate....

...Article 5 of the Statute includes Sierra Leonean domestic legal provisions on the abuse of girls and wanton destruction of property. However, to date none of the indictments encompasses charges of domestic crimes....

C. A Lower Budget and Voluntary Contributions

Another critical difference between the ad hoc tribunals and the Special Court lies in the latter's financial structure and management. The Special Court is funded from voluntary contributions, rather than the regular budget of the UN. More than 30 countries have contributed to the Special Court, although four of them (Canada, the Netherlands, the United Kingdom, and the United States) provided two-thirds of the Court's first-year budget. This has two consequences: the budget is tight overall, and these few states theoretically have great influence, although the Registrar has said that he has not experienced any interference.... Allowing the Court to be entirely reliant on donations from a small number of states makes it vulnerable and has potentially negative implications for its independence (a matter that defense counsel has already raised)....

D. State Cooperation

International tribunals depend on state cooperation in matters of enforcement, such as arrest and transfer of suspects, detention, witness protection, and so forth. The ICTY and ICTR have a Chapter VII mandate by virtue of being created pursuant to a UN Security Council Resolution under that Chapter, which makes it mandatory for all UN member states to cooperate. The Special Court for Sierra Leone was not created under a Chapter VII resolution but by an Agreement between Sierra Leone and the UN, and to date it has been at a disadvantage.... As to the arrest of suspects, when the arrests were first announced, the only accused not in Sierra Leone were thought to be in Liberia, a country then at war whose own head of state was indicted by the Special Court. It is worth noting, however, that once the Court failed to attain [Liberian head of state Charles] Taylor's arrest in Ghana, the

President wrote to the Secretary-General on June 10, 2003, requesting Chapter VII powers for the Court, but with no result.

…

The other ad hoc tribunals also may have been more inclined to keep Hinga Norman in detention if the Special Court had a similar mandate and powers.

A duty to cooperate would also assist in concluding agreements with states on the enforcement of sentences…

…

NANCY KAYMAR STAFFORD, A MODEL WAR CRIMES COURT: SIERRA LEONE

10 ILSA J. Int'l. & Comp. L. 117 (2003)

…Pierre Bourin, Justice of the Court, stated, "[t]he main objective of the court is to reestablish the rule of law in this country and then show to the people of Sierra Leone that justice can be done in this country." The judicial system has been decimated by 10 years of war….

…

…[T]he local population will have greater access to the proceedings of the Special Court if they are local….The entire population of Sierra Leone is a victim of the war. If the Special Court is not assisting in the healing of the nation, the people of Sierra Leone are present to "judge" the proceedings and ensure the Special Court does not deviate from its mandate or get bogged down in political issues or mismanagement….

…

…The most effective way for the people to reconcile with the past and start building a future is to see justice being done. Having the Special Court located in a third country deprives the local communities — the victims — of being a part of the judicial process….Every war is fought differently. Therefore "cookie cutter" justice is not always the best answer….Just because future atrocities do not fit neatly within the traditional mold of what constitutes a war crime, does not mean that the crimes should not be punished by tribunals….Future hybrid courts would be able to use the relevant aspects of their domestic laws to ensure the prosecutions cover all atrocities that were committed during their particular conflict….Sierra Leone is located in a hot bed of civil unrest. Liberia, Guinea, Burkina Faso and other countries in Western Africa have had tumultuous pasts. Obtaining sustained peace and the return to the rule of law in Sierra Leone would set an exceptional example for both the people and the governments of other West African nations….

There is a certain amount of concern that if the rebel commanders are tried for their crimes, their supporters may be angered and retaliate sending the country back into war….[T]he international community is keeping a close eye on Sierra Leone particularly since this is the first time post World War II, that a war crimes tribunal is being held in the country where the crimes were committed.... [T]his is an issue related to prosecution and not the structure of the hybrid court system. Presumably retaliation, if it were to occur, would be planned regardless of where the perpetrators were prosecuted....

The eight judges for the Special Court were sworn in on December 2, 2002. Five, from varying countries outside Sierra Leone, were appointed by the UN Secretary General and three by the Sierra Leone government. Some claim that the inclusion of judges from Sierra Leone renders the proceedings unfair. Issa Sesay, interim Chairperson of the RUF stated, "[i]f the Court is to be neutral then no Sierra Leonean judge should be included because they may have their prejudices."

...International judges from Britain, Canada, Austria, Nigeria, Gambia and Cameroon will be impartial and provide the necessary impediment to any prejudices the local judges may have. At the same time, the international judges will be reaffirming the rule of law and helping the local judges to reestablish a working judicial system in the country.

...International judges represent the majority in both chambers and therefore will be able to safeguard against any issues of impartiality. Significantly, public judgments subject to external scrutiny, will serve as an additional check on impartiality.

NOTE

The Special Court for Sierra Leone is expected to complete its mandate with the end of the Charles Taylor appeal process. The record of the Special Court includes several achievements, but also falls short of many expectations. A publication by the International Center for Transitional Justice (ICTJ), issued more than five years after the one excerpted above, acknowledged both sides of the record. The successes, according to the more recent report, include:

- Eight of those most responsible for the suffering of the Sierra Leonean people are now behind bars, with sentences ranging from 15 to 52 years.
- Liberian President Charles Taylor was indicted and now stands trial before the Court on 11 counts of war crimes, crimes against humanity and violations of international law.
- The Court established the legal precedent that the reasons for fighting are immaterial in determining where crimes against humanity have been committed; it ruled that members of the Civil Defence Forces — considered heroes by many — could not use a 'just cause' defence as a mitigating sentencing factor.
- The Court was the first international tribunal to convict people for crimes relating to the conscription and recruitment of children younger than 15 into hostile forces.
- Sexual conscriptions, or forced marriages, were also deemed a separate crime against humanity.

- With Taylor's indictment, the Court reaffirmed an important norm of dismissing head of state immunity for those who commit crimes against humanity.[21]

The report also acknowledges some of the concerns that have also been raised by many observers of the Court. One of the major concerns is the lack of a legacy effect. The question is whether the tribunal has conducted sufficient outreach to the citizenry or capacity-building of national and local institutions. The ICTJ report states:

> Through its legacy project, the court recently has attempted to provide capacity building for various institutions that promote accountability. But these initiatives came too late and seemed an afterthought, rather than a carefully planned policy priority. In addition, [u]ntil a few years ago, Sierra Leoneans only served in senior capacity on the defense team and no Sierra Leonean served in judicial management positions in the prosecution and registry, thus squandering the opportunity of local staff to develop and transfer valuable experience to the domestic justice sector. Similarly, the court's statute was carefully drafted to incorporate both national and international laws, but most of the charges proffered are pursuant to international law only, thus limiting the potential for domestic law reform'.

Significant advances were made in senior leadership positions, primarily when the Court began winding to a close.

Notably, with respect to the Special Court's relationship to national courts, political scientist Ellen Stensrud study concludes that this is a potential risk of the form of hybrid tribunals. Her research suggests that locating such tribunals within a country raises the expectations of the citizenry and introduces questions of legitimacy among the local population. She explains: 'Many of the problems of the mixed courts are inherent in the rationale of the model: it is employed in societies with dysfunctional judiciaries. Moreover, policymakers must understand the expectations these courts inevitably raise nationally, when an extremely expensive international institution is located *in situ*'; '[O]ther legitimacy problems have become apparent, that may potentially be as problematic as the ones faced by the purely international tribunals. In Sierra Leone, the mixed court has been criticized for having too little effect on the local judiciary. In Cambodia, on the other hand, the strong links to the national judiciary undermine trust in the mixed court'; 'based on the expectations expressed by civil society actors in Sierra Leone and Cambodia, ... the courts must fulfill certain forward-looking goals [which includes "a legacy for the national judiciary"] in order to be legitimate locally.' In short, the degree to which the Special Court failed to bolster the national judiciary is not simply a lost opportunity. It also

[21] M. Suma (Director of the Sierra Leone Court Monitoring Programme), 'The Charles Taylor Trial and Legacy of the Special Court for Sierra Leone', International Center for Transitional Justice (Sept. 2009).

compromises the legitimacy and thus the power of the Special Court to effectuate change among the national population.[22]

QUESTIONS

1. As the readings above suggest, the location of the Special Court in Freetown is considered a major advance in the development of international criminal tribunals. Yet in 2006 the Security Council, acting under Chapter VII, authorized the transfer of Charles Taylor to The Hague for trial by a 'special chamber' of the Special Court. Some consider this decision a major step backwards. Consider the following remarks by Sierra Leone's former Ambassador (1996–2002) to the United States:

> Mr. Taylor's forthcoming war crimes trial should not be transferred to The Hague, as Liberia's president and the court itself have requested.
>
> Such a transfer would defeat a principal purpose behind the establishment of the special court in Sierra Leone — namely, to teach Africans, firsthand and in their own countries, the fundamentals of justice and to drive home the democratic principle that no one is above the law. The special court has the potential to help raise West Africa's standards for accountability, transparency, fairness and the humane treatment of defendants.
>
> In countries where might makes right, demonstrating the proper administration of justice can be an unbeatable nation-building tool. This is a key part of what the special court was set up to do and has done quite well in Sierra Leone since it commenced operations in late 2002.
>
> ...
>
> True, fears that Mr. Taylor's trial in Freetown could cause instability in Sierra Leone, Liberia and elsewhere in the region have substantial merit....
>
> But the solution is not to rob Africans of the experience of seeing real justice administered to their most powerful tormentor. Potential instability should be addressed not by pandering to thuggish elements but by tightening security in both Sierra Leone and Liberia, under a robust United Nations peacemaking mandate.[23]

2. The purported virtues of the Special Court for Sierra Leone include the direct interactions between the OTP and the public. The ICTJ report refers to such interactions as 'another unique element of prosecutorial strategy in Sierra Leone'. These relationships, for example, are thought to make the Prosecutor more responsive to the people of Sierra Leone. Are these relationships and the expectations placed on the Prosecutor completely desirable? What are the costs and benefits of this arrangement?

3. Is it appropriate for a quasi-international institution to prosecute domestic crimes? Why should the Special Court have jurisdiction over such offences?

[22] Ellen Emilie Stensrud, 'New Dilemmas in Transitional Justice: Lessons from the Mixed Courts in Sierra Leone and Cambodia', 46 J. Peace Res. (2009), at 5–15 (Stensrud also suggests that 'on-the-ground legitimacy is a minimum criterion for positive learning effects').

[23] J. E. Leigh, Op-Ed, 'Bringing it all Back Home', *New York Times*, 17 Apr. 2006.

4. Nancy Stafford writes about the hybrid tribunal: 'International judges... will be impartial and provide the necessary impediment to any prejudices the local judges may have.' Doesn't the bias of even a single judge taint the entire judicial proceeding? Recall that in *İncal v. Turkey*, p. 470, *supra*, the presence of a single military judge impugned the fairness of that court system. The influence of the nonmilitary judges on their military colleague was not considered material. As another example, consider that the failure of one judge to recuse himself in *Ex parte Pinochet* required the UK House of Lords to rehear that case. Is the hybrid model for criminal tribunals in Sierra Leone distinguishable from these other situations? Do you agree with Stafford's reasoning?

D. ALTERNATIVE JUSTICE SYSTEMS: RWANDA'S GACACA COURTS

In addition to the ICTR, the Rwandan Government undertook a separate national effort to prosecute crimes related to the 1994 genocide. Several years after the genocide, more than 100,000 Rwandese were awaiting trial in national court, many of them since 1995. These individuals were held in severely overcrowded and abject detention conditions. Between 1996 and 2001, the national court system processed approximately 5,000 individual cases. At that rate, it would have taken several decades to clear the backlog of individuals awaiting trial.

By 2000, the Rwandan Government formulated a plan to transfer the majority of genocide cases to a new adjudicative system known as 'gacaca' courts. The concept of gacaca courts is borrowed from a traditional practice of community-based dispute resolution. The gacaca (roughly translated as 'grass') courts were intended to provide a participatory form of justice in which the general populace would participate. Local communities elected judges to sit on panels, and the hearings required a quorum of community members to be present. The stated purpose of this system was to achieve truth, accountability and reconciliation. The government formally launched the gacaca system in 2002 and introduced some legislative modifications in subsequent years. The implementing legislation established over 12,000 gacaca courts across the country. In 2005, gacaca courts began delivering their first judgments (hours after some of the trials began). In 2008, gacaca courts began to hear cases involving defendants accused of more significant crimes such as sexual violence and responsibility of local leaders of the genocide. Almost all the gacaca proceedings had officially drawn to a close by 2012.

The law classifies offenders into three broad categories. Category One includes planners, organizers, supervisors and leaders of the genocide or crimes against humanity as well as accomplices, and individuals who allegedly committed, or were accomplices in, torture, 'rape or acts of torture against sexual organs', particularly brutal or notorious killings or 'dehumanizing acts on the dead body'. Category Two includes perpetrators or accomplices of intentional homicides, serious assaults causing death or serious assaults without intending to cause death. Category Three includes perpetrators of property crimes. Gacaca courts have responsibility, in a pre-trial process, for classifying defendants according to these three groups. Category Two and Three defendants were then tried by gacaca courts. Category One defendants were then to be tried by regular national courts.

An official roster listed the names of all accused individuals, and the law provided incentives for confessions. It involved a complex scheme allowing individuals who confess to commute their sentences. For example, Category One offences carried a sentence of death or life imprisonment. Individuals who confessed to Category One offences received a prison sentence of 25–30 years. Individuals who confessed to Category One offences before being listed on the roster were eligible for partial commutation of sentence to community service. Category Two offences involving intentional homicides or serious assaults causing death carried a prison sentence of 25–30 years. Individuals who confessed to these offences after being listed on the roster received a prison sentence of 12–15 years with half of their sentence commuted to community service. Incentives related to other offences were similarly structured.

In practice, the process of making a confession frequently included the identification of additional suspects. The first wave of confessions resulted in the incrimination of thousands of additional individuals. By the end of the nationwide gacaca process, these courts had reportedly concluded over 1.2 million cases (one-eighth of the country's population).

A separate criticism of the law involved the concern that innocent individuals would be encouraged to confess to crimes they did not commit especially if their time already served in pre-trial detention satisfied half of the maximum prison penalty (such that the remaining time would be spent in community service). In addition to those concerns, consider the procedural fairness of trials before gacaca courts in light of the following material.

ORGANIC LAW NO 16/2004 OF 2004 ESTABLISHING THE ORGANIZATION, COMPETENCE AND FUNCTIONING OF GACACA COURTS CHARGED WITH PROSECUTING AND TRYING THE PERPETRATORS OF THE CRIME OF GENOCIDE AND OTHER CRIMES AGAINST HUMANITY, COMMITTED BETWEEN OCTOBER 1, 1990 AND DECEMBER 31, 1994

Article 29

Every Rwandan citizen has the duty to participate in the Gacaca courts activities.

Any person who omits or refuses to testify on what he or she has seen or on what he or [she] knows, as well as the one who makes a slanderous denunciation, shall be prosecuted by the Gacaca Court which makes the statement of it. He or she incurs a prison sentence from three (3) months to six (6) months. In case of repeat offence, the defendant may incur a prison sentence from six months (6) to one (1) year.

Is considered as refusing to testify on what he or she has seen or knows, any person who apparently knew something on a given matter denounced by others in his or her presence, without expressing his or her own opinion.

Is considered as refusing to testify:

1. Anyone who, once summoned to testify before the Court after knowing that he or she is holder of a testimony, refuses to declare by avoiding to speak or deliberately evading the question put to him or her;
2. Anyone who, once summoned by the Court and does not appear deliberately without reasons, avoiding to be questioned in as much as the summons is clearly notified to him or her.

Is considered as a perjurer, anyone who gives a testimony ascertaining that he or she is telling only the truth and holds evidences for that, takes an oath and signs it; but later on it appears to be false and done on purpose.

The perjury is prosecuted during the very hearing of the matter in which the prosecuted person has given the testimony, if it is discovered that the person did it on purpose.

Article 33

The General Assembly of the Gacaca Court of the Cell exercises the following attributions:

1. Electing Seat members of the Gacaca Court of the Cell and their deputies;
2. attending the activities of the Gacaca Court of the Cell for the nonmembers of the seat and take the floor only upon request;
3. assisting the Seat of the Gacaca Court in the establishment of a list of persons
   a. who resides in the Cell;
   b. who resided in the Cell before the genocide, locations they kept shifting to and routes they took;
   c. killed in their Cell of residence;
   d. killed outside their Cell of residence;
   e. killed in the Cell while they were not residing in it;
   f. victimized and their damaged property;
   g. alleged authors of the offences referred to in this organic law.
4. presenting evidences or testimonies on all persons suspected of having committed the crime of genocide and on others who took part;
5. examining and adopting activity report established by the Gacaca Court.

All residents of the Cell shall tell the facts of events which took place, especially in their home villages and give evidence, denounce the authors and identify the victims.

Article 34

The Seat for the Gacaca Court of the Cell exercises the following attributions:

1. With the participation of the General Assembly, to make up a list of persons:
   a. who reside in the Cell;
   b. who were residing in the Cell before the genocide, locations where they kept shifting to and routes they took;
   c. killed in their Cell of residence;
   d. killed outside their Cell of residence;
   e. killed in the Cell while they were not residing in it;
   f. victimized and their damaged property;
   g. who took part in the offences referred to in this organic law.
2. To receive confessions, guilt plea, repentance and apologies from the person who participated in genocide;
3. to bring together the files forwarded by the Public Prosecution;
4. to receive evidences and testimonies and other information concerning how genocide was planned and put into execution;
5. to investigate testimonies;
6. to categorize the accused as per the provisions of this organic law;
7. to put on trial and judges cases for the accused whose crimes classify them in the third category;
8. to give a ruling on objection to Seat members for the Gacaca Court of the Cell;
9. to forward to the Gacaca Court of the Sector, the files of the defendants classified in the second category;
10. to forward to the Public Prosecution, the files for the defendants classified in the first category;
11. to elect members of the Coordination Committee.

A victim referred to in point 1.f is anybody killed, hunted to be killed but survived, suffered acts of torture against his or her sexual parts, suffered rape, injured or victim of any other form of harassment, plundered, and whose house and property were destroyed because of his or her ethnic background or opinion against the genocide ideology.

Article 38

As regards offences relating to rape or acts of torture against sexual parts, the victim chooses among the Seat members for the Gacaca Court of the Cell, on or more to whom she submits her complaint or does it in writing. In case of mistrust in the Seat members, she submits it to the organs of investigations or the Public Prosecution.

. . .

It is prohibited to publicly confess such an offence. No body is permitted to publicly sue another party. All formalities of the proceedings of the that offence shall be conducted in camera.

Article 39

Gacaca Courts have competences similar to those of ordinary courts, to try the accused persons, on the basis of testimonies against or for, and other evidences that may be provided.

They may in particular:

1. Summon any person to appear in a trial;
2. order and carry out a search of or to the defendant's. This search must, however, respect the defendant's private property and basic human rights;
3. take temporary protective measures against the property of those accused of genocide crimes;
4. pronounce sentences and order the convicted person to compensate;
5. order the withdrawal of the distrait for the acquitted person's property;
6. prosecute and punish troublemakers in the court;
7. summon, if necessary, the Public Prosecution to give explanatory information on files it has investigated on;
8. issue summons to the alleged authors of offences and order detention or release on parole, if necessary.

Article 53

For the implementation of this organic law, the accomplice is the person who has, by any means, provided assistance to commit offences with persons referred to in Article 51 of this organic law.

Article 54

Any person who has committed offences aimed at in Article one of this organic law has right to have recourse to the procedure of confessions, guilt plea, repentance and apologies.

Apologies shall be made publicly to the victims in case they are still alive and to the Rwandan Society.

To be accepted as confessions, guilt plea, repentance and apologies, the defendant must:

1. Give a detailed description of the confessed offence, how he or she carried it out and where, when he or she committed it, witnesses to the facts, persons victimized and where he or she threw their dead bodies and damage caused;
2. reveal the co-authors, accomplices and any other information useful to the exercise of the public action;
3. apologise for the offences that he or she has committed.

AMNESTY INTERNATIONAL, RWANDA: THE TROUBLED COURSE OF JUSTICE

(26 Apr. 2000), at http://www.amnesty.org/en/library/info/AFR47/010/2000/en

Amnesty International delegates who visited Rwanda in late 1999 received both positive and negative reactions to the proposals from Rwandese of various backgrounds. Many people expressed a general sense of hope and optimism for the proposals. However, some families of victims of the genocide expressed fears that the gacaca jurisdictions would result in excessively light sentences for those who may have committed terrible crimes. Some of the accused, on the other hand, viewed the proposals as a way of legitimizing popular retribution on those presumed to be guilty for the genocide. Both groups expressed fears that the gacaca jurisdictions would be used as a way of settling personal scores, rather than extracting the truth or delivering justice....

...

Right to legal defence

The draft law on the gacaca jurisdictions does not make any explicit reference to the right of the accused to have access to legal representation. In view of existing safeguards of this right in national and international law, the accused should automatically enjoy this right in the gacaca trials. However, several senior Rwandese government officials, including the Minister of Justice, have stated explicitly and publicly that the accused in the gacaca trials would not be allowed representation by a defence lawyer. This would result in a serious disadvantage for the accused, especially as the majority are likely to have little or no formal education, limited awareness of their rights or knowledge of how to defend themselves in a formal or semi-formal context. The question of the right of defendants to legal assistance in the pre-trial period has not been addressed either.

...

Concerns relating to competence, independence and impartiality

Amnesty International is seriously concerned about the lack of legal training of members of the gacaca jurisdictions. The individuals who would be asked to try the cases which come before the gacaca jurisdictions would be elected into this role by the local population. They would have no prior legal background or training, and yet will be expected to hand down judgments in extremely complex and sensitive cases, with sentences as heavy as life imprisonment.... Even if these individuals are conscientious and striving to act in good faith, it is likely that they will be subjected to considerable pressures both from the accused and the complainants.... Government authorities have indicated that they would receive some "basic" training and have appealed for international assistance for this task, but have stressed that the rules governing the gacaca trials must be kept simple.

...

The search for the truth

One of the main hopes pinned on the gacaca jurisdictions is that they will succeed in revealing the truth — in a manner which the ordinary courts fail to do — by holding hearings at the grassroots level and encouraging people to testify to events they witnessed in their own community. However, it will not be sufficient to instruct people to tell the truth. The search for the truth is extremely important but should not be undertaken at the expense of justice....

International obligations

If the gacaca jurisdictions are set up as outlined in the draft law, the trials would clearly fail to meet basic international standards for fair trial....

A primary guarantee of a fair trial is that decisions will be made by competent, independent and impartial courts. This is reflected in Article 14(1) of ICCPR as well as Article 7 of the African Charter. Principle 2 of the Basic Principles on the Independence of the Judiciary states that "the judiciary shall decide matters before them impartially, on the basis of facts and in accordance with the law, without any restrictions, improper influences, inducements, pressures, threats or interferences, direct or indirect, from any quarter or for any reason". Judges should have legal training and experience (Principle 10 of the Basic Principles states "Persons selected for judicial office shall be individuals of integrity and ability with appropriate training or qualifications in law") and should be impartial: they should not have any interest or stake in a particular case and should not have pre-formed opinions about it.

Among the minimum guarantees for a fair trial, Article 14(3) of the ICCPR includes the right to defend oneself through legal counsel and to be informed of such a right, and the right to examine and call witnesses.

REPUBLIC OF RWANDA, REPLY TO AMNESTY INTERNATIONAL'S REPORT 'RWANDA: THE TROUBLED COURSE OF JUSTICE'

(May 2000), at www.gov.rw/government/06_11_00news_ai.htm#X.%20GACACA

...The observations of the report are critical of the proposed structures. The report, however, does not attempt to offer any alternative to Gacaca. Neither does it offer any practical solutions to the shortcomings that it claims to see in our proposal. The authors of the report are content merely to list a catalogue of things they are unhappy about. We are compelled to reply in detail to the report's comments on Gacaca tribunals.

...

We resolved, in particular, to let the existing court structures handle the genocide cases. The courts in charge of hearing genocide cases have now been in operation for more than three years....In 1997, they were only able to judge 346 persons. In 1999, the number had risen to 1318. The number for the first quarter of 2000 is almost 600.

In any other country, the successful conduct of 1500 murder trials would be an extraordinary achievement. In Rwanda, this is far from satisfactory in light of the large number of persons awaiting trial. Our court system is overwhelmed. Supporting institutions such as the parquets and police cannot cope. Our prisons are overcrowded. Although the conditions of detention are far from satisfactory for many detainees, the cost of maintaining these prisons takes a disproportionate portion of our budget. Part of this budget could be put to better use financing social programs.

Defendants and complainants alike are equally frustrated by the slow pace of justice. The problem is not the classical system of justice per se. The problem is that the system was never designed or intended to deal with accountability for crimes of such mass violence...

...

The system will encourage confessions by offering incentives to defendants who cooperate. The number of detainees in our overcrowded prisons will be reduced by substituting part of the sentence of every prisoner with a requirement to perform community service. This will reduce government expenditure on prisons and the savings made can help finance desirable social services. Conditions for detainees who will remain in prison will improve dramatically as the number of inmates goes down.... The system will, we strongly believe, produce a climate that will enhance the process for reconciliation.

...

Legal Representation

Rwanda has only around 60 lawyers in private legal practice. On account of various reasons, the majority of these advocates have shown little willingness to defend genocide suspects. We acknowledge the right of genocide suspects to legal defence. However, there should be no question that victims of genocide too are entitled to justice.

A position to the effect that the people who committed genocide in this country should not be tried because we lack lawyers to represent them would be indefensible in light of the crimes that were committed during the genocide. When we were drafting the legislation on the prosecution of genocide suspects in 1996, we chose to adopt the compromise position that legal representation is a right, but the state would not assume responsibility to finance it. We did not have the personnel to provide legal representation for all genocide suspects appearing before ordinary courts. We are unable to provide lawyers to represent genocide suspects whose cases will go to Gacaca tribunals.

Even on the assumption that enough lawyers were available, there would still be problems of financing. Who would bear the cost? And why has such financing not been available for the on-going trials?

...

The task of providing legal representation is already difficult as it is when there are only 12 court chambers specialising in handling genocide cases. There will be something in the range of 10,000 Gacaca tribunals. It is difficult to see how one could conceivably raise enough lawyers to appear in 10,000 jurisdictions across the country...

...

Concerns Relating Competence, Independence and Impartiality

...

There is concern, for example, that judges in Gacaca tribunals will not have any prior legal experience or training. The report misses the whole point about Gacaca tribunals. There would have been no need to turn to Gacaca tribunals in the first place if we had people with the necessary legal background in sufficient numbers to work in our courts.

The report expresses the fear that judges in Gacaca tribunals will be subjected to considerable pressure from both the accused and the complainants, as well as from political authorities. As Amnesty International itself acknowledges in the report, even judges in ordinary courts are themselves not immune to pressure. In any event, we are of the opinion that such pressure is less likely in Gacaca jurisdictions because of the large number of judges involved and the more transparent methods of operation that Gacaca tribunals will use.

The Amnesty International report criticises plans to keep the rules of procedure governing Gacaca simple. One of the reasons why it has become necessary to transfer genocide cases to Gacaca tribunals is because ordinary courts are burdened by cumbersome procedures. There would be absolutely no point in establishing Gacaca tribunals if the intention is to transform them into replicas of ordinary courts which are unable to help us resolve the problem at hand.

...

International Obligations

...

We acknowledge that Gacaca jurisdictions are tribunals to which the international human rights instruments, to which Rwanda is a party, apply. We undertake to honour our obligations under the treaties in question.

...The draft law conforms to the provisions of the requirements of the International Covenant on Civil and Political Rights on all essential issues generally, and the rights to a fair and public hearing and a competent, independent and impartial tribunal in particular.

Whereas there may be certain basic international standards that all parties to human rights treaties must adhere to, international human rights law recognises that circumstances in state parties differ in many respects. That is why many treaties permit states to make their signing of certain treaties subject to some reservations. Opt-out provisions are also common. Indeed, the framers of the International Covenant on Civil and Political Rights recognise that there should be room for exceptions.... [The government quotes Article 4(1)–(2) of the ICCPR.]

No one would doubt that the genocide, which Rwanda experienced in 1994, qualifies as a crisis that threatened the life of the nation.

The matters in respect of which the draft law on Gacaca jurisdictions does not, according to the Amnesty International report, conform to the International Covenant on Civil and Political Rights are matters covered by provisions from which Rwanda as a state party may derogate, and we do not have any doubt that the requisite circumstances that would entitle Rwanda to exercise the right of derogation exist.

...

AMNESTY INTERNATIONAL, RWANDA — GACACA: A QUESTION OF JUSTICE

(17 Dec. 2002), at www.amnesty.org/en/library/info/AFR47/007/2002/en

Despite the promise of gacaca, the legislation establishing the Gacaca Jurisdictions fails to guarantee minimum fair trial standards that are guaranteed in international treaties ratified by the Rwandese government.... If justice is not seen to be done, public confidence in the judiciary will not be restored and the government will have lost an opportunity to show its determination to respect human rights.... The laudable objectives of ending impunity and restoring the social fabric cannot be achieved without respecting human rights.

...

While the contemporary gacaca jurisdictions retain certain characteristics of the customary system — notably their location in the local community and the participation of community members, there are significant differences. Customary gacaca proceedings dealt with interfamily or intercommunity disputes. Offenders voluntarily appeared before *inyangamugayo*. Their appearance before community elders demonstrated their desire to be re-integrated into the community whose mores they had violated....

Contemporary Gacaca Jurisdictions deal, not with local disputes, but with a genocide organized and implemented by state authorities in which hundreds of thousands of individuals lost their lives. The new jurisdictions are state creations. Their operation and sentencing are dictated by national legislation.... If reconciliation is an essentially personal interaction between victim and perpetrator, one can see how gacaca, as previously practiced, would promote it. It is less clear that the state-mandated Gacaca Jurisdictions whose focus remains on retributive justice will achieve the same end.

...

The requirement of equal treatment by the courts in criminal cases demands that equality of arms must be observed throughout the trial process. It is essential that each party is afforded a reasonable opportunity to present its case, under conditions that do not place it at a substantial disadvantage vis-à-vis the opposing party. In criminal trials, where the prosecution has all the machinery of the state behind it, the principle of equality of arms is an essential guarantee of the right to defend oneself. It ensures among others that the defence has a reasonable opportunity to prepare and present its case on a footing equal to that of the prosecution; the right to adequate time and facilities to prepare a defence, including disclosure by the prosecution of material information; the right to legal counsel; the right to call and examine witnesses and the right to be present at the trial.

...

Thus, Article 14(1) of the ICCPR provides that "in the determination of any criminal charge against him, or of his rights and obligations in a suit at law, everyone shall be entitled to a fair and public hearing by a competent, independent and impartial tribunal established by law." The Human Rights Committee has stated that this right "is an absolute right that may suffer no exception". In fact, the right may not be suspended even in states of emergency under the African Charter on Human and Peoples' Rights.

...

Despite government disavowals, the prosecution enjoys a number of other advantages. A majority of cases will be judged on the basis of case-files prepared and passed on to the gacaca benches by the Public Prosecutor's Offices. Lay judges, with virtually no legal training, may be unwilling to challenge the information contained in them. Likewise, it will be difficult for defendants, without counsel, to effectively counter cases prepared by state authorities with infinitely more resources at their disposal...

...

Inyangamugayo were traditionally community elders whose status, experience and historical knowledge of the community gave them the independence, impartiality and competence required to arbitrate local conflicts. Contemporary gacaca judicial arbiters, "*les intègres*" (honest or upright individuals), represent the full spectrum within Rwandese communities. While this is advantageous and commendable, the gacaca judges do not occupy the same community standing as these inyangamugayo, which also calls into question their capacity to insure fair trial proceedings.

...

Cell-level Gacaca Jurisdictions operate at an administrative level small enough to enable community debate to take place. Ministry of Justice officials repeatedly told Amnesty International delegates that truth, if it can or will be told, is known at this level. The same cannot be said for province-level Gacaca Jurisdictions where the conceptualization of gacaca as a community forum breaks down. There is also more room for intervention both from the state and various pressure groups. Since all judges have the same amount of legal training, judges at the province-level would in most cases have neither the legal background nor legal knowledge to compensate for the loss of community discussion.

...

The Rwandese government has to further ensure that its own human rights violations during the genocide and armed conflict are investigated and tried. The Rwandese government can argue, as it does, that its crimes do not equal the magnitude and scale of those committed by the former government. Nonetheless, all human rights violations, regardless of who committed them or whether or not they constitute the crime of genocide have to be investigated and tried in a court of law.

...

IX. Recommendations

...

Amnesty International has already made some of the following recommendations; others are quite new.

...

…Relevant legislation regarding gacaca needs to ensure that:

…

- defendants and their lawyers have access to appropriate information, including documents, information and other evidence necessary to the preparation of their case;
- defendants and their lawyers should be given adequate time and facilities to prepare their defence at all stages of the proceedings. This is essential given the complexity of genocide cases and the fact that defendants will not have access to defence counsel;

…

- defendants have the opportunity to call and examine witnesses on their behalf and to examine witnesses against them;…
- each party in a gacaca hearing is afforded a reasonable opportunity to present its case under conditions that do not place it at a disadvantage;
- gacaca tribunals operate in an independent, impartial and competent manner;

…

- all gacaca sessions and hearings are open to the public, including human rights monitors, and operate in a transparent manner;…

…Amnesty International requests members of the international community to:

- use their political influence and financial resources to ensure that the Gacaca Jurisdictions respect international minimum fair trial standards…

PHIL CLARK, THE GACACA COURTS, POST-GENOCIDE JUSTICE AND RECONCILIATION IN RWANDA

(2010), at 154–64

First, the criticism that gacaca will weaken judicial safeguards as result of greater communal participation is highly flawed. The key problems with this complaint are that it ignores the various safeguards that are in place in gacaca to protect suspects from potential miscarriages of justice and how gacaca has operated in practice. Gacaca cannot protect against all miscarriages of justice but it is unjustified to argue that gacaca in no way protects individual rights. That judges are required to pass judgments and sentences on the basis of a consensus (or, when failing to achieve consensus, on a majority) of nine judges, rather than on the opinion of a single judge, constructs an important layer of protection for the accused. Judges must discuss cases in camera, where they are less influenced by the views of the community, before reaching a decision and communicating it to the general assembly. This forces judges to debate cases in private, often at great length, thus adding a crucial element of slow, critical consideration. My research indicates that, nationwide, approximately 25 per cent of gacaca cases have resulted in acquittals. The high acquittal rate may not be particularly surprising given that, reflecting the society as a whole, the majority of popularly elected gacaca judges are Hutu and may be inclined to judge their fellow Hutu sympathetically when they have been accused of genocide crimes. This situation is far from the brand of mob justice predicted by many human-rights observers of gacaca.

Furthermore, if individuals found guilty at gacaca believe they have not received a fair hearing, they may appeal the decision first to the jurisdiction where they were initially tried and, if still dissatisfied, to the next higher jurisdiction.... Twenty-nine of the eighty-two genocide suspects I interviewed around Rwanda after the commencement of the gacaca trial phase in 2005 said they had appealed their convictions or sentences. Twenty-four of these suspects, all of whom were subsequently either exonerated or had their sentences decreased, stated that they were satisfied with the decisions handed down at the appeals level.... Human-rights critics who equate popular participation in gacaca with lynch law ignore these protective features that are central to the gacaca process.

The Gacaca Law and Gacaca Manual also afford judges significant powers to control the content and tenor of evidence given at gacaca, in order to maintain decorum and security during hearings. Judges may stop individual testimony, banish antagonistic participants or halt entire hearings if they believe that certain testimony damages the overall pursuits of gacaca, or if there is a threat of violence towards judges or members of the general assembly....

... The government's descriptions of a near-absolute degree of popular participation in gacaca exacerbate commentators' concerns over the potential for miscarriages of justice. The government may be its own worst enemy in defending gacaca against the criticisms of human-rights observers concerning due process....

Second, non-Rwandan commentators overstate the extent to which government officials interfere in gacaca hearings and jeopardise notions of popular participation. At the outset, this critique is inconsistent with the argument — often made by the same commentators, including AI and HRW — that gacaca is likely to result in mob justice, in which the state and other actors are powerless to intervene.... Waldorf meanwhile cites examples of state coercion only in high-profile cases such as those involving Major General Laurent Munyakazi, a high-ranking Hutu military official, and Father Guy Theunis, a Belgian priest. While my own observations, as highlighted above, indicate that state officials do from time to time intervene directly in hearings, this is a generally uncommon occurrence and usually confined to communities close to Kigali, where there is invariably a greater state presence. On three occasions that I have witnessed, government officials have intervened during hearings and been told by judges to desist from speaking on the grounds that the community should be free to debate the genocide evidence at hand. On all occasions, the officials followed the judges' orders. Such instances of judges standing their ground represent important moments of local agency that remain under-recognised in most non-Rwandan critiques of gacaca.

There is evidence, including from my own observations, that state officials in some locations actively encourage — or even coerce — the population to participate in gacaca hearings. However, there is little evidence to suggest that this is a widespread phenomenon — the large number of hearings that have been cancelled due to low turnouts suggests quite the opposite... Waldorf's argument regarding coercion is problematic: he argues first that low turnouts at hearings represent 'peasant resistance' to state compellance of participation in gacaca and then later that '[l]ow participation rates have forced the state to employ coercion.' He attributes the slowness of the initial information phase of gacaca to low participation during hearings. However, I observed substantial participation during the information phase, with some of the highest turnouts at any point in the gacaca process, given that the population during that period viewed gacaca as novel and a source of relief after the long absence of any accountability process for genocide crimes. From my observations, I concur with Waldorf that the information phase was very slow and this diminished the population's enthusiasm for participation in gacaca, at least until the beginning of trials....

There is a further problem with some observers' arguments concerning government coercion of popular participation, namely that they centre around how spontaneously the population chooses to attend hearings rather than how actively it provides and debates testimony once hearings are underway. It is unclear why a state that requires citizens to participate in a legal process to which they could directly provide evidence should be seen as engaging in unjustifiable coercion. In such cases, there appears to be little difference between the actions of the Rwandan government and the legal requirement in many countries for citizens with relevant evidence or who have been summoned to jury service to actively participate in trials.

The third major problem with non-Rwandan observers' criticisms of popular participation in gacaca is their proposed alternative modus operandi.... [T]he dominant discourse criticises gacaca for failing to provide for formal justice. This critique provides an implicit, alternative view of how gacaca should operate. The formal approach to gacaca would apply what human-rights critics consider a form of legal due process, such as the one assumed to operate in institutions such as the ICTR... Judges would limit interactions in the general assembly to discussions of facts considered critical to determining the guilt or innocence of suspects. Members of the general assembly would be encouraged to respond only to questions from judges and not to debate with one another during hearings. Lawyers in turn would be present to advise survivors and suspects on how best to construct their respective arguments and to intervene in hearings if they believe that judges are contravening the Gacaca Law. The claim concerning the need for lawyers at gacaca is the only part of this formal alternative that the dominant discourse on gacaca outlines explicitly and consistently....

The formal alternative to gacaca is inadequate for both political and practical reasons. At the political level, the main problem with the formal approach to gacaca is that it defies the spirit of gacaca discernible from the government's and population's views. The population expects to participate in largely open, undirected hearings, in front of judges they have elected, and to debate and discuss both legal and non-legal issues. The population expects that gacaca will function very differently from a conventional courtroom. The formal approach implied by human-rights critics would prove alienating, distancing the population from the workings of a judicial system in which it would be entitled to participate only when called as witnesses and only in response to questions from judges and lawyers. Such strictures would greatly limit interactions between participants in gacaca.

Embodied in the various Rwandan sources' interpretations of popular participation in gacaca is a discursive understanding of the way gacaca is expected to operate. According to the discursive view, participants in gacaca should feel free to discuss issues that are crucial to their personal and communal experiences during and after the genocide. Whatever 'truth' may be discovered in gacaca will be reached through communal dialogue, not through the views of elites imparted to the population. Such dialogue may be messy, may take a long time and may in the end produce rather inconclusive results; there can be no doubting the risks inherent in the discursive approach embodied in gacaca. However, much of the population views the action of communal dialogue as inherently valuable. It contends that gacaca draws together people who may have, for reasons of protracted conflict, found it difficult to discuss matters of individual and mutual importance in the past. In this view, gacaca encourages participants to discuss crucial issues in an open environment where the community as a whole may benefit from hearing, and contributing to, such dialogue.

Because the formal alternative seeks to minimise communal involvement by giving an increased role to judges and lawyers, it directly opposes most Rwandans' self-definitions and their dialogical interpretation of gacaca. Viewing the negotiated approach as a potential cause of further acrimony and violence, the formal version of gacaca advocates an alternative that would lack popular legitimacy.... Because the Gacaca Law and Gacaca Manual enshrine the centrality of the population's acceptance of, and involvement in, gacaca... the question of ensuring gacaca's popular legitimacy is of the utmost importance.

... To allow some individuals to benefit from the assistance of lawyers, while others, operating within the same hearing and who may be arguing against those acting on expert legal advice, are unable to gain access to lawyers for financial or other reasons, is to introduce an unacceptable form of inequality of assistance into the gacaca process. It is preferable therefore to remove lawyers completely from gacaca, thus ensuring that no participants in gacaca gain an advantage over others by having access to legal assistance that is not available to all participants.

...

[Additionally], the strictly formal approach to gacaca severely limits the range of issues that the community can discuss and debate during hearings. This narrower discourse is not only problematic because it fails to meet most Rwandans' expectations of how gacaca should operate, and therefore lacks popular legitimacy, but at a pragmatic level it means that the community cannot pursue certain objectives (particularly those that may not necessarily relate directly to formal justice). The formal approach would limit gacaca hearings to discussions of legal facts, to the exclusion of many emotionally motivated expressions which, as we have seen, much of the population considers valuable functions of gacaca.

The shrinking of the dialogical space inherent in the formal approach to gacaca would stymie gacaca's pursuit of both legal and non-legal ends. Regarding legal objectives, communal dialogue in an open forum, where issues can be debated and discussed, is important for gacaca judges to make reasoned decisions about genocide cases. Survivors in particular can ask questions directly of those who committed crimes, which rarely occurs in more conventional legal settings, and the accused are permitted to respond. Judges may also hear evidence in an open, communal setting that they would not necessarily glean if they were limited to hearing testimony only from witnesses whom they had called. This more fluid exchange of views, in which judges act as mediators, can provide crucial information for determining the guilt or innocence of genocide suspects. The human-rights interpretation, which holds that significant communal involvement in a dialogically based legal setting automatically leads to unfair or biased decision-making, therefore neglects several important ways in which the discursive approach to discovering legal 'facts' may not only be safeguarded against miscarriages of justice, as gacaca is designed to do, but may even in some instances be more legally beneficial than more conventional methods of criminal justice.

Concerning non-legal ends, the formal model of gacaca would bar participants from expressing views and emotions that do not necessarily concern judicial cases but are nonetheless considered important for other reasons.... [M]any survivors view this greater sense of freedom of expression during gacaca hearings, relative to those in conventional courtrooms, as important for fulfilling their emotional and psychological needs after the genocide. Furthermore, the presence of lawyers, as the formal approach to gacaca requires, would undermine the content and tone of open, largely undirected, communal discourse that is otherwise possible during gacaca hearings. The presence of lawyers would significantly alter the dynamic between members of the general assembly, increasing the use of technical legal language and modes of argumentation, and alter power dynamics as fully trained lawyers operate in a space where (often minimally trained) judges are supposed to be the primary facilitators of gacaca. In such a situation, the population would feel more inhibited and intimidated than in a forum where they are among their neighbours, giving evidence before judges whom they have elected. In advocating the inclusion of lawyers in the gacaca process, critics of the institution risk undermining the popular ethos of gacaca and the modes of dialogue that ensue at gacaca.

LARS WALDORF, LIKE JEWS WAITING FOR JESUS: POSTHUMOUS JUSTICE IN POST-CONFLICT RWANDA

in Rosalind Shaw & Lars Waldorf (eds.), Localizing Transitional Justice (2010)

pp. 186–8

Belgian colonial administrators had encouraged gacaca even though colonial law did not formally recognize it. Under their system of indirect rule, the Belgians favored the Tutsi elite, appointing them as chiefs and subchiefs to govern the Hutu majority. Those, in turn, often appointed the inyangamugayo. After independence in 1962, gacaca was transformed into a "semi-official and neo-traditional" institution used by local authorities to resolve minor conflicts outside the formal justice system (Reyntjens 1990).... Whereas customary gacaca usually involved the concerned parties, their family or clan members, and the inyangamugayo, this "semi-official" gacaca involved public hearings before the assembled local community. In a sample of 112 cases, Reyntjens found that 40 percent were quarrels, brawls, and public insults (some involving personal injuries), and 60 percent were between family members or immediate neighbors. Commune residents rarely appealed gacaca decisions to the canton courts (the lowest-level courts), but when they did, those courts took note of gacaca decisions. Reyntjens concluded that gacaca was "quick justice, a good bargain (for the public authorities as well as for those being judged), extremely accessible, understood and accepted by all, and involving a large popular participation" (Reyntjens 1990).

Following the genocide, gacaca was proposed as a mechanism for trying genocide cases. Several Rwandan scholars rejected the idea in 1995, observing, "The justice of gacaca would be incompetent in the matter of genocide because it cannot even judge a homicide case" (UN High Commissioner for Human Rights 1996: 20). Rather, they proposed that gacaca function as local truth commissions to distinguish the innocent from the guilty....

...

Gacaca is often portrayed as "traditional," much as the South African Truth and Reconciliation Commission supposedly reflected an authentic expression of African harmony (ubuntu). In his public speeches, President Kagame promoted gacaca as a "traditional participatory system" (Kagame, April 22, 2004) that "had served us well before colonialism" (Kagame 2005). At a July 2008 conference in Kigali, the Minister of Justice stated: "Rwanda had to step back into its past to find a solution for its present predicament" (Workshop on Rwanda's Move Towards Commonwealth Membership, Kigali, August 5, 2008). In fact, gacaca bore no resemblance to customary dispute resolution other than the name. For one thing, genocide gacaca was a state institution intimately linked to the state apparatus of prosecutions and incarceration, and applying codified, rather than customary, law. This was recognized by its official title: inkiko-gacaca, or gacaca courts. Second, modern gacaca courts were judging serious crimes and meting out prison sentences, whereas "traditional" gacaca mostly resolved minor civil disputes with restitution awards. Third, the inyangamugayo were elected, comparatively young, and nearly one-third women, rather than the male elders of the past. Fourth, traditional gacaca hearings involved only the parties and the inyangamugayo; they were not held before the entire community. Finally, "[t]he main difference between the traditional and the new systems is probably the destruction of the social capital that underlies the traditional system" (Reyntjens and Vandeginste 2005: 118).

pp. 194–5:

Gacacas' insistence on public truth telling was fundamentally at odds with rural Rwanda's "pervasive" culture of secrecy (Lame 2005: 14; Ingelaere 2007: 22–24). Practices of concealment and dissimulation have their origins in the region's turbulent history and remain a widespread means of responding to perceived danger in the present, as anthropologist Lame details:

> Secrecy persisted as a cultural habit well beyond pre-colonial and colonial Rwanda, where people, subjected to a climate of constant insecurity, were at the mercy of capricious chiefs whose intrigues affected their lives. ... The habit of secrecy continues in the most ordinary circumstances: one's dwelling place is mentioned evasively, and the rooms of a house are set up so as to conceal the state of one's provisions. (Lame 2005: 14–15)

"Ritualized dissimulation" (Wedeen 1999: 82) under successive authoritarian states also enabled people to keep their true thoughts private. Another anthropologist described Rwandan society as "administrative groupings of nuclear families, devoid of a collective spirit and rife with suspicion" (Pottier, quoted in Eltringham and Hoyweghen 2001: 218). Still today, most rural Rwandans prefer to live in scattered households on hillsides rather than in villages. Furthermore, transparency and directness are considered undesirable and foolish traits: they put oneself and others at risk and undermine social relations (Overdulve 1997: 279–80, 282).

Several authors claim that gacaca created space for local dialogical truths and reconciliation (e.g., Clark 2007: 55–58, 2009: 314–15; Ngoga 2009: 327; Wierzynska 2004: 1962). However, this ignores how gacaca testimonies and silences were shaped by "the micropolitics of local standing" (Moore 1992: 11, 42). On Rwanda's hills, people were more concerned with demonstrating loyalty to kin and patrons than with truth telling (PRI 2006: 1; see Moore 1992: 37–38). ... Such micropolitics played out against the backdrop of pervasive secrecy, mutual suspicion, and occasional denunciation. Thus, a team of Rwandan researchers found "the sentiment of not wanting to attract enemies (kutiteranya) prevailed within the general population" during gacaca sessions (Karekezi 2004: 79).

pp. 196–7:

A Special Representative of the UN Human Rights Commission put the issue starkly:

> The question facing Rwanda's international partners is relatively simple: Do they grasp the nettle and participate, on the grounds that anything is preferable to the abuse [of then 120,000 detainees] in prisons, or do they hold firm to established legal principles [for fair trials] and stay aloof, thus increasing the likelihood that gacaca will fail? (UN Commission on Human Rights 2000)

Most ordinary Rwandans I have met, whether in the capital or on the hills, do not believe that gacaca delivered justice. Many Tutsi survivors deeply resented gacaca. A representative of AVEGA, the leading organization of women genocide survivors, told a public gathering early on: "Gacaca is for liberating the prisoners. It's a sort of hidden amnesty" (Coexistence Network meeting, Kigali, July 23, 2002). Another Rwandan told me: "Rescapes [survivors] are convinced that there is no justice, because they wish that everyone is in prison. They think that the government has decided to give pardon. Rescapes have a spirit of resignation."Once on my way back from a gacaca, I gave a lift to an elderly survivor. When I asked him what survivors thought of gacaca, he responded, "We are waiting for gacaca like Jews waiting for Jesus."

Many Hutu also see gacaca as unjust, but for very different reasons. Some argue that gacaca elicited false confessions from innocent people grown weary of being unjustly detained for many years. Others see gacaca as "victor's justice," because it focused exclusively on the genocide against Tutsi (African Rights 2003: 24–26; Longman and Rutagengwa 2004: 176; PRI 2004: 44–47; Rettig 2008: 40)....

During gacaca, people occasionally talked about the suffering of Hutu refugees in the DRC, Hutu suspects in overcrowded prisons, and Hutu victims of RPF killings, only to be cut off by local officials and gacaca judges. In a gacaca I attended in 2002, two judges stood at the end of the session and described how RPF soldiers "disappeared" their family member. When they asked why gacaca could not try the case, an official explained, "Gacaca treats uniquely the question of genocide," and told them to take their complaint to the local officials or the military courts (Southern Province, July 2002).

p. 200:

According to the transitional justice paradigm, criminal trials are supposed to break the cycles of violence, because the individualization of responsibility avoids collective guilt. A Rwandan representative of Avocats Sans Frontieres captured this when he told me: "It is also good for peaceful coexistence when the truly guilty are known.... Those Hutu who did nothing... are now cleaned of the common feeling of guilt." In fact, however, gacaca trials appear to have reinforced each group's feelings of collective victimization, making it harder to see past their own suffering to comprehend the suffering of the other group.

Overall, gacaca imposed collective guilt by generating accusations of genocide against perhaps one million Hutu — a quarter of the adult Hutu population (SNJG 2008a: 19)...

pp. 201–2:

International donors and policymakers were largely inattentive or dismissive when it came to those local responses to gacaca. After the Rwandan government criticized Penal Reform International's action research on how local communities viewed gacaca, the UK's Department for International Development cut its funding to PRI. Even when it became apparent that gacaca would swell the ranks of the accused and worsen ethnic tensions, most donors kept on financing it. This perplexed a former head of mission for PRI: "Gacaca was designed in 1998–1999 to deal with 130,000

— no more. No one dared to think 1 million could be judged.... No one has been traumatized by this figure — not the government and not the donors."

Similarly, international policymakers continued lauding gacaca long after its failings came to light. The prosecutor of the International Criminal Court has repeatedly suggested that states might be able to preclude ICC investigations and prosecutions by adopting a gacaca-like model (see Colloquium of Prosecutors 2004). He gave a spirited defense of gacaca when I raised concerns about it at a workshop in late 2005 (Conflict-Mapping Workshop, Harvard Law School, November 2005). The United Nations also praised gacaca in 2006 for having "helped bring Rwandan society together to rebuild trust, share the truth about the genocide and provide access to justice to the public" (UN Office of the High Representative for Least Developed Countries 2006: 130).

International support for gacaca cannot be explained solely by reference to what has been cynically termed Rwanda's "genocide credit" (Reyntjens 2004: 199). It also reflects disillusionment with expensive and inefficient international tribunals, belated appreciation for national and local responses to mass violence, a romanticizing of the "traditional," and wishful thinking about an "African renaissance." President Kagame has skillfully played on all these themes in some of his speeches:

> First of all, we must recognize that... there can never be a "one-size-fits-all" prescription for conflict resolution.... Second, any approach to conflict resolution must be locally driven, people-centred and people-owned... Third, we Africans must learn to find African solutions to African problems, and only invite the international community to complement our own efforts. (Kagame 2005)

Seduced by such rhetoric, some policymakers and scholars have looked to gacaca for guidance on how to adapt local dispute-resolution mechanisms to accomplish transitional justice in other post-conflict African states, such as Burundi, Uganda, and the Democratic Republic of Congo.

Gacaca offers several lessons for transitional justice — although not the ones that most policymakers and scholars want to hear. First, it points up the need to interrogate local, populist mechanisms more closely and to distinguish clearly between those produced bottom-up by communities from those imposed top-down by states. Gacaca looks awfully familiar when compared to other disappointing experiments with state-imposed informalism in many postcolonial states in Africa and Asia, which also resulted in increased formalism, decreased popular participation, and increased state coercion (Merry 1993; Stevens 1999). Second, Rwanda's experiment with gacaca suggests that local dispute-resolution mechanisms will be driven in new — and often problematic — directions where they are captured and coopted by the state. Finally, where people have reason to fear the government and/or their neighbors following communal violence, and where constraints against truth telling have developed as a historical response to danger, public truth telling within communities may expose people to serious risks and will be subject to resistance and reworking.

QUESTIONS

1. Recall the discussion of derogation rules in Chapter 5, *supra*. Did the Government of Rwanda lawfully derogate from its international obligations? If the government plausibly satisfied the substantive requirements, does it indicate that those requirements are too weak?

2. In applying international legal standards, should greater deference be accorded to post-conflict societies to allow them to fashion approaches to such extraordinary situations? Conversely, should governmental decisions in post-conflict societies receive closer scrutiny and less deference given the politically charged atmosphere including the public's thirst for vengeance that often accompanies such situations?

3. Do the gacaca courts satisfy the standards of a fair trial? Should a different standard apply to extremely impoverished countries dealing with such a large number of cases? Do the gacaca courts satisfy the specific requirements for an independent and impartial hearing? How could the government create an 'impartial' proceeding in such a post-genocidal society?

4. Amnesty International makes a number of consequentialist claims such as '[i]f justice is not seen to be done, public confidence in the judiciary will not be restored' and that 'restoring the social fabric cannot be achieved without respecting human rights.' Are these propositions correct? What empirical assumptions underlie such claims (and is Amnesty International well suited to make such empirical assessments)? Do these types of consequentialist claims help or hurt efforts to promote human rights? What if the public demands trials that fall far short of international standards? For example, what if community leaders explicitly call for summary trials and executions 'to restore the "social fabric"'? Consider as well Phil Clark's contention that gacaca hearings need to remain free of formal human rights standards or else they would lack 'popular legitimacy'.

5. Who makes a more persuasive case — Clark or Waldorf? Do you agree with Clark that gacacas should be allowed to pursue other objectives that do not involve the assessment of guilt in the individual case? Are Clark's explanations of procedural safeguards associated with gacaca hearings satisfactory? What is the major concern outlined by Waldorf and other critics of gacacas — was the gacaca system too lenient and biased in favour of defendants or arbitrary and lacking due process protections for defendants?

ADDITIONAL READING

D. Cohen, 'Hybrid Justice in East Timor, Sierra Leone, and Cambodia: Lessons Learned and Prospects for the Future', 43 Stan. J. Int'l. L. 1 (2007); C. L. Sriram & S. Pillay (eds.), *Peace Vs. Justice? The Dilemma of Transitional Justice in Africa* (2011);

P. K. Mendez, 'The New Wave of Hybrid Tribunals: A Sophisticated Approach to Enforcing International Humanitarian Law or an Idealistic Solution with Empty Promises?', 20 Crim. L. Forum 53 (2009); J. R. W. D. Jones et al., 'The Special Court for Sierra Leone: A Defense Perspective', 2 J. Int'l. Crim. Justice 211 (2004); J. Stromseth (ed.), *Accountability for Atrocities: National and International Responses* (2003); E. Stover & H. M. Weinstein (eds.), *My Neighbor, My Enemy: Justice and Community in the Aftermath of Mass Atrocity* (2004); L. A. Dickinson, 'The Promise of Hybrid Courts', 97 Am. J. Int'l. L. 295 (2003).

E. PEACE VERSUS JUSTICE?

How should institutional efforts to remedy mass human rights violations address concerns that such interventions promote war or social conflict? Efforts to address past wrongdoing, for example, may threaten to unravel a fragile peace agreement or the transition from an authoritarian past. Concerns about such consequences often relate to the prospect of criminal trials. These concerns, however, can also apply to a range of other measures. For instance, a truth commission, under certain circumstances, could be more likely to rupture social relations and foster notions of collective guilt rather than encourage reconciliation. Lustration policies — precluding former perpetrators and their supporters from participating in a successor government — might obstruct social integration and political stability. Civil suits against particular individuals or organizations, such as companies formerly involved in apartheid South Africa, might undermine government efforts to encourage those and other actors to rebuild the country.

The important question may not be whether to adopt particular institutional devices. The most important question may be one of timing. When is it appropriate, or most feasible, to deal with the past through these justice and accountability mechanisms? A central question may also be about who decides. That is, what institution or set of actors should have the authority to decide whether to pursue various strategies? Are local actors best situated to make those decisions, international actors, judicial or political bodies? Does it matter if local actors generally prefer amnesties?[24] What if local actors prefer prosecution, especially for retributive or symbolic reasons, despite a more pragmatic judgement of international exports and institutions? Should the structure of international and domestic legal institutions include a presumption favouring (or disfavouring) certain justice and accountability mechanisms? What factors should overcome that presumption?

Finally, how should decision-makers weigh justice and peace in the instant case versus the precedent set and consequences for dealing with situations of mass

[24] In general, *amnesties* foreclose prosecutions for stated crimes (often by reference to crimes or conduct that took place before a stated date), whereas *pardons* release convicted human rights offenders from serving their sentences (or the remainders thereof if they are prisoners at the time of pardon). Nonetheless, usage often views these terms as interchangeable, so that persons not yet tried are 'pardoned' and prisoners serving sentences are granted an 'amnesty'.

violations in the future? For example, trials in the instant case may be important to promoting norms and expectations of punishment in other countries or in the same country's political future. Alternatively, trials might encourage repressive leaders or combatants in the future to conclude that amnesties are not reliable and that conceding political power is not in their best interest.

The following readings emphasize the institutional response that has received the most attention: criminal trials. Efforts to bring individuals to justice through international and domestic prosecutions have bumped up against concerns about endangering peace and stability. As the readings below explain, proponents of prosecution argue that states and international institutions have a legal obligation to punish gross violations of human rights. Recent controversies include the decision of ICTY officials to indict Bosnian Serb leaders during the final stages of peace negotiations in the Balkans, the subsequent decision of the ICTY to indict Slobodan Milosević while the US Government was encouraging him to leave office, Cambodian Prime Minister Hun Sen's warning that prospective trials of Khmer Rouge leaders could reignite a civil war, Charles Taylor's request to have his indictment by the Special Court for Sierra Leone vacated in exchange for his leaving office, the approval by popular referendum of a broad-based amnesty for serious crimes committed by armed rebel groups in Algeria, the retroactive abolition of amnesties in several Latin American countries, the establishment of the Iraqi Special Tribunal to prosecute former senior officials in Saddam Hussein's Baath Party regime in the midst of an insurgency, indictments of rebel leaders in Uganda by the ICC Prosecutor despite local efforts to achieve peace and reconciliation, Iraqi Prime Minister Nouri al-Maliki's plan to offer amnesty to insurgents in his country. The list is long, and there is no reason to think similar cases will not arise in the future. The following readings begin with a commentary on the indictment of Milosević in historical perspective. The section concludes by examining the particular case of the ICC and its provisions for deferring to national amnesties and local reconciliation processes.

MAX BOOT, WHEN 'JUSTICE' AND 'PEACE' DON'T MIX

Wall Street Journal, 2 Oct. 2000, at A34

...Is [Slobodan Milosević] guilty? Sure. Was the indictment smart? No.

...

There's a better way to deal with dictators who stay past their sell-by date. In fact, we saw an example of this other approach last week too. Vladimiro Montesinos, the much-feared spy chief of Peru, was fired after being taped offering a bribe to a congressman. In order to avert a military coup, the U.S. government pressured Panama to grant him exile.

The Clinton administration's handling of Mr. Montesinos follows in the best Ronald Reagan tradition. In 1986, President Reagan dispatched his friend, Sen.

Paul Laxalt, to Manila to inform Ferdinand Marcos, who had just stolen an election, that the jig was up. Sen. Laxalt did not tell Marcos that he would be headed for the slammer if he left Malacanang Palace. Instead, he offered the dictator and his wife the opportunity to move to Hawaii. They wisely accepted the invitation, letting the rightful election winner, Corazon Aquino, take power. The same year, the Reagan administration also helped engineer Jean-Claude "Baby Doc" Duvalier's voyage from Haiti to the French Riviera.

None of these deals was popular with human-rights campaigners, whose favorite slogan is, "No Justice, No Peace." They want to make dictators pay for their crimes. Hence the recent attempted prosecution of Augusto Pinochet. But justice, while a laudable concept, is hard to apply in the lawless realm of international affairs. If a war-crimes indictment keeps a Milosevic in power longer, allowing him to inflict greater suffering on his people and their neighbors, it's hard to see how this is more moral than letting him ride off into the sunset.

There's a place for war-crimes prosecutions — but they need to be smarter and more selective. During World War II, the Allies made no secret of their intention to hold top Germans and Japanese accountable for their atrocities. This helped fire up morale in Allied countries by transforming the war into a moral crusade, and it cost nothing. Since the Allies' stated war aim was unconditional surrender, throwing in war-crimes charges was not likely to make the enemy fight any harder. In 1946, war-crimes tribunals were convened at Nuremberg (19 Nazis were convicted, 12 hanged) and Tokyo (25 convictions, seven hanged). These trials helped Germany and Japan make a break with their nefarious pasts. But the Allies were careful not to go too far, for fear of making the occupied countries ungovernable.

Gen. Douglas MacArthur famously refused to prosecute Emperor Hirohito, even though he was arguably more complicit in war crimes than some subordinates who were hanged. MacArthur figured, probably rightly, that harming their revered emperor would hinder his efforts to transform the Japanese from foe to friend.

In short, the Allies realized after World War II that settling scores can sometimes conflict with the need to create a better world. "Justice" and "peace" aren't always compatible. And when those two imperatives clash [sic], morality dictates that the future win out over the past.

Applying those principles today, it's clear that war-crimes prosecutions make sense in Bosnia. Like post-1945 Germany or Japan, postwar Bosnia is run by an Allied army of occupation. Letting mass murderers like Radovan Karadzic run around loose makes it harder to build a democracy. Just imagine how difficult it would have been to create a free West Germany if Hermann Goring were hanging around Bonn.

It is equally clear that in the case of Slobodan Milosevic — who still holds sway over unconquered Serbia — a war-crimes indictment is counter-productive.... The West has made a mistake in letting the courts take the lead in Balkans policy. Tricky matters like easing dictators out of power should be left to politicians, diplomats and generals, not to lawyers....

ABDUL RAHMAN LAMIN, CHARLES TAYLOR . . . AND INTERNATIONAL POLITICS

in C. L. Sriram and S. Pillay (eds.), Peace Vs. Justice? The Dilemma of Transitional Justice in Africa (2011)

[In the case of the Special Court for Sierra Leone] . . . the prosecutor's failure and inability to take into account fully the political context and dynamics of the conflict led to his own questionable decision to bring indictments against CDF leaders [Civil Defence Forces, a pro-government military forces] alongside RUF leaders [Revolutionary United Front, rebel forces]. While it would have been controversial for the prosecution to bring indictments only against RUF leaders, especially given its broad mandate, one would have imagined that a clear understanding of the political dynamics of the conflict might have dissuaded it from bringing charges against the CDF leaders in particular, given the resentment that action caused. . . . [T]he fact that Norman's[25] role in the conflict continues to be celebrated by many in Sierra Leone, even after his unfortunate death, suggests that the 'victims' on whose behalf the prosecution claimed to be working did not share the same enthusiasm about categorising the CDF and RUF as 'two sides of the same coin'.

The Norman indictment still remains a polarising issue, to the point that it was partly responsible for the defeat of the ruling Sierra Leone People's Party (SLPP) in the recently concluded presidential and parliamentary elections. . . . This was largely because many voters in those regions blamed the former government for 'sacrificing' Norman and other CDF leaders in the interest of political expediency. Many voters in the southern and eastern regions of Sierra Leone simply heeded the call of the break-away third party . . . to vote the SLPP government out of office, for its complicity in the 'Norman affair'. As a result, the leading opposition party, the APC, benefited politically, winning both the presidential and parliamentary election. In essence then, rather than complementing the reconciliation process, the Court actually succeeded in further polarising Sierra Leonean society.

JACK SNYDER & LESLIE VINJAMURI, TRIALS AND ERRORS: PRINCIPLE AND PRAGMATISM IN STRATEGIES OF INTERNATIONAL JUSTICE

28 Int'l. Security 5 (2003/04), at 43–4

Advocacy groups such as Human Rights Watch and Amnesty International have made a historic contribution to the cause of international human rights

[25] The case of Hinga Norman is discussed elsewhere in this chapter. The leader of the Civil Defence Force and Interior Minister at the time of his arrest, Norman was considered a war hero by many in Sierra Leone for protecting civilians against rebel attacks.

by publicizing the need to prevent mass atrocities such as war crimes, genocide, and widespread political killings and torture. However, a strategy that many such groups favor for achieving this goal — the prosecution of perpetrators of atrocities according to universal standards — risks causing more atrocities than it would prevent...

Amnesties, in contrast, have been highly effective in curbing abuses when implemented in a credible way, even in such hard cases as El Salvador and Mozambique. Truth commissions, another strategy favored by some advocacy groups, have been useful mainly when linked to amnesties, as in South Africa. Simply ignoring the question of punishing perpetrators — in effect, a de facto amnesty — has also succeeded in ending atrocities when combined with astute political strategies to advance political reforms, as in Namibia.

...

Justice does not lead; it follows. We argue that a norm-governed political order must be based on a political bargain among contending groups and on the creation of robust administrative institutions that can predictably enforce the law. Preventing atrocities and enhancing respect for the law will frequently depend on striking politically expedient bargains that create effective political coalitions to contain the power of potential perpetrators of abuses (or so-called spoilers). Amnesty — or simply ignoring past abuses — may be a necessary tool in this bargaining. Once such deals are struck, institutions based on the rule of law become more feasible. Attempting to implement universal standards of criminal justice in the absence of these political and institutional preconditions risks weakening norms of justice by revealing their ineffectiveness and hindering necessary political bargaining...

...

Trials do little to deter further violence and are not highly correlated with the consolidation of peaceful democracy.... In contrast, the empirical hypotheses underpinning pragmatism... fare better. Amnesties or other minimal efforts to address the problem of past abuses have often been the basis for durable peaceful settlements. The main positive effect of truth commissions has probably been to give political cover to amnesties in transitional countries with strong reform coalitions. The international criminal justice regime should permit the use of amnesties when spoilers are strong and when the new regime can use an amnesty to decisively remove them from power. Deciding what approach to adopt in a particular case requires political judgment. Consequently, decisions to prosecute should be taken by political authorities, such as the UN Security Council or the governments of affected states, not by judges who remain politically unaccountable.

... [C]hoices about punishment of past abuses must be made through the application of resolutely forward-looking criteria designed to avert atrocities and secure human rights, not backward-looking strategies based on rigid rule following or on what "feels right."

HELENA COBBAN, THINK AGAIN: INTERNATIONAL COURTS

Foreign Policy, May 2006

…

"War Crimes Tribunals and Truth Commissions Advance Human Rights" Not always.

War crimes tribunals and truth commissions are well-meaning responses to ghastly atrocities. But the assumption that they advance human rights rests on a deep failure to recognize that nearly all of today's atrocities are committed in the anarchic, violent atmosphere of war zones. Any strategy for limiting atrocities must prioritize the pursuit of providing a stable, sustainable end to armed conflicts.

In some instances, threats of prosecution can actually impede peacemaking, prolong conflict, and multiply the atrocities associated with them. Consider Uganda. In July 2004, the ICC's chief prosecutor — responding to a request from the Ugandan government — launched a judicial investigation into the situation in the north of the country, where the Lord's Resistance Army (LRA) has sustained a barbaric insurgency for some 18 years. In April 2005, two dozen community leaders from northern Uganda went to The Hague to urge the prosecutor to hold off. One delegation member was David Onen Acana II, the chief of the dominant tribe in the war zone. He and his colleagues argued that their communities' traditional approaches would be far more effective than international prosecutions in ending the violence. In October, the Ugandan government, which had escalated its campaign against the LRA, announced that the ICC had issued arrest warrants against five top LRA leaders. LRA fighters responded by stepping up attacks against civilians and aid workers — just as Acana had warned.

Many successful, rights — respecting peace accords — including those in Spain and Mozambique — were built on tacit agreements not to look back. Is modern Spain weaker and less law-abiding because it did not engage in wrenching and divisive prosecutions of those who committed abuses during its decades of civil war and repression? The logic of prosecution-obsessed activists would say yes; common sense says no.

…

"Giving Amnesty to War Criminals Encourages Impunity"

Where's the proof? Post-genocide Rwanda has been dedicated in its pursuit of war crimes prosecutions. But it has borne that country little fruit. At one point when Rwanda was still trying to prosecute all those accused of participating in the 1994 genocide, more than 130,000 of its 8 million citizens were detained. Yet President Paul Kagame has also kept all major elements of society, including the judiciary, the government, and the media, completely under his thumb. That undermines the rule of law in Rwanda, no matter how dedicated the regime is to seeking justice. In

1994, Freedom House gave Rwanda a "Not Free" rating for its political rights and civil liberties — basic components of the rule of law anywhere. In 2004, Rwanda received the same rating.

By contrast, when Mozambique and South Africa ended their internal conflicts in the early 1990s, they enacted widescale amnesties — and in both countries, the rule of law quickly improved. In each of them, political leaders opted to move past the violence and injustices of the past and to focus on the tasks of social and political reconstruction. As part of that reconstruction, each country became a multiparty democracy in which the accountability of leaders and other key norms of the rule of law could finally take root. The restoration of public security, meanwhile, allowed the provision of basic services. And though their criminal-justice systems remained woefully underfunded, both were finally able to start providing citizens basic protections, such as an assurance of "habeas corpus." South Africa's Freedom House score made impressive improvements between 1994 and 2004. In poorer Mozambique, the improvement was smaller but still marked.

"The World Needs the International Criminal Court"

No. We can predict that the ICC will be no more effective than the international courts for the former Yugoslavia and Rwanda in improving the lives of war-zone residents who are its primary stakeholders. That is, not very effective at all.

In a criminal trial, two sets of facts — those of the prosecution and those of the defense — do public battle with each other. Those competing facts are probed and examined in detail and a winner and loser are ultimately decided. When such a trial concerns events that took place in recent memory, in a society that's still highly divided and deeply traumatized, the trial itself too often exacerbates existing political rifts.

That was the case with the ICTY and ICTR, and it risks being true of the ICC, too. The ICC shares with the two ad hoc courts the attribute that — unlike the Nuremberg and Tokyo tribunals — it exercises jurisdiction without being part of any broader administrative body that is responsible under international law for the welfare of the people within its domain....

Meanwhile, these war-shattered communities continue to live under the day-to-day control of their national governments. In the case of the former Yugoslavia, this fact has made it hard (and, in the case of wanted war criminals Radovan Karadzic and Ratko Mladic, impossible) for the ICTY to arrest some of its highest-ranking indictees. In the case of the ICTR, the Rwandan government's control over most of the witnesses and physical evidence involved in the court's cases has given the government a huge bargaining chip. It has used this power to force the ICTR to halt its investigations into well-founded accusations that Kagame's supporters also committed atrocities. In the ICC's work thus far on Uganda, the Ugandan government has similarly been able to deter the prosecutor from pursuing cases against pro-government forces. The idealists who supported the ICC's creation hoped that it would help check the power of governments and improve the well-being of much-abused people. There is little to suggest it will do either.

[The following exchange was published in a subsequent issue of the same journal in which Cobban's article appeared.[26]]

David Scheffer, Jostling over Justice

Helena Cobban misstates the intentions of international criminal tribunals.... They are convened to pursue justice and, over the long term, influence the attitudes of perpetrators and victims. No one ever assumed that they would have a significant short-term impact on warring parties.

After 1945, most Germans and Japanese despised the Nuremberg and Tokyo trials. But subsequent generations in both countries have absorbed the historical significance of these tribunals and become champions of human rights. Germany's support of the International Criminal Court (ICC) is second to none. When I was the U.S. ambassador at large for war crimes issues, I observed how often German negotiators invoked the memory of Nuremberg in advocating a permanent court. Decades from now, the same will be said of Serbs and Rwandans. Imagine how events would have unfolded if the atrocity lords of the Balkans, Rwanda, and West Africa had not been isolated and brought to credible justice by the international tribunals.

Michael P. Scharf, Jostling over Justice

A major war crimes trial — whether before an international or domestic tribunal — may cost upward of $100 million. But for someone accused of orchestrating the murder of 800,000 Tutsis in Rwanda, 250,000 Muslims in Bosnia, or 500,000 Northern Kurds and Marsh Arabs in Iraq, that is just a few hundred dollars per victim.

The former Yugoslavia is a case study in the benefits of international justice. The indictment of Slobodan Milosevic led to his removal from power and surrender to The Hague, where he no longer posed a threat to the region. During the war crimes trials, the NATO peacekeeping force in Bosnia has been reduced from 60,000 to just 7,000, as peace has taken hold. And though Milosevic's popularity may have climbed in the early days of his trial, it ultimately plummeted. The former Serb leader's nationalist policies were thoroughly discredited when the prosecution presented a graphic video of the genocidal acts committed at Srebrenica evidence that was subsequently broadcast countless times throughout Serbia and Bosnia.

It is impossible to prove that war crimes prosecutions deter future atrocities. Yet evidence presented at the recent tribunals strongly suggests that the failure to prosecute perpetrators such as Pol Pot, Idi Amin, Saddam Hussein, Augusto Pinochet, and Papa Doc Duvalier convinced the Serbs and Hutus that they could commit genocide with impunity.

Cobban is calling for a return to the days before international accountability, a time when a person stood a better chance of being tried for killing one person than for killing 1 million. There must be no going back.

[26] 154 Foreign Policy (May/June 2006), 4–10.

Helena Cobban, Jostling over Justice

People in conflict-plagued, low-income countries compare the expense of international courts with the development aid they receive. Viewed through this lens, courts look mind-bogglingly dear.

Throughout history, humans have fashioned many different social mechanisms for escaping conflict, and it seems strange that anyone should imagine that Western-style criminal trials can provide the answer around the globe....

...My colleagues in the human rights movement would make a greater contribution to attaining our shared goal of ending atrocities if they emphasized finding sustainable ends to conflicts and to righting the world's glaring economic imbalances.

KATHRYN SIKKINK, THE JUSTICE CASCADE

(2011), at 132–3, 148–50, 153–4

...[I]n another influential piece of realist scholarship from 2003, Jack Snyder-Columbia political science professor...wrote with Leslie Vinjamuri a rebuttal of the grand claims regarding the consequences of trial justice. They argued on the basis of thirty-two cases from around the world that under certain conditions, human rights trials can themselves increase the likelihood of future atrocities, exacerbate conflict, and under-mine efforts to build democracy.

The skeptics have been joined by another group of unlikely allies: culturally aware international lawyers, scholars, and activists concerned that 'one size fits all' models of transitional justice will not be sufficiently attentive to different cultural, political, and legal contexts. They question whether it is necessary to put into place "a model that mimics Western legal mechanisms." A single "template" for transitional justice can be problematic, they argue, since what is helpful in one place may be harmful someplace else.

...

What impact do human rights prosecutions have on democracy? Do prosecutions undermine democracy and lead to military coups, as the pessimists claim? If we compare regions that have made extensive use of prosecutions to regions that have not, we find that Latin America, which has made the most extensive use of human rights prosecutions of any region, has also made the most stable democratic transitions of any region. During the twentieth century, political instability and military coups were endemic in Latin America. Since 1980, however, the region has experienced the most profound transition to democracy in its history, and there have been very few reversals of democratic regimes. Ninety-one percent of the countries in the region are now considered democratic, well above the level for Eastern Europe and the former USSR (67 percent), Asia and Pacific (48 percent), or Africa (40 percent).

Since 1983, when the first prosecutions were initiated in the region, here have been only four successful anti-democratic coups in Latin America, and none was provoked by human rights prosecutions. These include the "self-coup" in 1992 in Peru, and coups in Haiti in 2004, Ecuador in 2000, and in Honduras in 2009, all of which have since reverted back to democracy. The remaining countries that used prosecutions have not had a successful coup attempt since the initiation of prosecutions, and in many cases, they are increasingly considered "consolidated" democratic regimes. No government in Latin America "committed suicide" by carrying out human rights prosecutions. The argument that prosecutions undermine democracy came largely from observations of a single case: the early coup attempts in Argentina against the Alfonsín government, after it completed the trial of the Juntas for past human rights violations and embarked upon far-reaching prosecutions of lower-level officials. But almost twenty years have passed since those failed coup attempts, and Argentina has had more transitional prosecutions than any other country in the world, all while enjoying the longest uninterrupted period of democratic rule in its history and weathering at least two major economic crises.

Some trial skeptics now argue that it is acceptable to hold prosecutions in 'consolidated democracies', but not in transitional democracies. This argument is difficult to test because political scientists don't have a good definition of when a democracy is consolidated. By whatever definition, it is clearly easier to wait until democracy appears to be strong and irreversible before a country holds prosecutions. For the most part, this is what Chile and Uruguay chose to do. But some Latin American countries like Argentina, Guatemala, and Peru have chosen to hold prosecutions before their democracies were consolidated, and there is not evidence that this choice undermined their path toward a stronger democracy. One could even argue that prosecutions helped consolidate democracy, by warning spoilers (leaders who use force to undermine political change) of the possible costs to them of another coup and an authoritarian interlude.

Looking at the Latin American cases, it is difficult to maintain the argument that human rights prosecutions destabilize democracy. Nor, it should be noted, do we yet have indisputable evidence indicating that human rights prosecutions promote or enhance democracy. Virtually all of the countries in the region, for complex reasons, have made a transition to democracy that appears to be sustained. All quantitative studies of the causes of repression show that democratic rule is clearly associated with the protection of human rights. We assume it is democratic practices that are responsible for the improved human rights scores in much of the region. Brazil, however, which is the only major transitional country in the region not to hold prosecutions for past violations, presents an interesting outlier among the Latin American cases. For example, Brazil's level of democracy is considered relatively high, and similar to that of Argentina, Peru, and Mexico, but its human rights record is not as strong as this would seem to suggest. I believe that Brazil's failure to hold state officials accountable may help explain why its human rights situation has not improved as much as some other countries in the region.

...

Another key claim circulating primarily among security specialists is that human rights prosecutions can lead to more conflict, Quantitative studies have demonstrated that civil war is the best predictor of violations. That is, if a country is embroiled in an armed internal war, innocent people are likely to be the target of systematic violence. Conflict indeed leads to human rights violations, but it is not clear that human rights prosecutions lead to an increase in conflict. This returns us to the "peace vs. justice" debate discussed above, where these two outcomes are presented as mutually exclusive. For example, some argue that Ugandans prefer peace and reconciliation to retributive justice (i.e., prosecutions), and since you can't have both, peace and reconciliation is the better and more culturally appropriate option. But this argument rests on the as-yet-unproven causal claim that prosecutions undermine peace-a causal argument that is not supported by evidence from Latin America.

Latin America experienced many internal conflicts between 1979 and 2008 — the years for which we have data on prosecutions. Seventeen Latin American countries experienced some form of internal or international conflict (from a minor conflict to a full-fledged war) in the period 1970–2008. In most cases, judicial proceedings followed rather than preceded violence. There is not a single transitional trial case in Latin America where it can be reasonably argued that the decision to undertake prosecutions extended or exacerbated conflict. Snyder and Vinjamuri argue that the decision *not* to hold more prosecutions in El Salvador contributed to less fighting there, but their argument — that if prosecutions had been undertaken, more conflict would have ensued — is not supported by evidence from other countries in the region. Figure 5.5 charts the number of conflict years in Latin America compared to the number of human rights prosecution years. We see that as prosecutions (the black line) increase in the region, the number of conflicts (the gray line) decreases. We can't make any causal claims that the rise in prosecutions leads to the decline in conflict; indeed, it could be the other way around, that the decline in conflicts has made it easier for countries to hold human rights prosecutions, But in the light of this trend, it is difficult to sustain that human rights prosecutions have led to an *increase* in conflict.

The striking feature of Latin American politics, in addition to the increase in democracy, is the overall decline in conflict in the region. After a history of fairly extensive internal conflict for decades, the region is now largely free of internal and international wars. With the dramatic regional trend toward human rights prosecutions, and only a single case (Columbia) where significant conflict continues to date, it is difficult to sustain the argument that prosecutions have entrenched conflict in the region.

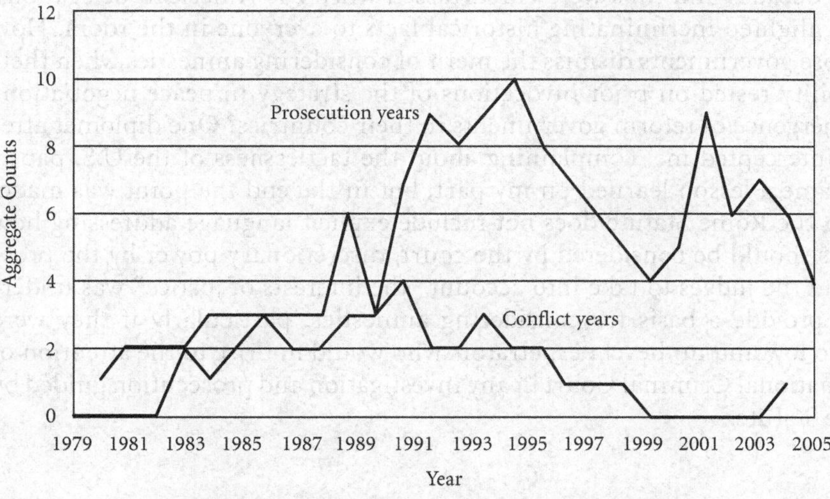

Figure 5.5. Regional Conflict Years and Prosecutions Years, 1979–2006

DAVID SCHEFFER, ALL THE MISSING SOULS: A PERSONAL HISTORY OF THE WAR CRIMES TRIBUNALS (2012)

[David Scheffer, the first US Ambassador-at-Large for War Crimes Issues, served as the head of the US delegation in negotiations on the ICC Statute. In this excerpt, Ambassador Scheffer recounts some of the backroom diplomacy in the final stages of negotiations concerning the issue of amnesties.]

...I had to make another pitch for Security Council control in th[e] floor statement because I was instructed to do so, but I knew the opposition to that position was so strong it was undermining our efforts on other negotiating fronts. I also circulated among all delegations a State Department paper on how amnesty deals with human rights abusers and war criminals in various countries, particularly in Latin America and Africa in recent years, had paved the way for peace agreements. I did so at the request of Sandy Berger, the national security adviser, who wanted me to explore an option for amnesties in the work of the International Criminal Court so that Washington had some flexibility to play that card in order to end conflicts through negotiated peace agreements. The idea of amnesties seemingly flew in the face of the entire purpose of the International Criminal Court, which was to end impunity for atrocity crimes and hold war criminals accountable before the bar of justice. My point in circulating the paper was to force the issue before all the negotiators so that we could decide how, if at all, to address the probability of future amnesties in the work of the court. I never proposed a formula for drafting other than to suggest enough discussion to structure some recognition of the option in the court's statute.

However, my initiative initially proved disastrous with other delegations particularly those representing governments that had caved in to amnesty deals in recent decades and thus were embarrassed when the American delegation's paper highlighted incriminating historical facts to everyone in the room. How could those governments dismiss the merit of considering amnesties when their own stability rested on prior invocations of the strategy in peace negotiations or the emergence of reform governments in their countries? One diplomat after another intercepted me, complaining about the tactlessness of the U.S. paper. That became a lesson learned on my part, but in the end the point was made. Although the Rome Statute does not include explicit language addressing how amnesties should be considered by the court, discretionary power by the prosecutor and the judges to take into account "the interests of justice" was understood to provide a basis for considering amnesties, particularly if they were granted to low and midlevel perpetrators who would not rise to the attention of the International Criminal Court in any investigation and prosecution guided by the Rome Statute.

DARRYL ROBINSON, SERVING THE INTERESTS OF JUSTICE: AMNESTIES, TRUTH COMMISSIONS AND THE INTERNATIONAL CRIMINAL COURT

14 Eur. J. Int'l. L. 481 (2003)

[Article 53 of the ICC Statute permits the Prosecutor, with the approval of a Pre-Trial Chamber, to forego investigations or prosecutions when doing so is 'in the interest of justice'. This provision is generally understood to permit the ICC to defer to a national amnesty or reconciliation programme. Under Article 16, the Security Council could also potentially preclude prosecutions in such circumstances.]

...Even among international lawyers who argue that prosecution should sometimes give way to alternative means of dealing with the past, many or most would also allow that there are exceptionally serious crimes for which prosecution may be required under international law. The first pertinent question is which crimes are covered by the duty. To summarize very briefly, it is relatively clear that states are under a duty to bring to justice those responsible for genocide, acts of torture, and grave breaches of the Geneva Conventions of 1949. These obligations are derived from treaties, but are now widely considered to be reinforced by equivalent customary international law obligations....

With respect to the other crimes in the ICC Statute (crimes against humanity and serious violations of the laws of armed conflict), the situation is less clear....In fact, it has often been noted that actual state practice has traditionally been distinctively unsupportive of such a duty, and tended in the past to condone the granting of amnesties. Nevertheless, there are convincing reasons to suggest that under current or emerging customary international law, there is a duty to bring to justice perpetrators of genocide, crimes against humanity and war crimes, at least with respect to crimes committed on the state's territory or by its nationals. First, there has been a marked revolution in state practice, decisively shifting from history's tacit endorsement of amnesties to today's consistent rejection of them for serious international crimes. This is illustrated by the disclaimer attached by the UN to the 1999 Lomé peace accord [for Sierra Leone] and the subsequent rejection of amnesties, and the exclusion of international crimes from the community reconciliation process in East Timor. Second, this practice is accompanied by numerous declarations affirming a duty to prosecute, in resolutions (such as the Resolution on Impunity adopted by the Commission on Human Rights), declarations (such as the Vienna Declaration and Programme of Action) and even the preamble of the ICC Statute. Without overstating the weight to be given to 'paper practice', these declarations are relevant in combination with the actual practice of states, as it shows that the practice of rejecting amnesties is accompanied by a sense of legal obligation. Third, a growing body of jurisprudence, generated by the Inter-American human rights system, the UN human rights system, and other national and international bodies, affirms that amnesties for serious violations also are incompatible with a state's basic human rights obligations....

The other major question is the extent of that duty. Those critical of the idea of a duty to prosecute have argued that it does not take account of the potentially precarious position of new fragile democracies, that it would be reckless to require fragile democracies to proceed with a course that may lead to their destruction and, in addition, that in situations involving thousands of perpetrators, prosecuting everyone may be logistically impossible, financially ruinous and socially divisive.

In response, many advocates of the duty have recognized two limitations. First, the duty does not necessarily require a transitional government to prosecute all offenders; the duty may be satisfied by prosecuting the ringleaders and persons most responsible. Second, the duty may be subject to an exception of 'necessity' in situations of a 'grave and imminent threat', such that governments would not be required 'to press prosecution to the point of provoking their own collapse'. Such an exception is not to be lightly invoked; the international duty is intended to provide a counterweight to pressure from groups seeking impunity and thereby help embolden fragile democracies to carry out prosecutions rather than seeking an 'easy escape route'. It is proposed... that these two suggested limitations provide a useful frame of reference for the ICC in deciding whether to defer to a national programme falling short of full prosecution.

...

It is often argued that amnesties are a practical necessity to stop a conflict or to secure and maintain a transition from a military regime to a democratic government....

However, any 'necessity' exception should be very carefully and narrowly construed.

...[G]ranting for the sake of argument that a 'necessity' exception is justified on consequentialist grounds, it is appropriate to weigh all of the consequences, including the long-term global consequences of granting impunity to violators. If governments adopt a general approach that 'impunity may be granted whenever expedient', then the consequence of giving into expediency in case after case will be impunity in case after case, thus reinforcing expectations of impunity and encouraging future violators.

Indeed, recent experience has tended to contradict the supposedly 'pragmatic' view that prosecution is destabilizing and that amnesties are necessary for peace, as indeed the very opposite propositions have been recently borne out. For example, in Sierra Leone, blanket amnesties were granted for horrific crimes against humanity in the belief that this was necessary for peace and reconciliation; instead this merely reinforced a culture of impunity in which brutal acts of mutilation and lawlessness continued. After more conflict and more atrocities, the policy was reversed in favour of prosecution and punishment of those bearing the greatest responsibility for international crimes. Likewise, many argued that the indictment of Slobodan Milosevic by the ICTY during the Kosovo conflict would only stiffen his resolve and prolong the conflict, and yet a peace agreement was reached shortly after the indictment, and Mr. Milosevic is now in The Hague facing trial. These and other cases cast considerable doubt on the received wisdom that peace and justice are somehow at odds.

...

This author would suggest that, in deciding whether a 'necessity exception' might apply, one should consider the balance between the extent of the departure from full prosecution, i.e., the quality of the measures taken, and the severity of the factors necessitating a deviation, to decide whether the society has done everything possible to advance accountability-related goals. Different authors have suggested different lists of criteria or factors to consider, but the following seem generally recognized as relevant:

- Was the measure adopted by democratic will?
- Is the departure from the standard of criminal prosecution of all offenders based on necessity, i. e. irresistible social, economic or political realities?
- Is there a full and effective investigation into the facts?
- Does the fact-finding inquiry 'name names'?
- Is the relevant commission or body independent and suitably resourced?
- Is there at least some form of punishment of perpetrators (are they identified, required to come forward, required to do community service, subject to lustration)?
- Is some form of remedy or compensation provided to victims?
- Does the national approach provide a sense of closure or justice to victims?

Is there a commitment to comply with other human rights obligations?
In the light of the core purpose of the ICC and its prior compact with the state concerned, a programme where even the persons most responsible may apply for amnesties should receive deference 'only in the most compelling of cases'.

QUESTIONS

1. Does the list of factors outlined by Robinson sufficiently resolve problems that might arise in the struggle for both peace and justice? Should some factors weigh more heavily than others? Are there factors that should be added or omitted?

2. What actors or institutions are best equipped to make the determination that amnesty is appropriate in a given case? Does international law, or the ICC structure in particular, place too much weight in favour of prosecutions?

3. Should states in all circumstances have an absolute duty to prosecute the commission of extreme crimes such as genocide and grave breaches of the Geneva Conventions? Or should the extent of the duty to punish, even for these offences, be qualified? Should any special exceptions be made for situations in which perpetrators and survivors must continue to coexist with one another in the same country?

4. 'Effective deterrence is predicated on strong and reliable incentives directed at rational actors. Some commentators claim it is most unlikely that the prospect of international criminal prosecution will deter future tyrants or genocidaires. Commentators who hold such a position, however, should not also claim that the existing threat of international criminal prosecution deters such individuals from relinquishing power or accepting a peace agreement. The two claims are inconsistent.' Comment.

ADDITIONAL READING

A. Laban Hinton, W. Babchuk, M. Bleeker & J. Burnet (eds.), *Transitional Justice: Global Mechanisms and Local Realities after Genocide and Mass Violence* (2010); Y. Naqvi, 'Amnesty for War Crimes: Defining International Recognition', 85 Int'l. Rev. Red Cross 583 (2003); D. Mendeloff, 'Truth-Seeking, Truth-Telling, and Postconflict Peacebuilding: Curb the Enthusiasm?', 6 Int'l. Stud. Rev. 355 (2004); E. Lutz & K. Sikkink, 'The Justice Cascade: The Evolution and Impact of Foreign Human Rights Trials in Latin America', 2 Chi. J. Int'l. L. 1 (2001); Robert I. Rotberg & Dennis Thompson (eds.), *Truth v. Justice* (2000).

F. TRUTH COMMISSIONS

Parts A–E examined the role of international, national and hybrid institutions in the prosecution of individuals accused of committing international crimes. The issues to be explored in Part F, like those in earlier parts, arise when systematic and gross human rights violations are committed internally by a controlling state regime (and in some cases by opposition groups as well). At a certain stage, whether because of a strengthening internal opposition, international pressures, economic deterioration or special international circumstances such as war, negotiations with opposing forces may start to displace the authoritarian regime in power by a popularly elected government committed to human rights. Alternatively, the (often military) regime in power may simply collapse.

The question then arises how the new regime should act towards those suspected of serious human rights violations in the prior period. Should there be trials and punishment of individuals or should other paths be followed? Part F examines one other path, that of truth commissions. It examines the attributes of such institutions on their own terms. It also explores their relationships with criminal tribunals, which are increasingly working alongside truth commissions in response to the same set of violations.

COMMENT ON THE RIGHT TO THE TRUTH

Between 1974—when Uganda established a Commission of Inquiry into Disappearances—and 2012, nearly 45 truth commissions have been created around the world. More than half of them came into existence during the last ten years. And the Arab Spring promises to bring new truth commissions online in the near future. Importantly, these institutional developments have occurred alongside an increasing recognition of a 'right to the truth' in international human rights law.

The right to the truth can be traced back to the law of armed conflict. In 1974, the UN General Assembly adopted a resolution on Assistance and Cooperation in

Accounting for Persons Who are Missing or Dead in Armed Conflicts. The resolution recognized that 'the desire to know the fate of loved ones in armed conflicts is *a basic human need*'. Building on this recognition, Article 32 of the 1977 First Additional Protocol to the Geneva Conventions provided for 'the *right* of families to know the fate of their relatives'. The reference to a 'right' was a subject of considerable debate in the drafting process. Upon acceptance of the text by the treaty negotiators, the Director of the UN Human Rights Division stated that the provision constituted 'an important step forward in the field of international efforts to protect human rights'.

Within institutions dedicated to human rights law, the right to the truth first found expression in the context of missing and disappeared persons. The Inter-American Commission on Human Rights and Court of Human Rights, the UN Working Group on Enforced or Involuntary Disappearances and the Human Rights Committee developed a doctrine recognizing the right of families to know the fate of their close relatives. Indeed, in its very first report (in 1981) the Working Group invoked Article 32 of Protocol I as a source of authority for recognizing the right in the human rights arena (E/CN.4/1435). More recently, the right to the truth has been codified in Article 24 of the 2006 International Convention for the Protection of All Persons from Enforced Disappearance. And, in 2010, the Working Group adopted a General Comment on the Right to the Truth characterizing it as 'both a collective and an individual right'.

Recognition of the right to the truth has expanded well beyond disappearances. In the late 1990s, the Commission on Human Rights initiated the development of a Set of Principles for the Protection and Promotion of Human Rights through Action to Combat Impunity, which were then updated in a 2005 Report submitted to the Commission by Independent Expert Diane Orentlicher (E/CN.4/2005/102/Add.1). The Principles set forth the 'inalienable right to know the truth about past events concerning the perpetration of heinous crimes and about the circumstances and reasons that led, through massive or systematic violations, to the perpetration of those crimes.' The Set of Principles as a whole were never formally endorsed by the Commission (see, e.g., Commission on Human Rights Resolution 2005/81); nor have they been endorsed by the Human Rights Council or General Assembly. The reluctance by those bodies may be due to other parts of the Set of Principles that concern more controversial topics such as the right to justice and the right to reparation and divisive sub-topics such as universal jurisdiction, military courts and amnesties. However, elements of the Principles, especially on the right to the truth, have been relied upon by the UN Secretary-General (A/66/335 (2 Sept. 2011)), the Office of the High Commissioner for Human Rights, the supervisory bodies of the American Convention on Human Rights, UN special procedures and national authorities.[27] Also, a separate set of UN principles, *inter alia*, recognizes the right to the truth. And the UN General Assembly has formally adopted those principles. That is, in 2005, the General Assembly adopted the Basic Principles and Guidelines on the Right to a Remedy and Reparation for Victims of Gross Violations of International Human Rights Law and Serious

[27] See, e.g., Report of the independent expert to update the Set of Principles E/CN.4/2004/88; E/CN.4/2006/91.

Violations of International Humanitarian Law. That body of norms considers 'full and public disclosure of the truth' a potential remedy, in the form of satisfaction, for a human rights violation (Art. 22). And Article 24 of the Principles on the Right to a Remedy and Reparation states: 'victims and their representatives should be entitled to seek and obtain information on the causes leading to their victimization and on the causes and conditions pertaining to the gross violations of international human rights law and serious violations of international humanitarian law and to learn the truth in regard to these violations.' In addition, beginning in 2005, the Commission on Human Rights passed resolutions recognizing the right to truth for serious human rights violations — not just disappearances. And the Human Rights Council followed in its footsteps. In 2009, the Council passed a resolution affirming the right to the truth:

> Stressing the importance for the international community to endeavour to recognize the right of victims of gross violations of human rights and serious violations of international humanitarian law, and their families and society as a whole, to know the truth regarding such violations, to the fullest extent practicable, in particular the identity of the perpetrators, the causes and facts of such violations, and the circumstances under which they occurred.

Reflecting these and related developments, in 2011, a report of the UN Secretary-General Ban Ki-moon stated, 'The right to the truth about serious violations of human rights and international humanitarian law…has taken on increasing importance in recent decades and has become recognized as a right also applicable with regard to other gross violations of human rights, such as extrajudicial executions, torture, and ill treatment, including sexual violence.'

In practice, the right to truth can have significant implications for international law and policy. The UN Secretary-General has insisted that the right to truth 'must be fully respected' as part of a peace agreement between warring authorities. (See, e.g., SG/SM/9400.) The European Union has also called for the inclusion of the right to truth in designing a comprehensive legal framework for the process of disarmament, demobilization and reintegration (Council Conclusion on Colombia, 3 Oct. 2005). The Inter-American Commission and Court have developed a robust case law overturning amnesty laws on the ground that such measures can 'eliminate[ ] the possibility of undertaking judicial investigations aimed at determining the responsibility of all those involved… [which] violate[s] the right of the victim's relatives and of society at large to know the truth about the events in question.' (See also Office of the High Commissioner for Human Rights, *Rule-of-Law Tools for Post-Conflict States: Amnesties* (2009).) And, in one of the boldest expressions, the Office of the High Commissioner for Human Rights stated: 'The right to the truth as a stand-alone right is a fundamental right of the individual and therefore should not be subject to limitations. Giving its inalienable nature and its close relationship with other non-derogable rights, such as the right not to be subjected to torture and ill-treatment, the right to the truth should be treated as a non-derogable right' (E/CN.4/2006/91; see also Guidance Note on National Human Rights Institutions and Transitional Justice 2008).

The right to the truth is now closely associated with the establishment of truth commissions. The Updated Set of Principles on Impunity recognizes the connection in several provisions that provide guidance for the design of independent and strong national truth commissions. The 2010 General Comment by the UN Working Group on Enforced or Involuntary Disappearances also discusses the scope of the right to the truth in general, and locates its pedigree as an international norm, in part, in the establishment of truth commissions: 'the existence of the right to the truth in international law is accepted by State practice consisting in both jurisprudential precedent and by the establishment of various truth seeking mechanisms in the period following serious human rights crises, dictatorships or armed conflicts. Those mechanisms include the launching of criminal investigations and the creation of "truth commissions"'. In 2010, the Inter-American Court on Human Rights examined Brazil's prospective national truth commission. The Court considered the commission 'an important mechanism... to comply with the obligation of the State to guarantee the right to the truth of what occurred', but 'the activities and information that this Commission will eventually obtain do not substitute the obligation of the State to establish the truth and ensure the legal determination of individual responsibility by means of criminal legal procedures' (*Lund et al. v. Brazil*, 24 Nov. 2010). In other words, a truth commission might be a necessary condition, but by no means would it constitute a sufficient condition, for satisfying the state obligation to fulfil the right to the truth.

It is important to consider how the right to the truth can conflict with other interests and rights. The obligation of a state to respect the right to the truth is often predicated on the notion that society's knowledge of past atrocities is critical to preventing their recurrence. For example, the Inter-American Court of Human Rights has stated: 'the State has the obligation... to ensure that these grave violations do not occur again. Therefore, the State must take all steps necessary to attain this goal. Preventive measures and those against recidivism begin by revealing and recognizing the atrocities of the past. . . . Society has the right to know the truth regarding such crimes, so as to be capable of preventing them in the future' (*Bámaca Velásquez Case*, Inter-Am. Ct. H. R. (Ser. C) No. 91 (2002); see also Principle 2 of the Set of Principles to Combat Impunity (E/CN.4/2005/102/Add.1)). In concrete cases, information about past atrocities can be important to stop ongoing or imminent violations. What if that information can be extracted only by releasing perpetrators from some form of criminal punishment? In such situations, international authorities are not clearly unified on how to balance the interests involved. In a General Comment on Article 18 of the Declaration on Disappearances, the Working Group stated that the Declaration:

> allows limited and exceptional measures that directly lead to the prevention and termination of disappearances... even if, prima facie, these measures could appear to have the effect of an amnesty law or similar measure that might result in impunity. Indeed... legislative measures that could lead to finding the truth and reconciliation through pardon might be the only option to terminate or prevent disappearances.

More recently, the Working Group both amplified and qualified aspects of its prior position stating:

> the realization of the right to the truth may in exceptional circumstances result in limiting the right to justice, within the strict limits contained in... the Working Group's general comment on article 18.... The Working Group in particular recalls that: 'Pardon should only be granted after a genuine peace process or bona fide negotiations with the victims have been carried out, resulting in apologies and expressions of regret from the State or the perpetrators, and guarantees to prevent disappearances in the future' (general comment on article 18, § 8-b). In addition, the Working Group is of the opinion that no such limitation may occur when the enforced disappearance amounts to a crime against humanity.[28]

In contrast, the Office of the High Commissioner for Human Rights (OHCHR) takes a different position: 'While the operation of a truth commission does not discharge a State's duty to ensure justice for gross violations of human rights and war crimes, a perpetrator's full disclosure of what he or she knows about such violations may justify a reduction in sentence, *as long as the sentence is still proportionate to the gravity of the crime*' (OHCHR, Rule-of-Law Tools for Post-Conflict States: Amnesties (2009)). Future commissions will thus have to grapple with this potential ambiguity in the law.

QUESTIONS

1. In 2010, the Supreme Court of the Philippines invalidated a 'truth commission' that had been created to investigate reports of widespread graft and corruption by the prior administration of former President Gloria Macapagal Arroyo. The Supreme Court held that the commission violated the Constitution's equal protection clause:

> [T]he Arroyo administration is but just a member of a class, that is, a class of past administrations.... Not to include past administrations similarly situated constitutes arbitrariness which the equal protection clause cannot sanction. Such discriminating differentiation clearly reverberates to label the commission as a vehicle for... selective retribution.... [T]o be true to its mandate of searching for the truth, [the Commission] must not exclude the other past administrations.

Earlier in this chapter we discussed selective justice with respect to criminal tribunals. Do the same concerns that animate that set of issues apply to truth commissions as well? What restrictions on a truth commission's jurisdiction are illegitimate such that the entire institution should be invalidated? Could the right to the truth help to draw the appropriate boundaries?

2. Do you agree with the Working Group's views on the relationship between the right to the truth and pardons? What justifies the distinction the Working Group makes for disappearances that amount to a crime against humanity?

[28] General Comment on the Right to the Truth (2010).

3. Other controversial aspects of the right to the truth involve the decision to publish names of perpetrators and the assumption that truth will always promote reconciliation. Both of those issues raise the question whether the right to the truth should be qualified in some circumstances. In its General Comment on the Right to the Truth, the Working Group on Disappearances addressed these issues:

> The right to know the truth about the circumstances of the disappearance, in contrast, is not absolute. State practice indicates that, in some cases, hiding parts of the truth has been chosen to facilitate reconciliation. In particular, the issue whether the names of the perpetrators should be released as a consequence of the right to know the truth is still controversial. It has been argued that it is inappropriate to release the names of the perpetrators in processes such as "truth commissions", when perpetrators do not benefit from the legal guarantees normally granted to persons in criminal processes, in particular the right to be presumed innocent.

Do you agree? Whether or not you agree, does the Working Group's statement contradict the OHCHR's position that the right to the truth 'should not be subject to limitations'. Note that the Working Group also stated, 'the right of the relatives to know the truth of the fate and whereabouts of the disappeared persons is an absolute right, not subject to any limitation or derogation. No legitimate aim, or exceptional circumstances, may be invoked by the State to restrict this right.'

HENRY STEINER, INTRODUCTION TO TRUTH COMMISSIONS

Harvard Law School Human Rights Program and World Peace Foundation, Truth Commissions: A Comparative Assessment (1997), at 7

The cause of the Irish problem, suggested William Gladstone, is that the Irish never forget, while the English never remember. Is there then a golden mean, some 'proper' degree of collective memory appropriate for bearing in mind the cruelties and lessons of a troubled past, while not so consuming as to stifle the possibilities of reconciliation and growth? How might one imprint such a memory on a people's or state's conscience? What kinds of institutions or processes would be appropriate? What purposes might be served by a detailed recording of gross abuses, not only for the collectivity but also for the individuals involved as victims or perpetrators?... In a brief fifteen years, 'truth commission' has become a familiar conception and institution for a state emerging from a period of gross human rights abuses and debating how to deal with its recent past. The term serves as the generic designation of a type of governmental organ that is intended to construct a record of this tragic history, and that has borne different titles in the many countries over several continents that have resorted to it. These commissions offer one among many ways of responding to years of barbarism run rampant, of horrific human rights violations that occurred while countries were caught up in racial, ethnic, class, and ideological conflict over justice and power. They may be alternative or complementary to other national responses, including the poles of amnesty and criminal prosecution.

The contemporary surge of truth commissions... started in Argentina after the country's defeat in the Falkland Islands war and the military's related retreat from political power. Other prominent examples of commissions that have effectively completed their work include Chile and El Salvador. In some countries such as Uruguay, commissions did not achieve a great deal. In others such as Uganda, hampered by a lack of political will and funds, they have been unable to complete their mission and issue a report. Among the commissions functioning today, the most discussed and — given the degree of reconstruction that will be necessary — potentially the most significant for a country's future operates in South Africa....

The truth commission has been a protean organ, not only in the many institutional forms it has assumed, but also in its varying membership, in the diverse functions that it serves, and in its range of powers, methods, and processes....

Although the general purposes and methods of truth commissions properly figure in a critical discussion of what they have achieved, what rapidly becomes apparent is that concrete examples drawn from different countries must inform abstract description. No architect of these institutions has proceeded by deduction from general principles. The effect of specific historical contexts on the kind of commission created is inconcealable. Consider, for example, one important explanation for the variations among commissions' mandates. When the military continues to hold considerable power as part of a negotiated move toward civilian rule (as in Chile where it retained its commander, the former political leader), severe constraints influence what a truth commission may be empowered to do, or the possibility of prosecution of military personnel. The Argentinian transition following a military disgrace enjoyed greater, though still limited, possibilities.

Commissions are official organs that are generally but not always staffed by citizens. They are organized for a time certain and for the specific purpose of examining through one or another method serious violations of personal integrity. Frequently, victims of gross violations testify before them, and alleged or confessed violators may testify as well. Invariably, the commissions receive or gather evidence of violations committed by state actors, and in some instances also of violations by nonstate actors such as insurgent groups. The investigative capacity given commissions has ranged from extensive staffs armed with legal powers, to reliance principally on voluntary testimony that may or may not be verified. Hearings have been both private and public. The reports of proceedings — including graphic evidence of abuses, sometimes the naming of victims and less frequently of perpetrators, summaries and conclusions, on occasion recommended changes in state institutions or structures — ultimately become public documents....

... [T]ruth commissions have addressed state conduct that raises the most politically and morally sensitive issues facing the country as a whole.

Commission's reports have implicated high reaches of state authority in raw and systematic violations of law that claimed victims into the many tens of thousands. This slaughter, rape, torture, imprisonment, and disappearance of victims occurred in the setting of consuming conflicts, sometimes decades long, over a country's basic nature and structure: ethnic hierarchy or equality, military or democratic rule, dictation or participation, repression or expression, mass murder or the rule of law, concentration of wealth and power within a given elite or broader distribution....

...[G]overnments have created these commissions principally at the time of a state's transition toward more participatory government expressing ideals of democracy, power bounded by law, formal legal equality, and social justice. Even when the moment of political change has been non-violent — as in Chile where the structural and substantive features of the change were discussed between an opposition and a government, or in South Africa where those features were submitted to the people for its approval — the term 'transition' may understate how radically the successor regime has departed from its predecessor with respect to moral principle and political ideology.

Realization of (or at least the aspiration toward) fundamental change appears to be an almost constant companion to the use of truth commissions. A repressive regime succeeding as repressive a government that it has ousted from power is unlikely to explore prior misdeeds that may be ideally suited to its own malign purposes. The movement toward democratic rule and associated human rights in the years since the Argentinean experiment has become more common in a world informed by the powerful ideals of the international human rights movement. Hence truth commissions have become more likely.

Second, the rules and principles drawn on by commissions in determining what is relevant testimony, in reaching conclusions about criminal conduct, or in making recommendations may be found directly in the international human rights movement. Or they may be found in a state's own internal law, a law that was violated by those holding power in the prior period. Even when the latter is the case, the impact on the national proceedings of such international norms (on murder, torture, disappearances, repression, ethnic discrimination, and so on) seems evident. South Africa offers a striking illustration of the powerful effect on a state of the international system's norms and pressures. Indeed, the term 'human rights' has figured as part of some commissions' titles....

Any assessment of truth commissions must involve comparisons between them and other approaches toward dealing with a tragic period of national history. At one extreme, a state may grant amnesty to those who committed defined crimes — say, crimes with a political objective — during a prior regime. At another, it may criminally prosecute (as did Argentina) a limited number of leading figures who are viewed as ultimately responsible....

Except where barred by amnesty provisions, victims' civil suits for compensatory damages first become possible as the repression lifts. The new government may develop a public program of systematic compensation or restitution. It may make public apology without fresh investigative proceedings — as, for example, the Czech and German governments have done in a recent joint declaration bearing on stated abuses during and after World War II. The so-called process of lustration (purification) may by law dismiss people from or make them ineligible for government or other positions because of their involvement in the criticized conduct of the prior regime.

Truth commissions can stand apart from all these approaches to dealing with the past, or they may be closely linked to one among them, perhaps to amnesty or to prosecution. In South Africa, for example, confession before a commission may lead to a grant of amnesty....

Some possibilities and purposes of truth commissions are distinctive to them; others characterize several of the alternative or complementary processes that have been noted....

[The author then notes some major issues about truth commissions.]

(1) Why should a state deal in some official way with its past? If it selects the path of truth commissions, what assurance can it have that major goals such as reconciliation among groups or catharsis for victims will be realized? For example, will the findings of a truth commission promote reconciliation without companion policies like compensation? Can the goal of deterrence of massive violations of human rights be realized through selective prosecutions of leaders, or through the narratives of truth commissions? (Consider in this respect the title, *Nunca Mas*, used for several reports of commissions.)

(2) What criteria and conditions should lead a state to resort to a truth commission rather than to alternative ways of dealing with the past like prosecution or lustration?

(3) Should commissions restrict themselves to recording facts developed through voluntary testimony or through investigative procedures? Should they also engage in broader causal analysis, as by advancing historical explanations of the sources of a conflict? Should a report include recommendations of structural and substantive changes in government with the purpose of avoiding mass recidivism?

(4) Can such questions be answered in general, or will answers necessarily depend on the particular close context for decision?...

JONATHAN D. TEPPERMAN, TRUTH AND CONSEQUENCES

Foreign Affairs, Mar./Apr. 2002, at 129–45

... [T]rials, the standard mechanism for arranging punishment, are a far from perfect way to establish transitional justice. The upper levels of the outgoing regime often demand immunity from prosecution as part of the transition deal. And even after repressive governments leave office, their civil servants — including judges, prosecutors, and police — usually remain in place. This makes practical sense, since new democracies cannot afford to purge all their experienced technocrats...Trials, moreover, with their high standard of proof and extensive evidentiary requirements, are complicated and expensive, and fledgling governments tend to be strapped for cash.

Even in countries eager to confront the past, trials have turned out not to be a good way of doing so. At their best, prosecutions for human rights crimes are limited in number and selective in scope. The Allied-sponsored Nuremberg trials, for example, covered 85, 882 individual cases but secured only 7,000 convictions — and this for the Holocaust and all other Nazi atrocities. Moreover, trials focus not on general social or economic forces, but on individuals, and one set of individuals at that: namely, the perpetrators and not their victims.

Truth commissions, in theory, are supposed to address all these shortcomings. By forgoing the right to dispense punishment they make themselves less objectionable to members of the old regime. By avoiding prosecutions, they can delve widely into institutional injustices in the past. And by broadening their focus, commissions allow victims, not just violators, to tell their stories — something thought to have a powerful healing effect on those who have suffered. This, at least, is how truth commissions are supposed to work...

...

Eyeing these mixed results in South Africa, Guatemala, or elsewhere, skeptics have raised four types of general objections to the work of truth commissions: that history is so murky and subjective that even well-intentioned investigations cannot establish anything that should actually be called, with a straight face, "truth"; that the panels too often focus on individual violations rather than broad structural problems; that their work does not lead to reconciliation; and that they interfere with, and distract attention from, the prosecution and punishment of past crimes. A close look at the South African and Guatemalan cases, however, shows that although some of these charges have merit, well-planned commissions can nevertheless make an essential contribution to justice and harmony in fragile societies.

The first question, whether historical truth is a reasonable goal, is crucial. In many cases a commission's actual findings are its sole lasting accomplishment.... And the value of revealing the truth is not abstract.... [I]t is argued, an honest accounting of past injustices is essential before shattered societies can start to rebuild.

Yet truth turns out to be a surprisingly elusive goal. One need not be a postmodernist to recognize that historical narratives are partly constructed rather than merely discovered, and that power and interests affect the process....

Furthermore, commissions have a bad habit of reflecting the prejudices and agendas of their framers. The TRC, for example, placed a disproportionate emphasis on crimes committed against nonblack South Africans. This slant was deliberate: even though blacks had suffered vastly more than other groups, [Chairperson of the TRC Archbishop Desmond] Tutu wanted the TRC to show how apartheid had affected all South Africans. As [Vice Chairperson of the TRC Alex] Boraine explained to me, "[Tutu] said that the major problem in our country is not a black problem, it's a white problem. It's a mixed race, a colored problem. So we mustn't go strictly on proportionality." However noble such a motive, unfortunately, giving nonblack victims more attention than they statistically "deserved" caused many blacks to angrily question the legitimacy of the TRC's findings....

Such criticisms, while serious, are best answered by the findings themselves. And there is abundant evidence that even imperfect truth commissions produce a wealth of previously unknown information regarding events that many people care about passionately. Families and friends have learned what happened to loved ones who "disappeared," and victims have had their charges legitimized. This can have a profound impact on sufferers.

...

Columbia University's Mahmood Mamdani, however, has leveled a somewhat different charge: that the [South African] TRC was not so much unable to locate the truth as it was unwilling to do so. The legislation that founded the commission, he notes, directed it to investigate only "gross violations of human rights." But the commission interpreted this mandate too narrowly, using it as an opportunity to avert its gaze from the broader criminality of the system itself and the racial inequities it perpetuated. Such choices explain why the TRC avoided economic injustice and documented only 21,000 victims — what Mamdani calls a "laughable" figure.

... [A]s Mamdani bitingly explains, "[it] ended up acknowledging as victims only political activists. But apartheid wasn't about political activists; it was about ordinary people. The only reconciliation the TRC can now expect is between two elites."

This hardly means that the TRC report was a total failure. The fact that both de Klerk and Mbeki challenged it in public and in court suggest that it got something right. But Mamdani's critique does highlight the consequences of the choices that commissions make and raises questions about what exactly is meant by all the talk of reconciliation...

...

Reconciliation, then, turns out to involve much more than mere forgiveness; to achieve it seems to require far more than truth telling. In fact, the reconciliation project could better be described as "nation building." Such a process involves addressing fundamental social inequalities. That is a task for politics, however, and not one that truth commissions — however broad their mandate — can hope to accomplish.

If truth commissions tend to achieve somewhat less than their advocates like to think, then the final charge against them — that they overshadow and undermine prosecutions — becomes more important....

...

Some governments, moreover, have turned to commissions precisely in order to put off — and eventually escape — formal legal proceedings that could spark confrontation with members or agents of the old regime....

Truth commission advocates such as Priscilla Hayner and Alex Boraine, both of whom are now professional truth-commission consultants at the [International Center for Transitional Justice], deny there is any necessary opposition between commissions and trials. The two processes, they argue, are complementary, not mutually exclusive. Hayner points to the fact that in both Argentina and Chad, evidence uncovered by truth commissions has been used in subsequent prosecutions. "You'll find that truth commissions increase the possibility of prosecutions rather than the other way around," she promises.

So far, at least, there is little evidence to support this claim.... Asked whether there is a causal connection between the work of the truth commission and the small number of prosecutions, Paul Seils, a Scottish human rights lawyer working in Guatemala, argues that the effect of the [Guatemalan Commission for Historical Clarification] report was to reduce international pressure on the country....

...

... Reconciliation turns out to be tremendously difficult to achieve or even understand. Truth too often remains elusive. The most appropriate response to such problems, however, should be not to blame the commissions for what they cannot accomplish, but to appreciate them for what they indisputably can. Although they may not have lived up to the giddy promises of their founders, for example, both the Guatemalan and the South African commissions made invaluable contributions to the health of those countries. Thanks to the TRC and the CEH, basic facts about apartheid in South Africa and the civil war in Guatemala are now part of the general historical record. De Klerk's political career has been ruined and he will never return to office. Even in Guatemala, a country slipping back toward chaos and gangsterism, the genocide of the 1980s is now impossible to deny.

And South Africa, at least, is a different country because of the TRC's collective national therapy. Harmony may not reign, but as Professor Jakes Gerwel, the chancellor of Rhodes University, argues, "notwithstanding the complex divisions and differences of various sorts, levels, and intensities, [it] is decidedly not an unreconciled nation in the sense of being threatened by imminent disintegration and internecine conflict." The fact that there have been no revenge killings in the country since the TRC started its work almost certainly says something about what kind of impact the commission has had.

VIEWS ON FUNCTIONS AND UTILITY OF TRUTH COMMISSIONS

Consider the following excerpts from the roundtable discussion in Truth Commissions: A Comparative Assessment, p. 1411, *supra*.

Bryan Hehir

I think that truth commissions function at three levels. The first entails catharsis.... The second level involves the process of moral reconstruction.... Society must pass judgment on what has been heard. It must establish a moral account of the historical record. The third level verges on the political — what is done with the process of truth telling? A number of options are available. A society may [even] choose to 'forget' or ignore the truth.

Tina Rosenberg

I am struck by how many comments outline the parallels between truth commissions and the therapeutic process of dealing with victims of post-traumatic stress disorder. The similarities are striking. People need to tell their story, but this is not all. Two other levels are important. People need to tell their stories to someone who is listening to them seriously and validating them. This is official acknowledgment. More importantly, victims must be able to reintegrate that narrative into their whole life story.

Lawrence Weschler (Staff Writer, *New Yorker*)

Furthermore, as the victims put their own lives together, they also pull the whole country together.

I detect three overlapping metaphors in our discussion — the realms of law, art and therapy. The most effective truth commissions carry on elements of the theatric, by being broadcast to the public on television for example. Artfulness of presentation makes the commission more effective. The public responds like an audience of a Greek tragedy. People must organize their lives in an artful way that lends them a cathartic life experience at the end.

[Use of truth commissions in the context of particular international disputes:]

Yael Tamir

Should Israel and Palestine establish a truth commission?...I can think of three kinds of justifications, which I have ordered from the most to the least convincing.

The first presupposes that we have a moral obligation to know and remember the wrongs that have occurred. If we ignore the injustice that has been done or forget it, we become in some sense accomplice to it. This implies that we have an obligation to know what has happened regardless of the social effects that this knowledge might produce. A truth commission contributes to our ability to reach this goal and is therefore welcome. It signals that no harm will go unnoticed and that those who bear responsibility will not go unpunished.

The second justification is instrumental. It is grounded in the psychological needs of the victims and their relatives: the need to talk about their harsh experiences and to have their suffering publicly acknowledged.... I am skeptical about the ability of truth commissions to serve this goal. I also have a deeper doubt about the psychological assumptions — for example, whether victims are better off if they are allowed to recount their experiences.

Truth commissions are also seen as instrumental in promoting reconciliation. I find this claim doubtful. In my experiences in Israeli-Palestinian workshops, I have found that an attempt to expose the facts is not particularly useful. It is often better to assume that injustices have been committed by both sides, and then focus on how to solve the conflict.

The most convincing justifications are then of the first kind, for the arguments for commissions that rest on instrumental justifications are very contingent on detailed contexts. I believe that a truth commission is unlikely to be helpful in the Israeli-Palestinian case.... To summarize, if the peace process is to move forward it cannot proceed on the basis of an investigation of the past. Rather, we must disassociate ourselves from the past and build a future based on an abstract acknowledgment of the injustice done by both sides, an injustice grounded in the fact that we share the same small piece of land for which both sides make claims of right. We must therefore reach an agreement regardless of past injustices. Peace cannot be grounded in competition over past suffering.

Fateh Azzam

Basically I agree with Yael Tamir's assessment of the situation and the potential for a truth commission. At the same time, I cannot help but note the urgency of dealing with issues of past injustices.

What should emerge from this strange animal called the peace process? I have some disagreement with Yael. Unless we acknowledge what happened in the past, it will continue to come up. Israelis and Palestinians must redefine their relationship, but not necessarily deny it. We must acknowledge one another in a way that lays a proper foundation for our future. This will take a very long time. The Palestinians need to hear some acknowledgment in order for them to admit that co-existence is possible.

For these reasons, I had thought a truth commission might be a useful exercise. But further reflection has made me realize how much the outcome of the peace process depends on politics and political desires. Our societies need to accept one another, and this has not yet happened. Perhaps it is a question of timing.

QUESTIONS

1. Are you satisfied with Jonathan Tepperman's exposition of the virtues of truth commissions? Do these benefits overcome the potential costs he identifies?

2. Some commentators have argued that a decision to 'name names' in a truth commission's report of those (in the armed forces, police) accused of committing serious human rights violations, as occurred in the Report on El Salvador, is justified in part by the fact that the state's justice system is incapable of honest investigation and impartial judgement. Do you agree? Are there other reasons pointing towards including names of violators? What form and methods of investigation would you recommend for a truth commission that intended to publish such names?

3. 'Truth commissions are particularly useful where the people involved — violators, victims, those just standing by — will (indeed must) live in close proximity to each other as members of the same state and society. Hence they are less necessary and less effective in many types of international conflicts where the peoples involved, the violators and the victims, will live separately after some accord and end to the conflict.' Do you agree?

COMMENT ON THE STANDARDIZATION OF TRUTH COMMISSIONS

An ideal often expressed for truth commissions is that states will tailor the general model to particular conditions within their country. The OHCHR, for example, states:

> It should be expected that every truth commission will be unique, responding to the national context and special opportunities present. While many technical

> and operational best practices from other commissions' experiences may usefully be incorporated, no one set truth commission model should be imported from elsewhere. This is true of the design of the commission's mandate as well as in specific operational aspects. Many key decisions should be based on local circumstance. This approach is likely to result in a stronger commission and enhance a sense of national ownership.[29]

How closely does practice approximate this ideal? That is, have truth commissions, which have now spread to all regions of the world, been adapted to the particularities of each context or has a more uniform model prevailed? The following readings provide diverse viewpoints in answer to that question.

That said, the readings arguably share a normative assumption that adaption and localization is best. After the readings, we turn to questions about the conditions under whether that assumption is valid. As you read the following materials consider whether some forms of standardization could be beneficial to the promotion of human rights. For instance, if a truth commission is tailored to the interests of powerful political elites, the design might not achieve the best results. Also recall our discussion of gacaca courts earlier in this chapter. Are there some standards and structural features which all truth commissions should share regardless of local interests? When should localization, even with its potential disadvantages, acquire primacy in setting up a transitional justice institution?

PRISCILLA B. HAYNER, UNSPEAKABLE TRUTHS: CONFRONTING STATE TERROR AND ATROCITY

(2nd edn. 2011), at 235–6

[T]ruth commissions are also changing over time. Early truth commissions largely focused on what happened, and usually on why it happened — in Argentina, Chile, El Salvador, Guatemala, Sri Lanka, Uganda. This moved to a period of commissions that not only concentrated on what and why, but also included a strong push for reconciliation, usually through public hearings: South Africa, Sierra Leone, Timor-Leste. Several bodies emerged that included a greater focus on perpetrators, giving the accused a more prominent platform in hearings but also usually naming those responsible in their reports: Ghana, Nigeria, Liberia, in addition of course to South Africa. A deeper analysis of historical and societal factors and consequences, such as racism and economic discrimination, and including robust research as well as legal analysis, seemed to set a new standard, in Peru and Guatemala. While some of the very early commissions included a prosecutions and reparations emphasis — and successfully influenced what followed — this emphasis has been even more pronounced in more recent bodies, such as those in Morocco and Peru. The inclusion of economic crimes (and possibly economic rights, more broadly) in the Kenyan commission is hinting at a new and challenging realm. The first bilateral

[29] OHCHR, *Rule-of-Law Tools for Post-Conflict States: Truth Commissions* (2008).

truth commission emerged—that between Indonesia and Timor-Leste—and, like that in Germany before it, relied more on documents and less on listening directly to victims. And, most recently, we are seeing the creation of truth commissions that reach back many generations and tackle fundamental historical issues that help define community relationships of today, in Mauritius and Canada.

...

The trend is toward broader inquiries with multifaceted mandates, covering longer periods of time. There is a greater use of public hearings, and higher public expectations for a commission's results. There has been some concern that the greater awareness of truth commissions, and an increase in the availability of international expertise and assistance, might be producing a standardized (and less nationally rooted) model, but in fact the opposite seems to be true. There is little tendency to copy or import models. There has been, rather, a healthy practice of closely studying other experiences, incorporating some of the more useful elements, while crafting something new and different, basing the new inquiries in national needs and historical context.

Thus, I am less worried about the increased use of truth commissions, the apparent quickening in pace of new commissions being created. Most of these seem to spring from national intention, and strong local demands for a recognition of the truth. Rather, my concern would be elsewhere: in the risk of the inquiries being weakened through rushed setting up, badly construed procedures for selecting members, or terms of reference that cut short their potential reach.

PATRICIA B. MINIKON, TRUTH COMMISSIONS IN AFRICA: LEARNING OVER A DECADE

(BiblioBazaar, Master's Dissertation) (2011)

The Liberian commission was similar to the Sierra Leonean commission in its format, mandate, and processes, although their amnesty-related powers differed in that the Liberian commission could recommend amnesty and the Sierra Leonean commission could not. Despite their many similarities, Sierra Leone's experience held limited guidance for Liberia. The Liberian commissioners visited their Sierra Leonean and South African peers, yet these learning opportunities did not provide an adequate roadmap. This is indicative of the limited role one commission's experience can play in establishing a roadmap for another.

The United Nations' involvement in the establishment of both commissions was pronounced, yet its toolkits for establishing truth commissions were not enough. Despite similar TRC Acts for both commissions, which indicate uniformity, collaboration, and referencing during the drafting stage, Liberia's TRC had to craft its own blueprint using the Liberian context. The pressure to behave as other TRCs had done was a source of frustration for the Liberian commission as expressed in Chairman Verdier's post to the Transitional Justice Network listserv:

> "Experts" will always have their prognosis and present the "best practices" that a [truth commission] should follow.... Without doubt, we have benefited

> enormously from all these engagements.... The TRC [adopted] practices, programs, and approaches that will best serve the Liberian situation and respond to the objectives of pursuing truth foremost and balancing reconciliation with justice. Every [truth commission], like every country, must find its own bearings and respond to the challenges that confront it. One size doesn't fit all. It is wrong when "experts" adopt the disposition that what is different... is wrong.

It is this tension between the standardization of truth commissions despite the unique circumstances of each country that I have examined in this study. My research and the case studies lead me to several conclusions:

The standardized organizational format of truth commissions affects how they learn, implement changes, and carry out their investigatory mandates. The move toward the standardization of truth commissions makes the process appear inorganic because the tools used to standardize them are usually created by external actors like the United Nations and technical advisors, without input from those within the affected countries. This external influence can weaken survivors' ownership of the process and create obstacles for the commission by making it seem externally imposed and inappropriate for the context. Further, the pressure to look similar stymies creative problem-solving by each commission that has been given a toolkit because the existence of the toolkit sends the signal that all there is to know is contained within it. Commissions are therefore discouraged from exploring organically generated knowledge to use in confronting the country's past. In addition, when U.N. agencies are involved in the standardization process, it creates a power imbalance because the U.N. also provides funding for the commissions. The commission is faced with a situation where it must challenge the utility of the proffered resource provided by a funder that is evaluating its continued investment in the project based on the commission's use of best practices the funder has generated.

My longitudinal analysis showed that acceptance of the South African commission by South Africans was easier because it was an organic process. The public hearings were innovative because they met a critical need in the post-apartheid era. They gave the populace the transparency they needed following the secrecy of apartheid. The conflicts in Sierra Leone and Liberia were not secretive dirty wars, yet there were public hearings. The violations that occurred in the civil wars in Liberia and Sierra Leone were openly conducted and no secret to survivors. In Sierra Leone, widespread amputations were done for that exact purpose — to intimidate the population by the visual image presented. In Liberia, public hearings were part of the commission's mandate, but there is no record of an assessment to determine that they were needed to meet a post-conflict need of the population. Assessments of this type must be conducted to ensure that truth commission processes are organic and meet the needs of the population. Theatre for the sake of theatre is not effective in the context of transitional justice and requires resources that could be expended on other, more needed programs.

Over the time period studied, the inclusion of processes without first ascertaining that it was appropriate and needed has led to less innovation by truth commissions. The commissions still innovate, but it is in more subtle ways, most likely due to the pressure to look and act the same as other commissions. Limited innovation may also restrict the effect of truth commissions on the affected populations. For example, if commissions were allowed to deviate from standardized practices, they could focus on the strength and resilience that allowed survivors to endure the conflict, thereby helping them regain their personal agency. Where the conflict had an ethnic dimension, in getting to the truth about violations that occurred, commissions could explore the fact that many went against expectations during the conflict to render lifesaving assistance to others, despite their ethnic identities. Reviewing the conflict from a different perspective could help rewrite the story and debunk myths, while contributing to a foundation for lasting peace by showing survivors that all who survived are united as fellow citizens, regardless of ethnic identities. As it stands now, commissions focus on the testimony of victimhood, which is not personally empowering, although it provides state acknowledgment of the atrocities committed.

Truth commissions rely heavily and exclusively on knowledge acquired by past commissions, technical advisors, and UN organs and this mode of knowledge transfer is limiting and has unintended consequences. Knowledge transfer is taking place, but it must be contextualized. The toolkits and resources attempt to standardized most processes of a truth commission, from enabling legislation to public hearings.... The knowledge acquired from past commissions is very useful in crafting future commissions, but that knowledge must be modified to accommodate the circumstances of different conflicts and countries.... The content of enabling legislation is not appropriate for standardization because it does not take into account the political or security realities in the country. When a commission is given robust powers that cannot be used due to political and security realities, it negatively affects public perception of the truth commission's effectiveness and its ability to bring perpetrators to account.

JAMES L CAVALLARO & SEBASTIAN ALBUJA, THE LOST AGENDA: ECONOMIC CRIMES AND TRUTH COMMISSIONS IN LATIN AMERICA AND BEYOND

in Kieran McEvoy & Lorna McGregor (eds.), Transitional Justice from Below: Grassroots Activism and the Struggle for Change (2008)

... [Truth and Reconciliation Commissions (TRCs)] have varied as to the scope of abuses addressed; the number gender and affiliation of commissioners; whether to include mechanisms to pardon violators in exchange for confession; whether to name the names of individuals responsible for abuse; whether to provide compensation and the measure of such compensations; duration; and the scope of investigative powers.

Yet these truth commissions, despite their heterogeneity, have consistently adopted a set of parameters established by the conventional understanding of the scope of human rights law and practice at the time of the creation of the first such bodies in Latin America. These constraints led to a focus on gross violations of civil and political rights, especially forced disappearances, execution, and torture.

Because of this reliance on the human rights framework, we argue, state-sponsored TRCs have failed to include in their mandates economic crimes and corruption — issues only recently embraced by mainstream human rights organisations. This is so, we contend, despite a marked grassroots condemnation of corruption and economic crimes and despite popular support for efforts to hold leaders accountable for economic crimes and corruption both in Latin America and Africa. . . .

. . .

. . . [O]nce the model for TRCs as a vehicle for denouncing only a limited set of human rights violations developed legitimacy in world society, modifying the script to include economic crimes and corruption — and thus undoing the process of socialisation of the model — became extremely difficult.

In practice, it is not difficult to identify the existence of personal and institutional links that have led to the development of this dominant script. While the first few truth commissions, such as the 1984 Argentine Commission, and the failed Bolivian commission of 1982, may have developed in relative isolation, subsequent TRCs have been the work of repeated information exchange and consultations with prior commission members and a cadre of international scholars and practitioners in the area. . . .

. . .

Further, there is good reason to believe that the forces leading to . . . adoption of 'world society' norms are present or perhaps intensified in situations of transition, in which states and their agents are particularly concerned, and their attention particularly focused, on the international community and its standards of legitimacy. . . .

. . .

Over the past 15 years, a second wave of states, primarily outside Latin America, has undergone transition from authoritarian and democratic rule. These states . . . have implemented transitional justice measures consistent with the growing international consensus, which provides a privileged place for truth commissions. As in Latin America, these states have, with some important exceptions, followed the dominant script with regard to economic crimes, even when this has differed significantly from indigenous demands. While TRC mandates have involved significant modifications and adaptations — such as naming perpetrators, expanding the range of civil and political rights covered, and providing pardon in exchange for confessions — they have consistently excluded economic crimes.

. . .

TRCs face a variety of constraints, related to political pressures, as well as limits on time, resources, and professional staff. Admittedly, the inclusion of corruption and economic crimes might serve to heighten these challenges. Nevertheless, investigating acts of economic malfeasance committed by authoritarian regimes may serve a variety of functions, rendering it a net gain for TRCs. First, investigation may provide a mechanism to address popular demands for accountability in an effective manner. Secondly, it may be highly functional to delegitimising authoritarian regimes — even more so than denouncing violations of civil and political rights. Finally, investigating this class of crimes may prove highly useful to the consolidation of burgeoning democracies.

The time may have come to rethink, at least in part, the prevailing TRC paradigm.

QUESTIONS

1. Have truth commissions remained relatively uniform? Have some features arisen and disappeared like fads over time? Cavallaro and Albuja suggest there has been heterogeneity along several dimensions except for the treatment of economic and social rights. If true, what would explain the uniform approach to economic and social rights but not other features of these institutions?

2. Do all the authors share a normative assumption that values localization over standardization in the design of truth commissions? Is such an assumption well founded? Recall our discussion of gacaca courts as a mechanism for effectuating transitional justice. Does a similar set of issues arise with respect to truth commissions? Under what conditions should international institutions defer to national-level actors in the design of truth commissions? Under what conditions should international institutions encourage a particular standard or common structural feature to guide the design of truth commissions across all countries?

3. In the same publication that the OHCHR expressed the ideal that 'every truth commission will be unique, responding to the national context and special opportunities present', the OHCHR stated the following with respect to economic and social rights:

> In some countries, economic crimes have been as prominent — and in the public's mind as egregious — as the civil and political rights violations by a prior regime. There may therefore be discussion of including corruption and other economic crimes within a truth commission's mandate, or broadening its terms of reference to include violations of social and economic rights. This decision, like most, must ultimately be taken by nationals, but those drafting the mandate should be conscious of the dangers and difficulties of including economic crimes within a truth commission's scope. The methodology and timing required for investigating corruption and economic crimes are quite different from those required for investigating individual or systematic practices of torture or killings, for example. Furthermore, a broad focus on "violations of economic and social rights" might suggest the need to look into poverty, homelessness, education policy failures and other social ills. Although these are critically important subjects, this could risk expanding the mandate of the commission so broadly that it may be impossible to reasonably complete its task. However, economic matters certainly should not be excluded per se. If there is a clear link between economic issues and violence — such as land conflicts that erupt in violence, or the State confiscates property when persons are arrested or disappear — then a truth commission should clearly recognize, inquire into and report on these matters.[30]

Does this statement substantiate the concerns outlined by Cavallaro and Albuja as well as by Minikon? Or are there valid reasons for the OHCHR to advise caution with respect to the inclusion of economic and social rights in the mandate of truth commissions?

[30] Ibid.

PROMOTION OF NATIONAL UNITY AND RECONCILIATION ACT OF SOUTH AFRICA, 1995

Definitions

...

1.

(ix) "gross violation of human rights" means the violation of human rights through—

(a) the killing, abduction, torture or severe ill-treatment of any person; or

(b) any attempt, conspiracy, incitement, instigation, command or procurement to commit an act referred to in paragraph (a), which emanated from conflicts of the past and which was committed during the period 1 March 1960 to the cut-off date within or outside the Republic, and the commission of which was advised, planned, directed, commanded or ordered, by any person acting with a political motive;

Functions of Commission

4. The functions of the Commission shall be to achieve its objectives, and to that end the Commission shall—

(a) facilitate, and where necessary initiate or coordinate, inquiries into—

(i) gross violations of human rights, including violations which were part of a systematic pattern of abuse;

(ii) the nature, causes and extent of gross violations of human rights, including the antecedents, circumstances, factors, context, motives and perspectives which led to such violations;

(iii) the identity of all persons, authorities, institutions and organisations involved in such violations;

(iv) the question whether such violations were the result of deliberate planning on the part of the State or a former state or any of their organs, or of any political organisation, liberation movement or other group or individual; and

(v) accountability, political or otherwise, for any such violation;

(b) facilitate, and initiate or coordinate, the gathering of information and the receiving of evidence from any person, including persons claiming to be victims of such violations or the representatives of such victims, which establish the identity of victims of such violations, their fate or present whereabouts and the nature and extent of the harm suffered by such victims;

(c) facilitate and promote the granting of amnesty in respect of acts associated with political objectives...;

...

(f) make recommendations to the President with regard to —
   (i) the policy which should be followed or measures which should be taken with regard to the granting of reparation to victims or the taking of other measures aimed at rehabilitating and restoring the human and civil dignity of victims;
   (ii) measures which should be taken to grant urgent interim reparation to victims;

…

(h) make recommendations to the President with regard to the creation of institutions conducive to a stable and fair society and the institutional, administrative and legislative measures which should be taken or introduced in order to prevent the commission of violations of human rights.

Powers of Commission

5. In order to achieve its objectives and to perform its functions the Commission shall have the power to —

…

(d) conduct any investigation or hold any hearing it may deem necessary and establish the investigating unit referred to in section 28;

…

(i) in consultation with the Minister [of Justice] and through diplomatic channels, obtain permission from the relevant authority of a foreign country to receive evidence or gather information in that country;

(j) enter into an agreement with any person, including any department of State, in terms of which the Commission will be authorized to make use of any of the facilities, equipment or personnel belonging to or under the control or in the employment of such person or department;

…

(l) hold meetings at any place within or outside the Republic;

(m) on its own initiative or at the request of any interested person inquire or investigate into any matter, including the disappearance of any person or group of persons.

…

[Article 31 provides the power of the Commission to subpoena individuals to testify.]

[Article 34 provides the power of the Commission to authorize entry into premises and the search and seizure of relevant evidence.]

Granting of amnesty and effect thereof

20. (1) If the Committee, after considering an application for amnesty, is satisfied that —

(a) the application complies with the requirements of this Act;

(b) the act, omission or offence to which the application relates is an act associated with a political objective committed in the course of the conflicts of the past in accordance with the provisions of subsections (2) and (3); and

(c) the applicant has made a full disclosure of all relevant facts, it shall grant amnesty in respect of that act, omission or offence.

(2) In this Act, unless the context otherwise indicates, "act associated with a political objective" means any act or omission which constitutes an offence or delict which, according to the criteria in subsection (3), is associated with a political objective, and which was advised, planned, directed, commanded, ordered or committed... by—

(a) any member or supporter of a publicly known political organisation or liberation movement on behalf of or in support of such organisation or movement, bona fide in furtherance of a political struggle waged by such organisation or movement against the State or any former state or another publicly known political organisation or liberation movement;

(b) any employee of the State or any former state or any member of the security forces of the State or any former state in the course and scope of his or her duties and within the scope of his or her express or implied authority directed against a publicly known political organisation or liberation movement engaged in a political struggle against the State or a former state or against any members or supporters of such organisation or movement, and which was committed bona fide with the object of countering or otherwise resisting the said struggle;

(c) any employee of the State or any former state or any member of the security forces of the State or any former state in the course and scope of his or her duties and within the scope of his or her express or implied authority directed—

(i) in the case of the State, against any former state; or

(ii) in the case of a former state, against the State or any other former state, whilst engaged in a political struggle against each other or against any employee of the State or such former state, as the case may be, and which was committed bona fide with the object of countering or otherwise resisting the said struggle;

(d) any employee or member of a publicly known political organisation or liberation movement in the course and scope of his or her duties and within the scope of his or her express or implied authority directed against the State or any former state or any publicly known political organisation or liberation movement engaged in a political struggle against that political organisation or liberation movement or against members of the security forces of the State or any former state or members or supporters of such publicly known political organisation or liberation movement, and which was committed bona fide in furtherance of the said struggle;

(e) any person in the performance of a coup d'etat to take over the government of any former state, or in any attempt thereto;
(f) any person referred to in paragraphs (a), (b), (c) and (d), who on reasonable grounds believed that he or she was acting in the course and scope of his or her duties and within the scope of his or her express or implied authority;

...

(3) Whether a particular act, omission or offence contemplated in subsection (2) is an act associated with a political objective, shall be decided with reference to the following criteria:

(a) The motive of the person who committed the act, omission or offence;
(b) the context in which the act, omission or offence took place, and in particular whether the act, omission or offence was committed in the course of or as part of a political uprising, disturbance or event, or in reaction thereto;
(c) the legal and factual nature of the act, omission or offence, including the gravity of the act, omission or offence;
(d) the object or objective of the act, omission or offence, and in particular whether the act, omission or offence was primarily directed at a political opponent or State property or personnel or against private property or individuals;
(e) whether the act, omission or offence was committed in the execution of an order of, or on behalf of, or with the approval of, the organisation, institution, liberation movement or body of which the person who committed the act was a member, an agent or a supporter; and
(f) the relationship between the act, omission or offence and the political objective pursued, and in particular the directness and proximity of the relationship and the proportionality of the act, omission or offence to the objective pursued, but does not include any act, omission or offence committed by any person referred to in subsection (2) who acted —
    (i) for personal gain: Provided that an act, omission or offence by any person who acted and received money or anything of value as an informer of the State or a former state, political organisation or liberation movement, shall not be excluded only on the grounds of that person having received money or anything of value for his or her information; or
    (ii) out of personal malice, ill-will or spite, directed against the victim of the acts committed.

...

(7)(a) No person who has been granted amnesty in respect of an act, omission or offence shall be criminally or civilly liable in respect of such act, omission or offence and no body or organisation or the State shall be liable, and no person shall be vicariously liable, for any such act, omission or offence.

...

[Sections 8–10 provide that amnesty shall result in the termination of any criminal prosecution for an act for which amnesty is granted and shall result in the nullification of any conviction and sentence for an offence for which amnesty is granted.]

REPORT OF TRUTH AND RECONCILIATION COMMISSION OF SOUTH AFRICA

5 vols (2003)

[Excerpts from the Report appear below. They are identified by volume, chapter number of the volume and paragraph number.]

Volume 1

Chapter 4: The Mandate

- *Why the South African Commission is different from other Commissions...*

25. The most important difference between the South African Commission and others was that it was the first to be given the power to grant amnesty to individual perpetrators. No other state had combined this quasi-judicial power with the investigation tasks of a truth-seeking body. More typically, where amnesty was introduced to protect perpetrators from being prosecuted for the crimes of the past, the provision was broad and unconditional, with no requirement for individual application or confession of particular crimes....

26. Another significant difference can be found in the Commission's powers of *subpoena*, search and seizure, which are much stronger than those of other truth commissions. This has led to more thorough internal investigation and direct questioning of witnesses, including those who were implicated in violations and did not apply for amnesty....

27. The very public process of the South African Commission also distinguishes it from other commissions.... The Latin American truth commissions heard testimony only in private, and information only emerged with the release of the final reports....

29. The South African Commission was the first to create a witness protection programme. This strengthened its investigative powers and allowed witnesses to come forward with information they feared might put them at risk.

30. Finally, the South African Commission was several times larger in terms of staff and budget than any commission before it....

- *Interpreting the mandate...*

34. It was recognised at the outset that the Commission could not carry out all the tasks required of it simultaneously. Thus, it first gave attention to the question of the restoration of the human and civil dignity of (individual) victims of past gross

human rights violations. It did so by creating opportunities for victims 'to relate their own accounts' of the violations they had suffered by giving testimony at public hearings across the length and breadth of South Africa between April 1996 and June 1997. These highly publicised hearings were coupled with an extensive statement-taking drive, investigations, research and so-called 'section 29' hearings (where witnesses and alleged perpetrators were *subpoenaed*) in order to 'establish the fate or whereabouts of victims' and the identity of those responsible for human rights violations.

35. During the second half of the Commission's life (from approximately the middle of 1997), the Commission shifted its focus from the stories of individual victims to an attempt to understand the individual and institutional motives and perspectives which gave rise to the gross violations of human rights under examination. It enquired into the contexts and causes of these violations and attempted to establish the political and moral accountability of individuals, organisations and institutions. The goal was to provide the grounds for making recommendations to prevent future human rights violations. Features of this phase were public submissions by, and questioning of, political parties, and a range of institutional, sectoral and special hearings that focused on the health and business sectors, the legal system, the media and faith communities, prisons, women, children and youth, biological and chemical warfare and compulsory national service. It was also during this period that the majority of amnesty hearings took place....

• *Who were victims of gross violations of human rights?...*

51. It is this systemic and all-pervading character of apartheid that provides the background for the present investigation. During the apartheid years, people did many evil things. Some of these are the gross violations of human rights with which this Commission had to deal. But it can never be forgotten that the system itself was evil, inhumane and degrading for the many millions who became its second and third class citizens. Amongst its many crimes, perhaps the greatest was its power to humiliate, to denigrate and to remove the self-confidence, self-esteem and dignity of its millions of victims....

55. ...[T]he Commission resolved that its mandate was to give attention to human rights violations committed as specific acts, resulting in severe physical and/or mental injury, in the course of past political conflict. As such, the focus of its work was not on the effects of laws passed by the apartheid government, nor on general policies of that government or of other organisations, however morally offensive these may have been. This underlines the importance of understanding the Commissions as but one of several instruments responsible for transformation and bridge-building in post-apartheid South Africa....

57. But bodily integrity rights are not the only fundamental rights. When a person has no food to eat, or when someone is dying because of an illness that access to basic health care could have prevented — that is, when subsistence rights are violated — rights to political participation and freedom of speech become meaningless.

58. Thus, a strong argument can be made that the violations of human rights caused by 'separate development' — for example, by migrant labour, forced removals, bantustans, Bantu education and so on — had, and continue to have, the most negative possible impact on the lives of the majority of South Africans. The

consequences of these violations cannot be measured only in the human lives lost through deaths, detentions, dirty tricks and disappearances, but in the human lives withered away through enforced poverty and other kinds of deprivation....

- *Just ends, just means and crimes against humanity*

64. In making judgments in respect of the above requirements, the Commission was guided by criteria derived from just war theory ..., international human rights principles and the democratic values inherent in the South African Constitution. By using these criteria, the Commission was able to take clear positions on the evils of apartheid, while also evaluating the actions of those who opposed it....

74. The Commission's confirmation of the fact that the apartheid system was a crime against humanity does not mean that all acts carried out in order to destroy apartheid were necessarily legal, moral and acceptable. The Commission concurred with the international consensus that those who were fighting for a just cause were under an obligation to employ just means in the conduct of this fight.

75. As far as justice in war is concerned, the framework within which the Commission made its findings was in accordance with international law and the views and findings of international organisations and judicial bodies. The strict prohibitions against torture and abduction and the grave wrong of killing and injuring defenceless people, civilians and soldiers 'out of combat' required the Commission to conclude that not all acts in war could be regarded as morally or legally legitimate, even where the cause was just.

76. It is for this reason that the Commission considered the concept of crimes against humanity at both a systemic level and at the level of specific acts. Apartheid as a system was a crime against humanity, but it was also possible for acts carried out by any of the parties to the conflicts of the past to be classified as human rights violations.

77. Thus, the Commission adopted the view that human rights violations could be committed by any group or person inside or outside the state: by persons within the Pan Africanist Congress (PAC), the IFP, the South African Police (SAP), the South African Defence Force (SADF), the ANC or any other organisation.

78. It is important to note, however, that this wider application of human rights principles to non-state entities is a relatively recent international development....

79. The Act establishing the Commission adopted this more modern position. In other words, it did not make a finding of a gross violation of human rights conditional on a finding of state action....

- *Racism*

127. There were cases in which people were victims of racist attack by individuals who were not involved with a publicly known political organisation and where the incident did not form part of a specific political conflict. Although racism was at the heart of the South African political order, and although such cases were clearly a violation of the victim's rights, such violations did not fall within the Commission's mandate.

128. Cases which were interpreted as falling inside the Commission's mandate included instances where racism was used to mobilise people through a political organisation as part of their commitment to a political struggle, or where racism was used by a political organisation to incite others to violence. Examples of these were instances when white 'settlers' or farmers were killed by supporters of the PAC or the ANC, or where black people were killed by supporters of white right-wing organisations....

- *Naming*

152. The Act required the publication of the names of those who received amnesty in the Government Gazette. These individuals had already identified themselves as perpetrators by applying for amnesty. The Commission had therefore, to resolve which of the other perpetrators identified in the course of its work should be named in accordance with its mandate — to enquire into 'the identity of all persons, authorities, institutions and organisations' involved in gross human rights violations, as well as the 'accountability, political or otherwise, for any such violation' (section 4(a)(iii), (V), the Act).

153. In fulfilling this part of its mandate, the Commission was again required to walk a tightrope. This time, it was faced with the tension between the public interest in the exposure of wrongdoing and the need to ensure fair treatment of individuals in what was not a court of law; between the rights of victims of gross violations of human rights to know who was responsible and the fundamentally important question of fairness to those who are accused of crimes or serious wrongdoing.

...

155. Given the investigative nature of the Commission's process and the limited legal impact of naming, the Commission made findings on the identity of those involved in gross violations of human rights based on the balance of probability. This required a lower burden of proof than that required by the conventional criminal justice system. It meant that, when confronted with different versions of events, the Commission had to decide which version was the more probable, reasonable or likely, after taking all the available evidence into account.

Volume 5

Chapter 6: Findings and conclusions...

The Commission's position on responsibility and accountability...

66. In the light of the above and of the evidence received, the Commission is of the view that gross violations of human rights were perpetrated or facilitated by all the major role-players in the conflicts of the mandate era. These include:

(a) The state and its security, intelligence and law-enforcement agencies, the SAP, the SADF and the NIS.

(b) Groups and institutions which, to a greater or lesser extent, were affiliated or allied to the state in an official capacity. These include homeland governments and their security forces as well as groups and institutions informally allied to the state....

(c) White right-wing organizations which, while actively opposing the state, actively and violently took action to preserve the *status quo* in the 1990s....

(d) Liberation movements and organizations which sought to bring about change through armed struggle and which operated outside South Africa and by covert and underground means inside the country.

(e) Organizations which sought to bring about change by non-violent means prior to and post-1990, including the United Democratic Front; and

(f) Non-state paramilitary formations such as the ANC's self-defence units and the IFP's self-protection units (SPUs)....

68. At the same time, the Commission is not of the view that all such parties can be held to be equally culpable for violations committed in the mandate period. Indeed, the evidence accumulated by the Commission and documented in this report shows that this was not the case. The preponderance of responsibility rests with the state and its allies....

71. ... [T]he evidence shows that the perpetration of gross violations of human rights by non-state actors often took place in circumstances where they were acting in opposition to the official state ideology and the policy of apartheid. In this sense, it was the state that generated violent political conflict in the mandate period — either through its own direct action or by eliciting reactions to its policies and strategies.

72. ... A state has powers, resources, obligations, responsibilities and privileges that are much greater than those of any group within that state. It must therefore be held to a higher standard of moral and political conduct than are voluntary associations...

...

74. It would, however, be misleading and wrong to assign blame for the gross violation of human rights only to those who confronted each other on the political and military battlefields, engaged in acts of commission. Others, like the church or faith groups, the media, the legal profession, the judiciary, the magistracy, the medical/health, educational and business sectors, are found by the Commission to have been guilty of acts of omission in that they failed to adhere or live up to the ethics of their profession and to accepted codes of conduct.

75. It is also the view of the Commission that these sectors failed not so much out of fear of the powers and wrath of the state — although those were not insignificant factors — but primarily because they were the beneficiaries of the state system. They prospered from it by staying silent. By doing nothing or not enough, they contributed to the emergence of a culture of impunity within which the gross violations of human rights documented in this report could and did occur.

[The balance of this section on Findings and Conclusions provides detailed findings against each of the state organs, government leaders, internal allies of the state, regional groups, liberation movements and sectors of civil society to which the earlier parts of this section refer.]

DECISIONS OF AMNESTY COMMITTEE, TRUTH AND RECONCILIATION COMMISSION

at www.justice.gov.za/trc/decisions/am98.htm

Ntamo, VS (4734/97); Peni, NA (5188/97); Nofemela, EM (5282/97); Manqina, MC (0669/96) (Heard in July 1997)

The Applicants were convicted and sentenced to imprisonment for 18 years for the murder of Amy Biehl.... The offence was committed on the NY1 Road in the Gugulethu Township, in Cape Town on the 25th August 1993. The applicants are young men whose ages, at the time of the commission of the offence ranged between 18 and 22 years. Except for Ntamo, whose education had not progressed beyond Std 4, the others were high school students.

They have applied for amnesty in terms of section 18 of the Promotion of National Unity and Reconciliation Act No. 34 of 1995.

Amy Biehl their victim was an American Citizen. She was on a Fulbright Scholarship and was affiliated to the Community Law Centre at the University of the Western Cape where she was pursuing her studies for a Ph. D in Political Science. On that fateful afternoon, she was conveying three colleagues in her car. She was on her way to drop some of them off in Gugulethu, when her vehicle came under attack by people who were running towards it and throwing stones at it. The stones smashed the windscreen and windows of the car. One of the stones hit Amy Biehl on her head, causing her to bleed profusely. She could not continue driving. She got out of her car and ran towards a garage across the road. Her attackers did not relent. They pursued her and continued throwing stones at her. Manqina tripped her, causing her to fall. She was surrounded by between 7 and 10 people and while she was being stoned, one of her attackers stabbed her. She died as a result of the injuries they inflicted on her.

According to the evidence of the applicants they were among those who were involved in the attack on Amy Biehl. Peni admitted throwing stones at his victim when he was three to four metres from her. Manqina stabbed her with a knife in addition to throwing stones at her. Nofemela threw stones at her and stabbed at her 3 or 4 times. Ntamo threw many stones at her head when he was only a metre away. They stopped attacking her when the police arrived on the scene.

The attack on the car driven by Amy Biehl was one of many incidents of general lawlessness in NY1 that afternoon. Bands of toyi-toying youths threw stones at delivery vehicles and cars driven by white people. One delivery vehicle was toppled over and set alight and only the arrival of the police prevented more damage....

The applicants explained their behavior by saying that earlier that day they had attended a meeting at the Langa High School where a Pan African Student organization (PASO) unit was relaunched. Peni was elected Chairperson at the meeting. Manqina was Vice Chairperson of the PASO unit at the Gugulethu Comprehensive School and Nofemela was a PASO organizer at the Joe Slovo High School.... The applicants said that speakers dealt with:

- the strike by Teachers in the Western Cape who demanded recognition for the South African Democratic Teachers Union (SADTU);

- the struggles of the Azanian Peoples Liberation Army (APLA) for the return of the land to the African People;
- APLA had declared 1993 as the 'Year of the Great Storm'. Reference was also made to the launching of 'OPERATION BARCELONA' to stop all deliveries into the townships.

The speakers urged the members of PASO to take an active part in the struggle of APLA by assisting APLA operators on the ground by making the country ungovernable.

The speeches were militant and punctuated by shouting the slogan 'ONE SETTLER ONE BULLET'.

Applicants said that they were all inspired by the speakers to such an extent that they left the meeting with many others in a militant mood. They marched through the township toyi-toying and shouting ONE SETTLER ONE BULLET, determined to put into effect what they had been urged to do. This is how they got involved in the activities briefly described above which led to the killing of Amy Biehl.... Although they did not act on the orders or instructions of APLA or PAC [Pan African Congress] on that day, they believed they owed loyalty to the same cause.... As members of PASO, which was a known political organization of students, they were active supporters of the PAC and subscribed to its political philosophy and its policies. By stoning company delivery vehicles and thereby making it difficult for deliveries into the townships, they were taking part in a political disturbance and contributing towards making their area ungovernable. To that extent, their activities were aimed at supporting the liberation struggle against the State. But Amy Biehl was a private citizen, and the question is why was she killed during this disturbance. Part of the answer may be that her attackers were so aroused and incited, that they lost control of themselves and got caught up in a frenzy of violence. One of the applicants said during his evidence that they all submitted to the slogan of ONE SETTLER, ONE BULLET. To them that meant that every white person was an enemy of the Black people. At that moment to them, Amy Biehl, was a representative of the white community. They believed that by killing civilian whites, APLA was sending a serious political message to the government of the day. By intensifying such activity the political pressure on the government would increase to such an extent that it would demoralize them and compel them to hand over political power to the majority of the people of South Africa.

When the conduct of the applicants is viewed in that light, it must be accepted that their crime was related to a political objective.

The PAC regarded the killing of Amy Biehl as a mistake committed by young people who were misguided. They nevertheless supported the application for amnesty.

The parents of Amy Biehl had come from America to attend the hearing. At the conclusion of the evidence Mr Biehl addressed the Amnesty Committee. Part of his speech reads as follows:

> ...We have the highest respect for your Truth and Reconciliation Commission and process. We recognise that if this process had not been a pre-negotiated condition your democratic free elections could not possibly have occurred.

> Therefore, and believing as Amy did in the absolute importance of those democratic elections occurring we unabashedly support the process which we recognize to be unprecedented in contemporary human history.
>
> At the same time we say to you it's your process, not ours. We cannot, therefore, oppose amnesty if it is granted on the merits. In the truest sense it is for the community of South Africa to forgive its own and this has its basis in traditions of ubuntu and other principles of human dignity. Amnesty is not clearly for Linda and Peter Biehl to grant.... We, as the Amy Biehl Foundation are willing to do our part as catalysts for social progress. All anyone need do is ask. Are you, the community of South Africa, prepared to do your part?

The applicants have made a full disclosure of all the relevant facts as required by section 20(1) of the Act. On a consideration of all the evidence placed before us, we have come to the conclusion that they be granted amnesty for the murder of Amy Biehl....

Dirk Coetzee (0063/96), David Tshikalange (0065/96), and Butana Almond Nofomela (0064/96) (Heard in November 1996 and January 1997)

...We are dealing now with the applications for amnesty made by the three Applicants in respect of the murder of Griffiths Mxenge. The three Applicants, who were at all relevant times serving members of the South African Police Force, have applied for amnesty in respect of many acts committed by them. [The three applicants had been convicted for one of the offences stated in their application, the murder of Mxenge.]...

The evidence led before us disclosed that the three Applicants were stationed at a place called Vlakplaas, which was a base established in the country where the police stationed what could perhaps fairly be described as hit squads....

At the relevant time all four groups from Vlakplaas were in Durban for various purposes. The First Applicant who was the commander reported, so he said, daily to Brigadier Van der Hoven, the regional security commander at about 7.30 am and again at 4 pm. On one such occasion, a few days before the 19th of November 1981, Brigadier Van der Hoven called him to make a 'plan' with Mxenge. He understood this to mean that he was to make arrangements to eliminate Mxenge. He was told in very brief terms that Mxenge, who was the victim in this application, was an ex-Robben Island prisoner and was an attorney practising in Durban. He acted on behalf of members of the liberation movement and others who were charged with criminal offences arising out of the struggle against apartheid, and a large amount of money was known to have gone through his account. There was no suggestion in the evidence before us that this money was improperly used in any way....

He was told that the security police had been unable to bring any charges against Mxenge and that he had accordingly become a thorn in their flesh by enabling persons charged with political offences to obtain the protection of the courts.

The First Applicant said that Brigadier Van der Hoven told him that they must not shoot or abduct Mxenge but that they should make it look like a robbery. He was then taken to Captain Taylor who gave him certain information about Mxenge. This information related to where his office was, where his house was, what car he drove and matters of that nature....

The First Applicant took charge of arrangements and set up a squad which was to be responsible for killing Mxenge, consisting of the Second and Third Applicants, [a certain] Mamasela, and a certain Brian Ngulunga, because he was from the Umlazi area and knew the vicinity well. The First Applicant took charge of the general planning of the murder.... He however left the details as to the actual killing to the four members of the squad he had appointed.... They intercepted the car in which Mxenge was travelling and dragged him out of it. While Brian Ngulunga stood by with a pistol in his hand, the others commenced to stab their victim.... The stabbing continued until he was dead. He had been disemboweled; his throat had been cut and his ears had been practically cut off. His body was found to have 45 lacerations and stab wounds.

It is quite clear from his evidence and from the evidence of the other two Applicants, that they considered this to be an act performed as part of their duties as policemen on the instructions of senior officers who would undoubtedly have satisfied themselves as to the necessity for it.

In this regard the First Applicant said the following during the course of his evidence before us:

> ...
> 'Do you still today believe that those were necessary or lawful orders?'
> 'Absolutely not.'
> 'Why do you think differently today?'
> 'Well, at the time, yes, but with hindsight absurd and absolutely — I mean unjustifiable.'

On the evidence before us we are satisfied that none of the Applicants knew the deceased, Mxenge, or had any reason to wish to bring about his death before they were ordered to do so. We are satisfied that they did what they did because they regarded it as their duty as policemen who were engaged in the struggle against the ANC and other liberation movements. It is, we think clear, that they relied on their superiors to have accurately and fairly considered the question as to whether the assassination was necessary or whether other steps could have been taken....

...With regard to the First Applicant, there was no direct evidence to confirm that he acted on the orders of Van der Hoven or Taylor. In fact, it is a matter of public knowledge that Van der Hoven and Taylor denied any involvement; they did so during their recent trial in which they were co-accused with the Applicants on a criminal charge in respect of this very incident. While there may be some doubt about the identity of the person or persons on whose advice, command or order, the First Applicant acted, the fact that he acted on the advice, command or order of one or more senior members of the security branch, admits of no doubt....

...We are accordingly of the view that the three Applicants are entitled to amnesty in respect of this offence, that is the murder of Griffiths Mxenge on the 19th of November 1981, and it will accordingly not be necessary for the Trial Court to proceed with the question of sentence.

NOTE

The Report stressed the role of the TRC in communicating to a relevant public the nature of amnesty and the process for submitting applications through visits of its members and staff to institutions such as prisons and through public talks. The amnesty hearings were open to all media, and television coverage became standard.

With respect to the procedure of the hearings, the Amnesty Committee took care to 'avoid overly formalising the process' and to retain flexibility. It took the view of the TRC that 'process should not be equated to that of a court of law and should not be overly regulated'. Nonetheless, the proceedings 'are largely judicial in nature' and included such rights as cross-examination 'within reasonable bounds'. Proceedings were recorded, and the Committee gave 'reasoned decisions' on all issues to be decided. All decisions were published.

Several legal challenges to the legislation underlying the amnesty provisions and the procedure governing the hearings were brought in the courts. The Constitutional Court resolved one such challenge in *Azanian Peoples Organisation (AZAPO) v. President of the Republic of South Africa*, CCT 17/96 (1996). The applicants claimed that certain provisions on amnesty of the Promotion of National Unity and Reconciliation Act 34 of 1995 were unconstitutional, since if amnesty were granted, a perpetrator would not be criminally or civilly liable in respect of the acts subject to the amnesty. The Court upheld the constitutionality of these provisions that limited applicants' right set forth in the Constitution to 'have justiciable disputes settled by a court of law'. The interim Constitution's epilogue on national unity and reconciliation sanctioned this limitation on the applicants' right of access to courts to bring a suit for damages. Absent such provisions, there would be no incentive for offenders to disclose the truth. Moreover, the amnesty provisions were a crucial part of the negotiated settlement leading to the Constitution. Parliament could always act to provide systematic reparations for victims of past abuses, and to provide for individualized reparations taking account of the claims of all victims, rather than preserving civil liability of the state and its officials for provable acts of wrongdoing. The Court also concluded that the amnesty provisions did not violate any international norms.

Upon the release of the TRC's final report, some pressure grew for a general amnesty. The ruling African National Congress, which along with other major political parties had key officials who could face prosecution because of the report, initially expressed willingness to consider another amnesty. In 2003, then-President Thabo Mbeki announced before Parliament that there would be no blanket amnesty. In 2004, charges brought against former security agents for the notorious 1985 killing of 'the Pebco Three' — three black South African anti-apartheid activists — appeared to signal the start of post-TRC prosecutions. All cases dealing with former abuses, however, were suspended in late 2004 while a new prosecutions policy was being developed.

In 2006, the Minister of Justice unveiled a new policy for prosecuting apartheid-era crimes.[31] The policy was highly controversial. Critics argued that it gave the National Prosecutions Authority wider powers than the TRC to grant amnesty and this time to individuals who were refused amnesty by the TRC or who failed to appear before the TRC. The new policy guidelines provided the National Director of Public Prosecutions discretion not to prosecute a person if the individual satisfied the former TRC's amnesty criteria such as providing 'full disclosure' of all relevant facts relating to the past acts and if the individual's commission of an alleged offence was associated with a 'political objective'. The guidelines also stipulated factors such as 'the degree of remorse shown by the alleged offender'; 'the degree of indoctrination to which the alleged offender was subjected', the extent to which prosecution would support or undermine 'nation-building through transformation [and] reconciliation' and '[i]f relevant, the alleged offender's role during the TRC process, namely, in respect of cooperation, full disclosure and assisting the process in general'. Opponents of the new policy included South African civil society organizations such as a survivor group Khulumani Support Group, TRC commissioners including the former head of the TRC Archbishop Desmond Tutu, Justice Richard Goldstone and the International Center for Transitional Justice. In December 2009, the High Court in Pretoria stuck down the new policy, and the National Prosecutions Authority was denied an application to appeal in 2009.

Notably in a separate case, in 2010, the South African Constitutional Court invalidated the President's procedures for granting pardons for political offences under a special dispensation that included criteria similar to the TRC's amnesty criteria. In late 2007, then-President Mbeki announced a special dispensation process for pardons of individuals convicted of crimes committed before 16 June 1999 who had not applied for amnesty before the TRC. The President explained: 'As a way forward and in the interest of nation-building, national reconciliation and the further enhancement of national cohesion, and in order to make a further break with matters which arise from the conflicts of the past, consideration has therefore been given to the use of the Presidential pardon to deal with this "unfinished business".' The Constitutional Court, in a unanimous vote, held that the procedures for granting pardons were unconstitutional because they excluded victim participation in the process.

31 See Prosecution Policy and Directives Relating to Prosecution of Criminal Matters Arising from Conflicts of the Past, http://us-cdn.creamermedia.co.za/assets/articles/attachments/02475_npaprosecutionpolicy.pdf.

QUESTIONS

1. Assuming that there were no serious political constraints in South Africa on one or another plan, what changes would you have made in the provisions for the TRC, including amnesty? What changes, if any, would you make to the 2006 guidelines for the National Prosecutions Authority?

2. The TRC required that acts eligible for amnesty be committed for a 'political motive'. Does the 'political motive' element make pragmatic sense? Is it normatively desirable? How does this requirement compare with the issues in *Tadic* concerning acts committed for 'purely personal motives' in association with a crime against humanity? Is the TRC category of eligible crimes too narrow or too broad?

3. Given the conditions for amnesty in the relevant legislation, do you agree with the decisions in the two amnesty cases? Do you agree with the Amnesty Committee's approach to the notion of a 'political motive', as applied in the Amy Biehl case?

4. What is your estimate of the long- or short-term consequences of the TRC for South African democracy, growth, political stability and social harmony among the different racial and ethnic groups? Do you view other factors as equally or more important to achieve these goals? How would you assess the significance of the TRC among those other factors?

5. Are the goals of truth and reconciliation necessarily complementary? Should there be any constraints on seeking the truth if doing so threatens to undermine social harmony? What actors or institutions should make these determinations?

COMMENT ON RELATIONSHIPS BETWEEN TRUTH COMMISSIONS AND CRIMINAL TRIBUNALS

In post-atrocity situations, criminal tribunals and truth commissions are increasingly being called on to operate alongside one another. Such situations are sometimes the result of deliberate planning and at other times the coincidence of separate political and institutional developments. Criminal tribunals and truth commissions are often thought to complement one another. Criminal prosecutions, for instance, may focus attention on personal guilt and away from structural or systemic causes, and trials lack opportunities for direct, broad-based public participation. Truth commissions potentially fill those gaps. Truth commissions, however, generally do not serve other objectives often associated with criminal justice such as deterrence and retribution. Truth commissions and criminal tribunals might also directly support each other's respective agendas. A truth commission can provide prosecutors and judges with valuable information on the nature of the atrocities and individuals involved. Criminal tribunals can, in turn, assist truth commissions. Indeed, without a conditional amnesty scheme and a credible threat of prosecution at the time, the South African TRC might have faltered.

Nevertheless, the two institutions could encounter conflict, if not fundamental incompatibility, with one another. Potential suspects may be reluctant to appear before a truth commission for fear that their testimony could be used against them by prosecutors. That is, the spectre of a criminal trial can potentially chill participation in a truth commission. In the reverse, witnesses and survivors who have already provided sworn testimony to a truth commission may undermine or complicate their value for prosecutors. Finally and perhaps most fundamentally, problems might arise if two institutions provide conflicting 'authoritative' accounts of the history of events and conclusions about the responsibility of various individuals and organizations. Such competing narratives can undermine the legitimacy of both institutions and the goals they serve.

As the following discussion by Priscilla Hayner explains, the operation of the International Criminal Court brings many of these issues to the fore. Some of these issues received attention in the context of the ICTY and a proposed truth commission for Bosnia and Herzegovina. Hayner discusses the ICTY experience and lessons for the ICC and other criminal tribunals. Following Hayner's discussion we turn to recent clashes between the truth commission and criminal tribunal operating in Sierra Leone.

PRISCILLA B. HAYNER, UNSPEAKABLE TRUTHS: CONFRONTING STATE TERROR AND ATROCITY

(2nd edn. 2011), at 110–20

Given the nature of the crimes that fall under the [ICC's] jurisdiction, it is logical that states in the midst of or emerging from war (or other violent conflict or repressive rule) will be the main target of the Court, and indeed this has been true in its first years. It is therefore likely that its investigations will overlap with those of truth commissions. This could raise some delicate legal and policy questions. These issues are not directly addressed in the Court's founding statute or rules of procedure. . . .

. . .

Two ideas in circulation should be dispensed with from the start. First, quite a number of observers — usually commenting from a distance — have suggested that any potential conflicts emerging in the simultaneous operation of a truth commission and the ICC (or other special tribunal) can be resolved through separating out the level of responsibility that would be targeted by the two institutions. A simple proposal has sometimes emerged: a special court should go after those most responsible, and a truth commission should handle "everyone else." Unfortunately, this makes no sense at the operational level, and misunderstands the role of a truth commission. It would be nonsensical for a truth commission to write the history of a conflict without analyzing and commenting on the role of senior officials, whether political or military, even if specific names are omitted.

It would be unfair to avoid interviewing those senior officials who wish to speak with the commission, or disallow them from taking part in public hearings. It is also impossible to know which persons will be considered by a prosecutor to be the "most responsible," and indeed only a few are likely to be prosecuted at the international level. Ignoring the upper ranks — with the idea that some of them might be targeted for prosecution — would be extraordinarily shortsighted, as well as impossible on a practical level, as their names will naturally come up in any regard in investigations and statement-taking.

Second, some have argued that possible tensions could be avoided by "sequencing" the work of a truth commission and prosecutions. In Liberia, it was understood that the TRC would be allowed to conclude its work before consideration was given to any prosecutions — a lesson the commission (and other authorities) said they learned from Sierra Leone. Elsewhere, as with the tribunal for the former Yugoslavia (described below), prosecutors may prefer that no truth commission is created until prosecutions have been completed, to avoid any complications of overlap. But neither of these approaches is a fair resolution. Asking either prosecutors or a proposed truth commission to hold off by several years risks both losing the momentum of transition (when there may be more political space for such investigations) and weakening the evidence base that is available, which is best assessed and protected as early as possible, before information might be corrupted.... Some of the difficult questions, such as whether a court can access confidential records of a commission, would remain even if a commission had concluded its work and boxed up its archives. Finally, prosecutions naturally carry on for many years (and generally do not have a clear ending point), so there is no reasonable way to undertake a truth commission "after" prosecutions. Instead, it must be acknowledged that in some cases a national truth commission will operate simultaneously with either domestic or international prosecutions, and a reasonable working relationship will have to be found.

Some of the troublesome issues that might arise were seen very early, in the discussions around a truth commission that was proposed for Bosnia in the mid-1990s, and especially in the strong response from the International Criminal Tribunal for the former Yugoslavia (ICTY), which opposed the idea of any commission that would overlap with its own investigations.

The idea for a truth commission in Bosnia was rooted in the recognition that three contradictory versions of history were being taught by the three ethnic communities of Bosnia — the Serbs, Muslims, and Croats — and that such radically different understandings of the war could well lead to future violence. The Tribunal's work, based in The Hague, the Netherlands, did not seem to be impacting these local perceptions. Those backing the idea of a truth commission argued that only by taking an assertive step toward reconciling such different conceptions of truth and history would Bosnians be able to find common ground and the relations between the three groups improved. The commission's supporters saw such a body as complementary to the Tribunal, and argued that a truth commission might enhance the Tribunal's reach by making more information available to it. For example, the commission could review and summarize thousands of local-language documents and videotapes that had been out of reach of the Tribunal.

But the leadership of the Tribunal was worried that a Bosnian truth commission could weaken the Tribunal by creating a parallel structure with overlapping interests, and the Tribunal's president and prosecutor openly opposed the idea of a truth commission while the Tribunal's work was under way. The concerns of the Tribunal's chief prosecutor and president were first outlined in November 1998. They argued that the existence of a truth commission could undermine the Tribunal's work by allowing individuals to cooperate with the commission while continuing to default on their obligations to the Tribunal; that the commission's findings of political responsibility might not be distinguished in the public's eye from those of criminal responsibility, thus leading to unreasonable demands for prosecutions; that there would be a danger that the commission and the Tribunal could arrive at contradictory findings of fact, given the commission's lower standards of evidence; that evidence could be contaminated by the commission, especially through repeated interviewing of witnesses; and that the Tribunal already was providing the historical truth, so that such a commission was unnecessary. They also argued that Bosnia was not ready for a truth commission and that the process would likely be manipulated by local political factions. In addition, advocates feared that a truth commission, which would have depended on international funding, could pull resources away from the Tribunal.

While these are legitimate concerns, they were not insurmountable, many observers insisted at the time. Whether political actors would try to use the truth commission as a means to avoid compliance with the Tribunal is not something the commission could control, except by making public statements to try to deter this ploy. Many countries work under different standards of evidence for different kinds of trials (criminal versus civil), and after mass crimes the public must appreciate that not all of the accused can be tried. The problem of a "contaminated" witness pool is also commonly confronted by prosecutors, and many argue that this should not be a formidable issue for the Tribunal; the commission could perhaps lessen this problem by avoiding taking testimony under oath. And finally, while the Tribunal's decisions include long descriptions of the historical context of each case, these decisions are not easily accessible or widely read, especially within the country.

The perspective of the ICTY changed over the next years, and it ultimately relaxed its position to accept that there may be a role for a truth commission. But this conflictive beginning seems to highlight the potential for the interests of a truth commission to clash with those of an international court....

But there are not only problems: the overlap between a truth commission and the ICC (or other international tribunal) could also result in benefits for both bodies. A commission report's outline of the broad pattern of crimes could help focus the court's investigations, especially if the commission concludes its work before the court's prosecutor begins investigations in the country. If information can be comfortably shared by the commission, its report, supporting materials, and interviews with thousands of victims could help identify witnesses and evidence for the prosecutor. Finally, a truth commission's detailed assessment of the strength and independence of the judiciary could help the Court determine whether the state is "unwilling or unable" to investigate and prosecute a case, a key test for the Court to gain jurisdiction over a matter.

Meanwhile, a truth commission is likely to appreciate the existence of an international court that could have jurisdiction over the crimes it is investigating. While some victims may request confidentiality, others will feel encouraged that information they provide might feed into criminal justice. Prospects that its documentation could be used for international prosecutions could add weight to a commission's work, focus its targeted investigations, and help shape or clarify its evidentiary standards. But regardless of these potential benefits, certain questions or tensions remain.

...

Where the ICC's engagement overlaps with a truth commission, will the Court have access to the information collected by the commission? This question of "information sharing" also arose in some national contexts... where commissions often provided information to prosecutors. Similar issues arise with the ICC, but there are also specific peculiarities to this different legal context.

Many truth commissions welcome the opportunity to pass information to a prosecutor, hoping to see justice done. But most truth commissions receive some information with a promise of confidentiality, and their governing mandate may even indicate that the commission "shall not be compelled to disclose any information given to it in confidence." If a commission cannot guarantee confidentiality — and indeed if its information might be passed directly to a prosecutor — surely there may be a chilling effect on the public's engagement with the commission, in particular by perpetrators who might be weighing the possibility of providing information to the commission.

Meanwhile, the Rome Statute requires state parties to cooperate fully with the Court, and to "comply with requests by the Court to provide... assistance in relation to investigations or prosecutions," including "the provision of records and documents, including official records and documents." Would a truth commission's information fall within the category of "official records and documents"? What about its archives, which are often handed to a government agency for safekeeping after the commission concludes?

...

William Schabas, who served as a member of the Sierra Leone truth commission, has written at length on this question of interrelationship and possible sharing of information. He concludes that information provided to a truth commission under a promise of confidentiality should be treated as "privileged," and consequently not subject to disclosure — equivalent to other respected categories, such as information shared between a lawyer and client, or doctor and patient. The ICC rules of procedure explicitly respect such privileged information. It would seem reasonable that much of the confidential information held by a truth commission would be dependent on a "professional or other confidential relationship" for which "confidentiality is essential to the nature and type of relationship between the person and the confidant," and thus protected under the ICC Rules of Procedure and Evidence. However, this has never been tested before the Court, and there is something inherently different between an exercise explicitly designed to collect thousands of testimonies about major crimes, and other commonly accepted privileged relationships.

On the other hand, Schabas identified the "most difficult issue" in the relationship between the two bodies in Sierra Leone as the question of admissibility in prosecutions of self-incriminating evidence produced before a truth commission. Some perpetrators were admitting to serious crimes in Sierra Leone, even in public hearings, and the legal framework or restrictions on the use of this information was unclear. (In other contexts, truth commission legislation allows deponents to receive "use immunity" such that information they provide cannot be used against them.)

In addition to the interest by a prosecutor, the defense counsel may have a strong interest in having wide access to truth commission records. It is possible they could find information in the commission records that directly challenges the accusations against their defendant (such as another person admitting to the crime, or other details which shed doubt on their client's involvement). More typically, defense counsel would be interested in analyzing the testimony given to the TRC by persons who are later witnesses in court....

...

The ICC prosecutor clearly appreciates the limitations of using confidential information. His 2009–2012 prosecutorial strategy states an explicit goal of "reducing reliance on confidential information." However, the assumption even here is that the office of the prosecutor will first have access to such documents, and then decide whether to make use of them, saying that it will be "developing an approach whereby the Office initially screens the [confidential] documents for relevance."

...

Various proposals have been put forward to address the kinds of complications that may emerge in the relationship between a truth commission and a judicial system, whether this be the ICC, national courts, or some form of special tribunal....

...[I]t is hard to envision...an advance agreement necessarily resolving the range of potential conflicts that may arise, or that either body would give up its rights or interests in an advance generic agreement.... It is also not clear with whom such a more universal agreement should be reached — given the varied interests of defense counsel, the prosecutor's office, and judges. The ICC prosecutor has signed memorandums of understanding with various non-governmental organizations, and thus such an agreement with a commission seems feasible on a practical level. But this would have no effect on defense counsel, for example....

PROSECUTOR v. NORMAN

(Decision on Appeal of TRC Request for Public Hearing with Chief Norman), Special Court for Sierra Leone, Case No. SCSL-2003–08-PT (2003)

[Sierra Leone provides a useful study of a truth commission operating alongside a criminal tribunal. The TRC of Sierra Leone was a product of the Lomé Peace

Agreement between the Government of Sierra Leone and the Revolutionary United Front. It was established as a national body by Parliament in 2000. Some impediments to the TRC involved its formal and informal relationships with the Special Court for Sierra Leone. Potential witnesses were reportedly unwilling to provide statements before the TRC for fear of subsequent prosecution. As one close observer explained:

> The Prosecutor, David Crane ... stated publicly that the court has its own investigative procedures and that it will not use evidence presented to the TRC. It has also been suggested that TRC evidence would be inadmissible in court. Unfortunately this message appears not to have reached everyone in Sierra Leone. Some Sierra Leoneans had difficulty distinguishing between the TRC and the court and feared that confessions to the TRC may lead to prosecution.... Arguably, only the Prosecutor's word stood between TRC testimony and court prosecutions, and it was highly likely that defense lawyers would mine TRC testimony, wherever possible, in support of their clients. Several of the people I spoke to ... mentioned the court as a deterrent to giving statements to the TRC.[32]

Paradoxically, the case that gave rise to a direct dispute between the TRC and Special Court involved the reverse situation: an accused who sought to provide testimony to the TRC.

Chief Sam Hinga Norman was one of the most prominent defendants in the custody of the Special Court. He was arrested in 2003 while serving as Minister of Internal Affairs. Norman was charged for his role as National Coordinator of the Civil Defence Forces, pro-government militias that fought during the civil war. The charges included his responsibility for militias that identified civilian 'collaborators' of rebel forces who were then 'unlawfully killed ... often shot, hacked to death, or burnt to death. Other practices included human sacrifices and cannibalism' and 'acts of terrorism' in particular regions of the country. Norman's arrest surprised many Sierra Leoneans who viewed him as a national hero.

The TRC approached the Special Court to seek the appearance of Norman before a public hearing. Norman formally notified the Court that he wanted to appear before the Commission. The ensuing confrontation between the TRC and Special Court created what William Schabas described as a 'most unfortunate ... quarrel between the [two institutions] ... at the close of what had otherwise been a cordial and uneventful relationship.' The Presiding Judge of the Trial Chamber rejected the TRC request. The TRC and Norman appealed to the President of the Special Court, Justice Geoffrey Robertson. Justice Robertson's decision follows.]

2. [This application raises], on any view, a novel and difficult question and one that is likely to recur for other indictees and in other post-war situations where the local or international community considers that the establishment of both a Special Court and a Truth Commission will assist in the restoration of peace and justice.

...

[32] Tim Kelsall, 'Truth, Lies, Ritual: Preliminary Reflections on the Truth and Reconciliation Commission in Sierra Leone', 27 Hum. R. Q. 361 (2005).

4. ...The Special Court was given, by Article 8 of its Statute, a primacy over the national courts of Sierra Leone (and, by implication, over national bodies like the TRC). It has an overriding duty to prosecute those alleged to bear the greatest responsibility for the war, with which duty the Government bound itself to co-operate. There was nothing in the Court's Agreement or Statute which required the Court to compromise its justice mission by deferring to local courts or national institutions.

...

6. The spirit of co-operation envisaged by the Secretary General had in fact resolved all problems without the need for any formal agreements, until this particular issue concerning whether indictees should give public testimony to the TRC arose late in October 2003. The Office of the Prosecutor, which has substantially more resources than the TRC, has followed a different and independent process of investigation. The Prosecutor even announced that he would not use any evidence collected or heard by the Commission, although this undertaking was made at a time when it was not envisaged that any indictee would testify (and the Prosecutor has made clear that he will not be constrained from using indictee testimony). Even so, this was a very considerable compromise by an organ of the Special Court: if crucial evidence against an author of a crime against humanity were to surface at a TRC hearing, one would expect the Prosecutor to obtain it (if a document) or to subpoena the witness, certainly if the testimony was given in public. Nonetheless, the Prosecutor is entitled to make agreements or announce self-denying ordinances and "no go" areas, and he gave this undertaking precisely to avoid any possible conflict with the TRC process. What he cannot do, of course, is bind defendants: if evidence vital for their defence is given at a TRC hearing, then the Trial Chamber would not be prevented from entertaining a defence application to obtain it.

...

8. ...The TRC, by this application, wishes to go towards the other extreme: it seeks not only to interview indictees, but to do so in public, in a courtroom over several days, in a form that will permit them to broadcast live to the nation, and then face sustained questioning shortly before their trial.

...

13. The TRC functions may broadly be divided, in accordance with its title, into those of providing an historical record ("truth") and those of assisting victims to come to terms with their perpetrators ("reconciliation"). The "truth" functions, described in Section 6(2)(a) of its Act, 19 could be interpreted as permitting findings about individual responsibility — the prime function of the Special Court. The "reconciliation" functions, described in Section 6(2)(b) are not so problematic, so long as they invite victims to reconcile with perpetrators who do not bear great responsibility and are not Special Court indictees. It is possible to envisage an indictee pleading guilty and then going before the TRC to beg his victims' forgiveness, and subsequently asking for any such forgiveness to be taken into account by the Court in mitigation of his sentence. But that is not this case and no indictee has yet evinced any intention to plead guilty...

...

15. ... I was told at the hearing by TRC representatives that the Commissioners are preparing to make some assessments of responsibility, and I have been given no assurance that indictees awaiting or undergoing trial will not be "judged" guilty or innocent by the Commissioners (who are not qualified judges), whether or not they testify to the TRC.... [I]ts publication may create expectations and anxieties among prospective witnesses and other defendants and prove indirectly damaging to either Prosecution or Defence. For the very reason that it would necessarily be a premature judgement, it might be shaken or reversed after all the evidence is heard and exposed to the test of cross-examination at the trial. Any such result might discredit the TRC report, but the Court must take no account of this: its judges remain committed by oath to reach their verdicts according to the evidence before them.

16. One solution to the problem could be for the TRC to issue a preliminary report in February and then suspend its operations until the trial process has been completed, when it would reconvene to consider the trial evidence and prepare and publish a final report, incorporating the results of the trials. But I am told that no such course can realistically be contemplated.

17. In these circumstances, a competent lawyer would be unlikely to advise an indicted client to run the risk of testifying before the TRC. There are no procedural safe-guards; he might make damaging admissions under questioning from the counsel to the Commission or from the Commissioners themselves and these admissions could be used by the Prosecution, whose self-denying ordinance does not extend to indictee testimony; he might be condemned in the Commission's report in a way which would create an expectation of his conviction by the Special Court and in consequence frighten off potential defence witnesses. When the TRC first approached a number of indictees, earlier in the year, they all declined a chalice that they were doubtless advised was poisoned. There came a point, however, when this applicant changed his mind.... Chief Sam Hinga Norman... [stated] since, almost 6 months after his arrest, "there is no news about the start of the trial...I would prefer to be heard by the people of Sierra Leone and also be recorded for posterity". He refers to the fact that President Kabbah has testified, as have other ministers of the Government.

18. ... He possesses, even as an indictee remanded in custody, a qualified right to freedom of speech. That right must be capable of assertion, in some meaningful way, to answer, if he wishes, any allegations that have been made against him in another forum: particular resonance attaches to free speech when it is sought as a "right of reply"....

19. To these claims of the indictee must be added the claim of the TRC itself to be put in a position to decide where the truth lies. The Commission states in paragraph 9 of its Application: The TRC perceives Chief Samuel Hinga Norman JP to have played a central role in the conflict in Sierra Leone. The Commission's report — insofar as it purports to present an impartial historical record — would not be complete without hearing from Chief Hinga Norman....

20. The Special Court was first approached by letter from the Executive Secretary of the TRC... The chief concern of the judges was that indictees should know what they were letting themselves in for if they gave interviews to the TRC, and to ensure that in that event they would be given every reasonable protection

against self-incrimination. Thus any prisoner who agreed to participate in the process had to signify his agreement in writing, confirmed by a lawyer who had advised him about it; he had to be provided with a list of written questions and told he was not obliged to answer any particular one; he had to be informed that his answers might be used against him by the Prosecution and that no "finding" by the TRC about him would sway the Court. Any interview had to be supervised by a lawyer appointed by the Registrar and had to be held in the presence of a lawyer for the indictee.

…

21. It must be understood that these were protections laid down not to obstruct the TRC but to provide fundamental protection for men facing charges alleging heinous crimes which if proved could lead to long years of imprisonment. That protection was essential where they were facing impromptu questioning by a skilled counsel for the TRC and by the commissioners themselves. There was not, indeed never has been, any inhibition against an indictee volunteering or communicating information to the TRC in writing, either directly or through his lawyers. The indictee retains freedom of speech to this very considerable extent, that he can write a book, if he wishes…and have it sent to the TRC — by his lawyers, who will sensibly vet it first. It is surprising that the TRC does not appear to have requested information in written form from this indictee. It is also surprising that it has shifted its request from a two day private interview with investigators to a full-scale public hearing broadcast "live" to the nation.

…

22. … [T]he promulgation of the Practice Direction was followed by TRC objections that it would infringe its powers to take evidence in confidence — powers that it seemed to want to use in respect of Chief Hinga Norman.…

26. The Prosecution opposes the joint application, despite admitting that the availability of evidence on oath from the defendant at an open hearing "had a certain appeal" — for reasons that are obvious. Nevertheless, it asserted that such a hearing would undermine the integrity of the Special Court, imperil the security situation in the country and could serve to intimidate witnesses given that the indictee has a large following, even if this was not his intention. The latter claim is always easy for prosecutors to make and often difficult for defendants to refute. It could have been discounted, but for the TRC's warning that if the Chief did not testify then his supporters might cause unrest and even "unleash powerful emotions" against the Special Court.… [T]he danger of unintended consequences, in a society where factions still have access to arms and where the war ended only last year, must be born in any judicial mind. To allow any accused to testify live-to-air, for several days in an uncontrolled environment, may be asking for unpredictable trouble.

…

30. What is actually proposed by this application may be described in different ways: it might appear as a spectacle. A man in custody awaiting trial on very serious charges is to be paraded, in the very court where that trial will shortly be held, before a Bishop rather than a presiding judge and permitted to broadcast live to the

nation for a day or so uninterrupted. Thereafter for the following day or days, he will be examined by a barrister and then questioned from the bench by the Bishop and some five or six fellow Commissioners. In the immediate vicinity will be press, prosecutors and "victims". His counsel will be present and permitted to interject but there are no fixed procedures and no Rules of Evidence. The event will have the appearance of a trial, at least the appearance of a sort of trial familiar from centuries past, although the first day of uninterrupted testimony may resemble more a very long party political broadcast. It is not necessary to speculate on the consequences of this spectacle: there may be none. There may be those the Prosecution fears which could lead to intimidation of witnesses and the rally of dormant forces. There may be those that doubtless informed the original advice of his lawyers against testifying — namely fodder for the Prosecution, an adverse effect on public perceptions of his innocence and a consequent disheartening of potential defence witnesses. There will probably, I fear, be this consequence, namely intense anxiety amongst other indictees, especially from rival factions, and concerns over whether they should testify to the TRC as well, or in rebuttal. The spectacle of the TRC sitting in court may set up a public expectation that it will indeed pass judgement on indictees thus confronted and questioned, whose guilt or innocence it is the special duty of the Special Court to determine.

31. . . . If it is the case that local TRCs and international courts are to work together in efforts to produce post-conflict justice in other theatres of war in the future, I do not believe that granting this application for public testimony would be a helpful precedent.

. . .

33. Let me to return to first principles. Truth Commissions and International Courts are both instruments for effectuating the promise made by states that victims of human rights violations shall have an effective remedy. Criminal courts offer the most effective remedy — a trial, followed by punishment of those found guilty, in this case of those who bear the greatest responsibility. TRC reports can assist society to move forward and beyond the hatreds that fuelled the war. Truth commissions offer two distinct prospects for victims — of truth, i.e. learning how and why they or their loved ones were murdered or maimed or mutilated, and of reconciliation, through understanding and forgiveness of those perpetrators who genuinely confess and regret. It seems to me that these are separate and severable objectives.

34. In what has been termed "transitional justice" periods, truth commissions may be the only option for weak governments. In this context they were common in South America in the 1980s — in Bolivia, Chile, El Salvador, Haiti, Argentina and so forth. They were usually accompanied by blanket amnesties and were not permitted to "name names" of those who might be identified as perpetrators of crimes against humanity, not to avoid prejudice to trials (which were not in prospect), but to avoid political embarrassment. The reports nonetheless shed light on abuses — in some cases, as with "Nunca Mas", very great light. They achieved a degree of truth, but without justice and in many cases without reconciliation — see the recent public demands in these countries to vacate the amnesties and prosecute the perpetrators. The Lomé Accord of 1999 offered both a blanket amnesty

and a TRC: only after that agreement was comprehensively violated did the international community deploy its muscle to insist on the prosecution of those bearing the greatest responsibility for the war.

...

36. In the case, as here, of Truth Commissions coinciding with court trials of alleged perpetrators, there is a dearth of precedent. In East Timor, a Memorandum of Understanding has been drawn up between the Office of the General Prosecutor (OGP) and the Commission (CAVR) which provides that: The OGP is able to provide information to the CAVR that is relevant to its truth-seeking function only in circumstances where this does not prejudice ongoing investigations or prosecutions or the confidentiality of witnesses or victims and is consistent with the mandate of the OGP. This does not address the specific issue of indictee testimony, although it demonstrates that in balancing the interests of the two processes, the value of fair trial must be overriding.

37. There is some assistance to be drawn from the experience of Peru, where the issue has arisen in relation to testimony by members of Shining Path who were awaiting trial. The TRC chose, I am told, to hear any testimony offered by such indictees in private, so as not to impact on their trial, even though the trial process there was to be inquisitorial rather than adversarial.... I note also that the TRC in that case wrestled with the difficulty inherent in public hearings for convicted perpetrators, namely that this can provide a "soapbox" or platform for justification of their crimes. It declined to provide such hearings for persons whose testimony (which it saw in written form in advance) was either self-promoting or at odds with other credible information it had gathered.... Despite some well-publicised confessions at the South African TRC, I am informed that it is rare for perpetrators, whether alleged or convicted, to use public hearings to make confessions: these are more likely to be forthcoming in private hearings....

...

39. It would clearly not be right that the TRC apply its "reconciliation" processes of public hearing, confrontation with victims, live broadcast and so on to Special Court indictees who have not pleaded guilty. This would, for the reasons given above, be wholly inappropriate.... I have to decide how to effectuate the wish to testify of an indictee who, his counsel tell me, intends to plead "not guilty" and to vigorously defend the legality of his actions in putting down an insurrection by use of what he will contend was reasonable force. His free speech entitlement may only be restricted — like his freedom of movement — to the extent that is consonant with his present status as an indictee.

40. That status does not only restrict his speech in the interests of security. It carries with it a host of considerations about ensuring the fairness of his trial (and "fairness" includes fairness to the Prosecutor and its witnesses) and fairness to other indictees who face trial....

41. In my judgement, Chief Sam Hinga Norman is entitled to testify to the TRC upon condition that he has been fully apprised and advised of the dangers of so doing. I am satisfied that he has been expertly warned. His testimony must, however, be provided in a manner that reduces to an acceptable level any danger that it will influence witnesses (whether favourably or adversely) or affect the integrity of

court proceedings or unreasonably affect co-defendants and other indictees. This in my judgement can be achieved by evidence prepared by him in writing (with the benefit of legal advice) and sworn in the form of an affidavit.... Should counsel for the TRC have any further questions, these may be put to the indictee in writing and his answers may be sworn and delivered in the same way. There shall be no public hearing of the kind requested or of any other kind prior to the conclusion of the trial. This is without prejudice to his right, if so advised, to make unsworn written statements to the TRC. It is without prejudice to his right to meet with commissioners in the Detention Unit, if they apply for that purpose, or to his right to meet them for a confidential session, if a joint application is made for that purpose.

42. ... Mr Tim Owen made the point that an affidavit would not be so beneficial as a radio broadcast in getting his message across to his followers, because many of them cannot read. But this begs the question of the legitimate purpose of the TRC hearing, which must be to get information across to the Commissioners for the purpose of their report, rather than to permit indicted political leaders to get messages to their followers. What is important is that followers should know that their leaders have been given an opportunity to put forward their version of events in full detail, and this is achieved by the affidavit method. The indictee will shortly address the Court either to have the seven charges against him dismissed (if his Preliminary Motions fail) or else to refute them by his own defence which he will be given every opportunity to develop under procedures that have been scrupulously laid down to achieve fairness. The time for him to give public testimony will be if and when he exercises his right to give evidence on oath.

44. The work of the Special Court and the TRC is complementary and each must accommodate the existence of the other. The TRC is not in a position to suspend its work once trials begin in order to issue a final report when they are over, taking the evidence and verdicts into account. It would be seemly if the report that the TRC is (I am told) to issue in February refrains from passing concluded judgement on the criminal responsibility of any person who is detained to face trial in this Court. Should comment or conclusion be passed, it will of course have absolutely no effect on the minds of the judges of this Court who sit to provide a fair trial according to international standards. That said, the Special Court respects the TRC's work and will assist it so far as is possible and proper, subject only to our overriding duty to serve the interests of justice without which there may not be the whole truth and there is unlikely to be lasting reconciliation.

FINAL REPORT OF THE TRUTH AND RECONCILIATION COMMISSION OF SIERRA LEONE: WITNESS TO TRUTH

Vol. 3B (2004)

1. ... In recent times, truth commissions have worked in tandem with national criminal justice processes and in one case a commission has functioned in parallel with a criminal tribunal established under UN regulations. However the Sierra

Leonean case has brought into sharp focus the different roles of these institutions and the potential pitfalls in their relationship....

43. ...While the Special Court has primacy over the national courts of Sierra Leone, the TRC does not fall within this mould. In any event, the relationship between the two bodies should not be discussed on the basis of primacy or lack of it. The ultimate operational goal of the TRC and the Court should be guided by the request of the Security Council and the Secretary-General to 'operate in a complementary and mutually supportive manner fully respectful of their distinct but related functions'.

64. ...For [there to be] any basis for [the] claim that the international Agreement [between Sierra Leone and the United Nations] took precedence over the powers of the TRC, further legislation specifically on that point would have had to [sic] enacted. No legislation was ever passed to require "full compliance" of the TRC with the "requests and orders" of the Special Court.

75. ...On 26 August 2003 Chief Samuel Hinga Norman, the former National Co-ordinator of the CDF, wrote a letter requesting his legal counsel to facilitate an appearance before the TRC....

76. Norman's application to testify to the TRC was followed by those of Augustine Bao and Issa Sesay, both members of the RUFP, formerly the RUF.

77. ...There was certainly nothing to prevent them recording their full testimonies in writing and submitting them through their lawyers. What these detainees were seeking, however, was a hearing; an opportunity to present testimony in person to the Commission and to answer questions posed by staff of the TRC. They were asserting their rights to be heard in a manner like that accorded to all other Sierra Leoneans who had so requested and so desired....

79. There is nothing unusual about a prisoner, either awaiting trial or convicted, testifying in proceedings in other cases and even in proceedings between other bodies. Such an occurrence happens regularly in national judicial systems and procedures exist in Sierra Leone and elsewhere to facilitate it. Indeed, the Special Court apparently gave its approval for certain detainees in its custody to give evidence in ongoing proceedings in the Sierra Leonean courts pertaining to charges of treason against other individuals.

80. More specifically, there is considerable precedent to be drawn from other truth and reconciliation commissions. In the South African Commission, both "awaiting-trial" and convicted prisoners appeared before hearings of the Human Rights Violations Committee in order to supply their versions of events. Prisoners and detainees also appeared before the Amnesty Committee of the South African Commission for purposes of having their amnesty applications heard. Indeed some prisoners and detainees appeared before both Committees. The Sierra Leone TRC was entrusted by the Parliament of Sierra Leone with the responsibility of hearing all relevant evidence and information concerning its mandate. Had Chief Hinga Norman or the other detainees been in prison in Sierra Leone awaiting trial before a national court, there can be no doubt that arrangements would have been made to have enabled them to be heard by the Commission. The TRC succeeded

in gaining access to several persons held in Freetown Central Prison in exactly this situation.

83. The Practice Direction was adopted by the Special Court for Sierra Leone on 9 September 2003. . . .

85. In requiring the Commission to make a substantive application to a Special Court Judge for permission to interview a detainee, the Practice Direction was inconsistent with the mandate and powers granted to the Commission under its founding statute. The Commission was granted the power to interview any individual within Sierra Leone at any place in the fulfilment of its mandate. There were no limitations, exceptions or qualifications on this power contained in the Truth and Reconciliation Commission Act 2000.

87. . . . The TRC routinely interviews awaiting trial prisoners before the criminal courts of Sierra Leone and there has been absolutely no question of monitoring our interviews or for that matter forwarding information to prosecutors. Indeed to do so would be regarded as an outrage. Our hope is that the Special Court, a body established through international co-operation and which subscribes to international human right standards, will not conduct itself in this way.

122. In an attempt to highlight the profound importance of the issue at hand, the Commission submitted that developments in national and international law created a presumption in favour of permitting Hinga Norman to appear before the Commission. Nationally, the established practice of the Truth and Reconciliation Commission had led to the recognition in national law of a de facto right to testify before the Commission. With regard to international practice, the Commission asserted the following: "In the light of developments in post-conflict societies in the late 20th and early 21st centuries in dealing with past human rights violations, there exists on the part of victims a right to know the truth. Truth Commissions have been created in several countries around the world to meet that recognised obligation. There is considerable weight to the argument that establishing the 'truth' is an essential component of the universally recognised 'right to an effective remedy.' The Special Court is duly bound to consider such a right in respect of the Sierra Leone population in its determination of the parameters of this request 'in the interests of justice'."

123. The Commission concluded its representations by suggesting that the historic moment had arrived whereby a decision had to be made as to whether these two institutions were indeed going to work together on a complementary basis or not. The outcome of this proceeding will in large measure determine whether two such institutions can in fact be complementary. The consequences for the people of Sierra Leone — and indeed for the people in all conflict zones which envisage similar mechanisms of transitional justice — will be far reaching.

140. The Commission submitted that the institutions of the Special Court and the TRC both had important roles to play in reaching the truth and addressing impunity in the context of post-conflict Sierra Leone. The Special Court seeks to prove and establish beyond reasonable doubt the elements of specifically-framed charges against individuals who are alleged to bear the greatest responsibility. It

endeavours to reach the truth in relation to the role of those individuals. In so doing it would hopefully provide a deterrent against future abuses.

141. The TRC, on the other hand, endeavours to establish the wider truth in relation to the roles of all key players and factions in the conflict. It was averred on behalf of the Commission that it was only when the full truth (or as close to the full truth as possible) was placed squarely before the public that society is able to examine itself honestly and robustly. It was this exercise that would permit society to take genuine measures to prevent repetition of the horrors of the past.

154. Judge Robertson then wished to know whether the Commission would "make a determination on the guilt or innocence of certain individuals": "Has the Commission addressed the issue of making judgements on people? Would the TRC make judgements?" Mr. Varney explained the nature of findings that truth commissions make and reminded the Judge that "the TRC is not a court". Judge Robertson indicated that it would be preferable if the Commission refrained from making pronouncements on the roles and responsibilities of the indictees held by the Special Court.

156. At this point Mr. Johnson on behalf of the Prosecution said that there were "ongoing efforts to intimidate and scare witnesses right now". He added: "I would hate to see this being used in some effort to promulgate that...."

157. The Judge and the Prosecution then engaged in a discussion on Hinga Norman and the potential volatility of his supporters:

160. The Judge then commented on the wisdom of having two institutions such as the Special Court and the Commission in operation at the same time: "It may be that our hope of working together and at the same time may not be possible." He suggested that the best resolution would be for the Commission to suspend the issuance of its report until all the trials at the Special Court were complete.

161. Mr. Varney pointed out to Judge Robertson that there was no prospect of securing a suspension of the Commission's proceedings. He also advised that it had always been open to the TRC to obtain Chief Norman's testimony by way of a written submission. No approval or intervention by the Special Court was ever required to obtain written testimony.

167. The decision of Judge Robertson was finally issued on 28 November 2003....

172. ...Extracts from the Commission's media statement of 1 December 2003 read as follows: "PRESS RELEASE BY THE TRC Freetown, Sierra Leone, 1 December 2003 SPECIAL COURT DENIES HINGA NORMAN'S RIGHT (AND THAT OF THE OTHER DETAINEES) TO APPEAR PUBLICLY BEFORE THE TRC...The ruling, in the view of the TRC, has dealt a serious blow to the cause of truth and reconciliation in Sierra Leone. As a citizen of Sierra Leone and as a key role-player in Sierra Leone's recent history, Chief Hinga Norman has a right to appear before the TRC to tell his story. All equivalent role-players have appeared before the TRC, including prisoners awaiting trial at Pademba Road Prison...."

192. The Judge's choice of words to describe the Commission's original approach to the detainees was unfortunate: "When the TRC first approached a number of indictees, earlier in the year, they all declined a chalice that they were doubtless advised was poisoned." The publication of such a theatrical metaphor in a decision under the hand of the President of the Court inferred that there was something poisonous about the agenda of the TRC, supposedly a "complementary" organisation.... According to the Judge, the Revised Practice Direction provided "for a confidential process of receiving information." In fact it provided for an official from the Registrar's office to monitor the interview within earshot. In addition, the monitoring officer had authority to intervene should the questions stray off the approved subject areas. In effect it was envisaged that a Court representative would sit at the interview table. The entire interview would be tape recorded and lodged at the Registrar's office. Parties to the proceedings could thereafter apply to the trial judge for the disclosure of the transcript "in the interests of justice"....

213. The achievement of "justice" may very well advance the cause of reconciliation. Whether it brings reconciliation in itself is debatable. Whether the kind of justice referred to by the Judge, namely the retributive justice pursued by the Special Court, is capable of producing national reconciliation is equally debatable. Confining the achievement of justice to retributive justice is a narrow interpretation of what justice has come to mean in recent times.

215. If Justice Robertson's proposition is correct then the achievement of reconciliation is presumably dependent on the "successful" outcome of the prosecutions before the Special Court. However, achieving justice and addressing impunity are difficult enough tasks. There are huge uncertainties inherent in criminal trials. Prosecutions fail as often as they succeed. To rest reconciliation on the successful outcome of a legal process is a risky endeavour. This point was made forcefully in a unanimous decision of the South African Constitutional Court in 1996. The applicants in the matter contested the denial of their rights to judicial redress under the amnesty provision of the truth and reconciliation process: "Every decent human being must feel grave discomfort in living with a consequence which might allow the perpetrators of evil acts to walk the streets of this land with impunity, protected in their freedom by an amnesty immune from constitutional attack; but the circumstances in support of this course require carefully [sic] to be appreciated. Most of the acts of brutality and torture [that] have taken place have occurred during an era in which neither the laws which permitted the incarceration of persons or the investigation of crimes, nor the methods and the culture which informed such investigations, were easily open to public investigation, verification and correction. Much of what transpired in this shameful period is shrouded in secrecy and not easily capable of objective demonstration and proof. Loved ones have disappeared, sometimes mysteriously and most of them no longer survive to tell their tales. Others have had their freedom invaded, their dignity assaulted or their reputations tarnished by grossly unfair imputations hurled in the fire and the cross-fire of a deep and wounding conflict. The wicked and the innocent have often both been victims. Secrecy and authoritarianism have concealed the truth in little crevices

of obscurity in our history. Records are not easily accessible; witnesses are often unknown, dead, unavailable or unwilling. All that often effectively remains is the truth of wounded memories of loved ones sharing instinctive suspicions, deep and traumatising to the survivors but otherwise incapable of translating themselves into objective and corroborative evidence which could survive the rigours of the law. The Act [that created the Truth and Reconciliation Commission] seeks to address this massive problem. [. . .] The alternative to the grant of immunity from criminal prosecution of offenders is to keep intact the abstract right to such a prosecution for particular persons without the evidence to sustain the prosecution successfully, to continue to keep the dependants of such victims in many cases substantially ignorant about what precisely happened to their loved ones; to leave their yearning for the truth effectively unassuaged; to perpetuate their legitimate sense of resentment and grief . . . ."

217. Judge Robertson's assertion of the power of the Court does not exclude other means of pursuing reconciliation, but his notion does not leave room for a lasting reconciliation to be built without resorting to criminal trials. Based on the practice of other countries, it does not appear to be accurate to say that criminal trials are a prerequisite for reconciliation. Mozambique, which experienced one of the bloodiest civil wars in the second half of the twentieth century, enjoys a measure of reconciliation even though there were no criminal trials, or for that matter a truth and reconciliation commission. South Africa, which deprived many victims of judicial redress, through its "truth for amnesty" formula, also enjoys a measure of reconciliation notwithstanding its bitter and divided past.

227. Ultimately where there is no harmonisation of objectives a criminal justice body will have largely punitive and retributive aims, whereas a truth and reconciliation body will have largely restorative and healing objectives. Where the two bodies operate simultaneously in an ad-hoc fashion, conflict between such objectives is likely. Confusion in the minds of the public is inevitable.

228. Harmonisation of objectives means that neither body can operate in a manner that is oblivious of the other. It is highly incongruous for one body to engage in intensive truth seeking and reconciliation exercises involving former participants in the conflict, while another body is independently pursing punitive actions against the same individuals. . . .

230. It is likely that in the future there will be more truth commissions that work alongside international judicial bodies. This will particularly be the case as the International Criminal Court commences operations in different post-conflict countries. . . .

233. In the light of developments in post-conflict societies in the late twentieth and early twenty-first centuries in dealing with past human rights violations, there exists on the part of victims a right to know the truth. Truth Commissions have been established in several countries around the world to meet this recognised obligation. The Commission finds that there is considerable weight to the argument that establishing the "truth" is an essential component of the universally recognised "right to an effective remedy".

234. The Commission also recognises that victims have a right to justice and to pursue this right through legal means.

QUESTIONS

1. What changes in structural design and legal rules could resolve the potential conflicts between truth commissions and criminal tribunals? Do the different goals of the two institutions make such conflicts likely, if not inevitable? Do Hayner's suggestions overcome the types of concern raised by ICTY officials? Are the concerns of the ICTY officials reasonable?

2. Truth commissions and criminal tribunals can also potentially benefit one another. What formal rules or procedures can improve upon the positive relationships between these institutions?

3. It is both explicit and implicit in Justice Robertson's reasoning that trials should have primacy over alternative remedial strategies in dealing with mass human rights violations. Does international law support his assessment? The TRC Final Report suggests that normative questions about whether such primacy is warranted might boil down to an empirical debate about the potential effectiveness of trials in different situations. Do you agree? What potential is there for trials ever to succeed in the aftermath of a collapsed state or where 'secrecy and authoritarianism have concealed the truth' for decades?

4. Is the Special Court the appropriate institution for addressing issues such as a defendant's rights before another body and the relative value of the TRC's work? Does the fact that the Special Court constitutes a quasi-international institution affect your evaluation?

5. Could permitting defendants to testify in public hearings before a truth commission be advantageous to criminal tribunals? For example, such an arrangement could provide an incentive for key suspects to offer important information about the history of events and their particular actions. Similarly, are there conditions under which a truth commission's exerting pressure on a tribunal to pursue convictions would be advantageous? What if the commission can be trusted to produce a fair and objective set of conclusions? What if a criminal tribunal would, in the absence of a commission's report, surrender to outside political pressure to acquit perpetrators?

ADDITIONAL READING

K. Ainley, 'Excesses of Responsibility: The Limits of Law and the Possibilities of Politics', 25 Ethics & Int'l. Affairs (2011); A. Laban Hinton, W. Babchuk, M. Bleeker & J. Burnet (eds.), *Transitional Justice: Global Mechanisms and Local Realities after Genocide and Mass Violence* (2010); E. Wiebelhaus-Brahm, *Truth Commissions and Transitional Societies: The Impact on Human Rights and Democracy* (2010); T. A. Olsen, L. A. Payne, A. G. Reiter & E. Wiebelhaus-Brahm, 'When Truth Commissions Improve Human Rights', 4 Int'l. J. Transitional Justice (2010), at

457–6; N. Kritz (ed.), *Transnational Justice: How Emerging Democracies Reckon with Former Regimes* (3 vols. 1995); Y. Naqvi, 'The Right to the Truth in International Law: Fact or Fiction?', 88 Int'l. Rev. Red Cross 245 (2006); N. Roht-Arriaza (ed.), *Impunity and Human Rights in International Law and Practice* (1995); M. Minow, *Between Vengeance and Forgiveness* (1998); Deborah Posel & Graeme Simpson (eds.), *Commissioning the Past: Understanding South Africa's Truth and Reconciliation Commission* (2003); Naomi Roht-Arriaza & Javier Mariezcurrena (eds.), *Transitional Justice in the Twenty-First Century: Beyond Truth versus Justice* (2006); J. Dugard, 'Possible Conflicts of Jurisdiction with Truth Commissions', in A. Cassese et al. (eds.), *The Rome Statute of the International Criminal Court: A Commentary* (2002); J. L. Gibson, *Overcoming Apartheid: Can Truth Reconcile a Divided Nation?* (2004); R. Shaw, 'Rethinking Truth and Reconciliation Commissions: Lessons from Sierra Leone', US Institute for Peace Report (2005); Ruti G. Teitel, *Transitional Justice* (2001).

16

Non-State Actors and Human Rights

One of the most dramatic developments within international human rights law over the past two decades has been the growing importance of a range of non-state actors. The centrality of the state is one of the defining features of international law and the human rights system builds upon this by seeking to bind states through a network of treaty obligations to which, in the vast majority of cases, only states can become parties. Non-state actors are thus, by definition, placed at the margins of the resulting legal regime. The problem is that actors such as transnational corporations, civil society groups, international organizations and armed opposition groups, to name just the most prominent among a wide range of potentially important non-state actors, have all assumed major roles in relation to the enjoyment of human rights, especially in recent years.

Various factors have contributed to this development. They include: (1) the privatization of functions previously performed by governments, including in relation to social welfare services, prisons, asylum processing, schools, adoptions, health-care provision for the poor, and the supply of water, gas and electricity; (2) the ever-increasing mobility of capital and the increased importance of foreign investment flows, facilitated by market deregulation and trade liberalization; (3) the expanding responsibilities of multilateral organizations, some of which have been called upon to exercise a wide range of governmental functions in areas ranging from Kosovo and East Timor to Afghanistan and Iraq; (4) the enormous growth in the role played by transnational civil society organizations, many of which now have multimillion dollar budgets, employ very large staffs, and perform public-type functions in a large number of countries; (5) the changing nature of conflicts, which has seen a growth in the number and proportion of internal conflicts and a subsequent rise in the importance of organized armed groups controlling territory and population and aspiring to gain international legitimacy; and (6) the growth of international terrorist networks such as Al Qaeda, and international criminal networks, such as drug cartels, which are not confined to any one state and some of whose activities have become global in scope.

These developments have increased the risk that a human rights regime that addresses itself effectively only to states will become increasingly marginalized in the years ahead. The phenomenon of privatizing security through the 'outsourcing' of military and military-support functions, even in wartime, provides a good illustration. As recently as the 1980s, there was widespread opposition to the role played by such 'mercenaries'. But the twenty-first century has witnessed a broad and potentially almost unlimited role being accorded to private contractors in conflict situations. In Iraq, for example, corporate contractors were accused of conspiring with US officials to humiliate, torture and abuse detainees, carrying out extrajudicial executions, and being involved in a range of other practices violating human rights standards.

This chapter looks at the role of non-state actors in three specific situations. The first concerns the attempts, primarily within the UNs setting, to articulate and implement human rights obligations for corporations, particularly those that operate transnationally. The second looks at the extent to which the existing framework of human rights law is capable of addressing the role of armed opposition groups and the third considers the issues involved in demands that international NGOs be held more accountable.

Before engaging with these specific contexts it is useful to set the scene with an excerpt from a General Comment adopted by the ICCPR Human Rights Committee in 2004 which addresses, albeit somewhat obliquely, the position of non-state actors:

> The article 2, paragraph 1, obligations ['to respect and to ensure to all individuals within its territory and subject to its jurisdiction the rights recognized …'] are binding on States Parties and do not, as such, have direct horizontal effect as a matter of international law. The Covenant cannot be viewed as a substitute for domestic criminal or civil law. However the positive obligations on States Parties to ensure Covenant rights will only be fully discharged if individuals are protected by the State, not just against violations of Covenant rights by its agents, but also against acts committed by private persons or entities that would impair the enjoyment of Covenant rights in so far as they are amenable to application between private persons or entities. There may be circumstances in which a failure to ensure Covenant rights as required by article 2 would give rise to violations by States Parties of those rights, as a result of States Parties' permitting or failing to take appropriate measures or to exercise due diligence to prevent, punish, investigate or redress the harm caused by such acts by private persons or entities. States are reminded of the interrelationship between the positive obligations imposed under article 2 and the need to provide effective remedies in the event of breach under article 2, paragraph 3. The Covenant itself envisages in some articles certain areas where there are positive obligations on States Parties to address the activities of private persons or entities. For example, the privacy-related guarantees of article 17 must be protected by law.
>
> It is also implicit in article 7 that States Parties have to take positive measures to ensure that private persons or entities do not inflict torture or cruel, inhuman or degrading treatment or punishment on others within their power. In fields affecting basic aspects of ordinary life such as work or housing, individuals are to be protected from discrimination within the meaning of article 26.[1]

QUESTION

Does it follow from the Human Rights Committee's interpretation of Article 2(1) that states' positive obligations to address non-state actors are limited to matters concerning privacy, torture or discrimination? Would this be a tenable reading of the Covenant? If not, what criteria might apply to determine the extent of such obligations?

[1] Human Rights Committee, General Comment No. 31 (2004) on (Art. 2) *The Nature of the General Legal Obligation Imposed on States Parties to the Covenant*, para. 8.

A. TRANSNATIONAL CORPORATIONS AND HUMAN RIGHTS

Globalization has contributed to, and in part been driven by, the increasingly central role of transnational corporations (TNCs) in the international economic order. This is not a new phenomenon, as illustrated by the diverse and powerful roles played since the seventeenth century by imperial trading companies such as the Dutch and British East India companies and the Hudson's Bay Company, a tradition continued far into the twentieth century by companies such as International Telephone and Telegraph and United Fruit Company.[2] But by the late twentieth century the number of TNCs and the range and scope of their activities had changed dramatically from earlier eras. As Macklem notes:

> Processes of economic globalization are dramatically enhancing technological, commercial and financial integration of national economies. Traditional geographical and political barriers are becoming increasingly irrelevant to the production, placement and sale of goods and services. States are gradually dismantling tariff barriers and actively seeking new forms of direct foreign investment. Multinational corporations, participating in spatially concentrated clusters often referred to as transnational production chains, are cutting across national economic and juridical boundaries, exploiting efficiency gains associated with economic globalization and technological innovation, and wielding unprecedented power and influence in local and global markets and domestic and international affairs.[3]

Along with greater power comes an enhanced potential to promote or undermine respect for human rights:

> The corporate world touches the lives of people more closely than any other constituency, giving it immense potential for good or harm.... [In addition to its great benefits] has come collateral damage — to individuals, to the environment, to communities. Whether directly or indirectly, companies encounter problems which we would now classify under the generic heading of human rights. In their supply chains they can meet exploitative child labour, discrimination, risks to health and life, forced labour. The extractive industries can be involved in the spoliation of the environment and the destruction of communities. In contexts of conflict and human rights violations they confront a need for security which is too often provided by ill-disciplined state security forces.
>
> Simply through their presence companies provide economic support and moral sanction to oppressive governments. If they lack appropriate policies and principles, companies risk the legitimate charge of complicity with oppression in pursuit of profit.[4]

[2] For a wide-ranging critique see A. Anghie, *Imperialism, Sovereignty and the Making of International Law* (2005), Ch. 4.

[3] Patrick Macklem, 'Corporate Accountability under International Law: The Misguided Quest for Universal Jurisdiction', 7 Int'l. L. Forum 281 (2005).

[4] G. Chandler, 'Corporate Liability: Human Rights and the Modern Business', Conference organized by JUSTICE and Sweet & Maxwell, 12 June 2006.

The scale of corporate power is illustrated by the case of one of the world's biggest companies (measured by sales), Wal-Mart. Its 2011 sales of $419 billion made it larger than the economies of all but the world's 24 richest nations. Its sales on a single day alone are greater than the annual Gross Domestic Product (GDP) of many countries in the world. In Mexico, for example, it is the largest private employer and accounts for 2 per cent of the country's GDP, but it also stands accused of covering up a major bribery scandal, and has consistently battled allegations of labour rights violations.[5]

1. ILLUSTRATING THE CHALLENGES

The types of human rights issues in which corporations are typically involved vary considerably, and particularly from sector to sector. The following examples illustrate the sort of cases that have been prominent in recent years.

The extractive industries have traditionally been at the heart of many alleged gross violations. Consider the following example involving Shell and the oil industry:

> SPDC [Shell Petroleum Development Company of Nigeria] has been engaged in oil exploration and production in the Ogoni region of Nigeria since 1958. In response to SPDC's activities residents of the Ogoni region organized a group named the "Movement for Survival of Ogoni People" to protest the environmental effects of oil exploration in the region. According to plaintiffs, in 1993 defendants responded by enlisting the aid of the Nigerian government to suppress the Ogoni resistance. Throughout 1993 and 1994, Nigerian military forces are alleged to have shot and killed Ogoni residents and attacked Ogoni villages — beating, raping, and arresting residents and destroying or looting property — all with the assistance of defendants. Specifically, plaintiffs allege that defendants, inter alia, (1) provided transportation to Nigerian forces, (2) allowed their property to be utilized as a staging ground for attacks, (3) provided food for soldiers involved in the attacks, and (4) provided compensation to those soldiers.
>
> ... [P]laintiffs brought claims of aiding and abetting (1) extrajudicial killing; (2) crimes against humanity; (3) torture or cruel, inhuman, and degrading treatment; (4) arbitrary arrest and detention; (5) violation of the rights to life, liberty, security, and association; (6) forced exile; and (7) property destruction.[6]

Mineral extraction companies have also been widely criticized. A Canadian company, Barrick Gold, is the world's largest gold miner and owns 95 per cent of the Porgera Joint Venture mine in Papua New Guinea. The mine contributes some 11 per cent of the country's GDP. Indigenous landowners and local organizations complained about abuses by Barrick's guards, environmental harms and the need for relocation. In 2009, in testimony to the Canadian Parliament, Sarah Knuckey

[5] D. Barstow, 'Vast Mexico Bribery Case Hushed Up by Wal-Mart After Top-Level Struggle', *New York Times*, 21 Apr. 2012, p. A1.

[6] *Kiobel v. Royal Dutch Pet. Co.*, 621 F.3d 111 (2d Cir. 2010); cert. granted 132 S. Ct. 472 (2011).

and Tyler Giannini, human rights lawyers from New York University School of Law and Harvard Law School, documented allegations of beatings and gang rapes by Barrick's guards.[7] Human Rights Watch also subsequently reported on the situation, and noted Barrick's 'history of angrily dismissing human rights and environmental concerns'.[8] Following years of local and international advocacy efforts, Barrick announced in 2010 that it would take measures to prevent future sexual assaults.[9]

Another mining industry example from another continent and involving a different type of TNC, concerns copper mining in Zambia by state-owned Chinese companies. Human Rights Watch (HRW)alleges that workers in the mines:

> suffer from abusive employment conditions that fail to meet domestic and international standards and fall short of practices among the copper mining industry elsewhere in Zambia. Miners...spoke of poor health and safety standards, including poor ventilation that can lead to serious lung diseases, hours of work in excess of Zambian law, the failure to replace workers' personal protective equipment that is damaged while at work, and the threat of being fired should workers refuse to work in unsafe places. Injuries and negative health consequences are not uncommon, although many incidents are not reported to the government, contrary to Zambian and international labor law....

As will almost always be the case, HRW added that primary responsibility in such cases 'rests with the Zambian government, which has largely failed to enforce the country's labor laws and mining regulations'.[10]

Information technology companies have also been involved in a wide range of issues ranging from freedom of information, through cooperation with repressive governments, to labour conditions. A prominent example of the latter concerns Apple, the consumer electronics giant. In January 2012 it was the world's largest corporation in terms of market capitalization ($419 billion). In the last quarter of 2011 it reported record profits of $13.06 billion on global sales of $46.3 billion, and in 2011 it paid just 9.8 per cent in taxes worldwide on its overall profits of $34.2 billion. In 2012, the *New York Times* reported that workers employed by Foxconn, a Chinese company which assembles Apple's iPhones, iPads and other such devices, work under harsh labour conditions: 'Employees work excessive overtime, in some cases seven days a week, and live in crowded dorms. Some say they stand so long that their legs swell until they can hardly walk.' The report also alleged improper disposal of hazardous waste and the use of poisonous chemicals in manufacturing processes.[11] While Apple declined to comment on the report, the story received extensive coverage and Apple subsequently announced that it had commissioned the Fair

[7] The testimony and reports are at www.business-humanrights.org/Documents/CanadaParliamentarytestimonyreBarrickPJV/.

[8] Human Rights Watch, 'Gold's Costly Dividend: Human Rights Impacts of Papua New Guinea's Porgera Gold Mine' (2011).

[9] Barrick's responses are at www.business-humanrights.org/Search/SearchResults?SearchableText=porgera&x=0&y=0.

[10] Human Rights Watch, '"You'll Be Fired if You Refuse": Labor Abuses in Zambia's Chinese State-owned Copper Mines', 4 Nov. 2011.

[11] C. Duhigg & D. Barboza, 'In China, Human Costs Are Built Into an iPad', *New York Times*, 25 Jan. 2012.

Labor Association, an NGO that sets voluntary standards and monitors compliance, to undertake an investigation. Its findings included:

> *A) Working Hours*
> During peak production, the average number of hours worked per week at Foxconn factories exceeded both the FLA Code standard and Chinese legal limits.... Some employees worked more than seven days in a row without the required minimum 24-hour break. The root causes include high labor turnover, which undermines efficiency, and gaps in production and capacity planning.
>
> Remedial Action: Foxconn has agreed to achieve full legal compliance regarding work hours by July 1, 2013, while protecting workers' pay....
>
> *B) Health and Safety*
> Our assessors identified numerous issues related to inconsistent policies, procedures and practices.... [W]orkers felt generally insecure regarding their health and safety....
>
> Remedial Action:... [I]ncreased worker involvement in formulating and implementing health and safety policy will help to ensure future compliance. Many... violations... have already been remedied. Additionally, Foxconn has agreed to change the system by which accidents are recorded. In the past, only those accidents that caused work stoppage were recorded as accidents....
>
> *C) Industrial Relations and Worker Integration*
> [W]orkers were largely alienated... from factories' safety and health committees and had little confidence in the management of health and safety issues....
>
> ... [M]anagement nominates candidates for election. The result is committees... dominated by management representatives. Moreover, committees are largely reactive, failing to monitor conditions in a robust manner....
>
> Remedial Action:... Foxconn has agreed to ensure elections of worker representatives without management interference....
>
> *D) Compensation and Social Security Insurance*
> ... 14 percent of the workers may not receive fair compensation for unscheduled overtime.... [In China, social security and related insurance] is set up on a provincial and city basis. This means that workers who migrate from other cities or provinces can't collect their insurance when they return home....
>
> Remedial Action: Foxconn has agreed that... workers will be paid fairly for all overtime and work-related meetings.... Foxconn will... investigate alternative private options to provide unemployment insurance to migrant workers, and work with government agencies to expedite the transportability of benefits. FLA will conduct a cost of living study... to assist Foxconn in determining whether worker salaries meet FLA requirements for basic needs, as well as discretionary income.[12]

In its *Annual Report 2012*, Amnesty International noted that '[d]igital and communications companies are coming under greater scrutiny as they face governments' demands to comply with patently illegal laws that violate human rights including the rights to freedom of expression, information and privacy. There is evidence that businesses ostensibly dedicated (and benefiting) from expression and sharing of opinion,

[12] Fair Labor Association, 'Independent Investigation of Apple Supplier, Foxconn Report Highlights', Mar. 2012.

including Facebook, Google, Microsoft, Twitter, Vodaphone and Yahoo are collaborating in some of these violations.' A related, but different challenge involving this sector is illustrated by allegations that Western companies have sold technologies that enable the Iranian and Syrian governments to disrupt and monitor the internet and track down government critics. In response, US President Obama issued an Executive Order in April 2012 authorizing the Treasury Secretary to sanction individuals and companies providing goods or services that can be used for such purposes.[13]

For human rights proponents, the growth of corporate power raises the question of how to ensure that the activities of transnational corporations in particular are consistent with human rights standards and of how to promote accountability when violations of those standards occur. In principle, the answer is straightforward. The human rights obligations assumed by each government require it to use all appropriate means to ensure that actors operating within its territory or otherwise subject to its jurisdiction comply with national legislation designed to give effect to human rights.

In practice, however, various problems arise: (1) governments are often loathe to take the measures necessary to ensure compliance by TNCs, especially, but not only, in relation to labour matters; (2) such measures are costly and perceived to be beyond the resource capabilities of governments in developing countries; (3) in the context of increasing global mobility of capital, competition among potential host countries discourages initiatives that may push up labour costs and make one country less attractive than others with lower regulatory standards (the so-called 'race to the bottom'); (4) the transnational complexity of manufacturing and related arrangements in an era of globalization makes it increasingly difficult to identify who is responsible for what activities and where; and (5) especially in the labour area, difficult issues arise about the different levels of minimum acceptable standards from one country to another.

Already in the 1970s, in the context of demands by developing countries for the establishment of a New International Economic Order, efforts were begun to draft a Code of Conduct for Transnational Corporations. Although a draft was completed in 1983, developed countries sought to circumvent the process by pursuing a separate initiative through the rich countries' club — the Organisation for Economic Co-operation and Development (OECD). The OECD adopted its Guidelines for Multinational Enterprises in 1976, and they continue to be regularly updated.[14] In the meantime, the Code, which reflected a much more stringent approach, was finally abandoned in 1992. The end of the Cold War brought much greater competition to attract foreign direct investment to developing countries and with it came increased pressure to accept the terms on offer from the TNCs rather than making human rights or related demands. Gradually, however, the pendulum has swung back again over the past decade or more. One prominent observer attributed the swing to 'reputational disasters' affecting prominent TNCs: 'It was the damaging experience of Shell and BP in Nigeria and Colombia respectively which proved the catalyst for a change of attitudes and provided a lesson about corporate responsibility which was reinforced

[13] www.whitehouse.gov/the-press-office/2012/04/23/executive-order-blocking-property-and-suspending-entry-united-states-cer.

[14] For the 2011 edition see www.oecd.org/dataoecd/43/29/48004323.pdf.

by the experience of Nike and other major international brands with reputations to protect.'[15] An additional element has been the rapid expansion of South-South investment by TNCs based in China, India and Brazil. As a result, the debate is no longer only about Northern corporations and their activities in the South. Four of the top 20 companies in the Forbes 2012 list are from China, one from Brazil and one from Russia. But eight are from the United States and the remaining six from Western Europe.[16]

2. TOWARDS 'REGULATION'

Codes of conduct have been adopted by thousands of TNCs and they vary hugely in their content, participation, arrangements for monitoring, follow-up, etc. For a compilation of corporate codes on human rights see http://business-humanrights.org/Documents/Policies. In 1999, then UN Secretary-General Kofi Annan launched the Global Compact designed to encourage corporations to commit to following a list of principles in their activities. In addition to principles governing the environment the Compact includes:

Human Rights

Principle 1: support and respect the protection of international human rights within their sphere of influence;

Principle 2: make sure their own corporations are not complicit in human rights abuses.

Labour Standards

Principle 3: freedom of association and the effective recognition of the right to collective bargaining;

Principle 4: the elimination of all forms of forced and compulsory labour;

Principle 5: the effective abolition of child labour;

Principle 6: the elimination of discrimination in respect of employment and occupation.

The Global Compact (www.unglobalcompact.org) has attracted significant corporate support but has generally elicited scepticism from human rights proponents because of their vagueness and their apparent failure to generate significant pressure upon corporations to improve their performance. As of May 2012 the Compact listed 6,978 business participants and 3,326 non-business participants. It also noted that 3,514 business participants had been delisted for failure to report over the period since the initiative was established. An Annual Review is undertaken to assess participation outcomes. The most recently available — the 2010 Review — notes that the best performers are large and publicly traded companies. While 'companies across the board report having anti-discrimination and equal opportunity policies…less than 20 percent of all respondents report conducting human rights impact assessments.' A recent

[15] Chandler, n. 4, above.

[16] www.forbes.com/global2000/.

scholarly study concluded that 'membership in the GC alone is unlikely to move a company in significant ways towards progressive and continuous implementation of the core GC principles.'[17] Regional and local Global Compact networks were seen to be especially important, and by 2011 almost 100 of these had been established.[18]

One of the most important international initiatives is the Voluntary Principles on Security and Human Rights (VPs) which were adopted in 2000 at the initiative of the US and UK Governments working with key TNCs and NGOs.[19] They aim 'to guide extractives companies in maintaining the safety and security of their operations within an operating framework that ensures respect for human rights.' They focus particularly on risk assessment, and interactions between companies and public and private security. In relation to effective risk assessment, for example, they call upon corporations to: (1) identify security risks; (2) estimate the potential for violence in a given area; (3) take account of the human rights records of public security forces, paramilitaries, local and national law enforcement and the reputation of private security; (4) take account of the local prosecuting authority and judiciary's capacity to hold actors accountable for human rights abuses; (5) identify the root causes and nature of local conflicts; and (6) consider the risks of transferring equipment to public or private security and the feasibility of measures to mitigate foreseeable negative consequences.

In addition to the United States and the United Kingdom, Canada, Colombia, the Netherlands, Norway and Switzerland have joined the initiative along with TNCs such as Amerada Hess, Anglo American, BHP Billiton, BP, Chevron, ExxonMobil, Freeport, Norsk Hydro, Occidental Petroleum, Rio Tinto, Shell, Statoil, Talisman Energy and Total. Key NGO participants include Amnesty International, Human Rights First, Human Rights Watch and Oxfam, and there are five observer organizations: Center for the Democratic Control of Armed Forces, International Committee of the Red Cross, International Council on Mining & Metals, International Finance Corporation and International Petroleum Industry Environmental Conservation Association.

Major NGOs have been critical of the extent to which TNCs, especially in the extractive industries, have taken the VPs seriously. In 2007 a UN expert called for: (1) adoption of 'internal and external reporting criteria, including specific performance measures'; (2) establishing 'a coherent and effective in-country presence' involving intensive interaction among all stakeholders; (3) systematic sharing of information and best practices; (4) supporting capacity-building in host countries; and (5) providing an adequately staffed Secretariat.[20] While there has been some progress in these areas, including the publication in 2011 of a volume on 'Implementation Guidance Tools', the degree of transparency exhibited by the publicly available information remains very limited (www.voluntaryprinciples.org).

National-level initiatives have also been important in this area. Perhaps the most important example is that of the Norwegian Government Pension Fund-Global

[17] W. Mwangi et al., 'Encouraging Greater Compliance: Local Networks and the United Nations Global Compact', in T. Risse, S. Ropp & K. Sikkink (eds.), *From Commitment to Compliance: The Persistent Power of Human Rights* (2012), Ch. 10.

[18] UN Global Compact, 'Local Network Report 2011'.

[19] See www.voluntaryprinciples.org.

[20] J. Ruggie, 'Voluntary Principles on Security and Human Rights', Remarks at Annual Voluntary Principles on Security and Human Rights Plenary (2007).

which receives all net government petroleum sector income, and invests all but the 4 per cent which goes to the national budget. In 2012 it had assets valued at $558 billion. In 2004 it adopted Ethical Guidelines to govern its investments. In addition to a commitment to sustainable development, the Fund is directed not to contribute to seriously unethical conduct. It should be guided by the various codes of conduct, including the Global Compact and the OECD Guidelines, and it should not invest in a company in relation to which there is 'an unacceptable risk that the company is complicit in or is responsible for: serious or systematic human rights violations...; serious violations of the rights of individuals in situations of war or conflict;...' A Council on Ethics reviews all investments and makes written recommendations on the exclusion of specific companies to the Ministry of Finance, which makes the final decision. So far only two companies — Wal-Mart and Wal-Mart de Mexico — have been excluded on the grounds of 'serious or systematic human rights violations', but others such as Barrick and Freeport McMoRan have been excluded on the grounds of 'serious environmental damage'. In 2010 the Council recommended the exclusion of PetroChina Co. Ltd on the grounds that there was 'an unacceptable risk of involvement in current and future human rights violations in connection with the construction of oil and gas pipelines in Burma.' The Ministry of Finance, however, rejected the recommendation on the grounds that the company and its subsidiary were not so closely connected that they should 'be regarded as a single entity'.[21]

But the problem with these diverse and rapidly proliferating 'voluntary' initiatives is that they generally lack meaningful forms of accountability and rely instead upon both public opinion and corporate altruism. The situation that often prevails is well illustrated by the case of another of the large global gold mining companies, with a major investment in West Papua, Freeport McMoRan. Since 2004 a Swiss NGO — the Berne Declaration — and Greenpeace Switzerland, have presented an annual 'Public Eye' award to the corporation voted to have shown the most 'contempt for the environment and human rights' in the world. In 2012, one of the six nominated companies was Freeport McMoRan. It was alleged by campaigners that the Grasberg mine had 'generated significant controversy because of its waste disposal methods, impacts on a sensitive ecosystem, lack of transparency, and conflicts with communities around human rights and other issues.' The corporation was said to have given $79.1 million to Indonesian police and military forces in the previous ten years in order to protect its operations, and those forces were said to have sometimes conducted themselves in a violent manner: 'According to community records, 160 people were killed in the mine area and surroundings between 1975 and 1997. Recently, the violence has continued.' It was also alleged that ten people had been killed in 2012 during and after a labour strike involving over 8,000 workers.[22]

The company responded as follows:

> Freeport-McMoRan condemns human rights violations of any form. We have a longstanding commitment to the protection of human rights and have been

[21] www.regjeringen.no. See also G. Nystuen et al. (eds.), *Human Rights, Corporate Complicity and Disinvestment* (2011).

[22] Nick Magel, 'Vote Freeport McMoRan for 2012's Worst Corporation on Earth', 19 Jan. 2012, at www.earthworksaction.org/earthblog/detail/vote_freeport_mcmoran_for_2012s_worst_corporation_on_earth.

> vigorous in communicating, enacting and enforcing our Human Rights Policy. Initially adopted in 1999, the Policy requires that we recognize and respect human rights and conduct business in a manner consistent with the Universal Declaration of Human Rights, educate our employees and protect any employee who reports suspected violations. It requires fair treatment and work conditions for all employees, including rights to freedom of association and collective bargaining, and prohibits forced, compulsory, and child labor.
>
> Freeport-McMoRan has been a member of the Voluntary Principles on Security and Human Rights [since] 2000. The Voluntary Principles have been an important cornerstone of our human rights and security program, providing guidance for our operations as well as a mechanism to promote engagement, awareness, and respect for human rights within our employee base as well as with our government and community partners. Each year, participants in this program meet to review implementation of the principles and to seek better ways to provide security for extractive industry operations around the world to protect employees and investments while assuring the highest level of human rights compliance. We post our annual Voluntary Principles on Security and Human Rights Report for stakeholders to understand our programs and performance....[23]

And there the debate rests with the views of neither the community groups nor the company being able to be vindicated except perhaps in the context of the battle for public opinion. In essence, the strategy reflected in the Voluntary Principles and in most of the codes is gradually to ratchet up the levels of commitment and accountability. Many in the human rights field, however, have expressed frustration with such incrementalism and have pressed instead for progress towards binding legal rules. This is the thrust of Howen's article, below. A first step in this direction was thought to have been the adoption of a set of Norms on the Responsibilities of Transnational Corporations and Other Business Enterprises with Regard to Human Rights (the so-called 'UN Norms'). The Norms were drafted by a working group of the UN Sub-Commission on the Promotion and Protection of Human Rights, chaired by David Weissbrodt. The Sub-Commission was abolished in 2006 and effectively replaced by the Human Rights Council Advisory Committee. The following draft was proposed for adoption by the Commission on Human Rights and perhaps ultimately the UN General Assembly. But governmental support in the Commission proved to be almost entirely lacking.

NORMS ON THE RESPONSIBILITIES OF TRANSNATIONAL CORPORATIONS AND OTHER BUSINESS ENTERPRISES WITH REGARD TO HUMAN RIGHTS

UN Doc. E/CN.4/Sub.2/2003/12/Rev.2 (2003)

Preamble

Bearing in mind the [UN Charter]...,

[23] www.business-humanrights.org/Documents/PublicEyenominations2012responses.

Recalling [the UDHR]...,

...

Realizing that transnational corporations and other business enterprises, their officers and persons working for them are also obligated to respect generally recognized responsibilities and norms contained in United Nations treaties and other international instruments such as the [Conventions on Genocide, Torture, Slavery, Racial Discrimination, Discrimination against Women, the Rights of the Child, and Migrant Workers; the two International Covenants; the four Geneva Conventions of 1949 and two Additional Protocols thereto; the Declaration on human rights defenders; the Rome Statute of the International Criminal Court; the UN Convention against Transnational Organized Crime; the Convention on Biological Diversity; the International Convention on Civil Liability for Oil Pollution Damage; the Declaration on the Right to Development; the Rio Declaration on Environment and Development; the UN Millennium Declaration; the WHO's Ethical Criteria for Medical Drug Promotion; conventions and recommendations of the International Labour Organization; the Refugee Convention and Protocol; the African Charter on Human and Peoples' Rights; the American Convention on Human Rights; the European Convention on Human Rights; the Charter of Fundamental Rights of the European Union; and other instruments],

...

Conscious also of the Commentary on [these UN Norms[24]], and finding it a useful interpretation and elaboration of the standards contained in the Norms,

...

Solemnly proclaims these Norms...and urges that every effort be made so that they become generally known and respected.

A. General obligations

1. States have the primary responsibility to promote, secure the fulfilment of, respect, ensure respect of and protect human rights recognized in international as well as national law, including ensuring that transnational corporations and other business enterprises respect human rights. Within their respective spheres of activity and influence, transnational corporations and other business enterprises have the obligation to promote, secure the fulfilment of, respect, ensure respect of and protect human rights recognized in international as well as national law, including the rights and interests of indigenous peoples and other vulnerable groups.

[Eds.: The Commentary to the Norms elaborates on this provision by stating:

> (b) Transnational corporations and other business enterprises shall have the responsibility to use due diligence in ensuring that their activities do not contribute directly or indirectly to human abuses, and that they do not directly or indirectly benefit from abuses of which they were aware or ought to have been aware. Transnational corporations and other business enterprises shall further

[24] UN Doc. E/CN.4/Sub.2/2003/38/Rev.2 (2003).

> refrain from activities that would undermine the rule of law as well as governmental and other efforts to promote and ensure respect for human rights, and shall use their influence in order to help promote and ensure respect for human rights. Transnational corporations and other business enterprises shall inform themselves of the human rights impact of their principal activities and major proposed activities so that they can further avoid complicity in human rights abuses. The Norms may not be used by States as an excuse for failing to take action to protect human rights, for example, through the enforcement of existing laws.]

B. Right to equal opportunity and non-discriminatory treatment

2. Transnational corporations and other business enterprises shall ensure equality of opportunity and treatment, as provided in the relevant international instruments and national legislation as well as international human rights law, for the purpose of eliminating discrimination based on race, colour, sex, language, religion, political opinion, national or social origin, social status, indigenous status, disability, age — except for children, who may be given greater protection — or other status of the individual unrelated to the inherent requirements to perform the job, or of complying with special measures designed to overcome past discrimination against certain groups.

C. Right to security of persons

3. Transnational corporations and other business enterprises shall not engage in nor benefit from war crimes, crimes against humanity, genocide, torture, forced disappearance, forced or compulsory labour, hostage-taking, extrajudicial, summary or arbitrary executions, other violations of humanitarian law and other international crimes against the human person as defined by international law, in particular human rights and humanitarian law.

4. Security arrangements for transnational corporations and other business enterprises shall observe international human rights norms as well as the laws and professional standards of the country or countries in which they operate.

D. Rights of workers

5. Transnational corporations and other business enterprises shall not use forced or compulsory labour....

6. Transnational corporations and other business enterprises shall respect the rights of children to be protected from economic exploitation....

7. Transnational corporations and other business enterprises shall provide a safe and healthy working environment....

8. Transnational corporations and other business enterprises shall provide workers with remuneration that ensures an adequate standard of living for them and their families. Such remuneration shall take due account of their needs for adequate living conditions with a view towards progressive improvement.

9. Transnational corporations and other business enterprises shall ensure freedom of association and effective recognition of the right to collective bargaining...as provided in national legislation and the relevant conventions of the International Labour Organization.

E. Respect for national sovereignty and human rights

10. Transnational corporations and other business enterprises shall recognize and respect applicable norms of international law, national laws and regulations, as well as administrative practices, the rule of law, the public interest, development objectives, social, economic and cultural policies including transparency, accountability and prohibition of corruption, and authority of the countries in which the enterprises operate.

. . .

12. Transnational corporations and other business enterprises shall respect economic, social and cultural rights as well as civil and political rights and contribute to their realization, in particular the rights to development, adequate food and drinking water, the highest attainable standard of physical and mental health, adequate housing, privacy, education, freedom of thought, conscience, and religion and freedom of opinion and expression, and shall refrain from actions which obstruct or impede the realization of those rights.

F. Obligations with regard to consumer protection

13. Transnational corporations and other business enterprises shall act in accordance with fair business, marketing and advertising practices and shall take all necessary steps to ensure the safety and quality of the goods and services they provide, including observance of the precautionary principle. Nor shall they produce, distribute, market, or advertise harmful or potentially harmful products for use by consumers.

G. Obligations with regard to environmental protection

14. Transnational corporations and other business enterprises shall carry out their activities in accordance with national laws, regulations, administrative practices and policies relating to the preservation of the environment of the countries in which they operate, as well as in accordance with relevant international agreements, principles, objectives, responsibilities and standards with regard to the environment as well as human rights, public health and safety, bioethics and the precautionary principle, and shall generally conduct their activities in a manner contributing to the wider goal of sustainable development.

H. General provisions of implementation

15. As an initial step towards implementing these Norms, each transnational corporation or other business enterprise shall adopt, disseminate and implement internal rules of operation in compliance with the Norms. Further, they shall periodically report on and take other measures fully to implement the Norms and to provide at least for the prompt implementation of the protections set forth in the Norms. Each transnational corporation or other business enterprise shall apply and incorporate these Norms in their contracts or other arrangements and dealings with contractors, subcontractors, suppliers, licensees, distributors, or natural or other legal persons that enter into any agreement with the transnational corporation or business enterprise in order to ensure respect for and implementation of the Norms.

16. Transnational corporations and other businesses enterprises shall be subject to periodic monitoring and verification by United Nations, other international and national mechanisms already in existence or yet to be created, regarding application of the Norms. This monitoring shall be transparent and independent and take into account input from stakeholders (including non governmental organizations) and as a result of complaints of violations of these Norms. Further, transnational corporations and other businesses enterprises shall conduct periodic evaluations concerning the impact of their own activities on human rights under these Norms.

17. States should establish and reinforce the necessary legal and administrative framework for ensuring that the Norms and other relevant national and international laws are implemented by transnational corporations and other business enterprises.

...

I. Definitions

20. The term "transnational corporation" refers to an economic entity operating in more than one country or a cluster of economic entities operating in two or more countries — whatever their legal form, whether in their home country or country of activity, and whether taken individually or collectively.

21. The phrase "other business enterprise" includes any business entity, regardless of the international or domestic nature of its activities, including a transnational corporation, contractor, subcontractor, supplier, licensee or distributor; the corporate, partnership, or other legal form used to establish the business entity; and the nature of the ownership of the entity. These Norms shall be presumed to apply, as a matter of practice, if the business enterprise has any relation with a transnational corporation, the impact of its activities is not entirely local, or the activities involve violations of the right to security as indicated in paragraphs 3 and 4.

22. The term "stakeholder" includes stockholders, other owners, workers and their representatives, as well as any other individual or group that is affected by the activities of transnational corporations or other business enterprises....

NICHOLAS HOWEN, BUSINESS, HUMAN RIGHTS AND ACCOUNTABILITY

Copenhagen (21 Sept. 2005), at www.icj.org/dwn/database/Nickspeech-Denmark-22092005.pdf

[The author was Secretary-General of the International Commission of Jurists.] ... I see at least seven reasons why there is need to develop clear, common and binding global rules on corporate accountability and human rights.

1. Documented abuses and complicity

... When we talk about accountability we must answer how to ensure the worst [corporations], and not only the best, respect the rules....

2. Market forces are not enough

Some have argued that we should leave it to the marketplace—economic forces—to regulate the behaviour of companies. This argument overlooks, however, that respecting human rights are not, unfortunately, always good for business. It is clear that companies can thrive in countries with abusive regimes, such as in South Africa under the *apartheid* regime, in Burma now, in Nigeria under military rule....

3. Need for binding, common benchmarks

We must go beyond voluntarism. Voluntary codes of conduct and initiatives have been important steps on the road to accountability but they're not enough. We need a mix of voluntary initiatives *and* legally binding rules.

Voluntary codes can be useful: individual company or industry-wide codes, ethical programmes. They can build a consensus around some rights, such as not using child labour. They can build a culture of compliance, to a certain extent. Some codes even go beyond the minimum human rights standards, which are set out in documents like the Universal Declaration of Human Rights. Voluntary codes are, however, only respected by those who want to respect them. Too often they fall by the wayside when there is a clash against hard commercial interests. They can be easily rejected when faced with the harsh competitiveness of the commercial world. Studies of voluntary codes have shown how most codes leave out the most difficult rights for business, such as the freedom of association and collective bargaining. There is a proliferation of voluntary standards that has brought confusion....

4. Victims' rights to remedy and reparation

Victims of human rights violations need rights and remedies, not merely charity or philanthropy.

We need to move from the good intentions of voluntary codes to the idea that if victims suffer and their rights are violated, they do have a right to compensation and restitution....

Providing remedies for victims is not about engaging in costly and drawn out court cases, but it is about building legal rights that encourage a culture of compliance....

5. Inability or failure of host states to hold business accountable

We need global rules because most large corporations have outgrown the ability of many individual states to regulate them effectively.

We find that the balance has often tilted in favour of transnational corporations. Often the government of a host country is worried that tough regulation will scare away foreign direct investment.... Governments in countries where multinationals have their headquarters have little interest in holding companies accountable for behaviour far away from home.

International law is not a substitute for effective national laws and policies. But international standards do help to provide common guidance to states, to harmonize rules at times of weak national regulation....

6. Why human rights standards?

...Aspects of consumer law, criminal law, environmental law or corporate law can all help companies decide what they should do and not do. But only human rights standards provide the comprehensive normative guide about how human beings should be treated.

7. Power needs to be constrained by law

A role of law is to balance power and obligations and to limit the arbitrary exercise of power. Large corporations are beginning to challenge the traditional economic and political dominance of governments.

Some states are dwarfed by the power of transnational corporations. Governments are losing authority up to supranational organisation bodies and internally as state functions are privatized.

...

QUESTIONS

1. 'In the truly problematic situations, where human rights are at great risk, host state governments will rarely be able or willing to stand up to enormous TNCs. The only realistic solution is for the governments of the corporations' home states to compel them to respect human rights wherever they operate.' Discuss.

2. What do you see as the major strengths and weaknesses of the Norms?

NOTE

Responses to the UN Norms varied dramatically. The most involved NGOs — notably Amnesty International, Human Rights Watch and the International Commission of Jurists — all endorsed them as an appropriate basis upon which to move forward to develop corporate accountability. While the views of scholars were deeply divided,[25] governmental reaction was largely negative. Most developing countries were not keen on intrusive regulation and most developed countries felt that the Norms were either unnecessary or overreaching. The United States, for example, spoke of an 'anti-business agenda'. The response of industry representatives was mixed, but most were hostile. In 2004, the UN Commission on Human Rights noted that the Norms contained 'useful elements and ideas', but stated that the draft had no legal standing. The following year, it opted (CHR Res. 2005/69) instead to appoint an independent expert as Special Representative of the Secretary-General (SRSG) with a mandate to:

[25] Cf. D. Kinley & R. Chambers, 'The UN Human Rights Norms for Corporations: The Private Implications of Public International Law', 6 Hum. Rts. L. Rev. 447 (2006) and U. Baxi, 'Market Fundamentalisms: Business Ethics at the Altar of Human Rights', 5 Hum. Rts. L. Rev. 1 (2005).

> (a) To identify and clarify standards of corporate responsibility and accountability ...; (b) To elaborate on the role of States in effectively regulating [corporations]..., including through international cooperation; (c) To research and clarify the implications...of concepts such as 'complicity' and 'sphere of influence'; (d) To develop materials and methodologies for undertaking human rights impact assessments of [corporate activities]; and (e) To compile a compendium of best practices of States and [corporations].

John Ruggie was appointed as SRSG on the issue of human rights and transnational corporations and other business enterprises. In his initial report (UN Doc. E/CN.4/2006/97), he was strongly critical of the Norms, characterizing it as an exercise that had 'became engulfed by its own doctrinal excesses'. He noted its 'highly contentious though largely symbolic proposal to monitor firms', but singled out 'its exaggerated legal claims and conceptual ambiguities'. In his view, the Norms had taken 'existing State-based human rights instruments and simply [asserted] that many of their provisions now are binding on corporations as well', an assertion which in his view had 'little authoritative basis in international law — hard, soft, or otherwise'.

Another problem was the imprecision of the Norms:

> in allocating human rights responsibilities to States and corporations.... By their very nature...corporations do not have a general role in relation to human rights as do States; they have a specialized one. The Norms...articulate no actual principle for differentiating human rights responsibilities based on the respective social roles performed by States and corporations. Indeed in several instances, and with no justification, the Norms end up imposing higher obligations on corporations than on States ...

As a result, he suggested that the 'concept of "spheres of influence" is left to carry the burden'. But it could not do so because of the elusive nature of its legal meaning.

A further criticism was that because 'corporations are not democratic public interest institutions, attempts to make them co-equal duty bearers for the broad spectrum of human rights...may undermine efforts to build indigenous social capacity and to make Governments more responsible to their own citizenry.' He concluded that the Norms' flaws made them 'a distraction' rather than a basis for moving forward.

Ruggie proceeded to adopt a very different approach. He assembled a staff of ten researchers/advisors, obtained free legal assistance from over 24 law firms worldwide, mobilized academic institutions and other researchers, engaged in 47 consultations with stakeholders around the world, conducted 20 site visits, drafted detailed studies and analyses of key issues and placed his mandate at the centre of most discussions about corporate human rights responsibilities. He raised millions of dollars from governments and corporations to facilitate his work, and he avoided explicit criticism of particular corporations. The intellectual framework that he developed was organized around the three principles of 'protect, respect and remedy'. In 2008, his mandate was renewed and expanded.

He was requested to elaborate on each of the elements of his framework, to 'identify, exchange and promote best practices and lessons learned' and to continue to consult with all stakeholders (HRC Res. 8/7). As a Special Procedures mandate-holder, Ruggie was limited to a total term of six years and thus submitted his final report in 2011. It consisted almost entirely of a set of Guiding Principles, on which comments from governments and other stakeholders had been solicited and reflected in advance.

GUIDING PRINCIPLES ON BUSINESS AND HUMAN RIGHTS: IMPLEMENTING THE UNITED NATIONS 'PROTECT, RESPECT AND REMEDY' FRAMEWORK

UN Doc. A/HRC/17/31, Annex (21 Mar. 2011)

General principles

These Guiding Principles are grounded in recognition of:

(a) States' existing obligations to respect, protect and fulfil human rights and fundamental freedoms;
(b) The role of business enterprises as specialized organs of society performing specialized functions, required to comply with all applicable laws and to respect human rights;
(c) The need for rights and obligations to be matched to appropriate and effective remedies when breached.

These Guiding Principles apply to all States and to all business enterprises, both transnational and others, regardless of their size, sector, location, ownership and structure.

...

Nothing in these Guiding Principles should be read as creating new international law obligations....

...

I. The State duty to protect human rights

A. Foundational principles

1. States must protect against human rights abuse within their territory and/or jurisdiction by third parties, including business enterprises. This requires taking appropriate steps to prevent, investigate, punish and redress such abuse through effective policies, legislation, regulations and adjudication.

...

2. States should set out clearly the expectation that all business enterprises domiciled in their territory and/or jurisdiction respect human rights throughout their operations.

Commentary

At present, States are not generally required under international human rights law to regulate the extraterritorial activities of businesses domiciled in their territory and/or jurisdiction. Nor are they generally prohibited from doing so....

There are strong policy reasons for home States to set out clearly the expectation that businesses respect human rights abroad, especially where the State itself is involved in or supports those businesses. The reasons include ensuring predictability for business enterprises by providing coherent and consistent messages, and preserving the State's own reputation.

...

B. Operational principles

General State regulatory and policy functions

3. In meeting their duty to protect, States should:

(a) Enforce laws that are aimed at, or have the effect of, requiring business enterprises to respect human rights, and periodically to assess the adequacy of such laws and address any gaps;

(b) Ensure that other laws and policies governing the creation and ongoing operation of business enterprises, such as corporate law, do not constrain but enable business respect for human rights;

(c) Provide effective guidance to business enterprises on how to respect human rights throughout their operations;

(d) Encourage, and where appropriate require, business enterprises to communicate how they address their human rights impacts.

Commentary

States should not assume that businesses invariably prefer, or benefit from, State inaction, and they should consider a smart mix of measures — national and international, mandatory and voluntary — to foster business respect for human rights.

The failure to enforce existing laws that directly or indirectly regulate business respect for human rights is often a significant legal gap in State practice....

...

Guidance to business enterprises on respecting human rights should indicate expected outcomes and help share best practices. It should advise on appropriate methods, including human rights due diligence....

...

The State-business nexus

4. States should take additional steps to protect against human rights abuses by business enterprises that are owned or controlled by the State, or that receive substantial support and services from State agencies such as export credit agencies and official investment insurance or guarantee agencies, including, where appropriate, by requiring human rights due diligence.

...

5. States should exercise adequate oversight in order to meet their international human rights obligations when they contract with, or legislate for, business

enterprises to provide services that may impact upon the enjoyment of human rights.

…

6. States should promote respect for human rights by business enterprises with which they conduct commercial transactions.

…

Supporting business respect for human rights in conflict-affected areas

7. Because the risk of gross human rights abuses is heightened in conflict-affected areas, States should help ensure that business enterprises operating in those contexts are not involved with such abuses, including by:

(a) Engaging at the earliest stage possible with business enterprises to help them identify, prevent and mitigate the human rights-related risks of their activities and business relationships;

(b) Providing adequate assistance to business enterprises to assess and address the heightened risks of abuses, paying special attention to both gender-based and sexual violence;

(c) Denying access to public support and services for a business enterprise that is involved with gross human rights abuses and refuses to cooperate in addressing the situation;

(d) Ensuring that their current policies, legislation, regulations and enforcement measures are effective in addressing the risk of business involvement in gross human rights abuses.

Commentary

Some of the worst human rights abuses involving business occur amid conflict over the control of territory, resources or a Government itself — where the human rights regime cannot be expected to function as intended. Responsible businesses increasingly seek guidance from States about how to avoid contributing to human rights harm in these difficult contexts. . . .

. . . In conflict-affected areas, the "host" State may be unable to protect human rights adequately due to a lack of effective control. Where transnational corporations are involved, their "home" States therefore have roles to play in assisting both those corporations and host States to ensure that businesses are not involved with human rights abuse, while neighboring States can provide important additional support.

To achieve greater policy coherence and assist business enterprises adequately in such situations, home States should foster closer cooperation among their development assistance agencies, foreign and trade ministries, and export finance institutions in their capitals and within their embassies, as well as between these agencies and host Government actors; develop early-warning indicators to alert Government agencies and business enterprises to problems; and attach appropriate consequences to any failure by enterprises to cooperate in these contexts, including by denying or withdrawing existing public support or services, or where that is not possible, denying their future provision.

States should warn business enterprises of the heightened risk of being involved with gross abuses of human rights in conflict-affected areas. They should review whether their policies, legislation, regulations and enforcement measures effectively address this heightened risk, including through provisions for human rights due diligence by business. Where they identify gaps, States should take appropriate steps to address them. This may include exploring civil, administrative or criminal liability for enterprises domiciled or operating in their territory and/or jurisdiction that commit or contribute to gross human rights abuses. Moreover, States should consider multilateral approaches to prevent and address such acts, as well as support effective collective initiatives.

All these measures are in addition to States' obligations under international humanitarian law in situations of armed conflict, and under international criminal law.

Ensuring policy coherence

8. States should ensure that governmental departments, agencies and other State-based institutions that shape business practices are aware of and observe the State's human rights obligations when fulfilling their respective mandates, including by providing them with relevant information, training and support.

...

9. States should maintain adequate domestic policy space to meet their human rights obligations when pursuing business-related policy objectives with other States or business enterprises, for instance through investment treaties or contracts.

Commentary

Economic agreements concluded by States, either with other States or with business enterprises — such as bilateral investment treaties, free-trade agreements or contracts for investment projects — create economic opportunities for States. But they can also affect the domestic policy space of governments. For example, the terms of international investment agreements may constrain States from fully implementing new human rights legislation, or put them at risk of binding international arbitration if they do so. Therefore, States should ensure that they retain adequate policy and regulatory ability to protect human rights under the terms of such agreements, while providing the necessary investor protection.

10. States, when acting as members of multilateral institutions that deal with business-related issues, should:

(a) **Seek to ensure that those institutions neither restrain the ability of their member States to meet their duty to protect nor hinder business enterprises from respecting human rights;**

(b) **Encourage those institutions, within their respective mandates and capacities, to promote business respect for human rights and, where requested, to help States meet their duty to protect against human rights abuse by business enterprises, including through technical assistance, capacity-building and awareness-raising;**

(c) **Draw on these Guiding Principles to promote shared understanding and advance international cooperation in the management of business and human rights challenges.**

Commentary

Greater policy coherence is also needed at the international level, including where States participate in multilateral institutions that deal with business-related issues, such as international trade and financial institutions. States retain their international human rights law obligations when they participate in such institutions.

…

II. The corporate responsibility to respect human rights

A. Foundational principles

11. Business enterprises should respect human rights. This means that they should avoid infringing on the human rights of others and should address adverse human rights impacts with which they are involved.

Commentary

The responsibility to respect human rights is a global standard of expected conduct for all business enterprises wherever they operate. It exists independently of States' abilities and/or willingness to fulfil their own human rights obligations, and does not diminish those obligations. And it exists over and above compliance with national laws and regulations protecting human rights.

Addressing adverse human rights impacts requires taking adequate measures for their prevention, mitigation and, where appropriate, remediation.

…

12. The responsibility of business enterprises to respect human rights refers to internationally recognized human rights — understood, at a minimum, as those expressed in the International Bill of Human Rights and the principles concerning fundamental rights set out in the International Labour Organization's Declaration on Fundamental Principles and Rights at Work.

…

13. The responsibility to respect human rights requires that business enterprises:

(a) **Avoid causing or contributing to adverse human rights impacts through their own activities, and address such impacts when they occur;**

(b) **Seek to prevent or mitigate adverse human rights impacts that are directly linked to their operations, products or services by their business relationships, even if they have not contributed to those impacts.**

Commentary

… [A] business enterprise's "activities" are understood to include both actions and omissions; and its "business relationships" are understood to include relationships with business partners, entities in its value chain, and any other non-State or State entity directly linked to its business operations, products or services.

14. The responsibility of business enterprises to respect human rights applies to all enterprises regardless of their size, sector, operational context, ownership and structure. Nevertheless, the scale and complexity of the means through which enterprises meet that responsibility may vary according to these factors and with the severity of the enterprise's adverse human rights impacts.

…

15. In order to meet their responsibility to respect human rights, business enterprises should have in place policies and processes appropriate to their size and circumstances, including:

(a) A policy commitment to meet their responsibility to respect human rights;

(b) A human rights due-diligence process to identify, prevent account for how they address their impacts on human rights;

(c) Processes to enable the remediation of any adverse human rights impacts they cause or to which they contribute.

…

B. Operational principles

Policy commitment

16. As the basis for embedding their responsibility to respect human rights, business enterprises should express their commitment to meet this responsibility through a statement of policy that:

(a) Is approved at the most senior level of the business enterprise;

(b) Is informed by relevant internal and/or external expertise;

(c) Stipulates the enterprise's human rights expectations of personnel, business partners and other parties directly linked to its operations, products or services;

(d) Is publicly available and communicated internally and externally to all personnel, business partners and other relevant parties;

(e) Is reflected in operational policies and procedures necessary to embed it throughout the business enterprise.

…

Human rights due diligence

17. In order to identify, prevent, mitigate and account for how they address their adverse human rights impacts, business enterprises should carry out human rights due diligence. The process should include assessing actual and potential human rights impacts, integrating and acting upon the findings, tracking responses, and communicating how impacts are addressed. Human rights due diligence:

(a) Should cover adverse human rights impacts that the business enterprise may cause or contribute to through its own activities, or which may be directly linked to its operations, products or services by its business relationships;

(b) Will vary in complexity with the size of the business enterprise, the risk of severe human rights impacts, and the nature and context of its operations;

(c) Should be ongoing, recognizing that the human rights risks may change over time as the business enterprise's operations and operating context evolve.

Commentary

…

Where business enterprises have large numbers of entities in their value chains it may be unreasonably difficult to conduct due diligence for adverse human rights impacts across them all. If so, business enterprises should identify general areas where the risk of adverse human rights impacts is most significant, whether due to certain suppliers' or clients' operating context, the particular operations, products or services involved, or other relevant considerations, and prioritize these for human rights due diligence.

Questions of complicity may arise when a business enterprise contributes to, or is seen as contributing to, adverse human rights impacts caused by other parties. Complicity has both non-legal and legal meanings. As a non-legal matter, business enterprises may be perceived as being "complicit" in the acts of another party where, for example, they are seen to benefit from an abuse committed by that party.

As a legal matter, most national jurisdictions prohibit complicity in the commission of a crime, and a number allow for criminal liability of business enterprises in such cases. Typically, civil actions can also be based on an enterprise's alleged contribution to a harm, although these may not be framed in human rights terms. The weight of international criminal law jurisprudence indicates that the relevant standard for aiding and abetting is knowingly providing practical assistance or encouragement that has a substantial effect on the commission of a crime.

…

18. In order to gauge human rights risks, business enterprises should identify and assess any actual or potential adverse human rights impacts with which they may be involved either through their own activities or as a result of their business relationships. This process should:

(a) Draw on internal and/or independent external human rights expertise;

(b) Involve meaningful consultation with potentially affected groups and other relevant stakeholders, as appropriate to the size of the business enterprise and the nature and context of the operation.

…

19. In order to prevent and mitigate adverse human rights impacts, business enterprises should integrate the findings from their impact assessments across relevant internal functions and processes, and take appropriate action.

(a) Effective integration requires that:
(i) Responsibility for addressing such impacts is assigned to the appropriate level and function within the business enterprise;
(ii) Internal decision-making, budget allocations and oversight processes enable effective responses to such impacts.
(b) Appropriate action will vary according to:
(i) Whether the business enterprise causes or contributes to an adverse impact, or whether it is involved solely because the impact is directly linked to its operations, products or services by a business relationship;
(ii) The extent of its leverage in addressing the adverse impact.

...

20. In order to verify whether adverse human rights impacts are being addressed, business enterprises should track the effectiveness of their response. Tracking should:

(a) Be based on appropriate qualitative and quantitative indicators;
(b) Draw on feedback from both internal and external sources, including affected stakeholders.

...

21. In order to account for how they address their human rights impacts, business enterprises should be prepared to communicate this externally, particularly when concerns are raised by or on behalf of affected stakeholders. Business enterprises whose operations or operating contexts pose risks of severe human rights impacts should report formally on how they address them. In all instances, communications should:

(a) Be of a form and frequency that reflect an enterprise's human rights impacts and that are accessible to its intended audiences;
(b) Provide information that is sufficient to evaluate the adequacy of an enterprise's response to the particular human rights impact involved;
(c) In turn not pose risks to affected stakeholders, personnel or to legitimate requirements of commercial confidentiality.

...

Remediation

22. Where business enterprises identify that they have caused or contributed to adverse impacts, they should provide for or cooperate in their remediation through legitimate processes.

...

Issues of context

23. In all contexts, business enterprises should:

(a) Comply with all applicable laws and respect internationally recognized human rights, wherever they operate;
(b) Seek ways to honour the principles of internationally recognized human rights when faced with conflicting requirements;
(c) Treat the risk of causing or contributing to gross human rights abuses as a legal compliance issue wherever they operate.

Commentary

...Where the domestic context renders it impossible to meet this responsibility fully, business enterprises are expected to respect the principles of internationally recognized human rights to the greatest extent possible in the circumstances, and to be able to demonstrate their efforts in this regard.

Some operating environments, such as conflict-affected areas, may increase the risks of enterprises being complicit in gross human rights abuses committed by other actors (security forces, for example). Business enterprises should treat this risk as a legal compliance issue, given the expanding web of potential corporate legal liability arising from extraterritorial civil claims, and from the incorporation of the provisions of the Rome Statute of the International Criminal Court in jurisdictions that provide for corporate criminal responsibility. In addition, corporate directors, officers and employees may be subject to individual liability for acts that amount to gross human rights abuses.

...

24. Where it is necessary to prioritize actions to address actual and potential adverse human rights impacts, business enterprises should first seek to prevent and mitigate those that are most severe or where delayed response would make them irremediable.

...

III. Access to remedy

A. Foundational principle

25. As part of their duty to protect against business-related human rights abuse, States must take appropriate steps to ensure, through judicial, administrative, legislative or other appropriate means, that when such abuses occur within their territory and/or jurisdiction those affected have access to effective remedy.

...

B. Operational principles

State-based judicial mechanisms

26. States should take appropriate steps to ensure the effectiveness of domestic judicial mechanisms when addressing business-related human rights abuses, including considering ways to reduce legal, practical and other relevant barriers that could lead to a denial of access to remedy.

…

State-based non-judicial grievance mechanisms

27. States should provide effective and appropriate non-judicial grievance mechanisms, alongside judicial mechanisms, as part of a comprehensive State-based system for the remedy of business-related human rights abuse.

…

Non-State-based grievance mechanisms

28. States should consider ways to facilitate access to effective non-State-based grievance mechanisms dealing with business-related human rights harms.

…

29. To make it possible for grievances to be addressed early and remediated directly, business enterprises should establish or participate in effective operational-level grievance mechanisms for individuals and communities who may be adversely impacted.

…

30. Industry, multi-stakeholder and other collaborative initiatives that are based on respect for human rights-related standards should ensure that effective grievance mechanisms are available.

…

Effectiveness criteria for non-judicial grievance mechanisms

31. In order to ensure their effectiveness, non-judicial grievance mechanisms, both State-based and non-State-based, should be:

(a) Legitimate: enabling trust from the stakeholder groups for whose use they are intended, and being accountable for the fair conduct of grievance processes;
(b) Accessible: being known to all stakeholder groups for whose use they are intended, and providing adequate assistance for those who may face particular barriers to access;
(c) Predictable: providing a clear and known procedure with an indicative timeframe for each stage, and clarity on the types of process and outcome available and means of monitoring implementation;
(d) Equitable: seeking to ensure that aggrieved parties have reasonable access to sources of information, advice and expertise necessary to engage in a grievance process on fair, informed and respectful terms;
(e) Transparent: keeping parties to a grievance informed about its progress, and providing sufficient information about the mechanism's performance to build confidence in its effectiveness and meet any public interest at stake;
(f) Rights-compatible: ensuring that outcomes and remedies accord with internationally recognized human rights;
(g) A source of continuous learning: drawing on relevant measures to identify lessons for improving the mechanism and preventing future grievances and harms;

Operational-level mechanisms should also be:

(h) Based on engagement and dialogue: consulting the stakeholder groups for whose use they are intended on their design and performance, and focusing on dialogue as the means to address and resolve grievances.

…

NOTE

In response to the SRSG's final report, the Council went as far as to 'endorse' the Guiding Principles (in marked contrast to the fate of the spurned Norms). It also commended Ruggie on the approach he had adopted, recognized the role of the Guiding Principles for the implementation of the overall Framework, 'on which further progress can be made', and stated that his work did not foreclose 'any other long-term development, including further enhancement of standards'. In his place, it appointed a five-member Working Group to promote the Principles, to gather good practices and lessons learned, to support capacity-building and, potentially most significantly, to 'explore options and make recommendations for enhancing access to effective remedies available to those whose human rights are affected by corporate activities, including those in conflict areas' (HRC Res. 17/4). While Ruggie explicitly disparaged suggestions that the next phase should include the drafting of a binding international legal instrument, he diplomatically suggested that 'a multilateral approach to providing greater legal clarification may be warranted in response to the diverging national interpretations of the applicability to business enterprises of international standards prohibiting 'gross' human rights abuses, possibly amounting to the level of international crimes.'[26] The Council chose to ignore this proposal.

The Working Group decided in 2012 to undertake two country missions per year focused on good practices, to receive information from all sources and to adopt a thematic focus for the annual Forum on Business and Human Rights authorized by the Council. It also stated that, '[g]iven the broad scope of its mandate, the vast scale and complexity of the issue at hand, and resource constraints, the Working Group is not in a position to investigate individual cases of alleged business-related human rights abuse.'[27]

Responses to the Guiding Principles have, predictably, been mixed. Business interests were generally very favourable. Governments were also, for the most part, satisfied with the outcome. Norway, a key sponsor, described the process as a 'fact based and incremental' one. The United Kingdom 'wholly embrace[d] the Principles from a policy perspective', but quickly added its 'understanding that the Principles do not all necessarily reflect the current state of international law.... In particular,... the

[26] www.business-humanrights.org/media/documents/ruggie-statement-to-un-human-rights-council-30-may-2011.pdf.

[27] UN Doc. A/HRC/20/29 (10 Apr. 2012), para. 89.

UK...does not consider that there is a general State duty to protect under the core United Nations human rights treaties, nor that such a duty is generally agreed to exist as a matter of customary international law. Equally, while certain treaty obligations contain a "due diligence" standard, this is not a general provision.' Ecuador also hedged its bets, but in a different direction. While it would 'not stand in the way of consensus', it regretted that the exercise had not addressed 'the creation of a binding international human rights legal framework', had not ensured accountability of TNCs for human rights violations and lacked 'a complaints mechanism independent of the companies themselves'. It added that since the Principles 'are not and do not aspire to be binding', 'we must continue to seek binding international standards'. Human rights groups were supportive of the Principles, but also critical.[28] Human Rights Watch, for example, noted that 'the Council missed an opportunity to take meaningful action to curtail business-related human rights abuses' and instead 'conformed to the status quo: a world where companies are encouraged, but not obliged, to respect human rights'.[29]

In evaluating the Principles, one approach is to compare them with the vacuum that existed following the rejection of the Norms and to marvel at the degree of relative consensus that has been achieved. A different approach is to compare them to Howen's list of 'requirements'. Do they, for example, transcend reliance on the market, supplement voluntarism with binding rules and ensure compensation and restitution for victims? The next two readings provide some critical perspectives on the Guiding Principles. A third reading, by Muchlinski, raises the question of whether the approach sought by human rights proponents is even possible without a fundamental change of paradigm in the way we think about the social role of corporations.

PENELOPE SIMONS, INTERNATIONAL LAW'S INVISIBLE HAND AND THE FUTURE OF CORPORATE ACCOUNTABILITY FOR VIOLATIONS OF HUMAN RIGHTS

3 J. Hum. Rts. & Env. 5 (2012), at 17

...

Leaving aside how [GP9] might be accomplished, or whether in the case of some states it is even feasible, protecting policy space for host states will not fully address the power differential or leverage that investors can have *vis-à-vis* a Third World host state by virtue of these agreements. Even the most powerful states have been subject to arbitral proceedings or threats of such proceedings with respect to the introduction of public interest legislation that would allegedly have an impact on

[28] For a statement on the penultimate draft, endorsed by 130 NGOs, see 'Joint Civil Society Statement on the draft Guiding Principles on Business and Human Rights', Jan. 2011, at www.escr-net.org/actions_more/actions_more_show.htm?doc_id=1473602.

[29] Human Rights Watch, 'Keeping the Momentum One Year in the Life of the UN Human Rights Council' (2011), 27.

investors' protected investment. Traditional BITs [bilateral investment treaties] and other international investment treaties provide the host state with few if any tools to ensure that the investment will support sustainable development. Host states have no means under these treaties to address investor conduct that has a negative impact on human rights. These agreements include no obligations for investors to comply with human rights standards and there are no mechanisms to regulate investor behaviour, nor are there any means for host states to counterclaim in any arbitral proceedings brought against them where the investor has committed, or been complicit in, grave violations of human rights.

One means of addressing the power imbalance between host states and investors would be to include in these BITs...legally binding human rights obligations for investors....

Regrettably the SRSG did not recommend such obligations....

Secondly, the SRSG's recommendations with respect to BITs...appear to ignore or to gloss over the power relations reflected in, and created by, these types of agreements, as well as the long history of exploitation of Third World states and facilitation of foreign corporate activity. For instance, in the 2008 report, he suggested that in drafting and negotiating BITs, '[s]tates, companies, the institutions supporting investments, and those designing arbitration procedures should work towards developing better means to balance investor interests and the needs of host States to discharge their human rights obligations'. This assumes that companies will change their modus operandi and support measures that may diminish their leverage with host states and increase the regulatory hold over their activities — something that companies have worked hard to avoid since the end of the colonial period.

...For...technical assistance to work, it cannot be left to the 'goodwill' of home states. Rather, a carefully conceived obligation on the home state would need to be embedded in a BIT....

...

CHRISTINE PARKER & JOHN HOWE, RUGGIE'S DIPLOMATIC PROJECT AND ITS MISSING REGULATORY INFRASTRUCTURE

in R. Mares (ed.), The UN Guiding Principles on Business and Human Rights: Foundations and Implementation (2012), at 273

...[T]he Framework could easily become the basis for a lukewarm, even counterproductive, set of practices around business and human rights. Yet it is also possible that the Framework might open up small opportunities for further contestation, crisis and hence political leverage that would make businesses transform their practices in substance...

...

We argue that Ruggie's Framework underestimates the radical nature of what is required for states to take "appropriate steps" to regulate business respect for human rights including the role of the state in "regulatory space" interacting with other actors especially where the state itself is directly involved in subsidising or operating business. Ruggie does recognise that the state's duty to protect should extend to where states are "doing business with business"; that is, outsourcing, procurement, investment and export promotion. We argue that states should use their role as market actors to subvert businesses' "economic licenses" by using the deployment of wealth and contractual provisions to regulate against human rights abuses. We go on to argue that Ruggie's Framework equally underestimates what is required for businesses to take "due diligence" to discharge their responsibility to respect (RtR) human rights, and provide victims with access to remedies. We argue that businesses will always seek to neutralise critiques of their adverse human rights impacts and to bring any new initiatives to regulate business and human rights back within the rubric of the "business case" and "risk management" since this provides greater opportunity for management discretion and profit-orientation in the way they respond to human rights concerns. We use literature on corporate self-regulation and compliance management systems to argue that the Framework underestimates the degree of corporate commitment, capacity and skill required to take due diligence processes seriously. More fundamentally, it ignores the need for due diligence processes to be designed and, importantly, implemented in such a way that they open themselves up to radical critique of the substantive injustices and human and environmental impacts of business. We argue that due diligence processes to protect human rights only have value to the extent that they continually make business managers more open to critique by local and international activists as well as "victims" of their whole model of business decision-making and its substantive results. If this does not occur, and often it does not, corporate management will tend to use due diligence as a risk management technique that papers over the conflict between "business as usual" and the steps that must be taken to change business operations and decision-making to address the injustices, inequalities and power differentials that allow human rights to be abused on a regular basis.

...

PETER MUCHLINSKI, IMPLEMENTING THE NEW UN CORPORATE HUMAN RIGHTS FRAMEWORK: IMPLICATIONS FOR CORPORATE LAW, GOVERNANCE, AND REGULATION

22 Business Ethics Q. 145 (2012), at 162

...

The corporate responsibility to respect human rights poses a challenge for corporate governance theory.... [T]he inclusion of a corporate responsibility to respect human rights suggests, at first glance, that a shareholder primacy model of corporate governance may be inadequate to deal with the complex changes in governance and regulation that such a responsibility would appear to impose on corporations. However, it may be equally difficult to reject outright a shareholder based model of corporate governance on this basis alone. Not only is this approach strongly embedded in the corporate laws of many countries, most notably those following the Anglo-American model, but it also contains a strong ethical foundation of its own so far as the preservation of the legitimate property rights of shareholders against corporate malpractice at the hands of managers is concerned. On the other hand it is hard to see how the existence of the corporate responsibility to respect human rights can become a significant element in corporate action unless a more stakeholder oriented approach is adopted in corporate governance and regulatory developments....

...

[T]he main thrust of agency based theories is the reduction of agency costs, that is, those costs which arise when managers fail to act in the best interests of the company and hence of the shareholders. The principal cost that needs to be controlled is the misallocation of funds away from the shareholder towards the enrichment of the manager.... [T]he main thrust of these arrangements is to enhance shareholder value. This is justified by the fact that shareholders take the greatest risks.... The main mechanism for controlling managers in this situation is the market itself. Inefficient firms will not attract shareholder interest, or will lead to takeovers by more efficient management teams.... Equally managers are placed under a moral imperative to protect the interests of shareholders as a result of their fiduciary duties towards them.

The value of these arguments can be questioned both from a regulatory and a business ethics perspective. As John Boatright has asked "what's so special about shareholders?" His answer is nothing much, given the erosion of shareholder power since the 1930s and the rise of public policy shareholder protection regulation. As a result he rejects, as an inadequate characterization of corporate governance law and practice, the notion that only shareholders can be the subject of fiduciary duties or that only fiduciary duties can cover shareholder interests, or that managers might not have responsibilities to other types of constituencies. Indeed given the limited nature of fiduciary obligations, pertaining to general matters of organisation and strategy, "in the ordinary conduct of business, where the business judgment rule applies, the interests of other constituencies may be taken into account without the possibility of a successful shareholder suit for the breach of any fiduciary duty." In addition the success of the company cannot be limited to the input of "specific capital" from shareholders, but is also dependant on the "opportunity capital" that society provides. Thus other interests apart from shareholders can and should be taken into account to ensure the success of the company, though shareholders remain special, "to the extent that public policy considerations support the continuation of the corporation as a private, profit-making institution, with strong accountability to shareholders."

Furthermore, the shareholder primacy approach has been criticised for limiting the scope for wider claims to be taken into account by corporate managers as a result of an unfortunate trend of analysis that has sought to overestimate the moral hazards arising out of the agency costs issue. In particular a crude kind of economic determinism has informed the content of agency theory leading to a reductionist tendency that seeks out underlying economic incentives to ethical choices and that regards economic self-interest and opportunism as the dominant motives for human behaviour. This in turn leads to the overemphasis on shareholder primacy even though there is no necessary causal relationship between agency cost problems and shareholder primacy. This approach is a caricature of human reality, and of corporate activity, and has serious implications in relation to corporate human rights responsibilities.

Crude... shareholder primacy arguments can be used to undermine attempts to add human rights obligations to the range of corporate duties. First, they can be used to prevent seeing the corporation as a collective actor based on co-ordinated management and so could justify the rejection of a responsibility to respect human rights since corporations are no more than, "legal fictions which serve as a nexus for a set of contracting relationships among individuals" and human rights victims by definition have no contractual nexus with the corporation. Secondly, a crude agency approach is likely to see a commitment to observe human rights as a threat to shareholder primacy. Should managers take steps to comply with any corporate responsibility to respect human rights this would be an illegitimate extension of their actions as it would fall outside the range of actions required to fulfil their agency obligations toward shareholders. It sets up a competing set of claimants whose risks in relation to the firm are virtually non-existent, at least in strict economic terms. The holders of human rights have invested nothing in the company and so require nothing from managers, while the latter have no right to exercise their managerial power to meet such third party claims.

In response to such arguments the stakeholder perspective recognises the company as an institution rather than a bundle of assets, one which has to consider the needs not only of internal stakeholders, such as the shareholders, managers and employees, but also the external stakeholders such as customers, suppliers, competitors and other special interest groups. Thus a more socially rooted approach to decision-making is required and more room is offered to ethical concerns.... This requires managers of investor-owned corporations to acknowledge that all corporate stakeholders have, "equal moral status and acknowledge that status in all their activities." In relation to actual or potential victims of corporate human rights violations the stakeholder model would appear to require that the interests of such constituents should be taken into account in the decision making processes of the firm....

The stakeholder approach has in turn been the subject of counter criticism. Thus Jensen sees it as flawed, "because it violates the proposition that any organization must have a single-valued objective as a precursor to purposeful or rational behavior" and that the corporation, "will be handicapped in the competition for survival because, as a basis for action, stakeholder theory politicizes the corporation, and it leaves its managers empowered to exercise their own preferences in spending the firm's resources." Jensen adds that organisations following a multiple objective policy, as stakeholder theory would require, cannot succeed and that in corporate life this is especially true if the value of profit maximization is displaced....

Jensen's ideas appear to be representative of what is actually taking place in corporate law developments related to stakeholder issues....

Other corporate governance mechanisms conducive to respecting human rights could be developed from existing models. For example continental European models of corporate governance often allow for worker participation in corporate affairs whether through works councils or through the use of co-determination laws that require a certain proportion of the board to be made up of worker representatives. Under the Anglo-American model wider stakeholder interests can be introduced through the appointment of suitable non-executive directors to the board. Equally the use of social accounting devices may assist. However, in relation to human rights concerns the relevant class of stakeholder is potentially very wide. It would encompass all those affected by corporate actions whether or not they can impact the corporation. For example it is highly unlikely that existing devices for widening stakeholder participation in companies could deal with aboriginal groups whose culture and way of life is threatened by an investment project. The identification of such potential stakeholders or their inclusion in corporate governance structures is hard to determine....

NOTE

One of the most controversial issues concerns extraterritorial obligations on the part of home states, to be exercised when host states are unable or unwilling to require a corporation to respect human rights. Consider the implications of GP2 and GP7 and their respective commentaries in this context.

One NGO commentary criticized the fact that 'the responsibility of the business enterprise's home State remains entirely vague and, as a result, abets home State inertia....[The relevant] Commentary is rudimentary, over-emphasizes obstacles which could in practice hardly become relevant, and leaves the reader with the overall impression that the approach of home State responsibility is not viable.'[30] Yet some General Comments by the UN Committee on ESCR have suggested that states do have certain extraterritorial obligations (see GC No. 12 (1999)). But developing country governments have suggested that imposing such obligations in this context would mark a return to the colonial era. Western governments have also strongly resisted the imposition of such legal obligations.

Consider Bill C-300 that was debated by Canada's House of Commons in 2009–10. The purpose of the proposed legislation was to 'ensure that corporations engaged in mining, oil or gas activities and receiving support from the Government of Canada act in a manner consistent with international environmental best practices and with Canada's commitments to international human rights standards.' It called for the adoption of 'guidelines that articulate corporate accountability standards for mining, oil or gas activities' and which would incorporate standards such as the Voluntary Principles on Security and Human Rights and other 'human rights provisions that ensure corporations operate in a manner that is consistent with international human rights standards.' It would have empowered the Ministers of Foreign Affairs and International Trade to receive complaints alleging contravention of those guidelines in relation to 'Canadian companies engaged in mining, oil or gas activities' and such complaints could be submitted by 'any Canadian citizen or permanent

[30] Position Paper, European Center for Constitutional and Human Rights, 27 Jan. 2011.

resident or any resident or citizen of a developing country in which such activities have occurred or are occurring.' The results of any investigations undertaken were required to be published within eight months and, if a violation was found, the Ministers were required to notify the President of Export Development Canada and the Chairperson of the Canada Pension Plan Investment Board. In other words, a violation would result in reputational costs and the possible reconsideration of financing assistance and public investment in the corporation's shares.

The Bill generated intense opposition from mining companies. Barrick Gold Corporation, Goldcorp Inc. and Kinross Gold Corporation claimed that the Bill would adversely affect the Canadian mining industry in five key ways. It would: '1. Risk the competitive position of Canadian companies; 2. Result in the reputational damage to Canadian companies; 3. Undermine the multi-stakeholder and collaborative approach to Corporate Social Responsibility (CSR); 4. Create incentive for companies to relocate; and 5. Ignore existing regulatory frameworks for CSR.'[31] In 2010 the Bill was defeated in a vote of 140 to 134.

Two other approaches to extraterritorial responsibility warrant mention. The first is the proposal for a World Court of Human Rights (p. 759, *supra*) which envisages that transnational corporations 'might be invited and encouraged to accept the binding jurisdiction' of the Court. The second relies upon the concept of universal jurisdiction and is inspired by the use of the Alien Tort Statute as a form of US civil litigation for foreign torts. See Chapter 13, *supra*. But Macklem argues that this is not the way to go:[32]

> What would universal jurisdiction add to [the law of state responsibility and state treaty obligations]? Universal jurisdiction would entitle a state — say, Belgium — to bring criminal proceedings against a multinational corporation that has no legal presence in Belgium for a small class of human rights violations it commits outside of Belgium....
>
> But by establishing independent multinational corporate liability in international law, the principle of universal jurisdiction would contribute to a conception in the field of multinational corporations as international legal actors with obligations owed to individuals and states. And with international corporate obligations comes international corporate rights. Such rights would emerge incrementally as corporations seek to defend themselves from criminal prosecution by states exercising universal jurisdiction. Prosecutions inevitably would require distinguishing between criminal and lawful activity, thereby producing over time a zone of freedom derived from international law itself — a realm of international corporate liberty — that would protect from state sanction a set of corporate actions that raise human rights concerns but which do not constitute criminal acts. This realm of international corporate liberty would combine easily with the emerging set of economic rights that multinational corporations enjoy under international economic law. Multinational corporations would possess even greater international economic freedom to exploit the opportunities afforded by globalization in ways that evade state efforts to promote human rights compliance.

[31] 'Barrick Gold Sets Out Position on Bill C-300 and Provides Facts', 26 Nov. 2009.
[32] Ibid.

QUESTIONS

1. What do you see as the principal strengths and weaknesses of the GP?

2. What significance, if any, do you attach to the Council's decision not to develop further standards in relation to 'international crimes' attributed to corporations, and to the Working Group's decision not to 'investigate' any alleged corporate violations?

3. How compelling are the arguments invoked by the mining companies to oppose Bill C-300? Would it help if other countries were persuaded to adopt comparable domestic legislation?

4. 'The term "stakeholders" is consistently used in this debate, but it is rarely defined in a meaningful way. At one level or another, we are all stakeholders in the role of large TNCs. Ultimately, it will be necessary to discard a shareholder-based corporate governance model and see corporations as civil entities performing essential societal functions.' Discuss.

ADDITIONAL READING

The best website is www.business-humanrights.org. See also J. Knox, 'The Ruggie Rules: Applying Human Rights Law to Corporations', 16 Aug. 2011, at http://ssrn.com/abstract=1916664; R. Mares (ed.), *The UN Guiding Principles on Business and Human Rights: Foundations and Implementation* (2011); Special issue, 22(1) Business Ethics Q. (2012); L. C. Backer, 'On the Evolution of the United Nations' "Protect-Respect-Remedy" Project', 9 Santa Clara J. Int'l. L. 37 (2011); D. Bilchitz, 'The Ruggie Framework: An Adequate Rubric for Corporate Human Rights Obligations?', 12 Sur 199 (2010); P. Alston (ed.), *Non-State Actors and Human Rights* (2005); S. Ratner, 'Corporations and Human Rights: A Theory of Legal Responsibility', 111 Yale L. J. 443 (2001).

B. ARMED OPPOSITION GROUPS

At one level, armed opposition groups are simply outlaws. They have rejected or resisted the authority of the state and opted to act outside the applicable legal framework. But at another level, such groups are often involved in a quest for legitimacy, designed to convince the relevant population and the world at large of the illegitimacy of the existing form of state power, and perhaps invoking by way of justification the state's violations of the rights of the group concerned. Two questions arise. First, should we seek to encourage such groups to accept human rights commitments? Second, what would the legal basis of any such obligations be?

One clear example of practical engagement is reflected in the work of the Special Representative of the UN Secretary-General for Children and Armed Conflict. Invoking the Convention on the Rights of the Child, as well as the Geneva Conventions, the Special Representative has sought and obtained commitments from groups as diverse as the Sudan People's Liberation Movement, the Revolutionary United Front in Sierra Leone, the Liberation Tigers of Tamil Eelam in Sri Lanka and the Revolutionary Armed Forces of Colombia.[33]

International humanitarian law (IHL) has long accepted that armed opposition groups engaged in an internal armed conflict are bound by IHL, even though they are not parties to the relevant treaties. Even though the structure and assumptions of human rights law are different there have been examples of governments and opposition groups combining both human rights and IHL commitments in a single agreement. Thus, in the context of peace negotiations, the Government of the Philippines, on one side, and the Communist Party of the Philippines and New Peoples' Army, on the other, jointly signed the Comprehensive Agreement on the Respect for Human Rights and International Humanitarian Law (CARHRIHL) in 1998.

In the readings that follow, Sivakumaran outlines the theoretical bases upon which the application of IHL to armed opposition groups might be grounded. Clapham then considers how the UN human rights regime has dealt with such groups.

SANDESH SIVAKUMARAN, BINDING ARMED OPPOSITION GROUPS

55 Int'l. & Comp. L. Q. 369 (2006)

The vast majority of conflicts being fought today are internal in character. Internal armed conflicts are fought between a state and an armed opposition group, or between two armed opposition groups, within the boundaries of a single state. Armed opposition groups are becoming increasingly sophisticated and are responsible for some of the most egregious atrocities committed in conflicts. Given the proliferation of internal armed conflicts, the number of armed opposition groups that take part in them, and the atrocities that are committed by such groups, it is essential that international humanitarian law regulates such conflicts and governs the behaviour of such groups.

There exist, however, only a minimum of international humanitarian law rules that pertain to armed conflict of an internal character. [They include, in particular, Common Article 3 of the four Geneva Conventions, and Additional Protocol II.] ...

A treaty binds parties to it, thus these instruments bind states parties fighting in an internal armed conflict. The language of these instruments also purports to bind armed opposition groups fighting in such a conflict. This raises the question of how armed opposition groups are bound by the law governing internal armed conflict when they are not party to the relevant treaties....

...

Four reasons that are commonly put forward to explain the binding nature of the rules governing internal armed conflict on armed opposition groups — customary international law; general principles; the rules governing the effect of treaties on

[33] www.un.org/children/conflict/english/conflicts.html.

third parties; and the principle of succession — are not in fact capable of binding all types of armed opposition groups by all the rules of internal armed conflict. This is so even when all four reasons are used in conjunction with one another. The legislative jurisdiction explanation — the principle whereby the state binds all individuals within its territory upon ratification of a treaty — is the only one that is capable of binding all types of armed opposition groups by all the rules that govern internal armed conflict.

There is a more fundamental theoretical difference between the four limited explanations on the one hand and the legislative jurisdiction explanation on the other hand. The four limited explanations apply the rules that are applied to states to armed opposition groups. In this way, they are treated like states. The legislative jurisdiction approach treats armed opposition groups as entities subordinate to states. The default positions of the two also differ. The four limited explanations start off from the position that armed opposition groups are not bound by the rules governing internal armed conflict while the legislative jurisdiction explanation begins from the view that armed opposition groups are so bound. Consequently, the four limited explanations are more attractive to armed opposition groups while the legislative jurisdiction approach is more appealing to states. As a result, a question that has to be asked is whether using the legislative jurisdiction approach will lead to a decrease in compliance with the rules on the part of the armed opposition group.

Compliance in this regard is likely affected more by the degree of legitimacy the armed opposition group sees in the rules than the precise manner in which they are bound. One of the threads underlying this article has been the degree of legitimacy of the rules from the perspective of the armed opposition group. In order to increase the degree of legitimacy of and foster a sense of respect for the laws governing internal armed conflict, participation of armed opposition groups in the formation of the rules is vital. Participation may range from the formal — for example involvement of armed opposition groups in the conclusion of new international humanitarian law treaties using their practice for the purposes of customary international law, concluding Common Article 3 agreements and encouraging unilateral declarations of acceptance — to the less formal — such as creating linkages with armed opposition groups that do respect international humanitarian law and pointing to the positive practice of other armed opposition groups.

That armed opposition groups are bound by the rules governing internal armed conflict is beyond doubt; quite how to increase their compliance with these rules is the next big question.

ANDREW CLAPHAM, HUMAN RIGHTS OBLIGATIONS OF NON-STATE ACTORS IN CONFLICT SITUATIONS

863 Int'l. Rev Red Cross 491 (2006), at 503

...For Dieter Fleck it is simply "logical" that if...insurgents can have obligations under humanitarian law they should also be able to bear human rights obligations.

From here it is a small step to suggest that such international human rights obligations apply at all times to all armed opposition groups (even before the appeals of the Security Council [which has frequently called upon such groups to respect IHL and sometimes human rights]). The resolution adopted by the distinguished expert body the Institute of International Law, at its Berlin session in 1999, stated that "All parties to armed conflicts in which non-State entities are parties, irrespective of their legal status...have the obligation to respect international humanitarian law as well as fundamental human rights." With regard to disturbances short of armed conflict the resolution includes an Article X to similar effect concerning fundamental human rights: "To the extent that certain aspects of internal disturbances and tensions may not be covered by international humanitarian law, individuals remain under the protection of international law guaranteeing fundamental human rights. All parties are bound to respect fundamental rights under the scrutiny of the international community."

To those who would still prefer to rely simply on humanitarian law I would respond as follows: first, humanitarian law does not usually apply in the absence of protracted armed conflict; second, even when there is a reasonable claim that there is a protracted armed conflict, governments have often denied the existence of a conflict, making dialogue with the parties about the application of humanitarian law rather problematic; and, third, the human rights framework allows for a wider range of accountability mechanisms, including monitoring by the Special Rapporteurs of the UN Commission of Human Rights and the field offices of the High Commissioner for Human Rights.

Most recently, the UN's Special Rapporteur on Extrajudicial, Summary or Arbitrary Executions, Philip Alston, grappled with the question in the context of his report on Sri Lanka [UN Doc. E/CN.4/2006/53/Add.5]. Alston concluded in the following terms:

> 25. Human rights law affirms that both the Government and the LTTE [Liberation Tigers of Tamil Eelam] must respect the rights of every person in Sri Lanka. Human rights norms operate on three levels — as the rights of individuals, as obligations assumed by States, and as legitimate expectations of the international community. The Government has assumed the binding legal obligation to respect and ensure the rights recognized in the International Covenant on Civil and Political Rights (ICCPR). As a non-state actor, the LTTE does not have legal obligations under ICCPR, but it remains subject to the demand of the international community, first expressed in the Universal Declaration of Human Rights, that every organ of society respect and promote human rights.
>
> 26. I have previously noted that it is especially appropriate and feasible to call for an armed group to respect human rights norms when it "exercises significant control over territory and population and has an identifiable political structure". This visit clarified both the complexity and the necessity of applying human rights norms to armed groups. The LTTE plays a dual role. On the one hand, it is an organization with effective control over a significant stretch of territory, engaged in civil planning and administration, maintaining its own form of police force and judiciary. On the other hand, it is an armed group that

has been subject to proscription, travel bans, and financial sanctions in various Member States. The tension between these two roles is at the root of the international community's hesitation to address the LTTE and other armed groups in the terms of human rights law. The international community does have human rights expectations to which it will hold the LTTE, but it has long been reluctant to press these demands directly if doing so would be to "treat it like a State".

27. It is increasingly understood, however, that the human rights expectations of the international community operate to protect people, while not thereby affecting the legitimacy of the actors to whom they are addressed. The Security Council has long called upon various groups that Member States do not recognize as having the capacity to formally assume international obligations to respect human rights. The LTTE and other armed groups must accept that insofar as they aspire to represent a people before the world, the international community will evaluate their conduct according to the Universal Declaration's "common standard of achievement".

Alston goes on to include specific human rights recommendations addressed to the non-state actor:

The LTTE should refrain from violating human rights, including those of non-LTTE-affiliated Tamil civilians. This includes in particular respect for the rights to freedom of expression, peaceful assembly, freedom of association with others, family life, and democratic participation, including the right to vote. The LTTE should specifically affirm that it will abide by the North-East Secretariat on Human Rights charter.

This approach is applied in the joint report on Lebanon and Israel by a group of four special rapporteurs [UN Doc. A/HRC/2/7 (2006)] [in dealing with the situation of Hezbollah, to the extent that it is a non-state actor].

...

The Office of the UN High Commissioner for Human Rights (OHCHR) has a human rights field operation in Nepal. The Office reports on the human rights situation. Reports include a special section on incidents involving the Communist Party of Nepal (Maoist) (CPN-M). Often these cannot be expressed in terms of violations of international humanitarian law since they took place during the cease-fire outside the context of an armed conflict. At one level there is apparently a commitment to human rights by the CPN-M, but this does not really seem dispositive to the UN's reporting. Another section in the report covered killings by an "illegal armed groups" known as Pratikar Samiti (retaliation groups) later renamed "Peace and Development Committees" as well as killings by a group known as the Special Tiger Force. The UN report does not allege that these groups were supported by the state. Their killings are simply detailed as part of the human rights situation....

To conclude this section, the assumption of many humanitarian law experts that human rights law applies only to governments, and not to unrecognized insurgents, is no longer a universally shared assumption.

NOTE

The trends described in relation to non-state armed groups have proved difficult to reconcile with some approaches to counter-terrorism.

> The extent of legitimacy and legal standing granted to non-state armed groups has varied enormously with the winds of international politics. National Liberation Movements achieved considerable rights of participation and much legitimation of their armed struggle, as a result of the geopolitical climate in which they emerged: the rise of the Third World majority in the General Assembly, and a Cold War dynamic in which each superpower sought to court, or avoid alienating, the newly emerging states, and so cooperated in different degrees with their normative agenda at the United Nations. In the contemporary world, the pendulum appears to have swung far in the other direction. The utility of declaring armed groups as 'terrorist' — and thus confining them categorically to the status of criminals — appears widely understood among states facing internal armed conflicts, with few states willing to contest such labels even if the facts are more complex. Thus, while there is no doubt that the Islamic Resistance Movement in Palestine (Hamas) engages in terrorist tactics, it is equally beyond doubt that they now effectively control the Gaza Strip and its population, and conduct a full range of governance functions. Continuing to label the group terrorist as a means of inducing compliance with humanitarian and human rights law has had limited success, and greatly limits the avenues through which 'carrots' can be used to induce moderation, compromise, and conflict resolution.[34]

Laws prohibiting the provision of 'material support' to terrorist groups can come into conflict with the humanitarian goal of engaging with non-state armed groups in order to protect civilian populations and seek an end to conflict. In *Holder v. Humanitarian Law Project*,[35] the HLP sought to train members of the Kurdistan Worker's Party (PKK) in international law for dispute resolution and for bringing petitions to UN bodies and to engage in political advocacy. The US Supreme Court held that while some US Government-designated Foreign Terrorist Organizations engage in political and humanitarian activities, they are nonetheless 'so tainted by their criminal conduct that any contribution to such an organization facilitates that conduct'. Three dissenting justices argued that the government should have to show that the 'defendants provided support that they knew was significantly likely to help the organization pursue its unlawful terrorist aims'. The contradictions between such criminal law approaches to counter-terrorism and initiatives to bring armed groups within the humanitarian umbrella have created serious unresolved dilemmas on the ground.[36]

[34] N. Bhuta, 'The Role International Actors Other Than States Can Play in the New World Order', in A. Cassese (ed.), *Realizing Utopia: The Future of International Law* (2012), 61 at 70.

[35] 130 S. Ct 2705 (2010).

[36] See N. K. Modirzadeh et al., 'Humanitarian Engagement Under Counter-Terrorism: A Conflict of Norms and the E.merging Policy Landscape', 93(883) Int'l. Rev. Red Cross 1 (2011).

QUESTIONS

1. In 2004, both the United States and the European Union voted against a resolution in the Commission on Human Rights because it referred to 'gross violations of human rights perpetrated by terrorist groups'. They did so on the ground that such a formulation equated states with terrorists, when the latter were in fact simply criminals. In response, India argued that 'non-state actors were armed groups that could be criminal, but in condemning them and asking them to follow international law, they were not being equated with States.' In light of such perceptions, how persuasive are the arguments recounted by Clapham in favour of attributing human rights obligations to certain non-state actors? What are the alternatives to such an approach?

2. 'Arguments based upon the approach of IHL to armed opposition groups have no relevance to human rights law. The latter's assumptions are fundamentally different and the label of human rights respecter is one that, by definition, can and should only be conferred on a legitimate state actor.' Discuss.

ADDITIONAL READING

See contributions to 'Engaging Armed Groups': 93(883) Int'l. Rev. Red Cross (2011); C. Ryngaert & A. van de Meulebroucke, 'Enhancing and Enforcing Compliance with International Humanitarian Law by Non-State Armed Groups: An Inquiry into Some Mechanisms', 16 J. Conflict & Security L. 443 (2012); A. Cassese, 'Should Rebels Be Treated as Criminals? Some Modest Proposals for Rendering Internal Armed Conflicts Less Inhumane', in A. Cassese (ed.), *Realizing Utopia: The Future of International Law* (2012), 519; D. PoKempner, 'The "New" Non-State Actors in International Humanitarian Law', 38 Geo. Wash. Int'l. L. Rev. 551 (2006); L. Zegveld, *Accountability of Armed Opposition Groups in International Law* (2002).

C. INTERNATIONAL NONGOVERNMENTAL ORGANIZATIONS

The non-state actors which have featured most prominently throughout this book are human rights NGOs, both domestic and international (INGOs). They were at the outset, and continue to be today, an indispensable component in the functioning of the international human rights regime. Their contributions are especially important in relation to fact-finding, reporting, standard-setting and the overall promotion, implementation and enforcement of human rights norms. They provoke and energize. They spread the message of human rights and mobilize people to realize that message. Decentralized and diverse, they proceed with a speed, decisiveness and range of concerns impossible to imagine in relation to most of the work of bureaucratic and politically constrained intergovernmental organizations.

NGOs operate on the basis of differing mandates, each responding to its own priorities and methods of action, bringing a range of viewpoints to the human rights movement. It is inconceivable that the state of human rights in the world, whatever its shortcomings, could have progressed as much since the Second World War without the spur and inventiveness of NGOs.

At the international level, and particularly in the UN context, the frequent reluctance of governmental actors to criticize their counterparts from other countries and the limited supply of independent sources of information have contributed to making NGOs the lynchpins of the system as a whole. In situations in which NGO information is not available or where the NGOs are either unable or unwilling to generate political pressures upon the governments concerned, the chances of a weak response by the international community, or of none at all, are radically increased. A high proportion of the most significant initiatives to draft new international instruments, to establish new procedures and machinery and to identify specific governments as violators have come as a result of concerted NGO campaigns designed to mobilize public opinion and lobby governmental support.

Human rights NGOs have experienced a quantum leap in their professionalism from the days of the 'amiable amateurs' importuning delegates for a brief chat to the high level of professionalism of many groups today. By comparison with the situation even as recently as 25 years ago, the output of the major INGOs is more visible and better marketed, their strategies are more clearly mapped out, their level of technical expertise is greater and their funding more adequate for the task. The communications revolution has assisted them in gathering timely and compelling information, in disseminating it, in running well-coordinated campaigns and in enlisting public opinion.

Moreover, their impact is often more obvious and tangible than it was in an earlier era. The 1997 Ottawa Conference to draft a Landmines Treaty, the 1998 Rome Conference to draft the Statute of an International Criminal Court and the drafting of the 2006 Convention on the Rights of Persons with Disabilities represent high-water marks in terms of NGO involvement and influence. Perhaps most significant is the blurring of the distinction between the insiders and the outsiders as NGO representatives have become part of governmental delegations. They have also increasingly become key partners in the delivery of humanitarian and other forms of development assistance, partners with government in performing a variety of functions such as human rights education, the monitoring of voluntary codes of conduct and even the delivery of basic social services, as well as partners with businesses and labour unions in various areas.

The crucial role played by INGOs is underscored by the extent to which NGOs at the national level are regularly under attack by governments, as this 2012 statement by the UN High Commissioner for Human Rights illustrates:

> Navi Pillay…expressed deep concern about current or recent moves in a number of countries to curtail the freedom of [NGOs] to operate independently and effectively.
>
> …

> Pillay expressed alarm at recent or ongoing attempts in a number of countries to tighten control over NGOs by restricting their sources of funding, and in particular foreign funding on which many very effective civil society organizations rely heavily.
>
> In Ethiopia, several human rights organizations have been forced to close due to a 2009 law preventing associations from receiving more than 10 percent of their overall resources from abroad.
>
> In Belarus, an amendment to the Criminal Code was adopted in October 2011 by the Parliament, establishing criminal liability for receiving foreign grants or donations in violation of Belarusian legislation....
>
> In Israel, the recently adopted Foreign Funding Law could have a major impact on human rights organizations, subjecting them to rigorous reporting requirements, forcing them to declare foreign financial support in all public communications, and threatening heavy penalties for non-compliance.
>
> In Venezuela, in January 2012, a new Organic Law against Terrorism and Organised Delinquency was adopted by Congress, but has not yet been signed into law by the President. The law establishes a broad definition of "terrorist acts" that may apply to legitimate acts of social protest or dissidence. It also places NGOs under the permanent surveillance of a State organ and imposes restrictions on foreign funding.
>
> And in Egypt, the authorities have been clamping down on foreign-funded civil society organizations, and the accompanying negative portrayal of Egyptian activists has led to them experiencing a surge in smear campaigns, threats and intimidation.[37]

The best resourced of the INGOs is Human Rights Watch. It reported a paid staff of 325 in 2011,[38] and assets of $215 million.[39] In 2010 Amnesty International reported that it had 3 million members worldwide, 1 million activists who participated in its 'actions', global income of €200 million and net assets of €108 million. In 2009, it sent 163 research missions into the field covering 87 countries/territories.[40]

But along with the growing influence of the international NGOs has come strong criticism, much of which is now expressed in terms of the debate over accountability and transparency. The question 'who elected the NGOs?' has become a rallying cry for those who feel that NGOs wield too much power and cannot be constrained by governmental actors. Many within the human rights field also consider that greater accountability and transparency will make the groups more effective and more strongly supported.

Attacks on the leading human rights NGOs are often led by officials and supporters of particular states whose policies have been criticized. Such attacks are, of course, evidence of the impact of the reports themselves, and the contested facts and

[37] OHCHR, 'New Restrictions on NGOs are Undermining Human Rights: Pillay', 25 Apr. 2012, at www.ohchr.org/EN/NewsEvents/Pages/DisplayNews.aspx?NewsID=12081&LangID=E.

[38] www.bbb.org/charity-reviews/national/civil-rights/human-rights-watch-in-new-york-ny-3452/all.

[39] Human Rights Watch Inc., Financial Statements, Year ended 30 June 2011.

[40] www.ingoaccountabilitycharter.org/wpcms/wp-content/uploads/AI-2010-Report-to-INGO-Accountability-Charter-GRI-NGO-Level-C-v09.pdf.

interpretations can be fought out in the public domain in light of constantly emerging new evidence. More problematic, from the perspective of NGOs in general, have been the generic critiques of the very legitimacy of such organizations. After the Seattle riots against the WTO in 1999 *The Economist* asked whether NGOs were 'the first steps towards an "international civil society" (whatever that might be)', or whether they instead represented 'a dangerous shift of power to unelected and unaccountable special-interest groups'.[41] A year later, the same magazine asked:

> who elected Oxfam ...? Bodies such as these are, to varying degrees, extorting admissions of fault from law-abiding companies and changes in policy from democratically elected governments. They may claim to be acting in the interests of the people—but then so do the objects of their criticism, governments and the despised international institutions. In the West, governments and their agencies are, in the end, accountable to voters. Who holds the activists accountable?[42]

The dilemma is straightforward. On the one hand, as Kingsbury has observed, '[i]nternational civil society in its widest sense is bound to be a largely unregulated free-for-all, with markets in prestige, influence, membership, fundraising capability, and other markers of organizational success.'[43] Efforts to regulate or control NGOs are in some respects contrary to their nature and ethos. They are inevitably suspect when coming from those who have been obliged to change their policies and practices as a result of NGO campaigning. On the other hand, the NGOs unyielding demands for accountability on the part of governments, corporations and INGOs like the World Bank and the World Trade Organization necessarily serve to focus attention on shortcomings in terms of their own accountability. In decades past, such demands have been shrugged off by most NGOs. Some have argued that they could not be held to the same standards of accountability as those who hold 'real' power. As one study put it,' [i]n the grand scheme of societal relations, NGOs ultimately have very little power. They do not have coercive power, financial power, or even the authority and power that derives from representation.'[44] Others note that they are in any event answerable to their supporters and funders, and that their impact and effectiveness is largely dependent upon their perceived legitimacy and credibility. Such responses have not satisfied the critics and as the impact of NGOs has become greater so too have the calls for enhanced accountability become stronger and more concerted.

The reluctance of many, although not all, human rights NGOs to come to grips with this issue is illustrated by the fate of a project launched in 2002 by the International Council on Human Rights Policy focusing on the Accountability of NGOs. It was designed to consider: (1) what are the essential elements of 'legitimacy' and 'accountability' for human rights NGOs; and (2) what benefits will human rights NGOs obtain by demonstrating clearly that they are accountable

41 'The Non-Governmental Order', *The Economist*, 18 Dec. 1999, p. 23.

42 'Angry and Effective, *The Economist*, 23 Sept. 2000.

43 B. Kingsbury, 'First Amendment Liberalism as Global Legal Architecture: Ascriptive Groups and the Problems of the Liberal NGO Model of International Civil Society', 3 Chicago J. Int'l. L.183 (2002), at 193.

44 Lisa Jordan, 'Mechanisms for NGO Accountability', Global Public Policy Institute, Research Paper Series No. 3 (2005), 13.

and legitimate — and what risks might they face? By 2007 the report had still not emerged. The group's website noted only that responses by NGOs and others to a first draft in 2003 had 'demonstrated both the sensitivity of this issue and the need to address it well'. In other words, the achievement of some sort of consensus position had proved elusive.

In the readings that follow, Anderson argues that INGOs are essentially elitist groups which lack democratic legitimacy. Jacques explores the sources of NGO legitimacy and Grant and Keohane suggest ways in which accountability is exacted in global politics. Finally, the INGOs' Accountability Charter illustrates one of the responses to the criticism of unaccountability.

KENNETH ANDERSON, THE OTTAWA CONVENTION BANNING LANDMINES, THE ROLE OF INTERNATIONAL NON-GOVERNMENTAL ORGANIZATIONS AND THE IDEA OF INTERNATIONAL CIVIL SOCIETY

11 Eur. J. Int'l. L. 92 (2000)

...The Ottawa Convention [on the Prohibition of the Use, Stockpiling, Production and Transfer of Anti-Personnel Mines and on their Destruction] represents the first time in over a century in which a major, traditional weapon system has been banned outright and not simply regulated in its use....

...

3. The Romance Between NGOs and International Organizations

A. Seven lessons from the Landmines Ban Campaign

[The author recalls the origin of the international campaign to ban landmines in the form of efforts by the ICRC. These were subsequently overtaken by a coalition of INGOs with diverse standpoints and coming together to form the International Campaign to Ban Landmines (ICBL).The groups that came together in 1992 included HRW, Handicap International (France), Medico International (Germany), Mines Awareness Group (United Kingdom), Physicians for Human Rights (United States) and Vietnam Veterans of America Foundation (United States). The campaign eventually numbered more than 1,200 NGOs in 60 countries. For mandate reasons, the ICRC was not a formal part of the coalition but actively supported the process leading to the Ottawa Convention.]

Second, governments were initially entirely uninterested; it was regarded by governments everywhere as pie-in-the-sky, even if they were not actively hostile to the idea....

Third, the ban campaign had a simple, easily understood message — a complete and comprehensive ban, nothing more, nothing less....

Fourth, although...the world's militaries [felt threatened, the campaign] did not represent an overwhelming economic threat to arms makers....As a consequence, no industrial and private sector groups had a strong incentive within the NATO countries to contribute money to a counter-campaign.

…

Fifth,…largely in response to [INGO] pressures [consensus was not the rule for negotiations. Instead,] sympathetic governments adopted a new principle of negotiating a treaty among 'like-minded' states …

Sixth, governments eventually began to come on board the landmines ban cause for three principal reasons. NGO pressure, first, brought them to an awareness of the genuine extent of the problem and put it on their policy agendas.…

Seventh,…the ban campaign [came to be seen as] a genuine partnership between NGOs, international organizations and sympathetic states.…

B. The partnership between 'international civil society', sympathetic states, and international organizations

…

The central assumption underlying the idea that the landmines campaign is a new and better way of doing international lawmaking is that international NGOs are somehow 'international civil society'.…

…[INGOs] are therefore a force for democratizing international relations and international institutions and, moreover, the authoritative bearers of 'world opinion'. They are therefore the legitimate representatives in the international sphere of 'people' in the world, in a way in which their states, even democratic states, and their state representatives, are not.…As [Canadian] Foreign Minister Axworthy put it in an address to NGOs in the midst of the Ottawa process:

> One can no longer relegate NGOs to simple advisory or advocacy roles in this process. They are now part of the way decisions have to be made. They have been the voice saying that government belongs to the people, and must respond to the people's hopes, demands and ideals.

…

C. But who elected the International NGOs?

…

…[The international bureaucracy] has adopted this theory of politics, of the legitimacy of the independent international NGO sector …[because] public international organizations *themselves* are in desperate need of legitimacy.…[I]nternational organizations have volunteered and been volunteered for a variety of tasks that, in a word, require forms of legitimacy that international organizations have never had.

By 'legitimacy' in this context I mean merely that institutions act and be understood to act with authority that is accepted as proper and moral and just.…[W]e call this apperception 'democracy' and the consent of the governed.

…[I]nternational lawyers…fundamentally believe that international organizations, and their underlying concept of 'world government' — what is today taken as the vision of Grotius — *are* legitimate, and deserve to be understood as the world's constitutionally supreme sources of authority and the exercise of power....

...[They] tend to form a church of those converted to belief in supranationalism....

...

...[But] the brutal fact remains that international organizations as they exist today do not have the perception of legitimacy to carry out the functions that international elites would assign to them....

...

...Yet now it is urgently needed, and where to get it?

...International organizations claim to have overcome the democratic deficit as an impediment to their legitimacy by having as their partners, and having the moral and political approval of, international NGOs, the voice of 'world opinion', and the loud and incessant invocation of 'international civil society'....

...

...International NGOs, for their part, are happy to accept the accolade of 'international civil society', the voice of the people, and so on, for the obvious reason that it increases their power and authority within international organizations, international elites, and beyond....

...

[The author suggests that some legitimacy might inhere in INGOs if they could claim to be] authentic intermediaries of the 'people'.... But this is implausible, for at least two reasons.

First, [INGOs] are not very often connected, in any direct way, to masses of 'people'. International NGOs, in virtue of their role to operate globally rather than locally, are fundamentally elite organizations. There are exceptions, to be sure, but they are prototypically large religious affiliations.... There are certain large secular exceptions, as well; Amnesty International is perhaps one, in that at least it has a large base membership. But that membership comes mostly from wealthy countries, and its membership even in those countries tends to be educated and at least middle class...[T]he far more typical 'international' NGO of the kind whose approval and favour international organizations seek is much closer to the model of Human Rights Watch — a relatively small, highly professional, entirely elite organization funded by foundations and wealthy individuals in the Western democracies, and having no discernible base outside international elites. This is not to denigrate Human Rights Watch or the vital work it does, but it would be the first to declare that its legitimacy is not based on democratic roots among the masses but on its fidelity to its own conception of the meaning of international human rights....

International NGOs collectively are not conduits from the 'people' or the 'masses' or the 'world citizenry' from the 'bottom up'. They are, rather, a vehicle for international elites to talk to other international elites about the things — frequently of undeniably critical importance — that international elites care about. The conversation is not vertical, it is horizontal. It has a worthwhile, essential function in making the world — sometimes at least, a better place — but it does not reduce the democratic deficit.

Second, if the idea of 'international civil society' is drawn by an analogy to civil society in domestic society, then it bears noting that at least in the United States, with its vigorous and diverse civil society, civil society is *not* conceived of as being a substitute for democratic processes, let alone conveying democratic legitimacy. On the contrary, the glory of civil society is precisely that it is something different from democracy and democratic processes....

Put bluntly, the glory of organizations of civil society is not democratic legitimacy, but the ability to be a pressure group....

ISOBELLE JAQUES, STRENGTHENING DEMOCRATIC GOVERNANCE: THE ROLE OF CIVIL SOCIETY

Report on Wilton Park Conference S06/10 (2006), at www.wiltonpark.org.uk/resources/en/pdf/22290903/22291321/wps06-10-report

...

The non-profit sector is coming under closer scrutiny, both from its proponents and those wishing to curtail its activities. Issue arising include: concern among donors wishing to engage with civil society organisations that transaction costs are too high; the relationship between northern and southern NGOs, and between international and national entities, with criticism that larger and northern-based organisations are not able fully to represent concerns of the South and, in some situations, adopt lifestyles inappropriate to local context; and the extent to which organisations can be professional yet able to represent, or facilitate the expression of, grassroots views. Undemocratic governments or emerging democracies are often uncomfortable with or, in some cases, hostile to the activity of civil society organisations.

There is overwhelming agreement that if the voluntary sector is to hold governments and business accountable, it needs to ensure its own legitimacy, openness and transparency. Legitimacy stems from several sources: firstly, from a strong moral conviction, through acting on the basis of universally-recognised rights and freedoms of speech, assembly and association to articulate public concerns inadequately addressed by government; secondly, a political legitimacy or credibility, through approval of the community or constituency represented by the voluntary association, asserting people's sovereignty and community control; thirdly, competence or performance legitimacy, by delivering results through being closer to local reality than governmental institutions, helping to bridge a government-community gap and promote social cohesion; fourthly, legal recognition, although in some countries, in the Middle East region for example, laws may prevent truly independent NGOs from functioning, or formal registration may undermine rather than enhance their reputation; and, most importantly, legitimacy comes from accountability and transparency.

NGOs should be accountable to a wide range of stakeholders: peoples whose rights they seek to protect and advance; their own members, supporters and staff; to those who contribute finance, goods or services; to partner institutions, both governmental and non-governmental; to regulatory bodies; to those whose policies, programmes or behaviour they wish to influence; and, more broadly, to the media and general public. They should be able to demonstrate a democratic structure, participative decision-making and non-partisan approach if they claim legitimacy on political grounds. They should focus on whatever is their primary agenda and not be diverted from this by demands of donors or obstacles in their operational environment. Some express concern that, in recent years, some civil society organisations, for example in the Philippines, have veered away from contentious issues like political reform and redistributive justice, with preference for 'doable' programmes such as delivery of social services. While there are urgent basic service needs which civil society organisations are equipped to fill, the need to address structural issues such as ineffectual government, distribution of resources and rampant corruption remains. Civil society organisations should pursue both. They should follow through on projects they undertake, conducting long-term programmes with sustainable results.

Fiscal accountability is, of course, vital, with effective reporting and monitoring systems, and sources of funding fully divulged. Some argue against accepting government support and foreign funding if civil society organisations are involved in promoting political and democratic reform; others, acknowledging the potential sensitivity of this, believe assuring a diversity of funding from public and private sources will overcome accusations of undue influence of donors.

The evolution towards national and international codes of conduct for voluntary self-regulation is regarded as a healthy development, although given the tremendous difference in size and scope of civil society organisations all cannot be brought under one approach. It will, however, introduce common principles which all can use in their work....

...

R. GRANT & R. KEOHANE, ACCOUNTABILITY AND ABUSES OF POWER IN WORLD POLITICS

99 Am. Pol. Sci. Rev. 29 (2005), at 35

...

...We have identified seven discrete accountability mechanisms that actually operate in world politics on the basis of which improved practices of accountability could be built....

Hierarchical accountability is a characteristic of bureaucracies and of virtually any large organization. Superiors can remove subordinates from office, constrain their tasks and room for discretion, and adjust their financial compensation. Hierarchical accountability as we use the term applies to relationships within organizations, including multilateral organizations such as the United Nations or the World Bank.

Supervisory accountability refers to relations between organizations where one organization acts as principal with respect to specified agents. For instance, the World Bank and IMF are subject to supervision by states and by institutions within states, such as courts....

Fiscal accountability describes mechanisms through which funding agencies can demand reports from, and ultimately sanction, agencies that are recipients of funding. This form of accountability... is particularly important for international organizations such as the United Nations and the World Bank, which rely on government appropriations to fund substantial parts of their activities.

Legal accountability refers to the requirement that agents abide by formal rules and be prepared to justify their actions in those terms, in courts or quasijudicial arenas. Public officials, like anyone else, can be "held accountable" for their actions both through administrative and criminal law. Courts do not have the broad general authority of governments or of electorates in democracies. Instead, the courts apply a narrow version of the trusteeship model, asking whether the power-wielders performed the duties of their offices faithfully in a limited sense: whether they obeyed the law. Legal accountability has long been important in constitutional democracies and has become increasingly important in world politics during recent years. The WTO Dispute Settlement Mechanism, the operations of the Hague Tribunal on the Former Yugoslavia, and the creation of a new International Criminal Court all illustrate the incursions that conceptions of legal accountability have made in world politics.

Market accountability is a less familiar category, but an important one. We want to emphasize that this form of accountability is not to an abstract force called "the market," but to investors and consumers, whose influence is exercised in whole or in part through markets....

Peer accountability arises as the result of mutual evaluation of organizations by their counterparts. NGOs, for example, evaluate the quality of information they receive from other NGOs and the ease of cooperating with them. Organizations that are poorly rated by their peers are likely to have difficulty in persuading them to cooperate and, therefore, to have trouble achieving their own purposes.

Public reputational accountability is pervasive because reputation is involved in all the other forms of accountability. Superiors, supervisory boards, courts, fiscal watchdogs, markets, and peers all take the reputations of agents into account. Indeed, reputation is a form of "soft power," defined as "the ability to shape the preferences of others". The category of public reputational accountability is meant to apply to situations in which reputation, widely and publicly known, provides a mechanism for accountability even in the absence of other mechanisms as well as in conjunction with them.

INTERNATIONAL NON-GOVERNMENTAL ORGANIZATIONS' ACCOUNTABILITY CHARTER

(2005), at www.ingoaccountabilitycharter.org

[The signatories include Amnesty International, Greenpeace, Oxfam International, International Save the Children Alliance, Terre des Hommes International, and Transparency International.]

We, international non-government organisations (INGOs) signatory to this Charter, are independent non-profit organisations that work globally to advance human rights, sustainable development, environmental protection, humanitarian response and other public goods.

…

Our right to act is based on universally-recognised freedoms of speech, assembly and association, on our contribution to democratic processes, and on the values we seek to promote.

Our legitimacy is also derived from the quality of our work, and the recognition and support of the people with and for whom we work and our members, our donors, the wider public, and governmental and other organisations around the world.

We seek to uphold our legitimacy by responding to inter-generational considerations, public and scientific concerns, and through accountability for our work and achievements.

By signing this Charter we seek to promote further the values of transparency and accountability that we stand for, and commit our INGO to respecting its provisions.

…

INGOs can complement but not replace the over-arching role and primary responsibility of governments….

We also seek to promote the role and responsibilities of the private sector….

We can often address problems and issues that governments and others are unable or unwilling to address on their own….

…

Wherever we operate, we seek to ensure that the high standards which we demand of others are also respected in our own organisations.

…

Our first responsibility is to achieve our stated mission effectively and transparently, consistent with our values. In this, we are accountable to our stakeholders. Our stakeholders include:

- Peoples, including future generations, whose rights we seek to protect and advance;
- Ecosystems, which cannot speak for or defend themselves;
- Our members and supporters;
- Our staff and volunteers;
- Organisations and individuals that contribute finance, goods or services;
- Partner organisations, both governmental and non-governmental, with whom we work;
- Regulatory bodies whose agreement is required for our establishment and operations;
- Those whose policies, programmes or behaviour we wish to influence;
- The media; and
- The general public.

…

INGOs are founded on the rights to freedom of speech, assembly and association in the Universal Declaration of Human Rights. We seek to advance international and national laws that promote human rights, ecosystem protection, sustainable development and other public goods.

Where such laws do not exist, are not fully implemented, or abused, we will highlight these issues for public debate and advocate appropriate remedial action.

…

We aim to be both politically and financially independent. Our governance, programmes and policies will be non-partisan, independent of specific governments, political parties and the business sector.

…

We will ensure that our advocacy is consistent with our mission, grounded in our work and advances defined public interests.

…

We are committed to openness, transparency and honesty about our structures, mission, policies and activities. We will communicate actively to stakeholders about ourselves, and make information publicly available.

…

We seek to comply with relevant governance, financial accounting and reporting requirements in the countries where we are based and operate.

…

We should be held responsible for our actions and achievements. We will do this by: having a clear mission, organisational structure and decision-making processes; by acting in accordance with stated values and agreed procedures; by ensuring that our programmes achieve outcomes that are consistent with our mission; and by reporting on these outcomes in an open and accurate manner.

The governance structure of each organisation will conform to relevant laws and be transparent. We seek to follow principles of best practice in governance. …

…

We seek continuously to improve our effectiveness. We will have defined evaluation procedures for our boards, staff, programmes and projects on the basis of mutual accountability.

…

We will be responsible in our public criticisms of individuals and organisations, ensuring such criticism amounts to fair public comment.

…

QUESTIONS

1. Does the INGOs' Accountability Charter respond adequately to the criticisms that have been made of the major human rights INGOs?

2. Is it reasonable to expect Amnesty International to deal with complaints, and to become transparent in all of its operations, when most of the governments and corporations which are subject to its criticism have not adopted comparable measures?

3. How would you analyse the accountability of human rights INGOs on the basis of the mechanisms described by Grant and Keohane?

ADDITIONAL READING

D. B. Reiser & C. R. Kelly, 'Linking NGO Accountability and the Legitimacy of Global Governance', 36 Brooklyn J. Int'l. L. 1011 (2011); S. Charnovitz, 'The Illegitimacy of Preventing NGO Participation', 36 Brooklyn J. Int'l. L. 891 (2011); K. Anderson, '"Accountability" as "Legitimacy": Global Governance, Global Civil Society and the United Nations', 36 Brooklyn J. Int'l. L. 841 (2011); S. Wheatley, 'Democratic Governance Beyond the State: The Legitimacy of Non-state Actors as Standard Setters', in A. Peters et al. (eds.), *Non-State Actors as Standard Setters* (2009), 215; D. Bell & J.-M. Coicaud (eds.), *Ethics in Action: The Ethical Challenges of International Human Rights Nongovernmental Organizations* (2007); International Council on Human Rights Policy, 'Human Rights Organisations: Rights And Responsibilities, Final Draft Report 2009', at www.ichrp.org/files/reports/67/119_report.pdf; M. Mutua, 'Standard Setting in Human Rights: Critique and Prognosis', 29 Hum. Rts. Q. 547 (2007).

17

Human Rights, Development and Climate Change

The past couple of decades have seen important efforts to apply human rights standards and obligations to activities in specific sectoral areas such as development, environment, trade, debt, migration, investment, labour and conflict prevention. Each of these different areas is complex and the challenge of making the relevant arrangements more human rights sensitive or compliant requires an understanding of the substantive issue areas and of the normative and institutional arrangements that govern. Rather than provide an inevitably superficial treatment of issues such as the relevance of human rights in the global trade and investments regimes, the role of human rights in relation to labour rights or the human rights responsibilities of key international economic actors such as the World Trade Organization, the World Bank or the International Monetary Fund, this chapter focuses primarily on the central issue of development. This involves looking at its relationship to human rights in general, the relevance of human rights to the Millennium Development Goals and the notion of the right to development. In addition, we consider whether the global climate change challenge can usefully be addressed through a human rights lens.

A. HUMAN RIGHTS AND DEVELOPMENT

Before the 1990s, human rights considerations were rarely addressed in the context of development policy. The reasons were diverse. Some economists considered human rights to be 'political' in contrast to the more 'technical' challenges of promoting economic development, some felt that many or even most human rights concerns were not able to be quantified effectively and thus could not be factored into the development equation, others were sympathetic to the idea that respect for civil and political rights was an issue that first required a significant degree of development to be attained, and some rejected the notion of economic and social rights as running counter to the functioning of free markets. It was only after the end of the Cold War that a more sophisticated debate began to take place. It was fuelled partly by the failure of old development models, and partly by the realization that notions of good governance, participation, accountability and transparency inevitably had human rights dimensions and could not be promoted adequately without addressing those dimensions. One of the most influential contributors to the debate has been Amartya Sen (whose related writings appear at pp. 305 and 311, *supra*). In the following reading, Sen argues that freedom should be seen as both the ends and the means of development.

AMARTYA SEN, DEVELOPMENT AS FREEDOM

(1999), at 35

Chapter 2: The Ends and the Means of Development

Let me start off with a distinction between two general attitudes to the process of development that can be found both in professional economic analysis and in public discussions and debates. One view sees development as a 'fierce' process, with much 'blood, sweat and tears' — a world in which wisdom demands toughness. In particular, it demands calculated neglect of various concerns that are seen as 'soft-headed'... [T]he temptations to be resisted can include having social safety nets that protect the very poor, providing social services for the population at large, departing from rugged institutional guidelines in response to identified hardship, and favoring — 'much too early' — political and civil rights and the 'luxury' of democracy. These things, it is argued in this austere attitudinal mode, could be supported later on, when the development process has borne enough fruit: what is needed here and now is 'toughness and discipline'. The different theories [diverge] in pointing to distinct areas of softness that are particularly to be avoided, varying from financial softness to political relaxation, from plentiful social expenditures to complaisant poverty relief.

This hard-knocks attitude contrasts with an alternative outlook that sees development as essentially a 'friendly' process. Depending on the particular version of this attitude, the congeniality of the process is seen as exemplified by such things as mutually beneficial exchanges (of which Adam Smith spoke eloquently), or by the working of social safety nets, or of political liberties, or of social development — or some combination or other of these supportive activities.

The approach of this book is much more compatible with the latter approach than with the former. It is mainly an attempt to see development as a process of expanding the real freedoms that people enjoy. In this approach, expansion of freedom is viewed as both (1) the *primary end* and (2) the *principal means* of development. They can be called respectively the 'constitutive role' and the 'instrumental role' of freedom in development. The constitutive role of freedom relates to the importance of substantive freedom in enriching human life. The substantive freedoms include elementary capabilities like being able to avoid such deprivations as starvation, undernourishment, escapable morbidity and premature mortality, as well as the freedoms that are associated with being literate and numerate, enjoying political participation and uncensored speech and so on. In this constitutive perspective, development involves expansion of these and other basic freedoms. Development, in this view, is the process of expanding human freedoms, and the assessment of development has to be informed by this consideration.

Let me refer here to an example.... Within the narrower views of development (in terms of say, [Gross Domestic Product] growth or industrialization) it is often asked whether the freedom of political participation and dissent is or is not 'conducive to development'. In the light of the foundational view of development as freedom, this question would seem to be defectively formulated, since it misses the crucial understanding that political participation and dissent are *constitutive* parts of development itself.... Development seen as enhancement of freedom cannot but address [deprivations of freedom]. The relevance of the deprivation of basic political freedoms or civil rights, for an adequate understanding of development, does not have to be established through their indirect contribution to *other* features of development (such as growth of GDP or the promotion of industrialization). These freedoms are part and parcel of enriching the process of development.

This fundamental development point is distinct from the 'instrumental' argument that these freedoms and rights may *also* be very effective in contributing to economic progress.... [T]he significance of the instrumental role of political freedom as *means* to development does not in any way reduce the evaluative importance of freedom as an *end* of development.

...The instrumental role of freedom concerns the way different kinds of rights, opportunities, and entitlements contribute to the expansion of human freedom in general, and thus to promoting development.... The effectiveness of freedom as an instrument lies in the fact that different kinds of freedom interrelate with one another, and freedom of one type may greatly help in advancing freedom of other types. The two roles are thus linked by empirical connections, as relating freedom of one kind to freedom of other kinds.

...

...I shall consider the following types of instrumental freedoms: (1) *political freedoms*,(2) *economic facilities*,(3) *social opportunities*,(4) *transparency guarantees*, and (5) *protective security*. These instrumental freedoms tend to contribute to the general capability of a person to live more freely, but they also serve to complement one another. While development analysis must, on the one hand, be concerned with the objectives and aims that make these instrumental freedoms consequentially important, it must also take note of the empirical linkages that tie the distinct types of freedom *together*, strengthening their joint importance. Indeed, these connections are central to a fuller understanding of the instrumental role of freedom. The claim that freedom is not only the primary object of development but also its principal means relates particularly to these linkages.

Let me comment a little on each of these instrumental freedoms. [Discussion of political freedoms omitted.]

Economic facilities refer to the opportunities that individuals respectively enjoy to utilize economic resources for the purpose of consumption, or production, or exchange. The economic entitlements that a person has will depend on the resources owned or available for use as well as on conditions of exchange, such as relative prices and the working of the markets. Insofar as the process of economic development increases the income and wealth of a country, they are reflected in corresponding enhancement of economic entitlements. It should be obvious that in the relation between national income and wealth, on the one hand, and the economic entitlements of individuals (or families), on the other, distributional considerations are important, in addition to aggregative ones. How the additional incomes generated are distributed will clearly make a difference.

…

Social opportunities refer to the arrangements that society makes for education, health care and so on, which influence the individual's substantive freedom to live better. These facilities are important not only for the conduct of private lives (such as living a healthy life and avoiding preventable morbidity and premature mortality), but also for more effective participation in economic and political activities. For example illiteracy can be a major barrier to participation in economic activities that require production according to specification or demand strict quality control (as globalized trade increasingly does). Similarly, political participation may be hindered by the inability to read newspapers or to communicate in writing with others involved in political activities.

…

Finally, no matter how well an economic system operates, some people can be typically on the verge of vulnerability and can actually succumb to great deprivation as a result of material changes that adversely affect their lives. *Protective security* is needed to provide a social safety net for preventing the affected population from being reduced to abject misery, and in some cases even starvation and death. The domain of protective security includes fixed institutional arrangements such as unemployment benefits and statutory income supplements to the indigent as well as ad hoc arrangements to generate income for destitutes.

These instrumental freedoms directly enhance the capabilities of people, but they also supplement one another, and can furthermore reinforce one another. These interlinkages are particularly important to seize in considering development policies.

…

Similarly the creation of social opportunities, through such services as public education, health care, and the development of a free and energetic press, can contribute both to economic development and to significant reductions in mortality rates. Reduction of mortality rates, in turn, can help to reduce birth rates, reinforcing the influence of basic education — especially female literary and schooling — on fertility behavior.

…

This approach goes against — and to a great extent undermines — the belief that has been so dominant in many policy circles that 'human development' (as the process of expanding education, health care and other conditions of human life is often called) is really a kind of luxury that only richer countries can afford. Perhaps the most important impact of the type of success that the East Asian economies, beginning with Japan, have had is the total undermining of that implicit prejudice. These economies went comparatively early for massive expansion of education, and later also of health care, and this they did, in many cases, *before* they broke the restraints of general poverty. And they have reaped as they have sown....

...

COMMENT ON THE MILLENNIUM DEVELOPMENT GOALS

Since 2001 the international community's dominant approach to poverty alleviation has been the implementation of the Millennium Development Goals (MDGs). These 'goals' grew out of the Millennium Declaration, adopted in 2000 by the UN General Assembly, in which 147 heads of state or government pledged to 'spare no effort to free our fellow men, women and children from the abject and dehumanizing conditions of extreme poverty.' In a Road Map produced by the UN Secretary-General, the various objectives were structured and developed into eight goals, 18 targets and 48 indicators. For example, Goal 1 concerns the eradication of extreme poverty and hunger and is broken down into three separate targets: A — to halve the proportion of people whose income is less than $1 a day (1990–2015); B — to achieve full and productive employment for all; and C — to halve the proportion of people who suffer from hunger (1990–2015). Goal 2 is universal primary education and the target is to ensure that, by 2015, all children will be able to complete a full course of primary schooling. Goal 3 is to promote gender equality and empower women; and Goal 4 is to reduce child mortality, specifically by reducing the under-5 mortality rate by two-thirds from 1990 to 2015.

Efforts to integrate human rights considerations into development strategies have been strongly affected by the international community's preoccupation with the MDGs. The following readings consider both the effectiveness of the MDG strategy and its implications for human rights.

CLAIRE MELAMED, AFTER 2015: CONTEXTS, POLITICS AND PROCESSES FOR A POST-2015 GLOBAL AGREEMENT ON DEVELOPMENT

Overseas Development Institute (4 Jan. 2012)

...

MDG 1: Behind the global figures on incomes

While the aggregate figures on income poverty are encouraging, the global figure masks considerable variation between countries and regions....

Figures on the incidence of poverty are particularly encouraging. The percentage of the world's population living on less than $1.25 a day has fallen from 42 per cent in 1990 to 25 per cent in 2005. It is projected to fall to 14 per cent in 2015. In absolute terms, these figures represent a fall from 1.8 billion poor people in 1990 to 1.4 billion in 2005 and a projected 0.9 billion in 2015.

However, the success on income poverty is very heavily concentrated in China, which, because of its size, dominates the global average.... The absolute number of poor people rose slightly in South Asia between 1990–2005 (although this is projected to fall significantly by 2015), and the number of poor people in Sub-Saharan Africa increased from 300 million in 1990 to almost 400 million in 2005. [Projected to decline to 350 million by 2015.]

The most significant rates of poverty reduction between 1990 and 2005 were achieved in East Asia and the Pacific. These regions saw reductions of nearly 70 per cent in the number of people living on less than $1.25 per day, and over 50 per cent reduction in the number of those with less than $2 a day. [By 2015 the figure] is predicted to be 119 million — just 13 per cent of the 1990 figure.

...

MDGs 2–7: Behind the global figures on health, nutrition, education and sanitation

[G]lobal progress on non-income poverty is distributed unevenly between regions. The proportion of children aged under 5 who are underweight has decreased across all regions of the world since 1990, with an average 23 per cent decrease in all developing countries. However, progress in Southern Asia and sub-Saharan [Africa] has been slower than the average, with less than a 20 per cent reduction in underweight, compared to an above-average 60 per cent decrease in Latin America and Eastern Asia.

Related data also shows that these two regions have achieved a 60 per cent reduction in deaths per 1000 live births between 1990 and 2009. In sub-Saharan Africa, the infant mortality rate remains above one in 10, nearly 20 times the number of deaths experienced in developed countries. Elsewhere, countries in Southern Asia have witnessed a decrease in the infant mortality rate from over 120 deaths per 1000 live births to under 70 over the last two decades. With the exception of these two regions and Oceania all other parts of the world have reduced child mortality rates by more than half....

Many regions of the developing world have now attained levels of primary education enrolment at between 90 and 95 per cent. However, the average enrolment rate across developing regions remains slightly lower due in particular to the effect of sub-Saharan Africa, which despite an increase of over 30 per cent in the decade leading to 2008/09 has an enrolment level of just 76 per cent.

Progress on access to water and sanitation presents a mixed picture. In most regions less than 15 per cent of the population lack access to unimproved water, a significant improvement on 1990. However, in sub-Saharan Africa forty per cent of the population are still using untreated water. Similar patterns are [in] evidence for sanitation. In every region apart from South Asia and sub-Saharan Africa more than half the population now has access to improved sanitation. In sub-Saharan Africa the proportion is just 31 per cent, while in South Asia it is 36 per cent.

...

4 Inequalities in MDG achievement

...

The people who have not benefitted from progress on MDGs 1–7 are not randomly distributed within countries — they tend to be from ethnic minorities, and/or to live in remote areas, and/or to be from religious groups who are discriminated against. Disability is another common and widely ignored source of inequality: UNESCO estimate that one third of the approximately 75 million children who do not attend school suffer some disability. Within these marginalised groups women and girls often fare worse than men and boys.

MDG indicators are consistently worse for disadvantaged groups in every region....

MAC DARROW, LIES, DAMNED LIES, AND THE MILLENNIUM DEVELOPMENT GOALS: HUMAN RIGHTS PRIORITIES FOR THE POST-2015 DEVELOPMENT AGENDA

15 Yale Hum. Rts. & Devt. L.J. 55 (2012)

B. Human rights critiques of the MDGs

...[C]ritics of the MDGs have pointed to the secretive circumstances of their birth, their technocratic and reductionist nature, their lack of ambition, their failure to address root causes of poverty, their failure to factor in legal obligations pertaining to social rights, their gender-blindness, their failure to address poverty in rich countries, their weak accountability mechanisms, their limited uptake by social movements in the global South, the potentially distorting character of target-driven policy-making, and the propensity of the MDGs to crowd out attention to important issues that didn't make it into the global list, for example, social security or social protection.

These critiques are relatively well rehearsed, however there are a number of [other] problems that deserve particular attention....

1. The MDGs can provide a figleaf for authoritarian regimes

...While no country has a clean human rights slate, lavishing praise [on authoritarian governments with good MDG records] offers a figleaf of legitimacy to authoritarian regimes, masks underlying inequalities and structural discrimination and oppression, and de-oxygenates local emancipatory struggles....

2. The MDGs emerged from a faulty process and are poorly specified

...[T]he MDGs [were] hatched behind closed doors and shaped by special interests and the proclivities of particular development agencies as much as by any coherent conceptual design or consistently rigorous statistical parameters.

The problem of poor specification is perhaps most notorious in connection with the income poverty target in MDG 1. Target 1.A commits states to halve, between 1990 and 2015, the proportion of people whose income is less than one dollar a day... The poor specification of Target 1.A has permitted a wide range of subjective interpretations, justifying a dramatic upward revision of headcount poverty estimates by the World Bank in 2008 at the same time that researchers elsewhere concluded that Sub-Saharan Africa's progress towards Target 1.A was on track. Clearer specification would reduce the range of such wildly different interpretations.

3. The definition of 'feasible' progress is arbitrary and unambitious

Other methodological ambiguities are equally troubling, relating to the baseline year for the MDGs and the assumptions underpinning their desired level of ambition. Target 1.A is, again, illustrative.... Target 1.A was preceded by a more ambitious pledge at the 1996 World Food Summit in Rome, to "halve the *number* [rather than proportion] of extremely poor people between 1996 [rather than 1990] and 2015".... The reformulation of this pledge in Target 1.A, [referred] to "proportion" rather than absolute numerical reduction, and [moved] the baseline year back to 1990 from 1996....

Second, moving the baseline back to 1990 makes it legitimate to measure the effects of income poverty reduction in China between 1990–1996, making the goal more achievable. Yet, China's large reduction was based upon strong growth performance and public policies that self-evidently preceded and had nothing to do with the MDGs. With these factors in view, Pogge argues that the re-calibrated MDG Target 1.A, if fulfilled, would reduce the number of extremely poor people by only twenty per cent between 1996 and 2015, compared with the target of a fifty per cent reduction under the 1996 World Food Summit. By lowering the MDG 1.A bar, the number of extremely poor people deemed morally acceptable in 2015 rises by 496 million (from 828 to 1,324 million) and shrinks by more than half (from 828 to 332 million) the reduction pledged in 1996. The result, in Pogge's assessment, is an additional six million morally acceptable deaths from poverty-related causes annually.

A further illustration of the feasibility concern, beyond Target 1.A, is MDG 5 on maternal health, which is the goal least likely to be met in global terms. Maternal deaths occur on a shocking scale in many countries, from 200 to over 1,000 deaths per 100,000 live births in various areas of Africa and South, East and Central Asia on best available estimates. This is largely preventable and occurs due to deeply ingrained discrimination, although rarely is adequate and disaggregated data collected and deaths investigated....

...

From a human rights perspective it can also be argued that ambitious targets are especially warranted for problems, such as maternal mortality and morbidity, that are determined more by deeply entrenched discrimination and inadequate political will than by resource constraints.... [U]nduly modest targets may constitute complicity in failure.

...

5. The MDGs are equity-blind and may have exacerbated global and country-level inequalities

The "equity-blindness" of the MDGs is probably the feature that has generated the strongest criticism. "[E]quity" refers generally to notions of fairness and distributive justice. The global MDGs provide global assessments of human development progress based upon average outcomes. As a result, the MDGs may inadvertently occlude analysis of differential outcomes for populations in the upper versus lower income quintiles, or overlook the particular barriers faced by women, children, indigenous peoples, minorities, persons with disabilities, and other groups who may face discrimination. Taken literally, the MDGs may easily be achieved in many countries without any effort to reach the most marginalised populations....

...

Gender equality is a particular concern. At the Millennium Summit, Member States committed themselves to promote "gender equality and the empowerment of women as effective ways to combat poverty, hunger and disease and to stimulate development that is truly sustainable." Seventy per cent of people living in poverty are women, and nearly two-thirds of the 780 million people who cannot read are women. However, MDG 3 ("promote gender equality and empower women"), Target 3.A, focuses only on eliminating gender disparities in primary and secondary education, "preferably by 2005," and in all areas of education by 2015. Two of the three indicators include the share of women in paid employment in the non-agriculture sector, and percentage of women in parliament. But this excludes many other areas — including the private sphere — where women and girls experience discrimination. Data shortages are certainly a critical constraint in many countries. But this is often more a matter of political will than resource constraints. Discrimination issues, including violence against women and other root causes of marginalisation, should be better reflected in the structure of the MDGs, within applicable statistical parameters, as well as in national reporting.

6. Certain MDGs may undermine international human rights law standards

In certain cases, the specific formulation of particular MDGs may conflict with or undermine international human rights treaty standards. For example, MDG 2 (universal primary education) omits the requirement that primary education be free-of-charge....

...

Target 7.D... commits states to "achieve a significant improvement in the lives of at least 100 million slum-dwellers," a mere ten per cent of those living in slums worldwide. U.N.-Habitat has reported that 227 million people have moved out of slum conditions since 2000; but at the same time, the total number of people living in slums has actually increased during this period, to over one billion in 2005, and 828 million in developing countries alone in 2010. Target 7.D fails to refer to secure tenure, which is the foremost consideration for most people in informal settlements, along with other important attributes of the right to housing....

...

7. MDGs have been co-opted by the growth and aid lobbies

... [T]he global development policy debate remains dominated by the implicit formula: "*faster economic growth + more foreign aid + better governance = MDGs*". The fact that inequality has increased in the majority of countries, for the majority of the MDGs, is... "dismissed as irrelevant or a passing phase".

...[G]lobal progress towards the MDGs...has been driven largely by aggregate gains through economic growth policies in China and India, based upon policies that pre-dated the MDGs....

C. Conclusions on the MDGs' impacts

...Human rights advocates have responded to the MDGs in different ways: some continue to condemn the MDGs, some ignore them entirely, and others pragmatically engage with the MDGs as potential vehicles for human rights realisation....
...

QUESTIONS

1. Can Sen's approach be characterized as a human rights-centred one? Does it matter if he does not specifically embrace the discourse of international human rights law in his analysis?

2. What, in your view, are the strengths and weaknesses of the approach of the MDGs, from a human rights perspective?

B. THE RIGHT TO DEVELOPMENT

Article 56 of the UN Charter commits all member states to take 'joint and separate action in co-operation' with the UN for the achievement of the purposes identified in Article 55, which includes human rights, 'higher standards of living...and conditions of economic and social progress and development' and 'solutions of international economic, social, health and related problems'. Similarly, Article 28 of the UDHR provides that '[e]very one is entitled to a social and international order in which the rights and freedoms set forth in this Declaration can be fully realized'. These provisions, although expressed at a level of great generality, have often been invoked by those who posit the existence of a broad international 'duty to cooperate' or a 'right to solidarity'. In a world of deep-rooted and growing inequalities among nations, the question inevitably arises whether the international community bears some responsibility for assisting states whose resources are inadequate to ensure the human rights of their own citizens, or for providing direct assistance to those individuals in dire need.

Since 1977 much of this debate has been pursued within the field of human rights under the rubric of the 'right to development'. The debate touches upon a number of themes raised in earlier chapters: the basis for recognition of new rights, the priority to be accorded to the different sets of rights, the links between human rights and democratic governance and the relationship between individual and collective rights (including peoples' rights).

The list of internationally recognized human rights is by no means immutable. Just as the British sociologist T. H. Marshall characterized the eighteenth century as the century of civil rights, the nineteenth as that of political rights and the twentieth as that of social rights so, too, have some commentators over the past three decades put forward claims for the recognition of the new rights, in particular a category known as the 'third generation of solidarity rights'. By analogy with the slogan of the French Revolution these rights have been said to correspond to the theme of *fraternité*, while first-generation civil and political rights correspond with *liberté* and second-generation economic and social rights with *egalité*. Karel Vasak's list of solidarity rights included 'the right to development, the right to peace, the right to environment, the right to the ownership of the common heritage of mankind, and the right to communication'.[1]

Far more significant has been the impact of the right to development. First recognized by the UN Commission on Human Rights in 1977 (CHR Res. 4 (XXXIII)), it was enshrined in the following very carefully negotiated Declaration.

DECLARATION ON THE RIGHT TO DEVELOPMENT

General Assembly Res. 41/28 (1986)

The General Assembly,

...

Proclaims the following Declaration on the Right to Development:

Article 1

1. The right to development is an inalienable human right by virtue of which every human person and all peoples are entitled to participate in, contribute to, and enjoy economic, social, cultural and political development, in which all human rights and fundamental freedoms can be fully realized.

2. The human right to development also implies the full realization of the right of peoples to self-determination, which includes, subject to the relevant provisions of both International Covenants on Human Rights, the exercise of their inalienable right to full sovereignty over all their natural wealth and resources.

Article 2

1. The human person is the central subject of development and should be the active participant and beneficiary of the right to development.

2. All human beings have a responsibility for development, individually and collectively, taking into account the need for full respect for their human rights and fundamental freedoms as well as their duties to the community, which alone can ensure the free and complete fulfilment of the human being, and they should therefore promote and protect an appropriate political, social and economic order for development.

[1] K. Vasak, 'For the Third Generation of Human Rights: The Rights of Solidarity', International Institute of Human Rights, July 1979, at 3.

3. States have the right and the duty to formulate appropriate national development policies that aim at the constant improvement of the well-being of the entire population and of all individuals, on the basis of their active, free and meaningful participation in development and in the fair distribution of the benefits resulting there from.

Article 3

1. States have the primary responsibility for the creation of national and international conditions favourable to the realization of the right to development.

2. The realization of the right to development requires full respect for the principles of international law concerning friendly relations and cooperation among States in accordance with the Charter of the United Nations.

3. States have the duty to co-operate with each other in ensuring development and eliminating obstacles to development. States should realize their rights and fullfil their duties in such a manner as to promote a new international economic order based on sovereign equality, interdependence, mutual interest and co-operation among all States, as well as to encourage the observance and realization of human rights.

Article 4

1. States have the duty to take steps, individually and collectively, to formulate international development policies with a view to facilitating the full realization of the right to development.

2. Sustained action is required to promote more rapid development of developing countries. As a complement to the efforts of developing countries, effective international co-operation is essential in providing these countries with appropriate means and facilities to foster their comprehensive development.

…

Article 6

…

2. All human rights and fundamental freedoms are indivisible and interdependent; equal attention and urgent consideration should be given to the implementation, promotion and protection of civil, political, economic, social and cultural rights.

…

Article 8

1. States should undertake, at the national level, all necessary measures for the realization of the right to development and shall ensure, inter alia, equality of opportunity for all in their access to basic resources, education, health services, food, housing, employment and the fair distribution of income. Effective measures should be undertaken to ensure that women have an active role in the development process. Appropriate economic and social reforms should be carried out with a view to eradicating all social injustices.

2. States should encourage popular participation in all spheres as an important factor in development and in the full realization of all human rights.

…

Article 10

Steps should be taken to ensure the full exercise and progressive enhancement of the right to development, including the formulation, adoption and implementation of policy, legislative and other measures at the national and international levels.

NOTE

The right to development has never ceased to be controversial among governments as well as among scholars and commentators. While the right is generally grounded in claims relating to the material conditions required to ensure realization of the full range of existing human rights, it is also sometimes grounded in claims of appropriate reparations for colonialism and other forms of exploitation of the South by the North, or on arguments that the existing international economic order is loaded against developing countries and that compensation should follow.[2]

The international community has underlined its importance on many occasions, including a statement endorsed by the 1993 Vienna World Conference on Human Rights to the effect that it is 'a universal and inalienable right and an integral part of fundamental human rights'. Despite such ringing endorsements, prolonged efforts to clarify its content and, more importantly, its implications, have yielded little agreement on concrete issues. Since the adoption of the Declaration, the UN Commission and its successor, the Human Rights Council, have employed various mechanisms designed to shed light on these issues. They include four different 'working groups', two composed of 'experts' and two of governmental representatives, as well as an independent expert. While a great many reports have been produced, they have yet to lead to any consensus about the practical consequences of the recognition of the right. Nevertheless, the right to development has achieved constitutional recognition in five countries (see p. 338, *supra*).

In the readings below Abi-Saab and Bedjaoui present the case for the existence in international law of a right to development, while Donnelly argues that the right is not only without foundation but is dangerous as well. Their analyses are followed by Moyn's reflection on the risk that the notion of human rights, especially through its embrace of a right to development, will succumb to the temptation to be all inclusive rather than narrowly focused on its original core, a risk that he sees as having dire consequences.

[2] These arguments were examined in detail in the first major UN report on the right to development. See UN Doc. E/CN.4/1334 (1978).

GEORGES ABI-SAAB, THE LEGAL FORMULATION OF A RIGHT TO DEVELOPMENT

in Hague Academy of International Law, The Right to Development at the International Level (1980), at 163

[Abi-Saab begins by noting that, for the right to development to be considered a legal right, it must be possible to identify the active and passive subjects of the right and its content. But those elements depend on the legal basis of the right, which in turn depends on whether the right is an individual or collective one.]

It is possible to think of different legal bases of the right to development as a collective right. The first possibility...is to consider the right to development as the aggregate of the social, economic and cultural rights not of each individual, but of all the individuals constituting a collectivity. In other words, it is the sum total of a double aggregation of the rights and of the individuals. This version...has the merit of shedding light on the link between the rights of the individual and the right of the collectivity; a link which is crucial....

Another way...is to approach it directly from a collective perspective...by considering it either as the economic dimension of the right of self-determination, or alternatively as a parallel right to self-determination, partaking of the same nature and belonging to the same category of collective rights.

...

As far as the beneficiaries or active subjects are concerned, the first answer that comes to mind is that they are those societies possessing certain characteristics which lead the international community to consider them wanting in terms of development and to classify them as 'developing' or 'less developed' countries (LDC)....

...

...Up to now, we have used societies, communities, countries and States as interchangeable, which they are not. In fact, here as with self-determination, the common denominator of these different ways of describing the beneficiary collectivity is the 'people' they designate, which constitutes the socially relevant entity or group in this context.... Suffice it to say here that the distinction between 'people' and 'State', though in theory it is as important in relation to the right to development as to the right of self-determination, in practice it is not....

...

... [T]he passive subject of the right to development can only be the international community as such. But as the international community does not have at its disposal the means (organs, resources) of directly fulfilling its obligations under the right to development, it can only discharge them through a category of its members, that of the 'developed' States....

...

... [S]atisfaction of the collective right is a necessary condition, a condition-precedent or a prerequisite for the materialization of the individual rights. Thus without self-determination it is impossible to imagine a total realization of the civil and political rights of the individuals constituting the collectivity in question. Such rights can be granted and exercised at lower levels, such as villages and municipalities, but they cannot reach their full scope and logical conclusion if the community is subject to colonial or alien rule.

...

The same with the right to development, which is a necessary precondition for the satisfaction of the social and economic rights of the individuals. And here, even more than in the case of self-determination, the causal link between the two levels is particularly strong; for without a tolerable degree of development, the society will not be materially in a position to grant and guarantee these rights to its members, i.e., of providing the positive services and securing the minimum economic standards which are required by these rights.

...

MOHAMMED BEDJAOUI, THE RIGHT TO DEVELOPMENT

in M. Bedjaoui (ed.), International Law: Achievements and Prospects (1991), at 1182

...

14. The right to development is a fundamental right, the precondition of liberty, progress, justice and creativity. It is the alpha and omega of human rights, the first and last human right, the beginning and the end, the means and the goal of human rights, in short it is the *core right* from which all the others stem....

...

15.... In reality the international dimension of the right to development is nothing other than *the right to an equitable share in the economic and social well-being of the world.* It reflects an essential demand of our time since four fifths of the world's population no longer accept that the remaining fifth should continue to build its wealth on their poverty.

...

IV. Basis of the Right to Development

19. The most essential human rights have, in a sense, a meta-juridical foundation. For example, the right to life is independent both of international law and of the municipal laws of States. It pre-exists law. In this sense it is a 'primary' or 'first' law, that is to say a law commanding all the others.... Thus the right to development imposes itself with the force of a self-evident principle and its natural foundation is as a corollary of the right to life....

...

22. The 'right to development' flows from this right to self-determination and has the *same nature.* There is little sense in recognizing self-determination as a superior and inviolable principle if one does not recognize *at the same time* a 'right to development' for the peoples that have achieved self-determination. This right to development can only be an 'inherent' and 'built-in' right forming an inseparable part of the right to self-determination.

23.... [This makes the right to development] much more a right of the State or of the people, than a right of the individual, and it seems to me that it is better that way.

...

26. The present writer considers that international solidarity means taking into account the interdependence of nations. One may identify three stages in this search for the foundation of the right to development based on international solidarity:

(i) interdependence, the result of the global nature of the world economy;
(ii) the universal duty of every State to develop the world economy, which makes development an international problem *par excellence*;
(iii) preservation of the human species as the basis of the right to development.

...

V. Content of the Right to Development

34.... [This right] has several aspects, the most important and comprehensive of which is the right of each people freely to choose its economic and social system without outside interference or constraint of any kind, and to determine, with equal freedom, its own model of development....

...

48.... [T]he State seeking its own development is entitled to demand that all the other States, the international community and international economic agents collectively *do not take away from it what belongs to it, or do not deprive it of what is or 'must be' its due in international trade.* In the name of this right to development, the State being considered may claim a '*fair price*' for its raw materials and for whatever it offers in its trade with the more developed countries.

...

49. This second meaning of the right to development which is due from the international community seems much more complex. It implies that the State is *entitled if not to the satisfaction of its needs at least to receive a fair share of what belongs to all, and therefore to that State also.*

...

50.... [T]he satisfaction of the needs of a people should be perceived as a right and not as an act of charity. It is a right which should be made effective by *norms and institutions.* The relation between the donor and the recipient States is seen in terms of responsibility and reciprocal rights over goods that are considered as belonging to all. There is no place in such an analysis for charity, the 'act of mercy', considered as being a factor of inequality from which the donor expects tokens of submissiveness or political flexibility on the part of the receiving State. The concept of charity thus gives place to that of justice. *The need,* taken as a criterion of equity, gives greater precision to the concept of '*equitable distribution*' which would otherwise be too vague.

...

VI. Degree of Normativity of the Right to Development

53. Learned opinion is divided in its view of the legal validity of the right to development. Many writers consider that while it is undoubtedly an inalienable

and imperative right, this is only in the moral, rather than in the legal, sphere. The present writer has, on the contrary, maintained that the right to development is, by its nature, so incontrovertible that it *should* be regarded as belonging to *jus cogens*.

...

55. It is clear, however, that a right which is not opposable by the possessor of the right against the person from whom the right is due is not a right in the full legal sense. This constitutes *the challenge which the right to development throws down to contemporary international law* and the whole of the challenge which the underdevelopment of four fifths of the globe places, in political terms, before the rulers of the world....

...

JACK DONNELLY, IN SEARCH OF THE UNICORN: THE JURISPRUDENCE AND POLITICS OF THE RIGHT TO DEVELOPMENT

15 Calif. Western Int'l. L. J. 473 (1985), at 482

III. Legal Sources of the Right to Development

...

...If the right to development means the right of peoples freely to pursue their development, then it can be plausibly argued to be implied by the Covenants' right to self-determination. However, such a right to development is without interest; it is already firmly established as the right to self-determination.

A substantially broader right to development, however, cannot be extracted from this right to self-determination. The right to self-determination recognized in the Covenants does not imply a right to live in a developing society; it is explicitly only a right to *pursue* development. Neither does it imply an *individual* right to development; self-determination, again explicitly, is a right of peoples only. In no sense does it imply a right to be developed. Thus the claim that the right to development is simply the realization of the right to self-determination is not based on the Covenants' understanding of self-determination.

It might also be argued that because development is necessary for self-determination, development is itself a human right. Such an argument, however, is fallacious. Since we will come across this form of argument again, let us look briefly at this 'instrumental fallacy'. Suppose that A holds mineral rights in certain oil-bearing properties. Suppose further that in order to enjoy these rights fully, she requires $500,000 to begin pumping the oil. Clearly A does not have a right to $500,000 just because she needs it to enjoy her rights....The same reasoning applies to the link between development and the right to self-determination. Even assuming that development is necessary for, rather than a consequence of, full enjoyment of the right to self-determination, it simply does not follow that peoples have a right to development.

Allowing such an argument to prevail would result in a proliferation of bizarre or misguided rights....

...

The second promising implicit source of a right to development is Article 28 of the [UDHR]...

...

[O]ne might question whether 'development' falls under the notion of a social and international order referred to in Article 28. 'Development' suggests a process or result; the process of development or the condition of being developed. 'Order', by contrast, implies a set of principles, rules, practices or institutions; neither a process nor a result but a structure. Article 28, therefore, is most plausibly interpreted as prohibiting *structures* that deny opportunities or resources for the realization of civil, political, economic, social or cultural human rights....

...

Suppose, though, that Article 28 *were* to be taken to imply a human right to development. What would that right look like? It would be an *individual* right, and only an individual right; a right of persons, not peoples, and certainly not States. It would be a right to the enjoyment of traditional human rights, not a substantively new right. It would be as much a civil and political as an economic and social right — Article 28 refers to *all* human rights — and would be held equally against one's national government and the international community...

...

[V. Subjects of the Right to Development]

...

If human rights derive from the inherent dignity of the human person, collective human rights are logically possible only if we see social membership as an inherent part of human personality, and if we argue that as part of a nation or people, persons hold human rights substantively different from, and in no way reducible to, individual human rights. This last proposition is extremely controversial....

The very concept of human rights, as it has heretofore been understood, rests on a view of the individual person as separate from, and endowed with inalienable rights held primarily in relation to, society, and especially the state. Furthermore, within the area defined by these rights, the individual is superior to society in the sense that ordinarily, in cases of conflict between individual human rights and social goals or interests, individual rights must prevail. The idea of collective *human* rights represents a major, and at best confusing, conceptual deviation.

I do not want to challenge the idea of collective rights *per se* or even the notion of peoples' rights; groups, including nations, can and do hold a variety of rights. But these are not *human* rights as that term is ordinarily understood....

...

A further problem with collective human rights is determining who is to exercise the right; the right-holder is not a physical person, and thus an institutional 'person'

must exercise it. In the case of a right held by a people, or by society as a whole, the most plausible 'person' to exercise the right is, unfortunately, the state. Again this represents a radical reconceptualization of human rights — and an especially dangerous one.
...

SAMUEL MOYN, THE LAST UTOPIA

(2010), at 222

Even as human rights continued to draw on the claim that their source of authority transcended politics, their transformation into the dominant framework of the government and improvement of human life in far-flung global locales changed them profoundly. The turn of the human rights movement to concerns with "governance" in postcolonial states around the world is perhaps the most vivid illustration of the embrace of politics. It seemed obvious that episodic kinds of concern, in reaction to episodic crises, would never solve the problems that gave rise to those wrongs in the first place. And the notion of "governance" as a move from spectacular to structural wrongs, besides illustrating the transition from antipolitics to program, is now frequently combined in the human rights movement with a revived and rethought version of a Cold War theory of social development once notorious for its disinterest in rights but now based on them. On reflection, this evolution is unsurprising. Much as in the original history of rights in the nineteenth century and domestic civil rights in a later age, the early assertion of abstract entitlements prompted their advocates to scrutinize conditions for the enjoyment of entitlements, which are unfailingly structural, institutional, economic, and cultural.

In this process, the star-crossed trajectory of the notion of a "right to development" to which suffering humanity might be entitled is especially thought provoking. Contrary to what is sometimes suggested, the content of such a right was not a fundamental departure, given that anticolonialism had long since redefined human rights in the direction of nationalistic self-determination and collective development. But it was a specific act of creative appropriation when . . . the phrase "right to development" [was coined] in 1972. To that point, not least during the heyday of Western and especially American Cold War doctrines of modernization and development, rights had not figured as central concepts. And while it was precisely in the 1970s that the high tide of anticolonialism found expression in the attempt to craft a subaltern politics of development, international agencies as well as state and private actors in the decades since have devised schemes of development in which honoring human rights is conceived as both the means and the end. Intellectually, the theoretical and doctrinal energy harnessed to the project of finding a vision of human rights adequate to global immiseration graphically illustrates the sheer distance from the landmark of their antitotalitarian invention that human rights have had to travel. The jury is clearly still out on whether a rights framework for global poverty is the right framework. But the verdict is debated only because human rights were forced to face –and it seemed believable that they might be able to face — problems that had been addressed by other schemes, and contending utopias, before.

Were human rights disabled by the circumstances of their birth from making precisely the moves they have made — and that so many demanded they make — from antipolitics to program? Was the movement too hobbled by its formulation of claims as individual entitlements, or its inattention to the relevance of economic and larger structural relationships for the realization of those entitlements, or was its challenge rather its far more general refusal of ideology? Is the process of its troubled expansion merely the story of the difficulty of combining cooperation with existing governmental and intergovernmental programs with criticism of them, or is its originally critical attitude toward power to blame? These are questions that are only beginning to be asked, based on perceived limitations of human rights as the best vessel of aspirations for a better world — dissatisfactions that are at the very least the burden of its success, but whose weighty consequences over the long term it is too soon to assess.

Instead of turning to history to monumentalize human rights by rooting them deep in the past, it is much better to acknowledge how recent and contingent they really are. Above all, it is crucial to link the emergence of human rights to the history of utopianism — the heartfelt desire to make the world a better place. That it is only one form of utopianism, indeed one that exists today because it weathered the recent storm in which others were shipwrecked, ought to be clear by now. But not every age need be as unsympathetic to political utopia as the recent one in which human rights came to the fore. And so the program of human rights faces a fateful choice: whether to expand its horizons so as to take on the burden of politics more honestly, or to give way to new and other political visions that have yet to be fully outlined.

In some ways, the choice has already been made: to the extent the human rights agenda has extended its purview or been forced to do so, it inevitably became something new. Yet this transformation is neither an easy nor an obvious process, and should happen consciously rather than inadvertently. Henry Steiner…lucidly cautioned the human rights movement that it needed to carefully distinguish two missions that it was apt to confuse: between human rights as catastrophe prevention and human rights as utopian politics. "The human rights corpus is very spacious in the rights, freedoms and liberties that it embraces," Steiner noted. "[Some] norms express what one could call the 'anti-catastrophe' goal or dimension of the human rights movement: stopping the massive disasters that have plagued humanity. That goal is complemented by another, related but distinct utopian dimension to human rights: giving people the freedom and capacity to develop their lives and the world.… When you get past the core, the absolute 'no's,' there is inevitable ambiguity and out-right conflict." Historically, Steiner's contrast is false. In fact, it was due to minimalism and utopianism, indissociably and together, that human rights made their way in the world. But the conditions for this combination were fleeting. And they are long since gone.

Today, these goals — preventing catastrophe through minimalist ethical norms and building utopia through maximalist political vision — are absolutely different. One remains more compatible with the moralized breakthrough of human rights in the first place; the other follows from aspirations human rights have incorporated since that time, aspirations that are emphatically visionary but also necessarily divisive. The first version can honestly confront its lack of answers and acknowledge that it must make room for the contest of genuinely political visions for the future: seeking ways to constrain the contest so it does not lead to disaster, perhaps, but playing no other role. Yet then human rights cannot be a general slogan or world-view or ideal. If it draws authority from its appeal to morality, the other, utopian version of human rights easily becomes a recipe for the displacement of politics, forcing aspirations for change to present themselves as less controversial than they really are, as if humanity were not still confused and divided about how to bring about individual and collective freedom in a deeply unjust world.

Born of the yearning to transcend politics, human rights have become the core language of a new politics of humanity that has sapped the energy from old ideological contests of left and right. With the advancement of human rights as their standard, a huge number of schemes of transformation, regulation, and "governance" contend with one another across the world. But if in the thirty years since their explosion in the 1970s human rights have followed a path from morality to politics, their advocates have not always forthrightly acknowledged that fact. Born in the assertion of the "power of the powerless," human rights inevitably became bound up with the power of the powerful. If "human rights" stand for an exploding variety of rival political schemes, however, they still trade on the moral transcendence of politics that their original breakthrough involved. And so it may not be too late to wonder whether the concept of human rights, and the movement around it, should restrict themselves to offering minimal constraints on responsible politics, not a new form of maximal politics of their own. If human rights call to mind a few core values that demand protection, they cannot be all things to all people....

QUESTIONS

1. Compare the different conceptions of the right to development put forward by Abi-Saab, Bedjaoui and Donnelly with the text of the 1986 General Assembly Declaration. Key concerns voiced by some of the governmental and other opponents of the right to development include objections to collective human rights and especially to any idea that a human right can be vested in a state, resistance to the idea that resource transfers from the North to the South are obligatory and fears that a right to development gives priority to development over human rights. To what extent does the Declaration provide a foundation for each of these concerns?

2. Do you agree with Moyn that the human rights movement's embrace of the right to development risks diluting the narrow focus that made it such a powerful tool and thus undermining its utility and effectiveness?

C. ENVIRONMENT, DEVELOPMENT AND HUMAN RIGHTS

The most contentious issue which emerges from the debates on the right to development is whether there is some sort of transnational obligation on the part of wealthy states to provide assistance to developing states to enable them to achieve the right to development. Consider the following instrumentalist case in favour of that proposition:

> The world's richest 500 individuals have a combined income greater than that of the poorest 416 million. Beyond these extremes, the 2.5 billion people living on less than $2 a day — 40% of the world's population — account for 5% of global income. The richest 10%, almost all of whom live in high-income countries, account for 54%. An obvious corollary of extreme global inequality is that even modest shifts in distribution from top to bottom could have dramatic effects on poverty. Using a global income distribution database, we estimate a cost of $300 billion for lifting 1 billion people living on less than $1 a day above the extreme poverty line threshold. That amount represents 1.6% of the income of the richest 10% of the world's population.[3]

Note that such analyses are usually based upon the notion that there is, or should be, a moral or ethical responsibility upon the rich to assist the poor. But many of the claims made in the name of the right to development go much further and posit a legal obligation requiring the provision of such assistance. Such an obligation could possibly be grounded in the framework of the (usually unspecified) obligation of 'international cooperation' which is reflected in the UN Charter and a range of human rights treaties, or in a provision such as Article 28 of the UDHR which provides that '[e]very one is entitled to a social and international order in which the rights and freedoms set forth in this Declaration can be fully realized'.

Other variations on this theme of international responsibility also warrant consideration. Two in particular will be dealt with here. The first is the argument that people in rich countries have an obligation to seek to improve the conditions of the workers in developing countries who produce the goods which the rich consume. The 'anti-sweatshop' movement has been especially prominent in recent years in asserting that the often exploitative working conditions in the factories of the global South that produce goods such as footwear, clothing and textiles for export to the North give rise to obligations upon Northern consumers. The principal objection to such claims is that the latter group have not themselves caused the relevant exploitation and thus could have no personal responsibility for improving the relevant conditions. The excerpt below from Iris Marion Young seeks to provide a philosophical justification for imposing a particular type of responsibility in such situations.

The second variation on the theme concerns claims upon the rich to compensate or assist those developing countries which are likely to be the worst affected by global climate change. These claims may be based either upon the specific attribution of responsibility to the countries of the North for the carbon emissions which are responsible for global warming, or upon a human rights-based claim that the wealthy must assist those who are at risk of large-scale rights deprivation and are effectively unable to help themselves. In each case the question arises as to the moral

[3] 'International Cooperation at a Crossroads: Aid, Trade And Security in an Unequal World', UNDP, Human Development Report 2005, p. 1.

and/or legal foundation of such a claim. In the materials that follow, consideration is given to the challenges stemming from climate change and to an analysis in which Iris Marion Young seeks to develop a philosophical argument that rejects a fault- or liability-based model as being inadequate and instead develops a political responsibility model which would have far-reaching implications in relation to all of the issues canvassed above.

INTERGOVERNMENTAL PANEL ON CLIMATE CHANGE, CLIMATE CHANGE 2007: IMPACTS, ADAPTATION AND VULNERABILITY

Working Group II Contribution to the Intergovernmental Panel on Climate Change, Fourth Assessment Report, Summary for Policymakers (Apr. 2007)

[Eds.: The IPCC's Fifth Assessment Report is scheduled to be completed in 2014.]

. . .

Africa

By 2020, between 75 and 250 million people are projected to be exposed to an increase of water stress due to climate change. If coupled with increased demand, this will adversely affect livelihoods and exacerbate water-related problems.

Agricultural production, including access to food, in many African countries and regions is projected to be severely compromised by climate variability and change. The area suitable for agriculture, the length of growing seasons and yield potential, particularly along the margins of semi-arid and arid areas, are expected to decrease. This would further adversely affect food security and exacerbate malnutrition in the continent. In some countries, yields from rain-fed agriculture could be reduced by up to 50% by 2020.

Local food supplies are projected to be negatively affected by decreasing fisheries resources in large lakes due to rising water temperatures, which may be exacerbated by continued over-fishing.

Towards the end of the 21st century, projected sea-level rise will affect low-lying coastal areas with large populations. The cost of adaptation could amount to at least 5–10% of Gross Domestic Product (GDP). Mangroves and coral reefs are projected to be further degraded, with additional consequences for fisheries and tourism.

New studies confirm that Africa is one of the most vulnerable continents to climate variability and change because of multiple stresses and low adaptive capacity. Some adaptation to current climate variability is taking place, however, this may be insufficient for future changes in climate.

Asia

Glacier melt in the Himalayas is projected to increase flooding, and rock avalanches from destabilised slopes, and to affect water resources within the next two to three decades. This will be followed by decreased river flows as the glaciers recede.

Freshwater availability in Central, South, East and Southeast Asia, particularly in large river basins, is projected to decrease due to climate change which, along with population growth and increasing demand arising from higher standards of living, could adversely affect more than a billion people by the 2050s.

Coastal areas, especially heavily-populated mega-delta regions in South, East and Southeast Asia, will be at greatest risk due to increased flooding from the sea and, in some mega-deltas, flooding from the rivers.

...

It is projected that crop yields could increase up to 20% in East and Southeast Asia while they could decrease up to 30% in Central and South Asia by the mid-21st century. Taken together and considering the influence of rapid population growth and urbanisation, the risk of hunger is projected to remain very high in several developing countries.

Endemic morbidity and mortality due to diarrhoeal disease primarily associated with floods and droughts are expected to rise...

...

Small islands

Small islands, whether located in the tropics or higher latitudes, have characteristics which make them especially vulnerable to the effects of climate change, sea level rise and extreme events.

Deterioration in coastal conditions, for example through erosion of beaches and coral bleaching, is expected to affect local resources, e.g., fisheries, and reduce the value of these destinations for tourism.

Sea-level rise is expected to exacerbate inundation, storm surge, erosion and other coastal hazards, thus threatening vital infrastructure, settlements and facilities that support the livelihood of island communities.

Climate change is projected by the mid-century to reduce water resources in many small islands, e.g., in the Caribbean and Pacific, to the point where they become insufficient to meet demand during low rainfall periods.

With higher temperatures, increased invasion by non-native species is expected to occur, particularly on middle and high-latitude islands.

...

...At present we do not have a clear picture of the limits to adaptation, or the cost, partly because effective adaptation measures are highly dependent on specific, geographical and climate risk factors as well as institutional, political and financial constraints.

The array of potential adaptive responses available to human societies is very large, ranging from purely technological (e.g., sea defences), through behavioural (e.g., altered food and recreational choices), to managerial (e.g., altered farm practices) and to policy (e.g., planning regulations)....For developing countries, availability of resources and building adaptive capacity are particularly important....

...

OPENING REMARKS BY Ms NAVI PILLAY, UN HUMAN RIGHTS COUNCIL SEMINAR ON THE ADVERSE IMPACTS OF CLIMATE CHANGE ON THE FULL ENJOYMENT OF HUMAN RIGHTS

(23 Feb. 2012), at www.ohchr.org/en/NewsEvents/Pages/DisplayNews.aspx?NewsID=11872&LangID=e

...

The effects of climate change will be most acutely felt by those segments of the population whose rights protections are already precarious due to factors such as poverty, gender, age, minority status, migrant status and disability. Certain groups, such as women, children, indigenous peoples and rural communities, are more exposed to climate change effects and risks. The poorest women and men in the developing South — who have contributed least to global warming — find their livelihoods most threatened, yet have the weakest voice and least influence on climate policy. As it happens, the most dramatic impacts of climate change are expected to occur in the world's poorest countries where rights protections are too often weak. Under international human rights law, States are legally bound to address such vulnerability in accordance with the human rights principle of equality and nondiscrimination.

The human rights perspective underlines the importance of empowerment and meaningful participation in decision-making processes. It also emphasizes the necessity of access to safe water, food, education, health services and adequate housing, all of which are important for reducing the vulnerability of individuals to climate change threats. There is no doubt that women and men do not experience climate change equally. In many developing countries, economic constraints and cultural norms that limit women's careers or even prohibit them from receiving paid employment mean that their livelihoods are particularly dependent on climate-sensitive sectors, such as subsistence agriculture or water collection. Women make up most of the world's farmers and produce more than half of the world's food, so their knowledge and capacity are crucial for successful climate change adaption policies.

However, gender inequality and discriminatory laws and practices in the distribution of assets and financial opportunities mean their choices are severely limited in the face of climate change. There is much work to be done to devise policies and measures to address discriminatory practices and to empower women so they become part of the solution to increasing their communities' capacity to cope with extreme weather events. Climate change policies and processes will be neither effective nor fair unless they become more gender aware.

While the precise relationship between climate change and migration is hard to quantify, there is no doubt that environmental factors are already affecting mobility patterns, particularly in relation to the movement of vulnerable and marginalized groups of people. Migrants who are compelled to leave their homes as a coping strategy will often remain in a precarious position throughout the cycle of their journey; they will be vulnerable to human rights violations as they move across borders, and they will frequently be in an irregular situation....

NOTE

Two questions that the preceding materials raise are: (1) whether climate change is appropriately addressed as a human rights issue and (2) what is the basis upon which the rich world might be required to assume particular financial and other responsibility for the resulting plight of the poorer countries?

(1) Climate Change as a Human Rights Issue

In 2006, former UN High Commissioner for Human Rights, Mary Robinson, had already made the case for treating climate change as a human rights concern:

> ... The human rights approach, emphasising the equality of all people, is a direct challenge to the power imbalances that allow the perpetrators of climate change to continue unchecked. And the human rights framework gives us the legal and normative grounds for empowering the poor to seek redress.
>
> ... [W]e can no longer think about climate change as an issue where the rich give charity to the poor to help them to cope with its adverse impacts. Rather, this has now become an issue of global injustice that will need a radically different framing to bring about global justice.
>
> ...
>
> There are strict limits to adaptation — the poor cannot buy their way out of trouble.... These [resulting] changes, in sum, will have a profound impact on the fulfilment of human rights: on people's right to food, right to water, right to health, and even to life itself....[4]

But responses have differed. In 2007, Kenneth Roth, Executive Director of Human Rights Watch, commented:

> ... I don't see a big advantage to calling this a human right issue.... [I]t's sufficient to say that global warming is an enormous environmental problem. It's something we need to deal with. I don't see huge value added to say, "Oh and by the way, it implicates the right to life, or the right to healthcare, or the right to this or that." Or even a right to a clean environment.... [A]dding that rhetorical rights language doesn't add appreciable weight to the arguments against global warming.[5]

Others have argued that international human rights machinery might actually offer the best hope of progress:

> Climate change represents an enormous threat to a whole host of human rights: the right to food, the right to water and sanitation, the right to development. There is therefore huge scope for human rights courts and non-judicial human rights bodies to treat climate change as the immediate threat to human rights that it is. Such bodies could therefore take government policy to task when it is too short-sighted, too unambitious, or too narrowly focused on its own constituents at the expense of those elsewhere. Fossil fuel mining, deforestation, the disturbance of carbon sinks, and the degradation of the oceans are developments that can be blocked on human rights grounds.

[4] Mary Robinson, 'Climate Change and Justice', Barbara Ward Lecture, London, 11 Dec. 2006.

[5] http://bigthink.com/ideas/4064.

> Human rights bodies can, and must, increasingly play this reactive role at the local level, in order to ward off the multitude of developments that simultaneously violate human rights and aggravate climate change. But that will not suffice. They must also become proactive and holistic in warding off human rights violations, and by extension, the advance of climate change at the global level.[6]

But perhaps the biggest challenge is to identify what a human rights approach to climate change might look like in practice. The following report represents one of the most sophisticated attempts to date to answer that question.

SIOBHAN MCINERNEY-LANKFORD, MAC DARROW & LAVANYA RAJAMANI, HUMAN RIGHTS AND CLIMATE CHANGE: A REVIEW OF THE INTERNATIONAL LEGAL DIMENSIONS

World Bank (2011), at 55

... Explicit human rights arguments are yet to gain traction to any appreciable extent within [international] climate change negotiations....

... However, if proper consideration is to be given to the interplay and coherence between the human rights and climate regimes, the normative premises must be clearly articulated together with a more tangible sense of practical implications....

A Frame for Policy Choices

... [T]he most important potential contributions of the international human rights framework in practical terms may be to help frame, rather than necessarily resolve, difficult policy choices and trade-offs....

... [T]here are three levels at which it might be useful to look at the more specific contributions of the human rights legal framework to climate change decision-making:

A Normative Focus on Human Welfare

A defining feature of a human rights approach is its normative focus on human welfare (i.e. "the dignity and worth of the human person.") ... The human rights framework can serve an important function in helping to draw attention to the human face of climate change harms and anthropogenic causes.

Procedural rights standards — improving decision-making processes

But what is it that constitutes "dangerous" anthropogenic interference with the climate system? And how is it to be determined? The IPCC notes that this is a value judgment determined through socio-political processes, taking into account considerations such as development, equity, and sustainability, as well as uncertainties and risk." ... [T]he human rights legal framework offers criteria for the *process* of negotiations, as well as decision-making on climate change policy issues more

[6] Olivier de Schutter, 'Climate Change is a Human Rights Issue – And That's How We Can Solve It, 24 Apr. 2012, at www.srfood.org/index.php/en/media/op-eds.

generally. While certain process guarantees enjoy firmer footing in international law than others,...active and informed participation — including by the most disadvantaged or vulnerable groups — can not only provide critical inputs to decision-making processes but also enhance the legitimacy and sustainability of outcomes. *Ex ante* human rights impact assessments, as part of environmental assessments, can help decision-makers and negotiators to identify in a more reliable, systematic and timely fashion the likely winners and losers of any proposed policy measure, as an operational expression of the "do no harm" principle. Whatever the eventual outcomes of a particular negotiation or policy-making process, the human rights legal framework urges that minimally effective and accessible redress mechanisms be in place to ensure that those whose human rights were overlooked or traded-off against other interests are adequately compensated.

Finally, the scheme of socio-economic rights obligations reflected in the ICESCR and CRC could add important qualitative dimensions to decision-making in the climate change context....

Substantive human rights standards — a focus on outcomes

...Conflicts between rights appear particularly pronounced in many developing countries.... The claims of some to development..., which might be indispensable for the progressive realisation of socio-economic rights in a given country, may directly conflict with the rights of others to their culture, livelihoods and territorial integrity. On what principled basis can one reconcile such claims?

[One approach is that of] "human rights thresholds"...in particular the idea of a "minimum core content" of socio-economic rights that should be respected at all times, and which should be prioritised in international assistance and cooperation....

...

Strengthening legal accountability

Courts are beginning to focus on climate litigation. In the Nigerian Gas Flaring Case the High Court of Nigeria held that the practice of gas flaring by Nigeria in the Niger Delta, violated guaranteed constitutional rights to life and dignity. Litigation under tort and administrative law has had impacts at the national level: the U.S. Supreme Court declared that carbon dioxide is an air pollutant under that country's Clean Air Act with the consequence that automobile emissions should be regulated; a ruling in Australia that GHG emissions from the burning of coal must be taken into account in a planning decision to approve a new coal mine; and a ruling in Germany requiring public disclosure of the climate change impacts of German export credits....

[F]uller exploration of administrative mechanisms is also needed, beginning with EIAs [environmental impact assessments] (informed by human rights concerns).... Practically, it may be that one way of integrating human rights considerations into responses to climate change would be to integrate them within EIAs....

While there is no template for a human rights impact assessment, the principal elements that emerge from the literature and practice include: (a) incorporating internationally recognized human rights as the explicit subject of the assessment; (b) identify indicators for the assessment that are consistent with relevant international human rights standards; (c) focusing upon people who are most excluded and marginalized along with responsible actors...; (d) striving to ensure that the assessment, as far as possible, contributes to building the capacities of relevant national stakeholders...; (e) ensuring that the process of carrying out the assessment respects "good process" principles...; and (f) seeking to involve human rights mechanisms and actors as far as possible, for example national human rights institutions, subject to their mandated functions and capacities. [The report also examines the importance of engaging the private sector, ensuring technology access and transfer to low income countries, and exploring the possibility of a new international instrument on climate-induced displacement.]

(2) The Responsibilities of the Rich

In 2007, President Museveni of Uganda characterized climate change as an act of aggression by the rich world against the poor and demanded compensation. In response, *The Economist* magazine argued that African governments had themselves done far less than they could have in response to the climate change crisis, the concluded that Africa 'should not expect much new [foreign aid] money to protect the environment. In the short run, Africa's own politicians need to take a lead, even if the people most culpable for the damage done by climate change live elsewhere.'[7]

And there are many philosophers who hold that arguments in favour of transnational justice are misplaced. For example, according to:

> Michael Walzer, there is no room for transnational distributive justice in international law because states ought to determine their own internal distributive arrangements. According to Walzer, each distinct society is engaged in an ongoing process of developing and revising shared social meanings that ground distinctive principles of distributive justice, and the identity and well-being of individuals depends upon their participation in this cultural project. The benefits that individuals derive from the process depend upon its integrity, and this in turn requires that their shared meanings be worked out among themselves without standards being imposed from outside. Thus, the whole enterprise of transnational distributive justice is illegitimate, because it is an attempt to impose an external conception of distributive justice, with the result that the integrity of the indigenous process will be undermined.[8]

Others have argued that fault- or liability-based arguments are unhelpful in resolving such issues and that a broader conception of political responsibility is necessary instead. Thus, for example, in addressing the question of how agents should think about responsibility in relation to structural social injustice Iris Marion Young distinguishes the liability and responsibility models in five respects:

> (1) Unlike responsibility as liability, political responsibility does not isolate some responsible parties in order to absolve others. (2) Whereas blame or liability seeks

[7] 'Global Warming in Africa: Drying Up and Flooding Out', *The Economist*, 12 May 2007, p. 43.

[8] A. Buchanan & D. Golove, 'The Philosophy of International Law', in J. Coleman and S. Shapiro (eds.), *Oxford Handbook on the Philosophy of Law* (2002), 808 at 900. In relation to Walzer, see his book *Spheres of Justice: A Defense of Pluralism and Equality* (1983).

> remedy for a deviation from an acceptable norm, usually by an event that has reached a terminus, with political responsibility we are concerned with structural causes of injustice that are normal and ongoing. (3) Political responsibility is more forward-looking than backward-looking. (4) What it means to take up or assign political responsibility is more open and discretionary than what it means to hold an agent blameworthy or liable. (5) An agent shares political responsibility with others whose actions contribute to the structural processes that produce injustice.

In Young's view, the political responsibility model she proposes is applicable to any issue of structural social injustice. She argues that only collective action can succeed in rectifying injustices that result from the product of the mediated actions of many. Her argument draws heavily upon Hannah Arendt's concept of political responsibility which envisaged:

> a kind of collective responsibility, and one where the responsibility borne collectively is not dissolvable to the self-conscious collaborative acts of individuals. Whereas responsibility as liability assigns responsibility according to what particular agents have done, on the model of political responsibility individuals are responsible precisely for things they themselves have *not* done. The reason to assume political responsibility involves not individual fault, but derives from "my membership in a group (a collective) which no voluntary act of mine can dissolve, that is, a membership which is utterly unlike a business partnership which I can dissolve at will." Arendt clearly takes the political community of a nation-state as her paradigm of such a collective.[9]

QUESTIONS

1. In what respects, if any, would you consider that the climate change crisis raises problems that are properly, or helpfully, classified as human rights issues? Does it necessarily reflect badly on the human rights regime if it has nothing much to add in relation to one of the most pressing problems of the twenty-first century?

2. Does Young's notion of collective action based on a concept of shared responsibility help in articulating a human rights-based theory for allocating international responsibilities for issues such as climate change?

3. Thomas Pogge has argued, primarily on the basis of Article 28 of the UDHR, that the global institutional order 'must afford the persons on whom it is imposed secure access to the objects of their human rights' and that there is 'a negative duty not to cooperate in the imposition of this global order if feasible reforms of it would significantly improve the realization of human rights'.[10] What are the reasonable limits of such an obligation? Do national boundaries make a major difference in terms of such obligations? Is it sufficient

[9] I. M. Young, 'Responsibility and Global Labor Justice', 12 J. Pol. Phil. 365 (2004), at 388. Young's reference is to Hannah Arendt, 'Collective Responsibility', in J. Bernauer (ed.), *Amor Mundi: Explorations in the Faith and Thought of Hannah Arendt* (1987), 45.

[10] T. Pogge, 'The International Significance of Human Rights', 4 J. Ethics 45 (2000).

for the international community to establish institutions devoted to the promotion of different aspects of development? Does it matter if some of these institutions, such as the WTO, explicitly exclude human rights from their fields of activity?

ADDITIONAL READING

International Council on Human Rights Policy, 'Beyond Technology Transfer: Protecting Human Rights in a Climate-Constrained World' (2011); Symposium: International Human Rights and Climate Change, 38 Georgia J. Int'l. & Comp. L. 511 (2010); J. McAdam (ed.), *Climate Change and Displacement: Multidisciplinary Perspectives* (2010); Report of the [UN OHCHR] on the Relationship Between Climate Change and Human Rights, UN Doc. A/HRC/10/61 (15 Jan. 2009); W. Burns & H. Osofsky (eds.), *Adjudicating Climate Change: State, National, and International Approaches* (2009); S. Humphreys (ed.), *Human Rights and Climate Change* (2010); P. Alston, 'Ships Passing in the Night: The Current State of the Human Rights and Development Debate', 27 Hum. Rts. Q. 755 (2005); B. A. Andreassen & S. P. Marks (eds.), *Development as a Human Right* (2006); P. Smith, *Liberalism and Affirmative Obligation* (1998); T. Nagel, 'The Problem of Global Justice', 33 Philosophy and Public Affairs 113 (2005); T. Pogge, *World Poverty and Human Rights: Cosmopolitan Responsibilities and Reforms* (2nd edn. 2008); P. Vizard, *Poverty and Human Rights* (2006); P. Uvin, *Human Rights and Development* (2004).

DOCUMENTS SUPPLEMENT

An Online Resource Centre, www.oxfordtextbooks.co.uk/orc/alston_goodman/, contains a documentary supplement for this course book. Part I of the supplement sets forth documents that are essential to an understanding of materials in different parts of the course book. Since they have been edited to delete provisions that are unnecessary for an understanding of those materials, you should not rely on any of them as full and official versions. Part II of the online supplement sets forth an extended set of documents. It contains additional conventions and protocols, including recently adopted instruments that have not yet entered into force. The list below comprises those documents found on the Online Resource Centre.

In the list below, after the official title of a document, there appear within parentheses the acronym or abbreviated name(s) by which the text is sometimes referred.

CONTENTS

Rome Statute of the International Criminal Court (ICC)

Geneva Convention (III) relative to the Treatment of Prisoners of War (POWs Convention)

Geneva Convention (IV) relative to the Protection of Civilian Persons in Time of War (Civilians Convention)

Protocol Additional to the Geneva Conventions of 12 August 1949, and relating to the Protection of Victims of International Armed Conflicts (Protocol I)

Protocol Additional to the Geneva Conventions of 12 August 1949, and relating to the Protection of Victims of Non-International Armed Conflicts (Protocol II)

Vienna Convention on the Law of Treaties

Constitution of the United States

II. Other important texts

Convention on the Elimination of All Forms of Racial Discrimination (CERD)

Convention on the Rights of the Child (CRC)

Convention on the Rights of Persons with Disabilities (CRPD)

Optional Protocol to the Convention on the Rights of Persons with Disabilities

Convention for the Protection of All Persons from Enforced Disappearance

Optional Protocol to the Convention against Torture and Other Cruel, Inhuman or Degrading Treatment or Punishments

Index of Topics

Index of Names

Note: This is not only an index of authors, but rather of all individuals cited in the book, except for: (a) those mentioned in the Additional Reading sections; (b) those referred to only in footnotes or questions; (c) editors or translators; (d) the authors of judgments; and (e) newspaper reporters.